BaseBall america®
2017 ALMANAC

BASEBALL AMERICA INC. · DURHAM, N.C.

EDITOR'S NOTE: Major league statistics are based on final, unofficial 2016 averages. >> The organization statistics, which begin on page 44, include all players who participated in at least one game during the 2016 season. >> Pitchers' batting statistics are not included, nor are the pitching statistics of field players who pitched in less than two games. >> For players who played with more than one team in the same league, the player's cumulative statistics appear on the line immediately after the player's statistics with each team. >> Innings pitched have been rounded off to the nearest full inning.

BaseBall america
2017 ALMANAC

Editor
JOSH NORRIS

Assistant Editors
BEN BADLER, HUDSON BELINSKY, TEDDY CAHILL,
J.J. COOPER, MATT EDDY, MICHAEL LANANNA,
VINCENT LARA-CINISOMO, JOHN MANUEL, JIM SHONERD

Database and Application Development
BRENT LEWIS

Contributing Writers
JOHN PERROTTO, TOM HAUDRICOURT

Photo Editor
JIM SHONERD

Editorial Assistants
JOSH LEVENTHAL

Design & Production
SARA HIATT MCDANIEL,
LINWOOD WEBB

Programming & Technical Development
BRENT LEWIS

Cover Photo
CHICAGO CUBS BY DIAMOND IMAGES

©2016 BASEBALL AMERICA INC. NO PORTION OF THIS BOOK MAY BE
REPRINTED OR REPRODUCED WITHOUT THE WRITTEN CONSENT OF THE
PUBLISHER. FOR ADDITIONAL COPIES, VISIT OUR WEBSITE AT
BASEBALLAMERICA.COM OR CALL
1-800-845-2726 TO ORDER. US $23.95-$26.95, PLUS SHIPPING
AND HANDLING PER ORDER. EXPEDITED SHIPPING AVAILABLE.

DISTRIBUTED BY SIMON & SCHUSTER ISBN-13: 978-1-932391-68-8

STATISTICS PROVIDED BY MAJOR LEAGUE BASEBALL ADVANCED MEDIA
AND COMPILED BY BASEBALL AMERICA

TABLE OF CONTENTS

Mike Trout, Baseball America's Major League Player of the Year

BILL NICHOLS

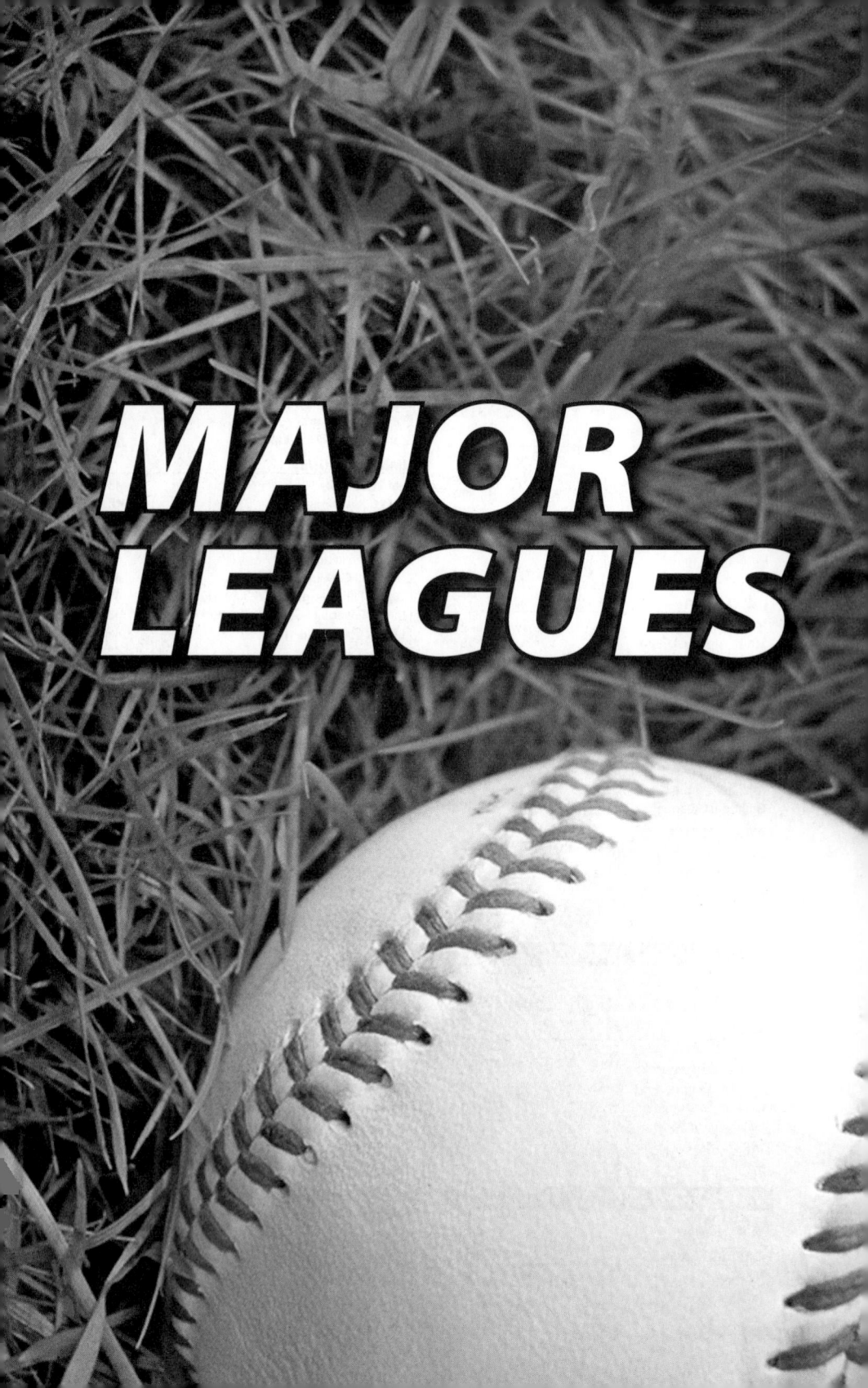

MAJOR
LEAGUES

Home runs, milestones provide 2016 highlights

BY JOHN PERROTTO

Big home run totals were supposed to be a thing of the past, tamped down by tougher testing for performance-enhancing drugs after the longball-happy era of mid 1990s-2000s.

Yet the homer-happy ways were back during the 2016 season. A total of 5,610 were hit, second only to 5,693 in 2000 during the height of the Steroids Era.

Many players felt the composition of the baseballs was different in years past, though Major League Baseball denied it had made any changes.

"I think the balls are harder," retiring Yankees first baseman Mark Teixeira said. "Definitely. I can just feel it. I can hear it off the bat."

Home runs had dropped from 4,661 in 2013 to 4,186 in 2014. The rise began in 2015, when the total increased to 4,909, then nearly reached a record level in 2016.

"We have tested the baseball. We are absolutely convinced that this issue is not driven by a difference in the baseball," commissioner Rob Manfred said. "My own view is that the spike is related to the way that the game is being played now, the way that we are training hitters from a very young age, and we have not been able to find any external cause that explains the spike in home runs."

In an era of power pitching, power hitting spiked. A total of 111 players hit 20 or more home runs, a major league record and up from 64 in 2016. And 35 of those players started at least 100 games at second base, third base or shortstop. The number of players with 30 or more home runs shot up to 38 in 2016 from 20 the year before.

Hitters also sold out at the plate to generate more power as the major leagues set a record for strikeouts for a ninth consecutive year with 38,982, an average of 8.02 a team per game. That was a 27-percent increase from 2007 when teams averaged 6.30 whiffs a game.

More and more, the game is a game of power. While home runs have ticked back up, extreme velocity also helped define baseball in 2016.

The average fastball velocity in the majors has been on a steady climb throughout the 21st century. In 2002, major league pitchers averaged 89.0 mph with their fastball. Since then, the average velocity for fastballs has either stayed the same or gotten faster in all but one of the past 15 years. In

DIAMOND IMAGES

No big league pitcher embodies the Age of Velocity like Aroldis Chapman

2016, the average major leaguer sat at 92.3 mph when throwing their fastball, a gain of more than three mph in the past 15 seasons. Changeups and sliders have shown similar velocity gains.

And the boon is not just being seen among relievers raring back and firing for an inning at a time. Mets righthander Noah Syndergaard's fastball averaged 98 mph. He threw 100 mph or harder at some point in most every start (he had 94 pitches clocked at 100 or better). Syndergaard's slider averaged 91 mph—two ticks harder than the average fastball in 2002.

More than 1,400 pitches clocked at 100 mph or harder during the 2016 major league season. Pitch f/x has tracked pitch velocities since 2007. Almost one-third (29.4 percent) of all 100 mph pitches Pitch f/x has tracked were thrown in 2016.

Even the hardest throwers keep throwing harder. Yankees/Cubs lefthander Aroldis Chapman has had the game's fastest fastball since the day he reached the majors. But in 2016, he threw harder than he ever had before.

Chapman came into 2016 as the only pitcher to have been clocked at 103 mph or harder by Pitch

f/x more than once. In 2016, 103 became almost routine for him.

After throwing 68 pitches of 103 or harder from 2010-2015 combined, Chapman touched 103 or better 101 times in 2016.

Also, Chapman now has some potential competition for the title of the fastest arm in the majors. Braves rookie reliever Mauricio Cabrera threw 344 pitches 100 mph or better in his debut season. That already puts him second to Chapman on the list for most 100 mph pitches of the Pitch f/x era. Cabrera became the only major league pitcher other than Chapman to have more than one pitch that has been clocked by Pitch f/x at 103 or better. Cabrera touched 104 on multiple occasions.

Are The Balls An Issue?

Teixeira's point about balls being hit harder was backed up by scientific evidence proving by Major League Baseball's Statcast. The average velocity of balls off the bat rose to 89.1 mph in 2016 from 88.5 mph in 2015.

"All of a sudden, did we get that much better? That much stronger?" Teixeira said.

It hasn't been sudden, but pitchers do throw harder in 2016 than ever before, and the game's approach is one of power, both at the plate and on the mound, more than ever before.

The baseballs used by MLB are manufactured by Rawlings in Costa Rica. They must weigh 5 to 5 1/4 ounces, have a circumference of 9 to 9 1/4 inches and a diameter of 2 7/8 to 3 inches. The company and MLB insisted nothing changed in 2016.

"We're not seeing anything outside our normal tolerance range and specification level," Rawlings spokeswoman Kathy Stephens told The Associated Press, adding the company conducts its own tests.

In a statement, MLB said: "We direct UMass-Lowell's Baseball Research Center to conduct periodic testing of baseballs throughout the regular season. Among the balls that are randomly tested are a sampling from the supplies of clubs. Balls are tested for weight, circumference, coefficient of restitution and other factors. Measurements are made to ensure compliance with our rules and are also compared to previous results. These reviews have found no differences to the ball that would have resulted in a change to its performance."

A spike in attendance in the late 1990s and early 2000s was attributed to the great home run feats of such sluggers as Barry Bonds, Mark McGwire and Sammy Sosa. Despite this year's power spike, MLB's average attendance dropped 1.1 percent in 2016, though it was still the sport's 11th-best year at the gate.

The 30 teams combined to draw 73,159,044 fans and average 30,169. That was down from 2015's total of 73.76 million and average of 30,517. The average was the lowest since 30,138 in 2010. The record total of 79.5 million and average of 32,785 were set in 2007, before the United States economy experienced a recession.

The National League West-champion Dodgers led in home attendance at 3.7 million, followed in the NL by the Cardinals (3.44 million), Giants (3.37 million) and Cubs (3.23 million).

The Blue Jays topped the American League at 3.39 million, followed by the Yankees (3.06 million) and Angels (3.02 million). The Angels (14 years) and Yankees (18 years) extended their streaks of exceeding 3 million in attendance.

The Rays had the lowest home attendance at 1.29 million, and the Athletics were 29th at 1.52 million. The Indians were 28th at 1.59 million while winning the American League Central for the first time since 2007. The Marlins drew an NL-low 1.71 million.

Time For Changes

MLB and Major League Baseball Players Association agreed to two rule changes prior to the start of the season

Rule 6.01(j) delineated criteria for a legal slide while trying to break up a double play, which is defined as making contact with the ground before reaching the base, being able to and attempting to reach the base with a hand or foot, being able to and attempting to remain on the base at the completion of the slide (except at home plate) and not changing his path for the purpose of initiating contact with a fielder. This is intended to protect infielders while still allowing for aggressive baserunning.

The World Umpires Association also approved the banishment of so-called block slides after Dodgers second baseman Chase Utley broke the leg of Mets shortstop Ruben Tejada on a takeout at second base in the 2015 postseason.

The second rule change limits managers and coaches visits to the mound to 30 seconds and shortens between innings break times by 20 seconds to match television commercial breaks.

While the slide rule created inconsistency in how it was called by the umpires early in the season, the attempts to speed up the pace of games failed miserably.

The average time of game in the regular season was 3 hours, 5 minutes, up four minutes from 3:01 in 2015. By comparison, games averaged 2:48 in 2006.

The A's were the only major league team to

ED WOLFSTEIN

Jose Fernandez already had established himself as one of baseball's best pitchers, but the Marlins star righthander died in late September in a boat crash off the coast of South Florida

post an average time of game less than three hours for both home and road games this season and had the lowest overall average time at 2:57. Just two other teams averaged under three hours as the Royals and Blue Jays were both at 2:59. The Diamondbacks played the longest games on average at 3:14, including 3:17 in home games at Chase Field.

One area in which MLB regressed was in the enforcement of the rule enacted in 2015 in which batters were required to keep at least one foot in the batter's box throughout his at-bat, the exceptions being a foul ball or a foul tip; a pitch forcing the batter out of the batter's box; "time out" being requested and granted; or a wild pitch or a passed ball.

"Last year the batter's box rule was new," Manfred said. "It was fresh in the players' minds. It was fresh in the umpires' minds. Everybody was focused on it. But a year goes by and things backslide a little bit."

Instant replay reviews have also added to the average time of game. When MLB first rolled out the replay system prior to the start of the 2014 season, it said five years would be needed to completely iron out the flaws. One tweak Manfred would like to see is a limit on the amount of time replays can be reviewed at the league office before a decision is made.

"Ninety seconds is around average, but the ones that attract a lot of attention are the 2 ½-minute, three-minute ones," Manfred said. "I do think it's possible that at some point we would give consideration to a cap. It is something we have to give consideration.

South Beach Tragedy

The most tragic story of the season came Sept. 25 when Marlins all-star righthander Jose Fernandez died in a boat accident along with two friends at age 24 when their 32-foot vessel slammed into a jetty off Miami Beach. It remained unclear who was piloting the boat.

The sad irony of his death was that it took him four tries as a teenager to escape communist Cuba by boat and when his mother fell out into the Yucatan Channel during that journey, he jumped into the water and pulled her out.

"All I can do is scream in disbelief," said Hall of Famer Tony Perez said, a Marlins executive and native of Cuba. "Jose won the love of all. I feel as if I had lost a son."

MLB, in a statement, said it was "stunned and devastated."

"He was one of our game's great young stars who made a dramatic impact on and off the field

CONTINUED ON PAGE 11

Trout blows away the field

BY TAYLOR WARD

For the fifth straight season, Angels center fielder Mike Trout is the best player in baseball. Now, for the third time in that span he is the Baseball America Major League Player of the Year.

The 25-year-old led the major leagues this season with 123 runs scored, 116 walks, a .441 on-base percentage and 10.6 wins above replacement, according to Baseball-Reference.com.

Trout is so good that we have run out of words to praise him. So we turn to the industry to learn what they're saying about the three-time POY.

Angels GM Billy Eppler

"How regularly that star level shows up is the main separator with a lot of high-end players, or guys who perform at their peak level. It's amazing how often (Trout) brings that peak level, and how many days that shows up over his 160 games.

"Getting to know him as a person, know what he means in that clubhouse and just his demeanor, (I admire) his energy, his looseness. When I met his parents I actually said that they did a great job raising him. They should be very proud of the man who he's become. That's my biggest takeaway from him."

Athletics Catcher Stephen Vogt

"Playing against Mike Trout is not the easiest thing in the world. In my opinion, he's the most complete player in baseball. He can

CLIFF WELCH

Teammates and rivals alike are in awe of Angels superstar Mike Trout

beat you with his glove, bat, speed, contact, power—you name it. He doesn't really have a hole in his swing.

"There's not really a good way to get him out. It's always a mind game trying to trick him or trying to get him to get out of his approach. That's not easy to do. He stays in his approach better than most people in baseball. He's a superstar.

"What's so great about him is his consistency. He used to swing in certain counts and maybe not swing in other counts and now you don't know. He's swinging at his pitch when he gets it. He's making adjustments as he's going, and he's getting better and better."

Astros Shortstop Carlos Correa

"His pitch selection (impresses me). He only swings at strikes that are right in the middle, and he does damage. He takes his walks. He has a .440 on-base percentage. That's absurd! He's having a great year. For me, he's the best player in the game right now.

"What I like about Mike is that he's one of the best players, but he's very humble."

PREVIOUS POY WINNERS

2005: Albert Pujols, 1b, Cardinals
2006: Johan Santana, lhp, Twins
2007: Alex Rodriguez, ss, Yankees
2008: C.C. Sabathia, lhp, Indians/Brewers
2009: Joe Mauer, c, Twins
2010: Roy Halladay, rhp, Phillies
2011: Matt Kemp, of, Dodgers
2012: Mike Trout, Angels
2013: Mike Trout, Angels
2014: Clayton Kershaw, Angels
2015: Bryce Harper, Nationals
2016: Mike Trout, Angels
Full list: BaseballAmerica.com/awards

CONTINUED FROM PAGE 9

since his debut in 2013," Manfred said.

The Marlins' game that day at home against the Braves was canceled. Within hours after the news broke, Marlins players gathered at the ballpark to grieve together.

"A lot of words were said—meaningful words and emotion and prayer," team president David Samson said. "Jose is a member of this family for all time."

Fernandez was on a vessel that hit a jetty near a harbor entrance. He died from trauma and not drowning, and traces of cocaine were found in his system; he also was legally drunk with a .147 blood alcohol content, nearly twice the legal limit. None of the three men in the boat was wearing life jackets.

Fernandez and his family settled in Tampa after finally reaching the U.S. and the Marlins selected him in the first round of the 2011 draft (14th overall). He reached the major leagues two years later, winning the 2013 National League Rookie of the Year award, and had a 38-17 career record over four seasons (missing a year with Tommy John surgery) while twice being selected to play in the All-Star Game.

A week before his death, posted a photo of his girlfriend sporting a "baby bump" on his Instagram page, announcing that the couple was expecting its first child.

"I'm so glad you came into my life," Fernandez wrote in that post. "I'm ready for where this journey is gonna take us together."

Fernandez became a U.S. citizen in 2015 and was highly popular in Miami because of his suc-

cess, high-energy personality and Cuban heritage.

"When I think about Josie, it's going to be thinking about a little kid," Marlins manager Don Mattingly said. "I see such a little boy in him. Kids play Little League, that's the joy Jose played with."

Next Year Arrives For Cubs

The Cubs dominated the regular season on their way to winning the franchise's first World Series title since 1908 as their 103-58 record was the best in the regular season.

They won the National League Central by a whopping 17 ½ games over the three-time defending champion Cardinals while ending St. Louis' streak of five consecutive playoff appearances, which had been the longest current streak in the major leagues.

The Cubs, who last won a division title in 2008, had entered the season with sky-high expectations after winning 97 games behind a youthful lineup in 2015. They added free-agent outfielder Jason Heyward on an eight-year contract, signed John Lackey as a free agent to bolster their rotation, then burnished their bullpen during the season with a pair of trades, adding lefthanders Mike Montgomery from the Mariners and, more significantly, closer Aroldis Chapman from the Yankees.

The new arms, plus strong campaigns from holdovers such as Kyle Hendricks, Jon Lester and Jason Hammel, helped the Cubs lead the majors with a 3.15 ERA. The Nationals finished a distant second at 3.51, and only the Dodgers and Nats struck out more batters as a staff than did Chicago.

While they led from start to finish and won the

CONTINUED ON PAGE 13

AMERICAN LEAGUE STANDINGS

EAST	W	L	PCT	GB	Manager	General Manager	Attendance	Average	Last Penn.
Boston Red Sox	93	69	.574	—	John Farrell	Mike Hazen	2,955,434	36,487	2013
* Toronto Blue Jays	89	73	.549	4	John Gibbons	Ross Atkins	3,392,099	41,878	1993
* Baltimore Orioles	89	73	.549	4	Buck Showalter	Dan Duquette	2,172,344	26,819	1983
New York Yankees	84	78	.519	9	Joe Girardi	Brian Cashman	3,063,405	37,820	2009
Tampa Bay Rays	68	94	.420	25	Kevin Cash	Matt Silverman	1,286,163	15,879	2008
CENTRAL	**W**	**L**	**PCT**	**GB**	**Manager**	**General Manager**	**Attendance**	**Average**	**Last Penn.**
Cleveland Indians	94	67	.584	—	Terry Francona	Mike Chernoff	1,591,667	19,650	2016
Detroit Tigers	86	75	.534	8	Brad Ausmus	Al Avila	2,493,859	31,173	2012
Kansas City Royals	81	81	.500	13 ½	Ned Yost	Dayton Moore	2,557,712	31,577	2015
Chicago White Sox	78	84	.481	16 ½	Robin Ventura	Rick Hahn	1,746,293	21,829	2005
Minnesota Twins	59	103	.364	35 ½	Paul Molitor	T. Ryan/R. Antony	1,963,912	24,246	1991
WEST	**W**	**L**	**PCT**	**GB**	**Manager**	**General Manager**	**Attendance**	**Average**	**Last Penn.**
Texas Rangers	95	67	.586	—	Jeff Banister	Jon Daniels	2,710,402	33,462	2011
Seattle Mariners	86	76	.531	9	Scott Servais	Jerry Dipoto	2,267,928	27,999	None
Houston Astros	84	78	.519	11	A.J. Hinch	Jeff Luhnow	2,306,623	28,477	2005 (NL)
Los Angeles Angels	74	88	.457	21	Mike Scioscia	Billy Eppler	3,016,142	37,236	2002
Oakland Athletics	69	93	.426	26	Bob Melvin	David Forst	1,521,506	18,784	1990

Wild Card Game: Blue Jays defeated Orioles. **Division Series:** Blue Jays defeated Rangers 3-0 and Indians defeated Red Sox 3-0 in best-of-five series. **Championship Series:** Indians defeated Blue Jays 4-1 in best-of-seven series.

ROOKIE OF THE YEAR

Seager dominates with L.A.

BY KYLE GLASER

Corey Seager saw all the draft reports out of high school listing him as a third baseman. He read every word questioning if he could stick at shortstop as he made his way up the minors.

At first, the questions confused and irritated him. As he got drafted and ascended the Dodgers system, they motivated him.

"That's kind of been something since I was drafted that's been brought up," Seager said by phone during the Dodgers penultimate regular-season series in San Diego. "'I wasn't going to play short. I was going to move to third,' so that was something that I always worked hard at. I kind of used it as a little edge to prove people wrong and prove that I could play there to people who really had never even seen me play."

Lost in all the criticism was year after year Seager made every play at shortstop, all the while showing an offensive skill set as gifted as any young prospect this side of Mike Trout or Kris Bryant.

In his first full season in the majors, Seager hit .308/.365/.512 with 26 homers and 72 RBIs. He finished in the top 10 in the National League in hits, doubles, runs, batting average and slugging percentage while hitting in the Nos. 2 and 3 spot all year for the NL West-champion Dodgers, and he did it all playing a solid, reliable shortstop. For all that, Seager is the easy choice for the Baseball America Rookie of the Year.

While Seager's defense proved sufficient, it was his offense that made him a star. One scout recalled putting an "80" grade on Seager's future hitting ability on the 20-to-80 scouting scale when he was a 19-year old in the high Class A California League, and Seager's career .891 OPS in the minors backed up every glowing report.

What was different, and slightly unexpected, was just how much power he showed as a rookie. Considered a 15-20-home run threat who might hit 25 in his prime, Seager instead hit 26 homers—more than he hit in any minor league season.

BILL MITCHELL

Corey Seager was a force in Los Angeles

"It just kind of happened," Seager said. "I never really ever hit this many home runs. It could be the more at-bats you're getting. You have a better gameplan coming into those. you know what pitchers do, you know what you want to do. It's an accumulation of everything."

Power, defense and a high batting average at shortstop. It's the recipe for a franchise player, which is exactly what Seager proved to be in his rookie season.

PREVIOUS ROY WINNERS

2004: Khalil Greene, ss, Padres
2005: Huston Street, rhp, Athletics
2006: Justin Verlander, rhp, Tigers
2007: Ryan Braun, 3b, Brewers
2008: Geovany Soto, c, Cubs
2009: Andrew McCutchen, of, Pirates
2010: Jason Heyward, of, Braves
2011: Jeremy Hellickson, rhp, Rays
2012: Mike Trout, of, Angels
2013: Jose Fernandez, rhp, Marlins
2014: Jose Abreu, 1b, White Sox
2015: Kris Bryant, 3b, Cubs
2016: Corey Seager, ss, Dodgers

World Series, their season wasn't without challenges. Outfielder/catcher Kyle Schwarber tore ligaments in his left knee on the season's second day and missed the rest of the regular season, only returning to the field in the World Series. and Heyward endured a truly awful season offensively, batting just .230/.306/.335 with a career-low seven home runs.

But president Theo Epstein, general manager Jed Hoyer and their staff had constructed a formidable, deep, athletic roster that was able to overcome Heyward's down season. Second-year third baseman Kris Bryant and first baseman Anthony Rizzo provided most of the thump, combining for 71 home runs and 211 RBIs.

The Dodgers overcame an injury-plagued season that included the loss of Clayton Kershaw for more than two months. However, L.A. went 38-24 without Kershaw under first-year manager Dave Roberts, catching rival San Francisco to win its fourth NL West championship in a row, finishing four games ahead of the Giants.

Meanwhile the Nationals overcame a down year by 2015 MVP Bryce Harper and late injury to Stephen Strasburg and finished eight games ahead of the defending NL champion Mets to finish first in the NL East for the second time in three years. Free-agent pickup Daniel Murphy (more on him later) and first-year manager Dusty Baker keyed the Nats, with Baker leading his fourth different team to the playoffs. (Davey Johnson, who was Baker's teammate with the Atlanta Braves in the early 1970s, managed the Nats to the 2012 NL East title, also skippered four different franchises to the postseason.)

The Mets and Giants won the two NL wild-card postseason berths. The Giants had surged late in the first half, entering the all-star break with the best record in baseball at 57-33. However, they lost 21 of their first 30 games in the second half and barely recovered to make the playoffs.

The Rangers were the only repeat division winner in the American League, finishing nine games ahead of the Mariners in the West. Texas had the best record in the AL at 95-67 even though the club finished with a run differential of just plus-eight. The team's Pythagorean Record—an estimate of a team's winning percentage given its runs scored and runs allowed—was just 82-80. The Rangers were 36-11 in one-run games and dominated the other contenders in the AL West, going 12-7 against the Mariners and 15-4 against the in-state rival Astros.

The Indians won the AL Central by eight games over the Tigers and the Red Sox won their first AL East since 2013—after finishing last the previous two seasons—by four games over both the Orioles and Blue Jays, who were the league's wild cards.

Boston led the big leagues with 878 runs scored, scoring 101 more than the Indians, who ranked second in the AL. Retiring DH David Ortiz led the Sox with 38 homers, and the lineup also got an MVP-caliber season by right fielder Mookie Betts (.318/.363/.534), who hit 31 homers and stole a club-high 26 bases, while Hanley Ramirez, moved from left field to first base, bounced back with his first 30-homer season since 2008.

Leaders In The Clubhouse

The Rockies' D.J. LeMahieu won his first

NATIONAL LEAGUE STANDINGS

EAST	W	L	PCT	GB	Manager	General Manager	Attendance	Average	Last Penn.
Washington Nationals	95	67	.586	—	Dusty Baker	Mike Rizzo	2,481,938	30,641	None
* New York Mets	87	75	.537	8	Terry Collins	Sandy Alderson	2,789,602	34,870	2015
Miami Marlins	79	82	.491	15 ½	Don Mattingly	Mike Hill	1,712,417	21,405	2003
Philadelphia Phillies	71	91	.438	24	Pete Mackanin	Matt Klentak	1,915,144	23,644	2009
Atlanta Braves	68	93	.422	26 ½	F. Gonzalez/B. Snitker	John Coppolella	2,020,914	24,950	1999

CENTRAL	W	L	PCT	GB	Manager	General Manager	Attendance	Average	Last Penn.
Chicago Cubs	103	58	.640	—	Joe Maddon	Jed Hoyer	3,232,420	39,906	2016
St. Louis Cardinals	86	76	.531	17 ½	Mike Matheny	John Mozeliak	3,444,490	42,525	2013
Pittsburgh Pirates	78	83	.484	25	Clint Hurdle	Neal Huntington	2,249,201	28,115	1979
Milwaukee Brewers	73	89	.451	30 ½	Craig Counsell	David Stearns	2,314,614	28,575	1982 (AL)
Cincinnati Reds	68	94	.420	35 ½	Bryan Price	Dick Williams	1,894,085	23,384	1990

WEST	W	L	PCT	GB	Manager	General Manager	Attendance	Average	Last Penn.
Los Angeles Dodgers	91	71	.562	—	Dave Roberts	Farhan Zaidi	3,703,312	45,720	1988
* San Francisco Giants	87	75	.537	4	Bruce Bochy	Bobby Evans	3,365,256	41,546	2014
Colorado Rockies	75	87	.463	16	Walt Weiss	Jeff Bridich	2,602,524	32,130	2007
Arizona Diamondbacks	69	93	.426	22	Chip Hale	Dave Stewart	2,036,216	25,138	2001
San Diego Padres	68	94	.420	23	Andy Green	A.J. Preller	2,351,422	29,030	1998

Wild Card Game: Giants defeated Mets. **Division Series:** Cubs defeated Giants 3-1 and Dodgers defeated Nationals 3-2 in best-of-five series. **Championship Series:** Cubs defeated Dodgers 4-2 in best-of-seven series.

National League batting title but it came with some controversy after manager Walt Weiss decided to hold the second baseman out of the final two games of the season to protect his lead over Nationals second baseman Daniel Murphy.

LeMahieu finished with a .348 average, one point better than Murphy. It was highest mark in the major leagues since 2008 when the Braves' Chipper Jones hit .354.

Murphy flied out in his lone at-bat on the last day of the season. He was limited to just three pinch-hitting appearances over the final 14 games because of a strained muscle in his buttocks.

"It was unique in that the other guy he was battling with wasn't playing," Weiss said. "If they're both playing and going at it, that's one thing. I didn't want him to lose it that way."

The Rockies, taking advantage of playing half their games in the mile-high altitude of Denver at Coors Field, won their ninth batting title in 19 seasons.

Astros second baseman Jose Altuve hit .338 and won his second American League batting title in three years. He won by 20 points over Red Sox second baseman Dustin Pedroia, who finished at .318.

"I have to thank all the guys on the team," Altuve said. "They went outside to the field and played hard, and that kind of encouraged me and pushed me to keep playing hard every day.

Right fielder Mark Trumbo made it four straight Orioles to lead the major leagues in home runs as he belted 47 in his first season after being acquired from the Mariners in a trade.

Trumbo followed Chris Davis (2013, 2015) and Nelson Cruz (2014) in pacing the AL in longballs. That is the longest stretch for one team's players to top the AL since the Yankees from 1923-31 with Babe Ruth, Lou Gehrig and Bob Meusel. Baltimore led the majors with 253 home runs as a team,

Rockies third baseman Nolan Arenado and Brewers first baseman Chris Carter tied for the NL homer lead with 41. Arenado also topped the NL with 133 RBIs while Blue Jays first baseman Edwin Encarnacion and Red Sox DH David Ortiz, who retired at the end of the season, had 127 each to tie for tops in the AL.

Blue Jays righthander Aaron Sanchez won the AL ERA title at 3.00, finishing in style as he allowed one run in seven innings on the season's finale day to beat the Red Sox and give Toronto the second AL wild-card berth. Sanchez's ERA was the highest for any league leader since the Angels' John Lackey had a 3.01 mark in 2007.

Cubs righthander Kyle Hendricks' 2.13 ERA

D.J. LeMahieu won the ninth batting title for the Rockies in the last 19 seasons

was the best in the major leagues. Eight qualifiers in the NL finished with sub-3.00 ERAs.

Red Sox righthander Rick Porcello led the majors in wins as he went 22-4 while Nationals righthander Max Scherzer went 20-7 to top the NL in victories. Scherzer also led the majors with 284 strikeouts, his first strikeout crown of his career, while former Tigers teammate Justin Verlander led the AL with 254, his fourth AL strikeout crown. On May 11, Scherzer became the fourth pitcher with 20 strikeouts in a nine-inning game. It marked the fifth time overall that a pitcher reached 20.

Mets closer Jeurys Familia led the major leagues in saves with 51 and the Orioles' Zach Britton topped the AL by going a perfect 47-for-47. Familia was then arrested after the season on a domestic violence charge.

Brewers infielder Jonathan Villar's 62 stolen bases were the most in the major leagues. On the down side, the Brewers' 1,543 strikeouts set a major league record as they had eight more than the Astros in 2013.

Indians outfielder Rajai Davis topped the AL with 43 (as Cleveland led the majors with 134 as a team). Davis' total was 24 more than the Orioles' team total of 19, which was the fewest by major league team since the Tigers had 17 in 1972.

Scully, Ortiz Call It Quits

One of baseball's greatest broadcasters and one

ALL-ROOKIE TEAM 2016

Pos	PLAYER, TEAM	AGE	AB	AVG	OBP	SLG	2B	HR	RBI	SB	RUNDOWN
C	Gary Sanchez, Yankees	23	201	.299	.376	.657	12	20	42	1	Looks like a perennial all-star catcher
1B	Tommy Joseph, Phillies	24	315	.257	.308	.505	15	21	47	1	Bat took off after concussions forced move off catcher
2B	Trea Turner, Nationals	23	307	.342	.370	.567	14	13	40	33	Blazing speed and surprising power made him a fixture
3B	Ryon Healy, Athletics	24	269	.305	.337	.524	20	13	37	0	Led the Athletics with an .861 OPS
SS	Corey Seager, Dodgers	22	627	.308	.365	.512	40	26	72	3	Top prospect led all rookies in average, slugging and more
CF	Tyler Naquin, Indians	25	321	.296	.372	.514	18	14	43	6	Stepped into a void to claim the Indians' center field job
OF	David Dahl, Rockies	22	222	.315	.359	.500	12	7	24	5	Tied rookie record with hits in his first 17 games
OF	Nomar Mazara, Rangers	21	516	.266	.320	.419	13	20	64	0	Known for power, produced 20 homers in debut season
DH	Trevor Story, Rockies	23	372	.272	.341	.567	21	27	72	8	27 homers topped all rookies despite missing two months

Pos	PITCHER, TEAM	AGE	W	L	SV	ERA	IP	SO	BB	RUNDOWN
SP	Tyler Anderson, Rockies	26	5	6	0	3.54	114	99	28	2011 first-round pick thrived on sharp control
SP	Jon Gray, Rockies	24	10	10	0	4.61	168	185	59	Led rookies in strikeouts thanks to fierce slider
SP	Michael Fulmer, Tigers	23	11	7	0	3.06	159	132	42	Stabilized Tigers' rotation behind Justin Verlander
SP	Kenta Maeda, Dodgers	28	16	11	0	3.48	176	179	50	Japanese import lived up to his billing in first season
SP	Steven Matz, Mets	25	9	8	0	3.40	132	129	31	Built on big-game experience from late 2015
RP	Chris Devenski, Astros	25	4	4	1	2.16	108	104	20	Limited opponents to a .206 average with a 0.91 WHIP

of the sport's top sluggers both retired at the end of the season.

Scully stepped down after 67 years as a Dodgers' play-by-play announcer, dating to 1950, which was eight years before the franchise moved to Los Angeles from Brooklyn.

Though the Dodgers won their fourth consecutive NL West title, Scully opted to call his last game in the regular-season finale Oct. 2, a 7-1 loss to the Giants at AT&T Park at San Francisco. The 88-year-old said he did not want to be a distraction to the team during the postseason.

Scully's final game came exactly 80 years to the day that the Bronx-born Scully became a Giants' fan in 1936.

"It was as if it was ordained," Scully said during the game. "I hope you're enjoying it and I hope I'm not interrupting it too much."

In that same spirit, Scully authored a very simple signoff, saying, "I have said enough for a lifetime, and for the last time, I wish you all a very pleasant good afternoon."

Red Sox DH David Ortiz headed the list of players who played their final seasons in 2016 and went out on top despite the Red Sox being swept by the Indians in three games in the American League Division Series.

The 40-year-old led the league in doubles (48), RBIs (127), slugging percentage (.620) and OPS (1.021). He also batted .315 with 38 home runs in 151 games.

Ortiz finished his career with a .286 batting average, 541 homers and 1,768 RBIs in 2,408 games over 20 seasons with the Twins (1997-2002) and Red Sox (2003-16). He was selected to play in 10 All-Star Games, won six Silver Sluggers, finished in the top five of AL MVP balloting on five different occasions and was the MVP of the 2013 World Series when the Red Sox beat the Cardinals

in six games.

Ortiz also helped the Red Sox win world titles in 2004, 2007 and 2013. Prior to that, the franchise's last World Series victory came in 1918. He also served as spokesman for the whole city for some after addressing the crowd following the 2013 Boston Marathon bombing and helped key the "Boston Strong" movement.

Ortiz was feted in a pregame ceremony before the Red Sox's season finale and the team announced it will retire his No. 34 next season.

During a pregame ceremony attended by Red Sox greats like Carl Yastrzemski and teammates from Ortiz's three World Series championships, the ballclub honored him by draping a Dominican flag over the Green Monster and bringing out his father to join him on the diamond.

Ortiz broke into tears when he mentioned his late mother before gathering himself to thank his teammates and various members of the organization from owner John Henry to clubhouse attendant Pookie Jackson.

He also thanked the fans by dropping to one knee and tipping his cap to the crowd before expressing his gratitude to Commissioner Manfred and Dominican Republic President Danilo Medina, who were both in attendance.

"I almost dropped to two knees but I would have had a hard time getting up at my age," Ortiz cracked.

"He changed the Red Sox," Manfred said. "He was a key part of the amazing three wins here. It changed the course of the franchise but I also think that he changed the city. He became a symbol of the strength of the city and will always be remembered for that."

While it wasn't officially announced as a retirement, Alex Rodriguez played his final game with the Yankees on Aug. 12 against the Rays, five days

after the team announced it was planning to release the 41-year-old DH.

The sellout Yankee Stadium crowd of 46,459 gave him standing ovations and chanted his name, admiration and perhaps even affection coming out after more than a decade of trouble and tension that included being suspended for the entire 2014 season for violating MLB's performance enhancing drug policy.

"I've given these fans a lot of headaches over the years and I've disappointed a lot of people," Rodriguez said after a 6-3 victory over the public-address system. "But like I've always said, you don't have to be defined by your mistakes. How you come back matters, too, and that's what New York's all about."

Rodriguez hit just .200 with nine home runs and 31 RBIs in 65 games in his 12th and final season with the Yankees. Though Rodriguez declined an offer to sign with the Marlins after his last game in New York, he left open the possibility of continuing to play in 2017.

Rodriguez's 696 home runs rank fourth on the career list behind Barry Bonds (762), Hank Aaron (755) and Babe Ruth (714).

The Yankees paid him $7,103,825 for the rest of 2016 and owe him $20 million for 2017, which would be the final year of his 10-year, $275-million contract.

The final day of the regular season also marked the end for first baseman Mark Teixeira as the 36-year-old decided to retire after 14 years. The 2000 College Player of the Year at Georgia Tech and the No. 5 overall pick in 2001, Teixeira won five Gold Gloves and three Silver Sluggers while being selected to three All-Star Games. He finished with a .268 batting average, 409 homers and 1,298 during a game spent with the Rangers (2003-07), Braves (2007-08), Angels (2008) and Yankees (2009-2016).

"Mentally and emotionally, I kind of prepared for it," Teixeira said after a 5-2 loss to the Orioles at Yankee Stadium in his finale. "It wasn't as weird as I thought it would be."

Rangers DH Prince Fielder was forced into retirement Aug. 10, 12 days after having a second cervical fusion surgery in his neck. The 32-year-old ended his career sooner than he wanted.

"To not be able to play, it's going to be tough," Fielder said.

When the Rangers acquired him in November 2013 from the Tigers for in a trade for Ian Kinsler, Fielder had played at least 157 games every year since 2006, and appeared in 809 of 810 possible games during the previous five seasons. However, Fielder was limited to 289 games in four seasons with the Rangers because of two neck surgeries in just more than two years.

Fielder finished his career with 319 home runs, the same number as his father Cecil Fielder though in 141 fewer games. The only other father-son duo with more than 300 homers each is Bobby and Barry Bonds.

Over 1,611 games with the Brewers (2005-11), Tigers (2012-13) and Rangers (2014-16), Fielder was a six-time All-Star who hit .283 with 1,028 RBIs.

White Sox first baseman Adam LaRoche opted to walk away from the White Sox on March 18 when club president Ken Williams asked the 36-year-old to limit the amount of time his 14-year-old son Drake spent in the team's clubhouse. LaRoche forfeited his $13-million salary by opting to retire. LaRoche and a group of ex-big leaguers including Josh Beckett, Roger Clemens, Tim Hudson and J.D. Drew did return to the field in August, playing in the National Baseball Congress World Series in Wichita, Kan. The club, called the Kansas Stars, lost in the NBC semifinals to the amateur Hays Larks.

Another Hall of Fame broadcaster, Dick Enberg, also retired after six seasons calling of Padres' games. He also was part of the Angels' broadcast team for 10 years and did the Game of the Week on NBC for six seasons.

Astros television play-by-play broadcaster Bill Brown retired after 30 seasons in Houston. He called major league games for a total of 38 seasons, including seven with the Reds and one with the Pirates.

Ryan, La Russa Out

It was a relatively quiet year for in-season firings as only one general manager and one manager got the axe, though another change happened soon after the season ended.

The Twins fired longtime GM Terry Ryan on July 17 with his team holding a 33-58 record that was the worst in the American League on their way to finishing with the worst mark in the major leagues at 59-103.

"Sometimes you may have to do things that are hard," Twins owner Jim Pohlad said. "I never try to shy away from hard decisions. I own this decision."

Rob Antony, in his 29th season with the organization and ninth as the team's assistant GM, took over on an interim basis through the end of the season. The Twins then hired Indians assistant GM Derek Falvey to oversee the baseball operations in the newly created post of chief baseball officer while Rangers assistant GM Thad Levine was hired to be GM.

Ryan spent two stints as GM, taking over in September 1994 and helping the franchise eventually become one of the models for small-market success in the early 2000s. He helped build one of baseball's strongest farm systems and made several shrewd trades that turned the Twins into a team that won four AL Central titles in five seasons.

The Braves fired manager Fredi Gonzalez on May 17 following a dismal 9-28 start, replacing him with Brian Snitker, a 40-year veteran of the organization and manager of their Triple-A Gwinnett farm club.

"It was wearing on (Gonzalez), how we were playing and what was going on," Braves director of baseball operations John Hart said. "We just thought this was the right thing to do."

Gonzalez went 434-413 in five-plus seasons in Atlanta, including leading the Braves to the NL East title in 2013, their 17th postseason appearance in 22 years. Yet what began as a slow slide in 2014 accelerated quickly over the last 10 months. Atlanta went 34-81 in Gonzalez's last 115 games, as the Braves traded many of their experienced players and began a youth movement.

The Braves went 59-65 under Snitker to finish 67-94 and he was named the permanent manager at the end of the season.

Meanwhile, manager Robin Ventura walked away from the White Sox at the end of the season while Walt Weiss was fired by the Rockies and Chip Hale was axed by the Diamondbacks, who had their own convulsions in the front office.

Arizona brought aboard Hall of Fame manager Tony La Russa as chief baseball officer two years ago, and La Russa hired Dave Stewart as GM and De Jon Watson as assistant GM. The trio's most notable moves included trading three players, including 2015 No. 1 draft pick Dansby Swanson, to the Braves for Shelby Miller, who flopped in his first season in the desert, as well as a mammoth six-year, $206.5 million deal for Zack Greinke.

The Diamondbacks went 69-93 in 2016, and ownership fired Stewart and Watson while shifting La Russa to a lesser role as chief baseball analyst. Mike Hazen, previously with the Red Sox, arrived as GM and brought former Boston scouting director Amiel Sawdaye with him as assistant GM. They tabbed Red Sox bench coach Torey Lovullo to replace Hale, who went 148-176 in his two-year stint.

"We feel very strongly that we have found the ideal candidate to lead our baseball operations," said Ken Kendrick, who has fired four general managers—Joe Garagiola Jr., Josh Byrnes, Kevin Towers and now Stewart—since taking over as managing general partner in 2004.

The White Sox promoted bench coach Rick

Renteria to replace Ventura, who had a 435-463 record in five seasons. Colorado tabbed former Padres manager Bud Black to take over for Weiss, who compiled a 283-365 mark over four years.

CONTINUED ON PAGE 19

AMERICAN LEAGUE BEST TOOLS

A Baseball America survey of American League managers, conducted at midseason 2016, ranked players with the best tools.

BEST HITTER
1. Mike Trout, Angels
2. Jose Altuve, Astros
3. Miguel Cabrera, Tigers

BEST CONTROL
1. Marco Estrada, Blue Jays
2. Josh Tomlin, Indians
3. Dallas Keuchel, Astros

BEST POWER
1. Mark Trumbo, Orioles
2. Chris Davis, Orioles
3. Edwin Encarnacion, Blue Jays

BEST PICKOFF MOVE
1. R.A. Dickey, Blue Jays
2. Nick Tropeano, Angels
3. Justin Verlander, Tigers

BEST BUNTER
1. Adam Eaton, White Sox
2. Billy Burns, Royals
3. Elvis Andrus, Rangers

BEST RELIEVER
1. Zach Britton, Orioles
2. Andrew Miller, Indians
3. Dellin Betances, Yankees

BEST STRIKE-ZONE JUDGMENT
1. Josh Donaldson, Blue Jays
2. David Ortiz, Red Sox
3. Mike Trout, Angels

BEST DEFENSIVE CATCHER
1. Salvador Perez, Royals
2. Yan Gomes, Indians
3. Russell Martin, Blue Jays

BEST HIT-AND-RUN ARTIST
1. Alcides Escobar, Royals
2. Jose Altuve, Astros
3. Elvis Andrus, Rangers

BEST DEFENSIVE 1B
1. Eric Hosmer, Royals
2. Mitch Moreland, Rangers
3. Mark Teixeira, Yankees

BEST BASERUNNER
1. Jose Altuve, Astros
2. Mookie Betts, Red Sox
3. Mike Trout, Angels

BEST DEFENSIVE 2B
1. Jose Altuve, Astros
2. Dustin Pedroia, Red Sox
3. Jason Kipnis, Indians

FASTEST BASERUNNER
1. Jarrod Dyson, Royals
2. Byron Buxton, Twins
3. Rajai Davis, Indians

BEST DEFENSIVE 3B
1. Manny Machado, Orioles
2. Adrian Beltre, Rangers
3. Josh Donaldson, Blue Jays

MOST EXCITING PLAYER
1. Mike Trout, Angels
2. Jose Altuve, Astros
3. David Ortiz, Red Sox

BEST DEFENSIVE SS
1. Andrelton Simmons, Angels
2. Francisco Lindor, Indians
3. Jose Iglesias, Tigers

BEST PITCHER
1. Chris Sale, White Sox
2. Danny Salazar, Indians
3. Cole Hamels, Rangers

BEST INFIELD ARM
1. Manny Machado, Orioles
2. Andrelton Simmons, Angels
3. Didi Gregorius, Yankees

BEST FASTBALL
1. Aroldis Chapman, Yankees
2. Zach Britton, Orioles
3. Chris Sale, White Sox

BEST DEFENSIVE OF
1. Jackie Bradley, Red Sox
2. Kevin Kiermaier, Rays
3. Kevin Pillar, Blue Jays

BEST CURVEBALL
1. Dellin Betances, Yankees
2. David Robertson, White Sox
3. Sonny Gray, Athletics

BEST OUTFIELD ARM
1. Kole Calhoun, Angels
2. Aaron Hicks, Yankees
3. Byron Buxton, Twins

BEST SLIDER
1. Andrew Miller, Indians
2. Chris Sale, White Sox
3. Michael Fulmer, Tigers

BEST MANAGER
1. Terry Francona, Indians
2. Buck Showalter, Orioles
3. John Gibbons, Blue Jays

BEST CHANGEUP
1. Marco Estrada, Blue Jays
2. Dallas Keuchel, Astros
3. Danny Salazar, Indians

Cubs' process gets results

BY KYLE GLASER

When team president Theo Epstein and general manager Jed Hoyer took over the Cubs' front office in Oct. 2011, their first item of business had nothing to do with the on-field product.

Every aspect of the Cubs baseball operations department, from the executives with corner offices at Wrigley Field to the scouts traversing the globe, was short-handed. Years of penny-pinching under Tribune Co. ownership had cut down the Cubs' number of scouts to 10 on the pro side and 47 on the amateur and international sides combined, limiting the franchise's ability to discover and evaluate talent, simply because they didn't have the manpower.

This, before anything else, was what Epstein and Hoyer, financed by new owner Tom Ricketts and family, knew they needed to address for the Cubs to ever become championship-caliber.

"It was a big priority for us," Hoyer said in November at the general manager meetings. "Everything—office staff, scouts, player development staff. Under Tribune they ran so lean it was kind of on us to push the numbers up a little bit."

Five years later, the front office overhaul was evident, with the Cubs' results on the field a direct result. The Cubs had 26 people in their pro scouting department in 2016. They also had 53 scouts on the amateur and international side, a modest but still notable increase.

The extra bodies allowed the Cubs to identify under-the-radar trade targets such as Kyle

BILL NICHOLS

Team president Theo Epstein helped build the Cubs into a winning franchise

Hendricks and Jake Arrieta, as well as make the accurate judgment that Anthony Rizzo and Addison Russell would be worth high prices in trades. It allowed them to take advantage of high draft position (and large bonus pools) resulting from five straight fifth-place finishes from 2010-2014 to nail Kris Bryant, Kyle Schwarber and Albert Almora with the new regime's first three first-round draft picks. It allowed them to correctly assess that Jon Lester, John Lackey and Ben Zobrist would be worthwhile veteran signings, even at a steep cost.

The infrastructure Epstein, Hoyer and Co. put in place culminated in the Cubs winning 103 games, making their first World Series appearance since 1945 and, of course, winning their first World Series since 1908. For that, the Cubs are Baseball America's Organization of the Year.

"It's over-talked about, but every team has their own way of doing things, and we were trying to make the 'Cubs Way' inclusive," Hoyer said. "Have everybody have their opinions heard and have it be sort of an organic thing. I think that was a big part of it. We weren't trying to dictate our own philosophy. We were trying to build a philosophy with the people here and I think that was effective."

PREVIOUS WINNERS

2003: Florida Marlins
2004: Minnesota Twins
2005: Atlanta Braves
2006: Los Angeles Dodgers
2007: Colorado Rockies
2008: Tampa Bay Rays
2009: Philadelphia Phillies
2010: San Francisco Giants
2011: St. Louis Cardinals
2012: Cincinnati Reds:
2013: St. Louis Cardinals
2014: Kansas City Royals
2015: Pittsburgh Pirates

Full list: BaseballAmerica.com/awards

Fort Bragg Game

One the most unique moments of the season occurred July 3 when the Braves and Marlins played in a temporary ballpark at Fort Bragg, N.C., marking the first regular-season game in any major North American professional sports league to be played at an active military installation. It also was the first MLB game ever played in the state of North Carolina.

The Marlins won 5-2 as lefthander Adam Conley pitched six innings in a game that was televised as part of ESPN's Sunday Night Baseball package.

"I know, for me, this has been my favorite place to ever pitch in my life," Conley said. "This is the most memorable place I've ever pitched."

J.T. Realmuto homered and drove in two runs and Christian Yelich also finished with two RBIs. He and Realmuto had run-scoring singles during a two-run fifth.

The ballpark was built from scratch in less than four months at the sprawling Army post that is home to 55,000 service members, including the famed paratroopers of the 82nd Airborne Division.

In a joint effort from by Major League Baseball and the Major League Baseball Players Association, an overgrown golf course was transformed into a major league-caliber field surrounded by temporary stands that were packed by 12,582 service members. Most of the seats closest to the action were reserved for disabled veterans.

"The bad part is, we lost the game," Braves manager Brian Snitker said. "The good part is, it's something I'll never forget the rest of my life."

Meanwhile the Braves said goodbye to Turner Field on the last day of the regular season following a 1-0 victory over the Tigers.

The Braves will move into SunTrust Park in suburban Cobb County, Ga., in 2017 after spending just 20 years at Turner Field, which was refitted as a baseball stadium after being built to host track and field events along with the opening and closing ceremonies of the 1996 Summer Olympics.

Turner Field will go through another conversion to become the downsized home of the Georgia State football team.

A sellout crowd of 51,220 attended the finale, including former President Jimmy Carter and his wife, Rosalynn. For a franchise known for its pitching—Hall of Famers Tom Glavine, Greg Maddux and John Smoltz all figured prominently in the pre-game ceremonies—it was only fitting that the Braves left with a shutout as Julio Teheran struck out 12 in seven innings while combining with Jose

Ramirez and Jim Johnson on a five-hitter.

Then it was on to a postgame ceremony that included the removal of home plate, which was taken by Braves great Hank Aaron and team chair-

CONTINUED ON PAGE 21

NATIONAL LEAGUE BEST TOOLS

A Baseball America survey of National League managers, conducted at midseason 2016, ranked players with the best tools.

BEST HITTER
1. Daniel Murphy, Nationals
2. Paul Goldschmidt, D-backs
3. Nolan Arenado, Rockies

BEST CONTROL
1. Clayton Kershaw, Dodgers
2. Zack Greinke, Diamondbacks
3. Johnny Cueto, Giants

BEST POWER
1. Giancarlo Stanton, Marlins
2. Kris Bryant, Cubs
3. Nolan Arenado, Rockies

BEST PICKOFF MOVE
1. Julio Teheran, Braves
2. Clayton Kershaw, Dodgers
3. Johnny Cueto, Giants

BEST BUNTER
1. Dee Gordon, Marlins
2. Billy Hamilton, Reds
3. Starling Marte, Pirates

BEST RELIEVER
1. Jeurys Familia, Mets
2. Kenley Jansen, Dodgers
3. Mark Melancon, Nationals

BEST STRIKE-ZONE JUDGMENT
1. Joey Votto, Reds
2. Ben Zobrist, Cubs
3. Matt Carpenter, Cardinals

BEST DEFENSIVE CATCHER
1. Yadier Molina, Cardinals
2. Buster Posey, Giants
3. Jonathan Lucroy, Brewers

BEST HIT-AND-RUN ARTIST
1. Martin Prado, Marlins
2. Yadier Molina, Cardinals
3. D.J. LeMahieu, Rockies

BEST DEFENSIVE 1B
1. Paul Goldschmidt, D-backs
2. Anthony Rizzo, Cubs
3. Brandon Belt, Giants

BEST BASERUNNER
1. Starling Marte, Pirates
2. Billy Hamilton, Reds
3. Dee Gordon, Marlins

BEST DEFENSIVE 2B
1. D.J. LeMahieu, Rockies
2. Brandon Phillips, Reds
3. Joe Panik, Giants

FASTEST BASERUNNER
1. Billy Hamilton, Reds
2. Dee Gordon, Marlins
3. Starling Marte, Pirates

BEST DEFENSIVE 3B
1. Nolan Arenado, Rockies
2. Anthony Rendon, Nationals
3. Matt Duffy, Giants

MOST EXCITING PLAYER
1. Bryce Harper, Nationals
2. Nolan Arenado, Rockies
3. Kris Bryant, Cubs

BEST DEFENSIVE SS
1. Brandon Crawford, Giants
2. Adeiny Hechavarria, Marlins
3. Zack Cozart, Reds

BEST PITCHER
1. Clayton Kershaw, Dodgers
2. Madison Bumgarner, Giants
3. Jake Arrieta, Cubs

BEST INFIELD ARM
1. Brandon Crawford, Giants
2. Nolan Arenado, Rockies
3. Danny Espinosa, Nationals

BEST FASTBALL
1. Noah Syndergaard, Mets
2. Max Scherzer, Nationals
3. Jeurys Familia, Mets

BEST DEFENSIVE OF
1. Starling Marte, Pirates
2. Jason Heyward, Cubs
3. Billy Hamilton, Reds

BEST CURVEBALL
1. Clayton Kershaw, Dodgers
2. Stephen Strasburg, Nationals
3. Adam Wainwright, Cardinals

BEST OUTFIELD ARM
1. Yasiel Puig, Dodgers
2. Yoenis Cespedes, Mets
3. Carlos Gonzalez, Rockies

BEST SLIDER
1. Jose Fernandez, Marlins
2. Clayton Kershaw, Dodgers
3. Max Scherzer, Nationals

BEST MANAGER
1. Bruce Bochy, Giants
2. Joe Maddon, Cubs
3. Mike Matheny, Cardinals

BEST CHANGEUP
1. Zack Greinke, Diamondbacks
2. Kyle Hendricks, Cubs
3. Fernando Rodney, Marlins

MAJOR LEAGUES

With David Ortiz retiring, Mookie Betts is primed to be the new face of the Red Sox

Max Scherzer led the majors in strikeouts in addition to winning 20 games

FIRST TEAM

Pos	Player, Team	AVG	OBP	SLG	AB	R	H	2B	3B	HR	RBI	BB	SO	SB	CS
C	Jonathan Lucroy, Brewers/Rangers	.292	.355	.500	490	67	143	24	3	24	81	47	100	5	0
1B	Anthony Rizzo, Cubs	.292	.385	.544	583	94	170	43	4	32	109	74	108	3	5
2B	Jose Altuve, Astros	.338	.396	.531	640	108	216	42	5	24	96	60	70	30	10
3B	Kris Bryant, Cubs	.292	.385	.554	603	121	176	35	3	39	102	75	154	8	5
SS	Manny Machado, Orioles	.294	.343	.533	640	105	188	40	1	37	96	48	120	0	3
CF	Mike Trout, Angels	.315	.441	.550	549	123	173	32	5	29	100	116	137	30	7
OF	Mookie Betts, Red Sox	.318	.363	.534	672	122	214	42	5	31	113	49	80	26	4
OF	Nelson Cruz, Mariners	.287	.360	.555	589	96	169	27	1	43	105	62	159	2	0
DH	David Ortiz, Red Sox	.315	.401	.620	537	79	169	48	1	38	127	80	86	2	0

Pos	Player, Team	W	L	ERA	G	GS	SV	IP	H	R	ER	HR	BB	SO	WHIP
SP	Madison Bumgarner, Giants	15	9	2.74	34	34	0	227	178	79	69	26	54	251	1.02
SP	Johnny Cueto, Giants	18	5	2.79	32	32	0	220	195	71	68	15	45	198	1.09
SP	Jon Lester, Cubs	19	5	2.44	32	32	0	203	154	57	55	21	52	197	1.02
SP	Max Scherzer, Nationals	20	7	2.96	34	34	0	228	165	77	75	31	56	284	0.97
SP	Justin Verlander, Tigers	16	9	3.04	34	34	0	228	171	81	77	30	57	254	1.00
RP	Zach Britton, Orioles	2	1	0.54	69	0	47	67	38	7	4	1	18	74	0.84

SECOND TEAM

Pos	Player, Team	AVG	OBP	SLG	AB	R	H	2B	3B	HR	RBI	BB	SO	SB	CS
C	Buster Posey, Giants	.288	.362	.434	539	82	155	33	2	14	80	64	68	6	1
1B	Freddie Freeman, Braves	.302	.400	.569	589	102	178	43	6	34	91	89	171	6	1
2B	Robinson Cano, Mariners	.298	.350	.533	655	107	195	33	2	39	103	47	100	0	1
3B	Josh Donaldson, Blue Jays	.284	.404	.549	577	122	164	32	5	37	99	109	119	7	1
SS	Corey Seager, Dodgers	.308	.365	.512	627	105	193	40	5	26	72	54	133	3	3
CF	Charlie Blackmon, Rockies	.324	.381	.552	578	111	187	35	5	29	82	43	102	17	9
OF	Yoenis Cespedes, Mets	.280	.354	.530	479	72	134	25	1	31	86	51	108	3	1
OF	Christian Yelich, Marlins	.298	.376	.483	578	78	172	38	3	21	98	72	138	9	4
DH	Daniel Murphy, Nationals	.347	.390	.595	531	88	184	47	5	25	104	35	57	5	3

Pos	Player, Team	W	L	ERA	G	GS	SV	IP	H	R	ER	HR	BB	SO	WHIP
SP	Jose Fernandez, Marlins	16	8	2.86	29	29	0	182	149	63	58	13	55	253	1.12
SP	Kyle Hendricks, Cubs	16	8	2.15	30	30	0	188	142	53	45	15	43	169	0.98
SP	Clayton Kershaw, Dodgers	12	4	1.69	21	21	0	149	97	31	28	8	11	172	0.72
SP	Corey Kluber, Indians	18	9	3.14	32	32	0	215	170	82	75	22	57	227	1.06
SP	Rick Porcello, Red Sox	22	4	3.15	33	33	0	223	193	85	78	23	32	189	1.01
RP	Andrew Miller, Yankees/Indians	10	1	1.45	70	0	12	74	42	13	12	8	9	123	0.69

EXECUTIVE OF THE YEAR

Chris Antonetti

After six seasons as the Indians' general manager, Antonetti was promoted to team president for the 2016 season. In the new role, the Georgetown product watched as the team he'd helped put together won the franchise's first pennant since 1997 and came a run away from its first World Series victory since 1948. Corey Kluber and Trevor Bauer—both integral parts of of the team's regular-season rotation—were acquired through Antonetti-authored trades. The Indians got close in 2015, but took the final leaps forward this season and dominated the American League Central en route to 94 wins, a total second only in the AL to the Rangers. Antonetti's other key move was the hiring of Terry Francona, the savvy skipper who piloted the team to the brink of October ecstacy.

PREVIOUS WINNERS

2004: Terry Ryan, Twins
2005: Mark Shapiro, Indians
2006: Dave Dombrowski, Tigers
2007: Jack Zduriencik, Brewers
2008: Theo Epstein, Red Sox
2009: Dan O'Dowd, Rockies
2010: Jon Daniels, Rangers
2011: Doug Melvin, Brewers
2012: Billy Beane, Athletics
2013: Dan Duquette, Orioles
2014: Dan Duquette, Orioles
2015: Sandy Alderson, Mets

Full list: BaseballAmerica.com/awards

MANAGER OF THE YEAR

Terry Francona

In his lengthy career, Terry Francona has managed Michael Jordan in the minors, led the Red Sox to their first two World Series titles since 1918, and then helped guide this year's Indians into the Fall Classic and nearly into the winner's circle. The four losses in this year's Series were, in fact, the first of his career. Part of what helped push the Indians over the edge this year was Francona's willingness to buck tradition. When the team acquired Andrew Miller from the Yankees at midseason, it would have been easy to plug him into the ninth and keep him there. In the postseason, however, Francona freestyled. He used the nearly unhittable Miller whenever the situation dictated, and the results were nearly perfect. With a few key moves, Francona nearly put his team on top.

PREVIOUS WINNERS

2004: Bobby Cox, Braves
2005: Ozzie Guillen, White Sox
2006: Jim Leyland, Tigers
2007: Terry Francona, Red Sox
2008: Ron Gardenhire, Twins
2009: Mike Scioscia, Angels
2010: Bobby Cox, Braves
2011: Joe Maddon, Rays
2012: Buck Showalter, Orioles
2013: Clint Hurdles, Pirates
2014: Buck Showalter, Orioles
2015: Joe Maddon, Cubs

Full list: BaseballAmerica.com/awards

CONTINUED FROM PAGE 19

man Terry McGuirk on a police-escorted ride to SunTrust Park.

"That's the way we all wanted to finish and close this book," Teheran said.

Milestone Stories

As usual, there were many milestones throughout the season, with three rookies who play up-the-middle positions impressing as much as any milestone makers.

Dodgers rookie Corey Seager set the single-season franchise record for home runs by a shortstop with his 23rd on Aug. 27. Seager hit .308/.365/.512 in his first full season with 40 doubles and 26 home runs, as he and his older brother, Mariners third baseman Kyle Seager, became the first brother tandem in MLB history to hit 25 home runs in the same season. Kyle hit a career-best 30 for Seattle.

Corey Seager set one record but still didn't lead NL shortstops in home runs, even though he played 157 games. That's because Rockies rookie shortstop Trevor Story started scorching hot, slowed only by a torn thumb ligament that ended his season two months early.

Story became the sixth player in major league history and first from the NL to hit two home runs in his debut. He was also the first to do so while

making his debut on Opening Day. Story homered again the next day to join Joe Cunningham of the 1954 Cardinals as the only players since 1900 with three home runs in his first two career games. Story became the first player in big league history to hit a home run in each of his first three games and have a homer as each of his four hits.

He hit two more home runs in his fourth game. That made him the first major leaguer ever with six home runs in his first four games and just the fifth major leaguer to homer in each of the first four games of the season.

Story hit yet another homer two games later. That made him the first player in big leaguer history seven homers in his first six games.

With his ninth home run on April 27, Story set an NL rookie record for home runs in April that had been set in 2001 by the Cardinals' Albert Pujols. Story went on to set the NL single-season record for home runs by a rookie shortstop when he connected for No. 25 on July 23, breaking the mark set by Troy Tulowitzki with the Rockies in 2007. He finished with 27.

The other notable rookie slugger was Yankees catcher Gary Sanchez, who became the fastest player in major league history to reach 11 home runs, doing so in his 23rd career game on Aug. 17. He became the first rookie to win consecutive player of the week awards, capturing honors for the weeks ending Aug. 21 and Aug. 28.

On Sept. 21. Sanchez became the quickest player in major League history to hit 19 home runs, doing so in his 45th game.

"We gave him first-round money for a reason," said Braves special assistant to the GM Gordon Blakely, who had been instrumental in signing Sanchez when he worked for the Yankees. The club gave Sanchez a $3 million bonus in 2009. "Personally, I thought he was going to be an all-star catcher and hit 25 home runs."

But he almost hit the 25 homers in half a season and almost singlehandedly got the Yankees, who embarked on a youth movement, back into the wild-card race in September.

Making a rookie splash is one thing, but doing it for 25 years is another, and no one has put up hits over a quarter-century like Marlins outfielder Ichiro Suzuki. He become the 30th member of the 3,000-hit club when he tripled against the Rockies on Aug. 7.

No other member of that exclusive club has Ichiro's resume, though, as he started his career in Japan's Nippon Professional Baseball, collecting 1,278 hits there before he came to the Mariners in 2001. The AL MVP and top rookie that year, he also reached the 500 stolen-base plateau in 2016,

With a triple in Colorado, Ichiro Suzuki reached 3,000 hits in his big league career

becoming the 38th player to do so, on April 29.

"Ichiro is one of the best hitters I've ever seen in my life," Mariners second baseman Robinson Cano said. "He's still impressive . . . not only the way he it hitting, but the way he's playing the outfield, his arm, and he can still run. He's fun to watch, and I love the way he plays."

Over 25 professional seasons between NPB and MLB, Ichiro finished the year with 4,308 career hits. "I think it would've been remarkable for him to play his whole career here," Cubs righthander Jake Arrieta said during the All-Star Game festivities, "just to see how many hits he could've actually had."

Arrieta couldn't quite repeat his Cy Young Award season of 2015, but he still pitched the lone no-hitter of the season—and second of his career—in a 16-0 rout of the Reds on April 21. He became the fourth reigning Cy Young Award winner to throw a no-hitter.

The Cubs' 16 runs were the most scored by the winning team in any no-hitter in the modern era (since 1900). The only no-hitter in which more runs were scored was in 1884, when the Buffalo Bisons defeated the Detroit Wolverines 18–0 behind a gem from Pud Galvin.

Arrieta also became the first pitcher to go unbeaten in the regular season between no-hitters since Johnny Vander Meer, who threw consecutive

CONTINUED ON PAGE 24

Hosmer leads AL to win

BY JOHN PERROTTO

Eric Hosmer was the first Royal to win All-Star Game MVP honors since 1989

BILL NICHOLS

SAN DIEGO

Eric Hosmer's first All-Star Game was memorable.

The Kansas City first baseman was named the game's MVP after he and Royals teammate Salvador Perez homered off of ex-teammate Johnny Cueto during a six-pitch span in the second inning to lead the American League to a 4-2 victory over the National League at Petco Park in San Diego on July 12.

Hosmer added an RBI single as the AL won for the fourth straight season.

"It's a great feeling," Hosmer said. "It's extremely humbling. Honestly, I was just so happy to be a part of all this and to be part of the team and make the All-Star Game for the first time. I never thought about becoming the MVP. I just wanted to soak up the whole experience, and it's everything and more you could every ask for."

The most touching moment was reserved for Red Sox DH David Ortiz, who was playing in his 10th and final All-Star Game before retiring at the end of the season.

The 40-year-old was embraced by his AL teammates near first base when he was lifted for pinch-runner Edwin Encarnacion of the Blue Jays in the third inning after drawing a walk from the Marlins' Jose Fernandez.

Fernandez, the 23-year-old wunderkind who would tragically die in a boating accident on Sept. 25, told Ortiz prior to the game that he would groove a fastball in hopes he would hit a home run in his last Midsummer Classic.

"My boy, on the first pitch, threw a change-up," Ortiz said with a smile. "Then 3-2 he threw me a slider and I'm like, 'Are you trying to break my back?' But he said it was the catcher's fault"

Indians righthander Corey Kluber pitched a perfect second inning for the win and Orioles closer Zach Britton was credited with the save.

Astros reliever Will Harris got the game's biggest out when he caught Cardinals rookie shortstop Aledmys Diaz looking on a 3-2 pitch with the bases loaded to end the eighth inning and preserve the AL's 4-2 lead.

2016 ALL-STAR GAME

JULY 12, 2016
AMERICAN LEAGUE 4, NATIONAL LEAGUE 2

National	AB	R	H	RBI	American	AB	R	H	RBI
Zobrist, 2B	2	0	0	0	Altuve, 2B	3	0	0	0
Murphy, PH-2B	3	0	2	0	Cano, 2B	0	0	0	0
Harper, RF	2	0	1	0	Nunez, 2B	0	0	0	0
Goldschmidt, PH-1B	3	0	0	0	Trout, CF	3	0	1	0
Bryant, 3B	2	1	1	1	Desmond, CF	1	0	0	0
Arenado, PH-3B	3	0	0	0	Machado, 3B	3	0	0	0
Myers, DH	3	0	1	0	Donaldson, 3B	1	0	0	0
Belt, PH-DH	1	0	0	0	Ortiz, DH	1	0	0	0
Posey, C	1	1	0	0	Encarnacion, PR-DH	1	1	0	0
Ramos, W, C	1	0	0	0	Bogaerts, SS	2	0	1	0
Lucroy, C	1	0	1	0	Lindor, PH-SS	2	0	0	0
Rizzo, 1B	2	0	1	0	Hosmer, 1B	3	1	2	2
Bruce, RF	2	0	0	0	Cabrera, M, 1B	1	0	0	0
Ozuna, CF	2	0	1	1	Betts, RF	2	1	1	0
Herrera, O, CF	1	0	0	0	Beltran, RF	1	0	0	0
Marte, S, PH-CF	1	0	1	0	Saunders, RF	1	0	0	0
Gonzalez, C, LF	2	0	1	0	Perez, S, C	2	1	1	2
Duvall, LF	1	0	0	0	Wieters, C	2	0	0	0
Russell, SS	2	0	0	0	Bradley Jr., LF	2	0	2	0
Seager, C, SS	1	0	0	0	Trumbo, LF	1	0	0	0
Diaz, A, PH-SS	1	0	0	0					
Totals	**32**	**4**	**8**	**4**	**Totals**	**37**	**2**	**10**	**2**

2B: Harper (1, Hamels); Myers (1, Quintana); Bogaerts (1, Fernandez). **HR:** Bryant (1, 1st inning off Sale, 0 on, 2 out); Hosmer (1, 2nd inning off Cueto, 0 on, 1 out); Perez, S (1, 2nd inning off Cueto, 1 on, 1 out). **RBI:** Bryant (1); Ozuna (1); Hosmer 2 (2); Perez, S 2 (2). **E:** Seager, C (1, fielding).; Altuve (1, fielding).

National	IP	H	R	SO	American	IP	H	R	SO
Cueto (L)	1.2	5	3	1	Sale	1.0	1	1	1
Fernandez	1.1	2	1	1	Kluber (W)	1.0	0	0	1
Pomeranz	1.0	1	0	0	Hamels	1.0	2	0	1
Teheran	1.0	0	0	0	Sanchez, Aa	1.0	2	1	0
Scherzer	1.0	0	0	1	Quintana	1.0	1	0	1
Lester	0.2	0	0	0	Herrera, K	1.0	0	0	1
Melancon	0.1	0	0	0	Betances	1.0	1	0	2
Rodney	0.2	0	0	1	Miller, A	0.2	2	0	1
Jansen	0.1	0	0	1	Harris	0.1	0	0	1
					Britton (S)	1.0	1	0	0

CONTINUED FROM PAGE 22

no-nos in 1938 for the Reds. Arrieta went 10-0 since no-hitting the Dodgers on Aug. 30, 2015.

In other milestones:

■ Tigers DH Victor Martinez became the first player in modern major league history to hit a pinch-hit home run in his team's first two regular-season games after connecting against the Marlins. Martinez also recorded his 1,000th career RBI on April 21 to become the 280th player and fifth Venezuelan-born player to reach the mark.

■ Nationals closer Jonathan Papelbon became the 11th major leaguer with 350 career saves April 4. However, the Nats released Papelbon in August.

■ Blue Jays lefthander Brett Cecil tied the major league record of 38 consecutive games pitched without allowing a run April 4 against the Rays. The reliever's streak ended the next day when the Rays' Logan Forsythe homered off Cecil.

■ Cubs righty John Lackey became the 16 pitcher to beat all 30 major league teams when he defeated the Cardinals on April 18. Lackey also recorded his 2,000th career strikeout May 6 to become the 75th pitcher to reach that milestone.

■ Braves catcher A.J. Pierzynski recorded his 2,000th career hit April 27 to become the 280th player to reach that plateau. He was expected to retire in the offseason.

■ Mets righthander Bartolo Colon became the oldest player to hit his first career home run when, at age 42 years, 349 days, he connected May 7 against the Padres. The previous oldest player was Randy Johnson at age 40 years, nine days.

■ Righthander Felix Hernandez became the Mariners' all-time winningest pitcher with his 146th career victory May 9 against the Rays. He broke Jamie Moyer's record. Hernandez notched

David Ortiz authored the best farewell season by a hitter in big league history

MIKE JULA, FOSTOFF PHOTOS

his 150th win Aug. 15 against the Angels, with three other veteran pitchers reaching the 150-win plateau for their careers during the season: Diamondbacks righthander Zack Greinke, Giants righthander Jake Peavy and Angels righthander Jered Weaver. Just 256 pitchers in MLB history have at least 150 career victories.

■ Red Sox DH David Ortiz belted his 600th career double May 14, becoming the 15th player to reach the milestone. He also became the third player to have at 500 home runs and 600 doubles in his career, joining Hank Aaron and Barry Bonds. Ortiz put up the best offensive season by a player in his final season, batting .315/.401/.620 to lead the AL in doubles (48) and slugging while belting 38 home runs.

■ Yankees DH Carlos Beltran became the 54th player reach 400 home runs May 5. He also became just the fourth switch-hitter to achieve that milestone. Beltran recorded his 2,500th career hit May 28. That made Beltran the 99th player, including the fourth born in Puerto Rico, to reach that mark. He also surpassed 1,500 runs scored, one of 72 players to do so, after being traded to the Rangers.

■ Tigers righthander Just Verlander became the 76th pitcher to get to 2,000 strikeouts when he whiffed the Twins' Eddie Rosario on May 18. Another Tigers star, first baseman Miguel Cabrera, hit his 500th career double May 23 to become the 62nd player to reach that mark then became

ACTIVE LEADERS

Career leaders among players who played in a game in 2016. Batters require 3,000 plate appearances and pitchers 1,000 innings to qualify for percentage titles.

BATTERS			PITCHERS		
AVG	Miguel Cabrera	.321	ERA	Clayton Kershaw	2.37
OBP	Joey Votto	.425	SO/9	Chris Sale	10.09
SLG	Albert Pujols	.573	BB/9	J. Zimmermann	1.85
OPS	Albert Pujols	.965	HR/9	Clayton Kershaw	0.54
R	Alex Rodriguez	2,021	W	CC Sabathia	223
H	Alex Rodriguez	3,115	L	CC Sabathia	141
2B	David Ortiz	632	SV	F. Rodriguez	430
3B	Jose Reyes	121	IP	CC Sabathia	3,168.1
HR	Alex Rodriguez	696	SO	CC Sabathia	2,726
RBI	Alex Rodriguez	2,086	BB	CC Sabathia	959
BB	Alex Rodriguez	1,338	AVG	Clayton Kershaw	.205
SO	Alex Rodriguez	2,287	G	F. Rodriguez	920
XBH	Alex Rodriguez	1,275	GS	CC Sabathia	482
SB	Ichiro Suzuki	508	HR	CC Sabathia	315

the 56th player to reach 1,500 RBIs on July 22. Finally, Cabrera became the 100th member of the 2,500-hit club Sept. 18.

■ Tigers closer Francisco Rodriguez became the sixth pitcher with 400 saves May 24.

■ Rangers third baseman Adrian Beltre drove in his 1,500th run May 28, becoming the 54th player to reach that plateau.

■ Giants shortstop Brandon Crawford became the sixth player in major league history to record seven hits in one game, during a 14-inning game against the Marlins on Aug. 8. The hits tied the NL record and set the franchise record.

■ Rockies outfielder David Dahl began his career with a 17-game hitting streak. His single on Aug. 11 against the Rangers tied the major-league record set by Chuck Aleno in 1941.

■ Blue Jays closer Roberto Osuna recorded his 47th career save on Aug. 17, setting a record for a pitcher under the age of 22.

■ Royals lefthander Danny Duffy set the franchise single-game record by striking out 16 on Aug. 1 against the Rays.

■ Pujols, the Angels' DH, recorded his 600th career double Sept. 16, becoming the 16th player to reach the. He also became the third player in major league history to amass 575 home runs and 600 doubles in his career, joining Aaron and Bonds.

Pujols became the fourth player to have 14 seasons with at least 30 home runs when he connected Sept. 17. He joined Aaron, Bonds and Alex Rodriguez in that club.

■ Rockies righthander Jon Gray, the No. 3 overall pick in the 2013 draft, set a franchise record with 16 strikeouts Sept. 17 against the Padres.

■ Rangers lefthander Cole Hamels recorded his 2,000th career strikeout June 12, getting Mariners center fielder Leonys Martin. Hamels became the 77th player to reach this mark.

■ Blue Jays righthander Marco Estrada had his 11th consecutive start allowing five hits or less while pitching at least six innings on June 21 to set the major league record.

■ Cubs third baseman Kris Bryant became the first player since at least 1913, the first year since records are available, to hit three homers and two doubles in one game, pulling off the feat June 27 against the Reds.

Numbers Game

All-time hits leader Pete Rose was among five players who had their numbers retired by their former teams, the Reds officially proclaiming that no would ever wear No. 14 again during a June 26 ceremony prior to a game against the Padres at

Closer Roberto Osuna led the Blue Jays back to the postseason with 36 saves

TOMASSO DEROSA

Great American Ball Park in Cincinnati.

Rose, a Cincinnati native, had 4,256 hits during his 24-year career from 1963-86, including 3,358 in 19 seasons with the Reds. He became the 10th player in team history to have his number retired and was inducted into the Reds' Hall of Fame.

Rose, of course, is ineligible for be considered for the National Baseball Hall of Fame in Cooperstown, N.Y, after being handed a lifetime ban from the sport in 1989 after an investigation by Major League Baseball found that he had bet on baseball games in violation of MLB rules.

"It solidifies what I've been saying for many, many, many years and will continue to say it: Cincinnati is the baseball capital of the world," Rose told the crowd.

Hall of Fame third baseman Wade Boggs' No. 26 was retired by the Red Sox on May 26 as he also became the 10th member of that organization to be bestowed with the honor.

Two players who won election to the Hall of Fame also had their numbers retired, Mike Piazza's No. 31 by the Mets on July 30 and Ken Griffey Jr.'s No. 24 by the Mariners on Aug. 6. Piazza was the fourth player to receive the honor from the Mets while Griffey's number became the first retired by the Mariners since their inception in 1977.

On a tragic note, the Marlins immediately retired righthander Jose Fernandez's No. 16 after the 24-year-old died Sept. 25 in a boating accident in Miami.

ARIZONA DIAMONDBACKS
Jake Barrett	April 4
Matt Buschmann	April 10
Zac Curtis	April 30
Braden Shipley	July 25
Steve Hathaway	July 31
Mitch Haniger	Aug. 16
Vicente Campos	Aug. 27
Kyle Jensen	Sept. 3
Matt Koch	Sept. 9

ATLANTA BRAVES
John Gant	April 6
Mallex Smith	April 11
Aaron Blair	April 24
Tyrell Jenkins	June 22
Mauricio Cabrera	June 27
Joel De La Cruz	June 29
Rob Whalen	Aug. 3
Madison Younginer	Aug. 7
Jason Hursh	Aug. 13
Dansby Swanson	Aug. 17
Rio Ruiz	Sept. 18

BALTIMORE ORIOLES
Joey Rickard	April 4
Hyun Soo Kim	April 10
Jayson Aquino	July 4
Donnie Hart	July 17
Parker Bridwell	Aug. 21
Jed Bradley	Sept. 3
Trey Mancini	Sept. 20

BOSTON RED SOX
Marco Hernandez	April 17
William Cuevas	April 21
Mike Miller	June 27
Andrew Benintendi	Aug. 2
Yoan Moncada	Sept. 2
Robby Scott	Sept. 2

CHICAGO CUBS
Albert Almora Jr.	June 7
Willson Contreras	June 17
Gerardo Concepcion	June 21
Jeimer Candelario	July 3
Felix Pena	Aug. 19
Rob Zastryzny	Aug. 19

CHICAGO WHITE SOX
Matt Purke	May 20
Jason Coats	June 4
Tim Anderson	June 10
Tyler Danish	June 11
Michael Ynoa	June 14
Carson Fulmer	July 17
Omar Narvaez	July 17
Charlie Tilson	Aug. 2
Juan Minaya	Sept. 1
Kevan Smith	Sept. 1
Blake Smith	Sept. 10

CINCINNATI REDS
Robert Stephenson	April 7
Tim Melville	April 10
Drew Hayes	April 21
Tim Adleman	May 1
Layne Somsen	May 14
Steve Selsky	May 20
Dayan Diaz	May 22
A.J. Morris	May 24
Cody Reed	June 18
Tony Renda	Aug. 2
Wandy Peralta	Sept. 4

CLEVELAND INDIANS
Tyler Naquin	April 5
Mike Clevinger	May 18
Ryan Merritt	May 30
Shawn Morimando	July 2

Joseph Colon	July 8
Erik Gonzalez	July 16
Perci Garner	Aug. 31
Adam Plutko	Sept. 24

COLORADO ROCKIES
Trevor Story	April 4
Tony Wolters	April 5
Carlos Estevez	April 23
Tyler Anderson	June 12
David Dahl	July 25
Matt Carasiti	Aug. 12
Jeff Hoffman	Aug. 20
Stephen Cardullo	Aug. 26
Raimel Tapia	Sept. 2
Pat Valaika	Sept. 6
German Marquez	Sept. 8
Jordan Patterson	Sept. 8

DETROIT TIGERS
Michael Fulmer	April 29
Warwick Saupold	May 14
Dustin Molleken	July 4
JaCoby Jones	Aug. 30
Joe Mantiply	Sept. 3

HOUSTON ASTROS
Tyler White	April 5
Chris Devenski	April 8
Tony Kemp	May 17
Colin Moran	May 18
A.J. Reed	June 25
Alex Bregman	July 25
Joe Musgrove	Aug. 2
James Hoyt	Aug. 3
Jandel Gustave	Aug. 11
Teoscar Hernandez	Aug. 12
Yulieski Gurriel	Aug. 21
Brady Rodgers	Sept. 3
David Paulino	Sept. 8

KANSAS CITY ROYALS
Whit Merrifield	May 18
Alec Mills	May 18
Brooks Pounders	July 5
Raul Mondesi	July 26
Matt Strahm	July 31
Kevin McCarthy	Sept. 9
Hunter Dozier	Sept. 12

LOS ANGELES ANGELS
Ji-Man Choi	April 5
Greg Mahle	April 13
Cody Ege	April 23
Daniel Wright	May 24
Ashur Tolliver	May 26
Juan Graterol	Sept. 2

LOS ANGELES DODGERS
Kenta Maeda	April 6
Ross Stripling	April 8
Julio Urias	May 27
Brock Stewart	June 29
Andrew Toles	July 8
Grant Dayton	July 22
Rob Segedin	Aug. 7
Jose De Leon	Sept. 4

MIAMI MARLINS
Hunter Cervenka	April 12
Nick Wittgren	April 19
Tayron Guerrero	May 17
Yefri Perez	July 17
Austin Brice	Aug. 12
Jake Esch	Aug. 31
Destin Hood	Sept. 2

MILWAUKEE BREWERS
Colin Walsh	April 4
Jacob Barnes	June 3
Orlando Arcia	Aug. 2
Damien Magnifico	Aug. 16
Brent Suter	Aug. 19

MINNESOTA TWINS
Byung Ho Park	April 4
Taylor Rogers	April 14
Pat Light	April 26
Jose Berrios	April 27
Pat Dean	May 11
J.T. Chargois	June 11
Adalberto Mejia	Aug. 20
Alex Wimmers	Aug. 26
James Beresford	Sept. 10

NEW YORK METS
Matt Reynolds	May 17
Ty Kelly	May 24
Brandon Nimmo	June 26
Seth Lugo	July 1
T.J. Rivera	Aug. 10
Gabriel Ynoa	Aug. 13
Josh Smoker	Aug. 19
Robert Gsellman	Aug. 23
Gavin Cecchini	Sept. 11

NEW YORK YANKEES
Johnny Barbato	April 5
Luis Cessa	April 8
Chad Green	May 16
Conor Mullee	May 16
Richard Bleier	May 30
Tyler Austin	Aug. 13
Aaron Judge	Aug. 13
Ben Heller	Aug. 26
Jonathan Holder	Sept. 2

OAKLAND ATHLETICS
Andrew Triggs	April 25
Sean Manaea	April 29
J.B. Wendelken	May 8
Zach Neal	May 11
Brett Eibner	May 27
Daniel Mengden	June 11
Dillon Overton	June 25
Ryon Healy	July 15
Bruce Maxwell	July 23
Chad Pinder	Aug. 20
Joey Wendle	Aug. 31
Raul Alcantara	Sept. 5
Jharel Cotton	Sept. 7
Renato Nunez	Sept. 12
Matt Olson	Sept. 12

PHILADELPHIA PHILLIES
Tyler Goeddel	April 6
Daniel Stumpf	April 7
Tommy Joseph	May 13
Zach Eflin	June 14
Edubray Ramos	June 24
Jake Thompson	Aug. 6
Roman Quinn	Sept. 11
Joely Rodriguez	Sept. 11
Jorge Alfaro	Sept. 12

PITTSBURGH PIRATES
Alen Hanson	May 16
Jameson Taillon	June 8
Jacob Stallings	June 19
Adam Frazier	June 24
Chad Kuhl	June 26
Steven Brault	July 5
Tyler Glasnow	July 7
Josh Bell	July 8
Max Moroff	July 31
Kelvin Marte	Sept. 3
Trevor Williams	Sept. 7

ST. LOUIS CARDINALS
Jeremy Hazelbaker	April 3
Seung Hwan Oh	April 3
Aledmys Diaz	April 5
Matt Bowman	April 6
Dean Kiekhefer	May 14
Alberto Rosario	July 9
Mike Mayers	July 24
Alex Reyes	Aug. 9
Luke Weaver	Aug. 13
Carson Kelly	Sept. 5
Jose Martinez	Sept. 6

SAN DIEGO PADRES
Jabari Blash	April 4
Luis Perdomo	April 4
Cesar Vargas	April 23
Ryan Schimpf	June 14
Buddy Baumann	July 16
Jose Rondon	July 29
Patrick Kivlehan	Aug. 20
Jake Smith	Sept. 7
Carlos Asuaje	Sept. 21
Manuel Margot	Sept. 21
Hunter Renfroe	Sept. 21
Jose Torres	Sept. 22

SAN FRANCISCO GIANTS
Derek Law	April 15
Steven Okert	April 19
Albert Suarez	May 8
Chris Stratton	May 30
Ty Blach	Sept. 5

SEATTLE MARINERS
Dae-Ho Lee	April 4
Ben Gamel	May 6
Edwin Diaz	June 6
Adrian Sampson	June 18
Ariel Miranda	July 3
Mike Freeman	July 17
Guillermo Heredia	July 29
Dan Altavilla	Aug. 27
Daniel Vogelbach	Sept. 12

TAMPA BAY RAYS
Blake Snell	April 23
Taylor Motter	May 16
Tyler Sturdevant	May 24
Ryan Garton	May 26
Dylan Floro	July 7
Eddie Gamboa	Sept. 2
Juniel Querecuto	Sept. 22

TEXAS RANGERS
Tony Barnette	April 5
Nomar Mazara	April 10
Brett Nicholas	April 11
Matt Bush	May 13
Jared Hoying	May 23
Jose Leclerc	July 6
Yohander Mendez	Sept. 5

TORONTO BLUE JAYS
Joe Biagini	April 8
Chad Girodo	April 22
Andy Burns	May 9
Dustin Antolin	May 16
Danny Barnes	Aug. 2
Matt Dermody	Sept. 3

WASHINGTON NATIONALS
Lucas Giolito	June 28
Reynaldo Lopez	July 19
Koda Glover	July 20
Brian Goodwin	Aug. 6
Spencer Kieboom	Oct. 2

CLUB BATTING

	AVG	G	AB	R	H	2B	3B	HR	RBI	BB	SO	SB	OBP	SLG
Boston	.282	162	5670	878	1598	343	25	208	836	558	1160	83	.348	.461
Detroit	.267	161	5526	750	1476	252	30	211	719	493	1303	58	.331	.438
Texas	.262	162	5525	765	1446	257	23	215	746	436	1220	99	.322	.433
Cleveland	.262	161	5484	777	1435	308	29	185	733	531	1246	134	.329	.430
Kansas City	.261	162	5552	675	1450	264	33	147	640	382	1224	121	.312	.400
Los Angeles	.260	162	5431	717	1410	279	20	156	686	471	991	73	.322	.405
Seattle	.259	162	5583	768	1446	251	17	223	735	506	1288	56	.326	.430
Chicago	.257	162	5550	686	1428	277	33	168	656	455	1285	77	.317	.410
Baltimore	.256	162	5524	744	1413	265	6	253	710	468	1324	19	.317	.443
New York	.252	162	5458	680	1378	245	20	183	647	475	1188	72	.315	.405
Minnesota	.251	162	5618	722	1409	288	35	200	690	513	1426	91	.316	.421
Toronto	.248	162	5479	759	1358	276	18	221	728	632	1362	54	.330	.426
Houston	.247	162	5545	724	1367	291	29	198	689	554	1452	102	.319	.417
Oakland	.246	162	5500	653	1352	270	21	169	634	442	1145	50	.304	.395
Tampa Bay	.243	162	5481	672	1333	288	32	216	647	449	1482	60	.307	.426

CLUB PITCHING

	ERA	G	CG	SHO	SV	IP	H	R	ER	HR	BB	SO	AVG
Toronto	3.79	162	0	0	43	1459	1340	666	615	183	461	1314	.242
Cleveland	3.86	161	5	3	37	1445	1330	676	619	186	461	1398	.243
Seattle	4.00	162	2	2	49	1457	1410	707	647	213	460	1318	.253
Boston	4.00	162	9	1	43	1440	1342	694	640	176	490	1362	.246
Houston	4.06	162	2	1	44	1468	1441	701	663	181	453	1396	.256
Chicago	4.12	162	7	1	43	1447	1422	715	662	185	521	1270	.257
New York	4.16	162	0	0	48	1428	1358	702	661	214	444	1393	.248
Tampa Bay	4.20	162	1	1	42	1426	1395	713	665	210	491	1357	.255
Kansas City	4.21	162	3	0	41	1440	1433	712	674	206	517	1287	.259
Baltimore	4.22	162	1	0	54	1432	1408	715	671	183	545	1248	.258
Detroit	4.24	161	3	1	47	1428	1417	721	673	182	462	1232	.260
Los Angeles	4.28	162	4	3	29	1421	1480	727	676	208	498	1136	.269
Texas	4.38	162	1	0	56	1443	1441	757	703	201	534	1154	.260
Oakland	4.51	162	2	1	42	1433	1459	761	719	185	464	1188	.263
Minnesota	5.09	162	4	1	26	1443	1617	889	816	221	479	1191	.283

CLUB FIELDING

	PCT	PO	A	E	DP		PCT	PO	A	E	DP
Houston	.987	4404	1599	77	359	Kansas City	.984	4320	1526	94	365
Detroit	.987	4284	1537	75	404	Chicago	.984	4340	1536	95	393
Boston	.987	4319	1427	75	379	Texas	.984	4329	1655	97	521
Baltimore	.987	4296	1579	80	452	Oakland	.984	4300	1630	97	412
Toronto	.986	4378	1622	88	392	Tampa Bay	.984	4279	1410	94	355
New York	.985	4285	1536	86	318	Los Angeles	.983	4264	1483	97	402
Seattle	.985	4371	1575	89	432	Minnesota	.979	4329	1610	126	469
Cleveland	.985	4335	1608	89	337						

INDIVIDUAL BATTING LEADERS

	AVG	G	AB	R	H	2B	3B	HR	RBI	BB	SO	SB
Altuve, Jose, Houston	.338	161	640	108	216	42	5	24	96	60	70	30
Betts, Mookie, Boston	.318	158	672	122	214	42	5	31	113	49	80	26
Pedroia, Dustin, Boston	.318	154	633	105	201	36	1	15	74	61	73	7
Cabrera, Miguel, Detroit	.316	158	595	92	188	31	1	38	108	75	116	0
Trout, Mike, Los Angeles	.315	159	549	123	173	32	5	29	100	116	137	30
Ortiz, David, Boston	.315	151	537	79	169	48	1	38	127	80	86	2
Ramirez, Jose, Cleveland	.312	152	565	84	176	46	3	11	76	44	62	22
Martinez, J.D., Detroit	.307	120	460	69	141	35	2	22	68	49	128	1
Escobar, Yunel, Los Angeles	.304	132	517	68	157	28	1	5	39	40	67	0
Andrus, Elvis, Texas	.302	147	506	75	153	31	7	8	69	47	70	24

INDIVIDUAL PITCHING LEADERS

	W	L	ERA	G	GS	CG	SV	IP	H	R	ER	BB	SO
Sanchez, Aaron, Toronto	15	2	3.00	30	30	0	0	192	161	69	64	63	161
Verlander, Justin, Detroit	16	9	3.04	34	34	2	0	228	171	81	77	57	254
Tanaka, Masahiro, New York	14	4	3.07	31	31	0	0	200	179	75	68	36	165
Kluber, Corey, Cleveland	18	9	3.14	32	32	3	0	215	170	82	75	57	227
Porcello, Rick, Boston	22	4	3.15	33	33	3	0	223	193	85	78	32	189
Happ, J.A., Toronto	20	4	3.18	32	32	0	0	195	168	72	69	60	163
Quintana, Jose, Chicago	13	12	3.20	32	32	0	0	208	192	76	74	50	181
Hamels, Cole, Texas	15	5	3.32	32	32	0	0	201	185	83	74	77	200
Sale, Chris, Chicago	17	10	3.34	32	32	6	0	227	190	88	84	45	233
Santana, Ervin, Minnesota	7	11	3.38	30	30	2	0	181	168	78	68	53	149

AWARD WINNERS

Selected by Baseball Writers Association of America

MOST VALUABLE PLAYER

Player	1st	2nd	3rd	Total
Mike Trout, Angels	19	8	1	356
Mookie Betts, Red Sox	9	17	4	311
Jose Altuve, Astros		2	15	227
Josh Donaldson, Blue Jays		2	9	200
Manny Machado, Orioles				150
David Ortiz, Red Sox	1		1	147
Adrian Beltre, Rangers	1		1	135
Robinson Cano, Mariners				79
Francisco Lindor, Indians				56
Miguel Cabrera, Tigers				56
Zach Britton, Orioles				11
Kyle Seager, Mariners				10
Brian Dozier, Twins				9
Edwin Encarnacion, Blue Jays				7
Nelson Cruz, Mariners				6
Chris Sale, White Sox				3
Jose Ramirez, Indians				2
Justin Verlander, Tigers				2
Adam Eaton, White Sox				1
Corey Kluber, Indians				1
Evan Longoria, Rays				1

CY YOUNG AWARD

Player	1st	2nd	3rd	Total
Rick Porcello, Red Sox	8	18	2	137
Justin Verlander, Tigers	14	2	5	132
Corey Kluber, Indians	3	6	12	98
Zach Britton, Orioles	5	3	2	72
Chris Sale, White Sox		1	4	40
J.A. Happ, Blue Jays			3	14
Aaron Sanchez, Blue Jays		1		6
Masahiro Tanaka, Yankees				6
Andrew Miller, Yankees/Indians			1	3
Michael Fulmer, Tigers				1
Jose Quintana, White Sox				1

ROOKIE OF THE YEAR

Player	1st	2nd	3rd	Total
Michael Fulmer, Tigers	26	4		142
Gary Sanchez, Yankees	4	23	2	91
Tyler Naquin, Indians		2	14	20
Chris Devenski, Astros		1	4	7
Edwin Diaz, Mariners			4	4
Nomar Mazara, Rangers			4	4
Tim Anderson, White Sox			2	2

MANAGER OF THE YEAR

Manager	1st	2nd	3rd	Total
Terry Francona, Indians	22	5	3	128
Jeff Banister, Rangers	4	12	8	64
Buck Showalter, Orioles	2	9	7	44
John Farrell, Red Sox	2	3	9	28
Joe Girardi, Yankees		1	2	5
Scott Servais, Mariners		1	1	

GOLD GLOVE WINNERS

Selected By AL Managers

P—Dallas Keuchel, Astros
C—Salvador Perez, Royals
1B—Mitch Moreland, Rangers
2B—Ian Kinsler, Tigers
3B—Adrian Beltre, Rangers
SS—Francisco Lindor, Indians
LF—Brett Gardner, Yankees
CF—Kevin Kiermaier, Rays
RF—Mookie Betts, Red Sox

DEPARTMENT LEADERS

BATTING

GAMES
Alcides Escobar, Kansas City	162
Jonathan Schoop, Baltimore	162
George Springer, Houston	162
Jose Altuve, Houston	161
Robinson Cano, Seattle	161

AT-BATS
Mookie Betts, Boston	672
Robinson Cano, Seattle	655
Xander Bogaerts, Boston	652
George Springer, Houston	644
2 players	640

PLATE APPEARANCES
George Springer, Houston	744
Mookie Betts, Boston	730
Xander Bogaerts, Boston	719
Jose Altuve, Houston	717
Robinson Cano, Seattle	715

RUNS
Mike Trout, Los Angeles	123
Mookie Betts, Boston	122
Josh Donaldson, Toronto	122
Ian Kinsler, Detroit	117
George Springer, Houston	116

HITS
Jose Altuve, Houston	216
Mookie Betts, Boston	214
Dustin Pedroia, Boston	201
Robinson Cano, Seattle	195
Xander Bogaerts, Boston	192

TOTAL BASES
Mookie Betts, Boston	359
Robinson Cano, Seattle	349
Manny Machado, Baltimore	341
Jose Altuve, Houston	340
Brian Dozier, Minnesota	336

DOUBLES
David Ortiz, Boston	48
Jose Ramirez, Cleveland	46
Jose Altuve, Houston	42
Mookie Betts, Boston	42
Melky Cabrera, Chicago	42

TRIPLES
Adam Eaton, Chicago	9
Jarrod Dyson, Kansas City	8
Elvis Andrus, Texas	7
Jackie Bradley Jr., Boston	7
5 players	6

EXTRA-BASE HITS
David Ortiz, Boston	87
Brian Dozier, Minnesota	82
Evan Longoria, Tampa Bay	81
Mookie Betts, Boston	78
Manny Machado, Baltimore	78

HOME RUNS
Mark Trumbo, Baltimore	47
Nelson Cruz, Seattle	43
Khris Davis, Oakland	42
Brian Dozier, Minnesota	42
Edwin Encarnacion, Toronto	42

RUNS BATTED IN
Edwin Encarnacion, Toronto	127
David Ortiz, Boston	127
Albert Pujols, Los Angeles	119
Mookie Betts, Boston	113
Hanley Ramirez, Boston	111

Mark Trumbo

SACRIFICES
Alcides Escobar, Kansas City	10
Jarrod Dyson, Kansas City	8
Carlos Perez, Los Angeles	8
4 players	7

SACRIFICE FLIES
Francisco Lindor, Cleveland	15
Jose Abreu, Chicago	9
Edwin Encarnacion, Toronto	8
Adam Jones, Baltimore	8
10 players	7

HIT BY PITCHES
Brandon Guyer, TB, Cleveland	31
Jose Abreu, Chicago	15
Adam Eaton, Chicago	14
Ian Kinsler, Detroit	13
2 players	11

WALKS
Mike Trout, Los Angeles	116
Josh Donaldson, Toronto	109
Carlos Santana, Cleveland	99
Chris Davis, Baltimore	88
George Springer, Houston	88

STOLEN BASES
Rajai Davis, Cleveland	43
Jose Altuve, Houston	30
Jarrod Dyson, Kansas City	30
Mike Trout, Los Angeles	30
Eduardo Nunez, Minnesota	27

STOLEN BASE PERCENTAGE
Brian Dozier, Minnesota	.900
Rajai Davis, Cleveland	.880
Kevin Kiermaier, Tampa Bay	.880
Mookie Betts, Boston	.870
Eduardo Nunez, Minnesota	.820

STRIKEOUTS
Chris Davis, Baltimore	219
Mike Napoli, Cleveland	194
Justin Upton, Detroit	179
Miguel Sano, Minnesota	178
George Springer, Houston	178

TOUGHEST TO STRIKE OUT
(AT-BATS PER STRIKEOUT)
Jose Iglesias, Detroit	9.34
Jose Altuve, Houston	9.14
Jose Ramirez, Cleveland	9.11
Adrian Beltre, Texas	8.83
Dustin Pedroia, Boston	8.67

GROUNDED INTO DOUBLE PLAYS
Miguel Cabrera, Detroit	26
Dustin Pedroia, Boston	24
Albert Pujols, Los Angeles	24
Edwin Encarnacion, Toronto	22
David Ortiz, Boston	22

MULTI-HIT GAMES
Mookie Betts, Boston	67
Jose Altuve, Houston	63
Robinson Cano, Seattle	59
Dustin Pedroia, Boston	57
2 players	56

ON-BASE PERCENTAGE
Mike Trout, Los Angeles	.441
Josh Donaldson, Toronto	.404
David Ortiz, Boston	.401
Jose Altuve, Houston	.396
Miguel Cabrera, Detroit	.393

ON-BASE PLUS SLUGGING
David Ortiz, Boston	1.021
Mike Trout, Los Angeles	.991
Miguel Cabrera, Detroit	.956
Josh Donaldson, Toronto	.953
Jose Altuve, Houston	.928

LOWEST AVERAGE
Alex Gordon, Kansas City	.220
Chris Davis, Baltimore	.221
Todd Frazier, Chicago	.225
Russell Martin, Toronto	.231
Mitch Moreland, Texas	.233

Brian Dozier

Rick Porcello

PITCHING

WINS

Rick Porcello, Boston	22
J.A. Happ, Toronto	20
Corey Kluber, Cleveland	18
David Price, Boston	17
Chris Sale, Chicago	17

LOSSES

Chris Archer, Tampa Bay	19
R.A. Dickey, Toronto	15
Ricky Nolasco, Minn., LAA	14
4 players	13

GAMES

Bryan Shaw, Cleveland	75
Dellin Betances, New York	73
Sam Dyson, Texas	73
3 players	72

GAMES STARTED

David Price, Boston	35
Justin Verlander, Detroit	34
Edinson Volquez, Kansas City	34
8 players	33

GAMES FINISHED

Zach Britton, Baltimore	63
Roberto Osuna, Toronto	61
Cody Allen, Cleveland	55
Francisco Rodriguez, Detroit	55
2 players	53

COMPLETE GAMES

Chris Sale, Chicago	6
Steven Wright, Boston	4
Corey Kluber, Cleveland	3
Rick Porcello, Boston	3
5 players	2

SHUTOUTS

Corey Kluber, Cleveland	2
13 players	1

SAVES

Zach Britton, Baltimore	47
Francisco Rodriguez, Detroit	44
Sam Dyson, Texas	38
Alex Colome, Tampa Bay	37
David Robertson, Chicago	37

INNINGS PITCHED

David Price, Boston	230
Justin Verlander, Detroit	228
Chris Sale, Chicago	227
Rick Porcello, Boston	223
Corey Kluber, Cleveland	215

HITS ALLOWED

David Price, Boston	227
Hisashi Iwakuma, Seattle	218
Edinson Volquez, Kansas City	217
Marcus Stroman, Toronto	209
Jered Weaver, Los Angeles	209

RUNS ALLOWED

Edinson Volquez, Kansas City	124
Martin Perez, Texas	110
Anibal Sanchez, Detroit	108
David Price, Boston	106
Jered Weaver, Los Angeles	106

HOME RUNS ALLOWED

Jered Weaver, Los Angeles	37
Josh Tomlin, Cleveland	36
Ian Kennedy, Kansas City	33
Hector Santiago, LAA, Minn.	33
Drew Smyly, Tampa Bay	32

WALKS ALLOWED

Hector Santiago, LAA, Minn.	79
Yordano Ventura, Kansas City	78
Cole Hamels, Texas	77
Edinson Volquez, Kansas City	76
Martin Perez, Texas	76

LOWEST WALKS PER NINE INNINGS

Josh Tomlin, Cleveland	1.04
Rick Porcello, Boston	1.29
Masahiro Tanaka, New York	1.62
Chris Sale, Chicago	1.79
David Price, Boston	1.96

HIT BATTERS

Chris Sale, Chicago	17
Ian Kennedy, Kansas City	13
Rick Porcello, Boston	13
Felix Hernandez, Seattle	10
4 players	9

STRIKEOUTS

Justin Verlander, Detroit	254
Chris Archer, Tampa Bay	233
Chris Sale, Chicago	233
David Price, Boston	228
Corey Kluber, Cleveland	227

STRIKEOUTS PER NINE INNINGS

Michael Pineda, New York	10.61
Chris Archer, Tampa Bay	10.42
Justin Verlander, Detroit	10.04
Corey Kluber, Cleveland	9.50
Chris Sale, Chicago	9.25

STRIKEOUTS PER NINE INNINGS (Relievers)

Dellin Betances, New York	15.53
Andrew Miller, NYY, Cleve.	14.89
Ken Giles, Houston	13.98
Michael Feliz, Houston	13.15
Mychal Givens, Baltimore	11.57

DOUBLE PLAYS

Martin Perez, Texas	36
Hisashi Iwakuma, Seattle	25
Mike Pelfrey, Detroit	24
Marcus Stroman, Toronto	22
6 players	21

PICKOFFS

6 players	4

WILD PITCHES

Mike Fiers, Houston	17
Sonny Gray, Oakland	15
Ken Giles, Houston	14
Yordano Ventura, Kansas City	13
3 players	11

WALKS PLUS HITS PER INNING

Justin Verlander, Detroit	1.00
Rick Porcello, Boston	1.01
Chris Sale, Chicago	1.04
Corey Kluber, Cleveland	1.06
Masahiro Tanaka, New York	1.08

OPPONENT AVERAGE

Chris Sale, Chicago	.227
Aaron Sanchez, Toronto	.224
Corey Kluber, Cleveland	.216
Justin Verlander, Detroit	.207
Marco Estrada, Toronto	.203

WORST ERA

Edinson Volquez, Kansas City	5.37
Wade Miley, Sea., Balt.	5.37
Jered Weaver, Los Angeles	5.06
Drew Smyly, Tampa Bay	4.88
Michael Pineda, New York	4.82

FIELDING

PITCHER

PCT	11 players	1.000
DP	Steven Wright, Boston	5
E	Yordano Ventura, Kansas City	5
A	Aaron Sanchez, Toronto	32
PO	Ervin Santana, Minnesota	20

CATCHER

PCT	3 players	.996
E	Matt Wieters, Baltimore	11
PO	Russell Martin, Toronto	989
	Salvador Perez, Kansas City	989
CS	Salvador Perez, Kansas City	37
PB	Ryan Hanigan, Boston	18
A	Salvador Perez, Kansas City	77
DP	James McCann, Detroit	9

FIRST BASE

PCT	Mitch Moreland, Texas	.998
PO	Chris Davis, Baltimore	1325
A	Miguel Cabrera, Detroit	95
DP	Chris Davis, Baltimore	138
	Mitch Moreland, Texas	138
E	Mike Napoli, Cleveland	13

SECOND BASE

PCT	Robinson Cano, Seattle	.996
PO	Robinson Cano, Seattle	311
A	Jonathan Schoop, Baltimore	447
DP	Rougned Odor, Texas	129
E	Rougned Odor, Texas	22

THIRD BASE

PCT	Manny Machado, Baltimore	.979
	Jose Ramirez, Cleveland	.979
PO	Josh Donaldson, Toronto	110

	Kyle Seager, Seattle	110
A	Kyle Seager, Seattle	373
DP	Kyle Seager, Seattle	46
E	Kyle Seager, Seattle	22

SHORTSTOP

PCT	Jose Iglesias, Detroit	.991
PO	Marcus Semien, Oakland	235
A	Marcus Semien, Oakland	477
DP	Marcus Semien, Oakland	109
E	Ketel Marte, Seattle	21
	Marcus Semien, Oakland	21

OUTFIELD

PCT	Mookie Betts, Boston	.997
PO	Adam Eaton, Chicago	417
A	Adam Eaton, Chicago	18
DP	3 players	4
E	Ian Desmond, Texas	12

MIKE JULA

MAJOR LEAGUES

CLUB BATTING

	AVG	G	AB	R	H	2B	3B	HR	RBI	BB	SO	SB	OBP	SLG
Colorado	.275	162	5614	845	1544	318	47	204	805	494	1330	66	.336	.457
Miami	.263	161	5547	655	1460	259	42	128	626	447	1213	71	.322	.394
Arizona	.261	162	5665	752	1479	285	56	190	709	463	1427	137	.320	.432
San Francisco	.258	162	5565	715	1437	280	54	130	675	572	1107	79	.329	.398
Pittsburgh	.257	162	5542	729	1426	277	32	153	696	561	1304	110	.332	.402
Chicago	.256	162	5503	808	1409	293	30	199	767	656	1339	66	.343	.429
Cincinnati	.256	162	5487	716	1403	277	33	164	678	452	1284	139	.316	.408
Washington	.256	162	5490	763	1403	268	29	203	735	536	1252	121	.326	.426
St. Louis	.255	162	5548	779	1415	299	32	225	745	526	1318	35	.325	.442
Atlanta	.255	161	5514	649	1404	295	27	112	615	502	1240	75	.321	.384
Los Angeles	.249	162	5518	725	1376	272	21	189	680	525	1321	45	.319	.409
New York	.246	162	5459	671	1342	240	19	218	649	517	1302	42	.316	.417
Milwaukee	.244	162	5330	671	1299	249	19	194	641	599	1543	181	.322	.407
Philadelphia	.240	162	5434	610	1305	231	35	161	574	424	1376	96	.301	.384
San Diego	.235	162	5419	686	1275	257	26	177	654	449	1500	125	.299	.390

CLUB PITCHING

	ERA	G	CG	SHO	SV	IP	H	R	ER	HR	BB	SO	AVG
Chicago	3.15	162	5	2	38	1460	1125	556	511	163	495	1441	.212
Washington	3.52	162	1	0	46	1460	1272	612	571	155	468	1476	.234
New York	3.58	162	1	1	55	1447	1397	617	575	152	439	1396	.254
San Francisco	3.69	162	10	3	43	1460	1334	631	599	158	439	1309	.243
Los Angeles	3.70	162	3	3	47	1453	1266	638	598	165	464	1510	.233
Miami	4.05	161	0	0	55	1435	1358	682	646	152	595	1379	.251
St. Louis	4.08	162	2	2	38	1448	1432	712	656	159	475	1290	.258
Milwaukee	4.10	162	0	0	46	1434	1450	733	653	178	532	1175	.263
Pittsburgh	4.22	162	5	1	51	1451	1490	758	681	180	533	1232	.267
San Diego	4.44	162	1	0	35	1440	1425	770	711	183	569	1222	.258
Atlanta	4.51	161	1	1	39	1448	1414	779	725	177	547	1227	.256
Philadelphia	4.64	162	4	3	43	1437	1468	796	741	213	466	1299	.265
Cincinnati	4.91	162	2	1	28	1442	1457	854	787	258	636	1241	.263
Colorado	4.92	162	2	2	37	1429	1532	860	781	181	547	1223	.274
Arizona	5.09	162	2	2	31	1451	1563	890	821	202	603	1318	.275

CLUB FIELDING

	PCT	PO	A	E	DP		PCT	PO	A	E	DP
San Francisco	.988	4381	1639	72	382	Atlanta	.983	4343	1565	101	355
Washington	.988	4379	1425	73	387	Cincinnati	.983	4326	1549	102	385
Los Angeles	.986	4359	1448	80	266	St. Louis	.983	4345	1747	107	470
Miami	.985	4305	1506	86	362	Pittsburgh	.982	4359	1745	111	469
New York	.985	4341	1519	90	369	Colorado	.982	4288	1749	110	397
Philadelphia	.984	4311	1503	97	393	San Diego	.982	4320	1623	109	453
Arizona	.983	4354	1663	101	391	Milwaukee	.978	4303	1671	136	385
Chicago	.983	4379	1635	101	313						

INDIVIDUAL BATTING LEADERS

	AVG	G	AB	R	H	2B	3B	HR	RBI	BB	SO	SB
LeMahieu, D.J., Colorado	.348	146	552	104	192	32	8	11	66	66	80	11
Murphy, Daniel, Washington	.347	142	531	88	184	47	5	25	104	35	57	5
Votto, Joey, Cincinnati	.326	158	556	101	181	34	2	29	97	108	120	8
Blackmon, Charlie, Colorado	.324	143	578	111	187	35	5	29	82	43	102	17
Segura, Jean, Arizona	.319	153	637	102	203	41	7	20	64	39	101	33
Marte, Starling, Pittsburgh	.311	129	489	71	152	34	5	9	46	23	104	47
Seager, Corey, Los Angeles	.308	157	627	105	193	40	5	26	72	54	133	3
Molina, Yadier, St. Louis	.307	147	534	56	164	38	1	8	58	39	63	3
Ramos, Wilson, Washington	.307	131	482	58	148	25	0	22	80	35	79	0
Braun, Ryan, Milwaukee	.305	135	511	80	156	23	3	30	91	46	98	16

INDIVIDUAL PITCHING LEADERS

	W	L	ERA	G	GS	CG	SV	IP	H	R	ER	BB	SO
Hendricks, Kyle, Chicago	16	8	2.13	31	30	2	0	190	142	53	45	44	170
Lester, Jon, Chicago	19	5	2.44	32	32	2	0	203	154	57	55	52	197
Syndergaard, Noah, New York	14	9	2.60	31	30	0	0	184	168	61	53	43	218
Bumgarner, Madison, San Fran.	15	9	2.74	34	34	4	0	227	179	79	69	54	251
Cueto, Johnny, San Francisco	18	5	2.79	32	32	5	0	220	195	71	68	45	198
Roark, Tanner, Washington	16	10	2.83	34	33	0	0	210	173	72	66	73	172
Fernandez, Jose, Miami	16	8	2.86	29	29	0	0	182	149	63	58	55	253
Scherzer, Max, Washington	20	7	2.96	34	34	1	0	228	165	77	75	56	284
Martinez, Carlos, St. Louis	16	9	3.04	31	31	0	0	195	169	68	66	70	174
Arrieta, Jake, Chicago	18	8	3.10	31	31	1	0	197	138	72	68	76	190

AWARD WINNERS

Selected by Baseball Writers Association of America

MOST VALUABLE PLAYER

Player	1st	2nd	3rd	Total
Kris Bryant, Cubs	29	1		415
Daniel Murphy, Nationals	1	11	10	245
Corey Seager, Dodgers		11	10	240
Anthony Rizzo, Cubs		3	4	202
Nolan Arenado, Rockies		3	6	199
Freddie Freeman, Braves		1		129
Joey Votto, Reds				100
Yoenis Cespedes, Mets				45
Justin Turner, Dodgers				44
Max Scherzer, Nationals				39
Paul Goldschmidt, Diamondbacks				18
Brandon Crawford, Giants				15
Jean Segura, Diamondbacks				14
Buster Posey, Giants				11
D.J. LeMahieu, Rockies				8
Madison Bumgarner, Giants				7
Jeurys Familia, Mets				6
Wilson Ramos, Nationals				6
Addison Russell, Cubs				5
Noah Syndergaard, Mets				5
Christian Yelich, Marlins				5
Yasmani Grandal, Dodgers				4
Kyle Hendricks, Cubs				2
Ryan Braun, Brewers				2
Yadier Molina, Cardinals				2
Charlie Blackmon, Rockies				1
Johnny Cueto, Giants				1

CY YOUNG AWARD

Player	1st	2nd	3rd	Total
Max Scherzer, Nationals	25	3	1	192
Jon Lester, Cubs	1	16	9	102
Kyle Hendricks, Cubs	2	7	8	85
Madison Bumgarner, Giants		2	6	46
Clayton Kershaw, Dodgers	2		1	30
Johnny Cueto, Giants			3	19
Jose Fernandez, Marlins		1	1	18
Noah Syndergaard, Mets		1	1	15
Jake Arrieta, Cubs				2
Tanner Roark, Nationals				1

ROOKIE OF THE YEAR

Player	1st	2nd	3rd	Total
Corey Seager, Dodgers	30			150
Trea Turner, Nationals		11	9	42
Kenta Maeda, Dodgers		11	4	37
Trevor Story, Rockies		7	3	24
Aledmys Diaz, Cardinals		1	11	14
Jon Gray, Rockies			1	1
Steven Matz, Mets			1	1
Seung Hwan Oh, Cardinals			1	1

MANAGER OF THE YEAR

Manager	1st	2nd	3rd	Total
Dave Roberts, Dodgers	16	7	7	108
Joe Maddon, Cubs	8	8	6	70
Dusty Baker, Nationals	4	12	10	66
Terry Collins, Mets	2	3	5	24
Don Mattingly, Marlins			2	2

GOLD GLOVE WINNERS

Selected By NL Managers

P—Zack Greinke, Diamondbacks
C—Buster Posey, Giants
1B—Anthony Rizzo, Cubs
2B—Joe Panik, Giants
3B—Nolan Arenado, Rockies
SS—Brandon Crawford, Giants
LF—Starling Marte, Pirates
CF—Ender Inciarte, Braves
RF—Jason Heyward, Cubs

DEPARTMENT LEADERS

BATTING

GAMES
Nolan Arenado, Colorado	160
Chris Carter, Milwaukee	160
Odubel Herrera, Philadelphia	159
Eugenio Suarez, Cincinnati	159
5 players	158

AT-BATS
Jean Segura, Arizona	637
Corey Seager, Los Angeles	627
Matt Kemp, San Diego, Atl.	623
Nolan Arenado, Colorado	618
Kris Bryant, Chicago	603

PLATE APPEARANCES
Paul Goldschmidt, Arizona	705
Kris Bryant, Chicago	699
Nolan Arenado, Colorado	696
Jean Segura, Arizona	694
Freddie Freeman, Atlanta	693

RUNS
Kris Bryant, Chicago	121
Nolan Arenado, Colorado	116
Charlie Blackmon, Colorado	111
Paul Goldschmidt, Arizona	106
Corey Seager, Los Angeles	105

HITS
Jean Segura, Arizona	203
Corey Seager, Los Angeles	193
D.J. LeMahieu, Colorado	192
Charlie Blackmon, Colorado	187
Daniel Murphy, Washington	184

TOTAL BASES
Nolan Arenado, Colorado	352
Freddie Freeman, Atlanta	335
Kris Bryant, Chicago	334
Corey Seager, Los Angeles	321
Charlie Blackmon, Colorado	319

DOUBLES
Daniel Murphy, Washington	47
Freddie Freeman, Atlanta	43
Anthony Rizzo, Chicago	43
Carlos Gonzalez, Colorado	42
2 players	41

TRIPLES
Brandon Crawford, San Fran.	11
Cesar Hernandez, Philadelphia	11
Chris Owings, Arizona	11
Jake Lamb, Arizona	9
3 players	8

EXTRA-BASE HITS
Freddie Freeman, Atlanta	83
Nolan Arenado, Colorado	82
Anthony Rizzo, Chicago	79
Kris Bryant, Chicago	77
Daniel Murphy, Washington	77

HOME RUNS
Nolan Arenado, Colorado	41
Chris Carter, Milwaukee	41
Kris Bryant, Chicago	39
Matt Kemp, San Diego, Atlanta	35
Freddie Freeman, Atlanta	34

Daniel Murphy

RUNS BATTED IN
Nolan Arenado, Colorado	133
Anthony Rizzo, Chicago	109
Matt Kemp, S.D., Atlanta	108
Daniel Murphy, Washington	104
Adam Duvall, Cincinnati	103

SACRIFICES
Max Scherzer, Washington	13
Johnny Cueto, San Francisco	11
Billy Hamilton, Cincinnati	11
Dan Straily, Cincinnati	11
Julio Teheran, Atlanta	11

SACRIFICE FLIES
Matt Kemp, San Diego, Atlanta	12
Chris Carter, Milwaukee	10
Bryce Harper, Washington	10
Brandon Crawford, San Fran.	9
Nick Markakis, Atlanta	9

HIT BY PITCH
Derek Dietrich, Miami	24
Danny Espinosa, Washington	20
Kris Bryant, Chicago	18
Starling Marte, Pittsburgh	16
Anthony Rizzo, Chicago	16

WALKS
Paul Goldschmidt, Arizona	110
Bryce Harper, Washington	108
Joey Votto, Cincinnati	108
Brandon Belt, San Francisco	104
Ben Zobrist, Chicago	96

STOLEN BASES
Jonathan Villar, Milwaukee	62
Billy Hamilton, Cincinnati	58
Starling Marte, Pittsburgh	47
Hernan Perez, Milwaukee	34
2 players	33

STOLEN BASE PERCENTAGE
Chris Owings, Arizona	.910
Billy Hamilton, Cincinnati	.880
Paul Goldschmidt, Arizona	.860
Keon Broxton, Milwaukee	.850
Trea Turner, Washington	.850

STRIKEOUTS
Chris Carter, Milwaukee	206
Danny Espinosa, Washington	174
Jonathan Villar, Milwaukee	174
Freddie Freeman, Atlanta	171
Adam Duvall, Cincinnati	164

TOUGHEST TO STRIKE OUT
(AT-BATS PER STRIKEOUT)
Joe Panik, San Francisco	9.87
Daniel Murphy, Washington	9.32
Martin Prado, Miami	8.70
Yadier Molina, St. Louis	8.48
Brandon Phillips, Cincinnati	8.09

GROUNDED INTO DOUBLE PLAYS
Martin Prado, Miami	24
Yadier Molina, St. Louis	22
Ryan Braun, Milwaukee	20
Howie Kendrick, Los Angeles	20
Christian Yelich, Miami	20

MULTI-HIT GAMES
D.J. LeMahieu, Colorado	59
Nolan Arenado, Colorado	57
Corey Seager, Los Angeles	57
Jean Segura, Arizona	57
Daniel Murphy, Washington	56

ON-BASE PERCENTAGE
Joey Votto, Cincinnati	.434
D.J. LeMahieu, Colorado	.416
Paul Goldschmidt, Arizona	.411
Freddie Freeman, Atlanta	.400
Brandon Belt, San Francisco	.394

ON-BASE PLUS SLUGGING
Daniel Murphy, Washington	.985
Joey Votto, Cincinnati	.985
Freddie Freeman, Atlanta	.968
Kris Bryant, Chicago	.939
Charlie Blackmon, Colorado	.933

Freddie Freeman

Jon Lester

PITCHING

WINS
Max Scherzer, Washington	20
Jon Lester, Chicago	19
Jake Arrieta, Chicago	18
Johnny Cueto, San Francisco	18
5 players	16

LOSSES
Jimmy Nelson, Milwaukee	16
Robbie Ray, Arizona	15
Jerad Eickhoff, Philadelphia	14
4 players	13

GAMES
Brad Hand, San Diego	82
Addison Reed, New York	80
Randall Delgado, Arizona	79
Hector Neris, Philadelphia	79
Jeurys Familia, New York	78

GAMES STARTED
Madison Bumgarner, San Fran.	34
Max Scherzer, Washington	34
5 players	33

GAMES FINISHED
Jeurys Familia, New York	67
Mark Melancon, Pitts., Wash.	67
Kenley Jansen, Los Angeles	63
Jeanmar Gomez, Philadelphia	59
A.J. Ramos, Miami	52

COMPLETE GAMES
Johnny Cueto, San Francisco	5
Madison Bumgarner, San Fran.	4
Clayton Kershaw, Los Angeles	3
Ivan Nova, NYY, Pitts.	3
3 players	2

SHUTOUTS
Clayton Kershaw, Los Angeles	3
Johnny Cueto, San Francisco	2
16 players	1

SAVES
Jeurys Familia, New York	51
Kenley Jansen, Los Angeles	47
Mark Melancon, Pitts., Wash.	47
A.J. Ramos, Miami	40
Jeanmar Gomez, Philadelphia	37

INNINGS PITCHED
Max Scherzer, Washington	228
Madison Bumgarner, San Fran.	227
Johnny Cueto, San Francisco	220
Tanner Roark, Washington	210
Jeff Samardzija, San Fran.	203

HITS ALLOWED
Adam Wainwright, St. Louis	220
Chad Bettis, Colorado	204
Mike Leake, St. Louis	203
Bartolo Colon, New York	200
Johnny Cueto, San Francisco	195

RUNS ALLOWED
Patrick Corbin, Arizona	109
Jimmy Nelson, Milwaukee	108
Adam Wainwright, St. Louis	108
Chad Bettis, Colorado	107
Robbie Ray, Arizona	105

HOME RUNS ALLOWED
Max Scherzer, Washington	31
Dan Straily, Cincinnati	31
Jerad Eickhoff, Philadelphia	30
Brandon Finnegan, Cincinnati	29
Chase Anderson, Milwaukee	28

WALKS ALLOWED
Jimmy Nelson, Milwaukee	86
Brandon Finnegan, Cincinnati	84
Tom Koehler, Miami	83
Jake Arrieta, Chicago	76
2 players	73

FEWEST WALKS PER NINE INNINGS
Bartolo Colon, New York	1.50
Mike Leake, St. Louis	1.53
Johnny Cueto, San Francisco	1.84
Jerad Eickhoff, Philadelphia	1.92
Julio Teheran, Atlanta	1.96

HIT BATTERS
Jimmy Nelson, Milwaukee	17
Tanner Roark, Washington	13
Jon Gray, Colorado	12
3 players	11

STRIKEOUTS
Max Scherzer, Washington	284
Jose Fernandez, Miami	253
Madison Bumgarner, San Fran.	251
Robbie Ray, Arizona	218
Noah Syndergaard, New York	218

STRIKEOUTS PER NINE INNINGS
Jose Fernandez, Miami	12.49
Robbie Ray, Arizona	11.25
Max Scherzer, Washington	11.19
Noah Syndergaard, N.Y.	10.64
Madison Bumgarner, San Fran.	9.97

STRIKEOUTS PER NINE INNINGS (RELIEVERS)
Kyle Barraclough, Miami	14.00
Kenley Jansen, Los Angeles	13.63
Tyler Thornburg, Milwaukee	12.09
David Phelps, Miami	11.84
SeungHwan Oh, St. Louis	11.64

DOUBLE PLAYS
Carlos Martinez, St. Louis	33
Tanner Roark, Washington	28
Adam Wainwright, St. Louis	27
Tyler Chatwood, Colorado	22
2 players	21

PICKOFFS
Julio Urias, Los Angeles	6
Johnny Cueto, San Francisco	5
5 players	4

WILD PITCHES
Jake Arrieta, Chicago	16
Mike Foltynewicz, Atlanta	13
Jonathon Niese, Pitts., NYM	11
Luis Perdomo, San Diego	10
Noah Syndergaard, New York	10

WALKS PLUS HITS PER INNING
Max Scherzer, Washington	0.97
Kyle Hendricks, Chicago	0.98
Jon Lester, Chicago	1.02
Madison Bumgarner, San Fran.	1.03
Julio Teheran, Atlanta	1.05

OPPONENT AVERAGE
Jake Arrieta, Chicago	.194
Max Scherzer, Washington	.199
Kyle Hendricks, Chicago	.207
Jon Lester, Chicago	.211
Madison Bumgarner, San Fran.	.213

WORST ERA
Robbie Ray, Arizona	4.90
Chad Bettis, Colorado	4.79
Mike Leake, St. Louis	4.69
Jaime Garcia, St. Louis	4.67
Adam Wainwright, St. Louis	4.62

FIELDING

PITCHER
PCT	7 players	1.000
DP	Jake Arrieta, Chicago	6
E	Jimmy Nelson, Milwaukee	5
A	Bartolo Colon, New York	40
	Jake Arrieta, Chicago	40
PO	Carlos Martinez, St. Louis	65

CATCHER
PCT	Yadier Molina, St. Louis	.998
E	J.T. Realmuto, Miami	10
PO	Yaider Molina, St. Louis	1113
CS	Tucker Barnhart, Cincinnati	34
PB	3 players	10
A	J.T. Realmuto, Miami	80
DP	Buster Posey, San Francisco	8
	J.T. Realmuto, Miami	8

FIRST BASE
PCT	Adrian Gonzalez, Los Angeles	.998
	Wil Myers, San Diego	.998
PO	Paul Goldschmidt, Arizona	1498
A	Anthony Rizzo, Chicago	125
DP	Wil Myers, San Diego	139
E	Chris Carter, Milwaukee	11
	Ryan Howard, Philadelphia	11

SECOND BASE
PCT	Joe Panik, San Francisco	.992
PO	D.J. LeMahieu, Colorado	276
A	D.J. LeMahieu, Colorado	422
DP	Cesar Hernandez, Philadelphia	102
E	Brandon Phillips, Cincinnati	14
	Scooter Gennett, Milwaukee	14

THIRD BASE
PCT	Anthony Rendon, Washington	.976
PO	Anthony Rendon, Washington	134
A	Nolan Arenado, Colorado	378
DP	Nolan Arenado, Colorado	39 E
	Eugenio Suarez, Cincinnati	23

SHORTSTOP
PCT	Freddy Galvis, Philadelphia	.987
PO	Freddy Galvis, Philadelphia	210
A	Brandon Crawford, SF	413
DP	Danny Espinosa, Washington	96
E	Corey Seager, Los Angeles	18
	Danny Espinosa, Washington	18

OUTFIELD
PCT	Curtis Granderson, New York	1.000
PO	Odubel Herrera, Philadelphia	372
A	Starling Marte, Pittsburgh	17
DP	4 players	4
E	Odubel Herrera, Philadelphia	9

BILL NICHOLS

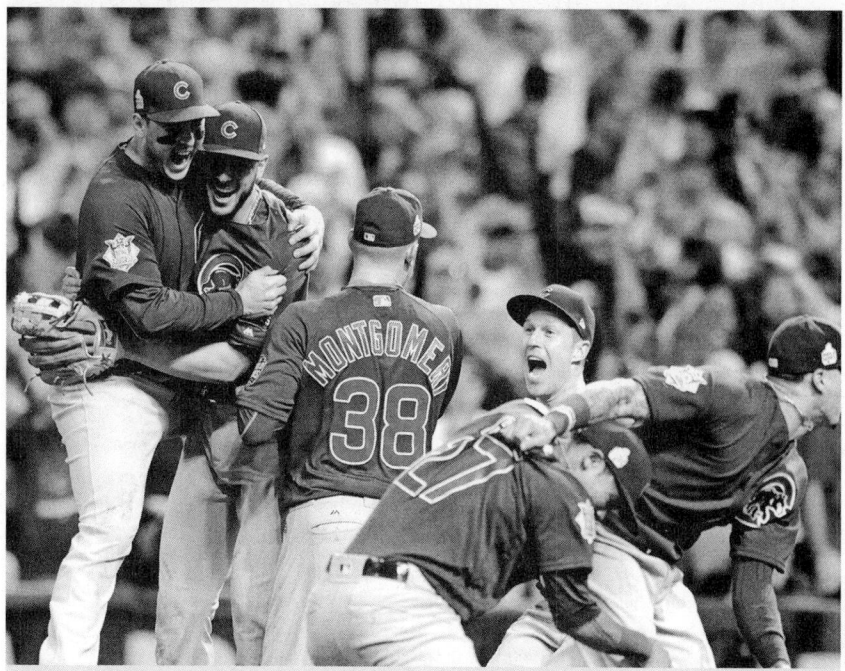

The Cubs celebrated on Cleveland's Progressive Field after coming back from a 3-1 deficit to win the World Series, capped by a thrilling, 10-inning 8-7 victory in Game Seven

After 108 long years, Cubs win World Series

BY TOM HAUDRICOURT

CLEVELAND

Curses are not easily broken, especially when they go back to 1908.

But they can be broken.

The Cubs finally showed it could be done in a Game Seven for the ages in the World Series. They survived a late rally by the Indians, a rain delay and an extra inning before finally prevailing, 8-7, at Cleveland's Progressive Field.

Nobody said it would be easy, and it certainly wasn't after the Cubs fell behind, three games to one. At that point, it seemed it was Cleveland's destiny to end a curse of its own, dating to the Indians' last title in 1948. Instead, it was heartbreak again, much like 1997 when the Indians bowed in Game Seven to the Marlins in 11 innings. "Wait 'til next year" stayed in play in Cleveland, but the 108-year

curse in Chicago finally came to an end.

No more talk of billy goats, black cats or Steve Bartman. The first World Series played at Wrigley Field since 1945 turned out to be the one that finally put the Cubs over the top.

As probably should have been expected after waiting so long, the Cubs had to do it the hard way. When the Indians took a 3-1 lead in the series by winning the first two World Series games at Wrigley Field in 71 years, Cubs fans began to think their supposedly cursed team would fall short again.

Then, in Game Five, the tide began to turn. The Cubs scored three times in the fourth inning off Indians starter Trevor Bauer, whose postseason was marred by slicing the pinkie finger on his pitching hand while working on a drone, of all things.

Before the World Series began, Indians manager

Terry Francona and his staff devised a pitching plan they thought provided the best chance to succeed. Having lost starting pitchers Carlos Carrasco (broken finger) and Danny Salazar (forearm) to injuries in early September, the decision was made to go with three starting pitchers—ace Corey Kluber, Josh Tomlin and Bauer.

The plan backfired in the final two games, however. Tomlin showed up with nothing in Game Six and the Cubs rolled to a 9-3 victory. Kris Bryant ignited a three-run rally in the first inning with a two-out home run and the Indians helped out with a miscue in the outfield.

Tomlin exited with the bases loaded in the third inning and 22-year-old shortstop Addison Russell greeted Dan Otero with a grand slam that broke open the game. Russell tied a single-game record with six RBIs while becoming the first Cubs player to hit a slam in the World Series.

The Fall Classic was tied, three games apiece, and the pressure shifted to the Indians. It was up to Kluber, who allowed just one run in his first two starts against the Cubs and was having a brilliant postseason. It became evident immediately that Kluber was vulnerable when Dexter Fowler led off the game with a home run.

Kluber also surrendered a home run to the last batter he faced, Javier Baez, leading off the fifth inning to put the Cubs on top, 4-1. With a 6-3 lead with two outs in the eighth, Maddon summoned closer Aroldis Chapman to replace Jon Lester, a starting pitcher working out of the bullpen on two days' rest.

Chapman, who was used in Game Six with the Cubs holding a five-run lead, was running low on gas. After Brandon Guyer delivered a run-scoring double, Rajai Davis shocked Chicago by driving a 97 mph fastball out to left field for a two-run homer that tied the game.

Just like that, it was 6-6, and Cubs fans no doubt wondered if all the curses in the franchise's past were combining to thwart their club once again. After a scoreless ninth inning, a rainstorm that had been forecast all day arrived and the tarp was rolled onto the field.

The stoppage of play lasted just 17 minutes but first baseman Anthony Rizzo called it "the most important rain delay" in team history. Right fielder Jason Heyward, who suffered through a miserable season after signing a $184 million free agent deal, took the opportunity to summon his teammates to the weight room and deliver a stirring speech.

When play resumed, the Cubs scored twice in the 10th off Indians reliever Bryan Shaw. Zobrist, who would be named World Series MVP, broke the deadlock with a RBI double and little-used

Anthony Rizzo went 17-for-50 with three homers between NLCS and World Series

DIAMOND IMAGES

catcher Miguel Montero added what would prove to be a huge run-scoring single.

The Indians cut the lead to one when Davis hit an RBI single off Carl Edwards Jr. Maddon summoned lefty Mike Montgomery, who never had saved a game in the majors, and he retired Michael Martinez on a grounder to Bryant at third to touch off a celebration 108 years in the making.

Pennant Paths

Chicago met stiff resistance in both the NLDS and NLCS, while the Indians rode fantastic pitching to cruise through the first two rounds.

The Cubs' path to the crown appeared in jeopardy when they trailed, 5-2, in the ninth inning of Game Four of the NLDS in San Francisco. All the Giants had to do was hold on for the victory to force a winner-take-all Game Five back in Chicago and a rematch of the Game One pitching pairing of Lester vs. Johnny Cueto, which the Cubs won, 1-0, on a late home run by Baez.

But the Cubs had other ideas, rallying for four runs off five Giants relievers to pull off a miraculous victory. Just like that, San Francisco's run of even-season magic came to a stunning end. The Giants had won the World Series in 2010, 2012 and 2014, but their bullpen was the end of them this time around.

The Cubs weren't finished with dramatic victories. In Game One of the NLCS, the game was knotted, 3-3, in the eighth inning when pinch-

hitter Montero crushed a grand slam off Dodgers reliever Joe Blanton that electrified the Wrigley Field crowd and led the way to an 8-4 triumph.

Then Chicago's offense went dry. Clayton Kershaw outpitched Kyle Hendricks in Game Two for a tense 1-0 victory, and Rich Hill followed suit in Game Three in Los Angeles as the Dodgers blanked the Cubs, 6-0.

Triggered by a bunt single by Zobrist, of all things, in the fourth inning of Game Four, the Cubs rallied for four runs off rookie lefty Julio Urias and cruised to a 10-2 victory. Chicago used that momentum to roll to an 8-4 romp in Game Five, taking them back to Wrigley with a three-games-to-two lead and another matchup with Kershaw.

The Dodgers ace didn't have it this time, however, as the Cubs scored three early runs and took control of the game behind brilliant pitching from Hendricks. It would be Chicago with the shutout by a 5-0 score, ending the 71-year drought since the team's last appearance in the World Series.

To get to that NLCS against the Cubs, the Dodgers had to survive a five-game dogfight against the Nationals in the Division Series. Not surprisingly, with two evenly matched clubs, that battle came down to a decisive Game Five at Nationals Park.

With ace Max Scherzer going for Washington, the Dodgers knew they had their work cut out on the road. The Nationals led 1-0 when Joc Pederson led off the seventh inning with an opposite-field home run, sending Scherzer from the game.

Nationals manager Dusty Baker ran through a parade of relievers, using five in the seventh but

the Dodgers scored four times before the inning was done. Carlos Ruiz put LA ahead with an RBI single and Justin Turner made it 4-1 with a two-run triple off Shawn Kelley.

That lead was quickly trimmed to one run when pinch-hitter Chris Heisey ripped a two-run homer in the bottom of the inning off Grant Dayton. Keeping with the theme of the postseason, Los Angeles manager Dave Roberts went out of the box to summon closer Kenley Jansen with nine outs needed to finish the game.

Throwing a career-high 51 pitches, Jansen made it to the ninth inning, when he ran out of steam and issued a pair of one-out walks. Roberts went even farther out of the box by summoning Kershaw, who had just one day of rest since his start in Game Four. Kershaw retired the next two hitters to record his first save in the major leagues.

Indians Roll

All Cleveland had to do to advance to the World Series was get past two of the top offenses in the AL—the Red Sox in the Division Series and the Blue Jays in the ALCS.

Francona showed immediately how he intended to move his team forward in the postseason when he went to Miller in the fifth inning of Game One with the Indians clinging to a 4-3 lead over the Red Sox. Bauer was at 78 pitches and there was still half the game to go but Francona decided it was time to use his best reliever and let him go as far as it made sense.

Francona didn't need to pull strings in Game Two as the Indians rolled to a 6-0 victory behind

AMERICAN LEAGUE CHAMPIONS, 1995–2016

American League postseason results in Wild Card Era, 1995-present, where (*) denotes wild card playoff entrant.

YEAR	CHAMPIONSHIP SERIES	ALCS MVP	DIVISION SERIES	DIVISION SERIES
2016	Cleveland 4, Toronto 1	Andrew Miller, lhp, Cleveland	Toronto* 3, Texas 0	Cleveland 3, Boston 0
2015	Kansas City 4, Toronto 2	Alcides Escobar, ss, Kansas City	Kansas City 3, Houston* 2	Baltimore 3, Texas 2
2014	Kansas City 4, Baltimore 0	Lorenzo Cain, of, Kansas City	Kansas City 3, Los Angeles 0	Baltimore 3, Detroit 0
2013	Boston 4, Detroit 2	Koji Uehara, rhp, Boston	Boston 3, Tampa Bay* 1	Detroit, 3, Oakland 2
2012	Detroit 4, New York 0	Delmon Young, of, Detroit	New York 3, Baltimore* 2	Detroit 3, Oakland 2
2011	Texas 4, Detroit 2	Nelson Cruz, of, Texas	Detroit 3, New York 2	Texas 3, Tampa Bay* 1
2010	Texas 4, New York 2	Josh Hamilton, of, Texas	Texas 3, Tampa Bay 2	New York* 3, Minnesota 0
2009	New York 4, Los Angeles 2	C.C. Sabathia, lhp, New York	New York 3, Minnesota 0	Los Angeles 3, Boston* 0
2008	Tampa Bay 4, Boston 3	Matt Garza, rhp, Tampa Bay	Boston* 3, Los Angeles 1	Tampa Bay 3, Chicago 1
2007	Boston 4, Cleveland 3	Josh Beckett, rhp, Boston	Boston 3, Los Angeles 0	Cleveland 3, New York* 1
2006	Detroit 4, Oakland 0	Placido Polanco, 2b, Detroit	Detroit* 3, New York 1	Oakland 3, Minnesota 0
2005	Chicago 4, Los Angeles 1	Paul Konerko, 1b, Chicago	Chicago 3, Boston* 0	Los Angeles 3, New York 2
2004	Boston 4, New York 3	David Ortiz, dh, Boston	Boston* 3, Anaheim 0	New York 3, Minnesota 1
2003	New York 4, Boston 3	Mariano Rivera, rhp, New York	New York 3, Minnesota 1	Boston* 3, Oakland 2
2002	Anaheim 4, Minnesota 1	Adam Kennedy, 2b, Anaheim	Anaheim* 3, New York 1	Minnesota 3, Oakland 2
2001	New York 4, Seattle 1	Andy Pettitte, lhp, New York	Seattle 3, Cleveland 2	New York 3, Oakland* 2
2000	New York 4, Seattle 2	David Justice, of, New York	New York 3, Oakland 2	Seattle* 3, Chicago 0
1999	New York 4, Boston 1	Orlando Hernandez, rhp, New York	Boston* 3, Cleveland 2	New York 3, Texas 0
1998	New York 4, Cleveland 2	David Wells, lhp, New York	Cleveland 3, Boston* 1	New York 3, Texas 0
1997	Cleveland 4, Baltimore 2	Marquis Grissom, of, Cleveland	Cleveland 3, New York* 2	Baltimore 3, Seattle 1
1996	New York 4, Baltimore 1	Bernie Williams, of, New York	Baltimore* 3, Cleveland 1	New York 3, Texas 1
1995	Cleveland 4, Seattle 2	Orel Hershiser, rhp, Cleveland	Cleveland 3, Boston 0	Seattle 3, New York* 2

seven shutout innings from Kluber and Lonnie Chisenhall's three-run homer off David Price. Price's postseason miseries continued as he fell to 0-8 in nine career starts.

Heading back to Boston, the Red Sox sought to turn the series around and extend the career of retiring DH David Ortiz. But there was no stopping the Indians, who got five gritty innings from Tomlin and a two-run homer by Coco Crisp to take a 4-3 nail-biter and sweep the Red Sox.

The other AL Division Series also resulted in a surprising sweep with the wild-card Blue Jays eliminating favored Texas. And it began with a stunning 10-1 rout of Rangers ace Cole Hamels.

The Blue Jays scored five runs in the fifth and cruised from there. It was a shocking beat down of Hamels, who posted a 3.32 ERA during an all-star regular season but didn't make it out of the fourth inning against Toronto, exiting with a 7-0 score.

For Texas, that set the tone for the remainder of the short series. The Blue Jays scored 12 runs over the next two games, winning by scores of 5-3 and 7-6 to sweep the shocked Rangers.

Toronto's bats quickly cooled off against Cleveland's strong pitching in the ALCS.

With Kluber pitching 6.1 scoreless innings, Miller striking out five hitters out of the pen and shortstop Francisco Lindor socking a two-run homer, Cleveland won Game One, 2-0. The next day, Tomlin and relief ace Andrew Miller did all of the heavy lifting in a 2-1 victory. For the second consecutive game, Miller struck out five.

The Blue Jays hoped for better things when play shifted to Toronto but the course of the series had been set. Not even the bloodied finger of Bauer, who hoped the stitches would hold up after his drone accident yet had to leave in the first inning, could stop the Indians from taking a 4-2 victory.

The Blue Jays ended Cleveland's six-game postseason winning streak with a 5-1 victory in Game Four, but it only postponed the inevitable. The Indians' dominant pitching returned with a 3-0 victory in Game Five, clinching the AL pennant and a trip to the World Series.

Where's Zach?

In a postseason highlighted by extraordinary bullpen work, it was ironic that it all began with a controversy over not using the best reliever in the AL. After Baltimore lost to Toronto, 5-2, in 11 innings in the wild-card game, the question everyone wanted to ask manager Buck Showalter was: "Where was Zach Britton?"

Britton put together a historic season for the Orioles, converting all 47 of his save opportunities with a 0.54 ERA in 69 appearances. Yet, Showalter found no spot he wanted to use Britton in the excruciating loss to the Blue Jays, who won on Edwin Encarnacion's walk-off, three-run homer off erstwhile starter Ubaldo Jimenez.

Unlike Showalter, Mets manager Terry Collins went to his closer in the ninth inning of a tied NL wild card game. It ended in the same result, when closer Jeurys Familia gave up a three-run home run to regular-season reserve Conor Gillaspie. That propelled the Giants to a 3-0 victory behind Madison Bumgarner's four-hit complete game.

NATIONAL LEAGUE CHAMPIONS, 1995–2016

National League postseason results in Wild Card Era, 1995-present, where (*) denotes wild card playoff entrant.

YEAR	CHAMPIONSHIP SERIES	NLCS MVP	DIVISION SERIES	DIVISION SERIES
2016	Chicago 4, Los Angeles 2	Javier Baez, 2b/Jon Lester, lhp, Chicago	Chicago 3, San Francisco* 1	Los Angeles 3, Washington 2
2015	New York 4, Chicago 0	Daniel Murphy, 2b, New York	New York 3, Los Angeles 2	Chicago* 3, St. Louis 1
2014	San Francisco 4, St. Louis 1	Madison Bumgarner, lhp, San Francisco	San Francisco 3, Washington 1	St. Louis 3, Los Angeles 1
2013	St. Louis 4, Los Angeles 2	Michael Wacha, rhp, St. Louis	St. Louis 3, Pittsburgh* 2	Los Angeles 3, Atlanta 1
2012	San Francisco 4, St. Louis 3	Marco Scutaro, 2b, San Francisco	St. Louis* 3, Washington 2	San Francisco 3, Cincinnati 2
2011	St. Louis 4, Milwaukee 2	David Freese, 3b, St. Louis	St. Louis* 3, Philadelphia 2	Milwaukee 3, Arizona 2
2010	San Francisco 4, Philadelphia 2	Cody Ross, of, San Francisco	Philadelphia 3, Cincinnati 0	San Francisco 3, Atlanta* 1
2009	Philadelphia 4, Los Angeles 1	Ryan Howard, 1b, Philadelphia	Los Angeles 3, St. Louis 0	Philadelphia 3, Colorado* 1
2008	Philadelphia 4, Los Angeles 1	Cole Hamels, lhp, Philadelphia	Los Angeles 3, Chicago 0	Philadelphia 3, Milwaukee* 1
2007	Colorado 4, Arizona 0	Matt Holliday, of, Colorado	Arizona 3, Philadelphia 0	Colorado* 3, Philadelphia 0
2006	St. Louis 4, New York 3	Jeff Suppan, rhp, St. Louis	New York 3, Los Angeles* 0	St. Louis 3, San Diego 1
2005	Houston 4, St. Louis 2	Roy Oswalt, rhp, Houston	St. Louis 3, San Diego 0	Houston* 3, Atlanta 1
2004	St. Louis 4, Houston 3	Albert Pujols, 1b, St. Louis	St. Louis 3, Los Angeles 1	Houston* 3, Atlanta 2
2003	Florida 4, Chicago 3	Ivan Rodriguez, c, Florida	Florida* 3, San Francisco 1	Chicago 3, Atlanta 2
2002	San Francisco 4, St. Louis 1	Benito Santiago, c, San Francisco	San Francisco* 3, Atlanta 2	St. Louis 3, Arizona 0
2001	Arizona 4, Atlanta 1	Craig Counsell, ss, Arizona	Atlanta 3, Houston 0	Arizona 3, St. Louis* 2
2000	New York 4, St. Louis 1	Mike Hampton, lhp, New York	St. Louis 3, Atlanta 0	New York* 3, San Francisco 1
1999	Atlanta 4, New York 2	Eddie Perez, c, Atlanta	Atlanta 3, Houston 1	New York* 3, Arizona 1
1998	San Diego 4, Atlanta 2	Sterling Hitchcock, lhp, San Diego	Atlanta 3, Chicago* 0	San Diego 3, Houston 1
1997	Florida 4, Atlanta 2	Livan Hernandez, rhp, Florida	Florida* 3, San Francisco 0	Atlanta 3, Houston 0
1996	Atlanta 4, St. Louis 3	Javy Lopez, c, Atlanta	St. Louis 3, San Diego 0	Atlanta 3, Los Angeles* 0
1995	Atlanta 4, Cincinnati 0	Mike Devereaux, of, Atlanta	Atlanta 3, Colorado* 1	Cincinnati 3, Los Angeles 0

Year	Winner	Loser	Result
1903	Boston (AL)	Pittsburgh (NL)	5-3
1904	NO SERIES		
1905	New York (NL)	Philadelphia (AL)	4-1
1906	Chicago (AL)	Chicago (NL)	4-2
1907	Chicago (NL)	Detroit (AL)	4-0
1908	Chicago (NL)	Detroit (AL)	4-1
1909	Pittsburgh (NL)	Detroit (AL)	4-3
1910	Philadelphia (AL)	Chicago (NL)	4-1
1911	Philadelphia (AL)	New York (NL)	4-2
1912	Boston (AL)	New York (NL)	4-3-1
1913	Philadelphia (AL)	New York (NL)	4-1
1914	Boston (NL)	Philadelphia (AL)	4-0
1915	Boston (AL)	Philadelphia (NL)	4-1
1916	Boston (AL)	Brooklyn (NL)	4-1
1917	Chicago (AL)	New York (NL)	4-2
1918	Boston (AL)	Chicago (NL)	4-2
1919	Cincinnati (NL)	Chicago (AL)	5-3
1920	Cleveland (AL)	Brooklyn (NL)	5-2
1921	New York (NL)	New York (AL)	5-3
1922	New York (NL)	New York (AL)	4-0
1923	New York (AL)	New York (NL)	4-2
1924	Washington (AL)	New York (NL)	4-3
1925	Pittsburgh (NL)	Washington (AL)	4-3
1926	St. Louis (NL)	New York (AL)	4-3
1927	New York (AL)	Pittsburgh (NL)	4-0
1928	New York (AL)	St. Louis (NL)	4-0
1929	Philadelphia (AL)	Chicago (NL)	4-1
1930	Philadelphia (AL)	St. Louis (NL)	4-2
1931	St. Louis (NL)	Philadelphia (AL)	4-3
1932	New York (AL)	Chicago (NL)	4-0
1933	New York (NL)	Washington (AL)	4-1
1934	St. Louis (NL)	Detroit (AL)	4-3
1935	Detroit (AL)	Chicago (NL)	4-2
1936	New York (AL)	New York (NL)	4-2
1937	New York (AL)	New York (NL)	4-1
1938	New York (AL)	Chicago (NL)	4-0
1939	New York (AL)	Cincinnati (NL)	4-0
1940	Cincinnati (NL)	Detroit (AL)	4-3
1941	New York (AL)	Brooklyn (NL)	4-1
1942	St. Louis (NL)	New York (AL)	4-1
1943	New York (AL)	St. Louis (NL)	4-1
1944	St. Louis (NL)	St. Louis (AL)	4-2
1945	Detroit (AL)	Chicago (NL)	4-3
1946	St. Louis (NL)	Boston (AL)	4-3
1947	New York (AL)	Brooklyn (NL)	4-3
1948	Cleveland (AL)	Boston (NL)	4-2
1949	New York (AL)	Brooklyn (NL)	4-1
1950	New York (AL)	Philadelphia (NL)	4-0
1951	New York (AL)	New York (NL)	4-2
1952	New York (AL)	Brooklyn (NL)	4-3
1953	New York (AL)	Brooklyn (NL)	4-2
1954	New York (NL)	Cleveland (AL)	4-0
1955	Brooklyn (NL)	New York (AL)	4-3
1956	New York (AL)	Brooklyn (NL)	4-3
1957	Milwaukee (NL)	New York (AL)	4-3
1958	New York (AL)	Milwaukee (NL)	4-3
1959	Los Angeles (NL)	Chicago (AL)	4-2
1960	Pittsburgh (NL)	New York (AL)	4-3
1961	New York (AL)	Cincinnati (NL)	4-1
1962	New York (AL)	San Francisco (NL)	4-3
1963	Los Angeles (NL)	New York (AL)	4-0
1964	St. Louis (NL)	New York (AL)	4-3
1965	Los Angeles (NL)	Minnesota (AL)	4-3
1966	Baltimore (AL)	Los Angeles (NL)	4-0
1967	St. Louis (NL)	Boston (AL)	4-3
1968	Detroit (AL)	St. Louis (NL)	4-3
1969	New York (NL)	Baltimore (AL)	4-1
1970	Baltimore (AL)	Cincinnati (NL)	4-1
1971	Pittsburgh (NL)	Baltimore (AL)	4-3
1972	Oakland (AL)	Cincinnati (NL)	4-3
1973	Oakland (AL)	New York (NL)	4-3
1974	Oakland (AL)	Los Angeles (NL)	4-1
1975	Cincinnati (NL)	Boston (AL)	4-3
1976	Cincinnati (NL)	New York (AL)	4-0

Cubs catcher David Ross went out a winner

MIKE JANES

Year	Winner	Loser	Result
1977	New York (AL)	Los Angeles (NL)	4-2
1978	New York (AL)	Los Angeles (NL)	4-2
1979	Pittsburgh (NL)	Baltimore (AL)	4-3
1980	Philadelphia (NL)	Kansas City (AL)	4-2
1981	Los Angeles (NL)	New York (AL)	4-2
1982	St. Louis (NL)	Milwaukee (AL)	4-3
1983	Baltimore (AL)	Philadelphia (NL)	4-1
1984	Detroit (AL)	San Diego (NL)	4-1
1985	Kansas City (AL)	St. Louis (NL)	4-3
1986	New York (NL)	Boston (AL)	4-3
1987	Minnesota (AL)	St. Louis (NL)	4-3
1988	Los Angeles (NL)	Oakland (AL)	4-1
1989	Oakland (AL)	San Francisco (NL)	4-0
1990	Cincinnati (NL)	Oakland (AL)	4-0
1991	Minnesota (AL)	Atlanta (NL)	4-3
1992	Toronto (AL)	Atlanta (NL)	4-2
1993	Toronto (AL)	Philadelphia (NL)	4-2
1994	NO SERIES		
1995	Atlanta (NL)	Cleveland (AL)	4-2
1996	New York (AL)	Atlanta (NL)	4-2
1997	Florida (NL)	Cleveland (AL)	4-3
1998	New York (AL)	San Diego (NL)	4-0
1999	New York (AL)	Atlanta (NL)	4-0
2000	New York (AL)	New York (NL)	4-1
2001	Arizona (NL)	New York (AL)	4-3
2002	Anaheim (AL)	San Francisco (NL)	4-3
2003	Florida (NL)	New York (AL)	4-2
2004	Boston (AL)	St. Louis (NL)	4-0
2005	Chicago (AL)	Houston (NL)	4-0
2006	St. Louis (NL)	Detroit (AL)	4-1
2007	Boston (AL)	Colorado (NL)	4-0
2008	Philadelphia (NL)	Tampa Bay (AL)	4-1
2009	New York (AL)	Philadelphia (NL)	4-2
2010	San Francisco (NL)	Texas (AL)	4-1
2011	St. Louis (NL)	Texas (AL)	4-3
2012	San Francisco (NL)	Detroit (AL)	4-0
2013	Boston (AL)	St. Louis (NL)	4-2
2014	San Francisco (NL)	Kansas City (AL)	4-3
2015	Kansas City (AL)	New York (NL)	4-1
2016	Chicago (NL)	Cleveland (AL)	4-3

WORLD SERIES BOX SCORES

GAME ONE *October 25, 2016*

CLEVELAND 6, CHICAGO 0

CHICAGO	AB	R	H	RBI	BB	SO	LOB	AVG
Fowler, CF	4	0	0	0	0	2	1	.000
Bryant, 3B	3	0	0	0	1	2	1	.000
Rizzo, 1B	4	0	0	0	0	0	1	.000
Zobrist, LF	4	0	3	0	0	0	0	.750
Schwarber, DH	3	0	1	0	1	2	3	.333
Baez, J, 2B	4	0	1	0	0	2	2	.250
Coghlan, RF	2	0	0	0	0	2	1	.000
a-Contreras, PH-C	2	0	1	0	0	0	3	.500
Russell, SS	4	0	0	0	0	3	4	.000
Ross, D, C	3	0	1	0	0	1	3	.333
Almora Jr., RF	0	0	0	0	0	0	0	.000
b-Montero, PH	1	0	0	0	0	1	1	.000
TOTALS	34	0	7	0	2	15	20	
CLEVELAND	AB	R	H	RBI	BB	SO	LOB	AVG
Davis, R, CF	5	0	1	0	0	1	0	.200
Kipnis, 2B	5	0	0	0	0	0	1	.000
Lindor, SS	4	1	3	0	0	0	0	.750
Napoli, 1B	3	1	0	0	1	2	2	.000
Santana, C, DH	2	0	0	0	2	2	0	.000
Ramirez, Js, 3B	4	0	3	1	0	0	0	.750
Guyer, LF	2	1	0	1	1	2	3	.000
Chisenhall, RF	4	1	1	0	0	1	4	.250
Perez, R, C	4	2	2	4	0	1	1	.500
TOTALS	33	6	10	6	4	9	11	
Chicago					000	000	000—0	
Cleveland					200	100	03x—6	

a-Flied out for Coghlan in the 7th. **b**-Struck out for Almora Jr. **in the 9th.**

2B: Zobrist, Schwarber, Contreras, Ramirez, Lindor, Davis. **HR:** Perez 2. **Chicago LOB:** 9. **Cleveland LOB:** 8. **SB:** Lindor. **CS:** Lindor.

CHICAGO	IP	H	R	ER	BB	SO	HR	ERA
Lester (L, 0-1)	5.2	6	3	3	3	7	1	4.76
Strop	0.2	0	0	0	0	1	0	0.00
Wood, T	0.1	0	0	0	0	0	0	0.00
Grimm	1.0	2	2	2	1	1	0	18.00
Rondon	0.1	2	1	1	0	0	1	27.00
CLEVELAND	IP	H	R	ER	BB	SO	HR	ERA
Kluber (W, 1-0)	6.0	4	0	0	0	9	0	0.00
Miller, A (H, 1)	2.0	2	0	0	2	3	0	0.00
Allen	1.0	1	0	0	0	3	0	0.00

Kluber pitched to 1 batter in the 7th. **Game Scores:** Lester 48; Kluber 77.

GAME TWO *October 26, 2016*

CHICAGO 5, CLEVELAND 1

CHICAGO	AB	R	H	RBI	BB	SO	LOB	AVG
Fowler, CF	5	0	1	0	0	2	4	.111
Bryant, 3B	5	1	1	0	0	1	3	.125
Rizzo, 1B	3	2	1	1	2	0	3	.143
Zobrist, LF	4	1	2	1	1	0	1	.625
Schwarber, DH	4	1	2	2	1	2	1	.429
Baez, J, 2B	5	0	1	0	0	2	5	.222
Contreras, C	3	0	0	0	2	0	2	.200
Soler, RF	2	0	0	0	1	0	2	.000
1-Heyward, PR-RF	2	0	0	0	0	1	0	.000
Russell, SS	4	0	1	1	1	0	2	.125
TOTALS	37	5	9	5	8	8	24	
CLEVELAND	AB	R	H	RBI	BB	SO	LOB	AVG
Santana, C, DH	4	0	0	0	0	2	2	.000
Kipnis, 2B	4	1	1	0	0	2	0	.111
Lindor, SS	3	0	0	0	1	1	1	.429
Napoli, 1B	3	0	2	0	1	0	0	.333
Ramirez, Js, 3B	3	0	0	0	1	1	4	.429
Chisenhall, RF	2	0	0	0	0	0	1	.167
a-Davis, R, PH-CF	2	0	0	0	0	2	0	.143
Crisp, LF	4	0	0	0	0	1	0	.000
Naquin, CF	2	0	0	0	0	2	0	.000
b-Guyer, PH-RF	1	0	0	0	1	0	0	.333
Perez, R, C	3	0	0	0	1	1	1	.286
TOTALS	31	1	4	0	5	12	9	
Chicago					101	030	000—5	
Cleveland					000	001	000—1	

1-Ran for Soler in the 5th. **a**-Struck out for Chisenhall in the 7th. **b**-Singled for Naquin in the 7th.

2B: Rizzo, Kipnis. **3B:** Zobrist. **Chicago LOB:** 13. **Cleveland LOB:** 8. **E:** Kipnis 2.

CHICAGO	IP	H	R	ER	BB	SO	HR	ERA
Arrieta (W, 1-0)	5.2	2	1	1	3	6	0	1.59
Montgomery	2.0	2	0	0	1	4	0	0.00
Chapman	1.1	0	0	0	1	2	0	0.00
CLEVELAND	IP	H	R	ER	BB	SO	HR	ERA
Bauer (L, 0-1)	3.2	6	2	2	2	2	0	4.91
McAllister	0.2	1	2	2	1	2	0	27.00
Shaw, B	0.2	1	1	0	2	2	0	0.00
Salazar	1.0	0	0	0	2	0	0	0.00
Manship	0.1	1	0	0	1	0	0	0.00
Otero	1.2	0	0	0	0	1	0	0.00
Clevinger	1.0	0	0	0	0	1	0	0.00

Game Scores: Arrieta 67; Bauer 42.

GAME THREE *October 28, 2016*

CLEVELAND 1, CHICAGO 0

CLEVELAND	AB	R	H	RBI	BB	SO	LOB	AVG
Santana, C, LF	1	0	0	0	2	1	0	.000
Miller, A, P	0	0	0	0	0	0	0	.000
a-Crisp, PH	1	0	1	1	0	0	0	.200
Shaw, B, P	0	0	0	0	0	0	0	.000
Guyer, LF	0	0	0	0	0	0	0	.333
Kipnis, 2B	3	0	1	0	0	1	2	.167
Lindor, SS	4	0	2	0	0	0	3	.455
Napoli, 1B	4	0	0	0	0	3	2	.200
Ramirez, Js, 3B	4	0	2	0	0	0	0	.455
Allen, P	0	0	0	0	0	0	0	.000
Chisenhall, RF	4	0	0	0	0	2	3	.100
Perez, R, C	3	0	1	0	0	1	3	.300
1-Martinez, M, PR-CF-3B	1	1	0	0	0	1	0	.000
Naquin, CF	2	0	1	0	0	0	0	.250
Gomes, C	1	0	0	0	0	0	0	.000
Tomlin, P	1	0	0	0	0	1	0	.000
Davis, R, LF-CF	0	0	0	0	1	0	0	.143
TOTALS	29	1	8	1	3	10	13	
CHICAGO	AB	R	H	RBI	BB	SO	LOB	AVG
Fowler, CF	4	0	1	0	0	1	0	.154
Bryant, 3B	3	0	0	0	1	2	1	.091
Rizzo, 1B	4	0	1	0	0	1	1	.182
3-Coghlan, PR	0	0	0	0	0	0	0	.000
Zobrist, LF	4	0	1	0	0	1	2	.500
Contreras, C	4	0	0	0	0	0	3	.111
Soler, RF	3	0	2	0	0	1	1	.400
2-Heyward, PR-RF	1	0	0	0	0	0	1	.000
Baez, J, 2B	4	0	0	0	0	1	5	.154
Russell, SS	3	0	0	0	0	1	1	.091
Hendricks, P	1	0	0	0	0	0	0	.000
Grimm, P	0	0	0	0	0	0	0	.000
b-Montero, PH	1	0	0	0	0	1	1	.000
Edwards Jr., P	0	0	0	0	0	0	0	.000
Montgomery, P	0	0	0	0	0	0	0	.000
Strop, P	0	0	0	0	0	0	0	.000
c-Schwarber, PH	1	0	0	0	0	0	0	.375
Chapman, P	0	0	0	0	0	0	0	.000
TOTALS	33	0	5	0	1	8	16	
Cleveland					000	000	100—1	
Chicago					000	000	000—0	

a-Singled for Miller, A in the 7th. **b**-Batted for Grimm in the 5th. **c**-Popped out for Strop in the 8th. **1**-Ran for Perez, R in the 7th. **2**-Ran for Soler in the 7th. **3**-Ran for Rizzo in the 9th.

3B: Soler. **Cleveland LOB:** 7. **Chicago LOB:** 7. **SB:** Heyward. **E:** Napoli.

CLEVELAND	IP	H	R	ER	BB	SO	HR	ERA
Tomlin	4.2	2	0	0	1	1	0	0.00
Miller, A (W, 1-0)	1.1	0	0	0	0	3	0	0.00
Shaw, B (H, 1)	1.2	2	0	0	0	1	0	0.00
Allen (S, 1)	1.1	1	0	0	0	3	0	0.00
CHICAGO	IP	H	R	ER	BB	SO	HR	ERA
Hendricks	4.1	6	0	0	2	6	0	0.00
Grimm	0.2	0	0	0	0	0	0	10.80
Edwards Jr. (L, 0-1)	1.2	2	1	1	1	1	0	5.40
Montgomery	0.2	0	0	0	0	1	0	0.00
Strop	0.2	0	0	0	0	1	0	0.00
Chapman	1.0	0	0	0	0	2	0	0.00

Game Scores: Tomlin 63; Hendricks 56. **HBP:** Kipnis (by Hendricks).

GAME FOUR October 29, 2016
CLEVELAND 7, CHICAGO 2

CLEVELAND	AB	R	H	RBI	BB	SO	LOB	AVG
Davis, R, LF-CF	4	1	0	0	0	0	2	.091
Kipnis, 2B	5	2	3	3	0	1	0	.294
Lindor, SS	4	1	2	1	1	1	0	.467
Santana, C, 1B	4	1	3	1	0	1	1	.273
Miller, A, P	0	0	0	0	0	0	0	.000
c-Martinez, M, PH	1	0	0	0	0	1	2	.000
Otero, P	0	0	0	0	0	0	0	.000
Ramirez, Js, 3B	5	0	0	0	0	1	6	.313
Chisenhall, RF	3	1	0	1	0	1	1	.077
Perez, R, C	3	0	0	0	1	1	1	.231
Naquin, CF	1	0	0	0	1	0	0	.200
a-Guyer, PH-LF	2	0	0	0	0	1	2	.200
Kluber, P	2	0	1	0	0	1	0	.500
b-Crisp, PH	1	1	1	0	0	0	0	.333
Napoli, 1B	1	0	0	0	0	0	0	.182
TOTALS	**36**	**7**	**10**	**6**	**3**	**10**	**15**	

CHICAGO	AB	R	H	RBI	BB	SO	LOB	AVG
Fowler, CF	4	2	2	1	0	0	0	.235
Bryant, 3B	3	0	0	0	1	0	1	.071
Rizzo, 1B	3	0	2	1	0	1	0	.286
Zobrist, LF	4	0	0	0	0	2	4	.375
Contreras, C	4	0	0	0	0	3	2	.077
Russell, SS	4	0	1	0	0	0	1	.133
Heyward, RF	4	0	2	0	0	0	1	.286
Baez, J, 2B	4	0	0	0	0	1	3	.118
Lackey, P	1	0	0	0	0	1	0	.000
d-Coghlan, PH	1	0	0	0	0	0	0	.000
Montgomery, P	0	0	0	0	0	0	0	.000
Grimm, P	0	0	0	0	0	0	0	.000
Wood, T, P	0	0	0	0	0	0	0	.000
e-Almora Jr., PH	1	0	0	0	0	0	0	.000
Rondon, P	0	0	0	0	0	0	0	.000
TOTALS	**33**	**2**	**7**	**2**	**1**	**8**	**12**	

Cleveland				021	001		300—7
Chicago				100	000		010—2

a-Batted for Naquin in the 6th. b-Doubled for Kluber in the 7th. c-Struck out for Miller, A in the 9th. d-Flied out for Lackey in the 5th. e-Lined out for Wood, T in the 7th.

2B: Kipnis, Crisp, Fowler, Rizzo. **HR:** Santana, Kipnis, Fowler. **Cleveland LOB:** 7. **Chicago LOB:** 6. **SB:** Rizzo. **E:** Bryant 2.

CLEVELAND	IP	H	R	ER	BB	SO	HR	ERA
Kluber (W, 2-0)	6.0	5	1	1	1	6	0	0.75
Miller, A	2.0	1	1	1	0	2	1	1.69
Otero	1.0	1	0	0	0	0	0	0.00

CHICAGO	IP	H	R	ER	BB	SO	HR	ERA
Lackey (L, 0-1)	5.0	4	3	2	1	5	1	3.60
Montgomery	0.2	1	1	1	2	0	0	2.70
Grimm	0.1	1	2	2	0	1	0	18.00
Wood, T	1.0	2	1	1	0	2	1	6.75
Rondon	2.0	2	0	0	0	2	0	3.86

Grimm pitched to 2 batters in the 7th. **Game Scores:** Kluber 67; Lackey 50. **IBB:** Naquin (by Lackey). **HBP:** Davis, R (by Grimm); Rizzo (by Kluber).

GAME FIVE October 30, 2016
CHICAGO 3, CLEVELAND 2

CLEVELAND	AB	R	H	RBI	BB	SO	LOB	AVG
Davis, R, CF	4	1	2	0	0	1	0	.200
Kipnis, 2B	4	0	0	0	0	2	2	.238
Lindor, SS	4	0	1	1	0	2	1	.421
Napoli, 1B	4	0	1	0	0	0	0	.200
Santana, C, LF	4	0	1	0	0	0	1	.267
Ramirez, Js, 3B	4	1	1	1	0	2	2	.300
Guyer, RF	2	0	0	0	1	1	1	.143
Perez, R, C	3	0	0	0	0	0	3	.188
Allen, P	0	0	0	0	0	0	0	.000
Bauer, P	1	0	0	0	0	0	0	.000
Clevinger, P	0	0	0	0	0	0	0	.000
a-Crisp, PH	1	0	0	0	0	0	0	.286
Shaw, B, P	0	0	0	0	0	0	0	.000
Gomes, C	1	0	0	0	0	1	0	.000
TOTALS	**32**	**2**	**6**	**2**	**0**	**9**	**10**	

GAME SIX November 1, 2016
CHICAGO 9, CLEVELAND 3

CHICAGO	AB	R	H	RBI	BB	SO	LOB	AVG
Fowler, CF	3	0	0	0	0	1	0	.200
Bryant, 3B	3	1	1	1	1	2	1	.118
Rizzo, 1B	3	1	1	0	1	0	1	.294
Zobrist, LF	3	1	1	0	1	0	2	.368
Russell, SS	4	0	2	1	0	1	2	.211
Heyward, RF	4	0	1	0	0	3	3	.273
Baez, J, 2B	4	0	1	0	0	3	2	.143
Ross, D, C	1	0	0	1	0	0	0	.250
b-Montero, PH	1	0	0	0	0	1	0	.000
Edwards Jr., P	0	0	0	0	0	0	0	.000
Chapman, P	1	0	0	0	0	1	1	.000
Lester, P	2	0	0	0	0	2	2	.000
Contreras, C	1	0	0	0	0	0	0	.071
TOTALS	**30**	**3**	**7**	**3**	**3**	**14**	**14**	

Cleveland				010	001		000—2
Chicago				000	300		00x—3

a-Grounded out for Clevinger in the 6th. b-Struck out for Ross, D in the 6th.

2B: Santana, Rizzo. **HR:** Ramirez, Bryant. **Cleveland LOB:** 4. **Chicago LOB:** 8. **SB:** Davis 3, Bryant, Fowler, Heyward 2. **CS:** Lindor. **E:** Perez.

CLEVELAND	IP	H	R	ER	BB	SO	HR	ERA
Bauer (L, 0-2)	4.0	6	3	3	0	7	1	5.87
Clevinger	1.0	0	0	0	2	0	0	0.00
Shaw, B	1.1	0	0	0	0	3	0	0.00
Allen	1.2	1	0	0	1	4	0	0.00

CHICAGO	IP	H	R	ER	BB	SO	HR	ERA
Lester (W, 1-1)	6.0	4	2	2	0	5	1	3.86
Edwards Jr. (H, 1)	0.1	1	0	0	0	0	0	4.50
Chapman (S, 1)	2.2	1	0	0	0	4	0	0.00

Game Scores: Bauer 44; Lester 61. **IBB:** Rizzo (by Allen). **HBP:** Guyer (by Chapman); Fowler (by Allen).

GAME SIX November 1, 2016
CHICAGO 9, CLEVELAND 3

CHICAGO	AB	R	H	RBI	BB	SO	LOB	AVG
Fowler, CF	5	0	0	0	0	1	1	.160
Schwarber, DH	4	1	1	0	1	0	0	.333
Bryant, 3B	5	2	4	1	0	0	1	.273
Rizzo, 1B	5	3	3	2	0	0	3	.364
Zobrist, LF	4	2	2	0	1	1	3	.391
Russell, SS	5	1	2	6	0	1	4	.250
Contreras, C	3	0	0	0	1	1	1	.059
Heyward, RF	4	0	0	0	0	0	1	.200
Baez, J, 2B	4	0	1	0	0	2	0	.160
TOTALS	**39**	**9**	**13**	**9**	**3**	**6**	**14**	

CLEVELAND	AB	R	H	RBI	BB	SO	LOB	AVG
Santana, C, DH	4	0	0	0	1	1	1	.211
Kipnis, 2B	5	2	3	1	0	0	1	.308
Lindor, SS	3	0	0	0	1	1	3	.364
Napoli, 1B	4	0	1	1	0	3	1	.211
Ramirez, Js, 3B	4	0	1	0	0	1	1	.292
Chisenhall, RF	1	0	0	0	1	1	0	.071
c-Gomes, PH	1	0	0	0	0	1	0	.000
Martinez, M, RF	0	0	0	0	0	0	0	.000
Crisp, LF	1	0	0	0	1	0	0	.250
a-Guyer, PH-LF	1	1	0	0	1	0	1	.125
Naquin, CF	2	0	0	0	0	2	3	.143
b-Davis, R, PH-CF	2	0	0	0	0	0	1	.176
Perez, R, C	3	0	1	1	1	1	0	.211
TOTALS	**31**	**3**	**6**	**3**	**6**	**10**	**13**	

Chicago				304	000		002—9
Cleveland				000	110		001—3

a-Grounded into a forceout for Crisp in the 6th. b-Lined out for Naquin in the 7th. c-Grounded into a double play for Chisenhall in the 8th.

2B: Russell, Kipnis. **HR:** Bryant, Russell, Rizzo, Kipnis. **Chicago LOB:** 6. **Cleveland LOB:** 8. **E:** Kipnis.

CHICAGO	IP	H	R	ER	BB	SO	HR	ERA
Arrieta (W, 2-0)	5.2	3	2	2	3	9	1	2.38
Montgomery	1.0	1	0	0	0	0	0	2.08
Chapman	1.1	1	1	1	1	1	0	1.42
Strop	0.2	1	0	0	1	0	0	0.00
Wood, T	0.1	0	0	0	0	0	0	5.40

CLEVELAND	IP	H	R	ER	BB	SO	HR	ERA
Tomlin (L, 0-1)	2.1	6	6	6	1	0	1	7.71
Otero	0.2	1	1	1	0	0	1	2.70
Salazar	2.0	1	0	0	0	4	0	0.00
Manship	0.2	1	0	0	0	1	0	0.00
McAllister	1.1	2	0	0	0	0	0	9.00
Clevinger	2.0	2	2	2	2	1	1	4.50

Chapman pitched to 1 batter in the 9th. **Game Scores:** Arrieta 59; Tomlin 16. **HBP:** Chisenhall (by Arrieta).

GAME SEVEN *November 2, 2016*
CHICAGO 8, CLEVELAND 7

CHICAGO	AB	R	H	RBI	BB	SO	LOB	AVG
Fowler, CF	5	1	3	1	0	0	1	.233
Schwarber, DH	5	0	3	0	0	0	2	.412
2-Almora Jr., PR-DH	0	1	0	0	0	0	0	.000
Bryant, 3B	4	2	1	0	1	1	3	.269
Rizzo, 1B	3	1	1	1	1	1	1	.360
Zobrist, LF	5	1	1	0	0	0	4	.357
Russell, SS	3	0	0	1	1	0	0	.222
Contreras, C	2	0	1	1	0	0	0	.105
Ross, D, C	1	1	1	1	0	0	0	.400
1-Coghlan, PR	0	0	0	0	0	0	0	.000
Montero, C	1	0	1	1	0	0	0	.250
Heyward, RF	5	0	0	0	0	1	5	.150
Baez, J, 2B	5	1	1	0	0	2	4	.167
TOTALS	**39**	**8**	**13**	**8**	**4**	**5**	**20**	
CLEVELAND	AB	R	H	RBI	BB	SO	LOB	AVG
Santana, C, DH	4	1	1	1	1	0	1	.217
Kipnis, 2B	5	1	1	0	0	3	2	.290
Lindor, SS	5	0	0	0	0	1	2	.296
Napoli, 1B	5	0	0	0	0	3	3	.167
Ramirez, Js, 3B	5	1	2	0	0	0	0	.310

CHICAGO								
Chisenhall, RF	2	0	1	0	0	0	0	.125
a-Guyer, PH-RF-LF	2	2	2	1	1	0	0	.300
Davis, R, CF	5	1	2	3	0	0	2	.227
Crisp, LF	4	1	2	0	0	0	0	.333
Martinez, M, RF	1	0	0	0	0	0	1	.000
Perez, R, C	1	0	0	0	0	1	1	.200
3-Naquin, PR	0	0	0	0	0	0	0	.143
Gomes, C	1	0	0	0	0	1	1	.000
TOTALS	**40**	**7**	**11**	**5**	**3**	**9**	**12**	

Chicago	100	221	000	2—8
Cleveland	001	020	030	1—7

1-Ran for Ross, D in the 9th. **2-**Ran for Schwarber in the 10th. **3-**Ran for Perez, R in the 7th.

a-Singled for Chisenhall in the 6th.

2B: Contreras, Zobrist, Crisp, Guyer. **HR:** Fowler, Baez, Ross, Davis. **Chicago LOB:** 7. **Cleveland LOB:** 7. **SB:** Schwarber, Heyward. **CS:** Fowler. **E:** Baez, Ross, Gomes.

CHICAGO	IP	H	R	ER	BB	SO	HR	ERA
Hendricks	4.2	4	2	1	1	2	0	1.00
Lester	3.0	3	2	1	1	4	0	3.68
Chapman (BS, 1)(W, 1-0)	1.1	3	2	2	0	2	1	3.52
Edwards Jr. (H, 2)	0.2	1	1	1	1	1	0	6.75
Montgomery (S, 1)	0.1	0	0	0	0	0	0	1.93
CLEVELAND	IP	H	R	ER	BB	SO	HR	ERA
Kluber	4.0	6	4	4	0	0	2	2.81
Miller, A	2.1	4	2	2	1	1	1	3.52
Allen	2.0	0	0	0	1	2	0	0.00
Shaw, B (L, 0-1)	1.0	3	2	2	1	0	0	3.86
Bauer	0.2	0	0	0	0	1	0	5.40

Kluber pitched to 1 batter in the 5th. **Game Scores:** Hendricks 54; Kluber 28. **IBB:** Rizzo (by Shaw, B); Russell (by Shaw, B). **HBP:** Rizzo (by Kluber).

AMERICAN LEAGUE WILD CARD GAME
TORONTO 5, BALTIMORE 2

BALTIMORE	AB	R	H	RBI	BB	SO	LOB	AVG
Jones, A, CF	5	1	1	0	0	1	0	.200
Kim, LF	4	0	0	0	0	0	1	.000
a-Reimold, PH-LF	1	0	0	0	0	1	0	.000
Machado, 3B	4	0	1	0	0	0	1	.250
Trumbo, DH	4	1	1	2	0	1	1	.250
Wieters, C	4	0	0	0	0	2	0	.000
Davis, C, 1B	3	0	0	0	1	2	0	.000
Schoop, 2B	4	0	0	0	0	1	1	.000
Bourn, RF	4	0	1	0	0	2	1	.250
Hardy, SS	4	0	0	0	0	2	1	.000
TOTALS	**37**	**2**	**4**	**2**	**1**	**12**	**6**	
TORONTO	AB	R	H	RBI	BB	SO	LOB	AVG
Travis, 2B	5	1	1	0	0	1	3	.200
Donaldson, 3B	5	1	2	0	0	1	0	.400
Encarnacion, 1B	4	1	1	3	1	0	1	.250
Bautista, RF	3	1	1	1	1	2	2	.333
Martin, R, C	4	0	0	0	0	0	3	.000
Tulowitzki, SS	4	0	0	0	0	1	0	.000
Saunders, DH	2	1	1	0	0	1	0	.500
b-Upton Jr., PH-DH	1	0	0	0	0	0	0	.000
c-Smoak, PH-DH	1	0	0	0	0	1	0	.000
Pillar, CF	4	0	1	0	0	1	0	.250
Carrera, LF	4	0	2	1	0	2	0	.500
TOTALS	**37**	**5**	**9**	**5**	**2**	**11**	**8**	

Baltimore	000	200	000	00—2
Toronto	010	010	000	03—5

One out when winning run scored.

a-Struck out for Kim in the 11th. **b-**Flied out for Saunders in the 7th. **c-**Struck out for Upton Jr. **in the 10th.**

2B: Saunders, Pillar, Donaldson. **HR:** Trumbo, Bautista, Encarnacion. **Baltimore LOB:** 3. **Toronto LOB:** 3. **SB:** Bourn.

BALTIMORE	IP	H	R	ER	BB	SO	HR	ERA
Tillman	4.1	4	2	2	1	4	1	4.15
Givens	2.1	0	0	0	0	3	0	0.00
Hart	0.1	0	0	0	0	0	0	0.00
Brach	1.1	2	0	0	1	2	0	0.00
O'Day	1.2	0	0	0	0	1	0	0.00
Duensing	0.1	0	0	0	0	1	0	0.00
Jimenez (L)	0.0	3	3	3	0	0	1	-.--
TORONTO	IP	H	R	ER	BB	SO	HR	ERA
Stroman	6.0	4	2	2	0	6	1	3.00
Cecil	0.1	0	0	0	1	0	0	0.00
Biagini	0.2	0	0	0	0	2	0	0.00
Grilli	1.0	0	0	0	0	1	0	0.00
Osuna	1.1	0	0	0	0	2	0	0.00
Liriano (W)	1.2	0	0	0	1	0	0	0.00

Game Scores: Tillman 48; Stroman 62. **IBB:** Encarnacion (by Brach).

AMERICAN LEAGUE DIVISION SERIES
TEXAS RANGERS VS. TORONTO BLUE JAYS

Toronto	AVG	G	AB	R	H	2B	3B	HR	RBI	BB	SO	SB
Darwin Barney, 2B	.000	3	7	0	0	0	0	0	0	0	0	0
Jose Bautista, RF	.167	3	12	3	2	0	0	1	4	2	3	0
Ezequiel Carrera, RF	.333	3	12	4	4	0	0	1	1	2	2	1
Josh Donaldson, 3B	.538	3	13	4	7	4	0	0	3	1	3	0
Edwin Encarnacion, DH	.417	3	12	4	5	0	0	2	4	2	0	0
Russell Martin, C	.083	3	12	2	1	0	0	1	1	2	5	0
Kevin Pillar, CF	.083	3	12	1	1	0	0	1	1	1	1	0
Michael Saunders, LF	.200	2	5	0	1	0	0	0	0	1	2	0
Justin Smoak, 1B	—	1	0	0	0	0	0	0	0	0	0	0
Devon Travis, 2B	.000	1	5	1	0	0	0	0	0	0	0	0
Troy Tulowitzki, SS	.462	3	13	2	6	0	1	1	5	0	1	0
Melvin Upton Jr., LF	.333	3	6	1	2	1	0	1	1	1	1	0
Totals	**.266**	**3**	**109**	**22**	**29**	**5**	**1**	**8**	**20**	**12**	**18**	**1**

Toronto	W	L	ERA	G	GS	SV	IP	H	R	ER	BB	SO
Joe Biagini	0	0	0.00	2	0	0	3.0	2	0	0	0	1
Brett Cecil	0	0	0.00	2	0	0	1.0	0	0	0	1	0
Marco Estrada	1	0	1.08	1	1	0	8.1	4	1	1	0	6
Jason Grilli	0	0	0.00	2	0	0	1.0	0	0	0	0	1
J.A. Happ	1	0	1.80	1	1	0	5.0	9	1	1	1	5
Francisco Liriano	0	0	54.00	1	0	0	0.1	2	2	2	1	0
Roberto Osuna	1	0	0.00	2	0	1	3.2	1	0	0	0	4
Aaron Sanchez	0	0	9.53	1	1	0	5.2	3	6	6	4	5
Ryan Tepera	0	0	0.00	1	0	0	0.2	0	0	0	0	0
Totals	**3**	**0**	**3.21**	**3**	**3**	**1**	**28.0**	**21**	**10**	**10**	**7**	**22**

Texas	AVG	G	AB	R	H	2B	3B	HR	RBI	BB	SO	SB
Elvis Andrus, SS	.364	3	11	2	4	0	1	1	1	0	0	0
Carlos Beltran, DH	.182	3	11	0	2	0	0	0	1	1	1	0
Adrian Beltre, 3B	.182	3	11	1	2	1	0	0	0	1	2	0
Robinson Chirinos, C	—	1	0	0	0	0	0	0	0	1	0	0
Shin-Soo Choo, RF	.000	1	3	0	0	0	0	0	1	0	2	0
Ian Desmond, CF	.214	3	14	0	3	1	0	0	2	0	3	0
Carlos Gomez, CF	.154	3	13	1	2	0	0	0	1	1	5	1
Jared Hoying, CF	.000	2	1	0	0	0	0	0	0	0	1	0
Jonathan Lucroy, C	.083	3	12	1	1	0	0	0	0	0	2	0
Nomar Mazara, RF	.167	2	6	1	1	0	0	0	0	0	3	0
Mitch Moreland, 1B	.250	3	8	1	2	2	0	0	2	1	1	0
Rougned Odor, 2B	.200	3	10	2	2	0	0	1	2	2	1	0
Ryan Rua, LF	.667	1	3	0	2	0	0	0	0	0	1	0
Totals	**.204**	**3**	**103**	**10**	**21**	**4**	**1**	**2**	**10**	**7**	**22**	**1**

Texas	W	L	ERA	G	GS	SV	IP	H	R	ER	BB	SO
Tony Barnette	0	0	0.00	3	0	0	4.0	3	0	0	0	1
Matt Bush	0	1	0.00	2	0	0	3.2	1	1	0	2	6
Alex Claudio	0	0	0.00	2	0	0	5.0	3	0	0	3	0
Yu Darvish	0	1	9.00	1	1	0	5.0	5	5	5	1	4
Jake Diekman	0	0	27.00	2	0	0	1.0	5	3	3	2	1
Sam Dyson	0	0	0.00	1	0	0	1.0	0	0	0	0	1
Cole Hamels	0	1	16.20	1	1	0	3.1	6	7	6	3	1
Jeremy Jeffress	0	0	0.00	1	0	0	1.0	1	1	0	1	1
Keone Kela	0	0	0.00	1	0	0	1.2	0	0	0	1	0
Colby Lewis	0	0	22.50	1	1	0	2.0	5	5	5	0	2
Totals	**0**	**3**	**6.18**	**3**	**3**	**0**	**27.2**	**29**	**22**	**19**	**12**	**18**

E: Andrus, Odor. **LOB:** Toronto 17, Texas 16. **DP:** Toronto 2, Texas 4. **GIDP:** Barney, Bautista, Travis, Tulowitzki, Beltre. **HBP:** Darvish (by Darvish). **IBB:** Encarnacion (by Bush), Pillar (by Diekman). **SB:** Carrera, Gomez. **CS:** Andrus. **WP:** Hamels. **PB:** Martin, Lucroy 2.

SCORE BY INNINGS

Toronto	327	231	003	1—22
Texas	101	302	021	0—10

CLEVELAND INDIANS VS. BOSTON RED SOX

Boston	AVG	G	AB	R	H	2B	3B	HR	RBI	BB	SO	SB
Andrew Benintendi, LF	.333	3	9	1	3	1	0	1	2	0	1	0
Mookie Betts, RF	.200	3	10	1	2	1	0	0	0	2	1	0
Xander Bogaerts, SS	.250	3	12	1	3	0	0	0	0	0	4	0
Jackie Bradley Jr., CF	.100	3	10	0	1	0	0	0	0	0	7	0
Marco Hernandez, SS	—	2	0	0	0	0	0	0	0	0	0	0
Aaron Hill, 3B	.000	1	1	0	0	0	0	0	0	0	1	0
Brock Holt, LF	.400	3	10	1	4	1	0	1	1	0	2	0
Sandy Leon, C	.100	3	10	1	1	0	0	1	1	1	5	0
David Ortiz, DH	.111	3	9	0	1	1	0	0	1	2	1	0
Dustin Pedroia, 2B	.167	3	12	2	2	1	0	0	0	2	5	0
Hanley Ramirez, 1B	.250	3	12	0	3	2	0	0	2	0	4	0
Travis Shaw, 3B	.500	1	2	0	1	0	0	0	0	0	0	0
Chris Young, LF	.000	1	1	0	0	0	0	0	0	1	0	0
Totals	**.214**	**3**	**98**	**7**	**21**	**7**	**0**	**3**	**7**	**8**	**31**	**0**

Boston	W	L	ERA	G	GS	SV	IP	H	R	ER	BB	SO
Matt Barnes	0	0	0.00	1	0	0	1.2	3	1	0	0	1
Clay Buchholz	0	1	4.50	1	1	0	4.0	6	2	2	1	4
Joe Kelly	0	0	0.00	3	0	0	3.2	0	0	0	0	3
Craig Kimbrel	0	0	0.00	2	0	0	1.1	0	0	0	0	3
Drew Pomeranz	0	0	4.91	2	0	0	3.2	4	2	2	2	7
Rick Porcello	0	1	10.38	1	1	0	4.1	6	5	5	0	6
David Price	0	1	13.50	1	1	0	3.1	6	5	5	2	3
Robbie Ross Jr.	0	0	0.00	1	0	0	0.1	0	0	0	0	1
Koji Uehara	0	0	0.00	2	0	0	2.0	1	0	0	0	1
Brad Ziegler	0	0	0.00	1	0	0	0.2	0	0	0	1	1
Totals	**0**	**3**	**5.04**	**3**	**3**	**0**	**25.0**	**26**	**15**	**14**	**6**	**30**

Cleveland	AVG	G	AB	R	H	2B	3B	HR	RBI	BB	SO	SB
Lonnie Chisenhall, RF	.300	3	10	2	3	0	0	1	4	1	3	0
Coco Crisp, LF	.167	2	6	1	1	0	0	1	2	0	1	0
Rajai Davis, CF	.000	3	6	0	0	0	0	0	1	0	3	0
Brandon Guyer, LF	.750	1	4	2	3	0	0	0	1	0	1	0
Jason Kipnis, 2B	.364	3	11	1	4	0	0	1	3	1	4	0
Francisco Lindor, SS	.250	3	12	1	3	1	0	1	1	0	5	0
Michael Martinez, 2B	.000	2	1	0	0	0	0	0	0	0	0	0
Mike Napoli, 1B	.167	3	12	0	2	1	0	0	0	0	4	1
Tyler Naquin, CF	.250	2	4	0	1	0	0	0	0	0	1	0
Roberto Perez, C	.222	3	9	3	2	0	0	1	1	2	2	0

Jose Ramirez, 3B	.500	3	10	4	5	1	0	0	0	2	1	0
Carlos Santana, DH	.182	3	11	1	2	0	0	0	0	0	2	0
Totals	**.271**	**3**	**96**	**15**	**26**	**3**	**0**	**5**	**15**	**6**	**30**	**1**

Cleveland	W	L	ERA	G	GS	SV	IP	H	R	ER	BB	SO
Cody Allen	0	0	0.00	2	0	2	3.0	4	0	0	2	5
Trevor Bauer	0	0	5.79	1	1	0	4.2	6	3	3	0	6
Corey Kluber	1	0	0.00	1	1	0	7.0	3	0	0	3	7
Andrew Miller	1	0	0.00	2	0	0	4.0	2	0	0	2	7
Dan Otero	0	0	0.00	1	0	0	1.0	0	0	0	0	1
Bryan Shaw	0	0	7.71	3	0	0	2.1	2	2	2	0	1
Josh Tomlin	1	0	3.60	1	1	0	5.0	4	2	2	1	4
Totals	**3**	**0**	**2.33**	**3**	**3**	**2**	**27.0**	**21**	**7**	**7**	**8**	**31**

E: Pedroia. **LOB:** Boston 20, Cleveland 16. **DP:** Boston 1, Cleveland 2. **GIDP:** Benintendi, Betts, Chisenhall. **SAC:** Chisenhall, Crisp. **SF:** Ortiz, Davis. **HBP:** Bradley Jr. (by Kluber), Santana (by Porcello). **IBB:** Ramirez (by Pomeranz). **SB:** Napoli. **CS:** Ramirez.

SCORE BY INNINGS

Boston	101	021	020—7
Cleveland	053	313	000—15

AMERICAN LEAGUE CHAMPIONSHIP SERIES

CLEVELAND INDIANS VS. TORONTO BLUE JAYS

Toronto	AVG	G	AB	R	H	2B	3B	HR	RBI	BB	SO	SB
Darwin Barney, 2B	.125	4	8	1	1	0	0	0	0	0	3	0
Jose Bautista, RF	.167	5	18	1	3	1	0	0	3	7	0	0
Ezequiel Carrera, RF	.235	5	17	2	4	0	2	0	1	0	4	0
Josh Donaldson, 3B	.333	5	18	1	6	1	0	1	2	2	3	0
Edwin Encarnacion, DH	.211	5	19	0	4	1	0	0	2	1	4	0
Ryan Goins, 2B	.200	3	5	1	1	0	0	0	1	1	2	0
Russell Martin, C	.118	5	17	0	2	0	0	0	1	9	0	0
Dioner Navarro, C	1.000	2	2	0	2	0	0	0	0	0	0	0
Kevin Pillar, CF	.063	5	16	0	1	0	0	0	1	1	4	1
Michael Saunders, LF	.429	5	14	1	6	0	0	1	0	7	0	0
Justin Smoak, 1B	.000	1	1	0	0	0	0	0	0	0	1	0
Devon Travis, 2B	.000	1	2	0	0	0	0	0	0	0	0	0
Troy Tulowitzki, SS	.111	5	18	1	2	0	0	0	0	2	2	0
Melvin Upton Jr., LF	.000	5	4	0	0	0	0	0	0	0	4	0
Totals	**.201**	**5**	**159**	**8**	**32**	**3**	**2**	**2**	**8**	**11**	**50**	**1**

Toronto	W	L	ERA	G	GS	SV	IP	H	R	ER	BB	SO
Joe Biagini	0	0	0.00	3	0	0	3.2	1	0	0	1	3
Brett Cecil	0	0	0.00	3	0	0	3.1	0	0	0	1	4
Marco Estrada	0	2	2.57	2	2	0	14.0	11	5	4	1	13
Jason Grilli	0	0	0.00	2	0	0	1.2	1	0	0	0	1
J.A. Happ	0	1	3.60	1	1	0	5.0	4	2	2	1	4
Roberto Osuna	0	0	0.00	4	0	0	4.0	3	0	0	0	4
Aaron Sanchez	1	0	1.50	1	1	0	6.0	2	1	1	2	5
Marcus Stroman	0	1	6.75	1	1	0	5.1	3	4	4	3	5
Totals	**1**	**4**	**2.30**	**5**	**5**	**0**	**43.0**	**25**	**12**	**11**	**9**	**39**

Cleveland	AVG	G	AB	R	H	2B	3B	HR	RBI	BB	SO	SB
Lonnie Chisenhall, RF	.250	5	16	0	4	0	0	0	0	0	5	0
Coco Crisp, LF	.250	4	8	2	2	0	0	1	1	2	1	1
Rajai Davis, CF	.000	5	6	1	0	0	0	0	0	0	5	0
Brandon Guyer, LF	.000	2	4	0	0	0	0	0	0	0	0	0
Jason Kipnis, 2B	.053	5	19	2	1	0	0	1	1	1	3	0
Francisco Lindor, SS	.368	5	19	2	7	1	0	1	3	1	5	0
Michael Martinez, 2B	—	1	0	0	0	0	0	0	0	0	0	0
Mike Napoli, 1B	.188	5	16	2	3	2	0	1	2	2	6	0
Tyler Naquin, CF	.167	4	12	0	2	0	0	0	1	0	2	0
Roberto Perez, C	.143	5	14	0	2	1	0	0	1	1	7	0
Jose Ramirez, 3B	.059	5	17	0	1	0	0	0	1	0	2	0
Carlos Santana, DH	.167	5	18	3	3	0	0	2	2	2	2	0
Totals	**.168**	**5**	**149**	**12**	**25**	**6**	**0**	**6**	**11**	**9**	**39**	**2**

Cleveland	W	L	ERA	G	GS	SV	IP	H	R	ER	BB	SO
Cody Allen	0	0	0.00	4	0	3	4.2	1	0	0	1	7
Trevor Bauer	0	0	0.00	1	1	0	0.2	0	0	0	2	1
Mike Clevinger	0	0	5.40	1	0	0	1.2	1	1	1	1	1
Corey Kluber	1	1	1.59	2	2	0	11.1	10	2	2	4	13
Jeff Manship	0	0	0.00	1	0	0	1.1	1	0	0	0	1
Zach McAllister	0	0	9.00	1	0	0	1.0	1	1	1	0	0
Ryan Merritt	0	0	0.00	1	1	0	4.1	2	0	0	0	3
Andrew Miller	0	0	0.00	4	0	1	7.2	3	0	0	0	14

Dan Otero	0	0	3.86	2	0	0	2.1	4	1	1	0	0
Bryan Shaw	2	0	2.70	4	0	0	3.1	6	2	1	1	4
Josh Tomlin	1	0	1.59	1	1	0	5.2	3	1	1	2	6
Totals	**4**	**1**	**1.43**	**5**	**5**	**4**	**44.0**	**32**	**8**	**7**	**11**	**50**

E: Carrera, Happ, Shaw. **LOB:** Toronto 31, Cleveland 20. **SAC:** Crisp 2,

Perez. **SF:** Pillar. **IBB:** Donaldson (by Shaw). **SB:** Pillar, Crisp, Davis. **CS:** Lindor. **WP:** Biagini, Happ, Sanchez, Stroman, Clevinger.

SCORE BY INNINGS

Toronto	012	110	210—8
Cleveland	212	214	000—12

NATIONAL LEAGUE WILD CARD GAME

SAN FRANCISCO 3, NEW YORK METS 0

SAN FRANCISCO	AB	R	H	RBI	BB	SO	LOB	AVG
Span, CF	4	0	1	0	1	1	1	.250
Belt, 1B	2	0	0	0	2	0	1	.000
Posey, C	3	0	0	0	1	0	1	.000
Pence, RF	4	0	0	0	0	2	4	.000
Crawford, B, SS	3	1	1	0	1	1	0	.333
Pagan, LF	4	0	1	0	0	3	1	.250
Panik, 2B	3	1	0	0	1	2	2	.000
Gillaspie, 3B	4	1	2	3	0	2	0	.500
Bumgarner, P	3	0	0	0	0	1	0	.000
TOTALS	**30**	**3**	**5**	**3**	**6**	**12**	**10**	
NEW YORK	AB	R	H	RBI	BB	SO	LOB	AVG
Reyes, 3B	4	0	0	0	0	0	1	.000
Cabrera, A, SS	3	0	1	0	1	0	1	.333
Cespedes, LF	4	0	0	0	0	2	2	.000
Granderson, CF	4	0	0	0	0	0	2	.000
Rivera, TJ, 2B	4	0	1	0	0	0	0	.250
Bruce, RF	3	0	0	0	0	1	1	.000
Rivera, Re, C	3	0	1	0	0	0	1	.333
Loney, 1B	3	0	0	0	1	0	1	.000
a-Campbell, PH-1B	1	0	0	0	0	1	0	.000
Syndergaard, P	2	0	0	0	0	2	2	.000
Reed, P	0	0	0	0	0	0	0	.000
b-Kelly, T, PH	1	0	1	0	0	0	0	1.000
Familia, P	0	0	0	0	0	0	0	.000
TOTALS	**30**	**0**	**4**	**0**	**2**	**6**	**11**	

San Francisco	000	000	003—3
New York	000	000	000—0

a-Struck out for Loney in the 8th. **b-**Singled for Reed in the 8th.
2B: Crawford, Rivera. **HR:** Gillaspie. **San Francisco LOB:** 7. **New York LOB:** 5. **SB:** Span. **CS:** Span.

SAN FRANCISCO	IP	H	R	ER	BB	SO	HR	ERA
Bumgarner (W)	9.0	4	0	0	2	6	0	0.00
NY METS	IP	H	R	ER	BB	SO	HR	ERA
Syndergaard	7.0	2	0	0	3	10	0	0.00
Reed	1.0	1	0	0	2	1	0	0.00
Familia (L)	1.0	2	3	3	1	1	1	27.00

Game Scores: Bumgarner 88; Syndergaard 82. **IBB:** Posey (by Reed); Loney (by Bumgarner).

NATIONAL LEAGUE DIVISION SERIES

CHICAGO CUBS VS. SAN FRANCISCO GIANTS

San Francisco	AVG	G	AB	R	H	2B	3B	HR	RBI	BB	SO	SB
Brandon Belt, 1B	.133	4	15	1	2	0	0	0	2	1	4	0
Gregor Blanco, RF	.125	4	8	1	1	1	0	0	1	1	2	0
Trevor Brown, C	.000	1	1	0	0	0	0	0	0	0	0	0
Madison Bumgarner, P	.000	2	2	0	0	0	0	0	0	0	0	0
Brandon Crawford, SS	.235	4	17	2	4	2	0	0	1	0	4	1
Johnny Cueto, P	.000	1	3	0	0	0	0	0	0	0	1	0
Conor Gillaspie, 3B	.400	4	15	2	6	0	1	0	3	0	3	0
Gorkys Hernandez, RF	.167	3	6	0	1	0	0	0	0	0	2	0
Matt Moore, P	.333	1	3	0	1	0	0	0	1	0	1	0
Eduardo Nunez, 3B	.000	3	0	0	0	0	0	0	0	0	0	0
Angel Pagan, LF	.333	2	6	0	2	1	0	0	0	0	0	0
Joe Panik, 2B	.600	3	10	2	6	2	0	0	2	2	2	0
Hunter Pence, RF	.222	4	18	1	4	0	0	0	0	3	0	0
Buster Posey, C	.333	4	15	1	5	1	0	0	2	2	1	0
Denard Span, CF	.267	3	15	3	4	2	1	0	1	0	3	0
Kelby Tomlinson, 2B	.000	1	0	0	0	0	0	0	0	0	3	0
Totals	**.252**	**4**	**143**	**13**	**36**	**9**	**2**	**0**	**13**	**6**	**29**	**1**

San Francisco	W	L	ERA	G	GS	SV	IP	H	R	ER	BB	SO
Ty Blach	1	0	0.00	2	0	0	3.1	2	0	0	0	3
Madison Bumgarner	0	0	5.40	1	1	0	5.0	7	3	3	1	4
Santiago Casilla	0	0	0.00	1	0	0	0.2	2	0	0	0	0
Johnny Cueto	0	1	1.13	1	1	0	8.0	3	1	1	0	10

Chicago	AVG	G	AB	R	H	2B	3B	HR	RBI	BB	SO	SB
George Kontos	0	0	4.50	1	0	0	2.0	1	1	1	0	1
Derek Law	0	0	3.86	3	0	0	2.1	1	1	1	1	3
Javier Lopez	0	0	13.50	2	0	0	0.2	0	1	1	1	0
Matt Moore	0	0	1.13	1	1	0	8.0	2	2	1	2	10
Sergio Romo	0	0	13.50	2	0	0	2.0	2	3	3	1	2
Jeff Samardzija	0	1	18.00	1	1	0	2.0	6	4	4	1	1
Will Smith	0	1	0.00	2	0	0	1.1	1	1	0	0	1
Hunter Strickland	0	0	0.00	3	0	0	2.2	1	0	0	1	3
Totals	**1**	**3**	**3.55**	**4**	**4**	**0**	**38.0**	**28**	**17**	**15**	**8**	**38**

Chicago	AVG	G	AB	R	H	2B	3B	HR	RBI	BB	SO	SB
Albert Almora Jr., CF	.000	2	3	0	0	0	0	0	0	0	1	0
Jake Arrieta, P	.333	1	3	1	1	0	0	1	3	0	1	0
Javier Baez, 3B	.375	4	16	4	6	0	0	1	2	1	4	0
Kris Bryant, 3B	.375	4	16	2	6	2	0	1	3	1	5	0
Chris Coghlan, LF	.000	3	2	0	0	0	0	0	0	0	1	0
Willson Contreras, C	.667	4	6	1	4	0	0	0	2	1	1	0
Dexter Fowler, CF	.133	4	15	2	2	1	0	0	0	2	6	0
Kyle Hendricks, P	1.000	1	1	0	1	0	0	0	2	0	0	0
Jason Heyward, RF	.083	4	12	2	1	1	0	0	0	3	0	0
Tommy La Stella, 3B	.000	1	1	0	0	0	0	0	0	0	1	0
John Lackey, P	.000	1	2	0	0	0	0	0	0	0	0	0
Jon Lester, P	.000	1	2	0	0	0	0	0	0	0	2	0
Miguel Montero, C	.000	2	4	0	0	0	0	0	0	0	0	0
Mike Montgomery, P	.000	2	1	0	0	0	0	0	0	0	0	0
Anthony Rizzo, 1B	.067	4	15	1	1	0	0	0	2	4	0	0
David Ross, C	.167	3	6	1	1	0	0	1	2	0	2	0
Addison Russell, SS	.067	4	15	1	1	0	0	0	2	0	0	0
Jorge Soler, LF	.000	2	4	0	0	0	0	0	0	1	1	0
Travis Wood, P	1.000	3	1	1	1	0	0	1	1	0	0	0
Ben Zobrist, 2B	.188	4	16	1	3	2	0	0	2	0	4	0
Totals	**.200**	**4**	**140**	**17**	**28**	**6**	**0**	**5**	**17**	**8**	**38**	**0**

Chicago	W	L	ERA	G	GS	SV	IP	H	R	ER	BB	SO
Jake Arrieta	0	0	3.00	1	1	0	6.0	6	2	2	1	5
Aroldis Chapman	0	0	2.70	4	0	3	3.1	3	1	1	1	7
Carl Edwards Jr.	0	0	0.00	2	0	0	2.0	1	0	0	0	0
Justin Grimm	0	0	18.00	2	0	0	1.0	2	2	2	0	0
Kyle Hendricks	0	0	4.91	1	1	0	3.2	4	2	2	0	0
John Lackey	0	0	6.75	1	1	0	4.0	7	3	3	2	4
Jon Lester	1	0	0.00	1	1	0	8.0	5	0	0	0	5
Mike Montgomery	0	1	1.69	2	0	0	5.1	5	1	1	1	2
Hector Rondon	1	0	5.40	3	0	0	1.2	1	1	1	1	2
Pedro Strop	0	0	0.00	1	0	0	0.2	0	0	0	0	0
Travis Wood	1	0	2.70	3	0	0	3.1	2	1	1	0	4
Totals	**3**	**1**	**3.00**	**4**	**4**	**3**	**39.0**	**36**	**13**	**13**	**6**	**29**

E: Crawford 2, Gillaspie, Panik, Bryant 2, Contreras 3. **LOB:** San Francisco 25, Chicago 19. **DP:** San Francisco 3, Chicago 3. **GIDP:** Blanco, Gillaspie, Ross 2, Russell. **SAC:** Blanco. **SF:** Belt 2, Panik, Posey, Ross. **HBP:** Russell (by Bumgarner). **SB:** Crawford. **CS:** Hernandez, Span.

SCORE BY INNINGS

San Francisco	103	230	030	000	1—13
Chicago	161	110	016	000	0—17

WASHINGTON NATIONALS VS. LOS ANGELES DODGERS

Los Angeles	AVG	G	AB	R	H	2B	3B	HR	RBI	BB	SO	SB
Austin Barnes, C	.000	2	1	1	0	0	0	0	0	0	1	0
Charlie Culberson, SS	.000	4	7	0	0	0	0	0	0	2	0	0
Andre Ethier, RF	.500	3	2	0	1	0	0	0	0	0	1	0
Adrian Gonzalez, 1B	.200	5	20	1	4	0	0	1	2	1	4	0
Yasmani Grandal, C	.125	5	16	0	2	0	0	0	0	3	6	0
Rich Hill, P	.333	2	3	0	1	0	0	0	0	0	1	0
Kenley Jansen, P	.000	4	1	0	0	0	0	0	0	0	0	0
Howie Kendrick, LF	.333	4	9	1	3	1	0	0	0	0	1	0
Clayton Kershaw, P	.333	3	3	1	1	1	0	0	0	0	1	0
Joc Pederson, CF	.333	5	15	2	5	1	0	1	3	2	6	0
Yasiel Puig, RF	.000	4	5	0	0	0	0	0	0	3	2	0
Josh Reddick, RF	.267	5	15	1	4	0	0	0	0	1	1	2

	AVG	G	AB	R	H	2B	3B	HR	RBI	BB	SO	SB
Carlos Ruiz, C	.500	3	4	2	2	0	0	1	3	0	1	0
Corey Seager, SS	.130	5	23	3	3	1	0	2	3	0	6	0
Andrew Toles, RF	.222	5	9	2	2	0	0	0	0	1	0	0
Justin Turner, 3B	.400	5	15	5	6	0	1	1	5	5	2	0
Chase Utley, 2B	.188	5	16	0	3	0	0	0	2	1	5	1
Totals	.261	5	23	5	6	1	1	2	5	5	6	1

Los Angeles	W	L	ERA	G	GS	SV	IP	H	R	ER	BB	SO
Luis Avilan	0	0	0.00	3	0	0	1.1	2	0	0	0	2
Pedro Baez	0	0	0.00	4	0	0	3.2	0	0	0	2	1
Joe Blanton	1	0	0.00	4	0	0	5.0	1	0	0	1	5
Grant Dayton	0	0	16.20	4	0	0	1.2	5	3	3	2	4
Josh Fields	0	0	0.00	2	0	0	1.0	0	0	0	1	3
Rich Hill	0	1	6.43	2	2	0	7.0	9	5	5	4	13
Kenley Jansen	0	0	6.75	4	0	2	5.1	4	4	4	5	9
Clayton Kershaw	1	0	5.84	3	2	1	12.1	15	8	8	3	19
Kenta Maeda	0	1	12.00	1	1	0	3.0	5	4	4	2	4
Ross Stripling	0	0	0.00	2	0	0	1.2	0	0	0	0	2
Julio Urias	1	0	0.00	1	0	0	2.0	1	0	0	2	1
Totals	3	2	4.91	5	5	3	44.0	42	24	24	22	63

Washington	AVG	G	AB	R	H	2B	3B	HR	RBI	BB	SO	SB
Wilmer Difo, SS	.000	2	2	0	0	0	0	0	0	0	1	0
Stephen Drew, 2B	.000	4	4	0	0	0	0	0	0	1	3	0
Danny Espinosa, SS	.143	5	14	3	2	0	0	0	1	1	8	0
Gio Gonzalez, P	.000	1	2	0	0	0	0	0	0	0	2	0
Bryce Harper, RF	.235	5	17	4	4	1	0	1	6	6	3	
Chris Heisey, LF	.250	5	4	1	1	0	0	1	3	0	2	0
Jose Lobaton, C	.222	4	9	1	2	0	0	1	3	0	2	0
Daniel Murphy, 2B	.438	5	16	3	7	0	0	0	6	5	1	2
Anthony Rendon, 3B	.150	5	20	1	3	0	0	1	4	1	6	0
Tanner Roark, P	.000	1	2	0	0	0	0	0	0	0	1	0
Clint Robinson, 1B	.667	3	3	0	2	1	0	0	0	0	1	0
Joe Ross, P	.000	2	1	0	0	0	0	0	0	0	0	0
Max Scherzer, P	.000	2	4	0	0	0	0	0	0	0	2	0
Pedro Severino, C	.100	4	10	1	1	0	0	0	0	0	3	0
Michael Taylor, CF	.000	3	2	0	0	0	0	0	0	0	1	0
Trea Turner, CF	.318	5	22	5	7	0	0	0	1	1	11	2
Jayson Werth, LF	.389	5	18	4	7	2	0	1	3	4	9	1
Ryan Zimmerman, 1B	.353	5	17	1	6	2	0	0	2	3	3	0
Totals	.251	5	167	24	42	7	0	4	24	22	63	8

Washington	W	L	ERA	G	GS	SV	IP	H	R	ER	BB	SO
Gio Gonzalez	0	0	6.23	1	1	0	4.1	4	3	3	1	4
Shawn Kelley	0	0	0.00	2	0	0	1.2	1	0	0	0	3
Reynaldo Lopez	0	0	4.50	1	0	0	2.0	2	1	1	1	3
Mark Melancon	0	0	0.00	4	0	1	4.1	3	0	0	2	5
Oliver Perez	0	0	0.00	3	0	0	3.1	1	0	0	1	3
Tanner Roark	0	0	4.15	1	1	0	4.1	7	2	2	3	1
Joe Ross	0	0	13.50	1	1	0	2.2	3	4	4	2	3
Marc Rzepczynski	0	1	4.50	3	0	0	2.0	0	1	1	4	3
Max Scherzer	0	1	3.75	2	2	0	12.0	10	5	5	2	12
Sammy Solis	1	0	1.93	5	0	0	4.2	3	1	1	2	2
Blake Treinen	1	1	6.75	3	0	0	2.2	3	2	2	2	5
Totals	2	3	3.89	5	5	1	44.0	37	19	19	18	44

E: Grandal, Utley. LOB: Los Angeles 39, Washington 41. DP: Los Angeles 2, Washington 3. GIDP: Gonzalez, Grandal, Toles, Lobaton. SAC: Jansen, Kershaw. SF: Heisey, Murphy, Turner. HBP: Pederson (by Ross), Toles 2 (by Roark, by Treinen), Turner 2 (by Scherzer, by Ross), Utley (by Perez), Espinosa 3 (by Hill 2, by Maeda), Harper (by Jansen), Werth (by Baez). IBB: Kendrick (by Melancon), Pederson (by Roark), Puig 2 (by Solis, by Melancon), Murphy 2 (by Hill, by Jansen). SB: Utley, Harper 3, Murphy 2, Turner 2, Werth. CS: Murphy. WP: Avilan, Scherzer.

SCORE BY INNINGS

Los Angeles	506	030	410—19
Washington	117	410	604—24

NATIONAL LEAGUE CHAMPIONSHIP SERIES
CHICAGO CUBS VS. LOS ANGELES DODGERS

Los Angeles	AVG	G	AB	R	H	2B	3B	HR	RBI	BB	SO	SB
Andre Ethier, RF	.250	5	4	2	1	0	0	1	1	1	1	0
Adrian Gonzalez, 1B	.190	6	21	2	4	0	0	1	4	2	4	1
Yasmani Grandal, C	.083	6	12	1	1	0	0	1	3	4	5	0
Enrique Hernandez, LF	.000	6	8	0	0	0	0	0	0	3	2	0
Rich Hill, P	.000	1	2	0	0	0	0	0	0	0	0	0
Howie Kendrick, LF	.154	5	13	1	2	1	0	0	0	0	3	1
Clayton Kershaw, P	.250	2	4	0	1	0	0	0	0	0	2	0
Kenta Maeda, P	.500	2	2	0	1	0	0	0	0	0	2	0
Joc Pederson, CF	.190	6	21	3	4	1	0	0	1	1	8	2
Yasiel Puig, RF	.286	6	14	1	4	0	0	0	0	0	1	0
Josh Reddick, RF	.364	5	11	1	4	0	0	0	0	0	3	0
Carlos Ruiz, C	.143	4	7	0	1	0	0	0	1	1	1	0
Corey Seager, SS	.286	6	21	6	6	0	0	0	1	2	7	0
Andrew Toles, RF	.462	6	13	4	6	2	0	0	2	1	2	0
Justin Turner, 3B	.200	6	20	1	4	0	0	1	3	2	3	1
Julio Urias, P	.000	1	1	0	0	0	0	0	0	0	0	0
Chase Utley, 2B	.000	5	12	1	0	0	0	0	0	2	1	0
Totals	.210	6	186	17	39	5	0	4	17	19	42	8

Los Angeles	W	L	ERA	G	GS	SV	IP	H	R	ER	BB	SO
Luis Avilan	0	0	0.00	2	0	0	2.1	2	0	0	1	1
Pedro Baez	0	0	5.40	3	0	0	3.1	6	6	2	2	4
Joe Blanton	0	2	21.00	3	0	0	3.0	7	7	7	2	3
Grant Dayton	0	0	0.00	3	0	0	1.2	1	0	0	0	2
Josh Fields	0	0	0.00	2	0	0	1.1	1	0	0	1	0
Rich Hill	1	0	0.00	1	1	0	6.0	2	0	0	2	6
Kenley Jansen	0	0	0.00	3	0	1	6.1	1	0	0	0	10
Clayton Kershaw	1	1	3.00	2	2	0	12.0	9	5	4	1	10
Kenta Maeda	0	0	4.70	2	2	0	7.2	7	4	4	5	8
Ross Stripling	0	0	13.50	2	0	0	2.2	6	5	4	1	0
Julio Urias	0	1	9.82	1	1	0	3.2	4	4	4	2	4
Alex Wood	0	0	0.00	2	0	0	2.0	2	0	0	0	1
Totals	2	4	4.33	6	6	1	52.0	48	31	25	16	50

Chicago	AVG	G	AB	R	H	2B	3B	HR	RBI	BB	SO	SB
Albert Almora Jr., CF	.000	4	6	0	0	0	0	0	0	0	1	0
Jake Arrieta, P	.000	1	2	0	0	0	0	0	0	0	2	0
Javier Baez, 3B	.318	6	22	3	7	4	0	0	5	1	4	2
Kris Bryant, 3B	.304	6	23	3	7	3	0	0	3	3	8	0
Chris Coghlan, LF	.000	2	2	1	0	0	0	0	0	1	0	0
Willson Contreras, C	.286	6	14	3	4	0	0	1	2	0	5	0
Dexter Fowler, CF	.333	6	27	6	9	3	0	1	4	0	4	0
Kyle Hendricks, P	.000	2	4	0	0	0	0	0	0	0	2	0
Jason Heyward, RF	.063	6	16	2	1	0	1	0	1	1	5	0
John Lackey, P	.000	1	2	0	0	0	0	0	0	0	0	0
Jon Lester, P	.000	2	3	0	0	0	0	0	0	0	2	0
Miguel Montero, C	.250	3	4	1	1	0	0	1	4	0	1	0
Mike Montgomery, P	1.000	4	1	1	1	0	0	0	0	0	0	0
Anthony Rizzo, 1B	.320	6	25	3	8	2	0	2	5	2	6	1
David Ross, C	.200	2	5	0	1	0	0	0	1	1	0	0
Addison Russell, SS	.273	6	22	5	6	1	0	2	4	0	5	0
Jorge Soler, LF	.000	4	4	0	0	0	0	0	0	1	2	0
Ben Zobrist, 2B	.150	6	20	3	3	1	0	0	1	4	3	0
Totals	.238	6	202	31	48	15	1	7	29	16	50	3

Chicago	W	L	ERA	G	GS	SV	IP	H	R	ER	BB	SO
Jake Arrieta	0	1	7.20	1	1	0	5.0	6	4	4	0	5
Aroldis Chapman	1	0	3.86	4	0	0	4.2	3	2	2	3	3
Carl Edwards Jr.	0	0	0.00	4	0	0	1.2	0	0	0	2	3
Justin Grimm	0	0	0.00	1	0	0	1.1	1	0	0	0	1
Kyle Hendricks	1	1	0.71	2	2	0	12.2	5	1	1	4	11
John Lackey	0	0	4.50	1	1	0	4.0	3	2	2	3	3
Jon Lester	1	0	1.38	2	2	0	13.0	9	2	2	9	9
Mike Montgomery	0	0	6.23	4	0	0	4.1	5	3	3	2	5
Hector Rondon	0	0	4.50	2	0	0	2.0	3	1	1	0	1
Pedro Strop	0	0	6.00	4	0	0	3.0	3	2	2	1	2
Travis Wood	0	0	0.00	3	0	0	1.1	1	0	0	2	1
Totals	4	2	2.89	6	6	0	53.0	39	17	17	19	42

E: Baez, Grandal, Hernandez, Pederson, Toles 2, Utley, Baez 2, Contreras. LOB: Los Angeles 35, Chicago 36. DP: Los Angeles 1, Chicago 7. GIDP: Gonzalez, Kendrick, Pederson, Puig, Seager 2, Almora Jr. SAC: Grandal, Almora Jr. SF: Toles, Baez, Zobrist. HBP: Seager (by Lackey), Turner 2 (by Strop 2), Bryant (by Wood), Heyward (by Maeda). IBB: Coghlan (by Blanton), Heyward (by Blanton). SB: Gonzalez, Kendrick, Pederson 2, Reddick 3, Turner, Baez 2, Rizzo. WP: Maeda. PB: Grandal.

SCORE BY INNINGS

Los Angeles	011	331	053—17
Chicago	430	527	0(10)0—31

ORGANIZATION STATISTICS

Arizona Diamondbacks

SEASON IN A SENTENCE: High hopes were dashed from the start as Arizona flopped despite adding Zack Greinke on a six-year, $206.5 million contract. At season's end, ownership fired GM Dave Stewart and manager Chip Hale while pushing aside chief baseball officer Tony La Russa, marking the fourth front-office change for Arizona since original GM Joe Garagiola was let go in 2005.

HIGH POINT: In late June, the D-backs won seven of eight, creeping within four games of .500 with a two-run, ninth-inning rally to beat the rival Rockies in Coors Field, 10-9. Yasmany Tomas, who led the team with 31 homers, tied the game with a solo shot, and center fielder Michael Bourn drove home Jean Segura, who led the National League with 203 hits, with the winning run.

LOW POINT: The broken right elbow of center fielder A.J. Pollock, incurred in the penultimate game of the Cactus League season, set the tone for Arizona's disaster. And just after the big win at Coors, offseason trade pickup Shelby Miller—acquired from Atlanta in a trade that cost righthander Aaron Blair, outfielder Ender Inciarte and 2015 No. 1 pick Dansby Swasnon—was rocked in Colorado the next night. Arizona went on a 7-25 stretch and started trading for prospects.

NOTABLE ROOKIES: Brandon Drury became a steady lineup presence, hitting .282/.329/.458 with 16 home runs. He played at least 15 games at four different defensive spots—left and right field, third base and second. Righthanders Jake Barrett, Enrique Burgos and Zack Godley all logged significant innings, with Barrett having the most success.

KEY TRANSACTIONS: The Miller trade worked out very poorly, helping lead the D-backs to sell veterans such as Bourn, closer Brad Ziegler and reliever Tyler Clippard for prospects in July. The organization's next leader, new GM Mike Hazen, was hired away from the Red Sox in October, with La Russa reassigned as chief baseball analyst.

DOWN ON THE FARM: Visalia had the second-best record in the high Class A California league and was league runner-up, but the system otherwise had a modest, .500 season. Top performers included lefthander Anthony Banda (10-6, 2.88), who finished the second half in Triple-A Reno, and outfielder Mitch Haniger, who finished the year in the big leagues and hit .321/.419/.581 with 25 homers in the minors.

OPENING DAY PAYROLL: $89,264,063 (23rd)

PLAYERS OF THE YEAR

MAJOR LEAGUE	MINOR LEAGUE
Paul Goldschmidt	**Anthony Banda**
1b	lhp
.297/.411/.489	(Double-A/Triple-A)
24 HR, 95 RBI	10-6, 2.88
33 2B, 32 SB	152 SO in 150 IP

ORGANIZATION LEADERS

BATTING		*Minimum 250 AB
MAJORS		
* AVG	Jean Segura	.319
* OPS	Paul Goldschmidt	.899
HR	Yasmany Tomas	31
RBI	Paul Goldschmidt	95
MINORS		
* AVG	Mitch Haniger, Mobile, Reno	.321
* OBP	Mitch Haniger, Mobile, Reno	.419
* SLG	Mitch Haniger, Mobile, Reno	.581
* OPS	Mitch Haniger, Mobile, Reno	.999
R	Dawel Lugo, Visalia, Mobile	85
H	Ildemaro Vargas, Mobile, Visalia, Reno	160
TB	Kyle Jensen, Reno	272
2B	Henry Castillo, Visalia	38
3B	Victor Reyes, Visalia	12
HR	Kyle Jensen, Reno	30
RBI	Kyle Jensen, Reno	120
BB	Mitch Haniger, Mobile, Reno	69
SO	Kyle Jensen, Reno	169
SB	Colin Bray, Kane County, Visalia	25
	Marcus Wilson, Hillsboro, Kane County	25

PITCHING		#Minimum 75 IP
MAJORS		
W	Zack Greinke	13
# ERA	Robbie Ray	4.90
SO	Robbie Ray	218
SV	Brad Ziegler	18
MINORS		
W	Justin Donatella, Kane County, Visalia	13
L	Carlos Hernandez, Kane County	11
	Josh Taylor, Visalia, Mobile	11
# ERA	Carlos Hernandez, Kane County	2.55
G	Bud Jeter, Visalia	52
	Joey Krehbiel, Mobile	52
	Gabriel Moya, Kane County, Visalia	52
	Jimmie Sherfy, Visalia, Mobile, Reno	52
GS	Taylor Clarke, Kane County, Visalia, Mobile	27
	Justin Donatella, Kane County, Visalia	27
SV	Jimmie Sherfy, Visalia, Mobile, Reno	30
IP	Anthony Banda, Mobile, Reno	150
BB	Carlos Hernandez, Kane County	69
SO	Anthony Banda, Mobile, Reno	152
# AVG	Carlos Hernandez, Kane County	.215

2016 PERFORMANCE

General Manager: Dave Stewart. **Farm Director:** Mike Bell. **Scouting Director:** Deric Ladnier.

Class	Team	League	W	L	PCT	Finish	Manager
Majors	Arizona Diamondbacks	National	69	93	.426	12th (15)	Chip Hale
Triple-A	Reno Aces	Pacific Coast	76	68	.528	4th (16)	Phil Nevin
Double-A	Mobile BayBears	Southern	65	73	.471	7th (10)	Robby Hammock
High A	Visalia Rawhide	California	81	59	.579	2nd (10)	J.R. House
Low A	Kane County Cougars	Midwest	65	75	.464	12th (16)	Mike Benjamin
Short season	Hillsboro Hops	Northwest	42	33	.560	3rd (8)	Shelley Duncan
Rookie	Missoula Osprey	Pioneer	33	42	.440	7th (8)	Joe Mather
Rookie	Diamondbacks	Arizona	27	29	.482	10th (14)	Darrin Garner
Overall 2016 Minor League Record			389	379	.507	T13th (30)	

ORGANIZATION STATISTICS

ARIZONA DIAMONDBACKS
NATIONAL LEAGUE

Batting	B-T	HT	WT	DOB	AVG	vLH	vRH	G	AB	R	H	2B	3B	HR	RBI	BB	HBP	SH	SF	SO	SB	CS	SLG	OBP
Ahmed, Nick	R-R	6-2	195	3-15-90	.218	.244	.208	90	284	26	62	9	1	4	20	15	4	2	3	58	5	2	.299	.265
Bourn, Michael	L-R	5-11	190	12-27-82	.261	.348	.240	89	329	43	86	12	6	3	30	22	0	6	1	83	13	5	.362	.307
Brito, Socrates	L-L	6-2	205	9-6-92	.179	.083	.193	40	95	10	17	3	1	4	12	2	0	0	0	23	2	0	.358	.196
Castillo, Welington	R-R	5-10	220	4-24-87	.264	.278	.259	113	416	41	110	24	0	14	68	33	4	0	4	121	2	0	.423	.322
Drury, Brandon	R-R	6-2	210	8-21-92	.282	.280	.283	134	461	59	130	31	1	16	53	31	3	0	4	100	1	1	.458	.329
Freeman, Mike	L-R	6-0	190	8-4-87	.000	—	.000	8	9	0	0	0	0	0	0	2	0	0	0	5	0	0	.000	.182
Goldschmidt, Paul	R-R	6-3	225	9-10-87	.297	.352	.282	158	579	106	172	33	3	24	95	110	7	0	8	150	32	5	.489	.411
Gosewisch, Tuffy	R-R	5-11	200	8-17-83	.156	.444	.083	33	90	8	14	1	1	3	7	7	1	1	0	22	0	0	.289	.224
Gosselin, Phil	R-R	6-0	200	10-3-88	.277	.288	.274	122	220	26	61	12	1	2	13	15	1	2	2	46	3	0	.368	.324
Haniger, Mitch	R-R	6-2	215	12-23-90	.229	.172	.250	34	109	9	25	2	1	5	17	12	1	0	1	27	0	0	.404	.309
Hernandez, Oscar	R-R	6-1	230	7-9-93	.182	.250	.143	4	11	1	2	0	0	1	1	0	0	0	0	6	0	0	.455	.182
Herrmann, Chris	L-R	6-0	200	11-24-87	.284	.381	.268	56	148	21	42	5	4	6	28	16	0	1	1	44	4	0	.493	.352
Jensen, Kyle	R-L	6-3	240	5-20-88	.194	.333	.063	17	31	5	6	0	1	2	7	2	1	0	0	13	0	0	.452	.265
Lamb, Jake	L-R	6-3	215	10-9-90	.249	.164	.271	151	523	81	130	31	9	29	91	64	3	0	4	154	6	1	.509	.332
O'Brien, Peter	R-R	6-4	235	7-15-90	.141	.136	.143	28	64	6	9	1	0	5	9	3	0	0	0	27	0	0	.391	.179
Owings, Chris	R-R	5-10	185	8-12-91	.277	.306	.267	119	437	52	121	24	11	5	49	20	5	2	2	87	21	2	.416	.315
Peralta, David	L-L	6-1	210	8-14-87	.251	.211	.263	48	171	23	43	9	5	4	15	8	3	0	1	42	2	0	.433	.295
Pollock, A.J.	R-R	6-1	195	12-5-87	.244	.125	.273	12	41	9	10	0	0	2	4	5	0	0	0	8	4	0	.390	.326
Segura, Jean	R-R	5-10	205	3-17-90	.319	.287	.333	153	637	102	203	41	7	20	64	39	12	4	2	101	33	10	.499	.368
Tomas, Yasmany	R-R	6-2	250	11-14-90	.272	.364	.242	140	530	72	144	30	1	31	83	31	1	0	1	136	2	4	.508	.313
Weeks, Rickie	R-R	5-10	220	9-13-82	.239	.284	.212	108	180	29	43	9	1	9	27	20	4	0	1	54	5	0	.450	.327

Pitching	B-T	HT	WT	DOB	W	L	ERA	G	GS	CG	SV	IP	H	R	ER	HR	BB	SO	AVG	vLH	vRH	K/9	BB/9
Barrett, Jake	R-R	6-2	240	7-22-91	1	2	3.49	68	0	0	4	59	47	25	23	6	28	56	.218	.222	.214	8.49	4.25
Bracho, Silvino	R-R	5-10	190	7-17-92	0	2	7.30	26	0	0	0	25	31	22	20	7	10	17	.295	.293	.297	6.20	3.65
Bradley, Archie	R-R	6-4	225	8-10-92	8	9	5.02	26	26	0	0	142	154	84	79	16	67	143	.276	.318	.235	9.08	4.24
Burgos, Enrique	R-R	6-4	250	11-23-90	1	2	5.66	43	0	0	1	41	38	27	26	5	23	43	.253	.236	.269	9.36	5.01
Buschmann, Matt	R-R	6-5	205	2-13-84	0	0	2.08	3	0	0	0	4	2	1	1	1	1	3	.143	.25	.100	6.23	2.08
Campos, Vicente	R-R	6-3	230	7-27-92	0	0	3.18	1	0	0	0	6	4	3	2	2	2	4	.182	.100	6.35	3.18
Chafin, Andrew	R-L	6-2	225	6-17-90	0	1	6.75	32	0	0	0	23	22	18	17	1	11	28	.259	.200	.311	11.12	4.37
Clippard, Tyler	R-R	6-3	200	2-14-85	2	3	4.30	40	0	0	1	38	34	18	18	7	15	46	.245	.247	.242	10.99	3.58
Collmenter, Josh	R-R	6-3	240	2-7-86	1	0	4.84	15	0	0	0	22	21	12	12	4	11	17	.253	.308	.205	6.85	4.43
2-team total (3 Atlanta)					3	0	3.70	18	3	0	0	41	36	17	17	7	16	33	—	—	—	7.19	3.48
Corbin, Pat	L-L	6-3	210	7-19-89	5	13	5.15	36	24	0	1	156	177	109	89	24	66	131	.286	.241	.300	7.57	3.82
Curtis, Zac	L-L	5-9	190	7-4-92	0	1	6.75	21	0	0	0	13	13	10	10	2	13	10	.253	.310	.182	6.75	8.78
De La Rosa, Rubby	R-R	6-0	210	3-4-89	4	5	4.26	13	10	0	0	51	43	26	24	8	20	54	.219	.198	.236	9.59	3.55
Delgado, Randall	R-R	6-4	220	2-9-90	5	2	4.44	79	0	0	0	75	77	39	37	8	36	68	.265	.284	.251	8.16	4.32
Drabek, Kyle	R-R	6-2	205	12-8-87	0	0	4.50	1	0	0	0	2	1	1	1	0	4	2	.143	.000	.250	9.00	18.00
Escobar, Edwin	L-L	6-2	225	4-22-92	1	2	7.23	25	2	0	0	24	33	21	19	4	12	17	.333	.280	.388	6.46	4.56
Godley, Zack	R-R	6-3	240	4-21-90	5	4	6.39	27	9	0	0	75	86	54	53	13	25	60	.289	.289	.288	7.23	3.01
Greinke, Zack	R-R	6-2	200	10-21-83	13	7	4.37	26	26	1	0	159	161	80	77	23	41	134	.262	.256	.269	7.60	2.33
Hathaway, Steve	L-L	6-1	185	9-13-90	0	0	4.91	24	0	0	0	15	18	8	8	1	6	15	.305	.333	.261	9.20	3.68
Hessler, Keith	L-L	6-4	240	3-15-89	0	0	9.00	2	0	0	0	3	5	3	3	0	2	2	.357	.750	.200	6.00	6.00
2-team total (15 San Diego)					1	0	4.15	17	0	0	0	22	24	10	10	2	13	11	—	—	—	4.57	5.40
Hudson, Daniel	R-R	6-3	230	3-9-87	3	2	5.22	70	0	0	5	60	65	40	35	6	22	58	.269	.283	.256	8.65	3.28
Koch, Matt	L-R	6-3	215	11-2-90	1	1	2.00	7	2	0	1	18	9	4	4	1	4	10	.145	.115	.167	5.00	2.00
Leone, Dominic	R-R	5-11	210	10-26-91	0	1	6.33	25	0	0	0	27	45	21	19	7	12	23	.391	.378	.400	7.67	4.00
Loewen, Adam	L-L	6-6	245	4-9-84	1	0	15.00	8	0	0	0	6	7	10	10	1	6	3	.318	.222	.385	4.50	9.00
Marshall, Evan	R-R	6-2	225	4-18-90	0	1	8.80	15	0	0	0	15	28	18	15	3	8	9	.400	.417	.391	5.28	4.70
Miller, Shelby	R-R	6-3	225	10-10-90	3	12	6.15	20	20	1	0	101	127	72	69	14	42	70	.310	.329	.285	6.24	3.74
Ray, Robbie	L-L	6-2	195	10-1-91	8	15	4.90	32	32	0	0	174	185	105	95	24	71	218	.267	.251	.272	11.25	3.67
Shipley, Braden	R-R	6-1	190	2-22-92	4	5	5.27	13	11	0	0	70	80	43	41	14	28	43	.293	.270	.325	5.53	3.60
Wagner, Tyler	R-R	6-2	205	1-24-91	1	0	1.80	3	0	0	0	10	9	3	2	0	2	7	.237	.190	.294	6.30	1.80
Ziegler, Brad	R-R	6-4	220	10-10-79	2	3	2.82	36	0	0	18	38	41	13	12	1	15	27	.281	.299	.266	6.34	3.52

Fielding

Catcher	PCT	G	PO	A	E	DP
Castillo	.992	107	799	72	7	7
Gosewisch	.996	31	241	20	1	1
Hernandez	1.000	4	25	0	0	0
Herrmann	.996	31	226	19	1	0

First Base	PCT	G	PO	A	E	DP
Drury	1.000	1	1	0	0	0
Goldschmidt	.997	157	1378	116	4	127
Gosselin	1.000	6	44	7	0	3
Herrmann	1.000	2	2	0	0	2
Jensen	1.000	4	10	0	0	1
O'Brien	1.000	1	0	1	0	0
Tomas	1.000	1	2	0	0	0

Second Base	PCT	G	PO	A	E	DP
Drury	.976	16	15	25	1	6
Gosselin	1.000	35	36	50	0	12
Owings	1.000	1	0	1	0	0
Segura	.985	142	219	382	9	80

Third Base	PCT	G	PO	A	E	DP
Drury	.952	29	17	42	3	4
Gosselin	1.000	10	3	7	0	0
Lamb	.945	142	92	251	20	13

Shortstop	PCT	G	PO	A	E	DP
Ahmed	.975	88	111	273	10	61
Owings	.971	70	92	175	8	43
Segura	.986	23	22	46	1	12

Outfield	PCT	G	PO	A	E	DP
Bourn	.965	86	188	4	7	0
Brito	.940	36	46	1	3	0
Drury	.986	89	140	0	2	0
Freeman	1.000	2	1	0	0	0
Gosselin	1.000	3	6	0	0	0
Haniger	.985	31	62	2	1	0
Herrmann	.909	9	9	1	1	0
Jensen	1.000	5	9	0	0	0
Miller	—	1	0	0	0	0
O'Brien	.944	16	17	0	1	0
Owings	1.000	49	93	4	0	1
Peralta	1.000	48	99	0	0	1
Pollock	1.000	12	31	1	0	0
Tomas	.966	137	192	7	7	2
Weeks	.927	38	36	2	3	0

RENO ACES
PACIFIC COAST LEAGUE
TRIPLE-A

Batting	B-T	HT	WT	DOB	AVG	vLH	vRH	G	AB	R	H	2B	3B	HR	RBI	BB	HBP	SH	SF	SO	SB	CS	SLG	OBP
Borenstein, Zach	L-R	6-0	225	7-23-90	.272	.180	.287	120	357	57	97	23	5	9	57	34	2	0	2	116	15	1	.440	.337
Bourgeois, Jason	R-R	5-9	195	1-4-82	.356	.529	.271	33	104	13	37	5	2	0	9	5	0	0	0	13	5	2	.442	.385
Brito, Socrates	L-L	6-2	205	9-6-92	.294	.276	.300	73	303	46	89	10	8	6	39	13	0	0	1	60	7	6	.439	.322
Drury, Brandon	R-R	6-2	210	8-21-92	.143	.200	.111	3	14	2	2	0	0	0	1	0	0	0	0	1	0	0	.143	.200
Freeman, Mike	L-R	6-0	190	8-4-87	.317	.341	.309	88	341	56	108	17	6	1	24	38	2	2	1	75	11	1	.411	.387
2-team total (26 Tacoma)					.314	—		114	446	71	140	23	6	4	39	51	2	2	2	94	12	1	.419	.385
Freeman, Ronnie	R-R	6-1	190	1-8-91	.286	.667	.240	10	28	4	8	1	0	1	3	0	0	0	0	8	0	0	.321	.355
Glaesmann, Todd	R-R	6-4	225	10-24-90	.274	.233	.293	74	223	36	61	15	4	6	31	9	2	0	2	47	2	1	.457	.305
Gosewisch, Tuffy	R-R	5-11	200	8-17-83	.342	.410	.312	58	199	33	68	13	1	9	26	15	4	1	0	30	0	0	.553	.399
Guerrero, Gabby	R-R	6-3	215	12-11-93	.212	.240	.203	34	99	10	21	5	1	1	9	6	0	0	2	25	0	0	.313	.273
Haniger, Mitch	R-R	6-2	215	12-23-90	.341	.438	.310	74	261	58	89	20	3	20	64	39	5	1	6	62	8	1	.670	.428
Hayes, Brett	R-R	6-1	210	2-13-84	.161	.133	.171	18	56	1	9	2	0	0	4	1	0	0	0	12	0	0	.196	.175
Herrmann, Chris	L-R	6-0	200	11-24-87	.087	.000	.091	7	23	3	2	1	0	0	3	3	1	0	1	8	0	0	.130	.214
Jamieson, Sean	R-R	6-0	195	3-2-89	.244	.241	.246	77	172	15	42	7	2	1	18	16	1	2	1	56	0	1	.326	.311
Jensen, Kyle	R-L	6-3	240	5-20-88	.289	.394	.253	133	498	77	144	34	2	30	120	44	6	0	7	169	1	1	.546	.350
Jones, Matt	R-R	6-0	195	4-14-92	1.000	—	1.000	1	1	1	1	0	0	0	0	0	0	0	0	0	0	0	2.000	1.000
Lucas, Ed	R-R	6-3	210	5-21-82	.250	.301	.224	82	220	27	55	11	2	2	12	26	1	0	0	59	1	0	.345	.332
2-team total (38 Tacoma)					.243	—		120	358	48	87	23	3	5	34	32	2	0	2	84	1	0	.366	.307
Marzilli, Evan	L-L	6-0	185	3-13-91	.209	.231	.204	21	67	11	14	5	2	0	1	9	1	1	0	20	3	1	.343	.312
McPhearson, Matt	L-L	5-8	175	4-18-95	.000	—	.000	3	1	0	0	0	0	0	0	0	0	0	0	1	0	0	.000	.000
Medrano, Kevin	L-R	5-11	155	5-21-90	.146	.000	.167	23	41	4	6	1	0	0	1	5	0	0	0	7	1	0	.171	.239
O'Brien, Peter	R-R	6-4	235	7-15-90	.254	.255	.253	105	406	64	103	20	5	24	75	23	2	0	3	147	2	0	.505	.295
Owings, Chris	R-R	5-10	185	8-12-91	.611	.667	.600	5	18	7	11	1	1	1	6	3	0	0	0	3	0	1	.944	.667
Peralta, David	L-L	6-1	210	8-14-87	.276	.214	.333	9	29	6	8	4	0	0	2	4	0	0	1	5	0	0	.414	.353
Pollock, A.J.	R-R	6-1	195	12-5-87	.444	.500	.429	4	18	6	8	4	0	1	8	2	0	0	1	1	1	.833	.500
Reinheimer, Jack	R-R	6-1	185	7-19-92	.288	.303	.283	132	500	64	144	28	7	2	48	48	4	4	4	93	20	11	.384	.353
Rivero, Carlos	R-R	6-3	230	5-20-88	.277	.221	.298	124	415	51	115	27	1	19	72	26	0	0	5	84	2	1	.484	.316
Rohlfing, Dan	R-R	6-0	205	2-12-89	.289	.259	.296	43	135	22	39	10	0	5	18	9	0	4	1	39	0	0	.474	.331
Thomas, Mark	R-R	6-1	220	5-5-88	.190	.160	.204	30	79	6	15	6	0	1	10	13	1	1	2	35	0	0	.304	.305
Vargas, Ildemaro	R-R	6-0	170	7-16-91	.354	.390	.344	49	198	35	70	13	0	2	18	20	2	4	0	13	13	1	.449	.418

Pitching	B-T	HT	WT	DOB	W	L	ERA	G	GS	CG	SV	IP	H	R	ER	HR	BB	SO	AVG	vLH	vRH	K/9	BB/9
Baker, Nick	R-R	6-1	190	8-2-92	0	1	12.00	1	1	0	0	3	7	4	4	1	2	1	.467	.444	.500	3.00	6.00
Banda, Anthony	L-L	6-2	190	8-10-93	4	4	3.67	13	13	0	0	74	73	36	30	6	27	68	.257	.282	.246	8.31	3.30
Barrett, Jake	R-R	6-2	240	7-22-91	1	0	0.00	3	0	0	1	3	2	0	0	0	1	3	.200	.167	.250	10.13	3.38
Bracho, Silvino	R-R	5-10	190	7-17-92	0	2	4.81	36	0	0	15	34	34	19	18	2	8	43	.256	.210	.296	11.50	2.14
Bradley, Archie	R-R	6-4	225	8-10-92	5	1	1.99	7	7	0	0	41	26	9	9	0	18	47	.191	.224	.150	10.40	3.98
Buckner, Billy	R-R	6-2	205	8-27-83	1	2	6.38	4	4	0	0	24	31	17	17	3	8	17	.323	.333	.315	6.38	3.00
Burgos, Enrique	R-R	6-4	250	11-23-90	3	0	1.95	24	0	0	1	28	23	7	6	1	17	29	.225	.146	.296	9.43	5.53
Buschmann, Matt	R-R	6-3	205	2-13-84	8	10	5.26	25	24	1	0	142	172	89	83	20	53	91	.306	.324	.288	5.77	3.36
Campos, Vicente	R-R	6-3	230	7-27-92	0	0	0.00	1	1	0	0	2	0	0	0	0	0	0	.000	.000	.000	0.00	0.00
Capps, Matt	R-R	6-2	250	9-3-83	4	0	5.15	39	1	0	3	51	54	34	29	7	21	47	.280	.317	.252	8.35	3.73
Chafin, Andrew	R-L	6-2	225	6-17-90	1	1	1.93	7	1	0	0	9	6	3	2	0	2	8	.188	.167	.200	7.71	1.93
Collmenter, Josh	R-R	6-3	240	2-7-86	0	0	1.23	3	2	0	0	7	7	1	1	5	6	.241	.375	.190	7.36	6.14
2-team total (4 Iowa)					1	0	1.93	7	6	0	0	23	20	5	5	1	13	15	—	—	—	5.79	5.01
Drabek, Kyle	R-R	6-2	205	12-8-87	3	6	6.68	15	11	0	0	69	91	54	51	4	33	41	.327	.326	.329	5.37	4.33
Escobar, Edwin	L-L	6-2	225	4-22-92	6	3	4.25	16	16	0	0	91	99	46	43	8	36	63	.284	.260	.293	6.23	3.56
Fleck, Kaleb	R-R	6-2	215	1-24-89	0	3	5.81	29	0	0	1	31	36	25	20	3	18	37	.279	.273	.284	10.74	5.23
Gann, Cameron	R-R	6-0	203	10-8-92	0	0	3.00	2	0	0	0	3	2	1	1	1	4	.182	.200	.167	12.00	3.00
Garcia, Edgar	R-R	6-2	190	9-20-87	3	6	7.59	12	10	0	0	62	75	55	52	9	29	37	.300	.295	.303	5.40	4.23
Gibson, Daniel	R-L	6-0	195	10-16-91	2	0	6.86	21	0	0	0	21	25	16	16	4	14	17	.298	.257	.327	7.29	6.00
Godley, Zack	R-R	6-3	240	4-21-90	2	1	3.31	7	6	0	0	33	37	16	12	3	15	38	.287	.276	.296	10.47	4.13
Greinke, Zack	R-R	6-2	200	10-21-83	0	1	9.00	1	1	0	0	5	9	5	5	2	2	5	.391	.368	.500	9.00	3.60

Pitching

Pitching	B-T	HT	WT	DOB	W	L	ERA	G	GS	CG	SV	IP	H	R	ER	HR	BB	SO	AVG	vLH	vRH	K/9	BB/9
Hall, Cody	R-R	6-4	235	1-6-88	0	0	7.98	12	0	0	0	15	23	13	13	2	7	10	.348	.367	.333	6.14	4.30
2-team total (4 New Orleans)					0	0	6.50	16	0	0	1	18	25	14	13	2	7	14	—	—	—	7.00	3.50
Hathaway, Steve	L-L	6-1	185	9-13-90	1	2	3.34	28	0	0	1	30	21	11	11	2	19	29	.210	.234	.189	8.80	5.76
Hernandez, Hector	B-L	6-1	190	2-20-91	0	0	2.25	2	0	0	0	4	1	1	1	1	0	2	.077	.143	.000	4.50	0.00
Irvine, Luke	R-R	6-1	200	12-1-88	0	0	3.38	1	0	0	0	3	2	1	1	0	0	2	.222	.200	.250	6.75	0.00
Johnson, Cole	R-R	6-3	200	10-6-88	0	0	9.00	3	0	0	0	3	5	3	3	0	0	3	.385	.333	.500	9.00	0.00
Koch, Matt	L-R	6-3	215	11-2-90	4	2	3.09	7	7	0	0	47	55	18	16	3	6	25	.294	.330	.250	4.82	1.16
Leone, Dominic	R-R	5-11	210	10-26-91	5	2	3.34	33	0	0	1	35	25	14	13	4	11	36	.202	.178	.215	9.26	2.83
Loewen, Adam	L-L	6-6	245	4-9-84	5	3	3.91	40	1	0	0	46	42	21	20	0	31	54	.249	.233	.260	10.57	6.07
Marshall, Evan	R-R	6-2	225	4-18-90	1	1	4.59	33	0	0	0	33	36	17	17	1	16	28	.281	.293	.276	7.56	4.32
Miller, Jared	L-L	6-7	240	8-21-93	0	0	6.00	5	0	0	0	6	5	4	4	2	2	3	.238	.286	.143	4.50	3.00
Miller, Shelby	R-R	6-3	225	10-10-90	5	1	3.91	8	8	1	0	51	55	24	22	4	10	55	.281	.278	.283	9.77	1.78
Muren, Drew	R-R	6-6	225	11-22-88	0	0	4.50	2	0	0	0	2	2	1	1	0	2	3	.286	1.000	.167	13.50	9.00
Nakaushiro, Yuhei	L-L	6-0	160	9-17-89	0	0	0.00	13	0	0	0	11	7	0	0	0	3	13	.189	.154	.273	10.97	2.53
Ogando, Alexi	R-R	6-4	200	10-5-83	1	0	13.50	6	0	0	0	5	10	8	8	0	7	2	.417	.417	.417	3.38	11.81
Omahen, Johnny	R-R	6-0	190	3-15-89	1	3	8.59	8	6	0	0	29	46	29	28	7	13	14	.374	.371	.377	4.30	3.99
Rice, Scott	L-L	6-6	230	9-21-81	0	0	5.68	9	0	0	0	6	7	5	4	1	9	3	.280	.267	.300	4.26	12.79
Sherfy, Jimmie	R-R	6-0	175	12-27-91	1	4	6.17	24	0	0	12	23	20	16	16	5	13	27	.247	.371	.152	10.41	5.01
Shipley, Braden	R-R	6-1	190	2-22-92	8	5	3.70	19	19	1	0	119	131	53	49	7	22	77	.281	.266	.294	5.81	1.66
Simmons, Seth	R-R	5-9	170	6-14-88	0	0	8.56	7	0	0	0	14	19	13	13	2	5	10	.333	.458	.242	6.59	3.29
Smith, Myles	R-R	6-1	175	3-23-92	0	0	47.25	1	0	0	0	1	7	7	7	1	3	2	.636	.714	.500	13.50	20.25
Smyth, Paul	R-R	5-11	210	4-1-87	0	0	18.00	1	0	0	0	2	4	4	4	1	1	2	.400	.286	.667	9.00	4.50
Stites, Matt	R-R	5-11	205	5-28-90	0	0	7.15	11	0	0	1	11	10	9	9	1	13	11	.244	.333	.192	8.74	10.32
Wagner, Tyler	R-R	6-3	205	1-24-91	1	4	3.04	5	5	1	0	27	29	15	9	1	11	15	.287	.320	.255	5.06	3.71

Fielding

Catcher	PCT	G	PO	A	E	DP	PB
Freeman	.973	10	65	8	2	0	0
Gosewisch	.993	57	419	34	3	5	4
Hayes	.980	16	84	14	2	1	0
Herrmann	1	3	23	0	0	0	1
Rohlfing	1	42	308	29	0	6	1
Thomas	.984	28	157	22	3	4	3

First Base	PCT	G	PO	A	E	DP
Freeman	1	4	14	0	0	1
Jensen	.991	105	921	46	9	104
Lucas	1	29	167	14	0	12
O'Brien	1	17	154	8	0	17
Rivero	.952	3	16	4	1	1

Second Base	PCT	G	PO	A	E	DP
Freeman	.986	71	130	235	5	70
Jamieson	.990	29	33	71	1	15

Lucas	1	10	16	28	0	6
Medrano	.923	4	3	9	1	1
Vargas	.987	45	84	138	3	29

Third Base	PCT	G	PO	A	E	DP
Drury	1	3	3	6	0	1
Jamieson	.971	13	7	27	1	2
Lucas	1	21	9	25	0	6
Medrano	1	8	5	18	0	2
Rivero	.987	110	57	174	3	15
Thomas	—	1	0	0	0	0

Shortstop	PCT	G	PO	A	E	DP
Jamieson	1	13	20	29	0	4
Owings	1	3	1	8	0	1
Reinheimer	.975	130	185	371	14	99
Vargas	1	6	8	26	0	4

Outfield	PCT	G	PO	A	E	DP
Borenstein	.936	77	87	1	6	0
Bourgeois	1	25	36	0	0	0
Brito	.987	72	151	5	2	1
Freeman	1	22	30	1	0	0
Glaesmann	1	63	132	1	0	1
Guerrero	.950	31	55	2	3	1
Haniger	.961	73	141	8	6	1
Herrmann	1	2	3	0	0	0
Jensen	1	10	23	2	0	0
Lucas	1	4	3	0	0	0
Marzilli	1	20	42	1	0	1
McPhearson	1	1	1	0	0	0
Medrano	—	1	0	0	0	0
O'Brien	.970	69	94	4	3	0
Owings	1	2	5	0	0	0
Peralta	1	9	15	0	0	0
Pollock	1	4	8	0	0	0

MOBILE BAYBEARS

SOUTHERN LEAGUE

DOUBLE-A

Batting	B-T	HT	WT	DOB	AVG	vLH	vRH	G	AB	R	H	2B	3B	HR	RBI	BB	HBP	SH	SF	SO	SB	CS	SLG	OBP
Belza, Tom	L-R	6-0	190	7-31-89	.232	.154	.244	40	95	10	22	7	0	0	4	10	1	1	0	24	3	2	.305	.311
2-team total (31 Biloxi)					.232	—	—	71	181	18	42	11	1	1	14	17	2	1	1	48	4	3	.320	.303
Bourn, Michael	L-R	5-11	190	12-27-82	.273	.333	.263	5	22	1	6	1	0	0	0	0	0	1	0	5	1	0	.318	.261
Cron, Kevin	R-R	6-5	245	2-17-93	.222	.198	.229	127	465	60	103	20	1	26	88	33	6	0	6	134	3	1	.437	.278
de Oleo, Eduardo	R-R	5-10	180	1-25-93	.500	.667	.400	2	8	2	4	0	0	1	7	0	0	0	0	1	0	0	.875	.500
Denker, Travis	R-R	5-9	205	8-5-85	.303	.349	.292	68	251	45	64	12	1	13	36	39	4	0	3	37	0	1	.555	.416
Flores, Rudy	L-R	6-3	205	12-12-90	.300	.300	.300	51	160	24	48	10	2	5	22	12	2	0	1	52	1	1	.481	.354
Freeman, Ronnie	R-R	6-1	190	1-8-91	.246	.267	.237	58	191	22	47	11	0	3	28	13	2	1	4	41	0	0	.351	.295
Glaesmann, Todd	R-R	6-4	225	10-24-90	.269	.196	.307	43	134	23	36	6	0	7	18	10	1	1	1	30	3	2	.470	.322
Guerrero, Gabby	R-R	6-3	215	12-11-93	.241	.203	.251	92	319	39	77	18	5	8	45	20	0	0	3	76	6	3	.404	.284
Haniger, Mitch	R-R	6-2	215	12-23-90	.294	.407	.252	55	197	21	58	14	2	5	30	30	8	0	1	37	4	3	.462	.407
Hernandez, Oscar	R-R	6-2	230	7-9-93	.194	.276	.174	42	144	12	28	6	0	7	18	5	1	0	0	27	3	0	.382	.227
Ijames, Stewart	L-R	6-0	220	12-8-88	.242	.182	.251	87	244	32	59	19	0	10	33	30	5	0	0	72	1	2	.443	.337
Jones, Matt	R-R	6-0	195	4-14-92	.129	.000	.133	9	31	3	4	2	0	0	2	0	0	0	1	9	0	0	.194	.125
Leyba, Domingo	B-R	5-11	160	9-11-95	.301	.303	.301	44	156	21	47	7	1	4	20	17	1	0	0	22	4	2	.436	.374
Lugo, Dawel	R-R	6-0	190	12-31-94	.306	.290	.310	48	173	24	53	9	2	4	20	4	0	0	1	15	1	1	.451	.322
Marzilli, Evan	L-L	6-0	185	3-13-91	.231	.214	.235	102	342	51	79	13	4	1	27	56	8	1	1	97	11	7	.301	.351
Medrano, Kevin	L-R	6-1	155	5-21-90	.285	.213	.304	68	228	29	65	12	2	0	24	13	1	6	4	26	4	4	.355	.321
Noriega, Gabriel	R-R	6-2	180	9-13-90	.211	.125	.228	31	95	9	20	2	0	1	5	6	0	1	2	24	2	1	.263	.252
2-team total (71 Biloxi)					.251	—	—	102	331	31	83	11	0	4	19	15	3	7	3	54	5	2	.320	.287
Oberacker, Chad	L-L	6-0	195	1-14-89	.184	.091	.211	20	49	6	9	1	1	0	6	9	3	1	1	10	3	1	.265	.339
Peralta, David	L-L	6-1	210	8-14-87	.167	.333	.000	2	6	1	1	1	0	0	1	0	0	0	1	0	1	0	.333	.286
Perez, Michael	L-R	5-11	180	8-7-92	.205	.000	.238	39	122	7	25	4	1	3	10	7	1	0	1	29	0	1	.328	.252
Regis, Cody	L-R	6-2	235	6-8-91	.194	.318	.140	32	72	7	14	2	0	2	10	1	0	2	1	21	0	2	.222	.294
Reyes, Robelys	B-R	5-9	150	7-25-90	.235	.500	.200	8	17	0	4	0	0	0	1	0	0	1	1	1	0	2	.235	.222

Batting	B-T	HT	WT	DOB	AVG	vLH	vRH	G	AB	R	H	2B	3B	HR	RBI	BB	HBP	SH	SF	SO	SB	CS	SLG	OBP
Rohlfing, Dan	R-R	6-0	205	2-12-89	.158	.167	.154	10	19	1	3	0	0	0	2	1	0	0	1	5	0	0	.158	.190
Taylor, Chuck	B-L	5-9	190	9-21-93	.238	.280	.220	41	84	11	20	6	0	1	11	6	3	0	1	15	1	0	.345	.309
Vargas, Ildemaro	R-R	6-0	170	7-16-91	.276	.385	.233	83	323	41	89	15	2	4	19	24	0	3	1	24	8	0	.372	.325
Westbrook, Jamie	R-R	5-9	170	6-18-95	.262	.238	.270	122	435	50	114	21	1	5	36	26	6	1	6	60	10	5	.349	.312

Pitching	B-T	HT	WT	DOB	W	L	ERA	G	GS	CG	SV	IP	H	R	ER	HR	BB	SO	AVG	vLH	vRH	K/9	BB/9
Banda, Anthony	L-L	6-2	190	8-10-93	6	2	2.12	13	13	0	0	76	70	23	18	4	28	84	.241	.264	.235	9.90	3.30
Brewer, Charles	R-R	6-3	210	4-7-88	0	0	1.04	3	2	0	0	9	7	1	1	1	4	8	.226	.214	.235	8.31	4.15
Buckner, Billy	R-R	6-2	205	8-27-83	4	6	3.22	16	11	1	1	73	66	32	26	4	26	70	.243	.231	.252	8.67	3.22
Campos, Vicente	R-R	6-3	230	7-27-92	1	2	3.60	4	4	0	0	20	22	9	8	0	5	15	.289	.371	.220	6.75	2.25
Clarke, Taylor	R-R	6-4	200	5-13-93	8	6	3.59	17	17	0	0	98	99	42	39	9	21	72	.261	.256	.265	6.63	1.94
Curtis, Zac	L-L	5-9	190	7-4-92	0	1	3.20	19	0	0	4	20	17	7	7	3	6	30	.227	.276	.196	13.73	2.75
Diaz, Miller	R-R	6-1	230	6-22-92	1	0	2.82	17	0	0	0	22	22	7	7	2	9	24	.253	.194	.294	9.67	3.63
Doyle, Terry	R-R	6-4	250	11-2-85	0	2	3.86	2	2	0	0	12	14	5	5	0	2	9	.292	.263	.310	6.94	1.54
Garcia, Edgar	R-R	6-2	190	9-20-87	4	3	2.77	14	8	1	1	62	55	25	19	3	20	56	.242	.233	.248	8.17	2.92
Gibson, Daniel	R-L	6-3	215	10-16-91	4	1	0.40	24	0	0	0	23	22	3	1	0	8	17	.262	.323	.226	6.75	3.18
Godley, Zack	R-R	6-3	240	4-21-90	2	5	3.83	8	8	1	0	49	48	27	21	4	11	31	.264	.241	.283	5.66	2.01
Hathaway, Steve	L-L	6-1	185	9-13-90	1	1	1.17	13	0	0	0	15	14	3	2	0	3	10	.250	.133	.293	5.87	1.76
Hernandez, Hector	B-L	6-1	190	2-20-91	1	0	2.45	3	0	0	0	4	2	1	1	0	4	3	.154	.000	.200	7.36	9.82
Hessler, Keith	L-L	6-4	240	3-15-89	0	0	5.06	7	0	0	1	5	7	3	3	0	3	5	.318	.333	.308	8.44	5.06
Irvine, Luke	R-R	6-1	200	12-1-88	1	3	5.76	6	4	0	0	30	31	19	19	4	16	24	.284	.327	.250	7.28	4.85
Johnson, Cole	R-R	6-3	200	10-6-88	4	4	4.01	9	8	1	0	49	50	29	22	4	9	36	.262	.263	.261	6.57	1.64
Koch, Matt	L-R	6-3	215	11-2-90	2	4	4.70	14	14	0	0	75	87	41	39	7	13	49	.295	.354	.248	5.91	1.57
Krehbiel, Joe	R-R	6-2	185	12-20-92	1	1	2.75	52	0	0	1	56	42	20	17	4	23	66	.207	.246	.187	10.67	3.72
Kussmaul, Ryan	R-R	6-4	190	9-19-86	1	0	4.96	3	3	0	0	16	20	9	9	1	5	14	.290	.321	.268	7.71	2.76
Locante, Will	L-L	6-0	205	2-2-90	0	1	11.25	4	0	0	0	4	3	5	5	1	9	5	.214	.000	.300	11.25	20.25
Lopez, Yoan	R-R	6-3	185	1-2-93	4	7	5.52	14	14	1	0	62	67	40	38	10	32	36	.277	.305	.259	5.23	4.65
Miller, Adam	R-R	6-1	210	12-28-89	0	3	4.44	21	0	0	3	24	27	12	12	1	15	24	.303	.306	.302	8.88	5.55
Miller, Jared	L-L	6-7	240	8-21-93	0	1	3.71	19	0	0	2	27	18	12	11	1	13	36	.188	.200	.183	12.15	4.39
Omahen, Johnny	R-R	6-0	190	3-15-89	8	6	4.79	18	18	0	0	98	112	56	52	7	32	62	.292	.309	.279	5.71	2.95
Ramirez, Luis	R-R	6-3	240	7-12-92	0	2	5.19	23	0	0	0	26	25	15	15	3	13	30	.253	.238	.263	10.38	4.50
Sarianides, Nick	R-R	6-1	200	8-29-89	0	0	3.65	8	0	0	0	12	15	7	5	1	5	11	.326	.333	.321	3.65	8.03
2-team total (22 Tennessee)					3	3	3.62	30	0	0	0	37	36	18	15	3	20	33	—	—	—	7.96	4.82
Sherfy, Jimmie	R-R	6-0	175	12-27-91	2	0	0.46	16	0	0	10	20	6	1	1	1	5	31	.092	.074	.105	14.19	2.29
Simmons, Seth	R-R	5-9	170	6-14-88	2	0	1.54	7	0	0	0	12	8	2	2	1	3	10	.195	.278	.130	7.71	2.31
Smith, Myles	R-R	6-1	175	3-23-92	0	1	4.78	18	1	0	0	32	33	17	17	4	20	27	.270	.317	.247	7.59	5.63
Solis, Jency	R-R	6-3	235	2-22-93	0	0	6.00	1	0	0	0	3	3	2	2	0	4	0	.273	.000	.500	0.00	12.00
Speier, Gabe	L-L	6-0	175	4-12-95	1	0	1.93	11	0	0	0	14	12	5	3	0	7	7	.250	.235	.258	4.50	4.50
Stites, Matt	R-R	5-11	205	5-28-90	5	2	1.54	36	0	0	15	41	31	8	7	0	11	35	.212	.231	.202	7.68	2.41
Taylor, Josh	L-L	6-5	225	3-2-93	3	4	4.94	11	11	1	0	55	63	32	30	4	18	46	.289	.290	.288	7.57	2.96
Wright, Austin	L-L	6-4	235	9-26-89	3	3	4.33	27	0	0	1	44	38	25	21	5	23	39	.235	.100	.295	8.04	4.74

Fielding

Catcher	PCT	G	PO	A	E	DP	PB
de Oleo	1	2	9	0	0	0	1
Freeman	.993	56	375	44	3	7	7
Hernandez	.983	40	304	44	6	2	4
Jones	.975	9	67	11	2	0	4
Perez	.993	36	226	40	2	4	1
Rohlfing	1	2	8	0	0	0	0

First Base	PCT	G	PO	A	E	DP
Belza	1	7	35	0	0	2
Cron	.989	124	966	64	11	98
Denker	1	1	13	0	0	2
Flores	1	7	61	9	0	2
Ijames	1	5	25	2	0	5
Regis	1	2	8	0	0	0

Second Base	PCT	G	PO	A	E	DP
Leyba	1	5	6	11	0	5
Medrano	.981	15	21	32	1	7

Noriega	1	3	2	9	0	2
Reyes	1	1	2	1	0	0
Vargas	1	4	7	10	0	2
Westbrook	.980	116	206	280	10	66

Third Base	PCT	G	PO	A	E	DP
Belza	0.84	12	6	15	4	1
Cron	—	1	0	0	0	0
Denker	.971	36	19	47	2	2
Lugo	.971	41	22	79	3	4
Medrano	.932	33	18	37	4	5
Noriega	.939	19	13	33	3	2
Regis	.966	14	9	19	1	3
Reyes	1	2	0	2	0	0

Shortstop	PCT	G	PO	A	E	DP
Leyba	.979	39	52	87	3	24
Lugo	.949	10	14	23	2	7
Medrano	1	7	7	15	0	1
Noriega	.939	8	6	25	2	6

Reyes	1	4	5	9	0	1
Vargas	.975	77	131	223	9	57

Outfield	PCT	G	PO	A	E	DP
Belza	1	17	24	0	0	0
Bourn	1	5	10	1	0	1
Denker	1	10	19	0	0	0
Flores	.933	24	28	0	2	0
Glaesmann	1	38	87	4	0	1
Guerrero	.974	86	172	12	5	2
Haniger	.981	52	94	7	2	4
Ijames	.948	54	91	1	5	0
Marzilli	.975	96	227	3	6	2
Medrano	1	13	20	1	0	0
Oberacker	.952	14	16	4	1	0
Peralta	1	1	2	0	0	0
Regis	1	11	30	0	0	0
Rohlfing	1	3	3	1	0	0
Taylor	1	34	39	1	0	0

VISALIA RAWHIDE

HIGH CLASS A

CALIFORNIA LEAGUE

Batting	B-T	HT	WT	DOB	AVG	vLH	vRH	G	AB	R	H	2B	3B	HR	RBI	BB	HBP	SH	SF	SO	SB	CS	SLG	OBP
Alcantara, Sergio	B-R	5-9	168	7-10-96	.267	.286	.250	4	15	2	4	1	0	0	0	3	1	0	0	2	0	1	.333	.421
Armstrong, Joey	R-R	6-0	200	8-20-93	.157	.200	.139	17	51	8	8	3	0	0	1	2	0	0	0	15	0	0	.216	.232
Baker, Tyler	L-R	5-9	179	3-8-93	.246	.241	.248	62	183	28	45	17	3	2	32	21	2	4	57	0	0	.404	.324
Bray, Colin	B-L	6-3	197	6-18-93	.240	.178	.263	109	400	65	96	18	5	9	40	39	7	12	3	127	16	11	.378	.316
Brito, Socrates	L-L	6-2	205	9-6-92	.111	.500	.000	2	9	1	1	0	0	1	2	0	0	0	2	0	0	.444	.111
Byler, Austin	L-R	6-3	225	10-15-92	.246	.214	.261	33	130	15	32	4	2	4	18	4	1	0	2	46	3	0	.400	.270

Batting	B-T	HT	WT	DOB	AVG	vLH	vRH	G	AB	R	H	2B	3B	HR	RBI	BB	HBP	SH	SF	SO	SB	CS	SLG	OBP
Castillo, Henry	B-R	5-11	189	12-8-94	.258	.236	.264	127	492	71	127	38	2	12	63	38	1	0	3	131	6	9	.417	.311
Cribbs, Galli	L-R	6-0	170	10-8-92	.176	.050	.207	33	102	10	18	3	4	1	13	7	2	3	0	35	2	1	.314	.243
Flores, Rudy	L-R	6-3	205	12-12-90	.292	.293	.291	66	257	36	75	15	0	14	50	22	2	1	5	82	0	1	.514	.346
Hernandez, Oscar	R-R		230	7-9-93	.295	.231	.314	34	112	15	33	10	0	3	15	18	2	1	0	26	1	0	.464	.402
Herum, Marty	R-R	6-3	214	12-16-91	.294	.330	.284	96	377	51	111	20	0	8	46	22	4	1	5	63	9	1	.411	.336
Heyman, Grant	L-R	6-4	222	11-7-93	.262	.086	.289	65	260	25	68	16	1	4	30	6	3	0	3	63	3	1	.377	.283
Jones, Matt	R-R	6-0	195	4-14-92	.229	.200	.233	13	35	2	8	4	0	0	2	6	0	0	0	6	0	1	.343	.341
Leonora, Ericson	R-R	5-11	175	8-25-92	.213	.226	.204	24	80	10	17	4	0	4	15	3	2	1	0	26	0	0	.413	.259
Leyba, Domingo	B-R	5-11	160	9-11-95	.294	.289	.295	86	340	48	100	25	1	6	40	29	0	1	4	62	5	1	.426	.346
Lugo, Dawel	R-R	6-0	190	12-31-94	.314	.169	.348	79	315	61	99	14	5	13	42	15	2	0	1	41	2	1	.514	.348
Mitsui, Trevor	R-R	6-5	225	10-1-92	.318	.368	.298	17	66	8	21	3	0	3	16	2	2	0	0	16	0	0	.500	.357
Munoz, Joe	R-R	6-3	195	12-28-93	.265	.286	.254	28	98	13	26	8	0	2	9	12	2	0	0	31	2	2	.408	.357
Nehrir, Zach	R-R	6-2	205	1-28-93	.227	.350	.182	18	75	12	17	3	0	4	1	2	1	1	1	19	3	2	.267	.253
Oberacker, Chad	L-L	6-0	195	1-14-89	.286	.333	.267	5	21	3	6	1	0	0	1	2	0	0	0	9	0	1	.333	.348
Perez, Michael	L-R	5-11	180	8-7-92	.256	.182	.276	47	156	17	40	10	1	7	19	15	0	0	2	33	1	0	.365	.318
Pollock, A.J.	R-R	6-1	195	12-5-87	.438	.400	.455	6	16	3	7	1	0	2	4	0	0	0	0	1	1	0	.875	.550
Regis, Cody	L-R	6-2	235	6-8-91	.272	.230	.284	81	283	37	77	14	5	1	34	33	2	3	2	59	3	2	.367	.350
Reyes, Robelys	B-R	5-9	150	7-25-90	.298	.322	.288	59	205	34	61	10	2	0	20	11	0	4	2	40	13	5	.366	.330
Reyes, Victor	L-R	6-3	170	10-5-94	.303	.367	.281	124	469	62	142	11	12	6	54	33	1	5	1	78	20	8	.416	.349
Taylor, Chuck	B-L	5-9	190	9-21-93	.273	.194	.293	42	154	27	42	5	4	3	19	26	1	1	2	39	1	3	.416	.377
Trahan, Stryker	L-R	6-0	232	4-25-94	.201	.167	.211	39	139	16	28	10	0	2	19	15	0	0	1	46	0	2	.317	.277
Vargas, Ildemaro	B-R	6-0	170	7-16-91	.250	—	.250	1	4	0	1	0	0	0	0	0	0	0	0	2	0	0	.250	.250

Pitching	B-T	HT	WT	DOB	W	L	ERA	G	GS	CG	SV	IP	H	R	ER	HR	BB	SO	AVG	vLH	vRH	K/9	BB/9
Baker, Nick	R-R	6-1	190	8-2-92	4	1	1.86	41	3	0	2	77	67	22	16	2	16	73	.232	.195	.257	8.50	1.86
Bellow, Kirby	L-L	6-1	220	11-14-91	0	0	1.00	7	0	0	0	9	5	1	1	1	5	11	.161	.143	.176	11.00	5.00
Chafin, Andrew	R-L	6-2	225	6-17-90	1	0	0.00	4	0	0	0	4	0	0	0	2	6	.000	.000	.000	13.50	4.50
Clarke, Taylor	R-R	6-4	200	5-13-93	1	1	2.74	4	4	0	0	23	19	7	7	3	7	22	.221	.273	.189	8.61	2.74
Collmenter, Josh	R-R	6-3	240	2-7-86	0	1	10.57	3	3	0	0	8	13	12	9	1	4	6	.382	.273	.435	7.04	4.70
Curtis, Zac	L-L	5-9	190	7-4-92	1	0	5.23	8	0	0	2	10	12	8	6	0	5	22	.279	.214	.310	19.16	4.35
De La Rosa, Rubby	R-R	6-0	210	3-4-89	0	0	0.00	2	2	0	0	3	1	0	0	0	6	.111	.333	.000	18.00	0.00
Diaz, Miller	R-R	6-1	230	6-22-92	1	1	6.00	24	3	0	0	39	60	36	26	4	19	41	.347	.367	.336	9.46	4.38
Donatella, Justin	R-R	6-6	236	9-16-94	6	4	3.03	12	12	0	0	65	58	31	22	7	16	54	.236	.196	.264	7.44	2.20
Duval, Max	R-R	6-3	235	4-15-91	1	0	9.64	1	0	0	0	5	7	5	5	2	2	3	.350	.455	.222	5.79	3.86
Elias, Ethan	R-R	6-3	180	4-27-93	5	4	5.53	15	15	0	0	72	86	46	44	6	25	60	.301	.265	.324	7.53	3.14
Gann, Cameron	R-R	6-0	203	10-8-92	2	2	3.60	28	0	0	6	30	27	14	12	2	10	21	.235	.333	.184	6.30	3.00
Huang, Wei-Chieh	R-R	6-1	170	9-26-93	1	1	6.49	6	0	0	0	26	33	20	19	5	12	25	.303	.447	.225	8.54	4.10
Irvine, Luke	R-R	6-1	200	12-1-88	4	0	2.32	7	5	0	0	31	26	10	8	2	8	26	.224	.159	.264	7.55	2.32
Jeter, Bud	R-R	6-3	205	10-27-91	9	3	3.08	52	0	0	14	61	51	23	21	3	31	74	.231	.276	.201	10.86	4.55
Keller, Brad	R-R	6-5	230	7-27-95	9	9	4.47	24	24	0	0	135	147	73	67	13	26	99	.281	.286	.278	6.60	1.73
Locante, Will	L-L	6-0	205	2-2-90	0	0	1.93	9	0	0	0	9	3	2	2	0	5	10	.107	.125	.100	9.64	4.82
Miller, Jared	L-L	6-7	240	8-21-93	0	1	1.88	12	0	0	1	14	9	3	3	0	3	20	.184	.313	.121	12.56	1.88
Miller, Shelby	R-R	6-3	225	10-10-90	2	0	0.75	2	2	0	0	12	8	3	1	0	1	19	.178	.176	.179	14.25	0.75
Moya, Gabriel	L-L	6-0	175	1-9-95	5	1	2.01	40	0	0	5	45	26	12	10	2	13	62	.167	.114	.188	12.49	2.62
Muren, Drew	R-R	6-6	225	11-22-88	0	0	3.04	20	0	0	0	24	19	9	8	1	9	33	.213	.188	.228	12.55	3.42
Nakaushiro, Yuhei	L-L	6-0	160	9-17-89	0	0	2.51	13	0	0	2	14	12	4	4	0	9	16	.218	.208	.226	10.05	5.65
Payamps, Joel	R-R	6-2	170	4-7-94	7	5	4.75	15	15	0	0	83	77	48	44	7	25	81	.245	.257	.236	8.75	2.70
Perry, Blake	R-R	6-5	190	2-3-92	0	1	4.63	18	0	0	0	23	23	13	12	0	6	32	.264	.462	.180	12.34	2.31
Pobereyko, Matt	R-R	6-3	232	12-24-91	0	0	2.08	2	0	0	0	4	3	1	1	0	2	7	.214	.500	.100	14.54	4.15
Ramirez, Luis	R-R	6-3	240	7-12-92	7	1	2.36	23	0	0	0	27	15	7	7	1	14	38	.170	.083	.203	12.83	4.73
Reed, Cody	L-L	6-3	245	6-7-96	0	5	6.06	8	7	0	0	36	40	26	24	4	17	29	.296	.242	.314	7.32	4.29
Sherfy, Jimmie	R-R	6-0	175	12-27-91	0	0	0.00	12	0	0	8	12	5	0	0	0	6	21	.128	.083	.148	15.32	4.38
Smith, Myles	R-R	6-1	175	3-23-92	1	2	3.04	18	0	0	0	24	21	11	8	2	14	33	.233	.289	.192	12.55	5.32
Solbach, Markus	R-R	6-5	205	8-26-91	5	2	3.56	12	10	0	0	66	74	34	26	4	15	58	.281	.257	.300	7.95	2.06
Solis, Ramon	R-R	6-3	235	2-22-93	2	1	6.08	35	0	0	0	47	54	33	32	4	19	35	.283	.294	.274	6.65	3.61
Speier, Gabe	L-L	6-0	175	4-12-95	1	0	4.50	9	0	0	1	14	14	7	7	2	5	9	.259	.190	.303	5.79	3.21
Takahashi, Bo	R-R	6-0	197	1-23-97	0	1	4.00	2	2	0	0	9	7	4	4	2	1	8	.206	.231	.190	8.00	1.00
Taylor, Josh	L-L	6-5	225	3-2-93	2	7	5.65	13	13	0	0	78	105	57	49	7	24	77	.335	.326	.339	8.88	2.77
Vargas, Emilio	R-R	6-3	200	8-12-96	0	0	7.80	4	3	0	0	15	20	14	13	2	7	15	.313	.190	.372	9.00	4.20
Wright, Austin	L-L	6-4	235	9-26-89	2	0	0.46	16	0	0	1	20	13	1	1	0	9	26	.188	.167	.200	11.90	4.12
Young, Alex	L-L	6-2	205	9-9-93	2	7	4.59	12	11	1	0	69	79	41	35	10	21	56	.289	.411	.245	7.34	2.75

Fielding

Catcher	PCT	G	PO	A	E	DP	PB
Baker	.992	62	439	78	4	5	8
Hernandez	.985	33	283	42	5	0	9
Jones	.991	12	96	12	1	2	1
Perez	.981	47	375	46	8	4	2

First Base	PCT	G	PO	A	E	DP
Byler	.990	25	191	10	2	16
Cribbs	—	1	0	0	0	0
Flores	.978	29	248	16	6	23
Herum	.990	58	442	43	5	38

	PCT	G	PO	A	E	DP
Mitsui	1.000	1	7	0	0	1
Munoz	1.000	2	18	0	0	0
Regis	.996	28	227	16	1	19

Second Base	PCT	G	PO	A	E	DP
Castillo	.971	99	182	257	13	60
Cribbs	1.000	2	4	10	0	0
Leyba	.985	17	28	39	1	9
Munoz	1.000	4	9	9	0	2
Regis	.977	10	18	24	1	5
Reyes	.981	15	19	32	1	6

Third Base	PCT	G	PO	A	E	DP
Armstrong	1	1	0	1	0	0
Baker	0.75	1	0	3	1	0
Castillo	0.833	13	6	14	4	0
Cribbs	—	1	0	0	0	0
Herum	0.944	39	25	59	5	7
Lugo	0.96	60	37	108	6	9
Munoz	0.86	17	11	26	6	3
Regis	0.889	13	9	23	4	3
Reyes	1	1	0	1	0	0

Shortstop	PCT	G	PO	A	E	DP
Alcantara	1	4	6	11	0	5
Castillo	0.75	1	2	1	1	0
Cribbs	0.943	28	38	78	7	11
Leyba	0.957	66	93	176	12	38
Lugo	0.952	14	19	41	3	10
Reyes	0.934	30	38	76	8	14
Vargas	1	1	1	2	0	1

Outfield	PCT	G	PO	A	E	DP
Armstrong	1	14	23	0	0	0
Bray	0.989	109	259	9	3	2
Brito	1	2	5	0	0	0
Cribbs	1	2	4	1	0	1
Heyman	1	46	57	3	0	0
Leonora	0.957	16	22	0	1	0
Nehrir	0.959	18	44	3	2	1

Oberacker	1	4	8	1	0	0
Pollock	1	2	6	0	0	0
Regis	0.909	23	27	3	3	1
Reyes	0.966	11	27	1	1	0
Reyes	0.972	121	202	5	6	1
Taylor	1	41	63	6	0	0
Trahan	0.878	23	38	5	6	1

KANE COUNTY COUGARS

MIDWEST LEAGUE — *LOW CLASS A*

Batting	B-T	HT	WT	DOB	AVG	vLH	vRH	G	AB	R	H	2B	3B	HR	RBI	BB	HBP	SH	SF	SO	SB	CS	SLG	OBP
Alcantara, Sergio	B-R	5-9	168	7-10-96	.267	.258	.268	53	180	15	48	6	1	1	16	14	0	2	4	26	3	2	.328	.313
Anderson, Josh	R-R	6-0	220	11-4-92	.254	.320	.237	35	122	11	31	7	0	1	10	6	4	0	1	29	1	2	.336	.308
Armstrong, Joey	R-R	6-0	200	8-20-93	.281	.394	.255	51	178	26	50	11	2	2	14	24	5	1	0	48	6	0	.399	.382
Basabe, Luis Alejandro	B-R	5-10	160	8-26-96	.217	.071	.248	45	161	16	35	4	2	3	13	29	1	0	1	60	3	6	.323	.339
Bracho, Didimo	R-R	5-11	170	9-2-96	.000	.000	.000	2	7	0	0	0	0	0	0	0	0	0	0	3	0	0	.000	.000
Bray, Colin	B-L	6-3	197	6-18-93	.253	.238	.258	20	87	10	22	5	1	3	9	8	1	1	0	21	9	2	.437	.323
Byler, Austin	L-R	6-3	225	10-15-92	.259	.179	.281	50	185	21	48	7	4	4	18	22	5	0	1	72	5	4	.405	.352
Cave, Jacy	R-R	6-0	190	1-21-95	.192	.000	.217	6	26	2	5	1	0	0	1	0	0	0	0	10	0	0	.231	.192
Christy, Francis	L-R	6-2	220	9-1-95	.244	.200	.250	59	201	20	49	11	2	2	17	22	0	0	1	61	0	3	.348	.317
Cribbs, Galli	L-R	6-0	170	10-8-92	.252	.174	.270	73	242	28	61	6	2	0	18	18	4	2	6	47	8	7	.293	.320
de Oleo, Eduardo	R-R	5-10	180	1-25-93	.216	.222	.214	15	51	6	11	3	0	1	7	1	2	0	0	13	0	0	.333	.259
Dezzi, Stephen	L-R	6-1	190	2-4-93	.226	.000	.241	17	62	5	14	0	1	0	7	7	0	1	1	14	0	1	.258	.300
Flores, Raymel	B-R	5-9	155	9-22-94	.212	.261	.198	90	311	39	66	9	3	1	18	28	5	5	1	96	11	7	.270	.287
Hernandez, Gerard	L-L	5-10	195	10-16-96	.211	.154	.221	55	175	19	37	8	1	5	21	3	1	0	1	44	2	1	.354	.228
Hernandez, Ramon	R-R	6-4	195	3-2-96	.267	.250	.269	23	86	9	23	5	2	0	10	2	2	0	0	20	0	0	.372	.300
Heyman, Grant	L-R	6-4	222	11-7-93	.263	.370	.236	36	137	18	36	2	2	6	16	6	1	0	0	31	4	1	.438	.299
Lopez, B.J.	R-R	5-9	185	9-29-94	.183	.042	.255	21	71	4	13	0	1	0	6	10	0	1	1	14	0	1	.211	.280
Lowery, Luke	R-R	6-2	230	12-8-93	.099	.063	.109	20	71	4	7	1	1	0	5	7	3	1	1	22	1	0	.141	.207
Mack, Quinnton	R-R	6-0	195	2-11-92	.167	.308	.122	19	54	6	9	1	1	0	1	5	2	0	0	20	0	0	.222	.262
McPhearson, Matt	L-L	5-8	175	4-18-95	.219	.200	.222	23	73	14	16	2	0	0	4	13	0	1	1	21	9	3	.247	.333
Mitsui, Trevor	R-R	6-5	225	10-1-92	.291	.227	.307	115	443	34	129	27	2	4	59	23	3	6	10	102	0	0	.388	.326
Morozowski, Jason	R-R	6-2	190	6-10-94	.215	.372	.176	61	219	27	47	6	3	3	12	27	3	1	2	65	6	4	.311	.307
Munoz, Joe	R-R	6-3	195	12-28-93	.232	.205	.238	62	220	26	51	12	4	5	28	19	6	0	1	57	3	1	.391	.309
Nehrir, Zach	R-R	6-2	205	1-28-93	.242	.254	.238	77	310	22	75	15	1	1	29	14	3	3	1	62	11	6	.306	.280
Ozuna, Fernery	B-R	5-8	170	11-9-95	.263	.333	.246	86	316	35	83	17	5	7	28	15	3	5	0	71	17	7	.415	.302
Queliz, Jose	R-R	6-2	224	8-7-92	.190	.163	.200	46	163	12	31	7	0	3	13	3	3	2	1	48	1	0	.288	.218
Railey, Matt	L-L	5-11	190	3-16-95	.136	.000	.163	20	59	6	8	0	0	0	1	7	2	0	1	13	3	1	.136	.246
Reyes, Robelys	B-R	5-9	150	7-25-90	.281	.300	.276	27	96	11	27	1	0	0	9	7	1	3	1	13	1	4	.292	.327
Smith, Jeff	R-R	6-0	180	10-2-92	.162	.000	.171	12	37	2	6	2	0	1	4	4	0	0	0	11	1	1	.297	.244
Trahan, Stryker	L-R	6-0	232	4-25-94	.200	.182	.202	27	100	7	20	5	1	2	10	3	0	0	0	30	1	0	.330	.223
Veras, Luis	R-R	6-1	180	11-4-93	.222	.333	.195	30	108	8	24	5	1	0	4	2	1	0	1	20	0	2	.287	.241
Wilson, Marcus	R-R	6-3	175	8-15-96	.253	.429	.224	26	99	11	25	8	1	1	5	13	3	0	0	32	7	2	.384	.357

Pitching	B-T	HT	WT	DOB	W	L	ERA	G	GS	CG	SV	IP	H	R	ER	BB	SO	AVG	vLH	vRH	K/9	BB/9
Almonte, Jose	R-R	6-2	185	9-8-95	2	4	3.23	11	11	0	0	56	48	27	20	4	22	59	.234	.223	.243	9.54	3.56
Bellow, Kirby	L-L	6-1	220	11-14-91	1	0	0.70	17	0	0	2	26	11	4	2	5	37	.124	.132	.118	12.97	1.75
Burr, Ryan	R-R	6-4	225	5-28-94	1	2	3.86	14	0	0	0	21	22	12	9	9	18	.265	.306	.234	7.71	3.86
Clark, Cody	R-R	6-2	215	7-22-93	4	1	2.14	25	0	0	3	46	32	12	11	2	14	49	.195	.254	.155	9.52	2.72
Clarke, Taylor	R-R	6-4	200	5-13-93	3	2	2.83	6	6	0	0	29	24	9	9	1	5	24	.222	.236	.208	7.53	1.57
Donatella, Justin	R-R	6-4	236	9-16-94	7	4	3.62	15	15	0	0	80	78	39	32	7	13	57	.254	.242	.263	6.44	1.47
Duval, Max	R-R	6-5	235	4-15-91	2	6	3.02	10	10	0	0	63	67	26	21	7	13	53	.271	.314	.233	7.61	1.87
Gann, Cameron	R-R	6-0	203	10-8-92	1	2	1.48	19	0	0	9	24	17	5	4	0	11	27	.191	.240	.128	9.99	4.07
Garcia, Junior	L-L	5-11	220	10-1-95	3	7	4.56	17	14	0	0	73	79	53	37	8	24	55	.274	.290	.267	6.78	2.96
Greer, Brody	R-R	6-2	198	5-15-91	0	1	6.23	6	0	0	0	9	10	6	6	2	13	.286	.389	.176	13.50	2.08
Gunn, Alex	L-L	6-4	210	9-8-91	2	0	3.00	2	2	0	0	12	15	4	4	2	1	4	.313	.273	.324	3.00	0.75
Hernandez, Carlos	R-R	5-9	171	4-26-94	7	11	2.55	26	22	0	1	123	94	46	35	5	69	122	.215	.236	.194	8.90	5.04
Hernandez, Hector	B-L	6-1	190	2-20-91	2	1	3.22	21	2	0	2	45	42	16	16	10	50	.237	.194	.261	10.07	2.01
Long, Keegan	R-R	6-2	190	8-27-93	1	1	1.87	43	0	0	7	67	45	19	14	3	12	47	.189	.168	.204	6.28	1.60
Mark, Tyler	R-R	6-1	195	10-18-94	0	5	8.03	7	4	0	0	25	34	22	22	2	13	25	.333	.306	.358	9.12	4.74
Martinez, Jose	R-R	6-1	160	4-14-94	0	0	4.80	14	0	0	0	15	15	9	8	0	21	17	.268	.194	.360	10.20	12.60
Mason, Austin	R-R	6-2	200	12-10-93	6	0	3.35	25	1	0	4	43	37	20	16	4	14	32	.236	.269	.211	6.70	2.93
McCullough, Mason	R-R	6-4	245	1-7-93	0	1	4.69	30	0	0	1	40	35	23	21	2	29	50	.243	.279	.217	11.16	6.47
McWilliams, Sam	R-R	6-7	190	9-4-95	3	6	3.98	15	15	0	0	75	86	43	33	4	18	43	.292	.319	.265	5.18	2.17
Mejia, Jefferson	R-R	6-7	195	8-24-94	0	1	2.70	5	0	0	0	10	5	3	3	0	3	16	.156	.059	.267	14.40	2.70
Miller, Jared	L-L	6-7	240	8-21-93	0	0	0.00	9	0	0	2	14	4	0	0	5	21	.085	.125	.065	13.19	3.14
Moya, Gabriel	L-L	6-0	175	1-9-95	1	0	0.47	12	0	0	0	19	12	2	1	0	4	20	.179	.200	.167	9.47	1.89
Muren, Drew	L-R	6-6	225	11-22-88	0	0	6.46	4	0	0	0	15	17	12	11	2	25	.279	.136	.359	14.67	5.28
Nakaushiro, Yuhei	L-L	6-0	160	9-11-89	0	0	0.00	3	0	0	0	3	1	0	0	1	3	.100	.000	.167	21.00	3.00
Payamps, Joel	R-R	6-2	170	4-7-94	3	3	2.36	13	4	0	0	50	40	15	13	1	11	47	.223	.270	.178	8.52	1.99
Perez, Julio	R-R	6-2	175	1-16-92	0	0	1.71	18	0	0	3	21	11	6	4	2	12	26	.149	.161	.140	11.14	5.14
Reed, Cody	L-L	6-3	245	6-7-96	5	2	1.82	7	7	0	0	40	32	9	8	1	3	55	.221	.222	.22	12.48	0.68
Solis, Jency	R-R	6-3	235	2-22-93	0	0	4.63	7	0	0	0	12	10	6	6	0	13	.233	.136	.333	10.03	3.09

ARIZONA DIAMONDBACKS

Pitching

Pitching	B-T	HT	WT	DOB	W	L	ERA	G	GS	CG	SV	IP	H	R	ER	HR	BB	SO	AVG	vLH	vRH	K/9	BB/9
Speier, Gabe	L-L	6-0	175	4-12-95	1	2	2.22	17	0	0	2	28	24	11	7	1	7	31	.224	.245	.207	9.85	2.22
Takahashi, Bo	R-R	6-0	197	1-23-97	1	1	3.00	7	5	0	0	24	23	10	8	1	11	19	.253	.327	.167	7.13	4.13
Vargas, Emilio	R-R	6-3	200	8-12-96	5	6	3.31	13	13	1	0	71	63	34	26	7	18	69	.234	.279	.197	8.79	2.29
Young, Alex	L-L	6-2	205	9-9-93	3	1	2.16	9	9	1	0	50	39	14	12	1	16	37	.217	.268	.194	6.66	2.88

Fielding

Catcher	PCT	G	PO	A	E	DP	PB
Christy	.988	58	445	54	6	2	7
de Oleo	1.000	12	78	11	0	0	1
Lopez	.977	21	188	28	5	2	7
Lowery	.991	11	94	13	1	0	3
Queliz	.988	43	361	37	5	7	5

First Base	PCT	G	PO	A	E	DP
Anderson	1.000	1	1	0	0	0
Armstrong	1.000	1	1	0	0	0
Byler	.987	43	363	25	5	36
Dezzi	.947	2	15	3	1	0
Hernandez	.985	21	178	13	3	23
Lowery	1	2	15	1	0	2
Mitsui	.991	67	485	41	5	38
Munoz	.980	6	45	4	1	3

Second Base	PCT	G	PO	A	E	DP
Alcantara	1.000	4	10	8	0	1
Basabe	.962	28	46	81	5	18
Bracho	.786	2	4	7	3	2

	PCT	G	PO	A	E	DP
Cribbs	1.000	22	38	40	0	11
Flores	.910	33	42	80	12	13
Munoz	1.000	3	7	5	0	2
Ozuna	.968	22	37	54	3	16
Reyes	.973	24	29	78	3	8
Smith	1.000	7	7	11	0	6

Third Base	PCT	G	PO	A	E	DP
Alcantara	.867	5	3	10	2	0
Anderson	.871	19	10	17	4	3
Armstrong	1.000	1	0	3	0	0
Cribbs	1.000	9	2	10	0	1
Hernandez	1.000	2	1	2	0	0
Munoz	.899	50	40	76	13	8
Ozuna	.950	61	36	97	7	11
Reyes	.800	2	2	2	1	0

Shortstop	PCT	G	PO	A	E	DP
Alcantara	.928	44	63	104	13	21
Basabe	.925	11	13	24	3	4
Cribbs	.947	39	56	88	8	16

	PCT	G	PO	A	E	DP
Flores	.958	50	63	118	8	25
Ozuna	1.000	1	0	2	0	1

Outfield	PCT	G	PO	A	E	DP
Armstrong	.967	48	84	4	3	0
Bray	.964	20	54	0	2	0
Cave	1.000	6	11	0	0	0
Cribbs	1.000	7	7	0	0	0
Dezzi	1.000	13	20	0	0	0
Hernandez	.913	46	77	7	8	1
Heyman	.985	34	64	2	1	1
Mack	.971	17	34	0	1	0
McPhearson	.974	21	37	0	1	0
Morozowski	.984	60	121	6	2	2
Munoz	—	1	0	0	0	0
Nehrir	.982	76	161	6	3	2
Ozuna	1.000	2	1	0	0	0
Railey	.933	14	26	2	2	2
Trahan	.973	23	35	1	1	0
Veras	1.000	24	46	3	0	0
Wilson	1.000	25	43	3	0	1

HILLSBORO HOPS
NORTHWEST LEAGUE

SHORT-SEASON

Batting	B-T	HT	WT	DOB	AVG	vLH	vRH	G	AB	R	H	2B	3B	HR	RBI	BB	HBP	SH	SF	SO	SB	CS	SLG	OBP
Alcantara, Sergio	B-R	5-9	168	7-10-96	.319	.429	.300	15	47	12	15	2	0	0	8	10	1	0	1	10	4	2	.362	.441
Anderson, Josh	R-R	6-0	220	11-4-92	.307	.341	.298	55	212	31	65	11	0	5	34	10	6	0	2	41	5	0	.429	.352
Brown, Max	R-R	6-6	200	4-30-93	.190	.200	.188	5	21	2	4	0	0	0	0	0	0	0	0	3	0	0	.190	.190
Chigbogu, Justin	L-L	6-1	240	7-8-94	.214	.219	.213	56	196	21	42	6	0	5	19	20	2	0	0	61	5	0	.321	.294
Coffman, Nic	R-R	6-3	180	12-15-92	.200	.333	.182	8	25	1	5	1	0	0	2	1	0	0	0	12	0	1	.240	.286
De La Garza, Paxton	R-R	6-0	200	12-17-93	.000	.000	.000	4	6	1	0	0	0	0	2	2	0	0	2	3	0	0	.000	.000
Deluzio, Ben	R-R	6-3	190	8-9-94	.313	.211	.344	30	80	23	25	2	2	0	7	10	5	2	0	15	14	2	.388	.421
Dezzi, Stephen	L-R	6-1	190	2-4-93	.167	—	.167	2	6	3	1	1	0	0	0	1	1	0	0	1	0	0	.333	.375
Endris, Billy	L-L	6-2	190	10-18-93	.267	.000	.333	4	15	2	4	1	0	1	3	0	0	0	2	1	0	1	.533	.389
Grier, Anfernee	R-R	6-1	180	10-13-95	.240	.211	.250	20	75	8	18	2	0	1	6	3	1	0	2	21	9	2	.307	.278
Heinrich, Jason	R-R	6-1	205	6-7-96	.000	.000	.000	1	3	1	0	0	0	0	1	0	0	0	0	0	0	0	.000	.250
Hernandez, Ramon	R-R	6-4	195	3-2-96	.253	.158	.281	22	83	8	21	4	2	2	13	4	2	0	1	19	0	0	.422	.300
Jefferson, Manny	R-R	6-3	170	3-5-95	.207	.300	.176	59	203	19	42	11	0	3	22	22	2	0	1	45	5	3	.305	.289
Karaviotis, Mark	R-R	185	10-12-95		.344	.455	.306	41	131	25	45	8	1	2	25	21	12	0	1	30	2	3	.466	.473
Lowery, Luke	R-R	6-2	230	12-8-93	.264	.262	.265	67	261	25	69	15	0	5	34	22	6	0	1	66	20	6	.379	.334
Martinez, Francis	B-R	6-4	187	6-28-97	.000	—	.000	1	1	0	0	0	0	0	0	0	0	0	0	0	0	0	.000	.000
McPhearson, Matt	L-L	5-8	175	4-18-95	.278	.000	.294	7	18	2	5	1	0	0	0	2	0	0	0	1	6	0	.333	.350
Morozowski, Jason	R-R	6-2	190	6-10-94	.291	.273	.297	38	134	33	39	8	3	9	27	12	6	0	2	34	3	2	.597	.370
Oberacker, Chad	L-L	6-0	195	1-14-89	.409	.444	.385	6	22	6	9	2	1	0	3	6	0	0	0	2	1	0	.591	.536
Olmeda, Alexis	R-R	6-0	225	4-5-94	.260	.260	.260	53	181	21	47	7	3	3	21	19	0	0	4	43	6	1	.381	.324
Owings, Connor	L-R	5-10	190	5-11-94	.175	.133	.185	26	80	13	14	2	1	1	8	12	0	0	1	20	2	2	.263	.280
Queliz, Jose	R-R	6-2	224	8-7-92	.200	.091	.235	14	45	4	9	1	0	2	6	2	0	1	0	11	0	1	.356	.234
Railey, Matt	L-L	5-11	190	3-16-95	.219	.000	.259	9	32	4	7	0	0	0	5	2	2	0	0	6	1	1	.219	.306
Rose, Joey	R-R	6-1	205	1-20-98	.000	.000	.000	2	2	0	0	0	0	0	0	1	0	0	0	2	0	0	.000	.333
Silverio, Luis	R-R	6-3	180	6-27-95	.185	.154	.214	7	27	2	5	1	0	0	7	4	1	0	0	6	2	0	.222	.313
Smith, Jeff	R-R	6-0	180	10-2-92	.107	.250	.050	8	28	3	3	0	0	0	1	3	0	0	0	8	0	0	.214	.133
Smith, Stephen	R-R	6-1	220	11-3-94	.203	.233	.194	37	128	19	26	4	1	2	10	19	6	0	1	39	2	0	.297	.331
Stupienski, Gavin	L-R	6-1	220	3-12-94	.250	1.000	.182	4	12	1	3	1	0	0	3	1	0	0	1	0	1	.333	.308
Veras, Luis	R-R	6-1	180	11-3-94	.222	.184	.236	43	144	21	32	10	1	0	10	11	2	0	2	27	0	0	.306	.283
Walton, Adam	R-R	6-1	190	9-22-93	.248	.229	.255	43	129	18	32	6	0	0	13	2	6	2	2	27	10	3	.295	.322
Wilson, Marcus	R-R	6-3	175	8-15-96	.252	.467	.190	43	135	24	34	5	2	0	15	38	2	0	2	40	18	3	.319	.418

Pitching	B-T	HT	WT	DOB	W	L	ERA	G	GS	CG	SV	IP	H	R	ER	HR	BB	SO	AVG	vLH	vRH	K/9	BB/9
Bellow, Kirby	L-L	6-1	220	11-14-91	1	0	0.00	5	0	0	0	4	4	0	0	0	0	10	.111	.429	22.50	0.00
Benitez, Anfernee	L-L	6-1	180	7-24-95	7	5	3.48	14	12	0	0	72	75	34	28	2	31	71	.273	.333	.246	8.83	3.86
Betts, Palmer	R-R	6-1	190	4-13-94	1	1	2.11	10	0	0	1	21	17	10	5	0	10	25	.224	.192	.240	10.55	4.22
Blackburn, Nick	R-R	6-2	205	7-10-94	0	0	0.00	3	0	0	0	3	2	0	0	0	0	0	.200	.250	.167	0.00	0.00
Duplantier, Jon	L-R	6-4	225	7-11-94	0	0	0.00	2	2	0	0	3	0	0	0	0	0	6	.000	.000	.000	18.00	0.00
Duval, Max	R-R	6-5	235	4-15-91	0	0	7.36	2	1	0	0	4	3	3	3	0	2	4	.214	.200	.222	9.82	4.91
Elias, Ethan	R-R	6-3	180	4-27-93	0	0	15.00	3	1	0	0	3	2	5	5	0	2	2	.182	.000	.286	6.00	6.00
Eveld, Tommy	R-R	6-5	195	12-30-93	2	1	1.86	24	0	0	2	29	17	6	6	0	8	31	.168	.205	.145	9.62	2.48
Garcia, Junior	L-L	5-11	220	10-1-95	4	1	4.47	9	9	0	0	46	51	26	23	3	17	37	.273	.233	.291	7.19	3.30

Pitching

Pitching	B-T	HT	WT	DOB	W	L	ERA	G	GS	CG	SV	IP	H	R	ER	HR	BB	SO	AVG	vLH	vRH	K/9	BB/9
Ginkel, Kevin	R-R	6-4	210	3-24-94	1	0	2.61	18	0	0	2	21	17	8	6	0	6	22	.224	.241	.213	9.58	2.61
Gouin, Alex	R-R	5-11	204	9-8-91	1	0	2.57	1	1	0	0	7	5	2	2	0	2	11	.192	.231	.154	14.14	2.57
Grey, Connor	R-R	6-0	180	5-6-94	0	0	0.00	6	0	0	0	10	4	0	0	0	2	14	.121	.000	.211	13.03	1.86
Huang, Wei-Chieh	R-R	6-1	170	9-26-93	2	2	5.34	9	4	0	0	30	33	19	18	4	11	42	.277	.226	.333	12.46	3.26
Jackson, Dean	R-R	6-7	225	2-23-94	0	0	0.00	1	0	0	0	2	0	0	0	0	1	2	.000	.000	.000	9.00	4.50
Lemieux, Mack	L-L	6-3	205	9-6-96	1	2	3.91	7	7	0	0	23	24	12	10	1	12	26	.270	.306	.245	10.17	4.70
Mark, Tyler	R-R	6-1	195	10-18-94	5	5	3.91	15	15	0	0	78	79	41	34	8	23	75	.258	.261	.256	8.62	2.64
Martinez, Jose	R-R	6-1	160	4-14-94	0	0	3.38	6	0	0	0	8	5	8	3	0	6	6	.172	.125	.190	6.75	6.75
Mason, Austin	R-R	6-2	200	12-10-93	0	0	0.00	1	0	0	1	1	0	0	0	0	1	2	.250	—	.250	18.00	9.00
Mejia, Jefferson	R-R	6-7	195	8-2-94	4	2	5.73	13	6	0	0	38	41	32	24	2	26	37	.268	.317	.237	8.84	6.21
Newton, Dallas	L-R	6-5	215	9-3-94	0	0	14.21	4	0	0	0	6	11	10	10	0	5	2	.393	.313	.500	2.84	7.11
Perez, Julio	R-R	6-2	175	1-16-92	0	0	3.00	3	0	0	1	3	3	1	1	0	0	1	.273	.000	.750	3.00	0.00
Pobereyko, Matt	R-R	6-3	232	12-24-91	0	2	11.42	5	0	0	0	9	12	12	11	2	2	9	.316	.091	.407	9.35	2.08
Poche, Colin	L-L	6-3	185	1-17-94	1	2	3.19	21	4	0	0	31	20	14	11	2	17	36	.194	.188	.197	10.45	4.94
Rodriguez, Wesley	R-R	5-10	210	12-4-96	0	0	0.00	1	0	0	0	1	0	0	0	0	1	1	.000	.000	.000	9.00	9.00
Simms, Trevor	R-R	6-5	205	3-15-92	2	2	3.94	10	1	0	0	30	25	19	13	1	16	22	.231	.333	.192	6.67	4.85
Smith, Riley	R-R	6-1	175	1-15-95	2	0	2.51	25	0	0	2	32	33	10	9	1	4	30	.268	.260	.274	8.35	1.11
Takahashi, Bo	R-R	6-0	197	1-23-97	5	2	2.50	10	10	0	0	50	39	17	14	0	17	40	.212	.226	.200	7.15	3.04
Taylor, Curtis	R-R	6-6	215	7-25-95	1	0	2.20	17	0	0	3	16	13	5	4	0	5	23	.213	.185	.235	12.67	2.76
Ward, Tucker	R-R	6-6	230	5-10-92	1	2	5.52	14	0	0	0	15	18	12	9	0	8	9	.290	.280	.297	5.52	4.91
Watson, Jordan	L-L	6-0	185	9-14-93	0	0	3.09	12	0	0	0	12	8	6	4	0	4	20	.182	.000	.222	15.43	3.09
Winston, Jake	R-R	6-3	194	9-13-93	1	1	2.87	28	0	0	5	31	31	14	10	0	15	31	.252	.283	.234	8.90	4.31
Wright, Taylor	R-R	6-2	190	11-23-92	0	3	6.86	5	4	0	0	21	30	16	16	2	3	16	.357	.317	.395	6.86	1.29

Fielding

C: Lowery 37, Olmeda 29, Queliz 14, Stupienski 1. **1B:** Chigbogu 42, Dezzi 2, Hernandez 10, Karaviotis 2, Lowery 6, Olmeda 18. **2B:** De La Garza 2, Jefferson 50, Karaviotis 3, Owings 1, Smith 6, Walton 18. **3B:** Anderson 47, Coffman 8, Hernandez 12, Olmeda 3, Rose 2, Smith 2, Walton 9. **SS:** Alcantara 15, De La Garza 2, Jefferson 9, Karaviotis 35, Walton 16. **OF:** Brown 5, DeLuzio 29, Endris 4, Grier 2, Heinrich 1, Lowery 1, McPhearson 5, Morozowski 34, Oberacker 6, Owings 22, Railey 9, Silverio 7, Smith 34, Veras 41, Wilson 43.

MISSOULA OSPREY   ROOKIE
PIONEER LEAGUE

Batting	B-T	HT	WT	DOB	AVG	vLH	vRH	G	AB	R	H	2B	3B	HR	RBI	BB	HBP	SH	SF	SO	SB	CS	SLG	OBP
Anderson, Josh	R-R	6-0	220	11-4-92	.500	—	.500	1	4	1	2	0	0	0	1	0	0	0	2	0	0	.500	.600
Araiza, Bryan	L-R	6-2	190	4-27-96	.254	.333	.234	32	118	14	30	8	1	1	13	12	0	1	0	32	3	1	.364	.323
Araujo, Juan	R-R	6-2	195	6-24-98	.222	1.000	.000	4	9	1	2	0	0	1	3	0	0	0	5	0	0	.556	.222
Bracho, Didido	R-R	5-11	170	9-2-96	.174	.118	.188	24	86	8	15	1	1	2	9	2	1	0	1	26	1	1	.279	.200
Branigan, Michael	R-R	5-10	175	1-9-96	.188	.143	.222	8	16	5	3	0	0	0	2	2	0	0	7	0	0	.188	.350
Brown, Max	R-R	6-6	200	4-30-93	.233	.000	.263	13	43	6	10	2	1	0	2	6	0	1	0	12	5	1	.326	.327
Cave, Jacy	R-R	6-2	190	1-21-95	.282	.270	.286	46	177	31	50	8	4	3	22	9	7	1	0	47	6	6	.424	.342
Chisholm, Jasrado	L-R	5-11	165	2-1-98	.281	.182	.302	62	249	42	70	12	1	9	37	19	1	0	1	73	13	4	.446	.333
De La Garza, Paxton	R-R	6-0	200	12-17-93	.394	.429	.385	25	99	15	39	5	2	5	31	9	2	0	0	23	1	5	.636	.455
Diaz, Eduardo	R-R	6-2	175	7-19-97	.000	.000	.000	3	2	0	0	0	0	0	0	0	0	0	0	1	0	0	.000	.000
Endris, Billy	L-L	6-2	190	10-18-93	.236	.103	.261	47	182	27	43	9	0	4	18	12	5	1	1	57	5	1	.352	.300
Grier, Anfernee	R-R	6-1	180	10-13-95	.214	.000	.231	4	14	2	3	1	0	1	2	0	1	0	0	5	0	0	.500	.267
Hernandez, Ramon	R-R	6-4	195	3-2-96	.337	.500	.314	25	98	16	33	3	3	4	8	2	4	0	0	16	0	0	.551	.375
Herrera, Jose	B-R	5-10	185	2-24-97	.277	.136	.304	36	137	23	38	5	1	5	18	15	1	0	1	27	1	2	.438	.351
Hill, Tanner	R-R	6-2	250	4-12-94	.303	.324	.298	44	155	24	47	15	1	7	29	18	4	0	3	38	2	2	.548	.383
January, Ryan	L-R	6-2	198	5-27-97	.273	.192	.287	51	183	34	50	6	0	10	26	24	4	0	0	63	0	1	.470	.376
Lopez, B.J.	R-R	5-9	185	9-29-94	.208	.250	.200	6	24	1	5	1	0	0	0	0	1	0	0	1	0	0	.250	.208
Maciel, Gabriel	B-R	5-10	170	1-10-99	.266	.417	.239	23	79	15	21	2	0	0	4	5	1	2	0	19	11	1	.291	.318
Marquez, Pedro	R-R	5-11	190	1-19-94	.284	.200	.312	30	102	18	29	5	0	3	11	10	1	0	0	18	2	4	.422	.354
Morozowski, Jason	R-R	6-2	190	6-10-94	.231	—	.231	3	13	4	3	0	0	1	0	0	0	0	2	1	0	.462	.231
Ramos, Eudy	R-R	6-1	195	2-19-96	.318	.333	.315	52	201	32	64	15	1	13	43	13	5	0	1	75	3	1	.597	.373
Sanchez, Yan	R-R	6-2	190	8-31-96	.276	.149	.312	60	217	30	60	13	1	5	36	16	1	1	3	54	12	1	.415	.325
Silverio, Luis	R-R	6-3	180	6-27-95	.263	.273	.261	22	80	18	21	5	1	6	14	5	2	2	0	19	2	1	.575	.298
Simmons, Kal	B-R	6-1	180	12-10-93	.367	.400	.353	16	49	13	18	5	0	2	9	5	0	0	0	12	1	2	.592	.426
Smith, Kyle	R-R	6-4	220	10-14-93	.244	.208	.253	33	119	21	29	6	2	8	24	4	10	0	0	47	1	0	.529	.323
Soole, Logan	L-L	6-0	185	3-8-96	.204	.318	.171	29	98	15	20	1	0	0	6	5	0	0	0	17	2	2	.214	.243
Veras, Luis	R-R	6-1	180	11-4-93	.154	.500	.091	4	13	2	2	2	0	0	3	0	1	0	0	5	0	0	.308	.214
Yerzy, Andy	L-R	6-3	215	7-5-98	.250	.071	.304	18	60	2	15	2	0	0	1	0	2	0	0	16	0	1	.283	.274

Pitching	B-T	HT	WT	DOB	W	L	ERA	G	GS	CG	SV	IP	H	R	ER	HR	BB	SO	AVG	vLH	vRH	K/9	BB/9
Atkinson, Ryan	R-R	6-3	218	5-10-93	1	4	3.38	7	6	1	0	29	29	21	11	3	11	33	.257	.257	.256	10.13	3.38
Becker, Cal	R-R	6-1	195	6-9-93	0	0	1.64	9	0	0	0	11	8	3	2	0	6	8	.216	.333	.160	6.55	4.91
Betts, Palmer	R-R	6-1	190	4-13-94	3	7	3.89	7	7	1	0	39	40	27	17	1	12	37	.248	.286	.229	8.47	2.75
Blackburn, Nick	R-R	6-2	205	7-10-94	0	0	3.38	2	0	0	0	3	3	3	1	0	1	2	.250	.000	.333	6.75	3.38
Castillo, Luis	R-R	6-2	180	3-10-95	0	3	4.04	19	3	0	0	38	37	22	16	3	13	38	.274	.283	.270	9.59	3.28
Duran, Jhoan	R-R	6-5	175	1-8-98	0	1	3.55	3	3	0	0	13	14	9	5	1	5	9	.250	.094	.458	6.39	3.55
Durruthy, Williams	R-R	6-4	225	10-11-94	1	1	6.32	15	1	0	0	31	32	25	22	2	24	34	.264	.350	.222	9.77	6.89
Galligan, Rob	R-L	6-4	218	7-1-93	0	0	6.92	12	0	0	0	13	18	15	10	0	7	7	.316	.286	.326	4.85	4.85
Gonzalez, Erbert	R-R	5-10	170	10-21-95	4	1	3.67	27	0	0	0	27	22	14	11	4	16	43	.216	.282	.175	14.33	5.33
Gonzalez, Gabe	R-R	6-4	210	8-16-96	2	2	8.23	17	0	0	0	27	35	30	25	8	18	23	.299	.405	.250	7.57	5.93

Pitching	B-T	HT	WT	DOB	W	L	ERA	G	GS	CG	SV	IP	H	R	ER	HR	BB	SO	AVG	vLH	vRH	K/9	BB/9
Gouin, Alex	R-R	5-11	204	9-8-91	2	6	4.60	10	10	1	0	59	74	38	30	9	10	46	.314	.260	.350	7.06	1.53
Grey, Connor	R-R	6-0	180	5-6-94	4	2	4.47	9	9	0	0	50	50	25	25	6	16	37	.262	.271	.258	6.62	2.86
Holtmann, Bryant	R-L	6-5	200	2-5-93	1	2	6.28	22	3	0	0	39	52	31	27	2	22	26	.329	.432	.298	6.05	5.12
Jackson, Dean	R-R	6-7	225	2-23-94	4	2	2.90	22	0	0	1	31	20	15	10	2	5	41	.177	.191	.167	11.90	1.45
Keele, Tyler	R-R	6-3	195	8-17-93	2	1	1.54	20	0	0	3	23	16	7	4	1	11	24	.195	.154	.214	9.26	4.24
Lin, Kai-Wei	R-R	5-11	165	3-19-96	1	3	6.90	6	6	1	0	30	45	28	23	5	5	25	.341	.250	.386	7.50	1.50
Lowman, Will	R-L	6-0	185	7-27-94	0	0	16.62	6	0	0	0	4	4	8	8	0	11	4	.267	.000	.286	8.31	22.85
Madero, Luis	R-R	6-3	175	4-15-97	0	2	11.07	5	5	0	0	20	32	26	25	3	15	9	.364	.371	.358	3.98	6.64
Mason, Austin	R-R	6-2	200	12-10-93	0	0	0.00	2	0	0	1	3	0	0	0	1	3	.000	.000	.000	9.00	3.00
Muhammad, Jay	R-R	6-2	195	11-14-94	0	0	13.50	2	0	0	0	2	2	3	3	0	1	4	.222	.000	.286	18.00	4.50
Newton, Dallas	L-R	6-5	215	9-3-94	2	0	8.00	8	0	0	0	9	10	12	8	1	9	8	.286	.214	.333	8.00	9.00
Pimentel, Chester	R-R	6-5	210	11-12-95	2	5	6.32	9	9	0	0	47	68	41	33	4	13	43	.333	.357	.321	8.23	2.49
Pujols, Rafael	R-R	6-6	175	8-21-95	3	0	3.83	21	0	0	1	40	33	23	17	2	19	46	.213	.200	.222	10.35	4.28
Romero, Pierce	R-R	6-3	200	5-12-94	1	4	9.14	13	9	0	0	42	67	50	43	7	23	22	.356	.368	.350	4.68	4.89
Simms, Trevor	R-R	6-4	205	3-15-92	0	1	3.92	4	4	0	0	21	24	11	9	0	3	19	.293	.333	.265	8.27	1.31
Torres, Juan	R-R	6-2	180	5-25-95	0	0	5.40	3	0	0	0	3	3	2	2	0	1	5	.231	.333	.200	13.50	2.70
Watson, Jordan	L-L	6-0	185	9-14-93	0	0	0.00	1	0	0	0	1	0	0	0	0	0	3	.000	.000	.000	27.00	0.00

Fielding

C: Branigan 5, Herrera 12, Hill 1, January 38, Lopez 6, Simmons 10, Yerzy 15. **1B:** Hernandez 5, Hill 42, Ramos 15, Simmons 1, Smith 17. **2B:** Bracho 23, Chisholm 1, De La Garza 23, Sanchez 34, Simmons 1. **3B:** Anderson 1, Hernandez 19, Ramos 37, Sanchez 12, Simmons 7, Smith 7. **SS:** Bracho 2, Chisholm 60, Sanchez 16, Simmons 3. **OF:** Araiza 32, Araujo 3, Brown 12, Cave 44, Diaz 3, Endris 44, Maciel 22, Marquez 20, Morozowski 3, Silverio 21, Simmons 1, Soole 27, Veras 3.

AZL DIAMONDBACKS   ROOKIE
ARIZONA LEAGUE

Batting	B-T	HT	WT	DOB	AVG	vLH	vRH	G	AB	R	H	2B	3B	HR	RBI	BB	HBP	SH	SF	SO	SB	CS	SLG	OBP
Alcantara, Sergio	B-R	5-9	168	7-10-96	.345	.333	.348	7	29	9	10	1	1	0	2	4	0	2	0	2	2	0	.448	.424
Araiza, Bryan	L-R	6-2	190	4-27-96	.500	.333	1.000	2	8	1	4	0	0	0	1	1	0	0	0	1	1	0	.500	.556
Araujo, Juan	R-R	6-2	195	6-24-98	.215	.245	.205	52	181	27	39	9	1	7	21	15	7	0	1	71	4	3	.392	.299
Babitt, Myles	L-L	5-9	180	3-17-93	.300	.267	.307	28	90	16	27	2	0	0	3	16	0	3	0	14	5	4	.322	.406
Bracho, Didimo	R-R	5-11	170	9-2-96	.167	.111	.185	13	36	2	6	3	0	0	2	6	0	0	0	14	1	0	.250	.211
Branigan, Michael	R-R	5-10	175	1-9-96	.207	.143	.227	10	29	1	6	1	0	0	5	2	1	0	0	6	0	0	.241	.281
Brito, Socrates	L-L	6-2	205	9-6-92	.143	.143	—	2	7	0	1	0	0	0	2	0	0	0	0	3	0	0	.143	.143
Coffman, Nic	R-R	6-3	180	12-15-92	.173	.000	.231	19	52	8	9	4	2	0	8	15	0	0	0	20	1	2	.327	.358
Comstock, Daniel	R-R	5-11	210	9-24-93	.200	.130	.259	19	50	3	10	6	0	0	7	7	0	1	0	19	2	0	.320	.298
De La Garza, Paxton	R-R	6-0	200	12-17-93	.321	.235	.360	28	109	14	35	12	1	1	14	8	3	0	0	28	5	3	.477	.383
de Oleo, Eduardo	R-R	5-10	180	1-25-93	.300	.250	.333	4	10	2	3	1	1	0	1	0	0	0	0	2	0	0	.600	.300
Deluzio, Ben	R-R	6-3	190	8-9-94	.364	.500	.286	4	11	1	4	0	0	0	1	0	0	0	0	2	0	0	.364	.364
Diaz, Eduardo	R-R	6-2	175	7-19-97	.229	.087	.274	26	96	7	22	2	1	0	7	10	2	2	1	24	4	2	.271	.312
Herrmann, Chris	L-R	6-0	200	11-24-87	.417	1.000	.300	4	12	2	5	3	0	0	1	1	0	0	0	1	0	0	.667	.500
Higuera, Walter	R-R	6-3	159	5-18-96	.167	.167	.167	20	30	8	5	1	0	0	3	7	5	0	0	11	2	1	.267	.405
Karaviotis, Mark	R-R	6-1	185	10-12-95	.361	.231	.435	13	36	9	13	4	0	1	8	7	0	0	0	8	0	3	.556	.549
Maciel, Gabriel	B-R	5-10	170	1-10-99	.289	.395	.245	37	149	28	43	3	0	0	10	12	1	3	2	22	11	4	.309	.341
Marquez, Pedro	R-R	5-11	190	1-19-94	.346	.308	.359	14	52	9	18	5	2	0	7	0	1	0	1	11	4	1	.519	.352
Martinez, Francis	B-R	6-4	187	6-28-97	.243	.226	.250	48	189	26	46	9	2	3	30	13	2	0	2	63	1	1	.360	.296
Morozowski, Jason	R-R	6-2	190	6-10-94	.429	—	.429	2	7	1	3	1	0	0	0	1	0	0	0	2	0	0	.571	.500
Novas, Joel	R-R	6-1	185	12-31-94	.260	.200	.283	21	73	9	19	0	0	3	7	0	0	0	0	10	0	1	.288	.325
Oberacker, Chad	L-L	6-0	195	1-14-89	.467	.375	.571	4	15	5	7	1	1	0	2	1	0	0	0	2	0	0	.667	.500
Ovalles, Adony	R-R	6-2	185	5-10-94	.154	.000	.167	7	13	1	2	0	0	0	1	1	0	0	0	6	0	0	.154	.267
Owings, Chris	R-R	5-10	185	8-12-91	.200	.000	.500	2	5	2	1	0	0	0	0	1	0	0	0	1	0	0	.200	.333
Peralta, David	L-L	6-1	210	8-14-87	.400	.667	.000	2	5	2	2	0	0	0	2	1	0	0	0	1	0	0	.400	.500
Pollock, A.J.	R-R	6-1	195	12-5-87	.333	.000	.667	2	6	2	2	0	0	0	0	0	1	0	0	0	0	0	.333	.429
Romero, Gerardo	B-R	5-9	160	10-5-95	.167	.227	.145	28	84	3	14	1	1	0	9	4	0	1	1	27	1	1	.202	.202
Rose, Joey	R-R	6-1	205	1-20-98	.229	.162	.250	47	153	19	35	10	4	1	9	13	5	1	0	55	2	0	.366	.310
Santana, Rafael	R-R	6-0	186	10-24-95	.217	.500	.158	7	23	3	5	1	0	0	3	5	0	0	0	9	0	0	.261	.333
Smith, Jeff	R-R	6-0	180	10-2-92	.185	.294	.146	21	65	6	12	0	0	2	4	3	2	0	1	21	0	0	.185	.264
Smith, Kyle	R-R	6-4	220	10-14-93	.424	.625	.360	9	33	7	14	5	1	1	9	5	2	0	1	9	0	1	.727	.512
Stupienski, Gavin	L-R	6-1	220	3-12-94	.250	.364	.222	22	56	6	14	5	0	1	6	12	6	0	2	8	2	0	.393	.323
Tejeda, Luis	R-R	6-3	195	7-11-95	.234	.263	.214	19	47	7	11	4	0	1	10	4	2	2	1	18	0	1	.383	.315
Van Rycheghem, Luke	L-R	6-3	210	2-9-98	.226	.333	.214	9	31	2	7	2	0	0	2	1	0	0	0	11	0	1	.290	.250
Walton, Adam	R-R	6-1	190	10-3-94	.000	.000	—	1	4	0	0	0	0	0	1	0	0	0	0	1	0	0	.000	.000
Yerzy, Andy	L-R	6-3	215	7-5-98	.196	.217	.190	27	102	5	20	3	0	1	15	4	0	1	5	30	1	0	.255	.220

Pitching	B-T	HT	WT	DOB	W	L	ERA	G	GS	CG	SV	IP	H	R	ER	HR	BB	SO	AVG	vLH	vRH	K/9	BB/9
Atkinson, Ryan	R-R	6-3	218	5-10-93	0	0	2.25	2	1	0	0	4	2	1	1	0	2	6	.143	.167	.125	13.50	4.50
Beato, Anyel	R-R	6-3	175	3-3-96	0	1	7.33	14	0	0	1	23	29	24	19	2	8	18	.315	.290	.328	6.94	3.09
Betts, Palmer	R-R	6-1	190	4-13-94	0	0	6.75	2	0	0	0	4	3	3	3	0	2	4	.188	.286	.111	9.00	4.50
Blackburn, Nick	R-R	6-2	205	7-10-94	0	1	12.27	3	0	0	0	4	5	6	5	0	4	2	.313	.500	.250	4.91	9.82
Burr, Ryan	R-R	6-4	225	5-28-94	0	0	0.00	2	0	0	2	6	0	0	0	0	2	6	.000	.000	.000	9.00	4.50
Chafin, Andrew	R-L	6-2	225	6-17-90	0	0	0.00	1	1	0	0	2	1	0	0	0	0	2	.286	1.000	.167	9.00	4.50
De La Rosa, Rubby	R-R	6-0	210	3-4-89	—	—	—	—	—	—	—	—	—	—	—	—	—	—	.375	.500	.357	—	—
Duran, Jhoan	R-R	6-5	175	1-8-98	1	2	5.85	4	4	0	0	20	24	13	13	1	5	13	.312	.190	.357	5.85	2.25

Pitching	B-T	HT	WT	DOB	W	L	ERA	G	GS	CG	SV	IP	H	R	ER	HR	BB	SO	AVG	vLH	vRH	K/9	BB/9
Duval, Max	R-R	6-5	235	4-15-91	1	1	1.13	2	1	0	0	8	6	2	1	0	3	15	.194	.167	.200	16.88	3.38
Elias, Ethan	R-R	6-3	180	4-27-93	1	0	4.91	3	1	0	0	4	3	2	2	0	0	2	.214	.333	.125	4.91	0.00
Fleck, Kaleb	R-R	6-2	215	1-24-89	0	0	0.00	3	0	0	1	3	1	0	0	0	1	6	.091	—	.091	16.20	2.70
Galligan, Rob	R-L	6-4	218	7-1-93	0	0	2.84	4	0	0	0	6	10	5	2	0	0	8	.313	.286	.320	11.37	0.00
Greinke, Zack	R-R	6-2	200	10-21-83	0	1	0.00	1	1	0	0	3	4	1	0	0	0	5	.308	.200	.375	15.00	0.00
Gunn, Alex	L-L	6-4	210		3	4	3.45	9	2	0	0	47	53	23	18	0	4	42	.275	.271	.276	8.04	0.77
Hernandez, Kenny	L-L	6-2	185	6-24-98	0	1	1.93	6	0	0	0	9	10	4	2	0	5	4	.270	.200	.396	3.86	4.82
Huang, Wei-Chieh	R-R	6-1	170	9-26-93	0	0	6.00	1	1	0	0	3	3	2	2	1	0	3	.273	.200	.333	9.00	0.00
Lemieux, Mack	L-L	6-3	205	9-6-96	1	0	1.42	7	4	0	0	13	8	2	2	1	3	17	.182	.333	.125	12.08	2.13
Lin, Kai-Wei	R-R	5-11	165	3-19-96	2	5	4.69	9	7	0	0	40	42	27	21	1	14	37	.258	.250	.261	8.26	3.12
Lopez, Yoan	R-R	6-3	185	1-2-93	0	0	0.00	2	2	0	0	3	3	0	0	0	0	4	.250	.400	.143	12.00	0.00
Madero, Luis	R-R	6-3	175	4-15-97	3	2	3.61	9	6	0	0	42	46	19	17	2	15	34	.275	.348	.248	7.23	3.19
Martinez, Edgar	R-R	6-0	175	11-2-97	2	0	5.46	14	0	0	0	28	30	19	17	2	8	17	.270	.238	.290	5.46	2.57
Miller, Adam	R-R	6-1	210	12-28-89	0	0	0.00	1	0	0	0	1	1	0	0	0	0	1	.000	—	.000	9.00	0.00
Muhammad, Jay	R-R	6-2	195	11-14-94	5	1	0.62	18	0	0	4	29	13	2	2	0	20	36	.137	.241	.091	11.17	6.21
Nakaushiro, Yuhei	L-L	6-0	160	9-17-89	0	0	0.00	1	0	0	0	1	1	0	0	0	0	4	.200	.333	.000	27.00	0.00
Ovalles, Melvin	R-R	6-2	180	11-21-96	0	1	7.71	3	2	0	0	7	10	11	6	1	6	8	.313	.500	.227	10.29	7.71
Ozuna, Bryan	R-R	6-1	215	3-13-94	0	0	21.60	2	0	0	0	2	5	5	4	0	1	2	.500	1.000	.444	10.80	5.40
Pobereyko, Matt	R-R	6-3	232	12-24-91	1	0	0.64	8	0	0	1	14	6	1	1	0	6	20	.125	.077	.143	12.86	3.86
Polancic, Jake	R-R	6-3	205	6-8-98	0	3	7.59	6	4	0	0	11	17	9	9	2	1	6	.347	.400	.310	5.06	0.84
Polanco, Oliver	R-R	6-3	210	5-13-97	1	0	2.76	8	2	0	0	16	11	5	5	0	5	16	.186	.300	.128	8.82	2.76
Rodriguez, Wesley	R-R	5-10	210	12-4-96	0	0	0.00	5	5	0	0	5	1	1	0	0	2	3	.063	.000	.143	5.40	3.60
Smith, Cameron	L-L	6-0	165	12-12-92	1	1	5.11	3	1	0	0	12	12	7	7	1	3	17	.245	.417	.189	12.41	2.19
Smith, Josh	R-R	6-3	185	7-8-96	0	0	14.54	4	0	0	0	4	4	7	7	1	9	5	.235	.200	.250	10.38	18.69
Soriano, Franklyn	L-L	6-2	173	7-21-95	2	3	5.08	13	8	0	0	57	71	39	32	2	27	48	.309	.260	.322	7.62	4.29
Speier, Gabe	L-L	6-0	175	4-12-95	1	0	0.00	2	0	0	0	2	0	0	0	0	1	2	.000	—	.000	9.00	4.50
Torres, Juan	R-R	6-4	200	9-11-92	1	0	4.00	2	1	0	0	9	10	6	4	0	2	8	—	—	—	8.00	2.00
Torres, Juan	R-R	6-2	180	5-25-95	2	1	3.72	16	2	0	2	36	34	20	15	0	17	37	.252	.250	.253	9.17	4.21

Fielding

C: Branigan 10, Comstock 7, de Oleo 4, Herrmann 1, Ovalles 5, Stupienski 11, Tejeda 19, Yerzy 18. **1B:** Coffman 8, Comstock 1, Martinez 46, Smith 1, Van Rycheghem 4. **2B:** Bracho 1, De La Garza 15, Novas 19, Romero 3, Smith 20, Walton 1. **3B:** Coffman 7, De La Garza 1, Rose 46, Smith 1, Smith 6. **SS:** Alcantara 7, Bracho 12, De La Garza 12, Karaviotis 6, Novas 2, Romero 24. **OF:** Araiza 2, Araujo 48, Babitt 25, Brito 1, Coffman 2, DeLuzio 4, Diaz 26, Herrmann 1, Higuera 15, Maciel 36, Marquez 11, Morozowski 2, Oberacker 4, Owings 1, Peralta 1, Santana 5.

DSL D-BACKS   ROOKIE
DOMINICAN SUMMER LEAGUE

Batting	B-T	HT	WT	DOB	AVG	vLH	vRH	G	AB	R	H	2B	3B	HR	RBI	BB	HBP	SH	SF	SO	SB	CS	SLG	OBP
Acosta, Enyor	L-R	6-2	165	1-28-99	.249	.291	.235	64	217	25	54	10	2	0	31	21	4	2	2	59	12	1	.313	.324
Arroyo, Mailon	B-R	6-0	200	1-2-98	.184	—	—	56	212	15	39	12	0	2	29	18	2	0	3	31	1	0	.269	.251
Bermudez, Miguel	R-R	5-10	155	8-20-99	.203	—	—	48	148	9	30	2	0	0	11	9	6	3	0	36	4	4	.216	.276
Bueno, Jonathan	R-R	6-1	168	10-4-98	.125	.221	—	49	149	17	33	3	3	1	12	19	7	2	2	36	9	4	.302	.333
Delgado, Roberto	L-R	6-1	165	8-28-98	.213	.200	.214	20	75	7	16	0	0	0	6	5	0	1	0	11	1	1	.213	.272
Diaz, Eduardo	R-R	6-2	175	7-19-97	.358	.333	.366	33	123	36	44	6	1	3	16	19	3	0	2	19	19	6	.496	.449
Federico, Randy	R-R	6-3	210	4-28-98	.197	.304	.181	57	178	21	35	5	0	0	26	21	6	0	4	59	5	4	.225	.297
Garcia, Andy	R-R	6-0	179	5-27-99	.098	.120	—	31	83	10	10	2	0	1	8	14	3	3	0	25	1	1	.181	.270
Garcia, Jorsan	R-R	5-11	220	4-16-99	.206	.286	.196	25	63	4	13	1	0	2	10	10	1	0	2	20	0	0	.317	.316
Gonzalez, Esmerlin	L-R	6-2	180	11-24-97	.175	.200	.173	38	80	8	14	1	0	0	6	12	1	0	0	29	3	3	.188	.290
Herize, Javier	L-R	5-11	180	2-1-99	.184	—	—	28	103	10	19	3	0	0	7	13	1	0	0	19	0	1	.214	.282
Hernandez, Eddie	B-R	5-9	160	4-18-99	.233	.200	.237	64	219	27	51	5	2	0	15	24	5	1	2	33	11	6	.274	.320
King, Jose	L-R	5-0	160	1-16-99	.350	.313	.364	61	240	51	84	7	4	0	27	21	2	8	3	36	21	3	.413	.402
Lanza, Douglas	R-R	6-1	180	3-14-98	.258	.313	.240	42	128	14	33	2	1	1	15	6	1	8	1	35	3	1	.313	.294
Lara, Luis	B-R	6-0	190	5-6-95	.315	.311	.316	67	251	47	79	14	5	6	51	37	2	0	7	34	9	2	.482	.397
Lemus, Edward	R-R	6-1	188	10-24-98	.265	.267	.265	42	113	10	30	2	0	0	11	8	6	0	0	20	1	1	.283	.346
Leyton, Brandon	R-R	5-10	165	12-17-98	.218	—	—	56	193	23	42	4	1	0	22	21	9	4	1	18	8	2	.249	.321
Machado, Gabriel	R-R	5-10	155	2-20-98	.142	.063	.156	40	106	9	15	1	0	1	9	18	1	0	1	38	2	1	.179	.270
Marriaga, Jesus	R-R	6-0	170	12-17-98	.299	—	—	64	234	42	70	10	4	0	23	32	4	1	1	72	25	10	.376	.391
Moreno, Oscar	R-R	6-0	180	12-10-97	.245	.200	.268	35	106	20	26	4	2	0	11	12	6	1	2	21	5	0	.321	.349
Munoz, Jesus	L-L	6-2	160	12-19-98	.269	.264	.271	60	197	26	53	3	1	1	16	16	3	1	2	38	12	6	.310	.330
Ovalles, Adony	R-R	6-2	185	5-10-94	.000	—	.000	1	3	0	0	0	0	0	0	0	0	0	0	0	1	0	.000	.000
Paulino, Yoneudi	R-R	6-2	200	5-26-95	.281	—	—	39	139	16	39	8	0	0	15	14	4	0	0	23	1	3	.338	.363
Perez, Jorge	L-L	5-8	165	1-18-98	.271	—	—	67	266	45	72	9	4	0	18	25	1	5	2	17	23	5	.335	.333
Ramirez, Waldy	R-R	6-4	175	6-16-97	.246	.125	.286	44	130	20	32	5	0	1	16	24	2	1	1	27	7	5	.308	.369
Reyes, Jose	R-R	5-9	160	10-11-98	.349	.292	.371	24	86	18	30	3	1	0	4	6	1	0	0	11	5	1	.407	.398
Rodriguez, Victor	L-L	5-9	157	1-31-97	.233	.320	.221	57	206	23	48	2	0	0	15	24	1	0	2	30	4	5	.262	.313
Sanchez, David	R-R	6-1	175	1-6-99	.245	.255	.241	57	192	21	47	7	1	0	29	12	4	0	1	36	8	2	.292	.301
Santana, Rafael	R-R	6-0	186	10-24-95	.250	.333	.000	3	4	1	1	0	0	0	0	0	0	0	0	0	1	0	.250	.250
Santilien, Osvaldo	R-R	6-3	195	6-23-98	.235	.318	.226	62	217	33	51	15	0	1	23	12	5	0	0	69	4	4	.318	.291
Sulbaran, Jose	R-R	6-0	175	5-19-99	.203	.125	.211	24	79	14	16	1	0	0	9	11	2	1	0	24	5	2	.215	.315
Valbuena, Luvin	R-R	5-9	165	5-7-99	.216	.200	.222	13	37	6	8	1	0	0	3	7	0	0	0	11	1	0	.243	.341

Pitching

Pitching	B-T	HT	WT	DOB	W	L	ERA	G	GS	CG	SV	IP	H	R	ER	HR	BB	SO	AVG	vLH	vRH	K/9	BB/9
Abreu, Oscar	L-L	6-4	185	12-19-94	0	0	4.15	12	0	0	0	17	14	9	8	0	19	11	.233	.143	.245	5.71	9.87
Almonte, Angelo	L-L	5-11	160	6-26-94	1	2	1.67	7	3	0	1	27	14	7	5	0	7	35	.154	.133	.158	11.67	2.33
Angel, Ricardo	R-R	6-2	175	2-18-98	2	1	1.56	20	0	0	2	35	25	11	6	0	11	32	—	—	—	8.31	2.86
Beriguete, Francis	L-L	6-3	165	8-11-99	0	0	0.00	2	0	0	0	3	1	0	0	0	1	4	.111	—	.111	12.00	3.00
Berroa, Silvestre	L-L	6-0	175	5-13-97	0	0	2.91	13	0	0	0	22	23	8	7	1	6	16	.271	.444	.250	6.65	2.49
Ceballos, Jesus	R-R	5-11	162	1-9-97	0	0	4.13	18	0	0	0	24	21	14	11	1	13	15	.239	.387	.158	5.63	4.88
Contreras, Christian	L-L	6-3	195	11-17-98	0	3	5.66	15	0	0	0	21	18	17	13	0	29	19	.247	.071	.288	8.27	12.63
Cruz, Wilfry	R-R	6-2	160	10-22-97	0	3	5.70	8	5	0	0	24	24	20	15	1	17	21	—	—	—	7.99	6.46
Cuevas, Felix	R-R	5-11	170	3-27-97	1	2	6.23	9	2	0	1	17	17	12	12	2	20	12	.270	.188	.298	6.23	10.38
De La Cruz, Carlos	R-R	6-4	178	5-7-98	0	0	10.43	7	2	0	0	15	15	18	17	1	21	16	.288	.118	.371	9.82	12.89
De Leon, Robert	R-R	6-5	200	12-18-97	0	0	54.00	1	0	0	0	0	0	2	2	0	2	0	.000	.000	—	0.00	54.00
De Leon, Yonal	R-R	6-2	186	8-6-97	2	7	7.83	13	10	0	0	46	64	51	40	1	28	26	.332	.288	.354	5.09	5.48
Defrank, Damian	R-R	6-3	200	2-1-95	3	4	3.60	23	0	0	7	30	27	18	12	0	20	15	.245	.313	.218	4.50	6.00
Despaigne, Jorge	R-R	6-3	242	1-28-91	3	0	3.19	6	6	0	0	31	17	12	11	0	10	39	.155	.120	.165	11.32	2.90
Done, Dawry	R-R	6-3	175	3-17-98	1	4	4.70	13	7	0	1	46	41	33	24	2	32	35	.248	.315	.196	6.85	6.26
Estepan, Luis	L-L	6-2	200	5-16-94	3	8	5.37	12	11	0	0	52	47	35	31	1	36	39	.235	.367	.212	6.75	6.23
Felix, Wellinton	R-R	6-1	185	11-25-94	2	0	3.66	15	0	0	2	20	17	9	8	2	11	16	—	—	—	7.32	5.03
Ferrand, Javier	L-L	6-0	185	4-26-96	0	0	5.68	6	0	0	0	6	3	4	4	0	16	8	.150	.333	.118	11.37	22.74
Frias, Luis	R-R	6-3	180	5-23-98	3	2	3.83	13	11	0	0	52	45	28	22	0	28	47	.231	.152	.255	8.19	4.88
Gomez, Jose	R-R	6-3	175	9-23-96	4	2	3.48	13	10	0	0	52	52	23	20	1	25	47	.264	.291	.254	8.19	4.35
Herman, Omar	R-R	5-10	170	3-21-97	4	3	3.68	13	7	0	0	51	51	25	21	0	18	41	.259	.264	.257	7.19	3.16
Hernandez, Juan	R-R	6-2	175	8-10-99	2	3	2.09	14	14	0	0	78	62	27	18	3	17	63	—	—	—	7.30	1.97
Herrera, Jhoendri	R-R	5-9	170	6-6-94	3	0	1.42	12	0	0	2	19	15	4	3	0	4	12	—	—	—	5.68	1.89
Javier, Joshua	L-L	6-3	185	12-16-98	2	4	6.00	14	9	0	0	42	40	33	28	0	43	42	—	—	—	9.00	9.21
Leal, Jhairon	L-L	6-2	175	8-21-98	1	2	8.68	6	3	0	0	19	19	20	18	1	11	20	.264	.176	.291	9.64	5.30
Martinez, Hector	R-R	6-1	180	12-28-98	0	0	16.20	16	0	0	0	10	19	24	18	0	23	4	.404	.333	.438	3.60	20.70
Montero, Merkis	R-R	6-2	155	12-1-95	3	1	1.89	18	0	0	0	38	24	11	8	0	18	26	.188	.276	.162	6.16	4.26
Olivero, Deyni	R-R	6-1	165	1-7-98	5	1	4.99	9	6	0	0	40	40	23	22	3	16	25	.268	.292	.264	5.67	3.63
Ramirez, Nestor	R-R	6-4	195	9-4-95	2	0	0.61	24	0	0	18	30	16	5	2	0	7	21	.150	.154	.148	6.37	2.12
Rodriguez, Diony	R-R	6-4	210	5-14-97	6	1	1.47	11	5	0	2	37	25	8	6	1	11	45	.197	.259	.180	11.05	2.70
Rodriguez, Joseph	R-R	6-1	180	9-5-98	1	0	2.04	20	0	0	0	40	35	13	9	0	20	29	.236	.178	.262	6.58	4.54
Sanchez, Geraldo	R-R	6-2	193	8-19-97	0	2	3.03	11	4	0	0	33	31	19	11	0	14	24	—	—	—	6.61	3.86
Santana, Yeison	R-R	6-0	160	10-25-96	4	2	0.58	21	0	0	5	46	25	6	3	0	6	59	.162	.256	.130	11.46	1.17
Valdez, Bryan	L-L	6-3	180	11-27-94	6	2	1.73	13	9	0	0	68	43	13	13	1	5	86	.180	.176	.180	11.44	0.67
Valdez, Jhonny	R-R	6-3	187	8-10-98	2	1	5.56	19	0	0	0	34	36	24	21	1	11	16	—	—	—	4.24	2.91
Zorrilla, Pedro	L-L	6-2	168	4-30-96	5	7	2.73	14	14	1	0	82	82	40	25	5	18	40	.255	.250	.256	4.37	1.97

Fielding

C: Arroyo 1, Garcia 20, Herize 1, Lanza 42, Paulino 1, Valbuena 13. **1B:** Arroyo 30, Bermudez 1, Lara 1, Paulino 25, Ramirez 24. **2B:** Bermudez 10, Bueno 6, King 28, Leyton 13, Ramirez 2, Reyes 16. **3B:** Bermudez 1, Lara 54, Leyton 1, Ramirez 17. **SS:** Bueno 9, King 32, Leyton 21, Reyes 8. **OF:** Acosta 49, Diaz 32, Marriaga 3, Moreno 25, Munoz 56, Perez 27, Sanchez 27, Santana 1.

Atlanta Braves

SEASON IN A SENTENCE: Atlanta wasn't supposed to contend this year and didn't, but after firing manager Fredi Gonzalez (9-28) and trading for Matt Kemp, the Braves became respectable, going 59-65 under longtime organizational soldier Brian Snitker.

HIGH POINT: The Braves played spoiler in their final series at Turner Field as they move out of the 20-year-old park in favor of new SunTrust Park next year. Detroit needed to win, but the Braves beat the Tigers in the last two games of the year, with Julio Teheran striking out 12 in seven innings to out-duel Justin Verlander in a 1-0 victory on the season's final day. Freddie Freeman had the lone RBI to cap a .304/.400/.569 season that included a 30-game hit streak and 34 homers.

LOW POINT: It was a brutal April as Atlanta lost its first nine games to open the season, and heralded Cuban import Hector Olivera was arrested for assaulting a woman in the same month. He was suspended and eventually traded to the Padres in a salary-dump deal that brought Kemp to Atlanta. The Padres immediately released Olivera, 31, who still had yet to find a new home as November arrived.

NOTABLE ROOKIES: Outfielder Mallex Smith tied for the team lead with 16 stolen bases in just 72 games and looks like at least a fourth outfielder going forward. Shortstop Dansby Swanson, who'll remain rookie-eligible in 2017, provided a glimpse into the future with a strong September. Atlanta's rookie pitchers almost uniformly struggled, particularly righthander Aaron Blair (2-7, 7.59), with hard-throwing reliever Mauricio Cabrera the notable exception.

KEY TRANSACTIONS: Trading for Kemp helped revitalize the offense as he provided needed power and protection for Freeman. The Shelby Miller trade in the offseason brought Swanson and Ender Inciarte, two key up-the-middle pieces for the future, as well as Blair, who showed flashes despite his struggles. Swanson came up after veteran Erick Aybar was traded to the Tigers.

DOWN ON THE FARM: A system burgeoning with talent showed up most at low Class A Rome, with a loaded pitching staff leading to a South Atlantic League title. Despite a 65-78 season, Gwinnett made the Triple-A International League playoffs and lost in the finals. The Braves went old-school in the draft, taking prep pitchers with each of their three selections in the top 44 picks.

OPENING DAY PAYROLL: $69,005,791 (29th)

PLAYERS OF THE YEAR

MAJOR LEAGUE	MINOR LEAGUE
Freddie Freeman	**Dansby Swanson**
1b	ss
.302/.400/.569	(High A/Double-A)
34 HR, 91 RBI	.275/.362/.426
3rd in NL in OPS	39 XBH, 13 SB

ORGANIZATION LEADERS

BATTING   *Minimum 250 AB

MAJORS

*	AVG	Freddie Freeman	.302
*	OPS	Freddie Freeman	.968
	HR	Freddie Freeman	34
	RBI	Freddie Freeman	91

MINORS

*	AVG	Emilio Bonifacio, Gwinnett	.298
*	OBP	Ray-Patrick Didder, Rome	.387
*	SLG	Austin Riley, Rome	.479
*	OPS	Austin Riley, Rome	.803
	R	Ray-Patrick Didder, Rome	95
	H	Ozzie Albies, Gwinnett, Mississippi	161
	TB	Austin Riley, Rome	237
	2B	Austin Riley, Rome	39
	3B	Ozzie Albies, Gwinnett, Mississippi	10
	HR	Austin Riley, Rome	20
	RBI	Dustin Peterson, Mississippi	88
	BB	Braxton Davidson, Carolina	71
	SO	Braxton Davidson, Carolina	184
	SB	Emilio Bonifacio, Gwinnett	37
		Ray-Patrick Didder, Rome	37

PITCHING   #Minimum 75 IP

MAJORS

	W	Mike Foltynewicz	9
#	ERA	Julio Teheran	3.21
	SO	Julio Teheran	167
	SV	Jim Johnson	20

MINORS

	W	Chris Ellis, Mississippi, Gwinnett	12
	L	Ryan Clark, Carolina	13
#	ERA	Rob Whalen, Mississippi, Gwinnett	2.40
	G	Madison Younginer, Mississippi, Gwinnett	46
	GS	Chris Ellis, Mississippi, Gwinnett	28
	SV	Madison Younginer, Mississippi, Gwinnett	15
	IP	Max Povse, Carolina, Mississippi	158
	BB	Lucas Sims, Gwinnett, Mississippi	92
	SO	Lucas Sims, Gwinnett, Mississippi	159
#	AVG	Patrick Weigel, Rome, Mississippi	.194

General Manager: John Coppolella. **Farm Director:** Dave Trembley. **Scouting Director:** Brian Bridges.

Class	Team	League	W	L	PCT	Finish	Manager
Majors	Atlanta Braves	National	68	93	.422	13th (15)	F. Gonzalez/B. Snitker
Triple-A	Gwinnett Braves	International	65	78	.455	10th (14)	B. Snitker/J. Moses
Double-A	Mississippi Braves	Southern	73	65	.529	5th (10)	Luis Salazar
High A	Carolina Mudcats	Carolina	52	87	.374	8th (8)	Rocket Wheeler
Low A	Rome Braves	South Atlantic	70	69	.504	9th (14)	Randy Ingle
Rookie	Danville Braves	Appalachian	31	36	.4th	7th (10)	Robinson Cancel
Rookie	Braves	Gulf Coast	28	28	.500	8th (17)	Nestor Perez Jr.
Overall 2016 Minor League Record			319	363	.468	23rd (30)	

ORGANIZATION STATISTICS

ATLANTA BRAVES
NATIONAL LEAGUE

Batting	B-T	HT	WT	DOB	AVG	vLH	vRH	G	AB	R	H	2B	3B	HR	RBI	BB	HBP	SH	SF	SO	SB	CS	SLG	OBP
Aybar, Erick	B-R	5-10	195	1-14-84	.242	.232	.246	97	335	27	81	14	2	2	26	20	6	3	4	59	3	5	.313	.293
Beckham, Gordon	R-R	6-0	190	9-16-86	.217	.233	.210	85	240	25	52	16	1	5	30	26	4	0	3	50	1	0	.354	.300
2-team total (3 San Francisco)					.212	—	—	88	245	25	52	16	1	5	31	26	4	0	4	52	1	0	.347	.294
Bonifacio, Emilio	B-R	5-10	210	4-23-85	.211	.333	.200	24	38	6	8	0	0	0	3	0	2	0	0	12	1	0	.211	.268
Brignac, Reid	L-R	6-3	210	1-16-86	.207	.333	.192	13	29	3	6	2	0	0	1	0	0	0	0	8	0	0	.276	.207
Castro, Daniel	R-R	5-11	190	11-14-92	.200	.216	.190	47	130	8	26	1	0	0	7	2	0	2	0	24	1	1	.208	.241
d'Arnaud, Chase	R-R	6-2	205	1-21-87	.245	.250	.242	84	233	24	57	14	2	1	21	23	3	0	3	50	9	3	.335	.317
Flowers, Tyler	R-R	6-4	260	1-24-86	.270	.258	.277	83	281	27	76	18	0	8	41	29	11	0	4	91	0	0	.420	.357
Francoeur, Jeff	R-R	6-4	225	1-8-84	.249	.273	.228	99	257	29	64	13	0	7	33	16	0	0	3	75	2	0	.381	.290
2-team total (26 Miami)					.254	—	—	125	307	33	78	15	1	7	34	20	0	1	3	90	2	2	.378	.297
Freeman, Freddie	L-R	6-5	220	9-12-89	.302	.301	.303	158	589	102	178	43	6	34	91	89	10	0	5	171	6	1	.569	.400
Garcia, Adonis	R-R	5-9	205	4-12-85	.273	.302	.262	134	532	65	145	29	0	14	65	24	6	0	0	93	3	2	.406	.311
Inciarte, Ender	L-L	5-11	190	10-29-90	.291	.319	.281	131	522	85	152	24	7	3	29	45	4	5	2	68	16	7	.381	.351
Johnson, Kelly	L-R	6-1	200	2-22-82	.215	.222	.213	49	121	8	26	6	0	1	10	10	0	0	1	25	1	0	.289	.273
2-team total (82 New York)					.247	—	—	131	304	25	75	14	0	10	34	25	2	0	2	65	4	0	.391	.306
Kemp, Matt	R-R	6-4	210	9-23-84	.280	.244	.289	56	214	35	60	15	0	12	39	20	1	0	6	56	1	0	.519	.336
2-team total (100 San Diego)					.268	—	—	156	623	89	167	39	0	35	108	36	1	0	12	156	1	0	.499	.304
Lalli, Blake	L-R	6-1	210	5-12-83	.154	.500	.091	10	13	0	2	1	0	0	1	0	0	0	0	3	0	0	.231	.154
Markakis, Nick	L-L	6-1	215	11-17-83	.269	.243	.280	158	599	67	161	38	0	13	89	71	5	0	9	101	0	2	.397	.346
Olivera, Hector	R-R	6-2	230	4-5-85	.211	.250	.200	6	19	2	4	1	0	0	2	1	0	0	1	5	0	0	.263	.238
Peterson, Jace	L-R	6-0	215	5-9-90	.254	.255	.254	115	350	45	89	16	1	7	29	52	1	2	3	69	5	5	.366	.350
Pierzynski, A.J.	L-R	6-3	250	12-30-76	.219	.108	.238	81	247	15	54	15	0	2	23	6	3	0	3	29	1	0	.304	.243
Recker, Anthony	R-R	6-2	240	8-29-83	.278	.292	.273	33	90	6	25	8	0	2	15	16	2	3	1	22	1	0	.433	.394
Ruiz, Rio	L-R	6-1	230	5-22-94	.286	—	.286	5	7	1	2	0	1	0	2	0	0	0	0	2	1	0	.571	.286
Smith, Mallex	L-R	5-9	180	5-6-93	.238	.080	.295	72	189	28	45	7	4	3	22	20	2	3	1	48	16	8	.365	.316
Snyder, Brandon	R-R	6-2	225	11-23-86	.239	.538	.121	37	46	8	11	5	1	4	9	1	0	0	0	16	0	0	.652	.255
Stubbs, Drew	R-R	6-4	205	10-4-84	.257	.263	.211	20	35	8	9	0	0	1	3	4	0	0	0	20	4	0	.316	.310
Swanson, Dansby	R-R	6-1	190	2-11-94	.302	.294	.304	38	129	20	39	7	1	3	17	13	0	1	2	34	3	0	.442	.361
Tuiasosopo, Matt	R-R	6-2	235	5-10-86	.000	.000	.000	3	3	0	0	0	0	0	0	0	0	0	0	1	0	0	.000	.000

Pitching	B-T	HT	WT	DOB	W	L	ERA	G	GS	CG	SV	IP	H	R	ER	HR	BB	SO	AVG	vLH	vRH	K/9	BB/9
Alvarez, Dario	L-L	6-1	170	1-17-89	3	1	3.00	16	0	0	0	15	11	5	5	3	5	28	.200	.217	.188	16.80	3.00
Blair, Aaron	R-R	6-4	250	5-26-92	2	7	7.59	15	15	0	0	70	82	61	59	14	34	46	.299	.323	.278	5.91	4.37
Bradley, Jed	L-L	6-3	225	6-12-90	1	1	5.14	6	0	0	0	7	4	4	4	0	6	4	.269	.400	.091	5.14	7.71
Cabrera, Mauricio	R-R	6-3	245	9-22-93	5	1	2.82	41	0	0	6	38	31	14	12	0	19	32	.225	.266	.189	7.51	4.46
Cervenka, Hunter	L-L	6-1	245	1-3-90	1	0	3.18	50	0	0	0	34	20	14	12	2	23	35	.175	.145	.212	9.26	6.09
2-team total (18 Miami)					1	0	3.53	68	0	0	0	43	31	19	17	3	28	42	—	—	—	8.72	5.82
Chacin, Jhoulys	R-R	6-3	215	1-7-88	1	2	5.40	5	5	0	0	27	29	17	16	4	8	27	.274	.229	.310	9.11	2.70
Collmenter, Josh	R-R	6-3	240	2-7-86	2	0	2.37	3	3	0	0	19	15	5	5	3	5	16	.221	.154	.262	7.58	2.37
2-team total (15 Arizona)					3	0	3.70	18	3	0	0	41	36	17	17	7	16	33	—	—	—	7.19	3.48
Cunniff, Brandon	R-R	6-0	185	10-7-88	2	0	4.24	15	0	0	0	17	14	9	8	2	9	16	.233	.240	.229	8.47	4.76
De La Cruz, Joel	B-R	6-1	240	6-9-89	0	7	4.88	22	9	0	0	63	65	40	34	10	22	37	.263	.260	.266	5.31	3.16
Foltynewicz, Mike	R-R	6-4	220	10-7-91	9	5	4.31	22	22	0	0	123	125	61	59	18	35	111	.263	.251	.273	8.10	2.55
Gant, John	R-R	6-3	200	8-6-92	1	4	4.86	20	7	0	0	50	54	32	27	7	21	49	.278	.248	.315	8.82	3.78
Grilli, Jason	R-R	6-5	235	11-11-76	1	2	5.29	21	0	0	2	17	16	11	10	2	13	23	.242	.333	.190	12.18	6.88
Harrell, Lucas	R-R	6-2	205	6-3-85	2	2	3.38	5	5	0	0	29	25	13	11	1	12	21	.234	.200	.263	6.44	3.68
Hernandez, Roberto	R-R	6-4	270	8-30-80	1	1	8.00	2	2	0	0	9	13	8	8	4	1	6	.351	.417	.320	6.00	1.00
Hursh, Jason	R-R	6-3	200	10-2-91	0	0	33.75	2	0	0	0	1	4	5	5	0	3	1	.500	.333	.600	6.75	20.25
Jenkins, Tyrell	R-R	6-4	210	7-20-92	2	4	5.88	14	8	0	0	52	55	35	34	11	33	26	.279	.286	.276	4.50	5.71
Johnson, Jim	R-R	6-6	250	6-27-83	2	6	3.06	65	0	0	20	65	57	23	22	3	20	68	.236	.218	.252	9.46	2.78
Kelly, Casey	R-R	6-3	215	10-4-89	0	3	5.82	10	1	0	0	22	30	14	14	1	7	7	.326	.361	.304	2.91	2.91
Krol, Ian	L-L	6-1	210	5-9-91	2	0	3.18	63	0	0	0	51	54	19	18	4	13	56	.271	.287	.259	9.88	2.29
Marksberry, Matt	L-L	6-1	180	8-25-90	0	0	5.40	4	0	0	0	5	5	2	2	1	1	2	.333	.200	.400	5.40	2.70
Norris, Bud	R-R	6-0	215	3-2-85	3	7	4.22	22	10	0	0	70	68	34	33	6	28	60	.257	.278	.242	7.68	3.58

Pitching

Pitching	B-T	HT	WT	DOB	W	L	ERA	G	GS	CG	SV	IP	H	R	ER	HR	BB	SO	AVG	vLH	vRH	K/9	BB/9
2-team total (13 Los Angeles)					6	10	5.10	35	19	0	0	113	116	67	64	14	49	102	—	—	—	8.12	3.90
O'Flaherty, Eric	L-L	6-2	210	2-5-85	1	4	6.91	39	0	0	0	29	39	25	22	3	11	22	.320	.288	.357	6.91	3.45
Ogando, Alexi	R-R	6-4	200	10-5-83	2	1	3.94	36	0	0	0	32	32	18	14	2	23	29	.274	.314	.256	8.16	6.47
Perez, Williams	R-R	6-0	240	5-21-91	2	3	6.04	11	11	0	0	54	57	37	36	7	15	27	.271	.295	.248	4.53	2.52
Ramirez, Jose	R-R	6-1	215	1-21-90	2	2	3.58	33	0	0	0	33	26	16	13	2	18	33	.220	.224	.217	9.09	4.96
Roe, Chaz	R-R	6-5	190	10-9-86	1	0	3.60	21	0	0	0	20	14	8	8	0	7	26	.200	.258	.154	11.70	3.15
Simmons, Shae	R-R	5-11	190	9-3-90	0	0	1.35	7	0	0	0	7	6	1	1	0	3	3	.240	.143	.364	4.05	0.00
Teheran, Julio	R-R	6-2	205	1-27-91	7	10	3.21	30	30	1	0	188	157	70	67	22	41	167	.223	.237	.212	7.99	1.96
Vizcaino, Arodys	R-R	6-0	230	11-13-90	1	4	4.42	43	0	0	10	39	37	25	19	3	26	50	.240	.205	.272	11.64	6.05
Weber, Ryan	R-R	6-1	180	8-12-90	1	1	5.45	16	2	0	0	36	46	22	22	7	5	23	.309	.333	.288	5.70	1.24
Whalen, Rob	R-R	6-2	220	1-31-94	1	2	6.57	5	5	0	0	25	20	20	18	4	12	25	.217	.189	.236	9.12	4.38
Winkler, Dan	R-R	6-3	205	2-2-90	0	0	0.00	3	0	0	0	2	0	0	0	0	1	4	.000	.000	.000	15.43	3.86
Wisler, Matt	R-R	6-3	205	9-12-92	7	13	5.00	27	26	0	1	157	159	90	87	26	49	115	.259	.257	.262	6.61	2.81
Withrow, Chris	R-R	6-3	240	4-1-89	3	0	3.58	46	0	0	0	38	29	16	15	5	17	28	.213	.192	.226	6.49	4.06
Younginer, Madison	R-R	6-4	205	11-3-90	0	0	6.43	8	0	0	0	7	12	5	5	0	4	4	.400	.364	.421	5.14	5.14

Fielding

Catcher	PCT	G	PO	A	E	DP	PB
Flowers	.995	81	607	29	3	1	7
Pierzynski	.992	64	457	23	4	5	5
Recker	.995	28	179	10	1	4	2

First Base	PCT	G	PO	A	E	DP
Freeman	.996	158	1305	107	5	116
Johnson	1.000	1	6	0	0	0
Lalli	1.000	4	10	0	0	5
Markakis	1.000	1	10	0	0	0
Snyder	1.000	1	1	2	0	0

Second Base	PCT	G	PO	A	E	DP
Aybar	1.000	1	1	6	0	2
Beckham	.989	51	61	118	2	17
Brignac	1.000	4	4	5	0	1
Castro	1.000	16	24	29	0	7

	PCT	G	PO	A	E	DP
d'Arnaud	.976	10	13	27	1	1
Johnson	.942	26	33	64	6	11
Peterson	.972	87	150	235	11	54

Third Base	PCT	G	PO	A	E	DP
Beckham	.952	15	7	13	1	3
Brignac	.944	5	4	13	1	1
Castro	1.000	9	4	9	0	1
d'Arnaud	1.000	19	12	24	0	1
Garcia	.939	123	79	199	18	17
Peterson	—	1	0	0	0	0
Ruiz	1.000	2	0	5	0	0
Snyder	.875	2	5	2	1	0

Shortstop	PCT	G	PO	A	E	DP
Aybar	.964	93	109	241	13	46
Beckham	.971	11	11	23	1	7
Castro	1.000	20	15	48	0	10

	PCT	G	PO	A	E	DP
d'Arnaud	.983	21	20	38	1	7
Swanson	.953	37	44	79	6	17

Outfield	PCT	G	PO	A	E	DP
Bonifacio	1.000	13	17	0	0	0
d'Arnaud	1.000	13	27	1	0	0
Francoeur	.968	62	82	8	3	1
Garcia	1.000	4	6	0	0	0
Inciarte	.989	129	351	14	4	4
Johnson	1.000	6	9	0	0	0
Kemp	.991	54	110	1	1	1
Markakis	.988	150	311	5	4	2
Olivera	1.000	5	7	0	0	0
Peterson	.931	16	27	0	2	0
Smith	.992	56	122	5	1	0
Snyder	—	1	0	0	0	0
Stubbs	1.000	13	20	0	0	0

ATLANTA BRAVES

GWINNETT BRAVES

INTERNATIONAL LEAGUE

TRIPLE-A

Batting

Batting	B-T	HT	WT	DOB	AVG	vLH	vRH	G	AB	R	H	2B	3B	HR	RBI	BB	HBP	SH	SF	SO	SB	CS	SLG	OBP
Albies, Ozzie	B-R	5-9	160	1-7-97	.248	.253	.245	56	222	27	55	11	3	2	20	19	1	3	2	39	9	4	.351	.307
Aybar, Erick	B-R	5-10	195	1-14-84	.172	.125	.231	7	29	3	5	1	0	0	2	2	0	0	0	2	2	0	.207	.226
Beckham, Gordon	R-R	6-0	190	9-16-86	.333	.000	.364	3	12	2	4	2	0	0	1	1	0	0	0	1	0	0	.500	.385
Bonifacio, Emilio	B-R	5-10	200	4-23-85	.298	.266	.311	107	420	57	125	14	5	2	40	39	1	7	4	70	37	9	.369	.356
Brignac, Reid	L-R	6-3	210	1-16-86	.264	.167	.291	102	363	56	96	21	1	8	42	52	4	3	2	91	6	3	.394	.361
Castro, Daniel	R-R	5-11	190	11-14-92	.257	.222	.266	61	214	29	55	10	0	3	20	8	0	3	4	25	0	1	.346	.279
d'Arnaud, Chase	R-R	6-2	205	1-21-87	.255	.217	.268	22	94	11	24	6	1	1	4	6	0	0	0	16	7	0	.372	.300
Flowers, Tyler	R-R	6-4	260	1-24-86	.429	—	.429	2	7	1	3	0	0	0	1	0	0	0	0	1	0	0	.429	.500
Garcia, Adonis	R-R	5-9	205	4-12-85	.356	.414	.318	19	73	14	26	7	0	4	18	3	4	0	0	12	2	1	.616	.413
Gaylor, Stephen	L-R	6-1	180	10-4-91	.333	.000	.500	1	3	1	1	0	0	0	0	1	0	0	0	0	0	0	.333	.500
Hyams, Levi	L-R	6-2	210	10-6-89	.130	.000	.167	9	23	0	3	1	0	0	1	1	0	0	0	7	0	0	.174	.167
Inciarte, Ender	L-L	5-11	190	10-29-90	.333	.000	.667	2	6	0	2	0	0	0	0	1	0	0	0	0	0	0	.333	.429
Infante, Omar	R-R	5-11	195	12-26-81	.209	.143	.225	27	110	8	23	5	1	1	9	3	0	1	2	16	0	1	.300	.226
Kazmar, Sean	R-R	5-9	180	8-5-84	.263	.337	.230	93	327	35	86	16	1	5	37	16	1	1	2	52	1	5	.364	.298
Kottaras, George	L-R	6-0	200	5-10-83	.196	.143	.205	18	51	5	10	2	0	1	8	10	0	0	0	15	0	0	.294	.328
Kubitza, Kyle	L-R	6-3	210	7-15-90	.157	.111	.167	20	51	7	8	1	1	0	4	9	0	0	0	15	0	0	.216	.283
Lalli, Blake	L-R	6-2	235	5-12-83	.256	.250	.257	109	348	28	89	22	0	1	36	22	2	4	4	60	1	1	.328	.301
Landoni, Emerson	B-R	5-11	189	2-19-89	.261	.273	.257	49	111	10	29	4	0	0	5	2	2	0	0	20	1	0	.297	.287
Lavarnway, Ryan	R-R	6-4	240	8-7-87	.276	.286	.271	25	98	7	27	8	0	0	8	1	0	0	0	18	0	1	.357	.336
Lipka, Matt	R-R	6-1	200	4-12-92	.238	.226	.241	56	164	19	39	7	4	2	14	10	3	0	2	36	3	0	.366	.291
McKenry, Michael	R-R	5-10	205	3-4-85	.267	.154	.313	14	45	6	12	2	0	1	3	7	0	0	0	16	0	0	.378	.365
Moore, Tyler	R-R	6-2	220	1-30-87	.229	.200	.239	25	96	10	22	5	0	3	14	7	0	1	2	28	0	0	.375	.276
Mustelier, Ronnier	R-R	5-10	210	8-8-84	.291	.308	.284	117	426	49	124	21	4	5	50	39	2	1	1	49	6	1	.394	.353
Olivera, Hector	R-R	6-2	230	4-5-85	.114	.000	.154	9	35	1	4	1	0	0	1	0	0	0	1	5	0	0	.143	.135
Pacheco, Jordan	R-R	6-1	200	1-30-86	.125	—	.125	2	8	1	1	0	0	0	0	1	0	0	0	0	0	0	.125	.222
2-team total (5 Louisville)					.045	—	—	7	22	1	1	0	0	0	1	1	0	0	0	7	0	0	.045	.125
Peterson, Jace	L-R	6-0	215	5-9-90	.186	.139	.213	26	97	8	18	3	2	0	6	11	1	1	0	15	2	2	.258	.275
Recker, Anthony	R-R	6-2	240	8-29-83	.243	.333	.210	40	136	20	33	6	0	6	18	16	1	0	1	45	0	0	.419	.325
2-team total (19 Columbus)					.244	—	—	59	197	30	48	11	0	8	28	30	2	0	1	62	1	0	.421	.348
Rojas Jr., Mel	B-R	6-2	225	5-24-90	.270	.240	.278	64	230	27	62	11	5	10	34	29	0	0	2	49	9	2	.491	.349
2-team total (12 Indianapolis)					.258	—	—	76	256	30	66	11	6	10	37	31	0	0	2	56	9	3	.469	.354
Ruiz, Rio	L-R	6-1	230	5-22-94	.271	.203	.294	133	465	52	126	24	3	10	62	61	3	4	5	116	1	4	.400	.355
Schlehuber, Braeden	R-R	6-2	210	1-7-88	.236	.321	.207	40	110	12	26	7	0	0	14	2	1	2	1	27	0	0	.300	.254
Smith, Mallex	L-R	5-9	180	5-6-93	.400	.143	.625	3	15	5	6	2	1	0	0	0	1	0	0	3	1	0	.667	.438

Batting	B-T	HT	WT	DOB	AVG	vLH	vRH	G	AB	R	H	2B	3B	HR	RBI	BB	HBP	SH	SF	SO	SB	CS	SLG	OBP
Snyder, Brandon	R-R	6-2	225	11-23-86	.327	.294	.344	43	147	19	48	8	0	3	26	8	1	1	3	35	6	0	.442	.358
Tuiasosopo, Matt	R-R	6-2	235	5-10-86	.246	.262	.240	64	211	33	52	17	0	11	28	32	3	0	2	71	0	0	.483	.351

Pitching	B-T	HT	WT	DOB	W	L	ERA	G	GS	CG	SV	IP	H	R	ER	HR	BB	SO	AVG	vLH	vRH	K/9	BB/9
Alvarez, Dario	L-L	6-1	170	1-17-89	0	0	1.13	8	0	0	0	8	4	1	1	0	4	14	.143	.250	.063	15.75	4.50
Banuelos, Manny	L-L	5-10	215	3-13-91	0	2	4.75	9	9	0	0	30	31	19	16	2	22	21	.270	.205	.303	6.23	6.53
Blair, Aaron	R-R	6-4	250	5-26-92	5	4	4.65	13	13	0	0	72	77	38	37	4	32	71	.278	.302	.261	8.92	4.02
Boscan, Wilfredo	R-R	6-2	175	10-26-89	0	2	8.00	3	2	0	0	9	18	10	8	1	7	7	.419	.667	.323	7.00	7.00
2-team total (17 Indianapolis)					6	9	4.16	20	18	1	0	93	115	49	43	6	21	58	—	—		5.61	2.03
Bradley, Jed	L-L	6-3	225	6-12-90	2	0	1.50	3	3	0	0	18	14	3	3	0	11	19	.219	.000	.292	9.50	5.50
Burawa, Danny	R-R	6-3	220	12-30-88	1	0	5.14	7	0	0	1	7	8	6	4	0	11	5	.320	.167	.368	6.43	14.14
Burnett, Sean	L-L	5-11	185	9-17-82	0	0	0.00	6	0	0	0	5	3	0	0	0	1	5	.158	.250	.091	8.44	1.69
3-team total (29 Rochester, 5 Syracuse)					0	3	2.27	40	0	0	3	40	30	12	10	2	8	27	—	—		6.13	1.82
Chacin, Jhoulys	R-R	6-3	215	1-7-88	1	0	0.00	1	1	0	0	8	5	0	0	0	2	7	.192	.222	.176	8.22	2.35
Cleto, Maikel	R-R	6-3	250	5-1-89	2	0	2.14	20	0	0	4	21	20	6	5	3	13	31	.250	.188	.292	13.29	5.57
Cunniff, Brandon	R-R	6-0	185	10-7-88	3	3	4.01	35	0	0	2	43	35	20	19	3	19	39	.232	.279	.193	8.23	4.01
De La Cruz, Joel	B-R	6-1	240	6-9-89	1	3	4.68	21	5	0	0	58	62	32	30	5	24	44	.287	.333	.252	6.87	3.75
Ellis, Chris	R-R	6-5	205	9-22-92	4	7	6.52	15	15	2	0	68	68	50	49	4	52	65	.269	.231	.303	8.65	6.92
Foltynewicz, Mike	R-R	6-4	220	10-7-91	1	2	1.67	5	5	0	0	27	13	7	5	0	14	25	.149	.088	.189	8.33	4.67
Gant, John	R-R	6-3	200	8-6-92	3	3	4.18	12	10	0	0	56	58	29	26	5	22	57	.262	.279	.252	9.16	3.54
Harrell, Lucas	B-R	6-2	205	6-3-85	2	1	2.81	9	5	0	0	32	35	13	10	1	19	27	.282	.308	.239	7.59	5.34
2-team total (1 Toledo)					3	1	2.92	10	6	0	0	37	40	15	12	1	21	31	—	—		7.54	5.11
Hernandez, Roberto	R-R	6-4	270	8-30-80	1	2	5.52	3	3	0	0	15	21	10	9	1	3	11	.339	.310	.364	6.75	1.84
2-team total (13 Buffalo)					4	6	4.60	16	16	0	0	86	95	47	44	11	26	59	—	—		6.17	2.72
Hursh, Jason	R-R	6-3	200	10-2-91	0	0	1.69	8	0	0	0	16	15	3	3	0	8	8	.273	.350	.229	4.50	4.50
Janas, Steve	R-R	6-5	210	4-21-92	3	2	3.31	26	1	0	1	52	48	23	19	4	12	31	.247	.213	.276	5.40	2.09
Jenkins, Tyrell	R-R	6-4	210	7-20-92	9	3	2.47	17	12	0	0	84	86	30	23	3	35	55	.272	.301	.250	5.92	3.76
Johnson, Jim	R-R	6-6	250	6-27-83	0	0	0.00	2	0	0	0	2	2	0	0	0	0	1	.286	1.000	.167	4.50	0.00
Kelly, Casey	R-R	6-3	210	10-4-89	3	6	3.53	15	12	0	0	74	64	33	29	6	28	47	.237	.250	.228	5.72	3.41
Kent, Steve	L-L	6-0	200	5-8-89	0	0	36.00	1	0	0	0	1	4	4	4	0	2	0	.571	.500	.600	0.00	18.00
Krol, Ian	L-L	6-1	210	5-9-91	1	2	4.38	12	0	0	1	12	10	6	6	1	6	14	.213	.136	.280	10.22	4.38
Marksberry, Matt	L-L	6-1	180	8-25-90	4	2	2.65	28	0	0	0	34	34	10	10	2	15	32	.260	.244	.267	8.47	3.97
Mateo, Victor	R-R	6-5	225	7-27-89	0	1	15.00	5	2	0	0	9	20	17	15	1	8	5	.465	.263	.625	5.00	8.00
Moran, Brian	L-L	6-3	210	9-30-88	0	0	5.06	6	0	0	0	5	6	3	3	1	0	1	.300	.500	.167	1.69	0.00
O'Flaherty, Eric	L-L	6-2	210	2-5-85	0	0	0.00	1	0	0	0	1	0	0	0	0	0	0	.000	.000	.000	9.00	0.00
Perez, Williams	R-R	6-0	240	5-21-91	1	2	2.59	4	4	2	0	24	15	9	7	2	7	24	.183	.167	.192	8.88	2.59
Peterson, Dave	R-R	6-5	205	1-4-90	0	2	9.17	15	0	0	3	18	26	19	18	3	14	15	.333	.364	.311	7.64	7.13
Portuondo, Carlos	R-R	6-2	235	11-9-87	1	1	2.70	5	0	0	0	10	13	3	3	0	4	4	.317	.286	.333	3.60	3.60
Ramirez, Jose	R-R	6-1	215	1-21-90	3	2	2.18	36	0	0	6	41	34	10	10	3	18	45	.228	.254	.207	9.80	3.92
Rogers, Chad	R-R	5-11	205	8-3-89	1	0	11.74	4	0	0	0	8	12	11	10	3	3	6	.343	.400	.267	7.04	3.52
2-team total (30 Louisville)					3	4	4.76	34	3	0	0	62	58	34	33	9	25	55	—	—		7.94	3.61
Roney, Bradley	R-R	6-2	200	9-1-92	3	0	3.57	27	0	0	4	45	34	18	18	3	39	55	.213	.328	.135	10.92	7.74
Simmons, Shae	R-R	5-11	190	9-3-90	0	0	1.50	12	4	0	1	12	7	2	2	0	4	9	.167	.211	.130	10.50	6.75
Sims, Lucas	R-R	6-2	220	5-10-94	2	6	7.56	11	10	0	0	50	56	44	42	12	37	58	.280	.375	.217	10.44	6.66
Teheran, Julio	R-R	6-2	205	1-27-91	0	1	1.80	1	1	0	0	5	3	2	1	0	0	5	.167	.200	.125	9.00	0.00
Texeira, Kanekoa	R-R	6-2	190	2-6-86	1	7	4.97	27	8	0	0	63	88	39	35	3	29	34	.337	.299	.368	4.83	4.12
Thayer, Dale	R-R	6-0	210	12-17-80	0	0	20.25	2	0	0	0	1	5	3	3	0	1	1	.714	1.000	.600	0.00	6.75
Weber, Ryan	R-R	6-1	180	8-12-90	2	3	2.76	26	5	0	1	62	65	21	19	1	14	41	.265	.271	.261	5.95	2.03
Whalen, Rob	R-R	6-2	220	1-31-94	0	1	1.93	3	3	0	0	19	12	4	4	0	7	18	.188	.241	.143	8.68	3.38
Wisler, Matt	R-R	6-3	205	9-12-92	2	1	3.71	4	4	1	0	27	27	13	11	3	5	22	.257	.259	.255	7.43	1.69
Withrow, Chris	R-R	6-3	240	4-1-89	0	1	4.50	11	0	0	5	10	7	6	5	1	6	12	.194	.182	.200	10.80	5.40
Wooten, Rob	R-R	6-1	200	7-21-85	3	5	3.58	35	6	0	1	73	75	31	29	9	11	60	.260	.296	.232	7.40	1.36
Younginer, Madison	R-R	6-4	205	11-3-90	0	0	7.24	11	0	0	1	14	18	16	11	1	11	13	.305	.167	.400	8.56	7.24

Fielding

Catcher	PCT	G	PO	A	E	DP	PB
Flowers	1.000	2	13	2	0	0	1
Kottaras	.968	11	59	2	2	0	1
Lalli	.991	45	318	25	3	2	5
Lavarnway	.994	22	166	8	1	0	1
McKenry	.983	7	55	2	1	0	2
Recker	.985	34	239	25	4	2	7
Schlehuber	1.000	32	232	17	0	0	3
Recker	1.000	1	2	0	0		1
Schlehuber	1.000	1	9	0	0		1
Snyder	1.000	2	10	1	0		1
Tuiasosopo	.995	27	199	11	1		21

First Base	PCT	G	PO	A	E	DP
Brignac	1.000	28	213	22	0	31
Hyams	1.000	1	3	0	0	0
Kazmar	.995	25	177	17	1	22
Kottaras	1.000	2	13	2	0	0
Kubitza	1.000	4	38	2	0	4
Lalli	.989	60	419	33	5	60
Landoni	1.000	3	5	1	0	1
Moore	.991	12	100	6	1	12
Pacheco	.957	2	22	0	1	1

Second Base	PCT	G	PO	A	E	DP
Albies	.965	23	45	91	5	17
Beckham	1.000	2	1	4	0	0
Bonifacio	1.000	2	3	7	0	1
Brignac	.991	40	94	129	2	44
Castro	1.000	1	2	2	0	1
Hyams	.950	6	13	25	2	9
Infante	.980	26	38	61	2	14
Kazmar	1.000	19	29	49	0	13
Landoni	.985	19	22	43	1	15
Peterson	1.000	16	26	48	0	10

Third Base	PCT	G	PO	A	E	DP
Beckham	1.000	1	1	2	0	0
Kazmar	.944	11	4	13	1	1
Kubitza	1.000	5	1	5	0	1
Landoni	.875	10	3	11	2	2
Mustelier	.923	7	10	14	2	1
Ruiz	.974	119	81	180	7	31

Shortstop	PCT	G	PO	A	E	DP
Albies	.931	33	52	97	11	28
Aybar	.971	6	11	22	1	8
Brignac	.959	25	45	72	5	18
Castro	.960	59	72	170	10	37
d'Arnaud	1.000	3	4	9	0	0
Kazmar	.970	23	20	45	2	14
Landoni	1.000	2	3	7	0	1

Outfield	PCT	G	PO	A	E	DP
Bonifacio	.990	100	194	5	2	0
Brignac	1.000	6	11	0	0	0
d'Arnaud	.977	19	41	1	1	0

Outfield	PCT	G	PO	A	E	DP
Garcia	1.000	17	29	0	0	0
Gaylor	1.000	1	2	0	0	0
Hyams	—	1	0	0	0	0
Inciarte	1.000	2	3	0	0	0
Kubitza	.933	8	14	0	1	0
Landoni	.909	7	9	1	1	0
Lipka	.992	54	118	6	1	0
Moore	1.000	7	9	1	0	0
Mustelier	.964	82	121	12	5	0
Olivera	1.000	8	14	0	0	0
Peterson	.957	10	22	0	1	0
Rojas Jr.	.976	63	117	4	3	1
Schlehuber	1.000	2	3	0	0	0
Smith	1.000	3	6	0	0	0
Snyder	1.000	37	62	2	0	0
Tuiasosopo	1.000	30	45	1	0	0

MISSISSIPPI BRAVES
SOUTHERN LEAGUE

DOUBLE-A

ATLANTA BRAVES

Batting	B-T	HT	WT	DOB	AVG	vLH	vRH	G	AB	R	H	2B	3B	HR	RBI	BB	HBP	SH	SF	SO	SB	CS	SLG	OBP
Albies, Ozzie	B-R	5-9	160	1-7-97	.321	.429	.296	82	330	56	106	22	7	4	33	33	6	0	2	57	21	9	.467	.391
Astudillo, Willians	R-R	5-9	225	10-14-91	.267	.328	.252	89	322	24	86	9	0	4	30	5	9	1	5	11	1	1	.332	.293
Camargo, Johan	B-R	6-0	160	12-13-93	.267	.320	.256	126	446	46	119	26	6	4	43	24	1	7	3	82	1	2	.379	.304
Franco, Carlos	R-R	6-3	208	12-20-91	.255	.135	.280	121	424	37	108	14	3	4	53	53	2	1	2	134	3	4	.330	.339
Gaylor, Stephen	L-R	6-1	180	10-4-91	.250	.111	.263	49	108	16	27	1	0	1	7	6	0	3	0	28	4	3	.287	.289
Godfrey, Sean	R-R	6-2	180	1-2-92	.304	.286	.313	11	23	2	7	2	1	0	3	1	0	1	0	7	1	0	.478	.333
Harper, Reed	R-R	6-2	200	12-21-90	.235	—	.235	6	17	0	4	0	0	0	2	1	0	0	0	4	0	0	.235	.278
Hyams, Levi	L-R	6-2	210	10-6-89	.237	.077	.259	82	219	20	52	10	2	5	26	10	1	2	2	60	0	4	.370	.272
Kennelly, Matt	R-R	6-1	200	3-21-89	.155	.105	.173	20	71	5	11	2	0	1	4	6	0	0	0	12	0	1	.225	.221
Landoni, Emerson	B-R	5-11	189	2-19-89	.222	.313	.150	14	36	3	8	1	0	0	5	3	1	0	1	3	0	0	.250	.293
Lien, Connor	R-R	6-3	225	3-15-94	.233	.296	.224	64	223	29	52	7	7	6	17	23	6	5	1	85	12	6	.408	.320
Lipka, Matt	R-R	6-1	200	4-15-92	.248	.245	.248	60	214	28	53	10	4	1	14	20	5	4	1	60	13	6	.346	.325
Meneses, Joey	R-R	6-3	190	5-6-92	.234	.233	.234	63	222	16	52	9	3	2	15	15	2	1	0	40	0	0	.329	.289
Odom, Joseph	R-R	6-2	225	1-9-92	.259	.412	.237	39	135	10	35	7	0	1	9	7	0	0	1	27	0	0	.333	.294
Peterson, Dustin	R-R	6-2	210	9-10-94	.282	.283	.282	132	524	65	148	38	2	12	88	45	5	0	4	100	4	1	.431	.343
Rodriguez, Steven	L-R	6-1	200	1-8-90	.209	.286	.194	14	43	2	9	0	0	0	3	3	0	0	1	12	0	0	.209	.255
Rojas Jr., Mel	R-R	6-2	225	5-24-90	.244	.292	.232	35	123	15	30	8	0	2	9	9	0	0	1	33	3	1	.358	.293
Schrader, Jake	R-R	6-2	220	3-1-91	.232	.286	.216	104	341	38	79	18	0	12	38	28	3	1	2	113	2	0	.390	.294
Scivicque, Kade	R-R	6-0	225	3-22-93	.182	—	.182	3	11	0	2	0	0	0	1	0	0	0	0	3	0	0	.182	.182
Smith, Mallex	L-R	5-9	180	5-6-93	.438	—	.438	5	16	4	7	0	1	0	4	0	0	0	0	5	3	1	.563	.550
Swanson, Dansby	R-R	6-1	190	2-11-94	.261	.279	.257	84	333	54	87	13	5	8	45	35	7	0	2	71	6	2	.402	.342
Toscano, Dian	L-L	5-11	200	3-9-89	.226	.241	.223	58	177	16	40	2	3	0	10	22	1	0	3	53	2	0	.271	.310

Pitching	B-T	HT	WT	DOB	W	L	ERA	G	GS	CG	SV	IP	H	R	ER	HR	BB	SO	AVG	vLH	vRH	K/9	BB/9
Banuelos, Manny	L-L	5-10	215	3-13-91	0	2	5.40	4	4	0	0	18	23	12	11	4	8	19	.311	.154	.344	9.33	3.93
Barker, Brandon	R-R	6-3	210	8-20-92	3	2	2.00	9	8	0	0	45	35	10	10	3	12	40	.217	.214	.220	8.00	2.40
Belicek, Trevor	L-L	6-3	215	12-10-92	0	0	0.00	1	0	0	0	3	3	1	0	0	0	3	.231	.000	.333	9.00	0.00
Bradley, Jed	L-L	6-3	225	6-12-90	4	3	2.35	15	10	0	0	65	59	24	17	0	23	69	.242	.169	.272	9.55	3.18
2-team total (17 Biloxi)					7	5	3.41	32	10	0	0	90	92	42	34	2	29	89	—			8.93	2.91
Burawa, Danny	R-R	6-3	220	12-30-88	2	0	6.75	9	0	0	0	12	14	9	9	0	11	4	.304	.450	.192	3.00	8.25
Cabrera, Mauricio	R-R	6-3	245	9-22-93	3	3	3.21	25	0	0	4	34	20	15	12	0	22	35	.165	.185	.149	9.36	5.88
Cervenka, Hunter	L-L	6-1	245	1-3-90	0	0	0.00	2	0	0	0	3	1	0	0	0	1	2	.111	.000	.200	6.00	3.00
2-team total (1 Jacksonville)					0	0	2.25	3	0	0	0	4	1	1	1	0	2	4	—			9.00	4.50
Cunniff, Brandon	R-R	6-0	185	10-7-88	0	1	0.71	8	0	0	2	13	6	1	1	0	5	10	.143	.091	.200	7.11	3.55
Dirks, Caleb	R-R	6-3	220	6-9-93	2	1	0.91	21	0	0	2	30	18	7	3	0	11	32	.173	.184	.167	9.71	3.34
Ellis, Chris	R-R	6-5	205	9-22-92	8	2	2.75	13	13	0	0	79	54	24	24	2	35	61	.201	.180	.215	6.98	4.00
Hursh, Jason	R-R	6-3	200	10-2-91	3	2	2.05	35	0	0	3	57	42	16	13	0	23	42	.204	.181	.220	6.63	3.63
Janas, Steve	R-R	6-5	210	4-21-92	3	2	1.89	18	0	0	3	33	24	9	7	1	4	25	.200	.167	.222	6.75	1.08
Kent, Steve	L-L	6-0	200	5-8-89	2	3	3.36	41	0	0	2	56	61	26	21	5	19	61	.276	.247	.293	9.75	3.04
Kinman, Kyle	L-L	5-11	185	9-25-90	1	2	3.07	13	0	0	1	15	12	6	5	2	9	15	.235	.150	.290	9.20	5.52
Lara, Jordy	R-R	6-3	215	5-21-91	0	0	0.00	1	0	0	0	1	0	0	0	0	0	1	.000	.000	.000	9.00	0.00
Lewis, Taylor	R-R	6-1	170	10-4-93	1	0	2.08	9	1	0	0	13	13	3	3	1	2	9	.255	.292	.222	6.23	1.38
Mader, Michael	L-L	6-2	195	2-18-94	0	3	2.40	5	5	1	0	30	27	8	8	0	6	26	.233	.258	.224	7.80	1.80
Marksberry, Matt	L-L	6-1	180	8-25-90	0	0	1.04	6	0	0	2	9	3	1	1	0	2	7	.115	.077	.154	7.27	2.08
Mateo, Victor	R-R	6-5	225	7-27-89	1	2	4.93	17	6	0	0	42	55	27	23	6	20	26	.324	.325	.322	5.57	4.29
Minter, A.J.	L-L	6-0	205	9-2-93	1	0	2.41	18	0	0	0	19	13	5	5	0	6	31	.188	.200	.184	14.95	2.89
Morris, Akeel	R-R	6-1	195	11-14-92	3	1	2.27	25	0	0	9	36	27	9	9	0	21	50	.209	.277	.171	12.62	5.30
Newcomb, Sean	L-L	6-5	255	6-12-93	8	7	3.86	27	27	1	0	140	113	62	60	4	71	152	.224	.257	.216	9.77	4.56
O'Neal, Michael	R-L	6-1	215	6-5-92	0	0	1.80	2	1	0	0	5	2	1	1	0	2	1	.125	.000	.167	1.80	3.60
Parsons, Wes	R-R	6-5	190	9-6-92	0	0	0.00	1	0	0	0	4	1	0	0	0	2	2	.091	.333	.000	4.50	4.50
Peterson, Dave	R-R	6-5	205	1-4-90	2	3	3.93	27	0	0	7	34	40	18	15	0	10	28	.278	.200	.326	7.34	2.62
Pfeifer, Phil	L-L	6-0	190	7-15-92	1	0	4.35	11	0	0	0	10	9	6	5	0	6	8	.243	.286	.217	6.97	5.23
Phillips, Reid	R-R	6-2	215	9-11-94	6	3	4.46	22	0	0	2	34	33	21	17	2	16	43	.262	.240	.276	11.27	4.19
Povse, Max	R-R	6-8	185	8-23-93	4	1	2.93	11	11	0	0	71	61	25	23	7	12	48	.236	.195	.265	6.11	1.53
Roney, Bradley	R-R	6-2	200	9-1-92	1	0	2.82	17	0	0	2	22	17	8	7	1	16	33	.210	.300	.122	13.30	6.45
Sims, Lucas	R-R	6-2	220	5-10-94	5	5	2.67	17	17	0	0	91	64	34	27	3	55	101	.203	.181	.220	9.99	5.44
Sobotka, Chad	R-R	6-3	205	7-10-93	0	0	0.00	2	0	0	0	2	0	0	0	0	0	2	.000	.000	.000	9.00	0.00
Thurman, Andrew	R-R	6-3	225	12-10-91	1	7	6.89	19	13	0	0	63	65	50	48	9	47	52	.270	.255	.281	7.47	6.75
Weigel, Patrick	R-R	6-6	220	7-8-94	1	2	2.18	3	3	0	0	21	9	6	5	2	8	17	.132	.161	.108	7.40	3.48
Whalen, Rob	R-R	6-2	220	1-31-94	7	5	2.49	18	18	0	0	101	87	35	28	4	37	94	.232	.234	.230	8.35	3.29
Younginer, Madison	R-R	6-4	205	11-3-90	0	3	2.98	35	0	0	14	42	33	14	14	1	12	47	.219	.200	.233	9.99	2.55

Fielding

Catcher	PCT	G	PO	A	E	DP	PB
Astudillo	.997	75	578	79	2	5	11
Kennelly	.993	16	132	7	1	1	0
Odom	.992	37	345	20	3	2	2
Rodriguez	1.000	12	88	7	0	0	0
Scivicque	1.000	3	27	4	0	0	0

First Base	PCT	G	PO	A	E	DP
Astudillo	.977	8	40	2	1	8
Franco	.987	18	151	5	2	9
Hyams	.981	32	245	16	5	28
Kennelly	.920	3	23	0	2	4
Lara	.981	16	101	5	2	8
Meneses	.992	17	114	7	1	10
Schrader	.989	63	491	28	6	43

Second Base	PCT	G	PO	A	E	DP
Albies	.992	60	101	158	2	30
Camargo	.977	64	115	183	7	42
Harper	1.000	1	1	3	0	2
Hyams	1.000	12	17	21	0	2
Landoni	1.000	3	4	10	0	4

Third Base	PCT	G	PO	A	E	DP
Camargo	.967	29	13	46	2	5
Franco	.913	93	52	115	16	8
Hyams	.857	11	9	15	4	0
Landoni	.857	6	3	9	2	0
Lara	1.000	9	7	9	0	2

Shortstop	PCT	G	PO	A	E	DP
Albies	.962	22	30	70	4	16

Camargo	.958	32	51	86	6	14
Harper	.800	3	3	5	2	1
Swanson	.980	83	128	271	8	56

utfield	PCT	G	PO	A	E	DP
Astudillo	1.000	2	1	0	0	0
Gaylor	.945	46	50	2	3	0
Godfrey	1.000	5	7	0	0	0
Lara	.935	24	37	6	3	3
Lien	.987	61	151	6	2	1
Lipka	.993	56	125	9	1	4
Meneses	1.000	46	78	0	0	0
Peterson	.983	129	228	4	4	4
Rojas Jr.	1.000	31	63	2	0	0
Smith	.947	5	17	1	1	0
Toscano	.957	49	87	3	4	0

CAROLINA MUDCATS
CAROLINA LEAGUE

HIGH CLASS A

Batting	B-T	HT	WT	DOB	AVG	vLH	vRH	G	AB	R	H	2B	3B	HR	RBI	BB	HBP	SH	SF	SO	SB	CS	SLG	OBP
Beckham, Gordon	R-R	6-0	190	9-16-86	.625	.750	.500	3	8	3	5	1	0	1	3	4	0	0	0	1	0	0	1.125	.750
Curcio, Keith	L-R	5-10	170	12-28-92	.271	.253	.280	124	458	67	124	29	8	3	54	54	7	4	7	64	24	6	.389	.352
Daris, Joseph	L-R	5-10	170	11-22-91	.226	.222	.228	73	239	29	54	13	2	2	17	22	3	1	1	67	5	5	.322	.298
Davidson, Braxton	L-L	6-2	230	6-18-96	.224	.195	.237	128	428	53	96	24	2	10	63	71	10	2	5	184	4	3	.360	.344
Demeritte, Travis	R-R	6-0	180	9-30-94	.250	.179	.271	35	124	21	31	9	5	3	11	26	1	1	0	50	4	1	.476	.384
Edgerton, Jordan	R-R	6-1	190	8-30-93	.215	.255	.195	121	451	37	97	27	2	5	55	20	2	0	7	131	2	1	.317	.248
Fernandez, Jose	R-R	6-1	190	8-30-93	.125	.133	.120	15	40	8	5	1	1	0	3	15	0	0	1	16	3	1	.200	.357
Gaylor, Stephen	L-R	6-1	180	10-4-91	.241	.243	.240	59	191	29	46	4	1	0	9	24	2	2	1	38	14	5	.272	.330
Gebhardt, Ryan	R-R	5-11	195	10-5-91	.259	.231	.269	57	197	15	51	10	1	1	19	14	1	0	4	23	0	2	.335	.306
Giardina, Sal	B-R	6-4	215	4-30-92	.246	.190	.267	67	228	20	56	9	2	3	19	9	0	0	1	56	1	1	.342	.302
Godfrey, Sean	R-R	6-2	180	1-2-92	.269	.250	.281	14	52	5	14	3	1	1	7	2	0	2	0	11	1	0	.423	.296
Harper, Reed	R-R	6-2	200	12-21-90	.218	.192	.229	76	266	25	58	12	1	1	33	21	0	5	5	45	0	2	.282	.271
Mendez, Erison	R-R	5-11	170	5-4-92	.253	.261	.248	66	198	24	50	12	0	1	9	1	1	1	8	0	38	3	4	.328	.295
Meneses, Joey	R-R	6-3	190	5-6-92	.342	.351	.337	66	243	31	83	19	1	5	31	24	1	0	1	38	2	1	.490	.401
Moore, Dylan	R-R	6-0	185	8-2-92	.343	.167	.435	10	35	4	12	4	0	0	4	4	1	0	1	6	2	0	.457	.415
Moss, J.B.	R-R	6-0	185	6-21-93	.195	.200	.193	25	77	8	15	4	0	0	7	8	0	2	2	18	0	0	.247	.264
Murphy, Tanner	R-R	6-1	215	2-27-95	.214	.222	.209	90	281	34	60	9	0	6	28	42	4	3	4	55	0	1	.310	.320
Obregon, Omar	B-R	5-10	150	4-18-94	.247	.173	.280	87	312	41	77	12	4	0	27	24	0	13	3	53	12	4	.311	.298
Odom, Joseph	R-R	6-2	225	1-9-92	.292	.318	.278	52	192	30	56	12	2	8	29	15	3	1	2	40	0	0	.500	.349
Scivicque, Kade	R-R	6-0	225	3-22-93	.179	.222	.158	8	28	1	5	0	0	0	1	3	0	0	0	5	0	0	.179	.258
Swanson, Dansby	R-R	6-1	190	2-27-94	.333	.333	.333	21	78	14	26	12	0	1	10	15	0	0	0	13	7	1	.526	.441
Tejeda, Isaias	R-R	6-0	195	10-28-91	.256	.217	.273	43	156	25	40	10	2	4	30	16	2	0	5	32	0	1	.423	.324
Valenzuela, Luis	L-R	5-10	150	8-25-93	.270	.308	.255	44	189	17	51	11	3	1	19	5	1	1	2	23	1	1	.376	.289

Pitching	B-T	HT	WT	DOB	W	L	ERA	G	GS	CG	SV	IP	H	R	ER	HR	BB	SO	AVG	vLH	vRH	K/9	BB/9
Beech, Caleb	R-R	6-4	215	4-18-93	2	9	4.98	13	13	0	0	69	92	43	38	2	13	41	.317	.303	.331	5.37	1.70
Bird, Zack	R-R	6-4	205	7-14-94	3	3	8.87	28	2	0	0	48	62	48	47	4	39	34	.320	.260	.378	6.42	7.36
Clark, Ryan	R-R	6-5	220	12-9-93	2	13	5.75	26	25	1	0	135	151	94	86	16	46	95	.282	.302	.262	6.35	3.07
Franco, Enderson	R-R	6-2	170	12-29-92	6	12	4.69	26	25	1	0	144	164	79	75	7	46	97	.288	.320	.250	6.06	2.88
Johnson-Mullins, Chasel	L	6-8	270	7-19-94	0	4	3.78	25	0	0	8	33	28	15	14	0	20	31	.239	.259	.233	8.37	5.40
Kennedy, Jon	L-L	6-5	215	9-20-95	0	0	0.00	1	0	0	0	2	2	0	0	0	0	4	.250	.000	.333	18.00	0.00
Lawlor, Ryan	R-L	6-1	185	1-8-94	1	5	4.95	14	7	0	0	44	36	24	24	3	29	41	.226	.233	.224	8.45	5.98
Lewis, Taylor	R-R	6-1	170	10-4-93	4	1	0.53	19	0	0	0	34	27	8	2	0	6	34	.220	.203	.237	9.09	1.60
McLaughlin, Sean	L-R	5-11	195	5-16-94	4	6	3.08	41	0	0	7	61	57	31	21	3	23	41	.248	.248	.248	6.02	3.38
Minter, A.J.	L-L	6-0	205	9-2-93	0	0	0.00	8	0	0	0	9	3	0	0	0	4	10	.100	.000	.125	9.64	3.86
Moran, Jimmy	R-R	6-1	180	6-7-90	0	0	14.40	5	0	0	0	5	11	8	8	1	6	3	.440	.500	.400	5.40	10.80
Navarro, Raymar	R-R	6-1	205	3-19-91	5	3	5.78	28	8	0	0	67	77	49	43	5	31	52	.301	.320	.284	6.99	4.16
O'Neal, Michael	R-L	6-1	215	6-5-92	3	4	5.27	27	2	0	0	41	45	28	24	2	16	36	.288	.293	.286	7.90	3.51
Parsons, Wes	R-R	6-5	190	9-6-92	0	2	3.86	16	7	0	0	56	56	30	24	0	18	44	.264	.248	.279	7.07	2.89
Peterson, Dave	R-R	6-5	205	1-4-90	0	0	0.00	4	0	0	0	4	2	0	0	0	1	1	.154	.333	.000	2.25	0.00
Pfeifer, Phil	L-L	6-0	190	7-15-92	0	0	2.57	6	0	0	2	7	3	2	2	0	4	10	.130	.111	.143	12.86	5.14
Phillips, Evan	R-R	6-2	215	9-11-94	2	1	1.27	21	0	0	8	28	18	6	4	0	8	19	.180	.120	.240	6.04	2.54
Portuondo, Carlos	R-R	6-2	235	11-9-87	1	0	4.01	12	1	0	1	25	17	11	11	2	13	21	.195	.100	.324	7.66	4.74
Povse, Max	R-R	6-8	185	8-23-93	5	5	3.71	15	15	0	0	87	89	44	36	5	17	91	.262	.321	.210	9.38	1.75
Quintana, Zach	R-R	5-11	180	4-15-94	1	6	4.93	22	5	0	1	46	59	27	25	6	20	36	.322	.360	.289	7.09	3.94
Salazar, Carlos	R-R	6-0	200	11-23-94	3	4	4.06	39	0	0	1	51	36	28	23	5	58	72	.198	.189	.207	12.71	10.24
Sobotka, Chad	R-R	6-7	200	7-10-93	1	1	2.04	13	0	0	3	18	12	4	4	0	3	24	.190	.123	.250	12.23	1.53
Thurman, Andrew	R-R	6-3	215	12-10-91	0	2	9.25	6	5	0	0	24	28	27	25	8	18	23	.292	.273	.308	8.51	6.66
Trepagnier, Bryton	R-R	6-6	208	9-18-91	0	0	9.00	2	0	0	0	2	1	2	2	0	4	2	.167	.000	.500	9.00	18.00
Withrow, Matt	R-R	6-5	235	9-23-93	9	6	3.80	25	24	0	0	121	100	60	51	11	68	131	.225	.238	.214	9.77	5.07

Fielding

Catcher	PCT	G	PO	A	E	DP	PB
Giardina	.986	30	186	33	3	3	3
Murphy	.992	79	554	62	5	4	10
Odom	.978	30	200	21	5	1	5
Scivicque	1.000	5	42	4	0	1	0
Tejeda	1.000	1	6	2	0	0	0

First Base	PCT	G	PO	A	E	DP
Edgerton	.971	5	34	0	1	5
Gebhardt	1.000	2	7	1	0	0
Giardina	.982	30	206	16	4	18
Harper	1.000	3	17	1	0	4
Mendez	1.000	7	38	3	0	0
Meneses	.991	63	524	31	5	40
Moore	.977	6	41	1	1	4
Tejeda	.981	31	237	18	5	15

Second Base	PCT	G	PO	A	E	DP
Demeritte	.985	30	49	82	2	17

	PCT	G	PO	A	E	DP	PB
Fernandez	.895	6	8	9	2	0	
Gebhardt	.973	26	37	71	3	14	
Harper	.966	19	36	49	3	10	
Mendez	.887	19	22	33	7	5	
Obregon	.972	43	64	109	5	17	
Valenzuela	1.000	2	1	2	0	0	

Third Base	PCT	G	PO	A	E	DP
Edgerton	.944	109	61	173	14	13
Gebhardt	.947	7	3	15	1	0
Giardina	.857	3	1	5	1	1
Harper	.842	5	7	9	3	1
Mendez	1.000	2	2	4	0	0
Moore	1.000	2	0	4	0	0
Valenzuela	.846	12	11	11	4	2

Shortstop	PCT	G	PO	A	E	DP
Beckham	1.000	2	3	3	0	0
Demeritte	—	1	0	0	0	0

	PCT	G	PO	A	E	DP
Gebhardt	.938	5	6	9	1	1
Harper	.953	48	83	118	10	26
Mendez	—	1	0	0	0	0
Moore	1.000	3	5	7	0	1
Obregon	.961	44	54	119	7	22
Swanson	.970	21	36	60	3	17
Valenzuela	.938	18	21	40	4	5

Outfield	PCT	G	PO	A	E	DP
Curcio	.986	117	282	7	4	3
Daris	.938	69	114	6	8	1
Davidson	.945	113	182	8	11	1
Fernandez	—	1	0	0	0	0
Gaylor	.985	54	129	2	2	2
Gebhardt	1.000	2	2	0	0	0
Godfrey	1.000	9	10	1	0	0
Mendez	.966	39	82	4	3	0
Moss	1.000	22	41	0	0	0

ROME BRAVES

LOW CLASS A

SOUTH ATLANTIC LEAGUE

Batting	B-T	HT	WT	DOB	AVG	vLH	vRH	G	AB	R	H	2B	3B	HR	RBI	BB	HBP	SH	SF	SO	SB	CS	SLG	OBP
Acuna, Ronald	R-R	6-0	180	12-18-97	.311	.409	.294	40	148	27	46	2	2	4	18	18	1	3	1	28	14	7	.432	.387
Baez, Leudys	B-R	6-0	160	6-26-96	.228	.129	.247	61	189	17	43	6	1	3	16	3	1	0	62	4	3	.286	.298
Castro, Carlos	R-R	6-1	195	5-24-94	.266	.200	.275	84	305	43	81	15	4	17	57	13	3	0	1	76	5	0	.508	.301
Didder, Ray-Patrick	R-R	6-0	170	10-1-94	.274	.293	.270	132	478	95	131	15	9	6	35	50	39	2	2	100	37	12	.381	.387
Dykstra, Luke	R-R	6-1	195	11-7-95	.304	.277	.309	81	322	32	98	17	1	0	41	6	9	2	3	31	7	3	.363	.332
Ellison, Justin	L-L	6-2	175	2-6-95	.247	.240	.248	121	433	49	107	25	8	4	54	37	0	2	4	88	18	8	.370	.304
Flowers, Tyler	R-R	6-4	260	1-24-86	.000	.000	—	1	4	0	0	0	0	0	0	0	0	0	1	0	0	.000	.000
Gaylor, Stephen	L-R	6-1	180	10-4-91				1	0	0	0	0	0	0	0	1	0	0	0	0	0	—	1.000
Grullon, Yeudi	B-R	6-1	170	7-18-94	.219	.192	.224	56	160	12	35	2	1	0	14	16	0	2	31	1	5	.244	.287
Herbert, Lucas	R-R	6-0	200	11-28-96	.185	.200	.182	96	335	29	62	11	1	6	30	18	5	4	5	96	2	4	.278	.234
James, Jared	L-R	6-1	185	2-22-94	.302	.263	.313	27	86	14	26	4	2	3	16	8	4	1	2	11	5	1	.500	.380
Josephina, Kevin	B-R	6-0	170	10-2-96	.267	.385	.238	37	131	14	35	7	1	2	12	0	1	4	26	6	2	.382	.259
Keller, Brad	R-R	6-1	195	12-15-96	.172	.240	.161	53	180	21	31	13	1	3	16	8	1	1	75	2	2	.306	.211
McLemore, Darien	R-R	5-8	180	12-11-93	.233	.286	.222	23	86	11	20	4	0	1	4	4	0	1	0	15	2	0	.314	.267
Mendez, Erison	R-R	5-11	170	5-4-92	.196	.000	.250	14	46	3	9	3	1	0	3	2	1	1	0	6	0	2	.304	.245
Morales, Jonathan	R-R	5-11	180	1-29-95	.269	.359	.249	113	424	49	114	25	0	4	55	25	5	2	6	55	3	4	.356	.313
Neslony, Tyler	L-R	6-1	190	2-13-94	.257	.129	.291	41	148	18	38	6	1	1	12	10	3	0	3	29	1	2	.331	.311
Nevarez, Wigberto	R-R	6-3	230	7-17-91	.164	.100	.175	44	134	6	22	7	0	1	12	11	1	2	0	43	0	0	.239	.233
Riley, Austin	R-R	6-3	220	4-2-97	.271	.315	.263	129	495	68	134	39	2	20	80	39	3	0	6	147	3	3	.479	.324
Salazar, Alejandro	R-R	6-0	100	10-5-96	.279	.244	.284	87	312	32	87	8	1	0	29	12	1	8	3	62	6	7	.311	.305
Seymour, Anfernee	B-R	5-11	165	6-24-95	.266	.286	.259	21	79	11	21	1	0	0	5	4	0	1	1	22	6	0	.278	.298
2-team total (104 Greensboro)					.257	—		125	491	72	126	14	3	1	31	26	2	16	2	118	43	13	.303	.296
Tellor, Matt	B-R	6-5	210	9-24-91	.171	.267	.149	23	82	4	14	2	0	1	3	1	0	1	0	31	0	0	.232	.181
Yepez, Juan	R-R	6-1	200	2-19-98	.261	.292	.250	23	92	10	24	5	0	1	7	7	1	0	0	23	0	0	.348	.320

Pitching	B-T	HT	WT	DOB	W	L	ERA	G	GS	CG	SV	IP	H	R	ER	HR	BB	SO	AVG	vLH	vRH	K/9	BB/9
Allard, Kolby	L-L	6-1	180	8-13-97	5	3	3.73	11	11	1	0	60	54	27	25	5	20	62	.244	.204	.257	9.25	2.98
Banuelos, Manny	L-L	5-10	215	3-13-91	0	1	13.50	1	1	0	0	2	5	5	3	0	2	4	.455	—	.455	18.00	9.00
Beech, Caleb	R-R	6-4	215	4-18-93	0	0	3.27	4	1	0	0	11	10	4	4	0	1	8	.233	.167	.258	6.55	0.82
Belicek, Trevor	L-L	6-3	215	12-10-92	3	0	2.49	11	0	0	0	25	19	8	7	2	1	29	.209	.200	.212	10.30	0.36
Caicedo, Oriel	L-L	5-11	190	1-14-94	3	5	4.26	32	6	0	3	89	89	49	42	4	13	67	.263	.319	.242	6.80	1.32
Clouse, Corbin	B-L	6-0	230	6-26-95	4	0	1.52	15	0	0	4	24	13	4	4	1	13	37	.160	.136	.169	14.07	4.94
Custred, Matt	R-R	6-6	240	9-8-93	5	3	3.18	40	1	0	2	57	34	22	20	3	36	64	.173	.155	.186	10.16	5.72
Fried, Max	L-L	6-4	185	1-18-94	8	7	3.93	21	20	0	0	103	87	52	45	10	47	112	.236	.233	.237	9.79	4.11
Gamez, Luis	R-R	6-2	175	6-25-96	0	0	0.00	1	0	0	0	3	0	0	0	0	2	3	.000	.000	.000	13.50	9.00
Gant, John	R-R	6-3	200	8-6-92	0	0	0.00	1	0	0	0	3	1	0	0	0	1	2	.111	.500	.000	6.00	3.00
Geekie, Dalton	R-R	6-5	200	10-3-94	2	4	5.16	31	0	0	1	45	43	35	26	5	17	31	.247	.171	.298	6.15	3.38
Graham, Josh	R-R	6-1	215	10-14-93	1	2	3.40	35	0	0	6	42	35	20	16	4	12	50	.217	.206	.224	10.63	2.55
Johnson, Jim	R-R	6-6	250	6-27-83	0	0	0.00	1	1	0	0	1	1	0	0	0	2	2	.250	.000	.500	18.00	18.00
Johnson-Mullins, Chase	L-L	6-8	270	7-19-94	2	0	1.29	14	0	0	2	21	18	3	3	0	6	19	.240	.176	.259	8.14	2.57
Jones, Grayson	R-R	6-2	220	8-22-94	2	2	4.58	40	0	0	2	57	58	34	29	4	34	30	.270	.325	.235	4.74	5.37
Kennedy, Jon	L-L	6-5	215	9-20-95	0	0	2.74	14	0	0	0	23	22	10	7	3	3	18	.237	.087	.286	7.04	1.17
Lewis, Taylor	R-R	6-1	170	10-4-93	0	3	4.66	13	0	0	1	19	24	11	10	0	6	20	.308	.323	.298	9.31	2.79
Matos, Bladimir	R-R	6-0	190	1-20-94	1	1	6.43	27	0	0	2	35	31	26	25	3	20	33	.240	.259	.225	8.49	5.14
McCreery, Adam	L-L	6-8	195	12-31-92	0	3	4.60	11	0	0	0	16	18	14	8	0	7	14	.295	.300	.293	8.04	4.02
Minter, A.J.	L-L	6-0	205	9-2-93	0	0	0.00	5	0	0	2	7	2	0	0	0	1	6	.091	.200	.059	8.10	1.35
O'Flaherty, Eric	L-L	6-2	210	2-5-85	0	0	0.00	4	1	0	0	4	6	2	0	0	0	5	.375	.333	.400	11.25	0.00
Perez, Williams	R-R	6-0	240	5-21-91	0	1	18.00	1	1	0	0	3	7	6	6	0	2	2	.467	.800	.300	6.00	6.00
Sanchez, Ricardo	L-L	5-11	170	4-11-97	7	10	4.75	24	23	0	0	119	119	72	63	14	54	103	.268	.250	.274	7.77	4.07

Pitching

Pitching	B-T	HT	WT	DOB	W	L	ERA	G	GS	CG	SV	IP	H	R	ER	HR	BB	SO	AVG	vLH	vRH	K/9	BB/9
Simmons, Shae	R-R	5-11	190	9-3-90	0	0	0.00	4	3	0	0	3	2	3	0	0	1	4	.167	.200	.143	10.80	2.70
Sobotka, Chad	R-R	6-7	200	7-10-93	1	2	4.26	15	0	0	0	19	23	11	9	1	12	19	.303	.432	.179	9.00	5.68
Soroka, Mike	R-R	6-4	195	8-4-97	9	9	3.02	25	24	1	0	143	130	58	48	3	32	125	.244	.260	.233	7.87	2.01
Toussaint, Touki	R-R	6-3	185	6-20-96	4	8	3.88	27	24	0	0	132	105	66	57	13	71	128	.217	.218	.217	8.71	4.83
Vizcaino, Arodys	R-R	6-0	230	11-13-90	0	0	9.00	1	1	0	0	1	2	1	1	0	0	1	.500	.000	.667	9.00	0.00
Watts, Devan	R-R	6-0	205	4-21-95	3	1	0.92	16	0	0	8	20	11	2	2	0	6	23	.169	.083	.220	10.53	2.75
Webb, Jacob	R-R	6-1	200	8-15-93	0	0	16.20	2	0	0	0	2	3	3	3	0	2	3	.429	.333	.500	16.20	10.80
Weigel, Patrick	R-R	6-6	220	7-8-94	10	4	2.51	22	21	1	0	129	92	44	36	7	47	135	.203	.190	.213	9.42	3.28
Withrow, Chris	R-R	6-3	240	4-1-89	0	0	0.00	1	0	0	0	1	1	0	0	0	0	3	.250	.000	.333	27.00	0.00

Fielding

Catcher	PCT	G	PO	A	E	DP	PB
Flowers	1.000	1	13	2	0	0	0
Herbert	.988	65	497	66	7	3	5
Morales	.992	64	536	90	5	9	8
Nevarez	.981	14	88	15	2	1	0

First Base	PCT	G	PO	A	E	DP
Castro	.985	72	574	37	9	47
Grullon	1.000	1	1	0	0	0
Mendez	1.000	4	17	3	0	1
Nevarez	.983	31	214	16	4	14
Tellor	.995	23	185	15	1	4
Yepez	.989	20	171	11	2	8

Second Base	PCT	G	PO	A	E	DP
Dykstra	.974	77	113	186	8	33

(2B)	PCT	G	PO	A	E	DP
Grullon	1.000	15	22	38	0	8
Josephina	.987	24	29	45	1	11
McLemore	.943	21	40	42	5	8
Mendez	.947	3	14	4	1	1
Salazar	.900	3	3	6	1	1
Seymour	1.000	1	3	3	0	1

Third Base	PCT	G	PO	A	E	DP
Grullon	1.000	13	11	22	0	1
Josephina	.600	3	2	1	2	0
Mendez	1.000	3	1	3	0	1
Morales	1.000	2	2	1	0	0
Riley	.910	122	92	213	30	12
Yepez	1.000	4	0	2	0	0

Shortstop	PCT	G	PO	A	E	DP
Grullon	.976	26	26	54	2	8

(SS2)	PCT	G	PO	A	E	DP
Josephina	.911	9	10	31	4	8
Mendez	.962	5	9	16	1	1
Salazar	.959	83	127	177	13	28
Seymour	.878	20	20	45	9	8

Outfield	PCT	G	PO	A	E	DP
Acuna	1.000	34	78	2	0	0
Baez	.901	53	98	2	11	0
Didder	.979	129	263	20	6	7
Ellison	.949	99	158	8	9	3
Gaylor	—	1	0	0	0	0
James	.969	24	30	1	1	0
Keller	.968	52	89	3	3	0
Morales	1.000	1	2	0	0	0
Neslony	.983	36	58	1	1	0

DANVILLE BRAVES

APPALACHIAN LEAGUE

ROOKIE

Batting	B-T	HT	WT	DOB	AVG	vLH	vRH	G	AB	R	H	2B	3B	HR	RBI	BB	HBP	SH	SF	SO	SB	CS	SLG	OBP
Arias, Elias	L-L	6-1	180	6-30-94	.223	.048	.264	40	112	13	25	4	2	2	13	10	1	1	0	33	4	3	.348	.293
Cruz, Derian	B-R	6-1	180	10-3-98	.183	.226	.164	25	104	10	19	4	3	0	5	3	0	0	1	28	3	2	.279	.204
Cumberland, Brett	B-R	5-11	205	6-25-95	.216	.167	.233	45	162	11	35	11	0	3	30	14	11	0	2	49	0	4	.340	.317
Gonzalez, Matt	R-R	5-11	193	11-30-93	.302	.189	.327	51	199	23	60	5	4	2	19	6	2	3	1	39	7	3	.397	.327
Hearn, Matt	L-R	5-9	165	2-29-96	.228	.286	.203	34	92	9	21	0	0	3	7	0	3	0	1	24	1	4	.228	.283
James, Jared	L-R	6-1	185	2-22-94	.298	.292	.299	33	121	15	36	5	0	1	17	13	4	1	2	19	6	3	.364	.379
Josephina, Kevin	B-R	6-0	170	10-2-96	.300	.333	.269	13	50	6	15	3	0	1	8	2	1	0	1	7	0	4	.420	.333
Keegan, Trey	R-R	5-10	205	5-11-93	.200	.182	.205	20	56	5	11	2	0	0	5	7	2	0	0	17	3	0	.236	.313
Keller, Brad	R-R	6-1	195	12-15-96	.203	.273	.176	35	118	15	24	3	1	1	8	7	0	1	1	47	4	1	.271	.246
Lee, Alex	L-R	6-1	195	10-23-93	.262	.304	.253	40	122	14	32	6	0	4	15	8	0	0	1	24	0	2	.410	.305
Martinez, Carlos	R-R	5-11	204	5-2-95	.224	.261	.213	30	98	8	22	2	0	1	3	2	0	4	8	0	0	.245	.252
McLemore, Darien	B-R	5-8	180	12-11-93	.161	.105	.186	19	62	4	10	2	0	0	5	10	0	0	16	0	1	.194	.278
Mooney, Marcus	R-R	5-7	160	1-20-94	.264	.263	.264	62	239	44	63	13	1	0	16	14	21	3	1	25	6	4	.326	.356
Moss, J.B.	R-R	6-0	185	6-21-93	.333	.278	.347	24	93	18	31	7	0	1	12	7	0	3	0	19	2	2	.441	.380
Neslony, Tyler	L-R	6-1	190	2-13-94	.500	.556	.429	5	16	5	8	3	0	1	3	1	3	0	1	0	1	.875	.571
O'Malley, Ryan	L-R	6-2	205	2-2-94	.188	.179	.191	42	138	20	26	6	0	5	19	14	3	0	3	47	4	4	.341	.272
Osuna, Ramon	L-R	6-2	245	6-27-95	.276	.171	.311	47	163	17	45	12	0	4	28	18	0	0	3	54	3	1	.423	.342
Pache, Cristian	R-R	6-2	185	11-19-98	.333	.333	.333	30	114	12	38	2	3	0	10	7	0	1	0	13	4	2	.404	.372
Pina, Jose	R-R	6-2	180	4-22-96	.000	—	.000	2	6	0	0	0	0	0	0	0	0	0	2	0	0	.000	.000
Wilson, Isranel	L-R	6-3	185	3-6-98	.192	.107	.216	38	130	19	25	8	1	2	12	14	1	1	0	51	6	2	.315	.276
Yelich, Collin	L-R	6-2	180	10-1-93	.154	.000	.182	11	26	3	4	1	0	0	1	5	4	1	0	8	0	0	.192	.371

Pitching	B-T	HT	WT	DOB	W	L	ERA	G	GS	CG	SV	IP	H	R	ER	HR	BB	SO	AVG	vLH	vRH	K/9	BB/9
Allard, Kolby	L-L	6-1	180	8-13-97	3	0	1.32	5	5	0	0	27	18	4	4	0	5	33	.186	.167	.192	10.87	1.65
Anderson, Ian	R-R	6-3	170	5-2-98	0	2	3.74	5	5	0	0	22	19	10	9	1	8	18	.244	.135	.341	7.48	3.32
Avalos, Gabino	R-R	6-2	185	8-15-94	0	1	27.00	1	0	0	0	1	4	4	4	0	1	3	.500	.500	.500	20.25	6.75
Carroll, Dalton	R-R	6-0	195	5-18-94	1	0	2.93	16	0	0	1	28	27	10	9	0	7	26	.265	.233	.288	8.46	2.28
Clouse, Corbin	B-L	6-0	230	6-26-95	1	0	0.00	4	0	0	1	7	0	0	0	0	2	16	.000	.000	.000	21.60	2.70
Cockrell, Taylor	R-L	6-3	175	6-21-94	0	0	3.47	14	0	0	0	23	23	12	9	0	5	19	.258	.333	.200	7.33	1.93
Feigl, Brady	R-L	6-4	195	12-27-90	0	0	0.00	3	0	0	0	3	2	0	0	0	1	4	.182	.000	.222	12.00	3.00
Gamez, Luis	R-R	6-2	175	6-25-96	2	4	2.93	6	6	0	0	28	22	18	9	1	15	16	.210	.176	.241	5.20	4.88
Gilmore, Connor	R-R	6-5	220	12-10-93	2	1	2.50	13	0	0	0	18	17	7	5	0	2	19	.246	.360	.182	9.50	1.00
Grosser, Alec	R-R	6-4	205	1-12-95	0	0	18.90	3	0	0	0	3	4	8	7	1	6	2	.308	.000	.400	5.40	16.20
Harrington, Drew	L-L	6-2	225	3-30-95	1	0	2.45	9	1	0	0	15	14	4	4	1	5	15	.237	.263	.225	9.20	3.07
Hellinger, Jarret	R-L	6-4	170	11-18-96	2	4	4.50	13	13	0	0	62	63	39	31	3	28	47	.273	.273	.273	6.82	4.06
Hyssong, Taylor	L-L	6-4	190	1-4-94	0	0	1.56	11	0	0	1	17	17	6	3	0	7	14	.246	.263	.240	7.27	3.63
Kennedy, Jon	L-L	6-5	215	9-20-95	0	0	4.76	4	0	0	0	6	11	5	3	0	1	7	.407	1.000	.304	11.12	1.59
Lara, Jordy	R-R	6-3	215	5-21-91	1	0	3.52	7	0	0	0	8	6	3	3	0	5	9	.214	.429	.143	10.57	5.87
Martinez, Jhon	L-L	6-0	165	2-9-95	4	6	3.21	12	12	0	0	62	68	31	22	3	16	45	.278	.275	.278	6.57	2.34
Matos, Bladimir	R-R	6-0	190	1-20-94	1	0	2.30	10	0	0	1	16	10	5	4	0	16	17	.189	.222	.171	9.77	9.19
McCreery, Adam	L-L	6-8	195	12-31-92	0	3	3.86	11	0	0	0	19	15	12	8	0	6	19	.208	.238	.196	9.16	2.89

Pitching

Pitching	B-T	HT	WT	DOB	W	L	ERA	G	GS	CG	SV	IP	H	R	ER	HR	BB	SO	AVG	vLH	vRH	K/9	BB/9
Mora, Luis	R-R	6-4	160	6-17-95	1	6	7.42	10	7	0	0	30	31	28	25	4	18	35	.261	.341	.218	10.38	5.34
Orozco, Evertz	R-R	6-5	192	9-16-94	1	1	4.66	15	0	0	0	29	33	18	15	1	9	19	.292	.304	.284	5.90	2.79
Ratcliffe, Sean	L-R	6-4	200	4-11-95	0	0	9.00	2	0	0	0	1	1	2	1	0	6	0	.250	.500	.000	0.00	54.00
Rice, Zach	L-L	6-2	205	10-15-95	2	1	8.66	15	0	0	1	18	22	19	17	2	18	20	.324	.308	.333	10.19	9.17
Schlosser, Ryan	R-R	6-4	190	1-31-96	0	0	7.71	2	0	0	0	2	3	2	2	0	1	1	.300	.333	.286	3.86	3.86
Stanton, Cameron	R-R	6-0	170	6-20-94	1	1	2.57	14	5	0	0	35	36	17	10	0	8	20	.269	.224	.294	5.14	2.06
Walker, Jeremy	R-R	6-5	205	6-12-95	3	3	3.18	13	5	0	0	40	40	17	14	2	8	37	.252	.267	.238	8.39	1.82
Watts, Devan	R-R	6-0	205	4-21-95	0	0	0.00	4	0	0	1	4	0	0	0	0	0	3	.000	.000	.000	6.75	0.00
Webb, Jacob	R-R	6-1	200	8-15-93	0	0	3.18	12	0	0	2	11	7	4	4	1	7	28	.171	.250	.138	22.24	5.56
Wentz, Joey	L-L	6-5	210	10-6-97	1	4	5.06	8	8	0	0	32	31	18	18	0	20	35	.265	.440	.217	9.84	5.63
White, Brandon S.	R-R	6-2	215	12-21-94	2	2	2.30	15	0	0	7	16	11	5	4	1	5	24	.204	.188	.211	13.79	2.87
White, Brandon T.	B-R	6-3	205	12-6-92	0	0	0.00	1	0	0	0	1	1	0	0	0	0	0	—	—	—	0.00	0.00

Fielding

C: Cumberland 33, Keegan 14, Martinez 23, Yelich 3. **1B:** Arias 1, Lee 32, Osuna 40, Yelich 3. **2B:** Gonzalez 35, Josephina 10, McLemore 12, Mooney 12. **3B:** Gonzalez 11, Martinez 2, McLemore 4, Mooney 12, O'Malley 42. **SS:** Cruz 24, Josephina 3, McLemore 1, Mooney 39, O'Malley 1. **OF:** Arias 26, Gonzalez 5, Hearn 28, James 19, Keller 33, Moss 23, Neslony 4, Pache 29, Pina 2, Wilson 36.

GCL BRAVES
GULF COAST LEAGUE

ROOKIE

Batting

Batting	B-T	HT	WT	DOB	AVG	vLH	vRH	G	AB	R	H	2B	3B	HR	RBI	BB	HBP	SH	SF	SO	SB	CS	SLG	OBP
Acuna, Ronald	R-R	6-0	180	12-18-97	.333	1.000	.200	2	6	1	2	0	0	0	1	1	1	0	0	1	0	0	.333	.500
Aquino, Alex	R-R	6-2	165	7-6-96	.274	.348	.259	43	135	17	37	11	0	1	19	9	3	5	2	25	5	1	.378	.329
Beckham, Gordon	R-R	6-0	190	9-16-86	.200	.000	.286	3	10	0	2	1	0	0	1	0	0	0	1	3	0	0	.300	.182
Benson, Griffin	B-R	6-5	210	9-28-97	.223	.152	.250	50	166	16	37	5	0	1	13	14	2	1	2	40	0	0	.271	.288
Boeldak, Sander	L-L	5-10	185	7-17-96	.250	.125	.300	23	56	10	14	2	2	1	9	3	0	3	0	15	1	1	.411	.288
Concepcion, Anthony	R-R	6-1	200	3-23-95	.272	.333	.255	53	180	25	49	12	3	4	36	22	5	0	5	35	5	2	.439	.358
Contreras, William	R-R	6-0	180	12-24-97	.261	.211	.283	30	72	8	19	5	0	1	8	7	2	1	0	15	0	1	.375	.346
Crowley, Alan	R-R	6-2	210	3-4-96	.327	.333	.324	26	52	7	17	0	0	1	3	4	0	0	0	9	0	0	.385	.375
Cruz, Derian	B-R	6-1	180	10-3-98	.309	.320	.306	26	110	11	34	7	1	2	16	2	3	1	1	16	4	1	.445	.336
Fernandez, Jeremy	R-R	6-1	185	7-11-94	.244	.241	.245	36	123	15	30	3	1	0	8	4	4	3	0	20	7	0	.285	.290
Flowers, Tyler	R-R	6-4	260	1-24-86	.000	—	.000	1	2	0	0	0	0	0	0	0	0	0	0	0	0	0	.000	.000
Foley, Matt	R-R	6-4	230	4-15-94	.333	.000	.333	1	3	1	1	0	0	0	0	0	0	0	0	2	0	0	.333	.333
2-team total (12 Marlins)					.258	—	—	13	31	7	8	0	0	0	2	5	2	0	1	9	0	1	.258	.385
Godfrey, Sean	R-R	6-2	180	1-2-92	.250	.400	.200	6	20	2	5	1	0	1	3	2	0	0	0	5	0	0	.450	.318
Hoekstra, Kurt	L-R	6-2	190	6-27-93	.091	.000	.111	4	11	2	1	1	0	0	1	1	1	0	0	3	0	0	.182	.231
Howell, Gabe	R-R	6-1	180	3-12-98	.150	.200	.133	7	20	4	3	0	0	0	0	2	2	0	0	11	1	0	.150	.292
Mejia, Luis	B-R	5-10	180	3-8-97	.242	.226	.247	35	120	14	29	2	1	0	11	5	0	4	1	18	3	1	.275	.270
Michel, Shean	R-R	5-11	170	9-26-97	.195	.100	.224	26	87	12	17	1	0	0	8	7	0	2	0	18	3	1	.207	.255
Moore, Tyler	R-R	6-2	220	1-30-87	.214	.500	.100	4	14	2	3	0	0	1	3	0	0	0	0	5	0	0	.429	.214
Olivera, Hector	R-R	6-2	230	4-5-85	.714	1.000	.500	3	7	3	5	1	0	1	3	2	1	0	0	1	0	0	1.286	.800
Ovando, Luis	R-R	6-1	160	10-3-96	.306	.444	.259	11	36	7	11	1	0	0	4	1	0	2	0	8	1	0	.333	.324
Pache, Cristian	R-R	6-2	185	11-19-98	.283	.259	.291	27	106	16	30	2	4	0	11	6	1	0	1	11	7	3	.377	.325
Perez, Ruben	R-R	6-0	180	9-21-95	.200	.167	.214	15	20	4	4	0	0	0	2	3	1	1	0	5	0	0	.400	.333
Pierzynski, A.J.	R-R	6-3	250	12-30-76	.444	1.000	.375	3	9	3	4	1	0	0	1	0	0	0	0	2	0	0	.556	.545
Pokorney, Jackson	L-R	6-2	205	4-28-98	.259	.263	.258	28	85	9	22	3	1	0	8	9	2	0	1	28	1	2	.318	.340
Rodriguez, Ricardo	R-R	5-10	175	12-20-97	.225	.250	.221	29	80	9	18	4	0	0	7	5	2	0	1	10	0	0	.275	.284
Salazar, Alejandro	R-R	6-0	170	10-5-96	.200	.000	.250	2	5	2	1	0	0	0	0	2	0	0	0	1	0	0	.200	.429
Shumpert, Nick	R-R	5-11	180	11-11-96	.189	.053	.236	26	74	12	14	5	0	1	7	4	1	0	1	25	3	1	.297	.238
Valenzuela, Luis	L-R	5-10	150	8-25-93	.143	.333	.000	2	7	0	1	0	0	0	0	1	0	0	0	3	0	0	.143	.250
Ventura, Randy	B-R	5-9	165	7-11-97	.284	.209	.305	53	194	34	55	2	4	1	32	25	1	6	6	31	15	6	.351	.358
Yelich, Colin	L-R	6-2	180	10-1-93	.211	.400	.143	19	57	9	12	4	0	0	3	1	0	1	0	9	0	0	.281	.233
Yepez, Juan	R-R	6-1	200	2-19-98	.200	—	.200	3	10	0	2	0	0	0	0	0	0	0	0	5	0	0	.200	.200

Pitching

Pitching	B-T	HT	WT	DOB	W	L	ERA	G	GS	CG	SV	IP	H	R	ER	HR	BB	SO	AVG	vLH	vRH	K/9	BB/9
Anderson, Ian	R-R	6-3	170	5-2-98	1	0	0.00	5	5	0	0	18	14	2	0	0	4	18	.222	.238	.214	9.00	2.00
Barrios, Luis	L-L	6-4	210	3-4-97	0	1	21.60	4	0	0	0	3	8	8	8	0	3	3	.500	.429	.556	8.10	8.10
Danciu, Parker	L-L	6-4	215	3-22-94	3	2	2.43	13	1	0	2	30	33	13	8	1	10	26	.292	.258	.305	7.89	3.03
Davidson, Tucker	L-L	6-2	215	3-25-96	0	3	1.52	11	1	0	0	30	32	9	5	1	4	32	.271	.242	.282	9.71	1.21
De La Cruz, Jasseel	R-R	6-1	175	6-26-97	2	0	0.00	6	0	0	0	15	4	0	0	0	1	12	.085	.118	.067	7.20	0.60
Feigl, Brady	R-L	6-4	195	12-27-90	0	0	0.00	3	0	0	0	3	1	0	0	0	2	2	.100	.000	.125	6.00	0.00
Greene, Tyler	R-R	6-2	200	12-14-94	1	0	2.53	10	0	0	1	11	8	3	3	1	4	6	.195	.294	.125	5.06	3.38
Guardado, Anthony	R-R	6-1	185	11-14-97	0	1	1.17	8	0	0	0	8	5	1	1	0	6	5	.200	.231	.167	5.87	7.04
Heredia, Jesus	R-R	6-2	175	1-21-95	1	3	3.77	12	3	0	0	31	19	15	13	4	20	29	.178	.140	.203	8.42	5.81
Javier, Odalvi	R-R	6-0	180	9-4-96	5	1	2.62	12	6	0	0	45	36	16	13	1	12	34	.216	.250	.196	6.85	2.42
Johnson-Mullins, Chase	L-L	6-8	270	7-19-94	0	0	0.00	1	0	0	0	1	0	0	0	0	1	0	.000	.000	.000	0.00	9.00
Lawlor, Ryan	R-L	6-1	185	1-8-94	0	0	0.00	2	0	0	0	2	1	0	0	0	0	3	.143	.333	.000	13.50	0.00
Mejia, Dilmer	L-L	5-11	160	7-9-97	3	1	3.06	11	5	0	0	35	39	18	12	0	10	29	.281	.357	.247	7.39	2.55
Muller, Kyle	R-L	6-6	225	10-7-97	1	0	0.65	10	9	0	0	28	14	3	2	0	12	38	.144	.121	.156	12.36	3.90
O'Flaherty, Eric	L-L	6-2	210	2-5-85	0	1	9.00	1	1	0	0	2	1	1	1	0	0	2	.333	.500	.000	18.00	0.00
Parsons, Wes	R-R	6-5	190	9-6-92	0	0	2.70	4	1	0	0	7	8	2	2	0	0	9	.296	.571	.200	12.15	0.00
Perez, Luis	R-R	6-1	195	4-7-97	0	1	9.64	5	0	0	0	5	7	6	5	1	4	3	.350	.400	.300	5.79	7.71
Perez, Williams	R-R	6-0	240	5-21-91	0	0	0.00	1	0	0	0	2	0	0	0	0	0	3	.182	.333	.000	9.00	0.00

Pitching	B-T	HT	WT	DOB	W	L	ERA	G	GS	CG	SV	IP	H	R	ER	HR	BB	SO	AVG	vLH	vRH	K/9	BB/9
Rangel, Alan	R-R	6-2	170	8-21-97	3	1	3.28	12	9	0	0	47	42	17	17	2	10	47	.241	.293	.216	9.06	1.93
Rodriguez, Alberto	L-L	6-5	205	12-13-95	1	0	2.95	13	0	0	0	18	10	6	6	1	8	15	.164	.316	.095	7.36	3.93
Schlosser, Ryan	R-R	6-4	190	1-31-96	1	2	1.04	17	0	0	6	17	13	6	2	1	1	12	.206	.188	.213	6.23	0.52
Simmons, Shae	R-R	5-11	190	9-3-90	0	0	6.00	3	3	0	0	3	2	2	2	0	2	5	.167	.400	.000	15.00	6.00
Suarez, Gilbert	R-R	6-2	215	6-19-97	1	1	0.76	13	0	0	0	24	15	7	2	0	5	16	.183	.211	.159	6.08	1.90
Tavers, Ramon	R-R	6-1	200	8-31-95	2	4	5.20	11	2	0	1	28	34	22	16	2	10	18	.304	.371	.273	5.86	3.25
Vega, Bredio	R-R	6-3	185	4-8-96	1	2	6.35	11	0	0	0	23	26	21	16	4	17	18	.289	.378	.200	7.15	6.75
Vizcaino, Arodys	R-R	6-0	230	11-13-90	0	0	0.00	1	1	0	0	1	0	0	0	0	0	2	.000	.000	.000	18.00	0.00
Wentz, Joey	L-L	6-5	210	12-21-97	0	0	0.00	4	4	0	0	12	3	0	0	0	5	18	.083	.111	.074	13.50	3.75
White, Brandon S.	R-R	6-2	215	12-21-94	—	—	—	—	—	—	—	—	—	—	—	—	—	—	—	—	—	—	—
White, Brandon T.	B-R	6-3	205	12-6-92	1	3	3.86	17	0	0	3	19	14	11	8	1	7	12	.203	.258	.158	5.79	3.38
Wilson, Bryse	R-R	6-1	225	12-20-97	1	1	0.68	9	6	0	0	27	16	4	2	0	8	29	.172	.229	.138	9.79	2.70

Fielding

C: Contreras 28, Crowley 21, Flowers 1, Perez 14, Pierzynski 1, Rodriguez 26, Yelich 5. **1B:** Benson 49, Concepcion 9, Moore 1, Yelich 2, Yepez 2. **2B:** Beckham 1, Fernandez 34, Mejia 10, Ovando 10, Shumpert 4. **3B:** Aquino 27, Beckham 2, Hoekstra 1, Howell 7, Mejia 1, Mejia 24. **SS:** Aquino 12, Cruz 24, Hoekstra 1, Mejia 1, Salazar 2, Shumpert 21, Valenzuela 1. **OF:** Acuna 1, Boeldak 10, Concepcion 38, Godfrey 4, Michel 26, Moore 2, Olivera 3, Pache 26, Pokorney 18, Ventura 51.

DSL BRAVES
DOMINICAN SUMMER LEAGUE
ROOKIE

Batting	B-T	HT	WT	DOB	AVG	vLH	vRH	G	AB	R	H	2B	3B	HR	RBI	BB	HBP	SH	SF	SO	SB	CS	SLG	OBP
Adrianza, Andres	R-R	6-0	190	2-6-99	.219	.250	.211	29	96	10	21	5	0	0	7	10	2	2	2	24	0	0	.271	.300
Bermudez, Jose	B-R	6-2	160	7-9-97	.258	.111	.288	52	159	28	41	6	1	0	17	17	5	5	0	47	11	2	.308	.348
Blanco, Reilys	B-R	5-10	150	7-30-96	.307	.333	.297	29	88	17	27	2	0	0	9	10	0	3	1	7	3	1	.330	.374
Borrego, Carlos	R-R	6-0	182	3-26-99	.224	.200	.229	32	85	10	19	0	0	0	6	6	1	0	2	18	5	2	.224	.277
Carrillo, Franger	R-R	6-1	185	11-7-98	.000	.000	.000	5	14	0	0	0	0	0	0	1	0	0	0	3	0	0	.000	.067
Centeno, Carlos	R-R	5-9	180	11-19-97	.225	.343	.187	46	142	16	32	5	1	0	20	15	4	2	1	29	2	1	.275	.315
De Hoyos, Victor	R-R	5-9	170	2-23-98	.163	.091	.188	13	43	2	7	1	0	0	2	1	1	2	0	7	0	0	.186	.200
Encarnacion, J.C.	R-R	6-3	195	1-17-98	.264	.273	.263	37	140	19	37	3	3	0	16	11	5	0	0	30	4	0	.329	.340
Estrada, Richard	R-R	5-10	172	4-4-98	.167	.000	.188	12	18	0	3	2	0	0	2	1	0	0	0	4	0	0	.278	.211
Figueroa, Brian	R-R	6-0	180	4-5-99	.000	.000	.000	5	5	2	0	0	0	0	0	1	3	0	0	1	0	0	.000	.444
Guitian, Emmanuel	R-R	5-11	165	9-14-98	.167	.500	.000	2	6	1	1	0	0	0	1	0	0	0	0	2	0	0	.167	.286
Isea, Emmanuel	R-R	6-1	180	12-2-98	.125	.125	.125	9	24	2	3	2	0	0	2	2	2	0	0	6	1	0	.208	.250
Lopez, Yoeli	R-R	5-10	167	7-31-97	.240	.216	.247	68	221	38	53	11	3	3	33	33	19	1	2	78	11	5	.357	.382
Lora, Eudis	L-R	6-2	180	10-8-97	.209	.205	.210	57	182	14	38	6	2	1	19	24	3	0	4	40	3	3	.280	.305
Martina, Ildion	R-R	5-11	195	5-24-97	.171	.667	.125	15	35	5	6	2	0	0	4	3	1	0	0	5	0	0	.229	.256
Michel, Shean	R-R	5-11	170	9-26-97	.316	.395	.289	39	152	26	48	5	5	0	19	15	3	0	4	17	9	4	.414	.379
Morales, Juan	R-R	6-2	165	11-17-98	.148	.176	.138	36	128	12	19	4	2	0	13	13	6	4	2	32	1	2	.211	.255
Olmos, Luis	R-R	6-0	175	8-28-97	.103	.000	.114	15	39	5	4	1	0	0	3	4	3	1	0	12	0	0	.128	.239
Ovando, Luis	R-R	6-1	160	10-29-98	.263	.303	.254	47	175	22	46	5	5	1	15	16	4	0	1	32	7	4	.366	.337
Ramos, Jeffrey	R-R	6-1	185	2-10-99	.230	.192	.240	33	126	19	29	8	1	1	12	9	1	0	2	27	3	2	.333	.283
Rojas, Romer	R-R	6-1	180	1-8-98	.174	.138	.188	36	109	10	19	3	0	0	9	10	2	0	2	34	4	0	.257	.252
Salazar, Danyer	R-R	6-1	180	2-19-98	.258	.143	.282	46	159	21	41	10	1	3	19	16	4	1	0	34	1	2	.390	.341
Vasquez, Braulio	B-R	6-0	170	4-13-99	.333	.231	.370	28	99	14	33	2	1	0	6	11	3	0	0	22	11	6	.374	.416

Pitching	B-T	HT	WT	DOB	W	L	ERA	G	GS	CG	SV	IP	H	R	ER	HR	BB	SO	AVG	vLH	vRH	K/9	BB/9
Abreu, Erick	L-R	6-3	180	1-1-98	1	1	5.52	16	1	0	0	31	26	23	19	1	27	31	.236	.261	.230	9.00	7.84
Bautista, Gregory	R-R	6-4	180	4-28-93	3	5	2.50	18	7	0	1	50	42	24	14	2	20	48	.227	.182	.252	8.58	3.58
De La Cruz, Jasseel	R-R	6-1	175	6-26-97	2	0	3.42	12	3	0	0	26	23	11	10	1	14	20	.247	.243	.250	6.84	4.78
Diaz, Jhonny	L-L	6-0	180	6-22-96	1	1	4.67	17	0	0	2	35	31	19	18	0	14	22	.250	.346	.224	5.71	3.63
Gil, Frank	R-R	6-2	165	9-24-96	1	1	3.86	9	1	0	0	16	14	9	7	0	13	13	.222	.250	.209	7.16	7.16
Hernandez, Servando	R-R	6-3	210	11-25-96	0	3	5.76	15	15	0	0	30	35	24	19	0	18	19	.292	.140	.377	5.76	5.46
Javier, Ciriaco	R-R	6-3	185	1-1-96	1	4	4.50	14	3	0	0	24	19	14	12	1	19	20	.211	.217	.209	7.50	7.13
Jerez, Miguel	L-L	5-11	180	10-13-97	1	0	1.64	11	0	0	0	22	21	11	4	2	8	23	.241	.182	.262	9.41	3.27
Joaquin, Victor	R-R	6-5	220	12-29-93	1	2	2.61	15	1	0	1	21	24	13	6	0	14	17	.279	.321	.259	7.40	6.10
Julian, Deyvis	R-R	6-2	165	4-10-96	0	8	2.68	17	15	0	0	40	30	21	12	3	14	37	.205	.211	.202	8.26	3.12
Laguna, Jason	R-R	5-11	170	1-8-96	0	0	2.76	10	0	0	2	16	18	5	5	0	2	18	.265	.318	.239	9.37	1.10
Lopez, Carlos	R-R	6-4	175	3-20-98	0	3	1.53	10	0	0	0	18	15	3	3	0	14	14	.238	.250	.231	7.13	7.13
Pantoja, Ali	R-R	6-4	180	1-31-97	0	4	10.58	15	4	0	0	25	31	36	29	2	32	28	.320	.300	.333	10.22	11.68
Rodriguez, Kelvin	L-L	6-5	195	12-31-93	3	2	2.60	17	6	0	2	52	55	19	15	1	6	33	.267	.277	.264	5.71	1.04
Sanchez, Filyer	L-L	6-1	175	2-8-97	3	1	2.01	19	0	0	5	45	38	15	10	0	10	30	.232	.231	.232	6.04	2.01
Santos, Lisandro	L-L	6-1	170	7-24-98	0	1	0.00	4	0	0	0	7	5	4	0	0	2	4	.192	.143	.211	5.40	2.70
Sepulveda, Jhoniel	R-R	6-2	175	5-15-97	3	3	2.93	18	3	0	0	43	46	39	14	0	25	32	.260	.259	.261	6.70	5.23
Vasquez, Williams	R-R	6-1	200	5-7-97	6	1	2.95	17	0	0	1	43	31	14	14	0	14	27	.196	.213	.189	5.70	2.95
Volquez, Albinson	B-R	6-3	185	8-16-97	3	3	3.50	20	1	0	1	44	42	26	17	6	13	36	.243	.211	.259	7.42	2.68
Zuniga, Guillermo	R-R	6-3	195	10-10-98	1	0	2.61	5	0	0	0	10	12	5	3	2	2	9	.308	.214	.360	7.84	1.74

Fielding

C: Adrianza 5, Centeno 43, De Hoyos 10, Estrada 6, Figueroa 3, Guitian 2, Martina 13. **1B:** Adrianza 22, Borrego 1, Lora 22, Salazar 29. **2B:** Blanco 5, Lora 10, Olmos 3, Ovando 42, Vasquez 13. **3B:** Adrianza 1, Blanco 20, Encarnacion 19, Lora 22, Olmos 6, Salazar 8. **SS:** Encarnacion 16, Morales 36, Olmos 6, Ovando 3, Rojas 1, Vasquez 13. **OF:** Bermudez 48, Blanco 4, Borrego 14, Carrillo 2, Isea 7, Lopez 64, Michel 38, Ramos 29, Rojas 16.

Baltimore Orioles

SEASON IN A SENTENCE: Baltimore led the majors with 253 home runs, had the big leagues' best closer, Zach Britton, and rode those bombs and their bullpen to a wild-card spot, their third playoff trip in five seasons.

HIGH POINT: The Orioles won seven straight at the end of June, including the first two games of a nine-game West Coast road trip. The winning streak started and finished with games against . . . the Padres? Mark Trumbo homers—two of his MLB-high 47—helped key both, a 7-2 home win on June 22 and a 12-6 win at San Diego on June 29. The latter gave the Orioles their biggest lead in the American League East all season at 5½ games.

LOW POINT: Baltimore and Toronto battled all season before matching up in the wild-card game, which the Blue Jays won, 5-2, in 11 innings. Both the Orioles' runs came on a Trumbo homer, but Britton never factored into the game, as manager Buck Showalter gambled and held his closer back, waiting for a lead that never came. Instead, Ubaldo Jimenez gave up a season-ending, three-run homer to Edwin Encarnacion.

NOTABLE ROOKIES: Righthander Dylan Bundy, out of options, had to make the big league roster or risk being exposed to waivers. He did much more, working from a relief role to a rotation spot. He ranked second on the team in wins, while fellow righty Mychal Givens became a crucial setup man in a boffo bullpen. Rule 5 pick Joey Rickard provided an early-season spark as a starting outfielder while Korean Hyun Soo Kim got his bearings; Kim wound up being a key offensive piece in left field, leading the team with a .382 OBP. Lefty Donnie Hart had a great September as a relief specialist.

KEY TRANSACTIONS: The offseason acquisition of Trumbo worked out spectacularly, while late free-agent pickup Pedro Alvarez also worked out well, smashing 22 homers in a part-time role. Late-August trade pickup Michael Bourn started the wild-card game, but a straight pitcher swap of Ariel Miranda for Wade Miley (2-5, 6.17 for Baltimore) failed to pay dividends.

DOWN ON THE FARM: Only low Class A Delmarva posted a winning record, but no Orioles affiliate made the playoffs, and the organization's top performers, such as Yermin Mercedes (the high Class A Carolina League batting champ), Conor Bierfeldt (20 homers) and Aderlin Rodriguez, were old for their leagues.

OPENING DAY PAYROLL: $145,533,782 (8th)

PLAYERS OF THE YEAR

MAJOR LEAGUE	MINOR LEAGUE
Manny Machado, 3b/ss	**Chance Sisco, c**
.294/.343/.533	(Double-A/Triple-A)
37 HR, 96 RBI	.317/.403/.430
40 2B, 105 R	6 HR, 51 RBI, 61 BB

ORGANIZATION LEADERS

BATTING   *Minimum 250 AB

MAJORS			
*	AVG	Manny Machado	.294
*	OPS	Manny Machado	.876
	HR	Mark Trumbo	47
	RBI	Mark Trumbo	108
MINORS			
*	AVG	Yermin Mercedes, Delmarva, Frederick	.345
*	OBP	Wynston Sawyer, Frederick, Bowie	.422
*	SLG	Yermin Mercedes, Delmarva, Frederick	.570
*	OPS	Yermin Mercedes, Delmarva, Frederick	.974
	R	Cedric Mullins, Delmarva	79
	H	Garabez Rosa, Norfolk, Bowie	155
	TB	Aderlin Rodriguez, Frederick	263
	2B	Dariel Alvarez, Norfolk	38
	3B	Cedric Mullins, Delmarva	10
	HR	Aderlin Rodriguez, Frederick	26
	RBI	Aderlin Rodriguez, Frederick	93
	BB	D.J. Stewart, Delmarva, Frederick	78
	SO	Trey Mancini, Bowie, Norfolk	140
	SB	Jay Gonzalez, Bowie, Frederick	43

PITCHING   #Minimum 75 IP

MAJORS			
	W	Chris Tillman	16
#	ERA	Kevin Gausman	3.61
	SO	Kevin Gausman	174
	SV	Zach Britton	47
MINORS			
	W	Matthew Grimes, Frederick, Bowie	11
	L	Joe Gunkel, Bowie, Norfolk	14
#	ERA	Brian Gonzalez, Bowie	2.50
	G	Pedro Beato, Norfolk	65
	GS	Joe Gunkel, Bowie, Norfolk	28
	SV	Jason Stoffel, Bowie, Norfolk	24
	IP	Joe Gunkel, Bowie, Norfolk	161
	BB	Ofelky Peralta, Delmarva	60
	SO	Cristian Alvarado, Delmarva	148
#	AVG	Francisco Jimenez, Delmarva	.246

2016 PERFORMANCE

General Manager: Dan Duquette. **Farm Director:** Brian Graham. **Scouting Director:** Gary Rajsich.

Class	Team	League	W	L	PCT	Finish	Manager
Majors	Baltimore Orioles	American	89	73	.549	t-4th (15)	Buck Showalter
Triple-A	Norfolk Tides	International	62	82	.431	13th (14)	Ron Johnson
Double-A	Bowie Baysox	Eastern	56	86	.394	12th (12)	Gary Kendall
High A	Frederick Keys	Carolina	68	72	.486	5th (8)	Keith Bodie
Low A	Delmarva Shorebirds	South Atlantic	73	66	.525	6th (14)	Ryan Minor
Short season	Aberdeen IronBirds	New York-Penn	32	43	.427	11th (14)	Luis Pujols
Rookie	Orioles	Gulf Coast	27	32	.458	11th (17)	Orlando Gomez
Overall 2016 Minor League Record			318	381	.455	25th (30)	

ORGANIZATION STATISTICS

BALTIMORE ORIOLES
AMERICAN LEAGUE

Batting	B-T	HT	WT	DOB	AVG	vLH	vRH	G	AB	R	H	2B	3B	HR	RBI	BB	HBP	SH	SF	SO	SB	CS	SLG	OBP
Alvarez, Dariel	R-R	6-2	180	11-7-88	.333	.333	—	2	3	0	1	1	0	0	0	1	0	0	0	0	0	0	.667	.500
Alvarez, Pedro	L-R	6-3	250	2-6-87	.249	.237	.251	109	337	43	84	20	0	22	49	37	0	0	2	97	1	0	.504	.322
Borbon, Julio	L-L	6-0	195	2-20-86	.308	.500	.222	6	13	1	4	0	0	0	0	0	0	2	0	3	0	1	.308	.308
Bourn, Michael	L-R	5-11	190	12-27-82	.283	.500	.262	24	46	5	13	1	0	2	8	6	0	2	1	9	2	0	.435	.358
Davis, Chris	L-R	6-3	230	3-17-86	.221	.216	.223	157	566	99	125	21	0	38	84	88	8	0	3	219	1	0	.459	.332
Flaherty, Ryan	L-R	6-3	220	7-27-86	.217	.300	.204	74	157	16	34	7	0	3	15	17	0	1	1	48	2	0	.318	.291
Hardy, J.J.	R-R	6-1	200	8-19-82	.269	.269	.269	115	405	43	109	29	0	9	48	26	0	1	6	68	0	0	.407	.309
Janish, Paul	R-R	6-2	200	10-12-82	.194	.235	.143	14	31	3	6	1	0	0	3	1	0	0	0	3	0	0	.226	.286
Jones, Adam	R-R	6-2	215	8-1-85	.265	.218	.280	152	619	86	164	19	0	29	83	39	5	1	8	115	2	0	.436	.310
Joseph, Caleb	R-R	6-3	180	6-18-86	.174	.083	.208	49	132	7	23	3	0	0	7	0	2	0	28	0	0	.197	.216
Kim, Hyun Soo	L-R	6-2	210	1-12-88	.302	.000	.321	95	305	36	92	16	1	6	22	36	4	0	1	51	1	3	.420	.382
Machado, Manny	R-R	6-3	185	7-6-92	.294	.329	.283	157	640	105	188	40	1	37	96	48	3	0	5	120	0	3	.533	.343
Mancini, Trey	R-R	6-4	215	3-18-92	.357	.400	.250	5	14	3	5	1	0	3	5	0	1	0	0	4	0	0	1.071	.400
Pearce, Steve	R-R	5-11	200	4-13-83	.217	.179	.250	25	60	9	13	2	0	3	6	8	2	0	1	14	0	0	.400	.329
2-team total (60 Tampa Bay)					.288	—	—	85	264	35	76	13	1	13	35	34	3	0	1	54	0	3	.492	.374
Pena, Francisco	R-R	6-2	230	10-12-89	.200	.333	.120	14	40	5	8	0	0	1	3	2	0	1	0	14	0	0	.275	.238
Reimold, Nolan	R-R	6-4	205	10-12-83	.222	.183	.263	104	203	25	45	9	1	6	15	22	1	0	1	62	1	2	.365	.300
Rickard, Joey	R-L	6-1	185	5-21-91	.268	.313	.247	85	257	32	69	13	0	5	19	18	2	3	2	54	4	1	.377	.319
Schoop, Jonathan	R-R	6-1	225	10-16-91	.267	.243	.274	162	615	82	164	38	1	25	82	21	8	0	3	137	1	2	.454	.298
Stubbs, Drew	R-R	6-4	205	10-4-84	.136	.133	.143	20	22	1	3	0	0	0	1	4	1	0	0	11	1	1	.136	.296
2-team total (19 Texas)					.214	—	—	39	42	7	9	0	0	2	4	8	1	0	1	18	5	1	.357	.346
Trumbo, Mark	R-R	6-4	225	1-16-86	.256	.173	.284	159	613	94	157	27	1	47	108	51	3	0	0	170	2	0	.533	.316
Wieters, Matt	B-R	6-5	230	5-21-86	.243	.229	.248	124	423	48	103	17	1	17	66	32	5	1	3	85	1	0	.409	.302

Pitching	B-T	HT	WT	DOB	W	L	ERA	G	GS	CG	SV	IP	H	R	ER	HR	BB	SO	AVG	vLH	vRH	K/9	BB/9
Aquino, Jayson	L-L	6-1	225	11-22-92	0	0	0.00	3	0	0	0	2	1	0	0	0	0	3	.125	.167	.000	11.57	0.00
Brach, Brad	R-R	6-6	215	4-12-86	10	4	2.05	71	0	0	2	79	57	23	18	7	25	92	.201	.288	.126	10.48	2.85
Bridwell, Parker	R-R	6-4	185	8-2-91	0	0	13.50	2	0	0	0	3	5	5	5	2	1	3	.357	.600	.222	8.10	2.70
Britton, Zach	L-L	6-3	195	12-22-87	2	1	0.54	69	0	0	47	67	38	7	4	1	18	74	.162	.185	.155	9.94	2.42
Bundy, Dylan	B-R	6-1	200	11-15-92	10	6	4.02	36	14	0	0	110	109	52	49	18	42	104	.257	.256	.259	8.53	3.45
Despaigne, Odrisamer	R-R	6-0	200	4-4-87	0	2	5.60	16	0	0	0	27	32	18	17	3	15	17	.305	.298	.310	5.60	4.94
Drake, Oliver	R-R	6-4	215	1-13-87	1	0	4.00	14	0	0	0	18	11	11	8	2	7	21	.167	.154	.175	10.50	3.50
Duensing, Brian	L-L	6-0	200	2-22-83	1	0	4.05	14	0	0	0	13	13	6	6	2	3	10	.250	.190	.290	6.75	2.03
Gallardo, Yovani	R-R	6-2	205	2-27-86	6	8	5.42	23	23	0	0	118	126	74	71	16	61	85	.276	.270	.281	6.48	4.65
Gausman, Kevin	R-R	6-3	190	1-6-91	9	12	3.61	30	30	0	0	180	183	76	72	28	47	174	.262	.232	.288	8.72	2.35
Givens, Mychal	R-R	6-0	210	5-13-90	8	2	3.13	66	0	0	0	75	59	28	26	6	36	96	.220	.366	.156	11.57	4.34
Hart, Donnie	L-L	5-11	180	9-6-90	0	0	0.49	22	0	0	0	18	12	1	1	1	6	12	.194	.132	.292	5.89	2.95
Hunter, Tommy	R-R	6-3	250	7-3-86	0	0	2.19	12	0	0	0	12	14	3	3	0	3	6	.304	.333	.290	4.38	2.19
2-team total (21 Cleveland)					2	2	3.18	33	0	0	0	34	35	13	12	1	8	23	—	—	—	6.09	2.12
Jimenez, Ubaldo	R-R	6-5	210	1-22-84	8	12	5.44	29	25	1	1	142	150	93	86	16	72	125	.268	.294	.249	7.90	4.55
Matusz, Brian	L-L	6-5	190	2-11-87	0	0	12.00	7	0	0	0	6	8	8	8	1	7	1	.407	.455	.375	1.50	10.50
McFarland, T.J.	L-L	6-3	220	6-8-89	2	2	6.93	16	0	0	0	25	33	19	19	3	10	7	.340	.367	.313	2.55	3.65
Miley, Wade	L-L	6-0	220	11-13-86	2	5	6.17	11	11	0	0	54	70	38	37	7	15	55	.315	.222	.333	9.17	2.50
2-team total (19 Seattle)					9	13	5.37	30	30	1	0	166	187	100	99	25	49	137	—	—	—	7.43	2.66
Miranda, Ariel	L-L	6-2	190	1-10-89	0	0	13.50	1	0	0	0	2	4	3	3	0	0	4	.364	.429	.250	18.00	0.00
2-team total (11 Seattle)					5	2	3.88	12	10	0	0	58	47	28	25	12	18	44	—	—	—	6.83	2.79
O'Day, Darren	R-R	6-4	220	10-22-82	3	1	3.77	34	0	0	3	31	25	13	13	6	13	38	.214	.243	.200	11.03	3.77
Ondrusek, Logan	R-R	6-8	230	2-13-85	0	0	9.95	7	0	0	0	6	9	7	7	1	3	4	.346	.545	.200	5.68	4.26
Roe, Chaz	R-R	6-5	190	10-9-86	1	0	3.72	9	0	0	0	10	8	4	4	2	7	11	.216	.333	.105	10.24	6.52
Tillman, Chris	R-R	6-5	200	4-15-88	16	6	3.77	30	30	0	0	172	155	73	72	19	66	140	.244	.240	.247	7.33	3.45
Tolliver, Ashur	L-L	6-0	170	1-24-88	1	0	5.79	5	0	0	0	5	5	4	3	1	3	5	.263	.250	.273	9.64	5.79
Wilson, Tyler	R-R	6-2	185	9-25-89	4	6	5.27	24	13	0	0	94	110	57	55	15	24	55	.288	.283	.293	5.27	2.30
Worley, Vance	R-R	6-2	250	9-25-87	2	2	3.53	35	4	0	1	87	84	37	34	11	35	56	.261	.264	.259	5.82	3.63
Wright, Mike	R-R	6-6	215	1-3-90	3	4	5.79	18	12	0	0	75	81	53	48	12	26	50	.282	.345	.238	6.03	3.13

Fielding

Catcher	PCT	G	PO	A	E	DP	PB
Joseph	.994	48	322	24	2	4	2
Pena	1.000	14	76	5	0	1	1
Wieters	.988	117	871	50	11	6	1

First Base	PCT	G	PO	A	E	DP
Davis	.993	152	1325	62	10	138
Flaherty	1.000	7	18	3	0	3
Joseph	1.000	2	1	0	0	0
Pearce	1.000	10	42	3	0	4
Trumbo	1.000	6	30	2	0	4

Second Base	PCT	G	PO	A	E	DP
Flaherty	1.000	1	0	1	0	0

	PCT	G	PO	A	E	DP
Pearce	1.000	1	2	2	0	1
Schoop	.989	162	277	447	8	123

Third Base	PCT	G	PO	A	E	DP
Alvarez	.556	12	0	5	4	0
Flaherty	.969	40	17	78	3	9
Janish	1.000	9	11	12	0	0
Machado	.979	114	86	236	7	26

Shortstop	PCT	G	PO	A	E	DP
Flaherty	1.000	13	12	17	0	4
Hardy	.987	115	140	326	6	80
Janish	1.000	6	2	6	0	2
Machado	.971	45	76	125	6	33

Outfield	PCT	G	PO	A	E	DP
Alvarez	1.000	1	1	0	0	0
Borbon	1.000	6	11	0	0	0
Bourn	1.000	24	21	2	0	0
Davis	1.000	3	5	0	0	0
Flaherty	1.000	9	6	0	0	0
Jones	.994	152	349	4	2	1
Kim	1.000	91	110	4	0	0
Pearce	1.000	12	12	1	0	0
Reimold	.992	95	117	3	1	1
Rickard	1.000	82	127	6	0	0
Stubbs	.917	18	11	0	1	0
Trumbo	.967	96	166	10	6	1

NORFOLK TIDES
INTERNATIONAL LEAGUE

TRIPLE-A

Batting	B-T	HT	WT	DOB	AVG	vLH	vRH	G	AB	R	H	2B	3B	HR	RBI	BB	HBP	SH	SF	SO	SB	CS	SLG	OBP
Almanzar, Michael	R-R	6-3	190	12-2-90	.241	.284	.227	118	410	42	99	23	2	10	41	31	3	2	4	106	1	2	.380	.297
Alvarez, Dariel	R-R	6-0	180	11-7-88	.288	.323	.278	130	524	53	151	38	0	4	49	28	2	2	4	80	7	2	.384	.324
Avery, Xavier	L-L	6-0	190	1-1-90	.248	.182	.262	101	303	38	75	15	1	6	19	37	2	4	1	123	18	2	.363	.332
Flaherty, Ryan	L-R	6-3	220	7-27-86	.421	.500	.385	5	19	3	8	1	0	0	1	3	0	0	0	5	0	0	.474	.500
Hoes, L.J.	R-R	6-0	200	3-5-90	.242	.252	.239	102	396	45	96	13	2	6	33	43	2	0	2	58	8	8	.331	.318
Janish, Paul	R-R	6-2	200	10-12-82	.248	.121	.287	76	246	26	61	8	0	0	18	28	4	4	1	33	1	3	.280	.333
Joseph, Caleb	R-R	6-3	180	6-18-86	.250	.167	.286	9	40	2	10	0	0	4	2	0	0	5	0	0	.250	.286	
Joseph, Corban	L-R	6-0	185	10-28-88	.305	.163	.331	85	285	36	87	14	1	7	34	26	0	1	1	32	4	0	.435	.362
Mancini, Trey	R-R	6-4	215	3-18-92	.280	.283	.278	125	483	60	135	22	5	13	54	48	4	0	1	123	2	2	.427	.349
Marte, Alfredo	R-R	5-11	200	3-31-89	.000	.000	.000	2	5	0	0	0	0	0	0	0	0	0	0	2	0	0	.000	.000
2-team total (10 Lehigh Valley)					.139	—		12	36	1	5	0	0	0	1	1	0	0	0	8	0	0	.139	.162
Martinez, Ozzie	R-R	5-10	200	5-7-88	.236	.286	.216	94	343	26	81	9	2	4	34	17	0	3	2	54	7	2	.309	.271
O'Brien, Chris	B-R	5-11	225	7-24-89	.156	.188	.138	13	45	6	7	1	0	0	3	6	0	0	0	9	0	0	.178	.255
Paredes, Jimmy	B-R	6-3	200	11-25-88	.333	.000	.375	8	27	5	9	2	0	1	3	2	1	0	1	8	2	0	.519	.387
Pena, Francisco	R-R	6-2	230	10-12-89	.246	.275	.238	54	191	17	47	11	1	4	23	15	0	0	2	25	0	1	.377	.298
Perez, Audry	R-R	6-2	220	12-23-88	.291	.318	.283	84	306	30	89	11	0	6	38	21	4	0	1	53	0	1	.386	.343
Rosa, Garabez	R-R	6-2	166	10-12-89	.234	.250	.230	20	77	4	18	1	0	1	3	1	0	0	0	12	0	1	.286	.244
Schoop, Sharlon	R-R	6-2	190	4-15-87	.236	.317	.210	46	165	13	39	6	1	4	22	13	1	1	0	40	0	1	.358	.296
Sisco, Chance	L-R	6-2	195	2-24-95	.200	.000	.267	4	16	4	4	0	0	2	7	2	0	0	5	0	0	.625	.333	
Terdoslavich, Joey	B-R	6-2	200	9-9-88	.140	.400	.115	17	57	5	8	0	0	1	12	0	1	1	13	1	0	.140	.286
Tolleson, Steve	R-R	5-11	185	11-1-83	.100	—	.100	8	20	3	2	0	0	0	6	0	0	0	5	0	0	.100	.308
Urrutia, Henry	L-R	6-5	200	2-13-87	.245	.167	.256	32	102	9	25	4	0	0	11	6	0	0	0	21	0	1	.304	.347
Walker, Christian	R-R	6-0	220	3-28-91	.264	.265	.264	131	504	64	133	29	2	18	64	40	4	0	4	138	1	3	.437	.321
Wynns, Austin	R-R	6-2	205	12-10-90	.278	.750	.143	8	18	3	5	1	0	0	1	4	0	0	0	2	0	0	.500	.278
Yastrzemski, Mike	L-L	5-11	180	8-23-90	.221	.141	.245	94	339	41	75	21	4	7	32	42	3	0	1	98	10	3	.369	.312

Pitching	B-T	HT	WT	DOB	W	L	ERA	G	GS	CG	SV	IP	H	R	ER	HR	BB	SO	AVG	vLH	vRH	K/9	BB/9
Additon, Nick	L-L	6-5	215	12-16-87	1	10	3.81	16	13	0	0	80	86	36	34	7	23	50	.281	.267	.286	5.60	2.58
Aquino, Jayson	L-L	6-1	225	11-22-92	2	0	2.08	5	0	0	0	13	12	3	3	0	3	12	.250	.154	.286	8.31	2.08
Beato, Pedro	R-R	6-6	230	10-27-86	5	5	2.65	65	0	0	4	68	59	29	20	6	24	62	.231	.279	.207	8.21	3.18
Bridwell, Parker	R-R	6-4	185	8-2-91	1	0	1.80	4	0	0	0	10	4	2	2	1	1	14	.121	.143	.105	12.60	0.90
Bundy, Bobby	R-R	6-2	215	1-13-90	0	0	0.00	1	0	0	0	1	1	0	0	0	0	1	.250	.333	.000	0.00	0.00
Cabral, Cesar	L-L	6-3	250	2-11-89	1	0	9.72	7	0	0	0	8	13	10	9	0	5	4	.361	.308	.391	4.32	5.40
Cortright, Garrett	R-R	6-5	210	10-2-91	0	0	27.00	1	0	0	0	2	1	1	0	1	0	1.000	1.000	—	0.00	27.00	
Despaigne, Odrisamer	R-R	6-0	200	4-4-87	1	9	3.87	18	17	0	0	88	91	39	38	5	27	70	.265	.260	.270	7.13	2.75
Doyle, Terry	R-R	6-4	215	11-2-85	0	2	5.87	4	4	0	0	23	29	15	15	0	6	12	.319	.300	.333	4.70	2.35
Drake, Oliver	R-R	6-4	215	1-13-87	1	4	2.72	47	1	0	10	56	44	20	17	5	25	79	.215	.171	.244	12.62	3.99
Duensing, Brian	L-L	6-0	200	2-22-83	0	0	0.00	3	0	0	0	3	4	0	0	0	0	6	.308	.400	.250	18.00	0.00
Gallardo, Yovani	R-R	6-2	205	2-27-86	1	0	3.60	2	2	0	0	5	4	4	2	4	10	.143	.167	.130	9.00	3.60	
Gausman, Kevin	R-R	6-3	190	1-6-91	0	1	4.76	1	1	0	0	6	4	3	3	0	2	9	.200	.222	.182	14.29	3.18
Gorzelanny, Tom	L-L	6-2	210	7-12-82	0	0	4.50	7	0	0	0	6	11	7	3	0	5	5	.355	.250	.391	7.50	7.50
2-team total (19 Columbus)					1	1	3.65	26	0	0	1	25	24	15	10	0	16	24	—	—	—	8.76	5.84
Gunkel, Joe	R-R	6-5	225	12-30-91	8	11	4.08	24	24	1	0	141	156	68	64	14	18	94	.281	.260	.294	5.99	1.15
Hale, David	R-R	6-2	210	9-27-87	4	7	5.84	20	20	0	0	94	133	65	61	10	23	56	.331	.386	.288	5.36	2.20
Lobstein, Kyle	L-L	6-3	220	8-12-89	0	0	0.00	1	0	0	0	1	0	0	0	0	1	0	.000	—	.000	0.00	9.00
2-team total (19 Indianapolis)					1	3	4.03	20	0	0	1	51	55	26	23	3	18	42	—	—	—	7.36	3.16
McFarland, T.J.	L-L	6-3	200	6-8-89	1	1	4.44	8	4	0	0	26	33	13	13	3	7	11	.314	.282	.333	3.76	2.39
McGough, Scott	R-R	5-11	190	10-31-89	2	3	4.72	26	2	0	0	48	50	27	25	5	19	36	.273	.325	.236	6.80	3.59
Miranda, Ariel	L-L	6-2	190	1-10-89	4	7	3.93	19	19	0	0	101	95	47	44	11	31	87	.249	.283	.238	7.78	2.77
Oliver, Andy	L-L	6-3	205	12-3-87	3	2	3.43	28	14	0	0	87	85	35	33	6	36	84	.261	.264	.260	8.73	3.74
Olmos, Edgar	L-L	6-4	220	4-12-90	4	4	2.88	42	0	0	0	69	63	26	22	4	28	76	.249	.217	.261	9.96	3.67
Phillips, Zach	L-L	6-1	200	9-21-86	3	3	4.45	49	0	0	1	61	60	32	30	3	30	84	.261	.294	.247	12.46	4.45
2-team total (2 Indianapolis)					9	3	4.35	51	0	0	2	62	60	32	30	3	33	85	—	—	—	12.34	4.79
Redmond, Todd	R-R	6-3	240	5-17-85	0	2	27.00	2	0	0	0	5	18	15	14	0	3	6	.563	.500	.611	10.80	5.40
Rodriguez, Richard	R-R	6-4	205	3-4-90	6	2	2.53	48	2	0	2	82	65	23	23	5	25	81	.216	.208	.221	8.93	2.76

Pitching	B-T	HT	WT	DOB	W	L	ERA	G	GS	CG	SV	IP	H	R	ER	HR	BB	SO	AVG	vLH	vRH	K/9	BB/9
Roe, Chaz	R-R	6-5	190	10-9-86	1	2	2.39	33	0	0	4	38	27	10	10	1	10	45	.205	.241	.176	10.75	2.39
Stoffel, Jason	R-R	6-1	230	9-15-88	0	2	1.78	28	0	0	12	30	22	8	6	2	11	37	.214	.213	.214	10.98	3.26
Tolliver, Ashur	L-L	6-0	170	1-24-88	0	0	1.42	11	0	0	0	13	11	2	2	0	6	16	.234	.111	.263	11.37	4.26
Wilson, Tyler	R-R	6-2	185	9-25-89	2	0	4.56	6	6	0	0	24	26	12	12	1	3	20	.289	.326	.250	7.61	1.14
Wright, Mike	R-R	6-6	215	1-3-90	4	4	3.07	13	13	0	0	76	72	30	26	8	14	48	.250	.309	.197	5.66	1.65
Zouzalik, Michael	L-R	6-3	195	7-13-90	0	0	3.12	3	0	0	0	9	6	3	3	1	2	4	.194	.154	.222	4.15	2.08

Fielding

Catcher	PCT	G	PO	A	E	DP	PB
Joseph	1.000	7	52	4	0	0	0
O'Brien	1.000	8	55	4	0	0	0
Pena	.991	51	416	31	4	5	5
Perez	.992	75	559	38	5	2	5
Sisco	1.000	4	22	2	0	0	0
Wynns	1.000	6	27	2	0	0	0

First Base	PCT	G	PO	A	E	DP
Mancini	.995	121	1067	62	6	99
O'Brien	1.000	2	13	0	0	2
Terdoslavich	1.000	17	110	9	0	15
Walker	1.000	5	42	3	0	5

Second Base	PCT	G	PO	A	E	DP
Flaherty	1.000	3	10	9	0	4

	PCT	G	PO	A	E	DP
Hoes	1.000	1	2	3	0	0
Joseph	.982	79	150	225	7	56
Martinez	.978	28	55	78	3	16
Rosa	.980	10	20	28	1	0
Schoop	.991	25	49	65	1	14
Tolleson	1.000	6	6	10	0	1

Third Base	PCT	G	PO	A	E	DP
Almanzar	.939	118	108	214	21	25
Flaherty	1.000	2	3	3	0	0
Martinez	.957	9	8	14	1	0
Paredes	.923	4	3	9	1	0
Perez	—	1	0	0	0	0
Rosa	.947	7	3	15	1	2
Schoop	1.000	4	2	14	0	0
Tolleson	1.000	2	1	0	0	0

Shortstop	PCT	G	PO	A	E	DP
Janish	.993	76	95	200	2	48
Martinez	.990	53	69	128	2	30
Rosa	1.000	3	3	11	0	3
Schoop	.973	17	24	48	2	10

Outfield	PCT	G	PO	A	E	DP
Alvarez	.995	113	201	13	1	1
Avery	.979	76	138	3	3	1
Hoes	.983	76	165	5	3	2
Urrutia	.800	8	7	1	2	0
Walker	.978	90	129	3	3	1
Yastrzemski	.969	85	176	11	6	0

BOWIE BAYSOX

EASTERN LEAGUE

DOUBLE-A

Batting	B-T	HT	WT	DOB	AVG	vLH	vRH	G	AB	R	H	2B	3B	HR	RBI	BB	HBP	SH	SF	SO	SB	CS	SLG	OBP
Bierfeldt, Conor	R-R	6-2	220	4-2-91	.209	.100	.242	13	43	4	9	2	0	2	4	3	0	1	0	16	0	0	.395	.261
Borbon, Julio	L-L	6-0	195	2-20-86	.276	.287	.273	111	424	61	117	11	4	6	27	36	2	7	1	59	30	10	.363	.335
Caronia, Anthony	L-R	6-0	170	5-22-91	.167	—	.167	4	12	0	2	0	0	0	0	0	0	0	0	2	1	1	.167	.167
Davis, Glynn	R-R	6-3	170	12-7-91	.251	.333	.221	80	247	32	62	12	2	5	33	21	2	2	5	60	6	8	.377	.309
Dickerson, Chris	L-L	6-4	230	4-10-82	.322	.154	.370	15	59	10	19	4	2	3	10	6	0	0	0	16	2	0	.610	.385
Dosch, Drew	L-R	6-2	200	6-24-92	.261	.194	.281	113	422	54	110	19	9	9	55	29	2	3	8	92	1	1	.412	.306
Gonzalez, Jay	L-L	5-9	170	12-11-91	.246	.455	.200	19	61	6	15	0	0	0	9	0	1	0	15	2	1	.246	.343
Hardy, J.J.	R-R	6-1	190	8-19-82	.364	—	.364	3	11	1	4	0	0	0	1	0	0	0	1	0	0	.364	.417
Joseph, Caleb	R-R	6-3	180	6-18-86	.286	.500	.200	6	21	2	6	1	0	1	2	1	1	0	0	7	0	1	.476	.348
Joseph, Corban	L-R	6-0	185	10-28-88	.349	.235	.377	22	86	10	30	5	1	1	12	6	1	1	1	9	1	1	.465	.394
Kemp, Jeff	R-R	6-0	190	3-23-90	.183	.213	.170	45	153	20	28	4	0	4	15	18	2	0	2	55	4	1	.288	.274
Kim, Hyun Soo	L-R	6-2	210	1-12-88	.286	.000	.500	2	7	1	2	0	0	0	2	0	0	0	0	2	0	0	.714	.286
Latimore, Quincy	R-R	5-11	175	2-3-89	.209	.242	.199	115	392	60	82	16	1	14	45	49	4	2	1	112	3	2	.362	.303
Levy, Stuart	R-R	6-2	185	8-21-92	.000	—	.000	1	3	0	0	0	0	0	0	0	0	0	0	1	0	0	.000	.000
Mancini, Trey	R-R	6-4	215	3-18-92	.302	.500	.264	17	63	18	19	4	0	7	16	10	2	0	0	17	0	0	.698	.413
Marin, Adrian	R-R	6-0	180	3-8-94	.232	.202	.240	119	406	38	94	11	4	4	33	29	1	7	1	82	11	8	.308	.284
Nathans, Tucker	L-R	6-0	200	11-6-88	.250	.213	.261	61	212	21	53	8	1	4	26	14	1	1	2	42	1	1	.354	.297
O'Brien, Chris	B-R	5-11	225	7-24-89	.186	.207	.178	65	204	19	38	6	0	7	26	40	2	1	4	47	0	1	.319	.320
Paredes, Jimmy	B-R	6-3	200	11-25-88	.243	.250	.241	10	37	4	9	2	1	1	5	4	0	0	0	12	1	0	.378	.317
Rosa, Garabez	R-R	6-2	166	10-12-89	.303	.327	.296	110	452	45	137	21	2	8	62	14	4	1	5	104	2	4	.412	.326
Sawyer, Wynston	R-R	6-3	205	11-14-91	.444	.000	.500	3	9	2	4	1	0	1	3	1	0	0	1	0	0	0	.889	.455
Schoop, Sharlon	R-R	6-2	185	4-15-87	.214	.278	.192	40	140	17	30	6	2	1	7	16	1	3	1	31	0	1	.307	.297
Sisco, Chance	L-R	6-2	195	2-24-95	.320	.210	.347	112	410	53	131	28	1	4	44	59	4	1	5	83	2	2	.422	.406
Terdoslavich, Joey	B-R	6-2	200	9-9-88	.246	.233	.251	109	394	53	97	24	1	14	61	60	3	0	2	71	0	0	.419	.349
Urrutia, Henry	L-R	6-5	200	2-13-87	.316	.370	.296	75	294	38	93	15	1	5	38	19	0	0	3	41	1	0	.425	.354
Wilkerson, Steve	B-R	6-1	195	11-13-91	.222	.200	.250	3	9	1	2	0	0	0	0	1	0	0	0	1	0	0	.222	.222
Wynns, Austin	R-R	6-2	205	12-10-90	.247	.150	.283	21	73	11	18	7	0	0	10	7	0	1	1	12	1	0	.342	.309
Yastrzemski, Mike	L-L	5-11	180	8-23-90	.268	.130	.298	33	127	27	34	5	0	6	27	19	0	0	1	20	4	0	.449	.361

Pitching	B-T	HT	WT	DOB	W	L	ERA	G	GS	CG	SV	IP	H	R	ER	HR	BB	SO	AVG	vLH	vRH	K/9	BB/9
Aquino, Jayson	L-L	6-1	225	11-22-92	5	10	3.90	20	19	1	0	115	130	55	50	7	33	77	.286	.341	.266	6.01	2.58
Barker, Brandon	R-R	6-3	210	8-20-92	5	7	4.75	18	17	0	0	100	109	57	53	14	33	68	.276	.247	.302	6.10	2.96
Beliveau, Jeff	L-L	6-1	190	1-17-87	0	0	3.86	4	0	0	0	5	3	5	2	1	4	2	.158	.154	.167	3.86	7.71
Bridwell, Parker	R-R	6-4	185	8-2-91	1	1	4.53	18	7	0	1	56	56	33	28	7	28	38	.258	.227	.290	6.14	4.53
Bundy, Bobby	R-R	6-3	215	1-13-90	3	1	3.49	36	0	0	1	49	46	22	19	4	19	46	.245	.253	.238	8.45	3.49
Chleborad, Tanner	R-R	6-6	185	11-4-92	0	0	40.50	1	0	0	0	1	5	6	6	0	2	0	.625	.500	.667	0.00	13.50
Cortright, Garrett	R-R	6-5	210	10-2-91	0	1	5.73	10	0	0	0	11	15	7	7	1	4	6	.333	.333	.333	4.91	3.27
Crichton, Stefan	R-R	6-3	200	2-29-92	2	6	3.73	48	4	0	1	72	73	35	30	4	26	61	.262	.271	.253	7.59	3.24
Demny, Paul	R-R	6-2	200	8-3-89	0	0	9.00	1	0	0	0	1	2	1	1	0	1	1	.500	1.000	.333	9.00	0.00
Duensing, Brian	L-L	6-0	200	2-22-83	0	0	1.29	3	0	0	0	7	5	1	1	0	1	7	.192	.167	.200	9.00	1.29
Fornataro, Eric	R-R	6-2	230	1-2-88	2	1	8.10	10	0	0	0	10	14	9	9	1	6	10	.341	.348	.333	9.00	5.40
Garcia, Jason	R-R	6-0	185	11-21-92	6	10	4.73	24	24	1	0	124	137	73	65	5	54	71	.291	.315	.268	5.17	3.93
Gausman, Kevin	R-R	6-3	190	1-6-91	0	1	0.00	1	1	0	0	4	1	0	0	0	1	4	.364	.333	.375	9.00	9.00
Grimes, Matt	R-R	6-5	185	9-4-91	3	5	4.68	11	11	0	0	58	60	33	30	5	23	37	.267	.270	.264	5.77	3.59
Gunkel, Joe	R-R	6-5	225	12-30-91	0	3	3.66	4	4	0	0	20	26	14	8	2	3	15	.310	.333	.289	6.86	1.37

Pitching

Pitching	B-T	HT	WT	DOB	W	L	ERA	G	GS	CG	SV	IP	H	R	ER	HR	BB	SO	AVG	vLH	vRH	K/9	BB/9
Hart, Donnie	L-L	5-11	180	9-6-90	3	1	2.72	40	0	0	4	46	41	17	14	1	7	50	.236	.188	.267	9.71	1.36
Hess, David	R-R	6-2	180	7-10-93	5	13	5.37	25	24	1	0	127	162	90	76	19	39	85	.310	.345	.276	6.01	2.76
Keller, Jon	R-R	6-5	210	8-8-92	0	3	6.69	24	0	0	1	36	38	27	27	4	32	31	.273	.197	.342	7.68	7.93
Lee, Chris	L-L	6-3	180	8-17-92	5	0	2.98	8	7	0	0	51	41	17	17	4	13	19	.222	.155	.252	3.33	2.28
Liranzo, Jesus	R-R	6-2	175	3-7-95	1	1	3.38	11	0	0	0	19	8	8	7	3	12	20	.127	.034	.206	9.64	5.79
Matusz, Brian	L-L	6-5	190	2-11-87	0	0	21.00	3	1	0	0	3	8	7	7	2	1	4	.471	.250	.538	12.00	3.00
McFarland, T.J.	L-L	6-3	220	6-8-89	0	1	3.00	2	1	0	0	3	4	3	1	1	0	3	.286	.200	.333	9.00	3.00
McGough, Scott	R-R	5-11	190	10-31-89	2	2	5.68	15	1	0	0	25	37	16	16	3	4	21	.349	.365	.333	7.46	1.42
Means, John	L-L	6-3	195	4-24-93	4	8	4.69	18	18	0	0	96	113	53	50	7	25	51	.295	.310	.288	4.78	2.34
O'Day, Darren	R-R	6-4	220	10-22-82	0	0	0.00	1	1	0	0	1	0	0	0	0	0	2	.250	.250	—	18.00	0.00
Ondrusek, Logan	R-R	6-8	230	2-13-85	0	1	6.43	5	0	0	0	7	10	6	5	2	1	9	.333	.200	.467	11.57	1.29
Reyes, Genison	R-R	6-5	190	9-19-91	0	2	6.35	23	0	0	1	28	33	26	20	3	17	26	.289	.300	.278	8.26	5.40
Richardson, David	R-R	5-11	170	1-31-91	0	0	5.68	6	2	0	1	13	16	8	8	2	7	15	.302	.333	.276	10.66	4.97
Scott, Tanner	R-L	6-2	220	7-22-94	1	2	5.63	14	0	0	0	16	18	11	10	0	15	18	.305	.300	.308	10.13	8.44
Stoffel, Jason	R-R	6-1	230	9-15-88	3	3	3.14	27	0	0	12	29	25	13	10	4	9	41	.229	.196	.254	12.87	2.83
Tolliver, Ashur	L-L	6-0	170	1-24-88	1	1	2.42	18	0	0	2	26	22	9	7	4	8	25	.237	.212	.250	8.65	2.77
Torres, Dennis	R-R	6-3	200	5-17-90	0	0	27.00	1	0	0	0	2	2	5	5	1	2	2	.286	.000	.400	10.80	10.80
Worley, Vance	R-R	6-2	250	9-25-87	0	1	5.40	1	0	0	0	2	5	1	1	0	0	0	.500	.000	.625	0.00	0.00
Yacabonis, Jimmy	R-R	6-3	205	3-21-92	2	2	2.03	34	0	0	6	44	34	13	10	2	14	46	.211	.226	.202	9.34	2.84
Zouzalik, Michael	L-R	6-3	195	7-13-90	2	0	3.00	12	0	0	0	24	26	8	8	1	7	15	.268	.250	.277	5.63	2.63

Fielding

Catcher	PCT	G	PO	A	E	DP	PB
Levy	1.000	1	4	2	0	0	0
O'Brien	.981	37	238	24	5	2	3
Sawyer	1.000	3	26	2	0	0	0
Sisco	.987	83	546	50	8	1	4
Wynns	.993	20	130	11	1	3	2

First Base	PCT	G	PO	A	E	DP
Joseph	1.000	2	20	0	0	1
Mancini	1.000	15	116	11	0	15
O'Brien	.994	20	160	13	1	14
Rosa	1.000	25	194	12	0	24
Terdoslavich	.978	81	656	47	16	63

Second Base	PCT	G	PO	A	E	DP
Caronia	.947	3	6	12	1	2
Joseph	.958	13	28	41	3	12
Kemp	.983	31	65	108	3	24

	PCT	G	PO	A	E	DP
Marin	1.000	2	4	5	0	1
Nathans	.971	9	16	17	1	2
Rosa	.960	63	130	181	13	43
Schoop	.989	20	28	61	1	8
Wilkerson	1.000	3	6	6	0	2

Third Base	PCT	G	PO	A	E	DP
Caronia	—	1	0	0	0	0
Dosch	.950	112	71	195	14	12
Kemp	1.000	3	2	5	0	0
Nathans	.765	14	8	18	8	1
Paredes	.667	1	2	0	1	0
Rosa	.824	7	6	8	3	0
Schoop	.889	6	6	10	2	2

Shortstop	PCT	G	PO	A	E	DP
Hardy	1.000	3	3	8	0	1
Kemp	.977	11	11	31	1	3

	PCT	G	PO	A	E	DP
Marin	.964	115	176	305	18	77
Rosa	.818	4	14	4	4	2
Schoop	.978	14	18	27	1	2

Outfield	PCT	G	PO	A	E	DP
Bierfeldt	.909	8	8	2	1	0
Borbon	.988	106	233	5	3	0
Davis	.995	79	197	13	1	4
Dickerson	.913	10	21	0	2	0
Gonzalez	1.000	19	45	3	0	0
Kim	1.000	1	1	0	0	0
Latimore	.981	94	195	11	4	3
Nathans	1.000	17	30	0	0	0
Paredes	1.000	3	8	0	0	0
Rosa	1.000	12	31	0	0	0
Terdoslavich	.947	10	18	0	1	0
Urrutia	.964	53	102	5	4	0
Yastrzemski	.971	32	63	3	2	0

FREDERICK KEYS
CAROLINA LEAGUE

HIGH CLASS A

Batting	B-T	HT	WT	DOB	AVG	vLH	vRH	G	AB	R	H	2B	3B	HR	RBI	BB	HBP	SH	SF	SO	SB	CS	SLG	OBP
Bierfeldt, Conor	R-R	6-2	220	4-2-91	.264	.317	.239	70	258	45	68	19	0	18	53	25	4	1	2	58	1	2	.547	.336
Bosco, Jimmy	L-R	5-10	170	5-21-91	.194	.000	.250	12	36	4	7	2	0	0	1	2	2	0	0	16	1	0	.250	.275
Caronia, Anthony	L-R	6-0	170	5-22-91	.245	.300	.232	40	102	10	25	2	0	0	3	5	0	2	1	31	3	2	.265	.278
Gold, Tad	L-L	6-1	195	3-1-91	.158	.067	.190	20	57	7	9	3	0	0	4	8	0	0	1	19	2	2	.211	.258
Gonzalez, Jay	L-L	5-9	170	12-11-91	.253	.230	.259	85	289	52	73	16	3	1	30	46	0	5	1	66	41	8	.339	.354
Hart, Josh	L-L	6-1	180	10-2-94	.223	.222	.223	97	337	34	75	17	2	4	31	25	4	3	3	78	9	5	.320	.282
Heim, Jonah	B-R	6-4	205	6-27-95	.216	.241	.207	88	291	30	63	14	1	7	30	33	2	2	1	51	2	0	.344	.300
Joseph, Caleb	R-R	6-3	180	6-18-86	.294	.667	.091	6	17	4	5	1	0	1	5	2	1	0	3	4	0	0	.529	.348
Kapstein, Zach	R-R	6-2	195	5-28-92	.154	.200	.125	8	26	2	4	0	0	0	0	0	0	0	0	8	0	1	.154	.154
Kneeland, Cam	R-R	6-1	195	6-23-90	.245	.191	.266	118	400	56	98	33	2	12	61	49	10	6	4	76	6	2	.428	.339
McClanahan, Jerry	R-R	6-1	200	6-11-92	.000	.000	—	1	3	0	0	0	0	0	0	0	0	0	0	1	0	0	.000	.000
Mercedes, Yermin	R-R	5-11	175	2-14-93	.318	.387	.289	31	107	20	34	6	0	5	17	10	1	0	0	19	0	0	.542	.381
Olesczuk, T.J.	R-R	6-1	205	2-5-92	.210	.222	.205	37	100	6	21	3	0	1	6	2	1	0	25	1	4	.270	.269
Paredes, Jimmy	B-R	6-3	200	11-25-88	.750	1.000	.667	1	4	2	3	1	0	0	1	0	1	0	0	1	0	0	1.000	.800
Perez, Pedro	R-R	5-11	170	5-8-91	—	—	—	1	0	1	0	0	0	0	0	0	0	0	0	0	0	0	—	—
Reyes, Jonah	R-R	6-3	200	2-20-97	.228	.270	.213	126	464	53	106	16	2	10	51	25	4	0	5	102	3	0	.336	.271
Rifaela, Ademar	L-L	5-10	180	11-20-94	.167	.000	.200	5	18	2	3	1	0	1	3	2	0	0	5	1	0	.389	.250
Rodriguez, Aderlin	R-R	6-3	210	11-18-91	.304	.353	.285	130	494	71	150	23	6	26	93	36	8	1	3	112	3	1	.532	.359
Salcedo, Erick	B-R	5-10	155	6-28-93	.270	.263	.274	133	488	66	132	23	8	3	39	36	1	6	4	60	13	9	.369	.319
Sawyer, Wynston	R-R	6-3	205	11-14-91	.281	.237	.296	89	299	35	84	19	1	11	51	63	12	1	4	58	3	4	.462	.421
Stewart, D.J.	L-R	6-0	230	11-30-93	.279	.274	.281	59	201	41	56	12	2	6	30	36	1	1	1	46	10	3	.448	.389
Wilkerson, Steve	B-R	6-1	195	1-11-92	.251	.256	.249	114	402	49	101	17	4	4	36	45	6	6	2	98	18	6	.343	.334
Wynns, Austin	R-R	6-2	205	12-10-90	.303	.377	.286	51	188	23	57	10	0	5	20	21	1	1	2	32	0	0	.436	.351

Pitching	B-T	HT	WT	DOB	W	L	ERA	G	GS	CG	SV	IP	H	R	ER	HR	BB	SO	AVG	vLH	vRH	K/9	BB/9
Belicek, Trevor	L-L	6-3	215	12-10-92	4	5	6.15	20	7	0	0	60	72	49	41	6	24	52	.303	.329	.288	7.80	3.60
Beliveau, Jeff	L-L	6-1	190	1-17-87	4	0	2.40	27	0	0	4	45	24	18	12	2	25	64	.155	.167	.147	12.80	5.00
Burke, Mike	R-R	6-2	200	8-27-92	1	0	1.13	3	0	0	1	8	2	1	1	0	0	10	.077	.133	.000	11.25	0.00
Chleborad, Tanner	R-R	6-6	185	11-4-92	5	3	3.51	32	1	0	2	51	54	21	20	4	14	36	.271	.260	.282	6.31	2.45

Pitching	B-T	HT	WT	DOB	W	L	ERA	G	GS	CG	SV	IP	H	R	ER	HR	BB	SO	AVG	vLH	vRH	K/9	BB/9
Cleavinger, Garrett	L-L	6-1	210	4-23-94	2	3	4.82	20	0	0	0	37	35	21	20	2	23	49	.255	.268	.250	11.81	5.54
Cortright, Garrett	R-R	6-5	210	10-2-91	0	0	2.19	15	0	0	8	25	21	6	6	1	4	19	.239	.310	.174	6.93	1.46
Gallardo, Yovani	R-R	6-2	205	2-27-86	0	0	9.00	1	1	0	0	3	7	3	3	0	2	4	.467	.667	.167	12.00	6.00
Gausman, Kevin	R-R	6-3	190	1-6-91	0	1	2.70	1	1	0	0	3	4	2	1	0	2	8	.267	.300	.200	21.60	5.40
Gonzalez, Luis	L-L	6-2	170	1-17-92	1	2	3.13	13	0	0	2	32	21	11	11	4	8	43	.191	.270	.151	12.22	2.27
Grimes, Matt	R-R	6-5	185	9-4-91	8	4	1.45	14	13	0	0	81	69	20	13	3	16	54	.233	.237	.229	6.02	1.79
Hernandez, Ivan	R-R	6-2	249	7-28-91	3	2	3.67	28	1	0	1	61	66	27	25	3	20	37	.278	.305	.258	5.43	2.93
Horacek, Mitch	L-L	6-5	185	12-3-91	5	11	4.59	27	27	3	0	133	172	83	68	13	45	110	.311	.267	.325	7.43	3.04
Jones, Cory	R-R	6-5	225	9-20-91	2	4	3.79	14	12	0	0	57	60	27	24	7	16	54	.274	.301	.233	8.53	2.53
Keller, Jon	R-R	6-5	210	8-8-92	0	3	2.93	7	7	0	0	28	15	15	9	1	24	27	.152	.109	.205	8.78	7.81
Long, Lucas	R-R	6-0	195	10-7-92	7	7	4.27	24	24	0	0	129	149	77	61	17	31	112	.290	.278	.300	7.83	2.17
Matusz, Brian	L-L	6-5	190	2-11-87	0	0	1.29	2	0	0	0	7	3	1	1	1	0	12	.120	.333	.053	15.43	0.00
McFarland, T.J.	L-L	6-3	220	6-8-89	0	0	19.29	2	2	0	0	2	7	5	5	2	1	4	.500	.000	.636	15.43	3.86
Means, John	L-L	6-3	195	4-24-93	5	0	1.80	9	9	1	0	50	43	11	10	1	10	54	.228	.277	.211	9.72	1.80
Meisinger, Ryan	R-R	6-4	235	5-4-94	3	2	2.25	19	0	0	1	40	34	15	10	3	12	46	.233	.186	.276	10.35	2.70
Reyes, Genison	R-R	6-5	190	9-19-91	2	2	6.32	10	0	0	0	16	24	14	11	3	6	11	.369	.387	.353	6.32	3.45
Richardson, David	R-R	5-11	170	1-31-91	4	6	4.13	21	13	0	0	81	89	42	37	4	27	70	.285	.297	.274	7.81	3.01
Romero, Franderlyn	R-R	6-1	190	2-21-93	6	4	6.16	16	16	0	0	76	96	56	52	16	22	54	.307	.244	.376	6.39	2.61
Schuh, Max	L-L	6-4	210	3-13-92	0	3	9.95	14	2	0	0	19	28	26	21	2	17	21	.354	.231	.415	9.95	8.05
Scott, Tanner	R-L	6-2	220	7-22-94	4	2	4.47	29	0	0	5	48	22	33	24	1	42	63	.133	.145	.126	11.73	7.82
Smith, Chipper	L-L	6-2	195	1-22-90	0	1	7.27	2	2	0	0	9	8	7	7	2	6	14	.235	.444	.160	14.54	6.23
Urban, Austin	L-R	6-1	185	7-8-92	2	4	5.30	22	1	0	0	36	34	24	21	3	26	25	.246	.242	.250	6.31	6.56
Worley, Vance	R-R	6-2	250	9-25-87	0	0	0.00	1	1	0	0	3	0	0	0	0	0	2	.000	.000	.000	6.00	0.00
Yacabonis, Jimmy	R-R	6-3	205	3-21-92	0	2	3.98	16	0	0	5	20	17	9	9	2	6	21	.227	.250	.209	9.30	2.66
Zouzalik, Michael	L-R	6-3	195	7-13-90	0	1	3.95	29	0	0	11	41	38	21	18	5	11	39	.239	.299	.196	8.56	2.41

Fielding

Catcher	PCT	G	PO	A	E	DP	PB
Heim	.988	72	602	55	8	5	11
Joseph	1.000	3	18	2	0	0	0
McClanahan	1.000	1	6	0	0	0	1
Mercedes	1.000	8	76	10	0	1	1
Sawyer	.994	22	142	18	1	1	6
Wynns	.997	36	257	48	1	4	4

First Base	PCT	G	PO	A	E	DP
Kneeland	.995	32	191	17	1	19
Rodriguez	.985	102	814	49	13	75
Sawyer	.980	16	136	10	3	12

Second Base	PCT	G	PO	A	E	DP
Caronia	.933	14	22	34	4	9

	PCT	G	PO	A	E	DP
Kneeland	.988	16	30	49	1	13
Wilkerson	.975	112	202	298	13	70

Third Base	PCT	G	PO	A	E	DP
Caronia	1.000	1	0	1	0	0
Kneeland	1.000	2	3	7	0	0
Reyes	.914	122	72	195	25	19
Rodriguez	.929	17	7	32	3	4

Shortstop	PCT	G	PO	A	E	DP
Caronia	.907	13	15	24	4	0
Kneeland	.833	1	2	3	1	0
Salcedo	.962	131	208	374	23	88
Wilkerson	.900	1	2	7	1	2

Outfield	PCT	G	PO	A	E	DP
Bierfeldt	.949	65	84	10	5	0
Bosco	1.000	11	13	1	0	0
Caronia	1.000	2	4	0	0	0
Gold	1.000	19	30	1	0	0
Gonzalez	.976	85	163	2	4	0
Hart	.986	96	201	3	3	1
Kapstein	.857	5	6	0	1	0
Kneeland	.971	68	92	7	3	3
Mercedes	1.000	3	1	0	0	0
Olesczuk	1.000	34	52	1	0	0
Paredes	1.000	1	1	0	0	0
Rifaela	1.000	4	6	0	0	0
Rodriguez	1.000	2	1	0	0	0
Stewart	.948	52	89	2	5	0

DELMARVA SHOREBIRDS
SOUTH ATLANTIC LEAGUE

LOW CLASS A

Batting	B-T	HT	WT	DOB	AVG	vLH	vRH	G	AB	R	H	2B	3B	HR	RBI	BB	HBP	SH	SF	SO	SB	CS	SLG	OBP
Anderson, Austin	L-R	5-11	190	6-18-92	.249	.245	.250	53	189	17	47	7	2	4	21	13	3	1	0	39	2	0	.370	.307
Andujar, Ricardo	B-R	6-0	160	8-6-92	.251	.253	.250	101	383	40	96	11	3	3	24	25	3	3	1	76	16	10	.319	.301
Coluccio, Brandon	R-R	6-0	200	8-15-92	.000	—	.000	1	1	0	0	0	0	0	0	1	0	0	0	1	0	0	.000	.500
Delgado, Natanael	L-L	6-1	170	10-23-95	.250	.203	.263	88	320	34	80	16	0	8	36	27	0	0	4	100	2	1	.375	.305
Gassaway, Randolph	R-R	6-4	210	5-23-95	.330	.333	.329	50	182	21	60	12	0	7	17	13	0	0	1	36	2	0	.511	.372
Graham, Jack	R-R	5-9	190	9-10-92	.111	.091	.125	10	27	1	3	0	0	0	1	6	1	0	0	10	0	0	.111	.294
Grim, Gerrion	R-R	6-2	190	9-17-93	.193	.209	.186	69	223	20	43	11	1	5	25	18	2	0	3	94	2	0	.318	.256
Juvier, Alejandro	L-R	6-1	180	1-20-96	.198	.212	.192	30	111	8	22	2	1	0	5	8	0	0	0	34	2	0	.234	.252
Laurino, Steve	R-R	6-3	215	1-5-93	.188	.213	.180	98	330	33	62	14	0	4	25	42	4	0	2	84	0	1	.267	.286
Ledesma, Ronarsy	R-R	5-11	170	4-19-93	.200	.300	.178	17	55	11	11	3	0	1	3	3	2	0	0	25	0	0	.309	.267
Levy, Stuart	R-R	6-1	185	8-21-92	.195	.158	.206	28	87	10	17	4	0	6	17	5	0	0	24	2	1	.379	.358
Mercedes, Yermin	R-R	5-11	175	2-14-93	.353	.389	.340	91	340	58	120	25	5	14	60	34	3	0	5	63	1	1	.579	.411
Mountcastle, Ryan	R-R	6-3	195	2-18-97	.281	.379	.248	115	455	53	128	28	4	10	51	25	3	0	6	95	5	4	.426	.319
Mullins, Cedric	B-L	5-8	175	10-1-94	.273	.217	.290	124	517	79	141	37	10	14	55	37	1	1	3	101	30	6	.464	.321
Murphy, Alex	R-R	5-11	210	10-9-94	.252	.261	.249	124	456	54	115	28	1	16	63	49	9	0	2	138	0	0	.423	.335
Rifaela, Ademar	L-L	5-10	180	11-20-94	.239	.183	.254	92	343	41	82	14	6	12	45	27	2	1	2	97	2	3	.420	.297
Ring, Jake	L-L	5-11	175	8-11-94	.167	—	.167	3	12	2	2	1	0	0	1	0	0	0	0	3	0	0	.250	.167
Salas, Guillermo	B-R	6-0	175	4-21-94	.267	.400	.240	9	30	3	8	1	0	0	5	1	0	1	0	4	0	0	.300	.290
Stewart, D.J.	L-R	6-0	230	11-30-93	.230	.185	.245	62	213	27	49	12	1	4	25	42	5	0	2	58	16	6	.352	.366
Turbin, Drew	L-R	5-11	200	4-24-93	.211	.274	.196	100	317	36	67	10	2	6	31	39	9	2	2	90	2	2	.312	.313

Pitching	B-T	HT	WT	DOB	W	L	ERA	G	GS	CG	SV	IP	H	R	ER	HR	BB	SO	AVG	vLH	vRH	K/9	BB/9
Alvarado, Cristian	R-R	6-3	175	9-20-94	10	9	3.41	27	27	1	0	148	143	62	56	11	29	148	.250	.262	.241	9.00	1.76
Baker, Patrick	R-R	6-3	215	8-15-93	2	2	3.15	18	0	0	2	40	36	19	14	1	21	45	.243	.227	.256	10.13	4.73
Bray, Ryan	R-R	6-5	185	12-8-92	1	0	1.86	13	0	0	2	19	13	4	4	1	5	22	.194	.037	.300	10.24	2.33
Burke, Mike	R-R	6-2	200	8-27-92	0	3	4.31	21	0	0	3	40	42	21	19	4	8	46	.271	.177	.333	10.44	1.82
Cleavinger, Garrett	L-L	6-1	210	4-23-94	5	0	1.38	17	0	0	4	39	25	8	6	3	11	53	.185	.184	.186	12.23	2.54

Pitching

Pitching	B-T	HT	WT	DOB	W	L	ERA	G	GS	CG	SV	IP	H	R	ER	HR	BB	SO	AVG	vLH	vRH	K/9	BB/9
Costello, Mike	R-R	6-5	215	7-10-92	1	3	5.64	15	7	0	0	53	63	41	33	9	8	44	.290	.333	.262	7.52	1.37
Delgado, Dariel	R-R	5-11	185	8-24-93	2	0	3.10	10	2	0	0	29	27	10	10	0	11	26	.252	.349	.188	8.07	3.41
Flaa, Jay	R-R	6-3	225	6-10-92	5	1	3.50	28	0	0	2	46	41	21	18	4	21	50	.240	.266	.224	9.71	4.08
Gonzalez, Brian	R-L	6-3	230	10-25-95	10	8	2.50	27	27	0	0	148	135	52	41	9	58	111	.247	.193	.267	6.77	3.53
Jimenez, Francisco	R-R	6-1	160	10-4-94	9	9	4.27	26	20	1	0	129	117	67	61	11	45	96	.246	.230	.259	6.72	3.15
Jones, Cory	R-R	6-5	225	9-20-91	0	1	1.00	2	2	0	0	9	7	2	1	0	0	9	.226	.250	.200	9.00	0.00
Klimek, Steven	L-R	6-3	205	4-4-94	0	1	6.10	5	0	0	0	10	14	8	7	1	2	6	.326	.400	.286	5.23	1.74
Liranzo, Jesus	R-R	6-2	175	3-7-95	0	0	1.05	16	0	0	0	34	12	5	4	0	15	46	.109	.167	.074	12.06	3.93
Long, Lucas	R-R	6-0	195	10-7-92	0	0	0.50	3	3	0	0	18	10	1	1	0	1	17	.159	.261	.100	8.50	0.50
Love, Reid	R-L	5-11	195	5-15-92	9	10	3.29	27	25	0	0	139	134	63	51	11	33	106	.254	.221	.266	6.85	2.13
Meisinger, Ryan	R-R	6-4	235	5-4-94	3	2	0.78	16	0	0	4	35	24	4	3	0	9	48	.189	.268	.151	12.46	2.34
Peluffo, Jhon	R-R	6-3	140	6-16-97	0	3	13.50	3	3	0	0	11	21	23	16	4	8	1	.396	.375	.414	0.84	6.75
Peralta, Ofelky	R-R	6-5	195	4-20-97	8	5	4.01	23	23	1	0	103	87	53	46	3	60	101	.230	.237	.225	8.80	5.23
Pinales, Elias	L-L	6-4	155	11-7-92	4	2	2.03	16	0	0	0	31	37	14	7	0	10	24	.289	.333	.270	6.97	2.90
Rutledge, Lex	L-L	6-1	195	6-28-91	0	1	2.12	18	0	0	6	30	18	9	7	0	7	18	.175	.152	.186	5.46	2.12
Strader, Robert	R-L	6-5	225	3-15-94	1	2	5.09	24	0	0	2	41	42	26	23	0	30	23	.273	.137	.340	5.09	6.64
Turnipseed, Christian	R-R	5-11	214	5-30-92	3	4	3.12	40	0	0	17	52	40	21	18	4	25	57	.212	.258	.187	9.87	4.33

Fielding

Catcher	PCT	G	PO	A	E	DP	PB
Coluccio	1.000	1	2	0	0	0	0
Levy	.974	28	193	31	6	1	1
Mercedes	.989	54	481	66	6	1	23
Murphy	.984	57	379	50	7	4	12

First Base	PCT	G	PO	A	E	DP
Anderson	1.000	1	11	0	0	2
Laurino	.993	96	800	54	6	68
Murphy	.994	42	332	17	2	27

Second Base	PCT	G	PO	A	E	DP
Anderson	—	1	0	0	0	0

Third Base	PCT	G	PO	A	E	DP
Anderson	.959	51	29	89	5	10
Andujar	.916	43	21	77	9	10
Juvier	.956	30	17	48	3	4
Ledesma	.923	15	9	27	3	0
Turbin	.667	1	2	0	1	0

Andujar	.972	26	41	65	3	16
Graham	.951	9	15	24	2	3
Salas	.949	7	20	17	2	2
Turbin	.983	99	180	290	8	55

Shortstop	PCT	G	PO	A	E	DP
Andujar	.939	34	45	78	8	10
Mountcastle	.949	105	165	225	21	54
Salas	.833	2	0	5	1	0

Outfield	PCT	G	PO	A	E	DP
Delgado	.951	46	70	7	4	1
Gassaway	.977	44	85	1	2	1
Grim	.968	66	119	3	4	0
Mullins	.987	122	287	7	4	3
Rifaela	.977	84	155	12	4	3
Ring	.938	3	15	0	1	0
Stewart	.971	58	98	2	3	0

ABERDEEN IRONBIRDS
NEW YORK-PENN LEAGUE
SHORT-SEASON

Batting

Batting	B-T	HT	WT	DOB	AVG	vLH	vRH	G	AB	R	H	2B	3B	HR	RBI	BB	HBP	SH	SF	SO	SB	CS	SLG	OBP
Billingsley, Cole	L-L	5-10	165	5-29-94	.286	.256	.295	53	192	25	55	6	1	3	15	20	1	2	2	39	14	1	.375	.353
Clare, Chris	R-R	6-2	175	11-24-94	.242	.225	.248	47	153	20	37	7	0	2	14	20	5	1	2	35	2	2	.327	.344
Crinella, Frank	R-R	5-11	188	6-9-94	.192	.400	.170	17	52	6	10	1	1	0	1	5	0	0	0	17	0	1	.250	.263
Curran, Seamus	L-R	6-6	245	9-6-97	.080	.000	.095	9	25	2	2	0	0	0	0	4	0	0	0	1	1	0	.080	.207
Diaz, Carlos	L-L	6-2	220	12-16-96	.250	—	.250	1	4	0	1	0	0	0	0	0	0	0	0	1	0	0	.250	.250
Fajardo, Daniel	R-R	6-1	170	11-19-94	.200	.167	.214	25	80	6	16	3	0	2	7	0	0	1	0	22	0	0	.313	.200
Ferguson, Jaylen	R-R	6-2	180	7-21-97	.183	.154	.190	53	186	14	34	9	0	2	13	12	1	1	3	62	4	1	.263	.233
Franco, Daniel	R-R	6-0	165	10-31-94	.000	—	.000	1	3	0	0	0	0	0	0	0	0	0	0	0	0	0	.000	.000
Gassaway, Randolph	R-R	6-4	210	5-23-95	.444	.000	.471	5	18	1	8	4	1	0	4	2	0	0	0	4	0	1	.778	.500
Gonzalez, Alfredo	R-R	6-0	165	12-14-95	.000	—	.000	1	3	0	0	0	0	0	0	0	0	0	0	0	0	0	.000	.000
Hays, Austin	R-R	6-1	195	7-5-95	.336	.343	.333	38	140	14	47	9	2	4	21	11	1	0	1	32	4	3	.514	.386
Heinrich, Jason	R-R	6-1	205	6-7-96	.231	.200	.239	44	147	16	34	8	0	3	13	13	2	0	1	40	1	2	.347	.301
Juvier, Alejandro	L-R	6-1	180	1-20-96	.228	.238	.226	58	219	26	50	9	0	3	28	13	2	2	2	59	8	2	.311	.275
Kemp, Jeff	R-R	6-0	190	3-23-90	.071	.667	.000	8	28	1	2	1	0	0	1	1	1	0	0	5	0	0	.107	.133
Ledesma, Ronarsy	R-R	5-11	170	4-19-93	.223	.240	.217	28	94	4	21	4	1	0	10	10	2	0	0	31	1	0	.287	.311
Levy, Stuart	R-R	6-2	185	8-21-92	.206	.267	.189	22	68	7	14	3	2	0	7	8	3	0	0	18	0	1	.309	.316
McClanahan, Jerry	R-R	6-1	200	6-11-92	.197	.118	.224	24	66	3	13	0	0	1	11	3	0	0	0	17	0	1	.197	.338
McKenna, Ryan	R-R	5-11	185	2-14-97	.241	.214	.247	62	220	29	53	10	1	1	26	22	5	2	3	59	17	6	.309	.320
Moesquit, Kirvin	B-R	5-8	165	3-10-95	.250	.239	.254	53	188	33	47	5	3	0	10	21	3	1	2	47	12	2	.309	.332
Nathans, Tucker	L-R	6-0	200	11-6-88	.211	.000	.235	5	19	2	4	2	0	1	3	2	0	0	0	7	0	0	.474	.286
Odenwaelder, Mike	R-R	6-5	225	9-18-92	.205	.182	.214	26	78	4	16	4	0	2	8	1	1	0	1	24	1	0	.333	.222
Ortega, Irving	R-R	6-2	165	10-30-96	.207	.286	.182	8	29	1	6	1	0	0	3	0	0	0	0	6	1	1	.241	.281
Palmeiro, Preston	L-R	5-11	180	1-22-95	.258	.313	.240	34	128	13	33	6	1	0	8	0	0	0	0	36	2	2	.320	.301
Salas, Guillermo	B-R	6-0	175	4-21-94	.232	.190	.246	26	82	7	19	2	0	0	5	4	0	1	1	24	0	0	.256	.264
Shaw, Chris	R-R	6-0	165	4-25-94	.133	.176	.121	23	75	3	10	2	0	2	8	3	1	0	0	30	0	1	.240	.177
Soto, Ronald	R-R	6-4	220	10-5-94	.200	.000	.214	6	15	2	3	1	0	1	2	0	0	0	0	4	0	0	.467	.294
Woody, Collin	R-R	6-1	210	8-5-94	.126	.095	.136	34	87	6	11	2	0	1	3	7	5	1	0	29	0	1	.184	.232

Pitching

Pitching	B-T	HT	WT	DOB	W	L	ERA	G	GS	CG	SV	IP	H	R	ER	HR	BB	SO	AVG	vLH	vRH	K/9	BB/9
Akin, Keegan	L-L	6-0	225	4-1-95	0	1	1.04	9	9	0	0	26	15	4	3	0	7	29	.161	.129	.177	10.04	2.42
Ayers, Danny	L-L	6-3	210	3-24-95	1	1	4.57	16	0	0	1	22	25	16	11	0	11	15	.281	.310	.267	6.23	4.57
Borde, Xavier	L-L	6-2	225	4-12-93	2	1	3.67	15	0	0	0	34	42	16	14	4	18	29	.307	.341	.292	7.60	4.72
Bray, Jake	R-R	6-1	185	12-8-92	0	1	5.06	8	0	0	2	11	14	6	6	2	1	7	.333	.231	.379	5.91	0.84
Bridwell, Parker	R-R	6-4	185	8-2-91	1	1	5.40	2	0	0	0	5	2	3	3	1	0	4	.118	.125	.111	7.20	0.00
Brown, Lucas	R-R	6-0	185	11-11-93	0	2	9.00	7	0	0	0	9	15	10	9	1	5	3	.405	.450	.353	3.00	5.00
Burke, Mike	R-R	6-2	200	8-27-92	0	0	0.00	2	0	0	1	4	3	0	0	0	4	.200	.333	.167	8.31	0.00
Cortright, Garrett	R-R	6-5	210	10-2-91	0	0	2.70	8	0	0	1	13	12	5	4	1	0	11	.250	.278	.233	7.43	0.00

BALTIMORE ORIOLES

Pitching	B-T	HT	WT	DOB	W	L	ERA	G	GS	CG	SV	IP	H	R	ER	HR	BB	SO	AVG	vLH	vRH	K/9	BB/9
Delgado, Dariel	R-R	5-11	185	8-24-93	1	0	2.25	3	0	0	0	12	8	3	3	0	2	7	.205	.176	.227	5.25	1.50
Dietz, Matthias	R-R	6-5	220	9-20-95	0	3	4.82	7	7	0	0	19	22	14	10	0	10	8	.306	.375	.250	3.86	4.82
Dube, Cody	R-R	6-1	198	10-21-94	3	1	2.54	11	4	0	0	28	23	8	8	0	8	20	.219	.216	.222	6.35	2.54
Elliot, Andrew	R-R	6-0	200	2-4-92	0	3	3.90	20	0	0	3	30	24	16	13	2	11	29	.222	.231	.217	8.70	3.30
Erwin, Tyler	L-L	6-0	185	8-29-94	2	1	3.22	13	0	0	0	22	20	10	8	0	11	21	.244	.192	.268	8.46	4.43
Harvey, Hunter	R-R	6-3	175	12-9-94	0	1	3.52	3	3	0	0	8	9	5	3	0	6	7	.310	.417	.235	8.22	7.04
Humpal, Lucas	R-R	6-3	180	9-5-93	1	2	3.34	11	10	0	0	30	30	12	11	0	9	27	.270	.292	.254	8.19	2.73
Johnson, Joe	R-R	6-3	175	5-24-94	0	0	0.00	2	0	0	0	3	0	0	0	0	0	3	.000	.000	.000	10.13	0.00
Klimek, Steven	L-R	6-3	205	4-4-94	2	3	2.68	12	1	0	1	37	29	13	11	2	11	27	.213	.189	.229	6.57	2.68
Knutson, Max	L-L	6-2	205	4-1-95	0	1	3.60	16	0	0	1	30	26	14	12	2	16	25	.232	.250	.225	7.50	4.80
Lin, Yi-Hsiang	L-L	6-0	175	12-16-92	4	0	2.57	14	0	0	0	28	17	8	8	1	6	18	.168	.182	.162	5.79	1.93
Moseley, Ryan	R-R	6-3	190	10-6-94	0	1	3.20	12	0	0	4	20	13	7	7	1	9	18	.191	.091	.239	8.24	4.12
Muckenhirn, Zach	L-L	6-1	185	2-27-95	5	2	2.43	12	3	0	0	33	38	10	9	2	3	34	.299	.217	.346	9.18	0.81
Seabrooke, Travis	L-L	6-6	205	9-16-95	2	7	3.53	13	13	0	0	66	67	34	26	5	19	33	.269	.259	.274	4.48	2.58
Sedlock, Cody	R-R	6-3	190	6-19-95	0	1	3.00	9	9	0	0	27	16	11	9	1	13	25	.158	.170	.148	8.33	4.33
Shepley, Will	R-L	6-1	190	5-17-93	1	2	3.97	18	0	0	0	23	20	12	10	0	21	26	.241	.143	.291	10.32	8.34
Strader, Robert	R-S	6-5	225	3-15-94	0	1	9.00	1	1	0	0	2	3	3	2	0	2	0	.429	.333	.500	0.00	9.00
Teague, James	R-R	6-0	185	8-29-94	1	0	3.29	9	0	0	2	14	14	5	5	0	5	12	.269	.261	.276	7.90	3.29
Tolliver, Ashur	L-L	6-0	170	1-24-88	0	0	0.00	2	0	0	0	3	2	0	0	0	0	5	.182	.500	.000	15.00	0.00
Vespi, Nick	L-L	6-3	215	10-10-95	1	0	0.00	1	0	0	0	2	2	0	0	0	3	0	.250	.000	.333	0.00	11.57
Wells, Alex	L-L	6-1	190	2-27-97	4	5	2.15	13	13	0	0	63	48	17	15	1	9	50	.216	.194	.225	7.18	1.29
Yoon, Jeong-Hyeon	L-L	6-2	220	5-17-93	1	2	6.75	6	2	0	0	17	27	15	13	2	3	11	.351	.440	.308	5.71	1.56

Fielding

C: Fajardo 24, Gonzalez 1, Levy 17, McClanahan 20, Shaw 16, Soto 4. **1B:** Curran 7, Diaz 1, Ledesma 23, Palmeiro 31, Woody 15. **2B:** Juvier 56, Kemp 2, Moesquit 12, Salas 7. **3B:** Clare 5, Crinella 17, Moesquit 42, Woody 16. **SS:** Clare 41, Juvier 2, Kemp 6, Ortega 8, Salas 19. **OF:** Billingsley 46, Ferguson 48, Franco 1, Gassaway 2, Hays 26, Heinrich 27, McKenna 57, Odenwaelder 20.

GCL ORIOLES   *ROOKIE*
GULF COAST LEAGUE

Batting	B-T	HT	WT	DOB	AVG	vLH	vRH	G	AB	R	H	2B	3B	HR	RBI	BB	HBP	SH	SF	SO	SB	CS	SLG	OBP
Becker, Branden	L-R	6-1	175	9-13-96	.226	.148	.247	37	124	10	28	4	0	0	7	4	2	0	1	22	0	2	.258	.260
Blanco, Hernys	R-R	5-10	175	10-7-94	.133	.250	.000	7	15	2	2	1	0	0	0	4	1	0	0	6	0	0	.200	.350
Carrillo, Jean	R-R	6-0	200	6-16-97	.216	.208	.219	30	97	7	21	4	1	1	16	3	1	0	0	9	0	0	.309	.248
Copeland, Garrett	L-L	5-11	190	2-22-95	.227	.237	.223	44	141	27	32	7	0	1	14	22	4	1	3	34	4	2	.298	.341
Curran, Seamus	L-R	6-6	245	9-6-97	.283	.277	.286	43	145	22	41	9	1	5	30	20	2	0	0	33	0	1	.462	.377
Davis, Glynn	R-R	6-3	170	12-7-91	.200	.000	.238	6	25	1	5	0	0	1	5	1	0	0	0	7	1	0	.320	.231
Diaz, Carlos	L-L	6-2	220	12-16-96	.213	.194	.219	38	127	10	27	2	0	2	25	9	2	0	2	31	0	1	.276	.271
Estrada, Jaime	L-R	5-10	170	12-15-94	.250	.200	.260	30	92	16	23	6	0	4	14	0	1	0	19	0	0	.315	.349
Franco, Daniel	R-R	6-0	165	10-31-94	.274	.217	.308	17	62	10	17	4	0	0	5	6	0	1	1	11	2	2	.339	.333
Gonzalez, Alfredo	R-R	6-0	165	12-14-95	.265	.273	.263	18	49	7	13	1	0	0	6	1	0	0	1	3	1	0	.286	.275
Graham, Tristan	R-R	6-4	215	7-21-95	.230	.230	.230	54	196	22	45	8	1	1	26	13	5	0	1	60	4	2	.296	.293
Hernandez, Luis	R-R	6-2	175	5-13-98	.120	.000	.143	14	25	2	3	0	0	0	1	0	0	0	0	2	0	0	.120	.154
Jones, Markel	B-R	5-10	175	8-8-94	.187	.206	.180	39	134	21	25	6	1	0	6	18	0	0	0	41	6	6	.246	.283
Kirk, Tanner	R-R	5-11	183	8-14-93	.245	.250	.242	34	106	13	26	7	1	2	15	9	0	1	2	20	3	1	.387	.299
Ortega, Irving	R-R	6-2	165	10-30-96	.269	.342	.240	40	134	25	36	7	1	0	12	11	2	1	0	25	4	0	.336	.333
Ring, Jake	L-L	5-11	175	8-11-94	.278	.325	.264	51	169	24	47	8	1	0	21	22	3	3	3	45	15	3	.337	.365
Soto, Ronald	R-R	6-4	220	10-5-94	.180	.189	.173	25	89	6	16	3	0	2	8	2	2	0	1	28	0	0	.281	.213
Torres, Alexis	R-R	6-0	183	12-17-97	.183	.133	.200	37	115	14	21	5	0	1	12	15	3	0	0	30	3	1	.252	.293
Vizcaino, Fabian	R-R	5-11	178	5-27-95	.000	.000	.000	1	1	0	0	0	0	0	0	0	0	0	0	0	0	0	.000	.000
Xu, Gui Yuan	L-L	6-0	188	1-29-96	.247	.500	.211	33	81	11	20	3	0	0	9	2	1	0	1	20	2	1	.284	.271

Pitching	B-T	HT	WT	DOB	W	L	ERA	G	GS	CG	SV	IP	H	R	ER	HR	BB	SO	AVG	vLH	vRH	K/9	BB/9
Bridwell, Parker	R-R	6-4	185	8-2-91	2	0	0.00	3	0	0	0	6	3	0	0	0	3	7	.150	.125	.167	10.50	4.50
Brown, Lucas	R-R	6-0	185	11-11-93	0	1	2.60	4	3	0	0	17	18	6	5	2	1	15	.254	.222	.217	7.79	0.52
Bruner, Layne	L-L	6-3	175	9-24-94	1	4	2.38	13	10	0	0	45	40	17	12	1	19	47	.240	.286	.230	9.33	3.77
De La Rosa, Matt	L-R	6-2	210	11-15-93	1	0	2.49	16	0	0	0	22	22	10	6	1	15	22	.247	.219	.263	9.14	6.23
Deduno, Sam	R-R	6-3	210	7-2-83	3	1	1.50	10	1	0	0	18	8	4	3	1	3	23	.129	.226	.032	11.50	1.50
Dennis, Will	L-R	6-2	195	8-9-93	1	0	1.29	4	0	0	2	7	8	1	1	0	3	9	.267	.111	.333	11.57	3.86
Duensing, Brian	L-L	6-0	200	2-22-83	0	0	0.00	2	0	0	0	2	2	0	0	0	0	2	.286	.500	.000	9.00	0.00
Echevarria, Juan	R-R	6-3	195	6-25-97	2	2	2.86	13	0	0	0	22	14	10	7	3	6	23	.173	.130	.229	9.41	2.45
Garcia, Ruben	R-R	6-4	220	8-2-96	0	1	1.76	11	0	0	0	15	5	4	3	0	4	21	.100	.136	.071	12.33	2.35
Harvey, Hunter	R-R	6-3	175	12-9-94	0	0	0.00	2	2	0	0	5	3	0	0	0	0	11	.167	.300	.000	19.80	0.00
Jobst, Nick	R-R	6-2	260	10-14-93	0	0	3.54	18	0	0	0	20	13	8	8	0	17	30	.191	.097	.270	13.28	7.52
Johnson, Joe	R-R	6-3	175	5-24-94	2	1	2.96	18	0	0	4	24	17	8	8	2	9	32	.193	.167	.217	11.84	3.33
Marrugo, Yeizer	R-R	6-0	170	10-1-94	3	2	3.22	15	4	0	2	50	52	32	18	1	23	36	.271	.306	.234	6.44	4.11
Matson, Zach	L-L	6-3	225	10-24-95	0	4	2.97	17	0	0	0	30	32	21	10	2	13	29	.267	.306	.250	8.60	3.86
McCord, Rocky	R-R	6-2	170	11-16-92	0	1	4.63	12	0	0	0	23	25	16	12	0	8	17	.260	.300	.232	6.56	3.09
McFarland, T.J.	L-L	6-3	220	6-8-89	0	0	0.00	1	0	0	0	1	0	0	0	0	1	1	.000	.000	.000	9.00	9.00
McGranahan, Zeke	R-R	6-4	215	1-3-91	1	1	7.36	8	0	0	0	7	8	6	6	0	5	10	.276	.182	.333	12.27	6.14
Myers, Tobias	R-R	6-0	193	8-5-98	0	0	4.70	3	3	0	0	8	10	5	4	1	2	4	.303	.353	.250	4.70	2.35
Negrette, Alirio	L-L	6-0	210	3-29-95	0	3	3.94	4	4	0	0	16	15	8	7	0	5	13	.242	.235	.244	7.31	2.81
Peluffo, Jhon	R-R	6-3	140	6-16-97	3	0	1.89	8	8	0	0	38	26	9	8	0	7	40	.190	.194	.186	9.47	1.66

Pitching	B-T	HT	WT	DOB	W	L	ERA	G	GS	CG	SV	IP	H	R	ER	HR	BB	SO	AVG	vLH	vRH	K/9	BB/9
Ramirez, Victor	R-R	6-2	185	5-12-95	0	0	2.84	5	0	0	0	6	7	2	2	0	0	5	.280	.214	.364	7.11	0.00
Rios, Willie	B-L	5-11	190	2-6-96	0	5	12.41	7	7	0	0	12	18	21	17	3	11	11	.353	.250	.400	8.03	8.03
Rodriguez, Yelin	L-L	6-3	200	11-3-98	0	3	4.18	10	6	0	0	28	25	14	13	3	18	27	.253	.375	.194	8.68	5.79
Romero, Victor	R-R	6-3	170	2-17-95	0	0	1.50	2	0	0	0	6	6	1	1	0	1	5	.273	.300	.250	7.50	1.50
Rutledge, Lex	L-L	6-1	195	6-28-91	1	1	7.36	3	0	0	0	4	1	3	3	0	2	5	.091	.143	.000	12.27	4.91
Teague, James	R-R	6-0	185	8-29-94	3	1	2.50	11	0	0	1	18	13	7	5	0	6	19	.191	.160	.209	9.50	3.00
Trowbridge, Matt	L-L	5-10	175	3-24-93	0	0	13.50	2	0	0	0	1	4	2	2	0	1	2	.500	.333	.600	13.50	6.75
Vespi, Nick	L-L	6-3	215	10-10-95	4	1	1.97	12	10	0	0	50	46	18	11	2	8	41	.256	.220	.269	7.33	1.43

Fielding

C: Carrillo 28, Gonzalez 18, Soto 20, Vizcaino 1. **1B:** Copeland 1, Curran 37, Diaz 22, Xu 7. **2B:** Copeland 31, Estrada 11, Hernandez 2, Kirk 2, Torres 19. **3B:** Becker 33, Copeland 9, Estrada 9, Kirk 12. **SS:** Becker 2, Hernandez 6, Ortega 39, Torres 18. **OF:** Blanco 7, Davis 4, Franco 16, Graham 53, Jones 38, Kirk 12, Ring 50, Xu 5.

DSL ORIOLES
DOMINICAN SUMMER LEAGUE

ROOKIE

Batting	B-T	HT	WT	DOB	AVG	vLH	vRH	G	AB	R	H	2B	3B	HR	RBI	BB	HBP	SH	SF	SO	SB	CS	SLG	OBP
Acosta, Rauel	R-R	6-4	210	12-23-95	.275	.247	.288	66	229	28	63	11	2	3	23	34	0	0	2	40	0	1	.380	.366
Adames, Angel	R-R	6-0	179	5-22-96	.178	.286	.161	33	107	12	19	5	1	1	11	13	2	3	1	23	2	0	.271	.276
Alvarado, Jean	R-R	5-10	170	7-9-98	.094	.000	.119	29	53	2	5	0	0	0	2	5	1	0	0	18	1	0	.094	.186
Ayala, Fernando	R-R	5-10	175	3-31-97	.236	.429	.171	20	55	7	13	0	0	0	2	7	6	0	0	12	0	1	.236	.382
Barcenas, Richard	R-R	6-1	165	10-22-97	.228	—	—	45	162	15	37	3	3	1	17	11	1	0	0	38	2	1	.302	.282
Baez, Carlos	R-R	6-3	175	11-22-97	.207	.194	.209	62	208	25	43	7	2	0	14	14	8	2	2	46	2	1	.260	.282
Briceno, Kipper	R-R	6-1	160	1-14-97	.106	.000	.109	21	47	3	5	0	0	0	0	3	3	0	0	16	0	1	.106	.208
Chaves, Luis	R-R	6-2	190	11-26-94	.175	.267	.130	43	137	10	24	7	1	0	9	7	1	1	2	41	0	1	.241	.218
Ciriaco, Bryan	R-R	6-1	185	3-29-97	.172	.217	.158	30	99	11	17	4	1	0	8	3	1	2	3	31	1	0	.232	.250
De Los Santos, Manuel	R-R	6-0	180	1-15-96	.241	.143	.260	30	87	12	21	8	0	1	8	12	4	0	3	28	0	3	.368	.349
Dixon, Johnny	R-R	6-1	185	1-5-98	.256	.325	.243	65	242	27	62	7	2	3	31	18	8	1	2	56	1	1	.339	.326
Engelhardt, Rachid	R-R	5-11	190	11-9-95	.259	.289	.248	46	139	19	36	4	1	2	13	13	6	0	3	19	5	3	.345	.342
Estevez, Marcos	R-R	6-0	185	7-12-95	.211	.037	.243	53	175	19	37	12	3	4	31	31	9	0	2	59	9	1	.383	.355
Flores, Pedro	B-R	5-10	141	4-18-96	.267	.227	.276	66	240	39	64	5	2	0	14	48	4	4	0	19	13	5	.304	.39
Galastica, Gonzalo	B-R	5-11	160	5-15-96	.218	.266	.197	57	216	26	47	6	1	1	9	14	3	2	0	39	9	4	.269	.275
Garcia, Alejandro	R-R	6-3	185	2-24-97	.198	.231	.185	30	91	9	18	4	0	1	6	8	4	2	1	29	0	0	.275	.288
Gil, Jorge	R-R	6-4	200	4-13-94	.242	.250	.238	57	190	21	46	8	0	0	20	21	4	0	3	23	3	3	.284	.326
Gonzalez, Frank	L-R	5-11	195	3-5-97	.144	.242	.094	33	97	13	14	4	0	0	8	18	3	1	0	50	2	1	.186	.297
Grasso, Victor	R-R	6-2	245	8-28-96	.107	.120	.100	34	75	6	8	1	0	0	3	8	2	2	1	24	0	0	.120	.292
Jimenez, Gerson	R-R	6-1	200	12-2-94	.229	.258	.223	53	170	18	39	7	0	1	23	35	7	0	4	25	2	0	.288	.375
Jimenez, Hansel	L-L	5-11	170	7-10-96	.455	.500	.444	5	11	1	5	0	0	0	3	0	0	0	1	2	1	1	.455	.417
Laureano, Carlos	R-R	6-3	175	6-27-94	.229	.207	.235	46	144	25	33	4	2	0	7	24	4	1	1	35	14	8	.285	.330
Lizarraga, Jose	R-R	5-10	170	8-27-97	.221	.235	.216	23	68	8	15	3	0	0	8	11	2	0	0	11	0	0	.265	.346
Medina, Robertico	R-R	6-0	170	1-12-94	.228	.255	.217	55	167	22	38	7	0	1	14	43	1	0	0	65	2	2	.287	.389
Mendez, Carlos	R-R	6-4	215	2-20-96	.220	.250	.216	34	118	10	26	5	0	1	11	4	4	1	0	27	0	0	.288	.270
Montes, Juan	B-R	6-2	185	5-15-95	.234	.273	.214	46	158	23	37	5	1	2	14	13	12	0	1	23	14	4	.316	.337
Morillo, Antony	L-R	6-1	190	10-9-97	.243	.259	.240	51	181	20	44	13	2	2	23	27	3	0	0	61	2	1	.370	.351
Ramirez, Wagner	R-R	5-11	170	12-11-94	.200	.154	.209	29	80	14	16	2	0	1	8	9	4	3	0	21	0	0	.263	.312
Rivero, Leisxonyer	R-R	6-1	165	2-12-97	.173	.133	.188	40	110	10	19	1	2	0	2	16	1	3	0	34	4	5	.218	.283
Rodriguez, Carlos	R-R	6-1	160	3-22-95	.254	—	—	55	177	20	45	7	1	0	17	17	12	8	0	45	10	7	.305	.359
Ruiz, Miguel	B-R	6-1	170	11-5-96	.085	.000	.105	16	47	7	4	0	0	0	2	9	0	1	0	10	0	0	.085	.232
Sanchez, Jose	R-R	6-0	165	12-8-95	.202	.111	.250	41	129	12	26	3	2	0	11	18	4	0	0	48	1	2	.256	.304
Santa, Adelyn	R-R	6-1	195	6-1-94	.160	.417	.125	28	100	10	16	5	0	1	8	4	0	0	1	44	1	1	.240	.250
Tucen, Adony	R-R	6-0	175	5-10-95	.200	.194	.203	41	110	8	22	7	1	0	12	7	0	1	0	37	6	1	.282	.248
Vizcaino, Fabian	R-R	5-11	178	5-27-95	.136	.000	.188	10	22	1	3	0	0	0	4	3	0	0	1	3	1	1	.136	.231

Pitching	B-T	HT	WT	DOB	W	L	ERA	G	GS	CG	SV	IP	H	R	ER	HR	BB	SO	AVG	vLH	vRH	K/9	BB/9
Alcantara, Jose	R-R	6-1	190	11-29-92	4	3	2.86	18	0	0	4	35	21	18	11	0	16	28	.178	.229	.157	7.27	4.15
Bautista, Angel	R-R	6-3	190	4-25-95	3	1	4.42	17	0	0	1	37	34	20	18	0	17	35	.258	.238	.267	8.59	4.17
Bautista, Felix	R-R	6-5	190	6-20-95	0	0	6.75	5	0	0	1	7	6	5	5	0	6	4	.222	.267	.167	5.40	8.10
Bonilla, Miguel Angel	R-R	6-3	185	9-29-94	0	0	1.24	12	0	0	4	29	26	12	4	0	3	25	.234	.302	.191	7.76	0.93
Carrillo, Rohimard	R-L	5-11	175	8-19-94	2	4	2.28	18	2	0	2	51	44	23	13	0	15	43	.234	.214	.240	7.54	2.63
Cruz, Oscar	R-R	6-1	170	8-25-94	2	3	6.00	16	0	0	0	36	47	30	24	1	13	23	.311	.344	.287	5.75	3.25
Daza, Manuel	R-R	6-1	175	9-22-96	2	0	1.93	8	0	0	0	9	7	2	2	0	8	10	—	—	—	9.64	7.71
De La Cruz, Andy	L-L	6-1	185	8-29-94	2	1	0.93	19	0	0	5	39	25	12	4	0	16	33	.182	.138	.194	7.68	3.72
Diaz, Frandy	L-L	5-10	155	3-25-95	1	5	5.36	16	6	0	0	40	47	30	24	0	22	48	.290	.241	.301	10.71	4.91
Diaz, Jose	R-R	6-3	185	8-1-96	2	5	2.23	14	14	0	0	69	57	25	17	1	24	44	.227	.242	.218	5.77	3.15
Dominguez, Manuel	R-R	6-5	230	1-17-94	0	2	6.35	11	0	0	0	11	16	10	8	0	7	9	.348	.273	.371	7.15	5.56
Encarnacion, Erick	L-L	6-1	180	4-4-96	1	0	2.55	16	0	0	1	25	17	12	7	1	15	21	.193	.000	.207	7.66	5.47
Fabian, Edward	R-R	6-3	170	8-23-95	0	1	6.11	13	0	0	0	18	24	14	12	0	13	11	.316	.200	.373	5.60	6.62
Feliz, Henry	R-R	6-0	185	5-23-92	3	1	2.60	12	5	0	0	38	37	16	11	0	15	41	.216	.086	.267	9.61	3.63
Gonzalez, Miguel	R-R	6-3	185	9-29-95	3	8	9.89	10	6	0	0	24	36	30	26	0	27	21	.299	.370	.267	7.99	10.27
Guance, Hector	R-R	6-6	200	7-12-95	4	3	2.52	14	14	0	0	71	61	27	20	1	14	41	.234	.256	.222	5.17	1.77
Jador, Junior	R-R	6-1	175	4-25-96	0	0	18.00	3	0	0	0	3	4	6	6	0	5	3	.364	.600	.167	9.00	15.00
Jimenez, Hector	L-L	6-0	160	4-3-95	1	3	5.87	18	0	0	0	31	37	22	20	2	19	42	.296	.333	.290	12.33	5.58
Jimenez, Julin	R-R	6-1	200	1-29-93	1	0	5.40	11	0	0	0	15	18	16	9	0	15	11	.300	.217	.351	6.60	9.00

Pitching

Pitching	B-T	HT	WT	DOB	W	L	ERA	G	GS	CG	SV	IP	H	R	ER	HR	BB	SO	AVG	vLH	vRH	K/9	BB/9
Leoncio, Tomas	R-R	6-2	180	3-3-95	2	5	3.76	14	14	0	0	69	79	36	29	3	13	47	.285	.324	.263	6.10	1.69
Martinez, Leybi	R-R	6-4	180	1-20-95	1	0	1.38	10	0	0	0	13	11	5	2	0	10	11	.224	.125	.244	7.62	6.92
Mena, Francisco	R-R	6-4	195	11-4-93	4	3	2.88	22	0	0	5	34	26	14	11	1	15	24	.206	.216	.200	6.29	3.93
Pacheco, Johalis	L-L	6-0	170	3-29-94	3	1	1.82	13	13	0	0	54	53	17	11	0	26	56	.254	.333	.234	9.28	4.31
Palumbo, Angelo	R-R	6-3	180	11-10-95	1	6	3.47	13	13	0	0	60	71	34	23	1	12	41	.297	.207	.326	6.18	1.81
Perez, Luis	R-R	6-0	175	5-3-95	1	2	2.40	22	4	0	6	45	31	13	12	0	19	44	.203	.286	.171	8.80	3.80
Polanco, Miguel	L-L	6-4	200	1-28-94	5	4	3.73	15	0	0	0	31	32	18	13	2	13	26	.278	.304	.272	7.47	3.73
Rojas, Edwin	R-R	6-6	200	9-26-95	1	5	3.07	15	8	0	0	44	44	22	15	0	28	32	.265	.231	.287	6.55	5.73
Valdez, Juan	R-R	6-2	160	2-6-91	2	8	2.69	14	14	1	0	77	79	32	23	3	5	61	.259	.279	.253	7.13	0.58
Vizcaino, Dember	R-R	6-4	205	5-12-95	1	3	2.86	16	0	0	0	28	30	14	9	0	21	22	.283	.250	.295	6.99	6.67
Vrolijk, Wally	R-R	6-4	225	11-19-94	2	2	3.05	10	0	0	0	21	15	7	7	0	16	12	.205	.192	.213	5.23	6.97
Wernet, Gillian	R-R	6-3	210	10-1-98	2	2	2.81	14	14	0	0	58	58	23	18	1	15	32	.265	.229	.282	4.99	2.34

Fielding

C: Alvarado 18, Ayala 14, Gonzalez 1, Grasso 34, Lizarraga 23, Mendez 34, Ramirez 29, Vizcaino 10. **1B:** Acosta 51, Adames 6, De Los Santos 6, Engelhardt 15, Garcia 10, Gil 4, Jimenez 52, Santa 11. **2B:** Adames 1, Briceno 6, Flores 66, Galastica 54, Gonzalez 12, Rivero 7, Ruiz 1. **3B:** Ciriaco 28, Garcia 14, Gonzalez 8, Medina 52, Morillo 40, Rivero 2, Ruiz 7. **SS:** Baez 62, Briceno 3, Medina 1, Rivero 30, Ruiz 8, Sanchez 41. **OF:** Adames 10, Barcenas 42, Chaves 31, De Los Santos 18, Dixon 62, Engelhardt 34, Estevez 50, Gil 27, Jimenez 4, Laureano 43, Medina 1, Montes 45, Rodriguez 49, Tucen 39.

Boston Red Sox

SEASON IN A SENTENCE: The Red Sox made David Ortiz's final season a grand one by going from worst-to-first to claim the AL East title, but they were unceremoniously swept out of the ALDS by Cleveland.

HIGH POINT: The Red Sox were just one game up in the division on the morning of Sept. 15, when Hanley Ramirez gave them a dramatic 7-5 victory over the Yankees that night with a walkoff two-run home run in the bottom of the ninth. The victory kicked off an 11-game winning streak that pulled Boston away from the pack for the AL East crown.

LOW POINT: The Red Sox leaned on marquee offseason signee David Price to deliver in Game Two of the ALDS after they dropped the opener, but Price got shelled for six hits and five runs in 3.1 innings as the Indians rolled to a 6-0 victory and 2-0 series lead that all but shut the door.

NOTABLE ROOKIES: Andrew Benintendi raced through the minors and made his major league debut on Aug. 2, less than 14 months after the Red Sox drafted him No. 7 overall in 2015. He delivered immediately, hitting .295 with an .835 OPS down the stretch while taking over as the starting left fielder. Touted Cuban infielder Yoan Moncada also debuted after a stellar minor league season, but he struck out 12 times in 20 plate appearances.

KEY TRANSACTIONS: In need of rotation help, the Red Sox acquired lefthander Drew Pomeranz from the Padres two days after he pitched in the All-Star Game in exchange for highly-regarded minor league righthander Anderson Espinoza. Pomeranz was 8-7, 2.57 for the Padres but 3-5, 4.59 for Boston, which filed a complaint with Major League Baseball asserting it was not given all of the relevant information regarding Pomeranz's medical history. MLB suspended Padres general manager A.J. Preller 30 days over the incident.

DOWN ON THE FARM: Moncada was named MVP of the Futures Game and won BA's Minor League Player of the Year award after hitting .294/.411/.507 with 15 homers, 62 RBIs and 45 stolen bases combined for high Class A Salem and Double-A Portland. Salem posted the best record in the Carolina League, helped largely by Benintendi and Moncada early in the season and third baseman Rafael Devers (.282, 11 HR, 71 RBIs) and 100 mph-throwing righthander Michael Kopech (4-1, 2.25) late. Short-season Lowell won its division in the New York-Penn League

OPENING DAY PAYROLL: $188,545,761 (4th)

PLAYERS OF THE YEAR

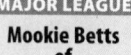

MAJOR LEAGUE	MINOR LEAGUE
Mookie Betts of	**Yoan Moncada,** 2b/3b
318/.363/.534	(High A/Double-A)
31 HR, 113 RBI	.294/.407/.511
42 2B, 26 SB	15 HR, 62 RBI, 45 SB.

ORGANIZATION LEADERS

BATTING *Minimum 250 AB

MAJORS

* AVG	Mookie Betts	.318
* OPS	David Ortiz	1.021
HR	David Ortiz	38
RBI	David Ortiz	127

MINORS

* AVG	Aneury Tavarez, Pawtucket, Portland	.330
* OBP	Yoan Moncada, Salem, Portland	.407
* SLG	Andrew Benintendi, Salem, Portland	.532
* OPS	Yoan Moncada, Salem, Portland	.918
R	Mauricio Dubon, Salem, Portland	101
H	Mauricio Dubon, Salem, Portland	157
TB	Chris Marrero, Pawtucket	242
2B	Nick Longhi, Salem	40
3B	Aneury Tavarez, Pawtucket, Portland	13
HR	Chris Marrero, Pawtucket	23
RBI	Nick Longhi, Salem	77
BB	Josh Ockimey, Greenville	88
SO	Josh Ockimey, Greenville	129
SB	Yoan Moncada, Salem, Portland	45

PITCHING #Minimum 75 IP

MAJORS

W	Rick Porcello	22
# ERA	Rick Porcello	3.15
SO	David Price	228
SV	Craig Kimbrel	31

MINORS

W	Logan Boyd, Greenville	14
L	Justin Haley, Portland, Pawtucket	10
	Dedgar Jimenez, Salem, Greenville	10
# ERA	Justin Haley, Portland, Pawtucket	3.01
G	Williams Jerez, Portland	40
	Chandler Shepherd, Portland, Pawtucket	40
	Luis Ysla, Portland, Pawtucket	40
GS	Matt Kent, Greenville, Salem	28
SV	Bobby Poyner, Greenville, Salem	15
IP	Matt Kent, Greenville, Salem	168
BB	Henry Owens, Pawtucket	81
SO	Mitch Atkins, Pawtucket, Portland	151
# AVG	Henry Owens, Pawtucket	.217

President: Dave Dombrowski. **GM:** Mike Hazen. **Farm Director:** Ben Crockett. **Scouting Director:** Mike Rikard.

Class	Team	League	W	L	PCT	Finish	Manager
Majors	Boston Red Sox	American	93	69	.574	3rd (15)	John Farrell
Triple-A	Pawtucket Red Sox	International	74	68	.521	5th (14)	Kevin Boles
Double-A	Portland Sea Dogs	Eastern	55	84	.396	11th (12)	Carlos Febles
High A	Salem Red Sox	Carolina	87	52	.626	1st (8)	Joe Oliver
Low A	Greenville Drive	South Atlantic	70	69	.504	t-8th (14)	Darren Fenster
Short season	Lowell Spinners	New York-Penn	47	29	.618	3rd(14)	Iggy Suarez
Rookie	Red Sox	Gulf Coast	33	28	.541	5th (17)	Tom Kotchman
Overall 2016 Minor League Record			366	330	.526	9th (30)	

ORGANIZATION STATISTICS

BOSTON RED SOX
AMERICAN LEAGUE

Batting	B-T	HT	WT	DOB	AVG	vLH	vRH	G	AB	R	H	2B	3B	HR	RBI	BB	HBP	SH	SF	SO	SB	CS	SLG	OBP
Benintendi, Andrew	L-L	5-10	170	7-6-94	.295	.179	.338	34	105	16	31	11	1	2	14	10	1	1	1	25	1	0	.476	.359
Betts, Mookie	R-R	5-9	180	10-7-92	.318	.264	.331	158	672	122	214	42	5	31	113	49	2	0	7	80	26	4	.534	.363
Bogaerts, Xander	R-R	6-1	210	10-1-92	.294	.304	.292	157	652	115	192	34	1	21	89	58	6	0	3	123	13	4	.446	.356
Bradley, Jackie	L-R	5-10	200	4-19-90	.267	.244	.277	156	558	94	149	30	7	26	87	63	10	0	5	143	9	2	.486	.349
Brentz, Bryce	R-R	6-0	210	12-30-88	.279	.286	.263	25	61	8	17	3	0	1	7	3	0	0	0	17	0	0	.377	.313
Castillo, Rusney	R-R	5-9	195	7-9-87	.250	.000	.286	9	8	4	2	1	0	0	0	0	0	0	0	3	0	0	.375	.250
Hanigan, Ryan	R-R	6-0	220	8-16-80	.171	.107	.195	35	105	9	18	4	0	1	14	7	1	0	0	27	0	0	.238	.230
Hernandez, Marco	L-R	6-0	200	9-6-92	.294	.500	.256	40	51	11	15	1	0	1	5	5	0	0	0	10	1	0	.373	.357
Hill, Aaron	R-R	5-11	200	3-21-82	.218	.286	.148	47	124	14	27	3	0	2	9	11	1	0	0	16	0	0	.290	.287
Holaday, Bryan	R-R	6-0	205	11-19-87	.212	.333	.143	14	33	3	7	1	0	0	1	2	0	0	0	12	0	0	.242	.257
2-team total (29 Texas)					.231	—		43	117	17	27	7	1	2	14	7	2	1	2	28	0	1	.359	.281
Holt, Brock	L-R	5-10	180	6-11-88	.255	.103	.279	94	290	45	74	16	0	7	34	27	3	1	3	58	4	3	.383	.322
LaMarre, Ryan	R-L	6-1	210	11-21-88	.000	.000	.000	5	5	1	0	0	0	0	0	1	0	0	0	2	0	0	.000	.167
Leon, Sandy	B-R	5-10	225	3-13-89	.310	.373	.286	78	252	36	78	17	2	7	35	23	2	4	2	66	0	0	.476	.369
Marrero, Deven	R-R	6-1	195	8-25-90	.083	.091	.000	13	12	0	1	0	0	0	0	2	0	0	0	5	0	0	.083	.214
Martinez, Michael	B-R	5-9	180	9-16-82	.167	.000	.250	4	6	1	1	0	0	0	0	1	0	0	0	2	0	0	.167	.286
2-team total (59 Cleveland)					.238	—		63	101	16	24	4	0	1	4	4	0	1	0	23	0	2	.307	.247
Miller, Mike	R-R	5-9	170	9-27-89	.000	.000	—	1	1	0	0	0	0	0	0	0	0	0	0	0	0	0	.000	.000
Moncada, Yoan	B-R	6-2	205	5-27-95	.211	.250	.200	8	19	3	4	1	0	0	1	1	0	0	0	12	0	0	.263	.250
Ortiz, David	L-L	6-3	230	11-18-75	.315	.313	.315	151	537	79	169	48	1	38	127	80	2	0	7	86	2	0	.620	.401
Pedroia, Dustin	R-R	5-9	175	8-17-83	.318	.305	.320	154	633	105	201	36	1	15	74	61	0	1	3	73	7	4	.449	.376
Ramirez, Hanley	R-R	6-2	235	12-23-83	.286	.346	.268	147	549	81	157	28	1	30	111	60	7	0	4	120	9	3	.505	.361
Rutledge, Josh	R-R	6-1	190	4-21-89	.265	.313	.242	28	49	9	13	6	0	0	3	6	0	1	0	19	2	0	.388	.345
Sandoval, Pablo	L-R	5-11	255	8-11-86	.000	—	.000	3	6	0	0	0	0	0	0	1	0	0	0	4	0	0	.000	.143
Shaw, Travis	L-R	6-4	230	4-16-90	.242	.187	.257	145	480	63	116	34	2	16	71	43	3	0	4	133	5	1	.421	.306
Swihart, Blake	B-R	6-1	200	4-3-92	.258	.800	.211	19	62	9	16	0	3	0	5	11	0	0	1	17	0	1	.355	.365
Vazquez, Christian	R-R	5-9	195	8-21-90	.227	.286	.212	57	172	21	39	9	1	1	12	10	2	0	0	39	0	0	.308	.277
Young, Chris	R-R	6-2	200	9-5-83	.276	.329	.246	76	203	29	56	18	0	9	24	21	3	0	0	54	2	0	.498	.352

Pitching	B-T	HT	WT	DOB	W	L	ERA	G	GS	CG	SV	IP	H	R	ER	HR	BB	SO	AVG	vLH	vRH	K/9	BB/9
Abad, Fernando	L-L	6-1	220	12-17-85	0	2	6.39	18	0	0	0	13	13	9	9	2	8	12	.255	.130	.357	8.53	5.68
2-team total (39 Minnesota)					1	6	3.66	57	0	0	1	47	40	20	19	4	22	41	—	—	—	7.91	4.24
Barnes, Matt	R-R	6-4	210	6-17-90	4	3	4.05	62	0	0	1	67	62	32	30	6	31	71	.248	.234	.256	9.59	4.19
Buchholz, Clay	L-R	6-3	190	8-14-84	8	10	4.78	37	21	0	0	139	130	80	74	21	55	93	.250	.280	.222	6.01	3.55
Cuevas, William	R-R	6-2	215	10-14-90	0	1	3.60	3	0	0	0	5	5	2	2	0	6	3	.294	.286	.300	5.40	10.80
Elias, Roenis	L-L	6-1	205	8-1-88	0	1	12.91	3	1	0	0	8	15	11	11	2	5	3	.417	.500	.375	3.52	5.87
Hembree, Heath	R-R	6-4	210	1-13-89	4	1	2.65	38	0	0	0	51	51	23	15	6	17	47	.249	.338	.201	8.29	3.00
Kelly, Joe	R-R	6-1	190	6-9-88	4	0	5.18	20	6	0	0	40	44	23	23	5	24	48	.278	.269	.283	10.80	5.40
Kimbrel, Craig	R-R	6-0	210	5-28-88	2	6	3.40	57	0	0	31	53	28	22	20	4	30	83	.152	.145	.158	14.09	5.09
Layne, Tommy	L-L	6-2	195	11-2-84	0	1	3.77	34	0	0	0	29	27	12	12	1	14	25	.260	.259	.260	7.85	4.40
2-team total (29 New York)					2	1	3.63	63	0	0	1	45	37	18	18	3	21	38	—	—	—	7.66	4.23
Light, Pat	R-R	6-5	220	3-29-91	0	0	23.63	2	0	0	0	3	7	8	7	2	1	2	.438	.333	.462	6.75	3.38
2-team total (15 Minnesota)					0	1	11.34	17	0	0	0	17	22	22	21	4	16	16	—	—	—	8.64	8.64
O'Sullivan, Sean	R-R	6-1	245	9-1-87	2	0	6.75	5	4	0	0	21	30	17	16	3	6	13	.337	.333	.341	5.48	2.53
Owens, Henry	L-L	6-6	220	7-21-92	0	2	6.95	5	5	0	0	22	23	17	17	5	20	21	.284	.250	.295	8.59	8.18
Pomeranz, Drew	R-L	6-6	240	11-22-88	3	5	4.59	14	13	0	0	69	70	35	35	14	24	71	.262	.286	.255	9.31	3.15
Porcello, Rick	R-R	6-5	205	12-27-88	22	4	3.15	33	33	3	0	223	193	85	78	23	32	189	.230	.225	.235	7.63	1.29
Price, David	L-L	6-5	215	8-26-85	17	9	3.99	35	35	2	0	230	227	106	102	30	50	228	.258	.275	.253	8.92	1.96
Ramirez, Noe	R-R	6-3	205	12-22-89	0	0	6.23	14	0	0	0	13	16	9	9	4	8	15	.327	.300	.333	10.38	5.54
Rodriguez, Eduardo	L-L	6-2	220	4-7-93	3	7	4.71	20	20	0	0	107	99	58	56	16	40	100	.241	.267	.235	8.41	3.36
Ross, Robbie	L-L	5-11	215	6-24-89	3	2	3.25	54	0	0	0	55	47	21	20	2	23	56	.228	.188	.254	9.11	3.74
Scott, Robby	B-L	6-3	220	8-29-89	1	0	0.00	7	0	0	0	6	6	0	0	0	2	5	.273	.250	.300	7.50	3.00
Smith, Carson	R-R	6-6	215	10-19-89	0	0	0.00	3	0	0	0	3	2	1	0	0	1	2	.200	.000	.286	6.75	3.38
Tazawa, Junichi	R-R	5-11	200	6-6-86	3	2	4.17	53	0	0	0	50	47	23	23	9	14	54	.245	.207	.273	9.79	2.54

Pitching

Pitching	B-T	HT	WT	DOB	W	L	ERA	G	GS	CG	SV	IP	H	R	ER	HR	BB	SO	AVG	vLH	vRH	K/9	BB/9
Uehara, Koji	R-R	6-2	195	4-3-75	2	3	3.45	50	0	0	7	47	34	18	18	8	11	63	.200	.139	.253	12.06	2.11
Wright, Steven	R-R	6-2	215	8-30-84	13	6	3.33	24	24	4	0	157	138	74	58	12	57	127	.235	.209	.254	7.30	3.27
Ziegler, Brad	R-R	6-4	220	10-10-79	2	4	1.52	33	0	0	4	30	26	8	5	1	11	31	.234	.229	.237	9.40	3.34

Fielding

Catcher	PCT	G	PO	A	E	DP	PB
Hanigan	1.000	34	258	26	0	3	18
Holaday	.989	13	76	10	1	2	0
Leon	.998	74	561	35	1	6	7
Swihart	1.000	6	59	3	0	0	3
Vazquez	.996	56	423	25	2	3	9

First Base	PCT	G	PO	A	E	DP
Ortiz	1.000	1	5	0	0	0
Ramirez	.996	133	1000	39	4	100
Shaw	1.000	50	251	19	0	27

Second Base	PCT	G	PO	A	E	DP
Hernandez	.955	14	9	12	1	4
Hill	1.000	4	1	5	0	1
Holt	1.000	8	10	11	0	1
Marrero	.875	6	2	5	1	1

(Second Base, cont.)	PCT	G	PO	A	E	DP
Miller	—	1	0	0	0	0
Pedroia	.990	152	245	362	6	98
Rutledge	1.000	5	6	7	0	3

Third Base	PCT	G	PO	A	E	DP
Hernandez	.938	10	5	10	1	4
Hill	.960	44	19	53	3	7
Holaday	1.000	1	0	1	0	1
Holt	.951	17	10	29	2	3
Marrero	1.000	4	0	5	0	0
Moncada	.933	5	2	12	1	0
Rutledge	.917	17	2	20	2	2
Sandoval	.800	2	1	3	1	0
Shaw	.945	105	76	197	16	20

Shortstop	PCT	G	PO	A	E	DP
Bogaerts	.979	157	195	355	12	73
Hernandez	1.000	2	0	2	0	0

(Shortstop, cont.)	PCT	G	PO	A	E	DP
Holt	1.000	7	6	12	0	1
Marrero	1.000	4	1	0	0	0
Martinez	—	1	0	0	0	0
Rutledge	—	1	0	0	0	0

Outfield	PCT	G	PO	A	E	DP
Benintendi	.982	32	55	0	1	0
Betts	.997	157	346	14	1	4
Bradley	.992	156	365	13	3	3
Brentz	.963	22	25	1	1	0
Castillo	1.000	4	6	0	0	0
Holt	.983	68	107	6	2	2
LaMarre	1.000	3	3	0	0	0
Martinez	1.000	2	5	0	0	0
Shaw	1.000	1	1	0	0	0
Swihart	1.000	13	30	1	0	0
Young	1.000	69	103	0	0	0

PAWTUCKET RED SOX
INTERNATIONAL LEAGUE

TRIPLE-A

Batting	B-T	HT	WT	DOB	AVG	vLH	vRH	G	AB	R	H	2B	3B	HR	RBI	BB	HBP	SH	SF	SO	SB	CS	SLG	OBP
Bethea, Danny	R-R	6-1	210	1-31-90	.000	—	.000	1	4	0	0	0	0	0	0	0	0	0	0	1	0	0	.000	.000
Boesch, Brennan	L-L	6-4	225	4-12-85	.221	.182	.238	38	145	15	32	6	0	4	15	9	1	0	3	24	2	1	.345	.266
Brentz, Bryce	R-R	6-0	210	12-30-88	.250	.333	.230	54	204	16	51	17	1	4	21	8	0	0	0	52	2	0	.402	.278
Butler, Dan	R-R	5-10	210	10-17-86	.308	.263	.324	48	146	14	45	12	0	3	16	20	2	1	0	34	0	0	.452	.399
Castillo, Rusney	R-R	5-9	195	7-9-87	.263	.304	.249	103	395	55	104	20	5	2	34	24	4	2	4	68	9	3	.354	.309
Court, Ryan	R-R	6-2	210	5-28-88	.279	.214	.298	18	61	8	17	3	1	0	7	5	0	0	1	8	1	1	.361	.328
Coyle, Sean	R-R	5-8	175	1-17-92	.125	.000	.167	24	72	6	9	1	0	2	4	6	0	2	0	30	1	0	.222	.192
Craig, Allen	R-R	6-2	215	7-18-84	.173	.158	.179	22	75	5	13	3	1	1	6	7	1	0	1	16	0	0	.280	.250
Dominguez, Chris	R-R	6-4	235	11-22-86	.241	.240	.241	77	278	35	67	12	2	13	39	11	4	0	5	70	7	3	.439	.275
Hanigan, Ryan	R-R	6-0	220	8-16-80	.200	.143	.222	8	25	2	5	1	0	0	3	3	2	0	1	7	0	0	.240	.323
Hernandez, Marco	L-R	6-0	200	9-6-92	.309	.328	.301	57	223	26	69	7	4	5	29	12	0	1	1	51	4	2	.444	.343
Holt, Brock	L-R	5-10	180	6-11-88	.320	.375	.294	8	25	2	8	2	0	0	2	5	0	0	0	5	0	0	.400	.433
LaMarre, Ryan	R-L	6-1	210	11-21-88	.303	.304	.303	86	317	44	96	15	0	10	41	28	8	0	5	80	17	6	.445	.369
Leon, Sandy	B-R	5-10	225	3-13-89	.243	.276	.233	36	115	12	28	3	1	2	13	11	2	0	2	24	0	0	.339	.315
Marrero, Chris	R-R	6-3	199	7-2-88	.284	.309	.275	131	490	63	139	30	2	23	71	46	2	0	6	85	0	0	.494	.344
Marrero, Deven	R-R	6-1	195	8-25-90	.198	.230	.186	96	363	30	72	11	1	1	27	22	1	0	2	90	10	3	.242	.245
Maxwell, Justin	R-R	6-4	225	11-6-83	.219	.193	.228	61	219	26	48	7	0	5	25	25	5	1	3	61	4	4	.320	.310
Miller, Mike	R-R	5-9	170	9-27-89	.228	.258	.220	90	312	38	71	13	1	1	20	27	3	5	2	40	12	4	.285	.294
Ramos, Henry	R-R	6-2	220	4-15-92	.247	.234	.252	57	190	18	47	8	3	5	29	11	1	2	5	44	4	2	.400	.285
Rosario, Rainel	R-R	6-1	190	3-29-89	.000	—	.000	2	7	0	0	0	0	0	1	0	0	0	3	1	0	0	.000	.125
Rutledge, Josh	R-R	6-1	190	4-21-89	.316	.375	.273	5	19	3	6	2	0	0	1	0	0	0	4	1	0	.421	.350
Solis, Ali	R-R	6-0	200	9-29-87	.270	.250	.273	13	37	1	10	1	0	1	5	1	0	0	2	5	0	0	.378	.275
Sturgeon, Cole	L-L	6-0	180	9-17-91	.333	—	.333	2	9	2	3	2	0	0	1	0	0	0	0	1	0	0	.556	.333
Swihart, Blake	B-R	6-1	200	4-3-92	.243	.294	.233	29	103	13	25	4	0	1	8	17	0	0	2	17	2	1	.311	.344
Tavarez, Aneury	L-R	5-9	175	4-14-92	.200	.500	.091	5	15	0	3	0	0	0	1	0	0	0	3	2	0	.200	.250
Travis, Sam	R-R	6-0	205	8-27-93	.272	.300	.263	47	173	26	47	10	0	6	29	15	1	0	1	40	1	0	.434	.332
Vazquez, Christian	R-R	5-9	195	8-21-90	.270	.214	.291	42	152	19	41	9	0	2	16	15	3	0	1	31	2	0	.368	.345
Vinicio, Jose	B-R	5-11	150	7-10-93	.269	.286	.265	48	167	17	45	4	3	1	13	5	1	5	0	34	6	2	.347	.295
Witte, Jantzen	R-R	6-2	195	11-28-89	.258	.297	.244	100	357	43	92	29	1	2	25	31	6	1	5	58	5	4	.361	.327
Young, Chris	R-R	6-2	200	9-5-83	.217	.167	.235	7	23	2	5	2	0	0	2	1	1	0	0	7	0	0	.304	.280

Pitching	B-T	HT	WT	DOB	W	L	ERA	G	GS	CG	SV	IP	H	R	ER	HR	BB	SO	AVG	vLH	vRH	K/9	BB/9
Atkins, Mitch	R-R	6-4	225	10-1-85	0	0	0.00	1	0	0	0	5	0	0	0	0	1	6	.000	.000	.000	11.57	1.93
Couch, Keith	L-R	6-2	210	11-5-89	1	3	4.31	6	4	0	0	31	38	17	15	3	6	17	.299	.375	.239	4.88	1.72
Cuevas, William	R-R	6-2	215	10-14-90	6	8	4.19	25	18	1	0	131	134	71	61	10	48	85	.264	.315	.228	5.84	3.09
Elias, Roenis	L-L	6-1	205	8-1-88	10	5	3.60	21	19	1	0	125	115	56	50	10	57	113	.250	.226	.260	8.14	4.10
Escobar, Edwin	L-L	6-2	225	4-22-92	0	0	0.00	3	1	0	0	7	6	3	0	0	1	2	.214	.250	.200	2.57	1.29
Haley, Justin	R-R	6-5	230	6-16-91	8	6	3.59	15	14	1	0	85	70	34	34	8	26	67	.230	.224	.236	7.07	2.74
Hembree, Heath	R-R	6-4	210	1-13-89	0	0	0.68	13	0	0	8	13	6	1	1	0	3	12	.130	.000	.207	14.85	2.03
Janssen, Casey	R-R	6-4	210	9-17-81	0	0	2.35	6	0	0	0	8	4	2	2	1	3	4	.148	.167	.143	4.70	3.52
Johnson, Brian	L-L	6-4	235	12-7-90	5	6	4.09	15	15	0	0	77	74	38	35	9	36	54	.258	.197	.278	6.31	4.21
Kelly, Joe	R-R	6-1	190	6-9-88	1	1	1.54	17	4	0	2	35	29	6	6	1	6	46	.230	.140	.289	11.83	1.54
Kimbrel, Craig	R-R	6-0	210	5-28-88	0	0	0.00	1	0	0	0	1	0	0	0	0	0	1	.000	.500	—	0.00	0.00
Light, Pat	R-R	6-5	220	3-29-91	1	1	2.32	25	0	0	7	31	21	8	8	1	17	36	.188	.136	.221	10.45	4.94
2-team total (6 Rochester)					2	1	2.37	31	0	0	9	38	26	10	10	1	19	42	—	—	—	9.95	4.50
Maddox, Austin	R-R	6-2	220	5-13-91	1	0	1.93	3	0	0	0	5	4	1	1	1	1	2	.222	.143	.273	3.86	1.93

Pitching	B-T	HT	WT	DOB	W	L	ERA	G	GS	CG	SV	IP	H	R	ER	HR	BB	SO	AVG	vLH	vRH	K/9	BB/9
Marban, Jorge	R-R	6-1	215	12-5-88	1	0	0.63	8	0	0	1	14	7	1	1	1	10	7	.152	.095	.200	4.40	6.28
Martin, Kyle	R-R	6-7	230	1-18-91	3	4	3.38	36	0	0	6	67	58	25	25	5	21	78	.239	.232	.243	10.53	2.84
McCarthy, Mike	R-R	6-3	200	11-18-87	0	1	16.20	1	1	0	0	3	9	7	6	1	2	0	.450	.333	.500	0.00	5.40
Mendez, Roman	R-R	6-3	235	7-25-90	4	2	3.38	32	0	0	2	64	49	26	24	6	27	59	.214	.193	.226	8.30	3.80
O'Sullivan, Sean	R-R	6-1	245	9-1-87	9	6	4.02	19	19	1	0	105	112	49	47	7	27	85	.280	.292	.268	7.26	2.31
Owens, Henry	L-L	6-6	220	7-21-92	10	7	3.53	24	24	1	0	138	107	60	54	13	81	135	.217	.208	.220	8.83	5.30
Ramirez, Noe	R-R	6-3	205	12-22-89	2	3	1.85	30	0	0	7	44	39	11	9	3	11	54	.238	.280	.219	11.13	2.27
Rodriguez, Eduardo	L-L	6-2	220	4-7-93	0	4	3.08	7	7	0	0	38	33	15	13	6	7	24	.231	.353	.193	5.68	1.66
Scott, Robby	B-L	6-3	220	8-29-89	4	3	2.54	32	6	0	0	78	57	22	22	9	14	73	.202	.147	.230	8.42	1.62
Shepherd, Chandler	R-R	6-3	185	8-25-92	1	2	3.71	18	1	0	1	34	28	14	14	3	8	23	.230	.200	.247	6.09	2.12
Varvaro, Anthony	R-R	6-0	190	10-31-84	3	2	2.83	18	0	0	1	29	21	10	9	2	13	31	.200	.150	.231	9.73	4.08
Wilkerson, Aaron	R-R	6-3	190	5-24-89	4	2	2.44	9	8	0	0	48	41	18	13	5	11	54	.223	.227	.220	10.13	2.06
Wright, Wesley	R-L	5-10	185	1-28-85	0	2	4.31	19	0	0	3	31	36	17	15	2	13	21	.288	.256	.305	6.03	3.73
Ysla, Luis	L-L	6-1	185	4-27-92	0	0	0.00	1	0	0	1	1	1	0	0	0	0	2	.250	.500	.000	18.00	0.00

Fielding

Catcher	PCT	G	PO	A	E	DP	PB
Butler	1.000	47	330	23	0	6	1
Hanigan	1.000	6	31	3	0	0	0
Leon	.996	29	216	19	1	2	4
Solis	1.000	13	96	8	0	0	0
Swihart	.983	15	108	10	2	1	1
Vazquez	.989	41	339	25	4	0	2

First Base	PCT	G	PO	A	E	DP
Court	.978	7	41	3	1	3
Craig	1.000	11	81	3	0	15
Dominguez	1.000	28	210	10	0	27
Leon	1.000	1	4	0	0	1
Marrero	.990	65	489	26	5	56
Travis	.973	34	237	20	7	22

Second Base	PCT	G	PO	A	E	DP
Court	.920	5	11	12	2	2
Coyle	.956	14	32	33	3	6
Hernandez	1.000	20	31	48	0	14
Marrero	1.000	2	7	6	0	1

	PCT	G	PO	A	E	DP	PB
Miller	.994	72	152	173	2	48	
Rutledge	1.000	2	2	2	0	0	
Vinicio	.974	27	55	59	3	18	
Witte	.833	1	3	2	1	2	

Third Base	PCT	G	PO	A	E	DP
Court	1.000	3	3	4	0	1
Coyle	1.000	3	5	5	0	0
Dominguez	.918	19	20	36	5	2
Hernandez	.955	10	7	14	1	0
Marrero	1.000	2	5	2	0	1
Miller	.971	10	10	23	1	1
Rutledge	1.000	3	6	7	0	0
Witte	.982	94	83	139	4	14

Shortstop	PCT	G	PO	A	E	DP
Court	1.000	4	1	4	0	2
Hernandez	.985	22	19	45	1	18
Holt	.857	2	2	4	1	1
Marrero	.964	92	132	247	14	61
Miller	1.000	6	10	12	0	4

	PCT	G	PO	A	E	DP
Vinicio	.940	21	26	52	5	13

Outfield	PCT	G	PO	A	E	DP
Boesch	.976	24	41	0	1	0
Brentz	.981	49	97	4	2	0
Castillo	.987	100	225	7	3	2
Court	—		1	0	0	0
Coyle	1.000	7	22	1	0	0
Craig	1.000	4	7	0	0	0
Dominguez	1.000	21	41	2	0	0
Hernandez	1.000	1	2	0	0	0
Holt	1.000	6	13	1	0	0
LaMarre	.989	83	169	5	2	3
Marrero	1.000	26	36	2	0	0
Maxwell	1.000	47	83	1	0	1
Ramos	.980	48	94	5	2	1
Rosario	1.000	2	4	0	0	0
Sturgeon	1.000	2	5	0	0	0
Swihart	.957	11	20	2	1	0
Tavarez	1.000	4	10	0	0	0
Young	1.000	4	11	1	0	0

PORTLAND SEA DOGS
EASTERN LEAGUE

DOUBLE-A

Batting	B-T	HT	WT	DOB	AVG	vLH	vRH	G	AB	R	H	2B	3B	HR	RBI	BB	HBP	SH	SF	SO	SB	CS	SLG	OBP
Benintendi, Andrew	L-L	5-10	170	7-6-94	.295	.326	.289	63	237	40	70	18	5	8	44	24	0	0	2	30	8	7	.515	.357
Bethea, Danny	R-R	6-1	210	1-31-90	.180	.205	.164	31	100	10	18	8	0	2	7	4	0	1	3	24	0	1	.320	.206
Betts, Jordan	R-R	6-3	220	10-6-91	.152	.143	.156	13	46	4	7	3	0	1	8	2	0	0	0	15	0	0	.283	.188
Brentz, Bryce	R-R	6-0	210	12-30-88	.200	.214	.192	12	40	5	8	2	0	1	3	7	1	0	0	14	1	0	.325	.333
Court, Ryan	R-R	6-2	210	5-28-88	.277	.357	.253	85	303	44	84	16	3	4	39	39	2	2	1	76	3	2	.389	.362
Coyle, Sean	R-R	5-8	175	1-17-92	.185	.200	.180	40	146	21	27	9	0	3	10	19	4	0	0	41	5	1	.308	.296
Decker, Cody	R-R	5-11	217	1-17-87	.232	.103	.258	63	233	39	54	14	1	14	37	16	3	0	5	79	1	1	.481	.284
Dubon, Mauricio	R-R	6-0	160	7-19-94	.339	.409	.324	62	251	48	85	20	6	6	40	11	3	2	2	36	6	3	.538	.371
Freiman, Nate	R-R	6-8	245	12-31-86	.277	.313	.267	90	311	39	86	17	2	11	60	43	5	0	9	68	0	2	.450	.364
Gragnani, Reed	B-R	5-11	180	9-5-90	.250	—	.250	2	8	1	2	1	0	0	0	0	0	0	0	0	0	0	.375	.250
Hanigan, Ryan	R-R	6-0	220	8-16-80	.333	.667	.000	2	6	0	2	0	0	0	1	2	0	0	0	1	0	0	.333	.500
Lin, Tzu-Wei	L-R	5-9	155	2-15-94	.223	.169	.237	108	372	39	83	16	5	2	27	34	0	4	1	55	10	7	.293	.287
Lovullo, Nick	R-R	6-0	180	3-29-89	.333	.333	.333	3	9	1	3	0	0	0	1	0	0	0	0	1	0	0	.333	.333
Madera, Chris	R-R	5-10	190	8-23-92	.000	.000	.000	1	5	0	0	0	0	0	0	0	0	0	0	0	0	0	.000	.000
Miller, Derek	R-R	6-2	180	7-18-92	.211	.267	.174	12	38	4	8	1	0	0	5	5	1	1	0	11	1	1	.237	.318
Miller, Mike	R-R	5-9	190	9-27-89	.217	.000	.313	6	23	3	5	2	0	0	3	2	0	0	1	1	0	0	.304	.269
Moncada, Yoan	B-R	6-2	205	5-27-95	.277	.167	.305	45	177	37	49	6	3	11	28	27	2	1	0	64	9	4	.531	.379
Ramos, Henry	B-R	6-2	220	4-15-92	.281	.333	.265	45	171	20	48	6	3	3	11	11	2	4	1	25	3	3	.404	.330
Ray, Jayce	L-R	6-0	195	11-26-89	.000	—	.000	2	6	0	0	0	0	0	0	1	0	0	0	1	0	0	.000	.000
Rijo, Wendell	R-R	5-11	170	9-4-95	.186	.120	.213	51	177	18	33	11	0	1	12	13	1	2	1	46	2	4	.266	.245
Roberson, Tim	R-R	5-10	215	7-10-89	.247	.234	.252	65	223	22	55	15	0	4	18	15	2	0	0	60	0	0	.368	.300
Romanski, Jake	R-R	5-11	200	12-22-90	.308	.319	.306	90	334	34	103	22	0	4	38	15	2	2	4	47	0	3	.410	.338
Rosario, Rainel	R-R	6-1	190	3-29-89	.254	.204	.274	101	323	36	82	15	2	2	42	25	1	1	4	43	2	2	.331	.306
Solis, Ali	R-R	6-0	200	9-29-87	.145	.273	.118	20	62	3	9	1	0	1	8	6	0	0	2	11	0	1	.210	.214
Sturgeon, Cole	L-L	6-0	180	9-17-91	.267	.218	.282	117	427	36	114	18	4	6	40	23	5	2	0	61	6	9	.370	.312
Tavarez, Aneury	L-R	5-9	175	4-14-92	.335	.313	.341	106	385	59	129	19	13	7	47	29	2	3	6	64	18	11	.506	.379
Vinicio, Jose	B-R	5-11	150	7-10-93	.230	.250	.216	22	61	6	14	0	0	1	3	0	4	1	9	1	2	.279	.262
Weems, Jordan	L-R	6-3	175	11-7-92	.119	.056	.143	22	67	4	8	1	0	0	1	11	0	0	1	24	0	0	.134	.241
Witte, Jantzen	R-R	6-2	195	1-4-90	.359	.375	.348	11	39	6	14	1	0	2	7	8	0	0	1	4	0	0	.538	.458

Pitching	B-T	HT	WT	DOB	W	L	ERA	G	GS	CG	SV	IP	H	R	ER	HR	BB	SO	AVG	vLH	vRH	K/9	BB/9
Atkins, Mitch	R-R	6-4	225	10-1-85	6	7	4.48	30	20	0	2	127	134	68	63	15	41	145	.275	.322	.233	10.30	2.91

Pitching

Pitching	B-T	HT	WT	DOB	W	L	ERA	G	GS	CG	SV	IP	H	R	ER	HR	BB	SO	AVG	vLH	vRH	K/9	BB/9
Beeks, Jalen	L-L	5-11	195	7-10-93	5	4	4.68	13	13	0	0	65	72	37	34	6	28	56	.283	.308	.273	7.71	3.86
Buttrey, Ty	L-R	6-6	230	3-31-93	9	0	4.44	33	9	0	0	79	80	52	39	6	46	52	.261	.237	.280	5.92	5.24
Couch, Keith	L-R	6-2	210	11-5-89	9	5	3.84	16	16	3	0	96	98	47	41	7	31	56	.262	.281	.245	5.25	2.91
Dahlstrand, Jacob	R-R	6-5	205	3-26-92	2	2	6.05	4	4	0	0	19	23	15	13	3	8	8	.299	.235	.349	3.72	3.72
Drehoff, Jake	L-L	6-4	195	6-25-92	0	1	5.55	22	0	0	1	36	43	24	22	6	22	32	.303	.250	.327	8.07	5.55
Grover, Taylor	R-R	6-3	195	4-22-91	2	5	5.00	21	0	0	0	45	53	34	25	5	16	42	.283	.276	.288	8.40	3.20
Haley, Justin	R-R	6-5	230	6-16-91	5	4	2.20	12	12	1	0	61	49	15	15	1	19	59	.219	.236	.198	8.66	2.79
Jerez, Williams	L-L	6-4	200	5-16-92	1	6	4.71	40	0	0	0	65	70	35	34	6	30	65	.282	.283	.282	9.00	4.15
Maddox, Austin	R-R	6-2	220	5-13-91	2	3	3.96	23	2	0	0	39	29	21	17	3	16	38	.207	.150	.250	8.84	3.72
McAvoy, Kevin	R-R	6-4	210	7-21-93	8	9	5.80	22	22	3	0	116	125	85	75	10	52	79	.282	.280	.285	6.11	4.02
McCarthy, Mike	R-R	6-3	200	11-18-87	0	2	4.38	12	5	0	0	37	43	18	18	4	14	12	.307	.342	.269	2.92	3.41
Mercedes, Simon	R-R	6-4	240	2-17-92	2	3	8.22	15	0	0	0	23	31	26	21	4	20	20	.323	.240	.413	7.83	7.83
Quevedo, Heri	R-R	6-2	225	6-7-90	0	2	5.02	4	1	0	0	14	15	8	8	0	10	8	.273	.286	.259	5.02	6.28
Shepherd, Chandler	R-R	6-3	185	8-25-92	1	1	1.80	22	0	0	6	30	14	8	6	1	10	39	.140	.153	.122	11.70	3.00
Smith, Carson	R-R	6-6	215	10-19-89	0	0	0.00	2	0	0	0	2	0	0	0	0	0	2	.000	.000	.000	10.80	0.00
Stankiewicz, Teddy	R-R	6-4	215	11-25-93	5	9	4.71	25	25	2	0	136	142	74	71	16	39	97	.274	.291	.255	6.43	2.59
Taylor, Ben	R-R	6-3	225	11-12-92	1	0	3.44	21	0	0	5	34	28	13	13	4	12	42	.222	.255	.197	11.12	3.18
Turley, Nik	L-L	6-4	195	9-11-89	1	2	4.29	20	2	0	2	36	26	20	17	3	28	48	.202	.159	.224	12.11	7.07
Wilkerson, Aaron	R-R	6-3	190	5-24-89	2	1	1.83	8	8	0	0	44	28	10	9	2	14	48	.175	.179	.169	9.74	2.84
Workman, Brandon	R-R	6-5	235	8-13-88	0	0	9.00	4	0	0	0	10	15	10	10	3	7	5	.333	.182	.478	4.50	6.30
Wort, Rob	R-R	6-1	155	2-7-89	0	4	6.75	17	0	0	1	28	33	23	21	3	17	27	.297	.267	.333	8.68	5.46
Ysla, Luis	L-L	6-1	185	4-27-92	2	5	4.07	39	0	0	3	55	54	28	25	4	27	60	.262	.316	.228	9.76	4.39

Fielding

Catcher	PCT	G	PO	A	E	DP	PB
Bethea	.987	31	214	15	3	1	2
Hanigan	1.000	1	4	0	0	0	0
Romanski	.993	89	676	77	5	5	7
Solis	.982	20	144	20	3	0	2

First Base	PCT	G	PO	A	E	DP
Court	.986	11	60	8	1	5
Decker	1.000	30	226	19	0	24
Freiman	.997	66	530	45	2	46
Roberson	.981	18	145	9	3	14
Rosario	1.000	1	1	0	0	0
Weems	.976	18	114	10	3	12
Witte	1.000	1	5	0	0	1

Second Base	PCT	G	PO	A	E	DP
Court	.938	9	18	27	3	5
Coyle	.949	9	12	25	2	2
Gragnani	1.000	2	3	5	0	0

	PCT	G	PO	A	E	DP
Lin	.973	27	39	71	3	16
Lovullo	1.000	2	4	3	0	0
Miller	1.000	3	5	3	0	0
Moncada	.957	34	60	73	6	21
Rijo	.963	51	95	137	9	36
Vinicio	1.000	8	15	19	0	6

Third Base	PCT	G	PO	A	E	DP
Betts	.966	13	9	19	1	3
Court	.987	59	45	104	2	13
Coyle	.952	28	19	40	3	2
Decker	1.000	1	0	1	0	0
Lin	.885	17	14	32	6	3
Miller	1.000	2	2	3	0	0
Moncada	.909	10	6	24	3	1
Vinicio	.636	3	1	6	4	0
Witte	.962	10	9	16	1	0

Shortstop	PCT	G	PO	A	E	DP
Court	.960	5	10	14	1	3

	PCT	G	PO	A	E	DP
Dubon	.967	62	99	137	8	29
Lin	.955	60	87	147	11	36
Miller	.600	1	1	2	2	1
Vinicio	.951	12	18	21	2	6

Outfield	PCT	G	PO	A	E	DP
Benintendi	1.000	57	138	5	0	1
Brentz	.900	9	9	0	1	0
Court	1.000	2	2	0	0	0
Coyle	1.000	1	5	0	0	0
Decker	1.000	9	9	0	0	0
Lin	1.000	5	12	0	0	0
Madera	1.000	1	4	0	0	0
Miller	1.000	12	16	2	0	0
Ramos	.968	40	88	3	3	0
Ray	1.000	1	1	0	0	0
Rosario	.967	85	114	3	4	2
Sturgeon	.985	112	253	11	4	6
Tavarez	.963	97	177	4	7	0

SALEM RED SOX
CAROLINA LEAGUE

HIGH CLASS A

Batting

Batting	B-T	HT	WT	DOB	AVG	vLH	vRH	G	AB	R	H	2B	3B	HR	RBI	BB	HBP	SH	SF	SO	SB	CS	SLG	OBP
Basabe, Luis Alexander	B-R	6-0	160	8-26-96	.364	.273	.455	5	22	5	8	2	1	0	1	0	0	0	3	0	0	.545	.391
Benintendi, Andrew	L-L	5-10	170	7-6-94	.341	.344	.340	34	135	30	46	13	7	1	32	15	3	0	2	9	8	2	.563	.413
Bethea, Danny	R-R	6-1	210	1-31-90	.250	—	.250	1	4	0	1	1	0	0	1	0	0	0	0	1	0	0	.500	.250
Betts, Jordan	R-R	6-3	220	10-6-91	.241	.284	.217	77	270	31	65	24	1	4	42	28	0	2	3	67	1	1	.381	.309
Chavis, Michael	R-R	5-10	190	8-11-95	.160	.111	.188	7	25	5	4	0	0	0	1	2	0	0	0	7	1	0	.160	.222
Devers, Rafael	L-R	6-0	195	10-24-96	.282	.278	.284	128	503	64	142	32	8	11	71	40	1	0	2	94	18	6	.443	.335
Dubon, Mauricio	R-R	6-0	160	7-19-94	.306	.328	.299	62	235	53	72	11	3	0	29	33	0	7	3	25	24	4	.379	.387
Gragnani, Reed	B-R	5-11	180	5-9-90	.244	.241	.246	22	86	11	21	2	1	1	7	12	0	2	1	20	0	0	.326	.333
Gunsolus, Mitchell	L-R	6-0	200	1-23-93	.043	.000	.050	7	23	1	1	1	0	0	2	6	0	1	0	5	1	0	.087	.241
Guzman, Franklin	R-R	5-11	185	2-4-92	.203	.158	.222	21	64	4	13	2	1	0	6	7	1	0	0	14	9	2	.266	.292
Hudson, Bryan	L-R	6-1	185	2-10-95	.269	.289	.265	83	249	45	67	12	2	0	26	59	1	3	1	60	26	6	.333	.410
Longhi, Nick	R-L	6-2	205	8-16-95	.282	.317	.267	124	471	56	133	40	3	2	77	50	3	2	9	106	2	3	.393	.349
Lopez, Deiner	B-R	6-0	165	5-30-94	.244	.182	.272	98	312	49	76	12	5	3	28	26	2	6	2	77	15	5	.343	.304
Mars, Danny	B-R	6-0	195	1-22-94	.293	.306	.288	108	409	60	120	18	10	2	54	36	4	2	4	84	31	13	.401	.353
Mesa, Carlos	R-R	6-2	215	2-10-88	.000	.000	—	2	5	0	0	0	0	0	0	0	0	0	0	2	0	0	.000	.000
Meyers, Mike	R-R	6-1	190	12-28-93	.272	.328	.248	111	419	53	114	17	9	4	66	36	3	0	9	116	26	5	.384	.328
Moncada, Yoan	B-R	6-2	205	5-27-95	.307	.286	.315	61	228	57	70	25	3	4	34	45	5	3	3	60	36	8	.496	.427
Monge, Joseph	R-R	6-0	170	5-18-95	.274	.276	.272	79	329	45	90	19	4	4	36	23	6	2	1	81	19	8	.392	.331
Moore, Ben	R-R	6-1	195	9-22-92	.221	.260	.202	49	154	12	34	7	0	2	17	7	5	2	2	30	2	3	.305	.274
Procyshen, Jordan	L-R	5-10	185	3-11-93	.249	.161	.283	61	221	29	55	16	0	4	29	14	4	2	3	56	3	0	.376	.302
Ray, Jayce	L-R	6-0	195	11-26-89	.343	.353	.338	33	105	19	36	6	1	0	13	19	2	0	0	13	6	1	.419	.452
Rijo, Wendell	R-R	5-11	170	9-4-95	.270	.000	.357	11	37	5	10	2	0	0	3	6	0	2	1	11	2	0	.324	.364
Sermo, Jose	B-R	6-0	190	3-22-91	.292	.375	.257	59	212	38	62	17	2	8	35	18	1	0	5	59	10	2	.505	.343
Sopilka, David	R-R	6-0	170	8-30-93	.273	.256	.281	42	139	17	38	7	1	1	14	12	1	4	2	30	1	0	.360	.331
Watkins, J.T.	R-R	6-0	190	8-30-89	.250	.000	.500	2	8	1	2	0	0	0	1	0	0	0	0	1	0	0	.250	.250

BOSTON RED SOX

Pitching

Pitching	B-T	HT	WT	DOB	W	L	ERA	G	GS	CG	SV	IP	H	R	ER	HR	BB	SO	AVG	vLH	vRH	K/9	BB/9
Alcantara, Mario	R-R	6-2	225	12-27-92	9	2	3.16	32	1	0	2	80	56	34	28	2	48	68	.206	.224	.188	7.68	5.42
Ball, Trey	L-L	6-6	185	6-27-94	8	6	3.84	23	23	0	0	117	121	61	50	8	68	86	.271	.297	.262	6.60	5.22
Beeks, Jalen	L-L	5-11	195	7-10-93	4	4	3.07	13	13	1	0	67	67	25	23	9	24	55	.259	.250	.262	7.35	3.21
Callahan, Jamie	R-R	6-2	230	8-24-94	5	3	3.29	36	0	0	7	66	53	30	24	1	38	63	.218	.240	.197	8.63	5.21
Cosart, Jake	R-R	6-2	175	2-11-94	0	0	1.00	8	0	0	0	18	7	2	2	0	11	28	.111	.125	.097	14.00	5.50
Drehoff, Jake	L-L	6-4	195	6-5-92	0	1	4.24	13	1	0	6	17	14	11	8	1	5	25	.209	.143	.239	13.24	2.65
Fernandez, Jeffry	R-R	6-1	220	3-25-93	2	1	5.79	9	1	0	0	19	19	13	12	1	10	15	.271	.282	.258	7.23	4.82
Grover, Taylor	R-R	6-3	195	4-22-91	1	1	2.67	17	0	0	3	30	25	9	9	1	9	31	.223	.265	.190	9.20	2.67
Jimenez, Dedgar	L-L	6-3	240	3-6-96	2	3	6.35	9	9	0	0	40	52	33	28	1	21	14	.317	.239	.347	3.18	4.76
Kelley, Trevor	R-R	6-2	210	10-20-93	0	0	0.00	1	0	0	0	2	0	0	0	0	0	3	.000	.000	.000	13.50	0.00
Kent, Matt	L-L	6-0	180	9-13-92	10	7	3.69	26	26	1	0	156	171	70	64	4	33	120	.280	.237	.298	6.92	1.90
Kopech, Michael	R-R	6-3	205	4-30-96	4	1	2.25	11	11	0	0	52	25	15	13	1	29	82	.147	.120	.186	14.19	5.02
Lakins, Travis	R-R	6-1	180	6-29-94	6	3	5.93	19	18	0	0	91	111	65	60	8	36	79	.299	.285	.314	7.81	3.56
Lau, Adam	R-R	6-2	210	7-5-94	3	0	4.35	5	0	0	0	10	4	5	5	1	6	10	.121	.100	.154	8.71	5.23
Leclerc, Angelo	R-R	6-0	170	10-9-91	4	3	4.04	14	9	0	0	56	56	27	25	6	23	43	.255	.250	.259	6.95	3.72
Maddox, Austin	R-R	6-2	220	5-13-91	2	0	3.33	13	0	0	5	24	29	10	9	0	8	24	.290	.310	.276	8.88	2.96
Marban, Jorge	R-R	6-1	215	12-5-88	1	0	5.94	9	0	0	1	17	23	11	11	3	7	9	.324	.278	.371	4.86	3.78
McEachern, Kuehl	R-R	6-4	195	5-7-93	0	0	0.00	1	0	0	0	1	0	0	0	0	0	1	.000	—	.000	9.00	0.00
McGrath, Daniel	R-L	6-3	205	7-7-94	8	6	4.11	19	19	2	0	103	80	54	47	12	43	62	.218	.182	.231	5.42	3.76
Mercedes, Simon	R-R	6-4	240	2-17-92	5	2	4.86	23	0	0	6	37	35	21	20	3	13	38	.246	.205	.290	9.24	3.16
Pimentel, Yankory	R-R	6-2	210	9-29-93	9	6	3.12	32	3	0	4	78	71	37	27	7	36	70	.242	.253	.231	8.08	4.15
Poyner, Bobby	L-L	6-0	205	12-1-92	3	1	4.99	23	1	0	4	40	44	24	22	4	11	30	.278	.309	.262	6.81	2.50
Taveras, German	R-R	6-2	180	2-15-93	1	0	9.38	25	1	0	0	47	59	53	49	6	34	33	.309	.347	.271	6.32	6.51
Taylor, Ben	R-R	6-3	225	11-12-92	0	2	2.60	15	3	0	3	45	35	14	13	0	10	56	.213	.194	.228	11.20	2.00

Fielding

Catcher	PCT	G	PO	A	E	DP	PB
Bethea	1.000	1	9	0	0	0	0
Moore	.984	44	287	27	5	1	4
Procyshen	.991	57	401	36	4	2	6
Sopilka	.997	42	316	40	1	5	9
Watkins	1.000	2	21	1	0	0	1

First Base	PCT	G	PO	A	E	DP
Betts	.997	40	308	19	1	2
Gunsolus	1.000	1	3	0	0	0
Longhi	.999	99	789	66	1	59

Second Base	PCT	G	PO	A	E	DP
Gragnani	.989	21	29	58	1	7
Lopez	.981	14	21	31	1	11

	PCT	G	PO	A	E	DP
Moncada	.958	58	109	140	11	23
Rijo	1.000	11	20	27	0	5
Sermo	.977	37	52	74	3	18

Third Base	PCT	G	PO	A	E	DP
Betts	.897	13	7	28	4	3
Chavis	.750	2	2	1	1	0
Devers	.960	117	104	258	15	19
Gunsolus	1.000	2	0	5	0	0
Lopez	.947	8	2	16	1	1
Sermo	1.000	1	2	0	0	0

Shortstop	PCT	G	PO	A	E	DP
Dubon	.941	61	86	136	14	24
Lopez	.951	69	112	160	14	31
Sermo	.980	13	21	29	1	6

Outfield	PCT	G	PO	A	E	DP
Basabe	1.000	4	20	0	0	0
Benintendi	.990	30	95	3	1	1
Betts	—	1	0	0	0	0
Guzman	.973	17	35	1	1	1
Hudson	.980	63	92	4	2	1
Longhi	1.000	12	22	2	0	0
Mars	.978	101	212	6	5	2
Mesa	—	1	0	0	0	0
Meyers	.973	94	176	7	5	0
Monge	.990	76	185	4	2	4
Ray	.977	26	42	1	1	0

GREENVILLE DRIVE

SOUTH ATLANTIC LEAGUE

LOW CLASS A

Batting	B-T	HT	WT	DOB	AVG	vLH	vRH	G	AB	R	H	2B	3B	HR	RBI	BB	HBP	SH	SF	SO	SB	CS	SLG	OBP
Baldwin, Roldani	R-R	5-11	175	3-16-96	.249	.270	.245	61	225	26	56	12	0	3	23	9	2	3	2	57	1	1	.342	.282
Basabe, Luis Alejandro	B-R	5-10	160	8-26-96	.310	.328	.304	64	229	39	71	16	4	4	25	37	4	3	2	58	14	6	.467	.412
Basabe, Luis Alexander	B-R	6-0	160	8-26-96	.258	.315	.245	105	403	61	104	24	8	12	52	40	2	2	4	116	25	5	.447	.325
Chavis, Michael	R-R	5-10	190	8-11-95	.244	.286	.233	74	279	30	68	11	3	8	35	22	10	0	1	74	3	1	.391	.321
De La Guerra, Chad	L-R	5-11	190	11-24-92	.250	.200	.259	66	240	40	60	8	4	1	20	31	2	2	4	57	7	2	.329	.336
Gunsolus, Mitchell	L-R	6-0	200	1-23-93	.223	.179	.231	100	346	37	77	12	0	11	45	50	3	3	3	98	4	6	.353	.323
Kemp, Trenton	R-R	6-2	195	6-5-94	.244	.258	.241	92	311	42	76	18	3	13	52	32	5	1	0	123	7	3	.447	.325
Lovullo, Nick	R-R	6-0	175	12-1-93	.163	.056	.180	37	129	15	21	4	0	0	4	9	1	3	0	33	0	1	.194	.223
Matheny, Tate	R-R	6-0	185	2-9-94	.277	.276	.278	105	411	59	114	20	4	5	52	28	4	4	7	104	21	12	.382	.324
Miller, Derek	R-R	6-2	180	7-18-92	.221	.308	.203	50	154	20	34	8	1	2	15	25	3	1	1	30	8	3	.325	.339
Monge, Joseph	R-R	6-0	170	5-18-95	.338	.310	.345	37	142	21	48	11	0	3	13	12	2	0	2	35	5	7	.479	.392
Nunez, Jhon	B-R	5-9	165	12-5-94	.316	.143	.417	4	19	1	6	2	0	0	1	1	0	0	0	2	0	1	.421	.350
Ockimey, Josh	L-R	6-1	215	10-18-95	.226	.192	.234	117	407	60	92	25	1	16	62	88	3	0	1	129	3	1	.425	.367
Ray, Jayce	L-R	6-0	195	11-26-89	.378	.333	.394	12	45	8	17	4	0	0	3	4	0	0	0	8	2	0	.467	.429
Rei, Austin	R-R	6-0	185	10-22-93	.212	.255	.205	91	311	50	66	13	1	6	33	41	15	0	2	82	1	4	.318	.331
Rivera, Jeremy	B-R	5-9	150	1-30-95	.260	.250	.262	111	365	42	95	19	4	0	36	19	3	8	3	54	9	5	.334	.300
Spoon, Tyler	R-R	5-11	190	9-28-92	.224	.533	.174	30	107	11	24	2	0	2	9	7	1	0	1	31	1	1	.299	.276
Washington, Kyri	R-R	5-11	220	7-11-94	.262	.258	.263	103	382	51	100	20	9	16	73	33	4	1	5	121	16	7	.487	.323
Watkins, J.T.	R-R	6-0	190	8-30-89	.135	.118	.139	29	89	7	12	0	1	0	7	8	0	1	0	21	0	1	.157	.206

Pitching	B-T	HT	WT	DOB	W	L	ERA	G	GS	CG	SV	IP	H	R	ER	HR	BB	SO	AVG	vLH	vRH	K/9	BB/9
Almonte, Jose	R-R	6-2	185	9-8-95	2	2	3.91	10	10	0	0	53	50	23	23	4	13	45	.249	.268	.238	7.64	2.21
Bautista, Gerson	R-R	6-2	170	5-31-95	1	4	3.24	15	0	0	1	25	20	11	9	3	11	23	.213	.250	.190	8.28	3.96
Boyd, Logan	L-L	6-2	205	11-26-93	14	7	4.78	27	27	0	0	139	169	83	74	10	31	112	.300	.279	.307	7.23	2.00
Brakeman, Marc	L-R	6-2	185	6-15-94	5	5	4.33	24	9	0	1	73	74	40	35	6	19	76	.261	.345	.207	9.41	2.35
Cosart, Jake	R-R	6-2	175	2-11-94	4	1	2.05	29	0	0	2	53	36	13	12	2	25	76	.193	.241	.157	12.99	4.27
De Jesus, Enmanuel	L-L	6-3	190	12-10-96	2	4	5.96	10	10	0	0	45	56	33	30	8	20	30	.313	.317	.312	5.96	3.97

Pitching

Pitching	B-T	HT	WT	DOB	W	L	ERA	G	GS	CG	SV	IP	H	R	ER	HR	BB	SO	AVG	vLH	vRH	K/9	BB/9
Diaz, Victor	R-R	6-3	190	5-24-94	2	5	3.88	37	0	0	10	60	65	30	26	2	25	63	.277	.368	.214	9.40	3.73
Espinoza, Anderson	R-R	6-0	160	3-9-98	5	8	4.38	17	17	0	0	76	77	39	37	2	27	72	.269	.209	.310	8.53	3.20
Fernandez, Jeffry	R-R	6-1	220	3-25-93	2	2	2.92	28	1	0	2	62	48	27	20	5	16	42	.217	.120	.275	6.13	2.34
Glorius, Austin	R-R	6-3	205	5-10-93	2	2	3.20	31	5	0	0	76	63	29	27	3	35	75	.222	.211	.229	8.88	4.14
Gonzalez, Daniel	R-R	6-5	180	2-9-96	5	5	3.70	16	16	0	0	88	88	42	36	5	17	69	.261	.265	.258	7.08	1.75
Jimenez, Dedgar	L-L	6-3	240	3-6-96	6	7	4.73	17	17	1	0	97	123	56	51	5	15	81	.311	.316	.309	7.52	1.39
Kelley, Trevor	R-R	6-2	210	10-20-93	1	3	1.93	21	0	0	3	37	34	9	8	2	5	40	.233	.333	.174	9.64	1.21
Kent, Matt	L-L	6-0	180	9-13-92	0	0	1.50	2	2	0	0	12	9	3	2	0	4	5	.220	.214	.222	3.75	3.00
Lau, Adam	R-R	6-2	210	7-5-94	3	2	3.54	29	1	0	4	53	36	22	21	4	36	58	.185	.167	.195	9.76	6.08
Leclerc, Angelo	R-R	6-0	170	10-9-91	3	1	1.77	21	0	0	8	41	24	10	8	2	12	42	.174	.150	.184	9.30	2.66
McEachern, Kuehl	R-R	6-4	195	5-7-93	2	3	5.68	24	0	0	1	52	66	38	33	4	13	55	.308	.291	.319	9.46	2.24
Nogosek, Steve	R-R	6-0	205	5-14-95	0	2	5.14	10	0	0	2	14	17	9	8	1	3	12	.293	.300	.289	7.71	1.93
Poyner, Bobby	L-L	6-0	205	12-1-92	0	0	0.35	16	0	0	11	26	11	2	1	0	0	32	.128	.087	.143	11.08	0.00
Raudes, Roniel	R-R	6-1	160	1-16-98	11	6	3.65	24	24	0	0	113	112	60	46	8	23	104	.260	.259	.261	8.26	1.83
Romero, Dioscar	R-R	6-3	230	4-17-95	0	0	4.08	8	0	0	0	18	20	9	8	1	7	16	.290	.208	.333	8.15	3.57

Fielding

Catcher	PCT	G	PO	A	E	DP	PB
Baldwin	.985	32	234	32	4	4	10
Nunez	1.000	4	39	7	0	0	0
Rei	.993	81	650	76	5	5	16
Spoon	.984	20	164	24	3	0	1
Watkins	1.000	7	37	5	0	0	1

First Base	PCT	G	PO	A	E	DP
Gunsolus	.984	23	182	8	3	12
Ockimey	.986	101	786	54	12	54
Watkins	1.000	20	162	12	0	9

Second Base	PCT	G	PO	A	E	DP
Basabe	.955	43	80	110	9	29
De La Guerra	.985	47	72	121	3	20
Gunsolus	.982	27	40	67	2	5
Lovullo	.973	28	46	63	3	9

Third Base	PCT	G	PO	A	E	DP
Baldwin	.892	23	21	45	8	5
Chavis	.945	68	40	131	10	4
De La Guerra	.917	6	4	7	1	2
Gunsolus	.952	45	29	71	5	4

Shortstop	PCT	G	PO	A	E	DP
Basabe	.836	17	20	31	10	8
De La Guerra	.966	8	5	23	1	4
Lovullo	.886	10	16	23	5	1
Rivera	.960	109	136	277	17	40

Outfield	PCT	G	PO	A	E	DP
Basabe	.992	98	252	8	2	1
Kemp	.983	74	108	8	2	1
Matheny	.990	96	192	15	2	4
Miller	.975	47	76	2	2	0
Monge	.987	33	74	4	1	3
Ray	1.000	7	6	0	0	0
Washington	.982	74	105	4	2	1

LOWELL SPINNERS
NEW YORK-PENN LEAGUE
SHORT-SEASON

Batting

Batting	B-T	HT	WT	DOB	AVG	vLH	vRH	G	AB	R	H	2B	3B	HR	RBI	BB	HBP	SH	SF	SO	SB	CS	SLG	OBP
Acosta, Victor	R-R	5-11	160	6-2-96	.274	.327	.254	50	186	35	51	7	3	0	21	11	1	4	2	36	5	2	.344	.315
Aybar, Yoan	L-L	6-2	165	7-3-97	.207	.192	.212	60	222	18	46	7	4	3	19	8	4	1	1	61	3	4	.315	.247
Baldwin, Roldani	R-R	5-11	175	3-16-96	.305	.375	.282	25	95	10	29	8	1	1	14	6	3	0	2	21	0	0	.442	.358
Chatham, C.J.	R-R	6-4	185	12-22-94	.259	.136	.291	27	108	19	28	4	1	4	19	8	2	2	1	20	0	1	.426	.319
Craig, Allen	R-R	6-2	215	7-18-84	.250	.333	.214	7	20	2	5	1	0	0	3	6	0	0	1	4	0	0	.300	.407
Dalbec, Bobby	R-R	6-4	225	6-29-95	.386	.343	.402	34	132	25	51	13	2	7	33	9	1	0	1	33	2	2	.674	.427
Downs, Jerry	L-L	6-4	215	12-22-93	.261	.235	.268	45	157	18	41	9	0	5	24	17	5	0	1	30	2	1	.414	.350
Hanigan, Ryan	R-R	6-0	220	8-16-80	.500	.500	.500	2	8	3	4	0	0	0	3	2	0	0	1	0	0	0	.500	.600
Hill, Tyler	R-R	6-0	195	3-4-96	.332	.339	.329	61	232	43	77	14	5	4	38	24	3	1	1	41	11	11	.487	.400
Lovullo, Nick	R-R	6-0	175	12-1-93	.268	.250	.273	18	56	9	15	1	1	0	5	8	1	2	1	10	1	1	.321	.364
Lucena, Isaias	R-R	5-11	180	11-15-94	.208	.333	.177	26	77	10	16	4	0	0	9	11	0	1	0	22	0	0	.260	.307
Madera, Chris	R-R	5-10	190	8-23-92	.259	.372	.220	48	166	26	43	6	2	2	20	24	2	3	1	23	12	4	.355	.358
McLean, Matt	L-R	5-11	190	9-15-93	.255	.279	.245	42	153	22	39	1	4	0	6	25	2	5	0	39	6	2	.314	.367
Nunez, Jhon	B-R	5-9	165	12-5-94	.286	.308	.273	12	35	6	10	2	1	0	6	3	1	0	0	5	2	0	.400	.359
Perez, Andy	R-R	6-0	175	2-23-93	.287	.300	.282	31	108	21	31	10	0	0	10	9	3	0	1	20	4	1	.380	.355
Reveles, Steven	R-R	5-8	170	1-8-93	.235	.292	.216	29	98	12	23	4	0	0	2	6	1	5	0	17	0	4	.276	.286
Rusconi, Jagger	B-R	5-11	165	7-18-96	.148	.000	.190	7	27	6	4	1	0	0	3	4	0	0	1	6	1	1	.185	.250
Sciortino, Nick	R-R	5-9	197	7-21-95	.217	.174	.232	29	92	7	20	2	0	1	5	10	2	2	1	29	0	0	.272	.305
Scott, Ryan	L-R	6-2	195	7-6-93	.276	.182	.308	49	174	28	48	11	3	4	33	13	5	0	4	42	0	2	.443	.337
Spoon, Tyler	R-R	5-11	190	9-28-92	.296	.143	.350	7	27	3	8	1	0	0	6	2	0	0	0	5	0	0	.333	.345
Tovar, Carlos	R-R	6-0	175	1-8-93	.287	.204	.313	58	209	28	60	14	2	2	28	11	2	2	4	42	1	3	.402	.323
Tubbs, Tucker	R-R	6-3	212	9-11-92	.238	.231	.240	42	143	20	34	11	1	6	23	20	3	0	2	31	1	1	.455	.339

Pitching

Pitching	B-T	HT	WT	DOB	W	L	ERA	G	GS	CG	SV	IP	H	R	ER	HR	BB	SO	AVG	vLH	vRH	K/9	BB/9
Anderson, Shaun	R-R	6-4	225	10-29-94	0	0	30.38	2	2	0	0	3	12	9	9	1	0	4	.571	.636	.500	13.50	0.00
Bautista, Gerson	R-R	6-2	170	5-31-95	0	0	0.87	8	0	0	5	10	5	1	1	0	2	13	.143	.176	.111	11.32	1.74
Dahlstrand, Jacob	R-R	6-5	205	3-26-92	0	2	1.50	2	2	0	0	12	12	2	2	0	2	4	.279	.250	.316	3.00	1.50
De Jesus, Enmanuel	L-L	6-3	190	12-10-96	2	1	2.42	4	4	0	0	22	16	7	6	0	11	16	.205	.105	.237	6.45	4.43
Goetze, Pat	R-R	6-6	200	3-3-94	4	1	3.72	20	1	0	2	46	55	28	19	2	9	36	.282	.380	.216	7.04	1.76
Gonzalez, Daniel	R-R	6-5	180	2-9-96	4	1	1.75	7	6	0	0	36	30	10	7	3	8	33	.226	.211	.237	8.25	2.00
Gorst, Matthew	R-R	6-1	205	8-24-94	1	0	2.67	13	0	0	2	27	21	9	8	2	6	27	.212	.278	.175	9.00	2.00
Groome, Jason	L-L	6-6	220	8-23-98	0	0	3.38	1	1	0	0	3	0	1	1	0	4	2	.000	.000	.000	6.75	13.50
Hernandez, Darwinzon	L-L	6-2	185	12-17-96	3	5	4.10	14	14	0	0	48	39	34	22	1	36	58	.217	.241	.205	10.80	6.70
Janssen, Casey	R-R	6-4	210	9-17-81	0	0	3.38	8	0	0	1	8	8	3	3	0	1	8	.250	.182	.286	9.00	1.13
Johnson, Brian	L-L	6-4	235	12-7-90	0	0	0.00	2	2	0	0	11	7	0	0	0	2	11	.184	.111	.207	9.00	1.64
Kelly, Joe	R-R	6-1	190	6-9-88	0	0	4.50	3	0	0	0	4	4	2	2	0	1	5	.250	.300	.167	11.25	2.25
Kopech, Michael	R-R	6-3	205	4-30-96	0	0	0.00	1	1	0	0	4	1	0	0	0	4	4	.250	.000	.400	8.31	8.31
Martinez, Algenis	R-R	6-1	185	9-12-93	1	1	1.94	18	0	0	3	42	26	10	9	2	11	41	.187	.259	.141	8.86	2.38

Pitching	B-T	HT	WT	DOB	W	L	ERA	G	GS	CG	SV	IP	H	R	ER	HR	BB	SO	AVG	vLH	vRH	K/9	BB/9
McEachern, Kuehl	R-R	6-4	195	5-7-93	1	0	0.36	11	0	0	2	25	22	1	1	0	3	23	.256	.400	.157	8.28	1.08
Nogosek, Steve	R-R	6-2	205	1-11-95	1	0	2.03	10	0	0	0	13	9	3	3	2	7	19	.196	.182	.208	12.83	4.73
Oliver, Jared	R-R	6-1	185	2-1-93	0	0	1.93	2	0	0	0	5	3	1	1	0	3	4	.200	.250	.182	7.71	5.79
Pennington, Josh	R-R	6-0	175	7-6-95	5	3	2.86	13	13	0	0	57	39	19	18	2	27	49	.200	.256	.156	7.78	4.29
Romero, Dioscar	R-R	6-3	230	4-17-95	4	2	3.31	20	0	0	6	35	36	16	13	2	15	38	.269	.327	.228	9.68	3.82
Shawaryn, Mike	R-R	6-2	200	9-17-94	0	1	2.87	6	6	0	0	16	15	6	5	0	7	22	.254	.241	.267	12.64	4.02
Smith, Dakota	R-R	5-10	195	10-25-92	5	2	1.77	9	7	0	0	46	41	13	9	2	11	35	.236	.258	.223	6.90	2.17
Smith, Hunter	R-R	6-3	195	3-18-94	2	0	4.09	3	1	0	0	11	9	5	5	1	2	12	.237	.267	.217	9.82	1.64
Steen, Kevin	R-R	6-1	170	7-24-96	3	5	5.37	14	14	0	0	67	70	44	40	4	42	41	.270	.327	.226	5.51	5.64
Stone, Brad	L-L	6-3	175	6-18-94	3	2	7.86	17	0	0	0	26	29	28	23	2	35	18	.293	.321	.282	6.15	11.96
Workman, Brandon	R-R	6-5	235	8-13-88	0	1	6.75	5	0	0	0	8	9	7	6	2	4	8	.273	.286	.263	9.00	4.50
Zandona, Danny	R-R	6-1	200	2-27-93	6	2	2.88	16	2	0	0	56	43	22	18	4	12	44	.207	.250	.172	7.03	1.92

Fielding

C: Baldwin 7, Hanigan 1, Lucena 26, Nunez 12, Sciortino 29, Spoon 5. **1B:** Craig 1, Downs 39, Tubbs 36. **2B:** Acosta 25, Lovullo 12, Madera 2, Perez 12, Reveles 5, Rusconi 5, Tovar 19. **3B:** Acosta 7, Baldwin 16, Dalbec 22, Lovullo 3, Perez 17, Reveles 12. **SS:** Chatham 26, Lovullo 2, Reveles 10, Tovar 40. **OF:** Acosta 10, Aybar 57, Craig 3, Hill 48, Madera 43, McLean 38, Scott 35.

GCL RED SOX   ROOKIE
GULF COAST LEAGUE

Batting	B-T	HT	WT	DOB	AVG	vLH	vRH	G	AB	R	H	2B	3B	HR	RBI	BB	HBP	SH	SF	SO	SB	CS	SLG	OBP
Abreu, Juan Carlos	R-R	6-0	175	5-30-97	.219	.188	.233	34	105	13	23	5	1	0	13	7	2	1	0	31	2	1	.286	.281
Barriento, Juan	R-R	6-2	201	4-28-96	.298	.294	.299	49	178	21	53	8	0	2	21	13	2	0	2	41	2	2	.376	.349
Boesch, Brennan	L-L	6-4	225	4-12-85	.222	—	.222	3	9	2	2	0	0	0	2	0	0	0	0	0	0	0	.222	.364
Campana, Marino	R-R	6-4	180	11-28-97	.182	.200	.176	12	44	4	8	0	0	1	1	0	0	0	0	15	0	2	.250	.182
Cedrola, Lorenzo	R-R	5-11	170	1-12-98	.290	.394	.243	53	214	33	62	14	1	2	21	11	10	1	2	28	9	4	.393	.350
Chatham, C.J.	R-R	6-4	185	12-22-94	.167	.167	.167	8	24	2	4	2	0	1	2	0	1	0	0	7	0	0	.375	.200
Cubillan, Ricardo	R-R	6-0	155	2-1-98	.000	.000	.000	2	6	2	0	0	0	0	1	2	0	0	0	2	0	0	.000	.250
Diaz, Imeldo	R-R	6-0	175	11-2-97	.234	.214	.240	46	171	11	40	4	1	0	14	5	2	1	24	0	3	.269	.263	
Espinal, Santiago	R-R	5-10	175	11-13-94	.244	.269	.233	26	86	8	21	2	0	0	10	10	1	2	0	11	1	0	.267	.330
Espinal, Stanley	R-R	6-2	190	11-15-96	.217	.231	.212	53	203	24	44	12	0	2	20	16	5	0	2	38	2	2	.305	.288
Gragnani, Reed	B-R	5-11	180	9-5-90	.233	.000	.292	7	30	2	7	2	0	0	1	1	0	0	5	0	0	.300	.258	
Hamilton, Nick	R-R	5-11	170	12-4-97	.190	.000	.235	14	42	10	8	3	0	0	1	7	3	1	0	11	3	1	.262	.346
Hardy, Chad	R-R	6-2	175	5-22-97	.163	.185	.153	27	86	6	14	0	0	2	5	3	0	1	0	32	1	0	.233	.191
Hernandez, Juan	L-R	5-10	155	4-9-96	.200	.000	.250	4	10	1	2	0	0	0	1	1	0	0	0	2	0	1	.200	.273
Houellemont, Ivan	B-R	6-2	170	9-10-98	.000	.000	.000	4	4	0	0	0	0	0	0	0	0	0	0	3	0	0	.000	.000
Lameda, Raiwinson	L-R	5-11	175	10-7-95	.238	.273	.228	54	193	16	46	9	2	0	21	14	3	2	1	40	3	2	.306	.299
Magee, Brandon	L-R	6-0	225	10-22-90	.240	.429	.167	8	25	2	6	0	1	0	4	1	0	0	10	1	1	.320	.367	
Marrero, Alan	R-R	5-10	155	2-28-98	.093	.083	.095	22	54	5	5	0	0	1	3	14	2	0	0	30	0	1	.148	.300
Miranda, Samuel	L-R	6-1	175	8-21-97	.291	.278	.294	27	86	5	25	6	0	2	16	5	3	1	1	16	0	0	.430	.347
Noviello, Andrew	L-R	6-0	195	10-24-96	.171	.100	.200	14	35	2	6	1	0	0	3	1	2	0	0	18	1	0	.200	.237
Nunez, Jhon	B-R	5-9	165	12-5-94	.400	.667	.000	2	5	1	2	1	0	0	0	0	0	0	0	1	1	0	.600	.400
Oliveras, Rafael	R-R	5-10	180	1-4-95	.275	.291	.268	45	182	20	50	6	0	0	9	14	5	0	6	20	6	0	.308	.343
Reveles, Steven	R-R	5-8	170	1-8-93	.303	.200	.348	10	33	6	10	0	0	0	4	3	1	0	0	4	3	0	.303	.378
Rusconi, Jagger	B-R	5-11	165	7-18-96	.292	.250	.313	7	24	1	7	2	0	0	3	1	0	0	0	3	1	0	.375	.320
Schmidt, Alberto	R-R	5-9	180	2-4-95	.195	.133	.231	15	41	3	8	3	0	0	8	10	1	2	0	14	0	0	.268	.365
Serven, Hemerson	R-R	5-11	210	11-11-97	.250	.000	.333	1	4	0	1	0	0	0	0	0	0	0	0	0	0	0	.250	.250
Studdard, Granger	L-R	6-1	200	2-14-95	.143	.333	.103	13	35	5	5	1	0	0	1	7	1	0	1	15	1	0	.171	.295
Valentin, Yomar	B-R	5-8	145	12-26-97	.220	.250	.209	33	91	13	20	4	1	1	10	12	0	1	3	19	2	2	.319	.302

Pitching	B-T	HT	WT	DOB	W	L	ERA	G	GS	CG	SV	IP	H	R	ER	HR	BB	SO	AVG	vLH	vRH	K/9	BB/9
Clemente, Nicolo	R-R	6-0	176	2-18-98	1	0	11.72	15	0	0	3	18	35	23	23	1	13	14	.407	.410	.404	7.13	6.62
Dahlstrand, Jacob	R-R	6-5	205	3-26-92	1	0	1.04	2	2	0	0	9	11	1	1	1	2	12	.314	.240	.500	12.46	2.08
Diaz, Jhonathan	L-L	6-0	170	9-13-96	4	4	2.85	13	12	0	0	60	52	28	19	2	18	57	.235	.197	.253	8.55	2.70
Espinoza, Junior	R-R	6-4	185	9-16-97	3	0	3.19	10	3	0	1	37	27	15	13	3	18	32	.205	.205	.203	7.85	4.42
Garcia, Victor	R-R	6-4	204	6-15-97	2	4	2.68	13	10	0	0	54	45	20	16	1	21	39	.231	.250	.203	6.54	3.52
Groome, Jason	L-L	6-6	220	8-23-98	0	0	2.25	2	2	0	0	4	3	1	1	0	0	8	.200	.500	.091	18.00	0.00
Hart, Kyle	L-L	6-5	170	11-23-92	0	2	2.31	4	4	0	0	12	12	5	3	0	2	19	.261	.231	.273	14.66	1.54
Johnson, Brian	L-L	6-4	235	12-7-90	0	1	3.86	2	2	0	0	7	7	4	3	0	2	9	.259	.375	.111	11.57	2.57
Lantigua, Marcos	R-R	6-3	200	12-14-95	1	0	11.25	13	0	0	0	16	33	21	20	0	8	15	.423	.442	.400	8.44	4.50
Marban, Jorge	R-R	6-1	215	12-5-88	0	0	10.13	3	0	0	0	3	5	4	3	0	2	1	.417	.429	.400	6.75	6.75
Oduber, Ryan	L-L	5-11	140	8-16-97	4	1	2.43	12	0	0	1	33	29	16	9	2	6	30	.228	.279	.202	8.10	1.62
Oliver, Jared	R-R	6-1	185	2-1-93	0	0	4.74	11	0	0	3	19	22	12	10	0	9	24	.286	.268	.306	11.37	4.26
Padron, Angel	L-L	5-11	175	9-16-97	2	3	3.86	13	1	0	4	26	18	12	11	1	19	26	.198	.147	.228	9.12	6.66
Pantoja, Yorvin	L-L	5-11	175	9-22-97	0	2	2.00	6	5	0	0	27	19	11	6	1	12	33	.188	.381	.138	11.00	4.00
Requena, Hildemaro	R-R	6-2	170	2-28-97	3	4	2.35	13	7	0	2	65	57	21	17	2	6	52	.234	.197	.254	7.20	0.83
Reyes, Denyi	R-R	6-4	209	11-2-96	4	1	2.34	9	3	0	0	35	30	13	9	3	4	25	.222	.227	.217	6.49	1.04
Sexton, Robby	L-L	6-0	225	4-29-94	0	1	1.80	6	0	0	0	20	15	4	4	1	2	23	.208	.100	.286	10.35	0.45
Smith, Hunter	R-R	6-3	195	3-18-94	2	0	0.00	8	0	0	1	15	11	2	0	1	20	.193	.120	.250	11.74	0.59
Soto, Francisco	R-R	6-5	220	12-18-96	2	1	6.75	9	0	0	0	12	12	9	9	2	8	.286	.348	.211	4.50	6.00
Taveras, German	R-R	6-2	180	2-15-93	0	0	0.87	5	0	0	0	10	10	3	1	0	0	9	.238	.200	.294	7.84	0.00
Watt, Max	R-R	6-8	250	8-9-94	2	2	4.76	9	3	0	0	17	16	14	9	0	14	16	.242	.216	.276	8.47	7.41
Workman, Brandon	R-R	6-5	235	8-13-88	0	1	4.50	1	1	0	0	2	2	1	1	0	0	3	.250	.000	.400	13.50	0.00

Fielding

C: Marrero 19, Miranda 26, Noviello 13, Nunez 2, Schmidt 13. **1B:** Barriento 1, Lameda 36, Oliveras 28, Serven 1. **2B:** Diaz 5, Espinal 14, Gragnani 5, Houellemont 1, Oliveras 12, Reveles 6, Rusconi 6, Valentin 21. **3B:** Barriento 1, Diaz 6, Espinal 47, Gragnani 1, Oliveras 6, Reveles 1. **SS:** Chatham 7, Cubillan 2, Diaz 32, Espinal 11, Houellemont 2, Reveles 1, Valentin 12. **OF:** Abreu 24, Barriento 35, Boesch 2, Campana 7, Cedrola 51, Espinal 1, Hamilton 13, Hardy 25, Hernandez 3, Lameda 19, Magee 8, Studdard 6.

DSL RED SOX   ROOKIE
DOMINICAN SUMMER LEAGUE

Batting	B-T	HT	WT	DOB	AVG	vLH	vRH	G	AB	R	H	2B	3B	HR	RBI	BB	HBP	SH	SF	SO	SB	CS	SLG	OBP
Andrade, Fabian	L-L	5-11	162	4-1-99	.204	.174	.213	61	201	22	41	6	1	0	14	27	4	1	0	37	5	1	.244	.310
Aponte, Dawill	L-L	6-0	155	8-19-97	.273	.333	.250	6	11	0	3	0	0	0	1	0	0	0	0	2	0	0	.273	.273
Berroa, Ramfis	R-R	6-2	190	11-2-95	.247	.175	.268	54	182	26	45	10	5	4	30	24	6	0	2	49	11	4	.423	.350
Campana, Marino	R-R	6-4	180	11-28-97	.267	.350	.243	25	90	11	24	4	3	2	12	7	3	0	1	18	2	3	.444	.337
Castellanos, Pedro	R-R	6-3	195	12-11-97	.326	.392	.308	62	236	28	77	23	4	3	47	20	7	0	1	25	2	5	.496	.394
Chacon, Jesus	R-R	5-11	167	5-27-99	.125	.067	.140	32	72	7	9	0	0	0	1	3	2	3	0	26	1	1	.125	.182
Coca, Yeison	R-R	5-5	155	5-22-99	.308	.302	.310	63	260	41	80	5	9	1	26	26	1	1	1	42	12	5	.408	.372
Conde, Eduard	L-R	5-9	155	2-13-98	.273	.286	.269	51	187	17	51	9	2	1	33	12	3	1	4	27	5	5	.358	.320
Cubillan, Ricardo	R-R	6-0	155	2-1-98	.231	.156	.250	50	160	40	37	6	2	0	17	38	2	3	3	21	13	3	.294	.379
Figueroa, Willis	B-R	5-10	165	12-31-94	.202	.162	.214	59	168	31	34	2	2	0	18	28	11	4	1	29	14	8	.238	.351
Guaimaro, Albert	R-R	6-0	180	1-17-99	.250	.050	.309	23	88	9	22	10	1	1	13	6	1	0	1	14	4	4	.420	.302
2-team total (19 Marlins)					.225	—	—	42	160	12	36	12	1	1	22	12	1	0	1	24	6	4	.331	.282
Hernandez, Angel	R-R	6-0	180	8-22-97	.000	.000	.000	2	5	0	0	0	0	0	0	0	0	0	0	4	0	0	.000	.000
Hernandez, Juan	L-R	5-10	155	4-9-96	.288	.161	.318	44	160	30	46	3	1	1	22	31	4	1	1	15	12	6	.338	.413
Hernandez, Luis	R-R	6-1	165	10-7-98	.231	.196	.241	65	212	38	49	7	0	0	11	47	8	4	1	43	9	7	.264	.388
Houellemont, Ivan	B-R	6-2	170	9-10-98	.171	.182	.167	13	35	9	6	1	0	0	1	9	2	0	0	12	1	1	.200	.370
Jimenez, Ivan	R-R	6-4	215	4-17-98	.161	.235	.133	23	62	5	10	2	0	0	2	8	2	0	0	19	0	0	.194	.278
Lozada, Everlouis	B-R	5-7	155	11-14-98	.298	.236	.316	62	248	48	74	12	4	1	30	35	3	2	1	56	17	6	.391	.390
Martinez, Alexander	R-R	6-0	170	9-6-96	.263	.200	.273	14	38	9	10	1	0	0	4	5	1	0	2	4	3	0	.289	.348
Martinez, Marcos	L-R	5-11	165	1-28-98	.191	.182	.193	40	110	15	21	1	0	0	6	19	1	2	0	27	4	1	.200	.315
Mejias, Jose	R-R	6-1	160	3-13-99	.138	.071	.159	43	116	10	16	1	0	1	6	14	2	1	3	39	4	4	.147	.237
Muzziotti, Simon	L-L	6-1	175	12-27-98	.317	.235	.349	17	60	9	19	2	1	0	4	0	0	1	6	1	1	.383	.354
2-team total (37 Phillies)					.256	—	—	54	203	21	52	6	2	0	22	15	0	2	1	16	8	4	.305	.306
Petit, Keibert	R-R	6-1	175	8-3-98	.208	.200	.211	18	48	9	10	1	0	0	4	12	3	0	0	11	2	1	.229	.397
Pinero, Antonio	B-R	6-1	155	3-15-99	.198	.200	.197	22	81	12	16	0	0	0	6	7	0	1	1	10	7	1	.198	.258
2-team total (28 Brewers)					.218	—	—	50	179	27	39	2	0	0	13	16	0	4	2	30	13	1	.229	.279
Pulgar, Ronaldo	R-R	5-10	158	1-2-97	.217	.208	.220	57	212	22	46	4	3	1	17	24	4	1	1	54	6	5	.278	.307
Pulido, Carlos	R-R	5-10	170	2-7-98	.283	.231	.298	66	223	36	63	9	1	1	27	35	12	0	4	24	1	2	.345	.401
Reynoso, Eddy	R-R	6-0	195	8-7-94	.278	.315	.267	64	245	28	68	16	3	3	44	12	1	0	6	43	0	3	.404	.309
Rincon, Daniel	R-R	6-0	160	1-22-99	.136	.063	.160	30	66	7	9	2	0	0	6	10	3	1	1	23	0	1	.167	.275
Rincones, Rafael	B-R	6-1	165	4-1-99	.275	.310	.264	40	120	26	33	5	1	1	20	21	4	2	0	43	6	2	.358	.400
Rodriguez, Kleiber	B-R	6-2	175	10-8-98	.160	.184	.152	61	200	19	32	4	3	0	22	35	4	0	1	44	1	2	.210	.296
Serven, Hemerson	B-R	5-11	210	11-11-97	.143	.500	.000	3	7	0	1	0	0	0	0	0	0	0	0	2	0	0	.143	.143
Suarez, Kervin	B-R	5-11	165	12-19-98	.274	.288	.269	66	259	40	71	11	3	1	25	21	7	1	0	58	18	7	.351	.345
Tejeda, Elwin	R-R	6-2	140	9-14-97	.148	.103	.160	43	135	9	20	2	0	0	14	8	4	0	4	38	4	4	.163	.237
Torrealba, Eduardo	R-R	5-8	140	3-26-99	.247	.389	.200	22	73	11	18	0	0	0	10	10	0	1	5	4	3	4	.247	.318
2-team total (21 Yankees2)					.253	—	—	43	150	26	38	3	0	1	21	23	5	1	6	13	11	6	.293	.359
Ugueto, Reinaldo	R-R	5-11	165	12-9-97	.310	.321	.307	44	129	24	40	7	0	0	12	8	12	2	1	20	11	6	.364	.400

Pitching	B-T	HT	WT	DOB	W	L	ERA	G	GS	CG	SV	IP	H	R	ER	HR	BB	SO	AVG	vLH	vRH	K/9	BB/9
Adames, Rayniel	L-L	6-6	175	9-7-97	2	1	2.74	12	12	0	0	46	32	17	14	1	24	38	.196	.217	.193	7.43	4.70
Batista, Edilson	L-L	6-3	210	7-7-97	5	2	2.39	13	13	0	0	53	40	17	14	0	20	37	.214	.125	.227	6.32	3.42
Bazardo, Eduard	R-R	6-0	155	9-1-95	6	2	0.79	17	1	0	4	45	23	7	4	0	18	48	.159	.14	.167	9.53	3.57
Caraballo, William	R-R	6-1	170	7-18-98	0	1	15.00	5	0	0	0	3	5	5	5	0	6	2	.357	.600	2.00	6.00	18.00
Calvo, Gary	R-R	6-3	180	10-4-96	1	1	1.74	5	1	0	0	10	4	3	2	0	11	.121	.000	.160	9.58	2.61
Cortes, Carlos	R-R	6-1	165	7-26-96	2	1	1.59	15	0	0	2	34	25	11	6	1	16	18	.208	.313	.170	4.76	4.24
Familia, Victor	R-R	6-0	170	4-3-98	3	0	4.50	19	0	0	1	34	37	22	17	0	15	27	.274	.256	.283	7.15	3.97
Figueroa, Junior	R-R	6-4	176	8-16-99	0	0	3.10	11	0	0	0	20	20	7	7	0	15	9	.267	.346	.224	3.98	6.64
Florentino, Juan	R-R	5-10	182	9-8-96	2	1	1.26	22	0	0	13	29	21	4	4	1	9	29	.216	.148	.243	9.10	2.83
Gomez, Rafael	R-R	5-11	167	4-17-98	1	0	1.29	8	0	0	3	14	8	2	2	0	5	15	.170	.143	.182	9.64	3.21
Gonzalez, Cesar	R-R	6-1	160	2-24-99	2	0	1.54	5	0	0	0	12	7	2	2	1	5	5	.171	.111	.188	3.86	3.86
2-team total (3 Padres)					2	0	1.53	8	0	0	0	18	8	3	3	1	14	8	—	—	—	4.08	7.13
Gonzalez, Jose	R-R	6-0	175	7-27-98	8	0	1.32	14	13	0	0	68	45	13	10	0	16	61	.189	.176	.195	8.07	2.12
Gutierrez, Ronald	R-R	6-2	175	4-22-99	1	2	11.12	9	0	0	0	11	13	16	14	1	16	12	.302	.294	.308	9.53	12.71
Guzman, Warlyn	R-R	6-2	196	9-9-95	6	1	1.41	21	5	0	3	57	39	16	9	0	21	43	.194	.169	.204	6.75	3.30
Jimenez, Andres	R-R	6-1	170	10-23-98	1	3	6.25	17	1	0	2	36	42	27	25	3	10	22	.300	.241	.337	5.50	2.50
Lacrus, Shair	R-R	6-1	170	12-22-96	3	1	3.11	18	0	0	3	38	34	15	13	0	35	26	.241	.256	.235	6.16	2.39
Martinez, Joan	R-R	6-3	195	8-29-96	1	2	1.88	18	0	0	9	29	17	7	6	1	8	26	.175	.200	.158	8.16	2.51
Mata, Bryan	R-R	6-3	160	5-3-99	4	4	2.80	14	14	0	0	61	54	23	19	2	19	61	.242	.301	.207	9.00	2.80
Medina, Roberto	R-R	6-3	160	1-13-95	2	0	3.08	21	0	0	2	45	46	17	15	1	19	16	.271	.344	.240	5.47	6.49
Mendoza, Ritzi	R-R	6-1	150	1-10-96	7	0	1.05	14	14	0	0	68	39	10	8	0	13	48	.166	.172	.164	6.32	1.71
Moreno, Rayniel	L-L	6-1	165	9-11-98	5	2	2.51	16	10	0	0	57	45	21	16	0	14	34	.222	.195	.228	5.34	2.20
Mosqueda, Oddanier	L-L	5-10	155	5-6-99	2	2	2.36	16	0	0	1	42	26	15	11	0	19	54	.183	.158	.187	11.57	4.07
Oduber, Ryan	L-L	5-11	140	8-16-97	2	0	0.00	4	0	0	0	15	7	0	0	0	2	15	.137	.111	.143	8.80	1.17
Padron, Angel	L-L	5-11	175	9-16-97	0	0	0.00	4	0	0	1	7	3	0	0	0	0	6	.143	.200	.125	7.71	0.00

Pitching	B-T	HT	WT	DOB	W	L	ERA	G	GS	CG	SV	IP	H	R	ER	HR	BB	SO	AVG	vLH	vRH	K/9	BB/9
Pantoja, Yorvin	L-L	5-11	175	9-22-97	0	1	3.86	3	3	0	0	14	12	6	6	1	7	13	.245	.357	.200	8.36	4.50
Perez, Geraldo	R-R	6-3	190	5-13-96	4	1	2.55	13	0	0	2	25	21	10	7	0	6	18	.231	.138	.274	6.57	2.19
Perez, Juan	R-R	6-1	198	8-30-96	5	2	2.35	15	14	0	0	69	51	24	18	1	11	42	.206	.247	.189	5.48	1.43
Police, Antonio	R-R	6-2	180	2-12-98	1	2	4.67	14	0	0	2	27	20	15	14	1	25	26	.204	.174	.213	8.67	8.33
Ramirez, Manuel	R-R	5-11	155	2-15-99	5	1	2.77	15	0	0	1	26	9	9	8	0	19	18	.111	.115	.109	6.23	6.58
Rivero, Luis	R-R	6-3	195	1-23-98	4	1	2.34	15	3	0	1	50	41	18	13	1	14	39	.218	.270	.192	7.02	2.52
Rodriguez, Alejandro	L-L	6-1	160	10-30-96	5	1	2.37	13	13	1	0	61	48	18	16	0	14	52	.215	.185	.219	7.71	2.08
Rosario, Ramses	R-R	6-3	180	10-18-95	2	1	2.63	14	1	0	0	41	35	22	12	0	17	34	.232	.158	.257	7.46	3.73
Santos, Gregory	R-R	6-2	190	8-28-99	3	3	4.17	16	10	0	1	41	40	27	19	1	26	25	.258	.261	.257	5.49	5.71
Tena, Francisco	L-L	6-3	160	3-4-95	0	0	2.70	2	0	0	0	3	5	3	1	0	2	2	.333	.000	.417	5.40	5.40
Zacarias, Jose	R-R	5-11	160	1-9-97	3	1	2.67	14	10	0	0	54	46	17	16	1	15	31	.238	.339	.197	5.17	2.50

Fielding

C: Conde 28, Jimenez 3, Martinez 28, Pulido 36, Reynoso 34, Rodriguez 20. **1B:** Andrade 3, Castellanos 37, Conde 1, Hernandez 18, Hernandez 1, Jimenez 8, Petit 1, Pulido 15, Reynoso 24, Rincon 1, Rincones 1, Rodriguez 32, Serven 2, Tejeda 13. **2B:** Chacon 20, Coca 5, Cubillan 7, Hernandez 13, Houellemont 5, Lozada 49, Pulgar 5, Suarez 30, Tejeda 1, Torrealba 3, Ugueto 13. **3B:** Castellanos 2, Chacon 5, Coca 16, Cubillan 6, Hernandez 33, Lozada 2, Pinero 9, Pulgar 44, Suarez 5, Tejeda 20, Torrealba 5. **SS:** Chacon 1, Coca 44, Cubillan 33, Hernandez 4, Houellemont 8, Lozada 5, Pinero 13, Suarez 12, Torrealba 14, Ugueto 13. **OF:** Andrade 58, Aponte 5, Berroa 49, Campana 23, Castellanos 22, Figueroa 54, Guaimaro 21, Hernandez 43, Martinez 13, Martinez 2, Mejias 40, Muzziotti 14, Petit 16, Pulgar 7, Pulido 1, Rincon 27, Rincones 39, Serven 1, Suarez 19, Ugueto 2.

Chicago Cubs

SEASON IN A SENTENCE: For the first time since 1908, the Cubs won the World Series. After posing the best record in baseball in the regular season—with 103 wins, a franchise-high since 1910—the North Siders staged a stirring ninth-inning comeback to eliminate the Giants, came back from 2-1 down to beat the Dodgers and won the last three games against the Indians to win the World Series in seven games.

HIGH POINT: Every clinch is special, especially clinching the World Series. The Cubs got to finish off the Dodgers in the National League Championship Series at Wrigley Field, though, winning their first pennant since 1945 in front of their home fans with a dominant 5-0 victory. Kyle Hendricks, who led the NL in ERA, out-dueled Clayton Kershaw, Anthony Rizzo and Willson Contreras homered, and the Cubs faithful got to celebrate at the friendly confines.

LOW POINT: In the season's second game, at Arizona, 2014 first-round pick Kyle Schwarber chased a fly ball into the left-center field gap and collided with center fielder Dexter Fowler. Schwarber went down in a heap and wound up with torn ligaments in his left knee. He missed the rest of the regular season, but after he tested the knee in two Arizona Fall League games, the Cubs activated him for the World Series, and he went 7-for-17 with three walks and two RBIs.

NOTABLE ROOKIES: Outfielder Albert Almora hit .277/.308/.455 in a part-time role and remains prospect-eligible for 2017. Contreras smacked 12 homers in the regular season while seeing time at catcher, left field and first base, and he played in every playoff game. Righthander Carl Edwards Jr. was one of Joe Maddon's more trusted relief options and pitched in eight playoff games.

KEY TRANSACTIONS: Fowler re-signed just as spring training was about to start and had a career-best .394 on-base percentage. The Cubs re-inforced their bullpen in July, first acquiring lefthander Mike Montgomery from the Mariners, then trading top prospect Gleyber Torres in a package to the Yankees for closer Aroldis Chapman.

DOWN ON THE FARM: The Cubs' winning culture extends to the minor leagues, as domestic affiliates went 373-319, with a .539 winning percentage that ranked sixth in baseball. Four Cubs affiliates made the playoffs, with high Class A Myrtle Beach (Carolina) and short-season Eugene (Northwest) winning league championships.

OPENING DAY PAYROLL: $ 154,575,168 (7th)

PLAYERS OF THE YEAR

MAJOR LEAGUE	MINOR LEAGUE
Kris Bryant	**Eloy Jimenez**
3b	**of**
.292/.385/.554	(low Class A)
39 HR, 102 RBI	.329/.369/.532
Led NL with 121 R	14 HR, 81 RBI

ORGANIZATION LEADERS

BATTING — *Minimum 250 AB

MAJORS

* AVG	Kris Bryant	.292
* OPS	Kris Bryant	.939
HR	Kris Bryant	39
RBI	Anthony Rizzo	109

MINORS

* AVG	Eloy Jimenez, South Bend	.329
* OBP	P.J. Higgins, South Bend	.389
* SLG	Eloy Jimenez, South Bend	.532
* OPS	Eloy Jimenez, South Bend	.901
R	John Andreoli, Iowa	96
H	Chesny Young, Tennessee	149
TB	Eloy Jimenez, South Bend	230
2B	Eloy Jimenez, South Bend	40
3B	Donnie Dewees, South Bend, Myrtle Beach	14
HR	Yasiel Balaguert, Myrtle Beach	19
RBI	Yasiel Balaguert, Myrtle Beach	96
BB	John Andreoli, Iowa	94
SO	John Andreoli, Iowa	162
SB	John Andreoli, Iowa	43

PITCHING — #Minimum 75 IP

MAJORS

W	Jon Lester	19
# ERA	Kyle Hendricks	2.13
SO	Jon Lester	197
SV	Hector Rondon	18

MINORS

W	Jonathan Martinez, Myrtle Beach, Tennessee	13
L	Drew Rucinski, Iowa	15
# ERA	Preston Morrison, South Bend, Myrtle Beach	2.11
G	Corey Black, Tennessee, Iowa	48
GS	Drew Rucinski, Iowa	28
SV	Ryan McNeil, Myrtle Beach	22
IP	Drew Rucinski, Iowa	155
BB	Tyler Skulina, Tennessee	71
SO	Trevor Clifton, Myrtle Beach	129
# AVG	Trevor Clifton, Myrtle Beach	.225

President: Theo Epstein. **GM:** Jed Hoyer. **Farm Director:** Jaron Madison. **Scouting Director:** Matt Dorey.

Class	Team	League	W	L	PCT	Finish	Manager
Majors	Chicago Cubs	National	103	58	.640	1st (15)	Joe Maddon
Triple-A	Iowa Cubs	Pacific Coast	67	76	.469	13st (16)	Marty Pevey
Double-A	Tennessee Smokies	Southern	58	81	.417	9th (10)	Mark Johnson
High A	Myrtle Beach Pelicans	Carolina	82	57	.590	3rd (8)	Buddy Bailey
Low A	South Bend Cubs	Midwest	84	55	.604	3rd (16)	Jimmy Gonzalez
Short season	Eugene Emeralds	Northwest	54	22	.711	1st (8)	Jesus Feliciano
Rookie	Cubs	Arizona	28	28	.500	9th (14)	Carmelo Martinez
Overall 2016 Minor League Record			373	319	.539	6th (30)	

ORGANIZATION STATISTICS

CHICAGO CUBS
NATIONAL LEAGUE

Batting	B-T	HT	WT	DOB	AVG	vLH	vRH	G	AB	R	H	2B	3B	HR	RBI	BB	HBP	SH	SF	SO	SB	CS	SLG	OBP
Almora, Albert	R-R	6-2	190	4-16-94	.277	.262	.286	47	112	14	31	9	1	3	14	5	0	0	0	20	0	0	.455	.308
Baez, Javier	R-R	6-0	190	12-1-92	.273	.311	.258	142	421	50	115	19	1	14	59	15	11	1	2	108	12	3	.423	.314
Bryant, Kris	R-R	6-5	230	1-4-92	.292	.314	.284	155	603	121	176	35	3	39	102	75	18	0	3	154	8	5	.554	.385
Candelario, Jeimer	B-R	6-1	210	11-24-93	.091	.000	.100	5	11	0	1	0	0	0	2	1	0	0	0	5	0	0	.091	.286
Coghlan, Chris	L-R	6-0	195	6-18-85	.252	.250	.253	48	103	21	26	7	2	1	16	22	2	0	1	26	1	0	.388	.391
Contreras, Willson	R-R	6-1	210	5-13-92	.282	.311	.270	76	252	33	71	14	1	12	35	26	4	0	1	67	2	3	.488	.357
Federowicz, Tim	R-R	5-10	215	8-5-87	.194	.455	.050	17	31	3	6	2	0	0	3	1	0	0	1	12	0	0	.258	.212
Fowler, Dexter	B-R	6-5	195	3-22-86	.276	.293	.270	125	456	84	126	25	7	13	48	79	11	1	4	124	13	4	.447	.393
Heyward, Jason	L-L	6-5	240	8-9-89	.230	.207	.238	142	530	61	122	27	1	7	49	54	5	1	2	93	11	4	.325	.306
Kalish, Ryan	L-L	6-0	215	3-28-88	.286	1.000	.167	7	7	1	2	0	0	0	2	1	1	1	0	0	0	0	.286	.444
Kawasaki, Munenori	L-R	5-11	175	6-3-81	.333	.000	.412	14	21	3	7	2	0	0	1	4	1	0	0	5	2	0	.429	.462
La Stella, Tommy	L-R	5-11	180	1-31-89	.270	.316	.264	74	148	17	40	12	1	2	11	18	2	0	0	27	0	1	.405	.357
Montero, Miguel	L-R	5-11	210	7-9-83	.216	.189	.221	86	241	33	52	8	1	8	33	38	3	0	2	58	1	0	.357	.327
Rizzo, Anthony	L-L	6-3	240	8-8-89	.292	.261	.305	155	583	94	170	43	4	32	109	74	16	0	3	108	3	5	.544	.385
Ross, David	R-R	6-2	230	3-19-77	.229	.283	.204	67	166	24	38	6	0	10	32	30	0	4	5	54	0	1	.446	.338
Russell, Addison	R-R	6-0	200	1-23-94	.238	.223	.244	151	525	67	125	25	3	21	95	55	12	0	6	135	5	1	.417	.321
Schwarber, Kyle	L-R	6-0	235	3-5-93	.000	—	.000	2	4	0	0	0	0	0	0	1	0	0	0	2	0	0	.000	.200
Soler, Jorge	R-R	6-4	215	2-25-92	.238	.267	.224	86	227	37	54	9	0	12	31	31	3	0	3	66	0	0	.436	.333
Szczur, Matt	R-R	6-0	200	7-20-89	.259	.225	.281	107	185	30	48	9	1	5	24	13	1	1	0	39	2	4	.400	.312
Zobrist, Ben	B-R	6-3	210	5-26-81	.272	.301	.261	147	523	94	142	31	3	18	76	96	4	4	8	62	6	4	.446	.386

Pitching	B-T	HT	WT	DOB	W	L	ERA	G	GS	CG	SV	IP	H	R	ER	HR	BB	SO	AVG	vLH	vRH	K/9	BB/9
Arrieta, Jake	R-R	6-4	225	3-6-86	18	8	3.10	31	31	1	0	197	138	72	68	16	76	190	.194	.194	.194	8.67	3.47
Buchanan, Jake	R-R	6-0	235	9-24-89	1	0	1.50	2	1	0	0	6	3	1	1	1	4		.150	.143	.154	6.00	1.50
Cahill, Trevor	R-R	6-4	240	3-1-88	4	4	2.74	50	1	0	0	66	49	22	20	7	35	66	.201	.206	.197	9.05	4.80
Chapman, Aroldis	L-L	6-4	215	2-28-88	1	1	1.01	28	0	0	16	27	12	4	3	0	10	46	.132	.105	.139	15.53	3.38
Concepcion, Gerardo	L-L	6-2	200	2-29-92	0	0	3.86	3	0	0	0	2	2	1	1	0	1	2	.250	.200	.333	7.71	3.86
Edwards, Carl	R-R	6-3	170	9-3-91	0	1	3.75	36	0	0	2	36	15	15	15	4	14	52	.123	.146	.108	13.00	3.50
Grimm, Justin	R-R	6-3	210	8-16-88	2	1	4.10	68	0	0	0	53	47	24	24	5	23	65	.234	.267	.209	11.11	3.93
Hammel, Jason	R-R	6-6	225	9-2-82	15	10	3.83	30	30	0	0	167	148	77	71	25	53	144	.239	.238	.238	7.78	2.86
Hendricks, Kyle	R-R	6-3	190	12-7-89	16	8	2.13	31	30	2	0	190	142	53	45	15	44	170	.207	.219	.198	8.05	2.08
Lackey, John	R-R	6-6	235	10-23-78	11	8	3.35	29	29	0	0	188	146	74	70	23	53	180	.218	.242	.201	8.60	2.53
Lester, Jon	L-L	6-4	240	1-7-84	19	5	2.44	32	32	1	0	203	154	57	55	21	52	197	.211	.200	.214	8.75	2.31
Matusz, Brian	L-L	6-5	190	2-11-87	0	0	18.00	1	1	0	0	3	6	6	6	3	2	2	.429	.500	.400	6.00	6.00
Montgomery, Mike	L-L	6-5	215	7-1-89	1	1	2.82	17	5	0	0	38	30	15	12	5	20	38	.217	.208	.222	8.92	4.70
Nathan, Joe	R-R	6-4	230	11-22-74	1	0	0.00	3	0	0	0	2	2	0	0	0	2	4	.250	.500	.167	18.00	9.00
2-team total (7 San Francisco)					2	0	0.00	10	0	0	0	6	5	0	0	0	4	9	—	—	—	12.79	5.68
Patton, Spencer	R-R	6-1	200	2-20-88	1	1	5.48	16	0	0	0	21	20	16	13	3	4	22	.233	.226	.236	9.28	5.91
Pena, Felix	R-R	6-2	185	2-25-90	0	0	4.00	11	0	0	1	9	5	4	4	1	3	13	.156	.000	.185	13.00	3.00
Peralta, Joel	R-R	5-10	210	3-23-76	0	1	9.00	5	0	0	0	4	6	5	4	2	1	5	.353	.400	.286	11.25	2.25
Ramirez, Neil	R-R	6-4	215	5-25-89	0	0	4.70	8	0	0	0	8	5	4	4	1	8	10	.200	.333	.125	11.74	9.39
2-team total (2 Milwaukee)					0	0	5.79	10	0	0	0	9	7	6	6	3	8	13	—	—	—	12.54	7.71
Richard, Clayton	L-L	6-5	240	9-12-83	0	1	6.43	25	0	0	1	14	23	14	10	0	7	7	.377	.412	.333	4.50	4.50
2-team total (11 San Diego)					3	4	3.33	36	9	0	1	68	81	35	25	4	31	41	—	—	—	5.45	4.12
Rondon, Hector	R-R	6-3	230	2-26-88	2	3	3.53	54	0	0	18	51	42	20	20	8	8	58	.225	.260	.200	10.24	1.41
Smith, Joe	R-R	6-2	205	3-22-84	1	1	2.51	16	0	0	0	14	11	4	4	4	5	15	.216	.118	.265	9.42	3.14
Strop, Pedro	R-R	6-1	220	6-13-85	2	2	2.85	54	0	0	0	47	27	16	15	4	15	60	.163	.143	.173	11.41	2.85
Warren, Adam	R-R	6-1	225	8-25-87	3	2	5.91	29	1	0	0	35	31	24	23	7	19	27	.238	.200	.256	6.94	4.89
Wood, Travis	R-L	5-11	175	2-6-87	4	0	2.95	77	0	0	0	61	45	24	20	8	24	47	.199	.128	.265	6.93	3.54
Zastryzny, Rob	R-L	6-3	205	3-26-92	1	0	1.13	8	1	0	0	16	12	3	2	0	5	17	.207	.138	.276	9.56	2.81

Fielding

Catcher	PCT	G	PO	A	E	DP	PB
Contreras	.986	57	389	31	6	0	6
Federowicz	.980	12	42	7	1	1	0
Montero	.988	71	550	37	7	2	4
Ross	.981	58	433	44	9	3	2

First Base	PCT	G	PO	A	E	DP
Baez	1.000	6	18	4	0	1
Bryant	1.000	9	35	3	0	3
Coghlan	1.000	6	19	0	0	2
Contreras	1.000	3	22	1	0	1
Rizzo	.996	154	1268	125	6	98
Zobrist	1.000	1	1	0	0	0

Second Base	PCT	G	PO	A	E	DP
Baez	.973	59	88	127	6	23
Kawasaki	.960	10	10	14	1	6

La Stella	.952	9	11	9	1	2
Rizzo	1.000	1	0	1	0	0
Zobrist	.984	119	177	250	7	52

Third Base	PCT	G	PO	A	E	DP
Baez	.944	62	27	91	7	4
Bryant	.953	107	58	187	12	18
Candelario	.800	3	1	3	1	0
Coghlan	.000	1	0	0	1	0
Kawasaki	—	1	0	0	0	0
La Stella	.917	33	12	32	4	4

Shortstop	PCT	G	PO	A	E	DP
Baez	.981	25	40	61	2	13
Bryant	—	1	0	0	0	0
Russell	.975	148	152	388	14	60
Zobrist	—	1	0	0	0	0

Outfield	PCT	G	PO	A	E	DP
Almora	1.000	41	74	1	0	2
Baez	—	2	0	0	0	0
Bryant	.989	69	83	3	1	0
Coghlan	1.000	31	40	2	0	0
Contreras	1.000	24	26	1	0	0
Fowler	.983	121	219	6	4	1
Heyward	.993	141	269	5	2	2
Kalish	1.000	3	3	0	0	0
Patton	—	1	0	0	0	0
Schwarber	1.000	2	1	0	0	0
Soler	.986	60	69	1	1	0
Strop	—	1	0	0	0	0
Szczur	1.000	70	83	0	0	0
Wood	1.000	3	1	0	0	0
Zobrist	1.000	46	43	1	0	0

IOWA CUBS
PACIFIC COAST LEAGUE

TRIPLE-A

Batting	B-T	HT	WT	DOB	AVG	vLH	vRH	G	AB	R	H	2B	3B	HR	RBI	BB	HBP	SH	SF	SO	SB	CS	SLG	OBP
Adams, Lane	R-R	6-3	220	11-13-89	.231	.250	.222	7	26	3	6	1	0	1	2	0	0	0	0	5	4	0	.385	.231
Alcantara, Arismendy	B-R	5-10	170	10-29-91	.263	.304	.246	54	198	32	52	9	5	5	21	15	0	0	1	61	21	0	.434	.313
2-team total (48 Nashville)					.276	—		102	398	60	110	19	10	11	48	29	1	2	3	118	32	6	.457	.325
Almora, Albert	R-R	6-2	190	4-16-94	.303	.241	.326	80	320	46	97	18	3	4	43	9	0	2	5	44	10	3	.416	.317
Andreoli, John	R-R	6-1	190	6-9-90	.256	.255	.257	140	507	96	130	21	7	12	61	94	5	4	7	162	43	12	.396	.374
Baez, Javier	R-R	6-0	190	12-1-92	.267	.333	.222	4	15	3	4	0	0	1	1	0	0	0	0	4	1	0	.467	.267
Bautista, Alex	R-R	6-0	200	9-6-93	.250	.500	.000	3	4	0	1	0	0	0	0	0	0	0	0	2	0	0	.250	.250
Bote, David	R-R	5-11	185	4-7-93	.364	.500	.313	12	22	4	8	0	0	1	3	2	0	0	0	5	0	0	.500	.417
Brockmeyer, Cael	R-R	6-5	235	10-8-91	.228	.286	.203	35	92	8	21	6	1	1	7	6	0	0	0	31	0	0	.348	.276
Bruno, Stephen	R-R	5-9	165	11-17-90	.188	.333	.100	7	16	1	3	1	0	1	0	0	0	0	5	1	0	.438	.188
Candelario, Jeimer	B-R	6-1	210	11-24-93	.333	.351	.326	76	264	44	88	22	3	9	54	38	3	0	4	53	0	2	.542	.417
Carhart, Ben	R-R	5-10	200	1-21-90	.111	.200	.000	4	9	2	1	0	0	0	0	0	0	0	0	1	0	0	.111	.111
Coghlan, Chris	L-R	6-0	195	6-18-85	.471	.333	.500	5	17	3	8	3	0	1	0	1	0	0	0	2	0	0	.647	.471
Contreras, Willson	R-R	6-1	210	5-13-92	.353	.377	.344	55	204	40	72	16	3	9	43	28	6	0	2	32	4	4	.593	.442
Davis, Taylor	R-R	5-10	200	11-28-89	.251	.284	.237	67	223	24	56	13	1	2	20	30	1	3	1	28	2	0	.345	.341
Federowicz, Tim	R-R	5-10	215	8-5-87	.293	.300	.289	65	229	25	67	12	0	8	39	18	4	0	2	51	3	0	.450	.352
Fowler, Dexter	B-R	6-5	195	3-22-86	.200	.000	.500	2	5	2	1	1	0	0	0	1	0	0	0	2	5	0	.400	.333
Freitas, David	R-R	6-3	225	3-18-89	.321	.211	.354	25	84	7	27	7	0	2	15	7	0	1	3	20	0	0	.476	.362
Gonzalez, Jose	R-R	6-1	160	1-12-96	.222	.200	.250	8	9	1	2	1	0	0	0	0	0	0	0	1	0	0	.333	.222
Kalish, Ryan	L-L	6-0	215	3-28-88	.368	.400	.362	21	57	15	21	4	2	0	4	10	2	0	1	9	3	1	.509	.471
Kawasaki, Munenori	L-R	5-11	175	6-3-81	.255	.213	.268	102	314	42	80	11	2	1	39	49	1	9	5	61	20	8	.312	.352
La Stella, Tommy	L-R	5-11	180	1-31-89	.273	.167	.313	12	44	6	12	2	0	1	3	2	0	0	0	9	0	0	.386	.304
Machin, Vimael	L-R	5-10	185	9-25-93	.278	.500	.214	14	18	7	5	0	0	0	1	7	0	0	0	4	0	1	.278	.480
Montero, Miguel	L-R	5-11	210	7-9-83	.200	.667	.000	3	10	0	2	0	0	0	2	0	0	0	0	3	0	0	.200	.200
Murton, Matt	R-R	6-1	220	10-3-81	.314	.385	.287	76	236	29	74	12	1	2	37	15	0	0	4	32	1	1	.398	.349
Negron, Kris	R-R	6-0	190	2-1-86	.256	.265	.252	117	375	47	96	20	4	9	46	20	11	7	6	90	23	6	.403	.308
Perez, Juan	R-R	5-11	185	11-13-86	.276	.360	.240	117	381	53	105	27	5	9	57	20	2	2	7	85	16	6	.444	.310
Rademacher, Bijan	L-L	6-0	200	6-15-91	.286	.294	.283	22	70	10	20	5	0	1	8	7	1	1	2	14	0	0	.400	.350
Soler, Jorge	R-R	6-4	215	2-25-92	.143	.250	.000	2	7	0	1	0	0	0	0	0	0	0	0	5	0	0	.143	.143
Victorino, Shane	B-R	5-9	190	11-30-80	.233	.250	.227	9	30	4	7	2	1	0	5	3	1	0	0	1	1	0	.367	.324
Vogelbach, Dan	L-R	6-0	250	12-17-92	.318	.259	.339	89	305	53	97	18	2	16	64	55	3	0	2	67	0	0	.548	.425
2-team total (44 Tacoma)					.292	—		133	459	79	134	25	2	23	96	97	4	0	3	101	0	0	.505	.417
Watkins, Logan	L-R	5-11	195	8-29-89	.261	.197	.280	108	337	45	88	14	7	1	42	26	2	8	5	67	15	7	.353	.314
Whiting, Sutton	B-R	5-8	170	5-13-92	.000	—	.000	1	1	0	0	0	0	0	0	0	0	0	0	1	0	0	.000	.000
Zagunis, Mark	R-R	6-0	205	2-5-93	.274	.196	.309	50	179	31	49	12	4	6	25	22	5	0	5	42	4	0	.486	.360

Pitching	B-T	HT	WT	DOB	W	L	ERA	G	GS	CG	SV	IP	H	R	ER	HR	BB	SO	AVG	vLH	vRH	K/9	BB/9
Barnes, Scott	L-L	6-4	200	9-5-87	1	3	7.02	9	2	0	0	17	21	13	13	3	10	18	.313	.308	.317	9.72	5.40
Beeler, Dallas	R-R	6-5	225	6-12-89	2	0	4.15	8	0	0	0	9	8	4	4	0	2	3	.258	.500	.174	3.12	2.08
Black, Corey	R-R	5-11	175	8-4-91	0	3	5.04	28	0	0	6	30	30	18	17	1	21	37	.254	.205	.284	10.98	6.23
Brooks, Aaron	R-R	6-4	225	4-27-90	1	1	7.71	5	4	0	0	16	23	15	14	5	4	12	.329	.306	.353	6.61	2.20
Buchanan, Jake	R-R	6-0	235	9-24-89	12	8	4.34	24	22	0	0	141	154	76	68	6	38	105	.278	.302	.263	6.70	2.43
Cahill, Trevor	R-R	6-4	240	3-1-88	0	3	4.58	6	6	0	0	20	25	12	10	3	12	25	.305	.343	.277	11.44	5.49
Collmenter, Josh	R-R	6-3	240	2-7-86	1	0	2.25	4	4	0	0	16	13	4	4	0	8	9	.224	.212	.240	5.06	4.50
2-team total (3 Reno)					1	0	1.93	7	6	0	0	23	20	5	5	1	13	15	—	—	5.79	5.01
Concepcion, Gerardo	L-L	6-2	200	2-29-92	2	4	7.29	32	0	0	1	42	57	36	34	6	24	35	.329	.211	.388	7.50	5.14
Edwards, Carl	R-R	6-3	170	9-3-91	1	1	4.26	24	0	0	1	25	17	12	12	1	17	35	.185	.179	.189	12.43	6.04
Fife, Stephen	R-R	6-3	225	10-4-86	3	4	4.61	7	7	0	0	27	28	14	14	1	10	25	.267	.316	.239	8.23	3.29
Gomes, Brandon	R-R	5-11	190	7-15-84	1	2	3.97	19	0	0	1	23	14	10	10	3	14	20	.182	.091	.250	7.94	5.56
Grimm, Justin	R-R	6-3	210	8-16-88	0	0	0.00	1	0	0	0	1	1	0	0	0	0	3	.250	.000	.500	27.00	0.00
Ihrig, Tyler	L-L	6-0	210	9-17-91	0	0	2.25	1	1	0	0	4	3	1	1	0	1	3	.214	.000	.250	6.75	2.25
Johnson, Pierce	R-R	6-3	200	5-10-91	4	6	6.14	22	11	0	0	63	60	44	43	8	43	75	.256	.323	.210	10.71	6.14

Pitching

Pitching	B-T	HT	WT	DOB	W	L	ERA	G	GS	CG	SV	IP	H	R	ER	HR	BB	SO	AVG	vLH	vRH	K/9	BB/9
Jokisch, Eric	R-L	6-2	205	7-29-89	0	1	16.62	1	1	0	0	4	11	8	8	2	2	3	.500	.500	.500	6.23	4.15
3-team total (18 New Orleans, 7 Round Rock)					3	2	4.27	26	5	0	1	59	70	33	28	5	24	37	—	—	—	5.64	3.66
Leathersich, Jack	R-L	6-0	205	7-14-90	0	0	0.00	5	0	0	0	6	0	0	0	0	6	6	.000	.000	.000	10.80	10.80
Machi, Jean	R-R	6-0	255	2-1-82	2	1	3.68	20	0	0	1	29	29	13	12	5	9	26	.271	.209	.313	7.98	2.76
2-team total (28 Sacramento)					4	3	3.65	48	0	0	13	62	59	30	25	9	17	53	—	—	—	7.74	2.48
Matusz, Brian	L-L	6-5	190	2-11-87	0	1	3.38	4	3	0	0	13	5	5	5	1	4	17	.235	.133	.278	11.48	2.70
Mejia, Miguel	R-R	6-2	210	1-19-88	1	1	5.70	30	0	0	0	47	56	31	30	3	17	43	.298	.250	.330	8.18	3.23
Nance, Tommy	R-R	6-6	235	3-19-91	0	0	27.00	1	0	0	0	1	4	3	3	1	1	0	.571	.667	.500	0.00	9.00
Nathan, Joe	R-R	6-4	230	11-22-74	0	0	6.75	4	0	0	0	3	0	2	2	0	5	3	.000	.000	.000	10.13	16.88
Patton, Spencer	R-R	6-1	200	2-20-88	1	0	0.75	35	0	0	11	36	21	4	3	0	15	59	.169	.145	.188	14.75	3.75
Pena, Felix	R-R	6-2	185	2-25-90	3	4	3.41	36	0	0	3	63	46	24	24	4	23	81	.203	.180	.217	11.51	3.27
Perakslis, Steve	R-R	6-1	185	1-15-91	0	1	4.00	5	3	0	0	18	15	10	8	3	3	14	.224	.222	.225	7.00	1.50
Peralta, Joel	R-R	5-10	210	3-23-76	0	0	4.50	5	0	0	2	4	3	5	2	0	4	4	.176	.200	.143	9.00	9.00
Peralta, Starling	R-R	6-4	210	11-11-90	1	2	6.48	3	1	0	0	8	11	6	6	0	4	4	.314	.368	.250	4.32	4.32
Pries, Jordan	R-R	6-0	190	1-27-90	5	2	5.21	9	9	0	0	47	48	28	27	7	23	35	.265	.231	.284	6.75	4.44
2-team total (7 Tacoma)					7	3	4.67	16	12	0	0	71	72	38	37	7	30	56	—	—	—	7.07	3.79
Richard, Clayton	L-L	6-5	240	9-12-83	0	0	0.00	2	2	0	0	5	1	0	0	0	2	2	.071	.000	.125	9.00	3.60
Riefenhauser, C.J.	L-L	6-0	195	1-30-90	2	1	4.55	28	0	0	1	28	17	15	14	2	18	26	.179	.132	.211	8.46	5.86
Rivero, Armando	R-R	6-4	190	2-1-88	5	3	2.13	43	0	0	1	68	41	19	16	3	35	105	.169	.146	.186	13.97	4.66
Rosario, Jose	R-R	6-1	170	8-29-90	1	1	2.95	22	0	0	5	21	26	7	7	0	6	18	.302	.333	.280	7.59	2.53
Rucinski, Drew	R-R	6-2	190	12-30-88	7	15	5.92	28	28	0	0	155	187	108	102	16	43	116	.301	.243	.342	6.74	2.50
Sanabia, Alex	R-R	6-2	210	9-8-88	2	2	9.59	6	5	0	0	25	35	27	27	5	10	15	.324	.318	.328	5.33	3.55
Smith, Joe	R-R	6-2	205	3-22-84	0	0	0.00	2	0	0	0	2	1	0	0	0	2	1	.167	.500	.000	9.00	9.00
Soto, Giovanni	L-L	6-2	210	5-18-91	1	3	5.14	33	0	0	0	49	51	32	28	3	31	55	.274	.254	.286	10.10	5.69
Thatcher, Joe	L-L	6-2	230	10-4-81	0	0	6.14	10	1	0	0	7	10	5	5	0	3	11	.333	.400	.300	13.50	3.68
2-team total (17 Oklahoma City)					0	0	4.43	27	1	0	0	22	24	11	11	0	8	32	—	—	—	12.90	3.22
Wagner, Michael	R-R	6-3	175	10-3-91	0	1	5.28	9	8	0	0	31	36	21	18	1	22	31	.295	.300	.292	9.16	6.46
Warren, Adam	R-R	6-1	225	8-25-87	0	0	4.15	2	2	0	0	9	4	4	4	1	4	6	.207	.143	.267	6.23	4.15
Williams, Ryan	R-R	6-4	220	11-1-91	4	1	3.27	9	9	0	0	44	43	18	16	4	12	30	.261	.352	.191	6.14	2.45
Zastryzny, Rob	R-L	6-3	205	3-26-92	7	3	4.33	15	14	0	0	81	67	42	39	7	31	77	.229	.190	.244	8.56	3.44

Fielding

Catcher	PCT	G	PO	A	E	DP	PB
Brockmeyer	.987	12	70	8	1	0	1
Carhart	1.000	1	3	0	0	0	1
Contreras	.995	45	360	38	2	7	7
Davis	.996	30	241	16	1	0	0
Federowicz	.993	42	372	33	3	2	5
Freitas	.993	20	135	9	1	1	1
Montero	1.000	2	9	0	0	0	0

First Base	PCT	G	PO	A	E	DP
Brockmeyer	.987	13	69	5	1	3
Candelario	1.000	10	57	5	0	5
Davis	.995	27	192	15	1	23
Federowicz	.986	10	67	1	1	5
Freitas	1.000	5	48	3	0	5
Murton	1.000	1	8	0	0	2
Negron	.983	15	50	7	1	3
Rademacher	1.000	1	2	0	0	0
Vogelbach	.992	76	585	49	5	58
Watkins	.967	5	29	0	1	4

Second Base	PCT	G	PO	A	E	DP

	PCT	G	PO	A	E	DP
Alcantara	.983	51	98	132	4	28
Baez	.750	1	2	1	1	0
Bruno	1.000	4	8	7	0	5
La Stella	1.000	4	3	7	0	1
Machin	.952	5	9	11	1	1
Negron	1.000	25	40	50	0	13
Perez	.957	11	18	27	2	10
Watkins	.974	68	97	124	6	30

Third Base	PCT	G	PO	A	E	DP
Baez	1.000	2	0	2	0	0
Bote	.800	1	3	1	1	0
Candelario	.963	67	41	114	6	10
Davis	1.000	7	1	9	0	0
Federowicz	—	2	0	0	0	0
La Stella	1.000	6	2	13	0	1
Negron	.952	27	20	40	3	3
Perez	.889	21	8	32	5	3
Watkins	.930	26	10	30	3	2

Shortstop	PCT	G	PO	A	E	DP
Baez	1.000	1	2	3	0	1
Kawasaki	.982	100	122	251	7	54

	PCT	G	PO	A	E	DP
Negron	.970	48	67	125	6	30
Watkins	1.000	3	3	9	0	1

Outfield	PCT	G	PO	A	E	DP
Adams	.875	5	7	0	1	0
Almora	.977	78	161	6	4	5
Andreoli	.977	135	246	4	6	0
Baez	1.000	2	1	1	0	0
Bautista	—	1	0	0	0	0
Coghlan	1.000	4	6	1	0	0
Fowler	1.000	1	2	0	0	0
Gonzalez	1.000	2	4	0	0	0
Kalish	.960	15	23	1	1	1
Murton	.986	49	67	2	1	1
Negron	1.000	13	10	1	0	1
Perez	.986	85	129	10	2	1
Rademacher	1.000	20	29	2	0	0
Soler	1.000	2	3	0	0	0
Victorino	1.000	8	14	0	0	0
Watkins	1.000	6	6	0	0	0
Zagunis	.977	48	81	3	2	0

TENNESSEE SMOKIES   DOUBLE-A
SOUTHERN LEAGUE

Batting	B-T	HT	WT	DOB	AVG	vLH	vRH	G	AB	R	H	2B	3B	HR	RBI	BB	HBP	SH	SF	SO	SB	CS	SLG	OBP
Adams, Lane	R-R	6-3	220	11-13-89	.325	.313	.328	22	83	12	27	6	0	3	19	5	2	1	0	20	9	0	.506	.378
Amaya, Gioskar	R-R	5-11	175	12-13-92	.183	.222	.163	44	131	12	24	2	1	1	8	13	2	0	0	43	0	1	.237	.267
Bautista, Alex	R-R	6-0	200	9-6-93	.000	—	.000	1	3	0	0	0	0	0	0	0	0	0	0	0	0	0	.000	.000
Bote, David	R-R	5-11	185	4-7-93	.200	.400	.150	7	25	1	5	0	0	0	1	2	0	0	0	6	0	0	.200	.259
Brockmeyer, Cael	R-R	6-5	235	10-8-91	.317	.313	.320	12	41	4	13	3	0	2	7	1	2	0	0	8	0	0	.537	.364
Bruno, Stephen	R-R	5-9	165	11-17-90	.263	.364	.200	22	57	7	15	2	1	0	5	4	3	0	1	18	1	0	.333	.338
Candelario, Jeimer	B-R	6-1	210	11-24-93	.219	.290	.184	56	210	30	46	17	1	4	23	32	1	0	1	46	0	0	.367	.324
Caratini, Victor	B-R	6-1	215	8-17-93	.291	.342	.271	115	412	57	120	25	2	6	47	54	6	0	8	80	2	1	.405	.375
Carhart, Ben	R-R	5-10	200	1-21-90	.259	.197	.289	58	201	26	52	13	0	6	28	15	5	1	1	35	1	0	.413	.309
Coghlan, Chris	L-R	6-0	195	6-18-85	.500	.333	.600	5	16	3	8	4	0	0	6	5	0	0	0	1	0	0	.750	.619
Davis, Taylor	R-R	5-10	200	11-28-89	.339	.313	.350	15	56	7	19	3	1	0	10	4	0	0	3	6	0	0	.429	.365
Dent, Ryan	R-R	6-0	190	3-15-89	.138	.071	.159	25	58	5	8	1	0	0	2	7	2	0	1	16	0	1	.155	.250
Dugan, Kelly	L-R	6-3	210	9-18-90	.266	.247	.274	96	274	43	73	17	0	13	50	29	11	0	5	63	1	1	.471	.354
Freitas, David	R-R	6-3	225	3-18-89	.286	.361	.256	66	248	37	71	20	1	4	38	21	1	0	0	47	0	0	.423	.344

CHICAGO CUBS

Batting	B-T	HT	WT	DOB	AVG	vLH	vRH	G	AB	R	H	2B	3B	HR	RBI	BB	HBP	SH	SF	SO	SB	CS	SLG	OBP
Giansanti, Anthony	R-R	5-10	195	9-28-88	.229	.111	.269	18	35	6	8	1	0	1	3	2	0	0	0	10	1	0	.343	.270
Hannemann, Jacob	L-L	6-1	200	4-29-91	.247	.267	.241	74	291	37	72	14	4	10	30	25	9	2	0	55	26	8	.426	.326
Happ, Ian	B-R	6-0	205	8-12-94	.262	.232	.274	65	248	35	65	14	0	8	31	20	2	0	4	60	6	2	.415	.318
La Stella, Tommy	L-R	5-11	180	1-31-89	.500	.500	.500	2	4	1	2	0	0	0	0	2	1	0	0	0	0	0	.500	.714
Lockhart, Danny	L-R	5-11	175	11-4-92	.213	.200	.216	52	155	12	33	7	0	1	16	10	1	3	3	35	2	1	.277	.260
Martin, Trey	R-R	6-2	190	12-11-92	.186	.217	.174	68	215	18	40	2	2	2	20	14	2	6	2	55	14	3	.242	.240
McKinney, Billy	L-L	6-1	205	8-23-94	.252	.255	.250	88	298	37	75	12	3	1	31	47	2	0	2	68	2	4	.322	.355
Penalver, Carlos	R-R	6-0	170	5-17-94	.211	.250	.195	118	407	36	86	21	1	0	33	29	2	4	3	73	2	2	.268	.265
Rademacher, Bijan	L-L	6-0	205	6-05-91	.313	.266	.328	86	256	43	80	17	0	9	36	35	1	0	2	49	0	0	.484	.395
Soler, Jorge	R-R	6-4	215	2-25-92	.167	.250	.136	9	30	4	5	0	0	0	2	11	0	0	1	11	0	0	.167	.381
Szczur, Matt	R-R	6-0	200	7-20-89	.000	—	.000	1	1	1	0	0	0	0	0	0	0	1	0	0	1	0	.000	.500
Vosler, Jason	L-R	6-1	190	9-6-93	.250	.091	.272	26	92	11	23	7	0	1	12	9	1	0	3	26	0	0	.359	.314
Young, Chesny	R-R	6-0	170	10-6-92	.303	.305	.303	126	491	60	149	25	2	4	37	57	2	0	3	64	16	14	.387	.376
Zagunis, Mark	R-R	6-0	205	2-5-93	.302	.345	.281	51	179	30	54	13	1	4	24	30	2	0	0	36	1	2	.453	.408

Pitching	B-T	HT	WT	DOB	W	L	ERA	G	GS	CG	SV	IP	H	R	ER	HR	BB	SO	AVG	vLH	vRH	K/9	BB/9
Acevedo, Andury	R-R	6-4	235	8-23-90	0	0	7.20	6	0	0	0	5	3	5	4	0	9	7	.167	.273	.000	12.60	16.20
Alvarez, R.J.	R-R	6-2	225	6-8-91	0	1	7.71	20	0	0	0	23	34	20	20	2	12	30	.330	.311	.345	11.57	4.63
Berg, David	R-R	6-1	210	3-28-93	2	4	6.28	34	0	0	4	43	67	35	30	0	11	30	.360	.395	.333	6.28	2.30
Black, Corey	R-R	5-11	175	8-4-91	0	3	3.18	20	0	0	8	23	18	9	8	0	15	25	.220	.176	.250	9.93	5.96
Blackburn, Paul	R-R	6-1	195	12-4-93	6	4	3.17	18	18	0	0	102	96	47	36	6	26	72	.251	.247	.254	6.33	2.29
2-team total (8 Jackson)					9	5	3.27	26	25	0	0	143	138	63	52	8	35	99	—			6.23	2.20
Concepcion, Gerardo	L-L	6-2	200	2-29-92	1	0	0.00	10	0	0	0	18	5	0	0	0	4	17	.089	.045	.118	8.66	2.04
Conway, Josh	R-R	6-1	190	4-12-91	1	5	5.40	22	0	0	0	23	18	14	14	1	28	18	.220	.212	.224	6.94	10.80
Farris, James	R-R	6-2	210	4-4-92	1	3	2.75	26	0	0	5	36	27	11	11	2	10	38	.209	.164	.243	9.50	2.50
Garner, David	R-R	6-1	180	9-21-92	1	6	4.19	43	0	0	3	54	54	31	25	2	35	56	.263	.220	.298	9.39	5.87
Hedges, Zach	R-R	6-4	210	10-21-92	3	3	2.47	8	8	0	0	47	45	18	13	2	9	32	.249	.238	.258	6.08	1.71
Jensen, Michael	R-R	6-1	185	12-10-90	2	0	8.27	12	0	0	1	21	25	21	19	3	15	15	.316	.265	.356	6.53	6.53
Leathersich, Jack	L-L	6-0	205	7-14-90	0	0	3.48	11	0	0	0	11	4	4	4	0	4	12	.282	.111	.429	10.45	3.48
Markey, Brad	R-R	5-11	185	3-3-92	8	7	3.17	26	23	1	0	131	129	54	46	13	45	65	.259	.280	.239	4.48	3.10
Martinez, Jonathan	R-R	6-1	205	6-27-94	1	1	5.25	2	2	0	0	12	13	7	7	3	1	15	.260	.360	.160	11.25	0.75
Matusz, Brian	L-L	6-5	190	2-11-87	0	0	2.70	1	0	0	0	3	2	1	1	0	2	6	.167	1.000	.091	16.20	5.40
Mejia, Miguel	R-R	6-2	210	1-19-88	1	2	2.70	8	0	0	1	13	13	4	4	1	1	17	.255	.269	.240	11.48	0.68
Nathan, Joe	R-R	6-4	230	11-22-74	0	1	2.70	7	0	0	0	7	3	2	2	0	6	6	.130	.000	.214	8.10	
Paniagua, Juan Carlos	R-R	6-1	200	4-4-90	3	3	4.04	41	0	0	4	65	49	31	29	5	39	62	.207	.207	.206	8.63	5.43
Perakslis, Steve	R-R	6-1	185	1-15-91	2	4	3.47	27	3	0	0	57	58	30	22	5	16	44	.260	.263	.258	6.95	2.53
Peralta, Starling	R-R	6-4	210	11-11-90	6	2	3.75	34	2	0	2	62	57	29	26	4	24	32	.244	.234	.250	4.62	3.47
Pugliese, James	R-R	6-3	220	8-12-92	0	0	2.25	2	0	0	0	4	1	1	1	0	3	1	.083	.143	.000	2.25	6.75
Richard, Clayton	L-L	6-5	240	9-12-83	0	1	3.52	2	2	0	0	8	7	3	3	0	0	5	.250	.000	.318	5.87	0.00
Rosario, Jose	R-R	6-1	170	8-29-90	0	0	2.76	11	0	0	4	16	11	5	5	1	3	15	.183	.231	.147	8.27	1.65
Sarianides, Nick	R-R	6-1	200	8-29-89	3	3	3.60	22	0	0	0	25	21	11	10	2	9	28	.231	.261	.200	10.08	3.24
2-team total (8 Mobile)					3	3	3.62	30	0	0	0	37	36	18	15	3	20	33	—			7.96	4.82
Skulina, Tyler	R-R	6-5	230	9-18-91	4	12	5.16	27	27	0	0	129	136	87	74	16	71	91	.270	.292	.252	6.35	4.95
Tseng, Jen-Ho	L-R	6-1	195	10-3-94	8	8	4.29	22	22	0	0	113	138	67	54	12	32	68	.308	.318	.300	5.48	2.54
Underwood, Duane	R-R	6-2	210	7-20-94	0	5	4.91	13	13	1	0	59	66	34	32	7	31	46	.280	.311	.254	7.06	4.76
Wagner, Michael	R-R	6-3	175	10-3-91	2	1	3.86	10	10	0	0	54	46	24	23	5	20	41	.235	.218	.246	6.88	3.35
Zastryzny, Rob	R-L	6-3	205	3-26-92	3	2	4.28	9	9	0	0	55	50	29	26	6	20	42	.245	.244	.245	6.91	3.29

Fielding

Catcher	PCT	G	PO	A	E	DP	PB
Amaya	.981	8	47	6	1	1	0
Brockmeyer	1.000	4	30	2	0	0	0
Caratini	.997	82	527	60	2	6	8
Carhart	.986	23	128	13	2	0	2
Davis	1.000	8	35	5	0	0	0
Freitas	.979	23	165	18	4	0	2

First Base	PCT	G	PO	A	E	DP
Amaya	1.000	15	112	9	0	12
Bote	.960	2	24	0	1	1
Brockmeyer	1.000	7	65	3	0	3
Candelario	1.000	2	13	1	0	0
Caratini	1.000	30	259	20	0	25
Carhart	.992	28	223	16	2	16
Davis	1.000	9	65	9	0	6
Dent	1.000	6	32	4	0	2
Dugan	.965	7	52	3	2	6
Freitas	.980	28	281	18	6	27
Giansanti	.952	6	20	0	1	4
Rademacher	.957	13	78	11	4	5
Vosler	1.000	1	8	0	0	0
Young	1.000	1	12	2	0	1

Second Base	PCT	G	PO	A	E	DP
Amaya	1.000	1	1	3	0	0
Bruno	.982	11	18	36	1	9
Carhart	1.000	1	2	1	0	0
Dent	1.000	5	3	16	0	1
Happ	.972	42	80	130	6	31
La Stella	.900	2	3	6	1	1
Lockhart	.982	24	36	71	2	12
Penalver	1.000	2	5	6	0	1
Young	.989	58	108	163	3	40

Third Base	PCT	G	PO	A	E	DP
Amaya	.875	11	4	24	4	2
Bote	1.000	5	3	12	0	1
Bruno	—	1	0	0	0	0
Candelario	.966	54	38	105	5	11
Carhart	.500	2	0	1	1	0
Dent	1.000	4	3	7	0	2
Giansanti	—	1	0	0	0	0
Lockhart	.870	8	4	16	3	0
Vosler	.967	25	12	46	2	3
Young	.935	35	16	56	5	5

Shortstop	PCT	G	PO	A	E	DP
Dent	.786	2	2	9	3	0
Lockhart	.949	8	12	25	2	6
Penalver	.937	117	150	308	31	69
Young	.958	17	22	47	3	10

Outfield	PCT	G	PO	A	E	DP
Adams	.978	21	44	1	1	0
Bautista	1.000	1	1	0	0	0
Coghlan	1.000	5	6	0	0	0
Dugan	.990	57	92	4	1	0
Giansanti	1.000	6	7	0	0	0
Hannemann	.973	73	178	5	5	3
Happ	.889	17	31	1	4	0
Lockhart	1.000	6	10	0	0	0
Martin	.994	67	152	3	1	1
McKinney	.968	77	147	6	5	1
Rademacher	.969	50	91	4	3	1
Soler	1.000	6	8	0	0	0
Szczur	—	1	0	0	0	0
Young	1.000	8	13	0	0	0
Zagunis	.991	48	105	2	1	1

MYRTLE BEACH PELICANS

HIGH CLASS A

CAROLINA LEAGUE

Batting	B-T	HT	WT	DOB	AVG	vLH	vRH	G	AB	R	H	2B	3B	HR	RBI	BB	HBP	SH	SF	SO	SB	CS	SLG	OBP
Amaya, Gioskar	R-R	5-11	175	12-13-92	.245	.262	.238	44	143	15	35	9	1	5	17	20	1	1	3	36	4	1	.427	.335
Baez, Jeffrey	R-R	6-0	180	10-30-93	.241	.296	.213	113	369	43	89	15	3	8	45	44	4	10	6	80	38	11	.363	.324
Balaguert, Yasiel	R-R	6-2	215	1-9-93	.263	.295	.251	135	533	62	140	25	2	19	96	43	1	0	6	125	5	1	.424	.316
Bote, David	R-R	5-11	185	4-7-93	.337	.293	.356	72	276	55	93	26	3	6	41	31	4	1	1	41	6	1	.518	.410
Brockmeyer, Cael	R-R	6-5	235	10-8-91	.190	.222	.180	24	79	9	15	2	0	4	12	10	2	0	1	19	2	0	.367	.293
Burks, Charcer	R-R	6-0	170	3-9-95	.247	.252	.245	124	445	71	110	28	5	11	43	66	11	6	3	116	23	7	.407	.356
Castillo, Erick	B-R	5-11	178	2-25-93	.185	.136	.206	43	151	17	28	2	0	1	8	7	5	1	0	29	0	0	.219	.245
Crawford, Rashad	B-R	6-3	185	10-15-93	.255	.321	.234	83	329	59	84	18	8	3	30	33	2	5	0	73	22	6	.386	.327
Dewees, Donnie	L-L	5-11	180	9-29-93	.289	.333	.269	35	149	25	43	10	2	2	19	10	3	2	3	36	14	0	.423	.339
Dunston Jr. Shawon	L-R	6-2	195	2-5-93	.219	.200	.222	37	114	11	25	6	4	0	5	11	2	1	0	31	7	1	.342	.299
Ely, Andrew	L-R	5-11	180	1-23-93	.237	.364	.204	60	211	19	50	7	0	1	16	23	3	2	3	55	2	3	.284	.317
Flete, Bryant	B-R	5-10	146	1-31-93	.285	.200	.312	34	123	22	35	6	2	2	18	19	4	0	1	21	1	1	.415	.395
Happ, Ian	B-R	6-0	205	8-12-94	.296	.279	.302	69	240	37	71	16	3	7	42	48	1	0	4	69	10	3	.475	.410
Hodges, Jesse	R-R	6-1	212	3-29-94	.186	.162	.200	29	102	12	19	5	0	1	11	7	2	1	2	33	0	1	.265	.248
Lockhart, Danny	L-R	5-11	175	11-4-92	.244	.286	.231	37	119	16	29	6	3	1	12	8	1	1	3	24	6	1	.370	.290
Martin, Trey	R-R	6-2	190	12-11-92	.233	.226	.237	29	90	10	21	3	0	0	12	11	0	1	3	30	2	1	.267	.308
Pearson, Tyler	R-R	6-0	185	4-15-92	.205	.267	.172	30	88	9	18	2	0	1	9	3	3	1	2	18	1	0	.261	.297
Rice, Ian	R-R	6-0	195	8-19-93	.238	.302	.211	58	210	33	50	13	0	6	31	36	4	0	2	55	2	2	.386	.357
Spingola, Daniel	L-L	6-1	180	5-5-93	.231	.091	.254	49	156	20	36	12	0	1	17	20	3	2	4	35	4	1	.327	.322
Torres, Gleyber	R-R	6-1	175	12-13-96	.275	.229	.292	94	356	62	98	23	3	9	47	42	5	5	1	87	19	10	.433	.359
Vosler, Jason	L-R	6-1	190	9-6-93	.254	.239	.260	93	334	32	85	25	2	2	39	33	5	0	6	52	1	2	.359	.325

Pitching	B-T	HT	WT	DOB	W	L	ERA	G	GS	CG	SV	IP	H	R	ER	HR	BB	SO	AVG	vLH	vRH	K/9	BB/9
Araujo, Pedro	R-R	6-3	214	7-2-93	0	2	5.21	13	0	0	1	19	18	12	11	2	13	22	.247	.286	.211	10.42	6.16
Berg, David	R-R	6-1	210	3-28-93	2	0	1.42	9	0	0	4	13	10	4	2	0	1	10	.208	.150	.250	7.11	0.71
Brooks, Craig	R-R	5-10	180	9-23-92	2	0	8.25	17	0	0	0	24	29	22	22	1	20	27	.296	.200	.396	10.13	7.50
Clifton, Trevor	R-R	6-1	170	5-11-95	7	7	2.72	23	23	0	0	119	97	42	36	4	41	129	.225	.205	.245	9.76	3.10
Effross, Scott	R-R	6-1	195	12-28-93	1	0	5.25	9	0	0	0	12	15	7	7	0	3	6	.313	.273	.346	4.50	2.25
Farris, James	R-R	6-2	210	4-4-92	1	2	2.40	17	0	0	8	30	21	8	8	0	7	36	.198	.192	.204	10.80	2.10
Hedges, Zach	R-R	6-4	210	10-21-92	7	8	2.89	16	16	1	0	97	92	46	31	4	18	63	.243	.313	.181	5.87	1.68
Ihrig, Tyler	L-L	6-0	210	9-17-91	0	0	0.00	3	0	0	0	7	1	1	0	0	4	4	.050	.091	.000	5.40	5.40
Leal, Erick	R-R	6-3	180	3-17-95	10	4	3.23	19	18	0	0	95	92	43	34	5	22	66	.253	.238	.270	6.27	2.09
Lewis, Daniel	R-R	6-0	200	3-26-91	5	0	2.59	20	0	0	0	31	30	9	9	0	16	20	.265	.327	.207	5.74	4.60
Maples, Dillon	R-R	6-2	225	5-9-92	0	1	7.71	9	0	0	0	7	9	7	6	0	7	6	.281	.176	.400	7.71	9.00
Martinez, Jonathan	R-R	6-1	205	6-27-94	12	6	4.19	23	23	1	0	131	129	64	61	13	43	77	.257	.247	.269	5.29	2.95
McNeil, Ryan	R-R	6-3	210	2-1-94	1	1	2.33	44	0	0	22	54	46	15	14	4	21	61	.231	.289	.176	10.17	3.50
Minch, Jordan	L-L	6-3	180	7-16-93	0	2	2.88	29	0	0	2	34	34	12	11	0	18	26	.276	.239	.299	6.82	4.72
Morrison, Preston	R-R	6-2	185	7-19-93	3	0	1.77	6	6	0	0	36	27	8	7	1	10	37	.218	.219	.217	9.34	2.52
Nance, Tommy	R-R	6-6	235	3-19-91	2	1	2.67	15	0	0	2	27	26	9	8	0	11	26	.257	.283	.229	8.67	3.67
Norwood, James	R-R	6-2	205	12-24-93	1	0	1.93	8	0	0	1	9	12	2	2	0	4	8	.300	.333	.273	7.71	1.93
Null, Jeremy	R-R	6-7	200	9-27-93	5	6	4.20	21	20	0	0	105	124	57	49	8	22	65	.295	.282	.309	5.57	1.89
Pugliese, James	R-R	6-3	220	8-12-92	7	5	3.83	28	7	0	0	85	80	40	36	3	31	83	.248	.215	.276	8.82	3.30
Rosario, Jose	R-R	6-1	170	8-29-90	1	0	1.65	12	0	0	5	16	15	3	3	0	8	14	.242	.241	.242	7.71	4.41
Stinnett, Jake	R-R	6-4	202	4-25-92	9	4	4.27	20	20	0	0	116	114	67	55	7	40	97	.263	.297	.235	7.53	3.10
Thorpe, Tommy	L-L	6-0	185	9-20-92	4	6	3.59	39	5	0	1	78	69	31	31	7	33	69	.239	.263	.226	8.00	3.82
Torrez, Daury	R-R	6-3	210	6-11-93	2	2	3.56	42	0	0	2	68	74	32	27	6	19	69	.275	.328	.231	9.09	2.50
Underwood, Duane	R-R	6-2	210	7-20-94	0	0	1.93	1	1	0	0	5	3	1	1	0	0	2	.176	.100	.286	3.86	0.00
Wagner, Michael	R-R	6-3	175	10-3-91	0	0	3.68	3	0	0	0	7	5	3	3	0	1	8	.185	.214	.154	9.82	1.23

Fielding

Catcher	PCT	G	PO	A	E	DP	PB
Amaya	.983	37	259	24	5	0	7
Brockmeyer	1.000	23	161	11	0	0	5
Castillo	.988	42	286	53	4	6	6
Pearson	1.000	28	226	20	0	2	3
Rice	.977	14	80	5	2	1	0

First Base	PCT	G	PO	A	E	DP
Amaya	1.000	1	5	1	0	0
Balaguert	.991	124	1019	92	10	87
Bote	.992	15	113	6	1	12
Brockmeyer	1.000	1	9	0	0	0
Rice	1.000	1	7	0	0	0

Second Base	PCT	G	PO	A	E	DP
Bote	.967	31	46	72	4	12
Ely	.976	21	29	51	2	13
Flete	1.000	27	39	56	0	15
Happ	.967	50	83	119	7	27
Lockhart	.980	14	19	30	1	3

Third Base	PCT	G	PO	A	E	DP
Amaya	1.000	1	0	1	0	0
Bote	.904	21	19	28	5	1
Hodges	.983	28	22	35	1	1
Lockhart	.833	4	2	3	1	0
Vosler	.929	89	69	141	16	8

Shortstop	PCT	G	PO	A	E	DP
Ely	.963	40	70	112	7	27
Flete	.933	6	7	7	1	4
Lockhart	.970	7	12	20	1	5
Torres	.951	87	135	230	19	50

Outfield	PCT	G	PO	A	E	DP
Baez	.978	103	208	16	5	1
Balaguert	1.000	3	6	0	0	0
Burks	.983	113	224	8	4	1
Crawford	.988	77	162	4	2	0
Dewees	.990	33	94	3	1	0
Dunston Jr.	1.000	21	39	1	0	0
Happ	1.000	6	11	0	0	0
Martin	1.000	29	64	1	0	0
Spingola	.944	39	65	2	4	1

SOUTH BEND CUBS

LOW CLASS A

MIDWEST LEAGUE

Batting

Batting	B-T	HT	WT	DOB	AVG	vLH	vRH	G	AB	R	H	2B	3B	HR	RBI	BB	HBP	SH	SF	SO	SB	CS	SLG	OBP
Alamo, Tyler	R-R	6-4	200	5-2-95	.243	.253	.239	85	309	28	75	12	0	5	50	16	3	2	4	71	0	0	.330	.283
Caro, Roberto	B-R	6-0	185	9-25-93	.231	.176	.252	59	182	18	42	4	3	0	18	18	2	4	2	62	4	5	.286	.304
Castillo, Erick	B-R	5-11	178	2-25-93	.000	.000	.000	3	8	0	0	0	0	0	0	1	0	0	0	1	0	0	.000	.111
Dewees, Donnie	L-L	5-11	180	9-29-93	.282	.243	.298	94	365	65	103	15	12	3	54	29	4	7	5	51	17	5	.414	.337
Ely, Andrew	L-R	5-11	180	1-23-93	.295	.214	.323	44	166	25	49	11	0	2	12	17	4	4	3	32	6	4	.398	.368
Flete, Bryant	B-R	5-10	146	1-31-93	.228	.159	.251	81	272	30	62	11	4	4	31	24	0	7	1	55	7	4	.342	.290
Fowler, Dexter	B-R	6-5	195	3-22-86	.000	—	.000	1	2	0	0	0	0	0	0	2	0	0	0	1	0	0	.000	.500
Higgins, P.J.	R-R	5-10	185	5-10-93	.283	.278	.285	121	445	57	126	30	1	0	40	72	8	8	4	75	3	1	.355	.389
Hodges, Jesse	R-R	6-1	212	3-29-94	.287	.200	.326	61	209	27	60	5	5	0	21	21	0	0	2	45	2	4	.359	.349
Jimenez, Eloy	R-R	6-4	205	11-27-96	.329	.258	.356	112	432	65	142	40	3	14	81	25	4	0	3	94	8	3	.532	.369
Machin, Vimael	R-R	5-11	185	9-25-93	.243	.115	.286	31	103	11	25	6	0	0	11	13	2	2	0	23	0	0	.301	.339
Martinez, Eddy Julio	R-R	6-1	195	1-18-95	.254	.226	.266	126	460	72	117	24	2	10	67	50	4	0	3	113	8	5	.380	.331
Mineo, Alberto	L-R	5-10	170	7-23-94	.243	.259	.240	40	152	21	37	7	0	2	26	13	0	3	0	46	0	0	.329	.298
Monasterio, Andruw	B-R	6-0	175	5-30-97	.216	.140	.241	48	176	25	38	5	1	0	11	10	3	3	0	33	7	5	.256	.270
Myers, Connor	R-R	5-11	170	2-3-94	.221	.259	.211	34	122	14	27	6	0	3	11	4	2	3	0	41	6	2	.344	.258
Paniagua, Jose	R-R	6-2	180	6-7-94	.095	.167	.067	6	21	1	2	0	0	0	2	1	0	0	1	6	0	0	.095	.130
Paredes, Isaac	R-R	5-11	175	2-18-99	.167	.500	.100	3	12	0	2	0	0	0	0	1	0	0	0	2	0	0	.167	.231
Paula, Adonis	R-R	6-1	185	6-21-94	.204	.270	.180	40	137	14	28	6	1	2	19	8	2	1	3	52	1	0	.307	.253
Rice, Ian	R-R	6-0	195	8-19-93	.310	.319	.304	39	126	24	39	8	0	9	27	26	0	0	4	27	0	0	.587	.417
Rose, Matt	R-R	6-4	195	8-2-94	.235	.300	.209	78	281	37	66	13	0	13	43	28	7	2	3	67	1	2	.420	.317
Sepulveda, Carlos	L-R	5-10	10	8-27-96	.310	.338	.302	80	332	55	103	14	2	1	26	34	3	4	0	41	4	11	.373	.366
Silver, Josh	R-R	6-1	200	4-24-90	.228	.286	.196	23	79	12	18	3	0	0	9	9	0	1	0	19	0	0	.266	.307
Spingola, Daniel	L-L	6-1	180	5-5-93	.309	.367	.292	38	136	20	42	6	1	0	10	12	3	2	0	25	4	3	.368	.377
Tidaback, Sam	R-R	6-0	210	10-6-93	.333	.250	.375	3	12	0	4	1	0	0	2	0	0	0	0	5	0	0	.417	.333
Whiting, Sutton	R-R	5-8	170	5-13-92	.247	.179	.283	26	81	12	20	2	0	0	7	14	0	3	1	20	1	3	.272	.354

Pitching

Pitching	B-T	HT	WT	DOB	W	L	ERA	G	GS	CG	SV	IP	H	R	ER	HR	BB	SO	AVG	vLH	vRH	K/9	BB/9
Alzolay, Adbert	R-R	6-0	179	3-1-95	9	4	4.34	22	20	0	0	120	119	61	58	9	28	81	.260	.271	.246	6.06	2.09
Araujo, Pedro	R-R	6-3	214	7-2-93	3	0	1.59	16	0	0	3	34	19	6	6	1	11	45	.161	.154	.170	11.91	2.91
Bloomquist, Casey	R-R	6-3	190	1-25-94	8	8	3.00	30	12	0	4	117	107	53	39	7	17	87	.239	.225	.253	6.69	1.31
Brooks, Craig	R-R	5-10	180	9-23-93	2	1	1.39	23	0	0	5	32	22	9	5	0	20	42	.196	.235	.164	11.69	5.57
Cheek, Jared	B-R	5-11	190	10-31-92	2	0	3.18	13	0	0	4	17	17	7	6	0	5	17	.279	.313	.241	9.00	2.65
De La Cruz, Oscar	R-R	6-4	200	3-4-95	1	2	3.25	6	6	0	0	28	22	10	10	0	8	35	.218	.222	.213	11.39	2.60
Effross, Scott	R-R	6-1	195	12-28-93	6	0	2.77	32	0	0	2	52	54	22	16	1	13	53	.267	.255	.278	9.17	2.25
Eregua, Greyfer	R-R	5-11	160	10-15-93	3	4	3.77	34	0	0	3	74	68	35	31	6	13	67	.247	.236	.260	8.15	1.58
Frazier, Scott	R-R	6-7	215	12-3-91	0	0	8.59	6	0	0	0	7	7	7	7	1	6	8	.241	.091	.333	9.82	7.36
Griggs, Tanner	R-R	6-5	165	6-14-94	2	2	2.67	14	0	0	0	30	26	10	9	0	7	27	.236	.281	.189	8.01	2.08
Kellogg, Ryan	R-L	6-6	230	2-4-94	9	7	3.03	24	23	1	0	131	115	51	44	8	26	107	.234	.258	.220	7.37	1.79
Malave, Mark	B-R	6-3	185	1-5-95	0	0	0.00	1	0	0	1	3	3	0	0	0	1	1	.300	.200	.400	3.00	3.00
Maples, Dillon	R-R	6-2	225	5-9-92	1	2	3.24	19	0	0	9	25	18	10	9	1	10	17	.198	.250	.140	6.12	3.60
Miller, Kyle	R-R	6-3	185	12-2-93	5	2	2.57	20	9	0	0	74	62	25	21	0	18	56	.235	.247	.227	6.84	2.20
Morrison, Preston	R-R	6-2	185	7-19-93	9	4	2.24	17	16	0	1	92	85	34	23	2	23	85	.241	.247	.235	8.29	2.24
Nance, Tommy	R-R	6-6	235	3-19-91	0	0	0.00	2	0	0	1	4	1	0	0	0	0	3	.091	.111	.000	7.36	0.00
Norwood, James	R-R	6-2	205	12-24-93	3	1	3.71	22	0	0	6	27	30	12	11	0	8	35	.273	.188	.339	11.81	2.70
Paulino, Jose	L-L	6-2	165	4-9-95	3	1	3.15	7	7	0	0	40	36	18	14	3	10	32	.234	.135	.284	7.20	2.25
Peitzmeier, Tyler	L-L	6-2	210	2-26-93	1	1	3.31	9	0	0	1	16	20	7	6	0	5	11	.317	.300	.333	6.06	2.76
Sands, Carson	L-L	6-3	205	3-28-95	7	4	5.91	21	14	0	1	75	79	50	49	4	42	51	.271	.298	.258	6.15	5.06
Steele, Justin	L-L	6-2	195	7-11-95	5	7	5.00	19	19	0	0	77	93	57	43	3	39	76	.305	.215	.344	8.84	4.54
Twomey, Kyle	L-L	6-3	165	12-29-93	2	3	3.44	19	10	0	1	73	67	33	28	5	28	75	.245	.232	.253	9.20	3.44
Underwood, Duane	R-R	6-2	210	7-20-94	0	1	2.08	3	3	0	0	9	5	2	2	0	4	12	.172	.222	.091	12.46	4.15
Wagner, Michael	R-R	6-3	175	10-3-91	1	0	3.38	2	0	0	1	3	2	1	1	0	2	2	.222	.500	.000	6.75	6.75
Williamson, John	L-L	6-1	195	9-27-92	2	1	2.37	37	0	0	0	57	45	18	15	1	20	53	.218	.146	.266	8.37	3.16

Fielding

Catcher	PCT	G	PO	A	E	DP	PB
Alamo	.996	25	198	26	1	0	2
Castillo	1.000	3	23	2	0	0	0
Higgins	.988	77	570	106	8	2	17
Mineo	.991	15	92	15	1	0	2
Rice	.987	17	126	21	2	0	0
Tidaback	.941	2	10	6	1	0	0

First Base	PCT	G	PO	A	E	DP
Alamo	.996	57	533	35	2	40
Higgins	.994	17	149	21	1	13
Mineo	.976	9	77	4	2	4
Paniagua	.955	6	41	1	2	3
Paula	.974	4	36	1	1	2
Rice	.900	1	9	0	1	1
Rose	.995	42	348	21	2	38
Silver	1.000	5	45	3	0	4

Second Base	PCT	G	PO	A	E	DP
Ely	.953	22	28	73	5	18
Flete	1.000	2	7	5	0	2
Machin	.968	15	19	41	2	6
Sepulveda	.976	78	133	226	9	56
Silver	.889	2	3	5	1	1
Whiting	.955	23	31	54	4	9

Third Base	PCT	G	PO	A	E	DP
Ely	.970	11	8	24	1	3
Flete	.889	2	2	6	1	0
Hodges	.910	56	35	96	13	7
Machin	1.000	10	7	19	0	5
Paula	.947	16	7	29	2	1
Rose	.907	33	17	61	8	7
Silver	.926	12	11	14	2	2
Whiting	1.000	1	0	1	0	0

Shortstop	PCT	G	PO	A	E	DP
Ely	.878	11	14	22	5	6
Flete	.943	72	97	182	17	40
Machin	1.000	5	6	7	0	4
Monasterio	.965	46	71	124	7	32
Paredes	.818	3	0	9	2	0
Silver	1.000	3	1	10	0	1

Outfield	PCT	G	PO	A	E	DP
Caro	.973	56	106	3	3	0
Dewees	.986	89	217	2	3	0
Jimenez	.988	97	164	1	2	1
Machin	1.000	3	2	0	0	0
Martinez	.978	120	208	12	5	1
Myers	1.000	34	73	1	0	0
Rose	1.000	1	2	0	0	0
Spingola	1.000	25	40	0	0	0
Whiting	1.000	1	1	0	0	0

EUGENE EMERALDS
NORTHWEST LEAGUE

SHORT-SEASON

Batting	B-T	HT	WT	DOB	AVG	vLH	vRH	G	AB	R	H	2B	3B	HR	RBI	BB	HBP	SH	SF	SO	SB	CS	SLG	OBP
Bautista, Alex	R-R	6-0	200	9-6-93	.167	.500	.000	2	6	0	1	0	0	0	1	1	0	0	0	3	0	0	.167	.286
Bruno, Stephen	R-R	5-9	165	11-17-90	.368	.500	.333	6	19	5	7	0	0	0	5	4	0	0	1	5	0	0	.368	.458
Davis, Taylor	R-R	5-10	200	11-28-89	.176	.400	.083	6	17	2	3	0	0	0	5	0	0	0	2	0	0	.176	.364
Foster, Michael	R-R	6-0	170	11-4-93	.176	.130	.214	20	51	6	9	3	0	0	5	7	0	0	0	12	2	2	.235	.276
Galindo, Wladimir	R-R	6-3	210	11-6-96	.243	.268	.236	66	247	46	60	19	4	9	40	33	2	0	0	81	3	0	.462	.337
Garcia, Robert	R-R	5-10	170	12-6-93	.283	.320	.269	49	184	29	52	13	3	2	19	15	3	2	1	53	5	1	.418	.345
Giambrone, Trent	R-R	5-8	175	12-20-93	.292	.267	.302	51	171	33	50	12	0	4	22	29	3	0	0	39	6	3	.433	.404
Gonzalez, Jose	R-R	6-1	160	1-12-96	.211	.091	.259	13	38	6	8	3	0	0	1	4	1	1	0	14	0	2	.289	.302
Machin, Vimael	L-R	5-10	185	9-25-93	.429	.375	.500	4	14	2	6	0	0	0	5	3	0	0	2	2	2	0	.429	.474
Marcano, Ricardo	L-R	6-2	190	10-18-94	.273	.500	.222	3	11	0	3	0	0	0	4	0	0	0	0	5	0	0	.273	.273
Mastrobuoni, Marcus	R-R	5-11	205	11-28-93	.227	.313	.200	39	132	21	30	6	1	3	19	17	1	1	3	19	2	1	.356	.314
Mineo, Alberto	L-R	5-10	170	7-23-94	.000	—	.000	1	4	0	0	0	0	0	0	0	0	0	0	0	0	0	.000	.000
Mitchell, Kevonte	R-R	6-4	185	8-12-95	.243	.203	.257	62	230	44	56	12	2	5	27	25	2	2	4	68	15	2	.378	.318
Monasterio, Andruw	B-R	6-0	175	5-30-97	.324	.429	.280	17	71	12	23	3	1	1	12	4	0	2	1	16	1	0	.437	.355
Myers, Connor	R-R	5-11	170	2-3-94	.265	.300	.250	10	34	9	9	2	1	0	7	5	1	1	1	11	2	0	.382	.366
Paniagua, Jose	R-R	6-2	180	6-7-94	.204	.243	.192	44	162	18	33	5	2	1	21	5	4	0	1	60	0	2	.278	.244
Payne, Tyler	R-R	5-11	210	10-25-92	.246	.250	.245	41	138	15	34	7	2	3	19	17	2	1	1	25	0	0	.391	.335
Peguero, Yeiler	B-R	5-10	150	9-20-97	.260	.270	.256	68	262	33	68	11	3	1	25	25	2	7	2	45	6	5	.336	.326
Pieters, Chris	L-L	6-3	185	9-21-94	.246	.261	.240	66	252	36	62	8	3	3	30	28	2	1	2	73	20	3	.337	.324
Rose, Matt	R-R	6-4	195	8-2-94	.241	.414	.148	23	83	13	20	5	0	4	16	12	1	0	0	30	3	0	.446	.344
Short, Zack	R-R	5-10	175	5-29-95	.236	.240	.235	39	127	22	30	6	1	1	23	33	4	1	3	24	10	5	.323	.401
Tidaback, Sam	R-R	6-0	210	10-6-93	.176	.150	.194	14	51	5	9	3	1	1	7	4	1	0	3	18	0	0	.333	.237
Wilson, D.J.	R-R	5-8	177	10-8-96	.257	.175	.282	64	245	37	63	15	2	3	29	20	4	2	3	56	21	8	.371	.320

Pitching	B-T	HT	WT	DOB	W	L	ERA	G	GS	CG	SV	IP	H	R	ER	HR	BB	SO	AVG	vLH	vRH	K/9	BB/9
Brink, Jordan	L-R	6-0	200	3-18-93	0	0	5.40	2	0	0	0	3	2	2	2	0	1	4	.167	.000	.222	10.80	2.70
Carter, Jed	R-R	6-0	190	1-26-95	3	1	5.68	8	0	0	0	6	7	8	4	0	5	11	.259	.200	.294	15.63	7.11
Castillo, Jesus	R-R	6-2	165	8-27-95	2	3	3.27	7	7	0	0	33	28	12	12	3	11	38	.224	.305	.152	10.36	3.00
Cease, Dylan	R-R	6-2	190	12-28-95	2	0	2.22	12	12	0	0	45	27	14	11	1	25	66	.175	.182	.172	13.30	5.04
Cheek, Jared	B-R	5-11	190	10-31-92	1	0	0.98	13	0	0	7	18	12	2	2	0	2	17	.185	.121	.250	8.35	0.98
Clark, Bailey	R-R	6-4	185	12-3-94	0	0	2.70	2	2	0	0	7	8	3	2	1	0	9	.276	.368	.100	12.15	0.00
Conway, Josh	R-R	6-1	190	4-12-91	0	0	4.15	4	0	0	0	4	5	2	2	1	6	8	.278	.300	.250	16.62	12.46
De La Cruz, Oscar	R-R	6-4	200	3-4-95	0	0	1.08	2	2	0	0	8	5	2	1	1	2	14	.167	.125	.214	15.12	2.16
De Los Rios, Enrique	R-R	6-1	175	5-2-95	4	4	4.21	14	0	0	0	26	22	18	12	1	25	26	.237	.262	.216	9.12	8.77
Diaz, Andin	L-L	6-0	182	9-2-92	2	0	4.50	12	0	0	1	20	18	11	10	0	8	23	.237	.190	.255	10.35	3.60
Frazier, Scott	R-R	6-7	215	12-3-91	1	0	9.00	12	0	0	1	15	13	15	15	2	16	15	.228	.250	.216	9.00	9.60
Hockin, Chad	R-R	6-2	200	10-7-94	0	0	6.00	12	0	0	0	12	14	10	8	0	4	14	.298	.350	.259	10.50	3.00
Huberman, Marc	L-L	6-2	180	1-10-94	3	0	1.72	8	0	0	0	16	9	3	3	0	10	17	.185	.000	.250	9.77	5.74
Hudson, Bryan	R-R	6-8	220	5-8-97	5	4	5.06	13	13	0	0	59	56	37	33	4	41	41	.262	.197	.288	6.29	6.29
Knighton, John Michael	R-R	6-2	190	4-30-94	2	0	1.72	18	1	0	4	37	28	8	7	0	9	27	.215	.173	.244	6.63	2.21
Lewis, Daniel	R-R	6-0	200	3-26-91	0	0	5.40	3	0	0	0	5	5	3	3	1	6	6	.278	.200	.375	10.80	10.80
Malave, Mark	B-R	6-3	185	1-5-95	0	1	3.81	21	0	0	8	26	22	13	11	2	13	33	.227	.286	.194	11.42	4.50
Mekkes, Dakota	R-R	6-7	252	11-6-94	1	1	2.12	9	0	0	0	17	11	7	4	1	4	21	.186	.296	.094	11.12	2.12
Miller, Tyson	R-R	6-5	200	7-29-95	1	1	3.97	6	4	0	0	23	26	11	10	4	4	14	.289	.343	.255	5.56	1.59
Minacci, M.T.	R-R	6-0	170	6-6-95	2	0	4.03	23	0	0	2	20	31	22	9	2	9	31	.254	.236	.266	6.25	4.03
Moreno, Erling	R-R	6-3	200	1-13-97	2	1	0.90	6	6	0	0	30	16	5	3	2	5	22	.150	.186	.125	6.60	1.50
Nance, Tommy	R-R	6-6	235	3-19-91	2	0	0.00	4	0	0	0	7	3	0	0	0	3	7	.143	.200	.125	9.45	4.05
Paulino, Jose	L-L	6-2	165	4-9-95	4	0	0.51	6	6	0	0	35	19	3	2	0	3	37	.156	.296	.116	9.51	0.77
Peitzmeier, Tyler	L-L	6-2	210	2-26-93	2	1	2.53	10	0	0	2	21	19	10	6	1	2	18	.226	.240	.220	7.59	0.84
Robinson, Duncan	R-R	6-6	220	12-5-93	2	1	4.19	7	0	0	0	19	24	10	9	0	6	17	.293	.275	.310	7.91	2.79
Rondon, Manuel	L-L	6-1	165	3-7-95	6	1	1.10	12	12	0	0	57	50	15	7	1	22	49	.233	.193	.247	7.69	3.45
Rucker, Michael	R-R	6-1	185	4-27-94	0	0	0.00	2	0	0	0	4	5	1	0	0	3	.313	.400	.273	15.75	0.00
Santana, Alex	R-R	6-1	170	10-3-93	1	1	7.57	18	0	0	0	27	28	26	23	2	25	22	.272	.306	.241	7.24	8.23
Short, Wyatt	L-L	5-8	180	10-14-94	1	0	0.00	15	0	0	7	15	5	1	0	0	7	14	.104	.000	.143	8.40	4.20
Silverio, Pedro	R-R	6-2	210	6-29-94	3	2	4.50	11	11	0	0	44	38	23	22	4	30	46	.233	.229	.237	9.41	6.14

Fielding

C: Davis 3, Foster 1, Mastrobuoni 33, Mineo 1, Payne 35, Tidaback 8. **1B:** Davis 2, Giambrone 10, Paniagua 23, Pieters 39, Rose 5. **2B:** Bruno 5, Giambrone 29, Machin 1, Monasterio 2, Peguero 42. **3B:** Galindo 59, Giambrone 4, Machin 3, Paniagua 1, Rose 10. **SS:** Monasterio 15, Peguero 24, Short 38. **OF:** Bautista 6, Foster 13, Garcia 48, Gonzalez 13, Marcano 2, Mitchell 57, Myers 8, Pieters 28, Wilson 64.

AZL CUBS
ARIZONA LEAGUE

ROOKIE

Batting	B-T	HT	WT	DOB	AVG	vLH	vRH	G	AB	R	H	2B	3B	HR	RBI	BB	HBP	SH	SF	SO	SB	CS	SLG	OBP
Ayala, Luis	R-L	6-0	176	12-21-95	.283	.275	.286	46	187	26	53	5	4	1	19	11	3	0	2	37	19	7	.369	.330
Bethencourt, Jhonny	R-R	5-11	160	2-12-97	.235	.182	.247	39	115	16	27	3	3	0	13	19	2	3	0	20	7	2	.313	.353
Cruz, Michael	L-R	5-11	210	1-13-96	.238	.286	.225	40	130	19	31	6	0	2	15	20	9	1	3	23	1	0	.331	.370
Davis, Zach	R-R	5-11	175	6-29-94	.188	—	.188	6	16	1	3	0	0	0	2	0	0	1	0	5	0	0	.188	.188
Diaz, Carlos	R-R	5-11	175	3-10-95	.121	.167	.111	9	33	4	4	1	1	0	2	0	0	0	0	9	1	0	.212	.171
Filotei, Tolly	L-R	5-6	155	11-28-95	.161	.154	.163	24	56	7	9	1	0	0	10	10	1	1	0	13	4	3	.179	.299
Gonzalez, Erick	R-R	5-10	175	9-2-96	.100	.000	.111	5	10	1	1	0	0	0	0	1	0	0	0	2	0	0	.100	.182

Batting	B-T	HT	WT	DOB	AVG	vLH	vRH	G	AB	R	H	2B	3B	HR	RBI	BB	HBP	SH	SF	SO	SB	CS	SLG	OBP
Gonzalez, Jose	R-R	6-1	160	1-12-96	.122	.095	.130	25	90	7	11	1	0	0	8	6	2	0	0	26	6	2	.133	.194
Kwon, Kwang-Min	L-L	6-2	210	12-12-97	.267	.500	.250	9	30	4	8	2	0	0	1	3	1	0	0	10	1	0	.333	.353
Matos, Yohan	R-R	6-0	175	10-6-96	.241	.208	.250	39	108	17	26	5	3	0	12	17	1	0	1	34	5	2	.343	.346
Mejia, Rafael	R-R	6-1	195	12-12-97	.203	.161	.216	36	128	11	26	6	1	2	10	3	1	0	1	34	0	0	.313	.226
Myers, Connor	R-R	5-11	170	2-3-94	.211	.000	.267	5	19	4	4	0	1	0	3	0	0	0	0	4	3	0	.316	.318
Paredes, Isaac	R-R	5-11	175	2-18-99	.305	.294	.308	47	167	23	51	14	3	1	26	13	2	0	2	20	4	0	.443	.359
Paula, Adonis	R-R	6-1	185	6-21-94	.250	—	.250	1	4	0	1	0	0	0	0	0	0	0	0	1	0	0	.250	.250
Pereda, Jhonny	R-R	6-1	170	4-18-96	.289	.269	.294	41	128	17	37	7	1	2	23	16	3	0	2	21	0	2	.406	.376
Polanco, Gustavo	R-R	6-0	190	6-13-97	.322	.353	.315	46	177	27	57	7	1	1	22	5	3	0	0	21	4	1	.390	.351
Reyes, Ruben	L-L	5-11	170	10-1-95	.245	.111	.276	42	143	16	35	7	0	0	11	6	1	5	2	38	1	2	.294	.276
Rondon, Edgar	L-R	5-7	170	1-14-95	.247	.304	.227	34	89	17	22	2	1	0	9	13	3	3	1	34	5	2	.292	.358
Short, Zack	R-R	5-10	175	5-29-95	.318	.167	.342	14	44	12	14	3	0	0	8	14	2	0	0	9	5	1	.386	.500
Tidaback, Sam	R-R	6-0	210	10-6-93	.300	.333	.286	3	10	3	3	2	0	0	1	0	0	0	0	2	0	0	.500	.364
Zamudio, Kevin	R-R	6-0	200	8-23-97	.237	.300	.221	45	152	22	36	14	1	4	23	10	2	0	1	48	0	0	.421	.291
Zinn, Delvin	R-R	5-10	170	5-29-97	.182	.000	.240	11	33	1	6	1	0	0	2	1	0	0	0	12	0	2	.212	.206

Pitching	B-T	HT	WT	DOB	W	L	ERA	G	GS	CG	SV	IP	H	R	ER	HR	BB	SO	AVG	vLH	vRH	K/9	BB/9
Albertos, Jose	R-R	6-1	185	11-7-98	0	0	0.00	1	1	0	0	4	1	0	0	0	1	7	.077	.000	.200	15.75	2.25
Aquino, Luis	R-R	6-1	170	6-30-93	0	3	5.01	19	0	0	6	32	32	20	18	0	6	38	.258	.156	.293	10.58	1.67
Assad, Javier	R-R	6-1	200	7-30-97	2	2	2.87	10	7	0	1	38	39	18	12	1	13	42	.267	.314	.242	10.04	3.11
Brink, Jordan	L-R	6-0	200	3-18-93	2	1	3.18	10	3	0	1	17	12	10	6	2	12	21	.203	.211	.200	11.12	6.35
Cammack, Holden	R-R	6-0	195	6-14-93	0	0	3.86	7	0	0	0	7	6	3	3	0	5	12	.222	.250	.211	15.43	6.43
Carter, Jed	R-R	6-0	190	1-26-95	0	0	0.00	3	0	0	0	3	3	0	0	0	1	6	.231	.333	.200	16.20	2.70
Clark, Bailey	R-R	6-4	185	12-3-94	0	0	0.00	2	2	0	0	5	3	0	0	0	0	4	.188	.333	.154	7.20	0.00
Conway, Josh	R-R	6-1	190	4-12-91	0	0	3.38	5	0	0	0	5	3	2	2	0	3	5	.263	.500	.200	8.44	5.06
Crow, Aaron	R-R	6-3	195	11-10-86	0	0	0.00	3	2	0	0	3	2	0	0	0	2	6	.200	.333	.143	6.00	3.00
De La Cruz, Oscar	R-R	6-4	200	3-4-95	0	1	6.00	1	1	0	0	3	3	3	2	0	1	2	.250	—	.250	6.00	3.00
De Los Rios, Enrique	R-R	6-1	175	5-2-95	1	1	1.98	5	0	0	0	14	12	7	3	1	5	14	.231	.167	.265	9.22	3.29
Diaz, Andin	L-L	6-0	182	9-2-92	1	0	1.23	6	2	0	0	7	6	1	1	0	2	7	.233	.333	.222	8.59	2.45
Fife, Stephen	R-R	6-3	225	10-4-86	0	0	4.50	3	3	0	0	8	9	5	4	0	3	5	.281	.250	.286	5.63	3.38
Freeman, Colton	L-L	6-1	210	12-18-93	0	0	14.73	4	0	0	0	4	7	6	6	0	2	4	.412	.667	.357	9.82	4.91
Gomez, Yapson	L-L	5-10	160	10-2-93	3	1	2.47	15	0	0	1	44	35	22	12	2	10	50	.208	.189	.214	10.31	2.06
Griggs, Tanner	R-R	6-2	165	6-14-94	1	0	3.60	6	0	0	0	10	9	4	4	0	3	10	.237	.182	.259	9.00	2.70
Huberman, Marc	L-L	6-2	180	1-10-94	1	0	2.08	3	0	0	0	4	4	1	1	0	1	5	.267	.200	.300	10.38	2.08
Leal, Erick	R-R	6-3	180	3-17-95	1	0	0.00	2	1	0	0	3	1	1	0	0	1	5	.111	.000	.143	15.00	3.00
Leathersich, Jack	R-L	6-0	205	7-14-90	1	0	1.13	10	1	0	0	8	4	1	1	0	3	16	.148	.000	.167	18.00	3.38
Leidenz, Jose	R-R	6-1	171	10-16-94	2	1	6.55	18	0	0	1	33	45	31	24	1	11	26	.338	.278	.361	7.09	3.00
Marte, Junior	R-R	6-0	170	6-6-95	0	5	5.77	12	5	0	0	34	31	30	22	2	20	45	.233	.267	.223	11.80	5.24
Matusz, Brian	L-L	6-5	190	2-11-87	0	0	1.29	4	4	0	0	7	3	1	1	0	1	10	.130	.143	.125	12.86	1.29
Mekkes, Dakota	R-R	6-7	252	11-6-94	0	0	0.00	2	0	0	0	3	1	0	0	0	0	6	.100	.000	.143	18.00	0.00
Miller, Tyson	R-R	6-5	200	7-29-95	1	0	0.00	2	1	0	0	6	2	2	0	0	3	3	.111	.000	.125	4.50	4.50
Moreno, Erling	R-R	6-3	200	1-13-97	2	2	2.78	6	4	0	0	32	31	11	10	1	4	33	.254	.243	.259	9.19	1.11
Ochoa, Pablo	L-L	6-0	180	1-11-98	1	6	5.79	12	6	0	1	37	57	33	24	2	8	28	.339	.321	.343	6.75	1.93
Palma, Eugenio	L-L	5-11	170	11-26-96	3	0	1.91	14	2	0	2	42	40	16	9	1	8	37	.242	.100	.262	7.87	1.70
Riefenhauser, C.J.	L-L	6-0	195	1-30-90	0	0	9.00	1	0	0	0	1	1	1	1	0	1	0	.250	—	.250	0.00	9.00
Robinson, Duncan	R-R	6-6	220	12-5-93	0	0	0.00	1	0	0	0	1	0	0	0	0	1	1	.400	.500	.333	9.00	0.00
Rondon, Andri	R-R	6-2	190	9-16-95	2	2	7.15	12	5	0	0	34	46	31	27	0	14	34	.324	.412	.275	9.00	3.71
Rucker, Michael	R-R	6-1	185	4-27-94	3	0	0.00	9	4	0	0	9	4	1	0	0	1	11	.138	.125	.143	11.42	1.04
Swarmer, Matt	R-R	6-5	175	9-25-93	0	1	3.38	8	5	0	0	19	20	9	7	0	9	23	.278	.348	.245	11.09	4.34
Sweeney, Nathan	R-R	6-4	185	8-21-97	0	1	12.46	5	0	0	0	4	5	7	6	1	4	1	.294	.167	.364	2.08	8.31
Underwood, Duane	R-R	6-2	210	7-20-94	0	0	0.00	1	1	0	0	1	1	0	0	0	0	2	.250	—	.250	18.00	0.00

Fielding

3B: Bethencourt 17, Mejia 35, Rondon 1, Zamudio 16. **SS:** Bethencourt 11, Paredes 45, Rondon 1, Short 3, Zinn 5. **OF:** Ayala 46, Cruz 1, Davis 6, Filotei 20, Gonzalez 24, Kwon 8, Matos 36, Myers 5, Reyes 41. **C:** Cruz 20, Diaz 5, Gonzalez 2, Pereda 23, Polanco 8, Tidaback 2. **1B:** Cruz 6, Mejia 1, Pereda 10, Polanco 18, Zamudio 26. **2B:** Bethencourt 18, Rondon 31, Short 10, Zinn 6.

DSL CUBS   ROOKIE
DOMINICAN SUMMER LEAGUE

Batting	B-T	HT	WT	DOB	AVG	vLH	vRH	G	AB	R	H	2B	3B	HR	RBI	BB	HBP	SH	SF	SO	SB	CS	SLG	OBP
Ademan, Aramis	L-R	5-11	160	9-13-98	.254	.333	.239	59	209	37	53	5	4	0	16	34	3	2	0	28	17	9	.316	.366
Amaya, Miguel	R-R	6-1	185	3-9-99	.245	.231	.249	58	208	29	51	12	0	1	22	21	11	1	1	27	9	3	.317	.344
Colasante, Moises	R-R	5-9	176	9-19-94	.165	.040	.202	46	109	10	18	3	3	0	6	16	5	1	2	46	10	4	.248	.295
Cuevas, Yovanny	R-R	6-0	170	7-28-98	.227	.200	.232	61	198	28	45	9	1	3	26	37	11	2	0	35	20	10	.328	.378
Diaz, Daniel	R-R	5-11	200	4-5-97	.178	.150	.184	37	107	10	19	3	0	0	11	18	6	2	0	32	3	1	.206	.328
Diaz, Luis	R-R	5-9	160	4-16-99	.251	.188	.267	64	239	37	60	9	3	0	21	22	8	0	0	60	23	11	.314	.335
Gonzalez, Erick	R-R	5-10	175	9-2-96	.278	.125	.321	12	36	2	10	2	0	0	5	3	0	0	0	2	1	0	.333	.333
Gutierrez, Jose	B-R	5-11	185	4-11-97	.241	.224	.246	65	261	33	63	6	11	2	20	17	2	2	2	43	12	9	.372	.291
Hidalgo, Luis	R-R	6-1	190	2-23-96	.216	.267	.203	48	153	22	33	7	0	9	30	18	6	0	1	35	10	4	.438	.320
Jules, Jose	R-R	6-2	170	10-13-97	.224	.325	.192	49	170	18	38	7	3	1	12	12	3	1	2	46	18	4	.318	.283
Kelli, Fernando	R-R	6-0	180	7-28-98	.240	.176	.259	44	150	18	36	1	0	0	8	15	5	0	0	40	23	11	.247	.329
Lara, Samir	R-R	6-0	165	10-29-96	.255	.250	.256	12	47	4	12	3	0	1	7	1	0	0	1	9	2	5	.383	.265
Lopez, Ronaldo	R-R	6-1	160	5-22-98	.149	.154	.148	53	168	16	25	3	0	1	13	18	2	2	0	35	5	2	.190	.239
Matos, Fidel	R-R	6-0	200	2-6-95	.217	.133	.239	46	143	15	31	2	2	3	23	17	4	0	3	22	2	6	.322	.311

Batting

Batting	B-T	HT	WT	DOB	AVG	vLH	vRH	G	AB	R	H	2B	3B	HR	RBI	BB	HBP	SH	SF	SO	SB	CS	SLG	OBP
Mejia, Fidel	B-R	5-11	160	8-30-98	.321	.333	.317	41	156	27	50	9	0	0	16	14	1	2	3	29	9	5	.378	.374
Narea, Rafael	R-R	5-10	160	4-3-98	.263	.216	.273	63	209	36	55	7	1	0	17	42	7	5	1	28	27	12	.306	.402
Nunez, Orian	R-R	5-10	160	9-3-98	.278	.333	.263	61	198	25	55	16	2	1	29	21	1	2	4	18	12	9	.394	.344
Nunez, Richard	R-R	5-10	170	3-14-95	.273	—	—	53	161	21	44	8	1	1	21	33	4	0	3	24	17	6	.354	.403
Pedra, Henrry	R-R	5-11	175	4-26-94	.211	—	—	21	57	15	12	3	0	1	8	11	5	0	1	7	7	3	.316	.378
Pena, Raymond	R-R	5-10	160	4-7-97	.143	.088	.167	40	112	7	16	4	0	1	5	14	1	1	0	26	3	4	.205	.244
Perez, Henderson	R-R	5-11	160	6-10-99	.226	.294	.207	46	155	15	35	9	0	0	9	18	4	0	1	45	9	4	.284	.320
Perez, Herson	B-R	5-11	175	12-19-96	.213	.190	.219	31	94	9	20	2	2	0	8	13	1	0	0	23	8	5	.277	.315
Perlaza, Yonathan	B-R	5-10	195	11-10-98	.256	.278	.249	60	223	29	57	12	4	3	18	18	1	1	2	50	17	11	.386	.311
Rijo, Tony	R-R	6-0	170	11-3-97	.161	.176	.158	41	118	16	19	8	1	1	15	20	4	0	0	50	6	2	.271	.303
Rodriguez, Abraham	L-L	5-11	175	3-9-99	.255	.286	.247	58	220	30	56	11	4	1	33	10	3	0	6	25	12	5	.355	.289
Rojas, Jose	R-R	5-11	210	4-1-94	.204	.231	.195	41	113	14	23	3	0	1	8	9	4	1	0	19	8	5	.257	.286
Sierra, Jonathan	L-L	6-3	190	10-17-98	.264	.205	.278	64	220	33	58	11	3	0	19	37	6	0	4	48	12	5	.341	.384
Tineo, Franklin	R-R	6-1	176	12-30-94	.235	—	—	49	162	19	38	7	1	2	21	16	1	1	2	31	10	3	.327	.304
Ubiera, Luis	R-R	6-2	170	9-17-96	.200	.208	.198	42	125	12	25	4	0	0	13	11	1	3	2	30	5	2	.232	.266

Pitching

Pitching	B-T	HT	WT	DOB	W	L	ERA	G	GS	CG	SV	IP	H	R	ER	HR	BB	SO	AVG	vLH	vRH	K/9	BB/9
Aguiar, Maikel	R-R	6-0	185	11-20-96	0	1	2.82	12	0	0	2	22	15	10	7	0	17	25	.190	.333	.102	10.07	6.85
Bonalde, Andres	L-L	6-6	198	12-12-97	2	6	4.84	13	12	0	0	58	67	41	31	1	22	35	—	—	—	5.46	3.43
Calderon, Fernando	R-R	6-0	170	10-22-96	0	3	9.92	11	0	0	0	16	25	23	18	0	12	9	.352	.313	.364	4.96	6.61
Carrera, Faustino	L-L	5-10	165	3-9-99	7	2	1.06	13	13	0	0	76	55	13	9	0	19	55	.208	.143	.221	6.48	2.24
Colorado, Alejandro	R-R	6-1	170	6-22-96	3	7	3.61	14	14	1	0	67	67	33	27	1	18	62	.264	.265	.289	8.29	2.41
De La Cruz, Yan	R-R	5-11	165	8-5-93	2	3	6.27	14	0	0	1	33	44	29	23	2	9	16	.321	.236	.378	4.36	2.45
Delgado, Wilfre	R-R	6-1	175	11-10-95	2	2	3.32	12	5	0	1	41	30	20	15	1	17	22	.201	.125	.238	4.87	3.76
Diaz, Elvis	R-R	6-3	185	2-6-93	4	1	1.67	16	0	0	4	38	31	15	7	0	7	39	.221	.231	.218	9.32	1.67
Escanio, Luiz	R-R	6-5	190	7-31-92	3	1	1.45	10	0	0	3	19	13	8	3	0	9	28	.194	.208	.186	13.50	4.34
Estevez, Miguel	R-R	6-3	160	10-31-93	0	0	4.85	12	0	0	0	26	16	18	14	3	19	17	.172	.278	.147	5.88	6.58
Fernandez, Riger	L-L	6-2	190	1-1-98	2	6	4.53	14	12	0	0	56	48	40	28	2	50	36	.231	.174	.247	5.82	8.08
Ferrebus, Emilio	R-R	6-2	165	11-25-97	2	6	4.25	14	14	0	0	66	74	43	31	1	29	47	.290	.267	.303	6.44	3.97
Garcia, Hector	R-R	6-0	157	5-30-98	5	1	1.67	13	13	0	0	75	55	18	14	1	14	62	.202	.304	.141	7.41	1.67
Guerrero, Fauris	R-R	5-11	180	10-5-96	4	4	2.68	18	0	0	1	44	38	14	13	3	10	46	.230	.263	.213	9.48	2.06
Mac Donna, Jose	L-L	6-2	195	9-3-95	5	3	2.06	15	8	0	0	57	46	19	13	0	17	33	.218	.444	.185	5.24	2.70
Marquez, Brailyn	L-L	6-4	185	1-30-99	4	2	1.48	12	12	0	0	55	44	24	9	1	23	48	.222	.167	.230	7.90	3.79
Medina, Ivan	R-R	6-3	162	2-26-96	4	0	4.30	14	0	0	0	29	34	16	14	0	17	14	.288	.289	.288	4.30	5.22
Molina, Bryan	R-R	6-1	187	3-21-95	0	1	1.37	12	0	0	0	20	14	9	3	0	17	12	—	—	—	5.49	7.78
Novas, Edison	R-R	6-0	150	2-8-97	2	1	4.12	17	0	0	2	44	33	21	20	1	16	25	.212	.290	.192	5.15	3.30
Ocampo, Carlos	R-R	6-2	181	9-3-98	1	2	3.56	9	9	0	0	30	20	14	12	0	25	29	.192	.194	.191	8.60	7.42
Ochoa, Pablo	L-L	6-0	180	1-11-98	0	1	8.53	3	3	0	0	6	9	6	6	0	4	5	.321	.000	.360	7.11	5.68
Perez, Yunior	R-R	6-4	190	12-19-98	0	2	4.13	9	9	0	0	28	31	19	13	1	8	21	.290	.250	.301	6.67	2.54
Ramirez, Moises	R-R	5-11	170	12-11-95	3	1	1.79	15	0	0	1	40	40	15	8	1	16	31	.265	.338	.239	6.92	3.57
Ramos, Eury	R-R	6-3	152	10-10-97	0	1	3.60	3	3	0	0	10	10	5	4	0	5	4	.286	.364	.25	3.60	4.50
Rengifo, Juan	R-R	6-3	206	6-12-94	3	2	4.54	18	0	0	1	42	38	27	21	2	26	29	.241	.277	.225	6.26	5.62
Romero, Jhon	R-R	5-10	195	1-17-95	0	0	5.06	5	0	0	3	5	4	3	3	0	2	5	.158	.000	.250	8.44	3.38
Rosario, Aneuris	R-R	6-0	165	3-4-95	1	3	2.42	17	0	0	3	26	21	9	7	3	2	30	.210	.211	.210	10.38	0.69
Severino, Robert	L-R	6-2	185	2-14-94	2	0	2.57	9	0	0	0	14	15	6	4	2	5	15	.294	.294	.294	9.64	3.21
Silva, Luis	L-L	5-11	165	6-6-97	0	1	7.02	11	0	0	1	17	12	14	13	0	21	13	.207	.111	.224	7.02	11.34
Tejada, Jesus	R-R	6-1	168	10-24-96	1	5	3.12	13	12	0	0	61	68	33	21	1	18	37	.281	.369	.249	5.49	2.67
Tineo, Freddy	R-R	6-0	160	11-22-97	3	3	3.76	18	1	0	1	41	36	20	17	2	27	29	.240	.273	.231	6.42	5.98
Torres, Deibi	R-R	6-3	190	12-8-94	0	0	0.00	2	0	0	0	4	1	0	0	0	3	5	.077	.000	.111	10.38	6.23
Valdez, Sucre	R-R	6-2	180	9-1-93	1	0	5.00	15	0	0	1	27	35	23	15	3	7	21	.302	.359	.273	7.00	2.33
Ventura, Omar	R-R	6-2	190	9-10-96	1	2	5.56	15	0	0	0	34	33	22	21	1	28	19	.260	.283	.243	5.03	7.41

Fielding

C: Amaya 33, Diaz 33, Gonzalez 9, Nunez 9, Pena 37, Perez 7, Perez 1, Rojas 1, Tineo 28. **1B:** Amaya 16, Diaz 4, Gonzalez 1, Hidalgo 42, Matos 25, Mejia 2, Nunez 6, Nunez 13, Pena 3, Rodriguez 12, Rojas 14, Tineo 19. **2B:** Diaz 48, Lopez 16, Mejia 6, Narea 4, Nunez 23, Pedra 2, Perez 21, Perlaza 26. **3B:** Rojas 15, Tineo 4, Diaz 9, Lopez 22, Mejia 17, Narea 9, Nunez 36, Nunez 16, Pedra 15, Perlaza 13. **SS:** Ademan 52, Lopez 11, Mejia 11, Narea 50, Nunez 2, Pedra 1, Perlaza 21, Rojas 1. **OF:** Colasante 45, Cuevas 58, Gutierrez 64, Jules 48, Kelli 42, Lara 10, Matos 11, Nunez 6, Rijo 36, Rodriguez 32, Rojas 8, Sierra 57, Ubiera 41.

Chicago White Sox

SEASON IN A SENTENCE: The song remained the same on the South Side, as a top-heavy pitching staff wasn't enough to drag a subpar offense to a winning record. The fourth straight losing season cost manager Robin Ventura his job at season's end.

HIGH POINT: The White Sox led the American League Central through most of the first two months of the season, starting with a 17-8 April. The Sox were 24-12 on May 13 after ace Chris Sale won his eighth straight decision to open the season, with a complete-game six-hitter in a 7-1 win at Yankee Stadium.

LOW POINT: The Sox went 9-24 after Sale's win before rallying to finish the first half above .500. But Chicago lost seven of its first eight after the break to become irrelevant in the division and wild-card races. A three-game sweep against the Angels in which the White Sox were shut out twice and scored one run in the other game confirmed that this team was not a contender.

NOTABLE ROOKIES: Chicago tried to buy time for shortstop Tim Anderson by signing Jimmy Rollins in the offseason, but the vet hit .221 and made way for Anderson, who played 99 games and showed athleticism, speed and a need for polish for his offensive approach. Catcher Omar Narvaez, still rookie-eligible for 2017, had a solid September. Four Sox rookies—catcher Kevan Smith, third baseman Matt Davidson and outfielders Jason Coats and Charlie Tilson—got injured either before or during their Sox big league debuts. All four remain rookie-eligible in 2017.

KEY TRANSACTIONS: The Sox improved their lineup a bit with offseason trades for second baseman Brett Lawrie (who was often hurt) and third baseman Todd Frazier, who hit a career-high 40 homers, but they weren't enough. Chicago gave up righty Erik Johnson as well as teen shortstop Fernando Tatis Jr. for James Shields when they were still in the race; Shields bombed for the Sox. Thereafter, the Sox traded for prospects, dealing lefty Zach Duke to the Cardinals for Chicago native Charlie Tilson.

DOWN ON THE FARM: White Sox domestic affiliates had the worst record in baseball collectively with a .427 winning percentage. Only Rookie-level Great Falls made the playoffs, but the system saw strong early results from its 2016 draft class, led by catcher Zack Collins and righthanders Alec Hansen and Zack Burdi.

OPENING DAY PAYROLL: $112,998,667 (16th)

PLAYERS OF THE YEAR

MAJOR LEAGUE	MINOR LEAGUE
Chris Sale	**Adam Engel**
lhp	of
17-10, 3.34	(High A, Double-A,
1.037 WHIP, 7.5 H/9	Triple-A)
233 SO in 226.2 IP	.259/.344/.406, 45 SB

ORGANIZATION LEADERS

BATTING		*Minimum 250 AB
MAJORS		
* AVG	Melky Cabrera	.296
* OPS	Jose Abreu	.820
HR	Todd Frazier	40
RBI	Jose Abreu	100
MINORS		
* AVG	Mason Robbins, Winston-Salem	.314
* OBP	Landon Lassiter, Kannapolis, Winston-Salem	.371
* SLG	Nicky Delmonico, Birmingham, Charlotte	.490
* OPS	Nicky Delmonico, Birmingham, Charlotte	.837
R	Adam Engel, W-S, Birmingham, Charlotte	90
H	Mason Robbins, Winston-Salem	159
TB	Mason Robbins, Winston-Salem	221
2B	Mason Robbins, Winston-Salem	33
	Toby Thomas, Winston-Salem	33
3B	Adam Engel, W-S, Birmingham, Charlotte	12
HR	Nicky Delmonico, Birmingham, Charlotte	17
RBI	Gerson Montilla, Winston-Salem	74
BB	Tyler Sullivan, Kannapolis	59
SO	Corey Zangari, Kannapolis, Great Falls	176
SB	Adam Engel, W-S, Birmingham, Charlotte	45

PITCHING		#Minimum 75 IP
MAJORS		
W	Chris Sale	17
# ERA	Jose Quintana	3.20
SO	Chris Sale	233
SV	David Robertson	37
MINORS		
W	Tanner Banks, Kannapolis, Winston-Salem	12
L	Spencer Adams, Winston-Salem, Birmingham	12
	Brandon Brennan, Winston-Salem, Birmingham	12
# ERA	Brannon Easterling, Kannapolis	1.86
G	Brad Goldberg, Birmingham, Charlotte	47
GS	David Holmberg, Birmingham, Charlotte	28
	Luis Martinez, Kannapolis	28
SV	Matt Foster, AZL White Sox, Great Falls	11
IP	Chris Volstad, Charlotte	177
BB	Jordan Guerrero, Birmingham	73
SO	Jordan Stephens, Winston-Salem	155
# AVG	Matt Cooper, Winston-Salem, Birmingham	.211

2016 PERFORMANCE

President: Kenny Williams. **GM:** Rick Hahn. **Farm Director:** Nick Capra. **Scouting Director:** Nick Hostetler.

Class	Team	League	W	L	PCT	Finish	Manager
Majors	Chicago White Sox	American	78	84	.481	11th (15)	Robin Ventura
Triple-A	Charlotte Knights	International	65	79	.451	11th (14)	Julio Vinas
Double-A	Birmingham Barons	Southern	49	91	.350	10th (10)	Ryan Newman
High A	Winston-Salem Dash	Carolina	56	83	.403	6th (8)	Joel Skinner
Low A	Kannapolis Intimidators	South Atlantic	58	82	.414	13th (14)	Cole Armstrong
Rookie	Great Falls Voyagers	Pioneer	47	28	.627	1st (8)	Tommy Thompson
Rookie	White Sox	Arizona	21	35	.375	13th (14)	Mike Gellinger
Overall 2016 Minor League Record			296	398	.427	30th (30)	

ORGANIZATION STATISTICS

CHICAGO WHITE SOX
AMERICAN LEAGUE

Batting	B-T	HT	WT	DOB	AVG	vLH	vRH	G	AB	R	H	2B	3B	HR	RBI	BB	HBP	SH	SF	SO	SB	CS	SLG	OBP
Abreu, Jose	R-R	6-3	255	1-29-87	.293	.262	.301	159	624	67	183	32	1	25	100	47	15	0	9	125	0	2	.468	.353
Anderson, Tim	R-R	6-1	185	6-23-93	.283	.326	.270	99	410	57	116	22	6	9	30	13	1	6	1	117	10	2	.432	.306
Avila, Alex	L-R	5-11	210	1-29-87	.213	.250	.208	57	169	19	36	6	0	7	11	38	1	0	1	78	0	0	.373	.359
Cabrera, Melky	B-L	5-10	210	8-11-84	.296	.322	.289	151	591	70	175	42	5	14	86	47	0	3	5	69	2	0	.455	.345
Coats, Jason	R-R	6-2	200	2-24-90	.200	.360	.040	28	50	8	10	4	0	1	4	5	2	1	0	12	1	0	.340	.298
Davidson, Matt	R-R	6-3	230	3-26-91	.500	.500	—	1	2	1	1	0	0	0	1	0	0	0	0	1	0	0	.500	.500
Eaton, Adam	L-L	5-8	185	12-6-88	.284	.282	.285	157	619	91	176	29	9	14	59	63	14	7	3	115	14	5	.428	.362
Frazier, Todd	R-R	6-3	220	2-12-86	.225	.217	.227	158	590	89	133	21	0	40	98	64	4	1	7	163	15	5	.464	.302
Garcia, Avisail	R-R	6-4	240	6-12-91	.245	.222	.252	120	413	59	101	18	2	12	51	34	4	0	2	115	4	4	.385	.307
Garcia, Leury	B-R	5-8	170	3-18-91	.229	.176	.258	18	48	6	11	1	1	1	5	1	1	0	0	13	2	1	.354	.260
Jackson, Austin	R-R	6-1	205	2-1-87	.254	.159	.285	54	181	24	46	12	2	0	18	17	1	2	2	39	2	1	.343	.318
Lawrie, Brett	R-R	6-0	210	1-18-90	.248	.284	.239	94	351	35	87	22	0	12	36	30	2	0	1	109	7	3	.413	.310
Morneau, Justin	L-R	6-4	220	5-15-81	.261	.278	.257	58	203	16	53	14	1	6	25	12	1	0	2	52	0	0	.429	.303
Narvaez, Omar	B-R	5-11	215	2-10-92	.267	.333	.250	34	101	13	27	4	0	1	10	14	0	0	2	14	0	0	.337	.350
Navarro, Dioner	B-R	5-9	215	2-9-84	.210	.232	.201	85	271	25	57	13	2	6	32	20	2	2	3	63	1	2	.339	.267
2-team total (16 Toronto)					.207			101	304	26	63	13	2	6	35	23	2	2	3	71	1	2	.322	.265
Rollins, Jimmy	B-R	5-7	175	11-27-78	.221	.455	.181	41	149	25	33	8	1	2	8	16	0	0	1	33	5	2	.329	.295
Saladino, Tyler	R-R	6-0	200	7-20-89	.282	.329	.265	93	298	33	84	14	0	8	38	13	3	2	3	62	11	5	.409	.315
Sanchez, Hector	B-R	6-0	235	11-17-89	.143	.000	.200	2	7	0	1	0	0	0	1	0	0	0	0	2	0	0	.143	.250
Sanchez, Carlos	B-R	5-11	195	6-29-92	.208	.167	.223	53	154	15	32	9	1	4	21	5	1	2	1	42	0	1	.357	.236
Sands, Jerry	R-R	6-4	225	9-28-87	.236	.222	.243	24	55	2	13	0	0	1	7	3	0	0	0	24	0	0	.291	.276
Shuck, J.B.	L-L	5-11	195	6-18-87	.205	.323	.187	80	224	27	46	5	2	4	14	12	1	3	1	21	3	3	.299	.248
Smith, Kevan	R-R	6-4	230	6-28-88	.125	.100	.167	7	16	2	2	0	0	0	0	0	0	0	0	6	0	0	.125	.125
Tilson, Charlie	L-L	5-11	195	12-2-92	.500	—	.500	1	2	0	1	0	0	0	0	0	0	0	0	0	0	0	.500	.500

Pitching	B-T	HT	WT	DOB	W	L	ERA	G	GS	CG	SV	IP	H	R	ER	HR	BB	SO	AVG	vLH	vRH	K/9	BB/9
Albers, Matt	L-R	6-1	225	1-20-83	2	6	6.31	58	1	0	0	51	67	44	36	10	19	30	.321	.308	.326	5.26	3.33
Beck, Chris	R-R	6-3	225	9-4-90	2	2	6.39	25	0	0	0	25	31	18	18	3	17	20	.301	.385	.250	7.11	6.04
Carroll, Scott	R-R	6-4	215	9-24-84	0	0	11.57	3	0	0	0	2	2	3	3	0	1	2	.250	.000	.400	7.71	3.86
Danish, Tyler	R-R	6-0	200	9-12-94	0	0	10.80	3	0	0	0	2	6	2	2	0	3	0	.667	—	.667	0.00	16.20
Danks, John	L-L	6-1	210	4-15-85	0	4	7.25	4	4	0	0	22	28	20	18	5	11	16	.322	.308	.324	6.45	4.43
Duke, Zach	L-L	6-2	210	4-19-83	2	0	2.63	53	0	0	1	38	31	11	11	2	16	42	.225	.264	.182	10.04	3.82
Fulmer, Carson	R-R	6-0	195	12-13-93	0	2	8.49	8	0	0	0	12	12	11	11	2	7	10	.273	.261	.286	7.71	5.40
Gonzalez, Miguel	R-R	6-1	170	5-27-84	5	8	3.73	24	23	0	0	135	132	61	56	11	35	95	.254	.237	.272	6.33	2.33
Jennings, Dan	L-L	6-3	210	4-17-87	4	3	2.08	64	0	0	1	61	57	18	14	1	28	46	.259	.217	.285	6.82	4.15
Johnson, Erik	R-R	6-3	230	12-30-89	0	2	6.94	2	2	0	0	12	14	9	9	5	6	11	.304	.222	.421	8.49	4.63
Jones, Nate	R-R	6-5	220	1-28-86	5	3	2.29	71	0	0	3	71	48	20	18	7	15	80	.190	.200	.184	10.19	1.91
Kahnle, Tommy	R-R	6-1	235	8-7-89	0	1	2.63	29	0	0	0	27	21	8	8	2	20	25	.212	.143	.250	8.23	6.59
Latos, Mat	R-R	6-6	245	12-9-87	6	2	4.62	11	11	0	0	60	63	33	31	10	25	32	.270	.227	.316	4.77	3.73
Minaya, Juan	R-R	6-4	210	9-18-90	1	0	4.35	11	0	0	0	10	10	6	5	0	5	6	.250	.200	.300	5.23	4.35
Petricka, Jake	R-R	6-5	220	6-5-88	0	0	4.50	9	0	0	0	8	8	5	4	1	8	7	.267	.250	.269	7.88	9.00
Purke, Matt	L-L	6-4	215	7-17-90	0	1	5.50	12	0	0	0	18	20	12	11	0	12	15	.278	.167	.300	7.50	6.00
Putnam, Zach	R-R	6-2	220	7-3-87	1	0	2.30	25	0	0	0	27	25	7	7	2	11	30	.248	.229	.258	9.88	3.62
Quintana, Jose	L-L	6-1	220	1-24-89	13	12	3.20	32	32	0	0	208	192	76	74	22	50	181	.246	.246	.247	7.83	2.16
Ranaudo, Anthony	R-R	6-7	240	9-9-89	0	1	8.46	7	5	0	0	28	34	26	26	9	10	16	.293	.250	.346	5.20	3.90
2-team total (2 Texas)					1	1	9.48	9	5	0	0	31	36	33	33	10	20	18	—	—	—	5.17	5.74
Robertson, David	R-R	5-11	195	4-9-85	5	3	3.47	62	0	0	37	62	53	24	24	6	32	75	.231	.212	.252	10.83	4.62
Rodon, Carlos	L-L	6-3	235	12-10-92	9	10	4.04	28	28	0	0	165	176	82	74	23	54	168	.273	.232	.283	9.16	2.95
Sale, Chris	L-L	6-6	180	3-30-89	17	10	3.34	32	32	6	0	227	190	88	84	27	45	233	.227	.197	.232	9.25	1.79
Shields, James	R-R	6-3	215	12-20-81	4	12	6.77	22	22	1	0	114	139	89	86	31	55	78	.296	.284	.307	6.14	4.33
Smith, Blake	L-R	6-2	220	12-9-87	0	0	6.23	5	0	0	0	4	7	3	3	1	0	1	.350	.375	.333	2.08	0.00
Turner, Jacob	R-R	6-5	215	5-21-91	1	2	6.57	18	2	0	0	25	33	27	18	5	16	18	.324	.250	.371	6.57	5.84
Webb, Daniel	R-R	6-3	215	8-18-89	0	0	0.00	1	0	0	0	1	2	0	0	0	1	3	.400	.500	.333	27.00	9.00
Ynoa, Michael	R-R	6-7	210	9-24-91	1	0	3.00	23	0	0	0	30	20	11	10	0	17	30	.183	.220	.153	9.00	5.10

Fielding

Catcher	PCT	G	PO	A	E	DP	PB
Avila	.995	54	414	21	2	3	4
Narvaez	.992	34	253	11	2	0	1
Navarro	.987	83	584	36	8	2	3
Sanchez	1.000	2	16	0	0	0	0
Smith	1.000	6	12	1	0	1	0

First Base	PCT	G	PO	A	E	DP
Abreu	.993	152	1243	84	10	131
Frazier	.984	7	59	3	1	4
Saladino	1.000	2	3	0	0	0
Sands	1.000	4	27	4	0	2

Second Base	PCT	G	PO	A	E	DP
Lawrie	.978	92	157	242	9	59
Saladino	.994	41	60	111	1	28
Sanchez	.977	33	50	75	3	14

Third Base	PCT	G	PO	A	E	DP
Frazier	.972	149	91	293	11	33
Saladino	.897	10	4	22	3	4
Sanchez	1.000	6	2	6	0	0

Shortstop	PCT	G	PO	A	E	DP
Anderson	.965	98	142	244	14	50
Rollins	.985	35	47	86	2	18
Saladino	.970	32	39	89	4	19
Sanchez	1.000	4	4	9	0	4

Outfield	PCT	G	PO	A	E	DP
Cabrera	.988	147	232	12	3	0
Coats	1.000	18	17	0	0	0
Eaton	.989	156	417	18	5	4
Garcia	.984	55	118	5	2	1
Garcia	1.000	16	30	0	0	0
Jackson	.984	54	118	3	2	2
Saladino	1.000	3	3	1	0	0
Sands	—	4	0	0	0	0
Shuck	.985	65	129	4	2	0
Tilson	1.000	1	1	0	0	0

CHARLOTTE KNIGHTS
INTERNATIONAL LEAGUE

TRIPLE-A

Batting	B-T	HT	WT	DOB	AVG	vLH	vRH	G	AB	R	H	2B	3B	HR	RBI	BB	HBP	SH	SF	SO	SB	CS	SLG	OBP
Alvarez, Eddy	B-R	5-9	180	1-30-90	.286	.600	.160	12	35	7	10	2	0	0	3	4	0	0	0	7	2	0	.343	.359
Anderson, Tim	R-R	6-1	185	6-23-93	.304	.346	.283	55	247	39	75	10	2	4	20	8	0	1	0	58	11	4	.409	.325
Avila, Alex	L-R	5-11	210	1-29-87	.333	.400	.316	9	24	4	8	1	0	1	3	6	0	0	0	7	0	0	.500	.467
Bourgeois, Jason	R-R	5-9	195	1-4-82	.272	.314	.259	89	345	36	94	20	2	3	38	23	1	2	3	32	14	3	.368	.317
Campana, Tony	L-L	5-8	170	5-30-86	.205	.150	.222	29	83	10	17	1	0	0	6	2	2	4	0	15	5	4	.217	.241
2-team total (43 Syracuse)					.217	—		72	203	20	44	3	0	0	13	15	2	12	0	29	10	6	.232	.277
Coats, Jason	R-R	6-2	200	2-24-90	.330	.359	.320	78	297	44	98	22	2	10	38	25	7	2	1	69	1	3	.519	.394
Davidson, Matt	R-R	6-3	230	3-26-91	.268	.312	.251	75	284	35	76	20	0	10	46	32	5	2	3	86	0	0	.444	.349
Delmonico, Nicky	L-R	6-2	230	7-12-92	.246	.158	.271	72	260	32	64	16	0	7	30	29	1	1	4	74	2	0	.388	.320
Engel, Adam	R-R	6-2	210	12-9-91	.242	.189	.259	41	149	19	36	6	2	3	16	10	2	0	0	50	8	5	.369	.298
Fields, Daniel	L-R	6-2	215	1-23-91	.216	.262	.189	32	116	14	25	1	1	1	15	16	0	0	0	51	4	0	.267	.311
Garcia, Avisail	R-R	6-4	240	6-12-91	.385	.500	.333	3	13	2	5	1	0	1	4	1	0	0	0	3	0	0	.692	.429
Garcia, Leury	B-R	5-8	170	3-18-91	.313	.298	.319	84	310	45	97	9	4	6	35	24	3	4	1	64	18	8	.426	.367
Gonzalez, Alfredo	R-R	6-1	225	7-13-92	.000	.000	.000	1	3	0	0	0	0	0	0	0	0	0	0	3	0	0	.000	.000
Hayes, Brett	R-R	6-1	210	2-13-84	.225	.417	.143	13	40	9	9	5	0	1	2	7	1	0	0	19	0	0	.425	.354
Hayes, Danny	L-R	6-4	230	9-21-90	.250	.286	.234	55	184	28	46	12	1	10	42	31	0	2	0	51	0	0	.489	.358
Heathcott, Slade	L-L	6-1	205	9-28-90	.258	.286	.250	34	93	19	24	1	2	2	7	8	2	2	1	30	1	1	.366	.407
2-team total (23 Scranton/W-B)					.244	—		57	180	33	44	7	2	2	14	27	3	2	4	61	3	2	.339	.346
Ishikawa, Travis	L-L	6-3	220	9-24-83	.201	.232	.184	40	154	24	31	4	0	6	18	14	3	2	2	54	0	1	.344	.277
Lemon, Marcus	L-R	5-11	175	6-3-88	.118	.118	.118	17	51	4	6	2	0	0	5	5	1	1	0	9	0	0	.157	.211
Leonards, Ryan	R-R	5-11	195	7-22-91	.200	.500	.125	4	10	0	2	0	0	0	1	0	0	0	0	4	0	1	.200	.273
May, Jacob	B-R	5-10	180	1-23-92	.266	.241	.275	83	301	38	80	19	2	1	24	15	4	1	0	72	19	8	.352	.309
Mendick, Danny	R-R	5-10	189	9-28-93	.000	—	.000	2	2	1	0	0	0	0	0	0	0	0	0	2	0	0	.000	.000
Morneau, Justin	L-R	6-4	220	5-15-81	.118	.250	.000	6	17	1	2	0	1	0	1	1	0	0	0	4	0	0	.235	.211
Muno, Danny	B-R	6-1	195	2-9-89	.211	.182	.224	33	109	9	23	8	0	1	14	14	1	1	0	28	1	1	.312	.306
Narvaez, Omar	B-R	5-11	215	2-10-92	.245	.257	.241	41	143	14	35	6	0	2	11	9	1	2	1	17	0	0	.329	.292
O'Connell, Sean	L-R	6-4	230	12-12-91	.111	.000	.125	4	9	0	1	0	0	0	1	0	1	0	0	2	0	0	.111	.200
O'Dowd, Chris	B-R	5-11	190	10-4-90	.000	—	.000	1	1	0	0	0	0	0	0	3	0	0	0	1	0	0	.000	.750
Parrino, Andy	B-R	6-0	185	10-31-85	.213	.258	.188	52	174	8	37	6	1	1	19	14	0	2	1	57	2	1	.276	.270
Peter, Jake	L-R	6-1	185	4-5-93	.259	.275	.254	62	228	30	59	13	0	2	24	17	3	1	1	44	3	1	.342	.317
Rottino, Vinny	R-R	6-1	215	4-7-80	.208	.224	.201	78	226	23	47	7	0	3	26	12	5	3	2	58	0	1	.279	.321
Sanchez, Hector	B-R	6-0	235	11-17-89	.143	.000	.182	8	28	2	4	1	0	2	3	1	0	0	0	6	0	0	.393	.200
Sanchez, Carlos	B-R	5-11	195	6-29-92	.255	.186	.278	61	235	31	60	11	2	8	29	17	2	4	2	55	10	4	.421	.309
Sands, Jerry	R-R	6-4	225	9-28-87	.252	.226	.260	73	270	32	68	12	1	8	37	26	1	2	2	62	0	1	.393	.318
Shuck, J.B.	L-L	5-11	195	6-18-87	.299	.315	.290	37	154	20	46	9	2	2	17	11	0	2	3	13	4	2	.422	.339
Silverio, Louis	R-R	6-3	215	12-15-93	.238	.286	.214	8	21	0	5	2	0	0	0	0	1	0	0	9	0	0	.333	.238
Smith, Kevan	R-R	6-4	230	6-28-88	.219	.265	.201	49	183	18	40	9	0	8	24	16	3	2	1	36	0	0	.399	.291

Pitching	B-T	HT	WT	DOB	W	L	ERA	G	GS	CG	SV	IP	H	R	ER	HR	BB	SO	AVG	vLH	vRH	K/9	BB/9
Aumont, Phillippe	L-R	6-7	240	1-7-89	0	2	12.27	10	0	0	0	11	18	15	15	1	11	14	.360	.368	.355	11.45	9.00
Barnette, Tyler	L-R	6-3	190	5-28-92	1	2	8.07	18	2	0	0	32	43	29	29	6	15	21	.333	.273	.378	5.85	4.18
Beck, Chris	R-R	6-3	225	9-4-90	5	4	4.21	22	7	0	0	66	77	32	31	5	25	50	.294	.208	.343	6.78	3.39
Burdi, Zack	R-R	6-3	205	3-9-95	1	0	2.25	9	0	0	1	16	9	4	4	0	11	22	.161	.160	.161	12.38	6.19
Carroll, Scott	R-R	6-4	215	9-24-84	2	8	5.55	16	12	0	0	60	78	48	37	8	25	31	.313	.336	.294	4.65	3.75
Clark, Brian	R-L	6-3	225	4-27-93	0	1	5.00	6	0	0	0	9	9	6	5	0	3	6	.265	.333	.227	6.00	3.00
Danish, Tyler	R-R	6-0	200	9-12-94	1	3	5.83	7	5	0	0	29	39	21	19	0	10	21	.320	.256	.354	6.44	3.07
Fulmer, Carson	R-R	6-0	195	12-13-93	2	1	3.94	4	4	0	0	16	14	7	7	1	5	14	.233	.250	.222	7.88	2.81
Goldberg, Brad	R-R	6-4	220	2-21-90	3	5	2.84	43	0	0	10	51	42	18	16	3	23	44	.227	.311	.171	7.82	4.09
Gonzalez, Miguel	R-R	6-1	170	5-27-84	1	1	4.64	5	5	0	0	21	27	12	11	5	4	25	.321	.348	.311	10.55	1.69
Holmberg, David	R-L	6-3	245	7-19-91	2	3	4.14	9	9	0	0	54	51	26	25	6	14	33	.254	.178	.276	5.47	2.32
Huntzinger, Brock	R-R	6-3	200	7-2-88	0	0	—	1	0	0	0	3	2	2	0	1	0	1.000	—1.000	—	—	
Johnson, Erik	R-R	6-3	230	12-30-89	2	1	2.94	8	8	1	0	49	44	18	16	7	17	35	.239	.244	.236	6.43	3.12
Kahnle, Tommy	R-R	6-1	235	8-7-89	1	1	3.00	23	0	0	7	27	17	9	9	0	12	36	.177	.267	.136	12.00	4.00
Lamb, Will	L-L	6-6	180	9-9-90	4	2	5.47	39	1	0	0	54	55	33	33	9	27	42	.259	.161	.295	6.96	4.47
Loe, Kameron	R-R	6-8	245	9-10-81	3	5	4.63	13	12	0	0	68	89	42	35	5	15	40	.322	.328	.317	5.29	1.99

Pitching	B-T	HT	WT	DOB	W	L	ERA	G	GS	CG	SV	IP	H	R	ER	HR	BB	SO	AVG	vLH	vRH	K/9	BB/9
Lollis, Matt	R-R	6-9	280	9-11-90	1	1	5.56	15	0	0	1	23	18	16	14	5	16	16	.204	.231	.200	6.35	6.35
Marin, Terance	R-R	6-1	170	8-21-89	8	7	4.66	26	16	1	0	110	118	58	57	13	34	59	.280	.272	.285	4.83	2.78
Minaya, Juan	R-R	6-4	210	9-18-90	4	3	3.38	17	0	0	1	27	23	11	10	2	10	28	.225	.333	.159	9.45	3.38
Purke, Matt	L-L	6-4	215	7-17-90	0	0	3.52	26	1	0	2	38	30	20	15	4	23	38	.210	.105	.248	8.92	5.40
Ranaudo, Anthony	R-R	6-7	240	9-9-89	6	5	3.35	16	16	2	0	97	92	38	36	15	11	65	.251	.243	.259	6.05	1.02
Rodon, Carlos	L-L	6-3	235	12-10-92	0	1	4.91	1	1	0	0	4	5	3	2	1	2	3	.313	.286	.333	7.36	4.91
Shirek, Charlie	R-R	6-3	205	10-25-85	0	0	18.00	1	0	0	0	1	3	2	2	0	0	0	.500	.000	.750	0.00	0.00
Smith, Blake	L-R	6-2	220	12-9-87	3	1	3.53	39	0	0	1	71	64	28	28	6	24	75	.242	.280	.215	9.46	3.03
Turner, Jacob	R-R	6-5	215	5-21-91	4	7	4.71	18	18	1	0	107	125	60	56	10	29	85	.297	.337	.267	7.15	2.44
Volstad, Chris	R-R	6-8	235	9-23-86	8	11	4.79	29	27	2	0	177	193	100	94	16	34	84	.279	.278	.280	4.28	1.73
Webb, Daniel	R-R	6-3	215	8-18-89	2	1	3.38	7	0	0	2	11	12	5	4	1	0	5	.279	.133	.357	4.22	0.00
Webb, Ryan	R-R	6-6	245	2-5-86	0	0	13.50	3	0	0	0	3	5	4	4	0	1	1	.500	.500	.500	3.38	3.38
2-team total (3 Durham)					0	1	9.53					6	9	7	6	0	3	4				6.35	4.76
Ynoa, Michael	R-R	6-7	210	9-24-91	1	3	4.56	18	0	0	4	24	25	12	12	2	12	20	.278	.353	.232	7.61	4.56

Fielding

Catcher	PCT	G	PO	A	E	DP	PB
Avila	1.000	5	21	2	0	0	0
Gonzalez	1.000	1	5	0	0	0	0
Hayes	.988	12	69	11	1	0	0
Narvaez	.993	39	251	21	2	2	3
O'Connell	1.000	3	14	1	0	0	0
O'Dowd	1.000	1	0	0	0	0	0
Rottino	.981	41	243	20	5	2	1
Sanchez	.971	8	63	3	2	2	1
Smith	.993	43	261	24	2	3	0

First Base	PCT	G	PO	A	E	DP
Davidson	1.000	6	27	1	0	3
Delmonico	1.000	16	146	9	0	13
Hayes	.997	37	347	29	1	36
Ishikawa	1.000	18	148	17	0	17
Rottino	1.000	6	49	3	0	5
Sands	.992	61	596	30	5	69
Shuck	1.000	8	57	4	0	6

Second Base	PCT	G	PO	A	E	DP
Garcia	.963	19	24	53	3	12
Lemon	.923	5	12	12	2	5

Leonards	1.000	3	1	4	0	1
Muno	.964	20	29	51	3	20
Parrino	.966	20	26	59	3	15
Peter	.994	34	52	124	1	30
Rottino	1.000	1	3	3	0	2
Sanchez	.987	45	83	142	3	44

Third Base	PCT	G	PO	A	E	DP
Davidson	.961	66	47	152	8	16
Delmonico	.968	39	36	84	4	14
Lemon	.714	3	1	4	2	0
Muno	.972	13	8	27	1	5
Parrino	.903	12	4	24	3	0
Peter	.931	9	5	22	2	2
Rottino	1.000	9	3	17	0	1

Shortstop	PCT	G	PO	A	E	DP
Alvarez	.981	11	16	36	1	6
Anderson	.962	52	89	164	10	42
Garcia	.952	25	41	79	6	22
Lemon	.891	9	10	31	5	9
Muno	1.000	1	0	1	0	0
Parrino	1.000	16	28	50	0	13

Peter	.943	19	25	57	5	15
Sanchez	.981	16	14	39	1	7

Outfield	PCT	G	PO	A	E	DP
Bourgeois	.980	63	93	3	2	1
Campana	1.000	25	38	2	0	1
Coats	.986	71	134	5	2	1
Delmonico	.935	17	27	2	2	0
Engel	.990	41	94	1	1	0
Fields	1.000	22	41	4	0	1
Garcia	1.000	2	3	0	0	0
Garcia	.988	39	74	6	1	0
Heathcott	.944	20	33	1	2	0
Ishikawa	1.000	5	7	0	0	0
Lemon	—	1	0	0	0	0
May	.995	82	184	7	1	2
Parrino	1.000	3	4	0	0	0
Peter	1.000	2	4	0	0	0
Rottino	1.000	17	24	0	0	0
Sands	.500	1	1	0	1	0
Shuck	1.000	27	53	6	0	0
Silverio	.941	7	15	1	1	0

BIRMINGHAM BARONS

DOUBLE-A

SOUTHERN LEAGUE

Batting	B-T	HT	WT	DOB	AVG	vLH	vRH	G	AB	R	H	2B	3B	HR	RBI	BB	HBP	SH	SF	SO	SB	CS	SLG	OBP
Alvarez, Eddy	B-R	5-9	180	1-30-90	.263	.196	.288	104	395	51	104	17	3	6	62	46	2	15	5	76	9	6	.367	.339
Barnum, Keon	L-L	6-5	225	1-16-93	.194	.194	.195	76	283	25	55	12	0	4	25	24	0	0	2	91	1	0	.279	.256
Basto, Nick	R-R	6-2	210	4-1-94	.188	.222	.177	22	80	6	15	4	0	0	8	7	0	1	0	11	0	0	.238	.253
Delmonico, Nicky	L-R	6-2	230	7-12-92	.338	.400	.321	38	142	25	48	14	2	10	31	13	1	3	0	33	1	0	.676	.397
DeMichele, Joey	L-R	5-11	190	2-5-91	.233	.144	.256	128	468	73	109	20	7	11	49	45	3	5	3	123	2	0	.376	.303
Dowdy, Jeremy	R-R	6-2	230	7-13-90	.246	.240	.248	54	183	18	45	9	1	4	25	24	1	2	0	28	0	0	.372	.337
Engel, Adam	R-R	6-2	210	12-9-91	.255	.279	.245	74	306	56	78	18	9	4	25	39	7	5	0	70	31	9	.412	.352
Gonzalez, Alfredo	R-R	6-1	225	7-13-92	.296	.424	.255	39	135	13	40	6	0	0	8	10	4	1	2	22	2	0	.341	.358
Hawkins, Courtney	R-R	6-3	245	11-12-93	.203	.181	.210	106	418	35	85	25	0	12	60	28	3	0	6	137	0	3	.349	.255
Jones, Hunter	R-R	6-2	185	8-17-91	.226	.368	.202	42	133	16	30	7	1	2	13	11	4	2	3	29	2	0	.338	.298
Lawrie, Brett	R-R	6-0	210	1-18-90	.313	—	.313	5	16	2	5	1	0	0	0	1	0	0	0	4	0	0	.375	.353
Lemon, Marcus	L-R	5-11	175	6-3-88	.242	.316	.228	67	227	20	55	6	4	1	24	21	5	12	2	55	1	1	.317	.318
Leonards, Ryan	R-R	5-11	190	7-22-91	.153	.267	.114	18	59	4	9	3	0	0	1	2	1	1	0	11	0	0	.203	.194
Michalczewski, Trey	B-R	6-3	210	2-27-95	.226	.256	.216	134	487	62	110	24	5	11	59	56	8	3	3	153	4	0	.363	.314
Morneau, Justin	L-R	6-4	220	5-15-81	.333	.667	.000	2	6	0	2	0	0	0	1	2	1	0	0	0	0	0	.333	.556
Narvaez, Omar	B-R	5-11	215	2-10-92	.222	.143	.237	13	45	4	10	2	0	0	5	4	0	0	0	6	0	0	.267	.286
O'Connell, Sean	L-R	6-4	230	12-12-91	.222	.188	.232	21	72	4	16	5	0	0	5	1	3	2	0	24	0	0	.292	.263
O'Dowd, Chris	B-R	5-11	190	10-4-90	.220	.000	.254	29	82	11	18	3	0	0	7	11	1	2	0	23	1	0	.256	.319
Peter, Jake	L-R	6-1	185	4-5-93	.304	.294	.308	68	253	27	77	14	0	4	29	31	2	0	5	52	5	1	.407	.378
Pina, Eudy	R-R	6-3	190	4-12-91	.249	.211	.260	105	382	38	95	10	2	4	39	24	6	2	4	90	6	2	.317	.300
Richmond, Josh	R-R	6-3	205	6-14-89	.256	.278	.250	23	78	10	20	3	1	2	11	7	2	0	0	22	0	0	.397	.333
Shoemaker, Brady	R-R	6-0	220	5-10-87	.229	.194	.244	29	109	13	25	6	0	2	5	12	1	0	0	28	0	0	.339	.311
2-team total (43 Jacksonville)					.217				72	258	32	56	11	0	6	29	35	5	0	2	64	0	0	.329	.320
Walker, Keenyn	B-R	6-3	190	8-12-90	.240	.208	.249	95	329	53	79	16	4	3	28	43	1	1	0	106	21	8	.340	.330

Pitching	B-T	HT	WT	DOB	W	L	ERA	G	GS	CG	SV	IP	H	R	ER	HR	BB	SO	AVG	vLH	vRH	K/9	BB/9
Adams, Spencer	R-R	6-3	171	4-13-96	2	5	3.90	9	9	0	0	55	59	29	24	2	10	26	.274	.253	.293	4.23	1.63
Barnette, Tyler	R-R	6-3	190	5-28-92	2	4	4.70	19	6	0	0	52	57	34	27	1	22	38	.281	.304	.266	6.63	3.83
Brennan, Brandon	R-R	6-4	220	7-26-91	2	8	8.09	24	8	0	0	66	90	63	59	5	29	54	.331	.315	.345	7.40	3.97
Burdi, Zack	R-R	6-3	205	3-9-95	0	0	3.94	12	0	0	0	16	7	3	7	2	9	24	.132	.167	.114	13.50	5.06
Clark, Brian	R-L	6-3	225	4-27-93	0	4	2.27	31	0	0	4	48	52	14	12	1	9	42	.284	.254	.298	7.93	1.70

Pitching	B-T	HT	WT	DOB	W	L	ERA	G	GS	CG	SV	IP	H	R	ER	HR	BB	SO	AVG	vLH	vRH	K/9	BB/9
Cooper, Matt	R-R	6-0	190	9-30-91	2	1	3.07	19	0	0	1	41	30	18	14	3	12	47	.207	.212	.203	10.32	2.63
Danish, Tyler	R-R	6-0	200	9-12-94	3	7	4.42	12	12	1	0	75	71	38	37	3	16	47	.246	.287	.213	5.62	1.91
Dykstra, James	R-R	6-4	195	11-22-90	4	9	4.93	28	15	0	0	102	129	64	56	4	39	66	.309	.277	.331	5.80	3.43
Fulmer, Carson	R-R	6-0	195	12-13-93	4	9	4.76	17	17	0	0	87	82	51	46	7	51	90	.248	.212	.276	9.31	5.28
Goldberg, Brad	R-R	6-4	220	2-21-90	0	0	1.50	4	0	0	0	6	4	3	1	0	3	7	.190	.333	.083	10.50	4.50
Guerrero, Jordan	L-L	6-3	195	5-31-94	7	8	4.83	25	25	0	0	136	133	76	73	13	73	108	.260	.244	.265	7.15	4.83
Hansen, Kyle	R-R	6-8	200	4-20-91	2	2	6.97	14	0	0	0	21	22	17	16	1	10	25	.268	.185	.309	10.89	4.35
Holmberg, David	R-L	6-3	245	7-19-91	6	6	3.70	19	19	0	0	114	112	57	47	7	28	74	.258	.271	.252	5.83	2.20
Huntzinger, Brock	R-R	6-3	200	7-2-88	0	0	7.90	9	0	0	0	14	21	16	12	1	7	15	.323	.276	.361	9.88	4.61
Kleven, Colin	R-R	6-5	220	4-15-91	0	3	5.29	13	0	0	0	17	19	11	10	1	3	19	.288	.143	.356	10.06	1.59
Krauss, Conor	R-R	6-5	235	6-14-93	0	1	12.00	4	0	0	0	3	4	4	4	0	5	4	.333	.200	.429	12.00	15.00
Leyer, Euclides	R-R	6-2	175	12-28-90	0	1	8.68	7	0	0	0	9	9	10	9	1	11	7	.250	.214	.273	6.75	10.61
Leyer, Robin	R-R	6-2	175	3-13-93	1	2	5.79	24	0	0	0	33	40	23	21	1	20	33	.308	.283	.325	9.09	5.51
Lollis, Matt	R-R	6-9	280	9-11-90	3	1	2.41	22	0	0	1	34	20	12	9	1	17	39	.169	.244	.130	10.43	4.54
Lowry, Thad	R-R	6-4	215	10-4-94	0	3	4.13	4	4	0	0	24	23	14	11	0	4	11	.245	.206	.267	4.13	1.50
Sanburn, Nolan	R-R	6-1	205	7-21-91	1	5	3.89	34	5	0	6	74	71	33	32	4	24	58	.254	.263	.248	7.05	2.92
Tago, Peter	R-R	6-3	215	7-5-92	6	4	4.37	38	0	0	7	60	47	32	29	3	33	78	.219	.226	.214	11.77	4.98
Turner, Colton	L-L	6-3	215	1-17-91	0	0	0.00	3	0	0	0	4	3	0	0	0	3	6	.231	.000	.300	13.50	6.75
Walsh, Connor	R-R	6-2	180	10-18-92	0	0	4.70	6	0	0	0	8	7	5	4	0	5	7	.233	.333	.167	8.22	5.87
Walters, Blair	L-L	6-0	200	11-8-89	4	8	4.54	21	20	0	0	101	103	62	51	6	54	85	.266	.250	.271	7.57	4.81
Wheeler, Andre	L-L	6-1	170	9-27-91	0	0	7.01	19	0	0	0	26	41	20	20	5	12	25	.360	.297	.390	8.77	4.21
Ynoa, Michael	R-R	6-7	210	9-24-91	0	0	0.00	3	0	0	0	4	0	0	0	0	0	4	.000	.000	.000	9.00	0.00

Fielding

Catcher	PCT	G	PO	A	E	DP	PB		Second Base	PCT	G	PO	A	E	DP		Shortstop	PCT	G	PO	A	E	DP
Dowdy	.987	53	434	35	6	3	3		DeMichele	.990	122	207	366	6	88		Alvarez	.941	104	128	286	26	66
Gonzalez	.975	35	243	25	7	4	7		Lawrie	.875	2	2	5	1	0		Lemon	.944	20	21	46	4	10
Narvaez	1.000	13	81	10	0	1	2		Lemon	.975	9	14	25	1	9		Leonards	1.000	5	3	14	0	2
O'Connell	.980	20	117	30	3	5	1		Leonards	1.000	7	7	9	0	4		Michalczewski	.957	12	15	29	2	8
O'Dowd	.970	25	153	8	5	1	5		Peter	1.000	7	9	11	0	3		Peter	1.000	1	0	2	0	0

First Base	PCT	G	PO	A	E	DP		Third Base	PCT	G	PO	A	E	DP		Outfield	PCT	G	PO	A	E	DP
Barnum	.991	70	627	33	6	57		Delmonico	1.000	3	1	5	0	1		Basto	1.000	11	17	1	0	0
Basto	.959	7	68	2	3	3		DeMichele	.900	4	2	7	1	0		Engel	.989	71	174	5	2	0
Delmonico	.989	30	254	22	3	26		Lemon	.737	6	4	10	5	0		Hawkins	.953	89	134	9	7	1
Lemon	1.000	3	26	1	0	2		Leonards	1.000	7	3	12	0	1		Jones	.962	42	99	3	4	1
Peter	.996	25	222	17	1	27		Michalczewski	.951	118	71	260	17	33		Lemon	.986	32	72	0	1	0
Shoemaker	.983	6	59	0	1	5		Peter	1.000	5	6	9	0	0		Peter	1.000	27	35	1	0	1
																Pina	.988	47	76	6	1	3
																Richmond	.917	15	30	3	3	1
																Walker	.958	93	195	11	9	3

WINSTON-SALEM DASH

HIGH CLASS A

CAROLINA LEAGUE

Batting	B-T	HT	WT	DOB	AVG	vLH	vRH	G	AB	R	H	2B	3B	HR	RBI	BB	HBP	SH	SF	SO	SB	CS	SLG	OBP
Austin, Brett	B-R	6-1	210	11-24-92	.205	.165	.220	89	302	34	62	14	1	9	45	40	2	1	2	81	0	0	.348	.301
Barnum, Keon	L-L	6-5	225	1-16-93	.256	.242	.262	30	117	7	30	5	0	1	9	7	0	0	3	25	0	0	.325	.291
Basto, Nick	R-R	6-2	210	4-1-94	.308	.341	.293	106	403	65	124	27	4	12	60	47	6	1	4	83	0	1	.484	.385
Collins, Zack	L-R	6-3	220	2-6-95	.258	.275	.250	36	120	24	31	7	0	6	18	33	0	0	0	39	0	0	.467	.418
Danner, Michael	L-R	5-10	186	9-18-91	.167	.500	.100	9	36	4	6	1	0	0	2	4	0	0	0	14	0	0	.194	.250
Davis, Marcus	L-L	6-3	200	4-26-92	.262	.206	.282	123	489	54	128	24	4	7	60	19	3	0	2	95	2	0	.370	.292
Engel, Adam	R-R	6-2	210	12-9-91	.327	.250	.349	14	55	15	18	6	1	0	5	7	1	1	0	11	6	0	.473	.413
Fish, Zach	R-R	6-0	215	11-5-92	.235	.267	.000	6	17	1	4	1	0	0	2	1	1	0	0	6	0	0	.294	.316
Flores, Dante	L-R	5-9	160	4-8-93	.179	.167	.182	9	28	4	5	0	1	1	5	3	1	1	1	9	0	0	.357	.273
Garcia, Joxelier	R-R	5-10	185	4-30-94	.000	.000	.000	1	3	0	0	0	0	0	0	0	0	0	0	0	0	0	.000	.000
Gonzalez, Daniel	R-R	6-1	190	12-6-95	.478	.375	.533	7	23	5	11	3	0	0	5	1	0	0	0	4	0	0	.609	.500
Jones, Hunter	R-R	6-2	185	8-17-91	.286	.314	.272	90	364	62	104	13	7	5	34	37	7	4	4	70	31	10	.401	.359
Lassiter, Landon	R-R	6-1	195	6-14-93	.271	.300	.260	38	140	27	38	7	1	0	8	20	4	0	2	41	5	1	.336	.373
Lechich, Louie	L-L	6-4	200	11-19-91	.159	.171	.155	39	138	8	22	4	0	0	7	8	0	0	0	42	0	0	.203	.205
Leonards, Ryan	R-R	5-11	195	7-22-91	.230	.238	.227	28	87	13	20	2	1	1	7	13	6	0	0	15	1	0	.310	.368
Massey, Grant	R-R	5-11	190	7-10-92	.158	.000	.375	6	19	1	3	0	0	0	2	1	0	1	0	5	0	0	.158	.200
Mendick, Danny	R-R	5-10	189	9-28-93	.125	.083	.139	15	48	6	6	2	0	0	2	5	0	0	0	10	0	0	.167	.208
Montilla, Gerson	R-R	5-10	170	11-13-89	.266	.323	.240	129	496	60	132	20	2	13	74	51	4	0	11	76	4	3	.393	.333
Nash, Telvin	R-R	6-1	248	2-20-91	.255	.318	.228	46	145	33	37	11	0	11	38	40	1	0	2	58	0	0	.559	.415
O'Connell, Sean	L-R	6-4	200	12-12-91	.167	.100	.200	10	30	1	5	1	0	0	1	1	0	0	0	5	0	0	.200	.194
O'Dowd, Chris	B-R	5-11	190	10-4-90	.284	.333	.259	23	81	11	23	4	0	1	9	11	3	0	1	17	3	1	.370	.385
Robbins, Mason	L-L	6-0	200	2-1-93	.314	.292	.324	123	507	57	159	33	7	5	62	14	2	1	6	87	3	2	.436	.331
Rondon, Cleuluis	R-R	6-0	155	4-30-94	.212	.195	.220	117	391	35	83	11	1	2	32	39	2	7	1	86	12	3	.261	.286
Silverio, Louis	R-R	6-3	215	12-15-93	.188	.100	.333	5	16	4	3	1	0	0	0	1	0	1	0	3	0	0	.250	.235
Suiter, Michael	R-R	6-1	200	4-9-92	.287	.322	.269	48	167	23	48	9	0	6	21	20	4	4	1	41	5	0	.449	.375
Thomas, Toby	R-R	5-11	185	12-9-93	.269	.296	.257	126	469	64	126	33	6	7	43	33	4	7	2	78	0	0	.409	.321

Pitching	B-T	HT	WT	DOB	W	L	ERA	G	GS	CG	SV	IP	H	R	ER	HR	BB	SO	AVG	vLH	vRH	K/9	BB/9
Adams, Spencer	R-R	6-3	171	4-13-96	8	7	4.01	18	18	1	0	108	120	50	48	7	21	74	.275	.308	.236	6.19	1.76

Pitching

Pitching	B-T	HT	WT	DOB	W	L	ERA	G	GS	CG	SV	IP	H	R	ER	HR	BB	SO	AVG	vLH	vRH	K/9	BB/9
Banks, Tanner	L-L	6-1	195	10-24-91	6	4	3.99	16	16	2	0	90	106	46	40	5	17	65	.291	.293	.291	6.48	1.69
Brennan, Brandon	R-R	6-4	220	7-26-91	1	4	4.54	7	7	2	0	38	44	19	19	1	11	24	.297	.317	.282	5.73	2.63
Bummer, Aaron	L-L	6-3	200	9-21-93	0	1	1.80	4	0	0	0	5	4	2	1	0	1	1	.200	.250	.188	1.80	1.80
Burdi, Zack	R-R	6-3	205	3-9-95	0	0	5.40	4	0	0	0	5	6	3	3	1	0	4	.316	.500	.111	7.20	0.00
Cherry, Taylore	R-R	6-9	290	6-24-93	0	2	7.41	10	0	0	0	17	26	14	14	0	8	12	.356	.293	.438	6.35	4.24
Cooper, Matt	R-R	6-0	190	9-30-91	4	5	3.36	13	13	1	0	78	60	30	29	7	21	95	.213	.244	.184	11.01	2.43
Dopico, Danny	R-R	6-2	190	12-18-93	0	3	7.80	25	0	0	2	30	29	30	26	3	33	39	.257	.321	.193	11.70	9.90
Hasler, Drew	R-R	6-6	245	8-14-93	1	1	2.00	13	0	0	1	27	20	6	6	2	3	11	.204	.174	.231	3.67	1.00
Katz, Alex	L-L	5-11	195	10-12-94	0	0	1.69	4	0	0	1	5	2	1	1	0	5	7	.118	.143	.100	11.81	8.44
Kleven, Colin	R-R	6-5	220	4-15-91	1	2	5.35	24	0	0	2	39	46	27	23	3	17	27	.299	.391	.224	6.28	3.96
Leyer, Euclides	R-R	6-2	175	12-28-90	0	4	4.69	28	0	0	1	40	34	23	21	3	31	34	.238	.219	.257	7.59	6.92
Leyer, Robin	R-R	6-2	175	3-13-93	3	4	4.21	13	10	1	0	51	57	27	24	4	29	42	.279	.242	.312	7.36	5.08
Lowry, Thad	R-R	6-4	215	10-4-94	8	8	4.06	24	23	0	0	135	143	69	61	8	38	90	.270	.311	.232	5.99	2.53
Martinez, Manny	R-R	6-1	155	12-31-91	1	6	6.17	27	0	0	1	47	45	37	32	6	29	44	.245	.272	.217	8.49	5.59
Morris, Jacob	R-R	6-3	215	12-19-90	2	4	4.11	34	0	0	3	46	31	25	21	2	40	53	.186	.194	.176	10.37	7.83
Peralta, Yelmison	R-R	6-2	210	3-3-95	0	2	3.57	16	0	0	4	23	19	11	9	1	11	21	.229	.225	.233	8.34	4.37
Quintero, Brandon	R-R	6-2	180	2-2-94	0	0	9.64	3	0	0	0	5	8	6	5	1	2	6	.421	.429	.417	11.57	3.86
Riga, Ryan	L-L	6-0	190	10-22-92	2	1	6.35	18	0	0	1	28	27	21	20	2	9	14	.252	.211	.275	4.45	2.86
Sanburn, Nolan	R-R	6-1	205	7-21-91	1	0	0.00	3	0	0	0	8	4	0	0	0	1	11	.148	.056	.333	12.91	1.17
Stephens, Jordan	R-R	6-1	190	9-12-92	7	10	3.45	27	27	0	0	141	129	59	54	12	48	155	.243	.281	.208	9.89	3.06
Thompson, Zach	R-R	6-7	230	10-23-93	3	5	5.60	10	10	0	0	55	66	37	34	7	15	40	.292	.276	.313	6.59	2.47
Valerio, Kelvis	R-R	6-1	190	9-26-91	3	6	4.62	32	9	0	3	90	105	54	46	7	28	58	.292	.294	.290	5.82	2.81
Walsh, Connor	L-R	6-2	180	10-18-92	2	2	3.40	25	0	0	5	40	28	17	15	1	19	41	.207	.194	.219	9.30	4.31
Walters, Blair	L-L	6-0	200	11-8-89	1	1	4.50	5	5	0	0	26	20	13	13	2	18	17	.230	.250	.224	5.88	6.23
Wheeler, Andre	L-L	6-1	170	9-27-91	2	1	2.20	16	1	0	2	33	25	11	8	3	16	33	.219	.200	.228	9.09	4.41

Fielding

Catcher	PCT	G	PO	A	E	DP	PB
Austin	.991	87	625	71	6	6	8
Collins	1.000	18	114	13	0	1	4
Garcia	1.000	1	5	1	0	0	0
Gonzalez	.983	7	54	4	1	0	0
O'Connell	.987	10	69	9	1	0	2
O'Dowd	1.000	20	128	25	0	0	4

First Base	PCT	G	PO	A	E	DP
Barnum	.985	27	239	18	4	32
Basto	.993	46	426	25	3	34
Davis	.982	36	297	22	6	21
Montilla	1.000	3	33	0	0	2
Nash	.989	28	254	14	3	15

Second Base	PCT	G	PO	A	E	DP
Flores	.976	8	15	26	1	7
Leonards	.977	10	18	24	1	3
Mendick	1.000	3	6	8	0	1
Montilla	1.000	15	25	44	0	11
Thomas	.972	105	199	327	15	65

Third Base	PCT	G	PO	A	E	DP
Leonards	.857	4	2	10	2	0
Massey	1.000	1	0	7	0	2
Mendick	1.000	2	3	4	0	0
Montilla	.944	110	78	228	18	25
O'Dowd	.857	4	0	6	1	0
Thomas	.945	20	5	47	3	4

Shortstop	PCT	G	PO	A	E	DP
Leonards	.949	9	15	22	2	4
Massey	1.000	5	4	13	0	1
Mendick	.905	9	5	14	2	1
Montilla	—	1	0	0	0	0
Rondon	.961	117	179	308	20	60

Outfield	PCT	G	PO	A	E	DP
Basto	.975	52	75	4	2	0
Danner	1.000	9	13	0	0	0
Engel	1.000	14	24	1	0	1
Fish	1.000	3	4	1	0	0
Jones	1.000	90	200	9	0	0
Lassiter	.958	37	65	3	3	0
Lechich	.950	39	72	4	4	0
Leonards	1.000	5	7	0	0	0
Robbins	.981	120	190	19	4	6
Silverio	1.000	5	11	4	0	2
Suiter	.989	47	91	2	1	0

KANNAPOLIS INTIMIDATORS
SOUTH ATLANTIC LEAGUE

LOW CLASS A

Batting	B-T	HT	WT	DOB	AVG	vLH	vRH	G	AB	R	H	2B	3B	HR	RBI	BB	HBP	SH	SF	SO	SB	CS	SLG	OBP
Adolfo, Micker	R-R	6-3	200	9-11-96	.219	.217	.219	65	247	30	54	13	1	5	21	14	3	1	0	88	0	1	.340	.269
Califano, Frank	L-L	5-11	185	3-31-94	.250	.000	.308	6	16	2	4	0	0	0	1	1	0	0	0	6	0	0	.250	.294
Call, Alex	R-R	6-0	188	9-27-94	.308	.400	.283	46	185	23	57	17	0	3	18	15	1	1	1	40	10	2	.449	.361
Cruz, Johan	R-R	6-2	188	10-8-95	.255	.386	.227	65	251	31	64	12	1	5	26	22	4	2	2	61	2	2	.371	.323
Daily, Cody	R-R	6-3	215	7-28-92	.281	.275	.283	118	423	46	119	26	4	4	44	46	6	2	3	72	1	0	.390	.358
Dexter, Sam	R-R	5-11	185	3-7-94	.000	.000	—	1	4	0	0	0	0	0	0	0	0	0	0	2	0	0	.000	.000
Dutto, Max	R-L	6-0	205	11-2-93	.218	.083	.256	19	55	7	12	2	1	0	4	10	4	0	0	22	1	1	.291	.377
Fincher, Jake	R-R	6-1	185	1-26-93	.256	.250	.259	11	39	4	10	1	1	0	5	4	0	1	0	9	4	0	.333	.326
Fish, Zach	R-R	6-0	215	11-5-92	.169	.118	.181	24	89	8	15	5	0	2	10	10	0	0	0	29	0	0	.292	.253
Flores, Dante	L-R	5-9	160	4-8-93	.250	.125	.281	12	40	4	10	2	1	0	8	10	0	0	0	6	1	0	.350	.400
Gonzalez, Daniel	R-R	6-1	190	12-6-95	.258	.200	.268	23	66	6	17	2	0	0	6	3	1	0	0	17	0	0	.288	.300
Lassiter, Landon	R-R	6-1	195	6-14-93	.283	.333	.268	77	286	35	81	13	1	2	24	31	9	2	1	78	9	6	.357	.370
Massey, Grant	R-R	5-11	190	7-10-92	.257	.333	.232	110	401	42	103	21	2	1	41	24	4	6	6	85	13	4	.327	.301
Mendick, Danny	R-R	5-10	189	9-28-93	.274	.293	.268	98	369	40	101	20	2	2	34	31	9	1	2	75	8	5	.355	.343
Nolan, Nate	R-R	6-1	210	10-11-94	.125	.091	.132	20	64	5	8	0	0	1	5	8	2	1	1	35	0	0	.172	.240
O'Connell, Sean	L-R	6-4	230	12-12-91	.333	.000	.500	1	3	0	1	0	0	0	1	0	0	0	1	0	0	0	.333	.250
Orvis, Sikes	L-R	6-3	235	11-12-92	.000	.000	.000	1	3	0	0	0	0	0	0	0	0	0	0	1	0	0	.000	.000
Perez, Carlos	R-R	5-11	160	9-10-96	.143	.000	.333	2	7	0	1	0	0	0	0	0	0	0	0	1	0	0	.143	.143
Remillard, Zach	R-R	6-1	200	2-20-94	.235	.231	.237	31	110	16	25	7	0	3	7	5	0	1	0	27	4	2	.373	.261
Rodriguez, Antonio	R-R	6-4	230	5-7-95	.237	.196	.248	123	472	40	112	18	3	5	46	19	3	1	6	104	8	3	.320	.268
Rondon, Cleuluis	R-R	6-0	155	4-13-94	.243	.429	.200	11	37	4	9	3	1	0	7	4	0	0	1	6	1	0	.378	.310
Ruchim, Kyle	R-R	5-10	180	8-11-92	.162	.364	.077	11	37	3	6	2	1	0	3	1	2	0	1	12	0	0	.270	.220
Schroeder, Casey	B-R	6-2	210	7-12-93	.077	.000	.125	5	13	2	1	0	0	1	1	4	0	0	0	5	0	0	.308	.294

Batting	B-T	HT	WT	DOB	AVG	vLH	vRH	G	AB	R	H	2B	3B	HR	RBI	BB	HBP	SH	SF	SO	SB	CS	SLG	OBP
Silverio, Louis	R-R	6-3	215	12-15-93	.136	.250	.000	6	22	0	3	0	0	0	1	1	0	0	0	12	0	0	.136	.174
Strong, Bradley	L-R	5-8	175	7-1-92	.259	.244	.263	65	216	28	56	8	2	5	19	17	1	2	2	36	11	3	.384	.314
Suiter, Michael	R-R	6-1	200	4-9-92	.243	.143	.267	11	37	5	9	1	0	0	2	2	1	0	1	7	0	0	.270	.293
Sullivan, Tyler	L-L	5-9	180	11-21-92	.255	.236	.260	130	510	65	130	21	5	2	40	59	7	9	4	91	31	11	.327	.338
Woods, K.J.	L-R	6-3	230	7-9-95	.259	.207	.274	40	135	17	35	6	1	6	18	26	2	0	1	50	0	0	.452	.384
Zangari, Corey	R-R	6-4	240	5-7-97	.166	.231	.146	57	223	22	37	9	0	8	24	20	4	1	0	106	0	2	.314	.247
Zavala, Seby	R-R	5-11	205	8-28-93	.253	.211	.264	93	360	40	91	19	3	7	49	35	7	1	1	108	1	1	.381	.330

Pitching	B-T	HT	WT	DOB	W	L	ERA	G	GS	CG	SV	IP	H	R	ER	HR	BB	SO	AVG	vLH	vRH	K/9	BB/9
Ball, Matt	R-R	6-5	200	1-23-95	0	1	4.50	10	0	0	1	16	17	15	8	1	5	24	.250	.393	.150	13.50	2.81
2-team total (21 Hickory)					4	2	2.30	31	4	0	4	67	68	26	17	3	22	63	—	—		8.51	2.97
Banks, Tanner	L-L	6-1	195	10-24-91	6	3	2.87	11	11	1	0	69	58	25	22	5	14	51	.228	.189	.244	6.65	1.83
Barrow, Dylan	R-R	6-3	195	7-29-93	3	3	3.43	24	0	0	0	39	37	16	15	3	15	33	.255	.293	.230	7.55	3.43
Beatty, Max	R-R	6-2	225	3-27-91	4	7	3.57	13	13	1	0	71	67	37	28	7	9	46	.247	.241	.252	5.86	1.15
Charleston, Jack	R-R	6-5	170	9-14-92	2	7	3.25	34	2	0	5	69	75	30	25	3	15	58	.277	.282	.273	7.53	1.95
Cherry, Taylore	R-R	6-9	290	6-24-93	1	4	2.42	30	0	0	7	45	40	15	12	2	8	51	.233	.176	.276	10.28	1.61
Comito, Chris	R-R	6-6	240	6-25-96	1	7	6.48	9	9	0	0	42	57	36	30	4	11	27	.310	.292	.321	5.83	2.38
Dopico, Danny	R-R	6-2	190	12-18-93	3	0	3.24	9	0	0	0	17	13	6	6	1	11	15	.217	.231	.206	8.10	5.94
Easterling, Brannon	R-R	6-4	240	8-1-90	7	3	1.86	34	18	0	2	126	103	36	26	4	31	88	.224	.229	.221	6.29	2.21
Frebis, Johnathan	L-L	6-3	230	9-24-92	8	10	4.79	29	25	0	0	124	137	71	66	5	48	71	.287	.243	.305	5.15	3.48
Hamilton, Ian	R-R	6-0	200	6-16-95	1	1	3.69	21	0	0	8	32	22	13	13	3	14	27	.202	.171	.221	7.67	3.98
Hansen, Alec	R-R	6-7	235	10-10-94	0	1	2.45	2	2	0	0	11	11	5	3	0	4	11	.262	.240	.294	9.00	3.27
Hasler, Drew	R-R	6-6	245	8-14-93	2	3	2.25	24	0	0	1	44	36	16	11	1	9	22	.222	.231	.216	4.50	1.84
Hinchley, Ryan	L-L	6-3	200	1-9-93	1	0	6.43	11	0	0	0	21	23	17	15	0	20	25	.280	.344	.240	10.71	8.57
Horejsei, Michael	L-L	5-10	195	8-5-92	0	0	1.32	15	0	0	2	27	19	4	4	1	9	30	.194	.103	.232	9.88	2.96
Katz, Alex	L-L	5-11	195	10-12-94	0	1	3.44	30	0	0	1	50	46	21	19	1	19	50	.249	.211	.266	9.06	3.44
Lambert, Jimmy	R-R	6-2	170	11-18-94	0	5	5.76	11	11	0	0	30	39	22	19	2	11	30	.315	.339	.290	9.10	3.34
Martinez, Luis	R-R	6-6	190	1-29-95	8	9	3.81	28	28	1	0	137	126	66	58	9	51	141	.244	.229	.255	9.26	3.35
Mendonca, Tanner	R-R	6-4	215	6-18-92	1	1	4.30	17	0	0	0	23	16	12	11	2	20	31	.205	.300	.146	12.13	7.83
Morrison, Mike	R-R	6-1	195	9-22-93	1	2	3.63	11	0	0	0	17	16	10	7	2	8	18	.235	.308	.190	9.35	4.15
Peralta, Yelmison	R-R	6-2	190	3-3-95	1	4	3.82	24	0	0	1	35	33	19	15	3	18	25	.241	.237	.244	6.37	4.58
Quintero, Brandon	R-R	6-2	180	2-2-94	0	0	0.00	1	0	0	0	1	0	0	0	0	1	1	.000	.000	.000	9.00	9.00
Riga, Ryan	L-L	6-0	190	10-22-92	0	3	4.84	19	5	0	0	48	50	27	26	4	19	46	.270	.218	.292	8.57	3.54
Rocha, Jaider	R-R	6-1	205	5-23-93	0	3	4.05	10	0	0	0	13	11	15	6	0	17	12	.224	.182	.259	8.10	11.48
Thompson, Zach	R-R	6-7	230	10-23-93	6	3	2.62	16	16	0	0	86	58	33	25	5	39	88	.193	.231	.156	9.21	4.08
Wright, Ben	R-R	6-0	185	6-21-94	1	1	4.99	17	0	0	3	31	37	19	17	1	6	22	.303	.320	.292	6.46	1.76

Fielding

Catcher	PCT	G	PO	A	E	DP	PB
Gonzalez	1.000	23	143	22	0	1	3
Nolan	.993	20	131	17	1	3	2
O'Connell	1.000	1	10	0	0	0	0
Perez	1.000	2	11	0	1	0	1
Schroeder	.977	5	40	2	1	0	1
Zavala	.984	92	692	93	13	6	14

First Base	PCT	G	PO	A	E	DP
Daily	.991	55	510	29	5	39
Fish	.971	7	66	2	2	4
Massey	1.000	1	5	0	0	0
Orvis	1.000	1	5	1	0	1
Woods	.986	28	261	14	4	18
Zangari	.978	51	515	30	12	38

Second Base	PCT	G	PO	A	E	DP
Cruz	1.000	1	1	3	0	1
Dexter	1.000	1	1	1	0	0
Dutto	1.000	8	16	23	0	6
Flores	.960	5	5	19	1	6
Massey	.980	42	71	125	4	22
Mendick	.969	30	50	74	4	16
Rondon	1.000	2	5	9	0	2
Strong	.977	56	99	158	6	32

Third Base	PCT	G	PO	A	E	DP
Daily	.908	43	29	80	11	6
Flores	1.000	4	3	15	0	1
Massey	.992	47	30	95	1	5
Mendick	.944	20	16	52	4	1
Remillard	.935	29	13	59	5	4

Shortstop	PCT	G	PO	A	E	DP
Cruz	.942	52	78	151	14	22
Dutto	.958	11	15	31	2	3
Massey	.976	23	31	91	3	15
Mendick	.969	48	62	155	7	25
Rondon	.972	9	6	29	1	5

Outfield	PCT	G	PO	A	E	DP
Adolfo	.969	63	120	5	4	1
Califano	1.000	5	11	1	0	1
Call	1.000	44	76	3	0	0
Fincher	1.000	11	19	2	0	1
Lassiter	.982	64	105	3	2	0
Rodriguez	.921	81	109	8	10	1
Ruchim	1.000	10	18	2	0	0
Silverio	.750	5	3	0	1	0
Suiter	1.000	11	15	3	0	1
Sullivan	.974	129	251	10	7	2

GREAT FALLS VOYAGERS
PIONEER LEAGUE

ROOKIE

Batting	B-T	HT	WT	DOB	AVG	vLH	vRH	G	AB	R	H	2B	3B	HR	RBI	BB	HBP	SH	SF	SO	SB	CS	SLG	OBP
Booker, Joel	R-R	6-1	190	11-1-93	.328	.435	.304	32	125	21	41	8	0	1	13	14	6	2	0	22	15	2	.416	.421
Califano, Frank	L-L	5-11	185	3-31-94	.240	.174	.252	46	154	24	37	3	4	0	13	11	0	2	1	32	12	4	.312	.289
Call, Alex	R-R	5-0	188	9-27-94	.308	.375	.297	27	107	19	33	3	1	3	17	19	7	1	0	18	4	4	.439	.444
Conlan, Brady	R-R	6-1	207	8-21-93	.281	.341	.270	67	274	38	77	15	1	8	41	12	5	3	2	50	4	0	.431	.321
Dexter, Sam	R-R	5-11	185	3-7-94	.237	.333	.219	37	114	11	27	4	1	1	12	5	5	6	1	14	3	1	.316	.296
Dutto, Max	R-L	6-0	205	11-2-93	.229	.235	.228	32	109	17	25	3	0	7	15	14	3	1	0	43	0	1	.450	.333
Fisher, Jameson	L-R	6-2	200	12-18-93	.342	.267	.357	50	187	39	64	13	1	4	25	27	4	1	0	43	13	7	.487	.436
Franco, J.J.	R-R	5-9	180	2-2-92	.206	.200	.208	18	63	7	13	5	0	0	4	5	1	2	1	13	0	1	.286	.268
Glines, Jackson	L-L	6-0	205	4-13-92	.243	.381	.209	34	107	21	26	8	2	2	15	18	9	1	1	15	4	1	.411	.393
Jarvis, Jake	R-R	5-10	175	2-23-95	.280	.231	.290	25	75	12	21	1	0	4	15	6	7	2	0	12	0	4	.453	.386
Nolan, Nate	R-R	6-1	210	10-11-94	.153	.000	.180	16	59	8	9	2	0	1	6	6	1	0	0	27	0	0	.237	.242
Perez, Carlos	R-R	5-10	160	9-10-96	.186	.308	.158	21	70	4	13	2	0	0	4	1	0	4	0	11	0	0	.214	.197
Pollakov, Steve	R-R	6-2	220	12-29-91	.278	.167	.300	17	36	7	10	1	0	1	7	4	0	1	0	11	0	0	.389	.350
Roman, Mitch	R-R	6-0	161	3-22-95	.332	.304	.338	67	256	52	85	10	6	0	33	21	6	2	3	42	26	6	.418	.392

Batting	B-T	HT	WT	DOB	AVG	vLH	vRH	G	AB	R	H	2B	3B	HR	RBI	BB	HBP	SH	SF	SO	SB	CS	SLG	OBP
Schnurbusch, Aaron	L-L	6-5	235	1-21-94	.357	.348	.359	66	238	53	85	14	6	6	44	47	4	2	0	69	19	8	.542	.471
Schroeder, Casey	B-R	6-2	210	7-12-93	.260	.200	.271	46	154	24	40	16	2	5	29	16	1	4	2	45	2	1	.487	.329
Silverio, Louis	R-R	6-3	215	12-15-93	.368	.500	.353	6	19	3	7	3	0	0	0	0	1	0	0	3	0	1	.526	.400
Villa, Anthony	R-R	6-3	220	3-29-94	.249	.222	.255	59	193	24	48	15	1	3	35	20	15	0	0	38	0	2	.383	.364
Zangari, Corey	R-R	6-4	240	5-7-97	.257	.325	.241	53	202	31	52	11	1	7	27	21	1	1	0	70	2	2	.426	.330

Pitching	B-T	HT	WT	DOB	W	L	ERA	G	GS	CG	SV	IP	H	R	ER	HR	BB	SO	AVG	vLH	vRH	K/9	BB/9
Beatty, Max	R-R	6-2	225	3-27-91	1	1	6.55	2	2	0	0	11	12	8	8	3	1	14	.267	.267	.267	11.45	0.82
Bummer, Aaron	L-L	6-3	200	9-21-93	1	1	3.38	7	0	0	0	8	7	3	3	0	4	11	.233	.400	.150	12.38	4.50
Comito, Chris	R-R	6-6	240	6-25-96	8	1	3.43	14	14	1	0	87	71	40	33	7	15	89	.217	.234	.205	9.24	1.56
Elliott, Jake	R-R	6-7	230	3-22-95	3	3	4.30	18	2	0	2	38	39	20	18	3	9	45	.273	.281	.267	10.75	2.15
Escorcia, Kevin	L-L	6-1	170	1-5-95	1	0	4.07	18	0	0	1	24	15	14	11	1	18	27	.176	.270	.104	9.99	6.66
Flores, Bernardo	L-L	6-3	170	8-23-95	6	1	3.66	11	11	0	0	59	63	28	24	4	12	45	.280	.241	.293	6.86	1.83
Foster, Matt	R-R	6-0	195	1-27-95	0	0	0.00	8	0	0	6	11	1	0	0	0	3	15	.029	.077	.000	11.91	2.38
Gallegos, Fernando	L-R	5-11	175	9-4-92	3	0	2.33	17	3	0	1	39	32	11	10	0	13	38	.229	.156	.263	8.84	3.03
Hansen, Alec	R-R	6-7	235	10-10-94	2	0	1.23	7	7	0	0	37	12	6	5	3	12	59	.102	.146	.071	14.48	2.95
Hinchley, Ryan	L-L	6-3	200	1-9-93	1	2	7.31	16	0	0	0	16	13	15	13	1	15	23	.213	.250	.195	12.94	8.44
Hobbs, Lane	R-R	6-5	235	5-22-95	1	0	5.24	18	0	0	3	22	31	17	13	0	2	21	.323	.368	.293	8.46	0.81
Horejsei, Michael	L-L	5-10	195	8-5-92	0	1	0.00	8	0	0	2	13	12	1	0	0	2	11	.250	.250	.250	7.82	1.42
Ledo, Luis	R-R	6-4	208	5-28-95	2	1	8.76	3	3	0	0	12	13	12	12	3	11	10	.265	.389	.194	7.30	8.03
Magallones, Brandon	R-R	6-3	205	1-19-93	0	2	3.20	17	0	0	1	20	11	9	7	3	3	27	.157	.125	.174	12.36	1.37
McRee, Aron	R-R	6-0	180	10-29-93	5	0	2.16	12	11	0	0	67	57	19	16	2	6	54	.226	.275	.193	7.29	0.81
McWilliams, Richard	R-R	6-4	210	4-21-93	0	3	4.18	19	0	0	0	24	20	12	11	1	8	25	.220	.257	.196	9.51	3.04
Panayotovich, Adam	R-R	5-11	180	9-3-91	4	6	4.26	16	6	1	0	57	61	35	27	3	9	48	.271	.313	.240	7.58	1.42
Rizzotti, Tony	R-R	6-4	205	4-21-92	0	0	18.00	1	1	0	0	2	3	5	4	0	3	1	.273	.333	.250	4.50	13.50
Rocha, Jaider	R-R	6-1	205	5-23-93	0	3	2.55	20	0	0	6	25	18	8	7	1	16	24	.217	.250	.206	8.76	5.84
Solorzano, Yosmer	R-R	6-2	181	2-11-97	9	3	4.11	15	15	2	0	81	85	43	37	1	18	81	.265	.302	.240	9.00	2.00
Wright, Ben	R-R	6-0	185	6-21-94	0	0	0.00	5	0	0	0	7	2	0	0	0	1	10	.077	.000	.100	12.27	1.23

Fielding

C: Nolan 15, Perez 20, Pollakov 6, Schroeder 41. **1B:** Pollakov 2, Villa 39, Zangari 37. **2B:** Conlan 1, Dexter 21, Dutto 9, Franco 13, Jarvis 18, Roman 19. **3B:** Conlan 65, Dexter 4, Franco 2, Villa 5. **SS:** Dexter 10, Dutto 20, Roman 46. **OF:** Booker 29, Califano 37, Call 25, Fisher 43, Franco 1, Glines 27, Jarvis 6, Roman 2, Schnurbusch 63, Silverio 4.

AZL WHITE SOX   ROOKIE
ARIZONA LEAGUE

Batting	B-T	HT	WT	DOB	AVG	vLH	vRH	G	AB	R	H	2B	3B	HR	RBI	BB	HBP	SH	SF	SO	SB	CS	SLG	OBP
Adolfo, Micker	R-R	6-3	200	9-11-96	.250	.000	.286	4	16	2	4	2	0	1	2	1	1	0	0	8	0	0	.563	.333
Booker, Joel	R-R	6-1	190	11-1-93	.296	.423	.266	33	135	30	40	8	1	1	18	13	7	0	0	27	26	1	.393	.387
Castillo, Luis	R-R	6-3	200	7-14-96	.000	—	.000	1	2	0	0	0	0	0	0	0	0	0	0	0	0	0	.000	.000
Collins, Zack	L-R	6-3	220	2-6-95	.091	.000	.100	3	11	1	1	0	0	0	0	0	0	0	0	7	0	0	.091	.091
Cooper, Jacob	R-R	5-10	221	6-1-96	.248	.259	.246	37	145	24	36	7	2	4	19	10	5	1	2	38	1	0	.407	.315
Curbelo, Luis	R-R	6-3	185	11-10-97	.226	.250	.219	45	164	20	37	6	2	2	14	15	4	0	2	42	4	0	.323	.303
Dexter, Sam	R-R	5-11	185	3-7-94	.258	.333	.188	9	31	5	8	2	0	1	5	4	0	0	0	3	1	0	.419	.343
Feliz, Maiker	R-R	6-0	195	8-17-97	.214	.316	.190	31	98	18	21	2	0	1	6	16	0	0	0	25	0	0	.265	.325
Fincher, Jake	R-R	6-1	185	1-26-93	.600	.833	.250	3	10	4	6	1	0	0	2	2	0	0	0	1	2	1	.700	.667
Flores, Dante	L-R	5-9	160	4-8-93	.226	.200	.231	10	31	4	7	2	2	0	3	3	0	0	3	11	1	1	.419	.270
Franco, J.J.	R-R	5-9	180	2-2-92	.158	.000	.200	6	19	1	3	0	0	0	1	3	0	0	0	3	0	1	.158	.273
Garcia, Joxelier	R-R	5-10	185	4-30-94	.250	.400	.211	9	24	3	6	2	0	0	5	4	3	0	0	5	0	0	.333	.419
Heathcott, Slade	L-L	6-1	205	9-28-90	.320	.429	.278	7	25	5	8	3	0	2	12	4	2	0	0	8	1	0	.680	.452
Hickman, Michael	L-R	6-1	215	11-5-96	.286	.100	.333	16	49	6	14	4	0	0	2	5	3	1	0	18	0	0	.367	.386
Mercedes, Felix	R-R	6-2	185	2-13-97	.276	.333	.267	34	116	18	32	7	1	2	12	10	5	0	2	32	0	0	.405	.353
Mota, Ricky	R-R	5-11	170	2-21-98	.244	.333	.222	23	78	11	19	2	0	3	6	4	0	1	0	31	1	1	.385	.280
Nunez, Amado	R-R	6-2	178	10-10-97	.287	.086	.326	52	216	19	62	11	2	1	26	10	1	4	1	52	9	2	.370	.320
Otano, Hanleth	R-R	6-3	195	7-16-96	.243	.296	.229	41	136	13	33	8	0	0	8	11	3	1	0	43	0	1	.301	.313
Perez, Carlos	R-R	5-10	160	9-10-96	.231	.250	.222	11	39	6	9	2	0	1	6	2	0	0	0	2	0	1	.359	.268
Remillard, Zach	R-R	6-0	205	2-21-94	.310	.571	.257	13	42	6	13	3	2	2	9	2	2	0	0	9	1	1	.619	.370
Reyes, Franklin	R-R	6-4	205	9-11-98	.171	.130	.182	52	211	20	36	10	2	1	16	5	0	0	1	71	0	0	.251	.189
Ruchim, Kyle	R-R	5-10	180	8-11-92	.000	.000	.000	2	5	0	0	0	0	0	2	0	0	0	0	2	0	0	.000	.286
Silverio, Louis	R-R	6-3	215	12-15-93	.267	.217	.282	27	101	15	27	4	1	4	21	2	1	3	0	20	2	1	.446	.288
Smith, Kevan	R-R	6-3	230	6-28-88	.200	—	.200	2	5	2	1	0	0	0	2	1	0	0	0	0	0	0	.800	.429
Sonnier, Trevin	R-R	5-10	185	8-8-92	.252	.259	.250	38	143	19	36	7	0	2	15	9	4	4	2	19	9	3	.343	.310
Villarroel, Ylexander	B-R	6-2	190	6-4-97	.220	.133	.250	17	59	8	13	3	0	0	7	4	3	0	0	12	0	0	.271	.303
Walker, David	L-R	5-9	180	3-24-92	.143	—	.143	3	7	1	1	0	0	0	0	0	0	0	0	2	0	0	.143	.143

Pitching	B-T	HT	WT	DOB	W	L	ERA	G	GS	CG	SV	IP	H	R	ER	HR	BB	SO	AVG	vLH	vRH	K/9	BB/9
Agar, Brandon	R-R	6-4	200	2-7-93	0	0	2.55	14	1	0	1	25	21	11	7	0	6	22	.226	.250	.210	8.03	2.19
Arias, Edinxon	R-R	6-2	155	12-5-97	2	7	6.50	13	11	0	0	44	66	49	32	6	16	27	.338	.290	.365	5.48	3.25
Bell, Evan	L-R	6-8	200	10-29-93	3	1	4.50	14	0	0	0	28	31	20	14	2	11	26	.270	.097	.333	8.36	3.54
Boelter, Ryan	L-L	6-2	240	12-28-93	1	0	4.12	14	0	0	0	20	22	11	9	2	5	23	.275	.000	.338	10.53	2.29
Bummer, Aaron	L-L	6-3	200	9-21-93	0	0	12.27	4	0	0	0	4	5	5	5	0	2	4	.313	.333	.308	14.73	4.91
Burdi, Zack	R-R	6-3	205	3-9-95	0	0	0.00	1	0	0	0	1	0	0	0	0	1	1	.000	.250	.333	.000	9.00	0.00
Cashman, Pat	R-R	6-0	185	11-1-92	0	1	27.00	2	0	0	0	1	5	4	3	0	0	1	.556	.750	.400	9.00	0.00
Diaz, Carlos	L-L	6-0	186	1-1-94	0	1	7.36	15	0	0	0	15	22	15	12	0	8	16	.355	.455	.333	9.82	4.91

Pitching	B-T	HT	WT	DOB	W	L	ERA	G	GS	CG	SV	IP	H	R	ER	HR	BB	SO	AVG	vLH	vRH	K/9	BB/9
Done, Victor	R-R	6-3	195	9-3-95	1	8	7.20	10	10	0	0	35	37	33	28	1	28	30	.272	.259	.280	7.71	7.20
Dopico, Danny	R-R	6-2	190	12-18-93	0	0	3.38	6	0	0	1	8	9	5	3	0	5	12	.265	.357	.200	13.50	5.63
Flores, Bernardo	L-L	6-3	170	8-23-95	0	1	1.50	3	0	0	0	6	4	1	1	0	0	7	.174	.143	.188	10.50	0.00
Foster, Matt	R-R	6-0	195	1-27-95	0	0	0.98	14	0	0	5	18	11	5	2	0	4	26	.169	.160	.175	12.76	1.96
Goossen-Brown, Josh	R-R	6-2	210	2-21-91	0	1	7.94	6	0	0	0	6	7	5	5	0	1	6	.280	.125	.353	9.53	1.59
Hamilton, Ian	R-R	6-0	200	6-16-95	0	0	0.00	1	0	0	0	1	0	0	0	0	1	2	.000	.000	.000	18.00	9.00
Hansen, Alec	R-R	6-7	235	10-10-94	0	0	0.00	3	3	0	0	7	1	0	0	0	4	11	.048	.000	.059	14.14	5.14
Haymes, Brad	R-R	6-3	205	3-22-94	0	0	5.84	10	0	0	0	12	20	11	8	1	2	14	.323	.263	.349	10.22	1.46
Heidenreich, Matt	L-R	6-5	185	1-17-91	0	0	3.00	1	1	0	0	3	2	1	1	1	1	4	.200	.333	.143	12.00	3.00
Holdzkom, John	R-R	6-9	245	10-19-87	0	0	54.00	1	1	0	0	1	3	4	4	0	2	0	.600	.000	.750	0.00	27.00
Krauss, Conor	R-R	6-5	235	6-14-93	0	0	1.93	4	0	0	0	5	2	1	1	0	4	4	.143	.250	.100	7.71	7.71
Lambert, Jimmy	R-R	6-2	170	11-18-94	1	1	3.38	4	2	0	0	8	5	5	3	1	2	13	.172	.167	.174	14.63	2.25
Ledo, Luis	R-R	6-4	208	5-28-95	4	3	1.19	11	9	0	0	45	34	14	6	0	12	36	.200	.167	.218	7.15	2.38
Percel, Eriberto	R-R	6-5	200	8-2-92	0	1	5.75	16	0	0	2	20	17	17	13	0	10	15	.224	.353	.119	6.64	4.43
Quijada, Jhoan	L-L	6-3	210	12-27-94	4	1	5.67	14	2	0	0	40	41	27	25	6	16	26	.259	.241	.270	5.90	2.27
Quintero, Brandon	R-R	6-2	180	2-2-94	1	0	0.00	5	2	0	0	13	6	0	0	0	1	11	.140	.000	.171	7.62	0.69
Renzi, Sean	R-R	6-3	245	2-14-93	1	1	4.70	16	0	0	0	23	24	17	12	2	7	29	.258	.265	.254	11.35	2.74
Sanchez, Andres	R-R	6-4	180	10-7-96	2	6	5.10	13	12	0	0	60	68	46	34	7	28	42	.283	.275	.289	6.30	4.20
Shearrow, Luke	R-R	6-4	225	2-10-91	0	0	3.38	5	0	0	0	5	3	2	2	0	2	6	.176	.333	.143	10.13	3.38
Villarreal, Salvador	R-R	6-1	165	2-5-98	0	0	5.68	14	1	0	0	25	27	26	16	1	23	18	.270	.258	.275	6.39	8.17
Walsh, Connor	L-R	6-2	180	10-18-92	0	0	0.00	1	0	0	0	1	0	0	0	0	0	3	.000	.000	.000	27.00	0.00
Winiarski, Cody	R-R	6-3	205	8-27-89	0	0	54.00	1	1	0	0	0	3	2	2	0	0	0	.750	.000	1.000	0.00	0.00

Fielding

C: Collins 3, Cooper 29, Garcia 7, Hickman 10, Perez 9, Smith 3. **1B:** Castillo 1, Mercedes 21, Reyes 20, Villarroel 16. **2B:** Curbelo 26, Flores 2, Franco 4, Mota 22, Sonnier 6. **3B:** Dexter 9, Feliz 29, Flores 4, Mercedes 6, Remillard 12. **SS:** Curbelo 14, Mota 1, Nunez 41. **OF:** Adolfo 4, Booker 33, Cooper 4, Fincher 2, Heathcott 4, Otano 39, Reyes 28, Ruchim 1, Silverio 26, Sonnier 31, Walker 3.

DSL WHITE SOX
DOMINICAN SUMMER LEAGUE

ROOKIE

Batting	B-T	HT	WT	DOB	AVG	vLH	vRH	G	AB	R	H	2B	3B	HR	RBI	BB	HBP	SH	SF	SO	SB	CS	SLG	OBP
Alfaro, Jhoandro	B-R	6-1	180	11-4-97	.238	.182	.243	41	126	17	30	4	0	1	8	18	11	1	0	19	1	1	.294	.381
Barreras, Robert	R-R	6-3	205	9-15-98	.179	.176	.180	26	78	6	14	3	1	0	8	6	1	0	0	17	0	0	.244	.247
Beltre, Ramon	R-R	5-11	160	10-18-96	.263	.229	.270	56	209	29	55	6	5	4	26	21	5	3	2	33	8	2	.397	.342
Cabral, Carlos	R-R	6-1	185	9-5-92	.158	.000	.176	21	19	1	3	0	0	0	3	5	0	0	0	7	0	0	.158	.333
Castillo, Luis	R-R	6-3	200	7-14-96	.247	.250	.246	23	77	8	19	3	0	2	15	9	1	0	1	18	0	0	.364	.330
Colina, Jose	R-R	6-0	180	3-26-98	.188	.095	.208	34	117	11	22	2	0	1	5	6	0	3	1	36	0	1	.231	.226
Felix, Enrique	R-R	6-3	188	1-7-99	.158	.105	.171	37	101	6	16	7	0	2	5	8	0	0	0	46	0	0	.287	.220
Gideon, Yolberth	R-R	5-11	155	2-6-96	.197	.250	.186	47	142	13	28	1	1	0	15	23	2	3	0	16	2	0	.218	.317
Hernandez, Nelson	L-R	6-0	180	2-29-96	.284	.385	.265	31	81	12	23	1	1	0	5	6	1	2	0	18	2	1	.321	.341
Martinez, Omar	R-R	6-2	192	12-23-98	.157	.167	.155	30	89	3	14	2	0	0	7	2	0	1	0	33	2	3	.180	.232
Martinez, Ulises	R-R	6-1	190	3-2-99	.306	.333	.302	19	49	5	15	4	2	0	7	4	1	2	0	12	0	0	.469	.370
Mejia, Carlos	R-R	6-3	190	9-27-95	.222	.292	.212	54	189	19	42	12	0	3	17	16	3	3	0	62	1	0	.333	.293
Mejia, Droherlin	R-R	6-1	180	8-20-94	.224	.130	.241	53	156	22	35	3	0	0	12	20	1	4	4	19	8	4	.244	.309
Mendoza, Harvin	L-L	6-2	185	2-18-99	.279	.367	.264	62	208	24	58	7	0	1	23	39	2	0	2	32	0	2	.327	.394
Nova, Brayant	B-R	6-0	170	8-25-98	.279	.222	.283	38	122	16	34	5	0	1	10	18	2	3	0	33	4	7	.344	.380
Requena, Carlos	R-R	6-0	170	4-8-97	.266	.455	.226	33	64	11	17	0	0	0	2	11	1	2	0	16	2	3	.266	.382
Reyes, Jose	B-R	6-0	155	9-24-96	.268	.500	.229	25	82	12	22	2	1	0	13	5	0	1	0	10	0	1	.317	.310
Rosas, Jorgen	R-R	5-9	160	1-10-98	.192	.294	.161	20	73	6	14	0	0	0	8	5	1	1	2	12	1	0	.192	.247
Tejeda, Anderson	L-R	6-0	165	8-1-98	.288	.167	.304	30	125	10	15	3	0	0	8	9	1	0	0	18	4	5	.346	.403
Vasquez, Santo	R-R	6-0	170	11-27-98	.233	.250	.230	50	180	27	42	8	2	0	8	13	6	4	1	52	10	2	.300	.305

Pitching	B-T	HT	WT	DOB	W	L	ERA	G	GS	CG	SV	IP	H	R	ER	HR	BB	SO	AVG	vLH	vRH	K/9	BB/9
Acosta, Nelson	R-R	6-3	195	8-22-97	2	4	2.31	11	11	0	0	47	36	16	12	1	8	45	.205	.262	.187	8.68	1.54
Arias, Yojensy	L-L	6-3	180	7-29-93	0	0	3.54	10	10	0	0	41	48	22	16	1	9	45	.294	.444	.265	9.96	1.99
Batista, Cristopher	R-R	6-3	180	11-1-98	1	5	2.94	14	10	0	1	52	44	28	17	1	22	28	.320	.197	.485	4.85	3.81
Caro, Fernando	R-R	6-2	192	2-25-97	5	5	3.73	21	0	0	1	41	45	20	17	1	16	34	.287	.341	.267	7.46	3.51
Coroba, Josbel	L-L	6-0	180	5-18-97	4	0	1.89	23	0	0	4	48	35	14	10	0	28	27	.205	.303	.181	5.10	5.29
De La Cruz, Leonardo	L-L	6-4	180	4-29-94	1	7	3.13	16	14	0	0	72	63	32	25	1	30	78	.235	.250	.234	9.75	3.75
Done, Victor	R-R	6-3	195	9-3-95	1	1	4.10	9	5	0	0	26	25	14	12	0	16	27	.258	.282	.241	9.23	5.47
Espinosa, Ramon	R-R	6-3	185	11-30-93	1	2	3.35	21	0	0	1	48	31	27	18	0	44	30	.180	.196	.175	5.59	8.19
Gerardo, Josue	R-R	6-3	180	3-27-93	5	2	3.38	21	1	0	2	45	26	19	17	2	38	53	.167	.205	.154	10.52	7.54
Herrera, Antonio	R-R	6-4	195	9-26-94	3	3	5.98	18	1	0	0	41	42	35	27	3	23	30	.271	.370	.250	6.64	5.09
Ledo, Luis	R-R	6-4	208	5-28-95	0	1	1.29	2	2	0	0	7	8	1	1	0	0	9	.333	.375	.313	11.57	0.00
Perez, Victor	L-L	6-3	195	8-11-95	0	1	4.50	12	1	0	0	20	27	23	10	0	19	12	.307	.412	.282	5.40	8.55
Pinales, Joselo	R-R	6-1	180	11-16-94	0	2	4.20	12	0	0	5	15	17	9	7	0	6	16	.288	.067	.364	9.60	3.60
Quijada, Jhoan	L-L	6-3	210	12-27-94	1	0	0.00	2	2	0	0	8	8	0	0	0	0	6	.195	.350	.048	4.63	0.00
Ramos, Jordis	L-L	6-10	194	6-15-96	1	3	3.31	14	1	0	0	35	25	17	13	0	22	34	.200	.318	.175	8.66	5.60
Rosario, Yordi	R-R	6-2	185	1-30-99	1	6	7.20	12	9	0	0	35	48	38	28	1	24	26	.320	.273	.347	6.69	6.17

Fielding

C: Alfaro 25, Cabral 21, Colina 29, Martinez 18. **1B:** Barreras 8, Castillo 11, Colina 3, Gideon 1, Mejia 1, Mendoza 54. **2B:** Beltre 3, Gideon 8, Nova 31, Reyes 13, Rosas 19. **3B:** Beltre 40, Castillo 2, Gideon 27. **SS:** Beltre 10, Gideon 12, Rosas 2, Vasquez 49. **OF:** Barreras 1, Beltre 1, Felix 37, Hernandez 27, Martinez 29, Mejia 49, Mejia 50, Requena 30, Tejeda 22.

Cincinnati Reds

SEASON IN A SENTENCE: In a year focused on the future, the Reds shed some contracts and tied for the National League lead with 94 losses, despite a monster season and particularly strong second half by first baseman Joey Votto.

HIGH POINT: The combination of better health on the pitching staff and Votto's nuclear production helped the Reds go 36-37 after the all-star break. Votto hit .408/.490/.668 in the last 72 games he played, adding seven homers in September and October. Overall, Votto hit .381/.498/.681 in 65 Reds victories.

LOW POINT: The Reds had won four straight to edge up to 13-17 when the wheels came off, with the club losing 18 of its next 22 games, including a season-long 11-game losing streak from May 16-27. The streak started with the Brewers putting up seven runs in the 10th inning of a 13-7 game the Reds once led 6-2; it ended with a 17-4 drubbing at Coors Field in which the Rockies slugged seven homers. Reds pitchers set a new single-season club record for home runs allowed with 258.

NOTABLE ROOKIES: Lefties John Lamb and Cody Reed and righty Tim Adleman, a former indy-ball find, got 37 starts among them, and both lefties struggled mightily. So did former No. 1 prospect Robert Stephenson, still rookie-eligible in 2017 after eight starts that covered just 37 innings. Rookie Reds hitters impressed a bit more, from outfielder Scott Schebler, who showed strong lefthanded power, to versatile Jose Peraza, whose speed and ability to play second base, shortstop and center field should come in handy.

KEY TRANSACTIONS: The Reds shed Jay Bruce's salary, trading their 2005 first-round pick to the Mets after he had a strong first half with 25 home runs. Righthander Dan Straily, a late-spring waiver claim, became the team's stalwart starter, going 14-8, 3.76 with 191.1 innings.

DOWN ON THE FARM: Reds affiliates barely peeked above .500, with two making the playoffs, led by Double-A Pensacola, which won 81 games. Outfielder Aristides Aquino was the MVP of the high Class A Florida State League after hitting .273/.327/.519 with 23 home runs. After loading up on arms in recent drafts, the Reds went hard after hitters in the draft, taking them with their first three selections, including No. 2 overall pick Nick Senzel. The Tennessee third baseman hit .305/.398/.514 in his pro debut with seven home runs and 18 stolen bases in just 68 games.

OPENING DAY PAYROLL: $89,955,059 (22nd)

PLAYERS OF THE YEAR

MAJOR LEAGUE

Joey Votto
1b
.326/.434/.550
29 HR, 97 RBI
Led NL in OBP

MINOR LEAGUE

Amir Garrett
lhp
(Double-A, Triple-A)
7-8, 2.55
132 SO in 144.2 IP

ORGANIZATION LEADERS

BATTING		*Minimum 250 AB
MAJORS		
* AVG	Joey Votto	.326
* OPS	Joey Votto	.985
HR	Adam Duvall	33
RBI	Adam Duvall	103
MINORS		
* AVG	Hernan Iribarren, Louisville	.327
* OBP	Jesse Winker, Louisville	.397
* SLG	Aristides Aquino, Daytona	.519
* OPS	Aristides Aquino, Daytona	.846
R	Blake Trahan, Daytona	90
H	Shed Long, Dayton, Daytona	140
TB	Aristides Aquino, Daytona	251
2B	Gavin LaValley, Dayton, Daytona	30
	Shed Long, Dayton, Daytona	30
3B	Aristides Aquino, Daytona	12
HR	Aristides Aquino, Daytona	23
RBI	Aristides Aquino, Daytona	79
BB	Brian O'Grady, Daytona	67
SO	Taylor Sparks, Daytona, Pensacola	141
SB	Phillip Ervin, Pensacola	36

PITCHING		#Minimum 75 IP
MAJORS		
W	Dan Straily	14
# ERA	Dan Straily	3.76
SO	Dan Straily	162
SV	Tony Cingrani	17
MINORS		
W	Tejay Antone, Daytona, Louisville	14
	Tyler Mahle, Daytona, Pensacola	14
L	Austin Orewiler, Dayton	14
# ERA	Amir Garrett, Pensacola, Louisville	2.55
G	Alejandro Chacin, Pensacola	52
GS	Tyler Mahle, Daytona, Pensacola	27
	Sal Romano, Pensacola	27
SV	Alejandro Chacin, Pensacola	30
IP	Tejay Antone, Daytona, Louisville	156
BB	Robert Stephenson, Louisville	71
SO	Jose Lopez, Dayton, Daytona	147
# AVG	Amir Garrett, Pensacola, Louisville	.192

2016 PERFORMANCE

General Manager: Dick Williams. **Farm Director:** Jeff Graupe. **Scouting Director:** Chris Buckley.

Class	Team	League	W	L	PCT	Finish	Manager
Majors	Cincinnati Reds	National	68	94	.420	14th (15)	Bryan Price
Triple-A	Louisville Bats	International	71	73	.493	6th (14)	Delino DeShields
Double-A	Pensacola Blue Wahoos	Southern	81	59	.579	2nd (10)	Pat Kelly
High A	Daytona Tortugas	Florida State	76	61	.555	4th (12)	Eli Marrero
Low A	Dayton Dragons	Midwest	47	93	.336	16th (16)	Dick Schofield
Rookie	Billings Mustangs	Pioneer	41	34	.547	2nd (8)	Ray Martinez
Rookie	Reds	Arizona	31	24	.564	2nd (14)	Jose Nieves
Overall 2016 Minor League Record			347	344	.502	15th (30)	

ORGANIZATION STATISTICS

CINCINNATI REDS
NATIONAL LEAGUE

Batting	B-T	HT	WT	DOB	AVG	vLH	vRH	G	AB	R	H	2B	3B	HR	RBI	BB	HBP	SH	SF	SO	SB	CS	SLG	OBP
Barnhart, Tucker	B-R	5-11	190	1-7-91	.257	.207	.271	115	377	34	97	23	1	7	51	36	2	2	3	72	1	0	.379	.323
Bruce, Jay	L-L	6-3	225	4-3-87	.265	.250	.271	97	370	60	98	22	6	25	80	27	2	0	3	83	4	2	.559	.316
2-team total (50 New York)					.250	—	—	147	539	74	135	27	6	33	99	44	3	0	3	126	4	2	.506	.309
Cabrera, Ramon	B-R	5-8	195	11-5-89	.246	.237	.248	61	171	11	42	10	0	3	23	8	1	2	3	30	1	1	.357	.279
Cozart, Zack	R-R	6-0	195	8-12-85	.252	.226	.260	121	464	67	117	28	2	16	50	37	2	1	4	84	4	1	.425	.308
De Jesus Jr. Ivan	R-R	5-11	200	5-1-87	.253	.186	.270	104	221	21	56	10	0	1	20	17	2	2	1	51	3	1	.312	.311
Duvall, Adam	R-R	6-1	220	9-4-88	.241	.238	.242	150	552	85	133	31	6	33	103	41	6	0	8	164	6	5	.498	.297
Hamilton, Billy	B-R	6-0	160	9-9-90	.260	.221	.275	119	411	69	107	19	3	3	17	36	1	11	1	93	58	8	.343	.321
Holt, Tyler	R-R	5-10	200	3-10-89	.235	.204	.246	106	179	21	42	5	3	0	13	23	2	3	1	48	4	3	.296	.327
Iribarren, Hernan	L-R	6-1	195	6-29-84	.311	.400	.300	24	45	6	14	0	3	0	2	0	0	0	0	11	1	0	.444	.311
Kivlehan, Patrick	R-R	6-2	215	12-22-89	.000	.000	.000	3	5	0	0	0	0	0	0	0	0	0	0	2	0	0	.000	.000
2-team total (5 San Diego)					.190	—	—	8	21	5	4	0	0	1	2	2	1	0	0	11	0	0	.333	.292
Lopez, Rafael	L-R	5-9	200	10-2-87	.000	.000	.000	8	7	0	0	0	0	0	0	0	0	0	0	3	0	0	.000	.000
Mesoraco, Devin	R-R	6-1	220	6-19-88	.140	.154	.135	16	50	2	7	1	0	0	1	5	0	0	0	10	0	1	.160	.218
Pacheco, Jordan	R-R	6-1	200	1-30-86	.157	.154	.158	31	51	1	8	4	0	0	0	0	0	0	0	14	0	0	.235	.157
Peraza, Jose	R-R	6-0	180	4-30-94	.324	.308	.328	72	241	25	78	8	2	3	25	7	5	0	3	33	21	10	.411	.352
Phillips, Brandon	R-R	6-0	210	6-28-81	.291	.256	.302	141	550	74	160	34	1	11	64	18	8	2	6	68	14	8	.416	.320
Renda, Tony	R-R	5-8	175	1-24-91	.183	.143	.196	32	60	4	11	2	0	0	3	5	0	2	0	11	0	0	.217	.246
Schebler, Scott	L-R	6-0	225	10-6-90	.265	.195	.278	82	257	36	68	12	2	9	40	19	6	0	0	59	2	4	.432	.330
Selsky, Steve	R-R	6-0	205	7-20-89	.314	.500	.268	24	51	9	16	2	0	2	7	2	0	1	0	22	1	0	.471	.340
Suarez, Eugenio	R-R	5-11	205	7-18-91	.248	.276	.240	159	565	78	140	25	2	21	70	51	8	0	3	155	11	5	.411	.317
Votto, Joey	L-R	6-2	220	9-10-83	.326	.314	.330	158	556	101	181	34	2	29	97	108	5	0	8	120	8	1	.550	.434
Waldrop, Kyle	L-L	6-2	215	11-26-91	.227	.000	.278	15	22	1	5	1	0	0	1	1	0	0	0	5	0	0	.273	.261

Pitching	B-T	HT	WT	DOB	W	L	ERA	G	GS	CG	SV	IP	H	R	ER	HR	BB	SO	AVG	vLH	vRH	K/9	BB/9
Adleman, Tim	R-R	6-5	225	11-13-87	4	4	4.00	13	13	0	0	70	64	32	31	13	20	47	.251	.256	.246	6.07	2.58
Bailey, Homer	R-R	6-4	225	5-3-86	2	3	6.65	6	6	0	0	23	35	19	17	2	7	27	.350	.429	.293	10.57	2.74
Cingrani, Tony	L-L	6-4	210	7-5-89	2	5	4.14	65	0	0	17	63	54	30	29	5	37	49	.236	.207	.252	7.00	5.29
Cotham, Caleb	R-R	6-3	215	11-6-87	0	3	7.40	23	0	0	0	24	32	21	20	3	12	21	.323	.348	.302	7.77	4.44
De Los Santos, Abel	R-R	6-2	195	11-21-92	0	0	11.12	5	0	0	0	6	7	7	7	1	4	2	.318	.455	.182	3.18	6.35
Delabar, Steve	R-R	6-5	215	7-17-83	0	0	6.75	7	0	0	0	8	5	6	6	1	10	10	.172	.000	.333	11.25	11.25
DeSclafani, Anthony	R-R	6-1	200	4-18-90	9	5	3.28	20	20	1	0	123	120	51	45	16	30	105	.259	.303	.206	7.66	2.19
Diaz, Dayan	R-R	5-10	195	2-10-89	0	0	9.45	6	0	0	0	7	10	9	7	2	7	3	.370	.412	.300	4.05	9.45
Diaz, Jumbo	R-R	6-4	280	2-27-84	1	1	3.14	45	0	0	0	43	36	20	15	8	19	37	.224	.197	.242	7.74	3.98
Finnegan, Brandon	L-L	5-11	200	4-14-93	10	11	3.98	31	31	1	0	172	150	86	76	29	84	145	.236	.218	.241	7.59	4.40
Hayes, Drew	R-R	6-1	205	9-3-87	0	0	8.38	6	0	0	0	10	15	10	9	3	6	8	.357	.476	.238	7.45	5.59
Hoover, J.J.	R-R	6-3	240	8-13-87	1	2	13.50	18	0	0	1	19	29	29	28	9	12	15	.345	.368	.326	7.23	5.79
Iglesias, Raisel	R-R	6-2	185	1-4-90	3	2	2.53	37	5	0	6	78	63	22	22	7	26	83	.216	.266	.171	9.54	2.99
Lamb, John	L-L	6-4	205	7-10-90	1	7	6.43	14	14	0	0	70	84	54	50	14	31	58	.303	.279	.311	7.46	3.99
Lorenzen, Michael	R-R	6-3	215	1-4-92	2	1	2.88	35	0	0	0	50	41	16	16	5	13	48	.224	.202	.245	8.64	2.34
Magill, Matt	R-R	6-3	210	11-10-89	0	0	6.23	5	0	0	0	4	5	3	3	1	5	1	.357	.400	.333	2.08	10.38
Melville, Tim	R-R	6-4	225	10-9-89	0	1	11.00	3	2	0	0	9	16	12	11	5	9	8	.381	.333	.400	8.00	9.00
Morris, A.J.	R-R	6-2	195	12-1-86	0	0	6.30	7	0	0	0	10	9	7	7	2	8	9	.237	.200	.278	8.10	7.20
Moscot, Jon	R-R	6-4	210	8-15-91	0	3	8.02	5	5	0	0	21	26	22	19	10	10	10	.292	.327	.250	4.22	4.22
Ohlendorf, Ross	R-R	6-4	240	8-8-82	5	7	4.66	64	0	0	0	66	59	35	34	14	32	68	.237	.198	.268	9.32	4.39
Peralta, Wandy	L-L	6-0	210	7-27-91	0	0	8.59	10	0	0	0	7	11	7	7	1	7	5	.355	.273	.400	6.14	8.59
Ramirez, J.C.	R-R	6-4	250	8-16-88	1	3	6.40	27	0	0	1	32	35	24	23	7	9	28	.278	.310	.250	7.79	2.51
Reed, Cody	L-L	6-5	225	4-15-93	0	7	7.36	10	10	0	0	48	67	47	39	12	19	43	.328	.304	.335	8.12	3.59
Sampson, Keyvius	R-R	6-2	225	1-6-91	0	1	4.35	18	2	0	0	39	40	24	19	9	27	42	.255	.216	.274	9.61	6.18
Simon, Alfredo	R-R	6-6	265	5-8-81	2	7	9.36	15	11	0	0	59	89	64	61	15	31	39	.349	.369	.331	5.98	4.76
Smith, Josh	R-R	6-2	220	8-7-87	3	3	4.68	32	2	0	0	60	57	32	31	11	26	48	.247	.287	.219	7.24	3.92
Somsen, Layne	R-R	6-0	190	6-5-89	0	0	19.29	2	0	0	0	2	6	5	5	2	3	2	.462	.333	.571	7.71	11.57
Stephenson, Robert	R-R	6-2	200	2-24-93	2	3	6.08	8	8	0	0	37	41	26	25	9	19	31	.279	.289	.268	7.54	4.62
Straily, Dan	R-R	6-2	215	12-1-88	14	8	3.76	34	31	0	0	191	154	80	80	31	73	162	.220	.191	.243	7.62	3.43

CINCINNATI REDS

Pitching	B-T	HT	WT	DOB	W	L	ERA	G	GS	CG	SV	IP	H	R	ER	HR	BB	SO	AVG	vLH	vRH	K/9	BB/9
Wood, Blake	R-R	6-5	240	8-8-85	6	5	3.99	70	0	0	1	77	72	38	34	9	38	81	.251	.213	.281	9.51	4.46
Wright, Daniel	R-R	6-2	205	4-3-91	0	2	7.62	4	2	0	0	13	25	16	11	2	2	6	.417	.447	.364	4.15	1.38

Fielding

Catcher	PCT	G	PO	A	E	DP	PB
Barnhart	.992	108	817	74	7	6	5
Cabrera	.989	48	333	17	4	2	2
Lopez	1.000	4	8	1	0	0	0
Mesoraco	.990	13	92	6	1	1	2

First Base	PCT	G	PO	A	E	DP
De Jesus Jr.	.978	12	44	0	1	5
Duvall	1.000	5	33	6	0	1
Iribarren	1.000	2	2	0	0	1
Lopez	1.000	1	1	0	0	0
Pacheco	1.000	3	7	0	0	0
Votto	.994	154	1168	107	8	124

Second Base	PCT	G	PO	A	E	DP
De Jesus Jr.	1.000	22	21	35	0	10

(Second Base cont.)	PCT	G	PO	A	E	DP
Iribarren	1.000	5	5	2	0	2
Pacheco	1.000	3	2	7	0	1
Peraza	.974	12	15	22	1	6
Phillips	.977	138	249	345	14	89
Renda	.964	9	8	19	1	4

Third Base	PCT	G	PO	A	E	DP
De Jesus Jr.	.955	14	5	16	1	1
Duvall	1.000	3	1	2	0	0
Pacheco	1.000	4	2	1	0	0
Renda	1.000	1	0	3	0	0
Suarez	.942	151	103	271	23	27

Shortstop	PCT	G	PO	A	E	DP
Cozart	.980	111	192	300	10	69
De Jesus Jr.	.991	30	41	73	1	16

(Shortstop cont.)	PCT	G	PO	A	E	DP
Peraza	.982	31	41	66	2	8
Suarez	1.000	2	3	3	0	1

Outfield	PCT	G	PO	A	E	DP
Bruce	.975	95	186	9	5	3
De Jesus Jr.	—	1	0	0	0	0
Duvall	.973	142	275	8	8	0
Hamilton	.990	115	276	9	3	4
Holt	.990	70	94	1	1	0
Iribarren	1.000	8	13	0	0	0
Kivlehan	1.000	2	2	0	0	0
Peraza	1.000	21	37	0	0	0
Renda	1.000	8	15	0	0	0
Schebler	.979	67	136	5	3	0
Selsky	1.000	15	29	1	0	0
Waldrop	1.000	4	4	0	0	0

LOUISVILLE BATS
TRIPLE-A
INTERNATIONAL LEAGUE

Batting	B-T	HT	WT	DOB	AVG	vLH	vRH	G	AB	R	H	2B	3B	HR	RBI	BB	HBP	SH	SF	SO	SB	CS	SLG	OBP
Allen, Brandon	L-R	6-2	230	2-12-86	.177	.154	.190	67	231	17	41	9	0	4	17	33	2	1	1	52	0	1	.268	.285
Amaral, Beau	L-L	5-10	177	2-11-91	.237	.200	.247	30	118	18	28	5	1	1	12	10	2	2	0	19	2	3	.322	.308
Berset, Chris	B-R	6-0	195	1-27-88	.249	.295	.223	85	289	34	72	7	0	2	28	25	0	3	3	57	1	0	.294	.306
Cabrera, Ramon	B-R	5-8	195	11-5-89	.259	.294	.243	15	54	3	14	1	0	0	2	1	0	0	1	6	0	0	.278	.268
Chang, Ray	R-R	6-1	195	8-24-83	.236	.208	.250	26	72	3	17	4	0	0	6	7	0	0	0	19	1	1	.292	.304
Curtis, Jermaine	R-R	5-11	190	7-10-87	.291	.337	.267	89	285	38	83	14	0	9	50	42	14	2	3	43	6	1	.435	.404
Herrera, Dilson	R-R	5-10	205	3-3-94	.266	.263	.267	24	64	10	17	0	2	2	9	11	1	2	2	15	1	2	.422	.372
Iribarren, Hernan	L-R	6-1	195	6-29-84	.327	.326	.327	101	373	46	122	20	1	3	35	33	0	2	2	60	3	5	.410	.380
Lopez, Rafael	L-R	5-9	200	10-2-87	.213	.233	.208	47	155	12	33	10	0	1	17	9	2	1	2	39	1	0	.297	.262
Lutz, Donald	L-R	6-3	240	2-6-89	.169	.182	.163	21	65	3	11	0	0	1	3	4	1	0	0	27	0	0	.215	.229
Mejias-Brean, Seth	R-R	6-2	216	4-15-91	.228	.246	.220	127	435	41	99	18	1	6	45	31	8	4	2	91	5	3	.315	.290
Pacheco, Jordan	R-R	6-1	200	1-30-86	.000	—	.000	5	14	0	0	0	0	0	1	1	0	0	0	5	0	0	.000	.067
2-team total (2 Gwinnett)					.045	—	—	7	22	1	1	0	0	0	1	1	1	0	0	7	0	0	.045	.125
Peraza, Jose	R-R	6-0	180	4-30-94	.281	.294	.274	71	288	40	81	15	3	2	21	21	2	10	1	43	10	7	.375	.333
Perez, Juan	L-R	5-11	185	11-1-91	.248	.233	.253	108	367	52	91	15	2	6	30	30	3	4	3	88	12	4	.349	.308
Renda, Tony	R-R	5-8	175	1-24-91	.276	.219	.301	30	105	13	29	3	1	1	9	10	2	4	0	16	2	3	.352	.350
Schebler, Scott	L-R	6-0	225	10-6-90	.311	.298	.319	75	289	40	90	18	8	13	43	19	9	0	2	59	2	0	.564	.370
Selsky, Steve	R-R	6-0	205	7-20-89	.280	.307	.264	85	296	40	83	24	1	9	37	29	11	0	3	74	2	1	.459	.363
Skipworth, Kyle	L-R	6-4	230	3-1-90	.182	.167	.188	7	22	3	4	2	0	0	3	1	0	0	1	9	0	0	.273	.208
Smith, Bryson	R-R	6-1	195	12-17-88	.174	.184	.167	49	121	12	21	2	0	0	6	9	4	3	0	31	1	0	.190	.254
Triunfel, Carlos	R-R	5-11	195	2-27-90	.278	.273	.280	105	378	36	105	29	1	4	40	3	7	5	1	70	1	1	.392	.296
Veras, Josciel	R-R	5-8	175	12-7-92	—	—	—	2	0	0	0	0	0	0	0	1	0	0	0	0	0	0	—	1.000
Waldrop, Kyle	L-L	6-2	215	11-26-91	.252	.290	.237	96	325	37	82	21	0	5	27	20	4	0	4	58	4	2	.363	.300
Winker, Jesse	L-L	6-3	215	8-17-93	.303	.260	.319	106	380	39	115	22	0	3	45	59	4	0	5	59	0	0	.384	.397

Pitching	B-T	HT	WT	DOB	W	L	ERA	G	GS	CG	SV	IP	H	R	ER	HR	BB	SO	AVG	vLH	vRH	K/9	BB/9
Adleman, Tim	R-R	6-5	225	11-13-87	4	4	4.00	13	13	0	0	70	64	32	31	12	20	47	.251	.256	.246	6.07	2.58
Bailey, Homer	R-R	6-4	225	5-3-86	2	3	6.65	6	6	0	0	23	35	19	17	2	7	27	0.35	.429	.293	10.57	2.74
Cingrani, Tony	L-L	6-4	210	7-5-89	2	5	4.14	65	0	0	17	63	54	30	29	5	37	49	.236	.207	.252	7.00	5.29
Cotham, Caleb	R-R	6-3	215	11-6-87	0	3	7.4	23	0	0	0	24	32	21	20	3	12	21	.323	.348	.302	7.77	4.44
De Los Santos, Abel	R-R	6-2	185	11-21-92	0	0	11.12	5	0	0	0	6	7	7	7	1	4	2	.318	.455	.182	3.18	6.35
Delabar, Steve	R-R	6-5	215	7-17-83	0	0	6.75	7	0	0	0	8	5	6	6	1	10	10	.172	.000	.333	11.25	11.25
DeSclafani, Anthony	R-R	6-1	200	4-18-90	9	5	3.28	20	20	1	0	123	120	51	45	16	30	105	.259	.303	.206	7.66	2.19
Diaz, Dayan	R-R	5-10	195	2-10-89	0	0	9.45	6	0	0	0	7	10	9	7	2	7	3	.37	.412	.340	.059	.450
Diaz, Jumbo	R-R	6-4	280	2-27-84	1	1	0.75	22	0	0	11	24	16	2	2	0	7	28	.186	.194	.180	10.50	2.63
Garrett, Amir	L-L	6-5	210	5-3-92	2	5	3.46	12	11	0	0	68	48	30	26	6	31	54	.202	.179	.206	7.18	4.12
Hayes, Drew	R-R	6-1	205	9-3-87	4	5	4.12	38	2	0	1	59	61	37	27	3	27	41	.270	.321	.239	6.25	4.12
Hoover, J.J.	R-R	6-3	240	8-13-87	4	2	3.52	32	0	0	4	38	39	15	15	2	11	50	.258	.271	.250	11.74	2.58
Johnson, Stephen	R-R	6-5	230	2-21-91	1	4	4.82	35	4	0	1	75	68	42	40	9	40	63	.244	.242	.245	7.59	4.82
Lamb, John	L-L	6-4	205	7-10-90	2	2	5.22	6	6	0	0	29	35	18	17	1	9	26	.299	.400	.256	7.98	2.76
Lorenzen, Michael	R-R	6-3	210	1-4-92	0	0	0.00	4	0	0	1	2	0	0	0	0	0	7	.000	.167	.143	15.70	0.00
Magill, Matt	R-R	6-3	210	11-10-89	4	1	4.46	29	0	0	0	42	40	24	21	6	21	43	.250	.208	.284	9.14	4.46
Mattheus, Ryan	R-R	6-3	220	11-10-83	1	1	6.43	6	0	0	0	7	8	6	5	0	4	6	.276	.200	.316	7.71	5.14
Mella, Keury	R-R	6-2	200	8-2-93	1	0	1.29	1	1	0	0	7	3	1	1	1	1	6	.130	.000	.231	7.71	1.29
Melville, Tim	R-R	6-4	225	10-9-89	1	1	4.32	6	0	0	0	8	10	7	4	1	5	7	.278	.222	.333	7.56	5.40
Morris, A.J.	R-R	6-2	195	12-1-86	0	2	3.96	18	6	0	0	39	46	24	17	5	11	32	.297	.323	.280	7.45	2.56
Moscot, Jon	R-R	6-4	210	8-15-91	4	4	5.26	9	9	0	0	50	58	29	29	9	16	31	.296	.304	.291	5.62	2.90
Muhammad, El'Hajj	R-R	6-2	219	7-7-91	0	0	6.00	1	0	0	0	3	6	2	2	0	4	2	.500	.667	.333	6.00	12.00
Peralta, Wandy	L-L	6-0	210	7-27-91	4	1	2.33	37	2	0	3	58	44	18	15	2	23	38	.216	.231	.211	5.90	3.57

Pitching

Pitching	B-T	HT	WT	DOB	W	L	ERA	G	GS	CG	SV	IP	H	R	ER	HR	BB	SO	AVG	vLH	vRH	K/9	BB/9
Ramirez, J.C.	R-R	6-4	250	8-16-88	0	0	0.00	5	0	0	0	6	4	0	0	0	3	10	.211	.333	.154	15.00	4.50
Reed, Cody	L-L	6-5	225	4-15-93	6	4	3.08	13	13	0	0	73	71	28	25	6	20	65	.259	.267	.256	8.01	2.47
Rogers, Chad	R-R	5-11	205	8-3-89	2	4	3.79	30	3	0	0	55	46	23	23	6	22	49	.225	.206	.235	8.07	3.62
2-team total (4 Gwinnett)					3	4	4.76	34	3	0	0	62	58	34	33	9	25	55	—	—	—	7.94	3.61
Routt, Nick	L-L	6-4	215	8-28-90	0	1	5.00	17	0	0	0	18	22	10	10	1	13	12	.314	.350	.300	6.00	6.50
Sampson, Keyvius	R-R	6-2	225	1-6-91	3	3	1.88	18	9	0	0	62	38	14	13	3	21	62	.174	.163	.181	8.95	3.03
Shackelford, Kevin	R-R	6-5	210	4-7-89	1	2	2.30	25	0	0	8	31	25	8	8	1	13	20	.214	.205	.219	5.74	3.73
Simon, Alfredo	R-R	6-6	265	5-8-81	0	2	4.80	5	5	0	0	15	17	8	8	1	6	7	.288	.318	.270	4.20	3.60
Smith, Josh	R-R	6-2	220	8-7-87	4	4	3.80	9	8	0	0	45	44	20	19	5	13	38	.262	.297	.240	7.60	2.60
Somsen, Layne	R-R	6-0	190	6-5-89	0	0	1.89	10	0	0	0	19	10	4	4	2	7	19	.154	.182	.140	9.00	3.32
2-team total (4 Scranton/W-B)					1	0	1.44	14	0	0	0	25	13	4	4	2	12	29	—	—	—	10.44	4.32
Stephenson, Robert	R-R	6-2	200	2-24-93	8	9	4.41	24	24	1	0	137	115	72	67	17	71	120	.228	.189	.251	7.90	4.68
Varner, Seth	L-L	6-3	225	1-27-92	0	2	24.75	2	2	0	0	4	16	14	11	1	4	3	.533	.333	.583	6.75	9.00
Villarreal, Pedro	R-R	6-1	235	12-9-87	0	0	4.05	4	0	0	0	7	7	3	3	0	3	4	.259	.417	.133	5.40	4.05
Wright, Daniel	R-R	6-2	205	4-3-91	6	5	6.13	17	12	2	0	84	109	66	57	10	25	65	.314	.319	.312	6.99	2.69

Fielding

Catcher	PCT	G	PO	A	E	DP	PB
Berset	.992	83	600	36	5	3	8
Cabrera	.985	14	124	5	2	1	
Lopez	.983	46	337	20	6	4	5
Skipworth	1.000	5	31	2	0	0	0

First Base	PCT	G	PO	A	E	DP
Allen	.996	54	442	25	2	40
Chang	1.000	18	128	9	0	13
Curtis	.986	9	65	4	1	7
Iribarren	.988	20	148	14	2	13
Mejias-Brean	.984	19	112	9	2	15
Pacheco	1.000	2	13	3	0	1
Selsky	.997	36	264	29	1	33

Second Base	PCT	G	PO	A	E	DP
Chang	.889	2	3	5	1	3
Curtis	1.000	8	14	18	0	4

	PCT/val	G	PO	A	E	DP
Herrera	1.000	16	23	37	0	10
Iribarren	.964	14	21	33	2	7
Pacheco	1.000	1	2	1	0	0
Peraza	1.000	5	15	11	0	4
Perez	.973	42	77	101	5	29
Renda	1.000	17	23	41	0	11
Triunfel	.983	53	99	136	4	36
Veras	1.000	1	0	1	0	0

Third Base	PCT	G	PO	A	E	DP
Chang	1.000	3	0	4	0	1
Curtis	.975	34	19	58	2	5
Iribarren	1.000	7	2	13	0	0
Mejias-Brean	.957	102	84	224	14	28
Pacheco	.667	2	0	4	2	0
Renda	1.000	6	2	8	0	1
Triunfel	.714	3	2	3	2	0

Shortstop	PCT	G	PO	A	E	DP
Iribarren	.942	14	16	33	3	6
Peraza	.951	58	74	157	12	31
Perez	.955	32	47	102	7	24
Triunfel	.970	44	59	105	5	25

Outfield	PCT	G	PO	A	E	DP
Amaral	.985	29	66	1	1	0
Iribarren	.969	42	91	2	3	0
Lutz	1.000	15	18	0	0	0
Peraza	1.000	6	16	0	0	0
Perez	1.000	25	51	3	0	0
Renda	1.000	7	14	1	0	0
Schebler	.994	73	176	0	1	0
Selsky	.987	39	71	6	1	4
Smith	.973	36	70	1	2	0
Veras	—	1	0	0	0	0
Waldrop	.962	83	141	10	6	1
Winker	.995	98	180	6	1	0

PENSACOLA BLUE WAHOOS — DOUBLE-A
SOUTHERN LEAGUE

Batting	B-T	HT	WT	DOB	AVG	vLH	vRH	G	AB	R	H	2B	3B	HR	RBI	BB	HBP	SH	SF	SO	SB	CS	SLG	OBP
Amaral, Beau	L-L	5-10	177	2-11-91	.246	.222	.258	38	138	17	34	4	2	3	17	13	3	3	3	33	2	2	.370	.318
Blandino, Alex	R-R	6-0	190	11-6-92	.232	.179	.253	113	401	52	93	18	0	8	37	55	7	0	2	114	14	5	.337	.333
Bueno, Ronald	B-R	5-10	154	10-4-92	.242	.000	.308	24	33	6	8	0	0	0	3	5	0	0	1	12	0	1	.242	.333
Chang, Ray	R-R	6-1	195	8-24-83	.269	.296	.246	46	119	13	32	5	0	0	14	9	1	1	1	28	0	0	.311	.323
Chen, Pin-Chieh	L-R	6-1	170	7-23-91	.182	.333	.095	14	33	4	6	1	0	0	0	7	0	1	0	6	1	0	.212	.325
Daal, Carlton	R-R	6-1	180	3-1-93	.310	.313	.310	40	116	15	36	3	1	1	6	9	1	1	0	26	5	1	.379	.365
Dixon, Brandon	R-R	6-2	215	1-29-92	.260	.256	.262	118	419	61	109	23	1	16	65	30	6	0	6	137	15	5	.434	.315
Duarte, Jose	R-R	6-2	222	4-23-93	.308	.500	.273	4	13	4	4	0	0	1	3	0	0	0	0	4	0	0	.538	.308
Duran, Juan	R-R	6-7	230	9-2-91	.217	.333	.176	16	46	3	10	2	0	0	6	4	0	0	1	19	0	0	.261	.275
Elizalde, Sebastian	L-R	6-0	175	11-20-91	.297	.268	.305	111	408	55	121	16	3	5	54	18	2	3	7	61	5	1	.387	.324
Ervin, Phillip	R-R	5-10	205	7-15-92	.239	.256	.232	123	419	71	100	22	3	13	45	65	18	0	3	88	36	10	.399	.362
Gelalich, Jeff	L-R	6-0	195	3-16-91	.249	.224	.257	75	237	28	59	12	5	2	21	15	1	3	1	93	10	0	.367	.295
Hudson, Joe	R-R	6-1	205	5-21-91	.203	.324	.135	67	207	21	42	12	0	2	16	31	3	1	0	59	0	0	.290	.315
Jagielo, Eric	L-R	6-3	210	5-17-92	.205	.153	.218	111	365	26	75	15	1	7	26	44	9	1	1	128	0	0	.310	.305
Lutz, Donald	L-R	6-3	240	2-6-89	.212	.222	.210	45	146	11	31	5	1	1	15	9	2	1	3	53	1	0	.281	.263
Parker, Kyle	R-R	6-0	205	9-30-89	.191	.235	.178	44	141	22	27	7	0	4	14	29	0	0	1	36	1	0	.326	.327
Renda, Tony	R-R	5-8	175	1-24-91	.326	.276	.346	68	261	36	85	25	3	2	28	14	5	0	2	20	15	1	.467	.369
Skipworth, Kyle	L-R	6-4	230	3-1-90	.143	.273	.123	28	84	10	12	1	0	4	9	12	1	1	1	32	0	0	.298	.255
Smith, Bryson	R-R	6-1	195	12-17-88	.200	.286	.161	12	45	4	9	1	1	0	5	3	1	0	1	6	0	0	.267	.260
Sparks, Taylor	R-R	6-4	200	2-23-93	.179	.163	.182	64	224	23	40	4	1	8	28	17	4	0	2	84	2	0	.313	.247
Vincej, Zach	R-R	5-11	177	5-1-91	.281	.222	.302	121	399	45	112	24	3	3	47	25	6	4	4	85	7	6	.378	.329
Wallach, Chad	R-R	6-3	230	11-4-91	.240	.256	.236	69	200	27	48	10	0	8	30	37	2	3	1	46	0	1	.410	.363

Pitching	B-T	HT	WT	DOB	W	L	ERA	G	GS	CG	SV	IP	H	R	ER	HR	BB	SO	AVG	vLH	vRH	K/9	BB/9
Astin, Barrett	R-R	6-1	200	10-22-91	9	3	2.26	37	11	0	0	103	74	31	26	8	25	96	.201	.222	.184	8.36	2.18
Bailey, Homer	R-R	6-4	225	5-3-86	0	1	2.25	1	1	0	0	4	6	5	1	0	2	3	.300	.333	.286	6.75	4.50
Chacin, Alejandro	R-R	6-0	204	6-24-93	5	2	1.78	52	0	0	30	61	51	12	12	2	26	75	.229	.248	.212	11.13	3.86
Cotham, Caleb	R-R	6-3	215	11-6-87	0	0	18.00	2	0	0	0	1	2	3	2	0	1	0	.333	.250	.500	0.00	9.00
Davis, Rookie	R-R	6-5	245	4-29-93	10	3	2.94	19	19	0	0	101	88	37	33	10	30	62	.237	.265	.211	5.52	2.67
De Los Santos, Abel	R-R	6-2	195	11-21-92	1	2	1.54	17	0	0	3	23	11	5	4	1	7	25	.134	.098	.171	9.64	2.70
DeSclafani, Anthony	R-R	6-1	200	4-18-90	0	0	6.75	1	1	0	0	4	4	3	3	2	1	5	.250	.333	.200	11.25	2.25
Ehret, Jake	R-R	6-3	190	3-18-93	3	2	5.40	22	0	0	0	30	29	20	18	2	21	31	.248	.275	.227	9.30	6.30
Garrett, Amir	L-L	6-5	210	5-3-92	5	3	1.75	13	12	0	0	77	51	20	15	0	28	78	.184	.194	.181	9.12	3.27

Pitching

Pitching	B-T	HT	WT	DOB	W	L	ERA	G	GS	CG	SV	IP	H	R	ER	HR	BB	SO	AVG	vLH	vRH	K/9	BB/9
Gonzalez, Carlos	R-R	6-1	213	6-12-90	7	3	3.77	49	0	0	8	62	50	28	26	4	22	57	.226	.240	.214	8.27	3.19
Iglesias, Raisel	R-R	6-2	185	1-4-90	0	0	0.00	3	2	0	0	5	3	0	0	1	5	.167	.143	.182	9.00	1.80
Magill, Matt	R-R	6-3	210	11-10-89	0	0	6.52	9	0	0	1	10	12	7	7	0	6	16	.308	.222	.381	14.90	5.59
Mahle, Tyler	R-R	6-4	200	9-29-94	6	3	4.92	14	14	0	0	71	78	45	39	12	20	65	.281	.278	.283	8.20	2.52
McMyne, Kyle	R-R	5-11	212	10-18-89	5	4	5.24	46	0	0	5	57	70	34	33	3	19	37	.310	.323	.299	5.88	3.02
Mitchell, Evan	R-R	6-2	175	3-18-92	4	1	2.70	33	0	0	0	47	38	14	14	2	15	32	.226	.205	.244	6.17	2.89
Moran, Jimmy	R-R	6-1	180	6-7-90	0	1	5.40	11	0	0	0	12	14	10	7	1	7	17	.280	.316	.258	13.11	5.40
Muhammad, El'Hajj	R-R	6-2	219	7-7-91	2	1	3.94	33	2	0	0	48	47	27	21	4	19	35	.254	.200	.295	6.56	3.56
Peralta, Wandy	L-L	6-0	210	7-27-91	0	1	3.06	13	0	0	0	18	17	6	6	1	3	20	.250	.350	.208	10.19	1.53
Romano, Sal	L-R	6-5	260	10-12-93	6	11	3.52	27	27	0	0	156	157	71	61	10	34	144	.260	.260	.261	8.31	1.96
Routt, Nick	L-L	6-4	215	8-28-90	2	0	0.89	33	0	0	0	50	29	5	5	1	12	46	.166	.190	.154	8.23	2.15
Shackelford, Kevin	R-R	6-5	210	4-7-89	1	0	1.38	10	0	0	0	13	11	4	2	1	4	11	.229	.300	.179	7.62	2.77
Stephens, Jackson	R-R	6-3	205	5-11-94	8	11	3.33	27	26	1	0	151	148	63	56	7	41	131	.254	.278	.235	7.79	2.44
Travieso, Nick	R-R	6-2	225	1-31-94	5	7	3.84	23	23	0	0	117	109	55	50	11	53	91	.248	.214	.278	6.98	4.07
Wright, Daniel	R-R	6-2	205	4-3-91	2	0	0.45	8	2	0	0	20	10	1	1	0	4	22	.145	.111	.167	9.90	1.80

Fielding

Catcher	PCT	G	PO	A	E	DP	PB
Duarte	1.000	3	17	3	0	0	1
Hudson	.995	66	512	67	3	2	12
Skipworth	.971	27	179	24	6	3	3
Wallach	.991	52	385	39	4	5	4

First Base	PCT	G	PO	A	E	DP
Chang	.996	37	236	16	1	18
Dixon	.985	11	63	1	1	5
Elizalde	1.000	1	5	1	0	1
Jagielo	.987	46	349	26	5	33
Lutz	.966	19	139	5	5	9
Parker	.994	38	303	33	2	18
Wallach	1.000	13	93	7	0	10

Second Base	PCT	G	PO	A	E	DP
Blandino	.977	74	123	173	7	37
Bueno	.909	6	5	5	1	1
Chang	.000	1	0	0	1	0
Dixon	.962	62	109	167	11	30
Renda	.923	6	12	12	2	2
Vincej	1.000	11	16	24	0	6

Third Base	PCT	G	PO	A	E	DP
Blandino	.966	30	17	40	2	3
Chang	1.000	2	0	5	0	0
Dixon	1.000	1	1	1	0	0
Jagielo	.902	49	19	73	10	3
Renda	.960	11	6	18	1	0
Sparks	.949	60	37	131	9	10
Vincej	1.000	1	1	1	0	0

Shortstop	PCT	G	PO	A	E	DP
Blandino	.962	16	19	32	2	7
Bueno	—	1	0	0	0	0
Daal	.922	31	38	69	9	11
Vincej	.991	105	137	282	4	54

Outfield	PCT	G	PO	A	E	DP
Amaral	1.000	37	74	1	0	0
Bueno	.500	2	1	0	1	0
Chen	1.000	9	16	1	0	0
Dixon	1.000	38	65	2	0	1
Duran	.933	10	14	0	1	0
Elizalde	.982	96	160	2	3	0
Ervin	.988	113	237	3	3	1
Gelalich	.992	63	130	2	1	0
Lutz	1.000	6	10	0	0	0
Parker	1.000	3	3	0	0	0
Renda	.955	47	82	3	4	0
Smith	1.000	12	24	2	0	1

DAYTONA TORTUGAS
FLORIDA STATE LEAGUE

HIGH CLASS A

Batting	B-T	HT	WT	DOB	AVG	vLH	vRH	G	AB	R	H	2B	3B	HR	RBI	BB	HBP	SH	SF	SO	SB	CS	SLG	OBP
Aquino, Aristides	R-R	6-4	190	4-22-94	.273	.240	.284	125	484	69	132	26	12	23	79	34	6	0	2	104	11	7	.519	.327
Boulware, Garrett	R-R	6-2	200	9-9-92	.223	.264	.211	70	233	23	52	10	0	3	23	21	2	4	1	49	0	0	.305	.292
Bueno, Ronald	B-R	5-10	154	10-4-92	.245	.217	.250	40	151	25	37	10	1	3	15	21	0	1	0	28	4	1	.384	.337
Butler, Blake	R-R	6-3	195	10-29-93	.222	.155	.246	87	320	28	71	12	0	5	28	15	8	3	4	58	4	2	.306	.271
Duran, Juan	R-R	6-7	230	9-2-91	.371	.350	.377	24	89	14	33	8	1	3	18	4	1	0	0	27	1	0	.584	.404
Gelalich, Jeff	L-R	6-0	210	3-16-91	.235	.444	.203	24	68	7	16	1	2	0	4	14	2	3	3	30	7	1	.309	.368
Gumbs, Angelo	R-R	6-0	175	10-13-92	.298	.295	.299	98	376	54	112	18	5	11	55	25	1	0	1	48	8	2	.460	.342
LaValley, Gavin	R-R	6-3	235	12-28-94	.275	.233	.290	92	338	50	93	29	2	11	61	29	3	0	4	72	0	0	.470	.334
Liberatore, Ernesto	R-R	6-0	180	3-26-96	.333	—	.333	1	3	0	1	0	0	0	0	0	0	0	0	0	0	0	.333	.333
Long, Shed	L-R	5-8	180	8-22-95	.322	.167	.363	38	143	22	46	6	4	4	30	10	3	0	3	35	5	1	.503	.371
Medina, Reydel	L-L	6-0	220	2-14-93	.309	.421	.288	36	123	21	38	12	3	3	19	3	0	0	4	44	2	1	.528	.325
O'Grady, Brian	L-R	6-2	215	5-17-92	.235	.291	.218	107	345	45	81	16	6	9	40	67	5	2	4	96	16	4	.394	.363
Pickens, Jimmy	L-R	6-0	220	3-18-92	.174	.200	.167	7	23	3	4	0	0	1	6	0	0	0	1	2	0	0	.174	.345
Rachal, Avain	R-R	6-0	195	2-11-94	.203	.184	.211	42	133	18	27	2	1	4	10	26	4	1	0	51	4	1	.323	.350
Rahier, Tanner	R-R	5-11	200	10-12-93	.286	.300	.278	8	28	1	8	1	0	0	3	0	1	0	1	3	0	1	.321	.300
Reynoso, Jonathan	R-R	6-3	177	1-7-93	.285	.235	.303	112	386	49	110	8	3	0	36	17	3	4	2	91	31	11	.321	.319
Rodriguez, Yorman	R-R	6-2	210	8-22-95	.346	.250	.364	11	26	3	9	1	0	0	1	0	6	0	0	9	0	0	.385	.370
Sparks, Taylor	R-R	6-4	200	4-3-93	.220	.227	.218	65	245	26	54	14	1	6	34	11	5	1	3	57	6	4	.359	.265
Trahan, Blake	R-R	5-9	180	9-5-93	.263	.303	.249	131	521	90	137	21	9	4	47	49	1	12	4	73	25	8	.361	.325
Tromp, Chadwick	R-R	5-9	180	3-21-95	.215	.230	.209	73	261	29	56	12	0	8	38	11	2	1	3	55	1	1	.352	.249
Washington, Ty	R-R	5-9	174	9-1-93	.238	.227	.242	68	240	37	57	14	2	5	11	18	1	4	0	57	3	1	.375	.293

Pitching	B-T	HT	WT	DOB	W	L	ERA	G	GS	CG	SV	IP	H	R	ER	HR	BB	SO	AVG	vLH	vRH	K/9	BB/9
Antone, Tejay	R-R	6-4	205	12-5-93	14	6	3.51	25	25	1	0	151	167	77	59	16	28	105	.280	.329	.244	6.24	1.67
Bautista, Wendolyn	R-R	6-0	185	3-27-93	3	1	2.01	10	10	0	0	45	34	15	10	2	16	19	.214	.275	.167	3.83	3.22
Becker, Nolan	R-L	6-6	225	6-13-91	0	2	2.96	31	1	0	1	46	50	17	15	4	13	36	.276	.269	.279	7.09	2.56
Bernardino, Brennan	L-L	6-4	180	1-15-92	5	3	3.71	50	0	0	1	61	62	25	25	5	25	61	.270	.288	.262	9.05	3.71
Brattvet, Scott	R-R	6-1	195	7-21-91	0	0	108.00	1	0	0	0	0	2	4	4	0	2	0	.667	1.000	.500	0.00	54.00
Crawford, Jonathon	R-R	6-2	205	11-1-91	1	3	6.35	6	6	0	0	23	28	19	16	1	13	9	.322	.425	.234	3.57	5.16
Ehret, Jake	R-R	6-3	190	3-18-93	1	2	2.59	23	0	0	6	31	27	9	9	2	7	32	.237	.289	.211	9.19	2.01
Guillon, Ismael	L-L	6-1	225	2-13-92	7	2	2.41	32	13	0	0	93	50	27	25	10	39	116	.162	.133	.174	11.19	3.76
Herget, Jimmy	R-R	6-3	170	9-9-93	4	4	1.78	50	0	0	24	61	47	16	12	3	21	86	.208	.226	.197	12.31	3.26
Hernandez, Ariel	R-R	6-3	180	3-2-92	3	1	1.76	25	0	0	3	31	18	8	6	1	19	34	.164	.125	.186	9.98	5.58

Pitching

Pitching	B-T	HT	WT	DOB	W	L	ERA	G	GS	CG	SV	IP	H	R	ER	HR	BB	SO	AVG	vLH	vRH	K/9	BB/9
Howard, Nick	R-R	6-4	215	4-6-93	0	1	6.75	25	0	0	1	20	20	18	15	1	31	20	.263	.265	.262	9.00	13.95
Kivel, Jeremy	R-R	6-1	200	10-16-93	0	0	10.80	9	0	0	0	7	9	9	8	0	10	5	.333	.308	.357	6.75	13.50
Klimesh, Ben	R-R	6-4	220	5-14-90	0	0	9.82	4	0	0	0	4	4	4	4	0	8	4	.083	.333	.000	9.82	19.64
Krauss, Conor	R-R	6-5	235	6-14-93	0	0	4.50	4	0	0	0	4	5	2	2	0	5	2	.313	.250	.375	4.50	11.25
Lopez, Jose	R-R	6-1	185	9-1-93	0	3	4.41	6	5	0	0	35	29	22	17	3	10	34	.227	.217	.232	8.83	2.60
Mahle, Tyler	R-R	6-4	200	9-29-94	8	3	2.50	13	13	1	0	79	58	24	22	1	17	76	.206	.200	.209	8.62	1.93
Martinez, Juan	L-L	6-2	175	7-15-92	1	1	5.16	22	0	0	0	30	34	17	17	1	16	19	.304	.297	.307	5.76	4.85
Mella, Keury	R-R	6-2	200	8-2-93	8	9	3.90	25	24	0	0	132	150	67	57	7	56	95	.290	.284	.294	6.49	3.83
Mitchell, Evan	R-R	6-2	175	3-18-92	1	1	3.38	12	1	0	1	16	13	6	6	0	6	18	.220	.238	.211	10.13	3.38
Moran, Jimmy	R-R	6-1	180	6-7-90	2	0	2.12	11	0	0	0	17	10	4	4	1	5	16	.172	.190	.162	8.47	2.65
Moscot, Jon	R-R	6-4	210	8-15-91	0	0	0.00	1	1	0	0	4	5	0	0	0	1	1	.333	.200	.400	2.45	2.45
Muhammad, El'Hajj	R-R	6-2	219	7-7-91	1	0	5.63	6	0	0	0	8	10	5	5	2	2	7	.303	.083	.429	7.88	2.25
Paulson, Jake	R-R	6-7	210	2-17-92	0	6	6.40	10	8	0	0	32	43	28	23	1	10	27	.307	.359	.263	7.52	2.78
Powers, Alex	R-R	6-4	180	2-26-92	9	0	3.13	48	0	0	1	63	51	27	22	1	20	66	.221	.291	.184	9.38	2.84
Strahan, Wyatt	R-R	6-3	220	4-18-93	0	1	3.80	4	4	0	0	24	26	10	10	0	8	15	.280	.325	.245	5.70	3.04
Sullivan, Michael	L-L	6-0	210	1-14-94	0	3	7.11	12	5	0	0	25	29	21	20	4	17	27	.293	.278	.296	9.59	6.04
Varner, Seth	L-L	6-3	225	1-27-92	8	9	3.83	29	21	1	0	134	151	63	57	10	27	100	.288	.268	.293	6.72	1.81
Williams, Greg	L-L	6-4	205	12-30-89	0	0	4.22	9	0	0	0	11	7	5	5	1	4	7	.179	.333	.133	5.91	3.38

Fielding

Catcher	PCT	G	PO	A	E	DP	PB
Boulware	.991	69	533	44	5	1	9
Tromp	.995	69	508	54	3	5	10

First Base	PCT	G	PO	A	E	DP
Gumbs	1.000	2	14	2	0	3
LaValley	.992	62	478	24	4	49
Medina	1.000	6	46	2	0	6
O'Grady	.989	31	246	17	3	26
Rachal	.995	41	359	30	2	27

Second Base	PCT	G	PO	A	E	DP
Bueno	.953	7	15	26	2	12
Butler	.983	66	112	182	5	36
Gumbs	1.000	2	1	5	0	0
Long	.971	38	65	103	5	29
Washington	.935	26	47	83	9	11

Third Base	PCT	G	PO	A	E	DP
Bueno	.920	23	22	47	6	4
Butler	.968	11	7	23	1	0
Gumbs	1.000	1	0	2	0	0
LaValley	.889	24	14	34	6	6
Rachal	.500	1	0	1	1	0
Rahier	1.000	8	3	13	0	1
Sparks	.942	62	37	124	10	10
Washington	.963	9	7	19	1	2

Shortstop	PCT	G	PO	A	E	DP
Bueno	.810	4	8	9	4	3
Butler	.967	8	9	20	1	3
Trahan	.974	124	186	368	15	76
Washington	.857	1	2	4	1	0

Outfield	PCT	G	PO	A	E	DP
Aquino	.970	123	234	28	8	4
Duran	1.000	6	11	0	0	0
Gelalich	1.000	20	28	0	0	0
Gumbs	.960	60	94	2	4	1
Medina	.900	27	35	1	4	1
O'Grady	.991	62	104	6	1	1
Pickens	1.000	5	5	0	0	0
Reynoso	.978	112	258	7	6	0
Rodriguez	1.000	5	2	0	0	0

DAYTON DRAGONS
MIDWEST LEAGUE

LOW CLASS A

Batting	B-T	HT	WT	DOB	AVG	vLH	vRH	G	AB	R	H	2B	3B	HR	RBI	BB	HBP	SH	SF	SO	SB	CS	SLG	OBP
Aldazoro, Argenis	L-L	6-2	160	9-17-92	.176	.222	.160	20	68	3	12	1	0	0	3	5	0	1	0	15	2	1	.191	.233
Bell, Brantley	R-R	6-3	185	11-16-94	.248	.203	.269	114	412	34	102	16	3	1	36	33	6	5	2	103	23	9	.388	.311
Charlton, Ed	R-R	6-1	190	11-20-92	.182	.238	.147	34	110	11	20	5	1	2	7	11	1	2	2	46	1	1	.300	.258
Chavez, Alberti	R-R	5-10	170	7-21-95	.333	1.000	.143	3	9	1	3	2	0	1	3	0	0	0	1	0	0	0	.889	.300
Crook, Narciso	R-R	6-3	220	7-12-95	.244	.167	.276	23	82	12	20	4	0	3	7	6	2	0	0	23	2	1	.402	.311
Duarte, Jose	R-R	6-2	222	4-23-93	.214	.115	.250	29	98	4	21	1	0	1	8	7	0	0	0	29	0	0	.255	.267
Duran, Juan	R-R	6-7	230	9-2-91	.158	.143	.167	5	19	1	3	1	0	0	0	0	0	0	0	5	0	0	.211	.158
Franklin, K.J.	R-R	6-1	220	11-24-94	.225	.300	.177	28	102	4	23	5	0	1	10	3	1	0	0	28	0	0	.304	.255
Garcia, Narciso	R-R	6-1	177	6-19-93	.187	.190	.184	25	91	5	17	2	0	0	5	6	0	1	0	15	2	1	.209	.237
Gonzalez, Luis	R-R	6-0	175	7-28-94	.228	.268	.209	105	381	30	87	23	2	3	36	18	0	2	3	87	4	1	.323	.261
LaValley, Gavin	R-R	6-3	235	12-28-94	.211	.000	.400	5	19	2	4	1	0	0	0	3	0	0	0	7	0	0	.263	.318
Liberatore, Ernesto	R-R	6-0	180	3-26-96	.111	.167	.000	3	9	0	1	0	0	0	0	0	0	0	0	2	0	0	.111	.111
Long, Shed	L-R	5-8	180	8-22-95	.281	.327	.261	94	335	47	94	24	1	11	45	44	5	4	1	85	16	3	.457	.371
Mardirosian, Shane	L-R	5-10	175	10-13-95	.226	.198	.233	111	394	39	89	13	5	2	24	29	8	0	2	79	9	9	.299	.291
Medina, Reydel	L-L	6-0	220	2-14-93	.235	.204	.246	54	187	17	44	9	4	5	20	4	2	0	2	79	8	4	.406	.256
Okey, Chris	R-R	5-11	195	12-29-94	.243	.286	.230	42	148	21	36	8	1	6	21	14	4	2	1	49	5	0	.432	.323
Piatnik, Mitch	B-R	6-0	170	9-12-94	.238	.303	.217	78	273	39	65	11	2	3	16	16	1	6	1	115	10	6	.326	.282
Rachal, Avain	R-R	6-0	195	2-11-94	.227	.143	.267	7	22	3	5	0	0	0	1	2	2	0	0	9	1	1	.227	.346
Rahier, Tanner	R-R	5-11	200	10-12-93	.221	.208	.227	16	68	8	15	2	0	1	6	3	2	0	1	16	0	1	.294	.243
Senzel, Nick	R-R	6-1	205	6-29-95	.329	.292	.340	58	210	38	69	23	3	7	36	32	2	1	4	49	15	7	.567	.415
Shields, Zach	L-R	6-2	160	5-12-93	.240	.306	.216	101	367	44	88	14	6	0	19	24	4	2	1	82	22	9	.311	.293
Siri, Jose	R-R	6-2	175	7-22-95	.145	.100	.170	27	83	5	12	3	0	0	3	2	0	1	1	34	3	2	.181	.163
Stephenson, Tyler	R-R	6-4	225	8-16-96	.216	.204	.200	39	139	17	30	4	1	3	16	12	0	2	0	45	0	3	.324	.278
Sweet, Daniel	B-L	6-0	190	12-28-94	.243	.172	.261	36	140	19	34	6	4	3	18	12	1	1	0	47	6	3	.407	.307
Thompson, Cory	R-R	5-11	180	9-23-94	.148	.143	.150	8	27	4	4	1	0	0	1	2	0	0	0	10	0	1	.185	.207
Trees, Mitch	R-R	6-0	200	7-18-95	.158	.173	.151	49	158	10	25	6	1	1	10	10	0	1	0	67	0	0	.228	.208
Vargas, Hector	R-R	6-2	170	1-27-95	.194	.185	.200	36	129	9	25	4	1	0	8	8	0	2	1	34	1	0	.240	.215
Vasquez, James	L-L	6-0	220	11-8-92	.223	.191	.235	130	475	46	106	20	1	14	66	43	7	0	4	92	2	1	.358	.295
Veras, Josciel	R-R	5-8	175	12-7-92	.216	.269	.188	26	74	12	16	4	0	2	9	6	2	1	0	21	1	0	.351	.293

Pitching	B-T	HT	WT	DOB	W	L	ERA	G	GS	CG	SV	IP	H	R	ER	HR	BB	SO	AVG	vLH	vRH	K/9	BB/9
Adams, Jesse	L-L	6-0	190	8-12-93	0	0	4.50	2	0	0	0	4	3	2	2	0	3	4	.214	.333	.182	9.00	6.75
Arias, Junior Joselin	R-R	6-3	170	11-10-93	0	0	13.50	4	0	0	0	3	6	5	5	1	1	2	.375	.429	.333	5.40	2.70

CINCINNATI REDS

Pitching	B-T	HT	WT	DOB	W	L	ERA	G	GS	CG	SV	IP	H	R	ER	HR	BB	SO	AVG	vLH	vRH	K/9	BB/9
Aybar, Manuel	R-R	6-3	240	1-6-93	3	5	4.19	40	0	0	2	58	45	35	27	4	43	75	.210	.255	.167	11.64	6.67
Bautista, Wendolyn	R-R	6-0	185	3-27-93	2	0	3.15	7	4	1	0	34	36	12	12	2	8	25	.281	.280	.283	6.55	2.10
Benenati, Lucas	R-R	6-2	215	5-27-93	0	2	2.77	14	0	0	0	26	28	13	8	2	1	25	.267	.250	.281	8.65	0.35
Boyles, Ty	R-L	6-3	270	9-30-95	6	8	4.81	24	22	0	0	122	131	69	65	7	49	98	.281	.300	.273	7.25	3.62
Constante, Jacob	L-L	6-4	235	3-22-94	4	9	4.50	26	18	0	0	108	112	65	54	2	51	68	.273	.258	.279	5.67	4.25
DeSclafani, Anthony	R-R	6-1	200	4-18-90	0	0	0.00	1	1	0	0	5	3	0	0	0	1	3	.176	.125	.222	5.40	1.80
Hendrix, Ryan	R-R	6-3	185	12-16-94	3	1	3.04	15	0	0	0	27	21	9	9	0	8	31	.212	.208	.216	10.46	2.70
Hernandez, Ariel	R-R	6-3	180	3-2-92	0	1	2.59	18	0	0	2	31	11	10	9	0	20	40	.107	.122	.097	11.49	5.74
Johnson, Jake	R-R	6-2	185	6-5-93	0	4	10.30	13	3	0	0	25	42	35	29	3	14	27	.365	.425	.333	9.59	4.97
Kivel, Jeremy	R-R	6-1	200	10-16-93	2	3	5.19	28	0	0	4	35	34	26	20	1	29	42	.260	.232	.280	10.90	7.53
Krauss, Conor	R-R	6-5	235	6-14-93	0	3	5.79	13	0	0	0	14	13	14	9	0	16	10	.236	.174	.281	6.43	10.29
Lopez, Jose	R-R	6-1	185	9-1-93	6	9	3.97	21	21	0	0	113	118	61	50	2	32	113	.262	.286	.238	8.97	2.54
Lugo, Sandy	R-R	6-0	170	3-26-94	1	1	2.45	30	0	0	2	55	46	22	15	6	13	77	.223	.260	.179	12.60	2.13
Martinez, Juan	L-L	6-2	175	7-15-92	3	2	1.60	25	0	0	0	34	37	9	6	0	8	27	.280	.273	.286	7.22	2.14
Moreta, Bernardo	R-R	6-2	180	2-2-93	0	1	5.19	6	0	0	0	9	10	6	5	0	7	7	.313	.350	.250	7.27	7.27
Ohanian, Sarkis	R-R	5-11	195	8-6-93	0	3	3.31	34	0	0	13	35	20	15	13	1	13	61	.159	.241	.097	15.54	3.31
Orewiler, Austin	R-R	6-2	220	5-18-93	3	14	4.05	28	23	1	0	131	150	75	59	3	40	79	.291	.293	.288	5.43	2.75
Ortiz, Braulio	R-R	6-7	253	12-20-91	0	1	6.06	12	0	0	0	16	16	14	11	2	5	23	.254	.154	.324	12.67	2.76
Rainey, Tanner	R-R	6-2	235	12-25-92	5	10	5.57	29	20	0	1	103	109	70	64	9	66	113	.273	.295	.252	9.84	5.75
Ramsey, Jordan	L-R	6-4	215	9-6-92	0	0	7.53	7	0	0	0	14	10	13	12	2	14	12	.185	.192	.179	7.53	8.79
Reyes, Jesus	R-R	6-2	180	2-21-93	5	5	2.40	30	10	0	2	94	73	31	25	3	37	68	.219	.253	.186	6.53	3.56
Romero, Franderlyn	R-R	6-1	190	2-21-93	1	4	2.87	8	8	0	0	47	46	22	15	1	9	42	.250	.265	.233	8.04	1.72
Santillan, Tony	R-R	6-3	240	4-15-97	2	3	6.82	7	7	0	0	30	27	23	23	3	24	38	.245	.226	.263	11.27	7.12
Sullivan, Michael	L-L	6-0	210	1-14-94	0	2	5.52	30	0	0	1	31	38	25	19	3	13	29	.288	.228	.333	8.42	3.77
Webb, Alex	R-R	6-3	210	7-19-94	1	2	4.15	3	3	0	0	13	13	8	6	0	2	7	.265	.227	.296	4.85	1.38

Fielding

Catcher	PCT	G	PO	A	E	DP	PB
Duarte	.984	27	224	23	4	3	4
Liberatore	1.000	2	4	2	0	0	0
Okey	.989	27	323	38	4	1	6
Stephenson	.987	27	213	23	3	3	5
Trees	.990	49	323	72	4	4	14

	PCT	G	PO	A	E	DP
Mardirosian	.975	22	41	77	3	15
Rahier	—	1	0	0	0	0
Vargas	.958	5	8	15	1	2
Veras	1.000	2	2	4	0	2

Third Base	PCT	G	PO	A	E	DP
Bell	.868	47	32	73	16	10
Duarte	1.000	1	0	1	0	0
Franklin	1.000	1	0	2	0	0
LaValley	—	1	0	0	0	0
Long	.800	3	2	2	1	2
Rahier	.921	13	8	27	3	2
Senzel	.945	56	30	108	8	12
Vargas	.828	13	8	16	5	3
Veras	1.000	7	3	12	0	1

	PCT	G	PO	A	E	DP
Piatnik	—	1	0	0	0	0
Thompson	.786	7	9	13	6	3
Vargas	.981	12	10	43	1	11

Outfield	PCT	G	PO	A	E	DP
Aldazoro	.957	11	20	2	1	0
Bell	1.000	1	3	0	0	0
Charlton	.978	26	44	0	1	0
Crook	.951	21	37	2	2	0
Duran	1.000	5	6	1	0	1
Franklin	1.000	3	3	0	0	0
Garcia	1.000	19	28	0	0	0
Mardirosian	.984	67	118	6	2	1
Medina	.942	48	77	4	5	1
Piatnik	.981	72	143	13	3	3
Shields	.944	85	163	6	10	1
Siri	.942	26	62	3	4	0
Sweet	.965	31	52	3	2	0
Veras	1.000	13	19	0	0	0

First Base	PCT	G	PO	A	E	DP
Aldazoro	.968	4	25	5	1	4
Franklin	.989	10	82	6	1	5
LaValley	.964	3	26	1	1	3
Medina	1.000	3	17	0	0	2
Rachal	.963	4	22	4	1	2
Vasquez	.988	120	998	70	13	97

Second Base	PCT	G	PO	A	E	DP
Bell	.941	28	47	80	8	20
Chavez	1.000	3	3	8	0	1
Long	.973	82	144	223	10	48

Shortstop	PCT	G	PO	A	E	DP
Bell	.958	21	38	53	4	13
Gonzalez	.959	101	160	265	18	63

BILLINGS MUSTANGS ROOKIE

PIONEER LEAGUE

Batting	B-T	HT	WT	DOB	AVG	vLH	vRH	G	AB	R	H	2B	3B	HR	RBI	BB	HBP	SH	SF	SO	SB	CS	SLG	OBP
Amaral, Beau	L-L	5-10	177	2-11-91	.389	.375	.393	11	36	6	14	1	0	1	5	6	0	0	1	8	1	1	.500	.465
Beltre, Michael	B-R	6-3	180	7-3-95	.309	.400	.268	22	81	14	25	9	0	3	13	15	1	0	0	13	4	1	.531	.423
Blankmeyer, Ty	R-R	5-7	170	10-12-93	.280	.308	.268	26	82	15	23	3	0	0	11	5	5	2	1	12	4	0	.317	.355
Brown, Cassidy	R-R	6-3	215	7-21-94	.322	.419	.297	43	149	28	48	6	0	1	25	20	4	2	3	32	4	1	.383	.409
Chavez, Alberti	R-R	5-10	170	7-21-95	.303	.400	.278	38	99	17	30	4	0	1	11	6	0	0	2	28	3	3	.374	.336
Friedl, T.J.	L-L	5-10	170	8-14-95	.347	.280	.365	29	121	24	42	11	2	3	17	13	3	0	0	25	7	2	.545	.423
Gordon, Miles	L-R	6-1	185	12-3-97	.262	.538	.192	22	65	11	17	3	2	0	11	11	1	2	1	14	3	2	.369	.372
Guerrero, Francis	R-R	6-3	185	11-16-94	.333	.500	.250	5	12	2	4	1	0	1	1	0	0	0	0	2	0	0	.667	.333
Lofstrom, Morgan	L-R	6-1	185	8-17-95	.197	.000	.260	22	66	5	13	4	0	1	8	4	2	2	0	26	0	1	.303	.264
Lopez, Alejo	B-R	5-10	170	5-5-96	.273	.226	.289	57	205	36	56	6	1	1	29	21	1	1	1	19	11	3	.327	.342
Marshall, Montrell	R-R	6-5	215	4-2-96	.246	.180	.264	59	224	37	55	14	0	1	26	29	3	0	1	76	3	1	.321	.339
McElroy, Satchel	R-R	5-10	170	8-13-96	.212	.100	.238	36	104	12	22	4	1	0	11	14	2	3	1	23	7	2	.269	.248
Okey, Chris	R-R	5-11	195	12-29-94	.162	.333	.147	9	37	5	6	1	0	0	1	1	0	0	1	8	0	0	.189	.179
Ovalle, Gabriel	B-R	6-2	170	10-28-94	.279	.125	.314	27	86	10	24	4	2	0	13	5	0	0	1	22	1	1	.372	.315
Piatnik, Mitch	R-R	6-0	170	9-12-94	.333	.200	.368	11	48	8	16	4	1	0	6	2	1	1	0	12	4	1	.458	.373
Rachal, Avain	R-R	6-0	195	2-11-94	.250	.500	.000	3	8	3	2	0	0	0	0	0	0	0	0	5	0	0	.250	.250
Sansone, John	R-R	5-11	200	9-15-93	.285	.366	.263	50	193	34	55	12	1	5	25	12	4	0	2	51	4	3	.435	.336
Senzel, Nick	R-R	6-1	205	6-29-95	.329	.263	.346	58	225	40	74	15	1	7	30	24	5	0	3	35	15	6	.567	.415
Siri, Jose	R-R	6-2	175	7-22-95	.320	.350	.309	59	241	52	77	12	8	10	35	8	3	2	1	66	17	4	.560	.348
Sweet, Daniel	B-L	6-0	190	12-28-94	.333	.400	.315	24	69	13	23	3	5	1	9	20	1	1	1	16	5	3	.565	.484
Trammell, Taylor	L-L	6-2	195	9-13-97	.303	.340	.292	61	228	39	69	9	6	2	34	23	4	0	4	55	24	7	.421	.374
Trees, Mitch	R-R	6-0	200	7-18-95	.194	.091	.225	27	93	12	18	1	1	4	13	7	1	0	0	37	4	1	.355	.257
Vargas, Hector	R-R	6-2	170	1-27-95	.352	.449	.323	57	210	32	74	17	2	6	41	6	0	3	3	19	12	3	.538	.365

Batting	B-T	HT	WT	DOB	AVG	vLH	vRH	G	AB	R	H	2B	3B	HR	RBI	BB	HBP	SH	SF	SO	SB	CS	SLG	OBP
Veras, Josciel	R-R	5-8	175	12-7-92	.333	.000	.400	2	6	2	2	1	0	1	1	0	0	0	0	1	0	0	1.000	.333
Wright, Colby	R-R	6-2	195	4-11-94	.225	.400	.179	39	120	23	27	6	0	5	32	19	9	0	5	29	6	2	.400	.359

Pitching	B-T	HT	WT	DOB	W	L	ERA	G	GS	CG	SV	IP	H	R	ER	HR	BB	SO	AVG	vLH	vRH	K/9	BB/9
Adams, Jesse	L-L	6-0	190	8-12-93	1	2	1.32	14	0	0	0	14	8	5	2	0	4	13	.157	.250	.114	8.56	2.63
Arias, Junior Joselin	R-R	6-3	170	11-10-93	1	0	2.18	16	0	0	3	21	15	5	5	0	7	19	.211	.231	.200	8.27	3.05
Benenati, Lucas	R-R	6-2	215	5-27-93	1	0	6.00	9	0	0	4	9	11	7	6	0	4	12	.306	.556	.222	12.00	4.00
Correll, Zac	R-R	6-6	230	1-28-96	5	0	2.64	18	3	0	0	44	37	14	13	1	8	51	.228	.241	.221	10.35	1.62
Cox, Andy	R-L	6-2	185	10-23-93	3	0	4.59	24	0	0	1	33	33	22	17	0	20	27	.258	.159	.310	7.29	5.40
Hendrix, Ryan	R-R	6-3	185	12-16-94	0	0	5.19	6	0	0	0	9	11	5	5	0	5	5	.333	.375	.320	5.19	5.19
Hunter, Brian	R-R	6-3	215	11-22-92	0	0	4.22	7	0	0	0	11	14	5	5	2	8	8	.333	.450	.227	6.75	1.69
Johnson, Jake	R-R	6-2	185	6-5-93	0	2	7.90	17	0	0	0	27	36	26	24	5	23	23	.321	.273	.353	7.57	7.57
Jordan, Andrew	R-R	6-2	180	8-3-97	1	6	5.43	13	12	0	0	55	63	37	33	6	21	59	.297	.342	.271	9.71	3.46
Kahaloa, Ian	R-R	6-1	185	10-3-97	2	2	2.82	10	10	0	0	45	38	20	14	4	13	42	.221	.208	.232	8.46	2.62
Kish, Keenan	L-R	6-3	205	11-21-91	1	0	8.44	5	0	0	0	5	6	5	5	0	6	7	.286	.333	.250	11.81	10.13
Kuhnel, Joel	R-R	6-5	260	2-19-95	0	1	3.43	18	0	0	4	21	28	11	8	1	1	14	.318	.263	.360	6.00	0.43
Machorro, Carlos	R-R	6-2	175	9-20-96	0	2	9.00	8	0	0	0	11	16	11	11	5	3	11	.348	.235	.414	9.00	2.45
Marquez, Soid	R-R	6-3	165	1-3-95	6	5	5.66	19	1	0	0	35	35	24	22	1	18	24	.267	.240	.284	6.17	4.63
Mena, Alfredo	R-R	6-3	205	12-6-93	3	3	6.75	20	2	0	0	40	57	38	30	4	14	36	.337	.312	.359	8.10	3.15
Moreta, Dauri	R-R	6-2	185	4-15-96	0	0	0.00	2	0	0	0	3	1	1	0	0	3	3	.143	—	.143	10.13	10.13
Moss, Scott	L-L	6-5	215	10-6-94	3	1	2.35	10	10	0	0	38	35	13	10	2	14	29	.241	.205	.255	6.81	3.29
Nova, Moises	R-R	6-3	190	8-2-95	0	7	4.80	15	15	0	0	54	46	40	29	5	33	51	.225	.203	.238	8.45	5.47
Quillen, Aaron	R-R	6-2	200	12-19-93	1	0	4.13	16	2	0	0	24	27	14	11	3	9	20	.284	.244	.315	7.50	3.38
Ramsey, Jordan	L-R	6-4	215	9-6-92	0	1	1.08	2	2	0	0	8	6	1	1	0	2	7	.207	.250	.190	7.56	2.16
Riehl, Patrick	R-R	6-5	230	5-19-94	5	2	3.76	22	0	0	2	38	33	19	16	3	12	36	.241	.298	.200	8.45	2.82
Rodriguez, Adrian	R-R	6-1	185	8-8-96	2	0	4.01	8	6	0	0	34	29	17	15	1	9	34	.228	.146	.267	9.00	2.41
Romero, Wennington	L-L	5-11	175	1-29-98	0	0	3.00	1	1	0	0	3	3	1	1	0	1	1	.250	.000	.300	3.00	3.00
Santillan, Tony	R-R	6-3	240	4-15-97	1	0	3.92	8	8	0	0	39	32	17	17	4	16	46	.221	.292	.186	10.62	3.69
Stallings, Jesse	R-R	6-2	198	10-27-94	1	2	5.09	19	0	0	5	23	24	16	13	3	13	21	.267	.200	.308	8.22	5.09
Webb, Alex	R-R	6-2	210	7-19-94	4	0	0.79	5	0	0	0	11	9	1	1	0	2	9	.209	.308	.167	7.15	1.59
Wotell, Max	R-L	6-3	195	9-13-96	0	1	15.00	3	3	0	0	6	10	10	10	1	7	5	.370	.300	.412	7.50	10.50

Fielding

C: Brown 37, Guerrero 4, Lofstrom 11, Okey 7, Trees 21. **1B:** Lofstrom 5, Marshall 57, Rachal 2, Wright 14. **2B:** Blankmeyer 22, Lopez 29, Sansone 22, Wright 5. **3B:** Chavez 18, Lopez 19, Ovalle 3, Sansone 20, Senzel 10, Veras 1, Wright 14. **SS:** Chavez 7, Lopez 1, Ovalle 20, Vargas 53. **OF:** Amaral 9, Beltre 20, Chavez 13, Friedl 23, Gordon 18, McElroy 34, Piatnik 10, Siri 56, Sweet 15, Trammell 51.

AZL REDS
ARIZONA LEAGUE

ROOKIE

Batting	B-T	HT	WT	DOB	AVG	vLH	vRH	G	AB	R	H	2B	3B	HR	RBI	BB	HBP	SH	SF	SO	SB	CS	SLG	OBP
Azcona, Francis	B-R	5-10	155	11-20-95	.179	.316	.108	17	56	8	10	2	0	1	4	12	1	0	0	17	4	0	.268	.333
Beltre, Michael	B-R	6-3	180	7-3-95	.292	.370	.266	29	106	23	31	4	6	0	10	11	4	1	0	25	9	0	.443	.380
Capitillo, Derik	R-R	5-11	205	4-11-95	.308	.455	.268	19	52	8	16	2	1	0	10	3	3	0	2	11	0	1	.385	.367
Conde, Mauro	R-R	6-0	20	6-1-97	.169	.167	.170	23	83	8	14	5	0	0	13	9	3	0	1	33	3	1	.229	.271
Cruz, Manny	R-R	5-11	170	8-29-95	.272	.324	.253	33	125	22	34	3	2	3	13	14	2	3	0	33	4	3	.400	.355
Herrera, Edgar	L-R	5-10	180	1-30-96	.274	.238	.288	21	73	10	20	5	1	1	11	6	1	0	0	17	1	1	.411	.338
Jimenez, Daniel	R-R	5-11	175	4-23-96	.284	.286	.284	30	109	13	31	3	3	0	12	7	4	0	0	17	3	1	.367	.350
Juaquin, Urwin	R-R	6-0	140	12-29-97	.100	.167	.063	15	50	4	5	1	0	0	1	2	0	0	0	16	0	0	.120	.135
Liberatore, Ernesto	R-R	6-0	180	3-26-96	.085	.105	.071	15	47	3	4	4	0	0	2	2	0	0	0	16	0	0	.170	.122
Ljatifi, Nadir	R-R	5-10	170	2-21-98	.244	.333	.192	23	82	11	20	2	0	1	8	8	2	1	0	20	0	1	.305	.326
Lofstrom, Morgan	L-R	6-1	185	8-17-95	.265	.429	.222	10	34	6	9	2	0	1	3	2	2	0	0	7	0	0	.412	.342
Manzanero, Pabel	R-R	6-0	170	1-30-96	.303	.405	.256	32	119	13	36	12	0	0	21	4	3	0	1	21	0	0	.403	.339
Martinez, Victor	R-R	6-1	170	1-29-97	.167	.250	.125	4	12	4	2	1	0	0	1	1	3	0	0	2	0	0	.250	.375
Munroe, Reshard	L-L	6-0	170	6-15-96	.157	.133	.167	21	51	11	8	0	3	0	5	10	1	0	0	11	7	1	.275	.306
Rivero, Carlos	L-R	6-0	175	4-30-97	.240	.217	.250	39	154	25	37	0	1	1	13	7	2	3	1	23	12	2	.273	.280
Salmon-Williams, J.D.	R-R	5-9	195	3-21-97	.272	.269	.273	30	103	16	28	2	4	2	10	14	1	0	1	30	3	1	.427	.361
Santana, Leandro	R-R	6-2	175	2-19-97	.228	.271	.209	44	158	28	36	8	2	3	20	20	0	0	3	58	2	2	.316	.317
Selsky, Steve	R-R	6-0	205	7-20-89	.556	.600	.500	3	9	2	5	1	0	0	4	2	0	0	0	3	0	0	.667	.636
Stephenson, Tyler	R-R	6-4	225	8-16-96	.250	.400	.200	5	20	4	5	1	0	1	2	2	1	0	0	7	0	0	.450	.348
Sugilio, Andy	B-R	6-2	170	10-26-96	.221	.233	.216	31	104	13	23	3	2	0	6	8	2	1	1	27	6	0	.288	.287
Turnbull, Jake	L-R	6-0	195	2-16-96	.167	.111	.185	12	36	6	6	3	0	0	3	4	0	0	0	12	1	0	.250	.250
Wallace, Raul	R-R	6-2	180	8-19-95	.228	.265	.213	35	123	19	28	10	1	1	14	10	2	0	2	46	8	2	.350	.292
Winker, Jesse	L-L	6-3	215	8-17-93	.462	.333	.571	4	13	6	6	0	0	2	6	2	0	0	0	4	0	0	.923	.533
Yari, Bruce	L-L	6-3	224	12-9-94	.270	.222	.287	35	137	13	37	2	3	1	17	12	1	0	2	29	1	0	.350	.329

Pitching	B-T	HT	WT	DOB	W	L	ERA	G	GS	CG	SV	IP	H	R	ER	HR	BB	SO	AVG	vLH	vRH	K/9	BB/9
Adleman, Tim	R-R	6-3	225	11-13-87	0	0	0.00	1	1	0	0	2	1	0	0	0	2	3	.143	—	.143	16.20	10.80
Aguilar, Miguel	R-R	6-0	180	7-25-95	5	0	4.18	17	0	0	0	24	32	11	11	0	6	27	.300	.257	.354	10.27	2.28
Alecis, Luis	R-R	6-3	190	6-7-97	2	2	3.26	12	7	0	0	47	44	25	17	2	19	50	.239	.149	.270	9.57	3.64
Anesty, Isaac	L-L	6-2	190	4-6-97	3	1	6.20	14	1	0	0	25	30	17	17	1	12	14	.306	.261	.320	5.11	4.38
Bennett, Connor	R-R	5-9	192	4-10-97	0	3	3.71	20	0	0	1	27	25	12	11	1	15	36	.255	.320	.233	11.81	3.71
Blandino, Matt	R-R	6-1	180	7-30-95	1	1	2.30	8	5	0	0	31	33	13	8	1	3	30	.266	.333	.235	8.62	0.86
Crawford, Jonathan	R-R	6-2	205	11-1-91	0	0	3.00	6	6	0	0	15	15	6	5	0	8	10	.278	.429	.225	6.00	4.80
Fossas, Aaron	R-R	6-2	200	9-2-92	2	0	2.55	18	2	0	2	25	12	11	7	0	8	31	.143	.100	.167	11.31	2.92

Pitching	B-T	HT	WT	DOB	W	L	ERA	G	GS	CG	SV	IP	H	R	ER	HR	BB	SO	AVG	vLH	vRH	K/9	BB/9
Hanson, Nick	R-R	6-6	205	6-10-98	0	2	9.18	8	8	0	0	17	25	19	17	1	15	15	.352	.323	.375	8.10	8.10
Hunter, Brian	R-R	6-3	215	11-22-92	0	0	1.93	4	0	0	0	5	3	2	1	0	1	1	.176	.167	.182	1.93	1.93
Kahaloa, Ian	R-R	6-1	185	10-3-97	1	0	0.00	2	1	0	0	8	2	0	0	0	1	10	.077	.000	.083	11.25	1.13
Kish, Keenan	L-R	6-3	205	11-21-91	0	0	0.00	3	2	0	0	3	0	0	0	0	2	2	.000	.000	.000	6.00	6.00
Klimesh, Ben	R-R	6-4	220	5-14-90	0	0	7.71	5	0	0	0	5	7	4	0	5	8	.263	.000	.333	15.43	9.64
Machorro, Carlos	R-R	6-2	175	9-20-96	1	0	1.52	15	0	0	5	24	18	5	4	0	1	19	.205	.200	.208	7.23	0.38
Melville, Tim	R-R	6-4	225	10-9-89	0	1	8.10	3	3	0	0	3	5	4	3	0	0	2	.357	.500	.333	5.40	0.00
Mondile, Tyler	L-R	6-2	175	11-4-97	0	0	3.60	4	3	0	0	10	10	5	4	1	1	6	.250	.267	.240	5.40	0.90
Moreta, Dauri	R-R	6-2	185	4-15-96	3	3	2.05	20	0	0	4	31	19	12	7	0	18	53	.170	.237	.135	15.55	5.28
Ortiz, Braulio	R-R	6-7	253	12-20-91	0	0	4.70	9	0	0	0	8	5	7	4	1	8	12	.172	.167	.176	14.09	9.39
Reinoso, Gregory	L-L	6-1	170	11-17-95	3	2	3.55	14	8	0	1	46	47	25	18	3	27	39	.258	.263	.257	7.69	5.32
Romero, Wennigton	L-L	5-11	175	1-29-98	3	3	1.93	10	7	0	0	47	39	16	10	1	8	46	.222	.250	.214	8.87	1.54
Rucker, Rock	L-L	6-5	220	3-24-93	0	0	0.00	2	0	0	0	2	1	0	0	1	3	.143	.000	.167	13.50	4.50
Santos, Yerry	R-R	6-4	194	11-30-94	3	1	4.42	15	0	0	1	37	34	23	18	1	27	44	.243	.268	.226	10.80	6.63
Shred, Darren	R-R	6-3	200	10-13-97	2	2	5.09	15	0	0	1	18	14	12	10	1	16	13	.222	.188	.234	6.62	8.15
Telleria, Adolfi	R-R	6-1	170	4-12-94	2	0	1.59	5	1	0	0	17	12	4	3	1	1	10	.197	.235	.182	5.29	0.53
Wright, Andrew	R-L	6-4	225	6-27-95	0	1	2.25	3	0	0	0	4	1	1	1	0	3	8	.083	.000	.125	18.00	6.75

Fielding

C: Capitillo 17, Liberatore 15, Lofstrom 3, Manzanero 23, Stephenson 4, Turnbull 4. **1B:** Herrera 1, Lofstrom 5, Manzanero 5, Santana 12, Turnbull 4, Yari 31. **2B:** Azcona 7, Cruz 29, Herrera 4, Juaquin 9, Ljatifi 3, Rivero 3, Salmon-Williams 2. **3B:** Azcona 1, Herrera 8, Ljatifi 11, Rivero 4, Salmon-Williams 1, Santana 33. **SS:** Azcona 7, Cruz 2, Juaquin 5, Ljatifi 7, Martinez 4, Rivero 30. **OF:** Beltre 28, Conde 23, Jimenez 25, Munroe 12, Salmon-Williams 20, Selsky 1, Sugilio 28, Wallace 34, Winker 4.

DSL REDS | ROOKIE

DOMINICAN SUMMER LEAGUE

Batting	B-T	HT	WT	DOB	AVG	vLH	vRH	G	AB	R	H	2B	3B	HR	RBI	BB	HBP	SH	SF	SO	SB	CS	SLG	OBP
Abreu, Felix	R-R	6-1	180	12-26-97	.215	.241	.211	60	200	29	43	4	4	2	22	27	4	1	1	47	7	2	.305	.319
Abreu, Hidekel	R-R	5-10	155	10-30-97	.322	.355	.317	57	214	40	69	8	4	3	35	30	2	3	0	37	11	5	.439	.411
Alegria, Benjamin	R-R	5-10	165	8-6-97	.259	.256	.259	65	259	44	67	12	1	0	25	29	4	2	2	31	8	8	.313	.340
Alvarez, Gabriel	L-L	6-2	195	7-11-97	.160	.059	.175	42	131	13	21	2	1	1	9	14	3	2	0	33	0	1	.214	.257
Bautista, Mariel	R-R	6-3	170	10-15-97	.333	.419	.314	62	237	40	79	16	4	3	35	22	10	0	3	36	13	4	.473	.408
Berroa, Melbin	R-R	6-4	175	3-10-97	.229	—	—	54	175	25	40	7	0	0	11	15	2	2	3	38	5	3	.269	.292
Cuevas, Abel	R-R	6-0	180	9-13-96	.071	.125	.000	4	14	0	1	0	0	0	0	0	0	0	0	4	0	0	.071	.071
De Los Santos, Tomas	L-R	6-3	180	4-16-95	.333	.333	.333	3	9	0	3	0	0	0	2	0	0	0	0	4	0	0	.333	.455
Diaz, Giovanni	R-R	6-1	150	5-5-99	.150	.143	.154	58	173	21	26	6	0	0	10	32	7	2	1	61	7	3	.185	.305
Doval, Sucre	R-R	6-3	175	9-6-96	.333	—	.333	6	15	3	5	1	1	0	3	3	0	1	1	4	2	1	.533	.421
Encarnacion, Johan	B-R	6-0	170	9-21-96	.206	.250	.192	12	34	5	7	1	0	0	1	7	0	1	0	9	2	0	.235	.341
Garzon, Angel	R-R	6-2	160	8-21-97	.073	.000	.075	13	41	1	3	0	0	0	2	4	0	0	0	18	1	0	.073	.156
Gomez, Elvis	R-R	6-0	170	5-27-99	.300	.000	.333	3	10	4	3	0	0	0	1	2	1	0	0	3	0	0	.300	.462
Hernandez, Miguel	R-R	6-0	170	4-13-99	.245	.175	.259	64	237	35	58	8	1	1	23	35	1	2	3	37	7	6	.300	.341
Martinez, Juan	R-R	6-0	179	11-8-98	.281	.250	.286	19	64	10	18	5	0	0	9	7	0	2	0	13	0	1	.359	.415
Juarez, Raul	R-R	6-1	165	7-9-97	.306	.339	.288	57	180	25	55	7	1	6	31	19	11	3	3	34	3	4	.456	.399
Martinez, Valentin	R-R	6-0	175	9-21-96	.257	.241	.265	52	167	26	43	3	0	2	17	11	8	0	1	28	9	1	.311	.332
Ochoa, Edwin	R-R	5-9	165	9-19-96	.189	.125	.216	23	53	4	10	0	0	0	5	10	1	0	0	21	5	2	.189	.328
Olivo, Cristian	L-L	6-2	170	9-30-98	.101	.053	.114	27	89	10	9	2	1	1	4	5	0	0	0	47	1	0	.180	.149
Ortiz, Leonardo	R-R	6-2	198	3-30-97	.242	.103	.301	42	132	15	32	4	0	0	11	10	2	1	2	19	5	2	.273	.301
Ozuna, Reniel	R-R	6-2	180	7-29-98	.268	.241	.281	51	179	27	48	13	1	4	24	11	7	0	2	39	6	3	.419	.332
Paulino, Alejandro	R-R	6-0	170	10-3-98	.260	.308	.251	68	250	41	65	19	5	1	31	27	4	6	5	47	14	7	.388	.336
Plaz, Peterson	L-L	5-10	155	3-6-99	.258	.221	.276	59	229	30	59	3	0	1	16	21	2	1	2	33	11	9	.284	.323
Reina, Carlos	B-R	6-0	175	12-11-98	.255	.235	.258	49	149	23	38	7	4	0	17	24	3	0	2	33	6	2	.356	.365
Remy, Daniel	R-R	6-1	170	5-5-98	.255	.250	.258	52	188	28	48	8	4	2	16	8	0	0	4	42	5	3	.372	.286
Rodriguez, Alfredo	R-R	6-0	190	6-17-94	.234	.258	.217	22	77	12	18	5	0	0	8	9	4	0	3	16	9	0	.299	.333
Salazar, Alexander	R-R	6-1	170	1-7-98	.182	.167	.189	48	132	16	24	4	1	1	16	20	3	3	2	35	2	3	.250	.299
Sanchez, Aristides	R-R	6-0	173	3-22-97	.155	.125	.160	37	97	7	15	2	0	1	8	16	5	2	1	30	0	1	.206	.303
Sequera, Jorge	R-R	6-0	175	3-20-99	.240	—	—	41	129	21	31	0	0	0	10	25	6	2	2	12	5	4	.240	.383
Sims, Johnny	R-R	6-3	192	10-29-96	.133	.180	.106	43	135	19	18	4	1	3	15	29	1	0	3	51	4	3	.244	.286
Tello, Jose	R-R	6-0	170	5-21-98	.265	.220	.289	49	147	14	39	10	1	1	20	14	6	1	1	27	2	2	.367	.351
Willems, Jonathan	R-R	5-11	180	11-7-98	.228	.212	.237	53	180	25	41	14	3	1	19	9	8	1	1	56	5	5	.356	.293
Yon, Edwin	R-R	6-5	180	7-24-98	.239	.258	.235	51	180	19	43	6	0	3	28	24	4	1	0	62	4	1	.322	.341

Pitching	B-T	HT	WT	DOB	W	L	ERA	G	GS	CG	SV	IP	H	R	ER	HR	BB	SO	AVG	vLH	vRH	K/9	BB/9
Carreno, Carlos	R-R	6-2	174	9-4-98	6	2	3.88	14	11	0	1	58	49	29	25	1	15	31	—	—	—	4.81	2.33
Castillo, Jose	R-R	6-4	190	6-10-96	2	4	3.10	13	12	0	1	58	54	24	20	1	15	41	.248	.237	.256	6.36	2.33
Centeno, Jaccen	L-L	5-11	170	7-3-99	1	1	3.38	14	0	0	2	21	13	9	8	0	20	23	.181	.200	.177	9.70	8.44
Conoropo, Omar	B-L	5-10	165	5-27-98	1	1	3.09	17	1	0	0	44	38	24	15	1	19	49	.225	.200	.230	10.10	3.92
Cuevas, Israel	R-R	6-1	180	9-19-93	1	2	4.18	12	0	0	4	28	22	15	13	1	22	21	.232	.231	.232	6.75	7.07
De Jesus, Jhon	R-R	6-4	180	1-9-97	4	4	2.85	13	13	0	0	73	68	33	23	2	18	49	.249	.274	.231	6.07	2.23
Diaz, Yoel	R-R	6-1	190	1-9-99	0	2	5.70	20	0	0	2	43	48	30	27	3	20	38	.279	.25	.298	8.02	4.22
Encarnacion, Marcos	R-R	6-2	180	11-28-95	0	1	16.88	1	1	0	0	3	5	6	5	0	3	4	.417	.500	.333	13.50	10.13
Escoboza, Edward	R-R	6-5	185	12-5-95	1	2	2.92	13	0	0	6	65	63	27	21	2	18	60	.252	.253	.252	8.35	2.51
Espinal, Jhon	R-R	5-9	170	2-9-96	1	1	5.82	13	0	0	0	17	17	11	11	1	14	7	—	—	—	3.71	7.41
Garcia, Eriberto	R-R	5-11	180	11-7-95	2	1	4.60	7	0	0	0	16	13	9	8	0	6	16	.232	.200	.244	9.19	3.45
Ismail, Ross	R-R	6-0	195	2-19-97	0	4	5.55	12	0	0	0	24	29	19	15	1	18	10	.309	.364	.279	3.70	6.66

Pitching	B-T	HT	WT	DOB	W	L	ERA	G	GS	CG	SV	IP	H	R	ER	HR	BB	SO	AVG	vLH	vRH	K/9	BB/9
Jimenez, Eury	R-R	5-11	175	1-9-98	1	3	8.64	13	0	0	1	17	21	17	16	1	15	13	.318	.350	.304	7.02	8.10
Jimenez, Felix	R-R	6-3	170	9-29-95	1	4	12.13	18	0	0	1	23	31	36	31	2	25	21	.320	.200	.404	8.22	9.78
Jones, Francis	R-R	6-4	200	12-6-96	5	8	3.87	14	14	1	0	74	70	43	32	2	24	64	.249	.228	.261	7.75	2.91
Mata, Jose	R-R	5-11	170	9-18-97	0	4	6.26	15	0	0	1	23	29	19	16	0	15	12	.341	.368	.319	4.70	5.87
Mateo, Marvin	R-R	6-3	170	1-8-98	2	4	4.04	13	13	0	0	49	66	32	22	1	24	36	.327	.455	.279	6.61	4.41
Mendez, Dawrin	L-L	6-3	170	2-21-98	0	1	6.75	4	0	0	0	5	5	4	4	0	5	4	.294	.500	.267	6.75	8.44
Morales, Enyer	R-R	6-2	175	9-14-97	4	3	4.14	12	12	0	0	59	67	29	27	1	23	42	.294	.341	.264	6.44	3.53
Nino, Jeffry	R-R	6-4	170	9-26-96	2	4	5.49	16	7	0	0	57	57	40	35	2	26	40	.263	.211	.299	6.28	4.08
Noriega, Orlando	R-R	6-0	175	5-15-99	2	3	4.06	22	0	0	3	31	24	26	14	2	34	36	.200	.205	.197	10.45	9.87
Perez, Geremi	R-R	5-11	180	8-3-97	0	0	0.93	6	0	0	2	10	7	3	1	0	4	11	.194	.167	.208	10.24	3.72
Pimentel, Samuel	R-R	6-1	190	12-16-96	0	0	47.25	1	0	0	0	1	5	7	7	0	2	1	.556	.667	.333	6.75	13.50
Rijo, Oliver	R-R	6-2	180	1-11-98	4	2	2.51	14	2	0	1	29	25	9	8	0	18	33	.245	.188	.271	10.36	5.65
Roman, Jesus	R-R	6-2	195	2-2-97	4	3	6.51	20	1	0	1	37	35	31	27	1	36	42	.248	.130	.305	10.13	8.68
Severino, Moises	R-R	5-11	185	9-20-97	1	3	4.76	15	8	0	2	40	27	26	21	2	37	34	.193	.207	.183	7.71	8.39
Smith, Ricardo	R-R	6-2	175	2-16-96	5	3	2.70	14	14	1	0	80	73	28	24	2	13	66	.247	.222	.253	7.43	1.46
Soleana, Cerilio	L-L	5-11	150	4-22-97	0	0	2.70	3	0	0	0	3	3	1	1	0	3	3	.231	.000	.250	8.10	8.10
Sosa, Francis	R-R	6-5	190	1-18-97	1	0	8.64	18	0	0	0	25	23	28	24	1	40	30	.250	.313	.217	10.80	14.40
Soto, Mario	R-R	6-3	180	7-29-94	0	4	19.02	13	0	0	0	15	20	36	31	1	20	12	.328	.375	.311	7.36	12.27
Sparles, Luis	R-R	6-3	170	5-1-97	1	0	17.55	13	0	0	0	13	15	29	26	0	32	11	.288	.313	.278	7.43	21.60
Telleria, Adolfi	R-R	6-1	170	4-12-94	1	3	2.93	11	3	0	2	43	52	24	14	1	6	32	.292	.328	.275	6.70	1.26
Valenzuela, Jose	R-R	6-1	190	5-5-98	2	3	2.04	13	13	0	0	66	60	22	15	1	13	61	.235	.229	.238	8.28	1.76
Zorrilla, Jose	L-R	6-1	180	10-2-98	1	2	7.77	18	0	0	0	24	32	25	21	1	12	19	.337	.458	.296	7.03	4.44

Fielding

C: Gomez 3, Martinez 30, Ortiz 22, Reina 47, Sanchez 20, Sequera 8, Tello 29. **1B:** Abreu 27, Garzon 5, Juarez 14, Martinez 18, Ortiz 11, Reina 1, Salazar 4, Sanchez 32, Sequera 14, Tello 20. **2B:** Abreu 11, Alegria 57, Diaz 8, Encarnacion 1, Ochoa 6, Paulino 5, Remy 47, Salazar 17. **SS:** Diaz 41, Encarnacion 3, Hernandez 61, Ochoa 5, Paulino 10, Remy 2, Rodriguez 21, Salazar 1. **OF:** Abreu 57, Alvarez 32, Bautista 62, Berroa 53, Cuevas 4, De Los Santos 3, Doval 6, Garzon 1, Olivo 3, Ozuna 50, Plaz 57, Salazar 17, Sims 40, Yon 50.

Cleveland Indians

SEASON IN A SENTENCE: Despite a spate of injuries to key performers such as outfielder Michael Brantley (out most of the year with a bad shoulder) and righthanders Carlos Carrasco (broken finger) and Danny Salazar (forearm), the Indians won the American League Central, then swept through two playoffs rounds before losing to the Cubs in seven games in the World Series.

HIGH POINT: The Indians won 10 of their first 12 playoff games. First, they swept the Red Sox in the Division Series, and they won the first three games of the League Championship Series before dropping one game to Toronto. The Tribe closed out the Blue Jays to claim its first pennant since 1997, then won three of the first four games against the Cubs. The Indians' high-water mark came with a 7-2 Game Four win at Wrigley Field as Corey Kluber and Andrew Miller shackled the Cubs.

LOW POINT: Down 5-1 in Game Seven, the Indians rallied, first with two runs scoring on a Jon Lester wild pitch, then with Rajai Davis tying the game at 6-6 in the bottom of the eighth with a dramatic home run off Cubs reliever Aroldis Chapman. But in the 10th, reliever Bryan Shaw gave up two runs, and while Davis had an RBI single in the bottom of the 10th to make it 8-7, reserve Michael Martinez grounded out to third base for the final out.

NOTABLE ROOKIES: Tyler Naquin took advantage of openings in the Cleveland outfield to seize the center field job and had one of the stronger years of any 2016 rookie, batting .296/.372/.514. His walk-off, inside-the-park home run on Aug. 19 against Toronto was one of the Indians' regular-season highlights.

KEY TRANSACTIONS: Instead of relying on their rotation in the postseason, the Indians tried to make every game Miller Time after dealing for lefthander Andrew Miller, giving up four prospects, including outfielder Clint Frazier and lefthander Justus Sheffield, for the dynamic reliever.

DOWN ON THE FARM: Indians domestic affiliates went 383-313, with a .550 winning percentage that ranked fourth in the minors, while four clubs made the playoffs. Akron won the Double-A Eastern League, while a passel of prospects helped high Class A Lynchburg go 84-56. Catcher Francisco Mejia authored a 50-game hitting streak, longest in the minors since 1954, while playing at two Class A levels. Mejia hit .342/.382/.514.

OPENING DAY PAYROLL: $ 74,311,900 (27th)

PLAYERS OF THE YEAR

MAJOR LEAGUE	MINOR LEAGUE
Corey Kluber rhp	**Francisco Mejia** c
18-9, 3.14	(Low A/High A)
227 SO in 222 IP	.342/.382/.514
Led AL in shutouts	50-game hit streak

ORGANIZATION LEADERS

BATTING		*Minimum 250 AB
MAJORS		
* AVG	Jose Ramirez	.312
* OPS	Carlos Santana	.865
HR	Mike Napoli	34
	Carlos Santana	34
RBI	Mike Napoli	101
MINORS		
* AVG	Francisco Mejia, Lake County, Lynchburg	.342
* OBP	Greg Allen, Lynchburg, Akron	.416
* SLG	Francisco Mejia, Lake County, Lynchburg	.514
* OPS	Francisco Mejia, Lake County, Lynchburg	.896
R	Greg Allen, Lynchburg, Akron	119
H	Greg Allen, Lynchburg, Akron	145
	Anthony Santander, Lynchburg	145
TB	Anthony Santander, Lynchburg	247
2B	Connor Marabell, Lake County, Lynchburg	45
3B	5 players	8
HR	Jesus Aguilar, Columbus	30
RBI	Bobby Bradley, Lynchburg	102
BB	Greg Allen, Lynchburg, Akron	77
	Bradley Zimmer, Akron, Columbus	77
SO	Nellie Rodriguez, Akron	186
SB	Greg Allen, Lynchburg, Akron	45
PITCHING		#Minimum 75 IP
MAJORS		
W	Corey Kluber	18
# ERA	Corey Kluber	3.14
SO	Corey Kluber	227
SV	Cody Allen	32
MINORS		
W	Shawn Morimando, Akron, Columbus	15
L	Shao-Ching Chiang, Lake County	12
	Casey Shane, Lake County	12
# ERA	Thomas Pannone, Lake County, Lynchburg	2.57
G	Shawn Armstrong, Columbus, Lake County	49
GS	Michael Peoples, Columbus, Akron	28
	Adam Plutko, Akron, Columbus	28
SV	Trevor Frank, Lynchburg	17
IP	Michael Peoples, Columbus, Akron	165
BB	Mitch Brown, Lynchburg	77
SO	Matt Esparza, Lake County, Lynchburg	141
# AVG	Thomas Pannone, Lake County, Lynchburg	.215

President: Chris Antonetti. **GM:** Mike Chernoff. **Farm Director:** Carter Hawkins. **Scouting Director:** Brad Grant.

Class	Team	League	W	L	PCT	Finish	Manager
Majors	Cleveland Indians	American	94	67	.584	2nd (15)	Terry Francona
Triple-A	Columbus Clippers	International	82	62	.569	3rd (14)	Chris Tremie
Double-A	Akron RubberDucks	Eastern	77	64	.546	3rd (12)	Dave Wallace
High A	Lynchburg Hillcats	Carolina	84	56	.600	2nd (8)	Mark Budzinski
Low A	Lake County Captains	Midwest	72	68	.514	7th (16)	Tony Mansolino
Short season	Mahoning Valley Scrappers	New York-Penn	37	38	.493	9th (14)	Edwin Rodriguez
Rookie	Indians	Arizona	31	25	.554	t-4th (14)	Anthony Medrano
Overall 2016 Minor League Record			383	313	.550	4th (30)	

ORGANIZATION STATISTICS

CLEVELAND INDIANS
AMERICAN LEAGUE

Batting	B-T	HT	WT	DOB	AVG	vLH	vRH	G	AB	R	H	2B	3B	HR	RBI	BB	HBP	SH	SF	SO	SB	CS	SLG	OBP
Aguilar, Jesus	R-R	6-3	250	6-30-90	.000	.000	.000	9	6	0	0	0	0	0	0	0	0	0	0	1	0	0	.000	.000
Almonte, Abraham	B-R	5-9	210	6-27-89	.264	.279	.254	67	182	24	48	20	1	1	22	8	1	0	3	42	8	0	.401	.294
Brantley, Michael	L-L	6-2	200	5-15-87	.231	.286	.219	11	39	5	9	2	0	0	7	3	0	0	1	6	1	0	.282	.279
Byrd, Marlon	R-R	6-0	245	8-30-77	.270	.368	.221	34	115	11	31	6	0	5	19	11	0	0	3	36	0	0	.452	.326
Chisenhall, Lonnie	L-R	6-2	190	10-4-88	.286	.217	.295	126	385	43	110	25	5	8	57	23	3	3	4	70	6	0	.439	.328
Cowgill, Collin	R-L	5-9	190	5-22-86	.083	.000	.333	9	12	0	1	0	0	0	0	2	0	0	0	7	0	0	.083	.214
Crisp, Coco	B-R	5-10	185	11-1-79	.200	.200	.211	20	53	9	11	3	0	2	8	9	0	2	0	13	3	0	.377	.323
2-team total (102 Oakland)					.231	—	—	122	446	54	103	27	4	13	55	46	0	4	2	78	10	5	.397	.302
Davis, Rajai	R-R	5-10	195	10-19-80	.249	.235	.258	134	454	74	113	23	2	12	48	33	5	1	2	106	43	6	.388	.306
Gimenez, Chris	R-R	6-2	230	12-27-82	.216	.229	.212	67	139	17	30	4	0	4	11	10	1	4	1	41	0	0	.331	.272
Gomes, Yan	R-R	6-2	215	7-19-87	.167	.271	.127	74	251	22	42	11	1	9	34	9	2	0	2	69	0	0	.327	.201
Gonzalez, Erik	R-R	6-3	195	8-31-91	.313	.200	.364	21	16	2	5	0	0	0	1	0	0	0	0	8	0	1	.313	.353
Guyer, Brandon	R-R	6-2	200	1-28-86	.333	.328	.348	38	81	12	27	5	0	2	14	7	8	0	0	13	1	1	.469	.438
2-team total (63 Tampa Bay)					.266	—	—	101	293	39	78	17	1	9	32	19	31	1	1	55	3	2	.423	.372
Kipnis, Jason	L-R	5-11	195	4-3-87	.275	.282	.272	156	610	91	168	41	4	23	82	60	6	5	7	146	15	3	.469	.343
Lindor, Francisco	B-R	5-11	190	11-14-93	.301	.292	.306	158	604	99	182	30	3	15	78	57	5	3	15	88	19	5	.435	.358
Martinez, Michael	R-R	5-9	180	9-16-82	.242	.265	.230	59	95	15	23	4	0	1	4	3	0	1	0	21	0	2	.316	.265
2-team total (4 Boston)					.238	—	—	63	101	16	24	4	0	1	4	4	0	1	0	23	0	2	.307	.267
Moore, Adam	R-R	6-3	220	5-8-84	.000	—	.000	9	5	0	0	0	0	0	0	0	0	0	0	4	0	0	.000	.000
Napoli, Mike	R-R	6-1	225	10-31-81	.239	.262	.229	150	557	92	133	22	1	34	101	78	5	0	5	194	5	1	.465	.335
Naquin, Tyler	L-R	6-2	195	4-24-91	.296	.250	.301	116	321	52	95	18	5	14	43	36	4	2	2	112	6	3	.514	.372
Perez, Roberto	R-R	5-11	220	12-23-88	.183	.240	.155	61	153	14	28	6	1	3	17	23	0	5	3	44	0	0	.294	.285
Ramirez, Jose	B-R	5-9	180	9-17-92	.312	.311	.312	152	565	84	176	46	3	11	76	44	4	1	4	62	22	7	.462	.363
Santana, Carlos	B-R	5-11	210	4-8-86	.259	.267	.256	158	582	89	151	31	3	34	87	99	2	0	5	99	5	2	.498	.366
Uribe, Juan	R-R	6-0	245	3-22-79	.206	.187	.215	73	238	19	49	9	0	7	25	15	3	0	3	49	0	0	.332	.259

Pitching	B-T	HT	WT	DOB	W	L	ERA	G	GS	CG	SV	IP	H	R	ER	HR	BB	SO	AVG	vLH	vRH	K/9	BB/9
Adams, Austin	R-R	5-11	200	8-19-86	0	0	9.82	19	0	0	0	18	27	22	20	5	7	17	.333	.375	.293	8.35	3.44
Allen, Cody	R-R	6-1	210	11-20-88	3	5	2.51	67	0	0	32	68	41	23	19	8	27	87	.177	.218	.139	11.51	3.57
Anderson, Cody	R-R	6-4	240	9-14-90	2	5	6.68	19	9	0	0	61	85	45	45	13	13	54	.333	.326	.342	8.01	1.93
Armstrong, Shawn	R-R	6-2	225	9-11-90	0	0	2.53	10	0	0	0	11	9	3	3	1	5	7	.237	.238	.235	5.91	4.22
Bauer, Trevor	R-R	6-1	200	1-17-91	12	8	4.26	35	28	1	0	190	179	96	90	20	70	168	.248	.239	.257	7.96	3.32
Carrasco, Carlos	R-R	6-4	210	3-21-87	11	8	3.32	25	25	1	0	146	134	64	54	21	34	150	.240	.235	.244	9.23	2.09
Chamberlain, Joba	R-R	6-3	245	9-23-85	0	0	2.25	20	0	0	0	20	12	6	5	1	5	11	.176	.172	.179	8.10	4.95
Clevinger, Mike	R-R	6-4	210	12-21-90	3	3	5.26	17	10	0	0	53	50	31	31	8	29	50	.246	.178	.301	8.49	4.92
Colon, Joseph	R-R	6-0	180	2-18-90	1	3	7.20	11	0	0	0	10	12	9	8	2	7	10	.279	.200	.348	9.00	6.30
Crockett, Kyle	L-L	6-2	175	12-15-91	0	0	5.06	29	0	0	0	16	16	9	9	0	7	17	.258	.256	.261	9.56	3.94
Detwiler, Ross	R-L	6-3	210	3-6-86	0	0	5.79	7	0	0	0	5	3	3	3	1	4	3	.188	.125	.250	5.79	7.71
2-team total (9 Oakland)					2	4	6.10	16	7	0	0	49	59	34	33	5	19	26	—	—	—	4.81	3.51
Garner, Perci	R-R	6-3	225	12-13-88	0	0	4.82	8	0	0	0	9	12	6	5	0	5	12	.308	.353	.273	11.57	4.82
Gorzelanny, Tom	L-L	6-2	210	7-12-82	1	0	21.00	7	0	0	0	3	4	7	7	1	5	4	.308	.111	.750	12.00	15.00
House, T.J.	R-L	6-1	205	9-29-89	0	0	3.38	4	0	0	0	3	6	1	1	0	0	2	.500	.800	.286	6.75	0.00
Hunter, Tommy	R-R	6-3	250	7-3-86	2	2	3.74	21	0	0	0	22	21	10	9	1	5	17	.256	.303	.224	7.06	2.08
2-team total (12 Baltimore)					2	2	3.18	33	0	0	0	34	35	13	12	1	8	23	—	—	—	6.09	2.12
Kluber, Corey	R-R	6-4	215	4-10-86	18	9	3.14	32	32	3	0	215	170	82	75	22	57	227	.216	.226	.206	9.50	2.39
Manship, Jeff	R-R	6-2	205	1-16-85	2	1	3.12	53	0	0	0	43	40	20	15	7	22	36	.241	.241	.241	7.48	4.57
McAllister, Zach	R-R	6-6	240	12-8-87	3	2	3.44	53	2	0	0	52	53	21	20	6	23	54	.256	.242	.269	9.29	3.96
Merritt, Ryan	L-L	6-0	180	2-21-92	1	0	1.64	4	1	0	0	11	6	2	2	0	0	6	.167	.286	.138	4.91	0.00
Miller, Andrew	L-L	6-7	205	5-21-85	4	0	1.55	26	0	0	3	29	14	5	5	3	2	46	.139	.161	.129	14.28	0.62
2-team total (44 New York)					10	1	1.45	70	0	0	12	74	42	13	12	8	9	123	—	—	—	14.89	1.09
Morimando, Shawn	L-L	6-0	200	11-20-92	0	0	11.57	2	0	0	0	5	9	6	6	2	5	5	.409	.429	.400	9.64	9.64
Otero, Dan	R-R	6-3	205	2-19-85	5	1	1.53	62	0	0	1	71	54	14	12	2	10	57	.211	.197	.223	7.26	1.27
Plutko, Adam	R-R	6-3	200	10-3-91	0	0	7.36	2	0	0	0	4	5	3	3	1	2	3	.313	.167	.400	7.36	4.91
Salazar, Danny	R-R	6-0	195	1-11-90	11	6	3.87	25	25	0	0	137	121	61	59	16	63	161	.235	.2	.264	10.55	4.13

Pitching

Pitching	B-T	HT	WT	DOB	W	L	ERA	G	GS	CG	SV	IP	H	R	ER	HR	BB	SO	AVG	vLH	vRH	K/9	BB/9
Shaw, Bryan	B-R	6-1	220	11-8-87	2	5	3.24	75	0	0	1	67	56	26	24	8	28	69	.230	.255	.214	9.32	3.78
Tomlin, Josh	R-R	6-1	190	10-19-84	13	9	4.40	30	29	0	0	174	187	97	85	36	20	118	.269	.229	.299	6.10	1.03

Fielding

Catcher	PCT	G	PO	A	E	DP	PB
Gimenez	.992	59	355	26	3	2	5
Gomes	.995	73	539	32	3	3	4
Moore	.958	9	21	2	1	1	0
Perez	.996	61	476	29	2	3	3

First Base	PCT	G	PO	A	E	DP
Aguilar	1.000	7	18	0	0	2
Chisenhall	1.000	3	8	0	0	0
Gimenez	1.000	4	3	0	0	1
Napoli	.985	98	831	52	13	64
Santana	.991	64	513	53	5	48

Second Base	PCT	G	PO	A	E	DP
Gonzalez	1.000	5	1	2	0	0

	PCT	G	PO	A	E	DP
Kipnis	.981	151	198	422	12	70
Martinez	.974	21	19	18	1	4
Ramirez	.938	9	5	10	1	1

Third Base	PCT	G	PO	A	E	DP
Chisenhall	1.000	1	1	0	0	0
Gimenez	1.000	3	1	2	0	1
Gonzalez	—	2	0	0	0	0
Martinez	.600	2	0	3	2	1
Ramirez	.979	117	54	174	5	16
Uribe	.961	68	43	128	7	12

Shortstop	PCT	G	PO	A	E	DP
Gonzalez	1.000	8	5	6	0	2
Lindor	.982	155	215	447	12	83
Martinez	.944	5	6	11	1	3

	PCT	G	PO	A	E	DP
Ramirez	1.000	5	5	6	0	2

Outfield	PCT	G	PO	A	E	DP
Almonte	.976	58	75	6	2	1
Brantley	1.000	11	18	1	0	0
Byrd	1.000	31	42	3	0	1
Chisenhall	.985	119	190	7	3	1
Cowgill	1.000	8	10	0	0	0
Crisp	1.000	13	22	0	0	0
Davis	.980	128	235	9	5	2
Gonzalez	1.000	2	1	0	0	0
Guyer	.982	33	53	2	1	0
Martinez	1.000	27	19	2	0	2
Naquin	.990	109	183	6	2	0
Ramirez	.986	48	72	1	1	0

COLUMBUS CLIPPERS   TRIPLE-A
INTERNATIONAL LEAGUE

Batting	B-T	HT	WT	DOB	AVG	vLH	vRH	G	AB	R	H	2B	3B	HR	RBI	BB	HBP	SH	SF	SO	SB	CS	SLG	OBP
Aguilar, Jesus	R-R	6-3	250	6-30-90	.247	.179	.266	137	515	62	127	26	0	30	92	53	4	1	5	110	0	0	.472	.319
Almonte, Abraham	B-R	5-9	210	6-27-89	.444	.200	.588	7	27	6	12	2	1	1	4	5	1	0	0	4	2	0	.704	.545
Brantley, Michael	L-L	6-2	200	5-15-87	.111	—	.111	3	9	2	1	1	0	0	1	1	0	0	1	1	0	0	.222	.182
Butler, Joey	R-R	6-2	220	3-12-86	.240	.289	.226	118	413	54	99	15	2	8	42	45	3	2	1	106	4	1	.344	.318
Castillo, Ivan	B-R	5-11	150	5-30-95	.000	.000	.000	2	3	0	0	0	0	0	0	0	0	0	1	0	0	0	.000	.000
Chisenhall, Lonnie	L-R	6-2	190	10-4-88	.000	.000	.000	3	8	0	0	0	0	0	2	2	0	0	1	3	0	0	.000	.182
Choice, Michael	R-R	6-0	230	11-10-89	.246	.276	.237	71	252	33	62	11	0	14	39	14	8	0	2	81	0	1	.456	.304
Cowgill, Collin	R-L	5-9	190	5-22-86	.234	.195	.246	103	359	46	84	17	1	4	30	34	7	5	2	85	7	2	.320	.311
Diaz, Yandy	R-R	6-2	185	8-8-91	.325	.381	.304	95	360	53	117	22	3	7	44	47	1	2	6	70	5	1	.461	.399
Frazier, Clint	R-R	6-1	190	9-6-94	.238	.250	.235	5	21	2	5	0	1	0	0	0	0	0	0	6	4	0	.333	.238
2-team total (25 Scranton/W-B)					.230	—	—	30	122	19	28	2	4	3	7	7	0	0	0	36	0	0	.385	.271
Gonzalez, Erik	R-R	6-3	195	8-31-91	.296	.260	.307	104	429	62	127	31	1	11	53	19	3	7	2	88	12	10	.450	.329
Grossman, Robbie	B-L	6-0	215	9-16-89	.256	.500	.206	34	117	14	30	5	0	6	14	21	0	1	0	25	3	1	.453	.370
2-team total (1 Rochester)					.256	—	—	35	121	15	31	5	0	6	14	21	0	1	0	26	4	1	.446	.366
Hankins, Todd	R-R	5-9	180	11-18-90	.321	.429	.286	7	28	7	9	1	1	0	2	1	0	0	0	11	3	0	.429	.345
Ison, Bobby	L-L	5-8	170	7-5-93	.143	—	.143	2	7	0	1	0	0	0	1	0	0	0	0	4	0	0	.143	.143
Lavisky, Alex	R-R	6-1	209	1-13-91	.167	.000	.200	2	6	0	1	0	0	0	1	0	0	0	0	5	0	0	.167	.286
Lucas, Jeremy	R-R	6-1	205	1-10-91	.250	.333	.231	4	16	2	4	1	0	0	0	0	0	0	0	5	0	0	.313	.250
Martinez, Michael	B-R	5-9	180	9-16-82	.288	.364	.280	27	104	12	30	8	1	2	12	9	1	0	0	21	2	2	.442	.351
Medina, Yhoxian	R-R	5-10	165	5-11-90	.257	.230	.267	67	222	28	57	13	1	3	20	8	6	5	2	32	5	2	.365	.298
Monsalve, Alex	R-R	6-2	225	4-22-92	.250	—	.250	1	4	0	1	0	0	0	0	0	0	0	0	1	0	0	.250	.250
Moore, Adam	R-R	6-3	220	5-8-84	.247	.254	.246	86	299	35	74	14	0	7	31	26	4	0	0	63	0	0	.365	.316
Myles, Bryson	R-R	5-11	230	9-18-89	.234	.167	.257	33	94	10	22	4	1	1	9	1	0	0	1	25	5	0	.330	.305
Naquin, Tyler	L-R	6-2	195	4-24-91	.286	.133	.327	17	70	6	20	3	1	1	8	8	0	0	1	15	1	2	.400	.354
Perez, Roberto	R-R	5-11	220	12-23-88	.400	.500	.333	2	5	1	2	1	0	0	2	0	0	0	0	0	0	0	.600	.571
Quiroz, Guillermo	R-R	6-1	215	11-29-81	.264	.250	.267	75	273	41	72	17	0	11	38	16	5	1	2	68	0	0	.447	.314
Recker, Anthony	R-R	6-2	240	8-29-83	.246	.333	.231	19	61	10	15	5	0	2	10	14	1	0	0	17	1	0	.426	.395
2-team total (40 Gwinnett)					.244	—	—	59	197	30	48	11	0	8	28	30	2	0	1	62	1	0	.421	.348
Rodriguez, Ronny	R-R	6-0	170	4-17-92	.258	.343	.231	116	450	58	116	24	5	10	59	22	2	10	4	88	4	4	.400	.293
Smith, Jordan	L-R	6-4	235	7-5-90	.189	.231	.175	17	53	6	10	3	0	1	3	5	0	1	0	13	2	0	.302	.259
Stamets, Eric	R-R	6-0	190	9-25-91	.164	.200	.151	22	73	7	12	0	1	1	9	3	3	1	3	28	1	0	.233	.220
Urshela, Giovanny	R-R	6-0	215	10-11-91	.274	.282	.271	117	468	54	128	24	1	8	57	15	1	1	6	58	0	0	.380	.294
Valdez, Ordomar	B-R	5-9	150	4-24-94	.111	.000	.125	3	9	2	1	0	0	0	3	0	0	0	1	2	0	0	.111	.100
Zimmer, Bradley	L-R	6-4	185	11-27-92	.242	.172	.263	37	128	18	31	5	0	1	9	21	0	0	0	56	5	1	.305	.349

Pitching	B-T	HT	WT	DOB	W	L	ERA	G	GS	CG	SV	IP	H	R	ER	HR	BB	SO	AVG	vLH	vRH	K/9	BB/9
Adams, Austin	R-R	5-11	200	8-19-86	2	4	4.54	34	0	0	8	38	44	21	19	1	9	41	.291	.290	.293	9.80	2.15
Anderson, Cody	R-R	6-4	240	9-14-90	0	2	3.62	13	6	0	1	32	32	15	13	4	10	40	.248	.273	.23	11.13	2.78
Angulo, Argenis	R-R	6-3	220	2-26-94	0	0	0.00	1	0	0	0	1	0	0	0	0	0	3	.200	1.000	.000	20.25	20.25
Armstrong, Shawn	R-R	6-2	225	9-11-90	3	1	1.84	47	0	0	9	49	27	11	10	0	29	72	.160	.122	.195	13.22	5.33
Brown, D.J.	R-R	6-6	205	11-28-90	0	0	7.20	1	1	0	0	5	9	4	4	2	3	3	.409	.400	.417	5.40	5.40
Clevinger, Mike	R-R	6-4	210	12-21-90	11	1	3.00	17	17	1	0	93	78	32	31	8	35	97	.229	.215	.239	9.39	3.39
Colon, Joseph	R-R	6-0	180	2-18-90	0	1	0.82	20	0	0	0	22	8	4	2	0	12	21	.114	.133	.100	8.59	4.91
Cooper, Jordan	R-R	6-2	190	5-10-89	1	0	3.00	3	0	0	0	3	3	1	1	0	1	2	.250	.200	.286	6.00	3.00
Crockett, Kyle	L-L	6-2	175	12-15-91	1	1	3.90	29	0	0	0	30	29	13	13	2	11	26	.248	.349	.189	7.80	3.30
Detwiler, Ross	R-L	6-3	210	3-6-86	2	4	4.60	12	12	0	0	63	64	33	32	6	21	41	.268	.250	.276	5.89	3.02
Garner, Perci	R-R	6-2	225	12-13-88	2	0	1.63	18	0	0	5	28	15	5	5	1	11	23	.156	.195	.127	7.48	3.58
Gorzelanny, Tom	L-L	6-2	210	7-12-82	1	1	3.38	19	0	0	1	19	13	8	7	0	19	19	.197	.156	.235	9.16	5.30
2-team total (7 Norfolk)					1	1	3.65	26	0	0	1	25	24	15	10	0	16	24	—	—	—	8.76	5.84

Pitching

Pitching	B-T	HT	WT	DOB	W	L	ERA	G	GS	CG	SV	IP	H	R	ER	HR	BB	SO	AVG	vLH	vRH	K/9	BB/9
Grube, Jarrett	R-R	6-4	220	11-5-81	0	3	4.43	11	7	0	0	45	48	25	22	7	10	37	.273	.325	.226	7.46	2.01
Haviland, Shawn	R-R	6-2	200	11-10-85	2	2	3.40	7	7	0	0	42	41	16	16	4	10	30	.258	.259	.257	6.38	2.13
Heller, Ben	R-R	6-3	205	8-5-91	2	2	2.49	28	0	0	5	25	20	7	7	1	7	25	.217	.108	.291	8.88	2.49
2-team total (6 Scranton/W-B)					2	3	2.27	34	0	0	6	32	23	8	8	1	9	32	—	—	—	9.09	2.56
Hill, Cameron	R-R	6-1	185	5-24-94	0	0	0.00	1	0	0	0	3	2	0	0	0	1	2	.222	.000	.333	6.75	3.38
House, T.J.	R-L	6-1	205	9-29-89	5	3	3.98	33	12	0	1	72	89	44	32	6	43	50	.304	.372	.279	6.22	5.35
Hunter, Tommy	R-R	6-3	250	7-3-86	2	1	3.00	14	2	0	1	15	14	5	5	2	2	10	.241	.261	.229	6.00	1.20
Hynes, Colt	L-L	5-11	200	6-28-85	0	0	13.50	1	0	0	0	1	3	2	2	1	0	1	.429	1.000	.333	6.75	0.00
2-team total (16 Buffalo)					2	0	5.71	16	0	0	1	17	26	14	11	3	1	22	—	—	—	11.42	0.52
Johnson, Jeff	R-R	6-0	185	2-9-90	4	1	2.87	48	0	0	2	53	45	22	17	3	24	57	.224	.284	.170	9.62	4.05
Maronde, Nick	B-L	6-3	210	9-5-89	0	0	4.24	17	2	0	1	23	25	12	11	1	11	16	.278	.258	.288	6.17	4.24
Martin, Josh	R-R	6-5	230	12-30-89	2	5	3.41	47	0	0	3	66	57	26	25	4	23	60	.230	.243	.219	8.18	3.14
McAllister, Zach	R-R	6-6	240	12-8-87	0	0	4.50	2	0	0	0	2	3	1	1	0	1	1	.333	.500	.200	4.50	0.00
Merritt, Ryan	L-L	6-0	180	2-21-92	11	8	3.70	24	24	2	0	143	156	67	59	15	23	92	.279	.250	.291	5.78	1.44
Morimando, Shawn	L-L	6-0	200	11-20-92	5	2	3.51	11	11	0	0	59	64	26	23	5	21	46	.281	.343	.255	7.02	3.20
Murata, Toru	L-R	6-0	175	5-20-85	9	4	3.78	33	10	0	4	102	102	47	43	7	24	62	.262	.283	.243	5.45	2.11
Olson, Tyler	R-L	6-3	195	10-2-89	1	0	5.91	9	0	0	0	11	12	9	7	1	6	10	.273	.235	.296	8.44	5.06
2-team total (11 Scranton/W-B)					2	2	5.45	20	3	0	0	38	43	26	23	3	14	31	—	—	—	7.34	3.32
Pasquale, Nick	R-R	6-0	190	10-27-90	1	0	0.00	1	1	0	0	7	2	0	0	0	3	2	.091	.167	.063	2.70	4.05
Paulino, Felipe	R-R	6-3	270	10-5-83	1	1	2.77	10	0	0	0	13	5	5	4	1	5	10	.122	.111	.130	6.92	3.46
Peoples, Scott	R-R	6-5	190	9-5-91	1	0	3.00	1	1	0	0	6	4	2	2	0	2	3	.182	.167	.250	4.50	3.00
Plutko, Adam	R-R	6-3	200	10-3-91	6	5	4.10	15	15	0	0	90	87	42	41	8	34	67	.256	.248	.262	6.70	3.40
Roberts, Will	L-R	6-5	220	8-14-91	6	6	4.70	16	15	0	0	88	89	46	46	12	38	42	.269	.318	.211	4.30	3.89
Speer, David	L-L	6-1	185	8-14-92	1	0	10.80	2	0	0	0	5	9	6	6	0	2	3	.429	.250	.471	5.40	3.60
Stammen, Craig	R-R	6-4	230	3-9-84	0	3	5.54	10	0	0	0	13	16	8	8	2	2	11	.302	.308	.296	7.62	1.38
Sulser, Cole	R-R	6-0	190	3-12-90	0	0	1.69	5	3	1	0	5	3	1	1	0	0	7	.158	.000	.231	11.81	0.00
Whitehouse, Matt	L-L	6-1	175	4-13-91	—	—	—	—	—	—	—	—	—	—	—	—	—	—	.000	.000	.000	—	—

Fielding

Catcher	PCT	G	PO	A	E	DP	PB
Lucas	1.000	2	16	0	0	0	0
Monsalve	1.000	1	6	0	0	0	0
Moore	.995	77	604	32	3	3	4
Perez	1.000	2	12	1	0	0	0
Quiroz	.997	55	335	21	1	1	0
Recker	1.000	12	80	5	0	0	0

First Base	PCT	G	PO	A	E	DP
Aguilar	.997	120	994	82	3	88
Lucas	1.000	2	20	0	0	0
Moore		1	0	0	0	0
Quiroz	.978	12	83	5	2	7
Recker	1.000	1	3	2	0	0
Rodriguez	.993	17	131	6	1	19

Second Base	PCT	G	PO	A	E	DP
Castillo	1.000	1	1	1	0	1
Diaz	.944	4	4	13	1	1
Gonzalez	.967	8	12	17	1	5
Hankins	1.000	2	2	6	0	1
Martinez	.983	14	25	34	1	11

	PCT	G	PO	A	E	DP	PB
Medina	.988	39	52	111	2	23	
Rodriguez	.984	85	149	226	6	48	
Valdez	1.000	1	0	2	0	0	

Third Base	PCT	G	PO	A	E	DP
Aguilar	1.000	2	2	1	0	1
Diaz	.955	30	28	56	4	5
Gonzalez	1.000	3	2	6	0	0
Hankins	1.000	3	1	9	0	0
Martinez	1.000	1	0	1	0	0
Medina	1.000	1	0	2	0	0
Rodriguez	.900	4	3	6	1	1
Urshela	.970	104	94	197	9	29
Valdez	.833	2	2	3	1	0

Shortstop	PCT	G	PO	A	E	DP
Castillo	1.000	1	0	1	0	0
Gonzalez	.961	90	125	243	15	49
Martinez	.960	6	5	19	1	3
Medina	.989	26	37	57	1	12
Rodriguez	1.000	1	0	2	0	0
Stamets	.959	22	41	77	5	11
Urshela	1.000	5	3	6	0	2

Outfield	PCT	G	PO	A	E	DP
Almonte	.941	6	15	1	1	0
Brantley	1.000	3	1	0	0	0
Butler	.995	97	192	7	1	0
Chisenhall	1.000	2	3	0	0	0
Choice	.974	28	33	4	1	1
Cowgill	.987	101	219	11	3	2
Diaz	.965	52	103	8	4	2
Frazier	.933	5	14	0	1	0
Gonzalez	1.000	3	5	1	0	0
Grossman	1.000	31	60	2	0	0
Hankins	1.000	3	3	1	0	1
Ison	.750	2	3	0	1	0
Martinez	1.000	5	11	1	0	1
Medina	1.000	1	2	0	0	0
Myles	.943	25	50	3	3	0
Naquin	1.000	17	37	1	0	0
Rodriguez	.968	13	26	4	1	1
Smith	1.000	17	35	0	0	0
Zimmer	1.000	36	87	3	0	1

AKRON RUBBERDUCKS

EASTERN LEAGUE

DOUBLE-A

Batting

Batting	B-T	HT	WT	DOB	AVG	vLH	vRH	G	AB	R	H	2B	3B	HR	RBI	BB	HBP	SH	SF	SO	SB	CS	SLG	OBP
Allen, Greg	B-R	6-0	175	3-15-93	.290	.421	.243	37	145	26	42	7	3	3	13	19	8	1	1	27	7	6	.441	.399
Bautista, Claudio	R-R	5-11	170	11-29-93	.127	.071	.143	19	63	2	8	1	0	1	4	0	0	0	0	20	1	0	.190	.127
Brantley, Michael	L-L	6-2	200	5-15-87	.211	.000	.235	6	19	1	4	1	0	0	1	2	0	0	1	0	0	0	.263	.286
Castillo, Ivan	B-R	5-11	150	5-30-95	.199	.259	.180	77	241	32	48	10	2	2	24	8	5	6	5	40	10	3	.282	.236
Chisenhall, Lonnie	L-R	6-2	190	10-4-88	.133	.000	.167	4	15	3	2	1	0	0	2	0	0	0	1	2	0	0	.200	.222
Diaz, Yandy	R-R	6-2	185	8-8-91	.286	.409	.242	26	84	13	24	0	1	2	14	24	1	0	1	16	6	2	.381	.445
Frazier, Clint	R-R	6-1	190	9-6-94	.276	.244	.286	89	341	56	94	25	1	13	48	41	3	3	3	86	13	4	.469	.356
Gallas, Anthony	R-R	6-2	210	12-14-87	.063	.000	.167	4	16	0	1	0	0	0	1	0	0	0	0	8	0	0	.063	.063
Gomes, Yan	R-R	6-2	215	7-19-87	.444	.000	.667	3	9	3	4	1	0	0	2	1	0	0	0	2	0	0	.556	.500
Haase, Eric	R-R	5-10	180	12-18-92	.208	.236	.199	63	226	28	47	14	1	12	33	17	1	1	1	75	0	2	.438	.265
Hankins, Todd	R-R	5-9	180	11-18-90	.221	.270	.205	121	456	56	101	16	7	9	55	34	5	7	2	126	18	6	.346	.282
Lucas, Jeremy	R-R	6-1	205	1-10-91	.252	.262	.249	95	341	44	86	21	1	12	48	45	8	1	3	74	1	3	.425	.350
Mathias, Mark	R-R	6-0	200	8-2-94	.067	.000	.083	5	15	1	1	0	0	0	1	0	0	0	0	6	0	0	.133	.125
Medina, Yhoxian	R-R	5-10	165	5-15-90	.212	.231	.200	10	33	4	7	2	1	0	1	3	0	0	0	5	0	0	.333	.297
Miguel, Angel	R-R	6-1	175	4-1-90	.138	.000	.167	12	29	0	4	1	0	0	1	2	0	0	0	8	0	1	.172	.194
Monsalve, Alex	R-R	6-2	225	4-22-92	.297	.278	.304	18	64	10	19	2	1	1	7	5	1	0	1	8	0	0	.406	.352
Murphy, Taylor	L-R	6-2	200	11-3-92	.235	.167	.246	21	81	14	19	6	0	2	7	13	4	0	0	27	2	0	.383	.367

Batting

Batting	B-T	HT	WT	DOB	AVG	vLH	vRH	G	AB	R	H	2B	3B	HR	RBI	BB	HBP	SH	SF	SO	SB	CS	SLG	OBP
Myles, Bryson	R-R	5-11	230	9-18-89	.228	.207	.235	36	114	17	26	6	1	6	16	16	3	0	0	27	5	4	.456	.338
Papi, Mike	L-R	6-2	190	9-19-92	.228	.273	.212	78	259	33	59	16	2	8	40	41	4	0	2	72	4	0	.398	.340
Rodriguez, Luigi	B-R	5-11	160	11-13-92	.222	.250	.214	42	158	16	35	5	2	3	18	8	2	1	1	55	6	1	.335	.266
Rodriguez, Nellie	R-R	6-2	225	6-12-94	.250	.220	.260	132	492	66	123	28	2	26	85	75	6	0	6	186	1	0	.474	.352
Salters, Daniel	L-R	6-3	210	2-5-93	.235	.324	.202	38	136	15	32	9	0	1	17	10	2	2	0	39	0	0	.324	.297
Sever, Joe	R-R	6-0	205	8-12-90	.251	.307	.233	114	419	44	105	20	1	4	35	24	7	4	2	111	2	2	.332	.301
Smith, Jordan	L-R	6-4	235	7-5-90	.271	.177	.299	97	350	53	95	26	3	7	49	38	2	0	2	75	15	6	.423	.344
Stamets, Eric	R-R	6-0	190	9-25-91	.258	.173	.281	69	244	47	63	17	2	6	28	21	9	2	4	67	8	1	.418	.335
Valdez, Ordomar	B-R	5-9	150	4-27-94	.250	.333	.222	5	12	2	3	0	0	0	0	1	1	0	0	1	0	1	.250	.357
Zimmer, Bradley	L-R	6-4	185	11-27-92	.253	.179	.277	93	340	58	86	20	6	14	53	56	8	3	0	115	33	13	.471	.371

Pitching

Pitching	B-T	HT	WT	DOB	W	L	ERA	G	GS	CG	SV	IP	H	R	ER	HR	BB	SO	AVG	vLH	vRH	K/9	BB/9
Angulo, Argenis	R-R	6-3	220	2-26-94	0	0	6.23	2	0	0	0	4	4	3	3	2	2	1	.222	.250	.200	2.08	4.15
Aviles, Robbie	L-R	6-4	200	12-17-91	2	2	4.39	32	1	0	1	55	67	28	27	5	19	34	.321	.303	.336	5.53	3.09
Brantley, Justin	R-R	5-11	167	3-5-91	1	0	7.47	12	0	0	0	16	21	16	13	3	14	14	.313	.256	.393	8.04	8.04
Brown, D.J.	R-R	6-6	205	11-28-90	8	8	4.78	27	20	0	0	132	139	73	70	14	42	117	.270	.276	.266	8.00	2.87
Carrasco, Carlos	R-R	6-4	210	3-21-87	0	0	2.25	1	1	0	0	4	7	2	1	1	1	6	.412	.333	.500	13.50	2.25
Castillo, Lendy	R-R	6-1	180	4-8-89	0	1	16.88	2	1	0	0	3	5	5	5	0	1	2	.385	.400	.375	6.75	3.38
2-team total (40 Erie)					3	4	5.68	42	1	0	0	51	34	32	4	27	52		—			9.24	4.80
Cooper, Jordan	R-R	6-2	190	5-10-89	0	0	18.00	1	0	0	0	1	3	2	2	1	1	0	.500	.500	.500	0.00	9.00
Cox, Cortland	R-R	6-1	185	11-3-94	0	0	7.27	3	0	0	0	9	12	7	7	0	3	9	.324	.182	.385	9.35	3.12
Feyereisen, J.P.	R-R	6-2	215	2-7-93	4	3	2.23	33	0	0	5	40	30	12	10	3	20	56	.205	.292	.136	12.50	4.46
2-team total (9 Trenton)					7	3	1.70	42	0	0	5	58	38	14	11	3	26	78		—			12.03	4.01
Garner, Perci	R-R	6-3	225	12-13-88	5	1	1.94	23	0	0	2	51	37	13	11	1	11	47	.202	.207	.198	8.29	1.94
Head, Louis	R-R	6-1	180	4-23-90	2	1	2.66	45	0	0	6	68	56	23	20	3	18	61	.228	.252	.209	8.11	2.39
Heller, Ben	R-R	6-3	205	8-5-91	1	0	0.55	15	0	0	7	16	3	1	1	1	5	23	.057	.065	.045	12.67	2.76
Hill, Cameron	R-R	6-1	185	5-24-94	0	0	2.51	10	0	0	3	14	11	4	4	2	1	10	.204	.200	.207	6.28	0.63
Hynes, Colt	L-L	5-11	200	6-28-85	1	0	5.00	8	0	0	1	9	10	6	5	0	2	8	.286	.167	.412	8.00	2.00
2-team total (13 New Hampshire)					1	1	2.51	21	0	0	1	29	24	9	8	1	8	29		—			9.10	2.51
Kaminsky, Rob	L-R	5-11	190	9-2-94	11	7	3.28	25	25	0	0	137	122	54	50	7	48	92	.241	.235	.243	6.04	3.15
Kime, Dace	R-R	6-4	200	3-6-92	1	3	11.32	4	4	0	0	10	8	13	13	0	16	5	.222	.313	.15	4.35	13.94
Maronde, Nick	B-L	6-3	210	9-5-89	0	1	2.19	21	0	0	4	25	24	7	6	2	3	23	.253	.205	.294	8.39	1.09
McAllister, Zach	R-R	6-6	240	12-8-87	0	0	0.00	2	0	0	0	2	1	0	0	0	0	3	.143	.000	.333	9.00	0.00
Merryweather, Julian	R-R	6-4	200	10-14-91	5	4	3.89	13	13	0	0	74	75	42	32	6	17	61	.255	.262	.248	7.42	2.07
Milbrath, Jordan	R-R	6-6	215	8-1-91	1	0	0.00	1	0	0	0	2	1	0	0	0	2	3	.143	.000	.333	11.57	7.71
Morimando, Shawn	L-L	6-0	200	11-20-92	10	3	3.09	16	16	0	0	93	77	34	32	5	36	73	.225	.177	.244	7.04	3.47
Pasquale, Nick	R-R	6-0	190	10-27-90	4	7	4.22	13	13	0	0	70	73	36	33	4	32	53	.266	.246	.288	6.78	4.09
Peoples, Scott	R-R	6-5	190	9-5-91	12	6	3.68	27	27	1	0	159	166	78	65	7	53	84	.275	.272	.279	4.75	3.00
Plutko, Adam	R-R	6-3	200	10-3-91	3	3	3.27	13	13	0	0	72	64	27	26	5	12	63	.238	.232	.243	7.91	1.51
Polanco, Anderson	L-L	6-3	190	6-6-92	1	5	8.06	6	5	0	0	22	29	22	20	2	14	21	.322	.250	.348	8.46	5.64
Roberts, Will	L-R	6-5	220	8-17-90	0	0	0.00	1	0	0	0	1	4	2	0	0	0	0	.667	.500	.750	0.00	0.00
Romero, Antonio	R-R	6-0	187	12-22-90	2	0	7.59	12	0	0	1	21	26	19	18	2	12	17	.292	.333	.25	7.17	5.06
Sides, Grant	R-R	6-4	215	6-22-89	2	1	3.36	42	0	0	3	62	41	26	23	4	27	69	.190	.177	.207	10.07	3.94
Speer, David	L-L	6-1	185	8-14-92	0	0	10.13	2	0	0	0	3	6	3	3	0	1	4	.429	.375	.500	13.50	3.38
Stammen, Craig	R-R	6-4	230	3-9-84	0	1	0.79	10	0	0	0	11	9	2	1	1	3	9	.214	.190	.238	7.15	2.38
Sulser, Cole	R-R	6-0	190	3-12-90	1	4	4.81	28	2	0	5	39	44	21	21	1	13	38	.280	.266	.290	8.69	2.97
Weathers, Casey	R-R	6-1	205	6-10-85	0	3	3.54	23	0	0	1	28	27	13	11	2	16	30	.252	.302	.204	9.64	5.14

Fielding

Catcher	PCT	G	PO	A	E	DP	PB
Haase	.995	46	338	34	2	1	4
Lucas	.997	45	328	40	1	2	3
Monsalve	.981	14	91	13	2	0	1
Salters	.993	37	274	21	2	1	2

First Base	PCT	G	PO	A	E	DP
Lucas	.989	10	80	11	1	4
Monsalve	1.000	1	7	1	0	1
Papi	1.000	2	14	1	0	1
Rodriguez	.993	123	1041	92	8	111
Sever	1.000	5	47	4	0	2

Second Base	PCT	G	PO	A	E	DP
Bautista	1.000	16	24	34	0	6
Castillo	.981	11	23	28	1	8
Diaz	1.000	1	1	2	0	1
Hankins	.985	98	172	282	7	68
Mathias	1.000	5	9	15	0	8
Medina	1.000	6	12	21	0	3
Miguel	1.000	2	0	2	0	1
Sever	.920	8	5	18	2	2
Stamets	.889	1	3	5	1	3
Valdez	1.000	5	5	14	0	3

Third Base	PCT	G	PO	A	E	DP
Bautista	.800	3	0	4	1	0
Castillo	.957	9	6	16	1	1
Diaz	.907	22	11	28	4	3
Haase	—	1	0	0	0	0
Hankins	1.000	6	3	7	0	1
Miguel	1.000	1	0	4	0	0
Sever	.920	101	64	154	19	16
Stamets	.917	3	4	7	1	2

Shortstop	PCT	G	PO	A	E	DP
Castillo	.971	57	76	159	7	38
Hankins	.973	18	20	51	2	6
Medina	.826	4	5	14	4	5
Miguel	.969	8	6	25	1	2
Stamets	.970	63	91	203	9	49

Outfield	PCT	G	PO	A	E	DP
Allen	1.000	36	87	6	0	2
Brantley	1.000	6	9	1	0	0
Chisenhall	1.000	4	11	0	0	0
Frazier	.950	75	144	9	8	0
Gallas	1.000	1	1	0	0	0
Hankins	.923	7	12	0	1	0
Murphy	1.000	19	40	1	0	0
Myles	1.000	22	33	0	0	0
Papi	.993	62	127	10	1	1
Rodriguez	.965	30	53	2	2	0
Smith	.983	87	166	5	3	1
Zimmer	.986	85	209	5	3	1

LYNCHBURG HILLCATS

CAROLINA LEAGUE

HIGH CLASS A

CLEVELAND INDIANS

Batting	B-T	HT	WT	DOB	AVG	vLH	vRH	G	AB	R	H	2B	3B	HR	RBI	BB	HBP	SH	SF	SO	SB	CS	SLG	OBP
Allen, Greg	B-R	6-0	175	3-15-93	.298	.264	.316	92	346	93	103	16	4	4	31	58	19	7	2	51	38	7	.402	.424
Armendariz, David	R-R	6-0	190	8-22-91	.252	.273	.243	30	103	18	26	8	1	4	13	5	2	0	1	24	0	1	.466	.297
Bautista, Claudio	R-R	5-11	170	11-29-93	.239	.183	.264	70	234	33	56	10	0	6	32	33	3	2	5	55	6	7	.359	.335
Bradley, Bobby	L-R	6-1	225	5-29-96	.235	.245	.230	131	485	82	114	23	1	29	102	75	8	0	4	170	3	0	.466	.344
Carter, Jodd	R-R	5-10	170	7-20-96	.333	—	.333	2	6	0	2	2	0	0	1	1	0	0	0	3	0	0	.667	.429
Castillo, Ivan	B-R	5-11	150	5-30-95	.174	.250	.151	19	69	9	12	1	0	1	11	5	1	2	1	12	6	0	.232	.237
Castro, Willi	B-R	6-1	165	4-24-97	.222	.000	.500	3	9	0	2	0	0	0	0	0	0	0	0	2	0	1	.222	.222
Cervenka, Martin	R-R	6-1	175	8-3-92	.545	.600	.500	4	11	3	6	2	0	1	2	1	0	0	0	3	0	1	1.000	.583
Chang, Yu-Cheng	R-R	6-1	175	8-18-95	.259	.252	.262	109	417	78	108	30	8	13	70	45	4	4	7	110	11	3	.463	.332
De La Cruz, Juan	B-R	6-1	195	8-5-93	.138	.000	.222	14	29	4	4	1	0	0	6	5	0	0	0	10	1	.172	.265
Hendrix, Paul	R-R	6-2	190	11-18-91	.216	.250	.200	65	213	29	46	11	0	4	29	34	2	1	5	76	2	3	.324	.323
Ison, Bobby	L-L	5-8	170	7-5-93	.250	.200	.300	6	20	3	5	3	0	0	4	0	0	1	0	4	0	0	.400	.250
Krieger, Tyler	B-R	6-2	170	1-16-94	.282	.317	.269	59	220	33	62	13	4	2	23	28	4	2	3	52	6	7	.405	.369
Loopstok, Sicnarf	R-R	5-11	195	4-26-93	.281	.309	.268	55	178	27	50	11	3	2	17	15	9	2	2	39	10	3	.410	.363
Lukes, Nathan	L-R	5-11	185	7-12-94	.261	.444	.143	5	23	3	6	1	0	0	1	0	0	0	0	5	1	0	.304	.261
Marabell, Connor	L-R	6-1	195	3-28-94	.266	.235	.277	35	128	11	34	13	1	1	19	6	4	0	2	17	1	1	.406	.284
Mathias, Mark	R-R	6-0	200	8-2-94	.274	.270	.275	115	427	70	117	39	1	5	60	48	10	2	3	87	9	1	.405	.359
Mejia, Francisco	B-R	5-10	175	10-27-95	.333	.286	.353	42	168	22	56	12	1	4	29	13	1	0	2	24	1	2	.488	.380
Mendoza, Yonathan	B-R	5-11	167	2-10-94	.327	.417	.302	17	55	6	18	2	0	0	4	6	2	1	0	12	1	0	.364	.413
Monsalve, Alex	R-R	6-2	225	4-22-92	.219	.292	.184	21	73	10	16	3	0	1	3	6	2	0	1	21	0	0	.301	.293
Murphy, Taylor	L-R	6-2	200	11-3-92	.267	.226	.282	99	359	51	96	22	3	12	55	46	4	0	4	110	3	5	.446	.354
Papi, Mike	L-R	6-2	190	9-19-92	.236	.206	.245	40	140	22	33	9	0	7	18	30	1	0	2	42	0	1	.450	.370
Paulino, Dorssys	R-R	6-0	175	11-21-94	.284	.292	.281	55	211	26	60	14	1	6	31	22	1	1	1	50	1	2	.445	.353
Rodriguez, Luigi	B-R	5-11	160	11-13-92	.330	.452	.270	24	94	18	31	5	1	3	26	6	1	0	4	32	6	2	.500	.362
Salters, Daniel	L-R	6-3	210	2-5-93	.281	.386	.244	48	167	22	47	7	0	4	17	20	2	2	1	35	1	0	.395	.363
Santander, Anthony	B-R	6-2	190	10-19-94	.290	.296	.287	128	500	90	145	42	0	20	95	54	12	1	7	118	10	5	.494	.368

Pitching	B-T	HT	WT	DOB	W	L	ERA	G	GS	CG	SV	IP	H	R	ER	HR	BB	SO	AVG	vLH	vRH	K/9	BB/9
Aviles, Robbie	L-R	6-4	200	12-17-91	2	0	2.16	6	0	0	0	8	8	3	2	1	2	7	.250	.200	.294	7.56	2.16
Brady, Sean	L-L	6-0	175	6-9-94	12	6	4.95	26	25	1	0	145	180	97	80	11	46	118	.304	.299	.306	7.31	2.85
Brown, Mitch	R-R	6-1	195	4-13-94	4	6	5.03	36	17	0	0	98	81	60	55	3	77	120	.229	.251	.206	10.98	7.05
DeMasi, Dominic	R-R	6-3	190	5-18-93	2	1	7.04	11	2	0	0	23	29	21	18	2	9	12	.290	.200	.380	4.70	3.52
Esparza, Matt	R-R	6-2	195	8-22-94	2	4	3.92	7	7	0	0	39	39	19	17	3	14	32	.252	.229	.278	7.38	3.23
Eubank, Luke	R-R	6-0	180	2-24-94	2	2	4.97	18	0	0	1	25	32	16	14	0	11	21	.327	.317	.333	7.46	3.91
Frank, Trevor	R-R	6-0	195	6-23-91	1	1	2.47	44	0	0	17	44	30	12	12	3	10	43	.191	.155	.212	8.86	2.06
Garcia, Justin	R-R	6-1	180	9-16-92	2	0	3.38	33	0	0	0	51	47	20	19	2	25	42	.255	.234	.746	4.44	4.44
Hartson, Brock	R-R	6-2	195	8-9-93	2	1	4.18	6	6	0	0	32	38	16	15	4	7	26	.290	.289	.291	7.24	1.95
Hill, Cameron	R-R	6-1	185	5-24-94	6	1	2.41	31	0	0	3	56	51	17	15	3	14	57	.245	.233	.257	9.16	2.25
Linares, Leandro	R-R	6-3	205	1-27-94	0	0	0.00	2	0	0	0	2	2	0	0	1	3	.222	.250	.200	11.57	3.86
Lugo, Luis	L-L	6-5	200	3-5-94	8	5	4.04	26	26	0	0	136	130	68	61	12	52	113	.253	.241	.258	7.48	3.44
Merryweather, Julian	R-R	6-4	200	10-14-91	8	2	1.03	11	11	0	0	61	47	14	7	4	15	58	.210	.220	.200	8.56	2.21
Milbrath, Jordan	R-R	6-6	215	8-1-91	3	5	5.43	41	0	0	4	60	59	49	36	6	35	62	.247	.240	.254	9.35	5.28
Pannone, Thomas	L-L	6-0	195	4-28-94	3	0	1.65	8	7	0	0	44	31	10	8	1	16	38	.200	.196	.202	7.83	3.30
Pasquale, Nick	R-R	6-0	190	10-27-90	2	1	2.03	8	5	0	0	27	25	8	6	0	7	25	.250	.222	.273	8.44	2.36
Polanco, Anderson	L-L	6-3	190	9-6-92	4	2	4.53	13	8	0	1	56	52	36	28	3	30	59	.249	.278	.234	9.54	4.85
Robinson, Jared	R-R	6-0	190	11-20-94	3	5	6.15	9	3	0	0	41	50	29	28	5	13	21	.301	.302	.300	4.61	2.85
Romero, Antonio	R-R	6-0	187	12-22-90	1	1	9.98	7	1	0	1	15	21	22	17	1	13	13	.313	.292	.326	7.63	7.63
Sheffield, Justus	L-L	5-10	195	5-13-96	7	5	3.59	19	19	0	0	95	91	40	38	6	40	93	.252	.242	.256	8.78	3.78
Speer, David	L-L	6-1	185	8-14-92	4	1	1.78	39	1	0	3	61	45	15	12	3	12	60	.201	.179	.212	8.90	1.78
Strode, Billy	L-L	6-0	180	8-10-92	2	1	2.08	18	0	0	0	26	22	6	6	0	6	24	.229	.231	.228	8.31	2.08
Sulser, Cole	R-R	6-0	190	3-12-90	1	1	4.12	12	0	0	2	20	21	12	9	1	4	25	.276	.244	.314	11.44	1.83
Whitehouse, Matt	L-L	6-1	175	4-13-91	3	4	3.44	24	2	0	1	50	50	22	19	2	22	49	.259	.255	.260	8.88	3.99

Fielding

Catcher	PCT	G	PO	A	E	DP	PB
Cervenka	.905	4	16	3	2	0	0
De La Cruz	1.000	10	55	5	0	1	4
Loopstok	.994	39	293	49	2	5	21
Mejia	.984	35	270	36	5	5	3
Monsalve	.982	14	102	9	2	2	3
Salters	.987	46	348	43	5	2	10

First Base	PCT	G	PO	A	E	DP
Bradley	.988	116	986	56	13	97
Hendrix	1.000	2	15	0	0	0
Loopstok	.953	4	40	1	2	4
Monsalve	1.000	1	6	0	0	0
Papi	1.000	9	74	7	0	7
Santander	.988	9	80	1	1	5

Second Base	PCT	G	PO	A	E	DP
Bautista	1.000	14	26	47	0	12
Castillo	1.000	1	4	4	0	0
Krieger	.980	56	100	141	5	36
Mathias	.983	69	103	193	5	41
Mendoza	1.000	1	4	1	0	1

Third Base	PCT	G	PO	A	E	DP
Bautista	.955	45	23	82	5	5
Castillo	.932	11	15	26	3	3
Hendrix	.944	51	29	89	7	3
Mathias	.946	26	20	50	4	8
Mendoza	1.000	9	7	13	0	1
Murphy	.667	1	0	2	1	0

Shortstop	PCT	G	PO	A	E	DP
Bautista	1.000	1	1	3	0	1
Castillo	1.000	7	9	16	0	2
Castro	1.000	1	1	0	0	0
Chang	.964	104	155	301	17	67
Hendrix	.938	4	6	9	1	2
Mathias	.933	19	26	57	6	9
Mendoza	.926	6	7	18	2	3

Outfield	PCT	G	PO	A	E	DP
Allen	.992	92	228	9	2	2
Armendariz	1.000	28	56	3	0	0
Carter	.667	2	2	0	1	0

	PCT	G	PO	A	E	DP
Ison	.941	6	16	0	1	0
Loopstok	1.000	2	3	0	0	0
Lukes	1.000	5	6	0	0	0
Marabell	.989	34	88	4	1	0
Murphy	.982	90	165	2	3	1

	PCT	G	PO	A	E	DP
Papi	.918	30	45	0	4	0
Paulino	.930	40	64	2	5	1
Rodriguez	.958	20	23	0	1	0
Santander	.981	75	99	2	2	0

LAKE COUNTY CAPTAINS

LOW CLASS A

MIDWEST LEAGUE

Batting	B-T	HT	WT	DOB	AVG	vLH	vRH	G	AB	R	H	2B	3B	HR	RBI	BB	HBP	SH	SF	SO	SB	CS	SLG	OBP
Armendariz, David	R-R	6-0	190	8-22-91	.238	.250	.233	55	210	16	50	14	2	3	25	4	2	1	0	58	0	0	.367	.259
Brantley, Michael	L-L	6-2	200	5-15-87	.667	—	.667	1	3	0	2	1	0	0	0	0	0	0	0	0	0	0	1.000	.667
Calica, Andrew	B-R	6-1	190	3-5-94	.359	.455	.321	10	39	5	14	3	0	1	5	1	2	0	0	11	1	1	.513	.405
Carter, Jodd	R-R	5-10	170	7-20-96	.276	.297	.269	38	145	18	40	5	0	2	11	20	2	0	0	36	2	0	.352	.371
Castro, Willi	B-R	6-1	165	4-24-97	.259	.233	.270	123	518	68	134	21	8	7	49	19	3	3	5	96	16	11	.371	.286
Cerda, Erlin	R-R	5-9	170	5-5-94	.182	.250	.167	7	22	0	4	1	0	0	2	2	0	1	0	10	0	0	.227	.250
Cervenka, Martin	R-R	6-1	175	8-3-92	.263	.276	.258	92	331	34	87	14	2	5	48	31	1	0	5	78	1	1	.363	.323
Chu, Li-Jen	R-R	5-11	200	3-13-94	.245	.292	.229	26	94	8	23	7	0	1	6	4	1	0	1	27	0	0	.351	.280
De La Cruz, Juan	B-R	6-1	195	8-5-93	.250	.167	.283	23	84	8	21	3	0	0	7	5	1	2	2	16	0	0	.286	.293
Goihl, Jack	R-R	6-2	215	3-2-93	.000	.000	.000	3	7	0	0	0	0	0	0	1	0	0	0	3	0	0	.000	.125
Haggerty, Sam	B-R	5-11	175	5-26-94	.230	.217	.236	100	344	56	79	15	2	4	39	45	5	5	6	105	12	2	.320	.323
Ison, Bobby	L-L	5-8	170	7-5-93	.225	.129	.256	90	285	34	64	9	2	3	31	25	3	3	3	55	6	7	.302	.291
Krieger, Tyler	B-R	6-2	170	1-16-94	.313	.316	.312	69	262	51	82	13	4	3	35	29	4	0	4	66	15	8	.427	.385
Loopstok, Sicnarf	R-R	5-11	195	4-26-93	.213	.200	.222	16	47	6	10	3	0	0	4	2	1	1	0	14	1	2	.277	.260
Lukes, Nathan	L-R	5-11	185	7-12-94	.301	.318	.293	89	342	54	103	21	8	5	32	37	6	4	4	60	14	8	.453	.375
Marabell, Connor	L-R	6-1	195	3-28-94	.311	.265	.333	95	338	41	105	32	4	6	50	33	1	2	6	50	11	3	.482	.368
Medina, Jose	L-L	6-1	185	2-14-95	.240	.195	.252	60	196	22	47	11	3	8	22	11	3	0	1	59	2	1	.449	.289
Mejia, Francisco	B-R	5-10	175	10-27-95	.347	.402	.318	60	239	41	83	17	3	7	51	15	1	1	3	39	1	0	.531	.384
Mendoza, Yonathan	B-R	5-11	167	2-10-94	.245	.246	.244	57	200	15	49	7	0	1	24	17	1	2	3	34	1	1	.295	.303
Miguel, Angel	R-R	6-1	175	4-1-90	.215	.250	.203	36	107	10	23	6	0	0	7	12	1	1	1	28	2	0	.271	.298
Miller, Anthony	L-R	6-4	240	10-4-94	.195	.198	.194	102	339	33	66	13	2	11	35	32	9	0	3	148	1	0	.342	.279
Perez, Roberto	R-R	5-11	220	12-23-88	.000	—	.000	1	2	0	0	0	0	0	0	1	0	0	0	0	0	0	.000	.333
Sayles, Silento	R-R	5-9	185	8-28-95	.188	.280	.128	18	64	6	12	3	0	0	1	5	3	0	0	21	4	4	.234	.278
Tom, Ka'ai	L-R	5-9	185	5-24-94	.323	.394	.288	28	99	20	32	6	1	1	11	21	1	2	0	13	3	3	.434	.446
Valdez, Ordomar	R-R	5-9	150	4-27-94	.181	.138	.199	61	204	12	37	5	2	0	7	8	1	6	2	47	9	1	.225	.214
Winfrey, Nate	R-R	6-2	205	9-29-94	.142	.178	.122	39	127	15	18	6	0	0	8	14	4	0	1	49	0	0	.189	.247

Pitching	B-T	HT	WT	DOB	W	L	ERA	G	GS	CG	SV	IP	H	R	ER	HR	BB	SO	AVG	vLH	vRH	K/9	BB/9
Algarin, Erick	R-R	6-1	195	3-31-95	0	1	3.27	22	0	0	3	33	25	15	12	1	11	47	.217	.241	.197	12.82	3.00
Angulo, Argenis	R-R	6-3	220	2-26-94	2	0	1.06	8	0	0	0	17	7	5	2	1	5	17	.130	.222	.037	9.00	2.65
Armstrong, Shawn	R-R	6-2	225	9-11-90	0	0	0.00	2	0	0	0	2	0	0	0	0	0	5	.000	.000	.000	22.50	0.00
Chiang, Shao-Ching	R-R	6-0	175	11-10-93	8	12	3.96	27	27	1	0	152	149	73	67	13	26	92	.258	.272	.246	5.44	1.54
Cox, Cortland	R-R	6-1	185	11-3-94	6	2	4.23	26	2	0	1	62	65	31	29	6	21	54	.277	.241	.307	7.88	3.06
DeMasi, Dominic	R-R	6-3	190	5-18-93	6	3	4.07	28	1	0	1	49	58	24	22	4	16	41	.293	.226	.342	7.58	2.96
Esparza, Matt	R-R	6-2	195	8-22-94	8	6	3.14	20	19	0	0	100	81	41	35	6	22	109	.221	.265	.183	9.78	1.97
Fitzsimmons, Jon	R-R	6-2	205	11-29-91	1	0	3.31	10	0	0	0	16	9	8	6	1	9	25	.158	.138	.179	13.78	4.96
Foss, Trevor	R-R	6-3	175	11-13-94	4	3	4.46	7	7	1	0	42	40	22	21	5	5	39	.252	.244	.261	8.29	1.06
Hartson, Brock	R-R	6-2	195	8-9-93	7	5	2.86	20	10	1	0	94	87	36	30	7	20	69	.243	.221	.262	6.58	1.91
Hentges, Sam	L-L	6-6	245	7-18-96	2	4	6.12	14	14	0	0	60	71	49	41	8	29	73	.296	.325	.281	10.89	4.33
Krauth, Ben	L-L	6-0	180	3-10-94	0	0	3.00	2	0	0	0	3	3	1	1	1	1	1	.300	.400	.200	3.00	3.00
Linares, Leandro	R-R	6-3	205	1-27-94	1	1	1.76	15	0	0	4	31	21	8	6	0	8	39	.194	.224	.169	11.45	2.35
Lovegrove, Kieran	R-R	6-4	185	7-28-94	4	3	4.25	39	0	0	6	49	47	29	23	2	22	44	.251	.250	.253	8.14	4.07
Marquina, Yoiber	R-R	5-10	190	2-3-96	1	1	3.16	28	0	0	7	31	27	11	11	7	14	43	.233	.240	.227	12.35	4.02
Mathews, Kenny	L-L	6-3	205	8-18-94	0	1	6.10	9	0	0	3	10	13	7	7	0	3	12	.317	.368	.273	10.45	2.61
McKenzie, Triston	R-R	6-5	165	8-2-97	2	2	3.18	6	6	0	0	34	27	12	12	2	6	49	.214	.183	.242	12.97	1.59
Meister, Christian	R-R	6-3	210	10-29-93	2	2	4.92	32	0	0	1	53	60	34	29	4	40	37	.294	.333	.263	6.28	6.79
Miniard, Micah	R-R	6-3	195	4-12-96	0	2	4.15	8	8	0	0	39	40	22	18	2	19	25	.263	.227	.299	5.77	4.38
Pannone, Thomas	L-L	6-0	195	4-28-94	5	5	3.02	17	17	0	0	89	73	33	30	7	25	84	.223	.248	.211	8.46	2.52
Robinson, Jared	R-R	6-0	190	11-20-94	2	2	5.63	18	2	0	2	62	80	40	39	7	21	50	.302	.295	.307	7.22	3.03
Shane, Casey	R-R	6-4	200	8-23-95	9	12	4.94	27	27	0	0	129	137	78	71	10	49	81	.273	.276	.271	5.64	3.41
Stewart, Devon	R-R	6-2	184	12-26-92	1	1	8.10	9	0	0	1	10	11	9	9	5	5	9	.268	.294	.250	8.10	4.50
Strode, Billy	L-L	6-0	180	8-10-92	1	0	0.68	21	0	0	5	27	9	3	2	2	2	27	.105	.093	.116	9.11	0.68
Whitehouse, Matt	L-L	6-1	175	4-13-91	1	0	0.98	12	0	0	2	28	18	6	3	1	6	33	.180	.233	.140	10.73	1.95

Fielding

Catcher	PCT	G	PO	A	E	DP	PB
Cervenka	.996	64	483	72	2	7	13
Chu	1.000	5	46	2	0	0	2
De La Cruz	.986	8	57	11	1	0	9
Goihl	1.000	1	3	0	0	0	0
Loopstok	.988	12	72	12	1	3	1
Mejia	.991	52	412	49	4	5	3
Perez	1.000	1	4	0	0	0	0

First Base	PCT	G	PO	A	E	DP
De La Cruz	1.000	5	35	2	0	3
Loopstok	1.000	4	31	1	0	0
Medina	.994	21	143	10	1	9
Mendoza	1.000	1	13	0	0	2
Miller	.984	97	773	51	13	67
Winfrey	.974	18	146	5	4	6

Second Base	PCT	G	PO	A	E	DP
Haggerty	.982	48	95	125	4	28
Krieger	.961	61	128	143	11	38
Mendoza	1.000	2	5	6	0	1
Miguel	1.000	22	29	61	0	12
Valdez	.968	10	12	18	1	5

Third Base	PCT	G	PO	A	E	DP
Cerda	.833	7	7	8	3	1
Haggerty	.948	33	24	67	5	4
Mendoza	.896	43	26	69	11	3
Miguel	1.000	5	3	11	0	0
Valdez	.939	50	24	83	7	5
Winfrey	.960	9	8	16	1	0

Shortstop	PCT	G	PO	A	E	DP
Castro	.951	119	187	295	25	71
Haggerty	.942	11	18	31	3	10
Mendoza	1.000	1	4	2	0	1
Miguel	1.000	9	7	27	0	3

Outfield	PCT	G	PO	A	E	DP
Armendariz	.986	47	69	0	1	0
Brantley	1.000	1	1	0	0	0

	PCT	G	PO	A	E	DP
Calica	1.000	10	27	0	0	0
Carter	.979	38	92	2	2	1
Haggerty	1.000	4	5	1	0	0
Ison	.985	86	128	4	2	1
Lukes	.995	83	180	3	1	2
Marabell	.995	87	180	6	1	1
Medina	.983	29	56	1	1	0
Sayles	1.000	17	45	2	0	2
Tom	1.000	26	45	8	0	3

MAHONING VALLEY SCRAPPERS
NEW YORK-PENN LEAGUE

SHORT-SEASON

Batting	B-T	HT	WT	DOB	AVG	vLH	vRH	G	AB	R	H	2B	3B	HR	RBI	BB	HBP	SH	SF	SO	SB	CS	SLG	OBP
Brantley, Michael	L-L	6-2	200	5-15-87	.500	1.000	.000	1	2	0	1	0	0	0	0	1	0	0	0	0	0	0	.500	.667
Calica, Andrew	B-R	6-1	190	3-5-94	.388	.324	.410	40	139	29	54	7	6	2	27	16	15	1	3	16	14	3	.568	.491
Carter, Jodd	R-R	5-10	170	7-20-96	.242	.310	.214	28	99	10	24	7	1	2	12	8	4	0	2	33	0	0	.394	.319
Cerda, Erlin	R-R	5-9	170	5-5-94	.233	.238	.231	59	206	25	48	8	1	5	35	16	5	0	6	50	8	6	.354	.296
Collins, Gavin	R-R	5-11	205	7-17-95	.260	.179	.284	48	173	19	45	8	1	0	19	22	2	0	1	28	0	0	.318	.348
Cruz, Grofi	R-R	6-2	175	4-3-96	.188	.000	.231	5	16	2	3	0	0	0	1	1	0	0	0	7	0	0	.188	.235
Eladio, Miguel	R-R	6-1	160	5-10-96	.313	.500	.286	4	16	2	5	2	0	1	4	2	0	0	1	2	0	0	.625	.368
Goihl, Jack	R-R	6-2	215	3-2-93	.160	.000	.195	18	50	6	8	2	1	2	9	7	0	0	2	13	0	0	.360	.254
Gomes, Juan	R-R	6-2	180	12-25-91	.000	.000	.000	3	4	0	0	0	0	0	0	0	1	0	0	3	0	0	.000	.200
Gonzalez, Gianpaul	R-R	6-0	185	1-11-96	.230	.160	.258	26	87	5	20	3	0	2	4	4	0	2	0	27	0	0	.264	.264
Gonzalez, Oscar	R-R	6-2	180	1-10-98	.000	.000	.000	1	3	0	0	0	0	0	0	1	0	0	0	1	0	0	.000	.250
Ice, Logan	B-R	5-10	195	5-27-95	.198	.172	.206	39	126	13	25	7	0	2	8	23	2	1	1	38	0	0	.302	.329
Isaacs, Todd	R-R	5-11	175	5-22-94	.333	.259	.350	44	144	24	48	6	1	6	20	8	5	6	2	45	14	2	.514	.384
Laureano, Jonathan	R-R	6-1	200	12-21-95	.104	.118	.100	23	77	3	8	0	0	1	10	3	1	2	3	15	0	0	.143	.143
Longo, Mitch	L-R	6-0	185	1-12-95	.307	.375	.298	38	137	21	42	9	1	1	15	8	2	0	2	17	4	0	.409	.349
Lucas, Simeon	L-R	6-2	195	2-7-96	.250	—	.250	1	4	1	1	0	0	0	1	1	0	0	0	1	0	0	.500	.400
Mejia, Gabriel	B-R	5-11	160	7-30-95	.322	.293	.330	65	264	55	85	8	3	0	16	24	0	5	0	51	28	9	.375	.378
Mendoza, Yonathan	B-R	5-11	167	2-10-94	.250	.333	.229	13	44	7	11	1	1	1	6	5	1	0	0	6	1	0	.386	.340
Pantoja, Alexis	B-R	5-11	150	1-18-96	.197	.132	.213	57	198	21	39	6	1	0	23	7	1	8	2	23	5	3	.237	.226
Rodriguez, Jorma	R-R	5-10	150	3-25-96	.213	.333	.184	18	61	9	13	4	0	1	5	5	2	1	0	16	0	0	.328	.294
Sayles, Silento	R-R	5-9	185	8-28-95	.202	.267	.178	53	163	28	33	6	4	2	17	22	4	1	2	57	5	2	.325	.309
Tapia, Emmanuel	L-L	6-3	215	2-26-96	.251	.170	.274	59	215	20	54	14	0	6	24	20	2	0	0	77	0	0	.400	.321
Tinsley, Michael	L-R	6-0	195	1-15-96	.214	.182	.235	8	28	3	6	2	0	0	2	5	0	0	0	7	3	0	.286	.333
Wakamatsu, Luke	B-R	6-3	185	10-10-96	.232	.158	.260	17	69	4	16	5	0	0	9	6	2	0	0	12	1	1	.304	.312
Winfrey, Nate	R-R	6-2	205	9-29-94	.187	.105	.218	43	139	18	26	6	1	3	20	17	5	0	2	56	1	1	.309	.294

Pitching	B-T	HT	WT	DOB	W	L	ERA	G	GS	CG	SV	IP	H	R	ER	HR	BB	SO	AVG	vLH	vRH	K/9	BB/9
Aiken, Brady	L-L	6-4	205	8-16-96	2	1	4.43	5	5	0	0	22	20	12	11	3	8	22	.233	.296	.203	8.87	3.22
Angulo, Argenis	R-R	6-3	190	2-26-94	1	0	1.19	11	0	0	1	23	10	3	3	1	8	28	.137	.103	.176	11.12	3.18
Bieber, Shane	R-R	6-3	195	5-31-95	0	0	0.38	9	0	0	0	24	10	2	1	0	2	21	.122	.175	.071	7.88	0.75
Chen, Ping-Hsueh	R-R	6-2	195	7-8-94	2	2	4.73	21	0	0	1	32	33	19	17	3	19	33	.260	.316	.214	9.19	5.29
Civale, Aaron	R-R	6-2	215	6-12-95	0	2	1.67	13	13	0	0	38	23	11	7	0	8	28	.180	.200	.155	6.69	1.91
Colegate, Ryan	R-R	6-5	195	11-12-93	6	2	3.22	19	3	0	0	50	46	25	18	1	15	44	.246	.231	.257	7.87	2.68
Herrera, Alsis	L-L	5-11	180	5-25-92	0	2	5.14	4	0	0	0	7	11	6	4	1	5	9	.367	.667	.292	6.43	1.29
Hillman, Juan	L-L	6-3	185	5-15-97	3	4	4.43	15	15	0	0	63	66	36	31	5	24	47	.268	.221	.290	6.71	3.43
Jimenez, Domingo	R-R	6-3	175	8-29-95	0	0	4.50	2	0	0	0	2	1	1	1	0	2	2	.143	.250	.000	9.00	9.00
Jimenez, Luis	R-R	6-4	170	1-2-95	1	5	5.24	14	7	0	0	55	48	39	32	4	31	38	.233	.289	.183	6.22	5.07
Kime, Dace	R-R	6-4	200	3-6-92	0	2	11.57	6	0	0	0	12	20	18	15	2	15	8	.377	.313	.476	6.17	11.57
Krauth, Ben	L-L	6-0	180	3-10-94	2	0	2.57	7	0	0	0	21	16	7	6	1	6	25	.213	.233	.200	10.71	2.57
Letkewicz, Michael	R-R	6-4	220	1-31-94	6	0	1.74	21	0	0	4	41	37	8	8	0	18	24	.252	.288	.223	5.23	3.92
Linares, Leandro	R-R	6-3	205	1-27-94	0	0	0.00	6	0	0	0	12	3	0	0	0	3	13	.083	.050	.125	10.03	2.31
Martinez, Henry	R-R	6-1	175	4-27-94	0	3	4.88	21	0	0	3	31	39	20	17	2	9	29	.300	.281	.315	8.33	2.59
Mathews, Kenny	L-L	6-3	205	8-6-93	1	0	1.54	6	0	0	2	12	6	3	2	1	4	10	.140	.091	.156	7.71	3.09
McKenzie, Triston	R-R	6-5	165	8-2-97	4	3	0.55	9	9	0	0	49	31	7	3	2	16	55	.180	.238	.099	10.03	2.92
Miniard, Micah	R-R	6-7	195	4-12-96	1	2	2.38	7	7	0	0	34	34	17	9	0	9	28	.264	.306	.224	7.41	2.38
Perez, Ryan	B-L	6-0	190	10-27-93	2	3	5.02	28	0	0	3	29	36	20	16	3	14	30	.310	.316	.308	6.28	4.40
Siri, Dalbert	R-R	6-2	190	7-19-95	0	0	0.00	2	0	0	0	5	1	0	0	0	3	7	.071	.000	.111	12.60	5.40
Stewart, Devon	R-R	6-2	184	12-26-92	0	3	4.30	9	0	0	0	15	15	7	7	0	6	11	.263	.143	.379	6.75	3.68
Tully, Tanner	L-L	6-0	200	11-30-94	4	1	1.17	13	7	0	0	46	32	11	6	0	26	9	.192	.120	.222	5.09	1.76
Valladares, Randy	L-L	5-11	155	7-6-94	2	3	6.39	21	0	0	0	25	39	20	18	0	11	30	.355	.389	.338	10.66	3.91
Ventura, Cesar	R-R	6-0	195	3-14-95	0	0	4.50	1	1	0	0	4	2	2	2	0	2	4	.154	.000	.222	9.00	4.50

Fielding

C: Goihl 15, Gomes 3, Gonzalez 25, Ice 36, Tinsley 1. **1B:** Collins 1, Goihl 1, Tapia 46, Winfrey 32. **2B:** Cerda 48, Mendoza 5, Pantoja 15, Rodriguez 11. **3B:** Cerda 9, Collins 41, Cruz 4, Laureano 21, Rodriguez 2, Winfrey 1. **SS:** Eladio 4, Mendoza 8, Pantoja 42, Rodriguez 5, Wakamatsu 17. **OF:** Brantley 1, Calica 35, Carter 21, Gonzalez 1, Isaacs 41, Laureano 1, Longo 18, Mejia 63, Sayles 45, Tinsley 6.

CLEVELAND INDIANS

AZL INDIANS ROOKIE
ARIZONA LEAGUE

Batting	B-T	HT	WT	DOB	AVG	vLH	vRH	G	AB	R	H	2B	3B	HR	RBI	BB	HBP	SH	SF	SO	SB	CS	SLG	OBP
Benson, Will	L-L	6-5	225	6-16-98	.209	.238	.198	44	158	31	33	10	3	6	27	22	4	0	0	60	10	2	.424	.321
Bradley, Kevin	B-R	6-0	195	1-9-94	.067	.000	.077	8	15	1	1	0	1	0	1	2	0	0	0	7	0	0	.200	.176
Brooks, Trenton	L-L	6-0	180	7-3-95	.222	.276	.206	35	126	12	28	9	0	0	10	8	1	3	3	18	3	2	.294	.268
Cantu, Ulysses	R-R	5-11	220	5-1-98	.202	.174	.209	30	109	11	22	2	0	1	9	12	3	1	0	42	0	0	.248	.298
Capel, Conner	L-L	6-1	185	5-19-97	.210	.138	.229	35	138	22	29	5	3	0	13	11	1	1	2	20	10	3	.290	.270
Cespedes, Cristopher	R-R	6-3	200	5-18-98	.111	.333	.000	2	9	0	1	0	0	0	1	0	0	0	0	2	0	0	.111	.200
Chu, Li-Jen	R-R	5-11	200	3-13-94	.500	.444	.520	10	34	11	17	6	1	1	7	3	2	0	0	6	1	0	.824	.564
Cruz, Grofi	R-R	6-2	175	4-3-96	.200	1.000	.000	2	5	1	1	0	0	0	1	1	0	0	0	2	0	0	.200	.333
Eladio, Miguel	R-R	6-1	160	5-10-96	.246	.241	.247	32	114	17	28	1	3	0	10	5	3	2	1	33	5	2	.307	.293
Garcia, Juan	R-R	6-3	195	8-17-97	.143	.000	.333	2	7	0	1	0	0	0	0	1	0	0	0	5	0	0	.143	.250
Gonzalez, Oscar	R-R	6-2	180	1-10-98	.303	.366	.279	40	145	30	44	10	2	8	26	8	1	0	1	57	4	0	.566	.342
Jones, Nolan	L-R	6-4	185	5-7-98	.257	.276	.250	32	109	10	28	5	2	0	9	23	1	0	1	49	3	1	.339	.388
Lucas, Simeon	L-R	6-2	195	2-7-96	.239	.130	.275	27	92	16	22	3	0	3	13	11	0	0	1	41	4	0	.370	.317
Nelson, Hosea	L-L	6-0	210	11-22-96	.222	.200	.230	30	99	15	22	5	4	2	11	11	2	0	1	45	13	0	.364	.310
Paulino, Dorssys	R-R	6-0	175	11-21-94	.393	.714	.286	9	28	8	11	2	0	0	5	6	1	0	0	5	3	1	.464	.514
Perez, Elvis	B-R	6-0	165	1-10-96	.288	.286	.289	36	132	24	38	10	1	1	22	14	1	0	2	31	5	1	.402	.356
Perez, Roberto	R-R	5-11	220	12-23-88	.333	.000	.375	6	9	4	3	0	0	0	3	5	0	0	0	1	0	0	.333	.571
Rodriguez, Jason	R-R	5-11	180	1-11-95	.205	.333	.148	24	78	7	16	2	0	0	12	3	2	1	2	18	0	0	.231	.247
Rodriguez, Jorma	R-R	5-10	150	3-25-96	.357	.368	.354	22	84	17	30	2	3	1	15	8	1	0	2	13	7	0	.488	.411
Rudledge, Jamal	R-R	6-2	170	11-22-95	.109	.333	.075	17	46	4	5	0	1	0	0	1	0	0	0	14	0	0	.152	.128
Soto, Junior	R-R	6-3	175	1-21-97	.282	.368	.258	26	85	14	24	11	1	2	14	4	1	0	1	27	1	0	.506	.319
Taylor, Samad	B-R	5-10	160	7-11-98	.293	.310	.287	32	116	25	34	5	1	1	14	11	2	4	2	24	6	2	.397	.359
Vicente, Jose	R-R	5-11	175	11-13-95	.280	.231	.297	41	157	23	44	9	1	3	28	12	2	0	3	40	2	1	.408	.333

Pitching	B-T	HT	WT	DOB	W	L	ERA	G	GS	CG	SV	IP	H	R	ER	HR	BB	SO	AVG	vLH	vRH	K/9	BB/9
Aiken, Brady	L-L	6-4	205	8-16-96	0	4	7.13	9	8	0	0	24	32	26	19	1	13	35	.308	.458	.263	13.13	4.88
Arias, Skylar	L-R	6-3	190	6-30-97	1	1	3.72	11	0	0	0	19	18	11	8	0	3	20	.234	.364	.212	9.31	1.40
Clemmer, Dakody	R-R	6-2	185	1-19-96	1	0	7.71	17	0	0	0	19	21	18	16	0	13	21	.288	.417	.262	10.13	6.27
Garza, Justin	R-R	5-10	170	3-20-94	0	2	7.00	6	4	0	0	9	12	8	7	0	7	9	.324	.357	.304	9.00	7.00
Herrera, Alsis	L-L	5-11	180	1-5-95	0	0	6.35	4	0	0	0	6	7	4	4	0	1	6	.318	.333	.316	9.53	1.59
Jimenez, Domingo	R-R	6-3	175	8-29-93	3	1	1.67	17	0	0	2	32	20	13	6	0	14	37	.174	.130	.203	10.30	3.90
Kime, Dace	R-R	6-4	200	3-6-92	0	0	9.00	2	0	0	0	4	5	4	4	0	3	2	.357	.333	.375	4.50	6.75
Krauth, Ben	L-L	6-0	180	1-10-94	2	0	0.00	7	0	0	2	14	9	1	0	0	0	20	.184	.154	.194	12.86	0.00
Marte, Randy	R-R	6-1	175	12-27-96	0	1	0.00	10	0	0	0	14	8	2	0	0	7	19	.167	.000	.250	11.93	4.40
Mathews, Kenny	L-L	6-3	205	8-6-93	0	1	3.38	6	1	0	0	13	13	3	0	1	8	.333	.143	.385	9.00	1.13
Mingo, Cameron	R-R	6-4	185	9-10-93	0	2	5.40	4	1	0	1	10	11	6	6	2	1	15	.268	.308	.250	13.50	0.90
Perez, Francisco	L-L	6-2	195	7-20-97	5	1	2.69	12	7	0	0	64	48	22	19	1	17	52	.203	.190	.208	7.35	2.40
Ryan, Ryder	R-R	6-2	205	5-11-95	0	1	3.86	15	0	0	1	19	21	9	8	1	9	24	.284	.214	.326	11.57	4.34
Salinas, Jhonleider	R-R	6-7	215	9-25-95	3	2	3.30	9	4	0	0	30	26	13	11	1	14	38	.232	.333	.200	11.40	4.20
Santos, Luis	R-R	6-4	180	9-18-94	0	2	0.00	0	0	0	1	29	34	24	20	2	6	33	.288	.292	.292	10.24	1.86
Siri, Dalbert	R-R	6-2	190	7-19-95	1	1	4.13	17	0	0	4	24	18	13	11	0	10	36	.200	.138	.230	13.50	3.75
Stammen, Craig	R-R	6-4	230	3-9-84	1	0	6.00	3	2	0	0	3	4	2	2	0	0	8	.308	.333	.286	24.00	0.00
Tati, Felix	R-R	6-2	190	4-1-97	5	2	6.04	12	10	0	0	54	67	37	36	2	17	48	.300	.347	.264	8.05	2.85
Vasquez, Gregori	R-R	6-1	185	9-8-97	5	2	3.18	12	8	0	0	57	54	27	20	3	17	44	.252	.256	.250	6.99	2.70
Ventura, Cesar	R-R	6-0	195	3-14-95	4	2	4.14	14	5	0	3	46	52	22	21	5	8	40	.287	.302	.302	7.88	1.58

Fielding

C: Capitillo 17, Liberatore 15, Lofstrom 3, Manzanero 23, Stephenson 4, Turnbull 4. **1B:** Herrera 1, Lofstrom 5, Manzanero 5, Santana 12, Turnbull 4, Yari 31. **2B:** Azcona 7, Cruz 29, Herrera 4, Juaquin 9, Ljatifi 3, Rivero 3, Salmon-Williams 2. **3B:** Azcona 1, Herrera 8, Ljatifi 11, Rivero 4, Salmon-Williams 1, Santana 33. **SS:** Azcona 7, Cruz 2, Juaquin 5, Ljatifi 7, Martinez 4, Rivero 30. **OF:** Beltre 28, Conde 23, Jimenez 25, Munroe 12, Salmon-Williams 20, Selsky 1, Sugilio 28, Wallace 34, Winker 4.

DSL INDIANS ROOKIE
DOMINICAN SUMMER LEAGUE

Batting	B-T	HT	WT	DOB	AVG	vLH	vRH	G	AB	R	H	2B	3B	HR	RBI	BB	HBP	SH	SF	SO	SB	CS	SLG	OBP
Cabrera, Julio	L-L	6-0	190	11-21-97	.167	.148	.172	40	120	12	20	4	2	0	10	13	6	0	1	17	2	0	.233	.279
Cespedes, Cristopher	R-R	6-3	200	5-18-98	.229	.235	.226	33	118	15	27	3	1	2	10	2	4	0	0	28	4	0	.322	.266
De Jesus, Christopher	R-R	5-11	170	9-24-96	.282	.316	.273	28	85	9	24	3	2	0	11	6	0	3	0	13	2	3	.365	.330
De La Rosa, Luis	R-R	6-4	170	8-31-98	.219	.167	.236	43	146	16	32	2	2	3	16	6	6	0	1	26	1	1	.301	.277
De Oleo, Henderson	R-R	6-4	210	2-11-98	.159	.167	.156	44	132	17	21	6	1	0	11	20	6	1	1	42	1	1	.220	.296
Dominguez, Ronny	R-R	6-0	175	6-5-97	.266	.220	.277	58	207	23	55	3	3	2	19	10	6	1	2	58	12	10	.338	.316
Fermin, Jose	R-R	5-11	160	3-29-99	.224	.250	.220	16	58	5	13	4	2	0	8	7	0	0	1	11	2	2	.362	.303
Fernandez, Felix	R-R	6-0	185	12-26-97	.256	.222	.267	35	117	8	30	6	0	0	15	8	0	1	2	22	1	5	.308	.299
Jerez, Miguel	R-R	6-1	178	10-24-97	.208	.167	.221	38	125	14	26	6	1	1	14	22	1	0	1	31	3	2	.296	.329
Jimenez, Pablo	R-R	6-2	175	2-6-99	.257	.217	.270	52	183	16	47	8	2	4	16	11	2	0	2	45	0	2	.388	.303
Lopez, Jonathan	B-R	6-2	175	8-13-99	.189	.048	.245	11	74	7	14	2	0	1	2	13	2	1	0	14	1	0	.216	.241
Mateo, Franklin	R-R	6-2	180	5-24-98	.146	.050	.177	30	82	6	12	3	1	1	7	11	2	0	0	50	1	2	.244	.263
Montero, Jean	R-R	5-11	175	2-26-99	.226	.303	.206	52	159	30	36	5	3	2	8	28	6	3	1	41	15	6	.333	.361
Pujols, Henry	R-R	6-3	195	12-10-98	.168	.231	.152	54	184	31	31	9	5	4	17	26	8	0	2	75	4	0	.337	.295
Rodriguez, Henry	R-R	6-0	190	3-26-99	.162	.250	.145	25	74	6	12	0	0	1	1	10	9	6	0	42	4	3	.162	.287
Rodriguez, Jhan	R-R	6-0	165	7-2-98	.214	.225	.210	51	159	14	34	8	1	1	10	9	6	0	0	42	4	3	.296	.282

Batting

Batting	B-T	HT	WT	DOB	AVG	vLH	vRH	G	AB	R	H	2B	3B	HR	RBI	BB	HBP	SH	SF	SO	SB	CS	SLG	OBP
Santiago, Wilbis	L-R	6-0	180	1-20-96	.320	.261	.333	39	125	19	40	6	2	1	17	5	8	0	1	10	5	1	.424	.381
Ventura, Carlos	L-R	6-0	180	2-22-98	.154	.000	.167	6	13	2	2	0	0	0	1	3	0	0	0	4	0	0	.154	.313

Pitching

Pitching	B-T	HT	WT	DOB	W	L	ERA	G	GS	CG	SV	IP	H	R	ER	HR	BB	SO	AVG	vLH	vRH	K/9	BB/9
Araujo, Luis	R-R	6-1	155	8-1-96	3	0	1.01	11	5	0	2	36	19	9	4	1	5	33	.158	.243	.120	8.33	1.26
Cedeno, Orlando	R-R	6-2	195	9-16-97	0	0	4.60	12	0	0	0	16	16	9	8	1	10	8	.281	.316	.263	4.60	5.74
Gutierrez, Jhonneyver	R-R	6-5	200	12-24-98	3	5	5.50	13	13	0	0	54	58	41	33	1	29	30	.271	.303	.254	5.00	4.83
Izaguirre, Alejandro	R-R	6-0	175	3-5-97	0	3	3.14	16	0	0	2	29	35	14	10	0	10	26	.315	.324	.311	8.16	3.14
Manzanillo, Maiker	R-R	6-2	190	10-14-96	2	3	3.00	14	0	0	0	21	18	10	7	1	6	16	.237	.208	.250	6.86	2.57
Mejia, Jean Carlos	R-R	6-4	205	8-26-96	2	4	3.48	17	1	0	5	34	33	21	13	0	5	22	.239	.302	.211	5.88	1.34
Meza, Wuilson	R-R	5-11	170	10-5-98	1	0	4.30	18	0	0	2	29	33	21	14	1	13	25	.292	.256	.314	7.67	3.99
Mota, Juan	R-R	6-4	190	5-4-96	5	4	3.15	13	13	0	0	60	50	32	21	0	28	41	.225	.203	.234	6.15	4.20
Nunez, Kenny	L-L	6-0	165	3-1-96	1	0	2.57	5	0	0	0	7	1	3	2	0	4	9	.045	.000	.053	11.57	5.14
Oca, Jose	R-R	6-0	150	2-28-99	1	2	3.82	17	2	0	1	38	38	21	16	0	10	32	.264	.280	.255	7.65	2.39
Oviedo, Luis	R-R	6-4	170	5-6-99	2	8	4.00	14	14	0	0	63	67	37	28	1	17	56	.276	.266	.279	8.00	2.43
Paredes, Juan	R-R	6-3	200	9-25-98	1	0	5.14	5	0	0	0	7	4	6	4	0	6	8	.174	.286	.125	10.29	7.71
Pereda, Leomar	R-R	6-1	160	9-27-97	0	1	10.29	9	0	0	0	14	21	20	16	0	6	9	.323	.556	.234	5.79	3.86
Perez, Eric	R-R	6-6	190	7-27-97	0	0	0.00	4	0	0	0	7	3	0	0	0	6	5	.120	.286	.056	6.43	7.71
Santana, Christophers	R-R	6-2	195	2-26-98	1	1	2.97	16	0	0	0	30	25	12	10	1	29	22	.231	.139	.278	6.53	8.60
Santos, Luis	R-R	6-4	180	9-18-94	0	2	3.00	3	0	0	0	6	7	3	2	1	1	3	.280	.333	.231	4.50	1.50
Tati, Felix	R-R	6-2	190	4-1-97	1	1	3.95	3	3	0	0	14	13	10	6	1	3	13	.228	.235	.225	8.56	1.98
Tineo, Ramon	R-L	6-0	170	1-31-96	1	0	2.57	4	0	0	0	7	6	2	2	0	1	11	.222	.000	.273	14.14	1.29
Valdez, Luis	R-R	6-3	170	10-14-96	0	4	3.40	12	12	0	0	45	37	27	17	2	30	24	.228	.188	.246	4.80	6.00
Varela, Jahir	L-L	5-10	175	2-7-98	0	2	6.45	17	0	0	0	22	19	18	16	0	24	19	.235	.143	.254	7.66	9.67
Ventura, Cesar	R-R	6-0	195	3-14-95	0	0	3.86	3	0	0	1	5	5	3	2	0	2	1	.278	.500	.250	1.93	3.86
Yannuzzi, Yeffersson	L-L	6-2	175	10-4-96	0	4	3.31	13	5	0	0	35	31	15	13	0	26	30	.242	.421	.211	7.64	6.62

Fielding

C: De Jesus 17, Fernandez 21, Jerez 36. **1B:** De Jesus 14, De Oleo 31, Fernandez 13, Jerez 2, Jimenez 8, Santiago 7. **2B:** Lopez 1, Montero 35, Rodriguez 14, Santiago 26. **3B:** De Oleo 11, Lopez 3, Pujols 53, Rodriguez 1, Santiago 4. **SS:** Fermin 15, Lopez 19, Montero 1, Rodriguez 38. **OF:** Cabrera 19, Cespedes 32, De La Rosa 24, Dominguez 57, Jimenez 39, Mateo 29, Montero 15, Ventura 4.

Colorado Rockies

SEASON IN A SENTENCE: For many teams, a 75-87 season is cause for alarm, but for the Rockies it's significant progress, seven games better than 2015 and the most wins for the franchise since 2010. Nevertheless, manager Walt Weiss stepped down at season's end when his contract expired.

HIGH POINT: Rookies provided most of them this year, from shortstop Trevor Story's four homers in his first four hits to righthander Jon Gray's club-record 16 strikeouts in a complete-game September shutout of the Padres. Lefty Tyler Anderson provided another, when he tossed seven strong innings to get the Rox over .500 on Aug. 3 in a 12-2 home win against the Dodgers. The game included five home runs, one by Nolan Arenado, who tied for the National League lead with 41, and another by D.J. LeMahieu, won the NL batting title by hitting .348.

LOW POINT: The Rockies had the majors' worst bullpen ERA, with a revolving door at closer. Rookie Carlos Estevez had his moments but also gave up four runs in the ninth in an Aug. 5 5-3 loss to the Marlins that dropped the Rockies back under .500. Seven different Rockies picked up a save.

NOTABLE ROOKIES: Story provided many of the other highlights in his first three months. While he struck out more than any Rockie despite playing just 97 games, he set an NL record for homers by a rookie shortstop with 27. Outfielder David Dahl, a 2012 first-rounder, stayed healthy and hit his way to Denver, hitting safely in his first 17 big league games in a strong debut. Anderson had the staff's best ERA by a starter with more than 75 innings while Gray struck out 185, a Rockies rookie record. Estevez finished second on the team in appearances (63) and saves (11).

KEY TRANSACTIONS: The biggest deal GM Jeff Bridich made came in January, when the Rockies acquired pitchers Jake McGee and German Marquez from the Rays for minor league third baseman Kevin Padlo and outfielder Corey Dickerson. Shortstop Jose Reyes started the year on the restricted list due to a domestic violence investigation; the Rockies wound up releasing him in June.

DOWN ON THE FARM: No Rockies farm team made the playoffs in a middling year in the minors, though low Class A Asheville had first baseman Brian Mundell set a modern (post-1963) minor league record with 59 doubles.

OPENING DAY PAYROLL: $112,645,071 (17th)

PLAYERS OF THE YEAR

MAJOR LEAGUE

Nolan Arenado
3b
.294/.362/.570
41 HR, 133 RBI
Led NL in HR, RBI

TONY FARLOW

MINOR LEAGUE

David Dahl
of
(Double-A/Triple-A)
.314/.394/.569
18 HR, 61 RBI

ORGANIZATION LEADERS

BATTING		*Minimum 250 AB
MAJORS		
* AVG	D.J. LeMahieu	.348
* OPS	Charlie Blackmon	.933
HR	Nolan Arenado	41
RBI	Nolan Arenado	133
MINORS		
* AVG	Raimel Tapia, Hartford, Albuquerque	.328
* OBP	David Dahl, Hartford, Albuquerque	.394
* SLG	David Dahl, Hartford, Albuquerque	.569
* OPS	David Dahl, Hartford, Albuquerque	.963
R	Brian Mundell, Asheville	94
H	Raimel Tapia, Hartford, Albuquerque	173
TB	Brian Mundell, Asheville	271
2B	Brian Mundell, Asheville	59
3B	Omar Carrizales, Modesto, Hartford	10
	Raimel Tapia, Hartford, Albuquerque	10
HR	Tom Murphy, Albuquerque	19
	Brendan Rodgers, Asheville	19
RBI	Sam Hilliard, Asheville	83
	Brian Mundell, Asheville	83
BB	Wes Rogers, Modesto	57
SO	Ryan McMahon, Hartford	161
SB	Wes Rogers, Modesto	43
PITCHING		#Minimum 75 IP
MAJORS		
W	Chad Bettis	14
# ERA	Jon Gray	4.61
SO	Jon Gray	185
SV	Jake McGee	15
MINORS		
W	Harrison Musgrave, Hartford, Albuquerque	13
	Jack Wynkoop, Asheville, Modesto	13
L	Carlos Hernandez, Albuquerque, Hartford	11
	Jesus Tinoco, Modesto, Asheville	11
# ERA	Parker French, Asheville, Modesto	2.63
G	Jerry Vasto, Modesto, Hartford	54
GS	Parker French, Asheville, Modesto	28
	Jack Wynkoop, Asheville, Modesto	28
SV	Matt Carasiti, Hartford, Albuquerque	31
IP	Parker French, Asheville, Modesto	178
BB	Yency Almonte, Modesto, Hartford	55
SO	Yency Almonte, Modesto, Hartford	156
# AVG	Helmis Rodriguez, Modesto	.231

2016 PERFORMANCE

General Manager: Jeff Bridich. **Farm Director:** Zach Wilson. **Scouting Director:** Bill Schmidt.

Class	Team	League	W	L	PCT	Finish	Manager
Majors	Colorado Rockies	National	75	87	.463	9th (15)	Walt Weiss
Triple-A	Albuquerque Isotopes	Pacific Coast	71	72	.497	7th (16)	Glenallen Hill
Double-A	Hartford Yard Goats	Eastern	74	67	.525	6th (12)	Darin Everson
High A	Modesto Nuts	California	60	80	.429	8th (10)	Fred Ocasio
Low A	Asheville Tourists	South Atlantic	66	72	.478	11th (14)	Warren Schaeffer
Short season	Boise Hawks	Northwest	33	43	.434	5th (8)	Andy Gonzalez
Rookie	Grand Junction Rockies	Pioneer	36	39	.480	6th (8)	Frank Gonzales
Overall 2016 Minor League Record			340	373	.477	21st (30)	

ORGANIZATION STATISTICS

COLORADO ROCKIES
NATIONAL LEAGUE

Batting	B-T	HT	WT	DOB	AVG	vLH	vRH	G	AB	R	H	2B	3B	HR	RBI	BB	HBP	SH	SF	SO	SB	CS	SLG	OBP
Adames, Cristhian	B-R	6-0	185	7-26-91	.218	.222	.216	121	225	25	49	7	3	2	17	24	4	3	0	47	2	3	.302	.304
Arenado, Nolan	R-R	6-2	205	4-16-91	.294	.267	.304	160	618	116	182	35	6	41	133	68	2	0	8	103	2	3	.570	.362
Barnes, Brandon	R-R	6-2	210	5-15-86	.220	.222	.219	48	100	10	22	6	2	0	8	3	1	5	0	30	1	2	.320	.250
Blackmon, Charlie	L-L	6-3	210	7-1-86	.324	.331	.320	143	578	111	187	35	5	29	82	43	13	3	4	102	17	9	.552	.381
Cardullo, Stephen	R-R	6-0	215	8-31-87	.214	.241	.185	27	56	5	12	3	1	2	6	3	0	0	0	12	0	0	.411	.254
Dahl, David	L-R	6-2	195	4-1-94	.315	.313	.316	63	222	42	70	12	4	7	24	15	0	0	0	59	5	0	.500	.359
Descalso, Daniel	L-R	5-10	190	10-19-86	.264	.233	.271	99	250	38	66	12	2	8	38	34	1	0	4	56	3	0	.424	.349
Garneau, Dustin	R-R	6-0	200	8-13-87	.235	.231	.238	24	68	7	16	6	0	1	6	6	0	0	1	22	0	0	.368	.293
Gonzalez, Carlos	L-L	6-1	220	10-17-85	.298	.273	.309	150	584	87	174	42	2	25	100	46	1	0	1	129	2	2	.505	.350
Hundley, Nick	R-R	6-1	205	9-8-83	.260	.333	.221	83	289	30	75	20	1	10	48	25	1	1	1	65	0	0	.439	.320
LeMahieu, D.J.	R-R	6-4	215	7-13-88	.348	.331	.354	146	552	104	192	32	8	11	66	66	3	6	6	80	11	7	.495	.416
Murphy, Tom	R-R	6-1	220	4-3-91	.273	.154	.323	21	44	8	12	2	0	5	13	4	1	0	0	19	1	0	.659	.347
Parra, Gerardo	L-L	5-11	210	5-6-87	.253	.258	.251	102	368	45	93	27	3	7	39	9	1	1	2	73	6	4	.399	.271
Patterson, Jordan	L-L	6-4	215	2-12-92	.444	.500	.438	10	18	1	8	1	0	0	2	1	0	0	0	1	0	1	.500	.474
Paulsen, Ben	L-R	6-4	210	10-27-87	.217	.375	.202	39	92	8	20	5	0	1	11	5	0	0	0	27	0	0	.304	.258
Raburn, Ryan	R-R	6-0	185	4-17-81	.220	.229	.213	113	223	30	49	10	2	9	30	28	2	0	3	80	0	0	.404	.309
Reynolds, Mark	R-R	6-2	220	8-3-83	.282	.250	.297	118	393	61	111	24	0	14	53	42	4	0	2	112	1	2	.450	.356
Story, Trevor	R-R	6-1	180	11-15-92	.272	.280	.268	97	372	67	101	21	4	27	72	35	5	2	1	130	8	5	.567	.341
Tapia, Raimel	L-L	6-2	160	2-4-94	.263	.250	.267	22	38	4	10	0	0	0	3	2	0	0	1	11	3	0	.263	.293
Valaika, Pat	R-R	5-11	200	9-9-92	.263	.286	.250	13	19	3	5	1	0	1	2	0	0	0	0	8	0	0	.474	.263
Wolters, Tony	L-R	5-10	200	6-9-92	.259	.225	.267	71	205	27	53	15	2	3	30	21	0	4	0	53	4	1	.395	.327
Ynoa, Rafael	R-R	6-0	190	8-7-87	.000	.000	.000	3	5	0	0	0	0	0	0	0	0	0	0	2	0	0	.000	.000

Pitching	B-T	HT	WT	DOB	W	L	ERA	G	GS	CG	SV	IP	H	R	ER	HR	BB	SO	AVG	vLH	vRH	K/9	BB/9
Anderson, Tyler	L-L	6-4	210	12-30-89	5	6	3.54	19	19	0	0	114	119	50	45	12	28	99	.272	.245	.281	7.79	2.20
Bergman, Christian	R-R	6-1	195	5-4-88	1	3	8.39	15	1	0	0	25	39	24	23	7	6	22	.355	.343	.36	8.03	2.19
Bettis, Chad	R-R	6-1	200	4-26-89	14	8	4.79	32	32	1	0	186	204	107	99	22	59	138	.278	.258	.297	6.68	2.85
Butler, Eddie	B-R	6-2	180	3-13-91	2	5	7.17	17	9	0	0	64	87	57	51	13	21	47	.328	.308	.342	6.61	2.95
Carasiti, Matt	R-R	6-3	205	7-23-91	1	0	9.19	19	0	0	0	16	25	17	16	1	11	17	.373	.548	.222	9.77	6.32
Castro, Miguel	R-R	6-5	190	12-24-94	0	0	6.14	19	0	0	0	15	18	10	10	3	5	12	.300	.389	.262	7.36	3.07
Chatwood, Tyler	R-R	6-0	185	12-16-89	12	9	3.87	27	27	0	0	158	147	75	68	15	70	117	.250	.256	.242	6.66	3.99
De La Rosa, Jorge	L-L	6-1	215	4-5-81	8	9	5.51	27	24	0	0	134	157	93	82	23	63	108	.293	.297	.291	7.25	4.23
Estevez, Carlos	R-R	6-4	210	12-28-92	3	7	5.24	63	0	0	11	55	50	32	32	6	28	59	.240	.181	.280	9.65	4.58
Flande, Yohan	L-L	6-2	180	1-27-86	0	0	12.27	2	0	0	0	4	8	6	5	0	3	0	.500	.400	.545	0.00	7.36
Germen, Gonzalez	R-R	6-1	200	9-23-87	2	1	5.31	40	0	0	1	41	41	25	24	5	25	32	.266	.328	.218	7.08	5.53
Gray, Jon	R-R	6-4	235	11-5-91	10	10	4.61	29	29	1	0	168	153	92	86	18	59	185	.243	.239	.248	9.91	3.16
Gurka, Jason	L-L	6-0	170	1-10-88	0	0	9.31	6	0	0	0	10	16	10	10	1	2	7	.381	.077	.517	6.52	1.86
Hale, David	R-R	6-2	210	9-27-87	0	0	13.50	2	0	0	0	2	4	3	3	1	2	1	.400	1.000	.333	4.50	9.00
Hoffman, Jeff	R-R	6-5	225	1-8-93	0	4	4.88	8	4	0	0	31	37	29	17	7	17	22	.287	.288	.286	6.32	4.88
Logan, Boone	R-L	6-5	215	8-13-84	2	5	3.69	66	0	0	1	46	27	23	19	4	20	57	.166	.142	.211	11.07	3.88
Lyles, Jordan	R-R	6-4	230	10-19-90	4	5	5.83	40	5	0	1	59	69	46	38	4	28	32	.291	.316	.275	4.91	4.30
Marquez, German	R-R	6-1	185	2-22-95	1	1	5.23	6	3	0	0	21	28	12	12	2	6	15	.326	.341	.310	6.53	2.61
McGee, Jake	L-L	6-3	230	8-6-86	2	3	4.73	57	0	0	15	46	56	25	24	9	16	38	.301	.297	.303	7.49	3.15
Miller, Justin	R-R	6-3	215	3-13-87	1	1	5.70	40	0	0	0	43	50	27	27	6	20	45	.298	.349	.267	9.49	4.22
Motte, Jason	R-R	6-0	205	6-22-82	0	1	4.94	30	0	0	0	24	28	15	13	6	8	24	.286	.295	.278	9.13	3.04
Oberg, Scott	R-R	6-2	205	3-13-90	1	1	5.19	24	0	0	1	26	26	15	15	3	11	20	.257	.361	.200	6.92	3.81
Ottavino, Adam	L-R	6-5	220	11-22-85	2	3	2.67	34	0	0	7	27	18	9	8	3	7	35	.184	.256	.116	11.67	2.33
Qualls, Chad	R-R	6-4	235	8-17-78	2	0	5.23	44	0	0	0	33	43	22	19	5	9	22	.305	.300	.307	6.06	2.48
Rusin, Chris	L-L	6-2	195	10-22-86	3	5	3.74	29	7	0	0	84	82	36	35	5	23	69	.259	.258	.259	7.36	2.45

Fielding

Catcher	PCT	G	PO	A	E	DP	PB
Garneau	.993	23	134	11	1	0	0
Hundley	.988	79	554	38	7	3	8
Murphy	.980	12	89	7	2	1	2
Wolters	.988	59	451	29	6	0	3

COLORADO ROCKIES

First Base	PCT	G	PO	A	E	DP
Cardullo	.982	15	104	8	2	7
Descalso	.973	16	106	3	3	14
Parra	1.000	19	120	7	0	11
Patterson	1.000	2	22	1	0	0
Paulsen	.993	23	145	5	1	10
Raburn	.950	5	14	5	1	2
Reynolds	.993	115	939	79	7	91

Second Base	PCT	G	PO	A	E	DP
Adames	.967	11	15	14	1	3
Descalso	.980	14	17	33	1	8
LeMahieu	.991	146	276	422	6	91
Reynolds	—	1	0	0	0	0

	PCT	G	PO	A	E	DP
Valaika	1.000	5	3	5	0	0
Wolters	1.000	7	0	8	0	0

Third Base	PCT	G	PO	A	E	DP
Adames	1.000	11	1	3	0	1
Arenado	.973	160	99	378	13	39
Descalso	1.000	4	3	0	0	0
Valaika	.667	6	1	1	1	0

Shortstop	PCT	G	PO	A	E	DP
Adames	.972	47	52	121	5	20
Descalso	.972	31	41	65	3	16
Story	.977	96	139	293	10	64
Valaika	1.000	2	1	1	0	0
Wolters	.667	3	0	2	1	1

Outfield	PCT	G	PO	A	E	DP
Barnes	.980	43	47	3	1	1
Blackmon	.990	138	293	4	3	0
Cardullo	1.000	4	6	1	0	0
Dahl	.976	59	79	4	2	0
Descalso	1.000	7	9	0	0	0
Gonzalez	.989	148	251	8	3	0
Parra	.962	79	116	9	5	0
Patterson	1.000	6	4	0	0	0
Paulsen	1.000	7	8	0	0	0
Raburn	.964	49	52	1	2	1
Tapia	1.000	11	14	0	0	0
Ynoa	.500	2	1	0	1	0

ALBUQUERQUE ISOTOPES — TRIPLE-A
PACIFIC COAST LEAGUE

Batting	B-T	HT	WT	DOB	AVG	vLH	vRH	G	AB	R	H	2B	3B	HR	RBI	BB	HBP	SH	SF	SO	SB	CS	SLG	OBP
Barnes, Brandon	R-R	6-2	210	5-15-86	.282	.250	.295	64	238	30	67	13	2	5	32	15	0	1	1	58	11	5	.416	.323
Bianchi, Jeff	R-R	5-11	185	10-5-86	.245	.268	.238	66	216	14	53	3	2	2	19	22	0	4	1	49	1	2	.306	.314
Cardullo, Stephen	R-R	6-0	215	8-31-87	.308	.328	.299	115	406	71	125	26	5	17	72	37	4	0	5	58	6	3	.522	.367
Casteel, Ryan	R-R	5-11	205	6-6-91	.230	.269	.222	43	152	19	35	8	2	3	20	10	0	0	0	47	0	1	.368	.273
Castellanos, Alex	R-R	6-0	200	8-4-86	.299	.370	.264	49	164	27	49	10	1	6	25	13	5	0	2	59	1	0	.482	.364
Ciriaco, Juan	R-R	5-9	165	7-6-90	.045	.000	.056	9	22	1	1	0	0	0	0	0	0	0	0	4	0	0	.045	.045
Cuevas, Noel	R-R	6-2	210	10-2-91	.234	.273	.221	44	137	13	32	4	3	1	8	8	4	1	1	28	4	2	.328	.293
Dahl, David	L-R	6-2	195	4-1-94	.484	.333	.532	16	62	17	30	6	2	5	16	6	0	0	0	11	1	2	.887	.529
Decker, Cody	R-R	5-11	217	1-17-87	.208	.364	.167	14	53	6	11	3	0	2	4	2	1	0	1	21	0	0	.377	.246
2-team total (7 Omaha)					.225	—		21	71	10	16	4	0	5	9	5	1	0	1	30	0	0	.493	.282
Descalso, Daniel	L-R	5-10	190	10-19-86	.400	.250	.455	4	15	1	6	1	0	0	1	3	0	0	0	2	0	1	.467	.500
Galvez, Cesar	B-R	5-9	145	7-24-91	.400	.000	.500	3	5	0	2	0	0	0	1	1	0	0	0	1	0	0	.400	.500
Garneau, Dustin	R-R	6-0	200	8-13-87	.292	.275	.299	52	185	31	54	11	0	15	35	16	7	1	2	43	2	0	.595	.367
Hundley, Nick	R-R	6-1	205	9-8-83	.182	1.000	.100	4	11	0	2	1	0	0	2	0	0	0	0	4	0	0	.273	.308
Murphy, Tom	R-R	6-1	220	4-3-91	.327	.341	.321	80	303	53	99	26	7	19	59	16	1	0	1	78	1	1	.647	.361
Nelson, Chris	R-R	5-11	205	9-3-85	.232	.281	.212	69	203	21	47	5	1	3	18	8	4	2	1	32	0	0	.310	.273
Parra, Gerardo	L-L	5-11	190	5-6-87	.150	.143	.154	5	20	2	3	0	0	0	3	0	0	0	0	5	0	0	.150	.150
Patterson, Jordan	L-L	6-4	215	2-12-92	.293	.245	.309	119	427	75	125	24	7	14	61	47	13	3	5	118	10	0	.480	.376
Paulsen, Ben	L-R	6-4	210	10-27-87	.278	.304	.265	78	288	44	80	17	5	6	40	24	0	0	2	64	1	0	.434	.331
Reyes, Jose	B-R	6-0	195	6-11-83	.303	.286	.316	9	33	7	10	0	0	2	2	7	0	0	0	4	3	0	.485	.425
Smalling, Tim	R-R	6-3	207	10-14-87	.233	.243	.228	76	232	27	54	4	1	3	27	15	1	4	0	36	0	2	.297	.282
Swanner, Will	R-R	6-2	195	9-10-91	.194	.200	.192	10	31	5	6	1	0	1	4	4	0	0	0	14	0	0	.323	.286
Tapia, Raimel	L-L	6-2	160	2-4-94	.346	.459	.284	24	104	14	36	5	0	4	15	6	2	1	0	32	12	6	.490	.355
Tauchman, Mike	L-L	6-2	200	12-3-90	.286	.225	.305	129	475	72	136	24	7	1	51	40	2	6	4	77	23	10	.373	.342
Valaika, Pat	R-R	5-11	200	9-9-92	.209	.194	.215	28	110	8	23	8	1	1	13	2	1	0	2	28	2	0	.327	.226
Vazquez, Jan	B-R	5-10	165	4-29-91	.000	.000	—	1	1	0	0	0	0	0	0	0	0	0	0	0	0	0	.000	.000
Williams, Jackson	R-R	5-11	200	5-14-86	.095	.000	.111	6	21	2	2	1	0	0	2	0	0	0	0	3	0	0	.143	.095
Wolters, Tony	L-R	5-10	200	6-9-92	.250	.000	.286	2	8	1	2	0	0	0	0	0	0	0	0	0	0	0	.250	.250
Wong, Joey	L-R	5-10	185	4-12-88	.233	.167	.245	91	258	26	60	11	2	1	28	42	3	4	3	52	1	1	.302	.343
Ynoa, Rafael	R-R	6-0	190	8-7-87	.262	.280	.255	121	481	65	126	30	3	3	33	45	2	2	2	86	7	4	.356	.326

Pitching	B-T	HT	WT	DOB	W	L	ERA	G	GS	CG	SV	IP	H	R	ER	HR	BB	SO	AVG	vLH	vRH	K/9	BB/9
Anderson, Tyler	L-L	6-4	210	12-30-89	1	1	2.12	3	3	0	0	17	15	4	4	1	6	13	.238	.529	.130	6.88	3.18
Arrowood, Ryan	R-R	6-3	190	8-24-90	1	1	3.48	6	0	0	1	10	10	4	4	1	4	10	.250	.300	.300	8.71	3.48
Bergman, Christian	R-R	6-1	195	5-4-88	3	3	3.66	10	10	0	0	52	52	24	21	8	12	33	.267	.225	.302	5.75	2.09
Burke, Devin	R-R	6-1	205	2-20-91	0	0	0.00	1	0	0	0	1	3	2	0	0	0	2	.429	.667	.250	18.00	0.00
Butler, Eddie	B-R	6-2	180	3-13-91	8	3	4.45	15	15	1	0	89	93	47	44	9	26	35	.267	.233	.301	3.54	2.63
Carasiti, Matt	R-R	6-3	205	7-23-91	0	0	0.00	6	0	0	2	7	2	0	0	0	2	5	.091	.333	.000	6.43	2.57
Carle, Shane	R-R	6-4	185	8-30-91	5	8	5.42	27	19	0	0	111	147	75	67	9	32	88	.324	.312	.333	7.11	2.59
Carpenter, Ryan	L-L	6-5	210	8-22-90	2	3	7.47	26	8	0	0	69	102	59	57	16	25	68	.349	.212	.406	8.91	3.28
Castro, Miguel	R-R	6-5	190	12-24-94	2	3	10.34	16	0	0	0	16	21	18	18	5	7	15	.328	.379	.286	8.62	4.02
Castro, Simon	R-R	6-5	230	4-9-88	0	5	3.38	50	0	0	10	53	52	21	20	5	12	58	.255	.303	.217	9.79	2.03
De La Rosa, Jorge	L-L	6-1	215	4-5-81	0	0	4.30	3	3	0	0	15	14	9	7	0	8	11	.255	.250	.255	6.75	4.91
Estevez, Carlos	R-R	6-4	210	12-28-92	1	0	3.18	5	0	0	0	6	4	2	2	1	3	4	.261	.111	.357	6.35	4.76
Flande, Yohan	L-L	6-2	180	1-27-86	3	3	4.25	18	1	0	0	42	52	22	20	2	14	27	.313	.271	.331	5.74	2.98
Flemer, Matt	R-R	6-2	210	11-22-90	6	4	3.74	24	11	0	0	96	96	41	40	12	24	63	.262	.244	.276	5.89	2.24
Freeland, Kyle	L-L	6-3	170	5-14-93	6	3	3.91	12	12	0	0	74	81	36	32	7	19	57	.284	.280	.291	6.96	2.32
Germen, Gonzalez	R-R	6-1	200	9-23-87	1	0	0.66	11	0	0	3	14	11	4	1	0	5	16	.212	.227	.200	10.54	3.29
Gonzalez, Nelson	R-R	6-1	170	2-15-90	3	3	5.09	28	0	0	0	35	39	21	20	7	15	32	.275	.274	.275	8.15	3.82
Gurka, Jason	L-L	6-0	170	1-10-88	0	1	1.69	18	0	0	4	21	25	6	4	3	6	31	.287	.200	.333	13.08	2.53
Hale, David	R-R	6-2	215	9-27-87	0	1	1.50	2	2	0	0	6	5	1	1	0	1	3	.217	.333	.190	10.50	3.00
Hernandez, Carlos	L-L	5-11	155	3-4-87	0	1	1.20	3	2	0	0	15	19	3	2	0	3	13	.311	.417	.243	7.80	1.80
Hoffman, Jeff	R-R	6-5	225	1-8-93	6	9	4.02	22	22	0	0	119	117	60	53	11	44	124	.261	.255	.266	9.40	3.34
House, Austin	R-R	6-4	200	1-24-91	0	0	7.56	13	0	0	0	17	25	19	14	3	7	15	.333	.394	.286	8.10	3.78
Logan, Boone	R-L	6-5	215	8-13-84	0	0	0.00	1	0	0	0	1	0	0	0	0	0	1	.000	—	.000	9.00	0.00

Pitching	B-T	HT	WT	DOB	W	L	ERA	G	GS	CG	SV	IP	H	R	ER	HR	BB	SO	AVG	vLH	vRH	K/9	BB/9
Lyles, Jordan	R-R	6-4	230	10-19-90	4	2	5.44	8	8	0	0	45	57	33	27	5	18	29	.322	.266	.367	5.84	3.63
Marquez, German	R-R	6-1	185	2-22-95	2	0	4.35	5	5	0	0	31	30	15	15	5	6	29	.254	.259	.250	8.42	1.74
McCoy, Pat	L-L	6-4	225	8-3-88	3	1	6.35	22	0	0	0	23	30	17	16	2	16	19	.341	.289	.380	7.54	6.35
Miller, Justin	R-R	6-3	215	6-13-87	0	0	6.75	12	0	0	0	12	15	10	9	0	4	8	.300	.240	.360	6.00	3.00
Moll, Sam	L-L	5-10	185	1-3-92	3	5	4.94	42	0	0	2	47	55	30	26	5	19	39	.296	.246	.320	7.42	3.61
Motte, Jason	R-R	6-0	205	6-22-82	0	0	3.18	6	0	0	0	6	3	2	2	1	3	5	.167	.000	.200	7.94	4.76
Musgrave, Harrison	L-L	6-1	205	3-3-92	8	7	4.30	19	19	0	0	113	118	57	54	17	40	79	.271	.319	.253	6.29	3.19
Oberg, Scott	R-R	6-2	205	3-13-90	1	0	2.43	27	0	0	9	30	16	8	8	1	11	36	.160	.133	.182	10.92	3.34
Ottavino, Adam	L-R	6-5	220	11-22-85	0	1	4.76	6	0	0	0	6	2	3	3	1	3	6	.111	.154	.000	9.53	4.76
Qualls, Chad	R-R	6-4	235	8-17-78	0	0	21.60	2	0	0	0	2	4	4	4	1	1	2	.444	.500	.400	10.80	5.40
Rusin, Chris	L-L	6-2	195	10-22-86	0	1	5.79	3	3	0	0	9	13	6	6	1	3	11	.325	.318	.333	10.61	2.89
Schlitter, Brian	R-R	6-5	235	12-21-85	1	2	3.64	36	0	0	8	42	42	19	17	2	21	43	.266	.225	.299	9.21	4.50

Fielding

Catcher	PCT	G	PO	A	E	DP	PB
Casteel	.986	20	129	7	2	1	1
Garneau	1.000	47	311	30	0	3	5
Hundley	.960	3	23	1	1	0	0
Murphy	.986	69	513	47	8	3	8
Vazquez	1.000	1	5	0	0	0	0
Williams	1.000	6	36	5	0	0	2
Wolters	1.000	2	14	1	0	1	0

First Base	PCT	G	PO	A	E	DP
Cardullo	1.000	3	22	1	0	2
Casteel	.993	16	132	14	1	13
Castellanos	1.000	2	24	0	0	3
Decker	.991	14	101	7	1	11
Patterson	.989	38	334	21	4	29
Paulsen	.991	64	518	33	5	67
Smalling	1.000	1	1	0	0	0
Swanner	1.000	7	58	3	0	7

Second Base	PCT	G	PO	A	E	DP
Bianchi	.983	48	87	139	4	41
Ciriaco	1.000	4	9	10	0	4
Descalso	1.000	1	0	4	0	0
Galvez	1.000	1	1	2	0	0
Nelson	1.000	3	4	6	0	0
Smalling	1.000	3	5	2	0	1
Valaika	1.000	9	14	37	0	9
Wong	.974	24	43	71	3	22
Ynoa	.975	55	97	133	6	27

Third Base	PCT	G	PO	A	E	DP
Castellanos	.961	39	31	67	4	8
Descalso	.000	1	0	0	1	0
Nelson	.924	39	24	61	7	5
Smalling	.978	32	19	71	2	8
Valaika	1.000	3	0	7	0	1
Wong	1.000	5	2	9	0	3
Ynoa	.946	31	19	51	4	3

Shortstop	PCT	G	PO	A	E	DP
Bianchi	1.000	11	13	25	0	6
Descalso	1.000	1	2	0	0	0
Reyes	.971	9	14	19	1	10
Smalling	.981	24	34	68	2	18
Valaika	.986	15	24	46	1	9
Wong	.976	54	79	162	6	31
Ynoa	.981	35	58	94	3	32

Outfield	PCT	G	PO	A	E	DP
Barnes	1.000	57	90	10	0	1
Cardullo	.974	90	141	8	4	1
Castellanos	1.000	5	9	0	0	0
Ciriaco	.750	1	2	1	1	0
Cuevas	.988	38	79	1	1	0
Dahl	.970	16	30	2	1	1
Parra	1.000	4	5	0	0	0
Patterson	.994	76	169	9	1	4
Paulsen	1.000	4	7	1	0	0
Swanner	—	1	0	0	0	0
Tapia	1.000	24	67	1	0	0
Tauchman	.982	122	273	7	5	2
Ynoa	1.000	2	3	0	0	0

HARTFORD YARD GOATS

DOUBLE-A

EASTERN LEAGUE

Batting	B-T	HT	WT	DOB	AVG	vLH	vRH	G	AB	R	H	2B	3B	HR	RBI	BB	HBP	SH	SF	SO	SB	CS	SLG	OBP
Benjamin Jr. Mike	R-R	6-0	190	3-18-92	.214	.150	.231	92	285	30	61	14	0	4	29	17	6	7	1	81	5	5	.305	.272
Carrizales, Omar	L-L	6-0	175	1-30-95	.250	.417	.221	21	80	14	20	2	0	0	4	4	0	0	0	17	5	2	.275	.286
Ciriaco, Juan	R-R	5-9	165	7-6-90	.280	.333	.267	65	218	28	61	8	1	3	14	5	1	6	1	25	10	7	.367	.298
Cuevas, Noel	R-R	6-2	210	10-2-91	.340	.277	.361	50	194	28	66	14	3	2	27	6	1	5	3	27	4	4	.474	.358
Dahl, David	L-R	6-2	195	4-1-94	.278	.313	.268	76	288	53	80	21	2	13	45	39	2	2	1	85	16	5	.500	.367
Galvez, Cesar	B-R	5-9	145	7-24-91	.292	.400	.263	9	24	2	7	1	0	0	5	0	0	0	0	5	1	1	.333	.292
Graeter, Ashley	R-R	6-1	190	10-3-89	.276	.353	.256	85	250	31	69	12	1	6	33	26	3	5	3	54	5	4	.404	.348
Herrera, Rosell	R-R	6-3	195	10-16-92	.292	.333	.279	126	425	61	124	16	3	5	66	36	2	7	4	79	36	8	.379	.374
McMahon, Ryan	L-R	6-2	185	12-14-94	.242	.283	.231	133	466	49	113	29	5	12	75	55	5	2	6	161	11	6	.399	.325
Osborne, Zach	R-R	5-8	175	4-2-90	.238	.209	.245	64	206	22	49	7	0	0	14	11	0	6	3	21	1	2	.272	.273
Parra, Gerardo	L-L	5-11	210	5-6-87	.333	—	.333	2	6	1	2	0	0	0	1	0	0	0	0	2	0	0	.333	.429
Prime, Correlle	R-R	6-5	222	2-18-94	.235	.261	.227	111	324	20	76	19	1	2	44	23	2	1	2	104	3	5	.318	.288
Soriano, Wilson	R-R	5-9	140	12-31-91	.317	.455	.286	20	60	4	19	2	1	0	7	3	0	1	0	21	1	1	.383	.349
Stein, Troy	R-R	6-1	210	4-17-92	.429	1.000	.333	3	7	1	3	2	0	0	1	0	0	0	0	1	0	1	.714	.500
Tapia, Raimel	L-L	6-2	160	2-4-94	.323	.309	.324	89	356	55	115	20	8	4	34	25	3	2	3	49	17	14	.450	.363
Thomas, Dillon	L-L	6-1	195	12-10-92	.289	.286	.290	111	374	39	108	37	1	4	46	28	11	2	4	97	13	8	.425	.353
Valaika, Pat	R-R	5-11	200	9-9-92	.269	.286	.264	108	431	66	116	33	3	13	67	28	2	9	4	95	8	9	.450	.314
Vazquez, Jan	B-R	5-10	165	4-29-91	.230	.130	.259	71	204	31	47	13	0	1	24	23	9	4	0	43	7	3	.309	.335
Williams, Jackson	R-R	5-11	205	11-14-86	.200	.283	.189	62	215	15	43	18	1	1	24	22	0	2	2	41	0	1	.274	.280

Pitching	B-T	HT	WT	DOB	W	L	ERA	G	GS	CG	SV	IP	H	R	ER	HR	BB	SO	AVG	vLH	vRH	K/9	BB/9
Almonte, Yency	B-R	6-3	205	6-4-94	3	1	3.00	5	5	1	0	30	22	11	10	4	16	22	.204	.250	.167	6.60	4.80
Anderson, Tyler	L-L	6-4	210	12-30-89	1	1	1.80	2	2	0	0	10	6	3	2	0	2	11	.167	.250	.100	9.90	1.80
Balog, Alex	R-R	6-5	210	7-16-92	5	2	4.77	11	11	0	0	55	68	34	29	9	21	31	.309	.341	.287	5.10	3.46
Broyles, Shane	R-R	6-1	180	8-19-91	0	1	5.65	36	0	0	1	51	45	32	32	4	33	69	.236	.216	.252	12.18	5.82
Burke, Devin	R-R	6-1	205	2-20-91	1	0	2.35	5	1	0	1	15	15	6	4	2	3	11	.268	.241	.296	6.46	1.76
Carasiti, Matt	R-R	6-3	205	7-23-91	0	2	2.31	38	0	0	29	39	28	13	10	5	7	43	.200	.222	.176	9.92	1.62
Chatwood, Tyler	R-R	6-0	185	12-16-89	0	0	0.00	1	1	0	0	4	4	2	0	1	1	2	.235	.000	.444	6.23	2.08
Flemer, Matt	R-R	6-2	210	11-22-90	1	0	1.50	1	1	0	0	6	5	1	1	1	1	0	.217	.308	.100	0.00	1.50
Freeland, Kyle	L-L	6-3	170	5-14-93	5	7	3.87	14	14	0	0	88	84	43	38	9	25	51	.254	.209	.271	5.20	2.55
Gonzalez, Rayan	R-R	6-3	175	10-18-90	2	2	3.12	46	0	0	1	52	44	18	18	2	23	49	.242	.250	.235	8.48	3.98
Hernandez, Carlos	L-L	5-11	155	3-4-87	6	10	5.15	25	20	1	0	115	166	77	66	10	16	81	.342	.363	.330	6.32	1.25

Pitching	B-T	HT	WT	DOB	W	L	ERA	G	GS	CG	SV	IP	H	R	ER	HR	BB	SO	AVG	vLH	vRH	K/9	BB/9
House, Austin	R-R	6-4	200	1-24-91	5	3	3.89	32	0	0	2	44	46	21	19	1	14	44	.264	.235	.283	9.00	2.86
Howard, Sam	R-L	6-3	170	3-5-93	5	6	3.99	16	16	0	0	90	113	51	40	11	28	67	.303	.339	.288	6.68	2.79
Jemiola, Zach	L-R	6-3	200	4-6-94	8	10	4.39	27	27	2	0	162	186	91	79	15	46	92	.292	.314	.270	5.11	2.56
Jiminian, Johendi	R-R	6-3	170	10-14-92	2	2	2.30	38	0	0	0	59	55	18	15	4	23	50	.255	.273	.236	7.67	3.53
Marquez, German	R-R	6-1	185	2-22-95	9	6	2.85	21	21	0	0	136	124	53	43	9	33	126	.245	.249	.242	8.36	2.19
Matzek, Tyler	L-L	6-3	230	10-19-90	0	1	14.29	8	0	0	0	6	8	9	9	0	14	5	.333	.231	.455	7.94	22.24
Musgrave, Harrison	L-L	6-1	205	3-3-92	5	1	1.79	6	6	0	0	40	20	9	8	1	8	30	.145	.224	.101	6.69	1.79
Niebla, Luis	R-R	6-4	185	1-4-91	0	1	5.40	9	0	0	0	13	11	8	8	1	10	6	.234	.182	.280	4.05	6.75
Pierpont, Matt	R-R	6-2	215	1-25-91	7	2	2.94	39	0	0	0	67	59	24	22	5	23	72	.232	.284	.188	9.62	3.07
Senzatela, Antonio	R-R	6-1	180	1-21-95	4	1	1.82	7	7	0	0	35	27	8	7	1	9	27	.218	.209	.228	7.01	2.34
Vasto, Jerry	L-L	6-2	195	2-12-92	4	3	3.03	31	0	0	10	30	28	13	10	2	15	34	.248	.200	.269	10.31	4.55
Wade, Konner	L-R	6-3	190	12-3-91	1	4	5.17	37	9	0	0	77	89	48	44	9	26	49	.287	.294	.280	5.75	3.05

Fielding

Catcher	PCT	G	PO	A	E	DP	PB
Graeter	.993	25	130	18	1	1	4
Stein	1.000	1	6	0	0	0	1
Vazquez	.994	59	422	39	3	5	1
Williams	1.000	59	417	50	0	7	0

First Base	PCT	G	PO	A	E	DP
Graeter	.988	7	73	10	1	3
McMahon	.988	67	527	30	7	51
Prime	.991	72	584	53	6	56
Thomas	.958	3	23	0	1	4

Second Base	PCT	G	PO	A	E	DP
Benjamin Jr.	.971	44	86	116	6	25
Ciriaco	.932	24	37	72	8	17
Galvez	1.000	8	10	20	0	2

Graeter	.950	28	46	68	6	12	
Osborne	.958	26	54	84	6	20	
Soriano	1.000	1	2	1	0	1	
Valaika	1.000	16	34	33	0	5	

Third Base	PCT	G	PO	A	E	DP
Benjamin Jr.	.945	42	30	74	6	6
Ciriaco	.500	1	0	1	1	0
Graeter	.667	1	2	0	1	0
McMahon	.920	67	50	146	17	15
Soriano	.926	8	8	17	2	4
Valaika	.924	29	16	57	6	4

Shortstop	PCT	G	PO	A	E	DP
Benjamin Jr.	1.000	1	2	5	0	1
Ciriaco	.957	37	52	81	6	19

Osborne	.970	35	39	92	4	20
Soriano	.938	6	5	10	1	1
Valaika	.971	65	90	181	8	41

Outfield	PCT	G	PO	A	E	DP
Carrizales	.976	20	41	0	1	0
Ciriaco	.500	2	0	1	1	0
Cuevas	.990	47	95	6	1	2
Dahl	.982	72	154	9	3	3
Herrera	.971	110	192	7	6	1
Parra	1.000	2	4	0	0	0
Soriano	1.000	4	8	0	0	0
Tapia	.992	99	236	9	2	2
Thomas	1.000	74	132	9	0	1

MODESTO NUTS

HIGH CLASS A

CALIFORNIA LEAGUE

Batting	B-T	HT	WT	DOB	AVG	vLH	vRH	G	AB	R	H	2B	3B	HR	RBI	BB	HBP	SH	SF	SO	SB	CS	SLG	OBP
Blackmon, Charlie	L-L	6-3	210	7-1-86	.125	.333	.000	2	8	1	1	0	0	0	0	0	0	0	0	1	0	0	.125	.125
Carrizales, Omar	L-L	6-0	175	1-30-95	.294	.260	.306	96	388	60	114	14	10	6	32	24	6	3	69	16	5	.428	.336
Daza, Yonathan	R-R	6-2	190	2-28-94	.242	.143	.269	8	33	1	8	2	0	0	3	1	2	0	7	1	1	.303	.306
Ferguson, Collin	L-L	6-2	215	2-9-93	.205	.222	.201	110	395	35	81	16	1	14	48	41	8	3	2	126	9	3	.357	.291
Fuentes, Josh	R-R	6-2	215	2-19-93	.278	.357	.253	77	291	44	81	15	4	9	44	16	3	13	3	2	54	1	1	.450	.342
Hoelscher, Shane	R-R	6-0	195	9-21-91	.274	.250	.282	114	446	61	122	23	6	11	62	29	10	6	5	122	8	2	.426	.329
Jean, Luis	R-R	6-1	150	8-17-94	.235	.239	.234	82	268	32	63	10	1	0	24	20	5	13	0	37	17	9	.280	.300
Jimenez, Emerson	L-R	6-1	160	12-16-94	.232	.217	.236	96	319	40	74	10	1	1	21	13	4	7	2	77	28	5	.279	.269
Nunez, Dom	L-R	6-0	175	1-17-95	.264	.269	.232	105	390	44	94	13	2	10	51	49	0	4	7	91	8	1	.362	.321
Perkins, Robbie	R-R	6-0	175	5-29-94	.238	.357	.179	15	42	4	10	1	1	0	1	11	0	0	0	23	0	1	.310	.396
Ramos, Roberto	L-R	6-5	220	12-28-94	.231	.100	.276	19	78	7	18	7	0	2	9	10	0	0	1	26	0	0	.397	.315
Rogers, Wes	R-R	6-3	185	3-7-94	.255	.315	.234	125	487	77	124	22	7	5	48	57	7	9	3	99	43	9	.359	.339
Soriano, Wilson	R-R	5-9	140	12-31-91	.178	.300	.132	22	73	8	13	1	0	0	2	2	1	2	0	14	1	1	.192	.211
Stein, Troy	R-R	6-1	210	4-17-92	.221	.245	.214	59	217	21	48	10	1	10	21	21	1	0	1	64	4	5	.415	.292
Stephens, Ryan	L-L	5-11	175	7-6-92	.158	.250	.133	11	38	5	6	0	0	0	3	3	1	0	1	12	0	1	.158	.233
Wall, Forrest	L-R	6-0	175	11-20-95	.264	.246	.270	120	459	57	121	16	4	6	56	41	6	10	5	97	22	11	.355	.329
Weeks, Drew	R-R	6-1	180	6-9-93	.233	.261	.224	111	424	52	99	16	4	8	57	35	0	6	7	101	11	10	.347	.288
White, Max	L-L	6-2	175	10-10-93	.238	.192	.249	109	407	43	97	20	7	8	39	38	6	2	2	139	36	7	.381	.311

Pitching	B-T	HT	WT	DOB	W	L	ERA	G	GS	CG	SV	IP	H	R	ER	HR	BB	SO	AVG	vLH	vRH	K/9	BB/9
Almonte, Yency	B-R	6-3	205	6-4-94	8	9	3.71	22	22	1	0	138	124	66	57	14	39	134	.237	.214	.249	8.72	2.54
Anderson, Tyler	L-L	6-4	210	12-30-89	0	0	4.91	1	1	0	0	4	2	2	2	0	5	6	.154	.167	.143	14.73	12.27
Balog, Alex	R-R	6-5	210	7-16-92	1	1	0.93	2	2	0	0	10	9	5	1	1	4	6	.237	.200	.261	5.59	3.72
Bello, Yoely	L-L	6-2	150	12-16-90	1	1	6.94	32	0	0	0	35	53	31	27	3	20	26	.342	.268	.384	6.69	5.14
Castellani, Ryan	R-R	6-3	193	4-1-96	7	8	3.81	26	26	1	0	168	156	79	71	8	50	142	.248	.248	.248	7.62	2.68
Chatwood, Tyler	R-R	6-0	185	12-16-89	0	0	0.00	1	1	0	0	5	1	0	0	0	2	3	.067	.000	.091	5.40	3.60
Cozart, Logan	R-R	6-2	215	1-27-93	2	6	4.69	45	0	0	3	56	57	36	29	2	28	51	.261	.209	.295	8.25	4.53
French, Parker	L-R	6-2	225	3-19-93	8	9	2.85	24	24	1	0	155	136	61	49	9	25	109	.237	.255	.217	6.34	1.45
Gray, Jon	R-R	6-4	235	11-5-91	0	1	2.08	2	2	0	0	9	8	5	2	0	1	11	.250	.200	.294	11.42	3.12
Howard, Sam	R-L	6-3	170	3-5-93	4	3	2.47	11	11	0	0	66	43	24	18	3	24	73	.184	.261	.165	10.01	3.29
Magliaro, Marc	R-R	5-11	175	2-17-90	0	2	6.91	11	0	0	0	14	17	11	11	1	6	8	.288	.355	.214	5.02	3.77
Matzek, Tyler	L-L	6-3	230	10-19-90	0	0	3.71	25	0	0	0	21	17	12	11	1	19	28	.233	.111	.273	12.00	8.14
McGee, Jake	L-L	6-3	230	8-6-86	1	0	0.00	2	0	0	0	2	0	0	0	0	0	2	.000	—	.000	9.00	0.00
Michalec, Josh	R-R	6-2	185	6-20-92	0	0	162.00	1	0	0	0	0	2	6	6	0	4	0	.667	—	.667	0.00	108.00
Neiman, Troy	R-R	6-6	230	11-13-90	7	4	3.55	45	0	0	2	71	65	32	28	10	23	83	.242	.244	.240	10.52	2.92
Niebla, Luis	R-R	6-4	185	1-4-91	2	1	1.69	32	0	0	17	37	28	9	7	1	14	40	.206	.200	.211	9.64	3.38
Ottavino, Adam	L-R	6-5	220	11-22-85	0	0	6.75	4	0	0	0	3	6	2	2	0	2	6	.429	.750	.300	20.25	6.75
Polanco, Carlos	R-R	6-2	175	2-18-94	2	7	4.57	18	15	0	0	69	68	51	35	2	50	61	.265	.221	.294	7.96	6.52
Rodriguez, Helmis	L-L	5-11	155	6-10-94	5	9	3.36	30	13	0	0	131	113	59	49	7	34	94	.231	.219	.237	6.44	2.33

Pitching

Pitching	B-T	HT	WT	DOB	W	L	ERA	G	GS	CG	SV	IP	H	R	ER	HR	BB	SO	AVG	vLH	vRH	K/9	BB/9
Sawyer, Logan	R-R	6-5	215	12-29-92	1	1	8.03	9	0	0	0	12	20	12	11	0	7	6	.370	.364	.375	4.38	5.11
Schlitter, Craig	R-R	6-0	195	5-16-92	2	2	4.26	38	0	0	1	51	41	31	24	4	30	66	.216	.191	.230	11.72	5.33
Schuh, Max	L-L	6-4	210	3-13-92	0	0	2.70	8	0	0	0	10	11	3	3	2	6	10	.297	.500	.200	9.00	5.40
Talley, Christian	R-R	6-4	190	9-22-91	1	1	10.80	5	1	0	0	12	22	16	14	3	6	6	.400	.483	.308	4.63	4.63
Tinoco, Jesus	R-R	6-4	190	4-30-95	0	3	14.85	4	4	0	0	13	37	23	22	3	3	8	.536	.400	.592	5.40	2.03
Vasto, Jerry	L-L	6-2	195	2-12-92	0	1	1.38	23	0	0	10	26	17	5	4	0	7	36	.181	.208	.171	12.46	2.42
Welmon, Colin	L-R	6-3	190	8-7-92	1	5	5.17	36	4	0	0	70	85	45	40	10	28	56	.305	.304	.306	7.23	3.62
Wynkoop, Jack	L-L	6-5	200	11-2-93	7	2	2.68	14	14	0	0	77	80	27	23	5	5	71	.270	.214	.288	8.26	0.58

Fielding

Catcher	PCT	G	PO	A	E	DP	PB
Nunez	.992	93	762	84	7	5	19
Perkins	1.000	10	63	11	0	1	1
Stein	.994	40	319	27	2	2	13

First Base	PCT	G	PO	A	E	DP
Ferguson	.984	102	911	89	16	82
Fuentes	.984	30	236	14	4	28
Ramos	.986	8	65	5	1	8
Soriano	1.000	2	6	1	0	1

Second Base	PCT	G	PO	A	E	DP
Jean	1.000	21	41	57	0	16
Soriano	.938	4	7	8	1	3
Wall	.943	117	209	318	32	74

Third Base	PCT	G	PO	A	E	DP
Fuentes	.922	41	31	88	10	10
Hoelscher	.927	82	63	153	17	18
Jean	.949	13	11	26	2	3
Soriano	1.000	7	4	20	0	1

Shortstop	PCT	G	PO	A	E	DP
Jean	.971	48	63	138	6	28
Jimenez	.922	95	166	261	36	57
Soriano	1.000	5	2	11	0	2

Outfield	PCT	G	PO	A	E	DP
Blackmon	1.000	2	6	0	0	0
Carrizales	.974	89	178	9	5	3
Daza	1.000	8	22	0	0	0
Rogers	.974	117	216	6	6	2
Soriano	1.000	4	10	1	0	0
Stephens	1.000	11	19	1	0	0
Weeks	.963	103	171	13	7	0
White	.918	88	130	4	12	1

ASHEVILLE TOURISTS
SOUTH ATLANTIC LEAGUE
LOW CLASS A

Batting

Batting	B-T	HT	WT	DOB	AVG	vLH	vRH	G	AB	R	H	2B	3B	HR	RBI	BB	HBP	SH	SF	SO	SB	CS	SLG	OBP
Burcham, Scotty	R-R	5-11	185	6-17-93	.271	.346	.245	61	207	25	56	15	1	2	22	19	2	7	2	51	7	4	.382	.335
Daza, Yonathan	R-R	6-2	190	2-28-94	.307	.333	.299	119	475	63	146	35	2	3	58	23	2	14	2	78	27	7	.408	.341
Fuentes, Josh	R-R	6-2	215	2-19-93	.398	.423	.388	28	93	18	37	14	0	4	20	4	5	4	2	22	2	4	.677	.442
George, Max	R-R	5-9	180	4-7-96	.248	.268	.242	111	347	48	86	25	2	8	39	54	17	20	4	104	10	8	.401	.372
Herrera, Carlos	L-R	6-0	145	9-23-96	.238	.218	.246	127	504	70	120	25	7	7	41	21	2	1	2	115	10	11	.357	.270
Hilliard, Sam	L-L	6-5	225	2-21-94	.267	.248	.274	127	461	71	123	23	5	17	83	56	3	4	3	150	30	12	.449	.348
Jones, Mylz	R-R	6-1	185	4-13-94	.270	.310	.257	124	511	64	138	22	5	8	49	22	6	10	3	106	28	14	.380	.306
Keck, Chris	L-R	6-2	180	9-2-92	.201	.208	.199	60	199	28	40	10	1	8	22	28	6	0	2	64	4	3	.382	.315
Marte, Hamlet	R-R	5-10	180	2-3-94	.237	.214	.243	62	241	29	57	15	2	6	32	12	0	4	4	83	6	4	.390	.268
McClure, Terry	R-R	6-2	190	9-29-95	.209	.200	.213	69	234	21	49	14	0	2	28	20	3	8	3	79	16	3	.295	.277
Mundell, Brian	R-R	6-3	230	2-28-94	.313	.317	.312	136	537	94	168	59	1	14	83	56	10	0	8	83	7	8	.505	.383
Piron, Jonathan	L-R	6-0	195	11-14-94	.187	.243	.165	37	134	11	25	6	2	2	14	3	4	3	2	36	1	1	.306	.224
Rabago, Chris	R-R	5-11	185	4-22-93	.272	.268	.274	77	279	35	76	13	2	0	32	27	5	5	2	50	12	6	.333	.345
Rodgers, Brendan	R-R	6-0	180	8-9-96	.281	.276	.282	110	442	73	124	31	0	19	73	35	8	2	4	98	6	3	.480	.342
Toole, Eric	L-R	6-0	180	2-8-93	.290	.100	.381	9	31	7	9	1	0	0	2	2	1	0	0	4	0	2	.323	.353

Pitching

Pitching	B-T	HT	WT	DOB	W	L	ERA	G	GS	CG	SV	IP	H	R	ER	HR	BB	SO	AVG	vLH	vRH	K/9	BB/9
Bowden, Ben	L-L	6-4	235	10-21-94	0	1	3.04	26	0	0	0	24	23	8	8	1	15	29	.261	.212	.291	11.03	5.70
Burke, Devin	R-R	6-1	205	2-20-91	4	6	3.77	17	12	1	1	72	68	32	30	8	12	54	.247	.202	.280	6.78	1.51
Craig, Dylan	R-L	6-2	210	5-1-93	3	1	6.10	11	8	0	1	49	57	35	33	3	15	33	.292	.339	.272	6.10	2.77
Franco, Kelvin	R-R	6-1	165	10-29-94	1	1	7.11	17	0	0	0	19	28	16	15	2	10	13	.346	.333	.354	6.16	4.74
French, Parker	L-R	6-2	225	3-19-93	2	1	1.17	4	4	0	0	23	17	6	3	0	4	13	.210	.275	.146	5.09	1.57
Guillen, Adonis	R-R	6-2	175	11-23-95	3	2	3.40	35	0	0	17	40	39	15	15	6	15	46	.252	.250	.253	10.44	3.40
Hill, David	R-R	6-2	195	5-27-94	4	4	4.48	14	14	0	0	82	95	42	41	8	14	81	.290	.307	.277	8.96	1.53
Johnson, Drasen	R-R	6-3	200	12-23-91	7	5	4.34	37	11	0	0	110	137	64	53	14	23	62	.309	.284	.328	5.07	1.88
Jones, Hayden	R-R	6-0	185	1-5-94	0	1	6.43	23	0	0	0	28	32	24	20	4	27	24	.281	.213	.328	7.71	8.68
Justo, Salvador	R-R	6-5	210	10-14-94	3	1	2.14	38	0	0	2	46	36	14	11	3	21	34	.225	.189	.256	6.60	4.08
Kenilvort, Alec	R-R	6-6	230	1-7-93	3	1	5.63	22	0	0	0	24	29	18	15	1	17	24	.290	.277	.302	9.00	6.38
Killian, Trey	R-R	6-3	190	3-24-94	12	6	3.87	26	26	0	0	146	144	69	63	14	36	136	.259	.250	.265	8.36	2.21
Koger, Daniel	R-L	6-6	185	8-12-93	0	2	7.62	19	0	0	0	26	40	22	22	5	7	21	.367	.270	.417	7.27	2.42
Lambert, Peter	R-R	6-2	185	4-18-97	5	8	3.93	26	26	0	0	126	125	58	55	7	33	108	.264	.211	.305	7.71	2.36
Lawrence, Justin	R-R	6-3	220	11-25-94	2	5	7.18	26	0	0	0	36	48	32	29	4	14	23	.327	.381	.286	5.70	3.47
McCormick, Ryan	R-R	6-2	205	3-15-94	0	2	18.90	5	2	0	0	10	22	22	21	5	6	3	.431	.391	.464	2.70	5.40
Palacios, Javier	R-R	6-1	165	9-29-93	1	6	6.51	34	5	0	0	55	76	47	40	14	33	44	.332	.324	.339	5.37	2.28
Pena, Juan	R-R	6-2	175	8-25-95	2	3	5.76	21	0	0	2	25	41	19	16	2	13	20	.387	.239	.500	7.20	4.68
Quintin, Cristian	R-R	6-3	165	12-27-93	4	5	3.93	41	0	0	0	55	56	25	24	5	20	50	.265	.286	.252	8.18	3.27
Sawyer, Logan	R-R	6-5	215	12-29-92	0	0	10.61	8	0	0	0	9	15	12	11	2	4	6	.366	.417	.294	5.79	3.86
Thoele, Sam	R-R	6-3	205	10-17-92	1	0	2.61	43	0	0	12	41	35	16	12	4	19	40	.223	.224	.222	8.71	4.14
Tinoco, Jesus	R-R	6-4	190	4-30-95	16	16	0	0	0	86	118	65	54	10	25	53	.324	.359	.294	5.53	2.61
Wynkoop, Jack	L-L	6-5	200	11-2-93	6	3	3.47	14	14	0	0	93	107	49	36	12	7	73	.294	.206	.328	7.04	0.68

Fielding

Catcher	PCT	G	PO	A	E	DP	PB
Marte	.990	61	417	78	5	5	13
Rabago	.992	77	533	78	5	5	9

First Base	PCT	G	PO	A	E	DP
Fuentes	.990	12	89	9	1	8
Keck	.977	15	120	9	3	8
Mundell	.992	112	1000	69	9	74

Second Base	PCT	G	PO	A	E	DP
Burcham	.959	14	17	30	2	3
George	.980	52	93	148	5	33
Herrera	.957	36	55	101	7	13
Piron	.974	15	30	46	2	12
Rodgers	.966	24	44	68	4	18

Third Base	PCT	G	PO	A	E	DP
Burcham	.944	37	43	59	6	7

	PCT	G	PO	A	E	DP
Fuentes	.949	10	12	25	2	1
George	.925	42	41	70	9	6
Jones	.818	8	2	7	2	0
Keck	.910	30	27	34	6	3
Piron	.857	15	14	28	7	3

Shortstop	PCT	G	PO	A	E	DP
Burcham	.889	12	19	37	7	7
Herrera	.967	71	123	199	11	40

	PCT	G	PO	A	E	DP
Jones	1.000	1	2	5	0	0
Rodgers	.933	56	71	151	16	31

Outfield	PCT	G	PO	A	E	DP
Daza	.988	116	230	22	3	1
Hilliard	.992	123	224	12	2	0
Jones	.990	113	282	20	3	6
McClure	.963	60	97	6	4	2
Toole	1.000	9	17	0	0	0

BOISE HAWKS
NORTHWEST LEAGUE

SHORT-SEASON

Batting	B-T	HT	WT	DOB	AVG	vLH	vRH	G	AB	R	H	2B	3B	HR	RBI	BB	HBP	SH	SF	SO	SB	CS	SLG	OBP
Abreu, Willie	L-L	6-4	225	3-21-95	.235	.157	.273	56	213	36	50	12	2	6	43	25	3	1	4	59	8	3	.394	.318
Bosiokovic, Jacob	R-R	6-5	240	12-21-93	.274	.270	.276	68	248	36	68	20	2	4	27	37	6	1	1	98	17	3	.419	.380
Brito, Antony	R-R	5-11	180	2-15-95	.242	.236	.244	54	190	17	46	10	0	0	24	18	1	1	3	36	1	2	.295	.307
Castro, Luis	R-R	6-1	187	9-19-95	.255	.237	.261	58	220	47	56	14	2	6	27	32	5	2	0	66	11	1	.418	.362
Follis, Tyler	L-R	6-2	200	7-19-93	.210	.278	.190	30	81	6	17	0	1	0	5	13	2	1	0	31	1	1	.235	.333
Hampson, Garrett	R-R	5-11	185	10-10-94	.301	.260	.318	68	256	43	77	14	8	2	44	48	1	0	7	56	36	4	.441	.404
Haynie, Will	R-R	6-5	222	6-12-94	.210	.300	.167	19	62	6	13	3	0	0	2	10	2	1	0	28	0	0	.258	.338
Jimenez, Wilkyns	R-R	6-2	180	7-18-95	.226	.250	.216	36	137	9	31	4	0	0	11	7	0	1	0	35	0	1	.255	.264
Jones, Wesley	R-R	6-2	180	8-12-95	.302	.233	.336	59	222	23	67	11	1	1	30	19	2	0	3	36	2	3	.374	.358
Linkous, Steven	L-R	6-0	171	9-28-94	.231	.229	.229	58	225	39	57	5	3	2	23	37	1	0	2	60	30	7	.329	.358
Nevin, Tyler	R-R	6-4	200	5-29-97	1.000	1.000	—	1	1	1	1	0	0	0	0	0	0	0	0	0	0	0	2.000	1.000
Orris, Tyler	R-R	5-9	175	8-3-94	.197	.184	.205	35	122	18	24	2	0	0	11	20	2	2	1	20	4	2	.213	.317
Stahel, Bobby	R-R	5-10	200	9-1-92	.214	.162	.238	34	117	20	25	6	3	2	12	10	6	1	2	41	6	2	.368	.304
Stephens, Ryan	L-L	5-11	175	7-6-92	.226	.200	.238	16	62	6	14	2	0	0	8	3	0	2	1	5	1	.258	.254
Suero, Daniel	L-L	6-0	165	9-21-93	.228	.203	.238	55	224	26	51	7	5	1	28	10	1	2	1	35	9	9	.317	.263
Toole, Eric	L-R	6-0	180	2-8-93	.253	.333	.222	26	99	13	25	2	1	0	3	6	0	0	0	23	7	2	.293	.339
Wear, Campbell	R-R	6-3	205	10-23-93	.145	.148	.143	28	83	7	12	3	1	0	5	13	4	1	1	29	0	1	.205	.287

Pitching	B-T	HT	WT	DOB	W	L	ERA	G	GS	CG	SV	IP	H	R	ER	HR	BB	SO	AVG	vLH	vRH	K/9	BB/9
Bunal, Mike	R-R	6-2	205	11-18-93	0	2	4.80	19	2	0	0	30	28	22	16	2	18	24	.250	.290	.235	7.20	5.40
Calomeni, Justin	R-R	6-3	210	10-13-95	2	1	2.33	15	0	0	0	19	17	5	5	0	7	25	.246	.250	.245	11.64	3.26
Cedotal, Kyle	L-L	6-1	190	9-19-93	1	2	4.37	17	3	0	0	35	38	18	17	1	16	24	.281	.227	.308	6.17	4.11
Eusebio, Breiling	L-L	6-1	175	10-21-96	2	5	5.26	13	13	0	0	63	78	46	37	6	30	42	.305	.344	.292	5.97	4.26
Fernandez, Julian	R-R	6-2	160	12-5-95	1	2	1.17	21	0	0	13	23	13	3	3	0	20	19	.163	.158	.167	7.43	7.83
Franco, Kelvin	R-R	6-1	165	10-29-94	0	0	0.00	2	0	0	0	3	3	1	0	0	4	2	.231	.250	.222	12.00	0.00
Garcia, Rico	R-R	5-11	190	1-10-94	0	4	4.57	16	8	0	0	35	50	35	25	1	17	35	.329	.309	.340	8.92	4.33
Gesell, Jared	R-R	6-3	185	3-20-94	2	0	2.36	23	0	0	0	27	15	14	7	1	13	39	.158	.207	.136	13.16	4.39
Gold, Brandon	R-R	6-3	203	9-16-94	1	2	4.01	15	0	0	0	25	30	15	11	3	2	23	.280	.244	.303	8.39	0.73
Jones, Hayden	R-R	6-0	185	1-5-94	0	0	1.80	3	0	0	0	5	4	1	1	0	2	4	.333	.182	.720	7.20	3.60
Julio, Erick	R-R	6-1	175	9-22-96	4	6	4.05	13	13	0	0	73	80	36	33	3	13	47	.277	.295	.263	5.77	1.60
Kenilvort, Alec	R-R	6-6	230	1-7-93	2	1	4.15	15	0	0	0	30	24	14	14	3	5	28	.222	.243	.211	8.31	1.48
Koger, Daniel	R-L	6-6	185	8-12-93	0	1	2.70	11	0	0	0	13	17	5	4	0	1	17	.298	.250	.324	11.48	0.68
Lawrence, Justin	R-R	6-3	220	11-25-94	2	1	2.20	23	0	0	8	29	27	8	7	0	6	40	.243	.345	.207	12.56	1.88
Magliaro, Marc	R-R	5-11	190	2-17-90	0	0	0.71	11	0	0	0	13	10	1	1	0	2	9	.222	.174	.273	6.39	1.42
McCormick, Ryan	R-R	6-2	205	3-15-94	1	0	9.37	11	0	0	0	16	30	21	17	2	10	8	.385	.406	.370	4.41	5.51
Medina, Javier	R-R	6-2	190	8-9-96	5	1	5.72	9	9	0	0	39	49	26	25	2	17	35	.312	.281	.333	8.01	3.89
Moore, Austin	R-R	6-2	230	6-21-94	0	0	6.53	14	0	0	0	21	18	16	15	5	6	13	.231	.214	.240	5.66	2.61
Santos, Antonio	R-R	6-3	180	10-6-96	6	4	4.16	13	13	0	0	71	85	42	33	5	14	53	.297	.301	.295	6.69	1.77
Talley, Christian	R-R	6-4	190	9-22-91	2	0	2.03	13	1	0	0	31	25	7	7	1	9	24	.219	.205	.229	6.97	2.61
Thanopoulos, George	R-R	6-1	205	1-18-93	1	1	4.30	18	0	0	0	23	20	14	11	0	15	21	.238	.231	.243	8.22	5.87
Tyler, Robert	R-R	6-4	226	6-18-95	0	2	6.43	5	5	0	0	7	2	11	5	0	16	5	.083	.000	.111	6.43	20.57
Zimmerman, Michael	L-L	6-3	185	8-13-96	1	8	6.52	9	9	0	0	39	54	48	28	4	29	20	.333	.400	.315	4.66	6.75

Fielding

C: Haynie 16, Jimenez 36, Wear 26. **1B:** Bosiokovic 42, Castro 34, Jones 1. **2B:** Brito 49, Castro 4, Hampson 1, Jones 5, Orris 22. **3B:** Brito 4, Follis 24, Jones 53, Nevin 1. **SS:** Hampson 64, Jones 2, Orris 10. **OF:** Abreu 50, Bosiokovic 7, Follis 3, Linkous 53, Stahel 27, Stephens 15, Suero 55, Toole 20.

GRAND JUNCTION ROCKIES
PIONEER LEAGUE

ROOKIE

Batting	B-T	HT	WT	DOB	AVG	vLH	vRH	G	AB	R	H	2B	3B	HR	RBI	BB	HBP	SH	SF	SO	SB	CS	SLG	OBP
Anderson, Cole	R-R	5-11	190	2-7-97	.222	.137	.254	52	185	30	41	7	2	3	12	20	2	1	0	90	9	4	.330	.304
Brito, Luis	L-L	6-0	185	1-28-96	.253	.320	.220	24	75	11	19	4	1	2	16	9	0	0	3	23	2	2	.413	.322
Bugner, Tyler	L-R	6-2	195	10-29-94	.328	.372	.305	34	125	24	41	7	1	1	21	15	1	0	3	24	9	6	.424	.396
Diaz, Joel	R-R	6-1	195	9-18-95	.301	.351	.284	40	153	20	46	7	2	3	18	12	1	1	0	36	4	2	.431	.355
Fernandez, Vince	L-R	6-3	210	7-25-95	.310	.281	.322	51	203	36	63	17	6	5	31	20	1	1	3	61	6	2	.527	.370
Galvez, Cesar	B-R	5-9	145	7-24-94	.346	.333	.350	8	26	4	9	0	0	4	0	0	0	0	6	1	1	.346	.346
Gomez, Jose	R-R	5-11	175	12-10-96	.367	.412	.352	66	267	54	98	14	2	3	51	23	6	6	2	24	23	13	.468	.426
Gonzalez, Pedro	R-R	6-5	190	10-27-97	.230	.245	.225	58	226	32	52	15	8	2	19	14	6	0	2	77	6	7	.394	.290
Leonard, Steven	R-R	5-11	185	12-30-92	.270	.368	.236	24	74	16	20	8	1	0	6	7	7	2	0	14	3	1	.405	.386
Melendez, Manuel	L-L	5-11	165	1-10-97	.294	.268	.304	60	265	53	78	10	3	7	33	11	7	4	2	42	24	6	.434	.337
Melton, Hunter	R-R	6-2	230	3-11-94	.237	.167	.265	51	186	29	44	11	1	5	29	26	4	0	2	55	3	2	.387	.339

Batting	B-T	HT	WT	DOB	AVG	vLH	vRH	G	AB	R	H	2B	3B	HR	RBI	BB	HBP	SH	SF	SO	SB	CS	SLG	OBP
Park, Jensen	R-R	5-10	168	12-10-92	.222	.000	.250	8	27	4	6	3	1	0	4	0	0	0	0	11	0	0	.407	.222
Piron, Jonathan	L-R	6-0	195	11-14-94	.299	.284	.305	57	231	28	69	11	4	5	42	13	0	4	2	60	16	11	.446	.333
Ramos, Roberto	L-R	6-5	220	12-28-94	.404	.316	.447	13	57	12	23	5	1	5	23	2	0	0	0	13	3	1	.789	.424
Rodriguez, Jose	L-R	5-10	160	2-23-96	.268	.318	.235	17	56	12	15	2	0	0	4	1	1	1	0	11	2	0	.304	.293
Serven, Brian	R-R	6-0	195	5-5-95	.203	.293	.163	34	133	11	27	7	0	1	16	7	1	1	1	22	0	3	.278	.246
Snyder, Taylor	R-R	6-2	165	9-28-94	.287	.273	.291	47	171	32	49	15	2	7	27	19	5	0	1	50	7	3	.520	.372
Welker, Colton	R-R	6-2	195	10-9-97	.329	.380	.313	51	210	38	69	15	2	5	36	13	1	0	3	28	6	4	.490	.366

Pitching	B-T	HT	WT	DOB	W	L	ERA	G	GS	CG	SV	IP	H	R	ER	HR	BB	SO	AVG	vLH	vRH	K/9	BB/9
Baker, Bryan	R-R	6-6	220	12-2-94	3	4	6.00	11	11	0	0	48	63	35	32	10	12	41	.320	.253	.364	7.69	2.25
Behr, Dakota	R-R	6-2	185	12-9-91	1	0	14.81	6	0	0	0	10	21	17	17	2	6	7	.420	.474	.387	6.10	5.23
Culbreth, Ty	L-L	5-11	175	4-9-94	3	4	5.33	11	11	0	0	49	68	35	29	4	10	28	.340	.305	.355	5.14	1.84
Dennis, Matt	R-R	6-1	210	1-3-95	5	2	3.27	23	0	0	2	33	39	16	12	2	4	37	.298	.271	.319	10.09	1.09
Guzman, Luis	L-L	6-1	180	2-27-96	5	2	3.97	18	9	0	0	59	66	32	26	6	12	55	.274	.246	.285	8.39	1.83
Hammer, J.D.	R-R	6-3	215	7-12-94	0	2	3.92	27	0	0	3	44	48	26	19	2	11	52	.274	.349	.202	10.72	2.27
Holder, Heath	R-R	6-6	211	8-23-92	2	0	2.83	22	0	0	0	35	28	13	11	3	12	46	.217	.281	.167	11.83	3.09
Humphreys, Reid	R-R	6-1	205	11-21-94	1	0	3.48	9	0	0	0	10	11	6	4	0	5	9	.250	.222	.269	7.84	4.35
Lopez, Carlos	R-R	6-2	187	4-24-96	0	0	6.31	20	0	0	0	26	35	21	18	3	17	22	.321	.311	.328	7.71	5.96
Luna, Ryan	R-R	5-11	190	9-21-93	0	2	8.10	24	0	0	0	30	48	31	27	3	13	30	.375	.370	.378	9.00	3.90
McCormick, Ryan	R-R	6-2	205	3-15-94	0	0	9.00	2	0	0	0	4	6	4	4	0	1	5	.353	.375	.333	11.25	2.25
Meier, Matt	R-R	6-1	190	5-6-92	0	0	7.88	6	0	0	0	8	11	7	7	0	4	4	.333	.385	.300	4.50	4.50
Michalec, Josh	R-R	6-2	185	6-20-92	0	0	13.50	1	0	0	0	1	1	1	1	1	3	2	.333	—	.333	27.00	40.50
Moll, Sam	L-L	5-10	185	1-3-92	0	0	0.00	2	0	0	0	2	0	0	0	0	0	5	.000	—	.000	22.50	0.00
Nikorak, Mike	R-R	6-5	205	9-16-96	1	0	3.68	7	7	0	0	29	33	16	12	2	19	20	.287	.300	.277	6.14	5.83
Oakley, Kenny	R-R	6-3	195	8-30-93	4	5	4.13	22	0	0	7	28	26	14	13	2	9	43	.239	.236	.241	13.66	2.86
Ozuna, Lorenz	R-R	6-0	175	9-22-94	1	1	3.97	20	1	0	1	34	43	24	15	0	5	27	.307	.347	.286	7.15	1.32
Pena, Juan	R-R	6-2	175	8-25-95	0	0	3.86	2	0	0	0	2	5	2	1	0	0	2	.455	.000	.556	7.71	0.00
Pint, Riley	R-R	6-4	195	11-6-97	1	5	5.35	11	11	0	0	37	43	28	22	3	36	30	.307	.314	.300	8.76	5.59
Quintana, Yohander	R-R	6-3	185	4-9-97	5	4	6.63	13	11	0	0	58	84	54	43	7	20	47	.337	.305	.366	7.25	3.09
Requena, Alejandro	R-R	6-2	200	11-29-96	3	6	4.97	13	13	0	0	67	80	51	37	15	19	59	.289	.269	.306	7.93	2.55
Sawyer, Logan	R-R	6-5	215	12-29-92	0	0	3.00	3	0	0	1	3	1	1	1	0	4	.250	.200	.286	12.00	4.50
Valdespina, Justin	R-R	6-0	200	3-20-95	0	0	0.00	3	0	0	0	3	0	0	0	0	2	.273	.500	.222	6.00	0.00
Valdez, Jefry	R-R	6-1	165	8-20-95	0	0	18.00	1	0	0	0	2	4	4	4	2	1	1	.444	.500	.333	4.50	4.50
Valek, John	L-L	6-0	175	1-31-94	0	0	5.68	8	0	0	0	13	20	10	8	1	4	9	.357	.190	.457	6.39	2.84
Westphal, Ethan	R-R	5-10	170	5-12-92	1	2	5.40	14	1	0	0	33	41	26	20	4	5	32	.311	.358	.278	8.64	1.35

Fielding

C: Diaz 23, Leonard 21, Serven 32. **1B:** Diaz 15, Melton 49, Ramos 11, Snyder 3. **2B:** Galvez 5, Gomez 8, Piron 49, Rodriguez 16, Snyder 4. **3B:** Piron 6, Snyder 24, Welker 48. **SS:** Galvez 2, Gomez 58, Snyder 17. **OF:** Anderson 44, Brito 14, Bugner 20, Fernandez 28, Gonzalez 57, Leonard 1, Melendez 60, Park 6.

DSL ROCKIES
DOMINICAN SUMMER LEAGUE

ROOKIE

Batting	B-T	HT	WT	DOB	AVG	vLH	vRH	G	AB	R	H	2B	3B	HR	RBI	BB	HBP	SH	SF	SO	SB	CS	SLG	OBP
Chal, Welington	L-R	6-1	170	11-18-97	.198	.200	.197	26	81	13	16	2	0	1	6	16	1	0	0	23	1	2	.259	.337
Corporan, Gabirel	R-R	6-1	195	8-11-98	.115	.000	.150	29	78	12	9	1	0	1	3	16	4	0	1	37	0	1	.167	.293
Garcia, Franklin	R-R	6-0	170	3-26-98	.280	.273	.281	47	161	19	45	6	1	0	11	13	3	6	0	27	7	4	.329	.337
Gonzalez, Hidekel	R-R	6-0	189	10-7-96	.325	.261	.343	59	212	41	69	13	4	4	31	17	9	1	5	31	7	3	.481	.391
Gonzalez, Pedro	R-R	6-5	190	10-27-97	.222	.286	.200	7	27	3	6	0	1	0	6	2	1	0	0	4	1	0	.296	.300
Grullart, Jose	L-L	6-1	175	6-21-99	.245	.243	.245	57	192	24	47	12	5	1	22	22	3	2	1	54	4	1	.375	.330
Guevara, Javier	R-R	5-11	165	9-25-97	.258	.235	.262	56	198	19	51	9	0	3	15	22	6	0	1	47	6	4	.348	.348
Marcelino, Ramon	L-R	6-1	175	12-23-98	.261	.220	.271	62	238	30	62	19	1	7	37	5	6	1	0	51	2	5	.437	.293
Mendoza, Shael	L-R	6-0	165	10-15-96	.272	.289	.269	58	224	30	61	4	4	1	19	8	2	2	3	36	25	10	.339	.300
Mezquita, Jonatan	R-R	6-0	180	11-1-99	.217	.160	.233	32	115	15	25	3	0	1	7	4	1	0	1	40	2	1	.348	.248
Montano, Daniel	L-R	6-0	170	3-31-99	.228	.250	.224	65	241	41	55	17	2	9	32	31	5	0	3	65	8	3	.427	.325
Navarro, Cristopher	R-R	6-0	152	6-14-99	.253	.194	.271	47	154	19	39	4	0	0	15	13	2	2	2	34	4	4	.279	.316
Peguero, Wasner	R-R	6-2	224	9-7-96	.202	.158	.211	36	109	9	22	8	0	2	15	10	3	0	1	32	1	0	.330	.285
Rosario, Yeremi	R-R	5-11	150	2-4-98	.233	.208	.239	39	116	18	27	7	0	0	9	7	2	5	0	33	2	7	.293	.288
Saldana, Enrique	R-R	5-11	155	6-26-99	.264	.222	.275	53	178	28	47	13	4	3	26	15	3	2	4	46	4	5	.433	.325

Pitching	B-T	HT	WT	DOB	W	L	ERA	G	GS	CG	SV	IP	H	R	ER	HR	BB	SO	AVG	vLH	vRH	K/9	BB/9
Alcantara, Jhosua	R-R	6-6	200	9-30-97	2	1	2.42	21	0	0	0	22	14	11	6	1	8	20	.179	.250	.148	8.06	3.22
Amarista, Anderson	R-R	6-1	185	11-9-98	3	3	3.52	13	10	0	0	46	40	20	18	4	16	46	.225	.207	.233	9.00	3.13
Cabrera, Wander	L-L	6-1	185	11-7-97	6	0	2.63	12	12	0	0	51	41	17	15	2	22	54	.216	.219	.215	9.47	3.86
Carrasco, Ronny	R-R	6-1	175	6-8-96	0	0	2.57	6	0	0	0	7	5	2	2	0	3	9	.185	.167	.190	11.57	3.86
Cespedes, Richard	R-R	6-0	185	8-29-97	3	0	2.95	11	4	0	0	37	30	19	12	3	11	11	.222	.133	.267	2.70	2.70
Duarte, Aneudy	R-R	6-3	170	10-20-97	2	0	2.75	12	6	0	0	39	40	15	12	3	16	23	.278	.323	.265	5.36	3.66
Estrada, Gabriel	R-R	6-2	180	5-28-99	3	1	2.45	12	10	0	0	40	30	12	11	0	13	42	.199	.212	.192	9.37	2.90
Filpo, Eris	R-R	6-3	170	5-3-98	1	0	4.15	14	0	0	0	22	26	11	10	1	8	14	.306	.304	.306	5.82	3.32
Garcia, Evaryn	R-R	6-0	192	6-13-96	2	0	3.09	9	0	0	0	12	11	5	4	1	3	9	.229	.333	.182	6.94	2.31
Goitia, Leonel	R-R	6-0	178	12-26-98	0	0	2.55	10	0	0	0	18	13	5	5	0	4	4	.200	.133	.220	6.11	2.04
Gonzalez, Carlos	R-R	6-2	180	12-11-98	4	3	4.55	13	3	0	0	30	47	23	15	1	4	15	.373	.286	.407	4.55	1.21
Julio, Erick	R-R	6-1	175	9-22-96	0	1	5.00	2	2	0	0	9	10	5	5	0	2	6	.286	.000	.323	6.00	2.00
Martinez, Alexander	R-R	6-1	165	12-28-96	4	0	2.02	34	0	0	22	36	27	10	8	0	11	28	.206	.316	.161	7.07	2.78

Pitching	B-T	HT	WT	DOB	W	L	ERA	G	GS	CG	SV	IP	H	R	ER	HR	BB	SO	AVG	vLH	vRH	K/9	BB/9
Moya, Ever	L-L	6-4	150	5-25-99	0	2	3.58	11	11	0	0	33	35	19	13	1	15	27	.276	.231	.287	7.44	4.13
Ocando, Jeffri	R-R	6-1	180	5-15-99	3	0	0.39	6	4	0	0	23	14	2	1	0	1	29	.171	.296	.109	11.35	0.39
Olivares, Keinter	L-L	6-0	170	12-1-97	5	2	1.55	15	5	0	1	52	39	14	9	1	6	34	.203	.432	.148	5.85	1.03
Oviedo, Jorge	L-L	6-2	180	10-6-96	7	1	1.05	18	0	0	1	43	31	6	5	1	11	40	.208	.172	.217	8.44	2.32
Paulino, Guillermo	R-R	6-4	180	3-30-97	2	0	0.79	10	0	0	0	11	7	6	1	0	10	9	.163	.211	.125	7.15	7.94
Perez, Esmerlin	R-R	6-0	165	1-8-96	1	2	2.05	21	0	0	1	26	21	8	6	1	6	24	.223	.308	.191	8.20	2.05
Pilar, Anderson	R-R	6-2	175	3-2-98	2	2	2.97	13	2	0	0	30	28	10	10	0	9	22	.248	.233	.253	6.53	2.67
Santos, Antonio	R-R	6-3	180	10-6-96	0	0	1.80	2	2	0	0	10	9	2	2	0	0	7	.250	.400	.192	6.30	0.00
Valdez, Jefry	R-R	6-1	165	8-20-95	1	2	2.43	29	0	0	6	33	23	11	9	1	9	32	.193	.233	.180	8.64	2.43

Fielding

C: Garcia 7, Gonzalez 37, Guevara 30. **1B:** Corporan 15, Garcia 20, Gonzalez 21, Guevara 21. **2B:** Garcia 1, Mendoza 52, Navarro 2, Rosario 13, Saldana 9. **3B:** Corporan 10, Garcia 15, Mezquita 27, Navarro 3, Rosario 10, Saldana 10. **SS:** Navarro 40, Rosario 2, Saldana 31. **OF:** Chal 10, Garcia 2, Gonzalez 7, Grullart 56, Marcelino 62, Montano 62, Peguero 25.

Detroit Tigers

SEASON IN A SENTENCE: Detroit bounced back from a brutal 2015 season, improving by 12 victories, but that wasn't enough to get back to the playoffs. Despite big years from usual suspects Miguel Cabrera and Justin Verlander, the Tigers fell just short of the American League wild card, losing their last two games in Atlanta to finish out of the money.

HIGH POINT: Detroit was just peeking over .500 late on June 30 when it went to Tampa and rallied after being down 7-2 entering the ninth inning. The Tigers used seven hits to score eight runs, including the last three on a bases-clearing Cameron Maybin double, to win 10-7, capping a 17-11 month that got them back in contention. Maybin's defense and bat provided a spark during a six-game winning streak.

LOW POINT: Any hopes of a division title were dashed fairly early, when Detroit lost seven straight and 11 of 12 in early May. The streak included a 10-5 loss to the Rangers as offseason acquisition Mike Pelfrey couldn't hold a 5-2 lead, and Texas slammed five homers. Veterans Pelfrey and Anibal Sanchez combined for an 11-23 mark and 45 home runs allowed in 48 starts.

NOTABLE ROOKIES: Pelfrey, oft-injured free-agent signee Jordan Zimmermann and Sanchez struggled in rotation, opening the door for Michael Fulmer, the club's top prospect, to make 26 starts. He thrived (11-7, 3.06) as the only Detroit rookie to exhaust his rookie eligibility. Former top prospect Steven Moya did show flashes in limited action, belting five home runs in 94 at-bats.

KEY TRANSACTIONS: Free-agent signee Justin Upton struggled in the first half but belted 22 homers after the break, including 13 after Sept. 1 to finish second on the team in homers (31) and RBIs (87). Zimmermann, the other big offseason pickup, got off to a 5-0, 0.55 start but struggled the rest of the way, missing time and losing effectiveness due to neck and lat muscle injuries. The only in-season trade of consequence involved acquiring Erick Aybar from the Braves to fill in at shortstop for the injured Jose Iglesias.

DOWN ON THE FARM: Low Class A West Michigan was the lone Tigers club to reach the playoffs in a season in which domestic affiliates posted a cumulative .474 winning percentage. Outfielder Christin Stewart hit 30 homers to rank fifth in the minors while ranking sixth in walks (86).

OPENING DAY PAYROLL: $194,876,481 (3rd)

PLAYERS OF THE YEAR

MAJOR LEAGUE	MINOR LEAGUE
Justin Verlander rhp	**Christin Stewart** of
16-9, 3.04	(High A, Double-A)
254 SO in 227.2 IP	.255/.386/.517
Led AL in SO, WHIP	30 HR, 87 RBI

ORGANIZATION LEADERS

BATTING

*Minimum 250 AB

MAJORS

* AVG	Miguel Cabrera	.316
* OPS	Miguel Cabrera	.956
HR	Miguel Cabrera	38
RBI	Miguel Cabrera	108

MINORS

* AVG	Will Maddox, West Michigan	.339
* OBP	Jeff McVaney, Erie, Toledo	.402
* SLG	Christin Stewart, Lakeland, Erie	.517
* OPS	Christin Stewart, Lakeland, Erie	.903
R	Chad Huffman, Toledo	78
H	Will Maddox, West Michigan	173
TB	Dean Green, Erie, Toledo	238
2B	Casey McGehee, Toledo	37
3B	Jose Azocar, West Michigan	8
HR	Christin Stewart, Lakeland, Erie	30
RBI	Dean Green, Erie, Toledo	108
BB	Christin Stewart, Lakeland, Erie	86
SO	Zac Shepherd, Lakeland	159
SB	Derek Hill, West Michigan	35

PITCHING

#Minimum 75 IP

MAJORS

W	Justin Verlander	16
# ERA	Justin Verlander	3.04
SO	Justin Verlander	254
SV	Francisco Rodriguez	44

MINORS

W	A.J. Ladwig, Lakeland	12
L	Josh Turley, Toledo, Erie	13
	Thad Weber, Toledo, Erie	13
# ERA	Tyler Alexander, Lakeland, Erie	2.44
G	Preston Guilmet, Toledo	65
GS	Myles Jaye, Erie, Toledo	28
SV	Joe Jimenez, Lakeland, Erie, Toledo	30
IP	Myles Jaye, Erie, Toledo	162
BB	Jairo Labourt, Lakeland	70
SO	Myles Jaye, Erie, Toledo	135
# AVG	Jeff Thompson, Lakeland	.231

General Manager: Al Avila. **Farm Director:** Dave Owen. **Scouting Director:** Scott Pleis.

Class	Team	League	W	L	PCT	Finish	Manager
Majors	Detroit Tigers	American	86	75	.534	6th (15)	Brad Ausmus
Triple-A	Toledo Mud Hens	International	68	76	.472	9th (14)	Lloyd McClendon
Double-A	Erie SeaWolves	Eastern	62	79	.440	t-9th (12)	Lance Parrish
High A	Lakeland Flying Tigers	Florida State	60	72	.455	10th (12)	Dave Huppert
Low A	West Michigan Whitecaps	Midwest	71	65	.522	6th (16)	Andrew Graham
Short season	Connecticut Tigers	New York-Penn	41	35	.539	5th (14)	Mike Rabelo
Rookie	Tigers East	Gulf Coast	21	37	.362	16th (17)	Rafael Gil
Rookie	Tigers West	Gulf Coast	30	28	.517	7th (17)	Rafael Martinez
Overall 2016 Minor League Record			353	392	.474	22nd (30)	

DETROIT TIGERS
AMERICAN LEAGUE

Batting	B-T	HT	WT	DOB	AVG	vLH	vRH	G	AB	R	H	2B	3B	HR	RBI	BB	HBP	SH	SF	SO	SB	CS	SLG	OBP
Aviles, Mike	R-R	5-10	205	3-13-81	.210	.203	.214	68	167	17	35	5	1	1	6	9	2	3	0	27	2	2	.269	.258
Aybar, Erick	B-R	5-10	195	1-14-84	.250	.250	.250	29	80	7	20	5	0	1	8	11	0	0	0	11	0	0	.350	.341
Cabrera, Miguel	R-R	6-4	240	4-18-83	.316	.302	.321	158	595	92	188	31	1	38	108	75	4	0	5	116	0	0	.563	.393
Castellanos, Nick	R-R	6-4	210	3-4-92	.285	.207	.315	110	411	54	117	25	4	18	58	28	3	0	5	111	1	1	.496	.331
Collins, Tyler	L-L	5-11	215	6-6-90	.235	.111	.266	56	136	14	32	2	3	4	15	13	1	0	1	38	1	1	.382	.305
Gose, Anthony	L-L	6-1	190	8-10-90	.209	.120	.242	30	91	11	19	2	2	2	7	9	1	0	0	38	0	1	.341	.287
Hicks, John	R-R	6-2	230	8-31-89	.500	.000	1.000	1	2	1	1	1	0	0	0	0	0	0	0	0	0	0	1.000	.500
Iglesias, Jose	R-R	5-11	185	1-5-90	.255	.254	.255	137	467	57	119	26	0	4	32	28	8	7	3	50	7	4	.336	.306
Jones, JaCoby	R-R	6-2	205	5-10-92	.214	.118	.364	13	28	3	6	3	0	0	2	0	0	0	0	12	0	0	.321	.214
Kinsler, Ian	R-R	6-0	200	6-22-82	.288	.309	.281	153	618	117	178	29	4	28	83	45	13	0	3	115	14	6	.484	.348
Machado, Dixon	R-R	6-1	170	2-22-92	.100	.200	.000	8	10	1	1	0	0	0	0	3	0	0	0	4	0	0	.100	.308
Martinez, J.D.	R-R	6-3	220	8-21-87	.307	.306	.307	120	460	69	141	35	2	22	68	49	3	0	5	128	1	2	.535	.373
Martinez, Victor	B-R	6-2	210	12-23-78	.289	.295	.287	154	553	65	160	22	0	27	86	50	4	0	3	90	0	0	.476	.351
Maybin, Cameron	R-R	6-3	215	4-4-87	.315	.296	.323	94	349	65	110	14	5	4	43	36	3	2	1	69	15	6	.418	.383
McCann, James	R-R	6-2	210	6-13-90	.221	.258	.201	105	344	31	76	9	1	12	48	23	2	1	3	109	0	1	.358	.272
McGehee, Casey	R-R	6-1	220	10-12-82	.228	.296	.200	30	92	4	21	1	0	0	1	3	1	0	0	14	0	0	.239	.260
Moya, Steven	L-R	6-7	260	8-9-91	.255	.600	.236	31	94	9	24	4	2	5	11	5	0	0	1	38	0	1	.500	.290
Presley, Alex	L-L	5-10	195	7-25-85	.200	.000	.250	3	5	0	1	0	0	0	0	0	0	0	0	0	0	0	.200	.200
Romine, Andrew	L-R	6-1	200	12-24-85	.236	.268	.226	108	174	21	41	5	2	2	16	13	4	3	0	38	8	0	.322	.304
Saltalamacchia, Jarrod	B-R	6-4	235	5-2-85	.171	.161	.174	92	246	30	42	5	1	12	38	41	0	0	5	104	0	0	.346	.284
Upton, Justin	R-R	6-2	205	8-25-87	.246	.236	.249	153	570	81	140	28	2	31	87	50	4	0	2	179	9	4	.465	.310
Wilson, Bobby	R-R	6-0	230	4-8-83	.154	.500	.091	5	13	0	2	0	0	0	2	1	0	0	1	3	0	0	.154	.200
3-team total (28 Tampa Bay, 42 Texas)					.237	—	—	75	228	25	54	6	0	7	33	11	1	7	4	64	0	0	.355	.270

Pitching	B-T	HT	WT	DOB	W	L	ERA	G	GS	CG	SV	IP	H	R	ER	HR	BB	SO	AVG	vLH	vRH	K/9	BB/9
Boyd, Matt	L-L	6-3	215	2-2-91	6	5	4.53	20	18	0	0	97	97	51	49	17	29	82	.258	.172	.276	7.58	2.68
Farmer, Buck	L-R	6-4	225	2-20-91	0	1	4.60	14	1	0	0	29	25	15	15	4	20	27	.231	.233	.229	8.28	6.14
Fulmer, Michael	R-R	6-3	210	3-15-93	11	7	3.06	26	26	1	0	159	136	57	54	16	42	132	.231	.222	.240	7.47	2.38
Greene, Shane	R-R	6-4	210	11-17-88	5	4	5.82	50	3	0	2	60	58	39	39	3	22	59	.257	.283	.233	8.80	3.28
Hardy, Blaine	L-L	6-2	215	3-14-87	1	0	3.51	21	0	0	0	26	25	11	10	2	12	20	.253	.200	.281	7.01	4.21
Kensing, Logan	R-R	6-1	190	7-3-82	0	0	1.93	5	0	0	0	5	8	1	1	0	2	1	.421	.300	.556	1.93	3.86
Lowe, Mark	R-R	6-3	210	6-7-83	1	3	7.11	54	0	0	0	49	57	41	39	12	21	49	.291	.253	.321	8.94	3.83
Mantiply, Joe	R-L	6-4	215	3-1-91	0	0	16.88	5	0	0	0	3	7	5	5	1	2	2	.538	.600	.500	6.75	6.75
Molleken, Dustin	L-R	6-4	230	8-21-84	0	0	4.32	4	0	0	0	8	12	4	4	0	5	8	.333	.267	.381	8.64	5.40
Norris, Daniel	L-L	6-2	195	4-25-93	4	2	3.38	14	13	0	0	69	75	30	26	10	22	71	.271	.214	.290	9.22	2.86
Parnell, Bobby	R-R	6-3	205	9-8-84	0	0	6.75	6	0	0	0	5	7	4	4	1	5	4	.318	.500	.278	6.75	8.44
Pelfrey, Mike	R-R	6-7	240	1-14-84	4	10	5.07	24	22	0	0	119	160	76	67	15	46	56	.332	.351	.312	4.24	3.48
Rodriguez, Francisco	R-R	6-0	195	1-7-82	3	4	3.24	61	0	0	44	58	45	24	21	6	21	52	.204	.225	.180	8.02	3.24
Rondon, Bruce	R-R	6-3	275	12-9-90	5	2	2.97	37	0	0	0	36	23	12	12	5	12	45	.181	.159	.207	11.15	2.97
Ryan, Kyle	L-L	6-5	215	9-25-91	4	2	3.07	56	0	0	0	56	48	21	19	2	15	35	.234	.225	.241	5.66	2.43
Sanchez, Anibal	R-R	6-0	205	2-27-84	7	13	5.87	35	26	0	0	153	171	108	100	30	53	135	.285	.261	.310	7.92	3.11
Saupold, Warwick	R-R	6-1	195	6-19-90	1	1	7.45	6	0	0	0	10	17	8	8	0	3	10	.395	.294	.462	9.31	2.79
VerHagen, Drew	R-R	6-6	230	10-22-90	1	0	7.11	19	0	0	0	19	28	15	15	3	7	10	.346	.438	.286	4.74	3.32
Verlander, Justin	R-R	6-5	225	2-20-83	16	9	3.04	34	34	2	0	228	171	81	77	30	57	254	.207	.187	.226	10.04	2.25
Wilson, Justin	L-L	6-2	205	8-18-87	4	5	4.14	66	0	0	1	59	61	29	27	6	17	65	.263	.308	.234	9.97	2.61
Wilson, Alex	R-R	6-0	215	11-3-86	4	0	2.96	62	0	0	0	73	68	26	24	5	21	49	.252	.239	.261	6.04	2.59
Zimmermann, Jordan	R-R	6-2	225	5-23-86	9	7	4.87	19	18	0	0	105	118	63	57	14	26	66	.284	.255	.309	5.64	2.22

Fielding

Catcher	PCT	G	PO	A	E	DP	PB
McCann	.995	99	756	44	4	9	4
Saltalamacchia	.994	68	471	19	3	3	1
Wilson	1.000	5	35	0	0	0	0

First Base	PCT	G	PO	A	E	DP
Cabrera	.995	147	1186	95	7	124
Hicks	1.000	1	3	1	0	0
Martinez	1.000	5	36	0	0	4
McGehee	1.000	1	3	0	0	0
Romine	1.000	20	60	1	0	5
Saltalamacchia	.966	11	53	3	2	4

Second Base	PCT	G	PO	A	E	DP
Aviles	1.000	10	7	21	0	3
Aybar	1.000	6	1	2	0	0
Kinsler	.988	151	303	432	9	109
Machado	—	2	0	0	0	0
Romine	1.000	12	16	16	0	6

Third Base	PCT	G	PO	A	E	DP
Aviles	.800	9	3	9	3	1
Aybar	1.000	12	4	9	0	1
Cabrera	1.000	1	2	0	0	0

	PCT	G	PO	A	E	DP
Castellanos	.965	108	66	184	9	12
Jones	1.000	6	1	6	0	0
McGehee	1.000	27	14	35	0	2
Romine	.977	44	7	35	1	1

Shortstop	PCT	G	PO	A	E	DP
Aviles	.846	6	4	7	2	4
Aybar	1.000	11	17	24	0	5
Iglesias	.991	136	180	389	5	92
Machado	1.000	6	5	12	0	1
Romine	.978	14	12	32	1	4

Outfield	PCT	G	PO	A	E	DP
Aviles	.977	39	40	2	1	0
Collins	.988	50	79	2	1	1
Gose	1.000	30	59	1	0	0
Jones	1.000	5	8	0	0	0
Martinez	.971	118	201	3	6	0
Maybin	.982	91	223	0	4	0
Moya	.933	26	38	4	3	2
Presley	1.000	2	5	0	0	0
Romine	1.000	25	35	1	0	1
Upton	.985	150	267	4	4	0

TOLEDO MUD HENS
INTERNATIONAL LEAGUE
TRIPLE-A

Batting	B-T	HT	WT	DOB	AVG	vLH	vRH	G	AB	R	H	2B	3B	HR	RBI	BB	HBP	SH	SF	SO	SB	CS	SLG	OBP
Bernard, Wynton	R-R	6-2	195	9-24-90	.235	.333	.207	46	149	18	35	5	1	1	11	10	1	1	1	30	10	3	.302	.286
Bortnick, Tyler	R-R	5-11	185	7-3-87	.222	.222	.222	17	45	7	10	1	1	1	6	7	0	1	0	10	0	2	.356	.327
Ciriaco, Pedro	R-R	6-0	180	9-27-85	.250	.250	.250	14	52	8	13	4	0	0	5	0	0	0	2	8	0	0	.327	.241
Collins, Tyler	L-L	5-11	215	6-6-90	.214	.159	.240	68	257	29	55	7	0	7	30	20	2	0	2	69	4	1	.323	.274
Diaz, Argenis	R-R	6-0	190	2-12-87	.241	.220	.250	111	323	32	78	13	0	3	32	21	0	5	1	58	1	3	.310	.287
Field, Tommy	R-R	5-10	185	2-22-87	.162	.000	.176	15	37	5	6	1	0	0	2	5	2	0	0	12	1	0	.189	.295
2-team total (82 Rochester)					.226	—	—	97	318	38	72	14	2	11	44	31	9	2	2	71	2	2	.387	.311
Gonzalez, Alberto	R-R	5-10	195	4-18-83	.091	.250	.000	3	11	0	1	0	0	0	0	0	0	0	0	0	0	0	.091	.091
Gonzalez, Miguel	R-R	5-11	220	12-3-90	.243	.304	.222	66	214	17	52	12	0	2	33	18	1	4	5	46	0	0	.327	.298
Gose, Anthony	L-L	6-1	190	8-10-90	.185	.195	.180	50	184	22	34	8	2	1	13	15	3	2	2	75	6	1	.266	.255
Green, Dean	L-R	6-4	255	6-30-89	.309	.390	.290	61	217	22	67	17	0	7	36	17	4	0	3	43	0	0	.484	.365
Greiner, Grayson	R-R	6-6	220	10-11-92	.000	—	.000	1	4	0	0	0	0	0	0	0	0	0	0	2	0	0	.000	.000
Hicks, John	R-R	6-2	230	8-31-89	.303	.290	.307	70	241	38	73	20	0	8	42	17	3	3	0	59	3	1	.485	.356
2-team total (9 Rochester)					.296	—	—	79	274	39	81	22	0	9	43	18	3	3	0	64	3	1	.474	.346
Huffman, Chad	R-R	6-1	215	4-29-85	.286	.278	.288	122	430	78	123	33	5	17	70	61	14	0	6	93	11	5	.505	.387
Iglesias, Jose	R-R	5-11	185	1-5-90	.375	.600	.273	4	16	2	6	1	0	1	1	0	0	0	0	0	0	0	.625	.375
Jones, Corey	L-R	6-0	205	9-14-87	.118	—	.118	14	34	2	4	2	1	0	2	4	0	0	0	7	0	0	.235	.211
Jones, JaCoby	R-R	6-2	205	5-10-92	.243	.269	.234	79	292	33	71	14	5	3	23	25	4	0	3	97	11	4	.356	.309
Krizan, Jason	L-R	6-0	185	6-28-89	.300	.294	.301	32	100	12	30	7	0	1	10	11	0	0	0	14	0	1	.400	.369
Longley, Andrew	R-R	6-3	215	10-5-88	.100	.000	.125	4	10	3	1	0	0	0	1	2	0	0	0	6	0	0	.100	.250
Machado, Dixon	R-R	6-1	170	2-22-92	.266	.298	.257	131	492	59	131	28	2	4	48	58	6	10	3	75	17	5	.356	.349
Martinez, J.D.	R-R	6-3	220	8-21-87	.278	.143	.310	8	36	3	10	3	0	0	5	1	0	0	0	11	1	0	.361	.316
Maybin, Cameron	R-R	6-3	215	4-4-87	.188	.250	.178	23	85	14	16	9	0	2	11	14	1	0	0	17	4	1	.365	.310
McCann, James	R-R	6-2	210	6-13-90	.091	.000	.095	6	22	2	2	0	0	0	2	0	0	0	0	6	0	0	.091	.259
McGehee, Casey	R-R	6-1	220	10-12-82	.317	.430	.281	116	438	56	139	37	0	6	50	38	2	0	2	73	6	3	.443	.373
McVaney, Jeff	R-R	6-2	210	1-16-90	.273	.314	.247	54	128	17	35	9	2	1	15	18	3	1	0	24	5	1	.398	.376
Moya, Steven	L-R	6-7	260	8-9-91	.284	.300	.281	97	409	60	116	23	3	20	66	15	1	0	1	96	3	0	.501	.310
Presley, Alex	L-L	5-10	195	7-25-85	.296	.279	.302	41	169	23	50	10	3	3	14	18	2	1	3	27	4	6	.444	.365
Quintero, Humberto	R-R	5-10	215	8-2-79	.244	.333	.212	15	45	0	11	2	0	0	3	2	0	1	0	11	1	0	.289	.277
2-team total (5 Buffalo)					.250	—	—	20	60	3	15	5	0	0	3	3	1	1	0	15	1	0	.333	.297
Schierholtz, Nate	L-R	6-2	215	2-15-84	.246	.150	.265	31	118	9	29	4	0	3	13	6	0	0	1	28	0	0	.356	.280
Valdespin, Jordany	L-R	6-0	190	12-23-87	.239	.226	.242	101	293	31	70	11	2	3	25	20	3	2	3	59	10	4	.321	.292
Wilson, Bobby	R-R	6-0	230	4-8-83	.333	—	.333	1	3	1	1	1	0	0	2	1	0	0	0	1	0	0	.667	.500

Pitching	B-T	HT	WT	DOB	W	L	ERA	G	GS	CG	SV	IP	H	R	ER	HR	BB	SO	AVG	vLH	vRH	K/9	BB/9
Alaniz, R.J.	R-R	6-4	219	6-14-91	0	1	2.52	18	0	0	0	25	22	8	7	0	11	25	.239	.143	.281	9.00	3.96
Bell, Chad	R-L	6-3	200	2-28-89	10	4	3.70	28	10	0	0	80	79	34	33	4	38	69	.259	.258	.259	7.73	4.26
Boyd, Matt	L-L	6-3	215	2-2-91	2	5	2.25	11	11	0	0	64	53	20	16	5	18	57	.224	.222	.224	8.02	2.53
Britton, Drake	L-L	6-2	215	5-22-89	0	3	4.57	37	0	0	0	41	43	22	21	3	21	17	.272	.241	.288	3.70	4.57
Crotta, Mike	R-R	6-6	235	9-25-84	0	1	7.36	7	0	0	0	7	7	6	6	1	5	7	.241	.267	.214	8.59	6.14
Crouse, Matt	L-L	6-4	190	7-1-90	6	5	3.66	20	13	0	0	93	91	42	38	7	33	57	.259	.214	.270	5.50	3.18
Farmer, Buck	L-R	6-4	225	2-20-91	5	6	3.96	20	20	0	0	100	106	48	44	11	28	93	.271	.267	.276	8.37	2.52
Ferrell, Jeff	R-R	6-4	205	11-23-90	2	1	7.36	6	0	0	0	7	16	6	6	1	2	13	.444	.533	.381	15.95	2.45
Fulmer, Michael	R-R	6-3	210	3-15-93	1	1	4.11	3	3	0	0	15	16	8	7	3	5	20	.258	.188	.333	11.74	2.93
Greene, Shane	R-R	6-4	210	11-17-88	0	0	1.13	2	2	0	0	8	9	1	1	0	2	12	.273	.200	.385	13.50	0.00
Guilmet, Preston	R-R	6-2	200	7-27-87	3	3	2.77	65	0	0	0	68	71	28	21	4	12	82	.270	.217	.306	10.80	1.58
Hardy, Blaine	L-L	6-2	215	3-14-87	1	0	1.72	32	0	0	1	31	20	6	6	1	5	19	.187	.200	.179	5.46	1.44
Harrell, Lucas	B-R	6-2	205	6-3-85	1	0	3.60	1	1	0	0	5	5	2	2	0	2	4	.278	.100	.500	7.20	3.60
2-team total (9 Gwinnett)					3	1	2.92	10	6	0	0	37	40	15	12	1	21	31	—	—	—	7.54	5.11
Jaye, Myles	B-R	6-3	170	12-28-91	1	4	3.69	7	7	0	0	39	30	18	16	2	12	31	.210	.289	.173	7.15	2.77
Jimenez, Joe	R-R	6-3	220	1-17-95	0	1	2.30	17	0	0	8	16	9	5	4	1	4	16	.164	.143	.176	9.19	2.30
Kensing, Logan	R-R	6-1	190	7-3-82	1	1	3.44	52	0	0	0	50	46	19	19	1	18	48	.245	.313	.210	8.70	3.26
Mantiply, Joe	R-L	6-4	215	3-1-91	1	1	4.32	7	1	0	0	8	11	4	4	1	1	7	.324	.250	.333	7.56	1.08
Molleken, Dustin	L-R	6-4	230	8-21-84	2	4	3.58	42	5	0	1	60	49	26	24	4	30	56	.227	.275	.199	8.35	4.48
Nesbitt, Angel	R-R	6-1	240	12-4-90	1	1	5.68	28	0	0	0	32	48	23	20	2	14	24	.356	.368	.345	6.82	3.98
Norris, Daniel	L-L	6-2	195	4-25-93	5	7	4.54	14	14	0	0	73	78	40	37	2	28	77	.272	.205	.297	9.45	3.44
Parnell, Bobby	R-R	6-3	205	9-8-84	2	1	3.95	44	0	0	12	43	43	20	19	6	18	30	.262	.297	.233	6.23	3.74
Pelfrey, Mike	R-R	6-7	240	1-14-84	0	0	8.53	2	2	0	0	6	12	6	6	0	1	3	.414	.333	.450	4.26	0.00
Ramos, Cesar	L-L	6-2	200	6-22-84	2	3	6.00	8	3	0	0	21	29	14	14	2	6	19	.333	.278	.348	8.14	2.57

DETROIT TIGERS

Pitching	B-T	HT	WT	DOB	W	L	ERA	G	GS	CG	SV	IP	H	R	ER	HR	BB	SO	AVG	vLH	vRH	K/9	BB/9
Riordan, Cory	R-R	6-4	200	5-25-86	1	2	3.58	5	5	0	0	33	32	15	13	4	3	24	.267	.324	.241	6.61	0.83
Roach, Donn	R-R	6-0	195	12-14-89	3	1	3.03	5	5	0	0	30	29	11	10	1	5	21	.257	.311	.221	6.37	1.52
Rondon, Bruce	R-R	6-3	275	12-9-90	2	2	3.74	22	0	0	9	22	23	9	9	1	16	30	.284	.342	.233	12.46	6.65
Ryan, Kyle	L-L	6-5	215	9-25-91	0	0	0.00	8	0	0	0	7	3	0	0	0	6	5	.130	.000	.188	6.43	7.71
Saupold, Warwick	R-R	6-1	195	1-16-90	7	2	2.30	18	11	1	0	74	64	20	19	3	22	50	.235	.209	.261	6.05	2.66
Spomer, Kurt	R-R	6-2	215	7-10-89	0	0	4.05	9	0	0	0	13	21	7	6	0	5	13	.396	.471	.361	8.78	3.38
Turley, Josh	L-L	6-0	185	8-26-90	2	3	4.68	6	6	0	0	33	42	20	17	3	12	24	.309	.263	.327	6.61	3.31
Valdez, Jose	R-R	6-1	200	3-1-90	0	0	3.48	8	0	0	0	10	7	4	4	2	5	8	.200	.200	.200	6.97	4.35
VerHagen, Drew	R-R	6-6	230	10-22-90	0	0	13.50	1	0	0	0	1	1	1	1	1	0	1	.333	.000	.500	13.50	0.00
Weber, Thad	R-R	6-2	205	9-28-84	7	11	4.44	22	20	3	0	130	149	72	64	12	32	65	.289	.326	.261	4.51	2.22
Wilson, Alex	R-R	6-0	215	11-3-86	0	0	5.40	2	0	0	0	2	2	1	1	0	1	3	.286	.333	.250	16.20	5.40
Zimmermann, Jordan	R-R	6-2	225	5-23-86	0	1	1.33	5	5	0	0	20	19	10	3	2	4	11	.257	.273	.250	4.87	1.77

Fielding

Catcher	PCT	G	PO	A	E	DP	PB
Gonzalez	.998	60	444	46	1	4	0
Greiner	1.000	1	8	2	0	0	0
Hicks	.992	66	482	37	4	5	7
Longley	1.000	3	16	3	0	0	2
McCann	1.000	4	24	2	0	0	0
Quintero	1.000	14	90	8	0	0	2
Wilson	1.000	1	9	0	0	0	0

First Base	PCT	G	PO	A	E	DP
Green	1.000	11	98	4	0	12
Huffman	.993	105	875	52	7	85
McGehee	.989	10	87	0	1	6
Valdespin	.995	25	187	11	1	17

Second Base	PCT	G	PO	A	E	DP
Bortnick	1.000	10	15	23	0	4
Ciriaco	1.000	3	5	12	0	6
Diaz	.981	96	128	242	7	57

Field	PCT	G	PO	A	E	DP
Field	.923	11	20	28	4	7
Gonzalez	1.000	3	4	7	0	2
Jones	.963	7	10	16	1	2
Krizan	1.000	2	2	2	0	0
Machado	1.000	4	8	10	0	2
Valdespin	.965	42	60	78	5	21

Third Base	PCT	G	PO	A	E	DP
Bortnick	1.000	3	1	4	0	0
Ciriaco	.923	5	2	10	1	1
Diaz	1.000	3	1	3	0	0
Hicks	—	0	0	0	0	0
Huffman	1.000	1	0	2	0	0
Jones	.898	22	13	31	5	2
McGehee	.980	100	48	153	4	16
Valdespin	.965	22	10	45	2	4

Shortstop	PCT	G	PO	A	E	DP
Ciriaco	1.000	5	4	13	0	1
Diaz	.948	16	17	38	3	4

	PCT	G	PO	A	E	DP
Iglesias	1.000	2	1	3	0	1
Machado	.973	130	207	403	17	85

Outfield	PCT	G	PO	A	E	DP
Bernard	.961	40	68	6	3	0
Ciriaco	—	1	0	0	0	0
Collins	.986	64	128	11	2	1
Gose	.983	48	113	3	2	1
Huffman	1.000	6	12	1	0	0
Jones	—	1	0	0	0	0
Jones	.985	61	135	0	2	0
Krizan	.947	19	18	0	1	0
Martinez	1.000	2	4	0	0	0
Maybin	1.000	9	24	0	0	0
McVaney	.975	40	74	3	2	0
Moya	.978	93	172	3	4	1
Presley	1.000	41	84	5	0	0
Schierholtz	.951	24	39	0	2	0
Valdespin	1.000	5	4	0	0	0

ERIE SEAWOLVES

DOUBLE-A

EASTERN LEAGUE

Batting	B-T	HT	WT	DOB	AVG	vLH	vRH	G	AB	R	H	2B	3B	HR	RBI	BB	HBP	SH	SF	SO	SB	CS	SLG	OBP
Bernard, Wynton	R-R	6-2	195	9-24-90	.308	.364	.286	58	227	38	70	8	4	6	22	27	1	5	2	39	13	2	.458	.381
Bortnick, Tyler	R-R	5-11	185	7-3-87	.279	.389	.233	33	122	14	34	5	2	4	22	13	1	1	2	24	4	0	.451	.348
Castro, Harold	L-R	6-0	165	11-30-93	.247	.165	.275	105	392	41	97	16	1	4	23	11	2	9	2	63	6	7	.324	.270
Eaves, Kody	L-R	6-0	175	7-8-93	.222	.167	.237	106	325	42	72	24	4	11	51	39	5	4	3	105	6	4	.422	.312
Ficociello, Dominic	B-R	6-4	200	4-10-92	.248	.221	.263	123	423	53	105	21	3	5	38	50	3	2	4	110	5	5	.348	.329
Frawley, Casey	R-R	5-11	170	9-17-87	.231	.200	.247	35	121	8	28	3	1	1	6	7	1	2	0	31	2	1	.298	.279
Gerber, Mike	L-R	6-0	190	7-8-92	.261	.162	.293	41	153	17	40	8	3	4	20	20	1	0	1	41	6	3	.431	.349
Gonzalez, Alberto	R-R	5-10	195	4-8-83	.258	.270	.250	24	97	10	25	4	0	1	8	2	2	1	0	5	1	0	.330	.287
Gose, Anthony	L-L	6-1	190	8-10-90	.224	.306	.200	40	156	16	35	4	0	6	27	17	0	0	0	54	11	4	.365	.301
Green, Austin	R-R	6-1	200	2-22-90	.231	.225	.235	53	186	17	43	9	0	4	27	6	2	1	3	31	0	0	.344	.259
Green, Dean	R-R	6-4	255	6-30-89	.286	.301	.276	69	259	33	74	11	0	16	72	22	6	0	6	43	2	0	.514	.348
Greiner, Grayson	R-R	6-6	220	10-11-92	.288	.286	.289	59	208	20	60	9	3	7	30	10	2	0	5	55	1	0	.462	.320
Harrell, Connor	R-R	6-3	215	3-24-91	.273	.328	.246	103	366	60	100	17	0	10	32	22	15	2	0	107	6	3	.402	.340
Hicks, John	R-R	6-2	230	8-31-89	.388	.353	.406	14	49	7	19	1	1	1	4	4	0	0	1	9	1	0	.510	.426
Jones, Corey	L-R	6-0	205	8-18-90	.252	.302		103	386	53	111	22	1	8	46	37	10	0	2	52	8	5	.412	.363
Jones, JaCoby	R-R	6-2	205	5-10-92	.312	.381	.286	20	77	11	24	6	2	4	20	10	1	0	1	23	2	1	.597	.393
Krizan, Jason	L-R	6-0	185	6-28-89	.292	.298	.290	95	356	46	104	24	6	9	55	45	0	0	5	27	2	3	.469	.367
Longley, Andrew	R-R	6-3	215	10-5-88	.147	.139	.151	34	109	12	16	7	0	3	10	11	1	0	0	43	0	0	.294	.231
Mattlage, Garrett	B-R	5-10	175	2-25-93	.167	.143	.200	4	12	1	2	0	0	0	1	0	0	0	0	4	0	0	.167	.231
McVaney, Jeff	R-R	6-2	210	1-16-90	.300	.378	.253	66	240	51	72	17	5	6	22	37	11	0	1	26	8	6	.488	.415
Nunez, Gustavo	B-R	5-10	170	2-8-88	.279	.255	.289	86	348	48	97	12	3	2	31	36	3	2	2	51	14	12	.348	.350
Pereira, Anthony	R-R	6-0	170	11-28-96	.200	.500	.000	4	10	0	2	0	0	0	0	0	0	1	0	3	0	0	.200	.200
Remes, Tim	R-R	6-0	205	6-17-92	.250	.333	.200	2	8	2	2	1	0	1	3	0	0	0	0	2	0	0	.750	.250
Salgado, Ismael	R-R	6-1	165	1-11-93	.100	.000	.125	8	20	1	2	0	0	0	2	0	2	0	0	6	0	0	.100	.182
Stewart, Christin	L-R	6-0	205	12-10-93	.218	.261	.203	24	87	17	19	2	0	6	19	12	0	0	0	36	0	0	.448	.310

Pitching	B-T	HT	WT	DOB	W	L	ERA	G	GS	CG	SV	IP	H	R	ER	HR	BB	SO	AVG	vLH	vRH	K/9	BB/9
Alaniz, R.J.	R-R	6-4	219	6-14-91	4	3	2.77	34	0	0	4	49	50	17	15	1	18	49	.269	.257	.270	9.06	3.33
Alexander, Tyler	R-L	6-2	200	7-14-94	2	1	3.15	6	6	0	0	34	36	13	12	4	4	23	.273	.214	.300	6.03	1.05
Castillo, Lendy	R-R	6-1	180	4-8-89	3	3	5.06	40	0	0	0	48	46	29	27	4	26	50	.254	.233	.269	9.38	4.88
2-team total (2 Akron)					3	4	5.68	42	1	0	0	51	51	34	32	4	27	52	—	—		9.24	4.80
Collier, Tommy	R-R	6-3	205	12-3-89	9	7	4.20	25	25	2	0	131	145	67	61	15	35	87	.280	.305	.254	5.99	2.41
Crotta, Mike	R-R	6-6	235	9-25-84	0	0	4.50	2	0	0	0	2	4	2	1	0	2	2	.400	.500	.250	9.00	0.00
Crouse, Matt	L-L	6-4	190	7-1-90	3	2	3.86	11	3	0	0	33	29	15	14	1	12	20	.238	.189	.259	5.51	3.31
Drummond, Calvin	R-R	6-3	200	9-22-88	0	2	4.97	13	3	0	0	25	26	19	14	2	18	26	.255	.220	.279	9.24	6.39

Pitching	B-T	HT	WT	DOB	W	L	ERA	G	GS	CG	SV	IP	H	R	ER	HR	BB	SO	AVG	vLH	vRH	K/9	BB/9
Fernandez, Anthony	L-L	6-4	215	6-8-90	0	3	5.18	5	5	1	0	24	26	18	14	3	7	16	.265	.300	.250	5.92	2.59
Garrido, Santiago	R-R	6-1	195	10-4-89	0	2	7.48	23	2	0	0	43	64	39	36	7	19	40	.344	.315	.371	8.31	3.95
Harrell, Lucas	B-R	6-2	205	6-3-85	2	1	3.28	5	5	0	0	25	24	11	9	1	14	16	.253	.167	.321	5.84	5.11
Hemmer, Gabe	R-R	6-3	220	6-22-90	1	0	5.21	13	0	0	0	19	17	14	11	0	13	18	.236	.200	.262	8.53	6.16
Jaye, Myles	B-R	6-3	170	12-28-91	4	8	4.04	21	21	1	0	123	127	60	55	11	29	104	.262	.269	.256	7.63	2.13
Jimenez, Joe	R-R	6-3	220	1-17-95	3	2	2.18	21	0	0	12	21	12	5	5	0	8	34	.171	.174	.17	14.81	3.48
Kubitza, Austin	R-R	6-5	225	11-16-91	2	3	5.40	7	4	0	0	20	22	17	12	1	16	11	.275	.205	.341	4.95	7.20
Lara, Confesor	R-R	6-2	170	8-7-90	1	2	8.47	12	1	0	0	17	24	16	16	2	7	15	.348	.269	.395	7.94	3.71
Lewicki, Artie	R-R	6-3	195	4-8-92	1	7	3.48	12	12	0	0	67	67	35	26	4	13	57	.256	.173	.31	7.62	1.74
Mantiply, Joe	R-L	6-4	215	3-1-91	3	1	2.47	49	0	0	1	51	40	17	14	1	11	62	.214	.143	.292	10.94	1.94
Martinez, David	R-R	6-2	220	8-4-87	2	3	5.62	12	5	0	0	42	46	33	26	6	10	34	.369	.406	.345	7.34	2.16
Nesbitt, Angel	R-R	6-1	240	12-4-90	1	1	3.65	11	0	0	0	12	13	5	5	1	2	13	.271	.333	.222	9.49	1.46
Norris, Daniel	L-L	6-2	195	4-25-93	1	0	4.05	1	1	0	0	7	5	3	3	2	3	7	.208	.000	.25	9.45	4.05
Ravenelle, Adam	R-R	6-3	185	10-5-92	1	1	4.85	27	0	0	1	30	30	18	16	4	16	23	.265	.231	.284	6.98	4.85
Riordan, Cory	R-R	6-4	200	5-25-86	5	8	5.21	22	19	0	0	121	153	73	70	14	27	89	.313	.284	.335	6.62	2.01
Rogers, Joe	L-L	6-1	205	2-18-91	1	0	5.06	7	0	0	0	11	17	6	6	1	7	8	.370	.375	.367	6.75	5.91
Shirley, Tommy	R-L	6-5	220	11-11-88	1	0	7.47	9	0	0	1	16	23	13	13	1	9	11	.359	.500	.304	6.32	5.17
Smith, Brennan	R-R	6-3	200	8-4-89	0	1	14.79	4	4	0	0	14	24	23	23	8	9	6	.375	.407	.351	3.86	5.79
Spomer, Kurt	B-R	6-2	215	7-10-89	2	1	2.51	32	0	0	0	43	39	15	12	3	9	36	.245	.333	.163	7.53	1.88
Turley, Josh	L-L	6-0	185	8-26-90	7	10	4.34	20	20	0	0	120	134	67	58	14	26	101	.282	.255	.295	7.55	1.94
Valdez, Jose	R-R	6-1	200	3-1-90	2	1	5.59	8	0	0	0	10	13	7	6	1	7	8	.351	.368	.333	7.45	6.52
Voelker, Paul	R-R	5-10	185	8-19-92	3	4	4.17	52	0	0	13	54	54	27	25	7	24	79	.269	.282	.262	13.17	4.00
Watkins, Spenser	R-R	6-1	190	8-27-92	0	0	6.75	1	1	0	0	4	7	3	3	1	3	4	.438	.444	.429	2.25	6.75
Weber, Thad	R-R	6-2	205	9-28-84	1	2	9.87	4	4	0	0	17	28	19	19	2	9	13	.364	.364	.364	6.75	4.67

Fielding

Catcher	PCT	G	PO	A	E	DP	PB
Green	.978	50	332	24	8	5	4
Greiner	1.000	56	424	38	0	3	3
Hicks	1.000	11	85	11	0	0	0
Longley	.982	28	201	15	4	3	2
Remes	.957	2	19	3	1	1	0

First Base	PCT	G	PO	A	E	DP
Ficociello	.998	98	755	47	2	74
Green	.994	20	162	10	1	17
Hicks	.957	2	18	4	1	3
Jones	.990	24	192	9	2	18
Jones	1.000	2	16	2	0	2

Second Base	PCT	G	PO	A	E	DP
Bortnick	.981	12	17	35	1	6
Castro	.975	68	133	184	8	44
Eaves	.939	31	49	74	8	15

	PCT	G	PO	A	E	DP
Frawley	.938	7	18	27	3	6
Gonzalez	.958	5	7	16	1	4
Jones	.969	24	32	62	3	12

Third Base	PCT	G	PO	A	E	DP
Bortnick	.919	12	9	25	3	1
Castro	1.000	8	5	10	0	1
Eaves	.943	67	43	105	9	7
Ficociello	.923	10	13	23	3	2
Frawley	1.000	1	2	2	0	0
Gonzalez	.972	15	13	22	1	2
Jones	.923	22	13	23	3	5
Jones	.929	9	2	11	1	2
Mattlage	1.000	1	2	4	0	1

Shortstop	PCT	G	PO	A	E	DP
Castro	.981	29	38	65	2	12
Frawley	.960	22	29	66	4	18
Gonzalez	1.000	1	1	2	0	1

	PCT	G	PO	A	E	DP
Mattlage	1.000	3	2	6	0	1
Nunez	.953	86	156	270	21	58
Pereira	1.000	3	2	5	0	1

Outfield	PCT	G	PO	A	E	DP
Bernard	.989	44	90	1	1	0
Bortnick	1.000	5	5	0	0	0
Ficociello	.950	15	18	1	1	1
Frawley	—	1	0	0	0	0
Gerber	1.000	39	84	4	0	1
Gose	.987	34	68	6	1	2
Harrell	.985	93	197	5	3	0
Jones	.963	18	26	0	1	0
Jones	1.000	9	32	0	0	0
Krizan	.988	79	155	7	2	1
McVaney	.972	64	135	5	4	0
Salgado	1.000	8	11	1	0	0
Stewart	1.000	22	33	4	0	0

LAKELAND FLYING TIGERS

FLORIDA STATE LEAGUE

HIGH CLASS A

Batting	B-T	HT	WT	DOB	AVG	vLH	vRH	G	AB	R	H	2B	3B	HR	RBI	BB	HBP	SH	SF	SO	SB	CS	SLG	OBP
Bortnick, Tyler	R-R	5-11	185	7-3-87	.302	.333	.290	22	86	11	26	5	0	1	6	7	1	1	0	14	3	1	.395	.362
Brown, Rashad	L-L	5-11	180	12-17-93	.229	.257	.216	25	109	12	25	5	2	0	6	4	1	0	0	27	1	0	.312	.263
Frawley, Casey	R-R	5-11	170	9-17-87	.311	.217	.353	19	74	9	23	6	0	4	13	3	0	0	0	16	0	0	.554	.338
Gerber, Mike	L-R	6-0	190	7-8-92	.282	.313	.270	91	351	52	99	22	3	14	60	32	2	0	3	111	2	3	.481	.343
Greiner, Grayson	R-R	6-6	220	10-11-92	.312	.214	.346	31	109	14	34	6	0	0	12	12	1	1	0	26	0	0	.367	.385
Hinkle, Wade	L-L	6-0	230	9-5-89	.295	.210	.324	120	420	62	124	26	1	11	66	44	9	0	6	98	0	0	.440	.370
Jones, Keaton	R-R	6-2	195	10-8-92	.000	—	.000	1	1	0	0	0	0	0	0	0	0	0	0	0	0	0	.000	.000
Kivett, Ross	R-R	6-1	195	10-19-91	.215	.200	.220	118	432	61	93	24	3	11	51	70	3	5	1	84	12	5	.361	.328
Longley, Andrew	R-R	6-3	215	10-5-88	.283	.278	.286	17	60	10	17	0	0	5	9	6	1	0	1	24	0	0	.533	.353
Mattlage, Garrett	B-R	5-10	175	2-25-93	.216	.243	.200	32	97	11	21	4	0	2	11	7	0	2	1	31	2	1	.320	.267
Maybin, Cameron	R-R	6-3	215	4-4-87	.231	.250	.222	4	13	3	3	2	0	0	2	0	0	0	0	2	1	0	.385	.333
Navarro, Franklin	R-R	5-10	181	10-17-94	.200	—	.200	1	5	0	1	0	0	0	0	0	0	0	0	0	0	0	.200	.200
Pankake, Joey	R-R	6-2	185	11-23-92	.215	.225	.211	96	354	47	76	10	0	15	45	33	3	0	6	95	1	1	.370	.284
Pereira, Anthony	R-R	6-0	200	11-28-96	.211	.250	.200	17	57	7	12	2	0	1	4	1	1	2	1	13	0	1	.298	.270
Pirtle, Brett	B-R	5-9	175	3-23-91	.130	.000	.150	7	23	1	3	0	0	0	2	0	0	0	0	3	0	0	.130	.200
Powell, Curt	R-R	6-0	180	4-30-91	.182	.286	.133	6	22	0	4	1	0	0	2	1	1	0	0	7	0	0	.227	.250
Presley, Alex	L-L	5-10	190	7-25-85	.571	1.000	.400	2	7	4	4	1	0	0	3	2	0	0	0	1	0	0	.714	.667
Reaves, Jared	R-R	5-10	185	7-20-90	.320	1.000	.261	8	25	4	8	1	0	1	5	3	1	0	0	4	0	0	.480	.414
Remes, Tim	R-R	6-0	205	6-17-92	.170	.300	.140	16	53	1	9	1	0	0	5	7	0	0	0	18	0	0	.358	.267
Salgado, Ismael	R-R	6-1	165	1-11-93	.213	.182	.225	36	122	12	26	4	2	0	8	2	3	1	1	29	1	2	.279	.242
Scivicque, Kade	R-R	6-0	220	3-22-93	.282	.268	.287	106	419	45	118	19	2	6	41	22	6	3	0	83	0	0	.379	.324
Serrano, Ariel	R-R	5-10	174	6-23-96	.214	.500	.167	4	14	0	3	0	0	0	2	0	0	0	0	5	0	0	.214	.214
Shepherd, Zac	R-R	6-3	185	9-14-95	.186	.171	.192	121	409	62	76	20	1	15	50	64	4	2	2	159	0	0	.350	.301
Simcox, A.J.	R-R	6-3	185	6-22-94	.262	.270	.259	127	527	76	138	19	5	5	51	28	2	4	7	108	7	5	.345	.298

Batting	B-T	HT	WT	DOB	AVG	vLH	vRH	G	AB	R	H	2B	3B	HR	RBI	BB	HBP	SH	SF	SO	SB	CS	SLG	OBP
Stewart, Christin	L-R	6-0	205	12-10-93	.264	.248	.271	104	356	60	94	22	1	24	68	74	10	0	2	105	3	1	.534	.403
Sthormes, Andres	R-R	5-10	171	8-7-96	.667	.667	—	1	3	0	2	0	0	0	1	0	0	0	0	1	0	0	.667	.667
Verlander, Ben	R-R	6-4	200	1-31-92	.252	.225	.264	80	286	33	72	18	2	5	39	22	1	0	5	59	3	1	.381	.303

Pitching	B-T	HT	WT	DOB	W	L	ERA	G	GS	CG	SV	IP	H	R	ER	HR	BB	SO	AVG	vLH	vRH	K/9	BB/9
Alexander, Tyler	R-L	6-2	200	7-14-94	6	7	2.21	19	18	0	0	102	87	36	25	7	16	82	.226	.274	.205	7.24	1.41
Belisario, Johan	R-R	5-11	165	8-13-93	0	2	5.82	10	0	0	1	17	17	11	11	1	10	14	.258	.391	.186	7.41	5.29
Briceno, Endrys	R-R	6-5	175	2-7-92	4	7	5.94	25	17	1	0	103	121	72	68	10	56	81	.303	.352	.275	7.08	4.89
De La Rosa, Edgar	R-R	6-8	235	11-12-90	0	1	5.09	12	0	0	1	18	17	12	10	4	7	18	.246	.250	.244	9.17	3.57
Drummond, Calvin	R-R	6-3	200	9-22-89	1	2	2.01	12	3	0	0	31	30	8	7	0	7	28	.250	.217	.270	8.04	2.01
Ferrell, Jeff	R-R	6-4	205	11-23-90	0	0	0.00	3	3	0	0	4	2	0	0	0	1	7	.143	.400	.000	15.75	2.25
Ford, Tyler	L-L	5-8	175	9-11-91	0	0	9.00	7	0	0	0	11	11	11	11	1	4	9	.262	.222	.273	7.36	3.27
Garrido, Santiago	R-R	6-1	195	10-4-89	2	1	2.81	10	0	0	5	16	15	5	5	0	5	15	.259	.158	.308	8.44	2.81
Gutierrez, Alfred	R-R	6-0	143	6-12-95	0	1	10.38	1	1	0	0	4	6	5	5	1	0	1	.316	.357	.200	2.08	0.00
Hall, Matt	L-L	6-0	200	7-23-93	3	2	4.15	12	11	1	0	61	61	34	28	6	28	54	.264	.200	.282	8.01	4.15
Hardy, Blaine	L-L	6-2	215	3-14-87	0	0	6.00	2	2	0	0	3	2	2	2	0	1	6	.167	.500	.100	18.00	3.00
Hemmer, Gabe	R-R	6-3	220	6-22-90	3	5	5.12	30	0	0	4	51	66	35	29	4	20	55	.311	.321	.306	9.71	3.53
Hicks, Taylor	R-R	6-3	230	2-26-92	0	0	18.00	2	0	0	0	3	5	6	6	2	6	3	.357	.286	.429	9.00	18.00
Jimenez, Joe	R-R	6-3	220	1-17-95	0	0	0.00	17	0	0	10	17	5	0	0	0	5	28	.089	.000	.119	14.54	2.60
Kubitza, Austin	R-R	6-5	225	11-16-91	2	1	4.60	22	0	0	1	43	46	31	22	3	26	35	.266	.235	.286	7.33	5.44
Labourt, Jairo	L-L	6-4	205	3-7-94	7	9	5.26	30	12	0	1	87	65	55	51	3	70	81	.202	.152	.229	8.35	7.21
Ladwig, A.J.	R-R	6-5	180	12-24-92	12	9	3.69	26	21	0	0	154	170	75	63	19	22	101	.279	.253	.297	5.92	1.29
Lara, Confesor	R-R	6-2	170	8-7-90	2	2	4.28	21	0	0	2	27	27	14	13	2	15	30	.250	.378	.183	9.88	4.94
2-team total (5 Fort Myers)					3	2	3.57	26	0	0	3	35	33	16	14	2	16	35	—	—	—	8.92	4.08
Lewicki, Artie	R-R	6-3	195	4-8-92	2	1	3.32	5	3	0	0	22	21	10	8	0	6	20	.250	.125	.279	8.31	2.49
Longwith, Logan	R-R	6-3	170	3-30-94	0	0	3.38	1	0	0	0	3	1	1	1	0	1	1	.111	.250	.000	3.38	3.38
Martinez, Malvin	R-R	6-0	170	4-19-95	1	1	6.00	12	0	0	1	24	24	21	16	4	12	26	.255	.311	.204	9.75	4.50
Moreno, Gerson	R-R	6-0	175	9-10-95	0	3	6.93	21	0	0	3	25	22	20	19	4	20	27	.232	.233	.231	9.85	7.30
Nesbitt, Angel	R-R	6-1	240	12-4-90	0	0	2.45	3	3	0	0	4	2	1	1	0	3	5	.182	.333	.125	12.27	7.36
Norris, Daniel	L-L	6-2	195	4-25-93	0	0	4.50	2	2	0	0	6	9	3	3	0	1	7	.346	.333	.350	10.50	1.50
Paredes, Willy	R-R	6-2	180	2-2-89	0	2	9.00	7	0	0	0	11	15	13	11	0	3	11	.349	.400	.333	9.00	2.45
Ravenelle, Adam	R-R	6-3	185	10-5-92	2	1	2.86	23	0	0	3	28	17	10	9	3	17	34	.168	.242	.132	10.80	5.40
Reininger, Zac	B-R	6-3	170	1-28-93	0	0	0.00	4	0	0	0	6	2	0	0	0	2	5	.111	.333	.000	7.94	3.18
Rogers, Joe	L-L	6-1	205	2-18-91	0	1	5.96	14	0	0	0	26	32	19	17	2	11	22	.302	.286	.308	7.71	3.86
Saupold, Warwick	R-R	6-1	195	1-16-90	0	0	1.59	2	2	0	0	6	7	5	1	0	4	1	.304	.385	.200	1.59	6.35
Sittinger, Brandyn	R-R	6-1	200	6-6-94	0	0	5.40	2	0	0	0	3	4	2	2	0	1	4	.286	.500	.125	10.80	2.70
Smith, Gage	R-R	6-2	185	2-13-91	1	0	3.32	9	0	0	0	19	18	7	7	1	4	16	.240	.500	.169	7.58	1.89
2-team total (7 Brevard County)					2	1	2.76	16	0	0	2	29	25	9	9	1	5	22	—	—	—	6.75	1.53
Smith, Slade	R-R	6-2	190	9-26-90	1	0	6.23	5	0	0	0	9	11	6	6	1	2	4	.324	.438	.222	4.15	2.08
Szkutnik, Trent	R-L	6-0	195	8-21-93	0	3	7.52	6	6	0	0	26	36	23	22	2	11	17	.340	.382	.319	5.81	3.76
Thompson, Jeff	R-R	6-6	245	9-23-91	7	7	3.49	27	20	0	1	119	99	54	46	6	67	100	.231	.263	.209	7.58	5.08
Turnbull, Spencer	R-R	6-3	215	9-18-92	1	1	3.00	6	6	0	0	30	24	12	10	1	10	27	.216	.214	.217	8.10	3.00
Verastegui, Adenson	R-R	5-11	205	2-19-93	1	1	3.38	7	0	0	0	8	6	3	3	0	9	11	.200	.125	.227	12.38	10.13
Warner, Burris	R-R	6-0	190	10-15-94	2	0	7.88	7	0	0	0	8	11	7	7	0	8	6	.314	.385	.273	6.75	9.00
Wilson, Alex	R-R	6-0	215	11-3-86	0	1	8.10	2	1	0	0	3	7	3	3	2	0	4	.412	.333	.455	10.80	0.00
Ziomek, Kevin	R-L	6-3	200	3-21-92	0	1	10.38	1	1	0	0	4	9	5	5	1	1	1	.450	.500	.429	2.08	2.08

Fielding

Catcher	PCT	G	PO	A	E	DP	PB
Greiner	.988	27	220	22	3	0	2
Longley	.986	16	131	6	2	2	1
Navarro	.933	1	14	0	1	0	1
Remes	.983	16	93	20	2	2	2
Scivicque	.989	72	501	44	6	2	4
Sthormes	1.000	1	8	0	0	0	0

First Base	PCT	G	PO	A	E	DP
Hinkle	.990	120	1065	66	12	92
Powell	.960	4	22	2	1	1
Reaves	1.000	1	1	0	0	0
Verlander	.987	8	71	3	1	7

Second Base	PCT	G	PO	A	E	DP
Bortnick	1.000	4	8	7	0	0
Frawley	1.000	7	6	23	0	6
Mattlage	.930	18	32	48	6	11
Pankake	.979	85	159	215	8	53
Pereira	.948	15	39	52	5	12
Pirtle	1.000	3	3	6	0	1
Reaves	1.000	2	4	7	0	1

Third Base	PCT	G	PO	A	E	DP
Bortnick	.952	6	6	14	1	1
Frawley	1.000	5	0	12	0	1
Mattlage	.750	2	0	3	1	0
Pirtle	1.000	2	1	1	0	0
Powell	1.000	2	2	4	0	0
Shepherd	.907	115	60	242	31	23

Shortstop	PCT	G	PO	A	E	DP
Frawley	1.000	2	2	6	0	1
Mattlage	1.000	5	7	13	0	6
Pereira	1.000	2	0	5	0	1
Reaves	.824	5	3	11	3	1
Simcox	.947	120	180	355	30	60

Outfield	PCT	G	PO	A	E	DP
Bortnick	—	1	0	0	0	0
Brown	1.000	25	36	1	0	0
Gerber	1.000	79	161	2	0	0
Kivett	.996	117	237	5	1	1
Maybin	1.000	2	1	0	0	0
Presley	1.000	2	2	0	0	0
Salgado	.973	33	72	1	2	0
Serrano	1.000	4	11	1	0	0
Stewart	.984	94	123	3	2	1
Verlander	.965	49	80	2	3	0

WEST MICHIGAN WHITECAPS

LOW CLASS A

MIDWEST LEAGUE

Batting	B-T	HT	WT	DOB	AVG	vLH	vRH	G	AB	R	H	2B	3B	HR	RBI	BB	HBP	SH	SF	SO	SB	CS	SLG	OBP
Allen, Will	R-R	6-3	220	3-25-92	.266	.355	.237	131	488	44	130	35	0	5	73	52	6	0	11	86	0	0	.369	.338
Azocar, Jose	R-R	5-11	165	5-11-96	.281	.275	.283	129	501	56	141	11	8	0	51	25	1	2	3	119	14	5	.335	.315
Brown, Rashad	L-L	5-11	180	12-17-93	.275	.310	.262	65	222	27	61	10	1	0	22	18	4	4	2	43	19	4	.329	.337
Fuentes, Steven	B-R	6-0	210	10-21-94	.165	.128	.186	33	109	12	18	1	3	0	13	13	0	1	4	39	1	0	.229	.246

Batting

Batting	B-T	HT	WT	DOB	AVG	vLH	vRH	G	AB	R	H	2B	3B	HR	RBI	BB	HBP	SH	SF	SO	SB	CS	SLG	OBP
Gibson, Cam	L-R	6-1	195	2-12-94	.221	.231	.217	119	394	59	87	11	7	6	40	42	4	6	1	110	26	9	.330	.302
Gonzalez, David	R-R	5-9	140	12-1-93	.248	.237	.252	113	404	54	100	21	3	2	34	42	3	5	3	59	15	7	.329	.321
Havrilak, Joey	L-R	6-1	195	11-25-91	.267	.133	.300	23	75	9	20	3	2	0	10	9	1	1	2	32	4	1	.360	.345
Hill, Derek	R-R	6-2	195	12-30-95	.266	.220	.284	93	384	66	102	17	6	1	31	24	3	2	2	105	35	6	.349	.312
Laffita, Leonardo	R-R	6-1	200	9-30-91	.213	.234	.207	76	272	27	58	15	1	2	26	12	5	1	3	43	6	4	.298	.257
Lester, Josh	L-L	6-3	216	7-17-94	.162	.083	.179	19	68	7	11	0	0	0	2	3	0	0	0	21	1	0	.162	.197
Maddox, Will	L-R	5-10	180	6-11-92	.339	.314	.348	127	511	59	173	23	3	1	58	32	5	5	5	89	28	12	.401	.380
Navarro, Franklin	B-R	5-10	181	10-17-94	.272	.250	.278	25	92	9	25	5	1	2	13	3	0	0	1	18	0	1	.413	.292
Padron, Victor	L-R	5-8	160	7-5-94	.135	.143	.133	11	37	4	5	0	0	0	3	7	0	0	0	12	1	0	.135	.273
Pereira, Anthony	R-R	6-0	170	11-28-96	.077	.000	.100	3	13	0	1	0	0	0	0	1	0	0	0	3	0	0	.077	.143
Perez, Arvicent	R-R	5-10	180	1-14-94	.303	.322	.297	74	271	28	82	16	4	0	30	7	2	6	4	36	1	0	.391	.320
Pirtle, Brett	B-R	5-9	175	3-23-91	.286	.297	.283	95	360	55	103	21	1	1	44	32	6	7	3	54	10	3	.358	.352
Salgado, Ismael	R-R	6-1	165	1-11-93	.375	.500	.333	4	16	2	6	1	0	0	1	0	0	0	0	3	0	0	.438	.412
Zambrano, Jose	B-R	5-7	155	11-4-93	.277	.189	.302	66	242	31	67	9	1	2	22	18	3	4	3	22	9	2	.347	.331
Zeile, Shane	R-R	6-1	195	6-14-93	.235	.235	.56	196	27	46	7	7	3	28	21	4	3	43	2	0	.388	.288	

Pitching

Pitching	B-T	HT	WT	DOB	W	L	ERA	G	GS	CG	SV	IP	H	R	ER	HR	BB	SO	AVG	vLH	vRH	K/9	BB/9
Baez, Sandy	R-R	6-2	180	11-25-93	7	9	3.81	21	21	0	0	113	125	54	48	7	28	88	.283	.298	.266	6.99	2.22
Boardman, Toller	L-L	6-3	210	11-15-92	8	3	2.10	38	1	0	1	86	85	26	20	2	18	57	.270	.278	.265	5.99	1.89
Burrows, Beau	R-R	6-2	200	9-18-96	6	4	3.15	21	20	0	0	97	87	38	34	2	30	67	.240	.206	.277	6.22	2.78
Cabrera, Yordy	R-R	6-1	205	9-3-90	1	3	6.16	12	0	0	1	19	19	13	13	1	15	19	.268	.353	.189	9.00	7.11
Castellanos, Ryan	R-R	6-3	215	4-15-94	1	0	1.50	1	1	0	0	6	7	1	1	0	0	4	.292	.188	.500	6.00	0.00
Dowdy, Kyle	R-R	6-1	195	2-3-93	10	3	2.84	23	16	1	0	108	109	38	34	6	24	86	.270	.25	.291	7.19	2.01
Ecker, Mark	R-R	6-0	180	5-27-95	0	0	1.86	9	0	0	5	10	9	2	2	1	2	10	.237	.300	.167	9.31	1.86
Garcia, Bryan	R-R	6-1	203	4-19-95	0	1	40.50	1	0	0	0	1	3	3	3	0	0	1	.600	.333	1.000	13.50	0.00
Greene, Shane	R-R	6-4	210	11-17-88	0	0	0.00	1	1	0	0	3	2	0	0	0	1	5	.182	.000	.167	15.00	3.00
Hall, Matt	L-L	6-0	200	7-23-93	8	0	1.09	12	12	0	0	66	49	10	8	0	21	72	.202	.165	.221	9.77	2.85
Houston, Zac	R-R	6-5	250	11-30-94	1	0	0.46	13	0	0	4	20	5	1	1	0	12	30	.082	.029	.148	13.73	5.49
Idrogo, Eudis	L-L	6-0	195	6-6-95	5	5	4.29	16	16	1	0	80	88	44	38	5	14	61	.285	.302	.276	6.89	1.58
Laxer, Josh	R-R	6-0	195	6-7-93	0	1	3.91	16	0	0	1	23	23	11	10	2	6	19	.284	.268	.300	7.43	2.35
Longwith, Logan	R-R	6-3	170	3-30-94	0	3	5.01	19	0	0	0	41	47	27	23	7	7	32	.281	.287	.275	6.97	1.52
Maciel, Jon	R-R	6-2	225	11-17-92	4	2	6.12	20	0	0	1	43	60	31	29	2	11	34	.343	.429	.276	7.17	2.32
Milton, Ryan	R-R	6-4	215	12-18-91	1	2	2.89	26	0	0	2	53	39	19	17	1	21	65	.203	.151	.245	11.04	3.57
Moreno, Gerson	R-R	6-0	175	9-10-95	1	1	1.08	23	0	0	11	25	19	5	3	0	8	27	.209	.268	.160	9.72	2.88
Perez, Fernando	R-R	6-3	181	12-17-93	4	7	5.53	18	18	0	0	85	100	57	52	4	37	71	.299	.313	.284	7.55	3.93
Shull, Jake	R-R	5-10	190	4-26-94	1	0	1.23	16	0	0	7	22	19	5	3	0	6	18	.232	.293	.171	7.36	2.45
Smith, Drew	R-R	6-2	190	9-24-93	1	2	2.96	35	0	0	4	49	34	18	16	0	23	62	.205	.244	.170	11.47	4.25
Smith, Jordan	R-R	6-1	210	4-23-92	4	7	4.48	26	9	0	1	74	83	43	37	6	23	52	.282	.329	.232	6.30	2.78
Szkutnik, Trent	R-L	6-0	195	8-21-93	3	4	2.64	22	10	0	1	80	80	33	25	6	20	68	.251	.267	.241	7.17	2.11
Verastegui, Adenson	R-R	5-11	205	2-19-93	0	5	6.27	22	0	0	3	33	40	25	23	2	20	33	.301	.348	.250	9.00	5.45
Watkins, Spenser	R-R	6-1	190	8-27-92	5	3	3.82	13	12	1	0	75	79	34	32	6	22	69	.270	.262	.279	8.24	2.63

Fielding

Catcher	PCT	G	PO	A	E	DP	PB
Allen	1.000	1	4	0	0	0	
Navarro	1.000	25	167	16	0	3	5
Perez	.987	68	531	80	8	3	11
Zeile	.995	49	321	43	2	2	1

First Base	PCT	G	PO	A	E	DP
Allen	.989	89	747	55	9	84
Lester	1.000	3	18	2	0	2
Maddox	.991	49	401	21	4	36

Second Base	PCT	G	PO	A	E	DP
Gonzalez	.982	59	114	161	5	46
Maddox	.975	30	71	84	4	25
Pereira	1.000	1	4	3	0	2
Pirtle	.975	53	82	149	6	29
Zambrano	1.000	1	2	4	0	1

Third Base	PCT	G	PO	A	E	DP
Fuentes	.918	33	25	42	6	7
Lester	.974	13	8	30	1	3
Pirtle	.967	28	15	44	2	7
Zambrano	.963	65	42	115	6	12

Shortstop	PCT	G	PO	A	E	DP
Gonzalez	.949	57	82	140	12	32
Laffita	.958	76	109	207	14	39
Pereira	.889	2	5	3	1	0
Pirtle	1.000	7	9	21	0	7

Outfield	PCT	G	PO	A	E	DP
Azocar	.951	127	255	16	14	3
Brown	.977	60	125	4	3	2
Gibson	.974	105	213	9	6	2
Havrilak	.974	22	37	1	1	0
Hill	.975	87	188	5	5	1
Padron	1.000	11	11	1	0	0
Salgado	1.000	4	4	0	0	0

CONNECTICUT TIGERS

NEW YORK-PENN LEAGUE

SHORT-SEASON

Batting

Batting	B-T	HT	WT	DOB	AVG	vLH	vRH	G	AB	R	H	2B	3B	HR	RBI	BB	HBP	SH	SF	SO	SB	CS	SLG	OBP
Athmann, Austin	R-R	6-2	210	4-27-95	.276	.268	.279	40	145	24	40	9	1	2	17	10	4	0	1	40	0	0	.393	.338
Bauml, Cole	L-R	6-3	205	11-2-92	.270	.290	.263	64	248	32	67	14	2	3	36	21	2	0	3	65	6	4	.379	.328
Donnels, Tanner	L-R	6-2	210	8-3-93	.195	.216	.190	53	174	12	34	3	1	1	19	18	2	0	1	36	0	2	.241	.277
Gonzalez, Cesar	R-R	6-2	175	5-31-95	.211	.158	.237	17	57	6	12	2	1	0	9	2	1	0	0	28	1	2	.281	.250
Havrilak, Joey	L-R	6-1	195	11-25-91	.270	.304	.256	45	163	31	44	10	2	3	24	26	3	2	3	31	8	0	.411	.376
Jones, Keaton	R-R	6-2	195	10-8-92	.176	.286	.148	10	34	3	6	0	0	0	5	2	0	2	1	8	1	1	.176	.216
Ledezma, Junnell	B-R	5-9	165	11-5-95	.204	.250	.187	38	103	16	21	4	0	0	5	18	3	1	0	25	0	1	.243	.339
Lester, Josh	L-L	6-3	216	7-17-94	.293	.273	.299	60	222	30	65	19	3	2	26	22	2	0	1	32	0	0	.432	.365
Machonis, Sam	B-L	6-1	195	6-16-94	.204	.216	.200	41	137	19	28	3	1	1	17	14	6	1	1	40	1	0	.263	.304
Navarro, Franklin	B-R	5-10	181	10-17-94	.364	.500	.333	3	11	0	4	0	0	0	2	0	0	0	0	2	0	0	.364	.364
Padron, Victor	L-R	5-8	160	7-5-94	.164	.143	.171	18	55	9	9	1	0	0	2	7	0	2	0	10	0	0	.182	.258
Pereira, Anthony	R-R	6-0	170	11-28-96	.240	.313	.206	14	50	4	12	6	0	0	7	5	0	0	0	12	1	0	.360	.309

Batting	B-T	HT	WT	DOB	AVG	vLH	vRH	G	AB	R	H	2B	3B	HR	RBI	BB	HBP	SH	SF	SO	SB	CS	SLG	OBP
Pinero, Daniel	R-R	6-5	210	5-2-94	.261	.343	.234	43	142	20	37	6	1	0	16	24	4	0	5	28	2	3	.317	.371
Policelli, Brady	R-R	5-11	195	6-24-95	.120	.000	.146	16	50	1	6	1	0	0	1	3	1	0	0	15	0	0	.140	.185
Robson, Jacob	L-R	5-10	175	11-20-94	.329	.250	.344	21	76	14	25	5	1	1	6	15	0	0	0	20	1	2	.461	.440
Salter, Blaise	R-R	6-5	245	6-25-93	.263	.288	.253	60	236	16	62	11	1	3	42	7	7	0	3	39	1	0	.356	.300
Sanjur, Mario	R-R	5-7	174	12-23-95	.221	.320	.186	31	95	8	21	3	0	0	8	3	0	3	0	13	0	0	.253	.294
Savage, Will	R-R	6-0	185	12-9-94	.200	.235	.185	47	175	26	35	2	2	1	21	23	4	1	2	35	15	1	.251	.304
Sedio, Chad	L-R	6-3	205	3-30-94	.125	.143	.118	7	24	4	3	1	0	0	2	0	2	0	1	9	1	0	.167	.185
Sthormes, Andres	R-R	5-10	171	8-7-96	.211	.333	.154	11	38	3	8	2	1	0	3	2	1	1	0	11	0	0	.316	.268
Swilling, Hunter	R-R	5-11	190	12-26-94	.207	.182	.214	29	92	13	19	3	0	1	6	1	1	1	2	25	0	2	.272	.257
Woodrow, Daniel	L-R	5-10	155	1-26-95	.276	.323	.263	36	145	21	40	5	1	0	13	12	0	0	1	32	8	2	.324	.329

Pitching	B-T	HT	WT	DOB	W	L	ERA	G	GS	CG	SV	IP	H	R	ER	HR	BB	SO	AVG	vLH	vRH	K/9	BB/9
Cabrera, Yordy	R-R	6-1	205	9-3-90	1	0	1.04	6	0	0	1	9	6	3	1	1	2	13	.176	.222	.160	13.50	2.08
Castellanos, Ryan	R-R	6-3	215	4-15-94	8	6	4.79	14	7	0	0	71	90	43	38	5	12	27	.311	.385	.257	3.41	1.51
Castillo, Oswaldo	R-R	6-0	193	8-18-96	2	1	6.39	8	0	0	0	13	12	10	9	1	7	11	.240	.063	.324	7.82	4.97
Chavez, Emanuel	R-R	6-3	175	1-19-95	2	1	8.05	16	0	0	1	19	28	20	17	1	12	22	.350	.417	.321	10.42	5.68
Ecker, Mark	R-R	6-0	180	5-27-95	2	0	0.50	11	0	0	4	18	7	1	1	0	3	21	.117	.167	.067	10.50	1.50
Foley, Jason	R-R	6-4	215	11-1-95	0	0	4.26	5	0	0	0	6	6	4	3	0	7	6	.240	.273	.214	8.53	9.95
Fuentes, Jose	R-R	6-1	165	10-6-94	1	0	6.00	3	0	0	0	3	2	2	2	0	5	3	.200	.500	.125	9.00	15.00
Funkhouser, Kyle	R-R	6-2	220	3-16-94	0	2	2.65	13	13	0	0	37	34	13	11	0	8	34	.246	.206	.286	8.20	1.93
Garcia, Bryan	R-R	6-1	203	4-19-95	0	1	1.00	16	0	0	6	18	13	7	2	1	3	21	.194	.179	.205	10.50	1.50
Gonzalez, Daniel	R-R	6-3	200	8-15-95	1	0	2.70	1	0	0	0	3	2	1	1	1	0	6	.167	.000	.250	16.20	0.00
Gutierrez, Alfred	R-R	6-0	143	6-12-95	1	4	3.16	15	11	0	0	63	60	25	22	2	11	41	.255	.211	.286	5.89	1.58
Hayes, John	R-R	6-6	225	1-7-93	2	2	1.80	19	0	0	0	15	7	5	0	10	16	.170	.211	.140	5.76	3.60
Hicks, Taylor	R-R	6-3	230	2-26-92	0	1	10.38	9	0	0	0	9	10	10	10	2	8	6	.294	.417	.227	6.23	8.31
Hill, Evan	L-L	6-4	175	8-18-93	0	0	4.50	2	0	0	0	2	3	1	1	0	0	1	.375	.500	.333	4.50	0.00
Houston, Zac	R-R	6-5	250	11-30-94	1	0	0.00	7	0	0	0	10	7	1	0	0	3	19	.189	.133	.227	17.10	2.70
Jimenez, Eduardo	R-R	6-0	183	4-4-95	0	0	2.70	14	0	0	5	13	12	4	4	0	5	18	.222	.118	.270	12.15	3.38
Lara, Carlos	R-R	6-2	170	3-2-94	0	0	0.00	1	0	0	0	1	0	0	0	0	0	1	.000	.000	.000	9.00	9.00
Longwith, Logan	R-R	6-3	170	3-30-94	0	0	5.06	4	0	0	0	5	5	3	3	0	2	4	.250	.300	.200	7.59	3.38
Martinez, Malvin	R-R	6-0	170	4-19-95	0	0	0.00	6	0	0	0	6	2	0	0	0	2	5	.105	.125	.091	7.50	3.00
Mueses, Victor	R-R	6-1	175	10-13-95	2	0	2.08	3	0	0	0	4	3	1	1	0	3	7	.188	.333	.154	14.54	6.23
Navilhon, Joe	R-R	6-0	200	7-13-93	2	0	0.34	16	0	0	2	26	22	3	1	0	7	29	.218	.152	.273	9.91	2.39
Schmidt, Clate	R-R	6-1	190	12-10-93	1	1	4.57	15	1	0	1	22	26	12	11	1	11	17	.299	.276	.31	7.06	4.57
Schreiber, John	R-R	6-3	215	3-5-94	2	3	2.76	18	0	0	0	29	23	14	9	0	9	24	.213	.152	.258	7.36	2.76
Sittinger, Brandyn	R-R	6-1	200	6-6-94	0	0	0.00	8	0	0	0	9	6	0	0	0	5	8	.194	.167	.211	8.31	5.19
Smith, Jordan	R-R	6-1	210	4-23-92	3	1	2.40	5	0	0	0	15	13	4	4	0	2	18	.228	.321	.138	10.80	1.20
Sodders, Austin	L-L	6-3	180	4-29-95	0	3	2.29	13	13	0	0	39	35	13	10	2	5	33	.230	.286	.204	7.55	1.14
Soto, Gregory	L-L	6-1	180	2-11-95	3	2	3.03	15	15	0	0	71	68	29	24	1	34	62	.256	.194	.292	7.82	4.29
St. John, Locke	L-L	6-3	180	1-31-93	6	7	2.12	15	15	0	0	89	78	32	21	3	26	71	.233	.218	.239	7.15	2.62
Vasquez, Jose	R-R	6-0	175	3-19-96	0	0	9.53	2	1	0	0	6	10	6	6	0	1	3	.400	.429	.389	4.76	1.59
Verastegui, Adenson	R-R	5-11	205	2-19-93	0	0	0.00	2	0	0	0	5	1	0	0	0	0	5	.100	.143	15.00	0.00	
Viloria, Felix	L-L	6-1	165	12-2-96	1	0	0.00	3	0	0	0	5	4	0	0	0	2	7	.222	.000	.308	12.60	3.60
Vinson, Mike	R-R	6-4	210	2-9-94	0	0	16.88	3	0	0	1	3	2	5	5	1	3	3	.200	.500	.125	10.13	10.13

Fielding

C: Athmann 28, Navarro 1, Policelli 12, Sanjur 29, Sthormes 10. **1B:** Donnels 48, Salter 32. **2B:** Ledezma 26, Savage 47, Sedio 2, Swilling 1. **3B:** Lester 55, Pereira 1, Swilling 20. **SS:** Jones 10, Ledezma 8, Pereira 13, Pinero 43, Sedio 2. **OF:** Bauml 60, Gonzalez 15, Havrilak 45, Machonis 37, Padron 14, Robson 21, Woodrow 36.

GCL TIGERS EAST   ROOKIE
GULF COAST LEAGUE

Batting	B-T	HT	WT	DOB	AVG	vLH	vRH	G	AB	R	H	2B	3B	HR	RBI	BB	HBP	SH	SF	SO	SB	CS	SLG	OBP
Arias, Franklin	R-R	6-0	165	3-3-97	.235	.333	.208	44	136	20	32	9	0	0	11	16	2	3	2	22	6	6	.301	.321
Aristigueta, Keyder	R-R	5-11	165	2-2-96	.245	.294	.232	49	159	16	39	6	1	1	18	19	4	1	2	35	1	1	.314	.337
Bello, Moises	R-R	5-10	160	6-13-97	.246	.318	.231	40	126	18	31	4	0	1	11	5	4	1	1	20	9	2	.302	.294
2-team total (5 Tigers West)					.245	—	—	45	143	19	35	5	0	1	13	5	4	2	1	25	11	2	.301	.288
Cortez, Johandry	R-R	5-10	170	5-24-98	.207	.154	.222	24	58	6	12	3	0	1	5	4	4	2	0	20	2	0	.310	.303
De La Cruz, Isrrael	R-R	6-0	150	6-15-97	.247	.367	.221	51	166	27	41	3	6	0	13	22	3	2	1	51	22	6	.337	.344
Escobar, Elys	R-R	6-0	190	9-21-96	.252	.308	.239	44	135	15	34	8	0	0	11	9	1	0	0	23	0	1	.311	.303
Garcia, Alexis	R-R	6-2	170	7-1-97	.250	.240	.254	36	88	12	22	4	0	0	10	10	1	3	1	22	4	2	.295	.330
Gonzalez, Gerardo	R-R	5-9	170	12-21-98	.194	.000	.255	30	67	13	13	1	0	0	5	8	2	0	0	17	2	1	.209	.299
Gonzalez, Jose	R-R	6-2	165	7-14-98	.211	.192	.215	43	133	12	28	3	1	0	6	9	4	2	1	35	5	3	.248	.279
Guzman, Carlos	R-R	6-1	170	5-16-98	.107	.167	.091	16	28	2	3	1	0	0	4	2	1	1	0	7	1	1	.143	.194
Hernandez, Hector	R-R	6-0	175	2-23-96	.178	.250	.145	41	101	13	18	2	2	0	7	16	1	2	3	39	5	1	.238	.289
2-team total (2 Tigers West)					.168	—	—	43	107	14	18	2	2	0	7	17	2	2	3	41	5	1	.224	.287
Nunez, Moises	R-R	6-2	190	2-7-97	.320	.316	.321	22	75	15	24	3	0	3	18	9	1	0	0	18	1	0	.480	.400
2-team total (16 Tigers West)					.275	—	—	38	109	19	30	4	0	4	24	13	1	0	0	34	1	0	.422	.358
Rodriguez, Alexander	R-R	5-11	170	3-13-98	.182	.222	.174	31	55	7	10	0	0	2	9	2	7	2	2	1	16	4	3	.182	.292
Salas, Jose	R-R	6-0	160	4-17-97	.222	.211	.225	48	158	19	35	5	2	0	14	11	5	3	1	25	1	6	.278	.291
Santos, Allan	R-R	6-1	180	6-5-98	.174	.192	.169	48	144	16	25	4	0	2	20	8	4	0	0	42	1	1	.243	.237
Tejeda, Bryan	R-R	6-0	190	1-17-96	.287	.316	.280	25	94	11	27	10	1	0	15	2	2	1	1	23	0	0	.415	.313
Torrealba, Luis	R-R	6-1	175	9-23-96	.178	.227	.162	37	90	10	16	1	1	0	9	17	1	3	0	22	5	0	.211	.315

Batting

Batting	B-T	HT	WT	DOB	AVG	vLH	vRH	G	AB	R	H	2B	3B	HR	RBI	BB	HBP	SH	SF	SO	SB	CS	SLG	OBP
Zeile, Shane	R-R	6-1	195	6-14-93	.857	1.000	.800	2	7	1	6	3	0	0	2	1	0	0	0	0	0	0	1.286	.875
2-team total (5 Tigers West)					.500	—	—	7	20	4	10	4	0	1	6	3	0	0	2	0	0	0	.850	.565

Pitching

Pitching	B-T	HT	WT	DOB	W	L	ERA	G	GS	CG	SV	IP	H	R	ER	HR	BB	SO	AVG	vLH	vRH	K/9	BB/9
Almonte, Yei	R-R	6-2	210	10-8-95	1	4	4.78	10	4	0	0	43	47	28	23	2	7	19	.273	.366	.208	3.95	1.45
Batista, Franchi	R-R	6-0	170	5-26-96	1	0	4.01	16	0	0	1	25	26	16	11	2	13	24	.274	.351	.224	8.76	4.74
Cabrera, Rusbell	R-R	6-3	170	9-29-95	0	0	5.63	4	0	0	0	8	13	5	5	0	4	4	.361	.231	.435	4.50	4.50
2-team total (8 Tigers West)					1	2	9.82	12	0	0	0	18	23	20	20	2	20	13	—	—	—	6.38	9.82
De La Rosa, Bairon	R-R	6-0	195	7-17-96	2	2	6.98	12	1	0	0	19	19	17	15	3	18	14	.264	.286	.243	6.52	8.38
Fuentes, Jose	R-R	6-1	165	10-6-94	0	1	4.13	6	5	0	0	24	29	14	11	2	8	21	.312	.353	.288	7.88	3.00
2-team total (5 Tigers West)					0	1	3.24	11	5	0	0	33	36	15	12	2	9	32	—	—	—	8.64	2.43
German, Francisco	R-R	6-2	160	12-26-96	0	2	2.40	7	6	0	0	30	22	12	8	2	15	33	.208	.225	.197	9.90	4.50
2-team total (1 Tigers West)					0	2	2.31	8	7	0	0	35	27	13	9	2	15	37	—	—	—	9.51	3.86
Javier, Xavier	R-R	6-4	170	2-9-98	0	4	3.67	9	9	0	0	34	25	20	14	2	14	31	.202	.266	.133	8.13	3.67
Lara, Carlos	R-R	6-2	170	3-2-94	2	3	2.08	19	0	0	5	26	20	7	6	0	11	37	.220	.290	.183	12.81	3.81
Lopez, Ronaldo	R-R	6-2	165	1-7-98	2	4	4.50	10	9	0	0	38	47	22	19	2	19	24	.313	.296	.329	5.68	4.50
Martinez, Stanley	R-R	6-3	185	11-29-94	1	4	4.93	10	9	0	0	38	30	22	21	3	19	41	.214	.259	.186	9.63	4.46
Mateo, Jhonny	R-R	6-3	170	8-19-94	1	2	2.45	8	3	0	0	26	28	10	7	0	7	19	.286	.375	.224	6.66	2.45
Morel, Melvin	L-L	6-2	185	12-14-93	0	3	5.91	15	0	0	0	21	23	18	14	2	15	30	.267	.192	.300	12.66	6.33
Pinto, Wladimir	R-R	5-11	170	2-12-98	1	1	2.66	16	0	0	1	24	11	8	7	0	10	32	.134	.073	.195	12.17	3.80
Rodriguez, Hector	R-R	6-4	210	12-4-96	5	0	1.95	16	0	0	0	28	21	11	6	0	16	23	.212	.257	.188	7.48	5.20
Rodriguez, Jesus	R-R	6-3	170	2-16-98	1	0	4.38	11	1	0	0	25	20	16	12	4	13	17	.215	.273	.163	6.20	4.74
Santana, Kilber	R-R	6-1	160	10-15-98	2	2	6.65	12	0	0	0	22	33	17	16	3	9	10	.351	.237	.429	4.15	3.74
Spomer, Kurt	R-R	6-2	215	7-10-89	0	1	6.00	2	2	0	0	3	4	3	2	0	0	2	.308	.333	.286	6.00	0.00
Tortosa, Cristhian	L-L	6-4	170	10-30-98	0	1	4.12	13	0	0	0	20	16	11	9	0	10	18	.222	.250	.212	8.24	4.58
Turnbull, Spencer	R-R	6-3	215	9-18-92	0	0	7.36	2	2	0	0	4	4	3	3	2	1	5	.267	.333	.167	12.27	2.45
2-team total (4 Tigers West)					0	1	4.40	6	6	0	0	14	7	7	7	2	6	12	—	—	—	7.53	3.77
Villarroel, Javier	R-R	6-1	180	10-31-97	2	3	4.68	10	7	0	0	33	33	19	17	1	9	15	.268	.259	.275	4.13	2.48

Fielding

C: Cortez 17, Escobar 41, Nunez 7, Tejeda 5, Zeile 1. **1B:** Aristigueta 20, Bello 4, De La Cruz 1, Nunez 18, Tejeda 15, Torrealba 10. **2B:** Aristigueta 24, Bello 10, De La Cruz 10, Garcia 1, Gonzalez 16, Salas 12. **3B:** Aristigueta 3, Bello 19, Garcia 25, Gonzalez 4, Guzman 14, Salas 9. **SS:** Bello 8, De La Cruz 37, Garcia 10, Guzman 2, Salas 20. **OF:** Arias 42, Bello 3, Gonzalez 43, Hernandez 39, Rodriguez 17, Santos 36, Torrealba 25.

GCL TIGERS WEST   ROOKIE
GULF COAST LEAGUE

Batting

Batting	B-T	HT	WT	DOB	AVG	vLH	vRH	G	AB	R	H	2B	3B	HR	RBI	BB	HBP	SH	SF	SO	SB	CS	SLG	OBP
Alcantara, Randel	L-R	6-1	220	5-13-97	.188	.152	.198	42	144	13	27	6	1	5	22	8	4	1	2	30	2	1	.347	.247
Azuaje, Jheyser	R-R	5-9	165	2-12-97	.253	.152	.333	27	75	5	19	4	0	0	6	1	5	1	0	16	4	2	.307	.309
Bello, Moises	R-R	5-10	160	6-13-97	.235	.400	.167	5	17	1	4	1	0	0	2	0	0	1	0	5	2	0	.294	.235
2-team total (40 Tigers East)					.245	—	—	45	143	19	35	5	0	1	13	5	4	2	1	25	11	2	.301	.288
Britt, Dalton	L-R	6-0	210	5-9-94	.271	.318	.254	28	85	4	23	5	1	1	9	10	0	1	2	13	3	2	.388	.340
Buentello, Niko	R-R	6-3	230	7-8-94	.236	.167	.258	52	174	23	41	13	0	5	17	23	5	0	2	46	4	0	.397	.338
Fernandez Jr. Alex	R-R	5-10	180	3-30-93	.238	.333	.206	30	84	11	20	6	0	2	10	11	1	1	2	24	7	0	.381	.365
Frailey, Dustin	R-R	5-10	180	2-19-94	.195	.292	.159	41	87	23	17	1	0	0	3	15	16	1	1	17	12	4	.207	.403
Fuentes, Steven	B-R	6-0	210	10-21-94	.133	.111	.148	17	45	5	6	2	0	0	2	5	1	0	1	14	2	2	.178	.231
Gonzalez, Cesar	R-R	6-2	175	5-31-95	.267	.167	.333	5	15	2	4	3	0	0	1	0	0	0	0	5	0	0	.467	.313
Hernandez, Hector	L-R	6-0	175	2-23-96	.000	.000	.000	2	6	1	0	0	0	0	1	1	0	0	0	2	0	0	.000	.250
2-team total (41 Tigers East)					.168	—	—	43	107	14	18	2	2	0	7	17	2	3	41	5	1	.224	.287
Martinez, Hector	R-R	5-11	175	11-7-96	.310	.265	.324	42	145	45	45	4	1	0	10	8	5	2	0	35	7	7	.352	.367
Martinez, Julio	R-R	6-2	195	12-15-97	.229	.225	.230	42	140	15	32	7	1	1	9	10	1	0	1	47	2	0	.314	.283
Nunez, Moises	R-R	6-2	190	2-7-97	.176	.000	.231	16	34	4	6	1	0	1	4	4	0	0	0	16	0	0	.294	.263
2-team total (22 Tigers East)					.275	—	—	38	109	19	30	4	0	4	24	13	1	0	34	1	0	.422	.358
Pinero, Daniel	R-R	6-5	210	5-2-94	.333	.000	.348	7	24	6	8	2	0	2	6	5	0	0	0	2	0	2	.667	.448
Policelli, Brady	R-R	5-11	195	6-24-95	.333	.000	.409	10	27	6	9	4	0	0	2	3	1	0	0	7	0	2	.481	.419
Robson, Jacob	L-R	5-10	175	11-20-94	.267	.280	.263	29	101	16	27	3	6	0	5	16	0	1	0	22	14	4	.347	.368
Santana, Felix	R-R	5-10	180	8-19-94	.167	.000	.185	10	30	3	5	1	1	1	3	2	1	0	0	6	0	0	.367	.242
Sedio, Chad	L-R	6-3	205	3-30-94	.275	.308	.263	43	153	15	42	10	5	2	29	11	8	1	3	29	8	1	.444	.349
Serrano, Ariel	R-R	5-10	174	6-23-96	.177	.172	.179	42	124	12	22	3	0	4	9	1	1	1	0	20	6	3	.202	.237
Sthormes, Andres	R-R	5-10	171	8-7-96	.254	.250	.255	20	59	7	15	3	1	1	11	3	0	0	0	7	1	0	.390	.277
Torres, Bryan	R-R	6-2	180	11-20-97	.055	.000	.064	24	55	6	3	1	0	0	1	12	0	0	0	30	0	1	.073	.224
Valdez, Ignacio	R-R	6-3	195	7-16-95	.219	.233	.214	46	160	25	35	7	2	11	26	17	3	0	0	48	0	1	.494	.306
Woodrow, Daniel	L-R	5-10	155	1-26-95	.351	.455	.326	18	57	10	20	7	0	0	9	1	1	1	2	12	5	0	.474	.441
Zeile, Shane	R-R	6-1	195	6-14-93	.308	—	.308	5	13	3	4	1	0	1	4	2	0	0	2	0	0	0	.615	.400
2-team total (2 Tigers East)					.500	—	—	7	20	4	10	4	0	1	6	3	0	0	2	0	0	0	.850	.565

Pitching

Pitching	B-T	HT	WT	DOB	W	L	ERA	G	GS	CG	SV	IP	H	R	ER	HR	BB	SO	AVG	vLH	vRH	K/9	BB/9
Baez, Jorge	R-R	6-2	185	5-9-95	2	4	6.95	13	0	0	0	22	20	18	17	1	16	24	.241	.344	.176	9.82	6.55
Cabrera, Rusbell	R-R	6-3	170	9-29-95	1	2	13.06	8	0	0	0	10	10	15	15	2	16	9	.250	.300	.233	7.84	13.94
2-team total (4 Tigers East)					1	2	9.82	12	0	0	0	18	23	20	20	2	20	13	—	—	—	6.38	9.82
Castillo, Oswaldo	R-R	6-0	193	8-18-96	3	0	0.00	4	0	0	0	11	4	0	0	0	2	12	.118	.083	.136	9.82	1.64
Castro, Anthony	R-R	6-0	174	4-13-95	3	3	4.26	11	10	0	0	51	52	26	24	0	16	54	.272	.288	.264	9.59	2.84
Chavez, Emanuel	R-R	6-3	175	1-19-95	0	0	0.00	2	0	0	0	3	1	0	0	0	4	.000	.000	.000	10.80	0.00
Figueroa, Ken	R-R	6-0	190	5-30-96	3	3	4.55	11	11	0	0	57	74	32	29	5	6	47	.307	.321	.299	7.38	0.94

Pitching

Pitching	B-T	HT	WT	DOB	W	L	ERA	G	GS	CG	SV	IP	H	R	ER	HR	BB	SO	AVG	vLH	vRH	K/9	BB/9
Foley, Jason	R-R	6-4	215	11-1-95	0	0	0.00	1	0	0	1	1	1	0	0	0	0	1	.250	.000	.333	9.00	0.00
Fuentes, Jose	R-R	6-1	165	10-6-94	0	0	0.96	5	0	0	0	9	7	1	1	0	1	11	.212	.333	.143	10.61	0.96
2-team total (6 Tigers East)					0	1	3.24	11	5	0	0	33	36	15	12	2	9	32	—	—	—	8.64	2.43
German, Francisco	R-R	6-2	160	12-26-96	0	0	1.80	1	1	0	0	5	5	1	1	0	0	4	.250	.286	.231	7.20	0.00
2-team total (7 Tigers East)					0	2	2.31	8	7	0	0	35	27	13	9	2	15	37	—	—	—	9.51	3.86
Gonzalez, Daniel	R-R	6-3	200	8-15-95	3	1	2.27	10	9	0	0	40	30	11	10	1	19	35	.211	.250	.176	7.94	4.31
Hill, Evan	L-L	6-4	175	8-18-93	1	3	2.45	12	0	0	0	22	19	10	6	2	13	19	.244	.143	.300	7.77	5.32
Lopez, Jose	R-R	5-9	174	6-21-95	1	0	2.75	17	0	0	6	20	20	8	6	1	6	14	.260	.464	.143	6.41	2.75
Lundeen, Dalton	L-L	6-3	210	10-10-93	1	0	6.12	13	0	0	1	25	37	22	17	2	7	18	.336	.308	.345	6.48	2.52
Manning, Matt	R-R	6-6	190	1-28-98	0	2	3.99	10	10	0	0	29	27	18	13	2	7	46	.237	.22	.247	14.11	2.15
Martinez, Malvin	R-R	6-0	170	4-19-95	1	0	1.74	6	0	0	3	10	3	2	2	0	2	11	.097	.000	.136	9.58	1.74
Mueses, Victor	R-R	6-1	175	10-13-95	0	2	3.32	13	0	0	0	22	22	16	8	1	16	23	.247	.175	.306	9.55	6.65
O'Connell, Colyn	R-R	6-5	215	7-19-93	4	1	3.90	14	0	0	0	30	35	15	13	1	12	28	.310	.234	.364	8.40	3.60
Ovalles, Noel	R-R	6-2	180	3-24-97	0	1	3.45	10	5	0	0	29	27	13	11	3	7	25	.237	.235	.238	7.85	2.20
Reininger, Zac	R-R	6-3	170	1-28-93	0	0	0.00	4	0	0	6	2	0	0	0	0	2	8	.000	.000	.333	12.00	3.00
Sittinger, Brandyn	R-R	6-1	200	6-6-94	0	1	2.08	6	0	0	2	9	11	3	2	0	3	12	.306	.417	.250	12.46	3.12
Turnbull, Spencer	R-R	6-3	215	9-18-92	0	1	3.38	4	4	0	0	11	3	4	4	0	5	7	.091	.100	.077	5.91	4.22
2-team total (2 Tigers East)					0	1	4.40	6	6	0	0	14	7	7	7	2	6	12	—	—	—	7.53	3.77
Vasquez, Jose	R-R	6-0	175	3-19-96	2	1	2.90	9	8	0	0	40	38	13	13	3	8	33	.250	.246	.253	7.36	1.79
Viloria, Felix	L-L	6-1	165	12-2-96	1	1	1.74	15	0	0	1	21	13	9	4	2	9	23	.178	.227	.157	10.02	3.92
Vinson, Mike	R-R	6-4	210	2-9-94	1	1	25.31	6	0	0	0	5	7	16	15	0	11	3	.318	.200	.353	5.06	18.56
Warner, Burris	R-R	6-0	190	10-15-94	3	1	0.69	9	0	0	1	13	5	1	1	0	3	14	.119	.176	.080	9.69	2.08

Fielding

C: Azuaje 27, Nunez 6, Policelli 10, Sthormes 16, Torres 15, Zeile 3. **1B:** Buentello 50, Nunez 11, Valdez 5. **2B:** Britt 2, Fernandez Jr. 20, Fuentes 3, Martinez 40. **3B:** Alcantara 39, Britt 9, Fernandez Jr. 2, Fuentes 14. **SS:** Bello 5, Britt 14, Fernandez Jr. 1, Pinero 7, Sedio 35. **OF:** Fernandez Jr. 5, Frailey 38, Gonzalez 5, Hernandez 2, Martinez 39, Robson 24, Santana 7, Serrano 37, Sthormes 1, Valdez 27, Woodrow 15.

DSL TIGERS ROOKIE

DOMINICAN SUMMER LEAGUE

Batting

Batting	B-T	HT	WT	DOB	AVG	vLH	vRH	G	AB	R	H	2B	3B	HR	RBI	BB	HBP	SH	SF	SO	SB	CS	SLG	OBP
Alvarado, Darwin	L-R	6-1	170	11-10-98	.247	.282	.238	55	190	37	47	3	2	0	18	31	6	1	0	49	10	1	.284	.370
Chirinos, Irwin	L-R	6-1	170	9-24-97	.216	.069	.274	37	102	17	22	1	2	0	7	17	5	0	0	22	4	2	.265	.355
Escalona, Ildemaro	R-R	6-0	170	2-12-99	.263	.321	.248	41	133	17	35	7	1	1	24	8	4	0	1	33	3	2	.353	.322
Figueroa, Gustavo	R-R	6-0	170	9-22-98	.336	.200	.364	39	119	16	40	6	1	0	13	13	6	1	1	20	4	2	.403	.424
Hernandez, Jhoan	R-R	6-0	145	4-21-99	.151	.059	.179	34	73	11	11	4	0	0	3	13	2	1	0	27	0	1	.205	.295
Hurtado, Pedro	B-R	5-11	160	3-1-99	.188	.176	.192	42	133	17	25	6	0	1	15	29	1	1	1	42	1	1	.256	.335
Laurencio, Luis	R-R	6-2	215	10-6-98	.209	.106	.244	57	182	23	38	12	0	6	32	23	6	0	1	68	1	2	.374	.316
Melo, Jeffrei	R-R	6-4	185	6-2-98	.211	.270	.194	52	166	25	35	9	2	0	21	21	2	1	2	72	2	1	.289	.304
Ortega, Marfrey	R-R	5-11	175	10-15-98	.177	.333	.157	32	79	10	14	5	0	0	6	14	4	1	0	28	1	1	.241	.330
Quero, Jose	L-L	6-0	190	9-5-98	.335	.333	.336	55	179	33	60	6	2	2	34	36	6	2	1	29	1	1	.425	.459
Ramirez, Juan	L-L	5-9	160	4-9-99	.297	.364	.281	57	222	44	66	12	5	0	29	39	3	2	1	71	7	5	.396	.408
Ramos, Melvin	R-R	5-11	155	12-26-98	.234	.324	.208	60	167	38	39	9	4	1	19	32	5	5	0	54	3	1	.353	.373
Silverio, Gresuan	B-R	6-0	175	1-5-99	.264	.220	.278	47	174	23	46	9	1	3	25	12	3	0	0	32	0	1	.379	.323
Torres, Melvin	R-R	5-10	140	2-10-98	.184	.179	.185	49	136	10	25	4	0	0	11	9	4	2	1	30	4	2	.213	.253
Vital, Santiago	R-R	6-2	145	1-15-99	.263	.222	.276	41	114	19	30	3	0	2	11	7	10	2	1	28	4	2	.325	.356
Ynirio, Jorge	R-R	5-11	170	10-19-97	.267	.308	.257	41	131	23	35	15	1	0	12	15	3	0	0	31	2	1	.397	.356

Pitching

Pitching	B-T	HT	WT	DOB	W	L	ERA	G	GS	CG	SV	IP	H	R	ER	HR	BB	SO	AVG	vLH	vRH	K/9	BB/9
Castro, Eddy	R-R	6-1	165	5-2-95	2	4	2.98	14	7	0	2	45	38	25	15	1	14	31	.225	.211	.229	6.15	2.78
De Jesus, Angel	R-R	6-4	185	2-13-97	0	2	7.08	9	3	0	0	20	25	16	16	0	9	28	.321	.222	.35	12.39	3.98
De Pena, Enrique	R-R	6-2	175	2-19-96	2	0	4.55	23	0	0	1	32	37	24	16	1	19	38	.287	.341	.259	10.80	5.40
Del Valle, Esmeiro	R-R	6-6	193	10-9-93	2	1	5.29	20	0	0	4	32	32	27	19	0	13	25	.244	.321	.223	6.96	3.62
Escalona, Edgar	R-R	6-4	193	3-30-98	3	4	3.46	14	12	1	0	55	53	24	21	1	16	35	.250	.250	.229	5.76	2.63
Figuera, Adonis	R-R	6-2	165	12-10-97	1	2	3.90	9	3	0	0	28	34	16	12	2	2	16	.301	.250	.325	5.20	0.65
Guante, Julio	R-R	6-3	180	5-29-97	4	2	2.17	17	6	0	1	50	44	19	12	0	22	37	.235	.156	.261	6.70	3.99
Matute, Marlon	L-L	6-1	170	6-10-97	0	2	5.85	15	6	0	1	32	27	28	21	0	26	25	.225	.200	.230	6.96	7.24
Moreno, Willians	R-R	6-0	182	3-30-96	1	3	7.36	14	0	0	1	18	15	16	15	2	18	21	.238	.214	.245	10.31	8.84
Munoz, Dionis	R-R	5-11	155	6-5-97	2	1	2.70	22	0	0	0	43	29	20	13	2	23	32	.191	.138	.203	6.65	4.78
Paricaguan, Jesus	R-R	6-0	165	12-3-95	4	4	3.11	16	11	0	1	55	50	31	19	1	15	44	.233	.267	.219	7.20	2.45
Paulino, Miguel	R-R	6-1	185	8-21-98	2	2	6.65	13	4	0	1	23	23	22	17	0	28	18	.258	.240	.266	7.04	10.96
Ramirez, Jose	R-R	6-1	170	8-18-97	2	2	8.28	16	0	0	0	25	22	33	23	1	30	20	.234	.105	.267	7.20	10.80
Reyes, Adonis	R-R	6-2	170	2-27-97	2	4	4.65	20	2	0	5	31	35	21	16	3	20	23	.307	.404	.239	6.68	5.81
Rodriguez, Perkyn	R-R	6-1	165	5-6-98	3	1	2.32	12	4	0	0	31	23	12	8	1	21	27	.202	.257	.177	7.84	6.10
Silva, Alfredo	L-L	6-3	180	7-27-98	1	2	2.81	14	11	0	0	48	44	27	15	1	26	51	.242	.214	.250	9.56	4.88
Valderrey, Rafael	R-R	6-2	155	5-31-99	0	0	7.50	9	0	0	0	12	17	10	10	1	13	9	.347	.353	.344	6.75	9.75
Yanez, Wildenson	R-R	6-1	165	11-23-96	2	0	3.24	6	0	0	0	8	7	4	3	0	3	10	.226	.375	.174	10.80	3.24

Fielding

C: Figueroa 27, Hurtado 25, Silverio 22. **1B:** Chirinos 1, Figueroa 1, Hernandez 1, Hurtado 3, Laurencio 15, Quero 48, Silverio 9, Ynirio 1. **2B:** Escalona 5, Hernandez 24, Ramos 22, Torres 4, Ynirio 18. **3B:** Laurencio 37, Ramos 1, Torres 25, Ynirio 21. **SS:** Escalona 35, Hernandez 10, Ramos 37. **OF:** Alvarado 51, Chirinos 26, Melo 43, Ortega 22, Quero 3, Ramirez 50, Vital 34.

Houston Astros

SEASON IN A SENTENCE: Houston dug itself a hole with a terrible start and ultimately took a step back, even though a small one, winning two fewer games and finishing in third place in the American League West.

HIGH POINT: The Astros started 7-17 in April but were 20 games over .500 for most of the next three months, culminating with a sweep of the lowly Angels and a 13-3 thrashing of Tim Lincecum on July 25. Jose Altuve, still swinging the bat at his best, slammed two homers in the game but his just seven the rest of the year.

LOW POINT: Houston couldn't beat rival Texas, which won the AL West and went 15-4 against the Astros. The last loss, a 3-2 defeat, was the eighth one-run Texas win and included two ninth-inning runs for the Rangers off Astros closer Ken Giles.

NOTABLE ROOKIES: Righthander Chris Devenski emerged early as a key force in the bullpen, and he delivered 108 innings and a 2.16 ERA, with 43 of his 48 appearances out of the bullpen. Houston relied heavily on rookies to boost the lineup in the second half, chief among them shortstop/third baseman Alex Bregman, who overcame a 2-for-36 start to hit .264/.313/.478. First base was a revolving door for the Astros, who tried both rookies Tyler White and A.J. Reed with little success. Righthanders Michael Feliz (8-1, 95 strikeouts in 65 innings) and Joe Musgrove (4-4, 4.06) showed flashes as well in the second half.

KEY TRANSACTIONS: Houston's key moves came in the offseason, with the exception of the July signing of Cuban free agent Yulieski Gurriel to a five-year, $47.5 million contract. The 32-year-old worked into the lineup in August and September and got 130 at-bats, leaving him prospect-eligible for 2017.

DOWN ON THE FARM: Houston ranked just 11th in organizational domestic winning percentage, its worst mark under GM Jeff Luhnow after having finished first in 2012, '13 and '15 and eighth in '14. Just two Astros affiliates made the playoffs; Corpus Christi had the best record in the Double-A Texas League (85-55), while Lancaster won the second half of the high Class A California League's South Division. Bregman (.306/.406/.580, 20 HR) was having one of the best seasons in the minors before his callup. Outfielder Myles Straw, who spent most of the season at low Class A Quad Cities, won the minor league batting title, hitting .358 in 346 at-bats.

OPENING DAY PAYROLL: $94,893,700 (21st)

PLAYERS OF THE YEAR

MAJOR LEAGUE

Jose Altuve
2b
.338/.396/.531
24 HR, 96 RBI, 30 SB
Led AL in AVG, hits

MINOR LEAGUE

Alex Bregman
ss
(Double-A/Triple-A)
.297/.415/.559
20 HR, 61 RBI

ORGANIZATION LEADERS

BATTING		*Minimum 250 AB
MAJORS		
* AVG	Jose Altuve	.338
* OPS	Jose Altuve	.928
HR	Evan Gattis	32
RBI	Jose Altuve	96
	Carlos Correa	96
MINORS		
* AVG	Myles Straw, Quad Cities, Lancaster	.358
* OBP	Ramon Laureano, Lancaster, Corpus Christi	.428
* SLG	Drew Ferguson, Lancaster, Corpus Christi	.542
* OPS	Ramon Laureano, Lancaster, Corpus Christi	.955
R	Ramon Laureano, Lancaster, Corpus Christi	89
H	Nick Tanielu, Lancaster, Corpus Christi	145
TB	J.D. Davis, Corpus Christi	235
2B	J.D. Davis, Corpus Christi	34
3B	Bobby Boyd, Lancaster, Corpus Christi	10
HR	J.D. Davis, Corpus Christi	23
	Jason Martin, Lancaster	23
RBI	J.D. Davis, Corpus Christi	81
BB	Derek Fisher, Corpus Christi, Fresno	83
	Jon Singleton, Fresno	83
SO	Derek Fisher, Corpus Christi, Fresno	154
SB	Ramon Laureano, Lancaster, Corpus Christi	43

PITCHING		#Minimum 75 IP
MAJORS		
W	Collin McHugh	13
# ERA	Collin McHugh	4.34
SO	Collin McHugh	177
SV	Luke Gregerson	15
	Ken Giles	15
MINORS		
W	Brady Rodgers, Fresno	12
	Cesar Valdez, Fresno	12
L	Yoanys Quiala, Quad Cities	12
# ERA	Brady Rodgers, Fresno	2.86
G	Brendan McCurry, Corpus Christi, Fresno	56
GS	Mike Hauschild, Fresno	24
SV	James Hoyt, Fresno	29
IP	Mike Hauschild, Fresno	140
BB	Albert Abreu, Quad Cities, Lancaster	58
SO	Rogelio Armenteros, Quad Cities, Lancaster, Corpus Christi	140
# AVG	Francis Martes, Corpus Christi	.222

2016 PERFORMANCE

General Manager: Jeff Luhnow. **Farm Director:** Allen Rowin. **Scouting Director:** Mike Elias.

Class	Team	League	W	L	PCT	Finish	Manager
Majors	Houston Astros	American	84	78	.519	t-8th (15)	A.J. Hinch
Triple-A	Fresno Grizzlies	Pacific Coast	73	70	.510	t-5th (16)	Tony DeFrancesco
Double-A	Corpus Christi Hooks	Texas	85	55	.607	1st (8)	Rodney Linares
High A	Lancaster JetHawks	California	77	63	.550	4th (10)	Ramon Vazquez
Low A	Quad Cities River Bandits	Midwest	61	78	.439	14th (16)	Omar Lopez
Short season	Tri-City ValleyCats	New York-Penn	38	38	.500	t-7th (14)	Lamarr Rogers
Rookie	Greeneville Astros	Appalachian	33	34	.493	6th (10)	Josh Bonifay
Rookie	Astros	Gulf Coast	22	31	.415	14th (17)	Marty Malloy
Overall 2016 Minor League Record			389	369	.513	11th (30)	

ORGANIZATION STATISTICS

HOUSTON ASTROS
AMERICAN LEAGUE

Batting	B-T	HT	WT	DOB	AVG	vLH	vRH	G	AB	R	H	2B	3B	HR	RBI	BB	HBP	SH	SF	SO	SB	CS	SLG	OBP
Altuve, Jose	R-R	5-6	165	5-6-90	.338	.306	.348	161	640	108	216	42	5	24	96	60	7	3	7	70	30	10	.531	.396
Bregman, Alex	R-R	6-0	180	3-30-94	.264	.250	.269	49	201	31	53	13	3	8	34	15	0	0	1	52	2	0	.478	.313
Castro, Jason	L-R	6-3	215	6-18-87	.210	.149	.231	113	329	41	69	16	3	11	32	45	1	0	1	123	2	1	.377	.307
Correa, Carlos	R-R	6-4	215	9-22-94	.274	.236	.287	153	577	76	158	36	3	20	96	75	5	0	3	139	13	3	.451	.361
Duffy, Matt	R-R	6-3	215	2-6-89	.000	.000	.000	3	3	0	0	0	0	0	0	0	0	0	0	2	0	0	.000	.000
Gattis, Evan	R-R	6-4	270	8-18-86	.251	.288	.230	128	447	58	112	19	0	32	72	43	4	0	5	127	2	1	.508	.319
Gomez, Carlos	R-R	6-3	220	12-4-85	.210	.221	.205	85	295	27	62	16	1	5	29	21	4	3	0	100	13	2	.322	.272
2-team total (33 Texas)					.231	—	—	118	411	45	95	22	1	13	53	34	5	3	0	136	18	5	.384	.298
Gonzalez, Marwin	B-R	6-1	205	3-14-89	.254	.253	.255	141	484	55	123	26	3	13	51	22	5	6	1	118	12	6	.401	.293
Gurriel, Yulieski	R-R	6-0	190	6-9-84	.262	.220	.281	36	130	13	34	7	0	3	15	5	1	0	1	12	1	1	.385	.292
Hernandez, Teoscar	R-R	6-2	180	10-15-92	.230	.278	.203	41	100	15	23	7	0	4	11	11	0	0	1	28	0	2	.420	.304
Kemp, Tony	L-R	5-6	165	10-31-91	.217	.143	.232	59	120	15	26	4	3	1	7	14	0	1	1	27	2	1	.325	.296
Kratz, Erik	R-R	6-4	245	6-15-80	.069	.125	.048	14	29	0	2	1	0	0	1	0	0	0	0	14	0	0	.103	.100
Marisnick, Jake	R-R	6-4	220	3-30-91	.209	.229	.197	118	287	40	60	18	1	5	21	16	3	4	1	83	10	5	.331	.257
Moran, Colin	L-R	6-4	204	10-1-92	.130	—	.130	9	23	1	3	1	0	0	2	1	1	0	0	8	0	0	.174	.200
Rasmus, Colby	L-L	6-2	195	8-11-86	.206	.136	.226	107	369	38	76	10	0	15	54	43	0	1	4	121	4	1	.355	.286
Reed, A.J.	L-L	6-4	275	5-10-93	.164	.067	.178	45	122	11	20	3	0	3	8	18	0	0	1	48	0	0	.262	.270
Springer, George	R-R	6-3	215	9-19-89	.261	.274	.256	162	644	116	168	29	5	29	82	88	11	0	1	178	9	10	.457	.359
Stassi, Max	R-R	5-10	200	3-15-91	.077	.000	.100	9	13	1	1	0	0	0	0	0	0	0	0	5	0	0	.077	.077
Tucker, Preston	L-L	6-0	215	7-6-90	.164	.105	.174	48	134	11	22	8	1	4	8	2	0	0	0	40	0	0	.328	.222
Valbuena, Luis	L-R	5-10	215	11-30-85	.260	.267	.258	90	292	38	76	17	1	13	40	44	1	3	2	81	1	1	.459	.357
White, Tyler	R-R	5-11	215	10-29-90	.217	.250	.199	85	249	24	54	16	0	8	28	23	2	0	2	65	1	0	.378	.286
Worth, Danny	R-R	6-1	195	9-30-85	.179	.200	.143	16	39	4	7	2	0	0	1	1	0	0	0	6	0	0	.231	.200

Pitching	B-T	HT	WT	DOB	W	L	ERA	G	GS	CG	SV	IP	H	R	ER	HR	BB	SO	AVG	vLH	vRH	K/9	BB/9
Chapman, Kevin	L-L	6-3	230	2-19-88	0	0	9.00	9	0	0	0	8	15	8	8	0	4	6	.395	.526	.263	6.75	4.50
Devenski, Chris	R-R	6-3	210	11-13-90	4	4	2.16	48	5	0	1	108	79	26	26	4	20	104	.206	.229	.185	8.64	1.66
Feldman, Scott	R-R	6-7	210	2-7-83	5	3	2.90	26	5	0	0	62	64	27	20	8	13	42	.264	.310	.232	6.10	1.89
2-team total (14 Toronto)					7	4	3.97	40	5	0	0	77	87	42	34	10	19	56	—	—	—	6.55	2.22
Feliz, Michael	R-R	6-4	230	6-28-93	8	1	4.43	47	0	0	0	65	55	33	32	10	22	95	.224	.237	.212	13.15	3.05
Fields, Josh	R-R	6-0	195	8-19-85	0	0	6.89	15	0	0	0	16	23	14	12	2	3	20	.343	.379	.316	11.49	1.72
Fiers, Mike	R-R	6-2	200	6-15-85	11	8	4.48	31	30	0	0	169	187	89	84	26	42	134	.280	.272	.287	7.15	2.24
Fister, Doug	L-R	6-8	210	2-4-84	12	13	4.64	32	32	0	0	180	195	98	93	24	62	115	.276	.321	.225	5.74	3.09
Giles, Ken	R-R	6-2	205	9-20-90	2	5	4.11	69	0	0	15	66	60	32	30	8	25	102	.234	.214	.254	13.98	3.43
Gregerson, Luke	L-R	6-3	205	5-14-84	4	3	3.28	59	0	0	15	58	38	23	21	5	18	67	.183	.212	.156	10.46	2.81
Gustave, Jandel	R-R	6-2	210	10-12-92	1	0	3.52	14	0	0	0	15	13	6	6	2	4	16	.232	.250	.219	9.39	2.35
Harris, Will	R-R	6-4	250	8-28-84	1	2	2.25	66	0	0	12	64	52	17	16	3	15	69	.220	.204	.236	9.70	2.11
Hoyt, James	R-R	6-6	230	9-30-86	1	1	4.50	22	0	0	2	16	12	11	5	9	28	.203	.212	.196	11.45	3.68
Keuchel, Dallas	L-L	6-3	205	1-1-88	9	12	4.55	26	26	1	0	168	168	88	85	20	48	144	.259	.237	.265	7.71	2.57
McCullers Jr. Lance	L-R	6-1	205	10-2-93	6	5	3.22	14	14	0	0	81	80	29	29	5	45	106	.261	.273	.248	11.78	5.00
McHugh, Collin	R-R	6-2	190	6-19-87	13	10	4.34	33	33	1	0	185	206	92	89	25	54	177	.282	.291	.274	8.63	2.63
Musgrove, Joe	R-R	6-5	265	12-4-92	4	4	4.06	11	10	0	0	62	59	28	28	9	16	55	.250	.270	.235	7.98	2.32
Neshek, Pat	B-R	6-3	220	9-4-80	2	2	3.06	60	0	0	0	47	33	17	16	6	11	43	.194	.250	.172	8.23	2.11
Paulino, David	R-R	6-7	215	2-6-94	0	1	5.14	3	1	0	0	7	6	4	4	0	3	2	.240	.278	.143	2.57	3.86
Peacock, Brad	R-R	6-1	210	2-2-88	0	1	3.69	10	5	0	0	32	21	15	13	6	14	28	.186	.200	.175	7.96	3.98
Rodgers, Brady	R-R	6-2	210	9-17-90	0	1	15.12	5	1	0	0	8	15	14	14	0	7	6	.385	.444	.333	3.24	7.56
Sipp, Tony	L-L	6-0	190	7-12-83	1	2	4.95	60	0	0	1	44	52	26	24	12	18	40	.297	.284	.310	8.24	3.71

Fielding

Catcher	PCT	G	PO	A	E	DP	PB
Castro	.996	111	865	53	4	8	12
Gattis	.996	55	448	34	2	4	5
Kratz	.986	13	64	7	1	0	0
Stassi	1.000	8	22	0	0	0	1

First Base	PCT	G	PO	A	E	DP
Castro	1.000	3	7	1	0	0
Gonzalez	.992	92	640	69	6	57
Gurriel	1.000	5	35	4	0	9
Reed	.991	35	214	13	2	20
Valbuena	1.000	8	61	6	0	4
White	.991	58	410	25	4	32

HOUSTON ASTROS

Second Base	PCT	G	PO	A	E	DP
Altuve	.988	148	206	361	7	73
Bregman	1.000	3	2	5	0	0
Gonzalez	.971	14	14	20	1	6
Kemp	.875	5	2	5	1	1
Valbuena	—	1	0	0	0	0
White	1.000	2	1	1	0	0
Worth	1.000	6	5	13	0	4

Third Base	PCT	G	PO	A	E	DP
Bregman	.931	40	28	80	8	8
Duffy	1.000	1	0	1	0	0

Gonzalez	.982	22	12	42	1	2
Gurriel	.977	21	13	30	1	1
Moran	.947	8	5	13	1	1
Valbuena	.970	81	54	143	6	17
White	—	3	0	0	0	0
Worth	.917	5	4	7	1	0

Shortstop	PCT	G	PO	A	E	DP
Altuve	1.000	1	0	2	0	0
Bregman	.938	6	6	9	1	4
Correa	.978	153	202	426	14	81
Gonzalez	1.000	11	9	18	0	3
Worth	1.000	2	0	3	0	1

Outfield	PCT	G	PO	A	E	DP
Bregman	.000	1	0	0	1	0
Gomez	.994	78	157	7	1	1
Gonzalez	1.000	19	26	1	0	0
Gurriel	—	1	0	0	0	0
Hernandez	.959	38	46	1	2	0
Kemp	.973	39	34	2	1	0
Marisnick	.995	105	203	9	1	1
Rasmus	1.000	103	173	13	0	2
Springer	.994	148	308	12	2	2
Tucker	.958	21	23	0	1	0

FRESNO GRIZZLIES

TRIPLE-A

PACIFIC COAST LEAGUE

Batting	B-T	HT	WT	DOB	AVG	vLH	vRH	G	AB	R	H	2B	3B	HR	RBI	BB	HBP	SH	SF	SO	SB	CS	SLG	OBP
Aplin, Andrew	L-L	6-0	205	3-21-91	.223	.240	.215	116	399	61	89	15	4	5	32	42	2	4	0	98	21	9	.318	.300
Ballard, Keach	L-R	6-0	180	7-16-92	.000	.000	.000	4	5	0	0	0	0	0	0	1	0	0	0	3	0	0	.000	.167
Bregman, Alex	R-R	6-0	180	3-30-94	.333	.289	.375	18	78	17	26	6	0	6	15	5	0	0	0	12	2	1	.641	.373
Duffy, Matt	R-R	6-3	215	2-6-89	.226	.247	.216	74	266	36	60	13	1	6	30	24	6	0	1	94	1	1	.350	.303
2-team total (35 Round Rock)					.229	—	—	109	401	53	92	17	2	14	52	30	10	0	3	124	1	1	.387	.297
Fisher, Derek	L-R	6-3	205	8-21-93	.290	.200	.325	27	107	17	31	8	0	5	17	9	1	0	1	26	5	0	.505	.347
Fontana, Nolan	L-R	5-11	195	6-6-91	.195	.240	.178	106	359	35	70	15	0	3	27	32	5	7	4	108	4	3	.262	.268
Garcia, Alejandro	R-R	5-10	182	6-9-84	.393	.474	.357	17	61	10	24	2	0	0	4	5	1	0	0	3	4	1	.426	.448
Gurriel, Yulieski	R-R	6-0	190	6-9-84	.222	.222	.222	4	18	3	4	1	0	1	2	1	0	0	0	4	0	0	.444	.263
Heineman, Tyler	B-R	5-11	205	6-19-91	.259	.256	.261	73	239	27	62	9	2	3	14	26	5	1	0	44	1	2	.351	.344
Heras, Leonardo	L-R	5-9	190	5-29-90	.000	.000	.000	2	5	0	0	0	0	0	0	0	0	0	0	3	0	0	.000	.000
Hernandez, Teoscar	R-R	6-2	180	10-15-92	.313	.294	.323	38	144	20	45	9	3	4	23	13	0	1	2	25	5	4	.500	.365
Kemmer, Jon	L-L	6-2	230	11-17-90	.265	.244	.276	120	407	53	108	24	4	18	69	38	5	0	2	128	8	10	.477	.334
Kemp, Tony	L-R	5-6	165	10-31-91	.306	.322	.298	69	255	36	78	9	4	2	24	34	2	8	2	34	10	8	.396	.386
Marisnick, Jake	R-R	6-4	220	3-30-91	.185	.250	.174	7	27	3	5	2	0	0	1	1	0	0	0	10	1	1	.259	.214
Mayfield, Jack	R-R	5-11	190	9-30-90	.197	.194	.198	45	132	10	26	5	0	2	8	11	0	3	3	27	2	1	.280	.253
Moon, Chan	R-R	6-0	185	3-23-91	.309	.323	.297	27	68	10	21	3	0	1	5	5	0	0	0	15	1	2	.397	.356
Moran, Colin	L-R	6-4	204	10-1-92	.259	.275	.250	117	459	59	119	18	1	10	69	47	2	1	0	8	0	3	.368	.329
Pena, Roberto	B-R	6-0	225	6-8-92	.226	.385	.175	15	53	4	12	1	0	0	5	5	1	1	0	8	0	0	.245	.305
Perez, Eury	R-R	6-0	190	5-30-90	.267	.306	.244	52	135	17	36	4	3	2	16	5	1	5	0	25	9	4	.385	.298
Reed, A.J.	L-L	6-4	275	5-10-93	.291	.256	.306	70	261	42	76	22	1	15	50	32	1	0	2	67	0	0	.556	.368
Singleton, Jon	L-L	6-2	230	9-18-91	.202	.194	.207	124	410	60	83	17	0	20	66	83	3	5	0	124	0	0	.390	.337
Stassi, Max	R-R	5-10	200	3-15-91	.230	.211	.240	69	243	21	56	12	1	7	32	20	2	1	0	65	1	0	.374	.294
Tucker, Preston	L-L	6-0	215	7-6-90	.301	.292	.307	53	209	35	63	14	3	8	29	15	2	0	3	49	1	1	.512	.349
White, Tyler	R-R	5-11	225	10-29-90	.241	.214	.260	44	174	18	42	13	1	4	13	29	16	0	0	30	1	1	.500	.305
Worth, Danny	R-R	6-1	195	9-30-85	.330	.361	.318	84	303	62	100	22	2	11	48	54	4	1	6	72	5	1	.525	.431

Pitching	B-T	HT	WT	DOB	W	L	ERA	G	GS	CG	SV	IP	H	R	ER	HR	BB	SO	AVG	vLH	vRH	K/9	BB/9
Cabrera, Edwar	L-L	6-0	195	10-20-87	0	1	7.94	11	0	0	0	11	9	10	10	2	12	13	.214	.389	.083	10.32	9.53
Chapman, Kevin	L-L	6-3	230	2-19-88	3	4	4.87	51	0	0	0	61	68	36	33	5	27	76	.272	.212	.311	11.21	3.98
Cotton, Chris	R-L	5-10	166	11-21-90	0	1	5.71	16	1	0	0	35	43	25	22	5	9	13	.299	.357	.275	3.38	2.34
De La Rosa, Eury	L-L	5-9	165	2-24-90	0	3	15.95	3	2	0	0	7	18	13	13	1	5	3	.462	.111	.567	3.68	6.14
Feliz, Michael	R-R	6-4	230	6-28-93	1	0	9.72	2	2	0	0	8	8	9	9	1	7	7	.258	.316	.167	7.56	7.56
Fields, Josh	R-R	6-0	195	8-19-85	1	0	1.65	23	0	0	1	27	19	6	5	0	7	32	.192	.213	.173	10.54	2.30
2-team total (2 Oklahoma City)					1	1	2.15	25	0	0	1	29	22	8	7	0	7	34	—	—	—	10.43	2.15
Frias, Edison	R-R	6-1	180	12-18-90	1	2	9.95	4	4	0	0	19	28	23	21	4	9	8	.341	.37	.327	3.79	4.26
Grills, Evan	L-L	6-4	210	6-13-92	1	2	2.55	3	3	0	0	18	21	8	5	3	1	10	.296	.385	.276	5.09	0.51
Guduan, Reymin	L-L	6-4	205	3-16-92	1	1	5.23	34	0	0	0	43	43	25	25	2	34	44	.256	.213	.28	9.21	7.12
Gustave, Jandel	R-R	6-2	210	10-12-92	3	3	3.79	47	0	0	3	57	46	27	24	1	23	55	.219	.244	.200	8.68	3.63
Hauschild, Mike	R-R	6-3	210	1-22-90	9	10	3.22	24	24	0	0	140	138	64	50	7	40	119	.259	.262	.257	7.67	2.58
Holmes, Brian	L-L	6-4	210	1-30-91	0	1	27.00	1	1	0	0	1	4	3	3	1	1	2	.571	.571	18.00	9.00
Hoyt, James	R-R	6-6	230	9-30-86	4	3	1.64	49	0	0	29	55	29	14	10	2	19	93	.154	.200	.117	15.22	3.11
Jankowski, Jordan	R-R	6-1	225	5-17-89	2	3	3.77	51	2	0	5	72	54	32	30	6	31	103	.206	.259	.169	12.93	3.89
McCullers Jr. Lance	L-R	6-1	205	10-2-93	0	0	0.00	1	1	0	0	2	1	0	0	0	2	7	.118	.143	.100	12.60	3.60
McCurry, Brendan	R-R	5-10	170	1-7-92	1	1	3.83	28	1	0	3	42	47	18	18	2	13	44	.283	.246	.307	9.35	2.76
Minaya, Juan	R-R	6-4	210	9-18-90	1	3	3.91	17	0	0	0	25	25	15	11	1	10	19	.266	.271	.261	6.75	3.55
Minnis, Albert	R-L	6-0	190	11-5-91	0	1	3.57	9	0	0	0	18	17	9	7	2	11	11	.266	.250	.273	5.60	5.60
Musgrove, Joe	R-R	6-5	265	12-4-92	5	3	3.81	10	10	0	0	59	60	26	25	8	7	57	.262	.312	.217	8.69	1.07
Paulino, David	R-R	6-7	215	2-6-94	0	2	3.86	3	3	0	0	14	16	9	6	1	6	20	.267	.250	.281	12.86	3.86
Peacock, Brad	R-R	6-1	210	2-2-88	5	6	4.23	22	21	1	0	117	122	64	55	11	40	119	.270	.302	.245	9.15	3.08
Rodgers, Brady	R-R	6-2	210	9-17-90	12	4	2.86	22	22	2	0	132	129	46	42	7	23	116	.257	.217	.300	7.91	1.57
Shirley, Tommy	R-L	6-5	220	11-11-88	7	7	5.38	18	18	0	0	92	102	54	54	14	32	61	.330	.321	.333	6.08	3.19
Valdez, Cesar	R-R	6-2	200	3-17-85	12	1	3.12	30	18	1	0	138	143	49	48	8	13	114	.267	.282	.257	7.42	0.85
West, Aaron	R-R	6-1	195	6-1-90	0	2	4.05	12	1	0	0	20	22	9	9	0	4	17	.278	.238	.293	7.65	1.80
Wojciechowski, Asher	R-R	6-4	235	12-21-88	2	2	5.33	5	5	0	0	25	29	21	15	1	13	22	.282	.283	.281	7.82	4.62
2-team total (13 New Orleans)					4	5	5.28	18	15	0	0	75	90	52	44	11	37	54	—	—	—	6.48	4.44
Yuhl, Keegan	R-R	6-0	220	1-23-92	0	3	8.20	5	5	0	0	26	40	24	24	5	6	28	.348	.295	.38	9.57	2.05

Fielding

Catcher

Catcher	PCT	G	PO	A	E	DP	PB
Heineman	.991	66	524	59	5	5	3
Pena	.952	15	128	12	7	2	1
Stassi	.998	66	553	46	1	9	9

First Base

First Base	PCT	G	PO	A	E	DP
Duffy	.986	13	64	5	1	4
Moran	1.000	2	13	0	0	3
Reed	.995	46	382	36	2	35
Singleton	.989	63	522	33	6	41
White	.995	24	200	14	1	19
Worth	.986	9	66	2	1	3

Second Base

Second Base	PCT	G	PO	A	E	DP
Ballard	.833	3	4	1	1	0
Fontana	.984	27	43	83	2	10
Kemp	.989	39	72	100	2	22
Mayfield	1.000	18	29	55	0	15
Moon	.951	18	29	48	4	8
Worth	.985	47	72	127	3	26

Third Base

Third Base	PCT	G	PO	A	E	DP
Bregman	1.000	2	1	3	0	0
Duffy	.948	29	14	59	4	5
Gurriel	1.000	2	3	3	0	1
Mayfield	1.000	2	1	4	0	0
Moran	.950	109	69	215	15	28
White	1.000	2	2	4	0	0
Worth	.750	3	1	2	1	0

Shortstop

Shortstop	PCT	G	PO	A	E	DP
Bregman	.965	14	9	46	2	2
Duffy	.976	10	15	26	1	4
Fontana	.966	77	88	199	10	41
Mayfield	.986	21	12	56	1	7
Moon	.938	5	3	12	1	3
Moran	1.000	2	3	4	0	2
White	.818	3	5	4	2	1
Worth	1.000	17	20	48	0	11

Outfield

Outfield	PCT	G	PO	A	E	DP
Aplin	.996	114	251	6	1	1
Bregman	1.000	3	3	0	0	0
Duffy	.943	21	31	2	2	0
Fisher	.982	26	54	1	1	0
Garcia	.963	14	24	2	1	0
Gurriel	—	1	0	0	0	0
Heras	1.000	2	2	0	0	0
Hernandez	.969	36	60	3	2	1
Kemmer	.964	105	159	3	6	0
Kemp	1.000	29	52	3	0	0
Marisnick	1.000	7	19	0	0	0
Perez	.983	50	54	4	1	1
Singleton	1.000	7	7	1	0	0
Tucker	1.000	48	52	3	0	0
White	1.000	3	1	0	0	0

CORPUS CHRISTI HOOKS

DOUBLE-A

TEXAS LEAGUE

Batting	B-T	HT	WT	DOB	AVG	vLH	vRH	G	AB	R	H	2B	3B	HR	RBI	BB	HBP	SH	SF	SO	SB	CS	SLG	OBP
Avea, Marlon	R-R	6-1	218	8-31-93	.000	—	.000	3	5	0	0	0	0	0	0	0	0	0	0	2	0	0	.000	.000
Ayarza, Rodrigo	B-R	5-8	145	2-20-95	.200	.000	.250	2	5	0	1	0	0	0	1	0	0	0	0	0	0	0	.200	.200
Boyd, Bobby	L-R	5-9	175	1-4-93	.211	.227	.204	21	76	11	16	2	3	0	3	7	1	3	1	22	4	1	.316	.282
Bregman, Alex	R-R	6-0	180	3-30-94	.297	.200	.311	62	236	54	70	16	2	14	46	42	6	1	0	26	5	3	.559	.415
Davis, J.D.	R-R	6-3	225	4-27-93	.268	.273	.267	126	485	61	130	34	1	23	81	45	5	0	4	143	1	3	.485	.334
Ferguson, Drew	R-R	5-11	180	8-3-92	.327	.313	.333	15	52	14	17	4	1	3	7	6	0	0	0	13	2	0	.615	.397
Fisher, Derek	L-R	6-3	205	8-21-93	.245	.306	.231	102	371	54	91	13	4	16	59	74	2	0	1	128	23	7	.431	.373
Fontana, Nolan	L-R	5-11	195	6-6-91	.278	.375	.250	10	36	4	10	4	0	0	2	8	0	0	0	5	1	0	.389	.409
Garcia, Alejandro	R-R	5-10	182	6-21-91	.271	.293	.265	51	192	24	52	9	0	3	20	6	1	0	0	30	6	3	.365	.296
Gattis, Evan	R-R	6-4	270	8-18-86	.375	.400	.371	11	40	8	15	2	0	5	10	1	1	0	0	4	0	0	.800	.405
Gomez, Carlos	R-R	6-3	220	12-4-85	.250	.400	.200	5	20	3	5	0	0	1	1	0	1	0	0	6	0	1	.400	.286
Gonzalez, Alfredo	R-R	6-1	225	7-13-92	.158	.115	.167	44	146	14	23	5	1	0	7	14	1	1	0	40	0	0	.205	.236
Gregor, Conrad	L-R	6-3	225	2-27-92	.211	.222	.209	106	370	36	78	18	3	9	43	48	0	1	3	64	0	1	.349	.299
Gurriel, Yulieski	R-R	6-0	190	6-9-84	.118	.400	.000	5	17	0	2	0	0	0	3	1	0	0	1	6	0	0	.118	.158
Hernandez, Teoscar	R-R	6-2	180	10-15-92	.305	.205	.323	69	279	53	85	19	6	3	30	32	5	3	2	55	29	11	.437	.384
Hyde, Mott	R-R	5-11	190	3-10-92	.218	.267	.205	86	280	27	61	11	3	2	26	26	4	3		85	2	3	.300	.286
Laureano, Ramon	R-R	5-11	185	7-15-94	.323	.355	.312	36	124	20	40	9	2	5	13	20	4	0	0	33	10	3	.548	.432
Mayfield, Jack	R-R	5-11	190	9-30-90	.237	.333	.220	33	118	21	28	7	0	9	26	8	3	0	2	27	2	0	.525	.298
McDonald, Chase	R-R	6-4	265	6-2-92	.227	.207	.232	109	392	40	89	12	0	17	53	36	1	0	5	120	0	0	.388	.290
Mitchell, Ronnie	L-L	5-11	200	6-21-91	.121	.000	.129	8	33	4	4	0	0	1	4	2	0	0	0	6	0	0	.212	.171
Moon, Chan	L-R	6-0	185	3-23-91	.237	.300	.229	40	93	15	22	1	0	1	2	11	2	2	0	24	5	4	.280	.330
Nunez, Antonio	R-R	5-9	165	1-10-93	.304	.364	.277	23	69	6	21	1	0	0	7	10	2	1	1	15	1	1	.319	.402
Pena, Roberto	B-R	6-0	225	6-8-92	.238	.261	.231	59	202	29	48	11	0	8	20	6	2	5	2	34	0	0	.411	.264
Ramsay, James	L-L	5-11	200	3-2-92	.195	.136	.208	97	338	44	66	17	2	4	24	40	4	7	2	67	4	4	.293	.286
Stubbs, Garrett	L-R	5-10	175	5-26-93	.325	.400	.305	31	120	23	39	9	1	4	16	14	2	0	1	11	5	0	.517	.401
Tanielu, Nick	R-R	5-11	215	9-4-92	.253	.276	.246	95	371	35	94	15	1	7	47	22	3	2	3	60	1	1	.356	.298
Tucker, Preston	L-L	6-0	215	7-6-90	.095	.000	.100	6	21	1	2	0	0	0	3	2	0	0	1	9	0	0	.095	.167
Vasquez, Danry	L-R	6-3	190	1-8-94	.265	.212	.275	60	211	20	56	12	1	3	20	17	1	3	1	24	8	5	.374	.322
Woodward, Trent	B-R	6-2	215	2-4-92	.250	.250	.250	13	48	5	12	4	0	1	3	5	0	0	0	12	0	0	.396	.321

Pitching	B-T	HT	WT	DOB	W	L	ERA	G	GS	CG	SV	IP	H	R	ER	HR	BB	SO	AVG	vLH	vRH	K/9	BB/9
Armenteros, Rogelio	R-R	6-1	215	6-30-94	2	0	1.96	3	3	0	0	18	17	5	4	1	4	13	.262	.273	.256	6.38	1.96
Comer, Kevin	R-R	6-3	205	8-1-92	0	0	3.68	8	0	0	1	15	17	6	6	2	6	18	.274	.211	.302	11.05	3.68
Cotton, Chris	R-L	5-10	166	11-21-90	1	1	1.71	16	0	0	2	26	29	7	5	0	7	18	.276	.237	.299	6.15	2.39
Deemes, Ryan	R-R	6-2	205	6-11-93	0	0	0.00	4	0	0	0	8	7	0	0	0	2	10	.233	.300	.200	10.80	2.16
Deetz, Dean	R-R	6-1	195	11-29-93	2	0	0.00	2	2	0	0	12	7	0	0	0	2	17	.175	.190	.158	12.75	1.50
Del Rosario, Yeyfry	R-R	6-2	182	4-27-94	1	0	0.00	1	0	0	0	1	0	0	0	0	0	2	.000	.000	.000	13.50	0.00
Dorris, Jacob	R-R	6-2	165	3-24-93	0	0	1.86	8	0	0	4	10	7	2	2	1	1	16	.200	.125	.222	14.90	0.93
Emanuel, Kent	L-L	6-5	225	6-4-92	6	4	5.23	17	16	0	1	83	97	51	48	8	20	58	.292	.300	.289	6.31	2.18
Freeman, Michael	R-L	6-8	235	10-7-91	3	4	7.19	37	0	0	2	56	79	50	45	5	36	29	.333	.213	.405	4.63	5.75
Frias, Edison	R-R	6-1	180	12-18-90	4	1	2.44	15	10	0	1	74	60	25	20	3	30	62	.222	.146	.269	7.57	3.67
Grills, Evan	L-L	6-4	210	6-13-92	5	5	3.99	16	13	1	1	95	94	47	42	13	16	69	.259	.266	.257	6.56	1.52
Guduan, Reymin	L-L	6-4	225	3-16-92	1	0	0.69	9	0	0	2	13	7	1	1	1	3	19	.156	.105	.192	13.15	2.08
Heredia, Angel	R-R	5-9	170	7-22-92	0	0	2.92	5	0	0	0	12	14	4	4	1	3	20	.286	.353	.250	14.59	2.19
Holmes, Brian	L-L	6-4	210	1-30-91	4	2	3.73	11	9	0	0	51	51	26	21	5	13	51	.258	.273	.255	9.06	2.31
Martes, Francis	R-R	6-1	225	11-24-95	9	6	3.30	25	22	0	0	125	104	53	46	4	47	131	.222	.222	.222	9.41	3.38
McCullers Jr. Lance	R-R	6-1	205	10-2-93	0	0	3.00	1	1	0	0	3	3	1	1	1	0	4	.273	.667	.125	12.00	0.00
McCurry, Brendan	R-R	5-10	170	1-7-92	2	4	2.27	28	0	0	13	28	20	12	7	1	8	50	.199	.171	.210	11.34	1.82
Minnis, Albert	R-L	6-0	190	11-5-91	2	1	4.74	12	0	0	1	19	18	10	10	2	6	11	.254	.200	.283	5.21	2.84

Pitching

Pitching	B-T	HT	WT	DOB	W	L	ERA	G	GS	CG	SV	IP	H	R	ER	HR	BB	SO	AVG	vLH	vRH	K/9	BB/9
Musgrove, Joe	R-R	6-5	265	12-4-92	2	1	0.34	6	4	0	0	26	19	2	1	1	3	30	.192	.154	.217	10.25	1.03
Paulino, David	R-R	6-7	215	2-6-94	5	2	1.83	14	9	0	1	64	47	16	13	3	11	72	.204	.213	.199	10.13	1.55
Peterson, Eric	R-R	6-4	195	3-8-93	6	3	3.69	27	0	0	3	54	52	29	22	4	9	55	.250	.235	.257	9.22	1.51
Sandoval, Edgardo	R-R	6-0	170	7-9-96	0	0	20.25	1	0	0	0	1	4	3	3	1	0	0	.500	.250	.750	0.00	4.50
Santos, Juan	R-R	6-4	240	8-30-95	0	1	9.00	1	0	0	0	2	2	2	2	0	1	2	.250	.250	.250	9.00	4.50
Sanudo, Gonzalo	L-R	6-3	235	1-10-92	0	0	4.05	4	0	0	0	7	7	3	3	0	3	5	.292	.250	.313	6.75	4.05
Schmidt, David	R-R	6-0	175	1-21-93	1	1	10.00	5	0	0	0	9	14	10	10	1	4	3	.350	.250	.417	3.00	4.00
Smith, Kyle	R-R	6-0	170	9-10-92	3	7	5.03	27	6	0	3	82	98	54	46	14	29	67	.294	.276	.306	7.32	3.17
Sneed, Cy	R-R	6-4	185	10-1-92	6	5	4.04	25	21	0	1	118	119	55	53	12	33	112	.259	.277	.250	8.54	2.52
Thompson, Ryan	R-R	6-6	221	6-26-92	3	1	1.80	23	0	0	3	40	32	9	8	0	10	23	.221	.209	.225	5.18	2.25
Thornton, Trent	R-R	6-0	175	9-30-93	1	1	2.35	7	7	0	0	46	42	12	12	5	5	35	.243	.237	.246	6.85	0.98
Weathersby, Scott	R-R	6-1	180	12-23-91	1	0	0.00	1	0	0	0	2	1	0	0	0	0	3	.143	.000	.167	13.50	0.00
West, Aaron	R-R	6-1	195	6-1-90	5	2	3.47	37	0	0	15	62	71	32	24	4	12	52	.285	.300	.278	7.51	1.73
Yuhl, Keegan	R-R	6-0	220	1-23-92	8	3	3.04	19	17	0	1	98	97	37	33	6	21	75	.258	.310	.225	6.91	1.94

Fielding

Catcher	PCT	G	PO	A	E	DP	PB
Avea	1.000	2	6	0	0	0	0
Gattis	1.000	4	34	4	0	1	0
Gonzalez	.993	44	370	38	3	4	8
Pena	.996	58	431	43	2	5	4
Stubbs	.992	30	225	23	2	1	3
Woodward	1.000	10	85	4	0	0	0

First Base	PCT	G	PO	A	E	DP
Gregor	.994	97	815	42	5	66
McDonald	.995	47	416	14	2	36
Tanielu	1.000	1	3	0	0	0

Second Base	PCT	G	PO	A	E	DP
Hyde	.967	38	62	83	5	18
Mayfield	.957	16	19	25	2	4
Moon	.980	24	39	60	2	17
Pena	1.000	1	1	3	0	1
Tanielu	.976	71	119	163	7	33

Third Base	PCT	G	PO	A	E	DP
Bregman	.970	11	6	26	1	0
Davis	.944	101	67	184	15	15
Gregor	1.000	1	0	2	0	0
Gurriel	.833	3	0	5	1	0
Mayfield	1.000	7	4	14	0	3
Moon	.667	1	1	1	1	0
Tanielu	.911	22	13	38	5	6

Shortstop	PCT	G	PO	A	E	DP
Bregman	.955	51	75	138	10	25
Fontana	1.000	9	8	32	0	6
Hyde	.959	50	63	124	8	19
Mayfield	.920	10	12	34	4	5
Moon	.906	6	10	19	3	3
Nunez	.957	23	29	61	4	12

Outfield	PCT	G	PO	A	E	DP
Ayarza	1.000	2	2	0	0	0
Boyd	1.000	19	34	4	0	1
Davis	1.000	4	4	0	0	0
Ferguson	.955	13	21	0	1	0
Fisher	.985	91	196	1	3	0
Garcia	.990	49	91	4	1	1
Gomez	1.000	3	6	3	0	1
Gregor	1.000	3	2	0	0	0
Hernandez	.978	67	125	7	3	0
Laureano	1.000	35	79	5	0	1
Mitchell	1.000	7	13	0	0	0
Ramsay	.990	90	189	6	2	3
Tucker	.750	3	3	0	1	0
Vasquez	.956	49	84	3	4	0

LANCASTER JETHAWKS   HIGH CLASS A
CALIFORNIA LEAGUE

Batting	B-T	HT	WT	DOB	AVG	vLH	vRH	G	AB	R	H	2B	3B	HR	RBI	BB	HBP	SH	SF	SO	SB	CS	SLG	OBP
Avea, Marlon	R-R	6-1	218	8-31-93	.000	.000	.000	1	3	0	0	0	0	0	0	0	1	0	0	0	0	0	.000	.250
Ballard, Keach	L-R	6-0	180	7-16-92	.211	.174	.218	44	147	22	31	8	0	3	25	22	4	1	1	46	1	3	.327	.328
Boyd, Bobby	L-R	5-9	175	1-4-93	.287	.293	.286	84	359	71	103	14	7	9	56	30	3	4	2	67	33	10	.440	.345
Correa, Christian	R-R	5-10	210	5-18-93	.227	.250	.214	7	22	5	5	2	0	3	5	4	0	0	0	4	0	0	.727	.346
Duarte, Osvaldo	R-R	5-9	160	1-18-96	.250	.387	.212	36	144	28	36	5	2	7	24	9	0	1	2	53	4	5	.458	.290
Ferguson, Drew	R-R	5-11	180	8-3-92	.313	.383	.290	90	326	70	102	25	2	14	69	45	13	2	6	82	28	9	.531	.410
Fernandez, Jose	R-R	6-1	190	5-20-93	.250	.000	.280	8	28	5	7	1	1	0	1	2	0	0	0	9	4	1	.357	.300
Garcia, Alejandro	R-R	5-10	182	6-21-91	.265	.308	.250	26	98	10	26	4	1	0	11	3	1	2	0	15	6	4	.327	.294
Gonzalez, Richard	R-R	5-8	180	11-18-93	.250	.000	.300	8	24	3	6	2	0	1	3	4	1	1	0	10	0	0	.458	.379
Gurriel, Yulieski	R-R	6-0	190	6-9-84	.429	.333	.455	4	14	2	6	2	0	1	9	0	0	0	2	3	0	0	.786	.375
Laureano, Ramon	R-R	5-11	185	7-15-94	.317	.322	.316	80	293	69	93	19	5	10	60	50	9	0	5	86	33	11	.519	.426
Marlow, Brooks	L-R	5-9	185	6-24-93	.205	.256	.195	74	258	38	53	12	1	6	45	33	4	1	3	70	1	2	.329	.302
Martin, Jason	L-R	5-11	190	9-5-95	.270	.159	.293	110	400	74	108	22	7	23	75	55	2	0	5	108	20	12	.533	.357
Mizell, Aaron	L-R	6-0	165	10-14-93	.268	.179	.288	61	209	42	56	8	3	8	31	29	1	3	2	55	8	2	.450	.332
Muniz, Bryan	R-R	6-0	210	6-5-93	.274	.298	.266	112	424	69	116	17	4	13	74	31	12	2	6	93	2	1	.425	.336
Nunez, Antonio	R-R	5-9	165	1-10-93	.273	.304	.262	54	176	40	48	7	2	0	20	31	0	3	2	45	11	4	.335	.378
Reynoso, Luis	R-R	6-1	190	9-2-94	.209	.290	.179	35	115	17	24	5	0	0	8	12	2	3	1	43	1	2	.252	.292
Ritchie, Jamie	R-R	6-2	205	4-9-93	.276	.309	.268	99	344	62	95	20	0	7	57	58	7	3	2	83	3	1	.395	.389
Sewald, Johnny	L-R	5-11	175	11-11-93	.287	.283	.288	79	293	58	84	16	3	6	35	45	7	6	3	71	23	7	.423	.391
Straw, Myles	R-R	5-10	180	10-17-94	.303	.368	.281	19	76	21	23	4	0	1	5	11	1	1	1	17	4	2	.395	.393
Stubbs, Garrett	L-R	5-10	175	5-26-93	.291	.278	.294	55	206	35	60	13	0	6	38	29	5	0	4	37	10	3	.442	.385
Tanielu, Nick	R-R	5-11	215	9-4-92	.372	.345	.380	35	137	23	51	9	2	4	29	7	2	0	2	22	5	1	.555	.405
Trompiz, Kristian	R-R	6-2	184	12-2-95	.190	.278	.164	46	158	19	30	8	1	0	17	14	2	1	4	54	4	2	.253	.258
Tucker, Kyle	L-R	6-4	190	1-17-97	.339	.222	.360	16	59	13	20	6	2	3	13	10	0	0	0	6	1	3	.661	.435
Wik, Marc	L-R	5-11	223	7-18-92	.248	.214	.256	67	214	29	53	10	3	5	30	30	2	2	3	55	6	4	.393	.341
Woodward, Trent	R-R	6-2	215	2-4-92	.263	.167	.287	54	179	31	47	11	0	6	36	31	1	2	2	48	1	1	.425	.371

Pitching	B-T	HT	WT	DOB	W	L	ERA	G	GS	CG	SV	IP	H	R	ER	HR	BB	SO	AVG	vLH	vRH	K/9	BB/9
Abreu, Albert	R-R	6-2	175	9-26-95	1	0	5.40	3	2	0	0	12	12	7	7	2	9	11	.267	.278	.259	8.49	6.94
Armenteros, Rogelio	R-R	6-1	215	6-30-94	3	4	4.18	19	16	0	1	90	87	47	42	13	37	107	.251	.220	.269	10.66	3.69
Bostick, Akeem	R-R	6-6	215	5-4-95	5	3	4.98	14	13	0	0	69	79	45	38	7	42	48	.293	.267	.309	6.29	5.50
Bower, Matt	R-L	6-5	190	6-16-94	2	3	9.32	7	5	0	0	28	46	38	29	7	14	33	.362	.325	.379	10.61	4.50
Comer, Kevin	R-R	6-3	205	8-1-92	2	2	4.30	21	0	0	3	29	31	16	14	4	11	37	.270	.208	.313	11.35	3.38
Deemes, Ryan	R-R	6-2	205	6-11-93	4	1	4.43	27	0	0	6	45	45	22	22	5	12	34	.266	.286	.250	6.85	2.42

Pitching

Pitching	B-T	HT	WT	DOB	W	L	ERA	G	GS	CG	SV	IP	H	R	ER	HR	BB	SO	AVG	vLH	vRH	K/9	BB/9
Deetz, Dean	R-R	6-1	195	11-29-93	6	5	4.24	23	16	0	1	93	86	58	44	9	45	86	.241	.252	.235	8.29	4.34
Del Rosario, Yeyfry	R-R	6-2	182	4-27-94	1	1	5.06	17	0	0	0	32	34	18	18	3	12	34	.274	.354	.224	9.56	3.38
Dorris, Jacob	R-R	6-2	165	3-24-93	1	0	3.43	23	0	0	10	42	34	20	16	6	21	65	.224	.278	.194	13.93	4.50
Dykxhoorn, Brock	R-R	6-8	250	7-2-94	10	4	5.02	24	21	0	0	124	142	81	69	21	31	91	.287	.326	.255	6.62	2.26
Ferrell, Riley	R-R	6-2	200	10-18-93	0	1	1.80	8	0	0	4	10	9	3	2	1	2	14	.237	.133	.304	12.60	1.80
Garza, Ralph	R-R	6-2	195	4-6-94	1	1	6.75	8	0	0	0	17	21	15	13	2	10	18	.296	.355	.250	9.35	5.19
Grills, Evan	L-L	6-4	210	6-13-92	3	1	3.47	5	3	0	0	23	16	10	9	4	6	21	.186	.238	.169	8.10	2.31
Heredia, Angel	R-R	5-9	170	7-22-92	0	3	6.57	10	0	0	1	12	13	11	9	2	11	17	.265	.188	.303	12.41	8.03
Hernandez, Elieser	R-R	6-0	210	5-3-95	2	5	6.93	13	10	0	0	51	66	46	39	11	23	39	.311	.278	.336	6.93	4.09
Hernandez, Jose	R-R	6-0	180	5-1-95	3	3	3.48	7	7	2	0	44	47	19	17	5	9	43	.269	.323	.236	8.80	1.84
James, Josh	R-R	6-3	206	3-8-93	9	5	4.81	23	19	0	1	110	120	64	59	11	40	121	.273	.257	.284	9.87	3.26
McCanna, Kevin	L-R	6-1	185	2-1-94	2	1	5.44	17	1	0	1	41	44	28	25	5	12	42	.273	.231	.302	9.15	2.61
Minnis, Albert	R-L	6-0	190	11-5-91	0	0	16.20	2	0	0	0	2	5	3	3	1	0	0	.500	.400	.600	0.00	0.00
Murphy, Chris	R-R	6-4	205	9-28-92	1	1	5.06	4	0	0	0	5	9	6	3	0	1	2	.391	.250	.467	3.38	1.69
Peterson, Eric	R-R	6-4	195	3-8-93	1	0	4.26	12	0	0	2	19	17	9	9	0	4	22	.239	.346	.178	10.42	1.89
Sandoval, Edgardo	R-R	6-0	170	7-9-96	0	1	27.00	3	0	0	0	2	5	5	5	1	3	3	.500	.500	.500	16.20	16.20
Santos, Juan	R-R	6-4	240	8-30-95	0	0	13.50	4	0	0	1	5	14	11	7	1	1	7	.467	.545	.421	13.50	1.93
Sanudo, Gonzalo	L-R	6-3	235	1-10-92	0	0	3.86	5	0	0	1	7	7	3	3	0	3	7	.250	.333	.154	9.00	3.86
Thome, Andrew	R-R	6-3	215	1-13-93	1	1	3.86	26	0	0	5	47	53	23	20	1	18	36	.288	.309	.276	6.94	3.47
Thompson, Ryan	R-R	6-6	221	6-26-92	2	1	5.09	20	0	0	2	35	41	21	20	3	9	42	.281	.305	.264	10.70	2.29
Thornton, Trent	R-R	6-0	175	9-30-93	7	4	4.12	17	14	1	0	90	91	46	41	14	16	89	.265	.292	.242	8.93	1.61
Valdez, Framber	L-L	5-11	170	11-19-93	0	1	4.76	1	1	0	0	6	8	5	3	0	2	1	.333	.250	.375	1.59	3.18
Walter, Andrew	R-R	6-4	200	10-18-90	0	0	7.00	4	1	0	0	9	8	7	7	5	4	11	.222	.313	.150	11.00	4.00
Weathersby, Scott	R-R	6-1	180	12-23-91	6	6	5.44	28	9	0	1	94	119	66	57	14	27	78	.308	.244	.358	7.44	2.58
Winkelman, Alex	L-L	6-2	180	2-8-94	1	5	8.79	15	2	0	0	29	40	32	28	3	25	26	.333	.351	.325	8.16	7.85

Fielding

Catcher	PCT	G	PO	A	E	DP	PB
Avea	1.000	1	3	0	0	0	1
Correa	1.000	4	29	1	0	0	0
Gonzalez	.967	7	54	4	2	0	1
Ritchie	.995	64	557	46	3	5	7
Stubbs	1.000	37	288	35	0	1	7
Woodward	.993	34	255	29	2	3	4

First Base	PCT	G	PO	A	E	DP
Laureano	—	1	0	0	0	0
Muniz	.984	101	736	81	13	62
Ritchie	.988	33	239	17	3	32
Wik	.984	8	56	5	1	11
Woodward	1.000	2	8	2	0	1

Second Base	PCT	G	PO	A	E	DP
Ballard	.912	9	11	20	3	8
Fernandez	.938	5	4	11	1	0
Marlow	.987	40	71	78	2	21

	PCT	G	PO	A	E	DP
Mizell	.941	45	63	111	11	24
Reynoso	1.000	12	20	24	0	3
Tanielu	1.000	11	21	35	0	7
Trompiz	1.000	6	10	14	0	5
Wik	.930	19	38	42	6	12

Third Base	PCT	G	PO	A	E	DP
Ballard	.930	15	12	28	3	1
Duarte	1.000	1	1	4	0	1
Fernandez	1.000	1	1	4	0	1
Gurriel	1.000	2	0	2	0	0
Marlow	.859	32	24	43	11	7
Nunez	.913	14	9	12	2	1
Reynoso	.903	13	6	22	3	2
Tanielu	.887	22	12	35	6	3
Trompiz	.857	8	4	14	3	1
Wik	.846	22	15	29	8	4
Woodward	.958	17	9	14	1	3

Shortstop	PCT	G	PO	A	E	DP
Ballard	.972	21	21	49	2	12
Duarte	.955	26	34	73	5	19
Fernandez	.786	2	4	7	3	2
Nunez	.940	38	50	75	8	17
Reynoso	.900	10	20	16	4	7
Trompiz	.943	32	38	95	8	12
Wik	.943	14	26	24	3	5

Outfield	PCT	G	PO	A	E	DP
Boyd	.964	61	129	6	5	1
Duarte	1.000	9	14	2	0	0
Ferguson	.992	61	116	7	1	2
Garcia	.960	15	24	0	1	0
Laureano	.984	75	178	7	3	1
Martin	.976	103	165	1	4	0
Mizell	.958	14	23	0	1	0
Sewald	1.000	57	108	10	0	1
Straw	.974	16	35	2	1	0
Tucker	1.000	13	27	2	0	0
Wik	1.000	3	5	0	0	0

QUAD CITIES RIVER BANDITS

LOW CLASS A

MIDWEST LEAGUE

Batting	B-T	HT	WT	DOB	AVG	vLH	vRH	G	AB	R	H	2B	3B	HR	RBI	BB	HBP	SH	SF	SO	SB	CS	SLG	OBP
Avea, Marlon	R-R	6-1	218	8-31-93	.185	.167	.200	8	27	3	5	2	0	0	3	1	0	0	0	7	0	0	.259	.214
Ballard, Keach	L-R	6-0	180	7-16-92	.229	.286	.217	26	83	12	19	7	0	1	8	9	2	2	0	16	0	0	.349	.319
Birk, Ryne	L-R	5-10	185	11-11-94	.323	.500	.310	7	31	4	10	4	1	0	8	1	0	0	0	4	0	1	.516	.344
Cameron, Daz	R-R	6-2	185	1-15-97	.143	.074	.180	21	77	5	11	2	2	0	6	8	0	1	1	33	4	3	.221	.221
Cesar, Randy	R-R	6-1	180	1-11-95	.205	.172	.214	36	146	14	30	2	1	3	14	6	0	1	1	47	0	0	.295	.235
Correa, Christian	R-R	5-10	210	5-18-93	.215	.289	.195	59	209	14	45	9	0	1	17	13	6	0	1	56	0	0	.273	.279
Duarte, Osvaldo	R-R	5-9	160	1-18-96	.272	.315	.257	76	287	41	78	20	7	3	23	22	0	6	3	86	15	9	.422	.321
Goedert, Connor	R-R	6-2	190	12-14-93	.216	.246	.207	69	255	23	55	19	0	5	33	17	0	6	7	90	0	2	.349	.259
Hermelyn, Anthony	R-R	6-1	210	11-18-93	.205	.250	.194	87	297	36	61	17	1	4	33	43	2	1	4	95	0	2	.310	.306
Johnson, Spencer	R-R	6-4	225	11-1-93	.149	.278	.107	21	74	5	11	4	0	2	5	11	0	0	0	29	0	0	.284	.160
Marlow, Brooks	L-R	5-9	185	6-24-93	.261	.148	.308	25	92	11	24	5	1	2	5	10	0	0	0	18	0	0	.402	.333
McCall, Dex	R-R	6-1	220	1-29-94	.286	.228	.300	108	399	45	114	21	3	9	58	39	4	0	4	87	0	0	.421	.352
Michelena, Arturo	R-R	5-11	165	10-15-94	.222	.143	.240	78	266	30	59	8	1	0	19	22	2	4	1	67	2	1	.259	.285
Mizell, Aaron	L-R	6-0	165	10-14-93	.252	.188	.270	39	147	15	37	8	4	2	13	6	2	3	0	43	5	3	.401	.281
Nunez, Antonio	R-R	5-9	165	1-10-93	.198	.200	.197	29	91	18	18	1	0	0	5	21	0	3	0	21	9	3	.209	.348
Porter, Pat	L-L	6-0	215	11-22-91	.185	.156	.192	96	335	36	62	10	6	9	37	38	10	2	1	105	7	5	.331	.286
Roa, Hector	R-R	6-0	195	3-1-95	.211	.224	.207	56	213	20	45	10	5	6	22	4	1	1	0	65	0	0	.390	.229
Rogers, Jake	R-R	6-1	200	4-18-95	.208	.222	.206	21	72	7	15	3	1	1	4	8	2	0	0	25	1	0	.319	.305
Sewald, Johnny	L-R	5-11	175	11-11-93	.219	.259	.205	29	105	19	23	4	0	1	8	16	5	1	1	35	16	4	.286	.346
Straw, Myles	R-R	5-10	180	10-17-94	.374	.449	.357	68	270	40	101	14	6	0	22	29	0	6	2	58	17	10	.470	.432
Trompiz, Kristian	R-R	6-1	184	12-2-95	.213	.280	.198	77	277	30	59	14	2	3	24	28	0	6	4	80	7	10	.310	.282

Batting	B-T	HT	WT	DOB	AVG	vLH	vRH	G	AB	R	H	2B	3B	HR	RBI	BB	HBP	SH	SF	SO	SB	CS	SLG	OBP
Tucker, Kyle	L-R	6-4	190	1-17-97	.276	.338	.259	101	373	43	103	19	5	6	56	40	6	0	9	75	31	9	.402	.348
Wernes, Bobby	R-R	6-3	200	7-4-94	.215	.238	.209	94	317	30	68	17	1	0	16	36	2	3	2	61	4	2	.274	.297
Wrenn, Stephen	R-R	6-2	185	10-7-94	.236	.292	.224	35	140	16	33	7	3	3	12	7	1	2	0	38	7	2	.393	.277

Pitching	B-T	HT	WT	DOB	W	L	ERA	G	GS	CG	SV	IP	H	R	ER	HR	BB	SO	AVG	vLH	vRH	K/9	BB/9
Abreu, Albert	R-R	6-2	175	9-26-95	2	8	3.50	21	14	0	4	90	62	40	35	5	49	104	.193	.220	.166	10.40	4.90
Armenteros, Rogelio	R-R	6-1	215	6-30-94	0	2	1.93	4	3	0	0	19	12	6	4	0	3	20	.179	.103	.237	9.64	1.45
Barrios, Agapito	R-R	6-2	201	11-30-93	1	0	2.00	2	2	0	0	9	4	2	2	1	2	5	.133	.158	.091	5.00	2.00
Bower, Matt	R-L	6-5	190	6-16-94	4	2	3.94	17	15	0	0	82	81	41	36	7	30	103	.251	.250	.251	11.26	3.28
Britton, Tyler	R-R	6-0	195	3-6-94	0	1	9.00	1	1	0	0	3	4	3	3	0	4	1	.333	.200	.429	3.00	12.00
Castro, Ricardo	R-R	6-3	187	1-12-96	0	0	7.71	1	0	0	0	2	5	2	2	0	2	2	.385	.444	.250	7.71	7.71
Chavez, Enrique	R-R	5-11	194	4-13-96	0	2	3.18	3	3	0	0	17	13	6	6	1	4	16	.213	.222	.200	8.47	2.12
Deemes, Ryan	R-R	6-2	205	6-11-93	1	0	0.87	9	0	0	1	21	11	2	2	1	4	19	.162	.152	.171	8.27	1.74
Dorris, Jacob	R-R	6-2	165	3-24-93	1	0	4.22	7	0	0	0	11	11	5	5	0	5	11	.268	.316	.227	9.28	4.22
Ferrell, Justin	R-R	6-7	205	4-21-94	5	6	4.74	22	7	0	2	63	54	35	33	6	34	56	.226	.226	.226	8.04	4.88
Garza, Ralph	R-R	6-2	195	4-6-94	5	4	2.33	32	0	0	6	58	56	15	15	3	16	46	.256	.280	.235	7.14	2.48
Hernandez, Elieser	R-R	6-0	210	5-3-95	4	3	2.37	11	9	0	0	57	54	19	15	3	12	68	.251	.259	.243	10.74	1.89
Hernandez, Jose	R-R	6-0	180	5-5-95	3	2	2.66	17	14	0	1	81	78	27	24	4	15	84	.248	.252	.246	9.30	1.66
Hernandez, Nick	R-R	6-1	212	12-30-94	0	1	1.35	4	0	0	0	7	10	3	1	0	4	7	.370	.300	.412	9.45	5.40
Kessay, Sebastian	L-L	6-2	215	6-19-93	1	3	5.40	7	3	0	0	20	16	15	12	0	16	23	.219	.364	.157	10.35	7.20
McCanna, Kevin	L-R	6-1	185	2-1-94	2	3	2.91	12	8	0	1	56	55	21	18	1	17	42	.262	.179	.346	6.79	2.75
Murphy, Chris	R-R	6-4	205	9-28-92	5	7	3.88	24	12	1	2	95	106	50	41	10	21	52	.288	.325	.254	4.93	1.99
Nelson, Makay	R-R	5-11	180	7-27-94	0	2	5.46	14	3	0	0	31	34	22	19	2	19	15	.291	.263	.317	4.31	5.46
Nicely, Austin	B-L	6-1	170	12-13-94	0	0	—	1	0	0	0	0	2	3	3	1	2	0	1.000	1.000	1.000	—	—
Perez, Franklin	R-R	6-3	197	12-6-97	3	3	2.84	15	10	0	1	67	63	24	21	1	19	75	.250	.258	.242	10.13	2.57
Perez, Hector	R-R	6-3	190	6-6-96	2	1	4.60	7	7	0	0	31	28	20	16	1	22	44	.246	.275	.200	12.64	6.32
Person, Zac	L-L	6-1	185	10-13-92	3	1	3.02	26	0	0	0	51	46	17	17	3	24	53	.238	.167	.271	9.41	4.26
Quiala, Yoanys	R-R	6-3	235	1-15-94	2	12	5.10	19	16	0	0	97	112	64	55	10	23	60	.289	.303	.274	5.57	2.13
Ramirez, Luis	L-L	5-10	160	11-27-95	0	0	9.00	1	0	0	0	2	1	1	1	0	0	2	.400	.500	.333	0.00	0.00
Saldana, Abdiel	R-R	5-11	195	3-13-96	0	0	2.25	1	1	0	0	4	3	1	1	0	3	4	.214	.333	.125	9.00	6.75
Santos, Juan	R-R	6-4	240	8-30-95	1	0	6.21	16	0	0	3	29	30	23	20	1	22	35	.278	.273	.283	10.86	6.83
Schmidt, David	R-R	6-0	175	1-21-93	4	3	3.50	24	0	0	3	46	43	18	18	2	23	35	.259	.263	.256	6.80	4.47
Sierra, Carlos	R-R	6-3	195	10-18-94	0	0	1.80	3	0	0	0	10	6	3	2	1	6	16	.182	.167	.200	14.40	5.40
Thome, Andrew	R-R	6-3	215	1-13-93	2	1	1.88	12	0	0	4	29	23	8	6	2	4	16	.221	.190	.242	5.02	1.26
Valdez, Framber	L-L	5-11	170	11-19-93	1	3	3.06	6	1	0	0	35	31	15	12	1	11	35	.244	.200	.264	8.92	2.80
Whitt, Adam	R-R	6-3	205	3-22-93	4	7	6.93	41	0	0	5	64	71	51	49	4	30	63	.278	.300	.259	8.91	4.24
Winkelman, Alex	L-L	6-2	180	2-8-94	5	1	3.72	8	5	0	0	36	31	16	15	1	15	37	.231	.167	.255	9.17	3.72

Fielding

Catcher	PCT	G	PO	A	E	DP	PB
Avea	1.000	4	20	2	0	0	1
Correa	.991	47	378	46	4	1	4
Hermelyn	.995	70	524	68	3	4	17
Rogers	.986	19	194	19	3	1	4

First Base	PCT	G	PO	A	E	DP
Goedert	.996	27	225	15	1	18
Johnson	1.000	5	31	3	0	2
McCall	.987	95	823	34	11	84
Porter	.933	3	27	1	2	1
Roa	.977	10	80	6	2	5

Second Base	PCT	G	PO	A	E	DP
Ballard	.985	16	25	40	1	6
Birk	1.000	6	8	17	0	3

	PCT	G	PO	A	E	DP
Duarte	1.000	1	0	4	0	0
Marlow	1.000	18	27	46	0	13
Michelena	.965	50	50	117	6	23
Mizell	.958	26	42	72	5	14
Trompiz	1.000	10	20	21	0	4
Wernes	.986	15	27	46	1	12

Third Base	PCT	G	PO	A	E	DP
Cesar	.900	30	31	50	9	8
Goedert	.903	12	8	20	3	3
Michelena	1.000	14	9	19	0	2
Nunez	.850	8	3	14	3	2
Trompiz	.857	2	0	6	1	0
Wernes	.975	74	67	129	5	12

Shortstop	PCT	G	PO	A	E	DP
Ballard	1.000	4	5	7	0	1

	PCT	G	PO	A	E	DP
Duarte	.967	42	55	120	6	21
Michelena	.903	14	17	39	6	8
Nunez	.963	21	30	73	4	12
Trompiz	.981	61	96	162	5	33

Outfield	PCT	G	PO	A	E	DP
Cameron	.921	19	34	1	3	0
Duarte	.977	29	75	9	2	0
Goedert	1.000	27	41	1	0	0
Johnson	.944	12	17	0	1	0
Mizell	1.000	13	23	1	0	0
Porter	.974	82	140	9	4	1
Roa	.980	28	45	3	1	0
Sewald	1.000	36	36	1	0	0
Straw	.975	60	145	9	4	4
Tucker	.984	92	170	10	3	0
Wrenn	.971	34	62	4	2	1

TRI-CITY VALLEYCATS

NEW YORK-PENN LEAGUE

SHORT-SEASON

Batting	B-T	HT	WT	DOB	AVG	vLH	vRH	G	AB	R	H	2B	3B	HR	RBI	BB	HBP	SH	SF	SO	SB	CS	SLG	OBP
Almonte, Marcos	R-R	5-10	163	3-28-96	.223	.222	.224	31	94	11	21	5	1	0	4	10	0	3	0	29	6	3	.298	.298
Ayarza, Rodrigo	B-R	5-8	145	2-20-95	.260	.143	.289	46	177	19	46	8	3	2	24	10	0	3	4	22	2	4	.373	.293
Birk, Ryne	L-R	5-10	185	11-11-94	.287	.179	.315	36	136	26	39	9	0	4	23	20	5	1	2	12	5	1	.441	.393
Bracamonte, Gabriel	R-R	5-9	165	5-15-95	.208	.250	.200	10	24	2	5	0	0	0	3	1	1	2	0	4	0	0	.208	.321
Cameron, Daz	R-R	6-2	185	1-15-97	.278	.350	.254	19	79	13	22	3	1	2	14	6	3	1	0	26	8	2	.418	.352
Carpenter, Kolbey	R-R	6-2	180	8-9-93	.158	.250	.133	5	19	5	3	0	0	0	0	6	2	0	0	7	0	1	.158	.407
Cesar, Randy	R-R	6-1	180	1-11-95	.389	.556	.356	30	108	21	42	7	1	1	15	14	0	2	2	30	0	0	.500	.452
Dawson, Ronnie	L-R	6-2	225	5-19-95	.225	.197	.236	70	244	41	55	13	1	7	36	41	6	0	0	66	12	6	.373	.351
De La Cruz, Bryan	R-R	6-2	175	12-16-96	.214	.000	.273	16	42	8	9	1	0	0	5	0	0	1	0	10	0	0	.238	.292
DeGoti, Alex	R-R	5-10	165	8-19-94	.228	.276	.211	63	219	36	50	13	3	2	21	25	6	6	3	54	9	6	.329	.320
Goedert, Connor	R-R	6-2	190	12-14-93	.182	.130	.209	19	66	4	12	3	0	2	4	2	1	0	1	16	2	0	.318	.214
Johnson, Spencer	R-R	6-4	225	11-1-93	.276	.071	.323	23	76	12	21	5	1	6	20	11	0	0	0	28	0	1	.605	.368
Jones, Taylor	R-R	6-7	225	12-6-93	.252	.212	.266	70	254	34	64	17	0	8	38	32	8	0	6	61	1	1	.413	.354

Batting

Batting	B-T	HT	WT	DOB	AVG	vLH	vRH	G	AB	R	H	2B	3B	HR	RBI	BB	HBP	SH	SF	SO	SB	CS	SLG	OBP
Martir, Kevin	R-R	5-11	210	2-11-94	.165	.227	.140	25	79	6	13	2	0	1	5	4	5	2	1	21	0	0	.228	.247
Mejia, Brauly	R-R	6-0	185	10-28-94	.257	.190	.279	49	171	17	44	8	0	1	21	15	7	0	2	42	1	0	.322	.338
Payano, Luis	R-R	6-1	175	5-12-96	—	—	—	1	0	0	0	0	0	0	0	0	0	0	0	0	0	0	—	—
Pineda, Andy	L-R	6-1	165	11-11-96	.400	.000	.667	2	5	0	2	0	0	0	0	0	0	0	0	2	0	.400	.400
Robinson, Chuckie	R-R	5-11	225	12-14-94	.275	.182	.310	45	160	25	44	13	0	2	18	19	2	2	0	48	0	1	.394	.359
Rogers, Jake	R-R	6-1	190	4-18-95	.253	.333	.240	25	87	11	22	7	1	2	12	13	3	1	0	18	0	2	.425	.369
Sierra, Miguelangel	R-R	5-11	165	12-2-97	.140	.080	.162	25	93	6	13	2	1	0	5	7	2	0	0	34	0	3	.183	.216
Wolfe, Tyler	R-R	6-0	190	9-21-93	.197	.200	.196	25	76	8	15	4	0	1	8	4	8	0	0	23	1	0	.289	.307
Wrenn, Stephen	R-R	6-2	185	10-7-94	.282	.240	.290	36	149	30	42	8	2	9	27	18	2	1	1	40	8	1	.544	.365

Pitching

Pitching	B-T	HT	WT	DOB	W	L	ERA	G	GS	CG	SV	IP	H	R	ER	HR	BB	SO	AVG	vLH	vRH	K/9	BB/9
Adcock, Brett	L-L	6-1	225	8-28-95	0	0	6.23	3	3	0	0	4	3	3	3	0	2	6	.188	.500	.143	12.46	4.15
Alcala, Jorge	R-R	6-3	180	7-28-95	0	1	5.27	3	3	0	0	14	20	15	8	1	4	15	.345	.393	.300	9.88	2.63
Barrios, Agapito	R-R	6-2	201	11-30-93	0	1	3.86	3	2	0	1	12	7	5	5	1	1	12	.171	.182	.158	9.26	0.77
Bostick, Akeem	R-R	6-6	215	5-4-95	1	1	3.27	2	2	0	0	11	10	4	4	1	0	7	.238	.250	.227	5.73	0.00
Brey, Howie	L-L	5-11	195	5-22-94	1	1	5.09	14	0	0	0	18	22	15	10	3	15	13	.310	.400	.275	6.62	7.64
Britton, Tyler	R-R	6-0	195	3-6-94	0	1	2.04	6	4	0	2	18	14	5	4	0	6	29	.209	.208	.209	14.77	3.06
Castro, Ricardo	R-R	6-3	187	1-12-96	0	0	4.50	2	0	0	0	8	5	4	4	0	4	10	.179	.235	11.25	4.50
Chavez, Enrique	R-R	5-11	194	4-13-96	3	2	2.78	11	7	0	1	45	34	17	14	1	11	35	.204	.164	.230	6.95	2.18
Cotton, Chris	R-L	5-10	166	11-21-90	0	0	0.00	4	0	0	0	5	2	0	0	1	6	.125	.125	.125	11.57	1.93
Hartman, Ryan	L-L	6-3	205	4-21-94	2	0	2.36	14	0	0	0	46	42	13	12	4	7	48	.240	.254	.232	9.46	1.38
Hernandez, Nick	R-R	6-1	212	12-30-94	1	1	1.86	15	0	0	6	19	17	5	4	2	5	23	.227	.276	.196	10.71	2.33
Hill, Kevin	R-R	6-0	230	8-12-92	1	4	4.37	13	5	0	1	35	44	19	17	3	7	22	.312	.271	.341	5.66	1.80
Hunt, Dustin	R-R	6-5	195	8-2-94	1	1	4.11	13	6	0	1	35	36	19	16	2	23	29	.261	.239	.282	7.46	5.91
James, Dylan	R-R	6-2	185	6-27-92	0	0	7.36	3	0	0	0	4	4	3	3	1	3	4	.286	.400	9.82	7.36
Kessay, Sebastian	L-L	6-2	215	6-19-93	3	1	4.12	12	7	0	1	44	39	21	20	3	23	62	.235	.138	.287	12.78	4.74
Minnis, Albert	R-L	6-0	190	11-5-91	0	0	0.00	1	0	0	0	2	0	0	0	0	0	4	.000	.000	.000	18.00	0.00
Montano, Salvador	L-L	6-3	150	7-14-94	2	0	5.25	5	0	0	0	12	7	8	7	0	23	13	.179	.250	.130	9.75	17.25
Nelson, Makay	R-R	5-11	180	7-27-94	2	1	3.76	7	3	0	0	26	19	11	11	1	13	21	.196	.205	.189	7.18	4.44
Nicely, Austin	B-L	6-1	170	12-13-94	5	4	6.80	14	7	0	1	49	59	37	37	7	16	22	.298	.309	.294	4.04	2.94
Perez, Hector	R-R	6-3	190	6-6-96	2	0	1.57	7	3	0	0	29	19	5	5	0	12	36	.181	.220	.156	11.30	3.77
Perez, Tyson	R-R	6-3	215	12-27-89	0	0	0.00	2	0	0	1	3	1	0	0	0	3	.091	.167	.000	9.00	0.00
Pinales, Erasmo	R-R	5-11	180	11-25-94	2	3	3.38	12	4	0	0	37	29	15	14	3	21	38	.210	.197	9.16	5.06
Raftery, Devin	R-R	5-10	205	9-21-92	0	1	5.68	4	0	0	0	6	9	4	4	1	2	10	.333	.462	.214	14.21	2.84
Ramirez, Luis	L-L	6-0	160	11-27-95	2	1	6.35	6	0	0	0	11	16	11	8	1	7	.348	.400	.333	5.56	8.74
Saldana, Abdiel	R-R	5-11	195	3-13-96	0	1	1.33	6	2	0	1	20	15	3	3	0	2	24	.200	.176	.220	10.62	0.89
Sanabria, Carlos	R-R	6-0	165	1-24-97	1	1	3.18	3	2	0	0	11	12	6	4	1	3	11	.267	.280	.250	8.74	2.38
Sandoval, Edgardo	R-R	6-0	170	7-9-96	1	3	3.98	13	6	0	0	41	39	18	18	3	15	34	.252	.204	.277	7.52	3.32
Santos, Juan	R-R	6-4	240	8-30-95	1	0	2.70	6	0	0	2	7	5	2	2	0	1	11	.192	.100	.250	14.85	1.35
Serrano, Angelo	R-R	6-3	190	5-18-92	2	2	5.25	9	0	0	1	12	13	9	7	1	7	15	.289	.167	.333	11.25	5.25
Sierra, Carlos	R-R	6-3	195	10-18-94	1	2	5.53	12	1	0	1	28	22	17	17	0	10	25	.227	.156	.262	8.13	3.25
Smith, Ben	L-L	6-2	195	1-20-93	0	1	25.31	4	1	0	0	5	12	19	15	1	11	5	.429	.571	.381	8.44	18.56
Stutzman, Sean	L-L	5-9	175	7-8-93	2	2	5.40	15	0	0	2	23	20	16	14	0	10	21	.230	.222	.233	8.10	3.82
Uribe, Josue	R-R	6-0	180	2-6-95	0	0	13.50	2	0	0	0	2	4	3	3	0	2	0	.444	1.000	.000	0.00	9.00
Valdez, Framber	L-L	5-11	170	11-19-93	2	1	3.74	5	2	0	0	22	22	10	9	0	7	28	.259	.350	.231	11.63	2.91
Winkelman, Alex	L-L	6-2	180	2-8-94	0	1	6.75	1	1	0	0	4	6	3	3	0	0	5	.333	.500	.286	11.25	0.00

Fielding

Catcher	PCT	G	PO	A	E	DP	PB
Bracamonte	1.000	10	62	10	0	2	1
Martir	.981	18	148	7	3	0	1
Robinson	.987	29	214	20	3	3	3
Rogers	.987	24	214	22	3	1	7

First Base	PCT	G	PO	A	E	DP
Benedetti	1.000	1	5	1	0	0
Cesar	.875	2	7	0	1	0
Goedert	.986	9	70	1	1	2
Johnson	1.000	5	42	1	0	0
Jones	.991	61	508	40	5	45

Second Base	PCT	G	PO	A	E	DP
Almonte	1.000	4	11	7	0	2

	PCT	G	PO	A	E	DP	PB
Ayarza	.923	19	24	48	6	3	
Birk	.984	35	50	71	2	19	
Carpenter	1.000	2	3	4	0	0	
DeGoti	.925	17	24	38	5	6	
Wolfe	1.000	2	4	1	0	1	

Third Base	PCT	G	PO	A	E	DP
Ayarza	.966	22	13	44	2	6
Carpenter	.857	3	3	3	1	0
Cesar	.966	27	22	64	3	8
Goedert	.800	3	4	4	2	0
Wolfe	1.000	23	15	43	0	0

Shortstop	PCT	G	PO	A	E	DP
Almonte	1.000	1	3	2	0	0

	PCT	G	PO	A	E	DP
Ayarza	1.000	6	6	13	0	2
DeGoti	.964	47	75	137	8	17
Sierra	.988	24	36	45	1	7

Outfield	PCT	G	PO	A	E	DP
Almonte	.978	24	43	1	1	1
Benedetti	1.000	27	40	3	0	2
Cameron	1.000	17	35	0	0	0
Dawson	.963	58	101	4	4	0
De La Cruz	1.000	14	18	1	0	1
Goedert	1.000	3	7	1	0	1
Johnson	.950	12	19	0	1	0
Mejia	.984	46	60	1	1	0
Pineda	1.000	2	3	1	0	0
Wrenn	.987	35	76	1	1	1

GREENEVILLE ASTROS

APPALACHIAN LEAGUE

ROOKIE

Batting

Batting	B-T	HT	WT	DOB	AVG	vLH	vRH	G	AB	R	H	2B	3B	HR	RBI	BB	HBP	SH	SF	SO	SB	CS	SLG	OBP
Almonte, Marcos	R-R	5-10	163	3-28-96	.238	.333	.222	23	84	13	20	5	2	1	4	2	4	1	1	16	8	3	.381	.286
Amador, Wilson	R-R	6-1	160	12-14-96	.143	.000	.200	2	7	1	1	0	0	0	1	0	0	0	3	0	0	.286	.250
Arauz, Jonathan	L-R	6-0	150	8-3-98	.249	.167	.279	53	201	26	50	10	1	2	18	19	4	3	2	45	1	3	.338	.323
Beltre, Reiny	R-R	6-0	180	7-16-96	.244	.259	.238	25	90	9	22	3	2	0	13	13	5	0	1	26	0	0	.322	.367
Bracamonte, Gabriel	R-R	5-9	165	5-15-95	.303	.389	.271	18	66	9	20	6	1	0	8	8	1	1	2	9	2	1	.424	.377
Campos, Oscar	R-R	5-10	170	12-8-96	.292	.286	.294	8	24	3	7	0	1	0	1	2	0	3	0	2	0	0	.375	.346

Batting

Batting	B-T	HT	WT	DOB	AVG	vLH	vRH	G	AB	R	H	2B	3B	HR	RBI	BB	HBP	SH	SF	SO	SB	CS	SLG	OBP
Castro, Ruben	L-R	5-10	182	7-10-96	.293	.286	.296	27	99	8	29	4	1	0	10	4	1	3	1	15	4	1	.354	.324
De La Cruz, Bryan	R-R	6-2	175	12-16-96	.250	.185	.277	28	92	21	23	3	4	3	13	14	0	1	0	23	0	0	.467	.349
Fernandez, Frankeny	R-R	6-1	170	12-7-96	.223	.279	.197	52	188	34	42	10	3	4	25	30	4	5	1	56	20	5	.372	.341
Franco, Wander	B-R	6-1	189	10-11-96	.200	.316	.139	14	55	3	11	2	0	1	7	2	0	0	1	18	0	1	.291	.224
Garcia, Justin	L-L	6-3	225	10-6-93	.174	.200	.167	6	23	3	4	1	0	1	2	0	2	0	0	8	0	0	.348	.240
Henderson, Ray	R-R	5-9	190	12-27-95	.223	.125	.257	26	94	10	21	7	0	3	16	9	1	0	2	24	0	0	.394	.292
Johnson, Spencer	R-R	6-4	225	11-1-93	.235	.333	.125	9	34	7	8	3	0	2	6	2	1	0	0	14	0	0	.500	.297
MacDonald, Connor	R-R	6-5	200	12-9-94	.267	.300	.252	43	161	22	43	8	1	6	22	10	4	0	2	63	1	2	.441	.322
Machado, Carlos	R-R	6-2	170	6-5-98	.252	.302	.221	29	111	12	28	1	0	0	8	5	3	0	0	21	4	1	.261	.303
Matute, Jonathan	R-R	6-0	170	4-28-97	.200	.130	.250	17	55	8	11	2	0	0	7	9	1	1	0	20	0	0	.236	.318
Pal, Chaz	R-R	6-0	200	5-6-93	.269	.333	.247	28	104	15	28	9	1	3	15	8	3	2	1	33	1	2	.462	.336
Payano, Luis	R-R	6-1	175	5-12-96	.228	.194	.242	38	127	18	29	1	1	6	16	7	3	1	4	31	7	3	.394	.277
Sanchez, Vicente	L-R	5-11	170	10-4-96	.198	.200	.197	35	101	14	20	5	1	2	12	14	3	0	1	39	3	3	.327	.311
Sieber, Troy	L-R	5-11	215	6-22-95	.242	.214	.250	33	124	12	30	9	0	1	10	20	2	0	0	41	1	1	.339	.356
Sierra, Miguelangel	R-R	5-11	165	12-2-97	.289	.278	.294	31	121	23	35	3	2	11	19	12	7	4	0	40	6	6	.620	.386
Toro, Abraham	B-R	6-1	190	12-20-96	.254	.283	.242	44	177	20	45	6	3	0	19	10	3	0	3	31	2	1	.322	.301
Van Der Meer, Stijn	L-R	6-3	170	5-1-93	.301	.435	.240	19	73	12	22	3	1	0	8	7	3	2	0	12	3	1	.370	.386
Wolfe, Tyler	R-R	6-0	190	9-21-93	.260	.320	.231	20	77	8	20	0	0	0	8	3	0	1	1	12	3	0	.260	.284

Pitching

Pitching	B-T	HT	WT	DOB	W	L	ERA	G	GS	CG	SV	IP	H	R	ER	HR	BB	SO	AVG	vLH	vRH	K/9	BB/9
Abreu, Bryan	R-R	6-1	175	4-22-97	0	1	11.81	3	1	0	0	5	6	8	7	0	5	6	.286	.375	.231	10.13	8.44
Alcala, Jorge	R-R	6-3	180	7-28-95	2	1	1.80	6	4	0	0	20	12	5	4	0	8	20	.174	.129	.211	9.00	3.60
Almengo, Diogenes	R-R	6-2	190	6-2-95	1	2	4.33	13	4	0	3	44	36	23	21	4	28	23	.229	.156	.259	4.74	5.77
Aquino, Dariel	R-R	6-1	190	1-30-96	0	0	2.70	3	0	0	1	3	3	3	1	0	4	3	.231	.000	.429	8.10	10.80
Brey, Howie	L-L	5-11	195	5-22-94	0	0	9.00	1	0	0	1	1	1	1	1	1	1	1	.250	—	.250	9.00	9.00
Britton, Tyler	R-R	6-0	195	3-6-94	3	1	2.66	7	3	0	0	20	19	9	6	1	2	33	.247	.250	.244	14.61	0.89
Carr, Devon	L-L	6-2	190	11-5-92	3	3	6.39	16	0	0	1	25	34	21	18	1	13	30	.312	.250	.338	10.66	4.62
Castro, Ricardo	R-R	6-3	187	1-12-96	3	2	2.38	13	6	0	2	53	53	22	14	4	13	44	.261	.239	.279	7.47	2.21
Chavez, Lupe	R-R	6-2	150	12-3-97	0	0	1.17	2	1	0	0	8	4	1	1	0	5	10	.154	.200	.000	11.74	5.87
Guzman, Jorge	R-R	6-2	182	1-28-96	2	3	4.76	9	4	0	0	23	25	15	12	1	7	29	.272	.200	.316	11.51	2.78
Hiraldo, Carlos	L-L	5-10	175	7-15-96	0	1	5.13	12	5	0	0	33	30	22	19	1	18	25	.242	.206	.256	6.75	4.86
Javier, Cristian	R-R	6-1	170	3-26-97	1	1	1.75	7	4	0	0	26	15	6	5	1	10	29	.170	.209	.133	10.17	3.51
Johnson, Reggie	R-R	6-4	205	10-28-93	3	3	3.27	15	0	0	0	22	29	15	8	2	10	15	.305	.324	.295	6.14	4.09
LaRue, Carson	R-R	6-1	175	3-6-96	0	0	0.00	1	0	0	0	2	0	0	0	0	0	3	.000	.000	.000	13.50	0.00
McKee, Colin	R-R	6-3	225	6-21-94	2	2	11.88	7	1	0	0	8	15	13	11	2	7	6	.375	.250	.500	6.48	7.56
Montano, Salvador	L-L	6-3	150	7-14-94	1	1	2.95	8	2	0	2	18	8	9	6	1	14	23	.129	.118	.133	11.29	6.87
Raftery, Devin	R-R	5-10	205	9-21-92	3	0	3.00	12	0	0	1	21	18	7	7	2	8	31	.231	.286	.211	13.29	3.43
Ramirez, Luis	L-L	5-10	160	11-27-95	1	1	5.06	10	0	0	0	16	18	11	9	2	3	12	.273	.250	.278	6.75	1.69
Robles, Juan	R-R	6-0	185	11-6-97	0	0	0.00	2	1	0	1	7	7	0	0	0	1	6	.269	.267	.273	7.71	1.29
Saldana, Abdiel	R-R	5-11	195	3-13-96	1	0	2.74	9	3	0	1	23	19	7	7	0	7	34	.224	.333	.164	13.30	2.74
Sanabria, Carlos	R-R	6-0	165	1-24-97	1	2	3.81	12	6	0	0	52	42	27	22	3	12	46	.221	.222	.221	7.96	2.08
Sandoval, Patrick	L-L	6-3	190	10-18-96	2	3	5.30	13	8	0	0	53	53	32	31	4	25	51	.266	.275	.264	8.72	4.27
Serrano, Angelo	R-R	6-3	190	5-18-92	1	1	2.25	9	0	0	1	16	13	4	4	1	7	18	.241	.294	.216	10.13	3.94
Smith, Ben	L-L	6-2	195	1-20-93	0	3	3.67	11	5	0	0	34	26	22	14	1	34	37	.210	.267	.191	9.70	8.91
Thompson, Nathan	L-L	6-1	170	11-14-93	2	1	5.01	10	3	0	1	23	26	13	13	2	7	23	.286	.259	.297	8.87	2.70
Uribe, Josue	R-R	6-0	180	2-6-95	1	0	0.00	1	0	0	0	1	1	0	0	0	1	1	.250	.500	.000	9.00	0.00
Valdez, Framber	L-L	5-11	170	11-19-93	1	0	1.69	2	2	0	0	11	7	2	2	0	3	15	.179	.200	.172	12.66	2.53
Whitley, Forrest	R-R	6-7	240	9-15-97	0	1	3.18	4	4	0	0	11	11	6	4	0	3	13	.244	.143	.333	10.32	2.38
Williams, Lucas	L-R	6-3	180	7-20-94	1	1	5.47	16	0	0	1	25	34	18	15	0	8	15	.340	.389	.313	5.47	2.92

Fielding

C: Bracamonte 18, Campos 8, Castro 27, Henderson 15. **1B:** Beltre 3, Garcia 6, Johnson 5, MacDonald 34, Sieber 22. **2B:** Almonte 5, Arauz 18, Beltre 2, Henderson 4, Matute 15, Sierra 10, van der Meer 10, Wolfe 7. **3B:** Almonte 2, Beltre 8, Franco 3, Henderson 2, Matute 1, Toro-Hernandez 41, van der Meer 1, Wolfe 10. **SS:** Almonte 3, Arauz 35, Sierra 21, van der Meer 10, Wolfe 1. **OF:** Almonte 13, Amador 2, De La Cruz 26, Fernandez 49, Johnson 2, Machado 28, Pal 26, Payano 36, Sanchez 26.

GCL ASTROS   ROOKIE
GULF COAST LEAGUE

Batting	B-T	HT	WT	DOB	AVG	vLH	vRH	G	AB	R	H	2B	3B	HR	RBI	BB	HBP	SH	SF	SO	SB	CS	SLG	OBP
Amador, Wilson	R-R	6-1	160	12-14-96	.268	.350	.252	38	127	18	34	6	3	1	14	8	4	3	1	35	7	5	.386	.329
Beltre, Reiny	R-R	6-0	180	7-16-96	.418	.500	.390	15	55	11	23	5	0	0	7	4	2	0	0	9	1	0	.509	.475
Benavente, Brandon	B-R	5-10	200	9-3-97	.333	.333	.333	7	12	0	4	1	0	0	1	0	0	0	0	3	0	1	.417	.385
Benjamin, Jose	R-R	6-2	170	12-16-95	.306	.000	.314	21	72	9	22	6	2	0	9	2	1	2	0	17	6	6	.444	.333
Campos, Oscar	R-R	5-10	170	12-4-96	.255	.333	.237	19	47	4	12	1	0	0	3	1	1	5	1	8	1	0	.277	.280
Celestino, Gilberto	R-R	6-0	170	2-13-99	.200	1.000	.185	18	55	7	11	3	1	0	2	8	1	0	1	16	6	1	.291	.308
Franco, Wander	B-R	6-1	189	10-11-96	.253	.333	.250	24	75	6	19	5	1	1	9	14	0	1	1	19	1	1	.387	.367
Gurriel, Yulieski	R-R	6-0	190	6-9-84	.286	—	.286	2	7	0	2	1	0	0	0	0	0	0	0	2	0	0	.429	.286
Heras, Bernardo	R-R	6-0	180	11-3-95	.278	.286	.278	7	18	1	5	0	0	0	2	2	0	0	0	3	0	0	.278	.350
Jimenez, Ronny	R-R	6-6	185	9-19-94	.263	.283	.263	5	19	2	5	1	0	0	2	0	0	0	1	5	1	1	.316	.333
Lorenzo, Edgar	R-R	5-11	160	1-15-97	.180	.000	.190	27	61	10	11	1	1	1	4	7	2	1	0	26	5	2	.279	.286
Luciano, Christopher	R-R	6-0	180	5-31-96	.111	.182	.100	28	81	5	9	1	0	1	5	20	1	1	0	29	0	0	.160	.294
Machado, Carlos	R-R	6-2	170	6-5-98	.327	.348	.320	26	98	13	32	3	1	0	12	2	1	0	0	13	4	5	.378	.347
Marquez, Orlando	R-R	5-10	180	3-12-96	.118	.077	.118	10	17	1	2	0	0	0	1	0	0	0	1	2	0	0	.118	.111
Martinez, Jorge	R-R	5-11	184	12-19-96	.036	.143	.000	16	28	3	1	0	0	0	0	5	0	1	0	15	0	0	.036	.182

Batting

Batting	B-T	HT	WT	DOB	AVG	vLH	vRH	G	AB	R	H	2B	3B	HR	RBI	BB	HBP	SH	SF	SO	SB	CS	SLG	OBP
Matute, Jonathan	R-R	6-0	170	4-28-97	.211	.077	.241	24	71	13	15	4	0	0	4	11	3	4	2	19	2	0	.268	.333
Mauricio, Joan	L-R	5-11	160	10-22-96	.182	.286	.169	43	132	3	24	3	2	0	16	10	6	2	2	23	5	5	.235	.236
Muriel, Nestor	R-R	6-2	170	6-11-98	.150	.167	.148	24	60	4	9	2	0	0	1	5	4	2	0	28	1	3	.183	.261
Pelletier, L.P.	R-R	5-10	195	2-1-96	.192	.250	.186	24	78	9	15	0	0	1	4	4	2	1	0	25	5	0	.231	.250
Pineda, Andy	L-R	6-1	165	10-11-96	.262	.158	.279	38	141	17	37	5	0	6	9	2	3	0	24	16	5	.298	.316
Pineda, Juan	R-R	5-10	145	1-31-98	.233	.071	.264	27	86	5	20	5	1	0	11	4	5	0	0	15	2	1	.314	.305
Sieber, Troy	L-R	5-11	215	6-22-95	.289	.375	.267	12	38	8	11	2	1	1	12	9	2	0	0	7	0	0	.474	.449
Toribio, Oliver	R-R	5-10	180	6-7-96	.000	.000	.000	8	10	0	0	0	0	0	0	2	0	0	0	5	0	0	.000	.167
Van Der Meer, Stijn	L-R	6-3	150	5-1-93	.667	—	.667	2	6	1	4	0	1	0	2	0	0	0	0	0	0	0	1.000	.667
Vasquez, Randy	R-R	5-10	190	3-13-96	.237	.000	.254	28	76	3	18	2	1	0	6	6	1	0	0	17	0	2	.289	.301
Westmoreland, Brody	R-R	6-3	185	8-22-95	.185	.158	.190	40	135	16	25	2	4	2	18	14	3	0	2	57	1	0	.304	.273

Pitching

Pitching	B-T	HT	WT	DOB	W	L	ERA	G	GS	CG	SV	IP	H	R	ER	HR	BB	SO	AVG	vLH	vRH	K/9	BB/9
Abreu, Bryan	R-R	6-1	175	4-22-97	2	4	3.78	10	3	0	0	33	33	20	14	0	15	35	.250	.171	.286	9.45	4.05
Acosta, Yhoan	L-L	6-1	175	6-17-95	0	0	0.00	2	0	0	0	2	1	0	0	0	1	2	.167	.000	.250	9.00	4.50
Alcala, Jorge	R-R	6-3	180	7-28-95	1	1	1.21	6	3	0	1	22	14	3	3	0	6	35	.175	.222	.151	14.10	2.42
Aquino, Dariel	R-R	6-1	190	1-30-96	1	2	3.78	13	0	0	3	17	18	7	7	0	7	17	.265	.154	.333	9.18	3.78
Barrios, Agapito	R-R	6-2	201	11-30-93	0	1	2.57	3	3	0	0	7	8	2	2	0	3	6	.320	.375	.294	7.71	3.86
Blanco, Ronel	R-R	6-0	180	8-31-93	0	0	0.00	2	1	0	0	6	3	0	0	0	3	5	.167	.143	.182	11.12	4.76
Chavez, Lupe	R-R	6-2	150	12-3-97	0	0	0.00	3	1	0	0	6	3	0	0	0	1	5	.150	.125	.167	7.50	1.50
2-team total (6 Blue Jays)					4	1	1.42	9	7	0	0	38	32	6	6	1	5	31	—	—	—	7.34	1.18
Del Rosario, Yeyfry	R-R	6-2	182	4-27-94	0	0	4.50	2	1	0	0	2	1	1	1	0	1	2	.167	.500	.000	9.00	4.50
Fidel, Edwin	R-R	6-3	200	12-14-94	0	0	6.75	2	0	0	0	3	1	2	2	0	1	7	.111	.250	.000	23.63	3.38
Garcia, Junior	R-R	6-3	175	1-29-96	0	0	21.00	4	0	0	0	3	8	7	7	0	8	4	.471	.500	.444	12.00	24.00
Gonzalez, Manuel	R-R	6-4	195	10-21-94	1	1	4.50	13	0	0	1	16	16	10	8	0	4	13	.262	.241	.281	7.31	2.25
Guzman, Jorge	R-R	6-2	182	1-28-96	1	1	3.12	7	4	0	0	17	4	7	6	0	10	25	.071	.059	.077	12.98	5.19
Hardman, Ian	R-R	6-5	240	9-16-95	0	0	7.31	11	0	0	0	16	19	14	13	0	11	17	.297	.400	.231	9.56	6.19
Holmes, Brian	L-L	6-4	210	1-30-91	0	0	1.17	3	3	0	0	8	8	1	1	1	2	5	.286	.455	.176	5.87	2.35
Javier, Cristian	R-R	6-1	170	3-26-97	3	1	2.84	6	2	0	1	25	19	9	8	1	8	37	.207	.222	.196	13.14	2.84
Johnson, Reggie	R-R	6-4	205	10-28-93	0	0	9.00	1	0	0	0	2	4	2	2	0	0	2	.444	1.000	.286	9.00	0.00
LaRue, Carson	R-R	6-1	175	3-6-96	0	0	1.35	3	0	0	0	7	7	1	1	0	0	5	.259	.125	.316	6.75	0.00
Martinez, Saul	R-R	6-2	185	6-21-95	0	0	1.29	5	0	0	0	7	4	1	1	0	4	9	.174	.111	.211	11.57	5.14
Paredes, Enoli	R-R	5-11	165	9-28-95	1	3	3.74	12	3	0	3	34	25	18	14	0	19	46	.207	.091	.250	12.30	5.08
Paulino, David	R-R	6-7	215	2-6-94	0	0	0.75	3	3	0	0	12	9	3	1	0	2	14	.196	.267	.161	10.50	1.50
Paulino, Hansel	R-R	6-7	170	1-3-96	1	1	5.04	12	1	0	0	30	37	22	17	1	14	33	.303	.364	.269	9.79	4.15
Perez, Tyson	R-R	6-3	215	12-27-89	0	0	0.00	1	1	0	0	1	1	0	0	0	1	1	.333	1.000	.000	9.00	9.00
Polanco, Moreno	R-R	6-3	180	7-29-94	0	1	216.00	2	2	0	0	0	2	9	8	0	4	1	.667	.667	—	27.00	108.00
Powell, Christian	L-R	6-4	225	7-3-91	0	0	5.40	2	1	0	0	2	1	2	1	0	2	2	.167	.000	.250	10.80	10.80
Ramirez, Yohan	R-R	6-4	190	5-6-95	1	0	2.25	2	0	0	0	4	5	3	1	0	2	3	.313	.167	.400	6.75	4.50
Ramos, Jose	R-R	6-1	160	8-4-96	0	1	13.50	4	0	0	1	5	5	7	7	0	3	5	.294	.167	.364	9.64	5.79
Robles, Juan	R-R	6-0	185	11-6-97	1	1	2.29	6	2	0	0	20	13	7	5	2	6	20	.186	.194	.179	9.15	2.75
Rodriguez, Leovanny	R-R	6-0	160	6-13-96	2	6	6.75	12	6	0	1	36	50	31	27	2	12	31	.321	.351	.303	7.75	3.00
Rosado, Cesar	R-R	6-1	172	6-22-96	3	3	3.00	12	6	0	0	39	32	15	13	0	18	41	.222	.231	.217	9.46	4.15
Santamaria, Cristhopher	L-L	5-11	175	6-19-96	0	0	0.00	4	0	0	0	5	1	0	0	0	4	2	.067	.125	.000	3.38	6.75
Tejada, Felipe	R-R	6-1	190	2-27-98	1	1	1.50	5	2	0	0	12	7	2	2	1	4	12	.159	.167	.156	9.00	3.00
Uribe, Josue	R-R	6-2	180	2-6-95	0	0	0.00	1	0	0	0	1	0	0	0	0	1	2	.000	.000	18.00	9.00
Valdez, Gabriel	R-R	6-2	185	10-25-95	2	2	4.05	9	2	0	0	20	18	11	9	0	1	19	.237	.107	.313	8.55	0.45
Whitley, Forrest	R-R	6-7	240	9-15-97	1	1	7.36	4	2	0	0	7	8	6	6	0	3	13	.267	.333	.238	15.95	3.68
Winkelman, Alex	L-L	6-2	180	2-8-94	0	0	0.00	2	1	0	0	7	4	0	0	0	1	9	.167	.000	.286	11.57	1.29

Fielding

C: Benavente 7, Campos 17, Heras 6, Marquez 9, Martinez 16, Toribio 8, Vasquez 21. **1B:** Luciano 25, Sieber 7, Vasquez 2, Westmoreland 19. **2B:** Matute 21, Mauricio 3, Pelletier 13, Pineda 18. **3B:** Beltre 14, Franco 23, Matute 1, Pineda 1, Westmoreland 14. **SS:** Jimenez 5, Mauricio 40, Pineda 7, van der Meer 2. **OF:** Amador 36, Benjamin 15, Celestino 16, Lorenzo 18, Machado 23, Muriel 23, Pineda 36, Pineda 1, Westmoreland 3.

DSL ASTROS

DOMINICAN SUMMER LEAGUE   ROOKIE

Batting	B-T	HT	WT	DOB	AVG	vLH	vRH	G	AB	R	H	2B	3B	HR	RBI	BB	HBP	SH	SF	SO	SB	CS	SLG	OBP
Alvarez, Alvaro	R-R	6-0	175	11-23-97	.105	—	—	25	57	7	6	1	0	1	6	9	2	0	0	21	0	0	.175	.250
Alvarez, Yordan	L-L	6-5	225	6-27-97	.341	.000	.357	16	44	7	15	2	1	1	4	12	0	0	1	7	2	1	.500	.474
Angarita, Alfredo	B-R	5-10	155	11-16-96	.207	.190	.212	55	174	31	36	3	3	1	12	41	4	4	3	37	18	9	.276	.365
Benavente, Brandon	B-R	5-10	200	9-3-97	.152	.167	.148	13	33	3	5	0	0	0	3	7	2	1	1	3	0	1	.152	.326
Benjamin, Jose	R-R	6-2	170	12-16-95	.257	.182	.277	42	152	25	39	9	0	2	24	18	7	0	4	29	8	6	.355	.354
Canelon, Carlos	R-R	5-11	170	12-14-94	.238	.375	.195	36	101	13	24	6	0	0	13	24	4	3	0	14	4	0	.297	.403
Caraballo, Samir	R-R	5-9	160	9-12-98	.228	—	—	46	167	19	38	8	0	0	17	14	4	3	9	45	9	5	.275	.303
Carrillo, Jose	R-R	6-0	165	1-24-98	.171	—	—	31	82	10	14	3	1	0	7	10	2	0	1	10	4	2	.232	.274
Castellanos, Norberto	L-L	6-0	185	12-3-93	.172	.182	.170	25	58	9	10	0	0	1	7	18	1	0	1	11	2	0	.224	.372
Castillo, Gerry	B-R	5-10	170	10-3-97	.103	.200	.088	26	39	3	4	0	0	0	0	8	0	0	0	13	0	0	.154	.255
Celestino, Gilberto	R-R	6-1	180	2-13-99	.279	.235	.286	38	136	22	38	9	3	2	17	25	1	0	3	29	14	9	.434	.388
Chavez, Euclides	L-L	6-1	170	7-1-97	.295	.000	.310	15	44	3	13	2	1	0	2	1	1	0	0	10	1	1	.386	.326
Coronel, Luis	B-R	5-11	150	7-11-97	.154	.000	.182	9	13	3	2	0	0	0	1	5	0	0	0	3	3	.154	.389
Cortez, Cesar	R-R	6-0	165	4-1-99	.228	.258	.220	48	149	24	34	6	4	0	15	23	4	6	2	30	9	3	.322	.343
De Leon, Angel	R-R	6-1	170	5-26-96	.213	.267	.201	52	164	21	35	9	4	2	27	35	3	1	2	46	5	4	.354	.358
Figueroa, Darlin	R-L	5-11	170	9-9-95	.136	.077	.161	22	44	6	6	2	1	0	3	4	0	1	0	13	1	1	.227	.208

Batting	B-T	HT	WT	DOB	AVG	vLH	vRH	G	AB	R	H	2B	3B	HR	RBI	BB	HBP	SH	SF	SO	SB	CS	SLG	OBP
Garcia, Michael	R-R	6-3	180	9-10-97	.109	—	—	18	46	1	5	0	0	1	3	1	2	0	0	18	0	0	.174	.163
Guzman, Eduardo	R-R	5-10	170	12-6-94	.156	—	—	18	32	2	5	0	0	0	1	2	1	0	0	11	0	0	.156	.229
Heras, Bernardo	B-R	6-0	180	11-3-95	.247	.286	.242	30	73	8	18	3	0	0	11	16	2	1	0	7	0	1	.288	.396
Hernandez, Jose	R-R	6-5	201	12-4-95	.222	.222	.222	26	72	10	16	1	0	2	11	8	6	1	2	24	3	0	.319	.341
Hernandez, Jose	R-R	6-3	185	3-12-96	.182	—	—	10	22	7	4	1	0	0	6	7	1	0	1	4	3	0	.227	.387
Infante, Juan	R-R	6-1	185	11-9-96	.164	.273	.143	35	67	8	11	3	2	0	6	8	2	0	1	12	3	1	.269	.269
Jimenez, Ronny	R-R	6-6	185	9-19-94	.230	.283	.210	56	191	35	44	7	3	1	17	27	4	1	4	39	6	3	.314	.332
Lucas, Felix	R-R	6-3	195	3-27-97	.250	.250	.250	16	52	7	13	1	0	1	3	5	1	0	0	22	0	1	.327	.328
Marquez, Orlando	R-R	5-10	180	3-12-96	.160	.077	.177	22	75	11	12	4	1	2	14	9	2	1	2	12	2	0	.320	.261
Martinez, Hector	R-R	6-1	185	7-6-98	.224	.050	.248	55	165	29	37	7	2	4	15	33	5	0	1	49	10	2	.364	.368
Martis, Renaigel	L-L	6-2	170	11-26-97	.258	.333	.247	39	97	13	25	2	3	3	14	20	1	1	0	27	8	4	.433	.390
Medina, Fredy	R-R	5-10	160	9-26-97	.267	1.000	.154	7	15	1	4	0	0	0	4	3	0	0	0	7	0	2	.267	.389
Miranda, Nicolas	R-R	5-10	160	12-9-96	.250	.237	.255	59	204	37	51	9	2	1	23	37	2	6	1	35	9	2	.328	.369
Mota, Vicente	R-R	6-3	195	6-8-94	.246	.333	.230	46	118	20	29	6	1	4	16	16	6	0	2	46	6	3	.415	.359
Moya, Kendy	R-R	5-10	150	12-4-98	.223	.167	.230	58	179	33	40	8	3	0	17	42	5	1	0	43	9	8	.302	.385
Peralta, Anardo	B-R	5-11	170	5-11-96	.000	.000	.000	7	13	3	0	0	0	0	0	2	0	0	0	6	0	0	.000	.133
Perez, Kelvin	R-R	5-11	180	12-8-98	.143	1.000	.100	14	21	1	3	0	0	0	1	1	0	1	5	2	0	.143	.208
Pineda, Juan	R-R	5-10	145	1-31-98	.314	.250	.333	11	35	3	11	2	0	0	6	2	1	0	3	7	0	1	.371	.341
Rafael, Ronny	R-R	6-2	185	10-14-97	.190	.138	.206	43	126	15	24	4	1	1	10	18	9	5	0	55	5	4	.262	.333
Ramirez, Yeuris	R-R	6-0	170	11-28-98	.178	.286	.171	40	118	14	21	5	2	0	5	18	5	1	0	38	11	2	.254	.312
Rodriguez, Anthony	R-R	6-2	195	7-23-96	.170	.043	.190	55	165	9	28	0	3	0	20	18	4	3	2	46	2	3	.273	.265
Rodriguez, Ramiro	L-L	5-10	145	2-2-98	.222	.143	.233	58	180	34	40	4	6	3	25	31	9	6	3	26	4	6	.361	.359
Sanchez-galan, Ozziel	R-R	5-11	160	10-30-97	.171	.182	.169	36	105	21	18	7	0	1	12	20	5	3	0	30	5	1	.267	.331
Sierra, Anibal	R-R	6-1	190	2-15-94	.316	.222	.344	23	79	17	25	5	2	2	11	18	4	0	0	20	3	4	.506	.465
Tejada, Nestor	L-L	5-11	175	4-17-97	.208	.167	.216	36	106	16	22	5	4	1	16	21	7	5	0	27	1	1	.358	.373
Tejeda, Angel	L-L	6-0	168	1-27-97	.296	.286	.299	45	152	19	45	8	1	0	16	22	3	3	1	29	7	6	.362	.393
Urdaneta, Ronaldo	B-R	5-10	155	11-18-98	.195	.182	.197	49	149	20	29	5	1	0	8	19	2	2	0	41	16	5	.242	.294
Valdez, Enmanuel	L-R	5-9	171	12-28-98	.245	—	—	55	192	32	47	16	3	5	34	27	5	0	7	35	5	1	.438	.342

Pitching	B-T	HT	WT	DOB	W	L	ERA	G	GS	CG	SV	IP	H	R	ER	HR	BB	SO	AVG	vLH	vRH	K/9	BB/9
Arias, Johnson	R-R	6-1	178	4-3-94	3	0	4.05	15	3	0	4	40	33	19	18	2	25	22	.232	.267	.216	4.95	5.63
Bernaez, Jesus	R-R	6-0	170	5-6-97	1	4	5.11	12	0	0	1	25	22	17	14	3	21	21	.237	.120	.279	7.66	4.38
Blanco, Ronel	R-R	6-0	180	8-31-93	7	1	2.40	12	0	0	0	45	32	14	12	1	15	52	.194	.256	.172	10.40	3.00
Bojorquez, Gerardo	R-R	6-3	195	10-23-97	3	5	4.93	14	6	0	0	49	54	33	27	5	18	39	.274	.205	.315	7.11	3.28
Bravo, Jose	R-R	6-3	185	6-10-97	2	2	2.90	7	6	1	0	31	37	12	10	2	2	25	—	—	—	7.26	0.58
Caraballo, Jheyson	R-R	6-0	170	10-16-95	3	0	2.85	13	8	0	3	54	38	22	17	2	11	46	.199	.234	.188	7.71	1.84
Castro, Luis	R-R	6-0	190	5-11-95	3	3	4.86	12	2	0	0	37	27	26	20	2	30	21	.203	.231	.191	5.11	7.30
Ceballos, Yeremi	L-L	6-2	165	12-21-98	2	1	0.79	19	0	0	1	34	21	6	3	0	18	30	.183	.250	.180	7.94	4.76
Collado, Willy	R-R	6-2	165	3-30-98	0	1	3.21	10	0	0	1	14	12	5	5	1	7	12	—	—	—	7.71	4.50
Corniel, Juan	R-R	6-2	175	1-2-96	0	4	3.12	12	6	0	1	40	28	22	14	2	24	36	.196	.205	.192	8.03	5.36
Corniel, Robert	R-R	6-3	190	6-23-95	1	2	3.00	18	0	0	0	36	29	17	12	2	19	29	.223	.182	.237	7.25	4.75
Cuevas, Juan	R-R	6-0	195	5-4-94	6	5	2.81	17	0	0	2	26	34	9	8	2	3	18	.312	.276	.325	6.31	1.05
2-team total (1 Marlins)					6	5	2.67	18	0	0	2	27	34	9	8	2	4	18	—	—	—	6.00	1.33
Espinoza, Carlos	L-L	6-1	180	8-16-94	0	0	4.80	11	0	0	3	15	13	10	8	1	11	12	.236	.333	.217	7.20	6.60
Fidel, Edwin	R-R	6-3	200	12-14-94	1	0	1.69	9	6	0	1	27	13	9	5	0	23	29	.146	.208	.123	9.79	7.76
Florencio, Harlen	R-R	6-4	210	9-24-95	0	0	27.00	1	0	0	0	1	3	3	3	0	2	0	.600	.667	.500	0.00	18.00
Frontado, Yulian	R-R	6-3	175	12-29-97	2	1	3.35	13	6	0	0	48	49	21	18	4	16	28	.274	.256	.279	5.21	2.98
Garcia, Freylin	R-R	6-3	170	12-6-97	1	0	1.86	5	1	0	0	9	2	2	0		4	4	.265	.167	.318	3.72	3.72
Garcia, Junior	R-R	6-3	175	1-29-96	0	1	4.32	3	2	0	0	8	14	4	4	0	4	7	.400	.278	.529	7.56	4.32
Gonzalez, Diosward	R-R	6-0	180	7-7-95	1	3	4.44	14	12	0	1	51	57	40	25	4	22	50	.277	.321	.261	8.88	3.91
Hernandez, Jose Antonio	R-R	6-0	165	6-18-99	0	0	0.73	8	0	0	1	12	7	1	1	0	9	8	.163	.231	.133	5.84	6.57
Javier, Christopher	R-R	6-4	170	7-16-98	0	0	9.00	2	0	0	0	2	3	2	2	1	2	1	.429	.000	.500	4.50	9.00
Kery, Adoni	R-R	6-0	170	2-18-96	0	0	0.00	2	0	0	0	2	3	0	0	0	3	2	.375	.500	.25	9.00	13.50
Lopez, Juan	R-R	6-2	175	6-25-97	2	0	3.24	12	4	0	4	33	27	13	12	0	25	33	.220	.162	.244	8.91	6.75
Madera, Ezequiel	R-R	6-2	180	3-22-96	0	2	7.43	6	3	0	0	13	19	16	11	0	11	7	—	—	—	4.73	7.43
Matos, Angel	R-R	6-2	225	7-21-97	0	0	4.26	6	0	0	0	6	4	3	3	0	8	3	.200	.000	.235	9.95	11.37
Matos, Miguel	R-R	5-11	165	9-29-96	3	1	4.10	11	0	0	0	26	22	15	12	1	18	30	.232	.385	.174	10.25	6.15
Mejias, Christian	R-R	6-0	160	5-19-99	1	0	3.00	2	0	0	0	3	2	1	1	1	3	2	.200	.000	.250	6.00	9.00
Melendez, Cristofer	R-R	6-3	170	9-16-97	4	2	3.86	14	0	0	2	35	34	17	15	1	18	35	.252	.244	.256	9.00	4.63
Navas, Javier	L-L	5-11	165	2-3-98	2	2	2.79	12	7	0	1	42	35	19	13	0	23	45	.233	.333	.227	9.64	4.93
Orta, Jose	L-L	5-10	150	5-22-99	0	1	19.29	4	0	0	0	2	4	5	5	0	7	4	.400	.500	.375	15.43	27.00
Paulino, Hansel	R-R	6-2	170	1-3-96	0	0	2.25	3	3	0	0	12	5	3	3	0	4	10	.132	.231	.080	7.50	3.00
Peralta, Kilvio	R-R	6-3	190	3-6-97	2	1	4.38	14	1	0	1	37	36	23	18	1	24	30	.252	.317	.225	7.30	5.84
Perdomo, Carlos	L-L	6-1	167	4-25-98	4	0	3.74	13	0	0	2	34	26	16	14	1	22	27	.220	.222	.220	7.22	5.88
Pirela, Gabriel	R-R	6-1	165	5-1-94	3	1	2.73	17	0	0	1	26	26	11	8	1	12	20	—	—	—	6.84	4.10
Quintin, Yonathan	R-R	6-1	170	11-18-96	3	1	1.74	12	0	0	1	21	11	4	4	1	4	11	.155	.250	.106	4.79	1.74
Ramirez, Yohan	R-R	6-4	190	5-6-95	1	1	2.39	10	4	0	1	26	20	9	7	0	12	26	.196	.268	.148	5.13	4.10
Ramos, Jose	R-R	6-1	160	8-4-96	2	0	0.00	3	0	0	1	11	7	2	0		6	13	.175	.100	.200	10.64	4.91
Reyes, Jean	R-R	6-0	180	12-1-97	0	0	0.00	2	0	0	0	3	4	0	0		2	4	.308	.000	.444	12.00	6.00
Richez, Michael	R-R	6-1	173	5-15-97	0	0	5.23	6	0	0	0	10	9	8	6	0	12	4	.231	.333	.185	3.48	10.45
Rodriguez, Leovanny	R-R	6-0	160	6-13-96	1	0	0.63	3	0	0	0	14	8	1	1	0	2	15	.157	.182	.162	9.42	1.26
Rodriguez, Nivaldo	R-R	6-0	170	4-16-97	1	0	1.17	5	0	0	0	15	6	2	1	0	4	8	.194	.182	.200	9.39	4.70
Rosado, Cesar	R-R	6-1	172	6-22-96	2	3	0.82	5	3	0	0	11	11	5	1	0	5	11	.244	.333	.212	9.00	4.09
Sambo, Jacques	R-R	6-2	185	7-27-98	1	0	12.00	8	0	0	0	9	8	12	12	0	11	8	.258	.400	.231	8.00	11.00

HOUSTON ASTROS

Pitching	B-T	HT	WT	DOB	W	L	ERA	G	GS	CG	SV	IP	H	R	ER	HR	BB	SO	AVG	vLH	vRH	K/9	BB/9
Sepulveda, Maikel	L-L	6-1	165	12-31-96	2	0	1.96	10	7	0	0	41	29	11	9	1	18	30	—	—	—	6.53	3.92
Tejada, Felipe	R-R	6-1	190	2-27-98	1	0	3.02	10	10	0	0	42	24	15	14	1	20	33	.174	.075	.214	7.13	4.32
Uribe, Asael	R-R	6-3	160	5-4-96	3	4	3.38	14	5	0	0	40	38	22	15	0	25	29	.244	.254	.237	6.53	5.63
Villegas, Francisco	L-L	6-2	175	8-31-97	0	3	2.81	12	8	0	0	42	38	22	13	2	22	37	.238	.162	.260	7.99	4.75
Zapata, Cosme	R-R	6-1	175	10-23-96	0	2	6.23	6	0	0	2	9	6	8	6	0	8	6	.188	.300	.136	6.23	8.31

Fielding

C: Alvarez 17, Benavente 12, Canelon 30, Carrillo 29, Castillo 26, Heras 19, Marquez 21, Mota 14, Perez 12, Rodriguez 1, Sanchez 5, Urdaneta 1, Valdez 1. **1B:** Alvarez 4, Benjamin 1, Castellanos 19, De Leon 40, Heras 1, Hernandez 1, Hernandez 21, Hernandez 2, Infante 1, Jimenez 21, Lucas 12, Mota 14, Peralta 2, Perez 2, Pineda 4, Rodriguez 26. **2B:** Angarita 24, Canelon 1, Caraballo 17, Carrillo 1, Cortez 1, Guzman 5, Guzman 7, Heras 1, Medina 1, Miranda 20, Moya 36, Peralta 1, Pineda 3, Ramirez 3, Sanchez-galan 5, Urdaneta 10, Valdez 29. **3B:** Alvarez 1, Caraballo 9, Garcia 12, Heras 10, Jimenez 21, Medina 5, Miranda 35, Moya 11, Peralta 3, Pineda 7, Ramirez 16, Rodriguez 23, Sanchez-galan 3, Urdaneta 14. **SS:** Angarita 17, Benavente 1, Caraballo 23, Guzman 4, Jimenez 8, Medina 1, Miranda 1, Moya 11, Ramirez 17, Sanchez-galan 29, Urdaneta 26, Sierra 20. **OF:** Angarita 12, Benjamin 33, Canelon 2, Castellanos 5, Celestino 37, Chavez 13, Coronel 7, Cortez 45, Figueroa 11, Hernandez 1, Hernandez 2, Hernandez 3, Infante 23, Jimenez 9, Martinez 52, Martis 31, Mota 4, Moya 5, Rafael 42, Rodriguez 58, Tejeda 72.

Kansas City Royals

SEASON IN A SENTENCE: The Royals followed their World Series championship with a season filled with injuries to top players, an anemic offense that resulted and their worst record since the 2012 season. Still, it was the Royals' fourth straight .500 or better record—the franchise's first such streak since 1975-80.

HIGH POINT: The Royals were in first place as late as mid-June and rode their bullpen to a nine-game August winning streak, part of a 20-9 month of August that got the team back into playoff contention. Royals pitchers limited opponents to a .232/.290/.341 line in August led by lefty Danny Duffy, who won five of six decisions and struck out 39 in 43 innings.

LOW POINT: The Royals entered a Sept. 12-15 four-game series at home against Oakland—which was 20 games under .500—just four games out of the wild-card race with 20 games to go. Four days later, they'd been swept by a combined score of 43-12, and trailed 14-0 in the finale before a five-run ninth. One of the losses included another blown save by Joakim Soria, the free-agent pickup who was on the mound 13 times when the Royals gave up the go-ahead or tying run.

NOTABLE ROOKIES: Injuries provided playing time for rookies all over the roster. Whit Merrifield and Cheslor Cuthbert played fairly regular roles at second and third base, Cuthbert replacing Mike Moustakas, who had knee surgery in May. Raul Adalberto Mondesi struggled in his stint at second base in 47 games.

KEY TRANSACTIONS: Signing Soria for a three-year, $25 million as a setup man didn't pay off, as he went 5-8, 4.05. The Royals missed left fielder Alex Gordon (wrist injury) for a month and tried two patchwork moves in left field, acquiring Billy Burns in July from Oakland and Daniel Nava in August to add outfield depth.

DOWN ON THE FARM: Double-A Northwest Arkansas and Rookie-level Burlington reached their league playoffs, but Royals domestic affiliates struggled overall, with a 342-414 mark. Lefthander Matt Strahm, who provided a September big league spark in the bullpen, and righty Josh Staumont, who finished second in the minors in strikeouts (167 in 123.1 innings), powered the Naturals' rotation. Meanwhile, 2011 first-round pick Bubba Starling endured a difficult season, hitting just .183/.236/.298 with 145 strikeouts between Northwest Arkansas and Triple-A Omaha.

OPENING DAY PAYROLL: $131,487,125 (15th)

PLAYERS OF THE YEAR

BRAD GLAZIER

MAJOR LEAGUE	MINOR LEAGUE
Danny Duffy	**Hunter Dozier**
lhp	3b
12-3, 3.51	(Double-A/Triple-A)
188 SO in 179.2 IP	.296/.366/.533
5th in AL in SO/9	23 HR, 75 RBI

ORGANIZATION LEADERS

BATTING   *Minimum 250 AB

MAJORS

*	AVG	Cheslor Cuthbert	.274
*	OPS	Kendrys Morales	.795
	HR	Kendrys Morales	30
	RBI	Eric Hosmer	104

MINORS

*	AVG	Hunter Dozier, NW Arkansas, Omaha	.296
*	OBP	Hunter Dozier, NW Arkansas, Omaha	.366
*	SLG	Hunter Dozier, NW Arkansas, Omaha	.533
*	OPS	Hunter Dozier, NW Arkansas, Omaha	.899
	R	Jorge Bonifacio, Omaha	82
		Corey Toups, Wilmington, NW Arkansas	82
	H	Samir Duenez, Lexington, Wilm., NW Arkansas	151
	TB	Hunter Dozier, NW Arkansas, Omaha	259
	2B	Hunter Dozier, NW Arkansas, Omaha	44
	3B	Corey Toups, Wilmington, NW Arkansas	7
	HR	Hunter Dozier, NW Arkansas, Omaha	23
	RBI	Samir Duenez, Lexington, Wilm., NW Arkansas	100
	BB	Cody Jones, Lexington, Wilmington	73
	SO	Brandon Downes, Wilmington, Omaha	175
	SB	Terrance Gore, NW Arkansas	44

PITCHING   #Minimum 75 IP

MAJORS

	W	Danny Duffy	12
#	ERA	Danny Duffy	3.51
	SO	Danny Duffy	188
	SV	Wade Davis	27

MINORS

	W	Jake Junis, NW Arkansas, Omaha	10
		Corey Ray, Lexington, Wilmington	10
	L	Ashton Goudeau, Wilmington, NW Arkansas	17
#	ERA	Yender Caramo, Omaha, NW Arkansas	2.45
	G	Kevin McCarthy, NW Arkansas, Omaha	47
	GS	4 players	27
	SV	Kevin McCarthy, NW Arkansas, Omaha	16
	IP	Eric Skoglund, NW Arkansas	156.3
	BB	Josh Staumont, Wilmington, NW Arkansas	104
	SO	Josh Staumont, Wilmington, NW Arkansas	167
#	AVG	Eric Skoglund, NW Arkansas	.23

2016 PERFORMANCE

General Manager: Dayton Moore. **Farm Director:** Ronnie Richardson. **Scouting Director:** Lonnie Goldberg.

Class	Team	League	W	L	PCT	Finish	Manager
Majors	Kansas City Royals	American	81	81	.500	10th (15)	Ned Yost
Triple-A	Omaha Storm Chasers	Pacific Coast	58	82	.414	16th (16)	Brian Poldberg
Double-A	NW Arkansas Naturals	Texas	65	75	.464	6th (8)	Vance Wilson
High A	Wilmington Blue Rocks	Carolina	54	84	.391	7th (8)	Jamie Quirk
Low A	Lexington Legends	South Atlantic	52	87	.374	14th (14)	Omar Ramirez
Rookie	Idaho Falls Chukars	Pioneer	40	36	.526	3rd (8)	Justin Gemoll
Rookie	Burlington Royals	Appalachian	42	26	.618	1st (10)	Scott Thorman
Rookie	Royals	Arizona	31	24	.564	t-2nd (14)	Darryl Kennedy
Overall 2016 Minor League Record			342	414	.452	27th (30)	

ORGANIZATION STATISTICS

KANSAS CITY ROYALS
AMERICAN LEAGUE

Batting	B-T	HT	WT	DOB	AVG	vLH	vRH	G	AB	R	H	2B	3B	HR	RBI	BB	HBP	SH	SF	SO	SB	CS	SLG	OBP
Burns, Billy	B-R	5-9	170	8-30-89	.243	.353	.150	24	37	7	9	0	0	0	1	0	2	0	1	7	3	2	.243	.275
2-team total (73 Oakland)					.235	—	—	97	311	39	73	11	4	0	13	10	6	3	2	37	17	5	.296	.271
Butera, Drew	R-R	6-1	200	8-9-83	.285	.179	.316	55	123	18	35	10	1	4	16	8	0	2	0	36	0	0	.480	.328
Cain, Lorenzo	R-R	6-2	205	4-13-86	.287	.371	.263	103	397	56	114	19	1	9	56	31	2	0	4	84	14	5	.408	.339
Colon, Christian	R-R	5-10	185	5-14-89	.231	.234	.230	54	147	13	34	6	0	1	13	11	2	1	0	31	0	1	.293	.294
Cruz, Tony	R-R	5-11	215	8-18-86	.000	—	.000	4	4	0	0	0	0	0	0	1	0	0	1	3	0	0	.000	.000
Cuthbert, Cheslor	R-R	6-1	190	11-16-92	.274	.320	.258	128	475	49	130	28	1	12	46	32	0	1	2	96	2	0	.413	.318
Dozier, Hunter	R-R	6-4	220	8-22-91	.211	.125	.273	8	19	4	4	1	0	1	2	0	0	0	0	8	0	0	.263	.286
Dyson, Jarrod	L-R	5-10	165	8-15-84	.278	.379	.267	107	299	46	83	14	8	1	25	26	3	8	1	39	30	7	.388	.340
Eibner, Brett	R-R	6-4	225	12-2-88	.231	.323	.170	26	78	11	18	6	0	3	10	6	0	1	0	23	0	0	.423	.286
2-team total (44 Oakland)					.193	—	—	70	187	21	36	10	1	6	22	19	0	1	1	50	0	2	.353	.266
Escobar, Alcides	R-R	6-1	185	12-16-86	.261	.222	.273	162	637	57	166	24	6	7	55	27	3	10	5	96	17	4	.350	.292
Fuentes, Reymond	L-L	6-0	160	2-12-91	.317	—	.317	13	41	2	13	1	0	0	5	3	0	0	0	2	3	0	.341	.364
Gordon, Alex	L-R	6-1	220	2-10-84	.220	.214	.223	128	445	62	98	16	2	17	40	52	8	0	1	148	8	1	.380	.312
Gore, Terrance	R-R	5-7	165	6-8-91	.000	.000	.000	17	3	6	0	0	0	0	0	0	0	0	0	1	11	2	.000	.000
Hosmer, Eric	L-L	6-4	225	10-24-89	.266	.233	.283	158	605	80	161	24	1	25	104	57	1	0	4	132	5	3	.433	.328
Infante, Omar	R-R	5-11	195	12-26-81	.239	.241	.238	39	134	16	32	9	1	0	11	9	0	2	4	23	0	0	.321	.279
Merrifield, Whit	R-R	6-0	195	1-24-89	.283	.351	.261	81	311	44	88	22	3	2	29	19	0	1	1	72	8	3	.392	.323
Mondesi, Raul A.	B-R	6-1	185	7-27-95	.185	.146	.202	47	135	16	25	1	3	2	13	6	2	6	0	48	9	1	.281	.231
Morales, Kendrys	B-R	6-1	225	6-20-83	.263	.330	.231	154	558	65	147	24	0	30	93	48	7	0	5	120	0	4	.468	.327
Moustakas, Mike	L-R	6-0	215	9-11-88	.240	.286	.229	27	104	12	25	6	0	7	13	9	0	0	1	13	0	1	.500	.301
Nava, Daniel	B-L	5-11	200	2-22-83	.091	.000	.100	9	11	1	1	1	0	0	1	0	0	0	0	4	0	0	.182	.167
2-team total (45 Los Angeles)					.223	—	—	54	104	11	29	6	0	1	13	10	5	0	3	30	0	0	.292	.297
Orlando, Paulo	R-R	6-2	210	11-1-85	.302	.307	.300	128	457	52	138	24	4	5	43	13	7	3	3	105	14	3	.405	.329
Perez, Salvador	R-R	6-3	240	5-10-90	.247	.247	.247	139	514	57	127	28	2	22	64	22	8	0	2	119	0	0	.438	.288

Pitching	B-T	HT	WT	DOB	W	L	ERA	G	GS	CG	SV	IP	H	R	ER	HR	BB	SO	AVG	vLH	vRH	K/9	BB/9
Alexander, Scott	L-L	6-2	190	7-10-89	0	0	3.32	17	0	0	0	19	24	7	7	1	7	16	.316	.353	.286	7.58	3.32
Davis, Wade	R-R	6-5	225	9-7-85	2	1	1.87	45	0	0	27	43	33	9	9	0	16	47	.210	.200	.221	9.76	3.32
Duffy, Danny	L-L	6-3	205	12-21-88	12	3	3.51	42	26	1	0	180	163	71	70	27	42	188	.241	.183	.252	9.42	2.10
Flynn, Brian	L-L	6-7	250	4-19-90	1	2	2.60	36	1	0	0	55	38	19	16	5	23	44	.198	.191	.202	7.16	3.74
Gee, Dillon	R-R	6-1	205	4-28-86	8	9	4.68	33	14	0	0	125	146	67	65	24	37	89	.291	.303	.280	6.41	2.66
Herrera, Kelvin	R-R	5-10	200	12-31-89	2	6	2.75	72	0	0	12	72	57	23	22	6	12	86	.214	.206	.223	10.75	1.50
Hochevar, Luke	R-R	6-5	225	9-15-83	2	3	3.86	40	0	0	0	37	31	17	16	6	9	40	.226	.164	.268	9.64	2.17
Kennedy, Ian	R-R	6-0	200	12-19-84	11	11	3.68	33	33	0	0	196	173	81	80	33	66	184	.236	.224	.249	8.46	3.04
McCarthy, Kevin	R-R	6-3	200	2-22-92	1	0	6.48	10	0	0	0	8	11	8	6	1	5	8	.314	.333	.294	7.56	5.40
Medlen, Kris	B-R	5-10	190	10-7-85	1	3	7.77	6	6	0	0	24	30	25	21	2	20	18	.309	.288	.333	6.66	7.40
Mills, Alec	R-R	6-4	190	11-30-91	0	0	13.50	3	0	0	0	3	5	5	5	0	5	4	.231	.286	.167	10.80	13.50
Moylan, Peter	R-R	6-2	225	12-2-78	2	0	3.43	50	0	0	0	45	42	19	17	4	16	34	.251	.333	.218	6.85	3.22
Pounders, Brooks	R-R	6-5	265	9-26-90	2	1	9.24	13	0	0	0	13	19	13	13	6	3	13	.352	.333	.370	9.24	2.13
Soria, Joakim	R-R	6-3	200	5-18-84	5	8	4.05	70	0	0	1	67	70	31	30	10	27	68	.271	.246	.297	9.18	3.65
Strahm, Matt	R-L	6-3	185	11-12-91	2	2	1.23	21	0	0	0	22	13	4	3	0	11	30	.173	.292	.118	12.27	4.50
Vargas, Jason	L-L	6-0	215	2-2-83	0	0	2.25	3	3	0	0	12	8	3	3	1	3	11	.182	.333	.158	8.25	2.25
Ventura, Yordano	R-R	6-0	195	6-3-91	11	12	4.45	32	32	2	0	186	190	96	92	23	78	144	.263	.249	.275	6.97	3.77
Volquez, Edinson	R-R	6-0	220	7-3-83	10	11	5.37	34	34	0	0	189	217	124	113	23	76	139	.286	.284	.288	6.61	3.61
Wang, Chien-Ming	R-R	6-4	225	3-31-80	6	0	4.22	38	0	0	0	53	60	27	25	6	18	30	.286	.232	.333	5.06	3.04
Young, Chris	R-R	6-10	255	5-25-79	3	9	6.19	34	13	0	1	89	104	63	61	28	43	94	.291	.340	.251	9.54	4.36

Fielding

Catcher	PCT	G	PO	A	E	DP	PB
Butera	.981	51	288	16	6	1	1
Cruz	1.000	4	9	0	0	0	1
Perez	.996	128	989	77	4	4	5

First Base	PCT	G	PO	A	E	DP
Butera	1.000	2	2	0	0	0
Hosmer	.995	154	1240	74	6	118
Merrifield	1.000	1	9	0	0	1

	PCT	G	PO	A	E	DP
Morales	1.000	7	46	3	0	4
Nava	1.000	6	17	2	0	2
Perez	1.000	1	3	0	0	0

Second Base	PCT	G	PO	A	E	DP
Colon	1.000	32	45	94	0	18
Infante	.977	39	66	102	4	17
Merrifield	.984	65	92	156	4	39
Mondesi	.983	42	75	96	3	23

Third Base	PCT	G	PO	A	E	DP
Colon	.967	15	8	21	1	0
Cuthbert	.948	127	77	216	16	15

	PCT	G	PO	A	E	DP
Merrifield	.900	5	1	8	1	2
Moustakas	.972	26	29	40	2	4

Shortstop	PCT	G	PO	A	E	DP
Colon	1.000	4	1	2	0	0
Escobar	.979	162	221	426	14	95
Mondesi	.889	7	3	5	1	1

Outfield	PCT	G	PO	A	E	DP
Burns	1.000	17	20	0	0	0

	PCT	G	PO	A	E	DP
Cain	.989	101	257	3	3	0
Dozier	1.000	7	13	0	0	0
Dyson	.990	95	196	11	2	0
Eibner	1.000	18	39	0	0	0
Fuentes	.960	12	23	1	1	0
Gordon	.991	126	222	6	2	1
Gore	1.000	2	3	0	0	0
Merrifield	1.000	16	28	3	0	2
Morales	1.000	5	8	0	0	0
Orlando	.984	122	235	6	4	2

OMAHA STORM CHASERS

TRIPLE-A

PACIFIC COAST LEAGUE

Batting	B-T	HT	WT	DOB	AVG	vLH	vRH	G	AB	R	H	2B	3B	HR	RBI	BB	HBP	SH	SF	SO	SB	CS	SLG	OBP
Barnes, Clint	R-R	6-1	200	3-6-79	.204	.233	.191	29	98	10	20	7	0	1	7	5	2	1	1	18	0	0	.306	.255
Bonifacio, Jorge	R-R	6-1	195	6-4-93	.277	.272	.279	134	495	82	137	22	6	19	86	51	7	3	2	130	6	2	.461	.351
Burns, Billy	B-R	5-9	170	8-30-89	.200	.000	.500	2	5	0	1	0	0	0	0	0	0	0	0	4	0	0	.200	.200
2-team total (10 Nashville)					.283	—	—	12	46	7	13	1	0	0	4	2	0	1	0	16	4	0	.304	.313
Cain, Lorenzo	R-R	6-2	205	4-13-86	.375	.000	.429	2	8	0	3	0	0	0	0	0	0	0	0	1	0	0	.375	.375
Calixte, Orlando	R-R	5-11	180	2-3-92	.265	.245	.275	88	332	48	88	17	5	9	29	28	0	5	2	68	5	4	.428	.320
Coleman, Dusty	R-R	6-2	205	4-20-87	.239	.214	.247	56	188	26	45	11	2	5	21	12	3	4	0	58	6	3	.399	.296
Colon, Christian	R-R	5-10	185	5-14-89	.273	.261	.278	19	77	9	21	5	0	1	5	6	1	1	0	11	2	0	.377	.333
Cruz, Tony	R-R	5-11	215	8-18-86	.264	.258	.267	92	318	32	84	18	0	7	55	41	1	0	3	74	2	1	.387	.347
Cuthbert, Cheslor	R-R	6-1	190	11-16-92	.333	.292	.348	24	93	15	31	4	1	7	28	11	1	0	2	14	0	1	.624	.402
De San Miguel, Allan	R-R	5-9	205	2-1-88	.200	.250	.167	10	30	6	6	3	0	0	2	1	1	0	1	5	0	0	.300	.242
Decker, Cody	R-R	5-11	217	1-17-87	.278	.333	.250	7	18	4	5	1	0	3	5	3	0	0	0	9	0	0	.833	.381
2-team total (14 Albuquerque)					.225	—	—	21	71	10	16	4	0	5	9	5	1	0	1	30	0	0	.493	.282
Diaz, Carlos	B-R	5-8	145	11-15-92	.133	.000	.286	6	15	1	2	0	0	0	0	0	0	0	0	1	0	0	.133	.133
Downes, Brandon	R-R	6-3	195	9-29-92	.308	.000	.333	5	13	2	4	2	0	0	1	0	0	0	0	5	0	0	.462	.357
Dozier, Hunter	R-R	6-4	220	8-22-91	.294	.367	.262	103	391	65	115	36	1	15	54	40	0	3		100	3	1	.506	.357
Dyson, Jarrod	L-R	5-10	165	8-15-84	.318	.429	.267	7	22	7	7	0	0	0	1	4	2	1	0	4	4	0	.318	.464
Eibner, Brett	R-R	6-4	225	12-2-88	.288	.311	.281	50	184	37	53	7	1	11	32	30	1	1	3	48	5	1	.516	.385
2-team total (4 Nashville)					.289	—	—	54	197	41	57	9	1	12	34	35	1	1	3	54	5	1	.528	.394
Evans, Zane	R-R	6-2	225	11-29-91	.250	.667	.111	4	12	2	3	0	0	0	1	0	0	0	0	0	0	0	.250	.308
Falu, Irving	B-R	5-9	185	6-6-83	.267	.186	.297	46	161	16	43	10	0	4	27	8	0	3		21	1	3	.404	.297
Franco, Angel	B-R	5-10	155	5-23-90	.220	.169	.246	68	209	20	46	9	4	1	15	14	1	9	0	32	0	0	.316	.272
Fuenmayor, Balbino	R-R	6-3	230	11-26-89	.291	.364	.253	101	358	27	104	23	0	6	42	17	3	0	3	77	0	0	.405	.325
Fuentes, Reymond	L-L	6-0	160	2-12-91	.254	.227	.267	65	240	32	61	9	3	0	14	23	4	1	4	62	17	5	.317	.325
Gordon, Alex	L-R	6-1	220	2-10-84	.429	.500	.000	2	7	0	3	0	0	0	3	0	0	0	0	0	0	0	.429	.600
Martinez, Jose	R-R	6-6	215	7-25-88	.298	.424	.259	37	141	18	42	10	0	3	18	14	1	0	4	24	2	0	.433	.356
2-team total (87 Memphis)					.278	—	—	124	442	52	123	28	1	11	60	39	2	1	5	74	11	1	.421	.336
Merrifield, Whit	R-R	6-0	195	1-24-89	.266	.200	.291	69	274	46	73	19	0	8	29	22	2	2	4	55	20	2	.423	.321
Mondesi, Raul A.	B-R	6-1	185	7-27-95	.304	.278	.316	14	56	9	17	2	4	1	9	2	4	1	0	19	5	0	.536	.328
Morin, Parker	L-R	5-11	195	7-2-91	.184	.214	.171	76	234	21	43	8	1	1	22	23	0	4	2	67	0	0	.239	.255
Nava, Daniel	B-L	5-11	200	2-22-83	.143	.200	.000	3	7	1	1	1	0	0	0	3	1	0	0	1	0	0	.286	.455
2-team total (22 Salt Lake)					.348	—	—	25	92	6	32	7	0	1	13	9	2	0	1	11	1	1	.457	.417
Pehl, Robert	R-R	6-1	205	9-23-92	.000	.000	.000	3	7	1	0	0	0	0	1	0	0	0	0	5	0	0	.000	.125
Snider, Travis	L-L	6-0	235	2-2-88	.245	.221	.257	84	277	36	68	16	2	3	29	39	2	1	3	63	0	1	.350	.340
Starling, Bubba	R-R	6-4	210	8-3-92	.181	.190	.177	47	166	14	30	8	2		17	7	0	2	1	64	1	0	.265	.213
Tolleson, Steve	R-R	5-11	185	11-1-83	.000	.000	.000	3	4	0	0	0	0	0	0	0	0	0	0	1	0	0	.000	.000
Torres, Ramon	B-R	5-11	170	1-22-93	.259	.286	.246	73	297	35	77	12	1	2	21	15	0	3	0	61	12	3	.327	.295
Villegas, Luis	R-R	5-10	170	12-2-92	.095	.100	.091	8	21	2	2	1	0	0	1	2	0	1		3	0	0	.143	.167

Pitching	B-T	HT	WT	DOB	W	L	ERA	G	GS	CG	SV	IP	H	R	ER	HR	BB	SO	AVG	vLH	vRH	K/9	BB/9
Alexander, Scott	L-L	6-2	190	7-10-89	2	0	3.00	22	0	0	1	30	32	16	10	2	10	24	.271	.231	.291	7.20	3.00
Almonte, Miguel	R-R	6-2	210	4-4-93	3	7	5.55	21	12	0	0	60	63	43	37	5	42	57	.274	.291	.258	8.55	6.30
Beal, Evan	R-R	6-5	195	8-2-93	0	0	4.50	2	0	0	0	4	4	2	2	1	2	3	.250	.333	.143	6.75	4.50
Beimel, Joe	L-L	6-3	205	4-19-77	0	0	4.30	12	0	0	0	15	20	8	7	1	6	6	.345	.304	.371	3.68	4.91
Binford, Christian	R-R	6-6	215	12-20-92	3	12	5.28	19	18	1	0	106	117	66	62	18	40	73	.281	.324	.251	6.22	3.41
Caramo, Yender	R-R	6-0	175	8-25-91	1	0	2.45	1	0	0	0	4	4	1	1	0	2	2	.308	.571	.000	4.91	0.00
Culver, Malcom	R-R	6-1	205	2-9-90	4	5	3.86	44	1	0	6	68	71	35	29	4	27	60	.268	.267	.268	7.98	3.59
Davis, Wade	R-R	6-5	225	9-7-85	0	0	0.00	2	0	0	0	2	2	0	0	0	3	3	.286	.333	.250	13.50	0.00
Duensing, Brian	L-L	6-0	200	2-22-83	1	0	3.10	12	0	0	2	16	7	7	0	5	19		.213	.219	.209	8.41	2.21
Dziedzic, Jonathan	R-L	6-1	190	2-4-91	5	10	4.05	26	25	0	0	140	134	77	63	12	63	107	.255	.235	.261	6.88	4.05
Edwards, Andrew	R-R	6-6	265	10-7-91	0	0	5.40	32	0	0	5	43	44	28	26	7	29	51	.267	.328	.234	10.59	6.02
Farrell, Luke	R-R	6-6	210	6-7-91	6	3	3.76	19	14	0	0	91	85	44	38	12	40	78	.249	.246	.253	7.71	3.96
Flynn, Brian	L-L	6-7	250	4-19-90	2	1	3.04	9	4	0	0	24	22	8	8	1	12	28	.247	.375	.200	10.65	4.56
Gee, Dillon	R-R	6-1	205	4-28-86	0	1	4.50	1	1	0	0	6	4	3	3	0	1	4	.182	.133	.286	6.00	1.50
Huff, David	L-L	6-1	210	8-22-84	1	1	4.18	12	0	0	0	24	29	11	11	3	2	29	.302	.333	.292	11.03	0.76
2-team total (6 Salt Lake)					2	3	5.68	18	6	0	1	52	71	34	33	8	11	52	—	—	—	8.94	1.89
Junis, Jake	R-R	6-2	215	9-16-92	1	3	7.20	6	6	0	0	30	39	24	24	6	7	26	.320	.290	.350	7.80	2.10
Lannan, John	L-L	6-4	235	9-27-84	7	8	5.24	25	19	1	0	132	166	91	77	15	43	55	.312	.267	.329	3.74	2.92
McCarthy, Kevin	R-R	6-3	200	2-22-92	2	4	2.97	25	0	0	5	33	28	15	11	4	16	30	.230	.273	.194	8.10	4.32
Medlen, Kris	B-R	5-10	190	10-7-85	2	0	3.69	8	5	0	0	20	25	20	19	9	7	18	.298	.263	.326	8.24	3.20

KANSAS CITY ROYALS

Pitching	B-T	HT	WT	DOB	W	L	ERA	G	GS	CG	SV	IP	H	R	ER	HR	BB	SO	AVG	vLH	vRH	K/9	BB/9
Mills, Alec	R-R	6-4	190	11-30-91	4	3	4.19	12	11	0	0	58	62	29	27	8	19	54	.272	.257	.285	8.38	2.95
Minor, Mike	R-L	6-4	210	12-26-87	0	4	6.23	8	8	0	0	35	38	25	24	7	17	33	.286	.353	.263	8.57	4.41
Mortensen, Clayton	R-R	6-4	185	4-10-85	3	5	5.65	32	3	0	0	64	75	42	40	9	30	70	.298	.252	.331	9.90	4.24
Moylan, Peter	R-R	6-2	225	12-2-78	1	1	0.71	12	0	0	5	13	8	2	1	0	5	10	.182	.150	.208	7.11	3.55
Mujica, Edward	R-R	6-3	220	5-10-84	1	0	8.25	9	0	0	2	12	17	11	11	2	2	14	.333	.375	.296	10.50	1.50
Murray, Matt	R-R	6-3	240	12-28-89	1	1	11.57	4	0	0	0	7	8	9	9	3	3	3	.286	.333	.250	3.86	3.86
Nina, Aroni	R-R	6-4	180	4-9-90	0	0	37.80	2	0	0	0	2	5	7	7	0	5	0	.556	1.000	.333	0.00	27.00
Olson, Tyler	R-L	6-3	195	10-2-89	0	0	2.84	5	0	0	0	6	10	3	2	1	2	2	.357	.300	.389	2.84	2.84
Peterson, Mark	R-R	6-0	190	9-7-90	1	2	5.83	15	0	0	2	29	38	19	19	5	17	20	.317	.283	.338	6.14	5.22
Pounders, Brooks	R-R	6-5	265	9-26-90	5	3	3.14	31	7	0	0	80	67	29	28	5	37	90	.226	.234	.219	10.08	4.15
Pruneda, Benino	R-R	5-9	170	8-8-88	4	1	3.89	19	1	0	0	35	21	21	15	3	21	42	.169	.161	.177	10.90	5.45
Tepesch, Nick	R-R	6-4	240	10-12-88	0	1	3.94	5	2	0	0	16	11	7	7	0	7	8	.204	.156	.273	4.50	3.94
4-team total																							
(3 Nashville, 3 Oklahoma City, 11 Round Rock)					8	4	3.96	22	19	0	0	116	121	56	51	7	28	62	—	—	—	4.81	2.17
Vargas, Jason	L-L	6-0	215	2-2-83	0	2	5.93	3	3	0	0	14	16	9	9	3	1	18	.291	.217	.344	11.85	0.66

Fielding

Catcher	PCT	G	PO	A	E	DP	PB
Cruz	.992	61	435	55	4	4	6
De San Miguel	.986	9	65	7	1	1	0
Evans	.947	3	15	3	1	0	1
Morin	.983	72	495	36	9	3	10
Villegas	1.000	5	34	3	0	3	1

First Base	PCT	G	PO	A	E	DP
Cruz	.989	22	172	12	2	13
Cuthbert	1.000	3	32	2	0	4
Decker	.952	2	20	0	1	2
Dozier	1.000	8	62	6	0	8
Evans	1.000	1	4	0	0	0
Fuenmayor	.988	77	557	34	7	72
Martinez	.988	20	162	9	2	14
Merrifield	1.000	9	40	0	0	2
Snider	.987	10	71	4	1	5
Villegas	1.000	2	8	1	0	1

Second Base	PCT	G	PO	A	E	DP
Barmes	1.000	5	8	14	0	5
Calixte	.967	17	22	36	2	11
Coleman	1.000	12	18	25	0	5
Colon	.958	6	9	14	1	4
Diaz	1.000	3	3	6	0	1

	PCT	G	PO	A	E	DP
Falu	.974	9	14	23	1	9
Franco	.984	32	45	76	2	18
Merrifield	.985	40	87	106	3	28
Mondesi	.929	2	6	7	1	3
Torres	.950	23	48	67	6	22

Third Base	PCT	G	PO	A	E	DP
Barmes	—	1	0	0	0	0
Calixte	1.000	15	10	24	0	1
Coleman	1.000	14	8	27	0	3
Colon	1.000	1	0	2	0	0
Cruz	—	1	0	0	0	0
Cuthbert	.887	21	13	42	7	4
Dozier	.949	63	56	94	8	14
Falu	1.000	4	6	3	0	0
Franco	1.000	23	9	36	0	11
Merrifield	1.000	4	1	3	0	0
Pehl	—	1	0	0	0	0
Tolleson	1.000	1	0	1	0	0

Shortstop	PCT	G	PO	A	E	DP
Barmes	1.000	22	22	73	0	12
Calixte	.949	11	13	24	2	8
Coleman	.947	26	22	85	6	15
Colon	.967	11	20	38	2	9
Diaz	.833	2	2	3	1	1

	PCT	G	PO	A	E	DP
Falu	1.000	4	3	7	0	2
Franco	1.000	7	13	15	0	4
Mondesi	1.000	12	26	28	0	8
Torres	.944	50	80	124	12	36

Outfield	PCT	G	PO	A	E	DP
Bonifacio	.971	121	254	17	8	6
Burns	.500	1	0	1	1	0
Cain	1.000	2	2	0	0	0
Calixte	.967	49	112	4	4	2
Coleman	—	1	0	0	0	0
De San Miguel	—	1	0	0	0	0
Downes	1.000	4	10	1	0	0
Dozier	.959	21	46	1	2	0
Dyson	1.000	7	9	1	0	0
Eibner	.989	46	92	2	1	1
Falu	1.000	6	13	0	0	0
Franco	.000	2	0	0	1	0
Fuentes	.983	53	113	3	2	1
Gordon	1.000	1	2	0	0	0
Martinez	1.000	15	21	1	0	0
Merrifield	.933	17	27	1	2	0
Nava	.500	2	1	0	1	0
Pehl	—	1	0	0	0	0
Snider	.978	49	85	3	2	0
Starling	1.000	44	103	7	0	3

NORTHWEST ARKANSAS NATURALS
DOUBLE-A

TEXAS LEAGUE

Batting	B-T	HT	WT	DOB	AVG	vLH	vRH	G	AB	R	H	2B	3B	HR	RBI	BB	HBP	SH	SF	SO	SB	CS	SLG	OBP
Arteaga, Humberto	R-R	6-1	160	1-23-94	.208	.293	.187	58	207	19	43	6	2	0	11	6	0	3	2	44	1	2	.256	.228
Calixte, Orlando	R-R	5-11	180	2-3-92	.295	.385	.286	38	139	26	41	9	0	2	14	9	0	2	2	31	14	3	.403	.333
De San Miguel, Allan	R-R	5-9	205	2-1-88	.180	.000	.200	20	61	5	11	1	0	1	5	5	1	1	1	11	0	0	.246	.250
Diaz, Carlos	R-R	5-8	145	11-15-92	.279	.200	.289	17	43	4	12	1	0	0	1	4	0	1	0	6	1	1	.302	.340
Dozier, Hunter	R-R	6-4	220	8-22-91	.305	.375	.299	26	95	14	29	8	0	8	21	14	1	0	0	23	4	0	.642	.400
Duenez, Samir	L-R	6-1	195	6-16-96	.278	.200	.308	14	54	4	15	5	0	0	9	5	0	0	0	12	2	0	.370	.339
Escalera, Alfredo	R-R	6-1	186	2-17-95	.277	.340	.258	50	202	25	56	14	0	2	23	6	2	3	4	51	5	1	.376	.299
Evans, Zane	R-R	6-2	225	11-29-91	.226	.250	.221	63	234	17	53	8	1	5	25	10	2	0	2	60	0	1	.333	.262
Gallagher, Cam	R-R	6-3	230	12-6-92	.259	.289	.255	91	301	23	78	16	1	4	24	37	5	0	2	52	2	2	.359	.348
Garcia, Carlos	R-R	5-10	172	3-18-92	.254	.261	.253	91	279	38	71	11	3	3	20	26	3	5	3	51	10	9	.348	.322
Gordon, Alex	L-R	6-1	220	2-10-84	.333	.000	.357	4	15	3	5	1	0	1	2	2	0	0	0	4	0	0	.600	.412
Gore, Terrance	R-R	5-7	165	6-8-91	.233	.237	.233	88	253	31	59	2	1	0	11	26	4	19	0	58	44	5	.249	.314
Lopez, Jose	R-R	5-9	165	12-16-92	.187	.242	.179	83	267	25	50	7	1	6	25	14	2	6	1	60	9	4	.288	.232
Mondesi, Raul A.	R-R	6-1	185	7-27-95	.259	.214	.265	29	116	20	30	5	1	5	17	13	0	1	1	30	17	1	.448	.331
Moon, Logan	R-R	6-2	195	2-15-92	.254	.264	.252	107	351	42	89	20	1	4	30	26	2	7	2	103	4	3	.350	.307
Moustakas, Mike	L-R	6-0	215	9-11-88	.250	.000	.333	2	8	0	2	0	0	0	0	0	0	0	0	3	0	0	.250	.250
O'Hearn, Ryan	L-L	6-3	200	7-26-93	.258	.280	.254	112	414	49	107	25	2	15	60	48	3	0	1	131	3	1	.437	.339
Ramos, Mauricio	R-R	6-1	185	2-2-92	.288	.190	.307	125	483	41	139	28	1	9	60	19	10	1	4	92	5	2	.406	.326
Schwindel, Frank	R-R	6-1	205	6-29-92	.270	.286	.268	120	455	57	123	20	0	20	68	18	5	0	7	86	1	1	.446	.301
Starling, Bubba	R-R	6-4	210	8-3-92	.185	.238	.179	62	233	28	43	15	1	5	23	15	6	0	1	81	10	1	.322	.251
Torres, Ramon	B-R	5-11	170	1-22-93	.268	.250	.270	41	164	20	44	5	1	1	8	18	0	2	1	18	9	4	.329	.339
Toups, Corey	R-R	5-10	170	2-12-93	.275	.355	.257	86	338	61	93	25	2	10	38	36	10	6	4	96	16	3	.450	.358
Villegas, Luis	R-R	5-10	170	12-2-92	.333	.500	.250	2	6	0	2	0	0	0	2	1	0	0	0	2	0	0	.333	.429

Pitching	B-T	HT	WT	DOB	W	L	ERA	G	GS	CG	SV	IP	H	R	ER	HR	BB	SO	AVG	vLH	vRH	K/9	BB/9
Almonte, Miguel	R-R	6-2	210	4-4-93	2	1	7.31	11	0	0	0	16	24	13	13	4	4	15	.348	.217	.413	8.44	2.25

Pitching

Pitching	B-T	HT	WT	DOB	W	L	ERA	G	GS	CG	SV	IP	H	R	ER	HR	BB	SO	AVG	vLH	vRH	K/9	BB/9
Alvarez, Matt	R-R	6-2	190	1-11-91	0	0	22.85	5	0	0	0	4	10	11	11	0	8	6	.476	.500	.467	12.46	16.62
Bartsch, Kyle	L-L	5-11	200	3-10-91	2	1	0.94	15	1	0	1	29	20	3	3	3	6	23	.200	.281	.162	7.22	1.88
2-team total (10 San Antonio)					2	1	3.72	25	1	0	1	46	52	22	19	5	16	33	—	—	—	6.46	3.13
Beal, Evan	R-R	6-5	195	8-2-93	3	2	3.81	29	0	0	1	54	51	23	23	9	19	44	.248	.215	.262	7.29	3.15
Binford, Christian	R-R	6-6	215	12-20-92	3	2	4.84	6	6	0	0	35	35	22	19	2	6	29	.261	.227	.294	7.39	1.53
Caramo, Yender	R-R	6-0	175	8-25-91	5	7	2.45	34	10	0	2	114	101	38	31	6	23	67	.233	.269	.212	5.29	1.82
Cordero, Estarlin	L-L	6-0	145	3-3-93	0	1	11.12	11	0	0	0	17	27	22	21	5	8	16	.365	.300	.389	8.47	4.24
Edwards, Andrew	R-R	6-6	265	10-7-91	0	0	0.50	10	0	0	2	18	14	2	1	0	4	23	.222	.250	.209	11.50	2.00
Ferguson, Andy	R-R	6-1	195	9-2-88	0	0	1.80	1	1	0	0	5	3	1	1	0	2	4	.167	.222	.111	7.20	3.60
Fernandez, Pedro	R-R	6-0	175	5-25-94	1	2	4.03	8	5	0	0	29	29	14	13	2	10	19	.261	.293	.243	5.90	3.10
Goudeau, Ashton	R-R	6-6	205	7-23-92	5	13	5.34	20	17	0	0	93	110	55	55	13	23	68	.296	.227	.335	6.60	2.23
Hill, Tim	L-L	6-2	200	2-10-90	2	2	3.02	31	0	0	1	45	41	17	15	6	17	48	.246	.258	.238	9.67	3.43
Junis, Jake	R-R	6-2	225	9-16-92	9	7	3.25	21	21	0	0	119	110	48	43	12	27	117	.246	.280	.225	8.85	2.04
McCarthy, Kevin	R-R	6-3	200	2-22-92	3	2	3.12	22	0	0	11	35	26	12	12	3	8	29	.208	.204	.211	7.53	2.08
Medlen, Kris	B-R	5-10	190	10-7-85	0	1	7.20	2	2	0	0	5	9	4	4	1	2	8	.391	.667	.294	14.40	3.60
Mills, Alec	R-R	6-4	190	11-30-91	1	2	2.39	12	12	0	0	68	57	19	18	2	12	68	.234	.261	.211	9.04	1.60
Minor, Mike	R-L	6-4	210	12-26-87	0	0	3.52	2	2	0	0	8	5	5	3	1	5	12	.185	.000	.192	14.09	5.87
Nina, Aroni	R-R	6-4	180	4-9-90	4	0	1.05	24	0	0	1	34	24	5	4	0	17	39	.198	.136	.234	10.22	4.46
Peterson, Mark	R-R	6-0	190	9-7-90	3	2	1.78	27	0	0	9	30	19	6	6	3	7	34	.177	.242	.151	10.09	2.08
Pruneda, Benino	R-R	5-9	170	8-8-88	2	2	3.13	14	1	0	1	23	17	9	8	1	13	33	.205	.273	.160	12.91	5.09
Redman, Reid	R-R	6-0	180	11-22-88	0	2	2.77	16	0	0	0	26	23	9	8	4	8	21	.245	.111	.299	7.27	2.77
Selman, Sam	L-L	6-3	190	11-14-90	0	0	14.46	9	0	0	0	9	17	17	15	3	10	8	.370	.273	.400	7.71	9.64
Skoglund, Eric	L-L	6-7	200	10-26-92	7	10	3.45	27	27	0	0	156	135	63	60	19	38	134	.230	.241	.227	7.71	2.19
Sparkman, Glenn	B-R	6-2	210	5-11-92	0	2	4.58	4	4	0	0	18	21	10	9	2	5	20	.296	.261	.313	10.19	2.55
Staumont, Josh	R-R	6-3	200	12-21-93	2	1	3.04	11	11	0	0	50	42	18	17	2	37	73	.232	.286	.198	13.05	6.62
Stout, Eric	L-L	6-3	185	3-27-93	6	4	3.86	42	0	0	2	72	68	32	31	3	25	69	.255	.181	.295	8.59	3.11
Strahm, Matt	R-L	6-3	185	11-12-91	3	8	3.43	22	18	0	0	102	102	47	39	14	23	107	.260	.260	.259	9.41	2.02
Stumpf, Daniel	L-L	6-2	200	1-4-91	2	0	2.11	14	0	0	1	21	14	5	5	0	4	26	.187	.222	.167	10.97	1.69
Vargas, Jason	L-L	6-0	215	2-2-83	0	0	7.71	1	1	0	0	2	4	3	2	2	0	1	.364	.500	.286	3.86	0.00
Zimmer, Kyle	R-R	6-3	225	9-13-91	0	1	0.00	1	1	0	0	1	1	1	0	0	2	2	.250	.500	.000	18.00	18.00

Fielding

Catcher

Catcher	PCT	G	PO	A	E	DP	PB
De San Miguel	1.000	17	164	8	0	1	1
Evans	.992	45	335	28	3	1	5
Gallagher	.996	80	648	62	3	9	7
Villegas	1.000	2	8	0	0	0	0

	PCT	G	PO	A	E	DP	PB
Lopez	.960	18	31	41	3		7
Mondesi	1.000	6	13	19	0		4
Torres	.990	22	35	64	1		15
Toups	.983	83	128	217	6		43

	PCT	G	PO	A	E	DP	PB
Garcia	1.000	1	0	1	0		0
Lopez	.980	42	79	114	4		25
Mondesi	.950	21	32	64	5		16
Torres	.936	17	20	53	5		11
Toups	1.000	1	1	0	0		0

First Base

First Base	PCT	G	PO	A	E	DP
Duenez	1.000	1	8	0	0	1
O'Hearn	.992	61	456	21	4	50
Ramos	.982	14	103	8	2	9
Schwindel	.991	69	539	32	5	45

Second Base

Second Base	PCT	G	PO	A	E	DP
Arteaga	1.000	4	8	10	0	2
Calixte	.882	3	5	10	2	2
Garcia	.957	7	6	16	1	2

Third Base

Third Base	PCT	G	PO	A	E	DP
Arteaga	1.000	4	2	2	0	0
Calixte	1.000	2	3	2	0	0
Diaz	1.000	3	1	2	0	0
Dozier	.972	19	14	21	1	3
Lopez	.903	17	9	19	3	2
Moustakas	1.000	1	0	3	0	0
Ramos	.964	105	73	165	9	15

Shortstop

Shortstop	PCT	G	PO	A	E	DP
Arteaga	.970	51	72	152	7	32
Diaz	.892	11	15	18	4	1

Outfield

Outfield	PCT	G	PO	A	E	DP
Calixte	.967	32	53	6	2	1
Dozier	1.000	6	7	0	0	0
Escalera	1.000	47	94	3	0	1
Garcia	.954	71	98	6	5	1
Gordon	1.000	3	7	0	0	0
Gore	.991	85	210	2	2	0
Lopez	1.000	3	5	0	0	0
Moon	.976	102	199	7	5	3
O'Hearn	.982	39	56	0	1	0
Starling	.973	58	137	6	4	1

WILMINGTON BLUE ROCKS

HIGH CLASS A

CAROLINA LEAGUE

Batting	B-T	HT	WT	DOB	AVG	vLH	vRH	G	AB	R	H	2B	3B	HR	RBI	BB	HBP	SH	SF	SO	SB	CS	SLG	OBP
Arteaga, Humberto	R-R	6-1	160	1-23-94	.286	.303	.280	67	266	35	76	8	2	2	24	7	1	10	1	46	14	5	.353	.305
Bailey, Austin	L-R	5-10	190	7-3-92	.256	.179	.280	106	363	41	93	14	4	2	31	28	3	0	4	65	3	4	.333	.312
Banuelos, Josh	R-R	6-2	215	9-3-91	.177	.179	.176	26	79	12	14	3	0	1	4	16	3	0	0	12	0	1	.253	.337
Bien, Brian	R-R	6-0	175	9-2-92	.246	.180	.279	62	183	13	45	7	0	0	13	10	2	5	4	30	10	4	.257	.286
Brontsema, John	R-R	6-2	187	12-13-94	.250	.333	.167	3	12	1	3	0	0	0	0	0	0	0	0	3	0	0	.250	.250
Collins, Roman	L-L	6-2	210	6-17-94	.222	.143	.231	21	72	6	16	3	0	0	5	5	0	0	1	10	2	0	.264	.269
Diaz, Carlos	B-R	5-8	145	11-15-92	.241	.304	.206	50	158	10	38	7	0	0	9	4	1	8	1	29	3	7	.285	.262
Dini, Nick	R-R	5-8	180	7-27-93	.208	.111	.267	7	24	2	5	1	0	0	1	0	1	0	0	3	0	0	.250	.240
Downes, Brandon	R-R	6-3	195	9-29-92	.230	.232	.229	130	478	56	110	34	3	12	66	41	11	1	7	170	19	6	.389	.302
Duenez, Samir	L-R	6-1	195	6-11-96	.300	.280	.312	56	213	30	64	13	2	7	42	19	2	1	0	34	10	2	.479	.363
Escalera, Alfredo	R-R	6-1	186	2-17-95	.269	.282	.263	73	283	37	76	10	1	3	30	21	7	0	0	75	5	3	.343	.334
Frabasilio, Colton	R-R	6-2	205	4-18-93	.167	.071	.227	10	36	3	6	3	1	0	3	0	0	0	0	8	0	0	.306	.231
Franco, Wander	R-R	6-2	170	12-13-94	.220	.294	.189	95	368	39	81	24	2	5	47	19	2	0	5	83	5	1	.337	.259
Hernandez, Elier	R-R	6-3	197	11-21-94	.226	.241	.220	134	500	51	113	28	4	2	43	30	10	1	5	120	8	5	.310	.281
Hill, Mike	L-R	6-2	195	1-29-92	.241	.258	.234	30	108	11	26	8	0	4	11	10	2	1	0	39	2	0	.426	.317
Johnson, Chad	R-R	6-0	190	5-31-94	.224	.159	.242	92	299	29	67	11	3	5	21	43	5	1	2	109	3	0	.331	.330
Jones, Cody	B-R	5-11	175	3-24-92	.216	.219	.215	78	287	36	62	10	1	0	12	57	4	2	1	71	22	5	.258	.352
Miller, Anderson	L-L	6-3	208	5-6-94	.201	.205	.200	38	144	18	29	8	3	3	16	12	1	2	1	50	5	0	.361	.266
Mondesi, Raul A.	B-R	6-1	185	7-27-95	.243	.133	.318	9	37	5	9	2	1	1	4	2	0	0	0	11	2	0	.432	.282
O'Hearn, Ryan	L-L	6-3	200	7-26-93	.352	.400	.342	22	88	13	31	7	0	7	18	8	1	0	1	27	0	0	.670	.408

Batting	B-T	HT	WT	DOB	AVG	vLH	vRH	G	AB	R	H	2B	3B	HR	RBI	BB	HBP	SH	SF	SO	SB	CS	SLG	OBP
Pehl, Robert	R-R	6-1	205	9-23-92	.268	.243	.278	83	261	41	70	25	0	1	40	36	7	2	3	66	2	1	.375	.368
Toups, Corey	R-R	5-10	170	2-12-93	.252	.190	.274	41	155	21	39	10	5	2	11	22	2	0	0	35	6	1	.419	.352
Villegas, Luis	R-R	5-10	170	12-2-92	.276	.265	.284	43	156	20	43	8	1	5	25	11	1	0	1	33	1	0	.436	.325

Pitching	B-T	HT	WT	DOB	W	L	ERA	G	GS	CG	SV	IP	H	R	ER	HR	BB	SO	AVG	vLH	vRH	K/9	BB/9
Alvarez, Matt	R-R	6-2	190	1-11-91	3	2	3.97	16	0	0	2	23	16	11	10	0	26	17	.200	.243	.163	6.75	10.32
Beal, Evan	R-R	6-5	195	8-2-93	0	0	1.23	9	0	0	1	15	8	3	2	0	6	12	.160	.148	.174	7.36	3.68
Bodner, Jacob	R-R	5-10	185	1-31-93	0	2	5.44	27	0	0	2	43	54	29	26	3	21	53	.295	.345	.253	11.09	4.40
Eaton, Todd	R-R	6-1	190	5-9-92	2	2	2.18	12	0	0	1	21	21	7	5	2	5	21	.263	.342	.190	9.15	2.18
Ferguson, Andy	R-R	6-1	195	9-2-88	0	3	3.72	4	4	0	0	19	13	9	8	1	8	20	.183	.154	.219	9.31	3.72
Fernandez, Pedro	R-R	6-0	175	5-25-94	3	1	2.14	6	6	1	0	34	24	8	8	0	11	31	.207	.219	.186	8.29	2.94
Gordon, Derek	R-R	6-6	220	6-14-91	2	2	4.38	34	6	0	7	76	73	39	37	9	26	83	.254	.285	.229	9.83	3.08
Goudeau, Ashton	R-R	6-5	205	7-23-92	2	4	5.14	7	5	0	0	35	41	23	20	2	9	35	.295	.329	.258	9.00	2.31
Griffin, Foster	L-L	6-3	200	7-27-95	5	10	6.23	20	20	0	0	95	130	79	66	9	43	76	.330	.353	.322	7.17	4.06
Henry, Brennan	L-L	6-4	200	10-23-91	1	0	4.63	33	0	0	3	56	66	37	29	4	31	50	.289	.217	.321	7.99	4.95
Hill, Tim	L-L	6-2	200	2-10-90	0	2	4.42	13	0	0	0	18	19	9	9	3	7	14	.279	.333	.250	6.87	3.44
Kalish, Jake	B-L	6-2	210	7-9-91	3	0	2.48	18	0	0	2	36	27	12	10	3	10	35	.201	.222	.191	8.67	2.48
Kubat, Kyle	L-L	6-1	195	12-4-92	4	1	4.28	25	2	0	0	55	65	29	26	2	19	43	.294	.233	.317	7.08	3.13
Lewis, Sam	R-R	6-4	195	10-9-91	2	0	3.00	5	0	0	0	9	7	3	3	1	2	6	.194	.222	.167	6.00	2.00
Lovvorn, Zach	R-R	6-0	185	5-26-94	2	15	3.95	25	23	0	0	128	134	70	56	8	44	107	.270	.284	.254	7.54	3.10
McCoy, Mark	L-L	6-2	200	4-30-94	0	3	8.44	11	0	0	0	16	22	17	15	0	18	12	.333	.333	.333	6.75	10.13
Newberry, Jake	R-R	6-2	195	11-20-94	3	2	3.00	29	0	0	3	57	48	22	19	4	16	51	.224	.240	.211	8.05	2.53
Ray, Corey	R-R	6-4	175	12-15-92	8	6	4.13	19	19	0	0	100	97	58	46	9	35	87	.246	.236	.259	7.80	3.14
Rico, Luis	L-L	6-1	175	11-29-93	2	0	4.37	26	0	0	7	47	40	29	23	8	25	51	.221	.268	.200	9.70	4.75
Rodgers, Colin	L-L	5-10	181	12-5-92	2	7	6.02	16	11	0	0	61	68	45	41	4	39	42	.282	.309	.272	6.16	5.72
Selman, Sam	R-L	6-3	190	11-14-90	0	0	4.00	5	0	0	0	9	7	4	4	0	5	12	.206	.286	.150	12.00	5.00
Sparkman, Glenn	B-R	6-2	210	5-11-92	1	0	3.86	2	2	0	0	12	9	5	5	1	1	9	.209	.158	.250	6.94	0.77
Staumont, Josh	R-R	6-3	200	12-21-93	2	10	5.05	18	15	0	0	73	62	49	41	3	67	94	.230	.188	.268	11.59	8.26
Tenuta, Matt	L-L	6-4	225	12-16-93	7	11	5.43	26	23	0	0	131	140	82	79	15	43	90	.282	.288	.280	6.18	2.95
Tompkins, Ian	L-L	6-0	195	3-23-93	0	0	8.44	7	0	0	0	11	9	11	10	0	12	12	.225	.267	.200	10.13	10.13
Zimmer, Kyle	R-R	6-3	225	9-13-91	0	1	1.93	2	2	0	0	5	3	1	1	0	4	9	.176	.182	.167	17.36	7.71

Fielding

Catcher	PCT	G	PO	A	E	DP	PB
Dini	.935	7	38	5	3	0	0
Frabasilio	1.000	2	14	0	0	0	1
Johnson	.984	89	680	57	12	2	9
Villegas	.984	41	323	40	6	4	6

First Base	PCT	G	PO	A	E	DP
Banuelos	.983	19	162	9	3	10
Duenez	.986	52	413	14	6	28
Frabasilio	1.000	1	6	0	0	0
O'Hearn	.989	21	173	8	2	16
Pehl	.975	45	333	25	9	31

Second Base	PCT	G	PO	A	E	DP
Arteaga	1.000	6	7	13	0	3

	PCT				
Bailey	.949	72	105	156	14	23
Bien	.978	39	56	78	3	23
Brontsema	1.000	1	3	2	0	1
Diaz	.923	4	4	4	1	3
Toups	.962	30	53	73	5	11

Third Base	PCT	G	PO	A	E	DP
Bailey	1.000	7	4	8	0	1
Bien	.875	1	3	4	1	0
Diaz	—	1	0	0	0	0
Franco	.930	89	51	148	15	11
Hill	.960	30	27	45	3	4
Pehl	.921	12	6	29	3	1

Shortstop	PCT	G	PO	A	E	DP
Arteaga	.970	61	79	147	7	26

	PCT	G	PO	A	E	DP
Bien	.911	23	30	42	7	7
Brontsema	1.000	1	1	5	0	1
Diaz	.934	45	57	99	11	21
Mondesi	1.000	6	4	19	0	4
Toups	.935	9	11	18	2	5

Outfield	PCT	G	PO	A	E	DP
Bailey	—	2	0	0	0	0
Collins	.979	17	45	1	1	0
Downes	.976	112	232	9	6	1
Escalera	.967	60	113	3	4	0
Hernandez	.979	117	226	7	5	1
Jones	.983	67	162	7	3	0
Miller	.976	37	79	2	2	1
Pehl	1.000	11	14	0	0	0

LEXINGTON LEGENDS

LOW CLASS A

SOUTH ATLANTIC LEAGUE

Batting	B-T	HT	WT	DOB	AVG	vLH	vRH	G	AB	R	H	2B	3B	HR	RBI	BB	HBP	SH	SF	SO	SB	CS	SLG	OBP
Banuelos, Josh	R-R	6-2	215	9-3-91	.241	.400	.158	9	29	4	7	0	0	1	2	3	1	0	0	7	0	0	.345	.333
Burt, D.J.	R-R	5-9	160	10-13-95	.257	.256	.258	125	474	74	122	16	5	4	59	51	7	5	5	108	43	17	.338	.335
Collins, Roman	L-L	6-2	210	6-17-94	.246	.219	.253	90	354	50	87	13	4	9	36	37	2	0	1	64	11	6	.381	.320
Dini, Nick	R-R	5-8	180	7-27-93	.333	.000	1.000	2	3	1	1	0	0	0	0	0	1	0	0	2	0	0	.333	.500
Duenez, Samir	L-R	6-1	195	6-11-96	.272	.215	.290	68	265	30	72	15	3	6	49	15	2	0	3	40	14	2	.419	.312
Dulin, Brandon	L-R	6-3	225	12-29-92	.254	.207	.268	66	248	28	63	11	1	7	31	17	4	0	0	70	1	1	.391	.312
Edwards, David	B-R	6-2	210	1-22-93	.263	.500	.200	5	19	2	5	0	1	0	0	1	0	0	0	5	0	0	.368	.300
Fernandez, Xavier	R-R	5-11	197	7-15-95	.259	.244	.264	92	328	37	85	15	0	9	42	30	1	1	3	51	1	0	.387	.320
Flores, Jeckson	R-R	5-11	145	10-28-93	.205	.180	.212	84	259	35	53	11	2	4	27	16	9	11	3	38	21	4	.309	.272
Frabasilio, Colton	R-R	6-2	205	4-18-93	.206	.143	.224	18	63	6	13	0	1	1	10	7	0	0	4	12	1	0	.286	.270
Fukofuka, Amalani	R-R	6-1	180	9-25-95	.200	.208	.198	110	404	45	81	14	0	5	34	29	6	2	4	136	24	6	.272	.262
Gasparini, Marten	B-R	6-0	195	5-24-97	.196	.194	.197	111	382	35	75	12	2	7	42	31	1	11	4	134	14	10	.293	.256
Hill, Mike	L-R	6-2	195	1-29-92	.263	.229	.271	61	205	30	54	15	0	6	21	20	2	1	1	60	2	5	.424	.333
Johnson, Ben	R-R	6-0	185	5-4-94	.213	.216	.211	112	381	49	81	27	2	6	45	36	6	2	2	162	7	6	.341	.289
Jones, Cody	B-R	5-11	175	5-25-93	.300	.278	.309	39	130	26	39	5	2	1	11	16	1	7	0	27	11	5	.392	.381
Maezes, Travis	L-R	6-2	195	12-10-93	.196	.145	.207	88	296	44	58	18	0	15	40	36	3	2	1	124	0	2	.409	.289
Miller, Anderson	L-L	6-3	208	5-6-94	.284	.370	.266	43	155	24	44	12	1	3	18	22	1	2	0	51	3	1	.432	.376
Stanley, Tanner	L-L	5-10	180	9-12-93	.233	.333	.217	61	176	20	41	2	0	1	8	23	1	7	1	22	3	2	.261	.323
Vallot, Chase	R-R	6-0	215	8-21-96	.246	.254	.244	82	272	37	67	20	0	13	44	39	15	0	4	118	0	0	.463	.367

Pitching	B-T	HT	WT	DOB	W	L	ERA	G	GS	CG	SV	IP	H	R	ER	HR	BB	SO	AVG	vLH	vRH	K/9	BB/9
Bayliss, Brian	R-R	6-2	200	8-4-94	0	1	5.14	6	0	0	0	14	15	9	8	3	6	14	.268	.273	.265	9.00	3.86
Blewett, Scott	R-R	6-6	210	4-10-96	8	11	4.31	25	25	2	0	129	138	72	62	10	51	121	.275	.312	.248	8.42	3.55
Bodner, Jacob	R-R	5-10	185	1-31-93	2	0	3.60	7	0	0	3	10	8	4	4	2	5	6	.222	.188	.250	5.40	4.50
Concepcion, Daniel	R-R	6-4	230	9-3-93	2	4	6.14	26	5	0	0	59	60	42	40	12	23	45	.263	.291	.246	6.90	3.53
Cramer, Gabe	R-R	6-2	205	11-1-94	3	2	4.12	27	0	0	4	44	38	22	20	4	23	57	.242	.271	.224	11.75	4.74
Deshazier, Torey	R-R	6-0	160	9-16-93	1	2	5.31	19	0	0	1	41	37	26	24	1	43	40	.250	.295	.218	8.85	9.52
Ditman, Matt	R-R	6-1	205	8-13-92	1	3	3.72	26	0	0	5	39	44	25	16	6	12	45	.288	.340	.264	10.47	2.79
Garabito, Gerson	R-R	6-0	160	8-19-95	2	11	4.80	18	18	0	0	81	78	50	43	9	35	61	.256	.261	.253	6.81	3.90
Griffin, Foster	L-L	6-3	200	7-27-95	1	4	3.38	7	7	0	0	37	35	25	14	3	9	29	.243	.163	.277	6.99	2.17
Kalish, Jake	B-L	6-2	210	7-9-91	0	0	2.38	5	0	0	1	11	6	3	3	0	1	13	.158	.235	.095	10.32	0.79
Kubat, Kyle	L-L	6-1	195	12-4-92	1	1	1.76	6	0	0	1	15	9	4	3	1	1	12	.158	.231	.097	7.04	0.59
Lewis, Sam	R-R	6-4	195	10-9-91	1	1	1.11	12	0	0	1	24	15	4	3	1	1	24	.169	.156	.175	8.88	0.37
Marte, Yunior	R-R	6-2	180	2-2-95	6	8	4.21	26	7	0	1	107	94	54	50	9	55	103	.234	.237	.233	8.66	4.63
McCoy, Mark	L-L	6-2	200	4-30-94	4	2	4.86	24	0	0	0	50	50	27	27	3	27	46	.265	.302	.246	8.28	4.86
Newberry, Jake	R-R	6-2	195	11-20-94	0	0	0.00	6	0	0	0	10	7	4	0	0	2	11	.179	.200	.167	10.24	1.86
Ogando, Emilio	L-L	6-2	180	8-13-93	7	10	3.80	25	20	0	0	133	126	71	56	14	35	130	.249	.170	.281	8.82	2.37
Pinto, Julio	R-R	6-3	185	11-18-95	2	4	5.84	16	11	0	1	49	49	34	32	4	30	40	.265	.284	.252	7.30	5.47
Puckett, A.J.	R-R	6-4	200	5-27-95	2	3	3.66	11	11	0	0	52	42	22	21	4	15	37	.227	.250	.214	6.45	2.61
Ray, Corey	R-R	6-4	175	12-15-92	2	1	3.92	8	8	1	0	39	46	26	17	3	10	32	.293	.206	.351	7.38	2.31
Redman, Reid	R-R	6-0	180	11-22-88	1	0	1.50	3	0	0	0	6	5	1	1	1	1	10	.217	.143	.250	15.00	1.50
Sparkman, Glenn	B-R	6-2	210	5-11-92	0	2	6.91	3	3	0	0	14	21	11	11	2	3	19	.350	.370	.333	11.93	1.88
Stephenson, Niklas	R-R	6-2	195	11-16-93	1	4	8.24	20	0	0	2	32	47	39	29	2	22	26	.338	.328	.346	7.39	6.25
Terrero, Franco	R-R	6-0	180	5-20-95	2	2	4.82	38	0	0	7	80	87	53	43	7	32	54	.281	.244	.304	6.05	3.59
Watson, Nolan	R-R	6-2	195	1-25-97	3	11	7.57	24	24	0	0	96	125	95	81	19	44	60	.314	.286	.333	5.61	4.11

Fielding

Catcher	PCT	G	PO	A	E	DP	PB
Dini	.917	2	10	1	1	0	0
Fernandez	.987	71	501	87	8	3	10
Frabasilio	1.000	2	23	6	0	0	0
Hill	.971	13	86	14	3	0	10
Vallot	.963	53	383	56	17	1	16

Second Base	PCT	G	PO	A	E	DP
Burt	.959	113	196	223	18	42
Edwards	1.000	3	7	5	0	1
Flores	1.000	8	18	22	0	7
Maezes	.967	19	27	31	2	10

Shortstop	PCT	G	PO	A	E	DP
Burt	.929	12	16	36	4	10
Flores	.941	23	39	72	7	13
Gasparini	.885	107	132	237	48	24
Hill	—	1	0	0	0	0

First Base	PCT	G	PO	A	E	DP
Banuelos	1.000	4	35	4	0	3
Duenez	.985	58	438	35	7	30
Dulin	.993	55	387	25	3	28
Frabasilio	1.000	12	109	9	0	10
Hill	.963	12	70	8	3	5

Third Base	PCT	G	PO	A	E	DP
Edwards	.833	2	0	5	1	0
Flores	.961	54	48	99	6	14
Hill	.907	37	25	53	8	5
Maezes	.933	51	28	69	7	5

Outfield	PCT	G	PO	A	E	DP
Collins	.995	87	179	9	1	0
Fukofuka	.992	101	233	6	2	2
Johnson	.978	94	169	6	4	1
Jones	.980	37	95	3	2	1
Miller	1.000	40	102	2	0	1
Stanley	.990	60	97	6	1	0

IDAHO FALLS CHUKARS   ROOKIE
PIONEER LEAGUE

Batting	B-T	HT	WT	DOB	AVG	vLH	vRH	G	AB	R	H	2B	3B	HR	RBI	BB	HBP	SH	SF	SO	SB	CS	SLG	OBP
Aracena, Ricky	B-R	5-8	160	10-2-97	.251	.263	.248	61	267	44	67	8	4	1	33	17	2	10	1	53	17	8	.322	.300
Castellano, Angelo	R-R	6-0	170	1-13-95	.283	.286	.282	64	237	50	67	10	4	2	47	21	6	5	4	26	11	5	.384	.351
Clemmons, Leland	R-R	5-9	170	6-17-93	.500	.500	.500	4	10	5	5	0	0	1	2	0	1	0	1	3	1	0	.800	.500
Dale, Ryan	R-R	6-3	180	3-16-96	.242	.161	.270	31	120	21	29	5	0	2	20	7	0	0	2	45	1	1	.333	.279
Dini, Nick	R-R	5-8	180	7-27-93	.378	.364	.385	9	37	7	14	2	0	0	7	2	0	0	0	3	1	1	.432	.410
Dudek, Joe	L-L	6-2	230	1-6-95	.346	.500	.305	30	104	19	36	11	0	6	29	24	0	0	0	27	0	0	.625	.469
Dulin, Brandon	L-R	6-3	225	12-29-92	.313	.200	.364	4	16	4	5	0	0	1	4	2	0	0	0	4	0	0	.500	.389
Ebert, Jordan	R-R	6-1	180	7-7-93	.299	.130	.337	32	127	16	38	7	1	1	22	4	2	1	1	21	8	2	.394	.328
Edwards, David	B-R	6-2	210	1-22-93	.284	.233	.298	51	194	37	55	14	1	8	35	18	2	1	3	52	8	1	.490	.346
Frabasilio, Colton	R-R	6-2	205	4-18-93	.348	.308	.364	12	46	14	16	7	0	0	5	8	0	0	1	10	0	0	.500	.436
Heath, Nick	L-L	6-1	187	11-27-93	.291	.333	.278	62	230	39	67	8	4	2	28	21	1	2	2	61	36	10	.387	.350
Martin, Rudy	L-L	5-7	150	1-31-96	.244	.263	.237	41	156	30	38	5	1	2	14	17	6	5	0	51	19	3	.327	.341
Melo, Yeison	R-R	6-1	180	7-30-95	.324	.294	.330	66	281	46	91	20	4	5	53	10	4	1	5	53	5	2	.477	.355
Olloque, Manny	R-R	6-2	165	5-11-96	.330	.351	.324	66	276	54	91	18	1	8	53	23	1	0	4	43	7	2	.489	.378
Sanchez, Jose	L-L	5-10	155	7-21-94	.438	1.000	.400	4	16	1	7	1	0	0	1	0	0	0	0	2	0	0	.500	.438
Sanchez, M.J.	L-R	5-10	197	8-17-94	.257	.231	.271	22	74	13	19	2	0	0	6	5	3	0	1	21	0	0	.284	.325
Stanley, Tanner	L-L	5-10	180	10-19-93	.337	.200	.377	21	89	19	30	6	2	1	14	10	0	1	1	7	1	3	.483	.400
Viloria, Meibrys	L-R	5-11	175	2-15-97	.376	.320	.392	58	226	54	85	28	3	6	55	20	8	5	0	36	1	1	.606	.436
Willis, Luke	R-R	5-11	190	11-9-92	.341	.509	.284	60	208	44	71	5	4	3	26	26	2	6	3	46	14	7	.447	.414

Pitching	B-T	HT	WT	DOB	W	L	ERA	G	GS	CG	SV	IP	H	R	ER	HR	BB	SO	AVG	vLH	vRH	K/9	BB/9
Andros, Nick	L-L	6-4	230	11-21-92	0	2	9.20	16	0	0	2	30	48	37	31	7	14	31	.364	.400	.341	9.20	4.15
Bayliss, Brian	R-R	6-2	200	8-4-94	4	1	3.18	11	0	0	2	17	20	7	6	1	5	14	.303	.409	.250	7.41	2.65
Camacho, Enmanuel	L-L	6-0	160	1-9-95	2	2	4.54	19	0	0	1	34	29	25	17	3	21	22	.223	.163	.259	5.88	5.61
Cepin, Reinaldo	L-L	6-1	160	1-10-94	1	4	3.86	15	4	0	1	44	46	24	19	2	18	31	.261	.316	.235	6.29	3.65
Feliz, Igol	R-R	6-3	195	5-31-93	3	5	5.08	13	13	0	0	73	90	50	41	9	23	32	.311	.276	.340	3.96	2.85
Flecha, Christian	L-L	6-2	150	5-9-95	1	1	6.03	17	0	0	1	31	34	22	21	2	19	37	.268	.262	.275	10.63	5.46
Freeman, Jason	L-R	6-4	200	10-3-91	2	2	4.75	18	0	0	2	36	42	26	19	3	11	46	.280	.217	.333	11.50	2.75
Hernandez, Arnaldo	R-R	6-0	175	2-9-96	5	2	5.86	14	14	0	0	71	99	54	46	7	18	63	.334	.331	.337	8.02	2.29
Lewis, Sam	R-R	6-4	195	10-9-91	0	0	6.75	2	0	0	0	4	5	3	3	1	0	3	.333	.429	.250	6.75	0.00

Pitching	B-T	HT	WT	DOB	W	L	ERA	G	GS	CG	SV	IP	H	R	ER	HR	BB	SO	AVG	vLH	vRH	K/9	BB/9
Lovelady, Richard	L-L	6-0	175	7-7-95	0	1	1.84	13	0	0	6	15	10	4	3	0	7	16	.200	.083	.237	9.82	4.30
Luna, Alex	R-R	6-5	205	2-11-93	5	1	3.90	12	8	0	0	55	68	25	24	4	9	55	.321	.299	.336	8.95	1.46
Machado, Andres	R-R	6-0	175	4-22-93	2	4	3.99	13	13	0	0	59	67	35	26	5	14	64	.283	.288	.278	9.82	2.15
Milligan, Drew	L-L	6-6	230	3-14-93	3	3	7.22	18	0	0	0	34	50	28	27	1	11	39	.338	.271	.370	10.43	2.94
Portland, Matt	R-L	6-3	225	2-11-94	4	3	5.25	13	13	0	0	60	63	50	35	5	37	57	.278	.250	.289	8.55	5.55
Redman, Reid	R-R	6-0	180	11-22-88	1	0	4.50	3	0	0	0	6	5	3	3	1	0	8	.227	.300	.167	12.00	0.00
Selman, Sam	L-L	6-3	190	11-14-90	0	0	9.00	4	0	0	0	6	11	9	6	0	4	10	.367	.444	.333	15.00	6.00
Vines, Jace	R-R	6-3	215	9-4-94	1	6	6.47	12	11	0	1	56	79	51	40	6	17	35	.329	.384	.291	5.66	2.75
Way, Cole	L-L	6-11	235	10-23-91	4	1	5.64	18	0	0	0	30	32	21	19	3	23	31	.278	.235	.296	9.20	6.82
Young, Paul	R-R	6-2	205	3-15-93	1	0	0.00	4	0	0	0	5	3	1	0	0	4	4	.176	.200	.167	7.20	7.20

Fielding

C: Dini 5, Frabasilio 1, Sanchez 22, Viloria 50. **1B:** Dale 24, Dudek 19, Dulin 4, Edwards 22, Frabasilio 7. **2B:** Castellano 36, Ebert 25, Edwards 16. **3B:** Castellano 13, Edwards 6, Olloque 58. **SS:** Aracena 61, Castellano 16. **OF:** Castellano 1, Clemmons 2, Heath 59, Martin 41, Melo 53, Sanchez 4, Stanley 18, Willis 56.

BURLINGTON ROYALS   ROOKIE
APPALACHIAN LEAGUE

Batting	B-T	HT	WT	DOB	AVG	vLH	vRH	G	AB	R	H	2B	3B	HR	RBI	BB	HBP	SH	SF	SO	SB	CS	SLG	OBP
Arroyo, Michael	R-R	6-0	181	12-31-95	.203	.333	.161	23	74	15	15	3	0	4	17	6	1	0	1	19	4	1	.405	.268
Cancel, Gabriel	R-R	6-1	185	12-8-96	.291	.304	.284	46	172	28	50	18	1	5	26	15	0	1	1	32	1	2	.494	.346
DeVito, Chris	L-R	6-2	220	12-1-94	.261	.179	.290	60	218	34	57	13	0	9	50	31	0	0	5	45	2	0	.445	.346
Esposito, Nate	R-R	5-11	180	6-25-93	.317	.261	.333	29	101	11	32	8	1	2	17	5	4	1	1	16	0	2	.475	.369
Evans, Zane	R-R	6-2	225	11-29-91	.350	.750	.250	6	20	3	7	1	0	1	3	1	0	0	1	5	0	0	.550	.364
Gray, Logan	R-R	6-1	180	1-12-95	.187	.158	.200	33	123	18	23	7	1	0	10	6	1	1	1	46	2	1	.260	.229
Livingston, Chase	R-R	6-1	203	4-6-94	.250	.400	.192	12	36	7	9	0	0	0	6	5	1	1	0	8	0	0	.250	.357
Lopez, Nicky	R-R	5-11	175	3-13-95	.281	.316	.270	62	231	54	65	6	5	6	29	35	10	3	4	30	24	4	.429	.393
McCray, Jonathan	B-R	5-10	180	1-8-95	.244	.200	.263	48	164	28	40	7	3	7	24	13	0	0	0	43	4	5	.451	.299
Nottebrok, Logan	R-R	6-4	230	3-24-92	.258	.200	.286	9	31	4	8	3	1	2	7	3	0	0	2	11	0	0	.613	.306
Peterson, Kort	L-R	6-1	195	4-29-94	.347	.360	.341	49	176	39	61	12	4	5	35	17	12	0	1	38	7	2	.545	.437
Rivera, Emmanuel	R-R	6-2	195	6-29-96	.249	.267	.242	58	217	25	54	13	4	2	27	21	2	0	3	44	7	3	.373	.317
Salva, Yordany	B-R	5-9	175	7-21-94	.313	.286	.333	6	16	3	5	1	0	1	3	3	1	1	0	4	0	0	.563	.450
Sanchez, Jose	L-L	5-10	155	7-21-94	.313	.167	.360	27	99	14	31	5	1	0	13	7	1	2	0	23	4	2	.384	.364
Straub, Tyler	R-R	6-4	205	7-8-93	.270	.219	.294	35	100	19	27	3	1	0	12	15	3	2	0	9	8	1	.320	.381
Vasquez, Cristhian	L-L	6-0	175	9-11-96	.164	.267	.116	41	140	20	23	3	3	3	12	13	4	2	2	31	2	2	.293	.252
Vazquez, Boo	L-R	6-4	212	8-4-92	.255	.250	.257	44	161	26	41	11	5	2	29	13	3	1	3	43	1	0	.422	.317
Vizcaino, Vance	R-R	6-3	215	8-1-94	.265	.321	.240	53	185	25	49	5	2	0	11	17	4	4	3	34	16	9	.314	.335

Pitching	B-T	HT	WT	DOB	W	L	ERA	G	GS	CG	SV	IP	H	R	ER	HR	BB	SO	AVG	vLH	vRH	K/9	BB/9
Bramblett, Geoffrey	R-R	6-2	200	4-26-95	6	1	2.17	11	10	0	0	50	34	13	12	3	9	43	.195	.208	.190	7.79	1.63
Camp, Justin	R-R	5-11	230	5-17-93	0	3	1.85	16	0	0	2	34	33	10	7	0	7	32	.252	.218	.276	8.47	1.85
Castillo, Cristian	L-L	6-0	185	9-25-94	3	3	3.13	12	12	1	0	72	57	28	25	3	14	73	.212	.271	.191	9.13	1.75
Davila, Garrett	L-L	6-2	180	1-17-97	7	0	2.77	12	12	0	0	65	56	21	20	2	27	55	.237	.206	.249	7.62	3.74
Davis, Andre	L-L	6-6	230	9-29-93	1	3	4.76	6	6	0	0	28	27	16	15	3	5	33	.252	.267	.247	10.48	1.59
Eckert, Travis	R-R	6-2	190	1-4-93	4	1	3.43	11	10	0	0	45	44	19	17	1	11	48	.262	.274	.247	9.67	2.22
Familia, Felix	L-L	6-0	170	11-28-95	1	0	13.50	7	0	0	0	9	15	14	14	3	10	5	.366	.286	.382	4.82	9.64
Gomez, Ofreidy	R-R	6-3	190	7-6-95	5	4	5.20	12	12	1	0	55	46	35	32	4	27	44	.236	.213	.250	7.16	4.39
Kidston, Anthony	R-R	6-2	185	5-18-93	0	1	4.70	16	0	0	0	23	20	12	12	4	14	36	.227	.250	.214	14.09	5.48
Massey, Alex	R-R	6-2	180	4-3-94	2	1	1.60	16	0	0	2	34	26	7	6	3	6	39	.211	.163	.238	10.43	1.60
McKay, David	R-R	6-3	205	3-31-95	3	3	2.64	12	5	0	0	44	38	14	13	3	15	41	.233	.246	.225	8.32	3.05
Sheller, Walker	R-R	6-3	195	5-21-95	0	0	2.95	17	0	0	6	21	13	10	7	0	15	18	.178	.242	.125	7.59	6.33
Silva, Michael	R-R	6-1	190	11-22-94	2	2	4.50	18	0	0	3	20	18	10	10	2	12	12	.250	.161	.317	5.40	5.40
Tatum, Vance	L-L	6-4	215	5-2-95	2	2	3.52	16	0	0	1	31	33	17	12	4	11	36	.266	.212	.286	10.57	3.23
Veras, Jose	R-R	6-1	170	7-15-94	1	2	3.24	14	1	0	1	33	32	14	12	5	5	30	.254	.308	.216	8.10	1.35

Fielding

C: Arroyo 21, Esposito 29, Evans 4, Livingston 12, Salva 6. **1B:** DeVito 57, Nottebrok 5, Straub 8. **2B:** Cancel 41, McCray 21, Straub 13. **3B:** Cancel 2, Gray 1, Nottebrok 1, Rivera 57, Straub 10. **SS:** Cancel 4, Lopez 62, Straub 6. **OF:** McCray 21, Peterson 43, Sanchez 27, Vasquez 42, Vazquez 30, Vizcaino 50.

AZL ROYALS   ROOKIE
ARIZONA LEAGUE

Batting	B-T	HT	WT	DOB	AVG	vLH	vRH	G	AB	R	H	2B	3B	HR	RBI	BB	HBP	SH	SF	SO	SB	CS	SLG	OBP
Arias, Joel	R-R	6-0	160	4-6-97	.229	.333	.207	25	70	6	16	3	0	1	9	1	0	0	1	31	1	1	.314	.236
Atencio, Jesus	R-R	5-10	165	8-22-96	.154	.167	.150	13	26	2	4	1	0	0	2	4	1	1	0	7	0	0	.192	.290
Brontsema, John	R-R	6-2	187	12-13-94	.343	.277	.367	47	175	34	60	9	1	0	24	13	4	0	3	30	9	4	.406	.395
Clemmons, Leland	R-R	5-9	170	6-17-93	.083	.000	.111	5	12	4	1	0	0	1	1	4	0	0	0	5	0	0	.333	.313
Coleman, Dusty	R-R	6-2	205	4-20-87	.280	.167	.316	7	25	5	7	2	1	1	5	3	0	0	1	5	2	0	.560	.345
Collado, Offerman	R-L	5-10	140	6-10-96	.250	.250	.250	22	80	5	20	3	0	0	9	3	1	2	0	12	0	1	.288	.286
Dini, Nick	R-R	5-8	180	7-27-93	.400	.000	.667	2	5	0	2	0	0	0	1	0	1	0	0	2	0		.400	.500
Ebert, Jordan	R-R	6-1	180	7-7-93	.300	.167	.324	10	40	11	12	2	1	0	3	2	2	0	0	6	6	1	.400	.364
Franco, Wander	R-R	6-2	180	12-13-94	.615	.500	.714	3	13	3	8	1	0	1	4	1	0	0	0	0	0	0	.923	.643
Griffin, Dalton	L-L	6-3	200	9-2-97	.179	.185	.177	40	140	14	25	5	0	0	13	10	0	3	2	36	3	0	.214	.230
Guzman, Jeison	B-R	6-2	180	10-8-98	.261	.304	.246	45	188	35	49	9	5	1	19	18	1	1	0	44	5	3	.378	.329

Batting

Batting	B-T	HT	WT	DOB	AVG	vLH	vRH	G	AB	R	H	2B	3B	HR	RBI	BB	HBP	SH	SF	SO	SB	CS	SLG	OBP
Jones, Cal	R-R	6-0	175	9-16-97	.232	.297	.212	39	155	27	36	4	1	4	19	14	3	1	1	54	7	3	.348	.306
Lee, Khalil	L-L	5-10	170	6-26-98	.269	.220	.284	49	182	43	49	9	6	6	29	33	6	0	1	57	8	4	.484	.396
Livingston, Chase	R-R	6-1	203	4-6-94	.316	.000	.429	8	19	3	6	0	0	0	3	0	1	0	0	3	0	0	.316	.409
Marquez, Jose	R-R	6-0	175	10-7-97	.220	.111	.250	36	123	16	27	3	2	1	17	9	1	1	2	34	4	1	.301	.274
Martin, Rudy	L-L	5-7	150	1-31-96	.313	—	.313	5	16	0	5	0	1	0	2	1	0	0	0	6	1	1	.438	.353
Matias, Seuly	R-R	6-3	200	9-4-98	.250	.250	.250	46	172	32	43	11	2	8	29	22	4	0	0	73	2	4	.477	.348
McCann, Mike	R-R	6-2	205	7-11-95	.200	.000	.250	5	15	2	3	0	0	0	3	2	0	0	1	2	0	0	.200	.278
Nunez, Oliver	B-R	5-10	170	2-21-95	.273	.235	.282	27	88	14	24	4	1	0	9	19	1	0	0	12	4	2	.341	.407
Rinn, Robby	L-L	6-1	205	10-17-92	.280	.256	.287	50	189	24	53	13	2	1	31	18	0	2	1	33	6	1	.386	.341
Rivero, Sebastian	R-R	6-1	180	11-16-98	.269	.129	.311	38	134	15	36	10	0	0	20	6	1	1	1	28	0	0	.343	.303
Vallot, Chase	R-R	6-0	215	8-21-96	.133	.000	.154	10	30	5	4	1	0	2	2	3	2	0	0	14	0	0	.367	.257
Wakamatsu, Jake	L-R	6-0	180	5-18-92	.364	.500	.286	3	11	2	4	0	0	0	1	0	0	0	0	2	0	0	.364	.364

Pitching

Pitching	B-T	HT	WT	DOB	W	L	ERA	G	GS	CG	SV	IP	H	R	ER	HR	BB	SO	AVG	vLH	vRH	K/9	BB/9
Alexander, Scott	L-L	6-2	190	7-10-89	0	0	4.91	5	2	0	0	7	8	4	4	0	2	12	.276	.000	.348	14.73	2.45
Bender, Anthony	R-R	6-4	205	2-3-95	2	0	3.03	9	5	0	2	33	31	15	11	0	4	32	.228	.229	.227	8.82	1.10
Davis, Wade	R-R	6-5	225	9-7-85	0	0	0.00	1	0	0	0	1	1	0	0	0	0	1	.250	.000	.500	9.00	0.00
Drabble, Dillon	R-R	6-2	190	7-12-96	4	2	3.88	14	7	0	0	60	71	33	26	3	9	51	.290	.248	.328	7.61	1.34
Eaton, Todd	R-R	6-1	190	5-9-92	0	0	4.50	5	0	0	1	8	7	4	4	0	0	9	.241	.167	.294	10.13	0.00
Fallwell, Tyler	R-R	6-5	210	11-8-95	0	0	2.08	2	0	0	0	4	5	2	1	0	0	6	.278	.429	.182	12.46	0.00
Familia, Felix	L-L	6-0	170	11-28-95	0	0	3.00	6	0	0	0	6	6	2	2	0	3	4	.240	.250	.238	6.00	4.50
Farrell, Luke	R-R	6-6	210	6-7-91	1	0	1.35	2	0	0	0	7	4	1	1	0	3	12	.167	.286	.118	16.20	4.05
Ferguson, Andy	R-R	6-1	195	9-2-88	0	1	2.03	4	4	0	0	13	10	6	3	0	1	13	.213	.176	.233	8.78	0.68
Gavin, Grant	R-R	6-2	185	7-10-95	3	1	2.01	13	4	0	1	49	41	17	11	0	5	47	.217	.221	.215	8.57	0.91
Gwinn, Jeremy	R-R	6-5	195	10-1-95	0	0	3.57	15	0	0	3	18	20	13	7	2	4	13	.286	.348	.255	6.62	2.04
Harris, Garrett	R-R	6-3	220	3-21-94	1	2	9.45	10	0	0	1	13	19	16	14	1	4	17	.339	.417	.281	11.48	2.70
Hill, Rex	L-L	6-3	200	9-8-93	2	2	4.04	11	2	0	0	36	42	24	16	2	12	42	.294	.235	.302	10.60	3.03
Howell, Colton	R-R	6-1	200	10-26-93	2	3	2.63	12	5	0	0	38	39	13	11	1	9	29	.264	.226	.284	6.93	2.15
Kaczmarek, Taylor	R-R	6-1	215	1-23-92	3	0	1.69	11	0	0	1	16	16	4	3	1	5	9	.262	.300	.306	5.06	2.81
Lovelady, Richard	L-L	6-0	175	7-7-95	2	0	1.74	8	0	0	3	10	4	5	2	0	2	14	.111	.000	.143	12.19	1.74
Maldonado, Ismael	R-R	6-4	170	9-28-95	1	2	6.90	13	2	0	0	30	33	35	23	3	20	22	.273	.259	.284	6.60	6.00
Medlen, Kris	B-R	5-10	190	10-7-85	0	0	0.00	1	1	0	0	3	3	0	0	0	0	2	.375	.000	.429	9.00	0.00
Messier, Mike	R-L	6-2	205	5-12-95	0	1	11.25	3	0	0	0	4	9	5	5	0	3	7	.350	.500	.286	15.75	6.75
Nesbit, Cody	R-R	6-3	175	3-5-96	0	0	3.18	5	0	0	0	6	5	2	2	0	4	4	.250	.167	.286	6.35	6.35
Pinto, Julio	R-R	6-3	185	11-18-95	0	0	4.91	5	4	0	0	11	11	9	6	1	7	10	.262	.111	.303	8.18	5.73
Puckett, A.J.	R-R	6-3	205	5-27-95	0	1	3.86	2	2	0	0	7	8	5	3	1	0	8	.258	.444	.182	10.29	0.00
Rodriguez, Jorge	L-L	6-0	160	6-30-96	3	2	2.63	7	6	0	0	24	17	7	7	1	6	19	.195	.059	.229	7.13	2.25
Russell, Ashe	R-R	6-4	201	8-28-96	0	1	9.00	2	2	0	0	2	1	2	2	0	2	1	.200	.333	.000	4.50	9.00
Selman, Sam	L-L	6-3	190	11-14-90	0	0	5.79	3	0	0	0	5	6	4	3	0	2	6	.273	.250	.278	11.57	3.86
Sparkman, Glenn	B-R	6-2	210	5-11-92	1	3	5.40	7	7	0	0	17	19	12	10	1	1	17	.279	.267	.289	9.18	0.54
Vargas, Jason	L-L	6-0	215	2-2-83	0	0	4.50	2	2	0	0	4	5	4	2	1	0	8	.278	.333	.267	18.00	0.00
Vines, Jace	R-R	6-3	215	9-4-94	0	0	10.80	1	0	0	0	3	2	2	2	0	1	2	.375	.333	.400	10.80	5.40
Webb, Nathan	R-R	6-2	215	8-20-97	1	1	5.06	12	0	0	0	16	14	9	9	0	12	16	.233	.192	.265	9.00	6.75
Wynne, Matt	R-R	6-4	235	7-5-93	3	0	1.74	14	0	0	2	21	20	9	4	0	4	15	.235	.185	.259	6.53	1.74
Young, Paul	R-R	6-2	205	3-15-93	0	0	0.00	1	0	0	0	1	0	0	0	0	0	1	.000	—	.000	6.75	0.00

Fielding

C: Atencio 12, Dini 2, Livingston 8, McCann 4, Rivero 37, Vallot 5. **1B:** Brontsema 5, Livingston 1, Rinn 50. **2B:** Brontsema 3, Coleman 1, Collado 11, Ebert 4, Marquez 34, Nunez 3, Wakamatsu 1. **3B:** Brontsema 32, Coleman 2, Collado 1, Ebert 3, Franco 1, Nunez 18. **SS:** Brontsema 2, Coleman 2, Collado 11, Guzman 44, Nunez 1. **OF:** Arias 22, Clemmons 3, Griffin 31, Jones 35, Lee 42, Martin 4, Matias 41.

DSL ROYALS

DOMINICAN SUMMER LEAGUE

ROOKIE

Batting

Batting	B-T	HT	WT	DOB	AVG	vLH	vRH	G	AB	R	H	2B	3B	HR	RBI	BB	HBP	SH	SF	SO	SB	CS	SLG	OBP
Bejaran, Leonel	B-R	5-9	160	7-23-97	.198	.294	.172	37	81	17	16	0	0	0	2	12	1	4	1	25	6	4	.198	.305
Caraballo, Jose	R-R	6-1	180	1-7-97	.287	.385	.244	48	171	28	49	9	1	6	26	13	3	3	1	40	2	3	.456	.346
Carrasco, Dennicher	R-R	5-11	195	10-12-95	.263	.242	.272	63	224	43	59	11	0	7	26	33	4	0	2	42	5	3	.406	.365
Fermin, Freddy	R-R	5-10	185	5-16-95	.273	.204	.301	52	172	18	47	9	0	0	17	21	3	1	6	23	1	2	.326	.351
Guzman, Jeison	B-R	6-2	180	10-8-98	.171	.200	.167	9	35	4	6	2	0	0	3	0	0	0	6	2	0	0	.229	.237
Jaquez, Rubendy	B-R	5-11	174	2-13-99	.240	.323	.214	47	129	20	31	5	0	0	9	22	5	1	0	20	5	6	.279	.372
Lopez, Raymond	B-R	6-1	155	12-4-98	.259	.279	.250	62	201	37	52	4	2	0	14	31	6	7	1	45	26	9	.299	.372
Martin, Andres	R-R	6-0	190	1-31-96	.257	.196	.277	56	187	23	48	2	2	0	26	20	4	8	3	27	8	3	.289	.336
Matias, Seuly	R-R	6-3	200	9-4-98	.125	.000	.167	7	24	2	3	1	0	0	2	2	1	0	0	13	0	0	.167	.222
Medina, Angel	R-R	6-1	180	11-2-98	.276	.214	.295	50	181	31	50	6	3	3	24	14	4	0	2	36	6	3	.392	.338
Mondesi, Paul	R-R	6-0	215	7-28-99	.239	.045	.333	28	67	2	16	6	0	0	16	8	1	0	1	7	2	0	.328	.325
Peguero, Juan	R-R	6-2	190	2-9-98	.243	.240	.244	38	111	14	27	5	1	0	14	10	9	1	0	29	2	1	.333	.354
Perez, Cristian	R-R	5-10	170	10-26-98	.251	.256	.250	59	175	24	44	7	0	0	36	26	4	8	7	20	10	5	.291	.349
Ramirez, Dagin	B-R	6-0	175	7-4-96	.150	.000	.194	22	40	5	6	1	0	0	2	5	1	1	0	8	0	3	.175	.261
Rivero, Sebastian	R-R	6-1	180	11-16-98	.333	.000	.375	8	27	3	9	0	0	0	4	1	0	0	0	4	0	0	.333	.357
Rodriguez, Ismaldo	B-R	6-0	175	7-3-98	.269	.429	.226	29	67	12	18	5	1	1	5	4	2	1	1	20	4	6	.418	.324
Romero, Rafael	B-R	5-10	155	11-14-98	.208	.172	.224	35	96	5	20	1	0	0	8	9	0	1	3	15	1	2	.219	.269
Ruiz, Esteury	R-R	6-0	150	2-15-99	.313	.236	.340	56	217	44	68	18	5	5	26	19	4	3	1	35	13	10	.512	.378
Torres, Jose	R-R	6-0	175	9-16-95	.250	.200	.263	17	24	6	6	1	0	0	4	6	0	0	1	4	3	1	.292	.387

Pitching

Pitching	B-T	HT	WT	DOB	W	L	ERA	G	GS	CG	SV	IP	H	R	ER	HR	BB	SO	AVG	vLH	vRH	K/9	BB/9
Acevedo, Randy	R-R	6-1	155	3-14-97	3	0	0.99	12	12	0	0	63	49	10	7	0	9	31	.216	.184	.225	4.41	1.28
Alcantara, Luis	R-R	6-0	150	11-1-97	1	2	2.04	12	0	0	2	18	18	8	4	1	6	13	.257	.250	.260	6.62	3.06
Castillo, Adriam	R-R	6-0	190	11-19-98	1	0	4.50	4	0	0	0	6	2	4	3	0	5	7	.095	.200	.063	10.50	7.50
Chavez, Francis	R-R	6-0	170	11-28-96	5	2	0.92	15	0	0	5	39	22	7	4	1	10	31	.165	.107	.181	7.09	2.29
De La Cruz, Joel	R-R	6-2	190	11-9-96	5	0	0.91	13	0	0	4	30	15	5	3	0	7	25	.146	.174	.138	7.58	2.12
De Leon, Jose	R-R	5-11	175	4-19-95	2	1	2.00	12	0	0	1	18	15	6	4	0	10	17	.242	.273	.225	8.50	5.00
Escotto, Jeicol	R-R	6-4	185	12-28-95	1	1	3.00	13	0	0	0	24	26	20	8	0	13	23	.274	.348	.250	8.63	4.88
Estevez, Emmanuel	R-R	6-3	210	8-22-96	2	2	3.86	11	0	0	1	19	15	13	8	1	11	18	.211	.222	.208	8.68	5.30
Fana, Jeisson	R-R	5-11	155	1-29-99	0	0	0.00	3	0	0	0	3	4	0	0	0	1	4	.308	.000	.333	12.00	3.00
Feliz, Darwin	R-R	6-1	175	9-19-96	3	0	1.30	13	13	0	0	55	37	12	8	0	9	45	.188	.240	.170	7.32	1.46
Garcia, Yerelmy	R-R	6-2	180	11-5-95	3	4	1.65	14	6	0	1	49	36	19	9	0	10	24	.209	.245	.193	4.41	1.84
Gonzalez, Kelvin	R-R	6-0	170	12-24-97	1	0	5.06	9	0	0	0	16	16	11	9	2	8	11	.246	.300	.236	6.19	4.50
Lara, Janser	R-R	6-0	170	8-10-96	1	2	4.09	12	7	0	1	33	33	17	15	4	21	45	.260	.244	.267	12.27	5.73
Marte, Christopher	R-R	6-1	190	7-9-96	8	2	1.89	14	11	0	0	67	54	20	14	3	16	39	.227	.266	.213	5.27	2.16
Medrano, Miguel	R-R	6-2	175	6-19-95	0	0	0.66	8	0	0	3	14	6	2	1	0	2	6	.130	.071	.156	3.95	1.32
Rodriguez, Enderson	R-R	6-3	180	3-21-96	3	1	1.87	13	7	0	0	43	33	13	9	1	16	20	.219	.348	.162	4.15	3.32
Sotillet, Andres	R-R	6-1	175	3-2-97	7	2	1.52	13	13	1	0	65	48	15	11	0	8	41	.210	.183	.219	5.68	1.11
Tapia, Jose	R-R	6-1	178	10-19-96	1	2	2.08	15	0	0	6	35	19	11	8	1	11	34	.162	.125	.182	8.83	2.86

Fielding

C: Fermin 43, Mondesi 27, Rivero 8, Torres 9. **1B:** Carrasco 57, Ramirez 2, Rodriguez 12, Torres 7. **2B:** Jaquez 38, Perez 6, Romero 7, Ruiz 26. **3B:** Medina 48, Ramirez 11, Rodriguez 3, Romero 24. **SS:** Guzman 7, Jaquez 1, Perez 52, Romero 8, Ruiz 10. **OF:** Bejaran 21, Caraballo 44, Lopez 59, Martin 54, Matias 7, Peguero 36.

Los Angeles Angels

SEASON IN A SENTENCE: Injuries riddled a thin pitching staff, from the rotation to the bullpen, and a lack of power stymied the offense as the Angels finished with their worst record in manager Mike Scioscia's 17 years at the helm.

HIGH POINT: As the big league team slipped, Mike Trout kept giving Angels fans a chance to come out, as the club surpassed 3 million fans for the 14th consecutive season, the second-best streak in the majors (after the Yankees, with 18). Trout won BA's Major League Player of the Year award for the third time in his five seasons, finishing one home run shy of his second 30-30 season. He led the majors in walks (116), runs (123) and on-base percentage (.441).

LOW POINT: The Angels' pitching staff had two major injuries, the biggest coming in May when Garrett Richards was diagnosed with a partially torn right ulnar collateral ligament. He didn't have Tommy John surgery and instead had stem cell therapy and platelet-rich plasma injections that had him throwing by instructional league. The second was on Sept. 4, when Mariners third baseman Kyle Seager hit a 105-mph line drive off the head of righthander Matt Shoemaker, fracturing his skull.

NOTABLE ROOKIES: Minor league free agents Jefry Marte (15 homers) and outfielder Rafael Ortega, as well as 2011 31st-round pick Jett Bandy all got time in the lineup, with Marte producing the most but Bandy performing well defensively.

KEY TRANSACTIONS: Hector Santiago, a 2015 all-star, was traded in July to the Twins for righthander Ricky Nolasco, a Southern California prep product, and righthander Alex Meyer, the 6-foot-9 former Nationals and Twins prospect. Meyer and Nolasco both could be in the 2017 rotation. Righthander Tim Lincecum tried to make a comeback with the Angels after signing in May, but the 32-year-old was rocked for 68 hits in 38 innings and posted a 9.16 ERA. Off the field, first-year GM Billy Eppler continued to put his stamp on the organization, reassigning scouting director Ric Wilson and hiring Matt Swanson, previously with the Cardinals, as scouting director.

DOWN ON THE FARM: While both Rookie-level affiliates made the playoffs—with Orem winning the Pioneer League title—the Angels' lack of farm system talent showed in its lack of big league reinforcements as well as a 313-381 record (.451) for domestic affiliates, 28th in baseball.

OPENING DAY PAYROLL: $137,251,333 (13th)

PLAYERS OF THE YEAR

MAJOR LEAGUE	MINOR LEAGUE
Mike Trout	**Jahmai Jones**
of	of
.315/.441/.550	(Rookie/Low A)
29 HR, 100 RBI,	.302/.379/.422
116 BB, 30 SB	4 HR, 30 RBI, 20 SB

ORGANIZATION LEADERS

BATTING   *Minimum 250 AB

MAJORS

*	AVG	Mike Trout	.315
*	OPS	Mike Trout	.991
	HR	Albert Pujols	31
	RBI	Albert Pujols	119

MINORS

*	AVG	Rafael Ortega, Salt Lake	.317
*	OBP	Michael Hermosillo, Burlington, Inland Empire	.402
*	SLG	Michael Hermosillo, Burlington, Inland Empire	.467
*	OPS	Michael Hermosillo, Burlington, Inland Empire	.869
	R	Hutton Moyer, Burlington, Inland Empire	75
	H	Alex Yarbrough, Salt Lake, Arkansas	139
	TB	Hutton Moyer, Burlington, Inland Empire	226
	2B	Kaleb Cowart, Salt Lake	34
	3B	Caleb Adams, Inland Empire, Arkansas	9
		Cal Towey, Arkansas, Salt Lake	9
	HR	Zachary Houchins, Inland Empire	18
	RBI	Zachary Houchins, Inland Empire	84
	BB	Cal Towey, Arkansas, Salt Lake	76
	SO	Cal Towey, Arkansas, Salt Lake	145
	SB	Quintin Berry, Salt Lake	35

PITCHING   #Minimum 75 IP

MAJORS

	W	Jered Weaver	12
#	ERA	Jered Weaver	5.06
	SO	Matt Shoemaker	143
	SV	Huston Street	9

MINORS

	W	Jordan Kipper, Arkansas	12
		Troy Scribner, Arkansas, Salt Lake	12
	L	Jake Jewell, Inland Empire	15
#	ERA	Jose Rodriguez, Burlington	3.14
	G	Eduardo Paredes, Inland Empire, Arkansas	54
	GS	5 players	27
	SV	Eduardo Paredes, Inland Empire, Arkansas	12
		Zach Hartman, Burlington, Inland Empire	12
		Javy Guerra, Salt Lake	12
	IP	Jordan Kipper, Arkansas	153
	BB	Ronnie Glenn, Burlington	66
	SO	Kyle McGowin, Arkansas, Salt Lake	130
#	AVG	Troy Scribner, Arkansas, Salt Lake	.206

General Manager: Billy Eppler. **Farm Director:** Bobby Scales. **Scouting Director:** Ric Wilson.

Class	Team	League	W	L	PCT	Finish	Manager
Majors	Los Angeles Angels	American	74	88	.457	12th (15)	Mike Scioscia
Triple-A	Salt Lake Bees	Pacific Coast	63	79	.444	15th (16)	Keith Johnson
Double-A	Arkansas Travelers	Texas	67	73	.479	5th (8)	Mark Parent
High A	Inland Empire 66ers	California	48	92	.343	10th (10)	Chad Tracy
Low A	Burlington Bees	Midwest	68	72	.486	10th (16)	Adam Melhuse
Rookie	Orem Owlz	Pioneer	38	38	.500	t-4th (8)	Dave Stapleton
Rookie	Angels	Arizona	29	27	.518	7th (14)	Elio Sarmiento
Overall 2016 Minor League Record			313	381	.451	28th (30)	

ORGANIZATION STATISTICS

LOS ANGELES ANGELS
AMERICAN LEAGUE

Batting	B-T	HT	WT	DOB	AVG	vLH	vRH	G	AB	R	H	2B	3B	HR	RBI	BB	HBP	SH	SF	SO	SB	CS	SLG	OBP
Bandy, Jett	R-R	6-4	235	3-26-90	.234	.203	.247	70	209	23	49	9	0	8	25	11	4	3	4	38	1	0	.392	.281
Buss, Nick	L-R	6-2	190	12-15-86	.198	.000	.242	36	81	7	16	7	1	1	8	6	0	1	2	24	2	1	.346	.247
Calhoun, Kole	L-L	5-10	205	10-14-87	.271	.290	.264	157	594	91	161	35	5	18	75	67	6	0	5	118	2	3	.438	.348
Choi, Ji-Man	L-R	6-1	230	5-19-91	.170	.000	.174	54	112	9	19	4	0	5	12	16	0	0	1	27	2	4	.339	.271
Cowart, Kaleb	B-R	6-3	225	6-2-92	.176	.294	.147	31	85	8	15	4	0	1	8	0	1	0	1	23	0	0	.259	.184
Cron Jr. C.J.	R-R	6-4	235	1-5-90	.278	.237	.290	116	407	51	113	25	2	16	69	24	7	0	5	75	2	3	.467	.325
Cunningham, Todd	B-R	6-0	205	3-20-89	.148	.500	.120	20	27	5	4	3	0	0	1	1	0	1	0	6	0	1	.259	.179
Escobar, Yunel	R-R	6-2	215	11-2-82	.304	.314	.301	132	517	68	157	28	1	5	39	40	3	3	4	67	0	3	.391	.355
Gentry, Craig	R-R	6-2	190	11-29-83	.147	.154	.125	14	34	2	5	1	0	0	2	3	1	1	0	6	0	0	.176	.237
Giavotella, Johnny	R-R	5-8	185	7-10-87	.260	.258	.261	99	346	44	90	20	1	6	31	13	1	4	3	39	4	3	.376	.287
Graterol, Juan	R-R	6-1	205	2-14-89	.286	.000	.308	9	14	2	4	2	0	0	3	0	0	1	0	3	0	0	.429	.286
Marte, Jefry	R-R	6-1	220	6-21-91	.252	.244	.256	88	258	38	65	14	0	15	44	18	5	0	3	59	2	2	.481	.310
Nava, Daniel	B-L	5-11	200	2-22-83	.235	1.000	.229	45	119	10	28	5	0	1	13	9	5	0	3	26	0	0	.303	.309
2-team total (9 Kansas City)					.223	—	—	54	130	11	29	6	0	1	13	10	5	0	3	30	0	0	.292	.297
Ortega, Rafael	L-R	5-11	160	5-15-91	.232	.200	.236	66	185	24	43	8	0	1	16	13	0	3	0	23	8	3	.292	.283
Pennington, Cliff	B-R	5-11	195	6-15-84	.209	.095	.225	74	172	18	36	4	2	3	10	13	0	3	0	55	1	0	.308	.265
Perez, Carlos	R-R	6-0	210	10-27-90	.209	.208	.209	87	268	25	56	16	0	5	31	12	1	8	2	49	1	0	.325	.244
Petit, Gregorio	R-R	5-10	200	12-10-84	.245	.222	.255	89	204	21	50	13	1	2	17	15	1	2	1	51	1	1	.348	.299
Pujols, Albert	R-R	6-3	240	1-16-80	.268	.279	.265	152	593	71	159	19	0	31	119	49	2	0	6	75	4	0	.457	.323
Robinson, Shane	R-R	5-9	170	10-30-84	.173	.185	.159	65	98	16	17	3	0	1	10	10	1	2	0	17	3	2	.235	.257
Ryan, Brendan	R-R	6-1	190	3-26-82	.077	.000	.111	17	13	1	1	0	0	0	0	0	1	0	7	0	0	.077	.077
Simmons, Andrelton	R-R	6-2	200	9-4-89	.281	.295	.277	124	448	48	126	22	2	4	44	28	2	1	4	38	10	1	.366	.324
Soto, Geovany	R-R	6-1	225	1-20-83	.269	.321	.240	26	78	11	21	5	0	4	9	6	0	2	0	21	0	0	.487	.321
Trout, Mike	R-R	6-2	235	8-7-91	.315	.323	.313	159	549	123	173	32	5	29	100	116	11	0	5	137	30	7	.550	.441

Pitching	B-T	HT	WT	DOB	W	L	ERA	G	GS	CG	SV	IP	H	R	ER	HR	BB	SO	AVG	vLH	vRH	K/9	BB/9
Achter, A.J.	R-R	6-5	215	8-27-88	1	0	3.11	27	0	0	0	38	43	13	13	7	12	14	.295	.288	.299	3.35	2.87
Alburquerque, Al	R-R	6-0	195	6-10-86	0	0	4.50	2	0	0	0	2	2	3	1	1	2	1	.200	.2	.2	4.50	9.00
Alvarez, Jose	L-L	5-11	190	5-6-89	1	3	3.45	64	0	0	0	57	71	29	22	4	15	51	.298	.283	.312	8.01	2.35
Bailey, Andrew	R-R	6-3	240	5-31-84	0	0	2.38	12	0	0	6	11	9	3	3	1	2	8	.214	.067	.296	6.35	1.59
Bedrosian, Cam	R-R	6-0	230	10-2-91	2	0	1.12	45	0	0	0	40	30	7	5	1	14	51	.207	.243	.173	11.38	3.12
Chacin, Jhoulys	R-R	6-3	215	1-7-88	5	6	4.68	29	17	1	0	117	124	64	61	10	47	92	.272	.276	.268	7.06	3.61
Ege, Cody	L-L	6-1	190	5-8-91	1	0	1.04	13	0	0	0	9	8	1	1	1	3	9	.250	.158	.385	9.35	3.12
Guerra, Deolis	R-R	6-5	245	4-17-89	3	0	3.21	44	0	0	0	53	52	23	19	6	7	36	.249	.21	.288	6.08	1.18
Guerra, Javy	R-R	6-1	225	10-31-85	0	0	5.68	7	0	0	0	6	5	4	4	1	7	4	.227	0	.263	5.68	9.95
Heaney, Andrew	L-L	6-2	195	6-5-91	0	1	6.00	1	1	0	0	6	7	4	4	2	0	7	.280	.167	.316	10.50	0.00
Huff, David	L-L	6-1	210	8-22-84	0	2	11.81	2	2	0	0	5	13	10	7	4	2	3	.464	.2	.522	5.06	3.38
Lincecum, Tim	L-R	5-11	170	6-15-84	2	6	9.16	9	9	0	0	38	68	41	39	11	23	32	.395	.367	.432	7.51	5.40
Mahle, Greg	L-L	6-2	230	4-17-93	1	0	5.40	24	0	0	0	18	23	13	11	4	10	14	.315	.333	.294	6.87	4.91
Meyer, Alex	R-R	6-9	225	1-3-90	1	2	4.57	5	5	0	0	22	17	11	11	2	13	24	.215	.29	.167	9.97	5.40
2-team total (2 Minnesota)					1	3	5.68	7	6	0	0	25	25	16	16	3	17	29	—	—	—	10.30	6.04
Morin, Mike	R-R	6-4	220	5-3-91	2	2	4.37	60	0	0	0	56	52	31	27	6	15	49	.250	.257	.246	7.92	2.43
Nolasco, Ricky	R-R	6-2	235	12-13-82	4	6	3.21	11	11	1	0	73	63	27	26	8	15	51	.232	.228	.234	6.29	1.85
2-team total (21 Minnesota)					8	14	4.42	32	32	1	0	198	202	104	97	26	44	144	—	—	—	6.56	2.00
Oberholtzer, Brett	L-L	6-1	225	7-1-89	1	1	8.55	11	2	0	0	20	27	19	19	7	9	16	.318	.32	.317	7.20	4.05
Ramirez, J.C.	R-R	6-4	250	8-16-88	2	1	2.91	43	0	0	1	46	42	17	15	5	13	31	.241	.205	.279	6.02	2.53
Rasmus, Cory	R-R	6-0	200	11-6-87	0	2	5.84	19	1	0	0	25	25	16	16	4	16	17	.260	.167	.333	6.20	5.84
Richards, Garrett	R-R	6-3	210	5-27-88	1	3	2.34	6	6	0	0	35	31	16	9	2	15	34	.238	.18	.29	8.83	3.89
Salas, Fernando	R-R	6-2	200	5-30-85	3	6	4.47	58	0	0	6	56	52	28	28	9	19	45	.248	.257	.238	7.19	3.04
Santiago, Hector	R-L	6-0	215	12-16-87	10	4	4.25	22	22	0	0	121	104	61	57	20	57	107	.233	.236	.232	7.98	4.25
2-team total (11 Minnesota)					13	10	4.70	33	33	0	0	182	169	100	95	33	79	144	—	—	—	7.12	3.91
Shoemaker, Matt	R-R	6-2	225	9-27-86	9	13	3.88	27	27	1	0	160	166	71	69	18	30	143	.266	.263	.27	8.04	1.69
Skaggs, Tyler	L-L	6-4	215	7-13-91	3	4	4.17	10	10	0	0	50	51	23	23	5	23	50	.267	.318	.252	9.06	4.17
Smith, Joe	R-R	6-2	205	3-22-84	1	4	3.82	38	0	0	6	38	36	16	16	4	13	25	.257	.246	.267	5.97	3.11

Pitching	B-T	HT	WT	DOB	W	L	ERA	G	GS	CG	SV	IP	H	R	ER	HR	BB	SO	AVG	vLH	vRH	K/9	BB/9
Street, Huston	R-R	6-0	205	8-2-83	3	2	6.45	26	0	0	9	22	31	16	16	5	12	14	.337	.279	.388	5.64	4.84
Tropeano, Nick	R-R	6-4	200	8-27-90	3	2	3.56	13	13	0	0	68	70	27	27	14	31	68	.270	.277	.264	8.96	4.08
Valdez, Jose	R-R	6-1	200	3-1-90	2	3	4.24	25	0	0	0	23	17	11	11	4	16	22	.202	.161	.226	8.49	6.17
Weaver, Jered	R-R	6-7	210	10-4-82	12	12	5.06	31	31	1	0	178	209	106	100	37	51	103	.297	.298	.296	5.21	2.58
Wright, Daniel	R-R	6-2	205	4-3-91	1	3	5.40	5	5	0	0	27	32	16	16	5	6	15	.314	.29	.324	5.06	2.03

Fielding

Catcher	PCT	G	PO	A	E	DP	PB
Bandy	.993	68	412	39	3	4	2
Graterol	1.000	9	31	3	0	0	0
Perez	.995	82	571	43	3	7	4
Soto	.993	23	145	6	1	0	1

First Base	PCT	G	PO	A	E	DP
Choi	.993	27	127	11	1	15
Cowart	1.000	1	3	0	0	1
Cron Jr.	.993	97	761	48	6	78
Marte	.989	29	169	14	2	18
Pennington	1.000	3	2	1	0	1
Perez	1.000	1	2	0	0	1
Pujols	.991	28	200	16	2	20
Soto	.750	1	2	1	1	0

Second Base	PCT	G	PO	A	E	DP
Cowart	.962	15	21	29	2	8
Giavotella	.986	97	165	186	5	54
Pennington	.994	58	66	98	1	27
Petit	.966	50	49	66	4	18

Third Base	PCT	G	PO	A	E	DP
Cowart	.974	21	8	30	1	3
Escobar	.937	129	95	188	19	22
Marte	.957	22	10	34	2	2
Pennington	1.000	1	1	0	0	0
Petit	.944	10	4	13	1	0
Soto	1.000	1	0	1	0	0

Shortstop	PCT	G	PO	A	E	DP
Pennington	.983	17	25	34	1	8
Petit	.973	32	31	78	3	13
Ryan	1.000	16	9	13	0	2
Simmons	.982	124	198	337	10	82

Outfield	PCT	G	PO	A	E	DP
Buss	1.000	31	39	1	0	0
Calhoun	.984	154	306	9	5	1
Choi	1.000	20	26	0	0	0
Cunningham	.955	18	19	2	1	1
Gentry	.967	13	28	1	1	0
Marte	.976	27	39	2	1	0
Nava	1.000	37	62	3	0	0
Ortega	.973	59	103	7	3	1
Petit	1.000	7	19	0	0	0
Robinson	.989	55	87	2	1	0
Ryan	1.000	1	1	0	0	0
Trout	.989	148	360	7	4	1

SALT LAKE BEES
PACIFIC COAST LEAGUE

TRIPLE-A

Batting	B-T	HT	WT	DOB	AVG	vLH	vRH	G	AB	R	H	2B	3B	HR	RBI	BB	HBP	SH	SF	SO	SB	CS	SLG	OBP
Allday, Forrestt	R-R	5-11	190	4-24-91	.227	.083	.281	14	44	3	10	0	0	0	1	4	0	1	0	7	1	0	.227	.292
Amendolare, Angelo	R-R	5-9	180	12-2-92	.000	—	.000	3	2	0	0	0	0	0	0	0	0	0	0	1	0	0	.000	.000
Arakawa, Tim	L-R	5-8	175	4-18-93	.176	.200	.167	16	51	3	9	1	1	0	4	4	0	1	1	13	1	0	.235	.232
Bandy, Jett	R-R	6-4	235	3-26-90	.274	.227	.288	24	95	13	26	7	0	2	21	2	5	0	3	19	2	1	.411	.314
Bayardi, Brandon	R-R	6-2	235	11-27-90	.333	—	.333	2	3	0	1	0	0	0	0	0	0	0	0	0	0	0	.333	.333
Bemboom, Anthony	L-R	6-2	195	1-18-90	.261	.235	.268	47	157	20	41	8	3	1	13	16	0	4	0	31	5	2	.369	.329
Berry, Quintin	L-L	6-1	195	11-21-84	.270	.274	.266	100	345	46	93	12	2	1	32	38	5	4	3	79	35	10	.325	.348
Briceno, Jose	R-R	6-1	210	9-19-92	.300	.250	.333	3	10	2	3	1	0	0	3	2	0	0	0	1	0	0	.400	.417
Buss, Nick	L-R	6-2	190	12-15-86	.290	.324	.275	87	331	49	96	23	8	6	46	30	0	7	4	66	8	5	.462	.345
Choi, Ji-Man	L-R	6-1	230	5-19-91	.346	.383	.328	53	188	31	65	17	1	5	31	31	2	1	5	34	4	3	.527	.434
Cousino, Austin	L-L	5-10	178	4-17-93	.172	.167	.174	10	29	3	5	0	1	0	4	1	0	1	0	11	3	1	.241	.200
Cowart, Kaleb	B-R	6-3	225	6-2-92	.280	.260	.289	107	414	58	116	34	5	9	58	37	2	1	3	100	18	4	.452	.340
Cron Jr. C.J.	R-R	6-4	235	1-5-90	.150	.333	.071	6	20	0	3	1	0	0	2	3	0	0	1	5	1	0	.200	.250
Cunningham, Todd	B-R	6-0	205	3-20-89	.278	.274	.280	99	349	66	97	16	2	6	43	51	7	3	5	56	23	5	.387	.378
Genao, Angel	R-R	6-2	180	3-22-93	1.000	—	1.000	1	1	1	1	0	0	0	1	0	0	0	0	0	0	0	2.000	1.000
Gentry, Craig	R-R	6-2	190	11-29-83	.129	.200	.115	8	31	6	4	1	0	0	1	5	0	0	1	8	4	0	.161	.243
Giavotella, Johnny	R-R	5-8	185	7-10-87	.296	.429	.250	7	27	2	8	3	0	0	1	3	0	0	0	3	1	0	.407	.367
Graterol, Juan	R-R	6-1	205	2-14-89	.300	.300	.299	68	227	24	68	10	0	2	23	10	5	2	2	27	2	1	.370	.340
Jackson, Ryan	R-R	6-2	180	5-10-88	.262	.339	.233	62	206	19	54	9	0	3	30	30	0	2	3	45	4	2	.306	.351
Johnson, Sherman	L-R	5-10	190	7-15-90	.226	.210	.233	108	394	54	89	17	3	8	45	60	5	3	5	85	16	3	.345	.332
Kratz, Erik	R-R	6-4	245	6-15-80	.231	.417	.148	12	39	6	9	3	0	0	7	1	0	0	0	12	0	0	.308	.268
Kubitza, Kyle	L-R	6-3	210	7-15-90	.253	.163	.285	54	186	22	47	5	5	2	19	27	1	0	1	60	6	3	.366	.349
2-team total (44 Round Rock)					.220	—	—	98	345	38	76	14	7	6	34	50	3	1	3	108	13	3	.354	.322
Marte, Jefry	R-R	6-1	220	6-21-91	.265	.293	.256	44	162	22	43	12	1	3	24	22	2	0	3	35	3	3	.407	.354
Nava, Daniel	B-L	5-11	200	2-22-83	.365	.280	.400	22	85	5	31	6	0	1	13	6	1	0	0	10	1	1	.471	.413
2-team total (3 Omaha)					.348	—	—	25	92	6	32	7	0	1	13	9	2	0	0	11	1	1	.457	.417
Navarro, Rey	B-R	5-10	185	12-22-89	.227	.295	.202	41	163	12	37	9	2	1	13	5	1	5	1	28	0	0	.325	.253
Ortega, Rafael	L-R	5-11	160	5-15-91	.317	.277	.335	78	322	47	102	18	7	4	31	15	1	2	1	39	14	8	.453	.348
Pennington, Cliff	B-R	5-11	195	6-15-84	.304	.000	.368	7	23	3	7	2	1	0	3	3	0	0	4	0	0	0	.478	.385
Perez, Carlos	R-R	6-0	210	10-27-90	.359	.300	.379	10	39	9	14	4	0	3	10	1	0	0	0	7	0	2	.692	.375
Petit, Gregorio	R-R	5-10	200	12-10-84	.327	.375	.308	17	55	7	18	3	0	2	5	0	1	1	3	13	2	0	.382	.377
Rivas, Webster	R-R	6-2	218	8-8-90	.286	.400	.000	3	7	0	2	0	0	0	0	0	0	0	0	2	0	0	.286	.286
Robinson, Shane	R-R	5-9	170	10-30-84	.315	.348	.300	19	73	14	23	4	0	4	3	12	1	2	1	8	4	0	.370	.346
Rosa, Angel	R-R	6-2	185	9-19-92	.203	.231	.192	47	143	13	29	3	2	4	15	12	2	2	1	44	6	0	.336	.272
Ryan, Brendan	R-R	6-2	190	3-26-82	.232	.240	.229	59	190	16	44	6	1	0	15	18	0	2	2	48	6	3	.274	.295
Simmons, Andrelton	R-R	6-2	200	9-4-89	.333	.750	.214	4	18	0	6	1	0	0	5	0	0	0	0	2	1	0	.389	.333
Soto, Geovany	R-R	6-1	225	1-20-83	.194	.182	.200	10	36	2	7	4	0	1	8	1	0	1	0	7	0	0	.389	.216
Towey, Cal	L-R	6-1	215	2-6-90	.244	.280	.230	78	258	37	63	9	4	9	32	42	4	1	1	94	9	5	.415	.357
Yarbrough, Alex	B-R	6-0	200	8-3-91	.214	.333	.125	4	14	0	3	0	0	0	0	1	1	0	0	0	1	0	0	.429	.200

Pitching	B-T	HT	WT	DOB	W	L	ERA	G	GS	CG	SV	IP	H	R	ER	HR	BB	SO	AVG	vLH	vRH	K/9	BB/9
Achter, A.J.	R-R	6-5	215	8-27-88	2	2	3.50	29	1	0	3	46	31	19	18	9	14	33	.187	.211	.168	6.41	2.72
Alburquerque, Al	R-R	6-0	195	6-10-86	1	0	3.80	24	0	0	8	24	24	12	10	0	13	26	.261	.200	.308	9.89	4.94
2-team total (6 Tacoma)					1	1	4.25	30	0	0	8	30	33	16	14	1	17	32	—	—	—	9.71	5.16
Alvarez, Jose	L-L	5-11	190	5-6-89	1	0	2.45	5	0	0	0	7	5	3	2	0	5	7	.208	.500	.15	8.59	6.14

Pitching

Pitching	B-T	HT	WT	DOB	W	L	ERA	G	GS	CG	SV	IP	H	R	ER	HR	BB	SO	AVG	vLH	vRH	K/9	BB/9
Bailey, Andrew	R-R	6-3	240	5-31-84	2	1	2.00	8	0	0	0	9	7	3	2	0	3	11	.212	.167	.238	11.00	3.00
Bedrosian, Cam	R-R	6-0	230	10-2-91	1	0	3.24	5	0	0	1	8	7	3	3	1	4	14	.212	.316	.071	15.12	4.32
Broussard, Geoff	R-R	6-0	185	9-21-90	2	4	7.25	29	2	0	0	45	60	40	36	8	20	40	.326	.253	.376	8.06	4.03
Brunnemann, Tyler	R-R	6-2	220	8-9-91	0	1	19.29	1	0	0	0	2	5	5	5	1	1	2	.417	.600	.286	7.71	3.86
Busenitz, Alan	R-R	6-1	180	8-22-90	0	1	7.62	10	0	0	0	13	16	13	11	1	5	13	.308	.360	.259	9.00	3.46
Carpenter, David	R-R	6-3	250	7-15-85	1	1	7.80	15	0	0	0	15	17	13	13	2	9	18	.293	.391	.229	10.80	5.40
Cotts, Neal	L-L	6-2	200	3-25-80	0	0	3.29	14	0	0	1	14	12	5	5	1	3	13	.235	.111	.303	8.56	1.98
2-team total (20 Round Rock)					2	2	3.62	34	0	0	1	37	35	15	15	3	13	36	—	—	—	8.68	3.13
DeLoach, Tyler	R-L	6-6	240	4-12-91	0	0	4.24	21	0	0	0	23	26	14	11	0	16	20	.277	.275	.278	7.71	6.17
Ege, Cody	L-L	6-1	190	5-8-91	0	0	4.91	6	0	0	0	7	6	4	4	1	2	11	.222	.300	.176	13.50	2.45
2-team total (36 New Orleans)					4	3	4.56	42	0	0	5	51	48	28	26	2	29	46	—	—	—	8.06	5.08
Guerra, Deolis	R-R	6-5	245	4-17-89	0	0	0.00	3	0	0	0	5	3	0	0	0	2	7	.167	.000	.214	12.60	3.60
Guerra, Javy	R-R	6-1	225	10-31-85	3	2	4.35	43	1	0	12	52	48	30	25	5	31	57	.239	.184	.281	9.93	5.40
Huff, David	L-L	6-1	210	8-22-84	1	2	6.91	6	6	0	0	29	42	23	22	5	9	23	.336	.366	.321	7.22	2.83
2-team total (12 Omaha)					2	3	5.68	18	6	0	1	52	71	34	33	8	11	52	—	—	—	8.94	1.89
Jones, Chris	L-L	6-2	205	9-19-88	7	11	6.46	23	21	0	0	118	155	91	85	10	39	80	.324	.346	.313	6.08	2.97
Kendrick, Kyle	R-R	6-3	220	8-26-84	6	5	4.73	16	15	0	0	93	101	50	49	13	19	67	.274	.215	.330	6.46	1.83
Lincecum, Tim	L-R	5-11	170	6-15-84	0	3	3.76	7	7	0	0	38	30	21	16	2	14	37	.213	.250	.178	8.69	3.29
Luetge, Lucas	L-L	6-4	205	3-24-87	1	1	4.85	48	0	0	2	56	58	32	30	4	26	58	.279	.284	.276	9.38	4.20
Mahle, Greg	L-L	6-2	230	4-17-93	1	1	7.71	30	0	0	2	33	48	29	28	7	12	24	.353	.370	.344	6.61	3.31
Maya, Yunesky	R-R	6-0	215	8-28-81	2	3	5.92	5	5	0	0	24	40	23	16	6	9	15	.377	.340	.415	5.55	3.33
McGowin, Kyle	R-R	6-3	195	11-27-91	6	12	6.11	22	22	0	0	116	144	86	79	16	46	98	.308	.308	.309	7.58	3.56
Meyer, Alex	R-R	6-9	225	1-3-90	0	0	0.00	1	1	0	0	4	2	0	0	0	0	6	.143	.250	.000	13.50	0.00
Middleton, Keynan	R-R	6-2	185	9-12-93	0	1	4.91	8	0	0	2	15	14	8	8	1	4	16	.250	.222	.276	8.59	2.45
Morin, Mike	R-R	6-4	220	5-3-91	0	1	3.60	11	0	0	2	10	8	4	4	2	1	11	.222	.250	.208	9.90	0.90
Nuding, Zach	R-R	6-4	260	3-29-90	2	7	6.51	14	13	0	0	66	81	51	48	11	31	41	.300	.331	.274	5.56	4.21
O'Grady, Chris	L-L	6-4	205	1-27-87	2	1	4.15	22	2	0	0	35	41	18	16	3	12	24	.311	.322	.301	6.23	3.12
Ramirez, Ramon	R-R	5-11	200	8-31-81	2	5	5.40	13	0	0	1	23	24	15	14	2	9	21	.270	.293	.250	8.10	3.47
Roenicke, Josh	R-R	6-3	205	8-4-82	0	0	23.63	4	0	0	0	3	10	7	7	0	3	1	.588	.600	.583	3.38	10.13
Satterwhite, Cody	R-R	6-4	235	1-27-87	3	1	1.80	18	0	0	0	25	19	10	5	2	8	22	.204	.209	.200	7.92	2.88
Scribner, Troy	R-R	6-3	190	7-2-91	4	2	3.30	8	7	2	0	46	34	18	17	4	22	35	.206	.217	.198	6.80	4.27
Shoemaker, Matt	R-R	6-2	225	9-27-86	1	0	1.00	1	1	0	0	6	6	1	1	1	2	8	.250	.111	.333	12.00	3.00
Skaggs, Tyler	L-L	6-4	215	7-13-91	3	2	1.67	7	7	0	0	32	19	9	6	2	8	45	.171	.226	.150	12.53	2.23
Smith, Nate	L-L	6-3	210	8-28-91	8	9	4.61	26	26	0	0	150	166	85	77	18	44	122	.283	.269	.290	7.30	2.63
Tropeano, Nick	R-R	6-4	200	8-27-90	1	0	2.70	1	1	0	0	7	3	2	2	1	1	7	.136	.100	.167	9.45	1.35
Valdez, Jose	R-R	6-1	200	3-1-90	0	1	0.70	22	0	0	5	26	13	3	2	1	11	28	.146	.097	.172	9.82	3.86
Weller, Blayne	R-R	6-5	220	1-30-90	0	3	15.00	4	4	0	0	15	30	29	25	6	13	14	.417	.394	.436	8.40	7.80

Fielding

Catcher	PCT	G	PO	A	E	DP	PB
Bandy	.983	21	164	14	3	2	3
Bemboom	.982	38	303	25	6	4	2
Briceno	.958	3	23	0	1	0	0
Graterol	.993	61	410	44	3	5	4
Kratz	.947	8	52	2	3	1	0
Perez	.988	9	79	4	1	0	1
Rivas	1.000	3	15	2	0	0	1
Soto	1.000	7	48	2	0	0	1

	PCT	G	PO	A	E	DP
Jackson	1.000	3	3	9	0	2
Johnson	.984	87	159	206	6	57
Kubitza	1.000	6	4	10	0	1
Navarro	1.000	11	19	22	0	3
Pennington	1.000	2	2	5	0	3
Petit	1.000	2	3	9	0	2
Rosa	1.000	5	1	5	0	0
Ryan	.917	2	5	6	1	2
Yarbrough	.933	4	6	8	1	3

Shortstop	PCT	G	PO	A	E	DP
Cowart	.979	10	17	30	1	6
Jackson	.974	38	49	98	4	22
Navarro	.935	16	25	33	4	7
Pennington	1.000	2	1	2	0	2
Petit	.960	15	25	47	3	9
Rosa	.929	16	26	39	5	9
Ryan	.970	49	73	119	6	33
Simmons	.933	3	6	8	1	2

First Base	PCT	G	PO	A	E	DP
Choi	1.000	28	220	11	0	21
Cowart	.992	15	116	5	1	13
Cron Jr.	.957	4	43	2	2	5
Jackson	.875	1	5	2	1	2
Kubitza	.962	12	92	9	4	7
Marte	.988	36	294	30	4	24
Nava	1.000	5	43	3	0	3
Rosa	1.000	19	133	12	0	21
Towey	.986	29	196	15	3	17

Third Base	PCT	G	PO	A	E	DP
Bemboom	—	1	0	0	0	0
Cowart	.953	65	48	115	8	7
Cunningham	1.000	1	2	2	0	0
Giavotella	.950	7	7	12	1	1
Jackson	.953	16	6	35	2	1
Johnson	.932	13	14	27	3	8
Kubitza	.917	14	12	21	3	0
Marte	1.000	6	2	16	0	1
Navarro	.969	11	7	24	1	2
Pennington	1.000	1	1	0	0	0
Rosa	.913	7	6	15	2	0
Ryan	1.000	4	3	6	0	1

Outfield	PCT	G	PO	A	E	DP
Allday	1.000	14	27	0	0	0
Arakawa	.833	6	5	0	1	0
Bayardi	1.000	2	1	0	0	0
Bemboom	1.000	1	1	0	0	0
Berry	.990	86	198	5	2	1
Buss	.988	71	156	4	2	0
Choi	.909	15	20	0	2	0
Cousino	.958	8	22	1	1	1
Cunningham	.973	89	175	7	5	0
Gentry	1.000	7	0	0	0	0
Kubitza	.964	14	26	1	1	0
Nava	1.000	8	13	2	0	0
Ortega	.978	69	122	10	3	2
Robinson	.969	13	30	1	1	0
Towey	.981	40	49	3	1	0

Second Base	PCT	G	PO	A	E	DP
Amendolare	—	0	0	0	0	0
Arakawa	1.000	11	23	28	0	10
Cowart	.947	14	20	34	3	6

ARKANSAS TRAVELERS
TEXAS LEAGUE

DOUBLE-A

Batting	B-T	HT	WT	DOB	AVG	vLH	vRH	G	AB	R	H	2B	3B	HR	RBI	BB	HBP	SH	SF	SO	SB	CS	SLG	OBP
Adams, Caleb	R-R	5-10	185	1-26-93	.228	.277	.216	70	246	28	56	5	3	4	24	18	3	6	2	82	9	4	.321	.286
Aguilera, Eric	L-L	6-2	218	7-3-90	.270	.238	.277	119	459	49	124	25	4	14	65	22	4	5	1	30	0	9	.434	.313
Allday, Forrestt	R-R	5-11	190	4-24-91	.281	.313	.274	28	89	11	25	8	0	0	7	12	3	2	0	13	4	2	.371	.385

Batting	B-T	HT	WT	DOB	AVG	vLH	vRH	G	AB	R	H	2B	3B	HR	RBI	BB	HBP	SH	SF	SO	SB	CS	SLG	OBP
Amendolare, Angelo	R-R	5-9	180	12-2-92	.167	—	.167	2	6	1	1	0	0	0	0	1	0	0	0	1	0	0	.167	.286
Arakawa, Tim	L-R	5-8	175	4-18-93	.173	.333	.151	27	98	8	17	4	0	0	7	13	1	4	0	18	6	1	.214	.277
Bayardi, Brandon	R-R	6-2	235	11-27-90	.246	.200	.262	18	57	5	14	3	0	1	7	1	3	1	0	15	0	1	.351	.295
Bemboom, Anthony	L-R	6-2	195	1-18-90	.146	.222	.125	25	82	6	12	3	0	0	1	7	1	0	0	17	0	2	.183	.222
Briceno, Jose	R-R	6-1	210	9-19-92	.225	.267	.214	62	227	25	51	12	2	3	21	11	0	1	1	42	2	2	.335	.259
Coyle, Sean	R-R	5-8	175	1-17-92	.204	.280	.189	40	157	20	32	6	1	3	13	14	2	3	0	56	7	3	.312	.277
Daniel, Andrew	R-R	6-1	195	1-27-93	.266	.259	.267	121	448	51	119	21	2	5	43	39	7	2	4	102	9	3	.355	.331
Fletcher, David	R-R	5-10	175	5-31-94	.300	.429	.273	20	80	10	24	6	0	0	6	3	0	0	0	13	1	0	.375	.325
Henry, Jabari	R-R	6-1	200	11-11-90	.213	.237	.207	102	352	42	75	11	1	15	51	36	7	0	2	110	2	8	.378	.297
Hinshaw, Chad	R-R	6-1	205	9-10-90	.190	.294	.170	57	205	26	39	6	1	5	23	20	9	0	2	69	14	6	.302	.288
Johnson, Sherman	L-R	5-10	190	7-15-90	.369	.300	.382	19	65	18	24	4	2	4	9	14	0	1	0	13	2	1	.677	.481
McGee, Stephen	R-R	6-3	215	2-7-91	.165	.241	.141	38	121	9	20	5	0	2	8	15	3	0	2	38	1	0	.256	.270
Phillips, Anthony	R-R	5-9	160	4-11-90	.259	.333	.241	114	347	43	90	11	3	1	37	37	4	11	6	79	9	11	.317	.332
Rosa, Angel	R-R	6-2	185	9-19-92	.182	.095	.211	54	165	16	30	5	2	2	11	11	1	2	5	52	2	0	.273	.239
Strentz, Michael	R-R	6-1	215	11-10-91	.083	.333	.000	4	12	0	1	0	0	0	0	2	0	0	0	6	0	1	.083	.214
Towey, Cal	L-R	6-1	215	2-6-90	.292	.152	.321	57	192	28	56	11	5	4	17	34	2	0	1	51	5	6	.464	.402
Wass, Wade	R-R	6-0	215	9-23-91	.189	.286	.170	41	127	13	24	2	1	1	13	19	3	1	3	49	4	2	.244	.303
Way, Bo	L-L	6-0	180	11-17-91	.261	.242	.264	130	425	41	111	11	4	2	36	31	6	8	1	87	21	14	.320	.320
Welz, Zach	R-R	6-1	190	5-7-92	.206	.182	.211	26	68	11	14	3	1	1	7	9	0	1	0	28	1	1	.324	.299
Yarbrough, Alex	B-R	6-0	200	8-3-91	.267	.238	.274	131	510	48	136	32	3	4	52	32	1	3	8	128	11	7	.365	.307

Pitching	B-T	HT	WT	DOB	W	L	ERA	G	GS	CG	SV	IP	H	R	ER	HR	BB	SO	AVG	vLH	vRH	K/9	BB/9
Adams, Austin	R-R	6-2	225	5-5-91	0	1	3.05	32	0	0	4	41	29	14	14	2	24	61	.199	.186	.204	13.28	5.23
Alcantara, Victor	R-R	6-2	190	4-3-93	3	7	4.30	29	20	0	0	111	106	62	53	9	57	79	.255	.307	.226	6.41	4.62
Alonzo, Eric	R-R	6-2	215	8-28-91	2	1	2.19	8	0	0	0	12	5	3	3	0	2	8	.125	.125	.125	5.84	1.46
Blackford, Alex	R-R	5-11	200	11-16-90	9	7	3.07	22	22	0	0	111	75	41	38	13	49	105	.189	.197	.184	8.49	3.96
Broussard, Geoff	R-R	6-0	185	9-21-90	0	0	4.58	15	0	0	3	18	11	9	9	5	5	24	.183	.120	.229	12.23	2.55
Brunnemann, Tyler	R-R	6-2	220	8-9-91	0	1	9.00	1	0	0	0	3	2	2	0	2	2	.333	.500	.200	9.00	9.00	
Busenitz, Alan	R-R	6-1	180	8-22-90	1	0	1.93	24	0	0	3	33	29	7	7	2	5	32	.244	.214	.260	8.82	1.38
Carpenter, Tyler	R-R	6-5	225	2-25-92	4	9	5.58	15	15	0	0	71	93	46	44	6	17	50	.323	.267	.353	6.34	2.15
DeLoach, Tyler	R-L	6-6	240	4-12-91	4	1	2.06	30	0	0	3	39	29	9	9	2	8	49	.213	.161	.257	11.21	1.83
Fury, Nate	R-R	5-11	200	2-6-91	0	1	2.16	7	0	0	0	8	5	2	2	0	9	8	.179	.000	.208	8.64	9.72
Grendell, Kevin	L-L	6-2	210	8-22-93	2	1	1.37	11	0	0	0	20	7	3	3	1	12	12	.091		.122	10.53	5.49
Johnson, D.J.	L-R	6-4	235	8-30-89	4	4	4.02	47	1	0	6	69	78	36	31	1	32	67	.291	.271	.301	8.70	4.15
Kipper, Jordan	R-R	6-4	185	10-6-92	12	7	3.35	25	25	2	0	153	147	63	57	10	41	85	.258	.252	.261	5.00	2.41
Klonowski, Alex	R-R	6-4	195	4-1-92	1	3	5.31	5	5	0	0	20	26	12	12	0	8	14	.321	.385	.291	6.31	3.54
McGowin, Kyle	R-R	6-3	195	11-27-91	3	2	4.56	5	5	1	0	26	22	17	13	4	9	32	.227	.257	.210	11.22	3.16
Middleton, Keynan	R-R	6-2	185	9-12-93	0	0	1.20	13	0	0	0	15	11	2	2	1	4	18	.196	.158	.216	10.80	2.40
Molina, Jose	L-L	5-11	160	6-26-91	0	3	5.55	25	8	0	0	62	78	39	38	5	23	48	.317	.228	.344	7.01	3.36
Nuding, Zach	R-R	6-4	260	3-29-90	2	3	2.97	13	5	0	0	39	43	16	13	3	10	28	.287	.235	.313	6.41	2.29
O'Grady, Chris	L-L	6-4	225	4-17-90	7	1	2.80	15	8	0	1	61	64	19	19	3	10	50	.276	.289	.269	7.38	1.48
Paredes, Eduardo	R-R	6-1	170	3-6-95	0	3	3.35	35	0	0	0	48	46	21	18	6	14	43	.247	.304	.223	8.01	2.61
Paredes, Edward	L-L	6-0	180	9-30-86	2	2	2.27	46	0	0	2	44	25	12	11	2	21	53	.167	.167	.167	10.92	4.33
Reynolds, Danny	R-R	6-0	190	5-2-91	1	3	5.61	22	0	0	0	34	27	21	21	2	24	31	.221	.244	.208	8.29	6.42
Roenicke, Josh	R-R	6-3	205	8-4-82	0	1	2.35	17	0	0	1	23	15	6	6	1	12	31	.192	.238	.175	12.13	4.70
Scribner, Troy	R-R	6-3	190	7-2-91	8	3	3.47	16	16	0	0	86	64	36	33	8	34	82	.206	.190	.215	8.61	3.57
Tolliver, Ashur	L-L	6-0	170	1-24-88	0	0	10.80	1	0	0	0	2	3	2	2	0	1	1	.429	.500	.400	5.40	5.40
Weller, Blayne	R-R	6-5	220	1-30-90	2	7	4.58	12	10	0	0	57	51	34	29	12	17	57	.237	.244	.233	9.00	2.68
Wood, Austin	R-R	6-4	230	7-11-90	1	1	4.76	19	0	0	3	17	17	13	9	1	14	12	.270	.333	.231	6.35	7.41

Fielding

Catcher	PCT	G	PO	A	E	DP	PB
Bemboom	.988	19	149	15	2	3	1
Briceno	.988	62	438	43	6	5	10
McGee	.987	25	210	15	3	1	11
Strentz	1.000	4	27	3	0	0	1
Wass	.997	35	279	20	1	2	8
Coyle	.995	38	92	106	1	29	
Daniel	1.000	20	42	51	0	12	
Johnson	.979	11	18	28	1	8	
Phillips	1.000	4	5	4	0	3	
Rosa	1.000	1	1	4	0	0	
Yarbrough	.996	59	100	138	1	36	
Fletcher	1.000	18	26	54	0	14	
Johnson	.923	5	4	8	1	2	
Phillips	.977	100	131	299	10	54	
Rosa	.976	17	29	52	2	14	

First Base	PCT	G	PO	A	E	DP
Aguilera	.993	99	798	43	6	75
Rosa	1.000	2	3	0	0	0
Towey	1.000	3	25	2	0	2
Yarbrough	1.000	38	293	13	0	31

Second Base	PCT	G	PO	A	E	DP
Amendolare	.750	2	5	1	2	1
Arakawa	1.000	7	13	14	0	6

Third Base	PCT	G	PO	A	E	DP
Daniel	.950	83	51	156	11	16
Johnson	.800	3	0	4	1	0
Phillips	1.000	1	1	2	0	2
Rosa	.986	32	22	49	1	3
Towey	.938	8	5	10	1	2
Yarbrough	.949	16	6	31	2	2

Shortstop	PCT	G	PO	A	E	DP
Arakawa	1.000	4	6	5	0	3

Outfield	PCT	G	PO	A	E	DP
Adams	1.000	68	115	4	0	1
Allday	1.000	28	68	3	0	0
Arakawa	1.000	16	22	0	0	0
Bayardi	1.000	15	24	1	0	0
Henry	1.000	53	89	4	0	2
Hinshaw	1.000	53	133	6	0	1
Phillips	1.000	11	23	0	0	0
Rosa	1.000	3	1	0	0	0
Towey	1.000	42	66	7	0	0
Way	.985	124	247	9	4	2
Welz	.962	23	50	1	2	0

INLAND EMPIRE 66ERS

HIGH CLASS A

CALIFORNIA LEAGUE

Batting	B-T	HT	WT	DOB	AVG	vLH	vRH	G	AB	R	H	2B	3B	HR	RBI	BB	HBP	SH	SF	SO	SB	CS	SLG	OBP
Adams, Caleb	R-R	5-10	185	1-26-93	.289	.227	.308	50	187	21	54	7	6	1	25	19	0	3	2	55	5	2	.406	.351

Batting

Batting	B-T	HT	WT	DOB	AVG	vLH	vRH	G	AB	R	H	2B	3B	HR	RBI	BB	HBP	SH	SF	SO	SB	CS	SLG	OBP
Allday, Forrestt	R-R	5-11	190	4-24-91	.278	—	.278	5	18	1	5	0	0	0	3	1	0	0	1	2	1	0	.278	.300
Allen, Trever	R-R	5-11	196	10-16-91	.157	.176	.151	22	70	10	11	2	1	0	2	6	0	0	0	22	0	0	.214	.224
Amendolare, Angelo	R-R	5-9	180	12-2-92	.278	.400	.231	5	18	7	5	0	1	0	2	7	0	0	0	3	1	0	.389	.480
Arakawa, Tim	L-R	5-8	175	4-18-93	.254	.271	.250	83	315	49	80	13	3	2	25	46	0	2	2	64	10	5	.333	.347
Baldoquin, Roberto	R-R	5-11	199	5-14-94	.198	.154	.211	64	227	19	45	6	1	0	15	21	3	3	1	62	3	3	.233	.274
Boehm, Jeff	L-L	6-1	215	11-4-92	.238	.139	.262	104	362	35	86	21	1	4	39	34	1	1	4	108	2	2	.334	.302
Briceno, Jose	R-R	6-1	210	9-19-92	.240	.250	.237	33	125	10	30	6	0	1	11	9	0	0	3	28	1	1	.312	.285
Delph, Josh	L-L	6-0	190	11-9-92	.206	.241	.196	44	136	8	28	3	0	0	7	18	2	2	1	37	1	1	.228	.306
Fletcher, David	R-R	5-10	175	5-31-94	.275	.313	.265	78	324	42	89	12	1	3	31	22	1	6	2	43	15	3	.346	.321
Foster, Jared	R-R	6-1	200	11-2-92	.294	.310	.290	40	160	23	47	7	2	4	23	4	4	2	4	33	6	2	.438	.320
Gentry, Craig	R-R	6-2	190	11-29-83	.227	.000	.250	7	22	3	5	1	0	0	3	5	1	0	0	4	2	0	.273	.393
Hermosillo, Michael	R-R	5-11	190	1-17-95	.309	.321	.306	40	149	36	46	7	4	4	17	16	6	1	2	30	6	7	.490	.393
Houchins, Zach	R-R	6-2	210	9-16-92	.262	.302	.252	134	511	69	134	24	2	18	84	35	4	0	5	94	2	0	.423	.312
Moyer, Hutton	B-R	6-1	185	4-30-93	.267	.190	.289	98	389	60	104	25	3	14	59	29	11	0	3	123	11	3	.455	.333
Nava, Daniel	B-L	5-11	200	2-22-83	.091	—	.091	4	11	1	1	0	0	0	0	2	0	0	0	1	0	0	.091	.231
Pennington, Cliff	B-R	5-11	195	6-15-84	.333	—	.333	2	6	0	2	0	1	0	1	0	0	0	0	1	0	0	.667	.429
Perez, Ayendy	L-R	5-9	170	10-9-93	.260	.286	.252	104	339	40	88	14	4	0	27	29	2	8	6	97	26	8	.324	.316
Rivas, Webster	R-R	6-2	218	8-8-90	.143	.000	.222	4	14	0	2	0	0	0	0	1	0	0	0	5	0	0	.143	.200
Robinson, Shane	R-R	5-9	170	10-30-84	.500	.500	.500	2	6	5	3	0	0	0	4	0	0	0	0	2	0	0	.500	.700
Rosa, Angel	R-R	6-2	185	9-19-92	.167	.333	.111	3	12	1	2	0	0	0	0	0	0	0	0	4	0	0	.167	.167
Sebra, Ryan	R-R	6-2	190	6-8-93	.175	.157	.182	58	183	16	32	5	2	0	22	13	3	2	2	37	4	1	.224	.239
Simmons, Andrelton	R-R	6-2	200	9-4-89	.333	—	.333	2	6	2	2	1	0	0	0	0	0	0	0	0	0	0	.500	.333
Strentz, Michael	R-R	6-1	215	11-10-91	.243	.209	.255	71	251	37	61	10	7	8	41	23	5	0	2	86	0	3	.434	.317
Towns, Kenny	R-R	5-11	180	12-19-92	.269	.400	.238	10	26	2	7	1	0	0	0	0	0	0	0	6	1	0	.308	.269
Ward, Taylor	R-R	6-1	185	12-14-93	.249	.274	.243	123	466	61	116	11	0	10	56	48	5	5	5	81	0	0	.337	.323
Wass, Wade	R-R	6-0	215	9-23-91	.259	.333	.242	53	193	25	50	15	1	8	32	22	8	0	1	71	2	1	.472	.357
Welz, Zach	R-R	6-1	190	5-7-92	.220	.297	.201	55	186	16	41	7	0	3	23	17	2	2	2	63	4	2	.306	.290

Pitching

Pitching	B-T	HT	WT	DOB	W	L	ERA	G	GS	CG	SV	IP	H	R	ER	HR	BB	SO	AVG	vLH	vRH	K/9	BB/9
Alonzo, Eric	R-R	6-2	215	8-28-91	1	1	3.58	18	1	0	1	33	38	15	13	1	8	32	.290	.224	.342	8.82	2.20
Anderson, Justin	L-R	6-3	220	9-28-92	8	12	5.70	28	27	0	0	145	193	99	92	15	48	107	.322	.347	.302	6.63	2.97
Carpenter, Tyler	R-R	6-5	225	2-25-92	2	0	0.82	5	5	0	0	33	19	3	3	1	3	27	.176	.135	.197	7.36	0.82
Cooney, Harrison	R-R	6-2	175	3-23-92	0	0	21.60	2	0	0	0	2	1	5	4	0	5	2	.167	.000	.333	10.80	27.00
Fury, Nate	R-R	5-11	200	2-6-91	1	2	3.21	30	0	0	0	42	34	21	15	7	21	49	.221	.200	.236	10.50	4.50
Grendell, Kevin	L-L	6-2	210	8-22-93	1	4	4.30	22	0	0	0	23	17	13	11	2	17	39	.202	.194	.208	15.26	6.65
Hartman, Zach	R-R	6-0	195	1-1-92	0	2	5.68	13	0	0	0	19	22	13	12	1	9	19	.286	.265	.302	9.00	4.26
Hofacket, Adam	R-R	6-1	195	2-18-94	1	2	6.03	26	0	0	2	34	38	24	23	4	13	37	.275	.286	.267	9.70	3.41
Holland, Sam	R-R	6-4	200	2-20-94	0	0	1.50	10	0	0	0	12	6	3	2	0	4	12	.158	.238	.059	9.00	3.00
Hoppe, Jason	R-R	6-1	170	6-13-92	1	2	4.22	25	5	0	0	49	56	26	23	3	18	47	.289	.293	.284	8.63	3.31
Jewell, Jake	R-R	6-3	200	5-16-93	2	15	6.31	28	27	0	0	137	191	110	96	10	65	104	.334	.333	.334	6.83	4.27
Karch, Eric	R-R	6-2	205	10-15-91	0	1	3.79	9	0	0	0	19	19	9	8	2	5	14	.257	.344	.190	6.63	2.37
Klonowski, Alex	R-R	6-4	195	4-1-92	8	11	5.57	23	22	0	0	128	127	82	79	15	38	106	.259	.285	.241	7.47	2.68
Lavendier, Winston	L-L	6-2	225	8-7-92	1	2	4.15	21	0	0	2	26	21	12	12	4	15	26	.221	.190	.245	9.00	5.19
Llorens, Dixon	R-R	5-10	170	11-18-92	3	1	5.57	12	0	0	0	21	26	17	13	2	14	21	.317	.321	.315	9.00	6.00
Loconsole, Brian	R-R	6-2	215	8-10-90	0	1	4.86	11	0	0	0	17	16	9	9	1	2	10	.262	.412	.205	5.40	1.08
Long, Grayson	R-R	6-5	230	5-27-94	2	1	5.14	3	3	0	0	14	14	9	8	5	4	15	.269	.357	.167	9.64	2.57
Meyer, Alex	R-R	6-9	225	1-3-90	0	0	11.57	1	1	0	0	2	3	3	3	0	1	3	.273	.250	.333	11.57	3.86
Middleton, Keynan	R-R	6-2	185	9-12-93	1	1	3.72	25	0	0	0	36	22	15	15	7	20	56	.172	.191	.160	13.87	4.95
Molina, Jose	L-L	5-11	160	6-26-91	3	2	2.53	16	0	0	0	21	19	6	6	1	6	17	.244	.24	.245	7.17	2.53
Muck, Ronnie	R-R	6-0	195	8-23-91	0	2	4.22	46	0	0	3	60	57	29	28	2	37	54	.257	.195	.293	8.15	5.58
Nuding, Zach	R-R	6-4	260	3-29-90	0	0	5.40	1	1	0	0	5	4	3	3	0	0	2	.222	.250	.200	12.60	0.00
Nuss, Garrett	R-R	6-1	180	4-15-93	3	3	5.82	9	9	0	0	43	48	31	28	3	19	34	.277	.232	.319	7.06	3.95
Paredes, Eduardo	R-R	6-1	170	3-6-95	1	2	3.27	19	0	0	4	22	18	9	8	2	6	32	.222	.308	.182	13.09	2.45
Piche, Jordan	R-R	6-1	180	9-3-91	2	5	4.39	44	0	0	1	55	63	36	27	4	17	34	.280	.298	.270	6.51	2.77
Rhoades, Jeremy	R-R	6-4	225	2-12-93	5	12	5.72	31	24	0	0	142	156	102	90	15	44	91	.277	.286	.270	5.78	2.80
Roenicke, Josh	R-R	6-3	205	8-4-82	1	1	2.65	10	0	0	0	17	9	6	5	0	8	17	.155	.211	.128	9.00	4.24
Ruxer, Jared	R-R	6-2	200	7-29-92	1	1	5.18	11	11	0	0	49	59	32	28	2	18	45	.306	.280	.333	8.32	3.33
Skaggs, Tyler	L-L	6-4	215	7-13-91	0	0	2.08	1	1	0	0	4	5	1	1	0	0	5	.294	.111	.500	10.38	0.00
Smith, Joe	R-R	6-2	205	3-22-84	0	0	0.00	2	1	0	0	2	0	0	0	0	0	2	.000	.000	.000	9.00	0.00
Trexler, David	R-R	6-3	185	9-4-90	0	0	6.75	3	0	0	0	4	2	3	3	2	4	7	.154	.667	.000	15.75	9.00
Tropeano, Nick	R-R	6-4	200	8-27-90	0	1	5.40	1	1	0	0	5	7	5	3	0	0	7	.318	.176	.800	12.60	0.00
Warmoth, Tyler	R-R	6-2	205	6-4-92	0	0	3.00	2	0	0	0	3	3	1	1	0	1	4	.250	.429	.000	3.00	3.00
Wilson, C.J.	L-L	6-1	210	11-18-80	0	0	2.25	1	1	0	0	4	5	1	1	0	0	4	.313	.143	.444	9.00	0.00

Fielding

Catcher	PCT	G	PO	A	E	DP	PB
Briceno	.984	18	157	22	3	1	4
Rivas	1.000	3	17	6	0	0	2
Strentz	.981	13	91	11	2	0	1
Ward	.994	90	685	93	5	3	19
Wass	.986	16	135	11	2	0	3

First Base	PCT	G	PO	A	E	DP
Boehm	.990	100	828	54	9	68
Houchins	1.000	16	140	13	0	15
Nava	1.000	1	5	0	0	0
Strentz	.989	12	88	6	1	12
Wass	.976	15	114	7	3	11

Second Base	PCT	G	PO	A	E	DP
Amendolare	.962	5	9	16	1	1
Arakawa	.981	34	61	91	3	18
Baldoquin	.991	25	44	70	1	11
Fletcher	.986	28	58	87	2	20
Moyer	.993	31	56	81	1	14
Rosa	1.000	2	5	2	0	0
Sebra	.933	19	36	47	6	11

Third Base	PCT	G	PO	A	E	DP
Baldoquin	.923	6	3	9	1	0
Houchins	.960	96	95	190	12	22
Moyer	.911	21	9	32	4	6
Sebra	.857	13	5	13	3	0
Towns	.923	9	3	9	1	0

Shortstop	PCT	G	PO	A	E	DP
Arakawa	.922	16	16	43	5	8
Baldoquin	.977	28	48	79	3	20
Fletcher	.979	47	76	115	4	23

	PCT	G	PO	A	E	DP
Houchins	.935	15	16	27	3	6
Moyer	.948	36	54	92	8	19
Pennington	1.000	1	1	5	0	1
Rosa	1.000	1	2	2	0	0
Simmons	1.000	2	1	3	0	1

Outfield	PCT	G	PO	A	E	DP
Adams	.987	48	74	1	1	0
Allday	1.000	5	13	2	0	0
Allen	1.000	22	33	3	0	2
Arakawa	.978	33	41	4	1	0

	PCT	G	PO	A	E	DP
Delph	.987	42	72	5	1	0
Foster	.969	37	89	6	3	1
Gentry	1.000	4	5	0	0	0
Hermosillo	.939	38	73	4	5	0
Nava	—	1	0	0	0	0
Perez	.933	102	174	8	13	2
Robinson	1.000	1	2	0	0	0
Sebra	1.000	19	32	5	0	1
Strentz	.896	31	39	4	5	0
Welz	.960	55	114	7	5	1

BURLINGTON BEES

LOW CLASS A

MIDWEST LEAGUE

LOS ANGELES ANGELS

Batting	B-T	HT	WT	DOB	AVG	vLH	vRH	G	AB	R	H	2B	3B	HR	RBI	BB	HBP	SH	SF	SO	SB	CS	SLG	OBP
Abbott, Alex	L-R	6-1	195	11-2-94	.138	.125	.143	28	87	9	12	2	0	0	7	10	4	1	0	27	0	2	.161	.257
Alberto, Ranyelmy	R-R	6-2	210	5-27-94	.231	.333	.204	73	281	20	65	11	1	2	27	11	0	0	1	87	1	0	.299	.274
Amendolare, Angelo	R-R	5-9	180	12-2-92	.280	.262	.287	44	157	24	44	8	0	0	10	19	5	1	0	33	5	3	.331	.376
Barash, Michael	R-R	6-1	200	10-12-94	.240	.455	.203	24	75	10	18	3	0	2	11	6	1	1	0	12	0	1	.360	.305
Delph, Josh	L-L	6-0	190	11-9-92	.255	.250	.256	35	106	14	27	4	0	0	12	18	1	4	0	21	6	4	.292	.368
Foster, Jared	R-R	6-2	200	11-2-92	.266	.339	.246	69	267	26	71	20	2	5	33	20	1	0	4	48	3	8	.412	.315
Genao, Angel	R-R	6-2	180	3-22-93	.171	.160	.178	21	70	8	12	2	2	0	3	3	1	3	0	24	1	2	.257	.216
Hermosillo, Michael	R-R	5-11	190	1-17-95	.326	.500	.286	37	138	22	45	8	1	2	22	18	2	2	0	22	4	3	.442	.411
Jones, Jahmai	R-R	6-0	215	8-4-97	.242	.273	.235	16	62	8	15	1	0	1	10	5	0	2	1	13	1	0	.306	.294
Justus, Connor	R-R	6-0	190	11-2-94	.230	.267	.226	42	139	19	32	3	1	2	9	14	11	2	1	34	1	2	.309	.345
Lubach, Tanner	R-R	6-0	190	11-21-92	.231	.214	.235	72	255	32	59	15	1	3	19	13	3	3	2	63	2	0	.333	.275
Lund, Brennon	L-R	5-10	185	11-27-94	.271	.400	.245	45	181	19	49	9	2	1	19	12	1	4	2	33	8	1	.359	.316
Montgomery, Troy	L-L	5-10	185	8-13-94	.261	.130	.286	38	142	15	37	7	2	3	13	16	2	4	2	30	3	2	.401	.340
Moreno, Juan	R-R	6-0	170	11-17-94	.167	.095	.194	40	150	10	25	2	0	0	9	1	7	0		34	5	5	.180	.219
Moyer, Hutton	B-R	6-1	185	4-30-93	.313	.158	.351	26	96	15	30	8	1	3	16	6	3	1	0	20	2	1	.510	.371
Pierson, Michael	L-R	5-11	200	5-3-92	.240	.309	.221	70	250	22	60	13	1	1	27	16	1	4	3	45	3	1	.312	.285
Rivas, Webster	R-R	6-2	218	8-8-90	.221	.176	.232	26	86	7	19	7	0	0	9	7	1	2	2	13	0	0	.302	.281
Rivera, Alexis	L-L	6-2	225	6-17-94	.290	.382	.276	71	259	26	75	17	0	6	36	17	1	0	0	49	5	4	.425	.336
Sanger, Brendon	L-R	6-0	195	9-11-93	.230	.221	.232	124	443	47	102	24	3	4	39	59	7	5	1	89	4	5	.325	.329
Serena, Jordan	R-R	6-2	220	8-4-92	.253	.299	.243	110	380	61	96	21	1	2	32	38	9	5	4	95	10	6	.329	.332
Thaiss, Matt	L-R	6-0	195	5-6-95	.276	.176	.297	52	199	24	55	12	3	4	31	22	2	1	2	28	1	0	.427	.351
Walsh, Jared	L-L	6-1	210	7-30-93	.290	.239	.301	109	393	55	114	30	1	7	36	31	2	3	1	81	2	0	.425	.344
Welz, Zach	R-R	6-1	190	5-7-92	.344	.545	.300	17	61	8	21	0	0	1	5	7	1	0	1	11	3	1	.393	.414
Yacinich, Jake	R-R	6-2	195	3-2-93	.241	.220	.247	51	199	21	48	7	0	4	27	8	3	2	0	34	5	2	.337	.281
Zimmerman, Jordan	R-R	6-1	195	11-21-94	.154	.250	.132	37	130	15	20	5	1	0	13	13	2	0	3	34	0	3	.208	.236

Pitching	B-T	HT	WT	DOB	W	L	ERA	G	GS	CG	SV	IP	H	R	ER	HR	BB	SO	AVG	vLH	vRH	K/9	BB/9
Alonzo, Eric	B-R	6-2	215	8-28-91	1	0	0.88	12	0	0	2	31	21	3	3	0	8	38	.189	.250	.143	11.15	2.35
Barria, Jaime	R-R	6-1	210	7-18-96	8	6	3.85	25	25	0	0	117	133	58	50	6	21	78	.282	.297	.260	6.00	1.62
Castillo, Jesus	R-R	6-2	165	8-27-95	3	2	2.43	6	6	0	0	30	33	11	8	1	7	23	.295	.349	.224	6.98	2.12
Cox, Aaron	R-R	6-3	205	8-5-94	3	2	3.94	33	0	0	10	48	47	22	21	1	14	40	.255	.325	.198	7.50	2.63
De Los Santos, Samil	R-R	6-4	175	1-8-94	0	0	10.80	3	0	0	0	3	7	6	4	1	3	4	.412	.600	.333	10.80	8.10
Gatto, Joe	R-R	6-3	220	6-14-95	3	8	7.03	15	15	0	0	64	88	62	50	5	33	54	.321	.339	.306	7.59	4.64
Glenn, Ronnie	L-L	6-3	230	7-15-93	3	7	4.55	27	20	0	2	113	123	65	57	8	66	70	.285	.294	.282	5.59	5.27
Grendell, Kevin	L-L	6-2	210	8-22-93	2	0	1.93	8	0	0	0	19	12	5	4	1	6	30	.188	.294	.149	14.46	2.89
Hartman, Zach	R-R	6-0	195	1-1-92	3	0	2.20	29	0	0	12	45	35	12	11	1	14	40	.213	.237	.193	8.00	2.80
Hofacket, Adam	R-R	6-1	195	2-18-94	1	1	2.53	15	0	0	7	21	20	6	6	2	2	24	.238	.286	.190	10.13	0.84
Holland, Sam	R-R	6-4	200	2-20-94	3	1	0.57	19	0	0	8	31	16	4	2	0	3	24	.148	.188	.117	6.89	0.86
Kaelin, Mike	R-R	5-9	185	3-30-94	1	1	2.16	18	0	0	0	33	39	11	8	1	8	25	.291	.255	.316	6.75	2.16
Karch, Eric	R-R	6-2	205	10-15-91	2	6	3.41	17	2	0	0	34	43	21	13	3	8	33	.297	.299	.295	8.65	2.10
Lavendier, Winston	L-L	6-2	225	8-7-92	1	2	3.16	24	0	0	0	43	46	21	15	2	14	45	.275	.286	.271	9.49	2.95
Lillis-White, Conor	L-L	6-4	220	7-22-92	1	0	3.00	6	0	0	0	9	7	3	3	1	6	15	.226	.333	.182	15.00	6.00
Long, Grayson	R-R	6-5	230	5-27-94	3	3	1.58	8	8	0	0	40	27	13	7	2	16	45	.190	.246	.148	10.13	3.60
Manoah, Erik	R-R	6-2	190	12-22-95	0	0	6.00	1	1	0	0	3	5	2	2	0	2	3	.385	.000	.455	9.00	6.00
McDavid, Jacob	R-R	6-5	210	2-20-93	0	1	10.13	3	0	0	0	5	6	6	6	0	5	5	.391	.357	.444	6.75	5.06
Pena, Luis	R-R	5-11	190	8-24-95	5	9	4.02	27	16	0	1	101	89	50	45	6	43	118	.239	.230	.246	10.55	3.84
Polanco, Jhonny	R-R	6-3	195	4-28-92	2	1	3.78	28	0	0	0	48	36	21	20	3	28	61	.202	.189	.216	11.52	5.29
Pope, Cody	R-R	6-4	220	5-13-93	0	1	6.23	7	0	0	0	9	11	11	6	0	10	5	.297	.263	.333	5.19	10.38
Robichaux, Austin	R-R	6-6	175	11-23-92	4	3	4.74	12	12	0	0	57	57	34	30	2	23	41	.264	.324	.207	6.47	3.63
Rodriguez, Jose	R-R	6-2	175	8-29-95	7	5	3.14	27	27	0	0	132	135	53	46	4	32	115	.263	.271	.254	7.86	2.19
Ruxer, Jared	R-R	6-3	200	7-29-92	3	2	1.44	18	8	0	0	62	59	19	10	3	13	54	.247	.206	.280	7.80	1.88
Sanchez, Eury	R-R	5-10	190	11-8-92	1	1	6.59	10	0	0	0	14	13	11	10	1	7	12	.255	.281	.217	7.90	4.61
Smith, Blake	R-R	6-5	240	8-12-92	4	2	1.52	15	0	0	1	30	20	6	5	1	7	19	.192	.137	.245	5.76	2.12
Vinson, Andrew	L-R	5-10	160	11-12-93	0	3	3.60	9	0	0	0	15	12	9	6	1	3	9	.214	.273	.176	5.40	1.80
Watson, Tyler	L-L	5-11	175	6-9-93	3	3	3.42	40	0	0	1	71	80	29	27	5	29	50	.286	.244	.305	6.34	3.68

Fielding

Catcher	PCT	G	PO	A	E	DP	PB
Barash	.985	24	176	18	3	3	3
Genao	.985	21	186	16	3	0	2
Lubach	.992	71	519	70	5	8	4
Rivas	.992	26	215	23	2	1	4

First Base	PCT	G	PO	A	E	DP
Pierson	.969	15	120	6	4	10
Rivera	.917	1	8	3	1	1
Serena	.971	5	31	2	1	4
Thaiss	.979	43	341	40	8	34
Walsh	.989	76	630	64	8	51

Second Base	PCT	G	PO	A	E	DP
Amendolare	.976	10	21	19	1	4
Moreno	1.000	2	3	3	0	2
Moyer	1.000	3	4	9	0	2
Sanger	.933	91	144	219	26	36
Yacinich	1.000	2	2	3	0	0
Zimmerman	.986	32	49	88	2	26

Third Base	PCT	G	PO	A	E	DP
Amendolare	.968	10	11	19	1	2
Moreno	.500	1	1	0	1	0
Moyer	.839	15	10	16	5	0
Pierson	.976	49	28	92	3	8
Sanger	.700	5	3	4	3	1
Serena	.942	57	42	88	8	8
Yacinich	.900	6	6	12	2	1

Shortstop	PCT	G	PO	A	E	DP
Amendolare	1.000	3	5	4	0	4
Justus	.954	41	74	114	9	27
Moreno	.950	37	50	84	7	19
Moyer	.885	6	13	10	3	4
Serena	.904	11	14	33	5	6
Yacinich	.953	43	75	109	9	18

Outfield	PCT	G	PO	A	E	DP
Abbott	1.000	19	31	2	0	1
Alberto	.977	67	121	9	3	1
Amendolare	—	1	0	0	0	0
Delph	.983	30	55	3	1	0
Foster	.986	68	139	5	2	1
Hermosillo	.969	37	60	3	2	0
Jones	.969	16	29	2	1	1
Lund	.989	45	88	5	1	2
Montgomery	1.000	37	81	4	0	2
Rivera	.970	37	63	2	2	0
Sanger	1.000	3	2	0	0	0
Serena	1.000	29	81	4	0	1
Walsh	.952	23	38	2	2	0
Welz	1.000	12	32	0	0	0

OREM OWLZ

ROOKIE

PIONEER LEAGUE

Batting	B-T	HT	WT	DOB	AVG	vLH	vRH	G	AB	R	H	2B	3B	HR	RBI	BB	HBP	SH	SF	SO	SB	CS	SLG	OBP
Abbott, Alex	L-R	6-1	195	11-2-94	.198	.179	.206	30	96	14	19	6	0	3	12	9	2	1	1	33	0	1	.354	.278
Allday, Forrestt	R-R	5-11	190	4-24-91	.200	.500	.125	3	10	2	2	1	0	0	2	1	0	1	0	2	0	0	.300	.273
Barash, Michael	R-R	6-1	200	10-12-94	.314	.458	.239	19	70	6	22	4	0	1	12	5	4	1	0	16	0	1	.414	.392
Flair, Nick	R-R	6-3	200	10-31-92	.348	.431	.316	54	210	40	73	23	1	8	47	8	0	2	3	51	3	1	.581	.367
Genao, Angel	R-R	6-2	180	3-22-93	.258	.133	.294	22	66	9	17	2	1	0	12	6	2	0	0	15	0	0	.318	.338
Gibbons, Zach	R-R	5-8	186	10-14-93	.351	.372	.345	50	191	37	67	12	2	5	30	29	2	1	0	22	17	9	.513	.441
Grieshaber, Keith	R-R	6-1	168	6-29-95	.295	.250	.313	37	132	15	39	7	3	0	17	6	5	1	6	27	7	3	.394	.336
Hinshaw, Chad	R-R	6-1	205	9-10-90	.167	—	.167	4	12	0	2	1	1	0	0	3	0	0	0	6	0	1	.417	.333
Jones, Jahmai	R-R	6-0	215	8-4-97	.321	.298	.331	48	196	49	63	12	3	3	20	21	7	1	1	29	19	6	.459	.404
Justus, Connor	R-R	6-0	190	11-2-94	.344	.387	.323	26	93	19	32	6	1	0	23	18	3	0	0	19	0	2	.430	.465
Kalawaia, L.J.	L-R	6-0	185	9-30-93	.268	.277	.263	41	142	24	38	7	0	1	16	14	6	1	0	33	4	1	.317	.346
Kruger, Jack	R-R	6-1	185	10-26-94	.330	.321	.333	27	103	14	34	7	1	0	14	6	1	0	2	11	6	1	.417	.366
Lund, Brennon	L-R	5-10	185	11-27-94	.397	.379	.409	18	73	15	29	3	0	2	11	7	2	2	0	11	7	2	.521	.463
McDonnell, Sam	L-R	6-0	190	8-10-95	.265	.175	.304	41	132	17	35	11	4	1	22	26	2	1	1	30	5	2	.432	.391
Montgomery, Troy	L-L	5-10	185	11-4-95	.341	.375	.321	26	88	16	30	3	2	4	17	15	3	7	0	20	10	4	.557	.453
Moreno, Juan	R-R	6-0	170	11-17-94	.198	.111	.231	48	162	18	32	4	0	2	10	3	2	6	1	24	1	1	.259	.220
Morgan, Brennan	R-R	6-4	230	4-13-94	.277	.319	.259	44	155	27	43	10	0	4	20	20	5	0	1	35	4	0	.419	.376
Navarro, Rey	B-R	5-10	185	12-22-89	.455	.667	.455	3	11	0	5	1	0	0	1	0	0	0	0	2	1	0	.545	.455
Pina, Keinner	R-R	5-10	165	2-12-97	.250	.429	.000	3	12	0	3	0	0	0	2	1	0	0	0	4	0	0	.250	.308
Ramer, Cody	L-R	5-8	178	11-24-93	.338	.407	.302	18	80	18	27	6	1	1	10	4	1	1	1	14	4	1	.475	.372
Rojas, Jose	L-R	6-0	200	2-24-93	.308	.322	.302	59	221	45	68	15	3	5	31	22	3	2	2	29	9	4	.471	.372
Schuknecht, John	R-R	6-0	200	7-12-94	.309	.417	.250	18	68	13	21	4	0	8	14	5	1	0	0	18	4	1	.721	.365
Scott, Ryan	R-R	6-1	180	2-7-95	.169	.077	.190	24	71	9	12	3	0	1	7	8	1	0	0	26	0	0	.254	.263
Thaiss, Matt	L-R	6-0	195	5-6-95	.338	.257	.433	15	65	16	22	7	1	2	12	4	2	0	0	4	2	4	.569	.394
Torres, Franklin	R-R	6-0	175	10-21-94	.255	.300	.183	29	111	17	25	5	0	0	16	12	0	3	1	24	2	2	.270	.298
Vega, Ryan	R-R	6-2	180	9-17-96	.191	.200	.189	12	47	4	9	2	0	2	7	5	0	0	0	10	0	0	.362	.269
Zimmerman, Jordan	R-R	6-1	195	11-21-94	.422	.469	.392	19	83	22	35	4	1	4	22	6	3	0	0	12	4	1	.639	.478

Pitching	B-T	HT	WT	DOB	W	L	ERA	G	GS	CG	SV	IP	H	R	ER	HR	BB	SO	AVG	vLH	vRH	K/9	BB/9
Barkell, Ty	R-R	6-3	225	3-12-93	3	3	4.50	17	7	0	0	44	53	29	22	5	11	38	.303	.378	.248	7.77	2.25
Bates, Nathan	R-R	6-8	205	3-1-94	1	0	0.00	3	0	0	0	3	3	0	0	2	1		.231	.333	.20	2.70	5.40
Belton, Greg	R-R	5-10	190	12-31-92	2	3	2.27	22	1	0	5	40	28	11	10	3	6	43	.193	.255	.160	9.76	1.36
Bertness, Nathan	L-L	6-6	205	8-4-95	5	1	3.64	12	10	0	0	54	61	22	22	2	15	41	.290	.396	.255	6.79	2.48
De Los Santos, Samil	R-R	6-4	175	1-8-94	0	0	8.31	13	0	0	1	13	18	13	12	3	6	21	.316	.269	.355	14.54	4.15
Geisler, Cory	R-L	6-4	190	7-22-92	0	0	2.13	4	0	0	0	13	18	3	3	0	4	9	.333	.280	.379	6.39	2.84
Glazer, Brandon	R-R	6-3	190	1-29-92	1	5	5.80	17	6	0	0	45	53	37	29	2	10	34	.285	.181	.369	6.80	2.00
Henson, Alex	L-L	6-5	235	2-7-92	1	1	3.00	22	0	0	1	33	29	16	11	0	17	30	.234	.234	.234	8.18	4.64
Herrin, Travis	R-R	6-2	220	4-29-95	3	4	5.67	14	14	0	0	60	82	40	38	6	15	50	.329	.330	.379	7.46	2.24
Isaac, Sean	R-R	6-4	225	12-17-92	0	1	6.75	3	0	0	0	4	5	3	3	2	2	5	.333	.250	.429	11.25	4.50
Kaelin, Mike	R-R	5-9	185	3-30-94	0	0	4.50	3	0	0	0	4	4	2	2	0	0	3	.235	.333	.182	6.75	0.00
Kelly, Justin	L-L	6-1	175	4-22-93	2	1	6.44	17	1	0	0	36	51	28	26	3	17	33	.345	.435	.304	8.17	4.21
Lillis-White, Conor	L-L	6-4	220	7-22-92	0	0	2.08	3	0	0	0	9	7	3	2	1		12	.206	.100	.250	12.46	1.04
Mieses, Crusito	R-R	6-5	224	9-15-96	1	0	8.18	5	5	0	0	11	17	10	10	0	6	11	.347	.32	.375	9.00	4.91
Nuss, Garrett	R-R	6-1	180	4-15-93	1	0	3.27	3	3	0	0	11	10	6	4	0	3	6	.256	.300	.241	4.91	2.45
Ovando, Ariel	L-L	6-4	250	9-15-93	0	2	8.13	23	0	0	1	28	39	25	25	4	19	28	.333	.342	.311	9.11	6.18
Pastrone, Sam	R-R	6-0	185	6-28-97	3	4	6.00	14	13	0	0	57	77	51	38	4	21	45	.322	.354	.300	7.11	3.32
Rasmus, Cory	R-R	6-0	200	11-6-87	0	0	0.00	1	0	0	0	1	0	0	0	0	0	0	.000	.000	.000	0.00	0.00
Robichaux, Austin	R-R	6-6	175	11-23-92	0	0	1.29	2	1	0	0	7	2	1	1	0	2	4	.095	.000	.133	5.14	2.57
Rodriguez, Ramon	R-R	5-11	185	9-27-95	0	1	8.10	5	1	0	1	7	12	8	6	2	11	9	.414	.636	.278	12.15	8.10
Smith, Blake	R-R	6-5	240	8-12-92	2	0	4.70	8	0	0	0	15	23	8	8	0	3	16	.348	.500	.250	9.39	1.76
Suarez, Jose	L-L	5-10	170	1-3-98	1	0	0.00	1	1	0	0	4	6	5	0	0	1	7	.300	.143	.385	14.54	2.08
Tolliver, Ashur	L-L	6-0	170	1-24-88	0	0	0.00	1	0	0	0	1	0	0	0	1	0	1	.250	.000	500	27.00	9.00
Trexler, David	R-R	6-3	185	9-4-90	1	1	3.12	13	0	0	0	26	21	11	9	2	10	30	.228	.211	.241	10.38	3.46
Tucker, Bo	L-L	6-4	210	5-23-95	3	3	5.17	17	0	0	0	31	36	25	18	2	12	29	.283	.265	.295	8.33	3.45

Pitching	B-T	HT	WT	DOB	W	L	ERA	G	GS	CG	SV	IP	H	R	ER	HR	BB	SO	AVG	vLH	vRH	K/9	BB/9
Vinson, Andrew	L-R	5-10	160	11-12-93	4	1	3.68	13	0	0	2	22	26	9	9	1	4	20	.292	.278	.302	8.18	1.64
Warmoth, Tyler	R-R	6-2	205	6-4-92	1	0	1.00	15	0	0	3	27	17	4	3	0	11	31	.185	.152	.203	10.33	3.67
Weller, Blayne	R-R	6-5	220	1-30-90	1	2	8.59	6	0	0	0	22	40	25	21	3	9	28	.396	.333	.446	11.45	3.68
Wesely, Jonah	L-L	6-1	215	12-8-94	0	2	6.62	12	5	0	0	18	22	13	13	2	8	31	.301	.259	.326	15.79	4.08
Willey, Doug	R-R	6-2	220	12-27-92	1	1	6.53	17	0	0	2	30	40	24	22	1	6	20	.308	.306	.309	5.93	1.78
Zarubin, Jackson	R-R	6-2	190	1-8-93	0	0	40.50	2	1	0	0	1	7	6	6	0	1	1	.636	.600	.667	6.75	6.75

Fielding

C: Barash 19, Genao 18, Morgan 21, Pina 3, Scott 23. **1B:** Flair 47, Morgan 19, Scott 2, Thaiss 15. **2B:** Grieshaber 17, Moreno 14, Ramer 18, Rojas 13, Torres 2, Zimmerman 15. **3B:** Flair 6, Moreno 1, Rojas 45, Torres 28. **SS:** Grieshaber 20, Justus 26, Moreno 33, Navarro 3. **OF:** Abbott 8, Allday 3, Gibbons 44, Hinshaw 3, Jones 47, Kalawaia 38, Lund 13, McDonnell 35, Montgomery 25, Schuknecht 15, Vega 11.

AZL ANGELS
ARIZONA LEAGUE

ROOKIE

Batting	B-T	HT	WT	DOB	AVG	vLH	vRH	G	AB	R	H	2B	3B	HR	RBI	BB	HBP	SH	SF	SO	SB	CS	SLG	OBP
Anderson, Brad	R-R	6-4	210	1-10-94	.216	.242	.195	23	74	8	16	6	0	0	10	9	5	1	0	21	0	1	.297	.341
Bates, Tyler	R-R	5-8	165	6-1-94	.284	.324	.262	31	95	16	27	8	0	0	17	15	4	2	2	19	5	4	.368	.397
Blumenfeld, Dalton	R-R	6-3	210	11-14-96	.269	.423	.115	16	52	3	14	3	0	0	11	2	0	1	0	6	0	0	.327	.291
Del Valle, Francisco	L-L	6-1	187	8-18-98	.250	.200	.259	9	32	4	8	2	0	0	3	2	1	1	0	6	0	0	.313	.294
Fecteau, Richard	L-R	5-10	190	3-17-94	.188	.188	.188	34	112	14	21	6	2	0	9	21	1	2	0	20	2	3	.277	.321
Fitzsimons, Connor	R-R	6-1	190	8-29-94	.103	.143	.091	11	29	1	3	1	0	0	1	2	1	0	0	7	0	0	.138	.188
Garcia, Julio	R-R	6-0	175	7-31-97	.149	.188	.129	14	47	2	7	3	0	0	7	4	0	0	0	13	1	0	.213	.216
Gentry, Craig	R-R	6-2	190	11-29-83	.000	—	.000	1	1	1	0	0	0	0	0	1	0	0	0	0	1	0	.000	.500
Grieshaber, Keith	R-R	6-1	168	6-29-95	.356	.375	.351	17	73	9	26	5	0	0	11	6	1	0	0	10	5	1	.425	.413
Hinshaw, Chad	R-R	6-1	205	9-10-90	1.000	—	1.000	1	3	2	3	1	0	1	2	1	0	0	0	1	0	0	2.333	1.000
Jenkins, Derek	R-R	5-8	155	2-11-94	.265	.213	.303	33	113	13	30	1	0	0	14	10	1	1	1	18	14	5	.274	.328
Kruger, Jack	R-R	6-1	185	10-26-94	.154	.333	.000	3	13	3	2	0	0	0	1	1	0	0	0	3	0	0	.154	.267
McGee, Stephen	R-R	6-3	215	2-7-91	.250	.333	.000	3	12	0	3	1	0	0	0	0	0	0	1	0	0	0	.333	.250
Navarro, Rey	B-R	5-10	185	12-22-89	.375	.667	.200	3	8	1	3	0	0	0	0	0	0	0	0	2	1	0	.375	.375
Pina, Keinner	R-R	5-10	165	2-12-97	.296	.250	.329	37	142	19	42	4	1	0	17	12	1	0	1	26	5	2	.338	.353
Pineda, Gleyvin	R-R	5-11	160	8-19-96	.236	.193	.264	40	148	25	35	3	0	0	13	20	3	1	1	40	12	4	.257	.337
Ramer, Cody	L-R	5-8	178	11-24-93	.412	.333	.455	5	17	2	7	2	1	0	4	3	0	0	0	3	0	1	.647	.500
Rivas, Leonardo	B-R	5-10	150	10-10-97	.253	.316	.208	26	91	22	23	5	0	1	4	16	0	1	0	16	6	3	.341	.364
Rodriguez, Jose	R-R	5-11	165	11-3-95	.196	.095	.257	19	56	9	11	3	1	1	10	11	2	1	0	23	2	0	.339	.348
Sanchez, Jeyson	R-R	5-10	174	7-4-94	.264	.342	.222	30	110	15	29	11	1	1	14	10	3	0	2	18	1	2	.409	.336
Santana, Gabriel	R-R	6-2	180	8-18-95	.236	.263	.224	36	123	18	29	8	0	0	13	8	5	1	1	32	1	1	.301	.307
Santana, Yefry	R-R	6-1	170	11-8-95	.250	.190	.282	38	120	19	30	2	5	0	12	15	1	0	3	44	11	6	.350	.331
Schuknecht, John	R-R	6-0	200	7-14-94	.318	.286	.333	33	110	22	35	16	1	0	18	13	4	0	3	28	6	3	.482	.400
Scott, Ryan	R-R	6-1	180	2-7-95	.000	—	.000	1	1	0	0	0	0	0	0	0	0	0	0	0	0	0	.000	.000
Strentz, Michael	R-R	6-1	215	11-10-91	.167	.000	.174	7	24	4	4	0	0	0	3	2	0	0	1	8	1	0	.167	.250
Vega, Ryan	R-R	6-2	180	9-17-96	.413	.350	.433	21	80	19	33	5	2	2	12	4	3	0	1	12	5	0	.600	.455
Williams, Cam	R-R	5-11	185	1-10-92	.235	.130	.289	23	68	7	16	3	1	0	10	12	1	1	1	26	2	9	.309	.354
Williams, Nonie	R-R	6-2	200	5-22-98	.244	.204	.262	38	156	23	38	4	1	0	8	8	0	0	0	40	8	3	.282	.280

Pitching	B-T	HT	WT	DOB	W	L	ERA	G	GS	CG	SV	IP	H	R	ER	HR	BB	SO	AVG	vLH	vRH	K/9	BB/9
Adams, Austin	R-R	6-2	225	5-5-91	0	0	3.00	2	0	0	0	3	1	1	1	0	0	2	.100	.000	.143	6.00	0.00
Alburquerque, Al	R-R	6-0	195	6-10-86	0	0	0.00	4	3	0	0	4	3	0	0	0	0	3	.214	.000	.333	6.75	0.00
Bates, Nathan	R-R	6-8	205	3-1-94	0	0	10.80	2	0	0	0	3	2	2	2	0	3	3	.375	.000	.600	16.20	0.00
Bethell, Max	L-L	6-3	225	5-8-94	3	2	2.09	14	3	0	1	52	35	12	12	0	9	41	.191	.179	.194	7.14	1.57
Broussard, Jason	L-R	6-4	215	4-9-93	2	0	3.24	8	0	0	1	17	12	7	6	2	6	11	.203	.083	.234	5.94	3.24
Davis, Erik	L-L	6-2	205	12-14-93	2	0	1.35	17	0	0	3	27	18	4	4	1	12	25	.191	.211	.187	8.44	4.05
Duensing, Cole	L-R	6-4	175	6-16-98	2	0	1.38	8	4	0	0	13	13	3	2	0	5	11	.250	.227	.267	7.62	3.46
Geisler, Cory	R-L	6-0	190	7-10-93	2	1	2.25	14	0	0	0	28	23	13	7	1	8	23	.219	.333	.204	7.39	2.57
Isaac, Sean	R-R	6-4	225	12-17-92	4	0	4.56	13	0	0	0	24	22	13	12	0	10	30	.247	.286	.235	11.41	3.80
Keinat, Taylor	L-L	6-0	170	2-4-93	0	0	1.93	4	0	0	0	5	2	1	1	0	4	4	.143	.500	.083	7.71	7.71
Kendrick, Kyle	R-R	6-3	220	8-26-84	1	1	2.31	4	4	0	0	12	13	7	3	1	0	3	.283	.417	.235	2.31	0.00
Lillis-White, Conor	L-L	6-4	220	7-22-92	0	0	1.93	8	0	0	0	19	19	6	4	0	4	28	.250	.059	.305	13.50	1.93
Long, Grayson	R-R	6-5	230	5-27-94	0	1	6.55	4	0	0	0	11	13	8	8	0	5	10	.295	.320	.263	8.18	4.09
Maya, Yunesky	R-R	6-0	215	8-28-81	0	0	0.00	1	1	0	0	1	1	0	0	0	0	0	.250	.000	.500	0.00	0.00
McDavid, Jacob	R-R	6-5	210	2-20-93	0	0	13.50	1	0	0	0	1	1	1	1	0	1	1	.333	.000	.500	13.50	13.50
Meyer, Alex	R-R	6-9	225	1-3-90	0	0	1.69	3	3	0	0	5	1	1	1	0	1	12	.273	.429	.200	20.25	1.69
Mieses, Crusito	R-R	5-5	224	9-15-96	1	0	9.00	4	0	0	0	8	14	10	8	0	2	11	.359	.357	.36	12.38	2.25
Molina, Cristopher	R-R	6-3	170	6-10-97	2	3	5.48	12	6	0	1	46	50	39	28	1	19	41	.276	.321	.256	8.02	3.72
Morell, Johnny	R-R	6-2	200	10-30-97	1	1	4.02	9	5	0	0	16	15	9	7	0	9	10	.263	.182	.314	5.74	5.17
Nielsen, J.D.	L-L	6-6	240	10-9-93	1	3	8.40	12	0	0	2	15	22	17	14	1	11	12	.333	.400	.314	6.60	6.60
Oquendo, Enrique	R-R	6-2	200	11-17-93	1	0	2.18	15	0	0	1	21	19	7	5	1	17	24	.257	.333	.232	10.45	7.40
Ortega, Oliver	R-R	6-0	165	10-2-96	2	3	2.83	8	5	0	0	29	15	9	9	1	10	27	.156	.135	.169	8.48	3.14
Parry, Turner	R-R	6-4	190	8-27-92	0	0	9.00	1	0	0	0	1	1	1	1	0	0	1	.333	.000	.500	9.00	0.00
Rodriguez, Chris	R-R	6-2	185	7-20-98	0	0	1.59	7	5	0	0	11	6	3	2	0	3	17	.154	.071	.200	13.50	2.38
Rodriguez, Elvin	R-R	6-3	160	3-31-98	2	2	1.57	7	5	0	0	29	18	6	5	1	6	23	.176	.133	.194	7.22	1.88
Skaggs, Tyler	L-L	6-4	215	7-13-91	0	0	0.00	1	1	0	0	3	2	0	0	0	0	3	.222	—	.222	10.13	0.00
Suarez, Jose	L-L	5-10	170	1-3-98	1	3	5.36	11	5	0	0	40	48	31	24	1	13	46	.296	.289	.298	10.26	2.90
Tindall, Matt	R-R	6-3	230	5-16-92	0	2	4.38	4	0	0	0	12	11	6	6	0	3	8	.256	.182	.281	5.84	2.19

Pitching	B-T	HT	WT	DOB	W	L	ERA	G	GS	CG	SV	IP	H	R	ER	HR	BB	SO	AVG	vLH	vRH	K/9	BB/9
Trexler, David	R-R	6-3	185	9-4-90	0	0	9.64	6	1	0	0	5	4	5	5	0	4	5	.250	.200	.273	9.64	7.71
Warmoth, Tyler	R-R	6-2	205	6-4-92	0	0	0.00	3	0	0	2	6	4	0	0	0	0	6	.190	.000	.308	9.00	0.00
Weller, Blayne	R-R	6-5	220	1-30-90	1	0	2.00	2	1	0	0	9	7	2	2	0	1	12	.206	.000	.280	12.00	1.00
Zarubin, Jackson	R-R	6-2	190	1-8-93	2	4	4.21	20	0	0	1	26	27	17	12	3	3	33	.265	.391	.228	11.57	1.05

Fielding

C: Fitzsimons 11, McGee 1, Pina 32, Sanchez 15, Strentz 3. **1B:** Anderson 23, Pina 1, Sanchez 4, Santana 34. **2B:** Fecteau 8, Garcia 1, Grieshaber 9, Pineda 26, Ramer 4, Rivas 10, Rodriguez 3. **3B:** Fecteau 26, Garcia 10, Rivas 5, Rodriguez 15, Sanchez 3. **SS:** Garcia 2, Grieshaber 5, Navarro 2, Pineda 12, Rivas 11, Rodriguez 1, Williams 28. **OF:** Bates 29, Blumenfeld 7, Del Valle 8, Gentry 1, Hinshaw 1, Jenkins 33, Santana 37, Schuknecht 27, Vega 21, Williams 14.

DSL ANGELS   ROOKIE
DOMINICAN SUMMER LEAGUE

Batting	B-T	HT	WT	DOB	AVG	vLH	vRH	G	AB	R	H	2B	3B	HR	RBI	BB	HBP	SH	SF	SO	SB	CS	SLG	OBP
Arias, Kevin	R-R	5-10	150	2-18-99	.218	.265	.206	53	165	19	36	6	0	1	8	15	6	4	0	40	12	5	.273	.306
Borges, Joel	R-R	6-0	170	7-13-98	.263	.444	.207	26	76	9	20	3	0	0	6	9	1	0	0	16	7	3	.303	.349
Carmona, Oliver	L-R	6-0	160	2-28-98	.214	.163	.229	55	187	20	40	7	2	0	23	24	4	4	2	28	9	4	.273	.313
Castillo, Oscateri	R-R	6-1	170	12-28-97	.277	.167	.298	49	148	26	41	6	1	1	8	14	5	1	1	38	16	4	.351	.357
De La Cruz, Miguel	B-R	5-11	170	12-4-97	.260	.313	.246	62	215	37	56	10	4	1	20	38	6	0	1	54	16	11	.358	.385
Garcia, Oswaldo	R-R	6-3	210	11-28-95	.227	.167	.238	25	75	13	17	2	0	1	13	10	1	0	0	12	3	3	.293	.326
Gomez, Cristian	L-R	6-2	190	10-29-96	.200	.233	.192	61	215	13	43	10	4	1	27	14	6	0	1	36	4	7	.298	.267
Mendoza, Willian	R-R	5-11	175	12-1-97	.240	.258	.235	45	150	13	36	5	0	1	11	7	4	0	1	43	3	2	.293	.290
Molina, Angel	R-R	6-0	175	8-20-97	.207	.176	.217	60	217	28	45	8	1	4	35	12	6	3	4	35	21	6	.309	.264
Mota, Darlyn	B-R	6-1	165	8-2-96	.147	.091	.158	32	68	9	10	2	0	0	1	12	3	3	0	18	2	0	.176	.301
Oliva, Osvaldo	R-R	6-0	165	12-10-97	.216	.250	.207	44	116	11	25	3	3	0	11	15	3	0	1	27	4	7	.293	.319
Pedie, Junior	R-R	6-3	185	6-17-97	.143	.250	.132	18	42	3	6	0	0	1	2	9	4	0	0	17	1	3	.214	.345
Rivas, Leonardo	B-R	5-10	150	10-10-97	.323	.304	.329	33	99	26	32	3	3	0	15	20	4	4	0	23	20	5	.414	.455
Rosario, Rayneldy	L-L	5-8	139	4-30-98	.315	.413	.288	63	216	44	68	6	2	0	16	17	7	0	0	38	25	11	.361	.383
Sala, Johan	R-R	6-1	175	12-17-97	.308	.175	.347	66	247	39	76	8	2	1	25	29	7	5	3	46	10	15	.368	.392

Pitching	B-T	HT	WT	DOB	W	L	ERA	G	GS	CG	SV	IP	H	R	ER	HR	BB	SO	AVG	vLH	vRH	K/9	BB/9
Arismendy, Samuel	L-L	5-11	183	1-30-97	0	0	14.40	13	0	0	0	10	12	23	16	0	28	15	.279	.455	.219	13.50	25.20
Arvelaez, Kiber	R-R	5-10	165	5-9-98	5	2	2.01	16	4	0	1	49	44	14	11	2	11	41	.243	.278	.228	7.48	2.01
Bonilla, Christopher	R-R	6-0	180	1-13-99	4	4	5.11	14	10	0	0	49	39	29	28	4	26	39	.219	.280	.195	7.11	4.74
Castro, Jesus	R-R	6-0	165	2-20-98	1	0	7.23	17	0	0	2	37	54	33	30	2	19	25	.338	.263	.379	6.03	4.58
De Los Santos, Richard	R-R	6-2	180	5-22-95	1	3	2.50	18	6	0	2	40	24	13	11	0	22	29	.176	.077	.216	6.58	4.99
Feliz, Jose	R-R	6-0	170	12-23-94	1	2	2.77	5	1	0	0	13	7	5	4	1	2	8	.152	.111	.179	5.54	1.38
Galan, Lianmy	R-R	6-3	165	8-23-96	4	2	4.18	16	2	0	0	52	57	35	24	1	20	33	.286	.250	.302	5.75	3.48
Hernandez, Wilkel	R-R	6-3	160	4-13-99	2	0	1.20	5	5	0	0	15	12	3	2	0	6	14	.231	.125	.278	8.40	3.60
Mendoza, Reyember	R-R	6-1	175	2-20-99	0	3	16.68	7	4	0	0	11	13	26	21	1	19	12	.295	.353	.259	9.53	15.09
Montilla, Anderson	R-R	6-4	180	10-23-95	0	0	7.94	7	0	0	0	6	5	7	5	0	7	8	.192	.000	.200	12.71	11.12
Perez, Melquicedec	R-R	6-0	180	3-1-97	1	1	5.27	6	1	0	0	14	9	11	8	0	13	18	.184	.357	.114	11.85	8.56
Pina, Shakiro	L-L	5-11	170	3-4-97	2	1	5.51	18	0	0	1	33	32	24	20	0	23	27	.267	.292	.260	7.44	6.34
Pineda, Roberto	R-R	6-3	190	6-2-96	3	2	3.31	16	7	0	1	49	48	22	18	0	19	45	.253	.338	.208	8.27	3.49
Portorreal, Samir	R-R	6-0	194	5-29-99	0	1	5.25	11	3	0	0	24	18	19	14	3	16	16	.198	.308	.154	6.00	6.00
Rodriguez, Elvin	R-R	6-3	160	3-31-98	2	0	1.50	7	6	0	0	30	14	5	5	2	8	34	.139	.077	.160	10.20	2.40
Soriano, Jose	R-R	6-3	168	10-20-98	3	5	1.58	14	14	0	0	57	37	22	10	2	30	45	.187	.190	.186	7.11	4.74
Tavarez, Jorge	R-R	5-10	150	8-4-95	4	3	2.05	21	0	0	9	44	35	15	10	0	7	49	.215	.132	.240	10.02	1.43
Yan, Hector	L-L	5-11	180	4-26-99	2	0	0.89	7	7	0	0	30	23	5	3	0	15	33	.217	.214	.217	9.79	4.45

Fielding

C: Borges 25, Garcia 9, Mendoza 44. **1B:** Garcia 8, Molina 60, Mota 6, Oliva 2. **2B:** Arias 36, De La Cruz 22, Oliva 14. **3B:** Arias 13, Carmona 18, De La Cruz 18, Garcia 1, Mota 12, Oliva 17, Rivas 1. **SS:** Arias 1, Carmona 39, Oliva 6, Rivas 31. **OF:** Castill 42, De La Cruz 3, Gomez 45, Rosario 61, Sala 66.

LOS ANGELES ANGELS

Los Angeles Dodgers

SEASON IN A SENTENCE: With first-year manager Dave Roberts handling an injury-riddled pitching staff, the Dodgers overcame their ever-changing roster to win the National League West for the fourth straight season. They beat the Nationals in a Division Series before losing in six games to the Cubs in the National League Championship Series.

HIGH POINT: Ace Clayton Kershaw, who missed more than two months with a herniated disc in his back, pitched in three of the five games of the Division Series, including coming out of the bullpen on one day's rest to save Game Five, a 4-3 win at Washington. He came in for reliever Kenley Jansen, who had entered the game in the seventh (his fourth outing of the series) and threw a career-high 51 pitches.

LOW POINT: On June 26, Kershaw took a 4-3 loss at Pittsburgh, just Kershaw's second loss in 13 decisions, and L.A. lost its third straight, putting it eight games behind the Giants in the NL West. However, even with Kershaw out, the Dodgers caught fire, taking over first place for good Aug. 21 and were well in front by the time Kershaw returned in September.

NOTABLE ROOKIES: The Dodgers used 13 rookies, led by shortstop Corey Seager, BA's Rookie of the Year and the Dodgers' top hitter all year. Among other key rookies, outfielder Trayce Thompson hit 13 homers in an 80-game audition before giving way to Andrew Toles, who started throughout the playoffs after being out of baseball in 2015. Kenta Maeda led the team in innings pitched (175.2), wins (16) and starts (32), while touted 19-year-old Julio Urias earned 15 starts and struck out 9.8 batters per nine innings.

KEY TRANSACTIONS: Most of the Dodgers' reinforcements came from within its deep farm system, which also was used for a key trade, as L.A. traded righthanders Jharel Cotton, Grant Holmes and Frankie Montas to Oakland for lefthander Rich Hill and outfielder Josh Reddick.

DOWN ON THE FARM: Four Dodgers affiliates reached the playoffs, with low Class A Great Lakes winning the Midwest League championship. Oklahoma City's Rob Segedin led the minors with a .598 slugging percentage, while righthander Brock Stewart had one of the best seasons of any minor league pitcher, going 9-4, 1.79 to rank third in ERA and first with a 0.88 WHIP. Both Segedin and Stewart also made their major league debuts.

OPENING DAY PAYROLL: $ 221,288,380 (2nd)

PLAYERS OF THE YEAR

MAJOR LEAGUE	MINOR LEAGUE
Corey Seager	**Brock Stewart**
ss	rhp
.308/.365/.512	(High A/Double-A/
26 HR, 72 RBI,	Triple-A)
54 BB, 105 R	9-4, 1.79, 129 SO

ORGANIZATION LEADERS

BATTING		*Minimum 250 AB
MAJORS		
* AVG	Corey Seager	.308
* OPS	Corey Seager	.877
HR	Justin Turner	27
	Yasmani Grandal	27
RBI	Adrian Gonzalez	90
	Justin Turner	90
MINORS		
* AVG	Rob Segedin, Okla. City	.319
* OBP	Rob Segedin, Okla. City	.392
* SLG	Rob Segedin, Okla. City	.598
* OPS	Rob Segedin, Okla. City	.989
R	Tim Locastro, Rancho Cucamonga, Tulsa	88
H	Tim Locastro, Rancho Cucamonga, Tulsa	151
TB	Kyle Garlick, Rancho Cucamonga, Tulsa	248
2B	Kyle Garlick, Rancho Cucamonga, Tulsa	42
3B	Erick Mejia, Rancho Cucamonga	12
HR	Johan Mieses, Rancho Cucamonga	28
RBI	Matt Beaty, Rancho Cucamonga	88
RBI	Willie Calhoun, Tulsa	88
BB	Cody Bellinger, Tulsa, Okla. City	60
SO	Corey Brown, Okla. City	155
SB	Micah Johnson, Okla. City	26

PITCHING		#Minimum 75 IP
MAJORS		
W	Kenta Maeda	16
# ERA	Kenta Maeda	3.48
SO	Kenta Maeda	179
SV	Kenley Jansen	47
MINORS		
W	Chase De Jong, Tulsa, Okla. City	15
L	Tommy Bergjans, Rancho Cucamonga	13
# ERA	Brock Stewart, Rancho, Okla. City, Tulsa	1.79
G	Jacob Rhame, Okla. City	54
GS	Chase De Jong, Tulsa, Okla. City	26
SV	Elio Serrano, DSL Dodgers1	15
IP	Trevor Oaks, Rancho, Tulsa, Okla. City	151
BB	Dennis Santana, Great Lakes	56
SO	Tommy Bergjans, Rancho Cucamonga	133
SO	Chase De Jong, Tulsa, Okla. City	133
# AVG	Brock Stewart, Rancho, Okla. City, Tulsa	.200

President: Andrew Friedman. **GM:** Farhan Zaidi. **Farm Director:** Gabe Kapler. **Scouting Director:** Billy Gasparino.

Class	Team	League	W	L	PCT	Finish	Manager
Majors	Los Angeles Dodgers	National	91	71	.562	3rd (15)	Dave Roberts
Triple-A	Oklahoma City Dodgers	Pacific Coast	81	60	.574	2nd (16)	Bill Haselman
Double-A	Tulsa Drillers	Texas	68	71	.489	4th (8)	Ryan Garko
High A	Rancho Cucamonga Quakes	California	79	61	.564	3rd (10)	Drew Saylor
Low A	Great Lakes Loons	Midwest	65	75	.464	11th (16)	Gil Velazquez
Rookie	Ogden Raptors	Pioneer	38	38	.500	4th (8)	Shaun Larkin
Rookie	Dodgers	Arizona	33	22	.600	1st (14)	John Shoemaker
Overall 2016 Minor League Record			364	327	.527	8th (30)	

ORGANIZATION STATISTICS

LOS ANGELES DODGERS
NATIONAL LEAGUE

Batting	B-T	HT	WT	DOB	AVG	vLH	vRH	G	AB	R	H	2B	3B	HR	RBI	BB	HBP	SH	SF	SO	SB	CS	SLG	OBP
Barnes, Austin	R-R	5-10	195	12-28-89	.156	.222	.130	21	32	3	5	1	0	0	2	5	0	0	0	9	0	0	.188	.270
Crawford, Carl	L-L	6-2	230	8-5-81	.185	.083	.203	30	81	8	15	2	1	0	6	4	1	0	1	11	0	1	.235	.230
Culberson, Charlie	R-R	6-0	200	4-10-89	.299	.333	.211	34	67	6	20	3	0	1	7	1	0	0	0	13	1	0	.388	.309
Ellis, A.J.	R-R	6-2	225	4-9-81	.194	.241	.160	53	139	8	27	5	0	1	13	16	2	3	1	24	1	1	.252	.285
2-team total (11 Philadelphia)					.216	—	—	64	171	11	37	8	0	2	22	19	2	3	1	31	2	1	.298	.301
Ethier, Andre	L-L	6-2	210	4-10-82	.208	.000	.217	16	24	2	5	1	0	1	2	2	0	0	0	6	0	0	.375	.269
Gonzalez, Adrian	L-L	6-2	215	5-8-82	.285	.244	.300	156	568	69	162	31	0	18	90	55	4	0	6	117	0	2	.435	.349
Grandal, Yasmani	B-R	6-1	235	11-8-88	.228	.224	.229	126	390	49	89	14	1	27	72	64	2	0	1	116	1	3	.477	.339
Hernandez, Enrique	R-R	5-11	200	8-24-91	.190	.189	.191	109	216	25	41	8	0	7	18	28	0	0	0	64	2	0	.324	.283
Johnson, Micah	L-R	6-0	210	12-18-90	.167	.000	.200	7	6	1	1	0	0	0	0	0	0	0	0	1	0	0	.167	.167
Kendrick, Howie	R-R	5-11	220	7-12-83	.255	.234	.264	146	487	65	124	26	2	8	40	50	3	0	3	96	10	2	.366	.326
Pederson, Joc	L-L	6-1	220	4-21-92	.246	.125	.269	137	406	64	100	26	0	25	68	63	4	1	2	130	6	2	.495	.352
Puig, Yasiel	R-R	6-2	240	12-7-90	.263	.261	.265	104	334	45	88	14	2	11	45	24	7	0	3	74	5	2	.416	.323
Reddick, Josh	L-R	6-2	195	2-19-87	.258	.121	.295	47	155	20	40	6	0	2	9	11	0	0	0	22	3	3	.335	.307
Ruiz, Carlos	R-R	5-10	215	1-22-79	.278	.308	.200	14	36	3	10	2	0	0	3	3	1	0	0	5	0	0	.333	.350
2-team total (48 Philadelphia)					.264	—	—	62	201	21	53	8	0	3	15	27	5	0	0	33	3	1	.348	.365
Seager, Corey	L-R	6-4	215	4-27-94	.308	.250	.334	157	627	105	193	40	5	26	72	54	4	0	2	133	3	3	.512	.365
Segedin, Rob	R-R	6-2	220	11-10-88	.233	.205	.265	40	73	9	17	2	1	2	12	6	2	0	2	22	0	0	.370	.301
Taylor, Chris	R-R	6-1	195	8-29-90	.207	.217	.200	34	58	8	12	2	2	1	7	4	0	0	0	13	0	0	.362	.258
Thompson, Trayce	R-R	6-3	225	3-15-91	.225	.219	.227	80	236	31	53	11	0	13	32	26	0	0	0	66	5	1	.436	.302
Toles, Andrew	L-R	5-10	185	5-24-92	.314	.231	.326	48	105	19	33	9	1	3	16	3	0	1	0	25	1	1	.505	.365
Turner, Justin	R-R	5-11	205	11-23-84	.275	.209	.305	151	556	79	153	34	3	27	90	48	10	0	8	107	4	1	.493	.339
Utley, Chase	L-R	6-1	195	12-17-78	.252	.154	.273	138	512	79	129	26	3	14	52	40	11	1	1	115	2	2	.396	.319
Van Slyke, Scott	R-R	6-4	215	7-24-86	.225	.243	.215	52	102	10	23	6	0	1	7	5	5	0	1	24	1	2	.314	.292
Venable, Will	L-L	6-3	205	10-29-82	.056	.000	.063	12	18	2	1	1	0	0	0	1	0	0	5	0	0	.111	.105
Walters, Zach	B-R	6-2	210	9-5-89	.000	.000	.000	3	5	0	0	0	0	0	0	0	0	0	2	0	0	.000	.000

Pitching	B-T	HT	WT	DOB	W	L	ERA	G	GS	CG	SV	IP	H	R	ER	HR	BB	SO	AVG	vLH	vRH	K/9	BB/9
Anderson, Brett	L-L	6-3	230	2-1-88	1	2	11.91	4	3	0	0	11	25	15	15	4	4	5	.446	.611	.368	3.97	3.18
Avilan, Luis	L-L	6-2	225	7-19-89	3	0	3.20	27	0	0	0	20	12	8	7	0	10	28	.176	.200	.143	12.81	4.58
Baez, Pedro	R-R	6-0	235	3-11-88	3	2	3.04	73	0	0	0	74	52	27	25	11	22	83	.195	.160	.214	10.09	2.68
Blanton, Joe	R-R	6-3	225	12-11-80	7	2	2.48	75	0	0	0	80	55	23	22	7	26	80	.194	.186	.198	9.00	2.93
Bolsinger, Mike	R-R	6-1	215	1-29-88	1	4	6.83	6	6	0	0	28	33	21	21	7	9	25	.303	.333	.286	8.13	2.93
Chavez, Jesse	R-R	6-2	175	8-21-83	1	0	4.21	23	0	0	0	26	28	14	12	3	8	21	.277	.314	.258	7.36	2.81
Coleman, Louis	R-R	6-4	205	4-4-86	2	1	4.69	61	0	0	0	48	45	27	25	5	24	45	.250	.316	.232	8.44	4.50
Dayton, Grant	L-L	6-2	195	11-25-87	0	1	2.05	25	0	0	0	26	14	7	6	4	6	39	.149	.140	.157	13.33	2.05
De Leon, Jose	R-R	6-2	190	8-7-92	2	0	6.35	4	4	0	0	17	19	17	12	5	7	15	.288	.212	.364	7.94	3.71
Fields, Josh	R-R	6-0	195	8-19-85	1	0	2.79	22	0	0	0	19	20	8	6	2	8	22	.256	.185	.294	10.24	3.72
Fien, Casey	R-R	6-2	210	10-21-83	0	1	4.21	25	0	0	0	26	24	12	12	8	7	23	.245	.270	.230	8.06	2.45
Frias, Carlos	R-R	6-4	195	11-13-89	0	0	0.00	1	0	0	0	4	2	0	0	0	1	3	.143	.200	.111	6.75	2.25
Garcia, Yimi	R-R	6-1	220	8-18-90	0	0	3.24	9	0	0	0	8	9	3	3	0	1	6	.310	.385	.250	4.32	1.08
Hatcher, Chris	R-R	6-1	200	1-12-85	5	4	5.53	37	0	0	0	41	40	26	25	8	21	43	.253	.150	.316	9.52	4.65
Hill, Rich	L-L	6-5	220	3-11-80	3	2	1.83	6	6	0	0	34	22	7	7	2	5	39	.182	.286	.160	10.22	1.31
Howell, J.P.	L-L	6-0	180	4-25-83	1	1	4.09	64	0	0	0	51	56	23	23	4	15	44	.281	.299	.265	7.82	2.66
Jansen, Kenley	B-R	6-5	270	9-30-87	3	2	1.83	71	0	0	47	69	35	14	14	4	11	104	.150	.191	.109	13.63	1.44
Kazmir, Scott	L-L	6-0	195	1-24-84	10	6	4.56	26	26	0	0	136	133	71	69	21	52	134	.253	.224	.264	8.85	3.43
Kershaw, Clayton	L-L	6-4	225	3-19-88	12	4	1.69	21	21	3	0	149	97	31	28	8	11	172	.184	.138	.201	10.39	0.66
Liberatore, Adam	L-L	6-3	240	5-12-87	2	2	3.38	58	0	0	0	43	34	16	16	2	17	47	.219	.171	.274	9.91	3.59
Maeda, Kenta	R-R	6-1	175	4-11-88	16	11	3.48	32	32	0	0	176	150	72	68	20	50	179	.229	.247	.213	9.17	2.56
McCarthy, Brandon	R-R	6-7	235	7-7-83	2	3	4.95	10	9	0	0	40	29	24	22	2	26	44	.207	.241	.183	9.90	5.85
Norris, Bud	R-R	6-0	215	3-2-85	3	3	6.54	13	9	0	0	43	48	33	31	8	21	42	.279	.325	.242	8.86	4.43
2-team total (22 Atlanta)					6	10	5.10	35	19	0	0	113	116	67	64	14	49	102	—	—	—	8.12	3.90
Ravin, Josh	R-R	6-4	215	1-21-88	0	0	0.93	10	0	0	0	10	2	1	1	1	4	13	.065	.222	.000	12.10	3.72
Ryu, Hyun Jin	L-L	6-3	250	3-25-87	0	1	11.57	1	1	0	0	5	8	6	6	1	2	4	.364	.200	.412	7.71	3.86

Pitching

Pitching	B-T	HT	WT	DOB	W	L	ERA	G	GS	CG	SV	IP	H	R	ER	HR	BB	SO	AVG	vLH	vRH	K/9	BB/9
Stewart, Brock	L-R	6-3	210	10-3-91	2	2	5.79	7	5	0	0	28	33	18	18	7	12	25	.292	.295	.290	8.04	3.86
Stripling, Ross	R-R	6-3	195	11-23-89	5	9	3.96	22	14	0	0	100	96	46	44	10	30	74	.250	.222	.272	6.66	2.70
Tepesch, Nick	R-R	6-4	240	10-12-88	0	1	11.25	1	1	0	0	4	7	5	5	1	0	3	.368	.400	.357	6.75	0.00
Tsao, Chin-Hui	R-R	6-1	210	6-2-81	0	1	5.40	2	0	0	0	2	1	1	1	0	3	0	.167	—	.167	0.00	16.20
Urias, Julio	L-L	6-0	215	8-12-96	5	2	3.39	18	15	0	0	77	81	32	29	5	31	84	.274	.234	.284	9.82	3.62
Wood, Alex	L-L	6-4	215	1-12-91	1	4	3.73	14	10	0	0	60	56	30	25	5	20	66	.245	.271	.235	9.85	2.98

Fielding

Catcher	PCT	G	PO	A	E	DP	PB
Barnes	1.000	9	47	1	0	0	0
Ellis	.998	46	380	28	1	2	2
Grandal	.995	115	1022	55	5	4	10
Ruiz	.988	9	73	10	1	3	1

First Base	PCT	G	PO	A	E	DP
Gonzalez	.998	151	1105	85	2	77
Grandal	1.000	4	24	1	0	1
Kendrick	.983	11	56	3	1	6
Segedin	.966	9	27	1	1	3
Turner	1.000	1	1	0	0	0
Van Slyke	.978	7	40	4	1	2
Walters	1.000	1	1	0	0	0

Second Base	PCT	G	PO	A	E	DP
Barnes	1.000	7	4	9	0	3
Culberson	.962	10	10	15	1	2
Hernandez	1.000	11	7	11	0	0
Johnson	1.000	3	2	0	0	0
Kendrick	.967	32	32	57	3	11
Taylor	.955	7	9	12	1	3
Utley	.989	134	195	266	5	49

Third Base	PCT	G	PO	A	E	DP
Barnes	—	1	0	0	0	0
Culberson	.833	4	2	3	1	0
Hernandez	.750	5	1	5	2	0
Kendrick	.969	17	5	26	1	2
Segedin	1.000	6	4	8	0	0
Taylor	1.000	10	2	5	0	0
Turner	.972	144	67	240	9	15
Utley	—	1	0	0	0	0

Shortstop	PCT	G	PO	A	E	DP
Culberson	1.000	11	8	16	0	3
Hernandez	1.000	2	0	1	0	0
Seager	.968	155	195	356	18	67
Taylor	1.000	5	8	9	0	0

Outfield	PCT	G	PO	A	E	DP
Crawford	1.000	21	28	0	0	0
Culberson	1.000	2	2	0	0	0
Ethier	1.000	4	5	0	0	0
Hernandez	1.000	62	78	4	0	1
Johnson	—	1	0	0	0	0
Kendrick	1.000	94	131	5	0	0
Pederson	.992	132	258	3	2	0
Puig	.978	95	172	6	4	0
Reddick	.953	42	79	3	4	0
Segedin	1.000	13	19	0	0	0
Thompson	.980	71	96	2	2	0
Toles	.967	32	55	3	2	0
Van Slyke	.973	29	36	0	1	0
Venable	1.000	5	6	0	0	0
Walters	1.000	1	1	0	0	0

OKLAHOMA CITY DODGERS

PACIFIC COAST LEAGUE

TRIPLE-A

Batting	B-T	HT	WT	DOB	AVG	vLH	vRH	G	AB	R	H	2B	3B	HR	RBI	BB	HBP	SH	SF	SO	SB	CS	SLG	OBP
Anderson, Lars	L-L	6-4	215	9-25-87	.208	.250	.200	8	24	4	5	1	0	1	2	5	0	0	0	9	2	0	.375	.345
Barnes, Austin	R-R	5-10	195	12-28-89	.295	.240	.318	85	336	59	99	22	5	6	39	43	4	1	1	53	18	3	.443	.380
Bellinger, Cody	L-L	6-4	210	7-13-95	.545	.667	.500	3	11	5	6	0	0	3	6	1	0	0	0	1	0	0	1.364	.583
Brown, Corey	L-L	6-1	200	11-26-85	.249	.200	.262	116	426	65	106	21	7	23	70	41	0	1	1	155	11	6	.493	.314
Cordero, Josmar	R-R	5-10	175	9-10-91	.000	—	.000	1	4	0	0	0	0	0	0	0	0	0	0	2	0	0	.000	.000
Crawford, Carl	L-L	6-2	230	8-5-81	.375	.000	.429	2	8	1	3	2	0	0	2	0	0	0	0	1	0	0	.625	.375
Culberson, Charlie	R-R	6-0	200	4-10-89	.260	.329	.234	70	265	32	69	17	2	4	33	18	1	1	0	61	6	5	.385	.310
Dickson, O'Koyea	R-R	5-11	220	2-9-90	.328	.327	.329	101	329	63	108	28	3	18	64	36	6	0	6	64	1	5	.596	.398
DiFazio, Vin	R-R	6-0	215	5-15-86	.200	.000	.250	4	15	1	3	1	0	0	0	0	0	0	0	5	0	0	.267	.200
Fields, Daniel	L-R	6-2	215	1-23-91	.250	.111	.304	10	32	7	8	2	1	0	3	4	0	0	1	14	2	2	.375	.324
Figueroa, Cole	L-R	5-10	185	6-30-87	.316	.000	.333	6	19	5	6	0	1	0	3	3	0	1	0	1	3	1	.421	.409
2-team total (41 New Orleans)					.240	—		47	154	19	37	7	2	0	14	18	1	1	3	18	3	2	.312	.318
Grandal, Yasmani	R-R	6-1	235	11-8-88	.333	1.000	.143	9	9	1	3	0	0	1	3	2	0	0	2	4	0	0	.667	.385
Guerrero, Alex	R-R	6-1	220	11-20-86	.125	.000	.167	2	8	0	1	0	0	0	0	0	0	0	0	6	0	0	.125	.125
Hassan, Alex	R-R	6-3	220	4-1-88	.232	.145	.270	88	254	28	59	7	0	1	20	39	4	1	3	60	2	0	.272	.340
Herrera, Elian	B-R	5-11	205	2-1-85	.218	.240	.211	28	101	15	22	2	0	0	10	14	0	0	2	28	0	0	.238	.308
Hicks, Brandon	R-R	6-2	215	9-14-85	.229	.182	.253	89	266	26	61	11	0	8	23	37	2	3	0	104	7	5	.361	.328
Johnson, Micah	L-R	6-0	210	12-18-90	.261	.174	.287	120	464	72	121	23	3	5	37	41	1	8	1	105	26	11	.356	.321
Maggi, Drew	R-R	6-0	192	5-16-89	.275	.333	.250	49	142	23	39	8	0	2	13	13	4	3	0	29	8	4	.373	.352
Murphy, Jack	B-R	6-4	235	4-6-88	.250	.194	.277	73	208	23	52	7	0	3	24	36	0	4	2	55	0	0	.327	.358
Noel, Rico	R-R	5-8	170	1-11-89	.230	.257	.220	47	126	13	29	5	2	0	14	6	2	2	0	31	8	3	.302	.276
Ogle, Tyler	R-R	5-10	210	8-9-90	.400	—	.400	2	5	1	2	1	0	0	2	0	0	0	0	2	0	0	.600	.400
Pederson, Joc	L-L	6-1	220	4-21-92	.625	.500	.750	3	8	1	5	0	0	0	4	0	0	0	1	0	0	0	.625	.750
Puig, Yasiel	R-R	6-2	240	12-7-90	.348	.333	.354	19	69	12	24	3	1	4	12	6	0	0	0	8	1	0	.594	.400
Ramsey, James	L-R	6-0	200	12-19-89	.264	.250	.268	83	254	33	67	13	3	8	38	24	5	1	0	80	5	4	.433	.339
2-team total (27 Tacoma)					.265	—		110	351	45	93	18	4	9	44	36	5	2	0	113	5	5	.416	.342
Richardson, Antoan	L-R	5-8	165	10-8-83	.146	.143	.148	15	41	7	6	1	0	0	1	4	0	0	0	16	3	0	.171	.222
Segedin, Rob	R-R	6-2	220	11-10-88	.319	.354	.307	103	373	71	119	23	9	21	69	40	7	0	4	81	3	4	.598	.392
Tabata, Jose	R-R	5-11	210	8-12-88	.244	.269	.234	30	90	9	22	5	0	1	18	11	3	0	2	16	3	1	.333	.340
Taylor, Chris	R-R	6-1	195	8-29-90	.368	.313	.390	15	57	7	21	6	2	0	8	6	1	0	0	16	5	0	.544	.438
2-team total (63 Tacoma)					.322	—		78	304	48	98	25	6	3	37	35	3	1	1	65	17	5	.474	.397
Toles, Andrew	L-R	5-10	185	5-24-92	.321	.273	.333	17	56	6	18	5	0	2	7	2	0	0	1	8	1	5	.518	.339
Van Slyke, Scott	R-R	6-4	215	7-24-86	.207	.286	.182	7	29	5	6	1	0	1	5	2	0	0	0	5	1	0	.345	.258
Venable, Will	L-L	6-3	205	10-29-82	.276	.213	.303	46	156	23	43	6	1	4	25	15	1	0	0	32	3	2	.404	.343
Walters, Zach	B-R	6-2	210	9-5-89	.276	.228	.297	94	333	45	92	18	4	10	53	25	2	1	5	63	3	1	.444	.326
Whiting, Brant	L-R	5-9	190	2-6-92	.250	—	.250	1	4	1	1	0	0	0	0	0	0	0	0	0	0	0	.250	.250
Zarraga, Shawn	R-R	6-0	255	1-21-89	.167	.154	.171	19	48	5	8	2	0	0	2	4	0	0	1	10	0	0	.208	.226

Pitching	B-T	HT	WT	DOB	W	L	ERA	G	GS	CG	SV	IP	H	R	ER	HR	BB	SO	AVG	vLH	vRH	K/9	BB/9
Anderson, Brett	L-L	6-3	230	2-1-88	0	1	3.60	1	1	0	0	5	6	2	2	0	0	2	.333	1.000	.294	3.60	0.00
Avilan, Luis	L-L	6-2	225	7-19-89	0	3	4.24	33	0	0	4	34	35	19	16	3	16	37	.265	.302	.247	9.79	4.24
Bawcom, Logan	R-R	6-2	220	11-2-88	6	5	1.92	31	12	0	1	89	70	28	19	5	32	69	.216	.244	.198	6.98	3.24
Bolsinger, Mike	R-R	6-1	215	1-29-88	2	1	3.41	13	2	0	0	29	32	12	11	2	10	34	.288	.190	.348	10.55	3.10
Bonilla, Lisalverto	R-R	6-0	225	6-18-90	4	5	4.28	24	6	1	2	74	76	39	35	4	27	79	.264	.287	.249	9.65	3.30
Broussard, Joe	R-R	6-1			0	0	4.50	2	0	0	1	2	1	1	1	0	0	3	.143	.000	.250	13.50	0.00
Burnett, Sean	L-L	5-11	185	9-17-82	0	0	2.35	7	0	0	0	8	8	3	2	1	6	5	.267	.143	.304	5.87	7.04
Cash, Ralston	R-R	6-3	215	8-20-91	4	0	2.63	17	0	0	1	24	15	8	7	1	11	28	.179	.182	.176	10.50	4.13
Choate, Randy	L-L	6-1	210	9-5-75	1	0	5.56	24	0	0	0	11	10	7	7	1	6	10	.238	.138	.462	7.94	4.76
Coleman, Louis	R-R	6-4	205	4-4-86	0	0	0.00	3	0	0	0	3	4	1	0	0	0	4	.308	.250	.333	12.00	0.00
Cotton, Jharel	R-R	5-11	195	1-19-92	8	5	4.90	22	16	1	0	97	80	59	53	17	32	119	.219	.207	.227	11.00	2.96
2-team total (6 Nashville)					11	6	4.31	28	22	2	0	136	108	71	65	20	39	155	—	—	—	10.28	2.59
Dayton, Grant	L-L	6-2	195	11-25-87	2	2	2.48	26	0	0	4	36	22	12	10	2	8	63	.169	.156	.176	15.61	1.98
De Leon, Jose	R-R	6-2	190	8-7-92	7	1	2.61	16	16	0	0	86	61	29	25	9	20	111	.194	.212	.184	11.57	2.08
DeJong, Chase	L-R	6-4	205	12-29-93	1	0	1.69	1	1	0	0	5	6	1	1	0	1	8	.273	.500	.083	13.50	1.69
Fields, Josh	R-R	6-0	195	8-19-85	0	1	9.00	2	0	0	0	2	3	2	2	0	0	2	.333	.333	.333	9.00	0.00
2-team total (23 Fresno)					1	1	2.15	25	0	0	1	29	22	8	7	0	7	34	—	—	—	10.43	2.15
Fien, Casey	R-R	6-2	210	10-21-83	1	0	4.35	8	0	0	1	10	11	5	5	1	2	13	.275	.304	.235	11.32	1.74
Figaro, Alfredo	R-R	6-0	190	7-7-84	1	0	1.89	3	0	0	0	19	18	4	4	0	4	8	.254	.333	.205	3.79	1.89
Frankoff, Seth	R-R	6-5	210	8-27-88	0	0	3.68	4	1	0	0	7	5	3	3	1	2	4	.200	.400	.067	4.91	2.45
Frias, Carlos	R-R	6-4	195	11-13-89	3	3	4.46	8	4	0	0	36	37	19	18	2	11	27	.274	.324	.224	6.69	2.72
Kehrt, Jeremy	R-R	6-2	190	12-21-85	4	5	5.11	12	9	0	0	56	63	35	32	4	23	42	.292	.258	.319	6.71	3.67
LeCure, Sam	R-R	6-0	210	5-4-84	5	5	4.55	31	12	0	2	91	97	48	46	10	15	72	.273	.288	.265	7.22	2.47
Lee, Zach	R-R	6-4	227	9-13-91	7	5	4.89	13	13	0	0	74	95	47	40	11	15	57	.315	.342	.288	6.96	1.83
2-team total (14 Tacoma)					7	14	6.14	27	27	0	0	148	193	111	101	22	39	107	—	—	—	6.51	2.37
Liberatore, Adam	L-L	6-3	240	5-12-87	0	0	0.00	4	0	0	1	5	0	0	0	0	2	10	.000	.000	.000	18.00	3.60
McCarthy, Brandon	R-R	6-7	235	7-7-83	0	0	2.45	1	1	0	0	4	3	1	1	0	2	4	.214	.000	.500	9.82	4.91
Merritt, Roy	L-L	6-0	170	9-22-85	0	0	4.26	3	2	0	0	13	13	6	6	1	4	8	.289	.167	.333	5.68	2.84
Montas, Frankie	R-R	6-2	255	3-21-93	0	0	2.38	4	3	0	0	11	12	3	3	0	2	15	.279	.211	.333	11.91	1.59
Oaks, Trevor	R-R	6-3	220	3-26-93	5	1	3.00	10	10	1	0	63	64	30	21	7	9	48	.262	.327	.206	6.86	1.29
Patterson, Red	R-R	6-3	220	5-11-87	0	1	9.00	2	0	0	0	3	5	3	3	2	2	1	.385	.444	.25	3.00	6.00
Ravin, Josh	R-R	6-4	215	1-21-88	0	0	0.00	2	0	0	0	4	1	0	0	0	1	7	.077	.125	.000	15.75	2.25
Rhame, Jacob	R-R	6-1	215	3-16-93	1	7	3.29	54	0	0	7	63	53	24	23	5	28	70	.231	.205	.248	10.00	4.00
Richardson, Dustin	L-L	6-6	220	1-9-84	0	0	0.00	3	0	0	0	0	0	0	0	0	2	1	.000	.000	.000	9.00	18.00
Rogers, Rob	R-R	6-0	205	10-25-90	0	1	10.38	3	0	0	0	4	5	6	5	0	1	5	.263	.222	.300	10.38	2.08
Ryu, Hyun Jin	L-L	6-3	250	3-25-87	0	1	8.38	3	3	0	0	10	17	9	9	2	0	8	.378	.350	.400	8.38	0.00
Schafer, Jordan	L-L	6-1	205	9-4-86	0	0	9.95	6	0	0	0	6	15	7	7	1	0	7	.455	.440	.478	9.95	0.00
Schlosser, Gus	R-R	6-4	225	10-20-88	1	1	9.15	12	1	0	0	21	33	23	21	3	10	19	.363	.452	.286	8.27	4.35
Shibuya, Tim	R-R	6-1	190	9-14-89	0	0	9.00	1	0	0	0	3	4	3	3	1	0	3	.333	.500	.250	9.00	0.00
Somsen, Layne	R-R	6-0	190	6-5-89	0	2	14.29	6	0	0	0	6	14	13	9	1	9	4	.438	.600	.364	6.35	14.29
Spitzbarth, Shea	R-R	6-1	195	10-4-94	0	0	19.29	1	0	0	0	2	5	5	5	1	3	2	.417	.500	.250	7.71	11.57
Stewart, Brock	L-R	6-3	210	10-3-91	4	0	2.49	9	9	0	0	51	41	14	14	4	6	54	.217	.197	.229	9.59	1.07
Stripling, Ross	R-R	6-3	210	11-23-89	0	2	3.78	5	4	0	0	17	20	7	7	2	2	17	.299	.227	.333	9.18	1.08
Tepesch, Nick	R-R	6-4	240	10-12-88	3	0	2.00	3	3	0	0	18	17	5	4	1	3	17	.254	.481	.100	8.50	1.50
4-team total (3 Nashville, 5 Omaha, 11 Round Rock)					8	4	3.96	22	19	0	0	116	121	56	51	7	28	62	—	—	—	4.81	2.17
Thatcher, Joe	L-L	6-2	230	10-4-81	0	0	3.60	17	0	0	0	15	14	6	6	0	5	21	.246	.167	.303	12.60	3.00
2-team total (10 Iowa)					0	0	4.43	27	1	0	0	22	24	11	11	0	8	32	—	—	—	12.90	3.22
Thomas, Ian	L-L	6-4	215	4-20-87	2	0	1.42	8	2	0	0	19	14	5	3	0	5	22	.209	.316	.167	10.42	2.37
Tsao, Chin-Hui	R-R	6-1	210	6-2-81	1	1	3.31	17	0	0	6	16	17	7	6	0	5	14	.266	.25	.275	7.71	2.76
Urena, Miguel	R-R	6-8	210	2-27-95	0	0	0.00	1	0	0	0	2	0	0	0	0	0	0	.000	.000	.000	0.00	0.00
Urias, Julio	L-L	6-0	215	8-12-96	5	1	1.40	11	7	0	0	45	31	7	7	2	8	49	.200	.250	.187	9.80	1.60
West, Matt	R-R	6-1	230	11-21-88	3	0	2.33	39	0	0	6	46	35	12	12	1	8	38	.219	.253	.188	7.38	1.55

Fielding

Catcher	PCT	G	PO	A	E	DP	PB
Barnes	.993	63	544	26	4	1	2
DiFazio	.976	4	39	2	1	1	0
Grandal	1.000	3	13	1	0	0	0
Murphy	.995	69	570	32	3	3	1
Whiting	1.000	1	9	0	0	0	0
Zarraga	1.000	11	72	12	0	1	0

First Base	PCT	G	PO	A	E	DP
Anderson	1.000	7	57	2	0	10
Bellinger	1.000	3	20	2	0	3
Cordero	1.000	1	11	0	0	1
Dickson	.975	31	215	15	6	28
Hassan	.977	46	342	37	9	40
Hicks	1.000	1	1	0	0	1
Ogle	1.000	1	11	1	0	0
Segedin	.996	36	249	9	1	28
Van Slyke	.933	2	14	0	1	1
Walters	.986	29	199	10	3	17
Zarraga	1.000	5	9	0	2	1

Second Base	PCT	G	PO	A	E	DP
Barnes	.949	15	27	47	4	13
Culberson	1.000	5	11	15	0	2
Figueroa	1.000	1	0	3	0	0
Herrera	1.000	3	6	7	0	5
Hicks	.935	22	29	43	5	12
Johnson	.958	84	134	212	15	59
Maggi	1.000	14	18	48	0	12
Segedin	1.000	1	2	2	0	0
Walters	.964	15	21	33	2	8

Third Base	PCT	G	PO	A	E	DP
Barnes	.905	9	7	12	2	2
Culberson	1.000	5	5	5	0	0
Figueroa	1.000	2	0	2	0	0
Hassan	.600	2	2	1	2	0
Herrera	.800	2	1	3	1	0
Hicks	.947	31	15	57	4	10
Johnson	1.000	2	2	4	0	0
Maggi	.963	17	15	37	2	3

	PCT	G	PO	A	E	DP
Segedin	.954	58	33	91	6	8
Taylor	1.000	2	1	3	0	0
Walters	.897	21	12	23	4	4

Shortstop	PCT	G	PO	A	E	DP
Culberson	.971	57	74	161	7	36
Figueroa	1.000	3	2	14	0	1
Herrera	.955	20	25	60	4	16
Hicks	.952	32	36	82	6	23
Maggi	.875	6	6	8	2	2
Segedin	1.000	1	3	1	0	2
Taylor	1.000	13	18	27	0	8
Walters	.931	18	24	43	5	14

Outfield	PCT	G	PO	A	E	DP
Anderson	—	1	0	0	0	0
Barnes	—	1	0	0	0	0
Brown	.991	105	208	4	2	0
Crawford	1.000	2	4	0	0	0
Culberson	—	1	0	0	0	0
Dickson	1.000	39	43	1	0	0
Fields	1.000	9	20	1	0	1

	PCT	G	PO	A	E	DP
Guerrero	1.000	2	6	0	0	0
Hassan	1.000	25	45	0	0	0
Herrera	1.000	3	3	0	0	0
Johnson	.975	40	78	0	2	0
Maggi	1.000	2	1	0	0	0
Noel	1.000	44	72	0	0	0
Pederson	1.000	3	3	0	0	0
Puig	1.000	17	33	1	0	0
Ramsey	.991	76	103	6	1	0

	PCT	G	PO	A	E	DP
Richardson	1.000	15	25	0	0	0
Schafer	1.000	3	4	0	0	0
Segedin	1.000	5	10	1	0	1
Tabata	1.000	17	27	1	0	1
Toles	1.000	14	30	1	0	0
Van Slyke	1.000	4	3	0	0	0
Venable	1.000	38	53	2	0	0
Walters	.944	12	16	1	1	0

TULSA DRILLERS
TEXAS LEAGUE

DOUBLE-A

LOS ANGELES DODGERS

Batting	B-T	HT	WT	DOB	AVG	vLH	vRH	G	AB	R	H	2B	3B	HR	RBI	BB	HBP	SH	SF	SO	SB	CS	SLG	OBP
Ahart, Devan	L-R	6-1	175	10-21-92	.215	.200	.219	24	79	9	17	4	0	1	7	4	0	0	2	17	1	0	.304	.247
Anderson, Lars	L-L	6-4	215	9-25-87	.271	.233	.282	88	262	40	71	18	0	7	46	38	0	0	2	48	1	0	.420	.361
Arruebarrena, Erisbel	R-R	6-1	230	3-25-90	.182	.455	.114	17	55	6	10	0	0	4	8	3	0	0	0	21	0	0	.400	.224
Bellinger, Cody	L-L	6-4	210	7-13-95	.263	.273	.260	114	399	61	105	17	1	23	65	59	3	0	4	94	8	2	.484	.359
Calhoun, Willie	L-R	5-8	187	11-4-94	.254	.219	.264	132	503	75	128	25	1	27	88	45	5	1	6	65	0	0	.469	.318
Curletta, Joey	R-R	6-4	245	3-8-94	.206	.208	.205	29	97	7	20	4	0	4	13	10	0	0	0	37	0	0	.371	.280
DiFazio, Vin	R-R	6-0	215	5-15-86	.244	.214	.258	15	45	4	11	0	0	4	9	1	0	0	13	0	1	.244	.382
Drake, Yadir	R-R	6-0	200	4-12-90	.109	.182	.091	19	55	4	6	1	0	0	2	3	0	1	0	11	1	0	.127	.155
Farmer, Kyle	R-R	6-0	205	8-17-90	.256	.269	.252	74	266	31	68	18	2	5	31	25	3	0	3	44	2	0	.395	.323
Fields, Daniel	L-R	6-2	215	1-23-91	.091	.000	.100	5	11	1	1	0	0	0	3	0	0	0	4	0	0	.091	.286
Garlick, Kyle	R-R	6-1	210	1-26-92	.284	.276	.287	79	292	42	83	29	2	8	39	18	6	0	3	83	1	0	.479	.335
Guerrero, Alex	R-R	6-1	220	11-20-86	.031	.000	.042	8	32	2	1	0	0	0	1	0	0	0	5	0	0	.031	.061
Henson, Jake	R-R	5-11	215	8-4-93	.000	.000	—	1	1	0	0	0	0	0	0	0	0	0	0	0	0	.000	.000
Hernandez, Enrique	R-R	5-11	200	8-24-91	.000	.000	.000	2	8	0	0	0	0	0	0	1	0	0	3	0	0	.000	.111
Hoenecke, Paul	L-R	6-2	205	7-8-90	.288	.188	.301	40	139	18	40	6	0	7	21	4	1	0	21	0	1	.482	.313
Law, Adam	R-R	6-0	193	2-5-90	.276	.235	.288	32	76	11	21	3	0	0	5	8	2	4	1	12	3	2	.316	.356
Locastro, Tim	R-R	6-1	200	7-14-92	.277	.286	.275	45	191	27	53	8	1	1	13	8	7	1	0	16	9	2	.346	.330
Maggi, Drew	R-R	6-0	192	5-16-89	.299	.333	.288	61	194	26	58	10	2	1	11	17	7	2	0	37	8	5	.402	.376
Ogle, Tyler	R-R	5-10	210	8-9-90	.213	.172	.224	49	136	13	29	6	1	4	18	13	4	0	2	32	0	1	.360	.297
Perio, Noah	L-R	6-0	170	11-14-91	.263	.200	.286	7	19	1	5	1	0	0	3	1	0	0	4	0	0	.316	.300
Rios, Edwin	L-R	6-3	220	4-21-94	.254	.250	.256	33	122	14	31	7	0	5	17	8	2	0	3	31	0	0	.434	.304
Scavuzzo, Jacob	R-R	6-4	185	1-15-94	.266	.260	.268	112	421	59	112	21	2	10	39	28	6	0	4	100	4	2	.397	.318
Tarsovich, Jordan	R-R	5-10	180	6-20-91	.219	.182	.228	59	169	23	37	9	0	4	16	26	1	1	1	32	6	2	.343	.325
Toles, Andrew	L-R	5-10	185	5-24-92	.314	.188	.343	43	175	27	55	14	3	5	22	12	2	0	1	30	13	5	.514	.363
Trinkwon, Brandon	L-R	6-1	170	3-30-92	.226	.244	.223	79	270	34	61	9	2	3	24	31	1	5	2	41	4	5	.307	.306
Verdugo, Alex	L-L	6-0	205	5-15-96	.273	.255	.278	126	477	58	130	23	1	13	63	44	4	0	4	67	2	6	.407	.336
Zarraga, Shawn	R-R	6-0	255	1-21-89	.306	.261	.323	27	85	9	26	5	0	0	14	12	0	0	3	12	0	1	.388	.384

Pitching	B-T	HT	WT	DOB	W	L	ERA	G	GS	CG	SV	IP	H	R	ER	HR	BB	SO	AVG	vLH	vRH	K/9	BB/9
Anderson, Chris	R-R	6-3	245	7-29-92	3	6	5.90	18	6	0	0	40	37	30	26	3	35	25	.248	.265	.240	5.67	7.94
Anderson, Isaac	R-R	6-2	185	9-4-93	0	3	6.65	5	5	0	0	22	27	16	16	3	6	16	.290	.333	.280	6.65	2.49
Barlow, Scott	R-R	6-3	170	12-18-92	4	7	3.98	24	23	0	0	124	125	63	55	9	52	102	.260	.306	.238	7.38	3.76
Bawcom, Logan	R-R	6-2	220	11-2-88	1	0	2.00	5	0	0	1	9	5	2	2	1	1	11	.156	.154	.158	11.00	1.00
Bonilla, Lisalverto	R-R	6-0	225	6-18-90	1	2	3.38	7	7	0	0	37	33	15	14	2	13	39	.237	.208	.253	9.40	3.13
Broussard, Joe	R-R	6-2	215	1-28-91	3	2	1.93	33	0	0	7	42	34	9	9	2	12	51	.222	.188	.238	10.93	2.57
Burgos, Alex	L-L	5-11	195	12-1-90	0	0	4.50	2	0	0	0	2	2	1	1	1	1	3	.250	—	.250	13.50	4.50
Cash, Ralston	R-R	6-3	215	8-20-91	5	3	3.00	29	0	0	1	45	36	20	15	1	22	56	.220	.236	.211	11.20	4.40
Choate, Randy	L-L	6-1	210	9-5-75	0	0	54.00	3	0	0	0	0	3	2	2	0	1	0	.750	.500	1.000	0.00	27.00
Corcino, Daniel	R-R	5-11	210	8-26-90	1	1	3.53	27	0	0	3	36	28	16	14	4	10	31	.211	.211	.211	7.82	2.52
Dayton, Grant	L-L	6-2	195	11-25-87	3	0	2.30	12	0	0	1	16	8	6	4	0	3	28	.148	.133	.154	16.09	1.72
DeJong, Chase	L-R	6-4	205	12-29-93	14	5	2.86	25	25	2	0	142	106	51	45	15	39	125	.207	.226	.199	7.94	2.48
Dirks, Caleb	R-R	6-3	220	6-9-93	3	2	1.44	28	0	0	6	31	25	10	5	3	7	35	.214	.194	.222	10.05	2.01
Figaro, Alfredo	R-R	6-0	190	7-7-84	2	0	3.50	5	3	0	0	18	17	9	7	2	3	10	.246	.318	.213	5.00	1.50
Frankoff, Seth	R-R	6-5	210	8-27-88	3	4	4.15	21	9	0	0	61	73	36	28	2	15	58	.297	.295	.298	8.60	2.23
Frias, Carlos	R-R	6-4	195	11-13-89	0	1	1.29	2	2	0	0	7	3	1	1	0	0	5	.130	.100	.154	6.43	0.00
Garcia, Yimi	R-R	6-1	220	8-18-90	0	1	10.80	3	0	0	0	3	4	4	4	1	5	.308	.400	.250	13.50	10.80	
Gonzalez, Felipe	R-R	6-1	200	8-15-91	0	4	9.37	5	4	0	0	16	24	17	17	3	12	13	.343	.267	.400	5.51	6.61
Griggs, Scott	R-R	6-4	215	5-13-91	0	2	4.54	31	0	0	5	34	33	20	17	3	20	21	.264	.282	.256	5.61	5.35
Hooper, Kyle	R-R	6-4	195	5-28-91	0	2	6.52	9	0	0	0	10	7	7	7	1	6	12	.212	.200	.214	11.17	5.59
Johnson, Dan	L-R	6-2	210	8-10-79	0	0	5.52	4	0	0	0	15	18	9	9	1	6	10	.305	.273	.313	6.14	3.68
Johnson, Michael	L-L	6-1	185	1-3-91	2	2	3.81	46	0	0	0	57	65	27	24	7	24	57	.289	.298	.286	9.05	3.81
Kehrt, Jeremy	R-R	6-2	190	12-21-85	4	6	6.03	13	13	0	0	66	83	46	44	6	15	38	.307	.368	.279	5.21	2.06
Malm, Jeff	L-L	6-2	225	10-31-90	1	1	2.79	17	0	0	1	19	19	6	6	2	6	17	.257	.389	.174	7.91	2.79
Montas, Frankie	R-R	6-2	255	3-21-93	0	0	1.93	3	1	0	0	5	2	1	1	1	1	7	.133	.200	.100	13.50	1.93
Oaks, Trevor	R-R	6-3	220	3-26-93	1	2	2.14	10	10	0	0	63	56	15	15	1	9	38	.239	.278	.219	5.43	1.29
Richardson, Dustin	L-L	6-6	220	1-9-84	0	0	7.36	7	0	0	0	7	9	8	6	2	4	11	.281	.000	.360	13.50	4.91
Rogers, Rob	R-R	6-0	205	10-25-90	1	0	3.09	16	0	0	3	23	18	9	8	0	10	16	.253	.167	.295	6.17	3.86
Sborz, Josh	R-R	6-3	225	12-17-93	0	1	3.78	10	0	0	1	17	17	10	7	2	6	17	.258	.333	.241	9.18	3.24
Schafer, Jordan	L-L	6-1	205	9-4-86	1	1	3.15	31	1	0	0	40	41	20	14	4	17	46	.261	.150	.299	10.35	3.83
Schlosser, Gus	R-R	6-4	225	10-20-88	0	1	2.05	14	0	0	4	22	20	7	5	2	0	23	.238	.190	.254	9.41	0.00
Shibuya, Tim	R-R	6-1	190	9-14-89	1	6	3.81	18	14	0	0	76	79	38	32	7	12	40	.267	.309	.248	4.76	1.43

LOS ANGELES DODGERS (side banner)

Pitching

Pitching	B-T	HT	WT	DOB	W	L	ERA	G	GS	CG	SV	IP	H	R	ER	HR	BB	SO	AVG	vLH	vRH	K/9	BB/9
Sierra, Yaisel	R-R	6-1	170	6-5-91	1	2	4.30	10	0	0	0	15	14	9	7	0	5	21	.237	.167	.255	12.89	3.07
Sopko, Andrew	R-R	6-2	205	8-7-94	2	2	4.94	6	6	0	0	31	35	17	17	4	11	25	.287	.405	.235	7.26	3.19
Stewart, Brock	L-R	6-3	210	10-3-91	3	4	1.37	10	10	1	0	59	41	12	9	4	11	65	.196	.157	.216	9.86	1.67
Thayer, Dale	R-R	6-0	210	12-17-80	1	1	6.75	7	0	0	0	8	16	10	6	2	2	10	.390	.385	.393	11.25	2.25

Fielding

Catcher	PCT	G	PO	A	E	DP	PB
DiFazio	.981	12	96	6	2	1	0
Farmer	.989	56	403	43	5	7	8
Hoenecke	.990	25	185	18	2	3	2
Ogle	.989	31	252	18	3	3	4
Zarraga	.994	23	152	21	1	3	2

First Base	PCT	G	PO	A	E	DP
Anderson	.997	52	355	33	1	27
Bellinger	.997	81	713	31	2	62
Hoenecke	1.000	1	6	1	0	0
Ogle	1.000	8	49	6	0	1
Rios	.973	4	34	2	1	2
Trinkwon	1.000	4	27	1	0	0
Zarraga	.667	1	4	0	2	0

Second Base	PCT	G	PO	A	E	DP
Calhoun	.957	119	200	263	21	60
Hernandez	1.000	1	2	5	0	1
Locastro	1.000	2	6	4	0	2

	PCT/AVG	G	PO	A	E	DP
Maggi	.889	2	4	4	1	2
Perio	1.000	1	1	2	0	0
Tarsovich	1.000	9	15	11	0	3
Trinkwon	.982	13	19	35	1	4

Third Base	PCT	G	PO	A	E	DP
Farmer	.889	16	6	26	4	2
Guerrero	1.000	4	2	6	0	1
Hoenecke	.947	8	4	14	1	1
Law	.921	15	10	25	3	1
Maggi	1.000	9	5	18	0	1
Perio	.800	3	2	2	1	0
Rios	.897	28	11	59	8	5
Tarsovich	.831	29	7	42	10	3
Trinkwon	.916	42	31	67	9	9

Shortstop	PCT	G	PO	A	E	DP
Arruebarrena	.914	14	14	39	5	2
Locastro	.957	40	52	128	8	23
Maggi	.966	48	48	153	7	19

	PCT	G	PO	A	E	DP
Tarsovich	.971	20	22	77	3	9
Trinkwon	.932	18	29	40	5	13

Outfield	PCT	G	PO	A	E	DP
Ahart	.966	14	28	0	1	0
Anderson	.964	16	25	2	1	1
Bellinger	1.000	34	53	2	0	0
Curletta	1.000	24	47	4	0	1
Drake	1.000	15	32	4	0	0
Fields	1.000	3	4	0	0	0
Garlick	.991	63	104	4	1	2
Guerrero	1.000	2	3	0	0	0
Hernandez	1.000	1	2	0	0	0
Law	1.000	11	15	0	0	0
Locastro	1.000	2	6	0	0	0
Maggi	1.000	1	4	0	0	0
Scavuzzo	.976	92	153	9	4	1
Tarsovich	1.000	1	1	0	0	0
Toles	.981	42	100	1	2	0
Verdugo	.963	121	249	13	10	2

RANCHO CUCAMONGA QUAKES — HIGH CLASS A
CALIFORNIA LEAGUE

Batting	B-T	HT	WT	DOB	AVG	vLH	vRH	G	AB	R	H	2B	3B	HR	RBI	BB	HBP	SH	SF	SO	SB	CS	SLG	OBP
Ahart, Devan	L-R	6-1	175	10-21-92	.274	.192	.285	62	212	35	58	12	2	3	28	22	2	0	2	49	8	1	.392	.345
Ahmed, Mike	R-R	6-2	195	1-20-92	.278	.284	.277	111	385	81	107	19	4	19	52	55	7	0	3	110	9	8	.496	.376
Beaty, Matt	L-R	6-0	210	4-28-93	.297	.330	.289	124	489	66	145	30	0	11	88	40	6	0	7	74	6	1	.425	.352
Chen, Pin-Chieh	L-R	6-1	170	7-23-91	.271	.375	.255	18	59	7	16	2	2	1	9	6	1	3	0	11	2	0	.424	.348
Crawford, Carl	L-L	6-2	230	8-5-81	.333	—	.333	1	3	0	1	0	0	0	1	1	0	0	0	1	0	0	.333	.500
Curletta, Joey	R-R	6-4	245	3-8-94	.267	.295	.261	77	270	40	72	13	5	13	54	27	3	0	2	87	0	2	.496	.338
Dean, Nick	R-R	6-1	190	5-11-92	.000	—	.000	3	5	1	0	0	0	0	1	4	0	1	0	2	0	0	.000	.444
Diaz, Yusniel	R-R	6-1	195	10-7-96	.272	.281	.270	82	316	47	86	8	7	8	54	29	1	0	2	71	7	8	.418	.333
Ethier, Andre	L-L	6-2	210	4-10-82	.290	.250	.304	9	31	7	9	4	0	0	3	1	2	0	1	6	0	0	.419	.343
Garlick, Kyle	R-R	6-1	210	1-26-92	.306	.350	.295	49	196	38	60	13	1	11	37	15	4	0	0	57	0	0	.551	.367
Guerrero, Alex	R-R	5-11	220	11-20-86	.269	—	.269	6	26	4	7	1	0	1	4	1	0	0	0	3	1	0	.423	.296
Henson, Jake	R-R	5-11	215	8-4-93	.400	—	.400	1	5	1	2	1	0	0	0	0	0	0	0	1	0	0	.600	.400
Hernandez, Enrique	R-R	5-11	200	8-24-91	.375	.000	.429	2	8	3	3	1	0	0	2	0	0	0	0	3	1	0	.500	.500
Hoenecke, Paul	L-R	6-2	205	7-8-90	.222	.300	.205	14	54	9	12	3	0	2	9	2	0	0	1	9	1	0	.389	.246
Kendrick, Howie	R-R	5-11	220	7-12-83	.333	.250	.364	4	15	2	5	3	0	0	4	0	1	0	0	3	1	1	.533	.375
Kennedy, Garrett	L-R	6-1	205	11-2-90	.182	.179	.182	63	220	20	40	11	1	3	21	18	1	2	6	67	0	1	.282	.245
Leon, Julian	R-R	5-11	200	1-24-96	.223	.182	.230	61	220	28	49	12	0	8	27	13	3	0	1	87	0	1	.386	.274
Locastro, Tim	R-R	6-1	200	7-14-92	.289	.259	.295	86	339	61	98	17	5	5	39	15	18	2	6	50	15	4	.413	.347
Mejia, Erick	B-R	5-11	155	11-9-94	.287	.165	.311	124	509	78	146	18	12	4	47	43	4	1	4	110	24	15	.393	.343
Mieses, Johan	R-R	6-2	185	7-13-95	.247	.250	.247	122	461	72	114	31	3	28	78	36	11	1	4	147	3	7	.510	.314
Navin, Spencer	R-R	6-1	185	8-11-92	.192	.000	.250	10	26	2	5	0	0	0	1	6	1	0	0	12	0	0	.192	.364
Perio, Noah	L-R	6-0	170	11-14-91	.355	.400	.347	30	121	23	43	9	2	6	24	6	1	0	1	14	1	0	.612	.388
Puig, Yasiel	R-R	6-2	240	12-7-90	.417	—	.417	5	12	2	5	0	0	1	2	3	0	0	0	3	1	2	.667	.533
Rios, Edwin	L-R	6-3	220	4-21-94	.367	.300	.381	42	177	37	65	11	1	16	46	8	1	0	2	35	0	0	.712	.394
Sandoval, Ariel	R-R	6-2	180	11-6-95	.229	.385	.204	50	188	23	43	9	2	3	21	11	4	1	2	59	5	1	.346	.283
Smith, Will	R-R	6-0	192	3-28-95	.216	.200	.220	25	97	13	21	4	0	2	12	14	3	0	1	31	1	0	.320	.330
Tarsovich, Jordan	R-R	5-10	180	6-20-91	.223	.130	.250	31	103	13	23	1	2	5	16	13	3	0	1	30	1	2	.417	.325
Tate, Donavan	R-R	6-3	200	9-27-90	.107	.111	.105	8	28	0	3	0	0	0	2	3	1	0	1	14	1	2	.107	.212
Toles, Andrew	L-R	5-10	185	5-24-92	.370	.188	.408	22	92	22	34	8	2	0	9	6	1	1	0	13	9	3	.500	.414
Toscano, Dian	L-L	5-11	190	3-9-89	.256	.238	.262	26	82	8	21	4	3	1	9	8	2	0	0	30	2	0	.415	.337
Trinkwon, Brandon	L-R	6-1	170	3-30-92	.286	.391	.258	30	112	19	32	4	0	1	18	15	1	0	1	17	1	1	.348	.372
Van Slyke, Scott	R-R	6-4	215	7-24-86	.500	—	.500	1	2	1	1	0	0	0	1	0	0	0	0	1	0	0	.500	.667

Pitching	B-T	HT	WT	DOB	W	L	ERA	G	GS	CG	SV	IP	H	R	ER	HR	BB	SO	AVG	vLH	vRH	K/9	BB/9
Anderson, Brett	L-L	6-3	230	2-1-88	0	1	6.00	3	2	0	0	9	17	9	6	0	2	10	.395	.273	.438	10.00	2.00
Anderson, Chris	R-R	6-3	245	7-29-92	1	2	3.25	18	2	0	0	28	20	16	10	3	11	26	.196	.250	.155	8.46	3.58
Anderson, Isaac	R-R	6-2	185	9-4-93	3	0	1.13	3	2	0	0	16	9	2	2	1	3	19	.155	.148	.161	10.69	1.69
Bergjans, Tommy	R-R	6-1	190	12-1-92	3	13	4.98	24	21	0	1	130	138	93	72	13	29	133	.268	.224	.298	9.21	2.01
Boyle, Michael	R-L	6-3	200	4-12-94	1	2	5.55	7	6	0	0	36	44	25	22	7	31	42	.308	.226	.330	7.82	1.77
Bray, Adam	R-R	6-3	210	4-14-93	1	0	3.70	19	4	0	2	49	44	25	20	8	7	51	.234	.261	.210	9.43	1.29
Broussard, Joe	R-R	6-1	220	1-28-91	1	0	1.38	15	0	0	1	26	21	4	4	1	4	27	.223	.139	.276	9.35	1.38
Brown, Kevin	R-R	6-3	220	6-9-92	0	1	2.52	18	0	0	2	25	18	8	7	0	11	26	.220	.205	.231	9.36	3.96
Burgos, Alex	L-L	5-11	195	12-1-90	4	0	2.79	22	0	0	1	39	30	14	12	2	18	32	.221	.188	.231	7.45	4.19

Pitching	B-T	HT	WT	DOB	W	L	ERA	G	GS	CG	SV	IP	H	R	ER	HR	BB	SO	AVG	vLH	vRH	K/9	BB/9
Copping, Corey	R-R	6-1	175	1-11-94	2	0	3.72	16	0	0	2	19	15	9	8	2	6	22	.211	.222	.205	10.24	2.79
Corcino, Daniel	R-R	5-11	210	8-26-90	0	0	1.80	3	0	0	0	5	6	1	1	0	2	4	.286	.091	.500	7.20	3.60
De Paula, Luis	L-L	6-1	170	4-23-92	2	2	5.74	26	0	0	1	31	27	26	20	5	23	34	.220	.179	.238	9.77	6.61
Fien, Casey	R-R	6-2	210	10-21-83	0	0	4.50	2	0	0	0	2	4	1	1	0	0	3	.400	.500	.333	13.50	0.00
Garcia, Yimi	R-R	6-1	220	8-18-90	0	0	6.00	2	2	0	0	3	3	2	2	2	0	5	.273	.400	.167	15.00	0.00
Gonzalez, Felipe	R-R	6-1	200	8-15-91	3	7	5.57	20	9	0	0	76	84	54	47	11	28	69	.283	.259	.298	8.17	3.32
Griggs, Scott	R-R	6-4	215	5-13-91	1	1	0.73	12	0	0	7	12	3	1	1	1	2	10	.073	.095	.050	7.30	1.46
Helsabeck, Wes	L-L	6-0	195	7-7-92	2	2	3.68	7	3	0	0	22	21	9	9	2	6	23	.263	.211	.279	9.41	2.45
Hermeling, Alex	R-R	6-5	230	3-22-93	0	1	8.74	7	0	0	0	11	17	11	11	1	7	6	.362	.500	.290	4.76	5.56
Holmes, Grant	L-R	6-1	215	3-22-96	8	4	4.02	20	18	0	1	105	103	60	47	6	43	100	.254	.265	.244	8.54	3.67
2-team total (6 Stockton)					11	7	4.63	26	23	0	1	134	147	85	69	10	53	124	—	—	—	8.33	3.56
Hooper, Kyle	R-R	6-4	195	5-28-91	1	2	3.14	19	0	0	2	29	23	10	10	0	11	28	.225	.205	.241	8.79	3.45
Kershaw, Clayton	L-L	6-4	225	3-19-88	0	0	0.00	1	1	0	0	3	1	0	0	0	0	5	.111	.000	.143	15.00	0.00
Kowalczyk, Karch	R-R	6-1	215	3-31-91	1	2	3.31	16	0	0	6	16	20	8	6	2	9	10	.313	.367	.265	5.51	4.96
Liberatore, Adam	L-L	6-3	240	5-12-87	0	0	18.00	1	0	0	0	1	3	2	2	0	0	0	.500	1.000	.000	0.00	0.00
Malm, Jeff	L-L	6-3	225	10-31-90	2	1	1.57	22	0	0	3	29	30	10	5	1	7	40	.270	.324	.243	12.56	2.20
McCarthy, Brandon	R-R	6-7	235	7-7-83	0	2	7.07	4	4	0	0	14	21	17	11	6	2	12	.333	.250	.444	7.71	1.29
Norris, Bud	R-R	6-0	215	3-2-85	1	1	1.59	1	1	0	0	6	4	1	1	0	1	4	.200	.083	.375	6.35	1.59
Oaks, Trevor	R-R	6-3	220	3-26-93	1	1	3.60	4	4	0	0	25	26	10	10	1	3	22	.280	.327	.220	7.92	1.08
Pfeifer, Phil	L-L	6-0	190	7-15-92	2	1	3.33	14	0	0	0	24	21	9	9	1	17	33	.241	.200	.263	12.21	6.29
Pittore, Gavin	R-R	6-3	230	9-18-93	1	0	3.55	6	0	0	0	13	10	7	5	0	5	13	.227	.217	.238	9.24	3.55
Powell, Chris	R-R	6-2	170	9-21-92	0	0	3.60	3	0	0	0	5	4	2	2	0	3	2	.222	.125	.300	3.60	5.40
Ravin, Josh	R-R	6-4	215	1-21-88	0	0	9.00	1	1	0	0	1	1	1	1	0	1	1	.250	.500	.000	9.00	0.00
Reid-Foley, David	L-R	6-3	190	1-2-91	1	3	7.16	21	0	0	0	33	36	27	26	8	11	31	.275	.232	.307	8.54	3.03
Rogers, Rob	R-R	6-0	205	10-25-90	1	1	4.82	6	0	0	0	9	9	7	5	0	5	6	.265	.400	.158	5.79	4.82
Rossman, Bubby	R-R	6-5	220	6-29-92	4	0	3.52	22	0	0	0	38	30	18	15	2	19	34	.210	.254	.171	7.98	4.46
Ryu, Hyun Jin	L-L	6-3	250	3-25-87	1	1	2.00	5	5	0	0	18	15	7	4	2	1	14	.214	.286	.184	7.00	0.50
Sborz, Josh	R-R	6-3	225	12-17-93	8	4	2.66	20	19	0	0	108	82	38	32	8	30	108	.207	.202	.211	8.97	2.49
Shibuya, Tim	R-R	6-1	190	9-14-89	4	0	2.51	5	4	0	0	29	25	8	8	3	11	15	.238	.244	.233	4.71	3.45
Sierra, Yaisel	R-R	6-1	170	6-5-91	5	5	6.20	20	13	0	0	74	87	51	51	9	25	65	.293	.352	.249	7.91	3.04
Sopko, Andrew	R-R	6-2	205	8-7-94	11	2	3.26	18	17	0	0	99	100	37	36	5	24	99	.264	.275	.255	8.97	2.17
Stewart, Brock	L-R	6-3	210	10-3-91	2	0	0.82	2	2	0	0	11	5	1	1	0	2	10	.135	.063	.190	8.18	1.64
Sylvester, Derrick	R-R	6-6	200	4-19-91	0	0	0.00	3	0	0	0	5	0	0	0	0	0	3	.000	.000	.000	5.40	0.00
Vanegas, A.J.	R-R	6-3	215	8-16-92	0	0	10.13	4	0	0	0	5	8	6	6	1	6	7	.348	.400	.308	11.81	10.13
White, Mitchell	R-R	6-4	207	12-28-94	1	0	0.00	1	0	0	0	2	1	0	0	0	0	2	.167	.200	.000	9.00	0.00

Fielding

Catcher	PCT	G	PO	A	E	DP	PB
Henson	1.000	1	11	0	0	0	2
Hoenecke	.979	10	83	10	2	0	1
Kennedy	.994	56	468	58	3	2	2
Leon	.980	52	396	47	9	3	7
Navin	1.000	10	76	10	0	0	1
Smith	1.000	16	115	17	0	3	2

First Base	PCT	G	PO	A	E	DP
Ahmed	.977	37	325	12	8	37
Beaty	.991	65	515	45	5	43
Garlick	1.000	8	61	6	0	5
Hoenecke	1.000	3	24	2	0	3
Leon	.974	9	68	6	2	4
Locastro	1.000	3	25	2	0	4
Rios	.987	18	141	11	2	9

Second Base	PCT	G	PO	A	E	DP
Ahmed	1.000	18	32	42	0	11
Kendrick	1.000	2	3	3	0	1
Locastro	.978	59	76	147	5	33
Mejia	.950	13	24	33	3	10
Perio	.988	21	33	52	1	11

Smith	1.000	2	2	6	0	0
Tarsovich	.984	11	24	39	1	8
Trinkwon	.986	18	31	42	1	8

Third Base	PCT	G	PO	A	E	DP
Ahmed	.952	36	20	60	4	6
Beaty	.930	51	31	75	8	9
Dean	1.000	3	0	3	0	1
Guerrero	1.000	2	0	6	0	0
Hoenecke	1.000	1	1	3	0	1
Kendrick	1.000	1	0	1	0	0
Perio	.857	5	2	10	2	0
Rios	.864	20	13	25	6	2
Smith	1.000	6	2	11	0	1
Tarsovich	.957	14	7	15	1	1
Trinkwon	.909	5	0	10	1	1

Shortstop	PCT	G	PO	A	E	DP
Ahmed	.929	5	2	11	1	1
Locastro	.937	17	18	41	4	7
Mejia	.922	110	181	267	38	59
Perio	1.000	1	1	6	0	0
Tarsovich	1.000	3	6	6	0	4
Trinkwon	.950	6	7	12	1	2

Outfield	PCT	G	PO	A	E	DP
Ahart	.982	56	103	4	2	1
Ahmed	.500	1	1	0	1	0
Chen	.962	15	25	0	1	0
Crawford	1.000	1	4	0	0	0
Curletta	.989	59	86	8	1	2
Diaz	.981	55	104	1	2	0
Ethier	1.000	5	7	0	0	0
Garlick	.981	31	52	1	1	0
Guerrero	1.000	2	4	0	0	0
Hernandez	1.000	2	2	0	0	0
Locastro	1.000	5	9	0	0	0
Mieses	.971	113	250	14	8	3
Puig	1.000	5	5	1	0	0
Rossman	1.000	1	4	0	0	0
Sandoval	.956	43	86	1	4	0
Tate	.909	7	10	0	1	0
Toles	.980	21	49	0	1	0
Toscano	1.000	15	18	0	0	0
Van Slyke	1.000	1	3	0	0	0

GREAT LAKES LOONS
MIDWEST LEAGUE

LOW CLASS A

Batting	B-T	HT	WT	DOB	AVG	vLH	vRH	G	AB	R	H	2B	3B	HR	RBI	BB	HBP	SH	SF	SO	SB	CS	SLG	OBP
Ayon, Andres	R-R	6-1	180	3-23-95	.125	.000	.143	2	8	1	1	0	0	0	0	0	0	0	0	1	0	0	.125	.125
Berman, Stevie	R-R	6-2	225	11-28-94	.190	.105	.231	20	58	7	11	1	0	0	4	10	2	0	0	16	0	0	.207	.329
Castillo, Deivy	L-L	6-3	170	7-21-95	.187	.095	.235	37	123	11	23	0	0	2	4	10	1	2	1	41	3	2	.236	.252
Celli, Federico	R-R	6-3	215	2-15-95	.091	.000	.125	6	22	0	2	0	0	0	1	2	0	0	0	13	0	0	.091	.167
Davis, Brendon	R-R	6-4	165	7-28-97	.241	.302	.219	109	398	51	96	18	2	5	49	29	3	2	4	118	8	3	.334	.295
Dean, Nick	R-R	6-1	190	5-11-92	.218	.237	.206	35	101	13	22	1	0	3	7	18	3	2	0	29	3	4	.317	.352
Estevez, Omar	R-R	5-10	168	2-25-98	.255	.218	.271	122	471	46	120	32	2	9	61	26	5	2	4	121	3	6	.389	.298
Fields, Daniel	L-R	6-2	215	1-23-91	.222	.222	.222	5	18	2	4	0	0	1	1	1	0	0	0	6	0	0	.389	.263

LOS ANGELES DODGERS

Batting	B-T	HT	WT	DOB	AVG	vLH	vRH	G	AB	R	H	2B	3B	HR	RBI	BB	HBP	SH	SF	SO	SB	CS	SLG	OBP
Gomez, Cristian	R-R	5-11	160	1-11-96	.168	.192	.159	62	190	19	32	10	1	2	20	11	1	1	1	60	4	2	.263	.217
Green, Gage	R-R	5-10	193	8-27-92	.210	.182	.218	100	315	33	66	7	1	7	24	32	12	10	2	88	11	9	.305	.305
Henson, Jake	R-R	5-11	215	8-4-93	.273	.359	.236	39	128	12	35	4	0	4	19	14	3	0	1	32	0	0	.398	.356
Hope, Garrett	R-R	6-3	245	12-27-93	.219	.227	.216	22	73	7	16	5	0	0	6	6	2	0	1	30	0	0	.288	.293
Isabel, Ibandel	R-R	6-4	225	6-20-95	.273	.357	.233	24	88	17	24	5	1	7	15	9	1	0	0	41	1	2	.591	.347
Jenco, Saige	L-L	5-10	175	8-7-94	.288	.370	.258	45	170	29	49	8	2	1	12	21	1	4	0	34	17	0	.376	.370
Jones, Matt	L-R	6-7	250	3-9-94	.219	.169	.238	89	283	42	62	11	2	9	38	51	8	0	2	112	2	3	.367	.352
Kennedy, Garrett	L-R	6-1	205	12-13-92	.255	.235	.267	16	47	11	12	3	0	2	4	11	0	0	0	12	1	0	.447	.397
Landon, Logan	R-R	6-2	180	2-17-93	.263	.308	.245	118	411	50	108	21	2	9	52	39	2	1	3	118	22	6	.389	.327
McKinstry, Zach	L-R	5-11	155	4-29-95	.261	.277	.253	41	142	18	37	5	2	0	14	15	5	2	1	29	6	1	.324	.350
Meza, Erick	L-L	6-1	245	3-5-98	.229	.135	.257	65	223	20	51	10	0	4	24	20	2	0	0	48	0	1	.327	.298
Paroubeck, Jordan	B-R	6-2	190	11-2-94	.200	.294	.163	17	60	8	12	2	1	1	3	5	0	0	0	33	1	0	.317	.262
Perez, Jimy	R-R	6-2	185	2-12-94	.114	.000	.135	13	44	4	5	1	0	0	1	4	0	0	0	20	0	0	.136	.188
Perio, Noah	L-R	6-0	170	11-14-91	.288	.261	.298	20	80	7	23	3	0	1	9	4	0	1	0	10	3	1	.363	.321
Raley, Luke	L-R	6-3	220	9-19-94	.245	.271	.237	56	200	24	49	11	4	2	17	15	9	2	5	47	4	4	.370	.319
Rios, Edwin	L-R	6-3	220	4-21-94	.252	.304	.219	33	119	17	30	8	1	6	13	8	1	0	0	44	3	1	.487	.305
Sandoval, Ariel	R-R	6-2	180	11-6-95	.244	.247	.243	79	287	39	70	20	3	11	43	15	4	0	3	77	9	8	.449	.288
Smith, Will	R-R	6-0	192	3-28-95	.256	.211	.270	23	82	12	21	1	0	1	7	11	4	0	0	18	2	1	.305	.371
Tate, Donavan	R-R	6-3	190	9-27-90	.286	—	.286	2	7	1	2	0	0	1	2	0	0	0	0	2	0	0	.714	.286
Toscano, Dian	L-L	5-11	200	3-9-89	.120	.000	.158	8	25	1	3	0	0	0	4	4	0	0	0	8	1	1	.120	.241
Tubbs, Darien	R-L	5-9	188	1-26-95	.234	.194	.252	59	222	27	52	12	0	2	19	22	3	2	0	43	14	3	.315	.312
Walker, Jared	L-R	6-2	195	2-4-96	.111	.000	.150	9	27	1	3	0	0	0	0	2	0	0	0	9	0	0	.111	.172
Whiting, Brant	L-R	5-9	190	2-6-92	.163	.238	.143	36	98	7	16	4	0	0	8	24	5	0	1	35	0	0	.204	.352

Pitching	B-T	HT	WT	DOB	W	L	ERA	G	GS	CG	SV	IP	H	R	ER	HR	BB	SO	AVG	vLH	vRH	K/9	BB/9
Abdullah, Imani	B-R	6-4	205	4-20-97	4	4	3.61	16	16	0	0	72	70	36	29	10	12	59	.251	.285	.211	7.34	1.49
Alvarez, Yadier	R-R	6-3	175	3-7-96	3	2	2.29	9	9	0	0	39	31	13	10	1	11	55	.214	.243	.183	12.58	2.52
Anderson, Isaac	R-R	6-2	185	9-4-93	5	5	4.22	16	16	0	0	81	74	41	38	8	16	82	.239	.244	.231	9.11	1.78
Bass, Brian	R-R	6-4	200	5-11-92	2	6	4.08	33	0	0	5	46	51	23	21	5	17	37	.288	.337	.235	7.19	3.30
Boyle, Michael	R-L	6-4	200	4-12-94	7	6	2.81	19	18	1	0	99	94	39	31	3	31	78	.251	.273	.240	7.07	2.81
Bray, Adam	R-R	6-3	210	4-14-93	2	0	3.20	15	0	0	2	25	27	11	9	2	4	29	.255	.333	.182	10.30	1.42
Brown, Kevin	R-R	6-3	220	6-9-92	0	0	2.86	13	0	0	1	22	24	9	7	0	7	26	.273	.230	.311	10.64	2.86
Buehler, Walker	R-R	6-2	175	7-28-94	0	0	0.00	2	1	0	0	3	0	0	0	0	3	3	.000	.000	.000	9.00	9.00
Burgos, Alex	L-L	5-11	195	12-1-90	1	0	0.00	3	0	0	0	8	7	0	0	0	3	6	.219	.214	.222	6.48	3.24
Crawford, Leonardo	L-L	6-0	180	2-9-97	4	1	2.20	6	5	0	0	29	22	7	7	3	9	24	.214	.103	.257	7.53	2.83
Crescentini, Marcus	R-R	6-4	240	12-26-92	0	2	7.71	16	0	0	4	16	21	15	14	3	11	22	.313	.400	.243	12.12	6.06
De Paula, Luis	L-L	6-1	170	4-23-92	2	0	1.15	8	0	0	1	16	12	4	2	0	7	12	.211	.125	.244	6.89	4.02
Ferguson, Caleb	R-L	6-3	215	7-2-96	1	4	2.68	10	10	0	0	50	49	17	15	3	4	41	.255	.218	.270	7.33	0.54
German, Angel	R-R	6-4	185	5-25-96	1	2	7.45	20	0	0	2	19	18	18	16	3	13	17	.254	.300	.194	7.91	6.05
Gonsolin, Tony	R-R	6-2	180	5-14-94	0	2	5.27	9	0	0	2	14	17	9	8	0	3	10	.309	.226	.417	6.59	1.98
Gonzalez, Victor	L-L	6-0	180	11-16-95	3	6	3.61	22	19	0	0	95	79	49	38	7	44	104	.224	.258	.206	9.89	4.18
Harrison, Garrett	L-L	6-3	200	8-14-93	2	3	4.75	16	1	0	0	36	47	22	19	2	11	16	.320	.358	.298	4.00	2.75
Helsabeck, Wes	L-L	6-0	195	7-7-92	3	0	1.62	14	3	0	0	39	19	9	7	1	8	45	.138	.148	.131	10.38	1.85
Hermeling, Alex	R-R	6-5	230	3-22-93	2	4	3.83	29	1	0	5	54	47	26	23	1	22	58	.228	.210	.245	9.67	3.67
Istler, Andrew	R-R	5-11	175	9-18-92	0	0	0.96	11	0	0	1	19	11	3	2	0	2	21	.167	.219	.118	10.13	0.96
Kowalczyk, Karch	R-R	6-1	215	3-31-91	1	0	4.50	2	0	0	0	2	1	1	1	0	1	2	.143	.250	.000	9.00	4.50
Kremer, Dean	R-R	6-3	180	1-7-96	2	0	0.59	6	0	0	0	15	4	1	1	0	4	22	.083	.042	.125	12.91	2.35
Long, Nolan	R-R	6-10	255	1-19-94	4	8	5.32	17	13	0	0	64	58	44	38	5	35	62	.241	.271	.205	8.67	4.90
McDonnell, Rob	L-L	6-2	190	4-28-92	0	0	16.88	2	0	0	0	3	6	5	5	1	2	4	.429	.800	.222	13.50	6.75
Pfeifer, Phil	L-L	6-0	190	7-15-92	1	0	0.00	3	0	0	0	6	2	1	0	0	1	9	.100	.167	.071	13.50	1.50
Pittore, Gavin	R-R	6-3	230	9-18-93	2	1	1.94	28	0	0	4	56	38	12	12	1	17	54	.195	.150	.256	8.73	2.75
Powell, Chris	R-R	6-2	170	9-21-92	3	3	3.44	16	2	0	0	34	27	14	13	2	9	31	.220	.227	.211	8.21	2.38
Reyes, Bernardo	R-R	6-0	175	7-22-95	0	0	0.00	1	0	0	0	1	0	0	0	0	1	1	.000	.000	.000	9.00	0.00
Santana, Dennis	R-R	6-2	160	4-12-96	5	9	3.07	25	14	0	0	111	84	51	38	2	56	124	.209	.239	.174	10.02	4.53
Santos, Jose	R-R	6-0	165	3-8-92	1	0	0.00	4	0	0	0	8	3	0	0	0	5	11	.111	.143	.077	11.88	5.40
Sheffield, Jordan	R-R	6-0	185	6-1-95	0	1	4.09	7	7	0	0	11	11	5	5	2	6	13	.275	.412	.164	10.64	4.91
Sopko, Andrew	R-R	6-2	205	8-7-94	0	0	0.00	1	0	0	0	5	4	0	0	0	0	8	.235	.000	.333	15.43	0.00
Soto, William	R-R	6-4	185	2-13-96	0	1	7.20	1	0	0	0	5	7	4	4	0	0	6	.368	.357	.400	0.00	0.00
Spitzbarth, Shea	R-R	6-1	195	10-4-94	0	1	1.91	17	0	0	6	28	22	6	6	2	7	43	.210	.200	.222	13.66	2.22
Vieitez, Ivan	L-R	6-2	170	5-8-93	4	4	3.86	28	0	0	3	56	54	28	24	3	12	43	.252	.229	.276	6.91	1.93
White, Mitchell	R-R	6-4	207	12-28-94	0	0	0.00	8	4	0	0	16	3	1	0	0	6	20	.058	.071	.042	11.25	3.38

Fielding

Catcher	PCT	G	PO	A	E	DP	PB
Berman	1.000	20	154	15	0	0	3
Green	1.000	13	81	10	0	0	1
Henson	.992	27	232	21	2	2	6
Hope	1.000	18	138	18	0	1	2
Kennedy	.993	15	131	10	1	0	1
Landon	1.000	1	5	0	0	0	0
Smith	.988	18	145	18	2	0	0
Whiting	.997	35	273	30	1	2	0

First Base	PCT	G	PO	A	E	DP
Celli	1.000	2	8	2	0	0
Dean	1.000	8	63	7	0	1
Green	1.000	3	16	2	0	1
Henson	—	1	0	0	0	0
Hope	.818	3	16	2	4	1
Isabel	1.000	15	102	7	0	11
Jones	.988	59	444	36	6	42
Meza	.984	44	331	27	6	28
Perez	1.000	2	3	1	0	0
Raley	.938	9	56	4	4	4
Rios	1.000	9	57	6	0	3

Second Base	PCT	G	PO	A	E	DP
Dean	.964	9	25	29	2	8
Estevez	.970	64	92	164	8	32
Gomez	.980	38	49	98	3	18
Green	1.000	2	0	1	0	0
McKinstry	.950	19	32	44	4	11
Perio	1.000	9	17	17	0	3
Smith	.909	3	4	6	1	1

Third Base	PCT	G	PO	A	E	DP
Davis	.979	19	17	30	1	3
Dean	1.000	17	10	20	0	2
Estevez	1.000	1	2	1	0	0
Gomez	.917	16	9	13	2	1
Green	.975	21	11	28	1	2
Henson	.600	2	0	3	2	1
Jones	.889	4	4	4	1	0
McKinstry	.965	18	17	38	2	5
Perez	.818	13	6	12	4	0
Perio	.929	9	4	9	1	1
Rios	.889	20	10	38	6	2
Smith	.750	2	0	6	2	0
Walker	.880	8	8	14	3	3

Shortstop	PCT	G	PO	A	E	DP
Davis	.932	80	101	172	20	35
Estevez	.959	46	59	128	8	25
Gomez	.864	8	9	10	3	3
McKinstry	.909	5	4	6	1	3
Perio	1.000	2	2	4	0	2

Outfield	PCT	G	PO	A	E	DP
Ayon	.857	2	6	0	1	0
Castillo	.959	36	69	2	3	2
Celli	1.000	1	2	0	0	0
Dean	—	1	0	0	0	0
Fields	1.000	5	5	0	0	0
Gonsolin	—	1	0	0	0	0
Green	.992	58	114	3	1	1

Outfield	PCT	G	PO	A	E	DP
Jenco	1.000	38	60	1	0	0
Jones	1.000	7	7	0	0	0
Landon	.973	104	207	7	6	1
Paroubeck	1.000	13	13	0	0	0
Raley	1.000	39	70	5	0	2
Sandoval	.961	71	120	3	5	1
Tate	1.000	2	1	0	0	0
Toscano	.917	7	10	1	1	1
Tubbs	.949	54	111	1	6	0

OGDEN RAPTORS   ROOKIE
PIONEER LEAGUE

Batting	B-T	HT	WT	DOB	AVG	vLH	vRH	G	AB	R	H	2B	3B	HR	RBI	BB	HBP	SH	SF	SO	SB	CS	SLG	OBP
Aquino, Carlos	B-R	6-0	175	10-20-95	.143	.000	.250	3	7	2	1	0	1	0	0	3	0	0	0	2	1	0	.429	.400
Carpenter, Brock	R-R	6-3	200	6-5-95	.241	.288	.223	55	191	32	46	11	2	5	30	34	6	0	4	55	1	1	.398	.366
Celli, Federico	R-R	6-3	215	2-15-95	.429	—	.429	2	7	0	3	0	1	0	1	0	0	0	0	1	0	0	.714	.429
Gomez, Cristian	R-R	5-11	160	1-11-96	.000	.000	.000	5	6	0	0	0	0	0	0	0	0	0	0	3	0	0	.000	.000
Hansen, Mitch	L-L	6-4	210	5-1-96	.311	.282	.321	70	293	55	91	8	6	11	50	22	3	0	8	70	11	4	.491	.356
Hope, Garrett	R-R	6-3	245	12-27-93	.167	.000	.273	6	18	2	3	1	0	1	2	2	0	0	0	3	0	1	.389	.250
Isabel, Ibandel	R-R	6-4	225	6-20-95	.351	.292	.367	32	114	19	40	6	2	5	29	15	2	0	1	36	0	2	.570	.432
Jenco, Saige	L-L	5-10	175	8-7-94	.390	.400	.387	11	41	10	16	5	2	0	5	8	1	1	1	7	5	1	.610	.490
Lux, Gavin	L-R	6-2	190	11-23-97	.387	.667	.273	8	31	7	12	3	0	0	3	3	0	0	0	8	1	0	.484	.441
Medina, Michael	R-R	6-0	210	8-24-96	.174	.000	.222	7	23	2	4	0	1	2	6	1	1	0	0	13	0	0	.522	.240
Montgomery, Brandon	R-R	6-0	180	2-12-96	.329	.356	.316	35	143	31	47	7	8	7	29	13	0	0	3	34	9	3	.636	.377
Ortiz, Samuel	B-R	5-10	191	8-4-96	.208	.214	.206	17	48	5	10	1	1	1	6	8	1	2	0	9	0	0	.333	.333
Paroubeck, Jordan	B-R	6-2	190	11-2-94	.231	.208	.238	30	104	13	24	4	0	5	15	12	0	1	0	50	4	1	.413	.308
Paz, Luis	L-R	6-1	190	7-5-96	.269	.154	.306	46	160	20	43	14	5	6	37	10	1	0	0	51	4	0	.531	.316
Perez, Moises	R-R	6-0	160	7-18-97	.246	.214	.256	50	175	28	43	12	2	5	15	10	0	3	2	58	2	1	.423	.295
Peters, D.J.	R-R	6-6	225	12-12-95	.351	.333	.358	66	262	63	92	24	3	13	48	35	5	0	0	66	5	3	.615	.437
Pitre, Gersel	R-R	6-0	203	7-23-96	.269	.294	.260	52	201	38	54	9	0	1	15	9	2	4	1	31	2	1	.328	.305
Raley, Luke	L-R	6-3	220	9-19-94	.417	.400	.421	5	24	6	10	2	2	1	5	1	0	0	0	1	0	0	.792	.440
Robinson, Errol	R-R	6-0	180	10-1-94	.282	.293	.278	55	220	40	62	17	1	2	26	17	2	2	2	42	18	2	.395	.336
Ruiz, Keibert	B-R	6-0	165	7-20-98	.354	.294	.377	48	189	28	67	18	2	3	33	12	2	0	3	23	0	0	.503	.393
Smith, Will	R-R	6-0	192	3-28-95	.321	.429	.286	7	28	4	9	0	0	1	5	4	0	0	1	1	0	0	.429	.394
Thomas, Cody	L-R	6-4	211	10-8-94	.276	.185	.308	52	210	41	58	9	3	16	44	18	10	0	1	84	9	3	.576	.360
Tubbs, Darien	R-L	5-9	188	1-26-95	.381	.000	.533	5	21	5	8	3	1	0	1	0	0	0	0	0	0	0	.619	.409
Walker, Jared	L-R	6-2	195	2-4-96	.260	.211	.272	29	100	16	26	6	0	4	15	12	0	1	1	31	0	1	.440	.336
Yarnall, Nick	L-L	6-0	200	10-17-94	.182	.143	.195	15	55	7	10	5	0	0	7	6	0	0	0	16	0	0	.273	.262

Pitching	B-T	HT	WT	DOB	W	L	ERA	G	GS	CG	SV	IP	H	R	ER	HR	BB	SO	AVG	vLH	vRH	K/9	BB/9
Bass, Brian	R-R	6-4	200	5-11-92	0	2	3.65	9	0	0	0	12	15	10	5	0	3	10	.313	.286	.333	7.30	2.19
Copping, Corey	R-R	6-1	175	1-11-94	0	2	6.23	6	0	0	0	9	8	6	6	1	7	13	.250	.300	.227	13.50	7.27
Costello, Connor	R-R	6-3	170	11-4-92	1	1	7.07	9	0	0	0	14	21	13	11	2	4	11	.350	.240	.429	7.07	2.57
Diaz, Johan	R-R	6-2	195	11-1-92	3	1	6.31	19	0	0	0	36	47	36	25	2	11	28	.309	.360	.284	7.07	2.78
Ferguson, Caleb	R-L	6-3	215	7-2-96	1	0	0.90	2	2	0	0	10	4	3	1	0	2	11	.114	.000	.174	9.90	1.80
Fernandez, Roberth	L-L	6-1	165	3-21-95	3	5	6.45	13	13	0	0	60	78	48	43	7	18	58	.321	.353	.304	8.70	2.70
French, Austin	R-L	6-4	220	9-14-93	1	2	9.00	13	6	0	0	25	31	27	25	5	17	31	.295	.265	.310	11.16	6.12
Gonsolin, Tony	R-R	6-2	180	5-14-94	1	0	2.60	10	0	0	0	17	12	5	5	1	5	15	.200	.308	.118	7.79	2.60
Gonzalez, Jorge	L-L	5-9	175	9-25-96	3	2	5.28	20	0	0	0	31	43	23	18	2	11	28	.331	.340	.325	8.22	3.23
Grotz, Zac	R-R	6-5	195	2-17-93	4	0	0.52	5	2	0	0	18	15	9	1	0	3	11	.211	.214	.209	5.50	1.50
Harcksen, Misja	R-R	6-2	165	4-19-95	0	1	6.94	9	0	0	0	12	18	9	9	0	7	11	.367	.385	.361	8.49	5.40
Harrison, Garrett	L-L	6-3	200	8-14-93	0	0	9.00	4	3	0	0	14	18	14	14	4	7	15	.316	.333	.310	9.64	4.50
Istler, Andrew	R-R	5-11	175	9-18-92	0	0	1.04	7	0	0	1	9	6	4	1	0	3	8	.188	.091	.238	8.31	3.12
Kimborowicz, Josh	R-R	6-3	215	3-17-92	2	1	6.38	6	4	0	0	24	34	20	17	4	9	26	.333	.375	.306	9.75	3.38
Kremer, Dean	R-R	6-3	180	1-7-96	0	1	3.86	6	0	0	0	16	15	7	7	0	3	13	.250	.208	.278	7.16	1.65
Long, Nolan	R-R	6-10	255	1-19-94	2	3	6.11	10	10	0	0	46	58	37	31	6	18	45	.312	.294	.322	8.87	3.55
Mathewson, Chris	L-R	6-1	200	5-26-96	0	1	8.10	8	0	0	1	10	14	9	9	1	1	11	.340	.474	.258	9.90	3.60
McDonnell, Rob	L-L	6-2	210	4-28-92	4	0	3.93	17	8	0	0	50	40	23	22	8	25	53	.226	.242	.217	9.48	4.47
Mora, Gregor	R-R	6-2	215	8-28-95	3	0	7.76	12	3	0	1	27	36	31	23	6	19	30	.321	.317	.324	10.13	6.41
Mortillaro, Joe	R-R	6-2	205	9-14-93	1	1	5.56	6	0	0	0	11	12	9	7	0	4	11	.250	.150	.321	8.74	3.18
Moyer, Dillon	R-R	6-0	200	7-18-91	1	0	9.00	5	0	0	0	7	10	7	7	1	4	7	.333	.364	.316	3.86	5.14
Pacheco, Jairo	L-L	6-0	165	7-6-96	1	5	7.08	12	5	0	0	34	54	32	27	6	10	26	.351	.339	.359	6.82	2.62
Palmer, Cameron	R-R	6-3	220	12-3-91	0	1	9.00	5	0	0	0	4	7	5	4	0	6	5	.412	.333	.455	11.25	13.50
Pena, Adalberto	R-R	6-2	173	3-11-95	1	0	7.71	2	0	0	0	3	2	3	2	1	5	3	.125	.333	.000	19.29	15.43
Ramirez, Osiris	R-R	6-3	185	9-14-95	0	0	10.80	2	0	0	0	3	4	4	1	1	3	4	.533	.667	.444	10.80	2.70
Reyes, Bernardo	R-R	6-0	175	7-22-95	1	1	4.79	12	0	0	0	21	27	14	11	4	5	19	.314	.303	.321	8.27	2.18
Santarsiero, Vince	R-R	6-7	185	12-10-93	1	2	0.00	8	0	0	2	7	4	2	0	0	5	6	.148	.250	.067	6.23	5.19
Santos, Jose	R-R	6-0	165	3-8-92	2	0	1.13	13	0	0	4	16	7	2	2	0	4	27	.127	.182	.091	15.19	2.25

Pitching	B-T	HT	WT	DOB	W	L	ERA	G	GS	CG	SV	IP	H	R	ER	HR	BB	SO	AVG	vLH	vRH	K/9	BB/9
Schuller, Sven	R-R	6-3	205	1-17-96	2	0	4.28	15	1	0	1	27	35	16	13	3	11	19	.330	.333	.329	6.26	3.62
Soto, William	R-R	6-4	185	2-13-96	3	1	4.80	14	8	0	0	45	55	31	24	3	13	39	.297	.373	.262	7.80	2.60
Spitzbarth, Shea	R-R	6-1	195	10-4-94	0	0	1.00	6	0	0	0	9	6	1	1	0	2	15	.200	.154	.235	15.00	2.00
Urena, Miguel	R-R	6-8	210	2-27-95	0	2	14.14	6	3	0	0	14	31	23	22	3	4	9	.431	.469	.400	5.79	2.57
Villegas, M.J.	R-R	6-2	190	9-6-94	0	0	2.79	9	2	0	0	19	24	9	6	2	6	11	.329	.452	.238	5.12	2.79

Fielding

C: Hope 3, Paz 2, Pitre 35, Ruiz 35, Smith 5. **1B:** Carpenter 12, Celli 1, Hope 1, Isabel 28, Paz 22, Yarnall 13. **2B:** Aquino 2, Gomez 2, Montgomery 18, Ortiz 13, Perez 31, Robinson 7, Smith 1, Walker 7. **3B:** Aquino 1, Carpenter 40, Montgomery 13, Ortiz 3, Pitre 6, Walker 16. **SS:** Gomez 2, Lux 8, Ortiz 1, Perez 19, Robinson 48. **OF:** Hansen 63, Jenco 10, Medina 6, Montgomery 5, Paroubeck 25, Paz 3, Peters 62, Raley 5, Thomas 49, Tubbs 5.

AZL DODGERS   ROOKIE
ARIZONA LEAGUE

Batting	B-T	HT	WT	DOB	AVG	vLH	vRH	G	AB	R	H	2B	3B	HR	RBI	BB	HBP	SH	SF	SO	SB	CS	SLG	OBP
Albert, Shakir	R-R	6-0	185	12-24-96	.269	.150	.298	37	104	13	28	1	2	4	21	6	2	0	1	28	1	1	.433	.319
Aquino, Carlos	B-R	6-0	175	10-20-95	.200	.353	.140	27	60	5	12	0	1	0	3	14	2	0	0	18	2	6	.233	.368
Ayon, Andres	R-R	6-1	180	3-23-95	.314	.368	.289	34	121	17	38	5	2	2	18	10	0	0	1	31	0	0	.438	.364
Berman, Stevie	R-R	6-2	225	11-28-94	.344	.444	.304	12	32	4	11	3	0	0	7	1	1	0	1	0	0	0	.438	.371
Clementina, Hendrik	R-R	6-0	165	6-17-97	.217	.229	.211	44	157	22	34	4	1	6	23	14	2	0	2	42	2	0	.369	.286
Cook, Dylan	R-R	6-4	195	4-7-94	.283	.385	.250	17	53	2	15	3	1	1	4	6	0	0	0	12	0	0	.434	.356
Cuadrado, Romer	R-R	6-4	185	9-12-97	.236	.167	.265	46	161	29	38	8	1	4	21	30	1	0	0	50	4	1	.373	.359
Diaz, Yusniel	R-R	6-1	195	10-7-96	.143	.000	.333	3	14	2	2	0	0	1	3	0	0	0	0	3	0	0	.357	.143
Farmer, Kyle	R-R	6-0	205	8-17-90	.294	.000	.333	4	17	4	5	0	0	2	4	1	0	0	0	1	0	0	.647	.333
Henson, Jake	R-R	5-11	215	8-4-93	.200	.000	.222	5	20	3	4	0	0	0	1	0	0	0	0	5	0	0	.200	.238
Hernandez, Enrique	R-R	5-11	200	8-24-91	.000	.000	.000	2	8	0	0	0	0	0	0	0	0	0	0	0	0	0	.000	.000
Hope, Garrett	R-R	6-3	245	12-27-93	.273	.333	.250	4	11	1	3	0	0	0	0	0	0	0	0	3	0	0	.273	.273
Lux, Gavin	L-R	6-2	190	11-23-97	.281	.238	.302	48	192	34	54	10	5	0	18	25	1	0	1	43	1	0	.385	.365
McKinstry, Zach	L-R	5-11	185	4-29-95	.176	.125	.222	4	17	1	3	0	1	0	0	0	0	0	0	3	0	1	.294	.176
Medina, Michael	R-R	6-4	210	8-24-96	.125	.000	.167	10	40	4	5	1	0	1	5	4	0	0	1	22	1	1	.225	.200
Montgomery, Brandon	R-R	6-0	180	2-12-96	.348	.400	.322	23	89	21	31	3	2	1	9	8	0	1	1	12	5	3	.461	.398
Morales, Brayan	R-L	6-1	170	12-8-95	.125	.000	.143	4	8	0	1	0	0	0	0	1	0	0	0	4	0	0	.250	.222
Mosquera, Carlos	B-L	5-9	150	1-18-96	.263	.263	.263	40	118	15	31	11	1	0	11	6	1	2	2	16	3	3	.373	.299
Noel, Rico	R-R	5-8	170	1-11-89	.091	—	.091	10	11	4	1	1	0	0	0	1	0	0	0	2	5	2	.182	.167
Ortiz, Samuel	B-R	5-10	191	8-4-96	.216	.067	.278	17	51	7	11	5	0	0	3	5	1	0	0	12	1	0	.314	.298
Raley, Luke	L-R	6-3	220	9-19-94	.625	.500	.667	5	16	4	10	1	0	1	2	2	1	0	2	0	0	0	.875	.684
Rincon, Carlos	R-R	6-3	190	10-14-97	.301	.379	.270	26	103	13	31	6	3	7	23	2	0	0	0	30	0	2	.621	.314
Rodriguez, Ramon	R-R	5-11	185	10-30-98	.000	—	.000	1	1	0	0	0	0	0	0	0	0	0	0	0	0	0	.000	.000
Ruiz, Keibert	B-R	6-0	165	7-20-98	.485	.571	.462	8	33	5	16	4	1	0	15	3	1	0	2	4	0	0	.667	.513
Santana, Cristian	R-R	6-2	175	2-24-97	.256	.314	.231	42	172	26	44	6	2	5	24	5	1	0	2	46	0	1	.453	.278
Souffront, Jefrey	R-R	6-1	190	5-23-97	.259	.389	.194	35	108	21	28	4	2	5	10	8	5	0	0	42	2	1	.472	.339
Thomas, Cody	L-R	6-4	211	10-8-94	.500	.000	.611	7	22	10	11	1	1	3	6	3	2	0	1	3	1	0	1.045	.571
Walker, Jared	L-R	6-2	195	2-4-96	.286	.000	.333	2	7	3	2	1	0	1	2	4	0	0	0	3	0	1	.857	.545
Whiting, Brant	L-R	5-9	190	2-6-92	.230	.182	.250	26	74	9	17	5	0	0	5	14	2	0	0	23	0	0	.297	.367
Yarnall, Nick	L-L	6-0	200	10-17-94	.293	.467	.210	26	92	19	27	3	2	1	12	16	1	0	1	21	1	1	.402	.400

Pitching	B-T	HT	WT	DOB	W	L	ERA	G	GS	CG	SV	IP	H	R	ER	HR	BB	SO	AVG	vLH	vRH	K/9	BB/9
Alexy, A.J.	R-R	6-4	195	4-21-98	1	0	4.61	7	3	0	0	14	17	8	7	2	3	12	.315	.353	.297	7.90	1.98
Alvarez, Yadier	R-R	6-3	175	3-7-96	1	1	1.80	5	5	0	0	20	9	4	4	0	10	26	.127	.103	11.70	4.50
Arzaga, Oscar	R-R	6-4	200	2-23-99	3	2	4.00	12	5	0	0	36	29	18	16	0	16	26	.210	.143	.227	6.50	4.00
Beachy, Brandon	R-R	6-2	220	9-3-86	0	0	0.00	1	1	0	0	1	1	0	0	0	0	1	.250	.000	.500	9.00	0.00
Buehler, Walker	R-R	6-2	175	7-28-94	1	0	0.00	1	0	0	0	2	0	0	0	0	0	3	.000	—	.000	13.50	0.00
Carter, James	R-R	6-3	185	3-10-94	0	0	9.00	1	0	0	0	1	1	1	1	0	2	1	.250	.000	.333	18.00	0.00
Castellanos, Saul	R-R	6-0	170	5-10-97	3	1	3.52	18	0	0	2	23	22	11	9	3	4	13	.250	.111	.286	5.09	1.57
Cespedes, Francis	L-L	6-4	185	9-28-94	0	0	9.42	10	0	0	0	14	19	21	15	0	13	27	.311	.250	.321	16.95	8.16
Choate, Randy	L-L	6-1	210	9-5-75	0	0	7.50	7	0	0	0	6	10	5	5	0	1	10	.370	.250	.391	15.00	1.50
Coleman, Louis	R-R	6-4	205	4-4-86	0	0	0.00	1	1	0	0	1	1	0	0	0	0	2	.250	.500	.000	18.00	0.00
Costello, Connor	R-R	6-3	170	11-4-92	1	0	2.70	3	0	0	0	3	3	1	1	1	2	3	.250	.000	.333	8.10	5.40
Crawford, Leonardo	L-L	6-0	180	2-2-97	2	1	2.58	8	4	0	0	38	31	14	11	1	7	39	.214	.237	.206	9.16	1.64
Crouse, Logan	R-R	6-6	225	12-24-96	2	5	4.78	13	6	0	0	53	62	40	28	4	14	38	.283	.224	.309	6.49	2.39
Felix, Carlos	R-R	6-2	240	11-6-95	0	0	3.00	2	1	0	0	3	2	1	1	0	4	.182	.500	.000	12.00	0.00
Ferguson, Caleb	R-L	6-3	215	7-2-96	1	0	1.50	2	0	0	0	6	4	3	1	0	0	11	.167	.000	.190	16.50	0.00
Fien, Casey	R-R	6-2	210	10-21-83	0	0	0.00	2	2	0	0	3	1	0	0	0	0	4	.111	—	.111	12.00	0.00
Figaro, Alfredo	R-R	6-0	190	7-7-84	0	0	3.00	2	2	0	0	3	4	1	1	0	1	2	.364	.600	.167	6.00	3.00
Forbes, Melvyn	R-R	6-3	185	12-2-93	1	1	9.64	4	0	0	0	5	5	7	5	0	8	5	.250	.375	.167	9.64	15.43
Frankoff, Seth	R-R	6-5	210	8-27-88	1	1	1.50	3	0	0	0	6	4	1	1	0	1	11	.182	.000	.235	16.50	1.50
Garcia, Yimi	R-R	6-1	180	8-18-90	0	0	0.00	1	0	0	0	1	0	0	0	0	0	0	.000	—	.000	0.00	0.00
German, Angel	R-R	6-4	185	5-25-96	1	0	2.45	5	0	0	2	7	5	4	2	0	3	6	.179	.250	.125	7.36	3.68
Harcksen, Misja	R-R	6-2	165	4-19-95	3	0	3.86	12	0	0	0	19	17	9	8	1	4	25	.246	.182	.259	12.05	1.93
Kowalczyk, Karch	R-R	6-5	215	3-31-91	0	0	3.00	2	2	0	0	3	1	1	1	0	1	6	.200	.200	18.00	3.00
Malisheski, Kevin	R-R	6-3	200	9-7-97	0	1	3.86	7	0	0	0	14	14	7	6	2	4	18	.255	.143	.324	11.57	2.57
Mathewson, Chris	L-R	6-1	200	5-26-96	0	1	9.00	0	0	0	0	2	2	2	2	1	1	3	.250	.500	.167	13.50	4.50
May, Dustin	R-R	6-6	180	9-6-97	0	1	3.86	10	6	0	0	30	37	16	13	0	4	34	.291	.333	.268	10.09	1.19
Osuna, Lenix	R-R	6-1	220	11-11-95	0	1	4.50	3	1	0	0	4	2	2	2	1	0	5	.143	.000	.200	11.25	0.00

Pitching	B-T	HT	WT	DOB	W	L	ERA	G	GS	CG	SV	IP	H	R	ER	HR	BB	SO	AVG	vLH	vRH	K/9	BB/9
Pacheco, Jairo	L-L	6-0	165	7-6-96	1	0	2.25	4	1	0	0	16	14	4	4	0	5	15	.233	.143	.245	8.44	2.81
Paschke, Jeff	R-R	6-5	215	12-19-94	0	0	9.00	1	0	0	0	1	1	1	1	0	1	2	.250	.000	.333	18.00	9.00
Pena, Adalberto	R-R	6-2	173	3-11-95	3	1	3.45	14	0	0	1	29	28	13	11	2	13	33	.257	.308	.229	10.36	4.08
Perkins, Jake	R-R	6-0	175	4-8-94	0	0	0.00	1	0	0	0	1	0	0	0	0	1	2	.000	.000	.000	18.00	9.00
Ramirez, Osiris	R-R	6-3	185	9-14-95	3	0	6.31	19	0	0	5	26	27	18	18	2	9	35	.276	.242	.292	12.27	3.16
Ravin, Josh	R-R	6-4	215	1-21-88	0	0	1.80	4	2	0	0	5	2	2	1	1	0	11	.105	.000	.125	19.80	0.00
Rodriguez, Hector	R-R	6-3	190	10-17-94	0	0	0.00	1	0	0	0	1	2	0	0	0	1	2	.400	—	.400	18.00	9.00
Rogers, Rob	R-R	6-0	205	10-25-90	1	0	3.00	2	1	0	0	3	4	1	1	0	5	333	.250	.375	15.00	0.00
Rossman, Bubby	R-R	6-5	220	6-29-92	0	0	0.00	1	0	0	0	1	0	0	0	0	1	0	.000	—	.000	0.00	9.00
Santos, Jose	R-R	6-0	165	3-8-92	1	0	3.18	5	0	0	3	6	2	2	2	0	2	10	.118	.400	.000	15.88	3.18
Schafer, Jordan	L-L	6-1	205	9-4-86	0	0	0.00	3	1	0	0	3	0	0	0	0	1	6	.000	.000	.000	18.00	3.00
Schuller, Sven	R-R	6-3	205	1-17-96	0	0	2.57	4	0	0	0	7	9	2	2	0	2	3	.360	.500	.267	3.86	2.57
Scrubb, Andre	R-R	6-4	265	1-13-95	2	1	2.13	10	0	0	0	13	9	5	3	1	7	18	.188	.222	.179	12.79	4.97
Sequera, Gregorio	R-R	6-1	165	12-9-97	0	0	2.87	9	0	0	0	16	12	11	5	0	11	23	.211	.133	.238	13.21	6.32
Sheffield, Jordan	R-R	6-0	185	6-1-95	0	0	0.00	1	1	0	0	1	0	0	0	0	0	0	—	.000	.000	0.00	0.00
Smeltzer, Devin	R-L	6-3	185	9-7-95	0	2	7.59	11	0	0	0	11	16	10	9	0	6	12	.390	.308	.429	10.13	5.06
Stripling, Ross	R-R	6-3	210	11-23-89	0	1	3.00	1	1	0	0	3	2	1	1	0	2	3	.182	.000	.250	9.00	6.00
Sylvester, Derrick	R-R	6-6	200	4-19-91	0	0	0.00	2	1	0	0	3	2	0	0	0	0	5	.182	.000	.286	15.00	0.00
Uter, Kam	R-R	6-3	200	1-26-96	2	2	4.05	15	0	0	0	20	17	12	9	0	13	26	.221	.182	.236	11.70	5.85
Vanegas, A.J.	R-R	6-3	215	8-16-92	0	0	0.00	3	0	0	0	5	2	0	0	0	0	8	.111	.000	.125	14.40	0.00
White, Mitchell	R-R	6-4	207	12-28-94	0	0	0.00	2	2	0	0	4	3	0	0	0	0	8	.200	.000	.3	18.00	0.00

Fielding

C: Berman 11, Clementina 16, Farmer 2, Henson 3, Hope 2, Rodriguez 1, Ruiz 7, Whiting 22. **1B:** Berman 1, Clementina 22, Cook 6, Hope 2, Ortiz 5, Raley 2, Whiting 1, Yarnall 23. **2B:** Aquino 24, Cook 4, Hernandez 1, McKinstry 2, Montgomery 15, Noel 1, Ortiz 8, Souffront 15. **3B:** Aquino 1, Cook 4, Ortiz 2, Santana 39, Souffront 13, Walker 2. **SS:** Lux 43, McKinstry 2, Montgomery 4, Ortiz 3, Souffront 10. **OF:** Albert 27, Ayon 27, Cuadrado 42, Diaz 2, Medina 10, Montgomery 2, Morales 4, Mosquera 38, Noel 3, Raley 3, Rincon 23, Thomas 6.

DSL DODGERS   ROOKIE
DOMINICAN SUMMER LEAGUE

Batting	B-T	HT	WT	DOB	AVG	vLH	vRH	G	AB	R	H	2B	3B	HR	RBI	BB	HBP	SH	SF	SO	SB	CS	SLG	OBP
Amon, Pascal	L-R	6-1	183	12-26-97	.199	.091	.215	55	166	31	33	8	3	0	19	31	3	0	1	37	6	4	.283	.333
Aponte, Kevin	R-R	6-2	175	10-26-97	.267	—	—	64	221	36	59	9	4	0	13	31	9	2	1	58	12	9	.344	.378
Asencio, Luis	R-R	6-2	160	9-9-97	.197	.208	—	53	192	26	40	8	2	1	22	6	6	1	2	45	8	6	.286	.252
Brito, Ronny	B-R	6-0	165	3-22-99	.228	—	—	59	206	38	47	11	5	1	30	36	5	0	3	53	9	7	.345	.352
Calderon, Jhoan	R-R	6-3	200	9-14-97	.187	—	—	45	123	13	23	7	0	2	10	17	2	0	0	53	13	3	.293	.296
Camargo, Jair	R-R	5-10	150	7-1-99	.250	—	—	41	136	16	34	4	3	1	13	6	6	2	1	28	7	3	.346	.309
Cruz, Oneil	R-R	6-1	150	10-4-98	.294	.200	.316	53	187	28	55	18	5	0	23	22	0	0	1	44	11	5	.444	.367
Espinoza, Aldo	R-R	6-0	148	9-11-98	.215	.147	.231	53	181	19	39	5	0	1	15	19	3	0	0	23	6	11	.260	.300
Estrella, Alberto	R-R	6-3	190	5-22-97	.223	.143	.246	46	157	16	35	8	2	2	23	22	4	0	0	51	3	1	.338	.333
Giordani, Federico	R-R	5-11	180	11-23-97	.220	.139	.250	42	132	22	29	5	1	2	20	19	3	1	3	40	5	9	.338	.325
Heredia, Starling	R-R	6-2	200	2-6-99	.258	—	—	64	240	42	62	13	4	5	40	24	5	0	0	51	10	6	.408	.338
Hernandez, Marco	R-R	6-2	170	6-22-98	.197	—	—	38	127	18	25	5	1	0	11	10	5	3	2	16	4	2	.252	.278
Lao, Sauryn	R-R	6-2	182	8-14-99	.201	.125	.221	50	154	19	31	1	1	1	10	20	3	0	1	49	8	3	.240	.303
Lebron, Rolando	R-R	5-9	170	5-10-98	.234	—	—	54	167	23	39	8	0	0	8	19	4	5	1	42	14	12	.281	.325
Loaisiga, Mike	B-R	5-11	167	8-29-99	.149	.250	.133	41	121	13	18	2	1	0	10	18	1	1	0	27	4	3	.182	.264
Medina, Michael	R-R	6-4	210	8-24-96	.000	.000	.000	1	1	0	0	0	0	0	0	0	0	0	1	0	0	.000	.000
Padilla, Daniel	R-R	6-2	175	2-16-97	.279	.333	.265	53	165	30	46	9	1	2	26	35	1	3	3	31	21	8	.345	.402
Pineda, Maikel	R-R	6-1	175	10-19-96	.239	.240	.239	59	209	34	50	10	2	1	21	26	5	0	3	30	7	6	.321	.333
Ramones, Gervin	R-R	6-2	180	5-15-99	.170	.250	.135	15	53	2	9	5	0	0	5	3	0	0	0	8	1	2	.264	.214
Reyes, Edwin	R-R	6-2	175	12-14-97	.108	.000	.121	13	37	4	4	1	0	1	4	7	2	0	0	26	0	1	.216	.283
Rincon, Carlos	R-R	6-3	190	10-14-97	.364	.000	.406	26	77	19	28	5	2	6	26	15	1	0	3	23	8	2	.714	.458
Rodriguez, Luis	B-R	6-0	150	3-2-99	.190	.150	.198	47	121	15	23	2	2	0	8	23	0	2	2	33	4	3	.240	.315
Romero, Mervin	B-R	5-11	138	8-7-99	.268	—	—	57	198	27	53	6	1	0	21	22	1	2	2	39	6	6	.308	.341
Rubi, Alvaro	R-R	6-2	185	2-16-97	.276	.148	.297	60	185	33	51	16	0	0	22	38	13	0	5	20	8	2	.362	.423
Sanchez, Frank	R-R	6-3	170	8-25-98	.186	—	—	45	129	12	24	1	0	1	11	10	4	3	1	28	7	3	.217	.264
Tirado, Lucas	L-R	6-2	180	11-13-96	.100	—	—	16	30	5	3	0	0	0	0	11	1	0	0	14	2	1	.100	.357
Valenzuela, Ronald	R-R	6-0	190	3-8-97	.233	—	—	34	120	12	28	9	1	0	14	4	2	1	3	14	2	2	.325	.264
Valera, Leonel	R-R	6-1	165	7-9-99	.228	—	—	55	171	24	39	4	4	0	13	24	2	0	1	42	16	9	.298	.328
Zabala, Juan	R-R	5-10	170	7-3-99	.195	.250	.183	28	87	9	17	3	1	0	10	8	6	2	1	20	5	2	.253	.304

Pitching	B-T	HT	WT	DOB	W	L	ERA	G	GS	CG	SV	IP	H	R	ER	HR	BB	SO	AVG	vLH	vRH	K/9	BB/9
Alejo, Carlos	R-R	6-1	165	8-23-99	0	1	4.50	13	2	0	0	24	23	19	12	0	19	10	—	—	—	3.75	7.13
Alvino, Jasiel	R-R	6-1	180	1-11-97	1	2	1.95	13	9	0	1	51	47	17	11	1	11	38	.244	.197	.265	6.75	1.95
Ascanio, Raul	R-R	6-1	180	11-18-96	3	2	3.22	18	0	0	1	36	25	20	13	0	29	32	—	—	—	7.93	7.18
Blanco, Leowis	R-R	5-11	190	3-20-95	3	2	6.03	20	0	0	0	31	26	27	21	0	29	20	.224	.167	.244	5.74	8.33
Castillo, Bryan	R-R	6-3	185	1-18-99	0	3	8.53	13	8	0	0	25	18	30	24	1	36	21	—	—	—	7.46	12.79
Castro, Jeronimo	R-R	6-4	200	9-3-96	3	3	3.78	14	8	0	0	50	52	30	21	0	15	38	—	—	—	6.84	2.70
Cespedes, Esmerlyn	R-R	6-3	195	3-10-98		0	4.80	8	0	0	0	15	11	12	8	1	8	13	—	—	—	7.80	4.80
Cespedes, Yeison	R-R	6-1	178	3-5-98	1	4	1.49	11	9	0	0	42	40	15	7	1	14	31	—	—	—	6.59	2.98
Chacin, Jose	R-R	6-4	168	3-25-97	7	1	1.71	12	12	0	0	63	53	17	12	1	10	51	.222	.132	.277	7.25	1.42
Flames, Celis	R-R	6-1	175	9-5-97	1	0	2.40	13	2	0	0	30	26	15	8	0	13	17	.236	.167	.270	5.10	3.90
Gooding, Max	L-L	5-11	165	3-7-96	3	2	1.31	19	0	0	2	34	34	13	5	0	6	24	.254	.233	.260	6.29	1.57

LOS ANGELES DODGERS

Pitching	B-T	HT	WT	DOB	W	L	ERA	G	GS	CG	SV	IP	H	R	ER	HR	BB	SO	AVG	vLH	vRH	K/9	BB/9
Herrera, Juan	R-R	6-3	170	1-28-96	4	2	3.07	13	9	0	0	59	33	25	20	0	26	62	—	—	—	9.51	3.99
Hernandez, Jose	L-L	6-2	170	12-31-97	2	1	6.75	7	0	0	0	9	10	8	7	0	11	8	.270	.200	.281	7.71	10.61
Inoa, Confesor	R-R	6-2	210	2-21-96	2	3	3.05	13	7	0	0	41	40	23	14	0	20	32	—	—	—	6.97	4.35
Jimenez, Melvin	B-R	6-0	170	7-23-99	4	3	1.47	12	12	0	0	55	35	14	9	0	18	66	.181	.186	.179	10.80	2.95
Lantigua, Dawlyn	R-R	5-11	165	7-28-98	6	3	3.34	18	0	0	1	30	22	16	11	1	13	18	—	—	—	5.46	3.94
Marcano, Enmanuel	R-R	6-1	185	12-4-98	2	2	4.04	13	9	0	0	42	41	22	19	2	15	25	—	—	—	5.31	3.19
Mateo, Santos	R-R	6-3	185	2-22-97	2	3	3.66	15	4	0	0	39	40	22	16	1	16	39	—	—	—	8.92	3.66
Mena, Johan	R-R	6-5	185	3-1-98	0	2	9.42	7	3	0	0	14	19	16	15	1	12	4	—	—	—	2.51	7.53
Morillo, Juan	R-R	6-1	150	3-19-99	2	3	3.79	13	8	0	0	40	33	18	17	0	25	18	—	—	—	4.02	5.58
Navarro, Orlandy	R-R	6-2	175	6-3-99	3	2	1.48	12	9	0	0	49	31	13	8	0	16	41	.191	.150	.216	7.58	2.96
Parra, Ronald	L-L	6-1	160	11-5-98	0	3	4.50	14	4	0	0	40	31	27	20	1	27	31	.205	.105	.220	6.98	6.08
Pasen, Luis	R-R	6-0	175	1-14-95	1	1	3.56	24	0	0	5	30	18	17	12	0	24	28	.176	.222	.160	8.31	7.12
Peralta, Rawel	R-R	6-4	190	6-3-97	0	0	0.00	3	0	0	0	5	4	2	0	0	4	3	.235	.286	.200	5.40	7.20
Perez, Edward	R-R	6-2	174	11-25-95	5	1	1.69	21	0	0	1	32	18	12	6	0	17	35	.158	.149	.164	9.84	4.78
Polanco, Oliver	R-R	6-2	180	3-3-96	0	1	2.84	15	0	0	2	19	14	6	6	0	13	15	.209	.045	.289	7.11	6.16
Pozo, William	R-R	6-3	200	3-4-97	2	1	3.20	15	0	0	1	25	17	13	9	0	17	20	—	—	—	7.11	6.04
Puello, Yariel	R-R	6-4	200	8-29-97	0	0	3.72	7	0	0	0	10	7	4	4	0	3	9	—	—	—	8.38	2.79
Serrano, Elio	R-R	5-11	160	8-2-98	0	2	1.75	24	0	0	15	26	19	8	5	0	13	28	.204	.207	.203	9.82	4.56
Soto, Algenis	R-R	6-4	185	5-24-96	2	1	3.38	14	0	0	1	24	21	10	9	0	10	18	—	—	—	6.75	3.75
Tavarez, Alfredo	R-R	6-5	190	11-27-97	3	0	1.53	12	11	0	0	53	24	12	9	1	15	35	—	—	—	5.94	2.55
Taveras, Raymond	R-R	6-1	170	11-7-94	0	1	7.27	6	0	0	0	9	12	8	7	1	3	3	.364	.273	.409	3.12	3.12
Uceta, Edwin	R-R	6-0	155	1-9-98	2	1	1.72	11	3	0	0	31	20	6	6	1	3	28	—	—	—	8.04	0.86
Urbina, Andres	R-R	6-1	175	3-29-96	3	2	3.27	23	0	0	4	33	27	19	12	0	27	19	—	—	—	5.18	7.36
Vargas, Jesus	R-R	6-2	175	8-18-98	6	3	1.83	11	8	0	0	54	52	18	11	0	9	34	.260	.281	.250	5.67	1.50

Fielding

C: Camargo 37, Hernandez 33, Ramones 14, Rubi 2, Valenzuela 32, Zabala 27. **1B:** Amon 1, Camargo 3, Estrella 39, Hernandez 1, Lao 27, Osorio 7, Padilla 12, Pineda 1, Reyes 5, Rubi 56. **2B:** Brito 5, Espinoza 47, Loaisiga 37, Pineda 13, Ramones 1, Rodriguez 17, Romero 21, Tirado 11, Valera 1. **3B:** Asencio 27, Brito 1, Cruz 32, Espinoza 2, Estrella 1, Lao 24, Loaisiga 2, Pineda 33, Rodriguez 11, Romero 7, Rubi 1, Valera 1. **SS:** Brito 46, Cruz 13, Lao 1, Loaisiga 2, Pineda 4, Rodriguez 20, Romero 23, Valera 41. **OF:** Alejo 1, Amon 49, Aponte 56, Asencio 22, Calderon 39, Giordani 37, Heredia 53, Lebron 46, Medina 1, Osorio 41, Padilla 35, Rincon 19, Sanchez 40.

Miami Marlins

SEASON IN A SENTENCE: A first-half surge that made the Marlins a playoff contender faded with a spate of second-half injuries, with the team finishing below .500, and the season ended in unbelievable sorrow with the death in a boating accident of star pitcher and staff ace Jose Fernandez, whose autopsy revealed he was drunk and had cocaine in his system at the time of his death.

HIGH POINT: The Marlins were above .500 every month through July and finished that month at 57-48, their high-water mark of the year. That July 31 victory, a 5-4 win against the Cardinals, came on a walk-off triple by Derek Dietrich. A week later, Miami hit another high note when 42-year-old outfielder Ichiro Suzuki got his 3,000th major league hit, a triple.

LOW POINT: The low point in franchise history came when Fernandez died early in the morning of Sept. 25 at age 24. That day's game was cancelled as the team and the sport reeled from the death of one of the game's biggest stars and most passionate players. Dee Gordon led off the next game on the 26th by taking the first pitch batting righthanded, mimicking Fernandez's stance, then hit a leadoff homer off Bartolo Colon from the left side, breaking into tears on his way around the bases.

NOTABLE ROOKIES: Miami relied heavily on rookies in the bullpen, as righty Kyle Barraclough led the club with 75 appearances and struck out 113 in a strictly relief role. Nick Wittgren (48 games) and Brian Ellington also pitched enough to exhaust their prospect eligibility.

KEY TRANSACTIONS: With the Marlins in the thick of the wild-card race in late July, they traded 2015 first-round pick Josh Naylor, plus righties Jarred Cosart, Carter Capps and Luis Castillo, to the Padres for righthanders Andrew Cashner, Tayron Guerrero and Colin Rea. When Rea's arm came up lame in his first Marlins start, Miami was able to trade him back to the Padres for Castillo after the Padres were revealed to have withheld injury information. After the season, Miami ended the one-year experiment of having Barry Bonds as hitting coach, firing him.

DOWN ON THE FARM: No Miami affiliate made the playoffs in the minors; cumulatively Marlins clubs went 311-374, 26th overall in the majors. Castillo emerged as the organization's top performer, reaching Double-A and going 8-6, 2.26 overall to rank in the top 10 in the minors in ERA and WHIP (1.07).

OPENING DAY PAYROLL: $ 77,314,202 (26th)

ORGANIZATION LEADERS

BATTING   *Minimum 250 AB

MAJORS

*	AVG	Martin Prado	.305
*	OPS	Christian Yelich	.859
	HR	Giancarlo Stanton	27
	RBI	Christian Yelich	98

MINORS

*	AVG	Xavier Scruggs, New Orleans	.290
*	OBP	Xavier Scruggs, New Orleans	.408
*	SLG	Xavier Scruggs, New Orleans	.565
*	OPS	Xavier Scruggs, New Orleans	.973
	R	Xavier Scruggs, New Orleans	69
	H	Brian Anderson, Jupiter, Jacksonville	128
	TB	Destin Hood, New Orleans	207
	2B	Destin Hood, New Orleans	29
	3B	6 players	5
	HR	Xavier Scruggs, New Orleans	21
	RBI	Destin Hood, New Orleans	80
	BB	Brian Anderson, Jupiter, Jacksonville	58
		Xavier Scruggs, New Orleans	58
	SO	Jeremias Pineda, Jacksonville, Jupiter	141
	SB	Yefri Perez, Jacksonville	39

PITCHING   #Minimum 75 IP

MAJORS

	W	Jose Fernandez	16
#	ERA	Jose Fernandez	2.86
	SO	Jose Fernandez	253
	SV	A.J. Ramos	40

MINORS

	W	Dillon Peters, Jupiter, Jacksonville	14
	L	Jorgan Cavanerio, Jupiter	12
#	ERA	Luis Castillo, Jupiter, Jacksonville	2.26
	G	Sean Donatello, Jacksonville	46
	GS	Jake Esch, Jacksonville, New Orleans	26
	SV	C.J. Robinson, Greensboro, Jupiter	22
	IP	Jake Esch, Jacksonville, New Orleans	142
	BB	Jeff Brigham, Jupiter	47
	SO	Patrick Johnson, Jacksonville	113
#	AVG	Luis Castillo, Jupiter, Jacksonville	.219

General Manager: Michael Hill. **Farm Director:** Marc DelPiano. **Scouting Director:** Stan Meek.

Class	Team	League	W	L	PCT	Finish	Manager
Majors	Miami Marlins	National	79	82	.491	7th (15)	Don Mattingly
Triple-A	New Orleans Zephyrs	Pacific Coast	69	70	.496	9th (16)	Arnie Beyeler
Double-A	Jacksonville Suns	Southern	63	76	.453	8th (10)	Dave Berg
High A	Jupiter Hammerheads	Florida State	68	69	.496	8th (12)	Randy Ready
Low A	Greensboro Grasshoppers	South Atlantic	65	75	.464	12th (14)	Kevin Randel
Short Season	Batavia Muckdogs	New York-Penn	22	53	.293	14th (14)	Angel Espada
Rookie	Marlins	Gulf Coast	24	31	.436	12th (17)	Julio Bruno
Overall 2016 Minor League Record			311	374	.454	26th (30)	

ORGANIZATION STATISTICS

MIAMI MARLINS
NATIONAL LEAGUE

Batting	B-T	HT	WT	DOB	AVG	vLH	vRH	G	AB	R	H	2B	3B	HR	RBI	BB	HBP	SH	SF	SO	SB	CS	SLG	OBP
Andino, Robert	R-R	5-11	185	4-25-84	.292	.273	.308	13	24	2	7	0	0	0	1	0	0	0	0	4	0	0	.292	.292
Arcia, Oswaldo	L-R	6-0	225	5-9-91	.000	—	.000	2	0	0	0	0	0	0	0	0	0	0	0	1	0	0	.000	.000
2-team total (14 San Diego)					.111	—	—	16	45	2	5	1	0	2	4	2	0	0	0	15	0	0	.267	.149
Bour, Justin	L-R	6-3	265	5-28-88	.264	.233	.268	90	280	35	74	12	1	15	51	38	0	0	3	56	0	0	.475	.349
Dietrich, Derek	L-R	6-0	205	7-18-89	.279	.200	.297	128	351	39	98	20	5	7	42	32	24	0	5	84	1	0	.425	.374
Francoeur, Jeff	R-R	6-4	225	1-8-84	.280	.250	.289	26	50	4	14	2	1	0	1	4	0	1	0	15	0	2	.360	.333
2-team total (99 Atlanta)					.254	—	—	125	307	33	78	15	1	7	34	20	0	1	3	90	2	2	.378	.297
Gillespie, Cole	R-R	6-2	215	6-20-84	.235	.200	.250	41	51	7	12	3	2	0	5	3	0	0	1	14	0	0	.373	.273
Gordon, Dee	L-R	5-11	170	4-22-88	.268	.260	.270	79	325	47	87	7	6	1	14	18	0	1	1	55	30	7	.335	.305
Hechavarria, Adeiny	R-R	6-0	195	4-15-89	.236	.207	.244	155	508	52	120	17	6	3	38	33	1	2	3	73	1	0	.311	.283
Hood, Destin	R-R	6-2	205	4-3-90	.240	.000	.286	13	25	3	6	1	0	1	2	0	0	0	0	11	0	1	.400	.240
Johnson, Chris	R-R	6-3	225	10-1-84	.222	.212	.229	113	243	20	54	11	0	5	24	19	1	1	0	78	0	0	.329	.281
Kelly, Don	L-R	6-4	215	2-15-80	.148	.000	.160	13	27	2	4	0	0	2	3	2	0	0	1	5	0	0	.296	.200
Mathis, Jeff	R-R	6-0	205	3-31-83	.238	.324	.202	41	126	12	30	4	1	2	15	4	1	1	0	36	0	0	.333	.267
Ozuna, Marcell	R-R	6-1	225	11-12-90	.266	.289	.259	148	557	75	148	23	6	23	76	43	4	0	4	115	0	3	.452	.321
Perez, Yefri	R-R	5-11	170	2-24-91	.667	—	.667	12	3	5	2	1	0	0	0	0	0	0	0	1	4	2	1.000	.667
Prado, Martin	R-R	6-0	215	10-27-83	.305	.424	.274	153	600	70	183	37	3	8	75	49	4	0	5	69	2	2	.417	.359
Realmuto, J.T.	R-R	6-1	210	3-18-91	.303	.215	.322	137	509	60	154	31	0	11	48	28	5	0	3	100	12	4	.428	.343
Rojas, Miguel	R-R	5-11	195	2-24-89	.247	.281	.234	123	194	27	48	12	0	1	14	11	1	6	2	27	2	1	.325	.288
Scruggs, Xavier	R-R	6-0	215	9-23-87	.210	.222	.208	24	62	1	13	3	0	1	5	2	5	2	0	20	0	0	.306	.290
Stanton, Giancarlo	R-R	6-6	245	11-8-89	.240	.273	.231	119	413	56	99	20	1	27	74	50	4	0	2	140	0	0	.489	.326
Suzuki, Ichiro	L-R	5-11	175	10-22-73	.291	.339	.280	143	327	48	95	15	5	1	22	30	3	3	2	42	10	2	.376	.354
Telis, Tomas	B-R	5-8	220	6-14-91	.308	.000	.364	10	13	1	4	0	0	1	4	0	0	0	0	2	0	0	.538	.308
Yelich, Christian	L-R	6-3	195	12-5-91	.298	.287	.301	155	578	78	172	38	3	21	98	72	4	0	5	138	9	4	.483	.376

Pitching	B-T	HT	WT	DOB	W	L	ERA	G	GS	CG	SV	IP	H	R	ER	HR	BB	SO	AVG	vLH	vRH	K/9	BB/9
Barraclough, Kyle	R-R	6-3	225	5-23-90	6	3	2.85	75	0	0	0	73	45	24	23	1	44	113	.176	.192	.160	14.00	5.45
Breslow, Craig	L-L	5-11	180	8-8-80	0	2	4.50	15	0	0	0	14	21	9	7	1	4	7	.362	.400	.333	4.50	2.57
Brice, Austin	R-R	6-4	235	6-19-92	0	1	7.07	15	0	0	0	14	9	12	11	2	5	14	.173	.194	.143	9.00	3.21
Cashner, Andrew	R-R	6-6	235	9-11-86	1	4	5.98	12	11	0	0	53	62	36	35	6	30	45	.301	.350	.255	7.69	5.13
2-team total (16 San Diego)					5	11	5.25	28	27	0	0	132	142	83	77	19	60	112	—	—	—	7.64	4.09
Cervenka, Hunter	L-L	6-1	245	1-3-90	0	0	4.82	18	0	0	0	9	11	5	5	1	5	7	.289	.348	.200	6.75	4.82
2-team total (50 Atlanta)					1	0	3.53	68	0	0	0	43	31	19	17	3	28	42	—	—	—	8.72	5.82
Chen, Wei-Yin	L-L	6-0	200	7-21-85	5	5	4.96	22	22	0	0	123	134	69	68	22	24	100	.276	.325	.266	7.30	1.75
Clemens, Paul	R-R	6-3	215	2-14-88	1	0	6.30	2	2	0	0	10	11	7	7	5	8	6	.289	.267	.304	5.40	7.20
2-team total (16 San Diego)					4	5	4.04	18	14	0	0	71	72	39	32	14	31	53	—	—	—	6.69	3.91
Conley, Adam	L-L	6-3	200	5-24-90	8	6	3.85	25	25	0	0	133	125	59	57	13	62	124	.250	.298	.235	8.37	4.19
Cosart, Jarred	R-R	6-3	205	5-25-90	0	1	5.95	4	4	0	0	20	19	14	13	0	16	11	.257	.220	.303	5.03	7.32
2-team total (9 San Diego)					0	4	6.00	13	13	0	0	57	61	41	38	4	39	38	—	—	—	6.00	6.16
Despaigne, Odrisamer	R-R	6-0	200	4-4-87	0	0	9.00	3	0	0	0	4	4	3	3	0	1	0	.364	.500	.000	0.00	3.00
Dunn, Mike	L-L	6-0	215	5-23-85	6	1	3.40	51	0	0	0	42	43	16	16	5	11	38	.270	.278	.263	8.08	2.34
Ege, Cody	L-L	6-1	190	5-8-91	0	0	12.00	5	0	0	0	3	8	4	4	1	2	2	.571	.400	.667	6.00	6.00
Ellington, Brian	R-R	6-3	215	3-26-90	4	2	2.45	32	0	0	0	33	27	10	9	2	16	32	.223	.288	.174	8.73	4.36
Esch, Jake	R-R	6-3	205	3-27-90	0	1	5.54	3	3	0	0	13	17	8	8	4	6	10	.327	.269	.385	6.92	4.15
Fernandez, Jose	R-R	6-3	240	7-31-92	16	8	2.86	29	29	0	0	182	149	63	58	13	55	253	.224	.244	.203	12.49	2.71
Flores, Kendry	R-R	6-2	195	11-24-91	0	0	0.00	1	1	0	0	3	1	0	0	0	3	1	.100	.250	.000	3.00	9.00
Hall, Cody	R-R	6-4	235	1-6-88	0	0	12.00	2	0	0	0	3	4	4	4	1	3	3	.308	.125	.000	9.00	9.00
Jackson, Edwin	R-R	6-2	215	9-9-83	0	1	5.91	8	0	0	0	11	13	7	7	2	6	7	.317	.357	.296	5.91	5.06
2-team total (13 San Diego)					5	7	5.89	21	13	0	0	84	92	56	55	14	41	61	—	—	—	6.54	4.39
Koehler, Tom	R-R	6-3	235	6-29-86	9	13	4.33	33	33	0	0	177	176	93	85	22	83	147	.261	.259	.263	7.49	4.23
McGowan, Dustin	R-R	6-3	235	3-24-82	1	3	2.82	55	0	0	1	67	49	26	21	7	33	63	.202	.290	.148	8.46	4.43
Morris, Bryan	L-R	6-3	220	3-28-87	0	0	3.06	24	0	0	1	18	15	7	6	4	10	13	.238	.222	.250	6.62	5.09
Narveson, Chris	L-L	6-3	205	12-20-81	1	0	8.64	6	0	0	0	8	10	8	8	3	2	6	.286	.333	.261	6.48	2.16
Nicolino, Justin	L-L	6-3	195	11-22-91	3	6	4.99	18	13	0	0	79	96	45	44	8	20	37	.307	.272	.319	4.20	2.27

Pitching

Pitching	B-T	HT	WT	DOB	W	L	ERA	G	GS	CG	SV	IP	H	R	ER	HR	BB	SO	AVG	vLH	vRH	K/9	BB/9
Ogando, Nefi	R-R	6-0	230	6-3-89	0	0	2.30	14	0	0	0	16	10	5	4	0	8	8	.179	.250	.107	4.60	4.60
Phelps, David	R-R	6-2	200	10-9-86	7	6	2.28	64	5	0	4	87	61	23	22	6	38	114	.197	.230	.172	11.84	3.95
Ramos, A.J.	R-R	5-10	200	9-20-86	1	4	2.81	67	0	0	40	64	52	21	20	1	35	73	.223	.213	.236	10.27	4.92
Rea, Colin	R-R	6-5	225	7-1-90	0	0	0.00	1	1	0	0	3	1	0	0	0	0	4	.100	.250	.000	10.80	0.00
2-team total (19 San Diego)					5	5	4.82	20	19	0	0	103	102	63	55	12	44	80	—	—	—	7.01	3.86
Reyes, Jo-Jo	L-L	6-2	230	11-20-84	0	0	9.00	1	0	0	0	2	3	2	2	0	1	0	.333	.000	.375	0.00	4.50
Rodney, Fernando	R-R	5-11	230	3-18-77	2	3	5.89	39	0	0	8	37	41	25	24	5	25	41	.289	.307	.269	10.06	6.14
2-team total (28 San Diego)					2	4	3.44	67	0	0	25	65	54	27	25	5	37	74	—	—	—	10.19	5.10
Urena, Jose	R-R	6-2	200	9-12-91	4	9	6.13	28	12	0	1	84	91	59	57	11	29	58	.275	.303	.242	6.24	3.12
Wittgren, Nick	R-R	6-2	210	5-29-91	4	3	3.14	48	0	0	0	52	50	18	18	6	10	42	.254	.242	.264	7.32	1.74

Fielding

Catcher	PCT	G	PO	A	E	DP	PB
Mathis	.991	38	304	32	3	3	1
Realmuto	.991	129	1069	80	10	8	8
Telis	1.000	3	8	2	0	0	0

First Base	PCT	G	PO	A	E	DP
Bour	.995	82	544	34	3	50
Dietrich	1.000	16	79	4	0	12
Gillespie	1.000	1	3	0	0	0
Johnson	.992	81	360	23	3	37
Kelly	1.000	12	63	9	0	5
Rojas	1.000	41	85	12	0	9
Scruggs	1.000	19	129	8	0	13

Second Base	PCT	G	PO	A	E	DP
Andino	1.000	3	4	5	0	1

	PCT	G	PO	A	E	DP
Dietrich	.986	75	120	165	4	33
Gordon	.980	78	150	186	7	51
Perez	1.000	1	2	1	0	0
Rojas	1.000	45	25	44	0	5

Third Base	PCT	G	PO	A	E	DP
Andino	—	1	0	0	0	0
Dietrich	1.000	13	5	14	0	2
Francoeur	—	1	0	0	0	0
Johnson	1.000	1	5	12	0	1
Prado	.972	150	73	240	9	30
Rojas	1.000	16	1	10	0	1

Shortstop	PCT	G	PO	A	E	DP
Andino	—	1	0	0	0	0
Hechavarria	.977	153	203	359	13	72

	PCT	G	PO	A	E	DP
Perez	1.000	2	1	1	0	0
Rojas	.968	33	46	76	4	18

Outfield	PCT	G	PO	A	E	DP
Andino	1.000	2	5	1	0	0
Dietrich	1.000	8	10	0	0	0
Francoeur	1.000	16	18	1	0	0
Gillespie	.933	8	13	1	1	0
Hood	1.000	7	11	0	0	0
Johnson	—	2	0	0	0	0
Ozuna	.985	142	310	8	5	0
Scruggs	1.000	2	2	0	0	0
Stanton	.982	106	215	5	4	0
Suzuki	.992	78	125	6	1	1
Yelich	.978	149	260	6	6	1

NEW ORLEANS ZEPHYRS   TRIPLE-A
PACIFIC COAST LEAGUE

Batting	B-T	HT	WT	DOB	AVG	vLH	vRH	G	AB	R	H	2B	3B	HR	RBI	BB	HBP	SH	SF	SO	SB	CS	SLG	OBP
Andino, Robert	R-R	5-11	185	4-25-84	.267	.340	.243	108	419	52	112	24	2	13	46	30	2	1	1	111	8	1	.427	.319
Arcia, Francisco	B-R	5-11	195	9-14-89	.213	.267	.196	18	61	2	13	1	0	0	2	2	2	1	0	14	0	0	.230	.262
Black, Dan	L-R	6-4	255	7-2-87	.214	.074	.281	33	84	5	18	1	0	2	8	7	0	0	0	25	1	0	.298	.275
Bour, Justin	L-R	6-3	265	5-28-88	.111	.250	.071	5	18	0	2	0	0	0	1	0	0	0	0	6	0	0	.111	.158
Ciriaco, Pedro	R-R	6-0	180	9-27-85	.221	.000	.259	23	68	4	15	2	0	0	2	1	1	0	1	13	4	0	.250	.239
2-team total (51 Round Rock)					.256	—	—	74	262	18	67	9	0	1	20	5	5	0	1	49	10	6	.302	.282
Corporan, Carlos	B-R	6-2	240	1-7-84	.195	.067	.239	37	118	12	23	6	0	4	16	5	3	0	0	34	0	0	.347	.246
Figueroa, Cole	L-R	5-10	185	6-30-87	.230	.171	.250	41	135	14	31	7	1	0	11	15	1	0	3	17	0	1	.296	.305
2-team total (6 Oklahoma City)					.240	—	—	47	154	19	37	7	2	0	14	18	1	1	3	18	3	2	.312	.318
Galloway, Isaac	R-R	6-2	205	10-10-89	.254	.200	.271	129	441	61	112	19	2	10	38	33	5	5	2	112	31	10	.374	.312
Gillespie, Cole	R-R	6-2	215	6-20-84	.190	.258	.167	37	121	7	23	5	0	1	11	14	1	0	0	23	1	0	.256	.279
Gordon, Dee	L-R	5-11	170	4-22-88	.257	.091	.333	9	35	9	9	1	1	0	2	1	0	0	0	5	3	0	.343	.278
Hood, Destin	R-R	6-2	205	4-30-90	.267	.331	.243	126	476	61	127	29	3	15	80	37	1	0	8	113	11	6	.435	.316
Juengel, Matt	R-R	6-2	185	1-13-90	.263	.309	.248	110	392	45	103	25	4	11	53	32	5	0	2	76	0	0	.431	.325
Kelly, Don	L-R	6-4	215	2-15-80	.198	.207	.194	72	202	19	40	2	1	1	19	24	1	1	2	40	1	1	.233	.284
Lough, David	L-L	5-10	175	1-20-86	.200	.111	.238	9	30	2	6	2	0	0	1	1	0	1	0	5	0	0	.267	.226
Lutz, Zach	R-R	6-1	220	6-6-86	.125	.053	.167	16	35	1	3	0	0	0	7	1	0	0	1	18	0	0	.086	.256
McGee, Stephen	R-R	6-3	215	2-7-91	.333	—	.333	1	3	1	1	0	0	1	1	0	0	0	1	0	0	.333	.333
Mooney, Peter	L-R	5-6	155	8-19-90	.286	.000	.333	2	7	1	2	0	0	0	3	1	0	0	2	0	0	.286	.375
Nieto, Adrian	B-R	5-10	205	11-12-89	.195	.111	.221	37	113	9	22	4	0	1	19	15	0	0	1	38	1	0	.257	.287
Nola, Austin	R-R	6-0	195	12-28-89	.261	.293	.250	113	372	34	97	23	1	6	44	24	2	8	1	56	4	1	.376	.308
Riddle, J.T.	L-R	6-1	180	10-12-91	.268	.250	.275	15	56	4	15	2	0	1	2	1	0	0	0	9	1	0	.357	.281
Scruggs, Xavier	R-R	6-0	215	9-23-87	.290	.253	.303	93	317	69	92	24	0	21	50	58	6	0	1	90	4	2	.565	.408
Shoemaker, Brady	R-R	6-0	220	5-10-87	.239	.292	.213	27	71	9	17	5	0	3	10	10	0	1	0	14	0	1	.437	.333
Soto, Elliot	R-R	5-9	160	8-21-89	.241	.410	.185	62	158	22	38	4	1	1	12	28	1	3	0	36	3	0	.297	.358
Telis, Tomas	B-R	5-8	220	6-18-91	.310	.321	.306	91	336	46	104	16	3	6	45	27	2	1	2	42	4	2	.429	.362
Weber, Garrett	R-R	5-10	165	3-29-89	.250	.667	.154	6	16	2	4	0	1	0	0	0	0	0	0	6	0	0	.375	.250
Wilson, Kenny	B-R	6-0	205	1-30-90	.219	.218	.220	93	310	37	68	14	0	1	20	39	7	0	2	75	26	8	.274	.318

Pitching	B-T	HT	WT	DOB	W	L	ERA	G	GS	CG	SV	IP	H	R	ER	HR	BB	SO	AVG	vLH	vRH	K/9	BB/9
Adkins, Hunter	R-R	6-4	190	9-20-90	2	1	6.75	5	1	0	0	15	13	11	11	2	15	10	.260	.200	.286	6.14	9.20
Axelrod, Dylan	R-R	5-10	195	7-30-85	9	7	4.19	26	25	1	0	133	140	65	62	13	33	86	.273	.293	.257	5.81	2.23
Barraclough, Kyle	R-R	6-3	225	6-18-90	1	0	1.50	3	0	0	1	6	2	1	1	0	1	9	.100	.250	.063	13.50	1.50
Bremer, Tyler	R-R	6-2	210	12-7-89	0	0	5.25	5	0	0	0	12	16	7	7	1	7	10	.333	.333	.333	7.50	5.25
Breslow, Craig	L-L	5-11	180	8-8-80	1	3	6.46	14	0	0	2	24	34	18	17	3	11	29	.330	.351	.318	11.03	4.18
2-team total (3 Round Rock)					1	3	7.01	17	0	0	2	26	39	21	20	3	13	29	—	—	—	10.17	4.56
Brice, Austin	R-R	6-4	235	6-19-92	0	0	1.04	5	0	0	2	9	3	1	1	1	1	10	.111	.071	.154	10.38	1.04
Cervenka, Hunter	L-L	6-1	245	1-3-90	0	0	0.00	2	0	0	1	2	1	0	0	0	4	1	.143	.333	.000	18.00	0.00
Chaffee, Ryan	R-R	6-2	195	5-18-88	0	0	12.46	2	0	0	0	4	8	6	6	2	4	2	.400	.500	.333	4.15	8.31
Clemens, Paul	R-R	6-3	215	2-14-88	6	4	4.30	14	14	2	0	75	66	38	36	6	25	66	.234	.211	.252	7.88	2.99
Cosart, Jarred	R-R	6-3	205	5-25-90	3	4	4.09	10	10	0	0	51	55	30	23	8	25	30	.279	.283	.276	5.33	4.44

Pitching

Pitching	B-T	HT	WT	DOB	W	L	ERA	G	GS	CG	SV	IP	H	R	ER	HR	BB	SO	AVG	vLH	vRH	K/9	BB/9
Ege, Cody	L-L	6-1	190	5-8-91	4	3	4.50	36	0	0	5	44	42	24	22	1	27	35	.256	.186	.295	7.16	5.52
2-team total (6 Salt Lake)					4	3	4.56	42	0	0	5	51	48	28	26	2	29	46	—	—	—	8.06	5.08
Ellington, Brian	R-R	6-3	215	8-4-90	1	0	3.12	32	0	0	2	35	17	12	12	2	26	54	.145	.160	.134	14.02	6.75
Esch, Jake	R-R	6-3	205	3-27-90	2	1	5.70	4	4	1	0	24	26	15	15	2	9	14	.299	.286	.311	5.32	3.42
Flores, Kendry	R-R	6-2	195	11-24-91	3	6	4.53	18	16	0	0	91	103	51	46	8	39	74	.289	.291	.286	7.29	3.84
Guthrie, Jeremy	R-R	6-1	205	4-8-79	3	3	8.44	6	6	0	0	27	45	27	25	5	14	16	.375	.386	.365	5.40	4.73
2-team total (11 El Paso)					6	8	7.17	17	17	0	0	87	120	74	69	10	33	53	—	—	—	5.50	3.43
Hall, Cody	R-R	6-4	235	1-6-88	0	0	0.00	4	0	0	1	3	2	1	0	0	0	4	.167	.000	.250	10.80	0.00
2-team total (12 Reno)					0	0	6.50	16	0	0	1	18	25	14	13	2	7	14	—	—	—	7.00	3.50
Jokisch, Eric	R-L	6-2	205	7-29-89	2	0	2.64	18	0	0	1	31	33	11	9	1	14	19	.277	.186	.329	5.58	4.11
3-team total (1 Iowa, 7 Round Rock)					3	2	4.27	26	5	0	1	59	70	33	28	5	24	37	—	—	—	5.64	3.66
Kinley, Tyler	R-R	6-4	205	1-31-91	0	2	7.45	8	0	0	1	10	13	14	8	1	9	12	.317	.350	.286	11.17	8.38
Lazo, Raudel	L-L	5-9	180	4-12-89	2	0	1.78	24	0	0	2	30	28	10	6	1	10	27	.237	.189	.259	8.01	2.97
Luebke, Cory	R-L	6-4	210	3-4-85	0	0	0.00	1	0	0	0	1	0	0	0	0	0	1	.000	.000	.000	9.00	0.00
McGough, Scott	R-R	5-11	190	10-31-89	0	1	13.50	2	0	0	0	3	6	4	4	0	3	1	.429	1.000	.385	3.38	10.13
McGowan, Dustin	R-R	6-3	235	3-24-82	0	0	0.00	4	0	0	2	7	1	0	0	0	6	7	.045	.083	.000	8.59	7.36
Nappo, Greg	L-L	5-10	195	8-25-88	5	6	4.63	26	1	0	0	68	69	37	35	10	33	60	.262	.304	.240	7.94	4.37
Narveson, Chris	L-L	6-3	205	12-20-81	4	6	3.41	20	15	0	0	90	76	36	34	10	30	68	.228	.206	.239	6.83	3.01
Nicolino, Justin	L-L	6-3	195	11-22-91	7	6	4.13	14	14	0	0	85	87	43	39	10	13	49	.270	.302	.263	5.19	1.38
Ogando, Nefi	R-R	6-0	230	6-3-89	0	0	3.33	22	0	0	2	24	18	9	9	2	11	19	.202	.194	.208	7.03	4.07
Pineyro, Ivan	R-R	6-1	200	9-29-91	0	2	5.06	5	3	0	0	16	12	9	9	0	10	13	.222	.294	.189	7.31	5.63
Reed, Chris	L-L	6-3	225	5-20-90	3	4	3.78	20	9	0	0	67	54	31	28	9	27	54	.220	.261	.205	7.29	3.65
Reyes, Jo-Jo	L-L	6-2	230	11-20-84	3	2	3.43	38	0	0	4	60	60	23	23	2	17	51	.259	.261	.258	7.61	2.54
Rienzo, Andre	R-R	6-2	195	7-5-88	2	1	2.51	27	0	0	8	32	25	9	9	1	18	33	.219	.217	.221	9.19	5.01
Steckenrider, Drew	R-R	6-5	215	1-10-91	0	1	5.40	10	0	0	7	12	11	9	7	1	7	15	.239	.263	.222	11.57	5.40
Tomshaw, Matt	L-L	6-2	200	12-17-88	0	1	2.12	8	0	0	0	17	15	5	4	3	2	16	.246	.217	.263	8.47	1.06
Urena, Jose	R-R	6-2	200	9-12-91	3	3	3.17	12	12	0	0	48	41	18	17	4	21	41	.234	.253	.219	7.63	3.91
Wittgren, Nick	R-R	6-2	210	5-29-91	1	0	1.42	10	0	0	2	13	6	2	2	1	4	11	.143	.250	.100	7.82	2.84
Wojciechowski, Asher	R-R	6-4	235	12-21-88	2	3	5.26	13	10	0	0	50	61	31	29	10	24	32	.305	.330	.277	5.80	4.35
2-team total (5 Fresno)					4	5	5.28	18	15	0	0	75	90	52	44	11	37	54	—	—	—	6.48	4.44

Fielding

Catcher	PCT	G	PO	A	E	DP	PB
Arcia	.993	18	131	11	1	0	2
Corporan	.981	34	238	18	5	1	3
McGee	1.000	1	14	0	0	0	0
Nieto	.996	34	225	17	1	3	5
Telis	.993	55	387	29	3	4	1

First Base	PCT	G	PO	A	E	DP
Black	1.000	18	139	5	0	11
Bour	1.000	4	25	0	0	2
Gillespie	1.000	11	93	8	0	11
Kelly	.993	19	141	10	1	12
Scruggs	.996	57	426	22	2	52
Shoemaker	1.000	16	119	8	0	10
Telis	.991	25	198	13	2	13
Weber	1.000	2	16	4	0	1

Second Base	PCT	G	PO	A	E	DP
Andino	1.000	11	22	21	0	7

	PCT	G	PO	A	E	DP
Ciriaco	.963	12	22	30	2	8
Figueroa	1.000	16	21	29	0	10
Gordon	.939	9	15	16	2	1
Kelly	.986	15	30	42	1	16
Lutz	1.000	2	0	1	0	0
Mooney	1.000	1	0	1	0	1
Nola	.981	56	102	151	5	36
Riddle	1.000	1	1	2	0	1
Soto	.973	36	64	81	4	19

Third Base	PCT	G	PO	A	E	DP
Ciriaco	1.000	2	1	1	0	0
Figueroa	—	1	0	0	0	0
Juengel	.954	99	66	183	12	21
Kelly	1.000	9	4	17	0	3
Lutz	1.000	7	5	15	0	2
Nola	.982	22	7	47	1	2
Soto	1.000	10	7	20	0	3

Shortstop	PCT	G	PO	A	E	DP
Andino	.967	83	117	238	12	51
Ciriaco	.923	3	2	10	1	1
Nola	.967	32	41	106	5	22
Riddle	.979	13	21	26	1	8
Soto	1.000	1	9	26	0	5

Outfield	PCT	G	PO	A	E	DP
Andino	1.000	12	25	0	0	0
Figueroa	.935	22	26	3	2	0
Galloway	.993	123	287	6	2	0
Gillespie	1.000	22	43	4	0	1
Hood	.987	122	216	8	3	2
Kelly	1.000	2	2	0	0	0
Lough	1.000	8	16	0	0	0
Scruggs	.981	30	50	3	1	0
Weber	—	1	0	0	0	0
Wilson	.986	90	206	8	3	0

JACKSONVILLE SUNS — DOUBLE-A
SOUTHERN LEAGUE

Batting	B-T	HT	WT	DOB	AVG	vLH	vRH	G	AB	R	H	2B	3B	HR	RBI	BB	HBP	SH	SF	SO	SB	CS	SLG	OBP
Anderson, Brian	R-R	6-3	185	5-19-93	.243	.350	.216	86	301	38	73	9	1	8	40	36	5	0	3	59	0	0	.359	.330
Arcia, Francisco	B-R	5-11	195	9-14-89	.232	.167	.250	75	250	15	58	11	1	1	18	25	7	1	1	60	0	1	.296	.318
Curley, Chris	R-R	6-0	185	5-25-87	.245	.188	.261	85	282	27	69	12	1	7	41	28	7	0	2	81	1	1	.369	.326
Dean, Austin	R-R	6-1	190	10-14-93	.238	.278	.226	130	480	60	114	23	5	11	67	48	2	1	5	110	1	2	.375	.307
Dietrich, Derek	L-R	6-0	205	7-18-89	.167	.000	.176	5	18	2	3	0	0	0	2	2	0	0	0	7	0	0	.167	.318
Glenn, Alex	L-L	5-11	180	6-11-91	.276	.235	.283	62	214	28	59	10	1	8	37	16	1	0	1	47	0	1	.444	.328
Juengel, Matt	R-R	6-2	185	1-13-90	.284	.200	.305	21	74	10	21	2	1	1	11	3	0	0	2	6	1	2	.378	.304
Maron, Cam	L-R	6-1	195	1-20-91	.302	.375	.290	61	162	17	49	8	0	1	23	24	0	2	0	33	1	4	.370	.392
Mitchell, Ronnie	L-L	5-11	200	6-21-91	.298	.259	.306	52	151	24	45	12	0	5	16	17	1	0	0	30	1	4	.477	.373
Mooney, Peter	L-R	5-6	155	8-19-90	.258	.250	.260	119	399	45	103	16	1	4	29	41	3	3	1	44	3	3	.333	.331
Muno, Danny	B-R	6-1	195	2-9-89	.222	.333	.200	8	18	2	4	0	0	0	4	0	0	0	0	4	0	0	.222	.364
Othman, Sharif	B-R	5-11	195	3-23-89	.176	.139	.197	35	102	9	18	4	2	0	8	8	0	2	0	30	0	0	.255	.236
Perez, Yefri	R-R	5-11	170	2-24-91	.259	.281	.250	84	328	49	85	7	3	1	28	39	1	3	6	66	39	11	.308	.334
Pineda, Jeremias	B-R	5-11	190	11-16-90	.182	.196	.178	61	203	24	37	4	1	0	9	22	3	6	1	77	17	8	.212	.271
Riddle, J.T.	L-R	6-1	180	10-12-91	.278	.313	.266	101	389	49	108	18	4	3	51	33	0	4	3	72	5	1	.368	.332
Roberts, James	R-R	6-2	180	12-11-91	.210	.222	.203	72	181	19	38	5	0	0	11	22	7	2	3	36	2	1	.238	.315
Romero, Avery	R-R	5-11	195	5-11-93	.190	.211	.185	36	100	13	19	3	2	1	10	15	1	0	1	17	2	0	.290	.299
Shoemaker, Brady	R-R	6-0	220	5-10-87	.208	.188	.214	43	149	19	31	5	0	4	24	23	4	0	2	36	0	0	.322	.326

BaseballAmerica.com

Batting

Batting	B-T	HT	WT	DOB	AVG	vLH	vRH	G	AB	R	H	2B	3B	HR	RBI	BB	HBP	SH	SF	SO	SB	CS	SLG	OBP
2-team total (29 Birmingham)					.217	—	—	72	258	32	56	11	0	6	29	35	5	0	2	64	0	0	.329	.320
Sierra, Moises	R-R	6-1	220	9-24-88	.336	.355	.330	82	268	44	90	16	3	9	37	30	7	0	2	45	6	3	.519	.414
Weber, Garrett	R-R	5-10	165	3-29-89	.208	.188	.213	56	154	12	32	4	1	2	16	16	1	0	1	36	0	0	.286	.285
Wilson, Kenny	B-R	6-0	205	1-30-90	.347	.286	.361	32	118	23	41	6	3	2	12	15	0	0	0	26	4	4	.500	.421

Pitching

Pitching	B-T	HT	WT	DOB	W	L	ERA	G	GS	CG	SV	IP	H	R	ER	HR	BB	SO	AVG	vLH	vRH	K/9	BB/9
Adkins, Hunter	R-R	6-4	190	9-20-90	2	5	5.04	22	11	0	1	70	70	42	39	12	22	60	.262	.270	.257	7.75	2.84
Araujo, Victor	R-R	5-11	170	11-9-92	1	1	3.38	9	0	0	1	16	18	7	6	1	11	12	.290	.310	.273	6.75	6.19
Ballew, Travis	R-R	6-0	160	5-1-91	1	1	5.28	11	0	0	0	15	10	10	9	1	9	8	.192	.182	.200	4.70	5.28
Berry, Tim	L-L	6-3	180	3-18-91	0	3	9.28	9	4	0	0	21	40	25	22	0	10	19	.404	.500	.362	8.02	4.22
Bremer, Tyler	R-R	6-2	210	12-7-89	5	4	3.08	36	0	0	3	61	48	25	21	5	24	49	.217	.182	.241	7.19	3.52
Brice, Austin	R-R	6-4	235	6-19-92	4	7	2.89	27	13	0	2	93	79	39	30	5	29	79	.231	.267	.203	7.62	2.80
Buckelew, James	L-L	6-2	155	8-4-91	0	0	0.00	1	0	0	0	1	2	0	0	0	1	0	.500	—	.500	0.00	9.00
Castillo, Luis	R-R	6-2	170	12-12-92	0	2	3.86	3	3	0	0	14	12	9	6	1	7	12	.218	.154	.276	7.71	4.50
Cervenka, Hunter	L-L	6-1	245	1-3-90	0	0	9.00	1	0	0	0	1	0	1	1	0	1	2	.000	.000	.000	18.00	9.00
2-team total (2 Mississippi)					0	0	2.25	3	0	0	0	4	1	1	1	0	2	4	—	—	—	9.00	4.50
Chaffee, Ryan	R-R	6-2	195	5-18-88	2	3	3.19	29	0	0	0	42	41	19	15	0	19	40	.258	.288	.240	8.50	4.04
De La Rosa, Esmerling	R-R	6-2	199	5-15-91	0	0	0.00	1	0	0	0	1	0	0	0	0	1	0	.000	—	.000	9.00	9.00
Donatello, Sean	R-R	6-2	205	8-24-90	3	1	3.40	46	0	0	7	50	48	19	19	1	12	26	.251	.314	.215	4.65	2.15
Esch, Jake	R-R	6-3	205	3-27-90	10	9	4.03	22	22	0	0	118	117	53	53	8	37	82	.264	.295	.239	6.24	2.81
Flores, Kendry	R-R	6-2	195	11-24-91	0	0	1.59	1	1	0	0	6	7	1	1	0	0	4	.292	.250	.333	6.35	0.00
Garcia, Jarlin	L-L	6-2	215	1-18-93	1	3	4.54	9	9	0	0	40	38	22	20	4	11	27	.253	.100	.292	6.13	2.50
Guerrero, Tayron	R-R	6-8	210	1-9-91	1	1	1.93	12	0	0	4	14	11	3	3	0	3	15	.212	.286	.161	9.64	1.93
Higgins, Tyler	R-R	6-3	215	4-22-91	3	5	3.45	44	0	0	9	73	65	31	28	6	19	45	.243	.204	.269	5.55	2.34
Johnson, Patrick	R-R	5-10	170	8-14-88	8	7	3.37	31	21	0	0	128	120	55	48	15	33	113	.253	.284	.228	7.92	2.31
Jokisch, Eric	R-L	6-2	205	7-29-89	0	0	0.00	1	1	0	0	4	2	0	0	0	0	5	.143	.000	.111	11.25	0.00
Jose, Jose	L-L	6-2	175	7-21-90	1	3	9.37	13	0	0	0	16	20	17	17	5	5	22	.290	.227	.319	12.12	2.76
Kinley, Tyler	R-R	6-4	205	1-31-91	2	2	3.96	36	0	0	5	50	44	23	22	3	20	51	.230	.333	.144	9.18	3.60
Lazo, Raudel	L-L	5-9	180	4-12-89	0	1	3.09	10	0	0	2	12	10	4	4	0	1	8	.238	.083	.300	6.17	0.77
Logan, Blake	R-R	6-1	245	1-12-92	0	0	9.00	3	1	0	0	6	7	6	6	1	3	3	.280	.231	.333	4.50	4.50
Luebke, Cory	R-L	6-4	210	3-4-85	0	0	0.00	2	0	0	0	4	5	0	0	0	0	3	.294	.500	.231	6.75	0.00
Lyman, Scott	R-R	6-4	215	3-21-90	0	2	5.09	11	1	0	0	18	18	11	10	0	10	11	.257	.188	.316	5.60	5.09
Mazza, Chris	R-R	6-4	180	10-17-89	6	5	4.16	19	14	0	0	80	78	41	37	8	28	51	.258	.318	.214	5.74	3.15
Newell, Ryan	R-R	6-2	215	6-18-91	0	0	9.39	2	2	0	0	8	12	8	8	3	3	3	.343	.313	.368	3.52	3.52
Peters, Dillon	L-L	5-9	180	8-31-92	3	0	1.99	4	4	0	0	23	17	5	5	2	4	16	.205	.133	.221	6.35	1.59
Pineyro, Ivan	R-R	6-1	200	9-29-91	0	2	11.57	3	3	0	0	9	18	12	12	2	4	1	.409	.389	.423	0.96	3.86
Ramsey, Matt	R-R	5-11	205	9-24-89	0	2	2.00	6	0	0	0	9	8	2	2	0	5	12	.250	.438	.063	12.00	5.00
Reed, Chris	L-L	6-3	225	5-20-90	1	0	3.07	4	2	0	0	15	12	5	5	0	5	11	.214	.250	.205	6.75	3.07
Rienzo, Andre	R-R	6-2	195	7-5-88	0	0	27.00	1	0	0	0	1	3	3	3	1	0	2	.429	.333	.500	18.00	—
Smith, Chipper	L-L	6-2	195	1-22-90	0	0	15.00	3	0	0	0	6	11	10	10	2	2	3	.367	.417	.333	4.50	3.00
Steckenrider, Drew	R-R	6-5	215	1-10-91	1	0	1.48	24	0	0	6	30	12	5	5	0	10	39	.120	.125	.117	11.57	2.97
Tomshaw, Matt	L-L	6-2	200	12-17-88	4	4	3.63	15	14	1	0	72	65	34	29	5	16	85	.236	.255	.231	10.63	2.00
Tracy, Matt	L-L	6-2	215	11-26-88	2	1	4.61	12	11	0	0	55	63	37	28	7	17	38	.288	.273	.291	6.26	2.80
Wojciechowski, Asher	R-R	6-4	235	12-21-88	1	0	2.53	2	2	0	0	11	9	3	3	0	1	9	.225	.231	.222	7.59	0.84

Fielding

Catcher

Catcher	PCT	G	PO	A	E	DP	PB
Arcia	.990	65	433	51	5	2	8
Maron	.994	49	292	35	2	2	4
Othman	.984	29	239	12	4	1	3

First Base

First Base	PCT	G	PO	A	E	DP
Arcia	1.000	5	26	2	0	1
Curley	.991	80	666	25	6	61
Dietrich	1.000	1	8	0	0	0
Juengel	1.000	4	30	2	0	2
Riddle	1.000	1	9	0	0	1
Roberts	1.000	2	9	0	0	3
Shoemaker	.988	39	325	15	4	26
Weber	.970	14	90	7	3	11

Second Base

Second Base	PCT	G	PO	A	E	DP
Dietrich	.944	4	8	9	1	1
Mooney	.996	51	100	135	1	39
Muno	.824	3	5	9	3	1
Perez	.951	13	26	32	3	3
Riddle	1.000	21	35	55	0	14
Roberts	.962	22	32	43	3	14
Romero	.948	16	24	31	3	10
Weber	.985	21	24	43	1	13

Third Base

Third Base	PCT	G	PO	A	E	DP
Anderson	.917	85	57	187	22	18
Curley	.500	1	0	1	0	0
Juengel	.919	14	10	24	3	3
Mooney	.714	5	1	4	2	0
Perez	1.000	2	1	1	0	0
Riddle	.875	6	2	12	2	2
Roberts	.980	18	21	28	1	3
Romero	.920	14	7	39	4	4
Weber	1.000	2	2	4	0	0

Shortstop

Shortstop	PCT	G	PO	A	E	DP
Mooney	.977	60	57	153	5	22
Muno	—	1	0	0	0	0
Perez	.939	8	13	18	2	3
Riddle	.982	71	93	187	5	43
Roberts	1.000	4	3	6	0	1

Outfield

Outfield	PCT	G	PO	A	E	DP
Curley	1.000	2	1	1	0	0
Dean	.977	116	207	7	5	2
Glenn	.975	56	118	1	3	0
Juengel	—	1	0	0	0	0
Mitchell	.972	39	66	3	2	1
Perez	.970	62	157	6	5	0
Pineda	1.000	51	98	2	0	0
Riddle	1.000	2	2	0	0	0
Roberts	1.000	9	12	0	0	0
Sierra	.967	71	166	8	6	4
Wilson	.984	30	60	0	1	0

JUPITER HAMMERHEADS

HIGH CLASS A

FLORIDA STATE LEAGUE

Batting	B-T	HT	WT	DOB	AVG	vLH	vRH	G	AB	R	H	2B	3B	HR	RBI	BB	HBP	SH	SF	SO	SB	CS	SLG	OBP
Anderson, Brian	R-R	6-3	185	5-19-93	.302	.250	.321	49	182	27	55	12	2	3	25	22	1	0	2	38	3	0	.440	.377
Aper, Ryan	R-R	6-3	175	6-6-93	.059	.250	.000	5	17	0	1	0	0	0	1	0	0	0	0	6	0	0	.059	.059
Ard, Taylor	R-R	6-2	230	1-31-90	.235	.269	.225	130	472	47	111	21	1	14	73	41	8	1	7	111	0	1	.373	.303
Bohn, Justin	R-R	6-0	180	11-2-92	.227	.233	.225	98	331	42	75	8	5	3	25	26	3	1	1	85	5	3	.308	.288
Cabrera, Rony	R-R	5-11	175	1-29-96	.208	.233	.198	46	154	9	32	5	0	0	12	9	0	5	0	44	2	1	.240	.252
Chavez, Joe	R-R	5-11	175	6-26-93	.167	.333	.000	3	6	0	1	0	0	0	0	3	0	0	0	3	0	0	.167	.444
Cordova, Rehiner	B-R	6-0	150	1-11-94	.165	.321	.126	56	139	22	23	1	0	0	11	19	1	6	0	22	1	1	.173	.270
Haynal, Brad	R-R	6-3	215	8-21-91	.251	.279	.241	92	335	26	84	17	0	3	48	23	4	3	3	66	2	3	.328	.304
Hoo, Chris	R-R	5-9	190	2-19-92	.210	.154	.227	77	233	19	49	6	0	2	14	17	10	3	1	48	0	0	.262	.291
Kjerstad, Dex	R-R	6-1	210	1-19-92	.227	.189	.239	124	462	64	105	17	5	15	55	29	14	5	4	132	9	7	.383	.291
Mitchell, Ronnie	L-L	5-11	200	6-21-91	.302	.444	.273	14	53	7	16	2	0	0	6	7	0	1	1	7	2	2	.340	.377
Norwood, John	R-R	6-1	185	9-24-92	.271	.255	.275	127	469	68	127	24	4	9	50	49	8	1	4	116	14	12	.397	.347
Othman, Sharif	B-R	5-11	195	3-23-89	.050	.167	.000	5	20	0	1	0	0	0	2	0	0	0	0	7	0	0	.050	.050
Pineda, Jeremias	B-R	5-11	190	11-16-90	.300	.267	.311	65	253	36	76	6	2	0	15	32	1	4	0	64	21	4	.340	.381
Ramirez, Yuniel	R-R	6-1	215	12-22-88	.185	.172	.190	33	108	11	20	3	1	2	9	4	0	0	1	18	2	4	.287	.212
Roberts, James	R-R	6-2	180	12-11-91	.400	.250	.500	3	10	1	4	0	0	1	4	2	0	0	0	1	1	1	.700	.500
Rodriguez, Arturo	R-R	6-0	235	10-3-91	.250	.259	.246	27	92	3	23	1	0	0	8	9	0	0	1	13	0	0	.261	.314
Romero, Avery	R-R	5-11	195	5-11-93	.253	.276	.246	75	269	28	68	13	0	3	27	20	4	0	3	39	1	0	.335	.311
Schales, Brian	R-R	6-1	170	2-13-96	.194	.174	.201	109	371	38	72	9	1	0	16	40	7	5	1	77	3	1	.224	.284
Sosa, Junior	L-L	5-10	180	10-3-90	.259	.222	.267	83	305	35	79	7	1	0	24	39	2	10	2	60	8	2	.289	.345
Vigil, Rodrigo	R-R	6-0	165	1-3-93	.250	.313	.235	24	84	4	21	2	3	0	8	2	2	1	0	12	0	0	.345	.284
Weber, Garrett	R-R	5-10	165	3-29-89	.250	.200	.267	6	20	3	5	0	0	0	2	4	1	0	0	3	0	0	.250	.400
Woods, K.J.	L-R	6-3	230	7-9-95	.155	.056	.182	24	84	6	13	1	0	2	7	8	2	0	0	34	0	0	.238	.245

Pitching	B-T	HT	WT	DOB	W	L	ERA	G	GS	CG	SV	IP	H	R	ER	HR	BB	SO	AVG	vLH	vRH	K/9	BB/9
Adames, Jose	R-R	6-2	165	1-17-93	1	5	6.00	36	0	0	7	48	51	33	32	2	27	43	.271	.256	.282	8.06	5.06
Adkins, Hunter	R-R	6-4	190	9-20-90	0	0	3.12	5	2	0	0	17	15	6	6	0	4	16	.242	.435	.128	8.31	2.08
Araujo, Victor	R-R	5-11	170	11-9-92	0	1	9.00	4	0	0	0	6	10	9	6	1	2	4	.370	.417	.333	6.00	3.00
Ballew, Travis	R-R	6-0	160	5-1-91	0	3	7.88	13	0	0	2	16	22	16	14	1	2	18	.297	.308	.292	10.13	1.13
Beltre, Andy	R-R	6-4	195	7-6-93	0	1	2.00	19	0	0	4	27	15	9	6	0	11	31	.156	.103	.193	10.33	3.67
Berry, Tim	L-L	6-3	180	3-18-91	1	0	2.08	5	1	0	0	13	6	3	3	1	3	7	.140	.250	.097	4.85	2.08
Brigham, Jeff	R-R	6-0	200	2-16-92	7	8	4.04	27	23	0	1	123	115	64	55	6	47	112	.246	.264	.231	8.22	3.45
Buckelew, James	L-L	6-2	155	8-4-91	5	2	2.74	31	9	0	0	95	87	43	29	0	30	69	.244	.262	.236	6.51	2.83
Castillo, Luis	R-R	6-2	170	12-12-92	8	4	2.07	23	21	1	0	118	95	29	27	2	18	91	.219	.229	.212	6.96	1.38
Cavanerio, Jorgan	R-R	6-1	155	8-18-94	8	12	4.70	26	24	0	0	128	156	76	67	12	21	73	.299	.319	.281	5.12	1.47
Cosart, Jarred	R-R	6-3	205	5-25-90	0	0	3.60	1	1	0	0	5	2	2	2	0	1	3	.250	.429	.154	5.40	1.80
De La Rosa, Esmerling	R-R	6-2	199	5-15-91	3	4	3.59	40	0	0	13	58	57	25	23	2	23	55	.259	.253	.263	8.58	3.59
Dunn, Mike	L-L	6-0	215	5-23-85	0	0	0.00	3	2	0	0	3	2	0	0	0	0	5	.167	.250	.125	15.00	0.00
Farnworth, Steven	R-R	6-2	175	9-6-93	1	0	3.60	5	0	0	2	10	10	4	4	2	3	5	.263	.294	.238	4.50	2.70
Fischer, Kyle	R-R	6-3	205	2-11-91	2	0	2.83	18	0	0	4	29	22	9	9	0	9	17	.210	.205	.213	5.34	2.83
Flores, Kendry	R-R	6-2	195	11-24-91	0	0	0.00	1	1	0	0	5	2	0	0	0	2	2	.125	.111	.143	3.60	0.00
Garcia, Jarlin	L-L	6-3	215	1-18-93	0	0	1.29	5	0	0	0	7	4	1	1	1	1	5	.154	.200	.125	6.43	1.29
Guillory, Preston	R-R	6-3	200	8-16-93	0	1	2.25	2	0	0	0	4	2	1	1	0	4	3	.167	.143	.200	6.75	9.00
Holmes, Ben	L-L	6-1	195	9-12-91	2	2	1.00	19	1	0	2	45	34	7	5	0	12	36	.213	.182	.224	7.20	2.40
Jackson, Edwin	R-R	6-2	215	9-9-83	0	1	6.75	2	2	0	0	4	5	3	3	0	1	3	.313	.250	.375	6.75	2.25
Jose, Jose	L-L	6-2	175	7-21-90	0	1	34.71	2	0	0	0	2	9	9	9	0	2	1	.600	.667	.500	3.86	7.71
Kinley, Jeff	L-L	6-1	195	2-15-92	0	0	16.20	1	0	0	0	2	5	3	3	1	0	1	.556	1.000	.500	5.40	0.00
Lazo, Raudel	L-L	5-9	180	4-12-89	0	1	5.40	8	2	0	0	8	9	5	5	1	1	9	.273	.263	.286	9.72	1.08
Luebke, Cory	R-L	6-4	210	3-4-85	0	0	0.00	1	1	0	0	1	0	0	0	0	2	2	.000	.000	.000	18.00	0.00
Lyman, Scott	R-R	6-4	215	3-21-90	1	0	0.00	11	0	0	1	19	13	0	0	0	6	6	.217	.269	.176	2.89	2.89
Mader, Michael	L-L	6-2	195	2-18-94	7	6	3.50	22	21	0	0	103	97	43	40	5	34	81	.251	.264	.247	7.08	2.97
Martinez, Juancito	R-R	6-1	170	6-10-89	0	4	4.63	26	0	0	0	35	37	20	18	5	17	22	.285	.235	.316	5.66	4.37
Mazza, Chris	R-R	6-4	180	10-17-89	1	0	1.20	7	0	0	0	15	12	3	2	1	2	8	.218	.333	.147	4.80	1.20
Morris, Bryan	L-R	6-3	220	3-28-87	0	0	0.00	1	0	0	0	1	0	0	0	0	0	0	.000	.000	.000	0.00	0.00
Ogando, Nefi	R-R	6-0	230	6-3-89	0	1	9.00	3	1	0	0	3	4	3	3	1	1	3	.333	.167	.500	9.00	3.00
Osoria, Aneury	R-R	6-7	170	11-15-93	0	0	0.00	1	0	0	0	1	0	0	0	0	0	0	.000	.000	.000	6.75	27.00
Peters, Dillon	L-L	5-9	195	8-31-92	11	6	2.46	20	20	0	0	106	102	36	29	2	16	89	.253	.286	.242	7.56	1.36
Quijada, Jose	L-L	6-0	175	11-9-95	2	2	4.41	9	0	0	0	16	13	8	8	1	3	25	.220	.095	.289	13.78	1.65
Ramsey, Matt	R-R	5-11	205	9-24-89	1	1	1.17	5	0	0	1	8	4	1	1	0	3	8	.154	.273	.067	9.39	3.52
Reid, Ryan	L-R	5-11	210	4-24-85	0	0	1.04	6	0	0	4	9	6	1	1	0	2	4	.200	.133	.267	4.15	2.08
Rienzo, Andre	R-R	6-2	195	7-5-88	0	0	5.40	1	0	0	0	2	0	1	1	0	2	2	.000	.000	.000	10.80	10.80
Robinson, C.J.	R-R	6-0	215	5-11-93	0	0	6.75	1	0	0	0	1	1	1	1	0	1	2	.429	.250	.667	13.50	6.75
Sadberry, Chris	L-L	6-0	195	11-8-91	0	0	6.75	3	0	0	0	4	5	3	3	0	3	3	.294	.000	.357	6.75	6.75
Smith, Chipper	L-L	6-2	195	1-22-90	0	0	0.00	1	0	0	0	2	0	0	0	0	0	1	.000	.500	.000	0.00	0.00
Squier, Scott	R-L	6-5	185	9-17-92	5	1	3.64	18	7	0	0	59	63	25	24	2	13	41	.273	.262	.277	6.22	1.97
Steckenrider, Drew	R-R	6-5	215	1-10-91	0	0	0.00	6	0	0	1	10	2	0	0	0	2	17	.065	.000	.105	15.30	1.80
Tanner, Cecil	R-R	6-6	240	10-3-90	0	0	15.88	5	0	0	0	6	7	11	10	0	14	3	.292	.462	.091	4.76	22.24
Tomshaw, Matt	L-L	6-2	200	12-17-88	1	0	0.00	1	0	0	0	3	2	0	0	0	0	3	.182	.667	.000	10.13	0.00
Tracy, Matt	L-L	6-3	215	11-26-88	1	0	0.00	1	0	0	0	3	2	0	0	0	0	3	.182	.667	.000	10.13	0.00
Velez, Jose	L-L	6-1	205	9-5-89	0	2	3.79	14	0	0	2	19	16	8	8	1	13	22	.219	.154	.255	10.42	6.16

Fielding

Catcher	PCT	G	PO	A	E	DP	PB
Haynal	.991	15	101	7	1	1	3
Hoo	.993	76	527	54	4	3	1
Othman	.974	5	35	3	1	0	0
Rodriguez	.993	22	139	9	1	1	3
Vigil	.994	24	151	15	1	1	1

First Base	PCT	G	PO	A	E	DP
Ard	.990	79	734	52	8	70
Cabrera	1.000	2	2	0	0	0
Cordova	1.000	5	13	0	0	1
Haynal	.989	40	346	22	4	29
Woods	.994	18	157	6	1	16

Second Base	PCT	G	PO	A	E	DP
Cabrera	.964	18	29	51	3	14
Chavez	1.000	1	2	2	0	1
Cordova	.981	11	20	31	1	7
Schales	.981	109	185	318	10	65

Third Base	PCT	G	PO	A	E	DP
Anderson	.966	47	34	109	5	11
Bohn	.950	6	6	13	1	3
Cabrera	1.000	1	1	0	0	0
Cordova	.957	10	7	15	1	3
Romero	.899	72	33	128	18	12
Weber	1.000	5	3	12	0	1

Shortstop	PCT	G	PO	A	E	DP
Bohn	.953	91	99	264	18	51
Cabrera	.949	26	32	79	6	15
Cordova	.900	23	26	73	11	13
Roberts	1.000	3	3	10	0	2

Outfield	PCT	G	PO	A	E	DP
Aper	1.000	4	2	0	0	0
Ard	1.000	12	24	0	0	0
Cordova	1.000	3	8	0	0	0
Kjerstad	.983	109	218	7	4	3
Mitchell	1.000	11	17	0	0	0
Norwood	.966	116	218	7	8	2
Pineda	.993	61	147	5	1	3
Ramirez	1.000	30	65	0	0	0
Sosa	.993	71	141	3	1	0

GREENSBORO GRASSHOPPERS   LOW CLASS A
SOUTH ATLANTIC LEAGUE

Batting	B-T	HT	WT	DOB	AVG	vLH	vRH	G	AB	R	H	2B	3B	HR	RBI	BB	HBP	SH	SF	SO	SB	CS	SLG	OBP
Alfonzo, Giovanny	R-R	5-11	185	12-19-92	.222	.213	.226	65	207	12	46	6	1	2	14	12	2	3	2	50	3	3	.290	.269
Barrett, Kyle	L-R	5-11	185	8-4-93	.282	.324	.266	101	354	39	100	10	3	2	32	25	4	6	4	67	17	5	.345	.333
Blanton, Aaron	R-R	6-2	175	9-1-93	.204	.229	.192	95	309	34	63	18	0	9	41	30	5	1	4	89	6	6	.350	.282
Cabrera, Rony	R-R	5-11	175	1-29-96	.184	.217	.173	27	98	5	18	3	1	0	12	6	0	0	0	23	1	1	.235	.231
Chavez, Joe	R-R	5-11	175	6-26-93	.188	.000	.250	4	16	2	3	1	0	0	0	1	0	0	1	7	0	0	.250	.235
Davis, Mason	B-R	5-9	175	1-11-93	.243	.333	.200	11	37	1	9	3	0	0	1	4	0	1	0	6	0	3	.324	.317
Dunbar, Korey	R-R	6-1	210	4-21-94	.188	.167	.196	22	69	6	13	0	0	1	5	12	0	1	0	32	0	0	.232	.305
Fernandez Jr. Alex	R-R	5-10	180	3-30-93	.211	.182	.217	16	57	7	12	2	1	0	2	8	2	0	0	19	4	0	.281	.328
Garrett, Stone	R-R	6-2	195	11-22-95	.213	.169	.235	52	197	21	42	9	2	6	16	11	3	1	0	71	1	2	.371	.265
Goodman, Kris	R-R	6-1	193	1-5-93	.154	.333	.081	20	52	4	8	0	0	0	1	7	1	1	0	15	2	0	.154	.267
Gould, J.J.	R-R	6-0	195	8-22-93	.154	.214	.120	11	39	4	6	0	0	3	7	2	1	0	0	19	0	0	.385	.214
Morales, Roy	R-R	6-2	195	6-25-95	.288	.277	.293	60	205	26	59	8	0	1	21	22	7	5	1	28	2	0	.341	.374
Munden, Taylor	R-R	5-10	185	7-7-93	.164	.150	.170	21	73	8	12	3	0	1	5	3	2	0	0	21	0	0	.247	.218
Naylor, Josh	L-L	6-0	225	6-22-97	.269	.212	.292	89	342	42	92	24	2	9	54	22	3	1	2	62	10	3	.430	.317
Pollman, Gunner	R-R	6-2	210	2-3-95	.114	.091	.125	12	35	1	4	0	0	1	3	1	0	0	0	20	0	0	.200	.139
Reyes, Angel	R-R	6-0	175	5-6-95	.252	.291	.234	122	445	51	112	22	2	6	55	36	5	3	7	97	1	2	.351	.310
Rodriguez, Arturo	R-R	6-0	235	10-3-91	.229	.286	.190	10	35	4	8	2	0	2	7	1	2	0	0	11	0	1	.457	.289
Santos, Jhonny	R-R	6-0	160	10-2-96	.125	.143	.118	7	24	1	3	0	0	0	1	3	0	1	0	5	1	0	.125	.222
Seymour, Anfernee	B-R	5-11	165	6-24-95	.255	.246	.259	104	421	61	105	13	3	1	26	22	2	15	1	96	37	13	.308	.295
2-team total (21 Rome)					.257	—	—	125	491	72	126	13	4	3	31	26	2	16	2	118	43	13	.303	.296
Silviano, John	L-R	5-11	190	7-11-94	.212	.091	.244	44	156	17	33	13	0	8	19	13	2	0	0	57	0	0	.449	.281
Soltis, Casey	L-L	6-1	185	6-8-95	.190	.184	.192	52	153	15	29	5	1	1	10	23	1	2	0	67	4	4	.255	.299
Soto, Isael	L-L	6-0	190	11-2-96	.247	.209	.262	113	401	51	99	24	5	9	38	43	1	1	2	115	3	0	.399	.320
Sullivan, Zach	R-R	6-3	180	11-26-95	.226	.281	.202	111	381	38	86	21	3	3	37	25	5	4	4	117	9	10	.320	.280
Tissenbaum, Maxx	B-R	5-10	185	7-25-91	.219	.143	.240	9	32	4	7	0	0	1	7	3	0	0	0	4	0	0	.313	.286
Twine, Justin	R-R	5-11	205	10-7-95	.249	.283	.235	99	353	42	88	17	2	3	33	19	12	0	2	116	8	6	.334	.308
Vigil, Rodrigo	R-R	6-0	165	1-3-93	.350	.400	.333	6	20	2	7	3	0	0	4	0	0	0	0	4	0	0	.500	.381

Pitching	B-T	HT	WT	DOB	W	L	ERA	G	GS	CG	SV	IP	H	R	ER	HR	BB	SO	AVG	vLH	vRH	K/9	BB/9
Adames, Jose	R-R	6-2	165	1-17-93	0	0	—	1	0	0	0	0	1	2	2	0	1	0	1.000	—	1.000	—	—
Bach, Connor	L-L	6-6	230	6-24-92	0	0	0.00	1	0	0	0	2	1	0	0	0	2	3	.143	.000	.167	13.50	9.00
2-team total (5 Hagerstown)					0	1	6.28	6	0	0	0	14	8	11	10	1	16	17	—	—		10.67	10.05
Bautista, Nestor	L-L	6-3	200	5-13-92	0	2	6.48	7	0	0	0	17	19	14	12	3	7	7	.297	.067	.367	3.78	3.78
Beltre, Andy	R-R	6-4	195	7-6-93	0	0	1.37	13	0	0	1	20	15	3	3	1	5	23	.205	.333	.143	10.53	2.29
Brewster, L.J.	R-R	6-2	205	5-2-94	4	7	5.26	29	12	0	0	79	101	61	46	5	33	44	.316	.341	.299	5.03	3.78
Bugg, Parker	R-R	6-6	210	10-26-94	1	0	3.77	8	0	0	0	14	10	6	6	0	5	11	.200	.217	.185	6.91	3.14
Castellanos, Gabe	L-L	6-1	165	12-28-93	3	1	3.78	12	10	0	0	48	53	28	20	4	25	45	.288	.279	.293	8.50	4.72
Crescentini, Marcus	R-R	6-4	240	12-26-92	2	3	1.48	20	0	0	4	30	21	7	5	2	12	47	.189	.244	.157	13.95	3.56
Delgado, Victor	R-R	6-3	185	2-3-95	0	0	0.00	1	0	0	0	2	2	0	0	0	0	1	.286	.500	.200	4.50	0.00
Effertz, Joel	R-R	6-3	235	9-27-90	0	1	7.50	2	0	0	0	12	22	10	10	2	5	7	.415	.636	.258	5.25	3.75
Farnworth, Steven	R-R	6-2	175	9-6-93	5	5	3.39	26	16	0	3	96	88	40	36	12	19	54	.240	.278	.210	5.08	1.79
Gil, Isaac	R-R	6-5	230	10-8-91	1	3	4.15	11	2	0	0	26	29	15	12	0	7	17	.293	.293	.293	5.88	2.42
Guillory, Preston	R-R	6-3	200	8-16-93	0	0	0.00	1	0	0	0	1	0	0	0	0	0	1	.000	.000	.000	9.00	0.00
Guzman, Kevin	R-R	6-3	165	11-6-94	1	4	3.90	7	5	0	0	28	22	18	12	1	8	28	.212	.262	.140	9.11	2.60
Hill, Trenton	L-R	6-4	210	3-10-94	1	0	36.00	1	0	0	0	1	2	4	4	1	0	2	.400	—	.400	18.00	0.00
Hillyer, Jordan	R-R	6-2	225	9-20-92	0	1	8.59	5	0	0	0	7	6	7	7	2	6	11	.207	.100	.263	13.50	7.36
Holloway, Jordan	R-R	6-4	190	6-13-96	2	4	6.16	8	8	0	0	31	31	23	21	8	15	24	.261	.298	.236	7.04	4.40
Holmes, Ben	L-L	6-1	195	9-12-91	5	0	1.36	16	0	0	2	46	24	8	7	4	20	43	.156	.143	.165	8.35	3.88
Jacome, Justin	L-L	6-6	230	10-19-93	1	5	3.72	21	16	0	0	73	69	35	30	5	36	47	.256	.265	.252	5.82	4.46
Keller, Kyle	R-R	6-4	200	4-28-93	3	2	3.35	29	0	0	1	46	41	19	17	4	13	57	.233	.266	.213	11.73	2.56
King, Mike	R-R	6-3	204	5-25-95	0	0	0.00	1	0	0	0	4	4	2	0	0	1	2	.235	.286	.200	4.15	2.08
Kinley, Jeff	L-L	6-1	195	2-15-92	5	2	2.77	32	0	0	0	55	39	17	17	5	27	49	.203	.196	.206	7.97	4.39
Lambert, Trey	R-R	6-4	205	6-5-91	0	0	3.68	8	0	0	0	15	15	8	6	1	3	8	.259	.350	.211	4.91	1.84

Pitching

Pitching	B-T	HT	WT	DOB	W	L	ERA	G	GS	CG	SV	IP	H	R	ER	HR	BB	SO	AVG	vLH	vRH	K/9	BB/9
2-team total (16 Hagerstown)					2	0	2.44	24	0	0	1	48	52	15	13	4	5	35	—	—	—	6.56	0.94
Lilek, Brett	L-L	6-4	220	8-10-93	0	1	5.06	7	5	0	0	16	19	11	9	1	16	13	.311	.375	.289	7.31	9.00
MacEachern, Ryley	R-R	6-2	213	5-27-94	2	1	4.19	20	0	0	0	34	32	20	16	3	13	30	.242	.192	.275	7.86	3.41
Mateo, Alex	R-R	6-2	200	1-18-94	0	0	4.50	4	0	0	0	8	6	4	4	0	4	4	.207	.182	.222	4.50	4.50
Meyer, Ben	R-R	6-5	180	1-30-93	4	11	3.62	33	10	0	1	97	93	45	39	11	21	94	.246	.237	.252	8.72	1.95
Newell, Ryan	R-R	6-2	215	6-18-91	0	2	3.60	2	2	0	0	5	5	2	2	1	1	4	.263	.375	.182	7.20	1.80
Paddack, Chris	R-R	6-4	195	1-8-96	2	0	0.95	6	6	0	0	28	9	3	3	2	2	48	.098	.143	.070	15.25	0.64
Poteet, Cody	R-R	6-1	190	7-30-94	4	9	2.91	24	24	0	0	117	108	53	38	5	44	106	.246	.266	.231	8.13	3.38
Quijada, Jose	L-L	6-0	175	11-9-95	3	0	1.32	19	0	0	2	34	17	5	5	1	7	44	.148	.212	.122	11.65	1.85
Richards, Trevor	R-R	6-2	190	5-15-93	2	3	2.68	8	8	0	0	44	29	17	13	3	14	38	.186	.169	.200	7.83	2.89
Robinson, C.J.	R-R	6-0	215	5-11-93	2	1	2.55	40	0	0	22	49	34	15	14	6	15	49	.195	.219	.178	8.94	2.74
Sawczak, Shane	L-L	6-0	188	11-20-95	0	1	22.50	2	0	0	0	2	6	5	5	0	4	1	.500	.667	.333	4.50	18.00
Squier, Scott	R-L	6-5	185	9-17-92	1	1	2.12	14	0	0	5	30	23	9	7	1	8	28	.215	.235	.205	8.49	2.43
Weaver, Chuck	R-R	6-4	200	1-4-91	9	5	3.02	17	14	0	0	83	77	37	28	7	10	72	.242	.229	.25	7.78	1.08

Fielding

Catcher	PCT	G	PO	A	E	DP	PB
Dunbar	.980	20	131	16	3	0	10
Morales	.992	57	450	34	4	1	7
Pollman	.987	12	66	10	1	0	2
Rodriguez	.989	9	85	9	1	0	1
Silviano	.969	32	205	16	7	2	6
Tissenbaum	.985	7	61	4	1	0	6
Vigil	1.000	6	45	6	0	1	1

Second Base	PCT	G	PO	A	E	DP
Alfonzo	.937	14	24	35	4	7
Cabrera	.965	21	35	75	4	22
Chavez	1.000	1	1	2	0	1
Davis	.923	2	6	6	1	1
Munden	.976	9	13	27	1	6
Twine	.985	96	180	265	7	68

Shortstop	PCT	G	PO	A	E	DP
Alfonzo	.942	27	36	62	6	15
Blanton	—		1	0	0	0
Cabrera	.818	5	6	12	4	1
Davis	1.000	2	2	4	0	2
Gould	.973	10	16	20	1	6
Seymour	.921	99	129	254	33	59

First Base	PCT	G	PO	A	E	DP
Alfonzo	1.000	5	43	6	0	6
Goodman	1.000	1	3	2	0	0
Munden	1.000	1	2	0	0	0
Naylor	.986	81	725	36	11	69
Reyes	.988	53	447	27	6	44
Rodriguez	1.000	1	11	0	0	0

Third Base	PCT	G	PO	A	E	DP
Alfonzo	.915	17	15	39	5	7
Blanton	.933	94	43	179	16	12
Cabrera	1.000	1	0	1	0	0
Chavez	1.000	2	4	4	0	1
Davis	1.000	2	1	0	0	0
Goodman	.727	8	3	13	6	0
Gould	1.000	1	1	1	0	0
Munden	.906	11	2	27	3	5
Reyes	.875	8	2	12	2	1

Outfield	PCT	G	PO	A	E	DP
Barrett	.982	91	161	1	3	0
Davis	1.000	4	5	0	0	0
Fernandez Jr.	.955	14	20	1	1	0
Garrett	.965	40	81	1	3	0
Goodman	1.000	7	5	1	0	0
Santos	1.000	7	21	0	0	0
Soltis	1.000	51	85	1	0	1
Soto	.972	101	162	10	5	3
Sullivan	.983	109	222	9	4	0

BATAVIA MUCKDOGS

NEW YORK-PENN LEAGUE

SHORT-SEASON

Batting

Batting	B-T	HT	WT	DOB	AVG	vLH	vRH	G	AB	R	H	2B	3B	HR	RBI	BB	HBP	SH	SF	SO	SB	CS	SLG	OBP
Anderson, Blake	R-R	6-3	180	1-5-96	.000	.000	.000	1	4	0	0	0	0	0	0	0	0	0	0	3	0	0	.000	.000
Berry, Branden	R-R	6-4	225	5-19-93	.227	.281	.186	21	75	7	17	4	0	2	6	4	4	0	0	14	0	0	.360	.301
Bird, Corey	L-L	6-1	185	8-11-95	.237	.328	.205	58	219	26	52	6	0	0	18	18	3	5	2	30	16	6	.265	.302
Cabrera, Rony	R-R	5-11	175	1-29-96	.308	.167	.350	15	52	5	16	1	0	0	2	3	1	0	0	8	1	1	.327	.357
Castro, Samuel	B-R	5-10	160	10-16-97	.180	.208	.166	66	217	20	39	4	1	1	17	20	2	7	2	51	3	4	.221	.253
Chavez, Joe	R-R	5-11	175	6-26-93	.139	.167	.125	11	36	3	5	0	0	0	4	5	1	0	0	15	0	0	.139	.262
Fernandez Jr. Alex	R-R	5-10	180	3-30-93	.111	.222	.000	5	18	0	2	1	0	0	1	1	0	0	0	7	0	1	.167	.158
Foley, Matt	R-R	6-4	230	4-15-94	.286	.500	.200	2	7	0	2	0	0	0	1	1	0	0	0	4	0	0	.286	.375
Garcia, Pablo	S-R	5-10	170	9-26-96	.228	.268	.211	39	136	12	31	8	0	0	23	10	0	2	3	19	0	0	.287	.275
Garzillo, Mike	R-R	5-11	185	2-11-94	.189	.167	.202	40	132	17	25	5	1	0	10	17	1	1	0	54	2	0	.242	.287
Gauntt, David	R-R	6-0	200	6-16-93	.100	.200	.067	6	20	1	2	1	0	0	3	1	0	0	7	0	0	.150	.250
Goodman, Kris	R-R	6-1	193	1-5-93	.256	.281	.239	22	78	9	20	3	0	0	3	11	0	0	0	19	2	2	.295	.348
Gould, J.J.	R-R	6-0	195	8-22-93	.241	.362	.191	53	199	22	48	15	0	6	20	18	6	1	0	55	1	3	.407	.323
Gutierrez, Eric	L-L	5-10	205	12-28-93	.218	.241	.209	54	202	18	44	12	1	5	34	16	9	0	3	46	2	0	.361	.300
Jones, Alex	R-R	6-2	215	2-16-93	.309	.294	.316	17	55	5	17	4	0	0	5	5	0	1	0	11	0	0	.382	.367
Knapp, Aaron	L-R	5-10	175	11-4-94	.253	.164	.288	60	217	31	55	7	2	1	21	25	4	5	2	56	19	7	.318	.339
Lara, Garvis	B-R	6-1	170	5-19-96	.065	.000	.074	9	31	2	2	0	0	0	1	3	0	1	0	11	0	0	.065	.147
Lopez, Javier	R-R	5-10	180	9-13-94	.221	.186	.235	45	145	13	32	4	3	0	12	10	2	2	1	27	3	1	.290	.278
Lusignan, Colby	L-R	6-4	230	11-15-92	.091	.077	.100	9	33	3	3	1	0	0	6	0	0	0	0	19	0	0	.121	.231
Munden, Taylor	R-R	5-10	185	7-7-93	.100	.333	.000	4	10	1	1	0	0	0	0	0	0	0	0	3	0	0	.100	.100
Olis, Walker	R-R	6-2	190	5-4-94	.247	.240	.250	26	97	11	24	3	2	0	5	10	2	4	1	22	9	2	.320	.327
Rindfleisch, Jarrett	R-R	6-1	225	9-4-95	.219	.182	.235	24	73	9	16	7	0	1	9	11	6	1	0	12	0	0	.356	.367
Santos, Jhonny	R-R	6-0	160	10-2-96	.203	.230	.191	52	192	23	39	8	0	2	9	19	1	1	2	43	6	1	.276	.276
White, Isaiah	R-R	6-0	170	1-7-97	.214	.146	.240	51	173	23	37	6	3	1	17	22	1	5	0	60	5	4	.301	.306
Whiting, Sutton	B-R	5-8	170	5-13-92	.143	.000	.167	6	21	3	3	0	0	1	2	0	0	0	0	6	1	1	.286	.217

Pitching

Pitching	B-T	HT	WT	DOB	W	L	ERA	G	GS	CG	SV	IP	H	R	ER	HR	BB	SO	AVG	vLH	vRH	K/9	BB/9
Bach, Connor	L-L	6-6	230	6-24-92	0	2	9.31	5	0	0	0	10	11	11	11	0	11	7	.316	.200	.357	6.52	10.24
Beggs, Dustin	R-R	6-3	180	6-14-93	2	3	5.23	16	3	0	0	31	42	20	18	2	5	20	.328	.429	.250	5.81	1.45
Bugg, Parker	R-R	6-6	210	10-26-94	0	0	3.66	11	0	0	4	20	13	8	8	0	3	16	.181	.237	.118	7.32	1.37
Crescentini, Marcus	R-R	6-4	240	12-26-92	0	0	2.25	4	0	0	0	4	3	1	1	0	2	5	.200	.250	.143	11.25	4.50
Delgado, Victor	R-R	6-2	185	2-3-95	0	1	15.19	5	0	0	0	5	13	11	9	0	5	3	.464	.250	.625	5.06	8.44
Diaz, Jose	R-R	6-2	180	5-7-93	0	7	6.51	15	12	0	0	47	49	36	34	3	22	24	.271	.260	.286	4.60	4.21
Diaz, Obed	R-R	6-2	185	5-5-97	0	1	8.10	2	0	0	0	3	8	4	3	1	2	2	.471	.714	.300	5.40	5.40
Effertz, Joel	R-R	6-3	235	9-27-90	0	0	7.36	5	0	0	0	7	7	6	6	0	5	3	.259	.357	.154	3.68	6.14

Pitching (Miami Marlins)

Pitching	B-T	HT	WT	DOB	W	L	ERA	G	GS	CG	SV	IP	H	R	ER	HR	BB	SO	AVG	vLH	vRH	K/9	BB/9
Garcia, Javier	R-R	6-2	230	2-26-98	0	4	4.20	14	3	0	0	30	32	18	14	4	18	13	.278	.267	.286	3.90	5.40
Hill, Trenton	L-L	6-4	210	3-10-94	3	1	2.05	17	0	0	0	26	17	7	6	0	16	25	.183	.130	.200	8.54	5.47
Hillyer, Jordan	R-R	6-2	225	9-22-93	0	1	4.76	4	0	0	0	6	4	3	3	1	1	8	.190	.125	.231	12.71	1.59
Holloway, Jordan	R-R	6-4	190	6-13-96	0	3	6.23	5	5	0	0	17	21	17	12	0	13	17	.280	.423	.204	8.83	6.75
Hoover, Chevis	R-R	6-3	240	10-18-93	0	0	2.45	7	0	0	0	11	11	3	3	0	5	10	.289	.357	.250	8.18	4.09
Hovis, Reilly	R-R	6-3	195	10-27-93	2	4	5.36	17	7	0	0	47	56	30	28	4	11	39	.287	.337	.237	7.47	2.11
King, Mike	R-R	6-3	204	5-25-95	2	2	3.38	10	1	0	1	21	22	8	8	0	6	15	.278	.390	.158	6.33	2.53
Langley, Justin	L-L	6-6	225	9-2-94	0	1	10.50	4	0	0	0	6	9	9	7	0	6	6	.346	.714	.211	9.00	9.00
Lee, Dylan	L-L	6-4	210	8-1-94	0	1	2.35	9	6	0	1	23	18	9	6	0	7	7	.220	.143	.259	2.74	2.74
MacEachern, Ryley	R-R	6-2	213	5-27-94	0	0	0.00	3	0	0	0	4	1	0	0	0	3	0	.083	.143	.000	0.00	7.36
Mateo, Alex	R-R	6-2	200	1-18-94	2	2	3.91	10	0	0	0	23	28	11	10	2	4	24	.301	.162	.393	9.39	1.57
McKay, Ryan	R-R	6-4	195	9-20-96	1	4	5.31	11	11	0	0	39	42	33	23	4	21	26	.282	.262	.298	6.00	4.85
Mejia, Humberto	R-R	6-3	175	3-3-97	1	2	4.82	3	2	0	0	9	10	6	5	1	2	15	.286	.250	.304	14.46	1.93
Mertz, Michael	R-R	6-2	220	9-24-93	1	2	4.44	10	5	0	0	24	24	13	12	0	18	11	.270	.262	.277	4.07	6.66
Neubeck, Travis	L-R	6-2	180	3-15-93	2	5	3.78	16	10	0	0	48	48	32	20	0	18	29	.264	.241	.283	5.48	3.40
Osoria, Aneury	R-R	6-7	170	11-15-93	0	0	7.56	5	0	0	0	8	13	9	7	0	10	3	.382	.267	.474	3.24	10.80
Peace, R.J.	R-R	6-2	175	6-24-97	1	0	6.00	2	0	0	0	3	4	2	2	1	0	3	.333	.500	.167	9.00	0.00
Perez, Sam	R-R	6-3	210	8-17-94	1	1	3.54	16	8	0	0	48	41	20	19	4	15	36	.234	.228	.240	6.70	2.79
Provencher, Ty	R-R	6-2	205	5-10-93	0	0	6.85	22	0	0	1	22	35	21	17	2	6	15	.368	.500	.255	6.04	2.42
Reed, Remey	R-R	6-5	230	5-5-95	0	0	0.00	1	0	0	0	1	0	0	0	0	1	2	.000	—	.000	13.50	6.75
Richards, Trevor	R-R	6-2	190	5-15-93	0	0	1.69	3	1	0	0	11	9	5	2	1	2	15	.225	.200	.250	12.66	1.69
Sawczak, Shane	L-L	6-0	188	11-20-95	1	1	1.93	17	1	0	0	33	23	7	7	3	13	26	.213	.263	.186	7.16	3.58
Smith, Chad	R-R	6-4	200	6-8-95	1	2	8.25	15	0	0	0	24	41	32	22	3	12	20	.360	.377	.344	7.50	4.50
Tanner, Cecil	R-R	6-6	240	4-23-90	0	0	13.50	2	0	0	0	3	1	5	5	0	8	3	.091	.167	.000	8.10	21.60
Wells, Hunter	R-R	6-2	170	5-22-95	2	0	6.30	6	0	0	1	10	13	7	7	0	5	5	.317	.350	.286	4.50	4.50
Wheatley, Brent	R-R	6-4	210	8-31-93	0	3	8.59	15	0	0	0	22	31	25	21	1	11	14	.333	.388	.273	5.73	4.50

Fielding

C: Anderson 1, Garcia 39, Gauntt 5, Jones 8, Rindfleisch 23. **1B:** Berry 8, Chavez 8, Foley 1, Goodman 2, Gutierrez 50, Lopez 5, Lusignan 2. **2B:** Cabrera 14, Castro 11, Chavez 3, Garzillo 39, Goodman 5, Gould 1, Whiting 5. **3B:** Cabrera 1, Gould 35, Lara 3, Lopez 39, Munden 1. **SS:** Castro 54, Gould 18, Lara 5, Whiting 1. **OF:** Bird 52, Fernandez Jr. 5, Goodman 9, Knapp 50, Olis 22, Santos 48, White 44.

GCL MARLINS
GULF COAST LEAGUE

ROOKIE

Batting

Batting	B-T	HT	WT	DOB	AVG	vLH	vRH	G	AB	R	H	2B	3B	HR	RBI	BB	HBP	SH	SF	SO	SB	CS	SLG	OBP
Bautista, Welbin	R-R	6-0	180	5-7-98	.000	.000	—	1	1	0	0	0	0	0	0	0	0	0	0	0	0	0	.000	.000
Bennett, Terry	L-L	5-11	195	9-3-96	.209	.150	.222	33	110	14	23	3	1	2	10	7	2	2	1	31	3	2	.309	.267
Berry, Branden	R-R	6-4	225	5-19-93	.313	.286	.318	22	80	11	25	5	0	2	19	9	3	0	0	12	2	2	.450	.402
Brooks, Matt	L-R	6-0	185	3-21-96	.197	.087	.218	42	142	24	28	4	0	0	12	18	3	4	1	45	2	2	.225	.299
Cohen, Justin	R-R	6-0	190	9-26-96	.267	.000	.286	4	15	2	4	1	0	0	1	2	0	1	0	6	0	1	.333	.353
Daly, Zach	L-L	6-3	175	12-13-93	.183	.000	.227	28	109	14	20	4	3	2	14	8	0	0	0	31	7	2	.330	.239
Davis, Mason	B-R	5-9	175	1-11-93	.375	.000	.500	4	8	3	3	1	1	0	0	1	0	0	0	1	0	1	.750	.444
Foley, Matt	R-R	6-4	230	4-15-94	.250	.000	.269	12	28	6	7	0	0	0	2	5	2	0	1	7	0	1	.250	.389
2-team total (1 Braves)					.258		—	13	31	7	8	0	0	0	2	5	2	0	1	9	0	1	.258	.385
Garrett, Stone	R-R	6-2	195	11-22-95	.143	—	.143	3	7	1	1	0	0	0	0	2	0	0	0	3	1	0	.143	.333
Garzillo, Mike	R-R	5-11	185	2-11-94	.313	.429	.280	9	32	4	10	1	1	0	2	5	1	0	0	7	1	2	.406	.421
Gauntt, David	R-R	6-0	200	6-16-93	.161	.214	.152	32	93	7	15	4	1	2	8	14	6	0	0	37	0	0	.290	.310
Gomes, Juan	R-R	6-2	180	12-25-91	.200	—	.200	3	5	2	1	0	0	0	1	0	1	0	1	1	0	0	.200	.286
Gutierrez, Eric	L-L	5-10	205	12-28-93	.600	1.000	.333	1	5	2	3	1	0	1	3	0	0	0	0	0	0	0	1.400	.600
Jones, Thomas	R-R	6-4	195	12-9-97	.234	.333	.230	19	64	11	15	3	1	0	6	11	4	1	0	20	6	2	.313	.380
Lovett, James	R-R	6-3	200	7-1-96	.000	—	.000	3	12	0	0	0	0	0	0	0	0	0	0	2	0	0	.000	.077
Lusignan, Colby	L-R	6-4	230	11-15-92	.319	.364	.314	31	113	15	36	9	1	2	17	20	1	1	1	35	1	2	.469	.422
Millan, J.C.	R-R	6-0	185	1-18-96	.177	.000	.182	24	79	9	14	2	1	0	8	5	3	1	1	9	2	1	.228	.250
Nelson, James	R-R	6-2	180	10-18-97	.284	.231	.294	43	162	26	46	10	0	1	24	14	2	0	2	30	7	3	.364	.344
Olis, Walker	R-R	6-2	190	5-4-94	.245	.158	.265	28	102	15	25	3	2	0	11	15	4	2	1	13	9	2	.314	.361
Pintor, Luis	R-R	5-9	170	6-6-95	.257	.364	.245	31	109	11	28	5	0	0	12	13	3	2	3	19	7	1	.303	.344
Pollman, Gunner	R-R	6-2	210	2-3-95	.250	.000	.286	14	32	4	8	1	0	0	7	6	2	0	0	10	0	0	.281	.400
Reyes, Yefry	L-R	5-10	160	12-10-96	.165	.100	.165	29	89	8	14	2	0	0	9	9	0	3	2	9	9	3	.180	.230
Reynolds, Sean	L-R	6-7	205	4-19-98	.155	.056	.169	42	148	17	23	2	2	0	11	22	0	1	2	64	3	3	.196	.262
Rindfleisch, Jarrett	R-R	6-1	225	9-4-95	.313	.000	.333	5	16	3	5	2	0	0	2	3	0	0	0	3	1	0	.438	.421
Rivera, Marcos	R-R	6-1	160	5-13-97	.203	.167	.212	43	123	17	25	3	1	0	7	19	1	0	0	41	2	1	.244	.315
Soto, Sleyter	R-R	6-2	195	8-14-97	.276	.167	.283	33	98	9	27	2	1	0	11	9	2	0	2	12	0	1	.316	.311
Vigil, Rodrigo	R-R	6-0	165	1-3-93	.182	.250	.143	4	11	1	2	1	0	0	1	1	0	0	0	2	0	0	.273	.308

Pitching

Pitching	B-T	HT	WT	DOB	W	L	ERA	G	GS	CG	SV	IP	H	R	ER	HR	BB	SO	AVG	vLH	vRH	K/9	BB/9
Beggs, Dustin	R-R	6-3	180	6-14-93	0	0	9.00	1	0	0	0	1	2	1	1	0	0	0	.667	—	.667	0.00	0.00
Cabrera, Edward	R-R	6-4	175	4-13-98	2	6	4.21	11	7	0	0	47	54	24	22	1	10	28	.289	.359	.252	5.36	1.91
Cosart, Jarred	R-R	6-3	205	5-25-90	0	1	6.00	1	1	0	0	3	5	2	2	0	1	2	.357	.000	.455	3.00	0.00
Cuello, Eliezer	R-R	6-2	195	11-18-96	1	1	2.65	11	4	0	0	37	36	13	11	0	13	30	.252	.212	.275	7.23	3.13
Delgado, Victor	R-R	6-2	185	2-3-95	1	1	5.79	5	1	0	0	9	12	6	6	0	3	6	.364	.333	.375	5.79	1.93
Diaz, Obed	R-R	6-2	185	5-5-94	0	2	5.40	12	0	0	0	17	19	10	10	0	5	12	.275	.222	.294	6.48	2.70
Effertz, Joel	R-R	6-3	235	9-27-90	0	1	1.50	5	2	0	0	6	4	1	1	0	2	5	.222	.250	.200	7.50	3.00
Fischer, Kyle	R-R	6-3	205	2-11-91	0	0	0.00	4	0	0	1	5	1	0	0	0	4	.063	.100	.000	7.20	0.00
Garcia, Jarlin	L-L	6-3	215	1-18-93	0	0	0.00	3	3	0	0	4	1	0	0	0	0	6	.077	.000	.091	13.50	0.00

MIAMI MARLINS

Pitching	B-T	HT	WT	DOB	W	L	ERA	G	GS	CG	SV	IP	H	R	ER	HR	BB	SO	AVG	vLH	vRH	K/9	BB/9
Garcia, Javier	R-R	6-2	230	2-26-98	1	0	0.00	1	0	0	0	4	4	0	0	0	1	0	.267	.500	.000	0.00	2.25
Guerrero, Alberto	R-R	6-3	192	12-13-97	4	3	2.63	11	4	0	0	41	32	14	12	1	18	32	.211	.213	.209	7.02	3.95
Guillory, Preston	R-R	6-3	200	8-16-93	0	0	0.68	7	0	0	3	13	7	1	1	1	1	15	.149	.133	.156	10.13	0.68
King, Mike	R-R	6-3	204	5-25-95	1	1	10.80	4	0	0	0	5	11	6	6	0	2	3	.440	.500	.400	5.40	3.60
Lee, Dylan	L-L	6-4	210	8-1-94	0	0	3.00	4	0	0	0	6	3	2	2	0	2	6	.136	.000	.150	9.00	3.00
Mateo, Alex	R-R	6-2	200	1-18-94	0	1	5.40	3	0	0	0	3	4	2	2	0	1	5	.286	.167	.375	13.50	2.70
Mazza, Chris	R-R	6-4	180	10-17-89	1	1	0.00	4	3	0	0	5	2	1	0	0	0	3	.125	.000	.182	5.40	0.00
McKay, Ryan	R-R	6-4	195	9-20-96	0	1	3.72	4	1	0	0	10	15	8	4	1	2	7	.385	.500	.320	6.52	1.86
Mejia, Humberto	R-R	6-3	175	3-3-97	3	3	2.45	10	2	0	0	40	38	15	11	1	8	34	.247	.167	.29	7.59	1.79
Mertz, Michael	R-R	6-2	220	9-24-93	0	0	0.00	3	0	0	0	4	1	0	0	0	0	4	.077	.000	.125	9.00	0.00
Mojica, Luis	R-R	6-1	190	2-18-98	0	1	2.70	13	0	0	0	20	20	7	6	1	7	13	.278	.318	.260	5.85	3.15
Morris, Bryan	L-R	6-3	220	3-28-87	0	1	5.40	3	3	0	0	5	7	3	3	1	0	3	.350	.500	.250	5.40	0.00
Newell, Ryan	R-R	6-2	215	6-18-91	0	0	0.00	6	4	0	0	9	5	3	0	0	4	11	.161	.286	.125	11.00	4.00
Osoria, Aneury	R-R	6-7	170	11-15-93	1	2	2.95	12	0	0	0	21	16	11	7	0	8	21	.208	.292	.170	8.86	3.38
Ovalle, Jeremy	R-R	6-3	185	1-17-97	1	0	1.27	11	2	0	2	28	18	5	4	1	9	19	.194	.219	.180	6.04	2.86
Peace, R.J.	R-R	6-2	175	6-24-97	0	2	2.60	11	0	0	1	28	22	10	8	4	6	17	.216	.159	.259	5.53	1.95
Pineyro, Ivan	R-R	6-1	200	9-29-91	0	0	0.00	3	3	0	0	3	3	0	0	0	0	5	.250	.200	.286	15.00	0.00
Ramsey, Matt	R-R	5-11	205	9-24-89	0	0	3.00	5	4	0	0	6	3	2	2	0	1	9	.150	.111	.182	13.50	1.50
Reed, Remey	R-R	6-5	230	5-5-95	1	0	5.79	3	0	0	0	5	7	3	3	1	1	2	.350	.167	.429	3.86	1.93
Rienzo, Andre	R-R	6-2	195	7-5-88	1	0	0.00	5	3	0	0	6	3	0	0	0	0	9	.143	.333	.067	13.50	0.00
Rodriguez, Manuel	L-L	6-2	160	12-23-96	1	2	5.80	12	4	0	1	36	42	24	23	0	13	23	.294	.167	.319	5.80	3.28
Sadberry, Chris	L-L	6-0	195	11-8-91	2	0	0.82	8	2	0	0	11	5	1	1	0	1	10	.125	.111	.129	8.18	0.82
Smith, Chad	R-R	6-4	200	6-8-95	0	0	7.71	3	0	0	0	2	3	6	2	0	3	3	.250	.200	.286	11.57	0.00
Suggs, Colby	R-R	5-11	235	10-25-91	0	0	6.35	6	2	0	0	6	4	4	4	0	6	3	.200	.444	.000	4.76	9.53
Wells, Hunter	R-R	6-2	170	5-22-95	0	0	0.00	4	0	0	0	4	2	0	0	0	0	2	.167	.25	.000	4.50	0.00
Wheatley, Brent	R-R	6-4	210	8-31-93	0	0	0.00	2	0	0	0	3	1	0	0	1	1	5	.143	.000	.200	15.00	3.00
Williams, Nick	R-R	6-2	225	11-15-91	0	0	36.00	2	0	0	0	1	5	4	4	0	2	0	.625	.750	.500	0.00	18.00

Fielding

C: Bautista 1, Bennett 1, Foley 6, Gauntt 31, Gomes 3, Lovett 1, Pollman 14, Rindfleisch 5, Vigil 3. **1B:** Berry 22, Foley 4, Lusignan 31. **2B:** Brooks 12, Davis 4, Garzillo 9, Millan 9, Pintor 18, Reyes 13. **3B:** Millan 5, Nelson 40, Pintor 1, Reyes 12. **SS:** Pintor 15, Reyes 2, Rivera 43. **OF:** Bennett 30, Daly 27, Garrett 2, Jones 19, Millan 5, Olis 28, Reynolds 41, Soto 26.

DSL MARLINS   ROOKIE
DOMINICAN SUMMER LEAGUE

Batting	B-T	HT	WT	DOB	AVG	vLH	vRH	G	AB	R	H	2B	3B	HR	RBI	BB	HBP	SH	SF	SO	SB	CS	SLG	OBP
Alfonzo, Ezequiel	R-R	5-10	165	8-31-99	.193	.163	.206	42	140	10	27	3	0	0	10	10	3	3	0	21	2	1	.214	.261
Arcaya, Luis	R-R	6-1	170	2-26-99	.157	.125	.167	32	102	5	16	4	0	0	8	12	0	0	1	25	1	0	.196	.243
Arosemena, Felix	R-R	5-9	150	1-17-97	.257	.317	.240	54	191	14	49	4	0	1	23	23	3	5	4	18	4	5	.293	.339
Bautista, Welbin	R-R	6-0	180	5-7-98	.234	.174	.250	33	111	6	26	2	0	0	5	8	2	0	0	23	1	1	.252	.298
Biegel, Bryan	R-R	6-1	170	6-19-98	.111	.000	.147	17	45	6	5	1	0	0	1	8	1	0	0	21	1	0	.133	.259
Borges, Juan	R-R	6-2	160	1-6-98	.100	.000	.125	9	20	2	1	0	0	0	0	5	0	0	0	2	0	1	.100	.400
Brito, Diego	R-R	5-11	190	9-12-98	.257	.263	.255	21	70	11	18	3	0	0	5	10	4	1	0	18	2	1	.300	.381
Capellan, Christian	R-R	6-4	210	12-5-97	.115	.100	.118	25	78	12	9	3	0	0	5	9	5	0	1	28	1	1	.154	.247
Castro, Anderson	R-R	6-3	200	1-10-98	.196	.136	.215	48	179	13	35	4	0	0	12	2	7	2	0	44	4	3	.218	.234
Encarnacion, Yeral	R-R	6-4	219	10-22-97	.218	.375	.154	14	55	6	12	2	1	1	7	1	0	1	0	11	0	0	.345	.232
Garcia, Jhon	R-R	6-0	170	6-18-99	.228	.200	.234	44	136	19	31	7	1	0	13	25	2	0	0	35	2	4	.294	.356
Guaimaro, Albert	L-R	6-0	180	1-17-99	.194	.105	.226	19	72	3	14	2	0	0	9	6	0	0	0	13	2	0	.222	.256
2-team total (23 Red Sox2)					.225	—	—	42	160	12	36	12	1	2	22	12	1	0	1	24	6	4	.331	.282
Nunez, Gerardo	R-R	6-1	180	2-6-98	.250	.000	.286	7	24	1	6	0	0	0	2	2	0	0	0	7	1	2	.250	.308
Prenza, Mario	R-R	6-0	160	2-3-99	.136	.192	.119	32	110	12	15	4	0	1	5	11	0	0	2	48	1	0	.200	.211
Rasquin, Wiklerman	L-L	5-9	145	12-5-98	.183	.167	.189	44	142	13	26	7	2	0	15	6	11	1	2	36	4	3	.261	.273
Reyna, Rosandel	R-R	5-10	165	6-5-97	.323	.321	.324	26	96	15	31	2	5	0	11	12	2	1	2	19	6	7	.448	.402
Reynoso, Ronal	L-R	6-1	165	5-23-98	.189	.100	.224	55	175	26	33	5	1	0	8	31	1	2	0	67	5	5	.229	.314
Rodriguez, Enmanuel	R-R	6-1	165	9-23-98	.165	.174	.163	37	103	6	17	3	0	0	9	11	1	0	0	38	0	0	.194	.252
Sacaria, David	R-R	6-3	195	11-25-96	.174	.174	.175	25	86	7	15	4	1	1	10	4	1	1	3	6	1	1	.279	.287
Vilera, Jose	R-R	5-11	155	11-24-98	.222	.316	.200	28	99	11	22	3	0	0	11	5	2	2	0	29	5	0	.253	.274
Villalobos, Andres	B-R	5-11	160	1-14-98	.206	.143	.222	23	68	3	14	1	0	0	3	8	1	0	0	8	1	1	.221	.299

Pitching	B-T	HT	WT	DOB	W	L	ERA	G	GS	CG	SV	IP	H	R	ER	HR	BB	SO	AVG	vLH	vRH	K/9	BB/9
Alcala, Elkin	R-R	5-11	175	8-2-97	1	1	4.74	4	4	0	0	19	16	10	10	2	2	15	.259	.209	.209	7.11	0.95
Baez, Gabriel	L-L	6-1	185	4-18-98	2	6	3.79	12	11	0	0	55	49	30	23	3	26	43	.239	.143	.242	7.08	4.28
Brito, Raul	R-R	6-1	180	5-23-97	0	0	0.00	3	0	0	0	6	4	2	0	0	2	5	.182	.125	.214	7.50	3.00
Cuevas, Juan	R-R	6-0	195	5-4-94	0	0	0.00	1	0	0	0	1	0	0	0	0	1	0	.000	.276	.000	0.00	6.75
2-team total (17 Astros Blue)					6	5	2.67	18	0	0	2	27	34	9	8	2	4	18	—	—	—	6.00	1.33
De Leon, Anderson	R-R	6-2	170	5-18-95	1	1	11.74	0	0	0	0	15	18	28	20	2	19	14	.273	.222	.292	8.22	11.15
De Oleo, Dailyn	R-R	6-2	190	11-27-97	0	0	9.00	3	0	0	0	4	6	6	4	0	3	4	.316	.143	.417	9.00	6.75
Frias, Julio	L-L	6-2	160	6-1-98	0	5	5.92	13	8	0	0	49	57	51	32	0	37	42	.284	.111	.292	7.77	6.84
Garcia, Willi	R-R	5-11	180	3-14-95	2	4	1.82	13	1	1	2	40	39	20	8	1	10	26	.264	.194	.282	5.90	2.27
Lara, Yeremin	R-R	6-1	160	11-6-98	0	5	2.73	11	0	0	1	30	36	23	9	1	10	20	.290	.268	.301	6.07	3.03
Liriano, Edin	B-L	6-4	185	6-25-97	0	6	3.75	11	9	0	0	50	52	28	21	0	14	32	.264	.300	.260	5.72	2.50
Martinez, Edgar	R-R	6-1	170	7-13-97	0	1	4.50	5	3	0	0	16	20	11	8	0	9	9	.313	.308	.314	6.75	5.06
Mejias, Juan	R-R	6-1	160	12-19-97	0	0	10.54	4	0	0	0	14	22	22	16	1	15	9	.355	.458	.289	5.93	9.88
Moya, Wandy	R-R	6-1	160	10-29-97	0	1	12.00	5	0	0	0	12	19	24	16	1	7	8	.339	.444	.289	6.00	5.25

Pitching	B-T	HT	WT	DOB	W	L	ERA	G	GS	CG	SV	IP	H	R	ER	HR	BB	SO	AVG	vLH	vRH	K/9	BB/9
Rodriguez, Rayner	R-R	6-1	170	9-16-98	0	1	2.84	4	0	0	0	6	4	2	2	0	6	4	.182	.286	.133	5.68	8.53
Sanchez, Jesus	R-R	5-11	150	4-8-99	0	0	23.40	4	1	0	0	5	14	14	13	0	6	2	.538	.500	.550	3.60	10.80
Soriano, George	R-R	6-2	170	3-24-99	1	6	3.56	17	9	0	2	56	49	33	22	3	28	56	.232	.175	.253	9.05	4.53
Suriel, Edison	L-L	5-10	160	10-24-98	1	8	3.50	14	8	0	0	46	39	27	18	1	36	47	.232	.478	.193	9.13	6.99
Vera, Anderson	R-R	6-3	185	10-14-97	1	4	4.70	11	5	0	0	44	47	29	23	3	13	33	.272	.320	.252	6.75	2.66
Villalobos, Hosnei	R-R	6-1	165	6-3-99	—	—	—	—	—	—	—	—	—	—	—	—	—	—	—	—	—	—	—
Villalobos, Jonaiker	L-L	6-0	160	7-11-99	1	2	4.76	16	1	0	0	40	46	26	21	1	13	32	.288	.400	.280	7.26	2.95
Wilmore, Luis	R-R	6-3	170	7-5-96	0	1	18.00	3	0	0	0	2	3	4	4	1	4	1	.375	.250	.500	4.50	18.00

Fielding

C: Arcaya 24, Bautista 18, Garcia 17, Guaimaro 9, Villalobos 10. **1B:** Alfonzo 3, Arcaya 6, Bautista 11, Capellan 13, Castro 4, Garcia 22, Rodriguez 3, Sacaria 10. **2B:** Alfonzo 14, Arosemena 42, Brito 8, Reyna 6. **3B:** Alfonzo 27, Arosemena 1, Bautista 4, Brito 13, Garcia 4, Nunez 2, Rodriguez 8, Villalobos 13. **SS:** Alfonzo 1, Arosemena 10, Nunez 3, Reynoso 54. **OF:** Bautista 1, Biegel 4, Borges 3, Capellan 5, Castro 39, Encarnacion 13, Guaimaro 8, Prenza 23, Rasquin 38, Reyna 20, Rodriguez 22, Sacaria 4, Vilera 27.

MIAMI MARLINS

Milwaukee Brewers

SEASON IN A SENTENCE: The Brewers weren't competing in 2016, not with the game's lowest payroll, but they found pieces who should be around when Milwaukee is ready to contend again.

HIGH POINT: Milwaukee was never at .500 after April 15, so the focus was more on individual highlights, such as first baseman Chris Carter, who tied for the National League lead with 41 homers, including two the final weekend at Colorado to tie the Rockies' Nolan Arenado. That same weekend, shortstop/third baseman Jonathan Villar stole two bases to finish with 62, which led the majors.

LOW POINT: Milwaukee never lost more than six games in a row, with both six-game skids coming in August, the team's worst month with a 10-20 record. The second skid included a 9-6 loss to the Pirates as Milwaukee blew a 5-1 lead that starter Jimmy Nelson, in the midst of a 16-loss season, couldn't hold.

NOTABLE ROOKIES: Veteran minor leaguer Junior Guerra, 31, unexpectedly became Milwaukee's top starter, going 9-3, 2.81 in a career-high 121.2 innings. Fellow rookie Zach Davies was the team's wins leader in an 11-7, 3.97 campaign. Top prospect Orlando Arcia pushed Villar to third base but had an uninspiring debut (.219/.273/.358), while 26-year-old rookie Keon Broxton looked like a potential keeper, showing power and speed in a 75-game trial.

KEY TRANSACTIONS: First-year GM David Stearns stayed busy, making 17 trades and 10 waiver claims in his first year on the job, among other moves. The biggest deal was his midseason trade of catcher Jonathan Lucroy and closer Jeremy Jeffress to the Rangers for a passel of prospects, including outfielders Lewis Brinson and Ryan Cordell and righthander Luis Ortiz. Milwaukee also got a two-time first-rounder, righthander Phil Bickford, plus catcher Andrew Susac, from the Giants for lefthander Will Smith.

DOWN ON THE FARM: After the farm system had a big year in 2015, Milwaukee stumbled in '16, with its domestic affiliates going just 302-379 (.443), second-worst in baseball. Prospects such as Arcia, righthander Jorge Lopez (3-11, 5.78 overall) and outfielder Brett Phillips (.229/.332/.397) faltered, while high Class A Brevard County lost a minor league-worst 97 games. Shortstop Isan Diaz led the low Class A Midwest League with 20 homers, while righthander Brandon Woodruff went 14-9, 2.68 and led the minors with 173 strikeouts.

OPENING DAY PAYROLL: $ 69,282,737 (28th)

PLAYERS OF THE YEAR

MAJOR LEAGUE
Ryan Braun
of
.305/.365/.538
30 HR, 91 RBI
23 2B, 16 SB

MINOR LEAGUE
Isan Diaz
ss
(low Class A)
.264/.358/.469
20 HR, 75 RBI

ORGANIZATION LEADERS

BATTING *Minimum 250 AB

MAJORS

* AVG	Ryan Braun	.305
* OPS	Ryan Braun	.903
HR	Chris Carter	41
RBI	Chris Carter	94

MINORS

* AVG	Kyle Wren, Biloxi, Col. Springs	.322
* OBP	Kyle Wren, Biloxi, Col. Springs	.412
* SLG	Isan Diaz, Wisconsin	.469
* OPS	Isan Diaz, Wisconsin	.827
R	Kyle Wren, Biloxi, Col. Springs	75
H	Dustin DeMuth, Brevard County, Biloxi	136
TB	Isan Diaz, Wisconsin	238
2B	Isan Diaz, Wisconsin	34
3B	Yadiel Rivera, Col. Springs	8
3B	Kyle Wren, Biloxi, Col. Springs	8
HR	Isan Diaz, Wisconsin	20
RBI	Isan Diaz, Wisconsin	75
BB	Michael Reed, Col. Springs	74
SO	Brett Phillips, Biloxi	154
SB	Johnny Davis, Brevard County, Biloxi	32

PITCHING #Minimum 75 IP

MAJORS

W	Zach Davies	11
# ERA	Zach Davies	3.97
SO	Jimmy Nelson	140
SV	Jeremy Jeffress	27

MINORS

W	Brandon Woodruff, Brevard County, Biloxi	14
L	Bubba Derby, Brevard County	13
# ERA	Brandon Woodruff, Brevard County, Biloxi	2.68
G	Stephen Peterson, Biloxi, Col. Springs	58
GS	Brandon Woodruff, Brevard County, Biloxi	28
SV	Nate Griep, Wisconsin	23
	Stephen Kohlscheen, Biloxi	23
IP	Brandon Woodruff, Brevard County, Biloxi	158
BB	Jorge Lopez, Col. Springs, Biloxi	71
SO	Brandon Woodruff, Brevard County, Biloxi	173
# AVG	Brandon Woodruff, Brevard County, Biloxi	.209

General Manager: David Stearns. **Farm Director:** Tom Flanagan. **Scouting Director:** Ray Montgomery.

Class	Team	League	W	L	PCT	Finish	Manager
Majors	Milwaukee Brewers	National	73	89	.451	10th (15)	Craig Counsell
Triple-A	Colorado Springs Sky Sox	Pacific Coast	67	71	.486	11th (16)	Rick Sweet
Double-A	Biloxi Shuckers	Southern	72	67	.518	6th (10)	Mike Guerrero
High A	Brevard County Manatees	Florida State	40	97	.292	12th (12)	Joe Ayrault
Low A	Wisconsin Timber Rattlers	Midwest	71	69	.507	8th (16)	Matt Erickson
Rookie	Helena Brewers	Pioneer	28	46	.378	8th (8)	Nestor Corredor
Rookie	Brewers	Arizona	24	29	.453	12th (14)	Tony Diggs
Overall 2016 Minor League Record			302	379	.443	29th (30)	

ORGANIZATION STATISTICS

MILWAUKEE BREWERS
NATIONAL LEAGUE

Batting	B-T	HT	WT	DOB	AVG	vLH	vRH	G	AB	R	H	2B	3B	HR	RBI	BB	HBP	SH	SF	SO	SB	CS	SLG	OBP
Arcia, Orlando	R-R	6-0	165	8-4-94	.219	.283	.200	55	201	21	44	10	3	4	17	15	0	0	0	47	8	0	.358	.273
Braun, Ryan	R-R	6-2	205	11-17-83	.305	.344	.293	135	511	80	156	23	3	30	91	46	4	0	3	98	16	5	.538	.365
Broxton, Keon	R-R	6-3	195	5-7-90	.242	.289	.210	75	207	28	50	10	1	9	19	36	0	1	0	88	23	4	.430	.354
Carter, Chris	R-R	6-4	245	12-18-86	.222	.224	.222	160	549	84	122	27	1	41	94	76	9	0	10	206	3	1	.499	.321
Elmore, Jake	R-R	5-10	180	6-15-87	.218	.255	.161	59	78	7	17	2	0	4	17	2	2	0	17	2	3	.244	.371
Flores, Ramon	L-L	5-10	190	3-26-92	.205	.226	.198	104	249	18	51	8	0	2	19	31	2	3	4	58	3	0	.261	.294
Gennett, Scooter	L-R	5-10	185	5-1-90	.263	.260	.264	136	498	58	131	30	1	14	56	38	2	1	2	114	8	1	.412	.317
Hill, Aaron	R-R	5-11	200	3-21-82	.283	.263	.292	78	254	34	72	11	0	8	29	30	2	0	4	43	4	2	.421	.359
Lucroy, Jonathan	R-R	6-0	200	6-13-86	.299	.238	.319	95	338	46	101	17	3	13	50	33	1	0	4	70	5	0	.482	.359
Maldonado, Martin	R-R	6-0	230	8-16-86	.202	.237	.188	76	208	21	42	7	0	8	21	35	6	3	1	56	1	0	.351	.332
Middlebrooks, Will	R-R	6-3	220	9-9-88	.111	.300	.000	10	27	2	3	0	0	1	4	0	0	0	3	13	0	0	.111	.226
Nieuwenhuis, Kirk	L-R	6-3	225	8-7-87	.209	.135	.218	125	335	38	70	18	1	13	44	56	1	0	0	133	8	9	.385	.324
Perez, Hernan	R-R	6-1	215	3-26-91	.272	.278	.269	123	404	50	110	18	3	13	56	18	1	3	4	94	34	7	.428	.302
Pina, Manny	R-R	6-0	215	6-5-87	.254	.200	.283	33	71	4	18	4	0	2	12	10	0	0	0	15	0	1	.394	.346
Pinto, Josmil	R-R	5-11	200	3-31-89	.000	—	.000	6	5	1	0	0	0	0	0	1	0	0	0	4	0	0	.000	.167
Presley, Alex	L-L	5-10	195	7-25-85	.198	.231	.189	47	116	12	23	2	0	3	11	11	1	0	1	25	0	2	.293	.271
Reed, Michael	R-R	6-0	215	11-18-92	.182	.167	.188	8	22	3	4	0	0	0	2	0	0	0	1	7	1	0	.182	.250
Rivera, Yadiel	R-R	6-3	185	5-2-92	.212	.208	.214	35	66	12	14	4	0	0	3	2	0	3	0	20	0	1	.273	.235
Santana, Domingo	R-R	6-5	220	8-5-92	.256	.312	.231	77	246	34	63	14	0	11	32	32	2	0	1	91	2	3	.447	.345
Susac, Andrew	R-R	6-1	215	3-22-90	.235	1.000	.188	9	17	3	4	1	0	1	2	2	0	0	0	5	0	0	.471	.316
Villar, Jonathan	B-R	6-1	215	5-2-91	.285	.309	.276	156	589	92	168	38	3	19	63	79	2	5	4	174	62	18	.457	.369
Walsh, Colin	B-R	6-1	200	9-26-89	.085	.000	.108	38	47	4	4	1	0	0	2	15	1	0	0	22	0	0	.106	.317
Wilkins, Andy	L-R	6-1	225	9-13-88	.125	.000	.150	26	24	3	3	1	0	0	2	2	0	0	0	9	0	0	.292	.222

Pitching	B-T	HT	WT	DOB	W	L	ERA	G	GS	CG	SV	IP	H	R	ER	HR	BB	SO	AVG	vLH	vRH	K/9	BB/9
Anderson, Chase	R-R	6-1	200	11-30-87	9	11	4.39	31	30	0	0	152	155	83	74	28	53	120	.266	.203	.313	7.12	3.15
Barnes, Jacob	R-R	6-2	220	4-14-90	0	1	2.70	27	0	0	1	27	24	9	8	1	6	26	.245	.318	.185	8.78	2.03
Blazek, Michael	R-R	6-0	205	3-16-89	3	1	5.66	41	0	0	0	41	52	31	26	7	27	36	.311	.292	.324	7.84	5.88
Boyer, Blaine	R-R	6-3	225	7-11-81	2	4	3.95	61	0	0	1	66	80	30	29	4	17	26	.305	.298	.312	3.55	2.32
Capuano, Chris	L-L	6-2	225	8-19-78	1	1	4.13	16	0	0	0	24	23	11	11	7	15	27	.256	.212	.281	10.13	5.63
Cravy, Tyler	R-R	6-2	220	7-13-89	0	1	2.86	20	2	0	0	28	21	9	9	3	12	22	.208	.25	.163	6.99	3.81
Davies, Zach	R-R	6-0	155	2-7-93	11	7	3.97	28	28	0	0	163	166	79	72	20	38	135	.263	.272	.255	7.44	2.09
Freeman, Sam	R-L	5-11	180	6-24-87	0	0	12.91	7	0	0	0	8	13	11	11	2	9	8	.394	.333	.429	9.39	10.57
Garza, Matt	R-R	6-4	220	11-26-83	6	8	4.51	19	19	0	0	102	117	67	51	11	36	70	.283	.292	.274	6.20	3.19
Goforth, David	R-R	5-10	205	10-11-88	0	0	10.97	10	0	0	0	11	18	14	13	3	4	9	.353	.381	.333	7.59	3.38
Guerra, Junior	R-R	6-0	205	1-16-85	9	3	2.81	20	20	0	0	122	94	40	38	10	43	100	.213	.191	.231	7.40	3.18
Jeffress, Jeremy	R-R	6-0	205	9-21-87	2	2	2.22	47	0	0	27	45	45	13	11	2	11	35	.262	.316	.215	7.05	2.22
Jungmann, Taylor	R-R	6-6	210	12-18-89	0	5	7.76	8	6	0	0	27	30	24	23	4	17	18	.291	.289	.293	6.08	5.74
Kirkman, Michael	L-L	6-4	215	9-18-86	0	0	9.00	1	0	0	0	1	1	1	1	0	1	1	.250	.5	0	9.00	9.00
2-team total (1 San Diego)					0	0	19.29	2	0	0	0	2	7	5	5	0	1	1	—	—	—	3.86	3.86
Knebel, Corey	R-R	6-4	220	11-26-91	1	4	4.68	35	0	0	2	33	32	20	17	3	16	38	.252	.172	.333	10.47	4.41
Magnifico, Damien	R-R	6-1	195	5-24-91	0	0	6.00	3	0	0	0	3	2	2	2	0	3	0	.200	.167	.25	0.00	9.00
Marinez, Jhan	R-R	6-1	200	8-12-88	0	1	3.22	43	0	0	0	59	60	24	21	3	21	47	.265	.26	.269	7.21	3.22
Nelson, Jimmy	R-R	6-6	250	6-5-89	8	16	4.62	32	32	0	0	179	186	108	92	25	86	140	.268	.252	.283	7.03	4.32
Pena, Ariel	R-R	6-3	245	5-20-89	0	0	27.00	1	0	0	0	2	5	5	5	3	2	0	.556	.6	.5	0.00	10.80
Peralta, Wily	R-R	6-1	255	5-8-89	7	11	4.86	23	23	0	0	128	152	73	69	19	43	93	.305	.307	.304	6.56	3.03
Ramirez, Neil	R-R	6-4	215	5-25-89	0	0	10.80	2	0	0	0	2	2	2	2	0	3	2	.286	.2	.5	16.20	9.00
2-team total (8 Chicago)					0	0	5.79	10	0	0	0	9	7	6	6	3	8	13	—	—	—	12.54	7.71
Rowen, Ben	R-R	6-4	200	11-15-88	0	0	15.00	4	0	0	0	3	10	6	5	0	0	2	.526	.25	.6	6.00	0.00
Scahill, Rob	R-R	6-2	220	2-15-87	0	0	2.45	16	0	0	0	18	16	5	5	1	3	14	.225	.323	.15	6.87	1.47
2-team total (15 Pittsburgh)					0	0	3.38	31	0	0	0	35	34	14	13	2	9	27	—	—	—	7.01	2.34
Smith, Will	R-L	6-5	265	7-10-89	1	3	3.68	27	0	0	0	28	13	13	9	3	22	48	.225	.316	.143	9.00	3.68
2-team total (26 San Francisco)					2	4	3.35	53	0	0	0	40	31	19	15	3	18	48	—	—	—	10.71	4.02
Suter, Brent	R-L	6-5	195	8-29-89	2	2	3.32	14	2	0	0	22	25	8	8	3	5	15	.298	.394	.235	6.23	2.08

Pitching

Pitching	B-T	HT	WT	DOB	W	L	ERA	G	GS	CG	SV	IP	H	R	ER	HR	BB	SO	AVG	vLH	vRH	K/9	BB/9
Thornburg, Tyler	R-R	5-11	190	9-29-88	8	5	2.15	67	0	0	13	67	38	19	16	6	25	90	.162	.130	.185	12.09	3.36
Torres, Carlos	R-R	6-1	180	10-22-82	3	3	2.73	72	0	0	2	82	65	26	25	8	30	78	.217	.222	.212	8.53	3.28

Fielding

Catcher	PCT	G	PO	A	E	DP	PB
Lucroy	.991	82	574	53	6	5	5
Maldonado	.987	69	486	39	7	3	5
Pina	.992	17	105	15	1	1	0
Susac	.969	6	28	3	1	1	0

First Base	PCT	G	PO	A	E	DP
Carter	.992	155	1316	73	11	122
Flores	1.000	2	3	0	0	0
Lucroy	1.000	6	40	0	0	2
Perez	1.000	6	35	9	0	5
Wilkins	.917	3	11	0	1	1

Second Base	PCT	G	PO	A	E	DP
Elmore	1.000	3	4	5	0	2
Gennett	.975	127	206	344	14	73

	PCT	G	PO	A	E	DP	PB
Hill	1.000	20	32	49	0	8	
Perez	.955	11	18	24	2	8	
Rivera	.962	13	21	29	2	7	
Villar	1.000	11	16	22	0	5	
Walsh	1.000	1	1	0	0	0	

Third Base	PCT	G	PO	A	E	DP
Elmore	.818	4	1	8	2	1
Hill	.985	59	38	97	2	10
Middlebrooks	1.000	8	6	19	0	3
Perez	.933	60	29	96	9	9
Rivera	.833	15	5	10	3	2
Villar	.881	42	30	59	12	3
Walsh	.958	11	6	17	1	2

Shortstop	PCT	G	PO	A	E	DP
Arcia	.981	53	98	160	5	31
Perez	1.000	3	1	5	0	0
Rivera	1.000	5	7	11	0	2
Villar	.965	108	152	321	17	67

Outfield	PCT	G	PO	A	E	DP
Braun	.987	127	209	12	3	3
Broxton	.973	68	143	0	4	0
Elmore	1.000	20	14	0	0	0
Flores	.993	83	134	4	1	0
Nieuwenhuis	.985	109	190	8	3	1
Perez	.979	46	94	1	2	0
Presley	.982	28	55	1	1	0
Reed	.950	7	18	1	1	0
Santana	.982	67	106	2	2	0
Walsh	—	2	0	0	0	0
Wilkins	—	1	0	0	0	0

COLORADO SPRINGS SKY SOX

TRIPLE-A

PACIFIC COAST LEAGUE

Batting	B-T	HT	WT	DOB	AVG	vLH	vRH	G	AB	R	H	2B	3B	HR	RBI	BB	HBP	SH	SF	SO	SB	CS	SLG	OBP
Arcia, Orlando	R-R	6-0	165	8-4-94	.267	.274	.265	100	404	59	108	19	6	8	53	29	3	2	2	77	15	8	.403	.320
Berberet, Parker	R-R	6-3	210	10-20-89	.125	.000	.143	4	8	0	1	0	0	0	0	0	0	0	0	3	0	0	.125	.125
Brinson, Lewis	R-R	6-3	195	5-8-94	.382	.300	.406	23	89	14	34	9	0	4	20	2	0	0	2	21	4	2	.618	.387
Broxton, Keon	R-R	6-3	195	5-7-90	.287	.319	.275	47	178	30	51	11	7	8	26	20	1	0	0	60	18	8	.562	.362
Cecchini, Garin	L-R	6-3	220	4-20-91	.271	.250	.278	126	424	50	115	21	5	5	52	33	4	2	6	64	13	5	.380	.325
Cooper, Garrett	R-R	6-6	230	12-25-90	.276	.323	.260	36	127	17	35	5	0	5	20	10	1	0	1	20	0	0	.433	.331
Elmore, Jake	R-R	5-10	180	6-15-87	.320	.344	.303	57	150	25	48	3	0	2	19	26	3	2	1	19	13	4	.380	.428
Flores, Ramon	L-L	5-10	190	3-26-92	.250	.167	.273	8	28	3	7	1	0	1	2	2	0	0	1	7	0	0	.393	.290
Garcia, Rene	R-R	6-0	205	3-21-90	.290	.267	.298	17	62	6	18	4	0	0	8	1	0	0	1	6	0	0	.355	.297
Guez, Ben	R-R	5-11	180	1-24-87	.171	.158	.182	19	41	3	7	3	0	1	6	7	1	0	1	23	3	1	.317	.300
Macias, Brandon	R-R	5-10	185	10-10-88	.203	.143	.233	31	64	5	13	1	0	2	10	2	1	1	0	9	0	0	.313	.239
McKenry, Michael	R-R	5-10	205	3-4-85	.250	.125	.292	14	32	6	8	2	0	1	6	15	1	0	0	8	0	0	.406	.500
3-team total (24 Memphis, 13 Round Rock)					.290	—		51	155	35	45	12	4	6	35	40	3	0	1	40	2	2	.535	.442
Middlebrooks, Will	R-R	6-3	220	9-9-88	.282	.227	.306	68	248	38	70	22	2	10	47	9	2	1	4	59	1	1	.508	.308
Orf, Nathan	R-R	5-9	180	2-2-90	.288	.246	.300	89	326	50	94	19	3	2	37	32	10	9	4	47	6	3	.383	.366
Perez, Hernan	R-R	6-1	215	3-26-91	.339	.440	.270	16	62	10	21	4	1	1	11	3	0	1	1	9	3	1	.484	.364
Peterson, Shane	L-L	6-0	225	2-11-88	.347	.412	.313	15	49	11	17	6	1	1	7	6	1	0	1	6	4	0	.694	.429
Pina, Manny	R-R	6-0	215	6-5-87	.329	.373	.312	63	237	35	78	21	3	5	43	17	1	3	4	39	1	1	.506	.371
Pinto, Josmil	R-R	5-11	225	3-31-89	.308	.241	.333	86	286	46	88	21	3	11	51	26	0	0	3	67	0	0	.517	.362
Presley, Alex	L-L	5-10	195	7-25-85	.344	.429	.320	9	32	5	11	2	1	1	3	3	0	0	0	7	1	0	.563	.400
Reed, Michael	R-R	6-0	215	11-18-92	.248	.227	.256	121	411	68	102	20	2	8	45	74	4	0	3	124	20	8	.365	.366
Rivera, Yadiel	R-R	6-3	185	5-2-92	.227	.177	.244	83	304	38	69	7	8	2	41	10	6	2	4	78	4	3	.322	.262
Santana, Domingo	R-R	6-5	220	8-5-92	.556	1.000	.500	3	9	5	5	2	0	0	5	0	0	0	0	3	0	0	.778	.714
Susac, Andrew	R-R	6-1	215	3-22-90	.125	.182	.103	11	40	2	5	1	0	0	3	2	0	0	1	16	0	0	.150	.163
2-team total (58 Sacramento)					.249	—		69	249	30	62	13	1	8	39	26	1	0	6	61	0	0	.406	.316
Weisenburger, Adam	R-R	5-10	185	12-13-88	.077	.000	.125	3	13	1	1	0	0	1	3	0	0	0	0	3	0	0	.308	.077
Wilkins, Andy	L-R	6-1	225	9-13-88	.235	.252	.227	91	327	44	77	20	2	12	56	41	2	0	4	91	3	0	.419	.321
Wren, Kyle	L-L	5-10	175	4-23-91	.339	.333	.341	77	271	54	92	10	6	1	29	42	0	5	2	52	20	4	.432	.425
Young Jr. Eric	B-R	5-10	195	5-25-85	.263	.218	.280	116	289	48	76	9	2	3	30	31	3	4	2	51	23	6	.339	.338

Pitching	B-T	HT	WT	DOB	W	L	ERA	G	GS	CG	SV	IP	H	R	ER	HR	BB	SO	AVG	vLH	vRH	K/9	BB/9
Barnes, Jacob	R-R	6-2	220	4-14-90	2	1	1.21	17	0	0	1	22	14	3	3	1	7	23	.184	.211	.158	9.27	2.82
Blazek, Michael	R-R	6-0	205	3-16-89	0	0	4.32	5	1	0	0	8	10	4	4	0	3	8	.313	.273	.333	8.64	3.24
Burgos, Hiram	R-R	5-11	210	8-4-87	10	10	4.40	27	25	1	0	143	157	76	70	12	55	115	.285	.278	.290	7.22	3.45
Chapman, Jaye	R-R	6-0	195	5-22-87	5	1	5.73	19	0	0	0	22	23	14	14	4	11	23	.261	.257	.264	9.41	4.50
Cravy, Tyler	R-R	6-2	220	7-13-89	3	3	5.91	21	9	0	0	56	56	40	37	5	28	65	.258	.308	.212	10.38	4.47
Davies, Zach	R-R	6-0	155	2-7-93	0	0	2.00	2	2	0	0	9	6	2	2	0	2	11	.176	.071	.250	11.00	2.00
Dillard, Tim	R-R	6-4	220	7-19-83	7	1	5.13	23	3	0	1	47	51	29	27	3	17	53	.277	.345	.216	10.08	3.23
Freeman, Sam	R-L	5-11	180	6-24-87	2	1	5.20	30	3	0	2	55	63	34	32	4	28	46	.293	.271	.303	7.48	4.55
Gagnon, Drew	R-R	6-4	195	6-26-90	2	1	5.56	31	4	0	0	55	60	38	34	4	21	48	.280	.276	.284	7.85	3.44
Goforth, David	R-R	5-10	205	10-11-88	3	4	4.91	42	0	0	2	51	56	30	28	3	35	38	.284	.230	.317	6.66	6.14
Guerra, Junior	R-R	6-0	205	1-16-85	0	2	4.05	5	5	0	0	27	18	12	12	2	11	25	.194	.162	.214	8.44	3.71
Hader, Josh	L-L	6-3	185	4-7-94	1	7	5.22	14	14	0	0	69	63	42	40	5	36	88	.245	.200	.259	11.48	4.70
Hall, Brooks	R-R	6-5	235	6-26-90	1	1	6.94	13	0	0	0	23	32	20	18	5	7	11	.344	.364	.333	4.24	2.70
Jones, Zack	R-R	6-1	195	12-4-90	0	0	18.00	2	0	0	0	1	2	2	2	0	3	0	.500	1.000	.333	0.00	27.00
Jungmann, Taylor	R-R	6-6	210	12-18-89	1	3	9.87	8	8	0	0	31	39	37	34	6	35	24	.312	.305	.318	6.97	10.16
Kirkman, Michael	L-L	6-4	215	9-18-86	1	0	2.81	42	0	0	0	32	40	12	10	2	17	34	.308	.246	.362	9.56	4.78

Pitching

Pitching	B-T	HT	WT	DOB	W	L	ERA	G	GS	CG	SV	IP	H	R	ER	HR	BB	SO	AVG	vLH	vRH	K/9	BB/9
2-team total (5 El Paso)					1	0	3.08	47	0	0	1	38	43	15	13	2	17	40	—	—	—	9.47	4.03
Knebel, Corey	R-R	6-4	220	11-26-91	1	0	1.32	11	2	0	2	14	5	2	2	0	3	14	.122	.077	.143	9.22	1.98
Lambson, Mitch	L-L	6-1	205	7-20-90	2	0	4.15	7	0	0	0	9	5	5	4	1	5	11	.167	.200	.15	11.42	5.19
Lopez, Jorge	R-R	6-3	195	2-10-93	1	7	6.81	17	16	0	0	79	101	66	60	12	55	66	.312	.313	.311	7.49	6.24
Magnifico, Damien	R-R	6-1	195	5-24-91	6	7	4.06	52	0	0	18	62	57	32	28	2	33	61	.246	.273	.226	8.85	4.79
Miller, Jim	R-R	6-1	200	4-28-82	1	0	7.41	10	0	0	0	17	20	16	14	3	11	19	.282	.29	.275	10.06	5.82
Pena, Ariel	R-R	6-3	245	5-20-89	2	2	8.36	16	5	0	0	38	51	36	35	7	32	35	.333	.369	.307	8.36	7.65
Peralta, Wily	R-R	6-1	255	5-8-89	1	3	6.31	10	10	0	0	41	55	31	29	5	17	39	.324	.338	.311	8.49	3.70
Peterson, Stephen	L-L	6-3	210	11-6-87	0	0	6.75	6	0	0	0	7	8	5	5	0	5	4	.296	.250	.316	5.40	6.75
Ross, Austin	R-R	6-2	200	8-12-88	6	2	3.89	47	1	0	0	72	65	32	31	8	23	79	.236	.193	.269	9.92	2.89
Rowen, Ben	R-R	6-4	200	11-15-88	0	0	1.69	8	0	0	0	11	11	2	2	0	3	12	.275	.412	.174	10.13	2.53
Scahill, Rob	R-R	6-2	220	2-15-87	0	0	4.82	8	0	0	0	9	11	5	5	1	5	4	.314	.313	.316	3.86	4.82
Suter, Brent	R-L	6-5	195	8-29-89	6	6	3.50	26	15	0	2	111	129	45	43	5	14	75	.301	.248	.321	6.10	1.14
Wang, Wei-Chung	L-L	6-2	185	4-25-92	1	3	4.85	13	0	0	0	26	32	16	14	2	2	23	.302	.250	.317	7.96	0.69
Wilkerson, Aaron	R-R	6-3	190	5-24-89	2	6	6.42	11	11	0	0	55	67	41	39	5	16	57	.302	.323	.286	9.38	2.63

Fielding

Catcher	PCT	G	PO	A	E	DP	PB
Berberet	1.000	2	15	1	0	0	0
Garcia	.974	17	127	25	4	0	1
McKenry	.991	11	101	6	1	0	1
Pina	.990	57	458	49	5	3	4
Pinto	.988	41	312	17	4	2	5
Susac	.987	10	72	3	1	1	0
Weisenburger	1.000	3	33	3	0	1	0

First Base	PCT	G	PO	A	E	DP
Cecchini	.994	64	474	31	3	52
Cooper	1.000	22	174	9	0	15
Flores	1.000	2	4	1	0	0
Macias	1.000	2	4	1	0	0
Middlebrooks	1.000	7	31	3	0	6
Peterson	1.000	1	2	0	0	0
Pinto	.992	31	225	17	2	20
Wilkins	.993	38	251	16	2	27

Second Base	PCT	G	PO	A	E	DP
Arcia	1.000	7	12	25	0	8
Cecchini	.667	2	2	0	1	0
Elmore	.992	32	55	66	1	19
Macias	1.000	9	7	11	0	0
Orf	.975	63	117	159	7	48
Perez	.969	10	14	17	1	3
Rivera	.962	32	47	103	6	20
Young Jr.	—	1	0	0	0	0

Third Base	PCT	G	PO	A	E	DP
Cecchini	.907	52	34	64	10	6
Elmore	.833	4	1	4	1	0
Macias	1.000	12	6	12	0	0
Middlebrooks	.971	54	33	103	4	5
Orf	.974	20	11	26	1	3
Perez	1.000	6	2	8	0	2
Rivera	.933	9	3	11	1	3
Wilkins	.941	9	5	11	1	1

Shortstop	PCT	G	PO	A	E	DP
Arcia	.965	92	141	272	15	65
Orf	1.000	9	8	33	0	5
Perez	.857	2	0	6	1	0
Rivera	.977	41	55	118	4	28

Outfield	PCT	G	PO	A	E	DP
Brinson	1.000	23	66	0	0	0
Broxton	.971	46	92	7	3	1
Cooper	.833	11	10	0	2	0
Elmore	1.000	17	19	0	0	0
Flores	1.000	8	10	0	0	0
Freeman	—	1	0	0	0	0
Guez	.900	14	18	0	2	0
Peterson	1.000	13	25	2	0	1
Presley	1.000	9	22	0	0	0
Reed	.978	114	177	4	4	1
Santana	.800	3	4	0	1	0
Wilkins	1.000	44	58	3	0	1
Wren	.980	71	93	2	1	0
Young Jr.	1.000	86	110	5	0	0

BILOXI SHUCKERS
SOUTHERN LEAGUE

DOUBLE-A

Batting	B-T	HT	WT	DOB	AVG	vLH	vRH	G	AB	R	H	2B	3B	HR	RBI	BB	HBP	SH	SF	SO	SB	CS	SLG	OBP
Belza, Tom	L-R	6-0	190	7-31-89	.233	.500	.226	31	86	8	20	4	1	1	10	7	1	0	1	24	1	1	.337	.295
2-team total (40 Mobile)					.232	—	—	71	181	18	42	11	1	1	14	17	2	1	1	48	4	3	.320	.303
Berberet, Parker	R-R	6-3	210	10-20-89	.111	.222	.056	12	27	2	3	2	0	1	2	3	0	2	0	10	0	0	.296	.200
Betancourt, Javier	R-R	6-0	180	5-8-95	.224	.213	.228	110	343	23	77	12	3	5	43	29	2	4	5	63	3	1	.321	.285
Cooper, Garrett	R-R	6-6	230	12-25-90	.299	.325	.290	92	301	27	90	22	1	4	49	20	5	0	3	55	3	3	.419	.350
Coulter, Clint	R-R	6-3	222	7-30-93	.337	.222	.364	28	95	16	32	4	0	2	12	4	3	0	0	16	1	0	.442	.382
Davis, Johnny	B-R	5-10	180	2-11-90	.200	.280	.169	69	218	32	57	4	4	1	6	14	2	4	0	63	16	5	.330	.312
DeMuth, Dustin	L-R	6-3	200	7-30-91	.270	.158	.292	34	115	14	31	4	2	0	8	7	5	0	1	32	0	0	.339	.336
Garcia, Omar	R-R	5-11	170	8-1-93	.185	.286	.150	19	27	8	5	0	0	0	2	9	0	1	0	10	5	1	.185	.389
Garcia, Rene	R-R	6-0	205	3-21-90	.225	.226	.225	38	120	9	27	3	0	0	7	0	1	0	1	14	1	2	.250	.268
Houle, Dustin	R-R	6-1	205	11-9-93	.167	—	.167	2	6	1	0	0	0	1	0	0	0	0	1	0	0	.167	.167
Macias, Brandon	R-R	5-10	185	10-10-88	.198	.118	.236	39	106	12	21	7	0	2	9	10	5	0	0	21	0	1	.321	.298
McFarland, Chris	R-R	6-0	190	11-24-92	.185	.162	.195	80	227	18	42	6	0	2	22	9	3	3	4	56	4	2	.238	.222
Middlebrooks, Will	R-R	6-3	220	9-9-88	.500	—	.500	1	2	0	1	0	0	0	1	0	0	0	0	1	0	0	.500	.500
Noriega, Gabriel	R-R	6-2	180	9-13-90	.267	.288	.260	71	236	22	63	9	0	3	14	9	3	6	1	30	3	1	.343	.301
2-team total (31 Mobile)					.251	—	—	102	331	31	83	11	0	4	19	15	3	7	3	54	5	2	.320	.287
Nottingham, Jacob	R-R	6-2	230	4-3-95	.234	.244	.231	112	415	46	97	14	0	11	30	29	8	1	3	138	9	2	.347	.295
Orf, Nathan	R-R	5-9	180	2-1-90	.211	.207	.212	38	128	18	27	4	0	0	5	18	7	1	2	16	3	2	.242	.335
Ortega, Angel	R-R	6-2	170	9-11-93	.235	.218	.240	66	247	15	58	10	0	3	21	3	3	0	1	41	4	3	.312	.252
Phillips, Brett	R-R	6-0	185	5-30-94	.229	.232	.228	124	441	60	101	14	6	16	62	67	2	5	2	154	12	7	.397	.332
Ramirez, Nick	L-L	6-3	225	8-1-89	.206	.098	.229	113	282	34	58	12	1	14	44	46	0	0	1	83	0	0	.404	.316
Roache, Victor	R-R	6-1	225	9-17-91	.243	.173	.281	51	148	19	36	11	1	4	15	21	0	0	0	41	2	0	.412	.337
Santana, Domingo	R-R	6-5	220	8-5-92	.333	.500	.250	3	6	2	2	0	0	1	1	4	0	0	0	1	1	0	.833	.600
Shaw, Nick	R-R	5-11	160	8-25-88	.250	.231	.252	39	116	9	29	4	1	0	14	11	1	2	2	28	2	0	.302	.315
Taylor, Tyrone	R-R	6-0	185	1-22-94	.232	.168	.253	134	465	51	108	15	1	9	34	38	9	7	0	73	9	5	.327	.303
Wren, Kyle	L-L	5-10	175	4-23-91	.283	.300	.280	50	127	21	36	4	2	1	10	21	0	2	1	20	9	8	.370	.383

Pitching	B-T	HT	WT	DOB	W	L	ERA	G	GS	CG	SV	IP	H	R	ER	HR	BB	SO	AVG	vLH	vRH	K/9	BB/9
Archer, Tristan	R-R	6-2	200	10-18-90	4	4	3.42	49	1	0	1	82	83	36	31	4	9	82	.259	.295	.233	9.04	0.99
Barnes, Jacob	R-R	6-2	220	4-14-90	0	0	0.00	3	0	0	0	3	2	0	0	0	4	.182	.167	.200	13.50	0.00	
Bradley, Jed	L-L	6-3	225	6-12-90	3	2	6.20	17	0	0	0	25	33	18	17	2	6	20	.314	.281	.329	7.30	2.19

Pitching	B-T	HT	WT	DOB	W	L	ERA	G	GS	CG	SV	IP	H	R	ER	HR	BB	SO	AVG	vLH	vRH	K/9	BB/9
2-team total (15 Mississippi)					7	5	3.41	32	10	0	0	90	92	42	34	2	29	89	—	—	—	8.93	2.91
Chapman, Jaye	R-R	6-0	195	5-22-87	1	0	0.00	12	0	0	10	11	2	0	0	0	0	15	.056	.000	.091	11.91	0.00
2-team total (22 Montgomery)					4	2	2.84	34	0	0	19	32	19	10	10	1	4	41	—	—	—	11.65	1.14
Gagnon, Drew	R-R	6-4	195	6-26-90	1	0	0.00	5	1	0	1	13	4	0	0	0	4	15	.095	.118	.080	10.13	2.70
Gainey, Preston	R-R	6-3	205	2-13-91	0	0	0.87	9	0	0	0	10	6	2	1	0	7	14	.158	.188	.136	12.19	6.10
Hader, Josh	L-L	6-3	185	4-7-94	2	1	0.95	11	11	0	0	57	38	7	6	1	19	73	.194	.075	.224	11.53	3.00
Hall, Brooks	R-R	6-5	235	6-26-90	5	2	3.48	20	7	0	1	75	64	29	29	6	18	59	.231	.205	.260	7.08	2.16
Houser, Adrian	R-R	6-4	235	2-2-93	3	7	5.25	13	13	0	0	70	76	42	41	5	22	56	.279	.293	.266	7.17	2.82
Johnson, Hobbs	R-L	5-11	230	4-29-91	1	0	6.04	16	0	0	0	25	30	19	17	2	20	19	.294	.219	.329	6.75	7.11
Jungmann, Taylor	R-R	6-6	210	12-18-89	3	4	2.51	13	13	0	0	75	53	24	21	2	35	81	.199	.203	.194	9.68	4.18
Kohlscheen, Stephen	R-R	6-6	235	9-20-88	2	3	2.54	50	0	0	23	50	41	15	14	3	17	67	.225	.294	.165	12.14	3.08
Lambson, Mitch	L-L	6-1	205	7-20-90	0	0	4.26	8	0	0	0	6	7	3	3	1	2	5	.280	.500	.176	7.11	2.84
Lee, Brett	L-L	6-4	210	9-20-90	2	1	7.20	18	0	0	0	20	29	16	16	3	13	8	.337	.219	.407	3.60	5.85
2-team total (6 Chattanooga)					2	1	7.57	24	0	0	0	27	41	25	23	3	16	15	—	—	—	4.94	5.27
Lopez, Jorge	R-R	6-3	195	2-10-93	2	4	3.97	8	8	0	0	45	45	21	20	5	16	47	.260	.197	.304	9.33	3.18
Ortega, Jorge	R-R	6-1	165	6-20-93	1	9	4.99	18	18	0	0	97	112	62	54	10	15	54	.284	.285	.282	4.99	1.39
Ortiz, Luis	R-R	6-3	230	9-22-95	2	2	1.93	6	6	0	0	23	26	7	5	2	10	16	.280	.405	.196	6.17	3.86
Perrin, Jon	R-R	6-5	220	5-23-93	0	1	24.30	1	1	0	0	3	8	10	9	1	3	2	.471	.556	.375	5.40	8.10
Peterson, Stephen	L-L	6-3	195	11-6-87	8	4	2.77	52	0	0	5	55	47	20	17	0	24	49	.239	.202	.272	7.97	3.90
Rincon, Junior	R-R	6-2	185	12-7-91	1	1	3.80	21	0	0	0	24	17	11	10	0	12	29	.198	.184	.208	11.03	4.56
Salas, Javi	R-R	6-4	210	3-20-92	3	2	5.13	13	12	0	0	47	34	30	27	1	38	35	.207	.217	.200	6.65	7.23
Scott, Tayler	R-R	6-3	185	6-1-92	3	2	4.39	24	0	0	1	27	21	15	13	3	14	21	.212	.171	.241	7.09	4.73
Smith, Gage	R-R	6-2	185	2-13-91	2	1	2.87	11	0	0	0	16	17	5	5	1	2	5	.283	.478	.162	2.87	1.15
Smith, Will	R-L	6-5	265	7-10-89	0	0	0.00	1	0	0	0	1	0	0	0	0	0	1	.000	.000	.000	9.00	0.00
Spurlin, Tyler	R-R	6-3	195	6-17-91	1	0	3.48	41	0	0	0	41	36	20	16	0	24	36	.234	.242	.228	7.84	5.23
Tillman, Daniel	R-R	6-1	195	3-14-89	3	0	0.46	14	0	0	6	20	17	1	1	1	6	25	.233	.265	.205	11.44	2.75
Uhen, Josh	R-R	6-4	185	4-7-92	1	0	4.00	4	0	0	0	8	8	0	0	0	2	4	.308	.556	.176	4.70	2.35
Ventura, Angel	R-R	6-2	185	4-7-93	2	4	4.09	11	9	0	1	55	50	30	25	9	25	52	.237	.242	.233	8.51	4.09
Viramontes, Martin	R-R	6-5	225	7-12-89	0	0	8.10	4	0	0	0	7	6	20	6	1	3	2	.167	.154	.182	2.70	10.80
Wang, Wei-Chung	L-L	6-2	185	4-25-92	6	5	3.52	19	19	0	0	107	102	45	42	7	33	91	.258	.220	.271	7.63	2.77
Woodruff, Brandon	R-R	6-4	215	2-10-93	10	8	3.01	20	20	1	0	114	88	39	38	4	30	124	.211	.217	.205	9.82	2.38

Fielding

Catcher	PCT	G	PO	A	E	DP	PB
Berberet	.973	8	66	5	2	0	1
Garcia	.993	37	247	38	2	1	3
Houle	1.000	2	12	1	0	0	0
Nottingham	.983	98	777	76	15	5	21

First Base	PCT	G	PO	A	E	DP
Cooper	.992	59	493	24	4	38
DeMuth	.986	26	205	11	3	17
Garcia	1.000	1	1	1	0	0
Nottingham	1.000	3	19	1	0	3
Ramirez	.994	70	471	37	3	38

Second Base	PCT	G	PO	A	E	DP
Belza	.976	12	15	25	1	5
Betancourt	.973	67	100	185	8	34
DeMuth	—	1	0	0	0	0

	PCT	G	PO	A	E	DP/PB
McFarland	.969	67	96	154	8	29
Noriega	—	1	0	0	0	0
Orf	1.000	9	11	22	0	3
Shaw	.700	2	4	3	3	2

Third Base	PCT	G	PO	A	E	DP
Belza	.889	17	5	11	2	0
Betancourt	.917	13	9	13	2	1
Macias	.959	35	16	54	3	1
Middlebrooks	1.000	1	1	0	0	0
Noriega	.937	57	27	92	8	10
Orf	.969	31	24	71	3	6
Shaw	1.000	1	0	3	0	0

Shortstop	PCT	G	PO	A	E	DP
Betancourt	.940	32	28	81	7	12
Noriega	.962	15	19	31	2	6

	PCT	G	PO	A	E	DP
Orf	1.000	3	3	3	0	1
Ortega	.958	66	93	156	11	41
Shaw	.948	35	30	97	7	14

Outfield	PCT	G	PO	A	E	DP
Belza	1.000	2	1	0	0	0
Cooper	1.000	27	33	2	0	1
Coulter	.956	25	42	1	2	0
Davis	.992	57	120	7	1	0
DeMuth	1.000	2	2	0	0	0
Garcia	1.000	10	8	0	0	0
Garcia	1.000	1	1	0	0	0
Phillips	.993	119	257	9	2	3
Roache	.984	40	60	2	1	0
Santana	1.000	3	3	1	0	0
Taylor	1.000	129	242	7	0	1
Wren	.961	39	45	4	2	1

BREVARD COUNTY MANATEES

HIGH CLASS A

FLORIDA STATE LEAGUE

Batting	B-T	HT	WT	DOB	AVG	vLH	vRH	G	AB	R	H	2B	3B	HR	RBI	BB	HBP	SH	SF	SO	SB	CS	SLG	OBP
Allemand, Blake	B-R	5-10	175	7-1-92	.238	.232	.240	71	265	23	63	7	1	4	31	20	9	2	2	50	2	1	.317	.311
Collymore, Malik	R-R	6-0	195	4-29-95	.167	.224	.136	59	192	22	32	8	0	0	14	1	1	0	84	9	1	.208	.227
Coulter, Clint	R-R	6-3	222	7-30-93	.220	.200	.228	87	327	26	72	13	3	6	32	20	11	0	4	71	2	1	.333	.285
Cuas, Jose	R-R	6-0	195	6-28-94	.170	.175	.168	120	388	35	66	13	1	4	27	44	5	4	0	144	5	1	.240	.263
Davis, Johnny	B-R	5-10	180	4-26-90	.295	.230	.321	58	217	35	64	6	2	0	14	31	3	3	0	50	16	10	.341	.390
DeMuth, Dustin	L-R	6-3	200	7-30-91	.287	.324	.273	96	366	42	105	21	2	6	43	28	14	0	3	104	2	4	.404	.358
Denson, David	L-R	6-3	254	1-17-95	.125	.190	.098	21	72	1	9	1	0	0	2	9	0	0	0	25	1	2	.139	.222
Diaz, Brandon	R-R	5-11	175	4-14-95	.166	.242	.119	57	163	16	27	4	0	0	9	19	2	2	0	68	7	4	.190	.261
Garcia, Omar	R-R	5-11	170	8-1-93	.213	.258	.202	45	150	15	32	1	1	0	6	12	2	4	0	23	6	4	.233	.280
Gennett, Scooter	L-R	5-10	185	5-1-90	.333	.000	.400	6	6	1	2	0	0	0	1	0	0	0	2	0	1	.333	.429
Ghelfi, Mitch	B-R	5-11	185	9-24-92	.248	.188	.290	30	117	9	29	10	0	0	12	1	3	0	22	1	0	.333	.273
Houle, Dustin	R-R	6-1	205	11-9-93	.202	.128	.233	94	317	18	64	10	1	1	38	6	2	6	1	1	1	1	.249	.293
Iskenderian, George	R-R	6-1	190	2-28-94	.260	.269	.256	90	331	36	86	9	1	5	24	21	4	0	0	63	8	5	.338	.312
McCall, Greg	L-R	6-1	195	12-25-91	.180	.167	.184	21	61	5	11	1	0	3	7	2	0	1	0	18	0	0	.344	.206
Ortega, Angel	R-R	6-2	170	9-11-93	.275	.308	.262	67	265	23	73	6	1	1	22	17	0	6	2	53	8	1	.317	.317
Pena, Fidel	R-R	5-11	170	7-19-91	.247	.278	.234	88	304	31	75	7	2	4	32	19	1	1	2	67	3	6	.322	.291
Ray, Corey	L-L	5-11	185	9-22-94	.247	.218	.261	57	231	24	57	13	2	5	17	20	1	0	2	54	9	5	.385	.307
Rijo, Wendell	R-R	5-11	170	9-4-95	.202	.161	.223	50	183	17	37	7	0	1	15	13	1	4	0	44	6	1	.257	.259
Rubio, Elvis	R-R	6-3	215	7-2-94	.216	.254	.199	108	393	29	85	12	0	6	38	20	8	1	1	95	6	1	.293	.268

Batting

Batting	B-T	HT	WT	DOB	AVG	vLH	vRH	G	AB	R	H	2B	3B	HR	RBI	BB	HBP	SH	SF	SO	SB	CS	SLG	OBP
Smith-Brennan, Taylor	R-R	6-0	210	1-31-92	.176	.217	.165	35	108	13	19	4	0	2	10	22	0	0	1	38	2	1	.269	.313
Weisenburger, Adam	R-R	5-10	185	12-13-88	.292	.500	.273	8	24	1	7	0	0	0	1	6	1	0	0	10	0	1	.292	.452
York, Trey	R-R	6-2	190	4-4-94	.333	.364	.300	7	21	5	7	1	2	0	1	4	0	0	0	2	1	1	.571	.440

Pitching

Pitching	B-T	HT	WT	DOB	W	L	ERA	G	GS	CG	SV	IP	H	R	ER	HR	BB	SO	AVG	vLH	vRH	K/9	BB/9
Bickford, Phil	R-R	6-4	200	7-10-95	2	1	3.67	6	5	0	0	27	26	12	11	1	15	30	.252	.19	.295	10.00	5.00
Derby, Bubba	L-R	5-11	185	2-24-94	6	13	5.59	26	25	0	0	132	165	91	82	17	47	109	.306	.297	.312	7.43	3.20
Diplan, Marcos	R-R	6-0	160	9-18-96	1	2	4.98	10	6	1	0	43	47	26	24	4	18	40	.276	.256	.295	8.31	3.74
Earls, Kaleb	R-R	6-5	185	3-17-93	0	0	7.71	18	0	0	0	21	19	22	18	1	22	16	.232	.212	.245	6.86	9.43
Gainey, Preston	R-R	6-3	205	2-13-91	0	0	1.04	7	0	0	1	9	6	1	1	0	6	9	.200	.267	.133	9.35	6.23
Hanhold, Eric	R-R	6-5	205	11-1-93	2	12	4.81	19	19	1	0	101	120	61	54	12	33	64	.300	.296	.302	5.70	2.94
Hirsch, Zach	L-L	6-4	220	7-6-90	0	6	3.68	20	1	0	0	59	52	27	24	2	11	52	.233	.270	.219	7.98	1.69
Jones, Zack	R-R	6-1	195	12-4-90	0	0	8.10	3	0	0	0	3	2	3	3	0	3	4	.182	.333	.000	8.10	8.10
Knebel, Corey	R-R	6-4	220	11-26-91	0	0	0.00	1	0	0	0	3	2	0	0	0	1	6	.182	.500	.111	18.00	3.00
Kuntz, Brad	L-L	6-0	180	5-14-92	3	4	3.43	31	0	0	5	42	42	16	16	0	14	40	.269	.159	.313	8.57	3.00
Lucroy, David	R-R	6-1	210	9-3-92	0	0	6.00	2	0	0	0	3	4	2	2	0	2	0	.333	.400	.286	0.00	6.00
Medeiros, Kodi	L-L	6-2	180	5-25-96	4	12	5.93	23	22	0	0	85	102	69	56	4	63	64	.300	.254	.312	6.78	6.67
Olczak, Jon	R-R	6-0	180	11-14-93	1	3	3.04	38	0	0	10	56	45	20	19	3	18	67	.216	.222	.214	10.70	2.88
Peralta, Freddy	R-R	5-11	175	6-4-96	0	3	5.73	8	2	0	0	22	27	14	14	4	12	20	.321	.250	.357	8.18	4.91
Perrin, Jon	R-R	6-5	220	5-23-93	2	8	2.60	19	16	1	0	111	108	39	32	4	19	95	.255	.281	.241	7.73	1.55
Ponce, Cody	R-R	6-6	240	4-25-94	2	8	5.25	17	17	0	0	72	84	52	42	6	17	69	.285	.267	.295	8.63	2.13
Rincon, Junior	R-R	6-2	185	12-7-91	0	2	3.50	19	0	0	1	36	32	17	14	1	20	33	.237	.241	.235	8.25	5.00
Salas, Javi	R-R	6-4	210	3-20-92	0	3	11.20	5	2	0	0	14	25	19	17	1	8	11	.403	.529	.356	7.24	5.27
Smith, Gage	R-R	6-2	185	2-13-91	1	1	1.74	7	0	0	2	10	7	2	2	0	1	6	.194	.267	.143	5.23	0.87
2-team total (9 Lakeland)					2	1	2.76	16	0	0	2	29	25	9	9	1	5	22	—		—	6.75	1.53
Smith, Will	R-L	6-5	265	7-10-89	0	0	0.00	2	0	0	0	3	1	0	0	0	0	4	.100	.000	.143	12.00	0.00
Spurlin, Tyler	R-R	6-3	195	6-17-91	0	1	1.69	9	0	0	4	11	8	2	2	0	1	9	.216	.182	.231	7.59	0.84
Terry, Clint	L-L	6-2	195	6-9-92	1	3	2.56	28	3	0	2	77	74	26	22	3	28	44	.255	.25	.257	5.12	3.26
Uhen, Josh	R-R	6-4	185	4-7-92	1	3	4.35	32	0	0	1	50	51	27	24	4	20	47	.266	.297	.250	8.52	3.62
Ventura, Angel	R-R	6-2	185	4-7-93	3	3	3.73	15	9	0	0	63	56	29	26	3	25	63	.237	.244	.233	9.05	3.59
Villegas, Kender	R-R	6-2	170	6-8-93	6	6	4.16	32	0	0	0	71	75	38	33	5	13	70	.269	.300	.251	8.83	1.64
Williams, Devin	R-R	6-3	165	9-21-94	1	2	4.32	5	2	0	0	25	27	15	12	2	12	20	.278	.324	.254	7.20	4.32
Woodruff, Brandon	R-R	6-4	215	2-10-93	4	1	1.83	8	8	0	0	44	33	12	9	2	10	49	.205	.184	.214	9.95	2.03

Fielding

Catcher	PCT	G	PO	A	E	DP	PB
Ghelfi	.989	11	82	9	1	0	1
Houle	.986	85	610	78	10	4	13
McCall	.968	21	135	15	5	1	2
Pena	.965	21	122	15	5	0	4
Weisenburger	.984	8	57	4	1	0	1

First Base	PCT	G	PO	A	E	DP
Cuas	1.000	11	83	6	0	9
DeMuth	.986	86	722	52	11	60
Denson	.963	4	26	0	1	2
Ghelfi	.980	19	142	7	3	14
Pena	.974	12	107	4	3	7
Smith-Brennan	1.000	11	64	5	0	3

Second Base	PCT	G	PO	A	E	DP
Allemand	.960	35	66	101	7	19
Gennett	1.000	2	3	5	0	3
Iskenderian	.941	49	82	110	12	20
Ortega	1.000	1	1	1	0	0
Pena	1.000	32	50	76	0	12
Rijo	.980	17	32	64	2	14
York	.947	5	6	12	1	2

Third Base	PCT	G	PO	A	E	DP
Allemand	.906	20	18	30	5	2
Cuas	.964	73	53	135	7	15
Iskenderian	.908	25	21	48	7	1
Pena	.950	5	4	15	1	0
Smith-Brennan	.967	16	6	23	1	3

Shortstop	PCT	G	PO	A	E	DP
Allemand	.824	3	6	8	3	3
Cuas	.981	37	51	102	3	24
Ortega	.965	67	76	172	9	28
Rijo	.972	33	52	87	4	20

Outfield	PCT	G	PO	A	E	DP
Collymore	.978	52	88	0	2	0
Coulter	.956	74	145	6	7	1
Davis	.987	55	150	2	2	0
Denson	.867	8	13	0	2	0
Diaz	.991	55	106	3	1	1
Garcia	.965	42	78	5	3	1
Ray	.972	40	104	0	3	0
Rubio	.975	91	151	5	4	0

WISCONSIN TIMBER RATTLERS
MIDWEST LEAGUE

LOW CLASS A

Batting

Batting	B-T	HT	WT	DOB	AVG	vLH	vRH	G	AB	R	H	2B	3B	HR	RBI	BB	HBP	SH	SF	SO	SB	CS	SLG	OBP
Allemand, Blake	B-R	5-10	175	7-1-92	.306	.261	.319	54	209	18	64	15	2	2	14	19	4	1	2	37	2	4	.426	.372
Aviles, Luis	R-R	6-1	170	3-16-95	.239	.260	.233	120	456	54	109	22	6	9	47	28	4	4	1	130	21	6	.373	.288
Belonis, Carlos	R-R	6-3	175	8-19-94	.255	.237	.260	100	353	39	90	10	1	3	33	16	3	5	0	107	13	5	.314	.293
Clark, Trent	L-L	6-0	205	11-1-96	.231	.300	.215	59	221	27	51	15	2	2	24	37	2	2	0	68	5	10	.344	.346
Denson, David	L-R	6-3	254	1-17-95	.231	.231	.231	93	325	32	75	18	0	10	43	46	1	0	1	103	2	1	.378	.327
Diaz, Brandon	R-R	5-11	175	4-14-95	.174	.143	.185	28	86	7	15	6	1	0	6	8	1	1	0	43	3	2	.267	.253
Diaz, Isan	L-R	5-10	185	5-27-96	.264	.242	.269	135	507	71	134	34	5	20	75	72	4	0	4	148	11	8	.469	.358
Erceg, Lucas	L-R	6-3	200	5-1-95	.281	.233	.292	42	167	17	47	9	3	7	29	12	0	0	1	38	1	3	.497	.328
Gatewood, Jake	R-R	6-5	190	9-25-95	.240	.310	.222	126	466	54	112	33	0	14	64	18	3	1	6	141	3	2	.391	.268
Ghelfi, Mitch	B-R	5-11	185	9-24-92	.326	.271	.341	73	285	44	93	15	1	5	32	23	6	0	1	58	3	2	.439	.387
Harrison, Monte	R-R	6-3	220	8-10-95	.221	.250	.213	75	267	34	59	11	1	6	37	20	8	2	1	97	8	3	.337	.294
Matos, Sthervin	R-R	6-1	200	2-13-94	.182	.281	.150	41	132	14	24	2	2	3	11	8	0	4	0	38	1	4	.295	.229
McDowell, Max	R-R	6-0	208	1-12-94	.270	.294	.264	98	345	48	93	21	1	1	27	33	17	2	3	62	21	3	.345	.359
Mejia, Natanael	R-R	6-0	175	7-10-92	.100	.000	.130	9	30	2	3	0	0	0	1	3	0	0	0	12	0	0	.100	.182
Middlebrooks, Will	R-R	6-3	220	9-9-88	.286	.000	.500	2	7	0	2	0	0	0	1	0	0	0	0	2	0	0	.286	.286
Neuhaus, Tucker	L-R	6-3	185	6-18-95	.370	.000	.417	8	27	3	10	2	1	0	3	1	0	0	0	8	0	0	.519	.393
Oquendo, Jonathan	B-R	6-3	170	3-21-96	.232	.091	.259	20	69	5	16	1	1	0	2	5	1	1	0	22	0	1	.275	.293
Ortiz, Juan	L-R	6-1	175	9-20-94	.168	.308	.146	29	95	12	16	1	0	2	4	13	2	0	1	37	2	1	.242	.279
Ray, Corey	L-L	5-11	185	9-22-94	.083	.000	.091	3	12	2	1	0	0	0	0	3	1	0	0	4	1	1	.083	.313

Batting

Batting	B-T	HT	WT	DOB	AVG	vLH	vRH	G	AB	R	H	2B	3B	HR	RBI	BB	HBP	SH	SF	SO	SB	CS	SLG	OBP
Rodriguez, Nathan	R-R	5-10	185	9-30-95	.111	.167	.083	4	18	0	2	0	0	0	1	1	0	0	0	3	0	0	.111	.158
Rubio, Elvis	R-R	6-3	215	7-2-94	.266	.429	.246	17	64	10	17	1	0	1	8	1	1	1	0	12	2	0	.328	.288
Santana, Domingo	R-R	6-5	220	8-5-92	.174	.333	.150	8	23	4	4	0	0	1	3	4	1	0	0	5	0	0	.304	.321
Sharkey, Alan	L-L	6-1	185	11-8-93	.182	.095	.190	71	231	29	42	5	1	2	24	19	5	2	1	43	4	1	.238	.258
Stokes, Troy	R-R	5-8	182	2-2-96	.268	.242	.274	86	314	50	84	20	4	4	29	36	10	3	3	62	20	4	.395	.358

Pitching

Pitching	B-T	HT	WT	DOB	W	L	ERA	G	GS	CG	SV	IP	H	R	ER	HR	BB	SO	AVG	vLH	vRH	K/9	BB/9
Brown, Zack	R-R	6-1	180	12-15-94	1	2	3.00	9	4	0	1	33	29	16	11	3	5	29	.221	.233	.207	7.91	1.36
Burkhalter, David	R-R	6-3	190	7-25-95	3	4	3.56	12	9	0	1	56	53	26	22	3	8	46	.247	.229	.261	7.44	1.29
Burnes, Corbin	R-R	6-3	205	10-22-94	3	0	2.20	9	5	0	0	29	20	8	7	1	16	31	.200	.164	.244	9.73	5.02
Desguin, Jordan	R-R	6-1	195	10-30-93	1	1	3.23	6	5	0	0	31	25	14	11	4	13	30	.221	.188	.265	8.80	3.82
Diaz, Miguel	R-R	6-1	175	11-28-94	1	8	3.71	26	15	0	3	95	83	49	39	7	29	91	.226	.204	.244	8.65	2.76
Diplan, Marcos	R-R	6-0	160	9-18-96	6	2	1.80	17	11	0	1	70	49	24	14	3	32	89	.191	.250	.154	11.44	4.11
Drossner, Jake	R-L	6-1	189	5-16-94	6	6	4.69	25	15	0	1	94	105	67	49	6	56	91	.279	.309	.265	8.71	5.36
Farina, Alex	L-R	6-0	230	5-30-93	5	2	2.83	33	0	0	0	54	53	19	17	2	26	39	.261	.316	.213	6.50	4.33
Garza, Matt	R-R	6-4	220	11-26-83	0	2	4.76	3	3	0	0	11	13	7	6	1	1	10	.295	.150	.417	7.94	0.79
Griep, Nate	R-R	6-2	190	10-11-93	2	2	2.05	49	0	0	23	57	41	18	13	0	18	54	.208	.235	.188	8.53	2.84
Grist, Scott	R-R	6-3	190	5-31-92	7	4	2.71	44	0	0	0	70	61	24	21	5	14	60	.238	.254	.225	7.75	1.81
Harber, Conor	R-R	6-2	205	12-18-93	4	3	3.02	20	7	0	1	57	45	23	19	2	19	67	.217	.232	.205	10.64	3.02
Jankins, Thomas	R-R	6-3	200	7-2-95	0	2	3.20	8	7	0	0	25	33	10	9	0	6	21	.327	.328	.326	7.46	2.13
Lucroy, David	R-R	6-1	210	9-3-92	2	7	4.83	31	2	0	1	60	67	35	32	5	41	60	.288	.267	.303	9.05	6.18
Owenby, Drake	L-L	6-2	205	1-7-94	3	1	2.67	17	7	0	2	67	64	28	20	6	21	65	.247	.233	.254	8.69	2.81
Peralta, Freddy	R-R	5-11	175	6-4-96	4	1	2.85	16	8	0	2	60	45	22	19	3	24	77	.202	.179	.219	11.55	3.60
Perrin, Jon	R-R	6-5	220	5-23-93	1	1	2.50	6	6	0	0	36	31	14	10	1	1	47	.223	.218	.230	11.75	0.25
Sanchez, Miguel	R-R	6-3	190	12-31-93	1	1	2.51	6	0	0	0	14	12	5	4	0	6	17	.235	.316	.188	10.67	3.77
Smith, Matt	R-R	6-3	215	8-27-93	0	2	5.74	5	2	0	0	16	20	10	10	2	5	12	.313	.333	.280	6.89	2.87
Supak, Trey	R-R	6-5	210	5-31-96	2	3	3.86	11	6	0	1	44	48	23	19	3	17	40	.274	.216	.346	8.12	3.45
Torres-Costa, Quintin	L-L	5-11	190	9-11-94	6	3	4.27	41	0	0	0	59	55	35	28	4	25	74	.253	.244	.260	11.29	3.81
Trent, Christian	L-L	6-0	190	9-10-92	0	0	4.26	3	0	0	0	6	9	4	3	2	1	11	.333	.286	.385	15.63	2.84
Williams, Chase	R-R	6-6	210	11-23-92	0	1	2.25	4	0	0	0	4	5	1	1	0	3	6	.294	.333	.273	13.50	6.75
Williams, Devin	R-R	6-3	165	9-21-94	6	3	3.61	17	10	0	2	72	64	32	29	4	34	74	.240	.243	.237	9.21	4.23
Yamamoto, Jordan	R-R	6-0	185	5-11-96	7	8	3.82	27	18	0	0	134	130	61	57	6	31	152	.252	.306	.201	10.18	2.08

Fielding

Catcher	PCT	G	PO	A	E	DP	PB
Ghelfi	.988	29	221	30	3	0	7
McDowell	.991	98	911	111	9	4	17
Mejia	.953	9	70	12	4	0	1
Rodriguez	1.000	4	44	3	0	0	0

First Base	PCT	G	PO	A	E	DP
Aviles	1.000	8	60	6	0	5
Gatewood	.978	26	200	18	5	19
Ghelfi	.997	33	278	17	1	27
Matos	.978	7	42	3	1	0
Ortiz	1.000	4	31	0	0	4
Sharkey	.998	70	523	49	1	57

Second Base	PCT	G	PO	A	E	DP
Allemand	.958	44	62	99	7	19

	PCT	G	PO	A	E	DP
Aviles	.965	38	62	104	6	28
Diaz	.960	41	71	119	8	28
Matos	1.000	1	0	1	0	0
Neuhaus	.889	8	15	17	4	3
Oquendo	.939	12	11	20	2	6

Third Base	PCT	G	PO	A	E	DP
Aviles	.933	7	4	10	1	0
Erceg	.956	37	35	52	4	9
Gatewood	.891	93	45	152	24	12
Middlebrooks	1.000	1	2	1	0	0
Oquendo	1.000	4	0	5	0	0

Shortstop	PCT	G	PO	A	E	DP
Aviles	.967	54	97	136	8	35
Diaz	.941	90	138	229	23	54

Outfield	PCT	G	PO	A	E	DP
Aviles	.974	18	35	3	1	0
Belonis	.946	96	153	5	9	1
Clark	.965	58	103	7	4	2
Denson	.981	33	50	3	1	0
Diaz	1.000	26	53	1	0	0
Gatewood	—		1	0	0	0
Harrison	.968	74	151	2	5	2
Matos	.981	32	52	1	1	0
Ortiz	1.000	2	1	0	0	0
Ray	1.000	3	7	0	0	0
Rubio	1.000	16	24	2	0	0
Santana	1.000	4	7	0	0	0
Stokes	.985	78	132	2	2	0

HELENA BREWERS

ROOKIE

PIONEER LEAGUE

Batting	B-T	HT	WT	DOB	AVG	vLH	vRH	G	AB	R	H	2B	3B	HR	RBI	BB	HBP	SH	SF	SO	SB	CS	SLG	OBP
Aguilar, Ryan	L-L	6-2	168	9-11-94	.248	.242	.250	40	145	30	36	11	0	2	14	28	0	2	0	37	6	2	.366	.370
Atencio, Johel	R-R	5-10	180	9-17-96	.160	.000	.174	8	25	3	4	0	0	0	2	0	1	0	4	0	1	.160	.222
Erceg, Lucas	L-R	6-3	200	5-1-95	.400	.524	.369	26	105	17	42	8	1	2	22	8	2	0	0	16	8	1	.552	.452
Galiano, Charles	R-R	6-1	200	5-23-94	.175	.000	.219	11	40	2	7	3	0	1	4	0	0	1	0	16	0	0	.325	.175
Gideon, Ronnie	R-R	6-2	225	9-20-94	.321	.340	.316	59	224	42	72	20	0	17	41	15	4	0	2	69	1	2	.638	.371
Hummel, Cooper	B-R	5-10	185	11-28-94	.176	.150	.183	35	102	16	18	5	1	1	17	27	2	2	0	25	4	0	.275	.359
Lara, Gilbert	R-R	6-2	190	10-30-97	.250	.261	.247	59	228	30	57	10	0	2	28	12	3	0	3	59	2	1	.320	.293
Mallen, Franly	R-R	6-1	160	5-27-97	.279	.194	.301	50	179	22	50	11	0	3	23	9	1	1	0	43	2	4	.391	.317
Martinez, Yerald	R-R	6-2	180	12-3-95	.198	.190	.200	52	187	26	37	5	0	10	26	23	0	2	2	87	3	2	.385	.283
Morrison, Trever	L-R	6-0	175	4-21-95	.265	.310	.252	37	132	17	35	3	0	0	10	9	1	3	1	31	5	3	.288	.315
Oquendo, Jonathan	B-R	6-3	170	3-21-96	.296	.200	.311	22	71	13	21	0	0	0	5	13	0	3	2	17	1	1	.296	.395
Orimoloye, Demi	R-R	6-4	225	1-6-97	.205	.209	.203	61	219	26	45	5	3	5	17	23	4	1	0	57	18	5	.324	.293
Ortiz, Juan	L-R	6-1	170	9-20-94	.362	.167	.390	12	47	10	17	4	1	1	12	4	0	1	0	2	0	0	.553	.404
Rodriguez, Nathan	R-R	5-10	185	9-30-95	.272	.346	.256	43	147	18	40	9	0	3	21	19	3	1	3	25	4	1	.395	.360
Segovia, Joantgel	R-R	6-1	175	11-8-96	.294	.283	.297	56	211	36	62	7	0	0	21	24	2	4	1	23	2	7	.327	.370
Vasquez, Yoel	R-R	6-1	180	8-20-96	.107	.286	.048	10	28	5	3	0	0	1	3	3	2	0	0	15	0	0	.214	.242
Whalen, Caleb	R-R	6-2	180	10-19-92	.222	.222	.222	47	153	25	34	12	0	1	18	14	3	1	4	36	8	0	.320	.293
Wilson, Weston	R-R	6-3	195	9-11-94	.318	.278	.330	62	233	38	74	16	7	4	38	23	7	2	4	33	5	4	.498	.390

Pitching

Pitching	B-T	HT	WT	DOB	W	L	ERA	G	GS	CG	SV	IP	H	R	ER	HR	BB	SO	AVG	vLH	vRH	K/9	BB/9
Benoit, Rodrigo	R-R	6-2	170	2-23-94	0	3	7.23	16	8	0	1	56	96	52	45	13	9	35	.381	.404	.364	5.63	1.45
Brown, Dalton	R-R	6-4	250	9-15-93	0	1	4.09	6	0	0	1	11	11	9	5	0	3	8	.262	.316	.217	6.55	2.45
Brown, Zack	R-R	6-1	180	12-15-94	0	2	13.50	3	2	0	0	5	11	8	8	0	5	5	.423	.200	.563	8.44	8.44
Clowers, Shawn	L-L	5-11	190	11-11-92	4	1	7.20	19	0	0	0	35	60	33	28	4	10	36	.385	.455	.357	9.26	2.57
Cross, Colton	R-R	6-0	200	3-24-93	0	2	1.82	20	0	0	10	25	17	8	5	1	8	33	.189	.200	.180	12.04	2.92
Desguin, Jordan	R-R	6-1	195	10-30-93	2	0	3.60	8	4	0	0	40	34	17	16	3	11	40	.233	.268	.211	9.00	2.48
Diaz, Juan	R-R	6-0	185	9-24-92	0	0	3.09	4	0	0	0	12	9	8	4	2	6	14	.200	.211	.192	10.80	4.63
Diplan, Nattino	R-R	6-3	180	12-30-93	0	5	7.24	13	7	0	0	46	72	44	37	4	22	28	.360	.378	.347	5.48	4.30
Finnegan, Jack	R-R	6-2	175	12-9-93	1	1	15.00	7	0	0	0	9	15	15	15	4	7	9	.375	.231	.444	9.00	7.00
Fortuno, Gentry	R-R	6-1	235	9-11-96	3	4	8.16	14	7	0	0	46	74	47	42	8	15	35	.366	.398	.339	6.80	2.91
Fox, Blake	L-L	6-4	220	6-17-93	0	1	2.57	6	0	0	0	7	5	2	2	0	2	9	.192	.000	.238	11.57	2.57
Gibbs, Emerson	R-R	6-2	200	6-25-94	1	2	5.49	6	3	0	0	20	33	12	12	1	3	18	.375	.257	.453	8.24	1.37
Jankins, Thomas	R-R	6-3	200	7-2-95	0	0	3.09	4	2	0	0	12	12	6	4	2	2	14	.255	.133	.313	10.80	1.54
Lindell, Karsen	R-R	6-3	190	6-2-96	1	4	8.89	7	4	0	0	26	34	27	26	3	21	8	.343	.426	.269	2.73	7.18
Myers, Aaron	R-R	6-3	225	9-2-93	3	1	1.38	11	2	0	1	33	16	6	5	1	7	44	.138	.156	.127	12.12	1.93
Petersen, Michael	R-R	6-7	195	5-16-94	1	3	7.71	10	5	0	0	23	41	24	20	4	13	19	.398	.455	.356	7.33	5.01
Rodriguez, Wuilder	R-R	6-2	180	1-21-93	5	4	4.48	17	7	0	1	60	65	39	30	11	11	41	.272	.318	.247	6.12	1.64
Roegner, Cam	L-L	6-6	205	6-19-93	2	3	3.66	10	4	0	0	32	30	18	13	1	14	20	.261	.214	.276	5.63	3.94
Saldivar, Santos	R-R	5-10	180	4-16-93	0	1	5.73	19	0	0	0	22	27	16	14	5	11	22	.303	.282	.320	9.00	4.50
Serigstad, Scott	R-R	6-1	190	11-2-94	2	4	10.59	14	9	0	0	43	74	57	51	10	14	35	.374	.367	.378	7.27	2.91
Smith, Matt	R-R	6-3	215	8-27-93	0	2	4.50	5	3	0	0	22	30	15	11	1	4	17	.323	.400	.250	6.95	1.64
Supak, Trey	R-R	6-5	210	5-31-96	1	1	1.29	4	2	0	0	14	10	3	2	0	1	11	.200	.294	.152	7.07	0.64
Torres-Costa, Quintin	L-L	5-11	190	9-11-94	0	0	0.00	4	0	0	1	5	3	1	0	0	4	7	.167	.000	.250	11.81	6.75
Walters, Nash	R-R	6-5	210	5-18-97	2	1	6.20	10	5	0	0	25	21	21	17	2	32	30	.241	.267	.228	10.95	11.68

Fielding

C: Atencio 4, Galiano 10, Hummel 28, Rodriguez 30, Vasquez 5. **1B:** Aguilar 10, Atencio 1, Gideon 52, Oquendo 3, Ortiz 8, Wilson 4. **2B:** Mallen 50, Morrison 11, Oquendo 4, Wilson 11. **3B:** Erceg 20, Hummel 1, Lara 2, Morrison 6, Oquendo 7, Wilson 41. **SS:** Lara 52, Morrison 19, Oquendo 5, Wilson 1. **OF:** Aguilar 32, Martinez 43, Orimoloye 49, Ortiz 1, Segovia 55, Whalen 45, Wilson 6.

AZL BREWERS   ROOKIE
ARIZONA LEAGUE

Batting

Batting	B-T	HT	WT	DOB	AVG	vLH	vRH	G	AB	R	H	2B	3B	HR	RBI	BB	HBP	SH	SF	SO	SB	CS	SLG	OBP
Aguilar, Ryan	L-L	6-2	168	9-11-94	.278	.167	.333	5	18	4	5	1	0	0	2	3	0	0	1	1	3	0	.333	.364
Atencio, Johel	R-R	5-10	180	9-17-96	.174	.188	.167	17	46	7	8	0	1	0	8	6	2	2	1	9	0	0	.217	.291
Cain, Nick	R-R	6-4	220	9-9-93	.183	.286	.159	34	109	12	20	4	2	0	11	11	2	0	0	40	1	0	.257	.270
Clark, Zach	R-R	6-2	200	12-5-95	.252	.182	.277	30	127	19	32	6	4	2	16	8	4	0	1	35	6	2	.409	.314
Cortes, Jomar	R-R	6-3	190	3-24-98	.091	.000	.111	4	11	0	1	0	0	0	0	0	0	0	0	5	0	0	.091	.091
Feliciano, Jay	R-R	6-2	215	9-28-95	.263	.207	.276	43	152	19	40	7	2	6	30	7	4	0	3	34	2	2	.454	.307
Feliciano, Mario	R-R	6-1	195	11-20-98	.265	.333	.241	29	117	16	31	5	3	0	16	7	1	0	2	19	2	2	.359	.307
Garcia, Gabriel	R-R	6-3	185	12-16-97	.300	.448	.257	37	130	24	39	12	4	2	27	17	3	0	0	34	4	2	.500	.393
Gomez, Jose	R-R	5-3	184	11-17-93	.280	.281	.279	45	161	26	45	3	1	2	15	23	2	2	2	36	8	4	.348	.372
Harrison, Monte	R-R	6-3	220	8-10-95	.211	.000	.267	5	19	4	4	1	1	0	1	4	1	1	0	4	0	0	.368	.375
Henry, Payton	R-R	6-2	215	6-24-97	.256	.273	.254	24	82	15	21	7	0	0	17	6	4	0	1	19	0	1	.341	.333
McClanahan, Chad	R-R	6-2	200	12-24-97	.208	.152	.225	35	144	22	30	7	1	3	14	11	3	0	1	45	1	2	.333	.277
Mendez, Julio	R-R	5-10	140	10-24-96	.231	.118	.253	32	104	16	24	5	1	0	11	9	4	2	0	19	4	2	.308	.316
Neuhaus, Tucker	L-R	6-3	190	6-18-95	.385	—	.385	4	13	3	5	0	1	0	2	2	1	0	0	3	0	0	.538	.500
Otano, Ignacio	R-R	6-0	175	7-16-97	.233	.190	.250	26	73	9	17	3	0	0	7	8	2	1	1	8	1	2	.274	.321
Perry, Tyrone	L-R	6-1	265	10-24-95	.235	.000	.250	4	17	1	4	1	0	0	1	1	0	0	0	7	0	0	.294	.278
Pierre, Nicolas	R-R	6-3	170	11-13-96	.237	.133	.262	21	76	4	18	6	0	0	8	3	0	0	2	16	2	1	.316	.259
Roscetti, Nick	R-R	6-3	190	11-6-93	.277	.250	.286	13	47	9	13	1	1	0	3	6	1	2	0	10	3	2	.340	.370
Taylor, Zach	R-R	6-1	220	10-29-95	.149	.143	.150	16	47	3	7	2	0	0	1	8	2	0	1	27	0	0	.191	.293
Thomas, Francisco	B-R	6-2	195	8-27-98	.110	.133	.103	23	73	12	8	1	0	0	1	13	1	1	0	23	0	2	.123	.253
Valderrey, Nicol	R-R	6-2	180	1-20-97	.220	.091	.250	18	59	10	13	5	0	0	5	8	1	0	0	20	1	0	.305	.324
Vasquez, Yoel	R-R	5-11	180	8-20-96	.200	.333	.000	3	5	1	1	0	0	0	1	0	0	1	0	1	0	0	.200	.200
York, Trey	R-R	6-2	190	4-4-94	.283	.268	.288	47	173	28	49	7	1	2	19	14	0	4	10	14	0	2	.387	.387

Pitching

Pitching	B-T	HT	WT	DOB	W	L	ERA	G	GS	CG	SV	IP	H	R	ER	HR	BB	SO	AVG	vLH	vRH	K/9	BB/9
Adams, Wilson	R-R	6-5	215	1-26-94	3	1	2.16	12	4	0	0	25	19	9	6	2	1	23	.207	.296	.169	8.28	0.36
Bean, Parker	R-R	6-6	185	3-7-95	0	0	4.50	2	2	0	0	2	1	1	1	0	2	1	.167	.000	.250	4.50	9.00
Brown, Daniel	L-L	5-10	185	3-22-95	0	0	6.23	3	1	0	0	4	5	3	3	0	1	5	.278	.333	.267	10.38	2.08
Brown, Dalton	R-R	6-4	250	9-15-93	1	0	0.00	6	0	0	0	9	3	0	0	0	2	4	.107	.000	.158	4.00	2.00
Burnes, Corbin	R-R	6-3	205	10-22-94	0	0	1.29	3	1	0	0	7	3	1	1	0	2	10	.125	.083	.167	12.86	2.57
De La Cruz, Joan	L-L	6-3	175	9-30-94	2	0	6.30	7	3	0	0	10	10	7	7	2	5	12	.256	.273	.250	10.80	4.50
Diaz, Juan	R-R	6-0	185	9-24-92	1	0	2.12	10	0	0	3	17	13	4	4	1	7	26	.203	.167	.225	13.76	3.71
Diaz, Victor	R-R	6-1	170	10-6-93	1	2	5.59	10	9	0	0	19	24	12	12	1	2	18	.304	.261	.321	8.38	0.93
Diplan, Nattino	R-R	6-3	180	12-30-93	1	2	4.91	4	1	0	0	11	15	12	6	1	2	10	.294	.294	.294	8.18	1.64
Earls, Kaleb	R-R	6-5	185	3-17-93	1	0	4.50	3	0	0	0	4	5	2	2	0	1	3	.333	.375	.286	6.75	2.25
Finnegan, Jack	R-R	6-2	175	12-9-93	1	3	3.79	8	0	0	0	19	16	10	8	1	9	15	.222	.200	.238	7.11	4.26
Flores, Junior	R-R	6-1	175	10-13-94	0	1	4.50	7	0	0	0	8	6	5	4	0	6	11	.214	.500	.100	12.38	6.75
Gainey, Preston	R-R	6-3	205	2-13-91	0	0	3.18	5	0	0	0	6	3	2	2	0	6	8	.150	.125	.167	12.71	9.53
Gibbs, Emerson	R-R	6-2	200	6-25-94	1	1	2.00	5	3	0	0	27	27	9	6	0	3	29	.265	.268	.262	9.67	1.00
Gonzalez, Michael	R-R	6-1	190	7-22-98	1	1	8.06	10	5	0	0	22	33	28	20	3	15	13	.344	.303	.365	5.24	6.04

Pitching	B-T	HT	WT	DOB	W	L	ERA	G	GS	CG	SV	IP	H	R	ER	HR	BB	SO	AVG	vLH	vRH	K/9	BB/9
Hernandez, Nelson	R-R	6-2	170	3-13-97	1	5	4.29	14	6	0	0	57	65	33	27	6	8	44	.286	.266	.294	6.99	1.27
Herrera, Carlos	R-R	6-2	150	10-26-97	3	6	4.50	14	6	0	0	50	52	35	25	4	12	49	.271	.300	.254	8.82	2.16
Lambson, Mitch	L-L	6-1	205	7-20-90	1	0	0.00	5	0	0	0	6	6	0	0	0	0	12	.240	.000	.316	18.00	0.00
Lillis, Blake	L-L	6-3	180	3-10-98	1	1	2.81	6	4	0	0	16	15	7	5	1	7	14	.250	.188	.273	7.88	3.94
Myers, Aaron	R-R	6-3	225	9-2-93	1	0	1.64	6	0	0	1	11	7	3	2	0	4	11	.175	.200	.160	9.00	3.27
Newton, Jeremy	R-R	6-2	200	6-1-93	0	2	10.80	6	0	0	2	8	17	10	10	1	1	5	.415	.333	.500	5.40	1.08
Nova, Boanerges	L-L	6-2	170	2-6-93	2	1	4.26	15	0	0	2	25	31	13	12	3	11	30	.298	.385	.269	10.66	3.91
Roegner, Cam	L-L	6-6	205	6-19-93	0	0	1.00	4	0	0	0	9	4	1	1	0	2	7	.143	.167	.136	7.00	2.00
Salas, Javi	R-R	6-4	210	3-20-92	0	0	9.53	3	3	0	0	6	8	7	6	0	5	7	.320	.000	.364	11.12	7.94
Sanchez, Miguel	R-R	6-3	190	12-31-93	1	1	3.44	10	0	0	1	18	19	10	7	0	2	20	.264	.241	.279	9.82	0.98
Smith, Jake	R-R	6-5	220	8-29-95	0	0	2.79	8	0	0	0	10	2	4	3	0	12	18	.065	.091	.050	16.76	11.17
Smith, Matt	R-R	6-3	215	8-27-93	1	0	0.87	6	0	0	0	10	6	2	1	0	2	10	.167	.222	.148	8.71	1.74
Trent, Christian	L-L	6-0	190	9-10-92	1	0	1.65	7	1	0	1	16	14	3	3	1	3	18	.230	.273	.220	9.92	1.65
Vernon, Andrew	R-R	6-4	232	1-17-94	0	3	2.55	14	0	0	3	18	23	9	5	0	6	23	.307	.324	.293	11.72	3.06
Walters, Nash	R-R	6-5	210	5-18-97	0	1	3.86	4	4	0	0	14	11	8	6	0	13	18	.204	.176	.216	11.57	8.36
Williams, Chase	R-R	6-6	210	11-23-92	0	0	0.00	2	0	0	0	4	2	0	0	0	2	4	.167	.000	.200	9.82	4.91

Fielding

C: Atencio 13, Feliciano 20, Garcia 1, Henry 18, Taylor 9, Vasquez 3. **1B:** Aguilar 3, Feliciano 9, Garcia 23, McClanahan 5, Perry 3, Valderrey 15. **2B:** Mendez 8, Neuhaus 4, Otano 2, York 43. **3B:** Garcia 8, McClanahan 29, Mendez 11, Roscetti 3, York 2. **SS:** Cortes 2, Garcia 1, Mendez 11, Otano 10, Roscetti 9, Thomas 23. **OF:** Aguilar 2, Cain 31, Clark 28, Feliciano 31, Gomez 45, Harrison 5, Otano 8, Pierre 21.

DSL BREWERS   ROOKIE
DOMINICAN SUMMER LEAGUE

Batting	B-T	HT	WT	DOB	AVG	vLH	vRH	G	AB	R	H	2B	3B	HR	RBI	BB	HBP	SH	SF	SO	SB	CS	SLG	OBP
Avalo, Luis	R-R	5-11	190	11-24-98	.202	.150	.220	50	163	19	33	4	1	1	16	10	2	0	1	24	4	1	.258	.256
Avila, Luis	R-R	5-11	150	3-5-99	.192	.098	.221	49	177	23	34	0	0	3	15	2	1	1	1	31	7	6	.192	.262
Castillo, Javier	R-R	5-11	160	4-4-98	.268	.370	.234	60	183	19	49	7	0	2	22	15	5	2	1	10	2	4	.339	.338
Connell, Bryan	R-R	6-3	195	11-9-98	.189	.122	.214	54	175	21	33	8	0	3	24	24	8	0	2	74	0	2	.286	.311
Familia, Aaron	R-R	6-2	170	3-16-99	.171	.258	.138	37	111	9	19	3	0	2	10	25	4	0	3	36	0	0	.252	.336
Feliciano, Jay	R-R	6-2	215	9-28-95	.156	.222	.130	9	32	6	5	3	0	1	3	3	4	0	0	13	2	0	.344	.308
Franco, Yorki	L-R	6-2	180	10-26-98	.192	.120	.216	33	99	10	19	6	1	0	4	9	0	0	0	26	2	2	.273	.259
Herrera, Josue	R-R	6-0	165	2-3-97	.293	.077	.393	12	41	7	12	3	0	0	9	3	1	0	0	10	1	0	.366	.356
Lujano, Jesus	L-L	5-10	160	2-18-99	.232	.213	.237	60	203	34	47	7	1	0	21	30	4	1	0	28	12	6	.276	.342
Manon, Luis	B-R	5-11	160	1-5-99	.211	.242	.200	41	123	16	26	4	1	0	9	25	1	5	0	38	7	5	.260	.349
Mendez, Melvin	R-R	6-4	195	10-7-97	.059	.077	.048	13	34	5	2	0	1	0	1	5	1	0	0	9	1	2	.118	.200
Pena, Jose	L-L	6-3	175	10-21-98	.220	.118	.243	30	91	11	20	4	0	0	5	6	1	0	1	26	1	1	.264	.273
Perez, Antonio	R-R	6-2	200	10-19-97	.125	.214	.095	21	56	5	7	0	0	1	2	4	2	0	0	18	1	0	.179	.210
Perez, Moises	R-R	6-1	190	8-17-98	.226	.226	.226	47	146	22	33	10	0	7	35	22	4	1	2	35	5	0	.438	.339
Pierre, Nicolas	R-R	6-3	170	11-13-96	.200	.167	.211	8	25	3	5	3	0	0	2	4	0	0	1	5	3	0	.320	.300
Pinero, Antonio	B-R	6-1	155	3-15-99	.235	.280	.219	28	98	15	23	2	0	0	7	9	0	3	1	20	6	0	.255	.296
2-team total (22 Red Sox2)					.218	—	—	50	179	27	39	2	0	0	10	16	0	4	2	30	13	1	.229	.279
Pinero, Marcos	R-R	6-1	200	.308	.165	43	105	23	21	4	1	0	10	17	13	1	0	39	3	4	.257	.378
Sano, Edwin	B-R	5-9	160	12-12-98	.236	.186	.257	43	148	25	35	9	0	2	19	14	6	0	0	16	2	2	.338	.327
Sibrian, Jose	R-R	5-11	175	10-24-98	.216	.111	.247	32	116	20	25	5	0	0	22	9	6	1	1	21	0	0	.259	.303
Torres, Bryan	L-R	5-11	165	7-2-97	.252	.143	.278	49	143	23	36	2	4	0	10	21	1	0	1	4	8	3	.322	.348

Pitching	B-T	HT	WT	DOB	W	L	ERA	G	GS	CG	SV	IP	H	R	ER	HR	BB	SO	AVG	vLH	vRH	K/9	BB/9
Acosta, Daniel	R-R	6-1	185	2-27-97	0	0	8.44	11	0	0	0	11	9	14	10	0	23	12	.250	.167	.292	10.13	19.41
Adames, Freisis	R-R	6-3	175	11-18-96	3	2	3.65	22	0	0	1	44	43	21	18	1	9	36	.250	.238	.254	7.31	1.83
Alberro, Jose	L-L	6-1	168	2-2-98	1	0	5.14	6	0	0	0	7	7	5	4	0	5	8	.250	.333	.227	10.29	6.43
Alvarado, Deymar	R-R	6-1	170	10-22-97	2	3	6.41	7	6	0	0	20	16	16	14	0	22	9	.242	.258	.229	4.12	10.07
Benitez, Luis	B-R	6-3	195	5-24-92	0	0	8.59	6	0	0	0	7	8	7	7	2	1	7	.286	.286	.286	8.59	1.23
Brea, Jesus	R-R	6-3	194	12-25-95	1	1	2.11	21	1	0	3	47	49	19	11	3	16	30	.269	.357	.230	5.74	3.06
Chirino, Harold	R-R	6-2	170	4-12-98	4	4	3.12	11	11	0	0	58	58	25	20	1	14	40	.269	.328	.242	6.24	2.18
Cordero, Luis	L-L	6-3	170	4-22-99	0	2	3.22	9	3	0	0	22	22	13	8	0	14	11	.268	.400	.239	4.43	5.64
Cruz, Axel	R-R	6-1	175	8-10-94	1	1	2.55	10	0	0	0	18	9	7	5	0	13	20	.155	.077	.178	10.19	6.62
Dominguez, Johan	R-R	6-4	190	1-18-96	4	5	2.78	16	8	0	0	58	37	22	18	1	24	62	.180	.186	.178	9.57	3.70
Duval, Starling	R-R	6-6	200	11-28-94	0	2	6.87	9	0	0	0	18	24	16	14	0	11	15	.324	.313	.328	7.36	5.40
Juan, Yunior	R-R	6-1	190	10-24-93	0	1	8.10	8	0	0	0	7	6	6	6	0	10	5	.250	.400	.211	6.75	13.50
Medina, Henry	R-R	6-0	175	9-5-97	4	4	4.04	13	7	0	0	56	53	28	25	0	15	30	.247	.185	.273	4.85	2.43
Montas, Jenri	R-R	6-2	200	8-10-96	2	7	5.24	12	10	0	0	46	50	37	27	1	22	37	.275	.262	.281	7.19	4.27
Paulino, Alberto	R-R	6-2	180	2-25-91	0	2	0.38	14	0	0	5	24	16	5	1	0	7	23	.193	.100	.222	8.75	2.66
Pena, Francisco	R-R	5-11	190	2-28-93	0	0	1.17	5	0	0	2	8	6	1	1	1	2	9	.214	.267	.154	10.57	2.35
Pinto, Maiker	R-R	6-3	180	9-25-96	2	5	6.24	12	12	0	0	53	71	42	37	2	18	34	.320	.375	.297	5.74	3.04
Salaman, Wilfred	L-L	5-11	210	10-5-97	0	0	2.60	9	0	0	0	17	18	12	5	2	13	15	.277	.000	.375	7.79	6.75
Sanchez, Miguel	R-R	6-3	190	12-31-93	0	0	6.75	2	1	0	0	7	5	5	5	0	5	10	.200	.444	.063	13.50	6.75
Tamares, Jefry	R-R	6-2	190	7-31-97	0	0	5.74	13	0	0	0	16	15	10	10	0	12	15	.259	.333	.233	8.62	6.89

Fielding

C: Avalo 26, Perez 18, Sibrian 25, Torres 15. **1B:** Avalo 21, Castillo 15, Feliciano 4, Herrera 7, Perez 30. **2B:** Avila 6, Castillo 5, Manon 28, Sano 33, Torres 5. **3B:** Castillo 37, Familia 32, Herrera 5, Pinero 5, Torres 4. **SS:** Avila 44, Castillo 6, Manon 8, Pinero 22. **OF:** Connell 45, Feliciano 3, Franco 30, Lujano 59, Mendez 12, Pena 28, Perez 10, Pierre 8, Pinero 38.

Minnesota Twins

SEASON IN A SENTENCE: The Twins had a winning record in 2015 and aimed to compete in 2016, but lost their first nine games and wound up losing 103 games, nine more than any club in the majors and the most losses since the franchise moved to Minnesota in 1961.

HIGH POINT: Second baseman Brian Dozier became just the second Twin to hit 40 homers in a season, joining Hall of Famer Harmon Killebrew on the list. From Sept. 2-6, he homered in five straight games, including three Sept. 5 against the Royals. Of course the Twins still lost that game 11-5, but Dozier wound up setting the single-season record for home runs by a second baseman.

LOW POINT: It never got much better after Minnesota lost its first nine games, scoring just 14 runs over that span while being shut out twice. But it did get worse, including a 13-game losing streak to end August that included a four-game sweep by the Royals in which the Twins were outscored 25-6.

NOTABLE ROOKIES: Five Twins rookies got significant playing time, with varying degrees of success. Byron Buxton used a retooled approach to hit nine of his 10 home runs in September, salvaging an otherwise disturbing season. Fellow outfielder Max Kepler ranked third on the team with 17 home runs, while Jorge Polanco hit .282/.332/.424 while manning shortstop for most of the final two months, with his bat ahead of his glove. However, righthander Jose Berrios (3-7, 8.02) struggled mightily with his command.

KEY TRANSACTIONS: In mid-July, ownership fired general manager Terry Ryan, who served from Sept. 1994 through Sept. 2007 and again from Nov. 2011-2016. After the regular season, the Twins hired Derek Falvey as chief baseball officer, after he most recently had served as director of baseball operations for the Indians. Interim GM Rob Antony swung minor deals in July, acquiring lefthander Adalberto Mejia for all-star Eduardo Nunez, then trading righthanders Ricky Nolasco and Alex Meyer for lefthander Hector Santiago.

DOWN ON THE FARM: Minnesota's domestic affiliates posted a .540 winning percentage, good for fifth in the game, even though just two made their playoffs. Twins farmhands peppered the minor league leaderboards, led by lefthander Stephen Gonsalves, who ranked among the top 15 in wins (13), ERA (2.06), WHIP (0.82) and opponents average (.179).

OPENING DAY PAYROLL: $105,333,200 (18th)

PLAYERS OF THE YEAR

MAJOR LEAGUE	MINOR LEAGUE
Brian Dozier **2b**	**Stephen Gonsalves** **lhp**
.268/.340/.546	(High A/Double-A)
42 HR, 99 RBI	13-5, 2.06
3rd in AL in HR	155 SO in 140 IP

ORGANIZATION LEADERS

BATTING   *Minimum 250 AB

MAJORS

*	AVG	Brian Dozier	.268
*	OPS	Brian Dozier	.886
	HR	Brian Dozier	42
	RBI	Brian Dozier	99

MINORS

*	AVG	Luis Arraez, Cedar Rapids	.347
*	OBP	LaMonte Wade, Cedar Rapids, Fort Myers	.402
*	SLG	Daniel Palka, Chattanooga, Rochester	.521
*	OPS	Daniel Palka, Chattanooga, Rochester	.848
	R	Zach Granite, Chattanooga	86
	H	Luis Arraez, Cedar Rapids	165
	TB	Daniel Palka, Chattanooga, Rochester	262
	2B	Luis Arraez, Cedar Rapids	31
	3B	Edgar Corcino, Fort Myers, Chattanooga	11
	HR	Daniel Palka, Chattanooga, Rochester	34
	RBI	Daniel Palka, Chattanooga, Rochester	90
	BB	Kennys Vargas, Rochester	66
	SO	Adam Walker, Rochester	202
	SB	Zach Granite, Chattanooga	56

PITCHING   #Minimum 75 IP

MAJORS

	W	Tyler Duffey	9
#	ERA	Ervin Santana	3.38
	SO	Ervin Santana	149
	SV	Brandon Kintzler	17

MINORS

	W	Stephen Gonsalves, Fort Myers, Chattanooga	13
	L	Dereck Rodriguez, Cedar Rapids, Fort Myers	13
#	ERA	Stephen Gonsalves, Fort Myers, Chattanooga	2.06
	G	Jake Reed, Chattanooga, Rochester	50
	GS	David Hurlbut, Chattanooga, Rochester	28
		Jason Wheeler, Chattanooga, Rochester	28
	SV	Trevor Hildenberger, Fort Myers, Chattanooga	19
	IP	Jason Wheeler, Chattanooga, Rochester	169
	BB	Sam Clay, Cedar Rapids, Fort Myers	67
	SO	Stephen Gonsalves, Fort Myers, Chattanooga	155
#	AVG	Stephen Gonsalves, Fort Myers, Chattanooga	.179

General Manager: Terry Ryan/Rob Antony. **Farm Director:** Brad Steil. **Scouting Director:** Deron Johnson.

Class	Team	League	W	L	PCT	Finish	Manager
Majors	Minnesota Twins	American	59	103	.364	15th (15)	Paul Molitor
Triple-A	Rochester Red Wings	International	81	63	.563	4th (14)	Mike Quade
Double-A	Chattanooga Lookouts	Southern	75	65	.536	4th (10)	Doug Mientkiewicz
High A	Fort Myers Miracle	Florida State	70	68	.507	7th (12)	Jeff Smith
Low A	Cedar Rapids Kernels	Midwest	78	61	.561	4th (16)	Jake Mauer
Rookie	Elizabethton Twins	Appalachian	36	31	.537	5th (10)	Ray Smith
Rookie	Twins	Gulf Coast	32	29	.525	6th (17)	Ramon Borrego
Overall 2016 Minor League Record			372	317	.540	5th (30)	

ORGANIZATION STATISTICS

MINNESOTA TWINS
AMERICAN LEAGUE

Batting	B-T	HT	WT	DOB	AVG	vLH	vRH	G	AB	R	H	2B	3B	HR	RBI	BB	HBP	SH	SF	SO	SB	CS	SLG	OBP
Arcia, Oswaldo	L-R	6-0	225	5-9-91	.214	.263	.202	32	103	8	22	4	0	4	12	10	1	0	0	46	0	0	.369	.289
2-team total (21 Tampa Bay)					.229	—	—	53	157	15	36	6	1	6	19	16	1	0	1	65	1	1	.395	.303
Beresford, James	L-R	6-1	170	1-19-89	.227	—	.227	10	22	0	5	1	0	0	0	1	0	1	0	6	0	0	.273	.261
Buxton, Byron	R-R	6-2	190	12-18-93	.225	.223	.225	92	298	44	67	19	6	10	38	23	3	4	3	118	10	2	.430	.284
Centeno, Juan	L-R	5-9	195	11-16-89	.261	.250	.265	55	176	16	46	12	1	3	25	12	1	3	0	38	0	0	.392	.312
Dozier, Brian	R-R	5-11	200	5-15-87	.268	.282	.264	155	615	104	165	35	5	42	99	61	8	2	5	138	18	2	.546	.340
Escobar, Eduardo	B-R	5-10	185	1-5-89	.236	.207	.249	105	352	32	83	14	2	6	37	21	1	2	1	72	1	3	.338	.280
Grossman, Robbie	B-L	6-0	215	9-16-89	.280	.344	.242	99	332	49	93	19	1	11	37	55	2	0	0	96	2	3	.443	.386
Kepler, Max	L-L	6-4	205	2-10-93	.235	.203	.248	113	396	52	93	20	2	17	63	42	3	1	5	93	6	2	.424	.309
Mastroianni, Darin	R-R	5-11	190	8-26-85	.000	.000	.000	7	9	1	0	0	0	0	0	2	0	0	0	4	1	0	.000	.182
Mauer, Joe	L-R	6-5	225	4-19-83	.261	.224	.272	134	494	68	129	22	4	11	49	79	1	0	2	93	2	0	.389	.363
Murphy, John Ryan	R-R	5-11	205	5-13-91	.146	.192	.125	26	82	4	12	3	0	1	3	5	0	2	1	19	0	0	.220	.193
Nunez, Eduardo	R-R	6-0	195	6-15-87	.296	.311	.292	91	371	49	110	15	1	12	47	15	3	2	5	58	27	6	.439	.325
Park, Byung Ho	R-R	6-1	220	7-10-86	.191	.170	.198	62	215	28	41	9	1	12	24	21	5	0	3	80	1	0	.409	.275
Plouffe, Trevor	R-R	6-2	215	6-15-86	.260	.240	.266	84	319	35	83	13	1	12	47	19	2	1	3	60	1	0	.420	.303
Polanco, Jorge	B-R	5-11	200	7-5-93	.282	.309	.271	69	245	24	69	15	4	4	27	17	3	2	3	46	4	3	.424	.332
Rosario, Eddie	L-R	6-1	180	9-28-91	.269	.263	.270	92	335	52	90	17	2	10	32	12	2	2	3	91	5	2	.421	.295
Sano, Miguel	R-R	6-4	260	5-11-93	.236	.227	.238	116	437	57	103	22	1	25	66	54	1	0	3	178	1	0	.462	.319
Santana, Danny	B-R	5-11	185	11-7-90	.240	.146	.265	75	233	29	56	10	2	2	14	12	1	1	1	55	12	9	.326	.279
Schafer, Logan	L-L	6-1	190	9-8-86	.238	.421	.159	26	63	8	15	3	1	0	1	8	2	1	0	16	0	0	.317	.342
Suzuki, Kurt	R-R	5-11	205	10-4-83	.258	.275	.250	106	345	34	89	24	1	8	49	18	5	1	4	48	0	0	.403	.301
Vargas, Kennys	B-R	6-5	290	8-1-90	.230	.378	.168	47	152	27	35	11	0	10	20	24	0	0	1	57	0	0	.500	.333

Pitching	B-T	HT	WT	DOB	W	L	ERA	G	GS	CG	SV	IP	H	R	ER	HR	BB	SO	AVG	vLH	vRH	K/9	BB/9
Abad, Fernando	L-L	6-1	220	12-17-85	1	4	2.65	39	0	0	1	34	27	11	10	2	14	29	.220	.163	.257	7.68	3.71
2-team total (18 Boston)					1	6	3.66	57	0	0	1	47	40	20	19	4	22	41	—	—	—	7.91	4.24
Albers, Andrew	R-L	6-1	200	10-6-85	0	0	5.82	6	2	0	0	17	27	16	11	5	6	16	.342	.176	.387	8.47	3.18
Berrios, Jose	R-R	6-0	185	5-27-94	3	7	8.02	14	14	0	0	58	74	56	52	12	35	49	.310	.29	.33	7.56	5.40
Boshers, Buddy	L-L	6-3	205	5-9-88	2	0	4.25	37	0	0	0	36	35	21	17	3	7	37	.248	.241	.253	9.25	1.75
Chargois, J.T.	B-R	6-3	200	12-3-90	1	1	4.70	25	0	0	0	23	25	12	12	0	12	17	.291	.281	.296	6.65	4.70
Dean, Pat	L-L	6-1	195	5-25-89	1	6	6.28	19	9	0	0	67	88	47	47	13	23	50	.321	.293	.329	6.68	3.07
Duffey, Tyler	R-R	6-3	220	12-27-90	9	12	6.43	26	26	0	0	133	167	103	95	25	32	114	.301	.266	.337	7.71	2.17
Fien, Casey	R-R	6-2	210	10-21-83	1	0	7.90	14	0	0	0	14	21	12	12	5	3	12	.350	.292	.389	7.90	1.98
Gibson, Kyle	R-R	6-6	215	10-23-87	6	11	5.07	25	25	1	0	147	175	89	83	20	55	104	.298	.326	.273	6.35	3.36
Graham, J.R.	R-R	5-11	195	1-14-90	0	0	10.80	1	0	0	0	2	3	2	2	0	1	2	.375	.000	.600	10.80	5.40
Hughes, Phil	R-R	6-5	240	6-24-86	1	7	5.95	12	11	1	0	59	76	40	39	11	13	34	.313	.385	.279	5.19	1.98
Jepsen, Kevin	R-R	6-3	235	7-26-84	2	5	6.16	33	0	0	7	31	42	22	21	7	12	22	.333	.370	.313	6.46	3.52
2-team total (25 Tampa Bay)					2	6	5.98	58	0	0	7	50	62	35	33	12	21	35	—	—	—	6.34	3.81
Kintzler, Brandon	R-R	6-0	190	8-1-84	2	2	3.15	54	0	0	17	54	59	22	19	5	8	35	.276	.250	.295	5.80	1.33
Light, Pat	R-R	6-5	220	3-29-91	0	1	9.00	15	0	0	0	14	15	14	14	2	15	14	.259	.182	.306	9.00	9.64
2-team total (2 Boston)					0	1	11.34	17	0	0	0	17	22	22	21	4	16	16	—	—	—	8.64	8.64
May, Trevor	R-R	6-5	240	9-23-89	2	2	5.27	44	0	0	0	43	39	26	25	7	17	60	.232	.153	.275	12.66	3.59
Mejia, Adalberto	L-L	6-3	195	6-20-93	0	0	7.71	1	0	0	0	2	5	2	2	0	1	0	.455	1.000	.333	0.00	3.86
Meyer, Alex	R-R	6-9	225	1-3-90	0	1	12.27	2	1	0	0	4	8	5	5	1	4	5	.421	.429	.417	12.27	9.82
2-team total (5 Los Angeles)					1	3	5.68	7	6	0	0	25	25	16	16	3	17	29	—	—	—	10.30	6.04
Milone, Tommy	L-L	6-0	220	2-16-87	3	5	5.71	19	12	0	0	69	84	53	44	15	22	49	.299	.276	.305	6.36	2.86
Nolasco, Ricky	R-R	6-2	235	12-13-82	4	8	5.13	21	21	0	0	125	139	77	71	18	29	93	.287	.267	.305	6.71	2.09
2-team total (11 Los Angeles)					8	14	4.42	32	32	1	0	198	202	104	97	26	44	144	—	—	—	6.56	2.00
O'Rourke, Ryan	R-L	6-3	230	4-30-88	0	1	3.96	26	0	0	0	25	18	13	11	3	10	24	.207	.077	.262	8.64	3.60
Perkins, Glen	L-L	6-0	205	3-2-83	0	0	9.00	2	0	0	0	2	5	2	2	0	1	3	.500	.400	.600	13.50	4.50
Pressly, Ryan	R-R	6-3	210	12-15-88	6	7	3.70	72	0	0	1	75	79	34	31	8	23	67	.266	.252	.275	8.00	2.75
Ramirez, Neil	R-R	6-4	215	5-25-89	0	0	6.14	8	0	0	0	15	15	10	10	5	10	11	.278	.308	.250	6.75	6.14
Rogers, Taylor	L-L	6-3	170	12-17-90	3	1	3.96	57	0	0	0	61	61	29	27	7	16	64	.260	.202	.291	9.39	2.35
Santana, Ervin	R-R	6-2	175	12-12-82	7	11	3.38	30	30	2	0	181	168	78	68	19	53	149	.245	.247	.244	7.40	2.63

MINNESOTA TWINS

Pitching	B-T	HT	WT	DOB	W	L	ERA	G	GS	CG	SV	IP	H	R	ER	HR	BB	SO	AVG	vLH	vRH	K/9	BB/9
Santiago, Hector	R-L	6-0	215	12-16-87	3	6	5.58	11	11	0	0	61	65	39	38	13	22	37	.267	.263	.268	5.43	3.23
2-team total (22 Los Angeles)					13	10	4.70	33	33	0	0	182	169	100	95	33	79	144	—	—	—	7.12	3.91
Tonkin, Michael	R-R	6-7	220	11-19-89	3	2	5.02	65	0	0	0	72	80	46	40	13	24	80	.280	.306	.266	10.05	3.01
Wimmers, Alex	L-R	6-2	215	11-1-88	1	3	4.15	16	0	0	0	17	14	8	8	2	11	14	.237	.2	.256	7.27	5.71

Fielding

Catcher	PCT	G	PO	A	E	DP	PB
Centeno	.983	53	321	34	6	3	5
Murphy	.995	25	187	12	1	0	3
Suzuki	.993	99	679	28	5	2	1

First Base	PCT	G	PO	A	E	DP
Beresford	.971	6	28	5	1	6
Kepler	1.000	2	5	0	0	0
Mauer	.998	95	811	53	2	91
Park	.995	24	189	17	1	25
Plouffe	.991	13	106	10	1	10
Vargas	.996	32	240	14	1	27

Second Base	PCT	G	PO	A	E	DP
Beresford	1.000	1	0	1	0	0
Dozier	.989	151	286	419	8	118
Escobar	1.000	6	5	8	0	3
Nunez	.882	5	7	8	2	2
Polanco	.958	5	9	14	1	3
Santana	—	3	0	0	0	0

Third Base	PCT	G	PO	A	E	DP
Beresford	1.000	3	1	5	0	2
Escobar	.980	23	13	35	1	4
Nunez	.957	33	25	42	3	7
Plouffe	.960	63	31	114	6	13
Polanco	.864	9	2	17	3	2
Sano	.896	42	35	94	15	10
Santana	.833	1	1	4	1	0

Shortstop	PCT	G	PO	A	E	DP
Escobar	.970	71	87	200	9	62
Nunez	.970	51	54	137	6	33
Polanco	.942	47	50	128	11	26
Santana	1.000	3	6	8	0	1

Outfield	PCT	G	PO	A	E	DP
Arcia	.963	29	50	2	2	0
Buxton	.984	92	243	2	4	0
Escobar	—	2	0	0	0	0
Grossman	.940	75	122	4	8	1
Kepler	.971	112	224	9	7	4
Mastroianni	1.000	6	4	0	0	0
Rosario	.979	89	176	10	4	0
Sano	.962	38	75	0	3	0
Santana	.979	61	136	2	3	1
Schafer	1.000	22	38	2	0	0

ROCHESTER RED WINGS
INTERNATIONAL LEAGUE

TRIPLE-A

Batting	B-T	HT	WT	DOB	AVG	vLH	vRH	G	AB	R	H	2B	3B	HR	RBI	BB	HBP	SH	SF	SO	SB	CS	SLG	OBP
Beresford, James	L-R	6-1	170	1-19-89	.269	.195	.294	122	465	63	125	14	3	0	35	43	1	4	3	78	2	1	.312	.330
Britton, Buck	L-R	6-0	170	5-16-86	.194	.156	.206	73	253	27	49	13	1	3	25	16	0	0	2	47	0	1	.289	.240
Buxton, Byron	R-R	6-2	190	12-18-93	.305	.277	.315	49	190	41	58	11	3	11	24	14	3	0	2	58	7	0	.568	.359
Centeno, Juan	L-R	5-9	195	11-16-89	.245	.385	.194	15	49	5	12	1	0	1	5	4	1	0	4	1	0	0	.327	.315
English, Tanner	R-R	5-10	160	3-11-93	.294	.000	.455	5	17	1	5	1	0	0	0	1	0	1	0	5	2	0	.353	.333
Field, Tommy	R-R	5-10	185	2-22-87	.235	.228	.238	82	281	33	66	13	2	11	42	26	7	2	2	59	1	2	.413	.313
2-team total (15 Toledo)					.226	—	—	97	318	38	72	14	2	11	44	31	9	2	2	71	2	2	.387	.311
Garver, Mitch	R-R	6-1	220	1-15-91	.329	.500	.229	22	76	6	25	5	0	1	8	7	0	0	1	21	0	0	.434	.381
Grossman, Robbie	B-L	6-0	215	9-16-89	.250	.500	.250	1	4	1	1	0	0	0	1	0	0	0	0	1	1	0	.250	.250
2-team total (34 Columbus)					.256	—	—	35	121	15	31	5	0	6	14	21	0	1	0	36	4	1	.446	.366
Hicks, John	R-R	6-2	230	8-31-89	.242	.250	.238	9	33	1	8	2	0	1	1	1	0	0	0	5	0	0	.394	.265
2-team total (70 Toledo)					.296	—	—	79	274	39	81	22	0	9	43	18	3	3	0	64	3	1	.474	.346
Kepler, Max	L-L	6-4	205	2-10-93	.282	.345	.259	30	110	16	31	4	6	1	19	16	0	0	2	14	1	1	.455	.367
Mastroianni, Darin	R-R	5-11	190	8-26-85	.256	.209	.270	51	180	20	46	6	1	6	15	18	2	1	2	39	8	3	.300	.327
Meneses, Heiker	R-R	5-9	200	7-1-91	.103	.091	.106	23	58	7	6	1	1	0	4	8	0	1	1	24	1	0	.155	.209
Murphy, David	L-L	6-3	210	10-18-81	.194	.250	.150	10	36	3	7	1	0	1	3	3	0	0	0	9	0	0	.306	.256
Murphy, John Ryan	R-R	5-11	205	5-13-91	.236	.258	.229	83	263	24	62	14	0	3	39	21	0	0	6	51	0	0	.323	.286
Olson, Brian	R-R	6-0	171	1-21-93	.000	—	.000	1	3	0	0	0	0	0	0	0	0	0	0	0	0	0	.000	.000
Palka, Daniel	L-R	6-2	220	10-28-91	.232	.236	.230	54	203	31	47	12	0	13	25	18	1	0	1	86	2	1	.483	.296
Park, Byung Ho	R-R	6-1	220	7-10-86	.224	.091	.255	31	116	18	26	5	0	10	19	6	6	0	0	32	0	0	.526	.297
Paulino, Carlos	R-R	6-0	175	9-24-89	.232	.368	.148	34	99	10	23	5	0	0	11	12	0	1	2	22	0	0	.283	.310
Plouffe, Trevor	R-R	6-2	215	6-15-86	.316	.333	.286	5	19	4	6	2	0	1	2	1	0	0	0	5	0	0	.579	.350
Polanco, Jorge	B-R	5-11	200	7-5-93	.276	.293	.271	75	293	32	81	14	6	9	39	27	1	0	4	51	5	4	.457	.335
Reginatto, Leonardo	R-R	6-2	180	4-10-90	.241	.321	.196	23	79	2	19	3	0	0	9	3	0	1	1	19	0	0	.278	.265
Rodriguez, Reynaldo	R-R	6-0	195	7-2-86	.220	.266	.193	50	173	21	38	7	0	4	12	21	0	0	0	45	3	0	.329	.304
Rosario, Eddie	L-R	6-1	180	9-28-91	.319	.294	.330	41	160	26	51	14	0	7	25	7	0	0	2	25	5	3	.538	.343
Sano, Miguel	R-R	6-4	260	5-11-93	.160	.100	.190	8	25	3	4	1	0	2	5	0	0	0	0	10	0	0	.440	.300
Santana, Danny	B-R	5-11	185	11-7-90	.364	.500	.286	3	11	3	4	0	0	0	0	0	0	0	0	2	1	0	.364	.364
Schafer, Logan	L-L	6-1	200	9-8-86	.264	.286	.256	64	216	29	57	7	1	4	19	22	3	0	3	35	5	2	.361	.340
Tovar, Wilfredo	R-R	5-10	185	8-25-91	.276	.239	.125	45	150	49	112	24	4	1	35	32	3	5	4	59	29	9	.327	.301
Vargas, Kennys	B-R	6-5	290	8-1-90	.233	.131	.283	96	330	41	77	16	1	15	58	66	2	0	4	89	1	0	.424	.361
Walker, Adam Brett	R-R	6-5	225	10-18-91	.243	.264	.235	132	478	61	116	22	5	27	75	44	2	0	7	202	7	4	.479	.305
Wickens, Stephen	R-R	5-10	170	3-5-89	.200	.091	.241	30	80	11	16	2	0	3	5	10	0	1	0	23	3	1	.338	.289

Pitching	B-T	HT	WT	DOB	W	L	ERA	G	GS	CG	SV	IP	H	R	ER	HR	BB	SO	AVG	vLH	vRH	K/9	BB/9
Albers, Andrew	L-L	6-1	200	10-6-85	10	6	3.69	21	21	2	0	124	150	53	51	10	30	84	.305	.353	.286	6.08	2.17
Baxendale, D.J.	R-R	6-2	190	12-8-90	2	1	1.29	23	0	0	0	35	28	9	5	1	8	40	.214	.224	.207	10.29	2.06
Bencomo, Omar	R-R	6-1	170	2-10-89	3	1	3.49	5	4	0	0	28	31	12	11	2	5	23	.277	.300	.250	7.31	1.59
Berrios, Jose	R-R	6-0	185	5-27-94	10	5	2.51	17	17	1	0	111	74	39	31	8	36	125	.191	.160	.216	10.10	2.91
Boshers, Buddy	L-L	6-3	205	5-9-88	1	1	3.52	22	0	0	2	26	18	8	1	1	11	29	.194	.182	.200	10.04	3.81
Burnett, Sean	L-L	5-11	185	9-17-82	0	3	2.15	29	0	0	3	29	20	9	7	1	7	18	.194	.150	.222	5.52	2.15
3-team total (6 Gwinnett, 5 Syracuse)					0	3	2.27	40	0	0	3	40	30	12	10	2	8	27	—	—	—	6.13	1.82
Busenitz, Alan	R-R	6-1	180	8-22-90	2	0	3.52	6	0	0	1	8	8	3	3	0	4	5	.267	.231	.294	5.87	4.70
Chargois, J.T.	B-R	6-3	200	12-3-90	2	1	1.29	28	0	0	9	35	27	7	5	1	8	41	.208	.216	.203	10.54	2.06
Darnell, Logan	L-L	6-2	220	2-2-89	8	8	3.53	18	18	2	0	110	105	47	43	7	36	53	.260	.225	.273	4.35	2.95
Dean, Pat	L-L	6-1	195	5-25-89	5	7	5.56	16	16	1	0	87	113	58	54	10	19	49	.309	.369	.291	5.05	1.96

Pitching	B-T	HT	WT	DOB	W	L	ERA	G	GS	CG	SV	IP	H	R	ER	HR	BB	SO	AVG	vLH	vRH	K/9	BB/9
Duffey, Tyler	R-R	6-3	220	12-27-90	1	1	2.93	5	5	1	0	31	24	10	10	4	12	25	.212	.206	.22	7.34	3.52
Gibson, Kyle	R-R	6-6	215	10-23-87	1	0	1.50	1	1	0	0	6	7	2	1	0	3	2	.292	.250	.375	3.00	4.50
Graham, J.R.	R-R	5-11	195	1-14-90	2	0	10.80	8	0	0	3	8	11	10	10	1	7	7	.324	.300	.333	7.56	7.56
2-team total (2 Scranton/W-B)					2	2	7.94	10	0	0	3	11	14	10	10	1	7	11	—	—	—	8.74	5.56
Greenwood, Nick	R-L	6-1	180	9-28-87	6	3	2.84	16	11	0	1	79	76	26	25	5	11	41	.261	.234	.274	4.65	1.25
Hurlbut, David	L-L	6-3	221	11-24-80	0	2	4.50	5	5	0	0	26	37	14	13	0	3	14	.336	.227	.364	4.85	1.04
Kintzler, Brandon	R-R	6-0	190	8-1-84	4	1	3.52	10	0	0	0	15	15	6	6	0	3	11	.273	.296	.250	6.46	1.76
Light, Pat	R-R	6-5	220	3-29-91	1	0	2.57	6	0	0	2	7	5	2	2	0	2	6	.200	.250	.176	7.71	2.57
2-team total (25 Pawtucket)					2	1	2.37	31	0	0	9	38	26	10	10	1	19	42	—	—	—	9.95	4.50
Martinez, David	R-R	6-2	220	8-4-87	1	3	6.23	19	6	0	0	52	64	37	36	8	13	41	.296	.194	.374	7.10	2.25
May, Trevor	R-R	6-5	240	9-23-89	0	1	2.45	4	0	0	1	4	1	1	1	0	1	6	.083	.000	.125	14.73	2.45
Mejia, Adalberto	L-L	6-3	195	6-20-93	2	2	3.76	4	4	0	0	26	28	11	11	3	3	25	.269	.226	.288	8.54	1.03
Meyer, Alex	R-R	6-9	225	1-3-90	1	1	1.04	3	2	0	1	17	11	2	2	0	4	19	.183	.111	.214	9.87	2.08
Milone, Tommy	L-L	6-0	220	2-16-87	4	0	1.66	7	7	0	0	49	41	11	9	4	4	41	.225	.170	.244	7.58	0.74
Mujica, Edward	R-R	6-3	220	5-10-84	0	0	1.35	6	0	0	3	7	6	1	1	0	2	8	.240	.300	.200	10.80	2.70
2-team total (36 Lehigh Valley)					0	3	3.35	42	0	0	26	46	48	20	17	3	6	35	—	—	—	6.90	1.18
O'Rourke, Ryan	R-L	6-3	230	4-30-88	1	1	1.93	33	0	0	1	28	26	9	6	1	6	29	.255	.255	.255	9.32	1.93
Ramirez, Neil	R-R	6-4	215	5-25-89	0	0	3.10	16	0	0	0	20	14	7	7	2	7	27	.197	.133	.244	11.95	3.10
Reed, Jake	R-R	6-2	190	9-29-92	1	1	1.69	9	0	0	0	11	8	2	2	0	2	8	.211	.231	.200	6.75	1.69
Rogers, Taylor	L-L	6-3	170	12-17-90	0	1	4.50	7	2	0	0	18	24	15	9	1	6	15	.316	.261	.340	7.50	3.00
Runzler, Dan	L-L	6-4	210	3-30-85	1	2	5.82	20	0	0	0	22	24	17	14	0	16	18	.273	.269	.274	7.48	6.65
Van Mil, Loek	R-R	7-1	260	9-15-84	0	1	23.63	5	1	0	0	5	17	15	14	1	6	4	.531	.500	.545	6.75	10.13
Walden, Marcus	R-R	6-0	195	9-13-88	1	1	2.54	36	0	0	5	46	41	15	13	1	13	33	.236	.190	.261	6.46	2.54
Wheeler, Jason	L-L	6-6	255	10-27-90	11	6	3.53	24	24	1	0	145	137	60	57	13	37	113	.245	.292	.230	7.00	2.29
Wimmers, Alex	L-R	6-2	215	11-1-88	2	1	3.62	39	0	0	11	50	42	22	20	2	24	50	.226	.205	.239	9.06	4.35

Fielding

Catcher	PCT	G	PO	A	E	DP	PB
Centeno	.971	14	61	7	2	0	0
Garver	1.000	14	96	9	0	1	1
Hicks	.985	9	63	2	1	0	1
Murphy	.997	80	590	31	2	5	9
Olson	1.000	1	9	1	0	0	0
Paulino	1.000	34	205	18	0	2	3

First Base	PCT	G	PO	A	E	DP
Beresford	1.000	25	201	14	0	15
Britton	1.000	6	54	2	0	2
Garver	.955	2	21	0	1	2
Park	.992	14	120	8	1	10
Plouffe	1.000	1	5	2	0	2
Rodriguez	.982	24	214	5	4	23
Vargas	.997	77	665	30	2	56

Second Base	PCT	G	PO	A	E	DP
Beresford	.994	42	82	97	1	24

	PCT	G	PO	A	E	DP
Britton	—	1	0	0	0	0
Field	.995	33	63	118	1	27
Meneses	.971	6	18	15	1	6
Polanco	.978	64	122	185	7	41
Tovar	1.000	1	2	1	0	1
Wickens	1.000	1	4	4	0	2

Third Base	PCT	G	PO	A	E	DP
Beresford	.972	52	23	82	3	9
Britton	1.000	16	6	37	0	3
Field	.957	26	19	47	3	3
Meneses	.952	8	5	15	1	1
Plouffe	1.000	2	1	3	0	1
Polanco	.857	2	0	6	1	0
Reginatto	.957	23	8	36	2	1
Sano	1.000	5	5	6	0	0
Wickens	.896	20	10	33	5	1

Shortstop	PCT	G	PO	A	E	DP
Field	.944	15	19	49	4	7

	PCT	G	PO	A	E	DP
Meneses	.960	7	7	17	1	0
Santana	1.000	1	0	1	0	0
Tovar	.971	125	178	400	17	85

Outfield	PCT	G	PO	A	E	DP
Britton	.982	35	53	2	1	1
Buxton	.991	47	103	2	1	0
English	1.000	5	11	0	0	0
Field	1.000	5	6	0	0	0
Grossman	—	1	0	0	0	0
Kepler	1.000	30	80	1	0	0
Mastroianni	1.000	50	126	1	0	0
Murphy	.952	8	19	1	1	0
Palka	.977	47	84	2	2	0
Rodriguez	.969	15	31	0	1	0
Rosario	.989	40	88	5	1	1
Sano	.000	1	0	0	1	0
Santana	1.000	3	5	0	0	0
Schafer	.984	63	113	7	2	0
Walker	.970	97	153	7	5	0

CHATTANOOGA LOOKOUTS
SOUTHERN LEAGUE

DOUBLE-A

Batting	B-T	HT	WT	DOB	AVG	vLH	vRH	G	AB	R	H	2B	3B	HR	RBI	BB	HBP	SH	SF	SO	SB	CS	SLG	OBP
Corcino, Edgar	B-R	6-1	210	6-7-92	.284	.250	.295	50	183	26	52	7	6	2	27	13	1	0	1	35	1	1	.421	.333
Garver, Mitch	R-R	6-1	220	1-15-91	.257	.161	.277	95	358	44	92	25	0	11	66	43	1	0	5	86	1	3	.419	.334
Goodrum, Niko	B-R	6-3	198	2-28-92	.275	.302	.264	49	182	25	50	10	2	6	28	22	2	0	1	52	8	2	.451	.357
Granite, Zack	L-L	6-1	175	9-17-92	.295	.291	.296	127	526	86	155	18	8	4	52	42	3	8	5	43	56	14	.382	.347
Harrison, Travis	R-R	6-1	215	10-17-92	.230	.260	.222	120	434	62	100	22	2	7	52	61	11	0	3	126	15	11	.339	.338
Hicks, D.J.	L-R	6-5	247	4-2-90	.264	.228	.274	111	420	47	111	27	0	6	59	52	3	0	2	109	2	0	.371	.348
Maloney, Joe	R-R	6-2	190	7-27-90	.241	.206	.252	39	145	12	35	11	1	1	16	14	3	0	0	51	1	1	.352	.321
Meneses, Heiker	R-R	5-9	200	7-1-91	.313	.400	.273	4	16	3	5	1	0	0	3	1	0	0	0	2	0	0	.375	.353
Michael, Levi	R-R	5-10	180	2-9-91	.215	.277	.189	96	316	41	68	4	7	2	27	23	12	6	1	83	5	2	.291	.293
Palka, Daniel	L-L	6-2	220	10-28-91	.270	.289	.263	79	300	42	81	12	4	21	65	38	1	0	6	100	7	4	.547	.348
Paulino, Carlos	R-R	6-0	175	9-24-89	.200	.333	.143	3	10	1	2	0	0	0	1	1	0	0	0	3	0	0	.200	.333
Reginatto, Leonardo	R-R	6-2	180	4-10-90	.270	.233	.280	109	404	44	109	17	2	2	37	31	7	5	6	66	9	3	.337	.328
Rodriguez, Jairo	R-R	5-11	180	8-24-88	.136	.222	.114	13	44	4	6	1	0	0	4	0	0	2	0	10	0	0	.159	.136
Turner, Stuart	R-R	6-2	220	12-27-91	.239	.371	.202	97	322	40	77	22	0	6	41	35	7	1	5	72	5	3	.363	.322
Vielma, Engelb	B-R	5-11	155	6-22-94	.271	.338	.249	90	314	47	85	7	4	0	21	34	3	13	3	62	10	8	.318	.345
Walker, Ryan	L-R	6-1	157	3-26-92	.274	.237	.289	79	296	49	81	10	4	2	30	32	4	3	3	63	13	5	.355	.349
White, T.J.	R-R	5-10	200	10-28-91	.218	.200	.225	58	197	29	43	6	4	0	22	16	6	0	2	48	9	9	.289	.294
Wilkerson, Shannon	R-R	6-0	200	7-20-88	.241	.321	.210	59	199	26	48	10	1	2	20	14	2	4	1	28	1	3	.332	.296
Witt, Tanner	R-R	6-0	195	1-25-91	.194	.000	.273	9	31	4	6	1	0	0	2	1	1	1	0	6	2	0	.226	.242

Pitching	B-T	HT	WT	DOB	W	L	ERA	G	GS	CG	SV	IP	H	R	ER	HR	BB	SO	AVG	vLH	vRH	K/9	BB/9
Bard, Luke	R-R	6-3	202	11-13-90	0	0	4.91	9	0	0	0	15	16	8	8	1	8	12	.281	.269	.290	7.36	4.91

Pitching

Pitching	B-T	HT	WT	DOB	W	L	ERA	G	GS	CG	SV	IP	H	R	ER	HR	BB	SO	AVG	vLH	vRH	K/9	BB/9
Baxendale, D.J.	R-R	6-2	190	12-8-90	6	7	3.44	14	14	1	0	81	82	32	31	4	16	59	.270	.221	.311	6.56	1.78
Bencomo, Omar	R-R	6-1	170	2-10-89	4	6	3.86	19	7	0	3	56	60	32	24	5	18	41	.279	.304	.260	6.59	2.89
Burdi, Nick	R-R	6-5	220	1-19-93	1	0	9.00	3	0	0	0	3	4	3	3	0	1	1	.308	.333	.250	3.00	3.00
Busenitz, Alan	R-R	6-1	180	8-22-90	0	0	3.52	5	0	0	0	8	9	3	3	0	1	5	.310	.250	.385	5.87	1.17
Chargois, J.T.	B-R	6-3	200	12-3-90	0	0	1.54	11	0	0	7	12	8	3	2	1	5	14	.190	.200	.182	10.80	3.86
Eades, Ryan	R-R	6-2	200	12-15-91	6	5	4.61	26	19	0	0	113	112	63	58	4	44	91	.264	.293	.239	7.23	3.49
Fernandez, Raul	R-R	6-2	180	6-22-90	3	2	3.55	26	0	0	6	38	35	15	15	2	15	29	.250	.226	.269	6.87	3.55
Gonsalves, Stephen	L-L	6-5	213	7-8-94	8	1	1.82	13	13	1	0	74	43	17	15	1	37	89	.171	.148	.178	10.78	4.48
Greenwood, Nick	R-L	6-1	180	9-28-87	3	1	4.09	5	5	0	0	33	37	15	15	4	2	16	.287	.238	.296	4.36	0.55
Hildenberger, Trevor	R-R	6-2	211	12-15-90	2	3	0.70	32	0	0	16	39	21	4	3	2	6	45	.157	.172	.145	10.47	1.40
Hurlbut, David	L-L	6-3	221	11-24-89	7	7	3.51	23	23	1	0	136	161	68	53	11	26	90	.295	.286	.298	5.96	1.72
Jay, Tyler	L-L	6-1	185	4-19-94	0	0	5.79	5	2	0	0	14	13	10	9	2	5	9	.245	.158	.294	5.79	3.21
Jones, Zack	R-R	6-1	195	12-4-90	2	2	2.53	21	0	0	2	32	22	9	9	1	15	46	.198	.170	.219	12.94	4.22
Jorge, Felix	R-R	6-2	170	1-2-94	3	5	4.12	11	11	1	0	74	83	34	34	7	12	32	.290	.294	.287	3.87	1.45
LeBlanc, Randy	R-R	6-4	185	3-7-92	1	0	0.00	2	1	0	1	10	5	0	0	0	4	9	.161	.235	.071	8.10	3.60
Lee, Brett	L-L	6-4	210	9-20-90	0	0	8.59	6	0	0	0	7	12	9	7	0	3	7	.364	.364	.364	8.59	3.68
2-team total (18 Biloxi)					2	1	7.57	24	0	0	0	27	41	25	23	3	16	15	—	—	—	4.94	5.27
Melotakis, Mason	R-L	6-2	220	6-28-91	1	2	2.97	36	0	0	0	33	36	12	11	3	12	42	.277	.231	.297	11.34	3.24
Peterson, Brandon	R-R	6-1	190	9-23-91	1	2	4.15	16	0	0	0	26	20	12	12	1	15	31	.211	.326	.102	10.73	5.19
Reed, Jake	R-R	6-2	190	9-29-92	3	3	3.90	41	0	0	3	60	51	29	26	2	22	64	.235	.256	.220	9.60	3.30
Rosario, Randy	L-L	6-1	200	5-18-94	0	1	10.50	4	0	0	0	6	6	7	7	1	5	10	.250	.333	.222	15.00	7.50
Slegers, Aaron	R-R	6-10	245	9-4-92	10	7	3.41	25	25	0	0	145	137	61	55	11	46	104	.258	.263	.254	6.44	2.85
Stewart, Kohl	R-R	6-3	195	10-7-94	9	6	3.03	16	16	1	0	92	91	40	31	4	44	47	.265	.265	.264	4.60	4.30
Strong, Mike	L-L	6-0	195	11-17-88	0	3	8.66	16	0	0	0	18	22	17	17	1	13	10	.314	.211	.353	5.09	6.62
Van Steensel, Todd	R-R	6-1	215	1-14-91	1	0	2.25	5	0	0	0	8	6	2	2	1	2	7	.207	.300	.158	7.88	2.25
Walden, Marcus	R-R	6-0	195	9-13-88	0	0	1.74	6	0	0	1	10	3	2	2	0	3	7	.091	.083	.095	6.10	2.61
Westphal, Luke	L-L	6-3	230	6-14-89	1	0	5.40	18	0	0	0	30	35	21	18	3	23	37	.294	.250	.310	11.10	6.90
Wheeler, Jason	L-L	6-6	255	10-27-90	1	1	1.88	4	0	0	0	24	20	9	5	0	3	22	.220	.350	.183	8.25	1.13
Williams, Corey	L-L	6-2	205	7-4-90	2	0	4.14	22	0	0	0	37	30	17	17	6	26	27	.231	.262	.216	6.57	6.32
Wimmers, Alex	L-R	6-2	215	11-1-88	0	1	6.43	6	0	0	0	7	10	5	5	0	1	6	.345	.533	.143	7.71	1.29

Fielding

Catcher	PCT	G	PO	A	E	DP	PB
Garver	.992	46	316	44	3	5	6
Paulino	.933	2	14	0	1	0	0
Rodriguez	.990	12	84	13	1	2	2
Turner	.994	83	590	55	4	4	8

First Base	PCT	G	PO	A	E	DP
Garver	.981	14	101	1	2	16
Goodrum	1.000	1	3	0	0	0
Harrison	1.000	1	14	0	0	2
Hicks	.997	101	935	56	3	102
Palka	1.000	3	18	0	0	2
Walker	1.000	8	73	1	0	11
White	1.000	13	107	6	0	8

Second Base	PCT	G	PO	A	E	DP
Meneses	1.000	1	2	3	0	0
Michael	.988	88	180	240	5	70
Reginatto	1.000	2	3	7	0	0
Vielma	.982	11	25	31	1	9
Walker	.990	43	84	116	2	33
Witt	1.000	1	2	2	0	0

Third Base	PCT	G	PO	A	E	DP
Goodrum	.899	24	14	48	7	4
Harrison	1.000	8	0	11	0	1
Meneses	1.000	1	1	1	0	0
Reginatto	.922	34	27	56	7	11
Vielma	.984	21	10	51	1	9
Walker	.936	15	6	38	3	4
White	.924	41	32	90	10	6
Witt	—	1	0	0	0	0

Shortstop	PCT	G	PO	A	E	DP
Goodrum	.982	12	17	38	1	12
Meneses	.750	2	1	5	2	2
Reginatto	.987	70	104	197	4	45
Vielma	.954	57	103	165	13	38

Outfield	PCT	G	PO	A	E	DP
Corcino	.978	49	83	5	2	2
Goodrum	.750	2	3	0	1	0
Granite	.997	125	291	13	1	2
Harrison	.989	99	172	9	2	2
Maloney	1.000	17	37	1	0	1
Palka	.962	66	97	5	4	0
Walker	1.000	17	7	1	0	0
Wilkerson	.979	52	93	0	2	0

FORT MYERS MIRACLE   HIGH CLASS A
FLORIDA STATE LEAGUE

Batting	B-T	HT	WT	DOB	AVG	vLH	vRH	G	AB	R	H	2B	3B	HR	RBI	BB	HBP	SH	SF	SO	SB	CS	SLG	OBP
Christensen, Chad	R-R	6-3	205	10-6-90	.190	.200	.184	42	116	13	22	1	1	2	7	8	2	4	0	34	6	3	.267	.254
Corcino, Edgar	B-R	6-1	210	6-7-92	.266	.319	.247	74	267	41	71	13	5	6	32	29	1	0	0	51	6	1	.419	.340
Diemer, Austin	R-R	6-1	195	4-28-93	.167	.174	.164	30	84	10	14	2	0	1	4	1	4	1	1	27	3	3	.226	.211
English, Tanner	R-R	5-10	160	3-11-93	.235	.417	.189	33	119	24	28	3	4	4	10	20	1	1	1	47	10	0	.429	.348
Escobar, Eduardo	B-R	5-10	185	1-5-89	.364	.500	.286	3	11	1	4	1	1	0	0	1	0	0	0	1	0	0	.636	.417
Garcia, Kevin	R-R	5-9	190	9-17-92	.250	.250	.250	16	44	4	11	3	0	0	8	3	3	0	1	9	0	0	.318	.333
Goodrum, Niko	B-R	6-3	198	2-28-92	.280	.250	.308	6	25	3	7	4	0	1	5	1	0	0	0	7	1	0	.560	.308
Gordon, Nick	L-R	6-0	160	10-24-95	.291	.220	.315	116	461	56	134	26	6	3	52	23	8	1	0	87	19	13	.386	.335
Hartong, Brad	R-R	6-4	215	2-4-92	.200	.154	.214	23	55	7	11	1	0	0	4	5	1	0	1	12	1	0	.218	.313
Ibarra, Chris	R-R	5-7	179	9-10-92	.203	.087	.250	21	79	9	16	5	1	1	9	6	1	0	0	12	0	0	.329	.267
Kihle, Daniel	R-L	6-0	190	10-1-93	.259	.080	.313	41	108	20	28	4	1	2	16	11	5	2	1	32	3	4	.370	.352
Maloney, Joe	R-R	6-2	190	7-27-90	.263	.351	.229	75	262	30	69	17	2	5	35	20	5	1	4	91	6	2	.401	.323
Martinez, Luis	B-R	5-11	170	10-25-95	.111	.333	.000	6	9	2	1	0	0	1	1	0	0	0	1	0	0	0	.111	.200
Miller, Sean	R-R	5-11	175	10-10-94	.186	.222	.171	18	59	7	11	3	0	0	5	1	1	1	1	12	1	1	.237	.210
Murphy, Max	R-R	5-11	195	11-17-92	.257	.314	.234	49	175	20	45	8	0	5	16	8	2	0	1	34	2	1	.389	.296
Murray, A.J.	R-R	6-2	215	4-4-93	.209	.225	.204	55	187	24	39	10	1	4	16	16	5	1	2	42	1	0	.337	.286
Navarreto, Brian	R-R	6-4	220	12-29-94	.197	.264	.176	72	229	20	45	8	0	2	21	11	5	1	2	51	0	0	.258	.247
Olson, Brian	R-R	6-0	171	1-21-93	.250	.250	.250	15	32	2	8	2	0	0	3	5	0	1	1	9	0	1	.313	.342
Paul, Chris	R-R	6-2	200	10-12-92	.219	.160	.237	92	338	33	74	14	3	2	36	22	5	2	5	86	4	0	.296	.273
Perez, Alex	L-R	5-10	180	10-24-92	.242	.250	.241	69	198	21	48	6	0	0	16	31	0	9	0	41	3	1	.273	.345

Batting	B-T	HT	WT	DOB	AVG	vLH	vRH	G	AB	R	H	2B	3B	HR	RBI	BB	HBP	SH	SF	SO	SB	CS	SLG	OBP
Plouffe, Trevor	R-R	6-2	215	6-15-86	.125	.000	.143	2	8	0	1	0	0	0	0	0	0	0	0	2	0	0	.125	.125
Real, Alex	R-R	6-0	210	1-19-93	.249	.318	.227	51	185	11	46	7	0	5	23	10	1	0	2	39	0	0	.368	.288
Rodriguez, Reynaldo	R-R	6-0	195	7-2-86	.308	1.000	.250	4	13	2	4	0	0	2	2	3	0	0	0	4	0	0	.769	.438
Santana, Danny	B-R	5-11	185	11-7-90	.200	.500	.125	3	10	2	2	0	0	1	1	0	0	0	0	2	1	0	.500	.200
Swim, Alex	B-R	5-0	185	3-26-91	.204	.143	.225	28	108	7	22	3	0	0	8	4	1	0	2	12	0	0	.231	.235
Vavra, Trey	R-R	6-2	185	9-17-91	.230	.243	.225	125	430	38	99	17	0	8	40	38	17	1	2	83	6	4	.326	.316
Vielma, Engelb	B-R	5-11	155	6-22-94	.200	.000	.238	8	25	5	5	0	0	0	0	5	0	0	8	2	0	.200	.333
Wade, LaMonte	L-L	6-1	189	1-1-94	.318	.286	.329	32	110	17	35	8	1	4	24	10	4	0	3	17	1	1	.518	.386
Wade, Logan	B-R	6-1	190	11-13-91	.209	.027	.250	55	201	14	42	6	4	1	19	10	1	1	2	48	4	3	.294	.248
Walker, Ryan	L-R	6-1	157	3-26-92	.262	.280	.254	24	84	10	22	0	2	0	6	5	0	1	0	10	1	1	.310	.340
White, T.J.	R-R	5-10	200	1-24-92	.274	.270	.275	59	234	37	64	12	2	7	30	18	8	1	1	51	3	3	.432	.345
Witt, Tanner	R-R	6-0	195	1-25-91	.246	.306	.222	67	224	25	55	11	1	2	20	25	2	3	5	42	2	0	.330	.320

Pitching	B-T	HT	WT	DOB	W	L	ERA	G	GS	CG	SV	IP	H	R	ER	HR	BB	SO	AVG	vLH	vRH	K/9	BB/9
Anderson, Nick	R-R	6-5	195	7-5-90	0	3	3.58	30	0	0	10	38	33	16	15	2	13	47	.241	.258	.227	11.23	3.11
Bard, Luke	R-R	6-3	202	11-13-90	3	1	3.40	35	0	0	2	50	47	21	19	0	20	45	.246	.322	.212	8.05	3.58
Booser, Cameron	L-L	6-3	225	5-4-92	0	2	4.85	9	0	0	0	13	8	7	7	2	8	20	.174	.154	.182	13.85	5.54
Clay, Sam	L-L	6-2	190	6-21-93	1	3	6.80	10	10	1	0	41	51	34	31	2	29	32	.315	.2	.336	7.02	6.37
Curtiss, John	R-R	6-4	200	4-5-93	0	2	3.06	38	0	0	3	53	42	20	18	0	23	68	.220	.217	.221	11.55	3.91
Fernandez, Raul	R-R	6-2	180	6-22-90	1	1	2.33	17	0	0	0	27	24	8	7	3	8	18	.235	.182	.261	6.00	2.67
Gibson, Kyle	R-R	6-6	215	10-23-87	0	0	0.96	2	2	0	0	9	9	1	1	0	1	8	.273	.2	.333	7.71	0.96
Gilbert, Brian	R-R	6-1	224	8-9-92	0	0	5.53	24	0	0	0	28	29	21	17	3	27	19	.282	.303	.271	6.18	8.78
Gonsalves, Stephen	L-L	6-5	213	7-8-94	5	4	2.33	11	11	1	0	66	43	19	17	2	20	66	.188	.255	.17	9.05	2.74
Hildenberger, Trevor	R-R	6-2	211	12-15-90	1	1	0.96	6	0	0	3	9	11	2	1	0	0	8	.282	.357	.24	7.71	0.00
Jay, Tyler	L-L	6-1	185	4-19-94	5	5	2.84	13	13	0	0	70	64	24	22	5	21	68	.248	.277	.242	8.78	2.71
Jorge, Felix	R-R	6-2	170	1-2-94	9	3	1.55	14	14	2	0	93	76	19	16	3	11	77	.226	.248	.208	7.45	1.06
Landa, Yorman	R-R	6-0	175	6-11-94	2	2	3.24	31	0	0	7	42	39	18	15	0	22	39	.257	.224	.272	8.42	4.75
Lara, Confesor	R-R	6-2	170	8-7-90	1	0	1.13	5	0	0	1	8	6	2	1	0	1	5	.200	0	.261	5.63	1.13
2-team total (21 Lakeland)					3	2	3.57	26	0	0	3	35	33	16	14	2	16	35	—	—		8.92	4.08
LeBlanc, Randy	R-R	6-4	185	3-7-92	5	7	4.70	13	13	1	0	69	79	40	36	3	22	41	.294	.353	.247	5.35	2.87
Lombana, Logan	R-R	6-3	225	7-17-94	0	0	3.38	1	0	0	0	3	5	1	1	0	2	1	.417	0	.455	3.38	6.75
Lujan, Hector	R-R	6-3	230	8-23-94	0	1	9.00	1	0	0	0	1	1	1	1	0	1	0	.250	1	0	9.00	0.00
Nordgren, Miles	R-R	6-2	190	6-12-92	1	5	5.50	7	7	0	0	38	43	27	23	3	13	17	.287	.274	.295	4.06	3.11
Peterson, Brandon	R-R	6-1	190	9-23-91	3	0	2.65	22	0	0	4	34	20	11	10	1	14	44	.171	.257	.134	11.65	3.71
Rodriguez, Dereck	R-R	6-1	180	6-5-92	1	2	2.56	5	5	0	0	32	29	12	9	4	2	18	.248	.212	.277	5.12	0.57
Romero, Fernando	R-R	6-0	215	12-24-94	5	2	1.88	11	11	0	0	62	48	15	13	1	10	65	.211	.244	.173	9.39	1.44
Rosario, Randy	L-L	6-1	200	5-18-94	6	6	3.34	21	16	0	1	94	102	47	35	3	34	68	.278	.282	.277	6.49	3.24
Stashak, Cody	R-R	6-2	169	6-4-94	2	0	0.54	3	3	0	0	17	13	1	1	0	3	10	.217	.163	.353	5.40	1.62
Steele, Keaton	R-R	6-3	225	10-30-91	8	11	3.60	23	23	1	0	132	137	61	53	3	40	85	.267	.265	.269	5.78	2.72
Stewart, Kohl	R-R	6-3	195	10-7-94	3	2	5.60	9	9	0	0	52	39	19	15	2	19	44	.207	.229	.195	7.66	3.31
Theofanopoulos, Mike	L-L	6-1	185	8-5-92	2	3	2.73	23	0	0	1	33	24	10	10	2	18	39	.205	.211	.203	10.64	4.91
Van Steensel, Todd	R-R	6-1	215	1-14-91	4	2	3.46	39	0	0	5	55	48	25	21	1	27	50	.238	.354	.182	8.23	4.45
Westphal, Luke	L-L	6-3	230	6-14-89	2	0	3.65	17	1	0	0	25	18	14	10	1	22	32	.207	.19	.212	11.68	8.03

Fielding

Catcher	PCT	G	PO	A	E	DP	PB
Garcia	.991	15	100	10	1	1	6
Murray	.993	37	249	16	2	0	6
Navarreto	.985	70	518	68	9	14	5
Olson	.985	10	59	8	1	1	2
Real	1.000	2	7	0	0	0	0
Swim	.968	13	87	4	3	0	3

First Base	PCT	G	PO	A	E	DP
Hartong	1.000	1	1	0	0	0
Murray	.983	6	51	6	1	3
Paul	.986	18	126	10	2	25
Real	.990	18	187	6	2	19
Rodriguez	1.000	2	16	1	0	0
Swim	1.000	2	15	2	0	4
Vavra	.990	83	685	44	7	66
Wade	1.000	3	10	0	0	0
White	.987	15	142	8	2	27

Second Base	PCT	G	PO	A	E	DP
Gordon	.923	2	5	7	1	5
Miller	1.000	8	15		0	3
Perez	.983	55	99	134	4	52
Vielma	1.000	3	10	2	0	1
Wade	.985	14	19	47	1	9
Walker	.972	22	47	59	3	16
White	1.000	1	2	3	0	1
Witt	.964	38	63	127	7	34

Third Base	PCT	G	PO	A	E	DP
Goodrum	1.000	1	2	4	0	1
Gordon	.667	1	1	1	1	0
Ibarra	.976	21	14	26	1	2
Miller	.889	3	2	6	1	2
Paul	.953	62	41	120	8	13
Plouffe	1.000	2	3	6	0	1
Santana	.800	1	1	3	1	0
Vavra	—	1	0	0	0	0
Vielma	.750	1	3	0	1	0
Wade	1.000	2	1	5	0	1
White	.871	40	17	71	13	10
Witt	1.000	6	7	6	0	0

Shortstop	PCT	G	PO	A	E	DP
Escobar	1.000	3	3	8	0	1
Goodrum	.857	2	1	5	1	0
Gordon	.952	103	157	322	24	85
Miller	.914	8	12	20	3	6
Perez	.974	9	8	29	1	3
Vielma	.900	4	4	14	2	5
Wade	.889	13	15	33	6	9

Outfield	PCT	G	PO	A	E	DP
Christensen	.984	37	61	0	1	0
Corcino	.968	66	118	3	4	0
Diemer	1.000	25	35	3	0	1
English	.982	28	51	3	1	1
Goodrum	1.000	2	2	0	0	0
Hartong	1.000	20	37	3	0	1
Kihle	.987	40	75	3	1	1
Maloney	.990	63	91	9	1	0
Martinez	1.000	5	3	0	0	0
Murphy	.988	45	77	4	1	1
Paul	1.000	10	15	1	0	0
Rodriguez	—	1	0	0	0	0
Santana	1.000	2	2	0	0	0
Swim	1.000	6	3	1	0	0
Vavra	.977	31	41	1	1	1
Wade	1.000	24	47	1	0	0
Wade	.968	24	29	1	1	0
Witt	1.000	10	13	0	0	0

Batting	B-T	HT	WT	DOB	AVG	vLH	vRH	G	AB	R	H	2B	3B	HR	RBI	BB	HBP	SH	SF	SO	SB	CS	SLG	OBP
Arraez, Luis	L-R	5-10	155	4-9-97	.347	.333	.351	114	475	67	165	31	3	3	66	31	1	4	3	51	3	3	.444	.386
Blankenhorn, Travis	L-R	6-2	208	8-3-96	.286	.227	.304	25	91	11	26	5	2	1	12	8	2	0	0	28	2	1	.418	.356
Cavaness, Christian	L-L	6-2	190	3-16-94	.201	.239	.191	68	219	28	44	2	3	0	18	13	0	3	1	65	4	4	.237	.294
Davis, Jaylin	R-R	6-1	190	7-1-94	.250	.255	.248	52	192	32	48	13	1	9	29	21	5	0	0	64	3	0	.469	.339
Diemer, Austin	R-R	6-1	195	4-28-93	.222	.333	.185	10	36	3	8	1	0	1	3	3	0	0	0	12	1	1	.333	.282
Fernandez, Jorge	B-R	6-3	188	3-30-94	.225	.272	.213	117	435	50	98	26	2	10	52	36	8	0	6	115	2	2	.363	.293
Garcia, Kevin	R-R	5-9	190	9-17-92	.248	.250	.248	38	145	12	36	8	0	1	11	7	2	0	0	39	4	0	.324	.292
Guzman, Manuel	B-R	5-9	160	2-10-95	.182	.250	.135	30	88	14	16	1	0	0	3	14	0	0	1	12	4	3	.193	.291
Hartong, Brad	R-R	6-4	215	2-4-92	.256	.348	.236	35	129	16	33	7	1	0	9	3	3	2	2	22	2	0	.326	.285
Hayman, Bryant	R-R	6-0	215	10-13-92	.121	.000	.182	12	33	2	4	0	0	2	4	1	0	1	5	0	0	.121	.231
Ibarra, Chris	R-R	5-7	179	9-10-92	.264	.217	.275	35	125	17	33	6	1	2	13	20	2	0	0	23	0	0	.376	.374
Kihle, Daniel	R-L	6-0	190	10-1-93	.259	.289	.252	49	193	35	50	5	0	2	17	14	3	1	1	50	5	2	.316	.318
Lopez, Brandon	R-R	6-1	190	9-9-93	.286	.385	.263	18	70	8	20	3	0	0	7	11	2	0	1	16	0	0	.329	.393
Miller, Sean	R-R	5-11	175	10-1-94	.263	.259	.264	90	361	48	95	17	4	4	50	10	5	5	7	56	7	5	.366	.287
Molina, Nelson	L-R	6-3	175	4-30-95	.300	.196	.321	94	333	37	100	15	3	2	43	38	3	5	3	53	5	1	.381	.374
Murphy, Max	R-R	5-11	195	11-17-92	.159	.118	.174	18	63	7	10	1	2	0	8	6	2	0	0	20	3	0	.238	.254
Murray, A.J.	R-R	6-2	215	4-4-93	.262	.356	.229	59	229	27	60	15	1	6	33	24	7	0	3	64	0	0	.415	.346
Olson, Brian	R-R	6-0	171	1-21-93	.211	.143	.236	21	76	13	16	6	0	0	10	7	0	0	1	24	0	0	.289	.274
Palacios, Jermaine	R-R	6-0	145	7-19-96	.222	.214	.224	71	261	34	58	8	3	1	28	18	3	2	4	39	3	4	.287	.276
Paul, Chris	R-R	6-2	200	10-12-92	.346	.286	.368	7	26	6	9	1	1	0	4	3	0	0	0	6	0	0	.462	.414
Perez, Alex	L-R	5-10	180	10-24-92	.262	.143	.298	18	61	8	16	1	1	0	10	14	1	1	1	11	0	0	.311	.403
Scoggins, Casey	L-L	5-10	185	3-14-94	.243	.154	.264	52	202	27	49	6	1	0	13	25	0	4	2	45	3	2	.282	.323
Silva, Rainis	R-R	6-1	185	3-20-96	.230	.367	.188	37	126	20	29	3	0	0	12	11	1	0	0	32	0	0	.254	.297
Valera, Rafael	R-R	5-11	180	8-15-94	.261	.321	.241	30	115	16	30	9	4	0	11	17	2	0	0	30	3	3	.409	.366
Wade, LaMonte	L-L	6-1	189	1-1-94	.280	.333	.265	56	207	32	58	6	3	4	27	44	5	0	5	27	5	3	.396	.410
Wiel, Zander	R-R	6-3	232	1-11-93	.259	.205	.275	128	501	75	130	27	8	19	86	55	3	3	6	125	7	1	.459	.333

Pitching	B-T	HT	WT	DOB	W	L	ERA	G	GS	CG	SV	IP	H	R	ER	HR	BB	SO	AVG	vLH	vRH	K/9	BB/9
Anderson, Brady	R-R	6-0	185	11-10-92	3	1	2.62	6	6	0	0	34	37	12	10	1	7	19	.285	.265	.296	4.98	1.83
Anderson, Nick	R-R	6-5	195	7-5-90	4	0	0.90	12	0	0	3	20	6	3	2	0	3	28	.090	.077	.098	12.60	1.35
Beardsley, Tyler	R-R	6-4	225	5-17-94	1	2	3.86	5	5	0	0	26	21	13	11	1	9	13	.219	.178	.255	4.56	3.16
Booser, Cameron	L-L	6-3	225	5-4-92	0	2	12.41	12	0	0	0	12	23	14	2	1	23	14	.267	.313	.241	10.22	16.78
Cederoth, Michael	R-R	6-6	195	11-25-92	4	0	2.45	30	0	0	0	48	35	15	13	3	33	61	.200	.214	.190	11.52	6.23
Clay, Sam	L-L	6-2	190	6-21-93	5	4	3.39	14	14	0	0	74	65	32	28	0	38	83	.240	.220	.249	10.05	4.60
Cordy, Max	R-R	6-4	220	6-9-93	1	2	3.00	15	0	0	1	27	23	12	9	1	15	33	.228	.236	.217	11.00	5.00
Curtiss, John	R-R	6-4	200	4-5-93	0	0	0.00	6	0	0	2	8	2	0	0	0	2	17	.077	.154	.000	19.13	2.25
Cutura, Andro	R-R	6-0	195	8-22-93	3	1	5.14	6	0	0	0	28	25	17	16	0	15	28	.231	.264	.200	9.00	4.82
Davis, Colton	R-R	6-1	190	1-5-94	0	0	0.00	2	0	0	0	2	0	0	0	0	2	3	.000	.000	.000	13.50	9.00
Del Rosario, Eduardo	R-R	6-0	145	5-19-95	6	2	3.67	16	16	0	0	83	75	34	34	7	32	81	.244	.248	.239	8.75	3.46
Gibbons, Sam	L-R	6-4	190	12-12-93	7	6	4.71	30	15	0	0	107	115	71	56	10	47	69	.276	.246	.301	5.80	3.95
Hackimer, Thomas	R-R	5-11	190	6-28-94	1	3	2.39	21	0	0	5	26	21	12	7	1	12	26	.223	.302	.157	8.89	4.10
Irby, C.K.	R-R	6-1	200	5-6-92	1	3	2.53	14	0	0	1	21	18	8	6	1	7	24	.240	.216	.263	10.13	2.95
LeBlanc, Randy	R-R	6-4	185	3-7-92	6	2	0.74	9	9	1	0	61	39	6	5	0	11	37	.189	.207	.176	5.46	1.62
Lo, Kuo	R-R	5-10	195	10-28-92	0	2	2.60	25	0	0	3	45	35	24	13	4	31	42	.213	.155	.275	8.40	6.20
Lombana, Logan	R-R	6-3	225	7-17-94	0	0	5.06	14	0	0	0	27	27	15	15	2	11	27	.262	.318	.220	9.11	3.71
McIver, Anthony	L-L	6-5	190	4-8-92	0	2	2.58	31	0	0	10	52	46	19	15	2	12	55	.238	.311	.193	9.46	2.06
Nordgren, Miles	R-R	6-2	190	6-12-92	4	6	2.91	17	13	1	0	90	92	39	29	2	22	80	.262	.260	.263	8.03	2.21
Poppen, Sean	R-R	6-4	195	3-15-94	1	1	2.12	4	3	0	0	17	11	4	4	1	6	19	.180	.115	.229	10.06	3.18
Ramirez, Williams	R-R	6-1	200	8-8-92	3	1	2.62	29	0	0	4	55	24	16	16	1	34	66	.134	.157	.111	10.80	5.56
Rodriguez, Dereck	R-R	6-4	185	5-28-92	4	11	5.08	18	18	0	0	101	98	64	57	7	38	93	.254	.260	.247	8.29	3.39
Romero, Fernando	R-R	6-0	215	12-24-94	4	1	1.93	5	5	0	0	28	19	7	6	1	5	25	.186	.152	.216	8.04	1.61
Stashak, Cody	R-R	6-2	169	6-4-94	8	5	3.16	18	17	0	1	105	90	38	37	4	30	80	.233	.263	.205	6.84	2.56
Theofanopoulos, Mike	L-L	6-1	185	8-5-92	3	0	1.67	21	0	0	2	32	18	8	6	1	16	45	.153	.139	.159	12.53	4.45
Tillery, Zach	R-R	6-3	210	1-12-93	1	1	8.10	6	0	0	0	10	12	9	9	0	10	12	.316	.267	.348	10.80	9.00
Vasquez, Andrew	B-L	6-6	228	9-14-93	1	0	1.59	13	0	0	1	28	13	7	5	0	12	36	.134	.077	.172	11.44	3.81
Wells, Lachlan	L-L	5-8	165	2-27-97	6	4	1.77	12	12	0	0	71	57	21	14	4	16	63	.218	.222	.216	7.95	2.02

Fielding

Catcher	PCT	G	PO	A	E	DP	PB
Fernandez	1.000	1	3	1	0	0	1
Garcia	.976	36	292	29	8	1	8
Hayman	1.000	9	69	7	0	0	1
Murray	.988	45	436	44	6	4	5
Olson	.993	15	120	13	1	1	2
Silva	.992	32	219	25	2	1	5
Valera	1.000	4	17	4	0	0	1

First Base	PCT	G	PO	A	E	DP
Fernandez	.979	17	124	14	3	11
Molina	1.000	1	0	1	0	1
Wiel	.985	123	1058	85	17	99

Second Base	PCT	G	PO	A	E	DP
Arraez	.976	82	133	239	9	57
Blankenhorn	1.000	8	10	22	0	2
Garcia	1.000	1	2	0	0	1
Guzman	.971	17	29	39	2	8
Miller	1.000	34	73	0	14	
Perez	.971	12	13	21	1	5
Valera	.923	4	6	6	1	3

Third Base	PCT	G	PO	A	E	DP
Arraez	.857	3	3	3	1	1
Blankenhorn	.667	1	1	1	1	0
Ibarra	.929	32	25	53	6	5

	PCT	G	PO	A	E	DP
Miller	.951	34	23	55	4	10
Molina	.946	67	53	106	9	14
Paul	.889	6	3	5	1	0
Valera	.750	3	0	6	2	0

Shortstop	PCT	G	PO	A	E	DP
Guzman	.976	9	10	31	1	6
Lopez	.946	18	18	52	4	6
Miller	.967	35	55	91	5	22
Molina	.917	15	17	38	5	5
Palacios	.952	69	110	167	14	38

Outfield	PCT	G	PO	A	E	DP
Arraez	1.000	1	1	1	0	1
Cavaness	.991	64	108	1	1	0
Davis	.956	50	85	2	4	0
Diemer	1.000	9	18	2	0	0
Fernandez	.970	87	151	8	5	2
Hartong	.984	34	57	4	1	2
Hayman	—	1	0	0	0	0
Kihle	.987	47	72	5	1	2
Murphy	1.000	17	20	2	0	0
Scoggins	.993	52	130	3	1	1
Valera	.895	10	15	2	2	0
Wade	.991	52	109	5	1	0

ELIZABETHTON TWINS   ROOKIE
APPALACHIAN LEAGUE

Batting	B-T	HT	WT	DOB	AVG	vLH	vRH	G	AB	R	H	2B	3B	HR	RBI	BB	HBP	SH	SF	SO	SB	CS	SLG	OBP
Blankenhorn, Travis	L-R	6-2	208	8-3-96	.297	.200	.344	34	138	30	41	7	1	9	29	8	2	0	1	33	3	0	.558	.342
Cabbage, Trey	L-R	6-3	204	5-3-97	.204	.192	.208	31	98	16	20	5	1	2	8	11	2	0	0	38	2	1	.337	.297
Carrier, Shane	R-R	6-2	220	6-8-96	.270	.280	.255	55	207	21	57	14	2	6	29	7	2	0	3	42	3	1	.449	.301
Cavaness, Christian	L-L	6-2	190	3-16-94	.235	.500	.200	6	17	4	4	0	0	0	0	3	0	0	0	4	0	0	.235	.350
Davis, Jaylin	R-R	6-1	190	7-1-94	.277	.313	.258	12	47	12	13	1	0	7	12	4	1	0	0	23	2	0	.745	.346
Diaz, Lewin	L-L	6-3	180	11-19-96	.310	.305	.313	46	174	26	54	15	2	9	37	12	0	0	1	35	0	0	.575	.353
Gonzalez, Roberto	L-L	6-0	195	3-14-95	.221	.500	.169	24	77	7	17	4	1	1	7	4	0	0	0	29	3	0	.338	.259
Guzman, Manuel	B-R	5-9	160	2-10-95	.333	.000	.429	5	18	1	6	1	0	0	1	2	0	0	0	2	0	0	.389	.400
Hamilton, Caleb	R-R	6-0	185	2-5-95	.207	.236	.188	45	140	25	29	7	2	2	15	28	3	1	0	44	2	1	.329	.351
Hayman, Bryant	R-R	6-0	215	10-13-92	.194	.188	.197	31	103	4	20	5	0	1	9	2	1	0	3	46	0	0	.272	.211
Jernigan, Andre	R-R	6-0	205	11-16-93	.243	.311	.194	36	107	16	26	6	1	2	15	13	2	0	0	41	1	1	.374	.336
Kiriloff, Alex	L-L	6-2	195	11-9-97	.306	.275	.324	55	216	33	66	9	1	7	33	11	2	0	3	32	0	1	.454	.341
Kranson, Mitchell	L-R	5-9	210	1-11-94	.245	.228	.255	43	163	23	40	6	0	4	15	13	2	0	0	40	0	0	.356	.309
Lopez, Brandon	R-R	6-1	190	9-9-93	.337	.306	.357	27	92	20	31	5	1	0	9	21	3	0	1	19	4	0	.413	.470
Martinez, Luis	B-R	5-11	170	10-25-95	.223	.333	.155	34	94	16	21	3	0	0	3	11	1	1	0	17	2	1	.255	.311
Minier, Amaurys	B-R	6-2	190	1-30-96	.222	.200	.234	48	167	20	37	8	0	10	32	24	0	0	1	62	0	0	.449	.318
Molina, Robert	R-R	5-11	175	9-16-96	.135	.103	.156	25	74	6	10	1	0	0	5	4	2	0	0	16	0	0	.149	.200
Montesino, Ariel	B-R	5-10	170	9-21-95	.299	.301	.298	47	187	33	56	4	1	0	13	13	0	1	1	34	7	6	.332	.343
Morrison, Hank	R-R	6-2	225	3-25-94	.148	.148	.147	20	61	9	9	1	2	0	3	7	1	0	0	18	0	0	.230	.246
Rortvedt, Ben	L-R	5-10	190	9-25-97	.250	.222	.273	13	40	2	10	0	0	0	7	5	1	1	0	2	0	0	.250	.348
Scoggins, Casey	L-L	5-10	185	3-14-94	.167	.333	.111	4	12	0	2	0	0	0	0	0	0	0	0	7	0	0	.167	.167

Pitching	B-T	HT	WT	DOB	W	L	ERA	G	GS	CG	SV	IP	H	R	ER	HR	BB	SO	AVG	vLH	vRH	K/9	BB/9
Beardsley, Tyler	R-R	6-4	225	5-17-94	2	0	2.65	7	5	0	1	34	32	12	10	2	6	33	.246	.269	.231	8.74	1.59
Beeker, Clark	R-R	6-3	205	11-22-92	0	1	2.38	2	2	0	0	11	7	3	3	2	2	12	.179	.167	.185	9.53	1.59
Carlini, Domenick	L-L	6-4	175	11-19-93	1	7	4.83	12	8	1	1	50	63	32	27	3	10	41	.310	.356	.297	7.33	1.79
Cordy, Max	R-R	6-4	220	6-9-93	1	0	3.18	3	0	0	0	6	9	2	2	0	4	9	.360	.400	.333	14.29	6.35
Davis, Colton	R-R	6-1	190	1-5-94	0	2	3.26	13	0	0	5	19	11	7	7	0	8	23	.169	.235	.146	10.71	3.72
De Jesus, Miguel	R-R	6-2	175	9-20-95	0	2	3.00	4	4	0	0	18	14	8	6	1	8	13	.222	.355	.094	6.50	4.00
Grogan, Quin	R-R	6-2	205	6-11-93	2	2	3.86	13	0	0	0	26	21	12	11	3	13	28	.223	.077	.279	9.82	4.56
Jax, Griffin	R-R	6-2	195	11-22-94	0	1	4.15	4	0	0	0	9	15	4	4	2	1	8	.385	.526	.250	8.31	1.04
Lujan, Hector	R-R	6-3	230	8-23-94	3	0	5.35	19	0	0	3	35	39	25	21	5	10	30	.271	.356	.232	7.64	2.55
Martinez, Jose	R-R	6-2	180	10-29-96	1	5	7.88	11	11	0	0	48	76	43	42	8	18	26	.365	.411	.341	4.88	3.38
Mason, Ryan	R-R	6-7	215	10-4-94	3	2	5.33	11	9	1	1	49	58	31	29	5	8	32	.297	.228	.326	5.88	1.47
McGuff, Patrick	L-R	6-2	200	3-30-94	2	0	2.77	18	0	0	9	26	23	9	8	1	10	33	.240	.314	.197	11.42	3.46
Poppen, Sean	R-R	6-4	195	3-15-94	2	3	2.97	8	8	0	0	36	34	18	12	2	18	38	.250	.219	.260	9.41	4.46
Quezada, Johan	R-R	6-6	200	8-25-94	2	1	5.04	19	0	0	3	30	24	21	17	1	21	29	.214	.189	.227	8.60	6.23
Robinson, Alex	L-L	6-3	217	8-11-94	0	1	3.00	15	0	0	0	33	19	15	11	2	34	52	.162	.118	.181	14.18	9.27
Schick, Alex	R-R	6-7	210	12-1-94	5	2	5.25	11	8	1	0	48	45	29	28	3	15	49	.247	.211	.264	9.19	2.81
Tribby, Austin	R-L	6-5	225	7-9-94	5	0	5.40	16	0	0	0	32	44	24	19	3	14	30	.333	.341	.330	8.53	3.98
Vasquez, Andrew	B-L	6-6	228	9-14-93	2	0	0.90	4	0	0	0	10	6	2	1	0	4	15	.182	.000	.240	13.50	3.60
Wells, Tyler	R-R	6-8	265	8-26-94	5	2	3.23	10	10	1	0	47	40	22	17	0	17	59	.223	.227	.221	11.22	3.23

Fielding

C: Hayman 24, Jernigan 1, Kranson 11, Molina 24, Rortvedt 13. **1B:** Diaz 39, Hayman 1, Kranson 3, Minier 26. **2B:** Blankenhorn 29, Guzman 3, Hamilton 6, Jernigan 29, Molina 1, Montesino 3. **3B:** Blankenhorn 2, Cabbage 30, Hamilton 13, Kranson 16, Montesino 9. **SS:** Cabbage 1, Guzman 2, Hamilton 1, Jernigan 3, Lopez 25, Montesino 35. **OF:** Carrier 49, Cavaness 5, Davis 11, Gonzalez 18, Hamilton 23, Kirilloff 49, Martinez 33, Minier 1, Morrison 18, Scoggins 4.

GCL TWINS   ROOKIE
GULF COAST LEAGUE

Batting	B-T	HT	WT	DOB	AVG	vLH	vRH	G	AB	R	H	2B	3B	HR	RBI	BB	HBP	SH	SF	SO	SB	CS	SLG	OBP
Aluko, Isaiah	L-L	6-4	230	11-24-93	.133	.000	.200	5	15	3	2	0	0	1	2	2	0	0	0	7	0	0	.333	.235
Alvarez, Jhonathan	R-R	6-0	190	2-18-96	.259	.318	.222	25	58	6	15	2	0	0	3	11	0	0	1	11	0	0	.293	.371
Andrade, Jorge	B-R	5-10	170	12-7-94	.239	.353	.172	14	46	8	11	4	1	0	6	9	0	2	1	16	5	2	.370	.357
Arias, Jean Carlos	L-L	5-11	170	1-14-98	.202	.167	.213	45	124	14	25	4	2	0	9	10	1	3	1	28	7	3	.266	.265
Baddoo, Akil	L-L	5-11	185	8-16-98	.178	.242	.149	38	107	15	19	0	2	2	15	18	1	0	1	36	8	1	.271	.299
Blanco, Dominic	L-R	6-2	215	11-10-95	.300	.375	.250	7	20	0	6	1	0	0	3	3	0	0	0	6	0	0	.350	.391
Cronin, Joe	R-R	5-10	185	5-15-94	.198	.160	.214	24	81	6	16	1	0	1	7	9	5	1	1	17	3	2	.247	.313
Davis, Tyree	B-R	6-3	175	9-4-95	.216	.244	.196	34	97	10	21	6	2	1	4	9	1	0	0	44	4	5	.351	.290
English, Tanner	R-R	5-10	160	3-11-93	.333	—	.333	3	9	1	3	0	0	1	3	2	0	0	0	5	0	0	.667	.455
Featherstone, Zach	L-L	6-2	215	12-18-95	.212	.107	.254	34	99	9	21	5	1	0	6	9	3	1	1	42	1	1	.283	.295
Guzman, Manuel	B-R	5-9	160	2-10-95	.200	.300	.160	11	35	4	7	0	0	0	3	1	0	0	1	6	5	4	.200	.282
Hartong, Brad	R-R	6-4	215	2-4-92	.333	.667	.000	2	6	2	2	0	0	0	1	0	0	0	1	2	0	0	.333	.429
Hazard, Justin	L-R	6-3	195	9-9-93	.280	.281	.279	25	93	9	26	6	0	1	8	1	0	1	1	16	1	1	.376	.284

Batting

Batting	B-T	HT	WT	DOB	AVG	vLH	vRH	G	AB	R	H	2B	3B	HR	RBI	BB	HBP	SH	SF	SO	SB	CS	SLG	OBP
Hutcheon, Dane	L-R	5-9	177	7-14-94	.216	.292	.192	34	97	15	21	2	0	0	6	14	1	3	0	21	5	2	.237	.321
Kendrick, Kolton	L-R	6-3	215	8-10-96	.073	.000	.100	14	41	1	3	0	0	1	1	7	1	0	0	24	0	1	.146	.224
Marrero, Lean	L-R	5-10	160	9-19-97	.290	.353	.260	36	107	10	31	6	1	2	12	5	0	2	1	16	5	3	.421	.319
Martinez, Luis	B-R	5-11	170	10-25-95	.357	.500	.333	4	14	2	5	3	0	0	2	2	0	0	0	4	1	1	.571	.438
Meneses, Heiker	R-R	5-9	200	7-1-91	.257	.125	.368	13	35	6	9	0	0	0	4	6	2	0	0	8	1	1	.257	.395
Miranda, Jose	R-R	6-2	180	6-29-98	.227	.224	.228	55	185	14	42	7	1	1	20	19	4	2	3	36	4	5	.292	.308
Morel, Emmanuel	R-R	5-10	150	5-4-97	.116	.139	.100	32	86	7	10	2	0	0	4	13	0	4	1	36	4	3	.140	.230
Munoz, Jorge	R-R	6-1	180	6-21-96	.256	.229	.271	54	199	23	51	13	1	2	18	13	6	1	5	37	13	3	.362	.314
Murphy, Max	R-R	5-11	195	11-17-92	.375	.000	.500	3	8	1	3	2	0	0	2	1	0	0	0	2	0	0	.625	.444
Olson, Brian	R-R	6-0	171	1-21-93	.217	.167	.235	10	23	1	5	3	0	0	5	0	0	0	0	9	0	0	.348	.357
Rortvedt, Ben	L-R	5-10	190	9-25-97	.203	.211	.200	20	59	3	12	3	0	0	3	5	1	1	0	8	0	0	.254	.277
Salva, Kidany	B-R	5-11	185	8-24-98	.179	.111	.191	18	56	4	10	1	1	0	6	3	0	0	1	13	1	0	.232	.217
Tapia, Roni	R-R	6-3	175	4-3-97	.127	.174	.094	20	55	5	7	1	0	3	5	3	0	0	0	29	0	1	.309	.172
Valera, Rafael	R-R	5-11	180	8-15-94	.250	.000	.333	1	4	1	1	0	0	0	1	0	0	0	0	2	1	0	.500	.400
Whitefield, Aaron	R-R	6-4	200	9-2-96	.298	.250	.325	51	191	30	57	7	0	2	17	19	4	1	2	47	31	9	.366	.370

Pitching

Pitching	B-T	HT	WT	DOB	W	L	ERA	G	GS	CG	SV	IP	H	R	ER	HR	BB	SO	AVG	vLH	vRH	K/9	BB/9
Anderson, Brady	L-R	6-0	185	11-10-92	2	0	0.98	8	0	0	0	28	18	3	3	0	2	25	.182	.239	.132	8.13	0.65
Balazovic, Jordan	R-R	6-4	175	9-17-98	2	1	1.97	8	6	0	1	32	26	9	7	0	5	16	.217	.213	.219	4.50	1.41
Beeker, Clark	R-R	6-3	205	11-22-92	2	1	2.51	12	1	0	2	32	27	11	9	2	8	40	.218	.196	.235	11.13	2.23
Clemensia, Taylor	L-L	6-1	185	2-20-97	1	4	2.47	11	10	0	0	44	27	24	12	0	26	47	.176	.212	.167	9.69	5.36
De Jesus, Miguel	R-R	6-2	175	9-20-95	3	1	2.06	7	7	0	0	35	23	8	8	2	11	34	.183	.132	.241	8.74	2.83
Farfan, Onas	L-L	5-11	185	6-23-93	1	2	3.48	19	0	0	4	31	23	13	12	1	12	36	.215	.241	.205	10.45	3.48
Fox, Tyler	R-R	6-1	177	11-22-93	2	3	3.10	13	0	0	1	52	42	20	18	1	11	36	.215	.258	.179	6.19	1.89
Gamez, Juan	R-R	5-11	220	3-7-94	0	0	2.45	3	0	0	0	4	2	1	1	0	3	2	.167	.000	.333	4.91	7.36
Gomez, Moises	R-R	6-1	192	2-8-97	4	0	1.19	14	1	0	0	38	34	7	5	0	12	27	.246	.259	.238	6.45	2.87
Grogan, Quin	R-R	6-2	205	6-11-93	0	1	2.25	1	1	0	0	4	3	1	1	0	1	4	.214	.286	.143	9.00	2.25
Hellquist, Bo	L-L	6-2	199	4-5-94	5	3	2.25	11	10	0	0	52	49	17	13	2	7	46	.245	.283	.231	7.96	1.21
Irby, C.K.	R-R	6-1	200	5-6-92	1	0	0.00	1	0	0	0	1	0	0	0	0	0	2	.000	—	.000	18.00	0.00
Jones, Matt	R-L	6-2	150	10-16-98	0	2	17.18	5	0	0	0	4	2	7	7	1	8	5	.182	.333	.125	12.27	19.64
Kelly, Garrett	R-R	6-1	210	8-2-94	1	3	3.67	18	0	0	3	27	24	11	11	0	11	29	.240	.214	.259	9.67	3.67
Martinez, Daniel	R-R	6-0	216	6-13-94	2	0	8.83	13	0	0	1	17	27	17	17	0	6	17	.342	.316	.366	8.83	3.12
McGuff, Patrick	L-R	6-2	200	3-30-94	0	0	0.00	4	0	0	2	6	3	0	0	0	0	6	.158	.125	.182	14.29	0.00
Pearce, Callan	R-R	6-3	190	8-1-95	2	2	1.99	18	0	0	2	32	27	13	7	0	12	28	.233	.220	.242	7.96	3.41
Schutte, Matz	R-R	6-3	185	10-4-97	1	0	3.00	13	0	0	0	21	16	9	7	0	7	11	.213	.182	.238	4.71	3.00
Strecker, Zach	R-R	6-4	225	9-30-93	0	1	3.27	17	0	0	6	33	35	15	12	1	8	28	.278	.271	.284	7.64	2.18
Ynoa, Huascar	R-R	6-3	175	5-28-98	3	5	3.18	11	11	0	0	51	44	21	18	1	12	51	.228	.167	.270	9.00	2.12

Fielding

C: Alvarez 25, Blanco 5, Gamez 7, Hazard 15, Olson 1, Rortvedt 17, Salva 1. **1B:** Cronin 1, Featherstone 28, Kendrick 10, Meneses 2, Olson 7, Tapia 1, Whitefield 26. **2B:** Andrade 1, Cronin 1, Guzman 6, Hutcheon 26, Meneses 3, Miranda 3, Morel 27, Munoz 4, Valera 1. **3B:** Andrade 3, Cronin 15, Guzman 1, Hutcheon 1, Meneses 5, Miranda 23, Munoz 15, Whitefield 7. **SS:** Hutcheon 5, Meneses 1, Miranda 22, Morel 1, Munoz 37. **OF:** Aluko 2, Andrade 10, Arias 40, Baddoo 35, Cronin 6, Davis 32, English 3, Featherstone 1, Hartong 2, Marrero 32, Martinez 4, Murphy 3, Tapia 12, Whitefield 27.

DSL TWINS
DOMINICAN SUMMER LEAGUE

ROOKIE

Batting	B-T	HT	WT	DOB	AVG	vLH	vRH	G	AB	R	H	2B	3B	HR	RBI	BB	HBP	SH	SF	SO	SB	CS	SLG	OBP
Calcano, Mariano	R-R	6-3	222	9-19-96	.206	.118	.224	32	102	9	21	4	1	4	15	9	3	0	1	41	0	0	.382	.287
Cuesto, Darling	R-R	6-0	175	10-12-97	.245	.200	.250	44	143	23	35	5	1	1	16	25	5	0	0	27	6	2	.315	.376
De La Cruz, Yeremi	R-R	5-11	180	7-15-97	.244	.227	.248	38	135	19	33	6	1	3	21	9	2	0	3	25	1	1	.370	.295
Duran, Moris	B-R	5-11	150	11-29-97	.208	.227	.203	34	101	17	21	6	1	1	9	14	2	2	2	28	5	3	.317	.311
Encarnacion, Yeltsin	L-R	6-0	155	6-28-98	.220	.304	.206	43	159	22	35	6	1	0	17	23	3	1	0	17	7	5	.270	.330
Henriquez, Zaino	R-R	5-11	165	6-7-98	.161	.143	.167	22	62	4	10	1	0	0	2	7	1	1	1	14	2	1	.177	.254
Herrera, Edgar	L-L	6-0	175	4-19-97	.317	.381	.309	51	186	32	59	11	3	0	14	15	2	0	0	14	2	3	.409	.374
Javier, Wander	R-R	6-1	165	12-29-98	.308	.000	.364	9	26	7	8	3	0	2	6	4	0	0	0	5	0	0	.654	.400
Maldonado, Humberto	B-R	6-3	202	12-30-97	.283	.286	.283	48	166	21	47	11	3	1	24	21	2	0	4	56	14	10	.404	.363
Marte, Agustin	B-R	5-11	160	12-9-98	.263	.368	.248	46	160	23	42	4	1	0	16	24	5	0	0	37	15	5	.300	.362
Martinez, Juan	R-R	6-1	190	9-30-96	.242	.250	.241	41	124	18	30	8	2	1	19	22	3	0	3	31	2	4	.363	.362
Parra, Jorge	R-R	6-0	170	6-14-95	.294	.235	.301	45	160	17	47	5	4	0	23	12	1	0	4	30	7	6	.375	.339
Perez, Yeison	R-R	6-0	185	4-9-96	.272	.143	.292	31	103	9	28	7	0	3	13	5	4	1	1	13	0	0	.427	.327
Santana, Ruben	B-R	5-9	165	11-30-97	.248	.241	.250	44	145	16	36	3	2	0	13	11	1	2	3	26	5	6	.297	.300
Tademo, Victor	R-R	6-1	170	7-9-99	.311	.300	.312	51	177	42	55	16	1	1	22	19	4	0	1	22	21	4	.429	.388
Tejada, Oliver	R-R	5-11	175	8-22-97	.273	.500	.222	3	11	0	3	0	0	0	0	0	0	0	0	1	0	0	.273	.273
Tovar, Antonio	R-R	6-0	197	6-1-96	.270	.455	.246	52	189	24	51	10	1	2	24	21	3	1	1	30	5	3	.365	.350
Vasquez, Samuel	L-L	5-9	160	1-15-97	.181	.280	.159	49	138	25	25	4	3	1	11	15	4	2	2	35	8	4	.254	.277

Pitching	B-T	HT	WT	DOB	W	L	ERA	G	GS	CG	SV	IP	H	R	ER	HR	BB	SO	AVG	vLH	vRH	K/9	BB/9
Acosta, Melvi	R-R	6-1	188	6-2-95	3	2	3.20	14	0	0	0	70	74	32	25	0	14	57	.273	.270	.275	7.29	1.79
Balbuena, Erick	R-R	6-2	175	6-4-96	0	1	11.00	7	0	0	0	9	12	12	11	1	10	6	.343	.500	.296	6.00	10.00
Bellorin, Luis	L-L	6-1	167	9-18-97	0	5	6.87	13	10	0	0	37	40	32	28	2	22	31	.278	.294	.276	7.61	5.40
Castro, Cristian	R-R	6-3	210	4-21-98	0	0	9.82	11	0	0	0	11	19	18	12	0	9	9	.388	.400	.400	5.73	7.36
Colina, Edwar	R-R	5-11	182	5-3-97	1	3	2.30	14	13	0	0	59	43	21	15	1	26	52	.200	.100	.248	7.98	3.99
Cruz, Amilcar	R-R	6-2	190	3-28-96	2	2	4.09	16	0	0	0	33	38	19	15	1	9	25	.284	.275	.287	6.82	2.45
Feliz, Danny	R-R	6-0	170	12-12-96	1	1	2.30	10	0	0	1	16	9	4	4	2	10	12	.164	.188	.154	6.89	5.74

Pitching	B-T	HT	WT	DOB	W	L	ERA	G	GS	CG	SV	IP	H	R	ER	HR	BB	SO	AVG	vLH	vRH	K/9	BB/9
Garcia, Pedro	R-R	6-2	180	7-21-95	5	1	2.17	14	14	0	0	62	39	17	15	1	24	69	.181	.250	.155	9.96	3.47
Marin, Andriu	R-R	6-1	183	7-6-98	4	3	2.88	20	0	0	4	41	40	16	13	2	15	36	.248	.227	.256	7.97	3.32
Mojica, Juan	R-R	6-3	195	7-27-95	5	2	2.47	14	13	0	0	62	43	17	17	3	22	73	.197	.234	.182	10.60	3.19
Pena, Juan	R-R	6-2	170	9-16-96	0	1	31.35	15	0	0	0	10	15	42	36	0	39	8	.349	.412	.308	6.97	33.97
Rivas, Elvis	R-R	5-11	200	2-16-96	2	1	3.90	19	0	0	1	28	18	12	12	1	25	22	.188	.156	.203	7.16	8.13
Soto, Fredderi	L-L	5-11	175	6-29-98	2	2	4.26	23	0	0	4	38	37	24	18	4	17	15	.264	.240	.270	3.55	4.03
Suniaga, Carlos	R-R	6-2	187	5-26-97	7	3	2.03	16	6	0	1	58	45	18	13	0	13	58	.209	.169	.229	9.05	2.03
Torres, Frandy	R-R	5-11	160	8-4-95	1	0	1.80	17	0	0	5	30	21	6	6	0	12	29	.198	.172	.208	8.70	3.60

Fielding

C: Cuesto 26, De La Cruz 26, Perez 24, Tejada 1. **1B:** Calcano 23, Cuesto 7, Henriquez 5, Herrera 26, Maldonado 1, Parra 19, Tademo 1, Vasquez 1. **2B:** Duran 23, Encarnacion 17, Henriquez 11, Marte 9, Santana 15, Tademo 1. **3B:** Cuesto 3, Duran 2, Encarnacion 18, Santana 17, Tademo 37. **SS:** Duran 1, Encarnacion 9, Javier 8, Marte 36, Santana 11, Tademo 12. **OF:** Calcano 1, Herrera 23, Maldonado 47, Martinez 39, Parra 22, Tovar 46, Vasquez 45.

New York Mets

SEASON IN A SENTENCE: Overcoming myriad injuries, the Mets ranked second in the National League in home runs and fourth in pitcher strikeouts to take a power-oriented roster to 87 wins and the Wild Card Game.

HIGH POINT: The Mets established a franchise record with 218 home runs—Asdrubal Cabrera, Yoenis Cespedes, Curtis Granderson and Neil Walker all topped 20—and qualified for the postseason in consecutive years for just the second time in franchise history, the first time coming in 1999 and 2000.

LOW POINT: After losing to the Giants on Aug. 19, and fresh off a 7-16 run, the Mets' record stood at just 60-62. They won 27 times in their final 40 games (.675) to claim the top wild card.

NOTABLE ROOKIES: While the Mets did not have a rookie class to rival the 2015 debuts of Noah Syndergaard and Michael Conforto, they received vital rookie reinforcements from right-handers Seth Lugo (5-2, 2.67 in 64 innings) and Robert Gsellman (4-2, 2.42 in 45 innings), a pair of 2011 draft picks taken after the 10th round. The duo helped support a rotation that lost Matt Harvey in July, Steven Matz in August and Jacob deGrom in September. Nondrafted free agent T.J. Rivera hit .333/.345/.476 in 33 games, mostly at second base as an injury replacement for Walker, while versatility allowed shortstop Matt Reynolds and outfielder Brandon Nimmo to serve as fill-ins.

KEY TRANSACTIONS: The Mets didn't have another Michael Fulmer-for-Cespedes blockbuster up their sleeve, but many of their smaller, around-the-margins transactions paid off. They purchased first baseman James Loney from the Padres to fill in for the injured Lucas Duda, while they signed Jose Reyes for the minimum and moved him to third base to spell David Wright. Minor trades for second baseman Kelly Johnson and reliever Fernando Salas were worth the price of admission.

DOWN ON THE FARM: Though the organization's domestic winning percentage fell from .532 in 2015 to .480 in 2016, the Mets had several top prospects show signs of development, including shortstop Amed Rosario and first baseman Dominic Smith, who both finished the year at Double-A. The Mets had batting champions at their three highest affiliates: Rivera (.353) in the Pacific Coast League, shortstop Phillip Evans (.335) in the Eastern League and catcher Tomas Nido (.320) in the Florida State League.

OPENING DAY PAYROLL: $133,889,129 (14th)

PLAYERS OF THE YEAR

MAJOR LEAGUE

Noah Syndergaard
rhp

14-9, 2.60
218 SO in 183.2 IP
3rd in NL in ERA

MINOR LEAGUE

P.J. Conlon
lhp

(Low A/High A)
12-2, 1.65 in 142 IP
Led minors in ERA

ORGANIZATION LEADERS

BATTING		*Minimum 250 AB
MAJORS		
* AVG	Asdrubal Cabrera	.280
* OPS	Yoenis Cespedes	.884
HR	Yoenis Cespedes	31
RBI	Yoenis Cespedes	86
MINORS		
* AVG	T.J. Rivera, Las Vegas	.353
* OBP	Brandon Nimmo, Las Vegas	.423
* SLG	Brandon Nimmo, Las Vegas	.541
* OPS	Brandon Nimmo, Las Vegas	.964
R	Travis Taijeron, Las Vegas	86
H	Amed Rosario, St. Lucie, Binghamton	155
TB	Travis Taijeron, Las Vegas	235
2B	Travis Taijeron, Las Vegas	42
3B	Amed Rosario, St. Lucie, Binghamton	13
HR	Johnny Monell, Las Vegas	19
	Travis Taijeron, Las Vegas	19
RBI	David Thompson, Columbia, St. Lucie	95
BB	Vinny Siena, Columbia, St. Lucie	69
SO	Champ Stuart, St. Lucie, Binghamton	168
SB	Champ Stuart, St. Lucie, Binghamton	40

PITCHING		#Minimum 75 IP
MAJORS		
W	Bartolo Colon	15
# ERA	Noah Syndergaard	2.60
SO	Noah Syndergaard	218
SV	Jeurys Familia	51
MINORS		
W	Ricky Knapp, St. Lucie, Binghamton, Las Vegas	13
L	Duane Below, Las Vegas	12
	Mickey Jannis, St. Lucie, Binghamton	12
# ERA	P.J. Conlon, Columbia, St. Lucie	1.65
G	Chasen Bradford, Las Vegas	56
	Paul Sewald, Las Vegas	56
	Jeff Walters, Las Vegas	56
GS	Tyler Pill, Binghamton, Las Vegas	27
SV	Corey Taylor, St. Lucie	20
IP	Tyler Pill, Binghamton, Las Vegas	166
BB	Mickey Jannis, St. Lucie, Binghamton	76
SO	Joe Shaw, Columbia, Binghamton	140
# AVG	P.J. Conlon, Columbia, St. Lucie	.220

General Manager: Sandy Alderson. **Farm Director:** Ian Levin. **Scouting Director:** Tommy Tanous.

Class	Team	League	W	L	PCT	Finish	Manager
Majors	New York Mets	National	87	75	.537	4th (15)	Terry Collins
Triple-A	Las Vegas 51s	Pacific Coast	70	74	.486	10th (16)	Wally Backman
Double-A	Binghamton Mets	Eastern	63	77	.450	8th (12)	Pedro Lopez
High A	St. Lucie Mets	Florida State	74	61	.548	5th (12)	Luis Rojas
Low A	Columbia Fireflies	South Atlantic	67	73	.479	10th (14)	Jose Leger
Short season	Brooklyn Cyclones	New York-Penn	37	39	.487	10th (14)	Tom Gamboa
Rookie	Mets	Gulf Coast	26	29	.473	10th (17)	Jose Carreno
Overall 2016 Minor League Record			364	394	.480	20th (30)	

ORGANIZATION STATISTICS

NEW YORK METS
NATIONAL LEAGUE

Batting	B-T	HT	WT	DOB	AVG	vLH	vRH	G	AB	R	H	2B	3B	HR	RBI	BB	HBP	SH	SF	SO	SB	CS	SLG	OBP
Bruce, Jay	L-L	6-3	225	4-3-87	.219	.160	.244	50	169	14	37	5	0	8	19	17	1	0	0	43	0	0	.391	.294
2-team total (97 Cincinnati)					.250	—	—	147	539	74	135	27	6	33	99	44	3	0	3	126	4	2	.506	.309
Cabrera, Asdrubal	B-R	6-0	205	11-13-85	.280	.321	.269	141	521	65	146	30	1	23	62	38	7	0	2	103	5	1	.474	.336
Campbell, Eric	R-R	6-3	215	4-9-87	.173	.212	.143	40	75	9	13	1	0	1	9	10	2	0	1	24	1	0	.227	.284
Cecchini, Gavin	R-R	6-2	200	12-22-93	.333	.500	.250	4	6	2	2	2	0	0	2	0	1	0	0	2	0	0	.667	.429
Cespedes, Yoenis	R-R	5-10	220	10-18-85	.280	.341	.266	132	479	72	134	25	1	31	86	51	7	0	6	108	3	1	.530	.354
Conforto, Michael	L-R	6-1	215	3-1-93	.220	.104	.242	109	304	38	67	21	1	12	42	36	5	0	3	89	2	1	.414	.310
d'Arnaud, Travis	R-R	6-2	210	2-10-89	.247	.190	.264	75	251	27	62	7	0	4	15	19	3	2	1	50	0	0	.323	.307
De Aza, Alejandro	L-L	6-0	195	4-11-84	.205	.195	.207	130	234	31	48	9	0	6	25	26	5	1	1	67	4	3	.321	.297
Duda, Lucas	L-R	6-4	255	2-3-86	.229	.133	.252	47	153	20	35	7	0	7	23	15	2	0	2	36	0	0	.412	.302
Flores, Wilmer	R-R	6-3	205	8-6-91	.267	.340	.232	103	307	38	82	14	0	16	49	23	2	0	3	48	1	1	.469	.319
Granderson, Curtis	L-R	6-1	200	3-16-81	.237	.226	.241	150	545	88	129	24	5	30	59	74	9	0	5	130	4	2	.464	.335
Johnson, Kelly	L-R	6-1	200	2-22-82	.268	.269	.268	82	183	17	49	8	0	9	24	15	2	0	1	40	3	0	.459	.328
2-team total (49 Atlanta)					.247	—	—	131	304	25	75	14	0	10	34	25	2	0	2	65	4	0	.391	.306
Kelly, Ty	L-R	6-0	180	7-20-88	.241	.368	.179	39	58	9	14	1	1	1	7	11	0	0	2	9	0	0	.345	.352
Lagares, Juan	R-R	6-1	215	3-17-89	.239	.260	.217	79	142	15	34	7	2	3	9	11	2	4	1	27	4	2	.380	.301
Loney, James	L-L	6-3	235	5-7-84	.265	.173	.282	100	343	30	91	16	1	9	34	16	5	1	1	37	0	0	.397	.307
Nimmo, Brandon	L-R	6-3	205	3-27-93	.274	.286	.273	32	73	12	20	1	0	1	6	6	1	0	0	20	0	0	.329	.338
Plawecki, Kevin	R-R	6-2	210	2-26-91	.197	.250	.177	48	132	6	26	6	0	1	11	17	2	0	0	33	0	0	.265	.298
Reyes, Jose	B-R	6-0	195	6-11-83	.267	.380	.239	60	255	45	68	13	4	8	24	23	0	0	1	49	9	2	.443	.326
Reynolds, Matt	R-R	6-1	200	12-3-90	.225	.296	.194	47	89	11	20	8	0	3	13	4	1	2	0	34	0	1	.416	.266
Rivera, Rene	R-R	5-10	215	7-31-83	.222	.314	.200	65	185	12	41	4	0	6	26	16	3	1	2	54	0	0	.341	.291
Rivera, T.J.	R-R	6-1	205	10-27-88	.333	.229	.386	33	105	10	35	4	1	3	16	3	1	0	4	17	0	0	.476	.345
Ruggiano, Justin	R-R	6-1	210	4-12-82	.350	.333	.400	8	20	4	7	0	0	2	6	2	0	0	0	9	0	1	.650	.409
Walker, Neil	B-R	6-3	210	9-10-85	.282	.330	.266	113	412	57	116	9	1	23	55	42	1	0	3	84	3	1	.476	.347
Wright, David	R-R	6-0	205	12-20-82	.226	.194	.238	37	137	18	31	8	0	7	14	26	0	0	0	55	3	2	.438	.350

Pitching	B-T	HT	WT	DOB	W	L	ERA	G	GS	CG	SV	IP	H	R	ER	HR	BB	SO	AVG	vLH	vRH	K/9	BB/9
Bastardo, Antonio	L-L	5-11	205	9-21-85	0	0	4.74	41	0	0	0	44	41	24	23	8	21	46	.244	.286	.214	9.48	4.33
2-team total (28 Pittsburgh)					3	0	4.52	69	0	0	0	68	60	37	34	11	32	74	—	—	—	9.84	4.26
Blevins, Jerry	L-L	6-6	190	9-6-83	4	2	2.79	73	0	0	2	42	36	14	13	4	15	52	.229	.255	.182	11.14	3.21
Colon, Bartolo	R-R	5-11	285	5-24-73	15	8	3.43	34	33	0	0	192	200	81	73	24	32	128	.268	.270	.267	6.01	1.50
deGrom, Jacob	L-R	6-4	180	6-19-88	7	8	3.04	24	24	1	0	148	142	53	50	15	36	143	.255	.241	.269	8.70	2.19
Edgin, Josh	L-L	6-1	245	12-17-86	1	0	5.23	16	0	0	0	10	10	6	6	1	6	11	.270	.235	.300	9.58	5.23
Familia, Jeurys	R-R	6-3	240	10-10-89	3	4	2.55	78	0	0	51	78	63	25	22	1	31	84	.220	.239	.204	9.73	3.59
Gilmartin, Sean	L-L	6-2	200	5-8-90	0	1	7.13	14	1	0	0	18	21	14	14	4	7	11	.300	.226	.359	5.60	3.57
Goeddel, Erik	R-R	6-3	190	12-20-88	2	2	4.54	36	0	0	0	36	33	20	18	5	14	36	.234	.231	.236	9.08	3.53
Gsellman, Robert	R-R	6-4	205	7-18-93	4	2	2.42	8	7	0	0	45	42	12	12	1	15	42	.258	.230	.281	8.46	3.02
Harvey, Matt	R-R	6-4	215	3-27-89	4	10	4.86	17	17	0	0	93	111	55	50	8	25	76	.302	.321	.282	7.38	2.43
Henderson, Jim	L-R	6-5	220	10-21-82	2	2	4.11	44	0	0	0	35	34	17	16	7	14	40	.248	.245	.250	10.29	3.60
Lugo, Seth	R-R	6-4	225	11-17-89	5	2	2.67	17	8	0	0	64	49	19	19	7	21	45	.220	.196	.240	6.33	2.95
Matz, Steven	R-L	6-2	200	5-29-91	9	8	3.40	22	22	0	0	132	129	53	50	14	31	129	.257	.269	.253	8.77	2.11
Montero, Rafael	R-R	6-0	185	10-17-90	0	1	8.05	9	3	0	0	19	23	17	17	4	16	20	.299	.424	.205	9.47	7.58
Niese, Jon	L-L	6-3	215	10-27-86	0	1	11.45	6	2	0	0	11	13	14	14	4	9	12	.289	.500	.243	9.82	7.36
2-team total (23 Pittsburgh)					8	7	5.50	29	20	0	0	121	145	77	74	25	47	88	—	—	—	6.55	3.50
Reed, Addison	L-R	6-4	230	12-27-88	4	2	1.97	80	0	0	1	78	60	18	17	4	13	91	.210	.210	.210	10.55	1.51
Robles, Hansel	R-R	5-11	185	8-13-90	6	4	3.48	68	0	0	1	78	69	32	30	7	36	85	.240	.179	.281	9.85	4.17
Salas, Fernando	R-R	6-2	200	5-30-85	0	1	2.08	17	0	0	0	17	11	4	4	3	0	19	.177	.154	.194	9.87	0.00
Smoker, Josh	L-L	6-2	250	11-26-88	3	0	4.70	20	0	0	0	15	16	10	8	4	4	25	.267	.360	.200	14.67	2.35
Syndergaard, Noah	L-R	6-6	240	8-29-92	14	9	2.60	31	30	0	0	184	168	61	53	11	43	218	.243	.262	.228	10.68	2.11
Verrett, Logan	R-R	6-2	190	6-19-90	3	8	5.20	35	12	0	0	92	100	55	53	16	43	66	.283	.276	.291	6.48	4.22
Ynoa, Gabriel	R-R	6-2	205	5-26-93	1	0	6.38	10	3	0	0	18	26	13	13	0	7	13	.333	.359	.308	8.35	3.44

Fielding

Catcher	PCT	G	PO	A	E	DP	PB
d'Arnaud	.998	73	608	36	1	4	4
Plawecki	.988	45	321	20	4	2	1
Rivera	.996	59	495	37	2	5	3

First Base	PCT	G	PO	A	E	DP
Campbell	.992	21	114	12	1	11
Duda	.991	45	313	23	3	26
Flores	.993	27	135	15	1	14
Johnson	1.000	2	6	1	0	1
Kelly	1.000	1	3	0	0	0
Loney	.989	97	664	62	8	72
Rivera	1.000	1	1	1	0	0
Rivera	1.000	1	2	1	0	0

Second Base	PCT	G	PO	A	E	DP
Campbell	1.000	1	1	0	0	0
Flores	.971	18	24	42	2	8

Johnson	1.000	26	36	31	0	6
Kelly	—	2	0	0	0	0
Reynolds	1.000	4	1	3	0	0
Rivera	1.000	26	30	48	0	12
Walker	.986	111	181	297	7	65

Third Base	PCT	G	PO	A	E	DP
Campbell	1.000	7	2	6	0	0
Flores	.938	51	36	55	6	8
Johnson	.949	21	10	27	2	6
Kelly	1.000	10	4	11	0	0
Reyes	.948	50	26	83	6	6
Reynolds	1.000	7	2	5	0	0
Rivera	.786	9	4	7	3	1
Wright	.953	36	23	58	4	5

Shortstop	PCT	G	PO	A	E	DP
Cabrera	.986	135	175	329	7	77
Cecchini	1.000	2	0	1	0	0

Flores	.944	8	9	8	1	1
Johnson	1.000	1	1	0	0	0
Reyes	1.000	13	9	26	0	5
Reynolds	.972	21	23	47	2	13

Outfield	PCT	G	PO	A	E	DP
Bruce	.988	43	79	1	1	0
Campbell	1.000	2	2	0	0	0
Cespedes	.981	122	250	9	5	0
Conforto	.979	87	134	4	3	1
De Aza	.981	76	106	0	2	0
Granderson	1.000	140	273	8	0	1
Johnson	1.000	9	8	0	0	0
Kelly	1.000	10	9	3	0	1
Lagares	.990	71	100	1	1	0
Nimmo	.967	22	29	0	1	0
Reynolds	1.000	1	2	0	0	0
Ruggiano	.938	6	15	0	1	0

LAS VEGAS 51S
PACIFIC COAST LEAGUE

TRIPLE-A

Batting	B-T	HT	WT	DOB	AVG	vLH	vRH	G	AB	R	H	2B	3B	HR	RBI	BB	HBP	SH	SF	SO	SB	CS	SLG	OBP
Ashley, Nevin	R-R	6-1	245	8-14-84	.240	.257	.227	63	167	26	40	10	0	5	28	27	3	0	3	45	1	1	.389	.350
2-team total (3 Round Rock)					.232	—	—	66	177	28	41	10	0	5	29	27	5	0	3	48	1	1	.373	.344
Bernadina, Roger	L-L	6-2	210	6-12-84	.292	.321	.284	114	387	65	113	29	4	10	55	48	5	4	2	93	20	5	.465	.376
Campbell, Eric	R-R	6-3	215	4-9-87	.301	.265	.320	83	302	63	91	15	4	7	47	41	6	0	5	55	7	3	.447	.390
Carrillo, Xorge	R-R	6-1	235	4-12-89	.333	.000	.455	5	15	0	5	0	0	1	0	0	0	1	0	1	0	0	.333	.333
Cecchini, Gavin	R-R	6-2	200	12-22-93	.325	.328	.324	117	446	71	145	27	2	8	55	48	0	3	1	55	4	1	.448	.390
Conforto, Michael	L-R	6-1	215	3-1-93	.422	.488	.391	33	128	30	54	8	2	9	28	13	2	0	0	18	2	2	.727	.483
d'Arnaud, Travis	R-R	6-2	210	2-10-89	.333	.333	.333	3	12	2	4	2	0	0	2	2	0	0	0	3	0	0	.500	.429
Glenn, Jeff	R-R	6-3	210	9-22-91	.400	—	.400	6	5	1	2	0	0	1	3	0	0	0	0	2	0	0	1.000	.400
Herrera, Dilson	R-R	5-10	205	3-3-94	.276	.271	.278	86	359	61	99	24	2	13	55	27	1	1	1	72	6	7	.462	.327
Johnson, Kyle	R-R	5-10	195	11-9-89	.244	.296	.216	26	78	6	19	4	0	1	6	6	1	0	0	22	0	0	.333	.298
Kelly, Ty	L-R	6-0	180	7-20-88	.328	.325	.330	81	271	45	89	21	1	2	35	38	1	3	3	42	5	6	.435	.409
Krauss, Marc	L-R	6-2	245	10-5-87	.214	.114	.238	84	229	42	49	9	0	14	39	38	2	0	3	79	2	0	.437	.327
Mazzilli Jr. L.J.	R-R	6-0	200	9-6-90	.229	.267	.212	13	48	5	11	5	0	1	7	4	0	0	3	7	1	1	.396	.273
Monell, Johnny	L-R	6-1	210	3-27-86	.276	.261	.280	113	417	69	115	22	1	19	75	37	3	0	4	76	2	0	.470	.336
Muno, Danny	B-R	6-2	195	2-9-89	.239	.250	.233	47	88	12	21	3	2	0	10	20	2	0	0	22	0	2	.318	.391
Nimmo, Brandon	L-R	6-3	205	3-27-93	.352	.358	.349	97	392	72	138	25	8	11	61	46	3	2	1	73	7	8	.541	.423
Plawecki, Kevin	R-R	6-2	210	2-26-91	.300	.281	.308	55	190	27	57	11	0	8	40	13	2	0	2	19	0	1	.484	.348
Reynolds, Matt	R-R	6-1	200	12-3-90	.264	.240	.273	71	269	43	71	15	2	2	24	26	3	1	0	64	9	2	.357	.336
Rivera, Rene	R-R	5-10	215	7-31-83	.280	.222	.313	8	25	3	7	1	0	0	5	2	1	1	0	3	0	0	.320	.357
Rivera, T.J.	R-R	6-1	205	10-27-88	.353	.323	.363	105	405	67	143	31	1	11	85	23	7	2	5	54	3	5	.516	.393
Romero, Niuman	B-R	6-1	215	1-24-85	.226	.216	.230	49	124	11	28	6	0	0	9	16	0	1	2	21	1	1	.274	.310
2-team total (44 Round Rock)					.229	—	—	47	175	28	40	11	1	0	13	23	24	1	0	2	56	1	1	.423	.322
Taijeron, Travis	R-R	6-2	220	1-20-89	.275	.222	.294	129	459	86	126	42	5	19	88	67	8	0	7	166	1	3	.512	.372

Pitching	B-T	HT	WT	DOB	W	L	ERA	G	GS	CG	SV	IP	H	R	ER	HR	BB	SO	AVG	vLH	vRH	K/9	BB/9
Alvarez, Dario	L-L	6-1	170	1-17-89	0	1	9.98	17	0	0	0	15	22	19	17	3	10	27	.324	.25	.375	15.85	5.87
2-team total (6 Round Rock)					2	1	7.33	23	0	0	1	23	30	22	19	4	13	37	—	—	—	14.27	5.01
Barbosa, Andrew	R-L	6-8	230	11-18-87	0	0	1.80	1	1	0	0	5	7	1	1	1	0	6	.333	.286	.429	10.80	0.00
Below, Duane	L-L	6-3	210	11-15-85	5	12	5.27	24	23	1	0	140	179	91	82	23	30	103	.311	.358	.286	6.62	1.93
Bradford, Chase	R-R	6-1	225	8-5-89	5	3	4.80	56	0	0	5	66	84	39	35	5	13	54	.311	.339	.289	7.40	1.78
Church, Andrew	R-R	6-2	200	10-7-94	0	1	6.75	1	0	0	0	4	7	3	3	0	1	4	.368	.250	.455	9.00	2.25
Edgin, Josh	L-L	6-1	245	12-17-86	2	2	3.24	37	0	0	2	33	35	13	12	2	20	38	.287	.311	.262	10.26	5.40
Gilmartin, Sean	L-L	6-2	200	5-8-90	9	7	4.86	19	18	1	0	107	122	63	58	12	31	94	.283	.245	.301	7.88	2.60
Goeddel, Erik	R-R	6-3	190	12-20-88	1	1	4.08	24	1	0	1	29	28	15	13	2	15	34	.262	.271	.254	10.67	4.71
Gorski, Darin	L-L	6-4	215	10-6-87	6	4	5.90	15	13	0	0	69	74	46	45	8	29	53	.268	.240	.279	6.95	3.80
Gsellman, Robert	R-R	6-4	205	7-18-93	1	5	5.73	9	9	0	0	49	56	35	31	8	16	40	.286	.321	.241	7.40	2.96
Henderson, Jim	L-R	6-5	220	10-21-82	0	2	4.50	8	0	0	2	8	8	4	4	1	4	10	.286	.308	.267	11.25	4.50
Herron, Tyler	R-R	6-2	210	8-5-86	1	0	2.70	1	1	0	0	7	3	2	2	2	3	7	.143	.250	.118	9.45	4.05
Huchingson, Chase	L-L	6-5	215	4-14-89	1	1	5.93	22	0	0	0	27	31	23	18	2	21	26	.282	.286	.279	8.56	6.91
Knapp, Ricky	R-R	6-1	215	5-20-92	0	1	5.50	3	3	0	0	18	22	11	11	2	7	11	.306	.296	.311	5.50	3.50
Lara, Rainy	R-R	6-4	240	3-14-91	1	0	3.18	2	1	0	0	5	5	2	2	0	2	4	.227	.250	.167	6.35	3.18
Lugo, Seth	R-R	6-4	225	11-17-89	3	4	6.50	21	14	0	0	73	103	63	53	10	20	62	.329	.295	.356	7.61	2.45
Mateo, Luis	R-R	6-3	200	3-22-90	1	0	0.00	3	0	0	0	4	7	0	0	0	3	3	.368	.182	.625	6.23	0.00
McGowan, Kevin	R-R	6-5	235	10-18-91	0	0	5.40	1	0	0	0	2	1	1	1	1	2	.286	.500	.000	10.80	5.40
Montero, Rafael	R-R	6-0	185	10-17-90	4	6	7.20	16	16	0	0	80	111	70	64	12	40	68	.329	.387	.263	7.65	4.50
Pill, Tyler	R-R	6-2	200	5-29-90	1	1	5.60	5	5	0	0	27	41	18	17	5	6	22	.360	.238	5.70	7.24	1.98
Pimentel, Stolmy	R-R	6-3	230	2-1-90	0	4	10.45	14	5	0	0	31	53	37	36	3	18	29	.379	.404	.361	8.42	5.23
Sewald, Paul	R-R	6-3	205	5-26-90	5	3	3.29	56	0	0	19	66	58	31	24	9	21	80	.232	.209	.250	10.96	2.88

Pitching

Pitching	B-T	HT	WT	DOB	W	L	ERA	G	GS	CG	SV	IP	H	R	ER	HR	BB	SO	AVG	vLH	vRH	K/9	BB/9
Smoker, Josh	L-L	6-2	250	11-26-88	3	2	4.11	52	0	0	3	57	66	32	26	5	18	81	.287	.282	.291	12.79	2.84
Thornton, Zach	R-R	6-3	215	5-19-88	0	3	7.03	35	0	0	0	40	54	33	31	4	15	25	.325	.308	.341	5.67	3.40
Verrett, Logan	R-R	6-2	190	6-19-90	2	0	1.50	2	2	0	0	12	8	2	2	1	8	5	.186	.222	.125	3.75	6.00
Walters, Jeff	R-R	6-3	220	11-6-87	4	3	5.89	56	0	0	1	66	70	48	43	10	28	48	.275	.303	.253	6.58	3.84
Wheeler, Beck	R-R	6-3	215	12-13-88	0	1	7.23	19	0	0	0	24	27	20	19	5	16	28	.284	.175	.364	10.65	6.08
Ynoa, Gabriel	R-R	6-2	205	5-26-93	12	5	3.97	25	25	0	0	154	170	77	68	15	40	78	.285	.331	.241	4.55	2.33
Zeid, Josh	R-R	6-4	220	3-24-87	3	2	5.54	7	7	0	0	37	45	24	23	7	18	33	.298	.291	.308	7.96	4.34

Fielding

Catcher	PCT	G	PO	A	E	DP	PB
Ashley	.980	38	232	18	5	2	5
Carrillo	1.000	4	28	0	0	0	1
d'Arnaud	1.000	2	15	0	0	0	0
Glenn	1.000	1	2	0	0	0	0
Monell	.985	62	439	34	7	2	9
Plawecki	1.000	41	305	26	0	5	4
Rivera	1.000	8	64	3	0	0	3

First Base	PCT	G	PO	A	E	DP
Ashley	1.000	7	63	5	0	4
Campbell	.984	44	322	38	6	38
Glenn	—	1	0	0	0	0
Kelly	1.000	3	15	0	0	0
Krauss	.989	69	477	47	6	40
Monell	.967	22	159	15	6	16
Plawecki	1.000	5	35	4	0	3
Rivera	1.000	9	59	8	0	9
Romero	1.000	3	9	0	0	1

Second Base	PCT	G	PO	A	E	DP
Campbell	—	2	0	0	0	0
Cecchini	.933	3	6	8	1	1
Herrera	.984	75	155	218	6	48
Kelly	1.000	24	31	64	0	15
Mazzilli Jr.	.903	12	21	35	6	4
Muno	.944	6	5	12	1	1
Reynolds	.959	9	13	34	2	9
Rivera	.983	14	19	40	1	8
Romero	1.000	6	9	14	0	3

Third Base	PCT	G	PO	A	E	DP
Campbell	.972	17	14	21	1	1
Kelly	1.000	9	5	12	0	1
Muno	.865	17	8	24	5	1
Reynolds	.947	30	25	47	4	7
Rivera	.960	69	34	134	7	15
Romero	1.000	15	7	19	0	2

Shortstop	PCT	G	PO	A	E	DP
Cecchini	.931	105	172	270	33	63
Kelly	1.000	4	0	9	0	0
Muno	1.000	1	2	4	0	0
Reynolds	.971	29	27	72	3	12
Romero	.977	13	17	26	1	8

Outfield	PCT	G	PO	A	E	DP
Bernadina	.982	104	213	9	4	1
Campbell	.976	21	38	3	1	0
Conforto	.930	30	50	3	4	0
Johnson	1.000	23	42	1	0	0
Kelly	1.000	44	74	3	0	0
Krauss	—	1	0	0	0	0
Nimmo	.986	94	212	5	3	1
Reynolds	1.000	4	8	0	0	0
Rivera	1.000	9	12	1	0	0
Ruggiano	1.000	3	3	0	0	0
Taijeron	.972	122	233	8	7	3

BINGHAMTON METS

EASTERN LEAGUE

DOUBLE-A

Batting

Batting	B-T	HT	WT	DOB	AVG	vLH	vRH	G	AB	R	H	2B	3B	HR	RBI	BB	HBP	SH	SF	SO	SB	CS	SLG	OBP
Boyd, Jayce	R-R	6-1	210	12-30-90	.259	.302	.246	77	270	19	70	14	1	2	26	31	1	0	2	51	2	2	.341	.336
Burdick, Dale	R-R	6-0	185	10-12-95	.000	.000	.000	4	6	0	0	0	0	0	0	0	0	0	0	1	0	0	.000	.000
Carrillo, Xorge	R-R	6-1	235	4-12-89	.269	.250	.275	80	275	28	74	14	0	4	24	29	5	0	2	48	0	1	.364	.347
Cruzado, Victor	R-R	6-0	210	6-30-92	.261	.278	.256	111	364	41	95	13	2	8	53	51	2	1	2	83	6	6	.374	.353
de la Cruz, Maikis	R-R	5-10	195	9-6-90	.227	.256	.217	102	330	36	75	16	0	4	34	26	0	1	1	75	6	6	.312	.283
Evans, Phillip	R-R	5-9	220	9-10-92	.335	.330	.337	96	361	50	121	30	0	8	39	49	4	1	1	60	1	1	.485	.374
Flores, Wilmer	R-R	6-3	205	8-6-91	.235	.273	.167	5	17	1	4	0	0	0	1	0	0	0	1	2	0	0	.235	.263
Gibson, Derrik	R-R	6-1	195	12-5-89	.281	.318	.270	107	392	65	110	18	4	2	35	44	7	2	1	70	14	4	.362	.363
Gomez, Raywilly	B-R	5-11	205	1-25-90	.182	.000	.214	13	33	2	6	2	0	0	4	3	0	1	0	5	0	0	.242	.250
Johnson, John	L-R	5-7	160	10-27-88	.500	.000	.667	1	4	1	2	0	0	0	1	0	0	0	0	0	1	0	.500	.600
Johnson, Kyle	R-R	5-10	195	11-9-89	.199	.278	.178	51	171	21	34	7	0	2	11	20	3	1	1	50	3	4	.292	.292
King, Jared	B-L	5-11	200	10-12-91	.188	.313	.159	32	85	10	16	7	0	0	3	10	0	0	0	24	3	1	.271	.274
Lagares, Juan	R-R	6-1	215	3-17-89	.333	.250	.400	4	18	2	6	0	1	0	2	0	1	0	0	5	0	0	.444	.368
Mazzilli Jr. L.J.	R-R	6-0	200	9-6-90	.240	.274	.230	109	366	47	88	13	6	4	36	48	0	2	3	66	7	3	.342	.326
McNeil, Jeff	L-R	6-1	165	4-8-92	.250	.250	.250	3	12	2	3	1	0	1	2	2	0	0	1	1	0	0	.583	.357
Oberste, Matt	R-R	6-2	240	8-9-91	.283	.323	.271	124	413	53	117	21	2	9	54	38	2	0	9	80	1	2	.409	.340
Plaia, Colton	R-R	6-2	225	9-25-90	.236	.255	.230	64	216	17	51	9	0	1	17	17	3	3	2	55	0	2	.292	.298
Reyes, Jose	R-R	6-0	195	6-11-83	.207	.214	.200	9	29	6	6	1	0	0	2	3	0	0	1	3	1	1	.241	.273
Romero, Niuman	B-R	6-1	215	1-24-85	.266	.250	.269	41	154	18	41	10	0	1	12	19	1	0	1	28	0	1	.351	.349
Rosario, Amed	R-R	6-2	190	11-20-95	.341	.333	.343	54	214	38	73	14	5	2	31	19	1	0	3	51	6	2	.481	.392
Sabol, Stefan	R-R	6-0	230	2-2-92	.229	.278	.213	72	218	20	50	12	1	5	24	27	2	0	3	86	3	2	.362	.316
Smith, Dominic	L-L	6-0	250	6-15-95	.302	.261	.314	130	484	64	146	29	2	14	91	50	3	0	5	74	2	1	.457	.367
Stuart, Champ	R-R	6-0	185	10-11-92	.201	.150	.215	43	184	23	37	3	1	2	10	14	2	2	1	73	15	3	.261	.264

Pitching

Pitching	B-T	HT	WT	DOB	W	L	ERA	G	GS	CG	SV	IP	H	R	ER	HR	BB	SO	AVG	vLH	vRH	K/9	BB/9
Baldonado, Alberto	L-L	6-4	250	2-1-93	0	1	5.13	34	0	0	0	40	48	25	23	5	23	47	.291	.296	.287	10.49	5.13
Barbosa, Andrew	R-L	6-8	230	11-18-87	2	0	2.33	7	7	0	0	39	22	12	10	1	16	36	.167	.125	.180	8.38	3.72
Crismatt, Nabil	R-R	6-1	200	12-25-94	0	1	1.50	1	1	0	0	6	5	1	1	1	1	7	.227	.250	.000	10.50	1.50
Delgado, Casey	R-R	5-10	185	6-15-90	4	5	4.84	10	10	0	0	58	71	33	31	5	20	46	.303	.301	.306	7.18	3.12
Gsellman, Robert	R-R	6-4	205	7-18-93	3	4	2.71	11	11	0	0	66	57	23	20	2	15	48	.233	.186	.273	6.51	2.04
Henderson, Jim	L-R	6-5	230	10-21-82	0	1	15.43	5	3	0	0	5	8	8	8	0	5	4	.421	.500	.364	7.71	9.64
Hepple, Mike	R-R	6-5	235	6-5-90	2	3	6.30	16	0	0	0	20	18	14	14	3	20	17	.269	.258	.278	7.65	9.00
Herron, Tyler	R-R	6-2	210	8-5-86	2	6	6.32	11	11	0	0	57	86	53	40	7	17	45	.351	.353	.349	7.11	2.68
Jannis, Mickey	R-R	5-9	195	12-16-87	3	11	5.65	23	22	0	0	121	120	82	76	9	66	71	.260	.271	.258	5.24	4.91
Knapp, Ricky	R-R	6-1	215	5-20-92	4	1	2.90	6	6	2	0	40	31	15	13	0	10	40	.209	.280	.137	8.93	2.23
Lara, Rainy	R-R	6-4	240	3-14-91	7	11	5.27	23	21	0	0	108	118	71	63	13	40	67	.278	.321	.245	5.60	3.34
Mateo, Luis	R-R	6-3	200	3-22-90	3	4	2.87	48	0	0	1	63	61	25	20	3	20	49	.262	.245	.274	7.04	2.87
McGowan, Kevin	R-R	6-5	235	10-18-91	4	1	3.26	26	2	0	0	50	48	20	18	5	17	48	.258	.238	.275	8.70	3.08
Montero, Rafael	R-R	6-0	185	10-17-90	4	3	2.20	9	9	1	0	49	35	17	12	4	19	40	.200	.181	.217	7.35	3.49
Morris, Akeel	R-R	6-1	195	11-14-92	2	2	4.62	22	0	0	1	25	19	13	13	4	16	36	.207	.182	.229	12.79	5.68
Paez, Paul	L-L	5-7	210	4-29-92	2	1	9.15	14	0	0	0	20	29	20	20	1	7	27	.333	.308	.354	12.36	3.20

Pitching	B-T	HT	WT	DOB	W	L	ERA	G	GS	CG	SV	IP	H	R	ER	HR	BB	SO	AVG	vLH	vRH	K/9	BB/9
Peterson, Tim	R-R	6-1	225	2-22-91	3	1	4.09	36	0	0	1	44	47	20	20	4	14	53	.275	.306	.253	10.84	2.86
Pill, Tyler	R-R	6-2	200	5-29-90	9	10	4.02	22	22	3	0	139	138	67	62	8	34	110	.261	.294	.227	7.14	2.21
Regnault, Kyle	L-L	6-2	215	12-13-88	0	0	3.92	15	1	0	0	21	27	10	9	1	3	18	.314	.364	.283	7.84	1.31
Roseboom, David	L-L	6-2	225	5-17-92	1	1	1.87	52	0	0	14	58	34	13	12	5	18	54	.170	.141	.189	8.43	2.81
Secrest, Kelly	L-L	6-0	225	9-13-91	0	1	5.51	12	0	0	0	16	14	12	10	1	10	20	.222	.120	.289	11.02	5.51
Shaw, Joe	R-R	6-3	228	12-20-93	0	1	5.40	1	1	0	0	5	6	3	3	1	3	6	.316	.286	.333	10.80	5.40
Tapia, Domingo	R-R	6-3	250	8-4-91	0	0	3.86	1	0	0	0	2	2	1	1	1	1	1	.250	.000	.500	3.86	3.86
Taylor, Logan	R-R	6-4	250	12-13-91	4	2	3.99	44	5	0	0	86	85	42	38	5	39	99	.261	.236	.281	10.40	4.10
Wheeler, Beck	R-R	6-3	215	12-13-88	0	2	5.06	28	0	0	6	32	29	18	18	2	18	47	.246	.271	.220	13.22	5.06
Zeid, Josh	R-R	6-4	220	3-24-87	4	4	3.98	9	8	0	0	54	42	25	24	5	26	40	.211	.193	.224	6.63	4.31

Fielding

Catcher	PCT	G	PO	A	E	DP	PB
Carrillo	.998	79	577	65	1	5	6
Gomez	.967	7	53	6	2	0	1
Plaia	.992	61	443	41	4	3	11

First Base	PCT	G	PO	A	E	DP
Flores	1.000	3	27	1	0	1
Oberste	.989	35	257	14	3	24
Romero	1.000	1	1	0	0	1
Smith	.987	106	847	72	12	72

Second Base	PCT	G	PO	A	E	DP
Burdick	1.000	2	2	0	0	0
Evans	.970	32	62	66	4	15
Flores	.833	2	2	3	1	1

	PCT	G	PO	A	E	DP
Gibson	1.000	5	8	16	0	2
Johnson	1.000	1	3	2	0	0
Mazzilli Jr.	.978	102	177	274	10	49
McNeil	1.000	2	5	10	0	2

Third Base	PCT	G	PO	A	E	DP
Evans	.980	24	8	40	1	5
Gibson	.943	69	39	109	9	9
Mazzilli Jr.	1.000	2	2	1	0	1
McNeil	1.000	1	0	1	0	0
Oberste	.963	35	21	58	3	7
Reyes	1.000	7	3	11	0	1
Romero	.939	13	7	24	2	3

Shortstop	PCT	G	PO	A	E	DP
Evans	.959	39	56	109	7	19
Gibson	.972	27	34	69	3	16
Romero	.952	25	45	73	6	16
Rosario	.941	53	67	126	12	20

Outfield	PCT	G	PO	A	E	DP
Boyd	.991	68	106	1	1	0
Cruzado	.984	98	176	7	3	1
de la Cruz	.985	89	185	10	3	2
Johnson	.984	48	117	4	2	0
King	1.000	25	42	2	0	0
Lagares	1.000	4	11	1	0	0
Sabol	.965	61	105	6	4	3
Stuart	.990	43	100	4	1	0

ST. LUCIE METS　　　　　　　　　　　HIGH CLASS A
FLORIDA STATE LEAGUE

Batting	B-T	HT	WT	DOB	AVG	vLH	vRH	G	AB	R	H	2B	3B	HR	RBI	BB	HBP	SH	SF	SO	SB	CS	SLG	OBP
Becerra, Wuilmer	R-R	6-3	225	10-1-94	.312	.204	.338	65	247	27	77	17	0	1	34	9	3	2	2	52	7	1	.393	.341
Biondi, Patrick	L-R	5-8	170	1-9-91	.271	.195	.295	99	340	47	92	17	2	0	34	39	6	6	4	69	26	9	.332	.352
Brosher, Brandon	R-R	6-3	235	2-17-95	.000	.000	.000	1	4	0	0	0	0	0	0	0	0	0	0	2	0	0	.000	.000
Cabrera, Asdrubal	B-R	6-0	205	11-13-85	.333	.000	.400	2	6	2	2	2	0	0	2	0	0	0	1	2	0	0	.667	.286
Cespedes, Yoenis	R-R	5-10	220	10-18-85	.222	.000	.286	3	9	1	2	1	0	0	2	0	0	0	0	2	0	0	.333	.222
d'Arnaud, Travis	R-R	6-2	210	2-10-89	.310	.000	.346	8	29	3	9	2	0	0	5	9	0	0	0	5	1	0	.379	.474
Evans, Phillip	R-R	5-9	220	9-10-92	.143	.250	.063	9	28	3	4	0	0	0	2	5	0	0	0	3	0	0	.143	.273
Guillorme, Luis	L-R	5-9	190	9-27-94	.263	.280	.257	123	441	47	116	16	2	1	46	43	4	13	3	63	4	2	.315	.332
Johnson, John	L-R	5-7	160	10-27-88	.249	.225	.254	61	217	38	54	7	3	1	14	38	5	3	2	35	12	6	.323	.370
Kaczmarski, Kevin	L-R	6-0	195	12-31-91	.301	.302	.300	42	153	28	46	10	3	0	18	21	0	0	1	26	8	0	.405	.383
Katz, Michael	R-R	6-3	235	8-6-92	.219	.224	.217	92	329	34	72	15	0	2	35	29	5	0	4	115	5	2	.283	.289
Mora, John	L-L	5-11	195	5-31-93	.246	.204	.257	128	439	63	108	15	7	5	42	60	4	2	1	72	8	6	.346	.341
Nido, Tomas	R-R	6-0	205	4-12-94	.320	.361	.309	90	344	38	110	23	2	7	46	19	3	0	4	42	0	1	.459	.357
Ramirez, Raphael	L-L	5-11	170	12-15-95	.095	.111	.083	8	21	0	2	0	0	0	0	0	0	0	0	7	0	0	.095	.095
Ricardo, Lednier	R-R	5-10	195	1-13-88	.205	.140	.231	46	151	13	31	9	0	2	14	12	1	2	1	48	0	0	.305	.267
Rodriguez, Dionis	R-R	6-0	205	2-15-95	.000	.000	.000	1	3	0	0	0	0	0	0	0	0	0	0	0	0	0	.000	.000
Rosario, Amed	R-R	6-2	190	11-20-95	.309	.232	.330	66	265	27	82	10	8	3	40	21	1	0	3	36	13	6	.442	.359
Siena, Vinny	R-R	5-10	200	12-24-93	.236	.197	.260	45	161	20	38	7	0	0	14	18	3	1	1	44	2	0	.280	.322
Stuart, Champ	R-R	6-0	185	10-11-92	.265	.274	.263	71	275	49	73	9	6	6	24	31	4	4	1	95	25	3	.407	.347
Taylor, Kevin	L-R	6-0	195	7-13-91	.288	.284	.289	112	399	59	115	20	1	8	58	56	8	0	1	55	0	0	.404	.386
Tharp, Tucker	R-R	6-0	195	11-26-91	.264	.188	.297	15	53	8	14	1	0	0	7	4	1	0	0	15	1	0	.283	.328
Thompson, David	R-R	6-0	220	8-28-93	.265	.255	.268	55	204	29	54	12	0	5	30	15	3	1	2	41	3	0	.412	.321
Urena, Jhoan	B-R	6-1	230	9-1-94	.225	.227	.223	115	383	52	86	17	2	9	53	42	1	0	3	75	0	1	.350	.301

Pitching	B-T	HT	WT	DOB	W	L	ERA	G	GS	CG	SV	IP	H	R	ER	HR	BB	SO	AVG	vLH	vRH	K/9	BB/9
Baldonado, Alberto	L-L	6-4	250	2-1-93	0	1	0.93	13	0	0	0	19	15	3	2	0	8	21	.221	.250	.208	9.78	3.72
Barbosa, Andrew	R-L	6-8	230	11-18-87	1	0	0.40	5	5	0	0	22	14	4	1	0	3	25	.173	.115	.200	10.07	1.21
Bashlor, Ty	R-R	5-11	195	4-16-93	0	1	5.06	4	0	0	0	5	3	3	2	0	2	5	.200	.091	.333	8.44	3.38
Church, Andrew	R-R	6-2	200	10-7-94	2	1	3.60	6	6	1	0	35	31	16	14	1	14	22	.242	.219	.266	5.66	3.60
Coles, Robby	R-R	6-0	190	8-20-91	3	2	4.26	36	0	0	3	51	53	25	24	3	19	28	.272	.308	.254	4.97	3.38
Conlon, P.J.	L-L	5-11	190	11-11-93	4	1	1.41	12	11	0	1	64	47	10	10	1	14	51	.203	.232	.194	7.21	1.98
Delgado, Casey	R-R	5-10	180	6-15-90	8	3	3.39	14	13	0	0	88	83	33	33	5	26	67	.251	.256	.248	6.88	2.67
Duff, Jimmy	R-R	6-6	200	11-15-93	2	2	7.31	22	0	0	1	32	50	29	26	5	14	24	.365	.488	.309	6.75	3.94
Edgin, Josh	L-L	6-1	245	12-17-86	0	0	2.08	6	3	0	0	4	2	1	1	0	1	7	.133	.000	.200	14.54	2.08
Flexen, Chris	R-R	6-3	235	7-1-94	10	9	3.56	25	25	1	0	134	125	62	53	6	51	95	.249	.249	.249	6.38	3.43
Griset, Ben	L-L	6-0	190	3-12-92	4	2	1.80	32	3	0	3	60	42	19	12	3	20	66	.193	.157	.204	9.90	3.00
Henderson, Jim	L-R	6-5	220	10-21-82	0	0	0.00	1	0	0	0	1	1	0	0	0	0	1	.250	.000	.500	9.00	0.00
Henry, Taylor	L-L	6-2	235	7-6-93	0	0	9.00	1	0	0	0	1	2	1	1	0	2	1	.333	.000	.500	9.00	0.00
Hepple, Mike	R-R	6-5	235	6-5-90	1	2	3.96	24	0	0	0	39	35	19	17	2	24	20	.252	.196	.280	4.66	5.59
Huchingson, Chase	L-L	6-5	215	4-14-89	0	0	0.00	1	0	0	0	1	1	0	0	0	0	2	.333	—	.333	18.00	0.00
Jannis, Mickey	R-R	5-9	195	12-16-87	2	1	5.95	4	3	0	0	20	24	14	13	0	10	11	.316	.400	.261	5.03	4.58
Knapp, Ricky	R-R	6-1	215	5-20-92	9	4	2.14	16	15	1	0	105	95	31	25	4	22	64	.243	.278	.226	5.47	1.88

Pitching

Pitching	B-T	HT	WT	DOB	W	L	ERA	G	GS	CG	SV	IP	H	R	ER	HR	BB	SO	AVG	vLH	vRH	K/9	BB/9
McGowan, Kevin	R-R	6-5	235	10-18-91	1	0	0.82	15	2	0	2	33	20	4	3	1	4	33	.175	.111	.205	9.00	1.09
Oswalt, Corey	R-R	6-5	245	9-3-93	4	2	4.12	14	13	0	0	68	73	34	31	4	18	68	.271	.253	.281	9.04	2.39
Paez, Paul	L-L	5-7	210	4-29-92	2	0	1.00	20	0	0	3	36	26	8	4	1	5	28	.208	.216	.205	7.00	1.25
Palsha, Alex	R-R	6-1	190	5-10-92	3	1	2.91	14	0	0	4	22	21	8	7	2	9	19	.250	.200	.266	7.89	3.74
Peterson, Tim	R-R	6-1	225	2-22-91	1	0	0.49	12	0	0	2	18	8	1	1	1	3	32	.127	.118	.130	15.71	1.47
Prevost, Josh	R-R	6-7	230	1-15-92	4	8	4.26	14	13	0	0	76	100	42	36	4	16	54	.324	.355	.307	6.39	1.89
Reyes, Scarlyn	R-R	6-2	215	12-10-89	8	10	5.90	24	21	0	0	119	128	85	78	8	55	96	.276	.321	.247	7.26	4.16
Secrest, Kelly	L-L	6-0	225	9-13-91	1	4	2.77	22	1	0	1	39	30	12	12	3	19	37	.216	.106	.272	8.54	4.38
Tapia, Domingo	R-R	6-3	250	9-3-91	0	2	3.54	19	0	0	0	28	35	15	11	2	13	24	.310	.359	.284	7.71	4.18
Taylor, Corey	R-R	5-11	245	1-8-93	4	5	1.87	45	0	0	20	53	53	21	11	1	13	45	.252	.219	.270	7.64	2.21
Wheeler, Zack	R-R	6-4	195	5-30-90	0	0	0.00	1	1	0	0	1	0	1	0	0	1	0	.000	.000	.000	9.00	9.00

Fielding

Catcher	PCT	G	PO	A	E	DP	PB
Brosher	1.000	1	9	0	0	0	0
d'Arnaud	1.000	3	23	2	0	0	0
Nido	.987	88	608	86	9	3	9
Ricardo	.985	46	292	32	5	5	3
Rodriguez	1.000	1	4	2	0	0	1

First Base	PCT	G	PO	A	E	DP
Katz	.997	72	598	53	2	73
Taylor	1.000	48	375	26	0	30
Urena	.983	21	162	14	3	10

Second Base	PCT	G	PO	A	E	DP
Evans	1.000	2	6	12	0	4
Guillorme	.977	52	103	149	6	42

	PCT	G	PO	A	E	DP
Johnson	.984	39	82	100	3	31
Siena	.983	43	74	100	3	16
Taylor	1.000	1	0	3	0	0

Third Base	PCT	G	PO	A	E	DP
Evans	.857	3	1	5	1	0
Johnson	.906	13	6	23	3	1
Taylor	1.000	1	0	3	0	0
Thompson	.918	46	26	86	10	5
Urena	.892	76	46	128	21	14

Shortstop	PCT	G	PO	A	E	DP
Cabrera	.750	2	0	3	1	1
Guillorme	.960	72	90	195	12	36
Johnson	.929	4	5	8	1	2

	PCT	G	PO	A	E	DP
Rosario	.962	60	93	189	11	44
Siena	.500	1	1	0	1	0

Outfield	PCT	G	PO	A	E	DP
Becerra	.938	13	30	0	2	0
Biondi	.996	99	221	5	1	2
Cespedes	1.000	2	3	0	0	0
Johnson	1.000	4	6	0	0	0
Kaczmarski	1.000	41	68	1	0	1
Katz	1.000	19	30	1	0	0
Mora	.973	127	248	9	7	0
Ramirez	1.000	6	15	0	0	0
Stuart	.994	70	154	3	1	1
Taylor	.975	27	38	1	1	0
Tharp	1.000	15	31	2	0	1

COLUMBIA FIREFLIES   LOW CLASS A
SOUTH ATLANTIC LEAGUE

Batting	B-T	HT	WT	DOB	AVG	vLH	vRH	G	AB	R	H	2B	3B	HR	RBI	BB	HBP	SH	SF	SO	SB	CS	SLG	OBP
Barring, Will	R-R	6-1	215	4-24-93	.176	—	.176	6	17	4	3	0	0	0	3	0	0	0	0	6	0	1	.176	.300
Brosher, Brandon	R-R	6-3	235	2-17-95	.167	.167	.167	12	30	3	5	0	0	1	2	8	0	0	0	11	3	0	.267	.342
Burdick, Dale	R-R	6-0	185	10-12-95	.229	.129	.260	40	131	14	30	8	4	1	13	12	1	0	1	47	5	2	.374	.297
Diehl, Jeff	R-R	6-5	195	9-30-93	.234	.286	.217	59	201	26	47	5	2	9	32	29	2	0	1	80	1	0	.413	.335
Garcia, Eudor	L-R	6-0	240	5-17-94	.275	.200	.302	55	204	27	56	14	1	5	31	16	1	0	3	44	1	0	.426	.326
Garcia, Jose	B-R	5-11	200	11-3-94	.200	.200	.200	22	70	7	14	2	0	0	3	8	0	0	0	27	0	1	.229	.282
Kaczmarski, Kevin	L-R	6-0	195	12-31-91	.268	.304	.260	69	261	41	70	19	7	2	28	29	4	4	3	50	6	6	.418	.347
Lupo, Vicente	R-R	5-11	235	11-27-93	.221	.169	.241	83	262	36	58	16	2	5	34	39	4	1	1	106	3	8	.355	.330
Mazeika, Patrick	L-R	6-3	210	10-14-93	.305	.308	.305	70	239	34	73	14	0	3	35	38	10	1	5	39	2	0	.402	.414
Moore, Tyler	L-R	6-1	215	8-8-93	.218	.140	.237	70	229	30	50	9	2	1	22	24	0	2	3	54	1	2	.288	.289
Ortega, Luis	R-R	5-10	210	4-5-93	.240	.224	.244	68	225	23	54	4	1	4	31	16	5	2	3	47	5	6	.320	.301
Ramos, Milton	R-R	5-11	180	10-26-95	.220	.179	.232	107	363	31	80	15	2	0	35	32	5	3	1	88	5	4	.273	.292
Ramos, Natanael	R-R	5-11	225	6-19-93	.297	.231	.333	12	37	3	11	2	1	0	3	4	1	2	0	11	1	0	.405	.381
Rodriguez, Jean	B-R	6-1	190	9-3-92	.237	.156	.256	124	469	66	111	18	4	9	49	44	2	6	3	87	18	7	.350	.303
Siena, Vinny	R-R	5-10	200	12-24-93	.291	.275	.297	66	223	53	65	16	4	0	13	51	8	3	3	66	8	1	.399	.435
Tharp, Tucker	R-R	6-0	195	11-26-91	.210	.216	.207	54	186	28	39	6	2	2	14	19	1	1	3	56	6	3	.296	.282
Thompson, David	R-R	6-0	208	8-28-93	.294	.349	.281	61	228	45	67	22	2	5	58	14	7	0	7	49	3	0	.474	.344
Tuschak, Joe	R-R	6-0	200	10-17-92	.199	.130	.213	98	326	42	65	14	2	6	28	30	1	3	8	83	6	2	.310	.281
Wilson, Ivan	R-R	6-3	220	5-26-95	.197	.075	.225	64	213	25	42	15	0	6	22	23	0	0	0	80	5	6	.352	.275
Winningham, Dash	L-L	6-2	225	10-11-95	.234	.231	.235	125	465	41	109	31	2	12	69	29	5	0	5	108	0	1	.387	.284
Zabala, Enmanuel	R-R	6-0	195	9-29-94	.280	.263	.287	50	186	25	52	4	2	1	11	11	4	1	2	41	8	3	.339	.330

Pitching	B-T	HT	WT	DOB	W	L	ERA	G	GS	CG	SV	IP	H	R	ER	HR	BB	SO	AVG	vLH	vRH	K/9	BB/9
Almonte, Gaby	R-R	6-0	190	8-15-92	4	5	4.78	14	14	2	0	81	106	51	43	10	16	44	.318	.320	.318	4.89	1.78
Badamo, Tyler	R-R	6-1	220	8-8-92	3	4	3.92	13	13	0	0	78	90	38	34	6	13	49	.290	.267	.301	5.65	1.50
Bashlor, Ty	R-R	5-11	195	4-16-93	4	2	2.50	34	0	0	3	50	35	16	14	2	28	68	.193	.152	.217	12.16	5.01
Beeler, Bryce	L-R	6-2	190	3-9-93	1	1	2.20	4	3	0	0	16	17	4	4	1	3	15	.270	.267	.273	8.27	1.65
Blank, Nicco	R-R	5-9	170	10-29-92	0	0	5.97	25	0	0	0	32	27	21	21	5	18	42	.231	.189	.266	11.94	5.12
Canelon, Kevin	L-L	5-11	180	1-16-94	6	11	3.64	25	25	1	0	143	139	65	58	15	28	119	.256	.270	.251	7.47	1.76
Church, Andrew	R-R	6-2	200	10-7-94	5	2	2.22	9	9	1	0	57	38	16	14	4	10	52	.191	.167	.203	8.26	1.59
Conlon, P.J.	L-L	5-11	190	11-11-93	8	1	1.84	12	12	0	0	78	68	19	16	4	10	61	.233	.203	.242	7.01	1.15
Crismatt, Nabil	R-R	6-1	200	12-25-94	1	2	1.88	4	3	0	0	29	20	8	6	1	2	32	.192	.139	.221	10.05	0.63
Davis, Seth	L-L	5-9	200	5-8-93	2	3	2.31	36	1	0	1	70	60	22	18	4	28	64	.237	.155	.278	8.23	3.60
De Los Santos, Luis	R-R	5-10	175	11-27-94	0	1	5.73	4	2	0	0	11	15	9	7	1	5	8	.326	.261	.391	6.55	4.09
Duff, Jimmy	R-R	6-6	200	11-15-93	2	2	2.92	17	0	0	7	25	27	9	8	2	6	22	.270	.257	.277	8.03	2.19
Feliz, Gabriel	L-R	5-11	160	11-12-92	0	0	0.00	2	0	0	0	2	0	0	0	0	2	2	.000	.000	.000	9.00	9.00
Haggard, Witt	R-R	6-2	205	12-9-91	3	4	3.58	24	0	0	0	38	36	17	15	2	27	38	.267	.308	.241	9.08	6.45
Ingram, Chase	R-R	6-3	215	4-16-94	8	9	4.60	25	25	0	0	131	141	78	67	8	57	132	.274	.278	.272	9.07	3.92
Jacobson, Raul	R-R	6-1	220	4-12-92	0	1	16.20	2	2	0	0	7	13	12	12	1	6	6	.406	.462	.368	8.10	8.10
Magliozzi, Johnny	R-R	5-8	195	7-21-91	5	4	2.70	40	0	0	5	63	52	21	19	7	14	51	.225	.247	.212	7.25	1.99
McIlrath, Thomas	R-R	6-3	200	2-17-94	1	4	6.23	7	7	1	0	35	37	27	24	5	15	25	.291	.271	.304	6.49	3.89

Pitching	B-T	HT	WT	DOB	W	L	ERA	G	GS	CG	SV	IP	H	R	ER	HR	BB	SO	AVG	vLH	vRH	K/9	BB/9
Missigman, Craig	R-R	6-2	190	8-5-93	3	4	2.89	37	0	0	2	72	56	31	23	5	30	78	.215	.220	.213	9.80	3.77
Montgomery, Christian	R-R	6-1	230	11-20-92	1	1	3.34	19	0	0	2	30	27	16	11	2	20	45	.235	.313	.179	13.65	6.07
Palsha, Alex	R-R	6-1	190	5-10-92	2	3	3.03	28	0	0	14	36	25	13	12	2	13	46	.197	.289	.146	11.61	3.28
Shaw, Joe	R-R	6-3	228	12-20-93	8	9	4.46	23	23	0	0	135	150	82	67	11	37	134	.279	.348	.238	8.91	2.46
Silva, Luis	R-R	6-0	210	11-17-96	0	0	2.08	1	1	0	0	4	2	1	1	0	3	3	.143	.250	.000	6.23	6.23

Fielding

Catcher	PCT	G	PO	A	E	DP	PB
Brosher	1.000	6	40	7	0	0	0
Garcia	1.000	21	171	22	0	1	3
Mazeika	.990	46	363	26	4	1	1
Moore	.988	59	466	42	6	1	15
Ortega	.923	2	9	3	1	2	1
Ramos	1.000	11	82	8	0	1	0

First Base	PCT	G	PO	A	E	DP
Diehl	.987	20	145	7	2	13
Garcia	1.000	10	83	4	0	7
Garcia	1.000	1	1	0	0	0
Moore	1.000	5	28	5	0	3
Ortega	.963	9	73	4	3	7
Winningham	.990	105	824	62	9	77

Second Base	PCT	G	PO	A	E	DP
Burdick	.993	35	63	72	1	20
Moore	1.000	4	5	8	0	2
Ortega	1.000	4	5	5	0	0
Rodriguez	.968	45	76	104	6	21
Siena	.970	59	110	150	8	37

Third Base	PCT	G	PO	A	E	DP
Burdick	.923	5	6	6	1	0
Diehl	—	1	0	0	0	0
Garcia	.932	29	21	47	5	7
Ortega	.932	43	32	77	8	5
Ramos	—	1	0	0	0	0
Rodriguez	.938	27	16	74	6	5
Thompson	.952	46	38	119	8	10

Shortstop	PCT	G	PO	A	E	DP
Ramos	.932	104	129	254	28	62
Rodriguez	.958	40	63	74	6	19

Outfield	PCT	G	PO	A	E	DP
Barring	1.000	6	13	0	0	0
Diehl	.981	29	52	1	1	0
Kaczmarski	.983	68	114	5	2	3
Lupo	.948	74	124	3	7	1
Rodriguez	1.000	1	2	0	0	0
Tharp	.988	52	81	2	1	1
Tuschak	.979	93	140	2	3	1
Wilson	.963	64	130	1	5	0
Zabala	.983	50	107	6	2	2

BROOKLYN CYCLONES
NEW YORK-PENN LEAGUE

SHORT-SEASON

Batting	B-T	HT	WT	DOB	AVG	vLH	vRH	G	AB	R	H	2B	3B	HR	RBI	BB	HBP	SH	SF	SO	SB	CS	SLG	OBP
Alonso, Peter	R-R	6-3	225	12-7-94	.321	.409	.262	30	109	20	35	12	1	5	21	11	1	0	2	22	0	1	.587	.382
Berrios, Arnaldo	B-R	5-9	190	1-15-96	.185	.114	.225	37	124	8	23	4	0	0	13	8	2	1	4	39	0	1	.218	.239
Brosher, Brandon	R-R	6-3	235	2-17-95	.194	.250	.175	30	108	13	21	2	0	5	17	10	3	0	1	46	3	1	.352	.279
Burdick, Dale	R-R	6-0	185	10-12-95	.113	.125	.111	14	53	2	6	0	0	0	3	6	0	0	0	17	3	0	.113	.230
Carpio, Luis	R-R	6-0	165	7-11-97	.140	.154	.133	12	43	4	6	2	0	0	1	8	1	0	0	10	0	0	.186	.288
Cone, Gene	L-L	6-0	175	9-21-94	.227	.284	.204	60	229	35	52	6	1	1	17	28	1	0	2	45	9	4	.275	.312
Correa, Franklin	R-R	5-9	195	1-1-96	.261	.111	.357	7	23	0	6	1	0	0	2	2	1	0	0	5	2	0	.304	.346
De Aza, Yeffry	R-R	6-0	205	1-14-97	.000	.000	.000	2	11	0	0	0	0	0	0	0	0	0	0	4	0	0	.000	.000
Dimino, Anthony	L-R	5-11	175	8-5-93	.364	.571	.308	10	33	4	12	2	0	0	4	7	0	0	0	5	1	1	.424	.475
Jabs, Jay	L-R	6-0	195	9-30-94	.177	.196	.168	52	175	13	31	6	1	0	12	21	3	0	1	47	2	3	.223	.275
Knight, Darryl	R-R	6-2	225	2-26-93	.200	.210	.193	41	150	18	30	4	2	1	13	18	1	1	0	50	3	3	.273	.290
Lindsay, Desmond	R-R	6-0	200	1-15-97	.297	.368	.260	32	111	18	33	5	0	4	17	20	3	0	0	26	3	1	.450	.418
Lupo, Vicente	R-R	5-11	235	11-27-93	.000	—	.000	1	3	0	0	0	0	0	0	0	0	0	0	1	0	0	.000	.000
Marte, Santo	R-R	5-9	185	9-30-93	.000	.000	.000	1	6	0	0	0	0	0	0	0	0	1	0	2	0	0	.000	.143
Paez, Michael	R-R	5-8	175	12-8-94	.190	.206	.180	46	179	18	34	11	0	2	11	18	2	1	1	43	8	6	.285	.270
Paulino, Dionis	L-L	6-3	225	6-20-94	.300	—	.300	5	10	1	3	0	0	0	0	0	0	0	0	5	0	1	.300	.364
Reyes, Jose	B-R	6-0	195	6-11-95	.182	.333	.125	4	11	3	2	1	0	0	1	3	0	0	0	4	2	0	.273	.357
Rizzie, Dan	R-R	6-2	200	11-26-93	.162	.200	.138	33	105	10	17	3	1	0	8	14	5	0	2	9	3	2	.210	.286
Rojas, Hengelbert	R-R	6-1	210	10-27-93	.170	.189	.158	29	94	8	16	4	0	0	9	15	4	0	1	29	2	0	.213	.307
Sanchez, Ali	R-R	6-1	200	1-20-97	.216	.224	.212	46	171	15	37	10	0	0	11	10	0	0	0	26	2	0	.275	.260
Sergakis, Nick	R-R	5-8	175	4-6-93	.250	.252	.207	38	143	21	36	10	0	2	15	16	7	0	1	27	11	0	.364	.353
Tiberi, Blake	L-R	5-11	205	2-16-95	.235	.327	.199	56	196	21	46	6	2	2	24	22	3	0	4	32	2	6	.316	.316
Woodmansee, Colby	R-R	6-3	190	8-27-94	.257	.267	.252	64	249	30	64	11	0	2	29	19	1	1	6	75	4	3	.325	.305
Zabala, Enmanuel	R-R	6-0	195	9-29-94	.132	.083	.154	8	38	3	5	0	0	1	3	2	1	0	0	9	1	3	.211	.195
Zanon, Jacob	R-R	6-1	180	6-25-95	.197	.236	.176	44	157	19	31	6	1	2	18	21	0	1	5	25	20	2	.287	.284

Pitching	B-T	HT	WT	DOB	W	L	ERA	G	GS	CG	SV	IP	H	R	ER	HR	BB	SO	AVG	vLH	vRH	K/9	BB/9
Almeida, Adrian	L-L	6-0	160	2-25-95	0	1	3.86	3	0	0	0	2	3	1	1	0	3	5	.273	.333	.25	19.29	11.57
Atkins, Adam	R-R	6-3	210	9-8-93	0	2	3.71	19	0	0	0	17	16	9	7	0	9	22	.246	.222	.255	11.65	4.76
Becker, Dillon	R-R	6-3	205	1-21-94	1	0	6.45	15	0	0	0	22	16	20	16	1	26	17	.200	.200	.200	6.85	10.48
Beeler, Bryce	L-R	6-2	190	3-9-93	0	0	0.00	2	0	0	1	7	0	0	0	0	1	7	.000	.000	.000	9.00	1.29
Blank, Nicco	R-R	5-9	170	10-29-92	0	0	2.45	2	0	0	0	4	2	1	1	0	2	7	.167	.200	.143	17.18	4.91
Castro, Alejandro	R-R	5-11	200	1-15-93	1	2	4.82	26	0	0	0	28	29	15	15	1	10	26	.271	.237	.290	8.36	3.21
Cornish, Gary	R-R	6-3	225	1-21-94	0	0	2.16	14	0	0	3	25	24	6	6	1	3	44	.250	.250	.250	15.84	1.08
Crismatt, Nabil	R-R	6-1	200	12-25-94	0	1	3.19	8	3	0	1	31	26	11	11	4	4	35	.218	.140	.263	10.16	1.16
Dunn, Justin	R-R	6-2	185	9-22-95	1	1	1.50	11	8	0	0	30	25	11	5	1	10	35	.227	.226	.228	10.50	3.00
Estevez, Gregorix	R-R	6-5	240	4-12-94	0	0	3.38	2	0	0	0	3	1	1	1	0	3	3	.111	.000	.200	10.13	0.00
Feliz, Gabriel	L-L	5-11	160	11-12-92	1	1	4.78	22	0	0	0	26	26	17	14	0	13	28	.257	.205	.290	9.57	4.44
Gonzalez, Harol	R-R	6-0	170	3-2-95	7	3	2.01	14	13	0	0	85	69	20	19	7	17	88	.223	.258	.185	9.32	1.80
Gonzalez, Merandy	R-R	6-1	195	10-9-95	6	3	2.87	14	14	0	0	69	65	29	22	2	27	71	.254	.284	.231	9.26	3.52
Henry, Taylor	L-L	6-2	235	7-6-93	2	1	1.71	24	0	0	4	37	28	8	7	2	8	28	.237	.111	.293	7.96	2.56
Huertas, Joel	B-L	6-3	215	2-14-96	2	3	8.03	6	4	0	0	25	37	23	22	0	7	22	.356	.393	.342	8.39	2.55
Humphreys, Jordan	R-R	6-2	225	6-11-96	0	1	1.50	1	1	0	0	6	7	1	1	0	1	9	.292	.231	.364	13.50	1.50
Jacobson, Raul	R-R	6-1	220	4-12-92	3	2	2.31	12	4	0	2	51	40	13	13	1	9	43	.214	.181	.264	7.64	1.60
Llanes, Gabe	R-R	6-4	205	1-15-96	4	8	3.94	14	13	0	0	80	95	51	35	6	8	37	.289	.282	.294	4.16	0.90
Manoah, Erik	R-R	6-2	190	12-22-95	5	5	5.37	13	12	0	0	62	71	40	37	4	27	63	.291	.288	.293	9.15	3.92
McGeorge, Austin	R-R	6-2	215	11-27-94	0	1	2.84	16	0	0	1	19	22	8	6	1	6	18	.301	.344	.268	8.53	2.84

Pitching	B-T	HT	WT	DOB	W	L	ERA	G	GS	CG	SV	IP	H	R	ER	HR	BB	SO	AVG	vLH	vRH	K/9	BB/9
Regnault, Kyle	L-L	6-2	215	12-13-88	1	0	0.00	3	0	0	1	3	1	0	0	0	2	4	.111	.250	.000	13.50	6.75
Szapucki, Thomas	R-L	6-2	205	6-12-96	2	2	2.35	4	4	0	0	23	10	7	6	0	11	39	.130	.188	.115	15.26	4.30
Williams, Ty	R-R	6-2	195	2-21-94	0	0	3.00	7	0	0	0	6	2	2	2	0	6	3	.105	.000	.200	4.50	9.00
Zanghi, Joe	R-R	6-3	195	12-1-94	1	0	1.23	23	0	0	8	29	20	6	4	0	15	45	.196	.093	.271	13.81	4.60

Fielding

Catcher	PCT	G	PO	A	E	DP	PB
Brosher	.994	17	152	12	1	0	8
Knight	1.000	1	7	2	0	0	0
Rizzie	.996	29	243	38	1	4	8
Sanchez	.982	33	301	32	6	5	8

First Base	PCT	G	PO	A	E	DP
Alonso	1.000	27	224	19	0	15
Burdick	1.000	2	16	1	0	1
Dimino	.990	10	93	3	1	5
Knight	.985	35	298	26	5	24
Paulino	.966	4	26	2	1	1

Second Base	PCT	G	PO	A	E	DP
Burdick	1.000	4	4	7	0	0
Correa	1.000	4	4	15	0	1
Jabs	.818	4	6	3	2	0
Marte	.875	1	2	5	1	1
Paez	.956	36	63	110	8	22
Sergakis	.966	28	63	80	5	20

Third Base	PCT	G	PO	A	E	DP
Burdick	1.000	2	3	9	0	0
Correa	1.000	3	0	4	0	1
De Aza	1.000	1	1	8	0	0
Jabs	.850	12	4	13	3	2
Reyes	.857	4	4	2	1	0
Sergakis	1.000	8	2	16	0	2
Tiberi	.930	51	40	93	10	9

Shortstop	PCT	G	PO	A	E	DP
Burdick	1.000	6	13	24	0	4
De Aza	.800	1	0	4	1	0
Paez	1.000	8	13	14	0	2
Woodmansee	.970	61	86	174	8	26

Outfield	PCT	G	PO	A	E	DP
Berrios	1.000	36	35	4	0	0
Cone	.982	60	104	4	2	0
Jabs	.978	28	40	4	1	0
Lindsay	.935	29	42	1	3	0
Lupo	1.000	1	5	0	0	0
Rojas	.974	28	36	2	1	1
Zabala	.955	8	19	2	1	1
Zanon	.946	44	84	3	5	1

KINGSPORT METS   ROOKIE
APPALACHIAN LEAGUE

Batting	B-T	HT	WT	DOB	AVG	vLH	vRH	G	AB	R	H	2B	3B	HR	RBI	BB	HBP	SH	SF	SO	SB	CS	SLG	OBP
Aybar, Cecilio	R-R	6-0	170	11-23-93	.300	.250	.315	22	70	18	21	4	0	1	10	5	2	2	0	20	5	2	.400	.364
Barring, Will	R-R	6-1	215	4-24-93	.232	.222	.237	27	95	14	22	2	1	0	9	18	0	1	1	31	5	3	.274	.351
Cespedes, Ricardo	L-L	6-1	200	8-24-97	.322	.280	.342	56	227	30	73	4	3	1	16	9	3	2	0	36	7	7	.379	.356
Correa, Franklin	R-R	5-9	195	1-1-96	.214	.222	.211	34	126	17	27	7	2	3	25	3	2	4	1	34	1	1	.373	.242
De Aza, Yeffry	R-R	6-0	205	1-14-97	.199	.229	.186	45	161	9	32	7	1	0	12	5	3	0	1	52	0	4	.255	.235
Dimino, Anthony	L-R	5-11	175	8-5-93	.325	.378	.300	37	117	19	38	7	0	1	15	22	2	2	1	20	7	2	.410	.437
Gamache, Reed	R-R	6-0	185	1-3-94	.279	.300	.269	50	179	31	50	14	0	1	19	35	0	0	2	39	1	1	.374	.394
Manea, Scott	R-R	5-11	205	12-21-95	.100	.100	.100	10	30	4	3	1	0	0	3	6	2	0	0	4	0	0	.133	.289
Manzanarez, Angel	R-R	6-0	170	5-19-97	.139	.059	.211	11	36	3	5	0	0	0	1	4	0	2	0	6	3	1	.139	.225
Maria, Jose	R-R	5-9	215	11-30-94	.306	.318	.301	43	157	28	48	18	0	3	31	11	4	0	2	32	0	1	.478	.362
Marte, Santo	R-R	5-9	185	9-30-93	.231	.231	.231	12	39	5	9	2	0	1	3	8	0	0	0	10	1	1	.359	.362
Medina, Jose	R-R	6-3	180	10-21-96	.286	.329	.265	63	231	34	66	9	2	4	33	27	0	0	2	46	8	3	.394	.358
Pascual, Oliver	R-R	5-10	180	11-16-96	.167	.250	.125	4	12	2	2	0	0	0	1	1	1	0	3	0	1	.167	.286
Ramirez, Raphael	L-L	5-11	170	12-15-95	.160	.133	.169	36	119	11	19	2	1	1	13	7	0	4	0	44	5	3	.235	.206
Rasquin, Walter	R-R	5-9	200	3-21-96	.294	.375	.252	49	187	24	55	3	3	2	20	16	1	0	0	31	8	3	.374	.353
Rodriguez, Dionis	R-R	6-0	205	2-15-95	.246	.256	.242	41	134	18	33	10	0	2	21	23	3	2	0	35	0	2	.366	.369
Strom, Ian	R-L	6-2	205	12-12-94	.228	.278	.198	37	145	19	33	9	2	0	10	20	0	0	1	33	9	4	.317	.319
Wolf, Jeremy	L-R	6-2	200	11-2-93	.290	.275	.295	50	183	31	53	12	1	5	33	19	2	0	2	37	0	1	.448	.359

Pitching	B-T	HT	WT	DOB	W	L	ERA	G	GS	CG	SV	IP	H	R	ER	HR	BB	SO	AVG	vLH	vRH	K/9	BB/9
Almeida, Adrian	L-L	6-0	160	2-25-95	0	3	6.14	18	0	0	2	22	21	18	15	3	13	29	.247	.267	.236	11.86	5.32
Buchmann, Connor	R-R	6-1	190	7-11-93	0	1	4.76	3	0	0	0	6	5	5	3	0	7	3	.263	.167	.308	4.76	11.12
Carreno, Luis	R-R	5-11	205	8-12-95	0	0	5.00	5	0	0	0	9	7	6	5	1	9	5	.219	.176	.267	5.00	9.00
Estevez, Gregorix	R-R	6-5	240	4-12-94	1	1	4.29	17	0	0	0	21	20	10	10	3	8	27	.244	.229	.255	11.57	3.43
German, Edwin	R-R	6-3	175	9-10-92	0	0	6.00	1	0	0	0	3	4	2	2	2	0	3	.308	.375	.200	9.00	0.00
Guedez, Ronald	R-R	6-1	170	1-26-96	2	0	1.08	10	0	0	2	17	14	6	2	0	6	13	.219	.281	.156	7.02	3.24
Holderman, Colin	R-R	6-6	215	10-8-95	1	0	3.86	13	0	0	3	19	17	10	8	1	11	13	.236	.364	.128	6.27	5.30
Horne, Kurtis	L-L	6-5	215	8-5-96	1	0	8.78	13	0	0	0	13	18	14	13	2	6	5	.327	.308	.333	3.38	4.05
Huertas, Joel	B-L	6-3	215	2-4-96	0	0	5.32	6	4	0	0	24	22	17	14	1	13	26	.247	.200	.261	9.89	4.94
Humphreys, Jordan	R-R	6-2	225	6-11-96	3	5	3.76	12	12	0	0	69	65	35	29	3	15	76	.247	.218	.277	9.87	1.95
Johnson, Trent	R-R	6-5	190	8-12-96	0	3	6.61	14	0	0	0	16	21	14	12	0	4	14	.300	.344	.263	7.71	2.20
Kuhns, Max	R-R	6-3	205	8-11-94	0	0	6.28	13	0	0	1	14	12	10	10	1	8	15	.218	.333	.107	9.42	5.02
Medina, Jose	L-L	6-2	210	3-31-96	2	3	3.86	15	0	0	0	23	28	12	10	3	3	21	.295	.296	.294	8.10	1.16
Napolitano, Joe	R-R	6-3	210	2-10-92	2	2	6.00	12	0	0	0	12	15	10	8	0	5	12	.306	.381	.250	9.00	3.75
Ramos, Darwin	R-R	6-2	210	11-23-95	0	3	5.31	13	5	0	1	39	44	33	23	2	16	42	.273	.182	.321	9.69	3.69
Simon, Jake	L-L	6-2	190	1-21-97	2	5	4.83	12	12	0	0	63	70	49	34	5	31	66	.271	.277	.269	9.38	4.41
Szapucki, Thomas	R-L	6-2	205	6-12-96	2	1	0.62	5	5	0	0	29	16	5	2	2	9	47	.157	.172	.151	14.59	2.79
Taylor, Blake	L-L	6-3	220	8-17-95	0	0	4.15	5	0	0	1	9	5	4	4	0	8	12	.167	.273	.105	12.46	8.31
Torres, Placido	L-L	5-11	165	5-17-93	2	2	3.38	13	0	0	0	19	22	12	7	2	6	26	.286	.444	.237	12.54	2.89
Torres, Sixto	L-L	6-3	225	3-31-96	2	4	2.70	7	7	0	0	37	44	21	11	1	12	30	.289	.333	.277	7.36	2.95
Uceta, Adonis	R-R	6-1	225	5-10-94	3	6	4.99	12	11	0	0	61	77	44	34	5	16	63	.301	.317	.289	9.24	2.35
Viall, Chris	R-R	6-9	230	9-28-95	0	2	6.75	9	6	0	0	20	18	19	15	2	17	27	.228	.182	.261	12.15	7.65
Wotell, Max	R-L	6-3	195	9-13-96	3	1	3.94	6	6	0	0	30	24	14	13	1	12	31	.220	.185	.232	9.40	3.64

Fielding

C: Dimino 19, Manea 8, Maria 15, Rodriguez 30. 1B: Dimino 11, Gamache 1, Maria 21, Wolf 38. 2B: Correa 2, Gamache 17, Manzanarez 6, Marte 11, Rasquin 34. 3B: Correa 23, De Aza 13, Gamache 33, Rasquin 1. SS: Aybar 22, Correa 9, De Aza 30, Manzanarez 5, Pascual 4. OF: Barring 18, Cespedes 56, Medina 62, Ramirez 35, Strom 37, Wolf 1.

GCL METS
ROOKIE
GULF COAST LEAGUE

Batting	B-T	HT	WT	DOB	AVG	vLH	vRH	G	AB	R	H	2B	3B	HR	RBI	BB	HBP	SH	SF	SO	SB	CS	SLG	OBP
Adon, Ranfy	R-R	6-3	185	8-2-97	.195	.222	.191	40	133	22	26	4	0	2	12	16	2	1	1	37	9	4	.271	.289
Bautista, Kenneth	R-R	6-3	220	8-7-97	.159	.143	.162	25	88	4	14	5	0	0	9	6	3	1	2	38	0	0	.216	.232
Carpio, Luis	R-R	6-0	165	7-11-97	.290	.000	.300	8	31	3	9	1	1	0	2	1	2	0	0	11	0	0	.387	.353
Dirocie, Anthony	R-R	6-0	170	4-24-97	.253	.211	.259	44	162	32	41	10	5	2	18	25	4	1	2	52	7	2	.414	.363
Gamache, Reed	R-R	6-0	185	1-3-94	.455	1.000	.429	6	22	6	10	1	1	0	3	3	0	0	2	6	0	1	.591	.481
Garcia, Eudor	L-R	6-0	240	5-17-94	.429	.000	.500	2	7	0	3	0	0	0	1	2	0	0	0	1	0	0	.429	.556
Hall, Kevin	R-R	6-3	210	11-13-93	.158	.000	.176	16	38	1	6	1	0	0	1	6	1	0	0	15	0	0	.184	.289
Hernandez, Kenny	L-R	6-1	200	8-13-98	.203	.222	.200	16	59	5	12	2	0	1	3	5	0	0	1	20	0	0	.288	.262
Jimenez, Grabiel	L-L	6-0	205	1-16-95	.206	.143	.219	37	126	13	26	4	1	0	12	13	1	1	1	32	1	1	.254	.284
Lagrange, Wagner	R-R	6-0	195	9-6-95	.231	.176	.237	46	186	16	43	10	0	1	21	11	1	0	1	25	1	1	.301	.276
Lindsay, Desmond	R-R	6-0	200	1-15-97	.364	.667	.250	5	11	3	4	1	0	0	5	0	0	0	0	5	0	0	.455	.563
Manea, Scott	R-R	5-11	205	12-21-95	.125	—	.125	3	8	0	1	0	0	0	0	1	0	0	0	2	0	0	.125	.222
Manzanarez, Angel	R-R	6-0	170	5-19-97	.233	.231	.234	28	90	11	21	3	0	0	4	7	1	2	0	15	1	2	.267	.296
Montero, Luis	R-R	6-3	210	1-16-96	—	—	—	1	0	0	0	0	0	0	0	0	0	0	0	0	0	0	—	—
Moscote, Victor	R-R	6-2	225	5-10-94	.293	.286	.293	40	147	19	43	8	0	1	16	15	7	0	0	26	0	2	.367	.385
Pascual, Oliver	B-R	5-10	180	11-16-96	.241	.167	.252	40	133	21	32	7	0	0	9	14	1	1	1	24	1	2	.293	.315
Patino, Miguel	R-R	6-2	170	12-17-95	.268	.000	.288	40	149	16	40	5	2	0	18	5	4	4	2	27	3	1	.329	.306
Ramos, Natanael	R-R	5-11	225	6-19-93	.000	—	.000	1	1	0	0	0	0	0	0	0	0	0	0	0	0	0	.000	.000
Sanchez, Carlos	R-R	6-0	210	6-6-96	.317	.500	.294	38	142	16	45	8	2	2	16	12	3	0	0	23	2	1	.444	.382
Terrazas, Rigoberto	B-R	6-2	180	4-11-96	.220	.200	.222	42	150	16	33	3	1	0	17	13	0	3	1	23	0	1	.253	.280
Uriarte, Juan	R-R	6-3	180	9-17-97	.236	.176	.245	37	123	9	29	5	0	1	13	7	6	1	2	29	3	0	.301	.304
Ventura, Pedro	R-R	6-1	180	3-14-97	.500	—	.500	2	2	0	1	0	0	0	0	0	0	0	0	0	0	0	.500	.500

Pitching	B-T	HT	WT	DOB	W	L	ERA	G	GS	CG	SV	IP	H	R	ER	HR	BB	SO	AVG	vLH	vRH	K/9	BB/9
Barbosa, Andrew	R-L	6-8	230	11-18-87	0	0	0.00	3	2	0	0	6	3	0	0	0	0	4	.167	.000	.231	6.35	0.00
Berihuete, Enmanuel	R-R	6-1	200	11-5-93	2	1	4.91	17	0	0	1	26	26	20	14	1	9	23	.265	.242	.277	8.06	3.16
Bryant, Garrison	L-R	6-3	190	12-3-98	0	0	9.72	7	0	0	0	8	15	9	9	0	2	5	.395	.438	.364	5.40	2.16
Buchmann, Connor	R-R	6-1	190	7-11-93	0	0	3.00	1	1	0	0	3	3	1	1	0	3	3	.273	.000	.375	9.00	9.00
Carreno, Luis	R-R	5-11	205	8-12-95	1	0	2.35	9	0	0	0	15	7	4	4	0	5	16	.130	.158	.114	9.39	2.93
Cleveland, Matt	R-R	6-5	190	3-18-98	0	1	12.27	7	0	0	0	7	12	12	10	1	6	2	.375	.400	.353	2.45	7.36
Colon, Yeudy	R-R	6-2	235	6-9-95	4	2	4.84	16	0	0	1	22	17	13	12	0	18	25	.218	.148	.255	10.07	7.25
De Los Santos, Luis	R-R	5-10	175	1-27-94	3	4	2.62	10	7	0	0	55	53	22	16	3	7	37	.252	.253	.252	6.05	1.15
Debora, Nicolas	R-R	6-4	185	12-6-93	4	2	4.46	11	7	0	0	40	39	21	20	4	12	41	.257	.214	.281	9.15	2.68
Geraldo, Jose	R-R	6-2	200	7-14-95	2	0	1.31	5	3	1	0	21	15	7	3	0	3	15	.205	.167	.224	6.53	1.31
Hernandez, Carlos	R-R	5-11	170	11-3-94	1	8	5.07	11	10	0	0	55	58	33	31	3	15	43	.282	.25	.302	7.04	2.45
Huchingson, Chase	L-L	6-5	215	4-14-89	0	0	3.38	3	1	0	0	3	4	1	1	0	1	5	.364	.25	.429	16.88	3.38
James, Christian	R-R	6-3	210	5-24-98	0	1	0.52	14	0	0	3	17	11	2	1	0	5	15	.177	.200	.167	7.79	2.60
Montijo, Marbin	R-R	6-2	185	7-4-96	1	2	3.05	11	5	0	1	38	32	13	13	4	19	17	.241	.250	.235	3.99	4.46
Napolitano, Joe	R-R	6-3	210	2-10-92	1	0	0.00	3	0	0	1	4	2	0	0	0	1	3	.143	.167	.125	6.75	2.25
Olivo, Aneury	L-L	6-1	170	10-24-94	0	0	4.76	1	1	0	0	6	5	3	3	0	3	3	.238	.286	.214	4.76	4.76
Oswalt, Corey	R-R	6-5	245	9-3-93	0	0	0.00	1	1	0	0	1	0	0	0	0	0	3	.000	.000	.000	27.00	0.00
Prevost, Josh	R-R	6-7	230	1-15-92	0	0	4.76	2	2	0	0	6	7	5	3	0	1	4	.292	.444	.2	6.35	1.59
Regnault, Kyle	L-L	6-2	215	12-13-88	0	0	1.80	4	2	0	0	5	3	1	1	1	1	8	.167	.000	.188	14.40	1.80
Reina, Richard	R-R	6-2	220	2-7-95	2	1	6.32	15	0	0	0	16	13	11	11	1	16	9	.232	.200	.244	5.17	9.19
2-team total (3 Blue Jays)					2	1	6.30	18	0	0	0	20	18	14	14	1	16	11	—	—	—	4.95	7.20
Rivera, Dariel	R-R	6-3	160	10-1-97	0	0	2.79	8	0	0	1	10	7	5	3	0	5	3	.206	.083	.273	2.79	4.66
Sanchez, Ronald	R-R	6-6	195	9-20-93	1	2	5.23	10	1	0	2	21	21	13	12	0	12	20	.266	.357	.216	8.71	5.23
Silva, Luis	R-R	6-0	210	11-17-96	2	1	3.06	9	7	0	0	35	30	16	12	2	15	24	.238	.255	.228	6.11	3.82
Torres, Sixto	L-L	6-3	225	3-31-96	2	1	1.89	4	2	0	0	19	14	4	4	1	7	21	.203	.294	.173	9.95	3.32
Villanueva, Eric	R-R	6-2	165	3-19-98	0	1	6.97	10	0	0	0	10	11	11	8	1	13	5	.268	.353	.208	4.35	11.32
Zabaleta, Ezequiel	R-R	6-0	175	8-20-95	0	2	3.28	9	3	0	1	25	23	12	9	2	2	20	.232	.333	.175	7.30	0.73

Fielding

C: Hall 5, Moscote 3, Ramos 1, Sanchez 16, Uriarte 32. **1B:** Hall 6, Montero 1, Moscote 33, Sanchez 18, Terrazas 1. **2B:** Gamache 4, Manzanarez 12, Pascual 4, Patino 32, Sanchez 1, Terrazas 5, Uriarte 1. **3B:** Gamache 1, Garcia 2, Hernandez 8, Manzanarez 7, Moscote 5, Sanchez 1, Terrazas 37. **SS:** Hall 1, Hernandez 5, Manzanarez 8, Pascual 36, Patino 7, Terrazas 2. **OF:** Adon 40, Bautista 15, Dirocie 43, Jimenez 25, Lagrange 42, Lindsay 4.

DSL METS
ROOKIE
DOMINICAN SUMMER LEAGUE

Batting	B-T	HT	WT	DOB	AVG	vLH	vRH	G	AB	R	H	2B	3B	HR	RBI	BB	HBP	SH	SF	SO	SB	CS	SLG	OBP
Araujo, Yordin	R-R	6-2	165	3-30-96	.202	.194	.204	46	124	17	25	5	1	1	9	20	3	1	1	43	2	3	.282	.324
Beracierta, Raul	R-R	6-2	205	5-24-99	.327	—	—	62	211	31	69	7	3	1	23	19	6	1	1	35	8	1	.403	.397
Bohorquez, Anderson	R-R	5-11	175	10-3-97	.294	.436	.237	46	136	33	40	1	0	0	13	31	3	1	2	26	16	8	.301	.391
Cedeno, Daniel	R-R	5-11	190	3-11-98	.173	—	—	31	81	2	14	1	0	0	4	3	3	1	0	17	0	1	.185	.230
De Oleo, Enmanuel	R-R	6-2	195	9-5-96	.265	.111	.320	11	34	5	9	0	0	1	7	3	0	0	0	9	0	1	.353	.324
Diaz, Alejandro	B-R	6-1	165	3-26-96	.116	.125	.114	14	43	4	5	2	0	0	4	2	1	0	8	1	1	.163	.224
Espinoza, Gilberto	R-R	6-0	200	11-8-98	.185	.000	.245	20	65	4	12	0	0	1	6	3	3	0	0	19	2	3	.231	.254
Fermin, Edgardo	R-R	6-2	170	5-28-98	.230	.286	.212	57	174	18	40	5	5	0	22	32	4	1	4	27	10	2	.316	.355
Garcia, Tulio	L-R	6-2	220	7-3-98	.140	—	—	43	114	20	16	3	0	0	6	30	4	0	0	53	4	2	.167	.338
Geraldo, Claudio	L-L	6-2	200	4-28-97	.265	.263	.265	40	117	13	31	5	2	0	17	12	2	1	2	31	3	3	.342	.338
Gil, Edy	R-R	5-9	195	9-3-95	.070	—	—	23	43	5	3	1	0	0	0	5	2	2	0	18	1	1	.093	.200

Batting	B-T	HT	WT	DOB	AVG	vLH	vRH	G	AB	R	H	2B	3B	HR	RBI	BB	HBP	SH	SF	SO	SB	CS	SLG	OBP
Gimenez, Andres	L-R	6-0	165	9-4-98	.350	—	—	62	214	52	75	20	4	3	38	46	8	0	7	22	13	8	.523	.469
Granadillo, Guillermo	R-R	6-0	190	2-12-97	.286	.220	.303	68	248	26	71	15	0	2	33	25	3	3	2	33	22	8	.371	.356
Guerrero, Gregory	R-R	6-0	180	1-20-99	.247	.281	.237	64	247	32	61	10	0	0	20	28	2	1	4	51	10	2	.287	.324
Lebron, Luis	R-R	6-0	190	1-6-97	.240	.184	.253	57	192	26	46	13	0	4	18	13	5	0	0	43	6	2	.370	.305
Lozano, David	R-R	5-11	170	5-11-98	.283	—	—	40	99	19	28	3	1	0	7	15	8	1	2	9	9	4	.333	.411
Martinez, Domingo	R-R	6-0	200	4-2-95	.216	.210	.218	68	268	33	58	17	2	6	46	19	6	0	6	45	3	2	.362	.278
Mena, Jose	R-R	5-11	200	12-22-96	.205	—	—	25	73	6	15	1	0	0	8	3	2	0	3	13	0	1	.219	.247
Moreno, Hansel	B-R	6-4	180	11-3-96	.317	.379	.298	64	249	53	79	8	9	3	28	21	1	1	4	43	14	8	.458	.367
Newton, Shervyen	B-R	6-4	180	4-24-99	.169	.217	.158	35	118	18	20	5	1	0	5	22	10	0	0	32	0	5	.229	.347
Nolasco, Pedro	L-R	6-2	180	5-16-97	.167	—	—	31	90	11	15	5	0	1	7	6	2	0	0	41	1	1	.256	.235
Ortiz, Hanser	L-R	6-2	205	6-2-94	.212	—	—	52	170	24	36	5	3	2	27	26	3	0	5	24	7	2	.312	.319
Pena, Ezequiel	R-R	6-0	190	5-25-99	.103	.000	.130	10	29	1	3	1	0	0	2	1	1	0	0	15	0	2	.138	.161
Pujols, Cristopher	R-R	6-3	180	8-19-97	.271	—	—	47	155	15	42	10	2	0	9	10	4	0	0	32	5	3	.361	.331
Regnault, Andres	R-R	6-2	225	12-21-98	.132	.158	.126	39	106	11	14	3	0	0	9	17	2	1	0	39	2	0	.160	.264
Reyes, Wilmer	R-R	6-2	190	12-22-97	.264	.216	.278	58	220	27	58	7	3	2	20	11	3	1	2	25	5	3	.350	.305
Rodriguez, Jeison	R-R	6-2	185	1-27-98	.213	—	—	42	136	19	29	5	1	2	14	23	1	0	1	40	7	6	.309	.329
Romero, Yoel	R-R	6-3	170	4-10-98	.170	.143	.177	49	141	14	24	4	1	0	11	12	2	2	1	27	8	3	.213	.244
Santana, Luis	R-R	5-9	165	7-20-99	.293	—	—	22	75	3	22	4	2	0	11	3	4	0	0	7	0	2	.400	.354
Valdez, Edinson	R-R	6-2	195	1-22-99	.307	—	—	58	218	28	67	12	1	1	34	15	2	0	0	28	5	4	.385	.357
Valdez, Rafael	R-R	5-11	165	4-19-97	.271	.154	.304	54	177	24	48	10	1	0	20	19	2	0	0	35	8	7	.339	.348
Valdez, Wilmy	R-R	6-9	205	7-3-97	.222	.150	.237	31	117	10	26	3	2	1	11	11	1	0	0	28	3	2	.282	.266

Pitching	B-T	HT	WT	DOB	W	L	ERA	G	GS	CG	SV	IP	H	R	ER	HR	BB	SO	AVG	vLH	vRH	K/9	BB/9
Acosta, Daison	R-R	6-3	170	8-24-98	0	1	3.86	3	3	0	0	12	14	6	5	0	6	8	.311	.238	.375	6.17	4.63
Advincola, Gregori	R-R	6-3	170	2-18-98	0	3	4.88	13	4	0	0	28	33	18	15	1	12	14	.292	.300	.290	4.55	3.90
Angela, Nelmerson	L-L	6-2	155	2-20-98	3	0	1.88	14	6	0	2	53	31	15	11	1	16	37	—	—	—	6.32	2.73
Batista, Brian	L-L	6-0	205	8-27-95	1	2	3.28	12	0	0	1	25	22	13	9	0	17	17	—	—	—	6.20	6.20
Campos, Yeizo	R-R	5-11	175	4-29-96	3	3	2.15	12	4	0	1	38	36	15	9	0	9	47	—	—	—	11.23	2.15
Campusano, Briam	R-R	6-1	175	3-26-96	4	4	1.76	13	12	0	0	61	49	27	12	1	12	59	.210	.188	.216	8.66	1.76
Cespedes, Jorge	L-R	6-4	215	6-26-95	3	1	2.74	13	6	0	2	46	43	20	14	3	19	32	—	—	—	6.23	3.70
Chalas, Angel	R-R	6-2	200	7-6-96	1	2	9.49	14	4	0	0	19	29	26	21	1	41	23	.224	.212	.231	8.39	14.96
Chourio, Jhoander	R-R	5-11	185	4-5-98	1	1	2.25	19	0	0	3	36	23	11	9	1	20	21	—	—	—	5.25	5.00
Colon, Yeudy	R-R	6-2	235	6-9-95	0	1	3.60	3	2	0	0	5	6	3	2	0	4	6	.316	.429	.250	10.80	7.20
De Los Santos, Luis	R-R	5-10	175	1-27-94	0	0	0.00	1	1	0	0	2	1	0	0	0	1	1	.167	—	.167	4.50	4.50
Encarnacion, Rafael	L-L	6-1	190	9-2-94	0	1	5.58	16	0	0	3	31	32	26	19	2	9	29	—	—	—	8.51	2.64
Familia, Misael	R-R	6-1	215	1-27-95	1	0	3.09	16	0	0	3	23	26	8	8	1	9	15	—	—	—	5.79	3.47
Felipe, Yom	L-L	5-11	180	9-18-96	0	0	7.04	8	0	0	0	8	6	7	6	0	14	4	.240	.500	.158	4.70	16.43
Fernandez, Wuender	R-R	6-2	180	1-15-97	1	0	7.30	11	0	0	0	12	15	12	10	0	13	5	.336	.188	.400	3.65	9.49
Gutierrez, Miguel	L-L	6-1	195	12-3-94	2	6	5.86	18	7	0	0	43	37	37	28	0	31	40	.230	.192	.237	8.37	6.49
Guzman, Daniel	R-R	6-0	205	2-16-98	3	2	3.38	20	3	0	1	56	53	24	21	2	15	33	—	—	—	5.30	2.41
Hernandez, Carlos	R-R	5-11	170	11-3-94	1	0	3.00	3	3	0	0	15	11	6	5	1	3	11	.208	.182	.226	6.60	1.80
Isturiz, Victor	R-R	6-1	205	3-8-97	0	2	2.76	12	3	0	0	16	16	7	5	0	23	11	—	—	—	6.06	12.67
Jimenez, Jurgen	R-R	6-4	190	1-14-96	0	4	5.18	16	7	0	0	40	50	36	23	0	20	32	.305	.219	.360	7.20	4.50
Laguerre, Ramon	R-R	6-2	185	4-28-96	2	2	2.97	7	7	0	0	33	27	15	11	0	15	22	.221	.182	.244	5.94	4.05
Leon, Nelson	R-R	6-0	185	3-1-95	0	1	2.73	17	0	0	4	33	18	11	10	1	12	28	.158	.171	.152	7.64	3.27
Martinez, Juan	R-R	6-2	185	2-14-96	0	2	7.23	11	2	0	0	19	18	20	15	0	17	9	.257	.194	.308	4.34	8.20
Martinez, Michael	L-L	6-3	175	6-30-97	0	0	8.64	8	0	0	0	8	6	11	8	0	18	6	—	—	—	6.48	19.44
Mata, Miguel	R-R	6-5	165	5-5-97	1	3	3.16	8	0	0	0	20	9	9	1	0	14	21	.213	.108	.281	4.91	3.51
Mateo, Luis	R-R	6-7	190	4-7-93	3	1	6.09	16	2	0	3	34	36	25	23	1	23	33	.305	.464	.256	8.74	6.09
Nieves, Kerwin	L-L	6-2	190	10-22-95	1	1	0.95	9	0	0	0	19	12	5	2	0	17	21	—	—	—	9.95	8.05
Otanez, Michel	R-R	6-2	209	7-8-97	1	1	4.64	5	5	0	0	21	23	11	11	0	6	21	.288	.300	.286	8.86	2.53
Pena, Luis	L-L	5-11	175	2-8-97	0	3	9.86	14	0	0	0	21	24	31	23	3	32	16	—	—	—	6.86	13.71
Ramirez, Miguel	R-R	6-0	145	3-10-97	0	7	5.14	16	9	0	2	42	38	35	24	2	30	37	.236	.222	.245	7.93	6.43
Romero, Joel	R-R	6-2	200	2-13-97	1	5	3.74	18	0	0	1	34	34	18	14	3	12	17	.270	.240	.289	4.54	3.21
Rondon, Ygnacio	R-R	6-4	185	5-16-95	8	2	2.17	15	12	0	1	71	64	25	17	2	23	50	.246	.215	.260	6.37	2.93
Sanchez, Boris	L-R	6-2	180	6-20-97	1	3	3.57	12	5	0	1	35	32	16	14	0	18	22	.260	.216	.279	5.60	4.58
Santana, Ivan	B-L	6-1	210	9-14-93	1	1	1.89	17	6	0	0	62	43	18	13	1	33	82	.155	.182	.152	11.90	4.79
Silva, Luis	R-R	6-0	210	11-17-96	0	2	5.19	2	2	0	0	9	8	6	5	0	4	4	.242	.429	.192	6.23	4.15
Taveras, Willy	R-R	5-11	155	1-20-98	2	2	3.35	13	5	0	2	38	43	18	14	0	5	26	.291	.407	.213	6.21	1.19
Tejada, Renlly	L-L	6-3	185	6-3-95	1	2	4.50	19	4	0	1	48	53	37	24	2	19	29	—	—	—	5.44	3.56
Vallejo, Bladimil	R-R	6-0	180	10-10-91	2	2	7.47	10	0	0	0	16	17	16	13	1	9	15	.266	.286	.256	8.62	5.17
Vilera, Jaison	R-R	6-2	200	6-19-97	5	1	1.59	13	10	0	1	57	38	11	10	1	20	44	—	—	—	6.99	3.18
Zabaleta, Ezequiel	R-R	6-0	175	8-20-95	2	0	0.60	3	3	0	0	15	8	2	1	0	3	12	.154	.091	.200	7.20	1.80

Fielding

C: Cedeno 30, Lebron 56, Lozano 1, Martinez 2, Mena 23, Ortiz 21, Regnault 31, Valdez 1. **1B:** Cedeno 1, Diaz 5, Fermin 3, Garcia 2, Martinez 65, Newton 1, Ortiz 25, Regnault 1, Romero 1, Valdez 22, Valdez 24. **2B:** Bohorquez 10, Diaz 1, Fermin 34, Gimenez 12, Lozano 29, Moreno 9, Reyes 16, Romero 23, Santana 13, Valdez 18. **3B:** Diaz 6, Fermin 13, Guerrero 14, Lozano 4, Lozano 2, Martinez 2, Moreno 37, Newton 11, Pujols 30, Reyes 18, Romero 20, Valdez 4. **SS:** Fermin 1, Gimenez 48, Guerrero 48, Moreno 9, Newton 18, Pujols 4, Reyes 19, Romero 4. **OF:** Araujo 44, Beracierta 59, Bohorquez 27, De Oleo 5, Espinoza 15, Fermin 8, Garcia 33, Geraldo 32, Gil 12, Granadillo 67, Mena 1, Moreno 1, Nolasco 11, Ortiz 1, Pena 9, Rodriguez 34, Romero 1, Sanchez 53, Valdez 24, Valdez 28, Valdez 5.

New York Yankees

SEASON IN A SENTENCE: The Yankees took the unusual step of selling off their veterans to embark on a rebuilding phase, but the young players they brought up provided more immediate impact than expected and kept the team in playoff contention until the season's final week.

HIGH POINT: Tyler Austin and Aaron Judge got their first big-league callups on Aug. 13 and did something never before done, hitting back-to-back homers in their first career at-bats to lead an 8-4 win over Tampa Bay. It was a historic moment and symbolic of the promise of the franchise's future.

LOW POINT: The Yankees hovered around .500 all year but could never get much over it, and the result was a firesale that saw Aroldis Chapman, Carlos Beltran, Andrew Miller and Ivan Nova all dealt for prospects at the trade deadline. It was the first time in baseball's collective memory the Yankees were active sellers at the deadline, an emblem of how far the franchise had fallen in baseball's pecking order.

NOTABLE ROOKIES: Catcher Gary Sanchez put on a historic performance with 20 home runs in 52 games after an August callup to thrust himself into Rookie of the Year contention despite playing less than one-third of the season. Infielders Austin, Rob Refsnyder and Ronald Torreyes and outfielder Judge all received their first significant big-league time but made minimal impact. Righthanders Luis Cessa (4-4, 4.35) and Chad Green (2-4, 4.73) were serviceable swingmen in the rotation and bullpen.

KEY TRANSACTIONS: The Yankees acquired multiple high-profile prospects from their summer trades, including shortstop Gleyber Torres from the Cubs as part of the Chapman deal, outfielder Clint Frazier and lefthander Justus Sheffield from the Indians in the Miller trade, and 2015 fourth overall pick Dillon Tate from the Rangers in the Beltran trade. The Yankees released Alex Rodriguez in August but retained him as a special advisor.

DOWN ON THE FARM: Buoyed by some of the franchise's midseason acquisitions, Scranton/Wilkes-Barre won the International League title and Triple-A National Championship. Double-A Trenton and high Class A Tampa made the Eastern and Florida State League finals, respectively, and all four full-season Yankees affiliates posted winning records. Pitching dominated up and down the system, with starters Jordan Montgomery (14-5, 2.13), Chance Adams (13-1, 2.33) and Domingo Acevedo (5-4, 2.61) leading the way.

OPENING DAY PAYROLL: $222,997,792 (1st)

PLAYERS OF THE YEAR

DAVID SCHOFIELD

MAJOR LEAGUE	MINOR LEAGUE
Gary Sanchez c	**Chance Adams, rhp**
.299/.376/.657	(high A/Double-A)
20 HR, 42 RBI in 53 G	13-1, 2.33, 127.1 IP,
41% CS rate	144 SO, 39 BB

ORGANIZATION LEADERS

BATTING		*Minimum 250 AB
MAJORS		
* AVG	Didi Gregorius	.276
* OPS	Didi Gregorius	.751
HR	Carlos Beltran	22
RBI	Starlin Castro	70
	Didi Gregorius	70
MINORS		
* AVG	Donovan Solano, Scranton/W-B	.319
* OBP	Tyler Austin, Trenton, Scranton/W-B	.392
* SLG	Tyler Austin, Trenton, Scranton/W-B	.524
* OPS	Tyler Austin, Trenton, Scranton/W-B	.916
R	Tyler Wade, Trenton	90
H	Donovan Solano, Scranton/W-B	163
TB	Dustin Fowler, Trenton	248
2B	Tyler Austin, Trenton, Scranton/W-B	34
3B	Dustin Fowler, Trenton	15
HR	Chris Gittens, Charleston	21
	Kyle Higashioka, Trenton, Scranton/W-B	21
RBI	Dustin Fowler, Trenton	88
BB	HoyJun Park, Charleston	67
SO	Chris Gittens, Charleston	126
SB	Jorge Mateo, Tampa	36

PITCHING		#Minimum 75 IP
MAJORS		
W	Masahiro Tanaka	14
# ERA	Masahiro Tanaka	3.07
SO	Michael Pineda	207
SV	Aroldis Chapman	20
MINORS		
W	Dietrich Enns, Trenton, Scranton/W-B	14
	Jordan Montgomery, Trenton, Scranton/W-B	14
L	Raynel Espinal, DSL, GCL, Pulaski, Staten Island	10
# ERA	Dietrich Enns, Trenton, Scranton/W-B	1.73
G	Andrew Schwaab, Tampa, Charleston	43
GS	Jordan Montgomery, Trenton, Scranton/W-B	25
SV	Andrew Schwaab, Tampa, Charleston	21
IP	Daniel Camarena, Tampa, Scranton/W-B, Trenton	142
BB	Daris Vargas, Charleston	57
SO	Chance Adams, Tampa, Trenton	144
# AVG	Chance Adams, Tampa, Trenton	.169

General Manager: Brian Cashman. **Farm Director:** Gary Denbo. **Scouting Director:** Damon Oppenheimer.

Class	Team	League	W	L	PCT	Finish	Manager
Majors	New York Yankees	American	84	78	.519	t-8th (15)	Joe Girardi
Triple-A	Scranton/W-B RailRiders	International	91	52	.636	1st (14)	Al Pedrique
Double-A	Trenton Thunder	Eastern	87	55	.613	2nd (12)	Bobby Mitchell
High A	Tampa Yankees	Florida State	77	58	.570	2nd (12)	Patrick Osborn
Low A	Charleston RiverDogs	South Atlantic	76	63	.547	t-2nd (14)	Luis Dorante
Short season	Staten Island Yankees	New York-Penn	44	31	.587	4th (14)	Dave Bialas
Rookie	Pulaski Yankees	Appalachian	29	37	.439	8th (10)	Tony Franklin
Rookie	Yankees East	Gulf Coast	19	36	.345	17th (17)	Raul Dominguez
Rookie	Yankees West	Gulf Coast	24	31	.436	t-12th (17)	Julio Mosquera
Overall 2016 Minor League Record			447	363	.552	3rd (30)	

ORGANIZATION STATISTICS

NEW YORK YANKEES
AMERICAN LEAGUE

Batting	B-T	HT	WT	DOB	AVG	vLH	vRH	G	AB	R	H	2B	3B	HR	RBI	BB	HBP	SH	SF	SO	SB	CS	SLG	OBP
Ackley, Dustin	L-R	6-1	205	2-26-88	.148	.154	.146	28	61	6	9	0	0	0	4	8	0	0	1	9	0	0	.148	.243
Austin, Tyler	R-R	6-2	220	9-6-91	.241	.348	.200	31	83	7	20	3	0	5	12	7	0	0	0	36	1	0	.458	.300
Beltran, Carlos	B-R	6-1	215	4-24-77	.304	.351	.282	99	359	50	109	21	0	22	64	22	2	0	4	70	0	0	.546	.344
2-team total (52 Texas)					.295	—	—	151	552	73	163	33	0	29	93	35	2	0	4	101	1	0	.513	.337
Butler, Billy	R-R	6-0	260	4-18-86	.345	.364	.286	12	29	3	10	2	0	1	4	2	0	0	1	8	0	0	.517	.375
2-team total (85 Oakland)					.284	—	—	97	250	27	71	18	0	5	35	21	0	0	3	42	0	0	.416	.336
Castro, Starlin	R-R	6-2	230	3-24-90	.270	.265	.272	151	577	63	156	29	1	21	70	24	3	1	5	118	4	0	.433	.300
Davis, Ike	L-L	6-4	220	3-22-87	.214	.000	.231	8	14	2	3	0	0	0	1	1	0	0	0	5	0	0	.214	.267
Ellsbury, Jacoby	L-L	6-1	195	9-11-83	.263	.247	.271	148	551	71	145	24	5	9	56	54	2	4	3	84	20	8	.374	.330
Gamel, Ben	L-L	5-11	185	5-17-92	.125	.000	.143	6	8	1	1	0	0	0	0	1	0	1	0	1	0	0	.125	.222
2-team total (27 Seattle)					.188	—	—	33	48	9	9	2	0	1	5	6	0	3	0	16	0	0	.292	.278
Gardner, Brett	L-L	5-11	195	8-24-83	.261	.247	.268	148	547	80	143	22	6	7	41	70	8	4	5	106	16	4	.362	.351
Gregorius, Didi	L-R	6-3	205	2-18-90	.276	.324	.258	153	562	68	155	32	2	20	70	19	6	5	5	82	7	1	.447	.304
Headley, Chase	B-R	6-2	215	5-9-84	.253	.277	.240	140	467	58	118	18	1	14	51	51	6	0	5	118	8	2	.385	.331
Hicks, Aaron	B-R	6-1	205	10-2-89	.217	.161	.249	123	327	32	71	13	1	8	31	30	0	1	3	68	3	4	.336	.281
Judge, Aaron	R-R	6-7	275	4-26-92	.179	.067	.203	27	84	10	15	2	0	4	10	9	1	0	1	42	0	1	.345	.263
McCann, Brian	L-R	6-3	225	2-20-84	.242	.218	.249	130	429	56	104	13	0	20	58	54	7	2	0	99	1	0	.413	.335
Parmelee, Chris	L-L	6-1	220	2-24-88	.500	1.000	.429	6	4	4	1	0	2	4	0	0	0	0	3	0	1	0	1.375	.500
Refsnyder, Rob	R-R	6-0	200	3-26-91	.250	.274	.233	58	152	25	38	9	0	0	12	18	1	0	3	30	2	1	.309	.328
Rodriguez, Alex	R-R	6-3	230	7-27-75	.200	.211	.195	65	225	19	45	7	0	9	31	14	1	0	3	67	3	0	.351	.247
Romine, Austin	R-R	6-1	220	11-22-88	.242	.274	.200	61	165	17	40	11	0	4	26	7	0	1	3	31	1	0	.382	.269
Sanchez, Gary	R-R	6-2	230	12-2-92	.299	.189	.338	53	201	34	60	12	0	20	42	24	2	0	2	57	1	0	.657	.376
Solano, Donovan	R-R	5-10	205	12-17-87	.227	.250	.214	9	22	5	5	2	0	1	2	1	0	0	0	3	0	0	.455	.261
Teixeira, Mark	B-R	6-3	225	4-11-80	.204	.227	.195	116	387	43	79	16	0	15	44	47	2	0	2	105	2	0	.362	.292
Torreyes, Ronald	R-R	5-10	150	9-2-92	.258	.186	.286	72	155	20	40	7	4	1	12	10	1	1	1	20	2	1	.374	.305
Williams, Mason	L-R	6-1	185	8-21-91	.296	.250	.316	12	27	4	8	1	0	0	2	1	0	1	0	12	0	0	.333	.321
Young Jr. Eric	B-R	5-10	195	5-25-85	.000	—	.000	6	1	2	0	0	0	0	0	0	0	0	0	0	1	0	.000	.000

Pitching	B-T	HT	WT	DOB	W	L	ERA	G	GS	CG	SV	IP	H	R	ER	HR	BB	SO	AVG	vLH	vRH	K/9	BB/9
Barbato, Johnny	R-R	6-1	235	7-11-92	1	2	7.62	13	0	0	0	13	13	11	11	2	5	15	.260	.391	.148	10.38	3.46
Betances, Dellin	R-R	6-8	265	3-23-88	3	6	3.08	73	0	0	12	73	54	31	25	5	28	126	.201	.233	.176	15.53	3.45
Bleier, Richard	L-L	6-3	215	4-16-87	0	0	1.96	23	0	0	0	23	20	6	5	0	4	13	.233	.150	.304	5.09	1.57
Cessa, Luis	R-R	6-0	205	4-25-92	4	4	4.35	17	9	0	0	70	64	36	34	16	14	46	.241	.234	.245	5.89	1.79
Chapman, Aroldis	L-L	6-4	215	2-28-88	3	0	2.01	31	0	0	20	31	20	8	7	2	8	44	.179	.167	.181	12.64	2.30
Clippard, Tyler	R-R	6-3	200	2-14-85	2	3	2.49	29	0	0	2	25	20	9	7	3	11	26	.211	.233	.192	9.24	3.91
Coke, Phil	L-L	6-1	210	7-19-82	0	0	6.00	3	0	0	0	6	7	5	4	1	4	1	.292	.222	.333	1.50	6.00
Eovaldi, Nate	R-R	6-2	225	2-13-90	9	8	4.76	24	21	0	0	125	123	66	66	23	40	97	.255	.268	.245	7.00	2.89
Goody, Nick	B-R	5-11	195	7-6-91	0	0	4.66	27	0	0	0	29	30	15	15	7	12	34	.265	.375	.205	10.55	3.72
Green, Chad	L-R	6-3	210	5-24-91	2	4	4.73	12	8	0	1	46	49	26	24	12	15	52	.272	.291	.255	10.25	2.96
Heller, Ben	R-R	6-3	205	8-5-91	1	0	6.43	10	0	0	0	7	11	5	5	3	4	6	.324	.200	.421	7.71	5.14
Holder, Jonathan	R-R	6-2	235	6-9-93	0	0	5.40	8	0	0	0	8	8	5	5	1	4	5	.258	.143	.292	5.40	4.32
Layne, Tommy	L-L	6-2	195	11-2-84	2	0	3.38	29	0	0	1	16	10	6	6	2	7	13	.175	.147	.217	7.31	3.94
2-team total (34 Boston)					2	1	3.63	63	0	0	1	45	37	18	18	3	21	38	—	—	—	7.66	4.23
Miller, Andrew	L-L	6-7	205	5-21-85	6	1	1.39	44	0	0	9	45	28	8	7	5	7	77	.174	.195	.167	15.29	1.39
2-team total (26 Cleveland)					10	1	1.45	70	0	0	12	74	42	13	12	8	9	123	—	—	—	14.89	1.09
Mitchell, Bryan	L-R	6-3	210	4-19-91	1	2	3.24	5	5	0	0	25	26	13	9	1	12	11	.277	.270	.281	3.96	4.32
Mullee, Conor	R-R	6-4	195	2-25-88	0	0	3.00	3	0	0	0	3	0	1	1	0	4	4	.000	.000	.000	12.00	12.00
Nova, Ivan	R-R	6-5	240	1-12-87	7	6	4.90	21	15	0	1	97	107	54	53	19	25	75	.276	.283	.271	6.93	2.31
Olson, Tyler	R-L	6-3	195	10-2-89	0	0	6.75	1	0	0	0	3	3	2	2	0	2	0	.300	.000	.750	0.00	6.75
Parker, Blake	R-R	6-3	225	6-19-85	0	0	4.96	16	0	0	1	16	16	9	9	1	8	15	.250	.259	.243	8.27	4.41
2-team total (1 Seattle)					1	0	4.67	17	0	0	1	17	17	9	9	1	9	15	—	—	—	7.79	4.67
Pazos, James	R-L	6-2	235	5-5-91	1	0	13.50	7	0	0	0	3	7	5	5	2	1	3	.438	.500	.375	8.10	2.70

Pitching

Pitching	B-T	HT	WT	DOB	W	L	ERA	G	GS	CG	SV	IP	H	R	ER	HR	BB	SO	AVG	vLH	vRH	K/9	BB/9
Pinder, Branden	R-R	6-4	215	1-26-89	0	0	18.00	1	0	0	0	1	3	2	2	0	1	1	.600	.5	.667	9.00	9.00
Pineda, Michael	R-R	6-7	260	1-18-89	6	12	4.82	32	32	0	0	176	184	98	94	27	53	207	.266	.272	.261	10.61	2.72
Sabathia, C.C.	L-L	6-6	300	7-21-80	9	12	3.91	30	30	0	0	180	172	83	78	22	65	152	.250	.209	.26	7.61	3.26
Severino, Luis	R-R	6-2	215	2-20-94	3	8	5.83	22	11	0	0	71	78	48	46	11	25	66	.275	.263	.286	8.37	3.17
Shreve, Chasen	L-L	6-4	195	7-12-90	2	1	5.18	37	0	0	1	33	29	19	19	8	13	33	.232	.275	.212	9.00	3.55
Swarzak, Anthony	R-R	6-4	215	9-10-85	1	2	5.52	26	0	0	0	31	28	19	19	10	7	31	.243	.25	.24	9.00	2.03
Tanaka, Masahiro	R-R	6-3	215	11-1-88	14	4	3.07	31	31	0	0	200	179	75	68	22	36	165	.236	.237	.235	7.44	1.62
Warren, Adam	R-R	6-1	225	8-25-87	4	2	3.26	29	0	0	0	30	28	13	11	4	10	25	.250	.159	.309	7.42	2.97
Yates, Kirby	R-R	5-10	210	3-25-87	2	1	5.23	41	0	0	0	41	41	24	24	5	19	50	.258	.204	.286	10.89	4.14

Fielding

Catcher	PCT	G	PO	A	E	DP	PB
McCann	.995	92	773	36	4	4	6
Romine	.997	50	318	22	1	2	2
Sanchez	.991	36	304	34	3	1	6

First Base	PCT	G	PO	A	E	DP
Ackley	1.000	13	80	7	0	7
Austin	1.000	27	166	15	0	17
Butler	.947	3	16	2	1	2
Davis	1.000	8	39	3	0	2
McCann	1.000	3	5	0	0	0
Parmelee	1.000	6	21	4	0	0
Refsnyder	.983	25	166	5	3	11
Romine	1.000	6	18	1	0	1
Teixeira	.997	110	867	39	3	65

Second Base	PCT	G	PO	A	E	DP
Ackley	—	1	0	0	0	0
Castro	.980	150	221	377	12	70
Refsnyder	.875	8	5	9	2	2
Solano	1.000	6	12	13	0	3
Torreyes	1.000	14	14	15	0	9

Third Base	PCT	G	PO	A	E	DP
Headley	.974	140	90	278	10	25
Refsnyder	—	1	0	0	0	0
Rodriguez	—	1	0	0	0	0
Solano	.000	2	0	0	1	0
Torreyes	.978	34	12	76	2	9

Shortstop	PCT	G	PO	A	E	DP
Castro	1.000	3	6	6	0	2
Gregorius	.974	153	180	380	15	68
Torreyes	.971	15	12	22	1	1

Outfield	PCT	G	PO	A	E	DP
Ackley	1.000	9	9	1	0	1
Austin	1.000	5	4	0	0	0
Beltran	.989	60	84	3	1	1
Ellsbury	.989	148	272	5	3	1
Gamel	1.000	5	3	0	0	0
Gardner	.989	147	250	9	3	2
Hicks	.995	119	186	3	1	1
Judge	.974	27	35	2	1	0
Refsnyder	1.000	27	28	3	0	0
Torreyes	1.000	2	1	0	0	0
Williams	1.000	11	18	0	0	0
Young Jr.	1.000	2	3	0	0	0

SCRANTON/WILKES-BARRE RAILRIDERS — TRIPLE-A
INTERNATIONAL LEAGUE

Batting	B-T	HT	WT	DOB	AVG	vLH	vRH	G	AB	R	H	2B	3B	HR	RBI	BB	HBP	SH	SF	SO	SB	CS	SLG	OBP
Adams, Lane	R-R	6-3	220	11-13-89	.267	.308	.235	8	30	2	8	1	0	0	3	2	0	0	0	10	0	0	.300	.313
Austin, Tyler	R-R	6-2	220	9-6-91	.323	.365	.304	57	201	39	65	24	0	13	49	32	0	0	1	59	5	0	.637	.415
Cave, Jake	L-L	6-0	200	12-4-92	.261	.256	.263	89	322	47	84	18	6	5	38	26	4	1	1	78	3	3	.401	.323
Culver, Cito	R-R	6-0	205	8-26-92	.263	.387	.184	24	80	10	21	1	0	1	11	7	0	0	1	21	1	0	.313	.318
Davis, Ike	L-L	6-4	220	3-22-87	.217	.000	.290	26	92	11	20	1	0	5	16	14	0	0	1	32	0	0	.391	.318
Diaz, Francisco	B-R	5-11	185	3-21-90	.167	.000	.250	2	6	1	1	0	0	0	1	0	0	0	0	3	0	0	.167	.286
Diaz, Jonathan	R-R	5-9	155	4-10-85	.207	.215	.202	101	305	42	63	8	1	1	25	47	2	16	1	63	4	2	.249	.315
Fiorito, Dan	R-R	6-4	215	8-20-90	.143	.143	.143	9	28	0	4	0	0	0	0	4	0	0	0	12	0	0	.143	.250
Frazier, Clint	R-R	6-1	190	9-6-94	.228	.161	.257	25	101	17	23	2	3	3	7	7	0	0	0	30	0	0	.396	.278
2-team total (5 Columbus)					.230	—		30	122	19	28	2	4	3	7	7	0	0	0	36	0	0	.385	.271
Gamel, Ben	L-L	5-11	185	5-17-92	.308	.314	.306	116	483	80	149	26	5	6	51	43	2	1	4	94	19	8	.420	.365
Heathcott, Slade	L-L	6-1	205	9-28-90	.230	.211	.245	23	87	14	20	5	1	0	7	5	1	1	3	31	2	1	.310	.271
2-team total (34 Charlotte)					.244	—		57	180	33	44	7	2	2	14	27	3	2	4	61	3	2	.339	.346
Higashioka, Kyle	R-R	6-1	200	4-20-90	.250	.304	.225	39	148	24	37	9	0	10	30	12	0	0	0	31	0	1	.514	.300
Judge, Aaron	R-R	6-7	275	4-26-92	.270	.279	.266	93	352	62	95	18	1	19	65	47	8	0	3	98	5	0	.489	.366
Kozma, Pete	R-R	6-0	190	4-11-88	.209	.203	.212	130	445	48	93	19	0	2	32	31	6	3	3	91	11	4	.265	.268
Parmelee, Chris	L-L	6-1	220	2-24-88	.248	.264	.242	64	214	29	53	10	0	11	29	29	0	0	2	42	0	0	.449	.335
Payton, Mark	L-L	5-7	180	12-7-91	.429	.250	.667	2	7	1	3	1	0	0	2	0	0	0	0	1	0	0	.571	.556
Puello, Cesar	R-R	6-2	220	4-1-91	.283	.289	.279	78	230	35	65	13	0	5	31	35	18	3	3	56	18	3	.404	.413
Refsnyder, Rob	R-R	6-0	205	3-26-91	.316	.225	.362	54	209	25	66	11	0	1	22	20	17	1	0	30	6	0	.402	.365
Rodriguez, Eddy	R-R	6-0	220	12-1-85	.214	.242	.192	44	140	11	30	7	0	3	13	8	2	2	1	60	0	1	.329	.265
Romero, Deibinson	R-R	6-1	220	9-24-86	.132	.077	.150	17	53	3	7	0	1	1	6	8	0	0	1	13	0	0	.226	.242
Rosario, Jose	R-R	5-11	190	11-29-91	.301	.308	.296	24	93	14	28	4	1	2	12	3	0	1	2	19	1	2	.430	.316
Sanchez, Gary	R-R	6-2	230	12-2-92	.282	.288	.280	71	284	39	80	21	1	10	50	21	5	0	3	45	7	1	.468	.339
Solano, Donovan	R-R	5-10	205	12-17-87	.319	.404	.280	131	511	64	163	33	4	7	67	25	2	1	7	79	2	1	.436	.349
Swisher, Nick	B-L	6-0	195	11-25-80	.255	.357	.207	55	220	17	56	6	0	7	25	14	0	0	2	54	0	0	.377	.297
Teixeira, Mark	B-R	6-3	225	4-11-80	.111	.250	.000	3	9	0	1	0	0	0	1	1	0	0	1	1	0	0	.111	.182
Williams, Mason	L-R	6-1	185	8-21-91	.296	.235	.319	31	125	19	37	8	1	0	23	5	0	4	4	21	1	1	.376	.313

Pitching	B-T	HT	WT	DOB	W	L	ERA	G	GS	CG	SV	IP	H	R	ER	HR	BB	SO	AVG	vLH	vRH	K/9	BB/9
Barbato, Johnny	R-R	6-1	235	7-11-92	3	2	2.61	31	1	0	3	48	38	17	14	3	23	49	.213	.194	.226	9.12	4.28
Bleier, Richard	L-L	6-3	215	4-16-87	2	3	3.72	12	10	0	1	58	66	25	24	2	11	25	.292	.222	.325	3.88	1.71
Camarena, Daniel	L-L	6-0	200	11-9-92	0	1	6.00	2	0	0	0	6	9	5	4	1	2	4	.346	.333	.353	6.00	3.00
Campos, Vicente	R-R	6-3	230	7-27-92	0	0	1.80	1	1	0	0	5	8	1	1	0	1	1	.400	.333	.455	1.80	1.80
Cessa, Luis	R-R	6-0	205	4-25-92	6	3	3.03	15	14	1	0	77	66	33	26	8	23	69	.235	.225	.242	8.03	2.68
Cloyd, Tyler	R-R	6-3	210	5-16-87	1	1	1.37	4	3	0	0	20	13	7	3	1	10	17	.178	.190	.173	7.78	4.58
Coke, Phil	L-L	6-1	215	7-31-82	5	3	2.96	20	11	0	0	70	68	29	23	3	21	61	.252	.254	.251	7.84	2.70
Cortes, Nestor	R-L	5-11	190	12-10-94	1	0	0.00	1	1	0	0	6	0	0	0	0	3	4	.000	.000	.000	6.35	4.76
Cotts, Neal	L-L	6-2	200	3-25-80	0	0	4.91	7	0	0	0	7	8	5	4	2	1	2	.286	.167	.318	2.45	1.23
Enns, Dietrich	L-L	6-1	210	5-16-91	7	2	1.52	14	10	0	1	65	47	13	11	3	26	50	.208	.115	.236	6.92	3.60

Pitching

Pitching	B-T	HT	WT	DOB	W	L	ERA	G	GS	CG	SV	IP	H	R	ER	HR	BB	SO	AVG	vLH	vRH	K/9	BB/9
Gallegos, Giovanny	R-R	6-2	210	8-14-91	5	1	1.40	25	0	0	2	45	28	7	7	4	10	53	.178	.119	.222	10.60	2.00
Goody, Nick	B-R	5-11	195	7-6-91	0	1	1.93	18	0	0	5	23	12	5	5	4	4	35	.146	.240	.105	13.50	1.54
Graham, J.R.	R-R	5-11	195	1-14-90	2	0	0.00	2	0	0	0	3	3	0	0	0	0	4	.273	.333	.200	12.00	0.00
2-team total (8 Rochester)					2	2	7.94	10	0	0	3	11	14	10	10	1	7	11	—	—	—	8.74	5.56
Green, Chad	L-R	6-3	210	5-24-91	7	6	1.52	16	16	0	0	95	68	21	16	3	21	100	.200	.261	.150	9.51	2.00
Haynes, Kyle	R-R	6-2	200	2-11-91	5	5	4.61	18	18	1	0	96	105	60	49	13	42	72	.283	.286	.281	6.77	3.95
Heller, Ben	R-R	6-3	205	8-5-91	0	1	1.42	6	0	0	1	6	3	1	1	0	2	7	.136	.000	.250	9.95	2.84
2-team total (28 Columbus)					2	3	2.27	34	0	0	6	32	23	8	8	1	9	32	—	—	—	9.09	2.56
Herrera, Ronald	R-R	5-11	185	5-3-95	0	1	9.00	1	1	0	0	5	7	5	5	1	3	8	.333	.444	.250	14.40	5.40
Holder, Jonathan	R-R	6-2	235	6-9-93	2	0	0.89	12	0	0	6	20	7	2	2	1	0	35	.103	.083	.114	15.49	0.00
Lail, Brady	R-R	6-2	205	8-9-93	7	6	5.07	17	17	0	0	92	97	57	52	11	30	58	.277	.258	.294	5.65	2.92
Mitchell, Bryan	R-R	6-3	210	4-19-91	0	0	1.00	2	2	0	0	9	8	2	1	0	2	14	.235	.222	.240	14.00	2.00
Montgomery, Jordan	L-L	6-6	225	12-27-92	5	1	0.97	6	6	0	0	37	28	4	4	0	9	37	.212	.209	.213	9.00	2.19
Montgomery, Mark	R-R	6-0	200	8-30-90	1	0	2.92	18	0	0	2	25	16	8	8	2	11	32	.184	.103	.224	11.68	4.01
Moreno, Diego	R-R	6-1	180	7-21-87	6	1	5.14	28	2	0	1	49	55	32	28	5	17	52	.278	.297	.269	9.55	3.12
Mullee, Conor	R-R	6-4	195	2-25-88	4	0	0.99	25	0	0	6	36	21	5	4	1	11	45	.169	.300	.107	11.15	2.72
Olson, Tyler	R-L	6-3	195	10-2-89	1	2	5.27	11	3	0	0	27	31	17	16	2	8	21	.290	.250	.329	6.91	2.63
2-team total (9 Columbus)					2	2	5.45	20	3	0	0	38	43	26	23	3	14	31	—	—	—	7.34	3.32
Pazos, James	R-L	6-2	235	5-5-91	2	2	2.63	23	0	0	1	27	19	8	8	1	19	41	.194	.063	.258	13.50	6.26
Pestano, Vinnie	R-R	6-0	210	2-20-85	1	1	3.38	8	0	0	0	11	8	4	4	0	1	16	.200	.273	.172	13.50	0.84
Pinder, Branden	R-R	6-4	215	1-26-89	0	0	0.00	2	0	0	1	5	2	0	0	0	0	8	.118	.000	.167	14.40	0.00
Rumbelow, Nick	R-R	6-0	190	9-6-91	0	0	0.00	1	0	0	0	1	2	0	0	0	0	0	.400	.000	.500	0.00	0.00
Ruth, Eric	R-R	6-0	195	9-26-90	2	0	1.98	2	2	0	0	14	10	3	3	0	2	12	.200	.219	.167	7.90	1.32
Severino, Luis	R-R	6-2	215	2-20-94	8	1	3.49	13	12	0	0	77	75	31	30	4	18	78	.249	.230	.265	9.08	2.09
Shreve, Chasen	L-L	6-4	195	7-12-90	0	0	1.62	13	1	0	0	17	4	3	3	1	7	20	.075	.059	.083	10.80	3.78
Somsen, Layne	R-R	6-0	190	6-5-89	1	0	0.00	4	0	0	0	6	3	0	0	0	5	10	.136	.000	.158	15.00	7.50
2-team total (10 Louisville)					1	0	1.44	14	0	0	0	25	13	4	4	2	12	29	—	—	—	10.44	4.32
Swarzak, Anthony	R-R	6-4	215	9-10-85	1	4	3.86	15	6	1	7	47	47	20	20	4	8	43	.263	.333	.212	8.29	1.54
Webb, Tyler	R-L	6-6	225	7-20-90	4	3	3.59	36	5	0	1	73	67	31	29	5	23	82	.245	.215	.258	10.16	2.85
Wotherspoon, Matt	R-R	6-1	210	10-6-91	2	0	2.01	10	1	0	3	22	20	5	5	1	7	14	.244	.229	.255	5.64	2.82
Yates, Kirby	R-R	5-10	210	3-25-87	0	1	1.62	14	0	0	4	17	12	3	3	0	6	19	.197	.148	.235	10.26	3.24

Fielding

Catcher	PCT	G	PO	A	E	DP	PB
Diaz	1.000	2	17	1	0	0	1
Higashioka	1.000	36	329	15	0	4	4
Rodriguez	.997	44	353	24	1	0	7
Sanchez	.991	64	505	31	5	5	10

First Base	PCT	G	PO	A	E	DP
Austin	.988	39	305	11	4	29
Culver	.987	12	74	2	1	10
Davis	1.000	14	125	3	0	16
Fiorito	1.000	1	6	0	0	0
Kozma	1.000	5	33	1	0	1
Parmelee	.992	48	353	37	3	37
Romero	1.000	3	20	1	0	3
Swisher	.991	25	209	23	2	25
Teixeira	1.000	2	16	1	0	1

Second Base	PCT	G	PO	A	E	DP
Culver	1.000	3	6	6	0	2

Third Base	PCT	G	PO	A	E	DP
Diaz	.982	51	90	132	4	27
Kozma	.969	18	38	57	3	18
Refsnyder	.983	16	29	30	1	6
Rosario	1.000	2	5	5	0	0
Solano	.963	55	86	150	9	43

Third Base	PCT	G	PO	A	E	DP
Austin	1.000	3	3	5	0	0
Culver	1.000	2	1	3	0	0
Fiorito	.867	8	5	21	4	3
Kozma	.945	23	14	38	3	5
Refsnyder	.903	26	17	39	6	2
Romero	.968	13	5	25	1	2
Rosario	.944	8	8	9	1	2
Solano	.969	65	31	125	5	11

Shortstop	PCT	G	PO	A	E	DP
Culver	.977	10	13	29	1	9
Diaz	.969	47	67	123	6	31

	PCT	G	PO	A	E	DP
Kozma	.974	84	101	239	9	50
Solano	1.000	7	9	25	0	4

Outfield	PCT	G	PO	A	E	DP
Adams	1.000	7	15	1	0	0
Austin	1.000	6	9	0	0	0
Cave	1.000	83	159	7	0	1
Diaz	1.000	3	5	0	0	0
Frazier	.911	22	39	2	4	0
Gamel	.989	103	181	5	2	0
Heathcott	1.000	19	36	1	0	1
Judge	.983	76	163	7	3	4
Parmelee	1.000	2	2	0	0	0
Payton	1.000	2	1	0	0	0
Puello	.956	62	106	2	5	0
Refsnyder	1.000	5	10	0	0	0
Rosario	.966	14	26	2	1	0
Swisher	1.000	7	17	0	0	0
Williams	1.000	23	41	0	0	0

TRENTON THUNDER   DOUBLE-A
EASTERN LEAGUE

Batting	B-T	HT	WT	DOB	AVG	vLH	vRH	G	AB	R	H	2B	3B	HR	RBI	BB	HBP	SH	SF	SO	SB	CS	SLG	OBP
Adams, Lane	R-R	6-3	220	11-13-89	.253	.229	.262	84	289	49	73	12	1	6	32	36	5	0	2	84	31	5	.363	.343
Andujar, Miguel	R-R	6-0	175	3-2-95	.266	.246	.272	72	282	28	75	16	2	2	42	21	7	0	9	42	2	1	.358	.323
Austin, Tyler	R-R	6-2	220	9-6-91	.260	.152	.298	50	177	22	46	10	1	4	29	30	1	0	2	46	1	1	.395	.367
Avelino, Abiatal	R-R	5-11	186	2-14-95	.244	.263	.236	33	127	15	31	11	0	0	14	10	2	1	1	19	1	2	.331	.307
Bichette Jr. Dante	R-R	6-1	210	9-26-92	.243	.247	.241	114	367	45	89	19	1	9	49	53	4	0	3	81	4	1	.373	.342
Bolasky, Devyn	L-L	5-11	185	1-24-93	.333	—	.333	2	6	0	2	0	0	0	1	1	0	0	0	2	0	0	.333	.429
Cave, Jake	L-L	6-0	200	12-4-92	.288	.190	.313	27	104	12	30	8	3	3	17	10	1	0	1	28	3	4	.510	.353
Conde, Vince	R-R	6-0	195	10-13-93	.192	.000	.278	8	26	5	5	1	0	0	2	4	0	0	0	6	1	0	.231	.300
Culver, Cito	R-R	6-0	205	8-26-92	.252	.286	.239	93	318	38	80	19	3	3	40	30	0	1	2	98	1	2	.358	.314
Diaz, Francisco	B-R	5-11	185	3-21-90	.250	.143	.286	26	84	8	21	2	1	0	2	12	0	1	0	8	0	1	.298	.344
Fiorito, Dan	R-R	6-4	215	8-20-90	.198	.179	.206	28	91	7	18	4	0	1	9	5	1	0	0	24	0	1	.275	.247
Fleming, Billy	R-R	6-1	200	9-20-92	.242	.367	.204	37	128	12	31	7	1	1	15	14	1	0	1	23	0	0	.336	.319
Ford, Mike	L-R	6-0	225	7-4-92	.280	.250	.288	42	143	21	40	10	0	5	26	34	1	0	2	25	0	0	.455	.417
Fowler, Dustin	L-L	6-0	195	12-29-94	.281	.324	.265	132	541	67	152	30	15	12	88	22	4	2	5	86	25	11	.458	.311
Haddad, Radley	L-R	6-0	190	5-11-90	.000	—	.000	1	2	0	0	0	0	0	0	0	0	0	0	2	0	0	.000	.000
Higashioka, Kyle	R-R	6-1	200	4-20-90	.293	.409	.244	63	222	31	65	15	0	11	51	26	0	0	8	42	0	1	.509	.355
McKinney, Billy	L-L	6-1	205	8-23-94	.234	.161	.258	35	128	15	30	7	1	3	13	12	2	0	0	29	2	2	.375	.310

Batting

Batting	B-T	HT	WT	DOB	AVG	vLH	vRH	G	AB	R	H	2B	3B	HR	RBI	BB	HBP	SH	SF	SO	SB	CS	SLG	OBP
Mitchell, Jared	L-L	6-0	205	10-13-88	.250	.313	.232	20	72	7	18	3	1	1	7	10	0	0	1	25	5	1	.361	.337
O'Neill, Michael	R-R	6-1	195	6-12-92	.233	.317	.207	60	176	25	41	8	2	1	15	12	3	2	3	49	4	4	.318	.289
Payton, Mark	L-L	5-7	180	12-7-91	.272	.287	.266	97	338	53	92	15	5	7	47	31	3	7	2	50	8	2	.408	.337
Rodriguez, Alex	R-R	6-3	230	7-27-75	.500	.333	.667	2	6	1	3	0	0	1	3	0	0	0	0	0	0	0	1.000	.500
Rosario, Jose	R-R	5-11	190	11-29-91	.261	.229	.274	45	165	20	43	7	1	2	15	2	3	0	0	33	3	2	.352	.282
Silva, Juan	L-L	6-0	200	1-8-91	.220	.240	.215	38	118	12	26	6	0	1	14	18	1	1	2	30	2	3	.297	.324
Skole, Jake	L-R	6-1	195	1-17-92	.333	—	.333	2	6	2	2	1	0	0	0	2	0	0	0	2	0	0	.500	.500
Snyder, Matt	L-R	6-5	230	6-17-90	.211	.000	.235	5	19	1	4	0	0	0	2	1	0	0	0	5	0	0	.211	.250
Valle, Sebastian	R-R	6-1	215	7-24-90	.202	.300	.167	68	228	25	46	11	0	4	18	13	0	1	2	72	0	0	.303	.243
Wade, Tyler	L-R	6-1	185	11-23-94	.259	.259	.260	133	505	90	131	16	7	5	27	66	7	4	1	103	27	8	.349	.352

Pitching

Pitching	B-T	HT	WT	DOB	W	L	ERA	G	GS	CG	SV	IP	H	R	ER	HR	BB	SO	AVG	vLH	vRH	K/9	BB/9
Adams, Chance	R-R	6-0	215	8-10-94	8	1	2.07	13	12	0	0	70	35	20	16	5	24	71	.145	.179	.110	9.17	3.10
Camarena, Daniel	L-L	6-0	200	11-9-92	9	6	3.68	25	22	1	1	130	126	60	53	12	21	106	.252	.233	.261	7.36	1.46
Campos, Vicente	R-R	6-3	230	7-27-92	5	1	3.02	9	9	1	0	57	45	19	19	1	14	48	.220	.230	.210	7.62	2.22
Carter, Will	L-R	6-3	190	1-18-93	1	4	4.40	8	8	0	0	43	43	25	21	1	18	28	.264	.313	.213	5.86	3.77
Cortes, Nestor	R-L	5-11	190	12-10-94	0	0	4.50	1	0	0	1	4	1	2	2	1	2	5	.077	.000	.100	11.25	4.50
Coshow, Cale	R-R	6-5	260	7-16-92	3	8	4.03	36	9	0	4	89	84	47	40	6	50	70	.250	.266	.236	7.05	5.04
Enns, Dietrich	L-L	6-1	210	5-16-91	7	2	1.93	12	12	1	0	70	55	15	15	3	30	74	.221	.267	.201	9.51	3.86
Feyereisen, J.P.	R-R	6-2	215	2-7-93	3	0	0.50	9	0	0	0	18	8	2	1	0	6	22	.136	.172	.100	11.00	3.00
2-team total (33 Akron)					7	3	1.70	42	0	0	5	58	38	14	11	3	26	78	—	—	—	12.03	4.01
Foley, Jordan	R-R	6-4	215	7-12-93	0	0	0.00	1	0	0	0	1	0	0	0	0	1	0	.000	.000	.000	0.00	13.50
Gallegos, Giovanny	R-R	6-2	210	8-14-91	2	1	1.09	17	0	0	2	33	20	6	4	1	7	53	.171	.140	.200	14.45	1.91
Graham, J.R.	R-R	5-11	195	1-14-90	2	1	1.82	17	0	0	5	30	26	7	6	1	9	33	.234	.265	.210	10.01	2.73
Haynes, Kyle	R-R	6-2	200	2-11-91	1	3	7.39	5	5	0	0	28	33	25	23	1	9	28	.292	.296	.288	9.00	2.89
Herrera, Ronald	R-R	5-11	185	5-3-95	10	7	3.75	23	23	0	0	132	131	61	55	9	35	123	.258	.229	.285	8.39	2.39
Hissong, Travis	R-R	6-0	195	7-19-91	3	0	2.70	15	0	0	1	33	26	12	10	3	7	32	.218	.271	.183	8.64	1.89
Holder, Jonathan	R-R	6-2	235	6-9-93	3	1	2.20	28	0	0	10	41	27	10	10	2	7	59	.188	.216	.172	12.95	1.54
Jones, Tyler	R-R	6-4	240	9-5-89	6	2	2.17	33	0	0	11	46	45	14	11	1	11	67	.249	.260	.240	13.20	2.17
Kubiak, Dave	R-R	6-7	230	8-3-89	0	0	1.42	3	0	0	0	6	3	1	1	0	5	4	.150	.143	.154	5.68	7.11
Lail, Brady	R-R	6-2	205	8-9-93	1	2	3.69	6	6	1	0	32	33	15	13	2	12	17	.270	.238	.305	4.83	3.41
Marsh, Matt	R-R	6-3	190	7-10-91	0	0	0.00	2	0	0	0	3	0	0	0	0	2	2	.000	.500	.125	6.00	6.00
McNamara, Dillon	R-R	6-5	220	10-6-91	0	0	4.50	1	0	0	0	2	3	1	1	0	1	2	.375	.333	.400	9.00	4.50
Mitchell, Bryan	L-R	6-3	210	4-19-91	0	1	5.40	2	2	0	0	7	6	5	4	1	3	6	.231	.143	.333	8.10	4.05
Montgomery, Jordan	L-L	6-6	225	12-27-92	9	4	2.55	19	19	1	0	102	94	35	29	5	36	97	.239	.240	.239	8.53	3.17
Montgomery, Mark	R-R	6-0	200	8-30-90	1	0	2.14	15	0	0	5	21	15	5	5	0	11	31	.195	.111	.268	13.29	4.71
Moreno, Diego	R-R	6-1	180	7-21-87	1	0	2.57	4	0	0	0	7	10	2	2	0	2	12	.333	.231	.412	15.43	2.57
Mullee, Conor	R-R	6-4	195	2-25-88	0	0	6.75	1	0	0	0	1	2	1	1	0	3	2	.333	.200	1.000	13.50	0.00
Reeves, James	R-L	6-5	195	6-7-93	0	0	0.00	3	0	0	0	4	4	1	0	0	1	8	.267	.167	.333	18.00	2.25
Rutckyj, Evan	R-L	6-5	225	1-31-92	0	0	13.50	4	0	0	0	2	5	3	3	0	6	2	.417	.750	.250	9.00	27.00
Ruth, Eric	R-R	6-0	195	9-26-90	2	1	2.97	13	5	0	0	33	26	12	11	1	14	32	.210	.224	.197	8.64	3.78
Sheffield, Justus	L-L	5-10	195	5-13-96	0	0	0.00	1	1	0	0	4	2	1	0	0	3	9	.125	.000	.182	20.25	6.75
Smith, Alex	R-R	6-3	235	9-29-89	0	2	3.41	22	0	0	2	32	26	13	12	1	18	29	.230	.229	.231	8.24	5.12
Smith, Caleb	R-L	6-2	205	7-28-91	3	5	3.96	27	7	0	3	64	66	34	28	4	20	70	.265	.297	.247	9.90	2.83
Tracy, Matt	L-L	6-3	215	11-26-88	3	1	5.11	13	0	0	0	25	30	14	14	0	10	23	.316	.182	.387	8.39	3.65
Wotherspoon, Matt	R-R	6-1	210	10-6-91	4	2	2.66	26	2	0	5	68	46	23	20	3	27	74	.189	.205	.176	9.84	3.59

Fielding

Catcher	PCT	G	PO	A	E	DP	PB
Diaz	1.000	26	222	20	0	2	2
Haddad	1.000	1	6	0	0	0	0
Higashioka	.985	61	532	51	9	4	6
Valle	.996	59	468	39	2	5	8

First Base	PCT	G	PO	A	E	DP
Austin	.990	37	273	17	3	21
Bichette Jr.	.987	57	417	41	6	45
Fiorito	.992	15	125	6	1	12
Fleming	.977	5	41	1	1	0
Ford	.995	25	176	18	1	12
Snyder	1.000	1	7	1	0	1
Valle	.985	9	63	3	1	2

Second Base	PCT	G	PO	A	E	DP
Avelino	.935	23	29	57	6	11
Conde	1.000	5	12	15	0	2
Culver	.966	36	62	107	6	21
Fiorito	1.000	5	5	9	0	2
Fleming	1.000	21	24	30	0	2
Rosario	.966	19	29	56	3	12
Wade	.959	38	57	85	6	18

Third Base	PCT	G	PO	A	E	DP
Andujar	.897	64	30	101	15	2
Bichette Jr.	.963	41	24	55	3	4
Conde	.500	3	0	1	1	0
Culver	.938	13	10	20	2	2
Fiorito	.955	10	2	19	1	1
Fleming	1.000	6	6	6	0	1
Rosario	.944	10	4	13	1	1

Shortstop	PCT	G	PO	A	E	DP
Avelino	.912	9	10	21	3	5
Culver	.955	44	56	115	8	22
Wade	.943	91	122	210	20	48

Outfield	PCT	G	PO	A	E	DP
Adams	1.000	73	146	2	0	0
Austin	1.000	7	3	0	0	0
Bolasky	1.000	2	3	0	0	0
Cave	.978	26	43	2	1	1
Fowler	.981	124	259	4	5	1
McKinney	.987	33	76	2	1	0
Mitchell	.960	14	23	1	1	1
O'Neill	.978	47	85	4	2	1
Payton	.994	85	153	11	1	2
Rosario	1.000	6	9	1	0	0
Silva	.926	14	25	0	2	0
Skole	—	1	0	0	0	0

TAMPA YANKEES   *HIGH CLASS A*
FLORIDA STATE LEAGUE

Batting	B-T	HT	WT	DOB	AVG	vLH	vRH	G	AB	R	H	2B	3B	HR	RBI	BB	HBP	SH	SF	SO	SB	CS	SLG	OBP
Amburgey, Trey	R-R	6-2	210	10-24-94	.279	.375	.239	47	190	26	53	9	1	1	22	6	3	0	5	45	4	3	.353	.304
Andujar, Miguel	R-R	6-0	175	3-2-95	.283	.193	.312	58	230	34	65	10	2	10	41	18	3	0	0	30	1	3	.474	.343
Aparicio, Jesus	R-R	5-11	186	8-18-94	.069	.125	.048	9	29	3	2	1	0	1	2	5	0	0	0	11	0	0	.207	.206

Batting

Batting	B-T	HT	WT	DOB	AVG	vLH	vRH	G	AB	R	H	2B	3B	HR	RBI	BB	HBP	SH	SF	SO	SB	CS	SLG	OBP
Aune, Austin	L-R	6-2	190	9-6-93	.241	.200	.257	85	315	31	76	13	2	5	38	33	0	0	3	116	0	1	.343	.311
Avelino, Abiatal	R-R	186	2-14-95	.266	.327	.241	93	357	54	95	17	2	6	34	29	4	0	4	63	20	13	.375	.325
Barrios, Daniel	R-R	5-11	183	4-18-95	.100	.250	.000	3	10	0	1	0	0	0	0	0	0	0	0	4	0	0	.100	.100
Bolasky, Devyn	L-L	5-11	185	1-24-93	.306	.317	.302	46	170	19	52	8	3	0	9	10	2	0	1	14	3	4	.388	.350
Conde, Vince	R-R	6-0	195	10-13-93	.193	.250	.163	48	140	18	27	8	2	1	21	24	0	4	3	36	0	2	.300	.305
Cornelius, Kevin	R-R	6-1	180	8-28-92	.277	.261	.284	43	148	18	41	9	1	7	27	22	1	0	0	45	0	0	.493	.374
Crawford, Rashad	B-R	6-3	185	10-15-93	.291	.364	.260	29	110	10	32	2	0	2	18	15	1	1	0	27	4	1	.364	.381
Diaz, Cesar	B-R	5-10	165	4-12-93	.167	.333	.111	4	12	3	2	1	0	0	2	5	0	0	1	1	0	0	.250	.412
Diaz, Francisco	R-R	5-11	195	3-21-90	.194	.115	.221	34	103	10	20	1	0	0	3	8	1	3	0	14	0	1	.204	.259
Estrada, Thairo	R-R	5-10	155	2-22-96	.292	.317	.283	83	315	52	92	15	1	3	30	29	3	2	2	46	7	5	.375	.355
Fleming, Billy	R-R	6-1	200	9-20-92	.329	.333	.327	38	146	18	48	13	0	3	27	15	1	0	0	33	0	1	.479	.395
Florial, Estevan	L-R	6-1	185	11-25-97	.125	—	.125	2	8	0	1	0	0	0	0	0	0	0	0	2	0	0	.125	.125
Ford, Mike	L-R	6-0	225	7-4-92	.371	.500	.345	10	35	3	13	1	0	2	14	5	0	0	1	4	0	1	.571	.439
Hendrix, Jeff	L-R	6-0	195	7-16-93	.284	.219	.303	35	141	17	40	5	3	0	14	13	2	0	0	24	6	2	.362	.353
Mateo, Jorge	R-R	6-0	190	6-23-95	.254	.301	.238	113	464	65	118	16	9	8	47	33	3	3	4	108	36	15	.379	.306
Nessy, Santiago	R-R	6-2	230	12-8-92	.202	.133	.222	38	129	13	26	5	0	1	11	15	0	0	0	28	0	0	.264	.285
O'Neill, Michael	R-R	6-1	195	6-12-92	.276	.342	.247	35	127	25	35	7	1	2	10	10	2	3	2	33	7	1	.394	.333
Oliver, Connor	L-R	6-0	180	10-13-93	.154	.167	.150	8	26	1	4	0	1	0	3	3	0	1	0	9	2	0	.231	.241
Payton, Mark	L-L	5-7	180	12-7-91	.309	.154	.382	24	81	15	25	2	1	3	15	16	0	0	1	18	2	3	.469	.418
Polo, Tito	R-R	5-9	185	8-23-94	.250	.260	.250	2	8	2	2	0	0	0	1	0	0	0	0	0	0	0	.250	.333
2-team total (55 Bradenton)					.275	—	—	57	222	42	61	3	0	4	29	22	5	5	2	47	17	7	.342	.351
Seitz, Jerry	R-R	5-10	180	9-27-94	.048	.000	.067	8	21	0	1	0	0	0	0	2	1	0	0	10	0	0	.048	.167
Skole, Jake	L-R	6-1	195	1-17-92	.202	.132	.225	65	213	27	43	6	1	6	27	21	2	1	1	72	6	1	.324	.278
Snyder, Matt	L-R	6-5	230	6-17-90	.500	—	.500	3	14	2	7	0	0	0	2	1	0	0	0	2	0	0	.500	.533
Spencer, Connor	L-R	6-2	215	1-22-93	.289	.171	.331	48	159	17	46	6	1	0	16	26	1	0	1	23	0	1	.340	.390
Thompson, Bo	R-R	5-10	255	1-27-93	.163	.087	.190	24	86	4	14	1	0	0	7	7	1	0	0	19	0	0	.174	.234
Torres, Gleyber	R-R	6-1	175	12-13-96	.254	.226	.264	31	122	19	31	6	2	2	19	16	0	0	0	23	2	3	.385	.341
Vidal, Carlos	L-L	5-11	160	11-29-95	.000	.000	.000	2	2	0	0	0	0	0	0	0	0	0	0	0	0	0	.000	.000
Williams, Mason	L-R	6-1	185	8-21-91	.333	.300	.364	11	42	2	14	2	1	0	1	1	0	0	0	4	0	0	.429	.349
Wilson, Wes	R-R	6-0	210	8-18-89	.236	.359	.200	49	174	16	41	5	0	1	19	6	1	0	3	43	0	0	.282	.261
Zehner, Zach	R-R	6-4	215	8-8-92	.278	.257	.286	109	385	50	107	24	2	3	35	63	3	0	0	90	1	4	.374	.384

Pitching

Pitching	B-T	HT	WT	DOB	W	L	ERA	G	GS	CG	SV	IP	H	R	ER	HR	BB	SO	AVG	vLH	vRH	K/9	BB/9
Acevedo, Domingo	R-R	6-7	190	3-6-94	2	3	3.22	10	10	1	0	50	49	19	18	3	15	54	.261	.263	.259	9.66	2.68
Adams, Chance	R-R	6-0	215	8-10-94	5	0	2.65	12	12	0	0	58	41	18	17	4	15	73	.196	.222	.182	11.39	2.34
Bisacca, Alex	R-R	6-2	205	6-23-93	0	1	9.00	1	0	0	0	1	3	1	1	0	0	0	.600	—	.600	0.00	0.00
Camarena, Daniel	L-L	6-0	200	11-9-92	1	0	1.50	2	0	0	0	6	2	1	1	1	1	4	.100	.000	.154	6.00	1.50
Campos, Vicente	R-R	6-3	230	7-27-92	4	2	3.49	10	10	0	0	59	50	24	23	3	23	56	.235	.250	.227	8.49	3.49
Carley, Sean	R-R	6-4	230	12-28-90	1	0	0.90	3	2	0	0	10	5	2	1	0	2	10	.152	.250	.095	9.00	1.80
Carter, Will	L-R	6-3	180	11-3-93	2	3	4.85	12	12	0	0	59	65	33	32	1	18	33	.277	.315	.253	5.01	2.73
Clarkin, Ian	L-L	6-2	190	2-14-95	6	9	3.31	18	18	2	0	98	100	44	36	4	30	72	.265	.329	.249	6.61	2.76
Cortes, Nestor	R-L	5-11	190	12-10-94	4	2	3.21	6	3	0	0	28	24	13	10	1	4	31	.224	.250	.215	9.96	1.29
Drozd, Jonny	L-L	6-7	200	9-17-91	0	1	3.12	11	0	0	0	17	19	7	6	5	14	.271	.313	.259	7.27	2.60
Encinas, Gabe	R-R	6-3	195	12-21-91	2	3	6.21	18	4	0	0	33	28	28	23	1	46	26	.233	.364	.158	7.02	12.42
Foley, Jordan	R-R	6-4	215	7-12-93	4	0	3.06	35	0	0	2	65	51	24	22	4	32	88	.215	.247	.197	12.25	4.45
Frare, Caleb	L-L	6-1	195	7-8-93	3	3	0.92	32	0	0	0	49	33	11	5	0	23	52	.198	.152	.215	9.55	4.22
Gabay, Willie	R-R	6-0	180	7-1-93	1	1	7.00	14	0	0	0	18	22	15	14	6	16	21	.293	.370	.250	10.50	8.00
German, Domingo	R-R	6-2	175	8-4-92	0	2	3.04	5	5	0	0	24	26	10	8	1	9	20	.283	.333	.250	7.61	3.42
Hissong, Travis	R-R	6-0	195	7-19-91	3	1	1.64	14	0	0	3	22	15	6	4	2	2	29	.181	.304	.133	11.86	0.82
Hodson, Chase	R-R	6-1	205	7-10-90	0	0	0.00	2	0	0	1	4	2	0	0	0	1	4	—	.000	.222	9.82	2.45
Holder, Jonathan	R-R	6-2	235	6-9-93	0	0	0.00	2	0	0	0	4	2	0	0	0	0	7	.154	.000	.250	15.75	0.00
Kamplain, Justin	R-L	6-0	175	2-13-93	0	0	0.00	1	0	0	0	2	1	0	0	0	2	2	.125	.000	.143	9.00	9.00
Kaprielian, James	R-R	6-4	200	3-2-94	2	1	1.50	3	3	0	0	18	8	6	3	1	3	22	.136	.200	.069	11.00	1.50
Koerner, Brody	R-R	6-1	190	10-17-93	1	0	2.03	2	2	0	0	13	9	3	3	0	2	8	.184	.136	.222	5.40	1.35
Lindgren, Jacob	L-L	5-11	210	3-12-93	1	0	2.57	6	0	0	1	7	0	4	2	0	9	8	.000	.000	.000	10.29	11.57
Maher, Joey	R-R	6-5	200	8-5-92	1	2	4.37	19	3	0	1	47	62	26	23	2	17	48	.320	.292	.333	9.13	3.23
Marsh, Matt	R-R	6-3	190	7-1-91	7	2	2.77	33	0	0	6	55	43	19	17	4	17	61	.211	.257	.187	9.92	2.77
McNamara, Dillon	R-R	6-5	220	10-6-91	5	3	1.86	38	0	0	13	58	43	15	12	3	20	50	.203	.145	.235	7.76	3.10
Mesa Jr. Jose	R-R	6-4	215	8-13-93	0	0	11.57	7	0	0	0	12	9	16	15	4	17	11	.205	.211	.200	8.49	13.11
Mitchell, Bryan	R-R	6-3	210	4-19-91	0	0	7.71	1	1	0	0	2	5	3	2	0	0	2	.417	.500	.400	7.71	0.00
Ramirez, Yefrey	R-R	6-2	165	11-28-93	3	7	2.84	11	11	0	0	63	34	23	20	5	18	66	.156	.139	.165	9.38	2.56
Reeves, James	R-L	6-3	195	6-7-93	5	1	2.27	25	12	0	1	83	53	23	21	4	26	94	.182	.160	.189	10.15	2.81
Rincon, Angel	R-R	6-1	180	9-26-92	0	3	2.04	10	0	0	1	18	17	4	4	1	2	10	.266	.292	.250	5.09	1.02
Rivera, Eduardo	R-R	6-5	190	9-24-92	0	0	3.86	5	0	0	0	7	7	5	3	0	8	13	.250	.400	.167	16.71	10.29
Rogers, Josh	L-L	6-3	185	7-10-94	10	5	2.53	20	20	2	0	114	111	35	32	5	20	90	.256	.266	.254	7.13	1.58
Ruth, Eric	R-R	6-0	195	9-26-90	1	0	4.29	8	0	0	0	21	18	10	10	1	4	23	.217	.286	.182	9.86	1.71
Schwaab, Andrew	R-R	6-1	185	2-8-93	0	0	3.86	8	0	0	1	14	14	8	6	1	11	18	.259	.261	.258	11.57	7.07
Severino, Luis	R-R	6-2	215	2-20-94	0	0	0.00	1	1	0	0	3	2	0	0	0	2	2	.182	.000	.286	6.00	0.00
Sheffield, Justus	L-L	5-10	195	5-13-96	3	1	1.73	5	5	0	0	26	14	6	5	0	10	27	.157	.105	.171	9.35	3.46
Tarpley, Stephen	R-L	6-1	180	2-17-93	0	1	9.00	1	1	0	0	5	7	5	5	0	2	3	.333	.000	.389	5.40	3.60
2-team total (20 Bradenton)					6	5	4.54	21	21	0	0	105	100	58	53	8	39	93	—	—	—	7.97	3.34
Walby, Philip	L-R	6-2	190	7-24-92	0	1	3.86	12	0	0	0	16	19	10	7	0	8	10	.302	.273	.317	5.51	4.41

Fielding

Catcher	PCT	G	PO	A	E	DP	PB
Aparicio	.989	9	86	3	1	0	4
Diaz	.983	34	261	35	5	3	5
Nessy	.985	38	304	34	5	3	9
Seitz	1.000	8	53	3	0	1	1
Wilson	.992	49	432	37	4	1	5

First Base	PCT	G	PO	A	E	DP
Barrios	1.000	1	7	0	0	0
Conde	.982	21	154	11	3	16
Cornelius	.993	20	141	9	1	15
Fleming	.988	18	151	12	2	12
Ford	.988	10	76	4	1	7
Snyder	.950	2	19	0	1	1
Spencer	.992	46	346	20	3	30
Thompson	.985	21	174	17	3	16

Second Base	PCT	G	PO	A	E	DP
Avelino	.972	44	76	98	5	18
Barrios	1.000	1	1	3	0	0

	PCT	G	PO	A	E	DP
Conde	.960	7	12	12	1	4
Estrada	.974	36	53	95	4	24
Fleming	1.000	10	12	18	0	4
Mateo	.994	40	80	94	1	26
Torres	1.000	1	1	2	0	0

Third Base	PCT	G	PO	A	E	DP
Andujar	.947	51	24	100	7	10
Barrios	.800	1	0	4	1	0
Conde	1.000	16	3	41	0	3
Cornelius	.809	22	13	25	9	2
Estrada	.971	38	23	77	3	6
Fleming	.957	8	5	17	1	0

Shortstop	PCT	G	PO	A	E	DP
Avelino	.962	43	56	123	7	23
Conde	1.000	3	3	10	0	1
Estrada	.917	3	3	8	1	5
Mateo	.937	62	104	148	17	26
Torres	.959	27	33	60	4	10

Outfield	PCT	G	PO	A	E	DP
Amburgey	1.000	35	58	5	0	2
Aune	.974	76	147	2	4	1
Bolasky	1.000	36	64	2	0	0
Crawford	1.000	27	69	2	0	0
Diaz	.875	3	7	0	1	0
Florial	1.000	2	4	0	0	0
Hendrix	.988	30	78	2	1	0
O'Neill	1.000	30	55	1	0	1
Oliver	1.000	6	19	0	0	0
Payton	1.000	17	29	5	0	1
Polo	1.000	2	5	0	0	0
Skole	.982	52	104	4	2	0
Spencer	—	1	0	0	0	0
Vidal	1.000	2	1	0	0	0
Williams	1.000	4	15	0	0	0
Zehner	.988	90	154	7	2	1

CHARLESTON RIVERDOGS
SOUTH ATLANTIC LEAGUE

LOW CLASS A

Batting	B-T	HT	WT	DOB	AVG	vLH	vRH	G	AB	R	H	2B	3B	HR	RBI	BB	HBP	SH	SF	SO	SB	CS	SLG	OBP
Afenir, Audie	R-R	6-2	215	2-15-92	.242	.262	.235	63	231	25	56	10	0	3	21	12	0	1	2	49	0	1	.325	.278
Aguilar, Angel	R-R	6-0	170	6-13-95	.220	.215	.222	64	227	23	50	11	1	8	28	13	2	2	1	58	8	2	.383	.267
Alvarez, Mandy	R-R	6-1	205	7-14-94	.274	.246	.285	53	208	25	57	12	0	5	29	6	0	0	4	23	0	2	.404	.289
Amburgey, Trey	R-R	6-2	210	10-24-94	.281	.286	.279	16	64	11	18	7	2	1	10	6	1	0	1	5	7	0	.500	.347
Bridges, Drew	L-R	6-4	230	2-3-95	.192	.400	.143	8	26	2	5	0	1	1	2	1	0	1	0	9	0	0	.385	.222
Coleman, Kendall	L-L	6-4	190	5-22-95	.202	.036	.253	37	119	10	24	1	1	2	17	17	0	1	0	44	1	5	.277	.301
Conde, Vince	R-R	6-0	195	10-13-93	.296	.250	.314	28	98	13	29	2	1	0	9	13	0	0	0	26	3	0	.337	.378
Diaz, Cesar	B-R	5-10	165	4-12-93	.258	.270	.252	66	217	24	56	10	1	3	21	22	2	2	1	35	12	8	.355	.331
Estrada, Thairo	R-R	5-10	155	2-22-96	.286	.243	.301	35	140	11	40	3	1	5	19	8	0	0	0	21	11	3	.429	.324
Ferreira, Ricardo	B-R	5-11	175	2-3-95	.256	.333	.219	44	168	22	43	5	2	2	15	13	1	2	1	42	14	2	.345	.311
Florial, Estevan	L-R	6-1	185	11-25-97	.300	.000	.333	5	20	4	6	0	1	1	5	2	0	0	1	5	0	0	.550	.348
Gittens, Chris	R-R	6-4	250	2-9-94	.253	.324	.225	107	383	57	97	23	0	21	70	56	9	0	3	126	4	2	.478	.359
Godinez, Chris	R-R	5-8	185	4-20-93	.462	.667	.400	8	26	4	12	1	0	0	1	4	0	0	4	1	1	1	.500	.533
Haddad, Radley	L-R	6-1	190	5-11-90	.296	.250	.304	8	27	2	8	1	0	0	2	2	1	0	7	1	0	.333	.367
Hendrix, Jeff	L-R	6-0	195	7-16-93	.299	.359	.290	62	234	36	70	16	1	1	25	35	5	1	3	62	11	3	.389	.397
Holder, Kyle	L-R	6-1	185	5-25-94	.290	.273	.295	88	352	40	102	13	2	1	18	15	3	2	2	53	8	6	.347	.323
Jackson, Jhalan	R-R	6-3	220	2-12-93	.236	.180	.253	103	386	48	91	28	4	11	50	38	5	0	2	114	6	8	.415	.311
Katoh, Gosuke	L-R	6-2	180	10-8-94	.229	.314	.204	65	218	30	50	14	3	1	25	26	4	3	2	66	6	1	.335	.320
Mikolas, Nathan	L-L	6-0	200	12-30-94	.225	.120	.250	39	129	14	29	5	0	3	10	10	4	0	2	35	3	1	.333	.297
Molina, Leonardo	R-R	6-2	180	7-31-97	.198	.304	.175	36	126	12	25	5	1	2	13	8	1	0	1	34	0	2	.302	.250
Navas, Eduardo	B-R	5-10	180	4-5-96	.184	.189	.182	43	136	11	25	3	0	0	9	8	4	1	0	35	2	0	.206	.268
Palma, Alexander	R-R	6-0	201	10-18-95	.265	.260	.267	64	238	31	63	17	1	6	37	9	1	1	2	35	5	4	.420	.292
Park, Hoy Jun	L-R	6-1	175	4-7-96	.225	.228	.224	116	435	60	98	15	12	2	34	67	7	5	3	120	32	3	.329	.336
Spencer, Connor	L-R	6-2	215	1-22-93	.253	.250	.254	45	158	23	40	10	0	5	19	19	3	0	1	35	2	0	.411	.343
Sweeney, Kane	L-R	6-3	220	10-6-92	.253	.214	.262	21	75	13	19	4	0	2	13	9	0	0	1	26	1	0	.387	.329
Torrens, Luis	R-R	6-0	175	5-2-96	.230	.237	.228	40	139	9	32	6	0	2	10	22	3	0	1	24	1	1	.317	.348
Vidal, Carlos	L-L	5-11	160	11-29-95	.143	.250	.100	4	14	0	2	0	0	0	2	0	0	0	5	0	0	.143	.143

Pitching	B-T	HT	WT	DOB	W	L	ERA	G	GS	CG	SV	IP	H	R	ER	HR	BB	SO	AVG	vLH	vRH	K/9	BB/9
Acevedo, Domingo	R-R	6-7	190	3-6-94	3	1	1.90	8	8	0	0	43	34	13	9	1	7	48	.221	.230	.215	10.13	1.48
Carley, Sean	R-R	6-4	230	12-28-90	0	1	2.28	11	0	0	0	28	20	9	7	3	9	22	.204	.286	.159	7.16	2.93
Carroll, Cody	R-R	6-5	200	10-15-92	4	4	3.15	26	6	0	3	91	89	45	32	3	41	90	.259	.318	.214	8.87	4.04
Carter, Will	L-R	6-3	190	1-18-93	0	0	3.60	1	1	0	0	5	5	2	2	0	1	7	.294	.286	.300	12.60	1.80
Cedeno, Luis	R-R	5-11	154	7-14-94	9	9	3.68	20	20	0	0	108	99	49	44	7	36	95	.249	.220	.270	7.94	3.01
Cortes, Nestor	R-L	5-11	190	12-10-94	6	2	0.79	13	8	0	2	68	36	10	6	3	15	75	.157	.115	.169	9.88	1.98
Custodio, Claudio	R-R	5-10	155	10-30-90	3	1	2.70	7	0	0	0	10	11	6	3	0	4	8	.275	.267	.280	7.20	3.60
De la Rosa, Simon	R-R	6-3	185	5-11-93	1	3	6.10	10	5	0	1	31	32	22	21	0	27	38	.262	.241	.281	11.03	7.84
Gabay, Willie	R-R	6-0	180	7-3-91	2	1	4.44	14	0	0	0	24	15	13	12	0	13	27	.179	.216	.149	9.99	4.81
German, Domingo	R-R	6-2	175	8-4-92	1	1	3.12	5	5	0	0	26	15	11	9	2	2	18	.167	.143	.188	6.23	0.69
Gomez, Anyelo	R-R	6-1	175	3-1-93	4	3	4.36	22	9	0	1	76	68	39	37	6	34	76	.237	.213	.255	8.96	4.01
Green, Nick	R-R	6-1	165	3-25-95	3	0	1.06	3	3	0	0	17	8	3	2	0	3	14	.210	.091	.275	7.41	1.59
Hamlin, Cody	R-R	6-3	190	2-9-93	1	0	0.00	2	0	0	0	4	1	0	0	0	1	11	.091	.000	.111	4.91	2.45
Harris, Hobie	R-R	6-3	200	6-23-93	2	4	2.60	23	0	0	1	52	43	19	15	2	21	59	.225	.228	.223	10.21	3.63
Hissong, Travis	R-R	6-0	195	7-19-91	0	0	0.54	6	0	0	1	17	9	1	1	0	3	23	.150	.161	.138	12.42	1.62
Hodson, Chase	R-R	6-1	205	7-10-92	0	0	0.00	2	0	0	0	3	1	1	0	0	1	4	—	.000	.167	12.00	3.00
Kamplain, Justin	R-L	6-0	175	2-13-93	0	0	5.52	6	0	0	1	15	17	10	9	2	16	15	.283	.056	.381	9.82	4.30
Koerner, Brody	R-R	6-1	190	10-17-93	1	0	1.74	3	3	0	0	21	13	5	4	1	3	21	.176	.190	.170	9.15	1.31
Loaisiga, Jonathan	R-R	5-11	165	11-2-94	0	0	7.71	1	1	0	0	2	2	2	2	1	1	2	.222	.000	.333	7.71	3.86
Mesa Jr. Jose	R-R	6-4	215	8-13-93	1	3	2.97	14	0	0	1	30	28	12	10	1	13	48	.239	.152	.296	14.24	3.86

Pitching	B-T	HT	WT	DOB	W	L	ERA	G	GS	CG	SV	IP	H	R	ER	HR	BB	SO	AVG	vLH	vRH	K/9	BB/9
Mitchell, Bryan	L-R	6-3	210	4-19-91	0	0	9.00	1	1	0	0	3	3	3	3	2	0	2	.250	.333	.167	6.00	0.00
Morris, Christian	R-R	6-4	195	1-23-94	8	5	2.99	22	22	0	0	120	105	44	40	7	24	99	.236	.213	.255	7.40	1.80
Mundell, Garrett	R-R	6-6	245	2-16-93	1	2	4.26	9	0	0	0	13	14	7	6	0	5	21	.264	.348	.200	14.92	3.55
Palladino, David	R-R	6-8	235	3-15-93	1	1	15.58	6	0	0	0	9	13	17	15	2	11	16	.333	.438	.261	16.62	11.42
Ramirez, Yefrey	R-R	6-2	165	11-28-93	4	2	2.80	11	11	0	0	61	48	20	19	4	14	66	.209	.264	.173	9.74	2.07
Reeves, James	R-L	6-3	195	6-7-93	1	1	2.70	4	0	0	0	10	2	3	3	0	3	15	.065	.000	.087	13.50	2.70
Reyes, Manolo	R-R	6-1	190	11-14-89	0	0	5.40	6	0	0	0	7	5	7	4	0	8	6	.208	.300	.143	8.10	10.80
Rivera, Eduardo	R-R	6-5	190	9-24-92	0	0	1.26	6	0	0	1	14	7	2	2	0	5	21	.140	.176	.121	13.19	3.14
Rogers, Josh	L-L	6-3	185	7-10-94	2	1	1.59	4	4	0	0	23	14	6	4	1	2	25	.171	.200	.158	9.93	0.79
Rosa, Adonis	R-R	6-0	160	11-17-94	2	5	2.86	8	0	0	0	44	40	20	14	2	8	46	.238	.242	.235	9.41	1.64
Schwaab, Andrew	R-R	6-1	185	2-8-93	4	1	2.27	35	0	0	20	40	32	12	10	1	11	43	.218	.229	.212	9.76	2.50
Sosebee, David	R-R	6-1	200	8-25-93	0	2	3.60	8	0	0	0	10	11	5	4	1	8	7	.297	.400	.176	6.30	7.20
Swanson, Erik	R-R	6-3	220	9-4-93	0	1	3.60	5	2	0	0	15	14	7	6	0	5	15	.246	.222	.267	9.00	3.00
2-team total (19 Hickory)					6	5	3.46	24	17	0	1	96	91	44	37	4	30	93	—	—	—	8.69	2.80
Tate, Dillon	R-R	6-2	165	5-1-94	1	0	3.12	7	0	0	0	17	21	10	6	1	6	15	.292	.250	.325	7.79	3.12
2-team total (17 Hickory)					4	3	4.70	24	16	0	0	82	99	49	43	6	33	70	—	—	—	7.65	3.61
Vargas, Daris	R-R	6-3	195	8-12-92	10	8	2.95	27	21	0	2	131	106	51	43	6	57	108	.225	.245	.209	7.40	3.91
Weissert, Greg	R-R	6-2	215	2-4-95	0	1	4.26	12	0	0	3	13	14	9	6	1	10	16	.286	.238	.321	11.37	7.11
Widener, Taylor	L-R	6-0	195	10-24-94	1	0	0.78	7	1	0	3	23	15	2	2	2	3	34	.188	.258	.143	13.30	1.17

Fielding

Catcher	PCT	G	PO	A	E	DP	PB
Afenir	.998	50	420	30	1	3	6
Haddad	1.000	8	89	16	0	0	2
Navas	.991	43	363	59	4	5	14
Torrens	.990	40	339	46	4	3	16

First Base	PCT	G	PO	A	E	DP
Afenir	.992	15	106	11	1	4
Conde	.964	6	46	8	2	0
Gittens	.977	79	619	56	16	41
Spencer	.984	24	183	1	3	11
Sweeney	.988	18	151	14	2	10

Second Base	PCT	G	PO	A	E	DP
Aguilar	.971	6	14	20	1	2
Conde	1.000	5	3	20	0	0
Estrada	.938	21	36	40	5	8

Godinez	.950	8	6	13	1	0
Holder	.983	24	46	68	2	12
Katoh	.982	45	74	94	3	20
Park	.959	32	44	73	5	11

Third Base	PCT	G	PO	A	E	DP
Aguilar	.950	56	47	106	8	5
Alvarez	.984	49	38	85	2	5
Bridges	.882	7	3	12	2	0
Conde	1.000	9	10	18	0	0
Estrada	.882	9	2	13	2	1
Katoh	1.000	10	4	18	0	0
Spencer	1.000	1	0	1	0	1

Shortstop	PCT	G	PO	A	E	DP
Conde	.941	4	9	7	1	1
Estrada	.909	5	4	6	1	1
Holder	.970	55	71	152	7	22

Katoh	.933	5	7	7	1	1
Park	.927	73	93	162	20	27

Outfield	PCT	G	PO	A	E	DP
Amburgey	1.000	13	20	1	0	0
Coleman	.984	32	58	4	1	1
Diaz	.991	60	114	1	1	0
Ferreira	.909	39	88	2	9	1
Florial	1.000	5	9	0	0	0
Hendrix	.991	58	114	2	1	1
Jackson	.969	85	146	11	5	2
Mikolas	.981	33	52	1	1	0
Molina	1.000	35	75	1	0	0
Palma	.981	57	94	10	2	4
Spencer	.750	2	3	0	1	0
Sweeney	—	1	0	0	0	0
Vidal	1.000	4	9	0	0	0

STATEN ISLAND YANKEES
NEW YORK-PENN LEAGUE

SHORT-SEASON

Batting	B-T	HT	WT	DOB	AVG	vLH	vRH	G	AB	R	H	2B	3B	HR	RBI	BB	HBP	SH	SF	SO	SB	CS	SLG	OBP
Aguilar, Angel	R-R	6-0	170	6-13-95	.222	.210	.228	51	189	24	42	11	0	5	19	8	3	1	0	63	6	1	.360	.265
Alvarez, Mandy	R-R	6-1	205	7-14-94	.339	.235	.381	13	59	11	20	4	0	0	11	4	0	0	3	3	0	0	.407	.364
Argomaniz, Manny	R-R	6-0	200	4-4-93	.000	.000	.000	2	7	0	0	0	0	0	0	1	0	0	1	0	0	0	.000	.000
Baez, Yancarlos	B-R	6-2	165	9-21-95	.041	.095	.000	15	49	3	2	1	0	0	2	1	1	0	0	20	0	0	.061	.078
Blaser, Dalton	L-L	6-1	200	1-31-94	.223	.167	.246	55	202	23	45	7	0	2	21	23	5	0	1	29	0	1	.287	.316
Bridges, Drew	R-R	6-4	230	2-3-95	.258	.221	.273	67	260	23	67	14	1	5	32	27	0	0	6	68	2	1	.377	.321
Coleman, Kendall	L-L	6-4	190	5-22-95	.194	.170	.203	55	186	14	36	4	2	0	18	31	1	0	3	55	1	1	.237	.308
Ferreira, Ricardo	B-R	5-11	175	2-3-95	.221	.235	.217	23	86	20	19	4	0	1	2	13	4	3	1	23	12	4	.302	.346
Fleming, Billy	R-R	6-1	200	9-20-92	.320	.429	.278	7	25	4	8	1	0	0	5	3	1	0	1	4	0	1	.360	.400
Ford, Mike	L-R	6-0	225	7-4-92	.167	.143	.200	4	12	2	2	1	0	1	3	2	0	0	1	0	0	0	.500	.267
Godinez, Chris	R-R	5-8	185	4-20-93	.205	.095	.250	24	73	13	15	3	0	1	4	11	8	1	2	17	7	0	.288	.362
Haddad, Radley	L-R	6-1	195	5-11-90	.130	.000	.158	8	23	2	3	1	0	0	1	2	2	0	0	10	0	1	.174	.259
Mateo, Welfrin	R-R	5-10	170	9-8-95	.444	1.000	.375	2	9	0	4	0	1	0	3	0	0	0	0	2	0	0	.667	.444
Mikolas, Nathan	L-L	6-0	200	12-30-93	.175	.083	.200	16	57	7	10	3	0	0	5	5	0	0	1	15	0	0	.228	.238
Navas, Eduardo	B-R	5-10	180	4-5-96	.231	.231	.231	29	91	9	21	4	0	0	3	6	6	0	1	22	0	0	.275	.317
Perez, Danienger	R-R	6-0	155	11-6-94	.162	.300	.130	19	68	5	11	0	0	0	2	5	1	0	0	20	2	2	.162	.219
Robinson, Timmy	R-R	6-1	225	6-17-94	.265	.227	.284	63	230	30	61	18	4	8	52	24	6	0	5	58	9	4	.483	.343
Rodriguez, Yonauris	R-R	6-1	155	3-10-97	.000	.000	.000	2	7	0	0	0	0	0	0	0	0	0	0	2	0	0	.000	.000
Rosario, Jose	R-R	5-11	190	11-29-91	.667	—	.667	2	6	3	4	3	0	0	2	3	2	0	0	0	3	0	1.167	.750
Ruta, Ben	R-L	6-3	195	6-8-94	.157	.129	.173	25	83	10	13	1	0	1	9	5	1	1	2	18	0	3	.205	.209
Seitz, Jerry	R-R	5-10	180	9-27-94	.239	.313	.196	25	88	3	21	7	0	0	7	7	1	0	0	25	0	1	.318	.302
Skinner, Keith	L-R	6-1	200	4-14-94	.222	.333	.190	8	27	1	6	0	0	1	1	0	0	0	0	4	0	0	.259	.250
Solak, Nick	R-R	5-11	175	1-11-95	.321	.311	.325	64	240	48	77	13	1	3	25	30	6	4	3	39	8	0	.421	.412
Sweeney, Kane	L-R	6-3	220	10-6-92	.277	.267	.281	39	141	14	39	6	1	0	21	28	1	0	0	41	0	1	.333	.400
Thompson-Williams, DomL	L-L	6-0	185	4-21-95	.246	.222	.253	56	195	30	48	8	1	3	16	28	4	0	3	43	15	5	.344	.348
Torrens, Luis	R-R	6-0	175	5-2-96	.311	.333	.308	12	45	6	14	4	0	0	5	4	0	0	1	7	1	1	.400	.360
Vazquez, Chucky	R-R	6-1	200	9-24-93	.231	1.000	.167	4	13	1	3	1	0	0	1	0	0	1	0	0	0	0	.308	.231
Vidal, Carlos	L-L	5-11	160	11-29-95	.216	.176	.235	13	51	6	11	1	0	0	7	1	0	0	1	12	1	1	.275	.322

Pitching	B-T	HT	WT	DOB	W	L	ERA	G	GS	CG	SV	IP	H	R	ER	HR	BB	SO	AVG	vLH	vRH	K/9	BB/9
Custodio, Claudio	R-R	5-10	155	10-30-90	3	0	2.95	19	0	0	0	37	32	19	12	2	9	26	.235	.275	.212	6.38	2.21
De la Rosa, Simon	R-R	6-3	185	5-11-93	6	4	3.38	13	13	0	0	69	54	28	26	3	29	76	.214	.210	.218	9.87	3.76
DeCarr, Austin	R-R	6-3	218	3-14-95	2	0	4.12	10	10	0	0	39	46	20	18	3	17	31	.293	.352	.244	7.09	3.89
Diehl, Phillip	L-L	6-2	180	7-16-94	1	0	0.00	1	0	0	0	2	1	0	0	0	0	3	.143	.500	.000	13.50	0.00
Espinal, Raynel	R-R	6-3	199	10-6-93	0	1	14.73	2	0	0	0	4	8	6	2	1	4	4	.444	.333	.556	9.82	2.45
Finley, Drew	R-R	6-3	200	7-10-96	0	3	4.28	6	6	0	0	27	21	16	13	2	9	20	.212	.200	.219	6.59	2.96
Gomez, Anyelo	R-R	6-1	175	3-1-93	2	1	3.48	5	4	0	0	21	19	12	8	0	8	17	.268	.259	.273	7.40	3.48
Graham, J.R.	R-R	5-11	195	1-14-90	0	0	0.00	2	1	0	0	3	0	0	0	0	0	3	.000	.000	.000	9.00	0.00
Green, Nick	R-R	6-1	165	3-25-95	1	1	1.69	2	2	0	0	11	7	3	2	1	3	7	.184	.133	.217	5.91	2.53
Harvey, Joe	R-R	6-2	220	1-9-92	0	0	1.04	6	0	0	0	9	11	1	1	0	4	14	.297	.250	.333	14.54	4.15
Kamplain, Justin	R-L	6-0	175	2-13-93	1	1	1.21	15	0	0	6	22	11	4	3	0	1	21	.145	.143	.145	8.46	0.40
Keller, Brian	R-R	6-3	170	6-21-94	0	0	0.00	1	0	0	1	2	0	0	0	0	1	3	.000	.000	.000	13.50	4.50
Kriske, Brooks	R-R	6-3	190	2-3-94	0	0	2.25	13	0	0	4	16	12	8	4	0	6	16	.214	.238	.200	9.00	3.38
Lane, Trevor	L-L	5-11	185	4-26-94	0	0	0.00	3	0	0	0	4	2	0	0	0	1	3	.154	.000	.200	6.75	2.25
Mahoney, Kolton	R-R	6-1	195	5-20-92	4	4	2.92	12	8	1	0	62	65	25	20	2	16	47	.275	.204	.341	6.86	2.34
Martin, Chad	R-R	6-4	215	1-2-94	4	0	2.73	6	5	0	0	33	25	12	10	0	17	31	.212	.206	.218	8.45	4.64
Padilla, Jonathan	R-R	5-10	175	3-30-93	3	2	2.37	14	6	0	0	57	53	23	15	0	12	57	.244	.278	.217	9.00	1.89
Palladino, David	R-R	6-8	235	3-15-93	3	2	2.43	18	0	0	5	33	18	9	9	1	25	42	.153	.245	.077	11.34	6.75
Pazos, James	R-L	6-2	235	5-5-91	0	0	0.00	2	0	0	0	6	1	0	0	0	1	6	.231	.167	.286	14.73	2.45
Perez, Freicer	R-R	6-8	190	3-14-96	2	4	4.47	13	13	0	0	52	51	34	26	3	25	49	.245	.241	.248	8.43	4.30
Rivera, Eduardo	R-R	6-5	190	9-24-92	0	0	0.00	7	0	0	2	12	8	0	0	0	6	13	.182	.263	.120	9.49	4.38
Roeder, Josh	R-R	6-0	175	12-2-92	3	1	3.38	16	0	0	0	43	43	19	16	1	7	47	.259	.235	.276	9.91	1.48
Rosa, Adonis	R-R	6-1	160	11-17-94	2	1	1.32	6	5	0	1	34	23	5	5	2	7	27	.189	.159	.205	7.15	1.85
Rutckyj, Evan	R-L	6-5	225	1-31-92	1	0	0.00	1	0	0	0	2	0	0	0	0	0	2	.286	.000	.500	9.00	0.00
Schaub, Mike	R-R	6-2	210	5-31-92	0	0	3.00	2	0	0	0	6	5	2	2	0	2	5	.238	.250	.235	7.50	3.00
Sosebee, David	R-R	6-1	200	8-25-93	2	2	2.03	21	0	0	2	31	30	11	7	0	10	27	.259	.269	.250	7.84	2.90
Taylor, Chad	R-R	6-0	180	8-29-90	2	1	2.08	10	0	0	2	13	2	4	3	0	6	12	.050	.063	.042	8.31	4.15
Trieglaff, Brian	R-R	6-1	190	6-13-94	0	1	4.40	14	0	0	0	14	16	7	7	0	8	10	.296	.348	.258	6.28	5.02
Widener, Taylor	L-R	6-0	195	10-24-94	2	0	0.00	6	1	0	1	15	2	0	0	0	4	25	.043	.000	.071	14.67	2.35

Fielding

C: Argomaniz 1, Haddad 7, Navas 29, Seitz 23, Skinner 8, Torrens 11, Vazquez 4. **1B:** Blaser 23, Bridges 18, Fleming 2, Ford 2, Haddad 1, Sweeney 32. **2B:** Baez 2, Fleming 1, Godinez 9, Perez 3, Rodriguez 2, Rosario 1, Solak 59. **3B:** Alvarez 12, Baez 10, Bridges 48, Fleming 2, Godinez 4, Mateo 1. **SS:** Aguilar 50, Baez 1, Godinez 9, Mateo 1, Perez 16. **OF:** Blaser 18, Coleman 42, Ferreira 21, Mikolas 8, Robinson 56, Rosario 1, Ruta 22, Thompson-Williams 51, Vidal 10.

PULASKI YANKEES   ROOKIE
APPALACHIAN LEAGUE

Batting	B-T	HT	WT	DOB	AVG	vLH	vRH	G	AB	R	H	2B	3B	HR	RBI	BB	HBP	SH	SF	SO	SB	CS	SLG	OBP
Argomaniz, Manny	R-R	6-0	200	4-4-93	.149	.136	.156	25	67	12	10	1	1	0	2	14	1	0	0	19	0	0	.194	.305
Cabrera, Oswaldo	R-R	5-10	145	3-1-99	.240	.219	.250	26	96	9	23	4	1	1	7	8	1	0	0	13	4	1	.333	.305
Cornelius, Kevin	R-R	6-1	180	8-28-92	.367	.300	.414	13	49	12	18	5	1	6	21	7	1	0	1	11	0	0	.878	.448
Diaz, Andy	L-L	5-11	190	11-21-95	.197	.300	.157	23	71	11	14	3	3	3	12	3	1	0	1	25	2	0	.451	.237
Florial, Estevan	L-R	6-1	185	11-25-97	.225	.186	.247	60	236	36	53	10	1	7	25	28	3	1	0	78	10	2	.364	.315
Garcia, Dermis	R-R	6-3	200	1-7-98	.206	.250	.175	57	194	31	40	9	0	13	24	32	3	0	1	79	0	2	.454	.326
Garcia, Wilkerman	B-R	6-0	176	4-1-98	.198	.226	.178	54	222	21	44	10	3	1	13	15	2	0	0	44	4	5	.284	.255
Gardiner, Josh	R-R	5-10	180	6-19-93	.250	.273	.238	25	64	16	16	3	1	0	4	10	3	0	0	15	4	0	.328	.377
Gilliam, Isiah	B-R	6-3	220	7-23-96	.239	.300	.195	57	218	32	52	14	0	10	33	17	3	0	1	64	3	0	.440	.301
Lynch, Tim	L-R	6-2	220	4-3-93	.229	.171	.266	29	105	13	24	10	2	3	13	17	0	0	0	19	0	0	.362	.336
Mateo, Welfrin	R-R	5-10	170	9-8-95	.289	.180	.348	45	142	11	41	7	2	2	21	4	2	1	9	29	5	6	.408	.315
Mendez, Erick	R-R	6-0	185	4-7-96	.119	.118	.120	14	42	2	5	0	0	2	3	1	0	1	23	1	0	.119	.191
Molina, Leonardo	R-R	6-2	180	7-31-97	.246	.268	.235	49	175	23	43	9	2	7	23	19	0	1	1	45	4	3	.440	.318
Rey, Victor	R-R	6-2	178	6-29-95	.180	.139	.203	30	100	11	18	5	0	1	11	16	0	1	0	31	1	0	.260	.293
Reyes, Brian	R-R	6-0	190	6-28-95	.269	.300	.241	29	104	12	28	8	0	1	13	12	0	0	0	20	0	0	.375	.345
Ruta, Ben	R-L	6-3	195	6-8-94	.283	.313	.267	13	46	8	13	1	1	1	8	6	0	1	0	9	2	1	.413	.365
Rutherford, Blake	L-R	6-3	195	5-2-97	.382	.406	.368	25	89	13	34	7	1	2	9	9	1	0	1	24	0	2	.618	.440
Sands, Donny	R-R	6-2	190	5-16-96	.300	.350	.275	16	60	7	18	1	0	2	10	6	0	0	2	9	1	0	.417	.353
Wagner, Brandon	L-R	6-0	210	8-24-95	.247	.211	.258	25	81	8	20	5	0	3	7	16	0	1	0	28	2	0	.420	.371

Pitching	B-T	HT	WT	DOB	W	L	ERA	G	GS	CG	SV	IP	H	R	ER	HR	BB	SO	AVG	vLH	vRH	K/9	BB/9
Alvarez, Daniel	R-R	6-3	228	6-28-96	1	0	0.00	1	1	0	0	5	1	0	0	0	2	1	.059	.000	.167	1.80	3.60
Aybar, Julian	R-R	6-1	188	2-13-92	0	2	10.38	6	4	0	0	22	30	28	25	5	15	14	.341	.488	.200	5.82	6.23
Bisacca, Alex	R-R	6-2	205	6-23-93	0	0	3.72	13	0	0	2	29	25	12	12	2	6	24	.248	.275	.230	7.45	1.86
Bristo, Braden	R-R	6-0	180	11-1-94	0	2	6.00	10	0	0	0	15	21	10	10	1	6	17	.333	.280	.368	10.20	3.60
Chambers, Miles	R-R	6-2	205	10-22-93	2	1	5.92	15	0	0	1	24	26	17	16	6	12	30	.268	.233	.230	11.10	4.44
Degano, Jeff	R-L	6-4	215	10-30-92	0	0	27.00	7	2	0	0	6	3	19	17	0	25	12	.143	.000	.189	19.06	39.71
Diehl, Phillip	L-L	6-2	180	7-16-94	0	0	2.56	14	1	0	1	32	23	11	9	1	6	38	.197	.333	.136	10.80	1.71
Duarte, Abel	R-R	6-1	190	5-20-94	1	6	3.60	10	9	1	0	50	61	40	20	4	13	38	.298	.305	.295	6.84	2.34
Espinal, Raynel	R-R	6-3	199	10-6-93	1	3	4.12	4	4	0	0	20	17	11	9	4	5	23	.227	.310	.174	9.15	2.29
Flemming, Icezack	R-R	6-2	200	6-24-92	0	1	3.18	7	0	0	0	11	4	4	4	1	10	13	.108	.200	.045	10.32	7.94
Hamlin, Cody	R-R	6-1	190	2-9-93	1	2	6.14	10	0	0	0	29	34	21	20	3	4	23	.288	.269	.303	7.06	1.23
Honahan, Tyler	R-L	6-2	175	1-5-94	2	0	2.48	13	0	0	1	29	26	9	8	0	12	30	.158	.140	.172	9.31	3.72
Jimenez, Juan	R-R	6-2	190	10-6-93	4	3	3.57	12	10	1	1	58	51	29	23	9	26	56	.243	.284	.209	8.69	4.03
Jones, Will	R-R	6-1	190	3-15-93	2	3	7.20	15	0	0	0	20	27	17	16	3	5	18	.303	.324	.291	8.10	2.25

Pitching	B-T	HT	WT	DOB	W	L	ERA	G	GS	CG	SV	IP	H	R	ER	HR	BB	SO	AVG	vLH	vRH	K/9	BB/9
Keller, Brian	R-R	6-3	170	6-21-94	1	0	1.89	5	2	0	0	19	17	6	4	0	5	25	.239	.200	.268	11.84	2.37
Lara, Rafael	R-R	5-10	166	6-10-95	3	6	5.80	12	7	0	0	50	50	37	32	12	25	49	.255	.295	.222	8.88	4.53
Mahoney, Spencer	L-R	6-4	205	6-10-93	2	3	2.52	12	6	0	1	39	29	11	11	1	11	57	.199	.102	.264	13.04	2.52
Martin, Chad	R-R	6-4	215	1-2-94	3	2	2.55	7	7	0	0	35	30	16	10	2	7	24	.226	.243	.206	6.11	1.78
Nelson, Nick	R-R	6-1	195	12-5-95	0	3	3.38	10	10	0	0	21	14	14	8	0	22	19	.200	.227	.188	8.02	9.28
Pena, Jose	R-R	6-0	190	3-22-91	0	0	0.00	2	0	0	0	2	0	0	0	0	3	4	.000	.000	.000	15.43	11.57
Wasserman, Zak	L-L	6-6	225	8-30-90	2	0	4.91	13	3	0	0	33	35	19	18	2	14	25	.267	.289	.258	6.82	3.82
Weissert, Greg	R-R	6-2	215	2-4-95	0	0	0.00	5	0	0	2	6	4	0	0	0	1	9	.182	.286	.133	12.79	1.42

Fielding

C: Argomaniz 10, Rey 27, Reyes 16, Sands 14. **1B:** Argomaniz 5, Cornelius 8, Gardiner 1, Lynch 26, Rey 3, Reyes 3, Wagner 22. **2B:** Cabrera 18, Gardiner 22, Mateo 29. **3B:** Argomaniz 2, Cornelius 2, Garcia 55, Mateo 12. **SS:** Cabrera 7, Garcia 54, Mateo 6. **OF:** Argomaniz 2, Diaz 21, Florial 51, Gilliam 50, Mendez 10, Molina 42, Ruta 10, Rutherford 16.

GCL YANKEES EAST   ROOKIE
GULF COAST LEAGUE

Batting	B-T	HT	WT	DOB	AVG	vLH	vRH	G	AB	R	H	2B	3B	HR	RBI	BB	HBP	SH	SF	SO	SB	CS	SLG	OBP
Amburgey, Trey	R-R	6-2	210	10-24-94	.000	—	.000	1	3	0	0	0	0	0	0	0	0	0	0	1	0	0	.000	.000
2-team total (4 Yankees2)					.188	—	—	5	16	3	3	1	0	0	0	1	1	0	0	4	0	0	.250	.278
Baez, Yancarlos	B-R	6-2	165	9-21-95	.143	.286	.119	14	49	3	7	0	0	0	2	3	0	0	1	20	3	0	.143	.189
Blanco, Lisandro	R-R	6-1	180	1-13-97	.111	.167	.095	26	81	7	9	3	0	1	6	17	0	1	0	36	1	1	.185	.265
Bossi, Aaron	R-R	5-11	205	10-22-93	.333	.364	.326	22	57	9	19	5	0	1	4	6	0	0	1	6	0	0	.474	.391
Cabrera, Oswaldo	R-R	5-10	145	3-1-99	.455	.333	.500	7	33	9	15	6	0	2	6	1	0	0	0	2	1	1	.818	.471
Corredera, Yeison	R-R	175	1-30-94	.207	.125	.224	40	140	15	29	4	1	2	13	9	1	0	1	30	3	2	.293	.258
Cuevas, Frederick	L-L	5-11	185	10-27-97	.231	.000	.261	9	26	3	6	1	0	0	1	1	0	0	0	5	0	1	.269	.259
2-team total (21 Yankees2)					.256	—	—	30	86	11	22	1	1	1	9	4	0	0	0	17	5	2	.326	.289
Emery, Brayan	B-R	6-3	185	3-15-98	.208	.263	.195	32	106	8	22	2	0	1	5	18	1	0	0	32	3	3	.255	.328
Graterol, Jesus	R-R	5-11	175	4-11-97	.263	.258	.265	37	133	17	35	6	1	0	9	8	4	0	1	33	3	4	.323	.322
Krill, Ryan	L-R	6-4	205	3-17-93	.500	.500	.500	1	4	2	2	1	0	1	3	1	0	0	0	0	0	0	1.500	.600
2-team total (17 Yankees2)					.379	—	—	18	58	13	22	5	0	3	15	9	2	0	1	11	1	0	.621	.471
Liranzo, Ozzie	B-R	5-8	182	1-26-93	.404	.429	.400	15	47	8	19	2	0	1	8	4	0	1	1	3	0	1	.511	.442
2-team total (20 Yankees2)					.323	—	—	35	96	10	31	6	0	1	17	7	0	1	3	6	0	1	.417	.358
Luaces, Edel	R-R	6-5	205	5-14-94	.241	.317	.218	50	174	23	42	11	6	5	26	23	3	0	0	79	4	3	.460	.340
Lynch, Tim	L-R	6-2	220	6-3-93	.286	.333	.277	18	56	9	16	7	1	1	9	10	1	0	0	8	0	0	.500	.403
Mateo, Algeni	R-R	5-9	170	8-1-95	.232	.250	.227	31	95	4	22	1	4	0	10	3	1	0	0	7	0	2	.295	.263
2-team total (4 Yankees2)					.231	—	—	35	108	5	25	4	1	0	12	5	1	0	0	9	0	3	.287	.272
Mendez, Erick	R-R	6-0	185	4-7-96	.296	.222	.313	26	98	15	29	10	1	3	26	9	3	0	0	31	2	2	.510	.373
Polonia, Jose	R-R	5-11	170	12-11-95	.205	.200	.207	23	78	4	16	1	0	0	4	2	0	0	0	12	4	0	.218	.225
2-team total (2 Yankees2)					.188	—	—	25	85	4	16	1	0	0	5	2	0	0	0	12	4	0	.200	.207
Robertson, Terrance	L-L	6-0	175	11-18-96	.258	.211	.279	22	62	22	16	2	2	0	5	18	0	0	0	18	10	3	.355	.425
2-team total (16 Yankees2)					.250	—	—	38	116	30	29	2	2	0	9	24	2	0	0	33	13	7	.302	.387
Rodriguez, Brayan	R-R	5-11	191	4-26-97	.222	.188	.234	27	63	3	14	4	0	0	4	2	2	0	0	18	0	0	.286	.269
Rodriguez, Yonauris	R-R	6-1	155	3-10-97	.176	.214	.165	44	131	8	23	5	1	0	6	5	1	1	0	32	5	3	.229	.212
Sands, Donny	R-R	6-2	190	5-16-96	.250	.000	.333	1	4	0	1	0	0	0	0	0	0	0	0	1	0	0	.250	.250
2-team total (13 Yankees2)					.269	—	—	14	52	3	14	3	0	0	3	1	1	0	0	4	1	0	.327	.296
Scott, Jordan	B-R	6-0	210	5-23-97	.209	.200	.211	46	163	19	34	5	1	5	17	18	5	1	1	40	9	5	.344	.305
Suarez, Ronaldo	R-R	5-10	165	8-30-97	.045	.000	.063	14	22	1	1	0	0	1	1	1	1	1	0	8	0	0	.091	.125
Urena, Pedro	R-R	6-1	195	6-1-95	.254	.444	.220	18	59	5	15	5	0	1	6	5	1	0	1	15	0	0	.390	.318
Wagner, Brandon	L-R	6-0	210	8-24-95	.283	.174	.313	29	106	16	30	7	1	5	17	12	2	0	0	18	0	3	.509	.367
Williams, Mason	L-R	6-1	185	8-21-91	.000	.000	.000	1	4	0	0	0	0	0	0	0	0	0	0	1	0	0	.000	.000

Pitching	B-T	HT	WT	DOB	W	L	ERA	G	GS	CG	SV	IP	H	R	ER	HR	BB	SO	AVG	vLH	vRH	K/9	BB/9
Alvarez, Daniel	R-R	6-3	228	6-28-96	5	1	1.74	11	9	0	0	57	51	18	11	0	13	48	.238	.240	.237	7.58	2.05
Brito, Jhony	R-R	6-2	160	2-17-98	1	3	5.59	4	4	0	0	19	25	13	12	0	1	14	.325	.313	.333	6.52	0.47
Burgos, Havid	L-L	6-0	186	8-6-94	1	2	7.98	13	0	0	0	15	19	14	13	5	14	15	.317	.267	.333	9.20	8.59
Cedeno, Moises	R-R	6-0	202	8-29-95	0	0	10.64	12	0	0	1	11	11	13	13	1	13	11	.262	.167	.300	9.00	10.64
Escorcia, Juan	R-R	6-1	161	5-16-96	1	3	6.29	10	2	0	0	34	42	28	24	3	14	26	.300	.289	.305	6.82	3.67
Espinal, Carlos	R-R	5-11	175	10-21-97	—														—	—	—		
Espinal, Raynel	R-R	6-3	199	10-6-93	0	4	4.26	6	4	0	0	32	35	21	15	2	0	30	.273	.268	.278	8.53	0.00
Garcia, Jairo	R-R	5-11	182	1-25-95	1	4	3.68	11	4	0	0	51	56	30	21	3	8	32	.276	.229	.301	5.61	1.40
Garcia, Rony	R-R	6-3	200	12-19-97	2	2	2.89	5	4	0	0	28	24	10	9	0	4	17	.238	.258	.229	5.46	1.29
Halbohn, Kyle	R-R	6-8	230	1-19-93	0	3	3.54	13	0	0	0	20	22	15	8	1	3	18	.272	.333	.246	7.97	1.33
Harvey, Joe	R-R	6-2	220	1-9-92	0	1	0.84	4	4	0	0	11	6	1	1	0	0	5	.167	.294	.053	4.22	0.00
2-team total (1 Yankees2)					0	1	0.71	5	5	0	0	13	6	1	1	0	0	5	—	—	—	3.55	0.00
Hodson, Chase	R-R	6-1	205	7-10-92	2	0	0.89	12	0	0	2	20	14	2	2	0	5	29	—	.258	.133	12.84	2.21
Holmes, Tim	R-R	6-2	200	10-16-93	0	0	0.59	14	0	0	0	15	14	1	1	0	6	15	.237	.375	.186	8.80	3.52
Lake, Deshorn	R-R	6-1	237	10-29-93	0	1	2.95	13	0	0	2	18	14	8	6	1	10	13	.212	.192	.225	6.38	4.91
Lane, Trevor	L-L	5-11	185	4-26-94	0	1	0.79	10	0	0	1	11	8	1	1	0	3	10	.200	.222	.194	7.94	2.38
Magallanes, Kelvin	R-R	6-1	201	7-15-94	0	4	6.42	11	7	0	0	34	36	31	24	0	18	27	.267	.255	.273	7.22	4.81
Marsh, Matt	R-R	6-3	190	7-10-91	0	0	2.35	3	0	0	1	8	4	3	2	0	1	8	.160	.143	.167	9.39	1.17
Martinez, Nolan	R-R	6-2	165	6-30-98	0	1	3.86	3	3	0	0	5	5	3	2	0	2	5	.261	.143	.385	3.86	5.14
Mendez, Bringnel	R-R	6-0	239	1-31-94	1	0	3.77	9	0	0	2	14	14	8	6	0	4	12	.280	.294	.273	7.53	2.51
2-team total (6 Yankees2)					2	0	4.30	15	0	0	3	23	27	13	11	0	7	18	—	—	—	7.04	2.74
O'Brien, Paddy	R-R	6-5	230	10-7-93	0	2	12.60	6	0	0	0	5	6	9	7	0	4	4	.286	.000	.333	7.20	7.20

Pitching

Pitching	B-T	HT	WT	DOB	W	L	ERA	G	GS	CG	SV	IP	H	R	ER	HR	BB	SO	AVG	vLH	vRH	K/9	BB/9
Ordaz, Rafael	R-R	6-6	235	2-17-95	0	0	0.00	1	0	0	0	1	0	0	0	0	0	1	.000	—	.000	9.00	0.00
Pena, Jose	R-R	6-0	190	3-22-91	0	0	0.00	1	0	0	0	1	1	1	0	0	0	2	.250	1.000	.000	18.00	0.00
2-team total (6 Yankees2)					0	0	1.93	7	0	0	0	9	6	3	2	1	2	13	—	—	—	12.54	1.93
Pomeroy, Curtiss	R-R	6-1	200	5-5-93	0	0	—	1	0	0	0	0	0	3	3	0	3	0	—	—	—	—	—
Rutckyj, Evan	R-L	6-5	225	1-31-92	0	0	1.50	5	3	0	0	6	4	2	1	0	3	9	.182	.000	.211	13.50	4.50
Taylor, Chad	R-R	6-0	180	8-29-90	0	0	2.25	3	3	0	0	4	3	1	1	0	1	4	.200	.143	.250	9.00	2.25
2-team total (3 Yankees2)					0	0	0.90	6	5	0	0	10	5	1	1	0	1	8	—	—	—	7.20	0.90
Yajure, Miguel	R-R	6-1	175	5-1-98	1	2	2.87	9	6	0	0	31	24	10	10	1	5	21	.211	.324	.163	6.03	1.44

Fielding

C: Bossi 9, Liranzo 2, Mateo 31, Rodriguez 27, Suarez 13. **1B:** Blanco 6, Krill 1, Liranzo 5, Lynch 12, Urena 14, Wagner 18. **2B:** Bossi 11, Corredera 6, Graterol 33, Polonia 6, Rodriguez 4, Wagner 2. **3B:** Baez 10, Corredera 27, Polonia 17, Rodriguez 2. **SS:** Baez 4, Cabrera 7, Corredera 7, Graterol 5, Rodriguez 34. **OF:** Amburgey 1, Blanco 15, Cuevas 9, Emery 24, Luaces 44, Mendez 20, Robertson 21, Scott 41, Wagner 1.

GCL YANKEES WEST   ROOKIE
GULF COAST LEAGUE

Batting	B-T	HT	WT	DOB	AVG	vLH	vRH	G	AB	R	H	2B	3B	HR	RBI	BB	HBP	SH	SF	SO	SB	CS	SLG	OBP
Alexander, Evan	L-L	6-2	175	2-26-98	.253	.227	.262	32	87	15	22	1	1	1	5	14	2	0	2	33	6	0	.322	.362
Amburgey, Trey	R-R	6-2	210	10-24-94	.231	—	.231	4	13	3	3	1	0	0	1	1	1	0	0	3	0	0	.308	.333
2-team total (1 Yankees1)					.188			5	16	3	3	1	0	0	1	1	1	0	0	4	0	0	.250	.278
Aparicio, Jesus	R-R	5-11	186	8-18-94	.000	.000	.000	8	15	0	0	0	0	0	1	1	1	0	1	6	0	0	.000	.111
Barrios, Daniel	R-R	5-11	183	4-18-95	.220	.294	.205	33	100	10	22	6	0	1	9	11	2	1	0	29	1	3	.310	.310
Burton, Joe	R-R	6-4	240	12-18-95	.238	.300	.226	36	126	20	30	1	0	2	11	10	2	0	0	48	1	1	.365	.304
Cabrera, Leobaldo	R-R	6-1	170	1-21-98	.196	.100	.221	43	143	13	28	1	0	1	11	11	2	1	1	32	3	4	.224	.261
Castillo, Diego	R-R	6-0	170	10-28-97	.267	.344	.248	44	165	14	44	7	0	1	8	14	3	0	2	21	5	3	.327	.332
Cuevas, Frederick	L-L	5-11	185	10-27-97	.267	.222	.286	21	60	8	16	0	1	1	8	3	0	0	0	12	5	1	.350	.302
2-team total (9 Yankees1)					.256			30	86	11	22	1	1	1	9	4	0	0	0	17	5	2	.326	.289
De Leon, Juan	R-R	6-2	185	9-13-97	.212	.000	.250	13	33	4	7	2	0	1	4	4	1	0	1	12	0	0	.364	.308
Flames, Miguel	R-R	6-2	210	9-14-97	.263	.188	.281	47	160	19	42	7	1	1	16	9	2	1	0	16	0	0	.338	.310
Gallardo, Carlos	R-R	5-10	160	1-26-97	.130	.091	.140	27	54	3	7	0	0	0	2	1	3	0	1	24	1	0	.130	.186
Garabito, Griffin	R-R	5-11	180	8-2-97	.182	.143	.194	36	121	7	22	5	0	0	7	6	3	1	0	31	6	3	.223	.238
Gomez, Nelson	R-R	6-1	220	10-8-97	.194	.186	.196	54	191	24	37	11	1	9	37	8	6	0	0	55	0	0	.403	.249
Krill, Ryan	L-R	6-4	205	3-17-93	.370	.500	.325	17	54	11	20	4	0	2	12	8	0	2	1	11	1	0	.556	.462
2-team total (1 Yankees1)					.379			18	58	13	22	5	0	3	15	9	2	0	1	11	1	0	.621	.471
Liranzo, Ozzie	B-R	5-8	182	1-26-93	.245	.200	.256	20	49	2	12	4	0	0	9	3	0	0	2	3	0	0	.327	.278
2-team total (15 Yankees1)					.323			35	96	10	31	6	0	1	17	7	0	1	3	6	0	1	.417	.358
Lopez, Jason	R-R	5-10	160	3-16-98	.192	.000	.294	11	26	2	5	1	0	1	7	1	2	0	1	8	1	0	.346	.267
Mateo, Algeni	R-R	5-9	170	8-1-95	.231	.000	.250	14	13	1	3	0	0	0	2	2	0	0	2	0	1	.231	.333
2-team total (31 Yankees1)					.231			35	108	5	25	4	1	0	12	5	1	0	0	9	0	3	.287	.272
Olivares, Pablo	R-R	6-0	160	1-27-98	.285	.289	.283	47	158	26	45	13	2	0	15	10	1	2	2	25	7	2	.392	.378
Perez, Danienger	R-R	5-10	155	11-6-96	.271	.333	.250	16	59	8	16	7	1	0	7	1	0	2	0	20	4	1	.424	.283
Polonia, Jose	R-R	5-11	170	12-11-95	.000	—	.000	2	7	0	0	0	0	0	0	0	0	0	0	0	0	0	.000	.000
2-team total (23 Yankees1)					.188			25	85	4	16	1	0	0	5	2	0	0	0	12	4	0	.200	.207
Robertson, Terrance	L-L	6-0	175	11-18-96	.241	.077	.293	16	54	8	13	0	0	0	4	6	2	0	0	15	3	4	.241	.339
2-team total (22 Yankees1)					.250			38	116	30	29	2	2	0	9	24	2	0	0	33	13	7	.302	.387
Rutherford, Blake	L-R	6-3	195	5-2-97	.240	.333	.227	8	25	3	6	1	0	1	3	4	0	0	1	6	0	0	.400	.333
Sands, Donny	R-R	6-2	190	5-16-96	.271	.267	.273	13	48	3	13	3	0	0	3	1	1	0	0	3	1	0	.333	.300
2-team total (1 Yankees1)					.269			14	52	3	14	3	0	0	3	1	1	0	0	4	1	0	.327	.296
Vazquez, Chucky	R-R	6-1	200	9-24-93	.368	.000	.412	17	19	5	7	2	0	1	4	2	0	0	4	0	0	.474	.520

Pitching	B-T	HT	WT	DOB	W	L	ERA	G	GS	CG	SV	IP	H	R	ER	HR	BB	SO	AVG	vLH	vRH	K/9	BB/9
Aybar, Julian	R-R	6-1	188	2-13-92	2	1	3.00	5	3	0	1	21	21	10	7	0	6	18	.256	.200	.274	7.71	2.57
Bryson, Woody	R-L	6-3	201	2-19-93	1	0	3.60	10	0	0	0	10	7	5	4	0	6	16	.179	.364	.107	14.40	5.40
Garcia, Leonardo	R-R	6-0	160	12-31-93	0	2	6.46	11	0	0	2	24	23	23	17	2	15	19	.253	.259	.25	7.23	5.70
Harvey, Joe	R-R	6-2	220	1-9-92	0	0	0.00	1	0	0	0	2	0	0	0	0	0	0	.000	.000	.000	0.00	0.00
2-team total (4 Yankees1)					0	1	0.71	5	0	0	0	13	6	1	1	0	0	5	—	—	—	3.55	0.00
Hernandez, Tony	L-L	6-2	215	8-8-96	2	2	5.73	11	6	0	0	33	39	25	21	3	12	17	.287	.333	.264	4.64	3.27
Jones, Connor	R-L	6-2	195	11-17-94	0	1	2.31	4	4	0	0	12	11	3	3	0	3	13	.250	.154	.29	10.03	2.31
Keller, Brian	R-R	6-3	170	6-21-94	0	0	0.00	7	0	0	1	20	11	1	0	0	1	23	.159	.138	.175	10.35	0.45
Lail, Brady	R-R	6-2	205	8-9-93	0	0	0.00	1	0	0	0	3	2	0	0	0	0	3	.273	.286	.250	0.00	0.00
Mendez, Brignel	R-R	6-0	239	1-31-94	1	0	5.19	6	0	0	1	9	13	5	5	0	3	6	.406	.200	.500	6.23	3.12
2-team total (9 Yankees1)					2	0	4.30	13	0	0	3	23	27	13	11	0	7	18	—	—	—	7.04	2.74
Montas, Kenlly	R-R	6-0	187	5-31-96	1	2	5.87	4	3	0	0	15	12	11	10	1	5	17	.222	.143	.25	9.98	2.93
Ovalles, Jordan	R-R	6-1	193	1-17-94	5	0	6.04	13	0	0	1	25	31	17	17	3	7	22	.304	.314	.294	7.82	2.49
Padilla, Isaac	R-R	6-4	277	6-14-96	1	1	2.10	6	3	0	1	26	22	7	6	3	8	23	.232	.146	.296	8.06	2.81
Pena, Jose	R-R	6-0	190	3-22-91	0	0	2.16	6	0	0	0	8	5	2	2	1	2	11	.167	.000	.238	11.88	2.16
2-team total (1 Yankees1)					0	0	1.93	7	0	0	0	9	6	3	2	1	2	13	—	—	—	12.54	1.93
Pujols, Jose	R-R	6-6	183	11-19-92	3	1	1.17	14	0	0	3	23	12	4	3	0	13	25	.154	.182	.143	9.78	5.09
Ramirez, Jean	R-R	6-4	180	3-1-93	1	1	4.82	4	0	0	0	9	9	6	5	1	3	10	.237	.154	.28	9.64	2.89
Ramos, Daniel	R-R	5-11	184	3-6-95	0	3	5.40	7	6	0	0	18	32	14	11	0	9	13	.395	.385	.400	6.38	4.42
Rosario, Alexander	R-R	6-3	185	1-19-95	0	4	3.88	11	8	0	0	46	62	32	20	2	6	32	.320	.313	.327	6.22	1.17
Ruth, Eric	R-R	6-0	195	9-26-90	0	0	3.86	1	1	0	0	2	1	0	0	0	2	2	.222	.000	.400	7.71	0.00
Severino, Anderson	L-L	5-10	165	9-17-94	1	4	6.29	11	8	0	0	49	61	37	34	3	21	34	.311	.326	.307	6.29	3.88
Stenhouse, Brandon	R-R	6-0	179	9-19-96	1	0	1.86	11	0	0	0	19	11	7	4	1	7	20	.155	.037	.227	9.31	3.26

Pitching	B-T	HT	WT	DOB	W	L	ERA	G	GS	CG	SV	IP	H	R	ER	HR	BB	SO	AVG	vLH	vRH	K/9	BB/9
Strzalka, Artur	R-L	5-11	180	8-19-95	2	2	5.40	11	0	0	0	17	14	13	10	0	17	12	.233	.200	.244	6.48	9.18
Tavares, Orby	L-L	6-4	278	9-16-94	1	2	8.31	8	0	0	2	13	16	13	12	4	5	15	.296	.267	.308	10.38	3.46
Taylor, Chad	R-R	6-0	180	8-29-90	0	0	0.00	3	2	0	0	6	2	0	0	0	0	4	.105	.100	.111	6.00	0.00
2-team total (3 Yankees1)					0	0	0.90	6	5	0	0	10	5	1	1	0	1	8	—	—	—	7.20	0.90
Troya, Gilmael	R-R	6-0	196	4-4-97	1	5	3.78	12	10	0	0	50	49	34	21	6	11	39	.249	.234	.258	7.02	1.98

Fielding

C: Aparicio 8, Flames 10, Gallardo 27, Liranzo 8, Lopez 11, Mateo 4, Sands 6, Vazquez 12. **1B:** Barrios 6, Flames 36, Krill 14, Liranzo 6, Vazquez 3.
2B: Barrios 16, Garabito 36, Perez 8, Polonia 1. **3B:** Barrios 11, Flames 1, Gomez 49, Polonia 1. **SS:** Barrios 6, Castillo 44, Perez 8. **OF:** Alexander 29, Amburgey 2, Burton 15, Cabrera 43, Cuevas 20, De Leon 10, Olivares 44, Robertson 13, Rutherford 6.

DSL YANKEES   ROOKIE
DOMINICAN SUMMER LEAGUE

Batting	B-T	HT	WT	DOB	AVG	vLH	vRH	G	AB	R	H	2B	3B	HR	RBI	BB	HBP	SH	SF	SO	SB	CS	SLG	OBP
Alvarez, Nelson	L-L	6-3	210	3-10-96	.290	.356	.271	56	200	37	58	12	2	3	27	34	4	0	1	38	1	2	.415	.402
Amundaray, Jonathan	R-R	6-2	215	5-11-98	.269	.409	.232	29	104	11	28	7	0	2	18	5	3	0	0	21	0	1	.394	.321
Arias, Antonio	R-R	6-2	180	6-12-98	.239	.086	.275	51	184	24	44	5	0	0	12	26	6	1	1	39	5	3	.266	.350
Bastidas, Jesus	R-R	5-10	145	9-14-98	.247	.250	.246	57	235	35	58	9	1	1	22	19	4	1	2	36	10	7	.306	.312
Cabrera, Oswaldo	R-R	5-10	145	3-1-99	.441	.600	.396	19	68	15	30	5	3	1	12	5	3	1	2	6	2	1	.647	.487
Chaparro, Andres	R-R	6-1	200	5-4-99	.238	.289	.224	50	185	25	44	9	5	0	26	25	1	0	2	43	2	2	.341	.329
Corredera, Yeison	R-R	5-11	175	1-30-94	.000	—	.000	1	1	0	0	0	0	0	0	0	0	0	0	0	0	0	.000	.000
De La Cruz, Samuel	R-R	5-11	180	10-18-97	.235	.231	.235	27	81	5	19	2	0	0	4	15	3	0	0	25	1	0	.259	.374
Delgado, Jonaikel	R-R	6-0	171	9-12-97	.243	.188	.259	33	74	16	18	2	0	0	5	9	5	0	1	14	10	0	.270	.360
Diaz, Fernando	R-R	6-0	185	10-14-94	.213	.211	.214	38	89	14	19	1	0	1	9	25	7	0	0	15	7	0	.258	.421
Duran, Diego	L-R	5-10	145	2-14-98	.214	.263	.200	48	168	21	36	2	2	1	21	16	4	2	3	13	11	2	.268	.293
Espinosa, Roberto	R-R	5-10	170	12-28-98	.242	.100	.278	31	99	13	24	3	1	1	17	4	7	1	5	16	0	1	.323	.304
Fernandez, Andres	R-R	6-1	165	12-10-98	.226	.138	.246	46	155	14	35	5	1	0	18	6	1	5	3	37	3	3	.271	.321
Gallardo, Carlos	R-R	5-10	160	1-26-97	.222	.000	.286	6	18	4	4	1	0	0	3	2	1	0	1	4	0	0	.278	.318
Graterol, Jesus	R-R	5-11	175	4-11-97	.214	.182	.222	16	56	10	12	2	2	0	6	3	1	1	0	8	3	2	.321	.274
Jimenez, Brayan	R-R	6-0	140	5-31-99	.230	.097	.265	40	148	23	34	3	2	0	15	22	3	0	0	30	4	3	.277	.341
Lobo, Moises	R-R	5-10	200	6-24-97	.213	.154	.235	17	47	4	10	2	0	1	3	3	1	0	0	13	0	0	.319	.275
Maneiro, Kleiber	R-R	5-10	155	2-24-97	.281	.227	.299	33	89	14	25	5	0	0	5	2	1	0	0	17	7	0	.337	.304
Martinez, Luis	R-R	5-11	170	11-24-98	.228	.200	.239	46	149	29	34	8	5	1	21	13	7	0	1	52	5	1	.369	.318
Medina, Brallan	R-R	5-10	180	6-9-97	.155	.133	.159	36	84	8	13	4	0	0	13	11	1	0	0	20	3	0	.202	.276
Mendez, Borinquen	R-R	5-11	165	2-1-98	.224	.289	.205	50	170	33	38	0	1	0	11	27	5	3	2	36	27	5	.235	.343
Moreno, Raymundo	R-R	6-1	185	3-9-98	.284	.243	.293	56	204	34	58	10	0	0	21	25	11	0	7	28	17	3	.333	.381
Moronta, Jhon	R-R	6-3	180	5-17-99	.267	.256	.270	52	165	20	44	8	1	0	15	30	3	0	1	37	2	2	.327	.387
Mota, Sandy	R-R	6-0	170	9-25-96	.251	.344	.231	56	179	24	45	3	3	2	21	23	6	1	2	48	15	5	.335	.352
Narvaez, Carlos	R-R	6-0	190	11-26-98	.338	.379	.327	35	133	17	45	9	1	1	24	8	3	0	0	8	0	0	.444	.389
Pena, Enrique	R-R	5-10	170	2-23-99	.137	.091	.145	31	73	8	10	1	0	0	3	12	2	0	0	26	5	3	.151	.276
Pena, Ysaac	L-R	5-9	180	6-19-98	.292	.217	.304	45	161	18	47	9	2	1	25	8	3	0	3	30	0	0	.391	.331
Polonia, Jose	R-R	5-11	170	12-11-95	.351	.167	.400	19	57	7	20	2	0	0	11	9	1	1	0	3	4	1	.386	.448
Pujols, Alfred	R-R	6-2	10	11-5-98	.167	.333	.133	5	18	2	3	1	0	0	0	1	0	0	0	6	0	0	.222	.211
Rodriguez, Ezequiel	R-R	6-0	175	6-22-96	.155	.136	.160	41	116	15	18	3	1	3	10	14	7	0	1	37	3	0	.276	.283
Rodriguez, Meure	R-R	6-2	200	5-20-99	.185	.227	.174	37	108	14	20	2	0	0	7	19	1	0	2	34	2	1	.204	.303
Rojas, Simon	R-R	5-10	160	1-20-98	.250	.176	.271	49	152	22	38	4	0	0	14	24	2	2	0	32	5	0	.276	.360
Sanchez, Luis	R-R	5-11	160	5-5-97	.238	.111	.274	38	122	16	29	7	0	1	18	15	3	0	0	28	2	1	.320	.336
Tatis, Carlos	R-R	6-3	185	12-19-96	.272	.233	.285	45	173	16	47	12	4	1	33	15	2	0	1	31	1	1	.405	.335
Torres, Saul	R-R	6-2	190	2-19-99	.154	.217	.119	19	65	2	10	0	0	2	0	5	2	2	0	19	0	0	.215	.203
Unda, Dario	L-L	5-11	168	5-24-96	.322	.324	.322	58	205	35	66	17	1	4	29	25	2	0	4	30	7	4	.473	.394
Vergel, David	R-R	6-0	165	1-13-97	.345	.409	.330	37	113	21	39	9	0	1	15	10	13	2	0	10	1	0	.451	.456

Pitching	B-T	HT	WT	DOB	W	L	ERA	G	GS	CG	SV	IP	H	R	ER	HR	BB	SO	AVG	vLH	vRH	K/9	BB/9
Alcantara, Brayan	R-R	6-1	170	8-6-93	3	6	2.63	16	0	0	1	27	29	10	8	0	6	18	.276	.194	.311	5.93	1.98
Barrios, Pedro	R-R	6-1	155	3-27-99	1	4	1.76	10	10	0	0	46	37	13	9	1	14	28	.222	.227	.217	5.48	2.74
Brito, Jhony	R-R	6-2	160	2-17-98	0	3	6.81	9	9	0	0	36	47	32	27	4	8	34	.318	.333	.314	8.58	2.02
Caceres, Wellington	R-R	5-11	185	1-29-96	6	3	3.91	14	7	0	1	53	52	26	23	4	11	44	.260	.333	.233	7.47	1.87
Cadette, Luis	L-L	6-3	175	8-26-95	0	0	3.18	13	0	0	1	17	15	10	6	1	11	9	.238	.308	.220	4.76	5.82
Campusano, Arcadio	R-R	6-6	206	12-21-97	3	4	6.14	13	8	0	0	51	59	42	35	3	23	39	.289	.271	.297	6.84	4.03
Cedeno, Moises	R-R	6-0	202	8-29-95	0	1	1.59	3	0	0	0	6	3	1	1	0	2	5	.167	.200	.154	7.94	3.18
Cortez, Rodrigo	R-R	6-1	174	1-11-97	0	0	2.45	3	3	0	0	4	3	1	1	0	3	1	.231	.286	.167	2.45	7.36
Diaz, Anderson	L-L	6-2	190	12-19-93	0	0	4.00	5	0	0	0	9	10	5	4	1	3	6	.263	.333	.250	6.00	3.00
Diaz, Deivi	L-L	6-0	160	6-9-99	3	3	4.06	14	2	0	0	38	43	23	17	0	32	26	.307	.333	.304	6.21	7.65
Espinal, Raynel	R-R	6-3	199	10-6-93	2	3	3.60	4	4	0	0	15	22	10	6	0	3	11	.344	.321	.361	6.60	1.80
Garcia, David	R-R	5-9	140	5-19-99	1	5	2.61	12	12	0	0	48	23	17	14	1	32	61	.149	.163	.144	11.36	5.96
Garcia, Rodrigo	R-R	6-2	185	3-13-99	0	0	0.00	1	1	0	0	3	1	0	0	0	0	0	.100	.333	.000	0.00	0.00
Garcia, Rony	R-R	6-3	200	12-19-97	1	3	1.88	9	9	0	0	43	35	20	9	1	9	39	.208	.295	.177	8.16	1.88
Gonzalez, Gabriel	R-R	5-11	150	10-13-98	4	5	4.99	13	2	0	0	40	30	26	22	0	36	42	.219	.286	.196	9.53	8.17
Herrera, Argelis	L-L	6-5	165	10-17-98	0	1	6.89	14	8	0	1	31	25	29	24	0	38	41	.212	.071	.256	11.78	10.91
Jaime, Leo	R-R	5-11	200	8-24-97	0	1	6.23	7	0	0	0	13	13	11	9	1	7	11	.277	.250	.290	7.62	4.85
Marten, Daniel	R-R	6-0	165	5-7-97	2	3	4.21	13	3	0	0	47	49	27	22	3	17	37	.278	.313	.271	7.09	3.26
McCoy, Corby	L-L	6-3	180	10-5-95	3	1	3.43	16	0	0	2	21	18	10	8	0	15	29	—	—	—	12.43	6.43
Medina, Luis	R-R	6-1	155	5-3-99	0	0	1.93	3	3	0	0	5	2	1	1	0	4	4	.118	.200	.111	7.71	7.71
Mejias, Alex	R-R	6-0	165	11-26-96	3	1	2.86	12	6	0	0	50	48	19	16	2	21	33	.259	.266	.256	5.90	3.75

Pitching	B-T	HT	WT	DOB	W	L	ERA	G	GS	CG	SV	IP	H	R	ER	HR	BB	SO	AVG	vLH	vRH	K/9	BB/9
Mendez, Bringnel	R-R	6-0	239	1-31-94	0	0	2.70	2	0	0	1	3	2	1	1	0	2	5	.167	.333	.111	13.50	5.40
Montas, Kenlly	R-R	6-0	187	5-31-96	4	2	3.15	10	0	0	1	34	29	22	12	1	16	32	.215	.184	.233	8.39	4.19
Moreno, Heiner	L-L	6-0	181	7-24-98	2	1	6.37	12	5	0	1	30	35	28	21	0	33	32	.315	.500	.289	9.71	10.01
Munoz, Jhonatan	R-R	6-0	180	8-10-99	3	3	3.50	15	9	0	0	54	44	22	21	2	21	57	.214	.238	.203	9.50	3.50
Naranjo, Edintson	L-L	5-11	170	11-6-96	0	0	0.00	1	1	0	0	1	1	0	0	0	0	1	.250	—	.250	9.00	0.00
Ojeda, Luis	R-R	5-11	180	1-10-97	1	0	7.15	11	5	0	0	39	47	33	31	3	12	32	.309	.426	.245	7.38	2.77
Padilla, Isaac	R-R	6-4	277	6-14-96	3	1	1.89	4	1	0	0	19	8	7	4	0	5	23	.123	.154	.103	10.89	2.37
Paredes, Edward	R-R	6-0	160	1-7-99	1	2	3.69	11	2	0	0	32	36	24	13	2	12	22	.281	.279	.282	6.25	3.41
Peguero, Elvis	R-R	6-3	185	3-20-97	2	7	4.39	14	9	0	0	53	50	41	26	3	27	43	.238	.250	.231	7.26	4.56
Peluso, Eduardo	L-L	6-0	175	8-29-98	0	0	5.21	14	0	0	0	19	16	13	11	0	11	21	.239	.222	.241	9.95	5.21
Peralta, Jean	R-R	6-1	170	1-7-94	0	0	3.97	6	0	0	0	11	10	10	5	0	4	5	.244	.333	.219	3.97	3.18
Polanco, Jean	R-R	5-11	175	4-3-97	2	0	2.51	9	0	0	1	14	12	5	4	0	8	17	.231	.214	.237	10.67	5.02
Ramirez, Jean	R-R	6-4	180	3-1-93	1	0	0.00	1	0	0	0	5	1	0	0	0	4	1	.071	.000	.100	1.80	7.20
Reynoso, Anderson	R-R	6-2	180	11-25-97	2	4	4.53	14	5	0	2	54	56	34	27	4	14	52	.264	.258	.267	8.72	2.35
Rijo, Luis	R-R	5-11	165	9-6-98	1	2	1.67	9	6	0	0	32	30	10	6	2	2	30	.240	.262	.229	8.35	0.56
Rodriguez, Carlos	R-R	6-0	155	12-13-98	0	2	9.00	5	0	0	0	11	22	16	11	0	1	9	.431	.429	.432	7.36	0.82
Rodriguez, Edison	R-R	6-1	180	7-6-92	0	0	3.98	11	0	0	1	20	22	21	9	0	9	19	.244	.214	.258	8.41	3.98
Rodriguez, Juan	R-R	6-5	228	9-20-96	2	0	4.09	15	0	0	0	22	22	15	10	1	18	19	.262	.292	.250	7.77	7.36
Rodriguez, Luis	R-R	6-4	190	10-10-96	1	1	3.77	10	0	0	2	14	12	7	6	0	6	11	.235	.214	.243	6.91	3.77
Rojas, Adonny	R-R	6-0	170	1-3-96	0	0	0.00	1	0	0	0	1	0	0	0	0	1	4	.000	—	.000	27.00	6.75
Rosario, Alexander	R-R	6-3	185	1-19-95	0	0	0.69	3	2	0	0	13	8	1	1	0	3	8	.174	.091	.200	5.54	2.08
Solano, Jose	R-R	6-0	180	1-21-94	3	1	1.00	17	0	0	8	27	21	6	3	1	5	16	.223	.238	.219	5.33	1.67
Soto, Wandy	R-R	6-0	175	1-27-96	0	1	10.45	8	0	0	0	10	16	12	12	1	12	6	—	—	—	5.23	10.45
Tavares, Orby	L-L	6-4	278	9-16-94	0	0	4.09	6	0	0	1	11	6	5	5	0	10	18	—	—	—	14.73	8.18
Thomas, Luigence	R-R	6-3	160	10-12-94	2	3	3.57	17	0	0	2	23	24	14	9	0	10	22	.255	.161	.302	8.74	3.97
Vizcaino, Alexander	R-R	6-2	160	5-22-97	0	5	4.89	11	6	0	0	35	40	27	19	4	13	27	.290	.227	.302	6.94	3.34

Fielding

C: De La Cruz 18, Espinosa 13, Gallardo 6, Lobo 5, Narvaez 29, Pena 20, Rodriguez 36, Sanchez 2, Torres 16, Vergel 14. **1B:** Alvarez 52, De La Cruz 2, Polonia 2, Rodriguez 8, Sanchez 28, Tatis 38, Vergel 19. **2B:** Cabrera 2, Duran 44, Graterol 12, Jimenez 22, Maneiro 4, Medina 23, Mendez 16, Mota 13, Pena 19, Polonia 1. **3B:** Chaparro 50, Corredera 1, Delgado 1, Duran 1, Graterol 2, Maneiro 11, Medina 7, Mota 32, Pena 1, Polonia 9, Pujols 5, Rodriguez 32. **SS:** Bastidas 55, Cabrera 14, Graterol 1, Jimenez 14, Maneiro 2, Mendez 34, Mota 6, Pena 5, Torrealba 20. **OF:** Amundaray 26, Arias 51, Delgado 19, Diaz 37, Fernandez 44, Maneiro 9, Martinez 44, Moreno 56, Moronta 47, Mota 4, Polonia 5, Rodriguez 1, Rojas 48, Tatis 2, Unda 50.

Oakland Athletics

SEASON IN A SENTENCE: With ace Sonny Gray enduring a lost season and the roster enduring an Oakland-record 27 disabled-list stints, the Athletics traded off most of the remaining members of its 2012-14 playoff run and finished in last place in the American League West.

HIGH POINT: Acquired in Febuary for prospects Bubba Derby and Jacob Nottingham, outfielder Khris Davis became the first A's hitter to reach 40 home runs in a season since Jason Giambi in 2000. He had five multi-homer games, including three on May 17 in an 8-5 win against the Rangers.

LOW POINT: Oakland showed it wasn't ready for prime time in a six-game road trip in early May to Baltimore and Boston. In the last four games of the 1-5 trip, Oakland gave up 51 runs, including Gray blowing a 4-1 lead and giving up five doubles among his eight hits and seven runs in 3.2 innings. Another low point was the late-August pre-game fight between veterans Danny Valencia and Billy Butler that resulted in Butler having a concussion; he was released less than a month later.

NOTABLE ROOKIES: The A's relied on veterans early before giving rookies more playing time in the second half. Ryon Healy made the Futures Game in the first half, then hit a 480-foot homer while batting .305/.337/.524 with 13 bombs as the primary third baseman in the second half. Lefty Sean Manaea wound up second on the team in starts and innings pitched after making his debut in late April. Righty Daniel Mengden (2-9, 6.50) had less success in his rookie season.

KEY TRANSACTIONS: The A's got a strong return for their late-July trade with the Dodgers, sending outfielder Josh Reddick and lefty Rich Hill to L.A. for righthanders Jharel Cotton, Frankie Montas and 2014 first-round pick Grant Holmes. Cotton and Montas should be part of next season's staff. The A's also traded Coco Crisp and lefty Marc Rzepczynski in late August, getting prospects back in lefty Colt Hynes and second baseman Max Schrock.

DOWN ON THE FARM: A's domestic affiliates posted a .488 winning percentage, with Double-A Midland winning the Texas League title with an intriguing playoff roster that included prospects such as Schrock, third baseman Yairo Munoz and 2015 first-rounder Richie Martin at shortstop. Third baseman Matt Chapman, a 2014 first-rounder who spent most of the year at Midland, finished third in the minors with 36 home runs.

OPENING DAY PAYROLL: $86,806,234 (24th)

PLAYERS OF THE YEAR

MAJOR LEAGUE	MINOR LEAGUE
Khris Davis	**Ryon Healy**
of	3b/1b
.247/.307/.524	(Double-A/Triple-A)
42 HR, 101 RBI	.326/.382/.558
3rd in AL in HR	14 HR, 64 RBI

ORGANIZATION LEADERS

BATTING   *Minimum 250 AB

MAJORS

*	AVG	Danny Valencia	.287
*	OPS	Khris Davis	.831
	HR	Khris Davis	42
	RBI	Khris Davis	102

MINORS

*	AVG	James Harris, Stockton, Midland	.297
*	OBP	Beau Taylor, Midland	.383
*	SLG	Matt Chapman, Midland, Nashville	.519
*	OPS	Matt Chapman, Midland, Nashville	.847
	R	Matt Chapman, Midland, Nashville	92
	H	James Harris, Stockton, Midland	157
	TB	Matt Chapman, Midland, Nashville	267
	2B	Trent Gilbert, Beloit	35
	3B	Justin Higley, Beloit, Stockton	9
		Joey Wendle, Nashville	9
	HR	Matt Chapman, Midland, Nashville	36
	RBI	Matt Chapman, Midland, Nashville	96
	BB	Viosergy Rosa, Midland	74
	SO	Matt Chapman, Midland, Nashville	173
	SB	Franklin Barreto, Midland, Nashville	30

PITCHING   #Minimum 75 IP

MAJORS

	W	Kendall Graveman	10
#	ERA	Kendall Graveman	4.11
	SO	Sean Manaea	124
	SV	Ryan Madson	30

MINORS

	W	Dillon Overton, Nashville	13
	L	Casey Meisner, Stockton	14
#	ERA	Evan Manarino, Beloit, Stockton	1.98
	G	Ryan Brasier, Nashville	46
		Aaron Kurcz, Midland, Nashville	46
		Jared Lyons, Beloit, Stockton	46
	GS	Daniel Gossett, Stockton, Midland, Nashville	27
	SV	Bobby Wahl, Stockton, Midland, Nashville	14
	IP	James Naile, Nashville, Beloit, Stockton, Midland	157
	BB	Casey Meisner, Stockton	59
	SO	Daniel Gossett, Stockton, Midland, Nashville	151
#	AVG	Daniel Gossett, Stockton, Midland, Nashville	.221

General Manager: David Forst. **Farm Director:** Keith Lieppman. **Scouting Director:** Eric Kubota.

Class	Team	League	W	L	PCT	Finish	Manager
Majors	Oakland Athletics	American	69	93	.426	13th (15)	Bob Melvin
Triple-A	Nashville Sounds	Pacific Coast	83	59	.585	1st (16)	Steve Scarsone
Double-A	Midland RockHounds	Texas	78	62	.557	2nd (8)	Ryan Christenson
High A	Stockton Ports	California	60	80	.429	t-8th (10)	Rick Magnante
Low A	Beloit Snappers	Midwest	59	80	.424	15th (16)	Fran Riordan
Short season	Vermont Lake Monsters	New York-Penn	28	48	.368	13th (14)	Aaron Nieckula
Rookie	Athletics	Arizona	29	24	.547	6th (14)	Webster Garrison
Overall 2016 Minor League Record			337	353	.488	18th (30)	

ORGANIZATION STATISTICS

OAKLAND ATHLETICS
AMERICAN LEAGUE

Batting	B-T	HT	WT	DOB	AVG	vLH	vRH	G	AB	R	H	2B	3B	HR	RBI	BB	HBP	SH	SF	SO	SB	CS	SLG	OBP
Alcantara, Arismendy	B-R	5-10	170	10-29-91	.211	.167	.231	16	19	2	4	1	0	0	2	0	0	0	0	8	3	3	.263	.211
Alonso, Yonder	L-R	6-1	230	4-8-87	.253	.227	.257	156	482	52	122	34	0	7	56	45	1	0	4	74	3	1	.367	.316
Burns, Billy	B-R	5-9	170	8-30-89	.234	.258	.226	73	274	32	64	11	4	0	12	10	4	3	1	30	14	3	.303	.270
2-team total (24 Kansas City)					.235	—	—	97	311	39	73	11	4	0	13	10	6	3	2	37	17	5	.296	.271
Butler, Billy	R-R	6-0	260	4-18-86	.276	.262	.288	85	221	24	61	16	0	4	31	19	0	0	2	34	0	0	.403	.331
2-team total (12 New York)					.284	—	—	97	250	27	71	18	0	5	35	21	0	0	3	42	0	0	.416	.336
Canha, Mark	R-R	6-2	210	2-15-89	.122	.158	.091	16	41	4	5	0	0	3	6	0	1	1	1	20	0	1	.341	.140
Coghlan, Chris	L-R	6-0	195	6-18-85	.146	.059	.156	51	158	14	23	5	0	5	14	13	1	0	0	47	1	1	.272	.215
Crisp, Coco	B-R	5-10	185	11-1-79	.234	.217	.239	102	393	45	92	24	4	11	47	37	0	2	2	65	7	5	.399	.299
2-team total (20 Cleveland)					.231	—	—	122	446	54	103	27	4	13	55	46	0	4	2	78	10	5	.397	.302
Davis, Khris	R-R	5-10	195	12-21-87	.247	.267	.241	150	555	85	137	24	2	42	102	42	8	0	5	166	1	2	.524	.307
Eibner, Brett	R-R	6-4	225	12-2-88	.165	.143	.183	44	109	10	18	4	1	3	12	13	0	0	1	27	0	2	.303	.252
2-team total (26 Kansas City)					.193	—	—	70	187	21	36	10	1	6	22	19	0	1	1	50	0	2	.353	.266
Healy, Ryon	R-R	6-5	225	1-10-92	.305	.313	.302	72	269	36	82	20	0	13	37	12	1	1	0	60	0	0	.524	.337
Ladendorf, Tyler	R-R	5-11	195	3-7-88	.083	.000	.182	44	48	6	4	0	0	0	1	1	0	1	0	13	2	0	.083	.102
Lambo, Andrew	L-L	6-3	220	8-11-88	.000	—	.000	1	1	0	0	0	0	0	0	0	0	0	0	0	0	0	.000	.000
Lowrie, Jed	B-R	6-0	180	4-17-84	.263	.298	.252	87	338	30	89	12	1	2	27	26	1	0	4	65	0	0	.322	.314
Maxwell, Bruce	L-R	6-1	250	12-20-90	.283	.200	.306	33	92	8	26	6	1	1	14	8	0	0	1	24	0	0	.402	.337
McBride, Matt	R-R	6-2	215	5-23-85	.209	.269	.118	20	43	4	9	3	0	0	2	1	0	0	0	10	0	0	.279	.227
Muncy, Max	L-R	6-0	210	8-25-90	.186	.200	.185	51	113	13	21	2	0	2	8	20	0	0	4	20	0	0	.257	.308
Nunez, Renato	R-R	6-1	220	4-4-94	.133	.167	.000	9	15	0	2	0	0	0	1	0	0	0	0	3	0	0	.133	.133
Olson, Matt	L-R	6-5	230	3-29-94	.095	.000	.111	11	21	3	2	1	0	0	0	7	0	0	0	4	0	0	.143	.321
Phegley, Josh	R-R	5-10	230	2-12-88	.256	.250	.262	25	78	11	20	6	0	1	10	5	2	0	1	13	0	0	.372	.314
Pinder, Chad	R-R	6-2	195	3-29-92	.235	.286	.174	22	51	4	12	4	0	1	4	3	0	0	1	14	0	0	.373	.273
Reddick, Josh	L-R	6-2	195	2-19-87	.296	.172	.341	68	243	33	72	11	1	8	28	28	0	0	1	34	5	0	.449	.368
Semien, Marcus	R-R	6-0	195	9-17-90	.238	.257	.231	159	568	72	135	27	2	27	75	51	0	1	1	139	10	2	.435	.300
Smolinski, Jake	R-R	5-11	205	2-9-89	.238	.276	.216	99	290	28	69	6	2	7	27	19	7	1	2	44	1	2	.345	.299
Valencia, Danny	R-R	6-2	210	9-19-84	.287	.318	.275	130	471	72	135	22	1	17	51	41	3	0	2	115	1	1	.446	.346
Vogt, Stephen	L-R	6-0	225	11-1-84	.251	.196	.264	137	490	54	123	30	2	14	56	35	4	0	3	83	0	0	.406	.305
Wendle, Joey	L-R	6-1	190	4-26-90	.260	.333	.247	28	96	11	25	5	1	0	1	6	0	0	2	16	2	0	.302	.298

Pitching	B-T	HT	WT	DOB	W	L	ERA	G	GS	CG	SV	IP	H	R	ER	HR	BB	SO	AVG	vLH	vRH	K/9	BB/9
Alcantara, Raul	R-R	6-4	220	12-4-92	1	3	7.25	5	5	0	0	22	31	18	18	9	4	14	.333	.306	.364	5.64	1.61
Axford, John	R-R	6-5	220	4-1-83	6	4	3.97	68	0	0	3	66	65	30	29	6	30	60	.258	.256	.259	8.22	4.11
Bassitt, Chris	R-R	6-5	220	2-22-89	0	2	6.11	5	5	0	0	28	35	20	19	5	14	23	.294	.210	.386	7.39	4.50
Cotton, Jharel	R-R	5-11	195	1-19-92	2	0	2.15	5	5	0	0	29	20	10	7	4	4	23	.185	.146	.217	7.06	1.23
Coulombe, Daniel	L-L	5-10	190	10-26-89	3	1	4.53	35	0	0	0	48	37	24	24	6	17	54	.216	.227	.208	10.20	3.21
Detwiler, Ross	R-L	6-3	210	3-6-86	2	4	6.14	9	7	0	0	44	56	31	30	4	15	23	.306	.267	.314	4.70	3.07
2-team total (7 Cleveland)					2	4	6.10	16	7	0	0	49	59	34	33	5	19	26	—	—	—	4.81	3.51
Doolittle, Sean	L-L	6-2	210	9-26-86	2	3	3.23	44	0	0	4	39	33	14	14	6	8	45	.231	.206	.250	10.38	1.85
Dull, Ryan	R-R	5-9	175	10-2-89	5	5	2.42	70	0	0	3	74	50	23	20	10	15	73	.186	.244	.156	8.84	1.82
Graveman, Kendall	R-R	6-2	200	12-21-90	10	11	4.11	31	31	2	0	186	196	87	85	22	47	108	.271	.272	.270	5.23	2.27
Gray, Sonny	R-R	5-10	190	11-7-89	5	11	5.69	22	22	0	0	117	133	80	74	18	42	94	.286	.286	.286	7.23	3.23
Hahn, Jesse	R-R	6-4	215	7-30-89	2	4	6.02	9	9	0	0	46	57	32	31	8	19	23	.313	.361	.273	4.47	3.69
Hendriks, Liam	R-R	6-0	200	2-10-89	0	4	3.76	53	0	0	0	65	69	31	27	6	14	71	.270	.228	.297	9.88	1.95
Hill, Rich	L-L	6-5	220	3-11-80	9	3	2.25	14	14	0	0	76	55	22	19	2	18	90	.201	.197	.202	10.66	3.32
Madson, Ryan	L-R	6-6	225	8-28-80	6	7	3.62	63	0	0	30	65	63	27	26	7	20	49	.257	.244	.270	6.82	2.78
Manaea, Sean	R-L	6-5	245	2-1-92	7	9	3.86	25	24	0	0	145	135	65	62	20	37	124	.248	.180	.263	7.71	2.30
Mengden, Daniel	R-R	6-2	190	2-19-93	2	9	6.50	14	14	0	0	72	83	54	52	9	33	71	.284	.283	.286	8.88	4.13
Neal, Zach	R-R	6-3	220	11-9-88	2	4	4.24	24	6	0	2	70	72	35	33	9	6	27	.265	.235	.294	3.47	0.77
Overton, Dillon	L-L	6-2	175	8-17-91	1	3	11.47	7	5	0	0	24	48	31	31	12	7	17	.407	.375	.415	6.29	2.59
Rodriguez, Fernando	R-R	6-3	235	6-18-84	2	0	4.20	34	0	0	0	41	30	19	19	3	17	37	.210	.313	.158	8.19	3.76
Rzepczynski, Marc	L-L	6-2	190	8-29-85	1	0	3.00	56	0	0	0	36	38	14	12	1	24	37	.266	.296	.226	9.25	6.00
Schuster, Patrick	R-L	6-2	190	10-30-90	0	0	10.80	5	0	0	0	7	8	8	8	0	6	6	.321	.111	.421	8.10	8.10
Smith, Chris	R-R	6-0	190	4-9-81	0	0	2.92	13	0	0	0	25	14	9	8	2	13	29	.165	.188	.151	10.58	4.74

Pitching

Pitching	B-T	HT	WT	DOB	W	L	ERA	G	GS	CG	SV	IP	H	R	ER	HR	BB	SO	AVG	vLH	vRH	K/9	BB/9
Surkamp, Eric	L-L	6-5	220	7-16-87	0	5	6.98	9	9	0	0	39	55	32	30	8	21	22	.327	.310	.333	5.12	4.89
Triggs, Andrew	R-R	6-4	220	3-16-89	1	1	4.31	24	6	0	0	56	56	30	27	5	13	55	.255	.277	.235	8.79	2.08
Wendelken, J.B.	R-R	6-0	220	3-24-93	0	0	9.95	8	0	0	0	13	18	15	14	3	9	12	.327	.333	.321	8.53	6.39

Fielding

Catcher	PCT	G	PO	A	E	DP	PB
Maxwell	.995	29	178	9	1	1	0
McBride	1.000	16	81	5	0	0	3
Phegley	1.000	25	164	13	0	1	3
Vogt	.991	113	766	45	7	5	5

	PCT	G	PO	A	E	DP
Ladendorf	.987	30	32	44	1	8
Lowrie	.984	82	141	235	6	60
Muncy	1.000	21	24	51	0	9
Pinder	.914	13	9	23	3	1
Wendle	.983	28	45	71	2	20

	PCT	G	PO	A	E	DP
Pinder	1.000	7	6	10	0	3
Semien	.971	159	235	477	21	109

First Base	PCT	G	PO	A	E	DP
Alonso	.997	145	1155	70	4	118
Butler	.981	22	97	7	2	8
Canha	.974	5	31	7	1	3
McBride	1.000	1	2	0	0	0
Olson	1.000	4	24	0	0	2
Valencia	.993	18	134	9	1	8
Vogt	1.000	1	1	0	0	0

Third Base	PCT	G	PO	A	E	DP
Alonso	.917	7	2	9	1	0
Canha	1.000	3	3	1	0	1
Coghlan	1.000	17	11	28	0	5
Healy	.954	72	42	144	9	9
Ladendorf	1.000	3	2	7	0	0
Muncy	.750	1	0	3	1	0
Valencia	.926	68	41	122	13	9

Outfield	PCT	G	PO	A	E	DP
Alcantara	1.000	5	5	0	0	0
Burns	.987	70	151	4	2	1
Canha	1.000	5	6	0	0	0
Coghlan	1.000	15	20	0	0	0
Crisp	.982	88	157	4	3	1
Davis	.970	93	159	4	5	3
Eibner	.987	38	72	2	1	1
Ladendorf	—	2	0	0	0	0
McBride	—	1	0	0	0	0
Muncy	1.000	21	29	1	0	0
Olson	1.000	5	7	0	0	0
Reddick	.985	68	126	5	2	1
Smolinski	.995	93	181	3	1	1
Valencia	1.000	38	67	6	0	1

Second Base	PCT	G	PO	A	E	DP
Alcantara	1.000	3	6	5	0	1
Coghlan	.986	20	19	51	1	12

Shortstop	PCT	G	PO	A	E	DP
Alcantara	1.000	2	1	4	0	0
Lowrie	1.000	2	0	1	0	0

NASHVILLE SOUNDS   TRIPLE-A
PACIFIC COAST LEAGUE

Batting	B-T	HT	WT	DOB	AVG	vLH	vRH	G	AB	R	H	2B	3B	HR	RBI	BB	HBP	SH	SF	SO	SB	CS	SLG	OBP
Alcantara, Arismendy	B-R	5-10	170	10-29-91	.290	.230	.317	48	200	28	58	10	5	6	27	14	1	2	2	57	11	6	.480	.336
2-team total (54 Iowa)					.276	—	—	102	398	60	110	19	10	11	48	29	1	2	3	118	32	6	.457	.325
Anderson, Bryan	L-R	6-1	200	12-16-86	.210	.179	.220	36	119	16	25	6	2	3	16	7	3	1	1	38	0	0	.370	.269
Barreto, Franklin	R-R	5-10	190	2-27-96	.353	1.000	.154	4	17	2	6	0	1	1	3	0	1	0	0	4	0	2	.647	.389
Blair, Carson	R-R	6-2	210	10-18-89	.222	.500	.143	3	9	2	2	0	0	1	1	0	0	0	0	3	0	0	.222	.300
2-team total (3 Round Rock)					.176	—	—	6	17	2	3	0	0	1	1	0	0	0	0	9	0	0	.176	.222
Boyd, B.J.	L-R	5-11	230	7-16-93	.267	.143	.304	7	30	2	8	0	0	0	1	2	0	0	0	3	0	0	.267	.313
Brugman, Jaycob	L-L	6-0	195	1-18-92	.295	.255	.308	94	386	50	114	26	4	7	67	36	2	1	8	88	5	3	.438	.352
Burns, Billy	B-R	5-9	170	8-30-89	.293	.308	.286	10	41	7	12	1	0	0	4	2	0	1	0	12	4	0	.317	.326
2-team total (2 Omaha)					.283	—	—	12	46	7	13	1	0	0	4	2	0	1	0	16	4	0	.304	.313
Chapman, Matt	R-R	6-0	210	4-28-93	.197	.250	.188	18	76	14	15	1	1	7	13	9	0	0	0	26	0	0	.513	.282
Devencenzi, Jordan	R-R	5-11	190	6-26-93	—	—	—	1	0	0	0	0	0	0	0	1	0	0	0	0	0	0	—	1.000
Eibner, Brett	R-R	6-4	225	12-2-88	.308	.250	.333	4	13	4	4	2	0	1	2	5	0	0	0	6	0	0	.692	.500
2-team total (50 Omaha)					.289	—	—	54	197	41	57	9	1	12	34	35	1	1	3	54	5	1	.528	.394
Healy, Ryon	R-R	6-5	225	1-10-92	.318	.400	.293	49	192	33	61	16	1	6	30	13	2	0	3	40	0	1	.505	.362
Ladendorf, Tyler	R-R	5-11	195	3-7-88	.234	.200	.247	35	128	17	30	5	0	1	6	7	0	2	0	26	0	0	.297	.274
Lambo, Andrew	L-L	6-3	220	8-11-88	.255	.240	.259	56	216	29	55	10	3	4	30	21	1	0	2	43	1	0	.384	.321
Lowrie, Jed	B-R	6-0	180	4-17-84	.250	—	.250	1	4	1	1	0	0	0	1	0	0	0	0	0	0	0	.250	.400
Maxwell, Bruce	L-R	6-1	250	12-20-90	.321	.297	.327	60	193	27	62	12	0	10	41	24	0	0	2	38	1	0	.539	.393
McBride, Matt	R-R	6-2	215	5-23-85	.267	.311	.249	70	247	33	66	20	1	7	30	26	1	0	0	49	0	1	.441	.339
Muncy, Max	L-R	6-0	210	8-25-90	.251	.225	.257	64	223	34	56	7	2	8	26	35	5	1	4	54	5	0	.408	.360
Nunez, Renato	R-R	6-1	220	4-4-94	.228	.198	.237	128	505	61	115	20	2	23	75	31	7	0	7	119	2	0	.412	.278
Olson, Matt	L-R	6-5	230	3-29-94	.235	.167	.256	131	464	69	109	34	1	17	60	71	0	2	3	132	1	0	.422	.335
Phegley, Josh	R-R	5-10	230	2-12-88	.316	.286	.333	5	19	2	6	1	0	0	1	4	0	0	0	6	0	0	.368	.435
Pinder, Chad	R-R	6-2	195	3-29-92	.258	.273	.253	107	426	72	110	23	3	14	51	25	9	1	4	108	5	1	.425	.310
Ravelo, Rangel	R-R	6-1	225	4-24-92	.262	.286	.253	106	367	60	96	23	1	8	54	34	8	3	4	63	1	1	.395	.334
Reddick, Josh	L-R	6-2	195	2-19-87	.120	.125	.118	6	25	2	3	1	0	1	1	0	0	0	0	6	0	0	.280	.154
Rodriguez, Josh	R-R	6-0	185	12-18-84	.264	.276	.260	36	106	18	28	7	0	5	23	24	1	2	1	25	1	1	.472	.402
Smolinski, Jake	R-R	5-11	205	2-9-89	.248	.226	.254	39	145	20	36	14	0	3	15	11	2	1	0	23	6	1	.407	.310
Walsh, Colin	B-R	6-1	200	9-26-89	.259	.280	.252	59	201	31	52	12	1	4	26	41	1	0	2	63	0	0	.388	.384
Wendle, Joey	L-R	6-1	190	4-26-90	.279	.303	.271	125	491	81	137	31	9	12	61	26	7	1	1	112	14	4	.452	.324

Pitching	B-T	HT	WT	DOB	W	L	ERA	G	GS	CG	SV	IP	H	R	ER	HR	BB	SO	AVG	vLH	vRH	K/9	BB/9
Alcantara, Raul	R-R	6-4	220	12-4-92	4	0	1.18	8	8	0	0	46	38	7	6	1	3	32	.229	.210	.240	6.31	0.59
Alvarez, Henderson	R-R	6-0	205	4-18-90	1	0	3.86	5	5	0	0	19	17	9	8	3	6	17	.239	.278	.200	8.20	2.89
Alvarez, R.J.	R-R	6-2	225	6-8-91	1	0	0.00	1	0	0	0	2	0	0	0	0	3	0	.000	.000	.000	16.20	0.00
Brasier, Ryan	R-R	6-0	225	8-26-87	5	3	3.56	46	0	0	1	61	50	25	24	6	19	70	.226	.256	.207	10.38	2.82
Castro, Angel	R-R	5-11	240	11-14-82	2	8	5.15	37	10	1	2	93	107	59	53	13	36	58	.292	.287	.297	5.63	3.50
Cotton, Jharel	R-R	5-11	195	1-19-92	3	1	2.82	6	6	1	0	38	28	12	12	3	7	36	.201	.151	.233	8.45	1.64
2-team total (22 Oklahoma City)					11	6	4.31	28	22	2	0	136	108	71	65	20	39	155	—	—	—	10.28	2.59
Coulombe, Daniel	L-L	5-10	190	10-26-89	0	0	1.08	20	0	0	0	25	18	4	3	0	6	35	.200	.179	.216	12.60	2.16
Detwiler, Ross	R-L	6-3	210	3-6-86	4	0	3.86	4	3	0	0	23	20	10	10	4	4	24	.225	.318	.194	9.26	1.54
Doolittle, Ryan	R-R	6-1	215	3-25-88	1	2	4.05	17	0	0	0	27	29	13	12	3	10	19	.279	.348	.226	6.41	3.38
Doolittle, Sean	L-L	6-2	210	9-26-86	0	0	1.50	6	0	0	0	6	1	1	1	0	1	10	.182	.143	.200	15.00	1.50
Gossett, Daniel	R-R	6-2	185	11-13-92	1	0	1.98	2	2	0	0	14	10	3	3	0	3	4	.213	.150	.259	2.63	1.98
Hahn, Jesse	R-R	6-4	215	7-30-89	1	7	4.32	15	15	0	0	75	74	41	36	8	34	46	.276	.304	.255	6.21	4.59
Healy, Tucker	L-R	6-1	210	6-15-90	4	3	3.61	44	0	0	8	52	38	25	21	3	26	76	.202	.257	.140	13.07	4.47

Pitching	B-T	HT	WT	DOB	W	L	ERA	G	GS	CG	SV	IP	H	R	ER	HR	BB	SO	AVG	vLH	vRH	K/9	BB/9
Hendriks, Liam	R-R	6-0	200	2-10-89	0	0	3.86	3	0	0	0	5	4	2	2	0	2	3	.222	.500	.000	5.79	3.86
Hynes, Colt	L-L	5-11	200	6-28-85	0	0	0.00	1	0	0	0	2	0	0	0	0	0	0	.000	.000	.000	0.00	0.00
Jensen, Chris	R-R	6-4	200	9-30-90	2	6	4.53	11	10	0	0	60	59	36	30	8	22	31	.262	.302	.227	4.68	3.32
Kurcz, Aaron	R-R	6-0	175	8-8-90	5	1	3.50	35	1	0	1	54	46	27	21	2	17	43	.231	.278	.200	7.17	2.83
Manaea, Sean	R-L	6-5	245	2-1-92	2	0	1.50	3	3	0	0	18	16	3	3	1	4	21	.232	.077	.268	10.50	2.00
Mann, Brandon	L-L	6-2	200	5-16-84	0	0	9.00	1	1	0	0	5	5	5	1	4	3	.250	.250	.250	5.40	7.20
Mengden, Daniel	R-R	6-2	190	2-19-93	8	2	1.67	13	13	0	0	75	54	15	14	4	17	67	.200	.204	.198	8.00	2.03
Naile, James	R-R	6-4	185	2-8-93	1	1	5.73	2	2	0	0	11	11	7	7	1	5	4	.256	.333	.125	3.27	4.09
Navas, Carlos	R-R	6-1	170	8-13-92	0	0	2.70	4	0	0	1	7	5	2	2	0	1	5	.208	.300	.143	6.75	1.35
Neal, Zach	R-R	6-3	220	11-9-88	7	2	3.21	11	11	0	0	62	62	27	22	5	8	32	.259	.233	.279	4.67	1.17
Overton, Dillon	L-L	6-2	175	8-17-91	13	5	3.29	21	20	1	0	126	132	50	46	6	31	105	.268	.314	.249	7.52	2.22
Santos, Eduard	R-R	6-2	240	10-22-89	3	3	3.43	45	2	0	5	63	42	25	24	3	39	66	.196	.179	.210	9.43	5.57
Schuster, Patrick	R-L	6-2	190	10-30-90	1	0	1.16	32	0	0	7	39	27	5	5	0	12	39	.194	.183	.203	9.08	2.79
Smith, Chris	R-R	6-0	190	4-9-81	6	8	3.93	22	22	0	0	131	120	64	57	11	45	121	.239	.223	.252	8.33	3.10
Stull, Cody	L-L	6-2	160	3-23-92	0	0	4.50	2	0	0	0	4	4	2	2	1	2	1	.267	.000	.400	2.25	4.50
Surkamp, Eric	L-L	6-5	220	7-16-87	3	1	3.07	5	5	0	0	29	22	12	10	3	10	34	.206	.125	.229	10.43	3.07
Tepesch, Nick	R-R	6-4	240	10-12-88	1	1	5.51	3	3	0	0	16	18	11	10	1	7	6	.277	.212	.344	3.31	3.86
4-team total					8	4	3.96	22	19	0	0	116	121	56	51	7	28	62	—	—	—	4.81	2.17
(3 Oklahoma City, 5 Omaha, 11 Round Rock)																							
Triggs, Andrew	R-R	6-4	220	3-16-89	2	1	2.95	16	0	0	2	18	16	7	6	0	5	21	.225	.130	.271	10.31	2.45
Wahl, Bobby	R-R	6-2	210	3-21-92	1	0	2.79	9	0	0	4	10	7	3	3	0	6	14	.200	.429	.048	13.03	5.59
Wendelken, J.B.	R-R	6-0	220	3-24-93	1	4	4.11	39	0	0	5	46	48	25	21	5	26	65	.259	.264	.257	12.72	5.09

Fielding

Catcher	PCT	G	PO	A	E	DP	PB
Anderson	.993	35	245	22	2	1	3
Blair	1.000	3	22	1	0	0	0
Devencenzi	1.000	1	1	1	0	0	0
Maxwell	.990	60	440	52	5	2	3
McBride	.998	46	382	27	1	0	4
Phegley	1.000	3	15	4	0	0	0

First Base	PCT	G	PO	A	E	DP
Healy	.981	19	139	15	3	9
McBride	1.000	1	11	2	0	1
Muncy	1.000	3	26	2	0	6
Olson	1.000	49	427	25	0	36
Ravelo	.995	71	588	29	3	51

Second Base	PCT	G	PO	A	E	DP
Alcantara	.875	5	5	9	2	2
Healy	—	1	0	0	0	0

	PCT	G	PO	A	E	DP
Lowrie	1.000	1	3	0	0	0
Muncy	1.000	3	7	8	0	2
Pinder	1.000	4	6	11	0	2
Rodriguez	1.000	3	2	7	0	1
Walsh	1.000	5	10	12	0	3
Wendle	.986	122	219	338	8	75

Third Base	PCT	G	PO	A	E	DP
Chapman	.984	18	22	38	1	6
Healy	.952	15	6	14	1	0
Muncy	.967	13	7	22	1	3
Nunez	.904	89	47	150	21	11
Walsh	.938	7	1	14	1	2

Shortstop	PCT	G	PO	A	E	DP
Alcantara	.925	12	21	28	4	9
Barreto	1.000	4	6	12	0	2
Ladendorf	.939	8	10	21	2	3
Pinder	.931	98	141	250	29	44

	PCT	G	PO	A	E	DP
Rodriguez	.948	22	40	51	5	13

Outfield	PCT	G	PO	A	E	DP
Alcantara	.977	23	40	2	1	0
Boyd	1.000	7	23	0	0	0
Brugman	1.000	93	204	5	0	1
Burns	1.000	10	21	0	0	0
Eibner	1.000	4	8	0	0	0
Ladendorf	.952	26	60	0	3	0
Lambo	1.000	27	50	0	0	0
McBride	1.000	21	45	2	0	0
Muncy	1.000	36	58	3	0	0
Nunez	.955	12	21	0	1	0
Olson	.966	81	141	1	5	0
Ravelo	1.000	13	20	0	0	0
Reddick	1.000	3	12	0	0	0
Rodriguez	1.000	10	13	0	0	0
Smolinski	1.000	38	67	2	0	1
Walsh	.930	27	53	0	4	0

MIDLAND ROCKHOUNDS   DOUBLE-A
TEXAS LEAGUE

Batting	B-T	HT	WT	DOB	AVG	vLH	vRH	G	AB	R	H	2B	3B	HR	RBI	BB	HBP	SH	SF	SO	SB	CS	SLG	OBP
Anderson, Bryan	L-R	6-1	200	12-16-86	.211	.000	.235	5	19	1	4	2	0	0	1	2	0	0	1	3	0	0	.316	.273
Barreto, Franklin	R-R	5-10	190	2-27-96	.281	.259	.288	119	462	63	130	25	3	10	50	36	6	1	2	90	30	15	.413	.340
Bennie, Joe	R-R	6-0	200	5-7-91	.176	.235	.158	21	74	9	13	0	0	2	7	9	1	0	0	18	0	0	.257	.274
Blair, Carson	R-R	6-2	210	10-18-89	.339	.450	.278	16	56	13	19	1	0	3	12	8	1	0	0	17	0	0	.518	.431
2-team total (19 Frisco)					.244	—	—	35	123	21	30	5	0	4	19	17	3	0	0	43	1	1	.382	.350
Brugman, Jaycob	L-L	6-0	195	1-18-92	.261	.257	.262	38	157	27	41	7	3	5	20	16	2	0	1	33	2	3	.439	.335
Chapman, Matt	R-R	6-0	210	4-28-93	.244	.286	.232	117	438	78	107	26	4	29	83	59	3	0	4	147	7	4	.521	.335
Harris, James	R-R	6-1	180	8-7-93	.216	.250	.200	11	37	8	8	1	0	0	5	2	0	0	1	11	2	1	.243	.250
Healy, Ryon	R-R	6-5	225	1-10-92	.338	.364	.330	36	145	27	49	12	3	8	34	18	0	0	1	35	1	0	.628	.409
Kirkland, Wade	R-R	5-11	200	4-4-89	.215	.230	.209	74	256	29	55	9	2	2	16	11	1	5	1	83	2	4	.289	.249
Marincov, Tyler	R-R	6-2	205	10-20-91	.267	.315	.253	101	374	54	100	15	3	10	56	40	3	2	4	91	7	6	.404	.340
Martin, Richie	R-R	5-11	190	12-22-94	.333	.000	.417	5	15	1	5	1	1	0	7	3	0	0	0	2	2	1	.533	.444
Munoz, Yairo	R-R	6-1	165	1-23-95	.240	.313	.216	102	387	44	93	16	3	9	39	23	2	1	0	76	6	7	.367	.286
Nogowski, John	R-L	6-2	210	1-5-93	.130	.250	.105	7	23	1	3	1	0	1	1	3	0	0	0	3	0	0	.304	.231
Oh, Danny	L-L	6-0	185	12-28-89	.236	.176	.249	85	276	34	65	11	0	0	16	22	6	6	0	52	12	2	.275	.306
Paz, Andy	R-R	6-0	170	1-5-93	.320	.358	.299	46	150	24	48	9	0	2	12	18	0	1	0	22	2	0	.420	.393
Rodriguez, Josh	R-R	6-0	185	12-18-84	.263	.237	.276	52	175	15	46	6	2	4	30	30	0	1	2	51	3	1	.389	.367
Rosa, Viosergy	L-L	6-3	185	6-16-90	.255	.265	.251	127	459	50	117	32	0	9	58	74	1	0	1	140	1	2	.383	.359
Schrock, Max	L-R	5-8	180	10-12-94	.391	.750	.316	6	23	3	9	1	0	0	3	1	0	0	0	1	0	0	.435	.375
Sportman, J.P.	R-R	5-9	190	1-26-92	.267	.275	.264	120	483	63	129	29	5	5	59	26	4	1	1	82	18	6	.379	.309
Taylor, Beau	L-R	6-0	205	2-13-90	.280	.318	.271	95	339	50	95	25	0	5	53	54	4	1	3	86	1	1	.398	.383
Vertigan, Brett	L-L	5-9	175	8-21-90	.246	.250	.245	110	415	47	102	19	2	2	25	40	2	3	2	90	14	1	.316	.314

Pitching	B-T	HT	WT	DOB	W	L	ERA	G	GS	CG	SV	IP	H	R	ER	HR	BB	SO	AVG	vLH	vRH	K/9	BB/9
Alcantara, Raul	R-R	6-4	220	12-4-92	5	6	4.80	17	17	0	0	90	100	52	48	11	27	73	.284	.277	.288	7.30	2.70
Avila, Andres	R-R	6-0	185	6-20-90	6	3	3.59	40	1	0	1	73	68	35	29	9	21	77	.245	.235	.250	9.54	2.60
Bracewell, Ben	R-R	6-0	195	9-19-90	8	3	2.14	29	10	0	2	88	70	23	21	4	25	59	.225	.228	.223	6.01	2.55

Pitching

Pitching	B-T	HT	WT	DOB	W	L	ERA	G	GS	CG	SV	IP	H	R	ER	HR	BB	SO	AVG	vLH	vRH	K/9	BB/9
Bragg, Sam	R-R	6-2	190	3-23-93	4	4	4.29	36	1	0	1	65	60	37	31	9	19	68	.238	.221	.248	9.42	2.63
Cochran-Gill, Trey	R-R	5-10	190	12-10-92	4	5	3.07	42	0	0	0	73	71	31	25	6	25	58	.259	.304	.236	7.12	3.07
Covey, Dylan	R-R	6-2	195	8-14-91	2	1	1.84	6	6	0	0	29	21	14	6	2	17	26	.200	.156	.219	7.98	5.22
Doolittle, Ryan	R-R	6-1	215	3-25-88	2	1	1.04	13	0	0	1	17	11	2	2	1	4	10	.186	.200	.179	5.19	2.08
Fillmyer, Heath	R-R	6-1	180	5-16-94	2	0	2.54	8	8	1	0	39	31	11	11	3	8	29	.223	.237	.213	6.69	1.85
Finnegan, Kyle	R-R	6-2	170	9-4-91	1	3	2.14	30	0	0	6	42	31	13	10	3	20	41	.208	.193	.217	8.79	4.29
Friedrichs, Kyle	R-R	6-1	195	1-22-92	0	0	9.00	1	0	0	0	2	4	2	2	0	2	2	.444	.667	.333	9.00	9.00
Gorton, Ryan	R-R	6-2	220	2-27-90	0	0	15.00	2	0	0	0	3	7	5	5	0	2	1	.500	.667	.455	3.00	6.00
Gossett, Daniel	R-R	6-2	185	11-13-92	5	5	2.49	16	16	0	0	94	75	37	26	4	25	94	.220	.221	.219	9.00	2.39
Hall, Kris	R-R	6-3	215	6-8-91	1	3	6.88	27	0	0	0	34	35	26	26	6	32	26	.271	.306	.250	6.88	8.47
Jensen, Chris	R-R	6-4	200	9-30-90	7	4	4.62	16	16	0	0	88	82	52	45	11	23	72	.246	.241	.250	7.39	2.36
Kurcz, Aaron	R-R	6-0	175	8-8-90	4	0	1.26	11	0	0	4	14	6	2	2	2	0	12	.125	.095	.148	7.53	0.00
Mann, Brandon	L-L	6-2	200	5-16-84	3	4	4.48	11	11	0	0	62	64	32	31	9	19	63	.263	.242	.271	9.10	2.74
Mengden, Daniel	R-R	6-2	190	2-19-93	2	0	0.78	4	4	0	0	23	15	2	2	0	12	28	.188	.154	.220	10.96	4.70
Naile, James	R-R	6-4	185	2-8-93	1	1	4.76	3	3	0	0	17	20	9	9	1	3	11	.303	.304	.302	5.82	1.59
Sanchez, Jake	R-R	6-1	205	8-19-89	7	5	3.11	44	1	0	8	67	59	30	23	2	18	72	.233	.232	.234	9.72	2.43
Seddon, Joel	R-R	6-1	165	7-13-92	9	9	4.40	27	26	0	0	143	149	84	70	13	48	75	.268	.255	.276	4.71	3.01
Stull, Cody	L-L	6-2	160	3-23-92	0	0	0.00	1	0	0	0	2	4	0	0	0	1	1	.444	.000	.571	4.50	4.50
Trivino, Lou	R-R	6-5	225	10-1-91	1	1	2.45	12	0	0	1	18	14	7	5	1	7	12	.209	.250	.186	5.89	3.44
Wagman, Joey	L-R	6-0	185	7-25-91	1	1	6.38	4	4	0	0	18	28	15	13	1	4	9	.368	.290	.422	4.42	1.96
Wahl, Bobby	R-R	6-2	210	3-21-92	0	1	2.21	33	0	0	10	41	26	11	10	3	17	48	.188	.118	.230	10.62	3.76
Walter, Corey	R-R	6-3	215	8-11-92	3	2	2.15	29	16	0	1	100	91	32	24	2	15	54	.244	.235	.249	4.84	1.35

Fielding

Catcher

Catcher	PCT	G	PO	A	E	DP	PB
Anderson	.969	4	29	2	1	0	0
Blair	1.000	14	108	9	0	0	2
Kirkland	—	1	0	0	0	0	0
Paz	.991	43	308	24	3	3	3
Taylor	.989	83	592	58	7	8	6

First Base	PCT	G	PO	A	E	DP
Healy	.988	25	235	16	3	27
Kirkland	1.000	15	81	7	0	11
Nogowski	1.000	6	53	4	0	5
Rodriguez	.983	11	105	9	2	8
Rosa	.989	91	803	45	9	72

Second Base	PCT	G	PO	A	E	DP
Barreto	.971	33	60	76	4	23
Bennie	.957	8	7	15	1	2

	PCT	G	PO	A	E	DP
Kirkland	.978	46	76	145	5	31
Munoz	.979	27	52	85	3	25
Rodriguez	.965	21	27	55	3	7
Schrock	1.000	6	7	11	0	1
Sportman	.966	7	14	14	1	2

Third Base	PCT	G	PO	A	E	DP
Bennie	.778	3	3	4	2	0
Chapman	.971	100	87	245	10	41
Healy	.909	7	7	13	2	0
Kirkland	.923	6	4	8	1	1
Munoz	.956	25	27	60	4	10
Rodriguez	.800	2	1	3	1	0
Taylor	1.000	1	1	1	0	0

Shortstop	PCT	G	PO	A	E	DP
Barreto	.950	81	88	200	15	37

	PCT	G	PO	A	E	DP
Chapman	.911	10	15	36	5	10
Kirkland	.960	10	7	17	1	4
Martin	.821	5	6	17	5	2
Munoz	.937	41	48	129	12	24

Outfield	PCT	G	PO	A	E	DP
Bennie	1.000	3	4	0	0	0
Brugman	.974	38	73	2	2	0
Harris	.933	11	13	1	1	0
Kirkland	1.000	3	2	0	0	0
Marincov	.977	88	165	6	4	0
Oh	.992	72	122	3	1	0
Rodriguez	1.000	4	10	0	0	0
Sportman	.982	101	151	17	3	4
Vertigan	.989	107	274	4	3	1

STOCKTON PORTS　　　　　　　　HIGH CLASS A
CALIFORNIA LEAGUE

Batting	B-T	HT	WT	DOB	AVG	vLH	vRH	G	AB	R	H	2B	3B	HR	RBI	BB	HBP	SH	SF	SO	SB	CS	SLG	OBP
Akau, Iolana	R-R	5-11	180	8-31-95	.214	.208	.216	64	206	13	44	8	0	1	24	16	7	3	3	79	0	2	.267	.289
Alcantara, Arismendy	B-R	5-10	170	10-29-91	.308	.333	.294	6	26	4	8	3	1	1	8	1	0	0	0	9	0	0	.615	.333
Bennie, Joe	R-R	6-0	200	5-7-91	.302	.340	.290	111	434	64	131	31	0	11	69	48	5	1	2	116	6	7	.449	.376
Boyd, B.J.	L-R	5-11	230	7-16-93	.288	.339	.270	101	413	48	119	14	3	8	58	34	4	4	3	74	8	6	.395	.346
Brizuela, Jose	L-R	6-0	180	8-31-92	.254	.207	.271	100	354	42	90	18	1	16	54	41	5	0	3	110	2	4	.446	.337
Brown, Seth	L-L	6-3	220	7-13-92	.241	.193	.257	127	453	83	109	21	5	8	53	65	6	2	6	124	13	2	.362	.340
Glenn, Alex	L-L	5-11	180	6-11-91	.333	.000	.444	3	12	3	4	2	1	0	1	1	0	0	0	2	0	0	.667	.385
Harris, James	R-R	6-1	180	8-7-93	.303	.254	.320	119	492	81	149	30	4	7	53	54	8	2	3	118	21	9	.423	.379
Higley, Justin	L-R	6-4	200	12-25-92	.360	.353	.364	12	50	7	18	5	2	0	6	5	0	0	0	20	2	1	.540	.418
Iriart, Chris	R-R	6-2	230	10-7-94	.311	.471	.250	16	61	14	19	3	0	6	15	9	2	0	0	15	0	0	.689	.417
Marincov, Tyler	R-R	6-2	205	10-6-91	.259	.250	.261	36	147	26	38	11	0	9	32	15	4	1	0	38	5	2	.517	.343
Martin, Richie	R-R	5-11	190	12-22-94	.230	.198	.243	86	330	46	76	14	2	3	31	36	10	3	3	73	12	8	.312	.322
Mercedes, Melvin	B-R	5-8	170	1-13-92	.260	.213	.277	106	358	52	93	12	5	1	30	56	2	10	0	71	7	8	.330	.363
Nogowski, John	R-L	6-2	210	1-5-93	.285	.239	.306	84	288	35	82	15	0	7	37	25	7	3	2	37	0	1	.410	.354
Paz, Andy	R-R	6-0	170	1-5-93	.421	.000	.471	6	19	1	8	1	1	0	2	4	0	0	0	1	1	0	.579	.522
Pimentel, Sandber	L-L	6-3	220	9-12-94	.237	.240	.237	117	417	61	99	18	1	21	66	60	7	0	1	145	1	0	.436	.342
Raga, Argenis	R-R	6-1	176	7-22-94	.263	.259	.265	84	289	40	76	19	1	2	41	29	2	5	5	62	5	1	.356	.329
Schrock, Max	L-R	5-8	180	8-30-94	.111	.111	.292	2	9	0	1	0	0	0	0	0	0	0	0	0	0	0	.111	.111
Sogard, Eric	L-R	5-9	180	5-22-86	.286	—	.286	2	7	1	2	0	0	0	1	0	0	0	0	0	0	0	.286	.286
Valencia, Danny	R-R	6-2	210	9-19-84	.143	.167	.000	2	7	1	1	0	0	1	1	0	0	0	0	0	0	0	.571	.143
White, Mikey	R-R	6-1	200	9-3-93	.247	.284	.233	124	469	65	116	25	3	6	50	40	7	3	2	130	4	2	.352	.315

Pitching	B-T	HT	WT	DOB	W	L	ERA	G	GS	CG	SV	IP	H	R	ER	HR	BB	SO	AVG	vLH	vRH	K/9	BB/9
Alvarez, Henderson	R-R	6-0	205	4-18-90	0	1	4.73	5	5	0	0	13	17	8	7	1	2	7	.315	.29	.348	4.73	1.35
Alvarez, R.J.	R-R	6-2	225	6-8-91	0	0	4.50	2	0	0	0	2	2	1	1	1	0	2	.250	.25	.25	9.00	0.00
Bracewell, Ben	R-R	6-0	195	9-19-90	1	1	12.60	5	0	0	1	5	6	8	7	0	3	5	.300	.375	.25	9.00	5.40
Butler, Brendan	L-R	6-3	217	5-2-93	1	0	8.10	2	0	0	0	3	6	3	3	0	3	3	.353	.333	.375	10.80	8.10
Erwin, Zack	L-L	6-5	193	1-24-94	3	10	6.53	18	16	0	0	80	109	70	58	11	32	58	.325	.289	.339	6.53	3.60
Fillmyer, Heath	R-R	6-1	180	5-16-94	5	6	3.60	18	16	0	0	95	101	53	38	4	31	89	.264	.268	.260	8.43	2.94

Pitching

Pitching	B-T	HT	WT	DOB	W	L	ERA	G	GS	CG	SV	IP	H	R	ER	HR	BB	SO	AVG	vLH	vRH	K/9	BB/9
Finnegan, Kyle	R-R	6-2	170	9-4-91	1	0	3.32	13	0	0	1	22	19	8	8	1	12	28	.235	.226	.240	11.63	4.98
Friedrichs, Kyle	R-R	6-1	195	1-22-92	3	7	4.29	18	18	0	0	101	109	54	48	10	10	86	.268	.267	.270	7.69	0.89
Gauna, Koby	R-R	6-3	225	9-10-93	3	0	3.54	44	0	0	1	69	86	34	27	8	24	35	.310	.330	.297	4.59	3.15
Gorton, Ryan	R-R	6-2	220	2-27-90	0	0	11.25	3	0	0	0	4	9	6	5	1	2	3	.450	.250	.583	6.75	4.50
Gossett, Daniel	R-R	6-2	185	11-13-92	4	1	3.33	9	9	0	0	46	40	20	17	4	13	53	.225	.244	.207	10.37	2.54
Graves, Brett	R-R	6-1	170	1-30-93	7	10	4.60	27	25	0	0	141	141	81	72	11	49	86	.262	.260	.264	5.49	3.13
Hendriks, Liam	R-R	6-0	200	2-10-89	0	0	0.00	1	0	0	0	1	0	0	0	0	0	1	.000	.000	—	9.00	0.00
Highberger, Nick	R-R	5-10	190	11-4-93	1	0	0.00	2	0	0	0	4	2	0	0	0	2	3	.154	.333	.000	6.75	4.50
Hill, Rich	L-L	6-5	220	3-11-80	0	0	3.00	1	1	0	0	3	4	1	1	0	0	6	.308	.333	.286	18.00	0.00
Holmes, Grant	R-R	6-1	215	3-22-96	3	3	6.91	6	5	0	0	29	44	25	22	4	10	24	.355	.447	.299	7.53	3.14
2-team total (20 R. Cucamonga)					11	7	4.63	26	23	0	1	134	147	85	69	10	53	124	—	—	—	8.33	3.56
Huber, Rob	R-R	5-11	200	1-8-92	0	1	10.45	15	0	0	0	21	30	28	24	4	19	18	.323	.333	.314	7.84	8.27
Jordan, Mitchell	R-R	6-2	205	4-10-95	1	0	6.43	2	1	0	0	7	7	5	5	2	4	5	.280	.250	.308	6.43	5.14
Lyons, Jared	L-L	6-0	190	5-18-93	1	0	4.91	5	0	0	0	7	5	4	4	0	4	10	.192	.000	.238	12.27	4.91
Manaea, Sean	R-L	6-5	245	2-1-92	0	0	4.91	1	1	0	0	4	2	2	2	1	2	3	.154	.000	.222	7.36	4.91
Manarino, Evan	L-L	6-1	195	12-28-92	2	1	1.27	6	3	0	0	28	23	6	4	0	8	18	.230	.207	.239	5.72	2.54
Meisner, Casey	R-R	6-7	190	5-22-95	1	14	4.85	28	19	0	1	117	126	76	63	12	59	100	.275	.250	.291	7.69	4.54
Miller, Corey	R-R	6-3	190	11-13-91	0	2	6.18	26	0	0	0	39	43	31	27	9	13	34	.269	.278	.261	7.78	2.97
Murray, Michael	R-R	6-3	215	9-26-93	1	2	7.62	3	3	0	0	13	16	13	11	3	7	9	.291	.237	.412	6.23	4.85
Naile, James	R-R	6-4	185	2-8-93	4	1	3.76	8	7	0	0	41	39	17	17	5	11	46	.257	.237	.288	10.18	2.43
Navas, Carlos	R-R	6-1	170	8-13-92	3	7	4.08	40	0	0	6	53	46	31	24	5	22	67	.230	.244	.219	11.38	3.74
Sergey, Matt	R-R	6-4	180	7-29-89	2	0	4.00	12	3	0	0	27	22	14	12	8	9	41	.220	.176	.242	13.67	3.00
Stalcup, Matt	L-L	6-2	195	7-6-90	3	1	7.23	22	6	0	0	56	72	48	45	10	29	39	.332	.270	.357	6.27	4.66
Stull, Cody	L-L	6-2	160	3-23-92	3	2	1.46	36	0	0	6	56	48	21	9	2	11	63	.231	.133	.270	10.19	1.78
Trivino, Lou	R-R	6-5	225	10-1-91	1	3	3.02	33	0	0	2	42	38	19	14	0	18	49	.239	.247	.232	10.58	3.89
Veliz, Victor	L-L	5-11	170	10-6-93	0	1	7.24	20	0	0	0	27	34	26	22	6	12	21	.298	.389	.256	6.91	3.95
Wagman, Joey	L-R	6-0	185	7-25-91	4	6	3.67	33	2	0	2	76	80	42	31	4	21	78	.269	.273	.266	9.24	2.49
Wahl, Bobby	R-R	6-2	210	3-21-92	0	0	6.75	3	0	0	0	4	3	3	3	0	5	3	.231	.200	.250	6.75	11.25

Fielding

Catcher	PCT	G	PO	A	E	DP	PB
Akau	.986	60	454	49	7	2	18
Brown	1.000	1	1	0	0	0	0
Mercedes	1.000	1	1	0	0	0	1
Nogowski	—	1	0	0	0	0	0
Paz	1.000	6	39	5	0	0	4
Raga	.985	79	599	61	10	5	19

First Base	PCT	G	PO	A	E	DP
Akau	1.000	1	1	0	0	1
Brown	1.000	1	3	0	0	0
Iriart	.992	12	114	8	1	11
Mercedes	1.000	1	2	0	0	0
Nogowski	.985	53	424	41	7	37
Pimentel	.975	83	664	49	18	53

Second Base	PCT	G	PO	A	E	DP
Alcantara	1.000	3	6	0	0	3

Bennie	.953	60	108	173	14	40
Brizuela	1.000	1	4	1	0	1
Mercedes	.984	15	24	38	1	7
Schrock	1.000	2	1	3	0	0
Sogard	1.000	1	2	2	0	0
White	.978	65	97	174	6	29

Third Base	PCT	G	PO	A	E	DP
Brizuela	.909	87	65	186	25	16
Mercedes	.927	50	30	85	9	10
Raga	1.000	3	0	2	0	1
Valencia	.667	2	0	4	2	0
White	.750	7	3	9	4	0

Shortstop	PCT	G	PO	A	E	DP
Alcantara	.500	1	1	0	1	0
Martin	.958	82	135	188	14	37
Mercedes	.912	11	7	24	3	5

Sogard	1.000	1	1	4	0	1
White	.975	50	72	126	5	32

Outfield	PCT	G	PO	A	E	DP
Akau	—	1	0	0	0	0
Alcantara	1.000	3	7	0	0	0
Bennie	.964	30	51	2	2	1
Boyd	.991	93	204	6	2	3
Brown	.944	108	183	4	11	1
Glenn	1.000	3	4	0	0	0
Harris	.949	112	222	3	12	0
Higley	1.000	12	12	0	0	0
Marincov	.979	30	44	3	1	0
Mercedes	.981	27	47	5	1	1
Nogowski	1.000	10	10	0	0	0

BELOIT SNAPPERS

LOW CLASS A

MIDWEST LEAGUE

Batting	B-T	HT	WT	DOB	AVG	vLH	vRH	G	AB	R	H	2B	3B	HR	RBI	BB	HBP	SH	SF	SO	SB	CS	SLG	OBP
Barrera, Luis	L-L	6-0	180	11-15-95	.286	.100	.317	19	70	8	20	4	2	1	4	4	0	1	1	17	3	1	.443	.320
Bolt, Skye	B-R	6-3	190	1-15-94	.231	.254	.225	101	342	34	79	20	2	5	37	42	7	0	11	88	10	5	.345	.318
Chavez, Jose	R-R	5-11	175	8-5-95	.207	.328	.171	80	251	19	52	9	0	0	15	12	2	5	3	51	0	0	.243	.246
Collins, Nick	L-R	6-2	218	4-13-94	.194	.000	.224	21	67	8	13	4	0	2	9	4	0	0	0	14	0	0	.343	.239
Devencenzi, Jordan	R-R	5-11	190	6-26-94	.281	.261	.286	38	114	11	32	6	0	0	8	12	1	2	1	17	1	1	.333	.352
Diaz, Edwin	R-R	6-2	195	8-25-95	.236	.292	.221	92	296	31	70	13	0	5	34	26	8	6	4	101	4	2	.331	.311
Gavitt, Tom	R-R	6-3	195	8-16-92	.250	.000	.364	5	16	2	4	1	0	0	2	1	0	0	0	5	0	0	.313	.294
Gilbert, Trent	L-R	6-1	175	3-17-93	.269	.256	.272	129	476	48	128	35	3	4	47	37	5	1	2	104	1	2	.380	.327
Gonzalez, Roger	R-R	5-9	190	11-2-93	.000	.000	.000	2	7	0	0	0	0	0	0	0	0	0	0	2	0	0	.000	.000
Guzman, Miguel	R-R	6-2	210	3-10-95	.300	.000	.333	3	10	1	3	1	0	0	0	0	0	0	0	0	0	0	.400	.300
Higley, Justin	L-R	6-4	200	12-25-92	.237	.125	.256	115	396	49	94	17	7	6	25	42	3	0	3	148	18	5	.361	.313
Howell, Ryan	R-R	6-2	205	10-30-92	.216	.247	.208	107	342	48	74	22	2	7	22	61	6	2	0	116	2	3	.354	.345
Iriart, Chris	R-R	6-2	230	10-7-94	.231	.265	.224	79	277	31	64	13	0	16	47	29	8	0	2	89	0	0	.451	.320
Loehr, Trace	L-R	5-10	175	5-23-95	.249	.279	.243	103	357	35	89	19	7	1	30	20	2	6	1	77	13	6	.350	.292
Lopez, Jesus	B-R	5-11	170	10-5-96	.202	.188	.206	89	302	31	61	13	2	2	24	4	0	3	2	88	2	1	.278	.259
Martin, Mike	R-R	6-0	175	9-29-92	.298	.250	.309	34	121	16	36	3	0	1	20	14	1	5	1	22	7	2	.347	.372
Martinez, Robert	R-R	6-1	180	2-8-94	.207	.250	.200	29	87	10	18	4	0	3	7	9	0	0	0	33	0	1	.356	.281
Pallares, Steven	R-R	6-2	185	4-26-93	.132	.125	.135	36	106	10	14	1	0	1	7	28	0	0	0	32	3	2	.170	.313
Paz, Andy	R-R	6-1	175	5-9-93	.250	.429	.111	4	16	2	4	0	0	0	3	1	0	0	0	4	0	0	.250	.294
Rodriguez, Jean Carlo	R-R	5-10	170	1-12-96	.232	.184	.243	55	190	25	44	16	1	2	19	17	3	3	1	33	0	5	.358	.303
Siddall, Brett	L-L	6-1	210	10-3-94	.241	.257	.237	135	481	50	116	24	2	9	60	47	11	0	3	98	5	6	.356	.321

Batting	B-T	HT	WT	DOB	AVG	vLH	vRH	G	AB	R	H	2B	3B	HR	RBI	BB	HBP	SH	SF	SO	SB	CS	SLG	OBP
Soto, Michael	R-R	6-3	215	11-17-91	.169	.136	.176	40	130	6	22	3	0	1	12	11	0	0	1	42	1	0	.215	.232
Theroux, Colin	R-R	6-2	220	3-10-94	.000	.000	.000	7	21	0	0	0	0	0	0	2	0	0	0	15	1	0	.000	.087

Pitching	B-T	HT	WT	DOB	W	L	ERA	G	GS	CG	SV	IP	H	R	ER	HR	BB	SO	AVG	vLH	vRH	K/9	BB/9
Alejo, Yordy	R-R	6-2	186	11-13-93	1	0	0.00	5	0	0	0	5	6	0	0	0	2	2	.353	.250	.444	3.86	0.00
Altamirano, Xavier	R-R	6-3	195	7-20-94	2	4	4.85	8	5	0	1	26	31	17	14	2	11	18	.304	.392	.216	6.23	3.81
Berube, Marc	L-R	6-2	180	2-12-93	0	1	15.43	3	0	0	0	2	4	4	4	0	4	4	.364	.250	.429	15.43	15.43
Biegalski, Boomer	R-R	6-2	165	7-13-94	8	8	3.70	28	25	0	0	153	144	72	63	14	38	115	.252	.236	.264	6.75	2.23
Blackwood, Nolan	R-R	6-5	185	3-16-95	2	2	4.05	13	0	0	2	20	21	9	9	1	5	20	.276	.300	.250	9.00	2.25
Butler, Brendan	L-R	6-3	217	5-2-93	1	5	3.14	9	9	1	0	52	44	22	18	4	15	46	.229	.234	.224	8.01	2.61
Driver, Dustin	R-R	6-2	210	10-11-94	0	2	9.47	13	2	0	0	19	23	21	20	2	23	11	.324	.370	.295	5.21	10.89
Duno, Angel	R-R	6-0	180	1-10-94	7	7	2.68	24	20	0	0	121	130	43	36	7	16	76	.273	.291	.259	5.65	1.19
Erwin, Zack	L-L	6-5	195	1-24-94	1	0	5.40	5	4	0	0	18	25	11	11	4	3	16	.316	.370	.288	7.85	1.47
Fagan, Mike	R-L	5-11	160	5-12-92	0	0	9.45	7	0	0	0	7	5	7	7	0	6	7	.208	.200	.211	9.45	8.10
Friedrichs, Kyle	R-R	6-1	195	1-22-92	3	2	1.25	10	8	0	0	50	38	10	7	2	6	31	.216	.247	.194	5.54	1.07
Huber, Rob	R-R	5-11	200	1-8-92	1	5	3.56	29	1	0	1	43	40	18	17	1	20	45	.252	.300	.213	9.42	4.19
Hurlbutt, Dustin	R-R	6-1	195	11-5-92	3	6	2.57	19	14	1	0	98	89	36	28	6	24	78	.248	.287	.213	7.16	2.20
Johnson, Kevin	R-R	6-3	175	4-5-91	0	1	3.42	12	4	0	1	26	31	12	10	3	12	16	.295	.278	.304	5.47	4.10
Kurz, Cody	R-R	6-4	225	9-13-92	3	7	4.89	40	0	0	6	42	32	25	23	2	37	36	.212	.221	.205	7.65	7.87
Lyons, Jared	L-L	6-0	190	5-18-93	5	3	1.72	41	0	0	7	52	42	13	10	1	16	61	.226	.205	.239	10.49	2.75
Manarino, Evan	L-L	6-1	195	12-28-92	8	5	2.15	22	18	0	0	122	112	37	29	1	20	103	.246	.206	.261	7.62	1.48
Miller, Corey	R-R	6-3	190	11-13-91	0	2	2.31	16	0	0	3	23	21	9	6	0	8	16	.241	.162	.300	6.17	3.09
Murray, Michael	R-R	6-3	215	9-26-93	4	2	4.28	12	12	0	0	61	72	31	29	6	13	53	.299	.283	.313	7.82	1.92
Naile, James	R-R	6-4	185	2-8-93	3	8	2.66	15	14	0	0	88	67	37	26	2	19	64	.211	.209	.212	6.55	1.94
Ruiz, Armando	R-R	5-9	185	7-19-93	3	4	3.46	39	1	0	3	52	42	20	20	0	25	50	.227	.247	.212	8.65	4.33
Schwartz, Jordan	R-R	6-2	195	2-28-92	0	1	4.98	9	0	0	0	22	20	13	12	2	8	14	.253	.219	.277	5.82	3.32
Tomasovich, Andrew	L-L	6-4	215	9-24-93	2	2	5.67	33	0	0	1	40	39	30	25	1	26	50	.257	.233	.272	11.34	5.90
Veliz, Victor	L-L	5-11	170	10-6-93	0	0	0.00	2	0	0	0	7	1	0	0	0	1	4	.043	.000	.048	4.91	1.23
Willman, Tyler	R-R	6-5	212	10-8-92	1	1	2.91	18	0	0	3	22	15	8	7	0	23	21	.188	.118	.239	8.72	9.55
Zambrano, Jesus	R-R	5-11	170	8-23-96	1	2	7.04	10	2	0	0	23	42	26	18	2	5	14	.393	.364	.413	5.48	1.96

Fielding

Catcher	PCT	G	PO	A	E	DP	PB
Chavez	.990	79	525	80	6	2	9
Collins	.973	18	97	12	3	1	1
Devencenzi	1.000	31	207	37	0	3	4
Gavitt	1.000	4	23	4	0	0	0
Gonzalez	.955	2	18	3	1	0	1
Guzman	.952	3	18	2	1	0	0
Paz	1.000	2	13	4	0	0	0
Rodriguez	1.000	3	24	2	0	0	0
Theroux	.957	6	41	4	2	0	0

First Base	PCT	G	PO	A	E	DP
Howell	.986	66	598	59	9	54
Iriart	.989	65	520	32	6	52
Paz	.938	2	15	0	1	1
Rodriguez	1.000	2	12	2	0	2
Soto	.977	12	77	7	2	7

Second Base	PCT	G	PO	A	E	DP
Diaz	1.000	2	4	5	0	2
Gilbert	.981	95	158	257	8	51
Loehr	1.000	10	14	15	0	5
Lopez	.957	29	60	75	6	20
Rodriguez	1.000	5	8	17	0	1

Third Base	PCT	G	PO	A	E	DP
Diaz	.944	63	41	127	10	8
Howell	.947	38	30	78	6	7
Loehr	.968	16	12	18	1	4
Lopez	1.000	13	6	18	0	1
Rodriguez	.871	25	19	35	8	4
Soto	1.000	1	3	4	0	0

Shortstop	PCT	G	PO	A	E	DP
Diaz	.951	30	49	87	7	21

	PCT	G	PO	A	E	DP
Loehr	.936	73	99	194	20	42
Lopez	.967	41	65	111	6	29
Rodriguez	—	3	0	0	0	0

Outfield	PCT	G	PO	A	E	DP
Barrera	.955	15	21	0	1	0
Bolt	.984	79	182	4	3	1
Higley	.983	108	175	2	3	0
Loehr	—	1	0	0	0	0
Martin	.986	33	66	6	1	2
Martinez	1.000	26	51	3	0	2
Pallares	.982	33	50	4	1	1
Rodriguez	.931	20	25	2	2	1
Siddall	.983	115	172	3	3	2

VERMONT LAKE MONSTERS   SHORT-SEASON
NEW YORK-PENN LEAGUE

Batting	B-T	HT	WT	DOB	AVG	vLH	vRH	G	AB	R	H	2B	3B	HR	RBI	BB	HBP	SH	SF	SO	SB	CS	SLG	OBP
Barrera, Luis	L-L	6-0	180	11-15-95	.321	.333	.317	41	159	26	51	10	4	2	18	16	0	0	2	29	5	2	.421	.379
Bennie, Rob	R-R	6-1	205	1-20-94	.169	.211	.154	22	71	5	12	1	1	0	3	5	0	0	0	32	0	0	.211	.224
Blair, Carson	R-R	6-2	210	10-18-89	.375	.667	.308	4	16	2	6	2	0	0	1	0	0	0	0	6	0	0	.500	.375
Collins, Nick	L-R	6-2	218	4-13-94	.136	.077	.151	23	66	3	9	5	0	0	7	11	1	0	1	18	1	0	.212	.266
Costa, Jarrett	R-R	5-11	225	4-23-93	.171	.083	.217	11	35	0	6	1	0	0	3	4	1	0	0	9	0	0	.200	.275
Godard, Javier	R-R	6-0	170	12-13-95	.000	.000	.000	3	13	1	0	0	0	0	0	0	0	0	0	3	0	0	.000	.000
Guzman, Miguel	R-R	6-2	210	3-10-95	.139	.235	.109	21	79	8	11	3	0	2	6	4	2	0	0	19	1	0	.264	.205
Lage, Jesus	B-R	6-1	155	12-1-97	.333	.333	.333	3	9	1	3	0	0	0	0	0	0	0	0	4	2	0	.333	.333
Lopez, Jesus	B-R	5-11	170	10-5-96	.133	.143	.132	13	45	3	6	1	0	1	1	6	0	0	0	11	1	1	.156	.235
Marinez, Eric	B-R	6-1	160	9-12-95	.251	.295	.236	60	235	18	59	10	3	1	19	4	0	0	2	47	1	5	.332	.261
Mercedes, Miguel	R-R	6-4	255	9-12-95	.258	.279	.250	67	248	32	64	9	1	12	43	23	3	0	4	74	0	0	.448	.324
Mondou, Nate	L-R	5-10	205	3-24-95	.298	.259	.311	60	225	27	67	11	2	0	24	24	4	1	0	37	6	6	.364	.375
Murphy, Sean	R-R	6-3	215	10-10-94	.237	.286	.218	22	76	10	18	1	0	2	7	9	0	0	0	12	1	0	.329	.318
Pallares, Steven	R-R	6-2	185	4-26-93	.190	.179	.195	57	174	20	33	2	0	0	10	28	3	2	2	28	14	1	.201	.309
Persico, Luke	R-R	6-3	180	10-4-95	.201	.214	.197	48	164	17	33	5	0	3	14	16	0	0	4	40	4	2	.287	.266
Proudfoot, Tim	R-R	5-10	180	3-23-93	.100	.000	.125	5	10	0	1	0	0	0	0	3	0	0	0	7	0	0	.100	.308
Ramirez, Tyler	L-L	5-9	185	2-21-95	.220	.194	.228	48	150	22	33	8	1	2	15	19	5	0	2	39	5	0	.327	.324
Rodriguez, Jhonny	L-L	6-3	170	7-20-96	.230	.240	.227	35	135	14	31	9	0	2	13	6	0	0	3	31	1	1	.341	.257
Shelby, JaVon	R-R	5-11	175	5-6-95	.186	.163	.193	56	194	16	36	9	0	5	18	25	0	0	5	51	5	4	.309	.279
Sunde, Brett	R-R	6-0	195	8-24-94	.250	.286	.237	27	80	7	20	2	1	0	5	8	1	2	1	23	0	1	.300	.322

Batting	B-T	HT	WT	DOB	AVG	vLH	vRH	G	AB	R	H	2B	3B	HR	RBI	BB	HBP	SH	SF	SO	SB	CS	SLG	OBP
Terrell, James	R-R	6-0	165	1-10-97	.220	.250	.206	26	91	8	20	2	0	1	6	4	2	2	0	39	3	0	.275	.268
White, Eli	R-R	6-2	175	6-26-94	.279	.269	.283	64	233	31	65	11	1	2	25	26	2	0	6	65	12	3	.361	.348

Pitching	B-T	HT	WT	DOB	W	L	ERA	G	GS	CG	SV	IP	H	R	ER	HR	BB	SO	AVG	vLH	vRH	K/9	BB/9
Alejo, Yordy	R-R	6-2	186	11-13-93	0	3	2.29	13	0	0	3	20	16	6	5	0	9	17	.222	.167	.262	7.78	4.12
Altamirano, Xavier	R-R	6-3	195	7-20-94	3	3	2.48	14	9	0	0	65	60	22	18	3	10	57	.242	.233	.250	7.85	1.38
Andueza, Ivan	L-L	5-11	180	2-7-95	2	3	4.68	13	7	0	0	58	54	36	30	4	29	43	.248	.283	.236	6.71	4.53
Bailey, Brandon	R-R	5-10	175	10-19-94	3	1	3.08	10	5	0	0	38	26	14	13	1	9	42	.193	.208	.184	9.95	2.13
Beasley, Derek	L-L	6-0	185	2-2-92	1	2	5.96	13	1	0	0	26	35	20	17	2	7	28	.315	.241	.341	9.82	2.45
Berube, Marc	L-R	6-2	180	2-12-93	0	1	4.85	7	0	0	0	13	7	8	7	0	10	8	.167	.059	.240	5.54	6.92
Blackwood, Nolan	R-R	6-5	185	3-16-95	0	0	2.84	5	0	0	4	6	3	2	2	0	1	5	.240	.300	.200	7.11	1.42
Bowers, Heath	R-R	6-4	190	7-25-93	3	7	4.31	15	10	0	0	71	71	44	34	2	28	44	.260	.218	.288	5.58	3.55
Butler, Brendan	L-R	6-3	217	5-2-93	2	1	1.95	7	5	0	0	37	31	9	8	1	8	32	.230	.242	.217	7.78	1.95
Chalmers, Dakota	R-R	6-3	175	10-8-96	5	4	4.70	15	13	0	0	67	55	41	35	8	37	62	.217	.237	.204	8.33	4.97
Damron, Ty	L-L	6-2	200	7-28-94	0	3	5.06	10	0	0	1	16	15	13	9	1	9	15	.238	.333	.190	8.44	5.06
Driver, Dustin	R-R	6-2	210	10-11-94	0	1	3.86	2	0	0	0	5	8	4	2	0	3	7	.364	.667	.250	13.50	5.79
Gilbert, Will	L-L	5-11	170	2-9-94	2	2	2.81	15	0	0	1	26	18	8	8	0	12	31	.194	.222	.182	10.87	4.21
Johnson, Kevin	R-R	6-3	175	4-5-91	0	1	7.71	1	1	0	0	5	4	4	4	0	4	3	.333	.300	.375	5.79	7.71
Kelliher, Branden	R-R	5-11	175	12-11-95	1	1	11.65	10	0	0	0	17	28	22	22	2	15	3	.368	.314	.415	1.59	7.94
Martinez, Jorge	L-L	5-11	170	1-5-96	0	1	6.00	2	0	0	0	3	4	3	2	1	0	4	.333	.500	.000	12.00	0.00
Milburn, Matt	R-R	6-3	210	7-29-93	1	2	6.92	5	0	0	0	13	22	11	10	0	0	14	.379	.333	.412	9.69	0.00
Painton, Tyler	L-L	6-5	195	2-20-92	0	1	3.69	15	0	0	1	32	31	14	13	1	15	18	.270	.289	.257	5.12	4.26
Puk, A.J.	L-L	6-7	220	4-25-95	0	4	3.03	10	10	0	0	33	23	18	11	0	12	40	.185	.257	.157	11.02	3.31
Sawyer, Dalton	L-L	6-5	210	11-22-93	0	3	3.38	14	0	0	3	19	15	9	7	1	10	26	.221	.190	.234	12.54	4.82
Schwartz, Jordan	R-R	6-2	195	2-28-92	1	0	2.45	8	1	0	1	15	11	10	4	1	12	19	.200	.148	.250	11.66	7.36
Shore, Logan	R-R	6-2	215	12-28-94	0	2	2.57	7	7	0	0	21	17	10	6	1	7	21	.207	.100	.269	9.00	3.00
Willman, Tyler	R-R	6-5	212	10-8-92	1	0	0.00	3	0	0	0	3	0	0	0	0	0	2	.000	.000	.000	6.75	0.00
Zambrano, Jesus	R-R	5-11	170	8-23-96	2	2	3.83	16	7	0	0	49	54	27	21	3	18	28	.271	.298	.248	5.11	3.28

Fielding

C: Argomaniz 1, Haddad 7, Navas 29, Seitz 23, Skinner 8, Torrens 11, Vazquez 4. **1B:** Blaser 23, Bridges 18, Fleming 2, Ford 2, Haddad 1, Sweeney 32. **2B:** Baez 2, Fleming 1, Godinez 9, Perez 3, Rodriguez 2, Rosario 1, Solak 59. **3B:** Alvarez 12, Baez 10, Bridges 48, Fleming 2, Godinez 4, Mateo 1. **SS:** Aguilar 50, Baez 1, Godinez 9, Mateo 1, Perez 16. **OF:** Blaser 18, Coleman 42, Ferreira 21, Mikolas 8, Robinson 56, Rosario 1, Ruta 22, Thompson-Williams 51, Vidal 10.

AZL ATHLETICS   ROOKIE
ARIZONA LEAGUE

Batting	B-T	HT	WT	DOB	AVG	vLH	vRH	G	AB	R	H	2B	3B	HR	RBI	BB	HBP	SH	SF	SO	SB	CS	SLG	OBP
Bennie, Rob	R-R	6-1	205	1-20-94	.336	.357	.329	29	110	21	37	8	5	0	26	9	1	0	1	32	3	2	.500	.388
Bittiger, Brett	R-R	5-10	175	10-23-92	.167	.000	.200	3	6	2	1	0	0	0	0	1	0	0	1	0	0	.167	.286
Churlin, Anthony	R-R	6-1	190	5-27-97	.236	.276	.217	27	89	7	21	2	1	0	4	9	1	1	0	28	2	2	.281	.313
Costa, Jarrett	R-R	5-11	225	4-23-93	.219	.286	.200	13	32	3	7	2	0	0	4	6	2	0	2	11	0	0	.281	.357
Godard, Javier	R-R	6-0	170	12-13-95	.277	.231	.297	36	130	22	36	6	1	0	16	12	4	3	4	21	9	4	.338	.347
Gonzalez, Roger	B-R	5-9	190	3-21-93	.357	.273	.412	9	28	3	10	3	0	1	4	5	1	0	0	5	0	0	.571	.471
Gould, Charley	R-R	6-2	220	12-3-92	.273	.200	.305	49	183	20	50	9	1	1	38	15	5	0	3	25	1	1	.350	.340
Gruber, Cole	L-L	6-0	190	3-31-94	.214	.270	.191	35	126	29	27	6	2	0	7	24	2	1	1	39	28	2	.294	.346
Guzman, Miguel	R-R	6-2	210	3-10-95	.357	.400	.344	10	42	2	15	3	0	1	9	0	1	0	0	4	0	1	.500	.372
Hiciano, Carlos	R-R	6-2	175	10-29-96	.116	.077	.133	11	43	5	5	0	0	0	2	0	0	0	0	18	3	0	.116	.116
Iriart, Chris	R-R	6-2	230	10-7-94	.500	.250	1.000	2	6	2	3	3	0	0	1	0	0	0	0	1	0	0	1.000	.500
Lage, Jesus	B-R	6-1	155	12-1-97	.172	.139	.188	34	116	20	20	4	2	0	11	13	3	2	0	42	4	1	.241	.273
Martinez, Robert	R-R	6-0	180	2-8-94	.353	.462	.286	9	34	8	12	6	0	1	6	4	0	0	0	9	1	0	.618	.421
McCray, Jeremiah	R-R	5-10	160	3-3-98	.202	.088	.250	32	114	17	23	3	5	0	15	8	1	0	0	36	8	2	.316	.260
Mondou, Nate	L-R	5-10	205	3-24-95	.000	.000	—	1	1	0	0	0	0	0	0	1	0	0	0	0	0	0	.000	.500
Mullen, Robert	R-R	6-0	170	5-23-96	.260	.226	.277	30	96	13	25	7	2	1	12	16	0	0	1	21	0	0	.406	.363
Murphy, Sean	R-R	6-3	215	10-10-94	.000	.000	.000	1	3	1	0	0	0	0	0	0	0	0	0	0	0	0	.000	.000
Nowlin, Kyle	R-R	6-0	240	3-4-94	.260	.245	.267	44	154	26	40	11	1	2	19	36	1	0	7	47	1	0	.383	.389
Persico, Luke	R-R	6-0	180	10-4-95	.111	.250	.071	6	18	3	2	0	1	0	3	0	0	0	3	2	0	.222	.238
Quintin, Christopher	R-R	6-0	135	6-7-99	.000	.000	.000	5	12	0	0	0	0	0	1	0	0	0	7	0	0	.000	.077
Ramirez, Tyler	L-L	5-9	185	2-21-95	.286	.250	.292	8	28	5	8	3	2	0	8	1	0	0	10	1	0	.536	.310
Rodriguez, Jhonny	L-L	6-3	170	7-20-96	.333	.200	.400	4	15	4	5	1	0	0	2	0	0	0	4	0	0	.400	.412
Shelby, JaVon	R-R	5-11	175	5-6-95	.667	1.000	.500	1	3	0	2	0	0	1	0	0	0	0	0	0	0	.667	.667
Terrell, James	R-R	6-0	165	1-10-97	.200	.188	.206	14	50	8	10	3	4	0	8	3	2	1	1	13	0	1	.420	.268
Theroux, Colin	R-R	6-2	220	3-10-94	.156	.222	.130	11	32	4	5	4	0	0	4	3	0	0	0	14	0	0	.281	.308
Thomas, Casey	R-R	5-10	160	3-16-93	.258	.235	.267	37	120	15	31	2	0	0	18	6	2	2	2	25	3	0	.275	.300
Vidales, Josh	B-R	5-8	164	8-6-93	.345	.367	.333	41	148	27	51	15	3	1	27	20	5	1	1	16	5	1	.507	.437
Weber, Skyler	R-R	5-10	176	6-6-95	.173	.188	.169	22	75	7	13	2	0	0	4	6	0	0	4	14	5	0	.200	.235
White, Eli	R-R	6-2	175	6-26-94	.000	.000	.000	1	3	0	0	0	0	0	0	0	0	0	0	0	0	0	.000	.000

Pitching	B-T	HT	WT	DOB	W	L	ERA	G	GS	CG	SV	IP	H	R	ER	HR	BB	SO	AVG	vLH	vRH	K/9	BB/9
Alvarez, Henderson	R-R	6-0	205	4-18-90	0	0	0.00	1	1	0	0	1	0	0	0	0	0	1	.250	.000	.333	9.00	0.00
Andueza, Ivan	L-L	5-11	180	2-7-95	0	0	0.00	1	1	0	0	5	4	1	0	0	1	4	.200	.000	.235	7.20	1.80
Bailey, Brandon	R-R	5-10	175	10-19-94	0	0	1.80	2	2	0	0	5	7	1	1	0	1	4	.333	.250	.381	7.20	1.80
Beasley, Derek	L-L	6-0	185	2-2-92	0	0	0.00	1	0	0	0	1	0	0	0	0	0	0	.000	—	.000	0.00	0.00
Blanco, Argenis	R-R	6-1	165	5-23-96	5	4	2.52	14	10	0	0	61	58	24	17	2	17	48	.250	.325	.208	7.12	2.52

Pitching	B-T	HT	WT	DOB	W	L	ERA	G	GS	CG	SV	IP	H	R	ER	HR	BB	SO	AVG	vLH	vRH	K/9	BB/9
Camacho, Joseph	R-R	5-9	175	6-23-94	2	3	3.03	19	0	0	3	30	27	11	10	1	6	22	.245	.281	.231	6.67	1.82
Charles, Wandisson	R-R	6-6	220	9-7-96	5	1	7.12	14	0	0	2	37	39	31	29	0	33	48	.277	.190	.313	11.78	8.10
De La Cruz, Frederick	R-R	6-3	170	9-13-96	1	1	8.82	11	0	0	0	16	19	22	16	0	19	11	.288	.182	.341	6.06	10.47
Driver, Dustin	R-R	6-2	210	10-11-94	0	1	3.12	4	3	0	0	9	9	3	3	0	7	7	.290	.364	.250	7.27	7.27
Duchene, Kevin	L-L	6-2	220	12-10-93	1	0	3.70	7	2	0	0	24	24	16	10	1	11	15	.253	.167	.273	5.55	4.07
Ferreras, Kevin	L-L	6-0	170	7-5-93	1	1	5.06	15	1	0	2	21	24	15	12	1	6	19	.279	.286	.278	8.02	2.53
Hall, Kris	R-R	6-3	215	6-8-91	0	0	0.00	4	0	0	0	5	4	0	0	0	2	3	.222	.222	.222	5.40	3.60
Highberger, Nick	R-R	5-10	190	11-4-93	2	2	3.38	17	0	0	3	27	33	15	10	1	7	18	.297	.270	.311	6.08	2.36
Jefferies, Daulton	L-R	6-0	180	12-2-95	0	0	2.38	5	5	0	0	11	11	3	3	0	2	17	.262	.167	.333	13.50	1.59
Jordan, Mitchell	R-R	6-2	205	4-10-95	1	1	3.08	12	11	0	0	38	39	14	13	2	8	33	.265	.373	.208	7.82	1.89
Kelliher, Branden	R-R	5-11	175	12-11-95	0	1	13.50	2	0	0	0	4	7	7	6	0	5	2	.389	.571	.273	4.50	11.25
Mann, Brandon	L-L	6-2	200	5-16-84	1	0	0.00	1	1	0	0	5	2	0	0	0	2	7	.118	—	.118	12.60	3.60
Martinez, Seth	R-R	6-2	200	5-29-94	0	0	3.86	3	0	0	1	2	3	1	1	0	2	2	.333	.333	.333	7.71	7.71
Milburn, Matt	R-R	6-3	210	7-29-93	0	0	3.42	9	2	0	0	24	23	14	9	0	2	30	.256	.250	.258	11.41	0.76
Minaya, Yeudy	R-R	6-4	195	5-11-96	1	0	2.03	6	1	0	1	13	6	4	3	0	4	8	.136	.143	.133	5.40	2.70
Nelo, Emerson	R-R	5-11	180	9-13-95	0	1	7.82	12	0	0	1	25	40	25	22	1	10	18	.360	.371	.355	6.39	3.55
Ortiz, Phillip	R-R	6-0	190	3-6-95	0	1	7.36	3	0	0	0	4	5	3	3	0	6	4	.357	.500	.300	9.82	14.73
Sanchez, Miguel	R-R	6-3	182	11-27-95	4	1	3.96	8	1	0	0	25	19	14	11	0	22	28	.226	.192	.241	10.08	7.92
Sheehan, Sam	R-R	6-3	195	8-8-93	2	1	3.20	14	0	0	3	20	17	10	7	0	12	29	.230	.185	.255	13.27	5.49
Szynski, Skylar	L-R	6-2	195	7-14-97	0	3	8.10	7	7	0	0	13	16	14	12	1	4	8	.296	.200	.333	5.40	2.70
Tovar, Oscar	R-R	6-1	160	3-19-98	3	2	3.56	10	5	0	0	43	41	20	17	0	17	31	.253	.220	.268	6.49	3.56

Fielding

C: Costa 12, Gonzalez 5, Guzman 4, Mullen 17, Murphy 1, Theroux 8, Weber 16. **1B:** Gould 47, Guzman 4, Iriart 2, Mullen 7. **2B:** Bittiger 1, Godard 10, Lage 2, Mondou 1, Quintin 2, Thomas 2, Vidales 41. **3B:** Bittiger 1, Godard 26, Hiciano 11, Lage 7, Mullen 1, Shelby 1, Thomas 8. **SS:** Bittiger 1, Lage 27, Quintin 3, Thomas 27, White 1. **OF:** Bennie 23, Churlin 25, Gruber 32, Martinez 6, McCray 32, Nowlin 26, Persico 6, Ramirez 6, Rodriguez 4, Terrell 13, Weber 1.

DSL ATHLETICS ROOKIE
DOMINICAN SUMMER LEAGUE

Batting	B-T	HT	WT	DOB	AVG	vLH	vRH	G	AB	R	H	2B	3B	HR	RBI	BB	HBP	SH	SF	SO	SB	CS	SLG	OBP
Agelvis, Javier	R-R	6-1	170	8-18-97	.133	.308	.085	22	60	6	8	1	0	0	4	14	2	1	2	13	2	3	.150	.308
Almanzar, Luis	R-R	6-1	170	5-11-99	.214	.241	.208	48	154	13	33	4	3	0	17	14	3	2	2	35	2	1	.279	.289
Alvarez, Wilson	R-R	5-10	150	5-19-98	.200	.130	.228	30	80	9	16	1	0	0	4	12	1	2	0	10	8	4	.213	.312
Arias, Jhoan	R-R	5-11	150	9-7-98	.207	.222	.203	51	164	15	34	3	2	0	8	15	7	1	2	33	6	2	.250	.298
De Los Santos, Martin	R-R	6-0	170	1-31-97	.148	.200	.161	50	137	27	23	3	2	4	14	25	3	2	0	41	11	7	.307	.309
Diaz, Cesar	R-R	6-0	170	1-8-97	.222	.267	.207	41	117	9	26	4	1	0	9	8	4	3	0	38	8	5	.274	.295
Gonzalez, Yhoelnys	R-R	6-0	170	10-30-96	.230	.353	.197	56	161	18	37	2	4	0	18	23	0	4	2	45	20	5	.292	.323
Gordon, Jorge	R-R	5-10	175	10-28-97	.153	.303	.094	38	118	9	18	3	0	0	4	15	0	0	1	19	1	1	.178	.246
Medina, Alonzo	R-R	6-2	190	2-2-99	.176	.294	.148	58	176	22	31	9	2	1	13	30	4	0	0	64	4	3	.267	.310
Monserratt, Jesus	R-R	6-0	180	1-3-97	.360	.333	.368	25	75	4	27	0	1	0	6	11	4	0	0	9	2	0	.387	.467
Mordock, Erick	R-R	5-11	165	9-9-97	.243	.244	.242	60	210	26	51	4	0	0	21	20	4	3	3	25	11	4	.262	.316
Paula, Jose	R-R	6-0	185	4-18-99	.224	.600	.146	24	58	5	13	0	0	0	4	10	4	0	0	17	1	1	.224	.375
Quintin, Christopher	R-R	6-0	135	6-7-99	.146	.095	.160	32	96	6	14	4	0	0	5	10	2	3	0	37	1	0	.188	.241
Rigby, Gean	R-R	6-0	180	1-7-97	.137	.154	.133	31	73	10	10	2	0	0	6	14	2	1	0	22	2	3	.164	.292
Rivas, Jose	R-R	5-11	190	8-5-98	.230	.174	.244	40	113	12	26	1	0	0	11	17	6	1	3	13	3	0	.239	.353
Serrano, Iraj	R-R	5-11	165	2-19-99	.180	.222	.168	58	161	24	29	7	1	0	15	28	5	2	1	24	9	2	.236	.318
Urena, Rafioby	L-L	6-4	210	9-22-98	.277	.250	.286	61	213	19	59	15	0	2	26	25	1	0	2	53	0	1	.376	.353

Pitching	B-T	HT	WT	DOB	W	L	ERA	G	GS	CG	SV	IP	H	R	ER	HR	BB	SO	AVG	vLH	vRH	K/9	BB/9
Aquino, Ruber	R-R	6-2	185	12-29-96	0	0	0.00	3	1	0	0	4	0	0	0	0	1	4	.000	.000	.000	9.00	2.25
Calderon, Alexander	L-L	6-3	170	2-23-96	1	3	3.07	14	9	0	0	59	55	32	20	1	30	53	.249	.125	.264	8.13	4.60
De La Cruz, Frederick	R-R	6-3	170	9-13-96	1	0	5.79	2	1	0	0	5	4	3	0	4	4	.294	.167	.364	7.71	7.71
Hernandez, Marcelo	R-R	6-1	160	1-23-99	3	2	2.33	17	0	0	1	27	13	7	7	2	7	25	.141	.172	.127	8.33	2.33
Herrera, Dennis	L-L	6-0	165	9-28-98	1	2	2.70	14	0	0	0	23	20	15	7	0	15	13	.233	.375	.218	5.01	5.79
Hurtado, Jhenderson	L-L	6-1	180	3-16-98	3	2	3.16	14	10	0	0	63	53	32	22	0	23	51	.227	.273	.232	7.32	3.30
Infante, Angello	R-R	6-1	180	4-16-99	3	1	2.12	18	0	0	2	34	34	9	8	1	4	22	.262	.313	.245	5.82	1.06
Magallanes, Wilfredo	R-R	6-2	185	11-15-95	1	3	6.59	17	0	0	0	29	30	26	21	1	22	19	.261	.273	.256	5.97	6.91
Mendoza, Abdiel	R-R	5-10	135	9-19-98	3	1	2.32	17	0	0	0	31	25	13	8	0	9	25	.223	.156	.250	7.26	2.61
Minaya, Yeudy	R-R	6-4	195	5-11-96	0	1	3.86	2	1	0	0	7	9	4	3	0	0	2	.321	.182	.412	2.57	0.00
Montilla, David	L-L	6-0	170	5-29-98	0	2	1.84	9	8	0	0	15	9	6	3	0	9	13	.170	.000	.180	7.98	5.52
Mora, Jose	R-R	6-3	185	10-1-97	0	5	3.55	13	8	0	0	46	41	28	18	0	18	27	.246	.224	.254	5.32	3.55
Morban, Jose	R-R	6-2	162	12-24-97	1	5	3.24	13	7	0	2	50	38	28	18	1	25	26	.209	.140	.240	4.68	4.50
Ramirez, Eliel	R-R	6-0	165	9-27-97	0	1	27.00	1	1	0	0	1	1	1	0	2	0	.500	1.000	.000	0.00	54.00
Rodriguez, Santiago	R-R	6-3	190	3-9-97	1	4	4.15	13	11	0	0	48	32	30	22	0	30	29	.186	.190	.185	5.48	5.66
Ruiz, Jean	R-R	6-1	165	9-6-96	4	2	1.70	13	7	0	1	58	45	19	11	0	14	50	.218	.184	.229	7.71	2.16
Sanchez, Carlos	R-R	5-11	150	12-26-97	3	0	2.86	17	0	0	3	35	34	11	11	0	2	21	.260	.286	.247	5.45	0.52
Sanchez, Miguel	R-R	6-3	182	11-27-95	0	3	6.16	7	4	0	0	19	23	16	13	0	15	20	.303	.182	.352	9.47	7.11
Sullivan, Enmanuel	R-R	6-3	195	6-24-96	1	4	7.17	16	0	0	3	21	31	24	17	1	13	9	.365	.429	.333	3.80	5.48

Fielding

C: Diaz 10, Gordon 32, Monserratt 9, Rivas 30. **1B:** Rigby 1, Serrano 20, Urena 61. **2B:** Agelvis 9, Almanzar 1, Alvarez 17, Arias 43, De Los Santos 9, Mordock 1, Quintin 1, Rigby 3. **3B:** Agelvis 13, Almanzar 16, Alvarez 1, Arias 7, De Los Santos 25, Diaz 15, Gordon 1. **SS:** Agelvis 4, Almanzar 27, Alvarez 11, Arias 1, De Los Santos 7, Quintin 30. **OF:** Diaz 2, Gonzalez 49, Gordon 1, Medina 55, Mordock 58, Paula 21, Rigby 21, Serrano 31.

Philadelphia Phillies

SEASON IN A SENTENCE: The Phillies' rebuild took a solid step forward, as the team improved by eight wins from the previous year despite a difficult offensive season. The Phils scored just 610 runs, tied for their fewest in a full season since 1988.

HIGH POINT: No one told Philadelphia it wasn't supposed to contend early on, as the Phillies got off to a 24-17 start. They were just a half-game back of first place as righthanders Jeremy Hellickson and Vince Velasquez won 11 of their first 14 decisions, and closer Jeanmar Gomez saved 16 of the club's first 24 victories. Velasquez provided the single-game highlight with an April 14 complete-game shutout with 16 strikeouts and no walks against the Padres.

LOW POINT: The Phillies ran out of gas and pitching in September, most exemplified by a late stretch including a series loss to the Mets with 10-5 and 17-0 losses sandwiched around a 10-8 win in which New York nearly rallied from a 10-0 deficit. Gomez posted a 19.13 ERA after Sept. 1 as the Phils went 11-18 to finish the season.

NOTABLE ROOKIES: With Ryan Howard ending his tenure in Philadelphia as his contract expires, rookie Tommy Joseph emerged as his platoon partner and hit 21 homers in a .257/.308/.505 campaign. The Phillies didn't get much out of rookie righthanders Zach Eflin (3-5, 5.54), Jake Thompson (3-6, 5.70) and Severino Gonzalez (1-2, 5.60), while Edubray Ramos (1-3, 3.83) had his moments in a relief role. Thompson has the highest expectations going into 2017.

KEY TRANSACTIONS: Philadelphia had traded its top pieces, with catcher Carlos Ruiz the last piece of the '08 World Series champions to be traded off, to the Dodgers in August. Howard finished his Phillies tenure with his 382 home runs ranking second in franchise history.

DOWN ON THE FARM: The Phillies' greatest progress came in the minors, where Philadelphia domestic affiliates finished with a .595 winning percentage, the best mark by a farm system since the 2007 Yankees. Four Phillies clubs made the playoffs, with three 80-win clubs at high Class A Clearwater, Double-A Reading and Triple-A Lehigh Valley. Reading had the minors' two top home run hitters, with outfielder Dylan Cozens edging first baseman Rhys Hoskins 40-38. Cozens also led the minors with 125 RBIs, while righthander Ben Lively went 18-5, 2.69 to lead the minors in wins.

OPENING DAY PAYROLL: $ 83,980,000 (25th)

2016 PERFORMANCE

President: Andy MacPhail. **GM:** Matt Klentak. **Farm Director:** Joe Jordan. **Scouting Director:** Johnny Almaraz.

Class	Team	League	W	L	PCT	Finish	Manager
Majors	Philadelphia Phillies	National	71	91	.438	11th (15)	Pete Mackanin
Triple-A	Lehigh Valley IronPigs	International	85	58	.594	2nd (14)	Dave Brundage
Double-A	Reading Fightin' Phils	Eastern	89	52	.631	1st (12)	Dusty Wathan
High A	Clearwater Threshers	Florida State	82	54	.603	1st (12)	Greg Legg
Low A	Lakewood BlueClaws	South Atlantic	74	65	.532	4th (14)	Shawn Williams
Short season	Williamsport Crosscutters	New York-Penn	39	36	.520	6th (14)	Pat Borders
Rookie	Phillies	Gulf Coast	43	15	.741	1st (17)	Roly De Armas
Overall 2016 Minor League Record			412	280	.595	1st (30)	

ORGANIZATION STATISTICS

PHILADELPHIA PHILLIES
NATIONAL LEAGUE

Batting	B-T	HT	WT	DOB	AVG	vLH	vRH	G	AB	R	H	2B	3B	HR	RBI	BB	HBP	SH	SF	SO	SB	CS	SLG	OBP
Alfaro, Jorge	R-R	6-2	225	6-11-93	.125	.000	.143	6	16	0	2	0	0	0	0	1	0	0	0	8	0	0	.125	.176
Altherr, Aaron	R-R	6-5	215	1-14-91	.197	.250	.184	57	198	23	39	6	0	4	22	23	6	0	0	69	7	2	.288	.300
Asche, Cody	L-R	6-1	205	6-30-90	.213	.227	.211	71	197	22	42	15	0	4	18	18	2	0	1	54	3	1	.350	.284
Blanco, Andres	B-R	5-10	195	4-11-84	.253	.211	.263	90	190	26	48	15	1	4	21	11	7	0	1	41	2	3	.405	.316
Bourjos, Peter	R-R	6-1	185	3-31-87	.251	.301	.235	123	355	40	89	20	7	5	23	17	4	6	1	91	6	4	.389	.292
Burriss, Emmanuel	B-R	6-0	190	1-17-85	.111	.000	.135	39	45	3	5	1	1	0	0	2	2	1	0	10	1	0	.178	.184
Ellis, A.J.	R-R	6-2	225	4-9-81	.313	.111	.391	11	32	3	10	3	0	1	9	3	0	0	0	7	1	0	.500	.371
2-team total (53 Los Angeles)					.216	—	—	64	171	11	37	8	0	2	22	19	2	3	1	31	2	1	.298	.301
Featherston, Taylor	R-R	6-1	185	10-8-89	.115	.083	.143	19	26	2	3	1	0	0	1	2	0	0	0	11	2	0	.154	.179
Franco, Maikel	R-R	6-1	215	8-26-92	.255	.286	.246	152	581	67	148	23	1	25	88	40	5	0	4	106	1	1	.427	.306
Galvis, Freddy	B-R	5-10	185	11-14-89	.241	.215	.250	158	584	61	141	26	3	20	67	25	3	8	4	136	17	6	.399	.274
Goeddel, Tyler	R-R	6-4	180	10-20-92	.192	.165	.216	92	213	17	41	3	3	4	16	17	2	1	1	52	3	0	.291	.258
Hernandez, Cesar	B-R	5-10	160	5-23-90	.294	.341	.279	155	547	67	161	14	11	6	39	66	2	5	2	116	17	13	.393	.371
Herrera, Odubel	L-R	5-11	205	12-29-91	.286	.236	.303	159	583	87	167	21	6	15	49	63	6	2	2	134	25	7	.420	.361
Howard, Ryan	L-L	6-4	250	11-19-79	.196	.121	.205	112	331	35	65	10	0	25	59	27	1	0	3	114	0	1	.453	.257
Hunter, Cedric	L-L	5-11	200	3-10-88	.088	.000	.091	13	34	3	3	0	0	1	1	2	0	0	0	6	0	0	.176	.139
Joseph, Tommy	R-R	6-1	255	7-16-91	.257	.281	.248	107	315	47	81	15	0	21	47	22	4	0	6	75	1	1	.505	.308
Lough, David	L-L	5-10	175	1-20-86	.239	.250	.238	30	67	6	16	3	1	0	4	9	2	0	1	8	1	2	.313	.342
Paredes, Jimmy	B-R	6-3	200	11-25-88	.217	.179	.231	76	143	13	31	7	0	4	17	5	0	1	1	44	0	1	.350	.242
Quinn, Roman	B-R	5-10	170	5-14-93	.263	.333	.238	15	57	10	15	4	0	0	6	8	2	2	0	19	5	1	.333	.373
Ruf, Darin	R-R	6-3	250	7-28-86	.205	.286	.164	43	83	8	17	2	0	3	9	4	0	0	2	25	0	1	.337	.236
Ruiz, Carlos	R-R	5-10	215	1-22-79	.261	.250	.264	48	165	18	43	6	0	3	12	24	4	0	0	28	3	1	.352	.368
2-team total (14 Los Angeles)					.264	—	—	62	201	21	53	8	0	3	15	27	5	0	0	33	3	1	.348	.365
Rupp, Cameron	R-R	6-2	260	9-28-88	.252	.324	.237	105	389	36	98	26	1	16	54	24	5	0	1	114	1	0	.447	.303

Pitching	B-T	HT	WT	DOB	W	L	ERA	G	GS	CG	SV	IP	H	R	ER	HR	BB	SO	AVG	vLH	vRH	K/9	BB/9
Araujo, Elvis	L-L	6-7	275	7-15-91	2	1	5.60	32	0	0	0	27	35	22	17	4	17	29	.313	.255	.361	9.55	5.60
Asher, Alec	R-R	6-4	230	10-4-91	2	1	2.28	5	5	0	0	28	22	11	7	1	4	13	.216	.241	.182	4.23	1.30
Bailey, Andrew	R-R	6-3	240	5-31-84	3	1	6.40	33	0	0	0	32	32	23	23	6	15	33	.260	.286	.243	9.19	4.18
Eflin, Zach	R-R	6-6	215	4-8-94	3	5	5.54	11	11	2	0	63	67	42	39	12	17	31	.269	.289	.250	4.41	2.42
Eickhoff, Jerad	R-R	6-4	245	7-2-90	11	14	3.65	33	33	0	0	197	187	88	80	30	42	167	.251	.278	.220	7.62	1.92
Garcia, Luis	R-R	6-3	230	1-30-87	1	1	6.46	17	0	0	0	15	21	11	11	2	8	14	.318	.378	.241	8.22	4.70
Gomez, Jeanmar	R-R	6-3	215	2-10-88	3	5	4.85	70	0	0	37	69	78	38	37	6	22	47	.289	.287	.290	6.16	2.88
Gonzalez, Severino	R-R	6-2	155	9-28-92	1	2	5.60	27	0	0	0	35	40	22	22	4	7	34	.286	.302	.273	8.66	1.78
Hellickson, Jeremy	R-R	6-1	190	4-8-87	12	10	3.71	32	32	1	0	189	173	86	78	24	45	154	.243	.257	.232	7.33	2.14
Hernandez, David	R-R	6-3	245	5-13-85	3	4	3.84	70	0	0	1	73	77	31	31	11	32	80	.270	.264	.276	9.91	3.96
Herrmann, Frank	L-R	6-4	220	5-30-84	1	2	8.40	14	0	0	0	15	20	16	14	7	5	14	.323	.269	.361	8.40	3.00
Hinojosa, Dalier	R-R	6-1	230	12-10-86	0	1	3.27	10	0	0	0	11	10	4	4	1	3	8	.250	.235	.261	6.55	2.45
Klein, Phil	R-R	6-7	255	4-30-89	0	0	8.44	4	0	0	0	11	15	10	10	0	7	7	.375	.417	.313	5.91	5.91
Mariot, Michael	R-R	6-0	190	10-20-88	1	0	5.82	25	0	0	0	22	18	14	14	5	14	23	.222	.311	.111	9.55	5.82
Morgan, Adam	L-L	6-1	200	2-27-90	2	11	6.04	23	21	0	0	113	141	81	76	23	29	95	.302	.257	.316	7.54	2.30
Morton, Charlie	R-R	6-5	235	11-12-83	1	1	4.15	4	4	0	0	17	15	8	8	1	8	19	.242	.258	.226	9.87	4.15
Murray, Colton	R-R	6-0	195	4-22-90	1	1	6.25	24	0	0	0	32	34	22	22	6	13	31	.276	.240	.301	8.81	3.69
Neris, Hector	R-R	6-2	215	6-14-89	4	4	2.58	79	0	0	2	80	59	26	23	9	30	102	.202	.210	.193	11.43	3.36
Nola, Aaron	R-R	6-2	195	6-4-93	6	9	4.78	20	20	0	0	111	116	68	59	10	29	121	.264	.241	.284	9.81	2.35
Oberholtzer, Brett	L-L	6-1	225	7-1-89	2	2	4.83	26	0	0	1	50	58	28	27	11	20	38	.284	.263	.297	6.79	3.58
Ramos, Edubray	R-R	6-0	160	12-19-92	1	3	3.83	42	0	0	0	40	36	18	17	5	11	40	.243	.260	.225	9.00	2.48
Rodriguez, Joely	L-L	6-1	200	11-14-91	0	0	2.79	12	0	0	0	10	8	3	3	0	4	7	.235	.333	.125	6.52	3.72
Russell, James	L-L	6-4	205	1-8-86	0	0	18.69	7	0	0	0	4	9	9	9	2	5	4	.429	.444	.417	8.31	10.38
Schuster, Patrick	R-L	6-2	190	10-30-90	0	1	45.00	6	0	0	0	2	6	11	10	1	4	2	.500	.286	.800	9.00	18.00
Stumpf, Daniel	L-L	6-0	200	1-4-91	0	0	10.80	7	0	0	0	5	9	6	6	1	2	2	.409	.429	.400	3.60	3.60
Thompson, Jake	R-R	6-4	235	1-31-94	3	6	5.70	10	10	0	0	54	53	34	34	10	28	32	.265	.284	.245	5.37	4.70
Velasquez, Vince	B-R	6-3	205	6-7-92	8	6	4.12	24	24	1	0	131	129	64	60	21	45	152	.263	.270	.255	10.44	3.09

Fielding

Catcher	PCT	G	PO	A	E	DP	PB
Alfaro	1.000	4	27	0	0	0	1
Ellis	1.000	11	67	5	0	1	1
Ruiz	.993	47	393	34	3	3	1
Rupp	.994	104	825	44	5	5	7

First Base	PCT	G	PO	A	E	DP
Blanco	1.000	19	35	4	0	5
Burriss	1.000	2	6	1	0	0
Howard	.982	83	557	45	11	47
Joseph	.989	97	612	36	7	69
Ruf	1.000	14	62	4	0	8

Second Base	PCT	G	PO	A	E	DP
Blanco	.971	20	28	38	2	7
Burriss	1.000	5	5	3	0	1
Featherston	1.000	4	9	6	0	3
Hernandez	.981	149	241	390	12	102
Paredes	1.000	1	1	0	0	0

Third Base	PCT	G	PO	A	E	DP
Blanco	.911	21	10	31	4	3
Franco	.960	148	93	223	13	16

Shortstop	PCT	G	PO	A	E	DP
Blanco	1.000	10	8	15	0	4
Burriss	1.000	3	0	1	0	0
Galvis	.987	156	210	407	8	93
Hernandez	1.000	4	6	6	0	3

Outfield	PCT	G	PO	A	E	DP
Altherr	.991	57	109	3	1	1
Asche	.991	57	104	3	1	0
Blanco	1.000	1	1	0	0	0
Bourjos	.995	119	202	2	1	0
Burriss	1.000	3	2	0	0	0
Goeddel	.969	77	88	5	3	3
Herrera	.977	155	372	11	9	4
Hunter	1.000	12	17	1	0	0
Lough	1.000	23	38	1	0	0
Paredes	.983	36	55	2	1	1
Quinn	.971	15	33	1	1	0
Ruf	.941	13	16	0	1	0

LEHIGH VALLEY IRONPIGS
INTERNATIONAL LEAGUE

TRIPLE-A

Batting	B-T	HT	WT	DOB	AVG	vLH	vRH	G	AB	R	H	2B	3B	HR	RBI	BB	HBP	SH	SF	SO	SB	CS	SLG	OBP
Aguila, Osmel	R-R	6-0	185	7-18-89	.400	1.000	.000	3	5	2	2	1	0	0	1	0	1	0	0	2	0	0	.600	.500
Alonso, Carlos	R-R	5-11	205	2-15-88	.224	.095	.297	21	58	9	13	4	0	1	8	9	0	1	0	16	1	0	.345	.328
Altherr, Aaron	R-R	6-5	215	1-14-91	.286	.500	.200	2	7	0	2	1	0	0	1	0	0	0	0	2	0	0	.429	.286
Arencibia, J.P.	R-R	6-1	210	1-5-86	.167	.167	.167	12	48	3	8	2	0	1	2	0	0	0	0	11	0	0	.271	.167
2-team total (78 Durham)					.241	—	—	90	357	37	86	16	0	16	49	9	5	0	1	104	1	1	.420	.269
Asche, Cody	L-R	6-1	205	6-30-90	.279	.229	.303	29	111	20	31	8	0	6	15	11	1	0	0	26	1	0	.514	.350
Bourjos, Peter	R-R	6-1	185	3-31-87	.278	.231	.400	5	18	2	5	0	0	1	2	1	0	0	0	5	0	0	.444	.316
Burriss, Emmanuel	R-R	6-0	190	1-17-85	.263	.267	.258	50	175	21	46	6	1	0	13	9	0	1	2	25	6	1	.309	.296
Crawford, J.P.	L-R	6-2	180	1-11-95	.244	.244	.244	87	336	40	82	11	1	4	30	42	1	4	2	59	7	4	.318	.328
Featherston, Taylor	R-R	6-1	185	10-8-89	.254	.240	.260	99	402	56	102	23	4	13	37	25	9	1	2	98	6	3	.428	.311
Hunter, Cedric	L-L	5-11	200	3-10-88	.294	.313	.284	98	330	33	97	16	0	10	53	15	0	4	1	56	6	3	.433	.324
Jackson, Ryan	R-R	6-2	180	5-10-88	.214	.148	.246	30	84	8	18	2	0	0	7	17	0	1	0	26	1	2	.238	.347
Joseph, Tommy	R-R	6-1	255	7-16-91	.347	.367	.338	27	95	11	33	7	0	6	17	4	0	0	1	12	0	1	.611	.370
Knapp, Andrew	R-R	6-1	185	11-9-91	.266	.277	.258	107	403	55	107	24	1	8	46	37	2	0	1	107	2	2	.390	.330
Lough, David	L-L	5-10	175	1-20-86	.270	.172	.299	45	126	17	34	7	1	1	9	11	1	0	1	17	2	0	.365	.331
Marte, Alfredo	R-R	5-11	200	3-31-89	.161	.222	.136	10	31	1	5	0	0	0	1	1	0	0	0	6	0	0	.161	.188
2-team total (2 Norfolk)					.139	—	—	12	36	1	5	0	0	0	1	1	0	0	0	8	0	0	.139	.162
Moore, Logan	R-R	6-3	220	8-22-90	.218	.200	.225	31	110	8	24	5	1	4	13	5	1	1	1	38	0	0	.391	.256
Nina, Angelys	R-R	5-11	165	11-16-88	.193	.216	.174	26	83	4	16	3	0	2	7	4	1	2	0	14	0	0	.301	.239
Perkins, Cam	R-R	6-5	195	9-27-90	.292	.316	.274	117	408	47	119	20	4	8	47	21	2	1	1	59	11	4	.419	.329
Ruf, Darin	R-R	6-3	250	7-28-86	.294	.331	.273	95	350	56	103	18	2	20	65	29	7	0	4	78	0	0	.529	.356
Stassi, Brock	L-L	6-2	190	8-7-89	.267	.293	.254	117	375	49	100	26	1	12	58	60	3	0	4	76	1	2	.437	.369
Sweeney, Darnell	B-R	6-1	195	2-1-91	.233	.242	.226	118	400	48	93	17	5	6	35	38	1	5	3	100	12	11	.345	.299
Valentin, Jesmuel	B-R	5-9	180	5-12-94	.248	.277	.224	36	105	17	26	2	0	4	14	12	0	6	0	24	0	1	.381	.325
Venable, Will	L-L	6-2	205	10-29-82	.205	.175	.218	41	127	12	26	7	0	2	19	17	2	1	2	28	2	2	.307	.304
Williams, Nick	L-L	6-3	195	9-8-93	.258	.231	.273	125	497	78	128	33	6	13	64	19	4	1	6	136	6	4	.427	.287

Pitching	B-T	HT	WT	DOB	W	L	ERA	G	GS	CG	SV	IP	H	R	ER	HR	BB	SO	AVG	vLH	vRH	K/9	BB/9
Appel, Mark	R-R	6-5	220	7-15-91	3	3	4.46	8	8	0	0	38	40	22	19	3	20	34	.267	.242	.284	7.98	4.70
Araujo, Elvis	L-L	6-7	275	7-15-91	1	0	2.18	18	0	0	1	21	15	7	5	2	6	19	.195	.207	.188	8.27	2.61
Asher, Alec	R-R	6-4	230	10-4-91	3	0	1.53	4	4	0	0	29	15	8	5	4	3	19	.144	.176	.129	5.83	0.92
Bailey, Andrew	R-R	6-3	240	5-31-84	0	1	1.50	5	0	0	1	6	4	1	1	0	2	12	.182	.273	.091	18.00	3.00
Bleich, Jeremy	L-L	6-2	200	6-18-87	0	0	0.00	1	0	0	0	1	0	0	0	0	0	1	.000	—	.000	9.00	0.00
Buchanan, David	R-R	6-3	200	5-11-89	10	9	3.98	27	26	1	0	167	163	81	74	15	40	95	.257	.239	.266	5.11	2.15
Cordero, Jimmy	R-R	6-3	215	10-19-91	0	1	27.00	1	0	0	0	1	4	4	4	0	2	1	.500	.000	.571	6.75	13.50
Eflin, Zach	R-R	6-6	215	4-8-94	5	2	2.90	11	11	0	0	68	49	24	22	2	11	55	.199	.202	.197	7.24	1.45
Garcia, Luis	R-R	6-3	230	1-30-87	6	3	2.14	48	0	0	13	55	38	13	13	3	24	53	.203	.203	.203	8.73	3.95
Gonzalez, Severino	R-R	6-2	155	9-28-92	0	1	3.31	15	1	0	0	35	37	14	13	3	6	26	.262	.274	.253	6.62	1.53
Herrmann, Frank	L-R	6-4	220	5-30-84	6	1	1.72	27	0	0	9	31	24	6	6	2	6	31	.205	.174	.225	8.90	1.72
Hinojosa, Dalier	R-R	6-1	230	2-10-86	1	3	2.96	22	0	0	1	24	25	9	8	2	14	23	.281	.316	.255	8.51	5.18
Hollands, Mario	L-L	6-5	230	8-26-88	0	0	2.31	8	0	0	0	12	11	5	3	1	4	8	.250	.333	.017	6.17	3.09
Infante, Greg	R-R	6-2	215	7-10-87	2	1	5.82	9	1	0	0	17	17	11	11	3	12	12	.279	.294	.273	6.35	6.35
Klein, Phil	R-R	6-7	255	4-30-89	5	1	1.52	14	10	0	0	65	44	13	11	4	13	76	.190	.210	.179	10.47	1.79
LaFromboise, Bobby	L-L	6-4	225	6-25-86	1	3	5.94	13	0	0	0	17	20	11	11	1	9	8	.387	.550	.327	4.32	4.86
Lively, Ben	R-R	6-4	190	3-5-92	11	5	3.06	19	19	1	0	118	83	45	40	10	27	90	.196	.245	.158	6.88	2.07
Mariot, Michael	R-R	6-0	190	10-20-88	1	2	2.23	26	0	0	1	32	16	8	8	3	13	24	.150	.222	.097	6.68	3.62
Milner, Hoby	L-L	6-2	165	1-13-91	0	1	4.50	11	0	0	1	16	19	8	8	2	3	22	.258	.333	.227	12.38	1.69
Morgan, Adam	L-L	6-1	200	2-27-90	6	1	3.04	8	7	0	0	50	48	19	17	4	10	52	.232	.157	.261	9.30	1.79
Mujica, Edward	R-R	6-3	220	5-10-84	0	3	3.69	36	0	0	23	39	42	19	16	3	4	27	.268	.300	.247	6.23	0.92
2-team total (6 Rochester)					0	3	3.35	42	0	0	26	46	48	20	17	3	6	35	—	—		6.90	1.18
Murray, Colton	R-R	6-0	195	4-22-90	2	2	2.95	27	0	0	0	37	31	14	12	2	15	36	.230	.213	.239	8.84	3.68
Pivetta, Nick	R-R	6-5	220	2-14-93	1	2	2.55	5	5	0	0	25	20	7	7	2	10	27	.233	.200	.255	9.85	3.65
Ramos, Edubray	R-R	6-0	160	12-19-92	1	0	0.38	15	0	0	3	24	15	1	1	0	3	26	.174	.129	.200	9.89	1.14

PHILADELPHIA PHILLIES

PHILADELPHIA PHILLIES

Pitching	B-T	HT	WT	DOB	W	L	ERA	G	GS	CG	SV	IP	H	R	ER	HR	BB	SO	AVG	vLH	vRH	K/9	BB/9
Rodriguez, Joely	L-L	6-1	200	11-14-91	0	0	2.79	13	0	0	0	19	16	6	6	0	6	18	.232	.200	.241	8.38	2.79
Roibal, Reinier	R-R	6-3	210	1-9-89	0	2	6.65	9	5	0	0	22	28	17	16	3	7	16	.311	.303	.316	6.65	2.91
Russell, James	L-L	6-4	205	1-8-86	3	5	4.29	29	13	0	0	80	88	43	38	11	19	49	.272	.176	.301	5.54	2.15
Schuster, Patrick	R-L	6-2	190	10-30-90	0	0	1.50	6	0	0	0	6	4	1	1	0	6	7	.182	.000	.250	10.50	9.00
Stumpf, Daniel	L-L	6-2	200	1-4-91	0	0	20.25	2	0	0	0	1	4	3	3	0	0	1	.500	.400	.667	6.75	0.00
Thompson, Jake	R-R	6-4	235	1-31-94	11	5	2.50	21	21	0	0	130	105	44	36	10	37	87	.225	.199	.243	6.04	2.57
Vasquez, Anthony	L-L	6-0	190	9-19-86	4	1	2.64	12	12	2	0	72	71	22	21	10	16	51	.257	.217	.269	6.40	2.01

Fielding

Catcher	PCT	G	PO	A	E	DP	PB
Arencibia	.988	10	75	7	1	2	0
Knapp	.991	104	712	56	7	1	16
Moore	.984	31	213	26	4	0	0

First Base	PCT	G	PO	A	E	DP
Asche	1.000	3	28	0	0	5
Joseph	.969	17	124	3	4	13
Knapp	1.000	1	3	0	0	0
Perkins	1.000	3	2	0	0	1
Ruf	1.000	47	379	20	0	38
Stassi	.999	86	701	41	1	71

Second Base	PCT	G	PO	A	E	DP
Alonso	1.000	2	1	1	0	0
Burriss	.984	25	44	78	2	22
Featherston	.966	28	39	76	4	23

Jackson	1.000	2	3	4	0	3	
Nina	1.000	1	3	2	0	1	
Sweeney	.980	54	91	155	5	26	
Valentin	.977	36	78	95	4	29	

Third Base	PCT	G	PO	A	E	DP
Alonso	1.000	17	7	25	0	2
Asche	.923	7	3	9	1	1
Burriss	1.000	9	6	15	0	0
Featherston	.930	50	35	85	9	7
Jackson	1.000	2	0	4	0	1
Nina	.968	22	19	42	2	6
Sweeney	.924	40	22	63	7	9

Shortstop	PCT	G	PO	A	E	DP
Burriss	.964	14	16	37	2	9
Crawford	.968	87	119	243	12	55

	PCT	G	PO	A	E	DP
Featherston	.945	17	24	62	5	10
Jackson	.979	26	32	63	2	16
Sweeney	1.000	1	1	2	0	0

Outfield	PCT	G	PO	A	E	DP
Aguila	1.000	1	1	0	0	0
Altherr	1.000	2	5	0	0	0
Bourjos	.973	16	35	1	1	0
Bourjos	1.000	3	6	0	0	0
Hunter	1.000	75	176	1	0	0
Lough	.974	40	74	2	2	1
Marte	1.000	8	17	0	0	0
Perkins	.972	103	237	3	7	0
Ruf	1.000	26	38	2	0	0
Sweeney	1.000	20	28	0	0	0
Venable	1.000	32	75	2	0	0
Williams	.989	122	255	6	3	1

READING FIGHTIN' PHILS — DOUBLE-A
EASTERN LEAGUE

Batting	B-T	HT	WT	DOB	AVG	vLH	vRH	G	AB	R	H	2B	3B	HR	RBI	BB	HBP	SH	SF	SO	SB	CS	SLG	OBP
Aguila, Osmel	R-R	6-0	185	7-18-89	.236	.250	.232	40	127	22	30	10	0	5	16	12	5	0	1	30	1	0	.433	.324
Alfaro, Jorge	R-R	6-2	225	6-11-93	.285	.213	.302	97	404	68	115	21	2	15	67	22	4	1	4	105	3	2	.458	.325
Alonso, Carlos	R-R	5-11	205	2-15-88	.178	.188	.172	16	45	4	8	3	0	0	3	4	1	0	0	9	0	0	.244	.260
Altherr, Aaron	R-R	6-5	215	1-14-91	.300	1.000	.222	3	10	3	3	0	0	1	1	2	0	0	2	2	0	0	.300	.462
Asche, Cody	L-R	6-1	205	6-30-90	.125	.000	.167	4	16	2	2	0	0	1	2	2	0	0	0	6	0	0	.313	.222
Brodzinski, Greg	B-R	6-2	220	7-23-91	.000	—	.000	1	1	0	0	0	0	0	0	0	0	0	1	0	0	0	.000	.000
Brown, Aaron	L-L	6-2	220	6-20-92	.224	.175	.234	74	228	39	51	14	4	3	27	22	8	6	1	63	2	4	.360	.313
Cozens, Dylan	L-L	6-6	235	5-31-94	.276	.197	.302	134	521	106	144	38	3	40	125	61	0	0	4	186	21	5	.591	.350
Crawford, J.P.	L-R	6-2	180	1-11-95	.265	.304	.257	36	136	23	36	8	0	3	13	30	0	0	0	21	5	3	.390	.398
Fisher, Joel	R-R	6-3	235	1-8-93	.300	.300	.300	8	20	3	6	2	0	2	7	3	0	1	0	6	0	0	.700	.391
Fox, Jake	R-R	6-0	220	7-20-82	.264	.280	.258	123	425	57	112	29	0	23	71	38	5	0	3	98	0	0	.494	.329
Hoskins, Rhys	R-R	6-4	225	3-17-93	.281	.277	.282	135	498	95	140	26	1	38	116	71	11	0	9	125	8	3	.566	.377
Kingery, Scott	R-R	5-10	180	4-29-94	.250	.206	.262	37	156	16	39	7	0	2	18	5	1	1	3	36	4	2	.333	.273
Lino, Gabriel	R-R	6-3	200	5-17-93	.317	.217	.375	18	63	12	20	4	0	3	8	7	3	0	3	10	0	0	.524	.411
Marrero, Christian	L-L	6-1	185	7-30-86	.282	.278	.283	82	195	36	55	11	0	8	32	46	2	0	1	38	0	1	.462	.422
Martinez, Harold	R-R	6-3	210	5-3-90	.275	.324	.257	78	255	35	70	15	0	9	44	18	1	2	4	59	0	1	.439	.320
Moore, Logan	L-R	6-3	220	8-22-90	.224	.313	.196	22	67	6	15	2	0	1	7	10	0	1	1	16	0	0	.299	.321
Mora, Angelo	B-R	5-11	150	2-25-93	.251	.250	.251	101	367	35	92	19	5	4	42	29	2	2	1	79	3	1	.362	.308
Pullin, Andrew	L-R	6-0	190	9-25-93	.346	.320	.355	46	188	32	65	10	0	10	32	13	3	0	2	36	0	0	.559	.393
Quinn, Roman	B-R	5-10	170	5-14-93	.287	.300	.282	71	286	58	82	14	6	6	25	30	4	1	1	68	31	8	.441	.361
Serna, K.C.	R-R	6-0	185	10-15-89	.295	.280	.300	108	336	57	99	18	0	4	35	39	3	1	2	58	6	6	.384	.371
Valentin, Jesmuel	B-R	5-9	180	5-12-94	.276	.278	.275	89	341	59	94	17	5	5	38	38	1	4	4	56	4	3	.399	.346
Walding, Mitch	L-R	6-3	190	9-10-92	.214	.286	.206	23	70	14	15	2	0	3	9	11	2	2	0	23	1	0	.371	.337

Pitching	B-T	HT	WT	DOB	W	L	ERA	G	GS	CG	SV	IP	H	R	ER	HR	BB	SO	AVG	vLH	vRH	K/9	BB/9
Arano, Victor	R-R	6-2	200	2-7-95	1	1	2.16	11	0	0	1	17	11	6	4	2	4	24	.177	.172	.182	12.96	2.16
Asher, Alec	R-R	6-4	230	10-4-91	1	2	3.38	5	5	0	0	29	29	12	11	1	5	21	.252	.241	.263	6.44	1.53
Bleich, Jeremy	L-L	6-2	200	6-18-87	4	2	4.14	29	1	0	1	41	52	22	19	4	14	23	.308	.303	.311	5.01	3.05
Cordero, Jimmy	R-R	6-3	215	10-19-91	1	1	3.46	11	0	0	1	13	13	5	5	0	1	6	.265	.190	.321	4.15	0.69
Denato, Joey	L-L	5-10	175	3-17-92	0	0	3.00	6	0	0	0	6	2	3	2	0	6	7	.105	.000	.200	10.50	9.00
Dygestile-Therrien, J.	R-R	6-2	200	3-18-93	1	1	3.71	11	0	0	0	17	20	7	7	2	5	22	.299	.313	.286	11.65	2.65
Eshelman, Tom	R-R	6-3	210	6-20-94	5	5	5.14	13	13	0	0	61	79	40	35	4	17	55	.307	.325	.291	8.07	2.49
Gonzalez, Severino	R-R	6-1	165	9-28-92	2	0	1.69	6	0	0	0	11	9	2	2	0	2	9	.220	.200	.238	7.59	1.69
Hockenberry, Matt	R-R	6-3	220	8-30-91	0	0	5.79	3	0	0	0	5	4	3	3	0	3	2	.250	.143	.333	3.86	5.79
Hollands, Mario	L-L	6-5	230	8-26-88	0	0	5.40	18	0	0	0	25	32	15	15	3	14	21	.314	.333	.298	7.56	5.04
Infante, Greg	R-R	6-2	215	7-10-87	4	2	4.84	30	1	0	0	45	49	25	24	4	23	53	.283	.254	.304	10.68	4.63
Joaquin, Ulises	R-R	5-11	165	6-11-92	1	0	9.45	6	0	0	0	7	13	7	7	1	2	5	.433	.500	.357	6.75	2.70
Leiter Jr. Mark	R-R	6-0	195	3-13-91	6	3	3.39	23	17	0	1	104	91	45	39	9	30	94	.240	.253	.229	8.16	2.60
Lively, Ben	R-R	6-4	190	3-5-92	7	0	1.87	9	9	0	0	53	35	11	11	1	15	49	.185	.168	.202	8.32	2.55
Mariot, Michael	R-R	6-0	190	10-20-88	0	0	4.50	3	0	0	0	4	6	2	2	1	1	4	.353	.500	.308	9.00	2.25
Milner, Hoby	L-L	6-2	165	1-13-91	5	3	1.84	38	0	0	5	49	41	12	10	3	12	54	.224	.207	.238	9.92	2.20
Morris, Will	L-R	6-4	180	5-2-93	0	1	4.63	3	2	0	0	12	13	6	6	1	4	8	.289	.353	.250	6.17	3.09
Nunez, Miguel	R-R	6-6	215	10-27-92	4	3	3.11	45	0	0	17	46	40	19	16	2	28	50	.242	.244	.241	9.71	5.44

Pitching	B-T	HT	WT	DOB	W	L	ERA	G	GS	CG	SV	IP	H	R	ER	HR	BB	SO	AVG	vLH	vRH	K/9	BB/9
Pinto, Ricardo	R-R	6-0	165	1-20-94	7	6	4.10	27	25	0	0	156	150	84	71	20	51	101	.253	.243	.261	5.83	2.94
Pivetta, Nick	R-R	6-5	220	2-14-93	11	6	3.41	22	22	1	0	124	108	50	47	10	41	111	.235	.255	.218	8.06	2.98
Ramos, Edubray	R-R	6-0	160	12-19-92	1	1	2.40	11	0	0	7	15	9	5	4	1	1	15	.170	.269	.074	9.00	0.60
Richy, John	R-R	6-4	215	7-28-92	4	4	5.11	13	13	0	0	69	74	43	39	7	28	45	.278	.224	.333	5.90	3.67
Rios, Yacksel	R-R	6-3	185	6-27-93	1	1	4.58	13	1	0	0	18	20	9	9	0	14	21	.294	.267	.316	10.70	7.13
Rivero, Alexis	R-R	6-0	180	10-18-94	1	0	4.05	23	0	0	1	33	38	17	15	4	14	32	.281	.379	.208	8.64	3.78
Rodriguez, Joely	L-L	6-1	200	11-14-91	7	0	2.57	33	0	0	2	49	46	18	14	3	16	41	.260	.194	.296	7.53	2.94
Roibal, Reinier	R-R	6-3	210	1-9-89	0	0	7.43	10	0	0	0	13	20	11	11	2	4	17	.328	.310	.344	11.48	2.70
Stumpf, Daniel	L-L	6-2	200	1-4-91	1	0	4.50	3	0	0	0	4	3	3	2	0	1	3	.188	.286	.111	6.75	2.25
Vasquez, Anthony	L-L	6-0	190	9-19-86	8	3	3.40	16	15	1	0	101	97	44	38	5	27	68	.264	.275	.258	6.08	2.41
Velasquez, Vince	B-R	6-3	205	6-7-92	1	0	1.80	1	1	0	0	5	2	1	1	1	1	3	.118	.000	.222	5.40	1.80
Viza, Tyler	R-R	6-3	170	10-21-94	4	6	4.69	16	16	0	0	94	100	50	49	12	23	58	.274	.292	.258	5.55	2.20
Windle, Tom	L-L	6-4	215	3-10-92	1	1	5.68	25	0	0	0	32	39	21	20	5	14	33	.312	.286	.329	9.38	3.98

Fielding

Catcher	PCT	G	PO	A	E	DP	PB
Alfaro	.993	95	736	71	6	7	7
Fisher	.983	7	54	4	1	0	0
Fox	1.000	2	8	0	0	0	0
Lino	.970	18	122	8	4	0	1
Moore	.994	22	137	23	1	1	0

First Base	PCT	G	PO	A	E	DP
Fox	.967	6	55	3	2	9
Hoskins	.988	129	1080	82	14	103
Marrero	.986	11	67	5	1	7
Martinez	1.000	2	4	0	0	0

Second Base	PCT	G	PO	A	E	DP
Alonso	1.000	3	6	4	0	1

	PCT	G	PO	A	E	DP
Kingery	.993	37	47	93	1	22
Mora	.967	18	35	54	3	11
Serna	.955	6	3	18	1	2
Valentin	.974	80	165	211	10	48

Third Base	PCT	G	PO	A	E	DP
Alonso	.958	11	8	15	1	2
Fox	.900	16	7	11	2	1
Martinez	.945	71	54	118	10	10
Mora	.907	24	10	29	4	2
Serna	.935	16	6	23	2	2
Walding	.961	23	13	36	2	3

Shortstop	PCT	G	PO	A	E	DP
Crawford	.963	36	56	128	7	28
Mora	.958	47	74	133	9	28

	PCT	G	PO	A	E	DP
Serna	.961	53	81	142	9	27
Valentin	.900	9	7	20	3	7

Outfield	PCT	G	PO	A	E	DP
Aguila	.978	39	86	1	2	0
Altherr	1.000	3	3	0	0	0
Asche	1.000	4	3	0	0	0
Brown	.973	70	140	3	4	0
Cozens	.982	128	254	12	5	4
Fox	1.000	3	2	0	0	0
Marrero	1.000	46	63	1	0	0
Mora	1.000	14	17	0	0	0
Pullin	.978	46	86	5	2	0
Quinn	.970	69	149	11	5	3
Serna	.982	28	53	3	1	1

CLEARWATER THRESHERS
FLORIDA STATE LEAGUE

HIGH CLASS A

Batting	B-T	HT	WT	DOB	AVG	vLH	vRH	G	AB	R	H	2B	3B	HR	RBI	BB	HBP	SH	SF	SO	SB	CS	SLG	OBP
Aguila, Osmel	R-R	6-0	185	7-18-89	.083	.200	.000	3	12	1	1	0	0	0	0	1	0	0	0	3	0	0	.083	.154
Altherr, Aaron	R-R	6-5	215	1-14-91	.375	—	.375	2	8	2	3	0	0	0	1	0	1	0	0	2	0	0	.375	.444
Asche, Cody	L-R	6-1	205	6-30-90	.167	.600	.000	5	18	2	3	0	0	1	2	1	0	0	0	6	0	0	.333	.211
Bossart, Austin	R-R	6-2	210	7-4-93	.340	.333	.342	18	53	6	18	4	0	0	9	3	0	0	1	9	0	0	.415	.368
Brown, Aaron	L-L	6-2	220	6-20-92	.304	.294	.308	20	69	9	21	0	0	2	12	11	1	0	1	19	3	0	.391	.402
Campbell, Derek	R-R	6-0	175	6-28-91	.263	.232	.276	63	190	32	50	8	1	11	31	12	11	4	1	43	1	1	.489	.341
Canelo, Malquin	R-R	5-10	156	9-5-94	.246	.202	.259	124	451	53	111	16	5	4	49	30	3	4	6	95	13	8	.330	.294
Coppola, Zach	L-R	5-10	160	5-19-94	.293	.286	.295	24	92	15	27	3	0	0	9	5	3	2	0	11	6	3	.326	.381
Green, Zach	R-R	6-3	210	3-7-94	.263	.330	.233	96	354	49	93	24	0	12	63	20	15	1	4	110	0	1	.432	.326
Hiciano, Samuel	R-R	6-1	205	1-25-94	.208	.273	.189	16	48	4	10	6	0	0	6	9	0	0	0	12	0	0	.333	.333
Kingery, Scott	R-R	5-10	180	4-29-94	.293	.383	.257	94	375	60	110	29	3	3	28	33	7	3	2	54	26	5	.411	.360
Lino, Gabriel	R-R	6-3	200	5-17-93	.199	.257	.178	40	136	10	27	5	0	2	6	10	2	0	0	33	0	0	.279	.264
Martin, Kyle	L-L	6-2	240	11-13-92	.250	.179	.277	121	448	68	112	23	1	19	82	47	6	1	9	117	5	3	.433	.324
Numata, Chace	B-R	6-0	175	8-14-92	.308	.253	.328	94	328	32	101	18	2	2	35	37	1	0	3	41	3	0	.393	.377
Pullin, Andrew	L-R	6-0	190	9-25-93	.293	.395	.250	36	147	21	43	11	2	4	19	5	1	0	0	19	0	0	.476	.320
Rivas, Raul	B-R	5-10	160	10-27-96	.333	1.000	.200	3	6	2	2	0	0	0	1	0	0	0	0	1	0	0	.333	.333
Rivero, Gregori	R-R	5-11	195	5-27-96	.000	—	.000	1	1	0	0	0	0	0	0	0	0	0	0	1	0	0	.000	.000
Rodriguez, Herlis	L-L	6-0	170	6-26-94	.213	.162	.231	48	141	11	30	2	2	1	11	10	4	1	1	19	3	3	.277	.282
Sandberg, Cord	L-L	6-3	215	1-2-95	.230	.164	.248	94	305	40	70	12	1	4	23	25	10	4	3	85	6	7	.315	.306
Stankiewicz, Drew	B-R	5-9	160	6-18-93	.204	.250	.185	53	167	19	34	7	3	1	17	27	0	1	2	36	2	0	.299	.311
Tobias, Josh	R-R	5-9	195	11-23-92	.254	.321	.235	34	126	21	32	7	0	2	14	12	3	1	4	30	4	1	.357	.324
Tocci, Carlos	R-R	6-2	160	8-23-95	.284	.235	.302	127	500	66	142	26	2	3	50	34	5	9	8	76	13	6	.362	.331
Tomscha, Damek	R-R	6-2	200	8-27-91	.105	.125	.091	6	19	0	2	0	0	0	0	0	0	0	0	4	0	0	.105	.105
Tromp, Jiandido	R-R	5-11	175	9-27-93	.240	.305	.215	59	217	34	52	13	2	10	36	14	3	0	4	42	5	2	.456	.290
Walding, Mitch	L-R	6-3	190	9-10-92	.280	.217	.302	100	350	46	98	18	4	10	53	52	4	2	8	111	2	3	.440	.372

Pitching	B-T	HT	WT	DOB	W	L	ERA	G	GS	CG	SV	IP	H	R	ER	HR	BB	SO	AVG	vLH	vRH	K/9	BB/9
Anderson, Drew	R-R	6-3	185	3-22-94	2	1	1.93	8	8	0	0	33	26	9	7	0	10	37	.217	.238	.205	10.19	2.76
Arano, Victor	R-R	6-2	200	2-7-95	4	1	2.29	35	0	0	4	63	52	21	16	4	15	71	.222	.193	.240	10.14	2.14
Bergjans, Tommy	R-R	6-1	190	12-1-92	1	0	1.35	1	0	0	0	7	3	1	1	1	1	5	.136	.167	.125	6.75	1.35
Cabrera, Ismael	R-R	6-1	185	6-19-94	0	0	18.00	1	0	0	0	2	4	4	4	1	1	2	.333	.600	.143	18.00	4.50
Casimiro, Ranfi	R-R	6-8	200	7-16-92	8	9	5.33	24	18	0	0	98	109	67	58	5	31	77	.280	.255	.295	7.07	2.85
Cordero, Jimmy	R-R	6-3	215	10-19-91	1	1	5.63	6	0	0	1	8	8	5	5	1	3	5	.267	.125	.429	5.63	3.38
Davis, Austin	L-L	6-4	245	2-3-93	0	1	5.28	11	1	0	1	15	16	10	9	0	4	18	.267	.250	.273	10.57	2.35
Denato, Joey	L-L	5-10	175	3-17-92	0	0	4.97	33	0	0	1	51	52	30	28	3	24	50	.278	.255	.287	8.88	4.26
Dygestile-Therrien, J.	R-R	6-2	200	3-18-93	2	2	2.21	27	0	0	4	37	24	16	9	3	22	52	.180	.184	.179	12.76	5.40
Eshelman, Tom	R-R	6-3	210	6-20-94	2	4	3.34	11	11	0	0	59	58	29	22	7	11	64	.251	.288	.232	9.71	1.67
Garcia, Elniery	L-L	6-0	155	12-24-94	12	4	2.68	20	19	0	0	118	94	41	35	8	36	91	.219	.215	.220	6.96	2.75

PHILADELPHIA PHILLIES

Pitching	B-T	HT	WT	DOB	W	L	ERA	G	GS	CG	SV	IP	H	R	ER	HR	BB	SO	AVG	vLH	vRH	K/9	BB/9
Harris, Scott	L-L	6-4	230	5-14-93	0	0	9.00	1	0	0	0	2	2	3	2	0	2	2	.250	.000	.400	9.00	9.00
Hinojosa, Dalier	R-R	6-1	230	2-10-86	0	0	2.25	3	0	0	0	4	4	1	1	0	2	10	.250	.125	.375	22.50	4.50
Hockenberry, Matt	R-R	6-3	220	8-30-91	3	1	1.39	41	0	0	7	58	39	9	9	1	23	54	.191	.167	.201	8.33	3.55
Hollands, Mario	L-L	6-5	230	8-26-88	0	0	2.25	3	0	0	0	4	2	1	1	0	6	1	.154	.000	.182	13.50	0.00
Imhof, Matt	L-L	6-5	220	10-26-93	4	3	3.91	14	9	0	0	53	42	27	23	4	43	48	.232	.222	.234	8.15	7.30
Joaquin, Ulises	R-R	5-11	165	6-11-92	3	2	2.62	46	0	0	10	65	49	20	19	7	19	57	.210	.218	.206	7.85	2.62
Leftwich, Luke	R-R	6-3	205	6-9-94	5	4	5.07	11	11	0	0	55	64	35	31	6	17	49	.292	.295	.291	8.02	2.78
Leibrandt, Brandon	L-L	6-4	190	12-13-92	4	1	2.25	6	6	0	0	28	21	7	7	1	10	21	.216	.250	.205	6.75	3.21
Mariot, Michael	R-R	6-0	190	10-20-88	0	1	14.54	3	2	0	0	4	7	7	7	2	2	4	.389	.500	.333	8.31	4.15
Morris, Will	L-R	6-4	180	5-2-93	9	3	3.56	25	12	1	0	96	97	40	38	10	21	51	.257	.221	.275	4.78	1.97
Munoz, Jairo	R-R	6-5	175	8-12-91	0	1	1.13	6	0	0	0	8	5	1	1	0	5	7	.222	.333	.167	7.88	5.63
Nin, Jose	R-R	6-2	170	6-20-95	0	0	5.40	1	0	0	0	2	3	1	1	0	0	0	.375	.500	.333	0.00	0.00
Nunez, Miguel	R-R	6-6	215	10-27-92	0	0	3.24	6	0	0	3	8	6	3	3	2	0	13	.200	.143	.217	14.04	0.00
Richy, John	R-R	6-4	215	7-28-92	4	4	3.53	10	10	0	0	51	49	22	20	5	14	33	.259	.233	.271	5.82	2.47
Rios, Yacksel	R-R	6-3	185	6-27-93	4	3	6.14	22	6	0	1	59	59	43	40	4	23	42	.269	.289	.259	6.44	3.53
Rivero, Alexis	R-R	6-0	180	10-18-94	4	1	1.13	23	0	0	5	32	18	4	4	2	7	34	.162	.143	.171	9.56	1.97
Rodriguez, Joely	L-L	6-1	200	11-14-91	0	0	0.00	7	0	0	3	8	3	0	0	0	1	10	.107	.200	.056	10.80	1.08
Singer, Jeff	L-L	6-0	200	9-13-93	0	1	4.97	10	0	0	0	13	13	7	7	1	6	10	.271	.375	.219	7.11	4.26
Stumpf, Daniel	L-L	6-2	200	1-4-91	0	0	3.00	2	0	0	0	3	2	1	1	0	0	1	.182	1.000	.100	3.00	0.00
Tirado, Alberto	R-R	6-0	180	12-10-94	0	0	16.20	2	0	0	0	3	6	6	6	0	6	6	.333	.333	.250	16.20	16.20
Viza, Tyler	R-R	6-3	170	10-21-94	6	2	2.54	9	9	1	0	50	55	19	14	5	8	55	.274	.333	.242	9.97	1.45
Watson, Shane	R-R	6-4	200	8-13-93	4	5	3.93	14	14	0	0	71	78	41	31	6	29	60	.282	.263	.294	7.61	3.68
Windle, Tom	L-L	6-4	215	3-10-92	0	1	4.09	14	0	0	1	22	17	10	10	1	10	21	.210	.333	.175	8.59	4.09

Fielding

Catcher	PCT	G	PO	A	E	DP	PB
Bossart	.984	18	115	11	2	3	0
Lino	.981	40	311	41	7	3	5
Numata	.986	85	609	86	10	3	14

First Base	PCT	G	PO	A	E	DP
Campbell	1.000	2	24	1	0	1
Green	.992	30	247	14	2	22
Martin	.998	104	886	44	2	65
Rodriguez	1.000	3	13	1	0	2

Second Base	PCT	G	PO	A	E	DP
Campbell	.917	8	9	13	2	2
Kingery	.975	88	149	237	10	52
Stankiewicz	.984	15	21	39	1	7
Tobias	.976	29	49	73	3	17

Third Base	PCT	G	PO	A	E	DP
Campbell	.919	24	12	45	5	5
Green	.727	6	2	6	3	0
Stankiewicz	.975	16	10	29	1	4
Walding	.935	96	60	169	16	13

Shortstop	PCT	G	PO	A	E	DP
Canelo	.948	124	174	319	27	61
Rivas	1.000	2	1	3	0	0
Stankiewicz	.922	12	15	32	4	5

Outfield	PCT	G	PO	A	E	DP
Aguila	1.000	3	5	0	0	0
Altherr	1.000	2	4	0	0	0
Asche	1.000	5	7	1	0	0
Brown	.889	16	24	0	3	0
Campbell	1.000	28	32	0	0	0
Coppola	1.000	24	39	0	0	0
Hiciano	1.000	12	20	0	0	0
Numata	1.000	1	1	0	0	0
Pullin	1.000	31	53	1	0	0
Rodriguez	.989	42	85	4	1	0
Sandberg	.994	93	154	4	1	0
Stankiewicz	1.000	3	4	0	0	0
Tobias	1.000	2	1	0	0	0
Tocci	.993	124	286	9	2	2
Tomscha	1.000	6	8	1	0	0
Tromp	1.000	44	93	2	0	0

LAKEWOOD BLUECLAWS — LOW CLASS A
SOUTH ATLANTIC LEAGUE

Batting	B-T	HT	WT	DOB	AVG	vLH	vRH	G	AB	R	H	2B	3B	HR	RBI	BB	HBP	SH	SF	SO	SB	CS	SLG	OBP
Biter, Venn	L-R	6-1	185	10-27-94	.231	.111	.267	20	39	6	9	0	0	0	3	3	1	1	1	13	1	2	.231	.295
Bossart, Austin	R-R	6-2	210	7-4-93	.263	.286	.254	30	99	18	26	5	0	1	9	8	3	2	0	12	0	0	.343	.336
Cabral, Edgar	R-R	5-11	210	9-12-95	.203	.273	.175	24	79	7	16	2	0	1	7	4	1	0	0	11	0	0	.266	.250
Coppola, Zach	L-R	5-10	160	5-9-94	.324	.315	.327	52	213	43	69	8	1	0	17	27	2	1	1	30	11	4	.371	.403
Cuicas, William	B-R	5-11	160	2-1-95	.122	.067	.147	19	49	5	6	0	0	0	4	5	1	1	0	15	1	0	.122	.218
Cumana, Grenny	B-R	5-5	145	11-10-95	.291	.311	.284	96	347	55	101	22	0	1	25	16	13	3	2	30	17	7	.363	.344
Duran, Carlos	R-R	6-2	170	11-22-94	.243	.241	.244	90	325	35	79	16	1	2	25	24	0	8	2	72	12	4	.317	.293
Espiritu, Luis	R-R	6-0	175	9-21-96	.200	.167	.222	6	15	1	3	0	0	0	2	0	1	0	4	0	0	.200	.294
Fisher, Joel	R-R	6-3	235	1-8-93	.188	.333	.154	6	16	3	3	1	0	0	1	0	1	1	0	7	0	0	.250	.278
Garcia, Wilson	B-R	5-11	180	1-11-94	.273	.259	.279	106	421	25	115	19	0	3	58	12	2	1	10	48	0	3	.340	.290
Grullon, Deivi	R-R	6-1	180	2-17-96	.256	.202	.277	87	320	29	82	20	0	6	45	30	2	0	4	83	0	3	.375	.320
Hayden, Brendon	L-R	6-5	215	12-26-92	.254	.236	.260	71	228	19	58	7	2	0	12	25	4	1	3	47	2	1	.303	.335
Hernandez, Jan	R-R	6-1	195	1-3-95	.255	.231	.263	86	310	47	79	15	3	10	31	23	3	1	0	100	1	3	.419	.313
Hiciano, Samuel	R-R	6-1	195	1-25-94	.182	.143	.189	13	44	5	8	4	0	2	7	3	1	1	0	14	0	0	.409	.250
Laird, Mark	L-L	6-2	180	3-29-93	.353	.290	.376	31	116	21	41	6	0	1	14	18	2	2	1	14	5	1	.431	.445
Marrero, Emmanuel	B-R	5-11	169	5-16-93	.248	.228	.255	113	415	54	103	15	1	4	33	32	3	7	3	84	6	7	.318	.305
Pujols, Jose	R-R	6-3	175	9-29-95	.241	.269	.231	128	498	67	120	21	3	24	82	44	4	0	3	179	5	3	.440	.306
Randolph, Cornelius	L-R	5-11	205	6-2-97	.274	.250	.281	63	241	33	66	12	1	2	27	26	6	0	3	57	5	4	.357	.355
Tobias, Josh	R-R	5-9	195	11-23-92	.304	.333	.295	93	365	49	111	24	3	7	55	31	13	2	4	59	6	4	.444	.375
Tomscha, Damek	R-R	6-2	200	8-27-91	.283	.282	.284	98	353	43	100	32	2	5	54	34	16	1	4	42	5	1	.428	.369
Tromp, Jiandido	R-R	5-11	177	9-27-93	.274	.220	.291	65	241	36	66	20	3	10	32	22	1	3	2	58	9	2	.506	.335

Pitching	B-T	HT	WT	DOB	W	L	ERA	G	GS	CG	SV	IP	H	R	ER	HR	BB	SO	AVG	vLH	vRH	K/9	BB/9
Anderson, Drew	R-R	6-3	185	3-22-94	1	3	3.38	7	7	0	0	37	29	17	14	3	12	41	.220	.148	.282	9.88	2.89
Arauz, Harold	R-R	6-2	185	5-29-95	6	6	3.18	19	19	1	0	99	79	39	35	4	24	85	.216	.215	.216	7.73	2.18
Arteaga, Alejandro	R-R	6-2	170	4-30-94	1	1	8.05	9	0	0	0	19	18	17	17	0	8	22	.349	.286	.396	10.42	3.79
Cabrera, Ismael	R-R	6-1	185	6-19-94	2	1	4.09	15	0	0	3	22	18	12	10	2	10	25	.217	.306	.149	10.23	4.09
Davis, Austin	L-L	6-4	245	2-3-93	1	0	0.00	7	0	0	1	13	6	2	0	0	2	17	.130	.077	.152	11.77	1.38

Pitching	B-T	HT	WT	DOB	W	L	ERA	G	GS	CG	SV	IP	H	R	ER	HR	BB	SO	AVG	vLH	vRH	K/9	BB/9
Dominguez, Seranthony	R-R	6-1	185	11-25-94	5	2	2.42	10	10	0	0	48	34	14	13	2	20	50	.202	.211	.196	9.31	3.72
Dyer, Grant	R-R	6-1	195	7-31-95	0	3	2.39	9	0	0	3	26	15	7	7	2	6	36	.163	.162	.164	12.30	2.05
Garcia, Edgar	R-R	6-1	180	10-4-96	4	1	2.80	27	4	0	2	61	59	30	19	6	15	59	.249	.288	.214	8.70	2.21
Gilbert, Tyler	L-L	6-3	190	12-22-93	7	9	3.98	23	23	0	0	131	136	65	58	10	26	106	.264	.266	.263	7.28	1.79
Gueller, Mitch	R-R	6-3	210	11-10-93	0	1	8.10	5	3	0	0	13	15	12	12	0	9	12	.288	.375	.214	8.10	6.08
Harris, Scott	L-L	6-4	230	5-14-93	1	0	0.96	7	0	0	1	9	10	1	1	1	3	8	.270	.313	.238	7.71	2.89
Hunter, Skylar	R-R	6-1	185	2-3-94	1	1	4.79	13	0	0	0	21	26	12	11	0	4	15	.295	.325	.271	6.53	1.74
Kilome, Franklyn	R-R	6-6	175	6-25-95	5	8	3.85	23	23	0	0	115	113	55	49	6	50	130	.259	.272	.247	10.20	3.92
Koplove, Kenny	R-R	6-2	170	8-2-93	0	1	15.43	10	0	0	0	2	5	4	4	0	4	9	.377	.400	.357	6.94	10.80
Leftwich, Luke	L-R	6-3	205	6-9-94	7	3	2.00	12	12	0	0	68	55	17	15	0	18	88	.223	.248	.201	11.70	2.39
McLoughlin, Sutter	R-R	6-6	230	9-24-93	1	3	2.51	34	0	0	14	47	33	14	13	0	10	42	.200	.253	.151	8.10	1.93
Morales, Luis	R-R	6-4	212	3-16-93	0	3	5.58	20	0	0	2	40	38	27	25	4	16	32	.250	.338	.173	7.14	3.57
Morris, Zach	L-L	6-4	195	3-6-93	8	3	2.57	43	0	0	5	67	63	25	19	1	22	55	.248	.25	.247	7.43	2.97
Quinn, Blake	R-R	6-4	222	8-29-94	0	0	1.50	3	0	0	0	6	3	1	1	0	1	8	.150	.143	.154	12.00	1.50
Sequeira, Anthony	L-R	6-6	235	9-16-92	0	0	21.00	3	0	0	0	3	7	7	7	2	2	2	.500	.500	.500	6.00	6.00
Singer, Jeff	L-L	6-0	200	9-13-93	2	0	0.43	9	0	0	0	21	9	2	1	0	6	27	.132	.000	.180	11.57	2.57
Tasin, Robert	R-R	6-0	190	9-18-91	1	3	4.93	28	0	0	6	35	41	21	19	1	18	44	.299	.381	.230	11.42	4.67
Taveras, Jose	R-R	6-4	210	11-6-93	8	8	3.28	25	20	1	0	137	116	60	50	15	26	154	.229	.230	.229	10.09	1.70
Tirado, Alberto	R-R	6-0	180	12-10-94	7	1	3.23	20	11	0	0	61	48	27	22	3	36	96	.214	.252	.182	14.09	5.28
Waguespack, Jacob	R-R	6-6	225	11-5-93	4	2	3.52	43	0	0	6	72	75	31	28	1	29	72	.265	.258	.271	9.04	3.64
Watson, Shane	R-R	6-4	200	8-13-93	2	2	3.20	7	7	0	0	39	32	18	14	3	11	32	.222	.148	.277	7.32	2.52

Fielding

Catcher	PCT	G	PO	A	E	DP	PB
Bossart	.990	29	253	30	3	3	1
Cabral	.996	24	219	15	1	0	1
Fisher	1.000	6	26	5	0	0	0
Garcia	.971	8	60	7	2	0	0
Grullon	.987	79	664	104	10	3	13

First Base	PCT	G	PO	A	E	DP
Garcia	.982	53	362	25	7	29
Hayden	.991	59	521	27	5	34
Hiciano	1.000	3	20	1	0	1
Tomscha	1.000	29	226	8	0	9

Second Base	PCT	G	PO	A	E	DP
Cuicas	.942	15	18	31	3	8

	PCT	G	PO	A	E	DP
Cumana	.961	41	64	85	6	9
Espiritu	1.000	3	9	5	0	3
Marrero	1.000	5	13	12	0	2
Tobias	.966	80	97	215	11	35

Third Base	PCT	G	PO	A	E	DP
Cuicas	1.000	3	0	1	0	0
Espiritu	1.000	3	1	1	0	0
Hernandez	.913	76	53	136	18	7
Marrero	.941	15	4	28	2	2
Tomscha	.963	46	28	77	4	5

Shortstop	PCT	G	PO	A	E	DP
Cumana	.944	47	66	85	9	20
Marrero	.963	95	112	203	12	27

Outfield	PCT	G	PO	A	E	DP
Biter	1.000	13	14	2	0	0
Coppola	.989	45	87	4	1	1
Cumana	1.000	6	8	0	0	0
Duran	.995	84	192	5	1	0
Hiciano	1.000	3	1	0	0	0
Laird	1.000	24	47	0	0	0
Pujols	.961	113	211	9	9	2
Randolph	.978	53	86	1	2	0
Tobias	1.000	5	6	0	0	0
Tomscha	.960	16	23	1	1	0
Tromp	.993	61	130	6	1	0

WILLIAMSPORT CROSSCUTTERS
NEW YORK-PENN LEAGUE

SHORT-SEASON

Batting	B-T	HT	WT	DOB	AVG	vLH	vRH	G	AB	R	H	2B	3B	HR	RBI	BB	HBP	SH	SF	SO	SB	CS	SLG	OBP
Alastre, Jesus	R-R	6-1	155	11-25-96	.290	.234	.313	50	162	25	47	4	1	0	16	7	7	2	1	23	14	4	.327	.345
Antequera, Jose	R-R	5-10	160	8-1-95	.151	.000	.200	16	53	3	8	0	0	0	3	1	2	3	16	4	3	.151	.200
Barbier, Brett	R-R	5-11	190	12-6-93	.282	.290	.278	32	110	14	31	8	1	2	10	8	1	0	1	28	0	0	.427	.333
Cuicas, William	B-R	5-11	160	2-1-95	.290	.385	.222	13	31	5	9	2	0	0	2	3	0	0	1	9	1	0	.355	.343
Duran, Rodolfo	R-R	5-9	170	2-19-98	.222	.400	.000	2	9	1	2	0	0	0	0	0	0	0	0	1	0	0	.222	.222
Encarnacion, Luis	R-R	6-2	185	8-9-97	.162	.265	.128	54	198	15	32	5	0	2	16	10	2	0	0	75	1	1	.217	.210
Espiritu, Luis	R-R	6-0	175	9-21-96	.230	.219	.234	44	139	13	32	6	0	0	9	15	1	4	1	31	4	2	.273	.308
Gamboa, Arquimedez	B-R	6-0	175	9-23-97	.200	.136	.213	35	130	15	26	6	0	2	15	9	1	5	2	28	5	1	.292	.254
Garcia, Enmanuel	R-R	6-0	180	7-23-94	.274	.256	.281	46	164	23	45	13	1	6	19	7	1	0	1	35	3	5	.476	.306
Hall, Chandler	R-R	5-11	157	2-27-95	.261	.154	.287	41	134	21	35	9	0	1	8	13	5	0	3	43	0	1	.351	.342
Hall, Darick	L-R	6-4	230	7-25-95	.282	.333	.261	57	195	27	55	19	0	9	29	13	16	0	2	57	0	2	.518	.372
Hernandez, Jan	R-R	6-1	195	1-3-95	.200	.500	.000	3	5	2	1	1	0	0	2	0	0	0	3	0	0	.400	.429
Kent, Tyler	R-R	6-0	205	8-26-93	.333	—	.333	2	9	0	3	1	0	0	0	0	0	0	0	0	0	0	.444	.333
Laird, Mark	L-L	6-2	180	3-29-93	.358	.167	.400	19	67	15	24	0	0	0	8	9	1	0	1	8	5	2	.358	.436
Lartigue, Henri	R-R	6-0	205	2-24-95	.212	.267	.189	41	151	12	32	7	1	1	15	12	0	1	3	27	2	0	.291	.265
Luis, Juan	L-R	6-4	175	3-23-96	.235	.132	.266	52	162	18	38	2	2	3	13	10	1	4	1	31	9	5	.327	.282
Maglich, Luke	L-R	6-3	210	7-20-93	.261	.250	.265	45	142	21	37	5	3	1	18	20	2	1	2	39	8	5	.359	.355
Martinelli, David	L-R	6-2	209	12-30-94	.235	.276	.220	54	217	21	51	8	0	4	25	6	2	0	5	57	7	5	.327	.281
Rivero, Gregori	R-R	5-11	195	5-27-96	.291	.200	.321	31	103	8	30	8	2	1	9	3	3	1	0	19	1	0	.437	.330
Rogers, Evan	R-R	5-11	175	4-29-94	.217	.250	.209	33	106	15	23	4	1	1	6	13	2	0	2	25	2	2	.302	.309
Sweaney, Jake	R-R	6-3	180	11-17-94	.500	.250	1.000	2	6	1	3	1	0	0	2	1	1	0	0	1	1	0	.667	.625
Williams, Lucas	R-R	6-1	180	8-9-96	.220	.240	.213	52	186	13	41	9	2	1	15	17	2	5	2	52	11	2	.301	.297

Pitching	B-T	HT	WT	DOB	W	L	ERA	G	GS	CG	SV	IP	H	R	ER	HR	BB	SO	AVG	vLH	vRH	K/9	BB/9
Alcantara, Randy	R-R	5-11	150	11-9-96	0	0	0.00	2	0	0	0	2	3	1	0	0	1	2	.375	.600	.000	10.80	5.40
Bettencourt, Trevor	R-R	6-0	195	7-21-94	0	0	0.00	2	0	0	0	2	0	0	0	0	1	2	.000	.000	.000	7.71	3.86
Dominguez, Seranthony	R-R	6-1	185	11-25-94	1	1	2.12	3	3	0	0	17	8	6	4	0	4	15	.136	.185	.094	7.94	2.12
Dyer, Grant	R-R	6-1	195	7-31-95	2	1	2.25	7	0	0	1	16	12	5	4	0	1	21	.207	.192	.219	11.81	0.00
Falter, Bailey	R-L	6-4	175	4-24-97	1	6	3.17	13	13	0	0	60	61	31	21	3	17	59	.257	.235	.266	8.90	2.56
Garcia, Julian	L-R	6-3	185	5-13-95	0	3	3.60	12	4	0	0	30	27	14	12	1	22	40	.233	.310	.189	12.00	6.60
Hallead, Tyler	R-R	6-5	190	5-17-95	2	2	4.91	14	0	0	2	26	23	16	14	1	10	13	.237	.152	.314	4.56	3.51

Pitching	B-T	HT	WT	DOB	W	L	ERA	G	GS	CG	SV	IP	H	R	ER	HR	BB	SO	AVG	vLH	vRH	K/9	BB/9
Harris, Scott	L-L	6-4	230	5-14-93	2	2	1.65	11	0	0	1	16	13	4	3	0	4	18	.220	.227	.216	9.92	2.20
Hennigan, Jonathan	L-L	6-4	185	8-27-94	1	0	1.88	13	0	0	0	14	8	4	3	1	6	19	.160	.000	.211	11.93	3.77
Hibbs, Will	R-R	6-7	245	10-27-93	3	4	1.44	19	0	0	4	31	17	8	5	1	10	27	.162	.194	.145	7.76	2.87
Indriago, Carlos	R-R	6-2	175	6-29-94	2	0	1.27	16	0	0	2	28	22	4	4	0	13	19	.212	.143	.273	6.04	4.13
Irvin, Cole	L-L	6-4	180	1-31-94	5	1	1.97	10	7	0	0	46	36	16	10	2	8	37	.209	.250	.192	7.29	1.58
Kelzer, Jake	R-R	6-8	230	6-30-93	1	1	4.34	13	0	0	3	19	23	11	9	0	7	19	.288	.242	.319	9.16	3.38
Kline, Alexander	L-L	6-4	200	5-27-94	2	0	2.88	15	0	0	3	25	15	10	8	0	17	28	.172	.115	.197	10.08	6.12
Koplove, Kenny	R-R	6-2	170	8-2-93	0	1	3.76	16	0	0	0	26	28	12	11	1	14	24	.267	.217	.305	8.20	4.78
Medina, Adonis	R-R	6-1	185	12-18-96	5	3	2.92	13	13	0	0	65	47	26	21	5	24	34	.203	.232	.176	4.73	3.34
Nin, Jose	R-R	6-2	170	6-20-95	0	0	2.70	3	0	0	0	3	3	1	1	0	2	3	.273	.167	.400	5.40	0.00
Ortiz, Geury	R-R	6-2	190	5-22-95	1	1	8.10	2	0	0	0	3	2	3	3	0	2	0	.167	.286	.000	0.00	5.40
Paulino, Felix	R-R	6-1	170	3-24-95	3	4	2.89	13	13	0	0	72	64	31	23	2	14	54	.238	.227	.248	6.78	1.76
Quinn, Blake	R-R	6-4	222	8-29-94	0	0	1.03	10	0	0	2	26	19	4	3	0	17	37	.202	.081	.281	12.65	5.81
Romero, JoJo	L-L	6-0	190	9-9-96	2	2	2.56	10	10	1	0	46	44	15	13	2	11	31	.256	.256	.256	6.11	2.17
Singer, Jeff	L-L	6-0	200	9-13-93	0	0	0.00	4	0	0	0	7	2	0	0	0	0	9	.087	.286	.000	12.15	0.00
Stubblefield, Gandy	R-R	6-5	190	7-23-92	0	0	9.00	2	0	0	0	2	3	2	2	0	2	1	.375	.500	.333	4.50	9.00
Suarez, Ranger	L-L	6-0	177	8-26-95	6	4	2.81	13	13	2	0	74	61	26	23	4	24	53	.223	.247	.214	6.48	2.93

Fielding

C: Barbier 7, Duran 2, Lartigue 39, Rivero 31. **1B:** Barbier 13, Cuicas 1, Encarnacion 23, Hall 43. **2B:** Antequera 15, Cuicas 3, Espiritu 41, Hall 5, Rogers 12. **3B:** Cuicas 2, Espiritu 1, Hall 5, Hernandez 1, Rogers 15, Williams 52. **SS:** Antequera 1, Cuicas 5, Gamboa 35, Hall 31, Rogers 6. **OF:** Alastre 39, Garcia 37, Kent 2, Laird 16, Luis 50, Maglich 41, Martinelli 53.

GCL PHILLIES | ROOKIE
GULF COAST LEAGUE

Batting	B-T	HT	WT	DOB	AVG	vLH	vRH	G	AB	R	H	2B	3B	HR	RBI	BB	HBP	SH	SF	SO	SB	CS	SLG	OBP
Alastre, Jesus	R-R	6-1	155	11-25-96	.316	1.000	.278	4	19	1	6	1	0	0	2	1	0	0	0	2	0	1	.368	.350
Altherr, Aaron	R-R	6-5	215	1-14-91	.375	.500	.357	6	16	5	6	1	0	1	3	6	1	0	0	2	0	0	.625	.565
Antequera, Jose	R-R	5-10	160	8-1-95	.299	.423	.264	33	117	21	35	13	2	0	7	9	2	1	0	12	8	1	.444	.359
Brito, Daniel	L-R	6-1	155	1-23-98	.284	.300	.280	47	190	35	54	10	5	2	25	21	1	1	2	27	7	2	.421	.355
Brown, Aaron	L-L	6-2	220	6-20-92	.273	.000	.300	3	11	0	3	0	0	0	1	0	0	0	0	2	0	0	.273	.273
Duran, Rodolfo	R-R	5-9	170	2-19-98	.315	.333	.310	32	73	14	23	2	1	3	14	4	0	0	1	14	1	1	.493	.346
Eldridge, Caleb	L-L	6-3	235	7-3-95	.159	.111	.171	12	44	6	7	2	0	0	4	9	1	0	0	18	0	0	.205	.315
Garner, Daniel	R-R	6-1	195	1-21-94	.310	.250	.320	15	29	4	9	2	0	0	4	2	0	0	0	10	0	0	.379	.394
Hall, Chandler	R-R	5-11	157	2-27-95	.250	.333	.200	5	8	2	2	0	0	0	0	1	0	0	0	1	0	0	.250	.333
Hernandez, Jan	R-R	6-1	195	1-3-95	.200	—	.200	2	5	0	1	0	0	0	1	0	0	0	0	2	0	0	.200	.200
Jimenez, Enger	R-R	6-1	187	7-4-95	.176	.000	.188	7	17	2	3	1	0	0	3	1	1	0	0	3	0	0	.235	.263
Martinez, Nerluis	L-R	6-2	175	4-10-96	.248	.357	.205	39	101	12	25	4	1	0	18	11	1	0	2	12	0	0	.307	.322
Matos, Malvin	R-R	6-3	170	8-19-96	.242	.323	.222	48	157	19	38	11	1	2	15	19	6	2	1	30	10	5	.363	.344
Moniak, Mickey	L-R	6-2	185	5-13-98	.284	.270	.288	46	176	27	50	11	4	1	28	11	5	0	2	35	10	4	.409	.340
Ortiz, Jhailyn	R-R	6-3	215	11-18-98	.231	.350	.195	47	173	29	40	9	1	8	27	17	7	0	0	53	8	2	.434	.325
Pelletier, Ben	R-R	6-2	190	8-22-98	.217	.167	.237	27	83	14	18	2	1	0	5	5	1	0	0	25	1	0	.265	.270
Quinn, Roman	B-R	5-10	170	5-14-93	.500	.667	.474	6	22	6	11	2	0	0	1	0	1	0	0	3	5	1	.591	.522
Randolph, Cornelius	L-R	5-11	205	6-2-97	.077	.125	.000	5	13	1	1	0	0	0	2	0	0	0	0	3	0	0	.077	.200
Rivas, Raul	B-R	5-10	160	10-27-96	.240	.222	.244	33	100	13	24	1	0	0	8	3	3	3	1	15	1	1	.250	.280
Rodriguez, Lenin	R-R	5-9	165	3-26-98	.340	.500	.282	24	53	6	18	3	0	1	5	9	1	0	1	8	0	0	.453	.438
Rogers, Evan	R-R	5-11	175	4-29-94	.389	.200	.462	7	18	5	7	3	1	2	10	1	0	0	0	4	0	0	1.000	.421
Stephen, Josh	L-L	6-0	185	9-22-97	.253	.194	.270	44	162	21	41	7	3	2	26	18	3	1	0	39	6	6	.370	.339
Stobbe, Cole	R-R	6-1	200	8-30-97	.270	.306	.259	44	148	23	40	8	0	4	13	14	2	2	2	30	3	6	.405	.337
Zardon, Danny	R-R	6-0	200	9-30-94	.260	.214	.274	36	123	16	32	13	1	1	17	16	0	0	1	17	1	1	.407	.343

Pitching	B-T	HT	WT	DOB	W	L	ERA	G	GS	CG	SV	IP	H	R	ER	HR	BB	SO	AVG	vLH	vRH	K/9	BB/9
Alcantara, Randy	R-R	5-11	150	11-9-96	0	0	1.65	14	0	0	0	16	13	4	3	1	1	16	.206	.207	.206	8.82	0.55
Arauz, Harold	R-R	6-2	185	5-29-95	0	0	6.48	3	3	0	0	8	12	7	6	0	2	8	.324	.333	.318	8.64	2.16
Asher, Alec	R-R	6-4	230	10-4-91	0	0	1.50	3	3	0	0	6	4	2	1	1	2	6	.200	.200	.200	9.00	3.00
Brown, Andrew	R-R	6-1	180	10-24-97	0	0	2.75	11	0	0	0	20	18	7	6	0	5	20	.257	.276	.244	9.15	2.29
Cabrera, Ismael	R-R	6-1	185	6-19-94	0	1	2.25	3	0	0	0	4	4	4	1	0	0	2	.250	.250	.250	4.50	0.00
Carrasco, Luis	R-R	6-3	170	9-11-94	7	2	2.18	11	5	0	0	41	35	18	10	0	14	50	.230	.271	.212	10.89	3.05
Cordero, Jimmy	R-R	6-3	215	10-19-91	0	0	1.93	4	0	0	0	5	2	1	1	0	4	7	.125	.250	.000	13.50	7.71
Davis, Austin	L-L	6-4	245	2-3-93	0	0	0.00	2	0	0	0	4	4	0	0	0	2	4	.286	.667	.182	9.00	4.50
Dygestile-Therrien, J.	R-R	6-2	200	3-18-93	0	0	0.00	1	0	0	0	2	1	0	0	0	0	2	.143	—	.143	9.00	0.00
Fanti, Nick	L-L	6-2	185	12-30-96	7	0	1.57	11	9	0	0	52	36	10	9	1	9	65	.191	.220	.184	11.32	1.57
Frohwirth, Tyler	R-R	6-1	165	9-13-93	1	1	2.08	18	0	0	10	17	12	4	4	3	14	14	.197	.136	.231	7.27	1.56
Fultz, Kale	R-R	6-5	225	3-31-94	0	1	4.61	10	0	0	0	14	13	8	7	1	3	6	.250	.353	.200	3.95	1.98
Gonzalez, Luis	R-R	6-3	179	7-6-94	4	0	4.40	11	0	0	0	14	16	10	7	0	11	12	.286	.273	.294	7.53	6.91
Gowdy, Kevin	R-R	6-4	170	11-16-97	0	1	4.00	4	4	0	0	9	9	5	4	0	2	9	.231	.250	.211	9.00	2.00
Kurokawa, Jordan	R-R	6-4	195	12-28-92	1	3	4.19	13	0	0	0	19	23	9	9	1	5	19	.291	.395	.195	8.84	2.33
Leibrandt, Brandon	L-L	6-4	190	12-13-92	0	0	2.30	4	4	0	0	16	14	5	4	1	4	13	.246	.250	.245	7.47	2.30
Llovera, Mauricio	R-R	5-11	200	4-17-96	7	1	1.87	11	10	0	0	53	39	12	11	0	12	56	.205	.243	.181	9.51	2.04
Medina, Yoervis	R-R	6-3	245	7-27-88	2	0	0.00	3	0	0	0	4	0	0	0	0	3	4	.000	.000	.000	9.00	6.75
Miller, Justin	R-R	6-4	183	5-17-98	1	0	2.03	8	0	0	0	13	10	3	3	0	11	7	.222	.278	.185	4.73	7.43
Munoz, Jairo	R-R	6-5	175	8-12-91	0	0	0.00	1	0	0	0	1	1	0	0	0	0	2	.250	.000	.333	18.00	0.00
Nin, Jose	R-R	6-2	170	6-20-95	1	1	1.02	16	0	0	7	18	12	4	2	1	5	15	.203	.238	.184	7.64	2.55
Nunez, Jhon	L-L	6-0	155	11-27-97	1	1	3.10	14	0	0	3	20	17	9	7	1	8	22	.230	.182	.238	9.74	3.54

Pitching	B-T	HT	WT	DOB	W	L	ERA	G	GS	CG	SV	IP	H	R	ER	HR	BB	SO	AVG	vLH	vRH	K/9	BB/9
Ortiz, Geury	R-R	6-2	190	5-22-95	0	0	8.56	12	0	0	1	14	24	16	13	1	5	8	.381	.321	.429	5.27	3.29
Rios, Yacksel	R-R	6-3	185	6-27-93	0	0	4.50	2	0	0	0	2	1	1	1	0	1	1	.167	.000	.200	4.50	4.50
Sanchez, Oskerlly	L-L	6-3	172	8-28-95	0	0	5.14	6	0	0	0	7	8	4	4	0	3	6	.286	.000	.333	7.71	3.86
Sanchez, Sixto	R-R	6-0	185	7-29-98	5	0	0.50	11	11	0	0	54	33	4	3	0	8	44	.181	.192	.177	7.33	1.33
Stewart, Will	L-R	6-2	175	7-14-97	2	3	4.06	11	7	0	0	44	34	20	20	1	19	35	.217	.195	.224	7.11	3.86
Windle, Tom	L-L	6-4	215	3-10-92	0	0	0.00	4	0	0	0	4	4	0	0	0	2	5	.250	.500	.100	11.25	4.50
Young, Kyle	L-L	6-10	205	12-2-97	3	0	2.67	9	2	0	0	27	23	11	8	0	2	19	.228	.286	.213	6.33	0.67

Fielding

C: Duran 32, Garner 13, Martinez 32, Rodriguez 18. **1B:** Antequera 7, Eldridge 12, Martinez 7, Rodriguez 25, Zardon 13. **2B:** Antequera 6, Brito 47, Rivas 5, Zardon 1. **3B:** Antequera 14, Hall 1, Hernandez 2, Rivas 24, Rogers 1, Zardon 23. **SS:** Antequera 6, Hall 4, Rivas 4, Rogers 6, Stobbe 44. **OF:** Alastre 4, Altherr 5, Brown 3, Jimenez 6, Matos 44, Moniak 32, Ortiz 31, Pelletier 23, Quinn 6, Randolph 5, Stephen 34.

DSL PHILLIES

DOMINICAN SUMMER LEAGUE

ROOKIE

Batting	B-T	HT	WT	DOB	AVG	vLH	vRH	G	AB	R	H	2B	3B	HR	RBI	BB	HBP	SH	SF	SO	SB	CS	SLG	OBP
Alfonso, Victor	B-R	5-11	140	8-27-99	.143	.194	.129	44	147	16	21	4	0	0	14	15	6	1	5	33	3	2	.170	.243
Avila, Juanj	L-L	5-9	185	3-17-95	.257	.308	.246	65	222	31	57	14	4	0	20	29	2	3	4	44	7	9	.356	.342
Baez, Ricardo	R-R	6-2	195	8-28-98	.197	.276	.176	46	137	10	27	9	0	0	13	17	1	6	0	42	2	1	.263	.290
Bocio, Keudy	R-R	5-10	161	11-15-98	.226	.250	.219	61	186	28	42	6	1	2	18	49	13	9	0	36	28	13	.301	.419
Estrada, Jose	R-R	5-11	165	5-3-99	.223	.273	.213	50	130	20	29	2	0	0	10	24	10	1	0	28	7	3	.238	.384
Feliz, Alexito	R-R	5-11	160	8-6-96	.245	.267	.241	57	192	24	47	7	1	0	16	4	2	3	2	23	12	11	.292	.265
Gamboa, Rafael	R-R	5-11	190	5-14-96	.195	.161	.206	46	128	16	25	8	0	0	17	18	2	4	2	33	2	2	.258	.300
Gutierrez, Dixon	B-R	5-11	165	6-30-98	.257	.262	.255	62	230	25	59	6	2	0	13	19	3	3	1	31	11	10	.300	.320
Guzman, Jonathan	R-R	6-0	156	4-17-99	.300	.373	.280	64	240	27	72	11	0	0	13	21	7	7	2	25	13	13	.346	.370
Henriquez, Jesus	R-R	6-0	168	4-7-98	.337	.250	.358	68	264	43	89	8	0	0	26	32	2	8	1	13	12	6	.367	.411
Herrera, Jhon Meison	B-R	5-11	160	4-8-98	.143	.250	.118	8	21	3	3	0	0	0	2	3	2	2	0	6	1	2	.143	.308
Liriano, Luis	B-R	6-0	192	12-26-97	.169	.207	.161	50	166	7	28	1	0	0	13	14	2	2	0	20	4	2	.175	.242
Marchan, Rafael	R-R	5-9	170	2-25-99	.333	.370	.320	44	171	23	57	7	1	0	34	16	0	0	5	14	6	0	.386	.380
Marrero, Ronaldo	R-R	6-0	160	2-7-96	.259	.171	.281	54	212	25	55	11	1	0	20	12	2	2	1	19	14	5	.321	.304
Medina, Leandro	L-R	6-0	150	7-8-99	.079	.000	.086	12	38	2	3	0	0	0	4	4	1	0	0	10	0	1	.079	.186
Mendoza, Luis	L-R	6-1	165	8-7-97	.285	.290	.284	49	186	28	53	10	2	1	32	19	0	4	1	19	5	4	.376	.372
Mora, Jose	R-R	6-0	170	4-7-96	.093	.000	.125	18	43	4	4	0	0	0	4	9	3	0	2	13	1	1	.093	.281
Muzziotti, Simon	L-L	6-1	175	12-27-98	.231	.385	.197	37	143	12	33	4	1	0	12	11	0	2	0	10	7	3	.273	.286
2-team total (17 Red Sox)					.256	—	—	54	203	21	52	6	2	0	22	15	0	2	1	16	8	4	.305	.306
Noboa, Rony	R-R	6-1	200	7-21-95	.231	.000	.250	5	13	2	3	0	0	0	2	0	0	0	0	2	0	0	.231	.333
Nunez, Yeremy	B-R	5-10	153	12-13-97	.197	.259	.178	33	117	7	23	3	1	0	7	12	1	3	1	28	6	3	.239	.275
Omana, Enmanuel	R-R	6-0	148	9-23-97	.196	.220	.189	68	219	26	43	6	0	0	11	22	17	4	1	30	8	8	.224	.317
Oropeza, Carlos	R-R	6-0	170	12-22-98	.233	.238	.233	48	150	17	35	10	0	0	19	23	11	1	2	27	6	1	.300	.371
Paulino, Miguel	R-R	5-10	170	11-4-94	.253	.273	.247	33	99	7	25	9	0	0	11	10	4	0	0	22	7	1	.343	.345
Romero, Daniel	R-R	5-11	155	5-5-97	.245	.316	.227	52	188	23	46	4	0	1	17	9	5	6	0	25	16	3	.282	.297
Rosado, Ismael	R-R	5-11	185	12-14-96	.167	.150	.170	34	108	8	18	4	0	0	11	19	2	0	1	7	1	2	.204	.300
Santana, Henry	R-R	6-3	180	12-19-94	.262	.159	.290	56	206	24	54	10	3	2	22	11	1	2	5	25	16	5	.369	.333
Silva, Wilman	R-R	5-8	165	10-17-96	.247	.273	.239	50	182	19	45	13	3	1	20	14	3	0	0	23	1	1	.368	.312
Smith, Juan Carlos	R-R	6-1	181	8-22-97	.229	.429	.179	9	35	2	8	2	0	0	3	3	1	0	0	10	0	0	.286	.308
Tabares, Yorbys	R-R	6-0	165	1-24-97	.250	—	.250	6	16	1	4	0	0	0	2	2	0	1	0	9	0	1	.250	.333
Trejo, Yerwin	R-R	5-11	155	12-14-96	.257	.283	.251	64	237	45	61	13	2	1	16	34	9	3	2	29	21	8	.342	.349
Vasquez, Rusbel	B-R	5-11	165	11-14-98	.239	.000	.256	13	46	5	11	2	0	0	4	1	1	0	0	10	0	1	.283	.271

Pitching	B-T	HT	WT	DOB	W	L	ERA	G	GS	CG	SV	IP	H	R	ER	HR	BB	SO	AVG	vLH	vRH	K/9	BB/9
Aponte, Leonel	R-R	6-4	144	7-2-99	2	4	2.77	13	8	0	1	49	38	19	15	1	11	23	.222	.197	.240	4.25	2.03
Aris, Abdallah	R-R	5-11	155	10-8-96	4	1	2.25	18	0	0	0	36	25	11	9	1	19	40	.195	.170	.210	10.00	4.75
Armas, Gustavo	R-R	6-1	195	1-15-96	4	3	2.19	15	14	0	0	74	68	22	18	6	18	50	.247	.246	.248	6.08	2.19
Avendano, Eudiver	R-R	6-3	200	2-1-99	3	0	7.02	13	0	0	0	17	23	15	13	1	11	10	—	—	—	5.40	5.94
Bastidas, Miguelangel	R-R	6-1	170	8-3-95	6	3	3.30	14	14	0	0	79	73	34	29	1	36	47	.250	.298	.227	5.35	4.10
Benitez, Alfredo	L-L	5-10	165	8-13-96	2	3	2.14	17	0	0	2	34	20	9	8	0	11	40	.169	.250	.160	10.69	2.94
Canizales, Antonio	R-R	6-1	160	1-24-98	0	0	2.00	7	0	0	0	9	7	3	2	0	2	11	.219	.250	.200	11.00	2.00
Carmona, Steiner	R-R	6-3	195	2-14-96	1	4	3.52	16	0	0	6	31	24	16	12	1	19	25	.222	.188	.237	7.34	5.58
Carvajal, Rafael	R-R	6-0	170	11-15-96	2	0	0.84	8	5	0	0	32	17	5	3	0	4	22	.157	.152	.161	6.12	1.11
Ciarla, Alessandro	R-R	6-4	155	11-3-97	1	0	5.40	6	0	0	0	10	7	8	6	1	5	6	.200	.333	.100	5.40	4.50
Coveri, Ludovico	R-R	6-2	195	3-6-97	0	1	3.86	8	0	0	0	12	11	5	5	0	3	4	.256	.545	.156	3.09	2.31
De Los Santos, Jesus	R-R	6-2	165	12-23-95	6	0	1.49	13	13	0	0	73	60	17	12	0	12	43	—	—	—	5.33	1.49
Diaz, Wilerik	R-R	6-0	171	1-12-97	2	3	2.89	14	9	0	1	47	32	17	15	1	23	35	.195	.247	.139	6.75	4.44
Ferrer, Gustavo	B-L	5-11	160	11-16-98	0	2	5.59	8	0	0	0	10	11	11	6	1	6	8	.282	.000	.306	7.45	5.59
Gomez, Yeral	R-R	6-0	180	6-5-96	1	4	3.66	16	1	0	3	39	45	20	16	1	10	25	.285	.293	.282	5.72	2.29
Gonzalez, Reiwal	R-R	6-2	196	11-11-94	3	1	1.47	11	0	0	4	18	17	5	3	0	3	18	.233	.185	.261	8.84	1.47
Heredia, Erick	R-R	6-4	175	3-17-97	0	0	4.15	2	1	0	0	4	5	2	2	0	4	0	.294	.400	.250	0.00	8.31
Jimenez, Jose	L-L	5-11	175	9-25-97	2	0	1.84	15	0	0	1	29	26	13	6	0	13	22	.236	.259	.229	6.75	3.99
Marcelino, Oscar	R-R	6-3	166	6-8-97	1	9	3.15	14	14	0	0	66	62	26	23	1	32	56	—	—	—	7.68	4.39
Martinez, Denny	B-L	6-0	157	11-1-96	9	2	2.00	14	14	0	0	72	46	20	16	0	14	81	.178	.212	.169	10.13	1.75
Martinez, Robinson	R-R	6-0	190	3-20-98	1	1	7.91	12	0	0	0	19	28	19	17	0	20	20	.346	.389	.333	9.31	9.31
Mateo, Gregorix	R-R	6-1	200	8-25-96	0	0	4.50	2	0	0	0	2	1	1	1	0	3	1	.000	—	.000	4.50	13.50
Melendez, Orestes	L-L	5-11	180	6-8-95	1	1	2.04	13	0	0	4	35	19	11	8	0	9	35	.177	.179	.177	8.92	2.29
Mendoza, Roimy	L-L	6-3	170	12-18-96	1	2	4.80	14	2	0	0	30	31	17	16	1	30	23	.247	.300	.241	6.90	9.00

Pitching	B-T	HT	WT	DOB	W	L	ERA	G	GS	CG	SV	IP	H	R	ER	HR	BB	SO	AVG	vLH	vRH	K/9	BB/9
Mendoza, Williams	R-R	6-7	200	4-29-98	0	0	4.97	11	0	0	0	13	12	8	7	0	12	7	.267	.188	.310	4.97	8.53
Nolasco, Moises	R-R	6-4	170	2-2-97	3	2	7.58	10	3	0	0	30	34	26	25	2	20	25	.312	.324	.307	7.58	6.07
Nunez, Melvin	R-R	6-2	185	3-17-97	0	1	1.93	5	0	0	1	9	10	4	2	0	2	7	.278	.278	.278	6.75	1.93
Nunez, Anderson	R-R	5-10	180	5-24-94	0	0	2.31	6	0	0	0	12	6	4	3	0	4	16	—	—	—	12.34	3.09
Ramirez, Luis	R-R	5-11	175	9-14-97	1	0	1.04	23	0	0	11	26	18	8	3	0	11	26	.189	.269	.159	9.00	3.81
Rosario, Sandro	R-R	6-3	185	1-23-96	5	4	2.54	13	13	1	0	71	63	25	20	1	20	21	.240	.261	.232	2.66	2.54
Salazar, Carlos	R-R	6-1	155	11-19-96	0	2	4.45	16	0	0	2	30	28	18	15	1	20	21	.255	.280	.247	6.23	5.93
Santos, Juan	R-R	6-3	173	8-30-96	0	0	3.38	6	0	0	0	11	10	5	4	0	10	7	.270	.571	.200	5.91	8.44
Silva, Manuel	L-L	6-2	145	12-18-98	2	4	2.78	12	10	0	0	58	48	23	18	3	16	33	.230	.208	.232	5.09	2.47
Sobil, Victor	R-R	6-2	215	7-17-96	0	2	1.88	10	6	0	1	29	24	9	6	0	8	26	.218	.200	.240	8.16	2.51
Tejada, Junior	L-L	6-1	170	5-23-97	0	0	6.00	3	0	0	0	3	3	2	2	0	2	4	.333	.000	.429	12.00	6.00
Valdez, Jean Carlos	R-R	6-2	185	8-30-97	2	5	2.54	12	11	0	0	57	46	23	16	0	26	40	.223	.184	.236	6.35	4.13

Fielding

C: Gamboa 13, Liriano 24, Marchan 24, Marrero 1, Oropeza 25, Paulino 24, Rosado 25, Silva 16. **1B:** Baez 14, Feliz 11, Gamboa 26, Henriquez 19, Liriano 19, Marchan 6, Marrero 1, Oropeza 3, Romero 1, Santana 40, Silva 10. **2B:** Alfonso 39, Bocio 49, Henriquez 18, Marrero 2, Medina 6, Nunez 8, Omana 14, Romero 7, Vasquez 1. **SS:** Alfonso 1, Feliz 1, Guzman 64, Henriquez 5, Marrero 12, Medina 5, Omana 53, Romero 3. **3B:** Bocio 11, Feliz 17, Gamboa 1, Henriquez 28, Marrero 39, Noboa 1, Romero 39, Vasquez 5. **OF:** Avila 64, Baez 23, Estrada 40, Feliz 30, Gutierrez 61, Henriquez 1, Herrera 4, Mendoza 48, Muzziotti 37, Nunez 20, Paulino 3, Santana 16, Silva 17, Smith 3, Tabares 1, Trejo 64, Vasquez 1.

Pittsburgh Pirates

SEASON IN A SENTENCE: Three years of playoff appearances ended, as injuries, sketchy pitching and an off-year by star Andrew McCutchen dropped the Pirates to their first losing record since 2012.

HIGH POINT: Through the first two months, the Pirates stayed on schedule, with Jeff Locke tossing a three-hit shutout May 30 in a 10-0 win at Miami. The Pirates ended the month 29-22 as emerging star Gregory Polanco homered against the Marlins en route to a 22-homer breakout this season at age 24.

LOW POINT: The Pirates were still in the wild-card hunt in late August when they embarked on a season-long eight-game losing skid. The kickoff came Aug. 29, when the Cubs rallied from a 6-3 deficit with two runs off Neftali Feliz and one off Tony Watson—Mark Melancon's replacement at closer after a July 30 trade—in the ninth. Locke, shifted to the bullpen, gave up the game-losing run in the 13th inning and the Pirates were on their way to a losing streak that took them under .500.

NOTABLE ROOKIES: The No. 2 overall pick in 2010—between Bryce Harper and Manny Machado—rigthander Jameson Taillon finally got healthy and thrived, making 18 starts in Pittsburgh, posting a 3.38 ERA and showed durability, tossing 165 innings overall including the minors. Versatile Adam Frazier broke though in the first half and hit .301, becoming a valuable reserve who could play virtually any position.

KEY TRANSACTIONS: Pittsburgh's free-agent moves worked out fine, from David Freese and John Jaso on the corners to picking up Juan Nicasio, who struggled in the rotation but pitched well in relief, leading the team in strikeouts while ranking second in innings pitched. But trading Neil Walker for Jon Niese proved a lose-lose proposition, and trading Mark Melancon to the Nationals made the bullpen less effective.

DOWN ON THE FARM: Top prospects such as Josh Bell and righthander Tyler Glasnow (23 MLB innings) made their big league debuts, with Glasnow dominating the upper minors with an 8-3, 1.87 mark at Triple-A Indianapolis. The club's 2015 first-round pick Kevin Newman reached Double-A while hitting .320/.389/.426 overall. Newman had started the season at high Class A Bradenton, which won the Florida State League title riding 2014 second-round pick Mitch Keller, who enjoyed a breakthrough season (9-5, 2.35).

OPENING DAY PAYROLL: $103,778,833 (19th)

PLAYERS OF THE YEAR

MAJOR LEAGUE	MINOR LEAGUE
Starling Marte	**Mitch Keller**
of	rhp
.311/.362/.456	(Low A/High A)
9 HR, 46 RBI	9-5, 2.35
34 2B, 47 SB	138 SO in 130.1 IP

ORGANIZATION LEADERS

BATTING   *Minimum 250 AB

MAJORS

* AVG	Starling Marte	.311
* OPS	Starling Marte	.818
HR	Andrew McCutchen	24
RBI	Gregory Polanco	86

MINORS

* AVG	Kevin Newman, Bradenton, Altoona	.32
* OBP	Kevin Newman, Bradenton, Altoona	.389
* SLG	Barrett Barnes, Altoona	.477
* OPS	Barrett Barnes, Altoona	.853
R	Tito Polo, West Virginia, Bradenton	86
H	Jose Osuna, Altoona, Indianapolis	132
TB	Jose Osuna, Altoona, Indianapolis	216
2B	Jose Osuna, Altoona, Indianapolis	37
3B	Austin Meadows, Altoona, West Va., Indianapolis	11
HR	Danny Ortiz, Indianapolis	17
RBI	Jose Osuna, Altoona, Indianapolis	69
BB	Max Moroff, Indianapolis	90
SO	Casey Hughston, West Virginia	154
SB	Tito Polo, West Virginia, Bradenton	37

PITCHING   #Minimum 75 IP

MAJORS

W	Juan Nicasio	10
# ERA	Jameson Taillon	3.38
SO	Juan Nicasio	138
SV	Mark Melancon	30

MINORS

W	Austin Coley, Bradenton	12
	Frank Duncan, Altoona, Indianapolis	12
L	Dario Agrazal, West Virginia	12
# ERA	Tyler Glasnow, Altoona, Indianapolis	1.93
G	Montana DuRapau, Altoona	50
GS	Dario Agrazal, West Virginia	27
	Tyler Eppler, Altoona	27
	Alex McRae, Bradenton, Altoona	27
SV	Montana DuRapau, Altoona	22
IP	Tyler Eppler, Altoona	163
BB	Cody Dickson, Altoona	93
SO	Tyler Glasnow, Altoona, Indianapolis	144
# AVG	Tyler Glasnow, Altoona, Indianapolis	.176

General Manager: Neal Huntington. **Farm Director:** Larry Broadway. **Scouting Director:** Joe Delli Carri.

Class	Team	League	W	L	PCT	Finish	Manager
Majors	Pittsburgh Pirates	National	78	83	.484	8th (15)	Clint Hurdle
Triple-A	Indianapolis Indians	International	70	74	.486	7th (14)	Dean Treanor
Double-A	Altoona Curve	Eastern	76	64	.543	4th (12)	Joey Cora
High A	Bradenton Marauders	Florida State	70	66	.515	6th (12)	Michael Ryan
Low A	West Virginia Power	South Atlantic	71	68	.511	7th (12)	Brian Esposito
Short season	West Virginia Black Bears	New York-Penn	38	38	.500	8th (14)	Wyatt Toregas
Rookie	Bristol Pirates	Appalachian	25	43	.368	10th (10)	Edgar Varela
Rookie	Pirates	Gulf Coast	22	34	.393	15th (17)	Milver Reyes
Overall 2016 Minor League Record			372	387	.490	17th (30)	

ORGANIZATION STATISTICS

PITTSBURGH PIRATES
NATIONAL LEAGUE

Batting	B-T	HT	WT	DOB	AVG	vLH	vRH	G	AB	R	H	2B	3B	HR	RBI	BB	HBP	SH	SF	SO	SB	CS	SLG	OBP
Bell, Josh	B-R	6-2	240	8-14-92	.273	.211	.284	45	128	18	35	8	0	3	19	21	0	0	3	19	0	1	.406	.368
Cervelli, Francisco	R-R	6-1	210	3-6-86	.264	.385	.241	101	326	42	86	14	1	1	33	56	6	0	5	72	6	2	.322	.377
Diaz, Elias	R-R	6-0	210	11-17-90	.000	—	.000	1	4	0	0	0	0	0	1	0	0	0	0	1	0	0	.000	.000
Figueroa, Cole	L-R	5-10	185	6-30-87	.154	.167	.150	23	26	0	4	0	0	0	3	1	0	0	0	2	1	0	.154	.185
Florimon, Pedro	B-R	6-2	185	12-10-86	.208	.200	.211	18	24	4	5	1	1	0	4	1	0	0	0	12	0	1	.333	.240
Frazier, Adam	L-R	5-10	180	12-14-91	.301	.417	.279	66	146	21	44	8	1	2	11	12	1	0	1	26	4	1	.411	.356
Freese, David	R-R	6-2	225	4-28-83	.270	.337	.252	141	437	63	118	23	0	13	55	45	10	0	1	142	0	1	.412	.352
Fryer, Eric	R-R	6-2	215	8-26-85	.218	.364	.194	36	78	12	17	2	1	0	8	10	0	2	2	18	0	2	.269	.300
2-team total (24 St. Louis)					.267	—	—	60	116	19	31	4	1	0	13	13	0	2	2	25	0	3	.319	.336
Hanson, Alen	B-R	5-11	175	10-22-92	.226	.143	.250	27	31	5	7	1	0	0	1	2	0	0	5	2	1	.258	.273
Harrison, Josh	R-R	5-8	190	7-8-87	.283	.311	.277	131	487	57	138	25	7	4	59	18	5	4	8	76	19	4	.388	.311
Jaso, John	L-R	6-2	205	9-19-83	.268	.050	.281	132	380	45	102	25	3	8	42	45	5	1	1	74	0	4	.413	.353
Joyce, Matt	L-R	6-2	205	8-3-84	.242	.235	.244	140	231	45	56	10	1	13	42	59	3	0	0	67	1	1	.463	.403
Kang, Jung Ho	R-R	6-0	210	4-5-87	.255	.209	.267	103	318	45	81	19	0	21	62	36	14	0	2	79	3	1	.513	.354
Kratz, Erik	R-R	6-4	245	6-15-80	.107	.222	.053	18	56	3	6	1	0	1	4	0	0	1	0	18	0	0	.179	.107
Marte, Starling	R-R	6-1	190	10-9-88	.311	.292	.315	129	489	71	152	34	5	9	46	23	16	1	0	104	47	12	.456	.362
McCutchen, Andrew	R-R	5-10	195	10-10-86	.256	.229	.262	153	598	81	153	26	3	24	79	69	5	0	3	143	6	7	.430	.336
Mercer, Jordy	R-R	6-3	205	8-27-86	.256	.275	.252	149	519	66	133	22	3	11	59	51	5	7	2	83	1	1	.374	.328
Moroff, Max	B-R	5-10	185	5-13-93	.000	.000	—	2	2	0	0	0	0	0	0	0	0	0	0	2	0	0	.000	.000
Morse, Mike	R-R	6-5	245	3-22-82	.000	.000	.000	6	8	0	0	0	0	0	0	0	0	0	0	2	0	0	.000	.000
Polanco, Gregory	L-L	6-5	230	9-14-91	.258	.245	.261	144	527	79	136	34	4	22	86	53	0	1	6	119	17	6	.463	.323
Rodriguez, Sean	R-R	6-0	200	4-26-85	.270	.286	.265	140	300	49	81	16	1	18	56	33	5	1	3	102	2	1	.510	.349
Rogers, Jason	R-R	6-1	260	3-13-88	.080	.143	.000	23	25	2	2	0	1	0	2	7	1	0	0	9	0	0	.160	.303
Stallings, Jacob	R-R	6-5	220	12-22-89	.400	—	.400	5	15	0	6	1	0	0	2	0	0	0	0	4	1	0	.467	.400
Stewart, Chris	R-R	6-4	205	2-19-82	.214	.316	.190	34	98	10	21	4	0	1	7	12	3	0	0	15	0	0	.286	.319

Pitching	B-T	HT	WT	DOB	W	L	ERA	G	GS	CG	SV	IP	H	R	ER	HR	BB	SO	AVG	vLH	vRH	K/9	BB/9
Bastardo, Antonio	L-L	5-11	205	9-21-85	3	0	4.13	28	0	0	0	24	19	13	11	3	11	28	.216	.185	.230	10.50	4.13
2-team total (41 New York)					3	0	4.52	69	0	0	0	68	60	37	34	11	32	74	—	—	—	9.84	4.26
Boscan, Wilfredo	R-R	6-2	175	10-26-89	1	1	6.46	6	1	0	0	15	15	11	11	2	7	8	.254	.333	.172	4.70	4.11
Brault, Steven	L-L	6-0	200	4-29-92	0	3	4.86	8	7	0	0	33	45	26	18	5	17	29	.313	.318	.311	7.83	4.59
Caminero, Arquimedes	R-R	6-4	245	6-16-87	1	2	3.51	39	0	0	1	41	46	17	16	4	22	32	.289	.284	.294	7.02	4.83
Coke, Phil	L-L	6-1	210	7-19-82	0	0	0.00	3	0	0	0	4	3	0	0	0	3	3	.231	.400	.125	6.75	6.75
Cole, Gerrit	R-R	6-4	220	9-8-90	7	10	3.88	21	21	1	0	116	131	57	50	7	36	98	.289	.329	.253	7.60	2.79
Feliz, Neftali	R-R	6-3	235	5-2-88	4	2	3.52	62	0	0	2	54	40	21	21	10	21	61	.207	.180	.231	10.23	3.52
Glasnow, Tyler	L-R	6-8	220	8-23-93	0	2	4.24	7	4	0	0	23	22	13	11	2	13	24	.250	.308	.204	9.26	5.01
Hughes, Jared	R-R	6-7	240	7-4-85	1	1	3.03	67	0	0	1	59	62	24	20	6	22	34	.277	.278	.276	5.16	3.34
Hutchison, Drew	L-R	6-3	205	8-22-90	0	0	5.56	6	1	0	0	11	15	7	7	2	3	10	.341	.533	.241	7.94	2.38
Kuhl, Chad	R-R	6-3	220	9-10-92	5	4	4.20	14	14	0	0	71	73	34	33	7	20	53	.267	.301	.240	6.75	2.55
LeBlanc, Wade	L-L	6-3	210	8-7-84	1	0	0.75	8	0	0	1	12	7	3	1	0	2	10	.175	.200	.167	7.50	1.50
Liriano, Francisco	L-L	6-2	225	10-26-83	6	11	5.46	21	21	0	0	114	115	76	69	19	69	116	.264	.255	.267	9.18	5.46
Lobstein, Kyle	L-L	6-3	220	8-12-89	2	0	3.96	14	0	0	0	25	25	11	11	2	12	15	.263	.083	.324	5.40	4.32
Locke, Jeff	L-L	6-0	200	11-20-87	9	8	5.44	30	19	1	0	127	151	81	77	17	44	73	.298	.282	.305	5.16	3.11
Luebke, Cory	R-L	6-4	215	3-4-85	0	1	9.35	9	0	0	0	9	15	9	9	2	11	9	.385	.364	.393	9.35	11.42
Marte, Kelvin	L-L	5-9	170	11-24-87	0	0	0.00	2	0	0	0	3	5	5	0	2	2	1	.333	.000	.357	2.70	5.40
Melancon, Mark	R-R	6-2	210	3-28-85	1	1	1.51	45	0	0	30	42	31	10	7	2	9	38	.205	.215	.198	8.21	1.94
2-team total (30 Washington)					2	2	1.64	75	0	0	47	71	52	16	13	2	12	65	—	—	—	8.20	1.51
Nicasio, Juan	R-R	6-4	255	8-31-86	10	7	4.50	52	12	0	0	118	117	64	59	15	45	138	.261	.291	.235	10.53	3.43
Niese, Jon	L-L	6-3	215	10-27-86	8	6	4.91	23	18	0	0	110	132	63	60	21	38	76	.297	.291	.300	6.22	3.11
2-team total (6 New York)					8	7	5.50	29	20	0	0	121	145	77	74	25	47	88	—	—	—	6.55	3.50
Nova, Ivan	R-R	6-5	240	1-12-87	5	2	3.06	11	11	3	0	65	68	27	22	4	3	52	.273	.343	.222	7.24	0.42
Partch, Curtis	R-R	6-5	240	2-13-87	0	0	40.50	2	0	0	0	1	2	3	3	0	2	0	.500	1.000	.000	0.00	27.00
Phillips, Zach	L-L	6-1	200	9-21-86	0	0	2.70	8	0	0	0	7	8	2	2	1	1	6	.296	.500	.211	8.10	1.35

Pitching	B-T	HT	WT	DOB	W	L	ERA	G	GS	CG	SV	IP	H	R	ER	HR	BB	SO	AVG	vLH	vRH	K/9	BB/9
Rivero, Felipe	L-L	6-2	210	7-5-91	1	3	3.29	28	0	0	0	27	23	13	10	3	18	39	.221	.172	.240	12.84	5.93
2-team total (47 Washington)					1	6	4.09	75	0	0	1	77	66	39	35	7	33	92	—	—	—	10.75	3.86
Rondon, Jorge	R-R	6-1	215	2-16-88	0	0	17.18	2	0	0	0	4	9	7	7	1	1	4	.474	.636	.250	9.82	2.45
Scahill, Rob	R-R	6-2	220	2-15-87	0	0	4.41	15	0	0	0	16	18	9	8	1	6	13	.290	.320	.270	7.16	3.31
2-team total (16 Milwaukee)					0	0	3.38	31	0	0	0	35	34	14	13	2	9	27	—	—	—	7.01	2.34
Schugel, A.J.	R-R	6-0	200	6-27-89	2	2	3.63	36	0	0	1	52	41	22	21	4	13	46	.216	.161	.268	7.96	2.25
Taillon, Jameson	R-R	6-5	220	11-18-91	5	4	3.38	18	18	0	0	104	99	40	39	13	17	85	.252	.269	.234	7.36	1.47
Vogelsong, Ryan	R-R	6-4	215	7-22-77	3	7	4.81	24	14	0	0	82	80	51	44	11	40	61	.254	.285	.230	6.67	4.37
Watson, Tony	L-L	6-4	225	5-30-85	2	5	3.06	70	0	0	15	68	52	26	23	10	20	58	.215	.211	.216	7.71	2.66
Williams, Trevor	R-R	6-3	230	4-25-92	1	1	7.82	7	1	0	0	13	19	13	11	4	5	11	.339	.350	.333	7.82	3.55

Fielding

Catcher	PCT	G	PO	A	E	DP	PB
Cervelli	.991	95	693	71	7	7	8
Diaz	1.000	1	7	4	0	0	0
Fryer	.987	32	211	10	3	1	3
Kratz	.992	17	109	8	1	1	2
Stallings	1.000	4	28	0	0	0	0
Stewart	.990	31	193	10	2	1	4

First Base	PCT	G	PO	A	E	DP
Bell	.983	23	157	14	3	11
Cervelli	1.000	2	7	0	0	2
Freese	.992	58	344	31	3	42
Jaso	.994	108	749	46	5	81
Kratz	1.000	1	1	0	0	0
Morse	1.000	1	5	0	0	1
Rodriguez	.995	57	176	14	1	17
Rogers	1.000	5	20	0	0	3
Stewart	1.000	1	0	1	0	0

Second Base	PCT	G	PO	A	E	DP
Figueroa	1.000	5	2	5	0	1
Florimon	1.000	8	7	6	0	1
Frazier	.938	17	15	30	3	7
Freese	—	2	0	0	0	0
Hanson	.923	8	13	11	2	6
Harrison	.989	128	262	366	7	97
Rodriguez	1.000	29	45	60	0	17

Third Base	PCT	G	PO	A	E	DP
Figueroa	1.000	2	0	3	0	1
Frazier	.900	5	1	8	1	2
Freese	.961	78	40	157	8	17
Kang	.934	92	49	191	17	20
Rodriguez	.941	11	3	13	1	1
Rogers	1.000	4	1	1	0	0

Shortstop	PCT	G	PO	A	E	DP
Figueroa	1.000	2	0	2	0	0
Florimon	1.000	6	2	8	0	3
Mercer	.985	146	187	411	9	95
Rodriguez	.944	27	23	45	4	11

Outfield	PCT	G	PO	A	E	DP
Bell	.944	16	17	0	1	0
Frazier	.938	35	29	1	2	0
Harrison	—	1	0	0	0	0
Jaso	—	1	0	0	0	0
Joyce	1.000	66	81	1	0	0
Marte	.982	123	196	17	4	2
McCutchen	.991	151	317	6	3	0
Polanco	.977	134	246	10	6	4
Rodriguez	.968	32	30	0	1	0

INDIANAPOLIS INDIANS

TRIPLE-A

INTERNATIONAL LEAGUE

Batting	B-T	HT	WT	DOB	AVG	vLH	vRH	G	AB	R	H	2B	3B	HR	RBI	BB	HBP	SH	SF	SO	SB	CS	SLG	OBP
Bell, Josh	B-R	6-2	240	8-14-92	.295	.267	.307	114	421	57	124	23	4	14	60	57	4	0	2	74	3	7	.468	.382
Cervelli, Francisco	R-R	6-1	210	3-6-86	.400	1.000	.333	3	10	1	4	1	0	0	1	3	0	0	0	2	0	0	.500	.538
Diaz, Elias	R-R	6-0	210	11-17-90	.266	.423	.206	25	94	4	25	3	0	0	10	3	0	0	0	17	1	0	.298	.289
Easley, Ed	R-R	6-0	215	12-21-85	.174	.140	.194	36	115	7	20	1	0	1	11	13	1	1	2	20	0	0	.209	.260
Figueroa, Cole	L-R	5-10	185	6-30-87	.307	.333	.300	20	75	12	23	3	1	2	11	3	0	0	0	9	2	1	.453	.333
Florimon, Pedro	B-R	6-2	185	12-10-86	.255	.226	.266	107	298	36	76	12	4	5	36	33	1	4	4	87	14	4	.372	.327
Frazier, Adam	L-R	5-10	180	12-14-91	.333	.329	.335	68	261	34	87	16	4	0	22	29	2	5	2	27	17	15	.425	.401
Gamache, Daniel	L-R	5-11	205	11-20-90	.244	.167	.269	79	176	23	43	8	0	2	22	26	0	0	2	50	0	3	.324	.338
Garcia, Willy	R-R	6-2	215	9-4-92	.245	.226	.252	129	462	53	113	30	4	6	43	31	2	1	3	131	5	9	.366	.293
Hanson, Alen	B-R	5-11	175	10-22-92	.266	.278	.261	110	432	58	115	15	7	8	32	32	2	10	2	78	36	15	.389	.318
Jhang, Jin-De	L-R	5-11	220	5-17-93	.200	.333	.176	6	20	2	4	1	0	0	2	1	1	0	1	2	0	0	.250	.261
Kang, Jung Ho	R-R	6-0	210	4-5-87	.146	.158	.138	16	48	5	7	0	0	2	7	7	0	0	2	11	0	1	.271	.246
Maffei, Justin	R-R	5-11	173	8-27-91	.125	.000	.143	4	8	1	1	0	0	0	0	0	0	0	0	1	0	0	.125	.222
Meadows, Austin	L-L	6-3	200	5-3-95	.214	.250	.200	37	126	16	27	7	3	6	24	15	1	0	3	34	8	2	.460	.297
Morales, Tomas	R-R	6-0	190	7-30-91	.400	—	.400	2	5	2	2	1	0	0	0	0	0	0	0	0	1	0	.600	.400
Moroff, Max	B-R	5-10	185	5-13-93	.230	.217	.236	133	421	61	97	18	4	8	45	90	2	5	2	129	9	7	.349	.362
Ngoepe, Gift	B-R	5-8	200	1-18-90	.217	.259	.196	102	332	40	72	20	1	8	27	31	3	6	1	130	5	2	.355	.289
Ortiz, Danny	L-L	5-11	190	1-5-90	.236	.299	.213	130	436	41	103	19	4	17	57	25	1	1	7	91	6	8	.415	.275
Osuna, Jose	R-R	6-2	213	12-12-92	.291	.364	.267	63	220	27	64	19	1	7	31	13	1	0	0	36	2	3	.482	.333
Richardson, Antoan	R-R	5-8	165	10-8-83	.063	.125	.000	5	16	2	1	0	0	0	1	0	0	0	0	5	0	0	.063	.118
Rogers, Jason	R-R	6-1	260	3-13-88	.263	.300	.246	105	372	38	98	18	2	6	40	43	1	0	4	78	1	0	.371	.338
Rojas Jr. Mel	B-R	6-2	225	5-24-90	.154	.000	.222	12	26	1	4	1	0	3	2	0	0	0	7	0	1	.269	.214
2-team total (64 Gwinnett)					.258	—	—	76	256	28	66	12	6	10	37	31	0	0	2	56	9	3	.469	.336
Schwind, Jonathan	R-R	6-0	185	5-30-90	.000	.000	.000	3	5	0	0	0	0	0	0	0	0	0	0	1	0	0	.000	.000
Stallings, Jacob	R-R	6-5	220	12-22-89	.214	.273	.194	80	257	23	55	17	0	6	28	11	2	5	0	66	0	1	.350	.252
Tam Sing, Trace	R-R	6-0	175	12-7-91	.200	—	.200	3	5	1	1	0	0	1	0	0	0	0	0	2	0	0	.800	.200

Pitching	B-T	HT	WT	DOB	W	L	ERA	G	GS	CG	SV	IP	H	R	ER	HR	BB	SO	AVG	vLH	vRH	K/9	BB/9
Boscan, Wilfredo	R-R	6-2	175	10-26-89	7	7	3.75	17	16	1	0	84	97	39	35	5	14	51	.298	.297	.299	5.46	1.50
2-team total (3 Gwinnett)					6	9	4.16	20	19	1	0	93	115	49	43	6	21	58	—	—	—	5.61	2.03
Brault, Steven	L-L	6-0	200	4-29-92	2	7	3.91	16	15	0	0	71	66	35	31	6	35	81	.243	.246	.242	10.22	4.42
Caminero, Arquimedes	R-R	6-4	245	6-16-87	0	0	9.00	3	0	0	0	4	4	4	4	1	3	6	.250	.400	.182	13.50	6.75
Cole, Gerrit	R-R	6-4	220	9-8-90	0	0	0.00	2	2	0	0	8	4	0	0	0	0	12	.148	.250	.130	13.50	0.00
Creasy, Jason	R-R	6-4	197	5-13-92	0	0	0.00	2	0	0	0	4	0	0	0	0	4	1	.000	.000	.000	2.25	9.00
Duncan, Frank	R-R	6-4	215	1-30-92	9	6	2.33	20	20	0	0	112	106	34	29	4	29	92	.251	.287	.227	7.39	2.33
Fuller, Cody	L-L	5-10	190	6-1-87	0	1	5.00	3	0	0	0	3	4	2	2	0	4	2	.286	.200	.333	5.40	10.80
Glasnow, Tyler	R-R	6-8	220	8-23-93	8	3	1.87	20	20	0	0	111	65	29	23	4	62	133	.175	.170	.178	10.82	5.04
Haley, Trey	R-R	6-4	215	6-21-90	2	4	5.76	38	0	0	5	45	44	33	29	3	32	32	.260	.317	.229	6.35	6.35
Hughes, Jared	R-R	6-7	240	7-4-85	0	0	7.50	4	0	0	0	6	5	5	5	1	3	5	.292	.300	.286	7.50	4.50
Hutchison, Drew	L-R	6-3	205	8-22-90	1	1	4.50	7	6	0	0	36	37	23	18	5	15	28	.262	.224	.289	7.00	3.75

Pitching	B-T	HT	WT	DOB	W	L	ERA	G	GS	CG	SV	IP	H	R	ER	HR	BB	SO	AVG	vLH	vRH	K/9	BB/9
2-team total (18 Buffalo)					7	6	3.59	25	24	0	0	138	115	63	55	16	50	138	—	—	—	9.00	3.26
Knudson, Guido	R-R	6-1	185	8-5-89	1	2	3.08	19	0	0	0	26	16	9	9	3	13	22	.178	.111	.206	7.52	4.44
Kuchno, John	R-R	6-5	210	5-21-91	1	4	5.22	28	2	0	0	60	69	36	35	6	22	25	.294	.353	.260	3.73	3.28
Kuhl, Chad	R-R	6-3	220	9-10-92	6	3	2.37	16	16	0	0	84	81	27	22	9	16	66	.257	.297	.234	7.10	1.72
Lobstein, Kyle	L-L	6-3	220	8-12-89	1	3	4.11	19	6	0	1	50	55	26	23	3	17	42	.284	.298	.277	7.51	3.04
2-team total (1 Norfolk)					1	3	4.03	20	6	0	1	51	55	26	23	3	18	42	—	—	—	7.36	3.16
Luebke, Cory	R-L	6-4	210	3-4-85	0	1	2.45	11	0	0	1	18	17	5	5	2	3	29	.233	.160	.271	14.24	1.47
Marte, Kelvin	L-L	5-9	170	11-24-87	4	3	3.67	34	4	0	2	74	65	31	30	4	21	57	.236	.241	.234	6.96	2.57
Masterson, Justin	R-R	6-6	260	3-22-85	2	2	4.97	25	5	0	0	54	62	30	30	3	26	32	.300	.301	.299	5.30	4.31
Medina, Jhondaniel	R-R	5-11	158	2-8-93	1	1	2.63	9	0	0	0	14	12	5	4	1	7	10	.235	.158	.281	6.59	4.61
Neverauskas, Dovydas	R-R	6-3	175	1-14-93	3	4	3.60	25	0	0	4	30	36	14	12	1	11	24	.308	.347	.279	7.20	3.30
Outman, Josh	L-L	6-1	205	9-14-84	0	1	4.95	10	1	0	0	20	24	11	11	3	3	15	.308	.100	.379	6.75	1.35
Partch, Curtis	R-R	6-5	240	2-13-87	2	2	2.24	42	0	0	4	60	41	17	15	1	30	60	.196	.100	.245	8.95	4.48
Phillips, Zach	L-L	6-0	200	9-21-86	0	0	0.00	2	0	0	1	1	0	0	0	0	3	1	.000	.000	.000	6.75	20.25
2-team total (49 Norfolk)					9	3	4.35	51	0	0	2	62	60	32	30	3	33	85	—	—	—	12.34	4.79
Rondon, Jorge	R-R	6-1	215	2-16-88	6	4	2.67	43	0	0	12	57	45	19	17	2	24	37	.216	.185	.236	5.81	3.77
Santana, Edgar	R-R	6-2	180	10-16-91	0	0	5.06	13	0	0	1	16	22	9	9	1	6	12	.328	.290	.361	6.75	3.38
Scahill, Rob	R-R	6-2	220	2-15-87	0	2	4.00	13	0	0	3	18	23	13	8	0	8	18	.295	.323	.277	9.00	4.00
Schugel, A.J.	R-R	6-0	200	6-27-89	1	2	4.00	13	0	0	0	18	13	8	8	0	3	18	.206	.227	.195	9.00	1.50
Smith, Josh	L-L	6-3	200	10-11-89	0	2	7.36	7	0	0	0	7	13	9	6	1	4	7	.394	.389	.400	8.59	4.91
Taillon, Jameson	R-R	6-5	220	11-18-91	4	2	2.04	10	10	0	0	62	44	14	14	2	6	61	.196	.148	.224	8.90	0.88
Vogelsong, Ryan	R-R	6-4	215	7-22-77	0	2	3.27	2	2	0	0	11	9	4	4	3	1	4	.220	.381	.050	3.27	0.82
Williams, Trevor	R-R	6-3	230	4-25-92	9	6	2.53	20	19	0	0	110	103	43	31	5	30	74	.249	.306	.204	6.04	2.45

Fielding

Catcher	PCT	G	PO	A	E	DP	PB
Cervelli	1.000	3	12	2	0	0	0
Diaz	.974	25	172	16	5	1	1
Easley	.996	36	252	10	1	0	5
Jhang	1.000	5	32	2	0	0	0
Morales	1.000	6	2	0	1	0	1
Stallings	.994	80	579	72	4	3	2

First Base	PCT	G	PO	A	E	DP
Bell	.985	96	892	52	14	90
Gamache	.992	17	127	5	1	10
Osuna	.987	27	213	16	3	20
Rogers	1.000	10	82	3	0	12

Second Base	PCT	G	PO	A	E	DP
Figueroa	1.000	3	5	10	0	2
Florimon	1.000	3	6	6	0	0
Frazier	.978	8	17	27	1	7

	PCT	G	PO	A	E	DP	
Gamache	1.000	1	1	1	0	0	
Hanson	.990	67	126	172	3	47	
Moroff	.997	61	129	183	1	42	
Ngoepe	1.000	3	4	11	0	4	
Tam Sing	1.000	3	2	3	0	1	

Third Base	PCT	G	PO	A	E	DP
Figueroa	.833	8	3	7	2	1
Florimon	.984	26	7	55	1	2
Gamache	.947	11	5	13	1	2
Hanson	.969	14	3	28	1	2
Kang	.897	13	5	21	3	4
Moroff	.937	43	33	71	7	7
Rogers	.983	49	35	82	2	7

Shortstop	PCT	G	PO	A	E	DP
Figueroa	1.000	2	2	3	0	0
Florimon	.974	29	39	72	3	22
Frazier	.900	2	4	5	1	1

	PCT	G	PO	A	E	DP
Moroff	.952	20	24	55	4	11
Ngoepe	.984	99	135	298	7	53

Outfield	PCT	G	PO	A	E	DP
Bell	.875	4	6	1	1	0
Figueroa	—	1	0	0	0	0
Florimon	1.000	39	63	3	0	0
Frazier	.979	58	90	3	2	0
Garcia	.970	128	213	17	7	4
Hanson	.976	27	41	0	1	0
Maffei	1.000	2	4	0	0	0
Meadows	.967	34	55	3	2	0
Ortiz	.989	125	259	7	3	0
Osuna	.984	30	57	3	1	0
Richardson	1.000	5	11	1	0	0
Rogers	1.000	1	1	0	0	0
Rojas Jr.	1.000	7	7	0	0	0
Schwind	—	1	0	0	0	0

ALTOONA CURVE DOUBLE-A

EASTERN LEAGUE

Batting	B-T	HT	WT	DOB	AVG	vLH	vRH	G	AB	R	H	2B	3B	HR	RBI	BB	HBP	SH	SF	SO	SB	CS	SLG	OBP
Allie, Stetson	R-R	6-2	230	3-13-91	.247	.185	.264	111	365	53	90	20	2	16	63	42	2	0	5	110	1	2	.444	.324
Barnes, Barrett	R-R	5-11	209	7-29-91	.306	.342	.298	124	405	60	124	28	7	9	47	41	6	4	2	105	10	4	.477	.377
Diaz, Chris	R-R	5-10	186	11-9-90	.226	.210	.232	79	226	30	51	13	0	1	16	32	4	3	3	43	5	2	.296	.328
Diaz, Elias	R-R	6-0	210	11-17-90	.286	—	.286	2	7	0	2	0	0	0	1	1	0	0	0	1	0	0	.286	.375
Escobar, Elvis	L-L	5-8	169	9-6-94	.241	.000	.265	29	112	21	27	2	2	2	7	10	0	5	0	26	2	2	.348	.303
Espinal, Edwin	R-R	6-2	250	1-27-94	.289	.287	.290	111	394	33	114	25	1	7	56	19	4	0	6	67	0	1	.411	.324
Feliz, Anderson	B-R	6-0	175	5-11-92	.256	.197	.270	106	347	39	89	22	4	4	32	35	0	4	0	88	7	1	.378	.325
Jhang, Jin-De	L-R	5-11	220	5-17-93	.298	.317	.293	54	188	20	56	13	0	1	21	11	2	0	3	12	1	0	.383	.338
Maffei, Justin	R-R	5-11	173	8-21-91	.175	.077	.200	25	63	9	11	1	0	0	5	6	1	1	0	13	1	0	.190	.257
McGuire, Reese	L-R	5-11	215	3-2-95	.259	.215	.274	77	266	29	69	16	2	1	37	29	3	4	2	26	4	4	.346	.337
2-team total (15 New Hampshire)					.254	—	—	92	319	34	81	18	2	1	42	36	4	4	2	34	6	6	.332	.335
Meadows, Austin	L-L	6-3	200	5-3-95	.311	.297	.315	45	167	33	52	16	8	6	23	16	1	1	5	32	9	3	.611	.365
Morales, Tomas	R-R	6-0	190	7-30-91	.235	.167	.244	21	51	6	12	0	2	2	6	2	1	0	0	7	0	0	.431	.278
Newman, Kevin	R-R	6-1	180	8-4-93	.288	.250	.294	61	233	41	67	11	2	2	28	26	3	2	4	24	6	3	.378	.361
Osuna, Jose	R-R	6-2	213	12-12-92	.269	.343	.240	70	253	34	68	18	3	6	38	23	2	0	5	44	1	1	.435	.329
Ramirez, Harold	R-R	5-10	220	9-6-94	.306	.292	.310	98	379	58	116	16	7	2	49	21	9	2	3	66	7	10	.401	.354
2-team total (1 New Hampshire)					.311	—	—	99	383	60	119	17	7	2	50	22	9	2	3	66	7	10	.407	.360
Schwind, Jonathan	R-R	6-0	185	5-30-90	.236	.354	.188	75	165	22	39	7	1	3	21	21	2	3	2	40	2	1	.345	.326
Stewart, Chris	R-R	6-4	205	2-19-82	.200	.500	.174	10	25	5	5	0	0	0	3	8	1	0	1	0	0	0	.200	.400
Weiss, Erich	L-R	6-2	190	11-8-91	.276	.284	.274	127	456	56	126	24	9	4	65	49	5	8	2	90	6	3	.408	.352
Wood, Eric	R-R	6-2	195	11-22-92	.249	.273	.243	118	402	63	100	26	5	16	50	52	5	1	4	88	5	4	.443	.339

Pitching	B-T	HT	WT	DOB	W	L	ERA	G	GS	CG	SV	IP	H	R	ER	HR	BB	SO	AVG	vLH	vRH	K/9	BB/9
Creasy, Jason	R-R	6-4	197	5-13-92	4	1	6.07	8	5	0	0	30	34	24	20	2	10	16	.291	.205	.342	4.85	3.03
Dickson, Cody	L-L	6-3	180	4-27-92	10	5	3.66	28	26	1	1	140	127	60	57	8	93	105	.252	.262	.249	6.75	5.98
Duncan, Frank	R-R	6-4	215	1-30-92	3	2	2.36	7	2	0	0	27	23	8	7	0	7	24	.228	.326	.155	8.10	2.36

BaseballAmerica.com

Pitching

Pitching	B-T	HT	WT	DOB	W	L	ERA	G	GS	CG	SV	IP	H	R	ER	HR	BB	SO	AVG	vLH	vRH	K/9	BB/9
DuRapau, Montana	R-R	5-11	175	3-27-92	3	3	3.65	50	0	0	22	49	43	21	20	6	19	51	.229	.239	.220	9.30	3.47
Eppler, Tyler	R-R	6-6	220	1-5-93	9	10	3.99	27	27	1	0	162	176	78	72	14	33	106	.280	.290	.269	5.88	1.83
Glasnow, Tyler	L-R	6-8	220	8-23-93	0	0	3.00	2	2	0	0	6	4	2	2	1	6	11	.190	.200	.182	16.50	9.00
Haley, Trey	R-R	6-4	215	6-21-90	0	1	4.35	9	0	0	0	10	10	5	5	1	11	11	.270	.267	.273	9.58	9.58
Hirsch, Henry	R-R	6-3	185	9-29-92	0	0	0.00	1	0	0	0	1	1	0	0	0	0	1	.250	.000	.333	9.00	0.00
Holmes, Clay	R-R	6-5	230	3-27-93	10	9	4.22	26	26	0	0	136	138	70	64	10	64	101	.272	.288	.258	6.67	4.22
Kingham, Nick	R-R	6-6	225	11-8-91	1	1	5.73	2	2	0	0	11	6	7	7	1	4	10	.162	.143	.174	8.18	3.27
Kuchno, John	R-R	6-5	210	5-21-91	2	1	3.00	10	2	0	0	24	17	9	8	4	8	18	.198	.184	.208	6.75	3.00
Lakind, Jared	L-L	6-2	205	3-9-92	5	1	2.59	47	0	0	7	66	50	19	19	3	28	62	.216	.196	.230	8.45	3.82
Lopez, Junior	R-R	6-2	165	6-27-91	0	0	0.00	1	0	0	0	2	2	0	0	1	0	2	.250	.000	.286	0.00	4.50
McKinney, Brett	R-R	6-2	225	11-19-90	2	1	3.90	44	0	0	2	67	67	32	29	3	27	65	.260	.327	.212	8.73	3.63
McRae, Alex	R-R	6-3	185	4-6-93	8	6	4.79	16	15	1	0	88	114	54	47	7	25	67	.317	.309	.323	6.83	2.55
Medina, Jhondaniel	R-R	5-11	158	2-8-93	2	2	3.70	37	0	0	6	56	42	26	23	5	31	60	.211	.230	.192	9.64	4.98
Neverauskas, Dovydas	R-R	6-3	175	1-14-93	1	0	2.57	22	0	0	1	28	12	10	8	0	11	32	.129	.122	.135	10.29	3.54
Rosario, Miguel	R-R	6-0	182	1-30-93	2	2	1.87	23	0	0	0	34	19	7	7	1	13	29	.167	.116	.197	7.75	3.48
Santana, Edgar	R-R	6-2	180	10-16-91	2	1	2.83	21	0	0	2	41	32	13	13	4	11	39	.216	.175	.247	8.49	2.40
Smith, Josh	L-L	6-3	200	10-11-89	2	2	6.44	42	0	0	2	57	61	44	41	8	30	61	.284	.130	.370	9.58	4.71
Vogelsong, Ryan	R-R	6-4	215	7-22-77	1	0	2.45	2	2	0	0	11	8	3	3	1	2	4	.211	.353	.095	3.27	1.64
Waddell, Brandon	L-L	6-3	180	6-3-94	7	9	4.12	22	20	0	0	118	122	60	54	9	61	94	.271	.247	.283	7.17	4.65
Whitehead, David	R-R	6-4	215	4-21-92	2	6	7.83	11	11	0	0	46	52	45	40	5	47	24	.299	.299	.299	4.70	9.20

Fielding

Catcher	PCT	G	PO	A	E	DP	PB
Diaz	1.000	2	15	1	0	0	0
Jhang	.995	48	330	34	2	4	7
McGuire	.986	73	494	69	8	4	3
Morales	1.000	15	86	4	0	0	3
Stewart	.974	10	65	9	2	2	

First Base	PCT	G	PO	A	E	DP
Espinal	.997	84	665	61	2	75
Feliz	.970	18	118	12	4	16
Osuna	.989	55	444	19	5	39

Second Base	PCT	G	PO	A	E	DP
Diaz	.966	17	36	49	3	15
Feliz	.986	18	22	48	1	7
Weiss	.979	118	211	358	12	84

Third Base	PCT	G	PO	A	E	DP
Diaz	1.000	5	2	8	0	1
Espinal	.971	14	8	25	1	3
Feliz	.952	12	5	15	1	2
Wood	.948	113	72	184	14	19

Shortstop	PCT	G	PO	A	E	DP
Diaz	.959	55	79	152	10	39

	PCT	G	PO	A	E	DP
Feliz	.955	41	50	97	7	20
Newman	.992	60	88	167	2	42

Outfield	PCT	G	PO	A	E	DP
Allie	.974	93	144	6	4	0
Barnes	.994	105	175	4	1	0
Escobar	.968	29	59	2	2	1
Feliz	1.000	14	21	1	0	0
Maffei	1.000	19	44	1	0	1
Meadows	.982	41	105	2	2	0
Osuna	1.000	12	14	1	0	0
Ramirez	.978	91	177	3	4	0
Schwind	.971	47	62	5	2	2

BRADENTON MARAUDERS
FLORIDA STATE LEAGUE

HIGH CLASS A

Batting	B-T	HT	WT	DOB	AVG	vLH	vRH	G	AB	R	H	2B	3B	HR	RBI	BB	HBP	SH	SF	SO	SB	CS	SLG	OBP
Diaz, Elias	R-R	6-0	210	11-17-90	.391	.200	.444	7	23	6	9	0	0	1	5	4	0	0	1	2	0	1	.522	.464
Escobar, Elvis	L-L	5-8	169	9-6-94	.272	.235	.282	92	323	47	88	18	4	4	32	19	1	8	2	62	7	6	.390	.313
Gushue, Taylor	B-R	6-1	215	12-19-93	.226	.246	.221	90	328	42	74	17	1	8	38	23	4	1	3	69	0	0	.357	.282
Hernandez, Raul	R-R	6-0	182	12-20-95	.000	—	.000	1	3	0	0	0	0	0	0	0	0	0	0	0	0	0	.000	.250
Hill, Logan	R-R	6-3	230	5-26-93	.226	.261	.205	17	62	6	14	2	0	2	7	5	4	0	1	20	1	1	.355	.319
Joe, Connor	R-R	6-0	205	8-16-92	.277	.368	.243	107	390	49	108	26	2	5	52	45	2	0	5	84	2	4	.392	.351
Kelley, Christian	R-R	5-11	185	9-23-93	.355	.231	.444	9	31	7	11	2	0	0	5	2	0	0	2	9	0	0	.419	.371
Kramer, Kevin	L-R	6-1	190	10-3-93	.277	.211	.295	118	444	56	123	29	2	4	57	48	6	10	5	63	3	9	.378	.352
Lunde, Erik	L-R	5-9	180	1-14-92	.222	.154	.261	15	36	5	8	2	0	0	2	7	0	1	0	7	0	0	.278	.349
Luplow, Jordan	R-R	6-1	195	9-26-93	.254	.228	.267	104	354	63	90	23	3	10	54	60	4	1	6	78	6	2	.421	.363
Maffei, Justin	R-R	5-11	173	8-27-91	.344	.300	.353	17	61	7	21	4	1	1	12	5	0	1	1	13	1	1	.492	.388
Mathisen, Wyatt	R-R	6-0	227	12-30-93	.296	.308	.289	36	115	13	34	10	0	1	18	11	0	2	1	21	0	1	.409	.354
Morales, Tomas	R-R	6-0	190	7-30-91	.257	.261	.255	22	74	7	19	3	0	0	10	6	1	1	2	9	1	0	.297	.313
Newman, Kevin	R-R	6-1	180	8-4-93	.366	.333	.381	41	164	24	60	10	1	3	24	17	3	2	3	12	4	1	.494	.428
Polo, Tito	R-R	5-9	185	8-23-94	.276	.260	.280	55	214	40	59	3	0	4	28	21	5	5	2	47	17	7	.346	.351
2-team total (2 Tampa)					.275	—	—	57	222	42	61	3	0	4	29	22	5	5	2	47	17	7	.342	.351
Ratledge, Logan	R-R	5-11	190	7-20-92	.571	.500	.600	2	7	2	4	2	0	0	3	0	0	0	0	1	0	0	.857	.571
Reyes, Pablo	R-R	5-10	150	9-5-93	.265	.250	.271	89	306	41	81	20	1	5	45	37	1	6	5	47	13	8	.386	.341
Roy, Jeff	L-L	5-8	178	1-24-92	.259	.160	.286	42	116	22	30	2	0	0	7	19	4	3	0	32	9	2	.276	.381
Simpson, Chase	B-R	6-1	210	2-17-92	.235	.250	.231	84	302	51	71	18	5	8	47	38	5	1	2	76	3	1	.407	.329
Suchy, Michael	R-R	6-3	228	4-15-93	.246	.156	.282	115	386	55	95	15	3	7	47	49	6	3	2	104	8	7	.355	.339
Suiter, Jerrick	R-R	6-4	230	3-4-93	.265	.277	.260	118	442	52	117	16	0	5	63	40	3	2	6	80	7	3	.335	.326
Tam Sing, Trace	R-R	6-0	175	12-7-91	.222	.200	.238	14	36	7	8	3	0	0	3	9	1	0	0	13	1	1	.306	.391
Tucker, Cole	B-R	6-3	185	7-3-96	.238	.167	.258	65	269	36	64	12	1	1	25	29	0	6	0	62	5	6	.301	.312

Pitching	B-T	HT	WT	DOB	W	L	ERA	G	GS	CG	SV	IP	H	R	ER	HR	BB	SO	AVG	vLH	vRH	K/9	BB/9
Anderson, Tanner	R-R	6-2	195	5-27-93	1	1	3.76	17	2	0	1	41	49	22	17	2	9	17	.302	.352	.264	3.76	1.99
Borden, Buddy	R-R	6-3	210	4-29-92	1	6	7.23	13	12	0	0	47	63	46	38	3	27	34	.320	.295	.339	6.46	5.13
Brewer, Colten	R-R	6-3	225	10-29-92	3	7	4.09	18	13	0	2	70	82	45	32	5	27	66	.285	.273	.292	8.45	3.45
Brubaker, J.T.	R-R	6-4	175	11-17-93	2	6	5.32	14	14	1	0	68	77	43	40	6	22	43	.289	.308	.272	5.72	2.93
Coley, Austin	R-R	6-2	203	7-14-92	12	10	4.65	26	25	2	0	139	141	79	72	15	44	90	.262	.229	.243	5.81	2.84
Garcia, Yeudy	R-R	6-2	203	10-6-92	6	8	2.76	26	25	1	1	127	122	53	39	7	54	127	.248	.258	.241	8.98	3.82
Heredia, Luis	R-R	6-5	251	8-10-94	4	6	3.64	45	0	0	12	54	55	30	22	1	31	42	.261	.313	.227	6.96	5.13
Hirsch, Henry	R-R	6-3	185	9-29-92	6	3	3.75	38	0	0	1	62	59	26	26	3	27	54	.257	.227	.275	7.80	3.90
Keller, Mitch	R-R	6-3	195	4-4-96	1	0	0.00	1	1	0	0	6	5	0	0	0	1	7	.227	.000	.294	10.50	1.50

Pitching

Pitching	B-T	HT	WT	DOB	W	L	ERA	G	GS	CG	SV	IP	H	R	ER	HR	BB	SO	AVG	vLH	vRH	K/9	BB/9
Keselica, Sean	L-L	6-2	210	6-14-93	0	0	0.00	1	0	0	0	1	0	0	0	0	0	1	.000	—	.000	9.00	0.00
Kingham, Nick	R-R	6-6	225	11-8-91	2	0	0.00	2	2	0	0	11	8	0	0	0	1	10	.211	.182	.222	8.18	0.82
Lopez, Junior	R-R	6-2	165	6-27-91	3	4	4.25	38	0	0	2	66	65	42	31	4	25	59	.251	.228	.266	8.09	3.43
Masterson, Justin	R-R	6-6	260	3-22-85	1	0	3.60	1	1	0	0	5	2	2	2	1	3	8	.118	.125	.111	14.40	5.40
McRae, Alex	R-R	6-3	185	4-6-93	3	4	2.69	12	12	0	0	67	62	23	20	4	17	35	.241	.233	.248	4.70	2.28
Neumann, Nick	R-R	6-3	205	4-26-91	1	0	2.98	29	0	0	6	42	46	15	14	3	9	33	.277	.323	.250	7.02	1.91
Regalado, Jose	R-R	6-3	180	11-22-91	3	2	2.60	23	4	0	1	52	39	16	15	4	16	41	.209	.259	.167	7.10	2.77
Rosario, Miguel	R-R	6-0	182	1-30-93	1	1	2.64	19	0	0	0	31	26	11	9	0	11	26	.232	.267	.209	7.63	3.23
Santana, Edgar	R-R	6-2	180	10-16-91	2	0	0.81	9	0	0	0	22	13	2	2	0	2	20	.169	.100	.213	8.06	0.81
Scioneaux, Tate	R-R	6-1	200	12-14-92	4	3	3.06	32	0	0	2	68	54	24	23	7	18	64	.214	.186	.233	8.51	2.39
Street, Sam	R-R	6-3	215	3-18-92	3	2	2.26	27	0	0	1	56	46	21	14	2	23	38	.225	.221	.228	6.14	3.72
Tarpley, Stephen	R-L	6-1	180	2-17-93	6	4	4.32	20	20	0	0	100	93	53	48	8	37	90	.249	.211	.263	8.10	3.33
2-team total (1 Tampa)					6	5	4.54	21	21	0	0	105	100	58	53	8	39	93	—	—	—	7.97	3.34
Topa, Justin	R-R	6-4	200	3-7-91	0	0	3.86	4	0	0	0	5	6	2	2	0	1	2	.316	.333	.300	3.86	1.93
Waddell, Brandon	L-L	6-3	180	6-3-94	4	0	0.93	5	5	0	0	29	13	3	3	1	2	26	.133	.042	.162	8.07	0.62
Williams, Trevor	R-R	6-3	230	4-25-92	1	0	0.00	1	1	0	0	5	4	0	0	0	0	4	.235	.222	.250	7.20	0.00

Fielding

Catcher	PCT	G	PO	A	E	DP	PB
Diaz	.943	6	30	3	2	1	0
Gushue	.994	90	628	61	4	4	14
Hernandez	1.000	1	4	2	0	0	0
Kelley	1.000	9	59	10	0	2	3
Lunde	.986	14	60	9	1	0	2
Morales	.978	22	147	30	4	1	2

First Base	PCT	G	PO	A	E	DP
Mathisen	1.000	1	11	0	0	2
Simpson	.994	38	324	26	2	32
Suiter	.990	98	834	55	9	78

Second Base	PCT	G	PO	A	E	DP
Kramer	.983	103	181	289	8	68
Reyes	.981	35	66	92	3	19
Tam Sing	1.000	3	5	4	0	1

Third Base	PCT	G	PO	A	E	DP
Joe	.892	96	55	152	25	13
Mathisen	.937	26	18	41	4	3
Reyes	1.000	1	0	2	0	0
Simpson	.951	17	11	28	2	2

Shortstop	PCT	G	PO	A	E	DP
Newman	.963	38	50	107	6	23
Reyes	.957	36	51	103	7	16
Tam Sing	.955	5	6	15	1	6

Tucker	.956	61	86	199	13	39

Outfield	PCT	G	PO	A	E	DP
Escobar	.982	90	212	11	4	5
Hill	.917	12	22	0	2	0
Lunde	.500	1	1	0	1	0
Luplow	.988	81	151	8	2	1
Maffei	.969	17	31	0	1	0
Polo	.981	54	102	3	2	1
Ratledge	1.000	2	3	0	0	0
Reyes	1.000	5	15	0	0	0
Roy	.988	40	84	1	1	0
Suchy	.974	114	220	5	6	2
Tam Sing	1.000	2	4	0	0	0

WEST VIRGINIA POWER
SOUTH ATLANTIC LEAGUE

LOW CLASS A

Batting	B-T	HT	WT	DOB	AVG	vLH	vRH	G	AB	R	H	2B	3B	HR	RBI	BB	HBP	SH	SF	SO	SB	CS	SLG	OBP
Alemais, Stephen	R-R	6-0	190	4-12-95	.189	.100	.222	11	37	2	7	1	1	0	2	2	1	1	1	11	1	3	.270	.244
Arribas, Danny	R-R	6-0	212	9-30-92	.256	.259	.255	127	426	54	109	20	4	11	49	58	13	8	3	103	9	3	.399	.360
Bormann, John	R-R	6-0	205	4-4-90	.243	.265	.234	52	177	22	43	9	1	2	20	11	1	4	3	20	0	0	.339	.286
Filliben, Tyler	R-R	6-2	188	8-8-92	.172	.203	.159	70	221	22	38	8	3	1	20	12	9	2	3	52	4	5	.249	.241
George, Zach	B-R	6-2	200	7-16-92	.324	.357	.312	34	105	15	34	13	0	0	10	24	2	0	1	22	4	2	.448	.455
Hayes, Ke'Bryan	R-R	6-1	210	1-28-97	.263	.234	.273	65	247	27	65	12	1	6	37	16	6	3	4	51	6	5	.393	.319
Hernandez, Raul	R-R	6-0	182	12-20-95	.150	.222	.129	11	40	1	6	3	0	0	5	0	0	0	0	5	0	0	.225	.150
Hill, Logan	R-R	6-3	230	5-26-93	.254	.329	.228	93	335	45	85	19	5	11	40	29	6	0	1	97	13	6	.439	.323
Hughston, Casey	L-R	6-2	200	6-9-94	.190	.196	.188	102	400	49	76	11	7	11	35	30	3	6	2	154	16	8	.335	.251
Kelley, Christian	R-R	5-11	185	9-23-94	.236	.185	.249	77	259	26	61	12	0	2	28	25	4	4	2	55	0	5	.305	.310
Moore, Ty	L-R	6-0	190	7-26-93	.195	.174	.204	22	77	8	15	5	0	0	6	6	1	2	2	11	0	1	.260	.256
Munoz, Carlos	L-L	5-11	225	6-29-94	.261	.164	.292	126	452	54	118	28	4	7	67	51	8	6	8	54	2	4	.387	.341
Nagle, Ryan	L-R	6-1	200	8-7-94	.247	.191	.264	111	396	35	98	20	1	2	42	36	2	3	5	69	8	3	.318	.310
Polo, Tito	R-R	5-9	185	8-23-94	.302	.317	.297	54	225	46	68	14	3	12	37	13	11	1	1	47	20	10	.551	.368
Ratledge, Logan	R-R	5-11	190	7-20-92	.239	.299	.219	85	301	40	72	14	0	4	23	18	11	11	2	48	24	11	.326	.304
Reyes, Alfredo	R-R	6-2	160	10-4-93	.199	.266	.176	97	312	34	62	7	2	3	25	8	2	1	12	97	28	2	.263	.262
Tolman, Mitchell	L-R	5-11	195	4-6-93	.265	.223	.276	119	434	65	115	20	1	8	48	71	6	5	8	68	10	13	.371	.370
Tucker, Cole	R-R	6-3	185	7-3-96	.262	.143	.278	15	61	9	16	4	2	1	2	4	0	2	0	9	1	1	.443	.308

Pitching	B-T	HT	WT	DOB	W	L	ERA	G	GS	CG	SV	IP	H	R	ER	HR	BB	SO	AVG	vLH	vRH	K/9	BB/9
Agrazal, Dario	R-R	6-3	216	12-28-94	8	12	4.20	27	27	0	0	150	173	80	70	18	18	88	.294	.280	.304	5.28	1.08
Amedee, Jess	R-R	6-2	205	9-5-93	1	2	3.76	23	0	0	0	41	38	22	17	1	16	53	.244	.241	.247	11.73	3.54
Anderson, Tanner	R-R	6-2	195	5-27-93	2	2	3.42	19	1	0	0	47	37	19	18	0	13	33	.218	.225	.211	6.27	2.47
Brubaker, J.T.	R-R	6-4	175	11-17-93	4	5	3.48	12	12	0	0	62	56	30	24	9	24	77	.241	.284	.208	11.18	3.48
Burnette, Jake	R-R	6-3	210	8-10-92	3	0	7.71	5	0	0	0	9	11	9	8	2	7	5	.282	.438	.174	4.82	6.75
Eusebio, Julio	R-R	6-1	202	6-2-92	1	1	1.62	40	0	0	11	50	28	12	9	2	27	47	.165	.194	.143	8.46	4.86
Frawley, Matt	R-R	6-1	195	8-8-95	0	0	0.00	1	0	0	0	3	1	0	0	0	1	2	.111	.167	.000	6.00	3.00
Hearn, Taylor	L-L	6-5	210	8-30-94	1	1	1.99	8	3	0	0	23	15	6	5	2	10	36	.183	.296	.127	14.29	3.97
2-team total (8 Hagerstown)					2	1	2.58	16	5	0	0	45	40	19	13	5	17	67	—	—	—	13.30	3.38
Helton, Bret	R-R	6-3	215	7-25-93	8	9	4.44	26	26	0	0	136	130	72	67	13	52	101	.253	.265	.245	6.70	3.45
Hightower, Scooter	R-R	6-6	215	10-15-93	2	0	0.00	2	0	0	0	7	2	0	0	0	0	8	.087	.111	.071	10.29	0.00
Hinsz, Gage	R-R	6-4	210	4-20-96	6	8	3.66	17	17	0	0	93	93	39	38	8	25	67	.266	.229	.304	6.46	2.41
Karch, Eric	R-R	6-2	205	10-15-91	0	1	5.74	8	0	0	0	16	14	10	10	1	5	14	.250	.257	.10.34	2.82	
Keller, Mitch	R-R	6-3	195	4-4-96	8	5	2.46	23	23	0	0	124	96	36	34	4	18	131	.211	.175	.242	9.48	1.30
Keselica, Sean	L-L	6-2	210	6-14-93	2	1	1.41	14	0	0	2	51	32	9	8	1	14	54	.180	.196	.172	9.53	2.47
McGarry, Seth	R-R	6-0	180	1-5-94	4	4	3.79	38	0	0	9	59	58	27	25	4	27	59	.260	.235	.28	8.95	4.10
Montero, Yunior	R-R	6-4	175	2-9-93	1	1	3.96	13	3	0	1	36	23	20	16	2	15	44	.174	.213	.141	10.90	3.72

Pitching	B-T	HT	WT	DOB	W	L	ERA	G	GS	CG	SV	IP	H	R	ER	HR	BB	SO	AVG	vLH	vRH	K/9	BB/9
Pimentel, Cesilio	L-L	6-2	185	1-5-93	2	3	2.65	29	0	0	6	51	38	16	15	2	15	48	.210	.219	.205	8.47	2.65
Roth, Billy	R-R	6-3	184	6-5-95	2	3	8.47	8	1	0	0	17	21	18	16	0	20	13	.328	.303	.355	6.88	10.59
Scioneaux, Tate	R-R	6-1	200	12-14-92	1	0	1.13	7	0	0	3	16	5	3	2	0	5	24	.094	.125	.081	13.50	2.81
Sendelbach, Logan	R-R	6-3	185	5-5-94	8	8	3.75	26	26	1	0	139	126	62	58	11	31	98	.244	.214	.266	6.33	2.00
Vivas, Julio	R-R	6-2	227	10-1-93	3	0	4.17	20	0	0	0	50	50	27	23	5	22	45	.258	.244	.269	8.15	3.99
Zamora, Daniel	L-L	6-3	190	4-15-93	3	2	3.46	21	0	0	1	39	32	15	15	2	15	45	.219	.234	.212	10.38	3.46

Fielding

Catcher	PCT	G	PO	A	E	DP	PB
Bormann	.993	52	405	52	3	2	4
Hernandez	.989	11	74	16	1	1	3
Kelley	.990	77	552	114	7	2	7

First Base	PCT	G	PO	A	E	DP
Arribas	.997	71	607	49	2	67
George	.971	4	31	2	1	3
Munoz	.991	68	610	37	6	42

Second Base	PCT	G	PO	A	E	DP
Filliben	.978	21	42	45	2	12

Catcher	PCT	G	PO	A	E	DP	PB
Ratledge	1.000	1	1	0	0	0	
Tolman	.984	119	215	335	9	81	

Third Base	PCT	G	PO	A	E	DP
Arribas	.905	12	7	12	2	1
Filliben	.893	21	11	39	6	2
Hayes	.954	64	50	116	8	9
Ratledge	.936	46	26	76	7	8

Shortstop	PCT	G	PO	A	E	DP
Alemais	.979	11	11	35	1	7
Filliben	.923	27	31	53	7	8
Reyes	.963	89	132	237	14	62

	PCT	G	PO	A	E	DP
Tucker	.957	15	20	47	3	11

Outfield	PCT	G	PO	A	E	DP
Arribas	—		1	0	0	0
Filliben	1.000	1	1	0	0	0
George	.966	16	28	0	1	0
Hill	.970	86	124	5	4	0
Hughston	.987	102	229	4	3	1
Moore	.976	21	41	0	1	0
Nagle	.974	101	146	4	4	0
Polo	.992	53	116	3	1	1
Ratledge	.975	37	73	4	2	3
Reyes	1.000	4	5	0	0	0

WEST VIRGINIA BLACK BEARS

SHORT-SEASON

NEW YORK-PENN LEAGUE

Batting	B-T	HT	WT	DOB	AVG	vLH	vRH	G	AB	R	H	2B	3B	HR	RBI	BB	HBP	SH	SF	SO	SB	CS	SLG	OBP
Alemais, Stephen	R-R	6-0	190	4-12-95	.263	.283	.252	39	156	23	41	5	0	1	18	5	3	3	1	18	9	3	.314	.297
Arbet, Trae	R-R	6-0	185	7-1-94	.000	—	.000	2	4	0	0	0	0	0	0	0	0	1	0	2	0	0	.000	.000
Baur, Albert	L-R	6-4	215	3-22-92	.279	.250	.293	69	240	34	67	16	2	4	40	30	2	4	5	45	3	1	.413	.357
Craig, Will	R-R	6-3	212	11-16-94	.280	.314	.264	63	218	28	61	12	0	2	23	41	11	0	4	37	2	0	.362	.412
Diorio, Matt	L-R	6-1	195	7-24-95	.215	.250	.202	37	121	14	26	5	0	2	14	19	2	2	1	35	0	1	.306	.329
Eagan, Clark	L-R	6-1	195	3-13-95	.277	.341	.239	30	112	13	31	7	2	0	16	3	3	3	1	10	3	1	.375	.311
Forgione, Erik	B-R	6-0	160	9-9-92	.231	.154	.260	49	143	20	33	3	6	0	9	14	1	8	1	38	12	3	.336	.302
George, Zach	B-R	6-2	200	7-16-92	.267	.278	.263	23	75	10	20	6	3	0	11	21	3	1	1	12	1	1	.427	.440
Harvey, Chris	R-R	6-5	220	3-10-93	.301	.386	.258	36	133	11	40	9	0	1	20	8	2	2	2	36	0	0	.391	.345
King, Nick	R-R	6-0	190	11-12-93	.196	.152	.220	28	92	12	18	4	1	0	11	9	0	1	1	26	0	2	.261	.265
Krause, Kevin	R-R	6-2	200	11-23-92	.273	.259	.279	52	176	34	48	6	1	3	20	35	3	2	1	26	10	4	.369	.400
Leffler, Tyler	R-R	6-1	185	7-11-94	.227	.318	.182	20	66	9	15	2	0	0	3	4	3	2	0	9	0	0	.258	.301
Mahala, Kevin	R-R	6-3	180	7-19-94	.265	.286	.256	51	181	19	48	4	1	2	18	17	2	3	2	46	6	1	.331	.332
Meadows, Austin	L-L	6-0	200	5-3-95	.200	.000	.273	5	15	0	3	2	0	0	0	2	0	0	0	1	0	0	.333	.294
Moore, Ty	L-R	6-0	190	7-26-93	.288	.269	.294	58	205	32	59	5	1	1	17	13	13	2	0	18	9	6	.337	.368
Owen, Hunter	R-R	6-0	195	9-22-93	.257	.190	.290	52	187	31	48	10	2	5	34	11	6	3	4	49	4	1	.412	.313
Pabst, Arden	R-R	6-1	202	3-14-95	.225	.259	.215	34	120	14	27	2	0	7	11	2	2	1	25	0	1	.275	.299
Santos, Sandy	R-R	6-3	185	4-20-94	.281	.242	.295	63	228	26	64	16	4	2	34	20	1	5	4	64	7	10	.412	.336

Pitching	B-T	HT	WT	DOB	W	L	ERA	G	GS	CG	SV	IP	H	R	ER	HR	BB	SO	AVG	vLH	vRH	K/9	BB/9
Anderson, Matt	R-R	6-2	200	7-29-94	2	2	4.65	14	7	0	0	31	24	17	16	0	14	42	.214	.236	.193	12.19	4.06
Beddes, Danny	R-R	6-6	240	7-16-94	6	3	2.27	14	12	0	0	71	48	20	18	3	24	55	.195	.160	.228	6.94	3.03
Bingel, Brandon	R-R	5-10	185	2-2-95	0	2	2.91	16	0	0	4	22	19	10	7	1	9	16	.238	.289	.190	6.65	3.74
Brault, Steven	L-L	6-0	200	4-29-92	0	0	0.00	1	1	0	0	4	1	0	0	0	0	5	.077	.000	.083	11.25	0.00
Creasy, Jason	R-R	6-4	197	5-13-92	0	0	0.00	2	0	0	0	3	2	0	0	0	1	3	.200	.250	.160	10.13	3.38
Escobar, Luis	R-R	6-1	155	5-30-96	6	5	2.93	15	12	0	0	68	50	25	22	4	28	61	.208	.188	.228	8.11	3.72
Frawley, Mark	R-R	6-1	195	8-8-95	3	1	4.18	17	0	0	1	28	25	14	13	2	9	33	.234	.174	.279	10.61	2.89
Grullon, Adrian	R-R	6-0	180	9-17-92	1	1	7.50	5	0	0	0	6	7	5	5	1	2	7	.280	.267	.300	10.50	3.00
Hightower, Scooter	R-R	6-6	215	10-15-93	2	5	2.82	16	0	0	0	38	46	16	12	0	7	37	.295	.290	.299	8.69	1.64
Kozikowski, Neil	R-R	6-4	180	5-26-95	2	1	4.19	16	0	0	1	39	42	19	18	2	12	33	.286	.348	.231	7.68	2.79
Marvel, James	R-R	6-3	185	9-17-93	5	6	4.43	13	13	0	0	65	57	36	32	1	20	41	.235	.256	.211	5.68	2.77
Meyer, Stephan	R-R	6-4	190	5-11-94	2	6	4.50	16	16	0	0	82	84	46	41	7	22	50	.265	.292	.243	5.49	2.41
Montero, Yunior	R-R	6-4	175	2-9-93	1	1	2.25	4	0	0	1	8	5	2	2	1	6	8	.185	.167	.200	9.00	6.75
Mota, Cristian	L-L	5-10	150	9-26-91	2	1	3.23	18	0	0	1	31	29	14	11	1	21	20	.248	.242	.25	5.87	6.16
Paula, Luis	B-R	6-3	205	6-22-93	0	0	5.09	15	0	0	2	18	20	11	10	0	7	12	.274	.268	.281	6.11	3.57
Piechota, Evan	R-R	6-1	225	10-19-93	2	0	1.93	4	0	0	0	9	11	2	2	0	3	5	.306	.438	.200	4.82	2.89
Prohoroff, Dylan	R-R	6-3	215	11-29-94	0	1	3.45	21	0	0	2	29	23	17	11	1	13	28	.219	.208	.228	8.79	4.03
Roth, Billy	R-R	6-3	184	6-5-95	1	1	7.47	19	0	0	0	31	33	27	26	3	21	30	.266	.291	.246	8.62	6.03
Taylor, Jacob	R-R	6-3	205	7-5-95	0	1	27.00	1	1	0	0	2	6	5	5	0	2	1	.600	.500	.625	5.40	10.80
Vieaux, Cam	L-L	6-4	200	12-5-93	2	2	3.33	14	14	0	0	68	63	30	25	2	21	52	.246	.227	.253	6.92	2.79
Vivas, Julio	R-R	6-2	227	10-1-93	0	0	0.00	3	0	0	0	7	4	1	0	0	2	13	.167	.182	.154	17.55	2.70
Wallace, Mike	R-R	6-5	180	5-21-94	0	0	0.00	1	0	0	0	2	0	0	0	0	1	1	.000	.000	.000	4.50	0.00

Fielding

C: Harvey 25, Krause 18, Pabst 34. **1B:** Baur 67, Forgione 1, George 2, Harvey 8. **2B:** Arbet 2, Forgione 12, King 12, Leffler 14, Mahala 39, Owen 1. **3B:** Craig 46, George 10, King 14, Mahala 2, Owen 6. **SS:** Alemais 39, Forgione 34, King 2, Leffler 2, Mahala 2. **OF:** Diorio 28, Eagan 29, Forgione 3, George 3, Krause 24, Meadows 5, Moore 50, Owen 39, Santos 62.

BRISTOL PIRATES   ROOKIE
APPALACHIAN LEAGUE

Batting	B-T	HT	WT	DOB	AVG	vLH	vRH	G	AB	R	H	2B	3B	HR	RBI	BB	HBP	SH	SF	SO	SB	CS	SLG	OBP
Bastardo, Alexis	R-R	5-11	190	2-26-94	.205	.205	.206	45	151	17	31	4	1	0	19	15	4	2	4	37	7	2	.245	.287
Brown, Garrett	L-R	6-0	185	3-16-94	.259	.250	.262	54	205	24	53	5	3	1	19	9	5	4	2	43	8	1	.327	.303
Cucjen, Daniel	R-R	6-0	180	5-4-93	.248	.140	.300	39	133	17	33	3	1	0	9	14	1	1	1	28	9	1	.286	.322
De La Cruz, Julio	R-R	6-1	190	10-5-95	.209	.231	.198	47	163	17	34	5	0	4	15	15	2	0	0	49	1	1	.313	.283
de la Cruz, Michael	L-L	6-1	165	7-10-96	.220	.370	.161	51	164	25	36	4	2	0	11	26	1	2	1	52	10	0	.268	.328
Fernandez, Victor	R-R	5-11	175	10-17-94	.314	.400	.266	49	169	29	53	13	2	2	19	15	5	5	2	31	12	7	.450	.382
Fuentes, Huascar	R-R	6-2	195	6-2-92	.253	.277	.244	47	166	25	42	9	1	2	19	12	9	0	2	44	4	0	.355	.333
Garcia, Deybi	R-R	5-11	185	2-11-92	.195	.375	.152	24	82	6	16	3	1	1	8	1	0	1	2	22	0	0	.293	.200
Gibbs, Brent	R-R	6-1	215	9-27-94	.236	.250	.229	19	55	12	13	4	0	0	6	7	6	3	2	9	2	1	.309	.371
Gonzalez, Yoel	R-R	6-1	180	8-1-96	.218	.156	.268	31	101	7	22	3	0	1	14	11	0	1	1	32	2	0	.277	.292
Herrera, Jhoan	L-R	6-1	185	6-14-95	.252	.153	.291	57	210	24	53	15	1	4	21	21	2	1	0	53	1	1	.390	.326
Kennelly, Sam	R-R	6-2	190	1-9-96	.138	.217	.095	19	65	4	9	1	0	0	4	1	4	0	0	12	0	0	.154	.200
Rosario, Henrry	L-L	5-9	180	4-5-93	.238	.185	.263	24	84	14	20	1	0	3	10	12	2	4	2	18	4	3	.357	.340
Siri, Raul	R-R	5-9	175	10-21-94	.223	.250	.209	59	202	33	45	10	1	3	21	26	1	5	1	51	11	2	.327	.313
Valerio, Adrian	B-R	5-11	150	3-13-97	.247	.310	.216	64	251	21	62	11	1	2	29	7	3	5	2	46	7	4	.323	.274

Pitching	B-T	HT	WT	DOB	W	L	ERA	G	GS	CG	SV	IP	H	R	ER	BB	SO	AVG	vLH	vRH	K/9	BB/9
Cederlind, Blake	R-R	6-3	190	1-14-96	0	1	4.67	6	6	0	0	17	18	12	9	2	7	14	.277	.158	.444	7.27	3.63
Coursel, Robbie	R-R	6-2	195	12-12-93	0	3	4.26	15	0	0	0	25	29	19	12	1	16	21	.296	.308	.288	7.46	5.68
Eckelman, Matt	R-R	6-4	240	10-6-93	5	3	2.76	13	11	0	0	62	51	24	19	6	9	55	.223	.241	.213	7.98	1.31
Economos, Nick	R-R	6-6	215	6-27-95	2	5	5.65	13	13	0	0	57	65	41	36	6	20	39	.283	.247	.302	6.12	3.14
Hartlieb, Geoff	R-R	6-6	210	12-9-93	4	1	4.44	16	0	0	1	26	26	22	13	3	9	28	.252	.286	.240	9.57	3.08
Hutchings, Nick	R-R	6-2	165	2-10-96	0	4	7.56	15	0	0	1	25	37	29	21	3	17	22	.327	.275	.356	7.92	6.12
Jess, Jordan	L-L	6-3	240	1-29-93	2	2	2.55	17	0	0	7	25	29	9	7	1	7	27	.274	.269	.275	9.85	2.55
Kemp, Shane	R-R	6-3	180	7-12-94	2	1	3.82	18	0	0	1	35	37	18	15	6	7	28	.261	.245	.270	7.13	1.78
Mazzoccoli, Pasquale	B-R	6-5	200	3-28-92	0	0	4.39	16	0	0	0	27	36	17	13	1	6	21	.319	.349	.300	7.09	2.03
Oller, Adam	R-R	6-4	225	10-17-94	2	2	4.45	13	9	0	2	55	63	28	27	7	9	46	.285	.268	.298	7.57	1.48
Oronel, Nestor	L-L	6-1	175	12-13-96	0	6	5.53	15	8	0	0	42	52	41	26	9	14	36	.291	.310	.285	7.65	2.98
Paula, Luis	R-R	6-3	205	6-22-93	0	0	3.18	4	0	0	0	6	1	2	2	0	0	6	.053	.000	.091	9.53	0.00
Piechota, Evan	R-R	6-1	225	10-19-93	0	1	4.66	6	0	0	1	10	11	5	5	3	1	9	.282	.182	.321	8.38	0.93
Pomeroy, John	L-R	6-5	210	10-9-94	0	2	7.90	14	0	0	1	14	9	14	12	1	19	18	.191	.200	.188	11.85	12.51
Schlabach, Ike	R-L	6-5	185	12-27-96	1	6	5.22	13	13	0	0	60	67	41	35	6	22	31	.289	.186	.312	4.62	3.28
Wallace, Mike	R-R	6-5	180	5-21-94	4	4	3.10	14	6	1	0	52	37	21	18	3	13	42	.198	.200	.196	7.22	2.24
Whitehead, David	R-R	6-4	215	4-21-92	3	2	7.13	18	2	0	0	35	45	31	28	3	21	35	.313	.296	.322	8.92	5.35

Fielding

C: Bastardo 1, Garcia 24, Gibbs 15, Gonzalez 31. **1B:** De La Cruz 2, Fuentes 11, Herrera 45, Kennelly 10. **2B:** Cucjen 25, Siri 39, Valerio 5. **3B:** Cucjen 6, De La Cruz 42, Kennelly 6, Siri 16. **SS:** Cucjen 7, Siri 2, Valerio 59. **OF:** Bastardo 32, Brown 47, Cucjen 1, De La Cruz 50, Fernandez 43, Fuentes 12, Rosario 22, Siri 1.

GCL PIRATES   ROOKIE
GULF COAST LEAGUE

Batting	B-T	HT	WT	DOB	AVG	vLH	vRH	G	AB	R	H	2B	3B	HR	RBI	BB	HBP	SH	SF	SO	SB	CS	SLG	OBP
Anderson, Carl	L-L	6-0	185	9-1-92	.083	.111	.067	9	24	1	2	0	0	0	1	3	0	0	0	5	2	1	.083	.185
Benitez, Luis	B-R	5-10	165	8-12-93	.250	.182	.268	36	104	14	26	3	4	0	11	11	7	1	0	23	27	4	.356	.361
Brands, Paul	R-R	6-1	185	5-13-97	.252	.296	.238	31	107	11	27	3	1	0	9	11	4	1	1	37	3	1	.299	.341
Brito, Gabriel	R-R	5-9	170	11-3-97	.167	.348	.167	4	12	0	2	1	0	0	1	2	0	0	0	2	0	0	.250	.286
Contreras, Yondry	R-R	5-11	180	9-11-97	.177	.111	.193	47	181	16	32	7	0	1	8	12	5	5	1	63	5	3	.232	.246
De Jesus, Johan	R-R	6-0	165	8-1-96	.185	.176	.187	48	173	18	32	9	2	1	10	9	3	6	2	57	6	1	.277	.235
Granberry, Mikell	R-R	6-1	190	8-19-95	.261	.320	.245	32	119	14	31	9	1	2	19	5	2	0	2	38	3	3	.403	.297
Hayes, Ke'Bryan	R-R	6-1	210	1-28-97	.400	.000	.667	2	5	0	2	1	0	0	0	1	0	0	0	1	0	0	.600	.500
Hernandez, Raul	R-R	6-0	182	12-20-95	.222	.130	.254	25	90	13	20	2	0	3	16	10	2	3	0	11	4	4	.344	.314
Jimenez, Melvin	B-R	5-10	170	9-9-95	.236	.294	.222	24	89	12	21	2	0	0	10	10	1	1	2	13	3	3	.258	.307
Jorge, Nelson	B-R	5-11	175	12-14-95	.274	.136	.310	33	106	16	29	5	4	2	13	10	5	1	1	36	9	2	.453	.361
Kennelly, Sam	R-R	6-2	190	1-9-96	.207	.250	.190	16	58	9	12	0	0	2	4	8	0	0	0	13	2	1	.310	.303
Lantigua, Edison	L-L	6-0	175	1-9-97	.261	.189	.281	45	165	15	43	5	7	0	19	21	1	0	0	40	5	2	.376	.348
Lunde, Erik	L-R	5-9	180	1-14-92	.000	—	.000	2	5	0	0	0	0	0	0	2	0	0	0	2	0	0	.000	.286
Ngoepe, Victor	R-R	5-8	150	2-9-98	.219	.194	.226	44	151	18	33	4	2	0	10	14	4	1	0	39	9	5	.272	.302
Portorreal, Jeremias	R-R	6-3	195	8-7-97	.172	.000	.192	8	29	3	5	1	2	0	4	3	0	0	0	7	0	0	.345	.250
Rosario, Henrry	L-L	5-9	180	4-5-93	.368	.417	.355	29	117	25	43	8	6	5	20	14	1	1	1	18	7	3	.667	.436
Synek, Brett	L-R	5-9	185	6-9-93	.259	.211	.274	23	81	14	21	4	2	0	9	13	4	1	1	10	3	0	.358	.384
Vinicio, Felix	L-L	5-10	175	10-28-94	.261	.281	.255	36	138	13	36	4	0	0	12	10	1	1	2	6	2	2	.290	.311
Walker, Andrew	R-R	6-1	169	2-13-94	.190	.115	.216	34	100	16	19	4	1	0	8	16	2	1	3	17	8	1	.250	.306

Pitching	B-T	HT	WT	DOB	W	L	ERA	G	GS	CG	SV	IP	H	R	ER	HR	BB	SO	AVG	vLH	vRH	K/9	BB/9
Agustin, Ronny	L-L	6-2	185	9-18-94	2	1	3.77	13	1	0	1	29	25	14	12	2	9	39	.229	.286	.21	12.24	2.83
Cespedes, Ivan	R-R	6-0	165	10-3-94	1	0	2.57	7	0	0	0	14	13	4	4	1	4	9	.255	.357	.216	5.79	2.57
Deyzel, Vince	R-R	6-2	180	2-9-98	0	3	5.29	11	0	0	1	17	18	14	10	2	16	13	.277	.320	.25	6.88	8.47
Garcia, Hector	L-L	6-0	170	10-4-95	1	0	0.00	4	0	0	0	6	4	0	0	0	1	8	.182	.333	.158	12.00	1.50
Hernandez, Miguel	R-R	6-5	175	11-3-95	2	2	4.67	10	9	0	0	35	25	21	18	0	23	27	.207	.279	.167	7.01	5.97
Hiciano, Delvin	R-R	6-2	175	12-24-91	0	0	0.00	2	0	0	0	2	0	0	0	0	1	.250	.333	.200	4.50	0.00

Pitching	B-T	HT	WT	DOB	W	L	ERA	G	GS	CG	SV	IP	H	R	ER	HR	BB	SO	AVG	vLH	vRH	K/9	BB/9
Kingham, Nick	R-R	6-6	225	11-8-91	0	4	3.00	6	6	0	0	24	23	13	8	0	1	16	.256	.238	.271	6.00	0.38
Kranick, Max	R-R	6-3	175	7-21-97	1	2	2.43	9	6	0	0	33	31	13	9	1	4	21	.246	.395	.169	5.67	1.08
Luciano, Mister	R-R	6-0	170	3-6-96	2	0	8.66	13	0	0	0	18	23	21	17	2	5	18	.324	.370	.295	9.17	2.55
MacGregor, Travis	R-R	6-3	180	10-15-97	1	1	3.13	9	9	0	0	32	29	12	11	1	10	19	.248	.250	.247	5.40	2.84
Martinez, Alex	R-R	6-3	175	5-8-95	0	1	1.90	12	0	0	1	24	23	7	5	0	9	13	.264	.269	.262	4.94	3.42
McDonald, Chris	R-R	6-6	220	7-31-94	1	3	3.55	8	0	0	0	25	28	14	10	0	7	15	.277	.206	.313	5.33	2.49
Nunez, Oddy	L-L	6-5	180	12-20-96	3	3	2.34	11	0	0	1	35	26	11	9	1	12	27	.205	.147	.226	7.01	3.12
Ogle, Braeden	L-L	6-2	170	7-30-97	0	2	2.60	8	8	0	0	28	18	11	8	2	11	20	.188	.136	.203	6.51	3.58
Piechota, Evan	R-R	6-1	225	10-19-93	1	0	0.00	4	0	0	0	7	5	0	0	0	0	5	.208	.000	.278	6.75	0.00
Regalado, Jose	R-R	6-3	180	11-22-91	0	0	27.00	2	0	0	0	1	4	4	4	0	1		.500	.667	.400	6.75	0.00
Robles, Domingo	L-L	6-2	170	4-29-98	1	2	4.25	9	1	0	0	36	40	19	17	3	4	18	.280	.375	.243	4.50	1.00
Rodriguez, Francis	R-R	6-2	172	11-28-92	0	3	1.37	16	0	0	4	20	11	9	3	1	9	14	.167	.208	.143	6.41	4.12
Romano, Argenis	R-R	6-1	190	6-16-95	0	1	5.14	4	3	0	0	14	18	9	8	1	2	14	.310	.235	.341	9.00	1.29
Scotti, Claudio	R-R	6-4	210	7-8-98	0	1	3.18	5	0	0	0	6	6	4	2	0	4	4	.250	.222	.267	6.35	6.35
Shields, Austin	L-R	6-5	220	11-23-97	0	0	8.53	4	1	0	0	6	3	6	6	1	10	3	.150	.125	.167	4.26	14.21
Singh, Rinku	L-L	6-2	190	8-8-88	0	0	0.00	1	1	0	0	1	1	0	0	0	0	0	.250	.333	.000	0.00	0.00
Sousa, Brian	R-R	6-3	180	8-7-97	1	4	4.11	11	4	0	1	35	31	26	16	3	20	27	.237	.273	.224	6.94	5.14
Taylor, Jacob	R-R	6-3	205	7-5-95	0	2	5.79	4	4	0	0	9	6	8	6	3	6	9	.182	.154	.200	8.68	5.79
Topa, Justin	R-R	6-4	200	3-7-91	2	0	1.13	6	0	0	0	8	3	1	1	0	2	6	.111	.167	.095	6.75	2.25
Vera, Eduardo	R-R	6-2	185	7-3-94	0	1	4.15	7	0	0	1	9	6	4	4	0	2	4	.188	.143	.200	4.15	2.08
Villamar, Julian	R-R	6-5	190	4-23-94	1	0	5.51	12	0	0	0	16	13	10	10	1	19	14	.220	.222	.219	7.71	10.47

Fielding

C: Brands 18, Brito 3, Granberry 5, Hernandez 20, Lunde 2, Synek 10. **1B:** De Jesus 15, Granberry 26, Kennelly 15, Walker 1. **2B:** Benitez 2, De Jesus 2, Jimenez 14, Jorge 32, Ngoepe 2, Walker 8. **3B:** Brands 11, De Jesus 31, Hayes 2, Jimenez 5, Walker 10. **SS:** Jimenez 4, Ngoepe 42, Walker 11. **OF:** Anderson 9, Benitez 33, Contreras 43, Lantigua 36, Portorreal 7, Rosario 21, Vinicio 26, Walker 5.

DSL PIRATES   ROOKIE
DOMINICAN SUMMER LEAGUE

Batting	B-T	HT	WT	DOB	AVG	vLH	vRH	G	AB	R	H	2B	3B	HR	RBI	BB	HBP	SH	SF	SO	SB	CS	SLG	OBP
Alcime, Larry	R-R	6-2	200	10-15-98	.138	.214	.104	43	138	10	19	3	2	0	17	8	2	1	2	40	4	1	.188	.193
Apostel, Sherten	R-R	6-4	198	3-11-99	.205	.192	.210	48	171	24	35	7	1	1	9	24	3	1	1	61	1	1	.275	.308
Babilonia, Yair	R-R	6-1	195	8-25-97	.233	.286	.212	32	73	7	17	1	1	0	10	9	8	1	0	15	0	0	.274	.378
Brito, Gabriel	R-R	5-9	170	11-3-97	.256	.348	.218	26	78	8	20	6	0	0	11	13	3	1	0	21	2	0	.333	.383
Calderon, Williams	B-R	6-0	170	12-22-97	.173	.182	.170	45	127	15	22	5	6	0	16	18	2	1	4	37	1	2	.307	.278
Castro, Rodolfo	B-R	6-0	170	5-21-99	.271	.170	.309	56	192	27	52	15	3	2	29	27	3	2	6	48	2	1	.411	.360
De Jesus, Johan	B-R	6-0	165	8-1-96	.219	.000	.259	10	32	3	7	0	0	0	2	3	1	0	1	12	2	1	.219	.297
Garcia, Carlos	L-L	6-0	170	4-7-99	.206	.143	.232	34	97	11	20	3	3	0	14	11	0	1	3	45	1	1	.299	.279
Guzman, Rudy	B-R	6-0	175	7-28-91	.264	.222	.277	47	121	26	32	2	6	2	17	28	4	1	1	23	16	5	.430	.416
Inoa, Samuel	R-R	5-11	180	10-6-98	.220	.148	.240	37	127	15	28	3	2	1	14	10	4	0	2	25	1	3	.299	.294
Mepris, Francisco	B-R	5-11	165	10-10-97	.266	.286	.261	49	154	27	41	6	3	0	8	20	2	3	0	31	11	6	.344	.358
Perez, Christopher	R-R	6-0	170	8-7-97	.272	.283	.267	51	162	26	44	8	3	0	13	17	6	3	0	24	2	3	.358	.362
Perez, Ramy	R-R	6-0	170	9-29-94	.244	.250	.242	58	168	16	41	7	2	0	22	13	4	2	0	31	4	5	.310	.314
Portorreal, Jeremias	L-L	6-3	195	8-7-97	.272	.294	.265	44	151	24	41	9	4	0	21	28	4	1	1	28	3	3	.384	.397
Sanchez, Lolo	R-R	6-0	150	4-23-99	.235	.255	.224	45	153	19	36	4	1	0	10	24	6	6	1	18	4	8	.275	.359
Simmons, Kyle	R-R	6-0	170	12-16-96	.160	.207	.138	42	94	14	15	1	0	0	5	30	8	1	0	42	6	2	.170	.402
Vizcaino, Eddy	L-L	5-11	165	7-19-96	.277	.333	.263	43	119	17	33	6	5	0	17	22	0	3	2	11	4	3	.412	.385

Pitching	B-T	HT	WT	DOB	W	L	ERA	G	GS	CG	SV	IP	H	R	ER	HR	BB	SO	AVG	vLH	vRH	K/9	BB/9
Bustamante, Carlos	R-R	6-0	170	9-15-95	0	1	1.69	16	0	0	0	21	13	4	4	0	7	14	.181	.273	.140	5.91	2.95
Cesar, Joel	R-R	5-11	191	1-26-96	0	0	2.70	2	2	0	0	7	4	3	2	1	7	5	.174	.000	.222	6.75	9.45
Contreras, Wilmer	R-R	6-3	185	2-5-98	6	1	4.00	15	1	0	0	36	27	19	16	0	10	35	.197	.294	.165	8.75	2.50
Cubilete, Sergio	R-R	6-4	185	3-19-95	1	3	3.52	15	15	0	0	61	46	37	24	0	31	42	.207	.241	.196	6.16	4.55
Delgado, Jose	R-R	6-3	195	12-19-94	1	3	5.83	23	0	0	5	29	28	25	19	2	28	26	.257	.222	.268	7.98	8.59
Garcia, Oliver	R-R	6-3	167	1-8-98	4	3	2.61	17	0	0	0	41	38	20	12	1	17	24	.248	.242	.250	5.23	3.70
Garcia, Ramon	R-R	6-0	195	3-12-92	0	4	3.60	21	0	0	9	25	27	15	10	0	12	11	.287	.269	.294	3.96	4.32
Jimenez, Randy	L-L	6-3	190	6-21-98	2	4	6.33	16	0	0	0	21	21	19	15	0	19	22	.259	.500	.225	9.28	8.02
Leon, Edgardo	R-R	6-3	190	7-4-96	1	0	13.50	4	0	0	0	7	9	11	10	1	8	2	.310	.125	.381	2.70	10.80
Machado, Kleiner	R-R	5-11	180	3-8-99	2	2	4.24	16	0	0	0	34	28	20	16	1	24	14	.220	.188	.232	3.71	6.35
Manzanillo, Yeudry	R-R	6-1	175	12-7-98	2	5	5.46	14	14	0	0	59	65	44	36	4	24	23	.278	.302	.269	3.49	3.64
Martinez, Angel	L-L	6-3	198	11-14-96	1	1	2.31	6	0	0	0	12	12	7	3	0	9	8	.279	.250	.282	6.17	6.94
Pena, Reymundo	L-L	5-11	165	4-1-96	0	0	4.50	1	0	0	0	2	1	1	1	0	2	1	.167	.000	.200	9.00	0.00
Pichardo, Adonis	R-R	6-3	195	4-9-96	1	3	3.88	13	10	0	0	51	57	30	22	0	14	32	.279	.192	.309	5.65	2.47
Pina, Leandro	R-R	6-3	174	9-23-98	2	2	1.46	13	13	0	0	62	50	19	10	0	9	34	.216	.143	.239	4.96	1.31
Rodriguez, Raymond	L-L	6-1	175	3-13-97	0	1	22.85	11	0	0	0	9	18	24	21	1	9	4	.419	.500	.410	4.15	19.73
Santana, Roger	L-L	6-1	168	9-26-97	1	6	1.98	15	14	0	0	68	69	32	15	1	12	55	.254	.273	.252	7.24	1.58
Sepulveda, Eumir	R-R	6-2	170	2-14-96	2	2	4.91	18	0	0	2	33	43	22	18	1	11	16	.314	.310	.315	4.36	3.00

Fielding

C: Babilonia 27, Brito 25, Inoa 23, Perez 14. **1B:** Babilonia 1, Calderon 35, De Jesus 5, Perez 2, Perez 39. **2B:** Mepris 31, Perez 11, Simmons 40. **3B:** Apostel 21, Castro 1, De Jesus 4, Mepris 12, Perez 30, Perez 10. **SS:** Castro 52, De Jesus 1, Mepris 11, Perez 10, Simmons 1. **OF:** Alcime 41, Calderon 6, Garcia 24, Guzman 43, Portorreal 37, Sanchez 42, Vizcaino 41.

St. Louis Cardinals

SEASON IN A SENTENCE: St. Louis won 14 fewer games than it had in 2015, but unlike the last time it dropped off that severely—in 2006, when its 83-win team won the World Series—these Cardinals couldn't even make the playoffs, falling short of a wild-card berth.

HIGH POINT: The Cardinals never won more than five games in a row, but when they had longer streaks like that, they came on the road, where the team went 48-33. Such a peak came June 20-22, when the Cardinals had just lost five in a row at home, scoring just 10 runs, but then went to Wrigley Field and swept the first-place Cubs. Rookie shortstop Aledmys Diaz had three hits, including a homer, in the 7-2 victory that sealed the sweep.

LOW POINT: Losing five of six games in a tight wild-card race is never good, but having two of those losses come in desultory fashion at San Francisco when the Cards were chasing the Giants proved too much to overcome. Former Reds nemesis Johnny Cueto shackled them in a complete-game 6-2 victory on Sept. 15, and the next day the Giants put up six runs in the third off rookie Luke Weaver en route to an 8-2 victory. Another low point arrived in July when former scouting director Chris Correa was sentenced to 46 months in prison in the hacking scandal involving the Astros.

NOTABLE ROOKIES: Diaz, signed out of Cuba in 2014, stunned offensively with a .300/.369/.510 season including 17 homers. His defense at shortstop impressed less. Korean import Seung Hwan Oh lived up to his nickname, as the Final Boss emerged as St. Louis' closer in the second half and converted 19 of his 22 save tries. Older rookies Greg Garcia (.393 OBP) and Jeremy Hazelbaker (12 HRs) contributed in reserve roles.

KEY TRANSACTIONS: The Cardinals relied on their offseason moves, such as signing Oh and Jedd Gyorko, as well as their farm system.

DOWN ON THE FARM: While Cards affiliates finished 10th in winning percentage at .520, five of them made their league playoffs. St. Louis swept its lower levels, with the Rookie-level Gulf Coast League and Appalachian League (Johnson City) titles as well as short-season State College claiming the New York-Penn League. Weaver had a breakthrough season in the minors before breaking into the big league rotation, while top prospect Alex Reyes also made his big league debut, flashing 100 mph heat in a bullpen role.

OPENING DAY PAYROLL: $ 143,053,500 (9th)

PLAYERS OF THE YEAR

MAJOR LEAGUE

Carlos Martinez
rhp
16-9, 3.04
174 SO in 195.1 IP
4th In NL in HR/9

MINOR LEAGUE

Luke Weaver
rhp
(Double-A/Triple-A)
7-3, 1.30
92 SO, 12 BB in 83 IP

ORGANIZATION LEADERS

BATTING		*Minimum 250 AB
MAJORS		
* AVG	Yadier Molina	.307
* OPS	Matt Carpenter	.885
HR	Jedd Gyorko	30
RBI	Stephen Piscotty	85
MINORS		
* AVG	Eliezer Alvarez, Peoria	.323
* OBP	Eliezer Alvarez, Peoria	.404
* SLG	David Washington, Springfield, Memphis	.532
* OPS	David Washington, Springfield, Memphis	.891
R	Magneuris Sierra, Peoria	78
H	Magneuris Sierra, Peoria	161
TB	Luke Voit, Springfield	230
2B	Eliezer Alvarez, Peoria	36
3B	Charlie Tilson, Memphis	8
HR	David Washington, Springfield, Memphis	30
RBI	David Washington, Springfield, Memphis	77
BB	Casey Grayson, Palm Beach	94
SO	David Washington, Springfield, Memphis	169
SB	Eliezer Alvarez, Peoria	36

PITCHING		#Minimum 75 IP
MAJORS		
W	Carlos Martinez	16
# ERA	Carlos Martinez	3.04
SO	Carlos Martinez	174
SV	SeungHwan Oh	19
MINORS		
W	Ryan Helsley, Peoria	10
L	Matt Pearce, Palm Beach, Springfield, Memphis	12
# ERA	Austin Gomber, Palm Beach, Springfield	2.69
G	Corey Littrell, Springfield, Memphis	53
GS	Deck McGuire, Springfield, Memphis	27
	Daniel Poncedeleon, Springfield	27
	J.C. Sulbaran, Memphis, Springfield	27
SV	Sam Tuivailala, Memphis	17
IP	Matt Pearce, Palm Beach, Springfield, Memphis	164
BB	Sandy Alcantara, Peoria, Palm Beach	59
SO	Sandy Alcantara, Peoria, Palm Beach	153
# AVG	Austin Gomber, Palm Beach, Springfield	.220

General Manager: John Mozeliak. **Farm Director:** Gary LaRocque. **Scouting Director:** Randy Flores.

Class	Team	League	W	L	PCT	Finish	Manager
Majors	St. Louis Cardinals	National	86	76	.531	6th (15)	Mike Matheny
Triple-A	Memphis Redbirds	Pacifc Coast	65	77	.458	14th (16)	Mike Shildt
Double-A	Springfield Cardinals	Texas	75	65	.536	3rd (8)	Dann Billardello
High A	Palm Beach Cardinals	Florida State	58	79	.423	11th (12)	Oliver Marmol
Low A	Peoria Chiefs	Midwest	73	66	.525	5th (16)	Joe Kruzel
Short season	State College Spikes	New York-Penn	50	26	.658	1st (14)	Johnny Rodriguez
Rookie	Johnson City Cardinals	Appalachian	39	29	.574	2nd (10)	Chris Swauger
Overall 2016 Minor League Record			393	363	.520	10th (30)	

ORGANIZATION STATISTICS

ST. LOUIS CARDINALS
NATIONAL LEAGUE

Batting	B-T	HT	WT	DOB	AVG	vLH	vRH	G	AB	R	H	2B	3B	HR	RBI	BB	HBP	SH	SF	SO	SB	CS	SLG	OBP
Adams, Matt	L-R	6-3	260	8-31-88	.249	.283	.243	118	297	37	74	18	0	16	54	25	2	0	3	81	0	1	.471	.309
Carpenter, Matt	L-R	6-3	205	11-26-85	.271	.270	.271	129	473	81	128	36	6	21	68	81	5	3	4	108	0	4	.505	.380
Diaz, Aledmys	R-R	6-1	195	8-1-90	.300	.256	.317	111	404	71	121	28	3	17	65	41	7	2	6	60	4	4	.510	.369
Fryer, Eric	R-R	6-2	215	8-26-85	.368	.300	.393	24	38	7	14	2	0	0	5	3	0	0	0	7	0	1	.421	.415
2-team total (36 Pittsburgh)					.267	—	—	60	116	19	31	4	1	0	13	13	0	2	2	25	0	3	.319	.336
Garcia, Greg	L-R	6-0	190	8-8-89	.276	.233	.287	99	214	33	59	11	0	3	18	38	4	0	1	50	1	1	.369	.393
Grichuk, Randal	R-R	6-1	205	8-13-91	.240	.240	.240	132	446	66	107	29	3	24	68	28	3	0	1	141	5	4	.480	.289
Gyorko, Jedd	R-R	5-10	215	9-23-88	.243	.245	.241	128	400	58	97	9	1	30	59	37	0	0	1	96	0	0	.495	.306
Hazelbaker, Jeremy	L-R	6-3	190	8-14-87	.235	.195	.245	114	200	35	47	7	3	12	28	18	0	4	2	64	5	2	.480	.295
Holliday, Matt	R-R	6-4	240	1-15-80	.246	.233	.252	110	382	48	94	20	1	20	62	35	8	0	1	71	0	0	.461	.322
Kelly, Carson	R-R	6-2	220	7-14-94	.154	.667	.000	10	13	1	2	1	0	0	1	0	1	0	0	2	0	0	.231	.214
Martinez, Jose	R-R	6-6	215	7-25-88	.438	.500	.250	12	16	4	7	1	0	0	1	2	0	0	0	1	0	0	.500	.500
McKenry, Michael	R-R	5-10	205	3-4-85	.000	—	.000	3	1	0	0	0	0	0	0	1	0	1	0	0	0	0	.000	.000
Molina, Yadier	R-R	5-11	205	7-13-82	.307	.304	.308	147	534	56	164	38	1	8	58	39	6	0	2	63	3	2	.427	.360
Moss, Brandon	L-R	6-1	210	9-16-83	.225	.232	.223	128	413	66	93	19	2	28	67	39	7	0	5	141	1	0	.484	.300
Pena, Brayan	B-R	5-9	240	1-7-82	.154	.500	.091	9	13	0	2	1	0	0	1	0	0	0	2	0	0	.231	.214
Peralta, Jhonny	R-R	6-2	225	5-28-82	.260	.182	.288	82	289	37	75	17	1	8	29	20	1	0	3	56	0	0	.408	.307
Pham, Tommy	R-R	6-1	210	3-8-88	.226	.206	.240	78	159	26	36	7	0	9	17	20	3	1	0	71	2	2	.440	.324
Piscotty, Stephen	R-R	6-3	210	1-14-91	.273	.297	.265	153	582	86	159	35	3	22	85	51	12	1	2	133	7	5	.457	.343
Rosario, Alberto	R-R	5-10	190	1-10-87	.184	.000	.226	20	38	3	7	2	0	0	2	2	0	1	0	5	0	0	.237	.225
Tejada, Ruben	R-R	5-11	200	10-27-89	.176	.333	.091	23	34	6	6	2	0	0	3	2	1	0	3	8	0	0	.235	.225
2-team total (13 San Francisco)					.167	—	—	36	66	9	11	5	0	0	5	7	1	1	3	13	0	0	.242	.247
Wong, Kolten	L-R	5-9	185	10-10-90	.240	.242	.239	121	313	39	75	7	7	5	23	34	9	0	5	52	7	0	.355	.327

Pitching	B-T	HT	WT	DOB	W	L	ERA	G	GS	CG	SV	IP	H	R	ER	HR	BB	SO	AVG	vLH	vRH	K/9	BB/9
Bowman, Matt	R-R	6-0	175	5-31-91	2	5	3.46	59	0	0	0	68	59	31	26	4	20	52	.229	.178	.256	6.92	2.66
Broxton, Jonathan	R-R	6-4	285	6-16-84	4	2	4.30	66	0	0	0	61	52	32	29	7	24	57	.229	.230	.229	8.46	3.56
Duke, Zach	L-L	6-2	210	4-19-83	0	1	1.93	28	0	0	1	23	17	5	5	0	13	26	.205	.161	.231	10.03	5.01
Garcia, Jaime	L-L	6-2	215	7-8-86	10	13	4.67	32	30	1	0	172	179	94	89	26	57	150	.268	.246	.273	7.86	2.99
Kiekhefer, Dean	L-L	6-0	175	6-7-89	0	0	5.32	26	0	0	0	22	24	13	13	2	7	14	.273	.209	.333	5.73	2.86
Leake, Mike	R-R	5-10	170	11-12-87	9	12	4.69	30	30	0	0	177	203	101	92	20	30	125	.288	.269	.304	6.37	1.53
Lyons, Tyler	B-L	6-4	210	2-21-88	2	0	3.38	30	0	0	0	48	35	18	18	9	14	46	.205	.156	.234	8.63	2.63
Maness, Seth	R-R	6-0	190	10-14-88	2	2	3.41	29	0	0	0	32	34	14	12	2	8	16	.274	.244	.291	4.55	2.27
Martinez, Carlos	R-R	6-0	190	9-21-91	16	9	3.04	31	31	0	0	195	169	68	66	15	70	174	.233	.256	.207	8.02	3.23
Mayers, Mike	R-R	6-3	200	12-6-91	1	1	27.00	4	1	0	0	5	16	16	16	3	3	2	.533	.500	.563	3.38	5.06
Oh, Seung Hwan	R-R	5-10	205	7-15-82	6	3	1.92	76	0	0	19	80	55	20	17	5	18	103	.190	.176	.201	11.64	2.03
Reyes, Alex	R-R	6-3	175	8-29-94	4	1	1.57	12	5	0	1	46	33	8	8	1	23	52	.201	.243	.170	10.17	4.50
Rosenthal, Trevor	R-R	6-2	230	5-29-90	2	4	4.46	45	0	0	14	40	48	22	20	3	29	56	.293	.292	.293	12.50	6.47
Siegrist, Kevin	L-L	6-5	230	7-20-89	6	3	2.77	67	0	0	3	62	42	20	19	10	26	66	.193	.221	.180	9.63	3.79
Socolovich, Miguel	R-R	6-1	205	7-24-86	1	0	2.00	15	0	0	0	18	5	4	4	2	5	16	.086	.125	.059	8.00	2.50
Tuivailala, Sam	R-R	6-3	225	10-19-92	0	0	6.00	12	0	0	0	9	12	6	6	0	6	7	.308	.300	.316	7.00	6.00
Wacha, Michael	R-R	6-6	215	7-1-91	7	7	5.09	27	24	0	0	138	159	86	78	15	45	114	.289	.264	.307	7.43	2.93
Wainwright, Adam	R-R	6-7	235	8-30-81	13	9	4.62	33	33	1	0	199	220	108	102	22	59	161	.287	.306	.272	7.29	2.67
Weaver, Luke	R-R	6-2	170	8-21-93	1	4	5.70	9	8	0	0	36	46	29	23	7	12	45	.311	.377	.264	11.15	2.97
Williams, Jerome	R-R	6-3	260	12-4-81	0	0	5.71	11	0	0	0	17	22	15	11	4	6	8	.306	.120	.404	4.15	3.12

Fielding

Catcher	PCT	G	PO	A	E	DP	PB
Fryer	1.000	22	63	9	0	0	0
Kelly	1.000	10	30	2	0	0	0
Molina	.998	146	1113	60	2	5	8
Pena	.933	3	13	1	1	0	1
Rosario	1.000	17	82	8	0	1	1

First Base	PCT	G	PO	A	E	DP
Adams	.990	86	617	71	7	62
Carpenter	.997	45	304	16	1	38
Gyorko	1.000	11	61	5	0	6
Holliday	1.000	10	65	10	0	5
Martinez	1.000	1	4	0	0	0

Molina	1.000	2	10	1	0	0
Moss	.991	64	401	26	4	49
Pena	1.000	1	2	0	0	0
Piscotty	1.000	1	1	0	0	0

ST. LOUIS CARDINALS

Second Base	PCT	G	PO	A	E	DP
Carpenter	.976	40	60	103	4	22
Diaz	1.000	1	1	0	0	1
Garcia	.974	26	31	43	2	7
Gyorko	.995	46	63	136	1	32
Tejada	1.000	3	1	1	0	1
Wong	.980	88	132	256	8	67

Third Base	PCT	G	PO	A	E	DP
Carpenter	.935	54	20	95	8	12
Garcia	.966	31	6	22	1	4

Gyorko	.962	39	21	54	3	7
Peralta	.976	67	39	125	4	15
Rosario	1.000	1	0	1	0	0
Tejada	.867	10	1	12	2	1

Shortstop	PCT	G	PO	A	E	DP
Diaz	.961	106	122	275	16	68
Garcia	.951	30	19	78	5	17
Gyorko	.949	26	38	74	6	18
Peralta	1.000	7	11	18	0	6
Tejada	.882	7	1	14	2	2

Outfield	PCT	G	PO	A	E	DP
Grichuk	.996	119	232	8	1	1
Hazelbaker	.952	73	79	0	4	0
Holliday	1.000	85	111	2	0	0
Martinez	1.000	4	2	0	0	0
Moss	1.000	72	95	4	0	2
Pham	1.000	66	71	2	0	1
Piscotty	.986	150	272	7	4	1
Wong	1.000	16	26	0	0	0

MEMPHIS REDBIRDS

PACIFIC COAST LEAGUE

TRIPLE-A

Batting	B-T	HT	WT	DOB	AVG	vLH	vRH	G	AB	R	H	2B	3B	HR	RBI	BB	HBP	SH	SF	SO	SB	CS	SLG	OBP
Adams, Matt	L-R	6-3	260	8-31-88	.188	.000	.214	5	16	4	3	1	0	1	2	4	0	0	0	3	0	0	.438	.350
Anna, Dean	L-R	5-11	180	11-24-86	.266	.184	.296	106	334	48	89	17	1	2	39	42	0	2	5	55	4	3	.341	.344
Bader, Harrison	R-R	6-0	195	6-3-94	.231	.292	.202	49	147	22	34	7	1	3	17	11	3	0	0	38	2	3	.354	.298
Caldwell, Bruce	L-R	5-11	175	11-27-91	.200	.250	.188	6	20	3	4	0	1	0	2	2	0	1	0	8	0	0	.300	.273
Cruz, Luis	R-R	6-2	225	5-26-93	.143	.000	.167	7	7	2	1	0	0	0	1	0	0	0	0	1	0	0	.143	.143
Garcia, Anthony	R-R	6-0	180	1-4-92	.229	.296	.197	70	218	25	50	12	0	8	27	20	3	0	6	44	1	1	.394	.296
Garcia, Greg	L-R	6-0	190	8-8-89	.269	.143	.316	30	104	13	28	4	1	0	8	11	2	3	0	20	2	2	.327	.350
Grichuk, Randal	R-R	6-1	205	8-13-91	.272	.233	.294	30	81	12	22	4	1	6	18	2	2	0	1	14	0	0	.568	.302
Hazelbaker, Jeremy	L-R	6-3	190	8-14-87	.325	.333	.320	13	40	8	13	3	0	1	11	6	2	2	0	12	2	1	.475	.438
Jenner, Jesse	R-R	6-0	205	7-18-93	.300	.400	.200	4	10	1	3	0	0	0	2	0	0	0	0	3	0	0	.300	.417
Kelly, Carson	R-R	6-2	205	7-14-94	.292	.167	.326	32	113	14	33	10	0	0	14	11	0	1	1	17	0	0	.381	.352
Martinez, Jose	R-R	6-6	215	7-25-88	.269	.256	.275	87	301	34	81	18	1	8	42	25	1	1	1	50	9	1	.415	.326
2-team total (37 Omaha)					.278	—	—	124	442	52	123	28	1	11	60	39	2	1	5	74	11	1	.421	.336
Martini, Nick	L-L	5-11	205	6-27-90	.273	.221	.300	86	256	38	70	12	3	2	26	31	3	0	4	39	6	0	.367	.354
McKenry, Michael	R-R	5-10	205	3-4-85	.341	.250	.379	24	82	20	28	5	4	5	20	14	1	0	2	22	2	2	.683	.443
3-team total																								
(14 Colorado Springs, 13 Round Rock)					.290	—	—	51	155	35	45	12	4	6	35	40	3	0	1	40	2	2	.535	.442
Mejia, Alex	R-R	6-1	200	1-18-91	.273	.290	.265	34	99	9	27	7	2	0	10	4	2	3	0	12	0	0	.384	.314
Navarro, Efren	L-L	6-0	210	5-14-86	.320	.309	.324	54	197	28	63	5	0	2	17	15	0	0	1	21	0	0	.376	.366
2-team total (72 Tacoma)					.275	—	—	126	465	68	128	16	3	7	48	43	2	0	4	84	0	0	.368	.337
Ohlman, Mike	R-R	6-5	240	12-14-90	.280	.267	.285	54	168	34	47	9	2	6	28	15	0	0	3	53	1	0	.464	.333
Peguero, Carlos	L-L	6-5	260	2-22-87	.283	.364	.257	44	138	19	39	6	0	5	27	15	1	0	1	41	3	0	.435	.355
Pena, Brayan	B-R	5-9	240	1-7-82	.200	.000	.308	5	20	1	4	0	0	0	1	1	0	0	1	2	0	0	.200	.227
Pham, Tommy	R-R	6-1	210	3-8-88	.236	.265	.224	33	110	15	26	5	1	3	17	18	0	0	0	29	8	2	.382	.344
Rivera, Chris	R-R	5-11	190	5-30-93	.333	—	.333	1	3	2	1	0	0	1	2	0	0	0	0	1	0	0	1.333	.333
Rodriguez, Jonathan	R-R	6-2	250	8-21-89	.259	.400	.200	39	135	18	35	6	0	7	24	10	0	0	0	46	3	1	.459	.310
Rosario, Alberto	R-R	5-10	190	1-10-87	.281	.316	.263	39	114	8	32	5	0	0	13	6	2	0	2	20	0	0	.325	.323
Tilson, Charlie	L-L	5-11	195	12-2-92	.282	.380	.243	100	351	53	99	16	8	4	34	33	3	4	5	51	15	3	.407	.345
Valera, Breyvic	R-R	5-11	160	1-8-92	.341	.368	.329	73	217	32	74	14	1	0	31	31	1	3	5	22	8	4	.415	.417
Washington, David	L-L	6-5	260	11-20-90	.255	.211	.272	105	345	52	88	17	1	25	62	51	1	0	4	142	4	5	.528	.349
Williams, Matt	R-R	6-0	170	8-29-89	.263	.288	.250	113	338	46	89	19	3	1	35	49	1	3	4	67	11	7	.346	.355
Wilson, Jacob	R-R	5-11	205	7-29-90	.221	.244	.208	72	226	29	50	14	0	8	29	20	4	0	3	55	3	2	.389	.292
Wisdom, Patrick	R-R	6-2	220	8-27-91	.233	.154	.266	78	262	29	61	20	1	5	30	26	2	0	4	73	5	1	.374	.303
Wong, Kolten	L-R	5-9	185	10-10-90	.429	.333	.455	7	28	10	12	0	1	4	11	4	2	0	0	6	1	0	.929	.529

Pitching	B-T	HT	WT	DOB	W	L	ERA	G	GS	CG	SV	IP	H	R	ER	HR	BB	SO	AVG	vLH	vRH	K/9	BB/9
Baker, Corey	R-R	6-1	170	11-23-89	1	3	8.13	6	6	0	0	31	46	30	28	7	10	23	.336	.373	.308	6.68	2.90
Brebbia, John	R-R	6-1	185	5-30-90	2	3	6.23	19	0	0	0	30	41	22	21	3	13	30	.323	.327	.319	8.90	3.86
Church, John	R-R	6-2	250	11-4-86	0	1	3.34	25	0	0	1	30	25	18	11	0	13	25	.236	.258	.227	7.58	3.94
Echemendia, Pedro	R-R	6-2	185	6-14-91	1	0	2.37	11	0	0	0	19	16	5	5	3	7	15	.239	.219	.257	7.11	3.32
Gonzalez, Juan	R-R	6-2	260	4-5-90	3	1	5.48	39	0	0	4	43	43	27	26	3	30	39	.264	.242	.278	8.23	6.33
Hefner, Jeremy	R-R	6-4	205	3-11-86	3	6	5.25	18	18	0	0	98	103	59	57	12	39	82	.269	.270	.268	7.56	3.59
Herget, Kevin	R-R	5-10	185	4-3-91	0	0	0.00	1	0	0	0	1	2	0	0	0	1	1	.400	1.000	.250	6.75	6.75
Heyer, Kurt	L-R	6-2	185	1-23-91	2	5	6.13	22	10	0	0	72	92	53	49	6	23	49	.317	.372	.278	6.13	2.88
Kiekhefer, Dean	L-L	6-0	175	6-7-89	6	1	2.08	29	0	0	2	35	32	8	8	2	8	20	.252	.192	.293	5.19	2.08
Lee, Thomas	R-R	6-1	190	10-20-89	2	5	6.11	19	8	0	0	56	80	42	38	3	18	34	.333	.258	.385	5.46	2.89
Littrell, Corey	L-L	6-3	185	3-21-92	1	4	4.56	40	1	0	1	51	51	30	26	5	29	49	.259	.177	.314	8.59	5.08
Lucas, Josh	L-R	6-1	185	11-5-90	0	0	9.39	7	0	0	0	8	9	9	8	0	4	5	.290	.111	.364	5.87	4.70
Maness, Seth	R-R	6-0	190	10-14-88	0	0	0.00	2	1	0	0	2	1	0	0	0	0	2	.143	.250	.000	0.00	0.00
Mayers, Mike	R-R	6-3	200	12-6-91	4	8	3.73	16	16	1	0	89	87	44	37	8	31	84	.256	.213	.284	8.46	3.12
McGuire, Deck	R-R	6-6	220	6-23-89	7	11	5.10	26	26	1	0	134	134	79	76	22	50	111	.263	.255	.270	7.46	3.36
Nielsen, Trey	R-R	6-1	190	9-1-91	1	0	1.69	1	1	0	0	5	2	1	1	1	4	4	.125	.100	.167	6.75	6.75
Pearce, Matt	R-R	6-2	205	2-24-94	0	2	4.91	2	2	0	0	11	12	9	6	2	4	6	.267	.357	.118	4.91	3.27
Reyes, Alex	R-R	6-3	175	8-29-94	2	3	4.96	14	14	0	0	65	63	38	36	6	32	93	.252	.238	.262	12.81	4.41
Reyes, Artie	R-R	5-11	185	4-6-92	9	4	4.17	19	19	0	0	101	97	53	47	12	36	77	.255	.295	.228	5.40	3.20
Shaban, Ronnie	L-R	6-1	195	3-8-90	0	0	0.00	3	0	0	0	3	4	0	0	0	0	2	.286	.600	.111	5.40	0.00
Sherriff, Ryan	L-L	6-1	185	5-25-90	7	1	2.84	49	0	0	3	67	56	23	21	4	23	55	.256	.172	.303	7.43	3.11
Socolovich, Miguel	R-R	6-1	205	7-24-86	2	6	3.14	45	0	0	5	52	42	24	18	2	16	59	.219	.238	.205	10.28	2.79
Sulbaran, J.C.	R-R	6-2	205	11-9-89	2	6	7.69	11	11	0	0	50	68	47	43	8	23	38	.315	.316	.314	6.79	4.11

Pitching	B-T	HT	WT	DOB	W	L	ERA	G	GS	CG	SV	IP	H	R	ER	HR	BB	SO	AVG	vLH	vRH	K/9	BB/9
Tuivailala, Sam	R-R	6-3	225	10-19-92	3	2	5.21	42	0	0	17	47	47	27	27	3	22	72	.254	.264	.248	13.89	4.24
Weaver, Luke	R-R	6-2	170	8-21-93	1	0	0.00	1	1	0	0	6	2	0	0	0	2	4	.100	.000	.125	6.00	3.00
Williams, Jerome	R-R	6-3	260	12-4-81	5	3	4.89	9	9	2	0	57	64	31	31	11	15	34	.287	.194	.354	5.37	2.37
Wright, Justin	L-L	5-9	175	8-18-89	0	1	4.30	22	0	0	0	23	22	11	11	3	16	20	.242	.296	.219	7.83	6.26
Wyatt, Heath	R-R	6-2	185	8-27-88	1	1	6.00	17	0	0	0	21	27	15	14	1	12	19	.314	.308	.317	8.14	5.14

Fielding

Catcher	PCT	G	PO	A	E	DP	PB
Cruz	.957	2	21	1	1	0	0
Jenner	1.000	3	18	3	0	0	0
Kelly	1.000	32	263	14	0	0	1
McKenry	.994	22	160	6	1	1	0
Ohlman	.989	49	339	24	4	1	5
Pena	1.000	4	23	0	0	0	1
Rivera	1.000	1	4	1	0	0	0
Rosario	.993	35	243	24	2	1	0

First Base	PCT	G	PO	A	E	DP
Adams	1.000	4	25	5	0	4
Martinez	.987	23	141	16	2	14
Navarro	.994	44	317	21	2	37
Ohlman	1.000	2	4	0	0	0
Pena	1.000	1	11	2	0	1
Rodriguez	.983	33	270	23	5	25
Washington	.982	43	353	26	7	29
Wilson	1.000	3	6	0	0	0
Wisdom	1.000	4	39	1	0	3

Second Base	PCT	G	PO	A	E	DP
Anna	.984	96	143	218	6	59
Caldwell	1.000	4	9	12	0	5
Garcia	1.000	2	3	3	0	1
Mejia	1.000	1	0	3	0	0
Valera	.992	32	54	67	1	21
Williams	1.000	13	9	36	0	3
Wilson	.973	10	14	22	1	9
Wong	1.000	4	5	10	0	1

Third Base	PCT	G	PO	A	E	DP
Garcia	1.000	2	0	2	0	0
Mejia	1.000	11	8	8	0	1
Rodriguez	1.000	3	3	6	0	0
Valera	.976	21	9	31	1	4
Williams	1.000	3	2	2	0	1
Wilson	.935	53	27	102	9	15
Wisdom	.947	65	37	123	9	5

Shortstop	PCT	G	PO	A	E	DP
Anna	1.000	2	0	2	0	0

	PCT	G	PO	A	E	DP
Garcia	.957	24	29	60	4	16
Mejia	.968	22	19	42	2	6
Valera	.934	15	17	40	4	8
Williams	.952	89	123	232	18	56
Wisdom	.833	3	5	5	2	0

Outfield	PCT	G	PO	A	E	DP
Bader	.978	44	85	4	2	0
Garcia	.960	54	93	3	4	1
Grichuk	1.000	17	30	1	0	0
Hazelbaker	1.000	11	17	1	0	0
Martinez	.963	54	75	3	3	0
Martini	.993	66	133	4	1	1
Navarro	1.000	4	6	0	0	0
Peguero	.963	35	73	4	3	0
Pham	.980	29	46	2	1	0
Tilson	.969	93	153	2	5	1
Valera	1.000	5	5	0	0	0
Washington	.963	50	76	1	3	0
Williams	1.000	7	4	0	0	0
Wilson	—	1	0	0	0	0
Wong	1.000	3	3	1	0	0

SPRINGFIELD CARDINALS

DOUBLE-A

TEXAS LEAGUE

Batting	B-T	HT	WT	DOB	AVG	vLH	vRH	G	AB	R	H	2B	3B	HR	RBI	BB	HBP	SH	SF	SO	SB	CS	SLG	OBP
Acevedo, Jhohan	R-R	6-1	173	3-28-93	.128	.100	.148	18	47	2	6	0	0	0	2	2	0	0	0	10	0	1	.128	.163
Bader, Harrison	R-R	6-0	195	6-3-94	.283	.426	.249	82	318	48	90	12	4	16	41	25	10	0	3	93	11	10	.497	.351
Bryan, Vaughn	B-R	6-0	185	6-5-93	.227	.286	.212	19	66	13	15	1	0	0	7	11	0	2	1	21	5	3	.242	.333
Caldwell, Bruce	L-R	5-11	175	11-27-91	.251	.171	.270	99	355	47	89	18	1	11	52	41	1	0	6	116	1	1	.400	.325
Carpenter, Matt	L-R	6-3	205	11-26-85	.333	—	.333	4	12	2	4	1	0	1	1	1	0	0	0	4	0	0	.667	.385
Cruz, Luis	R-R	6-2	225	5-26-94	.256	.220	.268	53	168	24	43	6	1	3	20	11	2	3	2	53	1	3	.357	.306
DeJong, Paul	R-R	6-1	195	8-2-93	.260	.252	.263	132	496	62	129	29	2	22	73	40	10	0	6	144	3	2	.460	.324
Drake, Blake	R-R	6-1	175	7-11-93	.254	.217	.265	58	193	27	49	8	1	5	26	19	0	1	0	53	3	4	.383	.321
Garcia, Anthony	R-R	6-0	180	1-24-92	.250	.255	.255	37	122	17	31	6	0	3	16	11	3	1	0	24	2	2	.377	.331
Godoy, Jose	L-R	5-11	180	10-13-94	1.000	—	1.000	1	1	0	1	0	0	0	0	0	0	0	0	0	0	0	1.000	1.000
Hawkins, Joey	R-R	5-11	170	3-10-93	.050	.000	.063	7	20	1	1	0	0	0	1	3	0	0	0	9	0	0	.050	.174
Herrera, Juan	R-R	5-11	165	6-28-93	.167	.220	.147	46	150	13	25	5	0	0	9	5	1	3	1	35	2	2	.200	.197
Jacobs, Chris	R-R	6-5	260	11-25-88	.212	.172	.226	37	113	12	24	2	0	4	12	6	1	0	1	39	0	1	.336	.256
Jenner, Jesse	R-R	6-0	205	7-18-93	.296	.261	.306	28	108	14	32	7	0	2	9	4	1	1	0	20	0	1	.417	.327
Katz, Mason	R-R	5-10	190	8-23-90	.381	.500	.353	14	42	7	16	2	0	3	7	6	0	0	1	11	3	0	.643	.458
Kelly, Carson	R-R	6-2	220	7-14-94	.287	.419	.254	64	216	29	62	7	0	6	18	14	3	2	1	46	0	1	.403	.338
Lankford, Cole	L-R	6-0	185	3-9-92	.182	.000	.200	6	11	2	2	1	0	0	1	1	0	0	0	1	0	0	.273	.250
Martini, Nick	L-L	5-11	205	6-27-90	.234	.205	.248	40	145	21	34	5	0	3	13	24	2	0	1	27	4	1	.331	.349
McElroy Jr. C.J.	R-R	5-10	180	5-29-93	.262	.318	.250	43	130	16	34	3	0	1	9	13	4	2	0	29	9	4	.308	.347
Mejia, Alex	R-R	6-1	200	1-18-91	.218	.200	.221	44	170	16	37	7	0	1	14	13	1	1	2	26	1	1	.276	.274
Moss, Brandon	L-R	6-1	210	9-16-83	.000	.000	.000	3	8	0	0	0	0	0	1	1	0	0	1	1	0	0	.000	.100
Ohlman, Mike	R-R	6-5	240	12-14-90	.301	.385	.286	24	83	9	25	3	0	1	16	10	0	0	3	19	0	2	.373	.365
Pena, Brayan	B-R	5-9	240	1-7-82	.188	.250	.179	9	32	2	6	0	0	0	0	1	0	0	0	4	0	0	.188	.212
Peralta, Jhonny	R-R	6-2	225	5-28-82	.000	.000	.000	1	2	0	0	0	0	0	1	0	0	0	0	1	0	0	.000	.333
Pham, Tommy	R-R	6-1	210	3-8-88	.357	.500	.300	4	14	3	5	0	0	2	3	0	0	0	0	3	0	1	.571	.471
Radack, Collin	R-R	6-3	205	3-30-92	.269	.160	.294	48	134	12	36	2	0	0	13	15	2	2	1	32	4	0	.284	.349
Reynolds, Mikey	B-R	5-9	170	8-19-90	.125	.333	.000	3	8	1	1	0	0	0	0	0	0	0	1	0	0	0	.125	.125
Rodriguez, Jonathan	R-R	6-2	250	8-21-89	.255	.214	.267	81	302	43	77	14	1	8	36	40	3	0	2	86	1	4	.387	.346
Sohn, Andrew	R-R	5-11	185	5-8-93	.286	.167	.318	10	28	3	8	2	0	0	1	3	0	0	0	8	0	0	.357	.355
Spitz, Tom	R-R	6-1	180	4-16-92	.250	.333	.200	4	16	1	4	1	0	0	2	1	0	0	1	4	1	0	.313	.278
Staton, Allen	R-R	5-10	190	9-10-92	.278	.341	.259	53	180	23	50	8	2	3	20	16	3	4	2	35	2	0	.394	.343
Tejada, Ruben	R-R	5-11	200	10-27-89	.333	.000	.375	3	9	2	3	1	0	0	0	0	0	0	0	1	0	0	.444	.333
Thompson, Nick	R-R	6-1	210	11-13-92	.200	.286	.167	10	25	5	5	1	0	1	2	2	0	0	0	5	0	0	.360	.259
Turgeon, Casey	R-R	5-10	160	9-4-92	.179	.222	.158	10	28	3	5	1	0	0	2	6	1	1	0	4	0	0	.214	.343
Valera, Breyvic	B-R	5-11	160	1-8-92	.258	.308	.245	52	178	16	46	5	1	0	12	9	0	2	3	18	3	1	.298	.289
Voit, Luke	R-R	6-3	225	2-13-91	.297	.304	.294	134	482	70	143	20	5	19	74	52	8	0	4	83	1	2	.477	.372
Washington, David	L-L	6-5	260	11-20-90	.276	.222	.293	22	76	15	21	4	1	5	15	16	0	0	0	27	0	1	.553	.402
Wilson, Jacob	R-R	5-11	205	7-29-90	.226	.111	.258	50	84	14	19	3	0	6	18	12	0	3	2	26	0	0	.476	.316

Pitching	B-T	HT	WT	DOB	W	L	ERA	G	GS	CG	SV	IP	H	R	ER	HR	BB	SO	AVG	vLH	vRH	K/9	BB/9
Baker, Corey	R-R	6-1	170	11-23-89	4	8	4.91	23	20	0	0	99	108	63	54	19	42	87	.280	.290	.274	7.91	3.82
Brebbia, John	R-R	6-1	185	5-30-90	3	2	4.06	24	0	0	2	38	41	17	17	6	6	38	.273	.328	.229	9.08	1.43
Donofrio, Joey	R-R	6-3	185	5-10-89	1	1	3.97	15	0	0	0	23	20	11	10	2	13	19	.238	.242	.235	7.54	5.16
Echemendia, Pedro	R-R	6-2	185	6-14-91	2	1	4.25	19	2	0	1	30	27	16	14	4	11	20	.245	.271	.226	6.07	3.34
Frey, Nick	R-R	6-4	185	8-30-91	0	0	0.00	1	0	0	0	2	2	0	0	0	0	2	.286	.250	.333	9.00	0.00
Gomber, Austin	L-L	6-5	235	11-23-93	1	0	1.40	4	4	0	0	19	11	4	3	0	9	15	.167	.231	.151	6.98	4.19
Hawkins, Chandler	L-L	6-1	170	2-28-93	0	0	4.13	14	0	0	0	24	21	16	11	3	10	17	.226	.194	.246	6.38	3.75
Herget, Kevin	R-R	5-10	185	4-3-91	5	0	3.32	36	0	0	10	38	42	23	14	1	11	39	.275	.222	.311	9.24	2.61
Heyer, Kurt	R-R	6-2	185	1-23-91	2	2	2.82	12	2	0	1	22	20	8	7	2	3	18	.235	.171	.280	7.25	1.21
Littrell, Corey	L-L	6-3	185	3-21-92	1	0	1.72	13	0	0	1	16	8	3	3	2	1	14	.145	.160	.133	8.04	0.57
Lucas, Josh	R-R	6-6	185	11-5-90	4	2	3.25	38	0	0	16	53	47	20	19	5	12	61	.234	.321	.175	10.42	2.05
Lynn, Lance	R-R	6-5	280	5-12-87	0	0	0.00	1	1	0	0	3	3	0	0	0	0	3	.273	.000	.333	9.00	0.00
Maness, Seth	R-R	6-0	190	10-14-88	0	0	3.00	3	0	0	0	3	1	1	1	1	1	1	.111	.000	.333	3.00	3.00
Mayers, Mike	R-R	6-3	200	12-6-91	5	2	2.30	9	9	0	0	55	47	17	14	4	17	43	.229	.270	.198	7.08	2.80
McGuire, Deck	R-R	6-6	220	6-23-89	0	0	0.00	1	1	0	0	7	2	1	0	0	3	8	.091	.100	.083	10.29	3.86
McKinney, Ian	L-L	5-11	185	11-18-94	1	0	2.89	2	2	0	0	9	9	3	3	1	7	7	.273	.667	.185	6.75	6.75
McKnight, Blake	R-R	6-1	185	2-13-91	1	0	10.80	4	0	0	0	5	8	6	6	1	4	4	.364	.200	.500	7.20	7.20
Morales, Andrew	R-R	6-0	185	1-16-93	4	4	3.35	14	14	0	0	78	71	38	29	10	18	66	.237	.272	.215	7.62	2.08
Nielsen, Trey	R-R	6-1	190	9-1-91	8	8	3.84	23	19	2	1	122	131	59	52	13	38	81	.279	.303	.264	5.98	2.80
Pearce, Matt	R-R	6-3	205	2-24-94	1	2	7.88	3	3	0	0	16	21	14	14	3	7	16	.313	.444	.265	9.00	3.94
Perry, Chris	L-R	6-2	215	7-15-90	1	2	3.38	37	0	0	0	53	34	22	20	2	40	60	.184	.276	.119	10.13	6.75
Poncedeleon, Daniel	R-R	6-4	185	1-16-92	9	8	3.52	27	27	1	0	151	128	71	59	10	56	122	.231	.235	.229	7.27	3.34
Rowland, Robby	R-R	6-4	215	12-15-91	1	0	4.82	8	0	0	0	9	10	7	5	0	4	12	.263	.444	.207	11.57	3.86
Shaban, Ronnie	L-R	6-1	195	3-8-90	8	3	3.11	42	0	0	10	55	52	19	19	7	16	40	.251	.227	.265	6.55	2.62
Sulbaran, J.C.	R-R	6-2	205	11-9-89	3	4	3.95	17	16	0	0	96	82	45	42	10	32	78	.230	.217	.238	7.34	3.01
Thomas, Chris	R-R	6-2	200	3-16-88	2	2	6.75	14	0	0	0	17	23	16	13	3	6	16	.315	.303	.325	8.31	3.12
Walter, John	R-R	6-5	225	5-20-91	1	6	6.24	9	8	0	0	49	52	35	34	3	20	35	.269	.274	.266	6.43	3.67
Weaver, Luke	R-R	6-2	170	8-21-93	6	3	1.40	12	12	0	0	77	63	23	12	4	10	88	.214	.220	.209	10.29	1.17
Wick, Rowan	L-R	6-3	220	11-9-92	0	0	4.12	21	0	0	0	20	14	9	9	1	14	20	.197	.259	.159	9.15	6.41
Wright, Justin	L-L	5-9	175	8-18-89	0	4	5.59	25	0	0	1	29	30	19	18	0	16	21	.273	.271	.274	6.52	4.97
Wyatt, Heath	R-R	6-2	185	8-27-88	1	1	5.40	12	0	0	0	18	30	11	11	3	3	7	.380	.405	.357	3.44	1.47

Fielding

Catcher	PCT	G	PO	A	E	DP	PB
Cruz	.984	46	328	31	6	2	4
Jenner	.982	27	190	23	4	2	3
Kelly	.994	60	454	43	3	5	5
Ohlman	.966	8	55	2	2	0	1
Pena	1.000	5	42	2	0	0	0

First Base	PCT	G	PO	A	E	DP
Jacobs	.988	10	78	6	1	5
Moss	1.000	2	16	1	0	0
Ohlman	.982	12	101	6	2	17
Pena	1.000	1	2	0	0	0
Rodriguez	.984	18	116	8	2	13
Voit	.991	104	805	68	8	77
Washington	1.000	1	9	0	0	0

Second Base	PCT	G	PO	A	E	DP
Caldwell	.967	72	111	183	10	35
Carpenter	.923	3	5	7	1	1
Herrera	.913	3	8	13	2	5
Katz	.930	9	16	24	3	8
Mejia	1.000	3	4	4	0	1
Sohn	1.000	2	3	5	0	0
Staton	.964	25	51	56	4	13

Third Base	PCT	G	PO	A	E	DP
Turgeon	1.000	1	1	2	0	0
Valera	.969	15	28	34	2	9
Wilson	.986	19	23	46	1	12

Third Base	PCT	G	PO	A	E	DP
Caldwell	.933	7	2	12	1	2
Carpenter	1.000	1	0	1	0	0
DeJong	.945	112	73	200	16	18
Katz	.833	2	1	4	1	0
Rodriguez	.960	10	4	20	1	0
Staton	.800	4	1	7	2	1
Turgeon	1.000	5	4	10	0	0
Wilson	1.000	4	1	8	0	1

Shortstop	PCT	G	PO	A	E	DP
Caldwell	1.000	15	29	38	0	10
DeJong	.981	11	14	39	1	10
Hawkins	.917	7	7	15	2	4
Herrera	.930	41	46	100	11	21
Mejia	.954	43	57	110	8	26
Peralta	1.000	1	1	3	0	0
Reynolds	.900	3	3	6	1	3
Sohn	.900	5	5	13	2	2
Tejada	.833	3	2	3	1	1
Valera	.947	26	28	62	5	8

Outfield	PCT	G	PO	A	E	DP
Acevedo	.909	8	10	0	1	0
Bader	.990	81	189	6	2	2
Bryan	.963	15	25	1	1	0
Drake	.993	56	147	4	1	2
Garcia	1.000	32	68	1	0	1
Katz	1.000	1	1	0	0	0
Lankford	1.000	3	5	0	0	0
Martini	.978	38	89	1	2	0
McElroy Jr.	1.000	41	82	2	0	0
Moss	1.000	1	1	0	0	0
Pham	1.000	4	15	0	0	0
Radack	.982	35	55	1	1	1
Rodriguez	1.000	44	76	5	0	1
Shaban	—	1	0	0	0	0
Spitz	.833	4	5	0	1	0
Staton	.977	23	43	0	1	0
Thompson	1.000	8	13	0	0	0
Turgeon	1.000	2	3	0	0	0
Valera	1.000	18	25	0	0	0
Voit	1.000	12	23	2	0	0
Washington	.929	19	26	0	2	0
Wilson	1.000	2	3	0	0	0

PALM BEACH CARDINALS

FLORIDA STATE LEAGUE

HIGH CLASS A

Batting	B-T	HT	WT	DOB	AVG	vLH	vRH	G	AB	R	H	2B	3B	HR	RBI	BB	HBP	SH	SF	SO	SB	CS	SLG	OBP
Acevedo, Jhohan	R-R	6-1	173	3-28-93	.227	.250	.216	24	75	7	17	1	0	0	7	7	1	1	0	20	2	3	.240	.301
Aikin, Craig	L-L	5-10	175	8-19-93	.000	.000	—	1	3	0	0	0	0	0	0	0	0	0	0	1	0	0	.000	.000
Bean, Steve	L-R	6-2	205	9-15-93	.188	.146	.196	80	255	16	48	6	0	1	20	25	1	0	7	89	1	0	.224	.257
Brodbeck, Andrew	L-R	5-10	185	1-22-93	.206	.048	.247	30	102	8	21	2	1	1	13	10	3	1	3	22	5	4	.275	.288
Bryan, Vaughn	B-R	6-0	185	6-5-93	.252	.245	.255	48	163	22	41	5	1	3	10	15	1	5	0	43	15	3	.350	.318
Davis, Matt	R-R	5-10	175	12-8-94	.182	.000	.333	6	11	2	2	0	0	0	1	0	0	0	0	4	0	0	.182	.250
Diaz, Aledmys	R-R	6-1	195	8-1-90	.167	.500	.000	2	6	0	1	0	0	0	0	2	0	0	0	0	0	0	.167	.375
Diekroeger, Danny	L-R	6-2	205	5-25-92	.282	.229	.296	46	170	21	48	13	1	0	19	18	7	0	1	33	2	3	.371	.372
Drake, Blake	R-R	6-1	175	7-11-93	.233	.263	.224	71	253	24	59	14	3	1	26	24	5	0	5	43	11	3	.324	.307
Fernandez, Jose	R-R	6-1	190	5-20-93	.176	.000	.225	17	51	5	9	1	0	0	3	7	0	1	1	23	2	0	.196	.271
Franco, Bladimil	R-R	6-0	170	10-29-93	.300	.400	.200	3	10	1	3	0	0	0	1	0	0	0	0	3	0	0	.300	.300

Batting

Batting	B-T	HT	WT	DOB	AVG	vLH	vRH	G	AB	R	H	2B	3B	HR	RBI	BB	HBP	SH	SF	SO	SB	CS	SLG	OBP
Garcia, Erik	R-R	5-11	215	3-23-93	.000	.000	.000	1	3	0	0	0	0	0	1	0	0	0	1	1	0	0	.000	.000
Grayson, Casey	L-L	6-1	215	8-24-91	.267	.222	.281	126	435	50	116	19	0	2	44	94	1	0	10	91	2	1	.324	.391
Hawkins, Joey	R-R	5-11	170	3-10-93	.125	.200	.000	2	8	0	1	0	0	0	1	0	0	0	0	2	0	0	.125	.125
Herrera, Juan	R-R	5-11	165	6-28-93	.237	.333	.211	25	97	8	23	3	3	1	8	7	0	0	0	24	1	3	.361	.288
Jenner, Jesse	R-R	6-0	205	7-18-93	.206	.192	.214	20	68	4	14	3	0	1	5	5	0	0	0	10	0	0	.294	.260
Katz, Mason	R-R	5-10	190	8-23-90	.053	.000	.067	5	19	2	1	1	0	0	2	2	0	0	1	4	0	0	.105	.136
Lankford, Cole	L-R	6-0	185	9-3-92	.293	.212	.319	71	276	22	81	10	0	1	27	13	4	0	3	33	2	0	.341	.331
Lopez, Joshua	R-R	5-10	188	3-4-96	.200	.000	.500	1	5	0	1	0	0	0	3	1	0	0	0	1	0	0	.200	.333
Martinez, Jose	B-R	5-10	150	8-15-96	.280	.100	.400	5	25	3	7	0	0	0	1	2	0	0	4	0	0	0	.280	.333
Mercado, Oscar	R-R	6-2	175	12-16-94	.215	.250	.204	125	442	50	95	23	1	0	27	44	9	6	5	71	33	26	.271	.296
O'Keefe, Brian	R-R	6-0	210	7-15-93	.167	—	.167	8	24	3	4	2	0	0	1	8	0	0	0	5	0	0	.250	.375
Olivera, Orlando	R-R	6-0	230	10-17-90	.220	.123	.252	91	323	25	71	10	0	6	29	29	3	0	3	62	1	2	.307	.288
Pena, Brayan	B-R	5-9	240	1-7-82	.263	.167	.308	6	19	1	5	0	0	0	5	0	0	0	2	3	0	0	.263	.238
Peralta, Jhonny	R-R	6-2	225	5-28-82	.286	.333	.273	4	14	2	4	3	0	0	1	2	0	0	0	0	0	0	.500	.375
Pritchard, Michael	L-L	5-11	180	11-10-91	.256	.270	.253	65	227	29	58	10	1	0	13	42	3	1	2	26	1	4	.308	.376
Radack, Collin	R-R	6-3	205	3-30-92	.176	.000	.194	9	34	0	6	2	0	0	2	3	1	0	0	9	1	1	.235	.263
Reynolds, Mikey	B-R	5-9	170	8-19-90	.186	.235	.170	18	70	5	13	0	2	0	7	4	4	1	1	12	5	1	.243	.266
Rivera, Chris	R-R	5-11	150	3-10-95	.182	.128	.211	33	110	9	20	2	0	2	13	13	3	0	1	39	0	0	.255	.283
Seferina, Darren	R-R	5-9	175	1-24-94	.247	.295	.234	70	275	34	68	7	5	1	15	25	2	4	3	68	32	6	.320	.311
Sohn, Andrew	R-R	5-11	185	5-8-93	.194	.182	.199	72	211	21	41	4	0	3	22	32	5	2	1	47	13	5	.256	.313
Sosa, Edmundo	R-R	5-11	170	3-6-96	.294	.154	.381	9	34	3	10	0	2	0	4	1	0	0	0	8	0	0	.412	.314
Spitz, Tom	R-R	6-1	180	4-16-92	.247	.250	.246	47	166	21	41	8	1	3	26	22	2	2	2	28	4	5	.361	.349
Staton, Allen	R-R	5-10	190	8-15-96	.219	.255	.207	49	192	15	42	8	0	3	26	11	1	0	4	41	0	0	.307	.260
Thompson, Nick	R-R	6-1	210	11-13-92	.171	.214	.161	22	76	9	13	5	0	0	5	10	0	0	0	18	0	0	.237	.267
Tice, Dylan	B-R	5-8	190	12-15-92	.288	.243	.304	40	139	16	40	6	0	1	18	10	3	0	1	21	2	4	.353	.346
Turgeon, Casey	R-R	5-10	160	9-28-92	.290	.231	.309	28	107	19	31	10	2	3	13	20	1	0	1	21	1	2	.505	.403
Zavala, Stephen	R-R	5-8	175	5-2-93	.333	.000	.500	3	6	0	2	0	0	0	1	0	0	0	0	2	0	0	.333	.429

Pitching

Pitching	B-T	HT	WT	DOB	W	L	ERA	G	GS	CG	SV	IP	H	R	ER	HR	BB	SO	AVG	vLH	vRH	K/9	BB/9
Alcantara, Sandy	R-R	6-4	170	9-7-95	0	4	3.62	6	6	1	0	32	25	13	13	0	14	34	.216	.348	.183	9.46	3.90
Anderson, Will	R-R	6-3	205	8-26-92	0	1	12.27	3	0	0	0	4	4	5	5	1	6	4	.267	.250	.286	9.82	14.73
Bard, Daniel	R-R	6-4	215	6-25-85	1	2	24.00	8	0	0	0	3	3	8	8	0	13	1	.300	.500	.167	3.00	39.00
Beck, Landon	R-R	6-3	215	12-9-92	1	4	3.54	34	0	0	7	41	41	17	16	2	20	39	.272	.278	.266	8.63	4.43
Echemendia, Pedro	R-R	6-2	185	6-14-91	1	0	3.98	13	0	0	0	20	25	9	9	2	5	18	.301	.286	.309	7.97	2.21
Evans, Jacob	L-L	6-2	215	11-27-93	4	7	3.73	16	16	0	0	89	104	52	37	12	17	48	.290	.295	.288	4.84	1.71
Fernandez, Junior	R-R	6-1	180	3-2-97	2	2	5.36	10	6	0	0	44	48	29	26	4	20	25	.271	.253	.293	5.15	4.12
Flaherty, Jack	R-R	6-4	205	10-15-95	5	9	3.56	24	23	0	0	134	129	63	53	8	45	126	.254	.248	.258	8.46	3.02
Frey, Nick	R-R	6-4	185	8-30-91	0	1	6.08	8	0	0	0	13	24	9	9	0	0	7	.393	.368	.405	4.73	0.00
Garcia, Silfredo	R-R	6-2	170	7-19-91	1	3	3.07	11	0	0	3	15	11	5	5	1	4	12	.208	.188	.216	7.36	2.45
Gomber, Austin	L-L	6-5	235	11-23-93	6	8	2.93	17	17	1	0	108	91	38	35	5	24	101	.229	.225	.231	8.44	2.01
Gonzalez, Derian	R-R	6-3	190	1-31-95	1	2	1.46	4	4	0	0	25	16	9	4	0	11	24	.182	.227	.167	8.76	4.01
Grana, Kyle	R-R	6-4	245	4-26-91	5	1	3.12	43	0	0	6	52	39	20	18	2	27	63	.203	.221	.194	10.90	4.67
Hawkins, Chandler	L-L	6-1	170	2-28-93	0	1	4.73	20	0	0	0	27	25	14	14	3	9	15	.248	.231	.258	5.06	3.03
Heesch, Michael	R-L	6-5	265	5-15-90	2	2	5.08	30	0	0	0	44	60	29	25	4	16	30	.328	.370	.314	6.09	3.25
Herget, Kevin	R-R	5-10	185	4-3-91	0	0	0.00	12	0	0	6	23	5	0	0	0	1	21	.070	.111	.045	8.22	0.39
Holt, Harley	R-R	6-0	165	10-28-91	0	0	4.50	1	0	0	0	2	2	1	1	0	1	3	.250	.300		13.50	4.50
Hudson, Dakota	R-R	6-5	215	9-15-94	1	1	0.96	8	0	0	3	9	6	3	1	0	7	10	.188	.143	.250	9.64	6.75
Leitao, Brennan	R-R	6-1	205	6-21-93	0	1	3.86	4	0	0	0	23	25	11	10	1	8	12	.278	.200	.327	4.63	3.09
Lynn, Lance	R-R	6-5	280	5-12-87	0	0	2.45	2	2	0	0	4	4	3	1	0	0	4	.250	.273	.200	9.82	0.00
McKinney, Ian	L-L	5-11	185	11-18-94	7	10	4.17	23	22	0	0	123	139	66	57	10	50	101	.285	.351	.269	7.39	3.66
McKnight, Blake	R-R	6-1	185	2-13-91	3	6	3.11	33	11	0	2	93	94	44	32	3	40	37	.267	.250	.279	3.59	3.88
Pearce, Matt	R-R	6-3	205	2-24-94	8	8	2.37	20	20	4	0	137	114	43	36	9	15	81	.222	.202	.235	5.33	0.99
Rowland, Robby	R-R	6-3	215	12-15-91	1	1	2.45	7	0	0	1	7	5	2	2	0	4	4	.185	.091	.250	4.91	4.91
Schumacher, Cody	R-R	6-1	190	12-1-90	3	2	3.38	39	0	0	0	61	69	27	23	2	23	55	.285	.333	.258	8.07	3.38
Walter, John	R-R	6-5	225	5-20-91	2	3	3.58	6	6	0	0	33	36	13	13	0	9	21	.288	.230	.344	5.79	2.48
Ward, Davis	R-R	6-0	196	2-23-92	2	0	1.74	10	0	0	0	21	16	7	4	0	3	9	.211	.267	.174	3.92	1.31
Wick, Rowan	L-R	6-3	220	11-9-92	2	0	1.09	23	0	0	6	25	16	4	3	0	6	37	.178	.194	.167	13.50	2.19
Wirsu, Josh	R-R	6-0	190	9-4-93	0	0	7.36	5	0	0	0	7	9	6	6	1	7	7	.300	.200	.350	8.59	8.59

Fielding

Catcher	PCT	G	PO	A	E	DP	PB
Bean	.988	78	517	49	7	4	9
Garcia	1.000	1	5	0	0	0	0
Jenner	.985	20	120	10	2	1	0
Lopez	1.000	1	10	0	0	0	1
O'Keefe	.979	7	45	2	1	0	1
Pena	1.000	2	16	0	0	0	0
Rivera	.984	32	218	21	4	1	5
Zavala	1.000	3	13	2	0	0	0

First Base	PCT	G	PO	A	E	DP
Diekroeger	.975	14	108	11	3	14
Grayson	.995	114	979	68	5	83
Lankford	.985	9	63	4	1	7
Olivera	.800	1	4	0	1	1
Pena	1.000	1	9	0	0	2

Second Base	PCT	G	PO	A	E	DP
Brodbeck	.983	13	19	38	1	13
Lankford	1.000	1	2	1	0	0
Reynolds	.940	11	18	29	3	7
Seferina	.959	63	106	153	11	34
Sohn	.990	19	40	61	1	16
Tice	.956	29	41	68	5	13
Turgeon	.952	6	10	10	1	2

Third Base	PCT	G	PO	A	E	DP
Brodbeck	.920	12	4	19	2	0
Bryan	—	1	0	0	0	0

	PCT	G	PO	A	E	DP
Davis	.889	4	1	7	1	0
Diekroeger	.897	12	11	24	4	4
Fernandez	.833	2	2	3	1	1
Hawkins	.333	1	0	1	2	0
Katz	.938	4	5	10	1	2
Lankford	.926	23	12	38	4	3
Mercado	1.000	1	0	1	0	0
Olivera	1.000	1	2	0	0	0
Peralta	1.000	3	0	3	0	1
Reynolds	1.000	2	1	2	0	0
Sohn	.975	33	29	48	2	6
Sosa	1.000	1	1	4	0	0
Staton	.935	32	17	55	5	10
Tice	1.000	5	3	10	0	2
Turgeon	.926	9	3	22	2	2

Shortstop	PCT	G	PO	A	E	DP
Brodbeck	.833	1	2	3	1	1
Hawkins	.833	1	1	4	1	1
Herrera	.973	25	33	77	3	15
Martinez	1.000	6	6	13	0	1
Mercado	.928	81	143	232	29	48
Peralta	.900	2	2	1	1	1
Reynolds	.875	2	2	5	1	2
Sohn	.939	14	15	47	4	5
Sosa	1.000	9	8	22	0	2

Outfield	PCT	G	PO	A	E	DP
Acevedo	.984	24	56	4	1	0
Aikin	1.000	1	1	0	0	0
Bryan	.983	48	114	4	2	1
Drake	.990	71	193	10	2	2
Fernandez	1.000	15	25	0	0	0
Franco	1.000	2	6	0	0	0
Katz	1.000	1	1	0	0	0
Lankford	1.000	18	33	1	0	0
Mercado	.971	38	95	5	3	0

	PCT	G	PO	A	E	DP
Olivera	.993	73	148	1	1	1
Pritchard	.986	39	70	2	1	0
Radack	.950	9	18	1	1	0
Spitz	.980	45	95	3	2	0
Staton	1.000	9	20	1	0	1
Thompson	.973	20	35	1	1	1
Tice	1.000	1	3	0	0	0
Turgeon	.963	15	26	0	1	0

PEORIA CHIEFS
MIDWEST LEAGUE

LOW CLASS A

Batting	B-T	HT	WT	DOB	AVG	vLH	vRH	G	AB	R	H	2B	3B	HR	RBI	BB	HBP	SH	SF	SO	SB	CS	SLG	OBP
Acevedo, Jhohan	R-R	6-1	173	3-28-93	.160	.333	.063	9	25	1	4	0	0	0	0	2	1	0	0	5	0	0	.160	.250
Aikin, Craig	L-L	5-10	175	8-19-93	.239	.200	.248	109	348	57	83	16	4	1	30	38	5	4	2	93	8	7	.316	.321
Alvarez, Eli	L-R	5-11	165	10-15-94	.323	.347	.316	116	433	70	140	36	6	6	59	53	8	1	4	96	36	15	.476	.404
Becker, Dylan	L-R	6-0	205	1-6-93	.218	.125	.236	50	147	11	32	3	1	0	13	22	7	0	2	34	0	0	.252	.343
Bryan, Vaughn	R-R	6-0	185	6-5-93	.208	.275	.189	52	183	22	38	9	2	0	13	17	0	1	1	58	4	3	.279	.274
Chinea, Chris	R-R	5-11	220	5-3-94	.312	.333	.306	99	381	40	119	24	0	6	63	22	2	0	4	64	1	1	.423	.350
Davis, Matt	R-R	5-10	175	12-8-94	.179	.400	.130	17	56	3	10	0	0	0	2	5	2	0	0	16	0	0	.250	.270
Dennard, R.J.	L-R	6-3	230	10-27-92	.229	.284	.214	110	401	43	92	19	4	5	47	43	2	0	4	110	0	0	.334	.304
Drongesen, Riley	R-R	6-2	205	5-29-92	.250	—	.250	1	4	0	1	0	0	0	0	0	0	0	0	0	0	0	.500	.250
Franco, Bladimil	R-R	6-0	170	10-29-93	.218	.222	.217	25	87	9	19	2	0	0	4	3	1	0	0	16	2	1	.241	.253
Godoy, Jose	L-R	5-11	180	10-13-94	.293	.274	.298	80	287	36	84	11	0	1	31	29	8	1	2	34	1	1	.341	.371
Martinez, Jose	R-R	5-10	150	8-15-96	.273	.250	.280	39	161	25	44	8	0	1	18	13	2	2	2	35	0	0	.342	.331
McCarvel, Ryan	R-R	6-2	180	12-23-94	.056	.000	.077	5	18	1	1	1	0	0	1	0	0	0		5	0	0	.111	
.105 O'Keefe, Brian	R-R	6-0	210	7-15-93	.258	.311	.244	101	357	50	92	25	2	13	63	52	7	0	4	78	1	1	.448	.360
Olivera, Orlando	R-R	6-0	230	10-17-90	.273	.500	.188	6	22	2	6	2	0	0	2	0	0	0	0	2	1	0	.364	.273
Peralta, Jhonny	R-R	6-2	225	5-28-82	.231	.000	.273	5	13	2	3	1	0	0	0	0	0	0	0	0	0	0	.308	.231
Pina, Leobaldo	R-R	6-2	160	6-29-94	.245	.266	.238	105	375	41	92	11	3	7	41	28	2	1	3	77	2	1	.347	.299
Sierra, Magneuris	L-L	5-11	160	4-7-96	.307	.299	.310	122	524	78	161	29	4	3	60	22	3	7	6	97	31	17	.395	.335
Sosa, Edmundo	R-R	5-11	170	3-6-96	.268	.302	.257	88	351	42	94	13	1	3	30	19	2	3	3	71	5	4	.336	.307
Spitz, Tom	R-R	6-1	180	4-16-92	.261	.277	.257	67	218	33	57	5	2	1	23	24	3	4	2	37	9	6	.317	.340
Swirchak, Josh	R-R	5-11	180	4-2-93	.177	.125	.196	22	62	5	11	1	0	0	4	5	1	0	1	20	0	0	.194	.246
Tice, Dylan	B-R	5-8	190	12-15-92	.375	.444	.348	8	32	8	12	2	0	1	6	3	0	0	0	5	0	0	.531	.429
Torres, Carlos	R-R	6-3	160	10-11-92	.268	.296	.256	51	183	18	49	9	1	1	10	9	2	2	0	33	1	3	.344	.309
Turgeon, Casey	R-R	5-10	160	9-28-92	.229	.273	.216	16	48	5	11	4	0	0	6	7	1	0	1	7	1	0	.313	.333

Pitching	B-T	HT	WT	DOB	W	L	ERA	G	GS	CG	SV	IP	H	R	ER	HR	BB	SO	AVG	vLH	vRH	K/9	BB/9
Alcantara, Sandy	R-R	6-4	170	9-7-95	5	7	4.08	17	17	0	0	90	78	49	41	4	45	119	.228	.219	.235	11.86	4.48
Beck, Landon	R-R	6-3	215	12-9-92	0	2	2.70	10	0	0	4	13	9	5	4	0	4	20	.184	.300	.103	13.50	2.70
Bowen, Brady	R-L	6-1	160	7-24-92	0	0	8.31	6	0	0	0	9	16	10	8	0	2	6	.390	.333	.414	6.23	2.08
Bray, Tyler	R-R	6-5	200	10-3-91	3	5	3.84	42	0	0	7	61	58	32	26	1	25	73	.248	.361	.168	10.77	3.69
De La Cruz, Steven	R-R	6-1	185	4-26-93	8	1	3.30	49	0	0	7	60	48	24	22	4	31	57	.219	.260	.187	8.55	4.65
DeLorenzo, Jordan	L-L	6-1	205	9-8-92	0	0	16.20	2	0	0	0	2	5	3	3	1	1	0	.556	1.000	.500	0.00	5.40
Fernandez, Junior	R-R	6-1	180	3-2-97	6	5	3.33	14	14	0	0	78	71	37	29	3	34	63	.244	.230	.255	7.24	3.91
Frey, Nick	R-R	6-4	185	8-30-91	3	2	4.64	28	0	0	4	54	70	31	28	3	12	44	.313	.339	.287	7.29	1.99
Gallardo, Steven	R-R	5-11	180	10-28-92	1	3	5.32	17	0	0	1	24	26	14	14	3	5	28	.263	.362	.173	10.65	1.90
Gonzalez, Derian	R-R	6-3	190	1-31-95	5	5	2.39	15	15	0	0	75	65	24	20	1	33	70	.236	.242	.236	8.36	3.94
Harrison, Luke	R-R	6-1	225	2-25-93	3	2	2.42	26	0	0	4	45	34	13	12	4	15	43	.205	.211	.200	8.66	3.02
Hawkins, Chandler	L-L	6-1	170	2-28-93	0	0	2.38	8	0	0	0	11	10	3	3	0	3	14	.238	.188	.269	11.12	2.38
Helsley, Ryan	R-R	6-1	195	7-18-94	10	2	1.61	17	17	0	0	95	77	22	17	3	19	109	.216	.250	.186	10.33	1.80
Holt, Harley	R-R	6-0	165	10-28-91	0	5	2.96	23	2	0	1	49	52	22	16	1	8	36	.269	.299	.245	6.66	1.48
Kilichowski, John	L-L	6-5	217	5-17-94	1	3	3.74	6	1	0	0	34	32	16	14	4	4	31	.250	.438	.188	8.29	1.07
Kuebel, Sasha	R-L	6-1	200	7-28-92	0	0	3.97	12	0	0	0	11	12	8	5	2	1	6	.255	.333	.219	4.76	0.79
Leitao, Brennan	R-R	6-1	205	6-21-93	6	7	4.08	18	17	1	0	110	120	57	50	12	21	90	.276	.283	.259	7.34	1.71
Martinez, Dailyn	R-R	6-2	180	4-19-93	5	5	5.78	12	12	0	0	67	86	48	43	5	16	68	.314	.346	.285	9.13	2.15
Perez, Juan	R-R	6-2	195	7-22-95	3	3	5.05	20	8	0	1	57	61	34	32	7	33	54	.272	.240	.298	8.53	5.21
Rodriguez, Jorge L.	R-R	6-2	175	3-18-94	4	1	2.17	27	6	0	1	71	67	23	17	2	20	66	.252	.344	.167	8.41	2.55
Velazco, Gerwuins	R-R	6-1	190	10-7-91	2	1	6.75	6	0	0	0	11	15	9	8	1	4	5	.319	.231	.429	4.22	3.38
Ward, Davis	R-R	6-0	196	2-23-92	0	0	4.02	8	0	0	1	16	18	7	7	0	2	19	.281	.310	.257	10.91	1.15
Wheatley, Bobby	L-L	6-5	220	2-4-92	1	1	3.09	4	0	0	0	12	17	6	4	0	4	8	.378	.421	.346	6.17	3.09
Williams, Ronnie	R-R	6-0	170	1-6-96	1	3	4.29	6	6	0	0	36	31	19	17	7	17	36	.231	.181	.290	9.08	4.29
Wirsu, Josh	R-R	6-0	190	9-4-93	1	2	2.31	16	0	0	3	23	22	7	6	0	8	30	.244	.303	.211	11.57	3.09
Woodford, Jake	R-R	6-4	210	10-28-96	5	5	3.31	21	21	0	0	109	104	47	40	7	37	82	.254	.258	.251	6.79	3.06

Fielding

Catcher	PCT	G	PO	A	E	DP	PB
Chinea	.990	21	179	10	2	2	2
Godoy	.996	56	461	45	2	3	2
O'Keefe	.990	67	546	49	6	7	2

	PCT	G	PO	A	E	DP
Dennard	.989	104	824	50	10	89
McCarvel	1.000	2	15	1	0	1
Olivera	1.000	2	6	1	0	0

	PCT	G	PO	A	E	DP
Davis	.840	4	8	13	4	3
Godoy	1.000	1	1	1	0	0
Pina	—	1	0	0	0	0
Sosa	—	1	0	0	0	0
Swirchak	.938	12	9	21	2	4
Tice	1.000	5	8	17	0	1
Turgeon	1.000	3	4	10	0	2

First Base	PCT	G	PO	A	E	DP
Chinea	.971	35	255	11	8	22

Second Base	PCT	G	PO	A	E	DP
Alvarez	.947	113	173	305	27	69
Becker	.926	8	7	18	2	3

Third Base	PCT	G	PO	A	E	DP
Becker	.903	38	18	38	6	8
Davis	.947	7	3	15	1	1
Godoy	—	1	0	0	0	0
Peralta	1.000	2	0	1	0	1
Pina	.930	90	59	128	14	17
Swirchak	.875	3	2	5	1	1
Tice	.667	2	1	1	1	1
Turgeon	1.000	6	3	12	0	1

Shortstop	PCT	G	PO	A	E	DP
Martinez	.976	39	53	112	4	26
Peralta	1.000	2	2	4	0	0
Pina	.965	14	27	28	2	8
Sosa	.958	85	122	223	15	48
Turgeon	.800	4	0	4	1	0

Outfield	PCT	G	PO	A	E	DP
Acevedo	1.000	8	14	0	0	0
Aikin	.985	105	190	7	3	1
Becker	1.000	2	7	0	0	0

Bryan	.974	44	73	2	2	0
Davis	1.000	6	7	1	0	0
Franco	.917	19	33	0	3	0
Olivera	1.000	2	3	1	0	0
Pina	—	1	0	0	0	0
Sierra	.964	121	286	11	11	2
Spitz	.985	63	121	9	2	4
Swirchak	.923	8	11	1	1	0
Tice	1.000	2	0	2	0	0
Torres	.967	51	84	5	3	1

STATE COLLEGE SPIKES
NEW YORK-PENN LEAGUE

SHORT-SEASON

Batting	B-T	HT	WT	DOB	AVG	vLH	vRH	G	AB	R	H	2B	3B	HR	RBI	BB	HBP	SH	SF	SO	SB	CS	SLG	OBP
Bautista, Ricardo	L-R	6-0	185	12-27-95	.249	.224	.259	65	233	30	58	14	3	2	28	23	2	0	2	82	1	0	.361	.319
Davis, Matt	R-R	5-10	175	12-8-94	.211	.154	.240	9	38	4	8	0	0	0	3	1	1	0	0	8	1	0	.211	.250
Drongesen, Riley	R-R	6-2	205	5-29-92	.179	.059	.213	25	78	10	14	5	1	1	9	8	1	0	1	16	1	0	.308	.261
Edman, Tommy	B-R	5-10	180	5-9-95	.286	.351	.258	66	255	61	73	14	5	4	33	48	3	0	4	29	19	3	.427	.400
Fennell, Mick	L-R	5-10	190	4-30-94	.256	.212	.273	42	121	22	31	7	1	0	11	18	3	5	0	13	1	1	.331	.366
Franco, Bladimil	R-R	6-0	170	10-29-93	.213	.179	.231	22	80	9	17	4	0	0	8	6	0	0	0	15	0	1	.263	.267
Gonzalez, Yariel	B-R	6-1	190	6-1-94	.260	.250	.263	22	77	3	20	4	0	0	9	10	0	1	2	15	2	0	.312	.337
Hawkins, Joey	R-R	5-11	170	3-10-93	.429	.500	.400	3	7	0	3	1	0	0	2	0	0	0	0	1	0	0	.571	.429
Hudzina, Danny	R-R	5-11	185	2-27-94	.239	.234	.241	56	205	21	49	13	0	4	24	13	2	2	1	23	1	0	.361	.290
Jackson, Vince	L-L	6-4	190	2-4-94	.233	.284	.214	70	266	39	62	13	4	4	45	26	9	0	4	58	16	7	.357	.318
Martin, Daniel	R-R	5-11	180	8-5-94	.286	.000	.357	13	35	11	10	4	0	0	3	6	0	0	2	5	2	0	.400	.432
Martinez, Jeremy	R-R	5-11	195	12-29-94	.325	.356	.311	57	194	28	63	14	2	1	32	32	3	1	5	16	1	1	.433	.419
Martinez, Jose	B-R	5-10	150	8-15-96	.276	.250	.288	26	98	15	27	2	0	1	9	13	0	0	1	12	0	4	.327	.357
McCarvel, Ryan	R-R	6-2	230	12-23-94	.224	.192	.238	65	237	31	53	8	1	10	45	26	6	0	3	62	1	1	.392	.313
Ray, Anthony	L-R	6-1	165	3-3-95	.257	.389	.210	45	136	21	35	4	1	1	12	8	1	3	1	14	3	1	.324	.301
Rivera, Chris	R-R	5-11	150	3-10-95	.147	.182	.130	13	34	2	5	0	1	0	1	3	0	0	0	10	1	0	.206	.216
Rodriguez, Elier	R-R	6-2	215	2-15-95	.279	.229	.296	49	183	21	51	8	0	2	26	19	3	1	0	38	3	0	.355	.356
Swirchak, Josh	R-R	5-11	180	4-2-93	.186	.263	.150	16	59	8	11	2	0	0	5	5	1	0	0	9	0	0	.220	.262
Tice, Dylan	B-R	5-8	190	12-15-92	.281	.400	.234	20	89	16	25	6	0	2	10	5	4	1	0	14	2	1	.416	.347
Young, Andy	R-R	6-0	195	5-10-94	.261	.269	.257	42	161	26	42	3	5	3	19	10	6	2	3	44	3	0	.398	.322

Pitching	B-T	HT	WT	DOB	W	L	ERA	G	GS	CG	SV	IP	H	R	ER	HR	BB	SO	AVG	vLH	vRH	K/9	BB/9
Almonte, Max	R-R	6-1	205	3-4-92	3	1	2.75	18	0	0	1	36	34	16	11	0	11	27	.252	.302	.208	6.75	2.75
Bowen, Brady	R-L	6-1	160	7-24-92	0	0	3.23	18	0	0	9	31	30	11	11	2	5	32	.252	.250	.253	9.39	1.47
Carter, Eric	R-R	5-11	202	7-7-92	0	0	2.38	17	0	0	9	23	18	8	6	1	4	26	.212	.206	.216	10.32	1.59
Cross, Carson	R-R	6-5	205	1-24-92	5	6	3.24	14	14	0	0	81	80	39	29	4	27	53	.261	.242	.282	5.91	3.01
DeLorenzo, Jordan	L-L	6-1	205	9-8-92	1	2	2.90	15	1	0	1	31	28	11	10	2	12	38	.237	.265	.226	11.03	3.48
Dobzanski, Bryan	R-R	6-4	220	8-31-95	4	6	3.93	14	13	0	0	71	81	36	31	3	26	37	.286	.288	.285	4.69	3.30
Escudero, Jhonatan	R-R	6-1	165	7-7-93	1	0	1.04	10	0	0	0	17	10	4	2	1	9	25	.154	.227	.116	12.98	4.67
Farinaro, Steven	R-R	6-0	170	8-18-95	9	1	3.46	14	14	0	0	83	100	38	32	0	18	53	.301	.319	.288	5.72	1.94
Hicks, Jordan	R-R	6-2	185	9-6-96	4	1	1.76	6	6	0	0	31	25	8	6	0	16	22	.217	.231	.200	6.46	4.70
Holt, Harley	R-R	6-0	165	10-28-91	1	0	5.06	4	2	0	0	16	16	7	6	1	3	4	.364	.462	.323	3.38	2.53
Jones, Connor	R-R	6-3	200	10-10-94	0	0	4.22	7	0	0	1	11	15	6	5	0	2	8	.341	.211	.440	6.75	1.69
Kilichowski, John	L-L	6-5	217	5-17-94	1	1	0.92	5	4	0	0	20	15	4	2	0	11	20	.214	.267	.200	9.15	5.03
Martinez, Dailyn	R-R	6-2	170	4-19-93	2	1	0.96	3	3	0	0	19	17	6	2	0	3	17	.233	.034	.364	8.20	1.45
Medina, Yeison	R-R	6-2	210	10-2-92	1	0	0.00	1	0	0	0	2	1	0	0	0	1	1	.167	.500	.000	4.50	4.50
Perez, Dewin	L-L	6-0	175	9-29-94	3	5	5.02	14	8	0	1	52	47	36	29	1	35	43	.242	.158	.277	7.44	6.06
Rowland, Robby	B-R	6-4	215	12-15-91	0	0	4.50	3	0	0	0	4	3	2	2	0	1	5	.214	.143	.286	11.25	2.25
Tomchick, Greg	R-R	6-4	200	12-30-92	1	1	5.57	17	3	0	1	32	30	21	20	2	13	20	.259	.326	.219	5.57	3.62
Trayner, Spencer	R-R	6-0	160	12-22-94	1	0	0.52	18	1	0	4	34	23	4	2	3	5	21	.190	.176	.200	5.50	1.31
Velazco, Gerwuins	R-R	6-1	190	10-7-91	3	0	3.38	13	0	0	2	37	34	16	10	2	7	23	.309	.419	.239	7.76	2.36
Wheatley, Bobby	L-L	6-5	220	2-4-92	3	0	0.50	9	0	0	1	18	18	5	1	0	7	14	.269	.440	.167	7.00	3.50
Williams, Ronnie	R-R	6-0	170	1-6-96	4	2	2.72	7	7	0	0	46	37	17	14	1	7	33	.213	.205	.218	6.41	1.36

Fielding

C: Drongesen 15, Martinez 48, McCarvel 8, Rivera 13. 1B: Drongesen 5, Gonzalez 1, McCarvel 46, Rodriguez 30. 2B: Davis 2, Edman 18, Gonzalez 8, Martin 10, Martinez 2, Swirchak 9, Tice 5, Young 24. 3B: Davis 6, Gonzalez 8, Hudzina 53, Rodriguez 1, Swirchak 2, Tice 7. SS: Edman 42, Hawkins 2, Martinez 22, Young 12. OF: Bautista 62, Drongesen 1, Fennell 36, Franco 16, Gonzalez 6, Jackson 62, Martin 1, Ray 43, Swirchak 1, Tice 8, Young 6.

JOHNSON CITY CARDINALS
APPALACHIAN LEAGUE

ROOKIE

Batting	B-T	HT	WT	DOB	AVG	vLH	vRH	G	AB	R	H	2B	3B	HR	RBI	BB	HBP	SH	SF	SO	SB	CS	SLG	OBP
Asbury, De'Andre	R-R	6-3	170	8-5-95	.247	.293	.229	47	150	23	37	8	3	2	16	13	5	3	2	46	4	2	.380	.324
Bandes, Luis	R-R	6-1	200	5-15-96	.231	.200	.245	44	156	22	36	7	0	4	17	5	5	0	1	29	0	1	.353	.275
Billings, Shane	R-L	5-11	190	12-14-94	.241	.208	.254	50	191	27	46	4	1	0	18	8	0	0	2	34	8	6	.272	.269
Brodbeck, Andrew	L-R	5-10	185	1-22-93	.273	.167	.313	6	22	3	6	1	0	1	2	3	2	0	0	2	1	2	.455	.407
Cordoba, Allen	R-R	6-1	175	12-6-95	.362	.345	.369	50	196	49	71	16	5	0	18	21	2	0	1	19	22	4	.495	.427
Davis, J.R.	R-R	5-10	190	8-10-94	.333	.204	.380	46	186	40	62	10	2	3	13	5	4	0	1	22	11	6	.457	.362
Denton, Bryce	R-R	6-0	190	8-1-97	.282	.161	.329	54	202	34	57	7	0	4	26	20	3	0	0	37	2	1	.376	.356

ST. LOUIS CARDINALS

Batting	B-T	HT	WT	DOB	AVG	vLH	vRH	G	AB	R	H	2B	3B	HR	RBI	BB	HBP	SH	SF	SO	SB	CS	SLG	OBP
Fiedler, Matt	R-R	5-10	195	3-22-95	.325	.339	.319	52	197	30	64	20	0	4	31	19	2	0	2	32	8	1	.487	.386
Garcia, Erik	R-R	5-11	215	3-23-93	.213	.200	.220	25	89	10	19	5	0	1	12	6	0	0	0	36	0	0	.303	.263
Gonzalez, Yariel	B-R	6-1	190	6-1-94	.308	.333	.300	19	78	10	24	9	0	1	11	6	0	0	1	10	0	0	.462	.353
Hawkins, Joey	R-R	5-11	170	3-10-93	.120	.250	.073	23	75	7	9	2	0	1	4	5	0	1	1	28	0	1	.187	.173
Knizner, Andrew	R-R	6-1	200	2-3-95	.319	.333	.314	53	185	35	59	12	1	6	42	21	14	0	2	21	0	0	.492	.423
Lopes, Caleb	R-R	5-8	195	7-21-95	.336	.333	.337	40	131	19	44	11	0	0	22	30	10	2	1	24	2	0	.420	.488
Lopez, Joshua	R-R	5-10	188	3-4-96	.305	.239	.333	42	154	22	47	6	2	5	33	20	2	0	2	41	1	0	.468	.388
Newman, Hunter	R-R	6-2	210	12-20-93	.279	.412	.227	15	61	11	17	4	0	1	11	3	1	0	1	12	0	0	.393	.318
Rivera, Jonathan	R-R	6-1	185	4-27-97	.257	.256	.257	41	144	18	37	7	3	3	24	4	0	0	0	51	2	0	.410	.277
Torres, Carlos	R-R	6-3	160	10-1-92	.240	.667	.182	7	25	3	6	0	0	0	3	0	0	0	1	7	1	0	.240	.231
Zavala, Stephen	R-R	5-8	175	5-2-93	.141	.105	.154	24	71	10	10	3	0	1	3	12	4	1	0	18	1	0	.225	.299

Pitching	B-T	HT	WT	DOB	W	L	ERA	G	GS	CG	SV	IP	H	R	ER	HR	BB	SO	AVG	vLH	vRH	K/9	BB/9
Arias, Estarlin	R-R	6-1	175	5-22-94	4	0	2.15	19	0	0	6	29	22	7	7	1	9	27	.206	.220	.193	8.28	2.76
Castano, Daniel	L-L	6-4	230	9-17-94	2	5	6.19	12	11	0	0	48	63	40	33	6	12	34	.317	.231	.347	6.38	2.25
Gonzalez, Noel	R-R	5-11	190	2-27-94	3	1	3.05	18	0	0	1	21	24	11	7	1	11	20	.286	.316	.261	8.71	4.79
Hicks, Jordan	R-R	6-2	185	9-6-96	2	1	4.20	6	6	0	0	30	33	20	14	1	13	20	.292	.322	.259	6.00	3.90
Mateo, Julio	R-R	6-3	180	9-29-95	1	2	8.03	16	0	0	0	25	26	24	22	7	12	23	.274	.188	.317	8.39	4.38
MaVorhis, Levi	R-R	6-2	215	7-31-94	2	0	3.09	18	1	0	2	35	28	14	12	3	9	22	.220	.137	.276	5.66	2.31
Medina, Yeison	R-R	6-2	210	10-2-92	4	2	3.58	18	0	0	3	33	39	23	13	1	10	28	.289	.286	.292	7.71	2.76
Oca, David	L-L	5-10	165	7-4-95	2	3	5.96	10	10	0	0	45	64	43	30	1	19	38	.330	.333	.328	7.54	3.77
Oxnevard, Ian	R-L	6-4	205	10-3-96	5	3	3.38	12	12	0	0	72	80	32	27	7	13	57	.283	.318	.267	7.13	1.63
Parra, Frederis	R-R	6-3	162	10-22-94	3	5	2.53	11	10	1	0	64	68	33	18	3	7	36	.269	.319	.229	5.06	0.98
Santos, Ramon	R-R	6-2	160	9-20-94	3	3	4.53	13	8	0	1	50	59	38	25	5	20	44	.282	.248	.320	7.97	3.62
Sexton, Austin	R-R	6-2	185	7-17-94	0	1	3.32	6	6	0	0	19	19	10	7	1	5	13	.260	.241	.273	6.16	2.37
Shew, Anthony	R-R	6-2	191	11-3-93	0	1	6.66	15	1	0	0	26	43	22	19	3	7	21	.374	.340	.397	7.36	2.45
Siomkin, Keaton	R-R	5-11	205	6-17-92	2	1	3.60	15	0	0	0	20	19	11	8	0	3	26	.247	.314	.190	11.70	1.35
Tilley, Leland	R-R	6-3	215	1-9-92	2	0	3.09	18	0	0	4	23	25	9	8	0	12	25	.281	.302	.250	9.64	4.63
Tomchick, Greg	R-R	6-4	200	12-30-92	1	1	4.15	2	0	0	0	4	5	2	2	0	0	4	.238	.200	.250	8.31	0.00
Vance, Ross	L-L	6-0	180	12-7-91	3	0	2.48	14	3	0	0	40	34	14	11	2	8	54	.225	.164	.267	12.15	1.80

Fielding

C: Garcia 8, Knizner 21, Lopez 21, Zavala 20. **1B:** Bandes 18, Garcia 13, Gonzalez 5, Knizner 19, Newman 15. **2B:** Brodbeck 6, Davis 46, Gonzalez 1, Hawkins 1, Lopes 18. **3B:** Denton 41, Gonzalez 12, Hawkins 3, Lopes 13. **SS:** Cordoba 50, Gonzalez 1, Hawkins 20, Lopes 1. **OF:** Asbury-Heath 46, Bandes 20, Billings 49, Fiedler 52, Rivera 36, Torres 7.

GCL CARDINALS   ROOKIE
GULF COAST LEAGUE

Batting	B-T	HT	WT	DOB	AVG	vLH	vRH	G	AB	R	H	2B	3B	HR	RBI	BB	HBP	SH	SF	SO	SB	CS	SLG	OBP
Balbuena, Starlin	R-R	6-2	175	3-4-98	.253	.263	.252	45	154	36	39	9	2	3	23	9	3	3	0	45	2	2	.396	.307
Carlson, Dylan	B-L	6-3	195	10-23-98	.251	.238	.253	50	183	30	46	13	3	3	22	16	1	0	1	52	4	2	.404	.313
Figuera, Edwin	R-R	5-10	160	9-2-97	.271	.357	.260	40	118	12	32	3	0	0	10	7	5	0	1	19	0	2	.297	.363
Flores, Luis	B-R	6-0	190	10-22-96	.263	.000	.278	33	76	11	20	4	0	0	5	6	1	2	1	23	1	2	.316	.321
Lancaster, Tyler	L-R	6-4	195	8-1-94	.148	.000	.160	19	54	9	8	1	0	3	6	8	1	0	1	9	0	0	.333	.266
Murders, J.D.	L-R	6-2	180	10-6-97	.219	.000	.239	24	73	7	16	4	1	0	7	6	0	0	0	20	0	0	.301	.278
Newman, Hunter	R-R	6-2	210	12-20-93	.297	.286	.299	21	74	11	22	4	1	2	11	8	4	0	1	13	0	0	.459	.391
Ortega, Dennis	R-R	6-2	180	6-11-97	.357	.500	.337	36	115	23	41	4	2	0	16	15	2	1	0	13	7	4	.426	.439
Pena, Brayan	B-R	5-9	240	1-7-82	.333	—	.333	3	9	3	3	1	0	1	3	0	0	0	0	1	0	0	.778	.333
Perez, Delvin	R-R	6-3	175	11-24-98	.294	.176	.308	43	163	19	48	8	4	0	19	12	3	1	1	28	12	1	.393	.352
Robbins, Walker	L-L	6-3	215	11-18-97	.185	.000	.220	30	108	8	20	1	0	0	6	5	1	0	1	31	3	0	.194	.226
Rodriguez, Carlos	B-R	6-2	215	1-6-97	.242	.231	.244	28	95	12	23	2	3	1	7	14	0	0	0	30	0	1	.358	.333
Rosendo, Sanel	R-R	6-2	205	5-7-97	.177	.091	.196	24	62	4	11	2	0	1	5	10	3	0	1	21	0	0	.258	.316
Talavera, Carlos	B-R	6-1	175	9-20-96	.221	.222	.221	40	95	12	21	2	1	0	8	7	0	1	0	22	2	2	.263	.275
Trosclair, Stefan	B-R	6-2	195	7-24-94	.279	.385	.267	40	129	20	36	6	0	5	22	13	8	0	3	25	2	2	.442	.373
Whalen, Brady	B-R	6-4	180	1-15-98	.178	.000	.191	25	73	7	13	2	0	1	8	11	0	1	0	9	0	1	.247	.265
Wilson, Irving	R-R	5-10	168	8-13-96	.223	.167	.232	30	94	9	21	6	0	0	11	10	4	0	1	23	0	0	.287	.321
Wisdom, Patrick	R-R	6-2	220	8-27-91	.500	.000	.600	3	6	2	3	0	0	0	3	3	0	0	0	1	0	0	.500	.667
Ynfante, Wadye	R-R	6-0	160	8-15-97	.059	.342	.059	6	17	1	1	0	0	0	0	1	0	1	0	6	0	1	.059	.111
Young, Andy	R-R	6-0	175	5-10-94	.323	.400	.308	11	31	7	10	2	1	0	5	7	4	1	0	3	0	0	.452	.500

Pitching	B-T	HT	WT	DOB	W	L	ERA	G	GS	CG	SV	IP	H	R	ER	HR	BB	SO	AVG	vLH	vRH	K/9	BB/9
Alvarez, Juan	R-R	6-4	180	12-28-96	4	2	2.63	11	6	0	1	48	43	15	14	1	20	30	.243	.250	.238	5.63	3.75
Anderson, Will	R-R	6-3	205	8-26-92	3	0	2.00	7	1	0	0	9	9	2	2	1	0	6	.265	.286	.250	6.00	0.00
Bohannan, Silas	R-R	6-3	245	1-26-93	2	1	5.57	18	0	0	0	21	35	19	13	0	12	12	.393	.394	.393	5.14	5.14
Calvano, Robert	R-R	6-2	225	2-27-93	1	1	6.06	15	0	0	1	16	16	16	11	2	9	14	.254	.280	.237	7.71	4.96
Casadilla, Franyel	R-R	6-3	175	4-5-97	5	2	2.32	11	9	1	0	50	50	16	13	1	16	35	.263	.254	.268	6.26	2.86
Changarotty, Will	R-R	6-0	165	10-19-95	1	0	2.37	16	1	0	3	30	29	13	8	3	7	31	.244	.256	.238	9.20	2.08
Ciavarella, Anthony	L-L	6-2	180	8-13-93	2	3	2.09	11	8	0	0	39	40	20	9	3	12	36	.263	.273	.259	8.38	2.79
Evans, Jacob	L-L	6-2	215	11-27-93	0	0	0.00	2	1	0	0	5	5	1	0	0	0	5	.238	.286	.214	9.00	0.00
Gallen, Zac	R-R	6-2	191	8-3-95	0	0	1.86	6	3	0	1	10	7	2	2	0	0	15	.194	.083	.250	13.97	0.00
Gordon, Robbie	R-R	6-2	205	6-8-93	4	1	2.45	16	0	0	2	22	16	6	6	1	9	27	.203	.182	.217	11.05	3.68
Hefner, Jeremy	R-R	6-4	180	3-11-86	0	1	3.00	2	2	0	0	6	4	2	2	2	0	9	.182	.143	.200	13.50	0.00
Hudson, Dakota	R-R	6-5	215	9-15-94	1	0	0.00	4	1	0	0	4	1	0	0	0	0	9	.235	.600	.083	20.25	0.00
Jones, Connor	R-R	6-3	200	10-10-94	0	0	2.25	4	0	0	0	4	3	1	1	0	1	3	.231	.500	.111	6.75	2.25

Pitching	B-T	HT	WT	DOB	W	L	ERA	G	GS	CG	SV	IP	H	R	ER	HR	BB	SO	AVG	vLH	vRH	K/9	BB/9
Lee, Thomas	R-R	6-1	190	10-20-89	1	0	0.00	3	0	0	0	6	8	3	0	0	1	5	.296	.000	.381	7.50	1.50
Morales, Andrew	R-R	6-0	185	1-16-93	0	1	5.79	2	2	0	0	5	5	3	3	1	3	10	.263	.500	.154	19.29	5.79
Mulford, Jonathan	R-R	6-2	210	8-16-94	1	2	2.29	16	0	0	6	20	13	6	5	0	5	19	.188	.160	.205	8.69	2.29
O'Reilly, Mike	R-R	5-11	180	9-3-94	3	1	2.48	11	4	0	1	40	35	12	11	1	5	38	.240	.236	.242	8.55	1.13
Reyes, Artie	R-R	5-11	185	4-6-92	0	1	4.26	2	2	0	0	6	8	4	3	0	1	5	.320	.500	.286	7.11	1.42
Salazar, Paul	R-R	6-2	195	5-23-97	0	0	11.88	7	0	0	0	8	12	12	11	0	15	6	.364	.333	.381	6.48	16.20
Schlesener, Jacob	L-L	6-3	175	10-8-96	1	3	9.00	11	5	0	0	19	15	22	19	0	34	19	.224	.211	.229	9.00	16.11
Seijas, Alvaro	R-R	5-8	175	10-10-98	3	2	3.06	10	9	0	0	50	48	21	17	4	13	33	.249	.231	.258	5.94	2.34
Then, Jery	R-R	6-2	195	5-6-95	0	0	3.00	3	0	0	0	3	1	1	1	0	1	1	.111	.000	.200	3.00	3.00
Thompson, Colton	L-L	6-0	190	7-22-92	1	0	1.03	16	0	0	5	26	16	5	3	0	10	29	.182	.179	.183	9.91	3.42
Wirsu, Josh	R-R	6-0	190	9-4-93	0	0	0.00	3	0	0	0	2	0	0	0	0	0	1	.000	.000	.000	4.50	0.00

Fielding

C: Lancaster 7, Ortega 29, Pena 1, Wilson 24. **1B:** Lancaster 5, Newman 11, Rodriguez 11, Trosclair 31. **2B:** Figuera 18, Flores 16, Murders 10, Talavera 1, Trosclair 3, Whalen 14, Young 4. **3B:** Balbuena 39, Figuera 5, Murders 1, Trosclair 5, Whalen 5, Wisdom 3, Young 2. **SS:** Balbuena 7, Figuera 13, Perez 40, Whalen 1. **OF:** Carlson 50, Figuera 7, Flores 15, Ortega 2, Perez 1, Robbins 29, Rodriguez 17, Rosendo 19, Talavera 36, Ynfante 5, Young 2.

DSL CARDINALS
ROOKIE
DOMINICAN SUMMER LEAGUE

Batting	B-T	HT	WT	DOB	AVG	vLH	vRH	G	AB	R	H	2B	3B	HR	RBI	BB	HBP	SH	SF	SO	SB	CS	SLG	OBP
Castillo, Moises	R-R	6-1	170	7-14-99	.244	.271	.236	62	209	41	51	11	2	0	23	35	5	5	2	47	4	2	.316	.363
Cedeno, Leandro	R-R	6-2	195	8-22-98	.290	.278	.293	47	193	32	56	15	4	4	30	12	1	0	2	42	0	0	.472	.332
Cotes, Oscar	R-R	6-2	165	3-31-97	.240	.158	.259	33	100	16	24	5	2	1	12	5	3	4	0	27	2	0	.360	.296
Del Rio, Diomedes	L-L	5-10	160	9-15-97	.163	.160	.164	31	86	11	14	2	2	0	8	12	4	3	1	25	3	0	.233	.291
Delgado, Esequiel	B-R	6-1	185	10-20-97	.205	.204	.205	59	195	37	40	3	3	2	18	47	3	2	1	38	9	3	.282	.366
Gomez, Dariel	L-R	6-4	190	7-15-96	.234	.235	.234	43	141	13	33	14	1	0	24	25	1	0	1	25	0	0	.348	.351
Jimenez, William	R-R	5-11	180	1-23-96	.236	.080	.282	41	110	22	26	2	1	0	16	18	2	5	1	20	8	2	.273	.351
Linares, Hector	R-R	6-0	160	1-13-97	.273	.385	.238	18	55	5	15	1	1	1	9	5	0	1	0	18	0	0	.382	.333
Luis, Carlos	R-R	6-4	180	8-22-96	.313	.355	.300	37	131	26	41	4	3	1	16	11	3	0	2	35	0	0	.412	.374
Luna, Andres	R-R	5-10	175	7-17-97	.353	.500	.308	5	17	4	6	2	0	0	1	3	1	0	0	2	0	2	.471	.476
Machado, Jonathan	L-L	5-9	155	1-21-99	.209	.400	.175	17	67	10	14	4	1	0	7	7	0	0	0	10	2	1	.299	.284
Montero, Elehuris	R-R	6-3	195	8-17-98	.260	.269	.257	61	227	41	59	14	2	1	26	28	4	1	2	51	2	1	.352	.349
Ozuna, Raffy	R-R	6-2	180	9-6-98	.181	.220	.171	50	193	27	35	12	2	2	18	26	0	1	1	74	0	2	.295	.277
Rodriguez, Julio	R-R	6-0	197	6-11-97	.322	.216	.358	40	143	30	46	10	3	7	37	19	3	0	5	19	0	0	.580	.400
Sanchez, Brian	R-R	6-2	180	4-18-96	.349	.385	.339	61	232	49	81	13	5	15	76	31	7	0	5	65	0	1	.642	.433
Soto, Carlos	L-R	6-2	220	4-27-99	.303	.161	.368	30	99	17	30	6	0	1	10	25	1	0	2	17	0	0	.394	.441
Wilson, Irving	R-R	5-10	168	8-13-96	.231	.000	.273	11	39	6	9	1	0	0	7	9	0	0	1	6	0	0	.256	.367
Ynfante, Wadye	R-R	6-0	160	8-15-97	.331	.342	.329	49	181	51	60	15	2	1	27	29	4	0	3	40	9	0	.453	.429

Pitching	B-T	HT	WT	DOB	W	L	ERA	G	GS	CG	SV	IP	H	R	ER	HR	BB	SO	AVG	vLH	vRH	K/9	BB/9
Blanco, Fabian	L-L	6-0	165	12-22-97	4	2	2.15	21	0	0	8	29	11	8	7	1	17	45	.112	.150	.103	13.81	5.22
Cordero, Diego	L-L	6-3	165	9-8-97	1	0	3.57	10	7	0	1	35	31	20	14	1	13	36	.238	.208	.249	9.17	3.31
De Jesus, Noel	R-R	6-3	181	1-8-97	6	2	1.96	13	10	0	1	60	53	18	13	1	15	48	.237	.320	.195	7.24	2.26
Garcia, Jesus	R-R	6-4	185	10-24-97	4	0	6.63	15	0	0	0	19	30	22	14	1	15	13	.353	.406	.321	6.16	7.11
Gonzalez, Junior	R-R	6-3	175	11-7-96	4	5	5.20	15	13	0	0	64	74	41	37	4	11	44	.291	.255	.314	6.19	1.55
Lugo, Cristhian	R-R	6-3	190	5-5-97	1	0	4.91	20	0	0	0	26	26	17	14	1	9	26	.257	.343	.212	9.12	3.16
Madera, Wilman	R-R	6-3	175	3-10-99	1	2	5.40	17	0	0	1	22	24	15	13	0	16	20	.286	.261	.295	8.31	6.65
Nicacio, Winston	R-R	6-2	180	12-29-96	3	3	4.80	14	10	0	0	54	54	40	29	2	36	53	.251	.269	.243	8.78	5.96
Oviedo, Johan	R-R	6-6	210	3-2-98	0	1	1.66	7	7	0	0	22	19	8	4	0	6	29	.238	.148	.283	12.05	2.49
Pereira, Wilfredo	R-R	6-0	175	4-26-99	2	1	2.27	18	0	0	0	36	40	13	9	0	7	27	.288	.327	.264	6.81	1.77
Perez, Enrique	L-L	6-2	180	8-10-97	2	2	2.51	27	0	0	1	43	29	15	12	1	17	40	.191	.114	.214	8.37	3.56
Pirela, Brian	R-R	6-0	180	1-19-98	3	2	2.19	14	0	0	0	25	16	7	6	0	12	33	.180	.200	.169	12.04	4.38
Ramirez, Edwar	R-R	6-3	190	3-15-98	5	2	4.17	13	10	0	0	58	67	33	27	1	14	47	.289	.293	.287	7.25	2.16
Rondon, Angel	R-R	6-3	180	12-1-97	2	2	2.79	14	7	0	1	42	39	18	13	0	13	50	.236	.296	.207	10.71	2.79
Seijas, Alvaro	R-R	5-8	175	10-10-98	2	0	4.19	4	4	0	0	19	20	10	9	0	6	22	.260	.095	.321	10.24	2.79
Solano, Enmanuel	R-R	6-1	160	9-23-98	1	1	3.86	11	0	0	1	23	24	11	10	1	4	17	.267	.212	.298	6.56	1.54
Tejada, Estalin	R-R	6-4	200	6-23-95	1	0	4.00	16	0	0	4	18	20	10	8	0	7	24	.282	.348	.250	12.00	3.50
Ventura, Francis	R-R	6-2	195	7-22-99	3	1	1.86	9	3	0	2	29	21	10	6	0	9	25	.198	.257	.169	7.76	2.79

Fielding

C: Cedeno 13, Rodriguez 36, Soto 16, Wilson 11. **1B:** Cedeno 31, Cotes 3, Gomez 39, Rodriguez 4. **2B:** Castillo 16, Cotes 6, Delgado 54. **3B:** Cotes 12, Linares 2, Montero 60. **SS:** Castillo 45, Cotes 7, Ozuna 24. **OF:** Cotes 6, Del Rio 29, Jimenez 37, Luis 35, Luna 5, Machado 16, Sanchez 59, Ynfante 48.

San Diego Padres

SEASON IN A SENTENCE: San Diego hosted the All-Star Game and associated festivities, but the hometown fans had little to celebrate as the big league club tied for the second-worst record in baseball and endured a tumultuous season that saw general manager A.J. Preller suspended for failing to disclose player injuries in a trade with the Red Sox.

HIGH POINT: The Padres gave up Trea Turner and Joe Ross in the three-team deal that netted them Wil Myers, so seeing Myers play nearly every day and establish himself at first base—where he was a Gold Glove Award finalist—was a plus.

LOW POINT: While on the field the team provided plenty of low-lights, the true low points were off-the-field. Preller's late-September 30-game suspension provided one nadir; the Padres had to take back righthander Collin Rea from the Marlins, returning righty Luis Castillo, after Rea came up lame in his first start with the Marlins. Another came when the club let go of president and CEO Mike Dee in October. Worst of all, in September, the wife of third baseman Yangervis Solarte, Yuliette, died of cancer at age 31.

NOTABLE ROOKIES: Three lefthanded-hitting rookies became regulars in San Diego's second half lineup. Center fielder Travis Jankowski (30 stolen bases) and second baseman Ryan Schimpf (20 HRs) both flashed big league tools, though Jankowski showed little power and Schimpf hit just .217. Left fielder Alex Dickerson (.257/.333/.455) had the best approach.

KEY TRANSACTIONS: The Padres cleaned house, with Preller acquiring highly touted righty Anderson Espinoza from the Red Sox for Drew Pomeranz while sending Andrew Cashner to the Marlins in a haul that included 2015 first-round pick Josh Naylor. Preller also jettisoned two huge contracts, righty James Shields and outfielder Matt Kemp, who were his first key acquisitions.

DOWN ON THE FARM: Triple-A El Paso, led by Pacific Coast League MVP Hunter Renfroe, outfielder Manuel Margot, catcher Austin Hedges and second baseman Carlos Asuaje, won the PCL title. Overall, the Padres added talent across the board though trades, a draft class that included three first-round picks and an aggressive international program. That group included 17-year-old Cuban lefthander Adrian Morejon, Dominican shortstop Luis Almanzar and outfielder Jeisson Rosario, and Venezuelan infielder Gabriel Arias.

OPENING DAY PAYROLL: $101,424,814 (20th)

PLAYERS OF THE YEAR

MAJOR LEAGUE	MINOR LEAGUE
Wil Myers	**Hunter Renfroe**
1b	of
.259/.336/.461	(Triple-A)
28 HR, 94 RBI	.306/.336/.557
29 2B, 28 SB	30 HR, 105 RBI

ORGANIZATION LEADERS

BATTING		*Minimum 250 AB
MAJORS		
* AVG	Wil Myers	.259
* OPS	Wil Myers	.797
HR	Wil Myers	28
RBI	Wil Myers	94
MINORS		
* AVG	Luis Urias, El Paso, Lake Elsinore	.333
* OBP	Luis Urias, El Paso, Lake Elsinore	.404
* SLG	Hunter Renfroe, El Paso	.557
* OPS	Hunter Renfroe, El Paso	.893
R	Carlos Asuaje, El Paso	98
	Manuel Margot, El Paso	98
H	Carlos Asuaje, El Paso	172
TB	Hunter Renfroe, El Paso	297
2B	Nick Torres, San Antonio, El Paso	36
3B	Franchy Cordero, Lk. Elsinore, San Antonio, El Paso	16
HR	Hunter Renfroe, El Paso	30
RBI	Hunter Renfroe, El Paso	105
BB	Ty France, Fort Wayne, Lake Elsinore	59
	Kodie Tidwell, AZL Padres, Lake Elsinore, Ft. Wayne	59
SO	Brad Zunica, Fort Wayne	156
SB	Michael Gettys, Fort Wayne, Lake Elsinore	33

PITCHING		#Minimum 75 IP
MAJORS		
W	Luis Perdomo	9
# ERA	Drew Pomeranz	2.47
SO	Drew Pomeranz	115
SV	Fernando Rodney	17
MINORS		
W	Dinelson Lamet, Lake Elsinore, San Antonio, El Paso	12
	Carlos Pimentel, El Paso	12
L	Jerry Keel, Fort Wayne, Lake Elsinore, San Antonio	14
# ERA	Walker Lockett, FW, LE, San Antonio, El Paso	2.96
G	Derek Eitel, El Paso	54
GS	5 players	28
SV	Jason Jester, San Antonio, El Paso	14
IP	Walker Lockett, FW, LE, San Antonio, El Paso	164
BB	Dinelson Lamet, Lk. Elsinore, San Antonio, El Paso	61
	Carlos Pimentel, El Paso	61
SO	Dinelson Lamet, Lk. Elsinore, San Antonio, El Paso	158
# AVG	Dinelson Lamet, Lk. Elsinore, San Antonio, El Paso	.229

General Manager: A.J. Preller. **Farm Director:** Sam Geaney. **Scouting Director:** Mark Conner.

Class	Team	League	W	L	PCT	Finish	Manager
Majors	San Diego Padres	National	68	94	.420	15th (15)	Bud Black
Triple-A	El Paso Chihuahuas	Pacific Coast	73	70	.510	5th (16)	Rod Barajas
Double-A	San Antonio Missions	Texas	58	82	.414	8th (10)	Phil Wellman
High A	Lake Elsinore Storm	California	69	71	.493	6th (10)	Francisco Morales
Low A	Fort Wayne Tincaps	Midwest	62	78	.443	13th (16)	Anthony Contreras
Short season	Tri-City Dust Devils	Northwest	34	42	.447	4th (8)	Ben Fritz
Rookie	Padres	Arizona	25	30	.455	11th (14)	Michael Collins
Overall 2016 Minor League Record			321	373	.463	24th (30)	

ORGANIZATION STATISTICS

SAN DIEGO PADRES
NATIONAL LEAGUE

Batting	B-T	HT	WT	DOB	AVG	vLH	vRH	G	AB	R	H	2B	3B	HR	RBI	BB	HBP	SH	SF	SO	SB	CS	SLG	OBP
Amarista, Alexi	L-R	5-6	160	4-6-89	.257	.150	.275	65	140	9	36	2	0	0	11	8	0	1	1	26	9	2	.271	.295
Arcia, Oswaldo	L-R	6-0	225	5-9-91	.116	.000	.147	14	43	2	5	1	0	2	4	2	0	0	0	14	0	0	.279	.156
2-team total (2 Miami)					.111	—	—	16	45	2	5	1	0	2	4	2	0	0	0	15	0	0	.267	.149
Asuaje, Carlos	L-R	5-9	160	11-2-91	.208	.222	.200	7	24	2	5	2	0	0	2	1	0	0	0	4	0	0	.292	.240
Bethancourt, Christian	R-R	6-2	210	9-2-91	.228	.244	.224	73	193	20	44	9	0	6	25	10	0	0	1	56	1	2	.368	.265
Blash, Jabari	R-R	6-5	235	7-4-89	.169	.118	.185	38	71	7	12	2	0	3	5	11	2	0	0	34	1	0	.324	.298
Dickerson, Alex	L-L	6-3	235	5-26-90	.257	.267	.254	84	253	39	65	16	2	10	37	26	4	0	2	44	5	1	.455	.333
Hedges, Austin	R-R	6-1	210	8-18-92	.125	.400	.053	8	24	2	3	1	0	0	1	0	1	0	1	7	0	1	.167	.154
Jankowski, Travis	L-R	6-2	185	6-15-91	.245	.155	.275	131	335	53	82	13	2	2	12	42	2	3	0	100	30	12	.313	.332
Jay, Jon	L-L	5-11	195	3-15-85	.291	.311	.282	90	347	49	101	26	1	2	26	19	6	1	0	78	2	0	.389	.339
Kemp, Matt	R-R	6-4	210	9-23-84	.262	.333	.241	100	409	54	107	24	0	23	69	16	0	0	6	100	0	0	.489	.285
2-team total (56 Atlanta)					.268	—	—	156	623	89	167	39	0	35	108	36	1	0	12	156	1	0	.499	.304
Kivlehan, Patrick	R-R	6-2	215	12-22-89	.250	.200	.273	5	16	5	4	0	0	1	2	1	0	0	9	0	0	.438	.368
2-team total (3 Cincinnati)					.190	—	—	8	21	5	4	0	0	1	2	2	1	0	0	11	0	0	.333	.292
Margot, Manuel	R-R	5-11	180	9-28-94	.243	.308	.208	10	37	4	9	4	1	0	3	0	0	0	0	7	2	0	.405	.243
Myers, Wil	R-R	6-3	205	12-10-90	.259	.261	.258	157	599	99	155	29	4	28	94	68	4	0	5	160	28	6	.461	.336
Noonan, Nick	L-R	6-1	185	5-4-89	.167	.000	.176	7	18	0	3	0	0	0	1	1	0	0	1	5	0	1	.167	.200
Norris, Derek	R-R	6-0	230	2-14-89	.186	.203	.178	125	415	50	77	17	0	14	42	36	4	0	3	139	9	2	.328	.255
Pirela, Jose	R-R	6-0	220	11-21-89	.154	.222	.133	15	39	2	6	2	0	0	0	1	0	1	0	9	0	1	.205	.175
Ramirez, Alexei	R-R	6-2	180	9-22-81	.240	.299	.217	128	421	33	101	19	2	5	41	17	4	0	2	56	6	9	.330	.275
Renfroe, Hunter	R-R	6-1	220	1-28-92	.371	.333	.385	11	35	8	13	3	0	4	14	1	0	0	0	8	0	0	.800	.389
Rondon, Jose	R-R	6-1	195	3-3-94	.120	.000	.136	8	25	1	3	0	0	0	1	1	0	0	0	4	0	0	.120	.154
Rosales, Adam	R-R	6-2	200	5-20-83	.229	.237	.222	105	214	37	49	12	3	13	35	29	1	0	4	88	4	0	.495	.319
Sanchez, Hector	R-R	6-0	235	11-17-89	.286	.200	.297	26	42	3	12	1	0	3	7	3	1	0	0	8	0	0	.524	.348
Sardinas, Luis	B-R	6-1	180	5-16-93	.287	.344	.263	34	108	13	31	6	1	2	13	11	0	1	0	23	3	1	.417	.353
Schimpf, Ryan	L-R	5-9	180	4-11-88	.217	.157	.231	89	276	48	60	17	5	20	51	42	9	0	3	105	1	1	.533	.336
Solarte, Yangervis	B-R	5-11	205	7-7-87	.286	.271	.291	109	405	55	116	26	1	15	71	30	5	0	3	63	1	1	.467	.341
Spangenberg, Cory	L-R	6-0	195	3-16-91	.229	.333	.182	14	48	6	11	1	1	1	8	4	1	0	0	13	1	0	.354	.302
Upton, Melvin	R-R	6-3	185	8-21-84	.256	.282	.247	92	344	46	88	11	2	16	45	23	2	1	3	106	20	5	.439	.304
Wallace, Brett	L-R	6-2	250	8-26-86	.189	.284	.171	119	217	19	41	10	0	6	20	29	9	0	1	83	0	0	.318	.309
Weeks, Jemile	B-R	5-9	170	1-26-87	.140	.143	.139	17	50	5	7	1	1	0	2	3	1	3	0	14	1	0	.200	.204

Pitching	B-T	HT	WT	DOB	W	L	ERA	G	GS	CG	SV	IP	H	R	ER	HR	BB	SO	AVG	vLH	vRH	K/9	BB/9
Baumann, Buddy	L-L	5-11	195	12-9-87	1	0	3.72	11	0	0	0	10	7	4	4	0	4	10	.200	.071	.286	9.31	3.72
Buchter, Ryan	L-L	6-4	250	2-13-87	3	0	2.86	67	0	0	1	63	34	20	20	4	31	78	.160	.147	.168	11.14	4.43
Campos, Leonel	R-R	6-2	215	7-17-87	1	0	5.73	18	0	0	0	22	18	16	14	3	14	24	.222	.219	.224	9.82	5.73
Cashner, Andrew	R-R	6-6	235	9-11-86	4	7	4.76	16	16	0	0	79	80	47	42	13	30	67	.264	.253	.275	7.60	3.40
2-team total (12 Miami)					5	11	5.25	28	27	0	0	132	142	83	77	19	60	112	—	—	—	7.64	4.09
Clemens, Paul	R-R	6-3	215	2-14-88	3	5	3.67	16	12	0	0	61	61	32	25	9	23	47	.257	.175	.314	6.90	3.38
2-team total (2 Miami)					4	5	4.04	18	14	0	0	71	72	39	32	14	31	53	—	—	—	6.69	3.91
Cosart, Jarred	R-R	6-3	205	5-25-90	0	3	6.03	9	9	0	0	37	42	27	25	4	23	27	.278	.203	.341	6.51	5.54
2-team total (4 Miami)					0	4	6.00	13	13	0	0	57	61	41	38	4	39	38	—	—	—	6.00	6.16
Dominguez, Jose	R-R	6-0	200	8-7-90	1	0	5.05	34	0	0	0	36	34	23	20	5	17	20	.258	.277	.247	5.05	4.29
Erlin, Robbie	L-L	6-0	190	10-8-90	1	2	4.02	3	2	0	0	16	12	7	7	3	3	13	.218	.125	.256	7.47	1.72
Friedrich, Christian	R-L	6-4	215	7-8-87	5	12	4.80	24	23	0	0	129	131	74	69	13	52	100	.259	.239	.265	6.96	3.62
Guerrero, Tayron	R-R	6-8	210	1-9-91	0	0	4.50	1	0	0	0	2	3	1	1	0	1	0	.375	.400	.333	0.00	4.50
Hand, Brad	L-L	6-3	220	3-20-90	4	4	2.92	82	0	0	1	89	63	32	29	8	36	111	.195	.125	.236	11.18	3.63
Hessler, Keith	L-L	6-4	240	3-15-89	1	0	3.38	15	0	0	0	19	19	7	7	2	11	9	.257	.219	.286	4.34	5.30
2-team total (2 Arizona)					1	0	4.15	17	0	0	0	22	24	10	10	2	13	11	—	—	—	4.57	5.40
Jackson, Edwin	R-R	6-2	215	9-9-83	5	6	5.89	13	13	0	0	73	79	49	48	12	35	54	.278	.250	.303	6.63	4.30
2-team total (8 Miami)					5	7	5.89	21	13	0	0	84	92	56	55	14	41	61	—	—	—	6.54	4.39
Johnson, Erik	R-R	6-3	230	12-30-89	0	4	9.15	4	4	0	0	20	32	20	20	9	5	10	.372	.324	.408	4.58	2.29
Kirkman, Michael	L-L	6-4	215	9-18-86	0	0	27.00	1	0	0	0	1	6	4	4	0	0	0	.600	.500	.667	0.00	0.00
2-team total (1 Milwaukee)					0	0	19.29	2	0	0	0	2	7	5	5	0	1	1	—	—	—	3.86	3.86

Pitching

Pitching	B-T	HT	WT	DOB	W	L	ERA	G	GS	CG	SV	IP	H	R	ER	HR	BB	SO	AVG	vLH	vRH	K/9	BB/9
Maurer, Brandon	R-R	6-5	230	7-3-90	0	5	4.52	71	0	0	13	70	65	37	35	7	23	72	.238	.213	.263	9.30	2.97
Morrow, Brandon	R-R	6-3	205	7-26-84	1	0	1.69	18	0	0	0	16	19	4	3	2	3	8	.306	.318	.3	4.50	1.69
Perdomo, Luis	R-R	6-2	185	5-9-93	9	10	5.71	35	20	1	0	147	187	99	93	23	46	105	.310	.310	.309	6.44	2.82
Pomeranz, Drew	R-L	6-6	240	11-22-88	8	7	2.47	17	17	0	0	102	67	30	28	8	41	115	.184	.212	.173	10.15	3.62
Quackenbush, Kevin	R-R	6-4	235	11-28-88	7	7	3.92	60	0	0	2	60	55	27	26	8	22	42	.242	.295	.209	6.34	3.32
Rea, Colin	R-R	6-5	225	7-1-90	5	5	4.98	19	18	0	0	99	101	63	55	12	44	76	.262	.259	.265	6.89	3.99
2-team total (1 Miami)					5	5	4.82	20	19	0	0	103	102	63	55	12	44	80	—	—	—	7.01	3.86
Richard, Clayton	L-L	6-5	240	9-12-83	3	3	2.52	11	9	0	0	54	58	21	15	4	24	34	.278	.167	.301	5.70	4.02
2-team total (25 Chicago)					3	4	3.33	36	9	0	1	68	81	35	25	4	31	41	—	—	—	5.45	4.12
Rodney, Fernando	R-R	5-11	230	3-18-77	0	1	0.31	28	0	0	17	29	13	2	1	0	12	33	.137	.122	.148	10.36	3.77
2-team total (39 Miami)					2	4	3.44	67	0	0	25	65	54	27	25	5	37	74	—	—	—	10.19	5.10
Ross, Tyson	R-R	6-6	245	4-22-87	0	1	11.81	1	1	0	0	5	9	8	7	0	1	5	.375	.412	.286	8.44	1.69
Shields, James	R-R	6-3	215	12-20-81	2	7	4.28	11	11	0	0	67	69	33	32	9	27	57	.272	.291	.25	7.62	3.61
Smith, Jake	R-R	6-4	190	6-2-90	1	0	4.50	4	0	0	0	4	5	2	2	1	1	3	.333	.375	.286	6.75	2.25
Thornton, Matt	L-L	6-6	235	9-15-76	1	0	5.82	18	0	0	0	17	22	12	11	2	6	9	.314	.300	.32	4.76	3.18
Torres, Jose	L-L	6-2	175	9-24-93	0	0	0.00	4	0	0	0	3	3	0	0	0	2	3	.250	.375	0	9.00	6.00
Vargas, Cesar	R-R	6-2	220	12-30-91	0	3	5.03	7	7	0	0	34	41	19	19	5	15	28	.301	.271	.333	7.41	3.97
Villanueva, Carlos	R-R	6-2	220	11-28-83	2	2	5.96	51	0	0	1	74	89	50	49	17	14	61	.297	.267	.315	7.42	1.70

Fielding

Catcher	PCT	G	PO	A	E	DP	PB
Bethancourt	.993	41	248	32	2	3	5
Hedges	.980	7	47	2	1	1	0
Norris	.990	116	875	58	9	5	8
Sanchez	.970	12	61	4	2	1	0

First Base	PCT	G	PO	A	E	DP
Myers	.998	149	1246	76	3	139
Norris	1.000	3	7	0	0	0
Rosales	—	1	0	0	0	0
Solarte	1.000	2	23	1	0	5
Wallace	.993	20	127	7	1	11

Second Base	PCT	G	PO	A	E	DP
Amarista	.988	28	33	50	1	11
Asuaje	.971	6	14	19	1	3
Bethancourt	1.000	1	0	0	0	0
Noonan	1.000	2	1	4	0	0
Pirela	.963	12	10	16	1	4
Rosales	.957	36	36	53	4	16
Sardinas	1.000	1	5	4	0	2

	PCT	G	PO	A	E	DP
Schimpf	.980	68	106	193	6	50
Solarte	.964	15	20	34	2	8
Spangenberg	.919	13	22	35	5	12
Weeks	.988	17	36	48	1	10

Third Base	PCT	G	PO	A	E	DP
Amarista	1.000	5	6	5	0	2
Myers	—	1	0	0	0	0
Rosales	.949	41	12	62	4	7
Schimpf	1.000	14	6	23	0	0
Solarte	.965	95	59	190	9	19
Wallace	.915	42	18	36	5	4
Weeks	—	1	0	0	0	0

Shortstop	PCT	G	PO	A	E	DP
Amarista	.967	12	12	17	1	6
Noonan	.964	5	10	17	1	4
Ramirez	.969	111	152	283	14	76
Rondon	.943	7	9	24	2	6
Rosales	1.000	15	6	31	0	4
Sardinas	.964	32	41	93	5	25

Outfield	PCT	G	PO	A	E	DP
Amarista	1.000	10	10	0	0	0
Arcia	1.000	13	26	1	0	0
Bethancourt	.938	12	15	0	1	0
Blash	1.000	21	43	1	0	0
Dickerson	.972	68	104	0	3	0
Jankowski	.995	114	221	0	1	0
Jay	.995	86	190	4	1	1
Kemp	.989	97	165	8	2	2
Kivlehan	.857	5	12	0	2	0
Margot	1.000	10	31	0	0	0
Myers	1.000	10	15	0	0	0
Pirela	—	1	0	0	0	0
Ramirez	1.000	3	3	0	0	0
Renfroe	.882	9	14	1	2	0
Rosales	1.000	3	2	0	0	0
Schimpf	1.000	1	2	0	0	0
Upton	.989	90	165	8	2	2

EL PASO CHIHUAHUAS   TRIPLE-A
PACIFIC COAST LEAGUE

Batting	B-T	HT	WT	DOB	AVG	vLH	vRH	G	AB	R	H	2B	3B	HR	RBI	BB	HBP	SH	SF	SO	SB	CS	SLG	OBP
Amarista, Alexi	L-R	5-6	160	4-6-89	.333	.385	.314	13	48	9	16	3	0	1	4	4	1	0	2	8	1	0	.458	.382
Asencio, Yeison	R-R	6-1	225	11-14-89	.364	.400	.353	5	22	1	8	0	0	0	4	1	0	0	0	0	0	0	.364	.391
Asuaje, Carlos	L-R	5-9	160	11-2-91	.321	.333	.316	134	535	98	172	32	11	9	69	49	3	5	5	82	10	5	.473	.378
Blanco, Felipe	R-R	6-1	175	12-9-93	.182	.000	.286	7	11	3	2	0	0	1	2	1	0	0	0	7	0	0	.455	.250
Blash, Jabari	R-R	6-5	235	7-4-89	.260	.302	.237	62	177	30	46	12	0	11	30	41	8	0	3	66	1	2	.514	.415
Bousfield, Auston	R-R	5-11	185	7-5-93	.204	.261	.188	38	103	12	21	6	0	1	6	10	2	0	1	31	1	0	.291	.284
Cordero, Franchy	L-R	6-3	175	9-2-94	.077	.200	.000	4	13	1	1	0	0	0	0	3	0	0	0	4	0	0	.077	.250
Del Castillo, Miguel	R-R	5-10	170	10-14-91	.225	.250	.219	20	40	5	9	0	0	0	5	0	0	0	0	10	0	0	.225	.279
Dickerson, Alex	L-L	6-3	235	5-26-90	.382	.456	.341	62	217	50	83	16	3	10	51	14	5	0	4	27	0	0	.622	.425
Gale, Rocky	R-R	6-1	185	2-22-88	.278	.341	.250	44	144	16	40	2	0	3	14	5	5	2	3	19	0	0	.354	.318
Goris, Diego	R-R	5-10	200	11-8-90	.260	.273	.256	84	273	30	71	11	1	7	35	14	1	7	1	49	0	2	.385	.298
Hagerty, Jason	B-R	6-3	230	9-13-87	.271	.268	.273	45	129	19	35	10	1	4	18	11	5	0	0	28	0	0	.457	.352
Hedges, Austin	R-R	6-1	210	8-18-92	.326	.350	.318	82	313	55	102	20	1	21	82	13	3	0	5	51	1	1	.597	.353
3-team total (37 Round Rock, 43 Tacoma)					.254	—	—	100	370	46	94	18	3	12	49	24	2	0	1	108	5	4	.416	.302
Kivlehan, Patrick	R-R	6-2	215	12-22-89	.306	.333	.298	20	72	8	22	2	1	3	8	5	0	0	0	23	1	0	.486	.351
Lindsey, Taylor	L-R	6-0	195	12-2-91	.276	.286	.274	38	105	13	29	7	1	2	9	12	0	0	1	20	0	1	.419	.347
Loney, James	L-L	6-3	235	5-7-84	.342	.343	.341	43	158	22	54	7	0	2	28	9	0	0	2	12	0	0	.424	.373
Margot, Manuel	R-R	5-11	180	9-28-94	.304	.358	.282	124	517	98	157	21	12	6	55	36	4	5	4	64	30	11	.426	.351
McElroy, Casey	L-R	5-8	180	12-28-89	.260	.273	.69	222	30	63	17	2	1	28	21	1	2	3	35	0	0	.392	.344
Noonan, Nick	L-R	6-1	185	5-4-89	.301	.294	.304	99	342	49	103	28	0	5	43	21	0	7	4	70	0	1	.427	.338
Olt, Mike	R-R	6-2	210	8-27-88	.200	—	.200	3	5	0	1	0	0	0	0	0	0	0	0	3	0	0	.200	.200
Pirela, Jose	R-R	6-0	220	11-21-89	.248	.216	.260	35	137	16	34	7	3	2	16	9	0	0	0	21	1	1	.387	.295
Renfroe, Hunter	R-R	6-1	220	1-28-92	.306	.345	.291	133	533	95	163	34	5	30	105	22	4	0	4	115	5	2	.557	.336
Rondon, Jose	R-R	6-1	195	3-3-94	.300	.350	.283	24	80	8	24	4	0	1	9	1	0	0	1	12	0	1	.388	.305
Sanchez, Hector	B-R	6-0	235	11-17-89	.324	.300	.329	55	176	25	57	16	0	13	40	20	1	0	2	40	0	0	.636	.392
Sardinas, Luis	B-R	6-1	180	5-16-93	.263	.333	.231	5	19	5	5	2	0	0	1	0	0	0	0	3	0	0	.368	.364
2-team total (44 Tacoma)					.253	—	—	49	182	22	46	6	0	0	18	12	2	1	2	23	8	4	.286	.303
Satin, Josh	R-R	6-2	215	12-23-84	.182	.222	.154	18	44	/3	8	4	0	0	4	2	2	1	0	11	0	0	.273	.250

Batting	B-T	HT	WT	DOB	AVG	vLH	vRH	G	AB	R	H	2B	3B	HR	RBI	BB	HBP	SH	SF	SO	SB	CS	SLG	OBP
Schimpf, Ryan	L-R	5-9	180	4-11-88	.355	.362	.353	51	166	36	59	17	0	15	48	21	2	0	1	33	0	1	.729	.432
Solarte, Yangervis	B-R	5-11	205	7-7-87	.714	—	.714	2	7	3	5	1	2	0	2	2	0	0	0	0	0	0	1.429	.778
Torres, Nick	R-R	6-1	220	6-30-93	.308	.324	.302	36	130	15	40	8	0	6	18	5	2	1	0	35	0	2	.508	.343
Urias, Luis	R-R	5-9	160	6-3-97	.444	.500	.429	3	9	6	4	0	0	1	3	5	1	0	0	1	1	0	.778	.667
Valenzuela, Ricardo	R-R	6-0	190	8-4-90	.188	.200	.182	12	32	2	6	0	0	0	4	2	1	1	0	7	0	0	.188	.257
Weeks, Jemile	B-R	5-9	170	1-26-87	.306	.000	.344	10	36	7	11	1	3	0	1	6	0	0	0	3	2	0	.500	.405

Pitching	B-T	HT	WT	DOB	W	L	ERA	G	GS	CG	SV	IP	H	R	ER	HR	BB	SO	AVG	vLH	vRH	K/9	BB/9
Baumann, Buddy	L-L	5-11	195	12-9-87	1	1	3.14	24	0	0	2	29	22	10	10	3	12	31	.214	.191	.232	9.73	3.77
Buchter, Ryan	L-L	6-4	250	2-13-87	0	0	18.00	1	0	0	0	1	2	2	2	0	1	1	.400	.333	.500	9.00	9.00
Campos, Leonel	R-R	6-2	215	7-17-87	2	1	4.32	37	0	0	1	50	47	25	24	2	30	62	.255	.250	.260	11.16	5.40
Castillo, Fabio	R-R	6-1	235	2-19-89	0	3	4.66	7	6	0	0	39	46	21	20	3	17	26	.309	.339	.289	6.05	3.96
Cimber, Adam	R-R	6-4	180	8-15-90	0	1	17.36	4	0	0	0	5	15	9	9	3	1	4	.556	.647	.400	7.71	1.93
De Paula, Rafael	R-R	6-2	215	3-24-91	0	0	9.00	1	0	0	0	5	5	5	4	0	3	13	.395	.25	.556	13.00	3.00
Dimock, Michael	R-R	6-2	195	10-26-89	1	1	5.36	26	1	0	3	40	34	25	24	6	16	52	.225	.25	.209	11.60	3.57
Distasio, Lou	R-R	6-4	195	2-5-94	0	0	13.50	1	0	0	0	1	1	2	2	1	2	1	.200	.000	1.000	6.75	13.50
Dominguez, Jose	R-R	6-0	200	8-7-90	3	3	3.79	27	0	0	6	36	28	17	15	1	25	36	.217	.250	.192	9.08	6.31
Eitel, Derek	R-R	6-4	200	11-21-87	5	1	3.67	54	0	0	1	69	55	30	28	5	40	71	.226	.246	.209	9.31	5.24
Friedrich, Christian	R-L	6-4	215	7-8-87	0	1	4.66	2	2	0	0	10	12	5	5	1	4	6	.300	.250	.333	5.59	3.72
Garces, Frank	L-L	5-11	175	1-17-90	6	8	4.41	37	18	0	1	114	129	63	56	16	39	98	.279	.192	.321	7.71	3.07
Guerrero, Tayron	R-R	6-8	210	1-9-91	0	0	6.00	13	0	0	0	12	12	9	8	2	9	11	.250	.136	.346	8.25	6.75
Guthrie, Jeremy	R-R	6-1	205	4-8-79	3	5	6.60	11	11	0	0	60	75	47	44	5	19	37	.314	.304	.323	5.55	2.85
2-team total (6 New Orleans)					6	8	7.17	17	17	0	0	87	120	74	69	10	33	53	—	—	—	5.50	3.43
Hancock, Justin	R-R	6-4	185	10-28-90	0	2	12.00	2	2	0	0	6	16	11	8	0	1	5	.485	.538	.450	7.50	1.50
Hellweg, Johnny	R-R	6-7	235	10-29-88	0	1	10.80	4	0	0	0	3	6	4	4	0	5	5	.375	.500	.300	13.50	13.50
Hessler, Keith	L-L	6-4	240	3-15-89	1	1	2.95	28	0	0	2	37	32	13	12	1	12	42	.237	.143	.319	10.31	2.95
Jackson, Edwin	R-R	6-2	215	9-9-83	0	1	7.11	3	3	0	0	13	20	13	10	2	6	9	.357	.478	.273	6.39	4.26
Jester, Jason	R-R	5-11	205	5-4-91	2	2	4.67	13	0	0	0	17	21	14	9	2	6	14	.292	.270	.314	7.27	3.12
Kelly, Mike	R-R	6-4	185	9-6-92	6	3	4.89	10	10	0	0	50	50	29	27	4	23	41	.273	.323	.222	7.43	4.17
Kirkman, Michael	L-L	6-4	215	9-18-86	0	0	4.50	5	0	0	1	6	3	3	3	0	0	6	.143	.111	.167	9.00	0.00
2-team total (42 Colorado Springs)					1	0	3.08	47	0	0	1	38	43	15	13	2	17	40	—	—	—	9.47	4.03
Lamet, Dinelson	R-R	6-4	187	7-18-92	0	2	4.22	2	2	0	0	11	13	7	5	2	4	13	.302	.368	.250	10.97	3.38
Lockett, Walker	R-R	6-5	225	5-3-94	1	2	4.50	3	3	0	0	18	23	10	9	2	2	12	.319	.370	.231	6.00	1.00
Maton, Phil	R-R	6-3	220	3-25-93	1	0	1.50	5	0	0	1	6	1	1	1	1	2	12	.053	.125	.000	18.00	3.00
Mazzoni, Cory	R-R	6-1	210	10-19-89	0	0	0.00	2	0	0	1	1	1	0	0	0	1	0	.200	.000	.250	0.00	6.75
McCutchen, Daniel	R-R	6-2	215	9-26-82	10	9	6.48	25	25	0	0	135	198	109	97	19	36	76	.349	.382	.321	5.08	2.41
McGrath, Kyle	L-L	6-2	185	7-31-92	0	0	0.00	1	0	0	0	2	1	2	0	0	1	2	.143	.25	.000	10.80	5.40
Morrow, Brandon	R-R	6-3	205	7-26-84	0	0	6.43	12	2	0	2	21	29	15	15	2	9	21	.322	.349	.298	9.00	3.86
Moskos, Daniel	R-L	6-1	200	4-28-86	5	2	3.39	53	0	0	0	61	71	33	23	2	22	47	.293	.257	.323	6.93	3.25
Northcraft, Aaron	R-R	6-4	230	5-28-90	5	1	5.04	21	6	0	1	50	61	33	28	5	21	46	.302	.333	.280	8.28	3.78
Pimentel, Carlos	R-R	6-3	215	12-1-89	12	8	5.65	28	28	1	0	145	174	93	91	17	61	121	.297	.332	.265	7.51	3.79
Quackenbush, Kevin	R-R	6-4	235	11-8-88	1	0	2.08	9	0	0	2	13	12	3	3	0	2	16	.240	.190	.276	11.08	1.38
Rea, Colin	R-R	6-5	225	7-1-90	0	0	9.00	1	1	0	0	1	1	1	1	0	1	2	.250	.000	.500	18.00	9.00
Reynolds, Greg	R-R	6-7	225	7-3-85	1	3	7.30	5	5	0	0	25	36	22	20	5	8	5	.346	.255	.421	1.82	2.92
Rodriguez, Bryan	R-R	6-5	180	7-6-91	4	8	5.11	16	16	1	0	86	108	52	49	10	26	51	.311	.322	.300	5.32	2.71
Rosin, Seth	R-R	6-6	265	11-2-88	0	0	8.31	5	0	0	0	9	14	8	8	3	3	4	.400	.533	.300	4.15	3.12
Torres, Jose	L-L	6-2	175	9-24-93	0	0	3.38	3	0	0	0	3	4	1	1	0	1	2	.333	.667	.000	6.75	3.38
Yardley, Eric	R-R	6-0	165	8-18-90	3	0	2.85	37	2	0	3	54	58	19	17	5	13	37	.286	.321	.262	6.20	2.18

Fielding

Catcher	PCT	G	PO	A	E	DP	PB
Del Castillo	.971	10	66	2	2	2	1
Gale	.997	36	257	30	1	3	2
Hagerty	1.000	12	65	4	0	0	1
Hedges	.991	73	578	54	6	9	3
Sanchez	.973	10	69	2	2	0	3
Valenzuela	1.000	8	49	8	0	0	0

First Base	PCT	G	PO	A	E	DP
Del Castillo	1.000	3	5	0	0	1
Dickerson	1.000	10	78	7	0	5
Goris	.978	16	85	5	2	10
Hagerty	.989	24	168	16	2	16
Kivlehan	1.000	11	78	5	0	10
Lindsey	.964	18	123	10	5	16
Loney	.993	35	277	27	2	31
Olt	1.000	1	4	1	0	0
Pirela	.978	4	40	4	1	4
Sanchez	.989	27	178	8	2	16
Satin	1.000	10	80	7	0	8
Schimpf	.975	6	36	3	1	3

Second Base	PCT	G	PO	A	E	DP
Amarista	1.000	2	2	4	0	2
Asuaje	.981	119	209	312	10	64
Blanco	.000	2	0	0	1	0
Goris	1.000	7	16	17	0	9
Lindsey	1.000	2	0	4	0	0
McElroy	.978	12	10	34	1	6
Pirela	1.000	3	3	10	0	2
Schimpf	1.000	3	5	5	0	1
Solarte	1.000	1	0	1	0	1
Urias	1.000	3	4	12	0	2
Weeks	1.000	1	2	1	0	0

Third Base	PCT	G	PO	A	E	DP
Amarista	1.000	1	1	3	0	0
Asuaje	.800	3	5	3	2	1
Blanco	1.000	3	1	4	0	1
Gale	1.000	4	3	5	0	0
Goris	.947	40	21	69	5	12
Kivlehan	.833	2	0	5	1	0
Lindsey	.952	17	2	18	1	3

(Second Base cont.)	PCT	G	PO	A	E	DP
McElroy	.974	32	20	56	2	6
Noonan	.962	17	6	19	1	1
Olt	1.000	1	0	2	0	0
Pirela	1.000	3	3	4	0	1
Rondon	.941	7	4	12	1	2
Schimpf	.957	33	11	56	3	4
Solarte	1.000	2	0	3	0	0
Weeks	.818	4	2	7	2	0

Shortstop	PCT	G	PO	A	E	DP
Amarista	.977	9	16	26	1	7
Goris	.937	18	18	41	4	10
McElroy	.966	20	25	32	2	9
Noonan	.971	79	125	243	11	51
Rondon	.932	17	28	40	5	10
Sardinas	1.000	5	8	13	0	4
Schimpf	.750	1	0	3	1	1
Weeks	1.000	5	7	8	0	1

Outfield	PCT	G	PO	A	E	DP
Amarista	1.000	1	2	0	0	0
Asencio	1.000	5	7	2	0	0
Asuaje	1.000	7	10	1	0	0
Blash	.990	49	93	3	1	0
Bousfield	.987	31	71	6	1	0

	PCT	G	PO	A	E	DP
Cordero	.889	4	8	0	1	0
Dickerson	.981	36	51	2	1	1
Goris	—	1	0	0	0	0
Hagerty	.000	2	0	0	1	0
Kivlehan	1.000	8	10	0	0	0
Loney	1.000	2	3	0	0	0

	PCT	G	PO	A	E	DP
Margot	.985	122	311	18	5	3
Pirela	1.000	23	39	0	0	0
Renfroe	.987	123	219	17	3	1
Schimpf	1.000	2	2	0	0	0
Torres	1.000	35	54	5	0	2
Weeks	1.000	1	2	0	0	0

SAN ANTONIO MISSIONS   DOUBLE-A
TEXAS LEAGUE

Batting	B-T	HT	WT	DOB	AVG	vLH	vRH	G	AB	R	H	2B	3B	HR	RBI	BB	HBP	SH	SF	SO	SB	CS	SLG	OBP
Allen, Austin	L-R	6-4	225	1-16-94	.273	.667	.125	3	11	1	3	0	0	1	1	0	0	0	0	0	0	0	.545	.273
Amarista, Alexi	L-R	5-6	160	4-6-89	.400	—	.400	1	5	0	2	0	0	0	1	0	0	0	0	0	0	0	.400	.400
Asencio, Yeison	R-R	6-1	225	11-14-89	.254	.297	.242	45	169	16	43	6	2	1	11	5	0	0	1	25	3	3	.331	.274
Blanco, Felipe	R-R	6-1	175	12-9-93	.125	.158	.111	23	64	4	8	4	0	0	3	2	0	2	0	21	0	0	.188	.152
Bousfield, Auston	R-R	5-11	185	7-5-93	.170	.163	.172	71	264	29	45	10	1	3	14	32	4	4	3	76	9	2	.250	.267
Cordero, Franchy	L-R	6-3	175	9-2-94	.306	.328	.298	59	245	31	75	8	8	6	19	17	2	0	0	67	12	6	.478	.356
Del Castillo, Miguel	R-R	5-10	170	10-14-91	.200	.167	.211	8	25	1	5	2	0	0	1	0	1	0	0	9	0	0	.280	.231
Gale, Rocky	R-R	6-1	185	2-22-88	.219	.231	.216	63	210	21	46	8	1	2	20	29	4	2	2	38	1	0	.295	.322
Goris, Diego	R-R	5-10	200	11-8-90	.217	.222	.216	22	69	4	15	2	0	2	9	2	0	1	0	11	2	0	.333	.239
Jensen, Chase	R-R	6-4	195	1-29-91	.141	.042	.185	27	78	9	11	2	0	3	9	4	1	2	0	29	2	0	.282	.193
Jones, Duanel	R-R	6-3	220	5-11-93	.000	.000	.000	4	8	0	0	0	0	0	0	0	0	0	0	3	0	0	.000	.000
Kennedy, A.J.	R-R	6-0	190	1-23-94	.161	.000	.238	10	31	0	5	0	0	0	2	4	0	0	1	12	0	2	.161	.250
Lindsey, Taylor	L-R	6-0	195	12-2-91	.202	.138	.221	86	287	33	58	11	2	8	26	29	2	3	3	71	4	2	.338	.277
Martinez, Alberth	R-R	6-1	170	1-23-91	.156	.000	.200	11	32	3	5	2	0	0	4	1	0	0	2	6	0	0	.219	.171
Miller, Ryan	R-R	6-2	200	11-17-92	.232	.296	.208	58	198	27	46	13	2	7	32	12	2	1	0	60	3	0	.424	.283
Olt, Mike	R-R	6-2	210	8-27-88	.255	.190	.277	49	161	25	41	9	0	5	25	31	0	1	55	1	0	0	.404	.373
Quintana, Gabriel	R-R	6-3	215	9-7-92	.241	.204	.253	130	456	53	110	28	2	20	73	20	7	2	2	138	5	3	.443	.282
Rondon, Jose	R-R	6-1	195	3-3-94	.279	.326	.266	96	376	45	105	21	2	5	44	15	3	12	3	66	13	4	.386	.310
Santos, Trae	L-L	6-1	235	10-11-92	.141	.067	.161	21	71	3	10	5	0	0	5	1	1	1	0	26	0	0	.268	.153
Schulz, Nick	R-R	6-3	210	5-3-91	.282	.317	.273	106	393	41	111	23	1	10	50	43	9	1	0	101	5	4	.422	.366
Smith, Mason	R-R	6-2	195	3-16-95	.083	.000	.118	9	24	1	2	1	0	0	3	2	0	0	0	10	0	0	.125	.241
Stevens, River	L-R	6-0	185	1-10-92	.232	.194	.244	78	276	32	64	6	2	4	26	19	3	5	5	53	5	3	.312	.284
Tejada, Luis	R-R	6-3	175	10-12-92	.256	.229	.265	63	195	26	50	13	3	4	25	22	2	2	1	41	4	2	.415	.336
Torres, Nick	R-R	6-1	220	6-30-93	.282	.329	.269	93	373	40	105	28	2	6	40	16	6	0	1	96	10	4	.416	.321
Valenzuela, Ricardo	R-R	6-0	190	8-4-90	.214	.250	.200	5	14	0	3	0	0	0	1	3	0	0	0	3	0	0	.214	.353
VanMeter, Josh	L-R	5-11	195	3-6-95	.198	.130	.217	29	106	10	21	2	0	2	5	7	0	1	0	18	2	2	.274	.248
Vilter, Nick	R-R	6-4	220	10-6-93	.000	.000	.000	1	3	0	0	0	0	0	0	0	0	0	0	0	0	0	.000	.000
Ward, Nelson	L-R	5-11	175	8-6-92	.221	.250	.212	123	453	55	100	15	2	6	28	56	7	8	4	126	31	9	.302	.313

Pitching	B-T	HT	WT	DOB	W	L	ERA	G	GS	CG	SV	IP	H	R	ER	HR	BB	SO	AVG	vLH	vRH	K/9	BB/9
Alger, Brandon	L-L	6-3	190	7-4-91	0	1	8.71	14	0	0	0	21	24	20	20	5	14	21	.304	.214	.353	9.15	6.10
Bartsch, Kyle	L-L	6-3	200	3-10-91	0	0	8.31	10	0	0	0	17	32	19	16	2	10	16	.390	.355	.412	5.19	5.19
2-team total (15 NW Arkansas)					2	1	3.72	25	1	0	1	46	52	22	19	5	16	33			—	6.46	3.13
Benjamin, Ramon	R-L	6-1	195	6-14-87	0	2	6.65	15	0	0	0	22	25	19	16	7	11	19	.278	.343	.236	7.89	4.57
Berry, Tim	L-L	6-3	180	3-18-91	2	4	6.80	10	10	0	0	48	64	41	36	9	33	30	.330	.364	.320	5.66	6.23
Brasoban, Yimmi	R-R	6-1	185	6-22-94	5	2	3.03	29	0	0	4	36	27	13	12	1	16	35	.216	.268	.190	8.83	4.04
Castillo, Fabio	R-R	6-1	235	2-19-89	3	4	4.38	7	7	0	0	39	35	21	19	6	16	40	.243	.246	.241	9.23	3.69
Cimber, Adam	R-R	6-4	180	8-15-90	3	2	2.56	42	0	0	3	53	41	19	15	1	14	27	.216	.260	.200	4.61	2.39
De Paula, Rafael	R-R	6-2	215	3-24-91	4	2	2.44	37	0	0	0	55	42	17	15	2	19	74	.233	.238	.201	12.04	3.09
Diaz, Luis	R-R	6-4	290	4-9-92	2	5	5.79	10	10	0	0	56	68	37	36	8	18	47	.301	.317	.287	7.55	2.89
Dimock, Michael	R-R	6-2	195	10-26-89	1	0	3.00	5	0	0	1	6	4	2	2	1	0	5	.200	.333	.143	7.50	0.00
Distasio, Lou	R-R	6-4	195	2-5-94	0	0	0.00	1	0	0	0	1	0	0	0	0	2	2	.000	—	.000	18.00	18.00
Guerrero, Tayron	R-R	6-8	210	1-9-91	0	3	4.94	19	0	0	0	24	20	14	13	2	10	25	.235	.247	.218	9.51	3.80
Hellweg, Johnny	R-R	6-7	235	10-29-88	1	4	10.97	6	6	0	0	21	32	27	26	2	14	12	.372	.400	.353	5.06	5.91
Jester, Jason	R-R	5-11	205	5-4-91	2	1	2.54	34	0	0	14	39	39	17	11	2	7	53	.253	.290	.228	12.23	1.62
Keel, Jerry	L-L	6-6	240	9-26-93	0	2	6.88	3	3	0	0	17	24	15	13	2	8	11	.338	.333	.339	5.82	4.24
Kelly, Mike	R-R	6-4	185	9-6-92	2	2	2.90	9	9	0	0	50	42	17	16	3	17	49	.237	.240	.235	8.88	3.08
Lamet, Dinelson	R-R	6-4	187	7-18-92	5	7	3.39	14	14	0	0	74	57	32	28	2	31	91	.207	.208	.206	11.02	3.75
Lemond, Zech	R-R	6-1	170	10-9-92	1	0	24.00	1	1	0	0	3	9	8	8	0	3	3	.529	.286	.700	9.00	9.00
Lloyd, Kyle	R-R	6-4	220	10-16-90	7	7	3.31	30	20	0	0	130	124	54	48	9	38	99	.252	.240	.258	6.84	2.62
Lockett, Walker	R-R	6-5	225	5-3-94	4	1	2.08	6	4	0	0	35	27	8	8	2	2	26	.216	.173	.247	6.75	0.52
McCutchen, Daniel	R-R	6-2	215	9-26-82	1	2	4.50	4	3	0	0	20	20	12	10	4	4	11	.256	.194	.298	4.95	1.80
McGrath, Kyle	L-L	6-2	185	7-31-92	1	2	1.29	33	0	0	1	49	32	8	7	4	8	50	.188	.125	.219	9.25	1.48
McNutt, Trey	R-R	6-2	220	8-2-89	0	0	1.50	6	0	0	0	6	2	1	1	0	1	7	.105	.000	.167	10.50	1.50
Morris, Elliot	R-R	6-4	210	4-26-92	0	0	4.91	4	0	0	0	7	9	6	4	1	3	3	.300	.308	.294	3.68	3.68
Morrow, Brandon	R-R	6-3	205	7-26-84	1	0	7.84	2	2	0	0	10	18	10	9	3	4	4	.391	.400	.387	3.48	3.48
Morrow, Bryce	R-R	6-2	200	1-2-88	1	7	5.94	9	9	0	0	50	62	35	33	6	22	28	.320	.400	.284	5.04	3.96
Northcraft, Aaron	R-R	6-4	230	5-28-90	2	2	2.88	7	7	0	0	41	33	15	13	4	9	27	.228	.222	.230	5.98	1.99
Paullus, Ben	R-R	6-1	190	8-31-89	0	0	0.00	1	0	0	0	1	0	0	0	0	0	0	.000	—	.000	0.00	0.00
Rodriguez, Bryan	R-R	6-5	180	7-6-91	3	5	3.51	10	10	0	0	59	67	29	23	5	18	32	.295	.307	.286	4.88	2.75
Sanchez, Elier	L-L	6-2	230	10-4-86	0	1	9.00	2	1	0	0	4	5	4	4	0	3	4	.313	.000	.333	9.00	6.75
Seidenberger, Trevor	L-L	6-2	200	6-9-92	0	0	12.00	1	0	0	0	3	5	4	4	1	3	3	.385	.000	.625	9.00	9.00
Simmons, Seth	R-R	5-9	170	6-14-88	3	4	2.35	20	15	0	0	96	72	27	25	9	29	88	.207	.190	.216	8.28	2.73
Smith, Jake	R-R	6-4	190	6-2-90	0	1	1.59	6	0	0	1	6	3	1	1	0	2	4	.150	.143	.154	6.35	3.18

Pitching

Pitching	B-T	HT	WT	DOB	W	L	ERA	G	GS	CG	SV	IP	H	R	ER	HR	BB	SO	AVG	vLH	vRH	K/9	BB/9
Torres, Jose	L-L	6-2	175	9-24-93	1	2	1.24	25	0	0	2	36	20	5	5	1	12	36	.165	.171	.163	8.92	2.97
Vargas, Cesar	R-R	6-2	220	12-30-91	0	0	1.42	2	2	0	0	13	5	2	2	0	1	14	.122	.143	.111	9.95	0.71
Weir, T.J.	R-R	6-0	205	9-15-91	3	4	6.02	16	7	0	0	49	54	35	33	6	19	45	.283	.235	.300	8.21	3.47
Wieck, Brad	L-L	6-9	255	10-14-91	1	0	0.44	15	0	0	0	20	10	1	1	0	8	31	.152	.200	.130	13.72	3.54
Wingenter, Trey	R-R	6-7	200	4-15-94	0	0	0.00	1	0	0	1	3	0	0	0	0	1	5	.000	.000	.000	15.00	3.00
Yardley, Eric	R-R	6-0	165	8-18-90	0	2	3.18	12	0	0	1	17	17	7	6	0	3	10	.274	.409	.200	5.29	1.59

Fielding

Catcher	PCT	G	PO	A	E	DP	PB
Allen	1.000	2	13	2	0	0	0
Del Castillo	.973	8	68	5	2	0	2
Gale	.989	62	496	40	6	2	4
Goris	1.000	6	46	10	0	3	2
Kennedy	.968	10	81	11	3	1	4
Miller	.984	49	340	40	6	3	7
Valenzuela	.974	5	32	6	1	2	2

First Base	PCT	G	PO	A	E	DP
Goris	1.000	9	70	3	0	13
Jensen	.971	6	31	3	1	2
Jones	1.000	2	14	2	0	1
Lindsey	.988	33	236	21	3	26
Olt	.994	42	334	11	2	43
Quintana	.971	9	60	7	2	5
Santos	.994	18	166	7	1	18
Tejada	1.000	28	234	18	0	27
Vilter	1.000	1	11	0	0	2

Second Base	PCT	G	PO	A	E	DP
Amarista	1.000	1	1	2	0	0
Blanco	1.000	6	6	11	0	4
Bousfield	1.000	1	1	0	0	0
Jensen	.926	8	10	15	2	4
Lindsey	.957	21	36	52	4	16
Ward	.972	109	199	286	14	80

Third Base	PCT	G	PO	A	E	DP
Amarista	1.000	1	1	1	0	0
Blanco	1.000	2	1	3	0	1
Goris	1.000	6	1	14	0	1
Jensen	1.000	4	3	6	0	1
Lindsey	.947	9	1	17	1	1
Olt	.800	2	1	3	1	0
Quintana	.947	52	18	89	6	9
Stevens	.962	40	28	74	4	7
VanMeter	.873	29	16	46	9	4
Ward	.750	1	1	2	1	0

Shortstop	PCT	G	PO	A	E	DP
Blanco	.972	9	9	26	1	7
Jensen	.857	2	1	5	1	2
Rondon	.977	93	154	265	10	76
Stevens	.992	32	53	75	1	16
Ward	.966	8	11	17	1	8

Outfield	PCT	G	PO	A	E	DP
Asencio	1.000	39	68	4	0	1
Bousfield	1.000	70	181	10	0	3
Cordero	.975	59	152	1	4	1
Jensen	1.000	3	5	0	0	0
Lindsey	—	1	0	0	0	0
Martinez	.923	9	12	0	1	0
Quintana	1.000	15	20	1	0	1
Schulz	1.000	100	197	1	0	0
Smith	1.000	4	6	1	0	0
Stevens	.500	1	1	0	1	0
Tejada	.983	29	55	3	1	1
Torres	.981	93	151	8	3	1
Ward	1.000	5	9	0	0	0

SAN DIEGO PADRES

LAKE ELSINORE STORM   HIGH CLASS A
CALIFORNIA LEAGUE

Batting	B-T	HT	WT	DOB	AVG	vLH	vRH	G	AB	R	H	2B	3B	HR	RBI	BB	HBP	SH	SF	SO	SB	CS	SLG	OBP
Amarista, Alexi	L-R	5-6	160	4-6-89	.250	.286	.000	2	8	1	2	0	0	0	0	0	0	0	0	1	0	0	.250	.250
Blanco, Felipe	R-R	6-1	175	12-9-93	.172	.300	.114	22	64	3	11	2	0	1	6	1	1	0	0	21	0	4	.203	.254
Bravo, Daniel	R-R	6-0	160	2-16-95	.234	.333	.211	30	94	13	22	3	0	0	6	5	1	3	0	21	2	1	.266	.280
Cordero, Franchy	L-R	6-3	175	9-2-94	.286	.373	.265	74	297	47	85	16	8	5	35	19	5	0	1	83	11	8	.444	.339
Del Castillo, Miguel	R-R	5-10	170	10-14-91	.200	.000	.222	3	10	0	2	0	0	0	1	0	0	0	0	5	0	0	.200	.200
France, Ty	R-R	6-0	205	7-13-94	.304	.366	.290	60	224	39	68	16	0	9	38	15	12	1	4	47	3	4	.496	.373
Gettys, Michael	R-R	6-1	203	10-22-95	.306	.341	.299	60	248	40	76	13	0	9	33	17	3	2	2	77	9	6	.468	.356
Giron, Ruddy	R-R	5-11	175	1-4-97	.426	.700	.351	14	47	7	20	7	1	1	5	3	0	0	0	13	1	0	.681	.460
Greene, Marcus	R-R	5-11	175	4-1-94	.143	.000	.196	18	63	5	9	1	0	1	4	6	2	0	0	20	0	0	.206	.239
Guerra, Javier	L-R	5-11	155	9-25-95	.202	.156	.213	105	391	49	79	19	1	9	41	34	0	3	3	141	4	4	.325	.264
Jay, Jon	L-L	5-11	195	3-15-85	.300	.000	.375	3	10	3	3	1	0	0	0	1	0	0	0	1	2	1	.400	.364
Jensen, Chase	R-R	6-4	195	1-29-91	.228	.125	.254	24	79	15	18	6	0	5	8	0	0	0	2	23	6	1	.304	.299
Kennedy, A.J.	R-R	6-0	190	1-23-94	.226	.176	.237	52	186	27	42	11	0	1	17	10	3	1	2	52	0	2	.301	.274
Kohlwey, Taylor	L-L	6-3	200	7-20-94	.302	.182	.333	13	53	8	16	2	2	0	3	3	1	0	0	16	0	1	.415	.351
Magdaleno, Westhers	R-R	6-1	190	10-30-96	.056	.250	.000	5	18	1	1	0	0	0	0	1	0	0	0	6	0	0	.056	.105
Moreno, Edwin	L-L	6-1	190	6-27-94	.267	.289	.261	109	405	54	108	18	11	14	63	15	1	4	3	126	4	4	.469	.292
Naylor, Josh	L-L	6-0	225	6-22-97	.252	.258	.250	33	139	17	35	5	0	3	21	3	0	0	2	22	1	1	.353	.264
Perez, Fernando	L-R	6-0	210	9-13-93	.213	.192	.217	44	169	22	36	5	1	9	28	12	3	1	1	49	1	1	.414	.276
Redman, Hunter	R-R	5-10	180	8-25-92	.000	.000	.000	4	8	0	0	0	0	0	0	1	0	0	0	4	0	0	.000	.111
Reyes, Franmil	R-R	6-5	240	7-7-95	.278	.267	.280	130	493	63	137	32	3	16	83	47	2	0	5	108	2	3	.452	.340
Santos, Trae	L-L	6-1	235	10-11-92	.209	.204	.211	90	301	30	63	20	4	7	35	35	11	0	1	97	0	0	.372	.313
Schulz, Nick	R-R	6-3	210	5-3-91	.231	.222	.233	13	39	2	9	2	0	0	2	4	0	0	0	3	0	1	.282	.302
Stevens, River	L-R	6-0	185	1-10-92	.240	.269	.230	31	100	10	24	9	0	2	10	7	0	0	1	18	1	2	.390	.287
Tejada, Luis	R-R	6-3	175	10-23-91	.223	.297	.200	46	157	21	35	5	1	6	20	16	5	0	2	23	3	2	.382	.311
Tidwell, Kodie	L-R	6-1	195	8-3-94	.219	.333	.192	9	32	5	7	1	0	1	3	4	0	0	0	8	3	0	.344	.306
Urias, Luis	R-R	5-9	160	6-3-97	.330	.299	.339	120	466	71	154	26	5	5	52	40	13	8	3	36	7	13	.440	.397
Valenzuela, Ricardo	R-R	6-0	190	8-4-90	.252	.409	.220	36	131	14	33	5	1	3	11	11	0	2	0	19	0	0	.313	.310
VanMeter, Josh	L-R	5-11	165	3-10-95	.267	.227	.277	95	348	51	93	21	2	12	51	48	1	1	3	64	9	2	.443	.355
Vilter, Nick	R-R	6-4	220	10-6-93	.000	.000	.000	8	20	3	0	0	0	0	0	1	0	0	0	9	0	0	.000	.048
Weeks, Jemile	B-R	5-9	170	1-26-87	.222	.000	.500	3	9	2	2	0	0	0	3	1	0	0	0	1	0	0	.222	.300

Pitching	B-T	HT	WT	DOB	W	L	ERA	G	GS	CG	SV	IP	H	R	ER	HR	BB	SO	AVG	vLH	vRH	K/9	BB/9
Alger, Brandon	L-L	6-3	190	7-4-91	3	1	5.51	12	0	0	0	16	15	11	10	2	7	14	.250	.167	.306	7.71	3.86
Arias, Martires	R-R	6-10	215	11-10-90	2	4	5.79	35	5	0	0	56	62	48	36	3	37	70	.274	.266	.280	11.25	5.95
Ashbeck, Elliott	L-R	6-3	215	11-16-93	0	1	0.00	1	1	0	0	3	2	1	0	0	1	.182	.000	.222	2.70	2.70
Bachar, Lake	R-R	6-3	210	6-3-95	1	0	3.60	4	0	0	0	5	4	2	2	0	0	5	.250	.000	.333	9.00	0.00
Blueberg, Colby	R-R	6-0	195	5-11-93	2	3	3.17	45	0	0	12	60	58	25	21	5	26	60	.254	.284	.236	9.05	3.92
Brasoban, Yimmi	R-R	6-1	185	6-22-94	0	0	0.68	10	0	0	5	13	8	1	1	1	1	13	.163	.071	.200	8.78	0.68
Cashner, Andrew	R-R	6-6	235	9-11-86	0	0	0.00	1	1	0	0	3	2	0	0	0	1	.182	.200	.167	3.00	0.00
Castillo, Jose	L-L	6-4	200	1-10-96	1	0	1.59	7	0	0	0	11	15	9	2	1	5	7	.326	.444	.250	5.56	3.97

Pitching

Pitching	B-T	HT	WT	DOB	W	L	ERA	G	GS	CG	SV	IP	H	R	ER	HR	BB	SO	AVG	vLH	vRH	K/9	BB/9
Cox, Taylor	L-L	6-3	210	7-2-93	1	2	5.68	12	0	0	0	19	16	14	12	3	14	13	.225	.158	.250	6.16	6.63
Cressley, Aaron	L-R	6-1	175	9-2-92	0	0	0.00	2	0	0	0	1	0	0	0	0	3	1	.000	—	.000	6.75	20.25
De Los Santos, Enyel	R-R	6-3	170	12-25-95	5	3	4.35	15	15	0	0	68	70	35	33	11	24	52	.267	.248	.281	6.85	3.16
Diaz, Luis	R-R	6-4	290	4-9-92	0	0	3.29	3	2	0	0	14	13	7	5	4	1	17	.250	.207	.304	11.20	0.66
Distasio, Lou	R-R	6-4	195	2-5-94	0	0	8.59	6	0	0	0	7	10	7	7	0	4	8	.323	.100	.429	9.82	4.91
Dorminy, Thomas	L-L	6-0	190	6-1-92	1	8	9.94	12	12	0	0	48	93	63	53	3	21	40	.415	.442	.407	7.50	3.94
Edwards, Jon	R-R	6-5	235	1-8-88	0	0	0.00	1	0	0	0	1	0	0	0	0	0	3	.000	—	.000	27.00	0.00
Friedrich, Christian	R-L	6-4	215	7-8-87	0	0	2.00	2	2	0	0	9	7	3	2	1	0	7	.206	.143	.222	7.00	0.00
Huffman, Chris	R-R	6-1	205	11-25-92	10	5	3.78	28	23	0	0	131	126	70	55	7	43	98	.251	.223	.269	6.73	2.95
Keel, Jerry	L-L	6-6	240	9-26-93	2	2	6.14	4	4	0	0	22	23	16	15	5	9	16	.277	.185	.321	6.55	3.68
Kelly, Mike	R-R	6-4	185	9-6-92	1	3	5.83	6	6	0	0	29	33	23	19	2	12	25	.275	.217	.311	7.67	3.68
Kennedy, Brett	R-R	6-0	200	8-4-94	6	10	3.80	22	22	0	0	114	114	57	48	9	44	109	.266	.275	.249	8.63	3.48
Kimber, Corey	R-R	6-1	175	6-28-94	0	0	8.53	3	0	0	0	6	8	5	5	1	3	3	.292	.125	.375	4.26	1.42
Lamet, Dinelson	R-R	6-4	187	7-18-92	7	1	2.35	12	12	0	0	65	56	17	17	4	26	54	.241	.250	.237	7.48	3.60
Lemond, Zech	R-R	6-1	170	10-9-92	6	5	6.66	19	13	0	0	78	104	60	58	7	14	57	.324	.306	.339	6.55	1.61
Lockett, Walker	R-R	6-5	225	5-3-94	4	3	2.98	11	10	0	0	66	57	28	22	3	12	56	.225	.237	.212	7.60	1.63
Maton, Phil	R-R	6-3	220	3-25-93	3	2	1.91	25	0	0	9	33	17	9	7	2	8	47	.149	.191	.119	12.82	2.18
McGrath, Kyle	L-L	6-2	185	7-31-92	1	0	0.00	11	0	0	1	17	8	1	0	1	1	26	.138	.111	.150	13.50	0.52
Mejia, Angel	R-R	6-0	160	2-10-95	0	0	0.00	1	0	0	1	3	0	0	0	0	2	2	.000	.000	.000	6.00	6.00
Morrow, Brandon	R-R	6-3	205	7-26-84	0	1	6.94	2	2	0	0	12	15	9	9	1	3	8	.319	.333	.313	6.17	2.31
Paullus, Ben	R-R	6-1	190	8-31-89	3	1	4.86	32	0	0	1	50	59	30	27	8	18	39	.299	.337	.272	7.02	3.24
Reyes, Gerardo	R-R	5-11	160	5-13-93	1	3	5.00	22	0	0	1	27	24	18	15	2	14	29	.242	.275	.220	9.67	4.67
Rogers, Blake	R-R	6-2	200	2-23-94	0	0	3.60	2	0	0	1	5	3	3	2	1	0	2	.176	.200	.167	3.60	0.00
Ross, Tyson	R-R	6-6	245	4-22-87	0	1	54.00	1	1	0	0	1	3	4	4	0	2	1	.750	1.000	.500	13.50	27.00
Ruiz, Jose	R-R	6-1	190	10-21-94	0	0	0.00	1	0	0	0	1	0	0	0	0	1	1	.000	.000	.000	9.00	9.00
Sanchez, Elier	L-L	6-2	230	10-4-86	0	2	8.74	3	3	0	0	14	18	14	13	11	3	7	6	.311	.333	.306	4.76	5.56
Scholtens, Jesse	R-R	6-4	230	4-6-94	0	0	0.00	1	1	0	0	5	4	2	0	0	1	2	.235	.200	.250	3.86	1.93
Seidenberger, Trevor	L-L	6-2	200	6-9-92	1	2	7.05	40	0	0	1	52	59	44	41	8	32	42	.282	.254	.295	7.22	5.50
Stoops, Dylan	L-L	6-4	235	1-27-92	0	1	7.94	3	2	0	0	6	13	5	5	0	1	9	.448	.417	.471	14.29	1.59
Thornton, Matt	L-L	6-6	235	9-15-76	0	1	6.00	3	0	0	0	3	4	3	2	1	0	3	.333	.000	.500	9.00	3.00
Torres, Jose	L-L	6-2	175	9-24-93	0	2	3.55	20	0	0	1	25	21	11	10	2	10	25	.223	.286	.197	8.88	3.55
Verbitsky, Bryan	R-R	5-11	205	6-11-92	0	0	0.00	2	0	0	0	3	4	0	0	0	1	3	.286	.500	.250	9.00	3.00
Weir, T.J.	R-R	6-0	205	9-15-91	3	2	1.50	18	3	0	0	36	26	8	6	1	10	45	.205	.195	.209	11.25	2.50
Wieck, Brad	L-L	6-9	255	10-14-91	3	1	1.54	26	0	0	1	41	34	9	7	0	16	62	.224	.286	.203	13.61	3.51
Wingenter, Trey	R-R	6-7	200	4-15-94	2	1	2.03	30	0	0	4	44	36	10	10	0	17	46	.229	.194	.259	9.34	3.45
Zimmerman, Mark	L-R	6-0	195	3-29-94	0	0	2.20	12	0	0	0	16	12	6	4	2	4	14	.200	.115	.265	7.71	2.20

Fielding

Catcher	PCT	G	PO	A	E	DP	PB
Del Castillo	.933	3	25	3	2	0	2
Greene	.982	17	153	9	3	1	2
Kennedy	.994	52	427	39	3	3	9
Redman	1.000	3	22	3	0	0	1
Ruiz	.988	49	361	59	5	5	7
Valenzuela	1.000	19	163	12	0	1	3

First Base	PCT	G	PO	A	E	DP
France	.988	9	75	6	1	6
Jensen	.882	3	14	1	2	2
Naylor	.970	32	241	15	8	31
Santos	.984	83	686	64	12	59
Tejada	.984	9	59	1	1	6
Valenzuela	.987	10	71	7	1	5

Second Base	PCT	G	PO	A	E	DP
Blanco	.974	18	26	50	2	10
Bravo	.941	15	19	29	3	7
Giron	—	1	0	0	0	0
Jensen	.909	3	6	4	1	2
Magdaleno	1.000	1	0	1	0	0
Perez	.889	6	5	11	2	2

	PCT	G	PO	A	E	DP	PB
Stevens	1.000	1	2	1	0	0	
Tidwell	.973	7	16	20	1	5	
Urias	.978	80	137	224	8	51	
VanMeter	.933	17	29	41	5	6	
Vilter	1.000	3	4	5	0	0	
Weeks	1.000	3	1	2	0	1	

Third Base	PCT	G	PO	A	E	DP
Blanco	.500	1	0	2	2	0
France	.878	35	22	50	10	3
Giron	.750	2	3	3	2	1
Greene	—	1	0	0	0	0
Jensen	1.000	6	3	12	0	3
Magdaleno	1.000	1	1	0	0	0
Perez	.714	6	0	5	2	1
Stevens	.944	15	4	30	2	2
Urias	.914	15	4	28	3	3
VanMeter	.907	61	31	106	14	9
Vilter	1.000	4	4	1	0	0

Shortstop	PCT	G	PO	A	E	DP
Amarista	1.000	2	4	4	0	1
Bravo	1.000	1	1	0	0	0

	PCT	G	PO	A	E	DP
Giron	.952	14	16	24	2	6
Guerra	.940	102	176	294	30	63
Jensen	.917	3	4	7	1	1
Magdaleno	1.000	3	5	10	0	0
Stevens	1.000	2	3	3	0	0
Urias	.947	22	38	51	5	18
Weeks	1.000	1	2	1	0	1

Outfield	PCT	G	PO	A	E	DP
Bravo	.955	13	20	1	1	0
Cordero	.962	72	143	7	6	1
Gettys	.993	58	139	4	1	1
Jay	1.000	2	2	0	0	0
Jensen	1.000	10	14	2	0	0
Kohlwey	.909	12	20	0	2	0
Moreno	.979	106	173	10	4	2
Reyes	.975	113	226	12	6	6
Schulz	1.000	10	15	0	0	0
Stevens	1.000	3	3	0	0	0
Tejada	.933	28	51	5	4	1
Tidwell	1.000	2	2	0	0	0
VanMeter	—	1	0	0	0	0

FORT WAYNE TINCAPS
MIDWEST LEAGUE

LOW CLASS A

Batting	B-T	HT	WT	DOB	AVG	vLH	vRH	G	AB	R	H	2B	3B	HR	RBI	BB	HBP	SH	SF	SO	SB	CS	SLG	OBP
Allen, Austin	L-R	6-4	225	1-16-94	.320	.362	.301	109	409	52	131	22	0	7	61	29	5	0	10	69	0	0	.425	.364
Baker, Chris	R-R	6-1	180	11-29-94	.286	.000	.367	17	63	9	18	3	3	3	11	7	1	2	0	18	0	0	.571	.366
Belen, Carlos	R-R	6-1	213	2-28-96	.222	.254	.210	114	436	49	97	25	7	12	72	32	4	0	7	132	1	4	.394	.278
Boykin, Rod	R-R	6-1	175	4-17-95	.187	.155	.205	62	198	21	37	5	3	0	7	18	6	9	0	77	13	3	.242	.275
Bravo, Daniel	R-R	6-0	160	2-16-95	.154	.214	.083	8	26	2	4	1	0	0	2	2	0	0	0	7	1	0	.192	.214
Del Castillo, Miguel	R-R	5-10	170	10-14-91	.111	—	.111	2	9	0	1	0	0	0	0	1	0	0	0	3	0	0	.111	.200
France, Ty	R-R	6-0	205	7-13-94	.237	.228	.243	68	219	35	52	8	0	5	35	44	16	1	1	49	3	3	.342	.400
Garcia, Alan	L-L	6-0	220	1-31-97	.222	.116	.255	52	180	13	40	6	0	1	6	7	0	3	1	53	0	0	.272	.250

Batting

Batting	B-T	HT	WT	DOB	AVG	vLH	vRH	G	AB	R	H	2B	3B	HR	RBI	BB	HBP	SH	SF	SO	SB	CS	SLG	OBP
Gettys, Michael	R-R	6-1	203	10-22-95	.304	.303	.304	68	257	37	78	10	5	3	27	18	10	2	2	69	24	10	.416	.369
Giron, Ruddy	R-R	5-11	175	1-4-97	.222	.230	.218	106	401	49	89	23	2	2	20	34	1	10	0	74	8	7	.304	.284
Greene, Marcus	R-R	5-11	195	8-19-94	.217	.263	.191	31	106	10	23	5	0	5	13	10	1	1	2	31	0	2	.406	.286
Kennedy, A.J.	R-R	6-0	190	1-23-94	.233	.267	.214	16	43	5	10	3	0	0	2	4	0	1	0	9	0	2	.302	.298
Kohlwey, Taylor	L-L	6-3	200	7-20-94	.357	.333	.360	7	28	3	10	1	0	0	2	2	1	1	0	6	4	1	.393	.419
Moore, Tyler	R-R	5-8	165	5-28-93	.240	.246	.237	63	221	24	53	8	1	1	13	19	3	5	1	52	4	3	.299	.307
Overstreet, Kyle	R-R	5-11	205	9-4-93	.267	.273	.263	11	30	3	8	2	0	0	2	5	0	0	0	5	0	0	.333	.371
Pena, Jhonatan	R-R	6-2	180	4-18-94	.200	.239	.183	96	350	26	70	11	2	7	32	12	3	0	3	93	1	1	.303	.231
Redman, Hunter	R-R	5-10	180	8-25-92	.333	.167	.500	4	12	0	4	1	0	0	1	3	0	0	0	2	0	0	.417	.467
Selesky, Tyler	L-R	6-0	192	10-6-93	.296	.333	.281	35	125	9	37	5	1	1	9	14	1	0	0	39	1	2	.376	.371
Smith, Mason	R-R	6-2	195	3-16-95	.135	.050	.188	17	52	5	7	3	0	0	5	3	3	1	1	21	0	0	.192	.220
Stevens, River	L-R	6-0	185	11-10-92	.286	.000	.400	21	7	1	7	6	2	0	2	3	1	1	4	0	3	4	.667	.348
Tejada, Luis	R-R	6-3	175	10-12-92	.323	.391	.282	16	62	9	20	8	1	1	18	5	0	0	0	12	1	0	.532	.373
Tidwell, Kodie	L-R	6-1	195	8-3-94	.242	.272	.231	94	326	45	79	16	2	4	23	53	2	7	1	99	7	9	.340	.351
Urena, Jose	R-R	6-3	180	1-14-95	.246	.268	.237	39	138	12	34	4	0	4	14	10	3	0	4	47	0	0	.362	.311
Van Gansen, Peter	L-R	5-9	175	3-4-94	.237	.203	.254	125	459	53	109	15	2	1	31	54	2	13	4	80	1	5	.285	.318
Vilter, Nick	R-R	6-4	220	10-6-93	.218	.231	.212	29	78	9	17	6	0	2	11	17	6	3	2	29	0	0	.372	.388
Zunica, Brad	L-R	6-6	254	10-21-95	.242	.224	.250	110	401	48	97	22	0	14	61	25	6	0	3	156	0	0	.401	.294

Pitching

Pitching	B-T	HT	WT	DOB	W	L	ERA	G	GS	CG	SV	IP	H	R	ER	HR	BB	SO	AVG	vLH	vRH	K/9	BB/9
Allen, Logan	R-L	6-3	200	5-23-97	3	4	3.33	15	11	0	0	54	48	22	20	2	22	47	.242	.194	.265	7.83	3.67
Ashbeck, Elliott	L-R	6-3	215	11-16-93	2	1	1.71	6	1	0	1	21	10	4	4	0	2	15	.143	.184	.094	6.43	0.86
Bachar, Lake	R-R	6-3	210	6-3-95	0	0	0.00	1	0	0	0	3	0	0	0	0	1	1	.000	.000	.000	3.00	3.00
Bednar, David	L-R	6-1	205	10-10-94	3	4	3.43	15	0	0	2	21	20	10	8	0	4	25	.244	.319	.143	10.71	1.71
Castillo, Jose	L-L	6-4	200	1-10-96	1	1	2.28	9	4	0	1	24	23	7	6	0	4	35	.256	.212	.281	13.31	1.52
Cosme, Jean	R-R	6-2	155	5-24-96	8	8	3.22	28	18	0	0	106	112	47	38	3	23	94	.267	.294	.242	7.96	1.95
Cox, Taylor	L-L	6-3	210	7-2-93	1	0	3.27	6	0	0	0	11	11	8	4	0	4	8	.268	.250	.276	6.55	3.27
Cressley, Aaron	L-R	6-1	175	9-2-92	1	0	4.05	13	0	0	0	20	23	12	9	0	10	18	.267	.267	.268	8.10	4.50
De Los Santos, Enyel	R-R	6-3	170	12-25-95	3	2	2.91	11	7	0	0	53	38	20	17	2	14	45	.199	.222	.178	7.69	2.39
Distasio, Lou	R-R	6-4	195	2-5-94	1	2	3.55	24	0	0	3	38	39	16	15	2	5	41	.262	.311	.213	9.71	1.18
Dorminy, Thomas	L-L	6-0	190	6-1-92	4	5	3.10	16	16	2	0	93	88	38	32	2	22	55	.256	.268	.250	5.32	2.13
Espinoza, Anderson	R-R	6-0	160	3-9-98	1	3	4.73	8	7	0	0	32	38	17	17	1	8	28	.290	.282	.300	7.79	2.23
Foriest, Nathan	R-L	6-2	190	1-28-92	0	0	4.34	12	0	0	1	19	13	9	9	2	18	24	.191	.276	.128	11.57	8.68
Headean, Will	R-L	6-4	230	10-11-93	1	0	5.00	8	0	0	0	18	20	12	10	0	7	12	.270	.313	.238	6.00	3.50
Keel, Jerry	L-L	6-6	240	9-26-93	5	10	2.97	25	9	0	0	76	79	35	25	1	21	62	.262	.186	.298	7.37	2.50
Kennedy, Brett	R-R	6-0	200	8-4-94	2	1	2.54	6	6	0	0	28	29	11	8	2	7	38	.269	.357	.212	12.07	2.22
Kimber, Corey	R-R	6-1	175	6-28-94	3	2	4.00	18	0	0	1	45	40	23	20	5	18	39	.240	.263	.220	7.80	3.60
Lauer, Eric	L-L	6-3	205	6-3-95	0	0	0.00	1	1	0	0	2	0	0	0	0	1	2	.000	.000	.000	9.00	4.50
Liriano, Elvin	L-L	6-3	190	10-17-92	2	3	3.38	21	0	0	4	48	37	19	18	6	17	44	.209	.189	.223	8.25	3.19
Lockett, Walker	R-R	6-5	225	5-3-94	1	3	3.00	8	8	0	0	45	43	20	15	0	8	29	.244	.286	.203	5.80	1.60
Lorenzini, Braxton	R-R	6-4	172	4-5-95	0	0	2.45	1	0	0	0	4	2	1	1	1	0	3	.154	.222	.000	7.36	0.00
Lucchesi, Joey	L-L	6-5	204	6-6-93	0	0	0.00	1	0	0	0	2	0	0	0	0	1	3	.444	.500	.429	13.50	4.50
Maton, Phil	R-R	6-3	220	3-25-93	1	1	1.42	8	0	0	1	13	14	3	2	0	1	19	.269	.261	.276	13.50	0.71
Mejia, Angel	R-R	6-0	160	2-10-95	1	3	6.92	5	2	0	0	13	25	15	10	0	5	5	.397	.378	.423	3.46	3.46
Miller, Evan	R-R	6-2	185	5-23-95	0	1	1.93	4	0	0	0	5	4	1	1	0	2	4	.250	.200	.333	7.71	3.86
Monroe, Nick	R-R	6-4	235	3-6-94	3	2	6.54	24	0	0	1	43	59	32	31	2	20	50	.330	.345	.316	10.55	4.22
Morris, Elliot	R-R	6-4	210	4-26-92	1	1	5.87	3	0	0	0	8	7	5	5	2	0	7	.226	.278	.154	8.22	0.00
Nix, Jacob	R-R	6-4	220	1-9-96	3	7	3.93	25	25	0	0	105	115	54	46	5	20	90	.280	.302	.255	7.69	1.71
Paddack, Chris	R-R	6-4	195	1-8-96	0	0	0.64	3	3	0	0	14	11	1	1	0	3	23	.212	.250	.188	14.79	1.93
Quantrill, Cal	L-R	6-2	165	2-10-95	0	1	17.36	2	2	0	0	5	12	9	9	1	4	2	.522	.500	.545	3.86	7.71
Ramirez, Emmanuel	R-R	6-2	190	7-15-94	2	3	4.71	16	7	0	1	57	58	32	30	5	21	54	.264	.297	.235	8.48	3.30
Reyes, Gerardo	R-R	5-11	160	5-13-93	3	2	2.10	18	0	0	5	26	23	8	6	1	10	18	.247	.261	.234	6.31	3.51
Rogers, Blake	R-R	6-2	200	2-23-94	1	3	5.58	21	2	0	0	61	78	44	38	6	20	36	.310	.368	.244	5.28	2.93
Scholtens, Jesse	R-R	6-4	230	4-6-94	0	0	3.00	1	0	0	0	3	3	1	1	0	0	1	.250	.500	.000	3.00	0.00
Smith, Austin	R-R	6-4	220	7-9-96	4	6	5.26	25	15	0	1	91	104	60	53	6	46	63	.294	.343	.244	6.25	4.57
Stillman, Will	R-R	6-4	175	11-2-93	0	0	5.54	7	0	0	0	13	14	8	8	0	9	15	.286	.296	.273	10.38	6.23
Wingenter, Trey	R-R	6-7	200	4-15-94	1	0	0.82	8	0	0	4	11	6	3	1	0	2	14	.162	.125	.190	11.45	1.64

Fielding

Catcher	PCT	G	PO	A	E	DP	PB
Allen	.991	89	679	82	7	6	11
Del Castillo	1.000	2	15	1	0	0	2
Greene	.971	21	151	18	5	2	6
Kennedy	.981	16	92	11	2	1	1
Overstreet	.957	10	59	8	3	1	0
Redman	1.000	4	27	3	0	0	1
Vilter	1.000	7	45	4	0	0	4

First Base	PCT	G	PO	A	E	DP
Belen	1.000	1	1	1	0	0
France	.992	40	348	24	3	27
Selesky	.978	11	88	3	2	7
Vilter	1.000	8	90	0	0	9
Zunica	.985	87	714	50	12	49

Second Base	PCT	G	PO	A	E	DP
Bravo	.939	7	9	22	2	3
Moore	.953	8	10	31	2	8
Tidwell	.961	20	27	47	3	6
Van Gansen	.981	106	148	320	9	54
Vilter	.909	2	1	9	1	2

Third Base	PCT	G	PO	A	E	DP
Belen	.917	101	80	152	21	13
France	.909	12	6	14	2	0
Selesky	.857	3	0	6	1	0
Stevens	1.000	2	2	0	0	0
Tidwell	.936	19	11	33	3	2
Vilter	1.000	6	4	13	0	2

Shortstop	PCT	G	PO	A	E	DP
Baker	.957	16	30	37	3	14
Giron	.946	103	160	277	25	56
Tidwell	.800	2	3	5	2	3
Van Gansen	.952	19	24	56	4	6

Outfield	PCT	G	PO	A	E	DP
Boykin	.993	62	134	6	1	0
Garcia	.955	50	100	5	5	0
Gettys	.976	68	150	11	4	1
Kohlwey	1.000	7	15	0	0	0
Moore	.973	55	100	8	3	1
Pena	.948	83	146	0	8	0
Selesky	1.000	7	10	1	0	0
Smith	1.000	16	26	1	0	0
Stevens	1.000	3	3	0	0	0
Tejada	1.000	13	25	1	0	0
Tidwell	.950	34	53	4	3	0
Urena	.986	32	64	4	1	2

TRI-CITY DUST DEVILS   SHORT-SEASON
NORTHWEST LEAGUE

Batting	B-T	HT	WT	DOB	AVG	vLH	vRH	G	AB	R	H	2B	3B	HR	RBI	BB	HBP	SH	SF	SO	SB	CS	SLG	OBP
Asuncion, Luis	R-R	6-4	205	2-27-97	.241	.286	.227	58	199	21	48	12	0	1	21	21	7	0	0	54	0	1	.317	.335
Baker, Chris	R-R	6-1	180	11-29-94	.303	.281	.313	54	201	33	61	11	0	2	27	23	7	0	3	49	14	4	.388	.389
Burgos, Aldemar	R-R	6-0	165	1-23-97	.189	.156	.203	31	106	10	20	4	1	0	7	5	1	6	0	36	1	5	.245	.232
De La Cruz, Wilfri	R-R	5-11	180	12-29-93	.284	.235	.300	21	67	11	19	2	0	1	9	6	2	1	0	19	1	1	.358	.360
Del Castillo, Miguel	R-R	5-10	170	10-14-91	.000	.000	.000	1	4	0	0	0	0	0	0	0	0	0	0	2	0	0	.000	.000
DeLeon, Manny	L-R	6-1	195	4-11-93	.214	.000	.273	15	42	4	9	1	0	0	4	8	1	0	1	14	2	1	.238	.346
Easley, Nate	R-R	5-10	170	1-11-96	.261	.297	.249	67	241	44	63	6	5	1	18	46	3	3	1	59	13	4	.340	.385
Garcia, Alan	L-L	6-0	200	1-31-97	.263	.444	.100	6	19	2	5	2	0	0	4	4	0	0	0	5	0	0	.368	.391
Kohlwey, Taylor	L-L	6-3	200	7-20-94	.220	.265	.204	33	127	14	28	4	4	1	20	19	1	0	1	27	8	3	.339	.324
Magdaleno, Westhers	R-R	6-1	190	10-30-96	.247	.233	.256	21	73	4	18	3	0	0	5	6	1	0	1	21	0	1	.288	.309
Magee, Josh	R-R	5-10	180	2-13-97	.187	.171	.192	47	166	20	31	2	1	0	10	18	5	2	1	56	4	3	.211	.284
Mattison, Chris	R-R	6-4	215	4-16-94	.162	.242	.125	32	105	12	17	3	0	2	10	12	1	1	1	43	0	0	.248	.252
Moore, Tyler	R-R	5-8	165	5-28-93	.237	.400	.179	11	38	3	9	0	0	1	8	1	0	0	0	13	0	2	.237	.383
Overstreet, Kyle	R-R	5-11	205	9-4-93	.253	.250	.254	64	241	25	61	7	1	0	28	21	1	1	5	40	1	0	.290	.310
Potts, Hudson	R-R	6-2	180	10-28-98	.233	.167	.250	16	60	7	14	0	1	0	6	9	2	1	0	13	2	1	.267	.352
Redman, Hunter	R-R	5-10	180	8-25-92	.182	.300	.147	15	44	0	8	0	0	0	5	8	1	0	0	12	0	1	.182	.321
Reed, Buddy	B-R	6-4	210	4-27-95	.254	.268	.248	51	205	31	52	9	4	0	13	22	1	0	2	53	15	5	.337	.326
Savinon, Jose	L-R	6-0	160	2-17-96	.238	.182	.246	26	80	9	19	2	1	0	4	7	0	1	0	12	3	1	.288	.299
Smith, Mason	R-R	6-2	195	3-16-95	.267	.333	.250	5	15	3	4	0	0	1	3	2	2	0	0	5	0	0	.467	.421
Sosa, Carlos	R-R	6-1	190	8-7-95	.175	.083	.214	13	40	3	7	1	0	0	6	3	4	0	0	15	0	0	.200	.298
Tatis Jr. Fernando	R-R	6-3	185	1-2-99	.273	.250	.278	12	44	4	12	4	2	0	5	3	0	0	2	13	1	1	.455	.306
White, Boomer	R-R	5-10	195	7-28-93	.213	.213	.213	61	230	25	49	11	1	0	21	19	4	0	2	34	3	3	.270	.282
Young, G.K.	L-R	6-1	225	10-17-94	.209	.208	.209	47	177	13	37	8	0	4	22	21	1	0	3	63	1	0	.322	.292

Pitching	B-T	HT	WT	DOB	W	L	ERA	G	GS	CG	SV	IP	H	R	ER	HR	BB	SO	AVG	vLH	vRH	K/9	BB/9
Allen, Logan	R-L	6-3	200	5-23-97	0	1	7.71	1	1	0	0	2	4	2	2	0	1	4	.364	.333	.375	15.43	3.86
Bednar, David	L-R	6-2	205	10-10-94	1	0	0.00	8	0	0	2	10	7	0	0	0	0	15	.184	.154	.208	13.50	0.00
Berry, Tim	L-L	6-3	180	3-18-91	0	1	1.42	2	2	0	0	6	6	1	1	0	1	3	.273	.333	.263	4.26	1.42
Castillo, Jose	L-L	6-4	200	1-10-96	0	1	1.80	4	0	0	1	5	5	1	1	1	3	7	.278	.200	.308	12.60	5.40
Cressley, Aaron	L-R	6-1	175	9-2-92	0	0	1.59	9	0	0	4	11	3	2	2	0	5	8	.083	.083	.083	6.35	3.97
De Horta, Adrian	R-R	6-3	185	3-13-95	2	2	3.95	9	1	0	0	27	24	18	12	1	7	25	.229	.244	.217	8.23	2.30
DiSabatino, Dom	R-R	6-5	190	3-21-96	0	0	0.00	2	0	0	0	2	0	0	0	0	1	2	.000	.000	.000	7.71	3.86
Erb, Dalton	R-R	6-8	250	5-13-94	2	1	2.70	19	0	0	0	40	37	16	12	0	14	17	.255	.295	.226	4.95	3.15
Ford, Chasen	R-R	6-3	200	7-18-95	0	1	7.31	13	0	0	0	16	34	19	13	1	14	17	.493	.483	.444	9.56	7.88
Foriest, Nathan	R-L	6-2	190	1-28-92	1	1	2.87	13	0	0	0	16	13	7	5	1	17	21	.210	.083	.289	12.06	9.77
Garcia, Jean	R-R	6-5	220	12-7-95	0	0	27.00	1	2	0	0	1	2	4	4	0	5	2	.400	1.000	.353	33.75	33.75
Guerrero, Jordan	R-R	6-5	260	8-1-96	4	5	4.34	10	7	0	0	37	39	27	18	2	22	23	.265	.260	.268	5.54	5.30
Headean, Will	R-L	6-4	230	10-11-93	4	5	4.32	15	14	0	0	73	75	43	35	4	26	77	.263	.250	.267	9.49	3.21
Lauer, Eric	R-L	6-3	205	6-3-95	1	0	1.44	7	7	0	0	25	17	4	4	0	7	28	.191	.240	.172	10.08	2.52
Lopez, Diomar	R-R	6-0	165	12-15-96	4	1	2.98	20	0	0	2	42	39	19	14	2	10	38	.239	.187	.284	8.08	2.13
Lorenzini, Braxton	R-R	6-4	172	4-5-95	3	5	6.15	13	5	0	0	45	47	38	31	2	22	43	.267	.258	.273	8.54	4.37
Lucchesi, Joey	L-L	6-5	204	6-6-93	0	2	1.35	14	10	0	1	40	27	7	6	0	2	53	.189	.174	.196	11.93	0.45
Mejia, Angel	R-R	6-0	160	2-10-95	1	2	4.58	8	7	0	0	37	39	24	19	2	15	26	.269	.291	.256	6.27	3.62
Miller, Evan	R-R	6-2	185	5-23-95	1	3	2.08	15	0	0	2	26	16	9	6	1	15	25	.163	.209	.127	8.65	5.19
Monroe, Nick	R-R	6-4	235	3-6-94	0	1	12.10	8	0	0	0	10	17	13	13	0	10	11	.405	.538	.345	10.24	9.31
Perez, Mayky	R-R	6-5	235	9-26-96	0	0	2.57	4	0	0	0	7	10	7	2	0	4	7	.303	.333	.267	9.00	5.14
Quantrill, Cal	R-R	6-2	165	2-10-95	0	0	1.93	5	5	0	0	19	15	7	4	0	2	28	.205	.171	.237	13.50	0.96
Ramirez, Emmanuel	R-R	6-2	190	7-15-94	4	1	2.62	8	4	0	0	45	36	16	13	0	13	42	.218	.246	.204	8.46	2.62
Rodriguez, Hansel	R-R	6-2	170	2-27-97	0	2	6.97	6	6	0	0	21	25	17	16	2	12	13	.298	.229	.389	5.66	5.23
Ruiz, Jose	R-R	6-1	190	10-21-94	2	0	0.00	9	0	0	2	11	3	0	0	0	2	12	.094	.118	.067	10.13	1.69
Sanchez, Elier	L-L	6-2	230	10-4-86	1	1	5.74	3	3	0	0	16	15	10	10	1	9	12	.259	.125	.310	6.89	5.17
Scholtens, Jesse	R-R	6-4	230	4-6-94	0	1	1.65	17	0	0	4	27	26	6	5	0	6	36	.258	.195	.281	11.85	1.98
Seidenberger, Trevor	L-L	6-2	200	6-9-92	0	0	1.17	5	0	0	0	8	5	2	1	0	2	6	.172	.333	.100	7.04	2.35
Sheckler, Ben	L-L	6-8	240	5-12-95	0	1	2.25	2	0	0	0	4	2	1	1	1	1	6	.167	.500	.000	9.00	2.25
Stillman, Will	R-R	6-4	175	11-2-93	2	0	0.61	11	0	0	0	15	4	1	1	0	6	17	.083	.125	.063	10.43	3.68
Weickel, Walker	R-R	6-6	195	11-14-93	0	1	3.86	4	0	0	0	7	7	4	3	0	3	5	.269	.500	.167	6.43	3.86
Zimmerman, Mark	L-R	6-0	195	3-29-94	1	2	0.86	10	0	0	0	21	15	4	2	0	4	31	.197	.222	.184	13.29	1.71

Fielding

C: De La Cruz 18, Del Castillo 1, Mattison 16, Overstreet 35, Redman 11. **1B:** De La Cruz 3, Mattison 12, Overstreet 17, Redman 1, Sosa 10, Young 36.
2B: Easley 64, Magdaleno 1, Overstreet 3, Potts 2, Savinon 5, Tatis Jr. 1. **3B:** Magdaleno 10, Overstreet 1, Potts 3, Savinon 4, Sosa 2, Tatis Jr. 3, White 56.
SS: Baker 54, Magdaleno 4, Potts 10, Savinon 3, Tatis Jr. 7. **OF:** Asuncion 53, Burgos 27, DeLeon 10, Easley 1, Garcia 5, Kohlwey 30, Magee 45, Moore 9, Reed 50, Smith 3.

Batting	B-T	HT	WT	DOB	AVG	vLH	vRH	G	AB	R	H	2B	3B	HR	RBI	BB	HBP	SH	SF	SO	SB	CS	SLG	OBP
Amarista, Alexi	L-R	5-6	160	4-6-89	.000	—	.000	1	1	1	0	0	0	0	1	1	0	0	1	0	0	0	.000	.333
Anguizola, Luis	R-R	5-11	210	2-27-94	.279	.192	.308	31	104	19	29	5	0	1	18	17	3	0	2	24	3	0	.356	.389
Aragon, Bryant	L-R	6-2	160	4-10-98	.234	.214	.238	20	77	8	18	3	1	1	12	5	1	0	1	17	0	0	.338	.286
Burgos, Aldemar	R-R	6-0	165	1-23-97	.164	.133	.174	18	61	8	10	2	1	1	5	3	0	2	0	15	1	1	.279	.203
Carter, Tre	L-R	6-2	181	3-22-97	.298	.250	.308	12	47	7	14	0	2	0	10	9	0	0	0	10	3	2	.383	.411
Contreras, Ronaldo	R-R	6-3	195	7-15-96	.154	.250	.111	3	13	1	2	0	0	0	1	0	0	0	0	6	0	0	.154	.154
De La Cruz, Wilfri	R-R	5-11	180	12-29-93	.313	.667	.231	5	16	3	5	2	0	0	1	0	1	0	0	1	0	0	.438	.353
DeLeon, Manny	L-R	6-1	195	4-11-93	.212	.222	.209	32	118	14	25	4	3	0	6	12	0	0	1	39	8	1	.297	.282
Gowdy, Denzell	R-R	6-2	185	11-30-96	.256	.321	.237	37	121	17	31	6	1	1	13	15	5	1	1	38	3	1	.347	.359
Ilarraza, Reinaldo	B-R	5-10	150	1-12-99	.179	.400	.103	13	39	7	7	0	0	0	2	7	2	0	1	20	0	1	.179	.327
Jensen, Chase	R-R	6-4	195	1-29-91	.000	.000	.000	2	7	1	0	0	0	0	0	1	1	0	0	2	0	0	.000	.222
Lezama, Jose	R-R	6-1	195	2-19-98	.259	.258	.259	35	116	17	30	4	0	0	13	19	4	2	3	14	2	2	.293	.373
Magdaleno, Westhers	R-R	6-1	190	10-30-96	.259	.286	.250	7	27	0	7	0	0	0	2	3	0	0	1	10	0	1	.259	.323
Magee, Josh	R-R	5-10	180	2-13-97	.263	.500	.154	5	19	3	5	0	1	0	2	2	1	0	0	7	2	2	.368	.364
Mattison, Chris	R-R	6-4	215	4-16-94	.500	.500	.500	2	6	4	3	1	0	0	2	0	0	0	0	1	0	0	.667	.625
Minaya, Euri	R-R	6-4	205	10-11-95	.169	.125	.179	22	83	6	14	1	3	1	9	0	1	0	1	44	1	0	.289	.176
Olmo, Dayon	B-R	5-11	165	11-15-96	.288	.323	.277	34	132	29	38	8	3	4	18	7	2	0	0	36	4	2	.485	.333
Ortega, Ariel	R-R	5-10	150	6-20-97	.231	.217	.235	29	91	10	21	4	0	0	8	8	1	0	0	34	2	1	.275	.300
Pennell, Tucker	R-R	6-2	200	4-7-94	.260	.364	.231	15	50	8	13	3	0	0	7	9	3	0	0	6	1	2	.320	.403
Potts, Hudson	R-R	6-2	180	10-28-98	.295	.279	.300	43	183	35	54	12	2	1	21	9	2	0	1	34	8	4	.399	.333
Rosario, Eguy	R-R	5-9	150	8-25-99	.379	.250	.429	7	29	3	11	3	0	1	2	1	0	0	7	1	1	.483	.438
Savinon, Jose	L-R	6-0	160	2-17-96	.364	.000	.444	4	11	1	4	0	1	0	2	2	0	0	1	4	1	0	.545	.429
Selesky, Tyler	L-R	6-0	192	10-6-93	.299	.286	.304	22	77	19	23	4	3	0	17	11	3	0	2	10	1	0	.429	.398
Sosa, Carlos	R-R	6-1	190	8-7-95	.236	.286	.220	16	55	10	13	2	0	1	9	6	1	0	0	12	0	0	.327	.323
Sotillo, Jose	R-R	6-1	175	5-13-96	.214	.000	.261	8	28	2	6	2	0	0	6	1	0	0	1	9	0	0	.286	.241
Suwinski, Jack	L-L	6-2	200	7-29-98	.231	.244	.30	108	12	26	5	0	0	10	12	2	0	1	19	3	0	.287	.325
Tatis Jr. Fernando	R-R	6-3	185	1-2-99	.273	.216	.288	43	176	35	48	13	1	4	20	10	0	1	0	44	14	2	.426	.312
Tidwell, Kodie	L-R	6-1	195	8-3-94	.143	.000	.200	2	7	1	1	1	0	0	2	0	0	0	0	0	0	0	.286	.333
Weeks, Jemile	B-R	5-9	170	1-26-87	.556	.600	.500	3	9	1	5	2	0	0	2	1	0	0	0	1	0	0	.778	.600
Williams, Jaquez	L-R	6-3	215	11-16-97	.169	.083	.200	26	89	11	15	5	2	1	12	9	0	0	0	40	0	0	.303	.245

Pitching	B-T	HT	WT	DOB	W	L	ERA	G	GS	CG	SV	IP	H	R	ER	HR	BB	SO	AVG	vLH	vRH	K/9	BB/9
Allen, Logan	R-L	6-3	200	5-23-97	0	0	3.00	3	3	0	0	6	5	2	2	0	1	8	.217	.333	.200	12.00	1.50
Arias, Juan	R-R	6-2	175	5-6-95	1	1	10.02	17	0	0	0	21	39	25	23	2	6	15	.394	.324	.435	6.53	2.61
Bachar, Lake	R-R	6-3	210	6-3-95	1	2	3.45	10	5	0	0	29	25	11	11	1	6	35	.231	.262	.212	10.99	1.88
Clase, Emmanuel	R-R	6-2	150	3-18-98	2	0	4.01	8	2	0	0	25	22	18	11	0	12	23	.227	.143	.274	8.39	4.38
Cordero, Starlin	R-R	6-7	220	7-21-98	2	1	2.84	15	2	0	0	25	22	16	8	0	17	31	.227	.263	.203	11.01	6.04
Dallas, Dan	L-L	6-2	180	12-24-97	1	2	3.09	5	3	0	0	12	11	6	4	0	7	16	.234	.125	.290	12.34	5.40
De Horta, Adrian	R-R	6-3	185	3-15-95	0	0	0.00	2	0	0	0	4	2	0	0	0	2	4	.154	.167	.143	9.82	4.91
Diaz, Luis	R-R	6-4	290	4-9-92	0	1	3.00	3	1	0	0	6	6	7	3	2	0	1	4	.292	.182	.385	6.00	1.50
DiSabatino, Dom	R-R	6-5	190	3-21-96	0	1	9.58	12	0	0	0	10	15	13	11	1	4	13	.319	.294	.333	11.32	3.48
Ford, Chasen	R-R	6-3	200	7-18-95	0	0	8.31	3	0	0	0	4	8	4	4	0	2	5	.421	.500	.400	10.38	4.15
Garcia, Jason	R-R	6-5	220	12-7-96	1	4	3.66	11	8	0	0	47	45	23	19	0	15	36	.257	.290	.239	6.94	2.89
Gauthier, Kyle	R-R	6-4	220	4-8-94	1	3	6.49	17	0	0	1	26	36	23	19	1	6	30	.324	.283	.354	10.25	2.05
Guzman, Jonathan	R-R	5-10	180	2-8-95	2	2	7.18	17	1	0	0	26	32	24	21	2	13	21	.299	.321	.291	7.18	4.44
Henry, Henry	R-R	6-3	178	12-17-98	1	4	5.28	9	4	0	0	29	35	24	17	0	13	29	.292	.359	.259	9.00	4.03
Lauer, Eric	R-L	6-3	205	6-3-95	0	1	6.75	2	2	0	0	4	7	5	3	1	1	7	.368	.333	.375	15.75	2.25
Lawson, Reggie	R-R	6-4	205	8-2-97	0	0	8.31	5	3	0	0	9	12	8	8	0	3	7	.316	.353	.286	7.27	3.12
Lucio, Seth	R-R	5-10	180	4-30-93	1	0	5.06	7	0	0	0	5	6	4	3	0	2	7	.261	.154	.400	11.81	3.38
McDade, Jim	L-R	6-5	190	12-1-92	5	1	1.59	18	0	0	2	34	25	9	6	0	6	27	.205	.205	.205	7.15	1.59
McNutt, Trey	R-R	6-4	220	8-2-89	0	0	0.00	2	0	0	0	1	1	2	0	0	1	0	.167	.000	.250	0.00	6.75
Morrow, Brandon	R-R	6-3	205	7-26-84	1	0	1.80	4	0	0	0	5	8	3	1	0	0	6	.364	.286	.400	10.80	0.00
Munoz, Andres	R-R	6-2	165	1-16-99	1	1	5.49	16	1	0	0	16	16	12	1	16	26	.213	.281	.163	11.90	7.32
Perez, Mayky	R-R	6-5	235	9-26-96	2	2	3.94	9	6	0	0	30	30	23	13	1	15	31	.250	.341	.197	9.40	4.55
Quantrill, Cal	L-R	6-2	165	2-10-95	0	2	5.27	5	5	0	0	14	12	8	8	0	2	16	.231	.125	.321	10.54	1.32
Ruiz, Jose	R-R	6-1	190	10-21-94	0	0	0.00	1	0	0	0	1	0	0	0	0	2	1	.000	—	.000	13.50	27.00
Sheckler, Ben	L-L	6-8	240	5-15-95	1	2	4.25	16	2	0	2	30	33	17	14	1	12	25	.280	.227	.292	7.58	3.64
Smith, Jake	R-R	6-4	190	6-2-90	0	0	0.00	1	0	0	0	1	1	0	0	0	0	2	.250	1.000	.000	18.00	0.00
Thompson, Mason	R-R	6-7	186	2-20-98	0	0	2.25	5	5	0	0	12	8	3	3	0	5	12	.186	.200	.182	9.00	3.75
Torres, Wilmer	R-R	6-3	190	5-31-96	1	0	2.49	20	0	0	9	22	15	6	6	0	13	27	.195	.133	.234	11.22	5.40
Weickel, Walker	R-R	6-6	195	11-14-93	0	0	12.00	1	2	0	0	3	4	4	4	2	0	2	.333	.250	.375	6.00	0.00
Zawadzki, Grant	R-R	5-10	200	4-27-92	0	0	6.26	23	0	0	0	23	25	18	16	1	12	25	.275	.258	.283	9.78	4.70

Fielding

C: Anguizola 1, Aragon 10, De La Cruz 1, Lezama 34, Mattison 2, Pennell 10. 1B: Anguizola 26, De La Cruz 4, Lezama 1, Selesky 1, Sosa 5, Williams 25. 2B: Gowdy 10, Ilarraza 9, Ortega 24, Potts 4, Rosario 5, Savinon 2, Tatis Jr. 8, Weeks 1. 3B: Gowdy 26, Magdaleno 3, Potts 4, Rosario 3, Selesky 12, Sosa 10, Tatis Jr. 2, Tidwell 1. SS: Amarista 1, Ilarraza 2, Jensen 1, Magdaleno 6, Ortega 4, Potts 14, Savinon 1, Tatis Jr. 29, Weeks 2. OF: Anguizola 3, Burgos 17, Carter 10, Contreras 3, DeLeon 32, Gowdy 2, Jensen 1, Magee 5, Minaya 22, Olmo 33, Savinon 1, Selesky 11, Sotillo 7, Suwinski 27.

SAN DIEGO PADRES

DSL PADRES   ROOKIE
DOMINICAN SUMMER LEAGUE

Batting	B-T	HT	WT	DOB	AVG	vLH	vRH	G	AB	R	H	2B	3B	HR	RBI	BB	HBP	SH	SF	SO	SB	CS	SLG	OBP
Alarcon, Kelvin	B-R	6-1	155	3-6-99	.254	.250	.256	58	169	34	43	4	1	0	19	58	2	3	0	43	16	4	.290	.450
Aragon, Bryant	L-R	6-2	160	4-10-98	.263	.000	.294	11	38	5	10	0	1	2	10	4	0	0	1	10	0	0	.474	.326
Burgos, Edward	L-L	6-2	175	8-24-96	.308	.342	.298	51	159	25	49	4	1	0	17	21	4	3	0	39	11	6	.346	.402
Fernandez, Juan	R-R	5-11	180	3-7-99	.353	.083	.459	33	85	13	30	3	1	1	17	17	4	1	2	16	0	1	.447	.472
Francisco, Yordi	L-R	6-1	175	3-14-97	.204	.207	.204	47	142	18	29	4	4	0	12	19	3	0	1	61	8	5	.289	.309
Garcia, Jaffe	R-R	6-1	175	3-13-96	.247	.152	.274	46	146	18	36	8	2	2	22	32	5	1	1	49	0	0	.370	.397
Guzman, Luis	R-R	6-2	175	6-20-98	.301	.344	.288	45	136	26	41	2	1	1	21	24	11	1	0	14	6	4	.353	.444
Martinez, Alam	R-R	6-2	208	6-13-97	.130	.043	.167	27	77	9	10	0	0	0	4	15	0	1	1	45	1	1	.130	.269
Melean, Kelvin	R-R	6-0	165	9-5-98	.291	.225	.311	49	172	30	50	8	3	0	24	27	6	1	2	28	9	6	.372	.401
Perez, Blinger	R-R	6-0	170	8-21-98	.202	.150	.219	25	84	7	17	3	0	0	6	13	1	0	0	18	1	0	.238	.316
Rosario, Eguy	R-R	5-9	150	8-25-99	.341	.280	.363	53	185	42	63	19	1	1	24	23	5	0	3	31	21	9	.470	.421
Sabala, Elvis	R-R	6-1	178	9-26-97	.232	.293	.215	53	185	19	43	7	0	2	30	16	2	3	3	45	4	3	.303	.296
Santos, Angel	L-R	6-4	170	1-13-96	.259	.226	.269	44	135	24	35	6	3	0	11	35	1	3	0	43	17	3	.348	.415
Sotillo, Jose	R-R	6-1	175	5-13-96	.300	.000	.333	3	10	0	3	2	0	0	0	1	0	0	0	5	0	0	.500	.364
Suarez, Felix	R-R	6-0	180	1-9-96	.194	.231	.179	39	134	17	26	6	0	0	8	12	2	0	0	34	16	0	.239	.270
Taveras, Carlos	B-R	5-11	165	4-17-97	.250	.353	.220	25	76	9	19	1	0	0	7	15	2	1	2	17	5	6	.263	.379
Tovar, Danny	L-L	5-11	180	11-2-98	.287	.324	.269	40	101	15	29	5	1	1	9	19	3	0	2	26	7	4	.386	.408

Pitching	B-T	HT	WT	DOB	W	L	ERA	G	GS	CG	SV	IP	H	R	ER	HR	BB	SO	AVG	vLH	vRH	K/9	BB/9
Acevedo, Angel	R-R	6-1	180	9-19-98	4	2	2.86	13	7	0	1	50	61	23	16	2	18	33	.293	.262	.301	5.90	3.22
Bencomo, Edwuin	R-R	6-2	165	4-14-99	0	2	5.24	19	0	0	6	22	27	20	13	1	10	26	.290	.333	.278	10.48	4.03
Cabrera, Jose	L-L	6-0	170	9-26-98	2	2	2.79	13	13	0	0	52	32	18	16	0	33	48	.174	.136	.179	8.36	5.75
Fernandez, Omar	L-L	5-11	160	4-20-99	3	0	0.76	12	12	0	0	59	33	6	5	1	11	30	.162	.188	.157	4.55	1.67
Gonzalez, Cesar	R-R	6-1	160	2-24-99	0	0	1.50	3	0	0	0	6	1	1	1	0	9	3	.059	.333	.000	4.50	13.50
2-team total (5 Red Sox)					2	0	1.53	8	0	0	0	18	8	3	3	1	14	8	—	—	—	4.08	7.13
Grullart, Oliver	R-R	6-1	165	3-23-97	0	0	5.19	6	0	0	1	9	12	5	5	1	4	6	.333	.143	.379	6.23	4.15
Guzman, Jonathan	R-R	5-10	180	2-8-95	1	0	0.75	4	1	0	0	12	9	1	1	0	3	12	.209	.111	.235	9.00	2.25
Guzman, Oliber	R-R	5-11	180	3-15-97	5	1	2.70	18	1	0	0	37	28	16	11	1	13	24	.214	.152	.235	5.89	3.19
Henry, Henry	R-R	6-4	178	12-17-98	0	0	3.00	2	2	0	0	6	5	2	2	0	0	8	.227	.250	.214	12.00	0.00
Hernandez, Adolfo	L-L	5-11	165	7-23-97	0	2	1.36	11	4	0	0	33	28	8	5	1	15	37	.230	.333	.218	10.09	4.09
Hernandez, Jose	R-R	6-1	165	8-6-98	3	2	4.10	15	0	0	0	26	26	27	12	0	24	14	.252	.345	.216	4.78	8.20
Lezama, Aaron	L-L	6-5	180	4-22-97	0	0	6.16	9	3	0	1	19	19	16	13	0	12	13	.247	.444	.221	6.16	5.68
Machuca, Cristian	L-L	6-1	165	4-24-97	3	5	4.15	13	11	1	0	61	77	39	28	1	13	40	.313	.389	.307	5.93	1.93
Martinez, Luis	R-R	5-11	184	12-1-95	3	2	12.05	12	0	0	1	19	22	27	25	3	25	13	.297	.313	.293	6.27	12.05
Polanco, Anderson	L-L	6-3	175	2-5-98	3	3	3.95	12	6	0	1	41	40	19	18	1	17	38	.263	.227	.269	8.34	3.73
Powell, Evan	R-R	6-9	246	11-18-96	0	2	19.41	12	0	0	0	11	20	26	23	1	20	9	.400	.455	.385	7.59	16.88
Ramos, Jordis	L-L	6-10	194	6-15-96	0	1	27.00	1	0	0	0	1	0	2	2	0	4	1	.000	—	.000	13.50	54.00
2-team total (14 White Sox)					1	4	3.75	15	1	0	0	36	25	19	15	0	26	35	—	—	—	8.75	6.50
Rivera, Carlos	R-R	6-3	190	6-8-95	0	0	0.00	1	0	0	1	0	0	0	0	0	0	0	.000	—	.000	0.00	0.00
Roman, Miguel	R-R	6-1	170	2-23-97	0	0	7.50	5	0	0	1	6	6	6	5	0	3	7	.240	.200	.250	10.50	4.50
Santana, Adonis	R-R	6-1	160	9-10-98	2	5	7.27	12	0	0	0	17	25	22	14	1	17	16	.329	.263	.351	8.31	8.83
Solano, Eduardo	L-L	6-3	203	5-22-97	3	1	4.05	18	0	0	2	33	33	22	15	0	27	40	.258	.294	.252	10.80	7.29
Valdez, Dauris	R-R	6-8	221	10-22-95	4	3	3.51	14	9	0	0	56	50	29	22	1	14	56	.238	.226	.246	8.95	2.24

Fielding

C: Aragon 10, Fernandez 21, Perez 19, Villalobos 7. **1B:** Fernandez 2, Francisco 2, Garcia 1, Sabala 31, Suarez 37. **2B:** Alarcon 28, Guzman 21, Rosario 26. **3B:** Alarcon 29, Guzman 1, Rosario 26, Sabala 20. **SS:** Alarcon 1, Guzman 24, Melean 47, Sabala 2. **OF:** Burgos 44, Fernandez 1, Francisco 38, Garcia 41, Martinez 18, Santos 41, Sotillo 2, Taveras 12, Tovar 33.

San Francisco Giants

SEASON IN A SENTENCE: For half a season, the Giants' even-year magic appeared to be holding, as San Francisco entered the all-star break with baseball's best record at 57-33. A shattered bullpen and punchless lineup led to a 30-42 second half, however, and Division Series loss to the Cubs.

HIGH POINT: The Giants heated up most in late June, winning 13 of 15 with two of the losses coming in Madison Bumgarner starts. The first winin the streak was a walk-off win over the Dodgers that included a four-hit, two-run rally off L.A. closer Kenley Jansen, capped by a groundball RBI single by Buster Posey for a 6-5 victory.

LOW POINT: The Giants managed to win five of their last six to claim a wild-card berth and advanced past the Mets with a complete-game shutout by Bumgarner, but the bullpen that led the majors in blown saves in the regular season lived up to that reputation in Game Four of the Division Series against the Cubs. Leading Chicago 5-2 in the ninth, the Giants used five pitchers, who combined to give up four hits, a walk and four runs as the Cubs eliminated the Giants. It was an all-too-familiar way for the Giants to lose a game.

NOTABLE ROOKIES: As expected, Jarrett Parker and Mac Williamson both saw time and showed power in the Giants' outfield, combining for 11 homers, though neither sewed up a regular spot. Righty Derek Law became a key bullpen piece, posting a 2.13 ERA while ranking fourth with 61 appearances.

KEY TRANSACTIONS: After signing Johnny Cueto and Jeff Samardzija in the offseason, the Giants still needed pitching help in the rotation and used infielder Matt Duffy as part of a package to acquire lefty Matt Moore, who was erratic as a Giant. They also used prospects to pick up infielder Eduardo Nunez from the Twins (he mostly played third base for the Giants) and lefty Will Smith from the Brewers, who came in a deal that cost former top prospect Andrew Susac and 2015 first-rounder Phil Bickford.

DOWN ON THE FARM: Only one Giants full-season affiliate, low Class A Augusta, managed a winning record and made its league playoffs. However, the system had strong individual performances, including having four members of its 2015 draft class—lefty Andrew Suarez, first baseman Chris Shaw, shortstop C.J. Hinojosa and outfielder Steve Duggar—finish the season in Double-A.

OPENING DAY PAYROLL: $ 172,253,778 (6th)

PLAYERS OF THE YEAR

MAJOR LEAGUE	MINOR LEAGUE
Madison Bumgarner lhp	**Tyler Beede** rhp
15-9, 2.74	(Double-A)
251 SO in 226.2 IP	8-7, 2.81
4th in NL in WHIP	135 SO in 147.1 IP

ORGANIZATION LEADERS

BATTING		*Minimum 250 AB
MAJORS		
* AVG	Buster Posey	.288
* OPS	Brandon Belt	.868
HR	Brandon Belt	17
RBI	Brandon Crawford	84
MINORS		
* AVG	Miguel Gomez, Augusta, San Jose	.330
* OBP	Austin Slater, Richmond, Sacramento	.393
* SLG	Dylan Davis, Augusta, San Jose	.521
* OPS	Austin Slater, Richmond, Sacramento	.893
R	Steven Duggar, San Jose, Richmond	78
H	Steven Duggar, San Jose, Richmond	153
TB	Dylan Davis, Augusta, San Jose	252
2B	Chris Shaw, San Jose, Richmond	38
3B	Steven Duggar, San Jose, Richmond	8
HR	Dylan Davis, Augusta, San Jose	26
RBI	Dylan Davis, Augusta, San Jose	92
BB	Steven Duggar, San Jose, Richmond	72
SO	Ronnie Jebavy, San Jose	153
SB	Johneshwy Fargas, San Jose, Augusta	41

PITCHING		#Minimum 75 IP
MAJORS		
W	Johnny Cueto	18
# ERA	Madison Bumgarner	2.74
SO	Madison Bumgarner	251
SV	Santiago Casilla	31
MINORS		
W	Ty Blach, Sacramento	14
L	Kyle Crick, Richmond	11
# ERA	Sam Coonrod, San Jose, Richmond	2.55
G	Reyes Moronta, San Jose	60
GS	Ty Blach, Sacramento	26
	Joan Gregorio, Richmond, Sacramento	26
SV	Rodolfo Martinez, San Jose, Richmond	24
IP	Ty Blach, Sacramento	163
BB	Kyle Crick, Richmond	67
SO	Joan Gregorio, Richmond, Sacramento	152
# AVG	Sam Coonrod, San Jose, Richmond	.209

President: Brian Sabean. **GM:** Bobby Evans. **Farm Director:** Shane Turner. **Scouting Director:** John Barr.

Class	Team	League	W	L	PCT	Finish	Manager
Majors	San Francisco Giants	National	87	75	.537	5th (15)	Bruce Bochy
Triple-A	Sacramento River Cats	Pacific Coast	69	75	.479	12th (16)	Jose Alguacil
Double-A	Richmond Flying Squirrels	Eastern	62	79	.440	10th (12)	Miguel Ojeda
High A	San Jose Giants	California	68	72	.486	9th (12)	Lipso Nava
Low A	Augusta Greenjackets	South Atlantic	76	63	.547	2nd (14)	Nestor Rojas
Short season	Salem-Keizer Volcanoes	Northwest	32	42	.432	6th (8)	Kyle Haines
Rookie	Giants	Arizona	28	27	.509	8th (14)	Henry Cotto
Overall 2016 Minor League Record			335	358	.483	19th (30)	

ORGANIZATION STATISTICS

SAN FRANCISCO GIANTS
NATIONAL LEAGUE

Batting	B-T	HT	WT	DOB	AVG	vLH	vRH	G	AB	R	H	2B	3B	HR	RBI	BB	HBP	SH	SF	SO	SB	CS	SLG	OBP
Adrianza, Ehire	B-R	6-1	170	8-21-89	.254	.353	.138	40	63	3	16	2	0	2	7	2	2	4	0	13	0	1	.381	.299
Beckham, Gordon	R-R	6-0	190	9-16-86	.000	.000	.000	3	5	0	0	0	0	1	0	0	0	0	1	2	0	0	.000	.000
2-team total (85 Atlanta)					.212	—	—	88	245	25	52	16	1	5	31	26	4	0	4	52	1	0	.347	.294
Belt, Brandon	L-L	6-5	220	4-20-88	.275	.279	.273	156	542	77	149	41	8	17	82	104	5	0	4	148	0	4	.474	.394
Blanco, Gregor	L-L	5-11	175	12-24-83	.224	.242	.218	106	241	28	54	10	4	1	18	29	1	1	1	51	6	3	.311	.309
Brown, Trevor	R-R	6-2	195	11-15-91	.237	.254	.227	75	173	17	41	7	0	5	19	10	1	0	0	39	0	1	.364	.283
Crawford, Brandon	L-R	6-2	215	1-21-87	.275	.276	.274	155	553	67	152	28	11	12	84	57	4	0	9	115	7	0	.430	.342
Duffy, Matt	R-R	6-2	170	1-15-91	.253	.290	.239	70	257	32	65	11	2	4	21	20	4	2	3	40	8	4	.358	.313
Gillaspie, Conor	L-R	6-1	195	7-18-87	.262	.227	.266	101	191	24	50	8	4	6	25	12	1	0	1	28	1	2	.440	.307
Green, Grant	R-R	6-3	180	9-27-87	.261	.321	.167	18	46	7	12	2	0	1	7	3	0	0	1	8	0	0	.370	.300
Hernandez, Gorkys	R-R	6-1	190	9-7-87	.259	.273	.238	26	54	7	14	5	0	2	4	3	0	0	0	11	0	1	.463	.298
Nunez, Eduardo	R-R	6-0	195	6-15-87	.269	.174	.301	50	182	24	49	9	3	4	20	14	2	0	1	30	13	4	.418	.327
Pagan, Angel	B-R	6-2	200	7-2-81	.277	.266	.282	129	495	71	137	24	5	12	55	42	0	0	3	66	15	4	.418	.331
Panik, Joe	L-R	6-1	190	10-30-90	.239	.226	.245	127	464	67	111	21	7	10	62	50	4	3	5	47	5	0	.379	.315
Parker, Jarrett	L-L	6-4	210	1-1-89	.236	.108	.289	63	127	22	30	3	1	5	14	19	5	0	0	44	0	1	.394	.358
Pena, Ramiro	B-R	5-11	200	7-18-85	.299	.273	.308	30	87	9	26	6	1	1	10	2	2	0	0	16	0	0	.425	.330
Pence, Hunter	R-R	6-4	220	4-13-83	.289	.256	.302	106	395	58	114	23	1	13	57	43	1	0	3	95	1	1	.451	.357
Posey, Buster	R-R	6-1	215	3-27-87	.288	.312	.277	146	539	82	155	33	2	14	80	64	3	0	8	68	6	1	.434	.362
Span, Denard	L-L	6-0	210	2-27-84	.266	.217	.289	143	572	70	152	23	5	11	53	53	4	6	2	79	12	7	.381	.331
Tejada, Ruben	R-R	5-11	200	10-27-89	.156	.222	.071	13	32	3	5	3	0	0	2	5	0	1	0	5	0	0	.250	.270
2-team total (23 St. Louis)					.167	—	—	36	66	9	11	5	0	0	5	7	1	1	3	13	0	0	.242	.247
Tomlinson, Kelby	R-R	6-3	180	6-16-90	.292	.306	.265	52	106	13	31	4	0	0	6	12	1	1	0	18	5	1	.330	.370
Williamson, Mac	R-R	6-4	240	7-15-90	.223	.212	.239	54	112	14	25	3	0	6	15	13	2	0	0	35	0	1	.411	.315

Pitching	B-T	HT	WT	DOB	W	L	ERA	G	GS	CG	SV	IP	H	R	ER	HR	BB	SO	AVG	vLH	vRH	K/9	BB/9
Blach, Ty	R-L	6-2	200	10-20-90	1	0	1.06	4	2	0	0	17	8	2	2	1	5	10	.143	.130	.152	5.29	2.65
Broadway, Mike	R-R	6-5	215	3-30-87	0	0	11.81	8	0	0	0	5	9	7	7	2	1	4	.375	.455	.308	6.75	1.69
Bumgarner, Madison	R-L	6-5	250	8-1-89	15	9	2.74	34	34	4	0	227	179	79	69	26	54	251	.213	.178	.221	9.97	2.14
Cain, Matt	R-R	6-3	230	10-1-84	4	8	5.64	21	17	0	0	89	103	58	56	16	32	72	.299	.322	.281	7.25	3.22
Casilla, Santiago	R-R	6-0	210	7-25-80	2	5	3.57	62	0	0	31	58	50	23	23	8	19	65	.235	.265	.215	10.09	2.95
Cueto, Johnny	R-R	5-11	220	2-15-86	18	5	2.79	32	32	5	0	220	195	71	68	15	45	198	.238	.255	.224	8.11	1.84
Gearrin, Cory	R-R	6-3	200	4-14-86	3	2	4.28	56	0	0	3	48	42	24	23	4	14	45	.233	.209	.241	8.38	2.61
Heston, Chris	R-R	6-3	195	4-10-88	1	1	10.80	4	0	0	0	5	9	6	6	0	6	3	.409	.300	.500	5.40	10.80
Kontos, George	R-R	6-3	215	6-12-85	3	2	2.53	57	0	0	0	53	42	19	15	3	20	35	.219	.243	.203	5.91	3.38
Law, Derek	R-R	6-2	210	9-14-90	4	2	2.13	61	0	0	1	55	44	13	13	3	9	50	.215	.188	.232	8.18	1.47
Lopez, Javier	L-L	6-4	220	7-11-77	1	3	4.05	68	0	0	1	27	24	13	12	3	15	15	.240	.208	.348	5.06	5.06
Mazzaro, Vin	R-R	6-2	220	9-27-86	1	0	54.00	2	0	0	0	1	7	9	6	0	1	0	.636	.600	.667	0.00	9.00
Moore, Matt	L-L	6-3	210	6-18-89	6	5	4.08	12	12	0	0	68	59	31	31	5	32	69	.233	.241	.231	9.09	4.21
Nathan, Joe	R-R	6-4	230	11-22-74	1	0	0.00	7	0	0	0	4	3	0	0	0	2	5	.188	.143	.222	10.38	4.15
2-team total (3 Chicago)					2	0	0.00	10	0	0	0	6	5	0	0	0	4	9	—	—	—	12.79	5.68
Okert, Steven	L-L	6-3	210	7-9-91	0	0	3.21	16	0	0	0	14	14	5	5	2	4	14	.259	.259	.259	9.00	2.57
Osich, Josh	L-L	6-2	230	9-3-88	1	3	4.71	59	0	0	0	36	31	20	19	7	19	25	.228	.156	.322	6.19	4.71
Peavy, Jake	R-R	6-1	195	5-31-81	5	9	5.54	31	21	0	0	119	134	76	73	18	36	102	.282	.302	.266	7.74	2.73
Reynolds, Matt	L-L	6-5	240	10-2-84	0	1	7.50	8	0	0	0	6	7	5	5	0	5	3	.292	.462	.091	4.50	7.50
Romo, Sergio	R-R	5-11	185	3-4-83	1	0	2.64	40	0	0	4	31	26	9	9	5	7	33	.236	.242	.234	9.68	2.05
Samardzija, Jeff	R-R	6-5	225	1-23-85	12	11	3.81	32	32	1	0	203	190	88	86	24	54	167	.249	.272	.225	7.39	2.39
Smith, Will	R-L	6-5	265	7-10-89	1	1	2.95	26	0	0	0	18	13	6	6	0	9	26	.197	.125	.265	12.76	4.42
2-team total (27 Milwaukee)					2	4	3.35	53	0	0	0	40	31	19	15	3	18	48	—	—	—	10.71	4.02
Stratton, Chris	R-R	6-3	190	8-22-90	1	0	3.60	7	0	0	0	10	11	4	4	1	5	6	.289	.211	.368	5.40	4.50
Strickland, Hunter	R-R	6-4	220	9-24-88	3	3	3.10	72	0	0	3	61	50	21	21	4	19	57	.221	.270	.197	8.41	2.80
Suarez, Albert	R-R	6-3	235	10-8-89	3	5	4.29	22	12	0	0	84	84	42	40	11	26	54	.264	.253	.274	5.79	2.79

Fielding

Catcher

Catcher	PCT	G	PO	A	E	DP	PB
Brown	.994	60	316	26	2	0	4
Posey	.997	123	1003	65	3	8	2

First Base

First Base	PCT	G	PO	A	E	DP
Belt	.994	151	1284	94	8	110
Gillaspie	1.000	7	29	2	0	3
Posey	.990	15	95	8	1	11

Second Base

Second Base	PCT	G	PO	A	E	DP
Adrianza	1.000	7	3	8	0	2
Green	.953	15	17	24	2	6
Nunez	1.000	1	1	0	1	
Panik	.992	126	233	363	5	82
Pena	.944	17	16	35	3	8
Tejada	1.000	1	1	1	0	1
Tomlinson	.985	19	21	43	1	9

Third Base

Third Base	PCT	G	PO	A	E	DP
Adrianza	1.000	7	0	1	0	0
Beckham	1.000	3	2	3	0	0
Brown	—	1	0	0	0	0
Duffy	.974	69	43	142	5	5
Gillaspie	.973	45	11	62	2	6
Nunez	.983	48	23	92	2	12
Pena	.889	12	5	11	2	2
Tejada	.931	13	6	21	2	3
Tomlinson	1.000	3	1	3	0	0

Shortstop

Shortstop	PCT	G	PO	A	E	DP
Adrianza	.941	13	8	24	2	2
Crawford	.983	155	209	413	11	90
Nunez	1.000	4	4	1	0	0
Pena	1.000	4	4	7	0	2
Tomlinson	.846	7	2	9	2	2

Outfield

Outfield	PCT	G	PO	A	E	DP
Belt	1.000	3	1	0	0	0
Blanco	.991	75	111	2	1	0
Gearrin	—	1	0	0	0	0
Hernandez	1.000	22	28	2	0	0
Pagan	.975	127	230	5	6	2
Parker	1.000	37	53	1	0	0
Pence	1.000	102	193	7	0	0
Span	.997	137	286	3	1	1
Tomlinson	1.000	3	5	1	0	0
Williamson	.969	36	62	1	2	0

SACRAMENTO RIVER CATS

PACIFIC COAST LEAGUE — TRIPLE-A

Batting	B-T	HT	WT	DOB	AVG	vLH	vRH	G	AB	R	H	2B	3B	HR	RBI	BB	HBP	SH	SF	SO	SB	CS	SLG	OBP
Adrianza, Ehire	B-R	6-1	170	8-21-89	.257	.364	.208	8	35	6	9	2	0	1	3	2	0	0	0	4	1	3	.400	.297
Arias, Junior	R-R	6-1	195	1-9-92	.100	.000	.167	5	10	1	1	0	0	0	0	0	1	0	0	3	0	0	.100	.182
Bennett, T.J.	L-R	6-3	215	7-22-92	.250	—	.250	4	8	1	2	1	0	0	1	1	1	0	0	3	0	0	.375	.400
Carbonell, Daniel	R-R	6-3	195	3-29-91	.667	1.000	.000	2	3	0	2	0	0	0	1	0	1	0	0	1	0	0	.667	.750
Castillo, Ali	R-R	5-10	165	6-19-89	.309	.333	.301	49	181	24	56	6	1	0	14	8	1	1	0	20	4	3	.354	.342
Ciriaco, Juan	R-R	6-0	160	8-15-83	.269	.284	.260	84	201	29	54	12	1	4	26	19	0	2	4	37	5	2	.398	.326
Delfino, Mitch	R-R	6-2	210	1-13-91	.242	.222	.248	58	186	20	45	4	0	3	23	16	0	1	1	39	0	1	.312	.300
Denorfia, Chris	R-R	6-0	195	7-15-80	.255	.273	.247	36	110	11	28	2	0	4	15	9	0	0	1	17	2	0	.382	.308
Duffy, Matt	R-R	6-2	170	1-15-91	.333	.000	.400	2	6	2	2	1	0	0	1	0	0	0	0	1	0	0	.500	.429
Ford, Darren	R-R	5-9	190	10-1-85	.250	.268	.243	49	152	17	38	3	2	1	9	12	2	4	1	23	8	6	.316	.311
Garvey, Robbie	L-L	5-8	165	4-26-89	.667	1.000	.500	3	9	4	6	0	0	1	3	0	0	0	0	3	0	0	1.000	.667
Gillaspie, Conor	L-R	6-1	195	7-18-87	.314	.261	.357	12	51	6	16	3	0	1	4	1	0	0	0	6	1	0	.431	.327
Green, Grant	R-R	6-3	180	9-27-87	.319	.275	.337	94	348	46	111	18	4	7	52	11	0	1	4	58	2	1	.454	.336
Hernandez, Gorkys	R-R	6-1	190	9-7-87	.302	.323	.294	116	437	74	132	22	3	8	51	52	6	5	3	77	20	13	.421	.382
Ishikawa, Travis	L-L	6-3	220	9-24-83	.257	.244	.263	76	268	31	69	13	0	12	55	29	8	0	3	81	0	0	.440	.344
Kottaras, George	L-R	6-0	200	5-10-83	.155	.083	.174	23	58	10	9	1	0	1	6	11	0	0	2	23	0	0	.224	.290
Lee, Hak-Ju	L-R	6-2	195	11-4-90	.265	.167	.283	47	162	19	43	7	1	3	12	17	3	3	1	49	4	3	.377	.344
Lollis, Ryan	L-L	6-0	190	12-16-86	.253	.184	.277	111	372	46	94	10	3	4	40	42	2	4	5	56	6	1	.320	.328
Moreno, Rando	R-R	5-11	165	6-6-92	.299	.386	.262	44	147	19	44	3	3	1	12	5	1	2	1	23	4	1	.381	.325
Olivo, Miguel	R-R	6-0	230	7-15-78	.246	.253	.242	81	289	41	71	12	4	10	34	18	1	2	3	90	1	0	.419	.289
Oropesa, Ricky	L-R	6-3	225	12-15-89	.158	.333	.125	14	19	0	3	0	0	0	2	4	1	0	0	6	0	0	.158	.333
Pagan, Angel	B-R	6-2	200	7-2-81	.364	1.000	.300	3	11	0	4	1	0	0	2	0	0	0	0	4	1	0	.455	.364
Panik, Joe	L-R	6-1	190	10-30-90	.231	.600	.000	4	13	2	3	1	0	0	1	0	0	0	0	0	0	0	.308	.286
Parker, Jarrett	L-L	6-4	210	1-1-89	.273	.243	.290	53	194	44	53	8	2	16	35	26	2	0	0	66	1	1	.582	.365
Pena, Ramiro	B-R	5-11	200	7-18-85	.296	.242	.320	57	216	24	64	12	1	5	24	21	2	4	2	35	5	6	.431	.361
Pence, Hunter	R-R	6-4	220	4-13-83	.417	.500	.357	7	24	6	10	2	0	3	7	0	1	0	0	3	0	0	.875	.440
Rodriguez, Rich	R-R	6-1	170	10-3-92	1.000	1.000	—	1	1	0	1	0	0	0	0	0	0	0	0	0	0	0	1.000	1.000
Sanchez, Tony	R-R	5-11	220	5-20-88	.200	.286	.167	16	50	6	10	1	0	2	5	8	1	0	1	12	0	1	.340	.317
Schroder, Myles	R-R	5-11	180	8-1-87	.221	.316	.187	49	145	15	32	7	2	1	13	6	2	2	3	27	3	3	.317	.256
Slater, Austin	R-R	6-2	215	12-13-92	.298	.412	.254	68	245	36	73	12	0	13	42	33	0	0	5	53	2	6	.506	.381
Susac, Andrew	R-R	6-1	215	3-22-90	.273	.302	.260	58	209	28	57	12	1	8	36	24	1	0	5	45	0	0	.455	.343
2-team total (11 Colorado Springs)					.249	—	—	69	249	30	62	13	1	8	39	26	1	0	6	61	0	0	.406	.316
Tejada, Ruben	R-R	5-11	200	10-27-89	.301	.278	.308	40	143	18	43	11	1	1	21	7	2	1	2	21	0	1	.413	.338
Tomlinson, Kelby	R-R	6-3	180	6-16-90	.286	.340	.268	49	185	28	53	8	1	0	20	22	3	1	1	26	12	3	.341	.370
Williamson, Mac	R-R	6-4	240	7-15-90	.269	.229	.281	54	208	35	56	14	0	11	42	12	3	0	3	53	2	1	.495	.314

Pitching	B-T	HT	WT	DOB	W	L	ERA	G	GS	CG	SV	IP	H	R	ER	HR	BB	SO	AVG	vLH	vRH	K/9	BB/9
Agosta, Martin	R-R	6-2	220	4-7-91	0	1	3.86	4	0	0	0	2	3	1	1	0	6	4	.300	.167	.500	15.43	23.14
Blach, Ty	R-L	6-2	200	10-20-90	14	7	3.43	26	26	3	0	163	147	65	62	9	38	113	.244	.197	.264	6.25	2.10
Blackburn, Clayton	L-R	6-3	230	1-6-93	7	10	4.36	25	23	0	0	136	142	76	66	18	35	101	.266	.266	.267	6.67	2.31
Broadway, Mike	R-R	6-5	215	3-30-87	0	3	3.94	26	0	0	5	30	32	14	13	4	11	30	.276	.356	.225	9.10	3.34
Cain, Matt	R-R	6-3	230	10-1-84	1	1	5.06	2	2	0	0	11	11	8	6	1	4	6	.262	.350	.182	5.06	3.38
Casilla, Jose	R-R	6-1	205	5-21-89	0	0	3.60	3	0	0	0	5	2	2	2	0	1	2	.316	.286	.333	3.60	1.80
Dunning, Jake	R-R	6-4	190	8-12-88	3	4	4.85	49	0	0	2	59	61	37	32	4	29	43	.266	.298	.244	6.52	4.40
Fleet, Austin	R-R	6-2	200	4-17-87	0	1	3.44	23	2	0	1	37	34	17	14	3	16	21	.248	.234	.260	5.15	3.93
Gearrin, Cory	R-R	6-3	200	4-14-86	0	0	1.13	8	0	0	0	8	5	1	1	0	2	9	.185	.222	.167	10.13	2.25
Gregorio, Joan	R-R	6-7	180	1-12-92	6	8	5.28	21	21	0	0	107	112	67	63	13	43	122	.267	.247	.281	10.23	3.61
Heston, Chris	R-R	6-3	195	4-10-88	2	9	4.54	15	14	0	1	81	87	42	41	8	32	53	.267	.315	.224	5.86	3.54
Kontos, George	R-R	6-3	215	6-12-85	0	0	2.45	4	0	0	0	4	5	1	1	0	0	2	.294	.333	.273	4.91	0.00
Lara, Braulio	L-L	6-1	180	12-20-88	1	1	3.90	25	0	0	1	28	27	15	12	3	13	25	.252	.244	.258	8.13	4.23
Law, Derek	R-R	6-2	210	9-14-90	0	0	0.00	3	0	0	0	3	1	0	0	0	1	2	.100	.000	.250	6.00	3.00
Lujan, Matt	L-L	6-1	210	8-23-88	0	5	4.04	12	11	0	0	49	52	28	22	8	23	45	.278	.241	.295	8.27	4.22
Machi, Jean	R-R	6-0	255	2-1-82	2	2	3.62	28	0	0	12	32	30	17	13	4	8	27	.246	.286	.219	7.52	2.23
2-team total (20 Iowa)					4	3	3.65	48	0	0	13	62	59	30	25	9	17	53	—	—	—	7.74	2.48

Pitching

Pitching	B-T	HT	WT	DOB	W	L	ERA	G	GS	CG	SV	IP	H	R	ER	HR	BB	SO	AVG	vLH	vRH	K/9	BB/9
Mazzaro, Vin	R-R	6-2	220	9-27-86	2	2	3.22	38	4	0	1	67	61	27	24	4	27	43	.248	.291	.213	5.78	3.63
McCormick, Phil	L-L	6-1	185	9-7-88	0	1	4.05	17	1	0	2	20	26	13	9	2	9	13	.333	.313	.348	5.85	4.05
Mejia, Adalberto	L-L	6-3	195	6-20-93	4	1	4.20	7	7	0	0	41	42	19	19	5	11	43	.263	.216	.284	9.52	2.43
Myers, D.J.	L-R	6-5	255	12-24-94	0	0	0.00	1	0	0	0	1	1	0	0	0	0	1	.250	.500	.000	9.00	0.00
Okert, Steven	L-L	6-3	210	7-9-91	4	3	3.80	41	0	0	3	47	53	27	20	2	11	60	.270	.235	.296	11.41	2.09
Osich, Josh	L-L	6-2	230	9-3-88	0	0	1.29	7	0	0	0	7	6	1	1	0	2	8	.222	.000	.286	10.29	2.57
Reynolds, Matt	L-L	6-5	240	10-2-84	1	0	0.00	12	0	0	0	14	5	0	0	0	2	12	.111	.105	.115	7.90	1.32
Rogers, Tyler	R-R	6-5	187	12-17-90	1	1	6.10	24	1	0	1	31	38	24	21	1	16	22	.297	.283	.309	6.39	4.65
Romero, Ricky	R-L	6-1	210	11-6-84	0	0	4.50	2	2	0	0	8	6	4	4	0	5	6	.207	.167	.217	6.75	5.63
Romo, Sergio	R-R	5-11	185	3-4-83	1	1	5.68	7	0	0	6	6	8	4	4	1	0	11	.296	.167	.400	15.63	0.00
Slania, Dan	R-R	6-5	275	5-24-92	2	0	1.38	2	2	0	0	13	8	2	2	0	4	14	.170	.182	.143	9.69	2.77
Stratton, Chris	R-R	6-3	190	8-22-90	12	6	3.87	21	20	1	0	126	120	57	54	6	39	103	.254	.220	.282	7.38	2.79
Suarez, Albert	R-R	6-3	235	10-8-89	4	3	4.34	9	7	0	0	46	46	26	22	3	14	39	.271	.254	.282	7.69	2.76
Torres, Alex	L-L	5-10	190	12-8-87	1	2	4.26	40	1	0	1	38	34	24	18	1	32	38	.236	.208	.253	9.00	7.58
Welker, Duke	L-R	6-7	240	2-10-86	1	3	3.86	31	0	0	2	35	49	20	15	3	16	30	.333	.328	.337	7.71	4.11

Fielding

Catcher

Catcher	PCT	G	PO	A	E	DP	PB
Kottaras	.991	15	106	4	1	3	1
Olivo	.988	65	452	35	6	3	3
Sanchez	1.000	16	136	9	0	0	1
Susac	.995	50	385	26	2	3	3

First Base

First Base	PCT	G	PO	A	E	DP
Ciriaco	1.000	15	97	7	0	11
Delfino	1.000	1	9	2	0	1
Gillaspie	1.000	1	12	0	0	1
Green	.992	28	228	12	2	18
Ishikawa	.996	57	448	46	2	44
Lollis	.994	46	339	18	2	32
Olivo	1.000	1	11	0	0	0
Oropesa	1.000	4	28	1	0	2

Second Base

Second Base	PCT	G	PO	A	E	DP
Castillo	.976	24	29	53	2	9
Ciriaco	.968	33	55	66	4	15
Green	.989	25	36	50	1	10
Moreno	.968	16	27	34	2	10
Panik	1.000	4	6	8	0	1

Third Base

Third Base	PCT	G	PO	A	E	DP
Adrianza	1.000	5	1	7	0	0
Castillo	.919	24	15	42	5	5
Ciriaco	1.000	4	1	6	0	0
Delfino	.953	44	28	73	5	18
Duffy	1.000	1	1	1	0	0
Gillaspie	.909	7	4	6	1	0
Green	.901	31	12	61	8	3
Lee	1.000	2	0	4	0	0
Schroder	.918	20	14	31	4	4
Tejada	1.000	2	0	8	0	0
Tomlinson	.956	14	5	38	2	2

Shortstop

Shortstop	PCT	G	PO	A	E	DP
Adrianza	.900	3	3	6	1	1
Castillo	1.000	2	1	3	0	0
Ciriaco	1.000	2	3	9	0	2
Lee	.972	45	66	142	6	22

(Catcher, continued)

	PCT	G	PO	A	E	DP
Pena	.989	42	86	101	2	28
Schroder	.846	3	6	5	2	2
Tomlinson	.986	16	32	40	1	7
Moreno	.982	28	39	70	2	16
Pena	1.000	12	18	33	0	4
Tejada	.971	37	38	97	4	19
Tomlinson	.975	20	33	45	2	8

Outfield

Outfield	PCT	G	PO	A	E	DP
Arias	1.000	2	5	0	0	0
Bennett	1.000	1	3	0	0	0
Carbonell	1.000	2	2	0	0	0
Denorfia	1.000	25	37	0	0	0
Ford	.979	43	89	3	2	0
Garvey	.800	3	4	0	1	0
Green	1.000	13	19	0	0	0
Hernandez	.993	113	261	8	2	1
Ishikawa	1.000	7	8	1	0	0
Lollis	.971	59	99	2	3	2
Pagan	1.000	3	2	0	0	0
Parker	.989	49	93	1	1	0
Pence	1.000	7	14	0	0	0
Schroder	1.000	22	38	2	0	0
Slater	.954	66	119	5	6	0
Williamson	.989	48	83	3	1	0

RICHMOND FLYING SQUIRRELS   DOUBLE-A

EASTERN LEAGUE

Batting

Batting	B-T	HT	WT	DOB	AVG	vLH	vRH	G	AB	R	H	2B	3B	HR	RBI	BB	HBP	SH	SF	SO	SB	CS	SLG	OBP
Amion, Richard	R-R	5-10	190	2-24-93	.167	.333	.000	3	6	1	1	0	0	0	1	4	0	1	0	4	1	0	.167	.500
Arnold, Jeff	R-R	6-2	205	1-13-88	.220	.188	.233	56	164	15	36	9	1	3	19	13	2	1	2	52	1	2	.341	.282
Arroyo, Christian	R-R	6-1	180	5-30-95	.274	.271	.275	119	474	57	130	36	1	3	49	29	3	4	7	72	1	1	.373	.316
Bednar, Brandon	R-R	6-4	195	3-21-92	.286	.306	.278	64	224	32	64	11	1	2	31	8	3	0	2	40	4	4	.371	.316
Bennett, T.J.	L-R	6-3	215	7-22-92	.250	—	.250	1	4	0	1	0	0	0	0	0	0	0	0	1	0	0	.500	.250
Castillo, Ali	R-R	5-10	165	6-19-89	.317	.271	.336	66	199	22	63	9	3	0	17	12	3	3	3	24	6	4	.392	.359
Cole, Hunter	R-R	6-1	190	10-3-92	.271	.313	.254	126	469	57	127	25	3	13	62	31	5	2	6	115	2	4	.420	.319
Duggar, Steven	L-R	6-2	195	11-4-93	.321	.277	.337	60	243	35	78	16	4	1	24	28	2	0	3	51	9	7	.432	.391
Ford, Darren	R-R	5-9	190	10-1-85	.238	.317	.209	70	223	36	53	8	2	0	15	30	0	3	2	56	13	4	.291	.325
Hinojosa, C.J.	R-R	5-10	175	7-15-94	.248	.254	.246	57	226	27	56	7	2	3	19	20	2	1	2	43	1	0	.336	.312
Horan, Tyler	L-R	6-2	230	12-2-90	.265	.280	.259	93	287	43	76	12	4	12	36	31	2	0	3	79	4	3	.460	.337
Jones, Ryder	L-R	6-3	215	6-7-94	.247	.265	.242	126	473	49	117	26	0	15	67	26	5	3	5	79	1	2	.397	.291
Lerud, Steve	L-R	6-1	220	3-29-84	.182	.246	.146	70	170	24	39	7	0	1	19	38	5	1	0	50	0	0	.288	.335
Moncrief, Carlos	L-R	6-2	220	11-3-88	.261	.333	.243	72	176	27	46	11	0	5	22	28	3	2	0	38	6	0	.409	.372
Moreno, Rando	R-R	5-11	165	6-6-92	.215	.245	.203	47	177	15	38	10	0	0	11	10	1	1	0	29	1	3	.271	.261
Oropesa, Ricky	L-R	6-3	225	12-15-89	.239	.233	.214	68	233	23	51	8	0	9	31	24	3	0	0	66	0	0	.369	.300
Polonius, John	R-R	6-1	160	1-13-91	.333	1.000	.200	3	6	2	2	0	1	0	0	1	0	0	0	2	0	0	.667	.429
Schroder, Myles	R-R	5-11	180	8-1-87	.272	.342	.241	66	250	28	68	12	1	2	45	11	11	2	2	45	5	1	.352	.328
Shaw, Chris	L-R	6-4	235	10-20-93	.246	.262	.240	60	232	26	57	16	4	5	30	20	2	0	2	55	0	0	.414	.309
Slater, Austin	R-R	6-2	215	12-13-92	.311	.311	.333	41	145	20	46	8	1	5	25	24	1	0	2	36	6	1	.490	.413
Turner, Ben	R-R	6-5	220	4-27-90	.176	.250	.154	5	17	2	3	0	0	0	1	0	0	0	0	2	0	0	.176	.222
Villalona, Angel	R-R	6-3	255	8-13-90	.143	.125	.156	24	56	4	8	2	0	1	5	6	2	0	0	20	0	0	.232	.250
Winn, Matt	R-R	6-3	200	8-5-92	.250	.250	.237	15	56	6	14	3	0	2	4	3	0	0	1	12	0	0	.411	.288
Zambrano, Eliezer	B-R	5-11	195	9-16-86	.185	.263	.161	33	81	5	15	3	0	4	4	0	0	0	1	12	0	1	.222	.224

Pitching

Pitching	B-T	HT	WT	DOB	W	L	ERA	G	GS	CG	SV	IP	H	R	ER	HR	BB	SO	AVG	vLH	vRH	K/9	BB/9
Alvarado, Carlos	R-R	6-4	175	10-22-89	1	0	2.79	16	0	0	0	19	13	7	6	2	0	24	.188	.200	.176	11.17	0.00
Beede, Tyler	R-R	6-3	210	5-23-93	8	7	2.81	24	24	1	0	147	136	58	46	9	53	135	.248	.272	.223	8.25	3.24
Black, Ray	R-R	6-5	225	6-26-90	1	4	4.88	35	0	0	6	31	17	17	17	1	32	53	.159	.182	.143	15.22	9.19
Casilla, Jose	R-R	6-1	205	5-21-89	2	3	3.59	32	0	0	0	48	53	22	19	5	17	33	.290	.383	.216	6.23	3.21
Claiborne, Preston	R-R	6-2	225	1-21-88	2	1	2.38	34	0	0	3	45	30	15	12	4	13	49	.186	.197	.180	9.73	2.58

Pitching	B-T	HT	WT	DOB	W	L	ERA	G	GS	CG	SV	IP	H	R	ER	HR	BB	SO	AVG	vLH	vRH	K/9	BB/9
Coonrod, Sam	R-R	6-2	225	9-22-92	4	3	3.03	13	13	0	0	77	59	33	26	7	38	52	.214	.216	.212	6.05	4.42
Crick, Kyle	L-R	6-4	220	11-30-92	4	11	5.04	23	23	0	0	109	110	72	61	8	67	86	.266	.261	.273	7.10	5.53
Gage, Matt	R-L	6-4	240	2-11-93	9	7	3.38	23	23	1	0	136	130	55	51	2	34	106	.248	.299	.226	7.01	2.25
Gregorio, Joan	R-R	6-7	180	1-12-92	0	2	2.33	5	5	0	0	27	15	7	7	1	6	30	.165	.105	.208	10.00	2.00
Johnson, Chase	R-R	6-3	190	1-9-92	1	4	3.27	24	7	0	5	52	47	21	19	2	18	37	.242	.322	.178	6.36	3.10
Jones, Christian	L-L	6-3	210	1-27-91	2	6	3.98	48	1	0	1	63	54	29	28	2	28	47	.235	.245	.228	6.68	3.98
Kickham, Mike	L-L	6-4	220	12-12-88	0	1	6.75	6	0	0	0	11	20	10	8	0	4	7	.392	.333	.410	5.91	3.38
Martinez, Rodolfo	R-R	6-2	180	4-4-94	0	3	6.65	25	0	0	3	23	29	31	17	1	15	17	.315	.347	.279	6.65	5.87
McCormick, Phil	L-L	6-1	185	9-7-88	1	0	2.38	9	0	0	0	11	10	4	3	0	3	5	.244	.235	.250	3.97	2.38
Mejia, Adalberto	L-L	6-3	195	6-20-93	3	2	1.94	11	11	0	0	65	48	16	14	4	16	58	.203	.161	.218	8.03	2.22
Mizenko, Tyler	R-R	6-1	200	4-9-90	2	7	4.31	51	0	0	2	54	61	32	26	7	25	41	.282	.247	.305	6.79	4.14
Molina, Nestor	R-R	6-1	220	1-9-89	2	0	2.95	4	3	0	0	18	16	8	6	2	3	13	.232	.300	.179	6.38	1.47
Nathan, Joe	R-R	6-4	230	11-22-74	1	0	0.00	6	0	0	2	6	3	0	0	0	1	7	.143	.111	.167	10.50	1.50
Osich, Josh	L-L	6-2	230	9-3-88	0	1	18.00	2	0	0	0	1	1	2	2	0	4	2	.250	.000	.500	18.00	36.00
Reynolds, Matt	L-L	6-5	240	10-2-84	0	0	0.00	8	0	0	0	5	2	0	0	0	1	7	.125	.250	.000	12.60	1.80
Rodriguez, Pedro	R-R	6-0	165	10-31-87	1	2	6.59	10	0	0	0	14	16	15	10	2	6	8	.296	.281	.318	5.27	3.95
Rogers, Tyler	R-R	6-5	187	12-17-90	1	1	0.77	35	0	0	10	35	25	8	3	0	8	24	.198	.235	.173	6.17	2.06
Slania, Dan	R-R	6-5	275	5-24-92	7	6	2.50	27	10	0	0	83	68	30	23	6	22	79	.223	.225	.222	8.60	2.40
Smith, Jake	R-R	6-4	190	6-2-90	2	1	7.08	22	0	0	1	20	17	19	16	1	23	26	.224	.179	.250	11.51	10.18
Suarez, Andrew	L-L	6-2	205	9-11-92	7	7	3.95	19	19	0	0	114	129	61	50	11	24	90	.292	.331	.275	7.11	1.89
Taylor, Cory	R-R	6-2	255	12-14-93	1	0	0.00	2	2	0	0	12	10	4	1	0	5	10	.227	.308	.111	7.50	3.75

Fielding

Catcher	PCT	G	PO	A	E	DP	PB
Arnold	1.000	51	352	35	0	4	6
Lerud	.998	57	426	27	1	7	8
Turner	1.000	3	16	2	0	0	0
Winn	.983	15	104	11	2	1	3
Zambrano	.995	27	173	11	1	2	2

Second Base	PCT	G	PO	A	E	DP
Amion	.923	2	4	8	1	4
Arroyo	1.000	19	33	53	0	11
Bednar	.988	50	94	147	3	37
Castillo	.996	54	98	139	1	37
Moreno	1.000	19	28	49	0	6

	PCT	G	PO	A	E	DP
Bednar	1.000	2	2	5	0	0
Castillo	.857	1	2	4	1	2
Hinojosa	.965	55	86	165	9	41
Moreno	.955	28	39	88	6	17
Polonius	.857	2	2	4	1	1
Schroder	.966	8	10	18	1	4

First Base	PCT	G	PO	A	E	DP
Bennett	1.000	1	4	0	0	0
Jones	.986	25	193	14	3	19
Oropesa	.994	56	483	29	3	42
Schroder	.989	10	83	5	1	13
Shaw	.986	48	394	21	6	46
Turner	1.000	1	10	0	0	2
Villalona	1.000	5	33	2	0	1

Third Base	PCT	G	PO	A	E	DP
Arroyo	.926	48	23	103	10	6
Bednar	.833	3	1	4	1	1
Jones	.907	91	43	151	20	13
Polonius	1.000	1	0	1	0	0
Shaw	—	1	0	0	0	0

Shortstop	PCT	G	PO	A	E	DP
Arroyo	.961	48	64	134	8	27

Outfield	PCT	G	PO	A	E	DP
Cole	.973	118	203	10	6	4
Duggar	.988	59	156	6	2	1
Ford	.985	62	128	0	2	0
Horan	.992	64	124	2	1	1
Moncrief	.971	39	57	9	2	1
Schroder	.981	50	97	9	2	4
Slater	1.000	40	60	0	0	0

SAN JOSE GIANTS
CALIFORNIA LEAGUE

HIGH CLASS A

Batting	B-T	HT	WT	DOB	AVG	vLH	vRH	G	AB	R	H	2B	3B	HR	RBI	BB	HBP	SH	SF	SO	SB	CS	SLG	OBP
Adrianza, Ehire	B-R	6-1	170	8-21-89	.333	.333	.333	9	33	8	11	3	0	5	11	2	0	0	1	6	0	0	.879	.361
Arenado, Jonah	R-R	6-4	230	2-3-95	.254	.246	.257	128	516	64	131	36	0	17	68	18	7	0	4	110	0	2	.422	.286
Arias, Junior	R-R	6-1	195	1-9-92	.179	.250	.167	9	28	3	5	0	0	0	1	3	0	0	0	12	2	0	.179	.258
Bednar, Brandon	R-R	6-4	195	3-21-92	.284	.281	.286	59	218	22	62	3	1	4	30	8	6	3	4	46	4	1	.362	.322
Bennett, T.J.	L-R	6-3	215	7-22-92	.284	.339	.265	65	222	32	63	15	1	9	28	20	6	1	1	67	2	1	.482	.357
Carbonell, Daniel	R-R	6-3	195	3-29-91	.284	.274	.289	64	211	28	60	12	0	3	20	17	4	2	1	51	11	5	.384	.348
Davis, Dylan	R-R	6-0	205	7-20-93	.278	.410	.235	63	248	36	69	10	1	18	49	22	4	0	2	61	1	0	.544	.344
Deacon, Jared	L-R	6-0	195	8-25-91	.143	.167	.125	5	14	0	2	1	0	0	3	0	1	0	0	5	0	0	.214	.294
Delfino, Mitch	R-R	6-2	210	1-13-91	.198	.273	.169	22	81	13	16	3	0	5	11	2	0	1	21	1	0	.235	.305
Duggar, Steven	L-R	6-2	195	11-4-93	.284	.273	.288	70	264	43	75	12	4	9	30	44	1	0	2	66	6	7	.462	.386
Fargas, Johneshwy	R-R	6-1	170	12-15-94	.172	.129	.184	36	134	14	23	0	3	0	9	12	3	4	0	40	9	7	.216	.255
Garcia, Aramis	R-R	6-2	220	1-12-93	.257	.226	.265	41	144	20	37	6	0	2	20	14	0	2	0	42	1	0	.340	.323
Garvey, Robbie	L-L	5-8	165	4-26-89	.269	.309	.257	69	242	34	65	10	4	1	17	27	0	4	2	48	11	7	.355	.339
Gomez, Miguel	B-R	5-10	185	12-17-92	.267	.171	.298	43	172	25	46	9	2	9	24	8	1	0	1	28	1	0	.500	.302
Hinojosa, C.J.	R-R	5-10	175	7-15-94	.296	.304	.293	69	260	45	77	14	3	6	34	36	0	3	3	46	1	4	.442	.378
Jebavy, Ronnie	R-R	6-2	205	5-17-94	.247	.233	.251	127	535	76	132	28	5	12	47	34	12	2	3	153	24	14	.385	.305
Melendez, Rene	R-R	6-1	190	1-20-95	.210	.308	.139	18	62	4	13	1	0	0	4	2	0	2	0	16	0	1	.226	.234
Moreno, Rando	R-R	5-11	165	6-6-92	.248	.265	.242	32	125	15	31	5	0	0	7	11	2	1	1	17	1	3	.288	.317
Paulino, Cristian	R-R	5-10	190	9-4-91	.259	.246	.262	81	286	35	74	17	2	4	24	8	1	3	0	69	29	10	.374	.281
Quinn, Heath	R-R	6-2	190	6-7-95	.353	.667	.286	4	17	2	6	1	0	0	2	0	0	0	0	7	0	0	.412	.421
Rodriguez, Rich	R-R	6-1	170	10-3-92	.174	.000	.209	36	109	9	19	1	0	0	3	5	0	2	1	21	2	0	.183	.209
Ross, Ty	R-R	6-2	225	1-17-92	.224	.241	.219	75	259	24	58	18	0	4	38	23	2	1	3	49	0	1	.340	.289
Shaw, Chris	L-R	6-4	235	10-20-93	.285	.257	.295	72	270	47	77	22	0	16	55	28	4	0	3	70	0	0	.544	.357
Susac, Andrew	R-R	6-1	215	3-22-90	.364	.000	.500	3	11	2	4	1	0	0	2	1	0	0	0	1	0	0	.455	.417
Tomlinson, Kelby	R-R	6-3	180	6-16-90	.250	.000	.500	2	8	0	2	0	0	0	0	0	0	0	0	1	0	0	.250	.250
Turner, Ben	R-R	6-5	220	4-27-90	.000	.000	.000	3	10	0	0	0	0	0	0	2	0	0	1	1	0	0	.000	.154
Vizcaino Jr. Jose	R-R	6-2	220	4-5-94	.261	.269	.258	83	295	35	77	17	2	7	44	29	6	0	3	69	3	5	.403	.336

Pitching	B-T	HT	WT	DOB	W	L	ERA	G	GS	CG	SV	IP	H	R	ER	HR	BB	SO	AVG	vLH	vRH	K/9	BB/9
Agosta, Martin	R-R	6-2	220	4-7-91	3	1	3.18	10	6	0	0	40	28	14	14	4	9	25	.201	.224	.185	5.67	2.04
Baragar, Caleb	R-L	6-3	210	4-9-94	0	1	4.76	1	1	0	0	6	2	3	3	0	5	3	.105	.000	.111	4.76	7.94

Pitching

Pitching	B-T	HT	WT	DOB	W	L	ERA	G	GS	CG	SV	IP	H	R	ER	HR	BB	SO	AVG	vLH	vRH	K/9	BB/9
Bickford, Phil	R-R	6-4	200	7-10-95	2	2	2.73	6	6	1	0	33	21	10	10	3	12	36	.186	.224	.156	9.82	3.27
Bostic, Alex	L-L	6-3	195	11-14-94	0	1	6.35	2	0	0	0	6	5	4	4	1	4	7	.250	.143	.308	11.12	6.35
Cain, Matt	R-R	6-3	230	10-1-84	0	1	20.25	1	1	0	0	4	10	9	9	1	3	2	.476	.455	.500	4.50	6.75
Coonrod, Sam	R-R	6-2	225	9-22-92	5	3	1.98	11	11	0	0	64	46	19	14	3	22	42	.204	.222	.186	5.94	3.11
Cyr, Tyler	R-R	6-3	200	5-5-93	2	1	2.35	19	0	0	1	23	19	8	6	1	9	24	.232	.270	.200	9.39	3.52
Diaz, Carlos	L-L	6-2	225	11-18-93	0	3	10.54	11	0	0	0	14	25	16	16	2	11	13	.397	.238	.476	8.56	7.24
Fleet, Austin	R-R	6-2	200	4-17-87	0	1	5.32	11	1	0	0	22	26	13	13	4	10	20	.302	.179	.362	8.18	4.09
Forjet, Jason	R-R	6-2	185	1-4-90	10	7	4.84	19	18	0	0	102	91	62	55	13	20	87	.235	.235	.235	7.65	1.76
Heston, Chris	R-R	6-3	195	4-10-88	0	0	6.23	1	1	0	0	4	5	3	3	0	3	1	.294	.500	.267	2.08	6.23
Johnson, Jordan	R-R	6-3	200	9-15-93	8	9	5.33	22	22	0	0	120	133	78	71	24	39	111	.277	.249	.305	8.33	2.93
Knight, Dusten	R-R	6-0	185	9-2-90	3	1	5.02	43	0	0	2	81	90	49	45	11	20	90	.279	.257	.297	10.04	2.23
Martinez, Rodolfo	R-R	6-2	180	4-4-94	1	1	0.88	32	0	0	21	31	23	9	3	1	10	33	.205	.294	.131	9.68	2.93
Medina, Hengerber	R-R	5-11	160	10-12-94	1	0	3.86	4	0	0	0	9	8	5	4	1	5	17	.222	.133	.286	16.39	4.82
Menez, Conner	L-L	6-3	195	5-29-95	2	0	4.94	6	5	0	0	27	29	21	15	4	11	20	.266	.154	.301	6.59	3.62
Morel, Jose	R-R	6-2	190	9-6-93	2	6	5.40	27	6	0	0	58	59	38	35	8	25	46	.263	.300	.234	7.10	3.86
Moronta, Reyes	R-R	6-0	175	1-6-93	0	3	2.59	60	0	0	14	59	43	20	17	7	20	93	.195	.257	.131	14.19	3.05
Overton, Connor	R-R	6-0	190	7-24-93	0	0	54.00	1	0	0	0	1	2	2	1	2	1	0	.500	—	.500	27.00	54.00
Reyes, Jose	R-R	6-1	185	1-3-91	4	6	5.38	29	14	0	0	100	118	68	60	13	33	64	.296	.309	.285	5.74	2.96
Reyes, Mark	R-L	6-1	225	10-8-92	9	9	4.74	23	23	0	0	127	137	73	67	13	60	80	.279	.327	.255	5.65	4.24
Romo, Sergio	R-R	5-11	185	3-4-83	0	0	0.00	4	0	0	0	5	2	0	0	0	1	8	.118	.167	.091	14.40	1.80
Santos, Wilson	R-R	6-2	200	10-20-91	0	0	13.50	2	0	0	0	3	4	4	4	0	3	0	.400	.400	.400	0.00	10.13
Slania, Dan	R-R	6-5	275	5-24-92	2	2	5.25	5	4	0	0	24	27	17	14	3	9	18	.284	.379	.242	6.75	3.38
Snelten, D.J.	L-L	6-7	245	5-29-92	4	7	4.11	31	13	1	1	96	114	55	44	2	32	82	.302	.241	.328	7.66	2.99
Soptic, Jeff	R-R	6-6	230	4-8-91	1	3	6.75	41	0	0	0	68	78	55	51	8	43	57	.290	.328	.254	7.54	5.69
Suarez, Andrew	L-L	6-2	205	9-11-92	2	1	2.43	5	5	0	0	30	25	9	8	2	5	34	.225	.143	.263	10.31	1.52
Taylor, Cory	R-R	6-2	255	12-14-93	1	1	6.75	3	3	0	0	9	12	7	7	0	4	11	.300	.407	.077	10.61	3.86
Young, Pat	R-R	6-7	240	3-24-92	6	1	4.13	52	0	0	3	72	70	41	33	3	40	70	.255	.233	.271	8.75	5.00

Fielding

Catcher	PCT	G	PO	A	E	DP	PB
Deacon	.971	5	33	1	1	0	0
Garcia	1.000	41	329	39	0	2	7
Melendez	.993	18	137	5	1	0	3
Ross	.989	75	557	48	7	4	5
Susac	1.000	3	16	3	0	1	0
Turner	1.000	3	20	5	0	0	1

First Base	PCT	G	PO	A	E	DP
Arenado	.989	78	632	64	8	59
Bednar	1.000	1	13	2	0	1
Bennett	1.000	2	8	0	0	1
Delfino	1.000	1	9	0	0	0
Gomez	.962	7	48	2	2	6
Shaw	.996	52	426	29	2	44

Second Base	PCT	G	PO	A	E	DP
Bednar	.976	52	87	161	6	37

	PCT	G	PO	A	E	DP
Bennett	.978	43	70	106	4	19
Gomez	1.000	6	16	10	0	7
Paulino	.974	28	49	65	3	20
Rodriguez	.980	12	16	34	1	2
Vizcaino Jr.	.833	3	4	6	2	1

Third Base	PCT	G	PO	A	E	DP
Adrianza	—	1	0	0	0	0
Arenado	.954	30	20	42	3	8
Bednar	—	1	0	0	0	0
Bennett	.938	6	2	13	1	1
Delfino	1.000	18	13	34	0	4
Gomez	.867	20	8	31	6	1
Paulino	.944	7	5	12	1	1
Vizcaino Jr.	.864	59	50	77	20	8

Shortstop	PCT	G	PO	A	E	DP
Adrianza	1.000	5	5	13	0	3

	PCT	G	PO	A	E	DP
Bednar	.875	4	8	6	2	2
Bennett	1.000	14	27	45	0	13
Hinojosa	.966	68	113	201	11	43
Moreno	.938	32	60	92	10	12
Rodriguez	.949	23	27	47	4	11

Outfield	PCT	G	PO	A	E	DP
Arias	.909	4	9	1	1	0
Bennett	—	1	0	0	0	0
Carbonell	.973	34	72	1	2	0
Davis	.966	50	82	2	3	0
Duggar	.980	65	138	7	3	1
Fargas	.921	34	52	6	5	0
Garvey	.986	65	131	9	2	0
Jebavy	.977	127	291	4	7	0
Paulino	.974	42	65	9	2	1
Quinn	1.000	4	9	1	0	0

AUGUSTA GREENJACKETS

LOW CLASS A

SOUTH ATLANTIC LEAGUE

Batting	B-T	HT	WT	DOB	AVG	vLH	vRH	G	AB	R	H	2B	3B	HR	RBI	BB	HBP	SH	SF	SO	SB	CS	SLG	OBP
Amion, Richard	R-R	5-10	190	2-24-93	.203	.133	.220	51	148	16	30	4	0	0	11	14	2	1	2	30	10	0	.230	.277
Angomas, Jean	L-R	6-0	170	6-5-95	.260	.213	.275	95	342	35	89	17	5	1	45	19	1	5	3	39	14	9	.348	.299
Arias, Junior	R-R	6-1	195	1-9-92	.275	.357	.245	59	207	29	57	9	3	11	37	12	3	0	1	66	11	5	.507	.323
Beltre, Kelvin	R-R	5-11	170	9-25-96	.250	.294	.226	55	192	29	48	14	2	4	22	16	7	0	1	63	7	4	.406	.329
Bennett, T.J.	L-R	6-3	215	7-22-92	.250	.333	.000	1	4	1	1	1	0	0	2	0	0	0	0	0	0	0	.500	.250
Bowers, Zack	R-R	6-2	215	10-14-93	.170	.214	.152	14	47	5	8	2	0	0	3	3	0	1	0	20	0	1	.213	.220
Brown, Tyler	R-L	6-1	180	1-18-95	.269	.231	.308	8	26	4	7	1	0	0	2	4	0	0	1	6	2	0	.308	.355
Cabrera, Gustavo	R-R	6-2	190	1-23-96	.232	.231	.233	19	69	9	16	4	1	0	5	5	1	0	0	16	3	0	.319	.293
Davis, Dylan	R-R	6-0	205	7-20-93	.288	.243	.309	63	236	38	68	17	4	8	43	10	1	0	2	58	3	1	.496	.368
Dobson, Dillon	L-R	6-2	220	8-21-93	.273	.296	.263	106	396	52	108	27	5	13	60	31	5	0	7	99	2	0	.465	.328
Dunston Jr. Shawon	L-R	6-2	195	2-5-93	.284	.167	.304	24	81	10	23	7	0	1	7	6	3	0	2	11	6	1	.407	.348
Ewing, Skyler	R-R	6-1	225	8-22-92	.241	.345	.212	74	261	41	63	10	2	10	34	28	9	0	4	69	2	1	.410	.331
Fargas, Johneshwy	R-R	6-1	170	12-15-94	.275	.200	.306	83	291	40	80	11	3	2	25	24	5	2	1	57	32	9	.354	.340
Fox, Lucius	B-R	6-1	175	7-2-97	.207	.184	.217	75	285	46	59	6	4	2	16	37	4	3	2	76	25	7	.277	.305
Fulmer, Ashford	R-R	6-1	175	6-29-93	.077	.105	.061	17	52	5	4	0	1	0	4	5	2	0	0	21	3	2	.115	.186
Geraldo, Manuel	R-R	6-1	175	12-1-96	.162	.119	.180	43	142	12	23	2	0	0	7	4	4	1	1	51	9	2	.176	.205
Gomez, Miguel	B-R	5-10	185	12-17-92	.371	.403	.359	66	267	41	99	17	1	8	43	12	3	1	2	25	3	2	.532	.401
Harrison, Seth	R-R	6-0	200	7-22-92	.256	.310	.235	118	407	61	104	19	4	6	35	37	6	4	2	94	16	8	.366	.325
Miller, Jalen	R-R	5-11	175	12-19-96	.223	.213	.227	112	457	65	102	20	5	5	44	26	6	6	5	107	11	5	.322	.271
Pare, Matt	L-R	6-0	205	11-17-90	.222	.286	.207	44	144	21	32	4	1	6	19	13	7	0	0	36	0	0	.389	.317
Polonius, John	R-R	6-1	160	1-13-91	.218	.250	.205	34	110	8	24	7	0	0	11	8	2	1	0	19	10	5	.282	.283
Reynolds, Bryan	B-R	6-3	200	1-27-95	.317	.241	.382	16	63	11	20	5	0	1	8	3	0	0	0	20	1	0	.444	.348

Batting	B-T	HT	WT	DOB	AVG	vLH	vRH	G	AB	R	H	2B	3B	HR	RBI	BB	HBP	SH	SF	SO	SB	CS	SLG	OBP
Sonabend, Adam	R-R	6-0	200	5-12-92	.200	.176	.211	20	55	2	11	0	0	0	2	8	1	2	0	20	0	1	.200	.313
Winn, Matt	R-R	6-1	210	8-5-92	.230	.250	.221	95	331	45	76	13	1	13	49	44	4	3	2	110	1	1	.393	.325

Pitching	B-T	HT	WT	DOB	W	L	ERA	G	GS	CG	SV	IP	H	R	ER	HR	BB	SO	AVG	vLH	vRH	K/9	BB/9
Alvarado, Carlos	R-R	6-4	175	10-22-89	0	0	0.00	9	0	0	7	10	4	0	0	0	1	11	.121	.100	.130	10.24	0.93
Bickford, Phil	R-R	6-4	200	7-10-95	3	4	2.70	11	11	1	0	60	49	23	18	2	15	69	.220	.198	.232	10.35	2.25
Cabrera, Sandro	L-L	6-2	175	6-22-95	0	0	0.00	1	0	0	0	1	1	0	0	0	3	.250	1.000	.000	27.00	0.00
Connolly, Mike	R-R	6-1	205	10-31-91	11	7	3.05	25	18	1	0	136	134	59	46	8	31	107	.258	.286	.238	7.10	2.06
Cyr, Tyler	R-R	6-3	200	5-5-93	3	3	2.31	20	0	0	2	51	36	17	13	1	16	65	.201	.257	.162	11.55	2.84
Halstead, Ryan	L-R	6-5	220	5-13-92	4	3	3.83	40	0	0	4	54	52	26	23	3	9	62	.249	.268	.236	10.33	1.50
Kaden, Connor	R-R	6-4	200	10-27-92	6	3	3.71	44	0	0	3	87	86	41	36	3	26	80	.257	.268	.249	8.24	2.68
Koziol, Ryan	R-R	6-3	185	10-4-93	4	3	3.01	46	0	0	9	69	77	32	23	2	13	59	.277	.250	.295	7.73	1.70
Marshall, Mac	R-L	6-0	181	1-27-96	0	0	4.60	4	4	0	0	16	11	10	8	1	17	14	.193	.429	.116	8.04	9.77
Mazza, Domenic	R-L	6-1	195	7-29-94	8	3	3.93	14	14	0	0	85	98	42	37	6	16	79	.292	.271	.300	8.40	1.70
McCasland, Jake	R-R	6-2	215	9-13-91	8	5	1.65	27	13	1	3	109	77	23	20	4	24	107	.197	.242	.164	8.81	1.98
Owen, Dave	R-R	6-0	190	10-21-93	1	0	2.08	9	0	0	0	9	6	2	2	0	2	5	.200	.333	.143	5.19	2.08
Pino, Luis	R-R	6-0	175	11-4-94	2	1	3.77	17	4	0	0	45	37	21	19	6	23	42	.222	.231	.213	8.34	4.57
Pope, Matt	R-R	6-5	225	7-5-94	0	0	9.49	9	0	0	0	12	13	18	13	2	18	16	.271	.263	.276	11.68	13.14
Sabo, Nick	R-L	6-5	220	6-14-93	0	0	3.86	6	0	0	0	5	5	2	2	1	3	5	.278	.125	.400	9.64	5.79
Santos, Michael	R-R	6-4	205	5-29-95	4	2	2.91	10	10	1	0	59	61	24	19	0	5	44	.264	.182	.305	6.75	0.77
Slatton, Heath	L-R	6-3	200	9-17-93	2	4	2.37	27	5	0	4	49	48	20	13	2	23	44	.254	.309	.213	8.03	4.20
Smith, Caleb	R-R	6-2	205	10-4-92	1	2	2.35	38	0	0	6	38	20	13	10	0	22	54	.147	.167	.132	12.68	5.17
Solter, Matt	R-R	6-3	220	6-4-93	4	6	6.45	14	14	0	0	68	87	50	49	7	30	60	.315	.311	.318	7.90	3.95
Taylor, Cory	R-R	6-2	255	12-14-93	9	5	2.58	18	18	0	0	98	99	44	28	4	25	100	.261	.283	.242	9.22	2.30
Vizcaino, Raffi	R-R	6-1	195	12-2-95	1	1	3.27	2	2	0	0	11	9	5	4	1	0	11	.231	.231	.231	9.00	0.82
Watson, Grant	L-L	6-0	185	7-2-93	3	7	4.62	17	17	0	0	78	84	42	40	1	18	68	.275	.247	.286	7.85	2.08
Webb, Logan	R-R	6-2	195	11-18-96	2	3	6.21	9	9	0	0	42	54	31	29	7	12	30	.303	.307	.301	6.43	2.57
Yanez, Cesar	R-R	6-5	175	9-30-94	0	0	4.05	13	0	0	0	13	12	8	6	0	8	19	.226	.261	.200	12.83	5.40

Fielding

Catcher	PCT	G	PO	A	E	DP	PB
Bowers	.977	14	116	14	3	0	2
Pare	.994	22	148	15	1	2	2
Sonabend	.970	18	117	11	4	2	1
Winn	.988	94	765	90	10	11	13

First Base	PCT	G	PO	A	E	DP
Arias	.973	23	201	14	6	17
Dobson	.984	52	458	26	8	25
Ewing	.994	59	473	35	3	40
Gomez	.985	7	63	3	1	4
Winn	—	1	0	0	0	0

Second Base	PCT	G	PO	A	E	DP
Amion	.969	22	36	58	3	12
Brown	1.000	2	2	6	0	1
Geraldo	1.000	10	16	29	0	5

		G	PO	A	E	DP	PB
Gomez	1.000	2	3	3	0	1	
Miller	.957	104	169	274	20	49	
Polonius	.875	1	3	4	1	3	

Third Base	PCT	G	PO	A	E	DP
Amion	.833	2	2	3	1	0
Beltre	.933	42	25	86	8	3
Bennett	—	1	0	0	0	0
Brown	1.000	2	0	5	0	0
Dobson	.912	42	25	68	9	6
Geraldo	.920	10	4	19	2	2
Gomez	.950	31	7	50	3	7
Polonius	1.000	11	1	25	0	1

Shortstop	PCT	G	PO	A	E	DP
Amion	.895	17	24	44	8	12
Beltre	1.000	4	8	11	0	4

		G	PO	A	E	DP
Brown	1.000	3	2	5	0	0
Fox	.897	70	92	188	32	24
Geraldo	.957	20	29	59	4	7
Miller	1.000	7	5	13	0	2
Polonius	.952	23	16	64	4	7

Outfield	PCT	G	PO	A	E	DP
Amion	1.000	1	2	0	0	0
Angomas	.981	91	152	6	3	0
Arias	.973	22	36	0	1	0
Cabrera	1.000	18	29	1	0	0
Davis	.940	48	77	1	5	0
Dunston Jr.	1.000	20	44	0	0	0
Fargas	.982	83	158	3	3	0
Fulmer	1.000	16	30	1	0	0
Harrison	.944	113	193	10	12	0
Reynolds	1.000	11	28	1	0	0

SALEM-KEIZER VOLCANOES SHORT-SEASON
NORTHWEST LEAGUE

Batting	B-T	HT	WT	DOB	AVG	vLH	vRH	G	AB	R	H	2B	3B	HR	RBI	BB	HBP	SH	SF	SO	SB	CS	SLG	OBP
Angomas, Jean	L-R	6-0	170	6-5-95	.389	.400	.385	9	36	4	14	5	0	0	3	1	0	0	0	3	2	1	.528	.405
Bowers, Zack	R-R	6-2	215	10-14-93	.226	.256	.216	49	155	22	35	12	0	2	27	24	3	0	3	52	0	0	.342	.335
Brusa, Gio	B-R	6-3	220	7-26-93	.264	.219	.286	53	220	36	58	15	3	10	42	11	2	0	5	69	1	1	.495	.298
Cabrera, Gustavo	R-R	6-2	190	1-23-96	.246	.194	.264	33	122	25	30	9	1	4	13	5	2	0	1	42	1	0	.434	.285
Compton, Chase	L-R	6-2	210	9-26-91	.211	.188	.220	33	114	18	24	8	0	0	16	10	2	0	1	24	3	0	.281	.283
Edwards, Woody	R-R	5-10	155	4-2-95	.269	.286	.263	7	26	4	7	0	0	0	0	5	0	0	0	7	2	1	.269	.387
Fulmer, Ashford	R-R	6-1	175	6-29-93	.292	.415	.248	56	202	36	59	12	3	1	24	27	9	1	2	43	12	3	.396	.396
Geraldo, Manuel	R-R	6-1	170	9-23-96	.298	.266	.311	62	272	47	81	10	5	0	32	14	2	2	3	69	13	7	.371	.333
Heyward, Jacob	R-R	6-3	210	8-1-95	.286	.000	.308	4	14	4	4	2	0	0	4	3	1	0	0	3	1	0	.429	.444
Hill, Nick	R-R	6-4	190	8-2-94	.231	—	.231	3	13	1	3	1	0	0	0	0	0	0	0	2	1	0	.308	.231
Howard, Ryan	R-R	6-2	180	7-25-94	.272	.328	.252	59	224	33	61	10	0	4	31	13	2	3	4	24	2	2	.371	.313
Kirby, Ryan	L-R	6-2	180	1-25-95	.260	.182	.291	53	196	27	51	16	1	3	28	22	4	0	1	49	1	2	.398	.345
Pena, Julio	R-R	6-0	185	12-13-92	.222	.167	.235	20	63	12	14	3	1	2	9	2	0	0	1	20	1	0	.397	.242
Quinn, Heath	R-R	6-2	190	6-7-95	.337	.357	.326	54	205	37	69	19	1	9	34	26	6	0	2	50	3	0	.571	.423
Reynolds, Bryan	B-R	6-3	200	1-27-95	.312	.291	.323	40	154	28	48	12	1	5	30	11	4	0	2	41	2	0	.500	.368
Riley, John	R-R	6-0	210	2-14-94	.274	.319	.253	41	146	17	40	10	0	3	14	15	7	0	0	51	0	0	.404	.369
Rivera, Kevin	B-R	5-11	170	6-12-96	.320	.357	.306	66	253	41	81	14	3	3	31	11	2	1	1	47	4	0	.435	.352
Rodriguez, Juan	R-R	6-1	175	8-29-94	.171	.111	.192	9	35	6	6	0	1	0	2	0	1	0	0	4	0	1	.229	.194
Rojas, Leo	R-R	5-11	190	6-11-90	.213	.136	.239	24	89	9	19	4	0	3	20	5	2	0	0	18	0	0	.360	.271
Van Horn, Brandon	R-R	6-2	175	12-18-93	.286	—	.286	2	7	2	2	0	0	1	3	1	0	0	0	1	0	0	.714	.375

Pitching	B-T	HT	WT	DOB	W	L	ERA	G	GS	CG	SV	IP	H	R	ER	HR	BB	SO	AVG	vLH	vRH	K/9	BB/9
Adon, Melvin	R-R	6-3	195	6-9-94	5	5	5.48	14	14	0	0	67	85	53	41	3	34	55	.317	.29	.331	7.35	4.54

Pitching	B-T	HT	WT	DOB	W	L	ERA	G	GS	CG	SV	IP	H	R	ER	HR	BB	SO	AVG	vLH	vRH	K/9	BB/9
Alvarado, Carlos	R-R	6-4	175	10-22-89	0	0	0.00	2	0	0	1	2	2	1	0	0	0	2	.222	.250	.200	7.71	0.00
Brody, Greg	R-R	6-2	185	10-22-91	0	0	6.75	2	0	0	0	1	2	1	1	0	3	1	.400	.500	.000	6.75	20.25
Burke, Jeff	R-R	6-5	210	6-7-93	1	2	3.26	23	0	0	1	30	34	17	11	0	10	25	.276	.319	.250	7.42	2.97
Concepcion, Victor	R-R	6-0	170	11-23-96	4	7	6.40	15	10	0	0	58	73	50	41	9	24	46	.313	.259	.345	7.18	3.75
Diaz, Carlos	L-L	6-2	225	11-18-93	1	1	4.32	10	0	0	0	8	9	6	4	0	3	7	.290	.235	.357	7.56	3.24
Duprey, Sidney	L-L	6-3	230	11-15-96	0	0	5.06	2	0	0	0	5	5	3	3	1	0	5	.250	.286	.231	8.44	0.00
Falwell, Chris	L-L	6-7	210	4-14-95	0	0	5.40	1	0	0	0	2	1	1	1	0	0	2	.167	.500	.000	10.80	0.00
Gettman, C.J.	L-R	6-5	215	6-2-94	1	0	2.78	18	0	0	1	23	17	8	7	1	12	27	.207	.200	.212	10.72	4.76
Hernandez, Rayan	R-R	6-4	230	9-24-95	0	3	2.78	17	0	0	0	36	28	14	11	4	16	30	.217	.269	.182	7.57	4.04
Krook, Matt	L-L	6-4	195	10-21-94	1	3	6.17	11	10	0	0	35	35	27	24	2	33	39	.263	.250	.266	10.03	8.49
Marshall, Mac	R-L	6-0	181	1-27-96	1	6	4.73	13	13	0	0	51	49	34	27	3	48	54	.255	.214	.272	9.47	8.42
Medina, Hengerber	R-R	5-11	160	10-12-94	2	3	4.43	12	7	0	0	45	45	23	22	5	18	37	.257	.277	.245	7.46	3.63
Melo, Kendry	R-R	6-3	210	1-7-94	4	1	4.99	22	0	0	0	40	32	26	22	1	24	44	.213	.295	.179	9.98	5.45
Menez, Conner	L-L	6-3	195	5-29-95	0	1	7.20	1	1	0	0	5	5	4	4	0	1	4	.278	.250	.286	7.20	1.80
Pope, Matt	R-R	6-6	225	7-5-94	1	1	9.09	20	0	0	1	32	50	36	32	3	22	20	.355	.370	.347	5.68	6.25
Riggs, Nolan	R-R	6-8	235	5-22-93	3	0	4.24	21	0	0	0	47	47	26	22	7	12	36	.264	.226	.284	6.94	2.31
Ruotolo, Pat	R-R	5-10	218	1-15-95	2	2	1.42	15	0	0	4	19	13	5	3	0	14	35	.188	.240	.159	16.58	6.63
Sabo, Nick	R-L	6-5	220	6-14-93	2	1	4.70	15	0	0	0	23	25	15	12	1	11	19	.269	.212	.300	7.43	4.30
Simpson, William	R-R	6-3	210	9-15-91	1	0	4.05	6	0	0	0	7	3	3	3	0	6	8	.125	.000	.188	10.80	8.10
Timmins, John	R-R	6-6	215	1-20-94	0	0	8.16	10	0	0	0	14	26	17	13	3	6	3	.388	.391	.386	1.88	3.77
Vizcaino, Raffi	R-R	6-1	195	12-2-95	0	4	4.60	11	10	0	1	47	56	27	24	5	23	43	.298	.319	.286	8.23	4.40
Williams, Garrett	L-L	6-1	205	9-15-94	1	2	5.68	7	7	0	0	25	28	18	16	1	14	22	.275	.217	.291	7.82	4.97
Woods, Stephen	R-R	6-2	200	6-10-95	1	0	5.63	2	2	0	0	8	7	6	5	1	5	12	.233	.222	.238	13.50	5.63
Yanez, Cesar	R-R	6-5	175	9-30-94	1	0	0.60	12	0	0	4	15	11	2	1	0	7	16	.208	.158	.235	9.60	4.20

Fielding

C: Bowers 45, Manwaring 6, Riley 32. 1B: Bowers 4, Brusa 1, Kirby 48, Riley 10, Rojas 14. 2B: Geraldo 8, Rivera 66. 3B: Compton 33, Geraldo 40, Hill 3. SS: Geraldo 15, Howard 58, Van Horn 2. OF: Angomas 7, Brusa 38, Cabrera 16, Edwards 7, Fulmer 51, Heyward 4, Pena 13, Quinn 49, Reynolds 33, Rodriguez 9.

AZL GIANTS   ROOKIE
ARIZONA LEAGUE

Batting	B-T	HT	WT	DOB	AVG	vLH	vRH	G	AB	R	H	2B	3B	HR	RBI	BB	HBP	SH	SF	SO	SB	CS	SLG	OBP
Albertson, Will	R-R	5-11	190	6-26-94	.213	.417	.143	14	47	6	10	1	1	0	4	1	1	0	0	7	0	0	.277	.245
Beltre, Kelvin	R-R	5-11	170	9-25-96	.333	.167	.389	7	24	3	8	4	1	0	5	1	0	1	0	4	1	0	.583	.360
Bernal, Mike	R-R	5-11	190	9-6-92	.260	.188	.281	44	146	18	38	11	4	4	34	11	9	1	6	44	2	0	.473	.337
Bono, Chris	L-R	6-1	185	10-6-92	.194	.313	.152	25	62	3	12	2	1	0	3	8	5	2	0	21	4	1	.258	.333
Brickhouse, Cody	R-R	6-3	210	12-23-96	.271	.313	.250	17	48	7	13	1	0	0	6	11	1	1	0	9	0	0	.292	.417
Case, Bryan	R-R	6-3	205	8-12-92	.091	.200	.000	3	11	1	1	0	0	0	1	0	0	0	0	6	0	0	.182	.167
Denorfia, Chris	R-R	6-0	195	7-15-80	.350	.250	.417	6	20	2	7	4	0	0	1	2	1	0	0	4	0	0	.550	.435
Edie, Mikey	R-R	5-11	175	7-3-97	.217	.189	.226	35	143	22	31	5	2	0	11	8	6	3	0	44	10	4	.280	.287
Edwards, Woody	R-R	5-10	155	4-25-94	.294	.357	.278	21	68	6	20	2	0	0	6	5	2	0	0	11	8	2	.324	.360
Fabian, Sandro	R-R	6-1	180	3-6-98	.340	.290	.352	42	159	30	54	13	5	2	35	7	2	1	5	28	3	1	.522	.364
Garcia, Aramis	R-R	6-2	220	1-12-93	.227	.000	.263	6	22	1	5	1	0	0	4	0	0	0	1	1	0	0	.273	.217
Heyward, Jacob	R-R	6-3	210	8-1-95	.337	.368	.329	28	95	27	32	10	5	1	21	24	5	0	1	30	10	2	.579	.488
Hill, Nick	R-R	6-4	190	8-2-94	.263	.310	.253	45	175	31	46	8	3	0	16	9	9	0	1	47	17	2	.343	.330
Howard, Ryan	R-R	6-2	180	7-25-94	.250	.000	.286	2	8	1	2	0	0	0	2	0	0	0	0	0	0	0	.250	.400
Javier, Nathanael	R-R	6-3	185	10-10-95	.327	.235	.368	17	55	7	18	2	0	0	6	0	0	0	0	14	0	0	.364	.327
Kirby, Ryan	L-R	6-2	180	1-25-95	.375	.500	.333	2	8	3	3	0	0	0	2	0	0	0	0	1	0	0	.375	.333
Lacen, Luis	R-R	6-1	195	10-13-96	.056	.000	.077	7	18	0	1	0	0	0	1	0	0	0	0	7	2	0	.056	.105
Layer, Jose	R-R	6-0	160	5-28-97	.283	.100	.326	15	53	9	15	5	0	0	9	5	1	2	0	7	1	4	.377	.356
Matranga, Ryan	R-R	5-10	195	1-1-95	.333	—	.333	5	9	1	3	2	0	0	1	0	0	0	0	0	0	0	.556	.333
Medrano, Robinson	R-R	6-3	180	4-6-98	.222	.150	.239	34	108	11	24	7	2	1	13	10	1	0	2	30	2	4	.352	.289
Mendoza, Beicker	R-R	6-2	185	2-14-98	.272	.235	.288	30	114	12	31	5	0	0	12	4	1	0	1	31	1	0	.316	.300
Murray, Byron	R-R	5-10	195	7-26-95	.083	.000	.143	4	12	1	1	0	0	0	3	0	0	1	0	5	0	0	.083	.250
Parra, Jeffery	R-R	6-0	195	1-24-98	.275	.200	.300	16	40	6	11	1	0	1	2	3	3	0	0	8	0	1	.375	.354
Polonius, John	R-R	6-1	160	1-13-91	.400	.700	.280	10	35	10	14	0	2	1	4	3	1	0	0	8	2	0	.600	.462
Quinn, Heath	R-R	6-2	190	6-7-95	.600	1.000	.333	2	5	4	3	1	0	0	2	2	0	0	0	0	0	0	.800	.778
Ramirez, A.J.	R-R	6-0	190	4-4-93	.121	.000	.138	14	33	3	4	1	1	0	2	4	0	0	0	10	1	0	.212	.216
Sabanosh, Connor	R-R	6-1	200	8-6-93	.265	.222	.280	12	34	8	9	2	0	0	6	4	3	2	1	9	0	0	.324	.381
Santiago, Hector	R-R	6-3	185	11-18-97	.167	.000	.194	16	42	2	7	1	0	0	4	1	0	1	1	18	0	0	.190	.182
Tona, Jesus	R-R	5-10	170	3-30-96	.148	.000	.200	11	27	2	4	0	1	0	1	0	0	0	0	5	0	0	.222	.179
Van Horn, Brandon	R-R	6-2	175	12-18-93	.231	.179	.242	47	160	25	37	7	2	0	15	24	1	0	4	47	5	5	.300	.328
Ziegler, Malique	R-R	6-2	170	9-8-96	.290	.368	.256	18	62	11	18	4	2	0	5	10	0	0	1	15	4	1	.419	.384

Pitching	B-T	HT	WT	DOB	W	L	ERA	G	GS	CG	SV	IP	H	R	ER	HR	BB	SO	AVG	vLH	vRH	K/9	BB/9
Alleman, Justin	R-R	6-1	220	12-20-93	0	0	11.81	5	0	0	1	5	9	7	7	1	1	4	.360	.375	.353	6.75	1.69
Amaya, Luis	L-L	5-11	160	8-26-98	1	0	3.68	5	0	0	1	7	9	3	3	0	3	7	.290	.444	.227	8.59	3.68
Avila-Leeper, Cameron	L-L	5-11	210	2-21-96	0	0	0.00	2	0	0	0	3	1	0	0	0	0	4	.100	.333	.000	12.00	0.00
Baragar, Caleb	L-R	6-3	210	4-9-94	5	2	2.28	14	10	0	0	55	47	17	14	2	16	50	.236	.200	.245	8.13	2.60
Bazar, Reagan	R-R	6-7	250	6-27-95	2	2	4.91	16	0	0	0	18	23	13	10	0	13	15	.311	.367	.273	7.36	6.38
Benitez, Julio	R-R	6-3	185	11-1-94	3	2	3.79	15	1	0	3	38	37	22	16	2	11	31	.252	.246	.256	7.34	2.61
Bostic, Alex	L-L	6-3	195	11-14-94	2	4	5.59	13	10	0	0	47	51	36	29	2	27	39	.271	.211	.287	7.52	5.21
Brody, Greg	R-R	6-2	185	10-22-91	0	0	0.00	2	0	0	0	2	0	0	0	0	0	2	.000	.000	.000	9.00	0.00

Pitching	B-T	HT	WT	DOB	W	L	ERA	G	GS	CG	SV	IP	H	R	ER	HR	BB	SO	AVG	vLH	vRH	K/9	BB/9
Cabrera, Sandro	L-L	6-2	175	6-22-95	2	2	2.81	17	1	0	1	42	33	20	13	2	14	38	.209	.161	.22	8.21	3.02
Cain, Matt	R-R	6-3	230	10-1-84	0	0	5.40	1	1	0	0	3	3	2	2	1	0	6	.231	.125	.400	16.20	0.00
Deeg, Nick	L-L	6-5	225	6-26-95	1	1	4.12	8	3	0	0	20	23	9	9	1	7	19	.288	.250	.300	8.69	3.20
Duprey, Sidney	L-L	6-3	230	11-15-96	2	2	1.61	8	1	0	0	22	18	8	4	0	10	12	.207	.105	.235	4.84	4.03
Falwell, Chris	L-R	6-7	210	4-14-95	3	1	2.73	12	3	0	1	33	32	12	10	0	12	20	.256	.172	.281	5.45	3.27
Gettman, C.J.	L-R	6-5	215	6-2-94	0	0	0.00	2	0	0	1	1	0	0	0	0	0	1	.000	.000	.000	9.00	0.00
Greenwalt, Jake	R-R	6-1	170	4-30-98	0	1	5.79	16	0	0	1	19	23	17	12	4	10	13	.295	.345	.265	6.27	4.82
Heston, Chris	R-R	6-3	195	4-10-88	0	0	0.00	2	2	0	0	7	7	0	0	0	2	7	.259	.000	.304	9.45	2.70
Krook, Matt	L-L	6-4	195	10-21-94	0	1	1.59	2	1	0	0	6	4	1	1	0	2	2	.261	.400	.222	3.18	3.18
Menez, Conner	L-L	6-3	195	5-29-95	2	0	2.57	8	2	0	0	21	15	7	6	0	4	26	.190	.125	.206	11.14	1.71
Myers, D.J.	L-R	6-5	255	12-24-94	3	2	1.70	14	9	0	0	58	60	17	11	4	5	52	.260	.311	.227	8.02	0.77
Ortiz, Randy	R-R	5-11	185	6-15-93	0	1	10.13	2	0	0	0	3	3	3	3	0	6	3	.333	.400	.250	10.13	20.25
Owen, Dave	R-R	6-0	190	10-21-93	1	0	0.00	3	0	0	1	3	2	0	0	0	2	.182	.000	.333	5.40	0.00
Parra, Olbis	R-R	6-2	180	10-1-94	0	1	2.45	4	0	0	0	4	4	2	1	0	0	.267	.250	.273	0.00	0.00
Ruotolo, Pat	R-R	5-10	218	1-15-95	0	0	0.00	4	0	0	0	5	3	1	0	0	7	.167	.250	.143	12.60	0.00
Santos, Wilson	R-R	6-2	200	10-20-91	0	0	2.35	6	0	0	1	8	5	2	2	0	3	10	.192	.200	.188	11.74	3.52
Timmins, John	R-R	6-6	215	1-20-94	0	1	4.50	8	0	0	3	8	11	7	4	0	8	3	.333	.222	.375	3.38	9.00
Williams, Garrett	L-L	6-1	205	9-15-94	1	0	2.57	3	1	0	0	7	4	2	2	0	3	5	.174	.000	.200	6.43	3.86
Woods, Stephen	R-R	6-2	200	6-10-95	0	2	2.67	10	8	0	0	27	25	19	8	0	17	25	.236	.204	.263	8.33	5.67
Woods, Stetson	R-R	6-8	200	1-15-95	0	1	13.50	4	2	0	0	9	18	14	13	1	5	10	.429	.333	.481	10.38	5.19

Fielding

C: Albertson 12, Brickhouse 17, Case 3, Garcia 6, Matranga 1, Parra 15, Sabanosh 11. **1B:** Kirby 2, Medrano 32, Mendoza 20, Ramirez 5, Sabanosh 1. **2B:** Beltre 2, Bernal 40, Polonius 2, Santiago 9, Tona 11, Van Horn 1. **3B:** Beltre 4, Bernal 1, Drabek 7, Hill 23, Javier 1, Mendoza 3, Polonius 7, Ramirez 9. **SS:** Beltre 1, Bernal 3, Howard 2, Polonius 2, Santiago 8, Van Horn 46. **OF:** Bono 17, Denorfia 5, Edie 32, Edwards 12, Fabian 41, Heyward 20, Hill 13, Lacen 3, Layer 15, Quinn 2, Ziegler 15.

DSL GIANTS   ROOKIE
DOMINICAN SUMMER LEAGUE

Batting	B-T	HT	WT	DOB	AVG	vLH	vRH	G	AB	R	H	2B	3B	HR	RBI	BB	HBP	SH	SF	SO	SB	CS	SLG	OBP
Almanzar, Angeddy	R-R	6-2	180	6-30-98	.294	.154	.321	65	235	35	69	17	1	5	36	22	10	0	4	48	1	0	.438	.373
Angulo, Andres	R-R	5-10	181	9-5-97	.231	.231	.231	45	117	15	27	5	0	1	21	17	8	1	2	12	6	2	.299	.361
Batista, Robinson	B-R	5-11	167	10-11-98	.250	.667	.000	7	8	3	2	0	0	0	1	2	0	0	0	2	0	0	.250	.400
Cairo, Victor	R-R	6-0	180	9-10-97	.111	—	.111	16	18	3	2	0	0	0	0	4	0	1	0	4	0	0	.111	.273
De Leon, Wascar	B-R	5-11	180	1-8-98	.268	.100	.287	41	97	17	26	2	1	0	14	16	3	0	0	18	4	3	.309	.388
De Pena, Brayan	L-L	6-4	240	11-19-97	.188	.143	.191	39	96	9	18	2	1	2	8	7	0	0	0	37	0	0	.292	.243
Genoves, Ricardo	R-R	6-2	190	5-14-99	.256	.182	.270	59	207	24	53	13	0	1	18	22	5	1	0	34	0	0	.333	.342
Gutierrez, Nishell	R-R	5-10	165	5-4-99	.226	.121	.248	57	186	22	42	2	3	0	22	20	1	1	1	24	5	4	.269	.303
Labour, Franklin	R-R	6-1	190	5-11-98	.242	.258	.239	61	194	30	47	9	0	1	20	21	7	1	3	38	4	0	.304	.333
Medina, Francisco	R-R	6-1	165	3-20-98	.289	.293	.289	67	228	35	66	4	1	3	33	33	3	1	0	39	4	1	.355	.386
Munguia, Ismael	L-L	5-10	158	10-19-98	.274	.278	.274	62	237	35	65	13	4	0	26	30	2	3	1	15	8	8	.363	.359
Patino, Jose	B-R	6-0	160	12-11-97	.278	.300	.273	64	205	38	57	10	0	0	19	15	6	5	0	35	7	6	.327	.345
Perez, Joel	B-R	5-11	160	7-7-95	.114	.125	.111	17	44	3	5	0	1	0	1	7	0	0	0	17	0	1	.159	.235
Rincones, Diego	R-R	6-0	175	6-14-99	.244	.270	.238	58	201	27	49	12	1	2	30	29	3	2	1	32	1	0	.343	.346
Rivero, Jose	L-R	5-11	158	4-30-98	.253	.200	.262	55	198	39	50	9	1	0	24	33	1	1	1	36	6	2	.308	.361
Santana, Marcos	R-R	6-3	190	9-18-96	.000	.000	—	1	1	0	0	0	0	0	0	0	0	0	0	0	0	0	.000	.000
Santiago, Hector	R-R	6-3	185	11-18-97	.190	.111	.212	13	42	3	8	0	0	0	5	4	1	0	1	10	0	0	.190	.271

Pitching	B-T	HT	WT	DOB	W	L	ERA	G	GS	CG	SV	IP	H	R	ER	HR	BB	SO	AVG	vLH	vRH	K/9	BB/9
Acosta, Aneudy	R-R	5-11	180	4-7-96	3	3	3.99	13	9	1	0	47	42	27	21	0	19	46	.233	.284	.204	8.75	3.61
Adames, Abel	R-R	6-5	190	12-04-95	0	0	22.50	3	0	0	0	2	4	5	5	0	8	4	.364	.333	.375	18.00	36.00
Castro, Kervin	R-R	6-0	185	2-7-99	3	1	4.71	13	0	0	0	21	17	14	11	0	12	25	.233	.259	.217	10.71	5.14
De La Rosa, Alejandro	R-R	6-0	165	2-14-95	5	0	1.19	16	0	0	4	30	21	8	4	1	10	32	.198	.243	.174	9.49	2.97
Figueroa, Miguel	R-R	6-5	165	8-9-97	5	0	3.02	11	11	0	0	48	42	18	16	3	14	28	.249	.245	.250	5.29	2.64
Gonzalez, Marco	L-L	6-1	190	12-8-97	1	0	4.91	11	0	0	0	15	6	10	8	2	15	15	.118	.286	.091	9.20	9.20
Gudino, Norwith	R-R	6-2	200	11-22-95	3	3	2.84	12	12	0	0	51	45	23	16	0	13	40	.233	.241	.230	7.11	2.31
Herrera, Jasier	R-R	6-5	190	1-1-98	3	1	3.27	17	0	0	5	22	25	9	8	0	7	21	.291	.381	.262	8.59	2.86
Herrera, Jose	R-R	6-1	170	12-8-98	4	4	2.09	14	14	0	0	78	65	26	18	3	18	50	.230	.231	.230	5.79	2.09
Labrador, Jorge	R-R	6-1	180	3-9-99	0	3	8.17	13	4	0	0	25	38	24	23	3	21	21	.339	.349	.333	7.46	7.46
Maita, Jose	L-L	5-11	180	12-23-97	0	1	4.01	12	0	0	0	25	24	11	11	0	11	24	.260	.250	.262	8.76	4.01
Marte, Jose	R-R	6-3	180	6-14-96	1	1	1.89	5	5	0	0	19	12	10	4	0	10	18	.182	.087	.233	8.53	4.74
Pinto, Oliver	R-R	6-0	175	9-4-96	4	1	1.80	15	0	0	2	40	26	9	8	1	11	23	.193	.091	.242	5.18	2.48
Quiroz, Orleny	L-L	6-3	180	7-21-93	2	5	2.18	14	8	0	0	45	42	25	11	1	22	50	.233	.212	.238	9.93	4.37
Reyes, Jesus	R-R	6-4	176	7-31-96	1	1	1.51	17	0	0	3	36	21	12	6	0	17	46	.164	.051	.213	11.61	4.29
Severino, Jerson	R-R	6-3	191	7-30-98	0	4	3.15	12	7	0	0	34	24	17	12	1	13	13	.195	.163	.216	3.41	3.41
Suarez, Willian	R-R	6-3	175	3-21-98	0	0	3.38	4	0	0	0	5	7	3	2	0	4	3	.304	.333	.294	5.06	6.75
Villa, Eduin	R-R	6-2	170	3-12-96	0	0	6.43	11	0	0	1	14	13	12	10	2	10	10	.260	.176	.303	6.43	6.43
Yan, Jose	R-R	6-0	170	12-12-97	0	1	9.00	5	0	0	1	6	6	7	6	3	6	2	.261	.250	.267	3.00	9.00
Yan, Weilly	R-R	6-0	175	1-30-98	0	1	1.23	13	0	0	2	22	13	9	3	0	16	27	.171	.152	.186	11.05	6.55

Fielding

C: Angulo 41, Cairo 11, Genoves 36, Gutierrez 2. **1B:** Almanzar 60, De Pena 2, Genoves 11. **2B:** Batista 1, De Leon 2, Gutierrez 49, Perez 10. **3B:** Almanzar 1, De Leon 2, Gutierrez 8, Medina 64, Perez 2. **SS:** Batista 1, Medina 1, Perez 6, Rivero 55, Santiago 13. **OF:** De Pena 15, Labour 49, Munguia 56, Patino 61, Rincones 56, Santana 1.

Seattle Mariners

SEASON IN A SENTENCE: Shrewd roster management by new general manager Jerry DiPoto, a bounce-back season by Robinson Cano and a potent offense helped the Mariners matter, as they contended for a wild-card spot down to the final week of the season, though they finished three games out of the playoffs.

HIGH POINT: Seattle was on the fringes of the playoff race until a mid-September eight-game winning streak in which the pitching staff caught fire, giving up just 15 runs in wins against division rivals Texas (two wins), Oakland (three) and Los Angeles (three). The final win, a 2-1 decision against the Angels, embodied the best of the season—Nelson Cruz and Kyle Seager hit home runs, Hisashi Iwakuma pitched into the seventh inning for his 16th victory and rookie Edwin Diaz earned his 16th save.

LOW POINT: The Mariners had soared to 10 games over .500 before a late-August swoon in which they lost eight of nine, including a 1-6 road trip. The last game of the stretch was a dismal 14-1 loss to the Rangers in which ace Felix Hernandez, gave up six runs in four innings and walked four.

NOTABLE ROOKIES: Diaz entered the season as the Mariners' top pitching prospect and thrived after a shift to the bullpen that started at Double-A; he averaged 15.3 strikeouts per nine innings and racked up 18 saves. Korean first baseman Dae-ho Lee, 34, played a solid role as a power source, primarily against lefthanded pitching.

KEY TRANSACTIONS: Seattle's offseason moves, such as trading Brad Miller in a package to the Rays for inconsistent starter Nathan Karns, or trading Mark Trumbo to Baltimore for Steve Clevenger didn't work out at all. DiPoto massaged the margins of the roster constantly; some moves (trading Wade Miley for Ariel Miranda) worked, but the club probably could have used lefty Mike Montgomery, traded to the Cubs for DH/first baseman Dan Vogelbach, down the stretch.

DOWN ON THE FARM: New farm director Andy McKay had unmatched success in his first season. All six Mariners affiliates made the playoffs; they cumulatively posted a .581 winning percentage, second in baseball, and Double-A Jackson (Southern League) and the Rookie-level Arizona League Mariners won championships. Outfielder Tyler O'Neill earned Southern League MVP honors, batting .293/.374/.508 with 24 homers and a league-high 102 RBIs.

OPENING DAY PAYROLL: $ 141,683,339 (10th)

PLAYERS OF THE YEAR

MAJOR LEAGUE	MINOR LEAGUE
Robinson Cano	**Tyler O'Neill**
2b	of
.298/.350/.533	(Triple-A)
39 HR, 103 RBI	.293/.374/.508
195 hits, 107 runs	24 HR, 102 RBI

ORGANIZATION LEADERS

BATTING		*Minimum 250 AB
MAJORS		
* AVG	Robinson Cano	.298
* OPS	Nelson Cruz	.915
HR	Nelson Cruz	43
RBI	Nelson Cruz	105
MINORS		
* AVG	Stefen Romero, Tacoma	.304
* OBP	Guillermo Heredia, Jackson, Tacoma	.395
* SLG	Stefen Romero, Tacoma	.541
* OPS	Stefen Romero, Tacoma	.902
R	Drew Jackson, Bakersfield	87
H	Tim Lopes, Jackson	145
TB	Tyler O'Neill, Jackson	250
2B	Benji Gonzalez, Jackson	33
3B	Leon Landry, Jackson	9
HR	Tyler O'Neill, Jackson	24
RBI	Tyler O'Neill, Jackson	102
BB	Chantz Mack, Jackson, Bakersfield	83
SO	Austin Wilson, Bakersfield	157
SB	Ian Miller, Jackson	49

PITCHING		#Minimum 75 IP
MAJORS		
W	Hisashi Iwakuma	16
# ERA	Hisashi Iwakuma	4.12
SO	Hisashi Iwakuma	147
SV	Steve Cishek	25
MINORS		
W	Joe Wieland, Tacoma	14
L	Anthony Misiewicz, Bakersfield	10
# ERA	Andrew Moore, Bakersfield, Jackson	2.65
G	Paul Fry, Tacoma	48
G	Matt Walker, Clinton	48
GS	Anthony Misiewicz, Bakersfield	29
SV	Blake Parker, Tacoma	19
IP	Zack Littell, Clinton, Bakersfield	166
BB	Eddie Campbell, Bakersfield	100
SO	Zack Littell, Clinton, Bakersfield	156
# AVG	Tyler Pike, Bakersfield	.223

General Manager: Jerry Dipoto. **Farm Director:** Andy McKay. **Scouting Director:** Tom McNamara.

Class	Team	League	W	L	PCT	Finish	Manager
Majors	Seattle Mariners	American	86	76	.531	7th (15)	Scott Servais
Triple-A	Tacoma Rainiers	Pacific Coast	81	62	.566	3rd (16)	Pat Listach
Double-A	Jackson Generals	Southern	84	55	.604	1st (10)	Daren Brown
High A	Bakersfield Blaze	California	76	64	.543	5th (10)	Eddie Menchaca
Low A	Clinton LumberKings	Midwest	86	54	.614	1st (16)	Mitch Canham
Short season	Everett AquaSox	Northwest	45	31	.592	2nd (8)	Rob Mummau
Rookie	Mariners	Arizona	31	25	.554	t-4th (14)	Zac Livingston
Overall 2016 Minor League Record			403	291	.581	2nd (30)	

ORGANIZATION STATISTICS

SEATTLE MARINERS
AMERICAN LEAGUE

Batting	B-T	HT	WT	DOB	AVG	vLH	vRH	G	AB	R	H	2B	3B	HR	RBI	BB	HBP	SH	SF	SO	SB	CS	SLG	OBP
Aoki, Nori	L-R	5-9	180	1-5-82	.283	.227	.300	118	417	63	118	24	4	4	28	34	9	5	1	45	7	9	.388	.349
Cano, Robinson	L-R	6-0	210	10-22-82	.298	.275	.312	161	655	107	195	33	2	39	103	47	8	0	5	100	0	1	.533	.350
Clevenger, Steve	L-R	5-10	210	4-5-86	.221	.000	.234	22	68	7	15	3	0	1	7	8	0	0	0	14	0	0	.309	.303
Cruz, Nelson	R-R	6-2	230	7-1-80	.287	.293	.284	155	589	96	169	27	1	43	105	62	9	0	7	159	2	0	.555	.360
Freeman, Mike	L-R	6-0	190	8-4-87	.385	.667	.300	13	13	1	5	1	0	0	1	0	0	0	0	2	0	0	.462	.385
Gamel, Ben	L-L	5-11	185	5-17-92	.200	.333	.161	27	40	8	8	2	0	1	5	5	0	2	0	15	0	0	.325	.289
2-team total (6 New York)					.188	—		33	48	9	9	2	0	1	5	6	0	3	0	16	0	0	.292	.278
Gutierrez, Franklin	R-R	6-2	200	2-21-83	.246	.280	.145	98	248	33	61	9	0	14	39	29	3	0	3	85	1	0	.452	.329
Heredia, Guillermo	R-L	5-10	180	1-31-91	.250	.250	.250	45	92	12	23	3	0	1	12	12	2	1	0	15	1	1	.315	.349
Iannetta, Chris	R-R	6-0	230	4-8-83	.210	.248	.185	94	295	23	62	14	0	7	24	38	2	1	2	83	0	0	.329	.303
Lee, Dae Ho	R-R	6-4	250	6-21-82	.253	.261	.244	104	292	33	74	9	0	14	49	20	5	0	4	74	0	0	.428	.312
Lind, Adam	L-L	6-2	195	7-17-83	.239	.240	.239	126	401	48	96	17	0	20	58	26	1	0	2	89	0	1	.431	.286
Marte, Ketel	B-R	6-1	165	10-12-93	.259	.217	.279	119	437	55	113	21	2	1	33	18	2	3	6	84	11	5	.323	.287
Martin, Leonys	L-R	6-2	200	3-6-88	.247	.261	.240	143	518	72	128	17	3	15	47	44	3	4	7	149	24	6	.378	.306
O'Malley, Shawn	R-R	5-11	175	12-28-87	.229	.245	.214	89	210	24	48	9	2	2	17	18	1	1	0	59	6	2	.319	.299
Robertson, Dan	R-R	5-8	205	9-30-85	.263	.364	.125	9	19	1	5	1	0	0	1	1	0	1	0	3	0	1	.316	.300
Romero, Stefen	R-R	6-2	220	10-17-88	.235	.273	.167	9	17	1	4	1	0	0	3	1	0	0	1	4	0	0	.294	.263
Sardinas, Luis	B-R	6-1	180	5-16-93	.181	.258	.122	32	72	12	13	0	0	2	5	1	1	3	0	25	1	1	.264	.203
Seager, Kyle	L-R	6-0	210	11-3-87	.278	.227	.307	158	597	89	166	36	3	30	99	69	8	0	2	108	3	1	.499	.359
Smith, Seth	L-L	6-3	210	9-30-82	.249	.167	.256	137	378	62	94	15	0	16	63	48	8	0	4	89	0	0	.415	.342
Sucre, Jesus	R-R	6-0	225	4-30-88	.480	1.000	.350	9	25	4	12	2	0	1	5	2	2	0	0	5	0	0	.680	.552
Taylor, Chris	R-R	6-1	195	8-29-90	.333	.333	—	2	3	0	1	0	0	0	0	0	0	0	0	2	0	0	.333	.333
Vogelbach, Dan	L-R	6-0	250	12-17-92	.083	.000	.091	8	12	0	1	0	0	0	0	1	0	0	0	6	0	0	.083	.154
Zunino, Mike	R-R	6-2	220	3-25-91	.207	.200	.210	55	164	16	34	7	0	12	31	21	6	0	1	65	0	0	.470	.318

Pitching	B-T	HT	WT	DOB	W	L	ERA	G	GS	CG	SV	IP	H	R	ER	HR	BB	SO	AVG	vLH	vRH	K/9	BB/9
Altavilla, Dan	R-R	5-11	200	9-8-92	0	0	0.73	15	0	0	0	12	11	1	1	0	1	10	.244	.214	.258	7.30	0.73
Aro, Jonathan	R-R	6-0	235	10-10-90	0	0	0.00	1	0	0	0	1	1	0	0	0	1	0	.333	—	.333	0.00	13.50
Benoit, Joaquin	R-R	6-4	250	7-26-77	1	1	5.18	26	0	0	0	24	20	16	14	4	15	28	.215	.217	.213	10.36	5.55
2-team total (25 Toronto)					3	1	2.81	51	0	0	1	48	37	17	15	5	24	52	—	—		9.75	4.50
Caminero, Arquimedes	R-R	6-4	245	6-16-87	1	1	3.66	18	0	0	0	20	21	14	8	3	11	18	.263	.273	.255	8.24	5.03
Cishek, Steve	R-R	6-6	215	6-18-86	4	6	2.81	62	0	0	25	64	44	21	20	8	21	76	.190	.216	.169	10.69	2.95
Diaz, Edwin	R-R	6-3	165	3-22-94	0	4	2.79	49	0	0	18	52	45	16	16	5	15	88	.226	.195	.248	15.33	2.61
Guaipe, Mayckol	R-R	6-4	235	8-11-90	0	0	4.91	5	0	0	0	7	8	6	4	0	4	5	.276	.250	.286	6.14	4.91
Hernandez, Felix	R-R	6-3	225	4-8-86	11	8	3.82	25	25	0	0	153	138	76	65	19	65	122	.239	.252	.229	7.16	3.82
Iwakuma, Hisashi	R-R	6-3	210	4-12-81	16	12	4.12	33	33	0	0	199	218	95	91	28	46	147	.282	.290	.276	6.65	2.08
Johnson, Steve	R-R	6-1	220	8-31-87	1	0	4.32	16	0	0	0	17	13	8	8	3	11	17	.206	.208	.205	9.18	5.94
Karns, Nathan	R-R	6-3	225	11-25-87	6	2	5.15	22	15	0	1	94	95	55	54	11	45	101	.259	.206	.305	9.64	4.29
LeBlanc, Wade	L-L	6-3	210	8-7-84	3	0	4.50	11	8	0	1	50	52	27	25	14	9	41	.261	.231	.269	7.38	1.62
Martin, Cody	R-R	6-3	230	9-4-89	1	2	3.86	9	2	0	0	26	28	11	11	5	9	15	.298	.314	.288	5.26	3.16
Miley, Wade	L-L	6-0	220	11-13-86	7	8	4.98	19	19	1	0	112	117	62	62	18	34	82	.274	.239	.284	6.59	2.73
2-team total (11 Baltimore)					9	13	5.37	30	30	1	0	166	187	100	99	25	49	137	—	—		7.43	2.66
Miranda, Ariel	L-L	6-2	190	1-10-89	5	2	3.54	11	10	0	0	56	43	25	22	12	18	40	.214	.286	.199	6.43	2.89
2-team total (1 Baltimore)					5	2	3.88	12	10	0	0	58	47	28	25	12	18	44	—	—		6.83	2.79
Montgomery, Mike	L-L	6-5	215	7-1-89	3	4	2.34	32	2	0	6	62	49	18	16	3	18	54	.220	.164	.244	7.88	2.63
Nuno, Vidal	L-L	5-11	210	7-26-87	1	1	3.53	55	1	0	0	59	67	23	23	11	11	51	.289	.293	.287	7.82	1.69
Parker, Blake	R-R	6-3	225	6-19-85	0	0	0.00	1	0	0	0	1	1	0	0	0	1	0	.250	.000	.333	0.00	9.00
2-team total (16 New York)					0	0	4.67	17	0	0	1	17	17	9	9	1	9	15	—	—		7.79	4.67
Paxton, James	L-L	6-4	235	11-6-88	6	7	3.79	20	20	0	0	121	134	62	51	9	24	117	.279	.284	.278	8.70	1.79
Peralta, Joel	R-R	5-10	210	3-23-76	1	0	5.40	26	0	0	0	23	24	14	14	7	7	28	.261	.209	.306	10.80	2.70
Roach, Donn	R-R	6-0	195	12-14-89	2	0	8.44	4	0	0	0	5	7	5	5	1	2	2	.292	.400	.263	3.38	3.38
Rollins, David	L-L	6-1	210	12-21-89	1	0	7.71	11	0	0	0	9	12	8	8	2	7	6	.300	.200	.333	5.79	6.75
Sampson, Adrian	R-R	6-2	210	10-7-91	0	1	7.71	1	1	0	0	5	8	4	4	2	1	2	.400	.400	.400	3.86	1.93
Scribner, Evan	R-R	6-3	190	7-19-85	0	0	0.00	12	0	0	0	14	5	0	0	0	2	15	.111	.200	.067	9.64	1.29

SEATTLE MARINERS

Pitching

Pitching	B-T	HT	WT	DOB	W	L	ERA	G	GS	CG	SV	IP	H	R	ER	HR	BB	SO	AVG	vLH	vRH	K/9	BB/9
Storen, Drew	B-R	6-1	195	8-11-87	3	0	3.44	19	0	0	0	18	13	7	7	1	3	16	.191	.125	.212	7.85	1.47
2-team total (38 Toronto)					4	3	5.23	57	0	0	3	52	56	30	30	7	13	48	—	—		8.36	2.26
Venditte, Pat	R-B	6-1	185	6-30-85	0	0	6.08	7	0	0	0	13	13	10	9	4	7	12	.265	.200	.31	8.10	4.73
2-team total (8 Toronto)					0	0	5.73	15	0	0	0	22	24	18	14	5	11	19	—	—		7.77	4.50
Vincent, Nick	R-R	6-0	185	7-12-86	4	4	3.73	60	0	0	3	60	53	26	25	11	15	65	.231	.226	.234	9.70	2.24
Walker, Taijuan	R-R	6-4	235	8-13-92	8	11	4.22	25	25	1	0	134	129	75	63	27	37	119	.247	.206	.285	7.97	2.48
Wieland, Joe	R-R	6-2	205	1-21-90	0	1	10.80	1	1	0	0	5	9	6	6	1	0	3	.391	.364	.417	5.40	0.00
Wilhelmsen, Tom	R-R	6-6	220	12-16-83	0	1	3.60	29	0	0	1	25	22	10	10	4	10	17	.244	.212	.263	6.12	3.60
2-team total (21 Texas)					2	4	6.80	50	0	0	1	46	60	35	35	11	19	28	—	—		5.44	3.69
Zych, Tony	R-R	6-3	190	8-7-90	1	0	3.29	12	0	0	0	14	10	6	5	0	10	21	.208	.192	.227	13.83	6.59

Fielding

Catcher	PCT	G	PO	A	E	DP	PB
Clevenger	.988	20	152	11	2	0	1
Iannetta	.993	93	722	42	5	2	6
Sucre	1.000	9	59	2	0	0	1
Zunino	1.000	52	400	15	0	0	3

First Base	PCT	G	PO	A	E	DP
Lee	.997	84	554	28	2	68
Lind	.994	101	731	50	5	75
Romero	1.000	1	3	0	0	0
Sardinas	1.000	3	5	1	0	2
Vogelbach	1.000	4	20	1	0	3

Second Base	PCT	G	PO	A	E	DP
Cano	.996	157	311	429	3	123
Freeman	1.000	5	8	7	0	3
O'Malley	.955	12	8	13	1	2
Sardinas	1.000	3	2	3	0	0

Third Base	PCT	G	PO	A	E	DP
O'Malley	1.000	7	5	6	0	0
Sardinas	1.000	3	0	7	0	0
Seager	.956	156	110	373	22	46

Shortstop	PCT	G	PO	A	E	DP
Freeman	1.000	2	2	2	0	0
Marte	.956	119	140	315	21	69
O'Malley	.985	36	45	85	2	19

	PCT	G	PO	A	E	DP
Sardinas	.961	18	17	32	2	7
Taylor	.500	1	1	1	2	0

Outfield	PCT	G	PO	A	E	DP
Aoki	.995	113	188	5	1	2
Cruz	.987	48	76	2	1	1
Gamel	1.000	26	26	0	0	0
Gutierrez	1.000	70	105	1	0	0
Heredia	.986	43	66	3	1	1
Martin	.992	143	353	11	3	3
O'Malley	1.000	34	33	1	0	0
Robertson	.917	8	11	0	1	0
Romero	.900	8	8	1	1	0
Sardinas	—	1	0	0	0	0
Smith	.994	109	155	7	1	1

TACOMA RAINIERS   TRIPLE-A
PACIFIC COAST LEAGUE

Batting	B-T	HT	WT	DOB	AVG	vLH	vRH	G	AB	R	H	2B	3B	HR	RBI	BB	HBP	SH	SF	SO	SB	CS	SLG	OBP
Aoki, Nori	L-R	5-9	180	12-5-81	.323	.280	.353	24	96	17	31	5	0	1	7	8	1	1	2	13	4	0	.406	.374
Baron, Steve	R-R	6-0	205	12-7-90	—	—	—	1	0	0	0	0	0	0	0	0	0	0	0	0	0	0	—	—
Baxter, Mike	L-R	6-0	205	12-7-84	.241	.169	.269	69	232	36	56	13	2	7	36	30	6	0	2	51	8	0	.405	.341
Brantly, Rob	L-R	6-1	195	7-14-89	.244	.120	.269	85	303	34	74	13	1	14	43	8	2	1	1	53	0	1	.432	.268
Filia, Eric	L-R	6-0	189	7-6-92	.000	.000	—	1	1	1	0	0	0	0	1	0	0	0	0	0	0	0	.000	.500
Freeman, Mike	L-R	6-0	190	8-4-87	.305	.379	.276	26	105	15	32	6	0	3	15	13	0	0	1	19	1	0	.448	.378
2-team total (88 Reno)					.314	—	—	114	446	71	140	23	6	4	39	51	2	2	2	94	12	1	.419	.385
Heredia, Guillermo	R-L	5-10	180	1-31-91	.312	.189	.356	35	138	27	43	6	1	2	13	12	4	1	2	15	3	0	.413	.378
Jones, P.J.	R-R	5-10	190	2-25-93	.000	—	.000	1	1	0	0	0	0	0	0	0	0	0	0	0	0	0	.000	.000
Kivlehan, Patrick	R-R	6-2	215	12-22-89	.293	.327	.276	43	157	21	46	8	2	8	25	8	0	0	0	49	2	2	.522	.327
3-team total (20 El Paso, 37 Round Rock)					.254	—	—	100	370	46	94	18	3	12	49	24	2	0	1	108	5	4	.416	.302
Lee, Dae Ho	R-R	6-4	250	6-21-82	.519	.556	.500	7	27	3	14	4	0	2	6	2	0	0	0	2	0	0	.889	.552
Littlewood, Marcus	B-R	6-3	195	3-18-92	.045	.000	.083	8	22	1	1	0	0	0	1	3	0	1	0	7	0	0	.045	.160
Lucas, Ed	R-R	6-3	210	5-21-82	.232	.220	.237	38	138	21	32	12	1	3	22	6	1	0	2	25	0	0	.399	.265
2-team total (82 Reno)					.243	—	—	120	358	48	87	23	3	5	34	32	2	0	2	84	1	0	.366	.307
Marte, Ketel	B-R	6-1	165	10-12-93	.214	.500	.100	7	28	5	6	2	0	0	2	2	0	0	1	2	1	0	.286	.258
Navarro, Efren	L-L	6-0	210	5-14-86	.243	.221	.251	72	268	40	65	11	3	5	31	28	2	0	3	63	0	0	.362	.316
2-team total (54 Memphis)					.275	—	—	126	465	68	128	16	3	7	48	43	2	0	4	84	0	0	.368	.337
O'Malley, Shawn	R-R	5-11	175	12-28-87	.317	.370	.291	25	82	15	26	5	1	1	13	13	1	3	1	18	5	1	.439	.412
Peterson, D.J.	R-R	6-1	210	12-31-91	.253	.311	.233	46	178	26	45	7	1	8	35	11	3	0	0	51	0	1	.438	.307
Pizzano, Dario	L-R	5-11	200	4-25-91	.259	.192	.277	77	247	23	64	12	4	2	29	16	1	0	4	42	0	0	.364	.302
Powell, Boog	L-L	5-10	185	1-14-93	.270	.275	.268	64	248	39	67	9	2	3	27	22	0	4	3	42	10	6	.359	.326
Ramsey, James	L-R	6-0	200	12-19-89	.268	.158	.295	27	97	12	26	5	1	6	12	0	1	0	33	0	1	.371	.349
2-team total (83 Oklahoma City)					.265	—	—	110	351	45	93	18	4	9	44	36	5	2	0	113	5	5	.416	.342
Robertson, Dan	R-R	5-8	205	9-30-85	.287	.228	.316	114	408	50	117	19	7	6	46	42	4	3	3	41	13	2	.412	.357
Romero, Stefen	R-R	6-2	220	10-17-88	.304	.310	.302	106	418	70	127	24	6	21	85	36	4	0	4	67	1	1	.541	.361
Sardinas, Luis	B-R	6-1	180	5-16-93	.252	.333	.220	44	163	17	41	4	0	0	17	9	2	1	2	20	7	4	.276	.295
2-team total (5 El Paso)					.253	—	—	49	182	22	46	6	0	0	18	12	2	1	2	23	8	4	.286	.303
Shank, Zach	R-R	6-1	180	12-7-89	.292	.326	.276	81	281	41	82	16	2	3	22	23	3	3	2	55	1	5	.395	.350
Smith, Tyler	R-R	6-0	195	7-1-91	.268	.309	.249	114	392	42	105	20	0	5	37	20	4	2	2	68	6	2	.357	.309
Strausborger, Ryan	R-R	6-0	185	3-4-88	.153	.094	.177	40	111	12	17	2	0	2	11	12	0	2	0	41	6	1	.225	.244
2-team total (45 Round Rock)					.234	—	—	85	274	37	64	10	0	6	27	22	5	1	3	74	15	4	.339	.299
Sucre, Jesus	R-R	6-0	225	4-30-88	.273	.206	.308	29	99	7	27	4	1	0	11	3	1	1	0	15	0	1	.333	.301
Taylor, Chris	R-R	6-1	195	8-29-90	.312	.355	.292	63	247	41	77	19	4	3	29	29	2	1	1	49	12	5	.457	.387
2-team total (15 Oklahoma City)					.322	—	—	78	304	48	98	25	6	3	37	35	3	1	1	65	17	5	.474	.397
Vogelbach, Dan	L-R	6-0	250	12-17-92	.240	.175	.263	44	154	26	37	7	0	7	32	42	1	0	1	34	0	0	.422	.404
2-team total (89 Iowa)					.292	—	—	133	459	79	134	25	2	23	96	97	4	0	3	101	0	0	.505	.417
Zunino, Mike	R-R	6-2	220	3-25-91	.286	.215	.313	79	280	47	80	15	0	17	57	35	8	0	4	69	0	1	.521	.376

Pitching	B-T	HT	WT	DOB	W	L	ERA	G	GS	CG	SV	IP	H	R	ER	HR	BB	SO	AVG	vLH	vRH	K/9	BB/9
Alburquerque, Al	R-R	6-0	195	6-10-86	0	1	6.00	6	0	0	0	6	9	4	4	1	4	6	.346	.364	.333	9.00	6.00
2-team total (24 Salt Lake)					1	1	4.25	30	0	0	8	30	33	16	14	1	17	32	—	—		9.71	5.16

SEATTLE MARINERS

Pitching

Pitching	B-T	HT	WT	DOB	W	L	ERA	G	GS	CG	SV	IP	H	R	ER	HR	BB	SO	AVG	vLH	vRH	K/9	BB/9
Aro, Jonathan	R-R	6-0	235	10-10-90	3	2	2.48	24	1	0	1	36	29	13	10	2	10	25	.221	.255	.200	6.19	2.48
Brentz, Jake	L-L	6-2	195	9-14-94	0	0	16.20	2	0	0	0	2	2	4	3	0	2	1	.400	.667	.000	5.40	10.80
Coleman, Casey	L-R	6-0	185	7-3-87	2	0	2.08	27	0	0	4	39	27	12	9	2	12	38	.188	.233	.155	8.77	2.77
De Fratus, Justin	B-R	6-4	225	10-21-87	2	2	3.21	19	0	0	0	28	23	10	10	2	7	18	.221	.341	.143	5.79	2.25
2-team total (10 Round Rock)					3	2	2.89	29	0	0	0	37	31	14	12	2	16	25	—	—	—	6.03	3.86
Dugger, Robert	R-R	6-2	180	7-3-95	0	0	6.75	2	0	0	0	4	5	3	3	0	0	4	.294	.333	.273	9.00	0.00
Fry, Paul	L-L	6-0	190	7-26-92	3	1	2.78	48	1	0	0	55	48	23	17	1	31	65	.238	.242	.234	10.64	5.07
Furbush, Charlie	L-L	6-5	215	4-11-86	1	0	1.80	6	0	0	0	5	5	1	1	0	2	4	.278	.429	.182	7.20	3.60
Gaviglio, Sam	R-R	6-2	195	5-22-90	3	2	3.71	10	9	1	0	63	59	29	26	7	14	50	.243	.238	.246	7.14	2.00
Gorgas, Marvin	R-R	5-9	185	1-19-96	0	0	0.00	1	0	0	0	2	2	0	0	0	1	0	.333	.000	.400	0.00	5.40
Grube, Jarrett	R-R	6-4	220	11-5-81	1	4	3.62	15	13	0	0	75	63	34	30	10	24	69	.229	.256	.209	8.32	2.89
Guaipe, Mayckol	R-R	6-4	235	8-11-90	0	1	3.14	12	0	0	4	14	10	5	5	1	4	13	.196	.240	.154	8.16	2.51
Hernandez, Felix	R-R	6-3	225	4-8-86	1	0	1.59	1	1	0	0	6	5	1	1	1	1	7	.238	.167	.267	11.12	1.59
Hunter, Kyle	L-L	6-2	210	6-18-89	0	0	8.31	2	0	0	0	4	6	4	4	1	3	3	.333	.267	.667	6.23	6.23
Johnson, Steve	R-R	6-1	220	8-31-87	3	0	2.05	11	0	0	0	22	14	5	5	1	6	26	.184	.225	.139	10.64	2.45
Kittredge, Andrew	R-R	6-1	200	3-17-90	2	2	3.55	23	1	0	7	38	39	18	15	5	9	47	.258	.250	.264	11.13	2.13
Knudson, Guido	R-R	6-1	185	8-5-89	1	0	3.72	6	0	0	0	10	8	4	4	0	1	7	.229	.300	.200	6.52	0.93
Lee, Zach	R-R	6-4	227	9-13-91	0	9	7.39	14	14	0	0	74	98	64	61	11	24	50	.313	.308	.317	6.05	2.91
2-team total (13 Oklahoma City)					7	14	6.14	27	27	0	0	148	193	111	101	22	39	107	—	—	—	6.51	2.37
Martin, Cody	R-R	6-3	230	9-4-89	10	7	3.62	25	20	0	0	114	106	48	46	6	33	114	.249	.261	.237	8.97	2.60
Mills, Brad	L-L	6-0	190	3-5-85	3	3	5.28	9	9	0	0	44	48	26	26	8	22	32	.281	.296	.274	6.50	4.47
Munson, Kevin	R-R	6-2	215	1-3-89	2	1	4.44	19	0	0	0	26	26	15	13	1	17	28	.286	.367	.246	9.57	5.81
Pagan, Emilio	L-R	6-3	210	5-7-91	1	2	3.67	23	0	0	1	34	28	14	14	6	18	39	.222	.160	.263	10.22	4.72
Parker, Blake	R-R	6-3	225	6-19-85	1	2	2.72	38	0	0	19	40	24	13	12	4	11	56	.175	.135	.222	12.71	2.50
Paxton, James	L-L	6-4	235	11-6-88	4	3	3.73	11	11	0	0	51	43	24	21	6	15	53	.228	.149	.254	9.41	2.66
Pries, Jordan	B-R	6-0	190	1-27-90	2	1	3.65	7	3	0	0	25	24	10	10	0	7	21	.253	.282	.232	7.66	2.55
2-team total (9 Iowa)					7	3	4.67	16	12	0	0	71	72	38	37	7	30	56	—	—	—	7.07	3.79
Roach, Donn	R-R	6-0	195	12-14-89	6	6	4.08	22	17	0	1	108	116	57	49	7	19	62	.276	.278	.273	5.17	1.58
Rollins, David	L-L	6-1	210	12-21-89	5	0	3.77	37	0	0	2	45	39	20	19	4	6	32	.236	.247	.226	6.35	1.19
Sampson, Adrian	R-R	6-2	210	10-7-91	7	4	3.25	13	13	0	0	80	81	30	29	5	12	61	.266	.329	.203	6.83	1.34
Scribner, Evan	R-R	6-3	190	7-19-85	0	0	3.86	4	0	0	0	5	5	2	2	1	2	8	.278	.286	.273	15.43	3.86
Sitton, Kraig	L-L	6-5	190	7-13-88	1	2	2.93	35	1	0	0	43	42	15	14	2	7	31	.251	.237	.264	6.49	1.47
Snow, Forrest	R-R	6-6	220	12-30-88	1	1	3.94	4	3	0	0	16	14	7	7	3	6	13	.230	.043	.342	7.31	3.38
Storen, Drew	R-R	6-1	195	8-11-87	0	0	0.00	1	0	0	0	1	1	0	0	0	1	1	.250	1.000	.000	9.00	9.00
Venditte, Pat	R-B	6-1	185	6-30-85	1	0	1.08	5	0	0	0	8	7	1	1	0	3	11	.233	.250	.227	11.88	3.24
Walker, Taijuan	R-R	6-4	235	8-13-92	1	0	3.60	3	3	0	0	15	12	6	6	1	8	6	.211	.233	.185	3.60	4.80
Wieland, Joe	R-R	6-2	205	1-21-90	14	6	5.43	26	24	0	0	124	154	82	75	15	39	118	.302	.277	.323	8.54	2.82
Wilhelmsen, Tom	R-R	6-5	220	12-16-83	0	0	3.00	2	0	0	0	3	2	1	1	0	0	2	.182	.167	.200	6.00	0.00
2-team total (5 Round Rock)					0	1	1.64	7	0	0	0	11	7	2	2	1	1	7	—	—	—	5.73	0.82
Zych, Tony	R-R	6-3	190	8-7-90	0	0	0.00	3	0	0	0	3	0	0	0	0	0	6	.000	.000	.000	18.00	0.00

Fielding

Catcher	PCT	G	PO	A	E	DP	PB
Baron	1.000	1	2	0	0	0	0
Brantly	.987	60	435	29	6	0	7
Littlewood	.985	6	61	6	1	1	0
Sucre	.991	28	209	18	2	2	0
Zunino	.987	57	421	38	6	4	3

First Base	PCT	G	PO	A	E	DP
Baxter	1.000	2	14	1	0	1
Kivlehan	1.000	4	30	4	0	4
Lee	1.000	3	25	3	0	5
Littlewood	1.000	1	3	2	0	1
Navarro	.994	64	505	34	3	36
41 Peterson	.992	32	239	23	2	23
Romero	1.000	18	140	9	0	14
Vogelbach	.995	25	205	12	1	17

Second Base	PCT	G	PO	A	E	DP
Freeman	.964	21	48	58	4	14
Lucas	1.000	1	2	3	0	0
O'Malley	.979	13	19	27	1	2
Robertson	.980	38	50	95	3	17

	PCT	G	PO	A	E	DP
Sardinas	.929	4	5	8	1	2
Shank	.987	18	28	49	1	13
Smith	.985	48	73	120	3	19
Strausborger	1.000	1	0	2	0	1
Taylor	.889	7	10	14	3	6

Third Base	PCT	G	PO	A	E	DP
Brantly	1.000	1	1	2	0	0
Freeman	1.000	1	1	2	0	0
Kivlehan	.930	24	21	32	4	3
Lucas	.971	36	30	69	3	5
O'Malley	1.000	2	1	4	0	0
Peterson	.909	7	3	7	1	0
Sardinas	1.000	5	4	8	0	1
Shank	.962	56	50	102	6	15
Smith	.941	14	6	26	2	3
Taylor	.944	5	6	11	1	1

Shortstop	PCT	G	PO	A	E	DP
Freeman	1.000	3	6	18	0	2
Lucas	1.000	1	1	0	1	
Marte	1.000	5	8	14	0	2
O'Malley	1.000	5	6	7	0	2

	PCT	G	PO	A	E	DP
Sardinas	.990	30	40	59	1	14
Shank	1.000	1	0	3	0	0
Smith	.976	55	62	141	5	33
Taylor	.959	50	69	143	9	20

Outfield	PCT	G	PO	A	E	DP
Aoki	1.000	23	28	1	0	0
Baxter	1.000	50	80	5	0	0
Filia	—	1	0	0	0	0
Freeman	1.000	1	3	0	0	0
Heredia	.989	35	90	2	1	0
Kivlehan	1.000	13	19	2	0	0
Navarro	1.000	1	1	0	0	0
O'Malley	1.000	8	12	1	0	1
Pizzano	1.000	46	70	1	0	0
Powell	.981	61	148	5	3	1
Ramsey	.979	27	46	0	1	0
Robertson	.995	78	178	8	1	2
Romero	.992	69	130	0	1	0
Sardinas	1.000	5	7	1	0	1
Shank	1.000	7	14	0	0	0
Strausborger	1.000	36	72	4	0	4

JACKSON GENERALS — DOUBLE-A
SOUTHERN LEAGUE

Batting	B-T	HT	WT	DOB	AVG	vLH	vRH	G	AB	R	H	2B	3B	HR	RBI	BB	HBP	SH	SF	SO	SB	CS	SLG	OBP
Baron, Steve	R-R	6-0	205	12-7-90	.280	.182	.311	66	232	35	65	7	1	3	22	34	2	1	0	54	3	1	.358	.377
Brady, Patrick	R-R	5-10	176	2-5-88	.227	.226	.228	80	251	28	57	12	5	2	33	36	1	6	3	74	6	1	.339	.323
Capriata, Alexander	R-R	5-11	190	8-3-92	.111	.000	.125	6	18	2	2	0	0	0	0	1	1	1	0	4	0	0	.111	.200
Casteel, Ryan	R-R	5-11	205	6-6-91	.243	.256	.240	50	185	21	45	9	1	3	28	19	0	0	5	51	3	1	.351	.306

SEATTLE MARINERS

Batting	B-T	HT	WT	DOB	AVG	vLH	vRH	G	AB	R	H	2B	3B	HR	RBI	BB	HBP	SH	SF	SO	SB	CS	SLG	OBP
Clevenger, Steve	L-R	5-10	210	4-5-86	.750	—	.750	1	4	0	3	0	0	0	0	0	0	0	0	0	0	0	.750	.750
Gonzalez, Benji	R-R	5-11	160	1-16-90	.271	.289	.265	129	502	78	136	33	5	5	59	57	1	2	7	83	19	8	.386	.342
Hebert, Brock	L-R	5-10	180	5-11-91	.218	.069	.248	56	170	29	37	8	4	1	22	43	5	2	3	59	3	1	.329	.385
Heredia, Guillermo	R-L	5-10	180	1-31-91	.293	.346	.275	58	205	39	60	7	2	2	34	36	9	1	9	32	2	5	.376	.405
Landry, Leon	L-R	5-11	185	9-20-89	.230	.188	.242	120	465	52	107	14	9	6	56	37	4	0	9	75	4	5	.338	.287
Law, Adam	R-R	6-0	193	2-5-90	.321	.270	.336	47	162	20	52	9	1	3	19	20	4	2	3	31	10	3	.444	.402
Littlewood, Marcus	B-R	6-3	195	3-18-92	.307	.260	.324	56	192	28	59	21	0	0	23	32	0	0	1	41	2	0	.417	.404
Lopes, Tim	R-R	5-11	180	6-24-94	.284	.297	.281	131	510	74	145	23	5	1	49	54	7	5	5	88	26	6	.355	.358
Mack, Chantz	L-L	5-10	205	5-4-91	.250	.600	.133	5	20	4	5	0	1	0	3	0	0	0	0	2	0	0	.350	.348
Marlette, Tyler	R-R	5-11	195	1-23-93	.300	.500	.273	15	50	4	15	2	0	1	6	3	0	0	1	11	1	0	.400	.333
Miller, Ian	L-R	6-0	175	2-21-92	.253	.217	.263	114	430	64	109	8	7	0	28	45	7	8	4	54	49	3	.305	.331
O'Neill, Tyler	R-R	5-11	210	6-22-95	.293	.250	.306	130	492	68	144	24	4	24	102	62	9	0	12	150	12	2	.508	.374
Paolini, Dan	R-R	6-0	190	10-11-89	.202	.139	.238	28	99	10	20	2	0	0	7	11	0	0	0	26	0	0	.222	.282
Peterson, D.J.	R-R	6-1	210	12-31-91	.271	.289	.264	73	277	31	75	21	0	11	43	27	4	0	4	68	1	1	.466	.340
Petty, Kyle	R-R	6-5	215	3-1-91	.194	.231	.178	37	129	12	25	8	1	0	16	12	2	0	1	35	0	0	.271	.271
Pizzano, Dario	L-R	5-11	200	4-25-91	.164	.333	.141	22	73	6	12	2	2	0	8	11	1	0	1	9	0	0	.247	.279
Seager, Justin	R-R	6-1	215	5-15-92	.000	.000	.000	2	6	0	0	0	0	0	0	0	0	0	0	3	0	0	.000	.000
Shank, Zach	R-R	6-1	180	1-6-91	.286	.333	.268	39	133	20	38	3	2	0	17	12	4	3	0	35	0	1	.338	.362

Pitching	B-T	HT	WT	DOB	W	L	ERA	G	GS	CG	SV	IP	H	R	ER	HR	BB	SO	AVG	vLH	vRH	K/9	BB/9
Altavilla, Dan	R-R	5-11	200	9-8-92	7	3	1.91	43	0	0	16	57	40	15	12	3	22	65	.196	.238	.155	10.32	3.49
Anderson, Matt	R-R	6-1	210	11-18-91	3	1	3.65	41	0	0	4	62	63	26	25	3	16	56	.266	.250	.283	8.17	2.34
Ash, Brett	R-R	6-2	195	5-27-91	12	8	4.46	25	24	1	0	135	177	78	67	9	31	59	.324	.321	.326	3.92	2.06
Blackburn, Paul	R-R	6-1	195	12-4-93	3	1	3.54	8	7	0	0	41	42	16	16	2	9	27	.268	.286	.247	5.98	1.99
2-team total (18 Tennessee)					9	5	3.27	26	25	0	0	143	138	63	52	8	35	99	—	—	—	6.23	2.20
Brooks, Aaron	R-R	6-6	210	5-15-92	1	0	5.01	16	0	0	0	23	32	16	13	0	8	24	.320	.356	.291	9.26	3.09
Diaz, Edwin	R-R	6-3	165	3-22-94	3	3	3.21	16	6	0	1	41	32	13	10	3	7	54	.212	.206	.217	11.95	1.55
Evans, Bryan	R-R	6-2	200	2-25-87	0	1	3.44	3	3	0	0	18	17	7	7	3	4	20	.239	.200	.278	9.82	1.96
Gaviglio, Sam	R-R	6-2	195	5-22-90	5	5	4.15	18	17	0	0	102	104	51	47	7	22	73	.263	.270	.256	6.44	1.94
Harper, Ryne	R-R	6-3	215	3-27-89	4	5	2.51	42	0	0	6	68	52	23	19	2	25	95	.212	.223	.202	12.57	3.31
Herb, Tyler	R-R	6-2	175	4-28-92	2	3	5.04	11	11	0	0	55	57	35	31	4	27	41	.268	.265	.270	6.67	4.39
Horstman, Ryan	L-L	6-1	185	7-20-92	1	3	5.70	23	0	0	0	24	26	20	15	1	27	26	.286	.125	.373	9.89	10.27
Hunter, Kyle	L-L	6-2	210	6-18-89	3	4	4.25	27	4	0	0	72	74	39	34	5	29	43	.271	.298	.259	5.38	3.63
Kittredge, Andrew	R-R	6-1	200	3-17-90	1	1	3.44	14	4	0	0	34	37	17	13	0	10	37	.278	.290	.268	9.79	2.65
Knudson, Guido	R-R	6-1	185	8-5-89	1	0	5.91	6	0	0	0	11	12	7	7	2	6	11	.279	.286	.273	9.28	5.06
Landazuri, Steve	R-R	6-0	195	1-6-92	0	0	27.00	1	0	0	0	3	8	8	8	1	7	5	.500	.500	.333	16.88	23.63
Moore, Andrew	R-R	6-0	185	6-2-94	9	3	3.16	19	19	1	0	108	112	41	38	9	18	86	.274	.294	.251	7.14	1.50
Pagan, Emilio	L-R	6-3	210	5-7-91	4	1	1.17	18	0	0	9	31	19	4	4	1	11	45	.170	.135	.200	13.21	3.23
Pries, Jordan	R-R	6-2	190	1-27-90	5	2	5.46	13	9	0	0	59	75	38	36	8	14	62	.309	.33	.289	9.40	2.12
Sanchez, Isaac	R-R	6-0	170	10-14-92	0	1	4.82	5	0	0	0	9	10	5	5	1	2	8	.263	.400	.174	7.71	1.93
Schepel, Kyle	L-R	6-1	230	8-7-90	1	2	2.13	23	0	0	0	38	24	9	9	3	19	40	.183	.22	.153	9.47	4.50
Scribner, Evan	R-R	6-3	190	7-19-85	0	0	0.00	1	0	0	0	1	0	0	0	0	1	1	.000	.000	—	9.00	9.00
Sisk, Brandon	L-L	6-2	220	7-13-85	1	0	0.00	4	0	0	1	8	3	0	0	0	7	7	.125	.143	.118	8.22	3.52
Sitton, Kraig	L-L	5-9	190	7-13-88	1	0	0.00	4	0	0	0	9	4	1	0	0	1	7	.133	.071	.188	6.75	0.96
Snow, Forrest	R-R	6-6	220	12-30-88	2	3	2.37	24	0	0	0	38	29	10	10	0	9	48	.215	.246	.192	11.37	2.13
Unsworth, Dylan	R-R	6-1	175	9-23-92	3	1	1.16	9	9	1	0	47	42	9	6	2	7	35	.241	.313	.154	6.75	1.35
Yarbrough, Ryan	R-L	6-5	205	12-31-91	12	4	2.95	25	25	1	0	128	112	45	42	7	31	99	.232	.183	.251	6.94	2.17
Zych, Tony	R-R	6-3	190	8-7-90	0	0	0.00	1	1	0	0	1	0	0	0	0	0	2	.000	—	.000	18.00	9.00

Fielding

Catcher	PCT	G	PO	A	E	DP	PB
Baron	.993	66	522	54	4	2	8
Capriata	.976	6	36	5	1	0	0
Littlewood	.995	54	395	36	2	4	5
Marlette	.992	14	107	11	1	0	2

First Base	PCT	G	PO	A	E	DP
Brady	1.000	13	115	8	0	9
Casteel	.997	35	304	17	1	33
Paolini	.952	9	74	5	4	5
Peterson	.986	62	524	28	8	45
Petty	1.000	20	190	9	0	11
Seager	1.000	1	10	3	0	0

Second Base	PCT	G	PO	A	E	DP
Brady	1.000	7	10	26	0	2
Hebert	1.000	7	11	16	0	5
Law	1.000	4	11	12	0	2
Lopes	.985	124	180	363	8	78

Third Base	PCT	G	PO	A	E	DP
Brady	.910	26	21	40	6	6
Hebert	.956	45	34	75	5	5
Law	.970	29	12	52	2	3
Paolini	.600	2	1	2	2	0
Seager	.667	1	0	2	1	0
Shank	.955	36	24	81	5	3

Shortstop	PCT	G	PO	A	E	DP
Gonzalez	.971	129	178	365	16	80
Hebert	1.000	4	9	13	0	0
Lopes	.971	7	13	20	1	5
Shank	1.000	1	1	3	0	1

Outfield	PCT	G	PO	A	E	DP
Brady	.972	36	62	7	2	1
Heredia	.992	55	124	1	1	0
Landry	1.000	77	144	7	0	3
Law	.957	14	20	2	1	0
Mack	1.000	3	9	0	0	0
Miller	.988	112	248	5	3	0
O'Neill	.982	113	203	10	4	3
Paolini	—	1	0	0	0	0
Petty	1.000	1	4	0	0	0
Pizzano	1.000	12	18	1	0	0
Shank	—	1	0	0	0	0

BAKERSFIELD BLAZE

HIGH CLASS A

CALIFORNIA LEAGUE

Batting	B-T	HT	WT	DOB	AVG	vLH	vRH	G	AB	R	H	2B	3B	HR	RBI	BB	HBP	SH	SF	SO	SB	CS	SLG	OBP
Barbosa, Aaron	L-R	5-10	160	4-14-92	.247	.275	.242	70	255	34	63	3	2	0	21	25	2	7	1	50	14	4	.275	.318
Baum, Jay	R-R	6-0	190	10-25-92	.252	.310	.236	131	524	71	132	28	3	9	78	55	7	3	6	109	14	10	.368	.328
Bishop, Braden	R-R	6-1	190	8-22-93	.247	.318	.221	41	166	19	41	6	0	2	22	11	2	4	1	39	2	0	.319	.300

Batting	B-T	HT	WT	DOB	AVG	vLH	vRH	G	AB	R	H	2B	3B	HR	RBI	BB	HBP	SH	SF	SO	SB	CS	SLG	OBP
Cousino, Austin	L-L	5-10	178	4-17-93	.167	.100	.188	20	84	9	14	3	0	2	11	6	0	2	1	27	0	1	.274	.220
Cowan, Jordan	L-R	6-0	160	4-13-95	.306	.233	.321	43	170	25	52	6	1	3	21	14	0	2	1	32	3	3	.406	.357
Craig, Gus	L-L	6-2	220	4-10-93	.348	.200	.462	6	23	4	8	4	0	0	7	0	1	0	0	7	1	0	.522	.375
DeCarlo, Joe	R-R	5-10	210	9-13-93	.265	.282	.260	105	377	58	100	21	4	14	54	59	11	0	1	110	1	0	.454	.379
Fields, Arby	B-R	5-9	195	6-25-91	.227	.300	.206	57	181	29	41	5	2	1	17	38	5	0	0	62	5	5	.293	.375
Guerrini, Ray	R-R	6-1	195	10-22-93	.308	.000	.333	5	13	6	4	1	0	0	0	7	1	0	0	5	2	1	.385	.571
Hebert, Brock	R-R	5-10	180	5-11-91	.299	.278	.304	23	87	17	26	7	1	1	7	17	2	0	0	25	3	1	.437	.425
Jackson, Drew	R-R	6-2	200	7-28-93	.258	.272	.254	124	524	87	135	24	2	6	47	50	10	9	3	105	16	8	.345	.332
Mack, Chantz	L-L	5-10	205	5-4-91	.286	.228	.299	124	476	71	136	18	5	14	89	80	3	0	4	123	5	3	.433	.389
Marlette, Tyler	R-R	5-11	195	1-23-93	.273	.324	.258	83	326	42	89	21	1	14	53	30	1	0	1	82	5	3	.472	.335
Morales, Jhombeyker	R-R	6-0	170	7-17-94	.077	.000	.100	5	13	0	1	0	0	0	1	1	0	1	0	4	0	0	.077	.143
Morgan, Gareth	R-R	6-4	220	4-12-96	.385	.000	.455	3	13	3	5	3	0	0	4	0	1	0	0	7	0	0	.615	.429
Petty, Kyle	R-R	6-5	215	3-1-91	.329	.355	.323	86	353	65	116	24	1	14	62	42	8	0	3	91	12	6	.521	.409
Rosa, Joseph	B-R	5-10	165	3-6-97	.308	.000	.333	4	13	2	4	0	0	0	1	0	0	0	0	5	0	1	.308	.357
Seager, Justin	R-R	6-1	215	5-15-92	.222	.288	.201	80	275	56	61	8	1	13	49	38	9	0	4	77	0	0	.400	.331
Torres, Dan	R-R	6-0	175	5-29-92	.228	.283	.211	74	259	29	59	10	0	2	32	32	3	2	3	61	0	1	.290	.310
Wawoe, Gianfranco	B-R	5-11	170	7-25-94	.288	.330	.270	102	396	72	114	17	0	8	55	32	3	9	3	61	12	5	.391	.343
Wilson, Austin	R-R	6-4	250	2-7-92	.226	.313	.195	104	368	56	83	14	1	13	49	48	16	0	3	157	7	3	.375	.338

Pitching	B-T	HT	WT	DOB	W	L	ERA	G	GS	CG	SV	IP	H	R	ER	HR	BB	SO	AVG	vLH	vRH	K/9	BB/9
Brooks, Aaron	R-R	6-6	210	5-15-92	3	1	4.22	28	0	0	3	53	57	26	25	3	15	35	.271	.333	.228	5.91	2.53
Campbell, Ed	L-L	6-0	200	1-17-92	11	9	5.74	28	25	0	0	140	152	103	89	20	100	117	.282	.256	.295	7.54	6.44
Dominguez, Ronald	R-R	6-2	180	1-13-94	0	2	3.38	12	0	0	0	16	22	14	6	0	8	12	.328	.423	.268	6.75	4.50
Gillies, Darin	R-R	6-4	220	11-6-92	2	1	2.48	18	0	0	1	29	23	8	8	4	9	36	.221	.273	.163	11.17	2.79
Herb, Tyler	R-R	6-2	175	4-28-92	7	3	3.28	15	15	0	0	85	77	45	31	8	28	93	.241	.268	.216	9.85	2.96
Hermann, Spencer	L-L	6-4	235	8-6-93	0	0	4.50	9	0	0	0	14	18	7	7	1	8	13	.316	.143	.417	8.36	5.14
Horstman, Ryan	L-L	6-1	185	7-20-92	0	1	2.63	9	0	0	2	14	8	4	4	1	3	23	.170	.111	.207	15.15	1.98
Hunter, Kyle	L-L	6-2	210	6-18-89	0	0	1.04	5	0	0	0	9	4	1	1	0	0	7	.133	.182	.105	7.27	0.00
Kerski, Kody	R-R	5-10	185	4-18-92	3	2	3.75	41	0	0	2	70	76	32	29	3	20	62	.283	.344	.227	8.01	2.58
Littell, Zack	R-R	6-3	190	10-5-95	8	1	2.51	12	11	0	0	68	64	21	19	3	13	61	.246	.236	.256	8.07	1.72
Misiewicz, Anthony	R-L	6-1	190	11-1-94	7	10	4.79	29	29	1	0	158	166	91	84	21	47	115	.272	.207	.301	6.56	2.68
Moore, Andrew	R-R	6-0	185	6-2-94	3	1	1.65	9	9	0	0	55	36	14	10	2	13	47	.188	.204	.172	7.74	2.14
Morales, Osmel	R-R	6-3	196	10-30-92	5	6	3.69	25	14	1	1	102	101	44	42	7	25	118	.258	.199	.312	10.38	2.20
Morla, Ramon	R-R	6-1	205	11-20-89	2	3	6.10	22	0	0	0	31	30	22	21	4	13	32	.248	.266	.228	9.29	3.77
Nittoli, Vinny	R-R	6-1	210	11-11-90	4	5	4.30	31	0	0	3	52	46	29	25	7	19	63	.237	.299	.175	10.83	3.27
Pike, Tyler	L-L	6-1	190	1-10-94	6	5	4.01	25	25	0	0	126	99	59	56	11	68	134	.223	.228	.221	9.60	4.87
Pineda, Rafael	L-R	6-6	210	2-3-91	1	0	8.44	3	0	0	0	5	7	5	5	2	3	4	.304	.071	.667	13.50	3.38
Pistorese, Joe	L-L	6-2	175	10-15-92	2	2	6.43	10	0	0	0	14	19	10	10	4	2	20	.311	.467	.261	12.86	1.29
Sanchez, Isaac	R-R	6-0	170	10-14-92	3	5	2.97	34	0	0	2	64	63	31	21	4	24	73	.261	.299	.226	10.32	3.39
Schepel, Kyle	L-R	6-1	230	8-7-90	3	1	2.03	20	0	0	6	27	13	8	6	1	10	35	.138	.222	.061	11.81	3.38
Schiraldi, Lukas	R-R	6-6	210	7-25-93	0	3	7.77	7	5	0	0	22	29	19	19	0	24	27	.309	.342	.286	11.05	9.82
Scribner, Evan	R-R	6-3	190	7-19-85	0	0	0.00	1	1	0	0	1	0	0	0	0	0	2	.250	.000	.333	18.00	0.00
Vieira, Thyago	R-R	6-2	210	7-1-93	1	0	2.84	34	0	0	8	44	37	19	14	1	18	53	.222	.243	.206	10.76	3.65
Warren, Art	R-R	6-3	230	3-23-93	2	1	5.15	13	6	0	0	37	42	26	21	1	28	38	.284	.325	.239	9.33	6.87
Zokan, Jake	R-L	6-1	200	4-27-91	3	1	1.45	32	0	0	6	37	26	6	6	1	2	43	.195	.229	.176	10.37	0.48

Fielding

Catcher	PCT	G	PO	A	E	DP	PB
Guerrini	1.000	5	41	3	0	0	4
Marlette	.989	64	525	93	7	6	13
Torres	.988	74	628	88	9	2	4

First Base	PCT	G	PO	A	E	DP
Baum	.987	33	283	16	4	27
DeCarlo	.944	2	15	2	1	2
Petty	.989	72	682	39	8	56
Seager	.975	34	293	25	8	27

Second Base	PCT	G	PO	A	E	DP
Baum	1.000	14	24	38	0	10
Cowan	.974	18	32	44	2	13
DeCarlo	1.000	1	0	2	0	0
Hebert	.981	12	14	39	1	5

	PCT	G	PO	A	E	DP
Morales	1.000	4	9	12	0	4
Rosa	1.000	3	5	5	0	0
Wawoe	.950	92	156	228	20	56

Third Base	PCT	G	PO	A	E	DP
Baum	.939	31	25	68	6	6
Cowan	.941	6	6	10	1	0
DeCarlo	.960	102	57	180	10	16
Hebert	.857	2	1	5	1	1
Seager	1.000	1	2	0	0	0

Shortstop	PCT	G	PO	A	E	DP
Baum	1.000	8	15	16	0	7
Cowan	.958	9	21	25	2	10
Hebert	.692	4	3	6	4	2
Jackson	.946	120	179	351	30	71
Rosa	1.000	1	2	1	0	0

Outfield	PCT	G	PO	A	E	DP
Barbosa	.993	65	147	3	1	1
Baum	.939	43	60	2	4	0
Bishop	1.000	41	73	4	0	0
Cousino	1.000	20	39	0	0	0
Cowan	—	1	0	0	0	0
Craig	1.000	4	6	0	0	0
Fields	.973	47	68	3	2	0
Hebert	1.000	6	8	1	0	0
Mack	.988	95	156	5	2	0
Morgan	1.000	3	8	0	0	0
Petty	1.000	1	2	0	0	0
Wilson	.984	101	172	7	3	0

CLINTON LUMBERKINGS
MIDWEST LEAGUE

LOW CLASS A

Batting	B-T	HT	WT	DOB	AVG	vLH	vRH	G	AB	R	H	2B	3B	HR	RBI	BB	HBP	SH	SF	SO	SB	CS	SLG	OBP
Alfonso, James	R-R	5-10	195	9-3-91	.214	.169	.226	80	276	20	59	20	0	3	28	25	11	1	6	72	0	3	.304	.299
Ascanio, Rayder	B-R	5-11	155	3-17-96	.257	.258	.256	125	456	61	117	15	3	2	49	54	2	12	6	101	10	14	.316	.334
Barbosa, Aaron	L-R	5-10	160	4-14-92	.216	.333	.194	12	37	9	8	0	0	0	2	8	0	2	1	4	4	0	.216	.348
Bishop, Braden	R-R	6-1	190	8-22-93	.290	.205	.306	63	248	38	72	5	1	1	21	25	4	6	1	48	6	1	.331	.363
Cousino, Austin	L-L	5-10	178	4-17-93	.156	.000	.172	9	32	4	5	2	0	0	3	3	0	1	0	11	1	0	.219	.229

SEATTLE MARINERS

Batting	B-T	HT	WT	DOB	AVG	vLH	vRH	G	AB	R	H	2B	3B	HR	RBI	BB	HBP	SH	SF	SO	SB	CS	SLG	OBP
Craig, Gus	L-L	6-2	220	4-10-93	.225	.093	.251	74	258	26	58	8	2	6	20	17	1	1	0	74	7	6	.341	.275
Eusebio, Ricky	R-R	5-11	195	11-25-93	.232	.233	.232	111	383	47	89	15	2	6	39	37	8	6	0	87	6	7	.329	.313
Fernandez, Rafael	B-R	5-10	180	4-21-94	.218	.179	.224	85	285	24	62	6	0	1	30	35	2	10	2	36	2	4	.249	.306
Gonzalez, Ivan	R-R	6-0	175	10-28-95	.000	.000	.000	4	14	0	0	0	0	0	1	0	0	0	1	4	0	1	.000	.000
Hale, Conner	R-R	6-1	190	10-10-92	.261	.273	.258	109	402	51	105	13	1	7	43	22	0	4	4	95	3	2	.351	.297
Jackson, Alex	R-R	6-2	215	12-25-95	.243	.237	.245	92	333	43	81	20	1	11	55	34	11	1	2	103	2	1	.408	.332
Kelly, Dalton	L-L	6-3	180	8-4-94	.293	.256	.302	130	481	70	141	30	4	7	58	63	11	4	5	114	21	10	.416	.384
Liberato, Luis	L-L	6-1	175	12-18-95	.258	.233	.264	100	372	65	96	19	8	2	29	47	0	12	1	100	4	2	.368	.340
Mariscal, Chris	R-R	5-10	170	4-26-93	.301	.300	.301	97	336	42	101	23	2	3	41	35	6	2	5	100	9	0	.408	.372
Morales, Jhombeyker	R-R	6-0	170	7-17-94	.077	.250	.000	5	13	1	1	0	0	0	1	0	3	0	3	0	0		.154	.143
Nieto, Arturo	R-R	6-2	195	12-9-92	.228	.350	.207	80	272	24	62	10	0	2	18	15	3	4	0	78	0	1	.287	.276
Taylor, Logan	R-R	6-1	200	9-22-93	.268	.282	.265	118	406	59	109	23	2	10	75	60	8	4	8	118	5	8	.409	.367

Pitching	B-T	HT	WT	DOB	W	L	ERA	G	GS	CG	SV	IP	H	R	ER	HR	BB	SO	AVG	vLH	vRH	K/9	BB/9
Brentz, Jake	L-L	6-2	195	9-14-94	3	1	4.35	8	0	0	0	10	7	5	5	0	6	14	.179	.067	.25	12.19	5.23
Dominguez, Ronald	R-R	6-2	180	1-13-94	3	8	2.69	22	10	1	3	80	73	27	24	5	11	91	.241	.265	.218	10.20	1.23
Gadea, Kevin	R-R	6-5	188	12-6-94	3	0	2.15	10	6	0	1	50	41	15	12	4	11	72	.218	.222	.213	12.87	1.97
Gillies, Darin	R-R	6-4	220	11-6-92	5	2	1.19	21	0	0	7	38	21	6	5	3	9	39	.159	.167	.152	9.32	2.15
Gohara, Luiz	L-L	6-3	210	7-31-96	5	2	1.82	10	10	0	0	54	44	12	11	1	20	60	.223	.23	.22	9.94	3.31
Gorgas, Marvin	R-R	5-9	185	1-19-96	1	0	6.23	3	0	0	0	4	4	3	3	1	2	5	.235	.273	.167	10.38	4.15
Hermann, Spencer	L-L	6-4	235	8-6-93	0	0	1.73	28	0	0	3	42	28	10	8	1	23	45	.190	.161	.212	9.72	4.97
Hernandez, Carlos	R-R	6-2	196		0	0	0.00	1	0	0	0	1	0	0	0	0	0	1	.000	.000	0	9.00	0.00
Kiel, Nick	R-L	5-11	205	11-30-92	1	1	3.86	14	0	0	1	23	27	11	10	1	4	20	.297	.371	.25	7.71	1.54
Littell, Zack	R-R	6-3	190	10-5-95	5	5	2.76	16	16	2	0	98	94	35	30	5	21	95	.258	.264	.25	8.75	1.94
Lopez, Pablo	R-R	6-3	200	3-7-96	7	1	2.13	17	13	0	0	84	68	22	20	4	9	56	.219	.226	.212	5.98	0.96
Medina, Jefferson	R-R	6-2	184	5-31-94	0	6	6.75	16	7	0	1	45	77	41	34	3	18	29	.379	.333	.435	5.76	3.57
Morales, Osmel	R-R	6-3	196	10-30-92	0	0	0.63	7	0	0	0	14	10	1	1	0	2	16	.200	.238	.172	10.05	1.26
Neidert, Nick	R-R	6-1	180	11-20-96	7	3	2.57	19	19	0	0	91	75	26	26	7	13	69	.225	.205	.247	6.82	1.29
Nittoli, Vinny	R-R	6-1	210	11-11-90	1	0	2.13	9	0	0	3	13	10	6	3	1	4	11	.208	.308	.091	7.82	2.84
Peterson, Pat	R-L	6-3	190	3-8-93	0	0	4.91	3	0	0	0	4	5	2	2	0	1	3	.313	.500	.25	7.36	2.45
Pierce, Rohn	R-R	6-3	210	1-21-93	6	0	1.99	23	0	0	0	32	19	12	7	0	11	24	.171	.224	.113	6.82	3.13
Pistorese, Joe	L-L	6-2	175	10-15-92	1	0	0.49	12	0	0	1	18	10	1	1	0	2	23	.159	.154	.162	11.29	0.98
Schiraldi, Lukas	R-R	6-6	210	7-25-93	4	4	2.68	28	9	0	2	74	52	27	22	1	49	98	.197	.200	.194	11.92	5.96
Silva, Dylan	L-L	6-1	215	12-27-93	4	2	3.91	39	0	0	3	51	43	26	22	7	28	42	.230	.200	.255	7.46	4.97
Strain, Joey	R-R	6-1	200	1-17-94	7	3	2.56	43	1	0	9	70	68	24	20	5	8	54	.256	.266	.246	6.91	0.77
Vasquez, Pedro	R-R	6-4	190	9-23-95	3	2	2.28	8	8	1	0	43	35	13	11	3	4	30	.223	.218	.229	6.23	0.83
Walker, Matt	R-R	6-6	201	9-28-94	4	3	3.12	48	0	0	13	58	52	21	20	0	17	65	.237	.252	.224	10.14	2.65
Warren, Art	R-R	6-3	230	3-23-93	9	1	2.19	14	14	0	0	74	71	23	18	1	18	55	.253	.275	.23	6.69	2.19
Wells, Nick	L-L	6-5	185	2-21-96	1	9	5.55	18	18	0	0	84	95	61	52	9	38	60	.283	.270	.29	6.40	4.06
Wilcox, Kyle	R-R	6-3	195	6-14-94	4	5	7.11	36	9	0	0	76	73	64	60	2	68	80	.258	.226	.288	9.47	8.05

Fielding

Catcher	PCT	G	PO	A	E	DP	PB
Alfonso	.990	67	527	56	6	3	3
Nieto	.994	76	601	65	4	4	9

First Base	PCT	G	PO	A	E	DP
Hale	.996	54	448	35	2	31
Kelly	.991	89	725	57	7	64

Second Base	PCT	G	PO	A	E	DP
Fernandez	.988	64	89	157	3	36
Gonzalez	—	1	0	0	0	0
Mariscal	.973	75	101	185	8	35
Morales	1.000	3	7	12	0	2

Third Base	PCT	G	PO	A	E	DP
Fernandez	.917	6	3	8	1	1
Hale	.948	29	26	47	4	5
Mariscal	1.000	10	7	19	0	0
Morales	—	1	0	0	0	0
Taylor	.926	98	65	149	17	14

Shortstop	PCT	G	PO	A	E	DP
Ascanio	.958	124	189	331	23	62
Fernandez	.941	16	18	46	4	8
Gonzalez	1.000	1	2	2	0	0
Morales	.909	1	3	7	1	3

Outfield	PCT	G	PO	A	E	DP
Barbosa	1.000	12	23	0	0	0
Bishop	.977	59	127	3	3	0
Cousino	.938	8	14	1	1	0
Craig	.963	62	100	5	4	1
Eusebio	.984	100	186	0	3	0
Gonzalez	1.000	3	6	2	0	0
Hale	—	1	0	0	0	0
Jackson	.984	70	117	9	2	2
Kelly	1.000	30	56	1	0	0
Liberato	.990	84	184	9	2	1
Taylor	—	2	0	0	0	0

EVERETT AQUASOX   SHORT-SEASON
NORTHWEST LEAGUE

Batting	B-T	HT	WT	DOB	AVG	vLH	vRH	G	AB	R	H	2B	3B	HR	RBI	BB	HBP	SH	SF	SO	SB	CS	SLG	OBP
Andrade, Greifer	R-R	6-0	170	1-27-97	.000	.000	.000	4	6	1	0	0	0	0	0	0	2	0	0	3	1	0	.000	.250
Baxter, Mike	L-R	6-0	205	12-7-84	.364	1.000	.125	3	11	3	4	2	0	0	2	2	1	0	0	1	0	0	.545	.500
Brigman, Bryson	R-R	5-11	180	6-19-95	.260	.255	.262	68	265	51	69	6	1	0	19	41	6	4	2	43	17	12	.291	.369
Brito, Kristian	R-R	6-5	240	12-20-94	.298	.314	.294	46	178	19	53	12	0	7	46	18	1	1	3	53	0	2	.483	.360
Camacho, Juan	R-R	6-3	215	4-19-96	.000	—	.000	1	1	0	0	0	0	0	0	0	0	0	0	1	0	0	.000	.000
Cowan, Jordan	L-R	6-0	160	4-13-95	.370	.364	.371	12	46	10	17	4	0	1	6	3	1	0	2	5	1	0	.522	.473
Craig, Gus	L-L	6-2	220	4-10-93	.286	.286	.286	6	21	6	6	1	1	1	8	3	1	0	2	5	1	0	.571	.370
Filia, Eric	L-R	6-0	189	7-6-92	.362	.322	.374	68	246	43	89	19	1	4	46	39	3	1	3	19	10	5	.496	.450
Goldstein, Jason	R-R	5-11	195	3-9-94	.255	.250	.256	14	51	5	13	2	0	0	5	5	0	1	1	7	1	0	.294	.316
Gonzalez, Ivan	R-R	6-0	175	10-28-95	.000	.000	.000	2	6	0	0	0	0	0	0	0	0	0	0	0	0	0	.000	.000
Grebeck, Austin	R-S	5-8	155	8-8-94	.241	.283	.228	65	220	43	53	12	1	2	25	33	2	1		54	11	6	.332	.346
Greer, David	R-R	6-1	188	7-4-95	.274	.214	.284	25	95	17	26	9	0	2	14	13	1	0	0	32	3	0	.432	.367
Guerrini, Ray	R-R	6-1	195	10-22-93	.222	.125	.250	14	36	3	8	1	0	0	3	4	3	0	0	13	0	0	.250	.349
Leal, Jose	R-R	6-3	215	2-16-95	.253	.382	.221	51	170	18	43	7	1	3	24	14	1	1	2	62	4	2	.359	.310

Batting	B-T	HT	WT	DOB	AVG	vLH	vRH	G	AB	R	H	2B	3B	HR	RBI	BB	HBP	SH	SF	SO	SB	CS	SLG	OBP
Lewis, Kyle	R-R	6-4	210	7-13-95	.299	.280	.304	30	117	26	35	8	5	3	26	16	1	0	1	22	3	0	.530	.385
Marte, Ketel	B-R	6-1	165	10-12-93	.333	.000	.400	2	6	1	2	1	0	1	1	1	0	0	0	0	0	0	1.000	.429
Morales, Jhombeyker	R-R	6-0	170	7-17-94	.269	.213	.287	59	197	29	53	9	2	1	28	15	4	3	5	40	10	3	.350	.326
Ojeda, Dimas	L-L	6-1	195	9-19-95	.266	.267	.265	34	128	22	34	8	0	5	22	15	1	1	0	29	0	0	.445	.347
Quevedo, Yojhan	B-R	6-1	215	11-6-93	.225	.265	.214	45	151	18	34	6	1	0	13	6	0	4	0	23	0	0	.278	.255
Thurman, Nick	L-R	6-2	210	9-9-93	.267	.179	.288	44	146	21	39	9	1	2	18	18	3	1	2	40	3	0	.384	.355
Venturino, Joe	R-R	6-0	185	7-18-94	.298	.333	.284	32	94	14	28	5	0	0	10	11	2	0	0	19	1	0	.351	.383
Walton, Donnie	B-R	5-10	184	5-25-94	.281	.132	.321	43	178	43	50	8	1	5	23	22	1	1	1	24	6	0	.421	.361
Zammarelli, Nick	L-R	6-1	195	7-30-94	.329	.327	.330	65	255	44	84	18	1	5	43	25	2	0	2	67	3	2	.467	.391

Pitching	B-T	HT	WT	DOB	W	L	ERA	G	GS	CG	SV	IP	H	R	ER	HR	BB	SO	AVG	vLH	vRH	K/9	BB/9
Anderson, Jack	R-R	6-3	210	1-10-94	0	0	0.00	2	0	0	0	2	2	0	0	0	1	0	.333	.200	1.000	4.50	4.50
Brentz, Jake	L-L	6-2	195	9-14-94	1	0	5.08	10	7	0	0	34	34	22	19	3	28	35	.268	.250	.273	9.36	7.49
Burrows, Thomas	L-L	6-0	205	9-14-94	0	1	2.55	20	0	0	6	25	23	8	7	1	11	37	.240	.111	.290	13.50	4.01
Cano, Joselito	L-L	6-5	190	9-16-92	3	2	4.64	21	0	0	0	33	25	20	17	3	24	37	.197	.233	.186	10.09	6.55
Cishek, Steve	R-R	6-6	215	6-18-86	0	1	13.50	2	2	0	0	2	5	3	3	0	0	5	.455	.400	.500	22.50	0.00
Covelle, Paul	R-R	6-0	205	9-12-93	4	3	4.65	19	0	0	0	31	29	17	16	1	13	20	.244	.205	.267	5.81	3.77
Dugger, Robert	R-R	6-2	180	7-3-95	2	1	5.47	6	6	0	0	26	25	18	16	5	10	25	.250	.257	.246	8.54	3.42
Festa, Matt	R-R	6-2	195	3-11-93	6	2	3.73	14	8	0	0	60	60	29	25	3	14	58	.259	.323	.216	8.65	2.09
Furbush, Charlie	L-L	6-5	215	4-11-86	0	1	20.25	2	2	0	0	1	4	3	2	2	1		.400	.000	.500	6.75	13.50
Garcia, Danny	L-L	6-1	195	2-21-94	6	2	3.59	12	6	0	0	43	40	18	17	4	9	23	.250	.300	.238	4.85	1.90
Gohara, Luiz	L-L	6-3	210	7-31-96	2	0	1.76	3	3	0	0	15	13	5	3	1	3	21	.224	.214	.227	12.33	1.76
Gorgas, Marvin	R-R	5-9	185	1-19-96	1	1	2.33	19	0	0	5	27	13	7	7	2	10	29	.144	.222	.111	9.67	3.33
Hernandez, Felix	R-R	6-3	225	4-8-86	0	0	7.36	1	1	0	0	4	6	3	3	0	2	6	.353	.286	.400	14.73	4.91
Koval, Michael	R-R	6-0	180	4-20-95	3	2	2.29	24	0	0	7	35	37	13	9	0	10	25	.255	.385	.183	6.37	2.55
McClain, Reggie	R-R	6-2	180	11-16-92	3	3	4.47	13	7	0	0	48	45	24	24	5	5	55	.244	.247	.250	10.24	0.93
Medina, Jefferson	R-R	6-2	184	5-31-94	1	0	4.17	13	2	0	0	37	38	19	17	3	10	27	.270	.137	.344	6.63	2.45
Miley, Wade	L-L	6-0	220	11-13-86	0	0	0.00	1	1	0	0	4	0	0	0	0	0	7	.000	.000	.000	15.75	0.00
Miller, Brandon	R-R	6-4	210	6-16-95	4	2	2.72	14	13	0	0	56	47	18	17	3	7	51	.226	.236	.218	8.15	1.12
Moyer, Dillon	R-R	6-0	200	7-18-91	0	1	4.63	8	0	0	0	12	16	11	6	1	6	14	.314	.348	.286	10.80	4.63
Moyers, Steven	R-L	6-0	190	9-23-93	0	0	0.00	1	0	0	0	2	1	0	0	0	1	1	.143	.250	.000	4.50	0.00
Newsome, Ljay	R-R	5-11	210	11-8-96	6	3	4.30	14	11	0	0	61	59	33	29	11	15	58	.255	.202	.295	8.60	2.23
Ratliff, Lane	L-L	6-3	185	3-22-95	2	1	6.23	21	0	0	1	30	36	25	21	1	13	46	.288	.324	.273	13.65	3.86
Rivera, Michael	R-R	6-3	220	6-19-97	0	0	1.50	2	0	0	0	6	4	1	1	0	3	2	.211	.667	.125	3.00	4.50
Stephens, Brandon	R-R	6-3	185	5-27-92	0	0	5.40	2	0	0	0	3	5	2	2	0	2	2	.333	.200	.400	5.40	5.40
Surrey, Elliot	L-L	6-0	190	2-22-94	1	2	3.69	12	6	0	0	32	31	16	13	2	9	36	.250	.129	.29	10.23	2.56
Viehoff, Tim	L-L	6-4	200	12-17-93	0	2	2.77	12	6	0	0	39	17	13	12	3	23	55	.133	.263	.110	12.69	5.31
Vincent, Nick	R-R	6-0	185	7-12-86	0	0	0.00	1	0	0	1	1	0	0	0	0	0	3	.250	—	.250	27.00	—

Fielding

C: Camacho 1, Goldstein 12, Guerrini 13, Quevedo 42, Thurman 18. **1B:** Brito 45, Filia 5, Greer 3, Ojeda 10, Thurman 7, Zammarelli 8. **2B:** Andrade 4, Brigman 15, Cowan 10, Morales 17, Venturino 19, Walton 17. **3B:** Cowan 1, Gonzalez 1, Greer 4, Morales 32, Zammarelli 43. **SS:** Brigman 51, Cowan 2, Marte 1, Morales 4, Walton 20. **OF:** Baxter 2, Craig 6, Filia 50, Grebeck 65, Greer 15, Leal 40, Lewis 27, Ojeda 26, Zammarelli 10.

AZL MARINERS
ARIZONA LEAGUE

ROOKIE

Batting	B-T	HT	WT	DOB	AVG	vLH	vRH	G	AB	R	H	2B	3B	HR	RBI	BB	HBP	SH	SF	SO	SB	CS	SLG	OBP
Andrade, Greifer	R-R	6-0	170	1-27-97	.341	.294	.354	26	82	17	28	2	3	3	16	5	3	0	1	17	2	2	.549	.396
Blanco, Dominic	L-R	6-2	215	11-10-95	.286	.000	.500	5	7	0	2	1	0	0	1	0	0	0	0	1	0	0	.429	.375
Camacho, Juan	R-R	6-3	215	4-19-96	.338	.346	.336	39	133	19	45	8	0	2	12	5	0	0	0	14	1	2	.444	.362
Capriata, Alexander	R-R	5-11	190	8-3-92	.281	.357	.256	18	57	9	16	3	0	1	2	0	1	0	0	6	6	1	.333	.305
Clevenger, Steve	L-R	5-10	210	4-5-86	.250	.000	.333	2	4	0	1	1	0	0	1	0	0	0	0	0	0	0	.500	.400
Goldstein, Jason	R-R	5-11	195	3-9-94	.400	1.000	.333	5	10	2	4	0	0	0	1	0	0	0	0	2	0	0	.400	.400
Gonzalez, Ivan	R-R	6-0	175	10-28-95	.194	.313	.157	29	67	11	13	2	2	0	6	9	1	0	0	25	3	3	.284	.299
Guerrini, Ray	R-R	6-1	195	10-22-93	.267	.250	.273	8	15	2	4	0	1	0	2	1	2	1	0	6	0	0	.400	.389
Halamandaris, Nick	L-L	6-1	215	11-10-95	.105	.167	.077	13	38	2	4	0	0	0	2	3	2	1	0	9	0	0	.105	.209
Hernandez, Brayan	B-R	6-2	175	9-11-97	.285	.188	.316	33	130	13	37	8	2	1	19	7	1	1	3	36	9	3	.400	.324
Jimenez, Anthony	R-R	5-11	165	10-21-95	.312	.370	.293	53	186	30	58	11	5	1	22	12	2	1	1	43	14	6	.441	.358
Morgan, Gareth	R-R	6-4	220	4-12-96	.216	.229	.211	35	125	17	27	5	4	1	11	8	0	0	1	58	5	1	.344	.261
Moses, DeAires	L-L	5-9	170	11-30-95	.300	.300	.300	22	50	11	15	2	0	0	8	8	0	2	0	20	8	2	.340	.397
Mota, Ismerling	R-R	6-1	185	9-2-97	.150	.188	.136	22	60	9	9	3	0	0	2	0	0	0	0	13	0	0	.200	.177
Ojeda, Dimas	L-L	6-1	195	9-19-95	.260	.222	.268	17	50	9	13	6	1	1	6	4	2	0	1	15	1	0	.480	.333
Pena, Ismael	L-L	6-3	175	12-15-95	.287	.310	.281	42	143	11	41	8	1	1	19	10	0	2	2	21	3	3	.378	.329
Pena, Onil	R-R	6-0	180	11-6-96	.209	.190	.213	35	110	15	23	4	2	2	13	12	2	0	2	39	1	2	.336	.294
Perez, Taylor	R-R	5-9	170	12-26-93	.333	.500	.000	2	3	1	1	0	0	0	0	0	0	0	0	0	0	0	.333	.333
Rengifo, Luis	R-R	5-9	165	12-29-96	.239	.280	.226	34	109	16	26	7	2	1	9	13	1	1	0	31	22	3	.367	.325
Rivera, Jansiel	L-L	6-1	205	8-28-98	.244	.286	.237	14	45	8	11	2	1	0	3	9	1	0	0	17	2	1	.333	.370
Rizzo, Joe	L-R	5-9	194	3-31-98	.291	.258	.299	39	148	21	43	7	1	2	21	17	0	4	0	36	2	1	.392	.355
Rosa, Joseph	B-R	5-10	165	3-6-97	.305	.300	.307	43	154	17	47	7	5	2	10	9	1	4	1	26	12	7	.455	.345
Sucre, Jesus	R-R	6-0	225	4-30-88	.400	.000	.444	4	10	1	4	0	0	0	3	0	0	0	0	1	0	0	.400	.400
Torres, Christopher	B-R	5-11	170	2-6-98	.257	.178	.287	44	167	31	43	9	4	0	17	19	1	2	0	44	12	4	.359	.337
Uhl, Ryan	R-R	6-6	230	5-26-93	.136	.000	.200	10	22	4	3	1	0	1	4	4	0	0	0	7	1	0	.318	.269
Venturino, Joe	R-R	6-0	185	7-18-94	.167	.000	.222	7	12	3	2	0	0	0	1	1	0	0	0	2	0	0	.167	.286

Pitching	B-T	HT	WT	DOB	W	L	ERA	G	GS	CG	SV	IP	H	R	ER	HR	BB	SO	AVG	vLH	vRH	K/9	BB/9
Anderson, Jack	R-R	6-3	210	1-10-94	3	1	1.89	16	0	0	6	19	19	10	4	0	6	18	.232	.233	.231	8.53	2.84
Clancy, Matt	B-L	5-11	180	4-1-94	0	0	0.00	1	1	0	0	1	0	0	0	0	0	1	.000	—	0	9.00	0.00
Cleto, Ramire	R-R	6-0	220	4-4-93	0	0	15.88	5	0	0	0	6	7	12	10	0	10	6	.280	.333	.25	9.53	15.88
Cook, Ryan	R-R	6-2	215	6-30-87	0	0	0.00	1	1	0	0	1	0	0	0	0	0	0	.000	0	0	0.00	0.00
De Paula, Juan	R-R	6-3	165	9-22-97	1	2	3.07	11	7	0	0	41	41	18	14	2	11	53	.253	.291	.234	11.63	2.41
Dugger, Robert	R-R	6-2	180	7-3-95	0	0	1.04	4	0	0	2	9	6	1	1	0	1	9	.188	.167	.200	9.35	1.04
Ellingson, David	R-R	6-2	200	1-23-95	1	0	0.00	12	0	0	3	10	12	6	0	0	2	8	.279	.333	.250	6.97	1.74
Gadea, Kevin	R-R	6-5	188	12-6-94	1	1	2.95	5	2	0	1	18	15	7	6	1	3	23	.214	.143	.245	11.29	1.47
Guaipe, Mayckol	R-R	6-4	235	8-11-90	0	0	4.50	3	3	0	0	4	6	2	2	0	1	4	.333	.333	.333	9.00	2.25
Hammond, Ted	R-R	6-2	195	12-17-93	3	1	1.93	11	0	0	1	19	17	6	4	0	6	24	.233	.235	.231	11.57	2.89
Hernandez, Carlos	R-R	6-3	195	2-8-96	1	1	4.50	16	1	0	2	38	42	24	19	3	10	32	.273	.188	.311	7.58	2.37
Horstman, Ryan	L-L	6-1	185	7-20-92	0	0	27.00	1	0	0	0	1	1	1	0	0	3	0	.500	.000	1.000	0.00	81.00
Hultzen, Danny	L-L	6-3	210	11-28-89	0	0	4.50	2	2	0	0	2	3	1	1	0	1	0	.429	1.000	.200	0.00	4.50
Inman, Ryne	R-R	6-5	215	5-13-96	2	3	3.47	13	12	0	1	62	73	39	24	5	20	52	.291	.390	.247	7.51	2.89
Mobley, Cody	R-R	6-3	190	9-23-96	0	0	13.50	1	0	0	0	1	4	2	2	0	1	6	.500	—	.500	0.00	6.75
Morla, Ramon	R-R	6-1	205	11-20-89	0	0	0.00	3	0	0	0	4	1	0	0	0	0	8	.077	.000	.091	18.00	0.00
Moyers, Steven	R-L	6-0	190	9-23-93	2	2	4.57	14	4	0	1	41	46	26	21	2	12	29	.275	.246	.291	6.31	2.61
Orozco, Jio	R-R	6-1	208	8-15-97	2	2	4.07	12	5	0	0	49	46	28	22	3	16	63	.236	.167	.271	11.65	2.96
Peeler, Joe	R-R	6-4	175	12-2-96	1	0	10.80	15	0	0	0	15	16	23	18	0	25	10	.286	.348	.242	6.00	15.00
Pierce, Rohn	R-R	6-3	210	1-21-93	0	0	0.00	1	0	0	1	1	0	0	0	0	0	1	.000	.000	.000	9.00	0.00
Pineda, Rafael	L-R	6-6	210	2-3-91	2	0	0.00	3	1	0	0	4	3	0	0	0	0	5	.188	.250	.167	10.38	0.00
Pistorese, Joe	L-L	6-2	175	10-15-92	0	0	0.00	1	0	0	0	2	0	0	0	0	0	4	.000	—	.000	18.00	0.00
Ridings, Steven	R-R	6-4	210	2-28-94	1	0	0.00	1	0	0	0	1	0	0	0	0	0	2	.000	—	.000	18.00	0.00
Rivera, Michael	R-R	6-3	220	6-19-97	3	2	4.10	16	0	0	0	37	34	19	17	1	16	36	.238	.222	.245	8.68	3.86
Scribner, Evan	R-R	6-3	190	7-19-85	0	1	21.60	2	1	0	0	2	5	4	4	1	0	3	.500	.500	.5	16.20	0.00
Stephens, Brandon	R-R	6-0	185	5-27-92	0	0	0.00	1	0	0	0	1	1	0	0	0	2	1	.250	1.000	.000	18.00	0.00
Suarez, Michael	L-L	6-2	180	3-21-95	4	0	3.22	7	5	0	1	36	42	17	13	2	9	35	.302	.326	.292	8.67	2.23
Thompson, Dylan	L-R	6-2	180	9-16-96	0	1	5.79	3	1	0	0	5	6	3	3	0	4	6	.316	.333	.300	11.57	7.71
Vasquez, Pedro	R-R	6-4	190	9-23-95	2	2	2.22	5	4	0	0	28	24	7	7	1	5	22	.238	.321	.205	6.99	1.59
Wells, Nick	L-L	6-5	185	2-21-96	0	0	0.00	4	4	0	0	10	6	0	0	0	2	6	.171	.125	.185	5.40	1.80
Zabala, Aneurys	R-R	6-2	175	12-21-96	1	5	2.88	16	0	0	1	25	15	15	8	1	15	28	.167	.192	.156	10.08	5.40
Zych, Tony	R-R	6-3	190	8-7-90	0	0	0.00	1	1	0	0	1	0	0	0	0	0	1	.000	.000	.000	9.00	0.00

Fielding

C: Blanco 2, Camacho 31, Capriata 14, Goldstein 3, Guerrieri 4, Mota 19, Pena 1, Sucre 2. **1B:** Camacho 1, Guerrieri 1, Halamandaris 11, Pena 30, Pena 22, Uhl 5. **2B:** Andrade 18, Gonzalez 6, Perez 1, Rengifo 10, Rosa 29, Venturino 4. **3B:** Andrade 2, Gonzalez 4, Rengifo 12, Rizzo 39, Rosa 4. **SS:** Andrade 2, Rengifo 9, Rosa 7, Torres 44. **OF:** Gonzalez 17, Hernandez 31, Jimenez 51, Morgan 25, Moses 16, Ojeda 16, Pena 17, Rivera 14, Venturino 1.

DSL MARINERS
ROOKIE
DOMINICAN SUMMER LEAGUE

Batting	B-T	HT	WT	DOB	AVG	vLH	vRH	G	AB	R	H	2B	3B	HR	RBI	BB	HBP	SH	SF	SO	SB	CS	SLG	OBP
Almonte, Adalfi	R-R	6-1	170	4-19-96	.222	.167	.227	36	72	14	16	3	0	1	5	20	7	6	0	27	9	2	.306	.434
Benoit, Luis	L-R	5-10	165	11-29-94	.136	.111	.143	18	44	10	6	1	0	0	6	12	3	0	1	10	5	0	.159	.350
Branche, Steve	R-R	6-1	165	9-1-97	.137	.000	.171	24	51	3	7	1	0	0	2	4	0	0	4	1	1	.157	.228
Cano, Jose	R-R	5-11	190	12-18-96	.167	.071	.200	25	54	6	9	2	0	0	3	9	4	0	1	20	0	0	.204	.324
Contreras, Danny	L-L	6-3	195	5-21-98	.240	.200	.247	65	217	40	52	14	2	0	29	40	1	0	1	54	11	3	.323	.359
Dominguez, Anthony	R-R	6-2	170	6-6-96	.211	.250	.196	31	76	5	16	5	1	0	10	8	2	5	1	9	0	1	.303	.299
Gamboa, Miguel	B-R	5-11	175	10-22-97	.261	.333	.250	40	111	21	29	3	3	1	18	23	1	3	2	27	3	1	.369	.387
Gregorio, Osmy	R-R	6-2	175	5-27-98	.227	.240	.224	46	172	26	39	5	3	1	10	24	5	2	0	30	6	7	.308	.338
Helder, Eugene	R-R	5-11	165	2-26-96	.277	.263	.280	59	202	33	56	3	2	1	29	17	7	1	3	16	9	5	.327	.349
Hernandez, Brayan	B-R	6-2	175	9-11-97	.278	.286	.276	31	133	30	37	6	2	5	15	10	1	1	1	23	12	2	.466	.331
Joseph, Luis	B-R	5-9	160	9-20-96	.229	.357	.196	27	70	14	16	0	1	0	6	8	0	1	1	13	4	1	.257	.304
Montilla, Geoandry	R-R	6-0	165	5-14-96	.297	.333	.291	55	175	37	52	11	2	4	19	30	5	0	2	36	8	7	.451	.410
Ochoa, Sebastian	R-R	6-1	180	5-24-98	.271	.375	.245	37	118	8	32	6	0	1	12	12	3	1	1	18	4	3	.347	.351
Perez, Nolan	B-R	6-2	190	5-9-99	.197	.161	.209	36	117	17	23	4	1	2	12	7	0	1	2	32	4	3	.299	.307
Rivera, Jansiel	L-L	6-1	205	8-28-98	.198	.278	.179	32	96	11	19	1	3	1	12	20	3	0	2	27	4	4	.302	.347
Rosario, Ronald	L-L	6-2	165	5-27-99	.292	.161	.321	52	171	29	50	13	4	1	31	13	0	2	4	33	6	4	.433	.335
Sandoval, Jose	R-R	6-2	195	10-23-96	.264	.350	.248	43	125	23	33	3	2	2	17	5	5	5	3	35	8	1	.368	.316
Santos, Daniel	R-R	6-2	175	1-25-99	.167	.200	.162	27	78	9	13	1	0	0	7	12	1	0	0	20	3	0	.179	.286
Vargas, Carlos	R-R	6-3	170	3-18-99	.242	.158	.260	62	215	41	52	11	0	7	35	32	4	0	5	35	2	0	.391	.344

Pitching	B-T	HT	WT	DOB	W	L	ERA	G	GS	CG	SV	IP	H	R	ER	HR	BB	SO	AVG	vLH	vRH	K/9	BB/9
Acosta, Geovanny	R-R	6-2	165	8-15-93	0	0	1.86	7	0	0	2	10	7	4	2	0	1	9	.206	.077	.286	4.66	4.66
Bonilla, Feliberto	R-R	6-2	165	4-21-98	5	1	3.81	14	14	0	0	54	49	29	23	1	35	26	.250	.383	.191	4.31	5.80
Canela, Jose	R-R	6-0	167	12-10-95	0	1	6.35	14	0	0	0	23	25	17	16	2	17	10	.298	.346	.276	3.97	6.75
Cruz, Aronny	L-L	6-2	175	7-23-95	3	1	2.75	10	0	0	1	20	12	6	6	0	8	17	.179	.182	.179	7.78	3.66
Cuenca, Saul	R-R	6-5	195	3-22-98	0	1	8.41	14	0	0	0	20	15	19	19	3	20	23	.268	.250	.100	10.18	8.85
Encarnacion, Frank	R-R	6-3	195	2-13-95	4	3	2.37	17	3	0	4	57	34	17	15	2	27	51	.178	.225	.150	8.05	4.26
Espinal, Erik	R-R	5-9	155	11-14-96	2	1	2.22	16	0	0	1	24	20	7	6	1	10	22	.233	.222	.237	8.14	3.70
Fortunato, Ivan	R-R	6-1	170	12-1-98	0	0	11.37	3	0	0	0	6	10	11	8	1	6	7	.323	.429	.292	9.95	8.53
Guzman, Carlos	R-L	6-1	170	1-28-97	3	0	4.42	16	1	0	0	18	14	10	9	0	21	22	.212	.385	.170	10.80	10.31
Hernandez, Anjul	R-R	6-2	192	1-2-96	4	1	1.37	14	5	0	4	59	38	11	9	0	14	49	.184	.203	.174	7.47	2.14
Martinez, Edwin	R-R	6-6	240	7-31-95	1	1	2.84	12	0	0	0	19	16	11	6	0	17	9	.232	.150	.265	4.26	8.05
Munoz, Luis	R-R	6-1	220	11-4-96	3	2	2.61	13	12	0	0	52	40	19	15	2	19	35	.214	.227	.207	6.10	3.31

Pitching	B-T	HT	WT	DOB	W	L	ERA	G	GS	CG	SV	IP	H	R	ER	HR	BB	SO	AVG	vLH	vRH	K/9	BB/9
Perez, Ulises	R-R	6-3	160	7-14-97	3	1	3.49	14	14	0	0	59	49	39	23	0	34	43	.228	.250	.216	6.52	5.16
Salinas, Edward	R-R	6-2	175	1-3-96	0	1	5.40	3	0	0	2	2	3	2	1	0	0	0	.333	.333	.333	0.00	0.00
Suarez, Michael	L-L	6-2	180	3-21-95	1	2	2.15	8	8	0	0	46	36	11	11	1	7	50	.216	.231	.213	9.78	1.37
Taveras, Andy	R-R	6-2	185	4-30-96	1	3	6.98	15	0	0	0	19	18	19	15	2	14	12	.237	.182	.259	5.59	6.52
Torres, Andres	R-R	6-3	185	10-31-95	10	3	1.26	14	14	0	0	78	53	17	11	2	14	55	.191	.130	.220	6.32	1.61
Trinidad, Edinson	R-R	6-2	186	5-12-95	3	0	2.81	13	0	0	0	16	11	10	5	0	15	9	.193	.143	.222	5.06	8.44

Fielding

C: Dominguez 31, Montilla 25, Santos 27. **1B:** Cano 16, Contreras 56, Gamboa 1, Helder 8, Montilla 1. **2B:** Benoit 10, Branche 15, Gamboa 5, Gregorio 25, Helder 33, Joseph 1. **3B:** Benoit 1, Branche 3, Gamboa 32, Helder 8, Perez 34, Vargas 1. **SS:** Branche 4, Gregorio 21, Helder 3, Vargas 51. **OF:** Almonte 32, Contreras 3, Helder 2, Hernandez 30, Joseph 15, Ochoa 37, Rivera 32, Rosario 52, Sandoval 41.

Tampa Bay Rays

SEASON IN A SENTENCE: The Rays were the one team never in contention in the AL East as they posted a losing record in every month—save a 2-0 October—and ultimately finished with the second-worst record in the American League.

HIGH POINT: In an otherwise lost season, franchise icon Evan Longoria homered on three straight days from Sept. 15-17 to set a new career-high in home runs. Longoria's second blast gave him 34 longballs to surpass his previous best of 33 set in 2009, and he finished the year with 36.

LOW POINT: The Rays worked their way to just one game under .500 on June 15 at 31-32, but the bottom fell out dramatically. They went 4-25 over their next 29 games, including separate losing streaks of eight and 11 games, to virtually end their season by the all-star break. Rays pitchers had a 5.69 ERA during the miserable 29-game stretch while the offense hit .234 with a .288 OBP.

NOTABLE ROOKIES: Lefthander Blake Snell, the 2015 Minor League Player of the Year, made his MLB debut in April and came up for good in June. He went 6-8, 3.54, struck out 9.9 batters-per-nine innings and had the lowest ERA on the team among starters. Knuckleballer Eddie Gamboa made his debut in September at age 31.

KEY TRANSACTIONS: The Rays resisted a full firesale in spite of their record, trading lefty Matt Moore but holding onto rotation-mates Jake Odorizzi and Chris Archer. Moore was sent to the Giants in exchange for Matt Duffy and two of San Francisco's top prospects, infielder Lucius Fox and righthander Michael Santos. Outfielder Brandon Guyer was sent to the Indians for two minor leaguers and first baseman/outfielder Steve Pearce was traded to the Orioles in exchange for well-regarded minor league catcher Johan Heim.

DOWN ON THE FARM: Willy Adames continued to stake his claim as the Rays' shortstop of the future by showing power, speed, and defensive excellence at Double-A Montgomery. Adames, first baseman/outfielder Jake Bauers (.274, 14 HR), and righthanders Brent Honeywell (3-2, 2.28) and Chih-Wei Hu (7-8, 2.59) led the prospect-rich Biscuits to the Southern League playoffs. High Class A Bowling Green and Rookie-level Princeton reached the Midwest and Appalachian League playoffs respectively, while short-season Hudson Valley reached the New York-Penn League championship series, led by 2015 first-rounder Garrett Whitley (21 SB).

OPENING DAY PAYROLL: $ 57,097,310 (30th)

ORGANIZATION LEADERS

BATTING   *Minimum 250 AB

MAJORS

* AVG	Evan Longoria	.273
* OPS	Evan Longoria	.840
HR	Evan Longoria	36
RBI	Evan Longoria	98

MINORS

* AVG	Michael Russell, Bowling Green	.293
* OBP	Joe McCarthy, Bowling Green, Charlotte	.398
* SLG	Casey Gillaspie, Montgomery, Durham	.479
* OPS	Casey Gillaspie, Montgomery, Durham	.866
R	Willy Adames, Montgomery	89
H	Jake Bauers, Montgomery	135
TB	Casey Gillaspie, Montgomery, Durham	226
2B	Casey Gillaspie, Montgomery, Durham	34
	Brett Sullivan, Bowling Green	34
3B	Jesus Sanchez, GCL Rays, Princeton	8
HR	Casey Gillaspie, Montgomery, Durham	18
RBI	Brett Sullivan, Bowling Green	81
BB	Casey Gillaspie, Montgomery, Durham	80
SO	Patrick Leonard, Durham, Montgomery	136
SB	Jake Fraley, Hudson Valley	33

PITCHING   #Minimum 75 IP

MAJORS

W	Jake Odorizzi	10
# ERA	Jake Odorizzi	3.69
SO	Chris Archer	233
SV	Alex Colome	37

MINORS

W	Yonny Chirinos, Bowling Green, Char., Mont.	12
	Taylor Guerrieri, Montgomery	12
L	Justin Marks, Charlotte, Durham	12
	Chris Pike, Charlotte	12
# ERA	Brent Honeywell, Charlotte, Montgomery	2.34
G	Jeff Ames, Montgomery	48
GS	Austin Pruitt, Durham	28
SV	Diego Castillo, Bowling Green, Charlotte	10
IP	Austin Pruitt, Durham	163
BB	Jacob Faria, Montgomery, Durham	68
	Jaime Schultz, Durham	68
SO	Jaime Schultz, Durham	163
# AVG	Hunter Wood, Charlotte, Montgomery	.178

General Manager: Matthew Silverman. **Farm Director:** Mitch Lukevics. **Scouting Director:** Rob Metzler.

Class	Team	League	W	L	PCT	Finish	Manager
Majors	Tampa Bay Rays	American	68	94	.420	14th (15)	Kevin Cash
Triple-A	Durham Bulls	International	64	80	.444	12th (14)	Jared Sandberg
Double-A	Montgomery Biscuits	Southern	76	64	.543	3rd (10)	Brady Williams
High A	Charlotte Stone Crabs	Florida State	64	71	.474	9th (12)	Michael Johns
Low A	Bowling Green Hot Rods	Midwest	84	55	.604	t-2nd (16)	Reinaldo Ruiz
Short season	Hudson Valley Renegades	New York-Penn	47	27	.635	2nd (14)	Tim Parenton
Rookie	Princeton Rays	Appalachian	38	29	.567	3rd (10)	Danny Sheaffer
Rookie	Rays	Gulf Coast	28	31	.475	9th (17)	Jim Morrison
Overall 2016 Minor League Record			401	357	.529	7th (30)	

ORGANIZATION STATISTICS

TAMPA BAY RAYS
AMERICAN LEAGUE

Batting	B-T	HT	WT	DOB	AVG	vLH	vRH	G	AB	R	H	2B	3B	HR	RBI	BB	HBP	SH	SF	SO	SB	CS	SLG	OBP
Arcia, Oswaldo	L-R	6-0	225	5-9-91	.259	.222	.267	21	54	7	14	2	1	2	7	6	0	0	1	19	1	1	.444	.328
2-team total (32 Minnesota)					.229	—	—	53	157	15	36	6	1	6	19	16	1	0	1	65	1	1	.395	.303
Beckham, Tim	R-R	6-0	195	1-27-90	.247	.276	.225	64	198	25	49	12	5	5	16	14	1	2	0	67	2	1	.434	.300
Casali, Curt	R-R	6-2	230	11-9-88	.186	.233	.163	84	226	23	42	10	0	8	25	25	2	3	0	82	0	0	.336	.273
Conger, Hank	B-R	6-2	220	1-29-88	.194	.250	.190	49	124	6	24	5	0	3	10	12	0	1	0	40	0	0	.306	.265
Decker, Jaff	L-L	5-9	190	2-23-90	.154	.000	.186	19	52	1	8	1	0	0	1	4	0	0	1	14	1	0	.173	.211
Dickerson, Corey	L-R	6-1	205	5-22-89	.245	.241	.246	148	510	57	125	36	3	24	70	33	2	0	2	134	0	2	.469	.293
Duffy, Matt	R-R	6-2	170	1-15-91	.276	.174	.321	21	76	9	21	3	0	1	7	3	0	0	1	13	0	1	.355	.300
Forsythe, Logan	R-R	6-1	205	1-14-87	.264	.270	.263	127	511	76	135	24	4	20	52	46	8	0	2	127	6	6	.444	.333
Franklin, Nick	B-R	6-1	190	3-2-91	.270	.216	.285	60	174	18	47	10	1	6	26	12	3	2	0	42	6	1	.443	.328
Guyer, Brandon	R-R	6-2	200	1-28-86	.241	.344	.196	63	212	27	51	12	1	7	18	12	23	1	1	42	2	1	.406	.347
2-team total (38 Cleveland)					.266	—	—	101	293	39	78	17	1	9	32	19	31	1	1	55	3	2	.423	.372
Jennings, Desmond	R-R	6-2	210	10-30-86	.200	.194	.203	65	200	22	40	7	1	7	20	21	2	1	1	58	2	0	.350	.281
Kiermaier, Kevin	L-R	6-1	215	4-22-90	.246	.262	.241	105	366	55	90	20	2	12	37	40	7	0	1	74	21	3	.410	.331
Longoria, Evan	R-R	6-2	210	10-7-85	.273	.250	.280	160	633	81	173	41	4	36	98	42	3	0	7	144	0	3	.521	.318
Mahtook, Mikie	R-R	6-1	200	11-30-89	.195	.258	.160	65	185	16	36	9	0	3	11	7	2	1	1	68	0	1	.292	.231
Maile, Luke	R-R	6-3	225	2-6-91	.227	.242	.221	42	119	10	27	7	0	3	15	4	0	3	0	36	0	0	.361	.252
Miller, Brad	L-R	6-2	200	10-18-89	.243	.227	.247	152	548	73	133	29	6	30	81	47	3	0	3	149	6	4	.482	.304
Morrison, Logan	L-L	6-2	240	8-25-87	.238	.258	.234	107	353	45	84	18	1	14	43	37	6	0	2	89	4	2	.414	.319
Motter, Taylor	R-R	6-1	195	9-18-89	.188	.348	.123	33	80	11	15	3	0	2	9	11	1	0	1	19	0	1	.300	.290
Pearce, Steve	R-R	5-11	200	4-13-83	.309	.377	.285	60	204	26	63	11	1	10	29	26	1	0	1	40	0	3	.520	.388
2-team total (25 Baltimore)					.288	—	—	85	264	35	76	13	1	13	35	34	3	0	1	54	0	3	.492	.374
Querecuto, Juniel	B-R	5-9	155	9-19-92	.091	.000	.125	4	11	1	1	0	0	0	2	0	0	0	6	0	0	.273	.091
Ramirez, Alexei	R-R	6-2	180	9-22-81	.246	.429	.186	17	57	5	14	3	0	1	7	4	0	1	0	7	2	0	.351	.295
Shaffer, Richie	R-R	6-3	220	3-15-91	.250	.286	.235	20	48	5	12	6	0	1	4	5	0	0	1	18	0	1	.438	.315
Souza, Steven	R-R	6-4	225	4-24-89	.247	.237	.250	120	430	58	106	17	1	17	49	31	5	0	2	159	7	6	.409	.303
Wilson, Bobby	R-R	6-0	230	4-8-83	.230	.167	.246	28	87	14	20	2	0	4	9	5	0	3	0	28	0	0	.391	.272
3-team total (5 Detroit, 42 Texas)					.237	—	—	75	228	25	54	6	0	7	33	11	1	7	4	64	0	0	.355	.270

Pitching	B-T	HT	WT	DOB	W	L	ERA	G	GS	CG	SV	IP	H	R	ER	HR	BB	SO	AVG	vLH	vRH	K/9	BB/9
Andriese, Matt	R-R	6-3	215	8-28-89	8	8	4.37	29	19	1	1	128	131	64	62	17	25	109	.265	.242	.285	7.68	1.76
Archer, Chris	R-R	6-3	190	9-26-88	9	19	4.02	33	33	0	0	201	183	100	90	30	67	233	.238	.231	.244	10.42	3.00
Boxberger, Brad	R-R	6-2	225	5-27-88	4	3	4.81	27	0	0	0	24	23	13	13	3	19	22	.250	.244	.255	8.14	7.03
Cedeno, Xavier	L-L	6-0	215	8-26-86	3	4	3.70	54	0	0	0	41	36	17	17	2	13	43	.229	.197	.259	9.36	2.83
Cobb, Alex	R-R	6-3	205	10-7-87	1	2	8.59	5	5	0	0	22	32	22	21	5	7	16	.337	.404	.271	6.55	2.86
Colome, Alex	R-R	6-2	220	12-31-88	2	4	1.91	57	0	0	37	57	43	12	12	6	15	71	.206	.184	.221	11.28	2.38
Eveland, Dana	L-L	6-1	235	10-29-83	0	1	9.00	33	0	0	0	23	32	23	23	3	19	21	.333	.361	.317	8.22	7.43
Farquhar, Danny	R-R	5-9	185	2-17-87	1	0	3.06	35	0	0	0	35	33	14	12	8	15	46	.241	.235	.244	11.72	3.82
Floro, Dylan	L-R	6-2	175	12-27-90	0	1	4.20	12	0	0	0	15	23	8	7	0	5	14	.348	.346	.350	8.40	3.00
Gamboa, Eddie	R-R	6-1	215	12-21-84	0	2	1.35	7	0	0	0	13	9	3	2	1	8	11	.196	.238	.160	7.43	5.40
Garton, Ryan	R-R	5-11	185	12-5-89	1	2	4.35	37	0	0	1	39	44	20	19	5	11	33	.277	.315	.257	7.55	2.52
Geltz, Steve	R-R	5-10	210	11-1-87	0	2	5.74	27	0	0	0	27	24	17	17	11	9	23	.238	.174	.291	7.76	3.04
Jepsen, Kevin	R-R	6-3	235	7-26-84	0	1	5.68	25	0	0	0	19	20	13	12	5	9	11	.282	.269	.289	6.16	4.26
2-team total (33 Minnesota)					2	6	5.98	58	0	0	7	50	62	35	33	12	21	35	—	—	—	6.34	3.81
Marinez, Jhan	R-R	6-1	200	8-12-88	0	0	2.45	3	0	0	0	4	2	1	1	1	0	3	.154	.167	.143	7.36	0.00
Marks, Justin	L-L	6-3	205	1-12-88	0	0	1.00	4	0	0	0	9	7	1	1	1	6	11	.212	.313	.118	6.00	9.00
Moore, Matt	L-L	6-3	210	6-18-89	7	7	4.08	21	21	0	0	130	125	62	59	20	40	109	.251	.239	.254	7.55	2.77
Odorizzi, Jake	R-R	6-2	190	3-27-90	10	6	3.69	33	33	0	0	188	170	80	77	29	54	166	.241	.190	.277	7.96	2.59
Ramirez, Erasmo	R-R	5-11	200	5-2-90	7	11	3.77	64	1	0	2	91	90	39	38	14	26	63	.265	.290	.251	6.25	2.58
Romero, Enny	L-L	6-3	215	1-24-91	2	0	5.91	52	0	0	1	46	42	31	30	7	28	50	.244	.288	.177	9.85	5.52
Smyly, Drew	L-L	6-3	190	6-13-89	7	12	4.88	30	30	0	0	175	174	103	95	32	49	167	.259	.250	.262	8.57	2.52
Snell, Blake	L-L	6-4	180	12-4-92	6	8	3.54	19	19	0	0	89	93	44	35	5	51	98	.269	.264	.270	9.91	5.16
Sturdevant, Tyler	R-R	6-0	185	12-20-85	0	1	3.93	16	0	0	0	18	18	8	8	1	6	14	.273	.250	.283	6.87	2.95

TAMPA BAY RAYS

Pitching	B-T	HT	WT	DOB	W	L	ERA	G	GS	CG	SV	IP	H	R	ER	HR	BB	SO	AVG	vLH	vRH	K/9	BB/9
Webb, Ryan	R-R	6-6	245	2-5-86	0	0	5.19	18	0	0	0	17	27	11	10	2	3	11	.370	.389	.364	5.71	1.56
Whitley, Chase	R-R	6-3	215	6-14-89	0	0	2.51	5	1	0	0	14	13	7	4	2	3	15	.224	.143	.348	9.42	1.88

Fielding

Catcher	PCT	G	PO	A	E	DP	PB
Casali	.993	76	538	37	4	4	4
Conger	.991	47	300	16	3	1	2
Maile	.990	37	278	27	3	1	4
Wilson	.992	28	230	9	2	1	3

Catcher (cont.)	PCT	G	PO	A	E	DP
Franklin	.833	8	6	14	4	3
Motter	.960	6	6	18	1	4
Pearce	.983	14	21	38	1	9
Querecuto	1.000	2	2	2	0	0
Ramirez	1.000	1	1	1	0	0
Miller	.961	105	132	215	14	45
Motter	.947	9	3	15	1	4
Querecuto	—	1	0	0	0	0
Ramirez	1.000	16	10	34	0	8

First Base	PCT	G	PO	A	E	DP
Beckham	1.000	6	38	1	0	4
Franklin	1.000	9	58	4	0	7
Maile	1.000	4	12	1	0	1
Miller	.986	39	277	12	4	17
Morrison	.993	83	566	42	4	63
Motter	1.000	1	4	1	0	0
Pearce	.987	30	202	19	3	22
Shaffer	.986	11	64	7	1	6

Second Base	PCT	G	PO	A	E	DP
Beckham	1.000	19	30	44	0	12
Forsythe	.981	118	206	264	9	69

Third Base	PCT	G	PO	A	E	DP
Beckham	1.000	7	0	7	0	1
Duffy	1.000	1	1	0	0	0
Longoria	.975	152	103	254	9	30
Motter	1.000	4	2	11	0	4
Pearce	1.000	2	1	1	0	0
Querecuto	1.000	1	1	1	0	0
Shaffer	1.000	4	4	0	0	0

Shortstop	PCT	G	PO	A	E	DP
Beckham	.958	25	27	64	4	14
Duffy	1.000	18	15	40	0	8
Franklin	.923	5	3	9	1	1

Outfield	PCT	G	PO	A	E	DP
Arcia	1.000	14	29	0	0	0
Decker	1.000	16	28	3	0	1
Dickerson	.986	78	134	2	2	0
Franklin	.978	25	45	0	1	0
Guyer	.970	50	97	1	3	0
Jennings	.983	62	112	3	2	1
Kiermaier	.993	104	264	7	2	1
Mahtook	1.000	61	106	3	0	1
Miller	.000	1	0	0	1	0
Motter	1.000	13	15	1	0	0
Shaffer	1.000	2	1	0	0	0
Souza	.984	113	232	8	4	1

DURHAM BULLS   TRIPLE-A
INTERNATIONAL LEAGUE

Batting	B-T	HT	WT	DOB	AVG	vLH	vRH	G	AB	R	H	2B	3B	HR	RBI	BB	HBP	SH	SF	SO	SB	CS	SLG	OBP
Acosta, Mayo	R-R	6-1	220	11-20-87	.085	.333	.026	15	47	1	4	0	0	0	4	2	0	0	1	14	0	0	.085	.120
Arencibia, J.P.	R-R	6-1	210	1-5-86	.252	.289	.237	78	309	34	78	14	0	15	47	9	5	0	1	93	1	1	.443	.284
2-team total (12 Lehigh Valley)					.241	—	—	90	357	37	86	16	0	16	49	9	5	0	1	104	1	1	.420	.269
Beckham, Tim	R-R	6-0	195	1-27-90	.158	.222	.100	5	19	0	3	0	0	0	1	0	0	0	0	7	0	1	.158	.200
Casali, Curt	R-R	6-2	230	11-9-88	.254	.294	.239	20	63	5	16	1	0	2	15	15	2	0	1	12	0	0	.365	.407
Conger, Hank	B-R	6-2	240	1-7-84	.165	.107	.185	30	109	7	18	4	1	3	11	4	1	1	1	24	0	0	.303	.200
Corporan, Carlos	B-R	6-2	240	1-7-84	.200	.222	.191	20	65	3	13	1	0	2	9	3	1	0	0	20	0	0	.308	.246
Decker, Jaff	L-L	5-9	190	2-23-90	.255	.229	.265	99	349	55	89	18	2	12	35	59	4	2	3	79	18	7	.421	.366
Duffy, Matt	R-R	6-2	170	1-15-91	.182	.200	.167	3	11	0	2	0	0	0	1	0	0	0	0	2	0	0	.182	.250
Field, Johnny	R-R	5-10	180	2-20-92	.275	.281	.272	69	255	34	70	23	4	5	27	21	5	1	3	64	3	6	.455	.338
Forsythe, Logan	R-R	6-1	205	1-14-87	.400	—	.400	2	5	1	2	0	0	1	1	1	1	0	0	0	1	0	1.000	.571
Franklin, Nick	B-R	6-1	190	3-2-91	.254	.240	.261	64	240	26	61	16	1	5	28	26	0	0	4	56	10	1	.392	.322
Gillaspie, Casey	B-L	6-4	240	1-25-93	.307	.289	.313	47	179	27	55	13	2	7	23	22	2	0	0	38	0	1	.520	.389
Goebbert, Jake	L-L	6-0	210	9-24-87	.218	.167	.231	93	321	40	70	14	1	10	35	36	3	0	4	88	0	3	.361	.299
Hager, Jake	R-R	6-1	170	3-4-93	.228	.289	.204	71	272	28	62	18	1	2	21	16	0	3	2	60	3	2	.324	.269
Leonard, Patrick	R-R	6-4	225	10-20-92	.198	.276	.176	42	131	10	26	5	1	0	6	13	1	0	0	54	0	1	.252	.276
Mahtook, Mikie	R-R	6-1	200	11-30-89	.305	.167	.323	27	105	16	32	5	3	1	7	12	2	0	1	24	5	1	.438	.383
Maile, Luke	R-R	6-3	225	2-6-91	.242	.180	.271	58	194	13	47	13	0	2	12	16	3	1	0	36	0	1	.340	.310
Motter, Taylor	R-R	6-1	195	9-18-89	.229	.227	.229	88	350	44	80	17	0	13	46	33	2	0	2	65	19	4	.389	.297
Perez, Eury	R-R	6-0	190	5-30-90	.239	.174	.262	27	88	15	21	2	2	0	4	5	2	4	0	18	11	2	.307	.295
Querecuto, Juniel	B-R	5-9	155	9-19-92	.242	.258	.236	36	120	11	29	8	0	0	11	6	2	1	0	31	3	1	.308	.289
Robertson, Daniel	R-R	6-1	205	3-22-94	.259	.280	.250	118	436	50	113	21	3	5	43	58	11	2	4	100	2	1	.356	.358
Roller, Kyle	L-R	6-1	250	3-27-88	.216	.333	.175	50	162	13	35	9	1	5	12	20	4	0	1	59	0	0	.377	.316
Seitzer, Cameron	L-R	6-5	220	1-11-90	.178	.256	.146	40	135	7	24	3	0	3	9	3	0	0	0	37	0	0	.200	.229
Shaffer, Richie	R-R	6-3	220	3-15-91	.227	.288	.207	119	428	49	97	27	0	11	48	65	1	0	2	135	4	1	.367	.329
Sole, Alec	L-R	6-2	200	6-1-93	.000	—	.000	3	7	0	0	0	0	0	0	1	0	0	0	4	0	0	.000	.125
Varona, Dayron	R-R	5-11	185	2-24-88	.232	.281	.212	117	435	52	101	32	1	14	59	18	4	0	2	99	12	6	.407	.274

Pitching	B-T	HT	WT	DOB	W	L	ERA	G	GS	CG	SV	IP	H	R	ER	HR	BB	SO	AVG	vLH	vRH	K/9	BB/9
Andriese, Matt	R-R	6-3	215	8-28-89	1	2	3.41	6	6	1	0	34	32	14	13	2	7	44	.242	.215	.269	11.53	1.83
Bellatti, Andrew	R-R	6-1	190	8-5-91	0	1	8.44	6	0	0	0	5	8	5	5	0	5	10	.348	.385	.300	16.88	8.44
Boxberger, Brad	R-R	6-2	225	5-27-88	0	0	10.80	2	0	0	0	2	2	2	2	1	0	4	.286	.000	.667	21.60	0.00
Cobb, Alex	R-R	6-3	205	10-7-87	0	1	6.60	4	4	0	0	15	24	13	11	3	5	10	.387	.286	.439	6.00	3.00
Coleman, Casey	L-R	6-0	185	7-3-87	1	3	3.86	11	0	0	0	14	13	8	6	1	5	16	.241	.235	.243	10.29	3.21
Eveland, Dana	L-L	6-1	235	10-29-83	1	0	0.30	20	1	0	0	30	16	2	1	1	6	21	.160	.105	.194	6.37	1.82
Faria, Jacob	R-R	6-4	200	7-30-93	4	4	3.72	13	13	0	0	68	46	31	28	7	32	64	.190	.183	.197	8.51	4.26
Farquhar, Danny	R-R	5-9	185	2-17-87	4	2	3.32	32	0	0	2	38	33	16	14	2	9	34	.241	.262	.222	5.68	2.13
Floro, Dylan	R-R	6-2	175	12-27-90	1	2	2.88	32	0	0	7	50	53	21	16	6	9	40	.270	.271	.270	7.20	1.62
Gamboa, Eddie	R-R	6-1	215	12-21-84	6	4	2.68	27	12	0	0	94	65	36	28	0	39	89	.196	.212	.186	8.52	3.73
Garton, Ryan	R-R	5-11	185	12-5-89	4	0	3.09	22	0	0	2	32	31	14	11	1	10	39	.252	.273	.235	10.97	2.81
Geltz, Steve	R-R	5-10	210	11-1-87	0	2	3.03	31	0	0	3	36	30	13	12	3	17	40	.227	.352	.141	10.09	4.29
Harris, Greg	R-R	6-2	170	8-17-94	0	0	9.00	1	0	0	0	3	5	3	3	0	3	6	.357	.167	.500	18.00	9.00
Hu, Chih-Wei	R-R	6-1	230	11-4-93	0	1	7.71	1	0	0	0	5	7	4	4	1	2	7	.350	.500	.286	13.50	3.86
Kolarek, Adam	L-L	6-3	205	1-14-89	0	2	3.05	34	0	0	2	41	28	15	14	1	23	46	.194	.146	.219	10.02	5.01
Marinez, Jhan	R-R	6-1	200	8-12-88	2	1	2.25	6	0	0	1	8	10	2	2	0	3	9	.313	.294	.333	10.13	3.38
Markel, Parker	R-R	6-4	220	9-15-90	5	3	2.52	34	1	0	0	61	56	19	17	1	24	47	.247	.321	.203	6.97	3.56

Pitching	B-T	HT	WT	DOB	W	L	ERA	G	GS	CG	SV	IP	H	R	ER	HR	BB	SO	AVG	vLH	vRH	K/9	BB/9
Marks, Justin	L-L	6-3	205	1-12-88	7	11	3.86	25	23	1	0	140	125	70	60	14	53	127	.239	.191	.254	8.16	3.41
McPherson, Kyle	B-R	6-4	215	11-11-87	0	0	19.89	5	0	0	0	6	13	14	14	5	3	6	.406	.214	.556	8.53	4.26
Pruitt, Austin	R-R	5-11	165	8-31-89	8	11	3.76	28	28	2	0	163	166	73	68	21	27	149	.267	.267	.267	8.24	1.49
Sappington, Mark	R-R	6-5	210	11-17-90	1	2	4.86	29	0	0	1	37	33	23	20	2	29	36	.234	.213	.250	8.76	7.05
Schreiber, Brad	R-R	6-3	225	2-13-91	0	0	4.15	2	0	0	0	4	6	2	2	1	1	4	.316	.600	.214	8.31	2.08
Schultz, Jaime	R-R	5-10	200	6-20-91	5	7	3.58	27	27	0	0	131	113	57	52	12	68	163	.236	.237	.235	11.23	4.68
Snell, Blake	L-L	6-4	180	12-4-92	3	5	3.29	12	12	0	0	63	56	23	23	4	28	90	.234	.200	.246	12.86	4.00
Stanek, Ryne	R-R	6-4	180	7-26-91	2	4	5.92	16	0	0	1	24	22	17	16	3	13	22	.242	.263	.226	8.14	4.81
Sturdevant, Tyler	R-R	6-0	185	12-20-85	3	2	3.66	34	0	0	4	39	39	16	16	6	12	49	.267	.259	.272	11.21	2.75
Wagner, Neil	R-R	6-0	215	1-1-84	1	2	4.81	38	0	0	2	43	49	23	23	4	24	44	.292	.286	.296	9.21	5.02
Webb, Ryan	R-R	6-6	245	2-5-86	0	1	6.00	3	0	0	0	3	4	3	2	0	2	3	.308	.429	.167	9.00	6.00
2-team total (3 Charlotte)					0	1	9.53	6	0	0	0	6	9	7	6	0	3	4	—	—	—	6.35	4.76
Wilk, Adam	L-L	6-2	180	12-9-87	2	8	3.61	15	15	0	0	87	85	45	35	9	13	75	.259	.167	.282	7.73	1.34
Winkler, Kyle	R-R	5-11	195	6-18-90	1	0	6.75	1	0	0	0	1	2	2	1	0	2	0	.333	.000	.500	0.00	13.50

Fielding

Catcher	PCT	G	PO	A	E	DP	PB
Acosta	.980	11	85	11	2	1	1
Arencibia	.992	42	351	22	3	2	23
Casali	.974	13	102	10	3	1	5
Conger	.994	19	162	13	1	1	3
Corporan	.989	20	170	14	2	2	3
Maile	.993	46	407	36	3	1	2

First Base	PCT	G	PO	A	E	DP
Arencibia	1.000	11	81	2	0	7
Gillaspie	.998	45	389	17	1	41
Goebbert	.979	12	85	7	2	7
Leonard	.990	14	97	5	1	7
Motter	.923	1	12	0	1	2
Roller	.992	17	122	4	1	14
Seitzer	.990	38	290	20	3	32
Shaffer	.986	19	136	4	2	14

Second Base	PCT	G	PO	A	E	DP
Beckham	1.000	1	3	2	0	0
Forsythe	1.000	1	1	1	0	0
Franklin	.984	54	107	142	4	40
Hager	.972	40	72	104	5	27
Motter	.965	16	20	35	2	9
Querecuto	1.000	15	28	25	0	6
Robertson	1.000	21	40	58	0	11

Third Base	PCT	G	PO	A	E	DP
Franklin	.667	4	3	3	3	1
Hager	1.000	2	0	3	0	0
Leonard	.975	10	11	28	1	5
Motter	.983	25	17	41	1	5
Querecuto	.977	21	14	28	1	3
Robertson	.942	20	11	38	3	8
Seitzer	1.000	2	0	1	0	0
Shaffer	.941	67	38	106	9	14
Sole	1.000	3	0	3	0	0

Shortstop	PCT	G	PO	A	E	DP
Beckham	1.000	4	3	14	0	4
Duffy	1.000	3	1	10	0	1
Hager	.989	27	25	63	1	14
Motter	.957	37	40	95	6	22
Querecuto	.000	1	0	0	1	0
Robertson	.974	75	96	200	8	37

Outfield	PCT	G	PO	A	E	DP
Decker	.990	96	178	12	2	5
Field	1.000	66	130	1	0	0
Franklin	1.000	3	4	1	0	0
Goebbert	.972	67	98	5	3	1
Leonard	.926	16	25	0	2	0
Mahtook	.980	25	48	2	1	1
Motter	1.000	9	15	0	0	0
Perez	.983	25	57	1	1	0
Shaffer	.897	28	31	4	4	1
Varona	.991	113	203	12	2	2

MONTGOMERY BISCUITS
DOUBLE-A
SOUTHERN LEAGUE

Batting	B-T	HT	WT	DOB	AVG	vLH	vRH	G	AB	R	H	2B	3B	HR	RBI	BB	HBP	SH	SF	SO	SB	CS	SLG	OBP
Adames, Willy	R-R	6-1	180	9-2-95	.274	.324	.259	132	486	89	133	31	6	11	57	74	4	1	3	121	13	6	.430	.372
Araiza, Armando	R-R	5-11	185	6-19-93	.296	—	.296	9	27	3	8	2	0	0	7	4	1	3	0	7	0	0	.370	.406
Bauers, Jake	L-L	6-1	195	10-6-95	.274	.236	.284	135	493	79	135	28	1	14	78	73	6	2	7	89	10	6	.420	.370
Blair, Pat	R-R	5-10	180	10-1-91	.179	.036	.221	38	123	12	22	5	0	1	9	14	0	2	0	35	6	1	.244	.263
Coyle, Tommy	L-R	5-7	170	10-24-90	.177	.152	.182	57	181	20	32	6	2	1	11	19	0	1	3	50	10	3	.298	.251
DePew, Jake	R-R	6-1	210	3-1-92	.215	.246	.205	86	284	26	61	10	1	9	42	26	0	2	4	72	2	0	.352	.277
Field, Johnny	R-R	5-10	180	2-20-92	.272	.375	.238	45	195	26	53	10	2	7	29	9	0	0	2	42	13	2	.451	.301
Gillaspie, Casey	B-L	6-4	240	1-25-93	.270	.208	.290	85	293	51	79	21	0	11	41	58	1	0	5	79	5	1	.454	.387
Goetzman, Granden	R-R	6-4	200	11-14-92	.243	.246	.242	83	313	49	76	14	4	5	38	16	2	1	2	70	24	9	.361	.282
Gotta, Cade	R-R	6-2	205	8-1-91	.261	.408	.231	76	291	42	76	21	3	5	33	23	1	1	3	46	22	4	.405	.314
Hager, Jake	R-R	6-1	170	3-4-93	.240	.296	.216	43	179	20	43	10	1	2	17	7	1	3	0	35	4	1	.341	.273
Lee, Braxton	L-R	5-10	185	8-23-93	.209	.162	.219	110	387	35	81	12	3	0	25	30	2	11	1	58	13	10	.256	.269
Leonard, Patrick	R-R	6-4	225	10-20-92	.286	.481	.239	74	276	48	79	24	0	9	47	20	7	0	4	82	8	1	.471	.345
Marjama, Mike	R-R	6-2	205	7-20-89	.288	.234	.304	74	278	38	80	26	1	5	38	19	5	2	3	46	2	0	.442	.341
O'Conner, Justin	R-R	6-0	190	3-31-92	.160	.000	.211	8	25	2	4	0	0	1	3	0	0	0	1	9	0	0	.280	.154
Querecuto, Juniel	B-R	5-9	155	9-19-92	.241	.200	.251	60	220	26	53	11	3	3	27	21	0	2	3	43	0	0	.359	.303
Rapacz, Josh	R-R	6-2	205	7-10-90	.167	.000	.250	2	6	0	1	0	0	0	0	1	0	0	0	1	0	0	.167	.286
Sole, Alec	R-R	6-2	180	6-1-93	.158	.400	.071	6	19	4	3	0	0	1	2	2	0	0	0	7	0	0	.316	.238
Williams, Justin	L-R	6-2	215	8-20-95	.250	.192	.262	39	148	20	37	7	2	6	28	5	1	0	1	30	0	1	.446	.277
Wong, Kean	L-R	5-11	190	4-17-95	.276	.273	.277	117	446	52	123	22	2	5	56	31	2	10	3	72	10	10	.368	.324

Pitching	B-T	HT	WT	DOB	W	L	ERA	G	GS	CG	SV	IP	H	R	ER	HR	BB	SO	AVG	vLH	vRH	K/9	BB/9
Ames, Jeff	R-R	6-4	220	1-31-91	6	2	2.71	48	0	0	6	63	45	21	19	7	40	61	.200	.158	.231	8.71	5.71
Ascher, Steve	L-L	6-0	185	10-18-93	3	1	4.30	26	3	0	1	46	44	22	22	5	18	36	.254	.103	.330	7.04	3.52
Bellatti, Andrew	R-R	6-1	190	8-5-91	0	2	9.00	4	0	0	0	5	6	6	5	1	3	7	.273	.444	.154	12.60	5.40
Bird, Kyle	L-L	6-2	175	4-12-93	1	1	2.94	32	0	0	4	49	45	19	16	4	17	38	.260	.320	.236	6.98	3.12
Borden, Buddy	R-R	6-3	210	4-29-92	1	0	5.22	14	0	0	3	29	28	19	17	2	21	24	.259	.240	.276	7.36	6.44
Boxberger, Brad	R-R	6-2	225	5-27-88	0	0	0.00	2	0	0	0	2	2	0	0	0	0	2	.286	.667	.000	10.80	0.00
Chapman, Jaye	R-R	6-0	195	5-22-87	3	2	4.43	22	0	0	9	20	17	10	10	1	4	26	.230	.259	.213	11.51	1.77
2-team total (12 Biloxi)					4	2	2.84	34	0	0	19	32	19	10	10	1	4	41	—	—	—	11.65	1.14
Chirinos, Yonny	R-R	6-2	170	12-26-93	5	3	4.46	14	8	0	0	67	74	37	33	5	12	43	.276	.298	.257	5.81	1.62
Faria, Jacob	R-R	6-4	200	7-30-93	1	6	4.21	14	14	0	0	83	64	39	39	5	36	93	.211	.207	.213	10.04	3.89
Guerrieri, Taylor	R-R	6-3	195	12-1-92	12	6	3.76	28	26	0	1	146	130	67	61	11	46	89	.239	.221	.255	5.49	2.84
Harrison, Jordan	R-L	6-1	180	4-9-91	2	0	2.59	25	0	0	0	24	13	7	7	0	19	17	.159	.103	.189	6.29	7.03

Pitching	B-T	HT	WT	DOB	W	L	ERA	G	GS	CG	SV	IP	H	R	ER	HR	BB	SO	AVG	vLH	vRH	K/9	BB/9
Honeywell, Brent	R-R	6-2	180	3-31-95	3	2	2.28	10	10	0	0	59	51	16	15	4	14	53	.231	.176	.277	8.04	2.12
Hu, Chih-Wei	R-R	6-1	230	11-4-93	7	8	2.59	24	24	0	0	143	128	49	41	7	36	107	.241	.235	.246	6.75	2.27
Kirsch, Chris	L-L	6-2	185	11-15-91	7	7	3.22	25	25	1	0	145	139	60	52	8	57	114	.256	.259	.255	7.06	3.53
Kolarek, Adam	L-L	6-3	205	1-14-89	3	2	3.32	13	0	0	0	19	14	13	7	0	12	17	.194	.136	.220	8.05	5.68
Markel, Parker	R-R	6-4	220	9-15-90	2	0	4.22	9	0	0	0	11	15	5	5	0	2	11	.319	.409	.240	9.28	1.69
Marshall, Brett	R-R	6-1	195	3-22-90	2	2	8.24	15	0	0	0	20	29	22	18	1	17	13	.337	.350	.326	5.95	7.78
Mortensen, Jared	L-R	5-11	205	6-1-88	7	7	5.23	34	4	0	0	72	53	44	42	7	57	86	.209	.243	.182	10.70	7.09
Sappington, Mark	R-R	6-5	210	11-17-90	0	0	7.80	13	0	0	0	15	17	15	13	0	15	12	.283	.231	.324	7.20	9.00
Schreiber, Brad	R-R	6-3	225	2-13-91	1	2	6.06	28	0	0	7	33	43	24	22	4	12	26	.321	.317	.324	7.16	3.31
Stanek, Ryne	R-R	6-4	180	7-26-91	2	6	3.79	18	11	0	2	78	64	36	33	6	35	91	.227	.294	.164	10.46	4.02
Whitley, Chase	R-R	6-3	215	6-14-89	2	1	2.93	6	6	0	0	28	17	12	9	3	8	22	.177	.195	.164	7.16	2.60
Winkler, Kyle	R-R	5-11	195	6-18-90	0	2	2.59	29	0	0	8	31	21	10	9	3	11	36	.188	.154	.217	10.34	3.16
Wood, Hunter	R-R	6-1	175	8-12-93	6	2	3.28	10	9	0	0	49	36	21	18	5	20	49	.206	.165	.240	8.94	3.65

Fielding

Catcher	PCT	G	PO	A	E	DP	PB
Araiza	.987	9	65	9	1	2	3
DePew	.990	73	514	63	6	7	12
Marjama	.983	53	423	48	8	3	9
O'Conner	.963	8	47	5	2	1	0
Rapacz	1.000	1	8	0	0	0	1

First Base	PCT	G	PO	A	E	DP
Bauers	.984	57	466	25	8	40
Blair	1.000	5	31	2	0	1
Gillaspie	.988	77	633	45	8	64
Leonard	1.000	2	10	0	0	1
Sole	1.000	1	1	1	0	0

Second Base	PCT	G	PO	A	E	DP
Blair	.960	13	22	26	2	5
Coyle	.976	42	72	93	4	26
Hager	.950	9	18	20	2	3
Querecuto	.981	18	44	58	2	18
Sole	1.000	1	1	2	0	0
Wong	.978	58	110	151	6	29

Third Base	PCT	G	PO	A	E	DP
Blair	.833	2	1	4	1	1
Coyle	1.000	2	1	7	0	0
Hager	.935	18	15	28	3	2
Leonard	.948	56	28	100	7	10
Querecuto	.973	24	22	50	2	5
Wong	.940	40	30	64	6	8

Shortstop	PCT	G	PO	A	E	DP
Adames	.952	112	132	305	22	52
Blair	.769	3	4	6	3	0
Hager	.971	9	14	20	1	8
Querecuto	.969	14	24	38	2	10
Sole	1.000	3	3	10	0	1

Outfield	PCT	G	PO	A	E	DP
Bauers	.968	66	145	7	5	2
Blair	1.000	13	26	3	0	1
Coyle	1.000	11	16	1	0	0
Field	.976	42	77	4	2	2
Goetzman	.987	75	141	8	2	0
Gotta	1.000	66	173	12	0	5
Lee	.982	109	261	11	5	6
Leonard	1.000	7	14	1	0	0
Williams	.987	34	72	3	1	0

CHARLOTTE STONE CRABS   HIGH CLASS A
FLORIDA STATE LEAGUE

Batting	B-T	HT	WT	DOB	AVG	vLH	vRH	G	AB	R	H	2B	3B	HR	RBI	BB	HBP	SH	SF	SO	SB	CS	SLG	OBP
Araiza, Armando	R-R	5-11	185	6-19-93	.288	.421	.225	18	59	6	17	0	1	2	5	6	1	0	0	14	0	0	.424	.364
Arcia, Oswaldo	L-R	6-0	225	5-9-91	.286	.250	.300	9	28	6	8	0	1	3	7	2	0	0	0	7	0	0	.679	.333
Blair, Pat	R-R	5-10	180	10-1-91	.164	.136	.179	19	61	8	10	0	1	3	6	9	0	1	0	13	2	0	.344	.271
Ciuffo, Nick	L-R	6-1	205	3-7-95	.262	.300	.249	59	229	16	60	8	0	0	15	9	0	2	2	45	2	3	.297	.288
Conrad, Jace	L-R	5-11	195	12-15-92	.223	.263	.209	107	373	27	83	12	4	1	33	17	4	3	6	63	25	12	.284	.260
Cray, Landon	L-L	5-9	190	1-25-94	.200	.200	.200	15	45	2	9	1	1	0	6	4	1	0	1	5	0	2	.267	.275
Cronenworth, Jake	L-L	6-1	185	1-21-94	.171	.158	.174	35	111	15	19	3	1	1	9	13	2	0	0	26	2	1	.243	.270
Dominguez, Wilmer	R-R	5-10	180	6-19-91	.333	.667	.167	4	9	0	3	0	0	0	1	0	0	1	0	3	0	0	.333	.300
Duffy, Matt	R-R	6-2	170	1-15-91	.500	—	.500	2	6	0	3	1	0	0	1	0	0	0	0	0	0	0	.667	.500
Eureste, Matt	L-R	6-1	175	7-29-93	.333	.500	.250	4	12	0	4	1	0	0	1	0	0	0	1	0	0	0	.417	.333
Franklin, Nick	B-R	6-1	190	3-2-91	.750	—	.750	1	4	2	3	0	0	0	2	0	0	0	0	0	0	0	.750	.750
Gotta, Cade	R-R	6-4	205	8-1-91	.306	.280	.317	46	173	25	53	9	2	4	17	14	1	1	0	36	7	2	.451	.362
Guyer, Brandon	R-R	6-2	200	1-28-86	.167	.000	.286	9	12	2	2	1	0	0	1	0	0	0	0	2	0	0	.250	.167
Heim, Jonah	B-R	6-4	205	6-27-95	.222	.250	.216	14	45	4	10	1	0	1	3	2	0	0	0	11	0	0	.311	.255
Jackson, Bralin	R-L	6-2	183	12-2-93	.219	.262	.203	65	233	22	51	7	0	3	17	18	1	3	2	59	6	5	.288	.276
James, Mac	R-R	6-1	195	6-2-93	.239	.284	.222	98	356	34	85	11	1	1	30	30	3	2	3	54	1	3	.284	.301
Jennings, Desmond	R-R	6-2	210	10-30-86	.267	.125	.429	4	15	2	4	1	0	1	2	1	0	0	0	1	1	0	.533	.313
Kay, Grant	R-R	6-0	185	5-29-93	.242	.202	.257	115	405	50	98	14	1	8	45	30	6	2	6	77	14	8	.341	.300
Kiermaier, Kevin	L-R	6-1	215	4-22-90	.667	.667	—	2	3	2	2	1	0	0	2	0	0	0	0	0	0	0	1.000	.800
Lukes, Nathan	L-R	5-11	185	7-12-94	.194	.167	.197	21	67	5	13	1	0	1	4	3	0	1	0	9	0	1	.254	.229
Mahtook, Mikie	R-R	6-1	215	11-30-89	.400	1.000	.333	3	10	1	4	0	0	0	1	0	0	0	0	3	0	0	.400	.455
McCarthy, Joe	L-L	6-3	225	2-23-94	.283	.170	.324	61	198	20	56	9	3	5	31	28	5	0	6	38	8	3	.434	.376
Milone, Thomas	L-L	5-11	190	1-26-95	.206	.202	.207	115	355	36	73	11	5	2	22	36	8	6	3	98	15	11	.282	.291
Morrison, Logan	L-L	6-2	240	8-27-87	.231	.000	.250	4	13	1	3	1	0	0	2	0	0	0	0	0	0	0	.308	.333
Pearce, Steve	R-R	5-11	200	4-13-83	.429	—	.429	2	7	2	3	1	0	0	1	0	0	0	0	0	0	0	.571	.500
Seibert, Mac	R-R	6-0	195	11-17-93	.000	.000	.000	1	4	0	0	0	0	0	0	0	0	0	0	0	0	0	.000	.000
Sole, Alec	L-R	6-2	200	6-1-93	.281	.304	.275	89	320	41	90	12	5	5	36	21	2	5	1	63	14	3	.397	.328
Souza, Steven	R-R	6-4	225	4-24-89	.000	.000	.000	1	3	1	0	0	0	0	0	0	0	0	0	1	0	0	.000	.250
Toribio, Cristian	R-R	5-11	170	9-13-94	.233	.227	.236	98	343	29	80	13	2	3	19	15	0	1	1	64	5	1	.309	.265
Unroe, Riley	B-R	5-10	180	8-3-95	.220	.216	.221	105	369	42	81	12	3	4	31	47	4	8	5	91	18	10	.301	.311
Velazquez, Andrew	L-R	5-10	160	7-14-94	.262	.268	.260	75	286	31	75	6	2	1	14	21	1	3	2	71	11	6	.308	.313
Williams, Justin	L-R	6-2	215	8-20-95	.330	.333	.329	51	194	23	64	11	0	4	31	6	1	0	2	26	0	1	.448	.350

Pitching	B-T	HT	WT	DOB	W	L	ERA	G	GS	CG	SV	IP	H	R	ER	HR	BB	SO	AVG	vLH	vRH	K/9	BB/9
Alvarado, Jose	L-L	6-0	240	5-21-95	2	1	3.91	27	0	0	0	46	38	27	20	1	38	51	.222	.245	.212	9.98	7.43
Ascher, Steve	L-L	6-0	185	10-18-93	3	1	3.34	11	1	0	1	30	28	13	11	0	10	17	.252	.280	.244	5.16	3.03
Bellatti, Andrew	R-R	6-1	190	8-5-91	0	0	2.25	3	0	0	0	4	2	1	1	0	1	4	.143	.333	.000	9.00	2.25

Pitching

Pitching	B-T	HT	WT	DOB	W	L	ERA	G	GS	CG	SV	IP	H	R	ER	HR	BB	SO	AVG	vLH	vRH	K/9	BB/9
Bird, Kyle	L-L	6-2	175	4-12-93	2	1	0.50	11	0	0	3	18	11	1	1	0	1	22	.177	.120	.216	11.00	0.50
Bivens, Blake	R-R	6-2	205	8-11-95	0	0	6.35	2	0	0	0	6	13	6	4	0	0	6	.419	.143	.500	9.53	0.00
Boxberger, Brad	R-R	6-2	225	5-27-88	0	0	2.84	7	5	0	0	6	7	2	2	1	4	7	.280	.250	.294	9.95	5.68
Carroll, Damion	R-R	6-3	200	1-31-94	0	1	9.00	2	0	0	0	2	3	3	2	0	1	1	.300	.167	.500	4.50	4.50
Castillo, Diego	R-R	6-3	240	1-18-94	2	3	4.87	14	0	0	3	20	28	12	11	3	6	17	.326	.448	.263	7.52	2.66
Centeno, Henry	R-R	6-2	200	8-24-94	3	3	2.72	13	9	0	0	43	43	16	13	0	20	31	.274	.204	.306	6.49	4.19
Chirinos, Yonny	R-R	6-2	170	12-26-93	6	1	2.15	11	7	0	0	50	47	16	12	5	3	31	.240	.328	.203	5.54	0.54
Cobb, Alex	R-R	6-3	205	10-7-87	0	2	6.75	4	4	0	0	7	7	5	5	0	3	5	.259	.200	.333	6.75	4.05
Coleman, Casey	L-R	6-0	185	7-3-87	1	0	3.38	2	0	0	0	3	2	1	1	0	2	4	.182	.250	.000	13.50	6.75
Espinal, Yoel	R-R	6-2	200	11-7-92	0	0	2.70	2	0	0	0	3	3	1	1	1	1	3	.231	.333	.000	8.10	2.70
Fierro, Edwin	R-R	6-1	200	8-30-93	2	3	3.78	16	1	0	1	33	40	14	14	2	9	17	.305	.373	.263	4.59	2.43
Franco, Mike	R-R	5-11	200	11-30-91	7	5	1.89	33	3	0	4	71	48	23	15	3	35	73	.188	.183	.191	9.21	4.42
Garvin, Grayson	L-L	6-6	225	10-27-89	0	1	3.80	6	5	0	0	24	14	11	10	6	7	15	.173	.063	.200	5.70	2.66
Gibaut, Ian	R-R	6-3	250	11-19-93	1	2	2.85	27	0	0	3	47	45	20	15	2	19	45	.253	.278	.242	8.56	3.61
Harris, Greg	R-R	6-2	170	8-17-94	10	6	3.12	26	23	2	0	147	119	56	51	10	58	134	.228	.240	.221	8.20	3.55
Harrison, Jordan	R-L	6-1	180	4-9-91	0	1	2.77	8	0	0	0	13	17	6	4	0	6	10	.309	.136	.424	6.92	4.15
Honeywell, Brent	R-R	6-2	180	3-31-95	4	1	2.41	10	10	0	0	56	43	16	15	5	11	64	.211	.202	.222	10.29	1.77
Howell, Jeff	R-R	5-11	200	4-1-83	1	7	3.82	31	4	0	2	64	44	37	27	2	66	49	.205	.233	.190	6.93	9.33
Ingram, Tim	L-R	5-11	200	10-9-93	0	1	4.50	1	0	0	0	2	2	1	1	0	0	1	.250	.000	.333	4.50	0.00
Koch, Brandon	R-R	6-1	205	12-25-93	0	0	2.57	5	0	0	2	7	3	2	2	0	4	7	.130	.231	.000	9.00	5.14
Maisto, Greg	L-L	6-1	180	11-17-94	0	0	3.18	2	2	0	0	6	7	4	2	0	4	3	.333	.500	.316	4.76	6.35
Marks, Justin	L-L	6-3	205	1-12-88	0	1	1.80	1	1	0	0	5	3	1	1	0	1	4	.176	.000	.231	7.20	1.80
Miller, Brian	R-R	6-4	200	7-15-92	3	1	1.11	23	0	0	9	32	30	9	4	0	7	26	.248	.178	.289	8.35	1.95
Moss, Benton	R-R	6-2	193	2-21-93	7	10	3.72	26	21	1	0	138	132	67	57	11	39	118	.255	.284	.238	7.70	2.54
Pike, Chris	R-R	6-1	180	10-11-92	4	12	4.58	26	24	3	0	138	170	90	70	10	38	73	.311	.353	.286	4.77	2.48
Romero, Enny	L-L	6-3	215	1-24-91	0	0	0.00	1	1	0	0	1	0	0	0	0	0	2	.000	.000	.000	18.00	0.00
Sawyer, Nick	R-R	5-11	175	9-23-91	3	1	4.13	26	0	0	4	28	24	14	13	2	22	36	.214	.205	.221	11.44	6.99
Schreiber, Brad	R-R	6-3	225	2-13-91	0	2	2.45	11	1	0	2	18	10	8	5	1	6	21	.159	.200	.132	10.31	2.95
Smith, Alex	R-R	6-3	235	9-29-89	0	0	6.75	5	0	0	0	5	10	4	4	1	3	5	.435	.500	.364	8.44	5.06
Sweet, Austin	R-R	6-5	245	9-21-93	0	0	6.75	1	0	0	0	1	3	3	1	0	2	0	.375	.000	.500	0.00	13.50
Venters, Jonny	L-L	6-3	200	3-20-85	0	1	9.00	5	1	0	0	4	7	4	4	1	2	3	.412	.800	.250	6.75	4.50
Wagner, Neil	R-R	6-0	215	1-1-84	0	0	1.59	4	0	0	0	6	1	1	1	0	2	4	.059	.091	.000	6.35	3.18
Webb, Ryan	R-R	6-6	245	2-5-86	0	0	13.50	1	0	0	0	1	2	1	1	1	0	2	.500	—	.500	27.00	0.00
Whitley, Chase	R-R	6-3	215	6-14-89	0	0	0.00	3	3	0	0	9	6	0	0	0	1	10	.194	.111	.227	10.00	1.00
Wood, Hunter	R-R	6-1	175	8-12-93	3	3	1.70	11	9	0	0	64	34	15	12	2	24	56	.155	.149	.160	7.92	3.39

Fielding

Catcher	PCT	G	PO	A	E	DP	PB
Araiza	.961	17	108	16	5	2	3
Ciuffo	.981	50	351	69	8	5	7
Dominguez	1.000	3	20	2	0	1	0
Heim	.972	12	95	9	3	0	3
James	.980	55	363	68	9	3	13
Sole	1.000	1	2	0	0	0	1

First Base	PCT	G	PO	A	E	DP
Conrad	1.000	3	29	0	0	6
James	.995	28	201	20	1	24
Kay	.985	77	628	50	10	49
McCarthy	.985	20	122	9	2	13
Morrison	1.000	1	6	0	0	2
Pearce	1.000	1	3	0	0	0
Sole	.971	12	98	1	3	10

Second Base	PCT	G	PO	A	E	DP
Blair	.950	6	9	10	1	1
Conrad	1.000	17	33	37	0	8
Eureste	1.000	2	4	0	3	

Franklin	1.000	1	2	0	0	0
Kay	.941	5	8	8	1	3
Sole	.917	3	6	5	1	1
Unroe	.974	95	173	245	11	65
Velazquez	.971	11	12	22	1	5

Third Base	PCT	G	PO	A	E	DP
Blair	1.000	3	3	4	0	0
Conrad	.833	5	6	9	3	0
Eureste	1.000	2	1	3	0	0
Kay	.947	11	5	13	1	3
Sole	.930	18	11	29	3	6
Toribio	.896	88	53	136	22	10
Velazquez	.926	11	10	15	2	1

Shortstop	PCT	G	PO	A	E	DP
Blair	.943	8	10	23	2	8
Cronenworth	.959	29	38	78	5	21
Duffy	1.000	2	1	0	0	1
Kay	.800	1	2	2	1	0
Sole	.951	48	66	127	10	21

Unroe	1.000	1	1	3	0	0
Velazquez	.948	51	69	130	11	29

Outfield	PCT	G	PO	A	E	DP
Arcia	1.000	5	12	0	0	0
Conrad	.976	70	119	5	3	0
Cray	1.000	15	20	0	0	0
Franklin	.500	1	0	1	1	0
Gotta	.960	38	94	2	4	0
Guyer	1.000	1	3	0	0	0
Jackson	.981	59	100	3	2	0
Jennings	.800	2	4	0	1	0
Kay	.925	17	36	1	3	0
Kiermaier	1.000	1	2	0	0	0
Lukes	1.000	21	41	2	0	0
Mahtook	1.000	2	3	1	0	1
McCarthy	1.000	37	72	4	0	0
Milone	.993	110	274	7	2	4
Souza	1.000	1	1	0	0	0
Williams	.959	43	91	3	4	1

BOWLING GREEN HOT RODS
MIDWEST LEAGUE

LOW CLASS A

Batting

Batting	B-T	HT	WT	DOB	AVG	vLH	vRH	G	AB	R	H	2B	3B	HR	RBI	BB	HBP	SH	SF	SO	SB	CS	SLG	OBP
Cray, Landon	L-L	5-9	170	1-25-94	.275	.333	.265	25	80	7	22	6	0	1	14	8	1	2	0	12	1	1	.388	.348
Cronenworth, Jake	L-R	6-1	185	1-21-94	.322	.322	.321	81	314	66	101	15	6	3	48	54	7	2	3	57	12	7	.436	.429
De La Calle, Danny	R-R	6-3	220	9-18-92	.238	.222	.250	6	21	3	5	1	0	0	6	3	0	0	0	10	0	0	.286	.333
Eureste, Matt	L-R	6-1	175	7-29-93	.212	.150	.239	25	66	7	14	1	1	0	3	7	1	1	0	13	4	0	.258	.297
Law, Zac	R-R	6-0	190	7-8-96	.252	.254	.252	115	432	47	109	20	3	4	47	27	6	5	8	95	19	9	.340	.300
Lowe, Brandon	L-R	6-0	185	7-6-94	.248	.177	.272	107	379	61	94	15	3	5	42	60	5	3	2	77	6	3	.343	.357
Maris, Peter	L-R	5-10	175	9-16-93	.270	.208	.294	84	281	39	76	11	3	5	42	35	1	5	7	49	4	7	.384	.346
McCarthy, Joe	L-L	6-3	225	2-23-94	.288	.216	.310	43	153	31	44	12	0	3	29	33	5	0	2	30	11	2	.425	.425
Meyer, Kewby	L-L	6-1	195	10-27-92	.221	.389	.331	47	181	23	40	9	1	4	38	4	2	2	2	29	2	1	.446	.339
Moreno, Angel	R-R	6-2	200	7-31-96	.228	.247	.220	78	276	34	63	15	1	1	24	10	4	5	0	62	13	3	.301	.266
Olmedo-Barrera, David	L-R	6-1	195	6-22-94	.311	.324	.306	67	254	44	79	17	4	6	42	17	6	1	5	38	13	2	.480	.362

Batting	B-T	HT	WT	DOB	AVG	vLH	vRH	G	AB	R	H	2B	3B	HR	RBI	BB	HBP	SH	SF	SO	SB	CS	SLG	OBP
Padlo, Kevin	R-R	6-2	205	7-15-96	.229	.218	.234	115	414	71	95	22	3	16	66	79	7	2	6	134	14	9	.413	.358
Perez, Angel	R-R	6-2	200	1-10-95	.190	.278	.158	38	137	10	26	3	0	0	8	6	1	2	0	30	5	0	.212	.229
Rodriguez, David	R-R	6-1	215	2-25-96	.240	.276	.225	112	416	54	100	16	1	9	62	44	7	1	4	88	4	3	.349	.321
Russell, Michael	R-R	6-2	200	1-30-93	.293	.239	.315	109	396	76	116	28	5	8	48	45	13	1	3	64	29	9	.449	.381
Sanchez, Manny	R-R	6-2	225	10-6-95	.246	.301	.228	93	329	54	81	13	0	12	39	30	5	2	2	87	8	9	.395	.317
Sullivan, Brett	L-R	6-1	195	2-24-94	.283	.254	.293	118	470	75	133	34	0	13	81	24	0	1	6	70	17	4	.438	.314
Wiggins, Samm	R-R	5-8	185	12-29-92	.200	.000	.273	4	15	3	3	2	0	0	3	0	2	0	0	6	1	0	.333	.294

Pitching	B-T	HT	WT	DOB	W	L	ERA	G	GS	CG	SV	IP	H	R	ER	HR	BB	SO	AVG	vLH	vRH	K/9	BB/9
Alvarado, Jose	L-L	6-0	240	5-21-95	2	0	1.46	10	0	0	2	25	12	5	4	0	17	34	.150	.043	.193	12.41	6.20
Baez, Fernando	R-R	6-1	190	2-1-92	3	1	3.00	24	0	0	2	42	21	15	14	2	24	70	.145	.153	.137	15.00	5.14
Bastardo, Armando	R-R	6-0	175	7-11-94	1	2	3.53	29	0	0	3	66	65	30	26	4	24	52	.262	.244	.281	7.06	3.26
Bivens, Blake	R-R	6-2	205	8-11-95	8	4	2.52	16	16	0	0	93	75	30	26	3	34	96	.221	.163	.267	9.29	3.29
Bonnell, Bryan	L-R	6-5	210	9-28-93	4	2	4.59	24	0	0	2	51	49	26	26	5	23	63	.259	.192	.306	11.12	4.06
Brashears, Tyler	R-R	6-2	170	2-24-94	6	1	3.00	30	4	0	4	72	67	25	24	2	27	59	.252	.240	.262	7.38	3.38
Cabrera, Genesis	L-L	6-1	170	10-10-96	11	5	3.88	23	22	2	0	116	110	58	50	9	48	96	.255	.238	.264	7.45	3.72
Castillo, Diego	R-R	6-3	240	1-18-94	1	3	2.03	24	0	0	7	40	34	12	9	1	11	50	.221	.250	.192	11.25	2.48
Centeno, Henry	R-R	6-2	200	8-24-94	5	1	1.34	9	6	0	0	47	36	9	7	1	9	50	.214	.183	.237	9.57	1.72
Chirinos, Yonny	R-R	6-2	170	12-26-93	1	0	2.31	4	2	0	0	12	8	4	3	0	1	9	.182	.250	.143	6.94	0.77
Espinal, Yoel	R-R	6-2	200	11-7-92	5	0	1.84	26	1	0	4	59	32	16	12	3	41	71	.158	.194	.120	10.89	6.29
Gibaut, Ian	R-R	6-3	250	11-19-93	1	0	0.93	7	0	0	1	10	6	2	1	0	1	18	.171	.214	.143	16.76	0.93
Hawkins, Taylor	R-R	6-0	205	9-17-93	2	5	4.21	20	9	0	0	68	55	40	32	2	53	32	.231	.222	.241	4.21	6.98
Ingram, Tim	L-R	5-11	200	10-9-93	1	2	4.01	19	0	0	7	25	12	12	11	0	4	20	.239	.289	.191	7.30	1.46
Karalus, Reece	R-R	6-3	245	6-14-94	2	3	3.33	21	0	0	1	46	43	21	17	6	14	48	.246	.296	.202	9.39	2.74
Lopez, Eduar	R-R	6-0	180	2-21-95	5	2	3.05	8	8	1	0	44	41	22	15	0	15	34	.241	.280	.211	6.90	3.05
Mujica, Jose	R-R	6-2	235	6-29-96	8	4	3.46	24	24	0	0	130	127	54	50	13	35	100	.258	.258	.257	6.92	2.42
Ramirez, Roel	R-R	6-1	210	5-26-95	7	8	4.68	25	18	0	3	108	126	68	56	10	30	79	.291	.315	.266	6.60	2.51
Tapia, Alexis	R-R	6-2	240	8-10-95	0	1	8.10	2	2	0	0	10	14	10	9	1	4	10	.341	.381	.300	9.00	3.60
Torres, Elias	R-R	6-1	176	2-22-92	1	1	1.42	12	0	0	0	19	8	4	3	0	18	26	.125	.182	.065	12.32	8.53
Varga, Cameron	R-R	6-2	190	8-19-94	2	1	7.24	3	3	0	0	14	19	12	11	1	4	16	.322	.318	.324	10.54	2.63
Velasquez, Mike	L-L	6-1	215	2-28-93	8	9	4.86	24	22	0	0	113	133	76	61	10	28	113	.290	.338	.270	9.00	2.23
Yepez, Angel	R-R	6-1	225	4-27-95	0	0	8.22	2	2	0	0	8	13	7	7	2	3	3	.419	.538	.333	3.52	3.52

Fielding

Catcher	PCT	G	PO	A	E	DP	PB
De La Calle	1.000	2	11	1	0	0	0
Rodriguez	.977	69	567	74	15	8	11
Sullivan	.983	65	487	84	10	10	22
Wiggins	.968	3	27	3	1	0	1

First Base	PCT	G	PO	A	E	DP
De La Calle	.667	1	1	1	1	0
Eureste	.984	11	58	3	1	6
Maris	1.000	7	48	3	0	3
McCarthy	.988	40	301	22	4	25
Meyer	.992	44	346	29	3	34
Russell	.986	41	310	32	5	29

Second Base	PCT	G	PO	A	E	DP
Eureste	.955	7	10	11	1	3
Lowe	.960	88	135	203	14	46
Maris	.971	40	50	82	4	18
Russell	.971	10	16	18	1	3

Third Base	PCT	G	PO	A	E	DP
Eureste	1.000	3	1	3	0	1
Maris	.974	16	15	22	1	3
Padlo	.960	109	91	152	10	21
Russell	.929	11	12	27	3	5

Shortstop	PCT	G	PO	A	E	DP
Cronenworth	.956	81	105	176	13	32
Eureste	1.000	2	2	0	0	0
Maris	.952	18	21	38	3	9
Russell	.971	38	58	108	5	20

Outfield	PCT	G	PO	A	E	DP
Cray	1.000	25	53	1	0	0
Law	.993	115	286	11	2	2
Maris	—	1	0	0	0	0
McCarthy	1.000	1	3	0	0	0
Meyer	—	1	0	0	0	0
Moreno	.991	78	203	6	2	1
Olmedo-Barrera	.966	65	107	6	4	2
Perez	.986	37	68	5	1	2
Russell	1.000	6	10	0	0	0
Sanchez	.958	92	172	9	8	4

HUDSON VALLEY RENEGADES

SHORT-SEASON

NEW YORK-PENN LEAGUE

Batting	B-T	HT	WT	DOB	AVG	vLH	vRH	G	AB	R	H	2B	3B	HR	RBI	BB	HBP	SH	SF	SO	SB	CS	SLG	OBP
Astacio, Joseph	L-R	6-0	155	6-5-94	.228	.389	.154	16	57	6	13	0	0	0	4	0	0	2	0	15	5	1	.228	.228
Betts, Chris	L-R	6-2	215	3-10-97	.157	.034	.244	23	70	2	11	4	0	0	7	17	2	0	1	23	0	0	.214	.333
Boldt, Ryan	L-R	6-2	210	11-22-94	.218	.238	.211	43	170	17	37	5	1	1	15	10	5	0	1	24	8	9	.276	.280
Brujan, Vidal	B-R	5-9	155	4-9-98	.000	.000	.000	2	8	1	0	0	0	0	0	1	0	0	0	1	2	0	.000	.111
Butera, Blake	R-R	5-9	175	8-7-92	.154	.000	.222	4	13	0	2	0	0	0	2	0	1	0	0	4	0	0	.154	.214
Cray, Landon	L-L	5-9	170	1-25-94	.238	.375	.206	14	42	6	10	0	1	1	6	6	2	1	0	6	4	1	.357	.360
De La Calle, Danny	R-R	6-3	220	9-18-92	.205	.200	.207	43	151	11	31	7	1	0	12	8	3	1	2	60	0	2	.265	.256
Fraley, Jake	L-L	6-0	195	5-25-95	.238	.190	.259	55	206	34	49	9	7	1	18	26	6	0	1	34	33	9	.364	.339
Haley, Jim	R-R	6-1	195	2-23-95	.285	.264	.293	65	246	27	70	7	3	1	19	20	3	0	3	42	13	7	.350	.342
Hernandez, Miguel	R-R	6-2	175	12-28-95	.231	.000	.250	4	13	2	3	2	0	0	2	1	0	1	0	6	0	0	.385	.286
Lowe, Nathan	L-R	6-4	235	7-7-95	.300	.365	.277	67	247	26	74	18	2	4	40	30	5	0	3	39	1	0	.437	.382
Mastrobuoni, Miles	L-R	5-11	175	10-31-95	.267	.185	.301	61	221	26	59	11	3	0	21	25	1	2	1	41	9	7	.344	.343
Meyer, Kewby	L-L	6-1	195	10-27-92	.188	.400	.091	5	16	0	3	0	0	0	4	3	1	0	2	2	0	0	.188	.318
Olson, Joe	R-R	6-0	220	11-20-92	.270	.167	.320	15	37	3	10	2	0	0	5	4	1	1	1	9	0	0	.324	.349
Perez, Angel	R-R	6-2	200	1-10-95	.275	.308	.261	60	222	25	61	11	6	1	15	10	4	2	0	48	14	8	.392	.318
Popadics, Jon	R-R	5-10	180	9-17-92	.277	.276	.278	32	119	17	33	6	1	0	11	9	2	0	0	14	5	1	.345	.338
Pujols, Bill	R-R	5-11	160	7-19-94	.240	.297	.224	59	171	24	41	13	0	1	12	25	5	2	5	53	9	4	.333	.343
Rojas, Jose	R-R	6-2	180	8-15-93	.310	.273	.329	36	126	18	39	8	0	1	20	4	1	1	0	21	0	1	.397	.336
Rojas, Oscar	R-R	5-11	165	7-5-96	.188	.160	.205	17	64	3	12	1	0	0	6	3	1	1	1	21	0	4	.203	.232
Whitley, Garrett	R-R	6-1	205	3-13-97	.266	.299	.251	65	256	38	68	12	7	1	31	30	6	0	0	75	21	5	.379	.356

Pitching	B-T	HT	WT	DOB	W	L	ERA	G	GS	CG	SV	IP	H	R	ER	HR	BB	SO	AVG	vLH	vRH	K/9	BB/9
Alonzo, Jose	R-R	6-4	191	2-24-93	1	3	2.23	13	4	0	3	32	28	9	8	0	5	24	.239	.167	.280	6.68	1.39
Burke, Brock	L-L	6-4	190	8-4-96	3	3	3.39	13	13	0	0	61	53	25	23	1	29	61	.235	.241	.233	9.00	4.28
Busfield, J.D.	R-R	6-7	230	5-5-95	4	1	1.53	15	0	0	2	35	28	7	6	1	6	22	.214	.245	.192	5.60	1.53
Clayton, Porter	L-L	6-4	220	5-22-93	1	3	3.62	15	0	0	2	37	36	16	15	0	9	20	.252	.237	.257	4.82	2.17
Fulenchek, Garrett	R-R	6-4	205	6-7-96	1	3	4.62	15	2	0	0	25	27	19	13	1	27	12	.281	.211	.328	4.26	9.59
Ingram, Tim	L-R	5-11	200	10-9-93	0	0	3.60	6	0	0	0	10	9	4	4	0	2	12	.237	.231	.240	10.80	1.80
Jones, Spencer	R-R	6-5	205	9-22-94	3	0	2.67	15	0	0	1	34	27	11	10	1	8	36	.209	.123	.278	9.62	2.14
Lawson, Brandon	R-R	6-3	205	12-13-94	6	1	2.03	16	0	0	2	31	30	13	7	0	6	27	.244	.295	.215	7.84	1.74
Lopez, Eduar	R-R	6-0	180	2-21-95	3	1	2.00	5	5	0	0	27	20	8	6	0	4	18	.213	.146	.264	6.00	1.33
McKinley, Jayson	R-R	6-4	210	1-18-94	0	0	1.21	11	0	0	7	22	9	3	3	1	3	29	.122	.111	.128	11.69	1.21
Mendez, Deivy	R-R	6-2	165	10-27-95	1	3	2.65	17	0	0	0	37	16	15	11	2	26	51	.133	.148	.121	12.29	6.27
Moran, Spencer	R-R	6-6	200	4-2-96	4	1	2.64	14	12	0	0	61	44	20	18	7	28	38	.203	.198	.206	5.58	4.11
Navas, Adrian	R-R	6-2	150	4-13-96	5	2	2.39	12	12	0	0	60	46	19	16	4	13	45	.216	.200	.226	6.71	1.94
Nunez, Luis	R-R	5-10	185	10-29-91	0	1	6.00	2	0	0	0	3	4	2	2	0	2	3	.308	.400	.250	9.00	6.00
Ott, Travis	L-L	6-4	170	6-29-95	6	0	1.06	13	10	0	0	59	31	8	7	2	18	61	.153	.250	.112	9.25	2.73
Rodriguez, Noel	R-R	6-3	190	6-17-94	4	2	2.35	15	9	1	2	54	41	17	14	1	15	39	.215	.159	.262	6.54	2.52
Rosillo, Eduard	R-R	6-4	210	12-22-93	2	3	4.98	8	8	0	0	34	31	22	19	1	25	35	.240	.232	.232	9.17	6.55
Serrapica, Joe	L-R	6-1	215	5-25-94	1	0	0.00	16	0	0	8	22	13	0	0	0	5	28	.165	.194	.146	11.28	2.01
Torres, Elias	R-R	6-1	176	2-22-92	0	1	2.00	6	0	0	0	9	3	3	2	0	6	10	.107	.000	.188	10.00	6.00

Fielding

C: Grant-Parks 6, Lorenzo 33, Pinto 17, Ramirez 14. **1B:** Davis 19, Melley 51. **2B:** Butera 9, Stemp 1, Tenerowicz 58. **3B:** Butera 31, Lowe 23, Rodriguez 13. **SS:** Butera 8, Rondon 50, Tansel 11. **OF:** Benard 24, Cabrera 60, Calloway 5, Gustave 53, Rojas 26, Sanchez 14, Stemp 23.

PRINCETON RAYS
ROOKIE
APPALACHIAN LEAGUE

Batting	B-T	HT	WT	DOB	AVG	vLH	vRH	G	AB	R	H	2B	3B	HR	RBI	BB	HBP	SH	SF	SO	SB	CS	SLG	OBP
Benard, Isaac	L-R	5-10	225	1-2-96	.255	.206	.276	34	110	22	28	3	0	3	16	15	2	0	1	26	3	0	.364	.352
Butera, Blake	R-R	5-9	175	8-7-92	.255	.281	.241	49	165	23	42	12	1	2	23	18	9	7	3	40	5	3	.376	.354
Cabrera, Eleardo	L-R	5-11	195	11-8-95	.311	.333	.302	60	238	44	74	12	2	7	36	17	10	1	4	73	8	4	.466	.375
Calloway, Ryan	L-L	5-11	160	6-29-94	.250	.286	.231	6	20	3	5	0	0	0	1	0	0	0	0	5	2	1	.250	.286
Davis, Devin	R-R	6-3	215	2-14-97	.238	.107	.304	25	84	17	20	6	1	1	10	6	4	0	2	25	0	0	.369	.313
Grant-Parks, Blake	R-R	6-1	190	7-15-93	.298	.350	.259	15	47	7	14	5	0	1	7	1	0	0	0	5	0	0	.468	.313
Gustave, Emilio	R-R	6-2	200	1-26-95	.252	.297	.232	57	206	36	52	12	2	6	37	22	6	0	3	70	5	2	.417	.338
Lorenzo, Rafelin	R-R	6-2	218	1-15-97	.207	.293	.172	35	140	23	29	7	0	1	18	2	2	0	2	34	0	0	.279	.226
Lowe, Josh	L-R	6-4	190	2-2-98	.238	.182	.259	26	80	11	19	0	2	3	11	17	0	0	3	32	1	1	.400	.360
Melley, Bobby	L-R	6-3	230	4-10-94	.323	.290	.339	53	189	34	61	15	0	4	32	21	6	0	2	33	0	1	.466	.404
Pinto, Rene	R-R	5-11	195	11-2-96	.309	.188	.346	18	68	13	21	7	0	6	15	3	1	0	1	17	0	0	.676	.342
Ramirez, Jean	R-R	6-0	210	4-27-93	.246	.158	.286	19	61	7	15	0	0	2	6	4	0	0	0	11	0	1	.344	.313
Rodriguez, Juan	R-R	6-0	175	2-13-97	.171	.063	.240	13	41	6	7	1	0	1	3	5	1	0	0	10	0	0	.268	.277
Rojas, Oscar	R-R	5-11	165	1-24-95	.318	.422	.264	34	132	18	42	9	3	2	17	10	2	1	1	37	7	3	.477	.372
Rondon, Adrian	R-R	6-1	190	7-7-98	.249	.328	.209	52	193	29	48	10	2	7	36	13	2	1	1	58	1	5	.430	.301
Sanchez, Jesus	L-R	6-2	185	10-7-97	.347	.308	.361	14	49	8	17	4	0	3	8	3	0	1	0	12	1	0	.612	.385
Stemp, Trek	R-R	5-10	170	7-20-93	.280	.362	.222	41	168	25	47	7	1	0	9	9	5	3	0	29	7	2	.333	.335
Tansel, Deion	R-R	5-8	155	6-4-94	.314	.455	.250	11	35	6	11	2	0	1	4	1	1	1	0	3	0	0	.457	.351
Tenerowicz, Robbie	R-R	6-1	185	1-6-95	.291	.263	.301	58	203	31	59	17	0	6	38	15	5	2	1	47	1	5	.463	.353

Pitching	B-T	HT	WT	DOB	W	L	ERA	G	GS	CG	SV	IP	H	R	ER	HR	BB	SO	AVG	vLH	vRH	K/9	BB/9
Agosto, Edrick	R-R	6-4	245	11-28-96	3	3	5.96	11	10	0	0	48	53	41	32	6	12	39	.279	.286	.273	7.26	2.23
Bayer, Peter	R-R	6-4	195	3-6-94	2	1	0.83	10	7	0	0	33	18	4	3	1	3	45	.158	.115	.194	12.40	0.83
Brito, Sandy	R-R	6-1	170	7-19-96	3	0	4.00	15	0	0	0	27	17	12	12	3	13	27	.175	.205	.155	9.00	4.33
Clark, Ethan	R-R	6-5	235	10-26-94	7	2	2.91	12	9	0	1	59	47	22	19	7	15	44	.216	.152	.262	6.75	2.30
Diomartich, Eric	L-L	6-2	180	5-4-94	0	0	9.00	3	0	0	0	6	10	7	6	3	4	5	.385	.000	.417	7.50	6.00
Disla, Jose	R-R	6-2	165	3-11-96	0	2	4.94	8	7	0	0	27	24	15	15	3	12	26	.242	.216	.271	8.56	3.95
Estrella, Alex	L-L	5-11	170	9-12-93	1	1	5.47	13	0	0	2	25	26	16	15	4	10	25	.265	.333	.243	9.12	3.65
Letkeman, Reign	L-R	6-3	180	5-12-95	1	3	5.19	15	0	0	0	26	26	17	15	0	12	21	.252	.261	.246	7.27	4.15
Linares, Resly	L-L	6-2	170	12-11-97	2	3	5.34	8	7	0	0	32	40	21	19	6	8	30	.305	.242	.327	8.44	2.25
Long, Sam	L-L	6-1	185	7-19-95	1	1	3.12	10	3	0	1	26	26	12	9	0	8	33	.255	.208	.269	11.42	2.77
Lopez, Hector	R-R	6-4	190	6-10-95	1	3	3.96	12	9	0	1	52	45	26	23	3	18	61	.224	.263	.200	10.49	3.10
McAfee, Brian	R-R	6-3	210	9-30-92	1	1	1.88	11	2	0	3	29	26	8	6	0	2	24	.234	.258	.204	7.53	0.63
Moats, Dalton	L-L	6-3	175	5-24-94	3	2	2.40	17	0	0	2	30	34	13	8	2	5	29	.286	.176	.329	8.70	1.50
Ortiz, Willy	R-R	6-1	180	7-20-95	8	0	3.25	11	11	0	0	55	67	25	20	5	6	47	.307	.310	.305	7.64	0.98
Ramos, Reimin	R-R	6-1	190	4-27-96	0	2	3.03	16	0	0	7	30	26	12	10	1	7	37	.236	.239	.234	11.22	2.12
Romero, Orlando	R-R	6-0	211	9-26-96	3	3	4.45	14	1	0	0	30	31	17	15	0	17	27	.265	.294	.242	8.01	5.04
Rosenberg, Kenny	L-L	6-1	195	7-9-95	0	1	5.87	3	1	0	0	8	8	5	5	1	2	6	.286	.333	.280	7.04	2.35
Sweet, Austin	R-R	6-5	245	9-21-93	1	0	2.65	10	0	0	0	17	10	8	5	2	4	12	.164	.316	.095	6.35	2.12
York, Mikey	R-R	6-2	190	2-24-96	0	0	16.88	2	0	0	0	3	7	8	5	1	1	3	.438	.400	.455	10.13	3.38
Zak, Bryce	R-R	6-3	210	11-1-91	1	1	5.93	7	0	0	0	14	15	11	9	2	5	10	.273	.227	.303	6.59	3.29

Fielding

C: Grant-Parks 6, Lorenzo 33, Pinto 17, Ramirez 14. **1B:** Davis 19, Melley 51. **2B:** Butera 9, Stemp 1, Tenerowicz 58. **3B:** Butera 31, Lowe 23, Rodriguez 13. **SS:** Butera 8, Rondon 50, Tansel 11. **OF:** Benard 24, Cabrera 60, Calloway 5, Gustave 53, Rojas 26, Sanchez 14, Stemp 23.

GCL RAYS
GULF COAST LEAGUE
ROOKIE

Batting	B-T	HT	WT	DOB	AVG	vLH	vRH	G	AB	R	H	2B	3B	HR	RBI	BB	HBP	SH	SF	SO	SB	CS	SLG	OBP
Alvarez, Alexander	R-R	5-11	200	9-14-96	.169	.138	.183	32	89	7	15	1	1	1	9	7	1	0	2	28	1	0	.236	.232
Arias, Juan	R-R	6-3	199	9-16-95	.213	.200	.220	26	89	9	19	2	0	2	15	11	0	0	1	39	2	1	.303	.297
Arrowood, J.D.	L-L	6-6	225	3-18-94	.294	.360	.258	41	143	18	42	9	1	2	22	14	5	0	0	40	3	1	.413	.377
Betts, Chris	L-R	6-2	215	3-10-97	.214	.100	.250	16	42	5	9	2	1	0	6	10	1	0	2	13	2	0	.310	.364
Brosseau, Mike	R-R	5-10	185	3-15-94	.319	.394	.288	35	113	20	36	12	1	0	21	15	8	3	3	19	7	3	.442	.424
Brujan, Vidal	B-R	5-9	155	2-9-98	.282	.263	.294	49	202	41	57	12	5	1	8	14	5	1	0	15	8	5	.406	.344
Caldwell, Ryan	R-R	6-3	195	12-25-95	.151	.091	.176	26	73	5	11	0	0	0	9	6	0	2	0	30	3	1	.151	.215
Calloway, Ryan	L-L	5-11	160	6-29-94	.238	.313	.213	21	63	6	15	1	0	0	6	3	3	0	0	10	2	1	.254	.304
Ciuffo, Nick	L-R	6-1	205	3-7-95	.067	.000	.100	5	15	1	1	0	0	0	0	2	0	0	0	2	0	0	.067	.176
Dominguez, Wilmer	R-R	5-10	180	6-19-91	.500	—	.500	1	2	1	1	0	0	0	0	0	0	0	0	0	0	0	1.000	.500
Eureste, Matt	L-R	6-1	175	7-29-93	.077	.000	.100	6	13	2	1	0	0	0	0	2	0	0	2	0	0	0	.077	.200
Goetzman, Granden	R-R	6-4	200	11-14-92	.467	1.000	.333	4	15	4	7	0	0	0	2	1	0	0	0	5	2	0	.467	.500
Gomez, Moises	R-R	5-11	200	8-27-98	.220	.194	.238	47	168	20	37	9	3	1	10	12	1	0	2	37	4	3	.327	.273
Jackson, Bralin	R-L	6-2	183	12-2-93	.364	.273	.455	6	22	4	8	3	0	0	1	2	0	0	0	4	0	2	.500	.417
Kiermaier, Kevin	R-L	6-1	215	4-22-90	.000	.000	.000	1	2	0	0	0	0	0	0	0	0	0	0	1	0	0	.000	.333
Lowe, Josh	L-R	6-4	190	2-2-98	.258	.231	.269	28	93	14	24	6	1	2	15	20	0	0	1	27	1	1	.409	.386
Mahtook, Mikie	R-R	6-1	200	11-30-89	.333	.000	.500	1	3	0	1	0	0	0	1	0	0	0	0	1	0	0	.333	.500
Marrero, Gilbert	L-L	6-2	195	8-9-96	.202	.179	.212	28	94	9	19	6	0	0	7	7	0	1	0	35	1	0	.266	.257
O'Conner, Justin	R-R	6-0	190	3-31-92	.325	.429	.269	12	40	8	13	2	0	2	5	5	0	0	0	7	0	0	.525	.400
Parrett, David	R-R	6-0	200	1-17-94	.120	.000	.214	9	25	3	3	1	0	0	2	2	0	2	0	13	0	0	.160	.185
Pinto, Rene	R-R	5-11	195	11-21-96	.222	.185	.241	22	81	9	18	2	0	2	13	4	2	0	1	21	0	0	.321	.273
Roach, Joey	L-R	6-0	205	8-27-93	.171	.000	.226	14	41	5	7	1	1	0	7	2	1	1	0	4	1	1	.244	.227
Sanchez, Jesus	L-R	6-2	185	10-7-97	.323	.373	.301	42	164	25	53	6	8	4	31	6	0	0	3	31	1	5	.530	.341
Santana, Yerson	R-R	6-3	195	12-2-96	.100	.000	.133	7	20	0	2	0	0	0	1	2	3	0	0	11	0	1	.100	.280
Santiago, Kevin	B-R	6-0	170	9-28-97	.202	.261	.162	35	114	15	23	5	0	2	11	11	7	3	1	36	2	1	.298	.308
Seibert, Mac	R-R	6-0	195	11-17-93	.143	.000	.250	3	7	0	1	0	0	0	0	0	0	0	0	3	0	0	.143	.143
Tansel, Deion	R-R	5-8	155	6-4-94	.271	.125	.348	21	70	8	19	4	0	0	6	4	6	1	0	3	1	2	.329	.363
Vasquez, Jose	R-R	6-1	205	4-4-96	.200	.154	.219	39	135	18	27	5	1	2	15	13	7	1	1	56	4	2	.296	.301

Pitching	B-T	HT	WT	DOB	W	L	ERA	G	GS	CG	SV	IP	H	R	ER	HR	BB	SO	AVG	vLH	vRH	K/9	BB/9
Centeno, Henry	R-R	6-2	200	8-24-94	0	0	0.00	1	1	0	0	3	2	0	0	0	0	2	.200	.143	.333	6.00	0.00
Collins, V.J.	R-R	5-10	170	7-6-92	0	1	9.24	5	0	0	1	13	16	16	13	1	8	3	.302	.241	.375	2.13	5.68
Diomartich, Eric	L-L	6-2	180	5-4-94	0	5	3.26	9	6	0	0	30	24	17	11	0	9	17	.216	.250	.205	5.04	2.67
Estrella, Alex	L-L	5-11	170	9-14-94	0	0	0.00	2	0	0	1	4	4	4	0	0	2	5	.235	.500	.091	11.25	4.50
Franklin, Austin	R-R	6-3	215	10-2-97	1	2	2.70	11	9	0	1	43	30	16	13	0	16	40	.192	.183	.200	8.31	3.32
Garvin, Grayson	L-L	6-6	225	10-27-89	0	0	2.70	2	1	0	0	10	7	3	3	0	2	10	.206	.333	.136	9.00	1.80
Graziano, Joey	R-R	6-1	190	11-16-93	0	2	5.87	9	0	0	0	15	20	11	10	0	6	10	.323	.333	.587	3.52	3.52
House, Tyler	L-L	6-3	200	10-15-92	4	2	3.80	12	0	0	3	21	28	10	9	1	7	19	.329	.320	.333	8.02	2.95
Karalus, Reece	R-R	6-3	245	6-14-94	2	0	4.50	2	0	0	0	4	3	2	2	0	0	2	.214	.200	.250	4.50	0.00
Lebron, Thomas	R-R	6-2	160	8-8-95	0	1	3.93	6	4	0	0	18	27	11	8	0	10	12	.351	.400	.281	5.89	4.91
Long, Sam	L-L	6-1	185	7-8-95	0	0	9.00	1	0	0	0	1	1	1	1	1	2	1	.250	.000	.333	18.00	9.00
Maisto, Greg	L-L	6-1	180	11-17-94	0	0	1.69	5	4	0	0	11	7	2	2	0	3	13	.184	.273	.148	10.97	2.53
McGee, Easton	R-R	6-6	205	12-26-97	1	1	3.09	6	4	0	0	23	19	8	8	1	8	14	.218	.268	.174	5.40	3.09
McKinley, Jayson	R-R	6-4	210	1-18-94	1	2	5.63	5	0	0	1	8	7	5	5	1	1	11	.226	.200	.250	12.38	1.13
Nunez, Luis	R-R	5-10	185	10-29-91	2	0	1.13	12	1	0	2	16	7	6	2	1	5	17	.125	.083	.156	9.56	2.81
Ortiz, Jesus	R-R	6-2	185	8-4-97	3	3	3.48	12	7	0	0	44	41	19	17	1	10	26	.243	.253	.234	5.32	2.05
Padilla, Nicholas	R-R	6-2	220	12-24-96	0	2	2.01	8	0	0	0	22	22	10	5	0	7	19	.250	.233	.267	7.66	2.82
Parente, Anthony	R-R	6-2	210	5-29-94	3	1	4.87	12	0	0	0	20	16	13	11	0	17	9	.222	.138	.279	3.98	7.52
Rodriguez, Angel	R-R	6-2	187	5-13-93	1	3	3.00	9	0	0	0	21	24	12	7	0	3	12	.293	.308	.279	5.14	1.29
Rosenberg, Kenny	L-L	6-1	195	7-9-95	1	1	1.31	9	0	0	2	21	15	5	3	1	4	27	.208	.200	.213	11.76	1.74
Rosillo, Eduard	R-R	6-4	210	12-22-93	2	0	0.56	4	2	0	0	16	11	3	1	0	10	23	.200	.143	.235	12.94	5.63
Salinas, Jhonleider	R-R	6-7	215	9-25-95	1	0	1.93	5	5	0	0	23	15	8	5	0	10	14	.181	.184	.176	5.40	3.86
Sweet, Austin	R-R	6-5	245	9-21-93	0	0	1.50	8	0	0	1	12	8	2	2	1	5	12	.182	.154	.222	9.00	3.75
Trageton, Zach	R-R	6-1	225	9-2-98	3	1	2.36	10	7	0	0	42	36	15	11	2	6	29	.229	.205	.253	6.21	1.29
Vogel, Matt	R-R	6-0	185	7-27-95	3	2	3.54	14	0	0	1	28	16	12	11	2	14	28	.167	.104	.229	9.00	4.50
Williams, Kevin	L-L	6-1	220	4-12-91	0	1	3.38	11	0	0	0	19	22	13	7	0	14	12	.310	.259	.341	5.79	6.75
York, Mikey	R-R	6-2	190	2-24-96	0	1	10.80	4	0	0	0	7	14	8	8	1	2	5	.438	.533	.353	6.75	2.70
Zak, Bryce	R-R	6-3	210	11-1-91	0	0	2.35	8	0	0	2	15	7	5	4	1	7	17	.132	.091	.200	9.98	4.11

Fielding
C: Alvarez 25, Betts 10, Ciuffo 4, Dominguez 1, O'Conner 8, Parrett 1, Pinto 15, Roach 6, Seibert 2. **1B:** Arrowood 38, Marrero 22. **2B:** Arias 1, Brosseau 10, Brujan 49, Tansel 1. **3B:** Arias 19, Brosseau 19, Eureste 2, Lowe 22. **SS:** Brosseau 4, Eureste 3, Santiago 34, Tansel 19. **OF:** Caldwell 25, Calloway 20, Goetzman 3, Gomez 45, Jackson 5, Kiermaier 1, Marrero 2, Parrett 3, Sanchez 41, Santana 6, Tonton 39.

DSL RAYS
DOMINICAN SUMMER LEAGUE
ROOKIE

Batting	B-T	HT	WT	DOB	AVG	vLH	vRH	G	AB	R	H	2B	3B	HR	RBI	BB	HBP	SH	SF	SO	SB	CS	SLG	OBP
Alvarez, Roberto	R-R	5-11	151	7-28-99	.291	.250	.305	43	158	11	46	6	1	0	20	13	6	0	2	25	2	2	.342	.363
Aranda, Jonathan	R-R	5-10	173	5-23-98	.257	.303	.246	49	175	23	45	6	5	1	17	17	7	2	1	32	5	4	.366	.345
Arias, Luis	R-R	6-1	165	10-7-98	.195	.219	.188	40	128	13	25	7	0	2	8	18	0	0	0	52	2	0	.297	.295
Arrendoll, Johampher	L-R	6-2	165	10-15-98	.141	.091	.162	53	185	19	26	4	2	0	7	21	3	0	3	59	4	5	.184	.236

Batting

Batting	B-T	HT	WT	DOB	AVG	vLH	vRH	G	AB	R	H	2B	3B	HR	RBI	BB	HBP	SH	SF	SO	SB	CS	SLG	OBP
Balbuena, Alfredo	R-R	5-9	178	11-25-98	.251	.242	.254	48	175	32	44	10	2	2	16	19	3	2	1	28	6	5	.366	.333
Brito, Raider	R-R	6-1	164	5-17-99	.215	.120	.240	36	121	12	26	1	2	0	6	14	1	1	1	25	8	8	.256	.299
Cabrera, Moises	L-R	6-1	188	12-4-96	.256	.214	.268	56	199	19	51	11	2	1	29	11	5	0	3	28	5	5	.347	.332
Cervantes, Victor	R-R	6-0	180	4-6-99	.191	—	—	43	136	9	26	6	1	0	14	6	1	1	1	30	1	1	.250	.229
Contreras, Victor	R-R	6-2	170	10-28-97	.147	—	—	32	95	8	14	6	0	0	10	12	3	1	2	35	4	2	.211	.259
Del Palacio, Jose	L-R	6-0	185	10-14-98	.222	—	—	56	207	24	46	9	2	2	14	15	2	0	1	63	0	3	.314	.280
Diaz, Pedro	R-R	6-3	210	1-9-99	.349	.455	.327	18	63	7	22	4	0	2	12	7	3	0	2	19	1	3	.508	.427
Garcia, Juan	R-R	6-0	191	1-6-99	.178	.167	.183	57	202	21	36	4	0	2	15	15	2	1	1	30	5	5	.228	.241
Hernandez, Ronaldo	R-R	6-1	185	11-11-97	.340	.359	.335	54	206	34	70	12	0	6	35	20	3	0	0	12	3	5	.485	.406
Hernandez, Yeilin	B-R	5-11	180	3-12-96	.210	.195	.214	50	167	16	35	8	1	3	17	20	4	1	2	33	2	4	.323	.306
Leon, Luis	B-R	6-0	175	9-10-98	.227	.140	.250	55	207	23	47	12	1	1	24	20	1	1	1	39	3	3	.309	.297
Lugo, Henry	R-R	5-11	160	11-30-95	.237	.250	.235	41	118	15	28	3	2	0	16	17	1	2	1	15	4	3	.297	.336
Martinez, Yunior	B-R	6-1	166	12-24-98	.219	.206	.222	47	187	36	41	8	1	0	18	6	1	1	1	45	14	5	.273	.307
Parra, Darwin	R-R	6-0	160	9-21-96	.146	—	—	20	41	1	6	2	0	0	3	2	0	1	0	7	0	0	.195	.182
Pena, Tony	R-R	5-11	180	9-24-97	.312	.409	.287	30	109	24	34	9	1	3	13	15	4	0	0	29	3	1	.495	.414
Pereira, Jose	R-R	5-11	153	3-3-99	.168	.036	.193	53	173	18	29	5	1	0	13	14	5	1	2	37	3	3	.191	.247
Perez, Luis	R-R	6-0	241	6-16-97	.242	.294	.230	29	91	11	22	5	0	1	9	7	4	0	2	25	1	0	.330	.317
Pimentel, Luis	R-R	6-1	145	1-7-98	.206	.237	.197	47	155	16	32	4	2	0	14	16	4	1	3	40	3	5	.258	.292
Polanco, Sabriel	R-R	6-1	180	4-4-95	.284	.228	.302	60	229	40	65	15	2	6	37	24	6	0	0	28	6	0	.445	.367
Rincon, Santiago	L-L	6-0	195	12-20-96	.204	.250	.196	36	108	18	22	3	1	2	11	20	7	0	3	38	2	2	.306	.355
Rodriguez, Alex	L-L	6-4	210	9-14-93	.249	.262	.244	49	169	24	42	4	0	2	27	26	1	0	4	33	0	0	.308	.345
Silva, Darwin	R-R	6-0	187	4-29-97	.207	.120	.233	32	111	10	23	6	1	0	11	7	0	0	1	24	1	2	.279	.276
Tejeda, Gioser	R-R	5-11	204	9-23-97	.258	.273	.255	21	62	5	16	1	0	1	3	2	1	0	0	7	1	0	.323	.292
Torrealba, Jose	R-R	6-2	171	10-15-97	.234	.244	.232	60	192	24	45	6	3	2	21	22	10	3	1	51	18	4	.328	.342
Valera, Robert	R-R	6-0	165	9-6-98	.289	.235	.321	14	45	6	13	2	0	0	5	3	1	0	0	4	2	1	.333	.347
Vargas, Jhosner	B-R	5-11	158	1-24-99	.264	.231	.275	17	53	6	14	0	1	0	2	8	0	2	0	6	1	0	.302	.361

Pitching

Pitching	B-T	HT	WT	DOB	W	L	ERA	G	GS	CG	SV	IP	H	R	ER	HR	BB	SO	AVG	vLH	vRH	K/9	BB/9
Alejandro, Jose	R-R	6-3	190	6-20-95	0	0	0.00	1	0	0	0	1	0	0	0	0	0	0	.400	.500	.333	0.00	0.00
Arauz, Jaime	R-R	6-0	160	1-31-99	1	0	4.91	15	0	0	1	26	29	17	14	2	15	18	.305	.387	.266	6.31	5.26
Batista, Oliver	R-R	6-0	180	10-30-96	1	0	2.70	9	0	0	0	13	9	7	4	0	11	8	.196	.353	.103	5.40	7.43
Caba, Jairo	R-R	6-3	190	8-27-97	2	2	4.26	14	0	0	1	19	13	13	9	1	24	18	.200	.143	.227	8.53	11.3
Cedeno, Jhoanbert	R-R	6-6	170	2-12-98	1	2	0.94	16	0	0	3	29	14	7	3	0	22	28	.146	.040	.183	8.79	6.91
Cespedes, Ender	R-R	5-11	206	5-30-96	1	0	6.35	13	0	0	0	17	13	13	12	1	23	15	.210	.231	.204	7.94	12.18
Constante, Marlon	R-R	5-11	180	7-5-96	5	4	2.92	17	0	0	0	37	34	16	12	1	6	30	.246	.328	.188	7.30	1.46
Cordero, Dauris	R-R	6-3	186	7-18-99	2	0	6.56	13	0	0	2	23	29	17	17	3	9	21	.309	.267	.328	8.10	3.47
De Los Santos, Adrian	L-L	5-10	165	11-5-93	3	1	6.17	15	0	0	0	23	22	18	16	1	23	23	.242	.238	.243	8.87	8.87
Felipe, Angel	R-R	6-5	190	8-30-97	1	3	4.15	13	6	0	1	26	23	19	12	0	21	18	.258	.321	.230	6.23	7.27
Fernandez, Christian	R-R	6-2	170	8-11-99	1	3	4.84	16	0	0	1	35	30	20	19	3	21	34	.236	.289	.207	8.66	5.35
Gonzalez, Ender	R-R	6-2	175	2-26-97	4	1	2.81	17	0	0	2	32	20	15	10	3	16	26	.174	.237	.143	7.31	4.50
Gonzalez, Luis	R-R	6-2	190	4-27-96	2	2	3.78	13	12	0	0	52	44	26	22	1	24	39	.233	.250	.218	6.71	4.13
Hernandez, Ronal	R-R	6-1	175	7-8-94	4	4	2.77	14	12	1	1	62	49	27	19	1	21	49	.222	.246	.212	7.15	3.06
Herrera, Bryan	R-R	6-2	175	4-22-98	2	1	5.04	17	0	0	0	30	22	20	17	2	22	19	.206	.200	.200	5.64	6.53
Lara, Miguel	R-R	5-11	165	7-17-97	2	6	3.93	14	13	0	0	53	38	33	23	1	41	53	.213	.185	.226	9.06	7.01
Linares, Wanderson	R-R	6-1	160	9-28-96	0	1	7.94	4	1	0	0	6	13	6	5	0	3	1	.481	.000	.591	1.59	4.76
Lopez, Edward	R-R	6-1	165	1-29-99	0	1	63.00	2	0	0	0	1	4	7	7	0	8	0	.571	1.000	.000	0.00	72.00
Lugo, Enyerbeth	R-R	6-3	159	1-4-98	1	2	4.50	17	0	0	4	26	24	15	13	0	21	23	.255	.300	.222	7.96	7.27
Medina, Luis	R-R	6-2	175	6-18-95	2	2	3.63	14	0	0	1	22	23	14	9	0	15	27	.284	.250	.295	10.88	6.04
Moncada, Luis	L-L	6-1	150	2-28-98	0	6	2.19	14	14	0	0	62	49	21	15	1	29	51	.226	.341	.199	7.44	4.23
Montero, Reynier	R-R	6-2	165	10-29-96	2	2	2.63	18	0	0	3	38	23	14	11	2	14	24	.181	.179	.182	5.73	3.35
Mujica, Arturo	L-L	6-3	181	6-4-96	2	1	2.37	14	0	0	0	61	52	22	16	0	25	51	.240	.222	.243	7.57	3.71
Peguero, Joel	R-R	5-11	160	5-5-97	2	3	3.43	16	2	0	3	42	39	17	16	1	19	26	.244	.329	.178	5.57	4.07
Pilar, Daniel	R-R	6-4	185	6-4-96	5	2	2.59	13	11	0	0	66	62	31	19	1	14	45	.257	.281	.249	6.14	1.91
Pinero, Dilan	R-R	6-2	170	4-25-97	1	7	3.96	14	14	0	0	52	56	34	23	1	24	30	.290	.311	.277	5.16	4.13
Roca, Jose	R-R	6-0	195	8-27-96	2	1	1.36	15	0	0	1	33	25	8	5	0	17	13	.217	.219	.217	3.55	4.64
Rodriguez, Aldor	R-R	6-1	182	7-4-97	0	2	4.21	15	0	0	0	26	19	13	12	0	10	17	.204	.300	.159	5.96	3.51
Rodriguez, Angel	R-R	6-5	229	1-28-98	1	4	4.28	13	10	0	0	48	40	25	23	1	24	35	.235	.222	.246	6.52	4.47
Sabino, Stanly	L-L	6-0	150	9-26-97	4	1	2.97	17	1	0	0	33	24	14	11	1	14	31	.197	.059	.219	8.37	3.78
Sanchez, Cristopher	L-L	6-5	165	12-12-96	5	3	3.06	13	11	1	1	62	57	25	21	0	12	42	.238	.222	.241	6.13	1.75
Sanchez, Francisco	L-L	6-1	160	4-24-98	1	2	3.38	13	12	0	0	43	34	20	16	0	21	34	.227	.000	.248	7.17	4.43
Santos, Fraylin	R-R	6-3	195	10-3-98	1	0	2.33	10	0	0	1	19	18	6	5	0	16	16	.265	.160	.326	7.45	6.05
Sanz, Chander	R-R	6-4	185	7-10-96	0	2	7.66	17	0	0	0	25	22	23	21	1	26	23	.247	.273	.239	8.39	9.49
Tavera, Jose	R-R	6-4	215	4-30-96	0	1	20.77	4	2	0	0	4	3	10	10	0	16	3	.214	.250	.200	6.23	33.23
Trinidad, Luis	R-R	6-0	165	5-16-98	1	0	4.20	10	0	0	0	15	16	10	7	0	14	18	.276	.333	.243	10.80	8.40
Ventura, Heriberto	R-R	6-0	160	8-10-98	1	0	6.43	5	0	0	0	7	7	5	5	1	2	8	.269	.286	.263	10.29	2.57
Zerpa, Jose	R-R	6-4	185	3-29-97	0	3	3.16	6	3	0	0	26	23	14	9	1	2	19	.240	.192	.257	6.66	0.70

Fielding

C: Alvarez 36, Hernandez 32, Parra 17, Perez 24, Silva 26, Tejeda 16, Valera 7. **1B:** Cabrera 56, Del Palacio 4, Del Palacio 22, Lugo 11, Rodriguez 48, Valera 1. **2B:** Pimentel 12, Vargas 12, Aranda 38, Balbuena 19, Garcia 19, Lugo 5, Pedroza 33, Pereira 10. **3B:** Balbuena 28, Cervantes 1, Contreras 26, Lugo 16, Pedroza 20, Pereira 19, Pimentel 34. **SS:** Arias 35, Contreras 1, Garcia 33, Leon 47, Pereira 26, Pimentel 1, Vargas 3. **OF:** Arrendoll 53, Brito 33, Cervantes 34, Del Palacio 27, Diaz 16, Hernandez 47, Lugo 8, Martinez 46, Pena 28, Polanco 48, Rincon 27, Torrealba 59.

Texas Rangers

SEASON IN A SENTENCE: The Rangers continued the best stretch in franchise history, winning their fourth division series since 2010 and making their fifth playoff trip in that stretch. The year's bunch won 95 games, most in the American League and tied for second in baseball, but Texas lost again in the division series to the Blue Jays, getting swept this time in three games.

HIGH POINT: The Rangers owned the rival Astros, going 15-4 against their in-state and division foes. Texas opened September with a pair of big wins over Houston, with a 12-4 win Sept. 3 capping a season-high seven-game winning streak. Other highlights of the rivalry for Texas included a walk-off comeback 6-5 victory on June 6 on a Rougned Odor double and a three-game April 19-21 sweep.

LOW POINT: Texas' rivalry with Toronto, fueled in 2015 by Jose Bautista's bat flip after a game-winning homer, gained fuel when Odor and Bautista precipitated a benches-clearing brawl in the final regular-season matchup between the clubs on May 15. While Odor landed a clean punch to Bautista's jaw that thrilled Rangers fans, Bautista and the Blue Jays had the last laugh with an easy three-game playoff sweep, including a 10-1 loss in Arlington and finishing with a walk-off defeat.

NOTABLE ROOKIES: Nomar Mazara took over early in the season as the right fielder when Shin-Soo Choo was sidelined and stayed in the lineup most of the season, belting 20 home runs and flashing star-quality tools as a 21-year-old.

KEY TRANSACTIONS: Texas GM Jon Daniels was active and wound up trading three first-round picks to fortify the big league roster. The Rangers sent 2015 first-round pick Dillon Tate to the Yankees in the Carlos Beltran deal and acquired catcher Jonathan Lucroy and righthander Jeremy Jeffress from Milwaukee for outfielder Lewis Brinson (2012 first-rounder), righty Luis Ortiz ('13) and outfielder Ryan Cordell.

DOWN ON THE FARM: High Class A High Desert won the California League title in its final season as a franchise; the Rangers helped contract two teams from the California League and will move their new high Class A affiliate to Kinston, N.C., in the Carolina League. Rangers affiliates posted a .491 winning percentage cumulatively. Lefthander Yohander Mendez started the season at High Desert, and he earned a callup to the big leagues.

OPENING DAY PAYROLL: $186,038,723 (5th)

PLAYERS OF THE YEAR

MAJOR LEAGUE	MINOR LEAGUE
Adrian Beltre	**Yohander Mendez**
3b	**lhp**
.300/.358/.521	(High A/Double-A/
32 HR, 104 RBI	Triple-A)
48 BB, 66 SO	12-3, 2.19

ORGANIZATION LEADERS

BATTING		*Minimum 250 AB
MAJORS		
* AVG	Elvis Andrus	.302
* OPS	Adrian Beltre	.879
HR	Rougned Odor	33
RBI	Adrian Beltre	104
MINORS		
* AVG	Scott Heineman, High Desert	.303
* OBP	Scott Heineman, High Desert	.386
* SLG	Travis Demeritte, High Desert	.583
* OPS	Travis Demeritte, High Desert	.935
R	Scott Heineman, High Desert	96
H	Scott Heineman, High Desert	159
TB	Luke Tendler, High Desert	266
2B	Scott Heineman, High Desert	39
3B	Franklin Rollin, DSL Rangers1	11
HR	Travis Demeritte, High Desert	25
HR	Joey Gallo, Round Rock	25
RBI	Luke Tendler, High Desert	97
BB	Joey Gallo, Round Rock	68
SO	Eric Jenkins, Hickory, High Desert	157
SB	Eric Jenkins, Hickory, High Desert	51

PITCHING		#Minimum 75 IP
MAJORS		
W	Cole Hamels	15
# ERA	Cole Hamels	3.32
SO	Cole Hamels	200
SV	Sam Dyson	38
MINORS		
W	Yohander Mendez, High Desert, Frisco, Round Rock	12
L	ChiChi Gonzalez, Round Rock	10
# ERA	Michael Roth, Round Rock	2.97
G	Jimmy Reyes, Round Rock	43
GS	ChiChi Gonzalez, Round Rock	24
GS	David Ledbetter, High Desert	24
SV	John Fasola, High Desert, Frisco, Round Rock	11
IP	Michael Roth, Round Rock	145
BB	Victor Payano, Frisco, Round Rock	60
SO	Connor Sadzeck, Frisco	133
# AVG	Connor Sadzeck, Frisco	.244

General Manager: Jon Daniels. **Farm Director:** Mike Daly. **Scouting Director:** Kip Fagg.

Class	Team	League	W	L	PCT	Finish	Manager
Majors	Texas Rangers	American	95	67	.586	1st (15)	Jeff Banister
Triple-A	Round Rock Express	Pacific Coast	71	72	.497	t-7th (16)	Jason Wood
Double-A	Frisco RoughRiders	Texas	63	76	.453	7th (8)	Joe Mikulik
High A	High Desert Mavericks	California	82	58	.586	1st (10)	Howard Johnson
Low A	Hickory Crawdads	South Atlantic	74	66	.529	5th (14)	Spike Owen
Short season	Spokane Indians	Northwest	32	43	.427	7th (8)	Tim Hulett
Rookie	Rangers	Arizona	18	37	.327	14th (14)	Matt Siegel
Overall 2016 Minor League Record			340	352	.491	16th (30)	

ORGANIZATION STATISTICS

TEXAS RANGERS
AMERICAN LEAGUE

Batting	B-T	HT	WT	DOB	AVG	vLH	vRH	G	AB	R	H	2B	3B	HR	RBI	BB	HBP	SH	SF	SO	SB	CS	SLG	OBP
Alberto, Hanser	R-R	5-11	215	10-17-92	.143	.136	.147	35	56	2	8	1	0	0	5	0	0	2	0	17	1	0	.161	.143
Andrus, Elvis	R-R	6-0	200	8-26-88	.302	.348	.289	147	506	75	153	31	7	8	69	47	4	4	7	70	24	8	.439	.362
Beltran, Carlos	B-R	6-1	215	4-24-77	.280	.297	.276	52	193	23	54	12	0	7	29	13	0	0	0	31	1	0	.451	.325
2-team total (99 New York)					.295	—	—	151	552	73	163	33	0	29	93	35	2	0	4	101	1	0	.513	.337
Beltre, Adrian	R-R	5-11	220	4-7-79	.300	.331	.291	153	583	89	175	31	1	32	104	48	6	0	3	66	1	1	.521	.358
Chirinos, Robinson	R-R	6-1	210	6-5-84	.224	.174	.234	57	147	21	33	11	0	9	20	15	5	1	2	44	0	1	.483	.314
Choo, Shin-Soo	L-L	5-11	210	7-13-82	.242	.304	.220	48	178	27	43	7	0	7	17	25	7	0	0	46	6	3	.399	.357
DeShields, Delino	R-R	5-9	200	8-16-92	.209	.209	.209	74	182	36	38	7	0	4	13	15	2	3	1	54	8	3	.313	.275
Desmond, Ian	R-R	6-3	215	9-20-85	.285	.338	.269	156	625	107	178	29	3	22	86	44	5	0	3	160	21	6	.446	.335
Fielder, Prince	L-R	5-11	275	5-9-84	.212	.181	.224	89	326	29	69	16	0	8	44	32	7	0	5	63	0	0	.334	.292
Gallo, Joey	L-R	6-5	235	11-19-93	.040	.000	.045	17	25	2	1	0	0	1	5	0	0	0	0	19	1	0	.160	.200
Gomez, Carlos	R-R	6-3	220	12-4-85	.284	.385	.272	33	116	18	33	6	0	8	24	13	1	0	0	36	5	3	.543	.362
2-team total (85 Houston)					.231	—	—	118	411	45	95	22	1	13	53	34	5	3	0	136	18	5	.384	.298
Holaday, Bryan	R-R	6-0	205	11-19-87	.238	.241	.236	29	84	14	20	6	1	2	13	5	2	1	2	16	0	1	.405	.290
2-team total (14 Boston)					.231	—	—	43	117	17	27	7	1	2	14	7	2	1	2	28	0	1	.359	.281
Hoying, Jared	L-R	6-3	205	5-18-89	.217	.167	.225	38	46	8	10	2	0	0	5	3	0	0	0	8	1	0	.261	.265
Lucroy, Jonathan	R-R	6-0	200	6-13-86	.276	.219	.292	47	152	19	42	7	0	11	31	14	2	0	0	30	0	0	.539	.345
Mazara, Nomar	L-L	6-4	215	4-26-95	.266	.234	.274	145	516	59	137	13	3	20	64	39	6	0	7	112	0	2	.419	.320
Moreland, Mitch	L-L	6-2	230	9-6-85	.233	.277	.221	147	460	49	107	21	0	22	60	35	8	0	0	118	1	0	.422	.298
Nicholas, Brett	L-R	6-2	220	7-8-88	.275	.500	.219	15	40	5	11	5	0	2	4	4	1	0	0	9	0	0	.550	.356
Odor, Rougned	L-R	5-11	195	2-3-94	.271	.269	.272	150	605	89	164	33	4	33	88	19	4	0	4	135	14	7	.502	.296
Profar, Jurickson	B-R	6-0	190	2-20-93	.239	.197	.254	90	272	35	65	6	3	5	20	30	3	2	0	61	2	1	.338	.321
Rua, Ryan	R-R	6-2	205	3-11-90	.258	.277	.245	98	240	40	62	8	1	8	22	21	6	0	2	76	9	0	.400	.331
Ruggiano, Justin	R-R	6-1	210	4-12-82	.250	.333	.000	1	4	0	1	0	0	1	0	0	1	0	0	1	0	0	.500	.250
Stubbs, Drew	R-R	6-4	205	10-4-84	.300	.235	.667	19	20	6	6	0	0	2	3	4	0	0	1	7	4	0	.600	.400
2-team total (20 Baltimore)					.214	—	—	39	42	7	9	0	0	2	4	8	1	0	1	18	5	1	.357	.346
Wilson, Bobby	R-R	6-0	210	4-8-83	.250	.333	.217	42	128	11	32	4	0	3	22	5	1	4	3	33	0	0	.352	.277
3-team total (5 Detroit, 28 Tampa Bay)					.237	—	—	75	228	25	54	6	0	7	33	11	1	7	4	64	0	0	.355	.270

Pitching	B-T	HT	WT	DOB	W	L	ERA	G	GS	CG	SV	IP	H	R	ER	HR	BB	SO	AVG	vLH	vRH	K/9	BB/9
Alvarez, Dario	L-L	6-1	170	1-17-89	0	0	7.71	10	0	0	0	12	17	11	10	3	2	13	.362	.357	.364	10.03	1.54
Barnette, Tony	R-R	6-1	190	11-9-83	7	3	2.09	53	0	0	0	60	54	16	14	4	16	49	.242	.287	.205	7.31	2.39
Bush, Matt	R-R	5-9	180	2-8-86	7	2	2.48	58	0	0	1	62	44	18	17	4	14	61	.196	.238	.171	8.90	2.04
Claudio, Alex	L-L	6-3	180	1-31-92	4	1	2.79	39	0	0	0	52	55	19	16	2	10	34	.270	.177	.310	5.92	1.74
Darvish, Yu	R-R	6-5	220	8-16-86	7	5	3.41	17	17	0	0	100	81	43	38	12	31	132	.214	.207	.221	11.84	2.78
Diekman, Jake	L-L	6-4	200	1-21-87	4	2	3.40	66	0	0	4	53	36	22	20	4	26	59	.189	.212	.177	10.02	4.42
Dyson, Sam	R-R	6-1	205	5-7-88	3	2	2.43	73	0	0	38	70	63	19	19	5	23	55	.244	.274	.221	7.04	2.94
Faulkner, Andrew	R-L	6-3	205	9-12-92	0	0	6.75	9	0	0	0	7	8	7	5	3	4	1	.286	.250	.313	1.35	5.40
Gonzalez, Chi Chi	R-R	6-3	215	1-15-92	0	2	8.71	3	3	0	0	10	21	13	10	1	9	7	.404	.412	.389	6.10	7.84
Griffin, A.J.	R-R	6-5	230	1-28-88	7	4	5.07	23	23	0	0	119	116	68	67	28	46	107	.256	.286	.227	8.09	3.48
Hamels, Cole	L-L	6-4	205	12-27-83	15	5	3.32	32	32	0	0	201	185	83	74	24	77	200	.243	.208	.252	8.97	3.45
Harrell, Lucas	B-R	6-2	205	6-3-85	1	0	5.60	4	4	0	0	18	21	11	11	3	13	15	.309	.265	.353	7.64	6.62
Holland, Derek	B-L	6-2	215	10-9-86	7	9	4.95	22	20	0	0	107	116	62	59	15	35	67	.276	.247	.282	5.62	2.93
Jackson, Luke	R-R	6-2	210	8-24-91	0	0	10.80	8	0	0	0	12	22	14	14	4	8	3	.415	.462	.370	2.31	6.17
Jeffress, Jeremy	R-R	6-0	205	9-21-87	1	0	2.70	12	0	0	0	13	10	4	4	0	7	7	.227	.455	.152	4.73	4.73
Kela, Keone	R-R	6-1	215	4-16-93	5	1	6.09	35	0	0	0	34	30	23	23	6	17	45	.236	.175	.264	11.91	4.50
Klein, Phil	R-R	6-7	255	4-30-89	0	1	5.19	8	0	0	0	9	8	5	5	2	2	12	.242	.214	.263	12.46	2.08
Leclerc, Jose	R-R	6-0	190	12-19-93	0	0	1.80	12	0	0	0	15	11	4	3	0	13	15	.212	.294	.171	9.00	7.80
Lewis, Colby	R-R	6-4	240	8-2-79	6	5	3.71	19	19	0	0	116	103	53	48	19	28	73	.236	.229	.241	5.65	2.17
Lohse, Kyle	R-R	6-2	215	10-4-78	0	2	12.54	2	2	0	0	9	15	13	13	4	5	3	.357	.381	.333	2.89	4.82
Martinez, Nick	L-R	6-2	200	8-5-90	2	3	5.59	12	5	0	0	39	45	24	24	8	19	16	.290	.310	.274	3.72	4.42
Mendez, Yohander	L-L	6-5	200	1-17-95	0	0	18.00	2	0	0	0	3	5	6	6	0	2	0	.333	.400	.300	0.00	6.00
Perez, Martin	L-L	6-0	200	4-4-91	10	11	4.39	33	33	0	0	199	205	110	97	18	76	103	.270	.176	.291	4.67	3.44
Ramos, Cesar	L-L	6-2	200	6-22-84	3	3	6.04	16	4	0	1	48	60	34	32	12	20	27	.319	.280	.333	5.10	3.78

Pitching	B-T	HT	WT	DOB	W	L	ERA	G	GS	CG	SV	IP	H	R	ER	HR	BB	SO	AVG	vLH	vRH	K/9	BB/9
Ranaudo, Anthony	R-R	6-7	240	9-9-89	1	0	17.18	2	0	0	0	4	2	7	7	1	8	2	.167	0	.286	4.91	19.64
2-team total (7 Chicago)					1	1	9.48	9	5	0	0	31	36	33	33	10	20	18	—	—	—	5.17	5.74
Roth, Michael	L-L	6-1	210	2-15-90	0	0	14.73	1	0	0	0	4	10	6	6	3	1	3	.476	.375	.538	7.36	2.45
Scheppers, Tanner	R-R	6-4	200	1-17-87	1	1	4.15	10	0	0	1	9	6	4	4	0	3	5	.188	.167	.192	5.19	3.12
Tolleson, Shawn	R-R	6-2	225	1-19-88	2	2	7.68	37	0	0	11	36	53	32	31	8	10	29	.338	.318	.352	7.18	2.48
Wilhelmsen, Tom	R-R	6-6	220	12-16-83	2	3	10.55	21	0	0	0	21	38	25	25	7	9	11	.392	.375	.4	4.64	3.80
2-team total (29 Seattle)					2	4	6.80	50	0	0	1	46	60	35	35	11	19	28	—	—	—	5.44	3.69

Fielding

Catcher	PCT	G	PO	A	E	DP	PB
Chirinos	.997	54	287	23	1	2	3
Holaday	1.000	27	143	9	0	3	1
Lucroy	1.000	44	344	22	0	4	3
Nicholas	1.000	15	96	5	0	2	2
Wilson	.993	42	289	11	2	4	2

First Base	PCT	G	PO	A	E	DP
Alberto	1.000	4	13	1	0	2
Fielder	.970	9	60	4	2	9
Gallo	.917	1	11	0	1	3
Moreland	.998	139	1036	65	2	138
Profar	1.000	17	111	10	0	12
Rua	.994	31	152	4	1	12

Second Base	PCT	G	PO	A	E	DP
Alberto	.944	6	8	9	1	2
Odor	.970	146	283	428	22	129
Profar	.978	19	35	55	2	14

Third Base	PCT	G	PO	A	E	DP
Alberto	1.000	11	1	14	0	1
Beltre	.976	141	104	301	10	43
Gallo	1.000	5	3	6	0	0
Profar	.913	25	9	33	4	1
Rua	1.000	2	0	2	0	0

Shortstop	PCT	G	PO	A	E	DP
Alberto	1.000	9	13	33	0	10
Andrus	.974	147	229	413	17	105

Profar	.974	11	11	26	1	9

Outfield	PCT	G	PO	A	E	DP
Beltran	1.000	9	13	1	0	0
Choo	.967	43	85	4	3	0
DeShields	.972	59	102	1	3	0
Desmond	.966	156	330	8	12	2
Gomez	.986	33	68	0	1	0
Holaday	1.000	1	1	0	0	0
Hoying	.947	31	17	1	1	0
Mazara	.994	143	300	7	2	2
Profar	1.000	14	11	1	0	0
Rua	.989	65	85	4	1	2
Ruggiano	1.000	1	4	0	0	0
Stubbs	1.000	18	14	0	0	0

ROUND ROCK EXPRESS   TRIPLE-A
PACIFIC COAST LEAGUE

Batting	B-T	HT	WT	DOB	AVG	vLH	vRH	G	AB	R	H	2B	3B	HR	RBI	BB	HBP	SH	SF	SO	SB	CS	SLG	OBP
Adams, Trever	R-R	6-0	210	9-30-88	.184	.200	.174	10	38	6	7	1	1	2	12	1	2	0	0	13	0	0	.421	.244
Alberto, Hanser	R-R	5-11	215	10-17-92	.275	.282	.273	63	265	32	73	13	1	7	36	8	2	2	0	29	2	2	.411	.302
Alvarez, Jhonniel	R-R	5-9	195	2-15-93	.167	.500	.000	2	6	0	1	0	0	0	1	0	0	0	0	1	0	0	.167	.286
Arroyo, Carlos	L-R	5-11	150	6-28-93	.314	.429	.286	13	35	6	11	0	0	0	1	2	0	3	0	7	2	0	.314	.351
Ashley, Nevin	R-R	6-1	245	8-14-84	.100	.000	.111	3	10	2	1	0	0	0	1	0	2	0	0	3	0	0	.100	.250
2-team total (63 Las Vegas)					.232	—		66	177	28	41	10	0	5	29	27	5	0	3	48	1	1	.373	.344
Beck, Preston	L-R	6-2	190	10-26-90	.254	.243	.259	33	122	14	31	9	2	1	12	10	0	0	0	25	2	1	.385	.311
Bernier, Doug	R-R	6-1	185	6-24-80	.275	.327	.257	120	414	56	114	18	4	10	47	45	4	7	3	97	7	6	.411	.350
Blair, Carson	R-R	6-2	210	10-18-89	.125	.500	.125	3	8	0	1	0	0	0	0	0	0	0	0	6	0	0	.125	.125
2-team total (3 Nashville)					.176	—		6	17	2	3	0	0	0	1	1	0	0	0	9	0	0	.176	.222
Burg, Alex	R-R	6-0	190	8-9-87	.203	.269	.167	23	74	3	15	7	0	0	7	6	0	0	0	24	0	0	.297	.263
Cantwell, Pat	R-R	6-2	210	4-10-90	.262	.326	.243	54	183	16	48	8	0	1	15	11	3	0	1	49	4	4	.306	.327
Chirinos, Robinson	R-R	6-5	84	167	.000	.182	3	12	0	2	0	0	0	0	0	0	0	0	5	0	0	.167	.167
Choo, Shin-Soo	L-L	5-11	210	7-13-82	.545	1.000	.500	3	11	2	6	1	0	1	5	1	0	0	0	1	1	1	.909	.583
Ciriaco, Pedro	R-R	6-0	180	9-27-85	.268	.170	.305	51	194	14	52	7	0	1	18	4	4	0	0	36	6	6	.320	.297
2-team total (23 New Orleans)					.256	—		74	262	18	67	9	0	1	20	5	5	0	1	49	10	6	.302	.282
Davis, Ike	L-L	6-4	220	3-22-87	.268	.100	.313	39	142	21	38	12	0	4	25	19	0	0	2	37	0	0	.437	.350
DeShields, Delino	R-R	5-9	200	8-16-92	.261	.256	.262	54	207	37	54	10	0	3	17	35	1	4	2	60	21	7	.353	.367
Duffy, Matt	R-R	6-3	215	2-6-89	.237	.381	.172	35	135	17	32	4	1	8	22	6	4	0	0	30	0	0	.459	.286
2-team total (74 Fresno)					.229	—		109	401	54	92	17	2	14	52	30	10	0	3	124	1	1	.387	.297
Gallo, Joey	L-R	6-5	235	11-19-93	.240	.207	.255	102	359	71	86	17	6	25	66	68	5	0	1	150	2	0	.529	.367
Garcia, Edwin	B-R	6-1	185	3-1-91	.165	.227	.145	26	91	5	15	4	0	0	6	4	0	2	0	14	0	0	.209	.200
Gomez, Carlos	R-R	6-3	210	12-4-85	.200	.000	.375	3	13	1	4	1	1	0	2	1	0	0	0	5	0	0	.538	.357
Guzman, Ronald	L-L	6-5	205	10-20-94	.216	.208	.219	25	88	9	19	5	1	1	16	6	0	0	0	23	0	1	.330	.266
Holaday, Bryan	R-R	6-0	205	11-19-87	.324	.400	.292	9	34	6	11	1	1	2	8	3	1	0	0	9	0	0	.588	.395
Hoying, Jared	L-R	6-3	205	5-18-89	.269	.202	.297	100	390	62	105	20	6	16	66	37	4	4	0	78	18	4	.474	.336
Jones, James	L-L	6-4	200	9-24-88	.232	.143	.255	76	276	31	64	10	4	3	21	23	3	2	1	87	12	7	.330	.297
Kivlehan, Patrick	R-R	6-2	215	12-22-89	.184	.244	.160	37	141	17	26	8	0	1	16	11	2	0	1	36	2	2	.262	.252
3-team total (20 El Paso, 43 Tacoma)					.254	—		100	370	46	94	18	3	12	49	24	2	0	1	108	5	4	.416	.302
Kubitza, Kyle	L-R	6-3	210	7-15-90	.182	.209	.172	44	159	29	29	9	2	4	15	23	2	1	2	48	7	0	.340	.290
2-team total (54 Salt Lake)					.220	—		98	345	38	76	14	7	6	34	50	3	1	3	108	13	3	.354	.322
Mazara, Nomar	L-L	6-4	215	4-26-95	.500	.750	.375	3	12	4	6	0	0	1	4	1	0	0	0	1	0	0	.750	.538
McKenry, Michael	R-R	5-10	205	3-4-85	.220	.250	.207	13	41	9	9	5	0	0	3	5	1	0	1	13	0	0	.341	.389
3-team total																								
(14 Colorado Springs, 24 Memphis)					.290	—		51	155	35	45	12	4	6	35	40	3	0	1	40	2	2	.535	.442
Mendez, Luis	B-R	5-10	188	1-1-93	.273	—	.273	3	11	0	3	0	0	0	0	0	0	0	0	3	0	0	.273	.273
Nicholas, Brett	L-R	6-2	220	7-18-88	.287	.263	.298	101	400	57	115	27	1	13	58	38	3	3	3	88	2	2	.458	.351
Profar, Jurickson	B-R	6-0	190	2-20-93	.284	.302	.278	42	169	28	48	9	0	5	26	16	3	1	0	26	4	3	.426	.356
Robinson, Drew	L-R	6-1	200	4-20-92	.257	.219	.271	125	467	76	120	24	10	20	67	66	2	2	4	148	17	5	.480	.350
Rua, Ryan	R-R	6-2	210	3-11-90	.500	.286	.714	4	14	2	7	0	0	1	2	0	0	0	0	2	0	1	.714	.563
Ruggiano, Justin	R-R	6-1	210	4-12-82	.226	.269	.205	44	164	26	37	10	1	7	23	23	1	0	2	53	3	1	.427	.321
2-team total (3 Las Vegas)					.229	—		47	175	28	40	11	1	7	23	24	1	0	2	56	3	1	.423	.322
Strausborger, Ryan	R-R	6-0	185	3-4-88	.308	.388	.279	45	185	25	57	4	0	1	16	20	5	1	3	33	9	3	.411	.339
2-team total (40 Tacoma)					.234	—		85	274	37	64	10	0	7	31	30	6	1	4	74	15	4	.336	.299
Stubbs, Drew	R-R	6-4	205	10-4-84	.231	.250	.229	12	39	10	9	4	0	2	10	10	0	0	2	8	2	1	.487	.373

Pitching

Pitching	B-T	HT	WT	DOB	W	L	ERA	G	GS	CG	SV	IP	H	R	ER	HR	BB	SO	AVG	vLH	vRH	K/9	BB/9
Alvarez, Dario	L-L	6-1	170	1-17-89	2	0	2.25	6	0	0	1	8	8	3	2	1	3	10	.276	.231	.313	11.25	3.38
2-team total (17 Las Vegas)					2	1	7.33	23	0	0	1	23	30	22	19	4	13	37	—	—	—	14.27	5.01
Badenhop, Burke	R-R	6-5	205	2-8-83	0	0	9.64	3	0	0	0	5	8	5	5	1	3	3	.400	.500	.333	5.79	1.93
Bell, Chad	R-L	6-3	200	2-28-89	1	0	1.50	5	2	0	0	18	12	4	3	0	5	19	.194	.188	.196	9.50	2.50
Bibens-Dirkx, Austin	R-R	6-1	210	4-29-85	3	2	4.34	17	13	0	0	85	85	42	41	11	25	62	.256	.282	.233	6.56	2.65
Breslow, Craig	L-L	5-11	180	8-8-80	0	0	13.50	3	0	0	0	2	5	3	3	0	2	0	.455	.250	.571	0.00	9.00
2-team total (14 New Orleans)					1	3	7.01	17	0	0	2	26	39	21	20	3	13	29	—	—	—	10.17	4.56
Carroll, Scott	R-R	6-4	215	9-24-84	0	1	10.00	2	2	0	0	9	11	10	10	1	6	3	.297	.182	.346	3.00	6.00
Carter, Anthony	L-R	6-4	215	4-4-86	0	0	6.10	21	0	0	2	21	25	16	14	4	5	17	.294	.316	.277	7.40	2.18
Claudio, Alex	L-L	6-3	180	1-31-92	0	0	0.55	6	0	0	1	16	7	1	1	0	4	8	.135	.063	.167	4.41	2.20
Cotts, Neal	L-L	6-2	200	3-25-80	2	2	3.80	20	0	0	0	24	23	10	10	2	10	23	.264	.286	.25	8.75	3.80
2-team total (14 Salt Lake)					2	2	3.62	34	0	0	1	37	35	15	15	3	13	36	—	—	—	8.68	3.13
Darvish, Yu	R-R	6-5	220	8-16-86	0	1	2.57	2	2	0	0	14	6	4	4	3	1	17	.125	.200	.071	9.00	3.86
De Fratus, Justin	B-R	6-4	225	10-21-87	1	0	1.93	10	0	0	0	9	8	4	2	0	9	7	.242	.182	.273	6.75	8.68
2-team total (19 Tacoma)					3	2	2.89	29	0	0	0	37	31	14	12	2	16	25	—	—	—	6.03	3.86
Fasola, John	R-R	6-2	195	12-12-91	1	0	2.00	7	0	0	0	9	7	2	2	0	1	11	.212	.176	.250	11.00	1.00
Faulkner, Andrew	R-L	6-3	205	9-12-92	5	3	3.97	41	1	0	4	45	39	21	20	3	20	39	.234	.226	.238	7.74	3.97
Fisher, Carlos	R-R	6-4	220	2-22-83	5	7	4.40	42	0	0	8	47	45	24	23	1	22	63	.245	.268	.230	12.06	4.21
Garrett, Reed	R-R	6-2	170	1-2-93	0	1	7.20	1	1	0	0	5	8	4	4	0	1	1	.400	.400	.400	1.80	1.80
Gonzalez, Chi Chi	R-R	6-3	215	1-15-92	8	10	4.70	25	24	0	0	138	154	73	72	8	44	91	.290	.258	.311	5.93	2.87
Grullon, Juan	L-L	6-0	185	3-4-90	0	4	5.40	10	1	0	0	20	20	13	12	4	8	14	.270	.143	.321	6.30	3.60
Hernandez, Jefri	R-R	6-2	210	4-27-91	0	1	3.12	12	0	0	0	17	15	7	6	1	8	17	.242	.304	.205	8.83	4.15
Holland, Derek	B-L	6-2	215	10-9-86	0	0	4.50	3	3	0	0	10	11	5	5	1	4	8	.268	.182	.300	7.20	3.60
Jackson, Luke	R-R	6-2	210	8-24-91	1	0	2.45	16	0	0	2	22	13	7	6	2	15	27	.178	.136	.196	11.05	6.14
Jokisch, Eric	R-L	6-2	205	7-29-89	1	1	4.13	7	4	0	0	24	26	14	11	2	8	15	.283	.296	.277	5.63	3.00
3-team total (1 Iowa, 18 New Orleans)					3	2	4.27	26	5	0	1	59	70	33	28	5	24	37	—	—	—	5.64	3.66
Kela, Keone	R-R	6-1	215	4-16-93	0	0	0.00	1	0	0	0	1	1	0	0	0	0	3	.250	.000	.333	27.00	0.00
Klein, Phil	R-R	6-7	255	4-30-89	0	0	4.26	1	0	0	0	13	14	7	6	0	5	12	.275	.286	.267	8.53	3.55
Leclerc, Jose	R-R	6-0	190	12-19-93	2	2	2.72	29	0	0	1	43	23	13	13	3	28	50	.160	.193	.138	10.47	5.86
Lohse, Kyle	R-R	6-2	215	10-4-78	3	5	5.06	10	10	0	0	59	60	37	33	8	14	41	.299	.266	.273	6.29	2.15
Martinez, Nick	L-R	6-1	200	8-5-90	7	6	3.91	18	16	0	0	99	109	47	43	7	17	67	.285	.305	.268	6.09	1.55
Mendez, Yohander	L-L	6-5	200	1-17-95	4	1	0.57	7	4	0	0	31	12	2	2	0	16	22	.119	.074	.135	6.32	4.60
Mendoza, Francisco	R-R	6-0	205	12-7-87	2	3	6.20	42	0	0	7	54	60	38	37	4	18	47	.296	.377	.261	7.88	3.02
Monegro, Jose	R-R	6-3	200	9-19-89	1	3	6.67	9	5	0	0	27	32	22	20	6	12	21	.288	.390	.259	7.00	4.00
Payano, Victor	L-L	6-5	185	10-17-92	2	2	5.53	6	4	0	0	28	17	17	17	4	16	20	.181	.308	.132	6.51	5.20
Pena, Richelson	R-R	6-1	170	9-29-93	1	1	7.11	6	5	0	0	19	32	18	15	4	8	17	.372	.381	.364	8.05	3.79
Pirela, Jesus	R-R	6-0	155	3-13-89	0	0	5.40	3	0	0	0	3	3	3	2	2	1	3	.214	.500	.167	8.10	2.70
Ramos, Cesar	L-L	6-2	200	6-22-84	0	1	3.18	3	3	0	0	11	8	4	4	1	2	10	.195	.167	.200	7.94	1.59
Ranaudo, Anthony	R-R	6-7	240	9-9-89	1	1	2.03	3	3	0	0	13	6	5	3	0	4	18	.130	.182	.083	12.15	2.70
Reyes, Jimmy	L-L	5-10	200	3-7-89	0	2	4.14	43	2	0	5	72	78	38	33	5	19	51	.279	.235	.296	6.40	2.39
Richman, Jason	R-R	6-4	210	10-15-93	0	0	0.00	3	0	0	0	3	3	0	0	0	1	3	.273	.000	.500	8.10	2.70
Roth, Michael	L-L	6-1	210	2-15-90	11	5	2.97	28	23	1	0	145	136	50	48	9	42	94	.252	.271	.246	5.82	2.60
Scheppers, Tanner	R-R	6-4	200	1-17-87	0	0	0.00	6	1	0	0	6	4	0	0	0	2	6	.174	.429	.063	9.00	3.00
Smith, Chad	R-R	6-3	220	10-2-89	3	2	13.06	8	0	0	0	10	21	19	15	4	6	7	.420	.368	.452	6.10	5.23
Snodgrass, Jack	L-L	6-6	210	12-16-87	0	1	7.50	4	2	0	0	12	21	10	10	3	5	9	.396	.444	.386	6.75	3.75
Tepesch, Nick	R-R	6-4	240	10-12-88	4	2	4.11	11	11	0	0	66	75	33	30	5	11	31	.286	.264	.303	4.25	1.51
4-team total (3 Nashville, 3 Oklahoma City, 5 Omaha)					8	4	3.96	22	19	0	0	116	121	56	51	7	28	62	—	—	—	4.81	2.17
Tolleson, Shawn	R-R	6-2	225	1-19-88	0	0	12.46	4	0	0	1	4	6	6	6	2	3	7	.316	.111	.500	14.54	6.23
Valdespina, Jose	R-R	6-6	220	3-22-92	0	1	2.45	9	0	0	1	15	18	7	4	1	4	6	.310	.464	.167	3.68	2.45
Werner, John	R-R	6-2	210	1-3-92	0	0	3.00	1	0	0	0	3	1	1	1	1	1	3	.100	.200	.000	9.00	3.00
Wilhelmsen, Tom	R-R	6-6	220	12-16-83	0	1	1.13	5	0	0	0	8	5	1	1	1	1	5	.172	.143	.200	5.63	1.13
2-team total (2 Tacoma)					0	1	1.64	7	0	0	0	11	7	2	2	1	1	7	—	—	—	5.73	0.82

Fielding

Catcher	PCT	G	PO	A	E	DP	PB
Ashley	1.000	3	20	2	0	1	0
Blair	.833	1	5	0	1	0	0
Burg	1.000	7	52	4	0	0	0
Cantwell	.992	48	367	27	3	4	0
Chirinos	1.000	2	16	2	0	0	0
Holaday	1.000	5	28	5	0	0	1
McKenry	1.000	9	57	6	0	1	0
Nicholas	.990	70	470	38	5	3	7

First Base	PCT	G	PO	A	E	DP
Blair	.917	1	11	0	1	1
Burg	1.000	5	48	2	0	7
Davis	1.000	24	244	9	0	21
Duffy	1.000	3	26	4	0	4
Gallo	.990	32	285	24	3	29
Garcia	1.000	3	25	1	0	1
Guzman	.989	20	165	8	2	25
Kivlehan	.993	16	135	5	1	17

	PCT	G	PO	A	E	DP
Kubitza	.978	9	87	4	2	11
Nicholas	1.000	19	165	18	0	17
Robinson	.991	14	107	7	1	20
Rua	1.000	1	2	1	0	0

Second Base	PCT	G	PO	A	E	DP
Alberto	.976	6	25	16	1	6
Bernier	.993	61	111	178	2	55
Ciriaco	.961	27	42	82	5	22
Garcia	1.000	15	26	46	0	12
Kubitza	1.000	1	1	1	0	0
Mendez	1.000	2	5	2	0	1
Profar	1.000	6	9	25	0	4
Robinson	.959	27	49	67	5	22
Strausborger	1.000	3	5	7	0	0

Third Base	PCT	G	PO	A	E	DP
Bernier	.913	7	2	19	2	2
Ciriaco	1.000	10	8	22	0	3

	PCT	G	PO	A	E	DP
Duffy	.955	23	16	48	3	1
Gallo	.928	44	26	102	10	13
Garcia	.952	7	2	18	1	1
Kivlehan	.957	17	10	34	2	0
Kubitza	.915	13	15	28	4	1
Robinson	.952	27	13	46	3	5

Shortstop	PCT	G	PO	A	E	DP
Alberto	.967	57	85	182	9	48
Bernier	.987	53	79	151	3	41
Ciriaco	1.000	1	3	2	0	1
Garcia	1.000	1	0	1	0	1
Mendez	.800	1	3	1	0	0
Profar	.968	31	44	106	5	25
Robinson	1.000	1	3	2	0	2

Outfield	PCT	G	PO	A	E	DP
Adams	1.000	7	14	1	0	0
Alvarez	1.000	2	3	0	0	0
Arroyo	.875	11	18	3	3	1
Beck	1.000	32	48	5	0	0
Burg	1.000	6	6	2	0	0
Cantwell	1.000	5	8	0	0	0
Choo	1.000	3	3	0	0	0
DeShields	.972	49	101	2	3	0
Gallo	—	2	0	0	0	0
Gomez	.833	3	5	0	1	0
Hoying	.986	91	215	2	3	1
Jones	.994	76	150	6	1	0
Kubitza	1.000	17	32	2	0	1
Mazara	1.000	3	7	0	0	0
Robinson	.971	56	127	6	4	0
Rua	1.000	3	3	1	0	0
Ruggiano	1.000	31	59	1	0	1
Strausborger	.975	38	76	3	2	1
Stubbs	.971	11	33	0	1	0

FRISCO ROUGHRIDERS

DOUBLE-A

TEXAS LEAGUE

Batting	B-T	HT	WT	DOB	AVG	vLH	vRH	G	AB	R	H	2B	3B	HR	RBI	BB	HBP	SH	SF	SO	SB	CS	SLG	OBP
Arroyo, Carlos	L-R	5-11	150	6-28-93	.222	.250	.214	6	18	0	4	1	0	0	2	0	0	1	1	4	0	0	.278	.211
Beck, Preston	L-R	6-2	190	10-26-90	.289	.273	.293	68	235	35	68	13	5	7	30	21	4	1	0	41	4	1	.477	.358
Bell, Alexei	R-R	5-7	187	10-2-83	.263	.286	.259	27	95	8	25	11	0	1	10	9	1	0	1	15	1	1	.411	.330
Blair, Carson	R-R	6-2	210	10-18-89	.164	.133	.173	19	67	8	11	4	0	1	7	9	2	0	0	26	1	1	.269	.282
2-team total (16 Midland)					.244	—	—	35	123	21	30	5	0	4	19	17	3	0	0	43	1	1	.382	.350
Brinson, Lewis	R-R	6-3	195	5-8-94	.237	.264	.231	77	304	46	72	14	6	11	40	17	2	1	2	64	11	4	.431	.280
Burg, Alex	R-R	6-0	190	8-9-87	.219	.317	.194	56	196	22	43	12	0	7	31	16	4	0	3	43	1	0	.388	.288
Chirinos, Robinson	R-R	6-1	210	6-5-84	.000	—	.000	3	9	0	0	0	0	0	0	0	0	0	0	2	0	0	.000	.000
Choo, Shin-Soo	L-L	5-11	210	7-13-82	.300	.000	.316	6	20	0	6	1	0	0	3	1	0	0	7	0	1		.350	.417
Cone, Zach	R-R	6-2	212	12-14-89	.208	.235	.204	36	125	18	26	7	1	5	26	8	2	0	2	42	2	0	.400	.263
Cordell, Ryan	R-R	6-4	195	3-31-92	.264	.286	.260	107	405	69	107	22	5	19	70	32	3	0	5	97	12	4	.484	.319
Deglan, Kellin	L-R	6-2	205	5-3-92	.194	.227	.188	83	268	24	52	8	1	9	27	18	5	1	2	108	1	3	.332	.256
Garcia, Edwin	B-R	6-1	185	3-1-91	.250	.348	.228	34	124	9	31	4	0	0	9	8	0	0	1	19	5	1	.282	.293
Garia, Chris	B-R	6-0	165	12-16-92	.132	.500	.111	14	38	1	5	0	0	0	1	1	0	1	11	1	3	.132	.175
Gimenez, Chris	R-R	6-2	230	12-27-82	.240	.000	.286	7	25	3	6	0	0	1	4	3	1	0	0	8	0	0	.360	.345
Guzman, Ronald	L-L	6-5	205	10-20-94	.288	.343	.276	102	375	51	108	16	5	15	56	33	3	1	3	82	2	1	.477	.348
Hamilton, Josh	L-L	6-4	240	5-21-81	.000	—	.000	1	2	0	0	0	0	0	0	0	0	0	0	0	0	0	.000	.000
Ibanez, Andy	R-R	5-10	170	4-3-93	.261	.319	.244	81	307	36	80	18	2	6	31	25	2	3	3	47	5	2	.391	.318
Jackson, Joe	L-R	6-1	180	5-5-92	.269	.269	.269	113	413	41	111	23	3	5	52	28	7	1	4	88	2	4	.375	.323
Kiner-Falefa, Isiah	R-R	5-10	176	3-23-95	.256	.262	.255	108	402	55	103	8	2	1	31	27	4	11	2	1	51	6	6	.286	.341
Marte, Luis	R-R	6-1	188	12-15-93	.264	.288	.256	73	265	29	70	15	1	5	33	5	3	3	2	58	6	4	.385	.284
Mastroianni, Darin	R-R	5-11	190	8-26-85	.232	.231	.232	23	95	14	22	6	0	1	6	5	2	0	0	15	5	2	.326	.284
Matta, Shaquille	R-R	5-8	175	4-9-94	.071	.000	.083	6	14	0	1	0	0	0	0	0	0	0	0	6	0	0	.071	.071
Mendez, Luis	B-R	5-10	188	1-1-93	.212	.130	.232	73	231	29	49	6	0	1	21	25	2	3	1	52	6	4	.251	.293
Pinto, Eduard	L-L	5-11	150	10-23-94	.318	.381	.303	29	110	13	35	5	0	0	12	9	1	1	1	8	3	1	.364	.372
Silva, Luis	R-R	5-11	170	6-30-95	.077	—	.077	4	13	0	1	0	0	0	0	0	0	0	0	3	0	0	.077	.143
Triunfel, Alberto	R-R	5-11	160	2-1-94	.184	.167	.187	87	293	22	54	12	0	1	21	12	3	2	1	64	4	2	.235	.223
Van Hoosier, Evan	R-R	5-11	185	12-24-93	.263	.143	.274	23	80	8	21	1	2	0	4	4	0	1	0	14	1	1	.325	.298
Weber, Garrett	R-R	5-10	165	3-29-89	.288	.091	.319	22	80	13	23	1	0	1	10	4	0	1	0	18	1	0	.338	.360

Pitching	B-T	HT	WT	DOB	W	L	ERA	G	GS	CG	SV	IP	H	R	ER	HR	BB	SO	AVG	vLH	vRH	K/9	BB/9
Buckel, Cody	R-R	6-1	185	6-28-92	0	0	0.00	4	0	0	0	5	1	0	0	0	7	2	.071	.000	.111	3.86	13.50
Bush, Matt	R-R	5-9	180	2-8-86	2	1	2.65	12	0	0	5	17	9	5	5	1	4	18	.158	.211	.132	9.53	2.12
Carroll, Scott	R-R	6-4	215	9-24-84	2	1	2.92	7	7	0	0	37	27	12	12	2	7	24	.199	.188	.209	5.84	1.70
Darvish, Yu	R-R	6-5	220	8-16-86	1	1	2.25	5	5	0	0	20	14	7	5	1	7	24	.197	.050	.255	10.80	3.15
Fasola, John	R-R	6-2	195	12-12-91	3	1	3.73	22	0	0	5	31	32	17	13	2	9	35	.264	.184	.301	10.05	2.59
Filomeno, Joe	R-L	5-11	235	12-31-92	2	2	2.20	30	0	0	4	41	23	11	10	3	30	49	.172	.180	.167	10.76	6.59
Garrett, Reed	R-R	6-2	170	1-2-93	3	8	5.74	26	15	0	0	94	100	65	60	10	44	79	.273	.264	.278	7.56	4.21
Griffin, A.J.	R-R	6-5	230	1-28-88	0	1	3.48	3	3	0	0	10	12	5	4	0	4	13	.279	.412	.192	11.32	3.48
Grullon, Juan	L-L	6-0	185	3-4-90	3	3	3.48	22	0	0	0	41	37	16	16	3	19	48	.242	.245	.240	10.45	4.14
Hernandez, Jefri	R-R	6-2	210	4-27-91	1	0	3.00	12	0	0	1	15	13	7	5	0	12	15	.245	.211	.265	9.00	7.20
Jackson, Luke	R-R	6-2	210	8-24-91	0	1	4.81	20	0	0	1	24	27	18	13	4	17	32	.276	.270	.279	11.84	6.29
Jurado, Ariel	R-R	6-1	180	1-30-96	1	6	3.30	8	6	0	0	44	44	17	16	3	10	35	.263	.267	.261	7.21	2.06
Kela, Keone	R-R	6-1	215	4-16-93	0	0	0.00	3	0	0	0	3	1	0	0	0	4		.083	.000	.100	12.00	0.00
Leclerc, Jose	R-R	6-0	190	12-19-93	0	5	3.52	10	2	0	1	23	17	11	9	1	10	28	.210	.324	.114	10.96	3.91
Ledbetter, Ryan	R-R	6-1	190	2-13-92	0	3	5.79	19	0	0	0	28	32	20	18	5	15	26	.283	.200	.321	8.36	4.82
Lewis, Colby	R-R	6-4	240	8-2-79	0	0	9.00	2	2	0	0	6	12	6	6	0	2	2	.400	.500	.313	3.00	3.00
Lopez, Frank	L-L	6-1	175	2-18-94	5	5	5.28	23	14	1	0	92	110	55	54	9	34	77	.304	.338	.295	7.53	3.33
Martinez, Emerson	R-R	6-0	190	1-11-95	0	0	4.32	5	0	0	0	8	7	4	4	1	6	5	.233	.250	.227	5.40	6.48
Martinez, Nick	L-R	6-1	200	8-5-90	0	0	3.00	1	1	0	0	6	4	2	2	1	1	7	.182	.250	.167	10.50	1.50
Mendez, Yohander	L-L	6-5	200	1-17-95	4	1	3.09	10	10	0	0	47	39	18	16	2	14	46	.228	.190	.240	8.87	2.70
Monegro, Jose	R-R	6-3	200	9-19-89	0	1	12.79	4	0	0	0	6	11	10	9	1	5	6	.367	.308	.412	5.68	8.53
Ortiz, Connor	R-R	6-3	200	3-17-95	1	4	4.08	9	8	0	1	40	47	25	18	5	7	34	.296	.245	.318	7.71	1.59
Palmquist, Cody	R-R	6-5	190	4-8-94	1	0	0.69	7	0	0	1	13	8	1	1	0	1	9	.190	.231	.172	6.23	0.69
Parks, Adam	R-R	6-3	200	10-10-92	1	0	1.86	17	0	0	6	29	16	7	6	4	3	30	.134	.200	.106	13.97	1.40
Payano, Victor	L-L	6-5	185	10-17-92	7	6	4.05	19	19	0	0	100	106	51	45	12	44	96	.270	.336	.243	8.64	3.96
Pena, Richelson	R-R	6-1	170	9-29-93	3	3	4.07	16	4	0	0	42	35	20	19	6	18	38	.224	.214	.230	8.14	3.86
Perez, David	R-R	6-5	200	12-20-92	1	6	4.83	28	6	0	0	54	54	32	29	5	31	51	.270	.290	.261	8.50	5.17
Richman, Jason	L-L	6-4	210	10-15-93	0	1	2.55	12	0	0	0	18	10	5	5	1	7	8	.169	.071	.200	4.08	3.57
Sadzeck, Connor	R-R	6-7	240	10-11-91	10	8	4.16	25	23	2	0	141	127	68	65	18	52	133	.244	.270	.225	8.51	3.33
Scheppers, Tanner	R-R	6-4	200	1-17-87	0	0	4.50	2	1	0	0	2	2	1	1	0	1	2	.286	.000	.400	4.50	4.50
Shortslef, Jake	R-R	6-5	235	12-29-94	0	1	11.57	2	0	0	0	3	4	3	3	0	3	3	.364	.333	.400	11.57	11.57
Slack, Ryne	L-L	6-2	220	7-22-92	2	4	3.88	39	0	0	4	49	41	24	21	5	28	41	.225	.203	.236	7.58	5.18

Pitching

Pitching	B-T	HT	WT	DOB	W	L	ERA	G	GS	CG	SV	IP	H	R	ER	HR	BB	SO	AVG	vLH	vRH	K/9	BB/9
Snodgrass, Jack	L-L	6-6	210	12-16-87	3	1	3.78	6	6	0	0	33	28	14	14	3	14	30	.222	.265	.207	8.10	3.78
Valdespina, Jose	R-R	6-6	220	3-22-92	4	1	4.01	31	0	0	3	49	51	25	22	4	19	35	.266	.204	.290	6.39	3.47
Wolff, Sam	R-R	6-1	190	4-14-91	4	3	4.83	10	10	0	0	50	49	28	27	7	31	39	.250	.299	.225	6.97	5.54

Fielding

Catcher

Catcher	PCT	G	PO	A	E	DP	PB
Blair	.984	9	60	3	1	0	1
Burg	.969	16	120	5	4	0	4
Chirinos	1.000	2	12	2	0	0	0
Deglan	.985	79	626	49	10	3	6
Gimenez	1.000	5	32	2	0	0	0
Jackson	.875	1	7	0	1	0	0
Kiner-Falefa	.989	31	245	34	3	4	6
Matta	1.000	3	22	2	0	0	0

First Base

First Base	PCT	G	PO	A	E	DP
Beck	.980	7	49	1	1	8
Blair	1.000	4	29	3	0	1
Burg	.978	4	43	1	1	5
Garcia	.996	27	208	17	1	29
Guzman	.988	95	749	44	10	86
Kiner-Falefa	1.000	1	3	0	0	0
Mendez	1.000	5	6	0	0	2

Second Base

Second Base	PCT	G	PO	A	E	DP
Garcia	1.000	1	0	1	0	0

	PCT	G	PO	A	E	DP	PB
Ibanez	.964	63	104	138	9	34	
Kiner-Falefa	1.000	10	15	28	0	12	
Mendez	1.000	7	10	16	0	4	
Triunfel	.950	32	67	86	8	27	
Van Hoosier	.967	15	27	31	2	14	
Weber	1.000	14	17	24	0	6	

Third Base

Third Base	PCT	G	PO	A	E	DP
Burg	.941	6	7	9	1	2
Garcia	1.000	5	3	7	0	0
Ibanez	.951	14	14	25	2	1
Kiner-Falefa	.964	44	26	107	5	13
Marte	1.000	3	4	8	0	0
Mendez	.926	42	29	84	9	11
Silva	.818	4	1	8	2	1
Triunfel	.967	12	13	16	1	2
Van Hoosier	.750	5	4	8	4	2
Weber	.941	9	3	13	1	0

Shortstop

Shortstop	PCT	G	PO	A	E	DP
Kiner-Falefa	.974	19	31	43	2	13

	PCT	G	PO	A	E	DP
Marte	.962	68	112	164	11	47
Mendez	.985	19	28	37	1	9
Triunfel	.963	37	59	95	6	21

Outfield

Outfield	PCT	G	PO	A	E	DP
Arroyo	1.000	6	7	1	0	0
Beck	.988	51	80	4	1	1
Bell	1.000	15	29	0	0	0
Brinson	.988	75	165	3	2	1
Burg	1.000	5	11	0	0	1
Choo	1.000	3	5	0	0	0
Cone	.986	35	71	1	1	0
Cordell	.988	98	235	5	3	0
Garia	.941	13	16	0	1	0
Hamilton	1.000	1	1	0	0	0
Jackson	.975	64	78	1	2	0
Kiner-Falefa	1.000	1	1	0	0	0
Mastroianni	1.000	23	55	3	0	1
Pinto	1.000	29	42	0	0	0
Triunfel	1.000	5	8	1	0	0
Van Hoosier	1.000	2	2	0	0	0

HIGH DESERT MAVERICKS
CALIFORNIA LEAGUE

HIGH CLASS A

Batting

Batting	B-T	HT	WT	DOB	AVG	vLH	vRH	G	AB	R	H	2B	3B	HR	RBI	BB	HBP	SH	SF	SO	SB	CS	SLG	OBP
Altmann, Josh	R-R	6-3	190	7-6-94	.259	.600	.182	8	27	5	7	1	0	0	1	0	1	0	0	6	0	0	.296	.286
Arroyo, Carlos	L-R	5-11	150	6-28-93	.269	.000	.292	7	26	3	7	1	0	3	0	0	1	1	6	0	0	.423	.259
Beras, Jairo	R-R	6-6	195	12-25-94	.262	.297	.255	107	409	71	107	28	4	22	78	24	4	0	4	121	5	5	.511	.306
Castillo, Elio	R-R	6-1	160	3-1-94	.240	.231	.242	20	75	12	18	2	1	0	13	5	0	1	2	9	0	0	.293	.280
De Leon, Michael	B-R	6-1	160	1-14-97	.267	.338	.253	128	454	54	121	25	1	9	54	24	4	6	2	57	7	5	.385	.308
Demeritte, Travis	R-R	6-0	180	9-30-94	.272	.250	.277	88	331	73	90	20	4	25	59	41	2	0	4	125	13	3	.583	.352
Gonzalez, Jose	B-R	6-1	175	3-16-94	.300	.290	.301	101	397	81	119	23	0	14	48	42	5	6	3	66	13	4	.463	.371
Heineman, Scott	R-R	6-1	215	12-4-92	.303	.375	.290	133	525	96	159	39	8	17	80	59	16	4	6	120	30	14	.505	.386
Jenkins, Eric	L-R	6-1	170	1-30-97	.000	—	.000	1	4	0	0	0	0	0	0	0	0	0	0	3	0	0	.000	.000
Lyon, David	B-R	5-11	190	1-19-90	.228	.222	.230	56	197	34	45	13	0	13	36	33	2	0	3	72	0	1	.492	.340
Martin, Tripp	R-R	6-2	190	4-2-92	.182	.140	.191	70	242	35	44	15	0	13	37	16	13	1	1	110	1	2	.405	.268
Moore, Dylan	R-R	6-0	185	8-2-92	.351	.364	.349	17	74	18	26	7	0	5	14	5	1	0	0	12	3	2	.649	.400
Morgan, Josh	R-R	5-11	185	11-16-95	.300	.325	.295	128	470	74	141	19	2	7	64	44	10	1	7	61	4	2	.394	.367
Profar, Juremi	R-R	6-1	185	1-30-96	.300	.186	.321	103	383	66	115	23	2	13	58	33	2	5	5	47	1	3	.473	.355
Spivey, Seth	L-R	5-11	180	7-9-92	.204	.208	.202	33	113	16	23	5	0	3	17	11	1	2	0	24	1	1	.327	.280
Tendler, Luke	L-R	5-11	190	8-25-91	.297	.321	.292	132	508	92	151	38	4	23	97	64	11	3	5	107	5	8	.524	.384
Torres, Kevin	L-R	6-3	195	2-24-90	.253	.154	.262	49	162	15	41	6	0	3	21	16	2	0	1	23	0	1	.346	.326
Trevino, Jose	R-R	5-11	195	11-28-92	.303	.397	.285	109	433	67	131	30	0	9	68	26	2	0	4	49	2	1	.434	.342

Pitching

Pitching	B-T	HT	WT	DOB	W	L	ERA	G	GS	CG	SV	IP	H	R	ER	HR	BB	SO	AVG	vLH	vRH	K/9	BB/9
Blanco, Josh	L-L	6-2	190	11-16-89	0	0	13.50	7	0	0	0	7	9	12	11	0	13	9	.281	.333	.235	11.05	15.95
Carvallo, Felix	L-L	6-0	175	10-5-93	0	3	3.74	36	0	0	0	67	70	35	28	7	34	69	.267	.194	.311	9.22	4.54
Cook, Clayton	R-R	6-3	175	7-23-90	0	1	4.09	10	0	0	1	11	5	6	5	0	4	12	.132	.059	.190	9.82	3.27
Davis, Tyler	R-R	5-10	185	1-5-93	5	8	6.59	17	16	0	0	83	112	65	61	18	28	79	.321	.302	.333	8.53	3.02
Dula, Chris	R-R	6-2	200	8-6-92	0	0	7.94	4	0	0	0	6	7	5	5	1	6	4	.333	.500	.182	6.35	9.53
Fasola, John	R-R	6-2	195	12-12-91	1	0	2.53	9	0	0	6	11	11	5	3	1	2	12	.250	.200	.276	10.13	1.69
Filomeno, Joe	R-L	5-11	235	12-31-92	1	0	0.57	11	0	0	3	16	10	2	1	0	8	20	.189	.200	.184	11.49	4.60
Gardewine, Nick	R-R	6-1	160	8-15-93	5	1	2.47	29	0	0	7	55	39	15	15	5	14	60	.198	.250	.159	9.88	2.30
Garrett, Reed	R-R	6-2	170	1-2-93	1	0	10.13	2	2	0	0	11	14	12	12	3	5	6	.311	.333	.292	5.06	4.22
Jurado, Ariel	R-R	6-1	180	1-30-96	7	2	3.86	16	16	0	0	79	83	38	34	4	24	71	.272	.228	.308	8.05	2.72
Ledbetter, David	L-R	5-11	190	2-13-92	6	9	5.45	25	24	1	0	135	153	98	82	22	41	111	.285	.320	.256	7.38	2.73
Ledbetter, Ryan	R-R	6-1	190	2-13-92	1	0	2.43	20	0	0	4	30	29	11	8	3	13	35	.257	.302	.217	10.31	3.94
Martin, Brett	L-L	6-4	190	4-28-95	2	1	4.24	6	6	0	0	23	24	13	11	3	7	16	.270	.292	.262	6.17	2.70
McCain, Shane	L-L	6-1	210	8-4-91	7	4	3.39	41	0	0	3	74	64	35	28	10	25	75	.228	.175	.267	9.08	3.03
Mendez, Yohander	L-L	6-5	200	1-17-95	4	1	2.45	7	7	0	0	33	21	9	9	2	11	45	.176	.205	.163	12.27	3.00
Milroy, Matt	L-R	6-2	185	10-5-90	3	0	5.67	18	0	0	0	27	24	17	17	0	34	34	.238	.300	.197	11.33	9.00
Monegro, Jose	R-R	6-3	200	9-19-89	0	0	4.50	2	0	0	0	4	4	2	2	1	0	2	.250	.000	.444	4.50	0.00
Ortiz, Luis	R-R	6-3	230	9-22-95	3	2	2.60	7	6	0	0	28	23	14	8	4	6	28	.221	.178	.254	9.11	1.95
Palmquist, Cody	R-R	6-5	190	4-8-94	4	2	3.80	25	2	0	5	43	36	25	18	6	15	51	.229	.292	.195	10.76	3.16
Perez, David	R-R	6-5	200	12-20-92	2	0	0.75	4	0	0	1	12	12	1	1	0	3	10	.267	.231	.281	7.50	2.25
Pettibone, Austin	R-R	6-3	180	9-10-92	1	2	5.37	40	0	0	1	64	69	40	38	6	41	55	.280	.286	.277	7.77	5.80
Quintana, Adam	R-R	6-2	225	1-24-92	8	4	4.34	27	15	0	1	102	111	64	49	8	51	99	.277	.302	.256	8.76	4.51
Richman, Jason	L-L	6-4	210	10-15-93	1	0	5.14	6	0	0	0	7	7	4	4	0	4	6	.280	.167	.385	7.71	5.14

Pitching	B-T	HT	WT	DOB	W	L	ERA	G	GS	CG	SV	IP	H	R	ER	HR	BB	SO	AVG	vLH	vRH	K/9	BB/9
Springs, Jeffrey	L-L	6-3	180	9-20-92	2	2	5.36	13	9	0	0	49	52	33	29	9	21	52	.277	.265	.283	9.62	3.88
Vasquez, Kelvin	R-R	6-4	195	4-6-93	0	1	4.10	16	0	0	0	26	24	12	12	2	20	26	.245	.216	.262	8.89	6.84
Wiles, Collin	R-R	6-4	212	5-30-94	3	8	4.89	23	23	0	0	127	139	76	69	18	29	80	.285	.275	.293	5.67	2.06
Williams, Scott	R-R	6-2	200	11-17-93	1	2	4.54	27	0	0	4	34	27	17	17	5	13	37	.213	.167	.247	9.89	3.48
Wiper, Cole	R-R	6-4	185	6-3-92	7	4	4.38	16	14	0	0	74	68	41	36	10	30	64	.246	.198	.290	7.78	3.65

Fielding

Catcher	PCT	G	PO	A	E	DP	PB
Lyon	.981	24	196	16	4	4	1
Torres	.974	20	135	15	4	3	2
Trevino	.998	100	846	102	2	12	8

First Base	PCT	G	PO	A	E	DP
Altmann	1.000	2	5	0	0	1
Arroyo	1.000	6	54	4	0	5
Castillo	1.000	2	5	0	0	0
Lyon	.971	8	60	6	2	4
Martin	.988	46	377	28	5	38
Moore	.990	13	93	10	1	7
Profar	.991	46	407	28	4	34
Spivey	1.000	2	18	2	0	1
Torres	.975	23	142	12	4	11

Second Base	PCT	G	PO	A	E	DP
Altmann	1.000	6	13	24	0	5
Castillo	.951	10	13	26	2	4
De Leon	.976	19	31	51	2	8
Demeritte	.970	80	120	241	11	43
Moore	1.000	1	1	2	0	0
Morgan	.938	20	22	39	4	6
Profar	.923	10	12	24	3	8

Third Base	PCT	G	PO	A	E	DP
Castillo	.846	7	5	6	2	1
Demeritte	—	1	0	0	0	0
Martin	.972	10	12	23	1	2
Morgan	.932	84	72	146	16	11
Profar	.944	45	25	60	5	5

Shortstop	PCT	G	PO	A	E	DP
Castillo	1.000	2	6	0	0	0
De Leon	.964	111	179	300	18	65
Demeritte	1.000	1	0	3	0	0
Moore	1.000	2	3	3	0	2
Morgan	.970	29	45	83	4	17

Outfield	PCT	G	PO	A	E	DP
Beras	.941	81	121	7	8	0
Gonzalez	.991	98	209	9	2	2
Heineman	.992	132	229	8	2	3
Jenkins	1.000	1	1	0	0	0
Lyon	—	1	0	0	0	0
Martin	—	6	0	0	0	0
Spivey	1.000	21	30	1	0	0
Tendler	.968	91	142	7	5	1

HICKORY CRAWDADS — *LOW CLASS A*

SOUTH ATLANTIC LEAGUE

Batting	B-T	HT	WT	DOB	AVG	vLH	vRH	G	AB	R	H	2B	3B	HR	RBI	BB	HBP	SH	SF	SO	SB	CS	SLG	OBP
Almonte, Jose	R-R	6-3	205	9-9-96	.278	.212	.305	57	180	29	50	6	0	8	26	8	10	0	0	56	8	2	.444	.343
Altmann, Josh	R-R	6-3	190	7-6-94	.260	.353	.233	71	227	43	59	16	2	6	30	23	8	0	0	38	9	7	.427	.349
Arroyo, Carlos	L-R	5-11	150	6-28-93	.213	.136	.245	19	75	6	16	1	0	1	3	2	0	1	0	15	0	2	.267	.234
Clark, LeDarious	R-R	5-10	185	12-27-93	.242	.213	.252	82	314	43	76	20	3	12	34	14	2	4	0	99	25	10	.439	.279
Day, Darius	L-L	5-11	175	8-25-94	.170	.000	.211	16	47	1	8	3	1	0	10	7	1	2	1	25	2	2	.277	.286
De La Rosa, Frandy	B-R	6-1	180	1-24-96	.250	.198	.267	118	424	54	106	18	2	7	39	45	7	4	3	92	19	23	.351	.330
Forbes, Ti'quan	R-R	6-3	180	8-26-96	.251	.275	.243	120	427	50	107	16	4	4	44	25	11	2	2	106	6	5	.335	.308
Garia, Chris	B-R	6-0	165	12-16-92	.238	.128	.287	33	126	19	30	5	3	4	13	11	0	4	0	25	11	2	.421	.299
Ibanez, Andy	R-R	5-10	170	4-3-93	.324	.281	.344	49	185	28	60	18	1	7	35	29	1	2	3	28	10	8	.546	.413
Jenkins, Eric	L-R	6-1	170	1-30-97	.221	.200	.228	126	506	72	112	13	9	8	40	40	3	8	6	154	51	15	.330	.279
Lacrus, Sherman	R-R	5-11	180	12-23-93	.231	.200	.240	55	169	22	39	7	1	2	10	13	4	1	2	34	5	3	.320	.298
Lindley, London	R-R	5-11	160	6-12-93	.214	.333	.200	6	28	1	6	3	0	0	2	0	0	0	0	5	1	0	.321	.214
McKay, Connor	R-R	6-3	180	10-10-92	.152	.214	.138	47	158	16	24	4	0	4	7	14	0	0	1	49	5	2	.253	.220
Moore, Dylan	R-R	6-0	185	8-2-92	.244	.261	.238	101	340	55	83	18	3	9	45	54	17	0	3	77	37	9	.394	.372
Moorman, Chuck	R-R	5-11	200	1-9-94	.227	.242	.223	90	304	20	69	17	0	2	32	14	0	5	3	63	1	3	.303	.259
Perez, Brallan	R-R	5-10	165	1-27-96	.393	1.000	.370	10	28	1	11	1	0	1	5	2	0	0	0	2	2	2	.536	.433
Pinto, Eduard	L-L	5-11	150	10-23-94	.337	.277	.358	51	184	26	62	11	0	5	28	17	1	2	2	16	1	3	.478	.392
Sanchez, Tyler	R-R	6-2	190	5-30-93	.280	.337	.257	86	293	42	82	18	0	10	56	38	14	1	4	70	3	3	.444	.384
Silva, Luis	R-R	5-11	170	6-30-95	.222	.000	.240	8	27	5	6	2	0	0	2	2	1	0	0	10	0	0	.296	.300
Turner, Xavier	R-R	6-1	205	8-24-93	.214	.400	.111	5	14	4	3	0	0	2	2	2	2	0	0	5	0	0	.643	.389
Valencia, Ricardo	R-R	6-0	185	1-13-93	.244	.194	.260	41	127	12	31	5	0	4	21	16	3	0	0	31	0	0	.378	.342
Yrizarri, Yeyson	R-R	6-0	175	2-2-97	.269	.262	.271	118	450	53	121	27	3	7	53	9	8	6	6	91	20	15	.389	.292

Pitching	B-T	HT	WT	DOB	W	L	ERA	G	GS	CG	SV	IP	H	R	ER	HR	BB	SO	AVG	vLH	vRH	K/9	BB/9
Ball, Matt	R-R	6-5	200	1-23-95	4	1	1.60	21	4	0	3	51	51	11	9	2	17	39	.271	.263	.278	6.93	3.02
2-team total (10 Kannapolis)					4	2	2.30	31	4	0	4	67	68	26	17	3	22	63	—	—	—	8.51	2.97
Bass, Blake	R-R	6-7	250	6-3-93	6	3	2.63	36	5	0	2	86	99	35	25	7	21	57	.292	.331	.263	5.99	2.21
Benjamin, Wes	R-L	6-1	180	7-26-93	6	5	3.79	21	18	0	1	102	105	45	43	13	22	101	.268	.230	.283	8.91	1.94
Brummett, Garrett	R-R	6-0	185	4-9-94	1	0	5.25	8	0	0	2	12	14	8	7	1	3	9	.292	.182	.385	6.75	2.25
Choplick, Adam	L-L	6-9	250	11-18-92	2	2	3.32	35	0	0	1	60	52	23	22	1	38	74	.239	.323	.203	11.16	5.73
Davis, Tyler	R-R	5-10	185	1-5-93	2	0	3.68	6	0	0	1	15	11	8	6	1	3	18	.196	.222	.184	11.05	1.84
Dula, Chris	R-R	6-2	200	8-6-92	1	0	18.00	2	0	0	0	2	3	4	4	1	2	2	.333	.500	.2	9.00	9.00
Fairbanks, Peter	R-R	6-6	215	12-16-93	4	5	4.88	24	16	0	2	101	112	61	55	9	31	80	.281	.344	.227	7.11	2.75
Ferguson, Tyler	R-R	6-4	225	10-5-93	0	1	8.78	10	0	0	1	13	12	13	13	1	18	10	.261	.143	.36	6.75	12.15
Hernandez, Jonathan	R-R	6-2	175	7-6-96	10	9	4.56	24	22	1	0	116	110	67	59	14	49	85	.252	.227	.271	6.58	3.79
Juan, Johan	R-R	6-1	180	4-14-94	0	0	4.85	8	0	0	1	13	16	7	7	3	4	10	.296	.450	.206	6.92	2.77
Lanphere, Luke	R-R	6-2	175	9-30-95	2	2	3.78	6	6	0	0	33	39	16	14	5	6	31	.300	.211	.37	8.37	1.62
Lopez, Omarlin	R-R	6-3	175	10-8-93	8	5	3.38	38	0	0	3	75	75	38	28	7	29	82	.254	.276	.24	9.88	3.50
Martin, Brett	L-L	6-4	190	4-28-95	2	3	4.53	9	9	0	0	44	58	29	22	3	14	48	.317	.341	.309	9.89	2.89
Martinez, Emerson	R-R	6-0	190	1-11-95	0	6	3.36	19	6	1	0	56	54	27	21	2	22	48	.251	.278	.229	7.67	3.51
Palumbo, Joe	L-L	6-1	168	10-26-94	7	5	2.24	33	7	0	8	96	71	28	24	5	36	122	.202	.149	.221	11.40	3.36
Payano, Pedro	R-R	6-2	170	9-27-94	3	3	2.08	15	13	1	0	74	59	22	17	2	29	82	.219	.191	.239	10.02	3.54
Richman, Jason	L-L	6-4	210	10-15-93	1	0	3.38	15	0	0	3	27	24	12	10	2	14	12	.233	.152	.298	4.05	4.73
Shortslef, Jake	R-R	6-5	235	12-29-94	1	1	3.44	11	0	0	1	18	16	7	7	1	3	23	.222	.103	.364	11.29	1.47
Springs, Jeffrey	L-L	6-3	180	9-20-92	1	1	1.16	18	0	0	3	31	11	8	4	1	8	40	.106	.182	.085	11.61	2.32

Pitching

Pitching	B-T	HT	WT	DOB	W	L	ERA	G	GS	CG	SV	IP	H	R	ER	HR	BB	SO	AVG	vLH	vRH	K/9	BB/9
Swanson, Erik	R-R	6-3	220	9-4-93	6	4	3.43	19	15	0	1	81	77	37	31	4	25	78	.248	.207	.275	8.63	2.77
2-team total (5 Charleston, SC)					6	5	3.46	24	17	0	1	96	91	44	37	4	30	93	—	—	—	8.69	2.80
Tate, Dillon	R-R	6-2	165	5-1-94	3	3	5.12	17	16	0	0	65	78	39	37	5	27	55	.311	.333	.295	7.62	3.74
2-team total (7 Charleston, SC)					4	3	4.70	24	16	0	0	82	99	49	43	6	33	70	—	—	—	7.65	3.61
Torres, Christian	L-L	6-0	160	9-7-93	2	3	1.47	12	3	0	0	31	28	9	5	1	10	30	.235	.184	.259	8.80	2.93
Werner, John	R-R	6-2	210	1-3-92	2	2	4.78	26	0	0	8	38	33	26	20	6	12	45	.236	.255	.224	10.75	2.87

Fielding

Catcher	PCT	G	PO	A	E	DP	PB
Moorman	.994	71	557	76	4	7	10
Sanchez	.990	59	453	48	5	3	4
Valencia	.974	22	137	15	4	1	1

First Base	PCT	G	PO	A	E	DP
Almonte	—	1	0	0	0	0
Altmann	.993	37	263	25	2	30
Forbes	.800	1	4	0	1	1
McKay	1.000	1	7	2	0	1
Moore	.991	59	518	32	5	33
Moorman	1.000	16	113	9	0	12
Sanchez	1.000	24	191	17	0	17
Silva	.982	7	54	2	1	6
Turner	1.000	2	8	0	1	
Valencia	1.000	5	37	3	0	4

Second Base	PCT	G	PO	A	E	DP
Altmann	1.000	7	17	16	0	5
Arroyo	1.000	3	7	4	0	2
De La Rosa	.974	83	154	222	10	50
Ibanez	.958	40	82	102	8	24
Moore	1.000	10	20	21	0	7
Perez	1.000	3	6	5	0	1

Third Base	PCT	G	PO	A	E	DP
Altmann	1.000	1	0	3	0	2
Arroyo	1.000	1	1	2	0	2
De La Rosa	.818	25	8	46	12	4
Forbes	.948	108	71	220	16	33
Moore	1.000	5	2	8	0	0
Perez	.818	3	0	9	2	0

Shortstop	PCT	G	PO	A	E	DP
Altmann	.944	4	7	10	1	4

	PCT	G	PO	A	E	DP
De La Rosa	1.000	1	1	2	0	0
Moore	.951	18	26	32	3	8
Perez	1.000	4	3	9	0	3
Yrizarri	.965	116	155	342	18	49

Outfield	PCT	G	PO	A	E	DP
Almonte	.975	49	71	7	2	0
Altmann	1.000	18	32	2	0	0
Arroyo	.913	15	19	2	2	1
Clark	.939	75	127	11	9	3
Day	.969	13	30	1	1	0
Garia	.964	23	27	0	1	0
Jenkins	.984	118	241	9	4	1
Lacrus	.972	52	101	4	3	1
Lindley	1.000	5	8	0	0	0
McKay	.939	19	30	1	2	0
Moore	1.000	8	10	1	0	1
Pinto	1.000	38	57	10	0	0

SPOKANE INDIANS
NORTHWEST LEAGUE
SHORT-SEASON

Batting

Batting	B-T	HT	WT	DOB	AVG	vLH	vRH	G	AB	R	H	2B	3B	HR	RBI	BB	HBP	SH	SF	SO	SB	CS	SLG	OBP
Bolin, Travis	R-R	5-11	208	10-18-94	.231	.160	.296	16	52	9	12	3	2	1	9	9	2	0	0	21	0	1	.423	.365
Castillo, Elio	R-R	6-1	160	3-1-94	.327	.333	.324	14	49	5	16	3	0	1	11	4	0	1	0	4	0	1	.449	.377
Day, Darius	L-L	5-11	175	8-25-94	.237	.222	.242	53	186	27	44	7	3	3	19	34	3	2	1	70	2	4	.355	.362
Garay, Carlos	R-R	6-0	210	10-5-94	.282	.409	.232	22	78	6	22	2	0	0	11	4	0	0	1	5	0	0	.308	.313
Kowalczyk, Alex	R-R	6-3	205	10-17-93	.288	.235	.310	31	118	12	34	8	0	3	13	7	2	0	3	32	0	0	.432	.331
LeBlanc, Charles	R-R	6-3	195	6-3-96	.285	.342	.258	61	228	36	65	12	4	1	15	31	4	0	5	34	1	3	.386	.380
Lohr, Stephen	R-R	6-0	208	3-2-95	.232	.256	.222	40	138	18	32	4	0	2	13	19	1	1	0	43	0	0	.304	.329
McDonald, Todd	R-R	6-3	180	10-23-95	.223	.148	.241	39	139	19	31	6	0	3	18	10	1	0	1	37	0	0	.331	.278
Merrigan, Josh	L-R	6-2	172	9-15-93	.236	.294	.218	19	72	10	17	2	0	1	6	6	1	0	0	16	2	2	.306	.304
Middleton, Clay	R-R	6-0	205	10-8-93	.224	.316	.179	20	58	8	13	4	0	2	3	11	3	2	0	11	0	0	.397	.375
Perez, Brallan	R-R	5-10	165	1-27-96	.307	.320	.300	29	75	9	23	1	0	2	13	13	2	1	0	10	1	2	.400	.422
Scott, Preston	R-R	6-2	215	3-29-94	.239	.212	.252	47	163	28	39	6	1	0	14	30	9	0	2	49	3	1	.288	.382
Smith, Chad	L-L	6-2	200	9-30-97	.242	.256	.234	61	236	29	57	13	0	3	25	23	2	0	7	53	4	0	.335	.312
Spivey, Seth	L-R	5-11	180	7-6-92	.226	.182	.248	61	230	29	52	10	0	3	42	34	5	1	4	35	3	1	.309	.333
Taveras, Leody	B-R	6-1	170	9-8-98	.228	.179	.250	29	123	14	28	6	1	0	9	8	0	0	2	26	3	1	.293	.271
Tejeda, Anderson	L-R	5-11	160	5-1-98	.277	.276	.277	23	94	15	26	0	1	8	19	5	0	0		33	1	0	.553	.313
Terrero, Luis	R-R	6-0	215	11-11-95	.276	.276	.277	45	170	17	47	8	0	2	20	13	4	0	0	32	7	4	.359	.342
Terry, Curtis	R-R	6-2	255	10-6-96	.194	.200	.190	9	31	4	6	1	0	1	3	0	1	0	0	15	0	0	.323	.219
Turner, Xavier	R-R	6-1	205	8-24-93	.340	.250	.372	29	106	19	36	7	2	2	16	11	2	0	2	11	1	0	.462	.405

Pitching

Pitching	B-T	HT	WT	DOB	W	L	ERA	G	GS	CG	SV	IP	H	R	ER	HR	BB	SO	AVG	vLH	vRH	K/9	BB/9
Anderson, Reid	R-R	6-3	185	8-22-95	1	3	3.44	14	2	0	1	37	31	18	14	1	20	18	.238	.239	.238	4.42	4.91
Bruce, Steven	R-R	6-0	190	3-7-92	1	0	4.05	12	0	0	3	20	18	9	9	0	4	18	.237	.240	.235	8.10	1.80
Brummett, Garrett	R-R	6-0	185	4-9-94	0	0	6.10	7	0	0	1	10	11	7	7	0	4	16	.268	.250	.280	13.94	3.48
Cody, Kyle	R-R	6-7	245	8-9-94	2	5	5.13	12	9	0	0	47	56	32	27	4	13	53	.293	.313	.108	10.08	2.47
Daniele, Alex	R-R	6-5	225	4-7-94	0	5	4.15	16	5	0	1	39	24	25	18	1	25	34	.174	.167	.178	7.85	5.77
Dula, Chris	R-R	6-2	200	8-6-92	0	1	3.38	7	0	0	0	8	4	4	3	0	7	11	.148	.000	.174	12.38	7.88
Evans, Demarcus	R-R	6-4	240	10-21-96	0	1	2.77	6	6	0	0	26	20	13	8	1	19	31	.204	.226	.194	10.73	6.58
Ferguson, Tyler	R-R	6-4	225	10-5-93	2	0	1.78	13	0	0	2	30	18	8	6	1	10	46	.161	.233	.116	13.65	2.97
Fontenot, Kaleb	R-R	6-1	180	6-23-93	0	2	4.17	19	3	0	3	37	38	21	17	3	16	41	.266	.262	.268	10.06	3.93
Green, Nick	R-R	6-1	165	3-25-95	2	2	4.98	7	7	0	0	34	33	22	19	0	14	44	.243	.180	.293	11.53	3.67
Juan, Kevin	R-L	6-1	180	4-14-94	2	2	3.51	18	0	0	3	33	32	19	13	1	12	28	.246	.140	.299	7.56	3.24
Kendrick, Clyde	L-L	6-2	185	11-21-93	0	0	0.00	1	0	0	0	2	0	0	0		1		.000	—	.000	4.50	0.00
Lanphere, Luke	R-R	6-2	175	9-30-95	3	3	3.52	7	7	0	0	38	36	17	15	4	16	26	.247	.255	.242	6.10	3.76
Lenik, Kevin	R-R	6-5	225	8-9-91	1	2	5.17	10	0	0	0	31	35	21	18	1	16	32	.278	.267	.284	9.19	4.60
Lewis, Colby	R-R	6-4	240	8-2-79	0	0	7.20	1	1	0	0	5	8	4	4	0	3		.364	.400	.333	5.40	0.00
Matuella, Michael	R-R	6-6	220	6-3-94	0	0	0.00	1	1	0	0	3	1	0	0	0	2	1	.111	.333	.000	3.00	6.00
Mendez, Sal	R-L	6-4	180	2-25-95	6	4	3.75	14	9	0	0	58	63	30	24	5	24	46	.276	.382	.243	7.18	3.75
Pelham, C.D.	L-L	6-6	235	2-21-95	0	6	6.16	16	7	0	2	38	36	30	26	0	43	50	.243	.283	.211	11.84	10.18
Phillips, Tyler	R-R	6-5	200	10-27-97	4	7	6.44	13	13	0	0	59	78	49	42	2	20	57	.307	.308	.306	8.74	3.07
Sebald, Scott	L-L	6-5	230	6-16-94	1	0	0.00	5	0	0	0	8	5	3	0	0	3	14	.216	.167	.240	12.60	2.70
Shortslef, Jake	R-R	6-5	235	12-29-94	0	0	3.00	5	0	0	0	6	3	2	2	0	8	19	.233	.286	.200	7.13	3.00
Stubblefield, Tyler	R-L	6-1	215	10-19-93	0	1	5.60	12	0	0	1	18	22	14	11	2	5	23	.297	.267	.305	11.72	2.55

Pitching	B-T	HT	WT	DOB	W	L	ERA	G	GS	CG	SV	IP	H	R	ER	HR	BB	SO	AVG	vLH	vRH	K/9	BB/9
Torres, Christian	L-L	6-0	160	9-7-93	0	0	9.00	7	0	0	0	7	11	9	7	1	3	6	.393	.500	.350	7.71	3.86
Vasquez, Kelvin	R-R	6-4	195	4-6-93	0	0	6.75	3	0	0	0	5	6	4	4	0	3	9	.300	.250	.333	15.19	5.06
Vasquez, Mark	R-R	6-4	220	5-11-92	4	0	2.10	17	0	0	0	34	28	8	8	0	13	41	.217	.240	.203	10.75	3.41
Werner, John	R-R	6-2	210	1-3-92	0	1	9.00	3	0	0	0	2	3	2	2	0	1	1	.375	.500	.333	4.50	4.50

Fielding

C: Garay 13, Kowalczyk 22, Middleton 18, Spivey 25. **1B:** Garay 7, Lohr 7, McDonald 34, Spivey 9, Terrero 11, Terry 9, Turner 1. **2B:** Perez 17, Prescott 48, Tejeda 3, Terrero 10. **3B:** Castillo 1, Leblanc 15, Lohr 23, Perez 5, Tejeda 2, Terrero 6, Turner 28. **SS:** Castillo 13, Leblanc 45, Perez 3, Tejeda 17. **OF:** Bolin 16, Day 52, McDonald 1, Merrigan 19, Prescott 1, Scott 37, Smith 58, Spivey 9, Taveras 28, Terrero 12.

AZL RANGERS   *ROOKIE*
ARIZONA LEAGUE

Batting	B-T	HT	WT	DOB	AVG	vLH	vRH	G	AB	R	H	2B	3B	HR	RBI	BB	HBP	SH	SF	SO	SB	CS	SLG	OBP
Almonte, Jose	R-R	6-3	205	9-9-96	.267	.000	.286	4	15	4	4	2	1	0	1	1	0	0	0	3	0	0	.533	.313
Alvarez, Jhonniel	R-R	5-9	195	2-15-93	.250	.000	.333	5	8	0	2	0	0	0	1	0	0	0	1	2	0	0	.250	.222
Arroyo, Carlos	L-R	5-11	150	6-28-93	.250	.000	.500	1	4	1	1	0	0	0	0	0	0	0	0	0	0	0	.250	.250
Bell, Alexei	R-R	5-7	187	10-2-83	.250	.000	.308	4	16	1	4	0	0	0	0	1	0	0	0	0	0	0	.250	.294
Bolin, Travis	R-R	5-11	208	10-18-94	.300	.192	.364	18	70	9	21	5	2	0	10	3	2	0	2	20	7	1	.429	.338
Brinson, Lewis	R-R	6-3	195	5-8-94	.231	1.000	.167	4	13	3	3	1	0	0	1	2	0	0	0	2	2	0	.308	.333
Cantwell, Pat	R-R	6-2	210	4-10-90	.571	.500	.600	2	7	1	4	1	1	1	2	0	0	0	0	3	0	0	1.429	.571
Clark, LeDarious	R-R	5-10	185	12-27-93	.214	.250	.200	4	14	4	3	1	0	1	2	1	0	0	1	4	1	0	.500	.214
Diaz, Willy	R-R	6-3	200	4-19-94	.266	.311	.250	47	173	24	46	13	3	1	22	15	5	0	1	60	3	1	.393	.340
Enright, Kole	R-R	6-1	175	1-21-98	.313	.436	.270	42	150	22	47	13	0	1	17	14	4	0	4	33	3	1	.420	.378
Fajardo, Kelvin	R-R	5-11	160	3-8-96	.140	.200	.107	13	43	2	6	1	0	0	1	6	0	0	1	4	1	0	.163	.240
Huff, Sam	R-R	6-4	215	1-14-98	.330	.444	.304	28	97	19	32	10	1	1	17	16	3	0	1	29	0	0	.485	.436
Kaye, Nick	L-L	6-2	180	10-18-96	.250	.171	.289	40	124	14	31	6	2	0	21	22	2	0	1	44	1	1	.331	.369
Kiner-Falefa, Isiah	R-R	5-10	176	3-23-95	.100	.000	.143	3	10	2	1	0	0	0	1	0	0	0	1	1	0	0	.100	.182
Lindley, London	R-R	5-11	160	6-23-95	.240	.250	.236	34	100	10	24	3	1	0	7	2	2	1	0	28	8	2	.290	.269
Mack, Marcus	L-L	6-2	185	8-1-98	.000	.000	.000	9	20	2	0	0	0	0	0	4	0	0	0	12	4	0	.000	.167
Marte, Luis	R-R	6-1	188	12-15-93	.417	.000	.556	3	12	2	5	2	0	0	1	0	0	0	0	2	0	0	.583	.417
McReynolds, Jonah	R-R	5-11	165	12-16-95	.219	.297	.187	37	128	11	28	3	2	1	10	9	1	0	2	37	2	1	.297	.271
Merrigan, Josh	L-R	6-2	172	9-15-93	.192	.118	.229	14	52	8	10	1	0	0	3	0	0	0	16	4	1	.212	.236
O'Banion, Austin	R-R	6-3	215	7-12-95	.212	.200	.215	34	104	13	22	6	0	0	8	5	0	1	0	29	2	1	.298	.297
Pozo, Yohel	R-R	6-0	175	11-4-97	.343	.289	.360	48	181	25	62	12	2	1	22	13	1	0	4	10	1	0	.448	.382
Quiroz, Isaias	R-R	5-10	195	10-22-96	.222	.143	.255	25	72	6	16	2	0	2	10	9	3	0	0	27	0	1	.333	.333
Silva, Luis	R-R	5-11	170	6-30-95	.238	.625	.147	13	42	4	10	3	0	0	7	2	0	0	0	6	0	2	.310	.273
Strausborger, Ryan	R-R	6-0	185	3-4-88	.333	—	.333	1	3	1	1	0	1	0	0	0	0	0	0	1	0	0	1.000	.333
Stubbs, Drew	R-R	6-4	205	10-4-84	.250	.500	.143	3	9	2	0	0	1	1	0	0	3	0	0	3	0	0	.222	.300
Taveras, Leody	B-R	6-1	170	9-8-98	.278	.111	.316	33	144	22	40	6	3	1	15	11	0	0	0	24	11	4	.382	.329
Tejeda, Anderson	L-R	5-11	160	5-1-98	.293	.200	.315	32	133	22	39	12	6	1	21	8	0	0	1	36	1	0	.496	.331
Terry, Curtis	R-R	6-2	255	10-6-96	.305	.385	.275	39	141	20	43	17	1	4	23	9	3	0	1	30	0	0	.525	.357

Pitching	B-T	HT	WT	DOB	W	L	ERA	G	GS	CG	SV	IP	H	R	ER	HR	BB	SO	AVG	vLH	vRH	K/9	BB/9
Barlow, Joe	R-R	6-3	195	9-28-95	2	4	4.41	13	3	0	2	33	29	17	16	4	19	29	.242	.283	.216	7.99	5.23
Bice, Dylan	L-R	6-4	220	8-17-97	0	2	5.73	13	0	0	0	22	33	19	14	1	7	23	.337	.324	.344	9.41	2.86
Brito, Pedro	L-L	5-11	155	4-4-95	1	2	4.91	4	2	0	0	15	15	9	8	1	1	16	.254	.231	.261	9.82	0.61
Bruce, Steven	R-R	6-0	190	3-7-92	0	0	1.00	4	0	0	0	9	8	1	1	0	0	6	.258	.444	.182	6.00	0.00
Casanova, Jean	R-R	6-3	155	3-4-97	1	1	3.16	14	2	0	0	26	19	10	9	0	15	32	.196	.314	.129	11.22	5.26
Cruz, Israel	R-R	6-1	170	6-1-97	0	3	4.36	8	5	0	1	33	30	19	16	0	14	33	.256	.238	.267	9.00	3.82
Engler, Scott	R-R	6-4	220	12-12-96	0	1	9.00	4	1	0	0	7	11	8	7	2	1	7	.355	.375	.348	9.00	1.29
Evans, Demarcus	R-R	6-4	240	10-22-96	1	1	3.10	8	6	0	0	29	19	11	10	2	18	44	.183	.171	.190	13.66	5.59
Heffel, Derek	R-R	6-6	225	4-13-96	2	1	7.85	13	6	0	1	37	53	39	32	1	16	27	.335	.289	.354	6.63	3.93
Jacobsen, Lucas	L-L	6-5	190	7-1-95	1	0	6.75	7	0	0	0	9	13	8	7	2	4	12	.310	.000	.351	11.57	3.86
Kendrick, Clyde	L-L	6-2	185	11-21-93	2	0	3.65	7	0	0	0	12	10	5	5	1	3	13	.222	.200	.233	9.49	2.19
Martin, Brett	L-L	6-4	190	4-28-95	0	0	3.86	2	2	0	0	2	3	1	1	0	0	6	.273	.333	.250	23.14	0.00
Mendoza, Kenny	R-L	6-4	215	3-12-98	0	3	4.24	12	0	0	0	23	14	12	11	0	14	27	.171	.091	.183	10.41	5.40
Munoz, Yelfri	R-R	6-3	210	11-24-93	0	0	17.18	5	0	0	0	4	10	7	7	0	5	5	.500	.400	.400	12.27	12.27
Peltier, Reilly	R-R	6-5	215	8-17-95	2	2	4.81	13	3	0	0	24	22	13	13	0	17	20	.250	.282	.224	9.50	3.70
Pichardo, Yonelvy	L-L	6-2	165	7-12-96	1	4	6.28	13	6	0	0	43	52	35	30	2	19	41	.297	.289	.300	8.58	3.98
Ragans, Cole	L-L	6-4	190	12-12-97	0	0	4.70	4	2	0	0	8	11	4	4	0	6	9	.344	.500	.308	10.57	7.04
Roberts, Kyle	L-L	6-6	210	10-20-95	0	2	11.81	4	0	0	0	5	9	11	7	2	6	5	.360	.000	.455	8.44	10.13
Rodriguez, Argenis	R-R	6-3	190	3-7-96	4	3	4.76	14	9	0	0	57	64	36	30	4	5	54	.272	.198	.312	8.58	0.79
Sebald, Scott	L-L	6-5	230	6-16-94	0	0	3.86	9	3	0	1	21	21	11	9	1	7	20	.276	.231	.286	8.57	3.00
Simon, Bradley	R-R	6-4	220	4-22-97	1	1	4.32	11	0	0	0	17	13	10	8	1	9	17	.220	.200	.235	9.18	4.86
Speas, Alex	R-R	6-4	180	3-4-98	0	0	0.00	4	3	0	0	8	4	0	0	0	7	11	.138	.000	.211	11.88	7.56
Stubblefield, Tyler	R-L	6-5	215	10-19-93	0	0	6.23	4	0	0	0	4	8	4	3	0	3	7	.381	.167	.467	14.54	6.23
Thompson, Tyree	R-R	6-4	165	6-12-97	0	2	7.11	9	0	0	0	6	9	5	5	0	5	6	.231	.273	.200	8.53	7.11
Tiedemann, Tai	R-R	6-6	195	5-31-96	0	0	6.23	4	2	0	0	9	12	7	6	1	3	8	.333	.300	.375	8.31	3.12
Werner, John	R-R	6-2	210	1-3-92	0	0	0.00	3	0	0	1	4	3	0	0	0	4	7	.214	.250	.25	15.75	9.00

Fielding

C: Alvarez 5, Cantwell 1, Huff 14, Kiner-Falefa 2, Pozo 25, Quiroz 18. **1B:** Diaz 15, Kaye 12, Pozo 4, Terry 29. **2B:** Arroyo 1, Enright 6, Fajardo 13, McReynolds 14, Silva 13, Tejeda 12. **3B:** Diaz 33, Enright 23, McReynolds 3. **SS:** Enright 13, Marte 3, McReynolds 20, Tejeda 20. **OF:** Almonte 3, Bell 4, Bolin 18, Brinson 3, Clark 4, Kaye 28, Lindley 29, Mack 5, Merrigan 14, O'Banion 31, Strausborger 1, Stubbs 2, Taveras 33.

Batting	B-T	HT	WT	DOB	AVG	vLH	vRH	G	AB	R	H	2B	3B	HR	RBI	BB	HBP	SH	SF	SO	SB	CS	SLG	OBP
Almonte, Juan	R-R	6-0	168	4-13-97	.291	.226	.304	54	189	20	55	8	0	2	26	12	3	2	4	25	12	7	.365	.337
Alonzo, Yimmelvyn	R-R	6-1	185	3-10-97	.248	.324	.223	46	149	27	37	9	4	2	21	28	4	1	1	49	7	4	.403	.37
Aparicio, Miguel	L-L	6-0	165	3-17-99	.274	.182	.297	58	219	32	60	10	4	3	36	18	4	6	2	36	15	7	.397	.337
Aybar, Saury	R-R	6-1	170	7-25-95	.255	.270	.250	50	153	29	39	7	2	1	25	16	4	2	4	24	9	5	.346	.333
Barrios, Ciro	R-R	6-1	178	9-27-96	.220	.200	.225	23	50	8	11	1	0	0	4	8	2	2	0	8	3	1	.240	.350
Cabrera, Wanderley	R-R	5-10	180	2-27-95	.239	.379	.175	31	92	15	22	5	1	1	13	6	1	0	1	19	1	0	.348	.290
Carrillo, Jairo	R-R	6-0	150	6-15-99	.200	.167	.208	16	30	6	6	1	0	0	2	8	2	1	0	5	1	1	.233	.400
Castro, Rubell	R-R	6-3	180	8-13-96	.191	.273	.164	34	89	12	17	2	1	0	7	17	1	0	1	38	4	4	.236	.324
Cordero, Andretty	R-R	6-1	170	5-3-97	.290	.327	.278	59	224	36	65	12	2	5	48	18	3	1	4	29	7	3	.429	.345
Damian, Rayner	B-R	6-0	155	4-29-97	.197	.071	.231	30	66	10	13	2	1	0	5	9	1	0	0	21	4	2	.258	.303
Encarnacion, Cristian	R-R	6-3	185	9-9-96	.244	.182	.265	57	176	24	43	8	3	1	22	27	13	0	5	44	16	2	.341	.376
Fajardo, Kelvin	R-R	5-11	160	3-8-96	.318	.387	.289	29	107	15	34	5	0	0	9	11	3	1	0	8	4	4	.364	.397
Favela, Samuel	R-R	5-11	160	5-15-98	.250	.333	.222	9	12	3	3	0	0	0	3	3	0	0	0	3	0	0	.250	.52
Gutierrez, Beder	R-R	6-0	180	1-13-97	.228	.286	.224	31	92	17	21	5	2	1	4	16	7	3	0	17	3	3	.359	.383
Hernandez, Yonny	B-R	5-9	140	5-4-98	.293	.250	.308	61	215	55	63	4	6	0	31	37	6	8	6	22	32	9	.367	.402
Inoa, Cristian	R-R	5-10	165	7-4-99	.282	.227	.294	65	238	44	67	16	2	3	21	31	10	1	2	41	16	4	.403	.384
Joseph, Starling	R-R	6-3	180	8-1-98	.256	.194	.268	63	215	38	55	13	1	5	27	25	3	0	5	66	13	5	.395	.335
Linares, Angel	R-R	5-11	175	1-21-98	.400	.167	.448	20	35	5	14	1	0	0	4	2	2	0	0	7	1	1	.429	.462
Liriano, Welin	R-R	6-2	160	10-18-98	.220	.263	.209	53	177	23	39	5	0	1	28	21	2	0	1	61	5	4	.266	.308
Martinez, Stanly	R-R	6-0	176	1-5-97	.272	.263	.274	63	217	36	59	11	4	6	26	35	7	0	1	52	11	4	.387	.388
Mendez, Luis	R-R	5-10	180	3-30-95	.261	.264	.260	53	199	29	52	12	0	3	27	20	2	0	0	23	6	4	.367	.335
Morales, Max	R-R	6-0	190	9-28-97	.239	.265	.234	61	201	38	48	9	2	9	40	40	4	0	2	62	7	2	.438	.372
Ogando, Pedro	L-R	6-0	175	6-10-96	.279	.286	.277	24	86	10	24	2	1	0	10	4	0	0	2	14	8	6	.384	.304
Pena, Andrison	L-R	6-0	165	10-27-96	.385	.250	.412	39	117	26	45	14	3	2	27	14	3	1	1	12	7	4	.607	.459
Pernalete, Adrian	B-R	6-0	165	9-14-98	.263	.333	.241	15	38	5	10	2	0	1	2	5	3	0	0	10	2	2	.395	.391
Pineda, Edgar	R-R	5-11	140	2-12-98	.204	.195	.208	46	147	31	30	6	1	0	11	11	5	1	2	28	5	1	.259	.279
Rivera, Eudys	R-R	6-1	152	6-3-97	.207	.263	.196	38	111	21	23	4	0	0	12	13	1	3	2	26	6	2	.243	.291
Rojas, Alejandro	R-R	5-10	175	8-6-94	.317	.385	.298	23	60	12	19	3	0	0	8	6	2	2	2	5	0	1	.367	.386
Rollin, Franklin	R-R	5-11	165	8-26-95	.377	.351	.387	61	247	64	93	12	11	4	36	23	6	3	1	26	36	13	.563	.440
Taveras, Leody	B-R	6-1	170	9-8-98	.385	.500	.355	11	39	6	15	2	2	0	9	6	0	0	0	5	4	3	.538	.467
Tejeda, Anderson	L-R	5-11	160	5-1-98	.262	.286	.250	11	42	9	11	2	3	1	7	5	0	0	0	4	5	0	.524	.340
Valdez, Fernando	B-R	6-0	175	11-14-98	.247	.219	.253	58	178	25	44	13	2	1	21	39	1	1	1	66	8	4	.360	.384
Vazquez, Joenny	R-R	6-2	160	10-1-96	.208	.000	.263	13	24	3	5	1	0	0	1	0	0	0	1	0	0	0	.250	.240
Ventura, Francisco	R-R	5-9	175	11-19-98	.308	.220	.336	51	169	23	52	10	1	3	32	33	1	1	4	18	3	5	.432	.415
Ventura, Juan	R-R	6-0	165	6-15-98	.276	.105	.316	29	98	12	27	2	1	1	7	7	4	0	0	14	1	4	.347	.349
Villahermosa, Alex	R-R	5-11	160	10-10-97	.159	.077	.179	31	69	14	11	3	1	2	5	13	2	1	1	30	5	0	.319	.306
Villarreal, Guillermo	R-R	5-11	165	1-7-98	.164	.500	.106	21	55	4	9	1	2	0	5	5	1	1	1	17	0	0	.182	.258

Pitching	B-T	HT	WT	DOB	W	L	ERA	G	GS	CG	SV	IP	H	R	ER	HR	BB	SO	AVG	vLH	vRH	K/9	BB/9
Arredondo, Edgar	R-R	6-3	190	5-16-97	6	2	1.60	12	12	0	0	62	60	15	11	0	4	56	.260	.205	.285	8.13	0.58
Betances, Emmanuel	R-R	6-5	189	2-5-96	1	2	2.95	19	0	0	4	40	41	19	13	2	8	20	.272	.226	.303	4.54	1.82
Brito, Pedro	L-L	5-11	155	4-4-95	3	1	1.50	8	8	0	0	42	34	9	7	0	9	40	.225	.143	.238	8.57	1.93
Buitimea, Martin	R-R	6-1	155	4-14-98	0	0	4.62	12	0	0	1	25	26	16	13	1	8	18	.248	.282	.226	6.39	2.84
Castillo, Juan	R-R	6-3	166	9-18-95	3	4	4.09	12	10	0	1	51	53	32	23	3	20	21	.279	.259	.294	3.73	3.55
Castillo, Leudy	L-L	6-3	185	6-13-97	0	0	27.00	1	0	0	0	1	2	2	2	0	3	0	.500	—	.500	0.00	40.50
Castro, Ray	R-R	6-5	165	5-9-97	2	3	1.25	9	8	0	0	43	27	9	6	1	14	19	.184	.170	.191	3.95	2.9
Civil, Henry	R-R	6-5	194	12-14-94	1	0	10.29	14	0	0	0	14	10	17	16	0	28	14	.196	.238	.167	9.00	18.0
Cruz, Edwin	L-L	6-4	195	7-26-94	4	2	3.73	15	4	0	2	41	30	18	17	2	18	33	.201	.217	.198	7.24	3.95
Duarte, Daniel	R-R	6-0	170	12-4-96	6	3	3.05	12	11	1	0	59	66	24	20	2	13	44	.282	.324	.264	6.71	1.98
Encarnacion, Ediberto	R-R	5-11	170	2-9-94	2	1	4.43	12	0	0	0	20	20	10	10	2	5	16	.250	.259	.245	7.08	2.2
Encarnacion, Yohan	R-R	6-3	180	1-19-96	3	1	4.79	13	0	0	0	21	22	14	11	0	9	18	.265	.222	.298	3.92	7.40
Fernandez, Jeuyson	R-R	6-2	185	6-9-98	2	3	3.00	17	0	0	5	36	34	14	12	0	19	23	.250	.224	.269	5.75	4.75
Hernandez, Alexander	L-L	6-1	170	3-20-98	0	0	3.00	3	0	0	1	6	5	2	2	0	1	5	.227	.500	.200	7.50	1.50
Jasco, Yeison	R-R	6-0	160	8-5-96	0	0	9.00	1	0	0	0	5	9	5	5	0	2	3	.375	.300	.429	5.40	3.60
Lacle, Wily	R-R	6-2	175	5-30-96	0	0	3.00	2	0	0	0	3	5	5	1	2	0	1	.357	.500	.300	3.00	0.00
Leal, Werner	R-R	6-1	160	7-8-95	4	1	3.70	11	11	0	0	56	52	24	23	2	15	47	.251	.280	.242	7.55	2.41
Linares, Jesus	R-R	6-4	216	1-10-97	1	0	1.85	11	9	0	1	49	41	18	10	0	14	44	.233	.259	.220	8.14	2.59
Lopez, Ismel	R-R	6-1	190	8-24-94	3	1	2.51	19	0	0	4	43	40	14	12	2	11	43	.248	.231	.257	9.00	2.30
Lopez, Luis	R-R	6-4	185	7-25-96	5	3	3.53	12	12	0	0	66	63	30	26	3	13	40	.252	.203	.273	5.43	1.76
Martinez, Greidy	R-R	6-0	155	4-24-96	3	1	3.15	18	0	0	6	34	33	17	12	0	8	34	.256	.280	.241	8.91	2.10
Mavo, Daniel	L-L	5-10	170	7-20-95	4	1	2.00	17	0	0	1	36	38	23	8	1	20	32	.270	.263	.270	8.00	5.00
Medrano, Miguel	R-R	6-0	165	1-4-98	0	1	3.60	3	0	0	0	5	4	2	2	0	5	5	.222	.250	.214	9.00	9.00
Nunez, Jeifry	R-R	5-11	160	4-1-98	2	3	3.46	13	12	0	0	55	46	24	21	3	13	46	.229	.208	.242	7.57	2.14
Ontiveros, Felipe	R-R	6-2	185	9-2-93	5	1	3.10	18	0	0	2	29	19	10	10	0	18	22	.184	.182	.186	6.83	5.59
Pacheco, Sergio	R-R	6-1	170	8-17-99	2	0	2.13	10	0	0	1	25	23	8	6	0	4	14	.240	.281	.219	4.97	1.42
Pena, Domingo	R-R	6-2	171	4-7-97	2	1	3.88	11	8	0	0	49	45	23	20	1	8	24	.259	.174	.314	4.66	1.55
Rodriguez, Eury	R-R	6-1	195	9-17-97	0	0	0.00	2	0	0	0	4	0	0	0	0	3	4	.000	.000	.000	9.00	6.75
Rodriguez, Yerry	R-R	6-2	180	10-15-97	4	3	2.66	16	6	0	2	51	53	19	15	0	10	38	.270	.216	.303	6.75	1.7
Rosario, Luis	R-R	5-11	165	2-8-97	6	5	4.13	12	12	1	0	61	83	38	28	2	8	46	.313	.318	.310	6.79	1.18
Rovain, Hector	R-R	6-1	165	5-5-98	2	2	7.00	17	0	0	0	27	33	22	21	2	20	13	.297	.289	.301	4.33	6.67
Sanmartin, Reiver	L-L	6-2	160	4-15-96	7	1	2.35	12	12	0	0	61	61	21	16	2	6	56	—	—	—	8.22	0.8

TEXAS RANGERS

Pitching	B-T	HT	WT	DOB	W	L	ERA	G	GS	CG	SV	IP	H	R	ER	HR	BB	SO	AVG	vLH	vRH	K/9	BB/9
Suarez, Sergio	L-L	6-0	160	5-24-95	0	2	10.80	13	0	0	2	18	24	23	22	2	21	16	—	—	—	7.85	10.3
Torres, Darel	R-R	5-11	160	1-5-99	0	0	0.00	2	0	0	0	2	0	0	0	0	0	3	.000	.000	.000	13.50	0.0
Urriola, Elvis	L-L	5-11	180	9-9-97	1	1	5.81	14	5	0	0	26	20	18	17	0	29	18	—	—	—	6.15	9.91
Vivas, Samir	R-R	5-11	170	2-1-95	1	0	1.72	17	0	0	5	31	22	7	6	1	5	28	.196	.333	.132	8.04	1.4
Volquez, Rafael	R-R	6-5	200	4-25-95	1	1	3.75	6	0	0	0	12	16	6	5	0	0	12	—	—	—	9.00	0.00

Fielding

C: Cabrera 8, Damian 1, Favela 9, Morales 42, Pernalete 11, Rojas 19, Vazquez 2, Ventura 49, Villarreal 21, Zacarias 5. **1B:** Aybar 4, Cabrera 13, Castro 28, Cordero 38, Inoa 3, Liriano 5, Martinez 59, Pena 3, Valdez 3, Vazquez 3, Ventura 3. **2B:** Almonte 7, Aybar 1, Barrios 16, Carrillo 10, Encarnacion 1, Hernandez 50, Inoa 40, Linares 14, Liriano 7, Pena 5, Pernalete 1, Pineda 3, Valdez 10, Ventura 4, Zacarias 1. **3B:** Almonte 5, Aybar 29, Barrios 6, Carrillo 3, Cordero 11, Fajardo 27, Inoa 3, Liriano 28, Martinez 2, Pena 23, Pineda 4, Tejeda 1, Valdez 9, Ventura 6. **SS:** Almonte 38, Aybar 16, Barrios 2, Carrillo 2, Fajardo 1, Hernandez 11, Inoa 18, Linares 2, Liriano 11, Pineda 38, Rivera 1, Tejeda 8, Valdez 1, Ventura 11. **OF:** Alonzo 43, Aparicio 54, Aybar 1, Carrillo 1, Castro 1, Damian 21, Encarnacion 43, Gutierrez 27, Joseph 59, Linares 1, Mendez 35, Ogando 21, Pena 2, Rivera 15, Rollin 60, Taveras 10, Valdez 36, Villahermosa 30, Zacarias 1.

Toronto Blue Jays

SEASON IN A SENTENCE: The Blue Jays reached the ALCS for the second-straight year behind a pitching staff that led the AL in ERA and one of the games' most explosive offenses, but they once again fell a round short of reaching their first World Series since 1993.

HIGH POINT: Needing a win on the final day of the regular season to clinch a playoff spot as a wild card, emerging ace Aaron Sanchez pitched seven brilliant innings and Troy Tulowitzki delivered the tiebreaking RBI single in the eighth to lift the Blue Jays to a 2-1 win over the Red Sox and into the postseason.

LOW POINT: The Blue Jays' powerful offense fell silent at the worst time: the playoffs. They scored just three runs combined in the first three games of the ALCS to fall into a 3-0 hole against the Indians, from which they couldn't recover.

NOTABLE ROOKIES: Rule 5 draft selection Joe Biagini dominated out of the bullpen from day one and eventually took over as the setup man for closer Roberto Osuna. Biagini went 4-3, 3.06 with 62 strikeouts in 67.1 innings and pitched 7.1 more scoreless innings of relief in the postseason. Fellow righthanded reliever Danny Barnes struck out 14 in 13.2 innings and earned an ALDS roster spot, and lefthander Chad Girodo posted a 4.35 ERA out of the bullpen in his first MLB action.

KEY TRANSACTIONS: The Jays acquired veteran reliever Jason Grilli from the Braves in May in exchange for minor league righthander Sean Ratcliffe. The 39-year old Grilli went 6-4, 3.63 as a key part of the Jays bullpen and didn't allow a run in five postseason outings. The Blue Jays further rearranged their pitching staff during the summer, acquiring Joaquin Benoit for Drew Storen, Mike Bolsinger for Jesse Chavez, Scott Feldman for Lupe Chavez and Francisco Liriano and well-regarded prospects Harold Ramirez and Reese McGuire from Pittsburgh in exchange for Drew Hutchison.

DOWN ON THE FARM: High Class A Dunedin won a wild card spot in the Florida State League and was the only Blue Jays affiliate to make the playoffs, led by touted righthanders Connor Greene (4-4, 2.90), Sean Reid-Foley (6-2, 2.67) and Jon Harris (3-2, 3.60). Tellez was an offensive force at the upper levels of the system, while Vladimir Guerrero Jr. (12 2B, 8 HR) and Bo Bichette (1.182 OPS), the sons of former big leaguers Vladimir Guerrero and Dante Bichette, respectively, had big seasons in Rookie-ball.

OPENING DAY PAYROLL: $ 138,701,700 (12th)

PLAYERS OF THE YEAR

MAJOR LEAGUE

Josh Donaldson
3b
.284/.404/.559
37 HR, 109 BB, 99 RBI
2nd in AL in OBP

MINOR LEAGUE

Sean Reid-Foley
rhp
(High A/Double-A)
10-5, 2.81
130 SO in 115.1 IP

ORGANIZATION LEADERS

BATTING		*Minimum 250 AB
MAJORS		
* AVG	Josh Donaldson	.284
* OPS	Josh Donaldson	.953
HR	Edwin Encarnacion	42
RBI	Edwin Encarnacion	127
MINORS		
* AVG	Jesus Montero, Buffalo	.317
* OBP	Rowdy Tellez, New Hampshire	.387
* SLG	Rowdy Tellez, New Hampshire	.530
* OPS	Rowdy Tellez, New Hampshire	.917
R	Jonathan Davis, Dunedin	74
H	Jesus Montero, Buffalo	155
TB	Rowdy Tellez, New Hampshire	232
2B	Juan Kelly, Lansing	35
3B	Richard Urena, Dunedin, New Hampshire	12
HR	Rowdy Tellez, New Hampshire	23
RBI	Ryan McBroom, New Hampshire, Dunedin	85
BB	Jonathan Davis, Dunedin	70
SO	Jason Leblebijian, Dunedin, New Hampshire	139
SB	Roemon Fields, New Hampshire	44

PITCHING		#Minimum 75 IP
MAJORS		
W	J.A. Happ	20
# ERA	Aaron Sanchez	3
SO	Marcus Stroman	166
SV	Roberto Osuna	36
MINORS		
W	Conor Fisk, Lansing, Dunedin	12
L	Scott Diamond, Buffalo	15
# ERA	Jon Harris, Lansing, Dunedin	2.71
G	Dusty Isaacs, Lansing, Dunedin	49
GS	Scott Diamond, Buffalo	28
	Jeremy Gabryszwski, New Hampshire	28
	Casey Lawrence, New Hampshire, Buffalo	28
SV	Ryan Tepera, Buffalo	18
IP	Scott Diamond, Buffalo	166
BB	Shane Dawson, New Hampshire	72
SO	Angel Perdomo, Lansing	156
# AVG	Sean Reid-Foley, Lansing, Dunedin	.19

General Manager: Ross Atkins. **Farm Director:** Gil Kim. **Scouting Director:** Brian Parker.

Class	Team	League	W	L	PCT	Finish	Manager
Majors	Toronto Blue Jays	American	89	73	.549	t-4th (15)	John Gibbons
Triple-A	Buffalo Bisons	International	66	78	.458	10th (14)	Gary Allenson
Double-A	New Hampshire Fisher Cats	Eastern	69	73	.486	7th (12)	Bobby Meacham
High A	Dunedin Blue Jays	Florida State	76	59	.563	3rd (12)	Ken Huckaby
Low A	Lansing Lugnuts	Midwest	69	71	.493	9th (16)	John Schneider
Short season	Vancouver Canadians	Northwest	29	45	.392	8th (8)	John Tamargo Jr.
Rookie	Bluefield Blue Jays	Appalachian	37	31	.544	4th (10)	Dennis Holmberg
Rookie	Blue Jays	Gulf Coast	39	17	.696	2nd (17)	Cesar Martin
Overall 2016 Minor League Record			385	374	.507	13th (30)	

ORGANIZATION STATISTICS

TORONTO BLUE JAYS
AMERICAN LEAGUE

Batting	B-T	HT	WT	DOB	AVG	vLH	vRH	G	AB	R	H	2B	3B	HR	RBI	BB	HBP	SH	SF	SO	SB	CS	SLG	OBP
Barney, Darwin	R-R	5-10	180	11-8-85	.269	.306	.249	104	279	35	75	13	2	4	19	22	1	2	2	48	2	2	.373	.322
Bautista, Jose	R-R	6-0	205	10-19-80	.234	.220	.238	116	423	68	99	24	1	22	69	87	3	0	4	103	2	2	.452	.366
Burns, Andy	R-R	6-2	205	8-7-90	.000	.000	.000	10	6	2	0	0	0	0	0	0	1	0	0	2	0	0	.000	.143
Carrera, Ezequiel	L-L	5-11	185	6-11-87	.248	.329	.218	110	270	47	67	9	1	6	23	27	4	7	2	70	7	4	.356	.323
Ceciliani, Darrell	L-L	6-1	220	6-22-90	.111	.000	.150	13	27	2	3	2	0	0	1	1	1	0	0	14	0	0	.185	.172
Colabello, Chris	R-R	6-4	210	10-24-83	.069	.000	.105	10	29	0	2	0	0	0	1	2	1	0	0	9	0	0	.069	.156
Dominguez, Matt	R-R	6-2	220	8-28-89	.000	.000	.000	5	11	0	0	0	0	0	0	1	0	0	0	3	0	0	.000	.083
Donaldson, Josh	R-R	6-1	210	12-8-85	.284	.279	.286	155	577	122	164	32	5	37	99	109	9	2	3	119	7	1	.549	.404
Encarnacion, Edwin	R-R	6-1	230	1-7-83	.263	.242	.268	160	601	99	158	34	0	42	127	87	5	0	8	138	2	0	.529	.357
Goins, Ryan	L-R	5-10	180	2-13-88	.186	.167	.190	76	183	13	34	9	2	3	12	9	1	3	0	48	1	1	.306	.228
Lake, Junior	R-R	6-2	230	3-27-90	.200	.263	.125	22	35	5	7	3	0	1	2	4	0	0	0	11	0	0	.371	.282
Martin, Russell	R-R	5-10	215	2-15-83	.231	.220	.234	137	455	62	105	16	0	20	74	64	10	1	5	148	2	1	.398	.335
Navarro, Dioner	B-R	5-9	215	2-9-84	.182	.125	.200	16	33	1	6	0	0	0	3	0	0	0	0	8	0	0	.182	.250
2-team total (85 Chicago)					.207	—	—	101	304	26	63	13	2	6	35	23	2	2	3	71	1	2	.322	.265
Paredes, Jimmy	B-R	6-3	200	11-25-88	.267	.000	.286	7	15	2	4	1	0	1	2	2	0	0	0	4	0	0	.533	.353
Pillar, Kevin	R-R	6-0	205	1-4-89	.266	.283	.261	146	548	59	146	35	2	7	53	24	6	3	3	90	14	6	.376	.303
Pompey, Dalton	B-R	6-2	195	12-11-92	.000	—	.000	8	2	3	0	0	0	0	0	0	0	0	0	1	2	1	.000	.000
Saunders, Michael	L-R	6-4	225	11-19-86	.253	.275	.247	140	490	70	124	32	3	24	57	59	5	1	3	157	1	2	.478	.338
Smoak, Justin	B-L	6-4	220	12-5-86	.217	.209	.221	126	299	33	65	10	0	14	34	40	2	0	0	112	1	0	.391	.314
Thole, Josh	L-R	6-1	205	10-28-86	.169	.156	.174	50	118	7	20	3	0	1	7	13	1	2	2	28	0	0	.220	.254
Travis, Devon	R-R	5-9	190	2-21-91	.300	.260	.313	101	410	54	123	28	1	11	50	20	0	1	1	87	4	1	.454	.332
Tulowitzki, Troy	R-R	6-3	205	10-10-84	.254	.266	.251	131	492	54	125	21	0	24	79	43	5	0	4	101	1	0	.443	.318
Upton, Melvin	R-R	6-3	185	8-21-84	.196	.257	.177	57	148	18	29	4	1	4	16	14	0	0	3	49	7	3	.318	.261

Pitching	B-T	HT	WT	DOB	W	L	ERA	G	GS	CG	SV	IP	H	R	ER	HR	BB	SO	AVG	vLH	vRH	K/9	BB/9
Antolin, Dustin	R-R	6-2	230	8-9-89	0	0	13.50	1	0	0	0	2	4	3	3	1	1	1	.400	1.000	.333	4.50	4.50
Barnes, Danny	L-R	6-1	195	10-21-89	0	0	3.95	12	0	0	0	14	14	6	6	0	5	14	.275	.200	.323	9.22	3.29
Benoit, Joaquin	R-R	6-4	250	7-26-77	2	0	0.38	25	0	0	1	24	17	1	1	1	9	24	.205	.265	.163	9.13	3.42
2-team total (26 Seattle)					3	1	2.81	51	0	0	1	48	37	17	15	5	24	52	—	—	—	9.75	4.50
Biagini, Joe	R-R	6-5	240	5-29-90	4	3	3.06	60	0	0	1	68	69	28	23	3	19	62	.259	.288	.239	8.25	2.53
Cecil, Brett	R-L	6-3	235	7-2-86	1	7	3.93	54	0	0	0	37	39	17	16	6	8	45	.269	.258	.278	11.05	1.96
Chavez, Jesse	R-R	6-2	175	8-21-83	1	2	4.57	39	0	0	0	41	43	22	21	9	10	42	.269	.303	.245	9.15	2.18
Dermody, Matt	R-L	6-5	190	7-4-90	0	0	12.00	5	0	0	0	3	6	4	4	1	0	5	.400	.571	.250	15.00	0.00
Diamond, Scott	L-L	6-3	205	7-30-86	0	0	27.00	1	0	0	0	1	2	3	3	0	2	0	.400	.000	.500	0.00	18.00
Dickey, R.A.	R-R	6-3	215	10-29-74	10	15	4.46	30	29	0	0	170	169	97	84	28	63	126	.258	.250	.264	6.68	3.34
Estrada, Marco	R-R	6-0	200	7-5-83	9	9	3.48	29	29	0	0	176	132	73	68	23	65	165	.203	.190	.218	8.44	3.32
Feldman, Scott	L-R	6-7	210	2-7-83	2	1	8.40	14	0	0	0	15	23	15	14	2	6	14	.348	.391	.326	8.40	3.60
2-team total (26 Houston)					7	4	3.97	40	5	0	0	77	87	42	34	10	19	56	—	—	—	6.55	2.22
Floyd, Gavin	R-R	6-4	245	1-27-83	2	4	4.06	28	0	0	0	31	23	14	14	4	8	30	.205	.111	.269	8.71	2.32
Girodo, Chad	L-L	6-1	190	2-6-91	0	0	4.35	14	0	0	0	10	11	5	5	3	2	5	.268	.211	.318	4.35	1.74
Grilli, Jason	R-R	6-5	235	11-11-76	6	4	3.64	46	0	0	2	42	28	17	17	8	19	58	.189	.169	.205	12.43	4.07
Happ, J.A.	L-L	6-5	205	10-19-82	20	4	3.18	32	32	0	0	195	168	72	69	22	60	163	.231	.245	.228	7.52	2.77
Hutchison, Drew	L-R	6-3	205	8-22-90	1	0	4.97	3	2	0	0	13	13	7	7	4	4	12	.271	.200	.321	8.53	2.84
Leon, Arnold	R-R	6-1	210	9-6-88	0	0	7.71	2	0	0	0	2	3	2	2	1	1	2	.300	.000	.429	7.71	3.86
Liriano, Francisco	L-L	6-2	225	10-26-83	2	2	2.92	10	8	0	0	49	42	22	16	7	16	52	.222	.194	.229	9.49	2.92
Loup, Aaron	L-L	5-11	210	12-19-87	0	0	5.02	21	0	0	0	14	15	8	8	2	4	15	.288	.250	.321	9.42	2.51
Morales, Franklin	L-L	6-1	210	1-24-86	0	1	9.00	5	0	0	0	4	3	4	4	1	2	2	.214	.222	.200	4.50	4.50
Osuna, Roberto	R-R	6-2	215	2-7-95	4	3	2.68	72	0	0	36	74	55	23	22	9	14	82	.206	.237	.176	9.97	1.70
Sanchez, Aaron	R-R	6-4	220	7-1-92	15	2	3.00	30	30	0	0	192	161	69	64	15	63	161	.224	.217	.231	7.55	2.95
Schultz, Bo	R-R	6-3	230	9-25-85	0	1	5.51	16	0	0	0	16	17	10	10	3	3	10	.266	.320	.231	5.51	1.65
Storen, Drew	B-R	6-1	195	8-11-87	1	3	6.21	38	0	0	3	33	43	23	23	6	10	32	.309	.375	.265	8.64	2.70
2-team total (19 Seattle)					4	3	5.23	57	0	0	3	52	56	30	30	7	13	48	—	—	—	8.36	2.26
Stroman, Marcus	R-R	5-8	180	5-1-91	9	10	4.37	32	32	0	0	204	209	104	99	21	54	166	.264	.268	.26	7.32	2.38

Pitching	B-T	HT	WT	DOB	W	L	ERA	G	GS	CG	SV	IP	H	R	ER	HR	BB	SO	AVG	vLH	vRH	K/9	BB/9
Tepera, Ryan	R-R	6-2	195	11-3-87	0	1	2.95	20	0	0	0	18	17	8	6	1	8	18	.233	.212	.25	8.84	3.93
Venditte, Pat	R-B	6-1	185	6-30-85	0	0	5.19	8	0	0	0	9	11	8	5	1	4	7	.297	.4	.227	7.27	4.15
2-team total (7 Seattle)					0	0	5.73	15	0	0	0	22	24	18	14	5	11	19	—	—	—	7.77	4.50

Fielding

Catcher	PCT	G	PO	A	E	DP	PB
Martin	.996	127	989	55	4	3	9
Navarro	.981	7	49	4	1	0	3
Thole	.997	50	292	18	1	1	17

First Base	PCT	G	PO	A	E	DP
Bautista	1.000	1	3	0	0	0
Burns	—	1	0	0	0	0
Colabello	1.000	8	74	3	0	6
Dominguez	1.000	1	9	0	0	1
Encarnacion	.997	75	602	27	2	57
Goins	1.000	2	4	1	0	0
Lake	1.000	1	3	0	0	2
Smoak	.996	111	753	38	3	69

Second Base	PCT	G	PO	A	E	DP
Barney	.976	40	55	105	4	35

	PCT	G	PO	A	E	DP
Goins	.981	37	64	95	3	20
Martin	1.000	1	0	1	0	0
Paredes	.667	1	2	0	1	0
Travis	.975	99	150	276	11	59

Third Base	PCT	G	PO	A	E	DP
Barney	.939	32	14	48	4	4
Burns	1.000	4	0	6	0	1
Dominguez	1.000	3	7	4	0	0
Donaldson	.961	136	110	237	14	27
Goins	.857	6	2	4	1	0
Martin	1.000	1	0	1	0	0
Paredes	.875	2	3	4	1	0

Shortstop	PCT	G	PO	A	E	DP
Barney	1.000	25	23	57	0	6
Goins	.990	28	31	65	1	16

	PCT	G	PO	A	E	DP
Tulowitzki	.983	128	158	366	9	72

Outfield	PCT	G	PO	A	E	DP
Barney	1.000	5	4	0	0	0
Bautista	.987	91	149	5	2	0
Burns	—	1	0	0	0	0
Carrera	.993	100	132	8	1	3
Ceciliani	.923	12	12	0	1	0
Colabello	—	1	0	0	0	0
Goins	1.000	3	3	0	0	0
Lake	.941	19	16	0	1	0
Paredes	—	1	0	0	0	0
Pillar	.983	146	337	6	6	2
Pompey	1.000	2	1	0	0	0
Saunders	.990	128	188	5	2	0
Upton	.987	55	75	1	1	0

BUFFALO BISONS

INTERNATIONAL LEAGUE

TRIPLE-A

Batting	B-T	HT	WT	DOB	AVG	vLH	vRH	G	AB	R	H	2B	3B	HR	RBI	BB	HBP	SH	SF	SO	SB	CS	SLG	OBP
Adams, David	R-R	6-2	205	5-15-87	.243	.202	.270	68	206	20	50	16	0	2	21	29	1	0	0	46	3	0	.350	.339
Bautista, Jose	R-R	6-0	205	10-19-80	.091	—	.091	3	11	0	1	0	0	0	0	0	0	0	0	2	0	0	.091	.091
Berry, Quintin	L-L	6-1	195	11-21-84	.105	.000	.167	5	19	2	2	0	0	0	2	1	1	0	7	0	0	.105	.227
Berti, Jon	R-R	5-10	195	1-22-90	.150	.000	.188	7	20	4	3	1	0	1	1	2	0	0	3	2	0	.350	.227
Brown, Domonic	L-L	6-5	225	9-3-87	.239	.215	.255	126	464	37	111	24	0	7	41	38	5	0	2	99	5	3	.336	.303
Burns, Andy	R-R	6-2	205	8-7-90	.230	.243	.222	111	418	42	96	25	1	8	38	33	0	1	2	82	13	5	.352	.285
Carrera, Ezequiel	L-L	5-11	185	6-11-87	.071	.000	.091	4	14	1	1	0	1	0	0	2	0	0	4	0	0	.214	.188
Casilla, Alexi	B-R	5-9	170	7-20-84	.241	.207	.261	83	257	35	62	10	2	2	16	20	0	5	0	40	5	1	.319	.296
Castillo, Wilkin	B-R	6-0	200	6-1-84	.250	.429	.200	10	32	3	8	3	0	0	1	0	0	1	0	2	0	0	.344	.250
Ceciliani, Darrell	L-L	6-1	220	6-22-90	.266	.237	.285	82	304	40	81	17	3	10	40	26	1	0	3	52	11	5	.441	.323
Colabello, Chris	R-R	6-4	210	10-24-83	.180	.213	.163	40	139	14	25	0	0	5	11	11	2	0	1	46	0	0	.288	.248
Dominguez, Matt	R-R	6-2	220	8-28-89	.269	.275	.266	127	475	47	128	18	0	18	67	29	5	0	5	70	1	0	.421	.315
Goins, Ryan	L-R	5-10	180	2-13-88	.265	.184	.317	28	98	9	26	6	0	2	10	8	0	2	1	23	0	1	.388	.318
Jimenez, A.J.	R-R	6-0	195	5-1-90	.241	.266	.228	67	228	24	55	17	1	4	25	13	4	0	3	33	1	1	.377	.290
Kotchman, Casey	L-L	6-3	220	2-22-83	.256	.179	.287	102	332	36	85	18	0	8	34	36	8	0	0	32	1	0	.383	.343
Kratz, Erik	R-R	6-4	245	6-15-80	.155	.167	.150	19	58	6	9	1	0	1	7	2	1	0	1	0	0	0	.172	.269
Lake, Junior	R-R	6-2	230	3-27-90	.231	.216	.239	82	281	33	65	12	2	6	31	33	2	0	2	77	10	4	.352	.314
Mesa, Melky	R-R	6-1	190	1-31-87	.290	.200	.345	26	93	6	27	7	1	0	8	1	0	0	1	25	1	1	.387	.353
Mier, Jio	R-R	6-2	205	8-26-90	.219	.209	.225	76	224	21	49	11	1	3	18	21	1	2	1	44	2	3	.317	.287
Montero, Jesus	R-R	6-3	235	11-28-89	.317	.319	.315	126	489	46	155	24	1	11	60	23	3	0	3	78	1	0	.438	.349
Opitz, Shane	L-R	6-1	180	1-10-92	.200	.000	.286	3	10	1	2	0	0	0	1	1	0	0	0	2	0	0	.200	.273
Pompey, Dalton	B-R	6-2	195	12-11-92	.270	.246	.284	93	337	48	91	14	1	4	28	40	2	1	2	72	18	7	.353	.349
Quintero, Humberto	R-R	5-10	215	8-2-79	.267	.400	.200	5	15	3	4	3	0	0	1	1	0	0	0	4	0	0	.467	.353
2-team total (15 Toledo)					.250	—	—	20	60	3	15	5	0	0	3	3	1	1	0	15	1	0	.333	.297
Sanchez, Tony	R-R	5-11	220	5-20-88	.201	.229	.188	45	149	19	30	7	0	3	10	17	2	0	0	31	0	0	.309	.292
Travis, Devon	R-R	5-9	190	2-21-91	.273	.111	.385	5	22	3	6	2	0	0	3	0	0	0	0	4	0	0	.364	.273

Pitching	B-T	HT	WT	DOB	W	L	ERA	G	GS	CG	SV	IP	H	R	ER	HR	BB	SO	AVG	vLH	vRH	K/9	BB/9
Aardsma, David	R-R	6-3	215	12-27-81	0	1	5.27	14	0	0	6	14	11	8	8	1	9	14	.229	.158	.276	9.22	5.93
Anderson, John	L-L	6-2	200	11-9-88	1	3	7.03	6	5	0	0	24	39	19	19	4	11	13	.358	.280	.381	4.81	4.07
Antolin, Dustin	R-R	6-2	230	8-9-89	2	3	2.04	46	1	0	10	53	41	15	12	3	28	61	.214	.138	.268	10.36	4.75
Barnes, Danny	L-R	6-1	195	10-21-89	1	0	0.35	17	0	0	5	26	6	1	1	0	2	37	.071	.024	.119	12.97	0.70
Berken, Jason	R-R	6-0	210	11-27-83	0	2	4.50	6	2	0	0	26	32	17	13	3	12	17	.308	.333	.288	5.88	4.15
Bolsinger, Mike	R-R	6-1	215	1-29-88	1	4	6.04	6	6	0	0	25	29	19	17	4	11	27	.284	.298	.273	9.59	3.91
Browning, Wil	R-R	6-3	190	9-8-88	0	0	6.75	1	0	0	0	1	0	1	1	0	1	3	.000	.000	0	20.25	6.75
Cecil, Brett	R-L	6-3	235	7-2-86	0	0	0.00	2	0	0	0	2	1	0	0	0	0	5	.167	.000	.25	0.00	0.00
Copeland, Scott	R-R	6-3	220	12-15-87	3	4	3.04	9	9	0	0	50	45	19	17	3	17	33	.241	.256	.228	5.90	3.04
Dermody, Matt	R-L	6-5	190	7-4-90	0	0	2.76	15	0	0	0	16	22	9	5	0	5	6	.324	.308	.333	3.31	2.76
Diamond, Scott	L-L	6-3	205	7-30-86	9	15	4.50	28	28	0	0	166	191	92	83	11	32	100	.296	.291	.297	5.42	1.73
Font, Wilmer	R-R	6-4	265	5-24-90	1	2	4.19	4	3	0	0	19	20	9	9	1	5	8	.267	.324	.2	3.72	2.33
Girodo, Chad	L-L	6-1	190	2-6-91	2	1	3.79	29	0	0	1	36	45	16	15	5	13	24	.321	.279	.354	6.06	3.28
Hernandez, Roberto	R-R	6-4	270	8-30-80	4	4	4.42	13	13	0	0	71	74	37	35	10	23	48	.267	.254	.278	6.06	2.90
2-team total (3 Gwinnett)					4	4	4.60	16	16	0	0	86	95	47	44	11	26	59	—	—	—	6.17	2.72
Hutchison, Drew	L-R	6-3	205	8-22-90	6	5	3.26	18	18	0	0	102	78	40	37	11	35	110	.210	.237	.191	9.71	3.09
2-team total (7 Indianapolis)					7	6	3.59	25	24	0	0	138	115	63	55	16	50	138	—	—	—	9.00	3.26
Hynes, Colt	L-L	5-11	200	6-28-85	2	0	5.71	16	0	0	1	17	26	14	11	3	1	22	.338	.323	.348	11.42	0.52
2-team total (0 Columbus)					2	0	5.71	16	0	0	1	17	26	14	11	3	1	22	—	—	—	11.42	0.52

Pitching

Pitching	B-T	HT	WT	DOB	W	L	ERA	G	GS	CG	SV	IP	H	R	ER	HR	BB	SO	AVG	vLH	vRH	K/9	BB/9
Jenkins, Chad	R-R	6-4	230	12-22-87	3	4	5.16	20	2	0	0	30	41	20	17	1	17	21	.315	.256	.341	6.37	5.16
Korecky, Bobby	R-R	5-11	185	9-16-79	0	0	4.30	13	0	0	0	23	28	16	11	3	9	21	.292	.368	.241	8.22	3.52
Lawrence, Casey	R-R	6-2	170	10-28-87	5	6	3.83	15	15	1	0	87	87	47	37	5	24	58	.260	.227	.286	6.00	2.48
LeBlanc, Wade	L-L	6-3	210	8-7-84	7	2	1.71	14	14	0	0	90	84	20	17	3	21	85	.246	.226	.252	8.53	2.11
Leon, Arnold	R-R	6-1	210		0	0	2.25	3	2	0	0	12	11	3	3	1	2	16	.234	.143	.308	12.00	1.50
Leroux, Chris	L-R	6-6	225	4-14-84	8	11	4.87	26	24	0	0	140	149	87	76	13	46	93	.276	.311	.251	5.96	2.95
Loup, Aaron	L-L	5-11	210	12-19-87	3	0	1.83	20	0	0	1	20	21	4	4	0	3	26	.269	.188	.326	11.90	1.37
McCoy, Pat	L-L	6-4	225	8-3-88	0	1	4.64	17	0	0	0	21	22	12	11	1	12	17	.262	.214	.286	7.17	5.06
Morales, Franklin	L-L	6-1	210	1-24-86	1	0	2.00	9	0	0	0	9	6	2	2	1	4	6	.200	.125	.227	6.00	4.00
Rowen, Ben	R-R	6-4	200	11-15-88	0	4	2.47	37	0	0	1	47	46	13	13	1	11	33	.256	.220	.269	6.42	2.09
Schultz, Bo	R-R	6-3	230	9-25-85	3	2	3.74	26	0	0	2	34	30	15	14	2	7	21	.248	.211	.265	5.61	1.87
Smith, Chris	R-R	6-2	205	8-19-88	0	1	2.45	4	0	0	0	4	2	1	1	1	1	5	.182	.400	.000	12.27	2.45
Smith, Murphy	R-R	6-3	210	8-25-87	0	0	0.00	1	0	0	0	1	1	0	0	0	1	1	.250	.000	.333	9.00	9.00
Stilson, John	R-R	6-3	205	7-28-90	0	0	0.00	1	0	0	0	1	1	0	0	0	0	1	.250	—	.250	9.00	0.00
Tepera, Ryan	R-R	6-2	195	11-3-87	1	2	2.58	37	0	0	18	45	33	13	13	3	16	48	.205	.261	.163	9.53	3.18
Venditte, Pat	R-B	6-1	185	6-30-85	2	1	4.37	25	2	0	0	35	39	17	17	3	13	52	.271	.258	.282	13.37	3.34

Fielding

Catcher	PCT	G	PO	A	E	DP	PB
Castillo	.955	9	60	4	3	0	1
Jimenez	.992	67	484	34	4	7	1
Kratz	1.000	19	137	4	0	0	0
Quintero	1.000	5	44	2	0	0	0
Sanchez	.988	45	318	14	4	1	2

First Base	PCT	G	PO	A	E	DP
Colabello	.991	24	217	12	2	23
Dominguez	.986	16	131	7	2	14
Goins	1.000	1	5	2	0	1
Kotchman	.999	84	702	48	1	65
Montero	.991	25	223	5	2	23

Second Base	PCT	G	PO	A	E	DP
Adams	.995	47	84	123	1	30

Berti	1.000	1	4	3	0	2
Burns	.993	55	105	179	2	43
Casilla	.973	33	58	88	4	22
Goins	.949	10	15	41	3	8
Travis	1.000	4	11	6	0	3

Third Base	PCT	G	PO	A	E	DP
Adams	.923	17	6	30	3	2
Burns	.946	17	10	25	2	0
Casilla	1.000	3	2	3	0	0
Dominguez	.966	111	77	235	11	28
Opitz	1.000	1	1	2	0	1

Shortstop	PCT	G	PO	A	E	DP
Burns	.965	19	25	57	3	11
Casilla	.969	42	44	113	5	19
Goins	1.000	14	19	43	0	10

Mier	.951	76	83	230	16	49
Opitz	1.000	2	1	4	0	0

Outfield	PCT	G	PO	A	E	DP
Bautista	1.000	2	8	0	0	0
Berry	1.000	5	7	0	0	0
Berti	1.000	5	10	0	0	0
Brown	.956	116	190	7	9	0
Burns	1.000	24	45	1	0	0
Carrera	.800	3	4	0	1	0
Casilla	—	1	0	0	0	0
Ceciliani	.977	76	164	4	4	1
Colabello	1.000	11	18	0	0	0
Lake	.969	78	146	10	5	0
Mesa	1.000	26	48	4	0	1
Pompey	.974	92	182	4	5	1

NEW HAMPSHIRE FISHER CATS   DOUBLE-A
EASTERN LEAGUE

Batting

Batting	B-T	HT	WT	DOB	AVG	vLH	vRH	G	AB	R	H	2B	3B	HR	RBI	BB	HBP	SH	SF	SO	SB	CS	SLG	OBP
Berti, Jon	R-R	5-10	195	1-22-90	.254	.380	.202	73	272	37	69	10	7	2	26	36	9	1	1	56	29	9	.364	.358
Castillo, Wilkin	B-R	6-0	200	6-1-84	.225	.333	.194	41	138	13	31	8	0	1	11	8	2	3	1	15	2	4	.304	.275
Conner, Seth	R-R	6-2	205	1-29-92	.250	.000	.333	2	4	0	1	0	0	0	1	0	0	0	0	1	0	0	.250	.250
Dean, Matt	R-R	6-3	220	12-22-92	.215	.213	.215	65	233	27	50	8	0	5	28	23	4	0	2	84	1	0	.313	.294
Fields, Roemon	L-L	5-11	180	11-28-90	.227	.268	.214	130	497	65	113	12	5	4	32	45	3	10	1	98	44	16	.296	.295
Flores, Jorge	R-R	5-5	160	11-25-91	.187	.221	.174	82	252	24	47	8	0	2	24	21	6	7	6	38	4	6	.242	.260
Guerrero, Emilio	R-R	6-4	189	8-21-92	.282	.222	.301	43	149	22	42	8	2	5	20	10	1	1	2	35	3	0	.463	.327
Hobson, K.C.	L-L	6-2	205	8-22-90	.163	.122	.180	39	141	13	23	5	1	3	15	16	1	0	1	33	0	0	.277	.252
Lavarnway, Ryan	R-R	6-4	240	8-7-87	.262	.308	.249	66	233	33	61	13	0	6	38	34	2	0	3	47	1	0	.395	.357
Leblebijian, Jason	R-R	6-2	205	5-13-91	.293	.302	.290	75	270	40	79	19	1	7	37	28	3	0	5	80	5	2	.448	.359
Lopes, Christian	R-R	6-0	185	10-1-92	.295	.306	.291	108	404	56	119	30	2	3	46	33	8	2	3	71	9	4	.401	.357
Loveless, Derrick	L-R	6-1	200	3-7-93	.207	.280	.194	56	169	19	35	8	3	7	22	25	1	1	1	56	3	3	.414	.311
McBroom, Ryan	R-L	6-3	230	4-9-92	.138	.167	.130	9	29	3	4	0	0	1	2	3	1	0	1	6	0	0	.241	.235
McGuire, Reese	L-R	5-11	215	3-2-95	.226	.000	.250	15	53	5	12	2	0	0	5	7	1	0	0	8	2	2	.264	.328
2-team total (77 Altoona)					.254	—		92	319	34	81	18	2	1	42	36	4	4	2	34	6	6	.332	.335
Mesa, Melky	R-R	6-1	190	1-31-87	.213	.200	.218	43	160	21	34	7	1	5	14	8	4	0	0	49	4	1	.363	.267
Opitz, Shane	L-R	6-1	180	1-10-92	.230	.200	.221	81	230	22	50	11	1	2	16	20	1	4	3	41	7	3	.300	.280
Parmley, Ian	L-L	5-11	175	12-19-89	.294	.350	.279	92	282	49	83	6	6	2	26	28	0	10	2	75	13	7	.379	.356
Ramirez, Harold	R-R	5-10	220	9-6-94	.750	.292	.750	1	4	2	3	1	0	0	1	0	0	0	0	0	0	0	1.000	.800
2-team total (98 Altoona)					.311	—		99	383	60	119	17	7	2	50	22	9	2	3	66	7	10	.407	.360
Saez, Jorge	R-R	5-10	195	8-28-90	.232	.205	.247	40	125	15	29	7	0	6	20	10	1	2	2	39	0	1	.432	.290
Smith Jr. Dwight	L-R	5-11	195	10-26-92	.265	.258	.268	126	471	56	125	24	5	15	74	45	5	0	6	91	12	7	.433	.332
Tellez, Rowdy	L-L	6-4	220	3-16-95	.297	.264	.310	124	438	71	130	29	2	23	81	63	6	0	7	92	4	3	.530	.387
Urena, Richard	B-R	6-0	185	2-26-96	.266	.194	.290	30	124	16	33	6	6	0	18	4	0	1	3	21	4	2	.395	.282

Pitching

Pitching	B-T	HT	WT	DOB	W	L	ERA	G	GS	CG	SV	IP	H	R	ER	HR	BB	SO	AVG	vLH	vRH	K/9	BB/9
Anderson, John	L-L	6-2	200	11-9-88	3	6	5.08	24	14	0	1	90	117	58	51	9	32	81	.310	.380	.277	8.07	3.19
Barnes, Danny	L-R	6-1	195	10-21-89	2	1	1.01	24	0	0	1	36	17	5	4	3	4	40	.139	.148	.131	10.09	1.01
Berken, Jason	R-R	6-0	210	11-27-83	2	7	4.41	23	11	0	1	80	86	39	39	9	23	46	.277	.302	.250	5.20	2.60
Browning, Wil	R-R	6-3	190	9-8-88	3	2	1.94	46	0	0	10	51	41	13	11	3	14	61	.215	.310	.158	10.76	2.47
Cole, Taylor	R-R	6-1	200	8-20-89	3	4	3.79	12	11	0	0	62	70	32	26	6	17	54	.294	.294	.294	7.88	2.48
Cook, Ryan	R-R	6-1	210	5-4-93	0	0	0.00	1	0	0	0	1	0	0	0	0	0	0	.000	.000	.000	0.00	0.00
Dawson, Shane	R-L	6-1	200	9-9-93	10	4	4.22	26	26	0	0	134	134	69	63	10	72	95	.266	.234	.280	6.36	4.82
Dermody, Matt	R-L	6-5	190	7-4-90	2	0	0.92	16	0	0	0	20	12	3	2	1	2	21	.174	.226	.132	9.61	0.92

Pitching

Pitching	B-T	HT	WT	DOB	W	L	ERA	G	GS	CG	SV	IP	H	R	ER	HR	BB	SO	AVG	vLH	vRH	K/9	BB/9
Dragmire, Brady	R-R	6-1	185	2-5-93	4	6	4.38	45	0	0	1	72	78	37	35	10	28	41	.284	.323	.252	5.13	3.50
Font, Wilmer	R-R	6-4	265	5-24-90	3	2	3.47	8	0	0	0	47	41	19	18	7	7	47	.234	.255	.210	9.06	1.35
Gabryszwski, Jeremy	R-R	6-4	195	3-16-93	8	11	5.23	29	28	0	0	146	167	96	85	16	49	96	.288	.287	.290	5.90	3.01
Gonzalez, Alonzo	L-L	6-5	212	1-15-92	1	0	3.38	7	0	0	0	13	7	5	5	1	5	11	.146	.200	.107	7.43	7.43
Greene, Conner	R-R	6-3	185	4-4-95	6	5	4.19	12	12	1	0	69	57	36	32	5	33	48	.224	.221	.227	6.29	4.33
Hynes, Colt	L-L	5-11	200	6-28-85	0	1	1.37	13	0	0	0	20	14	3	3	1	6	21	.203	.080	.273	9.61	2.75
2-team total (8 Akron)					1	1	2.51	21	0	0	1	29	24	9	8	1	8	29	—	—	—	9.10	2.51
Lawrence, Casey	R-R	6-2	170	10-28-87	3	6	4.56	13	13	0	0	75	92	42	38	8	13	50	.311	.308	.313	6.00	1.56
Mayza, Tim	L-L	6-3	220	1-15-92	1	3	4.11	14	0	0	0	15	16	10	7	0	15	13	.281	.190	.333	7.63	8.80
Santos, Luis	R-R	6-0	185	2-11-91	5	3	4.28	17	15	0	0	82	87	42	39	8	22	75	.269	.308	.236	8.23	2.41
Schlereth, Daniel	L-L	6-0	210	5-9-86	0	2	4.32	15	0	0	0	17	18	11	8	0	13	11	.295	.296	.294	5.94	7.02
Schultz, Bo	R-R	6-3	230	9-25-85	0	0	10.80	2	0	0	0	2	2	2	2	1	2	3	.286	.250	.333	16.20	10.80
Smith, Chris	R-R	6-2	205	8-19-88	1	2	1.89	43	0	0	15	57	44	20	12	2	21	76	.208	.274	.164	12.00	3.32
Smith, Murphy	R-R	6-3	210	8-25-87	4	5	1.50	42	0	0	5	72	51	20	12	5	25	68	.202	.193	.210	8.50	3.13
Stilson, John	R-R	6-3	205	7-28-90	4	1	3.88	34	0	0	1	49	42	27	21	2	23	41	.236	.224	.245	7.58	4.25
Straka, John	L-R	6-2	215	1-19-90	4	1	4.68	5	4	0	0	25	24	13	13	2	8	22	.258	.297	.232	7.92	2.88
Suriel, Starlyn	R-R	5-11	180	11-17-93	0	0	4.50	1	0	0	0	2	1	1	1	1	0	2	.143	.333	.000	9.00	0.00
Turner, Colton	L-L	6-3	215	1-17-91	0	1	5.23	9	0	0	0	10	12	6	6	1	8	10	.308	.308	.308	8.71	6.97

Fielding

Catcher	PCT	G	PO	A	E	DP	PB
Castillo	.991	39	291	28	3	3	4
Lavarnway	.994	59	439	30	3	1	7
McGuire	.978	13	85	2	2	1	0
Saez	.993	37	242	28	2	2	2

First Base	PCT	G	PO	A	E	DP
Conner	1.000	1	6	0	0	3
Dean	.958	7	44	2	2	3
Guerrero	1.000	5	39	3	0	6
Hobson	.986	17	132	7	2	11
McBroom	1.000	8	66	5	0	5
Opitz	.986	10	69	3	1	8
Tellez	.992	101	841	49	7	86

Second Base	PCT	G	PO	A	E	DP
Berti	.976	28	47	76	3	19
Flores	.959	17	27	44	3	10
Leblebijian	1.000	4	7	3	0	1
Lopes	.957	83	127	232	16	61
Opitz	.973	14	20	51	2	11

Third Base	PCT	G	PO	A	E	DP
Berti	1.000	14	12	30	0	5
Dean	.933	40	25	59	6	8
Guerrero	.963	31	16	61	3	10
Leblebijian	.903	47	25	77	11	8
Opitz	1.000	16	5	16	0	0

Shortstop	PCT	G	PO	A	E	DP
Berti	1.000	4	8	18	0	-1

	PCT	G	PO	A	E	DP
Flores	.969	64	103	175	9	41
Leblebijian	.984	13	14	48	1	9
Opitz	.986	39	45	96	2	20
Urena	.949	29	50	80	7	20

Outfield	PCT	G	PO	A	E	DP
Berti	1.000	21	39	1	0	0
Fields	.997	124	308	7	1	0
Guerrero	1.000	5	6	0	0	0
Hobson	1.000	2	7	0	0	0
Loveless	1.000	48	86	1	0	0
Mesa	1.000	39	84	4	0	0
Opitz	1.000	1	1	0	0	0
Parmley	.953	81	153	8	8	1
Ramirez	1.000	1	3	0	0	0
Smith Jr.	.968	114	208	7	7	2

DUNEDIN BLUE JAYS
FLORIDA STATE LEAGUE

HIGH CLASS A

Batting	B-T	HT	WT	DOB	AVG	vLH	vRH	G	AB	R	H	2B	3B	HR	RBI	BB	HBP	SH	SF	SO	SB	CS	SLG	OBP
Alford, Anthony	R-R	6-1	215	7-20-94	.236	.255	.228	92	339	53	80	17	2	9	44	53	5	0	4	117	18	6	.378	.344
Almonte, Josh	R-R	6-3	210	1-28-94	.162	.206	.143	39	111	14	18	4	1	0	14	4	3	2	1	35	2	2	.216	.210
Attaway, Aaron	R-R	5-7	170	3-6-92	.218	.259	.196	26	78	16	17	4	0	0	8	8	1	2	1	25	4	1	.269	.295
Bautista, Jose	R-R	6-0	205	10-19-80	.333	.500	.000	1	3	1	1	0	0	1	1	0	0	0	0	1	0	0	1.333	.333
Bourn, Michael	L-R	5-11	190	12-27-82	.257	.167	.276	9	35	2	9	2	1	0	4	5	1	0	0	8	1	0	.371	.366
Colabello, Chris	R-R	6-4	210	10-24-83	.222	—	.222	5	18	2	4	2	0	0	1	2	0	0	0	5	0	0	.333	.300
Dantzler, L.B.	L-R	5-11	200	5-22-91	.235	.317	.213	55	196	16	46	10	0	1	18	18	0	1	2	39	0	4	.301	.296
Davis, D.J.	L-R	6-1	180	7-25-94	.197	.148	.211	83	274	35	54	9	3	1	15	36	2	5	0	99	22	6	.263	.295
Davis, Jonathan	R-R	5-8	190	5-12-92	.252	.224	.261	120	417	74	105	21	8	14	54	70	17	7	6	111	33	6	.441	.376
De La Cruz, Michael	R-R	5-10	190	5-15-93	.241	.217	.253	41	133	16	32	6	4	2	24	13	1	0	2	22	5	3	.391	.309
Dean, Matt	R-R	6-3	220	12-22-92	.237	.240	.235	17	59	10	14	1	0	1	6	7	1	0	1	28	1	2	.305	.324
Fermin, Andy	L-R	6-0	180	7-27-89	.200	.000	.238	7	25	4	5	2	0	0	0	0	0	0	0	6	0	0	.280	.200
Flores, Jorge	R-R	5-5	160	11-25-91	.263	.182	.311	32	118	21	31	7	2	1	11	11	0	3	0	20	5	2	.381	.326
Guerrero, Emilio	R-R	6-4	189	8-21-92	.284	.302	.277	43	162	25	46	15	1	8	36	15	1	1	3	32	3	1	.537	.343
Guillotte, Andrew	R-R	5-8	170	3-30-93	.152	.125	.158	14	46	6	7	2	0	0	2	5	1	0	0	9	1	0	.196	.250
Harris, David	R-R	6-1	190	8-10-91	.221	.343	.159	30	104	11	23	5	1	1	18	5	2	0	1	29	3	2	.317	.268
Heidt, Gunnar	R-R	6-0	200	9-12-92	.256	.271	.250	50	180	28	46	13	0	5	24	21	2	1	2	45	9	4	.411	.337
Jansen, Danny	R-R	6-2	225	4-15-95	.218	.222	.216	54	188	18	41	7	0	1	23	22	5	0	2	40	7	1	.271	.313
La Prise, Andy	L-R	6-2	180	8-24-93	.318	.143	.400	6	22	2	7	1	0	0	1	2	0	1	0	5	1	0	.364	.375
Leblebijian, Jason	R-R	6-2	205	5-13-91	.295	.286	.297	52	200	32	59	7	0	6	18	18	3	1	0	59	6	4	.420	.362
Lopes, Christian	R-R	6-0	185	10-1-92	.196	.154	.209	15	56	8	11	1	1	3	10	11	0	0	1	12	1	0	.411	.324
Loveless, Derrick	L-R	6-1	200	3-7-93	.266	.233	.273	49	173	23	46	11	3	3	21	27	0	2	2	55	8	3	.416	.361
McBroom, Ryan	R-L	6-3	230	4-9-92	.274	.282	.271	119	468	58	128	26	1	21	83	34	4	0	8	112	10	4	.468	.323
Metzler, Ryan	R-R	6-3	190	3-20-93	.182	.500	.000	3	11	1	2	0	0	0	2	0	0	0	0	3	0	0	.182	.308
Pentecost, Max	R-R	6-2	191	3-10-93	.245	.278	.226	12	49	6	12	2	0	3	7	3	0	0	0	17	1	1	.469	.288
Pillar, Kevin	R-R	6-0	205	1-4-89	.857	1.000	.833	2	7	3	6	1	0	0	2	0	0	0	0	0	0	0	1.000	.889
Reeves, Mike	L-R	6-2	195	9-16-90	.244	.214	.250	53	164	23	40	8	0	3	16	30	2	2	1	47	3	3	.348	.365
Saez, Jorge	R-R	5-10	195	8-28-90	.313	.263	.333	18	67	11	21	2	0	6	12	5	0	0	0	18	1	0	.612	.361
Thon, Dickie Joe	R-R	6-2	190	11-16-91	.258	.204	.248	111	380	57	98	20	2	10	42	35	10	0	4	100	23	9	.400	.333
Travis, Devon	R-R	5-9	190	2-21-91	.357	.400	.333	4	14	1	5	2	0	0	5	1	0	0	1	1	0	0	.500	.375
Tulowitzki, Troy	R-R	6-3	205	10-10-84	.250	—	.250	1	4	0	1	0	0	0	0	0	0	0	0	2	0	0	.250	.250
Urena, Richard	B-R	6-0	190	2-26-96	.305	.258	.320	97	394	52	120	18	7	8	41	25	4	6	2	64	9	6	.447	.351

Pitching

Pitching	B-T	HT	WT	DOB	W	L	ERA	G	GS	CG	SV	IP	H	R	ER	HR	BB	SO	AVG	vLH	vRH	K/9	BB/9
Abel, Nate	L-L	6-1	190	11-2-92	0	0	0.00	1	0	0	0	2	1	0	0	0	0	4	.125	.250	.000	15.43	0.00
Allen, Brad	L-R	6-4	220	3-26-89	5	7	5.50	33	9	0	0	87	83	59	53	12	47	75	.246	.243	.249	7.79	4.88
Borucki, Ryan	L-L	6-4	175	3-31-94	1	4	14.40	6	6	0	0	20	40	33	32	10	12	10	.421	.400	.429	4.50	5.40
Cardona, Adonys	R-R	6-2	200	1-16-94	2	2	5.02	41	0	0	0	38	38	23	21	1	31	26	.260	.205	.284	6.21	7.41
Cecil, Brett	R-L	6-3	235	7-2-86	0	0	4.50	2	0	0	0	2	2	1	1	0	0	4	.250	.000	.500	18.00	0.00
Cole, Taylor	R-R	6-1	200	8-20-89	1	0	4.70	3	3	0	0	15	20	8	8	0	3	8	.323	.219	.433	4.70	1.76
Cook, Ryan	R-R	6-1	210	5-4-93	0	1	13.50	2	0	0	0	2	5	4	3	1	0	1	.455	.500	.429	4.50	0.00
Dermody, Matt	R-L	6-5	190	7-4-90	1	1	1.96	16	0	0	3	18	21	4	4	0	1	20	.296	.280	.304	9.82	0.49
Encina, Geno	R-R	6-4	220	7-7-94	0	0	3.00	1	0	0	0	3	3	2	1	1	1	1	.231	.400	.125	3.00	3.00
Fernandez, Jose	L-L	6-3	170	2-13-93	1	1	4.12	29	0	0	0	44	29	24	20	5	34	41	.188	.188	.189	8.45	7.01
Fisk, Conor	R-R	6-2	210	4-4-92	10	3	3.25	25	11	1	0	105	90	42	38	10	24	81	.227	.252	.213	6.92	2.05
Gonzalez, Alonzo	L-L	6-5	212	1-15-92	6	5	2.48	34	0	0	0	58	43	19	16	3	33	55	.214	.133	.248	8.53	5.12
Greene, Conner	R-R	6-3	185	4-4-95	4	4	2.90	15	15	0	0	78	74	36	25	5	38	51	.252	.196	.286	5.91	4.40
Harris, Jon	R-R	6-4	175	10-16-93	3	2	3.60	8	8	1	0	45	37	19	18	2	14	26	.224	.190	.243	5.20	2.80
Higuera, Juliandry	L-L	6-1	180	9-6-94	0	1	8.71	4	3	0	0	10	13	12	10	1	7	5	.283	.286	.281	4.35	6.10
Isaacs, Dusty	R-R	6-1	190	8-7-91	3	0	1.14	22	0	0	5	24	15	3	3	2	8	28	.183	.161	.196	10.65	3.04
Loup, Aaron	L-L	5-11	210	12-19-87	0	1	18.00	3	0	0	0	2	3	4	4	0	4	2	.333	—	.333	9.00	18.00
Lowery, Jackson	R-R	6-0	175	7-23-92	0	0	3.38	1	0	0	0	3	1	1	1	0	2	1	.111	.200	.000	3.38	6.75
Mayza, Tim	L-L	6-3	220	1-15-92	2	0	1.66	28	0	0	4	49	36	16	9	1	15	52	.201	.208	.198	9.62	2.77
Morales, Franklin	L-L	6-1	210	1-24-86	0	0	0.00	2	0	0	0	2	1	0	0	0	2	3	.143	.000	.200	13.50	9.00
Ramirez, Carlos	R-R	6-5	205	4-24-91	3	0	2.20	30	0	0	9	41	32	10	10	2	21	41	.221	.224	.219	9.00	4.61
Reid-Foley, Sean	R-R	6-3	220	8-30-95	6	2	2.67	10	10	0	0	57	35	17	17	2	16	71	.172	.189	.163	11.15	2.51
Rios, Francisco	R-R	6-1	180	5-6-95	5	6	3.47	19	15	2	0	91	88	37	35	5	21	65	.257	.256	.257	6.45	2.08
Robson, Tom	R-R	6-4	210	6-27-93	1	2	6.48	6	5	0	0	17	17	20	12	1	22	12	.266	.130	.341	6.48	11.88
Rowley, Chris	R-R	6-2	195	8-14-90	10	3	3.49	31	14	0	1	124	128	54	48	14	30	86	.269	.311	.243	6.26	2.18
Santos, Luis	R-R	6-0	185	2-11-91	4	1	3.40	9	7	0	0	45	41	23	17	3	15	42	.238	.241	.237	8.40	3.00
Schultz, Bo	R-R	6-3	230	9-25-85	0	0	10.13	3	0	0	0	3	4	4	3	0	3	3	.333	.333	.333	10.13	10.13
Shafer, Justin	R-R	6-2	195	9-18-92	4	6	5.23	23	20	0	0	115	129	71	67	9	42	62	.278	.341	.240	4.84	3.28
Snead, Kirby	L-L	6-0	200	10-7-94	0	0	0.00	1	0	0	0	2	0	0	0	0	2	1	.000	.000	.000	4.50	9.00
Suriel, Starlyn	R-R	5-11	180	11-17-93	0	0	3.18	3	0	0	0	6	4	4	2	0	3	4	.190	.375	.077	6.35	4.76
Turner, Colton	L-L	6-3	215	1-17-91	3	0	0.57	26	0	0	8	32	19	2	2	0	9	47	.171	.265	.130	13.36	2.56
Westwood, Kyle	R-R	6-3	190	4-13-91	1	6	6.71	12	9	0	0	56	78	44	42	10	14	31	.328	.308	.338	4.95	2.24

Fielding

Catcher	PCT	G	PO	A	E	DP	PB
De La Cruz	.986	27	195	15	3	3	7
Jansen	.994	50	333	21	2	2	2
Reeves	.985	45	295	41	5	2	1
Saez	1.000	17	137	12	0	1	2

First Base	PCT	G	PO	A	E	DP
Colabello	1.000	2	17	0	0	2
Dantzler	.995	24	195	11	1	15
Dean	1.000	1	6	0	0	1
Guerrero	1.000	1	7	0	0	2
McBroom	.995	107	895	34	5	87
Reeves	.967	3	26	3	1	4
Thon	1.000	2	2	0	0	0

Second Base	PCT	G	PO	A	E	DP
Attaway	.989	25	35	54	1	9
Fermin	1.000	7	10	23	0	3
Flores	.973	12	8	28	1	6
Guillotte	.941	3	4	12	1	3
Heidt	1.000	3	3	6	0	2

(Catcher, cont.)	PCT	G	PO	A	E	DP
La Prise	1.000	6	6	14	0	0
Leblebijian	1.000	4	4	2	0	2
Lopes	.986	14	25	43	1	11
Metzler	1.000	1	3	9	0	3
Thon	.969	66	133	175	10	50
Travis	.900	3	6	3	1	0

Third Base	PCT	G	PO	A	E	DP
De La Cruz	1.000	9	5	5	0	1
Dean	.970	15	6	26	1	1
Guerrero	.919	27	11	46	5	6
Guillotte	1.000	1	0	2	0	0
Harris	1.000	1	1	1	0	0
Heidt	.935	17	9	34	3	4
Leblebijian	.906	38	17	70	9	14
Metzler	1.000	2	3	5	0	0
Reeves	.875	3	3	4	1	0
Thon	.893	28	17	58	9	5

Shortstop	PCT	G	PO	A	E	DP
Flores	.934	21	30	55	6	10
Heidt	.990	28	28	73	1	8

(Shortstop, cont.)	PCT	G	PO	A	E	DP
Leblebijian	.958	9	18	28	2	8
Thon	1.000	2	4	4	0	1
Tulowitzki	1.000	1	0	3	0	0
Urena	.937	79	107	236	23	52

Outfield	PCT	G	PO	A	E	DP
Alford	.979	91	230	7	5	3
Almonte	.965	35	78	5	3	1
Bautista	—	1	0	0	0	0
Bourn	1.000	9	17	0	0	0
Colabello	1.000	2	3	0	0	0
Dantzler	1.000	9	15	1	0	0
Davis	.963	79	154	4	6	3
Davis	.992	105	242	7	2	2
De La Cruz	—	1	0	0	0	0
Guerrero	1.000	11	29	1	0	0
Guillotte	1.000	9	24	1	0	0
Harris	.955	23	40	2	2	1
Loveless	1.000	40	87	5	0	0
McBroom	1.000	5	1	0	0	0
Pillar	1.000	2	4	0	0	0
Thon	1.000	4	0	0	0	0

LANSING LUGNUTS   LOW CLASS A
MIDWEST LEAGUE

Batting	B-T	HT	WT	DOB	AVG	vLH	vRH	G	AB	R	H	2B	3B	HR	RBI	BB	HBP	SH	SF	SO	SB	CS	SLG	OBP
Almonte, Josh	R-R	6-3	210	1-28-94	.221	.281	.196	56	195	23	43	7	2	2	19	9	3	4	0	53	9	4	.308	.266
Anderson, Jake	R-R	6-4	190	11-22-92	.146	.233	.106	27	96	4	14	4	1	1	10	6	0	0	0	34	0	0	.240	.196
Atkinson, Justin	R-R	6-1	218	7-24-93	.190	.202	.186	109	384	33	73	19	1	5	47	30	2	1	7	95	0	0	.284	.248
Attaway, Aaron	R-S	5-7	170	3-6-92	.195	.333	.161	25	77	12	15	4	1	1	4	9	1	1	0	20	1	0	.312	.287
Biggio, Cavan	L-R	6-1	203	4-11-95	.222	.429	.172	9	36	3	8	1	0	0	1	4	1	0	1	7	2	0	.250	.310
Cardenas, J.C.	B-R	6-0	185	6-27-94	.206	.207	.206	78	262	28	54	14	0	3	25	27	0	1	1	71	2	1	.294	.279
Davis, Austin	R-R	5-10	170	4-26-93	.176	.333	.161	33	102	5	18	4	0	1	4	10	0	0	0	30	0	1	.186	.250
Guillotte, Andrew	R-R	5-8	170	3-30-93	.253	.318	.232	115	455	65	115	27	3	4	44	39	9	2	3	77	20	10	.352	.322
Heidt, Gunnar	R-R	6-0	200	9-12-92	.270	.308	.258	57	211	29	57	15	3	4	21	22	5	2	1	56	13	8	.427	.351
Hissey, Max	R-R	6-0	175	4-8-94	.246	.278	.236	111	410	43	101	19	3	4	36	36	5	7	1	97	5	1	.337	.310
Kelly, Juan	R-R	5-10	155	7-16-94	.274	.311	.263	131	475	60	130	35	6	12	67	57	8	0	8	113	11	0	.448	.356
La Prise, John	L-R	6-2	180	8-24-93	.255	.311	.242	64	239	42	61	12	1	0	25	24	4	3	3	76	4	3	.314	.332
Maldonado, Alex	R-R	5-9	175	6-12-91	.125	.000	.143	3	8	0	1	0	0	0	0	2	0	0	0	1	0	0	.250	.300

Batting	B-T	HT	WT	DOB	AVG	vLH	vRH	G	AB	R	H	2B	3B	HR	RBI	BB	HBP	SH	SF	SO	SB	CS	SLG	OBP
Metzler, Ryan	R-R	6-3	190	3-20-93	.163	.186	.156	58	184	17	30	7	3	1	16	20	4	2	2	78	10	2	.250	.257
Palacios, Josh	L-R	6-1	193	7-30-95	.342	.556	.276	9	38	2	13	3	0	0	1	1	1	0	0	3	0	2	.421	.375
Panas, Connor	L-R	6-0	218	2-11-93	.231	.190	.240	98	321	46	74	10	3	16	50	45	12	1	4	97	3	4	.430	.343
Pentecost, Max	R-R	6-2	191	3-10-93	.314	.408	.289	62	239	36	75	15	3	7	34	21	4	0	3	51	4	2	.490	.375
Tejada, Juan	R-R	6-3	190	12-13-94	.154	.091	.179	25	78	9	12	1	1	1	6	4	1	0	1	23	2	0	.231	.202
Thomas, Jake	R-R	5-10	190	7-21-93	.244	.186	.259	57	213	24	52	7	4	0	17	24	2	1	1	49	4	3	.315	.325
Thomas, Lane	R-R	6-1	210	8-23-95	.216	.234	.211	81	282	50	61	14	1	7	27	45	3	2	0	107	17	5	.348	.330
Wise, Carl	R-R	6-1	215	5-25-94	.240	.186	.256	84	304	36	73	15	0	4	27	21	2	0	3	72	1	3	.329	.291
Woodman, J.B.	L-R	6-2	195	12-13-94	.441	.429	.444	9	34	5	15	2	0	1	5	4	0	0	1	13	0	1	.588	.487

Pitching	B-T	HT	WT	DOB	W	L	ERA	G	GS	CG	SV	IP	H	R	ER	HR	BB	SO	AVG	vLH	vRH	K/9	BB/9
Abel, Nate	L-L	6-1	190	11-2-92	3	0	3.31	10	0	0	0	16	18	7	6	1	8	12	.286	.208	.333	6.61	4.41
Borucki, Ryan	L-L	6-4	175	3-31-94	10	4	2.41	20	20	1	0	116	105	36	31	1	26	107	.247	.234	.255	8.33	2.02
Case, Andrew	R-R	6-2	190	1-6-93	0	2	2.28	22	0	0	10	24	20	9	6	0	6	19	.225	.308	.160	7.23	2.28
Cook, Ryan	R-R	6-1	210	5-4-93	1	6	5.30	26	7	0	0	70	75	44	41	2	14	56	.278	.291	.265	8.63	4.39
Degraaf, Josh	R-R	6-3	195	1-28-93	5	7	3.43	35	7	0	3	94	91	44	36	6	25	79	.265	.253	.276	7.54	2.39
Encina, Geno	L-R	6-4	220	7-7-94	0	0	0.00	2	0	0	0	3	2	0	0	0	1	4	.167	.286	.000	10.80	2.70
Fisk, Conor	R-R	6-2	210	4-4-92	2	2	4.91	7	1	0	0	22	21	13	12	3	8	26	.239	.262	.217	10.64	3.27
Glaude, Griffin	R-R	5-9	175	4-6-92	0	0	22.50	2	0	0	0	2	7	5	5	0	0	1	.583	1.000	.286	4.50	0.00
Harris, Jon	R-R	6-4	175	10-16-93	8	2	2.23	16	16	0	0	85	74	28	21	1	24	73	.232	.252	.214	7.76	2.55
Isaacs, Dusty	R-R	6-1	190	8-7-91	1	4	2.87	27	0	0	12	31	32	17	10	2	6	37	.250	.300	.206	10.63	1.72
Lietz, Daniel	L-L	6-2	200	6-1-94	6	3	4.20	35	0	0	0	64	59	34	30	4	28	50	.245	.217	.262	6.99	3.92
Lowery, Jackson	R-R	6-0	175	7-23-92	1	2	4.03	17	0	0	4	22	23	10	10	0	7	21	.280	.333	.233	8.46	2.82
Maese, Justin	R-R	6-3	190	10-24-96	2	4	3.36	10	10	0	0	56	59	22	21	2	14	44	.272	.301	.240	7.03	2.24
Murphy, Patrick	R-R	6-6	220	6-10-95	0	1	4.29	8	2	0	2	21	24	12	10	3	14	20	.286	.237	.326	8.57	6.00
Perdomo, Angel	L-L	6-6	220	5-7-94	5	7	3.19	27	25	0	1	127	101	57	45	4	54	156	.219	.193	.233	11.06	3.83
Pierre, Gustavo	R-R	6-2	202	12-28-91	1	1	10.97	8	0	0	0	11	13	13	13	0	11	3	.317	.313	.320	2.53	9.28
Reid-Foley, Sean	R-R	6-3	220	8-30-95	4	3	2.95	11	11	0	0	58	43	22	19	2	22	59	.208	.235	.183	9.16	3.41
Rios, Francisco	R-R	6-1	180	5-6-95	2	0	1.20	6	6	0	0	30	21	7	4	0	8	43	.193	.160	.222	12.90	2.40
Robson, Tom	R-R	6-4	210	6-27-93	0	4	7.50	21	3	0	1	54	78	47	45	6	29	40	.342	.356	.327	6.67	4.83
Romano, Jordan	R-R	6-4	200	4-21-93	3	2	2.11	15	14	1	0	73	49	24	17	3	27	72	.191	.178	.205	8.92	3.34
Saucedo, Tayler	L-L	6-5	185	6-18-93	8	11	5.91	28	16	1	0	120	151	89	79	14	41	71	.307	.329	.296	5.31	3.07
Smith, Evan	R-L	6-5	190	8-17-95	0	0	13.50	4	0	0	0	5	12	8	8	0	2	6	.414	.625	.333	10.13	3.38
Snead, Kirby	L-L	6-0	175	10-7-94	0	3	3.91	13	0	0	1	25	31	12	11	0	3	17	.307	.209	.379	6.04	1.07
Suriel, Starlyn	R-R	5-11	180	11-17-93	5	3	3.21	32	0	0	2	62	51	28	22	2	23	60	.221	.244	.196	8.76	3.36
Turner, Colton	L-L	6-3	215	1-17-91	0	0	0.00	9	0	0	5	12	8	0	0	0	3	13	.182	.333	.103	9.75	2.25
Young, Danny	L-L	6-3	200	5-27-94	2	1	2.70	21	0	0	0	23	25	11	7	2	10	18	.272	.268	.275	6.94	3.86
Zeuch, T.J.	R-R	6-7	225	8-1-95	0	1	9.00	2	2	0	0	8	10	8	8	1	2	14	.294	.471	.118	15.75	2.25

Fielding

Catcher	PCT	G	PO	A	E	DP	PB
Atkinson	.991	47	362	69	4	2	13
Hissey	.992	95	745	78	7	11	12

	PCT	G	PO	A	E	DP
La Prise	.970	58	91	166	8	36
Metzler	.952	10	19	21	2	7
Thomas	.913	10	21	21	4	2

	PCT	G	PO	A	E	DP
Cardenas	.927	73	127	151	22	39
Heidt	.966	20	34	50	3	9
Metzler	.963	43	58	125	7	22

First Base	PCT	G	PO	A	E	DP
Atkinson	.991	57	485	40	5	40
Kelly	.993	82	658	53	5	63
Panas	1.000	7	68	4	0	4

Third Base	PCT	G	PO	A	E	DP
Atkinson	1.000	5	3	7	0	0
Attaway	.900	5	1	8	1	0
Davis	1.000	3	0	1	0	0
Kelly	.955	44	33	73	5	7
Maldonado	1.000	3	2	2	0	0
Metzler	.938	5	2	13	1	2
Wise	.902	80	54	131	20	16

Outfield	PCT	G	PO	A	E	DP
Almonte	.965	56	106	5	4	2
Anderson	1.000	16	23	0	0	0
Davis	1.000	28	36	3	0	2
Guillotte	.987	106	211	15	3	5
Palacios	1.000	9	17	0	0	0
Panas	.993	68	129	5	1	0
Tejada	.939	21	29	2	2	0
Thomas	.969	54	90	4	3	1
Thomas	.993	68	128	10	1	4
Woodman	.889	9	8	0	1	0

Second Base	PCT	G	PO	A	E	DP
Attaway	.938	10	4	26	2	4
Biggio	.929	9	15	24	3	5
Cardenas	.909	5	9	11	2	2
Guillotte	1.000	3	5	6	0	0
Heidt	.971	37	65	102	5	19

Shortstop	PCT	G	PO	A	E	DP
Attaway	.941	10	14	34	3	8

VANCOUVER CANADIANS
NORTHWEST LEAGUE
SHORT-SEASON

Batting	B-T	HT	WT	DOB	AVG	vLH	vRH	G	AB	R	H	2B	3B	HR	RBI	BB	HBP	SH	SF	SO	SB	CS	SLG	OBP
Anderson, Jake	R-R	6-4	190	11-22-92	.226	.194	.242	49	190	23	43	8	0	3	26	15	3	0	1	36	1	0	.316	.292
Barreto, Deiferson	R-R	5-10	165	5-19-95	.215	.260	.197	46	177	15	38	11	2	2	20	9	2	0	1	30	2	2	.333	.259
Biggio, Cavan	L-R	6-1	203	4-11-95	.282	.222	.304	53	202	24	57	11	3	0	21	29	5	0	2	28	9	3	.366	.382
Clark, Gabe	R-R	6-0	220	10-5-94	.132	.143	.125	10	38	4	5	1	0	1	4	3	2	0	0	15	0	0	.237	.233
Gudino, Yeltsin	R-R	6-0	150	1-17-97	.226	.228	.225	54	186	18	42	4	1	0	15	29	4	2	3	43	0	1	.258	.338
Hernandez, Javier	R-R	6-1	180	7-21-96	.215	.189	.227	46	163	19	35	10	0	2	15	15	3	0	1	52	0	1	.313	.291
Jacob, David	L-L	6-4	225	6-19-95	.300	.400	.200	2	10	1	3	1	1	1	0	2	0	0	0	1	0	0	.600	.300
Jones, Lance	R-R	5-11	175	11-10-92	.247	.407	.172	25	85	13	21	3	2	0	8	12	3	1	1	19	6	2	.329	.356
Knight, Nash	L-R	6-0	195	9-20-92	.261	.250	.268	24	92	16	24	1	0	0	12	11	0	0	0	17	1	1	.272	.340
Lizardo, Brayan	B-R	6-0	205	7-26-97	.220	.240	.211	63	246	34	54	15	2	3	21	20	2	0	0	71	0	1	.333	.284
McKnight, D.J.	L-R	5-10	180	1-29-94	.228	.324	.189	40	127	18	29	7	5	2	13	14	1	3	0	58	2	1	.409	.310
Orozco, Rodrigo	B-R	5-11	155	4-2-95	.241	.220	.250	55	187	24	45	9	0	0	11	30	2	2	2	59	5	5	.289	.348
Palacios, Josh	L-R	6-1	193	7-30-95	.355	.500	.278	28	110	15	39	7	3	0	13	14	2	0	0	14	4	2	.473	.437
Reavis, Josh	R-R	6-2	200	9-11-91	.161	.154	.163	20	56	3	9	2	0	1	5	12	1	0	2	20	1	1	.250	.310

Batting	B-T	HT	WT	DOB	AVG	vLH	vRH	G	AB	R	H	2B	3B	HR	RBI	BB	HBP	SH	SF	SO	SB	CS	SLG	OBP
Romanin, Mattingly	R-R	5-10	185	2-27-93	.229	.286	.214	12	35	8	8	1	0	1	7	10	2	0	0	7	0	0	.343	.426
Sinay, Nick	R-R	5-10	175	11-4-93	.200	—	.200	1	5	0	1	0	0	0	1	0	1	0	0	2	0	0	.200	.333
Sotillo, Andres	R-R	5-11	180	12-28-93	.200	.222	.191	29	95	7	19	3	0	1	11	6	4	0	1	19	0	0	.263	.274
Spiwak, Owen	L-R	6-2	185	5-23-95	.000	.000	.000	1	3	0	0	0	0	0	0	0	0	0	0	2	0	0	.000	.250
Tejada, Juan	R-R	6-3	220	2-13-94	.239	.235	.241	12	46	5	11	5	1	1	5	4	0	0	0	9	1	0	.457	.300
Wellman, Brett	L-R	6-0	200	11-22-91	.167	—	.167	3	6	1	1	0	0	0	0	3	0	0	0	3	0	0	.167	.444
Williams, Christian	L-R	6-3	210	9-14-94	.236	.286	.218	60	212	29	50	10	4	3	20	31	4	0	2	55	0	0	.340	.341
Woodman, J.B.	L-R	6-0	195	12-13-94	.272	.293	.263	54	195	28	53	13	7	1	28	30	4	0	3	72	10	2	.421	.375

Pitching	B-T	HT	WT	DOB	W	L	ERA	G	GS	CG	SV	IP	H	R	ER	HR	BB	SO	AVG	vLH	vRH	K/9	BB/9
Abel, Nate	L-L	6-1	190	11-2-92	1	2	3.66	11	2	0	0	32	36	13	13	0	10	34	.281	.308	.270	9.56	2.81
Bergen, Travis	L-L	6-1	205	10-8-93	0	0	0.00	2	0	0	0	2	1	0	0	0	2	3	.143	.000	.200	13.50	9.00
Carkuff, Jared	R-R	6-3	180	8-25-93	0	0	6.75	1	0	0	0	1	3	1	1	0	1	2	.375	1.000	.167	13.50	6.75
Cox, Christian	L-L	6-0	190	4-22-92	0	0	9.00	1	0	0	0	1	2	1	1	0	1	1	.400	.000	.500	9.00	9.00
Diaz, Denis	R-R	6-1	180	11-20-94	1	5	7.71	7	7	0	0	28	30	25	24	2	28	14	.280	.233	.313	4.50	9.00
Durand, Taylor	L-L	6-6	225	1-24-94	0	0	0.00	1	0	0	0	1	1	3	0	0	2	0	.250	.000	.333	0.00	27.00
Ellenbest, Mike	R-R	6-4	205	8-20-94	1	3	4.45	11	5	0	1	30	40	17	15	1	9	21	.323	.283	.352	6.23	2.67
Encina, Geno	L-R	6-4	220	7-7-94	0	0	2.03	10	0	0	0	27	23	6	6	1	4	28	.223	.333	.164	9.45	1.35
Estevez, Mike	L-R	6-0	170	9-27-92	0	0	0.00	1	0	0	0	1	2	0	0	0	1	0	.667	1.000	.500	0.00	9.00
Glaude, Griffin	R-R	5-9	175	4-6-92	2	1	2.36	21	0	0	5	34	24	12	9	1	17	40	.194	.261	.154	10.49	4.46
Hartman, Nick	R-R	6-2	180	10-24-94	2	2	3.00	19	0	0	4	24	29	10	8	0	7	17	.299	.394	.250	6.38	2.63
Higuera, Juliandry	L-L	6-1	180	9-6-94	1	3	3.92	5	5	0	0	21	26	13	9	0	12	12	.329	.100	.362	5.23	5.23
Holmes, Stuart	L-L	6-1	180	1-5-93	0	1	9.60	12	0	0	0	15	26	20	16	0	9	10	.400	.350	.422	6.00	5.40
Huffman, Grayson	L-L	6-2	195	5-6-95	2	2	6.35	19	0	0	0	28	36	27	20	0	16	25	.321	.314	.325	7.94	5.08
Jackson, Zach	R-R	6-4	215	12-25-94	1	1	3.57	13	0	0	0	18	13	8	7	0	12	23	.206	.172	.235	11.72	6.11
Lietz, Daniel	L-L	6-2	200	6-1-94	1	0	1.69	3	0	0	0	5	5	1	1	0	2	5	.250	.286	.231	8.44	3.38
Lowery, Jackson	R-R	6-0	175	7-23-92	1	0	0.87	9	0	0	5	10	4	1	1	1	1	12	.171	.231	.136	10.45	0.87
Maese, Justin	R-R	6-3	190	10-24-96	2	2	2.05	5	5	0	0	26	20	16	6	1	1	20	.204	.200	.206	6.84	0.34
McClelland, Jackson	R-R	6-5	220	7-19-94	2	4	3.26	24	0	0	1	30	31	12	11	2	10	25	.277	.324	.256	7.42	2.97
Murphy, Patrick	R-R	6-4	220	6-10-95	4	5	2.84	13	13	0	0	70	71	28	22	0	23	48	.264	.284	.253	6.20	2.97
Noyalis, Gabe	R-R	6-3	220	11-17-91	0	1	7.43	19	0	0	0	27	26	23	22	3	21	26	.252	.265	.246	8.78	7.09
Ravel, Andy	R-R	6-2	165	10-12-94	3	1	5.12	11	5	0	0	32	40	18	18	5	9	18	.315	.426	.233	5.12	2.56
Rodriguez, Dalton	R-R	6-1	180	8-20-96	2	7	6.18	14	14	0	0	63	84	50	43	3	35	42	.332	.400	.294	6.03	5.03
Sanchez, Luis	R-R	6-3	200	2-20-94	1	3	4.61	12	12	0	0	53	56	29	27	3	32	27	.277	.352	.219	4.61	5.47
Smith, Evan	R-L	6-5	190	8-17-95	2	1	7.03	21	0	0	2	32	43	26	25	4	14	33	.328	.263	.355	9.28	3.94
Smoral, Matt	L-L	6-8	220	3-18-94	0	0	13.15	11	0	0	0	13	15	19	19	0	16	18	.294	.263	.313	12.46	11.08
Zeuch, T.J.	R-R	6-7	225	8-1-95	1	1	3.52	6	6	0	0	23	21	9	9	1	5	22	.247	.282	.217	8.61	1.96

Fielding

C: Hernandez 42, Reavis 13, Sotillo 21. **1B:** Barreto 2, Clark 4, Jacob 2, Knight 9, Reavis 1, Sotillo 1, Williams 58. **2B:** Barreto 15, Biggio 49, Knight 6, Romanin 5. **3B:** Barreto 7, Knight 1, Lizardo 62, Romanin 4, Williams 2. **SS:** Barreto 20, Gudino 54, Lizardo 1. **OF:** Anderson 31, Barreto 1, Jones 23, Knight 1, McKnight 37, Orozco 50, Palacios 26, Sinay 1, Tejada 12, Woodman 48.

BLUEFIELD BLUE JAYS   ROOKIE
APPALACHIAN LEAGUE

Batting	B-T	HT	WT	DOB	AVG	vLH	vRH	G	AB	R	H	2B	3B	HR	RBI	BB	HBP	SH	SF	SO	SB	CS	SLG	OBP
Burl, Earl	R-R	6-0	190	11-10-93	.211	.250	.195	37	114	16	24	2	0	1	8	17	0	2	1	35	6	4	.254	.311
Florides, Andrew	R-R	6-1	170	1-22-95	.100	.188	.059	18	50	2	5	1	0	0	2	2	0	1	0	22	1	0	.120	.135
Guerrero Jr. Vladimir	R-R	6-1	200	3-16-99	.271	.242	.282	62	236	32	64	12	3	8	46	33	2	0	5	35	15	5	.449	.359
Jones, Bradley	R-R	6-1	180	6-12-95	.291	.264	.303	61	237	41	69	18	1	16	55	17	0	0	2	71	16	4	.578	.336
Jones, Lance	R-R	5-11	175	11-10-92	.325	.406	.267	28	77	24	25	3	1	1	12	23	3	2	21	12	2	.429	.486
Knight, Nash	L-R	6-0	195	9-20-92	.402	.588	.302	25	97	16	39	7	1	3	23	12	1	0	0	16	1	1	.588	.473
May, Kalik	B-R	6-2	205	10-5-92	.218	.231	.214	44	156	19	34	8	3	2	23	17	5	0	2	61	7	4	.346	.311
Mendoza, Juandy	R-R	5-10	180	10-14-96	.194	.235	.180	40	134	19	26	11	0	3	15	9	5	4	0	39	5	0	.343	.270
Monzon, Javier	R-R	6-0	195	2-6-93	.261	.435	.174	21	69	18	18	0	4	3	16	9	1	0	1	29	3	1	.507	.350
Morgan, Matt	R-R	6-1	190	1-27-96	.179	.154	.192	36	112	13	20	3	0	3	8	21	1	1	0	45	1	2	.286	.313
O'Brien, Cam	B-R	6-0	215	8-9-92	.264	.250	.269	33	91	19	24	6	1	5	12	20	4	0	1	27	0	2	.516	.414
Olivares, Edward	R-R	6-2	186	3-6-96	.273	.167	.355	15	55	8	15	3	1	1	6	5	1	0	1	12	1	2	.418	.339
Pruitt, Reggie	R-R	6-0	169	5-7-97	.237	.213	.246	46	173	36	41	3	0	1	10	13	7	4	0	43	16	2	.266	.316
Scott, Levi	R-R	6-5	235	8-4-92	.253	.281	.239	48	170	22	43	12	0	5	28	16	0	0	3	55	0	0	.412	.312
Severino, Jesus	L-R	6-0	190	2-13-96	.127	.254	.54	169	23	36	6	1	1	19	23	4	1	51	9	0	.278	.320		
Sinay, Nick	R-R	5-10	175	11-4-93	.246	.254	.242	58	191	52	47	4	2	1	11	40	24	10	0	45	34	5	.304	.435
Smith, Ridge	R-R	5-10	190	4-26-95	.228	.310	.190	30	92	15	21	5	2	4	16	8	4	2	0	28	0	0	.457	.317

Pitching	B-T	HT	WT	DOB	W	L	ERA	G	GS	CG	SV	IP	H	R	ER	HR	BB	SO	AVG	vLH	vRH	K/9	BB/9
Alicea, Angel	R-R	6-1	200	8-29-94	2	1	2.76	17	0	0	4	33	27	11	10	1	10	45	.223	.196	.243	12.40	2.76
Barnett, Hunter	L-L	6-3	205	8-13-94	0	1	6.23	8	0	0	1	9	10	7	6	1	3	4	.278	.200	.308	4.15	3.12
Bouchey, Brayden	R-R	6-6	212	9-20-95	1	0	2.57	10	0	0	0	21	15	9	6	0	15	32	.190	.211	.171	13.71	6.43
Cox, Christian	L-L	6-0	190	4-22-92	1	1	4.13	14	0	0	0	24	22	13	11	4	3	17	.244	.300	.217	6.38	1.13
Deramo, Andrew	R-R	6-6	200	5-26-95	0	3	7.71	14	1	0	0	23	42	22	20	5	8	18	.408	.444	.388	6.94	3.09
Diaz, Denis	R-R	6-1	180	11-20-94	1	2	2.91	5	3	0	0	22	17	9	7	0	6	12	.215	.237	.195	4.98	2.49
Diaz, Yennsy	R-R	6-1	160	11-15-96	4	6	5.79	12	10	0	0	56	59	39	36	9	27	48	.267	.263	.271	7.71	4.34
Eller, Connor	R-R	6-2	195	1-23-94	2	1	2.60	17	2	0	7	35	23	13	10	3	9	33	.189	.173	.200	8.57	2.34
Espada, Jose	R-R	6-0	170	2-22-97	3	4	4.92	12	10	0	1	53	54	34	29	6	12	32	.262	.277	.252	5.43	2.04

Pitching	B-T	HT	WT	DOB	W	L	ERA	G	GS	CG	SV	IP	H	R	ER	HR	BB	SO	AVG	vLH	vRH	K/9	BB/9
Espinal, Joel	R-R	6-2	185	8-15-96	2	2	8.62	7	7	0	0	31	44	31	30	7	18	17	.338	.378	.286	4.88	5.17
Estevez, Mike	L-R	6-0	170	9-27-92	0	0	3.86	3	0	0	0	5	2	2	2	0	2	8	.125	.000	.182	15.43	3.86
Gillingham, Luke	L-L	6-3	200	3-4-94	1	0	2.79	4	1	0	1	10	8	3	3	0	3	11	.222	.385	.13	10.24	2.79
Gutierrez, Osman	R-R	6-4	185	12-15-94	4	3	3.88	12	11	1	0	65	69	36	28	5	21	66	.264	.266	.263	9.14	2.91
Hall, Chris	R-R	6-2	212	1-27-94	3	0	2.40	16	0	0	2	30	22	10	8	2	8	21	.198	.255	.156	6.30	2.40
Higuera, Juliandry	L-L	6-1	180	9-6-94	2	3	3.23	8	8	1	0	39	39	23	14	4	16	35	.250	.216	.261	8.08	3.69
Holmes, Stuart	L-L	6-1	180	1-5-93	1	1	1.93	8	0	0	0	14	6	3	3	1	5	12	.140	.167	.129	7.71	3.21
Jose, Kelyn	L-L	6-4	195	5-19-95	0	0	4.08	12	0	0	0	18	12	10	8	0	19	17	.185	.286	.136	8.66	9.68
Nova, Jose	L-L	6-1	170	4-6-95	0	1	5.16	7	2	0	0	23	27	15	13	3	12	12	.307	.294	.315	4.76	4.76
Rodriguez, Hansel	R-R	6-2	170	2-27-97	2	1	3.06	6	6	0	0	32	25	13	11	1	11	26	.203	.200	.206	7.24	3.06
Veglahn, Eric	L-L	6-0	180	1-9-94	1	0	3.97	2	2	0	0	11	12	6	5	0	4	7	.267	.222	.278	5.56	3.18
Weatherly, Kyle	R-R	6-4	200	10-3-94	4	0	4.06	10	5	0	0	38	37	19	17	2	9	33	.259	.258	.259	7.88	2.15

Fielding

C: Morgan 36, O'Brien 10, Smith 29. 1B: Jones 35, Knight 1, O'Brien 1, Scott 33. 2B: Knight 18, Mendoza 35, Monzon 18. 3B: Florides 1, Guerrero Jr. 50, Jones 16, Knight 2, Monzon 1. SS: Florides 16, Mendoza 4, Severino 54. OF: Burl III 34, Jones 25, May 41, Olivares 14, Pruitt 42, Sinay 57.

GCL BLUE JAYS   ROOKIE
GULF COAST LEAGUE

Batting	B-T	HT	WT	DOB	AVG	vLH	vRH	G	AB	R	H	2B	3B	HR	RBI	BB	HBP	SH	SF	SO	SB	CS	SLG	OBP
Abbadessa, Dom	R-R	5-10	185	12-8-97	.192	.200	.188	14	26	3	5	0	0	0	1	1	1	1	0	3	2	2	.192	.250
Almonte, Miguel	R-R	5-11	165	11-26-96	.192	.133	.206	28	78	8	15	1	1	2	11	7	2	0	0	29	3	2	.308	.276
Berti, Jon	R-R	5-10	195	1-22-90	.400	.000	.533	6	20	2	8	0	0	1	6	1	0	0	0	1	5	0	.550	.429
Bichette, Bo	R-R	6-0	200	3-5-98	.427	.350	.452	22	82	21	35	9	2	4	36	6	0	0	3	17	3	0	.732	.451
Bohorquez, Alfredo	B-R	5-9	190	9-16-90	.216	.238	.211	36	97	19	21	4	0	1	8	12	7	1	0	7	4	1	.289	.345
Daniels, D.J.	R-R	6-3	205	12-17-97	.100	.115	.096	36	120	8	12	0	0	1	11	8	3	0	0	48	3	0	.125	.176
Dean, Matt	R-R	6-3	220	12-22-92	.154	.400	.000	4	13	0	2	0	0	0	1	0	1	0	0	6	0	0	.154	.214
Fuentes, Antony	R-R	5-11	160	9-26-95	.246	.286	.233	36	114	14	28	4	4	2	16	5	4	0	0	10	7	1	.404	.301
Gold, Ryan	L-R	5-11	180	10-10-97	.280	.333	.259	29	82	14	23	5	1	1	10	10	0	0	0	18	0	0	.402	.359
Guzman, Sterling	R-R	5-11	175	2-2-98	.214	.194	.222	36	126	16	27	6	0	4	19	13	3	2	0	33	1	1	.357	.303
Herazo, Manuel	B-R	5-10	175	3-17-95	.257	.467	.200	38	70	7	18	3	0	1	8	2	3	1	1	17	0	0	.343	.303
Jacob, David	L-L	6-4	225	6-19-95	.304	.195	.342	46	161	28	49	9	0	6	29	21	4	0	3	24	3	0	.472	.392
Jansen, Danny	R-R	6-2	225	4-15-95	.222	.400	.000	3	9	0	2	0	0	0	2	1	1	0	0	2	0	0	.222	.364
May, Kalik	B-R	6-2	165	10-5-92	.333	.000	.400	3	12	1	4	1	2	0	4	1	0	0	0	5	0	0	.750	.385
Monzon, Javier	R-R	6-0	195	2-6-93	.232	.400	.185	22	69	12	16	3	2	3	11	11	3	0	2	18	4	1	.464	.353
Navarro, Jesus	R-R	5-11	160	1-13-98	.182	.375	.103	18	55	4	10	2	0	0	2	3	1	1	0	13	0	1	.218	.237
Nay, Mitch	R-R	6-3	190	9-20-93	.091	.000	.111	8	22	1	2	0	0	0	0	1	0	0	0	9	0	0	.091	.130
Obeso, Norberto	L-R	6-0	175	7-9-95	.316	.273	.333	44	152	31	48	11	0	1	18	29	6	0	1	15	4	1	.408	.441
Palacios, Josh	L-R	6-1	193	7-30-95	.265	.385	.222	13	49	10	13	3	0	0	4	3	1	0	0	6	4	1	.327	.321
Rodriguez, Francisco	R-R	6-1	220	9-22-94	.230	.289	.202	35	122	19	28	10	1	3	20	6	0	0	0	42	1	0	.402	.333
Rodriguez, Freddy	L-R	6-1	180	11-15-96	.400	.400	.133	7	25	4	6	1	0	0	4	2	0	0	0	6	0	0	.280	.296
Rodriguez, Yorman	R-R	5-10	160	7-23-97	.296	.364	.279	21	54	12	16	0	1	2	5	7	6	1	0	5	6	1	.444	.433
Spiwak, Owen	L-R	6-2	185	5-23-95	.164	.176	.158	24	55	6	9	2	0	1	4	14	0	0	0	25	0	0	.255	.333
Thomas, Lane	R-R	6-1	210	8-23-95	.429	.250	.471	6	21	8	9	5	0	1	4	2	0	0	0	6	2	1	.810	.478
Vicuna, Kevin	R-R	6-0	140	1-14-98	.258	.353	.220	48	178	31	46	5	1	0	14	12	11	2	0	39	11	3	.298	.343
Wellman, Brett	L-R	6-0	200	11-22-91	—	—	—	1	0	0	0	0	0	0	0	1	0	0	0	0	0	0	—	1.000
Young, Chavez	B-R	6-2	180	8-8-97	.274	.286	.269	21	73	9	20	8	2	0	6	6	2	0	0	26	6	1	.438	.346

Pitching	B-T	HT	WT	DOB	W	L	ERA	G	GS	CG	SV	IP	H	R	ER	HR	BB	SO	AVG	vLH	vRH	K/9	BB/9
Aleton, Wilfri	L-L	6-3	165	11-18-95	4	1	2.92	10	8	0	0	49	41	22	16	2	11	45	.229	.204	.240	8.21	2.01
Bergen, Travis	L-L	6-1	205	10-8-93	0	0	0.00	3	0	0	0	3	1	0	0	0	0	4	.100	.000	.125	12.00	0.00
Bouchey, Brayden	R-R	6-6	212	9-20-95	1	0	5.40	4	0	0	0	5	4	3	3	1	2	6	.222	.167	.250	10.80	3.60
Carkuff, Jared	R-R	6-3	180	8-25-93	4	0	1.42	17	0	0	7	25	20	5	4	0	3	35	.217	.143	.250	12.43	1.07
Case, Andrew	R-R	6-2	190	1-6-93	0	0	0.00	1	0	0	0	2	0	0	0	0	0	3	.000		.000	13.50	0.00
Castillo, Maximo	R-R	6-2	200	5-4-99	2	3	4.62	9	9	0	0	39	38	23	20	2	13	29	.257	.302	.238	6.69	3.00
Chavez, Lupe	R-R	6-2	150	12-3-97	4	1	1.69	6	6	0	0	32	29	6	6	1	4	26	.248	.242	.250	7.31	1.13
2-team total (3 Astros)					4	1	1.42	9	7	0	0	38	32	6	6	1	5	31	—			7.34	1.18
Espinal, Joel	R-R	6-2	185	8-15-96	3	0	0.62	6	5	0	0	29	14	2	2	1	4	30	.143	.133	.151	9.31	1.24
Eveld, Mark	L-R	6-5	200	12-4-91	0	0	13.50	2	0	0	0	1	4	2	2	0	1	1	.500	.333	.600	6.75	6.75
Fishman, Jake	L-L	6-3	195	2-8-95	0	1	4.80	7	1	0	0	15	21	13	8	1	4	13	.328	.286	.340	7.80	2.40
Galindo, Alvaro	R-R	6-2	170	2-25-98	1	2	6.23	6	2	0	0	22	19	17	15	1	12	13	.247	.294	.233	5.40	4.98
Herdenez, Yonardo	R-R	6-1	170	9-20-95	3	0	1.06	11	2	0	3	42	24	5	5	1	6	26	.164	.196	.144	5.53	1.28
Hosterman, Travis	L-L	6-3	190	8-19-98	0	0	4.91	8	5	0	0	18	19	13	10	2	10	14	.250	.389	.207	6.87	4.91
Jackson, Zach	R-R	6-4	215	12-29-96	0	0	0.00	1	0	0	0	1	0	0	0	0	0	0	.333	—	.333	0.00	0.00
Jimenez, Dany	R-R	6-3	190	12-23-93	3	2	3.29	9	0	0	0	38	25	15	14	1	18	40	.185	.265	.140	9.39	4.23
McKown, Mitch	R-R	6-4	195	5-21-96	0	1	17.61	9	0	0	1	8	9	16	15	1	18	6	.333	.333	.333	7.04	21.13
Meza, Juan	R-R	6-2	172	2-4-98	1	2	8.61	14	0	0	0	23	34	25	22	5	13	10	.343	.303	.364	3.91	5.09
Mora, Gregor	R-R	6-2	215	8-28-95	0	0	0.00	1	0	0	0	3	0	0	0	0	2	2	.286	.167	.315	4.91	4.91
Moritz, Daniel	L-L	6-2	200	7-5-94	0	0	0.00	1	0	0	0	3	3	0	0	0	3	1	.300	.000	.333	11.57	0.00
Nova, Jose	L-L	6-1	170	4-6-95	0	0	4.63	5	2	0	0	12	10	6	6	0	5	7	.233	.375	.200	5.40	3.86
Olander, Tyler	L-R	6-9	280	7-9-92	0	0	0.00	6	5	0	0	10	6	0	0	1	6	5	.171	.300	.120	5.23	5.23
Ouellette, William	R-R	6-1	195	6-30-93	1	0	3.22	13	0	0	0	8	7	4	4	0	1	15	.238	.357	.179	6.04	2.82
Pascual, Orlando	R-R	6-3	210	11-7-95	4	1	3.08	14	0	0	0	26	25	13	9	2	5	19	.243	.303	.214	6.49	1.71
Pondler, Randy	L-L	6-2	160	11-8-96	3	3	3.52	10	0	0	1	31	39	18	12	1	12	20	.320	.344	.311	5.87	3.52

Pitching	B-T	HT	WT	DOB	W	L	ERA	G	GS	CG	SV	IP	H	R	ER	HR	BB	SO	AVG	vLH	vRH	K/9	BB/9
Reina, Richard	R-R	6-2	220	2-7-95	0	0	6.23	3	0	0	0	4	5	3	3	0	0	2	.278	.429	.182	4.15	0.00
2-team total (15 Mets)					2	1	6.30	18	0	0	0	20	18	14	14	1	16	11	—	—	—	4.95	7.20
Rosario, Jairo	R-R	6-4	190	10-21-93	0	1	3.86	7	0	0	0	9	7	4	4	1	6	9	.212	.231	.200	8.68	5.79
Sterner, Ty	L-L	6-1	208	12-9-92	1	1	1.17	4	0	0	0	8	9	4	1	0	1	11	.273	.200	.286	12.91	1.17
Winckowski, Josh	R-R	6-3	185	6-28-98	2	2	4.61	5	3	0	0	14	16	9	7	2	4	13	.281	.136	.371	8.56	2.63
Zeuch, T.J.	R-R	6-7	225	8-1-95	0	0	0.00	1	1	0	0	3	0	0	0	0	0	2	.000	.000	.000	6.00	0.00

Fielding

C: Gold 20, Herazo 38, Jansen 2, Rodriguez 6, Spiwak 24, Wellman 1. **1B:** Dean 3, Jacob 41, Monzon 8, Rodriguez 1, Rodriguez 10. **2B:** Almonte 18, Berti 3, Bichette 6, Bohorquez 15, Guzman 1, Navarro 5, Vicuna 19. **3B:** Almonte 3, Bohorquez 14, Guzman 34, Monzon 7, Nay 4. **SS:** Almonte 1, Bichette 16, Bohorquez 4, Navarro 14, Vicuna 31. **OF:** Abbadessa 8, Berti 2, Daniels 35, Fuentes 33, May 3, Monzon 1, Obeso 40, Palacios 13, Rodriguez 20, Rodriguez 7, Thomas 5, Young 19.

DSL BLUE JAYS   ROOKIE
DOMINICAN SUMMER LEAGUE

Batting	B-T	HT	WT	DOB	AVG	vLH	vRH	G	AB	R	H	2B	3B	HR	RBI	BB	HBP	SH	SF	SO	SB	CS	SLG	OBP
Briceno, Jose	R-R	6-2	185	10-14-97	.219	.231	.213	43	128	21	28	1	1	1	9	15	4	2	0	34	3	2	.266	.320
Buelens, Sam	R-R	5-11	160	12-27-95	.132	.250	.081	22	53	17	7	1	0	0	1	13	3	2	0	15	7	2	.151	.333
Concepcion, Antonio	R-R	6-0	190	6-16-97	.202	.211	.200	38	109	13	22	7	0	0	12	17	8	2	0	31	0	2	.266	.351
Concepcion, Ronald	R-R	6-0	170	4-19-97	.108	.087	.117	26	83	10	9	3	0	1	7	11	2	0	1	27	0	1	.181	.227
Contreras, Mc Gregory	R-R	6-1	170	8-30-98	.273	.288	.267	63	216	45	59	10	7	2	22	41	8	1	0	59	10	4	.412	.408
De Los Santos, Luis	R-R	6-1	160	6-9-98	.291	.356	.262	52	189	22	55	7	1	1	16	10	9	3	0	32	5	2	.354	.356
Estevez, Yeison	R-R	6-0	180	4-29-96	.253	.190	.277	48	154	25	39	7	1	0	16	24	4	1	0	35	12	2	.312	.368
Figuereo, Victor	R-R	6-1	180	5-24-97	.200	.225	.190	45	145	17	29	4	3	2	14	18	2	6	0	57	5	5	.310	.297
Green, Anderson	B-R	6-1	170	1-2-97	.135	.161	.123	36	104	9	14	2	0	0	7	9	2	1	0	26	1	2	.154	.217
Guerra, Andres	R-R	5-11	175	6-3-97	.243	.294	.221	38	111	13	27	2	1	0	15	19	2	1	2	33	0	1	.279	.358
Kelly, Yhordegny	R-R	6-3	205	3-5-97	.283	.286	.281	60	205	27	58	11	0	4	29	38	13	0	1	62	1	1	.395	.424
Molina, Jonelvy	R-R	6-0	180	3-18-97	.245	.167	.279	29	98	8	24	4	0	0	14	5	0	1	1	15	0	0	.286	.279
Navarro, Jesus	R-R	5-11	160	1-13-98	.243	.240	.245	37	148	21	36	4	2	0	12	24	0	3	1	19	4	3	.297	.347
Ovando, Aldo	R-R	6-5	195	4-6-97	.260	.269	.256	47	169	17	44	13	0	0	14	13	2	0	2	50	1	1	.337	.317
Peguero, Cristian	R-R	6-2	190	11-16-95	.214	.364	.161	13	42	6	9	3	0	0	4	3	3	0	0	15	0	0	.286	.313
Rodriguez, Yorman	R-R	5-10	160	7-23-97	.324	.323	.325	46	188	29	61	14	2	1	35	9	4	1	4	17	8	2	.436	.361
Theran, Jose	R-R	5-10	155	6-2-98	.296	.118	.352	20	71	9	21	4	1	0	5	5	2	0	1	5	2	0	.380	.354

Pitching	B-T	HT	WT	DOB	W	L	ERA	G	GS	CG	SV	IP	H	R	ER	HR	BB	SO	AVG	vLH	vRH	K/9	BB/9
Bautista, Juan	R-R	5-11	190	12-26-95	1	1	2.83	14	0	0	3	29	31	10	9	0	12	19	.287	.342	.257	5.97	3.77
Brito, Oscar	R-R	6-5	195	12-25-95	2	2	3.66	19	0	0	2	32	29	18	13	1	15	20	.238	.190	.263	5.63	4.22
Cabarcas, Nicolas	R-R	6-2	181	11-30-98	0	0	—	1	0	0	0	0	2	2	1	0	1	0	.667	1.000	.500	—	—
Castillo, Maximo	R-R	6-1	200	5-4-99	0	0	2.45	4	3	0	0	11	7	3	3	0	3	11	.175	.250	.143	9.00	2.45
Colman, Jesus	R-R	6-1	175	3-11-98	2	3	2.05	15	2	0	4	26	15	8	6	1	13	19	.181	.233	.151	6.49	4.44
Cornelius, Felix	R-R	6-1	197	10-29-97	0	1	5.14	4	0	0	0	7	5	5	4	0	9	4	.208	.000	.263	5.14	11.57
Cuevas, Adams	R-R	6-0	192	2-2-96	3	3	0.55	12	3	0	2	49	26	7	3	1	12	45	.158	.195	.145	8.27	2.20
Dominguez, Jose	R-R	6-2	165	2-21-96	3	4	3.57	13	11	0	1	58	58	29	23	3	17	58	.253	.281	.236	9.00	2.64
Galindo, Alvaro	R-R	6-2	170	2-25-98	8	0	0.62	9	4	0	0	43	29	7	3	0	12	46	.190	.130	.215	9.55	2.49
Galva, Claudio	L-L	6-2	169	10-9-96	1	1	3.86	7	3	1	1	16	14	8	7	0	6	10	.233	.385	.191	5.51	3.31
Henriquez, Tommy	R-R	6-0	173	7-31-95	1	0	4.50	2	0	0	0	4	4	3	2	0	2	8	.250	.500	.214	18.00	4.50
Jimenez, Dany	R-R	6-3	190	12-23-93	0	0	0.00	2	2	0	0	8	3	0	0	0	8	.111	.000	.188	9.00	0.00
Loficial, Pedro	R-R	6-2	190	5-21-95	1	0	1.35	3	0	0	0	7	4	1	1	0	3	4	.190	.000	.235	5.40	4.05
Manzueta, Danilo	R-R	6-3	188	1-18-97	0	2	3.38	3	0	0	0	11	8	4	4	1	2	6	.216	.25	.207	5.06	1.69
Mendoza, Luis	R-R	6-3	175	10-4-95	3	5	3.07	19	5	0	2	56	50	30	19	2	16	26	.239	.308	.208	4.20	2.59
Mueses, Wilton	R-R	6-2	190	5-19-96	0	0	9.00	8	0	0	0	6	4	7	6	0	14	8	.174	.286	.125	12.00	21.00
Nunez, Anderson	R-R	6-1	190	12-23-97	1	1	3.49	9	4	0	0	28	25	15	11	1	9	16	.234	.265	.219	5.08	2.86
Pascual, Orlando	R-R	6-3	210	11-7-95	0	1	1.64	4	3	0	1	11	8	4	2	0	4	8	.205	.267	.167	6.55	3.27
Pondler, Randy	L-L	6-2	160	11-8-96	0	1	2.08	3	3	0	0	13	12	4	3	1	2	5	.261	.222	.270	3.46	1.38
Reyes, Emmanuel	L-L	6-0	185	12-14-97	2	2	2.68	17	3	0	2	37	31	16	11	1	22	34	.231	.273	.223	8.27	5.35
Reyes, Meliton	R-R	6-2	180	7-31-97	4	2	2.70	15	8	0	1	57	46	22	17	2	21	55	.227	.246	.216	8.74	3.34
Silva, Elio	L-L	5-11	160	8-21-95	4	2	2.05	14	11	0	0	61	48	15	14	1	13	54	.218	.244	.212	7.92	1.91
Ventura, Ruben	R-R	6-2	183	12-8-94	0	1	3.78	4	3	0	0	17	20	10	7	1	7	11	.303	.313	.300	5.94	3.78

Fielding

C: Concepcion 1, Guerra 22, Molina 28, Rodriguez 19. **1B:** Concepcion 33, Guerra 16, Rodriguez 26. **2B:** Concepcion 25, Estevez 30, Green 2, Theran 19. **3B:** Concepcion 1, De Los Santos 25, Estevez 15, Green 33. **SS:** De Los Santos 27, Estevez 4, Green 1, Navarro 37. **OF:** Briceno 36, Buelens 10, Contreras 63, Figuereo 34, Kelly 19, Ovando 45, Peguero 11.

Washington Nationals

SEASON IN A SENTENCE: The Nationals won 12 more games than they did in 2015 and wound up with the second-best record in baseball despite a down year by 2015 MVP Bryce Harper, getting 20 or more homers from six different players to win the National League East.

HIGH POINT: For all the offensive balance, Max Scherzer continued to be the team's ace, going 2007, 2.96 and leading the majors with 284 strikeouts in 228.1 innings. Scherzer had 13 double-digit strikeouts games, none better than his record-tying 20 strikeouts against his former team, Detroit, on May 11. Scherzer threw an absurd 96 strikes out of his 119 pitches, walking none.

LOW POINT: The Nats continued to struggle in the playoffs, losing their third division series in five years. This time, it was the Dodgers who did in the Nationals and Dusty Baker, the third manager to lose a playoff series for the franchise in D.C. Washington led the series two games to one but lost Game Four in L.A. 6-5, then lost 4-3 in Game Five when its offense couldn't dent Kenley Jansen and Clayton Kershaw, who got the final two outs on one day's rest to clinch the series.

NOTABLE ROOKIES: The Nats didn't open a spot for Trea Turner, but he seized one, shifting to second base and then center field. No matter where Turner played, he hit, igniting Washington's offense with blazing speed and surprising power. He led rookies with 33 stolen bases despite playing less than half the season in the majors, and his .567 slugging percentage ranked third, behind Gary Sanchez and Trevor Story, among rookies with 200 or more at-bats. Righty Reynaldo Lopez and lefty Sammy Solis logged key innings down the stretch.

KEY TRANSACTIONS: Offseason free-agent pickup Daniel Murphy (.347, 25 homers) was one of the majors' best hitters. GM Mike Rizzo's big in-season moves involved releasing Jonathan Papelbon and replacing him with Mark Melancon, acquired from the Pirates for lefthanders Taylor Hearn and Felipe Rivero. Washington also traded for lefty reliever Marc Rzepczynski, giving up top performer Max Schrock.

DOWN ON THE FARM: Washington affiliates posted a .508 winning percentage and had two playoff clubs, led by low Class A Hagerstown going 83-57, the South Atlantic League's best record. Double-A Harrisburg outfielder Rafael Bautista tied for the minor-league lead with 56 stolen bases during a .282/.344/.341 season.

OPENING DAY PAYROLL: $ 141,652,646 (11th)

PLAYERS OF THE YEAR

WILL BENTZEL/HARRISBURG SENATORS

MAJOR LEAGUE

Max Scherzer
rhp
20-7, 2.96
284 SO in 228.1 IP
Led NL in SO, WHIP

MINOR LEAGUE

Trea Turner
of/2b
(Triple-A)
.302/.370/.471
36 XBH, 25 SB

ORGANIZATION LEADERS

BATTING   *Minimum 250 AB

MAJORS

*	AVG	Daniel Murphy	.347
*	OPS	Daniel Murphy	.985
	HR	Daniel Murphy	25
	RBI	Daniel Murphy	104

MINORS

*	AVG	Max Schrock, Hagerstown, Potomac	.333
*	OBP	Victor Robles, Hagerstown, Potomac	.384
*	SLG	Jose Marmolejos, Potomac, Harrisburg	.475
*	OPS	Jose Marmolejos, Potomac, Harrisburg	.845
	R	Jose Marmolejos, Potomac, Harrisburg	87
	H	Max Schrock, Hagerstown, Potomac	167
	TB	Jose Marmolejos, Potomac, Harrisburg	240
	2B	Jose Marmolejos, Potomac, Harrisburg	45
	3B	Chris Bostick, Harrisburg, Syracuse	10
		Andrew Stevenson, Potomac, Harrisburg	10
	HR	Matt Skole, Syracuse	24
	RBI	Matt Skole, Syracuse	78
	BB	Matt Skole, Syracuse	66
	SO	Jason Martinson, Syracuse	179
	SB	Rafael Bautista, Harrisburg	56

PITCHING   #Minimum 75 IP

MAJORS

	W	Max Scherzer	20
#	ERA	Tanner Roark	2.83
	SO	Max Scherzer	284
	SV	Jonathan Papelbon	19

MINORS

	W	Tyler Mapes, Harrisburg	12
		Phillips Valdez, Potomac, Harrisburg	12
	L	Taylor Hill, Syracuse	13
		Austen Williams, Harrisburg, Potomac	13
#	ERA	Lucas Giolito, Harrisburg, Hagerstown, Syracuse	2.97
	G	Rafael Martin, Syracuse	50
	GS	Joan Baez, Hagerstown	27
		Taylor Hill, Syracuse	27
		Phillips Valdez, Potomac, Harrisburg	27
	SV	Rafael Martin, Syracuse	22
	IP	Austin Voth, Syracuse	157
	BB	Joan Baez, Hagerstown	64
	SO	Paolo Espino, Syracuse	133
		Austin Voth, Syracuse	133
#	AVG	Austin Voth, Syracuse	.232

General Manager: Mike Rizzo. **Farm Director:** Doug Harris. **Scouting Director:** Kris Kline.

Class	Team	League	W	L	PCT	Finish	Manager
Majors	Washington Nationals	National	95	67	.586	2nd (15)	Dusty Baker
Triple-A	Syracuse Chiefs	International	61	82	.427	14th (14)	Billy Gardner Jr.
Double-A	Harrisburg Senators	Eastern	76	66	.535	5th (12)	Matthew Lecroy
High A	Potomac Nationals	Carolina	73	65	.529	4th (8)	Tripp Keister
Low A	Hagerstown Suns	South Atlantic	83	57	.593	1st (14)	Patrick Anderson
Short season	Auburn Doubledays	New York-Penn	28	47	.373	12th (14)	Jerad Head
Rookie	Nationals	Gulf Coast	30	23	.566	4th (17)	Josh Johnson
Overall 2016 Minor League Record			351	340	.508	12th (30)	

ORGANIZATION STATISTICS

WASHINGTON NATIONALS
NATIONAL LEAGUE

Batting	B-T	HT	WT	DOB	AVG	vLH	vRH	G	AB	R	H	2B	3B	HR	RBI	BB	HBP	SH	SF	SO	SB	CS	SLG	OBP
den Dekker, Matt	L-L	6-2	210	8-10-87	.176	.000	.200	19	34	3	6	1	0	1	4	4	1	0	0	10	1	0	.294	.282
Difo, Wilmer	B-R	5-11	200	4-2-92	.276	.263	.282	31	58	14	16	3	0	1	7	8	0	0	0	12	3	0	.379	.364
Drew, Stephen	L-R	6-0	200	3-16-83	.266	.188	.276	70	143	24	38	11	1	8	21	16	2	0	4	31	0	1	.524	.339
Espinosa, Danny	B-R	6-0	205	4-25-87	.209	.202	.212	157	516	66	108	15	0	24	72	54	20	7	4	174	9	2	.378	.306
Goodwin, Brian	L-L	6-0	205	11-2-90	.286	.250	.289	22	42	1	12	4	1	0	5	2	0	0	0	14	0	0	.429	.318
Harper, Bryce	L-R	6-3	215	10-16-92	.243	.226	.250	147	506	84	123	24	2	24	86	108	3	0	10	117	21	10	.441	.373
Heisey, Chris	R-R	6-1	220	12-14-84	.216	.239	.204	83	139	18	30	3	1	9	17	13	2	0	1	44	0	1	.446	.290
Kieboom, Spencer	R-R	6-0	210	3-16-91	—	—	—	1	0	1	0	0	0	0	0	0	0	0	0	0	0	0	—	1.000
Lobaton, Jose	B-R	6-1	205	10-21-84	.232	.067	.262	39	99	10	23	3	1	3	8	12	1	1	0	18	0	0	.374	.319
Murphy, Daniel	L-R	6-1	220	4-1-85	.347	.329	.354	142	531	88	184	47	5	25	104	35	8	0	8	57	5	3	.595	.390
Ramos, Wilson	R-R	6-1	255	8-10-87	.307	.330	.301	131	482	58	148	25	0	22	80	35	2	0	4	79	0	0	.496	.354
Rendon, Anthony	R-R	6-1	210	6-6-90	.270	.276	.268	156	567	91	153	38	2	20	85	65	7	0	8	117	12	6	.450	.348
Revere, Ben	L-R	5-9	175	5-3-88	.217	.203	.220	103	350	44	76	9	7	2	24	18	3	2	2	34	14	5	.300	.260
Robinson, Clint	L-L	6-5	240	2-16-85	.235	.300	.223	104	196	16	46	4	0	5	26	20	2	1	5	38	0	0	.332	.305
Severino, Pedro	R-R	6-0	215	7-20-93	.321	.200	.348	16	28	6	9	2	0	2	4	5	1	0	0	3	0	0	.607	.441
Taylor, Michael A.	R-R	6-3	210	3-26-91	.231	.259	.214	76	221	28	51	11	0	7	16	14	1	0	1	77	14	3	.376	.278
Turner, Trea	R-R	6-1	185	6-30-93	.342	.317	.348	73	307	53	105	14	8	13	40	14	1	0	2	59	33	6	.567	.370
Werth, Jayson	R-R	6-5	235	5-20-79	.244	.322	.220	143	525	84	128	28	0	21	69	71	4	0	6	139	5	1	.417	.335
Zimmerman, Ryan	R-R	6-3	225	9-28-84	.218	.200	.222	115	427	60	93	18	1	15	46	29	5	0	6	104	4	1	.370	.272

Pitching	B-T	HT	WT	DOB	W	L	ERA	G	GS	CG	SV	IP	H	R	ER	HR	BB	SO	AVG	vLH	vRH	K/9	BB/9
Belisle, Matt	R-R	6-3	230	6-6-80	0	0	1.76	40	0	0	0	46	43	13	9	2	7	32	.244	.147	.317	6.26	1.37
Burnett, Sean	L-L	5-11	185	9-17-82	0	0	3.18	10	0	0	0	6	5	2	2	1	1	3	.238	.143	.429	4.76	1.59
Cole, A.J.	R-R	6-5	215	1-5-92	1	2	5.17	8	8	0	0	38	37	24	22	7	14	39	.248	.247	.25	9.16	3.29
Giolito, Lucas	R-R	6-6	255	7-14-94	0	1	6.75	6	4	0	0	21	26	18	16	7	12	11	.295	.277	.317	4.64	5.06
Glover, Koda	R-R	6-5	225	4-13-93	2	0	5.03	19	0	0	0	20	15	12	11	3	7	16	.200	.176	.22	7.32	3.20
Gonzalez, Gio	R-L	6-0	205	9-19-85	11	11	4.57	32	32	0	0	177	179	98	90	19	59	171	.262	.241	.267	8.68	2.99
Gott, Trevor	R-R	6-0	185	8-26-92	0	0	1.50	9	0	0	0	6	6	1	1	0	3	6	.250	.333	.2	9.00	4.50
Grace, Matt	L-L	6-4	215	12-14-88	0	0	0.00	5	0	0	0	3	1	0	0	0	4		.100	.167	0	12.00	0.00
Kelley, Shawn	R-R	6-2	230	4-26-84	3	2	2.64	67	0	0	7	58	41	19	17	9	11	80	.194	.225	.176	12.41	1.71
Latos, Mat	R-R	6-6	245	12-9-87	1	1	6.52	6	1	0	0	10	11	7	7	1	5	10	.289	.238	.353	9.31	4.66
Lopez, Reynaldo	R-R	6-0	185	1-4-94	5	3	4.91	11	6	0	0	44	47	27	24	4	22	42	.272	.193	.353	8.59	4.50
Martin, Rafael	R-R	6-3	225	5-16-84	0	0	2.45	8	0	0	0	4	0	1	1	0	1	5	.000	0	0	12.27	2.45
Melancon, Mark	R-R	6-2	210	3-28-85	1	1	1.82	30	0	0	17	30	21	6	6	1	3	27	.202	.229	.179	8.19	0.91
2-team total (45 Pittsburgh)					2	2	1.64	75	0	0	47	71	52	16	13	3	12	65	—	—	—	8.20	1.51
Papelbon, Jonathan	R-R	6-5	230	11-23-80	2	4	4.37	37	0	0	19	35	37	18	17	3	14	31	.270	.271	.269	7.97	3.60
Perez, Oliver	L-L	6-3	225	8-15-81	2	3	4.95	64	0	0	0	40	38	22	22	4	20	46	.248	.233	.269	10.35	4.50
Petit, Yusmeiro	R-R	6-1	255	11-22-84	3	5	4.50	36	1	0	1	62	67	33	31	12	15	49	.272	.275	.271	7.11	2.18
Rivero, Felipe	L-L	6-2	210	7-5-91	0	3	4.53	47	0	0	1	50	43	26	25	4	15	53	.236	.344	.182	9.60	2.72
2-team total (28 Pittsburgh)					1	6	4.09	75	0	0	1	77	66	39	35	7	33	92	—	—	—	10.75	3.86
Roark, Tanner	R-R	6-2	235	10-5-86	16	10	2.83	34	33	0	0	210	173	72	66	17	73	172	.228	.214	.241	7.37	3.13
Ross, Joe	R-R	6-4	225	5-21-93	7	5	3.43	19	19	0	0	105	108	43	40	9	29	93	.269	.317	.225	7.97	2.49
Rzepczynski, Marc	L-L	6-2	220	8-29-85	0	0	1.54	14	0	0	0	12	8	3	2	0	5	9	.216	.143	.313	6.94	3.86
Scherzer, Max	R-R	6-3	210	7-27-84	20	7	2.96	34	34	1	0	228	165	77	75	31	56	284	.199	.242	.156	11.19	2.21
Solis, Sammy	R-L	6-5	250	8-10-88	2	4	2.41	37	0	0	0	41	31	12	11	1	21	47	.211	.2	.218	10.32	4.61
Strasburg, Stephen	R-R	6-4	235	7-20-88	15	4	3.60	24	24	0	0	148	119	59	59	15	44	183	.218	.2	.235	11.15	2.68
Treinen, Blake	R-R	6-5	225	6-30-88	4	1	2.28	73	0	0	1	67	51	19	17	5	31	63	.224	.221	.225	8.46	4.16

Fielding

Catcher	PCT	G	PO	A	E	DP	PB
Lobaton	.997	38	293	16	1	1	6
Ramos	.997	128	1094	61	3	6	10
Severino	.989	15	84	7	1	0	1

First Base	PCT	G	PO	A	E	DP
Murphy	.993	21	134	16	1	14
Robinson	.993	46	279	12	2	30
Zimmerman	.996	114	852	44	4	88

Second Base	PCT	G	PO	A	E	DP
Difo	.962	9	6	19	1	1
Drew	.963	21	33	44	3	9
Murphy	.981	117	194	265	9	76
Turner	.992	30	52	71	1	19

Third Base	PCT	G	PO	A	E	DP
Difo	1.000	3	1	3	0	0
Drew	1.000	12	5	19	0	1
Murphy	.667	1	1	1	1	0
Rendon	.976	155	134	239	9	25

Shortstop	PCT	G	PO	A	E	DP
Difo	.933	5	5	9	1	1
Drew	1.000	12	11	13	0	4
Espinosa	.970	157	181	404	18	96
Turner	1.000	2	3	5	0	2

Outfield	PCT	G	PO	A	E	DP
den Dekker	1.000	12	24	0	0	0
Goodwin	1.000	14	14	0	0	0
Harper	.992	143	256	5	2	1
Heisey	1.000	44	59	0	0	0
Revere	.989	87	170	2	2	1
Robinson	1.000	3	6	0	0	0
Taylor	.992	69	125	5	1	0
Turner	.980	45	99	1	2	0
Werth	.995	133	201	5	1	1

SYRACUSE CHIEFS
INTERNATIONAL LEAGUE

TRIPLE-A

Batting	B-T	HT	WT	DOB	AVG	vLH	vRH	G	AB	R	H	2B	3B	HR	RBI	BB	HBP	SH	SF	SO	SB	CS	SLG	OBP
Ballou, Isaac	L-R	6-2	205	3-17-90	.296	.125	.368	9	27	2	8	3	0	0	2	4	0	0	0	8	0	0	.407	.387
Bostick, Chris	R-R	5-10	190	3-24-93	.203	.221	.191	64	222	27	45	11	2	2	18	16	2	1	1	67	3	2	.297	.261
Campana, Tony	L-L	5-8	170	5-30-86	.225	.158	.238	43	120	10	27	2	0	0	7	13	0	8	0	14	5	2	.242	.301
2-team total (29 Charlotte)					.217	—	—	72	203	20	44	3	0	0	13	15	2	12	0	29	10	6	.232	.277
Collier, Zach	L-L	6-2	200	9-8-90	.203	.207	.200	46	148	8	30	7	2	1	15	15	0	0	1	54	2	1	.297	.274
den Dekker, Matt	L-L	6-2	210	8-10-87	.207	.210	.206	106	372	41	77	14	1	8	44	40	6	0	3	110	20	5	.315	.292
Difo, Wilmer	B-R	5-11	200	4-2-92	.200	.000	.500	1	5	0	1	0	0	0	0	0	0	0	0	0	0	0	.200	.200
Freiman, Nate	R-R	6-8	245	12-31-86	.154	.167	.150	8	26	3	4	1	1	0	1	0	0	0	0	10	0	0	.269	.154
Goodwin, Brian	L-L	6-0	205	11-2-90	.280	.308	.264	119	436	51	122	25	1	14	68	46	3	2	5	106	15	3	.438	.349
Jeroloman, Brian	L-R	6-0	205	5-10-85	.190	.143	.214	7	21	3	4	1	0	0	4	1	0	0	0	8	0	0	.238	.346
Keyes, Kevin	R-R	6-3	225	3-15-89	.146	.235	.083	28	82	7	12	4	0	0	6	10	1	0	1	32	0	0	.195	.245
Lobaton, Jose	B-R	6-1	205	10-21-84	.385	.500	.333	3	13	1	5	0	0	0	1	1	0	0	0	6	1	0	.385	.429
Lombardozzi Jr. Steve	B-R	6-0	195	9-20-88	.253	.275	.239	62	225	24	57	7	1	0	7	15	0	5	1	27	3	0	.293	.299
Lozada, Jose	R-R	6-0	180	12-29-85	.157	.170	.149	53	121	7	19	2	1	0	6	5	0	6	0	27	1	1	.190	.190
Martinson, Jason	R-R	6-1	210	10-15-88	.218	.222	.215	132	455	44	99	21	6	12	58	34	10	4	4	179	11	2	.369	.284
Norfork, Khayyan	R-R	5-10	190	1-19-89	.000	.000	.000	1	3	1	0	0	0	0	0	1	0	0	0	1	0	0	.000	.250
Ramsey, Caleb	L-R	6-2	215	10-7-88	.265	.192	.302	124	427	46	113	25	2	4	36	36	0	3	2	85	5	0	.361	.320
Revere, Ben	L-R	5-9	175	5-3-88	.188	.250	.000	5	16	1	3	0	0	0	1	1	0	0	0	1	0	0	.188	.235
Rickles, Nick	R-R	6-3	220	2-2-90	.250	.000	1.000	1	4	0	1	0	0	0	0	0	0	0	0	2	0	0	.250	.250
Ryan, Brendan	R-R	6-1	190	3-26-82	.263	.321	.229	21	76	7	20	4	1	1	8	4	1	1	1	10	1	0	.382	.305
Sanchez, Adrian	R-R	6-0	160	3-16-90	.216	.176	.235	14	51	4	11	1	0	0	3	1	0	0	0	7	1	0	.235	.231
Severino, Pedro	R-R	6-0	215	7-20-93	.271	.315	.251	82	291	25	79	13	0	2	21	19	2	1	4	45	3	4	.337	.316
Sizemore, Scott	R-R	6-0	190	1-4-85	.205	.246	.187	60	195	29	40	8	0	5	18	42	3	2	1	52	2	0	.323	.353
Skole, Matt	L-R	6-4	220	7-30-89	.244	.297	.212	140	499	67	122	22	1	24	78	66	5	0	3	119	2	0	.437	.337
Solano, Jhonatan	R-R	5-9	205	8-12-85	.225	.328	.170	52	173	8	39	6	0	2	22	14	2	2	3	20	0	0	.260	.286
Soto, Neftali	R-R	6-1	210	2-28-89	.270	.309	.233	29	115	9	31	7	0	0	7	3	1	0	0	24	0	0	.330	.294
Taylor, Michael A.	R-R	6-3	210	3-26-91	.205	.217	.193	31	117	17	24	5	1	1	9	12	1	0	0	33	7	1	.291	.285
Turner, Trea	R-R	6-1	185	6-30-93	.302	.319	.295	83	331	61	100	22	8	6	33	37	0	1	2	72	25	2	.471	.370
Zimmerman, Ryan	R-R	6-3	225	9-28-84	.500	.333	.556	3	12	3	6	0	1	1	3	1	0	0	0	3	0	0	.917	.538

Pitching	B-T	HT	WT	DOB	W	L	ERA	G	GS	CG	SV	IP	H	R	ER	HR	BB	SO	AVG	vLH	vRH	K/9	BB/9
Belisle, Matt	R-R	6-3	230	6-6-80	0	1	3.00	3	0	0	0	3	4	1	1	0	0	4	.308	.333	.250	12.00	0.00
Brady, Michael	R-R	6-0	195	3-21-87	0	0	1.29	1	1	0	0	7	4	1	1	0	0	8	.160	.235	.000	10.29	0.00
Burnett, Sean	L-L	5-11	185	9-17-82	0	0	5.40	5	0	0	0	5	7	3	3	1	0	4	.318	.667	.188	7.20	0.00
3-team total (6 Gwinnett, 29 Rochester)					0	3	2.27	40	0	0	3	40	30	12	10	2	8	27	—	—	—	6.13	1.82
Cole, A.J.	R-R	6-5	215	1-5-92	8	8	4.26	22	22	2	0	125	131	64	59	16	35	109	.266	.304	.236	7.87	2.53
Davis, Erik	R-R	6-3	205	10-8-86	7	5	4.13	45	0	0	0	52	50	28	24	3	22	64	.248	.218	.270	11.01	3.78
De Fratus, Justin	R-R	6-4	225	10-21-87	2	3	9.00	9	0	0	0	16	16	10	16	2	4	10	.340	.267	.375	9.00	3.60
De Los Santos, Abel	R-R	6-2	195	11-21-92	1	1	3.54	15	0	0	0	20	25	8	8	0	13	26	.305	.324	.292	11.51	5.75
Espino, Paolo	R-R	5-10	215	1-10-87	8	11	3.30	26	24	1	0	153	146	60	56	13	29	133	.248	.246	.249	7.84	1.71
Giolito, Lucas	R-R	6-6	255	7-14-94	1	2	2.17	7	7	0	0	37	31	11	9	3	10	40	.225	.295	.191	9.64	2.41
Glover, Koda	R-R	6-5	225	4-13-93	1	1	2.25	16	0	0	2	24	16	6	6	2	3	22	.195	.161	.216	8.25	1.13
Gott, Trevor	R-R	6-0	185	8-26-92	3	3	4.35	33	0	0	7	39	44	20	19	2	13	31	.288	.350	.247	7.09	2.97
Grace, Matt	L-L	6-4	215	12-14-88	1	3	2.85	35	0	0	1	47	54	17	15	1	9	32	.287	.242	.310	6.08	1.71
Gutierrez, Juan	R-R	6-3	245	7-14-83	1	0	5.21	18	0	0	0	19	21	11	11	1	8	17	.296	.222	.341	8.05	3.79
Harper, Bryan	L-L	6-5	205	12-29-89	1	1	2.95	20	0	0	0	21	16	9	7	2	11	20	.203	.161	.229	8.44	4.64
Hill, Taylor	R-R	6-3	230	3-12-89	6	13	4.60	27	27	1	0	155	168	83	79	19	38	97	.275	.316	.251	5.64	2.21
Jordan, Taylor	R-R	6-5	210	1-17-89	0	0	1.72	3	3	0	0	16	16	3	3	0	5	12	.267	.208	.306	6.89	2.87
Laffey, Aaron	L-L	5-11	190	4-15-85	6	6	3.82	29	14	0	0	99	113	50	42	5	28	68	.292	.250	.302	6.18	2.55
Latos, Mat	R-R	6-6	245	12-9-87	1	0	1.06	3	3	0	0	17	16	4	2	1	7	10	.254	.250	.255	5.29	3.71
Long, Jaron	R-R	6-0	190	8-28-91	2	3	4.14	9	8	0	0	50	61	24	23	2	12	31	.293	.337	.264	5.58	2.16
Lopez, Reynaldo	R-R	6-0	185	1-4-94	2	7	3.27	5	5	1	0	33	31	12	12	6	10	26	.179	.204	.162	7.09	2.73
Martin, Rafael	R-R	6-3	205	5-16-84	2	4	4.56	50	0	0	22	49	43	26	25	7	25	50	.230	.311	.177	9.12	4.56
Masset, Nick	R-R	6-5	225	5-17-82	0	3	4.71	30	0	0	3	29	34	19	15	2	13	19	.301	.282	.311	5.97	4.03
Ross, Joe	R-R	6-4	225	5-21-93	0	2	4.35	4	4	0	0	10	14	5	5	1	9	.318	.313	.321	7.84	0.87
Runion, Sam	R-R	6-4	220	11-9-88	1	1	5.75	24	0	0	0	36	38	25	23	0	12	22	.270	.321	.239	5.50	3.00
Self, Derek	B-T	6-3	205	1-14-90	0	0	4.91	2	0	0	1	4	4	2	2	0	0	1	.286	.500	.250	2.45	0.00
Solis, Sammy	R-L	6-5	250	8-10-88	0	0	1.00	6	0	0	0	9	5	1	1	0	3	14	.167	.143	.174	14.00	3.00
Voth, Austin	R-R	6-2	215	6-26-92	7	9	3.15	27	25	0	0	157	138	63	55	11	57	133	.232	.235	.229	7.62	3.27

Fielding

Catcher	PCT	G	PO	A	E	DP	PB
Jeroloman	1.000	7	53	4	0	0	0
Lobaton	1.000	2	18	1	0	0	1
Rickles	1.000	1	9	0	0	0	0
Severino	.995	81	546	54	3	2	7
Solano	.990	52	363	34	4	1	5

First Base	PCT	G	PO	A	E	DP
Freiman	1.000	4	30	1	0	7
Keyes	1.000	3	19	3	0	5
Martinson	1.000	2	9	0	0	2
Ramsey	.993	18	132	10	1	16
Skole	.999	97	830	43	1	71
Soto	.995	24	193	12	1	12
Zimmerman	1.000	2	17	2	0	1

Second Base	PCT	G	PO	A	E	DP
Bostick	.967	47	90	115	7	26
Lombardozzi Jr.	.974	31	56	92	4	17

Second Base (cont.)	PCT	G	PO	A	E	DP
Lozada	.960	15	15	33	2	7
Martinson	1.000	2	3	3	0	1
Norfork	1.000	1	2	2	0	0
Ryan	.978	8	16	28	1	6
Sanchez	1.000	1	0	2	0	0
Sizemore	.970	38	71	123	6	28
Turner	1.000	5	4	15	0	3

Third Base	PCT	G	PO	A	E	DP
Bostick	.909	13	11	19	3	5
Lombardozzi Jr.	.857	3	4	8	2	0
Lozada	.800	11	0	8	2	1
Martinson	.957	64	45	110	7	9
Ryan	1.000	6	7	10	0	1
Sizemore	.913	10	6	15	2	2
Skole	.980	41	20	78	2	9

Shortstop	PCT	G	PO	A	E	DP
Difo	.667	1	1	1	1	0
Lozada	.875	2	3	4	1	1

Shortstop (cont.)	PCT	G	PO	A	E	DP
Martinson	.967	53	65	141	7	28
Ryan	1.000	3	8	12	0	1
Sanchez	.933	13	18	38	4	10
Turner	.973	71	94	229	9	43

Outfield	PCT	G	PO	A	E	DP
Ballou	1.000	8	16	0	0	0
Bostick	1.000	2	1	0	0	0
Campana	.985	35	66	1	1	0
Collier	.987	38	76	1	1	1
den Dekker	.981	85	148	3	3	2
Goodwin	.978	115	258	10	6	1
Keyes	—	1	0	0	0	0
Lozada	.952	15	19	1	1	0
Martinson	1.000	9	12	2	0	0
Ramsey	.963	91	177	4	7	1
Revere	1.000	5	13	0	0	0
Ryan	.500	2	1	0	1	0
Taylor	1.000	28	63	1	0	0
Turner	1.000	6	19	1	0	0

HARRISBURG SENATORS
DOUBLE-A
EASTERN LEAGUE

Batting	B-T	HT	WT	DOB	AVG	vLH	vRH	G	AB	R	H	2B	3B	HR	RBI	BB	HBP	SH	SF	SO	SB	CS	SLG	OBP
Ballou, Isaac	L-R	6-2	205	3-17-90	.255	.250	.256	108	373	49	95	13	9	6	59	42	4	3	6	77	7	3	.386	.332
Bautista, Rafael	R-R	6-2	165	3-8-93	.282	.289	.279	136	543	77	153	12	4	4	39	45	8	8	3	94	56	10	.341	.344
Bostick, Chris	R-R	5-10	190	3-24-93	.290	.232	.311	71	262	34	76	11	8	6	33	25	4	2	4	58	8	8	.462	.356
Collier, Zach	L-L	6-2	200	9-8-90	.285	.241	.300	64	214	35	61	9	6	3	16	15	2	1	1	61	5	3	.425	.336
Difo, Wilmer	B-R	5-11	200	4-2-92	.259	.274	.253	104	410	59	106	15	3	6	41	34	3	2	2	59	28	11	.354	.318
Dykstra, Cutter	R-R	6-0	190	6-29-89	.297	.242	.341	37	74	4	22	3	1	0	6	10	0	2	0	21	1	0	.365	.381
Jeroloman, Brian	L-R	6-0	205	5-10-85	.238	.172	.273	27	84	8	20	5	1	0	12	15	0	4	1	19	0	0	.321	.350
Keyes, Kevin	R-R	6-3	225	3-15-89	.223	.212	.229	82	242	28	54	13	0	12	39	33	4	0	2	76	1	1	.426	.324
Kieboom, Spencer	R-R	6-0	210	3-16-91	.230	.244	.225	94	309	27	71	11	0	5	31	43	2	1	4	61	0	0	.314	.324
Lowery, Jake	L-R	6-0	200	7-21-90	.000	.000	.000	2	4	1	0	0	0	0	1	2	0	0	1	1	0	0	.000	.286
Marmolejos, Jose	L-L	6-1	185	1-2-93	.299	.318	.289	33	127	15	38	9	0	2	15	5	2	0	1	29	0	1	.417	.333
Norfork, Khayyan	R-R	5-10	190	1-19-89	.164	.182	.150	35	73	8	12	3	0	0	4	7	4	0	1	21	1	0	.205	.271
Perez, Stephen	B-R	5-11	185	12-16-90	.249	.197	.264	106	301	39	75	9	2	3	28	47	2	3	5	59	12	3	.342	.351
Pleffner, Shawn	L-R	6-5	225	8-17-89	.262	.240	.270	100	301	42	79	14	2	3	34	32	1	0	3	58	1	2	.352	.332
Rickles, Nick	R-R	6-3	220	2-2-90	.227	.250	.219	24	88	9	20	3	0	4	10	3	0	0	1	20	0	0	.398	.250
Sanchez, Adrian	B-R	6-0	165	8-16-90	.254	.280	.243	97	299	24	76	17	3	0	25	14	5	4	3	42	6	1	.331	.296
Soto, Neftali	R-R	6-1	210	2-28-89	.276	.318	.261	93	341	40	94	20	2	10	55	25	2	0	3	69	2	0	.434	.326
Stevenson, Andrew	L-L	6-0	185	6-1-94	.246	.235	.250	65	256	38	63	11	2	2	16	20	1	2	1	51	12	5	.328	.302
Ward, Drew	L-R	6-3	215	11-25-94	.219	.185	.234	53	178	19	39	7	0	3	24	22	2	0	1	51	0	1	.309	.310
Webb, Brenden	L-L	6-1	185	2-24-90	.176	.000	.209	17	51	5	9	2	0	1	6	11	0	0	0	15	2	0	.275	.323

Pitching	B-T	HT	WT	DOB	W	L	ERA	G	GS	CG	SV	IP	H	R	ER	HR	BB	SO	AVG	vLH	vRH	K/9	BB/9
Bacus, Dakota	R-R	6-2	200	4-2-91	1	1	7.80	9	0	0	1	15	16	15	13	1	14	13	.276	.296	.258	7.80	8.40
Belisle, Matt	R-R	6-3	230	6-6-80	0	0	4.50	3	0	0	0	4	5	2	2	0	0	2	.313	.444	.143	4.50	0.00
Benincasa, Robert	R-R	6-2	180	9-5-90	1	1	4.50	21	0	0	3	30	31	16	15	5	14	35	.263	.236	.286	10.50	4.20
Blackmar, Mark	R-R	6-3	215	4-28-92	4	5	5.37	9	9	0	0	57	55	34	34	7	21	25	.252	.263	.24	3.95	3.32
Brady, Michael	R-R	6-0	195	3-21-87	3	6	3.04	17	11	1	0	74	68	28	25	6	13	64	.249	.239	.256	7.78	1.58
Brinley, Ryan	L-R	6-1	200	4-9-93	0	2	11.12	8	0	0	0	11	17	14	14	5	2	4	.362	.263	.429	3.18	1.59
De Fratus, Justin	B-R	6-4	225	10-21-87	0	1	1.69	7	0	0	1	16	6	3	2	0	4	8	.162	.000	.231	6.75	3.38
De Los Santos, Abel	R-R	6-2	195	11-21-92	0	0	3.86	14	0	0	5	14	9	6	6	2	10	13	.176	.238	.133	8.36	6.43
Fedde, Erick	R-R	6-4	180	2-25-93	2	1	3.99	5	5	1	0	29	33	13	13	1	10	28	.284	.298	.271	8.59	3.07
Fish, Robert	L-L	6-2	230	1-19-88	0	0	22.09	3	0	0	0	4	8	10	9	1	4	2	.444	.333	.467	4.91	9.82
Giolito, Lucas	R-R	6-6	255	7-14-94	5	3	3.17	14	14	0	0	71	67	37	25	2	34	72	.247	.206	.292	9.13	4.31
Glover, Koda	R-R	6-5	225	4-13-93	2	0	3.22	17	0	0	4	22	20	9	8	1	7	29	.238	.250	.225	11.69	2.82
Gutierrez, Juan	R-R	6-3	245	7-14-83	1	0	1.23	7	0	0	2	7	6	1	1	1	3	11	.222	.250	.211	13.50	3.68
Harper, Bryan	L-L	6-5	205	12-29-89	2	1	1.50	20	0	0	6	24	12	4	4	3	7	21	.146	.091	.184	7.88	2.63
Lee, Nick	L-L	5-11	205	1-13-91	3	1	4.32	45	0	0	2	50	43	27	24	5	42	55	.228	.195	.250	9.90	7.56
Lively, Mitch	R-R	6-5	250	9-7-85	1	0	5.79	6	0	0	1	5	5	3	3	0	4	6	.263	.111	.400	11.57	7.71
Long, Jaron	R-R	6-0	180	8-28-91	3	3	2.37	10	10	0	0	57	52	19	15	8	10	41	.239	.270	.206	6.47	1.58
Lopez, Reynaldo	R-R	6-0	185	1-4-94	3	5	3.18	14	14	0	0	76	69	35	27	7	25	100	.235	.222	.248	11.79	2.95
Mapes, Tyler	R-R	6-2	205	7-18-91	12	10	3.19	25	25	4	0	155	154	61	55	11	39	78	.263	.297	.231	4.53	2.26
Martin, J.D.	R-R	6-4	220	1-2-83	0	0	4.50	1	1	0	0	8	7	4	4	0	2	3	.259	.462	.071	3.38	2.25
Mayberry, Whit	R-R	6-1	200	5-29-90	0	0	11.25	1	1	0	0	4	5	5	5	1	2	5	.313	.500	.125	2.25	4.50
Mendez, Gilberto	R-R	6-0	165	11-17-92	0	2	7.09	13	1	0	0	27	33	21	21	6	15	24	.297	.283	.31	8.10	5.06
Papelbon, Jonathan	R-R	6-5	230	11-23-80	0	0	0.00	2	0	0	0	2	0	0	0	0	1	2	.000	.000	.000	9.00	4.50
Robinson, Andrew	R-R	6-1	185	2-13-88	4	1	2.01	35	1	0	9	58	42	15	13	5	17	65	.200	.253	.160	10.03	2.62
Ross, Greg	R-R	6-3	205	9-6-89	5	1	4.08	9	1	0	6	54	40	6	5	1	11	69	.208	.243	.169	5.33	1.83
Runion, Sam	R-R	6-4	220	11-9-88	2	1	7.43	9	0	0	0	13	14	11	11	1	4	10	.280	.261	.296	6.75	2.70
Self, Derek	R-R	6-3	205	1-14-90	4	2	4.10	30	0	0	0	53	60	25	24	5	18	43	.293	.264	.316	7.35	3.08

Pitching

Pitching	B-T	HT	WT	DOB	W	L	ERA	G	GS	CG	SV	IP	H	R	ER	HR	BB	SO	AVG	vLH	vRH	K/9	BB/9
Simms, John	R-R	6-3	205	1-17-92	8	5	3.30	29	11	0	2	93	72	39	34	8	28	79	.215	.247	.189	7.67	2.72
Suero, Wander	R-R	6-3	195	9-15-91	3	0	2.44	39	0	0	4	55	53	16	15	3	21	48	.257	.244	.267	7.81	3.42
Valdez, Phillips	R-R	6-2	160	11-16-91	6	4	4.62	16	16	1	0	88	100	49	45	7	36	57	.292	.354	.245	5.85	3.70
Whiting, Boone	R-R	6-1	175	8-20-89	0	3	5.84	5	5	0	0	25	31	21	16	3	14	14	.295	.333	.267	5.11	5.11
Williams, Austen	R-R	6-3	220	12-19-92	1	7	5.68	10	10	0	0	51	66	42	32	5	22	30	.313	.324	.303	5.33	3.91

Fielding

Catcher

Catcher	PCT	G	PO	A	E	DP	PB
Jeroloman	1.000	27	216	17	0	1	1
Kieboom	.993	93	607	82	5	5	9
Lowery	1.000	2	21	1	0	0	
Rickles	.994	24	154	19	1	1	0

First Base

First Base	PCT	G	PO	A	E	DP
Keyes	1.000	9	68	5	0	5
Marmolejos	.996	29	262	16	1	24
Perez	1.000	2	10	0	0	2
Pleffner	.990	62	557	35	6	49
Soto	.987	46	352	39	5	31

Second Base

Second Base	PCT	G	PO	A	E	DP
Bostick	.974	62	116	180	8	39
Dykstra	1.000	1	2	3	0	1
Norfork	.970	26	40	57	3	10
Perez	.965	40	69	122	7	30
Sanchez	.980	22	35	62	2	11
Soto	1.000	1	2	6	0	1

Third Base

Third Base	PCT	G	PO	A	E	DP
Norfork	—	1	0	0	0	
Perez	.844	18	9	29	7	2
Pleffner	.667	2	0	2	1	0
Sanchez	.976	64	48	117	4	9
Soto	.960	19	6	18	1	0
Ward	.918	51	21	91	10	8

Shortstop

Shortstop	PCT	G	PO	A	E	DP
Difo	.958	103	137	292	19	61
Perez	.986	35	52	92	2	17
Sanchez	1.000	12	16	37	0	7

Outfield

Outfield	PCT	G	PO	A	E	DP
Ballou	.988	104	154	4	2	1
Bautista	.971	133	294	9	9	2
Bostick	.846	6	10	1	2	0
Collier	.991	59	112	4	1	2
Dykstra	.952	19	20	0	1	0
Keyes	.984	37	60	0	1	0
Perez	.900	5	9	0	1	0
Pleffner	1.000	1	1	0	0	0
Sanchez	1.000	1	1	0	0	0
Stevenson	1.000	64	171	3	0	2
Webb	.957	11	21	1	1	1

WASHINGTON NATIONALS

POTOMAC NATIONALS

CAROLINA LEAGUE

HIGH CLASS A

Batting

Batting	B-T	HT	WT	DOB	AVG	vLH	vRH	G	AB	R	H	2B	3B	HR	RBI	BB	HBP	SH	SF	SO	SB	CS	SLG	OBP
Abreu, Osvaldo	R-R	6-0	170	6-13-94	.247	.310	.218	126	497	86	123	23	4	6	52	55	6	2	3	108	18	10	.346	.328
Carey, Dale	R-R	6-3	185	11-14-91	.209	.294	.170	107	326	36	68	11	4	7	29	63	4	5	3	84	5	10	.331	.341
Davidson, Austin	L-R	6-0	180	1-3-93	.258	.255	.260	47	151	28	39	7	2	4	21	28	5	2	1	20	2	0	.411	.389
DeBruin, Grant	R-R	6-3	225	6-28-90	.211	.500	.133	6	19	0	4	2	0	0	2	2	0	0	0	2	0	0	.316	.286
Dent, Cody	L-R	5-11	190	8-1-91	.000	.000	.000	6	16	1	0	0	0	0	0	2	0	0	0	3	0	0	.000	.111
Drew, Stephen	R-R	6-0	200	3-16-83	.250	.000	.273	5	12	0	3	1	0	0	2	2	1	0	0	1	0	0	.333	.400
Gutierrez, Kelvin	R-R	6-3	185	8-28-94	.237	.308	.200	10	38	7	9	1	0	1	2	3	2	1	0	5	2	2	.342	.326
Keller, Alec	L-R	6-2	200	5-13-92	.285	.300	.280	117	438	57	125	20	5	3	63	35	1	2	2	78	14	2	.374	.338
Lowery, Jake	L-R	6-0	200	7-21-90	.212	.235	.200	17	52	4	11	4	0	1	10	11	1	0	1	14	0	0	.346	.354
Marmolejos, Jose	L-L	6-1	185	1-2-93	.286	.292	.283	103	378	72	108	36	5	11	59	59	2	0	5	84	2	3	.495	.381
Masters, David	R-R	6-1	185	4-23-93	.174	.127	.197	76	236	27	41	5	1	6	33	23	5	1	2	56	1	0	.280	.259
Mejia, Bryan	B-R	6-1	175	3-24-94	.241	.231	.246	117	427	39	103	19	7	4	41	22	2	10	4	98	19	10	.347	.279
Mesa, Narciso	R-R	5-11	175	11-16-91	.194	.156	.211	34	103	10	20	4	3	1	8	5	1	1	2	27	5	1	.320	.234
Norfork, Khayyan	R-R	5-10	190	1-19-89	.252	.250	.253	42	135	16	34	5	0	0	16	34	5	3	2	29	5	0	.289	.338
Page, Matt	L-L	6-3	210	10-22-91	.231	.300	.203	30	104	14	24	1	1	4	8	1	1	1		28	0	0	.288	.289
Read, Raudy	R-R	6-0	190	10-22-91	.241	.262	.308	101	386	54	101	30	1	9	51	31	6	0	3	53	6	3	.415	.324
Reistetter, Matt	L-R	5-10	180	5-5-92	.247	.250	.246	31	89	9	22	4	0	2	9	11	1	1	1	15	2	0	.360	.333
Robles, Victor	R-R	6-0	185	5-19-97	.262	.320	.237	41	168	24	44	8	2	3	11	14	11	3	2	32	18	5	.387	.354
Ruiz, Adderling	R-R	6-1	175	5-3-91	.000	—	.000	1	4	0	0	0	0	0	0	0	0	0	0	1	0	0	.000	.000
Schrock, Max	L-R	5-8	180	10-12-94	.341	.292	.363	54	232	30	79	11	0	5	29	9	3	0	2	27	2	7	.453	.373
Stevenson, Andrew	L-L	6-0	185	6-1-94	.304	.329	.293	68	273	37	83	12	8	1	18	24	0	2	1	44	27	9	.418	.359
Vettleson, Drew	L-R	6-1	185	7-19-91	.221	.205	.227	79	276	28	61	15	1	9	42	24	0	4	3	89	6	2	.380	.281
Ward, Drew	L-R	6-3	215	11-25-94	.228	.206	.309	64	230	36	64	16	0	11	32	34	3	0	1	70	0	1	.491	.377
Zimmerman, Ryan	R-R	6-3	225	9-28-84	.417	—	.417	3	12	4	5	1	0	1	5	0	0	0	0	4	0	0	.750	.417

Pitching

Pitching	B-T	HT	WT	DOB	W	L	ERA	G	GS	CG	SV	IP	H	R	ER	HR	BB	SO	AVG	vLH	vRH	K/9	BB/9
Bacus, Dakota	R-R	6-2	200	4-2-91	3	2	3.77	13	6	0	0	45	39	22	19	1	18	49	.224	.220	.229	9.73	3.57
Belisle, Matt	R-R	6-3	230	6-6-80	0	0	4.50	3	0	0	0	4	6	2	2	1	1	5	.353	.333	.400	11.25	2.25
Benincasa, Robert	R-R	6-2	180	9-5-90	0	1	2.79	6	0	0	0	10	4	4	3	0	3	8	.125	.059	.200	7.45	2.79
Blackmar, Mark	R-R	6-3	215	4-28-92	2	0	1.29	2	2	0	0	14	6	2	2	0	7	7	.125	.176	.097	4.50	4.50
Brinley, Ryan	L-R	6-1	200	4-9-93	4	1	1.37	32	0	0	16	39	28	7	6	1	7	34	.196	.169	.218	7.78	1.60
Crownover, Matt	L-R	5-11	200	3-5-93	4	4	4.28	17	17	0	0	90	100	52	43	11	31	76	.280	.247	.291	7.57	3.09
Estevez, Wirkin	R-R	6-1	170	3-15-92	2	4	5.03	23	10	0	0	59	67	39	33	6	31	37	.290	.310	.271	5.64	4.73
Fedde, Erick	R-R	6-4	180	2-25-93	4	2	2.85	18	17	0	0	92	85	35	29	7	19	95	.244	.225	.263	9.33	1.87
Glover, Koda	R-R	6-5	225	4-13-93	0	0	0.00	7	0	0	2	10	4	0	0	0	4	15	.094	.143	.056	13.97	3.72
Holland, Neil	R-R	6-0	190	8-14-88	1	4	2.77	14	0	0	2	26	32	17	8	1	4	13	.302	.358	.245	4.50	1.38
Johansen, Jake	R-R	6-6	235	1-23-91	1	0	4.82	6	0	0	0	9	11	5	5	1	11	5	.297	.294	.300	4.82	10.61
Lambert, Trey	R-R	6-4	205	6-5-91	0	0	4.50	6	1	0	0	8	8	7	4	0	7	7	.279	.308	.257	3.94	3.94
Martin, J.D.	R-R	6-4	220	1-23-83	1	2	5.96	4	4	0	0	26	26	18	17	2	13	16	.263	.277	.250	5.61	4.56
Mayberry, Whit	R-R	6-1	200	5-29-90	4	2	3.14	14	9	0	1	66	57	27	23	5	12	56	.227	.280	.175	7.64	1.64
Mendez, Gilberto	R-R	6-0	165	11-17-92	2	4	2.01	29	0	0	8	49	44	13	11	0	13	39	.235	.247	.226	7.11	2.37
Orlan, R.C.	R-L	6-0	185	9-28-90	5	6	3.93	41	0	0	9	53	39	26	23	3	46	46	.211	.234	.198	7.86	7.86
Pantoja, Jorge	R-R	6-5	215	3-26-94	0	1	6.30	6	0	0	0	10	15	9	7	3	9	3	.349	.368	.333	2.70	8.10
Papelbon, Jonathan	R-R	6-5	230	11-23-80	0	0	0.00	1	1	0	0	1	0	0	0	0	0	1	.000	.000	.000	9.00	0.00
Peterson, Tommy	R-R	6-1	205	10-11-93	0	1	3.66	14	0	0	0	20	21	11	8	1	11	22	.276	.378	.179	10.07	5.03
Reyes, Luis	R-R	6-2	175	9-26-94	4	8	5.60	14	14	0	0	71	69	50	44	7	46	46	.260	.246	.273	5.86	5.86

Pitching

Pitching	B-T	HT	WT	DOB	W	L	ERA	G	GS	CG	SV	IP	H	R	ER	HR	BB	SO	AVG	vLH	vRH	K/9	BB/9
Robinson, Andrew	R-R	6-1	185	2-13-88	0	0	3.68	4	0	0	0	7	8	5	3	0	2	11	.276	.143	.400	13.50	2.45
Ross, Greg	R-R	6-3	205	9-6-89	2	2	1.45	10	4	0	0	31	25	8	5	1	12	20	.221	.283	.179	5.81	3.48
Sanchez, Mario	R-R	6-1	166	10-31-94	5	0	3.46	32	0	0	2	78	80	33	30	5	22	62	.264	.316	.222	7.15	2.54
Self, Derek	R-R	6-3	205	1-14-90	0	0	0.00	5	0	0	1	8	3	0	0	0	2	4	.120	.091	.143	4.70	2.35
Silvestre, Hector	L-L	6-3	180	12-14-92	0	0	2.08	3	3	0	0	13	12	3	3	0	10	8	.240	.429	.167	5.54	6.92
Solis, Sammy	R-L	6-5	250	8-10-88	0	0	0.00	1	0	0	0	1	1	0	0	0	1	3	.250	.000	.333	27.00	9.00
Spann, Matt	L-L	6-6	185	2-17-91	2	2	4.57	20	5	0	0	45	58	26	23	4	34	44	.310	.304	.313	8.74	6.75
Thomas, Justin	L-L	6-2	195	10-21-90	3	2	4.75	33	0	0	3	47	44	28	25	3	21	36	.243	.235	.248	6.85	3.99
Valdez, Phillips	R-R	6-2	160	11-16-91	6	3	3.74	11	11	0	0	65	60	30	27	3	15	52	.244	.267	.227	7.20	2.08
VanVossen, Mick	R-R	6-3	190	10-30-92	1	1	9.00	4	0	0	0	6	6	6	6	1	1	4	.250	.625	.063	6.00	1.50
Whiting, Boone	R-R	6-1	175	8-20-89	11	3	3.45	18	18	0	0	107	103	46	41	14	16	64	.249	.246	.252	5.38	1.35
Williams, Austen	R-R	6-3	220	12-19-92	4	6	5.32	16	16	2	0	90	113	57	53	8	26	48	.310	.328	.29	4.82	2.61

Fielding

Catcher	PCT	G	PO	A	E	DP	PB
Lowery	1.000	16	100	9	0	1	3
Read	.990	97	622	100	7	4	20
Reistetter	.994	29	156	18	1	1	2
Ruiz	1.000	1	11	0	0	0	0

First Base	PCT	G	PO	A	E	DP
DeBruin	1.000	3	20	1	0	3
Marmolejos	.989	89	772	44	9	72
Masters	.995	26	187	16	1	13
Page	.986	22	188	21	3	15
Zimmerman	1.000	2	12	0	0	2

Second Base	PCT	G	PO	A	E	DP
Davidson	.966	6	8	20	1	5
Dent	1.000	2	2	5	0	0

Drew	1.000	1	0	2	0	0
Masters	1.000	15	27	41	0	10
Mejia	.949	64	109	151	14	29
Norfork	.980	9	16	32	1	10
Schrock	.980	46	79	119	4	24

Third Base	PCT	G	PO	A	E	DP
Davidson	.950	15	13	25	2	5
Dent	1.000	1	1	1	0	0
Drew	1.000	2	1	0	0	0
Gutierrez	.875	9	10	11	3	1
Masters	.925	21	10	39	4	3
Mejia	.906	33	23	73	10	7
Norfork	.889	12	9	23	4	3
Ward	.968	49	29	93	4	7

Shortstop	PCT	G	PO	A	E	DP
Abreu	.957	119	159	314	21	53
Dent	1.000	1	0	1	0	1
Masters	.937	14	22	37	4	9
Mejia	.931	7	13	14	2	2

Outfield	PCT	G	PO	A	E	DP
Carey	.996	104	234	4	1	1
Keller	.990	101	196	6	2	1
Mejia	1.000	4	7	0	0	0
Mesa	.948	33	53	2	3	1
Page	1.000	7	10	0	0	0
Robles	.993	40	137	1	1	0
Stevenson	.988	66	163	4	2	1
Vettleson	.993	73	142	3	1	0

HAGERSTOWN SUNS   LOW CLASS A
SOUTH ATLANTIC LEAGUE

Batting	B-T	HT	WT	DOB	AVG	vLH	vRH	G	AB	R	H	2B	3B	HR	RBI	BB	HBP	SH	SF	SO	SB	CS	SLG	OBP
Agustin, Telmito	L-L	5-10	160	10-9-96	.265	.298	.257	72	238	35	63	12	1	5	30	16	0	3	2	71	14	9	.387	.309
Beckwith, Tyler	R-R	6-2	195	7-18-94	.200	.000	.222	10	40	3	8	3	0	0	4	2	2	0	1	12	1	0	.275	.238
Davidson, Austin	R-R	6-0	180	1-3-93	.285	.375	.256	49	165	29	47	14	1	5	22	21	2	1	4	26	3	3	.473	.365
DeBruin, Grant	R-R	6-3	225	6-28-90	.290	.255	.299	71	259	35	75	14	0	5	31	30	1	0	4	39	3	1	.402	.361
Dent, Cody	L-R	5-11	190	4-6-91	.195	.286	.167	43	118	18	23	2	1	0	10	22	0	1	0	35	4	3	.229	.321
Encarnacion, Randy	R-R	6-3	180	7-31-94	.208	.261	.194	56	221	29	46	6	0	5	17	17	3	3	0	67	21	12	.303	.274
Gardner, Jeff	L-R	6-2	210	1-21-92	.200	.200	.200	9	25	4	5	1	0	3	8	3	0	0	0	8	0	0	.600	.286
Gutierrez, Kelvin	R-R	6-3	185	8-28-94	.300	.355	.282	96	377	58	113	19	6	3	48	29	3	2	6	65	19	7	.406	.349
La Bruna, Angelo	R-R	5-10	175	4-15-92	.194	.125	.217	33	93	7	18	3	1	1	8	10	1	0	1	19	2	3	.280	.276
Lora, Edwin	R-R	6-1	150	9-14-95	.231	.234	.229	118	386	56	89	32	5	4	42	30	8	4	1	113	23	4	.370	.297
Mesa, Narciso	R-R	5-11	175	11-16-91	.202	.320	.165	30	104	9	21	7	1	2	11	7	2	1	0	27	5	2	.346	.265
Noll, Jake	R-R	6-2	195	3-8-94	.259	.172	.287	32	116	21	30	4	1	3	15	7	2	0	1	16	2	0	.388	.310
Page, Matt	L-L	6-3	210	10-22-91	.280	.217	.298	88	311	53	87	23	2	10	62	45	1	1	6	71	4	3	.463	.366
Perkins, Blake	B-R	6-1	165	9-10-96	.200	.000	.217	7	25	4	5	0	0	0	2	5	0	3	0	6	0	1	.200	.333
Reetz, Jakson	R-R	6-1	195	1-3-96	.230	.172	.247	88	283	41	65	24	0	4	38	38	15	1	5	79	4	1	.357	.346
Reistetter, Matt	L-R	5-10	180	5-5-92	.172	.000	.185	10	29	2	5	0	0	0	3	6	3	0	1	5	1	0	.172	.342
Ripken, Ryan	L-L	6-6	205	7-26-93	.190	.205	.185	43	163	10	31	5	0	1	21	5	0	0	2	38	0	0	.239	.212
Robles, Victor	R-R	6-0	185	5-19-97	.305	.327	.299	64	233	48	71	9	6	5	30	18	22	11	1	38	19	8	.459	.405
Ruiz, Adderling	R-R	6-1	175	5-8-94	.138	.143	.136	9	29	2	4	1	0	1	6	4	0	0	0	13	0	0	.276	.242
Sagdal, Ian	L-R	6-3	190	1-6-93	.303	.318	.299	108	409	71	124	30	5	10	59	36	4	1	4	90	6	2	.474	.362
Schrock, Max	L-R	5-8	180	10-12-94	.326	.273	.343	67	270	46	88	20	2	4	39	22	4	0	3	20	15	3	.459	.381
Sundberg, Jack	L-R	5-11	195	7-21-93	.242	.188	.261	20	62	7	15	4	0	0	7	7	0	0	0	18	5	1	.306	.319
Tillero, Sandy	R-R	5-11	160	2-11-93	.285	.242	.299	37	130	9	37	7	1	0	11	5	5	0	2	1	23	2	3	.354	.309
Wiseman, Rhett	L-R	6-0	200	6-22-94	.255	.198	.272	134	478	71	122	25	5	13	75	42	12	3	9	104	19	10	.410	.325

Pitching	B-T	HT	WT	DOB	W	L	ERA	G	GS	CG	SV	IP	H	R	ER	HR	BB	SO	AVG	vLH	vRH	K/9	BB/9
Acevedo, Carlos	R-R	6-3	200	9-27-94	0	1	4.50	2	0	0	0	4	6	5	2	0	1	0	.400	.800	.200	0.00	2.25
Avila, Pedro	R-R	5-11	170	1-14-97	7	7	3.48	20	20	0	0	93	86	41	36	10	38	92	.249	.254	.243	8.90	3.68
Bach, Connor	L-L	6-6	230	6-24-92	0	1	7.30	5	0	0	0	12	7	11	10	1	14	14	.167	.133	.185	10.22	10.22
2-team total (1 Greensboro)					0	1	6.28	6	0	0	0	14	8	11	10	1	16	17	—	—	—	10.67	10.05
Baez, Joan	R-R	6-3	190	12-26-94	9	7	3.94	27	27	0	0	126	120	66	55	5	64	119	.258	.288	.235	8.52	4.58
Borne, Grant	L-L	6-5	205	4-9-94	5	2	3.34	21	2	0	3	59	60	29	22	2	11	46	.261	.277	.246	6.98	1.67
Bourque, James	R-R	6-4	190	7-9-93	5	6	5.03	17	13	0	0	68	81	44	38	10	23	55	.293	.293	.294	7.28	3.04
Crownover, Matt	L-R	5-11	205	3-5-93	5	1	1.17	10	3	0	1	38	26	5	5	1	11	34	.204	.224	.193	7.98	2.58
Derosier, Matt	R-R	6-2	200	7-13-94	3	3	4.54	14	14	0	0	67	71	38	34	3	18	59	.268	.217	.310	7.89	2.41
Dickey, Robbie	R-R	6-3	205	4-6-94	1	0	5.68	6	0	0	0	13	9	8	8	1	15	16	.209	.200	.214	10.66	10.66
Giolito, Lucas	R-R	6-6	255	7-14-94	0	0	5.14	1	1	0	0	7	6	4	4	2	0	4	.231	.222	.235	5.14	0.00
Guilbeau, Taylor	L-L	6-4	180	5-12-93	5	3	3.61	28	13	0	1	107	126	61	43	6	27	99	.292	.207	.324	8.30	2.26
Hearn, Taylor	L-L	6-5	210	8-30-94	1	0	3.18	3	2	0	0	25	25	13	8	3	7	31	.278	.355	.237	12.31	2.78
2-team total (8 West Virginia)					2	1	2.58	16	5	0	0	45	40	19	13	5	17	67	—	—	—	13.30	3.38

Pitching	B-T	HT	WT	DOB	W	L	ERA	G	GS	CG	SV	IP	H	R	ER	HR	BB	SO	AVG	vLH	vRH	K/9	BB/9
Held, Sam	R-R	6-5	190	8-24-94	0	0	2.00	4	0	0	1	9	8	2	2	1	1	7	.242	.200	.278	7.00	1.00
Howell, Jacob	R-R	6-3	180	8-9-95	1	1	4.57	8	0	0	0	22	20	11	11	1	7	15	.238	.371	.143	6.23	2.91
Johansen, Jake	R-R	6-6	235	1-23-91	3	1	1.86	11	0	0	1	19	20	4	4	0	4	16	.263	.174	.302	7.45	1.86
Lambert, Trey	R-R	6-4	205	6-5-91	2	0	1.89	16	0	0	1	33	37	7	7	3	2	27	.280	.345	.234	7.29	0.54
2-team total (8 Greensboro)					2	0	2.44	24	0	0	1	48	52	15	13	4	5	35	—	—	—	6.56	0.94
Lee, Andrew	L-R	6-5	225	12-2-93	2	2	3.71	11	11	0	0	51	45	25	21	1	18	46	.243	.253	.235	8.12	3.18
Martin, J.D.	R-R	6-4	220	1-2-83	0	1	5.40	1	1	0	0	5	7	3	3	0	4	5	.318	.500	.250	9.00	7.20
Pantoja, Jorge	R-R	6-5	215	3-26-94	9	1	2.63	28	0	0	3	55	53	19	16	1	10	43	.249	.262	.240	7.08	1.65
Pena, Ronald	R-R	6-4	195	9-19-91	0	0	3.38	5	0	0	2	8	8	3	3	2	3	8	.242	.200	.278	3.38	3.38
Peterson, Tommy	R-R	6-1	205	10-11-93	4	1	2.11	24	0	0	8	38	31	9	9	2	3	34	.220	.290	.165	7.98	0.70
Reyes, Luis	R-R	6-2	175	9-26-94	0	2	2.81	3	3	0	0	16	17	9	5	2	7	7	.274	.258	.290	3.94	3.94
Rivera Jr. Mariano	R-R	5-11	155	10-4-93	5	1	4.04	39	0	0	8	69	71	37	31	8	22	52	.266	.295	.241	6.78	2.87
Rodriguez, Jefry	R-R	6-5	185	7-26-93	7	11	4.96	25	25	1	0	123	110	73	68	6	52	96	.240	.251	.231	7.01	3.79
Ross, Joe	R-R	6-4	225	5-21-93	0	0	0.00	1	1	0	0	3	2	0	0	0	0	3	.182	.143	.250	9.00	0.00
Silvestre, Hector	L-L	6-3	180	12-14-92	1	0	1.80	1	1	0	0	5	4	1	1	0	0	3	.222	.167	.250	5.40	0.00
Solis, Sammy	R-L	6-5	250	8-10-88	0	0	9.00	1	0	0	0	1	1	1	1	1	0	1	.250	.000	.333	9.00	0.00
Torres, Luis	R-R	6-3	190	6-4-94	2	2	4.62	22	0	0	0	37	32	22	19	4	21	23	.237	.214	.253	5.59	5.11
VanVossen, Mick	R-R	6-3	190	10-30-92	3	3	3.71	29	0	0	8	53	50	26	22	5	18	46	.240	.253	.231	7.76	3.04
Walby, Philip	L-R	6-2	190	7-24-92	2	0	3.29	24	0	0	7	27	23	10	10	0	16	33	.223	.125	.309	10.87	5.27
Watson, Tyler	R-L	6-5	200	5-22-97	1	1	4.80	3	3	0	0	15	16	8	8	0	6	16	.296	.313	.289	9.60	3.60

Fielding

Catcher	PCT	G	PO	A	E	DP	PB
Reetz	.992	88	620	80	6	6	13
Reistetter	1.000	10	73	8	0	1	2
Ruiz	.971	9	55	13	2	1	2
Tillero	.981	37	257	45	6	2	5

First Base	PCT	G	PO	A	E	DP
DeBruin	.992	56	491	28	4	43
Page	.981	33	289	16	6	22
Ripken	.985	39	298	24	5	23
Sagdal	.992	14	108	9	1	11

Second Base	PCT	G	PO	A	E	DP
Davidson	.921	10	15	20	3	4
Dent	1.000	1	0	1	0	0
La Bruna	1.000	19	33	56	0	11

	PCT	G	PO	A	E	DP	PB
Noll	.975	24	48	68	3	19	
Sagdal	.979	34	51	88	3	19	
Schrock	.967	54	100	136	8	33	

Third Base	PCT	G	PO	A	E	DP
Beckwith	.905	10	5	14	2	1
Davidson	.964	22	15	38	2	3
DeBruin	1.000	5	3	5	0	0
Dent	.923	7	2	10	1	1
Gutierrez	.928	95	86	184	21	17
La Bruna	1.000	1	0	3	0	0
Sagdal	.833	3	2	3	1	0

Shortstop	PCT	G	PO	A	E	DP
Davidson	1.000	2	1	2	0	1
Dent	.958	12	19	27	2	4

	PCT	G	PO	A	E	DP
La Bruna	1.000	11	9	33	0	7
Lora	.941	118	166	296	29	64
Schrock	1.000	2	1	2	0	0

Outfield	PCT	G	PO	A	E	DP
Agustin	.952	64	99	1	5	0
Dent	.977	22	41	1	1	0
Encarnacion	.956	50	105	3	5	2
Gardner	1.000	8	11	0	0	0
Mesa	1.000	29	62	1	0	1
Page	1.000	28	35	1	0	0
Perkins	1.000	7	11	0	0	0
Robles	.983	63	159	13	3	2
Sagdal	1.000	17	31	0	0	0
Sundberg	1.000	20	27	4	0	0
Wiseman	.987	128	220	10	3	2

AUBURN DOUBLEDAYS
NEW YORK-PENN LEAGUE

SHORT-SEASON

Batting	B-T	HT	WT	DOB	AVG	vLH	vRH	G	AB	R	H	2B	3B	HR	RBI	BB	HBP	SH	SF	SO	SB	CS	SLG	OBP
Banks, Nick	L-L	6-1	215	11-18-94	.277	.250	.287	60	231	18	64	8	1	0	19	11	1	4	2	37	7	2	.320	.310
Barrera, Tres	R-R	6-0	215	9-15-94	.244	.333	.216	48	164	19	40	9	1	3	17	15	9	0	2	22	0	0	.366	.337
Brandt, Clayton	R-R	5-11	180	8-6-92	.179	.188	.177	49	145	12	26	10	0	0	18	16	3	5	2	33	2	2	.248	.271
Dulin, Dalton	B-R	5-8	165	5-9-94	.186	.208	.180	40	113	12	21	3	3	0	9	13	2	3	2	34	7	1	.265	.277
Encarnacion, Randy	R-R	6-3	180	7-31-94	.258	.091	.350	9	31	2	8	0	0	1	4	6	0	0	0	12	7	1	.355	.378
Florentino, Darryl	L-R	6-2	175	1-1-96	.056	.000	.071	8	18	3	1	0	1	0	3	0	0	0	0	5	0	0	.167	.190
Gutierrez, Kelvin	R-R	6-3	185	8-28-94	.323	.100	.429	9	31	5	10	3	0	0	6	3	0	0	1	5	4	0	.419	.371
Jefferies, Jake	B-R	6-1	180	8-7-93	.208	.286	.176	6	24	3	5	1	0	0	3	0	1	0	0	2	0	0	.250	.240
Johnson, Daniel	L-L	5-10	185	7-11-95	.265	.250	.269	62	245	25	65	9	4	1	14	7	10	0	1	42	13	3	.347	.312
Kerian, David	B-R	6-3	200	2-9-93	.144	.108	.156	44	146	8	21	5	2	1	10	7	1	0	2	31	0	0	.226	.186
La Bruna, Angelo	R-R	5-10	175	4-15-92	.476	.300	.636	6	21	3	10	1	0	0	3	2	0	0	0	1	0	2	.524	.522
Martinez, Andres	R-R	6-1	170	7-7-95	.208	.250	.196	40	130	16	27	5	1	1	8	7	4	0	1	28	1	0	.285	.268
Neuse, Sheldon	R-R	6-0	195	12-10-94	.230	.286	.209	36	126	16	29	5	3	1	11	13	1	0	1	26	2	2	.341	.305
Noll, Jake	R-R	6-2	195	3-8-94	.318	.250	.348	18	66	7	21	2	1	1	7	2	1	0	1	8	1	0	.424	.343
Ortiz, Oliver	L-L	6-0	170	5-6-96	.250	.237	.254	47	160	12	40	6	0	2	18	15	3	0	0	46	0	2	.325	.326
Panaccione, Paul	R-R	5-10	190	12-6-93	.205	.190	.209	50	176	11	36	6	1	0	9	9	3	1	1	20	4	0	.250	.254
Perkins, Blake	B-R	6-1	165	9-10-96	.203	.306	.203	56	231	30	49	5	1	1	16	26	5	2	2	39	10	3	.281	.318
Ripken, Ryan	L-L	6-6	205	7-26-93	.209	.216	.206	58	211	11	44	8	0	2	13	15	1	0	2	35	1	0	.265	.262
Soto, Juan	L-L	6-1	185	10-25-98	.429	.000	.474	6	21	3	9	3	0	0	1	3	0	0	0	4	0	0	.571	.500
Sundberg, Jack	L-R	5-11	195	7-21-93	.269	.238	.283	19	67	5	18	0	2	0	5	9	0	0	1	9	4	1	.328	.351
VanMeetren, Erik	R-R	6-4	215	9-4-92	.176	.000	.188	9	17	1	3	0	0	0	1	5	0	0	0	8	0	0	.176	.364
Vilorio, Luis	R-R	6-1	180	8-28-93	.216	.226	.213	33	111	12	24	6	0	0	7	5	1	0	1	19	2	1	.270	.254

Pitching	B-T	HT	WT	DOB	W	L	ERA	G	GS	CG	SV	IP	H	R	ER	HR	BB	SO	AVG	vLH	vRH	K/9	BB/9
Acevedo, Carlos	R-R	6-3	200	9-27-94	2	5	3.45	11	7	0	0	44	47	18	17	1	11	18	.278	.358	.225	3.65	2.23
Bogucki, A.J.	R-R	6-3	187	5-2-95	0	6	8.20	10	6	0	1	26	38	27	24	1	14	17	.336	.339	.333	5.81	4.78
Cespedes, Angher	R-R	6-1	190	7-25-94	1	0	0.84	10	0	0	3	11	5	1	1	0	10	10	.143	.167	.130	8.44	8.44
Conner, Nick	R-R	5-11	190	5-16-93	1	2	8.31	11	0	0	0	13	15	12	12	0	9	17	.283	.240	.321	11.77	6.23
Davis, Weston	R-R	6-3	185	7-6-96	3	6	2.67	11	11	0	0	54	39	19	16	1	11	33	.201	.241	.151	5.50	1.83
Dickey, Robbie	R-R	6-3	205	4-6-94	1	0	0.00	3	0	0	0	8	1	0	0	0	3	11	.040	.000	.063	12.38	3.38
Dunning, Dane	R-R	6-4	200	12-20-94	3	2	2.14	7	7	1	0	34	24	8	8	1	7	29	.208	.250	.182	7.75	1.87

Pitching	B-T	HT	WT	DOB	W	L	ERA	G	GS	CG	SV	IP	H	R	ER	HR	BB	SO	AVG	vLH	vRH	K/9	BB/9
Fuentes, Steven	R-R	6-2	175	5-4-97	2	1	3.65	17	1	0	3	49	53	23	20	0	10	47	.275	.185	.339	8.57	1.82
Gott, Trevor	R-R	6-0	185	8-26-92	0	0	4.50	1	0	0	0	2	3	1	1	0	0	2	.375	.200	.667	9.00	0.00
Harmening, Russell	R-R	6-1	195	9-27-94	0	1	2.57	17	0	0	0	28	26	9	8	1	8	23	.241	.200	.265	7.39	2.57
Held, Sam	R-R	6-5	190	8-24-94	1	2	3.00	7	0	0	0	12	14	4	4	0	3	8	.304	.211	.37	6.00	2.25
Howard, Hayden	R-L	6-5	193	3-26-94	0	2	5.06	11	0	0	0	21	28	13	12	1	9	12	.322	.444	.267	5.06	3.80
Howell, Jacob	R-R	6-3	180	8-9-95	1	0	0.00	2	0	0	0	5	2	0	0	0	0	6	.118	.167	.091	10.80	0.00
Mills, McKenzie	L-L	6-4	205	11-19-95	4	5	3.71	12	12	0	0	53	43	28	22	3	28	46	.218	.213	.22	7.76	4.73
Mooney, Kevin	R-R	6-1	185	8-18-94	0	2	3.33	21	0	0	1	24	18	12	9	0	11	19	.209	.195	.222	7.03	4.07
Morse, Phil	R-R	6-2	195	5-23-94	1	0	7.71	19	0	0	3	21	34	21	18	0	13	23	.382	.432	.346	9.86	5.57
Peguero, Francys	R-R	6-2	170	10-4-95	0	1	6.14	6	0	0	0	15	22	15	10	2	1	18	.324	.394	.257	11.05	0.61
Pena, Wilber	R-R	6-2	185	9-14-95	1	1	6.75	4	3	0	0	15	14	12	11	1	10	8	.255	.281	.217	4.91	6.14
Pirro, Matt	R-R	6-2	185		1	2	4.00	7	0	0	0	9	6	4	4	1	7	7	.200	.118	.308	7.00	7.00
Ramirez, Yonathan	L-L	5-11	165	4-13-97	4	3	3.69	13	11	0	1	54	58	25	22	4	12	41	.276	.321	.261	6.88	2.01
Ramos, David	R-R	6-0	175	9-13-91	0	0	0.00	5	0	0	2	6	3	0	0	0	2	9	.150	.286	.077	12.79	2.84
Reid, Jonny	L-L	5-10	165	6-28-95	1	0	3.10	7	0	0	1	20	19	7	7	3	4	17	.250	.192	.28	7.52	1.77
Reyes, Luis	R-R	6-2	175	9-26-94	0	1	1.13	3	3	0	0	8	4	1	1	0	1	3	.200	.111	.333	3.38	1.13
Serrata, Brayan	R-R	6-3	175	6-17-94	0	2	3.58	16	0	0	0	28	31	17	11	1	9	15	.277	.269	.283	4.88	2.93
Sharp, Sterling	R-R	6-4	190	5-30-95	0	0	3.60	1	1	0	0	5	5	3	2	0	0	3	.316	.600	.214	5.40	0.00
Silvestre, Hector	L-L	6-3	180	12-14-92	0	0	0.00	1	0	0	0	4	5	1	0	0	1	3	.313	.500	.286	6.75	2.25
Simonds, Kyle	R-R	6-4	205	5-17-93	0	3	2.51	13	3	0	0	32	27	14	9	2	8	27	.229	.341	.162	7.52	2.23
Valerio, Maximo	R-R	6-2	175	7-22-95	0	0	10.80	3	0	0	0	5	5	6	6	0	7	2	.263	.600	.143	3.60	12.60
Watson, Tyler	R-L	6-5	200	5-22-97	1	2	1.88	9	9	0	0	43	30	10	9	1	9	48	.189	.182	.19	10.05	1.88

Fielding

C: Barrera 42, VanMeetren 4, Vilorio 33. **1B:** Kerian 30, Ortiz 4, Ripken 44. **2B:** Brandt 2, Dulin 38, Jefferies 1, La Bruna 5, Martinez 2, Noll 16, Panaccione 13. **3B:** Brandt 3, Gutierrez 8, Jefferies 2, Martinez 31, Neuse 26, Noll 1, Panaccione 11. **SS:** Brandt 44, La Bruna 2, Martinez 4, Neuse 6, Panaccione 24. **OF:** Banks 55, Encarnacion 8, Florentino 7, Johnson 57, Kerian 2, Ortiz 29, Panaccione 2, Perkins 52, Soto 6, Sundberg 18.

GCL NATIONALS — ROOKIE
GULF COAST LEAGUE

Batting	B-T	HT	WT	DOB	AVG	vLH	vRH	G	AB	R	H	2B	3B	HR	RBI	BB	HBP	SH	SF	SO	SB	CS	SLG	OBP
Agustin, Telmito	L-L	5-10	160	10-9-96	.000	—	.000	1	4	0	0	0	0	0	0	0	0	0	0	2	0	0	.000	.000
Baez, Jeyner	R-R	6-1	175	7-25-95	.550	.000	.647	6	20	4	11	4	0	0	4	3	0	0	1	1	1	0	.750	.583
Beckwith, Tyler	R-R	6-2	195	7-18-94	.270	.200	.279	35	126	23	34	5	1	1	10	14	3	0	0	32	4	0	.349	.357
Boggetto, Branden	R-R	6-0	190	11-10-93	.280	.100	.299	32	107	16	30	5	0	3	16	6	2	0	1	13	2	2	.411	.328
Corredor, Aldrem	L-L	6-2	202	10-27-95	.290	.278	.291	42	169	18	49	8	2	1	26	21	0	0	4	28	1	1	.379	.361
Evangelista, Juan	R-R	5-11	165	5-28-98	.296	.286	.298	16	54	11	16	4	1	0	9	3	1	0	1	9	1	0	.407	.339
Florentino, Darryl	L-R	6-2	175	1-1-96	.340	.357	.337	27	103	18	35	2	1	0	8	6	1	0	2	11	7	6	.379	.375
Franco, Anderson	R-R	6-3	190	8-15-97	.277	.286	.275	24	83	9	23	3	0	1	9	4	0	0	1	11	1	0	.349	.307
Harris, Joey	L-R	6-0	200	2-13-94	.301	.556	.266	26	73	7	22	0	0	0	10	9	5	1	0	15	1	1	.329	.414
Kieboom, Carter	R-R	6-2	190	9-3-97	.244	.200	.252	36	133	22	33	8	4	4	25	12	5	0	3	43	1	2	.452	.323
Meregildo, Omar	R-R	6-1	185	8-18-97	.149	.091	.159	28	74	7	11	1	0	4	6	6	0	1	1	16	2	1	.162	.210
Mota, Israel	R-R	6-2	165	1-3-96	.216	.200	.220	31	97	18	21	7	0	3	9	13	5	0	2	29	2	1	.381	.333
Noll, Jake	R-R	6-2	195	3-8-94	.240	.333	.227	7	25	3	6	1	0	1	6	6	1	1	2	0	0	0	.400	.394
Ortiz, Oliver	L-L	6-0	170	5-6-96	.281	.000	.321	8	32	5	9	1	0	1	8	1	0	0	0	7	0	0	.406	.303
Perdomo, Luis	L-L	5-11	170	5-21-97	.263	.333	.255	15	57	5	15	3	1	0	11	7	1	0	0	10	6	2	.351	.354
Picerni, C.J.	R-R	5-10	165	12-15-92	.250	.000	.286	4	8	2	2	0	0	1	1	0	0	0	0	2	0	0	.250	.333
Pimentel, Davison	R-R	5-9	170	2-12-97	.286	.091	.342	16	49	4	14	1	0	0	5	3	1	1	0	8	0	0	.306	.340
Ramirez, Joshual	R-R	6-2	185	5-20-96	.213	.200	.214	39	122	19	26	7	3	1	15	9	2	1	3	26	3	2	.344	.276
Robles, Victor	R-R	6-0	185	5-19-97	.150	.000	.188	5	20	3	3	0	0	1	0	1	0	0	1	7	0	1	.300	.190
Shepard, Chance	R-R	6-1	210	11-8-94	.188	.222	.183	28	80	14	15	2	0	3	9	12	1	0	4	33	0	0	.325	.289
Simonetti, Conner	L-L	6-1	205	2-10-95	.267	.282	.242	42	157	21	44	6	1	6	24	10	0	0	1	54	0	0	.446	.333
Soto, Juan	L-L	6-1	185	10-25-98	.361	.333	.365	45	169	25	61	11	3	5	31	14	0	0	0	25	5	2	.550	.410
Sundberg, Jack	L-R	5-11	195	7-21-93	.259	.400	.227	6	27	7	7	0	1	1	2	6	0	0	0	3	1	4	.444	.394
Tillero, Jorge	L-L	5-11	160	12-21-93	.167	—	.167	3	6	1	1	0	0	0	0	0	0	0	0	0	0	0	.167	.286
Upshaw, Armond	B-L	6-0	190	6-20-96	.325	.600	.286	13	40	6	13	1	1	0	2	3	2	1	2	12	3	2	.400	.391

Pitching	B-T	HT	WT	DOB	W	L	ERA	G	GS	CG	SV	IP	H	R	ER	HR	BB	SO	AVG	vLH	vRH	K/9	BB/9
Alastre, Tomas	R-R	6-4	170	6-11-98	0	3	5.21	7	4	0	0	19	21	15	11	0	14	12	.292	.304	.286	5.68	6.63
Arroyo, Bronson	R-R	6-4	190	2-24-77	1	1	4.66	2	2	0	0	10	13	5	5	0	2	8	.317	.211	.409	7.45	1.86
Bacus, Dakota	R-R	6-2	200		1	0	1.50	2	0	0	0	6	4	1	1	0	0	6	.190	.500	.158	9.00	0.00
Baltrip, Joseph	R-R	6-1	220	2-15-95	2	1	1.38	16	0	0	4	26	15	4	4	1	23	17	.174	.185	.169	5.88	7.96
Barnett, Jake	L-L	6-2	190	7-30-94	0	0	1.80	2	0	0	0	5	4	3	1	1	0	2	.211	.000	.286	3.60	0.00
Bogucki, A.J.	R-R	6-3	187	5-2-95	0	0	9.00	2	1	0	0	4	6	7	4	0	2	6	.400	.364		13.50	4.50
Braymer, Ben	L-L	6-2	210	4-28-94	0	2	4.12	8	2	0	0	20	13	9	9	0	13	24	.194	.150	.213	10.98	5.95
Conner, Nick	R-R	5-11	190	5-16-93	1	0	2.53	6	0	0	0	11	6	3	3	0	2	5	.158	.125	.182	4.22	1.69
Dunning, Dane	R-R	6-4	200	12-20-94	0	0	0.00	1	1	0	0	2	0	0	0	0	0	3	.000	.000	.00	13.50	0.00
German, Jhonatan	R-R	6-4	215	1-24-95	1	2	4.00	8	0	0	0	15	18	8	8	0	10	23	.295	.154	.333	13.50	5.87
Gott, Trevor	R-R	6-0	185	8-26-92	0	0	9.00	1	0	0	0	1	2	1	1	0	0	1	.500	1.500	.429	9.00	0.00
Grace, Matt	L-L	6-4	215	12-14-88	1	0	3.86	3	0	0	0	2	1	1	1	0	0	4	.125	.167	.1	7.71	0.00
Gunter, Cody	L-R	6-3	195	4-18-94	0	0	0.00	1	0	0	0	1	0	0	0	0	0	0	.000	—	.000	0.00	0.00
Hearn, Taylor	L-L	6-5	210	8-30-94	0	0	1.42	2	2	0	0	6	2	1	1	0	6	9	.105	.000	.143	11.37	8.53
Held, Sam	R-R	6-5	190	8-24-94	0	0	0.00	3	0	0	0	4	1	0	0	0	4	7	.111	.083	.133	7.88	4.50
Holland, Neil	R-R	6-0	190	8-14-88	0	0	1.35	3	0	0	0	7	10	1	1	0	1	10	.370	.111	.5	13.50	1.35

Pitching

Pitching	B-T	HT	WT	DOB	W	L	ERA	G	GS	CG	SV	IP	H	R	ER	HR	BB	SO	AVG	vLH	vRH	K/9	BB/9
Howard, Hayden	R-L	6-5	193	3-26-94	1	0	0.00	1	0	0	0	2	0	0	0	0	1	2	.000	—	.000	9.00	4.50
Howell, Jacob	R-R	6-3	180	8-9-95	0	0	0.00	1	0	0	0	2	0	0	0	0	0	1	.000	.000	.000	5.40	0.00
Johansen, Jake	R-R	6-6	235	1-23-91	0	0	4.50	7	0	0	0	8	7	7	4	0	7	8	.241	.250	.238	9.00	7.88
Latos, Mat	R-R	6-6	245	12-9-87	0	0	1.64	3	3	0	0	11	4	2	2	0	3	18	.108	.067	.136	14.73	2.45
Martin, J.D.	R-R	6-4	220	1-2-83	1	2	5.79	3	3	0	0	14	19	9	9	1	4	7	.328	.476	.243	4.50	2.57
McDonald, Jeremy	L-L	5-9	182	9-22-93	3	1	3.42	11	0	0	1	26	27	11	10	0	5	27	.255	.091	.298	9.23	1.71
Morse, Phil	R-R	6-2	195	5-23-94	0	0	0.00	1	0	0	0	2	0	0	0	0	0	5	.000	.000	.000	27.00	0.00
Peguero, Francys	R-R	6-2	170	10-4-95	3	0	2.20	8	5	0	1	33	31	12	8	2	5	34	.240	.325	.202	9.37	1.38
Pena, Carlos	R-R	6-5	240	4-3-94	2	2	2.95	11	7	0	1	40	35	18	13	0	16	28	.245	.241	.247	6.35	3.63
Pena, Ronald	R-R	6-4	195	9-19-91	0	0	4.50	4	0	0	0	6	6	4	3	0	1	5	.240	1.000	.333	7.50	1.50
Pirro, Matt	R-R	6-1	185	4-24-93	2	2	4.73	8	0	0	0	13	11	7	7	1	5	10	.234	.286	.212	6.75	3.38
Porter, Connor	R-R	6-8	230	4-12-92	0	0	3.00	2	0	0	0	3	4	1	1	0	1	1	.333	.500	.167	3.00	3.00
Reid, Jonny	L-L	5-10	165	6-28-95	2	1	1.72	6	0	0	0	16	8	3	3	0	3	7	.145	.000	.186	4.02	1.72
Rishwain, Michael	R-R	6-3	220	6-27-94	1	0	3.63	13	0	0	0	17	28	19	7	0	5	14	.337	.429	.291	7.27	2.60
Rosa, Jeffrey	R-R	6-3	189	6-5-95	0	4	4.91	11	11	0	0	40	38	23	22	1	20	34	.245	.245	.245	7.59	4.46
Sharp, Sterling	R-R	6-4	170	5-30-95	3	0	3.24	11	7	0	2	42	47	16	15	2	6	35	.287	.281	.290	7.56	1.30
Silvestre, Hector	L-L	6-3	180	12-14-92	0	0	0.93	4	4	0	0	10	10	3	1	0	3	11	.263	.333	.241	10.24	2.79
Simonds, Kyle	R-R	6-4	205	5-17-93	1	0	0.00	2	1	0	0	5	2	0	0	0	0	4	.133	.143	.125	7.71	0.00
Tindall, Matt	R-R	6-3	230	5-16-92	4	1	3.95	9	0	0	0	14	13	9	6	0	6	11	.255	.200	.278	7.24	3.95

Fielding

C: Baez 6, Harris 26, Picerni 4, Pimentel 11, Shepard 17, Tillero 3. **1B:** Corredor 21, Shepard 1, Simonetti 33. **2B:** Beckwith 6, Boggetto 30, Meregildo 3, Noll 7, Ramirez 18. **3B:** Beckwith 11, Boggetto 1, Franco 19, Meregildo 26, Ramirez 11. **SS:** Beckwith 18, Kieboom 31, Ramirez 15. **OF:** Agustin 1, Boggetto 3, Corredor 14, Evangelista 15, Florentino 27, Mota 28, Ortiz 8, Perdomo 11, Robles 5, Shepard 1, Soto 42, Sundberg 6, Upshaw 13.

DSL NATIONALS   ROOKIE
DOMINICAN SUMMER LEAGUE

Batting

Batting	B-T	HT	WT	DOB	AVG	vLH	vRH	G	AB	R	H	2B	3B	HR	RBI	BB	HBP	SH	SF	SO	SB	CS	SLG	OBP
Andujar, Yoel	R-R	6-3	185	10-29-97	.178	.118	.185	47	152	15	27	5	2	0	16	19	2	0	0	59	7	1	.237	.277
Aquino, Luis	R-R	6-1	170	4-28-99	.210	.222	.208	57	205	28	43	4	5	0	14	12	2	1	0	71	6	3	.278	.260
Bencosme, Bryan	R-R	6-1	175	12-18-97	.191	.182	.192	64	215	20	41	2	4	0	21	33	2	2	3	53	5	0	.237	.300
Cabello, Jose	R-R	5-11	185	12-12-96	.277	.273	.277	53	177	18	49	8	1	0	26	28	7	0	3	24	4	4	.333	.391
De Los Santos, Andri	R-R	6-4	190	5-25-96	.279	.381	.262	43	147	17	41	11	2	2	20	8	3	0	2	28	3	2	.422	.325
Falcon, Santo	R-R	6-0	190	3-28-97	.250	.105	.269	46	164	19	41	4	5	0	17	15	6	4	1	41	12	5	.335	.333
Jimenez, Carlos	R-R	5-11	180	10-2-96	.194	.143	.200	22	67	3	13	0	1	0	5	2	0	1	0	24	0	0	.224	.217
Martinez, Adanlis	R-R	6-2	170	1-31-98	.234	.200	.237	44	141	16	33	2	0	0	14	8	7	1	2	29	8	2	.248	.304
Medina, Roberto	R-R	5-11	185	9-24-97	.215	.300	.198	36	121	14	26	4	1	0	14	13	2	1	0	26	8	0	.264	.301
Mesa, Brailin	R-R	6-3	185	11-2-97	.257	.231	.261	58	214	25	55	16	1	1	19	11	4	1	3	48	4	1	.355	.302
Morales, Jesus	R-R	5-10	158	12-22-97	.261	.368	.249	58	188	25	49	5	1	0	10	13	2	2	0	28	10	3	.298	.312
Pascal, Juan	R-R	6-1	175	11-6-97	.239	.276	.233	57	209	29	50	6	0	0	17	17	7	1	2	35	10	7	.268	.315
Pena, Landerson	R-R	6-1	180	10-14-97	.210	.063	.233	34	119	13	25	4	1	0	14	9	5	1	3	36	9	3	.261	.287
Sierra, Franklin	B-R	5-10	180	2-15-96	.231	.368	.214	57	173	24	40	6	7	0	14	26	5	1	2	41	11	7	.347	.345

Pitching

Pitching	B-T	HT	WT	DOB	W	L	ERA	G	GS	CG	SV	IP	H	R	ER	HR	BB	SO	AVG	vLH	vRH	K/9	BB/9
Archibald, Michael	L-L	6-2	165	3-15-95	0	1	—	1	0	0	0	1	2	2	0	0	2	1	.000	1.000			
Chu, Gilberto	L-L	5-11	160	11-19-97	1	4	3.18	11	11	0	0	51	40	23	18	2	9	50	.215	.214	.215	8.82	1.59
Constanzo, Francisco	R-R	6-1	180	10-4-96	0	1	3.68	8	0	0	1	7	5	7	3	0	9	8	.200	.500	.000	9.82	11.05
De La Cruz, Gerald	L-L	6-3	180	8-19-96	1	2	4.50	11	9	0	0	36	27	27	18	0	29	39	.209	.294	.179	9.75	7.25
De Los Santos, Jose	R-R	6-3	190	1-14-97	1	1	4.01	15	1	0	1	34	41	19	15	1	14	23	.308	.375	.280	6.15	3.74
Duran, Warner	R-R	5-11	165	3-25-98	1	0	1.65	19	0	0	6	33	18	6	6	1	6	35	.158	.051	.213	9.64	1.65
Garcia, Yordani	R-R	6-5	180	2-19-96	0	2	12.27	7	0	0	0	7	16	11	10	0	8	6	.485	.333	.571	7.36	9.82
German, Jhonatan	R-R	6-4	215	1-24-95	2	0	0.50	11	0	0	4	18	6	3	1	0	4	28	.105	.200	.071	14.00	2.00
Gomez, Rafael	R-R	6-0	178	6-15-98	1	2	2.25	7	3	0	1	24	32	9	6	0	4	20	.323	.324	.323	7.50	1.50
Guillen, Angel	R-R	6-2	150	1-24-97	4	1	1.67	12	11	0	0	54	39	17	10	2	12	50	.205	.167	.229	8.33	2.00
Hernandez, Alfonso	L-L	5-11	144	8-3-99	2	1	1.32	8	0	0	1	14	3	2	2	0	5	14	.073	.286	.029	9.22	3.29
Infante, Darly	L-L	6-2	165	10-20-96	1	4	2.94	12	12	0	0	49	54	26	16	2	19	52	.281	.269	.283	9.55	3.49
Jimenez, Jose	L-L	6-1	190	12-7-96	2	4	3.25	20	0	0	5	36	44	22	13	0	12	24	.289	.323	.281	6.00	3.00
Martinez, Adrian	R-R	6-0	185	8-2-98	1	1	3.86	14	1	0	0	37	35	20	16	0	13	32	.252	.280	.236	7.71	3.13
Matheus, Juan	R-R	6-2	165	4-14-97	1	0	8.59	6	0	0	0	7	11	7	7	2	2	4	.333	.385	.300	4.91	2.45
Michel, Edwin	L-L	6-2	166	4-22-99	1	0	3.75	9	0	0	0	12	9	7	5	0	7	14	.191	.375	.154	10.50	5.25
Oropeza, Yonaiker	R-R	6-3	170	11-15-97	0	0	4.50	2	0	0	0	2	4	1	1	0	0	1	.444	.400	.500	4.50	0.00
Ortiz, Miguel	R-R	6-5	190	1-8-99	1	2	1.59	10	0	0	0	17	11	9	3	1	9	11	.193	.182	.200	5.82	4.76
Peguero, Jairon	L-L	6-0	170	6-14-97	0	5	4.91	13	1	0	0	33	34	24	18	0	14	31	.262	.300	.250	8.45	3.82
Pena, Malvin	R-R	6-2	180	6-24-97	0	2	11.37	2	2	0	0	6	6	9	8	0	7	5	.240	.083	.385	7.11	9.95
Pena, Yefri	R-R	6-2	175	2-8-95	1	2	3.45	16	0	0	2	31	31	14	12	0	14	20	.254	.139	.302	5.74	4.02
Ramirez, Hector	R-R	6-4	190	2-25-98	0	1	5.17	11	0	0	0	16	12	12	9	0	21	12	.222	.125	.263	6.89	12.06
Sisnero, Yelmery	L-L	6-1	195	9-9-97	4	3	0.43	19	0	0	2	42	29	9	2	0	9	41	.190	.108	.216	8.86	1.94
Taveras, Felix	R-R	6-2	155	7-11-95	4	2	4.61	10	10	0	0	41	38	24	21	3	18	48	.241	.333	.179	10.54	3.95

Fielding

C: Cabello 28, Jimenez 19, Jimenez 1, Medina 28. **1B:** Cabello 21, Martinez 25, Mesa 9, Morales 11, Sierra 17. **2B:** Aquino 50, Morales 16, Sierra 10. **3B:** Bencosme 55, Martinez 8, Morales 12. **SS:** Aquino 6, Bencosme 9, Morales 5, Pascal 56. **OF:** Andujar 45, De Los Santos 31, Falcon 42, Mesa 48, Morales 3, Pena 34, Sierra 25.

MINOR
LEAGUES

Heritage Field will be empty going forward as the California League dropped High Desert

New logos, franchises change landscape

BY JOSH NORRIS

After a year in 2015 that saw the (mostly) successful openings of new parks in Nashville, Morgantown, W.Va., and Biloxi, the minor leagues mostly failed to capitalize on that trend in 2016.

Columbia's Spirit Communications Park opened on time and was widely hailed as a success. The team, which had moved from Savannah to South Carolina's capital city and changed its name from the Sand Gnats to the Fireflies in the offseason, more than doubled its attendance.

That, however, was the end of the positive news.

The Hartford Yard Goats, the other team scheduled to open a new park, was stymied at every turn and became an unexpected team without a home. Dunkin' Donuts Park never opened, and the team spent the entire year playing either as the home team on the road or at neutral sites.

Officially, Hartford drew just 41,569 fans all year and played seven times in front of no fans at all, because conditions prevented visiting stadiums from opening their gates to the public.

The year also saw the long-rumored fracturing of the California League come to fruition. High Desert and Bakersfield were contracted and moved

to the Carolina League, where they will land in Kinston, N.C. and Fayetteville, N.C.

On the field, the Cubs previewed their long-awaited World Series win with a pair of minor league championships at high Class A Myrtle Beach and short-season Eugene. The latter salved a championship drought of its own, claiming its first NWL title since 1975.

Cal League Contracts

The 2016 season began ominously for the High Desert Mavericks. The embattled California League franchise was mired in a long-running legal battle with its home city of Adelanto, Calif., which claimed its $1 per year lease on Heritage Field amounted to a gift of public funds.

The Adelanto City Council voted in January to cancel the team's lease and evict the Mavericks from the stadium and was set to send the team on a season-long road trip. Team ownership won an injunction in court just before the season began, however, and the Mavericks were issued a reprieve.

Dave Heller, the head of the Mavericks' ownership group, was effusive in his praise for the court's ruling.

"It just shows that (the city's) legal case is

flimsier and has more holes in it," he said, "than the thinnest slice of Swiss cheese ever known to mankind."

And while that victory kept the Mavericks from becoming the minors' latest nomads, the victory was short-lived. The signs of the forthcoming mess began in June, when the California and Carolina Leagues announced that they would hold individual all-star games in 2017 for the first time in more than three decades.

Since 1996 the leagues had rotated the site of their midseason celebration between the leagues; the most recent version was held in Lake Elsinore, and included a home run derby held on the deck of the U.S.S. Midway, a decommissioned aircraft carrier.

Less than two months later, the big news dropped: The Mavericks and the Bakersfield Blaze were ceasing operations at season's end and moving to the Carolina League. The High Desert move had been in the works for some time–the Rangers had a deal with Kinston, N.C. and Grainger Stadium since 2015. Meanwhile, Bakersfield's Sam Lynn Ballpark, originally built in 1941, had long received waivers from Minor League Baseball for sub-standard lighting and playing conditions.

Both clubs gave their fan bases one final hurrah before heading west. The Blaze and Mavericks each made the Cal League playoffs, and Bakersfield made it to the semifinals before bowing out against Visalia.

The Mavericks, however, went out in style. They swept Visalia in three games to claim the franchise's first championship since 1997. The club, which did not put its games on the radio, even imported two rival broadcasters in anticipation of what became the ultimate walk-off victory.

LogoMania

Once High Desert and Bakersfield are settled in the Carolina League, they'll need new identities. And although they're the among the only teams on the move this offseason, they're far from the only clubs giving their brand a revamp.

The Florida State League's Brevard County club ended a run of more than two decades when announced it would moved across the state and into Osceola County Stadium. The move also triggered an affiliation shift when the Braves, seeing a chance to position their high Class A club just 20 minutes away from their spring training home on the campus of Walt Disney World, stepped up and snatched the club from the Brewers, with whom the team had affiliated since 2005.

Along with the physical move, the former Brevard County team dropped the Manatees name

that had been with the team since its inception. To find a replacement, the team held an online naming contest. Fans were invited to submit their ideas on the team's Facebook page, and club officials winnowed the entries down to the best six.

The result was the Florida Fire Frogs, with a logo and color scheme designed by minor league logo kingpin Brandiose. Notably, the Fire Frogs are the only club in Atlanta's system without Braves as its nickname.

Binghamton (Mets), New Orleans (Marlins) and Staten Island (Yankees) each opted for similar rebrands, complete with online name submissions. Binghamton became the Rumble Ponies, and New Orleans' and Staten Island's new names weren't available at press time. Jacksonville didn't previously announce its intention to rebrand, choosing instead for a surprise drop of its new identity—the Jumbo Shrimp—in the hours before Game Seven of the World Series.

Affiliation Shuffle

This past year also brought with it the bi-annual return of the Affiliation Shuffle, the period in which major league clubs can try to find new homes for their minor league teams. The previous incarnation saw 21 changes, but this year's version was far tamer.

There were just seven moves in total, and none at Triple-A, low Class A, short-season or the Rookie-levels. The level most affected was high Class A, which had four affiliation shifts.

The contraction of Bakersfield and High Desert started a small chain reaction. It was long known that the Rangers were going to shift their franchise to Kinston, N.C.—the team and the city had a contract in place prior to the 2015 season that gave the Rangers a two-year time frame to move a high

Class A team into Kinston's Grainger Stadium.

The Astros, too, were seeking a way out of the hitter-friendly California League, and they made a quick move to snap up the former Bakersfield franchise and shift it to Fayetteville, N.C. Those two moves left the Mariners holding the bag, but not for long.

The Mariners and new farm director Andy McKay had seen the writing on the wall and took steps to secure their high Class A team not only for the next two years, but for the long-term future by purchasing a controlling stake in the Cal League team in Modesto.

"The Mariners are committed to a strong minor league system," McKay said at the time. "That commitment, coupled with our desire to remain in the California League and the great opportunity to be affiliated with the Nuts and the city and fans of Modesto, has led us to this partnership. We are looking forward to many, many years of success here in Modesto."

The Mariners move to Modesto, combined with the Braves seizing Osceola County, meant that this year's Affiliation Shuffle would end the same way the previous version did: with two teams dueling for the right to affiliate with the Carolina Mudcats for the next two seasons.

The Braves won out in 2014, and likely would have stayed for another two seasons if the Osceola County opportunity hadn't presented itself. This year's duel came down to the wire, but Mudcats management ultimately chose the Brewers and the wealth of prospects that will likely populate the team's roster in 2017.

"Having met with the Brewers, and in looking at their system, we are confident that we are getting an organization that is loaded with young, talented prospects that we feel will enhance our program," Mudcats owner Steve Bryant said. "We are very impressed with the Brewers in that they share with us a desire to develop young talent at the minor league level."

That move left the Rockies with Lancaster, a fine park and operation but with howling winds that create extreme offensive conditions that aren't conducive to player development.

The Southern and Texas Leagues also saw a bit of shuffling. The Diamondbacks struck first by cutting a deal with Jackson in the SL. The Mariners responded by hooking on with Arkansas in the Texas League, and the Angels were left Mobile in the SL.

Promotion Commotion

As is tradition, the minor leagues in 2016 were filled with another round of zany, innovative pro-

ORGANIZATION STANDINGS

Cumulative domestic farm club records for major league organizations, with winning percentages going back five years. Most organizations have six affiliates.

	2016						
	W	L	PCT	2015	2014	2013	2012
1. Phillies	412	280	.595	.542	.435	.468	.498
2. Mariners	403	291	.581	.435	.475	.497	.528
3. Yankees	447	363	.552	.512	.509	.495	.529
4. Indians	383	313	.550	.509	.507	.445	.506
5. Twins	372	317	.540	.534	.528	.546	.525
6. Cubs	373	319	.539	.540	.522	.504	.470
7. Rays	401	357	.529	.502	.505	.524	.515
8. Dodgers	364	327	.527	.529	.458	.486	.528
9. Red Sox	366	330	.526	.469	.529	.504	.504
10. Cardinals	393	363	.520	.512	.545	.494	.505
11. Astros	389	369	.513	.565	.519	.570	.546
12. Nationals	351	340	.508	.469	.514	.550	.506
13. Blue Jays	385	374	.507	.485	.495	.493	.524
14. D-backs	389	379	.507	.509	.561	.510	.499
15. Reds	347	344	.502	.512	.489	.426	.449
16. Rangers	340	352	.491	.518	.546	.528	.517
17. Pirates	372	387	.490	.547	.450	.515	.505
18. Athletics	337	353	.488	.483	.513	.497	.496
19. Giants	335	358	.483	.504	.509	.564	.506
20. Mets	364	394	.480	.532	.568	.546	.509
21. Rockies	340	373	.477	.466	.466	.482	.540
22. Tigers	353	392	.474	.472	.516	.484	.482
23. Braves	319	363	.468	.489	.493	.485	.461
24. Padres	321	373	.463	.476	.472	.496	.455
25. Orioles	318	381	.455	.524	.465	.481	.456
26. Marlins	311	374	.454	.427	.498	.497	.524
27. Royals	342	414	.452	.497	.450	.463	.492
28. Angels	313	381	.451	.459	.486	.501	.449
29. Brewers	302	379	.443	.439	.508	.449	.459
30. White Sox	296	398	.427	.504	.456	.488	.504

POSTSEASON RESULTS

LEAGUE	CHAMPION	RUNNER-UP
International	Scranton/W-B	Gwinnett
Pacific Coast	El Paso	Oklahoma City
Eastern	Akron	Trenton
Southern	Jackson	Mississippi
Texas	Midland	NW Arkansas
California	High Desert	Visalia
Carolina	Myrtle Beach	Lynchburg
Florida State	Bradenton	Tampa
Midwest	Great Lakes	Clinton
South Atlantic	Rome	Lakewood
New York-Penn	State College	Hudson Valley
Northwest	Eugene	Everett
Appalachian	Johnson City	Burlington
Pioneer	Orem	Billings
Arizona	Mariners	Angels
Gulf Coast	Cardinals	Phillies

motions. The Fresno Grizzlies were at the forefront with ever-growing Fresno Tacos alter ego.

What started as a simple alternate-jersey night (Taco Tuesdays) mushroomed into a merchandise behemoth. The Grizzlies were still the Tacos every Tuesday night, but with a lot more variety. The Grizzlies held 10 more Taco Tuesday nights in 2016, and also debuted a corresponding website

devoted solely to Tacos gear.

To go with the standard Tacos hats, which came about in 2015, Fresno unveiled product lines for four different taco meats—lengua, al pastor, carnitas and asada—and designed pennants, shirts, hats, shot glasses and other accessories around that theme.

Beyond the tacos, the Grizzlies also earned plaudits for other original promotions. The team announced its alternate jerseys before the season, including versions honoring the state of California and the "Three Amigos" movie. Rival executives were impressed enough to vote the Grizzlies the winner of the Best Promotional Jerseys category in Baseball America's first Best of the Minors survey.

The Grizzlies also won the Best Promotion category for their Taco Tuesdays. Other winners of included Richmond's Jay Burnham for Best Broadcaster, Charlotte for Best Skyline, Durham's Wool E. Bull for Best Mascot and Lehigh Valley's various bacon-based creations for Best Food Item.

The promotion of the summer, however, unquestionably belonged to Pokemon Go, Nintendo's revamp of its hit game from the 1990s. Most every team in the minors took a chance to cash in on the craze with a promotional night.

The Lakewood BlueClaws blew out all the stops for their version of the celebration.

Some of the night's planned highlights included: a Snorlax-themed sumo match, Ratatta chasing Cheese (a normal participant in Lakewood's nightly Pork Roll, Egg and Cheese race), a Kangaskhan sack race and a Name That Pokemon guessing game. Fans also had a chance to take a picture at the stadium's photo booth that was then transformed into a personalized Pokemon card.

Yardless Goats

On July 22, the inevitable became official: The Hartford Yard Goats, Double-A affiliate of the Rockies, would not play a game in Hartford all season.

The Eastern League that day announced the sites of the remainder of the team's scheduled home dates for the season, all of which had to be moved to road cities after continued delays and turmoil in the construction of Hartford's new Dunkin' Donuts Park.

The ballpark was scheduled to open this April, after the team moved from New Britain, Conn., to Hartford and changed its name from the Rock Cats to the Yard Goats. After construction issues scuttled its plans for an on-schedule opening, the next tentative home opener was slated for May 31. Two weeks in advance of that date, the developers, DoNo Hartford and Centerplan Co., were

Fresno dominated the promotion scene in 2016 with its continued Taco Tuesdays

supposed to have turned the stadium over to the city to give it time to get everything prepared for the opener.

That did not happen. In fact, the developers reported to the city that the remaining work on the stadium would take at least 60 days to complete. Moreover, in addition to the extra time, the developers told the city that they'd need money in excess of the initial $47.05 million price tag.

Instead, Hartford mayor Luke Bronin and the city terminated their contract with Centerplan and DoNo Hartford, which also were scheduled to help oversee the development of the area surrounding the stadium, and brought in an insurance company to assess the rest of the work that needed to be completed. What was supposed to be Dunkin Donuts Park instead sat padlocked and empty, awaiting both a team and a resolution.

In the meantime, the Yard Goats spent the entire season playing as the home team in road or neutral-site Eastern League stadiums, or at Dodd Stadium, in Norwich, Conn., the home of the short-season Connecticut Tigers.

The dream of minor league baseball in Hartford in 2016 was officially dead. After taking months

CONTINUED ON PAGE 356

Moncada shows all of his skills

BY BEN BADLER

It didn't generate much attention at the time, but a youth tournament in the city of Lagos de Moreno in Mexico six years ago was filled with future major league talent.

It was October 2010 when scouts ventured to Mexico for the COPABE 16U Pan American Championship. At shortstop, the United States had Corey Seager, who finished second in the tournament in hitting, ranking behind only his double-play partner, second baseman Alex Bregman. Mexico's ace was Roberto Osuna.

The player in Lagos de Moreno who captivated the attention of scouts was Cuba's 15-year-old third baseman, Yoan Moncada. Despite being one of the youngest players in the tournament, Moncada showed dynamic athleticism, tools and feel for the game beyond his years. It was the first time Moncada had traveled out of Cuba, the first time international scouts had seen him play.

Since then, Moncada left Cuba and signed with the Red Sox in March 2015 for $31.5 million, with the Red Sox paying a total of $63 million including the 100 percent overage tax to the commissioner's office for exceeding their international bonus pool.

With the spotlight shining on him, Moncada has so far lived up to the hype. Between high Class A Salem and Double-A Portland this season, Moncada hit .294/.407/.511 in 491 plate appearances with 15 home runs, 45 stolen bases and 72 walks. At 21 years old, Moncada was the Futures Game MVP, the No. 1 prospect in baseball and is now a big leaguer, forcing his way to Boston as a September callup.

For Moncada's outstanding season, he is Baseball America's Minor League Player of the Year. Yet as talented as Moncada is right now and as productive as he's been already, the most tantalizing part about Moncada is how much better he still has a chance to become.

During Moncada's time with the Red Sox, the one part of his game that stood out from the start was his speed. Moncada is a 70 runner on the 20-80 scouting scale. This season in the

Yoan Moncada

minors, Moncada was successful in 79 percent of his stolen base attempts, with 45 steals (tied for fifth in the minors) in 57 tries.

Moncada doesn't look like your typical speedster—he's built for power. He has the legs of a running back and the explosive bat speed few others on the planet can match.

Except, early on, Moncada wasn't showing much over-the-fence power in games.

In mid-June, after Moncada arrived in Portland—a home park that suppresses run scoring and home runs—his power spiked, with 11 home runs in 45 games with the Sea Dogs. Moncada was already a productive hitter and a line-drive machine with a compact swing (more so from the left side than the right), but the Red Sox wanted to optimize his stroke to capitalize on his raw power.

As Moncada transitions from second base to third, the early returns have been encouraging. Moncada is still getting acclimated to the angles and fundamentals at third, but in limited time he's already made terrific plays with his range to both sides and charging in on slow rollers.

That's what makes Moncada such an exciting player. He's already proven himself to be one of the most productive hitters and baserunners in the minors, with the ability to make quick adjustments and rapid improvements.

As good as he is right now, Moncada is just beginning to tap into his potential.

PREVIOUS WINNERS

2006: Alex Gordon, 3b, Wichita (Royals)
2007: Jay Bruce, of, Sarasota/Chattanooga/Louisville (Reds)
2008: Matt Wieters, c, Frederick/Bowie (Orioles)
2009: Jason Heyward, Myrtle Beach/Mississippi (Braves)
2010: Jeremy Hellickson, Montgomery/Durham (Rays)
2011: Mike Trout, Arkansas (Angels)
2012: Wil Myers, Northwest Arkansas/Omaha (Royals)
2013: Byron Buxton, Cedar Rapids/Fort Myers (Twins)
2014: Kris Bryant, Iowa (Cubs)
2015: Blake Snell, Charlotte/Montgomery/Durham (Rays)

Full list: BaseballAmerica.com/awards

Kayser exits TL on a high note

After 25 years as the president of the Texas League, Tom Kayser made it known at last year's Winter Meetings that 2016 would be his final season. Former Rangers executive Tim Purpura is taking over in 2017, but it's clear that Kayser will leave a lasting imprint after a quarter century in the TL.

Throughout those 25 years, the Texas League and Minor League Baseball as a whole have seen an immeasurable amount of change.

"It's like going from the horseless carriage to interstellar travel," Kayser said, before noting how the sport has gone from an afterthought to, in some cases, the centerpieces of downtown rebirths.

"We went places because they would take us in, as opposed to places that were particularly attractive," he said. " . . . Now, my lord, everything that we have, for the most part, is just smaller versions of major league operations."

Kayser won't officially vacate his post until February, but he is looking forward to both getting time to enjoy life away from baseball, and also seeing where the league and the game itself goes in the future.

He departs as Baseball America's Executive of the Year, having strengthened the Texas League even as the league has gone through significant movement, including seeing Round Rock move up to Triple-A.

CONTINUED FROM PAGE 354

to assess the situation, the Yard Goats and the city announced a plan to have Dunkin Donuts Park finished in time for Opening Day in 2017, through Arch Insurance Group. According to reporting by the Hartford Courant, an architect hired by the city from the Kansas City-based Pendulum firm found myriad problems with the unfinished ballpark, and the cost to complete it had ballooned to $71 million. But work resumed Oct. 18 to meet the Opening Day goal.

Before the season, the Rockies and the Yard Goats extended their Player Development Contract through the 2018 season. Restall says the Rockies were understanding throughout the process and have made no effort to back out of the PDC.

"They understand. They took the best approach to this. When we first found out in January, we sat down with them," Restall said. "They've been great and understanding. They're frustrated as well, but they know that it's not us and they've been great partners. I couldn't even imagine doing this without a better partner."

Hitting And Slugging

The on-field stories in the minor leagues were centered in Reading, Pa., and Lynchburg, Va., where a pair of burly sluggers marauded the record books and a catcher made a run at history.

Reading's FirstEnergy Stadium is known for cozy dimensions that make it a power hitter's dream. It's a taste of the California League on the East Coast. So it was no surprise that Phillies prospects Dylan Cozens and Rhys Hoskins, already primo power purveyors, put together a summer to remember in their first taste of Double-A.

The pair combined for 78 home runs—more than 38 full-season teams—and 241 RBIs, and broke several franchise records along the way. Cozens' 40 homers broke the Reading record of 38 set by Darin Ruf in 2012, and his 125 RBIs broke Greg Luzinski's 46-year-old mark of 120. Both totals led the minors, while Hoskins (38 homers, 116 RBIs) ranked second and third in those categories. Cozens also swiped 21 bases in 22 tries, and Phillies farm director Joe Jordan counted him as the most improved player in the organization.

"Dylan's gotten better in multiple phases of the game," Jordan said, "(including) on the bases and in the outfield, and his throwing has improved. And obviously his power production has taken a big step forward. Everybody pays attention to the power, but he's gotten better in every aspect, and

Wallace steadies Akron to title

Winning a championship at any level is never easy. Any manager will say that. But the accomplishment becomes that much more difficult when a team goes through a prolonged losing streak. The Akron RubberDucks in 2016 lost 12 consecutive Eastern League games, one of the longest losing skids in the minors, but still rebounded enough to not only make the playoffs, but to win the franchise's third EL championship since 2007 with a sweep of Trenton in the finals.

That success is due in no small part to their manager, Dave Wallace, the 2016 Minor League Manager of the Year.

In three seasons with Akron, Wallace has piloted the RubberDucks to a 223-202 mark and this year had to rally his team back from its early doldrums.

"The staff and I just continued to believe in them and the work that they were doing," Wallace said. "We knew that it would that it would pay off, and they saw that we genuinely believed in them."

MANAGER OF THE YEAR

PREVIOUS 10 WINNERS

2006: Todd Claus, Portland (Red Sox)
2007: Matt Wallbeck, Erie (Tigers)
2008: Rocket Wheeler, Myrtle Beach (Braves)
2009: Charlie Montoyo, Durham (Rays)
2010: Mike Sarbaugh, Columbus (Indians)
2011: Ryne Sandberg, Lehigh Valley (Phillies)
2012: Dave Miley, Scranton/Wilkes-Barre (Yankees)
2013: Gary DiSarcina, Pawtucket (Red Sox)
2014: Mark Johnson, Kane County (Cubs)
2015: Tony DeFrancesco, Fresno (Astros)

Full list: BaseballAmerica.com/awards

Outfielder Greg Allen, who spent the second half with Akron, praised Wallace as the type of manager players love.

"He was fun to play for. You can tell he wanted the most for his players," Allen said. "Whether it was defensively, pitching, hitting, he wanted his players to succeed and the energy that he brought was always fun to play under."

that's exciting.

In Lynchburg, Indians top prospect Francisco Mejia shot to the forefront by making a run at Joe DiMaggio. On May 27, Mejia collected two hits with low Class A Lake County. He didn't stop hitting until Aug. 13. He collected hits in 50 straight games, the fourth-longest streak in the minors and the longest in 62 years.

In between hitless games Mejia was promoted to high Class A Lynchburg, had the streak revived after an official scorer reversed a decision, played in the Futures Game in San Diego and was nearly traded to the Brewers. None of those diversions were enough to stop him.

Lawsuit Hits Roadblock

In July, Major League Baseball had a ruling go in its favor in a potential class-action lawsuit filed by former minor leaguers seeking increased wages.

U.S. Magistrate Judge Joseph Spero of the U.S. District Court in San Francisco denied class certification for the players in the suit—which is officially filed as Senne vs. the Office of the Commissioner of Baseball. The ruling meant the players could not file a class-action lawsuit.

Spero found the players' cases were different enough from one another that they couldn't be treated as a collective. MLB had filed a motion seeking to prevent class certification because, "the Plaintiffs are not similarly situated." In essence, because some players train in Arizona while others train in Florida, and each plays in different sets of states, their claims would vary too widely to be considered uniform.

Moreover, MLB used the players' recent decision to not seek pay for their time in fall instructional league or the Arizona Fall League as a cudgel to prove that the group cannot agree on their own definition of work. Therefore, their situations do not meet the standards for a collective-action suit.

The players, however, believed their claims were deserving of class-action status because "MLB and its franchises have implemented uniform contracts and policies and major league rules 'to ensure similar conditions of employment' and the legal issues 'can be distilled to a few common issues.'"

As a result of the lack of the uniformity from one situation to the next, the court denied the players' motion to join as a class-action lawsuit. It also granted MLB's motion to decertify the Fair Labor Standards Act Collective and its request to exclude the testimony from J. Michael Dennis, PhD, and Brian Kriegler, PhD, in support of the players.

TRIPLE-A

Pos	Player, Team (Org) League	Age	AVG	OBP	SLG	G	AB	R	H	2B	3B	HR	RBI	BB	SO	SB
C	Tom Murphy, Albuquerque (Rockies)	25	.327	.361	.647	80	303	53	99	26	7	19	59	16	78	1
1B	Dan Vogelbach, Iowa/Tacoma (Cubs/Mariners)	23	.292	.417	.505	133	459	79	134	25	2	23	96	97	101	0
2B	Carlos Asuaje, El Paso (Padres)	24	.321	.378	.473	134	535	98	172	32	11	9	69	49	82	10
3B	Yandy Diaz, Columbus (Indians)	24	.325	.399	.461	95	360	53	117	22	3	7	44	47	70	5
SS	Trea Turner, Syracuse (Nationals)	23	.302	.370	.471	83	331	61	100	22	8	6	33	37	72	25
OF	Brandon Nimmo, Las Vegas (Mets)	23	.352	.423	.541	97	392	72	138	25	8	11	61	46	73	7
OF	Hunter Renfroe, El Paso (Padres)	24	.306	.336	.557	133	533	95	163	34	5	30	105	22	115	5
OF	Scott Schebler, Louisville (Reds)	25	.311	.370	.564	75	289	40	90	18	8	13	43	19	59	2
DH	Mitch Haniger, Reno (Diamondbacks)	25	.341	.428	.670	74	261	58	89	20	3	20	64	39	62	8

Pos	Pitcher, Team (Organization)	Age	W	L	ERA	G	GS	SV	IP	H	HR	BB	SO	AVG	SO/9	WHIP
SP	Jose De Leon, Oklahoma City (Dodgers)	23	7	1	2.61	16	16	0	86	61	9	20	111	.194	11.6	0.94
SP	Tyler Glasnow, Indianapolis (Pirates)	22	8	3	1.87	20	20	0	111	65	4	62	133	.175	10.8	1.15
SP	Chad Green, Scranton/W-B (Yankees)	25	7	6	1.52	16	16	0	95	68	3	21	100	.200	9.5	0.94
SP	Brady Rodgers, Fresno (Astros)	25	12	4	2.86	22	22	0	132	129	7	23	116	.257	7.9	1.15
SP	Jake Thompson, Lehigh Valley (Phillies)	22	11	5	2.50	21	21	0	130	105	10	37	87	.225	6.0	1.10
RP	James Hoyt, Fresno (Astros)	29	4	3	1.64	49	0	29	55	29	2	19	93	.154	15.2	0.87

Player of the Year: Hunter Renfroe, of, El Paso (Padres). **Pitcher of the Year:** Brady Rodgers, rhp, Fresno (Astros).

DOUBLE-A

Pos	Player, Team (Organization)	Age	AVG	OBP	SLG	G	AB	R	H	2B	3B	HR	RBI	BB	SO	SB
C	Chance Sisco, Bowie (Orioles)	21	.320	.406	.422	112	410	53	131	28	1	4	44	59	83	2
1B	Rhys Hoskins, Reading (Phillies)	23	.281	.377	.566	135	498	95	140	26	1	38	116	71	125	8
2B	Ozzie Albies, Mississippi (Braves)	19	.321	.391	.467	82	330	56	106	22	7	4	33	33	57	21
3B	Matt Chapman, Midland (Athletics)	23	.244	.335	.521	117	438	78	107	26	4	29	83	59	147	7
SS	Willy Adames, Montgomery (Rays)	20	.274	.372	.430	132	486	89	133	31	6	11	57	74	121	13
OF	Cody Bellinger, Tulsa (Dodgers)	20	.263	.359	.484	114	399	61	105	17	1	23	65	59	94	8
OF	Dylan Cozens, Reading (Phillies)	22	.276	.350	.591	134	521	106	144	38	3	40	125	61	186	21
OF	Tyler O'Neill, Jackson (Mariners)	21	.293	.374	.508	130	492	68	144	26	4	24	102	62	150	12
DH	Rowdy Tellez, New Hampshire (Blue Jays)	21	.297	.387	.530	124	438	71	130	29	2	23	81	63	92	4

Pos	Pitcher, Team (Organization)	Age	W	L	ERA	G	GS	SV	IP	H	HR	BB	SO	AVG	SO/9	WHIP
SP	Chase De Jong, Tulsa (Dodgers)	22	14	5	2.86	25	25	0	142	106	15	39	125	.207	7.9	1.02
SP	Stephen Gonsalves, Chattanooga (Twins)	21	8	1	1.82	13	13	0	74	43	1	37	89	.171	10.8	1.08
SP	Chih-Wei Hu, Montgomery (Rays)	22	7	8	2.59	24	24	0	142	128	7	36	107	.241	6.8	1.15
SP	German Marquez, Hartford (Rockies)	21	9	6	2.85	21	21	0	136	124	9	33	126	.245	8.4	1.16
SP	Jordan Montgomery, Trenton (Yankees)	23	9	4	2.55	19	19	0	102	94	5	36	97	.239	8.5	1.27
RP	Alejandro Chacin, Pensacola (Reds)	23	5	2	1.78	52	0	30	60	51	2	26	75	.229	11.3	1.27

Player of the Year: Tyler O'Neill, of, Jackson (Mariners). **Pitcher of the Year:** German Marquez, rhp, Hartford (Rockies).

HIGH CLASS A

CALIFORNIA · CAROLINA · FLORIDA STATE

Pos	Player, Team (Organization)	Age	AVG	OBP	SLG	G	AB	R	H	2B	3B	HR	RBI	BB	SO	SB
C	Tomas Nido, St. Lucie (Mets)	22	.320	.357	.459	90	344	38	110	23	2	7	46	19	42	0
1B	Chris Shaw, San Jose (Giants)	22	.285	.357	.544	72	270	47	77	22	0	16	55	28	70	0
2B	Luis Urias, Lake Elsinore (Padres)	19	.330	.397	.440	120	466	71	154	26	5	5	52	40	56	7
3B	Rafael Devers, Salem (Red Sox)	19	.282	.335	.443	128	503	64	142	32	8	11	71	40	94	18
SS	Gleyber Torres, Myrtle/Tampa (Cubs/Yankees)	19	.270	.354	.421	125	478	81	129	29	5	11	66	58	110	21
OF	Aristides Aquino, Daytona (Reds)	22	.273	.327	.519	125	484	69	132	26	12	23	79	34	104	11
OF	Anthony Santander, Lynchburg (Indians)	21	.290	.368	.494	128	500	90	145	42	0	20	95	54	118	10
OF	Christin Stewart, Lakeland (Tigers)	22	.264	.403	.534	104	356	60	94	22	1	24	68	74	105	3
DH	Bobby Bradley, Lynchburg (Indians)	20	.235	.344	.466	131	485	82	114	23	1	29	102	75	170	3

Pos	Pitcher, Team (Organization)	Age	W	L	ERA	G	GS	SV	IP	H	HR	BB	SO	AVG	SO/9	WHIP
SP	Ryan Castellani, Modesto (Rockies)	20	7	8	3.81	26	26	0	168	156	8	50	142	.248	7.6	1.23
SP	Luis Castillo, Jupiter (Marlins)	23	8	4	2.07	23	21	0	118	95	2	18	91	.219	7.0	0.96
SP	Trevor Clifton, Myrtle Beach (Cubs)	21	7	7	2.72	23	23	0	119	97	4	41	129	.225	9.8	1.16
SP	Felix Jorge, Fort Myers (Twins)	22	9	3	1.55	14	14	0	93	76	3	11	77	.226	7.5	0.94
SP	Josh Sborz, Rancho Cucamonga (Dodgers)	22	8	4	2.66	20	19	0	108	82	8	30	108	.207	9.0	1.03
RP	Jimmy Herget, Daytona (Reds)	22	4	4	1.78	50	0	24	61	47	3	22	83	.208	12.3	1.14

Player of the Year: Christin Stewart, of, Lakeland (Tigers). **Pitcher of the Year:** Trevor Clifton, Myrtle Beach (Cubs).

LOW CLASS A

MIDWEST · SOUTH ATLANTIC

Pos	Player, Team (Organization)	Age	AVG	OBP	SLG	G	AB	R	H	2B	3B	HR	RBI	BB	SO	SB
C	Yermin Mercedes, Delmarva (Orioles)	23	.353	.411	.579	91	340	58	120	25	5	14	60	34	63	1
1B	Brian Mundell, Asheville (Rockies)	22	.313	.383	.503	136	537	94	168	58	1	14	83	56	83	7
2B	Eli Alvarez, Peoria (Cardinals)	21	.323	.404	.476	116	433	70	140	36	6	6	59	53	96	36
3B	Austin Riley, Rome (Braves)	19	.271	.324	.479	129	495	68	134	39	2	20	80	39	147	3
SS	Isan Diaz, Wisconsin (Brewers)	20	.264	.358	.469	135	507	71	134	34	5	20	75	72	148	11
OF	Luis Alexander Basabe, Greenville (Red Sox)	19	.258	.325	.447	105	403	61	104	24	8	12	52	40	116	25
OF	Eloy Jimenez, South Bend (Cubs)	19	.329	.369	.532	112	432	65	142	40	3	14	81	25	94	8
OF	Myles Straw, Quad Cities (Astros)	21	.374	.432	.470	68	270	40	101	14	6	0	22	29	58	17
DH	Brendan Rodgers, Asheville (Rockies)	19	.281	.342	.480	110	442	73	124	31	0	19	73	35	98	6

Pos	Pitcher, Team (Organization)	Age	W	L	ERA	G	GS	SV	IP	H	HR	BB	SO	AVG	SO/9	WHIP
SP	Brian Gonzalez, Delmarva (Orioles)	20	10	8	2.50	27	27	0	148	135	9	58	111	.247	6.8	1.31
SP	Ryan Helsley, Peoria (Cardinals)	21	10	2	1.61	17	17	0	95	77	3	19	109	.216	10.3	1.01
SP	Mitch Keller, West Virginia (Pirates)	20	8	5	2.46	23	23	0	124	96	4	18	131	.211	9.5	0.92
SP	Nick Neidert, Clinton (Mariners)	19	7	3	2.57	19	19	0	91	75	7	13	69	.225	6.8	0.97
SP	Patrick Weigel, Rome (Braves)	21	10	4	2.51	22	21	0	129	92	7	47	135	.203	9.4	1.08
RP	Nate Griep, Wisconsin (Brewers)	22	2	2	2.05	49	0	23	57	41	0	18	54	.208	8.5	1.04

Player of the Year: Eloy Jimenez, of, South Bend (Cubs). **Pitcher of the Year:** Mitch Keller, rhp, West Virginia (Pirates).

SHORT-SEASON

NEW YORK-PENN · NORTHWEST

Pos	Player, Team (Organization)	Age	AVG	OBP	SLG	G	AB	R	H	2B	3B	HR	RBI	BB	SO	SB
C	Jeremy Martinez, State College (Cardinals)	21	.325	.419	.433	57	194	28	63	14	2	1	32	32	16	1
1B	Peter Alonso, Brooklyn (Mets)	21	.321	.382	.587	30	109	20	35	12	1	5	21	11	22	0
2B	Nick Solak, Staten Island (Yankees)	21	.321	.412	.421	64	240	48	77	13	1	3	25	30	39	8
3B	Bobby Dalbec, Lowell (Red Sox)	21	.386	.427	.674	34	132	25	51	13	2	7	33	9	33	2
SS	Garrett Hampson, Boise (Rockies)	21	.301	.404	.441	68	256	43	77	14	8	2	44	47	56	36
OF	Heath Quinn, Salem-Keizer (Giants)	21	.337	.423	.571	54	205	37	69	19	1	9	34	26	50	3
OF	Bryan Reynolds, Salem-Keizer (Giants)	21	.312	.368	.500	40	154	28	48	12	1	5	30	11	41	2
OF	Stephen Wrenn, Tri-City (Astros)	21	.282	.365	.544	36	149	30	42	8	2	9	27	18	40	8
DH	Tyler Hill, Lowell (Red Sox)	20	.332	.400	.487	61	232	43	77	14	5	4	38	24	41	11

Pos	Pitcher, Team (Organization)	Age	W	L	ERA	G	GS	SV	IP	H	HR	BB	SO	AVG	SO/9	WHIP
SP	Dylan Cease, Eugene (Cubs)	20	2	0	2.22	12	12	0	44	27	1	25	66	.175	13.4	1.16
SP	Harol Gonzalez, Brooklyn (Mets)	21	7	3	2.01	14	13	0	85	69	2	17	88	.223	9.3	1.01
SP	Joey Lucchesi, Tri-City (Padres)	23	0	2	1.35	14	10	1	40	27	0	2	53	.189	11.9	0.73
SP	Triston McKenzie, Mahoning Valley (Indians)	18	4	3	0.55	9	9	0	49	31	2	16	55	.180	10.0	0.95
SP	Manuel Rondon, Eugene (Cubs)	21	6	1	1.10	12	12	0	57	50	1	22	49	.233	7.7	1.26
RP	Mark Vasquez, Spokane (Rangers)	24	4	0	2.10	17	0	0	34	28	0	13	41	.217	10.8	1.19

Player of the Year: Heath Quinn, of, Salem-Keizer (Giants). **Pitcher of the Year:** Triston McKenzie, rhp, Mahoning Valley (Indians).

ROOKIE

APPALACHIAN · ARIZONA · GULF COAST · PIONEER

Pos	Player, Team (Organization)	Age	AVG	OBP	SLG	G	AB	R	H	2B	3B	HR	RBI	BB	SO	SB
C	Meibrys Viloria, Idaho Falls (Royals)	19	.378	.437	.613	57	222	53	84	28	3	6	55	20	34	1
1B	Ronnie Gideon, Helena (Brewers)	21	.323	.373	.632	58	220	41	71	20	0	16	40	15	67	1
2B	Miguelangel Sierra, Greeneville (Astros)	18	.289	.386	.620	31	121	23	35	3	2	11	19	12	40	6
3B	Vladimir Guerrero Jr., Bluefield (Blue Jays)	17	.271	.359	.449	62	236	32	64	12	3	8	46	33	35	15
SS	Allen Cordoba, Johnson City (Cardinals)	20	.362	.427	.495	50	196	49	71	16	5	0	18	21	19	22
OF	Alex Kirilloff, Elizabethton (Twins)	18	.306	.341	.454	55	216	33	66	9	1	7	33	11	32	0
OF	Khalil Lee, Arizona League (Royals)	18	.269	.396	.484	49	182	43	49	9	6	6	29	33	57	8
OF	Juan Soto, Gulf Coast League (Nationals)	17	.361	.410	.550	45	169	25	61	11	3	5	31	14	25	5
DH	D.J. Peters, Ogden (Dodgers)	20	.351	.437	.615	66	262	63	92	24	3	13	48	35	66	5

Pos	Pitcher, Team (Organization)	Age	W	L	ERA	G	GS	SV	IP	H	HR	BB	SO	AVG	SO/9	WHIP
SP	Lupe Chavez, GCL, G'ville (Blue Jays/Astros)	18	4	1	1.42	9	7	0	38	32	1	5	31	.234	7.3	0.97
SP	Garrett Davila, Burlington (Royals)	19	7	0	2.77	12	12	0	65	56	2	27	55	.237	7.6	1.28
SP	Alec Hansen, AZL/Great Falls (White Sox)	21	2	0	1.23	7	7	0	37	12	3	12	59	.102	14.5	0.65
SP	Sixto Sanchez, Gulf Coast League (Phillies)	17	5	0	0.50	11	11	0	54	33	0	8	44	.181	7.3	0.76
SP	Thomas Szapucki, Kingsport (Mets)	20	2	1	0.62	5	5	0	29	16	2	9	47	.157	14.6	0.86
RP	Matt Foster, AZL/Great Falls (White Sox)	21	0	0	0.61	22	0	11	30	12	0	7	41	.121	12.4	0.64

Player of the Year: Meibrys Viloria, c, Idaho Falls (Royals). **Pitcher of the Year:** Sixto Sanchez, rhp, Gulf Coast League (Phillies).

MINOR LEAGUES

Eloy Jimenez won Midwest League
MVP honors during a stellar season

Stephen Gonsalves allowed just 86 hits
over 140 innings at two levels

PAUL GIERHART; MIKE JANES

FIRST TEAM

Pos	Player, Organization (Level)	Age	AVG	OBP	SLG	G	AB	R	H	2B	3B	HR	RBI	BB	SO	SB
C	Francisco Mejia, Indians (LoA • HiA)	20	.342	.382	.514	102	407	63	139	29	4	11	80	28	63	2
1B	Rhys Hoskins, Phillies (AA)	23	.281	.377	.566	135	498	95	140	26	1	38	116	71	125	8
2B	Yoan Moncada, Red Sox (HiA • AA)	21	.294	.407	.511	106	405	94	119	31	6	15	62	72	124	45
3B	Ryon Healy, Athletics (AAA • AA)	24	.326	.382	.558	85	337	60	110	28	4	14	64	31	75	1
SS	Alex Bregman, Astros (AA • AAA)	22	.306	.406	.580	80	314	71	96	22	2	20	61	47	38	7
CF	David Dahl, Rockies (AA • AAA)	22	.314	.394	.569	92	350	70	110	27	4	18	61	45	96	17
OF	Eloy Jimenez, Cubs (LoA)	19	.329	.369	.532	112	432	65	142	40	3	14	81	25	94	8
OF	Tyler O'Neill, Mariners (AA)	21	.293	.374	.508	130	492	68	144	26	4	24	102	62	150	12
DH	Dylan Cozens, Phillies (AA)	22	.276	.350	.591	134	521	106	144	38	3	40	125	61	186	21

Pos	Pitcher, Organization (Level)	Age	W	L	ERA	G	GS	SV	IP	H	HR	BB	SO	AVG	SO/9	WHIP
SP	Chance Adams, Yankees (AA • HiA)	22	13	1	2.33	25	24	0	127	76	9	39	144	.169	10.2	0.90
SP	Stephen Gonsalves, Twins (AA • HiA)	22	13	5	2.06	24	24	0	140	86	3	57	155	.179	10.0	1.02
SP	Mitch Keller, Pirates (LoA • HiA)	20	9	5	2.35	24	24	0	130	101	4	19	138	.212	9.5	0.92
SP	Brock Stewart, Dodgers (AA • AAA • HiA)	24	9	4	1.79	21	21	0	121	87	4	19	120	.200	9.6	0.88
SP	Brandon Woodruff, Brewers (AA • HiA)	23	14	9	2.68	28	28	0	158	121	6	40	173	.209	9.9	1.02
RP	Joe Jimenez, Tigers (AA • HiA • AAA)	21	3	3	1.51	55	0	30	54	26	1	17	78	.144	13.1	0.80

SECOND TEAM

Pos	Player, Organization (Level)	Age	AVG	OBP	SLG	G	AB	R	H	2B	3B	HR	RBI	BB	SO	SB
C	Chance Sisco, Orioles (AA • AAA)	21	.317	.403	.430	116	426	57	135	28	1	6	51	63	88	2
1B	Rowdy Tellez, Blue Jays (AA)	21	.297	.387	.530	124	438	71	130	29	2	23	81	63	92	4
2B	Ozzie Albies, Braves (AA • AAA)	19	.292	.358	.420	138	552	83	161	33	10	6	53	52	96	30
3B	Hunter Dozier, Royals (AAA • AA)	25	.296	.366	.533	129	486	79	144	44	1	23	75	54	123	7
SS	Trea Turner, Nationals (AAA)	23	.302	.370	.471	83	331	61	100	22	8	6	33	37	72	25
CF	Andrew Benintendi, Red Sox (AA • HiA)	22	.312	.378	.532	97	372	70	116	31	12	9	76	39	39	16
OF	Brandon Nimmo, Mets (AAA)	23	.352	.423	.541	97	392	72	138	25	8	11	61	46	73	7
OF	Christin Stewart, Tigers (HiA • AA)	22	.255	.386	.517	128	443	77	113	24	1	30	87	86	131	3
DH	Mitch Haniger, Diamondbacks (AAA • AA)	25	.321	.419	.581	129	458	79	147	34	5	25	94	69	99	12

Pos	Pitcher, Organization (Level)	Age	W	L	ERA	G	GS	SV	IP	H	HR	BB	SO	AVG	SO/9	WHIP
SP	Luis Castillo, Marlins (HiA • AA)	23	8	6	2.26	26	24	0	132	107	3	25	103	.219	7.0	1.00
SP	Josh Hader, Brewers (AAA • AA)	22	3	8	3.29	25	25	0	126	101	6	55	161	.223	11.5	1.24
SP	German Marquez, Rockies (AA • AAA)	21	11	6	3.13	26	26	0	167	154	14	39	155	.247	8.4	1.16
SP	Yohander Mendez, Rangers (AA • HiA • AAA)	21	12	3	2.19	24	21	0	111	72	4	41	113	.184	9.2	1.02
SP	Sean Reid-Foley, Blue Jays (HiA • LoA)	21	10	5	2.81	21	21	0	115	78	4	38	130	.190	10.1	1.01
RP	James Hoyt, Astros (AAA)	29	4	3	1.64	49	0	29	55	29	2	19	93	.154	15.2	0.87

Young Rome was built in a half

W hen everyone looks back at the 2016 Rome Braves years from now, they may be remembered as one of the better minor league teams of the early 21st century. The rotation featured prospects in all six spots; that's because it had too many prospects to settle for a five-man rotation. With third baseman Austin Riley and outfielder Ronald Acuna, the team had position prospects as well, and the bullpen had a number of hard-throwring relief aces.

But midway through the 2016 season, those Rome Braves stunk.

When the baby Braves went their separate ways for the all-star break in late June, Rome was 27-42, having lost five of its last six. The Braves were closer to the bottom of the South Atlantic League than the top.

Acuna was hurt. Riley hadn't hit. And the pitching staff had not been nearly as reliable as expected.

What is apparent now is that those were growing pains. Rome had the youngest team in full-season ball in 2016, with a roster that averaged a year younger than the SAL average. In fact, Rome was the youngest team in the South Atlantic League in more than a decade. And after learning how to survive in the first half, they figured out how to dominate in the second half.

Lefthander Kolby Allard struggled in his first three starts in Rome, but after a short demotion he returned to show the dominant form the Braves expected when they drafted him in the first round in 2015. Once he found his form, he was one of four first-round picks in the Rome rotation.

In addition to Allard, Rome relied on right-hander Touki Toussaint (Diamondbacks' first-round pick in 2014), lefthander Max Fried (Padres' first-round pick in 2012) and right-hander Mike Soroka (Braves' first-round pick in 2015). But the best starter Rome had was a seventh-round steal.

Righthander Patrick Weigel had struggled during his college career, rarely finding the strike zone enough to be given much responsibility. But once the Braves signed him and

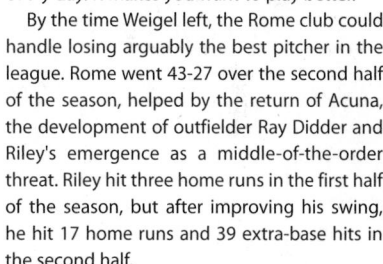

TEAM OF THE YEAR

developed him as a starter, Weigel proved he had four-pitches, including a mid- to high-90s fastball that was hard for low Class A hitters to hit.

Weigel went 10-4, 2.51 in 22 appearances with Rome. He earned a late-season promotion to Double-A Mississippi, leaving behind a group of teenage pitchers who had grown into the role.

MIKE JULA

Patrick Weigel

"Every day in the stands (when charting) it's a treat to watch. Whether it's Touki (Toussaint), Fried, Allard," Weigel said. "It's the best pitching staff I've seen. Every guy is good. You come away shaking your head. It creates a higher standard. You know those dudes are right behind you. It drives all of us to get better every day. It makes you want to play better."

By the time Weigel left, the Rome club could handle losing arguably the best pitcher in the league. Rome went 43-27 over the second half of the season, helped by the return of Acuna, the development of outfielder Ray Didder and Riley's emergence as a middle-of-the-order threat. Riley hit three home runs in the first half of the season, but after improving his swing, he hit 17 home runs and 39 extra-base hits in the second half.

Allard didn't allow a run in two playoff starts and Fried struck out 24 in 15 innings to win two playoff starts himself. Rome knocked off Charleston and Lakewood to win its first title since 2003.

PREVIOUS 10 WINNERS

2006: Tucson/Pacific Coast (Diamondbacks)
2007: San Antonio/Texas (Padres)
2008: Frisco/Texas (Rangers)
2009: Akron/Eastern (Indians)
2010: Northwest Arkansas/Texas (Royals)
2011: Mobile BayBears/Southern (Diamondbacks)
2012: Springfield Cardinals/Texas (Cardinals)
2013: Daytona Cubs/Florida State (Cubs)
2014: Portland Sea Dogs/Eastern League (Red Sox)
2015: Biloxi Shuckers/Southern League (Brewers)

Full list: BaseballAmerica.com/awards

MINOR LEAGUES

BY J.J. COOPER

SAN DIEGO

Yoan Moncada very rarely disappears into the background.

He has power. He has speed. He has a $31.5 million contract (which came with a $31.5 million, 100-percent overage tax penalty for the Red Sox). And he has a swagger to his game that the top prospects often have, though in pregame batting practice, while other World and U.S. hitters hit moonshots, Moncada worked on his lefthanded and righthanded swings. He hit no long drives, did nothing that drew any attention.

Once the game began, the game's best prospect grabbed the spotlight once again. After Astros shortstop Alex Bregman stole the show in the early innings with a triple, double and single, Moncada got the World team's first hit in the fourth inning. After his opposite-field single, he stole second and advanced to third on a throwing error before being stranded.

Four innings later, Moncada pulled a 405-foot, two-run home run to the second deck in left field. "I wasn't looking for anything in particular," he said. "I was just looking for contact and the contact happened to be a home run."

Moncada was named the MVP after going 2-for-5 with a run scored, two RBIs and a stolen base. Moncada's homer gave the World team a one-run lead it expanded into a 11-3 win to snap a six-game U.S. Futures Game win streak.

"I didn't know it had been that long, but it's pretty cool," said Marlins first baseman and Canadian representative Josh Naylor, who had just turned 12 the last time the World team won.

Cubs outfielder Eloy Jimenez was a star of both batting practice and the game. He showed massive raw power during a BP show that included balls that reached the second deck. Jimenez didn't enter the game until the fifth, but he then doubled and later made a dramatic diving catch down the right-field line where he threw his body into the fence to snag a foul ball.

Jimenez put the game away in the ninth inning with a massive three-run home run that reached the third deck in left field.

Moncada's home run swiped the game's MVP award from Bregman, and then Jimenez nearly stole it from Moncada with his massive home run, on the heels of a catch that will be replayed on Futures Game broadcasts for years to come.

There was plenty of defense, too, led by

Padres center fielder Manuel Margot's leaping catch to steal a home run from Cardinals catcher Carson Kelly.

FUTURES GAME BOX SCORE

WORLD 11, U.S. 3
JULY 10 IN SAN DIEGO

World	AB	R	H	RBI	U.S.	AB	R	H	RBI
Margot, CF	4	2	1	1	Benintendi, CF	3	0	0	0
Tapia, R, LF	5	2	1	2	Dahl, CF	2	0	0	0
Moncada, 2B	5	1	2	2	Bregman, 3B-SS	5	1	3	0
O'Neill, RF	2	0	0	0	Frazier, LF	3	1	2	1
Jimenez, RF	3	2	2	4	Stewart, LF	1	0	0	0
Guzman, R, 1B	1	0	0	0	Renfroe, RF	2	0	0	0
Naylor, J, 1B	3	0	2	1	Cozens, RF	1	0	0	0
Diaz, Y, 3B	2	0	1	0	Healy, R, DH	3	0	2	0
Asuaje, 3B	2	1	2	0	Smith, D, 1B	4	0	0	1
Sanchez, G, C	2	0	0	0	Swanson, SS	3	0	0	0
Mejia, F, C	3	1	1	0	Dozier, 3B	1	0	0	0
Bonifacio, J, DH	0	0	0	0	Demeritte, 2B	1	0	0	0
a-Herrera, D, PH-DH	2	1	1	1	Calhoun, 2B	2	0	0	0
Adames, SS	2	0	0	0	Sisco, C	2	1	1	1
Rosario, SS	2	1	1	0	Kelly, C, C	2	0	0	0
Totals	**38**	**11**	**14**	**11**	**Totals**	**35**	**3**	**8**	**3**

a-Struck out for Bonifacio, J in the 7th.

WORLD	000	002	027	11	14	1
UNITED STATES	002	100	000	3	8	2

World: 2B: Jimenez (1, Smith, N); Tapia, R (1, Stanek). **HR:** Moncada (1, 8th inning off Banda, 1 on, 1 out); Jimenez (1, 9th inning off Stanek, 2 on, 1 out). **RBI:** Jimenez 4 (4); Naylor, J (1); Moncada 2 (2); Herrera, D (1); Margot (1); Tapia, R 2 (2). **GIDP:** Diaz, Y; Adames; Mejia, F. **Team RISP:** 6-for-10. **Team LOB:** 5. **SB:** Moncada (1, 2nd base off Hoffman/Sisco). **E:** Moncada (1).

U.S.: 2B: Healy, R (1, Reyes, Al); Bregman (1, Perdomo, A); Frazier (1, Perdomo, A). **3B:** Bregman (1, Reyes, Al). **HR:** Sisco (1, 4th inning off Rios, 0 on, 1 out). **RBI:** Frazier (1); Smith, D (1); Sisco (1). **Team RISP:** 1-for-10. **Team LOB:** 8. **SB:** Frazier (1, 2nd base off Rios/Sanchez, G); Dozier (1, 2nd base off Neverauskas/Mejia, F). **E:** Sisco (1); Bregman (1). **Outfield assists:** Dahl (Naylor, J at home). **DP:** 3 (Demeritte-Smith, D; Bregman-Demeritte-Smith, D; Bregman-Smith, D).

World	IP	H	R	ER	BB	SO	U.S.	IP	H	R	ER	BB	SO
Reyes, Al	1.2	2	0	0	1	4	Musgrove	1	0	0	0	0	0
Jimenez	0.1	0	0	0	0	0	Garrett	2	0	0	0	2	0
Perdomo, A	0.2	2	2	2	2	0	Hoffman	1	1	0	0	0	1
Rios	1.1	3	1	1	0	0	Bickford	1	1	0	0	1	2
Hu	1	0	0	0	0	2	Smith, N	1	4	2	2	0	1
Pinto, R	0.2	0	0	0	0	0	Fulmer	1	0	0	0	0	2
Lopez, R	1	0	0	0	0	0	Banda (L)	0.2	1	2	1	0	0
Cotton (W)	0.1	0	0	0	0	0	Hader	0.1	0	0	0	1	0
Neverauskas	1	1	0	0	0	0	Chargois	0	2	3	3	1	0
Mejia	1	0	0	0	0	1	Stanek	1	5	4	4	1	1
Totals	**9**	**8**	**3**	**3**	**3**	**7**	**Totals**	**9**	**14**	**11**	**10**	**5**	**8**

Chargois pitched to 3 batters in the 9th.

Pitches-strikes: Reyes, Al 38-23; Jimenez 3-2; Perdomo, A 23-10; Rios 25-16; Hu 8-7; Pinto, R 7-2; Lopez, R 11-7; Cotton, J 3-1; Neverauskas 16-11; Mejia 12-9; Musgrove 11-8; Garrett 31-19; Hoffman 12-9; Bickford 20-12; Smith, N 15-10; Fulmer 11-9; Banda 17-9; Hader 5-3; Chargois 14-7; Stanek 31-22.
Inherited runners-scored: Jimenez 2-0; Rios 2-0; Stanek 2-2. **Weather:** 75 degrees, sunny. **Wind:** 9 mph, L to R. **First pitch:** 4:09 p.m.

TRIPLE-A: The lack of high-level bats was evident in the game, as the teams combined for just 11 hits in the International League's 4-2 win.

Travis Taijeron of Las Vegas (Mets) blasted a two-run homer to right-center in the second for both of the PCL's runs on the night, earning him the PCL Top Star Award. Chris Marrero homered to center in the eighth, clearing the shrubbery that's about 20 feet above the playing surface. The blast earned Marrero the IL Top Star Award.

EASTERN LEAGUE: Jorge Alfaro, Rhys Hoskins, Dylan Cozens and Jesmuel Valentin of Reading (Phillies) combined to go 7-for-13 with a home run and two doubles, scoring six runs and driving in three in the Eastern Division's 10-2 win. Binghamton's Matt Oberste (Mets) had four hits and four RBIs and was the game's MVP.

Bobby Bradley

SOUTHERN LEAGUE: Phillip Ervin (Reds) hit a towering grand slam to left center field as the South shut down the North at Trustman Park, home of the Shuckers, the Brewers' Double-A affiliate, to give the South a 5-1 win. Dansby Swanson (Braves) had two hits for the South. Willy Adames (Rays) and Kean Wong (Rays) had two hits for the North.

TEXAS LEAGUE: Headed for Triple-A Fresno, Alex Bregman's final act in Double-A was to play in the Texas League all-star game. He went out in style, blasting a two-run homer in the South's 8-5 win over the North. Ryan Cordell (Rangers) also homered and drove in four runs for the winners.

Frisco's Cordell was MVP after going 3-for-5. Springfield (Cardinals) second baseman Bruce Caldwell hit a three-run home run.

FLORIDA STATE LEAGUE: Dustin Houle's (Brewers) single scored Christin Stewart (Tigers), who had doubled earlier in the inning. That was the game's only run, and the bullpen combination of Adam Ravenelle (Tigers), Elniery Garcia (Phillies), Tim Mayza (Blue Jays), Adonys Cardona (Blue Jays), Alexis Rivero (Phillies), Jimmy Herget (Reds) and Jacob Ehret (Reds) made the lead stand up. Stewart was the MVP for driving in

the game's lone run. Jorge Mateo (Yankees) started the game at second base and had a hit in two trips and stole a base … Outfielder Carlos Tocci (Phillies) was the lone player with multiple hits.

CAROLINA/CALIFORNIA: Bobby Bradley hit a towering home run and fellow Indians farmhand Greg Allen scored three runs and stole two bases in the Carolina League's 6-4 win. Nationals prospect Andrew Stevenson hit two RBI triples, demonstrating the ability to drive the ball to both gaps and impressive speed flying around the bases. He finished 3-for-5 with two runs and two RBIs was named MVP.

MIDWEST LEAGUE: The East rallied from down 8-1 to beat the West 11-10, keyed by Eloy Jimenez's three-run, game-tying homer in the ninth. Jimenez drove in four runs and made a terrific catch against the left field wall in foul ground to start the ninth inning. Angel Perdomo (Blue Jays) relieved Lansing teammate Jon Harris and struck out catcher Mitch Ghelfi (Brewers).

SOUTH ATLANTIC LEAGUE: Max Schrock (Nationals) had two RBI hits to lead the North Division to a 2-1 win in a game that saw a combined 22 strikeouts. Schrock, the 2015 13th-round pick, drove in the first run with with a double to right and the second with a single to left in the fifth. Victor Robles (Nationals) had a single, a stolen base and scored on Schrock's double.

NORTHWEST/PIONEER: The Northwest League won a slugfest that saw both teams combine for 26 hits, pounding the Pioneer League, 11-5. Xavier Turner of Spokane (Rangers) went 3-for-3 with a homer and a pair of runs scored to lead the Northwest League. The former Vanderbilt third baseman was a 19th-round pick in 2015.

NEW YORK-PENN: The South Division scored a 9-5 win over the North Division. Erlin Cerda (Indians) was named the MVP of the game; he hit a go-ahead three-run home run. Williamsport's Adonis Medina (Phillies) allowed a single and then a ground rule double before proceeding to strike out the next three batters.

2016 OVERALL MINOR LEAGUE DEPARTMENT LEADERS

TEAM

WINS
Scranton/WB (International)................................91
Reading (Eastern)...89
Salem (Carolina)...87
Trenton (Eastern)..87
Clinton (Midwest)..86

LONGEST WINNING STREAK*
Akron (Eastern)...11
Columbus (International)..................................11
Corpus Christi (Texas)......................................11
High Desert (California)....................................11
Reading (Eastern)..11
Visalia (California)..11

LOSSES
Brevard County (Florida State)..........................97
Dayton (Midwest)..93
Inland Empire (California).................................92
Birmingham (Southern)....................................91
Carolina (Carolina)..87
Lexington (South Atlantic).................................87

LONGEST LOSING STREAK*
Greensboro (South Atlantic)...............................14

Richmond (Eastern)..14
Albuquerque (Pacific Coast).............................13
Brevard County (Florida State)..........................13
Akron (Eastern)..12
Birmingham (Southern)....................................12
Dayton (Midwest)..12
Wilmington (Carolina)......................................12

BATTING AVERAGE*
El Paso (Pacific Coast)....................................295
Las Vegas (Pacific Coast)................................291
Reno (Pacific Coast).......................................280
High Desert (California)...................................278
Iowa (Pacific Coast).......................................277

RUNS
Lancaster (California)......................................856
Las Vegas (Pacific Coast)................................821
High Desert (California)...................................812
Reading (Eastern)..790
El Paso (Pacific Coast)....................................786

HOME RUNS
Reading (Eastern)...185
High Desert (California)....................................177

El Paso (Pacific Coast)....................................156
Rancho Cucamonga (California)........................152
Nashville (Pacific Coast).................................148

STOLEN BASES
Salem (Carolina)..241
Hickory (South Atlantic)..................................216
Lancaster (California)......................................209
Modesto (California).......................................208
Dunedin (Florida State)...................................181

EARNED RUN AVERAGE*
Scranton/WB (International).............................2.98
Charleston (South Atlantic).............................3.03
Kane County (Midwest)..................................3.06
Tampa (Florida State).....................................3.08
Mississippi (Southern)....................................3.10

STRIKEOUTS
Wisconsin (Midwest)....................................1294
Durham (International)...................................1287
Bakersfield (California)..................................1267
Lakewood (South Atlantic).............................1267
Charleston (South Atlantic)............................1248

INDIVIDUAL BATTING

BATTING AVERAGE
Myles Straw (Quad Cities, Lancaster) 358
T.J. Rivera (Las Vegas).....................................353
Brandon Nimmo (Las Vegas)............................352
Luis Arraez (Cedar Rapids)...............................347
Yermin Mercedes (Delmarva, Frederick)............345

RUNS
Greg Allen (Lynchburg, Akron).........................119
Dylan Cozens (Reading)..................................106
Mauricio Dubon (Salem, Portland)....................101
Carlos Asuaje (El Paso).....................................98
Manuel Margot (El Paso)...................................98

HITS
Max Schrock (Hagerstown, Potomac, Stockton, Midland).177
Will Maddox (West Michigan)...........................173
Raimel Tapia (Hartford, Albuquerque)...............173
Carlos Asuaje (El Paso)...................................172
Brian Mundell (Asheville).................................168

TOP HITTING STREAKS
Alex Dickerson (El Paso)....................................29
Yandy Diaz (Columbus)....................................28
Francisco Mejia (Lynchburg)..............................26
J.T. Riddle (Jacksonville)...................................25
Mike Tauchman (Albuquerque)..........................25

MOST HITS (ONE GAME)
Danny Mars (Salem)...6
116 players..5

TOTAL BASES
Dylan Cozens (Reading)...................................308
Hunter Renfroe (El Paso)..................................297
Rhys Hoskins (Reading)...................................282
Kyle Jensen (Reno)..272
Brian Mundell (Asheville).................................271

EXTRA-BASE HITS
Dylan Cozens (Reading).....................................81
Brian Mundell (Asheville)..................................74
Hunter Renfroe (El Paso)...................................69
Matt Chapman (Midland, Nashville)....................68
Hunter Dozier (NW Arkansas, Omaha)................68

DOUBLES
Brian Mundell (Asheville)..................................59
Connor Marabell (Lake County, Lynchburg)..........45
Jose Marmolejos (Potomac, Harrisburg)..............45
Hunter Dozier (NW Arkansas, Omaha)................44
Kyle Garlick (Rancho Cucamonga, Tulsa)............42
Anthony Santander (Lynchburg).........................42
Travis Taijeron (Las Vegas)...............................42

TRIPLES
Franchy Cordero (Lake Elsinore, San Antonio, El Paso) 16
Dustin Fowler (Trenton)....................................15
Donnie Dewees (South Bend, Myrtle Beach).........14
Amed Rosario (St. Lucie, Binghamton).................13
Aneury Tavarez (Pawtucket, Portland).................13

HOME RUNS
Dylan Cozens (Reading)....................................40
Rhys Hoskins (Reading)....................................38
Matt Chapman (Midland, Nashville)....................36
Daniel Palka (Chattanooga, Rochester)...............34
Jesus Aguilar (Columbus)..................................30
Kyle Jensen (Reno)..30
Hunter Renfroe (El Paso)...................................30
Christin Stewart (Lakeland, Erie).........................30
David Washington (Springfield, Memphis)............30

RUNS BATTED IN
Dylan Cozens (Reading)...................................125
Kyle Jensen (Reno)..120
Rhys Hoskins (Reading)...................................116
Dean Green (Erie, Toledo).................................108
Hunter Renfroe (El Paso)..................................105

MOST RBIS (ONE GAME)
Bobby Boyd (Lancaster)......................................9
Adrian Rondon (Princeton)...................................9
Austin Hedges (El Paso)......................................8
Tyler O'Neill (Jackson)..8
Preston Tucker (Fresno).......................................8

WALKS
Daniel Vogelbach (Iowa, Tacoma).......................97
John Andreoli (Iowa)..94
Casey Grayson (Palm Beach)..............................94
Max Moroff (Indianapolis)...................................90
Josh Ockimey (Greenville)..................................88

INTENTIONAL WALKS
Josh Bell (Indianapolis).......................................8
Bobby Bradley (Lynchburg)..................................8
Derek Fisher (Corpus Christi, Fresno).....................7
Daniel Vogelbach (Iowa, Tacoma).........................7
Matt Chapman (Midland, Nashville).......................6
Alex Dickerson (El Paso)......................................6
Hernan Iribarren (Louisville).................................6
Jesse Winker (AZL Reds, Louisville).......................6

STRIKEOUTS
Adam Walker (Rochester)..................................202
Dylan Cozens (Reading)...................................186
Daniel Palka (Chattanooga, Rochester)...............186
Nellie Rodriguez (Akron)..................................186
Braxton Davidson (Carolina).............................184

STOLEN BASES
Rafael Bautista (Harrisburg)...............................56
Zach Granite (Chattanooga)...............................56
Eric Jenkins (Hickory, High Desert).....................51
Ian Miller (Jackson)...49
Greg Allen (Lynchburg, Akron)...........................45
Adam Engel (W-S, Birmingham, Charlotte)...........45
Yoan Moncada (Salem, Portland).......................45

CAUGHT STEALING
Frandy De La Rosa (Hickory)..............................23
Oscar Mercado (Palm Beach).............................20
Franklin Barreto (Midland, Nashville)..................17

D.J. Burt (Lexington)..17
Tito Polo (West Virginia, Bradenton, Tampa).........17
Magneuris Sierra (Peoria)..................................17
Raimel Tapia (Hartford, Albuquerque).................17

ON-BASE PERCENTAGE*
Ramon Laureano (Lancaster, Corpus Christi) 428
Brandon Nimmo (Las Vegas)...........................423
Myles Straw (Quad Cities, Lancaster).................423
Wynston Sawyer (Frederick, Bowie)...................422
Mitch Haniger (Mobile, Reno)...........................419

SLUGGING PERCENTAGE*
Rob Segedin (Oklahoma City) 598
Dylan Cozens (Reading)....................................591
Mitch Haniger (Mobile, Reno)............................581
Yermin Mercedes (Delmarva, Frederick)..............570
David Dahl (Hartford, Albuquerque)....................569

ON-BASE PLUS SLUGGING (OPS)*
Mitch Haniger (Mobile, Reno)............................999
Rob Segedin (Oklahoma City)............................989
Yermin Mercedes (Delmarva, Frederick)..............974
Xavier Scruggs (New Orleans)............................973
Brandon Nimmo (Las Vegas).............................964

HIT BY PITCH
Ray-Patrick Didder (Rome)..................................39
Victor Robles (Hagerstown, GCL Nationals, Potomac).34
Ty France (Fort Wayne, Lake Elsinore)..................28
Greg Allen (Lynchburg, Akron)...........................27
Tim Locastro (Rancho Cucamonga, Tulsa)............25
Nick Sinay (Vancouver, Bluefield)........................25

SACRIFICE BUNTS
Max George (Asheville).....................................20
Terrance Gore (NW Arkansas).............................19
Carlos Herrera (Asheville)..................................19
Johan Camargo (Mississippi)..............................17
Jonathan Diaz (Scranton/WB).............................16
Anfernee Seymour (Greensboro, Rome)...............16

SACRIFICE FLIES
Tyler O'Neill (Jackson).......................................12
Will Allen (West Michigan).................................11
Skye Bolt (Beloit)..11
Guillermo Heredia (Jackson, Tacoma)..................11
Gerson Montilla (Winston-Salem)........................11

GROUNDED INTO DOUBLE PLAY
Dawel Lugo (Visalia, Mobile)..............................22
Efren Navarro (Tacoma, Memphis).......................22
Henry Urrutia (Norfolk, Bowie)...........................22
Willy Garcia (Indianapolis).................................21
Diego Goris (San Antonio, El Paso).....................21
Casey Kotchman (Buffalo)..................................21
Jesus Montero (Buffalo)....................................21
Angel Ortega (Brevard County, Biloxi)..................21
Leobaldo Pina (Peoria)......................................21
Garabez Rosa (Norfolk, Bowie)...........................21
Neftali Soto (Harrisburg, Syracuse).....................21
Garrett Weber (Frisco, Jup., NO, Jax.)..................21

BATTING AVERAGE* BY POSITION

CATCHERS

Yermin Mercedes (Delmarva, Frederick) .345
Francisco Mejia (Lake County, Lynchburg) .342
Austin Allen (Fort Wayne, San Antonio) .319
Chance Sisco (Bowie, Norfolk) .317
Garrett Stubbs (Lancaster, Corpus Christi) .304

FIRST BASEMEN

Brian Mundell (Asheville) .313
Aderlin Rodriguez (Frederick) .304
Mitch Ghelfi (Wisconsin, Brevard County) .303
Dominic Smith (Binghamton) .302
Juremi Profar (High Desert) .300

SECOND BASEMEN

Luis Arraez (Cedar Rapids) .347
Luis Urias (El Paso, Lake Elsinore) .333
Max Schrock (Hag., Pot., Stockton, Midland) .331
Eliezer Alvarez (Peoria) .323
Carlos Asuaje (El Paso) .321

THIRD BASEMEN

T.J. Rivera (Las Vegas) .353
Miguel Gomez (Augusta, San Jose) .330
Rob Segedin (Oklahoma City) .319
Donovan Solano (Scranton/WB) .319
Yandy Diaz (Akron, Columbus) .318

SHORTSTOPS

Gavin Cecchini (Las Vegas) .325
Amed Rosario (St. Lucie, Binghamton) .324
Mauricio Dubon (Salem, Portland) .323
Phillip Evans (St. Lucie, Binghamton) .321
Kevin Newman (Bradenton, Altoona) .320

OUTFIELDERS

Myles Straw (Quad Cities, Lancaster) .358
Brandon Nimmo (Las Vegas) .352
Aneury Tavarez (Pawtucket, Portland) .330
Eloy Jimenez (South Bend) .329
Raimel Tapia (Hartford, Albuquerque) .328

DESIGNATED HITTERS

Will Maddox (West Michigan) .339
Jesus Montero (Buffalo) .317
Chris Chinea (Peoria) .312
Ian Sagdal (Hagerstown) .303
Dean Green (Erie, Toledo) .296

INDIVIDUAL PITCHING

EARNED RUN AVERAGE*

P.J. Conlon (Columbia, St. Lucie) 1.65
Dietrich Enns (Trenton, Scranton/WB) 1.73
Brock Stewart (Rancho Cuc., OKC, Tulsa) 1.79
Brannon Easterling (Kannapolis) 1.86
Tyler Glasnow (Altoona, Indianapolis) 1.93

WORST ERA*

Chris Jones (Salt Lake) 6.46
Jake Jewell (Inland Empire) 6.31
Daniel McCutchen (El Paso, San Antonio) 6.23
Zach Lee (Oklahoma City, Tacoma) 6.14
Drew Rucinski (Iowa) 5.92

WINS

Ben Lively (Reading, Lehigh Valley) 18
Chase De Jong (Tulsa, Oklahoma City) 15
Shawn Morimando (Akron, Columbus) 15
Tejay Antone (Daytona, Louisville) 14
Ty Blach (Sacramento) 14
Logan Boyd (Greenville) 14
Dietrich Enns (Trenton, Scranton/WB) 14
Tyler Mahle (Daytona, Pensacola) 14
Jordan Montgomery (Trenton, Scranton/WB) 14
Trevor Oaks (Rancho Cucamonga, Tulsa, Oklahoma City) 14
Dillon Peters (Jupiter, Jacksonville) 14
Joe Wieland (Tacoma) 14
Brandon Woodruff (Brevard County, Biloxi) 14

LOSSES

Ashton Goudeau (Wilmington, NW Arkansas) 17
Scott Diamond (Buffalo) 15
Jake Jewell (Inland Empire) 15
Zach Lovvorn (Wilmington) 15
Drew Rucinski (Iowa) 15

GAMES

Pedro Beato (Norfolk) 65
Preston Guilmet (Toledo) 65
Reyes Moronta (San Jose) 60
Tyler Rogers (Richmond, Sacramento) 59
Stephen Peterson (Biloxi, Colorado Springs) 58

GAMES STARTED

Anthony Misiewicz (Bakersfield) 29
25 tied 28

COMPLETE GAMES

Tyler Mapes (Harrisburg) 4
Matt Pearce (Palm Beach, Springfield, Memphis) 4
Tanner Banks (Kannapolis, Winston-Salem) 3
Ty Blach (Sacramento) 3
Keith Couch (Pawtucket, Portland) 3
Mitch Horacek (Frederick) 3
Felix Jorge (Fort Myers, Chattanooga) 3
Ricky Knapp (St. Lucie, Binghamton, Las Vegas) 3
Kevin McAvoy (Portland) 3
Chris Pike (Charlotte) 3
Tyler Pill (Binghamton, Las Vegas) 3
Anthony Vasquez (Reading, Lehigh Valley) 3
Thad Weber (Toledo, Erie) 3

SHUTOUTS

Ty Blach (Sacramento) 2
Jharel Cotton (Oklahoma City, Nashville) 2
Logan Darnell (Rochester) 2
Justin Haley (Portland, Pawtucket) 2
Greg Harris (Charlotte, Durham) 2
Josh Rogers (Charleston, Tampa) 2

GAMES FINISHED

Joe Jimenez (Lakeland, Erie, Toledo) 52
Jimmie Sherfy (Visalia, Mobile, Reno) 47
Alejandro Chacin (Pensacola) 46
Jimmy Herget (Daytona) 46
James Hoyt (Fresno) 44
Rafael Martin (Syracuse) 44
Jason Stoffel (Bowie, Norfolk) 44

HOLDS

Joey Krehbiel (Mobile) 21
Rayan Gonzalez (Hartford) 17
Reyes Moronta (San Jose) 17
Gabriel Moya (Kane County, Visalia) 17
Pedro Beato (Norfolk) 16
Tim Peterson (St. Lucie, Binghamton) 16
Nick Routt (Louisville, Pensacola) 16

SAVES

Matt Carasiti (Hartford, Albuquerque) 31
Alejandro Chacin (Pensacola) 30
Joe Jimenez (Lakeland, Erie, Toledo) 30
Jimmie Sherfy (Visalia, Mobile, Reno) 30
James Hoyt (Fresno) 29

INNINGS PITCHED

Parker French (Asheville, Modesto) 177.2
Chris Volstad (Charlotte) 176.2
Anthony Vasquez (Reading, Lehigh Valley) 172.1
Ben Lively (Reading, Lehigh Valley) 170.2
Jack Wynkoop (Asheville, Modesto) 170.2

WALKS

Josh Staumont (Wilmington, NW Arkansas) 104
Eddie Campbell (Bakersfield) 100
Cody Dickson (Altoona) 93
Lucas Sims (Gwinnett, Mississippi) 92
Chris Ellis (Mississippi, Gwinnett) 87

STRIKEOUTS

Brandon Woodruff (Brevard County, Biloxi) 173
Josh Staumont (Wilmington, NW Arkansas) 167
Jaime Schultz (Durham) 163
Josh Hader (Biloxi, Colorado Springs) 161
Lucas Sims (Gwinnett, Mississippi) 159
Aaron Wilkerson (Portland, Pawtucket, Col. Springs) 159

HITS ALLOWED

Daniel McCutchen (El Paso, San Antonio) 218
David Hurlbut (Chattanooga, Rochester) 198
Justin Anderson (Inland Empire) 193
Zach Lee (Oklahoma City, Tacoma) 193
Chris Volstad (Charlotte) 193

HOME RUNS ALLOWED

Corey Baker (Memphis, Springfield) 26
Jordan Johnson (San Jose) 24
Duane Below (Las Vegas) 23
Daniel McCutchen (El Paso, San Antonio) 23
David Ledbetter (High Desert) 22
Zach Lee (Oklahoma City, Tacoma) 22
Deck McGuire (Springfield, Memphis) 22

STRIKEOUTS PER NINE INNINGS (STARTERS)*

Josh Staumont (Wilmington, NW Arkansas) 11.90
Josh Hader (Biloxi, Colorado Springs) 11.50
Jaime Schultz (Durham) 11.23
Sandy Alcantara (Peoria) 11.23
Tyler Glasnow (Altoona, Indianapolis) 11.11

STRIKEOUTS PER NINE INNINGS (RELIEVERS)*

Reyes Moronta (San Jose) 14.19
Armando Rivero (Iowa) 13.97
Jonathan Holder (Trenton, Scranton/WB) 13.91
Brad Wieck (Lake Elsinore, San Antonio) 13.65
Kevin Grendell (Orem, Burlington, Inland Empire, Arkansas) 13.50

BATTING AVERAGE AGAINST (STARTERS)*

Chance Adams (Tampa, Trenton) .173
Tyler Glasnow (Altoona, Indianapolis) .176
Stephen Gonsalves (Fort Myers, Chattanooga) .179
Yefrey Ramirez (Charleston, Tampa) .183
Sean Reid-Foley (Lansing, Dunedin) .190

BATTING AVERAGE AGAINST (RELIEVERS)*

Danny Barnes (New Hampshire, Buffalo) .112
Ariel Hernandez (Dayton, Daytona) .136
Jose Leclerc (Frisco, Round Rock) .153
Yoel Espinal (Charlotte, Bowling Green) .155
Jonathan Holder (Trenton, Scranton/WB) .160

MOST STRIKEOUTS, ONE GAME

Emilio Vargas (Kane County) 17
Jose Taveras (Lakewood) 15
Sandy Alcantara (Peoria) 14
Matt Andriese (Durham) 14
Jose Berrios (Rochester) 14
Elieser Hernandez (Quad Cities) 14
Jon Perrin (Wisconsin) 14
Tyler Skaggs (Salt Lake) 14
Tyler Wells (Elizabethton) 14

WILD PITCHES

Jared Mortensen (Montgomery) 38
Adonis Santana (DSL Padres) 31
Lukas Schiraldi (Bakersfield, Clinton) 31
Juan Pena (DSL Twins) 28
Riger Fernandez (DSL Cubs1) 27
Argelis Herrera (DSL Yankees2) 27

BALKS

Chris Comito (Kannapolis, Great Falls) 6
Tony Santillan (Billings, Dayton) 6
Matt Andriese (Durham) 5
Vicente Campos (Tampa, Trenton, Scranton/ WB, Mobile, Reno) 5
Ronny Carvajal (DSL Rangers1, AZL Rangers) 5
Lendy Castillo (Erie, Akron) 5
Greg Harris (Charlotte, Durham) 5
Matt Meier (Grand Junction) 5
Julio Pinto (AZL Royals, Lexington) 5
Nolan Watson (Lexington) 5

HIT BATTERS

Santiago Rodriguez (DSL Athletics) 20
Blayne Weller (Arkansas, AZL Angels, Salt Lake, Orem) 19
Endrys Briceno (Lakeland) 18
Jared Mortensen (Montgomery) 17
Patrick Weigel (Rome, Mississippi) 17
Parker French (Asheville, Modesto) 16
Alex Klonowski (Inland Empire, Arkansas) 16

GROUND BALL DOUBLE PLAYS

Trevor Oaks (Rancho Cucamonga, Tulsa, Olla. City) 26
Zack Littell (Clinton, Bakersfield) 25
Jordan Kipper (Arkansas) 23
Michael Peoples (Columbus, Akron) 23
Aaron Slegers (Chattanooga) 23
Jake Thompson (Lehigh Valley) 23
Anthony Vasquez (Reading, Lehigh Valley) 23

INDIVIDUAL FIELDING

ERRORS

Marten Gasparini (Lexington) 48
Ricky Aracena (Idaho Falls) 38
Emerson Jimenez (Modesto) 36
Anfernee Seymour (Greensboro, Rome) 33
Lucius Fox (Augusta) 32
Ronal Reynoso (DSL Marlins) 32
Forrest Wall (Modesto) 32

MINOR LEAGUES

BY TEDDY CAHILL

A bumper crop of prospects called the International League home this season, including two of the last four Minor League Players of the Year. The IL was so deep this year that all 20 players that made the rankings have been ranked as Top 100 prospects in their career.

With so many talented players on the field, IL fans were treated to exciting baseball throughout the league. Scranton/Wilkes-Barre emerged as the best team in the league and among the best in the minors.

The RailRiders went 91-52 during the regular season, posting the best winning percentage and most victories of any team in full-season ball. Scranton/Wilkes-Barre followed that up by defeating Gwinnett in the IL finals to win the Governor's Cup. It finished the season with a 3-1 victory against El Paso in the Triple-A National Championship Game. It was the first national championship in franchise history, and the RailRiders were the first IL team in five years to win the title game.

Scranton/Wilkes-Barre had to finish the season without most of their best prospects, including Gary Sanchez and Aaron Judge, who were called up in August. They also lost IL MVP Ben Gamel, who was traded to the Mariners at the end of August.

Gwinnett was the IL runner-up, despite finishing the regular season 65-78. The Braves won the South Division, but were the first team since 1992 to reach the playoffs with a losing record. Their run to the championship series was led by manager John Moses, who began the season as the club's hitting coach. He took over as manager after Brian Snitker was called up to Atlanta to be the big

league team's interim manager.

Like Snitker many of the IL's best players went on to have success in the big leagues. Syracuse shortstop/outfielder Trea Turner was the league's top prospect and established himself as a National League rookie of the year candidate after earning a promotion to Washington.

Gamel was named MVP a year after he was named the league's rookie of the year. He became the 16th player to win both awards. Lehigh Valley righthander Jake Thompson was named most valuable pitcher and Columbus third baseman Yandy Diaz won rookie of the year honors.

Louisville outfielder Hernan Iribarren hit .327/.380/.410 to edge Diaz for the batting title. Columbus first baseman Jesus Aguilar hit 30 home runs and drove in 92 runs to lead the league in both categories. Thompson topped the circuit in ERA (2.50) and victories (11).

OVERALL STANDINGS

North Division	W	L	PCT	GB	Manager(s)	Attendance	Average	Last Pennant
Scranton/Wilkes-Barre RailRiders	91	52	.636	—	Al Pedrique	424,991	6,071	2016
Lehigh Valley IronPigs	85	58	.594	6	Dave Brundage	611,015	8,729	1995
Rochester Red Wings	81	63	.563	10 ½	Mike Quade	434,897	6,396	1997
Pawtucket Red Sox	74	68	.521	16 ½	Kevin Boles	407,097	6,076	2014
Buffalo Bisons	66	78	.458	25 ½	Gary Allenson	562,755	8,039	2004
Syracuse Chiefs	61	82	.427	30	Billy Gardner	274,427	4,158	1976

South Division	W	L	PCT	GB	Manager(s)	Attendance	Average	Last Pennant
Gwinnett Braves	65	78	.455	—	B. Snitker/R.Albert/J. Moses	225,259	3,218	2007
Charlotte Knights	65	79	.451	½	Julio Vinas	628,173	8,974	1985
Durham Bulls	64	80	.444	1 ½	Jared Sandberg	547,156	7,599	2013
Norfolk Tides	62	82	.431	3 ½	Ron Johnson	373,042	5,486	1999

West Division	W	L	PCT	GB	Manager(s)	Attendance	Average	Last Pennant
Columbus Clippers	82	62	0.569	—	Chris Tremie	602,171	8,855	2015
Louisville Bats	71	73	0.493	11	Delino Deshields	506,030	7,127	2001
Indianapolis Indians	70	74	0.486	12	Dean Treanor	636,888	8,970	2000
Toledo Mud Hens	68	76	0.472	14	Lloyd McClendon	532,008	7,824	2006

Semifinals: Gwinnett defeated Columbus 3-1 and Scranton/Wilkes-Barre 3-0 in best-of-five series. **Finals:** Scranton/Wilkes-Barre defeated Gwinnett 3-1 in a best-of-five series.

CLUB BATTING

	AVG	G	AB	R	H	2B	3B	HR	RBI	BB	SO	SB	OBP	SLG
Scranton/W-B	.266	143	4775	654	1272	245	25	113	611	446	1073	86	.333	.399
Toledo	.261	144	4854	603	1269	282	27	94	571	429	1057	98	.326	.389
Columbus	.260	144	4883	631	1270	253	21	129	592	400	1088	62	.320	.400
Gwinnett	.259	143	4810	566	1247	245	32	79	527	429	986	94	.322	.373
Louisville	.258	144	4822	539	1245	240	21	72	489	411	987	54	.324	.361
Norfolk	.257	144	4921	535	1264	232	21	94	498	439	1062	62	.320	.370
Lehigh Valley	.257	143	4753	599	1223	244	27	122	566	388	1046	64	.316	.397
Charlotte	.256	144	4799	598	1230	237	24	103	557	436	1146	105	.323	.380
Pawtucket	.254	142	4721	541	1198	234	26	94	502	368	993	93	.311	.374
Buffalo	.250	144	4695	499	1172	236	14	94	468	400	887	74	.313	.366
Indianapolis	.249	144	4738	548	1179	235	40	99	517	476	1135	110	.318	.378
Rochester	.248	144	4750	589	1178	220	34	129	557	452	1120	85	.315	.390
Durham	.238	144	4836	542	1149	264	23	115	507	473	1218	90	.311	.373
Syracuse	.238	143	4643	508	1103	211	29	81	475	444	1152	108	.307	.348

CLUB PITCHING

	ERA	G	CG	SHO	SV	IP	H	R	ER	HR	BB	SO	AVG
Scranton/W-B	2.98	143	3	1	45	1247	1081	469	413	86	387	1198	.234
Lehigh Valley	3.12	143	4	1	44	1262	1102	494	438	105	349	1009	.234
Indianapolis	3.30	144	1	0	34	1278	1184	528	469	79	456	1057	.248
Pawtucket	3.36	142	5	2	39	1247	1100	512	465	115	447	1100	.238
Rochester	3.43	144	8	2	43	1266	1233	540	482	87	349	1010	.256
Columbus	3.67	144	3	1	41	1278	1226	572	521	105	453	1035	.253
Durham	3.67	144	4	1	25	1284	1182	591	524	111	476	1287	.246
Toledo	3.68	144	4	1	31	1270	1288	581	520	87	424	1041	.265
Buffalo	3.74	144	1	0	45	1248	1261	586	519	97	392	1027	.263
Norfolk	3.78	144	1	0	33	1282	1288	585	538	102	395	1120	.263
Syracuse	3.79	143	5	1	30	1227	1236	566	516	101	368	1012	.260
Louisville	3.94	144	3	0	34	1274	1223	622	558	120	493	1068	.253
Gwinnett	4.05	143	5	2	31	1254	1267	626	564	92	588	1073	.265
Charlotte	4.50	144	8	2	29	1256	1328	680	628	131	414	913	.273

TEAM FIELDING

	PCT	PO	A	E	DP		PCT	PO	A	E	DP
Rochester	.985	3799	1455	80	345	Lehigh Valley	.981	3787	1408	99	368
Norfolk Tides	.985	3846	1432	83	365	Durham	.981	3852	1374	102	357
Columbus	.984	3835	1439	86	338	Gwinnett	.981	3761	1465	102	441
Pawtucket	.983	3742	1208	84	359	Indianapolis	.981	3833	1533	105	375
Toledo	.983	3811	1467	92	354	Charlotte	.981	3767	1633	106	456
Scranton/W-B	.982	3742	1360	91	363	Buffalo	.980	3745	1481	106	370
Syracuse	.981	3680	1426	97	329	Louisville	.979	3821	1410	113	365

INDIVIDUAL BATTING

Batter, Club	AVG	G	AB	R	H	2B	3B	HR	RBI	BB	SO	SB
Iribarren, Hernan, Louisville	.327	101	373	46	122	20	1	3	35	33	60	3
Diaz, Yandy, Columbus	.325	95	360	53	117	22	3	7	44	47	70	5
Solano, Donovan, Scranton/WB	.319	131	511	64	163	33	3	7	67	25	79	2
McGehee, Casey, Toledo	.317	116	438	56	139	37	0	6	50	38	73	6
Montero, Jesus, Buffalo	.317	126	489	46	155	24	1	11	60	23	78	1
Gamel, Ben, Scranton/WB	.308	116	483	80	149	26	5	6	51	43	94	19
Winker, Jesse, Louisville	.303	106	380	39	115	22	0	3	45	59	59	0
Bonifacio, Emilio, Gwinnett	.298	107	420	57	125	14	5	2	40	39	70	37
Gonzalez, Erik, Columbus	.296	104	429	62	127	31	1	11	53	19	88	12
Bell, Josh, Indianapolis	.295	114	421	57	124	23	4	14	60	57	74	3

INDIVIDUAL PITCHING

Pitcher, Club	W	L	ERA	G	GS	CG	SV	IP	H	R	ER	BB	SO
Thompson, Jake, Lehigh Valley	11	5	2.50	21	21	0	0	130	105	44	36	37	87
Lively, Ben, Lehigh Valley	11	5	3.06	19	19	1	0	118	83	45	40	27	90
Voth, Austin, Syracuse	7	9	3.15	27	25	0	0	157	138	63	55	57	133
Espino, Paolo, Syracuse	8	11	3.30	26	24	1	0	153	146	60	56	29	133
Wheeler, Jason, Rochester	11	6	3.53	24	24	1	0	145	137	60	57	37	113
Owens, Henry, Pawtucket	10	7	3.53	24	24	1	0	138	107	60	54	81	135
Schultz, Jaime, Durham	5	7	3.58	27	27	0	0	131	113	57	52	68	163
Hutchison, Drew, Buffalo, Indianapolis	7	6	3.59	25	24	0	0	138	115	63	55	50	138
Elias, Roenis, Pawtucket	10	5	3.60	21	19	1	0	125	115	56	50	57	113
Albers, Andrew, Rochester	10	6	3.69	21	21	2	0	124	150	53	51	30	84

ALL-STAR TEAM

C: Gary Sanchez, Scranton/WB. **1B:** Josh Bell, Indianapolis. **2B:** Donovan Solano, Scranton/WB.
3B: Casey McGehee, Toledo. **SS:** Trea Turner, Syracuse. **DH:** Jesus Montero, Buffalo. **OF:** Aaron Judge,
Scranton/WB; Chris Marrero, Pawtucket; Jake Thompson, Lehigh
Valley. **RP:** Edward Mujica, Lehigh Valley.
Most Valuable Pitcher: Jake Thompson, Lehigh Valley
Rookie of the Year: Yandy Diaz, Columbus
Manager of the Year: Al Pedrique, Scranton/WB.
Most Valuable Player: Ben Gamel, Scranton/WB.

DEPARTMENT LEADERS

BATTING

2B	Alvarez, Dariel, Norfolk	38
3B	Schebler, Scott, Louisville	8
	Turner, Trea, Syracuse	8
AB/SO	Mustelier, Ronnier, Gwinnett	8.69
BB	Moroff, Max, Indianapolis	90
CS	Frazier, Adam, Indianapolis	15
	Hanson, Alen, Indianapolis	15
H	Solano, Donovan, Scranton/WB	163
HBP	Puello, Cesar, Scranton/WB	18
HR	Aguilar, Jesus, Columbus	30
OBP	Diaz, Yandy, Columbus	.399
OPS	Huffman, Chad, Toledo	.892
R	Gamel, Ben, Scranton/WB	80
RBI	Aguilar, Jesus, Columbus	92
SAC	Diaz, Jonathan, Scranton/WB	16
SB	Bonifacio, Emilio, Gwinnett	37
SLG	Ruf, Darin, Lehigh Valley	.529
SO	Walker, Adam, Rochester	202
XBH	Aguilar, Jesus, Columbus	56

FIELDING

C PCT	Murphy, John Ryan, Rochester	.997
A	Stallings, Jacob, Indianapolis	72
PB	Arencibia, J.P., Lehigh Valley, Durham	23
DP	Jimenez, A.J., Buffalo	7
E	Knapp, Andrew, Lehigh Valley	7
PO	Knapp, Andrew, Lehigh Valley	712
1B PCT	Skole, Matt, Syracuse	.999
A	Aguilar, Jesus, Columbus	82
DP	Mancini, Trey, Norfolk	99
E	Bell, Josh, Indianapolis	14
PO	Mancini, Trey, Norfolk	1067
2B PCT	Diaz, Argenis, Toledo	.981
A	Diaz, Argenis, Toledo	242
DP	Diaz, Argenis, Toledo	57
E	Solano, Donovan, Scranton/WB	9
PO	Miller, Mike, Pawtucket	152
3B PCT	McGehee, Casey, Toledo	.980
A	Dominguez, Matt, Buffalo	235
DP	Ruiz, Rio, Gwinnett	31
E	Almanzar, Michael, Norfolk	21
PO	Almanzar, Michael, Norfolk	108
SS PCT	Ngoepe, Gift, Indianapolis	.984
A	Machado, Dixon, Toledo	403
DP	Machado, Dixon, Toledo	85
	Tovar, Wilfredo, Rochester	85
E	Machado, Dixon, Toledo	17
	Tovar, Wilfredo, Rochester	17
PO	Machado, Dixon, Toledo	207
OF PCT	Alvarez, Dariel, Norfolk	.995
A	Garcia, Willy, Indianapolis	17
DP	Decker, Jaff, Durham	5
E	Brown, Domonic, Buffalo	9
PO	Ortiz, Danny, Indianapolis	259

PITCHING

AVG	Lively, Ben, Lehigh Valley	.196
BB	Owens, Henry, Pawtucket	81
BB/9	Gunkel, Joe, Norfolk	1.15
BK	Andriese, Matt, Durham	5
CG	Weber, Thad, Toledo	3
ER	Volstad, Chris, Charlotte	94
G	Beato, Pedro, Norfolk	65
	Guilmet, Preston, Toledo	65
GF	Martin, Rafael, Syracuse	44
GS	Diamond, Scott, Buffalo	28
	Pruitt, Austin, Durham	28
H	Volstad, Chris, Charlotte	193
HB	Owens, Henry, Pawtucket	13
HR	Pruitt, Austin, Durham	21
IP	Volstad, Chris, Charlotte	176.2
L	Diamond, Scott, Buffalo	15
SO	Schultz, Jaime, Durham	163
SO/9	Schultz, Jaime, Durham	11.23
SO/9(RP)	Phillips, Zach, Nor., Ind.	12.34
SV	Mujica, Edward, LHV, Rochester	26
W	Clevinger, Mike, Columbus	11
	Lively, Ben, Lehigh Valley	11
	Merritt, Ryan, Columbus	11
	Thompson, Jake, Lehigh Valley	11
	Wheeler, Jason, Rochester	11
WP	Gamboa, Eddie, Durham	11

MINOR LEAGUES

BY KYLE GLASER

The El Paso Chihuahuas were unusually stacked with prospect talent for a Triple-A affiliate, and they rode it all the way to their first PCL title.

The "Core Four" of touted Padres minor leaguers Manuel Margot, Hunter Renfroe, Carlos Asuaje and Austin Hedges remained on El Paso's roster all season because of an organizational emphasis on winning in the minor leagues. Renfroe cruised to the PCL MVP award, Margot finished in the top five in the league in hits, runs and stolen bases despite being one of its youngest players, Asuaje was named Rookie of the Year after hitting .321, and Hedges had his best professional season offensively with .326 average, 21 homer and 82 RBIs.

With those four leading the way, El Paso won the Pacific Southern Division title and went 6-2 in the postseason, capped by a 4-3, 11-inning victory over Oklahoma City (Dodgers) in Game Four of the championship series. Shortstop Jose Rondon, another ranked Padres prospect, drove in the go-ahead run on a bunt single in the top of 11th, and Phil Maton, the organization's top relief prospect, closed it out with his third save of the postseason.

El Paso was hardly alone when it came top prospects performing in the league. Mets first-round selections Brandon Nimmo (2011) and Gavin Cecchini (2012) finished second and third in the league batting title race, hitting .352 and .325, respectively. They finished behind Las Vegas teammate T.J. Rivera, a 27-year old undrafted free agent who hit .353 to win the batting crown and earn his first major league callup. He made the most of it,

hitting .333 with an .821 OPS for the Mets in 33 games down the stretch to help them secure the top NL wild card spot.

Fresno righthander Brady Rodgers, the Astros third-round pick in 2012 out of Arizona State, won the ERA crown with a sterling 2.86 mark. Oklahoma City starters Julio Urias and Brock Stewart both dominated league hitters before earning promotions to Los Angeles, while Sacramento lefthander Ty Blach tied for the league lead with 14 wins and pitched three complete games to earn his first big league promotion for the Giants.

Rob Segedin, a minor league free agent pickup and third-round draft choice of the Yankees in 2010 out of Tulane, got his first big league callup after leading the PCL in slugging percentage.

TOP 20 PROSPECTS

1. Alex Reyes, rhp Memphis (Cardinals)
2. Willson Contreras, c, Iowa (Cubs)
3. Jose De Leon, rhp, Oklahoma City (Dodgers)
4. Orlando Arcia, ss, Colorado Springs (Brewers)
5. Jeff Hoffman, rhp, Albuquerque (Rockies)
6. Joey Gallo, 3b/1b, Round Rock (Rangers)
7. Hunter Renfroe, of, El Paso (Padres)
8. A.J. Reed, 1b, Fresno (Astros)
9. Joe Musgrove, rhp, Fresno (Astros)
10. Jharel Cotton, rhp, Okla. City (Dodgers)/Nash. (A's)
11. Josh Hader, lhp, Colorado Springs (Brewers)
12. Albert Almora, of, Iowa (Cubs)
13. Manuel Margot, of, El Paso (Padres)
14. Teoscar Hernandez, of, Fresno (Astros)
15. Hunter Dozier, 3b, Omaha (Royals)
16. Brock Stewart, rhp, Oklahoma City (Dodgers)
17. Jeimer Candelario, 3b, Iowa (Cubs)
18. Daniel Mengden, rhp, Nashville (Athletics)
19. Brandon Nimmo, of, Las Vegas (Mets)
20. Anthony Banda, lhp, Reno (Diamondbacks)

OVERALL STANDINGS

American Northern	W	L	PCT	GB	Manager(s)	Attendance	Average	Last Pennant
Oklahoma City Dodgers (Dodgers)	81	60	.574	—	Bill Haselman	437,905	6,536	1965
Colorado Springs Sky Sox (Brewers)	67	71	.486	12 ½	Rick Sweet	270,100	4,220	1995
Iowa Cubs (Cubs)	67	76	.469	15	Marty Pevey	504,160	7,414	Never
Omaha Storm Chasers (Royals)	58	82	.414	22 ½	Brian Poldberg	356,135	5,315	2014

American Southern	W	L	PCT	GB	Manager(s)	Attendance	Average	Last Pennant
Nashville Sounds (Athletics)	83	59	.585	—	Steve Scarsone	504,060	7,099	2005
Round Rock Express (Rangers)	71	72	.497	12 ½	Jason Wood	613,226	8,637	Never
New Orleans Zephyrs (Marlins)	69	70	.496	12 ½	Arnie Beyeler	339,400	5,142	2001
Memphis Redbirds (Cardinals)	65	77	.458	18	Mike Shildt	324,581	4,704	2009

Pacific Northern	W	L	PCT	GB	Manager(s)	Attendance	Average	Last pennant
Tacoma Rainiers (Mariners)	81	62	.566	—	Pat Listach	377,164	5,312	2010
Reno Aces (Diamondbacks)	76	68	.528	5 ½	Phil Nevin	365,883	5,227	2012
Fresno Grizzlies (Astros)	73	70	.510	8	Tony DeFrancesco	439,389	6,189	Never
Sacramento River Cats (Giants)	69	75	.479	12 ½	Jose Alguacil	609,666	8,587	2008

Pacific Southern	W	L	PCT	GB	Manager(s)	Attendance	Average	Last pennant
El Paso Chihuahuas (Padres)	73	70	.510	—	Rod Barajas	564,259	7,837	2016
Albuquerque Isotopes (Rockies)	71	72	.497	2	Glenallen Hill	522,266	7,795	1994
Las Vegas 51s (Mets)	70	74	.486	3 ½	Wally Backman	331,999	4,882	1998
Salt Lake Bees (Angels)	63	79	.444	9 ½	Keith Johnson	503,659	7,195	1979

Semifinals: Oklahoma defeated Nashville 3-2 and El Paso defeated Tacoma 3-1 in best-of-five series. **Finals:** El Paso defeated Nashville 3-1 in a best-of-five series.

CLUB BATTING

	AVG	G	AB	R	H	2B	3B	HR	RBI	BB	SO	SB	OBP	SLG
El Paso	.295	143	4975	786	1468	290	47	156	743	375	958	56	.348	.466
Las Vegas	.291	144	4994	821	1453	314	34	141	777	553	1052	73	.365	.452
Reno	.280	144	4970	726	1393	287	53	140	686	422	1262	93	.338	.444
Iowa	.277	143	4762	695	1320	260	52	102	648	495	1049	176	.347	.418
Colorado Springs	.274	139	4657	687	1274	246	52	98	643	454	1039	151	.341	.412
Sacramento	.272	144	4857	659	1320	213	30	120	621	430	1034	88	.334	.402
Tacoma	.272	144	4921	689	1338	248	39	124	658	446	943	81	.336	.414
Albuquerque	.270	143	4836	662	1306	248	56	111	625	393	1053	81	.329	.413
Salt Lake	.269	142	4739	615	1274	251	50	68	565	488	1007	180	.340	.386
Oklahoma City	.265	141	4752	680	1257	245	46	126	623	494	1208	122	.337	.415
Memphis	.264	142	4622	641	1222	238	33	107	605	490	1028	90	.336	.400
Nashville	.262	142	4843	715	1267	282	37	148	664	472	1144	57	.331	.427
Omaha	.260	140	4758	625	1235	261	31	109	573	427	1107	91	.322	.396
Fresno	.257	144	4818	659	1236	235	30	142	625	524	1198	85	.333	.406
Round Rock	.255	143	4887	681	1246	252	42	142	640	505	1247	123	.329	.411
New Orleans	.246	140	4559	549	1120	218	20	98	506	423	1046	103	.314	.367

TEAM PITCHING

	ERA	G	CG	SHO	SV	IP	H	R	ER	HR	BB	SO	AVG
Nashville	3.42	142	3	1	36	1251	1130	533	476	93	420	1113	.240
Oklahoma City	3.72	141	3	1	36	1251	1190	583	517	108	372	1245	.251
Tacoma	3.92	144	1	1	39	1269	1224	605	553	114	380	1127	.253
Sacramento	4.03	144	4	2	32	1254	1253	639	562	103	450	1048	.261
Fresno	4.08	144	4	3	41	1267	1302	641	574	100	405	1213	.265
New Orleans	4.11	140	4	2	43	1218	1189	608	556	120	496	982	.258
Round Rock	4.18	143	1	1	33	1287	1278	649	597	115	440	998	.262
Albuquerque	4.45	143	1	1	39	1250	1372	682	618	140	421	1034	.281
Omaha	4.67	140	2	0	29	1225	1285	713	635	146	521	1039	.271
Iowa	4.72	143	0	0	33	1238	1233	697	650	105	534	1197	.261
Reno	4.80	144	4	1	36	1296	1376	726	670	120	517	1029	.282
Memphis	4.80	142	4	2	33	1209	1281	709	645	127	481	1052	.272
El Paso	4.99	143	2	2	28	1250	1450	770	693	130	488	1039	.293
Colorado Springs	5.07	139	1	0	28	1203	1307	729	678	107	540	1111	.280
Salt Lake	5.10	142	2	1	39	1242	1356	780	703	146	473	1073	.279
Las Vegas	5.32	144	2	0	33	1258	1503	826	744	158	453	1075	.297

TEAM FIELDING

	PCT	PO	A	E	DP		PCT	PO	A	E	DP
New Orleans	.983	3653	1410	85	351	Colorado Springs	.980	3608	1411	103	365
Tacoma	.983	3807	1372	87	307	El Paso	.979	3751	1490	110	364
Reno	.983	3769	1510	91	425	Oklahoma	.978	3752	1366	113	386
Albuquerque	.982	3750	1434	94	397	Nashville	.978	3753	1336	115	296
Fresno	.982	3800	1472	97	323	Salt Lake	.978	3727	1359	117	339
Iowa	.981	3715	1371	96	333	Omaha Storm	.976	3675	1352	121	387
Sacramento	.980	3763	1405	103	319	Memphis	.976	3627	1372	121	341
Round Rock	.980	3860	1570	111	453	Las Vegas	.976	3773	1452	128	339

INDIVIDUAL BATTING

Batter, Club	AVG	G	AB	R	H	2B	3B	HR	RBI	BB	SO	SB
Rivera, T.J., Las Vegas	.353	105	405	67	143	31	1	11	85	23	54	3
Nimmo, Brandon, Las Vegas	.352	97	392	72	138	25	8	11	61	46	73	7
Cecchini, Gavin, Las Vegas	.325	117	446	71	145	27	2	8	55	48	55	4
Asuaje, Carlos, El Paso	.321	134	535	98	172	32	11	9	69	49	82	10
Segedin, Rob, Okla. City	.319	103	373	71	119	23	9	21	69	40	81	3
Freeman, Mike, Reno, Tacoma	.314	114	446	71	140	23	6	4	39	51	94	12
Cardullo, Stephen, Albuquerque	.308	115	406	71	125	26	5	17	72	37	58	6
Renfroe, Hunter, El Paso	.306	133	533	95	163	34	5	30	105	22	115	5
Romero, Stefen, Tacoma	.304	106	418	70	127	24	6	21	85	36	67	1
Margot, Manuel, El Paso	.304	124	517	98	157	21	12	6	55	36	64	30

INDIVIDUAL PITCHING

Pitcher, Club	W	L	ERA	G	GS	CG	SV	IP	H	R	ER	BB	SO
Rodgers, Brady, Fresno	12	4	2.86	22	22	2	0	132	129	46	42	23	116
Roth, Michael, Round Rock	11	5	2.97	28	23	1	0	145	136	50	48	42	94
Valdez, Cesar, Fresno	12	1	3.12	30	18	1	0	138	143	49	48	13	114
Hauschild, Mike, Fresno	9	10	3.22	24	24	0	0	140	138	64	50	40	119
Overton, Dillon, Nashville	13	5	3.29	21	20	1	0	126	132	50	46	31	105
Blach, Ty, Sacramento	14	7	3.43	26	26	3	0	163	147	65	62	38	113
Shipley, Braden, Reno	8	5	3.7	19	19	1	0	119	131	53	49	22	93
Stratton, Chris, Sacramento	12	6	3.87	21	20	1	0	126	120	57	54	39	103
Smith, Chris, Nashville	6	8	3.93	22	22	0	0	131	120	64	57	45	121
Tepesch, Nick, (Rr/Okc/ Nsh/Oma)	8	4	3.96	22	19	0	0	116	121	56	51	28	62

ALL-STAR TEAM

C: Austin Hedges, El Paso. **1B:** Kyle Jensen, Reno. **2B:** Carlos Asuaje, El Paso. **3B:** Rob Segedin, Okla. City. **SS:** Orlando Arcia, Col. Springs. **DH:** Daniel Vogelbach, Tacoma. **OF:** Hunter Renfroe, El Paso; Manuel Margot, El Paso; Stefen Romero, Tacoma. **SP:** Brady Rodgers, Fresno; Ty Blach, Sacramento. **RP:** James Hoyt, Fresno. **Most Valuable Player:** Hunter Renfroe, El Paso. **Pitcher of the Year:** Brady Rodgers, Fresno. **Rookie of the Year :** Carlos Asuaje, El Paso. **Manager of the Year:** Steve Scarsone, Nashville.

DEPARTMENT LEADERS

BATTING

2B Taijeron, Travis, Las Vegas	42
3B Margot, Manuel, El Paso	12
AB/SO Robertson, Daniel, Tacoma	9.95
BB Vogelbach, Daniel, Iowa, Tacoma	97
CS Hernandez, Gorkys, Sacramento	13
H Asuaje, Carlos, El Paso	172
HBP Patterson, Jordan, Albuquerque	13
HR Jensen, Kyle, Reno	30
Renfroe, Hunter, El Paso	30
OBP Nimmo, Brandon, Las Vegas	.423
OPS Segedin, Rob, Okla. City	.989
R Asuaje, Carlos, El Paso	98
Margot, Manuel, El Paso	98
RBI Jensen, Kyle, Reno	120
SAC Three tied with	9
SB Andreoli, John, Iowa	43
SLG Segedin, Rob, Okla. City	.598
SO Jensen, Kyle, Reno	169
XBH Renfroe, Hunter, El Paso	69

FIELDING

A Vogelbach, Daniel, Iowa, Tacoma	61
DP Jensen, Kyle, Reno	104
E Hassan, Alex, Okla. City	9
Jensen, Kyle, Reno	9
1B PCT Navarro, Efren, Tacoma, Memphis	.994
PO Jensen, Kyle, Reno	921
A Wendle, Joey, Nashville	338
DP Freeman, Mike, Reno, Tacoma	84
E Johnson, Micah, Okla. City	15
2B PCT Wendle, Joey, Nashville	.986
PO Wendle, Joey, Nashville	219
A Moran, Colin, Fresno	215
DP Moran, Colin, Fresno	28
E Nunez, Renato, Nashville	21
3B PCT Rivero, Carlos, Reno	.987
PO Moran, Colin, Fresno	69
A Heineman, Tyler, Fresno	59
PB Morin, Parker, Omaha	10
DP Hedges, Austin, El Paso	9
Stassi, Max, Fresno	9
E Morin, Parker, Omaha	9
C PCT Hedges, Austin, El Paso	.991
PO Hedges, Austin, El Paso	578
A Margot, Manuel, El Paso	18
DP Bonifacio, Jorge, Omaha	6
E Bonifacio, Jorge, Omaha	8
OF PCT Aplin, Andrew, Fresno	.996
PO Margot, Manuel, El Paso	311
A Reinheimer, Jack, Reno	371
DP Reinheimer, Jack, Reno	99
E Cecchini, Gavin, Las Vegas	33
SS FPCT Kawasaki, Munenori, Iowa	.982
PO Reinheimer, Jack, Reno	185

PITCHING

AVG Cotton, Jharel, Okla. City, Nashville	.214
BB Dziedzic, Jonathan, Omaha	63
BB/9 Valdez, Cesar, Fresno	0.85
BK Gregorio, Joan, Sacramento	4
CG Blach, Ty, Sacramento	3
ER Rucinski, Drew, Iowa	102
G Bradford, Chasen, Las Vegas	56
Sewald, Paul, Las Vegas	56
Walters, Jeff, Las Vegas	56
GF Hoyt, James, Fresno	44
GS Pimentel, Carlos, El Paso	28
Rucinski, Drew, Iowa	28
H McCutchen, Daniel, El Paso	198
HB Buchanan, Jake, Iowa	9
HR Below, Duane, Las Vegas	23
IP Blach, Ty, Sacramento	162.2
L Rucinski, Drew, Iowa	15
SO Cotton, Jharel, Okla. City, Nashville	155
SO/9 Cotton, Jharel, Okla. City, Nashville	10.28
SO/9(RP) Rivero, Armando, Iowa	13.97
SV Hoyt, James, Fresno	29
W Blach, Ty, Sacramento	14
Wieland, Joe, Tacoma	14
WP Magnifico, Damien, Colo. Springs	16

MINOR LEAGUES

BY JOSH NORRIS

As ever, the Eastern League was chock full of top-end prospects, but 2016's crop went beyond the usual motherlode.

Portland boasted two of the sport's best talents in infielder Yoan Moncada, who reigned as Baseball America's Minor League Player of the Year, and outfielder Andrew Benintendi, who ranked ahead of Moncada as the Red Sox's No. 1 prospect at season's end. Both players skipped over Triple-A en route to their major league debuts, and Benintendi earned a spot on Boston's American League Division Series roster.

Beyond those two, the EL's Top 20 prospects list featured six players who made their major league debuts in 2016, and 17 players who were featured on BA's Midseason Top 100 prospects. The four players who didn't make the list—Trenton's righthander Chance Adams and outfielder Dustin Fowler, Reading outfielder Dylan Cozens and Hartford righthander German Marquez—had some of the league's best individual campaigns.

Cozens, in particular, spent the season destroying the league. He finished the season hitting .276/.350/.591 with 40 home runs and 125 RBIs. The latter two marks broke franchise records set by Phillies great Ryan Howard and led the entire minor leagues. Cozens was complemented at the heart of Reading's murderer's row by first baseman Rhys Hoskins, who added 38 homers (second in the minors) and 116 RBIs (third) as the Fightins coasted to the EL's best record.

Success in the regular season, of course, doesn't guarantee anything in the playoffs. Reading's big boppers were cut off in the first round, where Trenton's strong pitching—particularly relievers J.P. Feyereisen and Tyler Jones—pushed it into the championship round.

The ELCS pitted Trenton against Akron, which battled through a 12-game losing streak in the middle of June to claim the Western Division's wild-card spot. It accomplished that, in part, by ripping off an 11-game winning streak in August.

The Rubber Ducks' most-important winning streak, however, came in the championship series. They swept Trenton in three games to claim the franchise's sixth championship since 2003 and fourth since 2007. Their last title, in 2012, also saw them clinch on Trenton's home turf of Arm & Hammer Park.

Off the field, the EL's season was dominated by the unending drama surrounding Hartford's Dunkin' Donuts Park. The park wasn't completed in time for the season to begin, and construction delays piled up all season long. The city wound up firing the original developer, Centerplan, and brought in their insurer to assess the remaining work and hire a new contractor to finish the job.

The Yard Goats spent the entire season on the road. With a new developer in place, Hartford is expected to begin 2017 where it should have begun 2016 if everything had gone to plan.

TOP 20 PROSPECTS

1. Yoan Moncada, 2b/3b, Portland (Red Sox)
2. Andrew Benintendi, of, Portland (Red Sox)
3. Austin Meadows, of, Altoona (Pirates)
4. David Dahl, of, Hartford (Rockies)
5. Lucas Giolito, rhp, Harrisburg (Nationals)
6. J.P. Crawford, ss, Reading (Phillies)
7. Amed Rosario, ss, Binghamton (Mets)
8. Clint Frazier, of, Akron (Indians)
9. German Marquez, rhp, Hartford (Rockies)
10. Reynaldo Lopez, rhp, Harrisburg (Nationals)
11. Raimel Tapia, of, Hartford (Rockies)
12. Jorge Alfaro, c, Reading (Phillies)
13. Dylan Cozens, of, Reading (Phillies)
14. Bradley Zimmer, of, Akron (Indians)
15. Dominic Smith, 1b, Binghamton (Mets)
16. Chance Sisco, c, Bowie (Orioles)
17. Tyler Beede, rhp, Richmond (Giants)
18. Chance Adams, rhp, Trenton (Yankees)
19. Kevin Newman, ss, Altoona (Pirates)
20. Dustin Fowler, of, Trenton (Yankees)

OVERALL STANDINGS

Eastern Division	W	L	PCT	GB	Manager(s)	Attendance	Average	Last Pennant
Reading Fightin Phils	89	52	.631	—	Dusty Wathan	420,320	6,092	2001
Trenton Thunder	87	55	.613	2½	Bobby Mitchell	347,661	5,039	2013
Hartford Yard Goats	74	67	.525	15	Darin Everson	41,569	799	2001
New Hampshire Fisher Cats	69	73	.486	20½	Bobby Meacham	338,387	4,834	2011
Binghamton Mets	63	77	.450	25½	Pedro Lopez	172,859	2,619	1994
Portland Sea Dogs	55	84	.396	33	Carlos Febles	374,746	5,354	2006

Western Division	W	L	PCT	GB	Manager(s)	Attendance	Average	Last Pennant
Akron RubberDucks	77	64	.546	—	Dave Wallace	350,077	5,074	2016
Altoona Curve	76	64	.543	½	Joey Cora	272,640	4,131	2010
Harrisburg Senators	76	66	.535	1½	Matt LeCroy	269,172	3,901	1999
Erie SeaWolves	62	79	.440	15	Lance Parrish	210,040	3,044	Never
Richmond Flying Squirrels	62	79	.440	15	Miguel Ojeda	390,693	5,745	2014
Bowie Baysox	56	86	.394	21½	Gary Kendall	236,349	3,528	Never

Semifinals: Akron defeated Altoona 3-1 and Trenton defeated Reading 3-1 in best-of-five series. **Finals:** Akron defeated Trenton 3-0 in a best-of-five series.

CLUB BATTING

	AVG	G	AB	R	H	2B	3B	HR	RBI	BB	SO	SB	OBP	SLG
Reading	.270	141	4854	790	1309	270	26	185	747	515	1181	91	.344	.450
Erie	.265	141	4737	618	1253	231	39	119	588	439	980	98	.333	.405
Altoona	.265	140	4638	616	1231	255	55	84	577	457	956	67	.335	.398
Hartford	.263	141	4608	577	1212	259	27	74	536	380	1047	145	.323	.379
Binghamton	.262	140	4724	571	1239	240	26	69	515	478	1030	72	.332	.368
Portland	.262	139	4580	579	1200	236	47	94	539	394	926	73	.322	.396
Bowie	.261	142	4771	608	1245	212	31	108	562	471	1010	73	.329	.386
Richmond	.257	141	4737	561	1217	243	29	83	523	405	1034	62	.320	.373
Trenton	.256	142	4668	611	1194	238	45	82	578	475	1014	120	.328	.379
Harrisburg	.253	142	4673	569	1183	190	43	72	494	458	997	142	.323	.358
New Hampshire	.251	142	4678	607	1173	222	41	99	557	468	1034	143	.323	.379
Akron	.242	141	4702	644	1138	256	37	132	603	507	1281	134	.324	.396

CLUB PITCHING

	ERA	G	CG	SHO	SV	IP	H	R	ER	HR	BB	SO	AVG
Trenton	3.13	142	5	2	50	1236	1079	491	430	65	420	1239	.233
Richmond	3.48	141	2	1	33	1229	1123	567	476	78	468	1048	.244
Harrisburg	3.75	142	8	2	40	1247	1199	591	520	111	454	1015	.253
Hartford	3.78	141	4	2	44	1224	1253	593	514	105	397	973	.266
Akron	3.83	141	1	0	39	1254	1202	594	533	84	445	1035	.253
Reading	3.85	141	2	1	36	1258	1245	598	538	108	422	1055	.260
New Hampshire	3.85	142	1	1	35	1246	1230	609	533	111	448	1033	.259
Altoona	4.05	140	3	0	37	1217	1164	598	547	93	547	993	.256
Binghamton	4.26	140	6	0	28	1223	1200	643	579	96	478	1076	.258
Bowie	4.45	142	3	1	30	1229	1329	690	608	114	450	924	.276
Portland	4.49	139	9	3	20	1197	1205	671	597	114	507	1040	.263
Erie	4.58	141	4	0	32	1232	1365	706	627	122	411	1059	.282

CLUB FIELDING

	PCT	PO	A	E	DP		PCT	PO	A	E	DP
Altoona	.980	3651	1482	105	381	Erie	.977	3695	1367	119	340
Akron	.980	3762	1495	110	367	Hartford	.976	3673	1440	124	337
Binghamton	.979	3668	1377	106	289	Trenton	.976	3708	1282	124	273
Richmond	.979	3688	1432	112	370	Reading	.975	3775	1423	132	344
Harrisburg	.979	3740	1495	115	334	Portland	.974	3592	1306	129	306
New Hampshire	.978	3737	1414	116	363	Bowie	.973	3688	1392	142	334

INDIVIDUAL BATTING

Batter, Club	AVG	G	AB	R	H	2B	3B	HR	RBI	BB	SO	SB
Evans, Phillip, Binghamton	.335	96	361	50	121	30	0	8	39	19	60	1
Tavarez, Aneury, Portland	.335	106	385	59	129	19	13	7	47	29	64	18
Tapia, Raimel, Hartford	.323	104	424	79	137	20	5	8	34	25	49	17
Sisco, Chance, Bowie	.320	112	410	53	131	28	1	4	44	59	83	2
Ramirez, Harold, Altoona, N.H.	.311	99	383	60	119	17	7	2	50	22	66	7
Barnes, Barrett, Altoona	.306	124	405	60	124	28	7	9	47	41	105	10
Rosa, Garabez, Bowie	.303	110	452	45	137	21	2	8	62	14	104	2
Smith, Dominic, Binghamton	.302	130	484	64	146	29	2	14	91	50	74	2
Tellez, Rowdy, New Hampshire	.297	124	438	71	130	29	2	23	81	63	92	4
Lopes, Christian, New Hampshire	.295	108	404	56	119	30	2	3	46	33	71	9

INDIVIDUAL PITCHING

Pitcher, Club	W	L	ERA	G	GS	CG	SV	IP	H	R	ER	BB	SO
Beede, Tyler, Richmond	8	7	2.81	24	24	1	0	147	136	58	46	53	135
Marquez, German, Hartford	9	6	2.85	21	21	0	0	136	124	53	43	33	126
Mapes, Tyler, Harrisburg	12	10	3.19	25	25	4	0	155	154	61	55	39	78
Kaminsky, Rob, Akron	11	7	3.28	25	25	0	0	137	122	54	50	48	92
Gage, Matt, Richmond	9	7	3.38	23	23	1	0	136	130	55	51	34	106
Pivetta, Nick, Reading	11	6	3.41	22	22	1	0	124	108	50	47	41	111
Dickson, Cody, Altoona	10	5	3.66	28	26	1	1	140	127	60	57	93	105
Camarena, Daniel, Trenton	9	6	3.68	25	22	1	1	130	126	60	53	21	106
Peoples, Michael, Akron	12	6	3.68	27	27	1	0	159	166	78	65	53	84
Herrera, Ronald, Trenton	10	7	3.75	23	23	0	0	132	131	61	55	35	123

ALL-STAR TEAM

C: Chance Sisco, Bowie. **1B:** Rhys Hoskins, Reading. **2B:** Erich Weiss, Altoona. **3B:** Eric Wood, Altoona. **SS:** Tyler Wade, Trenton. **DH:** Rowdy Tellez, New Hampshire. **OF:** Aneury Tavarez, Portland; Dylan Cozens, Reading; Raimel Tapia, Hartford. **IF:** Garabez Rosa, Bowie. **SP:** German Marquez, Hartford; Jordan Montgomery, Trenton. **RP:** Matt Carasiti, Hartford.
Manager of the Year: Dusty Wathan, Reading. **Most Valuable Player:** Dylan Cozen, Reading.
Pitcher of the Year: German Marquez, Hartford. **Rookie of the Year:** Rhys Hoskins, Reading.

DEPARTMENT LEADERS

BATTING

2B Cozens, Dylan, Reading	38
3B Fowler, Dustin, Trenton	15
AB/SO Krizan, Jason, Erie	13.19
BB Rodriguez, Nellie, Akron	75
CS Fields, Roemon, New Hampshire	16
H Bautista, Rafael, Harrisburg	153
HBP Harrell, Connor, Erie	15
HR Cozens, Dylan, Reading	40
OBP Sisco, Chance, Bowie	.406
OPS Hoskins, Rhys, Reading	.943
R Cozens, Dylan, Reading	106
RBI Cozens, Dylan, Reading	125
SAC Fields, Roemon, New Hampshire	10
Parmley, Ian, New Hampshire	10
SB Bautista, Rafael, Harrisburg	56
SLG Cozens, Dylan, Reading	.591
SO Cozens, Dylan, Reading	186
Rodriguez, Nellie, Akron	186
XBH Cozens, Dylan, Reading	81

FIELDING

A Rodriguez, Nellie, Akron	92
DP Rodriguez, Nellie, Akron	111
E Terdoslavich, Joey, Bowie	16
1B PCT Ficociello, Dominic, Erie	.998
PO Hoskins, Rhys, Reading	1080
TC Hoskins, Rhys, Reading	1176
A Weiss, Erich, Altoona	358
DP Weiss, Erich, Altoona	84
E Lopes, Christian, New Hampshire	16
2B PCT Hankins, Todd, Akron	.985
PO Weiss, Erich, Altoona	211
TC Weiss, Erich, Altoona	581
A Dosch, Drew, Bowie	195
DP Wood, Eric, Altoona	19
E Jones, Ryder, Richmond	20
3B PCT Dosch, Drew, Bowie	.950
PO Wood, Eric, Altoona	72
TC Dosch, Drew, Bowie	280
A Kieboom, Spencer, Harrisburg	82
PB Plaia, Colton, Binghamton	11
DP Three tied	7
E McGuire, Reese, Altoona, N.H.	10
C PCT Carrillo, Xorge, Binghamton	.998
PB Plaia, Colton, Binghamton	11
PO Alfaro, Jorge, Reading	736
TC Alfaro, Jorge, Reading	813
A Davis, Glynn, Bowie	13
DP Sturgeon, Cole, Portland	6
E Bautista, Rafael, Harrisburg	9
OF PCT Fields, Roemon, New Hampshire	.997
PO Fields, Roemon, New Hampshire	308
TC Fields, Roemon, New Hampshire	316
A Marin, Adrian, Bowie	305
DP Marin, Adrian, Bowie	77
E Nunez, Gustavo, Erie	21
SS PCT Marin, Adrian, Bowie	.964
PO Marin, Adrian, Bowie	176
TC Marin, Adrian, Bowie	499

PITCHING

AVG Pivetta, Nick, Reading	.235
BB Dickson, Cody, Altoona	93
BB/9 Hernandez, Carlos, Hartford	1.25
BK Castillo, Lendy, Erie, Akron	5
CG Mapes, Tyler, Harrisburg	4
ER Gabryszwski, Jeremy, New Hampshire	85
G Two tied wth	52
GF DuRapau, Montana, Altoona	43
GS Gabryszwski, Jeremy, New Hampshire	28
H Jemiola, Zach, Hartford	186
HB Holmes, Clay, Altoona	14
HR Pinto, Ricardo, Reading	20
IP Eppler, Tyler, Altoona	162.1
L Hess, David, Bowie	13
R Gabryszwski, Jeremy, New Hampshire	96
SHO 13 tied	1
SO Atkins, Mitch, Portland	145
SO/9 Atkins, Mitch, Portland	10.3
SO/9(RP) Feyereisen, J.P., Akron, Trenton	12.03
SV Carasiti, Matt, Hartford	29
W Two tied with	12
WP Beede, Tyler, Richmond	14

MINOR LEAGUES

BY MATT EDDY

The Mississippi double-play combination of shortstop Dansby Swanson and second baseman Ozzie Albies began the year not as teammates but as rivals for role of Braves shortstop of the future.

Swanson, who began the year at high Class A Carolina, took a clear and decisive lead in the race by manning shortstop for the five weeks in July and August that he and Albies were teammates at Mississippi. Swanson then reached the majors with Atlanta in mid-August and played well as a rookie.

Ultimately, Swanson and Albies are standout defenders who can hit toward the top of a big league lineup. Swanson batted .261/.342/.402 in 84 games and recorded the highest assist rate among full-season shortstops, while Albies hit .321/.391/.467 in 82 games and claimed the circuit's batting and on-base percentage titles.

Few leagues feature as little run-scoring as the Southern League, so pitchers tend to stand out. That was true in 2016, when Biloxi's Josh Hader (0.95 ERA in 11 starts) and Mississippi's Sean Newcomb (league-leading 152 strikeouts) showed the potential to be frontline starters.

The Braves and Rays each placed five players on the league's Top 20 Prospects ranking, and those clubs' affiliates each advanced to the SL playoffs, Mississippi on the strength of its pitching and Montgomery on the strength of its offense.

The Mississippi pitching staff brimmed with power arms, including Newcomb and righthanders Lucas Sims, Chris Ellis and Rob Whalen, and led the SL in ERA (3.10), strikeout rate (8.6 per nine innings) and opponent average (.228).

The M-Braves, minus Swanson and others, claimed a wild card and advanced to the SL finals, where they lost to Jackson, the Mariners affiliate that also bounced Montgomery in the first round.

Jackson recorded the league's best record at 84-55 (.604) and also featured the league's MVP (Tyler O'Neill) as well as its most outstanding pitcher (Ryan Yarbrough). O'Neill, a right fielder, finished fifth in the SL in average (.293), sec-

ond in home runs (24) and first in RBIs (102). Yarbrough, a control-oriented lefthander, went 12-4, 2.95 and finished second in the ERA race and also second in WHIP (1.11).

Montgomery led the SL in runs per game (4.59) and slugging percentage (.385) with a dynamic collection of position players, led by shortstop Willy Adames and first baseman/outfielder Jake Bauers, both of whom had been acquired by the Rays in headline-grabbing trades.

TOP 20 PROSPECTS

1. Dansby Swanson, ss, Mississippi (Braves)
2. Willy Adames, ss, Montgomery (Rays)
3. Ozzie Albies, 2b/ss, Mississippi (Braves)
4. Tyler O'Neill, of, Jackson (Mariners)
5. Jake Bauers, of/1b, Montgomery (Rays)
6. Josh Hader, lhp, Biloxi (Brewers)
7. Brent Honeywell, rhp, Montgomery (Rays)
8. Sean Newcomb, lhp, Mississippi (Braves)
9. Ian Happ, 2b/of, Tennessee (Cubs)
10. Anthony Banda, lhp, Mobile (Diamondbacks)
11. Amir Garrett, lhp, Pensacola (Reds)
12. Dustin Peterson, of, Mississippi (Braves)
13. Stephen Gonsalves, lhp, Chattanooga (Twins)
14. Chih-Wei Hu, rhp, rhp, Montgomery (Rays)
15. Casey Gillaspie, 1b, Montgomery (Rays)
16. Brandon Woodruff, rhp, Biloxi (Brewers)
17. Zach Granite, of, Chattanooga (Twins)
18. Lucas Sims, rhp, Mississippi (Braves)
19. Domingo Leyba, ss, Mobile (Diamondbacks)
20. Carson Fulmer, rhp, Birmingham (White Sox)

STANDINGS: SPLIT SEASON

FIRST HALF

NORTH	W	L	PCT	GB
Jackson	46	24	.657	—
Chattanooga	36	34	.514	10
Montgomery	34	36	.486	12
Birmingham	29	41	.414	17
Tennessee	28	42	.400	18

SOUTH	W	L	PCT	GB
Pensacola	41	29	.586	—
Biloxi	39	30	.565	1 ½
Mississippi	34	35	.493	6 ½
Mobile	32	38	.457	9
Jacksonville	30	40	.429	11

SECOND HALF

NORTH	W	L	PCT	GB
Montgomery	42	28	.600	—
Chattanooga	39	31	.557	3
Jackson	38	31	.551	3 ½
Tennessee	30	39	.435	11 ½
Birmingham	20	50	.286	22

SOUTH	W	L	PCT	GB
Pensacola	40	30	.571	—
Mississippi	39	30	.565	½
Mobile	35	35	.485	6
Jacksonville	33	36	.478	6 ½
Biloxi	33	37	.471	7

Playoffs—Semifinals: Jackson defeated Montgomery 3-1 and Mississippi defeated Pensacola 3-1 in best-of-five series. **Finals:** Jackson defeated Mississippi 3-0 in best-of-five series.

OVERALL STANDINGS

Division	W	L	PCT	GB	Manager(s)	Attendance	Average	Last Pennant
Jackson (Mariners)	84	55	.604	—	Daren Brown	126,116	2,002	2016
Pensacola (Reds)	81	59	.579	3 ½	Pat Kelly	302,340	4,319	Never
Montgomery (Rays)	76	64	.543	8 ½	Brady Williams	230,742	3,296	2007
Chattanooga (Twins)	75	65	.536	9 ½	Doug Mientkiewicz	223,517	3,193	2015
Mississippi (Braves)	73	65	.529	10 ½	Luis Salazar	190,130	2,838	2008
Biloxi (Brewers)	72	67	.518	12	Mike Guerrero	180,384	2,692	Never
Mobile (Diamondbacks)	65	73	.471	18 ½	Robby Hammock	96,185	1,527	2012
Jacksonville (Marlins)	63	76	.453	21	Dave Berg	264,401	4,197	2014
Tennessee (Cubs)	58	81	.417	26	Mark Johnson	293,694	4,319	2004
Birmingham (White Sox)	49	91	.350	35 ½	Ryan Newman	418,361	6,063	2013

MINOR LEAGUES

CLUB BATTING

	AVG	G	AB	R	H	2B	3B	HR	RBI	BB	SO	SB	OBP	SLG
Jackson	.263	139	4605	625	1211	215	50	62	572	555	985	141	.345	.372
Chattanooga	.257	140	4697	630	1206	211	45	72	572	473	1045	145	.331	.367
Tennessee	.257	139	4609	579	1184	249	20	80	528	482	958	84	.332	.372
Montgomery	.252	140	4670	642	1179	260	34	97	588	451	993	142	.320	.385
Mississippi	.250	138	4704	510	1177	211	44	71	472	369	1118	76	.309	.359
Mobile	.249	138	4517	559	1126	221	24	109	524	391	969	70	.314	.381
Jacksonville	.249	139	4510	538	1121	180	30	69	491	472	975	82	.325	.348
Birmingham	.241	140	4688	566	1130	225	39	80	520	461	1195	86	.314	.357
Pensacola	.240	140	4624	560	1111	212	25	89	496	456	1229	114	.316	.355
Biloxi	.235	139	4454	471	1048	167	24	81	437	390	1063	88	.304	.338

CLUB PITCHING

	ERA	G	CG	SHO	SV	IP	H	R	ER	HR	BB	SO	AVG
Mississippi	3.10	138	2	0	44	1252	1044	493	432	54	534	1196	.228
Pensacola	3.20	140	1	1	47	1242	1109	506	442	82	401	1104	.238
Jackson	3.49	139	4	3	41	1223	1198	532	474	74	367	1076	.257
Biloxi	3.59	139	1	0	44	1214	1100	533	484	74	434	1111	.242
Chattanooga	3.60	140	5	0	39	1242	1190	559	497	78	433	1009	.256
Mobile	3.68	138	6	2	39	1185	1156	545	485	89	432	1016	.257
Montgomery	3.73	140	1	1	41	1239	1096	574	513	89	512	1073	.238
Jacksonville	3.97	139	1	0	33	1195	1140	587	527	98	382	968	.252
Tennessee	4.05	139	2	0	32	1219	1204	637	549	100	496	938	.259
Birmingham	4.62	140	1	1	19	1228	1256	714	631	72	509	1039	.266

CLUB FIELDING

	PCT	PO	A	E	DP		PCT	PO	A	E	DP
Chattanooga	.984	3725	1468	87	414	Pensacola	.978	3726	1414	118	282
Jackson	.983	3668	1429	88	312	Montgomery	.977	3358	1118	325	
Mobile	.980	3556	1337	99	339	Jacksonville	.977	3586	1345	117	323
Mississippi	.979	3757	1358	111	320	Tennessee	.975	3656	1486	134	332
Biloxi	.978	3643	1402	115	284	Birmingham	.973	3685	1497	144	379

INDIVIDUAL BATTING

Batter, Club	AVG	G	AB	R	H	2B	3B	HR	RBI	BB	SO	SB
Albies, Ozzie, Mississippi	.321	82	330	56	106	22	7	4	33	33	57	21
Young, Chesny, Tennessee	.303	126	491	60	149	25	2	4	37	57	64	16
Elizalde, Sebastian, Pensacola	.297	111	408	55	121	16	3	5	54	18	61	5
Granite, Zach, Chattanooga	.295	127	526	86	155	18	8	4	52	42	43	56
O'Neill, Tyler, Jackson	.293	130	492	68	144	26	4	24	102	62	150	12
Caratini, Victor, Tennessee	.291	115	412	57	120	25	2	6	47	54	60	4
Lopes, Tim, Jackson	.284	131	510	74	145	23	5	1	49	54	88	26
Peterson, Dustin, Mississippi	.282	132	524	65	148	38	2	12	88	45	100	4
Vincej, Zach, Pensacola	.281	121	399	45	112	24	3	3	47	25	85	7
Riddle, J.T., Jacksonville	.278	101	389	49	108	18	4	3	51	33	72	5

INDIVIDUAL PITCHING

Pitcher, Club	W	L	ERA	G	GS	CG	SV	IP	H	R	ER	BB	SO
Hu, Chih-Wei, Montgomery	7	8	2.59	24	24	0	0	143	128	49	41	36	107
Yarbrough, Ryan, Jackson	12	4	2.95	25	25	1	0	128	112	45	42	31	99
Woodruff, Brandon, Biloxi	10	8	3.01	20	20	1	0	114	88	39	38	30	124
Markey, Brad, Tennessee	8	7	3.17	26	23	1	0	131	129	56	46	45	65
Kirsch, Chris, Montgomery	7	7	3.22	25	25	1	0	145	139	60	52	57	114
Blackburn, Paul, Tenn., Jackson	9	5	3.27	26	25	0	0	143	138	63	52	35	99
Stephens, Jackson, Pensacola	8	11	3.33	27	26	1	0	151	148	63	56	41	131
Johnson, Patrick, Jacksonville	8	7	3.37	31	21	0	0	128	120	55	48	33	113
Slegers, Aaron, Chattanooga	10	7	3.41	25	25	0	0	145	137	61	55	46	104
Hurlbut, David, Chattanooga	7	7	3.51	23	23	1	0	136	161	68	53	26	90

ALL-STAR TEAM

P: Chih-Wei Hu, Montgomery; Ryan Yarbrough, Jackson. **C:** Victor Caratini, Tennessee. **1B:** Jake Bauers, Montgomery. **2B:** Tim Lopes, Jackson. **3B:** J.T. Riddle, Jacksonville. **SS:** Willy Adames, Montgomery. **DH:** Kevin Cron, Mobile. **OF:** Daniel Palka, Chattanooga; Dustin Peterson, Mississippi; Tyler O'Neill, Jackson; Zach Granite, Chattanooga. **IF:** Chesny Young, Tennessee. **RP:** Alejandro Chacin, Pensacola; Cade Gotta , Montgomery.
Manager of the Year : Daren Brown , Jackson.
Most Outstanding Pitcher: Ryan Yarbrough Jackson.
Most Valuable Player: Tyler O'Neill, Jackson

DEPARTMENT LEADERS

BATTING

2B	Peterson, Dustin, Mississippi	38
3B	Engel, Adam, Birmingham	9
	Landry, Leon, Jackson	9
AB/SO	Granite, Zach, Chattanooga	12.23
BB	Adames, Willy, Montgomery	74
CS	Granite, Zach, Chattanooga	14
	Young, Chesny, Tennessee	14
H	Granite, Zach, Chattanooga	155
HBP	Ervin, Phillip, Pensacola	18
HR	Cron, Kevin, Mobile	26
OBP	Young, Chesny, Tennessee	.376
OPS	O'Neill, Tyler, Jackson	.882
R	Adames, Willy, Montgomery	89
RBI	O'Neill, Tyler, Jackson	102
SAC	Camargo, Johan, Mississippi	17
SB	Granite, Zach, Chattanooga	56
SLG	O'Neill, Tyler, Jackson	.508
SO	Phillips, Brett, Biloxi	154
TB	O'Neill, Tyler, Jackson	250
XBH	O'Neill, Tyler, Jackson	54

FIELDING

A	Cron, Kevin, Mobile	64
DP	Hicks, D.J., Chattanooga	102
E	Cron, Kevin, Mobile	11
FPCT	Hicks, D.J., Chattanooga	.997
PO	Cron, Kevin, Mobile	966
A	DeMichele, Joey, Birmingham	366
DP	DeMichele, Joey, Birmingham	88
E	Dixon, Brandon, Pensacola	11
FPCT	DeMichele, Joey, Birmingham	.990
PO	DeMichele, Joey, Birmingham	207
A	Michalczewski, Trey, Birmingham	260
DP	Michalczewski, Trey, Birmingham	33
E	Anderson, Brian, Jacksonville	22
FPCT	Michalczewski, Trey, Birmingham	.951
PO	Michalczewski, Trey, Birmingham	71
A	Astudillo, Willians, Mississippi	79
PB	Nottingham, Jacob, Biloxi	21
DP	DePew, Jake, Montgomery	7
DP	Freeman, Ronnie, Mobile	7
E	Nottingham, Jacob, Biloxi	15
C PCT	Astudillo, Willians, Mississippi	.997
PO	Nottingham, Jacob, Biloxi	777
A	Granite, Zach, Chattanooga	13
DP	Lee, Braxton, Montgomery	6
E	Walker, Keenyn, Birmingham	9
OF PCT	Taylor, Tyrone, Biloxi	1
PO	Granite, Zach, Chattanooga	291
A	Gonzalez, Benji, Jackson	365
DP	Gonzalez, Benji, Jackson	80
E	Penalver, Carlos, Tennessee	31
FPCT	Vincej, Zach, Pensacola	.991
PO	Gonzalez, Benji, Jackson	178

PITCHING

AVG	Woodruff, Brandon, Biloxi	.211
BB	Guerrero, Jordan, Birmingham	73
BB/9	Hurlbut, David, Chattanooga	1.72
BK	Guerrero, Jordan, Birmingham	3
BK	Kittredge, Andrew, Jackson	3
CG	24 tied with	1
ER	Skulina, Tyler, Tennessee	74
G	Chacin, Alejandro, Pensacola	52
	Krehbiel, Joey, Mobile	52
	Peterson, Stephen, Biloxi	52
GF	Chacin, Alejandro, Pensacola	46
GS	Newcomb, Sean, Mississippi	27
	Romano, Sal, Pensacola	27
	Skulina, Tyler, Tennessee	27
H	Ash, Brett, Jackson	177
HB	Mortensen, Jared, Montgomery	17
HR	Skulina, Tyler, Tennessee	16
IP	Romano, Sal, Pensacola	156
L	Skulina, Tyler, Tennessee	12
SO	Newcomb, Sean, Mississippi	152
SO/9	Woodruff, Brandon, Biloxi	9.82
SO/9(RP)	Harper, Ryne, Jackson	12.57
SV	Chacin, Alejandro, Pensacola	30
W	Three tied with	12
WP	Mortensen, Jared, Montgomery	38

MINOR LEAGUES

BY J.J. COOPER

The names keep changing but the Rockhounds keep winning.

Midland won its third straight Texas League title topping Northwest Arkansas 3-1 in the best-of-5 championship series. The win was also the team's fourth title in the past eight seasons. It was also the second straight year that Midland has topped Northwest Arkansas in the championship series.

Midland has won with a veteran club with few prospects (2014), they've won with a dominant lineup in 2015 and this year Brandon Mann's outstanding playoffs (1-1, 0.73) helped lead the Three-Peat.

This year's Rockhounds club was impressively loaded with prospects. First/third baseman Ryon Healy led the team in the first half before being promoted in a season that saw him reach the big leagues. Healy hit 13 home runs with the A's, including one against Kansas City that went 480 feet. It was the sixth longest home run of the year, as measured by Statcast. Third baseman Matt Chapman was consistent all season while shortstop/second baseman Franklin Barreto had a very strong second half. Yairo Munoz also provided plenty of power.

Midland's starting rotation was key in the championship series. Mann, James Naile, Joel Seddon and Cory Walter combined to allow four runs in 23 innings. Outfielder Tyler Marincov was 8-for-16 with a double and a home run to pace the RockHounds offense.

The league's overall talent couldn't compare to 2015 when Carlos Correa and Corey Seager made it a season for the ages, but Corpus Christi shortstop Alex Bregman was dominant in a 62-game stint before he was promoted out of the league.

Midland, Corpus Christi and Tulsa battled for the status as the league's most prospect-laden team. While Midland won the title, it was the Corpus Christi Hooks that had the league's best record at 85-55, seven games better than Midland. The Hooks were led by righthanders David Paulino

and Francis Martes and the power of third baseman J.D. Davis.

Overall, the league was particularly friendly to pitchers in 2016. No qualifying hitter topped .300 and the overall .249 batting average of the league was the worst mark of the past decade.

Arkansas' Jordan Kipper threw a nine-inning no hitter against Northwest Arkansas on May 17. It was the first no-hitter in the Texas League since Brooks Pounders' no-no in 2013. Davis provided the best offensive day the league saw with a three home run game against San Antonio on May 19.

TOP 20 PROSPECTS

1. Alex Bregman ss/3b, Corpus Christi (Astros)
2. Cody Bellinger 1b/of, Tulsa (Dodgers)
3. Francis Martes rhp, Corpus Christi (Astros)
4. Luke Weaver rhp, Springfield (Cardinals)
5. David Paulino rhp, Corpus Christi (Astros)
6. Matt Chapman 3b, Midland (Athletics)
7. Franklin Barreto ss/2b, Midland (Athletics)
8. Ryon Healy, 1b/3b, Midland (Athletics)
9. Teoscar Hernandez of, Corpus Christi (Astros)
10. Lewis Brinson of, Frisco (Rangers)
11. Carson Kelly, c, Springfield (Cardinals)
12. Andrew Toles, of, Tulsa (Dodgers)
13. Alex Verdugo, of, Tulsa (Dodgers)
14. Franchy Cordero, of, San Antonio (Padres)
15. Brock Stewart, rhp, Tulsa (Dodgers)
16. Willie Calhoun, 2b, Tulsa (Dodgers)
17. Matt Strahm, lhp, Northwest Arkansas (Royals)
18. Derek Fisher, of, Corpus Christi (Astros)
19. Yohander Mendez, lhp, Frisco (Rangers)
20. Harrison Bader, of, Springfield (Cardinals)

STANDINGS: SPLIT SEASON

FIRST HALF					SECOND HALF				
NORTH	W	L	PCT	GB	NORTH	W	L	PCT	GB
Springfield	41	29	.586	—	NW Arkansas	36	34	.514	—
Tulsa	37	32	.536	3½	Arkansas	35	35	.500	1
Arkansas	32	38	.457	9	Springfield	34	36	.486	2
NW Arkansas	29	41	.414	12	Tulsa	31	39	.443	5
SOUTH	W	L	PCT	GB	SOUTH	W	L	PCT	GB
Corpus Christi	47	23	.671	—	Midland	45	25	.643	—
Frisco	38	31	.551	8½	Corpus Christi	38	32	.543	7
Midland	33	37	.471	14	San Antonio	36	34	.514	9
San Antonio	22	48	.314	25	Frisco	25	45	.357	20

Playoffs—Semifinals: Midland defeated Corpus Christi 3-1 and NW Arkansas defeated Springfield 3-1 in best-of-five series. **Finals:** Midland defeated NW Arkansas 3-1 in a best-of-five series.

OVERALL STANDINGS

Team (Organization)	W	L	PCT	GB	Manager(s)	Attendance	Average	Last Pennant
Corpus Christi (Astros)	85	55	.607	—	Rodney Linares	350,964	5,161	2006
Midland (Athletics)	78	62	.557	7	Ryan Christenson	265,193	3,900	2016
Springfield (Cardinals)	75	65	.536	10	Dann Bilardello	316,990	4,731	2012
Tulsa (Dodgers)	68	71	.489	16½	Ryan Garko	366,734	5,393	1998
Arkansas (Angels)	67	73	.479	18	Mark Parent	306,570	4,716	2008
NW Arkansas (Royals)	65	75	.464	20	Vance Wilson	312,001	4,457	2010
Frisco (Rangers)	63	76	.453	21½	Joe Mikulik	463,564	7,024	2004
San Antonio (Padres)	58	82	.414	27	Phillip Wellman	317,607	4,603	2013

CLUB BATTING

	AVG	G	AB	R	H	2B	3B	HR	RBI	BB	SO	SB	OBP	SLG
Midland	.260	140	4763	641	1238	248	31	106	587	494	1132	110	.332	.392
Tulsa	.256	139	4652	615	1189	242	18	133	573	443	916	65	.325	.401
Springfield	.256	140	4661	598	1192	188	19	125	552	441	1154	57	.325	.385
NW Arkansas	.253	140	4719	552	1195	232	18	101	498	359	1106	157	.311	.374
Corpus Christi	.248	140	4750	626	1177	235	25	142	579	503	1071	109	.324	.397
Frisco	.246	139	4610	557	1134	208	33	96	527	341	993	79	.304	.368
Arkansas	.241	140	4538	509	1095	194	35	71	458	406	1199	110	.310	.346
San Antonio	.235	140	4647	512	1093	217	30	97	475	373	1182	112	.298	.357

CLUB PITCHING

	ERA	G	CG	SHO	SV	IP	H	R	ER	HR	BB	SO	AVG
Midland	3.48	140	1	1	36	1248	1149	570	482	104	395	1023	.246
Corpus Christi	3.50	140	1	1	55	1272	1244	564	495	102	345	1132	.255
Northwest Arkansas	3.56	140	0	0	32	1240	1159	534	490	122	373	1163	.248
Arkansas	3.67	140	3	2	40	1222	1109	547	498	99	464	1093	.245
Tulsa	3.70	139	3	1	33	1217	1171	581	501	97	398	1084	.252
Springfield	3.74	140	3	0	44	1239	1166	599	515	120	433	1058	.248
San Antonio	3.92	140	0	0	28	1236	1170	602	539	110	433	1077	.253
Frisco	4.09	139	3	0	32	1213	1145	613	552	117	519	1123	.250

CLUB FIELDING

	PCT	PO	A	E	DP		PCT	PO	A	E	DP
Arkansas	.987	3666	1317	65	333	Frisco	.976	3640	1286	119	373
NW Arkansas	.982	3720	1322	93	313	Midland	.976	3743	1503	131	377
San Antonio	.980	3708	1378	105	408	Springfield	.975	3717	1346	131	330
Corpus Christi	.978	3817	1367	114	294	Tulsa	.972	3652	1385	147	289

INDIVIDUAL BATTING

Batter, Club	AVG	G	AB	R	H	2B	3B	HR	RBI	BB	SO	SB
Voit, Luke, Springfield	.297	134	482	70	143	20	5	19	74	52	83	1
Guzman, Ronald, Frisco	.288	102	375	51	108	16	5	15	56	33	82	2
Ramos, Mauricio, NW Arkansas	.288	125	483	41	139	28	1	9	60	19	92	5
Schulz, Nick, San Antonio	.282	106	393	41	111	23	1	10	50	43	101	5
Torres, Nick, San Antonio	.282	93	373	40	105	28	2	6	40	16	96	10
Barreto, Franklin, Midland	.281	119	462	63	130	25	3	10	50	36	90	30
Taylor, Beau, Midland	.280	95	339	50	95	25	0	5	53	54	86	1
Rondon, Jose, San Antonio	.279	96	376	45	105	21	2	5	44	15	66	13
Toups, Corey, NW Arkansas	.275	86	338	61	93	25	2	10	38	36	96	16
Verdugo, Alex, Tulsa	.273	126	477	58	130	23	1	13	63	44	67	2

INDIVIDUAL PITCHING

Pitcher, Club	W	L	ERA	G	GS	CG	SV	IP	H	R	ER	BB	SO
Caramo, Yender, NW Arkansas	5	7	2.45	34	10	0	2	114	101	38	31	23	67
De Jong, Chase, Tulsa	14	5	2.86	25	25	2	0	142	106	51	45	39	125
Junis, Jake, NW Arkansas	9	7	3.25	21	21	0	0	119	110	48	43	27	117
Martes, Francis,, Corpus Christi	9	6	3.30	25	22	0	0	125	104	53	46	47	131
Lloyd, Kyle, San Antonio	7	7	3.31	30	20	0	0	130	124	54	48	38	99
Kipper, Jordan, Arkansas	12	7	3.35	25	25	2	0	153	147	63	57	41	85
Skoglund, Eric, NW Arkansas	7	10	3.45	27	27	0	0	156	135	63	60	38	134
Poncedeleon, Daniel, Springfield	9	8	3.52	27	27	1	0	151	128	71	59	56	122
Nielsen, Trey, Springfield	8	8	3.84	23	19	2	1	122	131	59	52	38	81
Barlow, Scott, Tulsa	4	7	3.98	24	23	0	0	124	125	63	55	52	102

ALL-STAR TEAM

P: Brendan McCurry, Corpus Christi; Chase De Jong, Tulsa; Eric Skoglund, NW Arkansas; Francis Martes, Corpus Christi; Jake Junis, NW Arkansas; Jason Jester, San Antonio; Jordan Kipper, Arkansas; Luke Weaver, Springfield. **C:** Beau Taylor, Midland. **1B:** Ronald Guzman, Frisco. **2B:** Willie Calhoun, Tulsa. **3B:** Matt Chapman, Midland. **SS:** Alex Bregman, Corpus Christi. **DH:** Luke Voit, Springfield. **OF:** Alex Verdugo, Tulsa; Ryan Cordell, Frisco; Teoscar Hernandez, Corpus Christi. **IF:** Franklin Barreto, Midland.
Manager of the Year : Ryan Christenson, Midland.
Pitcher of the Year: Chase De Jong ,Tulsa.
Player of the Year: Matt Chapman , Midland

DEPARTMENT LEADERS

BATTING

2B	Davis, J.D., Corpus Christi	34
3B	Cordero, Franchy, San Antonio	8
AB/SO	Kiner-Falefa, Isiah, Frisco	7.88
BB	Fisher, Derek, Corpus Christi	74
	Rosa, Viosergy, Midland	74
CS	Barreto, Franklin, Midland	15
H	Voit, Luke, Springfield	143
HBP	Kiner-Falefa, Isiah, Frisco	11
HR	Chapman, Matt, Midland	29
OBP	Taylor, Beau, Midland	.383
OPS	Chapman, Matt, Midland	.856
R	Chapman, Matt, Midland	78
RBI	Calhoun, Willie, Tulsa	88
SAC	Gore, Terrance, NW Arkansas	19
SB	Gore, Terrance, NW Arkansas	44
SLG	Chapman, Matt, Midland	.521
SO	Chapman, Matt, Midland	147
XBH	Chapman, Matt, Midland	59

FIELDING

A	Voit, Luke, Springfield	68
DP	Guzman, Ronald, Frisco	86
E	Guzman, Ronald, Frisco	10
1B PCT	Gregor, Conrad, Corpus Christi	.994
PO	Gregor, Conrad, Corpus Christi	815
A	Ward, Nelson, San Antonio	286
DP	Ward, Nelson, San Antonio	80
E	Calhoun, Willie, Tulsa	21
2B PCT	Ward, Nelson, San Antonio	.972
PO	Calhoun, Willie, Tulsa	200
A	Chapman, Matt, Midland	245
E	DeJong, Paul, Springfield	16
3B PCT	Chapman, Matt, Midland	.971
PO	Chapman, Matt, Midland	87
A	Gallagher, Cam, NW Arkansas	62
PB	McGee, Stephen, Arkansas	11
DP	Gallagher, Cam, NW Arkansas	9
E	Deglan, Kellin, Frisco	10
C PCT	Gallagher, Cam, NW Arkansas	.996
PO	Gallagher, Cam, NW Arkansas	648
A	Sportman, J.P., Midland	17
DP	Sportman, J.P., Midland	4
E	Verdugo, Alex, Tulsa	10
OF PCT	Schulz, Nick, San Antonio	1
PO	Vertigan, Brett, Midland	274
A	Phillips, Anthony, Arkansas	299
DP	Rondon, Jose, San Antonio	76
E	Barreto, Franklin, Midland	15
SS PCT	Phillips, Anthony, Arkansas	.977
PO	Rondon, Jose, San Antonio	154
TC	Phillips, Anthony, Arkansas	440

PITCHING

AVG	De Jong, Chase, Tulsa	.207
BB	Alcantara, Victor, Arkansas	57
BB/9	Caramo, Yender, NW Arkansas	1.82
BK	Four tied with	2
CG	Four tied with	2
ER	Seddon, Joel, Midland	70
G	Johnson, D.J., Arkansas	47
GF	Three tied with	25
GS	Poncedeleon, Daniel, Springfield	27
	Skoglund, Eric, NW Arkansas	27
H	Seddon, Joel, Midland	149
HB	Poncedeleon, Daniel, Springfield	15
HR	Baker, Corey, Springfield	19
	Skoglund, Eric, NW Arkansas	19
IP	Skoglund, Eric, NW Arkansas	156.1
L	Goudeau, Ashton, NW Arkansas	13
SO	Skoglund, Eric, NW Arkansas	134
SO/9	Martes, Francis, Corpus Christi	9.41
SO/9(RP)	Sanchez, Jake, Midland	9.93
SV	Lucas, Josh, Springfield	16
W	De Jong, Chase, Tulsa	14
WP	Sadzeck, Connor, Frisco	18

MINOR LEAGUES

BY KYLE GLASER

In their final season of existence, the High Desert Mavericks went out as champions.

Minor League Baseball announced in August the Cal League would contract by two teams—High Desert and Bakersfield—after the 2016 season.

Knowing this would be the end, High Desert, the Rangers affiliate, made sure to finish the season on a high note. The Mavericks won 13 of the final 20 games after the announcement was made they would be contracted, including a three-game sweep of Visalia (Diamondbacks) in the championship series. The won Game Three at home 7-4, clinching the title in grand style in front of the home fans one last time. Although the Mavericks went all season without radio broadcasters, the team imported two—Inland Empire's Mike Lindskog and Lake Elsinore's Sean McCall.

Lefthander Brett Martin, the Rangers fourth-round pick in 2014, was named Championship Series MVP after pitching seven no-hit innings with 15 strikeouts in Game 2. Catcher Jose Trevino, infielders Josh Morgan and Juremi Profar, and outfielders Luke Tendler, Scott Heineman and Jairo Beras all hit over .320 in the postseason after staying with High Desert all year to help it post an 82-58 regular-season record, best in the league. Top starting pitching prospects Luis Ortiz, Yohander Mendez and Ariel Jurado gave High Desert a boost earlier in the year before being promoted.

Bakersfield (Mariners) also had a Cinderella run in its final season, winning the North Division second-half title and reaching the semifinals before falling to Visalia. It was the final season after 75 years of minor league baseball in Bakersfield.

Youth was the theme of the league on an individual level. Modesto (Rockies) righthander Ryan Castellani, tied for the youngest pitcher in the league on Opening Day, led it in innings pitched and strikeouts. Lake Elsinore (Padres) second baseman Luis Urias, the youngest position player in

the league on Opening Day, won the batting title and was named League MVP. Rancho Cucamonga (Dodgers) righthander Josh Sborz, was named Pitcher of the Year. The 2015 College World Series Most Outstanding Player at Virginia led the league with a 2.66 ERA before being promoted to Double-A in his first full pro season.

To adjust to the contraction after the season, the Mariners purchased a controlling interest in Modesto and the Rockies affiliated with Lancaster.

TOP 20 PROSPECTS

1. Ryan Castellani, rhp, Modesto (Rockies)
2. Chris Shaw, 1b, San Jose (Giants)
3. Luis Urias, 2b/ss, Lake Elsinore (Padres)
4. Grant Holmes, rhp, Rancho/Stockton (Dodgers/A's)
5. Yusniel Diaz, of, Rancho Cucamonga (Dodgers)
6. Michael Gettys, of, Lake Elsinore (Padres)
7. Domingo Leyba, ss/2b, Visalia (Diamondbacks)
8. Travis Demeritte, 2b, High Desert (Rangers)
9. Dinelson Lamet, rhp, Lake Elsinore (Padres)
10. Ariel Jurado, rhp, High Desert (Rangers)
11. Andrew Moore, rhp, Bakersfield (Mariners)
12. Dawel Lugo, 3b, Visalia (Diamondbacks)
13. Johan Mieses, of, Rancho Cucamonga (Dodgers)
14. Yency Almonte, rhp, Modesto (Rockies)
15. Drew Jackson, ss, Bakersfield (Mariners)
16. Josh Sborz, rhp, Rancho Cucamonga (Dodgers)
17. Franchy Cordero, of, Lake Elsinore (Padres)
18. Jose Trevino, c, High Desert (Rangers)
19. Rodolfo Martinez, rhp, San Jose (Giants)
20. Ramon Laureano, of, Lancaster (Astros)

STANDINGS: SPLIT SEASON

FIRST HALF

NORTH	W	L	PCT	GB
Visalia	46	24	.657	—
San Jose	39	31	.557	7
Bakersfield	37	33	.529	9
Stockton	27	43	.386	19
Modesto	26	44	.371	20

SOUTH	W	L	PCT	GB
Bakersfield	39	31	.557	—
Visalia	35	35	.500	4
Modesto	34	36	.486	5
Stockton	33	37	.471	6
San Jose	29	41	.414	10

SECOND HALF

NORTH	W	L	PCT	GB
High Desert	43	27	.614	—
R. Cucamonga	42	28	.w600	1
Lancaster	35	35	.500	8
Lake Elsinore	32	38	.457	11
Inland Empire	23	47	.329	20

SOUTH	W	L	PCT	GB
Lancaster	42	28	.600	—
High Desert	39	31	.557	3
Lake Elsinore	37	33	.529	5
R. Cucamonga	37	33	.529	5
Inland Empire	25	45	.357	17

Playoffs—Semifinals: Visalia defeated Bakersfield 3-0 and High Desert defeated Lancaster 3-1 in best-of-five series. **Finals:** High Desert defeated Visalia 3-0 in a best-of-five series.

OVERALL STANDINGS

Division	W	L	PCT	GB	Manager(s)	Attendance	Average	Last Pennant
High Desert (Rangers)	82	58	.586	—	Howard Johnson	76,051	1,102	2016
Visalia (Diamondbacks)	81	59	.579	1	J.R. House	123,079	1,784	1978
Rancho Cucamonga (Dodgers)	79	61	.564	3	Drew Saylor	171,509	2,450	2015
Lancaster (Astros)	77	63	.550	5	Ramon Vazquez	165,947	2,405	2014
Bakersfield (Mariners)	76	64	.543	6	Eddie Menchaca	62,922	899	1989
Lake Elsinore (Padres)	69	71	.493	13	F. Morales/L. Burkhart	196,684	2,810	2011
San Jose (Giants)	68	72	.486	14	Lipso Nava	166,756	2,417	2010
Modesto (Rockies)	60	80	.429	22	Fred Ocasio	157,239	2,246	2004
Stockton (Athletics)	60	80	.429	22	Rick Magnante	188,732	2,735	2008
Inland Empire (Angels)	48	92	.343	34	Chad Tracy	190,933	2,728	2013

CLUB BATTING

	AVG	G	AB	R	H	2B	3B	HR	RBI	BB	SO	SB	OBP	SLG
High Desert	.278	140	4831	812	1345	295	26	177	748	443	1019	84	.345	.460
Rancho Cucamonga	.273	140	4867	762	1327	249	54	152	716	424	1210	100	.338	.440
Lancaster	.272	140	4709	856	1283	250	46	136	776	585	1183	209	.359	.432
Visalia	.270	140	4844	680	1310	268	48	101	602	390	1157	91	.328	.408
Stockton	.265	140	4841	691	1283	252	30	108	632	539	1226	87	.346	.396
Bakersfield	.262	140	4896	755	1284	223	24	116	680	583	1239	102	.349	.389
San Jose	.259	140	4776	636	1235	245	28	126	573	390	1122	109	.320	.401
Lake Elsinore	.257	140	4786	635	1228	255	39	111	580	376	1157	70	.318	.396
Inland Empire	.250	140	4712	599	1176	198	40	80	547	432	1162	102	.317	.360
Modesto	.246	140	4763	592	1174	196	49	90	521	411	1155	208	.313	.365

CLUB PITCHING

	ERA	G	CG	SHO	SV	IP	H	R	ER	HR	BB	SO	AVG
Modesto	3.89	140	3	1	34	1267	1221	655	548	89	445	1143	.253
Bakersfield	3.96	140	2	0	34	1272	1218	648	560	109	500	1267	.252
Rancho Cucamonga	3.97	140	0	0	29	1243	1189	647	548	114	401	1195	.251
Visalia	4.01	140	1	0	43	1244	1239	638	554	99	413	1234	.260
Lake Elsinore	4.24	140	0	0	38	1245	1260	690	586	101	456	1146	.263
High Desert	4.50	140	1	0	36	1242	1259	718	621	148	500	1170	.263
Stockton	4.59	140	0	0	20	1244	1334	764	634	129	455	1101	.273
San Jose	4.61	140	2	0	42	1239	1257	720	635	133	472	1096	.263
Inland Empire	4.93	140	0	0	15	1228	1318	753	673	114	470	1092	.275
Lancaster	4.99	140	3	2	40	1224	1350	785	678	161	461	1186	.278

CLUB FIELDING

	PCT	PO	A	E	DP		PCT	PO	A	E	DP
High Desert	.976	3726	1409	127	309	R. Cucamonga	.972	3728	1327	145	298
Visalia	.974	3731	1424	136	308	Lancaster	.970	3671	1263	151	303
Inland Empire	.974	3685	1432	136	303	Lake Elsinore	.967	3736	1446	175	338
San Jose	.974	3717	1375	138	321	Stockton	.967	3733	1442	176	305
Bakersfield	.972	3817	1490	152	328	Modesto	.967	3801	1514	183	357

INDIVIDUAL BATTING

Batter, Club	AVG	G	AB	R	H	2B	3B	HR	RBI	BB	SO	SB
Urias, Luis, Lake Elsinore	.330	120	466	71	154	26	5	5	52	40	36	7
Petty, Kyle, Bakersfield	.329	86	353	65	116	24	1	14	62	42	91	12
Ferguson, Drew, Lancaster	.313	90	326	70	102	25	2	14	69	45	82	28
Heineman, Scott, High Desert	.303	134	525	96	159	39	8	17	80	59	143	9
Harris, James, Stockton	.303	119	492	81	149	30	4	7	53	54	118	21
Reyes, Victor, Visalia	.303	124	469	62	142	11	12	6	54	33	78	20
Trevino, Jose, High Desert	.303	109	433	67	131	30	0	9	68	26	49	2
Bennie, Joe, Stockton	.302	111	434	64	131	31	0	11	69	48	116	6
Profar, Juremi, High Desert	.300	103	383	66	115	23	2	13	58	33	47	1
Morgan, Josh, High Desert	.300	128	470	74	141	19	2	7	64	44	61	4

INDIVIDUAL PITCHING

Pitcher, Club	W	L	ERA	G	GS	CG	SV	IP	H	R	ER	BB	SO
French, Parker, Modesto	8	9	2.85	24	24	1	0	155	136	61	49	25	109
Rodriguez, Helmis, Modesto	5	9	3.36	30	13	0	0	131	113	59	49	34	94
Almonte, Yency, Modesto	8	9	3.71	22	22	1	0	138	124	66	57	39	134
Huffman, Chris, Lake Elsinore	10	5	3.78	28	23	0	0	131	126	70	55	43	98
Kennedy, Brett, Lake Elsinore	6	10	3.80	22	22	0	0	114	114	57	48	44	109
Castellani, Ryan, Modesto	7	8	3.81	26	26	1	0	168	156	79	71	50	142
Pike, Tyler, Bakersfield	6	5	4.01	25	25	0	0	126	99	59	56	68	134
Keller, Brad, Visalia	9	7	4.47	24	24	0	0	135	147	73	67	26	99
Graves, Brett, Stockton	7	10	4.60	27	25	0	0	141	141	81	72	49	86
Holmes, Grant, , Rancho/Stockton	11	7	4.63	26	23	0	1	134	147	85	69	53	124

ALL-STAR TEAM

P: Andrew Sopko, Rancho Cucamonga. **P:** Joshua Sborz, Rancho Cucamonga. **P:** Parker French, Modesto. **P:** Yency Almonte, Modesto. **C:** Jose Trevino, High Desert. **1B:** Kyle Petty, Bakersfield. **2B:** Luis Urias, Lake Elsinore. **3B:** Matt Beaty, Rancho Cucamonga. **SS:** Erick Mejia, Rancho Cucamonga. **DH:** Johan Mieses, Rancho Cucamonga. **OF:** James Harris, Stockton. **OF:** Ramon Laureano, Lancaster. **OF:** Scott Heineman, High Desert. **IF:** Marty Herum, Visalia.
Manager-of-the-Year: Howard Johnson High Desert.
Most Valuable Player: Luis Urias Lake Elsinore.
Pitcher-of-the-Year: Joshua Sborz Rancho Cucamonga.
Rookie-of-the-Year: Luis Urias Lake Elsinore.

DEPARTMENT LEADERS

BATTING

2B	Heineman, Scott, High Desert	39
3B	Mejia, Erick, Rancho Cucamonga	12
	Reyes, Victor, Visalia	12
AB/SO	Urias, Luis, Lake Elsinore	12.94
BB	Mack, Chantz, Bakersfield	80
CS	Mejia, Erick, Rancho Cucamonga	15
H	Heineman, Scott, High Desert	159
HBP	Locastro, Tim, Rancho Cucamonga	18
HR	Mieses, Johan, Rancho Cucamonga	28
OBP	Ferguson, Drew, Lancaster	.41
OPS	Ferguson, Drew, Lancaster	.941
R	Heineman, Scott, High Desert	96
RBI	Tendler, Luke, High Desert	97
SAC	Jean, Luis, Modesto	13
SB	Rogers, Wes, Modesto	43
SLG	Demeritte, Travis, High Desert	.583
SO	Wilson, Austin, Bakersfield	157
XBH	Tendler, Luke, High Desert	65

FIELDING

A	Ferguson, Collin, Modesto	89
DP	Ferguson, Collin, Modesto	82
E	Pimentel, Sandber, Stockton	18
1B PCT	Boehm, Jeff, Inland Empire	.990
PO	Ferguson, Collin, Modesto	911
A	Wall, Forrest, Modesto	318
DP	Wall, Forrest, Modesto	74
E	Wall, Forrest, Modesto	32
2B PCT	Castillo, Henry, Visalia	.971
PO	Wall, Forrest, Modesto	209
A	Houchins, Zachary, Inland Empire	190
DP	Houchins, Zachary, Inland Empire	22
E	Brizuela, Jose, Stockton	25
3B PCT	Houchins, Zachary, Inland Empire	.960
PO	Houchins, Zachary, Inland Empire	95
A	Trevino, Jose, High Desert	102
PB	Three tied with	19
DP	Trevino, Jose, High Desert	12
E	Raga, Argenis, Stockton	10
C PCT	Trevino, Jose, High Desert	.998
PO	Trevino, Jose, High Desert	846
A	Mieses, Johan, Rancho Cucamonga	14
DP	Reyes, Franmil, Lake Elsinore	6
E	Perez, Ayendy, Inland Empire	13
OF PCT	Heineman, Scott, High Desert	.992
PO	Jebavy, Ronnie, San Jose	291
A	Jackson, Drew, Bakersfield	351
DP	Jackson, Drew, Bakersfield	71
E	Mejia, Erick, Rancho Cucamonga	38
SS PCT	De Leon, Michael, High Desert	.964
PO	Mejia, Erick, Rancho Cucamonga	181

PITCHING

AVG	Pike, Tyler, Bakersfield	.223
BB	Campbell, Eddie, Bakersfield	100
BB/9	French, Parker, Modesto	1.45
BK	11 tied with	2
CG	Hernandez, Jose, Lancaster	2
G	Moronta, Reyes, San Jose	60
GF	Blueberg, Colby, Lake Elsinore	33
GS	Misiewicz, Anthony, Bakersfield	29
H	Anderson, Justin, Inland Empire	193
HB	Klonowski, Alex, Inland Empire	14
	Polanco, Carlos, Modesto	14
IP	Castellani, Ryan, Modesto	167.2
L	Jewell, Jake, Inland Empire	15
SHO	Three tied with	1
SO	Castellani, Ryan, Modesto	142
SO/9	Pike, Tyler, Bakersfield	9.6
SO/9(RP)	Moronta, Reyes, San Jose	14.19
SV	Martinez, Rodolfo, San Jose	21
W	Three tied with	11
WHIP	French, Parker, Modesto	2.85
WP	Campbell, Eddie, Bakersfield	18
	Holmes, Grant, R. Cucamonga, Stockton	18

MINOR LEAGUES

BY LACY LUSK

Carolina League managers had little trouble rattling off a deep list of prospects this year, especially among position players. Starting with Baseball America Minor League Player of the Year Yoan Moncada, the league boasted two players who were fast to the big leagues, and it also had a strong mix of 20-and-under talent that included a catcher, Lynchburg's Francisco Mejia, who had a 50-game hitting streak.

This year's list started with two Red Sox—as in Boston Red Sox. The infielder Moncada and outfielder Andrew Benintendi made it all the way to the major leagues after leaving a lasting impression during their short time in the eight-team Carolina League.

"Moncada and Benintendi had the right approach every night," Lynchburg manager Mark Budzinski said. "Moncada is so impressive on the bases and Benintendi knows the game so well. They really separated themselves from the start."

Salem had the league's best regular-season record at 87-52, three more wins than Lynchburg, which had Mejia finish his 50-game hitting streak—longest in the minors since 1954—with the Hillcats. The 'Cats also sported first baseman Bobby Bradley, the league's MVP who led the CL with 29 homers and 102 RBIs. However, Cubs affiliate Myrtle Beach beat out Salem for the second-half South Division title, then beat Salem in the playoffs and finished it off by topping Lynchburg in four games to win the Mills Cup. The Pelicans have won back-to-back Carolina League titles in their first two seasons as a Cubs affiliate, becoming the first club to defend its Mills Cup title since Winston-Salem in 1985-86.

Righthander Trevor Clifton and corner infielder David Bote were the Pelicans' playoff heroes. Bote was the playoffs MVP after going 15-for-26 (.577) in seven games, driving home nine runs. The league's regular season pitcher of the year, Clifton won both his starts, tossing seven shutout innings in the pivotal Game Three of the Mills Cup finals.

The eight-team league was heavier in prospects than normal; Carolina manager Rocket Wheeler put his former shortstop, Braves rookie Dansby Swanson in the same category as Salem's Benintendi-Moncada duo. But the No. 1 pick from the 2015 draft only had 93 plate appearances for the Mudcats, short of the total needed to qualify (one per team game played)

The league will change in 2017, expanding by two teams after the California League contracted clubs in High Desert and Bakersfield. The new Carolina League franchises will be a Rangers affiliate in Kinston, which had a CL club from 1978-2011, and an Astros affiliate in Fayetteville.

— CONTRIBUTING: JOHN MANUEL.

TOP 20 PROSPECTS

1. Yoan Moncada, 2b, Salem (Red Sox)
2. Andrew Benintendi, of, Salem (Red Sox)
3. Victor Robles, of, Potomac (Nationals)
4. Gleyber Torres, ss, Myrtle Beach (Cubs)
5. Francisco Mejia, c, Lynchburg (Indians)
6. Rafael Devers, 3b, Salem (Red Sox)
7. Bobby Bradley, 1b, Lynchburg (Indians)
8. Michael Kopech, rhp, Salem (Red Sox)
9. Erick Fedde, rhp, Potomac (Nationals)
10. Ian Happ, 2b, Myrtle Beach (Cubs)
11. Justus Sheffield, lhp, Lynchburg (Indians)
12. Trevor Clifton, rhp, Myrtle Beach (Cubs)
13. Zack Collins, c, Winston-Salem (White Sox)
14. Mauricio Dubon, ss, Salem (Red Sox)
15. Yu-Cheng Chang, ss, Lynchburg (Indians)
16. Anthony Santander, of, Lynchburg (Indians)
17. Max Povse, rhp, Carolina (Braves)
18. Josh Staumont, rhp, Wilmington (Royals)
19. Travis Demeritte, 2b, Carolina (Braves)
20. Max Schrock, 2b, Potomac (Nationals)

STANDINGS: SPLIT SEASON

FIRST HALF

NORTH	W	L	PCT	GB
Lynchburg	45	25	.643	—
Frederick	36	34	.514	9
Potomac	34	34	.500	10
Wilmington	27	42	.391	17 ½

SOUTH	W	L	PCT	GB
Salem	43	26	.623	—
Myrtle Beach	36	34	.514	7 ½
Carolina	29	41	.414	14 ½
Winston	28	42	.400	15 ½

SECOND HALF

NORTH	W	L	PCT	GB
Lynchburg	39	31	.557	—
Potomac	39	31	.557	—
Frederick	32	38	.457	7
Wilmington	27	42	.391	11 ½

SOUTH	W	L	PCT	GB
Myrtle Beach	46	23	.667	—
Salem	44	26	.629	2.5
Winston	28	41	.406	18
Carolina	23	46	.333	23

Playoffs—Semifinals: Lynchburg defeated Potomac 2-1 and Myrtle Beach defeated Salem 2-1 in best-of-three series. **Finals:** Myrtle Beach defeated Lynchburg 3-1 in a best-of-five series.

OVERALL STANDINGS

Division	W	L	PCT	GB	Manager(s)	Attendance	Average	Last Pennant
Salem (Red Sox)	87	52	.626	—	Joe Oliver	200,478	3,084	2013
Lynchburg (Indians)	84	56	.600	3 ½	Mark Budzinski	122,929	1,863	2012
Myrtle Beach (Cubs)	82	57	.590	5	Buddy Bailey	227,491	3,500	2016
Potomac (Nationals)	73	65	.529	13 ½	Tripp Keister	195,448	3,054	2014
Frederick (Orioles)	68	72	.486	19 ½	Keith Bodie	314,443	4,838	2011
Winston-Salem (White Sox)	56	83	.403	31	Joel Skinner	295,411	4,476	2003
Wilmington (Royals)	54	84	.391	32 ½	Jamie Quirk	276,199	4,316	1999
Carolina (Atlanta)	52	87	.374	35	Rocket Wheeler	194,334	3,036	2006

CLUB BATTING

	AVG	G	AB	R	H	2B	3B	HR	RBI	BB	SO	SB	OBP	SLG
Salem	.274	139	4665	694	1280	286	62	51	625	495	1031	241	.346	.395
Lynchburg	.268	140	4685	763	1255	300	29	129	699	560	1164	116	.353	.427
Winston-Salem	.262	139	4691	618	1228	241	36	87	551	456	1001	72	.331	.384
Frederick Keys	.256	140	4581	629	1174	238	31	116	563	467	966	117	.331	.398
Potomac	.254	138	4602	619	1171	236	44	86	549	481	969	139	.330	.381
Myrtle Beach	.254	139	4617	639	1174	259	41	90	570	531	1075	169	.336	.387
Carolina	.249	139	4471	541	1112	247	38	56	488	439	1007	85	.321	.359
Wilmington	.244	138	4570	520	1116	239	33	62	476	404	1129	122	.312	.352

CLUB PITCHING

	ERA	G	CG	SHO	SV	IP	H	R	ER	HR	BB	SO	AVG
Myrtle Beach	3.48	139	2	0	48	1227	1176	545	474	65	411	1032	.253
Potomac	3.78	138	2	0	44	1209	1183	589	507	87	454	937	.255
Lynchburg	3.86	140	1	0	33	1220	1187	616	524	76	483	1124	.254
Frederick	4.06	140	4	2	38	1201	1214	645	541	108	440	1115	.263
Salem	4.07	139	4	0	42	1214	1157	624	549	79	527	1047	.251
Winston-Salem	4.27	139	7	2	26	1208	1204	638	573	88	471	1018	.259
Wilmington	4.55	138	1	1	28	1188	1204	692	600	91	534	1073	.262
Carolina	4.58	139	2	1	31	1168	1185	674	594	83	513	996	.265

CLUB FIELDING

	PCT	PO	A	E	DP		PCT	PO	A	E	DP
Salem	.978	3643	1330	111	255	Lynchburg	.975	3661	1441	130	336
Potomac	.977	3626	1382	118	296	Frederick	.972	3602	1403	146	331
Winston-Salem	.976	3624	1477	123	310	Carolina	.970	3503	1271	146	262
Myrtle Beach	.976	3681	1309	124	288	Wilmington	.969	3563	1234	153	248

INDIVIDUAL BATTING

Batter, Club	AVG	G	AB	R	H	2B	3B	HR	RBI	BB	SO	SB
Robbins, Mason, Winston-Salem	.314	123	507	57	159	33	7	5	62	14	87	3
Basto, Nick, Winston-Salem	.308	106	403	65	124	27	4	12	60	47	83	0
Rodriguez, Aderlin, Frederick	.304	130	494	71	150	23	6	26	93	36	112	3
Allen, Greg, Lynchburg	.298	92	346	93	103	16	4	4	31	58	51	38
Mars, Danny, Salem	.293	108	409	60	120	18	10	2	54	36	84	31
Santander, Anthony, Lynchburg	.290	128	500	90	145	42	0	20	95	54	118	10
Marmolejos, Jose, Potomac	.286	103	378	72	108	36	5	11	59	59	84	2
Jones, Hunter, Winston-Salem	.286	90	364	62	104	13	7	5	34	37	70	31
Keller, Alec, Potomac	.285	117	438	57	125	20	5	3	63	35	78	14
Longhi, Nick, Salem	.282	124	471	56	133	40	3	2	77	50	106	2

INDIVIDUAL PITCHING

Pitcher, Club	W	L	ERA	G	GS	CG	SV	IP	H	R	ER	BB	SO
Clifton, Trevor, Myrtle Beach	7	7	2.72	23	23	0	0	119	97	42	36	41	129
Stephens, Jordan, Winston-Salem	7	10	3.45	27	27	0	0	141	129	59	54	48	155
Kent, Matt, Salem	10	7	3.69	26	26	1	0	156	171	70	64	33	120
Withrow, Matt, Carolina	9	6	3.80	25	24	0	0	121	100	60	51	68	131
Ball, Trey, Salem	8	6	3.84	23	23	0	0	117	121	61	50	68	86
Lovvorn, Zach, Wilmington	2	15	3.95	25	23	0	0	128	134	70	56	44	107
Lugo, Luis, Lynchburg	8	5	4.04	26	26	0	0	136	130	68	61	52	103
Lowry, Thaddius, Winston-Salem	8	8	4.06	24	23	0	0	135	143	69	61	38	90
Martinez, Jonathan, Myrtle Beach	12	6	4.19	23	23	1	0	131	129	64	61	43	77
Long, Lucas, Frederick	7	7	4.27	24	24	0	0	129	149	77	61	31	112

ALL-STAR TEAM

C: Francisco Mejia, Lynchburg. **1B:** Bobby Bradley, Lynchburg. **2B:** Yoan Moncada, Salem. **3B:** Rafael Devers, Salem. **SS:** Yu-Cheng Chang, Lynchburg. **DH:** Aderlin Rodriguez, Frederick. **OF:** Anthony Santander, Lynchburg. **OF:** Greg Allen, Lynchburg. **OF:** Mason Robbins, Winston-Salem. **OF:** Nick Basto, Winston-Salem. **IF:** Mark Mathias, Lynchburg. **SP:** Trevor Clifton, Myrtle Beach. **RP:** Ryan Brinley, Potomac.
Manager of the Year: Mark Budzinski, Lynchburg.
Most Valuable Player: Bobby Bradley, Lynchburg.
Pitcher of the Year: Trevor Clifton, Myrtle Beach.

DEPARTMENT LEADERS

BATTING

2B	Santander, Anthony, Lynchburg	42
3B	Mars, Danny, Salem	10
AB/SO	Salcedo, Erick, Frederick	8.13
BB	Bradley, Bobby, Lynchburg	75
CS	Mars, Danny, Salem	13
H	Robbins, Mason, Winston-Salem	159
HBP	Allen, Greg, Lynchburg	19
HR	Bradley, Bobby, Lynchburg	29
OBP	Allen, Greg, Lynchburg	.424
OPS	Rodriguez, Aderlin, Frederick	.891
R	Allen, Greg, Lynchburg	93
RBI	Bradley, Bobby, Lynchburg	102
SAC	Obregon, Omar, Carolina	13
SB	Gonzalez, Jay, Frederick	41
SLG	Rodriguez, Aderlin, Frederick	.532
SO	Davidson, Braxton, Carolina	184
XBH	Santander, Anthony, Lynchburg	62

FIELDING

A	Balaguert, Yasiel, Myrtle Beach	92
DP	Bradley, Bobby, Lynchburg	97
E	Bradley, Bobby, Lynchburg	13
E	Rodriguez, Aderlin, Frederick	13
1B PCT	Longhi, Nick, Salem	.999
PO	Balaguert, Yasiel, Myrtle Beach	1019
A	Thomas, Toby, Winston-Salem	327
DP	Wilkerson, Stephen, Frederick	70
E	Thomas, Toby, Winston-Salem	15
2B PCT	Wilkerson, Stephen, Frederick	.975
PO	Wilkerson, Stephen, Frederick	202
A	Devers, Rafael, Salem	258
DP	Montilla, Gerson, Winston-Salem	25
E	Reyes, Jomar, Frederick	25
3B PCT	Devers, Rafael, Salem	.960
PO	Devers, Rafael, Salem	104
A	Read, Raudy, Potomac	100
DP	Austin, Brett, Winston-Salem	6
DP	Castillo, Erick, Myrtle Beach	6
E	Johnson, Chad, Wilmington	12
C PCT	Murphy, Tanner, Carolina	.992
PB	Loopstok, Sicnarf, Lynchburg	21
PO	Johnson, Chad, Wilmington	680
A	Robbins, Mason, Winston-Salem	19
DP	Robbins, Mason, Winston-Salem	6
E	Davidson, Braxton, Carolina	11
OF PCT	Carey, Dale, Potomac	.996
PO	Curcio, Keith, Carolina	282
TC	Curcio, Keith, Carolina	293
A	Salcedo, Erick, Frederick	374
DP	Salcedo, Erick, Frederick	88
E	Salcedo, Erick, Frederick	23
SS PCT	Chang, Yu-Cheng, Lynchburg	.964
PO	Salcedo, Erick, Frederick	208

PITCHING

AVG	Clifton, Trevor, Myrtle Beach	.225
BB	Brown, Mitch, Lynchburg	77
BB/9	Kent, Matt, Salem	1.9
BK	Four tied with	4
CG	Horacek, Mitch, Frederick	3
G	Frank, Trevor, Lynchburg	44
	McNeil, Ryan, Myrtle Beach	44
GF	Frank, Trevor, Lynchburg	35
GS	Horacek, Mitch, Frederick	27
	Stephens, Jordan, Winston-Salem	27
H	Brady, Sean, Lynchburg	180
HB	Kent, Matt, Salem	14
HR	Long, Lucas, Frederick	17
IP	Kent, Matt, Salem	156
L	Lovvorn, Zach, Wilmington	15
SO	Stephens, Jordan, Winston-Salem	155
SO/9	Stephens, Jordan, Winston-Salem	9.89
SO/9(RP)	Milbrath, Jordan, Lynchburg	9.35
SV	McNeil, Ryan, Myrtle Beach	22
W	Brady, Sean, Lynchburg	12
	Martinez, Jonathan, Myrtle Beach	12
WP	Brown, Mitch, Lynchburg	25

MINOR LEAGUES

BY JOHN MANUEL

No full-season league conspires to depress offense like the Florida State League, which combines big league spring training ballparks with Sunshine State heat and humidity to keep power at a minimum.

The environment challenges hitters, and often only the multi-tooled survive. That was the case in 2016, when the average FSL player slugged just .356—a 19-point improvement on 2015.

The league's best team, Clearwater, won 82 games but didn't win either half of the regular season and didn't make it into the playoffs, despite a roster deep with solid prospects. Instead, the league's top-scoring club, Bradenton, won the championship while hitting .311 with 10 homers in six postseason games. The Marauders, who won their first league title, also got a boost from right-hander Mitch Keller, who spent most of the season in low Class A but won two playoff starts.

Some power hitters figured out how to overcome the elements, but most of the top prospects were well-rounded middle infielders such as Newman, with shortstops like St. Lucie's Amed Rosario and Tampa's Gleyber Torres dominating the top of the rankings.

"Our league was loaded with shortstops," said Fort Myers manager Jeff Smith, who has piloted the Miracle for four of the last five seasons. "We'll see almost all of them in the major leagues, as shortstops, very soon."

The league had one new park in 2016, though it really was an old park. Due to renovations at Joker Marchant Stadium, the Lakeland Flying Tigers spent the season playing at the home of Florida Southern College, Henley Field. The ballpark played small; Lakeland hit 76 of its league-high 123 homers there, and an FSL-high 134 homers were hit there this season. Lakeland will return to Joker Marchant in 2017, and the ballpark will host the FSL all-star game as well.

The 2016 season proved to be the last season for the Brevard County Manatees, who will leave Space Coast Stadium. The Manatees lost a minor league-high 97 games before the franchise shut down and moved to Osceola County Stadium in Kissimmee. The city last had a franchise in that ballpark in 2000. The Braves will be the team's affiliate, their first time in the FSL since 1968.

TOP 20 PROSPECTS

1. Amed Rosario, ss, St. Lucie (Mets)
2. Gleyber Torres, ss, Tampa (Yankees)
3. Kevin Newman, ss, Bradenton (Pirates)
4. Nick Gordon, ss, Fort Myers (Twins)
5. Jorge Mateo, ss, Tampa (Yankees)
6. Corey Ray, of, Brevard County (Brewers)
7. Anthony Alford, of, Dunedin (Blue Jays)
8. Sean Reid-Foley, rhp, Dunedin (Blue Jays)
9. Aristides Aquino, of, Daytona (Reds)
10. Stephen Gonsalves, rhp, Fort Myers (Twins)
11. Luis Castillo, rhp, Jupiter (Marlins)
12. Brent Honeywell, rhp, Charlotte (Rays)
13. Fernando Romero, rhp, Fort Myers (Twins)
14. Scott Kingery, 2b, Clearwater (Phillies)
15. Christin Stewart, of, Lakeland (Tigers)
16. Brandon Woodruff, rhp, Brevard County (Brewers)
17. Conner Greene, rhp, Dunedin (Blue Jays)
18. Chance Adams, rhp, Tampa (Yankees)
19. Justin Williams, of, Charlotte (Rays)
20. Tomas Nido, c, St. Lucie (Mets)

STANDINGS: SPLIT SEASON

FIRST HALF

NORTH	W	L	PCT	GB
Tampa	42	27	.609	—
Clearwater	39	29	.574	2 ½
Daytona	36	33	.522	6
Lakeland	34	34	.500	7 ½
Dunedin	33	36	.478	9
Brevard Cty.	23	45	.338	18 ½

SOUTH	W	L	PCT	GB
Dunedin	43	23	.652	—
Clearwater	43	25	.632	1
Daytona	40	28	.588	4
Tampa	35	31	.530	8
Lakeland	26	38	.406	16
Brevard Cty.	17	52	.246	27 ½

SECOND HALF

NORTH	W	L	PCT	GB
Bradenton	38	30	.559	—
St. Lucie	35	32	.522	2 ½
Fort Myers	34	35	.493	4 ½
Charlotte	33	36	.478	5 ½
Palm Beach	32	36	.471	6
Jupiter	31	37	.456	7

SOUTH	W	L	PCT	GB
St. Lucie	39	29	.574	—
Jupiter	37	32	.536	2 ½
Fort Myers	36	33	.522	3 ½
Bradenton	32	36	.471	7
Charlotte	31	35	.470	7
Palm Beach	26	43	.377	13 ½

Playoffs—Semifinals: Bradenton defeated St. Lucie 2-0 and Tampa defeated Clearwater 2-1 in three-game series. **Finals:** Bradenton defeated Tampa 3-1 in a best-of-five series.

OVERALL STANDINGS

Division	W	L	PCT	GB	Manager(s)	Attendance	Average	Last Pennant
Clearwater (Phillies)	82	54	.603	—	Greg Legg	181,594	2,710	2007
Tampa (Yankees)	77	58	.570	4 ½	Pat Osborn	73,278	1,163	2010
Dunedin (Blue Jays)	76	59	.563	5 ½	Ken Huckaby	50,593	767	Never
Daytona (Reds)	76	61	.555	6 ½	Eli Marrero	112,053	1,672	2011
St. Lucie (Mets)	74	61	.548	7 ½	Luis Rojas	96,556	1,420	2006
Bradenton (Pirates)	70	66	.515	12	Michael Ryan	87,149	1,341	1963
Fort Myers (Twins)	70	68	.507	13	Jeff Smith	124,273	1,912	2014
Jupiter (Marlins)	68	69	.496	14 ½	Randy Ready	59,306	872	1991
Charlotte (Rays)	64	71	.474	17 ½	Michael Johns	95,588	1,593	2015
Lakeland (Tigers)	60	72	.455	20	Dave Huppert	20,387	334	2012
Palm Beach (Cardinals)	58	79	.423	24 ½	Oliver Marmol	70,991	1,076	2005
Brevard County (Brewers)	40	97	.292	42 ½	Joe Ayrault	85,032	1,308	2001

CLUB BATTING

	AVG	G	AB	R	H	2B	3B	HR	RBI	BB	SO	SB	OBP	SLG
Bradenton	.265	137	4486	638	1188	237	24	69	584	495	917	88	.341	.374
St. Lucie	.264	135	4501	588	1187	210	36	51	527	471	904	115	.338	.360
Clearwater	.261	136	4561	603	1192	232	28	91	557	403	979	92	.328	.384
Tampa	.260	135	4512	574	1174	193	36	67	515	458	992	101	.331	.363
Daytona	.259	137	4536	614	1174	221	52	102	553	382	997	130	.321	.398
Dunedin	.252	135	4496	629	1135	226	37	108	562	488	1167	181	.332	.391
Lakeland	.251	132	4434	601	1111	218	22	123	556	451	1122	37	.324	.393
Charlotte	.245	135	4348	455	1066	148	33	53	389	339	881	132	.303	.331
Fort Myers	.241	138	4490	515	1083	192	35	68	463	355	1014	86	.307	.345
Jupiter	.237	137	4469	496	1061	155	25	57	442	405	1006	74	.308	.322
Palm Beach	.235	137	4504	457	1057	178	23	43	412	513	936	137	.317	.306
Brevard County	.227	138	4501	427	1022	154	19	48	365	378	1153	95	.296	.302

CLUB PITCHING

	ERA	G	CG	SHO	SV	IP	H	R	ER	HR	BB	SO	AVG
Tampa	3.11	135	5	3	30	1191	1013	477	411	56	436	1162	.229
Fort Myers	3.21	138	6	1	37	1192	1088	496	425	47	430	1035	.245
Charlotte	3.25	135	6	3	34	1164	1057	520	420	71	461	982	.244
St. Lucie	3.29	135	3	2	40	1174	1118	508	429	57	384	946	.252
Palm Beach	3.44	137	6	1	34	1219	1185	550	466	70	406	950	.254
Jupiter	3.47	137	1	0	44	1200	1131	520	462	50	359	953	.249
Clearwater	3.56	136	2	0	41	1190	1085	541	470	92	406	1068	.244
Bradenton	3.59	137	4	1	29	1176	1130	558	469	76	411	938	.252
Daytona	3.62	137	3	1	38	1186	1139	551	477	82	438	1035	.254
Dunedin	3.94	135	4	0	30	1195	1133	597	523	100	474	959	.249
Brevard County	4.22	138	3	0	26	1193	1240	642	559	79	439	1041	.268
Lakeland	4.35	132	2	0	33	1143	1131	637	553	90	494	999	.257

CLUB FIELDING

	PCT	PO	A	E	DP		PCT	PO	A	E	DP
Clearwater	.977	3569	1303	113	274	Dunedin	.974	3584	1336	129	337
Jupiter	.977	3599	1448	120	342	Fort Myers	.973	3576	1481	138	443
St. Lucie	.975	3521	1406	126	331	Palm Beach	.973	3657	1356	138	320
Tampa	.975	3572	1275	124	280	Lakeland	.973	3430	1360	134	298
Bradenton	.975	3528	1408	128	330	Brevard County	.973	3579	1341	139	280
Daytona	.975	3558	1396	129	325	Charlotte	.970	3493	1308	151	316

INDIVIDUAL BATTING

Batter, Club	AVG	G	AB	R	H	2B	3B	HR	RBI	BB	SO	SB
Nido, Tomas, St. Lucie	.320	90	344	38	110	23	2	7	46	19	42	0
Urena, Richard, Dunedin	.305	97	394	52	120	18	7	8	41	25	64	9
Gumbs, Angelo, Daytona	.298	98	376	54	112	18	5	11	55	25	48	8
Hinkle, Wade, Lakeland	.295	120	420	62	124	26	1	11	66	44	98	0
Kingery, Scott, Clearwater	.293	94	375	60	110	29	3	3	28	33	54	26
Gordon, Nick, Fort Myers	.291	116	461	56	134	23	6	3	52	23	87	19
Taylor, Kevin, St. Lucie	.288	112	399	59	115	20	1	8	58	56	55	0
DeMuth, Dustin, Brevard County	.287	96	366	42	105	21	2	6	43	28	104	2
Reynoso, Jonathan, Daytona	.285	112	386	49	110	8	3	0	36	17	91	31
Tocci, Carlos, Clearwater	.284	127	500	66	142	26	2	3	50	34	76	13

INDIVIDUAL PITCHING

Pitcher, Club	W	L	ERA	G	GS	CG	SV	IP	H	R	ER	BB	SO
Castillo, Luis, Jupiter	8	4	2.07	23	21	1	0	118	95	29	27	18	91
Pearce, Matt, Palm Beach	8	8	2.37	20	20	4	0	137	114	43	36	15	81
Rogers, Josh, Tampa	10	5	2.53	20	20	2	0	114	111	35	32	20	90
Garcia, Elniery, Clearwater	12	4	2.68	20	19	0	0	118	94	41	35	36	91
Garcia, Yeudy, Bradenton	6	8	2.76	26	25	1	1	127	122	53	39	54	127
Harris, Greg, Charlotte	10	6	3.12	26	23	2	0	147	119	56	51	58	134
Thompson, Jeff, Lakeland	7	7	3.49	27	20	0	1	119	99	54	46	67	100
Rowley, Chris, Dunedin	10	3	3.49	31	14	0	1	124	128	54	48	30	86
Antone, Tejay, Daytona	14	6	3.51	25	25	1	0	151	167	77	59	28	105
Flaherty, Jack, Palm Beach	5	9	3.56	24	23	0	0	134	129	63	53	45	126
Flexen, Chris, St. Lucie	10	9	3.56	25	25	1	0	134	125	62	53	51	95

ALL-STAR TEAM

P: Corey Taylor, St. Lucie. **P:** Dillon Peters, Jupiter. **P:** Greg Harris, Charlotte. **P:** Jimmy Herget, Daytona. **P:** Luis Castillo, Jupiter. **P:** Matt Pearce, Palm Beach. **C:** Kade Scivicque, Lakeland. **C:** Tomas Nido, St. Lucie. **1B:** Ryan McBroom, Dunedin. **2B:** Scott Kingery, Clearwater. **3B:** Mitch Walding, Clearwater. **SS:** Richard Urena, Dunedin. **LF:** Christin Stewart, Lakeland. **CF:** Carlos Tocci, Clearwater. **RF:** Aristides Aquino, Daytona. **DH:** Kyle Martin, Clearwater. **OF:** Zack Zehner, Tampa. **IF:** Nick Gordon, Fort Myers.
Most Valuable Pitcher: Luis Castillo, Jupiter.
Most Valuable Player: Aristides Aquino, Daytona.

DEPARTMENT LEADERS

BATTING

2B	Three tied with	29
3B	Aquino, Aristides, Daytona	12
AB/SO	Gumbs, Angelo, Daytona	7.83
BB	Grayson, Casey, Palm Beach	94
CS	Mercado, Oscar, Palm Beach	20
H	Tocci, Carlos, Clearwater	142
HBP	Davis, Jonathan, Dunedin	17
	Vavra, Trey, Fort Myers	17
HR	Stewart, Christin, Lakeland	24
OBP	Stewart, Christin, Lakeland	.403
OPS	Stewart, Christin, Lakeland	.936
R	Trahan, Blake, Daytona	90
RBI	McBroom, Ryan, Dunedin	83
SAC	Guillorme, Luis, St. Lucie	13
SB	Mateo, Jorge, Tampa	36
SLG	Stewart, Christin, Lakeland	.534
SO	Shepherd, Zac, Lakeland	159
XBH	Aquino, Aristides, Daytona	61

FIELDING

A	Grayson, Casey, Palm Beach	68
DP	Hinkle, Wade, Lakeland	92
E	Hinkle, Wade, Lakeland	12
1B PCT	Martin, Kyle, Clearwater	.998
PO	Hinkle, Wade, Lakeland	1065
A	Schales, Brian, Jupiter	318
DP	Kramer, Kevin, Bradenton	68
E	Iskenderian, George, Brevard County	12
2B PCT	Kramer, Kevin, Bradenton	.983
PO	Schales, Brian, Jupiter	185
A	Shepherd, Zac, Lakeland	242
DP	Shepherd, Zac, Lakeland	23
E	Shepherd, Zac, Lakeland	31
3B PCT	Walding, Mitch, Clearwater	.935
PO	Shepherd, Zac, Lakeland	60
	Walding, Mitch, Clearwater	60
A	Nido, Tomas, St. Lucie	86
A	Numata, Chace, Clearwater	86
PB	Gushue, Taylor, Bradenton	14
	Numata, Chace, Clearwater	14
DP	Navarreto, Brian, Fort Myers	14
E	Houle, Dustin, Brevard County	10
	Numata, Chace, Clearwater	10
C PCT	Gushue, Taylor, Bradenton	.994
PO	Gushue, Taylor, Bradenton	628
A	Aquino, Aristides, Daytona	28
DP	Escobar, Elvis, Bradenton	5
E	Aquino, Aristides, Daytona	8
	Norwood, John, Jupiter	8
OF PCT	Kivett, Ross, Lakeland	.996
PO	Tocci, Carlos, Clearwater	286
A	Trahan, Blake, Daytona	368
DP	Gordon, Nick, Fort Myers	85
E	Simcox, A.J., Lakeland	30
SS PCT	Trahan, Blake, Daytona	.974
PO	Trahan, Blake, Daytona	186

PITCHING

AVG	Garcia, Elniery, Clearwater	.219
BB	Labourt, Jairo, Lakeland	70
BB/9	Pearce, Matt, Palm Beach	.990
BK	Campos, Vicente, Tampa	5
	Harris, Greg, Charlotte	5
CG	Pearce, Matt, Palm Beach	4
ER	Derby, Bubba, Brevard County	82
G	Bernardino, Brennan, Daytona	50
	Herget, Jimmy, Daytona	50
GF	Herget, Jimmy, Daytona	46
GS	Five tied with	25
H	Ladwig, A.J., Lakeland	170
	Pike, Chris, Charlotte	170
HB	Briceno, Endrys, Lakeland	18
HR	Ladwig, A.J., Lakeland	19
L	Derby, Bubba, Brevard County	13
SHO	Harris, Greg, Charlotte	2
	Rogers, Josh, Tampa	2
SO	Harris, Greg, Charlotte	134
SO/9	Garcia, Yeudy, Bradenton	8.98
SO/9(RP)	Herget, Jimmy, Daytona	12.31
SV	Herget, Jimmy, Daytona	24
W	Antone, Tejay, Daytona	14
WP	Reyes, Scarlyn, St. Lucie	22

MINOR LEAGUES

BY VINCE LARA-CINISOMO

Position players stood out in the low Class A Midwest League, despite its pitcher-friendly reputation. The league boasted the top bat in the 2016 draft (Nick Senzel), the top international talent from the 2013 class (Eloy Jimenez), the minor league all-star team catcher (Francisco Mejia) and the first high school position player popped in 2015 (Kyle Tucker).

Clinton, led by a staff that included Luiz Gohara and Nick Neidert compiled the league's best record and ran away with the Western Division title in the second half. In the Midwest finals, however, it was long shot Great Lakes that stole the show. The Loons, who finished sixth in the seven-team Eastern Division in the first half, had to win 15 of their final 22 games in the second half just to get into the playoffs. But once there, the Dodgers' affiliate beat Bowling Green (Rays) and West Michigan (Tigers) to get to the finals. The Loons finished their surprising season by beating Clinton for the franchise's first title.

As usual, the Midwest League saw the debut of some of the more advanced 2016 draft picks, such as Reds third baseman Senzel, the No. 2 overall pick out of Tennessee, and Angels first baseman Matt Thaiss, who went No. 16 overall out of Virginia.

Isan Diaz led the circuit in homers with 20 and extra-base hits with 59.

Unheralded $40,000 international signing Luis Arraez of Cedar Rapids (Twins) led the MWL in batting at .347 and finished second in hits to West Michigan's Will Maddox.

Lake County (Indians) catcher Francisco Mejia would have tied for the batting championship if he had the requisite at-bats, but he was promoted to high Class A in the middle of a 50-game hit streak.

TOP 20 PROSPECTS

1. Nick Senzel, 3b, Dayton (Reds)
2. Eloy Jimenez, of, South Bend (Cubs)
3. Francisco Mejia, c, Lake County (Indians)
4. Kyle Tucker, of, Quad Cities (Astros)
5. Sandy Alcantara, rhp, Peoria (Cardinals)
6. Marcos Diplan, rhp, Wisconsin (Brewers)
7. Isan Diaz, ss/2b, Wisconsin (Brewers)
8. Michael Gettys, of, Fort Wayne (Padres)
9. Sean Reid-Foley, rhp, Lansing (Blue Jays)
10. Franklin Perez, rhp, Quad Cities (Astros)
11. Luiz Gohara, lhp, Clinton (Mariners)
12. Magneuris Sierra, of, Peoria (Cardinals)
13. Jon Harris, rhp, Lansing (Blue Jays)
14. Albert Abreu, rhp, Quad Cities (Astros)
15. Matt Thaiss, 1b, Burlington (Angels)
16. Beau Burrows, rhp, West Michigan (Tigers)
17. Trent Clark, of, Wisconsin (Brewers)
18. Jake Cronenworth, ss, Bowling Green (Rays)
19. Eli Alvarez, 2b, Peoria (Cardinals)
20. Lucas Erceg, 3b, Wisconsin (Brewers)

STANDINGS: SPLIT SEASON

FIRST HALF					SECOND HALF				
EASTERN	W	L	PCT	GB	**EASTERN**	W	L	PCT	GB
South Bend	41	28	.594	—	Bowling Green	47	23	.671	—
W. Michigan	39	28	.582	1	South Bend	43	27	.614	4
Lake County	40	30	.571	1 ½	Great Lakes	36	34	.514	11
Bowling Green	37	32	.536	4	Lansing	33	37	.471	14
Fort Wayne	36	34	.514	5 ½	W. Michigan	32	37	.464	14 ½
Lansing	36	34	.514	5 ½	Lake County	32	38	.457	15
Great Lakes	29	41	.414	12 ½	Dayton	26	44	.371	21
Dayton	21	49	.300	20 ½	Fort Wayne	26	44	.371	21
WESTERN	W	L	PCT	GB	**WESTERN**	W	L	PCT	GB
Peoria	40	30	.571	—	Clinton	47	23	.671	—
Clinton	39	31	.557	1	Cedar Rapids	42	28	.600	5
Cedar Rapids	36	33	.522	3 ½	Wisconsin	37	33	.529	10
Wisconsin	34	36	.486	6	Burlington	36	34	.514	11
Kane County	33	37	.471	7	Peoria	33	36	.478	13 ½
Beloit	32	37	.464	7 ½	Kane County	32	38	.457	15
Burlington	32	38	.457	8	Quad Cities	30	40	.429	17
Quad Cities	31	38	.449	8 ½	Beloit	27	43	.386	20

Playoffs—Semifinals: Great Lakes defeated West Michigan 2-1 and Clinton defeated Cedar Rapids 2-1 in best-of-three series. **Finals:** Great Lakes defeated Clinton 3-1 in a best-of-five series.

OVERALL STANDINGS

Division	W	L	PCT	GB	Manager(s)	Attendance	Average	Last Pennant
Clinton (Mariners)	86	54	.614	—	Mitch Canham	124,154	1,910	2016
Bowling Green (Rays)	84	55	.604	1 ½	Reinaldo Ruiz	174,722	2,688	Never
South Bend (Cubs)	84	55	.604	1 ½	Jimmy Gonzalez	350,803	5,084	2005
Cedar Rapids (Twins)	78	61	.561	7 ½	Jake Mauer	166,413	2,484	1994
Peoria (Cardinals)	73	66	.525	12 ½	Joe Kruzel	230,277	3,489	2002
West Michigan (Tigers)	71	65	.522	13	Andrew Graham	386,416	5,683	2015
Lake County (Indians)	72	68	.514	14	Tony Mansolino	213,738	3,143	2010
Wisconsin (Brewers)	71	69	.507	15	Matt Erickson	243,767	3,585	2012
Lansing (Blue Jays)	69	71	.493	17	John Schneider	311,190	4,576	2003
Burlington (Angels)	68	72	.486	18	Adam Melhuse	75,429	1,109	2008
Great Lakes (Dodgers)	65	75	.464	21	Gil Velazquez	210,054	3,044	2000
Kane County (Diamondbacks)	65	75	.464	21	Mike Benjamin	400,931	5,811	2014
Fort Wayne (Padres)	62	78	.443	24	Anthony Contreras	413,701	6,084	2009
Quad Cities (Astros)	61	78	.439	24 ½	Omar Lopez	234,923	3,506	2013
Beloit (Athletics)	59	80	.424	26 ½	Fran Riordan	67,975	1,079	1995
Dayton (Cincinnati)	47	93	.336	39	Dick Schofield	548,574	8,188	Never

CLUB BATTING

	AVG	G	AB	R	H	2B	3B	HR	RBI	BB	SO	SB	OBP	SLG
Peoria	.266	140	4717	602	1255	236	30	49	526	417	996	103	.331	.360
South Bend	.266	139	4620	633	1227	229	35	68	576	439	1007	82	.333	.374
West Michigan	.266	137	4655	576	1236	206	48	25	500	353	937	172	.320	.347
Bowling Green	.264	139	4617	711	1220	240	31	90	642	486	951	163	.340	.388
Cedar Rapids	.259	139	4792	645	1241	223	44	65	572	471	1053	60	.330	.365
Lake County	.255	140	4648	573	1185	236	43	68	510	394	1123	102	.318	.368
Clinton	.253	140	4604	584	1166	210	26	61	512	481	1148	80	.330	.350
Burlington Bees	.250	140	4606	536	1151	239	23	53	462	404	980	75	.317	.346
Wisconsin	.247	140	4739	592	1170	241	32	92	518	426	1280	123	.317	.369
Fort Wayne	.243	140	4650	535	1131	215	29	75	481	429	1235	73	.315	.350
Kane County	.238	140	4650	474	1107	194	44	56	417	361	1216	113	.301	.335
Quad Cities	.237	139	4583	511	1086	227	50	61	450	423	1228	125	.305	.348
Lansing	.236	140	4643	572	1095	233	36	73	487	461	1223	108	.311	.349
Great Lakes	.234	140	4520	537	1057	203	24	90	481	439	1295	118	.311	.349
Beloit	.232	139	4475	475	1037	228	28	66	432	443	1184	71	.307	.339
Dayton	.231	140	4629	485	1070	213	36	70	431	350	1257	136	.290	.338

CLUB PITCHING

	ERA	G	CG	SHO	SV	IP	H	R	ER	HR	BB	SO	AVG
Kane County	3.07	140	2	1	40	1227	1072	517	419	69	409	1168	.234
Clinton	3.12	140	4	0	50	1234	1103	494	428	61	395	1157	.239
Cedar Rapids	3.19	139	2	1	33	1242	1035	524	440	54	499	1181	.227
Great Lakes	3.31	140	1	1	36	1207	1044	526	444	70	402	1193	.232
South Bend	3.35	139	1	0	43	1217	1122	538	453	52	364	1078	.245
Wisconsin	3.38	140	0	0	40	1255	1162	576	471	73	455	1294	.244
Beloit	3.41	139	2	0	28	1196	1140	535	453	64	385	972	.254
Burlington	3.48	140	0	0	44	1230	1226	575	476	61	431	1083	.259
West Michigan	3.49	137	3	1	42	1217	1214	538	472	60	369	1050	.263
Bowling Green	3.50	139	3	0	36	1218	1117	558	474	75	448	1150	.245
Peoria	3.58	140	1	0	34	1225	1209	571	487	75	406	1177	.256
Quad Cities	3.75	139	2	1	33	1221	1157	578	509	73	461	1147	.251
Lansing	3.78	140	3	1	41	1237	1206	609	519	62	439	1133	.256
Fort Wayne	3.78	140	2	1	28	1237	1261	608	519	57	380	1074	.263
Lake County	3.86	140	3	0	36	1226	1158	597	526	97	386	1109	.250
Dayton	4.28	140	2	2	27	1220	1208	697	580	59	528	1147	.258

CLUB FIELDING

	PCT	PO	A	E	DP		PCT	PO	A	E	DP
Clinton	.978	3701	1381	115	281	Lansing	.973	3712	1426	144	327
West Michigan	.977	3651	1389	117	354	Great Lakes	.972	3621	1277	141	354
Quad Cities	.977	3664	1390	118	305	Peoria	.971	3676	1308	148	336
South Bend	.976	3651	1463	128	316	Wisconsin	.971	3765	1361	154	320
Cedar Rapids	.975	3727	1421	131	329	Burlington	.970	3689	1373	156	297
Lake County	.975	3677	1348	128	303	Fort Wayne	.970	3711	1419	160	278
Bowling Green	.974	3653	1279	132	302	Dayton	.970	3661	1461	161	350
Beloit	.974	3588	1472	136	335	Kane County	.968	3682	1317	164	300

INDIVIDUAL BATTING

Batter, Club	AVG	G	AB	R	H	2B	3B	HR	RBI	BB	SO	SB
Arraez, Luis, Cedar Rapids	.347	114	475	67	165	31	3	3	66	31	51	3
Maddox, Will, West Michigan	.339	127	511	59	173	23	3	1	58	32	89	28
Jimenez, Eloy, South Bend	.329	112	432	65	142	40	3	14	81	25	94	8
Alvarez, Eliezer, Peoria	.323	116	433	70	140	36	6	6	59	53	96	36
Cronenworth, Jake, Bowling Green	.322	81	314	66	101	15	6	3	48	54	57	12
Allen, Austin, Fort Wayne	.320	109	409	52	131	22	0	7	61	29	69	0
Chinea, Chris, Peoria	.312	99	381	40	119	24	0	6	63	22	64	1
Marabell, Connor, Lake County	.311	95	338	41	105	32	4	6	50	33	50	11
Sierra, Magneuris, Peoria	.307	122	524	78	161	29	4	3	60	22	97	31
Lukes, Nathan, Lake County	.301	89	342	54	103	21	8	5	32	37	60	14

INDIVIDUAL PITCHING

Pitcher, Club	W	L	ERA	G	GS	CG	SV	IP	H	R	ER	BB	SO
Manarino, Evan, Beloit	8	5	2.15	22	18	0	0	122	112	37	29	20	103
Borucki, Ryan, Lansing	10	4	2.41	20	20	1	0	116	105	36	31	26	107
Hernandez, Carlos, Kane County	7	11	2.55	26	22	1	0	123	94	46	35	69	122
Duno, Angel, Beloit	7	7	2.68	24	20	0	0	121	130	43	36	16	76
Bloomquist, Casey, South Bend	8	8	3.00	30	12	0	4	117	107	53	39	17	87
Kellogg, Ryan, South Bend	9	7	3.03	24	23	1	0	131	115	51	44	26	107
Rodriguez, Jose, Burlington	7	5	3.14	27	27	0	0	132	135	53	46	32	115
Perdomo, Angel, Lansing	5	7	3.19	27	25	0	1	127	101	57	45	54	156
Mujica, Jose, Bowling Green	8	4	3.46	24	24	0	0	130	127	54	50	35	100
Biegalski, Boomer, Beloit	8	8	3.70	28	25	0	0	153	144	72	63	38	115

ALL-STAR TEAM

P: Spencer Herrmann, Clinton. **C:** Austin Allen, Fort Wayne. **1B:** Will Maddox, West Michigan. **2B:** Luis Arraez, Cedar Rapids. **3B:** Kevin Padlo, Bowling Green. **SS:** Isan Diaz, Wisconsin. **DH:** Trevor Mitsui, Kane County. **OF:** Connor Marabell, Lake County. **OF:** Eloy Jimenez, South Bend. **OF:** Magneuris Sierra, Peoria. **SP:** Angel Perdomo, Lansing. **SP:** Evan Manarino, Beloit. **SP:** Preston Morrison, South Bend. **RP:** Nate Griep, Wisconsin. **Most Valuable Player:** Eloy Jimenez, South Bend.

DEPARTMENT LEADERS

BATTING

2B	Jimenez, Eloy, South Bend	40
3B	Dewees, Donnie, South Bend	12
AB/SO	Arraez, Luis, Cedar Rapids	9.31
BB	Padlo, Kevin, Bowling Green	79
CS	Sierra, Magneuris, Peoria	17
H	Maddox, Will, West Michigan	173
HBP	McDowell, Max, Wisconsin	17
HR	Diaz, Isan, Wisconsin	20
OBP	Cronenworth, Jake, Bowling Green	.429
OPS	Jimenez, Eloy, South Bend	.901
R	Sierra, Magneuris, Peoria	78
RBI	Wiel, Zander, Cedar Rapids	86
SAC	Van Gansen, Peter, Fort Wayne	13
SB	Alvarez, Eliezer, Peoria	36
SLG	Jimenez, Eloy, South Bend	.532
SO	Zunica, Brad, Fort Wayne	156
TB	Diaz, Isan, Wisconsin	238

FIELDING

A	Wiel, Zander, Cedar Rapids	85
DP	Wiel, Zander, Cedar Rapids	99
E	Wiel, Zander, Cedar Rapids	17
1B PCT	Dennard, R.J., Peoria	.989
PO	Wiel, Zander, Cedar Rapids	1058
A	Van Gansen, Peter, Fort Wayne	320
DP	Alvarez, Eliezer, Peoria	69
E	Alvarez, Eliezer, Peoria	27
2B PCT	Van Gansen, Peter, Fort Wayne	.981
PO	Alvarez, Eliezer, Peoria	173
A	Three tied with	152
DP	Padlo, Kevin, Bowling Green	21
E	Gatewood, Jake, Wisconsin	24
3B PCT	Padlo, Kevin, Bowling Green	.960
PO	Padlo, Kevin, Bowling Green	91
A	McDowell, Max, Wisconsin	111
DP	Hissey, Ryan, Lansing	11
E	Rodriguez, David, Bowling Green	15
C PCT	Hermelyn, Anthony, Quad Cities	.995
PB	Sullivan, Brett, Bowling Green	22
PO	McDowell, Max, Wisconsin	911
A	Azocar, Jose, West Michigan	16
DP	Guillotte, Andrew, Lansing	5
E	Azocar, Jose, West Michigan	14
OF PCT	Law, Zacrey, Bowling Green	.993
PO	Law, Zacrey, Bowling Green	286
	Sierra, Magneuris, Peoria	286
A	Ascanio, Rayder, Clinton	331
DP	Castro, Willi, Lake County	71
E	Castro, Willi, Lake County	25
	Giron, Ruddy, Fort Wayne	25
SS PCT	Gonzalez, Luis, Dayton	.959
PO	Ascanio, Rayder, Clinton	189

PITCHING

AVG	Hernandez, Carlos, Kane County	.215
BB	Hernandez, Carlos, Kane County	69
BB/9	Duno, Angel, Beloit	1.19
BK	Nix, Jacob, Fort Wayne	4
CG	Three tied with	2
ER	Saucedo, Tayler, Lansing	79
G	De La Cruz, Steven, Peoria	49
	Griep, Nate, Wisconsin	49
GF	Griep, Nate, Wisconsin	39
GS	Three tied with	27
H	Saucedo, Tayler, Lansing	151
HB	Chiang, Shao-Ching, Lake County	15
HR	Biegalski, Boomer, Beloit	14
	Saucedo, Tayler, Lansing	14
IP	Biegalski, Boomer, Beloit	153.1
L	Orewiler, Austin, Dayton	14
SO	Perdomo, Angel, Lansing	156
SO/9	Perdomo, Angel, Lansing	11.06
SO/9(RP)	Aybar, Manuel, Dayton	11.64
SV	Griep, Nate, Wisconsin	23
W	Cabrera, Genesis, Bowling Green	11
WP	Rainey, Tanner, Dayton	25

MINOR LEAGUES

BY J.J. COOPER

Being loaded with prospects does not guarantee minor league success. But in 2016, the South Atlantic League Championship Series fittingly matched up the league's most prospect-laden team (Rome) vs. its second-best group of prospects (Lakewood).

And in the end, it was Rome, which fielded seven of the league's Top 20 prospects, that took home the title–the team's first since 2003.

Rome's combination of young, high-ceiling talent was most notable. The Braves had the youngest position players and pitching staff in the league, but also had the deepest starting rotation the league has seen in recent years. In the second half of the season until Patrick Weigel was promoted, Rome fielded a six-man rotation where all six were legitimate prospects.

Lakewood wasn't far behind with a pitching staff that was filled with pitchers with big fastballs and solid secondary pitches.

The Rome pitching staff was dominant in the championship series. Max Fried struck out 13 while allowing one run in seven innings in the deciding Game Four. Rome also got outstanding starts from Kolby Allard (six shutout innings) and Touki Toussaint (one run in seven innings).

There were other highlights around the league, including an outstanding year by league MVP Asheville first baseman Brian Mundell.

Mundell set a league record with 59 doubles, 20 more than anyone else in the league hit this year. Mundell's 59 doubles is also a modern-day minor league record, as no one else had hit that many in a season since the minors were reorganized into their current format in 1963.

Delmarva catcher Yermin Mercedes played just enough before his promotion to finish with a sabermetric Triple Crown as he led the league in batting (.353), on-base percentage (411) and slugging percentage (.579). West Virginia's Mitch Keller was named the league most valuable pitcher after going 8-5, 2.46 with 131 strikeouts in 124 innings in a breakout season.

TOP 20 PROSPECTS

1. Victor Robles, of, Hagerstown (Nationals)
2. Mitch Keller, rhp, West Virginia (Pirates)
3. Brendan Rodgers, ss/2b, Asheville (Rockies)
4. Anderson Espinoza, rhp, Greenville (Red Sox)
5. Kolby Allard, lhp, Rome (Braves)
6. Max Fried, lhp, Rome (Braves)
7. Mike Soroka, rhp, Rome (Braves)
8. Franklyn Kilome, rhp, Lakewood (Phillies)
9. Luis Alexander Basabe, of, Greenville (Red Sox)
10. Patrick Weigel, rhp, Rome (Braves)
11. Phil Bickford, rhp, Augusta (Giants)
12. Ronald Acuna, of, Rome (Braves)
13. Austin Riley, 3b, Rome (Braves)
14. Ke'Bryan Hayes, 3b, West Virginia (Pirates)
15. Touki Toussaint, rhp, Rome (Braves)
16. Max Schrock, 2b, Hagerstown (Nationals)
17. Gage Hinsz, rhp, West Virginia (Pirates)
18. Luis Alejando Basabe, 2b/ss, Greenville (Red Sox)
19. Jose Taveras, rhp, Lakewood (Phillies)
20. Joe Palumbo, lhp, Hickory (Rangers)

STANDINGS: SPLIT SEASON

FIRST HALF

NORTH	W	L	PCT	GB
Hagerstown	43	27	.614	—
Delmarva	42	27	.609	½
Greensboro	38	32	.543	5
Hickory	38	32	.543	5
West Virginia	35	34	.507	7 ½
Lakewood	29	40	.420	13 ½
Kannapolis	24	46	.343	19

SOUTH	W	L	PCT	GB
Lakewood	45	25	.643	—
Hagerstown	40	30	.571	5
Hickory	36	34	.514	9
West Virginia	36	34	.514	9
Kannapolis	34	36	.486	11
Delmarva	31	39	.443	14
Greensboro	27	43	.386	18

SECOND HALF

NORTH	W	L	PCT	GB
Charleston	42	27	0.609	—
Greenville	37	32	0.536	5
Augusta	36	34	0.514	6 ½
Columbia	36	34	0.514	6 ½
Asheville	34	35	0.493	8
Rome	27	42	0.391	15
Lexington	25	44	0.362	17

SOUTH	W	L	PCT	GB
Rome	43	27	0.614	—
Augusta	40	29	0.58	2 ½
Charleston	34	36	0.486	9
Greenville	33	37	0.471	10
Asheville	32	37	0.464	10 ½
Columbia	31	39	0.443	12
Lexington	27	43	0.386	16

Playoffs—Semifinals: Lakewood defeated Hagerstown 2-0 and Rome defeated Charleston 2-1 in best-of-three series. **Finals:** Rome defeated Lakewood 3-1 in a best-of-five series.

OVERALL STANDINGS

Division	W	L	PCT	GB	Manager(s)	Attendance	Average	Last Pennant
Hagerstown (Nationals)	83	57	.593	—	Patrick Anderson	82,526	1,250	Never
Augusta (Giants)	76	63	.547	6 ½	Nestor Rojas	169,421	2,606	2008
Charleston (Yankees)	76	63	.547	6 ½	Luis Dorante	293,161	4,311	Never
Lakewood (Phillies)	74	65	.532	8 ½	Shawn Williams	353,080	5,350	2010
Hickory (Rangers)	74	66	.529	9	Steve Mintz	150,110	2,176	2015
Delmarva (Orioles)	73	66	.525	9 ½	Ryan Minor	209,120	3,217	2001
West Virginia (Pirates)	71	68	.511	11 ½	Brian Esposito	143,755	2,212	1990
Greenville (Red Sox)	70	69	.504	12 ½	Darren Fenster	331,911	4,810	1998
Rome (Braves)	70	69	.504	12 ½	Randy Ingle	161,121	2,405	2016
Columbia (Mets)	67	73	.479	16	Jose Leger	261,134	3,785	2013
Asheville (Rockies)	66	72	.478	16	Warren Schaeffer	183,058	2,774	2014
Greensboro (Marlins)	65	75	.464	18	Kevin Randel	336,121	5,171	2011
Kannapolis (White Sox)	58	82	.414	25	Cole Armstrong	95,757	1,473	2005
Lexington (Royals)	52	87	.374	30 ½	Omar Ramirez	276,062	4,382	2001

CLUB BATTING

	AVG	G	AB	R	H	2B	3B	HR	RBI	BB	SO	SB	OBP	SLG
Asheville	.267	138	4695	657	1254	308	30	100	598	382	1123	141	.329	.409
Lakewood	.266	139	4734	598	1261	249	20	79	542	390	979	86	.330	.377
Hagerstown	.261	140	4564	668	1192	265	38	84	599	429	1003	172	.332	.391
Rome	.252	139	4669	565	1178	217	36	75	506	306	1058	122	.307	.362
Hickory	.251	140	4633	602	1161	229	32	103	537	385	1091	216	.318	.381
Delmarva	.251	139	4591	548	1153	236	36	112	497	427	1172	84	.320	.391
Charleston	.250	139	4594	560	1147	222	35	88	514	441	1100	139	.321	.371
Augusta	.250	139	4613	617	1152	217	42	91	534	389	1113	171	.316	.374
Greenville	.248	139	4596	620	1141	229	43	104	560	496	1236	127	.327	.385
Kannapolis	.248	140	4720	525	1171	228	30	62	465	422	1189	105	.317	.349
West Virginia	.242	139	4505	554	1088	220	35	81	496	432	973	146	.317	.360
Columbia	.241	140	4565	604	1101	234	40	72	533	487	1180	87	.319	.357
Greensboro	.236	140	4502	498	1064	207	26	69	447	354	1203	109	.299	.340
Lexington	.236	139	4443	577	1048	206	24	98	519	429	1231	159	.310	.359

CLUB PITCHING

	ERA	G	CG	SHO	SV	IP	H	R	ER	HR	BB	SO	AVG
Charleston	3.03	139	0	0	40	1223	1015	497	412	62	422	1248	.225
Delmarva	3.33	139	3	2	43	1204	1088	534	446	76	417	1098	.242
Greensboro	3.42	140	0	0	42	1203	1074	554	457	101	410	1063	.239
Augusta	3.43	139	4	2	39	1207	1163	555	460	60	361	1156	.251
Lakewood	3.53	139	2	2	43	1223	1110	554	480	69	399	1267	.241
West Virginia	3.55	139	1	0	33	1224	1086	535	482	88	381	1098	.239
Kannapolis	3.55	140	3	1	31	1234	1155	586	487	69	435	1053	.248
Hickory	3.57	140	3	1	41	1245	1223	592	494	97	445	1183	.257
Columbia	3.64	140	5	1	34	1222	1181	576	494	98	391	1136	.255
Rome	3.69	139	3	1	33	1220	1066	593	500	84	470	1162	.237
Hagerstown	3.77	140	1	0	44	1208	1180	595	506	81	423	1044	.256
Greenville	3.82	139	1	0	45	1214	1200	589	516	77	358	1128	.258
Asheville	4.60	138	1	0	35	1227	1388	710	627	136	371	980	.287
Lexington	4.66	139	3	0	22	1173	1182	723	608	120	486	1035	.263

CLUB FIELDING

	PCT	PO	A	E	DP		PCT	PO	A	E	DP
West Virginia	.979	3671	1464	111	333	Asheville	.973	3680	1477	144	292
Delmarva	.976	3612	1369	121	287	Columbia	.973	3666	1381	141	314
Hickory	.975	3736	1471	131	324	Hagerstown	.973	3624	1416	142	311
Charleston	.975	3669	1326	126	210	Greensboro	.969	3680	1383	160	345
Lakewood	.975	3670	1259	126	202	Rome Braves	.968	3661	1364	167	230
Greenville	.974	3643	1360	132	229	Lexington	.966	3519	1271	167	221
Kannapolis	.974	3701	1589	143	297	Augusta	.966	3622	1405	176	256

INDIVIDUAL BATTING

Batter, Club	AVG	G	AB	R	H	2B	3B	HR	RBI	BB	SO	SB
Mercedes, Yermin, Delmarva	.353	91	340	58	120	25	5	14	60	34	63	1
Mundell, Brian, Asheville	.313	136	537	94	168	59	1	14	83	56	83	7
Daza, Yonathan, Asheville	.307	119	475	63	146	35	2	3	58	23	78	2
Tobias, Josh, Lakewood	.304	93	365	49	111	24	3	7	55	31	59	6
Sagdal, Ian, Hagerstown	.303	108	409	71	124	30	5	10	59	36	90	6
Gutierrez, Kelvin, Hagerstown	.300	96	377	58	113	19	6	3	48	29	65	19
Cumana, Grenny, Lakewood	.291	96	347	55	101	22	0	1	27	16	30	17
Tomscha, Damek, Lakewood	.283	98	353	43	100	32	2	5	54	34	42	5
Barrett, Kyle, Greensboro	.282	101	354	39	100	10	3	2	32	25	67	17
Daily, Cody, Kannapolis	.281	118	423	46	119	26	4	4	44	46	72	1

INDIVIDUAL PITCHING

Pitcher, Club	W	L	ERA	G	GS	CG	SV	IP	H	R	ER	BB	SO
Easterling, Brannon, Kannapolis	7	3	1.86	34	18	0	2	126	103	36	26	31	88
Keller, Mitch, West Virginia	8	5	2.46	23	23	0	0	124	96	36	34	18	131
Gonzalez, Brian, Delmarva	10	8	2.50	27	27	0	0	148	135	52	41	58	111
Weigel, Patrick, Rome	10	4	2.51	22	21	1	0	129	92	44	36	47	135
Poteet, Cody, Greensboro	4	9	2.91	24	24	0	0	117	108	53	38	44	106
Vargas, Daris, Charleston	10	8	2.95	27	21	0	2	131	106	51	43	57	108
Morris, Christian, Charleston	8	5	2.99	22	22	0	0	120	105	44	40	24	99
Soroka, Mike, Rome	9	9	3.02	25	24	1	0	143	130	58	48	32	125
Connolly, Michael, Augusta	11	7	3.05	25	18	1	0	136	134	59	46	31	107
Taveras, Jose, Lakewood	8	8	3.28	25	20	1	0	137	116	60	50	26	154

ALL-STAR TEAM

P: Brian Gonzalez, Delmarva. **C:** Yermin Mercedes, Delmarva. **1B:** Brian Mundell, Asheville. **2B:** Josh Tobias, Lakewood. **3B:** Kelvin Gutierrez, Hagerstown. **SS:** Brendan Rodgers, Asheville. **DH:** Chris Gittens, Charleston. **OF:** Jose Pujols, Lakewood. **OF:** Luis Alexander Basabe, Greenville. **OF:** Tate Matheny, Greenville. **OF:** Yonathan Daza, Asheville. **IF:** Ian Sagdal, Hagerstown. **SP:** Mitch Keller, West Virginia. **RP:** C.J. Robinson, Greensboro.

Most Outstanding Pitcher: Mitch Keller, West Virginia.
Most Valuable Player: Brian Mundell, Asheville.

DEPARTMENT LEADERS

BATTING

2B	Mundell, Brian, Asheville	59
3B	Park, Hoy Jun, Charleston	12
AB/SO	Cumana, Grenny, Lakewood	11.57
BB	Ockimey, Josh, Greenville	88
CS	De La Rosa, Frandy, Hickory	23
H	Mundell, Brian, Asheville	168
HBP	Didder, Ray-Patrick, Rome	39
HR	Pujols, Jose, Lakewood	24
OBP	Mercedes, Yermin, Delmarva	.411
OPS	Mercedes, Yermin, Delmarva	.990
R	Didder, Ray-Patrick, Rome	95
RBI	Hilliard, Sam, Asheville	83
	Mundell, Brian, Asheville	83
SAC	George, Max, Asheville	20
SB	Jenkins, Eric, Hickory	51
SLG	Mercedes, Yermin, Delmarva	0.579
SO	Pujols, Jose, Lakewood	179
XBH	Mundell, Brian, Asheville	74

FIELDING

A	Mundell, Brian, Asheville	69
DP	Winningham, Dash, Columbia	77
E	Gittens, Chris, Charleston	16
1B PCT	Laurino, Steve, Delmarva	.993
PO	Mundell, Brian, Asheville	1000
A	Tolman, Mitchell, West Virginia	335
DP	Tolman, Mitchell, West Virginia	81
E	Miller, Jalen, Augusta	20
2B PCT	Twine, Justin, Greensboro	.985
PO	Tolman, Mitchell, West Virginia	215
A	Forbes, Ti'Quan, Hickory	220
DP	Forbes, Ti'Quan, Hickory	33
E	Riley, Austin, Rome	30
3B PCT	Forbes, Ti'Quan, Hickory	.948
PO	Riley, Austin, Rome	92
A	Kelley, Christian, West Virginia	114
PB	Mercedes, Yermin, Delmarva	23
DP	Winn, Matt, Augusta	11
E	Vallot, Chase, Lexington	17
C PCT	Moorman, Chuck, Hickory	.994
PO	Winn, Matt, Augusta	765
A	Daza, Yonathan, Asheville	22
DP	Didder, Ray-Patrick, Rome	7
E	Harrison, Seth, Augusta	12
OF PCT	Basabe, Luis Ax., Greenville	.992
PO	Mullins, Cedric, Delmarva	287
A	Yrizarri, Yeyson, Hickory	342
DP	Seymour, Anfernee, Greensboro, Rome	67
E	Gasparini, Marten, Lexington	48
SS PCT	Yrizarri, Yeyson, Hickory	.965
PO	Lora, Edwin, Hagerstown	166

PITCHING

AVG	Weigel, Patrick, Rome	.203
BB	Toussaint, Touki, Rome	71
BB/9	Agrazal, Dario, West Virginia	1.08
BK	Watson, Nolan, Lexington	5
CG	Almonte, Gaby, Columbia	2
	Blewett, Scott, Lexington	2
ER	Watson, Nolan, Lexington	81
G	Koziol, Ryan, Augusta	46
GF	Robinson, C.J., Greensboro	36
GS	Martinez, Luis, Kannapolis	28
H	Agrazal, Dario, West Virginia	173
HB	Helton, Bret, West Virginia	15
HR	Watson, Nolan, Lexington	19
IP	Agrazal, Dario, West Virginia	150
L	Agrazal, Dario, West Virginia	12
SO	Taveras, Jose, Lakewood	154
SO/9	Kilome, Franklyn, Lakewood	10.2
SO/9(RP)	Palumbo, Joe, Hickory	12.81
SV	Robinson, C.J., Greensboro	22
W	Boyd, Logan, Greenville	14
WP	Baez, Joan, Hagerstown	21

BY MICHAEL LANANNA

Johnny Rodriguez and the State College Spikes are on their way toward building a short-season New York-Penn League dynasty. For the second time in three years, the Spikes won the league title, dispatching Hudson Valley in two games to take home the crown.

"They were a good camaraderie group," Rodriguez said.

"You've got to have that. If we're winning by a lot, you look at them and they look at the same; we're losing by a lot, they look the same. They look the same every day. You do that in the big leagues, you have a dynasty."

The Spikes were led this season by 2016 Cardinals draftees Tommy Edman, a scrappy shortstop taken from Stanford in the sixth round, and catcher Jeremy Martinez, a fourth-rounder from Southern California who played a pivotal role for the Spikes as both a game-caller and middle-of-the-order bat. Meanwhile, the Spikes' pitching staff featured hard-throwing righthanders Jordan Hicks and second-rounder Connor Jones from Virginia, the latter of whom did not throw enough innings to qualify for the league's Top 20 Prospects list.

Jones was one of several high-profile arms who didn't qualify, including Brady Aiken (Indians), Logan Shore (Athletics), Jason Groome and Mike Shawaryn (Red Sox). Indians fourth-rounder Shane Bieber fell just an inning shy of qualifying. But the righthander drew rave reviews from opposing managers for his polish, sound mechanics and command, allowing just one earned run and striking out 21 to two walks in 24 innings with Mahoning Valley.

TOP 20 PROSPECTS

1. A.J. Puk, lhp, Vermont (Athletics)
2. Triston McKenzie, rhp, Mahoning Valley (Indians)
3. Justin Dunn rhp, Brooklyn (Mets)
4. Desmond Lindsay, of, Brooklyn (Mets)
5. Cody Sedlock, rhp, Aberdeen (Orioles)
6. Dane Dunning, rhp, Auburn (Nationals)
7. Will Craig, 3b, West Virginia (Pirates)
8. Peter Alonso, 1b, Brooklyn (Mets)
9. Bobby Dalbec, 3b, Lowell (Red Sox)
10. Jordan Hicks, rhp, State College (Cardinals)
11. Adonis Medina, rhp, Williamsport (Phillies)
12. Keegan Akin, lhp, Aberdeen (Orioles)
13. C.J. Chatham, ss, Lowell (Red Sox)
14. Austin Hays, of, Aberdeen (Orioles)
15. Tyler Hill, of, Lowell (Red Sox)
16. Josh Pennington, rhp, Lowell (Red Sox)
17. Aaron Civale, rhp, Mahoning Valley (Indians)
18. Garrett Whitley, of, Hudson Valley (Rays)
19. Daz Cameron, of, Tri-City (Astros)
20. Alex Wells, lhp, Aberdeen (Orioles)

As a whole, pitching dominated the league. Athletics first-rounder A.J. Puk, the No. 6 overall pick, continued to show the mid- to upper-90s lefthanded fastball he featured for three seasons at Florida. Mahoning Valley righthander Triston McKenzie was near unhittable as an 18-year-old, going 4-3, 0.55 to force a promotion to low Class A Lake County.

On the offensive side, Mets second-rounder Peter Alonso, from Florida, and Red Sox fourth-rounder Bobby Dalbec, from Arizona, made seamless transitions from the College World Series in Omaha to pro ball, with both showing plus power. Finally healthy from hamstring injuries in consecutive seasons, Mets prospect Desmond Lindsay flashed a glimpse of his five-tool potential with Brooklyn by hitting .297/.418/.450 with four home runs.

OVERALL STANDINGS

McNamara Division	W	L	PCT	GB	Manager(s)	Attendance	Average	Last Pennant
Hudson Valley (Rays)	47	27	.635	—	Tim Parenton	152,328	4,231	2012
*Staten Island (Yankees)	44	31	.587	3 ½	Dave Bialas	85,513	2,250	2011
Brooklyn (Mets)	37	39	.487	11	Tom Gamboa	207,702	5,614	2001
Aberdeen (Orioles)	32	43	.427	15 ½	Luis Pujols/Kevin Bradshaw	141,070	4,031	1983

Pinckney Division	W	L	PCT	GB	Manager(s)	Attendance	Average	Last Pennant
State College (Cardinals)	50	26	.658	—	Johnny Rodriguez	125,875	3,313	2016
Williamsport (Phillies)	39	36	.520	10 ½	Pat Borders	60,429	1,727	2003
West Virginia (Pirates)	38	38	.500	12	Wyatt Toregas	78,774	2,188	2015
Mahoning Valley (Indians)	37	38	.493	12 ½	Edwin Rodriguez	92,117	2,632	2004
Auburn (Nationals)	28	47	.373	21 ½	Jerad Head	52,811	1,427	2007
Batavia (Marlins)	22	53	.293	27 ½	Angel Espada	30,007	811	2008

Stedler Division	W	L	PCT	GB	Manager(s)	Attendance	Average	Last Pennant
Lowell (Red Sox)	47	29	.618	—	Iggy Suarez	139,943	3,782	Never
Connecticut (Tigers)	41	35	.539	6	Mike Rabelo	82,488	2,291	1998
Tri-City (Astros)	38	38	.500	9	Lamarr Rogers	149,847	4,281	2013
Vermont (Athletics)	28	48	.368	19	Aaron Nieckula	83,955	2,332	1996

Playoffs—Semifinals: Hudson Valley defeated Lowell 2-0 and State College defeated Staten Island 2-1 in best-of-three series. **Finals:** State College defeated Hudson Valley 2-0 in best-of-three series.

MINOR LEAGUES

CLUB BATTING

	AVG	G	AB	R	H	2B	3B	HR	RBI	BB	SO	SB	OBP	SLG
Lowell	.270	76	2525	370	683	131	30	39	330	237	538	51	.340	.392
West Virginia	.263	76	2472	330	649	114	25	23	295	263	498	66	.343	.357
Hudson Valley	.255	75	2455	286	626	116	32	12	250	232	537	125	.329	.343
State College	.254	76	2586	378	657	126	24	35	334	283	484	58	.335	.362
Tri-City	.252	76	2523	357	635	131	15	51	319	280	630	57	.339	.376
Mahoning Valley	.250	75	2464	326	615	112	22	35	285	232	601	84	.324	.356
Williamsport	.244	76	2479	288	605	118	12	35	244	192	608	78	.307	.344
Connecticut	.242	76	2472	312	598	110	18	18	289	247	556	46	.319	.323
Staten Island	.239	75	2522	312	602	120	12	30	272	277	605	67	.323	.331
Vermont	.233	76	2501	271	583	102	10	34	238	241	624	62	.304	.323
Auburn	.232	75	2464	235	571	95	23	12	199	191	466	65	.296	.304
Aberdeen	.228	75	2399	245	546	99	13	27	217	203	650	68	.296	.313
Batavia	.218	75	2442	264	532	100	13	20	226	240	602	70	.298	.294
Brooklyn	.216	76	2531	284	546	106	9	27	249	283	603	83	.301	.297

CLUB PITCHING

	ERA	G	CG	SHO	SV	IP	H	R	ER	HR	BB	SO	AVG
Hudson Valley	2.56	75	1	0	27	657	498	224	187	22	239	571	.210
Williamsport	2.70	76	3	2	18	656	541	250	197	24	228	564	.222
Staten Island	2.83	75	1	1	24	677	570	268	213	22	235	644	.228
Connecticut	3.06	76	0	0	21	653	605	274	222	22	209	562	.244
State College	3.06	76	0	0	30	679	662	295	231	23	223	522	.255
Mahoning Valley	3.23	75	0	0	15	654	581	295	235	29	246	558	.238
Aberdeen	3.27	75	0	0	16	641	586	277	233	28	219	508	.245
Lowell	3.30	76	0	0	22	659	584	293	242	34	273	597	.238
Brooklyn	3.32	76	0	0	21	690	641	305	255	27	230	706	.246
Auburn	3.66	75	1	0	15	650	624	319	264	24	218	522	.252
West Virginia	3.77	76	0	0	12	661	602	319	277	29	244	553	.243
Vermont	3.95	76	0	0	14	661	617	358	290	33	269	572	.244
Tri-City	4.11	76	0	0	22	667	628	345	305	40	278	654	.246
Batavia	5.02	75	0	0	11	651	709	436	363	41	290	469	.280

CLUB FIELDING

	PCT	PO	A	E	DP		PCT	PO	A	E	DP
Tri-City	.978	2002	708	62	132	State College	.971	2036	805	85	184
Connecticut	.975	1960	775	69	158	Auburn	.970	1950	768	84	152
Brooklyn	.974	2071	818	78	154	West Virginia	.969	1983	824	90	168
Staten Island	.973	2032	770	78	154	Mahoning Valley	.965	1962	788	101	180
Hudson Valley	.972	1971	786	79	177	Batavia	.964	1953	788	102	156
Aberdeen	.972	1922	807	80	197	Williamsport	.963	1967	860	108	151
Lowell	.971	1978	701	80	139	Vermont	.956	1982	751	127	151

INDIVIDUAL BATTING

Batter, Club	AVG	G	AB	R	H	2B	3B	HR	RBI	BB	SO	SB
Hill, Tyler, Lowell	.332	61	232	43	77	14	5	4	38	24	41	11
Martinez, Jeremy, State College	.325	57	194	28	63	14	2	1	32	32	16	1
Mejia, Gabriel, Mahoning Valley	.322	65	264	55	85	8	3	0	16	24	51	28
Solak, Nick, Staten Island	.321	64	240	48	77	13	1	3	25	30	39	8
Lowe, Nathaniel, Hudson Valley	.300	67	247	26	74	18	2	4	40	30	39	1
Mondou, Nate, Vermont	.298	60	225	27	67	11	2	0	24	24	37	6
Lester, Josh, Connecticut	.293	60	222	30	65	19	3	2	26	24	32	0
Moore, Ty, West Virginia	.288	58	205	32	59	5	1	1	17	13	18	9
Tovar, Carlos, Lowell	.287	58	209	28	60	14	2	2	28	11	42	1
Billingsley, Cole, Aberdeen	.286	53	192	25	55	6	1	3	15	20	39	14

INDIVIDUAL PITCHING

Pitcher, Club	W	L	ERA	G	GS	CG	SV	IP	H	R	ER	BB	SO
Gonzalez, Harol, Brooklyn	7	3	2.01	14	13	0	0	85	69	20	19	17	88
St. John, Locke, Connecticut	6	7	2.12	15	15	0	0	89	78	32	21	26	71
Wells, Alex, Aberdeen	4	5	2.15	13	13	0	0	63	48	17	15	9	50
Beddes, Danny, West Virginia	6	3	2.27	14	12	0	0	71	48	20	18	24	55
Altamirano, Xavier, Vermont	3	3	2.48	14	9	0	0	65	60	22	18	10	57
Moran, Spencer, Hudson Valley	4	1	2.64	14	12	0	0	61	44	20	18	28	38
Suarez, Ranger, Williamsport	6	4	2.81	13	13	2	0	74	61	26	23	24	53
Gonzalez, Merandy, Brooklyn	6	3	2.87	14	14	0	0	69	65	29	22	27	71
Paulino, Felix, Williamsport	3	4	2.89	13	13	0	0	72	64	31	23	14	54
Mahoney, Kolton, Staten Island	4	4	2.92	12	8	1	0	62	65	25	20	16	47

DEPARTMENT LEADERS

BATTING

2B	Hall, Darick, Williamsport	19
	Lester, Josh, Connecticut	19
3B	Fraley, Jake, Hudson Valley	7
	Whitley, Garrett, Hudson Valley	7
AB/SO	Martinez, Jeremy, State College	12.13
BB	Edman, Tommy, State College	48
CS	Hill, Tyler, Lowell	11
H	Mejia, Gabriel, Mahoning Valley	85
HBP	Hall, Darick, Williamsport	16
HR	Mercedes, Miguel, Vermont	12
OBP	Martinez, Jeremy, State College	.419
OPS	Hall, Darick, Williamsport	.890
R	Edman, Tommy, State College	61
RBI	Robinson, Timmy, Staten Island	52
SAC	Forgione, Erik, West Virginia	8
	Pantoja, Alexis, Mahoning Valley	8
SB	Fraley, Jake, Hudson Valley	33
SLG	Hall, Darick, Williamsport	.518
SO	Bautista, Ricardo, State College	82
XBH	Robinson, Timmy, Staten Island	30

FIELDING

A	Three tied with	40
DP	Lowe, Nathaniel, Hudson Valley	54
E	Tapia, Emmanuel, Mahoning Valley	15
1B PCT	Lowe, Nathaniel, Hudson Valley	.994
PO	Baur, Albert, West Virginia	609
A	Mastrobuoni, Miles, Hudson Valley	174
DP	Juvier, Alejandro, Aberdeen	40
E	Espiritu, Jr., Luis, Williamsport	15
2B PCT	Mastrobuoni, Miles, Hudson Valley	.993
PO	Juvier, Alejandro, Aberdeen	127
A	Haley, Jim, Hudson Valley	116
DP	Hudzina, Danny, State College	14
E	Craig, Will, West Virginia	16
3B PCT	Hudzina, Danny, State College	.968
PO	Haley, Jim, Hudson Valley	50
A	Navas, Eduardo, Staten Island	51
DP	Sanchez, Ali, Brooklyn	5
E	De La Calle, Daniel, Hudson Valley	8
	Martinez, Jeremy, State College	8
C PCT	Barrera, Tres, Auburn	.990
PB	Garcia, Pablo, Batavia	20
PO	De La Calle, Daniel, Hudson Valley	328
A	Banks, Nick, Auburn	10
DP	Banks, Nick, Auburn	4
E	Bautista, Ricardo, State College	7
	Rodriguez, Jhonny, Vermont	7
OF PCT	Perkins, Blake, Auburn	1
PO	Aybar, Yoan, Lowell	139
A	Woodmansee, Colby, Brooklyn	174
DP	Pujols, Bill, Hudson Valley	38
E	Castro, Samuel, Batavia	25
SS PCT	Woodmansee, Colby, Brooklyn	.970
PO	Woodmansee, Colby, Brooklyn	86

PITCHING

AVG	Beddes, Danny, West Virginia	.195
BB	Steen, Kevin, Lowell	42
BB/9	Llanes, Gabriel, Brooklyn	0.9
BK	Mota, Cristian, West Virginia	3
CG	Suarez, Ranger, Williamsport	2
ER	Meyer, Stephan, West Virginia	41
G	Perez, Ryan, Mahoning Valley	28
GF	Zanghi, Joseph, Brooklyn	17
GS	Meyer, Stephan, West Virginia	16
H	Farinaro, Steven, State College	100
HB	Bowers, Heath, Vermont	11
HR	Chalmers, Dakota, Vermont	8
IP	St. John, Locke, Connecticut	89.1
L	Llanes, Gabriel, Brooklyn	8
R	Llanes, Gabriel, Brooklyn	51
SO	Gonzalez, Harol, Brooklyn	88
SO/9	De la Rosa, Simon, Staten Island	9.87
SO/9(RP)	Mendez, Deivy, Hudson Valley	12.29
SV	Bowen, Brady, State College	9
	Carter, Eric, State College	9
W	Farinaro, Steven, State College	9
WP	Provenchen, Ty, Batavia	13
	Rosillo, Eduard, Hudson Valley	13

MINOR LEAGUES

MINOR LEAGUES

BY JOSH NORRIS

While their parent club was on a mission to end its 108-year World Series drought, the Eugene Emeralds vanquished some ghosts of their own.

The last time Eugene won a Northwest League title was 1975. Since that year, the Emeralds have moved from Civic Stadium to P.K. Park and changed affiliates many times over. They won a co-championship in 1980, but hadn't won a solo crown in more than four decades.

That changed in 2016, thanks to a prospect-packed roster and a season of dominance. The Emeralds broke a Northwest League record with 15 straight wins and finished with a league-best 54-22 mark before entering the postseason.

Although it didn't translate to success on the field, Salem-Keizer's squad was one of the most prospect-laden in the league. The Volcanoes' outfield comprised three college products in Bryan Reynolds (Vanderbilt), Heath Quinn (Samford) and Gio Brusa (Pacific) who each figured among the NWL's best hitters. Their rotation also featured flame-throwing but raw righthander Melvin Adon, a $20,000 signing from the Dominican Republic. His fastball touched triple-digits with regularity out of the rotation, which earned him a spot toward the back of the league's Top 20 prospects.

Spokane claimed two of the youngest and best prospects in the league in center field Leody Taveras and shortstop Anderson Tejeda. The pair of 17-year-olds was promoted late in the season and each made impact. Tejeda socked eight home runs in just 92 at-bats, and Taveras showed off five-tool potential day in and day out.

Although his season was cut short by a grisly knee injury, Everett outfielder Kyle Lewis—the No. 8 overall pick in the draft—impressed evaluators enough to take the No. 2 spot on the NWL Top 20.

League-champion Eugene placed four players on the Top 20, including high-octane righthander Dylan Cease, whose fastball peaked at 100 mph.

Everett advanced to the championship series by topping Spokane, but their division series featured

an intriguing wrinkle. Because of a rainout and some creative scheduling, Game Two of the series was played at Seattle's Safeco Field. Everett swept the set, which meant the Aquasox's players got to celebrate their victory in a major league ballpark.

Eugene and Everett alternated wins over the first two games of the series, setting up a winner-take-all showdown in Game Three. Lefthander Manuel Rondon spun six innings of one-run ball and Eugene's bullpen silenced Everett the rest of the way en route to the franchise's first outright title in 31 years and the first championship celebration at PK Park.

TOP 20 PROSPECTS

1. Leody Taveras, of, Spokane (Rangers)
2. Kyle Lewis, of, Everett (Mariners)
3. Dylan Cease, rhp, Eugene (Cubs)
4. Anderson Tejeda, ss, Spokane (Rangers)
5. Bryan Reynolds, of, Salem-Keizer (Giants)
6. J.B. Woodman, of, Vancouver (Blue Jays)
7. Garrett Hampson, ss, Boise (Rockies)
8. Justin Maese, rhp, Vancouver (Blue Jays)
9. Heath Quinn, of, Salem-Keizer (Giants)
10. Wladimir Galindo, 3b, Eugene (Cubs)
11. Joey Lucchesi, lhp, Tri-City (Padres)
12. Patrick Murphy, rhp, Vancouver (Blue Jays)
13. D.J. Wilson, of, Eugene (Cubs)
14. Gio Brusa, of, Salem-Keizer (Giants)
15. Bryson Brigman, ss/2b, Everett (Mariners)
16. Chris Pieters, 1b/of, Eugene (Cubs)
17. Matt Krook, lhp, Salem-Keizer (Giants)
18. Melvin Adon, rhp, Salem-Keizer (Giants)
19. Tyler Ferguson, rhp, Spokane (Rangers)
20. Buddy Reed, of, Tri-City (Padres)

STANDINGS: SPLIT SEASON

FIRST HALF				SECOND HALF			
NORTH	**W**	**L**	**PCT**	**GB**			

FIRST HALF					SECOND HALF				
NORTH	**W**	**L**	**PCT**	**GB**	**NORTH**	**W**	**L**	**PCT**	**GB**
Spokane	19	19	.500	—	Everett	27	11	.711	—
Tri-City	19	19	.500	—	Tri-City	15	23	.395	12
Everett	18	20	.474	1	Vancouver	13	23	.361	13
Vancouver	16	22	.421	3	Spokane	13	24	.351	13½
SOUTH	**W**	**L**	**PCT**	**GB**	**SOUTH**	**W**	**L**	**PCT**	**GB**
Eugene	28	10	.737	—	Eugene	26	12	.684	—
Hillsboro	19	19	.500	9	Hillsboro	23	14	.622	2½
Salem-Keizer	17	21	.447	11	Boise	17	21	.447	9
Boise	16	22	.421	12	Salem-Keizer	15	21	.417	10

Playoffs—Semifinals: Eugene defeated Hillsboro 2-1 and Everett defeated Spokane 2-0 in best-of-three-series. **Finals:** Eugene defeated Everett 2-1 in best-of-three-series.

OVERALL STANDINGS

Team (Organization)	W	L	PCT	GB	Manager(s)	Attendance	Average	Last Pennant
Eugene (Cubs)	54	22	.711	—	Jesus Feliciano	121,587	3,200	2016
Everett (Mariners)	45	31	.592	9	Rob Mummau	104,162	2,815	2010
Hillsboro (Diamondbacks)	42	33	.560	11½	Shelley Duncan	131,851	3,470	2015
Tri-City (Padres)	34	42	.447	20	Ben Fritz	86,886	2,286	Never
Boise (Rockies)	33	43	.434	21	Andy Gonzalez	114,476	3,094	2004
Salem-Keizer (Giants)	32	42	.432	21	Kyle Haines	80,469	2,175	2009
Spokane (Rangers)	32	43	.427	21½	Tim Hulett	187,848	5,077	2008
Vancouver (Blue Jays)	29	45	.392	24	John Tamargo	222,363	6,177	2013

CLUB BATTING

	AVG	G	AB	R	H	2B	3B	HR	RBI	BB	SO	SB	OBP	SLG
Everett	.282	76	2624	437	740	147	16	42	382	309	568	77	.363	.398
Salem-Keizer	.276	74	2583	412	712	163	20	50	363	206	634	49	.338	.412
Spokane	.258	75	2572	347	664	119	15	43	305	292	627	39	.342	.366
Hillsboro	.250	75	2482	353	621	112	17	42	301	274	598	120	.336	.360
Eugene	.250	76	2549	394	636	133	26	41	338	296	661	98	.332	.370
Boise	.247	76	2562	353	634	116	29	24	308	315	674	137	.335	.343
Vancouver	.238	74	2466	305	587	127	21	24	254	298	605	42	.329	.336
Tri-City	.234	76	2524	298	591	92	21	13	249	291	664	69	.322	.303

CLUB PITCHING

	ERA	G	CG	SHO	SV	IP	H	R	ER	HR	BB	SO	AVG
Eugene	3.24	76	0	0	30	687	576	306	247	34	316	680	.226
Tri-City	3.43	76	0	0	18	673	614	330	256	21	261	663	.241
Hillsboro	3.81	75	0	0	17	659	623	342	279	28	259	660	.249
Everett	3.86	76	0	0	16	669	614	329	287	54	230	679	.242
Spokane	4.26	75	0	0	17	658	643	378	311	27	301	672	.252
Boise	4.32	76	0	0	21	671	717	409	322	37	268	559	.273
Vancouver	4.63	74	0	0	16	647	710	382	333	28	300	526	.282
Salem-Keizer	4.88	74	0	0	15	645	688	423	350	50	346	592	.273

CLUB FIELDING

	PCT	PO	A	E	DP		PCT	PO	A	E	DP
Everett	.970	2011	718	84	143	Boise	.962	2013	855	112	241
Eugene	.968	2061	849	97	217	Salem-Keizer	.961	1936	724	107	165
Vancouver	.968	1940	801	92	178	Tri-City	.960	2018	785	117	164
Hillsboro	.964	1976	759	103	137	Spokane	.955	1973	781	131	197

INDIVIDUAL BATTING

Batter, Club	AVG	G	AB	R	H	2B	3B	HR	RBI	BB	SO	SB
Filia, Eric, Everett	.362	68	246	43	89	19	1	4	46	39	19	10
Quinn, Heath, Salem-Keizer	.337	54	205	37	69	19	1	9	34	26	50	3
Zammarelli, Nick, Everett	.329	65	255	44	84	18	1	5	43	25	67	3
Rivera, Kevin, Salem-Keizer	.320	66	253	41	81	14	3	3	31	11	47	4
Anderson, Josh, Hillsboro	.307	55	212	31	65	11	0	5	34	10	41	5
Baker, Chris, Tri-City	.303	54	201	33	61	11	0	2	27	23	49	14
Jones, Wesley, Boise	.302	59	222	23	67	11	1	1	30	19	36	2
Hampson, Garrett, Boise	.301	68	256	43	77	14	8	2	44	48	56	36
Geraldo, Manuel, Salem-Keizer	.298	62	272	47	81	10	5	0	32	14	69	13
Fulmer, Ashford, Salem-Keizer	.292	56	202	36	59	12	3	1	24	27	43	12

INDIVIDUAL PITCHING

Pitcher, Club	W	L	ERA	G	GS	CG	SV	IP	H	R	ER	BB	SO
Murphy, Patrick, Vancouver	4	5	2.84	13	13	0	0	70	71	28	22	23	48
Benitez, Anfernee, Hillsboro	7	5	3.48	14	12	0	0	72	75	34	28	31	71
Mark, Tyler, Hillsboro	5	5	3.91	15	15	0	0	78	79	41	34	23	70
Julio, Erick, Boise	4	6	4.05	13	13	0	0	73	80	36	33	13	47
Santos, Antonio, Boise	6	4	4.16	13	13	0	0	71	85	42	33	14	53
Headean, Will, Tri-City	4	5	4.32	15	14	0	0	73	75	43	35	26	77
Eusebio, Breiling, Boise	2	5	5.26	13	13	0	0	63	78	46	37	30	42
Adon, Melvin, Salem-Keizer	5	5	5.48	14	14	0	0	67	85	53	41	34	55
Rodriguez, Dalton, Vancouver	2	7	6.18	14	14	0	0	63	84	50	43	35	42

ALL-STAR TEAM

P: Anfernee Benitez, Hillsboro. **P:** Dylan Cease, Eugene. **P:** Joey Lucchesi, Tri-City. **P:** Manuel Rondon, Eugene. **P:** Patrick Murphy, Vancouver. **C:** Luke Lowery, Hillsboro. **1B:** Kristian Brito, Everett. **2B:** Kevin Rivera, Salem-Keizer. **3B:** Nick Zammarelli, Everett. **SS:** Garrett Hampson, Boise. **DH:** Jacob Bosiokovic, Boise. **OF:** Eric Filia, Everett. **OF:** Gio Brusa, Salem-Keizer. **OF:** Heath Quinn, Salem-Keizer. **Manager of the Year:** Jesus Feliciano, Eugene. **Most Valuable Player:** Eric Filia, Everett.

DEPARTMENT LEADERS

BATTING

2B	Bosiokovic, Jacob, Boise	20
3B	Hampson, Garrett, Boise	8
AB/SO	Filia, Eric, Everett	12.95
BB	Hampson, Garrett, Boise	48
CS	Brigman, Bryson, Everett	12
H	Filia, Eric, Everett	89
HBP	Karaviotis, Mark, Hillsboro	12
HR	Brusa, Gio, Salem-Keizer	10
OBP	Filia, Eric, Everett	.450
OPS	Quinn, Heath, Salem-Keizer	.993
R	Brigman, Bryson, Everett	51
RBI	Brito, Kristian, Everett	46
	Filia, Eric, Everett	46
SAC	Peguero, Yeiler, Eugene	7
SB	Hampson, Garrett, Boise	36
SLG	Quinn, Heath, Salem-Keizer	.571
SO	Bosiokovic, Jacob, Boise	98
XBH	Galindo, Wladimir, Eugene	32

PITCHING

A	Williams, Christian, Vancouver	33
DP	Williams, Christian, Vancouver	52
E	McDonald, Todd, Spokane	19
1B PCT	Williams, Christian, Vancouver	.990
PO	Williams, Christian, Vancouver	477
A	Rivera, Kevin, Salem-Keizer	185
DP	Rivera, Kevin, Salem-Keizer	41
E	Brito, Antony, Boise	16
2B PCT	Easley, Nate, Tri-City	.955
PO	Easley, Nate, Tri-City	121
A	Galindo, Wladimir, Eugene	120
DP	Jones, Wesley, Boise	13
E	Geraldo, Manuel, Salem-Keizer	17
3B PCT	Jones, Wesley, Boise	.940
PO	Galindo, Wladimir, Eugene	41
A	Hernandez, Javier, Vancouver	58
DP	Bowers, Zack, Salem-Keizer	7
E	Hernandez, Javier, Vancouver	10
	Quevedo, Johan, Everett	10
C PCT	Bowers, Zack, Salem-Keizer	.995
PB	Riley, John, Salem-Keizer	16
PO	Bowers, Zack, Salem-Keizer	351
A	Fulmer, Ashford, Salem-Keizer	8
DP	Asuncion, Luis, Tri-City	3
	Burgos, Aldemar, Tri-City	3
E	Wilson, D.J., Eugene	7
OF PCT	Grebeck, Austin, Everett	.993
PO	Grebeck, Austin, Everett	133
A	Hampson, Garrett, Boise	226
DP	Hampson, Garrett, Boise	50
E	Gudino, Yeltsin, Vancouver	22
SS PCT	Howard, Ryan, Salem-Keizer	.947
PO	Hampson, Garrett, Boise	102

PITCHING

AVG	Mark, Tyler, Hillsboro	.258
BB	Marshall, Mac, Salem-Keizer	48
BB/9	Julio, Erick, Boise	1.6
BK	Julio, Erick, Boise	4
ER	Rodriguez, Dalton, Vancouver	43
G	Winston, Jake, Hillsboro	28
GF	Fernandez, Julian, Boise	19
GS	Mark, Tyler, Hillsboro	15
H	Adon, Melvin, Salem-Keizer	85
	Santos, Antonio, Boise	85
HB	Melo, Kendry, Salem-Keizer	11
HR	Newsome, Ljay, Everett	11
IP	Mark, Tyler, Hillsboro	78.1
L	Zimmerman, Michael, Boise	8
SO	Headean, Will, Tri-City	77
SO/9	Headean, Will, Tri-City	9.49
SO/9(RP)	Ferguson, Tyler, Spokane	13.65
SO/9(RP)	Ratliff, Lane, Everett	13.65
SV	Fernandez, Julian, Boise	13
W	Benitez, Anfernee, Hillsboro	7
WP	Rodriguez, Dalton, Vancouver	16

MINOR LEAGUES

BY HUDSON BELINSKY AND JOHN MANUEL

For the fourth time in seven seasons, the Johnson City Cardinals won the Appalachian League title, powering past Elizabethton and Burlington by scoring 39 runs in five postseason games. The Cardinals got a playoff boost from 2015 second-round pick Bryce Denton, a third baseman who hit a three-run clinching shot in Game Two of the finals and went 9-for-20 with seven RBIs in the postseason.

The Appalachian League has hosted plenty of prospects in recent years, from the 2011 season, when 2016 Cy Young candidates Noah Syndergaard and Aaron Sanchez teamed for Bluefield, while burgeoning regulars in Miguel Sano and Brandon Drury were regulars for Elizabethton and Danville.

This year, the pool of talent was particularly deep, with a number of high draft picks stacking up against a stout international class. The highest picked player from the 2016 draft to play in the Appy League this summer was Ian Anderson, the Braves righthander picked No. 3 overall. He missed the innings requirement to qualify for BA's Top 20 Prospects list, finishing the year two outs from qualifying.

First-rounders picked after Anderson who played in the Appy League in 2016 included third baseman Josh Lowe (Rays), outfielders Alex Kirilloff (Twins) and Blake Rutherford (Yankees) and righthander Forrest Whitley (Astros), who were all among the top 17 picks in the draft, as well as Braves lefthander Joey Wentz, a sandwich pick. Kirilloff, who hit .306/.341/.454 with seven home runs, was named the league's player of the year.

Adrian Rondon and Vladimir Guerrero were each the No. 1 international prospect in their respective classes in 2014 and 2015, and they both made impressive strides forward this season in the Appy League. Other former highly-ranked international prospects also occupied the league,

with Braves outfielder Cristian Pache headlining a group that also included shortstop Derian Cruz (Braves), middle infielder Miguelangel Sierra (Astros), shortstop Wilkerman Garcia (Yankees), third baseman Dermis Garcia (Yankees) and first baseman Lewin Diaz (Twins). Rondon had one of the signature games of the season on June 24, hitting three homers and driving home nine, including an eighth-inning grand slam.

The league pitcher of the year was Mexican lefthander Cristian Castillo, who led Rookie-level Burlington to the league's best regular-season record. He led the league in opponents average (.212) while ranking second in strikeouts (73) and WHIP (0.99) while going 6-1, 3.13. He threw a complete-game one-hit shutout of Pulaski on July 29. In fact, after allowing a leadoff hit to Rutherford (who left the game immediately thereafter with a cramp), Castillo held Pulaski hitless the rest of the way. Lefty 19-year-old Garrett Davila (7-0, 2.77) and 21-year-old righty Geoffrey Bramblett (6-1, 2.17), a 30th-rounder out of Alabama, complemented him in the rotation.

TOP 20 PROSPECTS

1. Vladimir Guerrero Jr., 3b, Bluefield (Blue Jays)
2. Blake Rutherford, of, Pulaski (Yankees)
3. Estevan Florial, of, Pulaski (Yankees)
4. Kolby Allard, lhp, Danville (Braves)
5. Jordan Hicks, rhp, Johnson City (Cardinals)
6. Alex Kirilloff, of, Elizabethton (Twins)
7. Adrian Rondon, ss, Princeton (Rays)
8. Thomas Szapucki, lhp, Kingsport (Mets)
9. Cristian Pache, of, Danville (Braves)
10. Joey Wentz, lhp, Danville (Braves)
11. Josh Lowe, 3b, Princeton (Rays)
12. Derian Cruz, ss, Danville (Braves)
13. Allen Cordoba, ss, Johnson City (Cardinals)
14. Miguelangel Sierra, ss, Greeneville (Astros)
15. Ian Oxnevad, lhp, Johnson City (Cardinals)
16. Garrett Davila, lhp, Burlington (Royals)
17. Yennsy Diaz, rhp, Bluefield (Blue Jays)
18. Travis Blankenhorn, 2b, Elizabethton (Twins)
19. Nicky Lopez, ss, Burlington (Royals)
20. Brett Cumberland, c, Danville (Braves)

OVERALL STANDINGS

Eastern Division	W	L	PCT	GB	Manager(s)	Attendance	Average	Last Pennant
Burlington (Royals)	42	26	.618	—	Scott Thorman	49,227	1,492	1993
*Princeton (Rays)	38	29	.567	3 ½	Danny Sheaffer	14,635	457	1994
Bluefield (Blue Jays)	37	31	.544	5	Dennis Holmberg	22,651	731	2001
Danville (Braves)	31	36	.463	10 ½	Robinson Cancel	31,540	956	2009
Pulaski (Yankees)	29	37	.439	12	Tony Franklin	57,995	1,871	2013

Western Division	W	L	PCT	GB	Manager(s)	Attendance	Average	Last Pennant
Johnson City (Cardinals)	39	29	.574	—	Chris Swauger	51,855	1,673	2016
*Elizabethton (Twins)	36	31	.537	2 ½	Ray Smith	19,427	627	2012
Greeneville (Astros)	33	34	.493	5 ½	Josh Bonifay	41,651	1,262	2015
Kingsport (Mets)	27	41	.397	12	Luis Rivera	27,990	903	1995
Bristol (Pirates)	25	43	.368	14	Kory DeHaan	16,441	530	2002

Playoffs—Semifinals: Burlington defeated Princeton 2-1 and Johnson City defeated Elizabethton 2-1 in best-of-three series. **Finals:** Johnson City defeated Burlington 2-0 in a best-of-three series.

MINOR LEAGUES

CLUB BATTING

	AVG	G	AB	R	H	2B	3B	HR	RBI	BB	SO	SB	OBP	SLG
Johnson City	.281	68	2313	373	651	132	17	37	306	201	469	63	.350	.401
Princeton	.274	67	2229	363	611	129	14	56	326	185	567	41	.342	.420
Burlington	.264	68	2264	373	597	119	32	49	331	226	481	82	.339	.409
Kingsport	.262	68	2248	317	589	111	17	25	275	239	513	60	.338	.360
Elizabethton	.255	67	2232	323	569	102	15	60	282	203	565	29	.322	.395
Greeneville	.249	67	2288	311	569	102	25	46	267	211	602	66	.324	.375
Danville	.248	67	2220	272	550	99	15	27	239	170	527	52	.314	.342
Bluefield	.248	68	2223	375	551	104	21	57	310	285	634	118	.347	.390
Pulaski	.238	66	2161	288	514	112	22	60	258	242	585	43	.320	.393
Bristol	.237	68	2201	275	522	91	14	23	224	192	527	78	.309	.323

CLUB PITCHING

	ERA	G	CG	SHO	SV	IP	H	R	ER	HR	BB	SO	AVG
Burlington	3.38	68	2	1	15	593	517	256	223	41	204	571	.235
Danville	3.78	67	0	0	15	581	555	309	244	22	236	551	.251
Greeneville	3.87	67	0	0	16	609	568	322	262	34	266	605	.247
Princeton	3.92	67	0	0	21	576	556	300	251	50	164	551	.251
Johnson City	4.06	68	1	0	17	584	651	353	263	42	170	492	.280
Bluefield	4.23	68	2	1	16	592	574	329	278	54	223	508	.252
Elizabethton	4.36	67	4	2	23	568	580	325	275	42	221	560	.265
Pulaski	4.40	66	2	0	10	556	518	330	272	54	235	546	.245
Kingsport	4.45	68	0	0	10	575	589	370	284	40	235	606	.260
Bristol	4.66	68	1	1	14	578	615	376	299	61	200	480	.270

CLUB FIELDING

	PCT	PO	A	E	DP		PCT	PO	A	E	DP
Burlington	.980	1779	665	49	141	Pulaski	.960	1669	648	96	153
Greeneville	.971	1827	667	75	130	Danville	.958	1744	725	107	150
Bluefield	.965	1775	648	87	124	Bristol	.957	1734	696	110	146
Princeton	.964	1729	661	89	139	Kingsport	.953	1724	594	114	121
Elizabethton	.962	1705	632	93	136	Johnson City	.950	1751	730	130	171

INDIVIDUAL BATTING

Batter, Club	AVG	G	AB	R	H	2B	3B	HR	RBI	BB	SO	SB
Cordoba, Allen, Johnson City	.362	50	196	49	71	16	5	0	18	21	19	22
Peterson, Kort, Johnson City	.347	49	176	39	61	12	4	5	35	17	38	7
Davis, J.R., Johnson City	.333	46	186	40	62	10	2	3	13	5	22	11
Fiedler, Matt, Johnson City	.325	52	197	30	64	20	0	4	31	19	32	8
Melley, Bobby, Princeton	.323	53	189	34	61	15	0	4	32	21	33	0
Cespedes, Ricardo, Kingsport	.322	56	227	30	73	4	3	1	16	9	36	7
Knizner, Andrew, Johnson City	.319	53	185	35	59	12	1	6	42	21	21	0
Fernandez, Victor, Bristol	.314	49	169	29	53	13	2	2	19	15	31	12
Cabrera, Eleardo, Princeton	.311	60	238	44	74	12	2	7	36	17	73	8
Diaz, Lewin, Elizabethton	.310	46	174	26	54	15	2	9	37	12	35	0

INDIVIDUAL PITCHING

Pitcher, Club	W	L	ERA	G	GS	CG	SV	IP	H	R	ER	BB	SO
Parra, Frederis, Johnson City	3	5	2.53	11	10	1	0	64	68	33	18	7	36
Eckelman, Matt, Bristol	5	3	2.76	13	11	0	0	62	51	24	19	9	55
Davila, Garrett, Burlington	7	0	2.77	12	12	0	0	65	56	21	20	27	55
Clark, Ethan, Princeton	7	2	2.91	12	9	1	0	59	47	22	19	15	44
Castillo, Cristian, Burlington	6	3	3.13	12	12	1	0	72	57	28	25	14	73
Martinez, Jhon, Danville	4	6	3.21	12	12	0	0	62	68	31	22	16	45
Ortiz, Willy, Princeton	8	0	3.25	11	11	0	0	55	67	25	20	6	47
Oxnevad, Ian, Johnson City	5	3	3.38	12	12	0	0	72	80	32	27	13	57
Jimenez, Juan, Pulaski	4	3	3.57	12	10	1	1	58	51	29	23	26	56
Humphreys, Jordan, Kingsport	3	5	3.76	12	12	0	0	69	65	35	29	15	76

ALL-STAR TEAM

C: Andrew Knizner, Johnson City. **1B:** Bobby Melley, Princeton. **2B:** J.R. Davis, Johnson City.
3B: Vladimir Guerrero Jr., Bluefield. **SS:** Allen Cordoba, Johnson City. **DH:** Lewin Diaz, Elizabethton.
OF: Alex Kirilloff, Elizabethton. **OF:** Eleardo Cabrera, Princeton. **OF:** Kort Peterson, Burlington.
OF: Matt Fiedler, Johnson City. **IF:** Nicky Lopez, Burlington. **SP:** Cristian Castillo, Burlington. **SP:** Ethan
Clark, Princeton. **RP:** Patrick McGuff, Elizabethton.
Manager of the Year: Scott Thorman, Burlington.
Pitcher of the Year: Cristian Castillo, Burlington.
Player of the Year: Alex Kirilloff, Elizabethton.

DEPARTMENT LEADERS

BATTING

2B	Fiedler, Matt, Johnson City	20
3B	Three tied with	5
AB/SO	Cordoba, Allen, Johnson City	10.32
BB	Sinay, Nick, Bluefield	40
CS	Vizcaino, Vance, Burlington	9
H	Cabrera, Eleardo, Princeton	74
HBP	Sinay, Nick, Bluefield	24
HR	Jones, Bradley, Bluefield	16
OBP	Peterson, Kort, Burlington	.437
OPS	Peterson, Kort, Burlington	.982
R	Lopez, Nicky, Burlington	54
RBI	Jones, Bradley, Bluefield	55
SAC	Sinay, Nick, Bluefield	10
SB	Sinay, Nick, Bluefield	34
SLG	Jones, Bradley, Bluefield	.578
SO	Garcia, Dermis, Pulaski	79
XBH	Jones, Bradley, Bluefield	35

FIELDING

A	Osuna, Ramon, Danville	31
DP	DeVito, Chris, Burlington	42
E	Lee, Alex, Danville	12
1B PCT	DeVito, Chris, Burlington	.994
PO	DeVito, Chris, Burlington	453
A	Tenerowicz, Robbie, Princeton	137
DP	Tenerowicz, Robbie, Princeton	30
E	Davis, J.R., Johnson City	19
2B PCT	Tenerowicz, Robbie, Princeton	.996
PO	Tenerowicz, Robbie, Princeton	103
A	Rivera, Emmanuel, Burlington	98
DP	Garcia, Dermis, Pulaski	8
E	Denton, Bryce, Johnson City	21
3B PCT	Rivera, Emmanuel, Burlington	.940
PO	Toro-Hernandez, Abraham, Greeneville	36
A	Lorenzo, Rafelin, Princeton	49
DP	Gonzalez, Yoel, Bristol	7
E	Four tied with	7
C PCT	Morgan, Matt, Bluefield	.976
PB	Rodriguez, Dionis, Kingsport	22
PO	Rodriguez, Dionis, Kingsport	257
A	Cabrera, Eleardo, Princeton	12
DP	Cabrera, Eleardo, Princeton	4
E	De La Cruz, Michael, Bristol	7
	Gustave, Emilio, Princeton	7
OF PCT	Vizcaino, Vance, Burlington	.991
PO	Sinay, Nick, Bluefield	120
A	Valerio, Adrian, Bristol	200
DP	Cordoba, Allen, Johnson City	40
E	Cordoba, Allen, Johnson City	17
	Severino, Jesus, Bluefield	17
SS PCT	Lopez, Nicky, Burlington	.981
PO	Cordoba, Allen, Johnson City	88
TC	Valerio, Adrian, Bristol	297

PITCHING

AVG	Castillo, Cristian, Burlington	.212
BB	Robinson, Alex, Elizabethton	34
	Smith, Ben, Greeneville	34
BB/9	Ortiz, Willy, Princeton	0.98
BK	Jose, Kelyn, Bluefield	4
CG	12 tied with	1
ER	Martinez, Jose, Elizabethton	42
G	Three tied with	19
GF	Five tied with	14
GS	Three tied with	13
H	Oxnevad, Ian, Johnson City	80
HB	Schick, Alex, Elizabethton	9
HR	Lara, Rafael, Pulaski	12
IP	Castillo, Cristian, Burlington	72
	Oxnevad, Ian, Johnson City	72
L	Carlini, Domenick, Elizabethton	7
SO	Humphreys, Jordan, Kingsport	76
SO/9	Humphreys, Jordan, Kingsport	9.87
SO/9(RP)	Alicea, Angel, Bluefield	12.4
SV	McGuff, Patrick, Elizabethton	9
W	Ortiz, Willy, Princeton	8
WP	Three tied with	15

BY BILL MITCHELL

The Orem Owlz captured the Pioneer League championship despite a roster that turned over significantly during the course of the season with many of the Angels' affiliate's best players promoted to low Class A Burlington. Despite finishing the regular season with a 38-38 record, skipper Dave Stapleton's squad made up of later draft picks and Arizona League reinforcements raced through two playoff series. The Owlz swept the best-of-three championship series against Billings after dispatching intra-state rivals Ogden in the first round. The Owlz used strong outings from teenaged pitchers Sam Pastrone and Jose Suarez, the latter just up from the Arizona League, in the series against Billings.

The Great Falls Voyagers recorded the league's best regular season record at 47-28 before the White Sox affiliate lost two straight to Billings in the North Division opening playoff round. The Voyagers' success was primarily the result of a strong pitching staff that led the league with a 3.54 ERA, nearly a full run better than the next best team. For a league known more for its extreme hitter's parks, several Great Falls pitchers stood out for their exploits. Nondrafted free agent Aaron McRee (Great Falls) was named pitcher of the year after posting a 5-0, 2.16 ERA with an exemplary 54-to-6 strikeout-to-walk ratio. Teammate Yosmer Solorzano was part of two no-hitters within a 15-day span, the second of which was a rain-shortened five-inning game.

Idaho Falls catcher Meibrys Viloria (Idaho Falls) captured MVP honors while leading the league in batting average (.376), doubles (28) and RBIs (55). The 2016 season was a remarkable turnaround from the Viloria's 2015 Appalachian league season in which he hit a paltry .260/.335/.260 with no extra base hits in 150 at-bats. Helena first baseman Ronnie Gideon, Milwaukee's 23rd round pick from Texas A&M, led the circuit in slugging percentage (.638) and homeruns (17).

Kansas high school product Riley Pint and Oklahoma's Alec Hansen were two of the most frequently-mentioned names as possibilities for the first overall pick leading into 2016. While neither hurler went No. 1, both flashed big-time potential in their Pioneer League debuts to rank as the circuit's top two prospects.

In addition to Pint, three other first-round picks made their pro debuts in the league—third baseman Nick Senzel (Billings), first baseman Matt Thaiss (Orem) and catcher Will Smith (Odgen) —but did not get enough playing time to qualify for the prospect list. Another Dodgers first-round pick, shortstop Gavin Lux, finished his rookie season with eight games for Ogden after finishing his Arizona League season.

TOP 20 PROSPECTS

1. Riley Pint, rhp, Grand Junction (Rockies)
2. Alec Hansen, rhp, Great Falls (White Sox)
3. Taylor Trammell, of, Billings (Reds)
4. Lucas Erceg, 3b, Helena (Brewers)
5. Jahmai Jones, of, Orem (Angels)
6. Tony Santillan, rhp, Billings (Reds)
7. D.J. Peters, of, Ogden (Dodgers)
8. Gilbert Lara, ss, Helena (Brewers)
9. Jasrado Chisholm, ss, Missoula (Diamondbacks)
10. T.J. Friedl, of, Billings (Reds)
11. Pedro Gonzalez, of, Grand Junction (Rockies)
12. Meibrys Viloria, c, Idaho Falls (Royals)
13. Mitch Hansen, of, Ogden (Dodgers)
14. Cody Thomas, of, Ogden (Dodgers)
15. Colton Welker, 3b, Grand Junction (Rockies)
16. Keibert Ruiz, c, Ogden (Dodgers)
17. Jose Gomez, ss, Grand Junction (Rockies)
18. Ian Kahaloa, rhp, Billings (Reds)
19. Demi Orimoloye, of, Helena (Brewers)
20. Bernardo Flores, lhp, Great Falls (White Sox)

STANDINGS: SPLIT SEASON

FIRST HALF					SECOND HALF				
NORTH	W	L	PCT	GB	**NORTH**	W	L	PCT	GB
Billings	23	15	.605	—	Great Falls	26	11	.703	—
Great Falls	21	17	.553	2	Billings	18	19	.486	8
Missoula	16	22	.421	7	Missoula	17	20	.459	9
Helena	15	23	.395	8	Helena	13	23	.361	12½
SOUTH	W	L	PCT	GB	**SOUTH**	W	L	PCT	GB
Orem	22	16	.579	—	Ogden	21	17	.553	—
Idaho Falls	22	16	.579	—	Grand Junct.	20	17	.541	½
Ogden	17	21	.447	5	Idaho Falls	18	20	.474	3
Grand Junct.	16	22	.421	6	Orem	16	22	.421	5

Playoffs—Semifinals: Billings defeated Great Falls 2-0 and Orem defeated Ogden 2-1 in best-of-three series. **Finals:** Orem defeated Billings 2-0 in a best-of-three series.

OVERALL STANDINGS

Division	W	L	PCT	GB	Manager(s)	Attendance	Average	Last Pennant
Great Falls (White Sox)	47	28	.627	—	Tommy Thompson	43,500	1,243	2013
Billings (Reds)	41	34	.547	6	Ray Martinez	104,315	2,819	2014
Idaho Falls (Royals)	40	36	.526	7½	Justin Gemoll	96,866	2,549	2013
Ogden (Dodgers)	38	38	.500	9½	Shaun Larkin	124,200	3,450	Never
Orem (Angels)	38	38	.500	9½	Dave Stapleton	57,504	1,554	2016
Grand Junction (Rockies)	36	39	.480	11	Frank Gonzales	79,470	2,091	Never
Missoula (Diamondbacks)	33	42	.440	14	Joe Mather	73,207	1,979	2015
Helena (Brewers)	28	46	.378	18½	Nestor Corredor	37,624	1,075	2010

CLUB BATTING

	AVG	G	AB	R	H	2B	3B	HR	RBI	BB	SO	SB	OBP	SLG
Idaho Falls	.306	76	2714	517	831	157	29	49	454	235	563	132	.366	.440
Orem	.298	76	2700	466	804	166	25	56	407	261	518	116	.369	.440
Ogden	.292	76	2671	474	779	165	43	88	426	256	695	72	.359	.484
Grand Junction	.288	75	2670	446	769	158	37	54	392	212	647	124	.347	.436
Billings	.286	75	2616	443	747	137	32	47	385	241	606	127	.353	.416
Great Falls	.280	75	2542	415	713	137	26	53	369	267	567	105	.365	.417
Missoula	.275	75	2627	420	722	132	20	90	370	193	719	72	.336	.443
Helena	.264	74	2476	376	654	129	13	53	320	256	603	71	.338	.391

CLUB PITCHING

	ERA	G	CG	SHO	SV	IP	H	R	ER	HR	BB	SO	AVG
Great Falls	3.54	75	4	2	22	659	578	306	259	39	181	678	.233
Billings	4.41	75	0	0	19	661	663	385	324	49	270	613	.262
Orem	4.96	76	0	0	16	678	809	440	374	50	229	639	.296
Grand Junction	5.15	75	0	0	14	669	830	474	383	71	215	625	.305
Idaho Falls	5.22	76	0	0	17	665	801	475	386	60	255	598	.299
Missoula	5.31	75	4	0	7	655	739	489	387	65	279	600	.281
Ogden	5.48	76	0	0	12	661	797	498	403	76	255	627	.299
Helena	5.91	74	0	0	15	630	802	490	414	80	237	538	.312

CLUB FIELDING

	PCT	PO	A	E	DP		PCT	PO	A	E	DP
Billings	.969	1984	772	89	109	Helena	.958	1891	772	117	197
Great Falls	.968	1976	836	94	141	Missoula	.956	1966	706	123	134
Grand Junction	.962	2007	829	111	188	Ogdens	.955	1984	812	131	207
Orem	.958	2034	771	122	192	Idaho Falls	.944	1996	829	167	157

INDIVIDUAL BATTING

Batter, Club	AVG	G	AB	R	H	2B	3B	HR	RBI	BB	SO	SB
Viloria, Meibrys, Idaho Falls	.376	58	226	54	85	28	3	6	55	20	36	1
Gomez, Jose, Grand Junction	.367	66	267	54	98	14	2	3	51	23	24	23
Schnurbusch, Aaron, Great Falls	.357	66	238	53	85	14	6	6	44	47	69	19
Ruiz, Keibert, Ogden	.354	48	189	28	67	18	2	2	33	12	23	0
Vargas, Hector, Billings	.352	57	210	32	74	17	2	6	41	6	19	12
Peters, DJ, Ogden	.351	66	262	63	92	24	3	13	48	35	66	5
Gibbons, Zach, Orem	.351	50	191	37	67	12	2	5	30	29	22	17
Flair, Nick, Orem	.348	54	210	40	73	23	1	8	47	8	51	3
Fisher, Jameson, Great Falls	.342	50	187	39	64	13	1	4	25	27	43	13
Willis, Luke, Idaho Falls	.341	60	208	44	71	5	4	3	26	26	46	14

INDIVIDUAL PITCHING

Pitcher, Club	W	L	ERA	G	GS	CG	SV	IP	H	R	ER	BB	SO
McRee, Aron, Great Falls	5	0	2.16	12	11	0	0	67	57	19	16	6	54
Comito, Chris, Great Falls	8	1	3.43	14	14	1	0	87	71	40	33	15	89
Solorzano, Yosmer, Great Falls	9	3	4.11	15	15	2	0	81	85	43	37	18	81
Requena, Alejandro, Grand Junction	3	6	4.97	13	13	0	0	67	80	51	37	19	59
Feliz, Igol, Idaho Falls	3	3	5.08	13	13	0	0	73	90	50	41	23	32
Hernandez, Arnaldo, Idaho Falls	5	2	5.86	14	14	0	0	71	99	54	46	18	63

ALL-STAR TEAM

C: Meibrys Viloria, Idaho Falls. **1B:** Ronnie Gideon, Helena. **2B:** Jose Gomez, Grand Junction. **3B:** Manny Olloque, Idaho Falls. **SS:** Hector Vargas, Billings. **DH:** Eudy Ramos, Missoula. **OF:** Aaron Schnurbusch, Great Falls; DJ Peters, Ogden; Zach Gibbons, Orem. **P:** Alec Hansen, Great Falls. **P:** Aron McRee, Great Falls. **P:** Chris Comito, Great Falls. **P:** Wuilder Rodriguez, Helena. **P:** Yosmer Solorzano, Great Falls.
Most Valuable Player: Meibrys Viloria, Idaho Falls.
Pitcher of the Year: Aron McRee, Great Falls.

DEPARTMENT LEADERS

BATTING

2B	Viloria, Meibrys, Idaho Falls	28
3B	Three tied with	8
AB/SO	Gomez, Jose, Grand Junction	11.13
BB	Schnurbusch, Aaron, Great Falls	47
CS	Gomez, Jose, Grand Junction	13
H	Gomez, Jose, Grand Junction	98
HBP	Villa, Anthony, Great Falls	15
HR	Gideon, Ronnie, Helena	17
OBP	Schnurbusch, Aaron, Great Falls	.471
OPS	Peters, DJ, Ogden	1.052
R	Peters, DJ, Ogden	63
RBI	Viloria, Meibrys, Idaho Falls	55
SAC	Aracena, Ricky, Idaho Falls	10
SB	Heath, Nick, Idaho Falls	36
SLG	Gideon, Ronnie, Helena	.638
SO	Anderson, Cole, Grand Junction	90
XBH	Peters, DJ, Ogden	40

FIELDING

A	Marshall, Montrell, Billings	44
DP	Gideon, Ronnie, Helena	47
E	Zangari, Corey, Great Falls	14
1B PCT	Gideon, Ronnie, Helena	.992
PO	Marshall, Montrell, Billings	472
A	Piron, Jonathan, Grand Junction	135
DP	Piron, Jonathan, Grand Junction	31
E	Piron, Jonathan, Grand Junction	17
2B PCT	Mallen, Franly, Helena	.955
PO	Mallen, Franly, Helena	85
A	Conlan, Brady, Great Falls	160
DP	Olloque, Manny, Idaho Falls	12
E	Olloque, Manny, Idaho Falls	25
3B PCT	Conlan, Brady, Great Falls	.926
PO	Olloque, Manny, Idaho Falls	50
A	Viloria, Meibrys, Idaho Falls	69
DP	Brown, Cassidy, Billings	5
E	Viloria, Meibrys, Idaho Falls	14
C PCT	Schroeder, Casey, Great Falls	.992
PB	January, Ryan, Missoula	16
PO	Viloria, Meibrys, Idaho Falls	374
A	Siri, Jose, Billings	13
DP	Gonzalez, Pedro, Grand Junction	3
E	Heath, Nick, Idaho Falls	12
OF PCT	Trammell, Taylor, Billings	.990
PO	Gonzalez, Pedro, Grand Junction	123
A	Gomez, Jose, Grand Junction	195
DP	Gomez, Jose, Grand Junction	41
E	Aracena, Ricky, Idaho Falls	38
SS PCT	Lara, Gilbert, Helena	.941
PO	Chisholm, Jasrado, Missoula	105

PITCHING

AVG	Comito, Chris, Great Falls	.217
BB	Portland, Matt, Idaho Falls	37
BB/9	McRee, Aron, Great Falls	0.81
BK	Meier, Matt, Grand Junction	5
CG	Solorzano, Yosmer, Great Falls	2
ER	Serigstad, Scott, Helena	51
G	Gonzalez, Erbert, Missoula	27
	Hammer, J. D., Grand Junction	27
GF	Oakley, Kenny, Grand Junction	20
GS	Nova, Moises, Billings	15
	Solorzano, Yosmer, Great Falls	15
H	Hernandez, Arnaldo, Idaho Falls	99
HB	Diplan, Nattino, Helena	12
HR	Requena, Alejandro, Grand Junction	15
IP	Comito, Chris, Great Falls	86.2
L	Nova, Moises, Billings	7
SO	Comito, Chris, Great Falls	89
SO/9	Comito, Chris, Great Falls	9.24
SO/9(RP)	Jackson, Dean, Missoula	11.9
SV	Cross, Colton, Helena	10
W	Solorzano, Yosmer, Great Falls	9
WP	Quintana, Yohander, Grand Junction	13

MINOR LEAGUES

BY BILL MITCHELL

The 2016 Arizona League championship round was extended to a best-of-three series in 2016, but a strong Mariners squad needed only two games to capture the crown by defeating the Angels 4-2 and 3-1 on consecutive evenings. The Mariners got to the final round by disposing the Cubs and Reds in single-game qualifying rounds. First-time skipper Zac Livingston earned his first ring after spending the previous four years as a minor league catcher and coach in the Angels organization.

Two Mariners—Anthony Jimenez (.312) and Joseph Rosa (.305)—ranked among the top 10 AZL qualified hitters. Second-year hurler Ryne Inman topped Mariners pitchers with a 3.47 ERA while also earning the win in Game One of the championship round. Righthander Jio Orozco led the league in strikeouts with 63 prior to being traded to the Yankees just before the postseason.

Oscar Gonzalez (Indians) was voted the league MVP, leading all hitters in slugging percentage (.566) and tying for the lead in HRs (eight). Josh Vidales (Athletics) topped all hitters in batting average (.345), on-base percentage (.437) and OPS (.944). An undersized 23-year-old college grad, Vidales is not regarded as a top prospect although scouts foresee a possible big league bench role for him later in his career. White Sox righthander Luis Ledo led all pitchers with a 1.19 ERA. Padres closer Wilmer Torres saved nine games.

John Shoemaker was named manager of the year after his Dodgers squad posted the top regular-season record (33-22).

Hitters dominated the Arizona League top prospect list, with position players making up 17 of the top 20 players. Outfielder Leody Taveras (Rangers), 17, ranked as the league's top prospect Eight first-round picks from the 2016 draft made

their pro debuts during the season, with outfielder Will Benson (Indians), infielder Hudson Potts (Padres) and shortstop Gavin Lux (Dodgers) playing enough to qualify for the prospect list.

TOP 20 PROSPECTS

1. Leody Taveras, of, Rangers
2. Yadier Alvarez, rhp, Dodgers
3. Will Benson, of, Indians
4. Khalil Lee, of, Royals
5. Brady Aiken, lhp, Indians
6. Nolan Jones, 3b/ss, Indians
7. Hudson Potts, ss, Padres
8. Seuly Matias, of, Royals
9. Gavin Lux, ss, Dodgers
10. Fernando Tatis Jr., ss, Padres
11. Anderson Tejeda, ss, Rangers
12. Dustin May, rhp, Dodgers
13. Oscar Gonzalez, of, Indians
14. Sandro Fabian, of, Giants
15. Mario Feliciano, c, Brewers
16. Kole Enright, 3b/ss, Rangers
17. Joe Rizzo, 3b, Mariners
18. Gabriel Garcia, 1b, Brewers
19. Amado Nunez, ss, White Sox
20. Sebastian Rivero, c, Royals

STANDINGS: SPLIT SEASON

FIRST HALF					SECOND HALF				
EAST	**W**	**L**	**PCT**	**GB**	**EAST**	**W**	**L**	**PCT**	**GB**
Cubs	16	12	.571	—	Angels	17	11	.607	—
Athletics	15	13	.536	1	Giants	16	11	.593	½
D-backs	13	15	.464	3	Athletics	14	11	.560	1 ½
Angels	12	16	.429	4	D-backs	14	14	.500	3
Giants	12	16	.429	4	Cubs	12	16	.429	5

CENTRAL	**W**	**L**	**PCT**	**GB**	**CENTRAL**	**W**	**L**	**PCT**	**GB**
Indians	20	8	.714	—	Reds	19	8	.704	—
Dodgers	19	9	.679	1	Dodgers	14	13	.519	5
Brewers	12	16	.429	8	Brewers	12	13	.480	6
Reds	12	16	.429	8	Indians	11	17	.393	8 ½
White Sox	11	17	.393	9	White Sox	10	18	.357	9 ½

WEST	**W**	**L**	**PCT**	**GB**	**CENTRAL**	**W**	**L**	**PCT**	**GB**
Mariners	16	12	.571	—	Royals	17	10	.630	—
Royals	14	14	.500	2	Mariners	15	13	.536	2 ½
Padres	12	16	.429	4	Padres	13	14	.481	4
Rangers	12	16	.429	4	Rangers	6	21	.222	11

OVERALL STANDINGS

Division	W	L	PCT	GB	Manager(s)	Last Pennant
Dodgers	33	22	.600	—	John Shoemaker	2011
Reds	31	24	.564	2	Jose Nieves	Never
Royals	31	24	.564	2	Darryl Kennedy	Never
Indians	31	25	.554	2 ½	Anthony Medrano	2014
Mariners	31	25	.554	2 ½	Zac Livingston	2016
Athletics	29	24	.547	3	Webster Garrison	2001
Angels	29	27	.518	4 ½	Elio Sarmiento	Never
Giants	28	27	.509	5	Henry Cotto	2013
Cubs	28	28	.500	5 ½	Carmelo Martinez	2002
Diamondbacks	27	29	.482	6 ½	Darrin Garner	Never
Padres	25	30	.455	8	Michael Collins	2006
Brewers	24	29	.453	8	Tony Diggs	2010
White Sox	21	35	.375	12 ½	Ever Magallanes	2015
Rangers	18	37	.327	15	Matt Siegel	2012

Quarterfinals: Mariners defeated Cubs and Angels defeated Indians in one-game playoffs. **Semifinals:** Angels defeated Royals and Mariners defeated Reds in one-game playoffs. **Finals:** Mariners defeated Angels in a best-of-three series.

CLUB BATTING

	AVG	G	AB	R	H	2B	3B	HR	RBI	BB	SO	SB	OBP	SLG
Rangers	.269	55	1885	252	507	120	26	16	222	159	468	54	.333	.386
Mariners	.268	56	1937	274	520	97	34	18	214	162	489	104	.329	.382
Dodgers	.268	55	1912	298	513	87	28	48	249	189	480	32	.339	.418
Giants	.260	55	1868	275	486	102	32	10	232	167	477	73	.334	.365
Angels	.259	56	1910	289	495	103	16	6	235	208	454	97	.341	.339
Royals	.259	55	1908	302	494	90	23	27	255	189	494	60	.332	.373
Indians	.254	56	1895	303	482	96	26	29	248	183	560	77	.326	.378
Athletics	.253	53	1817	274	459	103	30	8	245	204	446	76	.336	.356
Padres	.252	55	1900	293	478	92	24	16	228	185	505	61	.326	.351
Diamondbacks	.250	56	1898	253	474	101	19	17	211	179	524	50	.326	.350
Cubs	.249	56	1869	255	465	87	20	13	214	174	423	66	.322	.338
White Sox	.247	56	1918	261	473	96	15	29	217	143	493	58	.312	.358
Reds	.243	55	1856	270	451	76	27	17	209	172	485	64	.318	.341
Brewers	.241	53	1803	264	435	90	22	17	219	190	455	52	.324	.344

CLUB PITCHING

	ERA	G	CG	SHO	SV	IP	H	R	ER	HR	BB	SO	AVG
Giants	3.36	55	0	0	15	482	473	245	180	20	180	414	.253
Reds	3.46	55	0	0	15	484	444	243	186	16	212	494	.241
Angels	3.48	56	0	0	14	497	448	243	192	14	166	486	.240
Mariners	3.65	56	0	0	19	495	492	272	201	22	180	490	.253
Royals	3.69	55	0	0	18	490	493	274	201	18	132	475	.255
Brewers	3.74	53	0	0	14	469	465	251	195	27	154	478	.256
Dodgers	3.82	55	0	0	14	488	456	259	207	23	172	555	.243
Cubs	3.88	56	0	0	14	488	489	287	210	17	158	519	.259
Athletics	4.13	53	0	0	17	469	478	268	215	10	206	417	.265
Indians	4.14	56	0	0	14	489	486	272	225	18	164	522	.256
Diamondbacks	4.23	56	0	0	12	492	501	286	231	17	188	469	.260
White Sox	4.60	56	0	0	9	485	501	338	248	30	195	442	.261
Padres	4.64	55	0	0	14	483	508	318	249	14	196	492	.265
Rangers	4.92	55	0	0	9	476	498	307	260	25	201	500	.267

CLUB FIELDING

	PCT	PO	A	E	DP		PCT	PO	A	E	DP
Dodgers	.962	1466	569	81	108	Cubs	.954	1464	618	101	106
Athletics	.961	1407	623	82	147	Giants	.953	1446	560	98	112
Rangers	.958	1429	541	86	100	Reds	.950	1453	556	105	121
Padres	.958	1449	589	89	126	Diamondbacks	.950	1476	579	108	121
Indians	.958	1467	572	90	125	Mariners	.949	1487	605	113	121
Brewers	.957	1406	544	87	110	Royals	.947	1471	572	114	100
Angels	.955	1491	616	100	130	White Sox	.934	1455	627	148	150

INDIVIDUAL BATTING

Batter, Club	AVG	G	AB	R	H	2B	3B	HR	RBI	BB	SO	SB
Vidales, Josh, Athletics	.345	41	148	27	51	15	3	1	27	20	16	5
Brontsema, John, Royals	.343	47	175	34	60	9	1	0	24	13	30	9
Pozo, Yohel, Rangers	.343	48	181	25	62	12	2	1	22	13	10	1
Fabian, Sandro, Giants	.340	42	159	30	54	13	5	2	35	7	28	3
Polanco, Gustavo, Cubs	.322	46	177	27	57	7	1	1	22	5	21	4
Enright, Kole, Rangers	.313	42	150	22	47	13	0	1	17	14	33	3
Jimenez, Anthony, Mariners	.312	53	186	30	58	11	5	1	22	12	43	14
Paredes, Isaac, Cubs	.305	47	167	23	51	14	3	1	26	13	10	4
Rosa, Joseph, Mariners	.305	43	154	17	47	7	5	2	23	9	26	12
Terry, Curtis, Rangers	.305	39	141	20	43	17	1	4	23	9	30	0

INDIVIDUAL PITCHING

Pitcher, Club	W	L	ERA	G	GS	CG	SV	IP	H	R	ER	BB	SO
Ledo, Luis, White Sox	4	3	1.19	11	9	0	0	45	34	14	6	12	36
Myers, D.J., Giants	3	2	1.70	14	9	0	0	58	60	17	11	5	52
Romero, Wennington, Reds	3	3	1.93	10	7	0	0	47	39	16	10	8	46
Gavin, Grant, Royals	3	1	2.01	13	4	0	1	49	41	17	11	5	47
Bethell, Max, Angels	3	2	2.09	14	3	0	1	52	35	12	12	9	41
Baragar, Caleb, Giants	5	2	2.28	14	10	0	1	55	47	17	14	16	50
Blanco, Argenis, Athletics	5	4	2.52	14	10	0	0	61	58	24	17	17	48
Perez, Francisco, Indians	5	1	2.69	12	7	0	0	64	48	22	19	17	52
Vasquez, Gregori, Indians	5	2	3.18	12	8	0	0	57	54	27	20	17	44
Alecis, Luis, Reds	2	2	3.26	12	7	0	0	47	44	25	17	19	50

ALL STAR TEAM

P: Luis Ledo, White Sox. **C:** Yohel Pozo, Rangers. **1B:** Charley Gould, Athletics. **2B:** Josh Vidales, Athletics. **3B:** John Brontsema, Royals. **SS:** Isaac Paredes, Cubs. **DH:** Gustavo Polanco, Cubs. **OF:** Joel Booker, White Sox. **OF:** Oscar Gonzalez, Indians. **OF:** Sandro Fabian, Giants. **SP:** Francisco Perez, Indians. **SP:** Grant Gavin, Royals. **SP:** Wennington Romero, Reds. **RP:** Eugenio Palma, Cubs. **RP:** Wilmer Torres, Padres.
Manager of the Year: John Shoemaker, Dodgers.
Most Valuable Player: Oscar Gonzalez, Indians.

DEPARTMENT LEADERS

BATTING

2B	Terry, Curtis, Rangers	17
3B	Three tied with	6
AB/SO	Pozo, Yohel, Rangers	18.1
BB	Nowlin, Kyle, Athletics	36
CS	Ayala, Luis, Cubs	7
	Rosa, Joseph, Mariners	7
H	Nunez, Amado, White Sox	62
	Pozo, Yohel, Rangers	62
HBP	Three tied with	9
HR	Three tied with	8
OBP	Vidales, Josh, Athletics	.437
OPS	Vidales, Josh, Athletics	.944
R	Lee, Khalil, Royals	43
RBI	Gould, Charley, Athletics	38
SAC	Reyes, Ruben, Cubs	5
SB	Gruber, Cole, Athletics	28
SLG	Gonzalez, Oscar, Indians	.566
SO	Matias, Seuly, Royals	73
XBH	Terry, Curtis, Rangers	22

FIELDING

A	Rinn, Robby, Royals	32
DP	Gould, Charley, Athletics	41
E	Rinn, Robby, Royals	11
1B PCT	Gould, Charley, Athletics	.984
PO	Martinez, Francis, D-backs	404
A	Vidales, Josh, Athletics	119
DP	Vidales, Josh, Athletics	24
E	Curbelo, Luis, White Sox	12
2B PCT	Vidales, Josh, Athletics	.991
PO	Vidales, Josh, Athletics	90
A	Rose, Joey, D-backs	100
DP	Feliz, Maiker, White Sox	8
	Rose, Joey, D-backs	8
E	Mejia, Rafael, Cubs	20
3B PCT	Rizzo, Joe, Mariners	.924
PO	Rose, Joey, D-backs	43
A	Pina, Keinner, Angels	50
DP	Pina, Keinner, Angels	5
E	Camacho, Juan, Mariners	8
	Cruz, Michael, Cubs	8
C PCT	Pina, Keinner, Angels	.990
PB	Mota, Ismerling, Mariners	12
PO	Rivero, Sebastian, Royals	299
A	Ayala, Luis, Cubs	8
DP	Three tied with	3
E	Otano, Hanleth, White Sox	8
OF PCT	Ayala, Luis, Cubs	.990
PO	Ayala, Luis, Cubs	89
	Edie, Mikey, Giants	89
TC	Ayala, Luis, Cubs	98
A	Paredes, Isaac, Cubs	140
DP	Nunez, Amado, White Sox	30
E	Nunez, Amado, White Sox	30
SS PCT	Paredes, Isaac, Cubs	.949
PO	Van Horn, Brandon, Giants	64

PITCHING

AVG	Bethell, Max, Angels	.191
BB	Charles, Wandisson, Athletics	33
BB/9	Gunn, Alex, D-backs	0.77
BK	Nova, Boanerges, Brewers	3
	Pinto, Julio, Royals	3
ER	Tati, Felix, Indians	36
G	Zawadzki, Grant, Padres	23
GF	Torres, Wilmer, Padres	20
GS	Inman, Ryne, Mariners	12
	Sanchez, Andres, White Sox	12
H	Inman, Ryne, Mariners	73
HB	Herrera, Carlos, Brewers	14
	Marte, Junior, Cubs	14
HR	Sanchez, Andres, White Sox	7
IP	Perez, Francisco, Indians	63.2
L	Done, Victor, White Sox	8
SO	Orozco, Jio, Mariners	63
SO/9	Orozco, Jio, Mariners	11.65
SO/9(RP)	Moreta, Dauri, Reds	15.55
SO/9(SP)	Tati, Felix, Indians	7.91
SV	Torres, Wilmer, Padres	9
W	Nine tied with	5
WP	Charles, Wandisson, Athletics	19

MINOR LEAGUES

BY JOHN MANUEL

Phillies affiliates posted the best cumulative record in baseball in 2016, and the Rookie-level Gulf Coast League Phillies were no exception. They went 43-15 in the GCL's Northwest Division, posting the league's best record even in a division with three of its four teams that finished above .500.

These Phillies included the No. 1 pick in the 2016 draft, outfielder Mickey Moniak, who had 15 multi-hit games to help the Phillies go 43-15. The roster also featured the Phillies' two other top picks from the top of the draft, supplemental first-rounder Kevin Gowdy, a righthander who made four starts, and second-round shortstop Cole Stobbe (.270/.337/.405), whose four homers ranked second on the team to high-priced international signee Jhailyn Ortiz, whose eight homers ranked third in the league.

Moniak played just two games in the playoffs due to what the organization termed tightness in his hips. On the mound, the Phillies featured the league's top two starters in terms of results, righthander Sixto Sanchez, who went 5-0, 0.50 to lead the league in ERA.

However, the GCL Cardinals held the Phillies in check in the league finals, shutting out the Phils in Game One, then getting a 4-2 victory in the rubber game of the best-of-three finals. So while Phillies farm teams nearly won 60 percent of their games, no Phils affiliate won a league championship.

The Cardinals, who won the GCL East with

TOP 20 PROSPECTS

1. Mickey Moniak of, Phillies
2. Matt Manning, rhp, Tigers
3. Juan Soto, of, Nationals
4. Bo Bichette, ss, Blue Jays
5. Delvin Perez, ss, Cardinals
6. Jesus Sanchez, of, Rays
7. Sixto Sanchez, rhp, Phillies
8. Josh Lowe, 3b, Rays
9. Alvaro Seijas, rhp, Cardinals
10. Cristian Pache, of, Braves
11. Kyle Muller, lhp, Braves
12. Daniel Brito, 2b, Phillies
13. Derian Cruz, ss, Braves
14. Carter Kieboom, ss, Nationals
15. Jhailyn Ortiz, of, Phillies
16. Dylan Carlson, of, Cardinals
17. Austin Franklin, rhp, Rays
18. Lorenzo Cedrola, of, Red Sox
19. Diego Castillo, ss, Yankees
20. Lupe Chavez, rhp, Astros

a 33-21 record, had their own draft star power, with 2016 first-rounders Delvin Perez and outfielder Dylan Carlson, and Perez crafted a strong debut, ranking seventh in the league in batting at .294/.352/.393.

A second-rounder, Blue Jays shortstop Bo Bichette, was a top performer despite missing more than a month with an appendicitis. Bichette, son of ex-big leaguer Dante, ranked second in the league in RBIs with 36 in just 22 games, batting .427/.451/.732. He had 15 extra-base hits in his 22 games and hit two grand slams.

The league expanded by one team in 2016 to 17, as the Tigers joined the Yankees in having two affiliates in the league.

OVERALL STANDINGS

Eastern Division

	W	L	PCT	GB	Manager(s)	Last Pennant
Cardinals	33	21	.611	—	Steve Turco	2016
Nationals	30	23	.566	2 ½	Josh Johnson	2009
Mets	26	29	.473	7 ½	Jose Carreno	Never
Marlins	24	31	.436	9 ½	Julio Bruno	Never
Astros	22	31	.415	10 ½	Marty Malloy	Never

Northeastern Division

	W	L	PCT	GB	Manager(s)	Last Pennant
Braves	28	28	.500	—	Nestor Perez	2003
Pirates	22	34	.393	6	Edgar Varela	2012
Tigers East	21	37	.362	8	Rafael Gil	Never
Yankees East	19	36	.345	8 ½	Raul Dominguez	Never

Northwestern Division

	W	L	PCT	GB	Manager(s)	Last Pennant
Phillies	43	15	.741	—	Roly de Armas	2010
Blue Jays	39	17	.696	3	Cesar Martin	Never
Tigers West	30	28	.517	13	Rafael Martinez	Never
Yankees West	24	31	.436	17 ½	Marc Bombard	2011

Southern Division

	W	L	PCT	GB	Manager(s)	Last Pennant
Red Sox	33	28	.541	—	Tom Kotchman	2015
Twins	32	29	.525	½	Ramon Borrego	Never
Rays	28	31	.475	3 ½	Jim Morrison	Never
Orioles	27	32	.458	4 ½	Orlando Gomez	Never

Playoffs—Semifinals: Phillies defeated Braves and Cardinals defeated Red Sox in one-game playoffs. **Finals:** Cardinals defeated Phillies 2-1 in a best-of-three series.

CLUB BATTING

	AVG	G	AB	R	H	2B	3B	HR	RBI	BB	SO	SB	OBP	SLG
Nationals	.273	53	1837	268	501	82	19	32	240	172	402	43	.341	.390
Phillies	.266	58	1934	294	514	109	21	30	247	193	385	61	.342	.390
Braves	.256	58	1839	248	471	74	17	16	218	145	373	56	.318	.341
Cardinals	.251	54	1729	223	434	74	18	20	200	168	393	34	.330	.349
Blue Jays	.250	56	1885	288	472	92	17	34	254	191	430	69	.339	.371
Mets	.243	55	1808	213	439	78	13	10	175	166	411	28	.317	.317
Rays	.242	59	1938	257	469	90	23	21	222	173	493	45	.319	.345
Red Sox	.237	61	2020	218	479	85	7	14	190	163	447	33	.307	.307
Yankees2	.236	56	1780	249	420	86	7	22	188	138	419	46	.305	.329
Pirates	.235	56	1854	228	436	72	32	16	184	185	438	98	.316	.334
Yankees1	.235	56	1794	210	422	92	16	29	188	176	456	48	.312	.353
Tigers West	.234	58	1854	233	434	96	15	33	197	192	455	79	.321	.355
Orioles	.232	59	1927	250	448	85	7	16	221	177	446	45	.304	.309
Astros	.231	53	1605	169	370	59	19	8	149	149	421	62	.308	.306
Tigers East	.229	58	1820	227	416	70	14	8	181	175	437	69	.309	.296
Marlins	.228	55	1793	236	408	69	16	12	197	214	448	54	.321	.304
Twins	.225	61	1970	212	444	80	12	18	169	205	530	107	.306	.306

CLUB PITCHING

	ERA	G	CG	SHO	SV	IP	H	R	ER	HR	BB	SO	AVG
Phillies	2.55	58	0	0	21	509	422	178	144	11	146	477	.226
Braves	2.64	58	0	0	13	492	408	193	144	20	163	447	.225
Twins	2.79	61	0	0	22	543	452	208	168	11	162	493	.225
Orioles	3.05	59	0	0	11	508	443	234	172	22	191	510	.233
Marlins	3.10	55	0	0	8	485	446	200	167	16	129	375	.245
Cardinals	3.16	54	1	1	20	465	442	215	163	21	181	421	.251
Rays	3.16	59	0	0	15	513	451	238	180	15	188	410	.236
Nationals	3.36	53	0	0	11	471	438	221	176	12	184	415	.247
Red Sox	3.45	61	0	0	17	535	494	257	205	21	177	503	.243
Blue Jays	3.47	56	0	0	16	499	447	236	192	26	167	410	.240
Pirates	3.73	56	0	0	11	493	439	261	204	26	195	368	.239
Tigers West	3.81	58	0	0	15	501	472	255	212	26	187	485	.248
Mets	3.82	55	1	0	11	474	431	239	201	24	181	374	.245
Yankees1	3.93	56	0	0	10	471	453	260	206	19	148	383	.251
Astros	4.02	53	0	0	14	439	395	234	196	9	194	490	.239
Yankees2	4.05	56	0	0	13	475	473	275	214	30	171	404	.258
Tigers East	4.15	58	0	0	7	490	471	279	226	30	218	419	.254

CLUB FIELDING

	PCT	PO	A	E	DP		PCT	PO	A	E	DP
Twins	.974	1628	640	61	121	Orioles	.964	1525	560	78	126
Marlins	.972	1455	621	60	139	Tigers West	.964	1503	610	80	133
Mets	.971	1421	609	60	140	Yankees2	.963	1426	570	77	118
Blue Jays	.971	1496	558	61	132	Nationals	.962	1414	579	78	125
Phillies	.970	1526	617	67	142	Cardinals	.961	1394	511	78	108
Braves	.967	1475	596	70	131	Pirates	.960	1478	632	87	141
Red Sox	.966	1605	648	79	138	Tigers East	.957	1469	550	90	125
Astros	.966	1316	484	64	93	Yankees1	.952	1414	590	100	137
Rays	.965	1538	626	78	112						

INDIVIDUAL BATTING

Batter, Club	AVG	G	AB	R	H	2B	3B	HR	RBI	BB	SO	SB
Soto, Juan, Nationals	.361	45	169	25	61	11	3	5	31	14	25	5
Sanchez, Jesus, Rays	.323	42	164	25	53	6	8	4	31	6	31	1
Obeso, Norberto, Blue Jays	.316	44	152	31	48	11	0	1	18	29	15	4
Jacob, David, Blue Jays	.304	46	161	28	49	9	0	6	29	21	24	3
Whitefield, Aaron, Twins	.298	51	191	30	57	7	0	2	17	19	47	31
Barriento, Juan, Red Sox	.298	49	178	21	53	8	0	2	21	13	41	2
Perez, Delvin, Cardinals	.294	43	163	19	48	8	4	0	19	12	28	12
Arrowood, Jonathon, Rays	.294	41	143	18	42	9	1	2	22	14	40	3
Moscote, Victor, Mets	.293	40	147	19	43	8	0	1	16	15	26	0
Corredor, Aldrem, Nationals	.290	42	169	18	49	8	2	1	26	21	28	1

INDIVIDUAL PITCHING

Pitcher, Club	W	L	ERA	G	GS	CG	SV	IP	H	R	ER	BB	SO
Sanchez, Sixto, Phillies	5	0	0.50	11	11	0	0	54	33	4	3	8	44
Fanti, Nick, Phillies	7	0	1.57	11	9	0	0	52	36	10	9	9	65
Alvarez, Daniel, Yankees East	5	1	1.74	11	9	0	0	57	51	18	11	13	48
Llovera, Mauricio, Phillies	7	1	1.87	11	10	0	0	53	39	12	11	12	56
Vespi, Nick, Orioles	4	1	1.97	12	10	0	0	50	46	18	11	8	41
Hellquist, Bo, Twins	5	3	2.25	11	10	0	0	52	49	17	13	7	46
Casadilla, Franyel, Cardinals	5	2	2.32	11	9	1	0	50	50	16	13	16	35
Requena, Hildemaro, Red Sox	3	4	2.35	13	7	0	2	65	57	21	17	6	52
De Los Santos, Luis, Mets	3	4	2.62	10	7	0	0	55	53	22	16	7	37
Alvarez, Juan, Cardinals	4	2	2.63	11	6	0	1	48	43	15	14	20	30

DEPARTMENT LEADERS

BATTING

2B	Cedrola, Lorenzo, Red Sox	14
3B	Sanchez, Jesus, Rays	8
AB/SO	Brujan, Vidal, Rays	13.47
BB	Obeso, Norberto, Blue Jays	29
CS	Whitefield, Aaron, Twins	9
H	Cedrola, Lorenzo, Red Sox	62
HBP	Frailey, Dustin, Tigers West	16
HR	Valdez, Ignacio, Tigers West	11
OBP	Obeso, Norberto, Blue Jays	.441
OPS	Soto, Juan, Nationals	.960
R	Brujan, Vidal, Rays	41
RBI	Gomez, Nelson, Yankees West	37
SAC	De Jesus, Johan, Pirates	6
	Mauricio, Joan, Astros	6
SB	Whitefield, Aaron, Twins	31
SLG	Soto, Juan, Nationals	.550
SO	Luaces, Edel, Yankees East	79
XBH	Luaces, Edel, Yankees East	22

FIELDING

A	Benson, Griffin, Twins	31
DP	Buentello, Niko, Tigers West	37
	Jacob, David, Blue Jays	37
E	Lameda, Raiwinson, Red Sox	9
1B PCT	Jacob, David, Blue Jays	.992
PO	Buentello, Niko, Tigers West	403
A	Brujan, Vidal, Rays	148
DP	Brito, Daniel, Phillies	30
E	Fernandez, Jeremy, Braves	14
2B PCT	Brito, Daniel, Phillies	.964
PO	Brito, Daniel, Phillies	101
A	Gomez, Nelson, Yankees West	91
DP	Four tied with	9
E	Espinal, Stanley, Red Sox	15
3B PCT	Gomez, Nelson, Yankees West	.919
PO	Terrazas, Rigoberto, Mets	38
A	Gauntt, David, Marlins	37
DP	Mateo, Algeni, Yankees West/East	5
	Miranda, Samuel, Red Sox	5
E	Four tied with	6
C PCT	Uriarte, Juan, Mets	1
PB	Three tied with	9
PO	Escobar, Elys, Tigers East	283
A	Frailey, Dustin, Tigers West	8
	Scott, Jordan, Yankees East	8
DP	Three tied with	3
E	Ring, Jake, Orioles	6
	Scott, Jordan, Yankees East	6
OF PCT	Seven tied with	1
PO	Carlson, Dylan, Cardinals	123
A	Rivera, Marcos, Marlins	144
DP	Castillo, Diego, Yankees West	27
E	Ngoepe, Victor, Pirates	20
SS PCT	Rivera, Marcos, Marlins	.958
PO	Castillo, Diego, Yankees West	80

PITCHING

AVG	Sanchez, Sixto, Phillies	.181
BB	Schlesener, Jacob, Cardinals	34
BB/9	Requena, Hildemaro, Red Sox	0.83
BK	Four tied with	3
CG	Casadilla, Franyel, Cardinals	1
	Geraldo, Jose, Mets	1
ER	Severino, Anderson, Yankees West	34
G	Farfan, Onas, Twins	19
	Lara, Carlos, Tigers East	19
GF	Frohwirth, Tyler, Phillies	18
GS	Diaz, Jhonathan, Red Sox	12
H	Figueroa, Ken, Tigers West	74
HB	Hernandez, Miguel, Pirates	14
HR	Troya, Gilmael, Yankees West	6
IP	Requena, Hildemaro, Red Sox	65
L	Hernandez, Carlos, Mets	8
SO	Fanti, Nick, Phillies	65
SO/9	Fanti, Nick, Phillies	11.32
SO/9(RP)	Lara, Carlos, Tigers East	12.81
SO/9(SP)	Llovera, Mauricio, Phillies	9.19
SV	Frohwirth, Tyler, Phillies	10
W	Three tied with	7
WP	Three tied with	13

Dominican Summer League

BY VINCE LARA-CINISOMO

I t was a season of extremes in the 42-team Dominican Summer League. The Red Sox, who fielded two teams in the league, had one team post a .735 win percentage, while the two entries were a combined 98-40. Meanwhile, the Marlins barely avoided an ignominious mark. Miami's DSL squad was just 10-56, a .152 win percentage that rivaled the 2007 Athletics2 team that went a DSL-worst 9-54 (.143).

Not surprisingly, the Red Sox1, the Northwest League champs, won the league championship. Boston's club beat the Rangers1 team, which tied the Rockies1 team for most victories during the regular season with 51. In the championship series, the Red Sox1 beat the Rangers1 in four games, closing out the finale 8-1 in a game that took two days to complete because of rain.

VSL Shuts Down

The Venezuelan Summer League, which first began operations in 1997, shut down before the 2016 season began.

With several teams having pulled out of their Venezuelan academies in recent years, the VSL was down to just four teams—the Cubs, Phillies, Rays and Tigers—in 2015.

When the Cubs decided to pull out of the VSL this year, leaving just three teams (down from a peak of 10 in 2006), the league was scrapped.

It's the latest move in a trend of teams reducing their presence in Venezuela, a oil-rich country deep in baseball talent, but one that has become more challenging and dangerous for teams to navigate. The South American nation has struggled with political turmoil, soaring inflation, shortages of basic goods and one of the world's highest homicide rates.

PLAYOFFS—Division Series: Mariners1 defeated Rockies 2-0 and Red Sox2 defeated D-Backs 2-0 in best-of-three series. **Semifinals:** Rangers1 defeated Red Sox2 2-0 and Red Sox1 defeated Mariners1 2-1 in best-of-three series. **Finals:** Red Sox1 defeated Rangers1 3-1 in a best-of-five series.

NORTH

TEAM	W	L	PCT	GB
Rangers1	51	19	.729	—
Mets1	45	26	.634	6 ½
Yankees1	33	36	.478	17 ½
Cubs1	29	42	.408	22 ½
Pirates	27	42	.391	23 ½
Indians	24	44	.353	26

SOUTH

TEAM	W	L	PCT	GB
Mariners1	48	23	.676	—
Dodgers1	42	27	.609	5
Giants	40	30	.571	7 ½
Cubs2	38	32	.543	9 ½
Twins	36	34	.514	11 ½
Orioles2	29	42	.408	19
Rojos	25	45	.357	22 ½
D-backs2	22	47	.319	25

NORTHWEST

TEAM	W	L	PCT	GB
Red Sox1	50	18	.735	—
Royals	48	21	.696	2 ½
Astros Blue	42	23	.646	6 ½
Rays1	34	35	.493	16 ½
Dodgers2	32	36	.471	18
Phillies	28	40	.412	22
Athletics	26	41	.388	23 ½
Marlins	10	56	.152	39

BASEBALL CITY

TEAM	W	L	PCT	GB
D-backs	49	20	.710	—
Blue Jays	36	32	.529	12 ½
Padres	36	33	.522	13
Reds	31	37	.456	17 ½
Orioles1	27	42	.391	22
White Sox	26	41	.388	22

SAN PEDRO

TEAM	W	L	PCT	GB
Rockies	51	20	.718	—
Cardinals	45	26	.634	6
Angels	39	31	.557	11 ½
Tigers	33	36	.478	17
Braves	30	40	.429	20 ½
Nationals	29	41	.414	21 ½
Yankees2	27	42	.391	23
Brewers	26	44	.371	24 ½

NORTHEAST

TEAM	W	L	PCT	GB
Red Sox2	48	22	.686	—
Phillies2	42	28	.600	6
Rangers2	38	32	.543	10
Astros Orange	31	37	.456	16
Rays2	29	40	.420	18 ½
Mets2	20	49	.290	27 ½

INDIVIDUAL BATTING LEADERS

PLAYER, TEAM	AVG	G	AB	R	H	2B	3B	HR	RBI	BB	SO	SB
Rollin, Franklin, Rangers1	.377	61	247	64	93	12	11	4	36	23	26	36
Gimenez, Andres, Mets	.350	62	214	52	75	20	4	3	38	46	22	13
King, Jose, D-backs	.350	61	240	51	84	7	4	0	27	21	36	21
Sanchez, Brian, Cardinals	.349	61	232	49	81	13	5	15	76	31	65	0
Rosario, Eguy, Padres	.341	53	185	42	63	19	1	1	24	23	31	21
Hernandez, Ronaldo, Rays1	.340	54	206	34	70	12	0	6	35	20	12	3
Henriquez, Jesus, Phillies2	.337	68	264	43	89	8	0	0	26	32	13	12
Quero, Jose, Tigers	.335	55	179	33	60	6	2	2	34	36	29	1
Bautista, Mariel, Rojos	.333	62	237	40	79	16	4	3	35	22	36	13
Ynfante, Wadye, Cardinals	.331	49	181	51	60	15	2	1	27	29	40	9

INDIVIDUAL PITCHING LEADERS

PLAYER, TEAM	W	L	ERA	G	GS	CG	SV	IP	H	R	ER	BB	SO
Fernandez, Omar, DSL Padres	3	0	0.76	12	12	0	0	59	33	6	5	11	30
Acevedo, Randy, DSL Royals	3	0	0.99	12	12	0	0	63	49	10	7	9	31
Mendoza, Ritzi, DSL Red Sox1	7	0	1.05	14	14	0	0	68	39	10	8	13	48
Carrera, Faustino, DSL Cubs2	7	2	1.06	13	13	0	0	76	55	13	9	19	55
Torres, Andres, DSL Mariners1	10	3	1.26	14	14	0	0	78	53	17	11	14	55
Gonzalez, Jose, DSL Red Sox2	8	0	1.32	14	13	0	0	68	45	13	10	16	61
Hernandez, Anjul, DSL Mariners1	4	1	1.37	14	5	0	4	59	38	11	9	14	49
Pina, Leandro, DSL Pirates	2	2	1.46	13	13	0	0	62	50	19	10	9	34
De Los Santos, Jesus, DSL Phillies2	6	0	1.49	13	13	0	0	73	60	17	12	12	43
Sotillet, Andres, DSL Royals	7	2	1.52	13	13	1	0	65	48	15	11	8	41

	INTERNATIONAL LEAGUE	PACIFIC COAST LEAGUE	EASTERN LEAGUE	SOUTHERN LEAGUE	TEXAS LEAGUE	CALIFORNIA LEAGUE	CAROLINA LEAGUE	FLORIDA STATE LEAGUE	MIDWEST LEAGUE	SOUTH ATLANTIC LEAGUE
Best Batting Prospect	Trea Turner, Syracuse	Hunter Renfroe, El Paso	Clint Frazier, Akron	Tyler O'Neill, Jackson	Alex Bregman, Corpus Christi	Luis Urias, Lake Elsinore	Yoan Moncada, Salem	Amed Rosario, St. Lucie	Eloy Jimenez, South Bend	Victor Robles, Hagerstown
Best Power Prospect	Aaron Judge, Scranton/W-B	Joey Gallo, Round Rock	Dylan Cozens, Reading	Daniel Palka, Chattanooga	Matt Chapman, Midland	Chris Shaw, San Jose	Bobby Bradley, Lynchburg	Christin Stewart, Lakeland	Eloy Jimenez, South Bend	Josh Ockimey, Greenville
Best Strike-Zone Judgment	Jermaine Curtis, Louisville	Dan Vogelbach, Iowa/Tacoma	Chance Sisco, Bowie	Casey Gillaspie, Montgomery	Alex Bregman, Corpus Christi	Steven Duggar, San Jose	Ian Happ, Myrtle Beach	Casey Grayson, Palm Beach	Jake Cronenworth, Bowling Green	Josh Ockimey, Greenville
Best Baserunner	Trea Turner, Syracuse	Arismendy Alcantara, Nashville	Rafael Bautista, Harrisburg	Zach Granite, Chattanooga	Teoscar Hernandez, Corpus Christi	Bobby Boyd, Lancaster	Yoan Moncada, Salem	Darren Seferina, Palm Beach	Kyle Tucker, Quad Cities	Eric Jenkins, Hickory
Fastest Baserunner	Trea Turner, Syracuse	Manuel Margot, El Paso	Rafael Bautista, Harrisburg	Yefri Perez, Jacksonville	Terrance Gore, Northwest Arkansas	Wes Rogers, Modesto	Greg Allen, Lynchburg	Jorge Mateo, Tampa	Derek Hill, West Michigan	Eric Jenkins, Hickory
Best Pitching Prospect	Tyler Glasnow, Indianapolis	Julio Urias, Oklahoma City	Lucas Giolito, Harrisburg	Josh Hader, Biloxi	Daniel Mengden, Midland	Phil Bickford, San Jose	Justus Sheffield, Lynchburg	Brent Honeywell, Charlotte	Sandy Alcantara, Peoria	Mitch Keller, West Virginia
Best Fastball	Luis Severino, Scranton/W-B	Alex Reyes, Memphis	Reynaldo Lopez, Harrisburg	Mauricio Cabrera, Mississippi	Connor Sadzeck, Frisco	Rodolfo Martinez, San Jose	Michael Kopech, Salem	Luis Castillo, Jupiter	Sandy Alcantara, Peoria	Anderson Espinoza, Greenville
Best Breaking Pitch	Tyler Glasnow, Indianapolis	Braden Shipley, Reno	Jordan Montgomery, Trenton	Carson Fulmer, Birmingham	Francis Martes, Corpus Christi	Josh Sborz, Rancho Cucamonga	Erick Fedde, Potomac	Jimmy Herget, Daytona	Jacob Nix, Fort Wayne	Touki Toussaint, Rome
Best Changeup	Jose Berrios, Rochester	Chris Smith, Nashville	Shawn Morimando, Akron	Jake Faria, Montgomery	Yohander Mendez, Frisco	Walker Lockett, Lake Elsinore	Ryan Brinley, Potomac	Brent Honeywell, Charlotte	Junior Fernandez, Peoria	P.J. Conlon, Columbia
Best Control	Austin Pruitt, Durham	Brady Rodgers, Fresno	Daniel Camarena, Trenton	David Hurlbut, Chattanooga	Jake Junis, Northwest Arkansas	Parker French, Modesto	Zach Hedges, Myrtle Beach	Felix Jorge, Fort Myers	Evan Manarino, Beloit	Mitch Keller, West Virginia
Best Reliever	Oliver Drake, Norfolk	James Hoyt, Fresno	Matt Carasiti, Hartford	Edwin Diaz, Jackson	Brendan McCurry, Corpus Christi	Rodolfo Martinez, San Jose	Ryan McNeil, Myrtle Beach	Jimmy Herget, Daytona	Gerson Moreno, West Michigan	Andrew Schwaab, Charleston
Best Defensive Catcher	Gary Sanchez, Scranton/W-B	Austin Hedges, El Paso	Jorge Alfaro, Reading	Stuart Turner, Chattanooga	Carson Kelly, Springfield	Jose Trevino, High Desert	Raudy Read, Potomac	Nick Ciuffo, Charlotte	Francisco Mejia, Lake County	Tyler Sanchez, Hickory
Best Defensive First Baseman	Jesus Aguilar, Columbus	Efren Navarro, Tacoma/Memphis	Dominic Ficociello, Erie	Casey Gillaspie, Montgomery	Cody Bellinger, Tulsa	Chris Shaw, San Jose	Nick Longhi, Salem	Casey Grayson, Palm Beach	Juan Kelly, Lansing	Dillon Dobson, Augusta
Best Defensive Second Baseman	Alen Hanson, Indianapolis	Mike Freeman, Reno	Jesmuel Valentin, Reading	Ozzie Albies, Mississippi	Franklin Barreto, Midland	Luis Urias, Lake Elsinore	Yoan Moncada, Salem	Luis Guillorme, St. Lucie	Eli Alvarez, Peoria	Luis Alejandro Basabe, Greenville
Best Defensive Third Baseman	Matt Dominguez, Buffalo	Carlos Rivero, Reno	Eric Wood, Altoona	Jeimer Candelario, Tennessee	Matt Chapman, Midland	Dawel Lugo, Visalia	Rafael Devers, Salem	Brian Anderson, Jupiter	Kevin Padlo, Bowling Green	Kelvin Gutierrez, Hagerstown
Best Defensive Shortstop	Deven Marrero, Pawtucket	Orlando Arcia, Colorado Springs	Amed Rosario, Binghamton	Dansby Swanson, Mississippi	Matt Chapman, Midland	Drew Jackson, Bakersfield	Gleyber Torres, Myrtle Beach	Amed Rosario, St. Lucie	Jake Cronenworth, Bowling Green	Kyle Holder, Charleston
Best Infield Arm	Erik Gonzalez, Columbus	Orlando Arcia, Colorado Springs	Wilmer Difo, Harrisburg	Johan Camargo, Mississippi	Matt Chapman, Midland	Javier Guerra, Lake Elsinore	Gleyber Torres, Myrtle Beach	Jorge Mateo, Tampa	Carlos Belen, Fort Wayne	Yeyson Yrizarri, Hickory
Best Defensive Outfielder	Byron Buxton, Rochester	Manuel Margot, El Paso	Bradley Zimmer, Akron	Jacob Hannemann, Tennessee	Bubba Starling, Northwest Arkansas	Ramon Laureano, Lancaster	Hunter Jones, Winston-Salem	Carlos Tocci, Clearwater	Derek Hill, West Michigan	Victor Robles, Hagerstown
Best Outfield Arm	Dariel Alvarez, Norfolk	Hunter Renfroe, El Paso	Bradley Zimmer, Akron	Tyler O'Neill, Jackson	Alex Verdugo, Tulsa	Austin Wilson, Bakersfield	Mason Robbins, Winston-Salem	Blake Drake, Palm Beach	Jose Azocar, West Michigan	Yonathan Daza, Asheville
Most Exciting Player	Trea Turner, Syracuse	Hunter Renfroe, El Paso	Austin Meadows, Altoona	Ozzie Albies, Mississippi	Alex Bregman, Corpus Christi	Travis Demeritte, High Desert	Yoan Moncada, Salem	Amed Rosario, St. Lucie	Eloy Jimenez, South Bend	Victor Robles, Hagerstown
Best Manager Prospect	Chris Tremie, Columbus	Pat Listach, Tacoma	Dave Wallace, Akron	Robby Hammock, Mobile	Ryan Christenson, Midland	J.R. House, Visalia	Tripp Keister, Potomac	Luis Rojas, St. Lucie	Mitch Canham, Clinton	Warren Schaeffer, Asheville

NOR LEAGUES

Successful franchises get their due

Triple-A

ROUND ROCK (PACIFIC COAST)

Round Rock has won a Freitas Award before, but not since shifting from the Double-A Texas League into the PCL. The Express led the league in attendance in 2016 with an average of 8,623 fans per game at Dell Diamond.

With Nolan Ryan as one of the team's co-owners, fans have flocked to the ballpark on a regular basis. PCL president Branch Rickey III says the Hall of Famer's impact can't be understated.

"I said when first came here, if Texans were polled to name the person they most admired, he would beat out any politician or religious leader or celebrity. That's true with movie stars or singers or whatever," Rickey said. "It's not true today because fame as a former athlete subsides a bit, but as he's moved into banking he's set up a parallel reputation there. He's not just idolized for his fastball. The residual is he's a Texan who shows what it means to be loyal to the state of Texas."

Double-A

PENSACOLA BLUE WAHOOS (SOUTHERN)

After five seasons in existence, it's clear that Pensacola has become one of the Southern League's destination teams. With superstar golfer Bubba Watson as a part owner and one the most picturesque parks in the country, it's easy to see why Pensacola earned this year's Double-A Freitas.

"They do put their fans first. Not to mention their great ballpark, which is a wonderful place to watch a ballgame," SL president Lori Webb said. "They have gotten their community behind them. They have such a great support base from the business folks, and that's fanned out to their regular baseball fans. They're always doing something in the community, or charity events. They donate a lot to charity."

Class A

INLAND EMPIRE 66ERS (CALIFORNIA)

Despite playing in the financially strapped city of San Bernardino, the 66ers have managed to remain among the Cal League's top three in attendance in each of the past three seasons. More than that, the team has been a pillar of a community that has gone through its share of tragedy in recent years.

"Especially with what happened a year ago with the terrorist attacks in San Bernardino, they hosted a memorial at the stadium, they stepped right up and were available to the community," Cal League president Charlie Blaney said. "They also were involved in fundraising—selling T-shirts—for that project."

Short-Season

PULASKI YANKEES (APPALACHIAN)

In two seasons since Pulaski switched affiliations from the Mariners to the Yankees, new operator David Hagan has bent over backward to reshape the team's image. Calfee Park was completely renovated, with the most striking addition being a 22.5-foot by 35-foot JumboTron. Suites, VIP areas, expanded seating areas and new parking lots were added. The total cost to upgrade the park before the 2015 season eclipsed $7 million.

"It's a very well-run club from the top on down. Mr. Hagan . . . purchased the ballpark from the city of Pulaski to keep baseball there, because Pulaski didn't have the financial means to get the stadium to meet facility standards from Minor League Baseball and also the league," Appalachian League president Lee Landers said. "He's done a marvelous job and he's a competitor in everything that he does. He doesn't take second place or third place in anything."

To wit, the club has led the Appy League in attendance in both seasons since Hagan took over.

PREVIOUS WINNERS

TRIPLE-A	DOUBLE-A	CLASS A	SHORT-SEASON
2006: Durham (International)	2006: Altoona (Eastern)	2006: Daytona (Florida State)	2006: Aberdeen (New York-Penn)
2007: Albuquerque (Pacific Coast)	2007: Frisco (Texas)	2007: Lake Elsinore (California)	2007: Missoula (Pioneer)
2008: Columbus (International)	2008: Birmingham (Southern)	2008: Greensboro (South Atlantic)	2008: Greeneville (Appalachian)
2009: Iowa (Pacific Coast)	2009: New Hamshire (Eastern)	2009: San Jose (California)	2009: Tri-City (New York-Penn)
2010: Louisville (International)	2010: Corpus Christi (Texas)	2010: Lynchburg (Carolina)	2010: Idaho Falls (Pioneer)
2011: Colo. Springs (Pacific Coast)	2011: Harrisburg (Eastern)	2011: Fort Wayne (Midwest)	2011: Vancouver (Northwest)
2012: Lehigh Valley (International)	2012: N-West Arkansas (Texas)	2012: Greenville (South Atlantic)	2012: Billings (Pioneer)
2013: Indianapolis (International)	2013: Tulsa (Texas)	2013: Clearwater (Florida State)	2013: State College (NY-Penn)
2014: Charlotte (International)	2014: Montgomery (Southern)	2014: West Michigan (Midwest)	2014: Brooklyn (NY-Penn)
2015: Salt Lake (Pacific Coast)	2015: Richmond (Eastern)	2015: Myrtle Beach (Carolina)	2015: Grand Junction (Pioneer)

BY BILL MITCHELL

The Mesa Solar Sox used the piggyback starter tandem of Dylan Covey and Frankie Montas to great success throughout the Arizona Fall League regular season, with the two Athletics righthanders combining for a 5-0 record.

That formula worked again in the league championship game in Scottsdale (Ariz.) Stadium, with Covey and Montas holding Surprise to one run and two hits over eight innings to lead the Solar Sox to a 6-1 victory in front of a crowd of 2,519. James Farris (Cubs) pitched a perfect ninth inning to preserve the win for Mesa.

Covey and Montas had previously been part of a combined no-hitter against the same team on Nov. 1—the first AFL no-hitter since 2001—and were nearly as effective in the championship gamer, with Surprise not getting its first hit and run until the fifth inning.

Covey, who went 4-0, 4.74 in the AFL, allowed just one hit and a run in five innings. Nevertheless, Covey, who missed most of the season because of an oblique injury, was not protected on the A's 40-man roster, announced the night before the championship game.

Montas allowed just a hit and walk in three innings, striking out five, with his fastball sitting 97-100 mph. During the AFL's regular season, Montas was 1-0, 0.53 and allowed just seven hits in 17 innings, although he walked eight and struck out nine.

All six Solar Sox runs came on home runs off the bats of the Nos. 3-4 in the order, with third baseman Brian Anderson (Marlins) striking the first blow with a three-run bomb to left field off Surprise starter Eric Stout (Royals) in the first inning.

For Anderson, it was a nice conclusion to a fall season in which he led the AFL in homers with five.

"I was just looking for something out over the plate from that guy," Anderson said. "He left a fastball up, kind of out over the plate, and I was able to put a good swing on it."

Switch-hitting Ian Happ (Cubs) added a two-run homer from the left side of the plate to right-center in the third inning. He hit a solo shot in the seventh inning, again to right center but this time while batting righthanded.

Happ added a double and single in a 4-for-4 game, and made a leaping grab in left field of a long line drive off the bat of Mitch Garver (Twins) in the fifth inning to keep Covey's no-hit bid alive

for one more hitter.

Happ played mostly at second base in 2016, but he was forced back into left field—the position he played in his first pro season—due to injuries to Anthony Alford (Blue Jays) and Yefri Perez (Marlins).

It was the first time that the Cubs' 2015 first-rounder homered from both sides of the plate in the same game.

Both teams had to wait until the last day of the regular season to qualify for the AFL championship game, but Surprise was most affected by the close races. The Saguaros had to use ace Michael Kopech (Red Sox) for their division-clinching win on the last day of the regular season, leaving the fireballing righthander unavailable to start the championship game.

Coupled with the unavailability of Josh Staumont (Royals), who was shut down by his parent organization after his final start, Saguaros manager Carlos Febles had to rely on a parade of middle relievers against Mesa. Stout had made just two starts as a pro prior to starting the AFL finale.

The Solar Sox squeaked into the championship game with a half-game lead over Salt River, finishing with a 16-15-1 record, with the Mesa hitters putting up a league-best 25 homers and .734 OPS.

"I didn't have to tell these guys anything," said Mesa manager Ryan Christenson. "They've always showed up to play, and I knew they'd be out here to play (in the title game)."

Gleyber Torres (Yankees) of Scottsdale was presented with the Joe Black MVP Award as the AFL's MVP prior to the championship game, as well as being honored as the league's leading hitter. The righthanded-hitting middle infielder batted .403/.513/.645, pacing all hitters in batting average, on-base average and OPS, and finishing second in slugging percentage. At 19, Torres is the youngest MVP in league history.

"Before I came here I prepared myself very well," Torres said through a translator. "Before every game this year I prepared myself, so right now the hard work is paying off . . . I was honored to come here and represent the Yankees."

Austin Nola (Marlins) was presented with the AFL's Dernell Stenson Sportsmanship Award prior to the championship game. The award, named in memory of the Reds farmhand player who was murdered in 2003 while in Arizona taking part in the AFL, has been given annually since 2004 to the player who best exemplifies unselfishness, hard work and leadership.

MINOR LEAGUES

STANDINGS

EAST	W	L	PCT	GB
Mesa Solar Sox	16	15	.516	—
Salt River Rafters	15	15	.500	½
Scottsdale Scorpions	13	18	.419	3

WEST	W	L	PCT	GB
Surprise Saguaros	17	14	.548	—
Glendale Desert Dogs	17	15	.531	½
Peoria Javelinas	14	15	.483	2

INDIVIDUAL BATTING LEADERS
(Minimum 2 Plate Appearances/League Games)

Player, Team	AVG	G	AB	R	H	HR	RBI
Gleyber Torres, Scottsdale	.403	18	62	15	25	3	11
Andrew Stevenson, Glendale	.353	21	85	18	30	2	12
Zach Vincej, Peoria	.352	20	71	10	25	4	18
Nick Gordon, Surprise	.346	21	81	15	28	0	7
Brandon Dixon, Peoria	.333	16	60	9	20	2	11
Eric Wood, Surprise	.330	23	88	17	29	3	20
JaCoby Jones, Salt River	.329	21	82	11	27	1	13
Dustin Peterson, Salt River	.324	18	68	9	22	1	9
Cody Bellinger, Glendale	.314	20	70	16	22	3	17
Kean Wong, Peoria	.313	22	80	10	25	0	8

INDIVIDUAL PITCHING LEADERS
(Minimum .4 Innings Pitched/League Games)

NAME	W	L	ERA	IP	H	BB	SO
Jared Miller, Salt River	1	0	0.00	18.1	6	4	30
Edgar Santana, Surprise	0	0	0.00	13.2	11	2	18
Frankie Montas, Mesa	1	0	0.53	17	7	8	9
Jason Jester, Peoria	0	0	0.71	12.2	8	5	13
Louie Lechich, Glendale	1	0	0.71	12.2	7	5	7
Jeff Singer, Scottsdale	0	0	1.42	12.2	9	5	10
Trey Cochran-Gill, Mesa	0	0	1.84	14.2	14	2	14
Tayler Scott, Salt River	1	0	1.88	14.1	12	6	11
Corey Taylor, Scottsdale	0	1	1.93	14	12	1	17
Sam Bragg, Mesa	1	1	1.98	13.2	11	1	12

GLENDALE DESERT DOGS

NAME	AVG	AB	R	H	2B	3B	HR	RBI	BB	SO	SB
Abreu, Osvaldo	.267	60	6	16	3	0	0	8	4	20	5
Bader, Harrison	.304	79	12	24	2	1	2	16	5	14	4
Bellinger, Cody	.314	70	16	22	8	0	3	17	14	18	0
Calhoun, Willie	.255	47	5	12	1	0	1	6	3	5	0
Collins, Zack	.227	22	6	5	0	0	2	5	6	8	0
DeJong, Paul	.232	69	4	16	1	0	1	9	3	21	1
Garcia, Alejandro	.200	20	1	4	0	0	0	1	2	3	0
Hawkins, Courtney	.219	73	7	16	5	0	1	9	5	23	0
Hayes, Danny	.161	62	6	10	0	0	1	3	6	20	0
Kelly, Carson	.286	77	12	22	4	0	3	18	13	4	2
Laureano, Ramon	.295	44	12	13	4	2	0	8	3	9	5
Locastro, Tim	.303	33	5	10	0	0	0	6	1	7	2
Martin, Jason	.194	31	9	6	3	0	0	2	8	4	2
Michalczewski, Trey	.185	54	7	10	4	0	0	4	10	17	1
Stevenson, Andrew	.353	85	18	30	4	2	2	12	10	17	9
Stubbs, Garrett	.171	70	13	12	4	0	1	6	10	10	2
Tanielu, Nick	.352	54	7	19	5	0	1	5	2	7	0
Verdugo, Alex	.140	43	3	6	2	1	0	2	4	8	0
Ward, Drew	.309	81	13	25	6	0	0	8	10	21	1

NAME	W	L	ERA	G	GS	SV	IP	H	BB	SO	AVG
Anderson, Chris	1	4	11.88	6	6	0	16.2	28	12	9	.364
Armenteros, Rogelio	0	0	11.05	8	0	1	7.1	10	4	8	.333
Brinley, Ryan	1	1	2.53	9	1	0	10.2	6	1	9	.167
Broussard, Joe	0	1	1.59	11	0	5	11.1	10	0	9	.227
Cash, Ralston	0	0	4.32	8	0	0	8.1	8	7	4	.258
Clark, Brian	0	0	2.08	8	0	0	13	12	6	13	.245
Copping, Corey	0	1	3.48	9	0	0	10.1	10	5	11	.244
Dorris, Jacob	1	1	3.38	8	0	0	8	9	10	15	.273
Gomber, Austin	5	1	2.14	7	7	0	33.2	26	12	33	.205
Johansen, Jake	0	0	2.13	9	0	0	12.2	13	3	5	.265
Lechich, Louie	1	0	0.71	10	0	0	12.2	7	5	7	.167
Lee, Nick	0	0	1.54	10	0	0	11.2	10	10	14	.238
Littrell, Corey	0	1	4.40	9	0	0	14.1	11	4	18	.200
Martes, Francis	2	1	3.22	6	6	0	22.1	20	9	25	.244
Paulino, David	0	0	0.00	5	0	1	5	2	1	1	.125

NAME	G		ERA				IP	H		SO	AVG
Sanburn, Nolan	2	0	4.81	6	6	0	24.1	23	12	18	.250
Sheriff, Ryan	0	1	5.79	9	0	0	9.1	13	7	9	.325
Turner, Colton	1	0	5.06	8	0	0	10.2	13	4	10	.289
Voth, Austin	3	2	5.16	7	7	0	29.2	23	11	23	.219
Wick, Rowan	0	1	4.50	9	0	0	10	11	6	8	.282

PEORIA JAVELINAS

NAME	AVG	AB	R	H	2B	3B	HR	RBI	BB	SO	SB
Ciuffo, Nick	.190	79	6	15	7	1	0	9	4	17	0
Cordero, Franchy	.203	74	11	15	3	0	1	9	7	26	4
Dixon, Brandon	.333	60	9	20	7	0	2	11	10	24	1
Gettys, Michael	.157	70	8	11	4	1	2	4	6	30	2
Heredia, Guillermo	.255	51	8	13	3	1	1	8	9	12	4
Jackson, Drew	.149	47	3	7	1	0	0	2	5	16	1
Marin, Adrian	.136	44	4	6	2	0	0	6	4	12	1
Marlette, Tyler	.267	45	8	12	3	0	2	10	2	15	0
O'Grady, Brian	.211	38	5	8	1	0	0	5	7	13	1
O'Neill, Tyler	.292	72	15	21	5	0	3	14	12	22	1
Stewart, D.J.	.244	78	7	19	6	1	1	9	19	21	4
VanMeter, Josh	.265	68	17	18	3	1	1	9	17	19	2
Vincej, Zach	.352	71	10	25	7	2	4	18	9	14	1
Wallach, Chad	.250	68	12	17	4	0	3	10	4	16	0
Williams, Justin	.219	64	9	14	6	3	0	5	3	14	0
Wong, Kean	.313	80	10	25	4	0	0	8	9	11	4
Wynns, Austin	.300	40	6	12	1	0	1	2	7	11	0

NAME	W	L	ERA	G	GS	SV	IP	H	BB	SO	AVG
Astin, Barrett	0	1	3.21	11	1	1	14	13	7	8	.255
Bird, Kyle	0	1	3.77	12	0	0	14.1	20	9	8	.351
Bridwell, Parker	0	0	2.57	4	0	0	7	8	2	2	.308
Castillo, Diego	1	1	4.38	10	0	0	12.1	13	5	11	.277
Crichton, Stefan	1	0	5.54	13	0	1	13	16	3	9	.308
Gohara, Luiz	1	0	3.86	9	0	0	11.2	14	3	19	.304
Harris, Greg	0	1	2.19	9	0	0	12.1	13	9	8	.250
Honeywell, Brent	1	0	5.40	5	5	0	15	11	4	14	.204
Jester, Jason	0	0	0.71	11	0	2	12.2	8	5	13	.170
Kittredge, Andrew	0	0	4.50	2	0	0	2	1	1	2	.143
Liranzo, Jesus	0	0	5.40	1	0	0	1.2	1	2	1	.167
Maton, Phil	2	0	2.92	10	0	0	12.1	13	1	15	.271
McGrath, Kyle	2	1	3.71	6	6	0	17	14	3	11	.219
Mitchell, Evan	1	1	5.52	11	0	0	14.2	12	5	13	.231
Pagan, Emilio	0	1	6.55	11	0	1	11	12	8	12	.286
Routt, Nick	0	0	3.00	11	0	0	9	3	12	12	.091
Scott, Tanner	0	2	6.32	7	7	0	15.2	17	7	17	.283
Torres, Jose	0	0	2.16	8	0	1	8.1	7	5	6	.241
Unsworth, Dylan	4	1	3.00	6	6	0	21	22	4	15	.272
Varner, Seth	1	2	7.11	6	6	0	19	27	3	14	.329
Vieira, Thyago	0	1	3.38	5	0	0	5.1	4	1	7	.211
Wieck, Brad	0	1	6.57	11	0	0	12.1	12	11	19	.267
Yacabonis, Jimmy	0	1	8.53	12	0	1	12.2	15	8	13	.288

SALT RIVER RAFTERS

NAME	AVG	AB	R	H	2B	3B	HR	RBI	BB	SO	SB
Cron, Kevin	.188	80	5	15	3	0	3	11	4	19	2
Cuevas, Noel	.196	56	9	11	0	0	0	2	7	10	1
Demeritte, Travis	.261	92	23	24	4	4	4	14	11	25	3
Diaz, Isan	.239	67	12	16	6	0	1	5	9	24	3
Greiner, Grayson	.205	44	7	9	4	0	1	6	5	13	0
Jones, JaCoby	.329	82	11	27	5	0	1	13	7	16	5
Lugo, Dawel	.267	90	9	24	6	0	1	13	1	10	1
McMahon, Ryan	.247	77	5	19	2	1	1	9	11	21	1
Moore, Dylan	.317	41	6	13	3	0	2	6	3	4	2
Nottingham, Jacob	.203	74	8	15	3	0	1	8	2	24	0
Peterson, Dustin	.324	68	9	22	5	1	1	9	3	13	2
Phillips, Brett	.210	62	14	13	3	1	0	9	18	23	6
Scivicque, Kade	.378	37	3	14	4	0	0	4	2	4	0
Stewart, Christin	.268	71	12	19	5	1	1	9	7	23	1
Valaika, Pat	.263	76	8	20	3	0	0	12	6	12	1
Westbrook, Jamie	.233	60	7	14	1	0	1	7	4	11	1

NAME	W	L	ERA	G	GS	SV	IP	H	BB	SO	AVG
Carle, Shane	1	0	4.19	10	0	0	19.1	19	6	19	.257
Ellis, Chris	1	1	5.03	6	6	0	19.2	19	12	17	.257
Gonzalez, Rayan	0	0	2.31	11	0	1	11.2	7	2	12	.175
Jemiola, Zach	1	3	5.64	7	7	0	22.1	26	4	19	.286
Krehbiel, Joey	3	1	2.70	12	0	0	13.1	6	6	20	.136

NAME	W	L	ERA	G	GS	SV	IP	H	BB	SO	AVG
Lewicki, Artie	1	0	5.68	9	0	0	12.2	18	3	12	.327
Miller, Jared	1	0	0.00	10	1	0	18.1	6	4	30	.103
Morris, Akeel	2	1	2.89	9	0	0	9.1	10	7	12	.263
Phillips, Evan	0	1	4.22	9	0	0	10.2	6	10	11	.162
Ravenelle, Adam	1	1	6.75	10	0	5	9.1	10	7	7	.270
Salas, Javier	0	2	7.63	6	5	0	15.1	16	11	10	.286
Scott, Tayler	0	1	1.88	9	0	0	14.1	12	6	11	.226
Speier, Gabe	1	1	3.97	10	0	0	11.1	11	3	6	.256
Spurlin, Tyler	1	0	2.81	11	0	1	16	9	4	14	.158
Taylor, Josh	1	0	3.57	6	6	0	22.2	21	5	20	.241
Thompson, Jeff	0	0	6.75	8	0	0	10.2	11	9	8	.282
Turnbull, Spencer	1	3	3.60	6	6	0	20	10	10	20	.250
Uhen, Josh	0	0					12.2	14	5	11	.269
Vasto, Jerry	0	0	8.31	9	0	1	8.2	14	2	9	.359

NAME	AVG	AB	R	H	2B	3B	HR	RBI	BB	SO	SB
Tebow, Tim	.194	62	6	12	3	0	0	2	8	20	1
Torres, Gleyber	.403	62	15	25	4	1	3	11	14	8	4
Wade, Tyler	.241	54	17	13	0	1	0	4	13	11	10
Walding, Mitch	.286	63	8	18	4	1	2	8	11	27	3
Ward, Taylor	.283	53	4	15	5	0	0	9	3	13	0
Zambrano, Eliezer	.316	19	1	6	0	0	0	0	0	4	0

NAME	W	L	ERA	G	GS	SV	IP	H	BB	SO	AVG
Alcantara, Victor	0	1	12.60	10	0	0	10	15	11	8	.357
Anderson, Justin	0	0	6.75	5	0	0	6.2	7	5	8	.269
Arano, Victor	0	0	2.79	8	0	0	9.2	5	6	9	.152
Cortes, Nestor	0	0	4.70	6	0	0	7.2	6	6	10	.214
Feyereisen, J.P.	2	1	2.57	10	0	1	14	15	7	18	.278
Hofacket, Adam	0	1	5.79	3	0	0	4.2	8	1	3	.364
Kaprielian, James	2	3	4.33	7	7	0	27	22	8	26	.218
Koerner, Brody	0	1	5.85	6	4	0	20	24	11	13	.308
Long, Grayson	2	2	6.75	6	6	0	17.1	18	16	18	.277
Martinez, Rodolfo	0	0	27.00	4	0	0	3	8	6	2	.500
Mizenko, Tyler	1	1	7.20	8	0	0	10	14	5	6	.333
Molina, Marcos	0	0	3.78	7	2	0	16.2	16	7	8	.250
Nunez, Miguel	0	0	3.60	9	0	3	10	9	4	7	.250
Oswalt, Corey	4	1	3.33	7	7	0	27	25	11	21	.245
Paredes, Eduardo	0	2	5.40	11	0	0	11.2	14	5	11	.298
Rogers, Tyler	0	1	6.23	9	0	1	8.2	13	2	9	.351
Roseboom, David	0	1	0.79	11	0	1	11.1	4	8	15	.108
Singer, Jeff	0	0	1.42	10	0	0	12.2	9	5	10	.205
Stratton, Chris	2	2	3.12	6	6	0	26	29	5	21	.269
Tate, Dillon	0	0	3.86	6	0	0	9.1	9	1	11	.265
Taylor, Corey	0	1	1.93	9	0	1	14	12	1	17	.222

SURPRISE SAGUAROS

NAME	AVG	AB	R	H	2B	3B	HR	RBI	BB	SO	SB
Dubon, Mauricio	.211	71	10	15	3	1	3	7	4	12	3
English, Tanner	.239	71	7	17	2	1	1	5	8	25	2
Escalera, Alfredo	.179	78	6	14	1	0	0	7	2	24	1
Garver, Mitch	.229	70	10	16	4	0	4	14	7	17	0
Gordon, Nick	.346	81	15	28	4	2	0	7	8	22	5
Heineman, Scott	.231	65	11	15	2	0	1	6	13	13	3
Ibanez, Andy	.281	64	8	18	7	0	0	8	4	6	2
Jhang, Jin-De	.319	47	5	15	3	0	0	7	6	5	0
Joe, Connor	.204	49	10	10	1	0	2	8	11	11	3
Kiner-Falefa, Isiah	.194	31	4	6	0	0	0	3	7	7	0
Mars, Danny	.259	58	4	15	2	0	0	4	3	13	3
Moncada, Yoan	.292	24	6	7	1	0	1	3	3	10	1
O'Hearn, Ryan	.291	86	12	25	4	0	1	11	13	26	0
Ramos, Mauricio	.228	57	7	13	4	0	2	7	3	11	0
Toups, Corey	.238	63	5	15	3	0	2	4	3	19	2
Trevino, Jose	.230	74	8	17	4	0	2	7	3	3	0
Wood, Eric	.330	88	17	29	5	0	3	20	8	28	1

NAME	W	L	ERA	G	GS	SV	IP	H	BB	SO	AVG
Anderson, Tanner	2	2	3.76	7	7	0	26.1	30	6	19	.294
Ball, Trey	1	1	6.08	11	0	0	13.1	10	13	9	.204
Beal, Evan	0	0	3.68	11	0	0	14.2	7	10	13	.143
Beeks, Jalen	0	1	6.57	10	0	0	12.1	16	5	13	.308
Callahan, Jamie	0	0	0.75	12	0	2	12	12	3	12	.250
Curtiss, John	0	0	2.84	11	0	1	12.2	13	4	18	.265
DuRapau, Montana	0	1	5.40	10	0	0	10	12	5	10	.300
Eaton, Todd	0	0	6.43	5	0	0	7	9	0	5	.310
Fasola, John	0	2	2.00	8	0	3	9	11	0	9	.297
Faulkner, Andrew	0	0	0.00	2	0	0	2	1	0	1	.167
Garrett, Reed	1	0	2.25	5	3	0	16	11	6	15	.204
Gonsalves, Stephen	0	2	8.31	4	4	0	8.2	10	4	7	.294
Juan, Johan	0	0	4.50	3	2	0	6	10	3	3	.370
Kopech, Michael	3	0	2.01	6	6	0	22.1	18	8	26	.231
Martin, Brett	1	1	2.89	3	3	0	9.1	12	2	7	.300
McCain, Shane	3	0	0.00	6	0	0	8.1	4	3	13	.133
McRae, Alex	0	1	3.38	10	0	0	16	15	4	9	.254
Melotakis, Mason	1	1	1.64	11	0	0	11	12	1	11	.299
Newberry, Jake	0	0	0.00	2	0	0	2	2	0	4	.250
Rosario, Randy	1	0	4.26	10	0	0	12.2	18	5	11	.333
Santana, Edgar	0	0	0.00	9	0	3	13.2	11	2	18	.220
Staumont, Josh	4	2	4.50	7	7	0	24	15	16	30	.179
Stout, Eric	0	0	2.77	9	0	1	13	10	6	13	.217

SCOTTSDALE SCORPIONS

NAME	AVG	AB	R	H	2B	3B	HR	RBI	BB	SO	SB
Andujar, Miguel	.284	67	10	19	2	2	0	5	9	11	0
Bird, Greg	.215	65	9	14	4	1	1	10	12	17	1
Bossart, Austin	.091	11	0	1	0	0	0	0	0	3	0
Brown, Aaron	.184	76	5	14	3	2	3	13	5	27	0
Cecchini, Gavin	.295	61	12	18	5	1	1	7	7	8	0
Cole, Hunter	.235	68	9	16	1	0	2	9	8	17	0
Fletcher, David	.250	60	10	15	2	1	1	7	5	4	2
Garcia, Aramis	.191	47	3	9	1	0	1	12	5	17	0
Hermosillo, Michael	.267	30	5	8	2	1	0	2	3	4	1
Jones, Ryder	.302	63	8	19	2	2	2	12	7	16	0
Kingery, Scott	.234	77	8	18	3	0	1	6	7	18	5
Oberste, Matt	.184	49	2	9	3	0	1	8	2	9	0
Stuart, Champ	.300	70	12	21	4	0	1	5	3	22	12

MESA SOLAR SOX

NAME	AVG	AB	R	H	2B	3B	HR	RBI	BB	SO	SB
Alford, Anthony	.253	75	15	19	3	1	3	15	11	24	6
Allen, Greg	.269	78	12	21	3	1	3	8	10	17	12
Anderson, Brian	.273	77	17	21	3	0	5	12	9	9	0
Barreto, Franklin	.261	88	15	23	6	0	0	8	2	21	3
Caratini, Victor	.226	62	2	14	3	0	0	4	10	14	0
Chang, Yu-Cheng	.304	56	4	17	5	0	0	7	3	21	1
Haase, Eric	.278	18	1	5	3	0	0	0	1	5	0
Happ, Ian	.236	72	12	17	4	1	2	8	15	22	0
Jansen, Danny	.282	71	6	20	0	2	0	9	9	10	0
Jimenez, Eloy	.255	55	6	14	4	0	3	10	6	11	0
Kelly, Juan	.283	46	5	13	0	0	1	6	1	10	1
Kjerstad, Dexter	.140	57	5	8	3	0	2	5	2	20	0
McBroom, Ryan	.250	28	4	7	2	0	2	10	1	6	0
Munoz, Yairo	.270	74	8	20	3	2	0	7	5	17	3
Nola, Austin	.273	22	5	6	1	0	0	2	6	1	0
Perez, Yefri	.270	74	14	20	0	1	0	2	9	16	7
Schrock, Max	.278	54	4	15	5	1	0	10	1	2	1
wSchwarber, Kyle	.167	6	1	1	1	0	0	0	2	0	0
Zimmer, Bradley	.257	74	25	19	7	0	4	16	19	26	8

NAME	W	L	ERA	G	GS	SV	IP	H	BB	SO	AVG
Bragg, Sam	1	1	1.98	8	0	0	13.2	11	1	12	.220
Brigham, Jeff	0	0	11.57	1	1	0	2.1	4	1	2	.333
Buckelew, James	0	2	4.29	8	5	0	21	32	7	20	.330
Cochran-Gaudet, Trey	0	0	1.84	10	0	0	14.2	14	2	14	.246
Covey, Dylan	4	0	4.74	6	6	0	24.2	28	8	17	.280
Dermody, Matt	1	0	5.40	8	0	0	10	10	3	8	.256
Farris, James	1	0	0.00	8	0	0	10	5	2	12	.147
Frank, Trevor	1	0	11.88	9	0	0	8.1	13	4	5	.342
Garcia, Jarlin	0	1	4.97	9	0	0	12.2	12	4	8	.245
Greene, Conner	0	1	5.40	4	4	0	10	6	11	5	.176
Hill, Cameron	0	1	4.80	9	1	1	15	14	7	13	.255
Mayza, Tim	0	0	6.14	10	0	0	14.2	15	8	15	.273
McNeil, Ryan	0	0	8.18	8	0	0	11	9	5	13	.220
Montas, Frankie	1	0	0.53	6	0	0	17	7	8	9	.132
Newell, Ryan	0	0	7.20	5	0	0	5	3	6	8	.167
Peoples, Michael	0	2	3.96	7	7	0	25	19	7	26	.200
Perakslis, Steve	1	0	0.00	6	0	1	6.1	3	1	6	.136
Shafer, Justin	1	3	8.71	7	6	0	20.2	29	16	14	.354
Speer, David	3	1	5.27	10	0	0	13.2	14	2	10	.269
Steckenrider, Drew	2	1	3.46	10	0	3	13	12	4	15	.245
Stilson, John	0	1	12.46	9	0	0	8.2	16	5	6	.400
Underwood Jr., Duane	0	1	9.00	2	2	0	6	8	2	5	.333

INDEPENDENT LEAGUES

Innovations helps indy ball roll along

BY J.J. COOPER

The independent leagues have always been innovative. They've had no choice.

The St. Paul Saints had immediate success, really birthing the indy ball movement, by rewriting the rules of baseball promotions. Playing it straight would not have sold the tickets, not have drawn the fans needed to make indy ball work.

And ever since, indy ball has thrown a lot of ideas against the wall to see what's worth keeping.

There have been leagues that tried a single-owner, franchise model. Others have tried a single-site approach. To try to win titles with limited rosters, indy ball managers have used strong-armed hitters as pitchers as well.

In the third decade of indy ball, the innovations keep happening and they keep changing.

Indy ball is an incubator, where new ideas can be tried outside of Organized Baseball on a smaller stage. The bad ideas often get thrown out. The good ones filter into other areas of the game.

The Atlantic League led the way on pace of play initiatives with moves such as pitch clocks and a limit on in-inning timeouts and mound visits. Major League Baseball took notice and adopted its own version of some of the Atlantic League's innovations at the minor league and big league levels.

In 2016, indy ball's desires to innovate traveled into additional directions. When it comes to women in baseball, indy ball is leading the way. The Normal Cornbelters hired Justine Siegal as a coach, marking the second time an indy ball team has hired Siegal, the only women to have coached in pro baseball this century. It won't be a surprise if an indy ball team has a female manager at some point in the not too-distant future.

The Pacific Association's Sonoma Stompers became the first pro team to have more than one female player on its roster in decades when it added a trio of women to its roster.

Across the country, the new United Shores Professional Baseball League worked on being innovative in a different way. The USPBL focused on being a developmental league for young, undrafted players. And it did so by using video analysis and a pitching development program called the Delivery Value System that attempted to improve pitchers deliveries both to keep them

Art Charles dominated the Can-Am League, winning its triple crown

healthy and to improve their stuff.

All of that innovation is doing much to keep indy ball around, but it's not drawing additional fans. Indy ball's attendance has dropped significantly since the start of the decade. In 2010, the independent leagues drew 8.1 million fans. In 2016, the four largest independent leagues drew just under 5.9 million fans. The biggest reason for the drop has been consolidation and the loss of some leagues—the United League, Golden League and Northern Leagues have all disappeared since the decade began.

INDEPENDENT ATTENDANCE, 2016

Announced attendance for the four largest independent leagues.

LEAGUE	TOTAL ATTENDANCE	AVERAGE
American Association	2,099,629	3,939
Atlantic League	1,833,503	3,156
Frontier League	1,285,885	2,390
Can-Am League	667,716	2,241

Charles wins Can-Am Triple Crown

Like many players before him, being released left Art Charles shocked.

The Phillies let him go during spring training in mid-March after he hit .215/.304/.367 with nine home runs in a part-time role for Double-A Reading in 2015. For a moment, Charles said he wondered what was going to happen next. He wondered if he was done. He wondered if he needed to start looking for a day job.

"I didn't know what was going to happen. It was the weirdest, most awkward feeling," Charles said. "But then I started to get calls from indy teams. It made me feel better because someone wants you."

New Jersey manager Joe Calfapietra believed. Charles responded by putting together one of the best seasons in Cam-Am League history, winning the league's triple crown by hitting .352-29-101 while setting league records in .699, total bases (248) and extra-base hits (60).

Charles won the league's batting title by 11 points. He hit eight more home runs than anyone else and finished with 22 more RBIs than the next best in the league.

There was little drama about whether Charles would win the Triple Crown heading into the final two games of the season, but he finished with a flurry anyway, going 5-for-8 with two doubles and a home run.

For all that, Charles is the 2016 Independent Leagues Player of the Year.

"The power, you were hoping for, but the all-around package ended up being unbelievable," Calfapietra said. "He has good plate discipline. He hit the ball the other way. He ran well. He did everything you could hope for."

And along the way, Charles found his footing. Being released leaves its marks. But Charles handed it in a positive way. He took it as a message of what he needed to improve.

No one had ever doubted Charles power. He was drafted in the 18th round by Toronto in 2010 because of that power.

He's a 6-foot-6, 260-pound hitter with long arms and massive raw power. For a long time he had known he needed to be a more consistent hitter. He finished second in the Florida State League in home runs in 2014 with 19 home runs–the most-ever for a Clearwater Thresher—and led the league in extra-base hits. But he also hit .229.

"It was nice to hit all those home runs, but I knew that I could do better," Charles said. "I knew I could hit more consistently and I knew if I put the bat on the ball more I'd have hit more home runs."

Being released gives that to-do list much added urgency.

"Teams are looking for more consistency. I had to put the bat on the ball more," Charles said. "I went with the approach that I have to get more consistent. It's shortening up with two strikes."

What Calfapietra and the Jackals could offer was everyday at-bats and a shot to build some confidence.

From day one, Charles' new approach seemed to work.

In March he heard from a farm director that he was being released. He hopes to get a call now that tells him he's been signed.

INDEPENDENT TOP 10 PROSPECTS

1. Dalton Wheat, of, Kansas City T-Bones (American Association)
2. Art Charles, 1b, New Jersey (Can-Am League)
3. Jose Nivar, rhp, Laredo (American Association)
4. Chad Nading, rhp, Wichita (American Association)
5. Jesse Beal RHP, Sussex (Can-Am)
6. Danny Reynolds, rhp, Laredo (American Association)
7. Lindsey Caughel, rhp, Lincoln (American Association)
8. Austin Crutcher, of, Utica (United Shore Professional Baseball League)
9. Andrew Potter, rhp, Utica (USPBL)
10. Jordan Mills, lhp, Quebec (Can-Am)

PREVIOUS WINNERS

2005: Eddie Lantigua, 3b, Quebec (Can-Am)
2006: Ian Church, of, Kalamazoo (Frontier)
2007: Darryl Brinkley, of, Calgary (Northern)
2008: Patrick Breen, of, Orange County (Golden)
2009: Greg Porter, of, Wichita (American Association)
2010: Beau Torbert, of, Sioux Falls (American Association)
2011: Chris Collabello, 1b, Worcester (Can-Am League)
2012: Blake Gailen, of, Lancaster (Atlantic)
2013: C.J. Ziegler, 1b, Wichita (American Association)
2014: Balbino Fuenmayor, 1b, Quebec (Can-Am League)
2015: Joe Maloney, of, Rockland (Can-Am League)
Full list:
BaseballAmerica.com/awards

AMERICAN ASSOCIATION

When discussing the greatest players in American Association history, Reggie Abercrombie is near the top of the list.

And that is even more true after Abercrombie almost single-handedly led Winnipeg to its third league title and its first since 2012. In the deciding Game Five of the championship series Abercrombie went 3-for-4 with a double, two home runs and seven RBIs in Winnipeg's 11-4 win over Wichita.

Abercrombie was named the league's first ever Scott Miller/Brian Rose Man of the Year for his community service during the season. He also took over the American Association career home run lead with 99. The 35-year-old former Marlin and Astros has yet to slow down; he hit .297/.359/.519 with 20 home runs. He ranked second in the league in home runs and third in total bases.

STANDINGS

NORTH DIVISION

	W	L	PCT	GB
St Paul Saints	61	39	.610	—
* Winnipeg Goldeyes	58	42	.580	3
Fargo-Moorhead RedHawks	52	48	.520	9
Sioux Falls Canaries	40	60	.400	21

CENTRAL DIVISION

	W	L	PCT	GB
Sioux City Explorers	54	46	.540	—
Gary SouthShore RailCats	52	48	.520	2
Lincoln Saltdogs	52	48	.520	2
Kansas City T-Bones	42	58	.420	12

SOUTH DIVISION

	W	L	PCT	GB
Wichita Wingnuts	61	39	.610	—
Laredo Lemurs	57	42	.576	3 ½
Joplin Blasters	36	64	.360	25
Texas AirHogs	34	65	.343	26 ½

*Wild Card

PLAYOFFS: SEMIFINALS—Winnipeg defeated St. Paul 3-2 and Wichita defeated Sioux City 3-1 in best-of-5 series. **CHAMPIONSHIP**—Winnipeg defeated Wichita 3-2 in best-of-5 series.

ATTENDANCE: St Paul Saints 413,482; Winnipeg Goldeyes 231,206; Kansas City T-Bones 213,165; Fargo-Moorhead RedHawks 180,345; Lincoln Saltdogs 169,750; Gary SouthShore RailCats 163,519; Wichita Wingnuts 150,929; Sioux Falls Canaries 125,591; Sioux City Explorers 68,278; Texas AirHogs 44,282; Laredo Lemurs 41,955; Joplin Blasters 31,001.

MANAGERS: Fargo-Moorhead—Doug Simunic; Gary SouthShore—Greg Tagert; Joplin—Gabe Suarez; Kansas City—John Massarelli; Laredo—Pete Incaviglia; Lincoln—Bobby Brown; Sioux City—Steve Montgomery; Sioux Falls—Chris Paterson; St. Paul—George Tsamis; Texas—James Frisbie; Wichita—Pete Rose; Winnipeg—Rick Forney.

ALL-STAR TEAM: C: Luis Alen, Lincoln. **1B:** David Rohm, Winnipeg. **2B:** Brett Wiley, Kansas City. **3B:** Josh Mazzola, Fargo-Moorhead. **SS:** Nate Samson, Sioux City. **OF:** Willie Cabrera, Winnipeg; Alonzo Harris, St. Paul and Keury De La Cruz, Fargo-Moorhead. **DH:** Curt Smith, Lincoln. **SP:** Lindsey Caughel, Lincoln. **RP:** Ryan Rodebaugh, St. Paul.

PLAYER OF THE YEAR: Nate Samson, SS, Sioux City. **MANAGER OF THE YEAR:** Greg Tagert, Gary SouthShore. **ROOKIE OF THE YEAR:** INF Matt Chavez, Wichita. **TOP DEFENDER:** C Jose Gonzalez, Gary SouthShore.

BATTING LEADERS

PLAYER	AVG	AB	R	H	HR	RBI	SB
Chavez, Matt, Wichita	.359	259	42	93	16	61	0
Kain, Harrison, Wichita	.358	240	38	86	3	48	15
Samson, Nate, SC	.350	391	68	137	6	68	31
Rohm, David, Winnipeg	.339	366	58	124	7	71	3
Smith, Curt, Lincoln	.331	314	50	104	17	60	0
Valentin, Geraldo, Joplin	.329	401	71	132	18	65	3
Schmit, Blake, Sioux Falls	.319	370	61	118	5	29	20
Cabrera, Willie, Winnipeg	.318	340	58	108	17	77	4
De La Cruz, Keury, Fargo	.316	433	76	137	18	72	19
Glasser, Mitch, Joplin	.314	350	66	110	3	47	16

PITCHING LEADERS

PLAYER	W	L	ERA	IP	H	BB	SO
Caughel, Lindsey, Lincoln	6	3	2.09	125	101	24	120
Bircher, Joe, Sioux Falls	6	6	2.55	124	119	34	108
Almarante, Jose, Fargo	4	2	2.74	115	99	39	86
Kickham, Mike, Kansas City	3	5	2.83	86	78	26	73
Beckman, Ryan, Lincoln	8	8	2.92	133	129	24	97
Rosario, Charle, Gary	11	4	3.13	155	141	46	120
Hamburger, Mark, St. Paul	12	6	3.29	159	165	22	100
Boshers, Alex, Wichita	12	3	3.29	123	147	21	66
Martis, Shairon, Lincoln	9	8	3.34	121	121	31	93
Alexander, Tyler, Fargo	12	5	3.45	143	132	48	156

FARGO-MOORHEAD REDHAWKS

PLAYER	AVG	AB	R	H	HR	RBI	BB	SO	SB	CS
Dustin Geiger, 1B	.329	228	40	75	9	36	21	40	0	1
# Charlie Valerio, C	.325	80	10	26	3	15	13	21	0	0
* Keury De La Cruz, OF	.316	433	76	137	18	72	18	87	19	10
* Brian Humphries, 1B	.293	406	59	119	13	66	16	75	5	2
* KD Kang, OF	.291	364	66	106	18	61	60	99	3	4
* Kes Carter, OF	.280	396	50	111	16	57	35	111	5	4
Ryan Wagner, C	.270	111	23	30	3	16	11	25	0	0
Ryan Pineda, 2B	.269	398	70	107	8	36	51	90	8	7
Josh Mazzola, 3B	.259	390	72	101	20	78	50	95	8	5
* Mike Gilmartin, SS	.242	132	13	32	4	21	9	33	0	0
Bryan Johns, SS	.219	183	21	40	1	20	20	37	1	1
* Chad Mozingo, OF	.194	170	25	33	2	13	21	32	4	4
Luke Bailey, C	.152	237	18	36	6	22	16	76	1	1

PLAYER	W	L	ERA	G	SV	IP	H	BB	SO
Tyler Herron	5	1	0.80	7	0	56	31	12	47
* Mike Mason	0	1	0.81	6	0	11	6	4	13
Travis Ballew	1	0	1.63	10	4	11	7	4	13
Jose Almarante	4	2	2.73	25	1	115	99	39	86
Richie Mirowski	1	2	2.79	4	0	19	14	7	22
Colton Reavis	2	6	3.37	42	12	53	46	19	66
* Tyler Alexander	12	5	3.45	22	0	143	132	48	156
Taylor Stanton	5	5	3.73	18	0	113	127	38	87
Cody Scarpetta	2	1	4.61	5	0	27	25	31	30
Patrick Mincey	2	3	4.70	22	1	36	35	14	27
Dylan Mouzakes	2	0	4.76	7	0	23	27	9	23
* Will Mathis	2	5	4.77	44	0	66	82	32	72
Dan Sattler	2	2	5.09	23	0	30	25	37	32
* Will Solomon	6	3	5.14	16	0	72	82	34	39
Roman Madrid	0	2	5.19	15	0	17	7	16	11
Brian Ernst	3	4	5.56	7	0	44	48	25	39
* Matt Snyder	1	3	6.04	12	0	42	42	33	41

GARY SOUTHSHORE RAILCATS

PLAYER	AVG	AB	R	H	HR	RBI	BB	SO	SB	CS
* Reggie Wilson, OF	.337	92	26	31	1	14	16	16	4	1
# Jose Sermo, IF	.311	106	14	33	5	24	20	29	2	2
* Cameron Newell, OF	.303	234	40	71	0	24	35	31	4	1
* John Holland, IF	.302	129	19	39	1	14	14	41	1	1
# Frank Martinez, IF	.301	266	45	80	7	56	36	37	10	3
* Anthony Cheky, IF	.300	120	19	36	0	16	15	11	8	5
Chase Harris, OF	.299	134	23	40	1	12	7	26	8	3
* Alex Crosby, IF	.293	311	31	91	3	44	28	38	6	2
# Jaime Del Valle, C	.270	100	12	27	0	9	22	14	1	1
Jarred Mederos, IF	.268	298	26	80	2	38	17	58	6	4
Brennan Metzger, OF	.265	189	30	50	1	23	36	58	6	3
# Andy DeJesus, IF	.262	84	11	22	2	13	2	19	4	1
# Elbert Devarie, IF	.244	308	39	75	0	26	54	59	5	7
Jose Gonzalez, C	.232	207	23	48	4	21	25	56	0	3
Tillman Pugh, OF	.232	198	27	46	8	31	24	56	11	3
* Colin Willis, OF	.227	44	3	9	0	5	6	7	2	0
* Jeremy Hamilton, 1B	.221	195	19	43	0	27	25	47	1	0
Randy Santiesteban, IF	.207	58	9	12	1	3	1	12	1	1
* Matt Petrone, IF	.188	112	17	21	1	11	23	27	6	1
Mike Falsetti, C	.172	58	3	10	0	6	3	21	3	1
* Masato Fukae, OF	.159	82	9	13	0	3	6	32	3	3

PLAYER	W	L	ERA	G	SV	IP	H	BB	SO
Conrad Wozniak	0	0	1.03	7	0	17	11	3	17
Jorge De Leon	0	2	1.70	21	11	32	24	17	32
Aryton Costa	1	0	2.36	6	0	19	10	4	10
*Lars Liguori	1	1	2.60	19	0	28	35	7	13
Santiago Rodriguez	6	5	2.60	36	3	48	47	24	39
Charle Rosario	11	4	3.12	24	0	155	141	46	120
*Andy Roberts	4	1	3.31	23	3	35	39	15	24
*Alex Gunn	2	0	3.37	12	1	43	38	11	23
Karl Triana	4	4	3.50	17	0	105	89	39	79
Richard Castillo	7	8	3.64	23	0	141	153	39	73
Manny Arciniega	0	0	4.67	11	0	17	24	7	17
John Kovalik	0	1	4.84	20	0	26	28	14	17
*Moises Melendez	4	1	4.90	21	1	33	39	18	32
Taylor Black	7	6	4.99	33	7	70	84	39	34
Zach Staniewicz	0	1	6.00	2	0	15	17	7	7
Travis McGee	4	8	6.47	25	0	72	82	32	69
Carlos Pinales	0	3	9.48	5	0	12	12	1	7

JOPLIN BLASTERS

PLAYER	AVG	AB	R	H	HR	RBI	BB	SO	SB	CS
# Oscar Mesa, OF	.356	90	21	32	2	8	9	10	7	4
Geraldo Valentin, IF	.329	401	71	132	18	65	27	33	3	2
Mitch Glasser, IF	.314	350	66	110	3	47	44	39	16	5
Willie Cabrera, OF	.311	161	19	50	8	43	18	25	2	0
Zack Burling, OF	.307	88	14	27	2	10	9	31	10	2
# Charlie Valerio, C	.297	219	29	65	6	32	18	38	0	2
Brandon Tierney, IF	.292	168	26	49	5	33	7	29	1	1
# Edwin Gomez, IF	.292	202	24	59	4	25	23	39	1	0
Juan Medina, C	.291	79	6	23	0	4	8	20	0	0
Jake Taylor, IF	.286	42	7	12	1	3	9	12	0	0
KC Huth, OF	.276	203	23	56	2	17	6	54	7	3
Jesus Solorzano, OF	.254	71	11	18	1	5	5	12	4	2
*Will Soto, IF	.250	140	8	35	1	17	10	26	3	6
*Axel Johnson, P	.246	61	10	15	0	3	6	15	0	1
Alex Polston, IF	.239	163	18	39	2	8	20	44	6	3
Sean Smith, OF	.227	97	18	22	5	13	12	37	7	3
*Conor Sullivan, C	.226	84	8	19	1	10	5	22	1	0
Cory Morales, IF	.218	119	7	26	1	8	5	16	0	2
Aaron Brill, IF	.210	62	10	13	0	4	5	15	1	0
Mark Krueger, OF	.209	153	16	32	2	20	16	49	1	1
Ermindo Escobar, C	.202	84	4	17	0	5	4	11	1	0
Ronnie Richardson, OF	.200	45	9	9	0	3	6	13	3	1
Greyson Bogden, SS	.191	47	6	9	0	4	1	12	1	0
Sergio Leon, IF	.175	80	6	14	2	8	3	27	1	1
Matt Martinez, OF	.167	42	4	7	1	2	2	15	0	1

PLAYER	W	L	ERA	G	SV	IP	H	BB	SO
Winston Abreu	0	0	1.50	11	4	12	9	2	21
Victor Capellan	2	1	2.36	32	7	38	22	18	44
Keith Picht	1	4	3.33	41	1	57	55	31	61
Jose Ortega	3	2	3.58	29	0	33	31	19	33
Mario Morales	2	3	3.78	7	0	36	41	5	20
Harrison Lee	0	1	3.95	3	0	14	12	2	3
Santos Arias	2	2	4.00	8	0	43	44	15	32
Roby Romero	2	2	4.23	27	3	34	34	7	22
Carlos Fuentes	2	5	4.59	28	1	82	90	39	67
*Axel Johnson	0	0	4.72	12	0	13	9	8	5
Victor Ramirez	2	0	4.83	11	0	22	18	6	20
*Wander Perez	3	4	4.88	10	0	55	55	13	47
Patrick Mincey	1	0	5.34	10	0	30	26	11	16
Matt Parish	2	1	5.40	8	0	13	16	10	15
*Noel Arguelles	1	2	5.40	5	0	25	30	16	22
Josh Hodges	2	4	5.44	9	0	45	44	21	20
*Luis Gonzalez	2	4	5.61	7	0	42	37	16	29
*Frank Del Valle	1	3	5.70	6	0	30	38	12	27
Alex De La Cruz	2	7	6.04	14	0	70	83	34	63
Tyler Herr	0	2	6.75	8	0	11	18	8	10
Raul Rivera	1	3	7.20	8	0	20	29	13	15
Ethan Rosebeck	0	1	7.97	6	0	15	17	6	8
*Alberto Castillo	1	2	8.10	14	0	17	22	6	9
*Josue Montanez	1	4	8.36	8	0	24	23	17	20
Jason Zgardowski	1	0	9.25	7	0	12	22	10	17
Josh Evans	0	3	11.11	4	0	11	19	6	7

KANSAS CITY T-BONES

PLAYER	AVG	AB	R	H	HR	RBI	BB	SO	SB	CS
* Dalton Wheat, OF	.335	206	28	69	0	27	24	36	9	3
Brandon Tierney, IF	.323	164	20	53	1	15	6	27	3	0
* Brett Wiley, IF	.305	364	46	111	5	45	32	74	3	0
Ryan Retz, OF	.298	47	2	14	2	9	3	15	1	0
* Tyler Massey, OF	.266	395	56	105	7	30	45	59	15	5
Jake Blackwood, IF	.259	390	45	101	14	66	27	72	2	1
Starlin Rodriguez, IF	.257	269	39	69	7	29	17	52	11	2
Brian Erie, C	.253	79	7	20	0	11	6	19	2	1
* Tyson Gillies, OF	.252	163	23	41	4	16	13	39	1	1
# Vladimir Frias, SS	.246	358	50	88	7	40	38	52	16	8
Robby Kuzdale, OF	.239	88	11	21	2	8	19	15	4	1
Tyler Moore, C	.234	64	6	15	1	5	9	11	0	0
Jimmy Mojica, SS	.222	81	7	18	1	11	10	16	0	2
Anthony Gallas, OF	.221	335	59	74	16	48	45	89	3	1
# Steven Swingle, C	.220	91	10	20	2	8	8	29	0	2
Christian Torres, OF	.205	44	5	9	1	5	2	7	0	1
Nolan Johnson, C	.191	47	2	9	0	0	1	12	0	0
Cole Leonida, C	.175	63	6	11	2	7	4	14	0	0
* Nate Tenbrink, IF	.167	30	4	5	0	0	3	9	2	0
Sergio Leon, IF	.139	79	4	11	2	6	2	32	0	0

PLAYER	W	L	ERA	G	SV	IP	H	BB	SO
*Tyler Ybarra	1	0	2.53	9	1	11	10	8	12
*Mike Kickham	3	5	2.82	14	0	86	78	26	73
Mark Haynes	5	2	3.24	40	15	44	32	31	50
*Evan DeLuca	3	3	3.78	41	0	52	55	33	46
Josh Hodges	3	4	4.02	13	0	78	80	26	66
Sean Furney	3	3	4.02	10	0	47	40	32	30
*Josh Tols	5	4	4.17	27	0	60	50	30	60
Jared Messer	5	4	4.25	24	0	104	107	40	62
David Holman	4	5	4.36	23	0	78	105	30	35
Jordan Cooper	3	6	4.58	19	0	112	125	34	55
Johnny Shuttlesworth	3	7	5.03	36	2	70	79	31	61
Aaron Baker	2	4	6.00	28	2	30	40	13	21
Casey Barnes	1	3	7.51	5	0	26	37	4	13
Brett Zawacki	0	3	7.60	26	0	34	42	19	37
Jeremy Strawn	0	4	7.76	6	0	24	29	7	17

LAREDO LEMURS

PLAYER	AVG	AB	R	H	HR	RBI	BB	SO	SB	CS
Leandro Castro, OF	.316	174	36	55	9	26	7	25	5	4
* Drew Martinez, OF	.309	307	41	95	0	31	34	35	16	7
Abel Nieves, IF	.290	259	39	75	3	19	41	39	3	3
Jesus Posso, C	.282	273	27	77	9	46	18	44	0	0
Denis Phipps, OF	.280	357	65	100	24	62	46	85	21	3
Cesar Valera, IF	.272	235	30	64	4	29	28	44	7	5
* Ty Morrison, OF	.270	356	57	96	5	40	44	83	13	5
# Alvaro Rondon, IF	.263	315	32	83	1	37	17	54	20	2
Travis Denker, IF	.263	76	15	20	7	17	15	10	1	0
* Zane Chavez, C	.260	273	36	71	6	38	26	39	5	1
J.D. Pulfer, IF	.237	371	54	88	9	58	38	57	11	3
Burt Reynolds, OF	.208	87	8	16	1	6	5	18	2	1
Matt Koch, C	.205	83	8	17	1	11	7	13	0	0
* Reggie Wilson, OF	.182	55	10	10	0	2	9	12	0	2
Brennan Metzger, RF	.150	60	9	9	0	2	6	19	0	1
Jimmy Norris, IF	.148	61	9	9	0	2	6	9	3	2

PLAYER	W	L	ERA	G	SV	IP	H	BB	SO
Matt Sergey	4	0	0.81	7	0	44	26	15	56
Kyle Winkler	4	0	0.84	8	0	11	5	4	7
*Zack Dodson	2	1	1.27	6	0	28	21	13	26
Dan Reynolds	2	0	1.68	14	0	16	9	3	27
Barret Loux	3	2	2.53	9	0	53	53	11	54
Manny Martinez	3	2	2.53	8	0	11	9	1	8
Luis De La Cruz	3	1	2.64	45	5	51	43	23	48
Jeff Inman	2	3	2.70	45	17	50	40	18	49
* Luis Pollorena	4	2	2.82	24	3	45	34	9	26
Ryan Beckman	8	8	2.91	21	0	133	129	24	97
Jose Nivar	3	2	3.15	34	0	66	68	33	76
Kamakani Usui	4	4	3.24	41	0	42	29	22	48
Troy Marks	8	4	3.83	24	1	99	93	34	94
Gabe Perez	1	1	4.21	8	0	24	24	10	38

PLAYER	W	L	ERA	G	SV	IP	H	BB	SO
*Harold Guerrero	1	0	4.53	39	1	48	43	27	64
Danny Moskovits	2	4	6.51	13	0	47	60	18	20
Kyle DeVore	0	1	6.53	6	0	21	24	11	13
Scott Garner	0	1	6.58	8	1	27	34	12	15
*Josue Montanez	0	2	7.04	4	0	15	26	8	7
*Joe Testa	1	2	8.30	6	0	13	15	6	14
*Matt Bywater	0	1	9.90	5	0	10	9	11	8

LINCOLN SALTDOGS

PLAYER	AVG	AB	R	H	HR	RBI	BB	SO	SB	CS
Christian Ibarra, IF	.371	70	15	26	5	13	13	13	0	0
* Austin Gallagher, IF	.349	63	8	22	1	6	3	6	0	0
Curt Smith, IF	.331	314	50	104	17	60	36	43	0	2
* Connor Teykl, IF	.323	31	1	10	0	6	5	9	0	0
Cesar Valera, IF	.307	75	9	23	0	6	6	12	0	2
Rene Leveret, 1B	.306	291	36	89	7	41	41	38	6	1
Luis Alen, C	.297	354	41	105	9	53	43	23	1	1
Brandon Jacobs, OF	.280	304	43	85	11	34	31	73	4	1
Dayner Moreira, IF	.274	164	13	45	0	5	0	13	4	6
Robby Kuzdale, OF	.263	240	43	63	2	17	37	48	9	7
Juan Martinez, IF	.260	50	5	13	1	8	5	15	0	0
# Tyler Urps, IF	.249	189	18	47	0	11	19	45	2	2
Dan Hennigan, IF	.243	70	12	17	0	5	14	9	1	1
* Jon Smith, OF	.241	295	35	71	12	52	34	65	5	5
* Austin Darby, OF	.225	178	27	40	2	22	13	42	2	1
Pat Kelly, IF	.194	155	12	30	1	8	8	27	4	2
Chase Harris, OF	.191	89	11	17	0	4	9	18	3	3
Pat McKenna, IF	.188	64	9	12	0	7	13	23	0	1
* Mike Gilmartin, IF	.175	57	5	10	1	4	9	11	0	0
Ryan Wiggins, C	.174	161	12	28	4	20	8	70	0	1
Freddy Flores, IF	.143	28	4	4	0	3	1	6	0	0
* Alexi Colon, OF	.121	33	3	4	0	1	5	6	0	2

PLAYER	W	L	ERA	G	SV	IP	H	BB	SO
Clayton Cook	1	0	0.90	10	0	10	6	2	16
Evan Reed	3	4	1.97	40	22	41	34	11	44
Lindsey Caughel	6	3	2.09	19	0	125	101	24	120
*Ryan Davis	0	1	2.28	23	0	20	11	14	19
J.R. Bunda	3	1	2.31	9	0	12	9	3	8
*Bennett Parry	1	0	3.24	4	0	17	10	11	13
Shairon Martis	9	8	3.33	24	0	121	121	31	93
Casey Barnes	2	1	3.66	7	0	39	52	10	20
Matt Larkins	7	7	3.69	21	1	124	156	28	73
Ryan O'Sullivan	4	3	4.15	40	3	43	43	15	49
*Jeffrey McKenzie	5	4	4.32	30	4	67	84	20	29
Zac Westcott	0	0	4.35	8	0	10	15	7	8
Brad Orosey	5	5	4.44	19	0	117	126	48	76
*Randy Zeigler	0	1	4.80	7	0	15	20	8	10
Matt Shepherd	0	4	5.34	10	0	32	38	22	22
Stephen Shackleford	4	4	5.69	31	2	36	42	22	36
Graham Johnson	0	1	6.75	3	0	11	18	5	6

SIOUX CITY EXPLORERS

PLAYER	AVG	AB	R	H	HR	RBI	BB	SO	SB	CS
Nate Samson, IF	.350	391	68	137	6	68	54	24	31	4
* Noah Perio, IF	.338	145	27	49	3	36	10	10	1	2
* LeVon Washington, OF	.336	149	23	50	0	30	33	7	1	
# Derrick Robinson, OF	.313	348	63	109	2	36	42	59	31	10
* Tim Colwell, OF	.301	392	59	118	3	55	31	64	28	12
Brendan Slattery, C	.292	154	31	45	2	19	17	30	0	0
# Ralph Henriquez, C	.267	345	44	92	6	46	47	63	7	2
# Matty Johnson, OF	.265	196	29	52	1	21	22	24	9	6
* Ino Patron, 1B	.264	144	19	38	2	19	11	30	3	0
Jarek Cunningham, IF	.261	234	31	61	4	33	25	61	5	4
* Tommy Mendonca, 3B	.254	347	55	88	8	61	56	88	3	2
Bryan Johns, SS	.215	93	13	20	2	13	9	22	2	1
Matt Koch, C	.205	132	17	27	3	23	17	43	1	1

PLAYER	W	L	ERA	G	SV	IP	H	BB	SO
Tayler Scott	1	0	1.88	17	0	29	23	6	32
Connor Overton	5	1	1.96	30	11	37	21	12	45
Jake Kuebler	3	2	2.15	35	0	75	55	29	49
Rob Wort	6	4	2.37	35	6	53	30	24	70

PLAYER	W	L	ERA	G	SV	IP	H	BB	SO
*Nick Lomascolo	0	1	3.72	11	0	10	6	8	11
Dylan Rheault	1	1	3.97	33	1	45	53	28	24
*Cody Forsythe	11	5	4.38	21	0	125	105	54	102
Graham Johnson	5	3	4.41	13	0	73	74	32	39
P.J. Francescon	5	7	4.82	23	2	41	46	16	36
Bubba Maxwell	1	1	5.00	8	0	27	31	8	21
Jordan Risse	2	1	5.31	24	1	61	63	36	45
Bryan Escanio	5	3	5.60	14	0	79	87	30	56
*Hobbs Johnson	1	2	5.60	9	0	18	17	18	18
James Walsh	2	2	6.10	10	0	38	43	12	32
Ryan Zimmerman	3	9	6.41	19	0	87	92	63	62
Michael Pereslucha	0	0	6.51	6	0	10	14	8	8
Eric Wordekemper	1	2	7.44	4	0	19	26	10	8
Trevor Bayless	0	2	8.80	12	0	15	16	12	18
Matt LeVert	0	0	10.80	8	0	12	16	12	8

SIOUX FALLS CANARIES

PLAYER	AVG	AB	R	H	HR	RBI	BB	SO	SB	CS
* Patrick Fiala, IF	.320	50	6	16	3	13	2	13	0	0
Blake Schmit, IF	.319	370	61	118	5	29	32	54	20	9
J.C. Linares, RF	.314	172	18	54	4	32	12	29	2	0
* B.J. Guinn, SS	.297	111	15	33	3	16	8	21	0	0
# Darwin Perez, IF	.292	226	39	66	3	22	27	35	12	5
Jake Taylor, IF	.270	244	43	66	12	38	33	67	6	2
David Bergin, 1B	.262	282	34	74	15	58	48	75	2	1
* Taylor Zeutenhorst, C	.261	69	11	18	2	9	6	23	2	0
* Rubi Silva, IF	.256	39	5	10	0	4	3	6	1	0
* Ethan Chapman, OF	.249	381	48	95	6	33	28	68	20	6
Cameron Monger, OF	.240	275	44	66	10	34	45	98	17	9
# Michael Pair, C	.238	105	12	25	6	16	16	22	1	0
* Chris Grayson, OF	.229	83	8	19	2	9	8	14	5	2
Nolan Johnson, C	.222	81	8	18	0	4	9	23	0	2
Ryan Lashley, 3B	.219	96	5	21	2	15	3	14	0	0
# Frank Martinez, IF	.215	79	13	17	4	15	6	8	0	0
# Jerome Pena, IF	.212	66	11	14	0	3	9	15	0	0
Aaron Owen, C	.206	180	26	37	3	15	17	62	9	5
Cameron Garfield, C	.158	38	4	6	0	4	2	6	0	0
Mike Falsetti, C	.088	114	14	10	0	7	18	40	1	2

PLAYER	W	L	ERA	G	SV	IP	H	BB	SO
Jose Ortega	0	0	0.87	11	5	10	4	4	11
*Joe Bircher	6	6	2.54	19	0	124	119	34	108
Dylan Thompson	5	2	3.30	22	0	68	76	16	49
*Billy Waltrip	3	1	3.69	34	3	39	24	29	51
*Kris Regas	5	7	4.07	28	0	102	128	41	87
*Josh Ferrell	3	1	4.15	43	0	61	56	23	66
James Jones	0	2	4.80	27	0	30	25	15	26
Jimmer Kennedy	1	0	5.94	17	1	17	20	12	9
Stephen Bougher	2	10	5.94	19	0	112	140	43	69
*Misael Siverio	3	6	6.27	10	0	57	77	19	53
Ray Hanson	1	7	6.90	10	0	57	77	24	37
Madison Boer	4	7	7.05	41	7	52	68	29	42
Shawn Blackwell	6	8	7.07	26	0	90	124	31	63
*Matt Bywater	0	2	7.64	4	0	18	14	21	17
Lance Fairchild	0	0	8.10	8	0	10	11	6	8

ST. PAUL SAINTS

PLAYER	AVG	AB	R	H	HR	RBI	BB	SO	SB	CS
* Mike Gilmartin, IF	.326	46	12	15	3	10	8	9	0	0
Alonzo Harris, OF	.307	391	67	120	15	58	27	73	43	9
Nate Hanson, IF	.304	322	63	98	12	63	33	28	0	0
Tony Thomas, IF	.296	375	63	111	13	65	39	87	7	3
Willie Argo, OF	.294	228	54	67	8	41	43	55	14	2
* Angelo Songco, 1B	.285	270	53	77	13	45	46	51	4	1
David Bergin, IF	.279	43	8	12	4	13	4	11	0	0
* Aaron Gretz, C	.277	191	21	53	3	25	15	22	0	0
* Dan Johnson, P	.277	65	12	18	6	15	9	8	0	0
* Brady Burzynski, IF	.271	144	27	39	0	12	24	22	7	2
Tanner Vavra, IF	.270	270	33	73	0	21	17	47	9	2
Breland Almadova, OF	.256	336	57	86	4	40	38	67	29	8
Tony Caldwell, C	.256	219	37	56	12	47	35	69	0	0

PLAYER	AVG	AB	R	H	HR	RBI	BB	SO	SB	CS
Trever Adams, IF	.253	95	17	24	8	19	13	31	0	1
# Ryan Cavan, IF	.231	39	7	9	0	4	10	6	0	0
Vinny DiFazio, C	.222	54	5	12	0	2	8	11	0	0
Bryson Myles, OF	.216	37	5	8	1	6	6	9	2	2
Chad Christensen, OF	.194	72	11	14	2	9	3	20	4	1
Maxx Garrett, C	.193	57	9	11	2	9	9	21	0	0
Sam Maus, IF	.193	109	8	21	0	16	15	40	0	0

PLAYER	W	L	ERA	G	SV	IP	H	BB	SO
Ryan Rodebaugh	3	2	1.84	38	23	39	29	8	52
* Caleb Thielbar	5	2	2.39	42	4	64	50	15	56
* Cody Wheeler	0	3	2.91	24	0	34	29	24	36
* Kramer Sneed	0	1	3.05	3	0	18	17	9	18
Mark Hamburger	12	6	3.29	21	0	159	165	22	100
Benji Waite	2	2	3.52	27	0	46	41	20	42
Robert Coe	11	3	4.23	21	0	119	115	68	75
Cody Scarpetta	1	0	4.30	5	0	23	20	17	19
* Eric Veglahn	3	4	4.38	10	0	53	50	18	32
John Straka	10	3	4.48	17	0	94	107	22	77
Dan Johnson	4	3	4.50	7	0	40	34	20	27
Gene Escat	0	0	4.50	15	0	16	14	24	14
* Kody Knaus	2	2	4.53	12	0	46	53	20	19
* Corey Williams	2	2	5.40	10	0	27	27	19	20
Jeff Shields	2	2	5.64	4	0	22	28	9	12
* Michael Strong	1	1	5.83	7	0	12	16	8	5
Alec Crawford	2	3	9.66	10	0	36	49	17	21
Zac Westcott	0	0	10.24	6	0	10	12	8	5
Chris Peacock	1	0	11.17	7	0	10	12	10	9

TEXAS AIRHOGS

PLAYER	AVG	AB	R	H	HR	RBI	BB	SO	SB	CS
Kenny Peoples-Walls, OF	.349	86	13	30	1	9	3	21	1	1
* Devon Rodriguez, 1B	.302	381	38	115	6	49	22	53	1	2
Brian Bistagne, IF	.285	355	47	101	8	36	27	53	24	1
# Leon Byrd, IF	.284	190	26	54	3	14	22	49	2	1
Michael Hur, IF	.266	364	48	97	4	35	35	71	5	4
* Cody Lenahan, IF	.264	329	45	87	12	49	14	90	4	2
Burt Reynolds, OF	.261	261	51	68	23	44	31	75	11	2
Juan Sanchez, IF	.253	395	44	100	11	51	21	71	6	6
Cory Morales, IF	.236	140	13	33	2	12	10	23	1	3
* Austin Gallagher, IF	.233	202	22	47	3	28	16	24	3	2
Michael Miller, C	.224	232	22	52	6	28	17	43	1	0
Nick Akins, RF	.215	195	23	42	6	14	13	65	1	1
K.J. Alexander, IF	.206	34	4	7	0	3	0	8	0	0
Mike Valadez, C	.191	115	4	22	1	10	3	25	0	0
* Will Dupont*, IF	.167	66	11	11	2	8	6	22	0	1

PLAYER	W	L	ERA	G	SV	IP	H	BB	SO
Roman Madrid	1	0	0.63	3	0	14.1	12	11	16
Jack Karraker	1	1	1.93	14	0	14	14	2	11
Trey Masek	1	0	2.05	20	1	22	18	15	16
* Ethan Carnes	2	0	3.45	5	0	31.1	30	10	18
Richard Suniga	0	0	3.78	15	0	16.2	13	14	13
Diego Ibarra	0	4	3.89	6	0	37	49	8	22
Alan Oaks	2	4	4.03	40	8	38	42	14	43
* Tyler Ihrig	2	3	4.14	34	0	45.2	60	15	44
* David Russo	3	7	4.28	35	0	69.1	72	25	52
* Derek Callahan	0	5	4.45	7	0	30.1	30	12	20
Tyler Harris	2	2	4.99	24	0	48.2	59	22	39
Matt Shepherd	3	5	5.45	14	0	76	77	36	63
* Griffin Russell	4	9	5.68	21	0	103	126	49	82
Carlos Misell	2	8	5.82	36	6	77.1	97	24	56
Cody Hebner	5	8	5.83	18	0	97.1	111	50	80
Palmer Betts	3	2	5.91	6	0	35	35	17	28
Cody Culp	0	1	6.57	23	0	24.2	39	1	13
Sam Martin	3	6	7.69	16	0	59.2	79	26	35

WICHITA WINGNUTS

PLAYER	AVG	AB	R	H	HR	RBI	BB	SO	SB	CS
Matt Chavez, 1B	.359	259	42	93	16	61	27	58	0	2
Harrison Kain, OF	.358	240	38	86	3	48	26	24	15	9
Nick Van Stratten, OF	.339	62	10	21	0	9	2	4	3	0
Brent Clevlen, OF	.313	348	66	109	17	63	38	82	5	2

PLAYER	AVG	AB	R	H	HR	RBI	BB	SO	SB	CS
* Zack Cox, 3B	.290	420	77	122	12	64	34	78	6	1
* T.J. Mittelstaedt, IF	.288	365	77	105	16	74	80	106	23	5
* Christian Stringer, IF	.287	411	82	118	1	34	56	39	22	8
* Brennen Salgado, OF	.276	156	20	43	3	30	20	49	1	1
Brent Dean, C	.258	225	27	58	3	31	14	40	13	3
Richard Prigatano, OF	.256	281	42	72	5	38	41	82	26	5
Leo Vargas, IF	.250	352	47	88	3	38	17	74	15	3
Martin Medina, C	.245	204	32	50	1	29	22	44	1	0
Dustin Geiger, 1B	.234	141	17	33	2	21	21	21	4	0
# Tyler Urps, IF	.176	34	2	6	0	1	3	8	0	0

PLAYER	W	L	ERA	G	SV	IP	H	BB	SO
Ryan Kussmaul	0	0	1.62	3	0	17	11	5	11
Tyler Kane	2	1	1.68	3	0	16	16	3	10
Gage Smith	1	0	1.80	10	0	10	8	2	2
Chad Nading	0	1	1.83	40	2	39	36	17	30
* Frankie Reed	6	3	1.86	48	21	53	42	17	53
Mike Devine	1	0	2.07	10	0	13	14	2	8
Seth Harvey	2	0	2.07	22	0	22	13	8	26
Luis Pardo	0	0	2.53	9	0	11	9	4	12
Chase Johnson	4	2	3.23	34	1	39	29	24	41
Alex Boshers	12	3	3.29	24	0	123	147	21	66
Garrett Gould	0	1	3.46	5	0	13	9	6	12
Jesse Pratt	6	2	3.47	35	1	78	85	18	49
Jon Link	7	5	3.72	14	0	89	104	15	66
Tim Brown	9	4	4.11	19	0	125	161	5	43
* Charles Leesman	2	2	5.18	7	0	33	39	15	18
Eddie Medina	6	6	5.56	20	0	100	117	40	63
Fabian Roman	2	1	6.39	22	0	25	26	19	13
* Todd Kibby	1	5	6.86	8	0	39	48	15	33
* Anthony Capra	3	9	9.91	8	0	26	25	53	22

WINNIPEG GOLDEYES

PLAYER	AVG	AB	R	H	HR	RBI	BB	SO	SB	CS
David Rohm, OF	.339	366	58	124	7	71	39	49	3	4
Willie Cabrera, OF	.324	179	39	58	9	34	23	31	2	0
* Josh Romanski, OF	.305	328	67	100	9	64	60	48	7	5
* Adam Heisler, OF	.300	330	60	99	8	49	48	63	27	7
Reggie Abercrombie, OF	.297	374	71	111	20	68	31	95	21	4
Casio Grider, IF	.279	348	61	97	11	68	43	97	22	5
* Jacob Rogers, 1B	.275	258	51	71	8	44	56	76	1	1
* Wes Darvill, IF	.262	340	51	89	2	41	41	47	18	0
Maikol Gonzalez, IF	.256	394	72	101	3	43	75	52	31	4
Carlton Tanabe, C	.250	228	30	57	3	38	10	45	0	2
Ridge Hoopii-Haslam, IF	.239	155	23	37	4	30	23	58	4	4
* Tanner Murphy, C	.208	144	10	30	1	18	13	37	0	0

PLAYER	W	L	ERA	G	SV	IP	H	BB	SO
* Eric Eadington	4	4	3.00	42	9	45	23	24	63
Cameron McVey	2	2	3.40	39	2	37	30	16	41
* Kyle Anderson	3	1	3.43	29	1	73	81	7	37
* Kevin McGovern	8	3	3.55	21	0	129	117	41	125
Victor Capellan	1	1	3.95	13	2	14	14	6	12
Mikey O'Brien	10	4	4.34	21	0	122	124	49	78
Brandon Shimo	2	2	4.44	43	2	51	55	15	38
Kyle Lotzkar	1	0	4.50	18	0	20	17	16	21
Robert Tasin	0	1	4.50	19	3	22	23	10	17
Edwin Carl	10	6	4.69	20	0	113	104	53	115
Duke von Schamann	8	7	4.87	22	0	116	135	23	66
Zachary Dando	0	2	5.40	11	0	22	28	8	9
Ethan Carnes	6	3	5.79	15	0	73	86	30	42
* Jailen Peguero	2	4	5.89	18	7	18	22	12	23
* Conor Spink	1	1	7.50	17	0	18	24	8	16

ATLANTIC LEAGUE

Perched by themselves, half a country away from the rest of the Atlantic League, the Sugar Land Skeeters turned themselves into one of the top teams in the league almost instantly.

But until this year, they didn't have a trophy. Sugar Land won an Atlantic League-record 95 games in 2013 but failed to make it to the championship series. A year later, the Skeeters made it to the championship series only to be swept by the Lancaster Barnstormers.

This year, the Skeeters finished the job. It wasn't the best Skeeters

team during the regular season, but a club led by Jeremy Barfield's 27 home runs and Roy Merritt's 8-2, 2.99 season on the mound, Sugar Land swept Long Island for the title.

FREEDOM DIVISION	W	L	PCT	GB
York Revolution	76	64	.543	—
* Sugar Land Skeeters	74	66	.529	2
Lancaster Barnstormers	67	73	.479	9
Southern Maryland Blue Crabs	57	83	.407	19

LIBERTY DIVISION	W	L	PCT	GB
Somerset Patriots	77	63	.550	—
* Long Island Ducks	72	68	.514	5
New Britain Bees	71	69	.507	6
Bridgeport Bluefish	66	74	.471	11

*Wild Card

PLAYOFFS: Semifinals—Sugar Land defeated York 3-0 and Long Island defeated Somerset 3-2 in best-of-5 series. **Finals**—Sugar Land defeated Long Island 3-0 in best-of-5 series.

ATTENDANCE: Somerset 360,755; Long Island 352,728; Sugar Land 300,331; Lancaster 247,943; York 237,433; New Britain 214,635; Southern Maryland 201,883; Bridgeport 183,921.

MANAGERS: Bridgeport—Luis Rodriguez; Lancaster—Butch Hobson; Long Island—Kevin Baez; New Britain—Stan Cliburn; Somerset—Brett Jodie; Southern Maryland—Jeremy Owens; Sugar Land—Gary Gaetti; York—Mark Mason.

ALL-STAR TEAM: C: James Skelton, New Britain. **1B:** K.C. Hobson, Lancaster. **2B:** Eric Farris, Somerset. **3B:** David Vidal, Somerset. **SS:** Luis Hernandez, Bridgeport. **OF:** Jeremy Barfield, Sugar Land; Caleb Gindl, Lancaster; Fehlandt Lentini, Long Island. **DH:** Joel Guzman, York. **SP:** Jonathan Albaladejo, Bridgeport. **RP:** Andrew Johnston, Sugar Land. **Closer:** Mike DeMark, York.

PLAYER OF THE YEAR: Jeremy Barfield, of, Sugar Land. **PITCHER OF THE YEAR:** Jonathan Albaladejo, Bridgeport. **MANAGER OF THE YEAR:** Stan Cliburn, New Britain. **DEFENSIVE PLAYER OF THE YEAR:** Eric Farris, INF, Somerset.

BATTING LEADERS

PLAYER	AVG	AB	R	H	HR	RBI	SB
Chavez, Endy, Bridgeport	.345	371	55	128	2	37	5
Dotel, Wellington, Bridgeport	.335	361	58	121	6	49	19
Cleary Jr., Delta, Long Island	.321	405	51	130	3	52	32
Hobson, K.C., Lancaster	.320	363	60	116	24	65	5
Lentini, Fehlandt, Long Island	.313	571	108	179	9	75	51
Hague, Rick, Sugar Land	.311	437	69	136	17	67	12
Eggleston, Aharon, Somerset	.310	458	73	142	8	55	9
Barfield, Jeremy, Sugar Land	.306	510	87	156	27	85	2
Maddox, Craig, New Britain	.306	510	56	156	10	56	1
Snyder, Michael, Southern Md.	.304	336	44	102	25	65	0

PITCHING LEADERS

PLAYER	W	L	ERA	IP	H	R	ER
Simon, Kyle, New Britain	8	6	2.77	120.1	113	49	37
Merritt, Roy, Sugar Land	8	2	2.99	120.1	117	45	40
Grening, Brian, Southern Md.	10	6	3.09	116.2	113	49	40
Gailey, Frank, York	5	3	3.14	123.1	109	55	43
Doyle, Terry, Lancaster	6	6	3.29	123	118	53	45
Brownell, John, Long Island	10	8	3.30	169	175	69	62
Burres, Brian, Southern Md.	11	9	3.33	156.2	151	70	58
Leverett, Jarret, Long Island	6	9	3.74	115.2	137	56	48
Gallagher, Sean, Sugar Land	10	8	3.79	154.1	169	80	65
Thompson, Aaron, Sugar Land	9	5	3.98	133.1	148	69	59

BRIDGEPORT BLUEFISH

PLAYER	AVG	AB	R	H	HR	RBI	BB	SO	SB
* Sean Burroughs, 3B	.369	141	21	52	1	18	11	13	0
* Endy Chavez, OF	.345	371	55	128	2	37	33	21	5
Welington Dotel, OF	.335	361	58	121	6	49	29	79	19
Jose Gil, C	.314	191	26	60	3	35	18	31	4
* Carlos Sosa, OF	.312	77	11	24	1	12	14	7	8
Angelys Nina, IF	.286	213	26	61	4	30	5	39	8
Jose Cuevas, IF	.286	482	77	138	10	65	48	74	4
Jonathan Galvez, OF	.283	318	54	90	9	50	42	68	10
# Luis Hernandez, IF	.283	565	78	160	1	56	30	64	10

PLAYER	AVG	AB	R	H	HR	RBI	BB	SO	SB
# Jiwan James, OF	.276	29	6	8	0	0	1	4	1
Geraldo Valentin, OF	.275	51	6	14	1	7	0	3	1
Wilkin Ramirez, OF	.274	84	8	23	1	8	3	18	2
* Rossmel Perez, C	.269	186	18	50	1	20	11	13	0
# Luis Rodriguez, IF	.259	243	26	63	2	23	27	22	1
# Ruben Sosa, IF	.255	51	5	13	0	4	3	15	1
Anthony Giansanti, OF	.247	291	41	72	6	35	13	57	8
* Connor David, C	.230	61	7	14	1	3	0	15	0
Luis Nunez, IF	.229	349	34	80	2	38	16	51	8
Josh Vitters, IF	.226	265	36	60	5	25	22	72	0
* Dan Johnson, IF	.223	139	21	31	5	27	14	27	0
* Adron Chambers, OF	.218	87	14	19	2	10	8	27	2
* Luis Domoromo, OF	.152	92	6	14	0	6	5	19	1
Alex Marquez, C	.150	40	2	6	0	5	3	13	0

PLAYER	W	L	ERA	G	SV	IP	H	BB	SO
* Chris Rearick	2	3	1.89	7	0	33	29	11	29
Sammy Gervacio	2	3	1.98	35	3	36	29	7	34
Taylor Thompson	3	2	1.98	36	6	36	24	8	44
Paul Demny	5	2	2.59	38	0	35	27	25	45
Scott Shuman	1	3	2.76	28	0	29	25	15	42
* Brian Moran	0	4	3.11	38	0	35	39	12	42
David Carpenter	1	0	3.28	36	6	36	34	16	39
John Church	1	2	3.50	24	0	26	28	8	21
David Kubiak	7	4	3.75	20	0	101	92	31	106
* Mike Antonini	4	7	3.91	17	0	87	90	37	59
Jonathan Albaladejo	15	6	4.06	28	0	173	194	34	164
* Jim Patterson	2	5	4.30	39	0	102	117	37	89
D.J. Mitchell	2	3	4.39	12	0	55	58	28	48
* Matthew Spann	3	1	4.44	6	0	26	32	21	21
Blake Beavan	5	4	4.59	18	0	92	126	16	61
Ross Seaton	1	3	4.82	9	0	50	53	20	24
Joe Kuzia	3	1	5.18	34	0	42	55	11	15
* Eric Niesen	2	3	5.20	29	2	28	35	8	33
Jose Veras	2	2	5.32	26	12	24	22	10	25
* Matt Iannazzo	1	4	5.78	29	0	37	47	17	30
David Anderson	1	2	6.64	9	0	22	37	7	12
R.J. Hively	1	4	6.79	16	0	49	67	20	48
Dan Johnson	0	2	7.50	9	0	18	16	15	14

LANCASTER BARNSTORMERS

PLAYER	AVG	AB	R	H	HR	RBI	BB	SO	SB
* K.C. Hobson, 1B	.320	363	60	116	24	65	42	67	5
* Logan Schafer, OF	.299	67	8	20	2	9	3	11	1
# Trayvon Robinson, OF	.298	171	37	51	6	20	24	32	13
# Josh Bell, IF	.296	476	71	141	19	87	71	105	1
Jeff Kobernus, IF	.295	224	32	66	1	22	6	43	22
* Caleb Gindl, OF	.295	539	65	159	10	72	58	94	7
Sean Halton, OF	.290	400	58	116	22	71	32	85	6
Josh Whitaker, OF	.285	228	33	65	6	30	15	55	5
* Charlie Cutler, C	.285	249	41	71	4	29	30	46	9
Kevin Ahrens, IF	.284	469	64	133	13	64	37	84	8
# Mike McDade, 1B	.281	424	45	119	15	53	22	70	0
* Blake Gailen, OF	.280	157	25	44	4	21	20	28	1
Mike Crouse, OF	.268	71	12	19	0	7	5	16	10
Travis Witherspoon, OF	.256	129	25	33	2	13	15	45	7
# Yusuke Kajimoto, 2B	.254	114	16	29	1	8	14	20	4
# Lance Zawadzki, SS	.240	96	11	23	7	18	7	29	2
* Mike Jacobs, 1B	.236	288	33	68	5	24	36	64	1
Dean Wilson, IF	.167	132	11	22	0	13	4	34	1
Chase Patterson, C	.131	99	11	13	2	5	9	53	1

PLAYER	W	L	ERA	G	SV	IP	H	BB	SO
Bryan Woodall	3	0	0.47	5	0	38	18	7	24
* Luis Gonzalez	1	0	0.83	4	0	22	15	7	11
* Matt Reynolds	1	0	1.63	26	0	22	13	4	32
Cory Burns	0	3	2.16	55	31	54	50	8	60
Kevin Munson	2	0	3.08	12	0	12	11	1	18
Pete Andrelczyk	9	2	3.09	65	4	67	67	26	57
Terry Doyle	6	6	3.29	19	0	123	118	34	72
* Kelvin De La Cruz	6	3	3.45	13	0	68	68	12	57
Justin Jackson	3	3	3.64	29	0	62	61	29	40
Austin Bibens-Dirkx	3	3	3.81	19	0	80	79	11	50

PLAYER	W	L	ERA	G	SV	IP	H	BB	SO
Scott Gracey	2	6	3.81	35	0	31	36	22	28
*Ryan Dennick	4	5	3.98	48	1	52	59	18	36
Joe Gardner	3	1	4.21	6	0	36	43	7	24
Tanner Peters	5	4	4.22	18	0	66	74	22	57
Bryan Evans	4	9	4.42	23	0	124	126	27	130
Hitoshi Fujie	1	0	4.50	22	0	26	28	3	31
Mike Lee	4	5	5.18	22	0	75	92	26	45
Joseph Maher	2	4	5.21	9	0	48	58	22	28
*Jonny Drozd	0	1	5.58	21	0	19	29	1	13
Connor Root	1	3	5.85	6	0	28	35	12	12
Josh Wall	0	1	6.00	20	0	18	19	13	16
RJ Hively	0	3	6.05	33	0	36	58	12	29
*Anthony Fernandez	1	2	6.09	8	0	21	26	8	17
*Al Yevoli	1	2	6.35	22	0	23	25	13	19
Evan Meek	1	2	7.24	15	0	14	13	8	17
J.D. Martin	1	2	7.80	6	0	28	45	11	22
Mark Lamm	0	0	9.22	16	0	14	21	8	4

LONG ISLAND DUCKS

PLAYER	AVG	AB	R	H	HR	RBI	BB	SO	SB
Mark Minicozzi, IF	.356	73	15	26	4	15	9	18	0
# Delta Cleary, OF	.321	405	51	130	3	52	28	72	32
Fehlandt Lentini, OF	.313	571	108	179	9	75	38	80	51
Lew Ford, OF	.305	223	30	68	5	30	16	40	0
Mike Dowd, C	.284	331	37	94	4	43	18	52	2
* Sean Burroughs, IF	.281	160	18	45	0	9	10	18	0
# Ruben Gotay, IF	.275	363	41	100	7	63	56	90	0
Dan Lyons, IF	.272	382	58	104	7	49	18	73	4
Cody Puckett, IF	.272	445	62	121	9	73	31	65	1
Mike Blanke, C	.253	375	37	95	10	50	30	92	0
* Anthony Vega, OF	.249	413	75	103	11	45	51	152	24
* Blake Tekotte, OF	.225	187	27	42	4	12	13	49	2
* Tyler Colvin, IF	.218	257	23	56	5	28	15	62	0
* Dan Johnson, IF	.217	46	5	10	2	7	10	9	0
Matt Wessinger, IF	.207	266	34	55	2	20	39	85	7
# Carlos Hughes, IF	.145	62	3	9	0	4	4	28	0
Chris Scura, OF	.114	44	5	5	0	1	4	11	1

PLAYER	W	L	ERA	G	SV	IP	H	BB	SO
Frank DeJiulio	2	0	1.03	22	0	17	5	9	17
*Patrick Crider	3	2	1.67	61	0	43	21	27	38
Amalio Diaz	5	2	2.09	52	5	52	37	10	69
Bruce Kern	4	1	2.16	18	0	62	60	18	61
Mark Blackmar	6	2	2.72	13	0	79	69	20	51
Todd Coffey	3	4	3.06	45	27	44	43	15	42
James Lomangino	0	0	3.09	29	1	32	31	16	35
Matt Larkins	1	0	3.21	2	0	14	12	3	10
*Eury De La Rosa	3	4	3.25	39	1	47	38	14	60
*Jarrett Casey	0	0	3.29	15	0	14	13	7	15
John Brownell	10	8	3.30	25	0	169	175	38	147
Nick Struck	4	5	3.34	39	0	75	70	30	60
Luis Perdomo	1	0	3.46	10	0	13	11	4	13
*Dustin Richardson	1	3	3.50	13	0	26	31	7	24
*Darin Downs	5	8	3.60	17	0	105	98	22	108
*Jack Snodgrass	6	6	3.79	14	0	78	85	27	85
*Danny Herrera	3	1	4.35	8	0	41	43	17	25
*Jarret Leverett	2	2	4.50	4	0	22	23	9	18
Danny Burawa	0	1	5.09	22	0	18	21	8	17
Kevin Vance	3	1	5.21	25	0	29	32	14	29
Bobby Blevins	2	12	5.51	23	0	127	154	28	79
Dan Blewett	0	1	7.36	19	0	15	20	6	17
Chris McCoy	1	2	7.83	3	0	10	18	2	6
Kyle Hansen	1	2	8.43	19	0	16	19	11	16
Mike Jackson	0	3	11.11	5	0	17	29	6	11

NEW BRITAIN BEES

PLAYER	AVG	AB	R	H	HR	RBI	BB	SO	SB
* Craig Maddox, IF	.306	510	56	156	10	56	20	84	1
Greg Golson, OF	.292	380	40	111	3	38	22	92	18
Mike Crouse, OF	.291	382	62	111	10	60	36	113	51
Jovan Rosa, 3B	.283	547	56	155	13	59	50	99	1
Jon Griffin, 1B	.274	452	60	124	12	67	28	140	0

PLAYER	AVG	AB	R	H	HR	RBI	BB	SO	SB
Jon Jones, OF	.269	264	32	71	5	33	12	37	24
* James Skelton, C	.266	402	67	107	10	40	91	114	16
Jonathan Roof, 2B	.251	435	59	109	4	40	33	97	13
* Kevin Rivers, OF	.246	130	16	32	1	7	20	36	3
Steve Carrillo, U	.246	276	25	68	3	25	17	67	1
Cole Garner, OF	.240	121	22	29	7	23	5	48	0
Anthony Hewitt, OF	.223	274	39	61	9	36	24	100	7
Jake McGuiggan, IF	.219	196	19	43	4	31	15	54	6
# Brandon Chaves, SS	.212	132	16	28	1	14	17	36	2
Nick Murphy, C	.196	107	10	21	1	6	9	15	0
* Jon Dziomba, IF	.192	26	2	5	0	1	3	8	1

PLAYER	W	L	ERA	G	SV	IP	H	BB	SO
* Nick Greenwood	3	0	0.00	3	0	19	13	4	17
*Shawn Gilblair	4	2	1.86	46	21	53	37	17	57
Mike Lee	5	0	2.45	8	0	44	41	15	29
Cole Johnson	7	6	2.70	14	0	87	72	13	48
Rob Bryson	2	2	2.73	18	5	23	19	10	23
Kyle Simon	8	6	2.76	20	0	120	113	24	67
Kevin Vance	2	1	2.85	13	0	28	22	12	22
* Anthony Marzi	5	1	3.02	36	1	77	70	48	49
Shawn Haviland	3	4	3.33	22	0	94	97	31	70
Grady Wood	3	2	3.49	22	1	28	20	10	27
*Jarret Leverett	4	7	3.55	28	0	94	114	19	68
*Josh Outman	3	3	4.23	14	0	85	85	23	55
Eric Fornataro	1	5	4.50	35	0	46	53	15	24
Brian Dupra	4	3	4.51	21	0	98	97	39	75
Dan Sattler	2	4	4.86	9	0	33	28	28	31
Dylan Thompson	0	1	4.90	3	0	11	11	8	8
Josh Zeid	2	3	5.06	8	0	37	42	16	43
*Brandon Fry	3	3	5.66	38	1	54	50	29	39
Nate Roe	5	3	5.87	12	0	57	67	22	21
Craig Stem	2	4	6.60	23	7	30	52	12	24
Sean Gleason	2	6	6.75	15	0	39	59	6	27
Joe Kuzia	1	0	6.88	13	0	17	24	9	12
Scott Patterson	0	1	7.26	16	0	17	24	6	16

SOMERSET PATRIOTS

PLAYER	AVG	AB	R	H	HR	RBI	BB	SO	SB
David Vidal, IF	.320	316	66	101	26	62	45	68	5
* Aharon Eggleston, OF	.310	458	73	142	8	55	49	71	9
Eric Farris, IF	.301	492	74	148	6	66	41	72	26
* Kyle Roller, IF	.284	194	27	55	10	40	32	49	0
* Vinny Zarrillo, IF	.282	277	37	78	2	32	40	62	0
* Bryan LaHair, IF	.279	476	59	133	10	86	56	83	1
* Brad Snyder, OF	.270	126	21	34	8	23	18	36	0
Scott Kelly, IF	.265	385	66	102	1	30	32	56	38
Yovan Gonzalez, C	.264	276	34	73	2	30	31	53	0
# Carlos Guzman, OF	.264	409	41	108	12	58	40	63	11
Mycal Jones, OF	.246	341	53	84	3	40	33	75	30
* Robert Kral, C	.236	220	36	52	4	24	38	47	3
# Trayvon Robinson, OF	.235	247	37	58	9	28	22	62	12
Brian Van Kirk, OF	.233	176	17	41	4	17	11	41	0
# Matt Fields, IF	.229	227	26	52	6	32	23	94	2
Luis Mateo, IF	.216	88	11	19	2	9	5	22	4
# Darwin Perez, IF	.192	52	7	10	0	5	9	12	6

PLAYER	W	L	ERA	G	SV	IP	H	BB	SO
Gus Schlosser	2	0	0.00	15	1	15	12	4	19
Jim Miller	1	0	0.00	26	0	25	8	2	24
Ryan Reid	0	0	0.00	14	0	14	8	7	9
*Brandon Sisk	3	4	1.94	45	0	46	38	18	62
* Nik Turley	5	1	2.02	10	0	49	32	13	66
*Jeremy Bleich	2	2	2.45	17	0	22	24	3	28
Kyler Newby	1	2	2.48	52	0	51	36	12	62
* Mike Thomas	5	1	2.73	55	1	49	48	20	45
*Efrain Nieves	3	0	3.08	9	0	35	30	11	30
Connor Little	5	0	3.25	46	0	64	57	17	67
Will Oliver	7	2	3.30	16	0	98	99	32	72
Scott McGregor	4	4	3.35	9	0	59	60	6	31
*Jeremy Horst	5	2	3.39	11	0	66	69	14	55
Jon Hunton	0	3	3.75	51	37	50	57	7	32
*Darin Gorski	4	2	3.87	11	0	60	53	30	49

PLAYER	W	L	ERA	G	SV	IP	H	BB	SO
*Rudy Owens	4	3	4.01	12	0	67	63	24	67
Bryce Morrow	4	2	4.55	18	0	28	32	3	21
Shaun Garceau	3	4	4.91	19	0	112	128	38	58
Alexis Candelario	2	1	5.01	8	0	38	40	14	47
Donovan Hand	4	8	5.15	24	0	103	125	19	77
Jeremy McBryde	6	5	5.40	35	2	38	38	8	38
*Matt Bywater	0	2	5.71	6	0	17	15	14	19
Mickey Storey	1	9	5.75	34	0	86	102	21	56
Randy Boone	3	3	6.38	10	0	31	39	11	20

SOUTHERN MARYLAND BLUE CRABS

PLAYER	AVG	AB	R	H	HR	RBI	BB	SO	SB
# Steve Lombardozzi, IF	.367	166	27	61	0	20	10	18	8
Michael Snyder, IF	.304	336	44	102	25	65	42	78	0
* Jamar Walton, OF	.284	436	49	124	13	49	16	112	2
Angel Sanchez, IF	.280	282	26	79	7	35	27	28	0
D'Arby Myers, OF	.280	382	42	107	7	44	14	54	29
# Bry Nelson, IF	.279	491	52	137	2	49	43	47	13
Zach Wilson, IF	.278	485	60	135	19	70	37	107	6
* Eric Garcia, IF	.261	436	56	114	3	50	39	84	7
* Fred Lewis, OF	.256	82	9	21	4	12	7	18	1
Gustavo Molina, C	.254	205	20	52	6	24	8	59	0
Gary Brown, OF	.249	401	62	100	10	40	22	75	21
* Kuan-Jen Chen, OF	.248	137	13	34	0	11	7	13	0
Angel Flores, C	.232	246	24	57	6	19	17	48	1
* Jon Dziomba, IF	.225	102	13	23	0	3	8	32	0
Alfredo Marte, IF	.220	186	32	41	10	21	16	43	7
Ryde Rodriguez, OF	.200	45	2	9	1	1	2	12	0
# Antoan Richardson, OF	.200	90	16	18	0	1	20	27	11
# Norberto Susini, C	.123	57	5	7	0	3	6	18	0

PLAYER	W	L	ERA	G	SV	IP	H	BB	SO
Cody Eppley	3	2	3.06	61	31	62	63	20	40
Brian Grening	10	6	3.08	39	0	117	113	22	114
* Brian Burres	11	9	3.33	28	0	157	151	55	139
* Robert Carson	1	5	3.49	36	0	46	37	18	54
* Scott Maine	1	3	3.52	50	0	38	40	16	42
Craig Stem	1	4	3.99	37	1	38	47	16	34
Navery Moore	2	2	4.55	61	0	53	60	36	56
Daryl Thompson	5	9	4.69	23	0	132	152	26	85
Gaby Hernandez	7	10	4.88	27	0	153	150	36	150
* Scott Snodgress	3	6	5.12	38	0	93	102	38	93
Shaun Garceau	1	2	5.19	6	0	26	35	6	16
Justin Berg	2	5	5.22	29	0	31	45	13	27
Ian Marshall	4	1	5.27	19	0	43	54	29	20
Jon Leicester	2	4	5.40	7	0	38	41	13	26
Joe Van Meter	0	0	5.72	9	0	11	13	8	12
Tim Sexton	3	10	6.28	27	0	125	170	32	80
* Jeff Urlaub	0	1	6.54	14	0	11	22	5	14
Orlando Santos	1	4	6.57	28	0	26	35	13	23

SUGAR LAND SKEETERS

PLAYER	AVG	AB	R	H	HR	RBI	BB	SO	SB
Rick Hague, IF	.311	437	69	136	17	67	21	91	12
Jeremy Barfield, OF	.306	510	87	156	27	85	62	108	2
* Rene Tosoni, OF	.301	356	49	107	7	41	33	55	14
# Delwyn Young, IF	.297	445	56	132	6	61	33	58	2
Wilfredo Rodriguez, C	.288	236	32	68	7	32	26	29	0
# Albert Cordero, C	.275	182	21	50	1	12	10	32	2
Andy LaRoche, IF	.269	52	4	14	0	6	4	5	0
# Lance Zawadzki, IF	.268	127	20	34	3	9	6	36	4
* Travis Scott, C	.264	405	48	107	16	67	42	71	2
* Tyson Gillies, OF	.261	46	7	12	0	5	3	19	3
* Johan Limonta, OF	.242	227	24	55	3	21	17	47	1
# Jeff Dominguez, IF	.242	492	69	119	11	54	45	96	13
Patrick Palmeiro, IF	.235	247	32	58	11	44	18	93	0
Beamer Weems, IF	.235	323	33	76	3	23	18	76	0
Kent Matthes, OF	.234	239	26	56	7	37	14	47	4
Josh Prince, IF	.230	317	58	73	5	25	67	73	24
# Brooks Conrad, IF	.161	62	7	10	1	5	15	17	0
Ben Guez, OF	.091	33	1	3	0	0	1	14	1

PLAYER	W	L	ERA	G	SV	IP	H	BB	SO
Andrew Johnston	5	2	1.78	61	4	61	45	8	47
*Dan Runzler	0	1	1.95	33	2	28	36	10	29
*Derrick Loop	2	3	1.98	57	32	59	58	23	70
Zech Zinicola	2	5	2.93	60	3	61	61	18	49
*Roy Merritt	8	2	2.99	25	1	120	117	25	93
Ryan Mattheus	3	2	3.00	38	0	42	37	22	28
Michael Nix	2	1	3.12	6	0	32	28	12	30
Chris Treibt	1	1	3.46	10	0	13	15	3	6
Jake Hale	6	3	3.73	19	0	104	111	14	58
Sean Gallagher	10	8	3.79	27	0	154	169	66	112
Robbie Weinhardt	6	7	3.96	56	2	59	60	22	61
*Aaron Thompson	9	5	3.98	25	0	133	148	33	102
Brett Marshall	6	6	4.33	17	0	81	86	34	67
Jon Velasquez	3	2	4.52	51	0	62	59	21	43
*Bryan Morgado	2	3	5.27	6	0	29	32	11	23
Parker Frazier	5	4	5.31	12	0	61	76	23	31
Sean Gleason	1	2	5.94	5	0	17	23	7	2
*Chris Rearick	3	2	6.61	35	0	33	37	17	34
Tim Alderson	0	1	7.36	12	0	18	22	17	19
Barret Loux	0	3	8.01	8	0	30	26	25	40
Ian Marshall	0	3	9.42	8	0	21	33	10	7

YORK REVOLUTION

PLAYER	AVG	AB	R	H	HR	RBI	BB	SO	SB
Isaias Tejeda, C	.356	270	40	96	9	38	17	41	2
Michael Rockett, OF	.295	458	65	135	7	50	23	117	8
Travis Witherspoon, OF	.293	328	57	96	8	34	36	102	34
Andres Perez, 1B	.289	481	66	139	14	63	34	93	2
* Jared Mitchell, OF	.285	270	47	77	8	39	40	81	26
Joel Guzman, IF	.278	503	64	140	16	85	25	106	2
* Michael Burgess, OF	.275	167	21	46	8	31	11	40	0
Telvin Nash, 1B	.275	193	29	53	15	28	33	79	0
Jason Repko, OF	.272	162	25	44	4	16	18	37	2
Alfredo Marte, OF	.258	132	20	34	5	14	11	32	2
Josh Wilson, IF	.255	420	59	107	8	39	22	98	14
* Kevin Rivers, OF	.254	248	38	63	8	39	38	79	2
# Keith Castillo, C	.251	191	27	48	5	28	16	53	0
Bryan Pounds, 3B	.250	424	53	106	13	69	47	123	1
# Brandon Chaves, SS	.235	204	25	48	0	22	25	48	2
James Simmons, OF	.219	146	16	32	3	14	3	53	0
Salvador Paniagua, C	.200	140	10	28	2	13	8	42	0
Alex Marquez, C	.148	27	3	4	0	1	3	5	0
Ryde Rodriguez, OF	.147	34	2	5	0	1	3	10	0

PLAYER	W	L	ERA	G	SV	IP	H	BB	SO
Mike DeMark	0	1	0.75	47	35	48	27	6	62
*Nate Reed	1	0	1.63	24	1	22	11	16	23
Jorge Martinez	3	2	1.80	7	0	40	27	15	23
Manny Corpas	3	1	2.18	34	0	33	32	12	27
Jose Arredondo	1	2	2.25	35	0	36	35	10	38
Ricardo Gomez	3	3	2.31	49	3	47	39	19	62
*Frank Gailey	6	5	3.13	26	0	123	109	44	100
Mariel Checo	4	1	3.52	19	1	23	16	11	23
Matt Neil	3	0	3.52	12	0	51	63	20	28
* Scott Rice	4	2	3.60	35	1	30	20	21	27
Micah Owings	7	6	4.30	23	0	107	108	38	81
James Simmons	11	9	4.36	26	0	161	189	37	118
Ty'Relle Harris	5	7	4.48	36	0	118	122	51	116
Julio DePaula	2	1	4.74	42	1	44	50	23	21
*Kelvin De La Cruz	3	6	5.21	10	0	48	70	16	30
Michael Click	7	3	5.25	48	1	62	66	17	59
Tony Pena	7	10	5.58	28	1	139	167	36	82
Luis Perdomo	3	1	5.70	22	0	24	23	19	19
*Ron Schreurs	1	0	5.75	26	0	20	24	14	18
Mike McClendon	0	2	5.85	6	0	28	37	8	17
Beau Vaughan	1	1	6.58	14	0	14	21	4	12

CAN-AM LEAGUE

In only their second year in the league, the Ottawa Champions lived up to their name.

The league made history as the Cuban National Team, admittedly much diminished from its status as the top team in international

baseball for decades, played 20 games in the league. Shikoku Island, a team made up of independent league players from Japan, also played 20 games against Can-Am League teams. Neither was eligible to win the championships, but their stats were treated the same as any other team in the league.

CAN-AM LEAGUE	W	L	PCT	GB
New Jersey Jackals	62	38	.620	—
Rockland Boulders	58	42	.580	4
Quebec Capitales	56	44	.560	6
# Cuban National Team	11	9	.550	11
Ottawa Champions	51	49	.510	11
# Shikoku Island	8	12	.400	14
Sussex County Miners	39	61	.390	23
Trois-Rivieres Aigles	35	65	.350	27

Not eligible for playoffs

PLAYOFFS: Semifinals—Ottawa defeated New Jersey 3: 1 and Rockland defeated Quebec 3: 2 in best: of: 5 series. **Finals**—Ottawa defeated Rockland 3-2 in best-of-5 series.

ATTENDANCE: Rockland 149,632; Quebec 146,946; Ottawa 127,618; Sussex County 90,237; Trois-Rivieres 78,948; New Jersey 74,335.

MANAGERS: New Jersey—Joe Calfapietra; Ottawa—Hal Lanier; Quebec—Pat Scalabrini; Rockland—Jamie Keefe; Sussex County—Bobby Jones; Trois-Rivieres—Pete LaForest.

ALL-STAR TEAM: C: Marcus Nidiffer, Rockland. **1B:** Art Charles, New Jersey. **2B:** Albert Cartwright, Ottawa. **3B:** Danny Mateo, Trois: Rivieres. **SS:** Junior Arrojo, Rockland. **OF:** Jay Austin, Sussex County; D'Vontrey Richardson, New Jersey; Michael O'Neill, New Jersey. **DH:** Chris Jacobs, Sussex County. **SP:** Austin Chrismon, Ottawa. **RP:** Jon Fitzsimmons, Quebec.

PLAYER OF THE YEAR: Art Charles, 1b, New Jersey. **ROOKIE OF THE YEAR:** Lee Sosa, rhp, New Jersey. **DEFENSIVE PLAYER OF THE YEAR:** Eddie Newton, IF, New Jersey. **MANAGER OF THE YEAR:** Hal Lanier, Ottawa.

BATTING LEADERS

PLAYER	AVG	AB	R	H	HR	RBI	SB
Charles, Art, New Jersey	.352	355	79	125	29	101	3
Austin, Jay, Sussex	.341	381	66	130	3	39	40
Arrojo, Junior, Rockland	.341	346	89	118	6	49	47
O'Neill, Mike, New Jersey	.338	397	76	134	3	45	9
Pyles, Derrick, Sussex	.328	268	45	88	2	26	2
Tissenbaum, Maxx, Quebec	.326	273	44	89	7	47	1
Gracial, Yurisbel, Quebec	.320	328	57	105	9	58	10
Calderon, Yeicok, Quebec	.319	288	45	92	6	40	1
Hirama, Hayato, Shikoku	.317	63	6	20	0	14	4
Alarcon, Yosvani, Cuba	.317	82	10	26	2	15	0

PITCHING LEADERS

PLAYER	W	L	ERA	IP	H	BB	SO
Domínguez, Yayfredo, Cuba	1	1	1.13	16	14	4	9
Harada, Yuki, Shikoku	2	0	1.88	24	16	9	20
Banos, Vladimir, Cuba	3	0	2.37	19	14	2	8
Chrismon, Austin, Ottawa	8	4	2.39	135	133	29	108
Sosa, Lee, New Jersey	9	6	2.51	111	99	57	84
Alvarez, Edilson, Trois-Rivieres	6	5	2.67	115	103	32	89
Blanco, Lazaro, Cuba	1	1	2.79	19	12	8	20
Fischer, David, Rockland	9	3	2.91	108	80	62	110
Salazar, Richard, Rockland	10	6	3.32	119	103	46	104
Parish, Matt, New Jersey	7	2	3.36	80	75	24	60

CUBA NATIONAL TEAM

PLAYER	AVG	AB	R	H	HR	RBI	BB	SO	SB
Juan Torriente, 2B	.333	27	5	9	0	4	0	2	1
Yoelvis Fiss, OF	.327	49	7	16	0	3	1	7	1
Yosvani Alarcon, C	.317	82	10	26	2	15	2	8	0
Yorbis Borroto, SS	.311	74	15	23	1	11	11	6	0
* Lazaro Ramirez, OF	.304	46	5	14	0	4	2	4	1
Jeferson Delgado, IF	.298	57	7	17	0	5	2	10	0
Raul Gonzalez, IF	.292	65	11	19	0	8	7	8	2
Luis Robert, IF	.289	83	8	24	0	13	4	11	1
Moiran, Luis, OF	.286	63	12	18	1	8	4	15	3
* Julio Martinez, OF	.231	78	10	18	1	9	0	16	4
Yunior Paumier, IF	.226	31	7	7	0	0	7	5	0

PLAYER	W	L	ERA	G	SV	IP	H	BB	SO
Miguel Lahera	0	0	0.90	6	2	10	6	2	12
Yaifredo Dominguez	1	1	1.12	5	0	16	14	4	9
* Livan Moinelo	0	1	1.88	9	3	14	8	7	19
Vladimir Banos	3	0	2.36	4	0	19	14	2	8
Lazaro Blanco	1	1	2.79	6	0	19	12	8	20
* Yoanni Yera	1	1	4.11	7	0	20	23	9	12
Vladimir Garcia	2	2	4.67	4	0	17	15	12	11
Freddy Alvarez	2	1	5.14	4	0	21	27	7	19

NEW JERSEY JACKALS

PLAYER	AVG	AB	R	H	HR	RBI	BB	SO	SB
Daniel Rockett, OF	.372	188	47	70	11	38	29	34	7
* Art Charles, 1B	.352	355	79	125	29	101	66	92	3
* Mike O'Neill, OF	.338	397	76	134	3	45	62	28	9
D'Vontrey Richardson, OF	.310	364	56	113	3	67	26	59	25
Johnny Bladel, IF	.293	283	62	83	3	33	42	74	17
* Robert Stock, C	.289	204	36	59	7	37	9	40	2
Rylan Sandoval, IF	.274	383	72	105	4	56	45	103	14
* Mike Schwartz, OF	.271	48	9	13	0	6	9	8	1
Dustin Lawley, IF	.263	76	14	20	4	22	6	22	3
Taylor Brennan, IF	.262	187	30	49	7	34	30	70	7
Cory Vaughn, OF	.256	324	57	83	9	57	46	104	13
Adam Martin, C	.249	169	25	42	4	20	23	57	2
Eddie Newton, IF	.244	287	39	70	5	50	38	70	5
* Jared Mitchell, OF	.190	42	6	8	0	4	7	19	3

PLAYER	W	L	ERA	G	SV	IP	H	BB	SO
John Walter	3	0	1.00	4	0	27	14	7	29
* Nick Gonzalez	0	1	1.21	28	2	37	24	6	42
* Jose Jose	2	2	2.42	21	5	30	18	9	38
Lee Sosa	9	6	2.50	23	0	111	99	57	84
Fernando Cruz	6	3	2.62	34	12	72	59	23	79
Whit Mayberry	3	0	2.82	7	0	22	19	6	15
Robert Stock	1	2	2.85	52	5	60	47	40	73
Matt Parish	7	2	3.36	15	0	80	75	24	60
Johnny Hellweg	3	1	3.42	20	1	21	25	14	30
Brian Ernst	5	4	3.67	13	0	69	71	25	69
James Stokes	2	3	3.94	28	0	43	44	26	44
Justin Brantley	0	3	4.35	19	0	21	25	20	18
* Isaac Pavlik	8	2	4.43	13	0	69	90	22	52
Matt Loosen	9	6	4.91	19	0	112	133	39	85
* Andres Caceres	1	2	6.42	10	0	14	13	14	13
David Anderson	1	1	7.64	6	0	18	27	7	8
Matt Alvarez	0	0	8.73	8	0	11	18	9	11
John Sheehan	0	0	8.77	10	1	13	11	9	15

OTTAWA CHAMPIONS

PLAYER	AVG	AB	R	H	HR	RBI	BB	SO	SB
Derrick Pyles, OF	.313	144	19	45	0	10	10	14	0
* Adron Chambers, OF	.304	102	13	31	1	10	8	11	2
Albert Cartwright, IF	.292	377	61	110	3	34	32	68	26
* Sebastien Boucher, CF	.291	347	62	101	8	55	87	58	16
Michael Mastroberti, IF	.279	197	22	55	0	15	9	43	1
Donal Duarte, 3B	.272	298	39	81	2	35	37	28	9
Ryan Brockett, U	.268	56	7	15	0	3	5	11	3
* Kenny Bryant, OF	.261	372	59	97	11	69	34	78	15
Brian Van Kirk, OF	.254	71	6	18	1	6	13	22	0
* Matt Helms, OF	.247	380	51	94	4	40	34	65	16
Jason Coker, IF	.239	46	6	11	0	7	9	10	1
* Alexander Malleta, 1B	.238	290	32	69	6	53	30	40	2
Daniel Bick, IF	.205	205	26	42	0	12	35	61	10
Robert Garza, IF	.197	66	7	13	0	5	4	23	3
Dan Grauer, C	.196	270	31	53	5	33	23	61	0
Brian Erie, C	.135	74	7	10	0	7	7	20	0

PLAYER	W	L	ERA	G	SV	IP	H	BB	SO
Tyler Wilson	3	4	2.07	42	14	48	32	24	60
Austin Chrismon	8	4	2.39	20	0	135	133	29	108
Wilmer Font	2	2	3.13	10	0	60	57	13	61
* Yean Carlos Gil	8	6	3.46	23	0	112	107	38	94
Daniel Cordero	10	4	3.79	20	0	116	113	39	86
* Miles Moeller	3	4	4.07	24	1	53	57	23	55
Calvin Rayburn	2	1	4.15	14	0	17	17	21	17

INDEPENDENT LEAGUES

PLAYER	W	L	ERA	G	SV	IP	H	BB	SO
Randy Hamrick	2	3	4.33	23	3	35	29	18	29
Andrew Cooper	2	2	4.35	33	1	52	57	27	41
Nick Cunningham	2	1	4.36	15	0	23	30	11	14
Steve Borkowski	1	2	4.43	4	0	22	23	5	14
Laetten Galbraith	3	7	5.01	23	0	97	104	29	43
Luis Munoz	3	3	5.44	11	0	41	46	23	43
*Josh Blanco	0	1	5.81	22	3	22	19	21	21
Kevin Perez	1	2	6.37	21	0	24	18	27	23
*Jarret Martin	0	1	6.96	3	0	10	6	16	9

QUEBEC CAPITALES

PLAYER	AVG	AB	R	H	HR	RBI	BB	SO	SB
Derrick Pyles, OF	.375	64	15	24	2	9	10	6	1
* Maxx Tissenbaum, C	.326	273	44	89	7	47	27	20	1
Yurisbel Gracial, IF	.320	328	57	105	9	58	27	56	10
Yeicok Calderon, OF	.319	288	45	92	6	40	26	60	1
* Adam Ehrlich, C	.305	259	42	79	4	28	28	41	0
Tanner Nivins, OF	.303	33	3	10	0	4	1	8	0
* Roel Santos, OF	.301	312	46	94	1	34	36	43	23
* Jordan Lennerton, 1B	.301	375	57	113	9	62	57	77	0
Jonathan Malo, 3B	.283	364	65	103	6	42	47	42	12
Kalian Sams, OF	.277	224	40	62	12	41	34	55	10
Marcus Knecht, OF	.259	344	49	89	8	49	39	95	9
* Lachlan Fontaine, IF	.239	197	27	47	3	32	10	52	1
* Trevor Gretzky, OF	.228	57	4	13	0	7	1	11	0
Josh Wong, IF	.220	50	8	11	2	3	1	12	0
* Scott David, C	.214	126	17	27	1	13	13	44	7

PLAYER	W	L	ERA	G	SV	IP	H	BB	SO
Jon Fitzsimmons	1	0	1.25	25	13	29	14	7	44
*Jordan Mills	6	0	1.96	44	3	55	44	20	51
Shaun Ellis	3	3	2.03	40	6	53	47	13	49
Sam Brunner	1	1	2.04	12	0	22	20	4	18
Ryan Leach	3	1	2.70	38	3	47	38	26	38
Karl Gelinas	7	7	3.68	16	0	103	110	15	61
Luis Pardo	0	0	4.32	11	0	17	15	12	20
*Martire Garcia	2	1	4.45	7	0	36	34	21	22
Mark Smyth	2	3	4.50	14	0	44	46	26	27
Steven Inch	1	1	4.62	2	0	12	10	5	6
Jasvir Rakkar	10	3	4.99	25	2	101	123	28	66
*Mac Acker	5	6	5.21	20	0	78	104	31	45
Nate Roe	4	2	5.32	11	0	47	49	26	29
Deryk Hooker	4	5	5.43	12	0	55	63	15	34
*Sheldon McDonald	3	7	5.52	25	0	88	108	18	66
Sean Gleason	1	2	6.09	5	0	31	51	12	15

ROCKLAND BOULDERS

PLAYER	AVG	AB	R	H	HR	RBI	BB	SO	SB
Junior Arrojo, IF	.341	346	89	118	8	49	62	55	47
Leandro Castro, RF	.316	76	13	24	2	10	3	4	3
* Mike Schwartz, OF	.312	109	15	34	0	20	23	12	1
* Mike Fransoso, IF	.291	313	54	91	6	43	49	57	21
* Jared McDonald, OF	.289	228	53	66	9	34	40	34	10
Devin Harris, OF	.283	205	31	58	12	50	24	46	1
Jared Schlehuber, OF	.274	354	45	97	15	73	59	70	0
Quinnton Mack, OF	.268	71	13	19	1	7	10	23	3
* Riley Palmer, IF	.258	66	7	17	1	9	5	23	4
Marcus Nidiffer, C	.255	329	62	84	20	79	44	80	3
# Elvin Soto, C	.254	209	28	53	4	25	12	65	1
Mike Montville, OF	.251	307	40	77	11	48	40	85	8
Pat McKenna, IF	.233	257	46	60	4	21	52	100	5
Alex DeBellis, C	.208	130	16	27	0	10	6	23	3
* Luis Parache, IF	.207	29	4	6	0	0	1	2	0
Ray Frias, IF	.194	72	12	14	0	6	12	25	2
Brian Ragira, OF	.184	49	5	9	1	5	5	11	0
Ed Charlton, OF	.172	58	10	10	0	2	4	22	2
* Brenden Webb, OF	.143	35	5	5	2	5	6	11	0
Aaron Wilson, IF	.103	39	6	4	0	0	3	9	0

PLAYER	W	L	ERA	G	SV	IP	H	BB	SO
Matt Kostalos	1	1	0.46	9	0	19	11	8	19
Markus Solbach	6	2	2.43	10	0	74	73	12	52
Hector Nelo	4	2	2.45	37	17	40	34	33	44

PLAYER	W	L	ERA	G	SV	IP	H	BB	SO
David Fischer	9	3	2.90	19	0	108	80	62	110
Alex Gouin	3	1	3.16	7	0	37	27	8	25
*Richard Salazar	10	6	3.31	19	0	119	103	46	104
*Jason Byers	3	1	3.49	10	0	49	51	19	24
Pat Butler	2	5	4.13	47	3	61	76	13	35
Edgar Valle	4	0	4.80	22	4	45	52	18	34
*Jarret Martin	0	2	5.11	7	0	32	33	16	33
Joey Ravert	1	1	5.27	7	0	29	31	17	17
Brett Palanski	4	2	5.51	6	0	31	36	18	13
Daniel Carela	1	1	5.76	36	1	39	34	42	44
Mike Adams	5	6	5.86	16	0	66	85	37	30
*Liarvis Breto	0	1	6.27	9	0	14	16	12	13
*Donnie Joseph	0	1	7.16	18	2	16	19	14	15
Bo Budkevics	5	5	7.29	12	0	58	94	7	51
Luis Sanz	0	2	12.51	7	0	14	18	18	11

SHIKOKU ISLAND ALL-STARS

PLAYER	AVG	AB	R	H	HR	RBI	BB	SO	SB
* Takaya Furukawa, OF	.393	28	3	11	0	4	1	5	4
* Naoto Kawada, OF	.345	29	5	10	0	4	0	6	1
* Hayato Hirama, IF	.317	63	6	20	0	14	2	15	4
* Zach Colby, IF	.304	79	11	24	1	16	12	9	2
Yuki Tarui, C	.289	38	2	11	0	2	6	6	1
* Jiro Kato, IF	.256	43	7	11	0	3	5	13	0
* Yoshihiro Kobayashi, IF	.256	82	12	21	1	9	5	18	1
* Yusuke Matsuzawa, OF	.241	87	8	21	0	5	5	19	1
Ryosuke Yotsuya, IF	.224	75	7	17	0	1	5	8	6
Masashi Muneyuki, OF	.209	43	5	9	1	3	6	15	0
* Takahiro Hayashi, IF	.205	83	13	17	1	6	9	19	5
Hiroki Tsuruta, C	.154	26	1	4	0	3	0	9	0

PLAYER	W	L	ERA	G	SV	IP	H	BB	SO
Yuki Harada	2	0	1.87	4	0	24	16	9	20
Osamu Taira	0	2	2.84	12	4	13	10	6	15
Junki Kishimoto	2	2	3.64	12	1	12	13	5	12
Hiroki Sato	0	1	3.85	6	0	16	15	6	19
Shungo Fukunaga	0	1	4.05	4	0	20	22	12	20
*Itsuki Shoda	0	0	4.32	4	0	17	29	5	8
Kouhei Maso	1	1	4.35	9	0	21	22	7	18
Hideaki Matsumoto	1	2	4.42	4	0	20	23	12	15
Yato Kakazu	1	1	4.76	9	0	11	9	5	7
*Barrett Phillips	0	0	6.75	7	0	11	15	4	5

SUSSEX COUNTY MINERS

PLAYER	AVG	AB	R	H	HR	RBI	BB	SO	SB
* Jay Austin, OF	.341	381	66	130	3	39	24	45	40
Alex DeBellis, C	.327	214	26	70	4	27	14	29	2
Derrick Pyles, OF	.317	60	11	19	0	7	2	4	1
Chris Jacobs, IF	.291	299	44	87	21	70	36	77	0
Nick Giarraputo, IF	.286	378	51	108	7	48	19	93	9
* Joe Dunigan, 1B	.276	29	6	8	1	3	3	7	0
Dominique Taylor, RF	.269	249	29	67	3	18	15	46	8
Ryan Dent, SS	.266	79	10	21	1	7	2	15	5
Carl Thomore, OF	.264	276	39	73	3	31	40	68	22
Steve Nyisztor, IF	.259	293	30	76	1	33	23	52	11
Gaby Juarbe, IF	.241	29	3	7	0	3	1	9	1
Dustin Lawley, IF	.238	105	17	25	1	15	5	24	0
# Elvin Soto, C	.231	104	9	24	1	14	17	25	0
Michael Antonio, OF	.227	66	6	15	0	3	5	10	0
* Brenden Webb, OF	.223	179	30	40	10	23	37	48	11
* Chris Chiaradio, IF	.195	133	13	26	1	13	11	30	11
Nate Irving, IF	.183	131	12	24	1	15	13	33	0
* John Brucker, IF	.171	76	7	13	0	4	2	23	0
* Chris Duffy, 1B	.140	50	5	7	2	7	4	21	1
Sean Hurley, OF	.138	58	4	8	0	3	9	25	2

PLAYER	W	L	ERA	G	SV	IP	H	BB	SO
Ivan Pineyro	1	0	0.77	3	0	11.2	6	3	4
*Stone Speer	0	2	2.00	18	0	18	13	8	14
Jesse Beal	2	0	2.59	22	5	24.1	18	8	31
Drew Cisco	0	5	2.83	19	1	35	37	5	20
Kaohi Downing	1	1	3.38	12	4	13.1	11	6	16
J.B. Kole	0	0	3.52	12	1	15.1	13	9	13

INDEPENDENT LEAGUES

PLAYER	W	L	ERA	G	SV	IP	H	BB	SO
Michael Tamburino	2	5	4.12	30	0	67.2	76	23	62
*Ryan Kulik	5	2	4.42	10	0	55	75	11	26
Andres Santiago	2	6	4.50	22	6	60	77	19	55
*Nick Gonzalez	2	1	4.59	15	0	17.2	17	8	14
*Francisco Rodriguez	7	3	4.63	15	0	83.2	87	42	65
Joey Donino	3	10	4.92	19	0	104.1	116	44	91
Michael Suk	7	8	5.10	26	0	97	121	36	73
Jamie Walczak	0	2	5.21	4	0	19	25	11	10
Ray Hanson	2	4	5.27	8	0	41	50	13	25
Danny Moskovits	1	4	5.98	9	0	49.2	66	16	26
Josh Wood	4	3	6.25	39	2	72	104	19	57
*Frank Del Valle	0	1	6.48	4	0	16.2	18	12	13
*Austin Solecitto	0	0	6.89	12	0	15.2	9	25	22

TROIS-RIVIERES AIGLES

PLAYER	AVG	AB	R	H	HR	RBI	BB	SO	SB
* Zach Colby, 1B	.397	58	3	23	0	7	7	2	0
# Daniel Mateo, IF	.315	390	46	123	8	56	15	41	8
* Ryan Bollinger, U	.292	120	27	35	0	11	18	19	4
Javier Herrera, OF	.290	200	38	58	8	36	29	69	2
* Mike Schwartz, OF	.288	153	20	44	0	17	18	19	0
* Danny Richar, IF	.286	119	14	34	0	10	13	22	0
Connor Crane, 1B	.286	255	37	73	3	33	15	81	11
Steve Brown, OF	.276	294	43	81	8	41	29	75	7
# Kori Melo, IF	.270	37	5	10	0	1	5	6	1
Jesus Merchan, IF	.270	148	22	40	1	13	15	18	0
# Yeixon Ruiz, IF	.266	316	45	84	2	22	24	38	22
Kyle Lafrenz, C	.250	284	33	71	2	40	38	83	2
# Jiwan James, CF	.236	89	9	21	3	12	5	19	1
Ryan Brockett, IF	.236	140	19	33	0	17	20	26	2
# Delvis Morales, IF	.232	246	25	57	0	15	16	69	11
Eric Grabe, IF	.222	72	8	16	1	2	5	12	1
Jalen Harris, IF	.211	38	1	8	0	1	2	11	1
* Reed Lavallee, C	.211	76	7	16	0	7	5	20	1
* Bobby Coyle, 1B	.208	48	3	10	2	7	2	11	0
Sam Judah, OF	.203	79	4	16	1	7	6	15	2
Simon Gravel, C	.187	107	7	20	1	5	5	18	1
Joel Carranza, IF	.113	53	5	6	1	2	1	14	0

PLAYER	W	L	ERA	G	SV	IP	H	BB	SO
Kaohi Downing	4	3	2.48	31	11	33	29	14	36
Edilson Alvarez	6	5	2.66	29	0	115	103	32	89
Matt Rusch	7	8	3.82	20	0	125	127	25	111
*Dennis Neal	1	1	3.94	32	0	57	69	29	41
Scott Kuzminsky	3	1	4.00	40	1	45	45	15	50
*Porfirio Lopez	5	9	4.51	19	0	108	108	59	95
*Ryan Bollinger	2	11	4.87	22	0	113	139	36	96
*Guillaume Blanchette	1	4	5.40	18	1	58	74	30	41
Dario Santangelo	0	1	5.74	14	1	16	9	21	13
Tyler Stirewalt	1	0	5.74	12	0	16	19	15	12
David Leblanc	2	2	5.93	31	0	30	29	19	23
Matt Horan	3	3	6.30	9	0	36	41	13	20
Luis Munoz	0	3	6.53	4	0	21	33	5	28
Charlie Gillies	0	5	7.22	6	0	29	43	19	15
Max Schonfeld	0	3	11.63	6	0	22	44	10	17
Edgar Valle	0	1	13.88	9	0	12	16	13	15

FRONTIER LEAGUE

Slowly and steadily, Andy McCauley built the Evansville Otters into a winner. When McCauley took over the Otters midway through the 2010 season, they were perennially a cellar dweller, having failed to post a .500 record nor topped 40 wins in the past five seasons. Under McCauley, Evansville topped .500 in 2012, topped 50 wins in 2013 and have been in playoff contention every year since.

But it wasn't until this year that the Otters put everything together. Led by second baseman Josh Allen, Evansville earned the top wild card spot, knocked off East division champ Joliet then held off River City in the championship series.

EAST DIVISION	W	L	PCT	GB
Joliet Slammers	51	45	.531	—
Lake Erie Crushers	48	48	.500	3
Washington Wild Things	46	49	.484	4 ½

EAST DIVISION	W	L	PCT	GB
Traverse City Beach Bums	42	52	.447	8
Windy City ThunderBolts	42	53	.442	8 ½
Schaumburg Boomers	41	55	.427	10

WEST DIVISION	W	L	PCT	GB
Southern Illinois Miners	63	33	.656	—
* Evansville Otters	55	40	.579	7 ½
* River City Rascals	49	47	.510	14
Florence Freedom	46	49	.484	16 ½
Normal CornBelters	45	50	.474	17 ½
Gateway Grizzlies	44	51	.463	18 ½

*Wild Card

PLAYOFFS: Semifinals—River City defeated Southern Illinois 3-1 and Evansville defeated Joliet 3-1 in best-of-5 series. **Finals**—Evansville defeated River City 3-2 in best-of-5 series.

ATTENDANCE: Schaumburg 172,996; Gateway 163,679; Southern Illinois 153,940; Traverse City 121,500; Normal 91,193; Joliet 90,458; Florence 88,438; Evansville 82,412; River City 82,061; Lake Erie 81,835; Washington 80,503; Windy City 76,870.

MANAGERS: Evansville—Andy McCauley; Florence—Dennis Pelfrey; Gateway—Phil Warren; Joliet—Jeff Isom; Lake Erie—Chris Mongiardo; Normal—Brooks Carey; River City—Steve Brook; Schaumburg—Jamie Bennett; Southern Illinois—Mike Pinto; Traverse City—Dan Rohn; Washington—Gregg Langbehn; Windy City-Ron Biga.

ALL-STAR TEAM: C: Mike Jurgella, River City. **1B:** Aaron Dudley, Normal. **2B:** Josh Allen, Evansville. **3B:** Steve Marino, Southern Illinois. **SS:** Santiago Chirino, Normal. **DH:** Craig Massey, Southern Illinois. **OF:** Nolan Meadows, Normal; Shane Kennedy, Southern Illinois; Andrew Godbold, Florence. **SP:** Trevor Foss, Washington. **RP:** Randy McCurry, Evansville.

MVP: Josh Allen, Evansville. **PITCHER OF THE YEAR:** Liam O'Sullivan, Joliet. **ROOKIE OF THE YEAR:** Shane Kennedy, Southern Illinois. **MANAGER OF THE YEAR:** Jeff Isom, Joliet.

INDIVIDUAL BATTING LEADERS

PLAYER	AVG	AB	R	H	HR	RBI	SB
Kennedy, Shane, Southern Ill.	.363	273	68	99	5	47	34
Allen, Josh, Evansville	.354	347	75	123	9	46	29
Silver, Josh, River City	.352	227	45	80	9	44	8
Chirino, Santiago, Normal	.334	398	53	133	4	41	4
Dudley, Aaron, Normal	.327	330	58	108	18	80	7
Oldham, Taylor, Florence	.324	330	71	107	14	65	25
Bell, Carter, Joliet	.312	346	57	108	13	73	3
Kelly, Dylan, Normal	.311	338	34	105	3	36	0
Gaedele, Kyle, River City	.308	302	60	93	14	50	24
Jurgella, Mike, River City	.304	260	48	79	5	41	10

INDIVIDUAL PITCHING LEADERS

PLAYER	W	L	ERA	IP	H	BB	SO
Foss, Trevor, Washington	8	3	2.50	101	90	14	66
Champlin, Kramer, Traverse City	5	7	2.81	125	112	23	95
Olson, Preston, Evansville	7	3	2.90	81	56	29	66
Kines, Gunnar, Schaumburg	5	6	2.96	113	81	37	104
Miller, Jarrett, Southern Ill.	8	4	3.05	127	130	34	93
Vail, Tyler, Evansville	6	3	3.12	101	91	36	94
Kraus, Jordan, Florence	7	8	3.15	120	95	38	70
Fraudin, Matt, Washington	7	8	3.17	114	101	46	94
Stoops, Dylan, Traverse City	8	3	3.18	91	77	28	79
Chapman, Clay, Windy City	9	7	3.30	125	104	47	93

EVANSVILLE OTTERS

PLAYER	AVG	AB	R	H	HR	RBI	BB	SO	SB
* Dane Phillips, C	.365	63	13	23	4	18	6	7	0
Josh Allen, IF	.354	347	75	123	9	46	59	86	29
* Rolando Gomez, IF	.290	317	54	92	5	30	28	70	33
* Nik Balog, 1B	.283	332	46	94	5	45	33	47	8
Julio Rodriguez, C	.281	263	29	74	0	26	7	15	5
Chris Riopedre, IF	.278	291	36	81	5	44	35	64	27
Chris Breen, 1B	.274	296	51	81	10	48	30	97	1
* Kaeo Aliviado, OF	.253	154	14	39	4	27	16	13	2
Denzel Richardson, OF	.245	143	22	35	5	23	12	50	14
* Jeff Gardner, OF	.242	149	20	36	6	24	14	45	2
* John Schultz, OF	.236	254	48	60	4	29	36	49	2

PLAYER	AVG	AB	R	H	HR	RBI	BB	SO	SB
Kurt Wertz, OF	.233	90	14	21	2	11	13	23	1
* Kolten Yamaguchi, C	.227	88	15	20	2	11	14	21	5
Chris Sweeney, OF	.224	232	39	52	11	38	31	78	7

PLAYER	W	L	ERA	G	SV	IP	H	BB	SO
*Kenny Frosch	5	4	1.50	47	0	48	23	21	37
Matt Wivinis	4	0	1.59	12	0	40	27	19	43
Randy McCurry	3	3	2.12	35	23	34	29	16	41
Tyler Thompson	4	3	2.18	41	0	45	43	11	40
Kevin Kleis	0	0	2.33	15	1	19	19	9	20
Preston Olson	7	3	2.90	13	0	81	56	29	66
Tyler Vail	6	3	3.12	17	0	101	91	36	94
Felix Baez	1	0	3.38	10	0	32	22	17	38
Shane Weedman	7	3	3.52	30	0	77	60	40	74
*Hunter Ackerman	7	6	3.77	19	0	117	124	29	87
Max Duval	4	1	4.40	7	0	43	32	10	42
J.R. Edwards	0	1	5.56	7	0	11	7	10	10
*Payton Baskette	2	1	5.58	6	0	31	39	16	21
Tyler Levine	0	1	6.10	7	0	10	16	6	5
*Dylan Badura	1	1	6.51	9	0	28	39	10	11
Luc Rennie	1	4	7.33	18	0	47	60	30	41
Andrew Potter	0	1	7.71	12	0	12	7	10	15
*Derrick Penilla	1	2	9.92	5	0	16	26	11	8
Trevor Walch	0	1	10.24	2	0	10	10	7	6

FLORENCE FREEDOM

PLAYER	AVG	AB	R	H	HR	RBI	BB	SO	SB
Taylor Oldham, IF	.324	330	71	107	14	65	45	39	25
* Richard Seigel, IF	.320	97	12	31	1	11	13	31	1
Shaun Cooper, OF	.313	64	13	20	2	12	7	21	9
* Jordan Brower, IF	.299	154	21	46	3	21	12	22	2
* Josh Henderson, OF	.298	245	36	73	2	31	19	43	3
Andrew Godbold, OF	.287	314	59	90	13	59	32	59	22
* Andre Mercurio, OF	.282	131	18	37	0	12	8	12	6
Garrett Vail, C	.272	158	21	43	3	18	16	37	5
* Austin Newell, OF	.259	359	48	93	4	48	37	42	18
Travis Weaver, IF	.258	310	41	80	4	29	24	59	15
Mason Salazar, IF	.250	44	7	11	1	6	2	8	0
* Daniel Fraga, IF	.239	339	67	81	1	27	60	76	28
Collins Cuthrell, OF	.233	313	46	73	13	60	45	67	8
* Isaac Wenrich, C	.224	196	23	44	9	29	23	47	1
Zach Mathieu, 1B	.146	41	1	6	0	2	3	9	0

PLAYER	W	L	ERA	G	SV	IP	H	BB	SO
Matt Pobereyko	0	2	1.33	20	0	20	10	10	31
Pete Levitt	3	1	2.33	52	1	27	15	14	15
Jordan Kraus	4	4	2.86	11	0	79	61	28	49
Cody Gray	7	3	3.18	14	0	74	72	30	55
*Braulio Torres-Perez	4	0	3.21	7	1	34	33	11	22
Tony Vocca	3	2	3.60	35	0	75	66	28	72
Jeremy Gooding	8	6	3.93	18	0	112	117	24	102
Ben Allison	1	1	4.20	6	0	15	18	8	6
*Stetson Nelson	2	3	4.54	8	0	36	39	15	32
*Zach Wendorf	1	4	4.86	19	0	33	33	19	36
Ethan Gibbons	2	3	4.91	44	14	44	41	23	54
Zach Isler	2	4	5.05	6	0	41	49	3	20
Davis Adkins	4	3	5.06	18	0	53	52	13	51
*Patrick McGrath	2	6	7.00	21	1	80	112	27	53
T.J. Bozeman	1	3	7.27	34	0	35	38	35	40
*Brandon Bargas	0	2	8.34	5	0	23	35	16	15

GATEWAY GRIZZLIES

PLAYER	AVG	AB	R	H	HR	RBI	BB	SO	SB
* Tyler Tewell, C	.288	250	34	72	11	31	14	41	1
* Logan Davis, IF	.270	319	34	86	2	29	29	40	18
* Cody Livesay, OF	.264	345	44	91	1	22	39	62	14
Josh Bunselmeyer, IF	.256	164	25	42	5	22	19	50	0
* Zach Lavy, IF	.254	126	20	32	6	22	7	42	0
Seth Heck, IF	.249	289	36	72	1	26	27	49	3
Craig Massoni, IF	.248	339	49	84	14	52	45	67	0
Brandon Thomas, OF	.241	328	57	79	11	42	51	101	18
Blake Brown, OF	.235	238	28	56	8	36	19	67	5
* Vincent Guglietti, IF	.234	107	13	25	1	15	11	22	0

PLAYER	AVG	AB	R	H	HR	RBI	BB	SO	SB
* Ben Waldrip, IF	.233	292	31	68	12	42	13	58	0
* Jason Scholl, C	.221	68	7	15	3	12	9	23	0
Sam Fischer, OF	.213	188	36	40	12	27	24	59	6
Tyler Nordgren, C	.125	32	1	4	0	1	1	9	0

PLAYER	W	L	ERA	G	SV	IP	H	BB	SO
Will LaMarche	1	2	2.01	29	6	31	23	18	26
Jordan Wellander	2	1	2.23	30	2	36	27	9	39
Dakota Smith	2	1	2.25	9	0	40	23	8	42
JaVaun West	3	5	3.02	37	5	60	44	23	73
Jon Pusateri	3	1	3.15	32	0	46	32	20	58
Trevor Richards	3	3	3.21	9	0	48	40	20	48
Vincent Molesky	5	8	3.70	18	0	117	111	25	110
*Corey Kimes	4	6	3.96	18	0	105	100	50	71
Adam Eggnatz	6	4	4.02	19	0	78	73	39	68
Will Landsheft	7	8	4.15	19	0	115	101	48	93
*Chris Scarlett	0	1	4.50	11	0	12	9	15	14
*Jon Jones	4	4	5.23	31	0	64	67	36	62
Nate Carter	2	2	5.56	10	1	11	12	4	11
Kevin Jefferis	1	2	6.44	25	6	29	39	8	33
*Sasha Kuebel	1	3	9.00	4	0	18	34	4	15

JOLIET SLAMMERS

PLAYER	AVG	AB	R	H	HR	RBI	BB	SO	SB
* Boo Vazquez, OF	.324	142	36	46	11	39	20	38	1
Carter Bell, IF	.312	346	57	108	13	73	32	58	3
Jake Gronsky, IF	.294	357	53	105	8	67	21	48	6
* Casey Fletcher, C	.281	167	23	47	1	25	23	33	9
Alfredo Rodriguez, IF	.281	370	74	104	3	28	51	45	21
Mike Garza, IF	.279	61	11	17	2	7	4	8	0
# Zarley Zalewski, U	.279	104	14	29	6	14	9	27	0
* Marc Flores, IF	.272	356	64	97	12	62	38	59	11
* Melvin Rodriguez, C	.260	285	30	74	6	32	22	62	4
* Charlie White, OF	.260	366	61	95	6	35	33	46	28
# Joe Staley, C	.257	214	37	55	10	38	24	50	0
# Sikes Orvis, IF	.250	84	10	21	2	13	13	26	0
Phillip Bates, OF	.224	241	32	54	4	21	15	58	10
* Rock Shoulders, OF	.194	31	6	6	0	7	5	11	0
Hunter Ridge, OF	.186	59	4	11	2	7	4	16	0

PLAYER	W	L	ERA	G	SV	IP	H	BB	SO
*Zach Hirsch	0	1	1.32	9	2	14	11	1	15
Tyler Levine	2	2	1.71	32	0	42	26	29	35
Kevin McNorton	2	1	2.82	17	6	22	20	7	12
Liam O'Sullivan	11	1	3.33	20	0	122	114	26	109
*Sean Townsley	7	8	3.75	19	0	103	98	42	80
Shane Bryant	5	2	3.86	13	0	72	63	34	50
*Chris Rice	4	4	4.08	26	0	64	56	36	63
*Brent Choban	4	8	4.32	36	6	50	35	30	50
Kevin Simmons	1	2	4.91	36	4	44	45	28	36
*Spencer Medick	8	4	5.27	18	0	96	110	48	49
Robert Robbins	0	0	5.71	12	0	17	18	10	15
Kaleb Ort	3	4	6.05	20	1	61	62	42	61
Marc Rutledge	2	5	6.45	30	1	53	63	25	33
Mitchell Osnowitz	1	0	8.1	8	1	10	15	2	7
Luke Crumley	0	1	11.5	7	0	18	28	21	11

LAKE ERIE CRUSHERS

PLAYER	AVG	AB	R	H	HR	RBI	BB	SO	SB
Eric Grabe, IF	.290	245	37	71	5	41	32	44	2
Juan Avila, OF	.276	98	14	27	5	19	2	22	0
* Connor Oliver, OF	.275	295	48	81	13	40	36	55	18
* Jose Barraza, C	.264	367	49	97	6	53	37	101	7
Bryan De La Rosa, C	.261	238	35	62	4	30	28	66	5
* Richard Seigel, IF	.257	140	17	36	1	17	22	54	6
Brendan Costantino, IF	.251	283	39	71	1	28	24	32	11
Sean Hurley, OF	.242	178	27	43	7	28	29	55	4
* William Beckwith, IF	.234	94	11	22	1	8	6	20	2
* Brady North, 1B	.229	48	3	11	0	2	10	11	0
Max Casper, SS	.229	301	26	69	0	29	21	56	2
* Robb Paller, OF	.223	112	26	25	2	16	28	15	1
* Parks Jordan, IF	.216	74	12	16	1	8	6	12	2
* Parker Norris, OF	.213	211	27	45	2	25	34	66	6

PLAYER	AVG	AB	R	H	HR	RBI	BB	SO	SB
Carlos Avila, 2B	.211	109	12	23	0	9	9	21	3
Marquis Riley, OF	.194	31	2	6	1	1	2	4	1
Nick Covello, 3B	.178	45	5	8	0	2	6	17	0
* Justin Byrd, OF	.173	75	11	13	0	4	10	16	9
* Daniel Aldrich, OF	.160	75	10	12	2	9	3	28	0
Cody Herald, OF	.133	30	1	4	0	1	2	8	1

PLAYER	W	L	ERA	G	SV	IP	H	BB	SO
Fernando Gallegos	2	1	0.36	6	1	25	14	2	21
Josh Laxer	1	0	1.84	13	0	15	10	4	9
Jordan McCoy	0	1	2.29	23	0	20	16	10	17
Chandler Jagodzinski	3	3	2.38	48	14	53	42	7	51
*Todd Kibby	2	4	2.70	10	0	57	45	18	56
Manny Arciniega	1	1	2.87	15	1	31	17	16	34
Brad Duffy	1	2	3.09	21	0	32	25	11	36
Steve Hagen	7	6	3.49	11	0	111	122	35	91
Juan Caballero	5	1	3.54	27	0	81	74	32	54
Jordan Kraus	3	4	3.70	7	0	41	34	10	21
*Connor Reed	4	2	3.70	17	0	58	52	16	32
Justin Sinibaldi	1	5	4.18	12	1	28	27	21	18
Keegan Ghidotti	2	1	4.34	39	0	37	52	13	24
*Stetson Nelson	5	3	4.37	10	0	58	66	21	40
Ryan Richardson	1	0	4.38	16	0	12	11	2	11
Mike Devine	7	6	4.56	29	3	81	87	18	67
Josh Heddinger	2	2	4.88	4	0	24	25	12	17
Trevor Longfellow	0	2	6.00	20	2	21	30	15	9
Devin Malone	1	0	7.11	16	1	13	14	13	10
Colin Feldtman	0	3	8.59	9	1	22	27	12	7

NORMAL CORNBELTERS

PLAYER	AVG	AB	R	H	HR	RBI	BB	SO	SB
Jacoby Middleton, OF	.410	39	8	16	0	3	6	10	1
Santiago Chirino, IF	.334	398	53	133	4	41	18	24	4
* Aaron Dudley, IF	.327	330	58	108	18	80	66	62	7
* Dylan Kelly, C	.311	338	34	105	3	36	18	60	0
* Nolan Meadows, OF	.277	361	64	100	27	76	36	94	0
# Ty Morris, IF	.271	214	42	58	4	26	22	64	23
* Craig Lepre, C	.268	149	11	40	3	21	18	20	1
RJ Perucki, IF	.267	180	22	48	6	26	10	31	0
Dillon Haupt, OF	.253	360	56	91	17	49	26	78	0
Mitch Elliott, OF	.247	93	14	23	1	3	8	30	4
Mike Fish, OF	.247	150	16	37	3	16	14	20	5
Justin Fletcher, IF	.236	148	22	35	0	7	10	13	8
Jesus Solorzano, OF	.235	51	5	12	1	3	0	11	1
Elvin Rodriguez, IF	.213	108	15	23	2	12	19	40	2
# Mike Skoller, IF	.209	91	10	19	0	5	5	22	1
Elijah Trail, IF	.202	104	14	21	3	9	12	29	0
Brandon Roberts, IF	.118	34	4	4	0	3	1	17	0

PLAYER	W	L	ERA	G	SV	IP	H	BB	SO
Brennan Smith	1	0	0.54	15	6	17	6	7	19
Francisco Carrillo	3	2	1.75	41	4	57	43	25	77
Horacio Acosta	9	4	3.64	26	0	96	92	17	67
Kevin Jefferis	1	0	3.68	11	1	15	15	5	21
*Max Homick	4	6	3.69	21	0	83	73	42	66
*Casey Brown	1	0	3.86	16	1	21	24	11	18
Charlie Gillies	6	4	3.99	11	0	68	63	37	58
Race Parmenter	3	3	4.27	35	6	53	49	25	48
Michael Schweiss	7	9	4.38	19	0	103	95	79	98
Chris Carmain	7	9	4.40	20	0	133	143	29	88
*Vince Apicella	1	1	5.21	5	0	19	18	10	18
Matt Chavarria	0	3	6.20	29	0	61	70	27	50
Jake Negrete	0	2	6.28	3	0	14	19	6	10
Mike Elwood	1	3	7.12	13	0	37	41	13	38
Quinn Pippin	1	0	7.30	8	0	12	14	8	7
Eddie Cody	1	1	8.16	3	0	14	22	4	7

RIVER CITY RASCALS

PLAYER	AVG	AB	R	H	HR	RBI	BB	SO	SB
Josh Silver, IF	.352	227	45	80	9	44	27	27	8
Dominique Taylor, OF	.315	92	13	29	1	9	2	20	4
Kyle Gaedele, OF	.308	302	60	93	14	50	37	80	24
Mike Jurgella, C	.304	260	48	79	5	41	33	47	10

PLAYER	AVG	AB	R	H	HR	RBI	BB	SO	SB
* Griff Gordon, OF	.297	118	18	35	1	15	12	14	7
Willi Martin, IF	.295	149	18	44	3	19	14	24	3
* Jason Merjano, IF	.291	354	47	103	5	51	14	53	17
Josh Ludy, C	.289	339	31	98	4	45	34	46	2
Johnny Morales, IF	.281	253	45	71	3	26	28	23	7
Robby Enslen, OF	.272	287	44	78	8	42	25	65	4
* Alexi Colon, OF	.266	263	58	70	17	42	65	54	22
* Clint Freeman, IF	.254	228	31	58	9	39	9	40	2
Steve Pascual, IF	.229	35	2	8	0	1	5	10	0
Danny Rosenbaum, IF	.214	28	2	6	0	4	0	6	0
Braxton Martinez, IF	.194	139	17	27	1	13	18	27	0

PLAYER	W	L	ERA	G	SV	IP	H	BB	SO
Zac Treece	3	1	1.86	41	22	48	37	15	75
*Dan Ludwig	3	1	2.41	5	0	34	30	6	28
Joe Pavlovich	4	2	2.81	19	0	64	63	21	44
Nick Kennedy	2	5	2.90	46	0	40	39	11	28
Dylan Brammer	2	1	3.06	4	0	18	15	8	13
Jake Negrete	0	2	3.18	3	0	11	12	3	5
Will Schierholz	4	1	3.46	35	1	39	46	13	29
Zeb Sneed	8	8	3.77	20	0	122	121	20	92
Jason Zgardowski	1	1	4.38	15	1	25	18	7	30
*Austin Warner	4	1	4.42	10	0	39	42	14	42
Shane Street	1	1	4.50	17	0	16	10	12	24
*Michael Gunn	3	1	4.68	33	0	25	26	21	24
Tim Koons	4	6	4.68	16	0	85	86	33	66
Josh Wright	3	2	5.36	15	0	49	63	17	35
Skylar Hunter	0	1	5.56	9	0	11	6	9	12
Reese Gregory	2	3	5.71	16	1	52	60	15	30
Joe Scanio	3	3	5.93	8	0	41	62	4	26
Jared Wilson	0	3	6.41	18	1	20	21	7	23
*Lucas Laster	0	0	6.61	14	0	16	25	9	13
*Jason Ziegler	1	1	6.66	6	0	26	34	3	16
Francis Ramirez	1	2	8.27	5	0	18	15	15	15

SCHAUMBURG BOOMERS

PLAYER	AVG	AB	R	H	HR	RBI	BB	SO	SB
Josh Gardiner, IF	.311	90	18	28	2	14	13	17	6
* Zack Weigel, OF	.297	111	15	33	0	7	23	25	4
Mike McClellan, IF	.286	77	9	22	2	11	11	22	0
Kenny Towns, IF	.283	233	23	66	3	17	15	39	6
* Ino Patron, 1B	.280	161	25	45	5	24	10	36	5
* Paul Kronenfeld, OF	.279	280	39	78	10	49	34	88	5
* Mark Nelson, IF	.260	342	26	89	2	32	46	46	2
Jordan Dean, IF	.256	395	56	101	3	38	21	48	14
* Tobias Moreno, IF	.254	59	5	15	0	4	8	15	3
Argenis Aldazoro, OF	.248	125	10	31	0	8	11	20	2
* Justin Byrd, OF	.237	97	11	23	0	7	15	23	7
Dusty Robinson, IF	.206	189	17	39	1	24	14	32	3
# Mikal Hill, IF	.203	202	14	41	1	27	19	52	3
* Matt Petrone, OF	.200	40	3	8	0		6	9	1
Nick Oberg, IF	.199	151	10	30	1	15	19	33	1
Chris Robinson, C	.197	117	21	23	2	10	17	29	2
* Griff Gordon, OF	.191	68	6	13	0	1	11	14	0
James Keller, C	.189	196	16	37	2	17	17	62	1
Shawn Payne, OF	.167	66	8	11	2	8	7	18	4
Mike Valadez, IF	.127	63	5	8	0	2	2	11	0
* Jack Cockrum, C	.070	43	2	3	0	1	3	6	0

PLAYER	W	L	ERA	G	SV	IP	H	BB	SO
Evan Boyd	2	0	1.05	28	4	34	19	3	30
Jake Joyce	7	3	2.35	33	1	42	31	30	64
Dexter Price	4	4	2.52	41	15	46	42	12	53
Patrick Dolan	0	1	2.72	29	0	36	28	13	36
*Gunnar Kines	5	6	2.95	18	0	113	81	37	104
Kagen Hopkins	5	6	3.84	20	0	98	106	31	71
Seth Webster	8	9	3.90	20	0	127	140	20	108
Derek DeYoung	2	2	4.46	31	0	42	40	23	41
Kenneth Knudsen	0	2	5.29	26	0	36	31	19	36
Scott Schultz	4	7	5.48	19	0	107	133	29	79
Josh Heddinger	2	4	5.64	10	0	45	53	19	29
*Lars Liguori	0	3	6.18	3	0	16	23	6	8
Brett Mabry	2	5	6.30	10	0	56	71	19	39
Kurt Lipscomb	0	2	6.55	16	1	34	50	12	19

SOUTHERN ILLINOIS MINERS

PLAYER	AVG	AB	R	H	HR	RBI	BB	SO	SB
Shane Kennedy, IF	.363	273	68	99	5	47	44	70	34
Craig Massey, OF	.295	295	58	87	5	40	48	37	19
* Nolan Earley, OF	.291	354	53	103	9	70	43	68	3
Steve Marino, IF	.288	371	53	107	16	79	22	49	0
* Aaron Gates, IF	.288	385	78	111	8	54	48	57	11
# Riley Moore, C	.281	135	14	38	3	13	18	28	0
* Brandon Cummins, OF	.269	67	13	18	3	8	16	12	6
Alex De Leon, IF	.256	332	50	85	14	72	53	90	0
Willi Martin, IF	.254	67	5	17	1	7	4	12	0
Julius Gaines, IF	.249	173	22	43	1	13	10	29	2
Edison Sanchez, IF	.238	63	7	15	1	6	8	15	0
Toby DeMello, C	.227	194	27	44	5	22	22	53	0
* Vincent Guglietti, IF	.215	93	9	20	3	11	3	11	0
Francisco Rosario, IF	.213	277	46	59	0	19	45	98	8
* Brendan O'Brien, OF	.183	60	11	11	0	4	11	18	5
* Jordan Brower, IF	.143	28	2	4	0	4	3	4	0
Brian Portelli, OF	.107	28	1	3	0	2	0	6	0

PLAYER	W	L	ERA	G	SV	IP	H	BB	SO
Adam Lopez	3	0	0.71	25	13	25	10	19	29
*Rich Mascheri	0	0	1.88	13	0	14	8	3	17
Evan Mott	3	1	2.09	46	1	47	37	12	39
Josh Kimborowicz	8	0	2.33	10	0	62	51	29	45
Kyle Tinius	4	1	2.51	38	0	43	41	19	29
Jarett Miller	8	4	3.04	20	0	127	130	34	93
Nick Palacios	4	1	3.61	29	1	32	35	15	25
Chris DeBoo	1	1	3.63	43	3	40	40	19	28
Corey Sessions	1	2	3.90	7	0	30	29	10	15
Jake Cose	0	2	4.05	24	7	20	20	20	21
Brooks Trujillo	4	4	4.17	17	0	65	66	20	27
*Dan Ludwig	7	2	4.23	13	0	79	85	13	50
Dyllon Nuernberg	6	5	4.36	17	0	91	78	45	69
*Rick Teasley	8	5	4.80	17	0	109	123	21	80
* Jake Pannunzio	0	0	6.51	9	0	10	16	3	8
Zach Cooper	0	1	10.12	15	2	11	15	13	9

TRAVERSE CITY BEACH BUMS

PLAYER	AVG	AB	R	H	HR	RBI	BB	SO	SB
Jose Vargas, IF	.298	329	47	98	13	52	24	71	0
* Steven Patterson, IF	.296	351	56	104	12	61	37	62	8
* Will Kengor, SS	.280	328	52	92	8	48	32	90	4
# Marcos Derkes, OF	.267	202	33	54	1	21	37	49	16
* Christian Santisteban, IF	.260	150	13	39	1	16	9	35	0
# Ryan Bottger, OF	.256	312	48	80	1	34	35	66	3
Kendall Patrick, IF	.247	146	13	36	4	20	9	36	0
Elijah Trail, U	.235	170	18	40	3	23	18	67	0
Gaby Juarbe, C	.229	131	9	30	0	10	7	29	1
Casey Rodrigue, U	.224	165	19	37	1	15	4	41	8
* Jeff DeBlieux, OF	.223	310	43	69	1	26	37	78	16
Brian Portelli, OF	.219	32	2	7	0	4	1	7	1
* Nate Causey, C	.208	48	3	10	0	7	5	15	0
Matt Burns, SS	.192	26	2	5	0	2	5	7	0
Brandon Thomasson, 1B	.186	118	14	22	1	16	5	28	0
Giancarlo Brugnoni, IF	.181	188	33	34	10	25	35	96	0
Tyler Peterson, IF	.179	28	1	5	1	2	2	6	1
Wes Wallace, OF	.050	40	6	2	1	1	5	12	0

PLAYER	W	L	ERA	G	SV	IP	H	BB	SO
Luke Barker	1	4	1.44	42	7	62	40	10	83
Augie Gallardo	3	0	1.45	4	0	25	15	12	21
Tucker Simpson	4	4	2.73	10	0	46	41	20	31
Kramer Champlin	5	7	2.80	19	0	125	112	23	95
*Joeanthony Rivera	0	2	3.00	31	0	27	38	8	30
Rob Blanc	1	1	3.06	24	0	50	37	30	41
*Dylan Stoops	8	3	3.17	16	0	91	77	28	79
James Ball	4	3	3.25	41	0	58	54	19	36
*Ben Libuda	4	5	3.95	31	0	64	61	32	47
Ashton Perritt	0	1	4.40	13	0	16	13	8	11
Jake Lanning	4	6	4.44	29	0	77	85	17	49
Michael Shreves	3	10	5.06	19	0	107	116	47	44
Andrew Brockett	3	4	6.56	26	5	25	35	7	18
*Sasha Kuebel	0	1	7.14	3	0	11	22	6	10
Austin Bembnowski	2	1	8.88	7	0	26	36	16	14

WASHINGTON WILD THINGS

PLAYER	AVG	AB	R	H	HR	RBI	BB	SO	SB
Ricky Rodriguez, OF	.289	318	50	92	9	35	24	76	2
* Chris Grayson, OF	.282	188	24	53	5	20	14	26	18
# David Popkins, OF	.281	306	45	86	15	48	60	85	5
Andrew Heck, OF	.275	255	32	70	0	16	32	55	8
Jamal Austin, OF	.272	151	23	41	0	8	11	23	13
Nick Ferdinand, LF	.263	57	6	15	1	11	6	15	2
* Logan Uxa, IF	.257	140	21	36	6	21	22	38	2
* Jimmy Yezzo, IF	.220	300	29	66	12	42	12	51	2
Kyle Pollock, C	.214	168	15	36	3	15	22	32	3
* Austin Wobrock, IF	.214	295	36	63	2	19	22	61	6
Bryan Haar, IF	.212	151	16	32	9	29	15	41	1
Alex McKeon, C	.198	91	6	18	1	5	2	17	0
Grant Fink, IF	.197	213	23	42	9	24	14	72	0
* Jamodrick McGruder, IF	.192	73	7	14	1	5	10	16	6
* Justin Garcia, OF	.190	42	3	8	1	4	3	17	0
Alvaro Gonzalez, IF	.167	42	5	7	1	7	2	18	0
Ryne Willard, IF	.156	32	2	5	0	0	2	16	0
* Scott Carcaise, IF	.129	31	2	4	0	3	6	10	0
Justin Fox, IF	.125	48	6	6	0	2	8	13	0
John Ziznewski, IF	.097	31	1	3	0	2	4	8	0

PLAYER	W	L	ERA	G	SV	IP	H	BB	SO
Zac Grotz	4	2	1.36	29	10	46	32	9	51
Trevor Foss	8	3	2.50	15	1	101	90	14	66
*Brandon Bixler	1	2	2.70	3	0	13	17	2	7
*Devon Davis	1	1	2.76	37	7	42	34	16	43
Kolin Stanley	3	1	2.96	37	5	52	42	14	42
Matt Fraudin	7	8	3.16	19	0	114	101	46	94
Andrew Woeck	2	1	3.29	35	4	44	28	15	46
Chase Cunningham	7	10	4.21	19	0	105	104	38	56
Luke Wilkins	4	7	4.24	18	0	104	101	49	79
*Brian O'Keefe	2	2	4.50	25	0	44	47	11	35
Sam Agnew-Wieland	2	3	5.51	10	1	31	37	16	18
Christian Powell	1	1	5.60	5	0	18	16	6	11
*Conner Kendrick	0	2	5.94	4	0	20	21	14	12
*Brandon Hinkle	2	3	6.03	7	0	28	30	21	13
*Matt Snyder	1	1	6.06	5	0	16	20	9	17
Ashton Perritt	1	0	10.63	9	0	11	12	11	6

WINDY CITY THUNDERBOLTS

PLAYER	AVG	AB	R	H	HR	RBI	BB	SO	SB
Tim Zier, IF	.275	374	47	103	0	34	23	61	23
Corey Bass, C	.256	281	43	72	11	42	39	99	3
* Cody Keefer, OF	.254	276	37	70	4	29	23	45	3
Coco Johnson, OF	.253	367	47	93	6	36	23	65	48
Ransom LaLonde, IF	.252	314	38	79	2	37	28	51	7
* Kyle Wood, IF	.246	130	20	32	3	23	17	36	2
Reggie Lawson, OF	.242	153	19	37	1	20	19	33	2
Taylor Smart, IF	.230	278	34	64	3	31	23	71	12
Larry Balkwill, C	.228	158	16	34	4	17	30	48	4
* John Williams, OF	.226	93	10	21	0	2	3	13	5
Blair Beck, IF	.205	259	26	53	5	31	29	76	15
* Charley Thurber, OF	.201	134	9	27	1	5	6	36	1
Johnny Eierman, IF	.198	192	20	38	3	19	17	68	6
Kevin Barker, OF	.158	57	7	9	1	8	6	18	2

PLAYER	W	L	ERA	G	SV	IP	H	BB	SO
Zac Westcott	1	0	1.36	20	0	40	24	8	32
*Jake Stolley	2	1	2.05	8	0	26	22	15	23
Austin Delmotte	3	0	3.00	21	0	18	14	12	21
*Jake Fisher	9	4	3.30	16	0	98	106	23	86
Clay Chapman	9	7	3.30	20	0	125	104	47	93
Joel Lima	0	1	3.57	24	1	23	19	7	21
Andrew Lowe	1	0	4.33	24	0	27	33	19	20
Brian Loconsole	1	3	4.33	38	9	37	34	15	32
Kyle Von Ruden	1	7	4.41	9	0	51	54	20	37
Jayson Yano	1	3	4.42	4	0	20	21	11	9
*Chris Chigas	1	2	4.47	34	1	58	48	26	49
*Brady Muller	3	9	4.48	15	0	84	78	35	67
Cameron Giannini	3	4	4.90	34	7	33	26	16	36
Tyler Murphy	2	5	5.34	21	0	64	73	21	53
Ryan Strombom	3	4	5.71	9	0	46	57	16	31

INDEPENDENT LEAGUES

PLAYER	W	L	ERA	G	SV	IP	H	BB	SO
Mitchell Cody	0	3	6.57	8	0	26	32	11	19
Brandon Boyle	4	1	8.25	9	0	12	17	8	9
Isaac Gil	0	0	10.12	13	5	11	17	7	16

PACIFIC ASSOCIATION

Since the Pacific Association sprung from the North American League, the San Rafael Pacifics have been the class of the league. But in 2016, the Sonoma Stompers finally caught their rival.

In a one-game championship, Sonoma knocked off San Rafael 5-4 to thwart the Pacifics try for a three-peat. Instead Sonoma got to celebrate its first title.

It was a momentous year for Sonoma. During the season the Stompers added a trio of women (Stacy Piagno, Kelsie Whitmore and Anna Kimbrell) to the roster to become the first U.S. men's professional team to have multiple women on the roster in decades.

PACIFIC ASSOCIATION	W	L	PCT	GB
Sonoma Stompers	47	31	.603	—
San Rafael Pacifics	41	37	.526	6
Pittsburg Diamonds	36	42	.462	11
Vallejo Admirals	32	46	.410	15

PLAYOFFS—Sonoma defeated San Rafael 5-4 in one-game championship.

ATTENDANCE: San Rafael 16,075; Sonoma 13,370; Vallejo 5,712; Pittsburg 2,608.

INDIVIDUAL BATTING LEADERS

PLAYER	AVG	AB	R	H	HR	RBI	SB
Carranza, Joel, Sonoma	.316	263	50	83	15	60	0
Williams, Tim, Vallejo	.312	269	42	84	7	48	14
Taylor, Jake, San Rafael	.307	316	48	97	16	74	9
Baptista, Daniel, Sonoma	.304	283	43	86	9	61	2
Bautista, Gerald, Vallejo	.302	225	32	68	4	38	0
Bekakis, Johnny, San Rafael	.301	196	28	59	1	18	6
Sandford, Darian, Vallejo	.293	290	57	85	0	30	99
Tucker, Chase, San Rafael	.293	294	54	86	4	36	14
Morioka, Mason, Sonoma	.292	226	44	66	5	31	2
Oddo, Nick, Pittsburg	.291	268	30	78	7	48	0

INDIVIDUAL PITCHING LEADERS

PLAYER	W	L	ERA	IP	H	BB	SO
Conroy, Patrick, San Rafael	5	2	2.12	102	105	28	71
Jackson Jr., Mike, Sonoma	8	2	2.84	76	59	27	61
Barnett, Patrick, San Rafael	4	5	2.87	85	85	20	70
Thurber, Taylor, Sonoma	7	5	2.95	85	82	16	70
Brammer, Dylan, Pittsburg	7	3	3.26	80	69	34	64
Cummins, Chris, Pittsburg	7	7	3.35	107	115	27	102
Garcia, Oliver, Sonoma	5	2	3.57	71	58	47	85
Hutchinson, Marquis, Vallejo	6	5	3.61	90	89	55	51
Espinosa, Juan, Sonoma	4	4	3.78	64	58	22	60
Polanco, Celson, San Rafael	6	5	4.13	98	105	33	77

PECOS LEAGUE

The Pecos League's footprint continued to grow in 2016 as the league moved further into Kansas, but the league's title stayed in Arizona as Tucson knocked off Trinidad.

NORTH	W	L	PCT	GB
Garden City Wind	38	26	.594	—
* Trinidad Triggers	35	29	.547	3
* Topeka Train Robbers	28	33	.459	8 ½
Salina Stockade	29	36	.446	9 ½
Great Bend Boom	19	43	.306	18

SOUTH	W	L	PCT	GB
Tucson Saguaros	51	14	.785	—
* Roswell Invaders	44	23	.657	8
* Alpine Cowboys	32	32	.500	18 ½
White Sands Pupfish	28	40	.412	24 ½
Santa Fe Fuego	19	47	.288	32 ½

*Wild Card

PLAYOFFS—Quarterfinals-Trinidad defeated Topeka 2-0 and Roswell defeated Alpine 2-0 in best-of-3 series. **Semifinals**—Trinidad defeated Garden City 2-1 and Tucson defeated Roswell 2-1 in best-of-3 series. Finals-Tucson defeated Trinidad 2-0 in best-of-3 series.

INDIVIDUAL BATTING LEADERS

PLAYER	AVG	AB	R	H	HR	RBI	SB
Maria, Eric, Santa Fe	.448	223	52	100	12	49	5
Bishop, Cody, Roswell	.429	203	67	87	16	61	5
Miller, Joey, Roswell	.427	199	60	85	21	75	0
Wharton, T.J., White Sands	.423	227	54	96	10	67	3
Coffman, Cody, Roswell	.418	239	80	100	22	76	2
Kalbfliesh, Eric, White Sands	.418	275	63	115	8	59	6
Baez, Dubal, White Sands	.408	179	70	73	2	20	21
Ardeeser, Clay, Garden City	.404	255	55	103	12	76	9
Epperson, C.J., Salina	.401	162	37	65	6	34	15
Ferguson, Eric, Alpine	.397	232	63	92	5	29	35

INDIVIDUAL PITCHING LEADERS

PLAYER	W	L	ERA	IP	H	BB	SO
Anderson, Marty, Garden City	4	2	2.64	58	44	26	72
Borkowski, Steve, Tucson	10	0	2.72	79	78	46	92
Swagerty, Stephen, Great Bend	3	4	3.42	76	73	48	61
Fuss, Skyler, Salina	3	5	3.64	54	68	12	40
Keen, Randy, Tucson	6	0	3.68	64	67	21	40
Lemmo, Pat, Alpine	2	4	4.01	52	69	10	43
Boyle, Austin, Garden City	8	3	4.03	87	82	36	77
Johnson, David, Roswell	9	2	4.43	81	94	9	81
Blackmon, Tim, Salina	4	2	4.50	62	50	45	86
Robinson, Joe, Trinidad	4	4	4.74	74	86	24	73

UNITED STATES PROFESSIONAL BASEBALL LEAGUE

The fledgling USPBL lived up to its promises in 2016. The league fielded three teams based at one new stadium. The league promised to work on player development and it did as multiple players were signed to affiliated contracts.

TEAM	W	L	PCT	GB
Birmingham Bloomfield Beavers	26	22	.542	—
East Side Diamond Hoppers	25	24	.510	1 ½
Utica Unicorns	22	27	.449	4 ½

PLAYOFFS: Wild Card—Utica defeated East Side in a one-game wild card game. **Finals**—Utica defeated Birmingham in one-game championship.

INDIVIDUAL BATTING LEADERS

PLAYER	AVG	AB	R	H	HR	RBI	SB
Wilson, Nic, Birmingham	.340	144	38	49	17	41	0
Power, Chris, East Side	.338	148	29	50	2	14	8
Ortel, Luke, East Side	.322	171	35	55	3	21	11
Stewart, Kameron, East Side	.306	157	26	48	5	30	6
Caswell, Corey, East Side	.301	173	24	52	2	31	0
Crutcher, Austin, Utica	.301	186	44	56	15	51	19
Ortega, Ray, Birmingham	.298	121	20	36	3	22	3
Williams, Miles, Birmingham	.292	168	22	49	8	33	2
Kennon, Dan, Birmingham	.291	172	37	50	2	21	3
Cruz, Chris, Utica	.287	174	23	50	9	40	8

INDIVIDUAL PITCHING LEADERS

PLAYER	W	L	ERA	IP	H	BB	SO
Nelson, Andrew, Birmingham	2	0	2.25	40	23	27	51
Murray, Donny, Utica	1	5	2.84	73	60	24	82
Wynne, Randy, Birmingham	5	4	3.08	61	75	8	55
Brenner, Seth, Utica	4	5	3.31	54	55	22	40
Root, Connor, East Side	3	2	3.62	50	41	20	48
Koumas, Forrest, Birmingham	4	2	3.65	49	33	30	47
Conley, Jeff, East Side	5	3	3.98	63	56	22	65
Kinch, Alex, Birmingham	2	4	4.82	52	77	29	46
Jensen-Clagg, Nick, Birmingham	3	3	5.28	51	66	26	57
Ezell, Jacob, Utica	1	4	5.29	48	52	20	42

INTERNATIONAL

Olympic return caps busy year around globe

COMPILED BY JOHN MANUEL

The World Baseball Classic field is set for 2017 after four qualifying tournaments were played in 2016.

And the events of the past year set the table for a more robust international calendar to come. For while the WBC has taken center stage for the last decade, it will have competition in the next three years after the International Olympic Committee agreed to put baseball and softball back on the program for the 2020 Games in Tokyo.

Approved in August during the 2016 Games in Rio de Janeiro, the proposal includes baseball and softball for six-nation tournaments in 2020 under the World Baseball Softball Confederation's one-sport, two-disciplines plan. Baseball and softball weren't permanently added to the Olympics, but current IOC policy allows host nations to tailor the Games to their fans and athletes. While baseball's place in the Games isn't secure for the long-term, it will be an Olympic sport for the first time since 2008 in Beijing.

"I would like to express our deepest gratitude to the Tokyo 2020 leadership for putting their faith in our sport to begin with," WBSC president Riccardo Fraccari said in August, when the inclusion became official.

Major League Baseball commissioner Rob Manfred added, "We are excited about the IOC's announcement restoring baseball and softball to the 2020 Olympics in Tokyo. Baseball and softball are global sports that belong in the Olympics."

Japan's baseball federation and Nippon Professional Baseball have promoted getting baseball back in the Olympics for years, and put money and time behind that effort, including playing host to the WBSC's inaugural Premier 12 tournament in November 2015. That event, won by South Korea with a 8-0 gold-medal game win against the United States, was the WBSC's top-level event, and while the caliber of its competition was modest, Japanese fans packed the Tokyo Dome for the semifinals and finals.

WBC Field Set

South Korea won the Premier 12 and also will server as a host site for the first time for World Baseball Classic games in 2017. The 16-team WBC had its field and sites set, first with four

Veteran big leaguer Jason Marquis helped Israel qualify for the World Baseball Classic

TOMASSO DEROSA

qualifying tournaments played in 2016, then with the dates set for the four edition of the event.

The Tokyo Dome and Seoul, South Korea's Gocheok Skydome will host Pools A and B of the 2017 WBC from March 7-10. Pool A in Tokyo will include China, Cuba, Japan and Australia, which won a qualifying tournament played in February 2016 in Sydney.

Pool B will include the Netherlands, South Korea, Taiwan and Israel, which won the Brooklyn qualifier played in September, besting a field that included Brazil, Great Britain and Pakistan. The Israeli team, which leaned almost exclusively on Americans of Jewish heritage, featured players with big league experience such as Ike Davis, Cody Decker, Ryan Lavarnway, Nate Freiman and Jason Marquis. The righthanded Marquis, who won 124 games in 15 big league seasons, pitched three innings in the semifinal against Great Britain, then

tossed four perfect innings in the finale, a rematch against the British that Israel won 9-1. Former indy leaguer Blake Gailen, Lavarnway and Decker all homered in the finale.

Pools C and D for the '17 WBC are scheduled for March 9-12 in North America. Miami's Marlins Park will host the Pool C with the U.S., Canada, Colombia and reigning champion Dominican Republic. Colombia qualified with a March 17-20 qualifier victory in Panama in an event that also included the host Panamanians, Spain and France. Mets second baseman Dilson Herrera hit a solo home run in the bottom of the eighth inning in the championship game to push Colombia past Panama 2-1.

Pool D in Guadalajara, Mexico, will include Mexico, which won a March 17-20 qualifier in Mexicali, beating out the Czech Republic, Germany and Nicaragua. Joining Mexico in Pool D are Italy, Puerto Rico and Venezuela.

Second-round WBC games will take place in Tokyo and San Diego at Petco Park before the four semifinalists advance to Dodger Stadium in Los Angeles, which hosts the semis and finals March 20-22.

The U.S. team announced Jim Leyland as its manager. He'll try to succeed where Buck Martinez (2006), Davey Johnson (2009) and Joe Torre (2013) have failed, as the U.S. has yet to even win a game in the WBC semifinal round, having reached that far only once, in 2009. American teams have won just nine games in three WBCs; six nations have won more.

Packed Calendar

The WBC qualifiers were just part of the 2016 international schedule. The WBSC held a 15U World Cup in Iwaki, Japan from July 29-Aug. 7, plus a Women's World Cup in September in Gijang, South Korea. The 18U and 12U age groups held continental qualifying tournaments, while the WBSC launched a new event, at the 23U level, in Monterrey, Mexico, though baseball nations such as the United States, Cuba, Dominican Republic and Canada did not participate. The 23U classification replaced a 21U level that was held in 2014.

Japan's reign as the top women's baseball team in the world continued in convincing fashion at the Women's World Cup. Japan beat Canada 10-0 in the championship game in a game that was cut short after seven innings because Japan held a double-digit lead. Ayami Sato picked up the win with seven shutout innings. She held Canada to two hits while striking out five.

Japan was 8-0 for the tournament with five

COPABE PAN AMERICAN CHAMPIONSHIP MONTERREY, MEXICO

FINAL STANDINGS

1. U.S.
2. Cuba
3. Mexico
4. Nicaragua
5. Panama
6. Brazil
7. Colombia
8. Honduras

FINAL STATISTICS

BATTING

PLAYER	AVG	AB	R	H	2B	3B	HR	RBI	BB	SO	SB
Royce Lewis	.500	18	4	9	2	0	0	3	8	3	3
Jarred Kelenic	.407	27	6	11	2	2	1	7	4	1	4
Ryan Vilade	.364	22	7	8	3	0	1	8	5	1	4
Calvin Mitchell	.364	11	3	4	1	0	0	1	3	2	1
Nick Allen	.346	26	13	9	2	1	0	2	7	3	9
Triston Casas	.333	24	7	8	2	0	2	11	4	5	0
Quentin Holmes	.333	9	3	3	1	0	0	0	2	2	2
Nick Pratto	.286	21	5	6	3	0	0	1	3	7	2
Hunter Greene	.261	23	2	6	3	0	0	6	2	5	1
Patrick Bailey	.222	9	5	2	0	0	1	5	1	2	1
M.J. Melendez	.182	11	1	2	0	0	0	3	2	2	0
Michael Siani	.133	15	4	2	0	0	0	2	3	2	3

PITCHING

PITCHERS	W	L	ERA	SV	G	IP	H	BB	SO
Blayne Enlow	0	1	0.00	0	2	13	5	3	9
Hans Crouse	2	0	0.00	0	2	12	3	5	12
Nick Pratto	2	0	0.00	0	2	9	2	0	13
Jordan Butler	1	0	0.00	0	2	5	2	2	4
Triston Casas	0	0	0.00	0	1	3	2	0	3
Michael Siani	0	0	0.00	0	1	3	1	1	1
C.J. Van Eyk	1	0	1.12	0	2	8	7	1	6
Hagen Danner	0	0	5.40	0	1	2	2	2	1
Logan Allen	0	0	6.00	0	1	3	7	1	2
Shane Baz	0	0	6.00	0	1	3	2	1	4
Mitchell Stone	0	0	9.00	0	2	2	6	2	3

shutouts. It outscored its opponents 70-5. Japan has now won the past five Women's World Cups, which are held every two years. USA Baseball won the first two World Cups, held in 2004 and 2006, but Japan has won every World Cup since 2008. Venezuela defeated Taiwan in the bronze medal game.

While Japan was once again a convincing champion, the American women finished seventh, their worst ever for a World Cup.

Cuba defeated Japan to win the 15U championship, winning 9-4 in the gold-medal game. Liodel Chapelli, a first baseman, went 5-for-5 in the title match and hit .444 in the tournament overall to win MVP honors.

Team USA, which went 7-2 in the event, took home the bronze with an 8-3 victory against Panama. American losses to Cuba and Colombia in the semifinal cost it a shot at gold.

America's 18U national team program got a new director in former Cardinals scout Matt Blood but kept up its winning ways, winning its sixth consecutive gold medal in international competition.

INTERNATIONAL

USA BASEBALL

Nick Pratto helped USA Baseball's 18U team win gold for a second straight year

earned tournament MVP honors by going 11-for-27 in the tournament with five extra-base hits (including a homer), seven RBIs and four stolen bases, as well as a powerful throwing arm in right field that throttled opposing baserunners. Infielder Royce Lewis (Aliso Viejo, Calif.) batted .500 (9-for-18) in the event, with eight walks, three hit by pitches and no strikeouts helping account for a .690 OBP in eight games.

International Incidents

■ Major League Baseball returned to Cuba for the first time since 1999 when the Tampa Bay Rays made a late March visit to the island for an exhibition game, bringing a special guest with them. President Barack Obama headed a list of dignitaries as part of his continued efforts to normalize relations with the Caribbean island nation, which included re-establishing an American embassy in Havana.

Cuban pitchers Pedro Luis Lazo, the all-time wins leader in Cuba's Serie Nacional, and ex-big leaguer Luis Tiant threw out the first pitches before the Rays, featuring Cuban player Dayron Varona, beat the Cuban national team 4-1. Commissioner Rob Manfred, union head Tony Clark, former Yankees shortstop Derek Jeter and Rachel Robinson (widow of Jackie Robinson) were among those in the official MLB traveling part at Estadio Latinamericano, often sitting in the same section as Cuban dictator Raul Castro and members of his government.

■ MLB, which had funded 75 percent of Australia Baseball League operations since it re-launched in 2010, decided to cuts its funding in August, but the six-team ABL made plans to go ahead with the 2016-17 season, though it reduced its league schedule from 55 to 40 games. MLB was expected to redirect funding to grassroots programs Down Under. Baseball Australia's chief executive Brett Pickett told Australian media, "There is no question their exit is going to have a material impact on the league, but they're still heavily committed to the game."

■ The Dutch National Team defended its European Baseball Championship by going a perfect 9-0 in the tournament, including a 3-2 win over Spain in the championship game. Yurendell DeCaster singled in the winning run in the bottom of the 10th in the deciding game. Loek Van Mil picked up the win with two scoreless innings of relief. This was Spain's first-ever appearance in the European Baseball Championship championship game. For the Netherlands, it was the 22nd Euro Baseball Championship. Italy finished third and Germany finished fourth.

The crown, won in Monterrey, Mexico, was in the 2016 Pan American championships, with Team USA going 7-1 in the tournament and topping Cuba 6-1 in the championship game.

Righthander Hans Crouse, out of Dana Point, Calif., no-hit Cuba into the fifth inning and struck out 11 over seven one-hit innings in the gold-medal game. The U.S. team, loaded with potential top draft picks for 2017 and beyond, hit six home runs in the tournament while the rest of the field hit only one.

The squad had four returnees from the 2015 roster that won the World Cup. Catcher/righthander Hagen Danner (Huntington Beach, Calif.), one of the returning veterans, drove in the game's first two runs with a double, then scored on an RBI double by Nick Pratto (Huntington Beach, Calif.), also a member of that 2015 team and his high school teammate in California. Another returnee, lefthander Jordan Butler (Odessa, Fla.), pitched the final two innings out of the bullpen to close out the victory.

Outfielder Jarred Kelenic (Waukesha, Wis.)

INTERNATIONAL

MLB vets lead Puebla to title

BY BRUCE BASKIN

The Mexican League has long served as a viable option for former major leaguers to extend their careers. Minnie Minoso hit .317 over seven years before retiring at age 51 and George Scott batted .302 in his five-year stint, to name two. However, rarely have as many ex-MLBers been important pieces to a team as the six who played for 2016 champion Puebla. A seventh piloted the Pericos to the crown after arriving in the colonial city under unusual circumstances.

In perhaps the strangest managerial firing among the eight skippers who were canned during the season (high turnover even by Mexican League standards), Puebla's Matias Carrillo was canned during June's all-star break despite holding the circuit's best record at 38-16. Cory Snyder was brought in and piloted the team to second place in the South Division with a 74-38 mark before beating defending champion Quintana Roo, top seed Yucatan (77-33) and North Division titlist Tijuana to claim the flag. Snyder could field an entirely ex-MLB outfield of Nyjer Morgan (.305 with 11 homers and 22 steals), Willy Taveras (.325) and Ruben Rivera, who hit .286 at age 42. Carlos Quentin hit .211 before being released. Lefthander Travis Blackley went 8-8, 3.92 during the season and went on to be playoff MVP while closer Chad Gaudin converted 33 saves with a 1.65 ERA. As prominent as the former MLBers were, it was a homegrown product who won both the batting title and regular season MVP honors.

Sonora-born Cesar Tapia topped the loop with a .383/.431/.662 slash line, adding 21 homers and 94 RBIs while collecting the MVP trophy. Tapia is a career .331 batter after 12 seasons. Alex Valdez of Monterrey led with 30 homers, Aguascalientes' Diory Hernandez was tops with 97 RBIs and Satillo teammates Justin Greene and Christian Zazueta each stole 39 bases to tie for first.

Among pitchers, while Puebla's Blackley, Gaudin and Mauricio Lara got most of the postseason ink, Yucatan's Yoanner Negrin dominated the regular campaign. The Cuban righty went 18-1, 2.29, recording 15 consecutive wins to end the schedule after a 5-4 loss to Puebla on May 1. Monclova's Josh Lowey challenged Negrin for pitcher of the year until signing a contract with

Korea's KT Wiz in early July. Despite missing the final month, Lowey still led the Mexican League with a 1.65 ERA and 131 strikeouts to augment his 13-3 record. Another Monclova hurler, Arcenio Leon, beat out Gaudin for the saves title with 36.

The Monterrey Sultanes easily led all teams in average attendance, drawing 12,783 per opening, but it was a tough season at the gate for the league. Monterrey, Tijuana (9,303 average) and Yucatan (9,101) all drew well. However, eight of the LMB's 16 teams averaged fewer than 3,000 a game, leading to rumbling among some observers about contraction heading into the offseason.

STANDINGS & LEADERS

NORTH	W	L	PCT	GB
Sultanes de Monterrey	72	39	.649	—
Acereros del Norte	69	43	.616	3 ½
Toros de Tijuana	64	48	.571	8 ½
Vaqueros de la Laguna	63	50	.558	10
Diablos Rojos del Mexico	57	54	.514	15
Rieleros de Aguascalientes	53	58	.477	19
Saraperos de Saltillo	50	61	.450	22
Broncos de Reynosa	24	88	.214	48 ½

SOUTH	W	L	PCT	GB
Leones de Yucatan	77	33	.700	—
Pericos de Puebla	74	38	.661	4
Tigres de Quintana Roo	68	45	.602	10 ½
Piratas de Campeche	57	51	.528	19
Olmecas de Tabasco	44	67	.396	33 ½
Rojos del Aguila de Veracruz	43	67	.391	34
Guerreros de Oaxaca	42	70	.375	36
Delfines de Ciudad del Carmen	31	76	.290	44 ½

PLAYER, TEAM	AVG	AB	R	H	2B	3B	HR	RBI	BB	SO	SB
Tapia, Cesar, PUE	.383	334	64	128	30	0	21	94	27	37	13
Sosa, Ruben, LAG	.371	259	67	96	12	10	2	29	41	47	22
Torres, Tim, OAX	.351	271	55	95	22	1	11	41	37	58	15
Alfonzo, Eliezer, SAL	.350	331	52	116	20	0	23	80	15	64	2
Lopez, Carlos, VER	.350	297	40	104	21	1	5	29	36	47	5
Rios, Ramon, MTY	.344	393	70	135	20	2	4	56	19	30	4
Castillo, Jesus, AGS	.342	392	73	134	24	1	12	56	67	75	14
Madera, Sandy, TAB	.340	365	58	124	17	0	17	67	30	49	1
Greene, Justin, SAL	.340	427	73	145	22	8	10	48	50	84	39
Beltre, Engel, CAM	.339	304	47	103	19	3	5	33	15	50	6
Quiroz, Esteban, TIG	.335	337	69	113	18	0	15	63	66	48	4
Ibarra, Walter, MTY	.329	410	78	135	25	3	6	62	24	60	10
Alvarez, Ricky, LAG	.329	435	69	143	31	1	24	91	13	79	8
Diaz, Frank, OAX	.326	414	73	135	22	3	13	75	31	48	1
Taveras, Willy, PUE	.325	329	68	107	13	9	4	44	26	47	16

PITCHER, TEAM	W	L	ERA	G	IP	H	R	ER	HR	BB	SO	AVG
Lowey, Josh, MVA	13	3	1.65	16	104	71	22	19	5	25	131	.196
Negrin, Yoanner, YUC	18	1	2.29	22	141	114	36	36	5	37	92	.224
Pena, Miguel, TIJ	9	3	2.43	17	107	103	32	29	6	15	72	.256
Velazquez, Hector, CAM	5	1	2.47	22	131	115	43	36	8	16	120	.236
Arballo, Julian, TIG	9	7	2.72	22	116	104	39	35	8	55	69	.249
Oyervides, Jose, MVA	10	2	2.78	19	104	91	36	32	7	33	120	.236
Delgado, Efren, MEX	11	1	2.83	24	102	92	34	32	5	38	92	.241
Campos, Francisco, CAM	8	6	2.88	21	122	116	44	39	13	22	68	.257
Castellanos, Jonathan, YUC	11	3	2.89	21	109	110	36	35	4	32	78	.270
Araiza, Angel, TAB	6	4	2.98	20	112	111	44	37	5	35	81	.261
Lara, Mauricio, PUE	13	3	3.14	22	112	112	47	39	5	34	64	.269
Castillo, Jorge, CAM	7	8	3.19	21	127	121	53	45	23	23	77	.244
Enright, Barry, TIJ	10	5	3.19	22	127	132	49	45	9	16	73	.270
Gonzalez, Edgar, MTY	10	2	3.20	21	121	124	48	43	9	25	57	.272
Solano, Javier, MTY	10	4	3.25	22	133	122	54	48	8	30	74	.248

Laird powers Fighters to the top

BY WAYNE GRACZYK

The Hokkaido Nippon Ham Fighters defeated the Hiroshima Carp in six games to win the best-of-seven 2016 Japan Series, capturing the Nippon Professional Baseball title for the first time since 2006. Guided by manager Hideki Kuriyama, the Pacific League champion Fighters overcame a double-digit games deficit at midseason to pass the Fukuoka SoftBank Hawks and win the pennant by two-and-a-half games.

Nippon Ham clinched a spot in the Japan Series after defeating SoftBank in the final stage of the PL Climax Series playoffs after the Hawks had knocked off the regular season third-place Chiba Lotte Marines in the first stage of the postseason.

Brandon Laird

The Fighters spoiled what had otherwise been a fantastic year for Hiroshima. The Carp won the Central League pennant by a whopping 17½ games and easily beat the third-place Yokohama DeNA Baystars in the Climax Series final stage. DeNA, managed by Alex Ramirez, had eliminated the second-place Yomiuri Giants in the first stage.

Based in Sapporo on Japan's northernmost main island of Hokkaido, the Fighters were led by American third baseman Brandon Laird. The ex-Yankee and Astro hit 39 regular season home runs to top the Pacific League. He also belted three home runs, including a grand slam, and had seven RBIs in the Japan Series, earning MVP honors.

U.S. teammate relief pitcher Anthony Bass made five appearances and was a three-game winner for the Fighters in the Japan Series.

Nippon Ham first baseman Sho Nakata's 110 regular season RBIs led the Pacific League, and the batting title in that division was won by Chiba outfielder Katsuya Kakunaka. Former major leaguer Tsuyoshi Wada, back with SoftBank, registered 15 wins to lead the PL, and Fukuoka closer Dennis Sarfate picked up 43 saves to lead both divisions.

The Fighters' highly touted two-way player, righthander/outfielder/DH Shohei Otani, drew more notice from MLB scouts. Just 22, Otani was 10-4, 1.89 on the mound in 21 appearances and registered a fastball clocked at 165 kph (102.5 mph). As a hitter, he batted .322 with 22 home runs and 67 RBIs. He hit just five homers in 2015. Because of rest days he was given after pitching, Otani did not reach the minimum number of innings or plate appearances required for listing among league leaders in pitching or batting.

Hiroshima, under manager Koichi Ogata, made it to the Japan Series for the first time in a quarter-century, having last played in the final in 1991. The Carp easily won the Central League with a star-studded lineup that included first baseman Takahiro Arai, second baseman Ryosuke Kikuchi, shortstop Kosuke Tanaka, center fielder Yoshihiro Maru and right fielder Seiya Suzuki.

Righthander Yusuke Nomura won a league-leading 16 games, and American lefty Kris Johnson chipped in with 15 victories. Johnson also had the second-best ERA in the league with a 2.15 and was given the Sawamura Award, the Japanese equivalent of the Cy Young, as the country's best pitcher.

First baseman/outfielder Brad "Big Country" Eldred and righthanded reliever Jay Jackson also made significant contributions to Hiroshima's successful season.

Yomiuri shortstop Hayato Sakamoto won the CL batting crown, and DeNA slugger Yoshitomo Tsutsugo hit the most home runs (44) and had the most RBIs (110). The Giants' Canadian relief pitcher Scott Mathieson accumulated 41 holds to lead both leagues in that category.

Tokyo Yakult Swallows second baseman Tetsuto Yamada turned in a second straight "triple three" season. He belted 38 homers, hit .304 and stole 30 bases.

A total of 77 foreigners played in Japan's Central and Pacific Leagues in 2016, coming from the U.S., Canada, Australia, South Korea, Taiwan, Mexico, Puerto Rico, Venezuela, the Dominican Republic, Cuba, the Netherlands and Curacao.

Japanese baseball saw an increase in attendance over 2015. A total of 11,132,526 fans attended Pacific League games in 2016, a 3.8 percent increase over the previous season. Average attendance was 25,950 per game. In the Central League, 13,848,988 spectators saw games in 2016. That was 2.5 percent more than in 2015. The average attendance at CL games was 32,282.

CENTRAL LEAGUE

	W	L	T	Pct.	GB
Hiroshima Carp	89	52	2	.631	—
Yomiuri Giants	71	69	3	.507	17 ½
Yokohama DeNA Baystars	69	71	3	.493	19 ½
Hanshin Tigers	64	76	3	.457	24 ½
Tokyo Yakult Swallows	64	78	1	.451	25 ½
Chunichi Dragons	58	82	3	.414	30 ½

CLIMAX SERIES PLAYOFFS—First Stage: Yokohama DeNA defeated Yomiuri 2-1 in best-of-three series. **Final Stage:** Hiroshima defeated Yokohama DeNA 4-1 in best-of-seven series.

INDIVIDUAL BATTING LEADERS
(Minimum 443 Plate Appearances)

	AVG	AB	R	H	2B	3B	HR	RBI	SB
Sakamoto, Hayato, Giants	.344	488	96	168	28	3	23	75	13
Suzuki, Seiya, Carp	.335	466	76	156	26	8	29	95	16
Tsutsugo, Yoshitomo, Baystars	.322	469	89	151	28	4	44	110	0
Kikuchi, Ryosuke, Carp	.315	574	92	181	22	3	13	56	13
Fukudome, Kosuke, Tigers	.311	453	52	141	25	3	11	59	0
Yamada, Tetsuto, Swallows	.304	481	102	146	26	3	38	102	30
Murata, Shuichi, Giants	.302	529	58	160	32	0	25	81	1
Kawabata, Shingo, Swallows	.302	420	48	127	22	1	1	32	3
Arai, Takahiro, Carp	.300	454	66	136	23	2	19	101	0
Sakaguchi, Tomotaka, Swallows	.295	526	74	155	14	5	0	39	7
Kuramoto, Toshihiko, Baystars	.294	534	38	157	19	2	1	38	2
Oshima, Yohei, Dragons	.292	599	80	175	27	9	3	27	26
Maru, Yoshihiro, Carp	.291	557	98	162	30	8	20	90	23
Kuwahara, Masayuki, Baystars	.284	462	80	131	23	2	11	49	19

REMAINING U.S., CANADIAN & LATIN PLAYERS

	AVG	AB	R	H	2B	3B	HR	RBI	SB
Eldred, Brad, Carp	.294	316	42	83	14	0	21	53	1
Nanita, Ricardo, Dragons	.285	319	32	91	16	0	8	35	0
Viciedo, Dayan, Dragons	.274	416	63	114	22	0	22	68	1
Luna, Hector, Carp	.272	243	35	66	8	1	5	34	6
Balentien, Wladimir, Swallows	.269	457	64	123	20	0	31	96	0
Lopez, Jose, Baystars	.263	483	66	127	27	1	34	95	0
Jones, Garrett, Giants	.258	422	48	109	22	1	24	68	0
Gomez, Mauro, Tigers	.255	498	58	127	20	0	22	79	2
Cruz, Luis, Giants	.252	298	26	75	14	0	11	37	0

INDIVIDUAL PITCHING LEADERS
(Minimum 143 Innings Pitched)

	W	L	ERA	G	SV	IP	H	BB	SO
Sugano, Tomoyuki, Giants	9	6	2.01	26	0	183	156	26	189
Johnson, Kris, Carp	15	7	2.15	26	0	180	154	49	141
Nomura, Yusuke, Carp	16	3	2.71	25	0	153	139	37	91
Taguchi, Kazuto, Giants	10	10	2.72	26	0	162	150	49	126
Iwasada, Yuta, Tigers	10	9	2.90	25	0	158	119	55	156
Messenger, Randy, Tigers	12	11	3.01	28	0	185	178	60	177
Kuroda, Hiroki, Carp	10	8	3.09	24	0	152	152	30	98
Ishida, Kenta, Baystars	9	4	3.12	25	0	153	128	36	132
Fujinami, Shintaro, Tigers	7	11	3.25	26	0	169	152	70	176
Ino, Shoichi, Baystars	7	11	3.50	23	0	152	156	47	113
Nomi, Atsushi, Tigers	8	12	3.67	26	0	147	140	52	126
Ogawa, Yasuhiro, Swallows	8	9	4.50	25	0	158	149	52	114

REMAINING U.S., CANADIAN, AUSTRALIAN & LATIN PLAYERS

	W	L	ERA	G	SV	IP	H	BB	SO
Jackson, Jay, Carp	5	4	1.71	67	0	68	46	23	89
Mateo, Marcos, Tigers	1	3	1.80	52	20	55	40	24	56
Dolis, Rafael, Tigers	3	3	2.12	34	8	34	19	16	36
Mathieson, Scott, Giants	8	4	2.36	70	1	80	65	22	98
Mikolas, Miles, Giants	4	2	2.45	14	0	93	84	23	84
Ondrusek, Logan, Swallows	3	1	2.45	30	11	29	23	11	29
Satterwhite, Cody, Tigers	1	1	2.57	20	0	21	19	8	18
Hagens, Bradin, Carp	7	3	2.92	50	0	83	71	33	33
Lueke, Josh, Swallows	6	6	3.06	69	0	65	66	20	60

PACIFIC LEAGUE

	W	L	T	Pct.	GB
Hokkaido Nippon Ham Fighters	87	53	3	.621	—
Fukuoka SoftBank Hawks	83	54	6	.606	2 ½
Chiba Lotte Marines	72	68	3	.514	15
Saitama Seibu Lions	64	76	3	.457	23
Tohoku Rakuten Golden Eagles	62	78	3	.443	25
Orix Buffaloes	57	83	3	.407	30

CLIMAX SERIES PLAYOFFS—First Stage: Fukuoka SoftBank defeated Chiba Lotte 2-0 in best-of-three series. **Final Stage:** Hokkaido Nippon Ham defeated Fukuoka SoftBank 4-2 in best-of-seven series.

INDIVIDUAL BATTING LEADERS
(Minimum 443 Plate Appearances)

	AVG	AB	R	H	2B	3B	HR	RBI	SB
Kakunaka, Katsuya, Marines	.339	525	74	178	30	5	8	69	12
Nishikawa, Haruki, Fighters	.314	493	76	155	18	4	5	43	41
Asamura, Hideto, Lions	.309	557	73	172	40	0	24	82	8
Itoi, Yoshio, Buffaloes	.306	532	79	163	24	1	17	70	53
Yanagita, Yuki, Hawks	.306	428	82	131	31	4	18	73	23
Uchikama, Seiichi, Hawks	.304	556	62	169	19	0	18	106	3
Akiyama, Shogo, Lions	.296	578	98	171	32	4	11	62	18
Yo, Daikan, Fighters	.293	495	66	145	24	1	14	61	5
Nakamura, Akira, Hawks	.287	488	69	140	21	1	7	50	6
Suzuki, Daichi, Lions	.285	501	62	143	30	2	6	61	3
Okada, Takahiro, Buffaloes	.284	454	56	129	25	0	20	76	5
Despaigne, Alfredo, Marines	.280	496	81	139	27	0	24	92	0
Kuriyama, Takumi, Lions	.279	477	52	133	30	2	3	41	0
Mogi, Eigoro, Eagles	.278	424	56	118	20	7	7	40	11

REMAINING U.S. & LATIN PLAYERS

	AVG.	AB	R	H	2B	3B	HR	RBI	SB
Peguero, Carlos, Eagles	.279	183	25	51	7	1	10	26	0
Wheeler, Zelous, Eagles	.265	517	74	137	25	2	27	88	2
Laird, Brandon, Fighters	.263	547	71	144	21	0	39	97	0
Amador, Japhet, Eagles	.258	132	15	34	3	2	9	19	0
Morel, Brent, Buffaloes	.244	308	29	75	13	0	8	38	2
Perez, Felix, Eagles	.239	88	8	21	2	0	5	15	0
Navarro, Yamaico, Marines	.217	286	38	62	6	1	10	44	0
Bogusevic, Brian, Buffaloes	.187	171	19	32	12	1	3	18	3

INDIVIDUAL PITCHING LEADERS
(Minimum 143 Innings Pitched)

	W	L	ERA	G	SV	IP	H	BB	SO
Ishikawa, Ayumu, Marines	14	5	2.16	23	0	162	142	22	104
Kikuchi, Yusei, Lions	12	7	2.58	22	0	143	117	67	127
Senga, Kodai, Hawks	12	3	2.61	25	0	169	125	53	181
Norimoto, Takahiro, Eagles	11	11	2.91	28	0	195	192	50	216
Arihara, Kohei, Fighters	11	9	2.94	22	0	156	150	38	103
Takeda, Shota, Hawks	14	8	2.95	27	0	183	163	70	144
Wakui, Hideaki, Marines	10	7	3.01	26	0	189	195	48	118
Wada, Tsuyoshi, Hawks	15	5	3.04	24	0	163	138	38	157
Standridge, Jason, Marines	8	8	3.56	27	0	162	168	45	99
Kaneko, Chihiro, Buffaloes	7	9	3.83	24	0	162	143	59	125
Shiomi, Takahiro, Eagles	8	10	3.89	24	0	148	145	37	111
Nishi, Yuki, Buffaloes	10	12	4.14	26	0	165	171	48	108

REMAINING U.S., EUROPEAN & LATIN PLAYERS

	W	L	ERA	G	SV	IP	H	BB	SO
Martin, Chris, Fighters	2	0	1.07	52	21	51	25	7	57
Sarfate, Dennis, Hawks	0	7	1.88	64	43	62	40	11	73
Mickolio, Kam, Eagles	5	1	2.38	45	0	45	37	6	29
Wolfe, Brian, Lions	4	0	3.04	4	0	24	26	4	8
Suarez, Robert, Hawks	2	6	3.19	58	1	54	49	18	64
Bass, Anthony, Fighters	8	8	3.65	37	0	104	102	47	71
Vanden Hurk, Rick, Hawks	7	3	3.84	13	0	82	64	15	92
Mendoza, Luis, Fighters	7	8	3.88	23	0	132	135	45	77
Dickson, Brandon, Buffaloes	9	11	4.36	27	0	171	183	71	139
Paulino, Felipe, Lions	0	6	4.70	9	0	44	44	25	32

KOREA

Doosan Sweeps

Leaning on a "Fantastic Four" rotation that included two ex-big league pitchers, the Doosan Bears won the Korean Baseball Organization championship in dominant fashion. The Bears swept second-place NC Dinos to win their second consecutive title after setting a KBO record with 93 regular-season victories.

Righthanders Dustin Nippert and Michael Bowden joined Korea natives Chang Won-jun and Yoo Hee-kwan in the Bears' rotation, the first in KBO history to feature four 15-game winners. Nippert, in his sixth KBO season, led the league with 22 wins and a 2.95 ERA. "We deserve the name," Bowden told the Yonhap News Agency. "We deserve that name. We have four guys who threw really well this year."

Outfielder Eric Thames continued his KBO dominance, tying for the league lead with 40 home runs in a .321/.433/.679 season. He ranked second in OPS after winning the triple crown in 2015.

STANDINGS & LEADERS

	W	L	T	PCT	GB
Doosan Bears	93	50	1	.650	—
NC Dinos	83	58	3	.589	9
Nexen Heroes	77	66	1	.538	16
LG Twins	71	71	2	.500	21 ½
Kia Tigers	70	73	1	.490	23
SK Wyverns	69	75	0	.479	24 ½
Hanwha Eagles	66	75	3	.468	26
Lotte Giants	66	78	0	.458	27 ½
Samsung Lions	65	78	1	.455	28
KT Wiz	53	89	2	.373	39 ½

INDIVIDUAL BATTING LEADERS

PLAYER, TEAM	AVG	AB	R	H	2B	3B	HR	RBI	SB	SO
Hyung-woo Choi, Samsung	.376	519	99	195	46	2	31	144	2	83
Tae-kyun Kim, Hanwha	.365	529	94	193	39	0	23	136	1	97
Yong-kyu Lee, Hanwha	.352	452	98	159	20	4	3	41	21	29
Joo-chan Kim, Kia	.346	511	97	177	37	3	23	101	9	68
Yong-taik Park, LG	.346	509	84	176	24	0	11	90	6	71
Ja-wook Koo, Samsung	.343	428	105	147	19	13	14	77	10	68
Min-woo Park, NC	.343	435	84	149	16	6	3	55	20	70
Han-joon Yoo, KT	.336	408	70	137	22	0	14	64	4	40
Jae-gyun Hwang, Lotte	.335	498	97	167	26	5	27	113	25	66
Kun-woo Park, Doosan	.335	484	95	162	36	4	20	83	17	86

INDIVIDUAL PITCHING LEADERS

PITCHER, TEAM	W	L	ERA	G	IP	H	R	ER	BB	SO
Dustin Nippert, Doosan	22	3	2.95	28	168	151	61	55	57	142
Won-jun Jang, Doosan	15	6	3.32	27	168	161	66	62	76	137
Hector Noesi, Kia	15	5	3.40	31	207	211	88	78	51	139
Eric Hacker, NC	13	3	3.45	23	141	132	57	54	31	119
Merill Kelly, SK	9	8	3.68	31	200	205	91	82	60	152
Hyun-jong Yang, Kia	10	12	3.68	31	200	191	96	82	77	146
Michael Bowden, Doosan	18	7	3.80	30	180	159	83	76	54	160
Kwang-hyun Kim, SK	11	8	3.88	27	137	139	68	59	41	116
Jae-young Shin, Nexen	15	7	3.90	30	169	192	76	73	21	99
Jae-kuk Ryu, LG	13	11	4.30	29	161	152	83	77	70	138

TAIWAN

Rhinos Beat Elephants In 6

The EDA Rhinos scored three runs in the ninth inning to rally for a 4-3 victory in Game Six of the championship series and beat the Brother Elephants. The Rhinos thought they won on a diving catch by ex-big leaguer Che Hsuan Lin in right field, but the catch was overturned and the Rhinos had to stop celebrating to get the final out.

Lin was named MVP of the series, going 11-for-26 as the Rhinos won the last four games. EDA trailed 5-1 in the fifth of Game Three when the Rhinos scored seven runs that inning. EDA outscored Chinatrust 35-9 the rest of the seres.

It's the team's last act as the Rhinos. Fubon Financial Services bought the team in September; the club won 15 of its last 21 games after the sale went through. The team was expected to move to Taipei from Kaohsiung and will get a new name.

Lamigo's Wang Po Jung set league records with a .414 average and 200 hits. He also ranked fourth in home runs (29), third in RBIs (105), second in stolen bases (24) and first in total bases (333).

STANDINGS & LEADERS

	W	L	T	PCT	GB
Chinatrust Brother Elephants	68	50	2	.576	—
EDA Rhinos	61	58	1	.513	7 ½
Uni-President 7-Eleven Lions	55	65	0	.458	14
Lamigo Monkeys	53	64	3	.453	14 ½

INDIVIDUAL BATTING LEADERS

PLAYER, TEAM	AVG	AB	R	H	2B	3B	HR	RBI	SB
Po Jung Wang, Lamigo	.414	483	130	200	40	3	29	105	24
Chih Hsien Chiang, BE	.402	351	85	141	28	0	30	104	2
Hung Yu Lin, Lamigo	.400	418	97	167	40	1	23	108	0
Chih Ping Lin, Lamigo	.365	351	80	128	16	0	4	43	26
Yi Chuan Lin, EDA	.350	417	67	146	24	0	17	81	1
Wu Hsiung Pan, Uni	.346	358	71	124	18	3	18	62	10
Che Hsuan Lin, EDA	.345	400	77	138	20	2	22	79	12
Ssu Chi Chou, BE	.342	409	83	140	30	3	17	103	6
Cheng Wei Chang, BE	.342	436	108	149	24	0	4	48	5
Cheng Min Peng, BE	.341	343	58	117	19	0	8	67	4

INDIVIDUAL PITCHING LEADERS

PITCHER, TEAM	W	L	ERA	G	IP	H	R	ER	BB	SO
Mike Loree, EDA	13	11	3.98	31	190	200	98	84	57	159
Kai Wen Cheng, BE	9	8	4.53	38	145	175	86	73	32	114
Nate Long, BE	11	3	4.62	21	111	131	70	57	46	82
Orlando Roman, Lamigo	12	7	4.64	34	157	167	97	81	58	154
Jared Lansford, EDA	6	4	4.75	24	108	121	61	57	30	119
Scott Richmond, EDA	9	9	4.78	29	153	157	96	81	61	117
Fu Te Ni, EDA	6	6	4.84	43	97	112	56	52	22	69
Bruce Billings, Uni	11	9	5.28	30	170	207	119	100	72	172
Jair Jurrjens, Uni	6	7	5.38	17	90	115	66	54	28	67
Wen Yang Liao, Uni	6	5	6.41	22	94	126	86	67	51	50

INTERNATIONAL

Cedeno pushes Bologna to top

BY HARVEY SAHKER

Bologna defeated Rimini in six games in the Italy Series, winning its second national title in three years. It was the third straight season in which the two clubs faced each other in the Italian club championships. Bologna advanced to the Italy Series by defeating Nettuno four games to one in their semi-final series. Rimini dispatched San Marino in the other semifinal, also in five games.

Former big leaguer Ronny Cedeno took over as Bologna's shortstop in 2016. The 33-year old Venezuelan led the Italian Baseball League in slugging and total bases and finished second in average, hits, doubles and homers.

Three other Bologna newcomers who played pro ball in North America made major contributions for the champs. Former Braves farmhand Osman Marval finished third in the batting race. Southpaw Matt Zielinski, a five-year independent league veteran, led the IBL with nine regular-season wins and a microscopic 0.53 ERA, the seventh-best in IBL history. Righty Brent Buffa, another former indy leaguer, had a 1.88 ERA in 24 innings.

Ronny Cedeno

San Marino outfielder Sebastiano Poma edged out Cedeno to win the IBL batting title by a single point. Poma, 23, enjoyed a breakout season after moving from Parma to San Marino. He hit .369, which was 117 points higher than his career batting average going into the 2016 campaign.

Last-place Novara began the year with a 16-game losing streak and finished it with 12 straight defeats. The team batted .181 collectively and its 5.79 ERA was more than two runs a game worse than any other IBL club, although Novara righty Jonnathan Aristil (0-10, 4.57) led the IBL in strikeouts. The 29-year old Dominican toiled in the Rockies and Astros systems for seven years. Aristil was a hard luck hurler for Novara. For example, on July 1 at Rimini. He held the home team to one hit and whiffed 11 in seven innings. The lone hit was a homer and Aristil lost the game 1-0.

Bologna right fielder and Novara native Claudio Liverziani became the third player to score 1,000 runs in his IBL career. He made his IBL debut in 1991 at the age of 17 and played two years in the Mariners' system from 1997-98. Liverziani led the league in walks and is the all-time IBL walks leader.

Italy finished a disappointing third in the European Championships, but they opened the tournament with a 21-2 rout of Greece in which catcher Mattia Reginato hit for the cycle, scored four runs and drove in six. Reginato has only three triples in his IBL career, which began in 2009

STANDINGS AND LEADERS

	W	L	PCT	GB
Bologna	27	9	.750	—
Rimini	22	14	.611	5
San Marino	22	14	.611	5
Nettuno	21	15	.583	6
Parma	18	18	.500	9
Padova	14	22	.389	13
Novara	2	34	.056	25

Semifinals (best-of-seven): Bologna defeated Nettuno 4-1, Rimini defeated San Marino 4-1. **Finals (best-of-seven):** Bologna defeated Rimini 4-2.

PLAYER, TEAM	AVG	AB	R	H	2B	3B	HR	RBI	BB
Poma, Sebastiano, RSM	.369	141	31	52	3	2	0	17	22
Cedeno, Ronny, BOL	.368	125	27	46	11	0	4	25	10
Marval, Osman, BOL	.354	130	22	46	8	0	2	21	34
Ambrosino, Paolino, BOL	.346	130	35	45	7	0	4	27	15
Alvarez, Luis, PDO	.331	130	12	43	9	0	1	16	8
Gomez, Adolfo, PAR	.329	73	9	24	5	0	0	9	12
Colmenares, Carlos, RSM	.326	92	17	30	5	2	0	12	12
Ferrini, Jose, PDO	.324	74	12	24	3	0	0	11	11
Mayora, Daniel, RIM	.313	131	16	41	10	1	3	22	24
Infante, Juan Carlos, BOL	.312	125	29	39	6	0	1	13	30
Mirabal, Charlie, PAR	.309	136	22	42	11	0	1	18	14
Nosti, Nick, PDO	.305	131	18	40	8	1	0	11	14
Vasquez, Wuillians, RSM	.297	128	22	38	7	1	3	27	34
Marquez, Jairo, NOV	.286	84	2	24	2	0	1	6	3
Flores, Jose, RIM	.283	145	24	41	11	0	2	23	15
Fondin, Onelio, NET	.280	82	12	23	4	1	0	8	11
Imperiali, Francesco, RSM	.279	86	15	24	3	0	3	21	18
Zappone, Lino, RIM	.278	90	6	25	4	0	0	7	7
Mazzuca, Joseph, RSM	.271	140	22	38	12	0	2	23	13
Retrosi, Ennio, RIM	.271	129	20	35	5	0	0	11	12

PITCHER, TEAM	W	L	ERA	SV	IP	H	R	ER	BB	SO
Zielinski, Matt, BOL	9	0	0.53	0	68	44	12	4	18	69
Camacho, Yoimer, RSM	7	2	0.58	1	62	29	7	4	19	72
Cubillan, Darwin, RSM	0	0	0.91	4	30	21	5	3	7	32
Gonzalez, Jose, PAR	2	2	0.98	4	37	19	4	4	12	44
De Santis, Riccardo, BOL	4	0	1.54	0	35	27	8	6	8	24
Oberto, Junior, RSM	1	1	1.55	1	29	21	6	5	9	20
Quevedo, Carlos, RSM	6	2	1.63	0	72	52	15	13	28	77
Rivero, Raul, BOL	5	2	1.64	3	60	46	16	11	8	60
Candelario, Alexis, RIM	4	2	1.88	0	38	25	10	8	15	54
Uviedo, Ronad, PAR	7	2	1.89	0	81	57	18	17	37	56
Fabiani, Diego, PDO	2	1	2.02	1	36	21	11	8	15	33
Ruiz, Raul, PDO	4	6	2.04	0	75	63	26	17	23	78
Rodriguez, Rodney, NET	4	0	2.08	3	39	26	12	9	14	47
Hernandez, Ricardo, RIM	7	3	2.42	0	63	45	23	17	17	83
De La Cruz, Eulogio, NET	4	4	2.52	0	75	72	27	21	31	63

INTERNATIONAL

Four straight for Neptunus

BY HARVEY SAHKER

Neptunus defeated the Amsterdam Pirates in six games in the Holland Series to claim its fourth consecutive national championship. It was the Rotterdam club's 17th title overall.

Rotterdam native Dwayne Kemp won the Holland Series MVP award. The 28-year-old Neptunus shortstop had eight hits and five RBIs in the Series, where four of the six games were decided by one run.

Veteran third baseman Raily Legito starred for Neptunus in the clinching Game Six. Legito doubled home the first run of the game in the bottom of the fourth frame. In the eighth inning with the score tied 3-3, he singled, stole second and scored what proved to be the winning run. Legito, 38, announced his retirement after the Series. Legito played a record 249 games for the Dutch national team, including in the Olympics and World Baseball Classic. He is an eight-time Holland Series champ who played 18 years in the Dutch Major League.

Orlando Yntema

Amsterdam shortstop Michael Duursma also retired after the Holland Series. Duursma, who played collegiately at Purdue, played in many of the same international competitions as Legito and appeared in 178 games for the Netherlands.

The Pirates qualified for the Holland Series because of bonus points awarded to them for their regular-season performance. This allowed them to leapfrog over the Hoofddorp Pioniers, who finished second, and into the finals.

Shortly after the Holland Series, former minor leaguer Evert Jan t'Hoen was replaced as Neptunus' manager. The club's new skipper is Ronald Jaarsma, who was previously the third-base coach for the Pirates.

The Holland Series opponents were combatants of another type during a regular season game. A bench clearing brawl between the clubs resulted in the suspensions of six players. Former Mets minor league Rien Vernooij, an infielder for Neptunus, was initially banned for a year. The suspension was later reduced to 23 games.

Orlando Yntema of Neptunus was one of three DML hurlers to throw a no-hitter in the regular season. The former Giants farmhand walked three batters in his early season no-no, an 11-0 win over Hoofddorp that was called after seven innings because of the league's 10-run mercy rule. It was his second no-hitter in as many seasons.

American lefthander Chris Pfau held HCAW hitless and whiffed 13 in a 3-0, nine-inning Pioniers victory. Pfau, who went to Lincoln (Mo.), threw 134 pitches in the game and walked five.

The Netherlands hosted and won its European Championships in September.

STANDINGS & LEADERS

	W	L	T	GB
Neptunus	34	7	1	—
Amsterdam Pirates	31	11	0	3½
Hoofddorp Pioniers	27	15	0	7½
Kinheim	24	17	1	10
HCAW	19	23	0	15½
Oosterhout Twins	16	26	0	18½
UVV	9	33	0	25½
DSS	7	35	0	27½

Semifinal Round	W	L	T	GB
Neptunus	6	3	0	—
Hoofddorp Pioniers	6	3	0	—
Amsterdam Pirates	5	4	0	1
Kinheim	1	8	0	5

PLAYER, TEAM	AVG	AB	R	H	2B	3B	HR	RBI	SB
Diaz, Christian, NEP	.382	152	29	58	12	1	0	23	8
Berkenbosch, Kenny, AMS	.356	104	23	37	10	1	0	23	6
Croes, Linoy, AMS	.355	110	26	39	8	3	3	19	8
Henrique, Roelie, HCA	.353	170	33	60	11	5	1	16	21
Dille, Benjamin, NEP	.351	97	25	34	3	0	0	19	4
Rooi, Vince, HCA	.336	143	29	48	8	1	2	25	1
Paap, Sander, KIN	.330	109	21	36	3	0	1	13	0
Dirksen, Kevin, PIO	.328	128	24	42	11	0	2	26	5
Leonora, Dudley, KIN	.327	162	22	53	11	3	3	39	4
Williams, Omar, UVV	.325	123	16	40	6	0	3	16	1
Lampe, Gilmer, AMS	.323	127	22	41	11	0	0	19	13
de Cuba, Quentin, PIO	.319	138	36	44	11	0	2	22	3
Hernandez, Julio, KIN	.314	140	19	44	5	2	0	24	3
Raap, Brian, PIO	.314	105	21	33	11	1	3	30	0
Gario, Mervin, PIO	.313	131	23	41	5	1	0	10	9

PITCHER, TEAM	W	L	ERA	SV	IP	H	R	ER	BB	SO
van den Branden, Kenny, NEP	9	0	0.62	0	73	43	6	5	22	73
de Blok, Tom, AMS	5	0	0.88	5	41	21	5	4	11	43
Veltkamp, Nick, KIN	6	0	1.13	1	48	39	11	6	22	29
Huijer, Lars, PIO	10	2	1.19	0	98	60	18	13	25	107
Yntema, Orlando, NEP	10	1	1.20	0	90	68	17	12	23	75
Uezono, Keiji, TWI	4	1	1.68	0	59	37	12	11	16	45
Heijstek, Kevin, AMS	5	1	1.80	0	45	34	12	9	6	33
Ward, Kyle, AMS	5	0	2.20	0	49	43	15	12	17	58
Burgersdijk, Dennis, AMS	8	3	2.25	0	76	66	26	19	28	50
Rietel, Maickel, PIO	5	1	2.47	1	47	31	15	13	20	34
Pfau, Chris, PIO	6	6	2.66	0	88	52	33	26	55	105
Figueroa Roman, Luis, KIN	6	2	2.66	0	74	56	30	22	39	54
Hendrix, Daan, AMS	2	2	2.74	4	46	38	15	14	11	30
Delemarre, Ian, HCA	6	4	2.78	3	65	66	30	20	24	40
Ploeger, Jim, HCA	6	5	3.00	0	84	64	32	28	37	76

Ciego repeats as champs

BY BEN BADLER

The rise of Cuban talent in Major League Baseball has come at the expense of Serie Nacional in Cuba. A massive escalation of players leaving Cuba, from veteran stars to rising teenage prospects, has drained the quality of play in Cuba's top league.

The biggest blow came in February, when Industriales third baseman Yulieski Gurriel, the best player in Cuba, left the Cuban team in the Dominican Republic after the Caribbean Series with his younger brother, Lourdes, to pursue major league contracts.

One club that wasn't hit as hard as others by players fleeing the island was Ciego De Avila, which repeated as Serie Nacional champions with an 8-0 victory over Pinar Del Rio in Game Seven of the championship series.

Yunier Cano

ALYSON BOYER RODE

Outfielder Jose Adolis Garcia, the younger brother of Braves third baseman Adonis Garcia, won the MVP award, hitting .315/.395/.517 and playing good defense in right field. After the season, however, Garcia became the latest Cuban player to leave the country to try to sign with an MLB team.

Ciego De Avila had one of the league's most exciting outfields with Garcia and Luis Robert, one of the top young players still in Cuba. The 6-foot-2, 175-pound Robert, in his age-18 season, hit .304/.382/.410 with a promising combination of size, power, speed and athleticism.

On the mound, righthander Vladimir Garcia, led the pitching staff, posting a 2.18 ERA that ranked third in the league. It was a bounce back year for Garcia, an experienced starter on the Cuban national team who missed much of the previous season due to injury.

Righthander Yunier Cano, 22, has a fastball that can reach 94 mph and was one of the league's best closers, posting an ERA of 0.91 with a 52-23 strikeout-to-walk mark in 69.1 innings for Ciego

De Avila.

The loss of the Gurriel brothers was a devastating blow to the Industriales, who finished third in the league but went just 22-20 in the second half. Despite his in-season departure, Yulieski won the batting title by hitting .500, while Lourdes tied for third in slugging (.560) and home runs (15). Ciego De Avila swept Industriales 4-0 in the semifinals.

Matanzas finished with the league's best regular-season record but lost 3-2 to Pinar Del Rio in Game Seven of the semifinals.

Catcher Yosvani Alarcon, who led the league with 17 home runs, hit a two-out, ninth-inning home run to break the 2-2 tie and push Pinar Del Rio to the victory.

STANDINGS & LEADERS

TEAM	SECOND HALF	FIRST HALF
Matanzas	55-30	26-19
Ciego De Avila	54-32	31-14
Industriales	52-35	30-15
Pinar Del Rio	51-35	29-16
Holguin	47-39	26-19
Las Tunas	43-43	26-19
Granma	43-44	28-17
Isla De La Juventud	40-45	25-20
Guantanamo	N/A	22-23
Villa Clara	N/A	22-23
Santi Spiritus	N/A	22-23
Cienfuegos	N/A	20-24
Santiago De Cuba	N/A	15-30
Artemisa	N/A	13-31
Camaguey	N/A	11-34
Mayabeque	N/A	11-34

INDIVIDUAL BATTING LEADERS

PLAYER, TEAM	AVG	AB	R	H	2B	3B	HR	RBI	BB	SO	SB
Yulieski Gurriel, IND	.500	174	55	87	20	0	15	51	38	3	3
Yosvani Alarcon, LTU/PRI	.371	259	56	96	16	2	17	60	38	33	4
Yohandry Urgelles, ART/HOL	.367	229	34	84	11	0	5	36	48	21	0
Yordanis Samon, GRA	.362	312	49	113	21	3	7	61	59	32	5
Ruben Paz, LTU	.361	252	54	91	14	3	3	32	17	38	3
Yorbis Borroto, CAV	.355	299	63	106	27	1	3	42	58	27	1
Rigoberto Gomez, IJV	.349	315	40	110	12	1	1	24	28	24	9
Guillermo Aviles, GRA/CAV	.347	300	49	104	18	5	5	58	47	49	2
Jefferson Delgado, MTZ	.347	222	30	77	6	2	4	40	25	17	4
Alexander Pozo, MAY/MTZ	.346	254	52	88	13	4	5	38	39	31	5

INDIVIDUAL PITCHING LEADERS

PLAYER, TEAM	W	L	ERA	G	GS	CG	SV	IP	H	HR	BB	SO
Freddy Alvarez, VCL/MTZ	9	2	1.48	18	17	0	0	104	87	3	25	61
Vladimir Banos, PRI	8	3	1.88	16	15	1	0	91	79	2	30	61
Vladimir Garcia, CAV	11	3	2.18	19	19	0	0	95	89	1	44	57
Yaifredo Dominguez, PRI	9	3	2.43	19	17	0	0	89	73	3	39	53
Leandro Martinez, GRA	6	3	2.55	17	17	0	0	106	106	5	27	41
Yosvani Torres, PRI	6	8	2.70	17	17	2	0	104	101	8	16	48
Erlis Casanova, PRI	7	6	2.80	17	17	1	0	96	104	3	33	73
Yoanni Yera, MTZ	11	6	2.84	22	21	0	0	124	102	4	27	114
Danny Betancourt, SCU/MTZ	8	6	2.89	17	16	1	0	90	88	6	31	49
Jonder Martinez, MTZ	12	5	2.90	19	16	2	0	109	89	8	22	62

Jorge Vazquez's walk-off homer lifted Mexico to another Caribbean Series title

DAVID SCHOFIELD

Mexico walks off in Caribbean Series final

Mexico has emerged as the Caribbean Series' dominant force in the first half of the 2010s, a run that continued with the Venados de Mazatlan becoming the fourth Mexican representative to win the title in six years.

This one didn't come easily, as Mazatlan trailed 4-2 entering the bottom of the seventh in the championship game against Venezuela's Tigres de Aragua, but a pair of unearned runs, driven home by Sebastian Valle, allowed Mazatlan to tie the score. That set the stage for a storybook ending, as Mexican DH Jorge Vazquez belted a walk-off home run in the bottom of the ninth to win the game 5-4.

Mexico finished the tournament a perfect 6-0, having defeated Cuba 7-2 in the semifinals and going undefeated in round robin play. It's the first undefeated run through the Caribbean Series since 2006.

Cuba, the defending champion and making its third appearance in the Series since ending a 50-year hiatus, went just 1-4, while the host Dominican Republic team disappointingly went 0-4 and was left out of the semifinal round.

AUSTRALIAN BASEBALL LEAGUE

TEAM	W	L	PCT	GB
Brisbane Bandits	37	19	.661	—
Canberry Cavalry	31	25	.554	6
Adelaide Bite	30	26	.536	7
Sydney Blue Sox	26	29	.473	10 ½
Perth Heat	23	33	.411	14
Melbourne Aces	20	35	.364	16 ½

Championship: Brisbane defeated Adelaide, 2-0.

BATTER, CLUB	AVG	AB	R	H	2B	3B	HR	RBI	BB	SO	SB
Harris, David, Can	.346	179	38	62	11	2	6	19	15	36	7
D'Antonio, Trent, Syd	.344	157	36	54	4	2	3	32	32	13	7
Williams, Justin, Bri	.342	184	33	63	12	1	10	33	12	25	8
Pounds, Bryan, Can	.325	163	28	53	11	0	7	35	30	30	1
Wik, Marc, Ade	.324	170	38	55	15	1	2	33	44	34	11
Unroe, Riley, Bri	.318	211	42	67	9	3	0	25	31	37	14
Petty, Kyle, Ade	.317	208	39	66	13	0	14	44	17	46	12
Wade, Logan, Bri	.315	130	21	41	8	0	5	20	9	28	5
Leblebijian, Jason, Can	.312	202	39	63	19	1	8	44	22	45	3
Vavra, Tanner, Mel	.309	165	31	51	10	1	2	22	18	25	11

PITCHER, CLUB	W	L	ERA	G	SV	IP	H	BB	SO	AVG
Searle, Ryan, Bri	5	2	0.40	31	17	45	26	9	54	.165
Balog, Alex, Syd	5	2	1.35	8	0	47	34	12	45	.204
Mitchinson, Scott, Per	3	2	1.83	25	6	39	39	18	40	.253
Tols, Josh, Ade	4	1	2.23	19	0	48	34	17	46	.200
Carl, Edwin, Per	4	2	2.95	14	0	85	62	28	85	.199
Teasley, Rick, Bri	7	4	3.01	14	0	78	81	20	63	.264
Kent, Steve, Can	6	4	3.04	14	0	77	75	23	79	.253
Larkins, Matthew, Mel	6	6	3.06	15	0	97	87	28	68	.237
Bailey, Tom, Per	4	2	4.14	14	0	52	51	19	47	.264
Grening, Brian, Can	6	4	3.47	15	0	86	84	24	83	.249

DOMINICAN LEAGUE

TEAM	W	L	PCT	GB
Estrellas de Oriente	29	21	.580	—
Tigres del Licey	29	21	.580	—
Leones del Escogido	25	25	.500	4
Toros del Este	23	27	.460	6
Aguilas Cibaenas	22	28	.440	7
Gigantes del Cibao	22	28	.440	7

Championship: Escogido defeated Licey, 5-1.

BATTER, CLUB	AVG	AB	R	H	2B	3B	HR	RBI	BB	SO	SB
Alberto, Hanser, EST	.364	154	21	56	8	1	1	21	9	17	5
Velez, Eugenio, TOR	.349	166	25	58	7	1	2	14	15	28	4
Ciriaco, Audy, EST	.314	175	21	55	10	1	2	25	7	34	2
Hernandez, Diory, LIC	.308	169	17	52	14	0	1	18	10	18	0
Almonte, Zoilo, LIC	.303	175	23	53	11	0	3	18	14	31	0
Moya, Steven, TOR	.298	131	14	39	8	1	4	27	10	34	0
White, Tyler, EST	.297	158	29	47	10	0	7	31	32	37	0
Rosario, Wilin, EST	.297	128	12	38	4	0	3	21	9	20	0
Rickard, Joey, ESC	.277	191	28	53	13	1	6	32	16	36	3
Rogers, Jason, LIC	.272	147	20	40	6	1	3	18	9	22	0

PITCHER, CLUB	W	L	ERA	G	SV	IP	H	BB	SO	AVG
Salcedo, Adrian, EST	3	1	1.71	9	0	42	34	16	35	.229
Maya, Yunesky, LIC	3	2	2.39	10	0	60	53	10	50	.243
Norberto, Jordan, ESC	2	4	2.68	11	0	50	37	15	37	.206
Owens, Rudy, TOR	2	3	2.88	11	0	50	48	19	37	.255
MacLane, Evan, EST	4	2	3.21	11	0	48	40	6	32	.222
Evans, Bryan, TOR	1	3	3.38	10	0	45	38	12	39	.221
Bierman, Sean, AGU	2	3	3.50	11	0	44	52	7	23	.295
Castro, Angel, AGU	3	1	3.50	9	0	44	51	7	20	.293
Villanueva, Elih, TOR	3	5	5.89	10	0	44	60	6	29	.335

PUERTO RICAN LEAGUE

TEAM	W	L	PCT	GB
Indios de Mayaguez	27	15	.643	—
Cangrejeros de Santurce	21	21	.500	6
Criollos de Caguas	21	21	.500	6
Gigantes de Carolina	15	27	.357	12

Championship: Santurce defeated Mayaguez, 4-2.

BATTER, CLUB	AVG	AB	R	H	2B	3B	HR	RBI	BB	SO	SB
Fuentes, Reymond, SAN	.326	129	18	42	4	3	1	14	13	16	8
Sosa, Ruben, SAN	.319	119	21	38	5	0	0	16	18	17	16
Lozada, Jose, SAN	.311	122	13	38	7	0	0	14	15	17	1
Vargas, Kennys, MAY	.308	120	21	37	5	0	7	20	15	24	0
Feliciano, Jesus, CAG	.300	140	21	42	7	1	0	10	12	7	1
Valentin, Jesmuel, MAY	.270	163	26	44	8	0	0	16	10	21	3
Vazquez, Christian, SAN	.269	108	10	29	6	1	0	12	5	16	0
Monell, Johnny, MAY	.268	123	20	33	8	1	3	16	22	21	4
Dominguez, Jeff, CAG	.268	153	16	41	6	1	2	9	13	31	4
Lopez, Felipe, CAR	.264	125	6	33	8	0	0	15	5	26	0

PITCHER, CLUB	W	L	ERA	G	SV	IP	H	BB	SO	AVG
Colon, Joseph, SAN	0	0	1.16	12	0	39	34	17	31	.245
Roibal, Reinier, SAN	3	1	1.58	9	0	40	37	9	27	.252
Flores, Adalberto, SAN	5	2	2.04	10	0	53	33	17	35	.178
Rivera, Raul, CAR	2	1	2.15	15	0	46	40	12	26	.241
Maldonado, Ivan, MAY	4	3	2.18	10	0	54	44	15	28	.227
Texeira, Kanekoa, MAY	5	0	2.30	9	0	43	42	16	26	.268
Blacksher, Derek, CAG	1	3	2.60	10	0	45	35	13	24	.219
Sanchez, Jonathan, MAY	1	1	2.72	11	0	36	25	20	32	.198
Brownell, John, CAG	4	2	3.43	8	0	39	35	8	22	.236
Gonzalez, Dicky, CAR	2	2	3.46	10	0	55	54	19	27	.258

MEXICAN PACIFIC LEAGUE

TEAM	W	L	PCT	GB
Yaquis de Obregon	39	29	.573	—
Aguilas de Mexicali	38	29	.567	½
Venados de Mazatlan	38	30	.559	1
Mayos de Navojoa	36	32	.529	3
Caneros de Los Mochis	35	33	.515	4
Charros de Jalisco	30	38	.441	9
Tomateros de Culiacan	28	40	.412	11
Naranjeros de Hermosillo	27	40	.403	11½

Championship: Mazatlan defeated Mexicali, 4-1.

BATTER, CLUB	AVG	AB	R	H	2B	3B	HR	RBI	BB	SO	SB
Valdez, Jesus, JAL	.347	222	36	77	14	2	5	31	11	26	2
Zazueta, Amadeo, JAL	.335	212	33	71	7	5	2	26	10	14	9
Dotel, Wellington, MXC	.326	258	37	84	12	8	2	38	16	64	22
Roberson, Chris, MXC	.325	212	24	69	10	2	2	23	12	24	10
Amador, Jose, NAV	.323	217	31	70	13	0	11	39	38	36	0
Villanueva, Christian, OBR	.322	227	43	73	9	0	9	38	41	31	3
Robles, Oscar, CUL	.319	110	23	35	0	2	21	34	24	0	
Quiroz, Esteban, MAZ	.317	227	37	72	12	0	7	39	25	49	4
Liddi, Alex, MXC	.312	231	30	72	17	0	7	36	16	61	3
Owens, Jerry, HER	.310	203	30	63	9	3	1	19	14	28	3

PITCHER, CLUB	W	L	ERA	G	SV	IP	H	BB	SO	AVG
Soto, Alejandro, MAZ	4	4	2.63	13	0	72	64	12	48	.237
Valdez, Rolando, OBR	6	4	2.81	14	0	77	69	19	56	.241
Gaxiola, Amilcar, MAZ	6	3	2.92	12	0	71	67	28	34	.262
Velazquez, Hector, NAV	5	2	2.92	13	0	71	60	21	36	.236
Rodriguez, Hector Daniel, CUL	3	3	3.00	14	0	78	65	23	62	.225
Reed, Nate, HER	3	6	3.10	16	0	81	78	42	65	.257
Gamboa, Eddie, NAV	5	2	3.12	13	0	81	88	15	60	.285
Miramontes, Derrick, MOC	5	6	3.19	13	0	73	74	14	47	.261
Solano, Javier, MXC	8	3	3.33	13	0	81	75	20	71	.244
Silva, Walter, MAZ	7	4	3.81	13	0	76	68	27	53	.254

VENEZUELAN LEAGUE

TEAM	W	L	PCT	GB
Navegantes de Magallanes	36	27	.571	—
Leones del Caracas	35	30	.538	2
Caribes de Anzoategui	34	30	.531	2½
Tiburones de La Guaira	33	31	.515	3½
Cardenales de Lara	33	31	.515	3½
Tigres de Aragua	31	32	.492	5
Bravos de Margarita	28	35	.444	8
Aguilas del Zulia	24	39	.380	12

Championship: Aragua defeated Magallenes, 4-2.

BATTER, CLUB	AVG	AB	R	H	2B	3B	HR	RBI	BB	SO	SB
Romero, Alex, MAG	.383	230	35	88	12	1	1	28	25	17	0
Mustelier, Ronnier, LAG	.360	189	25	68	10	1	1	21	17	26	0
Ravelo, Rangel, LAR	.354	178	29	63	13	0	8	38	41	32	7
Querecuto, Juniel, ARA	.352	165	28	58	11	3	0	19	12	16	2
Cabrera, Alex, LAR	.335	173	23	58	8	0	11	39	27	25	0
Vargas, Illdemaro, ARA	.335	197	37	66	7	5	0	20	22	13	6
Hernandez, Gorkys, ORI	.333	228	32	76	10	2	1	20	29	34	6
Perez, Felix, MAG	.332	202	28	67	20	1	7	34	33	30	2
Osuna, Jose, MAR	.330	212	31	70	13	0	9	30	22	37	2
Hazelbaker, Jeremy, ORI	.321	162	30	52	11	5	3	22	15	35	11

PITCHER, CLUB	W	L	ERA	G	SV	IP	H	BB	SO	AVG
Johnson, Patrick, ORI	2	1	1.57	10	0	52	43	16	46	.228
Rivero, Raul, LAR	7	4	2.03	13	0	80	74	16	54	.251
Zarate, Robert, ARA	3	1	2.12	11	0	51	45	16	36	.238
Candelario, Alexis, LAG	3	2	2.16	11	0	58	43	32	42	.211
Diaz, Luis, CAR	1	2	2.43	12	0	59	49	21	43	.229
Perez, Sergio, MAR	2	4	2.54	13	0	67	59	28	43	.243
Bencomo, Omar, MAR	5	3	2.58	13	0	70	64	15	28	.244
Molina, Nestor, LAR	4	3	2.69	13	0	67	65	17	45	.259
Guerra, Junior, LAG	4	2	2.86	12	0	57	53	17	49	.247
Gardner, Joe, CAR	4	5	3.36	15	0	64	61	25	25	.256

INTERNATIONAL

COLLEGE

Anthony Marks (29) and Coastal Carolina won the school's first national title in any sport

ANDREW WOOLLEY

Chants of a lifetime: Coastal wins it all

BY TEDDY CAHILL

OMAHA

Nothing about Coastal Carolina's journey to the College World Series was easy, so it was only fitting that the final out of the decisive third game of the CWS against Arizona was as stressful as possible.

With two outs in the bottom of the ninth, Arizona had the tying run on third base and the winning run on second. It was as close as the Wildcats could get to completing the comeback. Righthander Alex Cunningham blew a fastball by Ryan Haug to strike out the sophomore and clinch a 4-3 victory and the national championship.

The national championship. For Coastal Carolina, a school of 10,000 students in suburban Myrtle Beach, S.C., that wasn't even a four-year college until 1974, and didn't become autonomous under its current name until 1993.

Coastal's triumph came a day after the series was supposed to end. Bad weather in Omaha the night before forced Game Three to be pushed back a day. It proved to be worth the wait for the Chanticleers, who won their first Division I national championship in any sport.

Righthander Andrew Beckwith, who won Game Three and was named CWS most outstanding player, said the victory was the culmination of a long journey for the Chanticleers.

"Just the hard work we put in," he said. "The hard work the alumni have put in to get us to have these great facilities, and this coaching staff is just unbelievable. And the senior class pushed everyone from the start when they got back in the fall, and just one goal was to get to Omaha and win it all.

"And we got to Omaha and we won it all. We won a national championship."

Coastal's run to that national championship was improbable not because of its lack of pedigree—the Chanticleers won 55 games and have been to super regionals three times—but rather because of the road it faced to get here.

The Chanticleers had hoped to host a regional and went into Selection Monday ranked No. 12 in RPI. The selection committee followed RPI almost exactly when picking the 16 host sites. The only team ranked in the top 16 of the RPI not to host a regional: Coastal Carolina.

So the Chanticleers began a monthlong road trip that took them from North Carolina State

COACHING CAROUSEL

SCHOOL	IN (PREVIOUS JOB)	OUT (REASON/NEW JOB)
Alabama	Greg Goff (Louisiana Tech head coach)	Mitch Gaspard (resigned)
Alabama State	Jose Vazquez (Alabama State assistant)	Mervyl Melendez (Fla. International head coach)
Appalachian State	Kermit Smith (Lander, S.C., head coach)	Billy Jones (fired)
Army	Jim Foster (Boston College assistant)	Matt Reid (fired)
Butler	Dave Schrage (South Dakota State head coach)	Steve Farley (fired)
Central Florida	Greg Lovelady (Wright State head coach)	Terry Rooney (Alabama assistant)
Florida International	Mervyl Melendez (Alabama State head coach)	Turtle Thomas (resigned)
Furman	Brett Harker (Furman assistant)	Ron Smith (resigned)
Jacksonville	Chris Hayes (Jacksonville assistant)	Tim Montez (fired)
Kentucky	Nick Mingione (Mississippi State assistant)	Gary Henderson (resigned)
Lamar	Will Davis (Lamar assistant)	Jim Gilligan (retired)
Liberty	Scott Jackson (North Carolina assistant)	Jim Toman (resigned)
Long Island-Brooklyn	Dan Pirillo (Chicago State assistant)	Alex Trezza (Boston College assistant)
Louisiana Tech	Lane Burroughs (Northwestern State head coach)	Greg Goff (Alabama head coach)
Maryland-Eastern Shore	Charlie Goens (Davis & Elkins, W.Va., head coach)	John O'Neil* (remained on staff)
Mississippi State	Andy Cannizaro (Louisiana State assistant)	John Cohen (Miss. State athletics director)
Missouri	Steve Bieser (Southeast Mo. State head coach)	Tim Jamieson (resigned)
Nebraska-Omaha	Evan Porter* (Nebraska-Omaha assistant)	Bob Herold (fired)
Northwestern State	Bobby Barbier (Northwestern State assistant)	Lane Burroughs (Louisiana Tech head coach)
Oakland	J. Healy (Oakland asst.) /C. Kaline (Fla. Southern asst.)	John Musachio (fired)
Purdue	Mark Wasikowski (Oregon assistant)	Doug Schreiber (resigned)
Saint Peter's	Danny Ramirez (Monroe, N.Y., JC head coach)	T.J. Baxter (resigned)
San Jose State	Jason Hawkins (Utah assistant)	Dave Nakama (fired)
South Dakota State	Rob Bishop (Montana State-Billings head coach)	Dave Schrage (Butler head coach)
Southeast Mo. State	Andy Sawyers (Kansas State assistant)	Steve Bieser (Missouri head coach)
SIU-Edwardsville	Sean Lyons (Bradley assistant)	Tony Stoecklin (fired)
Texas	David Pierce (Tulane head coach)	Augie Garrido (resigned)
Tulane	Travis Jewett (Vanderbilt assistant)	David Pierce (Texas head coach)
Villanova	Kevin Mulvey (Villanova assistant)	Joe Godri (fired)
Wright State	Jeff Mercer (Wright State assistant)	Greg Lovelady (Central Florida head coach)
Youngstown State	Dan Bertolini (Mercyhurst North East, Pa., JC)	Steve Gillispie (fired)

*interim head coach

to Louisiana State to Omaha. In the Raleigh Regional, they fought off rain and were pushed to the brink by the host Wolfpack. In the second regional final game, rain forced the game to be suspended with one out in the ninth inning and Coastal trailing by two runs. The Chanticleers came back the next day and found a way to win. Emboldened, they went into Alex Box Stadium, one of the toughest venues for a visiting team, and swept LSU, the No. 8 national seed.

In Omaha, Coastal found itself in the tougher bracket, and opened its first CWS with Florida, the No. 1 national seed. Led by Beckwith, the Chanticleers knocked off the Gators, then fell into the loser's bracket with a loss to TCU. Coastal fought its way out, eliminating Texas Tech, the No. 5 national seed, and then beating TCU twice to reach the finals.

After losing the first game to Arizona, Coastal's back was again against the wall. But the Chanticleers again wouldn't be denied. They won Game Two, pushed through the rainout the next day, and again led by Beckwith, found a way to win the decisive third game.

"They never faltered," head coach Gary Gilmore said. "You look at who we had to beat. To do this is an incredible feat. I don't care what team you are.

To go through LSU and then come here, Florida, TCU, Texas Tech, TCU twice and (Arizona) three times, it's an incredible journey for any program."

It was a national championship a long time coming for Gilmore, who has been the head coach at his alma mater since 1996. The final win marked the 1,100th in his career, and he became the first coach to win the national championship in his first CWS appearance since 2008, when Mike Batesole led Fresno State to the title.

Batesole's Bulldogs did it at Rosenblatt Stadium in an offensive era. Gilmore's Chanticleers did it by grinding through TD Ameritrade Park in a challenging offensive atmosphere, where the teams combined to hit .232 with 10 home runs. They did it by beating teams from the SEC, Big 12 and Pacific-12 conferences.

They did it with grit from left fielder Anthony Marks, who hit .382 (13-for-34) to pace Coastal's offense and made a key defensive play in the bottom of the ninth, holding the tying runner, Ramer, at third on Ryan Aguilar's double. They won with offense from catcher David Parrett, who had four RBIs against Texas Tech and TCU in the loser's bracket, after entering the CWS hitting just .130 (9-for-69) on the year. And they triumphed with heroics from closer Mike Morrison, who started an

elimination game in Game Two and went a career-high 6⅔ innings, striking out 10 in a 5-4 victory.

Gilmore thanked God for the opportunity to coach these Chanticleers. "That's one of the greatest blessings," Gilmore said. "Whenever I die, I'll know that this group of guys here, they willed themselves to be national champions."

ACC, SEC Dominate RPI

The 2016 NCAA tournament field broke several precedents—yet there was little surprise at any of them.

The 64-team field was a bonanza for college baseball's two most powerful conferences, the Atlantic Coast and Southeastern. The ACC tied a record with 10 teams selected for the field, while the SEC broke the record for most regional hosts out of one conference with seven. The ACC had six hosts itself, the two leagues accounting for 13 of the 16 regional sites. All season, the top of the RPI has been chock full of ACC and SEC teams, those two conferences accounting the top 11 teams in the RPI on Selection Monday.

At the other end of the spectrum, no regionals were hosted west of Texas for the first time since 1994. No West Coast teams finished higher than 21st in the RPI (Arizona) at selection time, and the committee stuck close to the RPI in selecting its hosts—15 of the 16 were from the top 16 in the RPI, the lone exception being No. 17 Virginia getting one over No. 12 Coastal Carolina.

In the past, the committee might have shoe-horned in a West Coast regional or two in the name of geographic balance and saving on travel costs. One of the options might have been to ship a No. 1 seed out West, where a team like Arizona, Arizona State or Cal State Fullerton could host as a No. 2, but the selection committee chose not to go in that direction.

"I think it's fair to say it became apparent that the fairest thing to do was to not (make a No. 1 seed travel west)," said committee chairman Joel Erdmann, who is South Alabama's athletic director. "There were teams that had, through their performance and their resume this season, justified their case to let them play at home . . . Ultimately, I think it's fair to say the committee would've had a hard time taking the earned privilege of hosting away from somebody to balance things out regionally."

Busy Coaching Carousel

The end of the 2016 season brought more coaching upheaval than usual. Thirty one programs will have a new head coach next spring. That is 12 more changes than last offseason and is the most new head coaches in any year since

RPI RANKINGS

The Ratings Percentage Index is an important tool used by the NCAA in selecting at-large teams for the 64-team Division I tournament. The NCAA now releases its RPI rankings during the season. These were the top 100 finishers for 2016. A team's rank in the final Baseball America Top 25 is indicated in parentheses, and College World Series teams are in bold.

1. **Florida** (5)	52-16		51. Northwestern State	33-24
2. Louisville (11)	50-14		52. Washington	33-23
3. **Miami** (6)	48-14		53. Nebraska	37-22
4. Texas A&M (8)	49-16		54. West Virginia	36-22
5. **Coastal Carolina** (1)	55-18		55. Illinois	28-23
6. **Texas Christian** (3)	49-18		56. Brigham Young	37-17
7. Clemson (17)	44-20		57. Houston	36-23
8. N.C. State (25)	38-22		58. Southeast Mo. State	38-21
9. Mississippi (18)	43-19		59. Oral Roberts	38-21
10. Louisiana State (12)	45-21		60. Maryland	30-27
11. Florida State (13)	41-22		61. Saint Mary's	33-25
12. **Arizona** (2)	49-24		62. College of Charleston	31-26
13. South Carolina (14)	46-18		63. North Florida	39-19
14. **Texas Tech** (7)	47-20		64. Marshall	34-21
15. Mississippi State (10)	44-18		65. Alabama	32-26
16. Vanderbilt (20)	43-29		66. Hartford	37-18
17. La.-Lafayette (22)	43-21		67. Oklahoma	30-27
18. **UC Santa Barbara** (9)	43-20		68. California	32-21
19. North Carolina	34-21		69. Indiana State	35-21
20. Southern Miss. (24)	41-20		70. Kentucky	32-25
21. **Oklahoma State** (4)	43-22		71. Kent State	43-14
22. Georgia Tech	38-25		72. Xavier	32-30
23. Virginia (21)	38-22		73. Iowa	27-26
24. Rice	38-24		74. Stanford	31-23
25. Dallas Baptist	44-19		75. Va. Commonwealth	38-19
26. Boston College (16)	35-22		76. UNC Greensboro	38-21
27. East Carolina (15)	38-23		77. Lamar	35-19
28. Wake Forest	35-27		78. Michigan State	36-20
29. Duke	33-24		79. Southern California	28-28
30. UNC Wilmington	41-19		80. Oregon	29-26
31. Louisiana Tech	42-20		81. Georgia Southern	36-24
32. Tulane (19)	41-21		82. Old Dominion	32-24
33. Gonzaga	36-21		83. Missouri State	38-21
34. Florida Atlantic (23)	39-19		84. Jacksonville	33-22
35. Bryant	47-12		85. Pittsburgh	25-26
36. Ohio State	44-20		86. New Orleans	31-26
37. Wright State	46-17		87. Nevada	37-24
38. Arizona State	36-23		88. Tennessee	29-28
39. Michigan	36-21		89. William & Mary	31-31
40. Sam Houston State	42-22		90. Utah	26-29
41. Long Beach State	38-22		91. Pepperdine	29-24
42. Cal State Fullerton	36-23		92. Jacksonville State	34-24
43. South Alabama	42-22		93. Troy	32-26
44. Southeastern La.	40-21		94. Fresno State	36-22
45. Georgia	27-30		95. Mercer	38-23
46. Oregon State	35-19		96. Notre Dame	27-27
47. New Mexico	39-23		97. Western Carolina	31-31
48. Connecticut	38-25		98. Florida International	28-29
49. Creighton	38-17		99. Texas-Arlington	30-28
50. Minnesota	34-22		100. UCLA	25-31

Baseball America began cataloging the coaching carousel in the Almanac in 2002. In that time, there have been an average of 23.4 new coaches every spring.

This year's carousel saw Augie Garrido, the all-time winningest college baseball coach, step down at Texas after going 25-32 this spring. After winning the Big 12 Conference tournament to make regionals in 2015, Garrido entered the 2016 season on the hot seat in the minds of most college

baseball observers. Texas was never able to get on track and finished 25-32 and in seventh place in the Big 12. Its season ended with a loss to Texas Christian in the Big 12 tournament semifinals.

While Texas has scuffled by its lofty standards in recent years—it reached the College World Series in 2014 but has not hosted a regional since 2011—Garrido's career was exemplary. One of five coaches to have twice been named BA College Coach of the Year, Garrido, 76, has won five national championships and has a career record of 1,975-952 in 48 years as a head coach.

Garrido began his college coaching career at San Francisco State in 1969. After one season, he moved on to Cal Poly for three years. Then, in 1973 he arrived at Cal State Fullerton. It was at Fullerton that Garrido's legend was born. He helped the Titans transition to Division I, leading them to the CWS in 1975, their first season at the highest level. He won his first national championship in 1979 and added another in 1984.

Garrido became Illinois' coach in 1988, and spent three seasons in that role. He then returned to Fullerton and won another national championship in 1995, a team led by Mark Kotsay and named by Baseball America as the best college team of the 20th century. Garrido's second stint with the Titans ended after the 1996 season, when he took over at Texas. In 21 seasons at Fullerton, he went 929-391-6.

Other longtime coaches such as Jim Gilligan (Lamar), Tim Jamieson (Missouri) and Doug Schreiber (Purdue) also found themselves on the way out.

This year's hyperactive coaching carousel may end up proving to be an anomaly, brought on by a variety of factors including fewer changes in 2015 and a cascading effect of prominent programs such as Alabama, Kentucky, Missouri and Texas all making moves in the same summer. But many coaches think this year's activity is closer to the new normal than a one-time wonder.

"From the athletic director standpoint, you have the potential to make a lot of money in baseball as a result of what you're seeing around the country in facilities," longtime Florida State head coach Mike Martin said. "You have marketing of the program at the level now that's the highest I can remember it. Athletic directors are expecting a lot out of the program in order to meet their input into the program."

These developments are generally welcomed

COLLEGE WORLD SERIES CHAMPIONS

YEAR	CHAMPION	COACH	RECORD	RUNNER-UP	MOST OUTSTANDING PLAYER
1948	Southern California	Sam Barry	40-12	Yale	None selected
1949	Texas*	Bibb Falk	23-7	Wake Forest	Charles Teague, 2b, Wake Forest
1950	Texas	Bibb Falk	27-6	Washington State	Ray VanCleef, of, Rutgers
1951	Oklahoma*	Jack Baer	19-9	Tennessee	Sid Hatfield, 1b-p, Tennessee
1952	Holy Cross	Jack Barry	21-3	Missouri	Jim O'Neill, p, Holy Cross
1953	Michigan	Ray Fisher	21-9	Texas	J.L. Smith, p, Texas
1954	Missouri	Hi Simmons	22-4	Rollins	Tom Yewcic, c, Michigan State
1955	Wake Forest	Taylor Sanford	29-7	Western Michigan	Tom Borland, p, Oklahoma State
1956	Minnesota	Dick Siebert	33-9	Arizona	Jerry Thomas, p, Minnesota
1957	California*	George Wolfman	35-10	Penn State	Cal Emery, 1b-p, Penn State
1958	Southern California	Rod Dedeaux	35-7	Missouri	Bill Thom, p, Southern California
1959	Oklahoma State	Toby Greene	27-5	Arizona	Jim Dobson, 3b, Oklahoma State
1960	Minnesota	Dick Siebert	34-7	Southern California	John Erickson, 2b, Minnesota
1961	Southern California*	Rod Dedeaux	43-9	Oklahoma State	Littleton Fowler, p, Oklahoma State
1962	Michigan	Don Lund	31-13	Santa Clara	Bob Garibaldi, p, Santa Clara
1963	Southern California	Rod Dedeaux	37-16	Arizona	Bud Hollowell, c, Southern California
1964	Minnesota	Dick Siebert	31-12	Missouri	Joe Ferris, p, Maine
1965	Arizona State	Bobby Winkles	54-8	Ohio State	Sal Bando, 3b, Arizona State
1966	Ohio State	Marty Karow	27-6	Oklahoma State	Steve Arlin, p, Ohio State
1967	Arizona State	Bobby Winkles	53-12	Houston	Ron Davini, c, Arizona State
1968	Southern California*	Rod Dedeaux	42-12	Southern Illinois	Bill Seinsoth, 1b, Southern California
1969	Arizona State	Bobby Winkles	56-11	Tulsa	John Dolinsek, of, Arizona State
1970	Southern California	Rod Dedeaux	51-13	Florida State	Gene Ammann, p, Florida State
1971	Southern California	Rod Dedeaux	53-13	Southern Illinois	Jerry Tabb, 1b, Tulsa
1972	Southern California	Rod Dedeaux	50-13	Arizona State	Russ McQueen, p, Southern California
1973	Southern California*	Rod Dedeaux	51-11	Arizona State	Dave Winfield, of-p, Minnesota
1974	Southern California	Rod Dedeaux	50-20	Miami	George Milke, p, Southern California
1975	Texas	Cliff Gustafson	56-6	South Carolina	Mickey Reichenbach, 1b, Texas
1976	Arizona	Jerry Kindall	56-17	Eastern Michigan	Steve Powers, dh-p, Arizona
1977	Arizona State	Jim Brock	57-12	South Carolina	Bob Horner, 3b, Arizona State
1978	Southern California*	Rod Dedeaux	54-9	Arizona State	Rod Boxberger, p, Southern California
1979	Cal State Fullerton	Augie Garrido	60-14	Arkansas	Tony Hudson, p, Cal State Fullerton
1980	Arizona	Jerry Kindall	45-21	Hawaii	Terry Francona, of, Arizona
1981	Arizona State	Jim Brock	55-13	Oklahoma State	Stan Holmes, of, Arizona State

across the country. They mean fans are more engaged, bringing better facilities for the players and raising the salaries of coaches. But more attention also means more pressure to win, and that pressure leads to changes.

Baseball has long had powerhouses from outside the power structure that rule football and basketball, including the juggernaut Garrido built at Cal State Fullerton. Coastal Carolina's national championship this year, the first in any sport by a school in the Big South Conference, showed that remains true even in the era of Power Five autonomy. That Coastal was no Cinderella on the diamond makes the lesson more widely relevant: building a baseball power does not require membership in an elite conference. As more schools realize what is possible, more raise their expectations.

Whether this year's amount of coaching changes becomes standard or not, it is a profession that inherently will have a fair amount of yearly turnover. While baseball experienced one of its largest turnovers this offseason, it still lags behind other sports in the amount of change. The 31 changes mean 10.4 percent of Division I schools will have a new coach in 2017. Football (22.7 percent), men's basketball (14.8) and women's basketball (15.5) all had

a higher percentage of coaching changes this year.

Vandy's Everett Dies

The NCAA tournament began with a somber tone, as Vanderbilt freshman righthander Donny Everett lost his life June 2, the night before regionals were set to begin, in a drowning accident.

"We learned last night of the tragic death of Donny Everett, an outstanding young man who exemplified the best of our university," Vanderbilt athletics director David Williams said in a statement. "As you can imagine, the team, the athletic department and the university are trying to come to terms with this tragedy. His parents and loved ones are on our minds and in our prayers as we share in their grief."

Everett, a product of Clarksville (Tenn.) High, was a second-team Preseason High School All-American in 2015 and ranked between first-rounders Cornelius Randolph (Phillies) and Brady Aiken (Indians) on the final BA500. He had a stellar senior prep season and was a first-team All-American at season's end after going 9-1, 1.21 with 125 strikeouts in 67 innings.

The righthander was banged up early in the spring of 2016 but made his first collegiate start

YEAR	CHAMPION	COACH	RECORD	RUNNER-UP	MOST OUTSTANDING PLAYER
1982	Miami	Ron Fraser	57-18	Wichita State	Dan Smith, p, Miami
1983	Texas	Cliff Gustafson	66-14	Alabama	Calvin Schiraldi, p, Texas
1984	Cal State Fullerton	Augie Garrido	66-20	Texas	John Fishel, of, Cal State Fullerton
1985	Miami*	Ron Fraser	64-16	Texas	Greg Ellena, dh, Miami
1986	Arizona	Jerry Kindall	49-19	Florida State	Mike Senne, of, Arizona
1987	Stanford	Mark Marquess	53-17	Oklahoma State	Paul Carey, of, Stanford
1988	Stanford	Mark Marquess	46-23	Arizona State	Lee Plemel, p, Stanford
1989	Wichita State	Gene Stephenson	68-16	Texas	Greg Brummett, p, Wichita State
1990	Georgia	Steve Webber	52-19	Oklahoma State	Mike Rebhan, p, Georgia
1991	Louisiana State*	Skip Bertman	55-18	Wichita State	Gary Hymel, c, Louisiana State
1992	Pepperdine*	Andy Lopez	48-11	Cal State Fullerton	Phil Nevin, 3b, Cal State Fullerton
1993	Louisiana State	Skip Bertman	53-17	Wichita State	Todd Walker, 2b, Louisiana State
1994	Oklahoma*	Larry Cochell	50-17	Georgia Tech	Chip Glass, of, Oklahoma
1995	Cal State Fullerton*	Augie Garrido	57-9	Southern California	Mark Kotsay, of-p, Cal State Fullerton
1996	Louisiana State*	Skip Bertman	52-15	Miami	Pat Burrell, 3b, Miami
1997	Louisiana State*	Skip Bertman	57-13	Alabama	Brandon Larson, ss, Louisiana State
1998	Southern California	Mike Gillespie	49-17	Arizona State	Wes Rachels, 2b, Southern California
1999	Miami*	Jim Morris	50-13	Florida State	Marshall McDougall, 2b, Florida State
2000	Louisiana State*	Skip Bertman	52-17	Stanford	Trey Hodges, rhp, Louisiana State
2001	Miami*	Jim Morris	53-12	Stanford	Charlton Jimerson, of, Miami
2002	Texas*	Augie Garrido	57-15	South Carolina	Huston Street, rhp, Texas
2003	Rice	Wayne Graham	58-12	Stanford	John Hudgins, rhp, Stanford
2004	Cal State Fullerton	George Horton	47-22	Texas	Jason Windsor, rhp, Cal State Fullerton
2005	Texas*	Augie Garrido	56-16	Florida	David Maroul, 3b, Texas
2006	Oregon State	Pat Casey	50-16	North Carolina	Jonah Nickerson, rhp, Oregon State
2007	Oregon State*	Pat Casey	49-18	North Carolina	Jorge Reyes, rhp, Oregon State
2008	Fresno State	Mike Batesole	47-31	Georgia	Tommy Mendonca, 3b, Fresno State
2009	Louisiana State	Paul Mainieri	56-17	Texas	Jared Mitchell, of, Louisiana State
2010	South Carolina	Ray Tanner	54-16	UCLA	Jackie Bradley Jr., of, South Carolina
2011	South Carolina*	Ray Tanner	55-14	Florida	Scott Wingo, 2b, South Carolina
2012	Arizona*	Andy Lopez	48-17	South Carolina	Robert Refsnyder, of, Arizona
2013	UCLA*	John Savage	49-17	Mississippi State	Adam Plutko, rhp, UCLA
2014	Vanderbilt	Tim Corbin	51-21	Virginia	Dansby Swanson, 2b, Vanderbilt
2015	Virginia	Brian O'Connor	44-24	Vanderbilt	Josh Sborz, rhp, Virginia
2016	Coastal Carolina	Gary Gilmore	55-18	Arizona	Andrew Beckwith, rhp, Coastal Carolina

*Undefeated

FIRST TEAM

POS.	NAME	YEAR	AVG	OBP	SLG	AB	R	H	HR	RBI	BB	SO	SB
C	Zack Collins, Miami	Jr.	.357	.538	.649	185	53	66	15	57	75	51	1
1B	Eric Gutierrez, Texas Tech	Sr.	.333	.465	.581	234	54	78	13	60	42	37	3
2B	Ryne Birk, Texas A&M	Jr.	.310	.378	.478	255	52	79	7	45	29	34	9
3B	Boomer White, Texas A&M	R-Jr.	.386	.462	.517	259	49	100	5	46	33	16	10
SS	Taylor Walls, Florida State	So.	.355	.479	.516	248	72	88	6	46	59	45	14
OF	Seth Beer, Clemson	Fr.	.369	.535	.700	203	57	75	18	70	62	27	1
OF	Kyle Lewis, Mercer	Jr.	.395	.535	.731	223	70	88	20	72	66	48	6
OF	Anfernee Grier, Auburn	Jr.	.366	.457	.576	238	56	87	12	41	32	55	19
DH	Will Craig, Wake Forest	Jr.	.379	.520	.731	182	53	69	16	66	47	35	0
UT	Brendan McKay, Louisville	So.	.333	.414	.513	228	43	76	6	41	24	33	0

		YEAR	W	L	ERA	G	CG	SV	IP	H	BB	SO	AVG
SP	Eric Lauer, Kent State	Jr.	10	2	0.69	15	3	0	104	49	28	125	.141
SP	A.J. Puckett, Pepperdine	Jr.	9	3	1.27	14	1	0	99	65	26	95	.191
SP	Cody Sedlock, Illinois	Jr.	5	3	2.49	14	2	0	101	80	31	116	.219
SP	Logan Shore, Florida	Jr.	12	1	2.31	18	3	0	105	82	19	96	.215
RP	Troy Rallings, Washington	Sr.	4	1	0.89	28	0	16	61	32	12	60	.155
UT	Brendan McKay, Louisville	So.	12	4	2.30	17	1	0	110	89	42	128	.220

SECOND TEAM

POS.	NAME	YEAR	AVG	OBP	SLG	AB	R	H	HR	RBI	BB	SO	SB
C	Chris Okey, Clemson	Jr.	.339	.465	.611	239	61	81	15	74	51	54	4
1B	Jameson Fisher, Southeastern Louisiana	Jr.	.424	.558	.692	194	49	84	11	66	54	31	15
2B	Jake Noll, Florida Gulf Coast	R-Jr.	.367	.427	.620	237	58	87	12	61	20	29	9
3B	Nick Senzel, Tennessee	Jr.	.352	.456	.595	210	57	74	8	59	40	21	25
SS	C.J. Chatham, Florida Atlantic	Jr.	.357	.422	.554	249	48	89	8	50	23	36	2
OF	Heath Quinn, Samford	Jr.	.343	.452	.682	242	62	83	21	77	44	55	4
OF	Corey Ray, Louisville	Jr.	.310	.388	.545	268	55	83	15	60	36	41	44
OF	J.B. Woodman, Mississippi	Jr.	.323	.412	.578	232	53	75	14	55	33	48	12
DH	Matt Thaiss, Virginia	Jr.	.375	.437	.578	232	55	87	10	59	39	16	0
UT	Luken Baker, Texas Christian	Fr.	.379	.483	.577	248	59	94	11	62	45	39	1

		YEAR	W	L	ERA	G	CG	SV	IP	H	BB	SO	AVG
SP	Corbin Burnes, Saint Mary's	Jr.	9	2	2.48	16	3	0	102	76	33	120	.212
SP	Connor Jones, Virginia	Jr.	11	1	2.34	15	3	0	104	85	38	72	.225
SP	Brigham Hill, Texas A&M	Jr.	9	2	2.51	24	0	1	97	86	28	99	.234
SP	Dakota Hudson, Mississippi State	Jr.	9	5	2.55	17	3	0	113	106	35	115	.248
RP	Mark Ecker, Texas A&M	Jr.	4	2	0.39	25	0	8	47	24	7	56	.155
UT	Luken Baker, Texas Christian	Fr.	3	1	1.70	10	0	0	48	37	16	41	.213

THIRD TEAM

POS.	NAME	YEAR	AVG	OBP	SLG	AB	R	H	HR	RBI	BB	SO	SB
C	Nick Feight, UNC Wilmington	So.	.349	.412	.726	241	60	84	21	91	29	35	1
1B	Peter Alonso, Florida	Jr.	.374	.469	.659	211	51	79	14	60	31	31	2
2B	Nick Solak, Louisville	Jr.	.376	.470	.564	165	49	62	5	29	28	22	9
3B	Jake Burger, Missouri State	So.	.349	.420	.689	235	59	82	21	72	23	35	3
SS	Donnie Walton, Oklahoma State	Sr.	.337	.428	.447	246	45	83	3	44	32	36	14
OF	Ronnie Dawson, Ohio State	Jr.	.331	.419	.611	257	55	85	13	51	37	43	21
OF	Jake Mangum, Mississippi State	Fr.	.408	.458	.510	206	40	84	1	28	14	20	6
OF	David Oppenheim, Southern California	Sr.	.387	.500	.508	191	37	74	4	25	39	24	6
DH	Brett Cumberland, California	So.	.344	.480	.678	180	46	62	16	51	38	40	5
UT	Adam Haseley, Virginia	So.	.304	.377	.502	247	61	75	6	37	28	29	3

		YEAR	W	L	ERA	G	CG	SV	IP	H	BB	SO	AVG
SP	Keegan Akin, Western Michigan	Jr.	7	4	1.82	17	2	0	109	72	30	133	.192
SP	Justin Dunn, Boston College	Jr.	4	2	2.06	18	1	2	66	52	72	18	.214
SP	Joey Lucchesi, Southeast Missouri State	Sr.	10	5	2.19	17	2	1	111	96	37	149	.234
SP	Thomas Hatch, Oklahoma State	R-So.	9	3	2.14	19	4	0	130	108	33	112	.233
RP	Pat Krall, Clemson	Jr.	10	2	1.67	29	1	5	81	58	17	65	.203
UT	Adam Haseley, Virginia	So.	9	1	1.73	23	1	0	78	54	21	48	.194

on May 10 against Louisville, and overall was 0-1, 1.50 with 13 strikeouts in 12 innings.

The NCAA regional weekend, for Vanderbilt, was about healing, about finding some measure of solace between the lines at Hawkins Field. The Commodores honored Everett as best they could, hanging his No. 41 jersey in the dugout, leaving a space for him down the foul line during the national anthem, writing "DE41" on their hats and hanging the stadium flags at half staff.

As circumstances would dictate, the Commodores had to play twice, on a rainy, gray day. They lost the first game, 15-1, to No. 4 seed Xavier, as uncharacteristic errors led to a 13-run seventh inning and put Vanderbilt's season on the brink. In the second game, an elimination game, the Commodores established a five-run lead over No. 3 seed Washington in the sixth inning. But the Huskies were playing to extend their own season, too. They fought back. A two-run home run by Jack Meggs in the bottom of the eighth gave them a 9-8 lead, and they held it.

"The game in a lot of ways seems insignificant, but at the same time it provides some healing for the kids in the immediate moment," head coach Tim Corbin said. "Now that it's gone, then we'll delve into another level of emotions. They know that it's coming. They have a whole lot of weight on their shoulders right now. It's just very difficult to lose a teammate and for it to just happen during the time that you are supposed to compete.

"What is primary right now is how they feel about one another and what has happened and that this is tough to get over, and they probably won't get over it for quite some time."

North Dakota Folds Program

For the third straight year, a Division I baseball program was shut down, as North Dakota followed in the unfortunate footsteps of Temple (2014) and Akron (2015).

North Dakota's baseball program began in 1889. After spells without a team from 1917-1919 and 1921-1955, it had existed since 1956. North Dakota moved up to Division I in 2009 and had its best season in 2015, going 24-27.

North Dakota's administration originally announced its plans to drop baseball, along with men's golf, in April, citing revenue shortfalls and Title IX compliance. The cuts were made to save $2.4 million for the UND athletic department. A week after that original decision was made public, a glimmer of hope remained for baseball's survival, as UND officials met with supporters of the program to lay out plans for how it could keep going.

Chief among those plans was the need for the program to raise $530,958 by Aug. 30 to operate for the 2017 season, according to the Grand Forks (N.D.) Herald. Aside from the immediate need, the program would need to generate a similar amount each year to keep playing. Long term, the school felt the best path to keeping baseball alive was to build an endowment of more than $13 million.

UND interim president Ed Schafer initially expressed optimism that the program could be saved, but the baseball program's supporters argued

COLLEGE WORLD SERIES

STANDINGS

BRACKET ONE	W	L
Arizona	4	1
Oklahoma State	2	2
UC Santa Barbara	1	2
Miami	0	2
BRACKET TWO	**W**	**L**
Coastal Carolina	4	1
Texas Christian	2	2
Texas Tech	1	2
Florida	0	2

CWS FINALS (BEST OF THREE)
June 27: Arizona 3, Coastal Carolina 0
June 28: Coastal Carolina 5, Arizona 4
June 30: Coastal Carolina 4, Arizona 3

ALL-TOURNAMENT TEAM
C: David Parrett, Coastal Carolina. **1B:** Ryan Aguilar, Arizona. **2B:** Cody Ramer, Arizona. **3B:** Zach Remillard, Coastal Carolina. **SS:** Ryan Merrill, Texas Christian. **OF:** Anthony Marks, Coastal Carolina; Zach Gibbons, Arizona; Jared Oliva, Arizona. **DH:** Luken Baker, Texas Christian. **P:** *Andrew Beckwith, Coastal Carolina; J.C. Cloney, Arizona.

*Named Most Outstanding Player.

BATTING
(Minimum 8 PA)

PLAYER	AVG	AB	R	H	2B	3B	HR	RBI	SB
Zack Collins, Miami	.600	5	1	3	1	0	1	2	0
Eric Gutierrez, TTU	.500	10	1	5	0	0	1	2	0
Jacob Heyward, Miami	.429	7	0	3	0	0	0	0	0
Peter Alonso, Florida	.429	7	0	3	0	0	1	2	0
Zach Gibbons, Arizona	.419	31	4	13	3	0	0	9	0
Anthony Marks, Coastal	.387	31	4	12	1	0	0	4	1
Luken Baker, TCU	.375	16	3	6	1	0	2	5	0
Dane Steinhagen, TCU	.357	14	4	5	2	0	1	1	0
Evan Skoug, TCU	.333	18	1	6	1	0	0	0	0
Cory Raley, Texas Tech	.333	12	2	4	1	0	0	0	2

PITCHING
(Minimum 6 IP)

PITCHER	W-L	ERA	G	SV	IP	H	BB	SO
J.C. Cloney, Arizona	2-0	0.00	2	0	16	9	5	8
Tyler Buffett, Okla. State	1-0	0.00	2	0	9	3	2	6
Davis Martin, Texas Tech	1-0	0.00	1	0	7	3	3	3
Trey Cobb, Okla. State	0-0	0.00	2	1	6	4	2	5
Andrew Beckwith, Coastal	3-0	0.76	3	0	24	19	4	14
Bobby Dalbec, Arizona	1-2	0.87	3	0	21	13	6	26
Nathan Bannister, Arizona	1-0	0.93	2	0	10	8	4	16
Shane Bieber, UCSB	0-1	1.12	1	0	8	6	0	6
Noah Davis, UCSB	1-0	1.50	1	0	6	2	2	3
Alex Faedo, Florida	0-1	2.35	1	0	8	7	0	9

that UND should've lowered the fundraising targets, citing the program used only five scholarships, well below the maximum 11.7 allowed by the NCAA. When the administration and baseball supporters were unable to come to an agreement on the dollar amounts, the school announced its final decision on May 11, the same day UND took the field for a game against South Dakota State.

North Dakota played its final home game on May 15, losing 7-2 to New Mexico State. The team honored its senior class before the game, but as junior lefthander Zach Muckenhirn told the Herald, "We all feel like seniors."

REGIONALS

JUNE 3-6
64 teams, 16 four-team, double-elimination tournaments. Winners advance to super regionals.

GAINESVILLE, FLA.
Host: Florida (No. 1 national seed).
Participants: No. 1 Florida (47-13), No. 2 Georgia Tech (36-23), No. 3 Connecticut (37-23), No. 4 Bethune-Cookman (29-25).
Champion: Florida (3-0).
Runner-up: Georgia Tech (2-2).
Outstanding player: Peter Alonso, 1b, Florida.

TALLAHASSEE, FLA.
Host: Florida State.
Participants: No. 1 Florida State (37-20), No. 2 Southern Mississippi (40-18), No. 3 South Alabama (40-20), No. 4 Alabama State (38-15).
Champion: Florida State (3-0).
Runner-up: South Alabama (2-2).
Outstanding player: Dylan Busby, 1b, Florida State.

BATON ROUGE
Host: Louisiana State (No. 8 national seed).
Participants: No. 1 Louisiana State (42-18), No. 2 Rice (35-22), No. 3 Southeastern Louisiana (39-19), No. 4 Utah Valley (37-21).
Champion: Louisiana State (3-1).
Runner-up: Rice (3-2).
Outstanding player: Greg Deichmann, 1b, Louisiana State.

RALEIGH, N.C.
Host: North Carolina State.
Participants: No. 1 North Carolina State (35-20), No. 2 Coastal Carolina (44-15), No. 3 Saint Mary's (33-23), No. 4 Navy (42-14).
Champion: Coastal Carolina (3-1).
Runner-up: North Carolina State (3-2).
Outstanding player: Zach Remillard, 3b, Coastal Carolina.

COLLEGE STATION, TEXAS
Host: Texas A&M (No. 4 national seed).
Participants: No. 1 Texas A&M (45-14), No. 2 Minnesota (32-20), No. 3 Wake Forest (34-25), No. 4 Binghamton (30-23).
Champion: Texas A&M (3-0).
Runner-up: Minnesota (2-2).
Outstanding player: Jonathan Moroney, dh, Texas A&M.

FORT WORTH
Host: Texas Christian.
Participants: No. 1 Texas Christian (42-15), No. 2 Arizona State (34-21), No. 3 Gonzaga (35-19), No. 4 Oral Roberts (38-19).
Champion: Texas Christian (3-0).
Runner-up: Arizona State (2-2).
Outstanding player: Cam Warner, 2b, Texas Christian.

LUBBOCK, TEXAS
Host: Texas Tech (No. 5 national seed).

Participants: No. 1 Texas Tech (42-15), No. 2 Dallas Baptist (34-21), No. 3 New Mexico (35-19), No. 4 Fairfield (38-19).
Champion: Texas Tech (3-1).
Runner-up: Dallas Baptist (3-2).
Outstanding player: Hayden Howard, lhp, Texas Tech.

CHARLOTTESVILLE, VA.
Host: Virginia.
Participants: No. 1 Virginia (37-20), No. 2 Bryant (47-10), No. 3 East Carolina (34-21-1), No. 4 William & Mary (29-29).
Champion: East Carolina (3-0).
Runner-up: William & Mary (2-2).
Outstanding player: Travis Watkins, c, East Carolina.

CORAL GABLES, FLA.
Host: Miami (No. 3 national seed).
Participants: No. 1 Miami (43-11), No. 2 Florida Atlantic (38-17), No. 3 Long Beach State (36-20), No. 4 Stetson (29-29).
Champion: Miami (3-0).
Runner-up: Long Beach State (2-2).
Outstanding player: Carl Chester, of, Miami.

OXFORD, MISS.
Host: Mississippi.
Participants: No. 1 Mississippi (43-17), No. 2 Tulane (39-19), No. 3 Boston College (31-20), No. 4 Utah (25-27).
Champion: Boston College (3-0).
Runner-up: Tulane (2-2).
Outstanding player: Johnny Adams, ss, Boston College.

STARKVILLE, MISS.
Host: Mississippi State (No. 6 national seed).
Participants: No. 1 Mississippi State (41-16-1), No. 2 Cal State Fullerton (35-21), No. 3 Louisiana Tech (40-18), No. 4 Southeast Missouri State (38-19).
Champion: Mississippi State (3-0).
Runner-up: Louisiana Tech (2-2).
Outstanding player: Brent Rooker, dh, Mississippi State.

LAFAYETTE, LA.
Host: Louisiana-Lafayette.
Participants: No. 1 Louisiana-Lafayette (41-19), No. 2 Arizona (38-20), No. 3 Sam Houston State (41-20), No. 4 Princeton (24-19).
Champion: Arizona (4-1).
Runner-up: Louisiana-Lafayette(2-2).
Outstanding player: Nathan Bannister, rhp, Arizona.

LOUISVILLE
Host: Louisville (No. 2 national seed).
Participants: No. 1 Louisville (47-12), No. 2 Ohio State (43-18-1), No. 3 Wright State (44-15), No. 4 Western Michigan (22-32).
Champion: Louisville (3-0).
Runner-up: Wright State (2-2).
Outstanding player: Brendan McKay, lhp/1b, Louisville.

NASHVILLE
Host: Vanderbilt.

Participants: No. 1 Vanderbilt (43-17), No. 2 UC Santa Barbara (37-18-1), No. 3 Washington (32-21), No. 4 Xavier.
Champion: UC Santa Barbara (3-0).
Runner-up: Xavier (2-2).
Outstanding player: Austin Bush, 1b, UC Santa Barbara.

CLEMSON, S.C.
Host: Clemson (No. 7 national seed).
Participants: No. 1 Clemson (42-18), No. 2 Oklahoma State (36-20), No. 3 Nebraska (37-20), No. 4 Western Carolina (30-29).
Champion: Oklahoma State (3-0).
Runner-up: Clemson (2-2).
Outstanding player: Corey Hassel, of, Oklahoma State.

COLUMBIA, S.C.
Host: South Carolina.
Participants: No. 1 South Carolina (42-15), No. 2 UNC Wilmington (39-17), No. 3 Duke (33-22), No. 4 Rhode Island (30-25).
Champion: South Carolina (4-1).
Runner-up: UNC Wilmington (2-2).
Outstanding player: Tyler Johnson, rhp, South Carolina.

SUPER REGIONALS

JUNE 10-13
16 teams, best-of-three series. Winners advance to College World Series.

FLORIDA STATE AT FLORIDA
Site: Gainesville, Fla.
Florida wins 2-1, advances to CWS.

COASTAL CAROLINA AT LOUISIANA STATE
Site: Baton Rouge, La.
Coastal Carolina wins 2-0, advances to CWS.

TEXAS CHRISTIAN AT TEXAS A&M
Site: College Station, Texas.
Texas Christian wins 2-1, advances to CWS.

EAST CAROLINA AT TEXAS TECH
Site: Lubbock, Texas.
Texas Tech wins 2-1, advances to CWS.

BOSTON COLLEGE AT MIAMI
Site: Coral Gables, Fla.
Miami wins 2-1, advances to CWS.

ARIZONA AT MISSISSIPPI STATE
Site: Starkville, Miss.
Arizona wins 2-0, advances to CWS.

UC SANTA BARBARA AT LOUISVILLE
Site: Louisville
UC Santa Barbara wins 2-0, advances to CWS.

OKLAHOMA STATE AT SOUTH CAROLINA
Site: Columbia, S.C.
Oklahoma State wins 2-0, advances to CWS.

Lewis powers away from field

BY JIM SHONERD

As a recruit, Kyle Lewis didn't exactly fit Mercer's mold.

The Bears look for players ready to contribute quickly. Lewis wasn't going to be that guy, his attention always having been divided between baseball and basketball. Still, between his athleticism, his intelligence and his tools—even if he only showed them in flashes—Mercer coaches decided he was worth bringing in.

"He was just an athletic piece and his skill level wasn't there (as a high schooler)," Mercer head coach Craig Gibson said. "So he's generally not what we sign. We like more guys that are a little more skilled, that can come in and play immediately. But he was a guy we took a chance on—that we thought if his skill level ever caught up with his athleticism, he's going to be a good player."

The skill level did catch up. Three years later, Lewis will leave as the program's new gold standard. "He's the best player in school history," Gibson said.

Lewis' statistics read like something out of another era—a .395/.535/.731 slash line in 61 games. Although Mercer's season ended in the finals of the Southern Conference tournament, at the time, Lewis ranked among the top five nationally in total bases, slugging and on-base percentage. Mercer's coaches are quick to point out his 66 walks cost him roughly 15 games of at-bats too, meaning he did his greatest damage—his 20 homers and 72 RBIs—as if

Kyle Lewis

he played in 45 games.

With that level of domination, on top of being one of college baseball's premier talents, Lewis is the 2016 College Player of the Year.

Even though the thunderous power in his bat is usually the first thing mentioned in any Lewis scouting report, he doesn't think of himself as a home run hitter. For Lewis, home runs are just a by-product of trying to hit balls on a line, a mentality that would make any hitting coach proud.

"I'm not trying to go up there and just slug home runs and swing for the fences. I'm trying to put hard line drives in play consistently," Lewis said. "I think that if you try to hit low line drives consistently that you'll get the elevation and you'll get some balls out of the park, and I've been able to do that."

After not playing every day as a freshman, Lewis took off as a sophomore in 2015. He hit .367/.423/.677 with 17 homers in the spring for Mercer, then tore up the prestigious Cape Cod League over the summer, hitting .300/.344/.500.

"We'll have 15-30 or more scouts at each game," Mercer assistant coach and recruiting coordinator Brent Shade said. "He knows that they're there, but he puts it out of his mind and just goes about his business."

Lewis led the Bears to back-to-back SoCon regular-season titles in 2015 and 2016, winning conference player of the year honors in both. Suffice to say that chance the Bears took paid off. "I don't know what's to come," Lewis said, "but it's going to be fun."

PREVIOUS WINNERS

1982: Jeff Ledbetter, of/lhp, Florida State
1983: Dave Magadan, 1b, Alabama
1984: Oddibe McDowell, of, Arizona State
1985: Pete Incaviglia, of, Oklahoma State
1986: Casey Close, of, Michigan
1987: Robin Ventura, 3b, Oklahoma State
1988: John Olerund, 1b/lhp, Washington St.
1989: Ben McDonald, rhp, Louisiana State
1990: Mike Kelly, of, Arizona State
1991: David McCarthy, 1b, Stanford
1992: Phil Nevin, 3b, Cal State Fullerton
1993: Brooks Kieschnick, dh/rhp, Texas

1994: Jason Varitek, c, Georgia Tech
1995: Todd Helton, 1b/lhp, Tennessee
1996: Kris Benson, rhp, Clemson
1997: J.D. Drew, of, Florida State
1998: Jeff Austin, rhp, Stanford
1999: Jason Jennings, rhp, Baylor
2000: Mark Teixeira, 3b, Georgia Tech
2001: Mark Prior, rhp, Southern California
2002: Khalil Greene, ss, Clemson
2003: Rickie Weeks, 2b, Southern
2004: Jered Weaver, rhp, Long Beach State
2005: Alex Gordon, 3b, Nebraska

2006: Andrew Miller, lhp, North Carolina
2007: David Price, lhp, Vanderbilt
2008: Buster Posey, c/rhp, Florida State
2009: Stephen Strasburg, rhp, San Diego State
2010: Anthony Rendon, 3b, Rice
2011: Trevor Bauer, rhp, UCLA
2012: Mike Zunino, c, Florida
2013: Kris Bryant, 3b, San Diego
2014: A.J. Reed, 1b/lhp, Kentucky
2015: Andrew Benintendi, of, Arkansas

Schlossnagle turns TCU into force

COACH OF THE YEAR

BY TEDDY CAHILL

Coach Jim Schlossnagle said going into the fall that he thought his Texas Christian squad had the talent to get back to the NCAA Tournament, where its success would come down to how well it was playing in June. But a third straight College World Series appearance was not on his mind.

"I think three straight Omaha trips is absurd," Scholossnagle said. "Because everybody is so good in college baseball these days and they're trying to be good. The margin for error has never been thinner just to win a baseball game."

TCU rose to new heights in 2014 and 2015, producing the greatest two years in program history. The Horned Frogs made back-to-back College World Series appearances, won both a Big 12 Conference regular season and tournament championship and were twice awarded national seeds in the NCAA Tournament.

But the core of those teams broke up after TCU ended last season with a loss to Vanderbilt in the final four of the CWS. The Horned Frogs lost three of their four starting pitchers, their closer and five regulars from their lineup.

TCU did bring in the seventh-ranked recruiting class, but a step back seemed natural. Instead, the Horned Frogs made it back to Omaha for the third consecutive season. For those reasons, Schlossnagle is the 2016 College Coach of the Year.

TCU had success from the start of Schlossnagle's tenure. In his first year, the

Jim Schlossnagle

Horned Frogs won what was then a program record 39 games and claimed the CUSA Tournament championship (the first conference tournament title in program history) to reach the NCAA Tournament for the first time in a decade.

They would only build from there, bringing in better and better players, adding conference championships and win after win. Less than four years into his tenure, Schlossnagle was already the third-winningest coach in program history (he has since moved to No. 1 on TCU's all-time wins list).

Schlossnagle credits his assistant coaches throughout his tenure for helping him build the program. His current staff of associate head coach Bill Mosiello and pitching coach Kirk Saarloos is no different.

"I have an incredible amount of confidence in our coaching staff," Schlossnagle said. "This is the best coaching staff that I've ever been a part of."

Schlossnagle's vision has helped shape all aspects of TCU's program. Lupton Stadium opened the season before he was hired but has been added to several times to keep pace with the Horned Frogs' growth. The most recent addition, which was completed before this season, was for a new team facility, including a new locker room and coaches' offices.

"The mental part of the game is overcoming failure," TCU athletics director Chris Del Conte said. "Three out of 10, you bat .300, there's still failure. And how do you overcome failure? To be successful, every little thing, he's meticulous in all his details."

PREVIOUS WINNERS

1982: Gene Stephenson, Wichita State
1983: Barry Shollenberger, Alabama
1984: Augie Garrido, Cal State Fullerton
1985: Ron Polk, Mississippi State
1986: Skip Bertman, LSU/Dave Snow, LMU
1987: Mark Marquess, Stanford
1988: Jim Brock, Arizona State
1989: Dave Snow, Long Beach State
1990: Steve Webber, Georgia
1991: Jim Hendry, Creighton
1992: Andy Lopez, Pepperdine
1993: Gene Stephenson, Wichita State

1994: Jim Morris, Miami
1995: Pat Murphy, Arizona State
1996: Skip Bertman, Louisiana State
1997: Jim Wells, Alabama
1998: Pat Murphy, Arizona State
1999: Wayne Graham, Rice
2000: Ray Tanner, South Carolina
2001: Dave Van Horn, Nebraska
2002: Augie Garrido, Texas
2003: George Horton, Cal State Fullerton
2004: David Perno, Georgia
2005: Rick Jones, Tulane

2006: Pat Casey, Oregon State
2007: Dave Serrano, UC Irvine
2008: Mike Fox, North Carolina
2009: Paul Mainieri, Louisiana State
2010: Ray Tanner, South Carolina
2011: Kevin O'Sullivan, Florida
2012: Mike Martin, Florida State
2013: John Savage, UCLA
2014: Tim Corbin, Vanderbilt
2015: Brian O'Connor, Virginia

Tigers' Beer brews dream season

BY MICHAEL LANANNA

Seth Beer lined up all of his high school classes so he could enroll in Clemson a semester early, in January. Playing this spring as a Clemson freshman—when he should've been a senior in high school—Beer established himself as not only the country's top newcomer but one of its best players. Period.

Beer hit .369/.535/.700 with 70 RBIs and a Clemson freshman-record 18 home runs. In 203 at-bats, he struck out just 27 times to 62 walks. After going hitless in his first college game, Beer went on a 26-game hitting streak and reached base via a hit or a walk in each of his last 60 games, helping lead Clemson to an ACC tournament

Seth Beer

title and the No. 7 national seed.

Beer became the first freshman to ever win the ACC's player of the year award, and the national awards and recognition kept rolling in, capped off with Baseball America Freshman of the Year honors.

But as much as Beer's stats stand out, Tigers head coach Monte Lee said he was as much in awe by Beer's complete package. Despite all of the national attention and recognition Beer garnered, he kept a level head. Lee said Beer remained humble, meshed with his teammates and was able to balance the rigors of college life, earning his way onto the spring honor roll despite his early enrollment.

"He's a young man on a mission," Lee said. "And that's the best way to describe him. In one sentence: This is a man on a mission."

PREVIOUS WINNERS

1982: Cory Snyder, 3b, Brigham Young
1983: Rafael Palmeiro, of, Mississippi State
1984: Greg Swindell, lhp, Texas
1985: Jack McDowell, rhp, Stanford
1986: Robin Ventura, 3b, Oklahoma State
1987: Paul Carey, of, Stanford
1988: Kirk Dressendorfer, rhp, Texas
1989: Alex Fernandez, rhp, Miami
1990: Jeffrey Hammonds, of, Stanford
1991: Brooks Kieschnick, rhp/dh, Texas
1992: Todd Walker, 2b, Louisiana State
1993: Brett Laxton, rhp, Louisiana State
1994: R.A. Dickey, rhp, Tennessee
1995: Kyle Peterson, rhp, Stanford
1996: Pat Burrell, 3b, Miami
1997: Brian Roberts, ss, North Carolina
1998: Xavier Nady, 2b, California
1999: James Jurries, 2b, Tulane
2000: Kevin Howard, 3b, Miami
2001: Michael Aubrey, of/lhp, Texas
2002: Stephen Drew, ss, Florida State
2003: Ryan Braun, ss, Miami
2004: Wade LeBlanc, lhp, Alabama
2005: Joe Savery, lhp, Rice
2006: Pedro Alvarez, 3b, Vanderbilt
2007: Dustin Ackley, 1b, North Carolina
2008: Chris Hernandez, lhp, Miami
2009: Anthony Rendon, 3b, Rice
2010: Matt Purke, lhp, Texas Christian
2011: Colin Moran, 3b, North Carolina
2012: Carlos Rodon, lhp, N.C. State
2013: Alex Bregman, ss, Louisiana State
2014: Zack Collins, c, Miami
2015: Brendan McKay, lhp/1b, Louisville

FRESHMAN ALL-AMERICA TEAMS

FIRST TEAM

POS.		AVG	OBP	SLG	AB	R	H	HR	RBI	SB
C	Cal Raleigh, Florida State	.301	.412	.511	229	45	69	10	40	1
1B	Joe Davis, Houston	.331	.383	.577	239	33	79	14	58	0
2B	Nick Madrigal, Oregon State	.333	.380	.456	195	38	65	1	29	8
3B	Jonathan India, Florida	.303	.367	.440	234	43	71	4	40	13
SS	Ford Proctor, Rice	.336	.428	471	223	34	75	3	41	6
OF	Seth Beer, Clemson	.369	.535	.700	203	57	75	18	70	1
OF	Jake Mangum, Miss. State	.408	.458	.510	206	40	84	1	28	6
OF	Dwayna Williams-Sutton, ECU	.360	.455	.551	178	31	63	5	27	7
DH	Kevin Strohschein, Tenn. Tech	.393	.447	.707	229	57	90	15	73	2
UT	Luken Baker, Texas Christian	.379	.483	.577	248	59	94	11	62	1

		W	L	ERA	G	SV	IP	H	BB	SO	BAA
SP	Tristan Beck, Stanford	6	5	2.48	14	0	83	60	26	76	.205
SP	Colton Eastman, CS Fullerton	8	3	2.24	16	0	101	78	20	100	.218
SP	Davis Martin, Texas Tech	10	1	2.52	19	0	89	75	27	61	.233
SP	Braden Webb, South Carolina	10	6	3.09	18	0	102	80	48	128	.216
RP	Durbin Feltman, Texas Christian	3	0	1.56	27	9	35	15	11	49	.129
UT	Luken Baker, Texas Christian	3	1	1.70	10	0	48	37	16	41	.213

SECOND TEAM

C—Joey Bart, Georgia Tech (.299-1-31). **1B**—Grayson Jenista, Wichita State (.326-5-32). **2B**—Richie Palacios, Towson (.329-6-38). **3B**—Ivan Vera, West Virginia (.381-0-23). **SS**—Owen Miller, Illinois State (.328-5-44). **OF**—D.J. Artis, Liberty (.369-2-41); Darius Hill, West Virginia (.342-5-53); Josh Watson, Texas Christian (.280-11-44). **DH**—Alonzo Jones, Vanderbilt (.285-1-35). **UT**—Tyler Holton, Florida State (.214-2-7; 3-4, 2.79, 68 IP, 84 SO). **SP**—Tim Cate, Connecticut (5-1, 2.73, 82 IP, 101 SO); Jensen Elliott, Oklahoma State (9-3, 3.50, 87 IP, 71 SO); Ross Massey, Tulane (10-3, 2.29, 90 IP, 51 SO); Jacob Stevens, Boston College (4-4, 2.58, 74 IP, 70 SO). **RP**—Chad Luensmann, Nebraska (1-2, 1.18, 38 IP, 23 SO).

HITTING (Minimum 140 at-bats)

BATTING AVERAGE

RK.	PLAYER, TEAM	CLASS	AVG	OBP	SLG	G	AB	2B	3B	HR	RBI	BB	SO	SB
1.	Ryan Scott, Arkansas-Little Rock	Sr.	.435	.516	.713	54	216	20	2	12	66	27	33	7
2.	Jameson Fisher, Southeastern Louisiana	Jr.	.424	.558	.692	61	198	16	2	11	66	54	31	15
3.	Cornelius Copeland, Jackson State	Jr.	.422	.537	.631	54	187	18	3	5	38	26	16	8
4.	Mandy Alvarez, Eastern Kentucky	Sr.	.409	.455	.646	55	237	13	2	13	58	22	24	1
5.	Carlos Diaz, Jackson State	Jr.	.409	.465	.620	48	171	14	2	6	57	15	16	10
6.	Danny Hudzina, Western Kentucky	Sr.	.408	.470	.564	54	218	18	2	4	32	26	12	0
7.	Bradley Haslam, Air Force	Jr.	.408	.449	.558	57	233	22	2	3	57	16	17	4
8.	Jake Mangum, Mississippi State	Fr.	.408	.458	.510	62	206	12	3	1	28	14	20	6
9.	Daniel Barnett, Grambling State	Jr.	.408	.504	.647	48	184	15	1	9	60	34	17	0
10.	Charles LeBlanc, Pittsburgh	So.	.405	.494	.513	49	195	9	3	2	46	30	29	6
11.	T.J. Friedl, Nevada	So.	.401	.494	.563	58	222	9	9	3	35	32	26	13
12.	Andrew Moritz, UNC Greensboro	Fr.	.400	.454	.570	41	165	11	7	1	33	18	21	8
13.	L.J. Kalawaia, UNC Greensboro	Sr.	.396	.493	.578	56	225	11	6	6	65	40	32	23
14.	Deon Stafford Jr., St. Joseph's	So.	.395	.486	.702	54	215	10	1	18	49	36	45	4
15.	Kyle Lewis, Mercer	Jr.	.395	.535	.731	61	223	11	2	20	72	66	48	6
16.	Collin Thacker, Gardner-Webb	Jr.	.394	.452	.578	58	218	28	0	4	46	26	16	1
17.	Kevin Strohschein, Tennessee Tech	Fr.	.393	.447	.707	55	229	21	3	15	73	22	56	2
18.	David MacKinnon, Hartford	Jr.	.392	.471	.544	55	217	15	3	4	34	29	18	5
19.	Riley Delgado, Middle Tennessee State	Jr.	.388	.492	.437	55	206	10	0	0	18	34	12	4
20.	Ben Ellzey, Florida A&M	Jr.	.388	.467	.517	50	178	11	0	4	42	15	31	1
21.	Matt Smith, Western Carolina	Jr.	.388	.495	.582	62	232	11	2	10	55	43	30	6
22.	David Oppenheim, Southern California	Sr.	.387	.500	.508	53	191	9	1	4	25	39	24	6
23.	Brennon Lund, Brigham Young	Jr.	.387	.454	.531	54	243	19	5	2	34	23	37	15
24.	Boomer White, Texas A&M	Jr.	.386	.462	.517	65	259	19	0	5	46	33	16	10
25.	Shaine Hughes, Monmouth	So.	.385	.457	.522	39	161	15	2	1	34	17	6	1
26.	Zach Gibbons, Arizona	Sr.	.385	.460	.446	71	278	15	1	0	48	36	28	9
27.	Josh Palacios, Auburn	Jr.	.385	.463	.608	34	143	9	4	5	23	19	27	12
28.	Ben Spitznagel, UNC Greensboro	Jr.	.385	.459	.474	59	247	15	2	1	23	25	21	21
29.	Brett Netzer, Charlotte	So.	.384	.461	.555	53	211	17	2	5	35	25	20	6
30.	Will Smith, Louisville	Jr.	.382	.480	.567	55	157	8	0	7	43	19	14	9
31.	Keith Skinner, North Florida	Sr.	.382	.466	.486	57	212	16	0	2	40	36	14	2
32.	Daniel Johnson, New Mexico State	Jr.	.382	.434	.630	57	246	11	7	12	50	18	29	29
33.	Daulton Varsho, Milwaukee	So.	.381	.447	.610	57	231	17	6	8	51	29	41	16
34.	Luis Gonzalez, New Mexico	So.	.381	.470	.575	61	252	21	5	6	48	43	26	18
35.	Will Craig, Wake Forest	Jr.	.379	.520	.731	55	182	16	0	16	66	47	35	0
36.	Luken Baker, Texas Christian	Fr.	.379	.483	.577	67	248	16	0	11	62	45	39	1
37.	Tanner Gardner, Texas Tech	So.	.379	.484	.549	65	235	19	6	3	35	43	32	6
38.	Matt Gonzalez, Georgia Tech	Sr.	.378	.419	.577	59	246	16	0	11	54	18	39	10
39.	Alec Wong, Florida A&M	Sr.	.378	.504	.528	52	193	12	1	5	33	40	29	5
40.	Adam Groesbeck, Air Force	Jr.	.378	.453	.583	57	230	16	8	5	33	28	35	19
41.	Robby Rinn, Bryant	Sr.	.378	.442	.591	59	225	25	4	5	61	28	17	1
42.	Michael Tinsley, Kansas	Jr.	.377	.460	.495	56	212	15	2	2	32	32	18	9
43.	Caleb Stayton, Ball State	Jr.	.377	.482	.614	58	220	17	1	11	71	42	40	2
44.	Brandon Lopez, Miami	Sr.	.376	.449	.469	58	213	14	0	2	42	23	34	5
45.	Nick Solak, Louisville	Jr.	.376	.470	.564	47	165	14	1	5	29	28	22	9
46.	Jeremy Martinez, Southern California	Jr.	.376	.460	.563	56	213	18	2	6	42	19	12	1
47.	Evan White, Kentucky	So.	.376	.419	.535	54	226	15	3	5	40	14	42	10
48.	Stijn van der Meer, Lamar	Sr.	.376	.471	.441	54	213	9	1	1	20	38	15	7
49.	Cole Gruber, Nebraska-Omaha	Sr.	.376	.464	.466	56	221	13	2	1	30	32	34	43
50.	Dustin Frailey, Cal State Bakersfield	Jr.	.376	.479	.593	52	194	12	9	4	27	30	19	23
51.	Matt Thaiss, Virginia	Jr.	.375	.473	.578	60	232	13	2	10	59	39	16	0
52.	R.J. Devish, Rutgers	Sr.	.375	.524	.435	52	168	7	0	1	27	41	19	24
53.	Brady Policelli, Towson	Jr.	.375	.502	.620	55	200	14	4	9	45	45	42	22
54.	Chris DeVito, New Mexico	Jr.	.375	.444	.685	60	232	20	2	16	65	29	31	0
55.	Payton Squier, NevadaLas Vegas	So.	.375	.439	.431	55	216	9	0	1	28	26	23	8
56.	Dalton Thomas, Arkansas-Little Rock	Jr.	.375	.415	.582	54	232	19	1	9	52	12	37	2
57.	Jordan Zimmerman, Michigan State	Jr.	.374	.461	.594	56	219	17	2	9	37	32	33	10
58.	Steven Linkous, UNC Wilmington	Sr.	.374	.456	.492	60	254	13	7	1	43	35	51	29
59.	Nick Mascelli, Wagner	Jr.	.374	.414	.472	47	195	6	2	3	21	14	11	2
60.	Peter Alonso, Florida	Jr.	.374	.469	.659	58	211	18	0	14	60	31	31	2
61.	Hagen Owenby, East Tennessee State	So.	.374	.426	.660	57	235	16	0	17	60	23	30	1
62.	Matt Fiedler, Minnesota	Jr.	.372	.417	.534	58	234	12	1	8	38	18	28	14
63.	Cody Bruder, Michigan	Jr.	.372	.425	.485	57	231	18	1	2	53	15	40	7
64.	Clayton Daniel, Jacksonville State	So.	.372	.443	.480	58	250	20	2	1	54	34	13	7
65.	Bryson Brigman, San Diego	So.	.372	.428	.424	47	191	8	1	0	22	16	19	17
66.	Kevin LaChance, Maryland-Baltimore County	Sr.	.371	.450	.537	51	205	14	1	6	29	28	22	28
67.	Matt Parrish, Campbell	Sr.	.371	.448	.526	49	175	14	2	3	41	16	32	8
68.	Brian Mims, UNC Wilmington	So.	.371	.443	.614	60	259	17	2	14	64	33	68	4

RK.	PLAYER, TEAM	CLASS	AVG	OBP	SLG	G	AB	2B	3B	HR	RBI	BB	SO	SB
69.	John Sansone, Florida State	Sr.	.370	.455	.576	63	257	26	0	9	65	29	35	8
70.	Lee Solomon, Lipscomb	So.	.370	.471	.498	58	227	11	3	4	50	36	47	25
71.	Austin Athmann, Minnesota	Jr.	.370	.440	.615	51	192	14	0	11	40	14	34	0
72.	Joel Booker, Iowa	Sr.	.370	.421	.532	56	235	19	2	5	37	16	29	23
73.	Brian Davis, Florida A&M	So.	.370	.471	.566	51	189	14	1	7	44	28	20	1
74.	Chas Hadden, Belmont	Fr.	.370	.521	.495	58	192	11	2	3	37	61	32	8
75.	Seth Beer, Clemson	Fr.	.369	.535	.700	62	203	13	0	18	70	62	27	1
76.	Michael Morman, Richmond	Sr.	.369	.464	.544	49	195	20	1	4	48	25	16	6
77.	Alex Lewis, Longwood	Jr.	.369	.409	.528	57	233	22	0	5	45	13	31	5
78.	D.J. Artis, Liberty	Fr.	.369	.500	.464	59	222	9	3	2	41	52	28	23
79.	Sheldon Neuse, Oklahoma	Jr.	.369	.465	.646	55	198	15	5	10	48	39	43	12
80.	Keaton Kringlen, Brigham Young	Fr.	.369	.442	.560	42	141	12	0	5	34	18	23	2
81.	Jose Garcia, Texas-Rio Grande Valley	Jr.	.369	.447	.477	45	176	13	3	0	19	18	14	16
82.	Mark Osis, George Washington	So.	.368	.418	.420	48	174	5	2	0	26	11	17	15
83.	Cole Krzmarzick, Nevada	So.	.368	.426	.479	53	190	16	1	1	37	19	14	3
84.	Derek Hirsch, Wofford	Sr.	.368	.453	.439	52	171	4	1	2	27	25	28	9
85.	Jake Noll, Florida Gulf Coast	Jr.	.367	.427	.620	56	237	20	2	12	61	20	29	9
86.	Will Savage, Columbia	Jr.	.367	.463	.487	41	158	11	1	2	15	26	15	20
87.	Christian Santisteban, Manhattan	Sr.	.367	.453	.570	54	207	21	0	7	46	30	38	1
88.	Chris Osborne, Southeast Missouri State	Sr.	.367	.456	.741	49	166	11	3	15	44	16	39	2
89.	Reed Gamache, Binghamton	Sr.	.366	.452	.545	54	202	15	0	7	46	23	37	8
90.	Matt Albanese, Bryant	Jr.	.366	.471	.639	49	183	13	2	11	52	28	15	15
91.	Anfernee Grier, Auburn	Jr.	.366	.457	.576	56	238	8	3	12	41	32	55	19
92.	Tim Lynch, Southern Mississippi	Sr.	.365	.470	.545	61	233	12	0	10	59	39	13	0
93.	Brady Cox, Texas-Arlington	Jr.	.365	.427	.455	58	222	12	1	2	41	23	27	2
94.	Robbie Thorburn, UNC Wilmington	Jr.	.364	.427	.511	60	225	12	6	3	28	21	36	20
95.	Tim Graul, Penn	Jr.	.364	.443	.642	41	162	21	0	8	35	20	24	2
96.	Miles Mastrobuoni, Nevada	Jr.	.364	.458	.474	61	228	17	4	0	40	38	40	18
97.	Noah Cummings, Oral Roberts	So.	.364	.426	.527	58	220	18	0	6	44	22	30	6
98.	Chad Carroll, James Madison	Sr.	.363	.419	.470	42	168	9	3	1	24	14	25	23
99.	Gene Cone, South Carolina	Jr.	.363	.474	.498	59	215	13	2	4	30	45	26	7
100.	Cesar Trejo, UNC Greensboro	Fr.	.363	.415	.587	51	179	7	3	9	30	15	42	3

ON-BASE PERCENTAGE

RANK, PLAYER, POS., TEAM	OBP
1. Jameson Fisher, c, Southeastern La.	.558
2. Zack Collins, c, Miami	.544
3. Cornelius Copeland, inf, Jackson State	.537
4. Seth Beer, of, Clemson	.535
5. Kyle Lewis, of, Mercer	.535
6. R.J. Devish, c, Rutgers	.524
7. Chas Hadden, c, Belmont	.521
8. Will Craig, inf, Wake Forest	.520
9. Ryan Scott, of, Little Rock	.516
10. Daniel Barnett, inf, Grambling	.504

SLUGGING PERCENTAGE

RANK, PLAYER, POS., TEAM	SLG
1. Chris Osborne, of, Southeast Mo. St.	.741
2. Kyle Lewis, of, Mercer	.731
3. Will Craig, inf, Wake Forest	.731
4. Nick Feight, c, UNCW	.726
5. Ryan Scott, of, Little Rock	.713
6. Kevin Strohschein, of, Tennessee Tech	.707
7. Spencer Johnson, of, Missouri State	.707
8. Deon Stafford, Jr., c, Saint Joseph's	.702
9. Seth Beer, of, Clemson	.700
10. Tyler Jones, of, Air Force	.694

RUNS BATTED IN

RANK, PLAYER, POS., TEAM	RBI
1. Nick Feight, c, UNC Wilmington	91
2. Heath Quinn, of, Samford	77
3. Chris Okey, c, Clemson	74
4. Kevin Strohschein, of, Tennessee Tech	73
5. Jake Burger, inf, Missouri State	72
Darick Hall, inf, Dallas Baptist	72
Kyle Lewis, of, Mercer	72
Zach Remillard, inf, Coastal Carolina	72
G.K. Young, inf, Coastal Carolina	72
10. Caleb Stayton, c, Ball State	71

HOME RUNS

RANK, PLAYER, POS., TEAM	HR
1. Spencer Johnson, of, Missouri State	24
2. Jake Burger, inf, Missouri State	21
Nick Feight, c, UNC Wilmington	21
Kyle Nowlin, of, Eastern Kentucky	21
Heath Quinn, of, Samford	21
6. Darick Hall, inf, Dallas Baptist	20
Kyle Lewis, of, Mercer	20
8. Bryson Bowman, of, Western Carolina	19
Austin Edens, inf, Samford	19
Tyler Jones, of, Air Force	19
Zach Remillard, inf, Coastal Carolina	19
Gary Russo, of, Miami (Ohio)	19

DOUBLES

RANK, PLAYER, POS., TEAM	2B
1. Collin Thacker, c, Gardner-Webb	28
2. Weston Jackson, of, Presbyterian	27
Taylor Jones, inf, Gonzaga	27
4. John Sansone, inf, Florida State	26
5. Ronnie Dawson, of, Ohio State	25
Robby Rinn, 1b, Bryant	25
Nick Senzel, inf, Tennessee	25
Hunter Swilling, inf, Samford	25
9. Alex Call, of, Ball State	24
Nick Feight, c, UNC Wilmington	24
Tyler Zabojnik, inf, Air Force	24
Nick Zammarelli, inf, Elon	24

TRIPLES

RANK, PLAYER, POS., TEAM	3B
1. Chris Hess, inf, Rhode Island	10
2. Adam Bauer, of, Murray State	9
Dustin Frailey, of, Cal State Bakersfield	9
T.J. Friedl, of, Nevada	9
5. Andy DeJesus, inf, Indiana State	8
Adam Groesbeck, of, Air Force	8

Kyle Isbel, inf, UNLV	8
Jeren Kendall, of, Vanderbilt	8
Zach Lavy, inf, Missouri	8
Cody Ramer, inf, Arizona	8

STOLEN BASES

RANK, PLAYER, POS., TEAM	SB	CS
1. Derek Jenkins, of, Seton Hall	52	11
2. Corey Ray, of, Louisville	44	9
3. Cole Gruber, of, Omaha	43	7
4. Ryan Lazo, inf, Texas Southern	40	0
5. Jawuan Harris, of, Rutgers	37	7
6. Marquise Gill, inf, Eastern Michigan	35	14
Nick Heath, of, Northwestern State	35	7
8. Corey Bird, of, Marshall	34	4
Garrett Brown, of, Western Carolina	34	8
10. Chris Chiaradio, inf, Seton Hall	32	2
Richie Palacios, inf, Towson	32	9
Daniel Woodrow, of, Creighton	32	7

RUNS

RANK, PLAYER, POS., TEAM	R
1. Steven Linkous, inf, UNC Wilmington	78
2. Taylor Walls, inf, Florida State	72
3. Brian Mims, inf, UNC Wilmington	71
4. Trevor Ezell, inf, Southeast Mo. State	70
Kyle Lewis, of, Mercer	70
6. T.J. Friedl, of, Nevada	68
7. Adam Bauer, of, Murray State	67
Alex Call, of, Ball State	67
Daniel Johnson, of, New Mexico State	67
J.B. Moss, of, Texas A&M	67
Michael Paez, of, Coastal Carolina	67
Chase Pinder, of, Clemson	67

HITS

RANK, PLAYER, POS., TEAM	H
1. Zach Gibbons, of, Arizona	107
2. Cody Ramer, inf, Arizona	102
3. Boomer White, c, Texas A&M	100
4. Zach Remillard, inf, Coastal Carolina	99
G.K. Young, inf, Coastal Carolina	99
6. Mandy Alvarez, inf, Eastern Kentucky	97
7. Luis Gonzalez, of, New Mexico	96
Brian Mims, inf, UNC Wilmington	96
9. Bradley Haslam, inf, Air Force	95
Steven Linkous, inf, UNC Wilmington	95
John Sansone, inf, Florida State	95
Ben Spitznagel, inf, UNC Greensboro	95

TOTAL BASES

RANK, PLAYER, POS., TEAM	TB
1. Zach Remillard, inf, Coastal Carolina	177
2. Nick Feight, c, UNC Wilmington	175
3. G.K. Young, inf, Coastal Carolina	168
4. Heath Quinn, of, Samford	165
5. Kyle Lewis, of, Mercer	163
6. Jake Burger, inf, Missouri State	162
Alex Call, of, Ball State	162
Kevin Strohschein, of, Tennessee Tech	162
9. Connor Owings, inf, Coastal Carolina	161
10. Carl Stajduhar, inf, New Mexico	160

WALKS

RANK, PLAYER, POS., TEAM	BB
1. Zack Collins, c, Miami	78
2. Kyle Lewis, of, Mercer	66
3. Seth Beer, of, Clemson	62
4. Chas Hadden, c, Belmont	61
Ky Parrott, of, James Madison	61
6. Drew LaBounty, inf, South Alabama	59
Taylor Walls, inf, Florida State	59
8. Matt Hilston, of, UTSA	57
Austen Wade, of, TCU	57
10. Jake Placzek, inf, Nebraska	56

TOUGHEST TO STRIKE OUT

RANK, PLAYER, POS., TEAM	AB/SO
1. J.T. O'Reel, inf, Alabama A&M	34.2
2. Jacob Seward, of, Southeastern La.	26.0
3. Deion Tansel, inf, Toledo	24.8
4. Ernie Clement, inf, Virginia	21.8
5. Kyle Brey, inf, Wagner	20.7
6. Jeremy Ake, inf, Delaware	20.3
7. Brian Lamboy, inf, LIU-Brooklyn	20.1
8. Clayton Daniel, inf, Jacksonville State	19.2
9. C.J. Krowiak, of, Binghamton	18.6
10. Danny Hudzina, inf, Western Ky.	18.2

HIT BY PITCH

RANK, PLAYER, POS., TEAM	HBP
1. Cornelius Copeland, inf, Jackson State	26
2. Andrew Calica, of, UC Santa Barbara	24
3. Bryce Jordan, inf, LSU	23
4. Jake Bakamus, inf, Arkansas State	21
5. Chris Fornaci, inf, Pepperdine	20
Eric Gutierrez, inf, Texas Tech	20
Pete Guy, c, UNC Asheville	20
Tyler Langley, of, Central Arkansas	20
Christian Vangeison, of, Niagara	20
10. Jonah Bride, inf, South Carolina	19
Carl Chester, of, Miami	19

SACRIFICE BUNTS

RANK, PLAYER, POS., TEAM	SH
1. Jack Meggs, of, Washington	23
2. Zack Domingues, inf, Long Beach State	22
3. Corey Hassel, inf, Oklahoma State	21
4. Charlie Madden, c, Mercer	17
Mason Mamarella, of, Kent State	17
6. Ryan Heeke, inf, Central Michigan	16
Colby Higgerson, inf, Radford	16
Grayson Lewis, inf, Rice	16
Garrett Zech, of, South Florida	16
10. K.J. Brady, of, Washington	15
Carl Chester, of, Miami	15
Zach Janes, of, Western Kentucky	15
Luke Manzo, inf, Col. of Charleston	15
Hayden Martin, inf, Ark.-Little Rock	15
Cody Roberts, c, North Carolina	15
Lucas Sokol, c, Toledo	15

SACRIFICE FLIES

RANK, PLAYER, POS., TEAM	SF
1. Collin Woody, inf, UNC Greensboro	11
2. Connor Schaefbauer, inf, Minnesota	10
Harrison Wenson, c, Michigan	10
4. Ryan Aguilar, of, Arizona	9
Yamil Pagan, inf, Alabama State	9
Robby Rinn, 1b, Bryant	9
Josh Shaw, inf, St. John's	9
8. Cole Billingsley, of, South Ala.	8
Clayton Daniel, inf, Jacksonville State	8
Camden Duzenack, inf, Dallas Baptist	8
Cole Fabio, inf, Bryant	8
Connor Fikes, inf, S.F. Austin	8
Jameson Fisher, c, Southeastern La.	8
Connor Myers, of, Old Dominion	8
Colton Shaver, c, BYU	8
Pavin Smith, 1b, Virginia	8
Jamie Switalski, inf, UMBC	8
Spencer Thornton, of, San Diego State	8

PITCHING (Minimum 40 innings pitched)

EARNED RUN AVERAGE

RK.	PITCHER, TEAM	CLASS	W	L	ERA	G	GS	SV	IP	H	R	ER	BB	SO
1.	Mark Ecker, Texas A&M	Jr.	4	2	0.39	25	0	8	47	24	5	2	7	56
2.	Matthew Gorst, Georgia Tech	Jr.	2	1	0.55	28	0	12	49	30	5	3	13	55
3.	Ryan Wilson, Pepperdine	So.	2	0	0.63	14	3	6	43	18	5	3	14	46
4.	Eric Lauer, Kent State	Jr.	10	2	0.69	15	15	0	104	49	15	8	28	125
5.	Troy Rallings, Washington	Sr.	4	1	0.89	28	0	16	61	32	7	6	12	60
6.	Dylan Moore, Louisiana-Lafayette	So.	6	1	0.91	26	0	14	50	24	7	5	15	59
7.	Shaun Anderson, Florida	Jr.	3	0	0.97	36	1	13	46	31	6	5	7	60
8.	Austin McGeorge, Long Beach State	Jr.	1	1	1.02	33	0	5	53	35	6	6	14	76
9.	Daulton Jefferies, California	Jr.	7	0	1.08	8	8	0	50	34	12	6	8	53
10.	Stephen Nogosek, Oregon	Jr.	2	2	1.11	29	0	16	41	25	7	5	14	45
11.	Thomas Hackimer, St. John's	Sr.	7	3	1.17	28	0	8	54	24	7	7	19	71
12.	Adam Atkins, Louisiana Tech	Sr.	6	1	1.20	24	0	9	45	28	7	6	12	56
13.	Scott Serigstad, Cal State Fullerton	Jr.	2	1	1.22	27	0	4	52	30	12	7	20	55
14.	Adam Oller, Northwestern State	Jr.	8	1	1.23	15	15	0	110	81	24	15	32	73
15.	A.J. Puckett, Pepperdine	Jr.	9	3	1.27	14	14	0	99	65	22	14	26	95
16.	Trey Cumbie, Houston	Fr.	5	2	1.29	15	5	0	56	42	12	8	9	42
17.	Jake Kelzer, Indiana	Jr.	3	2	1.32	22	0	4	41	25	10	6	12	48
18.	Walker Sheller, Stetson	Jr.	2	3	1.38	35	0	12	46	38	14	7	21	44
19.	Nick Hernandez, Houston	Jr.	3	0	1.40	29	0	11	51	27	9	8	11	66
20.	Trevor Lane, Illinois-Chicago	Sr.	8	5	1.41	26	1	5	71	41	15	11	35	90
21.	Jake Meyers, Nebraska	So.	6	1	1.42	9	9	0	51	37	8	8	10	36
22.	Mike Morrison, Coastal Carolina	Sr.	8	1	1.50	34	1	11	72	41	15	12	27	94
23.	Michael Dailey, Virginia Commonwealth	Fr.	6	0	1.57	14	10	0	69	56	13	12	18	47
24.	Seth Kinker, Ohio State	So.	6	1	1.65	38	0	2	55	50	12	10	10	45
25.	Pat Krall, Clemson	Jr.	10	2	1.67	29	3	5	81	58	18	15	17	65
26.	Tyler Howe, Alabama State	Jr.	10	3	1.69	15	12	0	80	64	24	15	15	82
27.	Tyler Beardsley, Sacramento State	Sr.	4	2	1.71	30	0	11	47	36	10	9	16	24
28.	Tim Borst, Fresno State	Sr.	3	3	1.72	28	1	8	52	42	12	10	26	59
29.	Sam Sorenson, Navy	Sr.	5	2	1.72	25	0	6	47	38	14	9	11	44

RK.	PITCHER, TEAM	CLASS	W	L	ERA	G	GS	SV	IP	H	R	ER	BB	SO
30.	Adam Haseley, Virginia	So.	9	3	1.73	13	13	0	78	54	25	15	21	48
31.	Aaron Civale, Northeastern	Jr.	9	3	1.73	15	15	0	114	91	27	22	15	121
32.	Dakota Mekkes, Michigan State	So.	3	2	1.74	28	0	7	57	26	14	11	41	96
33.	Anthony Herrera, Louisiana-Monroe	Jr.	1	4	1.74	22	0	10	41	27	11	8	12	26
34.	Michael Baird, Southern Illinois	So.	9	4	1.76	15	15	0	102	75	22	20	26	58
35.	Mark Washington, Lehigh	So.	6	1	1.80	13	6	0	45	35	13	9	27	24
36.	Keegan Akin, Western Michigan	Jr.	7	4	1.82	17	17	0	109	72	24	22	30	133
37.	B.J. Butler, Ball State	Jr.	6	1	1.84	25	2	9	64	57	18	13	14	54
38.	Andrew Beckwith, Coastal Carolina	Jr.	15	1	1.85	26	10	2	117	113	34	24	18	75
39.	Reece Eddins, Nebraska	So.	4	3	1.85	26	0	1	49	43	15	10	21	30
40.	Burris Warner, Marshall	Jr.	3	1	1.88	26	0	11	43	37	14	9	15	34
41.	Garrett Schilling, Xavier	So.	4	3	1.91	29	0	14	42	38	12	9	17	34
42.	Casey Sutton, Louisiana Tech	Jr.	8	1	1.91	17	9	0	85	72	21	18	24	46
43.	Joe Napolitano, St. John's	Sr.	3	1	1.93	25	0	2	42	38	15	9	12	31
44.	Erik Dowse, Campbell	Jr.	2	2	1.93	24	0	6	47	38	18	10	29	59
45.	Marc Huberman, Southern California	Sr.	2	1	1.94	26	0	3	42	27	11	9	32	45
46.	Drew Harrington, Louisville	Jr.	12	2	1.95	17	17	0	111	92	25	24	25	92
47.	Robby Howell, Central Florida	Jr.	7	4	1.96	15	15	0	101	74	34	22	35	65
48.	Sean Labsan, Florida Atlantic	Jr.	5	1	1.96	11	10	1	46	40	18	10	17	39
49.	Chad Lee, Stony Brook	Sr.	6	4	1.97	16	10	1	82	68	24	18	21	56
50.	Ryan Brady, Evansville	So.	2	1	1.99	28	0	5	41	27	10	9	12	22
51.	Evan Kruczynski, East Carolina	Jr.	8	1	2.01	17	17	0	117	107	32	26	27	95
52.	Kaleb Fontenot, McNeese State	Sr.	6	5	2.02	15	15	0	107	80	32	24	34	108
53.	Darren McCaughan, Long Beach State	So.	10	1	2.03	16	16	0	111	76	31	25	16	84
54.	Colton Hock, Stanford	So.	4	5	2.03	27	0	6	58	37	17	13	24	61
55.	Hunter Martin, Tennessee	Jr.	3	3	2.03	21	5	1	40	48	17	9	18	20
56.	Domenick Carlini, Southeastern Louisiana	Sr.	8	2	2.03	16	16	0	97	71	35	22	36	63
57.	James Karinchak, Bryant	So.	12	3	2.00	15	15	0	95	70	23	21	43	112
58.	Corey Merrill, Tulane	Jr.	4	1	2.05	15	5	3	53	41	14	12	19	63
59.	Griffin Jax, Air Force	Jr.	9	2	2.05	15	15	0	105	94	35	24	20	90
60.	Justin Dunn, Boston College	Jr.	4	2	2.06	18	8	2	66	52	17	15	18	72
61.	Josh Reagan, South Carolina	Jr.	3	2	2.08	29	0	11	56	34	14	13	20	50
62.	Konnor Pilkington, Mississippi State	Fr.	3	1	2.08	14	11	0	43	38	13	10	15	42
63.	Eric Carter, Louisiana-Lafayette	Sr.	6	2	2.08	26	0	4	52	37	14	12	12	69
64.	John Gavin, Cal State Fullerton	So.	6	3	2.09	18	14	1	86	61	27	20	31	60
65.	Brandon Bielak, Notre Dame	So.	3	2	2.10	15	4	1	56	43	17	13	25	54
66.	Brandon Schlimm, St. Bonaventure	So.	7	5	2.11	13	13	0	94	71	35	22	23	64
67.	Tarik Skubal, Seattle	So.	6	1	2.11	8	8	0	43	32	13	10	17	50
68.	Michael Hearne, Notre Dame	Sr.	8	2	2.13	14	13	0	80	64	19	19	15	42
69.	Jack Anderson, Penn State	Sr.	4	2	2.14	29	0	13	55	50	19	13	19	43
70.	Thomas Hatch, Oklahoma State	So.	9	3	2.14	19	19	0	130	108	34	31	33	112
71.	Blake Quinn, Cal State Fullerton	Jr.	4	3	2.16	17	12	1	67	40	20	16	32	69
72.	Cody Culp, Hawaii	Sr.	3	1	2.16	31	0	5	50	51	15	12	5	37
73.	Ricky Tyler Thomas, Fresno State	So.	9	4	2.16	15	15	0	104	86	36	25	16	108
74.	James Taubl, Sacred Heart	So.	5	3	2.16	16	9	1	67	64	23	16	24	27
75.	Kyle Nelson, UC Santa Barbara	So.	7	2	2.18	33	1	10	74	56	24	18	18	87
76.	Jake Roehn, Ohio	So.	2	2	2.18	23	0	7	45	42	15	11	9	43
77.	Bret Clarke, Stony Brook	Fr.	6	2	2.19	15	13	0	62	55	19	15	34	55
78.	Joey Lucchesi, Southeast Missouri State	Sr.	10	5	2.19	17	16	1	111	96	36	27	37	149
79.	Jesse Lepore, Miami	So.	9	0	2.20	14	13	0	74	59	21	18	28	57
80.	Brad Haymes, Gardner-Webb	Sr.	11	3	2.20	15	15	0	111	87	34	27	16	115
81.	Tommy Eveld, South Florida	Jr.	0	3	2.21	26	1	9	53	36	15	13	24	67
82.	Max Kuhns, Santa Clara	Jr.	1	4	2.21	28	0	14	41	28	15	10	16	37
83.	Will Gilbert, North Carolina State	Sr.	5	1	2.22	24	0	6	53	48	13	13	11	62
84.	Colton Eastman, Cal State Fullerton	Fr.	8	3	2.24	16	15	0	101	78	28	25	20	100
85.	Gabe Kleiman, Penn	Jr.	3	3	2.24	9	9	0	52	43	13	13	17	27
86.	Patrick Ruotolo, Connecticut	Jr.	2	2	2.25	25	0	12	40	33	13	10	11	47
87.	Ryan Rigby, Mississippi State	So.	5	1	2.25	20	0	1	48	37	14	12	13	43
88.	Mac Sceroler, Southeastern Louisiana	So.	10	4	2.25	16	16	0	96	83	30	24	33	93
89.	Glenn Otto, Rice	So.	9	2	2.26	33	0	8	72	53	25	18	30	76
90.	Gunner Leger, Louisiana-Lafayette	So.	7	3	2.26	16	16	0	92	71	31	23	24	81
91.	Bryan Baker, North Florida	Jr.	6	4	2.27	14	14	0	83	65	28	21	28	80
92.	Jacob Moreland, Texas-Arlington	Sr.	6	1	2.27	30	0	5	71	63	25	18	19	40
93.	Dakota Forsyth, Penn State	Jr.	2	3	2.28	20	0	1	43	27	15	11	27	28
94.	Cam Vieaux, Michigan State	Jr.	7	4	2.28	15	14	0	87	77	32	22	19	77
95.	Seth Romero, Houston	So.	6	4	2.29	15	13	0	94	60	32	24	28	113
96.	Ross Massey, Tulane	Fr.	10	3	2.29	18	12	0	90	87	32	23	18	51
97.	Tyler Wilson, Rhode Island	So.	13	1	2.29	15	15	0	102	53	32	26	33	122
98.	Jonathan Mauricio, Norfolk State	Jr.	6	2	2.29	15	10	0	59	53	25	15	26	59
99.	Dane Dunning, Florida	Jr.	6	3	2.29	33	5	2	79	68	22	20	12	88
100.	Grant Bennett, Troy	Sr.	8	2	2.29	15	15	0	102	104	34	26	19	76

WINS

RANK, PITCHER, TEAM	W
1. Andrew Beckwith, Coastal Carolina	15
2. Tyler Wilson, Rhode Island	13
Ryan Foster, UNC Wilmington	13
Alex Faedo, Florida	13
5. Kade McClure, Louisville	12
Logan Shore, Florida	12
Nathan Bannister, Arizona	12
Drew Harrington, Louisville	12
James Karinchak, Bryant	12
Shane Bieber, UC Santa Barbara	12
Brendan McKay, Louisville	12

SAVES

RANK, PITCHER, TEAM	SV
1. Sam Donko, Virginia Commonwealth	20
2. Bryan Garcia, Miami	18
3. Iannick Remillard, Canisius	17
4. Troy Rallings, Washington	16
Stephen Nogosek, Oregon	16
6. Cameron Ragsdale, Florida Atlantic	15
7. Zach Willeman, Kent State	14
Troy Montemayor, Baylor	14
Dylan Moore, Louisiana-Lafayette	14
Max Kuhns, Santa Clara	14
Yianni Pavloupolos, Ohio State	14
Garrett Schilling, Xavier	14
Brady Womacks, Oral Roberts	14

STRIKEOUTS

RANK, PITCHER, TEAM	SO
1. Joey Lucchesi, Southeast Mo. State	149
2. Jon Duplantier, Rice	148
3. Keegan Akin, Western Michigan	133
Alex Faedo, Florida	133
5. Matt Anderson, Morehead State	130
6. Clarke Schmidt, South Carolina	129
7. Brendan McKay, Louisville	128
Braden Webb, South Carolina	128
9. Kevin Hill, South Alabama	126
10. Brandon Bailey, Gonzaga	125
Alex Lange, LSU	125
Eric Lauer, Kent State	125

STRIKEOUTS PER NINE

RANK, PITCHER, TEAM	SO/9
1. Dakota Mekkes, Michigan State	15.16
2. Matt Anderson, Morehead State	12.76
3. J.B. Bukauskas, North Carolina	12.75
4. A.J. Puk, Florida	12.34
5. Andrew Vernon, N.C. Central	12.34
6. Stephen Woods, Albany	12.25
7. Joey Lucchesi, Southeast Mo. State	12.08
8. Jon Duplantier, Rice	12.00
9. Aaron Leasher, Morehead State	11.94
10. Colton Davis, Western Carolina	11.90

FEWEST HITS PER NINE

RANK, PITCHER, TEAM	H/9
1. Dakota Mekkes, Michigan State	4.11
2. Eric Lauer, Kent State	4.24
3. Tyler Wilson, Rhode Island	4.66
4. Troy Rallings, Washington	4.72
5. Trevor Lane, Illinois-Chicago	5.25
6. Landon Hughes, Ga. Southern	5.37
7. Blake Quinn, Cal State Fullerton	5.40
8. Heath Holder, Georgia	5.45
9. Jeff Albrecht, Creighton	5.48
10. Kade McClure, Louisville	5.65

FEWEST WALKS PER NINE

RANK, PITCHER, TEAM	BB/9
1. Andrew Lantrip, Houston	0.50
2. Taylor Bloom, Maryland	0.79
3. Reggie McClain, Missouri	0.80
4. John Signore, Fairfield	0.86
5. Jeffrey Stovall, Northwestern State	0.87
6. Duncan Robinson, Dartmouth	0.92
7. Connor Seabold, Cal State Fullerton	0.97
8. Blake Redman, Loyola Marymount	0.98
9. J.D. Busfield, Loyola Marymount	1.02
10. Lucas Rollins, Saint Joseph's	1.05

TEAM LEADERS

SCORING

RANK, TEAM		G	R	R/G
1.	Alabama State	55	472	8.6
2.	Jackson State	60	507	8.5
3.	UNC Wilmington	60	505	8.4
4.	UNC Greensboro	59	492	8.3
5.	Jacksonville State	58	481	8.3
6.	Brigham Young	54	435	8.1
7.	Florida A&M	52	416	8.0
8.	Southeast Mo. State	60	474	7.9
9.	Bryant	59	465	7.9
10.	Tennessee Tech	55	430	7.8
11.	Austin Peay State	57	443	7.8
12.	Mercer	61	473	7.8
13.	Belmont	60	465	7.8
14.	Grambling	49	376	7.7
15.	East Tennessee State	57	430	7.5
16.	New Mexico	62	467	7.5
17.	Missouri State	59	440	7.5
18.	Morehead State	59	437	7.4
19.	Murray State	56	414	7.4
20.	Louisville	64	471	7.4
21.	Western Carolina	62	453	7.3
22.	Florida State	63	460	7.3
23.	Texas A&M	65	471	7.2
24.	Delaware	54	390	7.2
25.	Clemson	64	461	7.2
26.	North Florida	58	413	7.1
27.	Wright State	63	448	7.1
28.	Coastal Carolina	73	516	7.1
29.	Samford	61	428	7.0
30.	Texas Christian	67	467	7.0
31.	Texas Tech	67	462	6.9
32.	Hartford	55	379	6.9
33.	Southern Mississippi	61	419	6.9
34.	North Carolina State	60	411	6.9
35.	Air Force	57	390	6.8
36.	Virginia	60	410	6.8
37.	Miami	64	439	6.8
38.	Nevada	61	416	6.8
39.	Georgia Tech	63	429	6.8
40.	Dallas Baptist	63	428	6.8
41.	Little Rock	54	365	6.8
42.	North Carolina	55	370	6.7
43.	Southeastern Louisiana	61	410	6.7
44.	Richmond	52	349	6.7
45.	Vanderbilt	62	416	6.7
46.	Elon	54	362	6.7
47.	New Orleans	57	382	6.7
48.	Lipscomb	58	386	6.7
49.	Texas Southern	50	331	6.6
50.	Eastern Kentucky	55	362	6.6

BATTING AVERAGE

RANK, TEAM	AVG
1. UNC Greensboro	.346
2. BYU	.325
3. Air Force	.325
4. Jackson State	.322
5. Florida A&M	.322
6. Louisville	.322
7. Minnesota	.321
8. UNC Wilmington	.320
9. Nevada	.319
10. Bryant	.318

HOME RUNS

RANK, TEAM	HR
1. Coastal Carolina	96
2. Mercer	93
3. UNC Wilmington	87
4. Samford	83
5. Missouri State	80
6. Belmont	76
7. East Tennessee State	75
Clemson	75
9. Western Carolina	72
10. VMI	68
Tennessee Tech	68

DOUBLES

RANK, TEAM	2B
1. New Mexico	150
2. Texas Tech	146
3. UNC Greensboro	145
Jacksonville State	145
5. Florida State	142
6. Air Force	141
Louisville	141
8. Georgia Tech	139
TCU	139
Nevada	139

TRIPLES

RANK, TEAM	3B
1. UNC Greensboro	32
Oregon State	32
Nevada	32
4. Navy	31
5. Arizona	30
6. Wright State	27
Bucknell	27
8. Vanderbilt	26
Missouri State	26
10. New Orleans	25

SLUGGING PERCENTAGE

RANK, TEAM	SLG
1. UNC Greensboro	.538
2. UNC Wilmington	.517
3. Missouri State	.500
4. Jackson State	.500
5. New Mexico	.492
6. Louisville	.492
7. Mercer	.491
8. East Tennessee State	.491
9. Austin Peay State	.490
10. Belmont	.486

STOLEN BASES

RANK, TEAM	SB	CS
1. Seton Hall	183	34
2. Texas Southern	166	24
3. Eastern Michigan	127	40
4. Rutgers	121	25
5. Belmont	115	28
6. Southeastern Louisiana	113	45

7. Coastal Carolina	112	33
8. South Alabama	107	38
9. Jackson State	103	28
Wisconsin-Milwaukee	103	22

WALKS

RANK, TEAM	BB
1. Mercer	366

2. Clemson	359
3. Texas Tech	347
4. Coastal Carolina	342
5. Southeast Missouri State	335
6. Florida State	332
7. South Alabama	330
8. Belmont	327
9. Arizona	323
10. TCU	315

PITCHING

EARNED RUN AVERAGE

RANK, TEAM	ERA
1. Cal State Fullerton	2.22
2. Houston	2.48
3. Michigan State	2.75
4. St. Bonaventure	2.79
5. Louisville	2.82
6. Florida	2.91
7. Kent State	2.95
8. Southeastern Louisiana	3.01
9. Northwestern State	3.01
10. Texas A&M	3.05
11. Indiana	3.09
12. Creighton	3.15
13. North Carolina	3.16
14. Stanford	3.17
15. Long Beach State	3.17
16. Texas Christian	3.18
17. Arizona	3.18
18. California	3.20
19. Navy	3.20
20. Seton Hall	3.21
21. Oklahoma State	3.21
22. Bryant	3.22
23. Fla. Atlantic	3.24
24. Tulane	3.24

25. Vanderbilt	3.25
26. Louisiana-Lafayette	3.25
27. South Carolina	3.29
28. Cal State Northridge	3.29
29. Mississippi State	3.35
30. Ohio State	3.35
31. Coastal Carolina	3.41
32. Alabama	3.46
33. Wright State	3.49
34. Bradley	3.52
35. Oregon State	3.53
36. East Carolina	3.53
37. Mississippi	3.53
38. Iowa	3.56
39. Saint Mary's	3.58
40. Connecticut	3.58
41. Illinois	3.60
42. Pepperdine	3.60
43. Seattle	3.62
44. Miami	3.63
45. Southern Illinois	3.64
46. Norfolk State	3.66
47. North Florida	3.68
48. Florida State	3.69
49. Northeastern	3.71
50. Penn State	3.71

STRIKEOUTS PER NINE

RANK, TEAM	K/9
1. Florida	9.80
2. South Carolina	9.70
Vanderbilt	9.70
4. Morehead State	9.60
5. North Carolina	9.50
6. Alabama State	9.30
7. Southeast Missouri State	9.20
Texas A&M	9.20
South Florida	9.20
10. Mississippi State	9.10
Missouri State	9.10

FEWEST WALKS PER NINE

RANK, TEAM	BB/9
1. Houston	1.97
2. Indiana	2.31
3. Saint Joseph's	2.39
4. Florida	2.44
5. Wright State	2.45
6. Ohio State	2.47
7. Cal State Fullerton	2.54
8. Missouri	2.59
9. Maryland	2.59
10. Louisiana-Lafayette	2.65

FIELDING

FIELDING PERCENTAGE

RANK, TEAM	FPCT
1. Stanford	.983
2. Miami	.983
3. Florida	.982
4. Creighton	.981
5. Indiana State	.980
6. Stony Brook	.980
7. Minnesota	.980
8. Mercer	.980
9. Binghamton	.979
10. South Alabama	.979
11. Western Michigan	.978
12. South Carolina	.978
13. Northeastern	.978
14. Iowa	.978

15. Louisville	.978
16. Cal State Northridge	.978
17. Oklahoma State	.978
18. California	.978
19. Long Beach State	.977
20. Notre Dame	.977
21. Arizona	.977
22. Florida Atlantic	.977
23. Texas A&M	.977
24. Pepperdine	.977
25. Nevada	.977

DOUBLE PLAYS

RANK, TEAM	DP
1. Texas Tech	83
2. Georgia Tech	80
3. Oklahoma State	74
4. Northwestern State	71
5. New Mexico	66
Coastal Carolina	66
7. North Carolina State	63
8. Charlotte	61
Utah Valley	61
Saint Mary's	61

Batters: 10 or more at-bats. Pitchers: 5 or more innings.

1. COASTAL CAROLINA

Coach: Gary Gilmore. Record: 55-18.

PLAYER, POS., YEAR	AVG	OBP	SLG	AB	R	2B	3B	HR	RBI	SB
Beaird, Matt, c, So.	.208	.338	.233	120	17	3	0	0	17	0
Chadwick, Tyler, inf, Sr.	.268	.367	.463	205	38	14	1	8	44	1
Cooke, Billy, of, So.	.324	.415	.429	238	47	16	0	3	36	27
Crump, Josh, of, So.	.231	.500	.231	13	5	0	0	0	2	0
Ewing, Dalton, of, So.	.133	.341	.333	30	13	0	0	2	5	8
Issacson, Peyton, c, Fr.	.125	.222	.250	16	0	0	1	0	2	0
Lancaster, Seth, inf, So.	.326	.457	.509	175	44	11	0	7	35	15
Marks, Anthony, of, Sr.	.291	.408	.313	265	56	3	0	1	28	15
Owings, Connor, inf, Sr.	.352	.458	.636	253	64	20	2	16	57	14
Paez, Michael, of, Jr.	.276	.368	.514	290	67	18	3	15	52	7
Parrett, David, c, Sr.	.151	.325	.267	86	14	4	0	2	14	6
Pearcey, Cameron, inf, Fr.	.167	.326	.250	36	7	0	0	1	5	3
Remillard, Zach, inf, Sr.	.341	.391	.610	290	66	17	2	19	72	15
Rivers, Kieton, inf, Fr.	.308	.471	.538	13	3	0	0	1	5	0
Woodall Jr., Kevin, inf, So.	.207	.333	.326	92	15	2	0	3	17	0
Young, G.K., inf, Jr.	.337	.391	.571	294	60	11	2	18	72	1

PITCHER, YEAR	W	L	ERA	G	GS	SV	IP	H	BB	SO
Beckwith, Andrew, Jr.	15	1	1.85	26	10	2	117	113	18	75
Bilous, Jason, Fr.	3	1	4.43	16	10	0	45	46	35	47
Corbett, Patrick, Sr.	0	1	5.87	7	1	0	8	13	6	6
Cunningham, Alex, Jr.	10	4	3.62	22	17	1	119	116	40	98
Davidson, Chris, Fr.	0	1	15.88	5	1	0	6	9	6	1
Holmes, Bobby, So.	7	2	4.20	28	6	4	84	89	35	74
Hopeck, Zack, So.	3	4	3.70	16	10	1	56	46	14	39
Kitchen, Austin, Fr.	4	0	3.19	21	1	2	42	28	12	36
Miller, Brandon, Fr.	0	0	3.86	6	0	0	7	10	4	5
Morrison, Mike, Sr.	8	1	1.50	34	1	11	72	41	27	94
Poole, Tyler, Sr.	4	3	3.72	11	10	0	46	38	26	45
Schaefer, Cole, Jr.	1	0	4.04	11	5	0	36	46	13	23

2. ARIZONA

Coach: Jay Johnson. Record: 49-24.

PLAYER, POS., YEAR	AVG	OBP	SLG	AB	R	2B	3B	HR	RBI	SB
Aguilar, Ryan, of, Sr.	.310	.384	.495	287	52	23	3	8	56	12
Behnke, Justin, of, Sr.	.218	.406	.274	124	32	1	3	0	16	10
Boyd, Louis, inf, Jr.	.240	.378	.306	183	38	12	0	0	23	11
Dalbec, Bobby, inf, Jr.	.260	.370	.429	231	42	14	2	7	40	7
Gibbons, Zach, of, Sr.	.385	.460	.446	278	43	15	1	0	48	9
Gieseke, Sawyer, inf, Jr.	.182	.308	.273	11	3	1	0	0	1	0
Haug, Ryan, c, So.	.254	.390	.328	67	13	5	0	0	5	1
Lewis, Kyle, inf, Jr.	.258	.385	.292	89	13	3	0	0	12	1
Matijevic, J.J., inf, Jr.	.287	.331	.411	265	43	17	2	4	37	2
Oliva, Jared, of, So.	.240	.293	.378	217	27	4	7	4	36	13
Ramer, Cody, inf, Sr.	.348	.441	.485	293	64	18	8	2	40	9
Rivas, Alfonso, of, Fr.	.247	.329	.332	190	22	9	2	1	26	1
Salazar, Cesar, c, Fr.	.276	.329	.342	196	30	9	2	0	20	1

PITCHER, YEAR	W	L	ERA	G	GS	SV	IP	H	BB	SO
Bannister, Nathan, Sr.	12	2	2.59	22	20	0	142	104	33	114
Cloney, J.C., Jr.	8	4	2.45	18	18	0	110	100	22	61
Dalbec, Bobby, Jr.	11	6	2.50	29	8	7	101	82	37	96
Deason, Cody, Fr.	1	2	3.73	21	2	0	31	26	9	25
Flynn, Michael, Fr.	1	0	5.17	14	2	0	16	13	6	14
Ginkel, Kevin, Jr.	5	1	2.80	25	7	3	64	53	19	45
Gomez, Rio, So.	3	0	4.32	18	1	1	17	17	9	19
Hartman, Matt, So.	0	0	6.55	10	0	0	11	14	6	13
Medel, Robby, So.	1	3	5.71	12	0	0	17	21	5	14
Ming, Cameron, So.	3	3	3.59	32	8	4	80	76	22	59
Moffett, Cody, Sr.	1	1	4.38	14	1	0	12	9	7	12
Rivas, Alfonso, Fr.	2	1	3.50	16	1	3	18	14	15	15
Rubick, Austin, Fr.	0	1	8.10	11	0	0	10	10	5	5
Schnabel, Austin, Jr.	1	0	4.02	12	5	0	16	12	11	11

3. TEXAS CHRISTIAN

Coach: Jim Schlossnagle. Record: 49-18.

PLAYER, POS., YEAR	AVG	OBP	SLG	AB	R	2B	3B	HR	RBI	SB
Baker, Luken, inf, Fr.	.379	.483	.577	248	59	16	0	11	62	1
Barzilli, Elliott, inf, Jr.	.339	.418	.518	251	44	16	4	7	48	14
Hesse, Mason, inf, Jr.	.275	.407	.406	69	14	5	2	0	14	4
Johnson, Aaron, c, Jr.	.214	.290	.286	28	7	2	0	0	3	2
Landestoy, Michael, inf, So.	.290	.346	.362	69	13	0	1	1	14	1
Merrill, Ryan, inf, Jr.	.298	.353	.410	178	31	9	4	1	25	11
Plunkett, Zack, c, So.	.200	.355	.280	25	6	2	0	0	0	0
Skoug, Evan, c, So.	.301	.390	.502	249	54	21	1	9	51	7
Steinhagen, Dane, of, Sr.	.313	.379	.502	243	49	20	1	8	51	12
Wade, Austen, of, So.	.286	.434	.359	217	50	11	1	1	27	13
Wanhanen, Connor, of, So.	.231	.327	.290	186	39	7	2	0	23	9
Warner, Cam, inf, Jr.	.300	.346	.431	283	47	17	1	6	43	10
Watson, Josh, of, Fr.	.280	.398	.506	243	52	12	5	11	44	12

PITCHER, YEAR	W	L	ERA	G	GS	SV	IP	H	BB	SO
Baker, Luken, Fr.	3	1	1.70	10	10	0	48	37	16	41
Brown, Dalton, Fr.	0	1	5.00	10	0	0	9	11	2	11
Burnett, Ryan, So.	3	1	1.97	27	0	1	32	23	6	31
Feltman, Durbin, Fr.	3	0	1.56	27	0	9	35	15	11	49
Gooch, Drew, So.	0	0	2.01	16	0	0	22	25	7	17
Guillory, Preston, Jr.	4	2	4.35	28	0	1	41	41	12	34
Hill, Rex, Jr.	2	3	5.91	13	11	0	46	58	18	45
Horton, Dalton, Fr.	8	0	2.58	13	12	0	59	47	17	27
Howard, Brian, Jr.	10	2	3.19	17	17	0	99	80	30	93
Janczak, Jared, Fr.	7	4	2.61	26	7	0	83	76	26	80
Traver, Mitchell, Jr.	1	3	3.26	7	7	0	30	27	10	28
Trieglaff, Brian, Jr.	4	1	3.22	26	0	4	45	48	17	39
Wymer, Sean, Fr.	3	0	4.68	16	2	1	33	32	15	39

4. OKLAHOMA STATE

Coach: Josh Holliday. Record: 43-22.

PLAYER, POS., YEAR	AVG	OBP	SLG	AB	R	2B	3B	HR	RBI	SB
Benge, Garrett, inf, So.	.292	.380	.433	240	37	16	3	4	40	7
Chappell, Jacob, inf, So.	.190	.255	.190	42	3	0	0	0	4	2
Costello, Conor, of, Sr.	.351	.447	.595	111	16	10	1	5	31	4
Davis, J.R., inf, Jr.	.347	.422	.438	219	43	13	2	1	32	9
Hassel, Corey, inf, Jr.	.282	.356	.448	248	47	19	2	6	39	16
Littell, Jon, of, So.	.258	.332	.343	198	28	9	1	2	23	4
McCain, Garrett, of, So.	.203	.385	.243	74	22	3	0	0	6	11
Petrino, David, inf, Sr.	.146	.217	.195	41	4	2	0	0	3	0
Rosa, Andrew, inf, So.	.257	.388	.286	70	12	2	0	0	11	3
Simpson, Colin, c, Fr.	.212	.302	.341	85	15	3	1	2	9	0
Sluder, Ryan, of, Jr.	.197	.278	.322	183	31	9	1	4	18	7
Theroux, Collin, c, Jr.	.163	.312	.292	178	28	5	0	6	30	0
Walton, Donnie, inf, Sr.	.337	.428	.447	246	45	16	1	3	44	14
Williams, Dustin, inf, Jr.	.218	.320	.441	220	32	5	1	14	42	4

PITCHER, YEAR	W	L	ERA	G	GS	SV	IP	H	BB	SO
Battenfield, Blake, So.	1	0	3.68	24	0	2	29	32	16	16
Buffett, Tyler, Sr.	9	3	2.81	37	5	9	83	70	32	76
Cobb, Trey, Jr.	4	7	3.09	24	12	6	82	81	32	100
Costello, Conor, Sr.	1	0	5.68	3	0	0	6	9	1	6
Cowan, Jake, So.	0	0	3.72	7	0	0	10	6	8	12
Elliott, Jensen, Fr.	9	3	3.50	17	17	0	87	83	35	71
Hackerott, Alex, Sr.	1	0	4.05	12	0	0	7	7	3	11
Hatch, Thomas, So.	9	3	2.14	19	19	0	130	108	33	112
Leeper, Ben, Fr.	0	0	3.18	2	2	0	6	3	4	8
Lienhard, Joe, Fr.	1	0	3.38	15	2	0	19	14	12	18
Mertz, Michael, Jr.	3	4	4.33	23	7	3	52	42	39	58
Reed, Remey, Jr.	4	1	3.66	24	0	1	39	29	18	51
Teel, Carson, Fr.	1	0	2.70	17	0	0	17	15	10	17
Williams, Garrett, Jr.	2	0	6.08	14	1	0	13	12	11	20

5. FLORIDA

Coach: Kevin O'Sullivan. **Record:** 52-16.

PLAYER, POS., YEAR	AVG	OBP	SLG	AB	R	2B	3B	HR	RBI	SB
Alonso, Peter, 1b, Jr.	.374	.469	.659	211	51	18	0	14	60	2
Guthrie, Dalton, inf, So.	.305	.367	.366	279	47	14	0	1	22	8
Hicks, Christian, inf, So.	.118	.400	.176	17	3	1	0	0	0	1
Horvath, Nick, of, So.	.143	.333	.357	28	6	0	0	2	5	2
India, Jonathan, inf, Fr.	.303	.367	.440	234	43	16	2	4	40	13
Kolozsvary, Mark, c, So.	.235	.316	.588	17	3	0	0	2	5	1
Larson, Ryan, of, Jr.	.161	.245	.184	87	12	2	0	0	7	2
Liput, Deacon, inf, Fr.	.270	.363	.398	241	39	14	4	3	36	13
Maldonado, Nelson, inf, Fr.	.256	.350	.405	195	35	7	2	6	30	6
Reed, Buddy, of, Jr.	.262	.362	.391	256	57	9	6	4	32	24
Reyes, Daniel, of, Fr.	.269	.278	.423	52	6	3	1	1	11	1
Rivera, Mike, c, So.	.245	.347	.419	229	33	9	2	9	47	0
Schwarz, JJ, c, So.	.290	.397	.456	252	47	15	3	7	60	2
Vasquez, Jeremy, of, So.	.291	.387	.358	165	22	11	0	0	15	1

PITCHER, YEAR	W	L	ERA	G	GS	SV	IP	H	BB	SO
Anderson, Shaun, Jr.	3	0	0.97	36	0	13	46	31	7	60
Byrne, Michael, Fr.	0	1	3.94	13	0	0	16	11	3	15
Dunning, Dane, Jr.	6	3	2.29	33	5	2	79	68	12	88
Faedo, Alex, So.	13	3	3.18	17	17	0	105	87	21	133
Horvath, Nick, So.	2	1	2.08	15	0	1	13	13	5	8
Kowar, Jackson, Fr.	3	0	3.38	12	6	0	35	34	10	44
Moss, Scott, So.	3	0	1.57	14	5	0	23	15	9	31
Puk, A.J., Jr.	2	3	3.05	17	16	0	74	51	37	101
Rubio, Frank, Jr.	3	1	4.46	23	0	1	34	36	8	21
Shore, Logan, Jr.	12	1	2.31	18	18	0	105	82	19	96
Singer, Brady, Fr.	2	2	4.95	23	1	1	44	43	17	38
Snead, Kirby, Jr.	3	1	2.78	41	0	1	36	39	12	33

6. MIAMI

Coach: Jim Morris. **Record:** 48-14.

PLAYER, POS., YEAR	AVG	OBP	SLG	AB	R	2B	3B	HR	RBI	SB
Abreu, Willie, of, Jr.	.285	.353	.510	239	47	14	2	12	56	5
Alvarez, Ryan, of, Fr.	.400	.471	.467	15	1	1	0	0	1	0
Barr, Christopher, 1b, Sr.	.256	.336	.308	234	44	6	3	0	25	14
Batista, Randy, inf, Jr.	.272	.403	.361	147	29	3	2	2	26	7
Chester, Carl, of, So.	.336	.426	.395	253	56	9	0	2	29	16
Collins, Zack, c, Jr.	.363	.544	.668	190	54	10	0	16	59	1
Crocitto, Peter, c, So.	.218	.271	.255	55	8	2	0	0	2	0
Gomez, Joe, c, Jr.	.296	.394	.519	27	12	4	1	0	6	0
Gonzalez, Romy, 3b, Fr.	.173	.215	.280	75	11	5	0	1	10	0
Heyward, Jacob, of, Jr.	.242	.403	.372	215	43	10	0	6	39	7
Lopez, Brandon, inf, Sr.	.376	.449	.469	213	50	14	0	2	42	5
Michelangeli, Edgar, inf, Jr.	.269	.322	.384	219	35	8	1	5	40	1
Ruiz, John, inf, Jr.	.342	.431	.491	234	46	17	3	4	57	3

PITCHER, YEAR	W	L	ERA	G	GS	SV	IP	H	BB	SO
Bartow, Frankie, Fr.	6	0	2.72	43	0	0	56	56	10	29
Cabezas, Andrew, Fr.	3	1	5.07	28	3	0	55	45	24	54
Garcia, Danny, Jr.	9	5	3.57	18	18	0	98	101	35	52
Garcia, Bryan, Jr.	2	0	1.89	35	0	18	38	25	18	55
Guerra, Ryan, Jr.	2	1	7.36	10	0	0	11	12	6	9
Hammond, Cooper, Jr.	0	0	3.18	7	0	0	6	2	0	6
Lepore, Jesse, So.	9	0	2.20	14	13	0	74	59	28	57
Mediavilla, Michael, So.	11	2	3.40	18	18	0	103	88	43	85
Meyer, Devin, So.	1	1	3.26	13	0	0	19	15	10	11
Musa, Isaiah, Fr.	0	0	7.84	11	0	0	10	8	11	8
Pimentel, Keven, So.	2	0	3.67	18	1	2	34	45	13	20
Woodrey, Thomas, Sr.	5	4	4.98	18	11	0	69	82	30	40

7. TEXAS TECH

Coach: Tim Tadlock. **Record:** 47-20.

PLAYER, POS., YEAR	AVG	OBP	SLG	AB	R	2B	3B	HR	RBI	SB
Bernstein, Matt, c, Fr.	.263	.348	.368	19	6	2	0	0	5	0
Davis, Michael, inf, So.	.268	.346	.384	250	44	20	0	3	37	6
Davis, Zach, of, Sr.	.250	.444	.300	40	22	2	0	0	6	13
Farhat, Cody, of, Fr.	.167	.265	.267	30	4	0	0	1	6	0
Floyd, Tyler, c, Sr.	.217	.333	.294	143	28	6	1	1	18	2
Garcia, Orlando, inf, So.	.265	.378	.425	200	37	8	3	6	30	6
Gardner, Tanner, inf, So.	.379	.484	.549	235	55	19	6	3	35	6
Gutierrez, Eric, inf, Sr.	.333	.465	.581	234	54	17	1	13	60	3
Hargrove, Hunter, inf, Jr.	.305	.379	.000	105	14	10	0	2	28	2
Long, Ryan, inf, Jr.	.225	.339	.265	102	14	4	0	0	26	1
Lyons, Anthony, of, Jr.	.286	.407	.381	21	2	0	1	0	3	0
Neslony, Tyler, of, Sr.	.306	.400	.536	235	53	22	1	10	58	3
Ochoa, Trey, inf, Fr.	.212	.313	.235	85	9	2	0	0	7	2
Raley, Cory, inf, Sr.	.319	.408	.458	260	59	14	2	6	53	21
Sanchez, Kholeton, c, Jr.	.146	.260	.220	41	5	1	1	0	10	0
Smith, Stephen, of, Jr.	.309	.422	.511	272	55	19	3	10	42	8

PITCHER, YEAR	W	L	ERA	G	GS	SV	IP	H	BB	SO
Brown, Dalton, Sr.	0	1	4.11	14	0	0	15	17	5	12
Damron, Ty, Jr.	4	2	6.52	14	13	0	50	54	25	43
Dugger, Robert, Jr.	6	1	2.67	30	0	3	61	62	22	54
Eden, Chandler, Jr.	0	0	8.00	12	0	0	9	8	7	10
Gingery, Steven, Fr.	4	2	3.18	15	14	0	68	61	31	63
Harpenau, Ty, Fr.	1	0	6.85	15	9	0	45	58	24	32
Howard, Hayden, Jr.	9	3	2.98	35	1	9	85	76	20	54
Lanning, Erikson, Fr.	3	4	5.19	14	11	0	52	57	18	36
Martin, Davis, Fr.	10	1	2.52	19	14	2	89	75	27	61
Moseley, Ryan, Jr.	6	4	5.14	25	4	4	56	54	37	32
Mushinski, Parker, So.	0	0	1.93	21	0	1	14	7	12	15
Patterson, Jacob, So.	0	0	3.77	13	0	0	14	13	12	9
Shetter, Ryan, Fr.	4	2	4.02	19	1	1	31	31	10	18

8. TEXAS A&M

Coach: Rob Childress. **Record:** 49-16.

PLAYER, POS., YEAR	AVG	OBP	SLG	AB	R	2B	3B	HR	RBI	SB
Banks, Nick, of, Jr.	.280	.353	.473	239	48	13	3	9	49	7
Barash, Michael, c, Sr.	.324	.393	.444	216	45	11	0	5	43	1
Bedford, Cole, c, Fr.	.143	.286	.200	35	9	2	0	0	1	0
Birk, Ryne, inf, Jr.	.310	.378	.478	255	52	14	4	7	45	9
Choruby, Nick, inf, Jr.	.299	.364	.339	177	33	7	0	0	22	13
Davis, Joel, inf, Jr.	.293	.376	.504	123	18	9	4	3	22	2
Gideon, Ronnie, inf, Jr.	.284	.419	.597	67	14	6	0	5	20	1
Homan, Austin, inf, Jr.	.356	.392	.431	160	32	7	1	1	26	5
Janca, George, inf, Fr.	.231	.294	.269	78	11	1	1	0	11	1
Melton, Hunter, 1b, Sr.	.300	.375	.510	253	56	13	2	12	67	2
Moroney, Jonathan, of, Sr.	.319	.406	.549	91	21	4	1	5	26	3
Moss, J.B., of, Sr.	.318	.408	.483	261	67	17	4	6	43	16
Pennington, Walker, of, Jr.	.258	.347	.532	62	12	5	0	4	16	3
White, Boomer, c, Jr.	.386	.462	.517	259	49	19	0	5	46	10

PITCHER, YEAR	W	L	ERA	G	GS	SV	IP	H	BB	SO
Ecker, Mark, Jr.	4	2	0.39	25	0	8	47	24	7	56
Hendrix, Ryan, Jr.	0	1	6.39	20	0	5	25	20	20	36
Hill, Brigham, So.	9	2	2.51	24	13	1	97	86	28	99
Ivey, Tyler, Fr.	2	3	3.56	11	10	0	43	41	15	48
Kilkenny, Mitchell, Fr.	2	0	1.67	15	1	0	27	24	10	29
Kolek, Stephen, Fr.	3	0	3.30	12	3	0	30	28	13	21
Larkins, Turner, So.	3	0	2.51	19	6	1	43	34	16	39
Martin, Corbin, So.	2	1	5.47	16	3	0	26	29	21	33
Schlottmann, Ty, Sr.	1	0	2.25	14	0	0	8	12	4	13
Sherrod, Cason, So.	1	0	4.50	16	0	1	18	15	10	17
Simonds, Kyle, Sr.	11	3	2.61	17	17	0	100	81	26	80
Vines, Jace, So.	6	1	4.76	17	11	1	62	74	18	60
Vinson, Andrew, Sr.	4	3	2.32	22	1	2	50	33	10	57

9. UC SANTA BARBARA

Coach: Andrew Checketts. **Record:** 43-20.

PLAYER, POS., YEAR	AVG	OBP	SLG	AB	R	2B	3B	HR	RBI	SB
Adams, Josh, of, So.	.229	.325	.368	144	18	8	0	4	27	2
Bush, Austin, inf, So.	.265	.346	.465	230	32	11	1	11	49	0
Calica, Andrew, of, Jr.	.252	.427	.360	222	50	8	2	4	24	18
Clark, Ryan, inf, Sr.	.268	.329	.342	149	22	6	1	1	15	4
Cohen, Sam, c, Fr.	.357	.379	.679	28	3	3	0	2	11	1
Cumberland, Ryan, inf, Jr.	.292	.296	.292	24	2	0	0	0	5	0
Fisher, Clay, inf, So.	.285	.332	.377	239	32	15	2	1	24	14
Fredrick, Billy, inf, Jr.	.231	.318	.291	134	16	6	1	0	18	2
Gradford, Devon, inf, Jr.	.331	.412	.454	130	22	7	3	1	18	4
Grover, Dempsey, c, So.	.273	.386	.381	194	39	13	1	2	29	6
McAdoo, Michael, of, Fr.	.191	.307	.243	115	19	4	1	0	19	3
Mitchell, Tevin, inf, Fr.	.250	.300	.297	64	10	3	0	0	6	2
Muno, JJ, inf, So.	.294	.370	.450	231	44	15	3	5	31	17

	AVG	OBP	SLG	AB	R	2B	3B	HR	RBI	SB
Plantier, Kyle, inf, So.	.191	.312	.244	131	18	4	0	1	16	3
Rowan, Thomas, c, Fr.	.182	.246	.218	55	4	2	0	0	5	0

PITCHER, YEAR	W	L	ERA	G	GS	SV	IP	H	BB	SO
Bettencourt, Trevor, Jr.	4	2	3.43	24	1	4	42	36	21	46
Bieber, Shane, Jr.	12	4	2.74	18	18	0	135	126	16	109
Carter, James, Jr.	0	0	1.04	6	3	0	9	11	2	4
Chandler, Kevin, Fr.	1	0	3.68	18	0	0	29	31	12	19
Chapman, Kenny, So.	1	1	12.08	10	0	0	13	16	19	7
Clements, Chris, So.	0	0	10.13	7	2	0	13	22	8	13
Davis, Noah, Fr.	7	4	4.46	17	15	0	83	85	30	63
Dragmire, Grant, Fr.	0	0	5.40	4	0	0	5	6	4	4
Garcia, Alex, So.	0	0	2.38	10	0	0	11	12	6	12
Hatton, Kyle, Fr.	3	1	4.21	12	6	0	47	50	9	32
Kelly, Justin, Sr.	2	1	3.80	10	2	1	24	27	9	35
Nelson, Kyle, So.	7	2	2.18	33	1	10	74	56	18	87
Record, Joe, So.	6	5	3.91	16	16	0	90	91	38	63

10. MISSISSIPPI STATE

Coach: John Cohen. **Record:** 44-18.

PLAYER, POS., YEAR	AVG	OBP	SLG	AB	R	2B	3B	HR	RBI	SB
Alexander, Luke, inf, Jr.	.222	.342	.333	63	11	1	0	2	9	2
Brown, Cody, of, Jr.	.241	.388	.398	83	19	3	2	2	13	3
Collins, Gavin, c, Jr.	.302	.405	.516	215	43	14	1	10	39	0
Gordon, Cole, 1b, Fr.	.333	.429	.611	18	3	3	1	0	3	0
Gridley, Ryan, inf, So.	.284	.340	.345	229	30	8	0	2	32	1
Holland, John, inf, Sr.	.229	.276	.280	118	21	4	1	0	12	0
Humphreys, Reid, inf, Jr.	.310	.396	.492	187	32	15	2	5	44	0
Kruger, Jack, c, Jr.	.344	.435	.550	209	43	19	0	8	40	6
Lowe, Nathaniel, 1b, Jr.	.348	.423	.490	247	44	20	0	5	49	2
Mangum, Jake, of, Fr.	.408	.458	.510	206	40	12	3	1	28	6
Marrero, Elih, c, Fr.	.233	.286	.287	150	15	6	1	0	12	2
Robson, Jacob, of, Jr.	.321	.414	.413	184	42	6	4	1	24	18
Rooker, Brent, inf, So.	.324	.376	.578	204	34	15	2	11	54	2
Smith, Michael, of, Sr.	.214	.353	.286	14	11	1	0	0	2	1
Stovall, Hunter, inf, Fr.	.241	.313	.299	87	16	5	0	0	14	6

PITCHER, YEAR	W	L	ERA	G	GS	SV	IP	H	BB	SO
Billingsley, Jacob, So.	0	0	1.80	12	0	1	10	10	3	14
Breaux, Kale, Fr.	1	1	5.40	16	1	1	17	19	10	19
Brown, Daniel, Jr.	4	2	3.62	23	6	2	55	54	18	54
Cyr, Ryan, Fr.	1	1	1.04	12	1	0	17	14	7	11
Houston, Zac, Jr.	6	0	1.63	18	6	0	39	29	19	42
Hudson, Dakota, Jr.	9	5	2.55	17	17	0	113	106	35	115
Hughes, Noah, Fr.	0	0	8.22	8	0	1	8	9	4	6
Humphreys, Reid, Jr.	0	1	5.56	17	0	7	23	28	7	31
James, Keegan, Fr.	3	0	3.24	14	4	0	25	19	8	15
Pilkington, Konnor, Fr.	3	1	2.08	14	11	0	43	38	15	42
Rigby, Ryan, So.	5	1	2.25	20	0	1	48	37	13	43
Sexton, Austin, Jr.	8	3	3.56	17	17	0	101	104	25	98
Small, Ethan, Fr.	1	0	13.06	15	0	0	10	11	10	20
Smith, Blake, Jr.	2	2	2.93	20	0	5	28	17	15	31
Tatum, Vance, Jr.	0	0	5.24	17	0	1	22	22	7	23
Young, Paul, Jr.	0	0	8.53	10	0	0	6	7	9	10

11. LOUISVILLE

Coach: Dan McDonnell. **Record:** 50-14.

PLAYER, POS., YEAR	AVG	OBP	SLG	AB	R	2B	3B	HR	RBI	SB
Clemons, Austin, of, Fr.	.067	.263	.067	15	2	0	0	0	1	0
Ellis, Drew, 3b, Fr.	.309	.426	.468	94	19	6	0	3	22	3
Fitch, Colby, c, So.	.339	.451	.596	109	23	7	3	5	25	0
Hairston, Devin, ss, So.	.361	.415	.478	249	56	16	2	3	45	3
Lyman, Colin, of, Fr.	.301	.364	.392	153	31	6	4	0	30	9
Mann, Devin, inf, Fr.	.303	.414	.404	89	15	9	0	0	17	1
McKay, Brendan, 1b, So.	.333	.414	.513	228	43	19	2	6	41	0
Pinkham, Zeke, c, Fr.	.091	.286	.091	11	2	0	0	0	2	0
Ray, Corey, of, Jr.	.310	.388	.545	268	55	16	1	15	60	44
Rosenbaum, Danny, inf, Sr.	.287	.359	.510	202	36	13	1	10	42	0
Smith, Will, c, Fr.	.382	.480	.567	157	40	8	0	7	43	9
Solak, Nick, inf, Jr.	.376	.470	.564	165	49	14	1	5	29	9
Stowers, Josh, of, Fr.	.231	.333	.231	13	4	0	0	0	2	2
Summers, Ryan, of, So.	.195	.250	.220	41	9	1	0	0	3	1
Taylor, Logan, of, Jr.	.280	.354	.387	168	40	8	5	0	18	18
Tiberi, Blake, inf, So.	.340	.387	.553	244	47	18	2	10	51	2

12. LOUISIANA STATE

Coach: Paul Mainieri. **Record:** 45-21.

PLAYER, POS., YEAR	AVG	OBP	SLG	AB	R	2B	3B	HR	RBI	SB
Adams, Bryce, inf, Jr.	.150	.227	.350	20	1	1	0	1	6	0
Breaux, Brennan, of, Fr.	.139	.279	.167	36	12	1	0	0	5	3
Dawson, Trey, inf, Fr.	.111	.273	.111	18	1	0	0	0	1	0
Deichmann, Greg, inf, So.	.288	.346	.513	236	45	14	3	11	57	5
Duplantis, Antoine, of, Fr.	.327	.404	.419	272	45	9	5	2	39	13
Fraley, Jake, of, Jr.	.326	.408	.464	267	61	10	6	5	36	28
Freeman, Cole, inf, Jr.	.329	.427	.403	216	46	7	3	1	27	26
Jordan, Bryce, inf, So.	.293	.419	.410	188	40	7	0	5	33	0
Jordan, Beau, of, So.	.286	.354	.379	224	31	9	0	4	39	5
Lochridge, O'Neal, inf, Fr.	.229	.318	.486	35	10	3	0	2	10	0
Papierski, Michael, c, So.	.242	.358	.387	124	16	9	0	3	20	1
Reid, Chris, inf, Fr.	.287	.417	.371	167	27	9	1	1	14	0
Robertson, Kramer, inf, Jr.	.324	.417	.440	259	61	20	2	2	39	14
Romero, Jordan, c, Jr.	.297	.378	.545	145	24	9	0	9	41	0
Wofford, Brody, of, Fr.	.242	.254	.306	62	6	2	1	0	5	0

PITCHER, YEAR	W	L	ERA	G	GS	SV	IP	H	BB	SO
Bain, Austin, So.	4	0	4.60	20	2	0	29	27	14	32
Bugg, Parker, Jr.	1	2	3.63	28	0	4	40	31	16	36
Cartwright, Alden, So.	3	0	2.93	11	2	0	15	11	4	13
Devall, Hunter, Sr.	0	0	3.12	10	0	0	8	6	11	11
Gilbert, Caleb, Fr.	4	4	5.04	25	5	1	45	55	22	43
Lange, Alex, So.	8	4	3.79	17	17	0	112	92	49	125
Latz, Jake, Fr.	0	1	7.56	7	3	0	8	10	4	11
McKay, Cole, Fr.	0	1	6.75	8	0	0	8	12	11	12
Newman, Hunter, Jr.	1	1	2.13	28	0	8	38	31	15	40
Norman, Doug, So.	1	1	3.41	23	2	0	32	26	18	21
Poche', Jared, Jr.	9	4	3.35	19	17	0	102	106	37	87
Reynolds, Russell, Jr.	3	0	4.08	26	0	1	35	35	10	23
Smith, Riley, So.	2	1	7.66	12	1	0	22	25	11	11
Stallings, Jesse, So.	3	0	3.64	25	2	1	30	26	15	18
Valek III, John, Sr.	6	2	4.04	15	13	0	62	70	9	52

13. FLORIDA STATE

Coach: Mike Martin. **Record:** 41-22.

PLAYER, POS., YEAR	AVG	OBP	SLG	AB	R	2B	3B	HR	RBI	SB
Busby, Dylan, inf, So.	.323	.374	.597	248	49	16	5	14	55	11
Bussey, Bryan, c, Jr.	.167	.250	.250	24	2	2	0	0	6	0
DeLuzio, Ben, inf, Jr.	.237	.346	.333	198	40	12	2	1	25	15
Graganella, Nick, of, Sr.	.200	.317	.240	50	10	2	0	0	3	1
Henderson, Matt, inf, Jr.	.230	.420	.279	165	44	6	1	0	14	4
Holton, Tyler, of, Fr.	.214	.389	.500	28	7	2	0	2	7	0
Kelly, Hayden, inf, Sr.	.200	.500	.500	10	5	0	0	1	3	0
Lueck, Brett, of, Jr.	.379	.494	.576	132	33	10	2	4	35	2
Miller, Darren, inf, So.	.229	.375	.325	83	14	5	0	1	14	3
Nieporte, Quincy, inf, Jr.	.300	.354	.440	200	24	13	0	5	38	2
Petrey, Donovan, of, Fr.	.250	.382	.333	84	18	4	0	1	8	2
Raleigh, Cal, c, Fr.	.301	.412	.511	229	45	16	1	10	50	1
Sansone, John, inf, Jr.	.370	.455	.576	257	58	26	0	9	65	8
Truluck, Hank, inf, Jr.	.204	.344	.327	49	13	3	0	1	11	0
Walls, Taylor, inf, So.	.355	.479	.516	248	72	20	1	6	46	14
Wells, Jr., Steven, of, So.	.184	.333	.237	76	12	1	0	1	13	0
West, Gage, dh, Jr.	.293	.404	.387	75	14	4	0	1	12	1

PITCHER, YEAR	W	L	ERA	G	GS	SV	IP	H	BB	SO
Bordner, Sam, Fr.	1	0	4.15	16	0	1	22	15	10	22
Burdi, Zack, Jr.	1	3	3.30	27	0	11	30	17	9	47
Dale, Chandler, Fr.	0	0	2.16	7	0	0	8	4	7	4
Funkhouser, Kyle, Sr.	9	3	3.86	16	15	0	93	70	47	95
Harrington, Drew, Jr.	12	2	1.95	17	17	0	111	92	25	92
Henzman, Lincoln, So.	0	0	4.50	20	0	1	24	31	6	27
Hummel, Shane, Jr.	2	1	1.99	15	2	2	32	22	8	17
Kidston, Anthony, Sr.	1	0	2.63	14	0	0	14	11	13	13
Leland, Sean, So.	0	0	3.24	7	0	0	8	4	10	2
McClure, Kade, So.	12	0	2.54	15	13	0	78	49	20	77
McKay, Brendan, So.	12	4	2.30	17	17	0	110	89	42	128
Shoffner, Dylan, Jr.	0	0	2.45	8	0	0	7	10	2	9
Sparger, Jake, Jr.	0	1	5.12	19	0	0	19	17	9	21
Wolf, Adam, Fr.	0	0	1.38	15	0	0	13	13	4	14

PITCHER, YEAR	W	L	ERA	G	GS	SV	IP	H	BB	SO
Byrd, Alec, Jr.	1	0	2.20	28	0	0	33	18	10	32
Carlton, Drew, So.	8	3	3.94	17	17	0	94	93	23	76
Compton, Mike, Sr.	5	3	4.92	15	12	0	60	70	19	32
Haney, Chase, Fr.	5	0	2.78	31	0	0	32	29	19	37
Holton, Tyler, Fr.	3	4	2.79	18	10	1	68	60	33	84
Johnson, Cobi, So.	0	0	3.50	12	1	0	18	6	9	20
Karp, Andrew, So.	1	1	6.91	9	2	0	14	19	6	8
Kinney, Matthew, Sr.	3	0	2.49	27	0	0	25	16	12	16
Sands, Cole, Fr.	6	7	4.13	18	17	0	70	69	33	50
Voyles, Ed, So.	1	2	2.66	23	4	1	47	53	19	41
Voyles, Jim, Jr.	6	1	3.16	25	0	2	51	35	18	48
Warmoth, Tyler, Sr.	1	1	5.34	23	0	4	30	24	9	40
Zirzow, Will, So.	1	0	4.42	15	0	0	18	15	10	24

14. SOUTH CAROLINA

Coach: Chad Holbrook. **Record:** 46-18.

PLAYER, POS., YEAR	AVG	OBP	SLG	AB	R	2B	3B	HR	RBI	SB
Arendas, D.C., inf, Sr.	.245	.350	.391	151	23	5	1	5	24	3
Blair, Danny, of, Fr.	.250	.300	.321	28	8	2	0	0	4	1
Bride, Jonah, inf, So.	.283	.393	.363	226	41	12	0	2	32	8
Cone, Gene, of, Jr.	.363	.474	.498	215	53	13	2	4	30	7
Cullen, Chris, c, Fr.	.238	.337	.333	147	19	11	0	1	23	2
Destino, Alex, dh, So.	.321	.373	.509	234	40	14	0	10	59	2
Grosvenor, Ross, 1b, Jr.	.357	.400	.429	14	1	1	0	0	2	0
Hopkins, T.J., of, Fr.	.322	.388	.405	121	25	5	1	1	26	8
Jones, John, c, So.	.269	.372	.420	212	36	11	0	7	49	1
McIlwain, Brandon, of, Fr.	.100	.100	.100	10	0	0	0	0	1	0
Mooney, Marcus, inf, Sr.	.314	.413	.377	204	38	10	0	1	29	4
Scolamiero, Clark, of, So.	.206	.293	.206	34	6	0	0	0	5	2
Stokes, Madison, inf, So.	.304	.371	.382	102	16	5	0	1	12	5
Taylor, Hunter, c, So.	.226	.294	.290	31	2	2	0	0	4	2
Thompson-Williams, D., of, Jr.	.321	.418	.517	240	58	17	3	8	41	18
Tolbert, L.T., inf, Fr.	.229	.306	.323	192	32	7	1	3	27	5
Williams, Matt, inf, So.	.240	.321	.520	25	3	1	0	2	2	1

PITCHER, YEAR	W	L	ERA	G	GS	SV	IP	H	BB	SO
Bowers, Colie, Jr.	1	0	2.03	7	2	0	13	5	8	15
Cropper, Canaan, So.	0	0	5.14	5	2	0	7	10	5	10
Haswell, Tyler, Jr.	2	0	3.10	11	1	0	20	19	3	15
Hill, Adam, Fr.	7	0	3.53	14	14	0	66	49	28	72
Johnson, Tyler, So.	3	2	2.42	29	1	9	52	34	8	59
Murray, Brandon, So.	2	0	6.38	20	1	0	24	26	11	15
Provey, Colton, Jr.	0	0	10.13	5	0	0	5	8	6	6
Reagan, Josh, Jr.	3	2	2.08	29	0	11	56	34	20	50
Schmidt, Clarke, So.	9	5	3.40	18	17	0	111	107	27	129
Scott, Reed, Jr.	4	1	2.56	29	0	2	46	41	15	31
Vogel, Matthew, Jr.	1	0	3.86	9	0	0	7	6	12	11
Webb, Braden, Fr.	10	6	3.09	18	17	0	102	80	48	128
Widener, Taylor, Jr.	4	2	4.20	17	9	0	56	54	16	68

15. EAST CAROLINA

Coach: Cliff Godwin. **Record:** 38-23.

PLAYER, POS., YEAR	AVG	OBP	SLG	AB	R	2B	3B	HR	RBI	SB
Bolka, Luke, dh, Jr.	.317	.400	.463	82	13	3	0	3	12	3
Brooks, Garrett, of, So.	.308	.374	.420	169	29	14	1	1	20	6
Brown, Turner, inf, Fr.	.281	.379	.352	199	28	5	0	3	34	9
Harman, Bryce, 1b, Jr.	.242	.379	.376	178	27	8	2	4	25	2
Lamm, Parker, of, Sr.	.287	.332	.321	237	28	6	1	0	28	12
Littlefield, Ryan, 1b, Jr.	.267	.412	.400	15	2	0	1	0	1	0
Lloyd, Brady, inf, Fr.	.333	.385	.500	12	8	2	0	0	1	2
Morgan, Kirk, inf, Jr.	.299	.364	.342	117	9	5	0	0	19	2
Mozingo, Zack, of, Jr.	.243	.356	.365	74	9	3	0	2	12	0
Nelson, Jeff, of, Sr.	.250	.418	.368	76	21	4	1	1	5	8
Phillips, Wesley, inf, Jr.	.079	.122	.184	38	7	1	0	1	5	1
Tyler, Eric, of, Jr.	.306	.381	.426	242	37	14	0	5	36	9
Watkins, Travis, c, Jr.	.326	.407	.476	233	43	14	0	7	44	3
Williams-Sutton, Dwanya, of, Fr.	.354	.451	.545	178	31	11	4	5	27	7
Yorgen, Charlie, inf, Jr.	.262	.346	.326	233	33	12	0	1	22	6

PITCHER, YEAR	W	L	ERA	G	GS	SV	IP	H	BB	SO
Boyd, Jimmy, Sr.	7	5	2.83	18	16	0	102	84	21	61
Brady, Denny, Fr.	0	0	8.76	11	1	0	12	16	7	13
Bridges, Matt, Fr.	2	1	2.98	28	0	1	42	29	18	45

Colmore, Cam, Fr.	2	0	1.64	8	1	0	11	5	4	9
Durazo, Nick, Sr.	1	1	4.35	14	4	1	21	25	10	24
Holba, Chris, Fr.	3	1	6.23	25	1	1	30	36	10	19
Ingle, Joe, So.	6	3	3.59	32	0	12	53	36	40	75
Kirkpatrick, Davis, So.	0	3	6.48	14	3	1	25	37	12	14
Kruczynski, Evan, Jr.	8	1	2.01	17	17	0	117	107	27	94
Lanier, Sam, Fr.	2	2	4.15	34	0	0	35	33	15	40
Voliva, Evan, So.	0	2	5.63	12	1	0	16	19	7	9
Wolfe, Jacob, Jr.	6	4	2.95	17	17	0	88	81	32	57

16. BOSTON COLLEGE

Coach: Mike Gambino. **Record:** 34-22.

PLAYER, POS., YEAR	AVG	OBP	SLG	AB	R	2B	3B	HR	RBI	SB
Adams, Johnny, inf, Jr.	.286	.345	.384	203	33	17	0	1	26	6
Balogh, Chris, 1b, Jr.	.219	.342	.250	32	1	1	0	0	1	1
Bigras, Mitch, 1b, So.	.261	.353	.330	115	14	5	0	1	14	3
Braren, Scott, of, So.	.333	.422	.423	78	10	4	0	1	16	0
Casey, Donovan, of, So.	.273	.348	.364	121	23	6	1	1	14	4
Cronin, Joe, inf, Sr.	.267	.375	.429	210	33	16	3	4	36	11
Hardaway, Dominic, c, Fr.	.188	.220	.250	48	8	3	0	0	4	4
Hernandez, Gabriel, inf, Sr.	.220	.331	.320	100	13	4	0	2	7	6
Hoggarth, Logan, inf, Sr.	.280	.355	.335	161	21	3	0	2	20	10
Martellini, Jason, of, Jr.	.224	.294	.327	107	11	3	1	2	14	0
Maselli, Anthony, 3b, So.	.227	.346	.364	44	6	1	1	1	6	0
Palomaki, Jake, 2b, So.	.258	.400	.300	213	46	9	0	0	25	19
Sauter, Stephen, c, Sr.	.197	.288	.310	71	6	2	0	2	8	1
Sciortino, Nick, inf, Jr.	.271	.372	.349	166	22	7	0	2	22	1
Strem, Michael, of, Jr.	.301	.377	.384	219	30	13	1	1	32	7

PITCHER, YEAR	W	L	ERA	G	GS	SV	IP	H	BB	SO
Adams, Jesse, Sr.	5	5	4.41	23	7	6	51	39	28	38
Casey, Donovan, So.	0	0	1.17	8	0	1	8	6	5	3
Dunn, Justin, Jr.	4	2	2.06	18	8	2	66	52	18	72
Hughes, Sean, Fr.	1	0	9.00	8	0	0	5	4	9	7
King, Mike, Jr.	8	4	3.29	17	16	0	104	110	31	64
Lane, Thomas, Fr.	1	2	6.83	11	7	0	29	31	16	16
Metzdorf, Dan, Fr.	0	0	8.00	17	1	0	9	14	8	10
Nelson, Jack, Fr.	2	0	4.20	9	0	0	15	17	4	12
Nicklas, John, Sr.	3	1	6.75	20	0	0	24	16	13	23
Rapp, Brian, So.	3	2	5.67	20	1	1	27	25	17	39
Skogsbergh, Bobby, So.	1	1	2.61	24	0	4	38	32	11	28
Stevens, Jacob, Fr.	4	4	2.54	15	14	0	74	61	33	70
Stromberg, Zach, Fr.	1	0	3.49	17	3	0	28	26	17	20
Witkowski, John, Fr.	2	0	3.10	19	0	0	20	16	8	20

17. CLEMSON

Coach: Monte Lee. **Record:** 44-20.

PLAYER, POS., YEAR	AVG	OBP	SLG	AB	R	2B	3B	HR	RBI	SB
Batson, Glenn, inf, So.	.043	.080	.087	23	1	0	0	0	2	0
Beer, Seth, of, Fr.	.369	.535	.700	203	57	13	0	18	70	1
Bryant, K.J., of, Fr.	.257	.337	.351	74	18	1	0	2	8	1
Campana, Jackson, 1b, Jr.	.100	.100	.100	10	1	0	0	0	1	0
Cox, Andrew, inf, Jr.	.224	.284	.327	107	10	3	1	2	16	3
Gibson, Maleeke, of, Jr.	.167	.375	.167	18	8	0	0	0	0	1
Greene, Jordan, inf, Fr.	.235	.422	.321	81	22	4	0	1	7	3
Jolly, Robert, c, So.	.217	.339	.250	92	10	3	0	0	12	1
Okey, Chris, c, Jr.	.339	.465	.611	239	61	16	2	15	74	4
Pinder, Chase, of, So.	.294	.412	.471	255	67	8	2	11	46	7
Renwick, Adam, inf, So.	.139	.259	.153	72	14	1	0	0	7	2
Rohlman, Reed, of, So.	.274	.374	.383	248	40	21	0	2	43	1
Triller, Mike, of, Sr.	.269	.350	.654	52	11	5	0	5	14	0
Wharton, Drew, of, So.	.154	.324	.154	26	0	0	0	0	6	0
White, Eli, inf, Jr.	.272	.389	.380	250	57	13	1	4	30	24
Williams, Chris, inf, So.	.245	.342	.413	184	34	5	1	8	38	2
Wilson, Weston, inf, Jr.	.279	.343	.434	251	50	12	3	7	45	8

PITCHER, YEAR	W	L	ERA	G	GS	SV	IP	H	BB	SO
Andrews, Patrick, Sr.	1	0	2.31	19	0	0	23	21	8	23
Barnes, Charlie, So.	6	4	4.66	16	16	0	95	97	24	84
Bostic, Alex, Jr.	4	2	5.13	26	1	2	33	26	27	44
Campbell, Paul, So.	0	0	11.17	12	0	0	10	16	5	9
Crawford, Brooks, Jr.	3	0	3.66	26	2	1	47	45	19	26
Eubanks, Alex, Fr.	6	5	4.09	23	11	3	81	93	21	70
Gilliam, Ryley, Fr.	3	2	6.10	15	6	0	31	26	18	16

	W	L	ERA	G	GS	SV	IP	H	BB	SO
Higginbotham, Jake, Fr.	3	0	4.59	8	7	0	33	39	21	28
Krall, Pat, Jr.	10	2	1.67	29	3	5	81	58	17	65
Lovorn, Garrett, Jr.	0	0	2.35	10	0	0	15	16	9	4
Papp, Andrew, Fr.	0	0	1.69	6	0	0	5	4	5	5
Schmidt, Clate, Sr.	8	5	4.83	18	15	0	86	105	21	68
Schnell, Alex, So.	0	0	6.11	21	3	0	28	38	13	19

18. MISSISSIPPI

Coach: Mike Bianco. **Record:** 43-19.

PLAYER, POS., YEAR	AVG	OBP	SLG	AB	R	2B	3B	HR	RBI	SB
Alejo, Ray, inf, Fr.	.000	.214	.000	11	2	0	0	0	1	0
Blackman, Tate, inf, So.	.322	.392	.435	230	48	13	2	3	38	3
Bortles, Colby, inf, Jr.	.269	.379	.475	219	37	21	0	8	50	0
Cloyd, Connor, of, Sr.	.219	.333	.247	73	13	2	0	0	10	1
Dishon, Cameron, of, Sr.	.225	.338	.378	111	18	5	0	4	22	9
Fitzsimmons, Michael, inf, Fr.	.265	.342	.429	98	12	7	0	3	14	0
Fortes, Nick, c, Fr.	.194	.356	.194	36	7	0	0	0	1	0
Golsan, Will, inf, So.	.273	.345	.377	231	45	11	2	3	31	5
Lartigue, Henri, c, Jr.	.353	.414	.464	207	37	11	0	4	31	2
Miller, D.J., of, Fr.	.111	.273	.111	18	4	0	0	0	1	0
Olenek, Ryan, inf, Fr.	.265	.327	.324	185	31	5	0	2	28	2
Perdzock, Holt, c, Sr.	.253	.364	.330	91	13	4	0	1	17	3
Perkins, Nic, c, So.	.067	.067	.067	15	0	0	0	0	0	0
Robinson, Errol, inf, Jr.	.270	.326	.352	256	45	10	4	1	36	9
Watson, Kyle, inf, So.	.231	.322	.397	78	17	4	0	3	9	5
Woodman, J.B., of, Jr.	.323	.412	.578	232	53	15	1	14	55	12

PITCHER, YEAR	W	L	ERA	G	GS	SV	IP	H	BB	SO
Bramlett, Brady, Jr.	8	3	3.17	16	16	0	82	79	23	96
Denny, Matt, Sr.	0	1	9.00	9	0	0	6	9	4	6
Feigl, Brady, Fr.	4	0	3.76	26	0	0	41	44	14	39
Green, Connor, Fr.	0	0	2.73	20	0	0	33	26	19	37
Johnson, Sean, Jr.	3	1	4.96	10	9	0	33	38	18	18
Lowe, Andrew, Fr.	0	0	3.00	8	0	0	9	4	7	8
McArthur, James, Fr.	6	1	4.26	15	12	0	61	66	20	61
Pagnozzi, Andy, Fr.	8	2	3.31	22	3	1	49	44	9	39
Parkinson, David, So.	5	3	2.78	22	9	0	68	74	24	50
Short, Wyatt, Jr.	2	3	2.90	22	1	11	40	38	10	31
Smith, Chad, Jr.	4	4	4.22	15	12	0	60	64	39	62
Stokes, Will, So.	2	1	2.93	30	0	7	43	37	7	40
Woolfolk, Dallas, Fr.	1	0	2.55	18	0	1	18	20	8	8

19. TULANE

Coach: David Pierce. **Record:** 41-21.

PLAYER, POS., YEAR	AVG	OBP	SLG	AB	R	2B	3B	HR	RBI	SB
Alemais, Stephen, inf, Jr.	.311	.368	.401	212	37	14	1	1	28	19
Braud, Matt, inf, Sr.	.154	.316	.615	13	2	0	0	2	5	0
Brown, Grant, of, Jr.	.184	.315	.368	76	16	5	0	3	12	0
Burns, Cameron, c, Jr.	.375	.464	.417	24	2	1	0	0	4	0
Carthon, Richard, of, Sr.	.270	.319	.378	148	21	4	6	0	23	5
DeHart, Jarret, of, Jr.	.182	.347	.312	77	17	5	1	1	7	2
Edwards, Cade, inf, Jr.	.211	.338	.281	57	12	4	0	0	7	1
Hope, Hunter, inf, Jr.	.267	.357	.507	221	46	9	1	14	36	3
Kaplan, Lex, of, Jr.	.253	.324	.343	233	32	9	0	4	34	6
Montalbano, Jeremy, c, Jr.	.269	.345	.500	234	35	14	2	12	45	0
Pierce, Shea, inf, Sr.	.148	.233	.148	27	2	0	0	0	2	0
Rogers, Jake, c, Jr.	.261	.384	.403	211	46	9	0	7	28	13
Rowland, Matt, inf, So.	.324	.439	.353	34	5	1	0	0	7	1
Williams, Hunter, 1b, Jr.	.294	.345	.581	136	20	10	1	9	30	0
Willsey, Jake, inf, Jr.	.265	.377	.535	170	28	10	3	10	31	0
Witherspoon, Grant, of, Fr.	.270	.373	.360	211	33	6	2	3	25	5

PITCHER, YEAR	W	L	ERA	G	GS	SV	IP	H	BB	SO
Bjorngjeld, Sam, So.	1	0	3.15	22	0	1	20	15	9	19
Colletti, Christian, Jr.	0	0	4.97	15	0	1	13	15	4	9
Duester, Patrick, Jr.	0	1	4.46	25	1	2	34	26	23	33
France, J.P., Jr.	6	4	3.33	19	12	0	76	72	27	67
Gibbs, Emerson, Sr.	6	4	2.61	16	16	0	110	88	24	88
Massey, Alex, Sr.	6	4	4.22	15	14	0	81	76	28	71
Massey, Ross, Fr.	10	3	2.29	18	12	0	90	87	18	51
Merrill, Corey, Jr.	4	1	2.05	15	5	3	53	41	19	63
Montalbano, Jeremy, Jr.	0	1	2.57	9	0	0	7	8	0	10
Rankin, Daniel, Jr.	2	1	2.82	16	0	2	22	21	14	25
Simms, Trevor, Jr.	4	1	3.44	16	1	1	18	11	11	22

	W	L	ERA	G	GS	SV	IP	H	BB	SO
Steel, Eric, Jr.	0	0	4.15	12	0	0	13	17	2	14
Yandel, Tim, Sr.	2	1	6.11	13	1	0	18	19	10	19

20. VANDERBILT

Coach: Tim Corbin. **Record:** 43-19.

PLAYER, POS., YEAR	AVG	OBP	SLG	AB	R	2B	3B	HR	RBI	SB
Campbell, Tyler, inf, Sr.	.259	.333	.318	170	36	4	3	0	22	7
Coleman, Ro, inf, Jr.	.236	.317	.292	161	37	4	1	1	13	3
Delay, Jason, c, Jr.	.248	.296	.336	149	17	10	0	1	31	1
Ellison, Karl, c, Jr.	.213	.270	.388	80	12	6	1	2	11	0
Gristanti, Walker, of, Fr.	.349	.481	.605	43	14	2	1	1	10	0
Infante, Johnny, inf, Fr.	.259	.333	.541	85	17	4	1	6	20	1
Jones, Alonzo, inf, Fr.	.285	.371	.418	165	32	15	2	1	35	10
Kaiser, Connor, inf, Fr.	.261	.362	.311	119	23	4	1	0	19	3
Kendall, Jeren, of, So.	.332	.396	.568	250	63	16	8	9	59	28
Murfee, Penn, inf, Fr.	.290	.351	.377	69	7	4	1	0	12	1
Paul, Ethan, inf, Fr.	.305	.406	.485	167	33	14	2	4	31	9
Reynolds, Bryan, of, Jr.	.330	.461	.603	224	59	16	3	13	56	8
Rodgers, Nolan, of, Jr.	.185	.258	.259	27	4	2	0	0	6	1
Sabino, Liam, inf, So.	.302	.400	.419	43	7	2	0	1	8	4
Scott, Stephen, of, Fr.	.091	.200	.091	22	2	0	0	0	2	0
Smith, Kyle, of, Sr.	.227	.352	.364	88	15	3	0	3	12	3
Toffey, Will, inf, So.	.227	.387	.266	203	37	6	1	0	23	9

PITCHER, YEAR	W	L	ERA	G	GS	SV	IP	H	BB	SO
Abraham, Joey, So.	0	0	5.40	7	1	1	17	13	6	22
Bowden, Ben, Jr.	2	1	3.51	24	5	10	49	48	14	65
Conger, Maddux, Fr.	0	0	0.79	9	0	0	11	5	7	12
Day, Chandler, Fr.	2	1	4.26	10	3	0	25	30	12	26
Everett, Donny, Fr.	0	1	1.50	6	2	0	12	11	5	13
Johnson, Ryan, So.	4	0	4.26	14	2	0	32	39	7	12
Kilichowski, John, Jr.	1	2	5.06	10	2	2	27	29	9	21
McGarry, Matt, Fr.	1	0	3.27	7	2	0	11	12	9	12
Raby, Patrick, Fr.	7	1	2.61	15	10	2	59	35	19	63
Ruppenthal, Matt, So.	5	2	2.33	25	0	1	46	24	27	59
Sheffield, Jordan, So.	8	6	3.01	16	16	0	102	82	40	113
Snider, Collin, So.	4	0	2.57	23	0	0	35	37	6	30
Steele, Evan, Fr.	1	0	4.63	11	0	0	12	11	5	14
Stone, Hayden, Jr.	0	1	4.22	10	3	2	21	15	13	24
Wright, Kyle, So.	8	4	3.09	16	15	0	93	82	32	107

21. VIRGINIA

Coach: Brian O'Connor. **Record:** 38-22.

PLAYER, POS., YEAR	AVG	OBP	SLG	AB	R	2B	3B	HR	RBI	SB
Clement, Ernie, inf, So.	.351	.383	.443	262	62	13	4	1	30	6
Cody, Charlie, inf, So.	.220	.313	.402	82	12	6	0	3	18	0
Coman, Robbie, c, Sr.	.200	.333	.200	15	1	0	0	0	1	0
Doherty, Kevin, of, Sr.	.261	.280	.261	23	2	0	0	0	6	0
Dozier, Doak, of, Fr.	.217	.267	.333	69	9	2	0	2	6	1
Eikhoff, Nate, inf, Fr.	.284	.321	.441	102	10	7	3	1	17	2
Gerstenmaier, Jack, inf, So.	.284	.398	.365	74	13	3	0	1	12	2
Haseley, Adam, of, So.	.304	.377	.502	247	61	19	6	6	37	3
Karstetter, Ryan, inf, Fr.	.225	.254	.275	120	15	4	1	0	12	0
McCarthy, Jake, of, Fr.	.368	.429	.368	19	3	0	0	0	2	0
Novak, Justin, inf, So.	.274	.350	.335	164	26	4	0	2	29	1
Pinero, Daniel, inf, Jr.	.340	.441	.500	212	50	20	1	4	39	5
Simmons, Cameron, of, Fr.	.261	.313	.412	165	29	13	0	4	21	3
Smith, Pavin, 1b, So.	.329	.410	.513	228	43	16	1	8	57	2
Thaiss, Matt, c, Jr.	.375	.473	.578	232	55	13	2	10	59	0
Weber, Andy, inf, Fr.	.269	.314	.323	93	16	3	1	0	11	0

PITCHER, YEAR	W	L	ERA	G	GS	SV	IP	H	BB	SO
Bettinger, Alec, Jr.	3	5	5.43	23	8	7	61	59	30	53
Doherty, Kevin, Sr.	1	1	3.86	27	0	7	37	37	14	25
Doyle, Tommy, So.	2	7	5.06	22	7	3	64	63	19	51
Grounds, Holden, Jr.	0	0	2.79	6	1	0	10	8	7	7
Harrington, Chesdin, Fr.	1	1	9.00	11	0	0	11	15	10	7
Haseley, Adam, So.	9	3	1.73	13	13	0	78	54	21	48
Jones, Connor, Jr.	11	1	2.34	15	15	0	104	85	38	72
Lynch, Daniel, Fr.	1	3	5.49	13	9	0	41	44	15	37
Roberts, Jack, Jr.	0	0	3.26	15	0	0	19	7	19	24
Rosenberger, David, Sr.	2	0	7.76	17	2	0	31	42	8	26
Shambora, Tyler, Jr.	5	1	3.22	24	0	1	50	47	13	35
Sousa, Bennett, So.	3	0	7.92	16	3	0	25	30	19	23

22. LOUISIANA-LAFAYETTE

Coach: Tony Robichaux. **Record:** 43-21.

PLAYER, POS., YEAR	AVG	OBP	SLG	AB	R	2B	3B	HR	RBI	SB
Antchak, Brad, inf, Jr.	.246	.343	.336	122	22	8	0	1	12	5
Clement, Kyle, of, Sr.	.353	.415	.516	184	33	14	2	4	25	9
Conrad, Brenn, inf, Jr.	.280	.384	.411	214	30	16	0	4	43	5
Edwards, Ishmael, of, Jr.	.265	.347	.373	83	15	6	0	1	10	5
Fontenot, Kennon, inf, So.	.240	.354	.396	96	16	4	1	3	12	3
Herrington, Derek, of, Sr.	.225	.321	.324	71	16	5	1	0	8	1
Kasuls, Hunter, inf, Fr.	.234	.315	.289	128	22	2	1	1	11	4
Mills, Brian, of, Sr.	.269	.325	.383	175	31	8	0	4	37	5
Pinero, Alex, inf, Jr.	.312	.355	.406	138	17	5	1	2	24	1
Poncho, Dylon, inf, Fr.	.255	.417	.340	47	6	4	0	0	7	1
Rizer, Johnny, of, Fr.	-	.000	-	14	2	0	0	0	0	0
Robbins, Joe, inf, Jr.	.286	.387	.491	220	46	7	4	10	37	10
Sensley, Steven, inf, So.	.252	.349	.417	151	17	7	0	6	23	2
Thurman, Nick, c, Sr.	.281	.341	.380	221	32	16	0	2	29	1
Trosclair, Stefan, inf, Sr.	.277	.386	.468	231	48	13	5	7	39	7

PITCHER, YEAR	W	L	ERA	G	GS	SV	IP	H	BB	SO
Bacon, Will, Sr.	1	0	3.53	17	0	1	36	43	13	33
Bazar, Reagan, Jr.	1	0	1.93	9	0	0	9	4	5	3
Carter, Eric, Sr.	6	2	2.08	26	0	4	52	37	12	69
Charpentier, Chris, Jr.	0	0	4.80	12	0	0	15	12	4	15
Guillory, Evan, So.	5	6	4.34	16	15	0	75	69	15	58
Harris, Hogan, Fr.	2	0	3.90	16	2	1	28	29	11	26
Huval, Jevin, Sr.	3	1	3.11	24	0	3	38	33	15	32
Lee, Nick, Fr.	7	1	3.31	16	16	0	87	69	27	75
Leger, Gunner, So.	7	3	2.26	16	16	0	92	71	24	81
Marks, Wyatt, So.	5	7	4.50	15	15	0	76	75	20	80
Moore, Dylan, So.	6	1	0.91	26	0	14	50	24	15	59

23. FLORIDA ATLANTIC

Coach: John McCormack. **Record:** 39-19.

PLAYER, POS., YEAR	AVG	OBP	SLG	AB	R	2B	3B	HR	RBI	SB
Bonilla Traverso, Jose, of, So.	.179	.300	.224	67	7	3	0	0	4	2
Chatham, C.J., inf, Jr.	.357	.422	.554	249	48	17	4	8	50	2
Dicks, Christian, of, Sr.	.276	.382	.356	225	32	13	1	1	33	4
Endris, Billy, of, Sr.	.288	.367	.378	222	38	10	2	2	31	8
Frank, Tyler, inf, Fr.	.285	.401	.365	137	22	8	0	1	27	3
Kerr, Stephen, inf, Jr.	.252	.341	.368	242	47	11	1	5	37	17
Labsan, Sean, of, Jr.	.268	.349	.436	149	23	6	2	5	23	0
Lambert, Gunnar, c, So.	.306	.433	.449	98	22	9	1	1	11	1
Langham, Austin, inf, Jr.	.320	.421	.392	197	37	12	1	0	23	1
Lashley, Brett, inf, Jr.	.274	.370	.340	197	38	13	0	0	30	5
Puerta, Esteban, inf, Jr.	.307	.401	.500	228	39	14	0	10	52	2

PITCHER, YEAR	W	L	ERA	G	GS	SV	IP	H	BB	SO
Carr, Devon, Sr.	5	1	2.29	31	0	1	35	27	10	27
Coursel, Robbie, Sr.	5	3	2.73	18	1	0	33	27	10	30
House, Alex, So.	2	1	3.13	23	0	1	37	35	15	30
Labsan, Sean, Jr.	5	1	1.96	11	10	1	46	40	17	39
McKay, David, Jr.	3	6	3.74	14	14	0	75	62	26	66
Nowatnick, Mark, So.	1	1	3.38	13	1	0	21	27	5	14
O'Connell, Colyn, Jr.	2	1	2.00	22	0	0	27	24	10	19
Ragsdale, Cameron, Jr.	0	1	1.61	24	0	15	28	18	11	21
Rhodes, Brandon, Sr.	7	4	4.09	16	15	0	99	99	15	52
Stewart, Marc, Fr.	6	0	3.58	15	15	0	78	69	32	45
Swan, Nick, Fr.	3	0	3.09	19	2	0	35	38	10	22

24. SOUTHERN MISSISSIPPI

Coach: Scott Berry. **Record:** 41-20.

PLAYER, POS., YEAR	AVG	OBP	SLG	AB	R	2B	3B	HR	RBI	SB
Braley, Taylor, inf, So.	.323	.450	.688	96	23	5	0	10	31	0
Burdeaux, Dylan, of, Jr.	.331	.418	.525	257	59	13	2	11	41	8
Cooper, Storme, inf, Fr.	.237	.377	.275	131	26	5	0	0	25	2
Dawson, Nick, inf, Sr.	.328	.432	.473	201	43	19	2	2	37	6
Gilber, Michael, inf, Sr.	.194	.342	.274	62	9	2	0	1	10	0
Hadley, Tracy, inf, Jr.	.256	.338	.339	121	18	3	2	1	14	3
Keating, Daniel, inf, So.	.303	.401	.486	142	28	9	1	5	29	7
Lynch, Tim, inf, Sr.	.365	.470	.545	233	49	12	0	10	59	0
Robinson, Chuckie, c, Jr.	.288	.349	.433	208	31	7	1	7	44	0
Rubiera, Claudio, c, Jr.	.208	.286	.500	24	3	1	0	2	8	0
Sandlin, Jake, of, Sr.	.353	.436	.540	235	57	17	3	7	39	2
Scott, Chase, inf, Sr.	.240	.387	.433	171	36	12	0	7	29	0
Slater, Hunter, inf, Fr.	.314	.372	.458	153	28	10	0	4	26	1

PITCHER, YEAR	W	L	ERA	G	GS	SV	IP	H	BB	SO
Case, Houston, Jr.	0	1	7.94	3	1	0	6	4	4	5
Cockrell, Cord, Sr.	7	2	4.13	15	15	0	70	77	9	45
Coughlin, Bryan, Sr.	0	0	2.84	5	0	0	6	7	3	4
Johnson, Nick, Sr.	3	1	4.19	19	8	2	58	60	25	50
Livingston, Cody, Sr.	2	2	5.66	19	0	4	21	24	8	23
Lowery, Luke, Sr.	4	0	5.12	28	0	0	19	24	6	17
McCarty, Kirk, So.	8	1	3.15	17	16	0	89	100	27	89
Millet, Austin, Fr.	1	1	5.21	13	0	0	19	10	15	9
Powell, Walker, Fr.	4	3	3.46	18	4	0	39	44	9	32
Powers, Stevie, Fr.	1	1	4.64	18	5	0	33	25	22	26
Roberts, Hayden, So.	0	0	3.95	7	2	0	14	10	12	13
Sandlin, Nick, Fr.	3	3	2.38	26	0	12	42	32	20	44
Stevens, Hunter, Jr.	0	1	9.58	7	2	0	10	14	9	14
Tageant, Clay, Sr.	0	0	0.61	15	0	0	15	10	10	12
Walley, Sam, Jr.	1	2	5.57	9	3	1	21	26	14	18
Winston, Jake, Sr.	7	2	4.68	22	5	1	67	64	28	50

25. NORTH CAROLINA STATE

Coach: Elliott Avent. **Record:** 38-22.

PLAYER, POS., YEAR	AVG	OBP	SLG	AB	R	2B	3B	HR	RBI	SB
DeJuneas, Tommy, p, So.	.118	.211	.118	17	3	0	0	0	1	0
Deatherage, Brock, of, So.	.313	.391	.473	224	45	8	5	6	39	14
Dunand, Joe, inf, So.	.297	.345	.424	236	35	18	0	4	41	3
Edwards, Storm, of, Jr.	.333	.556	.333	12	6	0	0	0	2	0
Kinneman, Brett, of, Fr.	.296	.405	.526	135	33	13	0	6	32	2
Knizner, Andrew, 3b, Jr.	.292	.359	.388	240	40	5	0	6	30	3
LeGrant, Xavier, inf, Fr.	.245	.375	.358	53	12	3	0	1	5	2
McLain, Josh, inf, So.	.300	.359	.465	213	41	19	2	4	37	13
Mendoza, Evan, 3b, So.	.362	.417	.449	196	31	5	0	4	33	3
Palmeiro, Preston, 1b, Jr.	.337	.412	.539	243	53	20	1	9	55	1
Pitarra, Stephen, inf, So.	.291	.376	.347	199	36	9	1	0	25	2
Shepard, Shane, inf, So.	.258	.396	.461	89	12	8	2	2	13	1
Shepard, Chance, of, So.	.279	.384	.558	215	50	15	0	15	54	3
Suggs, Garrett, of, So.	.214	.353	.286	14	5	1	0	0	0	0
Willard, Ryne, inf, Sr.	.268	.289	.341	41	6	3	0	0	8	0

PITCHER, YEAR	W	L	ERA	G	GS	SV	IP	H	BB	SO
Adler, Sean, Jr.	0	1	6.94	19	1	0	23	24	21	26
Beckman, Cody, So.	2	0	6.05	16	0	0	19	14	8	23
Brabrand, Evan, So.	1	1	7.23	17	0	1	24	30	9	29
Brown, Brian, So.	7	3	3.70	17	17	0	88	84	32	79
DeJuneas, Tommy, So.	2	3	6.37	24	0	6	30	35	19	27
Demby, Christian, Fr.	0	1	7.27	7	1	0	9	12	4	9
Gilbert, Will, Sr.	5	1	2.22	24	0	6	53	48	11	62
Keglovits, Karl, Jr.	1	0	4.50	10	1	0	14	14	10	11
O'Donnell, Joe, Jr.	3	2	4.02	6	4	0	31	30	12	25
Orwig, Travis, Sr.	1	0	1.93	17	0	0	19	16	13	21
Piedmonte, Johnny, Jr.	1	3	5.56	13	8	1	34	35	22	28
Staley, Austin, Fr.	3	1	3.16	26	0	0	26	17	11	23
Wilder, Cory, Jr.	3	4	4.61	15	13	0	57	51	30	40
Williams, Chris, Sr.	2	0	2.51	22	0	1	32	39	7	14
Williamson, Ryan, Jr.	7	2	2.69	15	13	0	70	60	38	77

NCAA regional teams in bold. Conference category leaders in bold.
*Team won conference's automatic regional bid. #Category leader who did not qualify for batting or pitching title.

AMERICA EAST CONFERENCE

	Conference		Overall	
	W	L	W	L
*Binghamton	19	5	30	23
Hartford	14	9	37	18
Stony Brook	13	9	27	27
Maryland-Baltimore County	13	10	28	23
Albany	9	14	23	30
Maine	8	15	20	35
Massachusetts-Lowell	5	19	20	32

All-Conference Team: C—Hunter Dolshun, Jr., Maryland-Baltimore County. **1B**—David MacKinnon, Jr., Hartford. **2B**—Reed Gamache, Sr., Binghamton. **3B**—T.J. Ward, So., Hartford. **SS**—Ben Bengtson, So., Hartford. **OF**—C.J. Krowiak, So., Binghamton; Chris DelDebbio, Sr., Hartford; Anthony Gatto, Sr., Maryland-Baltimore County. **DH**—Kevin Lachance, Sr., Maryland-Baltimore County. **UTIL**—Eddie Posavec, Jr., Binghamton. **SP**—Mike Bunal, Sr., Binghamton; Logan Fullmer, Sr., Maine; Conrad Wozniak, Sr., Maryland-Baltimore County; Chad Lee, Sr., Stony Brook. **Player of the Year:** David MacKinnon, Hartford. **Pitcher of the Year:** Mike Bunal, Binghamton. **Rookie of the Year:** Bret Clarke, Stony Brook. **Coach of the Year:** Tim Sinicki, Binghamton.

INDIVIDUAL BATTING LEADERS
(Minimum 140 At-Bats)

	AVG	OBP	SLG	AB	2B	3B	HR	RBI	SB
David MacKinnon, Hartford	**.392**	**.471**	.544	217	15	3	4	34	5
Kevin Lachance, UMBC	.371	.450	.537	205	14	1	6	29	**28**
Reed Gamache, Binghamton	.366	.452	.545	202	15	0	7	46	8
Anthony Gatto, UMBC	.358	.429	.491	159	9	0	4	24	3
Aaron Wilson, Hartford	.349	.446	.497	195	8	**6**	3	17	20
Matt Hinchy, Albany	.349	.402	.429	175	9	1	1	34	2
Hunter Dolshun, UMBC	.345	.416	**.603**	174	6	0	**13**	47	1
Erik Ostberg, Hartford	.340	.444	.431	197	12	0	2	47	5
Eddie Posavec, Binghamton	.319	.403	.432	185	13	4	0	26	6
Ben Bengston, Hartford	.316	.385	.540	187	14	5	6	**51**	5
C.J. Krowiak, Binghamton	.314	.366	.368	**223**	10	1	0	27	16
Casey Baker, Stony Brook	.314	.392	.367	188	8	1	0	31	4
T.J. Ward, Hartford	.313	.378	.425	179	9	1	3	35	2
Kyle Sacks, Albany	.311	.382	.404	193	8	2	2	30	9
Danny Casals, Maine	.310	.404	.455	200	12	4	3	21	12
Brendan Skidmore, Binghamton	.307	.381	.521	192	10	2	9	42	0
Andruw Gazzola, Stony Brook	.304	.368	.411	207	12	2	2	22	3
Paul Rufo, Binghamton	.304	.388	.409	171	12	0	2	26	5
Chris Deldebbio, Hartford	.302	.405	.495	192	17	1	6	42	2
Colin Ridley, Maine	.299	.338	.497	177	13	2	6	42	3
Andrew Casali, UMBC	.296	.343	.451	162	10	**6**	1	27	7
Jamie Switalski, UMBC	.295	.365	.443	176	14	0	4	40	1
Toby Handley, Stony Brook	.288	.394	.377	191	6	4	1	21	12
Jack Parenty, Stony Brook	.286	.373	.354	189	8	1	1	31	6
Kevin Donati, Albany	.284	.335	.324	176	5	1	0	18	18
Tyler Schanwz, Maine	.267	.342	.451	195	**19**	1	5	25	8

INDIVIDUAL PITCHING LEADERS
(Minimum 40 Innings Pitched)

	W	L	ERA	G	SV	IP	H	BB	SO
Chad Lee, Stony Brook	6	4	**1.97**	16	1	82	68	21	56
Bret Clarke, Stony Brook	6	2	2.19	15	0	62	55	34	55
Logan Fullmer, Maine	4	2	2.55	17	3	71	62	17	70
Kyle Gauthier, Hartford	5	2	2.76	12	0	75	63	16	48
Cory Callahan, UMBC	0	3	2.89	20	1	53	53	17	28
Conrad Wozniak, UMBC	6	3	3.32	14	0	76	65	24	57
Mike Bunal, Binghamton	**8**	4	3.41	16	0	**90**	74	46	87
Brian Murphy, Hartford	7	2	3.48	14	1	75	70	31	49
Ryan Brendan, Albany	5	4	3.86	15	1	63	55	30	48
Rob Hardy, Binghamton	1	4	3.88	**21**	6	65	66	16	45
John Arel, Maine	2	**9**	3.94	15	0	75	76	20	77
Andrew Ryan, UMass-Lowell	3	7	4.11	12	0	70	69	30	54
Steve Xirinachs, UMass-Lowell	1	**9**	4.28	13	0	61	58	31	34
Jake Cryts, Binghamton	7	4	5.22	16	0	79	92	32	36

	W	L	ERA	G	SV	IP	H	BB	SO
Tyler Honahan, Stony Brook	5	6	5.25	14	0	70	70	36	62
Woods Stephen, Albany	3	5	5.57	14	0	65	69	41	**88**
Nick Kuzia, UMass-Lowell	3	6	5.88	13	0	64	74	28	40
Jake Wloczewski, Binghamton	4	0	3.06	10	1	50	37	17	17
Nick Wegmann, Binghamton	2	0	3.32	16	0	41	41	10	27
Sam McKay, Hartford	4	2	3.77	16	1	45	54	10	24
Jacob Christian, UMBC	3	1	4.17	16	0	50	44	19	38
Kendall Pomeroy, UMass-Lowell	4	0	4.24	20	0	40	50	**9**	25
Justin Courtney, Maine	2	3	4.30	8	0	44	48	12	30
Jonah Normandeau, Maine	1	2	4.50	13	0	42	44	18	36
Stinar Ryan, Albany	5	2	4.87	9	0	41	34	20	40
Nick Silva, Maine	3	4	5.89	**21**	7	65	66	16	45
Chris Murphy, Maine	0	4	6.05	13	0	42	**29**	45	54

AMERICAN ATHLETIC CONFERENCE

	Conference		Overall	
	W	L	W	L
Tulane	15	7	41	21
East Carolina	16	8	38	23
*Connecticut	14	9	38	25
Cincinnati	13	10	26	30
Houston	11	12	36	23
Memphis	9	15	22	39
Central Florida	8	16	26	33
South Florida	8	16	24	33

All-Conference Team: C—Jake Rogers, Jr., Tulane. **1B**—Joe Davis, Fr., Houston. **2B**—Kevin Merrell, So., South Florida. **3B**—Willy Yahn, So., Connecticut. **SS**—Stephen Alemais, Jr., Tulane. **OF**—Joe DeRoche-Duffin, Sr., Connecticut; Dwanya Williams-Sutton, Fr., East Carolina; Corey Julks, So., Houston. **DH**—Jeremy Montalbano, Jr., Tulane. **UTIL**—Connor Wong, So., Houston. **SP**—Andrew Zellner, Jr., Cincinnati; Anthony Kay, Jr., Connecticut; Evan Kruczynski, Jr., East Carolina; Emerson Gibbs, Sr., Tulane. **RP**—Nick Hernandez, Jr., Houston. **Player of the Year:** Joe DeRoche-Duffin, Connecticut. **Pitcher of the Year:** Anthony Kay, Connecticut. **Rookie Position Player of the Year:** Joe Davis, Houston. **Rookie Pitcher of the Year:** Tim Cate, Connecticut. **Coach of the Year:** Jim Penders, Connecticut.

INDIVIDUAL BATTING LEADERS
(Minimum 140 At-Bats)

	AVG	OBP	SLG	AB	2B	3B	HR	RBI	SB
Dwanya Williams-Sutton, ECU	**.360**	**.455**	.551	178	11	4	5	27	7
Corey Julks, Houston	.332	.409	.439	196	10	1	3	28	10
Joe Davis, Houston	.331	.383	**.577**	239	17	0	14	**58**	0
Travis Watkins, East Carolina	.326	.407	.476	233	14	0	7	44	3
Kevin Merrell, South Florida	.320	.418	.401	147	5	2	1	22	16
Willy Yahn, UConn	.319	.355	.453	**276**	**20**	4	3	46	7
Bobby Melley, UConn	.313	.438	.526	230	16	0	11	55	1
Stephen Alemais, Tulane	.311	.368	.401	212	14	1	1	28	19
Garrett Brooks, East Carolina	.308	.374	.420	169	14	1	1	20	6
Eric Tyler, East Carolina	.306	.381	.426	242	14	0	5	36	9
Connor Wong, Houston	.304	.415	.435	230	13	1	5	30	9
Darien Tubbs, Memphis	.304	.379	.441	227	12	5	3	24	22
John Toppa, UConn	.303	.383	.374	155	8	0	1	23	7
Jake Little, Memphis	.301	.384	.410	229	14	1	3	29	12
Brennan Bozeman, Central Fla.	.299	.389	.344	157	5	1	0	22	9
Connor Hollis, Houston	.294	.377	.350	180	6	2	0	16	2
Brandon Grudzielanek, Memphis	.292	.321	.373	236	8	1	3	32	10
Connor McVey, Cincinnati	.292	.379	.420	212	15	0	4	27	**27**
Bryan Daniello, UConn	.289	.353	.415	246	15	2	4	38	13
Parker Lamm, East Carolina	.287	.332	.321	217	6	1	0	28	12
Eli Putnam, Central Florida	.287	.340	.410	188	9	1	4	26	10
Kam Gellinger, Central Florida	.282	.365	.400	195	17	0	2	21	5
Michael Pyeatt, Houston	.282	.345	.333	177	5	2	0	10	0
Turner Brown, East Carolina	.281	.379	.352	199	5	0	3	34	9
Chris Carrier, Memphis	.280	.351	.467	214	16	3	6	38	15

	AVG	OBP	SLG	AB	2B	3B	HR	RBI	SB
Richard Carthon, Tulane	.270	.319	.378	148	4	6	0	23	5
Joe Deroche-Duffin, UConn	.266	.382	.549	233	15	0	17	55	1

INDIVIDUAL PITCHING LEADERS
(Minimum 40 Innings Pitched)

	W	L	ERA	G	SV	IP	H	BB	SO
Trey Cumbie, Houston	5	2	1.29	15	0	56	42	9	42
Nick Hernandez, Houston	3	0	1.40	29	11	51	27	11	66
Robby Howell, Central Florida	7	4	1.96	15	0	101	74	35	65
Evan Kruczynski, East Carolina	8	1	2.01	17	0	117	107	27	95
Corey Merrill, Tulane	4	1	2.05	15	3	53	41	19	63
Tommy Eveld, South Florida	0	3	2.21	26	9	53	36	24	67
Patrick Ruotolo, UConn	2	2	2.25	25	12	40	33	11	47
Seth Romero, Houston	6	4	2.29	15	0	94	60	28	113
Ross Massey, Tulane	10	3	2.29	18	0	90	87	18	51
Andrew Zellner, Cincinnati	7	4	2.32	15	0	109	91	29	66
Brandon Lawson, South Florida	5	5	2.50	15	0	101	83	30	111
Emerson Gibbs, Tulane	6	4	2.61	16	0	110	88	24	88
Anthony Kay, UConn	9	2	2.65	17	0	119	99	37	111
Andrew Lantrip, Houston	6	6	2.70	15	0	90	80	5	84
Tim Cate, UConn	5	1	2.73	14	0	82	55	27	101
Jimmy Boyd, East Carolina	7	5	2.83	18	0	102	84	21	61
Mitch Ullom, Houston	7	4	2.88	14	0	78	71	14	39
Bubba Maxwell, Houston	1	1	2.89	18	3	44	41	13	45
Jacob Wolfe, East Carolina	6	4	2.95	17	0	88	81	32	57
J.T. Perez, Cincinnati	6	5	2.97	14	0	91	97	14	58
Matt Bridges, East Carolina	2	1	2.98	28	2	42	29	18	45
William Montgomerie, UConn	6	3	3.04	16	0	74	64	24	87
A.J. Kullman, Cincinnati	4	3	3.20	19	3	56	47	21	33
J.P. France, Tulane	6	4	3.33	19	0	76	72	27	67
Harrison Hukari, Central Florida	3	3	3.38	33	3	53	49	39	44
Joe Ingle, East Carolina	6	3	3.59	32	12	53	36	40	75
Colton Hathcock, Memphis	5	8	3.94	15	0	82	77	37	71

	AVG	OBP	SLG	AB	2B	3B	HR	RBI	SB
Brandon Lopez, Miami	.376	.449	.469	213	14	0	2	42	5
Nick Solak, Louisville	.376	.470	.564	165	14	1	5	29	9
Matt Thaiss, Virginia	.375	.473	.578	232	13	2	10	59	0
John Sansone, Florida State	.370	.455	.576	257	26	0	9	65	8
Seth Beer, Clemson	.369	.535	.700	203	13	0	18	70	1
Evan Mendoza, N.C. State	.362	.417	.449	196	5	0	4	33	3
Devin Hairston, Louisville	.361	.415	.478	249	16	2	3	45	3
Zack Collins, Miami	.357	.538	.649	185	9	0	15	57	1
Taylor Walls, Florida State	.355	.479	.516	248	20	1	6	46	14
Trevor Craport, Georgia Tech	.352	.414	.543	199	15	1	7	31	4
Ernie Clement, Virginia	.351	.383	.443	262	13	4	1	30	6
Brian Miller, North Carolina	.345	.440	.469	226	12	5	2	33	21
Johnny Ruiz, Miami	.342	.431	.491	234	17	3	4	57	3
Blake Tiberi, Louisville	.340	.387	.553	244	18	2	10	51	2
Daniel Pinero, Virginia	.340	.441	.500	212	20	1	4	40	5
Nick Anderson, Virginia Tech	.339	.418	.483	174	13	0	4	30	0
Chris Okey, Clemson	.339	.465	.611	239	16	2	15	74	4
Preston Palmeiro, N.C. State	.337	.412	.539	243	20	1	9	55	1
Logan Warmoth, North Carolina	.337	.402	.481	208	14	2	4	53	8
Carl Chester, Miami	.336	.426	.395	253	9	0	2	29	16
Justin Bellinger, Duke	.336	.417	.571	140	10	1	7	32	1
Frank Maldonado, Pittsburgh	.330	.415	.449	185	5	7	1	25	5
Corey Ray, Louisville	.310	.388	.545	268	16	1	15	60	44

INDIVIDUAL PITCHING LEADERS
(Minimum 40 Innings Pitched)

	W	L	ERA	G	SV	IP	H	BB	SO
Matthew Gorst, Georgia Tech	2	1	0.55	28	12	49	30	13	55
Pat Krall, Clemson	10	2	1.67	29	5	81	58	17	65
Adam Haseley, Virginia	9	3	1.73	13	0	78	54	21	48
Drew Harrington, Louisville	12	2	1.95	17	0	111	92	25	92
Justin Dunn, Boston College	4	2	2.06	18	2	66	52	18	72
Brandon Bielak, Notre Dame	3	2	2.10	15	1	56	43	25	54
Michael Hearne, Notre Dame	8	2	2.13	14	0	80	64	15	42
Jesse Lepore, Miami	9	0	2.20	14	0	74	59	28	57
Will Gilbert, N.C. State	5	1	2.22	24	6	53	48	11	62
Brendan McKay, Louisville	12	4	2.30	17	0	110	89	42	128
Connor Jones, Virginia	11	1	2.34	15	0	104	85	38	72
Brandon Gold, Georgia Tech	9	3	2.48	16	0	105	109	31	81
Kade McClure, Louisville	12	0	2.54	15	0	78	49	20	77
Jacob Stevens, Boston College	4	4	2.54	15	0	74	61	33	70
Ed Voyles, Florida State	1	2	2.66	23	1	47	53	19	41
Zac Gallen, North Carolina	5	6	2.68	13	0	91	68	21	95
Ryan Williamson, N.C. State	7	2	2.69	15	0	70	60	38	77
Frankie Bartow, Miami	6	0	2.72	43	0	56	56	10	29
Tyler Holton, Florida State	3	4	2.79	18	1	68	60	33	84
A.J. Bogucki, North Carolina	5	5	2.86	28	1	50	39	25	53
Kellen Urbon, Duke	7	2	2.87	21	0	88	74	17	47
J.B. Bukauskas, North Carolina	7	2	3.10	13	0	78	68	29	111
T.J. Zeuch, Pittsburgh	6	1	3.10	10	0	70	61	19	74
Jim Voyles, Florida State	6	1	3.16	25	2	51	35	18	48
Parker Dunshee, Wake Forest	10	5	3.20	16	0	101	98	32	102
Donnie Sellers, Wake Forest	5	5	5.65	36	5	43	46	21	25

ATLANTIC COAST CONFERENCE

Atlantic Division	Conference		Overall	
	W	L	W	L
Louisville	22	8	50	14
Florida State	16	10	40	22
North Carolina State	15	13	38	22
*Clemson	16	14	44	20
Boston College	13	15	35	22
Wake Forest	13	13	35	27
Notre Dame	11	17	27	27

Coastal Division	Conference		Overall	
	W	L	W	L
Miami	21	7	50	14
Virginia	19	11	38	22
Duke	14	15	33	24
Georgia Tech	13	16	38	25
North Carolina	13	17	34	21
Pittsburgh	10	18	25	26
Virginia Tech	6	24	19	36

All-Conference Team: C—Chris Okey, Jr., Clemson; Zack Collins, Jr., Miami. **1B**—Tristin English, Fr., Georgia Tech. **2B**—Nate Mondou, Jr., Wake Forest. **3B**—Will Craig, Jr., Wake Forest. **SS**—Charles Leblanc, So., Pittsburgh. **OF**—Seth Beer, Fr., Clemson; Kel Johnson, So., Georgia Tech; Matt Gonzalez, Sr., Georgia Tech; Corey Ray, Jr., Louisville. **DH/UT**—Brendan McKay, So., Louisville. **SP**—Drew Harrington, Jr., Louisville; Brendan McKay, So., Louisville; Connor Jones, Jr., Virginia. **RP**—Zack Burdi, Jr., Louisville. **Player of the Year:** Seth Beer, Clemson. **Pitcher of the Year:** Drew Harrington, Louisville. **Freshman of the Year:** Seth Beer, Clemson. **Coach of the Year:** Dan McDonnell, Louisville.

INDIVIDUAL BATTING LEADERS
(Minimum 140 At-Bats)

	AVG	OBP	SLG	AB	2B	3B	HR	RBI	SB
Charles LeBlanc, Pittsburgh	.405	.494	.513	195	9	3	2	46	6
Will Smith, Louisville	.382	.480	.567	157	8	0	7	43	9
Will Craig, Wake Forest	.379	.520	.731	182	16	0	16	66	0
Matt Gonzalez, Georgia Tech	.378	.419	.577	246	16	0	11	54	10

ATLANTIC SUN CONFERENCE

	Conference		Overall	
	W	L	W	L
Kennesaw State	17	4	29	27
North Florida	15	6	39	19
Jacksonville	14	7	33	22
Lipscomb	12	9	31	27
*Stetson	9	12	29	30
Florida Gulf Coast	9	12	27	32
South Carolina-Upstate	5	15	22	30
NJIT	2	18	17	36

All-Conference Team: C—Keith Skinner, Sr., North Florida. **1B**—Adam Lee, Sr., Lipscomb. **2B**—Jake Noll, Jr., Florida Gulf Coast. **3B**—Tyler Selesky, Sr., Florida Gulf Coast. **SS**—J.J. Gould, Sr., Jacksonville. **OF**—Austin Hays, Jr., Jacksonville; Nick Karmeris, Sr., North Florida; Chris Thibideau, Jr., North Florida. **DH**—Corbin Olmstead, Sr., North Florida. **SP**—Brady Puckett, So., Lipscomb; Bryan Baker, Jr., North

Florida; Nathan Disch, Jr., Jacksonville. **RP**—Corbin Olmstead, Sr., North Florida. **Player of the Year:** Jake Noll, Florida Gulf Coast. **Pitcher of the Year:** Brady Puckett, Lipscomb. **Defensive Player of the Year:** Kyle Brooks, North Florida. **Freshman of the Year:** Devon Ortiz, South Carolina-Upstate. **Coach of the Year:** Mike Sansing, Kennesaw State.

INDIVIDUAL BATTING LEADERS
(Minimum 140 At-Bats)

	AVG	OBP	SLG	AB	2B	3B	HR	RBI	SB
Keith Skinner, North Florida	**.382**	.466	.486	212	16	0	2	40	2
Lee Solomon, Lipscomb	.370	**.471**	.498	227	11	3	4	50	**25**
Jake Noll, FGCU	.367	.427	.620	237	20	2	12	61	9
Matt Reardon, FGCU	.360	.418	.464	222	15	4	0	25	6
Corbin Olmstead, North Florida	.359	.438	.558	231	8	1	12	59	2
Corey Greeson, Kennesaw State	.356	.417	.521	163	10	1	5	29	5
Austin Hays, Jacksonville	.350	**.406**	**.655**	223	16	2	**16**	42	15
Austin Upshaw, Kennesaw State	.344	.411	.517	209	13	1	7	36	2
Chris Thibideau, North Florida	.344	.406	.561	189	13	2	8	32	12
Cody Brittain, USC Upstate	.343	.381	.547	181	12	**5**	5	36	4
John Fussell, Stetson	.341	.390	.439	205	8	0	4	32	6
J.J. Gould, Jacksonville	.332	.441	.564	202	18	1	9	37	10
Dakota Higdon, North Florida	.328	.403	.402	204	11	2	0	26	1
James Fowlkes, USC Upstate	.328	.401	.563	192	7	4	10	38	6
Tyler Selesky, FGCU	.317	.419	.543	230	16	0	12	54	2
Alex Merritt, North Florida	.316	.379	.479	215	14	0	7	48	2
Zeke Dodson, Lipscomb	.314	.422	.393	191	7	1	2	44	5
Adam Lee, Lipscomb	.311	.435	.466	206	11	0	7	**64**	22
Kirk Sidwell, Stetson	.308	.316	.379	169	9	0	1	23	1
Charlie Carpenter, USC Upstate	.306	.399	.474	196	13	1	6	24	1
Kyle Brooks, North Florida	.305	.387	.389	239	15	1	1	33	4
Nick Karmeris, North Florida	.305	.363	.464	233	7	0	10	51	4
Evan Pietronico, NJIT	.304	.386	.475	204	**21**	1	4	44	1
Tevin Symonette, Lipscomb	.304	.389	.500	184	8	2	8	37	4
Alex Liquori, Kennesaw State	.302	.386	.426	162	8	3	2	24	5
Vance Vizcaino, Stetson	.286	.378	.385	**262**	10	2	4	26	22

INDIVIDUAL PITCHING LEADERS
(Minimum 40 Innings Pitched)

	W	L	ERA	G	SV	IP	H	BB	SO
Walker Sheller, Stetson	2	3	**1.38**	35	**12**	46	38	21	44
Bryan Baker, North Florida	6	4	2.27	14	0	83	65	28	80
Mike Schappell, Jacksonville	5	2	2.34	21	1	42	**28**	15	29
Matthew Naylor, North Florida	5	3	2.52	30	3	50	44	12	56
Logan Gilbert, Stetson	2	1	2.74	21	0	49	44	27	43
Brooks Wilson, Stetson	5	6	2.90	12	0	68	72	23	55
Brady Puckett, Lipscomb	**9**	2	2.93	15	0	**108**	91	19	**101**
Richard Lovelady, Kenn. State	4	2	2.96	**37**	4	46	30	25	52
Spencer Stockton, Jacksonville	5	5	3.21	15	0	76	77	20	45
Jeffrey Passantino, Lipscomb	6	5	3.40	15	0	98	97	12	82
Josh Thorne, Stetson	3	4	3.47	32	0	47	40	8	39
Eric Birklund, USC Upstate	1	3	3.48	10	0	44	45	22	39
Nathan Disch, Jacksonville	5	4	3.74	14	0	84	76	24	62
Mitchell Jordan, Stetson	6	5	3.94	15	0	80	73	32	75
Brady Anderson, FGCU	5	7	3.97	15	0	100	127	21	62
Austin Drury, North Florida	6	1	4.02	15	0	72	63	24	48
Erik Wiebke, Stetson	1	2	4.03	19	0	45	47	13	33
Tyler Jackson, USC Upstate	4	3	4.10	13	0	75	77	17	86
Michael Baumann, Jacksonville	4	4	4.32	14	0	75	71	35	69
Mason Ward, Kennesaw State	3	2	4.34	19	0	48	52	13	33
Gabe Friese, Kennesaw State	6	2	4.35	13	0	72	86	24	61
Johnny Malatesta, NJIT	4	4	4.46	11	0	40	57	7	10
A.J. Moore, Kennesaw State	4	3	4.48	13	0	70	79	30	72
Matt Vaka, North Florida	3	1	4.63	14	0	47	61	14	21
Tony Dibrell, Kennesaw State	1	4	4.64	14	1	54	54	30	66
Tyler Dupont, North Florida	3	2	5.30	13	0	56	77	**6**	33
Sean Lubreski, NJIT	3	**9**	5.45	14	0	79	92	29	45

ATLANTIC 10 CONFERENCE

	Conference		Overall	
	W	L	W	L
* **Rhode Island**	18	6	31	25
Virginia Commonwealth	15	7	38	19
Saint Joseph's	15	9	31	23
Saint Louis	15	9	25	31
Fordham	14	10	29	29
Davidson	11	11	28	26
George Washington	12	12	24	33
Massachusetts	11	13	18	27
St. Bonaventure	11	13	26	22
Richmond	11	13	28	24
Dayton	8	16	19	36
George Mason	7	17	19	35
La Salle	6	18	15	39

All-Conference Team: C—Deon Stafford, So., St. Joseph's. **1B**—Bobby Campbell, Jr., George Washington. **2B**—Sam Foy, Sr., Davidson. **3B**—Michael Morman, Sr., Richmond. **SS**—Matt Davis, Jr., Virginia Commonwealth. **OF**—Joey Bartosic, Jr., George Washington; Trent Leimkuehler, Jr., Saint Louis; John Brue, Sr., St. Joseph's. **DH**—Kurtis Brown, Jr., Richmond. **SP**—Tyler Wilson, So., Rhode Island; Clark Beeker, Sr., Davidson. **RP**—Sam Donko, Jr., Virginia Commonwealth. **Player of the Year:** Deon Stafford, St. Joseph's. **Pitcher of the Year:** Tyler Wilson, Rhode Island. **Rookie of the Year:** Michael Dailey, Virginia Commonwealth. **Coach of the Year:** Raphael Cerrato, Rhode Island.

INDIVIDUAL BATTING LEADERS
(Minimum 140 At-Bats)

	AVG	OBP	SLG	AB	2B	3B	HR	RBI	SB
Deon Stafford, St. Joseph's	**.395**	.486	**.702**	215	10	1	**18**	49	4
Michael Morman, Richmond	.369	.464	.544	195	20	1	4	48	6
Mark Osis, GW	.368	.418	.420	174	5	2	0	26	15
Joey Bartosic, GW	.349	.375	.410	**249**	10	1	1	27	19
Jordan Powell, Rhode Island	.349	.402	.428	215	14	0	1	31	13
Kurtis Brown, Richmond	.341	.426	.480	179	16	0	3	35	1
Martin Figueroa, Rhode Island	.327	.388	.543	223	**22**	1	8	43	8
Parker Sniatynski, Saint Louis	.327	.375	.400	205	7	1	2	29	8
Tyler Walter, St. Bonaventure	.325	.395	.414	169	6	3	1	25	4
Josh Bunselmeyer, Saint Louis	.325	.429	.579	209	15	1	12	**54**	2
Brian Fortier, Davidson	.322	.375	.389	208	8	0	2	31	6
Kyle Adams, Richmond	.321	.425	.458	190	15	1	3	33	5
Matt Davis, VCU	.321	.385	.443	237	9	1	6	35	3
Tyler Beckwith, Richmond	.319	.401	.528	216	19	4	6	38	10
Jimmy Kerrigan, VCU	.318	.409	.438	217	14	0	4	35	15
Jared Melone, La Salle	.315	.383	.405	168	13	1	0	16	7
Mike Hart, UMass	.313	.414	.448	163	7	3	3	14	5
Jake Sidwell, Davidson	.309	.410	.360	175	6	0	1	23	4
Mark Donadio, Fordham	.306	.381	.393	206	9	3	1	34	8
Chris Hess, Rhode Island	.305	.378	.528	233	14	**10**	6	36	8
Daniel Brumbaugh, Richmond	.302	.383	.396	159	7	1	2	26	4
John Jennings, UMass	.298	.354	.538	171	10	2	9	32	1
Trent Leimkuehler, Saint Louis	.297	.326	.502	229	13	2	10	39	5
Doug Kraeger, Richmond	.297	.411	.456	182	7	2	6	40	3
Taishi Terashima, St. Bonaventure	.296	.371	.352	199	9	1	0	16	8
Michael Bozarth, Saint Louis	.274	.401	.360	175	10	1	1	18	**26**

INDIVIDUAL PITCHING LEADERS
(Minimum 40 Innings Pitched)

	W	L	ERA	G	SV	IP	H	BB	SO
Michael Dailey, VCU	6	0	**1.57**	14	0	69	56	18	47
Brandon Schlimm, St. Bona.	7	5	2.11	13	0	94	71	23	64
Tyler Wilson, Rhode Island	**13**	1	2.29	15	0	102	53	33	**122**
Matt Olson, Richmond	4	2	2.54	19	1	60	55	23	34
Clark Beeker, Davidson	9	4	2.55	15	0	**109**	108	19	73
Tim Brennan, St. Joseph's	7	2	2.59	14	0	87	73	15	72
Sam Donko, VCU	3	2	2.63	**30**	**20**	58	44	14	53
Connor Grey, St. Bonaventure	3	6	2.84	15	0	92	68	33	95
Reid Van Woert, St. Bonaventure	5	2	2.89	19	3	56	54	16	35
Aaron Phillips, St. Bonaventure	3	3	3.02	13	0	57	52	21	31
Matt Eckleman, Saint Louis	9	4	3.12	15	0	101	93	29	81
Miller Hogan, Saint Louis	3	**8**	3.27	15	0	72	71	22	59
Sean Thompson, VCU	6	1	3.28	11	0	60	48	33	44
Durin O'Linger, Davidson	7	5	3.39	15	0	85	89	20	54
Pat Vanderslice, St. Joseph's	7	3	3.44	19	0	71	71	17	49
Lucas Rollins, St. Joseph's	5	5	3.45	14	0	86	88	**10**	71
Devin Moloney, UMass	2	4	3.49	11	0	70	68	23	41
Luke Reilly, La Salle	2	4	3.49	12	0	59	59	16	50
Joseph Serrapica, Fordham	5	5	3.54	18	1	84	76	28	62
Brandon Walsh, UMass	5	1	3.54	7	0	48	**38**	22	54

	W	L	ERA	G	SV	IP	H	BB	SO
Devin Mahoney, Saint Louis	4	3	3.61	17	0	62	76	17	44
Tyler Zombro, George Mason	4	7	3.75	14	0	86	84	11	65
Matt Jamer, VCU	6	2	3.91	**30**	2	69	69	19	55
Austin Cline, Dayton	4	4	4.00	18	0	72	71	26	55
Steve Moyers, Rhode Island	6	7	4.00	15	0	97	98	24	78
Greg Weissert, Fordham	5	4	4.04	14	0	78	64	42	82

BIG EAST CONFERENCE

	Conference		Overall	
	W	L	W	L
*Xavier	14	4	32	30
Creighton	13	5	38	17
Seton Hall	10	8	38	20
St. John's	9	9	28	26
Georgetown	8	10	25	29
Villanova	5	13	20	32
Butler	4	14	14	40

All-Conference Team: C—Daniel Rizzie, Jr., Xavier. **1B**—Max Beermann, Sr., Villanova. **2B**—Todd Czinege, Jr., Villanova. **3B**—Rylan Bannon, So., Xavier. **SS**—Andre Jernigan, Jr., Xavier. **OF**—Daniel Woodrow, Jr., Creighton; Michael Donadio, Jr., St. John's; Derek Jenkins, Sr., Seton Hall. **DH**—Nate Soria, So., Xavier. **SP**—Rollie Lacy, So., Creighton; Simon Matthews, Jr., Georgetown; Shane McCarthy, So., Seton Hall; Hunter Schryver, Jr., Villanova. **RP**—Thomas Hackimer, Sr., St. John's. **Player of the Year:** Andre Jernigan, Xavier. **Pitcher of the Year:** Thomas Hackimer, St. John's. **Freshman of the Year:** Josh Shaw, St. John's. **Coach of the Year:** Scott Googins, Xavier.

INDIVIDUAL BATTING LEADERS
(Minimum 140 At-Bats)

	AVG	OBP	SLG	AB	2B	3B	HR	RBI	SB
Daniel Woodrow, Creighton	**.343**	.399	.430	230	9	4	1	22	32
Zach Weigel, Seton Hall	.333	**.458**	.420	207	11	2	1	33	25
Michael Derenzi, Georgetown	.332	.372	.459	205	7	5	3	21	26
Daniel Rizzie, Xavier	.317	.383	.472	**246**	9	1	9	36	7
Michael Donadio, St. John's	.315	.420	.452	197	16	1	3	31	8
Michael Hartnagel, Butler	.312	.319	.395	205	13	2	0	15	2
Mike Alescio, Seton Hall	.310	.367	.418	158	9	4	0	27	10
Tyler Houston, Butler	.309	.346	.404	178	8	3	1	27	9
Todd Czinege, Villanova	.307	.395	.460	202	11	1	6	32	2
Nicky Lopez, Creighton	.306	.417	.444	196	11	5	2	22	11
Kevin Connolly, Creighton	.301	.391	.417	156	6	3	2	20	11
Derek Jenkins, Seton Hall	.299	.341	.338	234	6	0	1	35	**52**
Jesse Berardi, St. John's	.298	.394	.455	191	7	4	5	40	7
Josh Shaw, St. John's	.297	.312	.367	229	10	0	2	42	7
Chris Givin, Xavier	.293	.384	.408	174	8	3	2	16	9
Jake Kuzbel, Georgetown	.293	.354	.402	174	9	2	2	27	3
Alex Caruso, St. John's	.288	.450	.346	191	9	1	0	24	6
Brett Murray, Creighton	.287	.337	.395	167	8	2	2	22	1
Chase Bushor, Georgetown	.287	.361	.377	167	12	0	1	21	1
Donovan May, Villanova	.287	.387	.346	188	7	2	0	29	6
Joe Gellenbeck, Xavier	.285	.348	.508	246	16	0	13	**51**	12
Jamie Galazin, St. John's	.283	.374	.375	152	7	2	1	23	14
Ryan Ramiz, Seton Hall	.275	.398	.295	193	2	1	0	13	15
Robbie Knightes, St. John's	.274	.293	.347	190	12	1	0	26	4
Rylan Bannon, Xavier	.273	.390	.473	205	**17**	0	8	32	7
Chris Chiaradio, Seton Hall	.265	.368	.363	223	10	6	0	22	32
Andre Jernigan, Xavier	.253	.363	**.557**	221	**17**	4	**14**	42	6

INDIVIDUAL PITCHING LEADERS
(Minimum 40 Innings Pitched)

	W	L	ERA	G	SV	IP	H	BB	SO
Thomas Hackimer, St. John's	7	3	**1.17**	28	8	54	**24**	19	71
Garrett Schilling, Xavier	4	3	1.91	**29**	**14**	42	38	17	34
Joe Napolitano, St. John's	3	1	1.93	25	2	42	38	12	31
Shane McCarthy, Seton Hall	6	4	2.38	15	0	**102**	87	18	**84**
Jeff Albrecht, Creighton	7	1	2.39	17	0	64	39	28	48
Simon Mathews, Georgetown	5	4	2.45	13	0	95	104	18	59
Hunter Schryver, Villanova	5	4	2.64	15	0	89	79	30	79
Cullen Dana, Seton Hall	7	2	2.75	13	0	72	52	24	66
Matt Leon, Seton Hall	2	1	2.88	26	2	41	31	**9**	28
Connor Miller, Creighton	1	1	3.02	24	2	45	35	16	36
Zac Lowther, Xavier	7	5	3.09	16	0	**102**	87	30	**84**

	W	L	ERA	G	SV	IP	H	BB	SO
Rollie Lacy, Creighton	**9**	2	3.15	16	0	91	87	24	58
Jeff Schank, Butler	2	**7**	3.16	14	0	91	89	27	59
Keith Rogalla, Creighton	5	3	3.21	15	0	73	55	35	59
Woody Bryson, Villanova	4	3	3.35	26	3	40	33	18	48
Trey Schramm, Xavier	4	0	3.65	27	2	57	48	27	21
Kevin Torres, St. John's	3	2	3.91	18	0	48	53	**9**	23
Taylor Williams, Xavier	0	3	3.91	27	1	46	41	17	39
Zach Prendergast, Seton Hall	5	**7**	3.97	15	0	82	82	22	67
Nick Morton, Butler	2	**7**	4.04	14	0	91	100	16	43
Damien Richard, Xavier	4	3	4.14	15	0	46	44	31	29
Ryan McAuliffe, St. John's	5	2	4.32	15	0	77	77	23	44
Zach Schellenger, Seton Hall	4	4	4.34	30	6	46	44	21	70
Matt Smith, Georgetown	3	6	4.52	13	0	82	82	28	64
Jack Cushing, Georgetown	3	5	4.58	17	0	57	66	17	27

BIG SOUTH CONFERENCE

	Conference		Overall	
	W	L	W	L
*Coastal Carolina	21	3	53	17
High Point	14	10	32	24
Longwood	14	10	32	27
Gardner-Webb	14	10	37	21
Campbell	13	11	26	27
Presbyterian	12	12	27	30
Liberty	12	12	31	28
Winthrop	12	12	28	27
Radford	9	15	19	39
Charleston Southern	6	18	19	34
UNC Asheville	5	19	16	38

All-Conference Team: C—Justin Kunz, Fr., Gardner-Webb. **INF**—Zach Remillard, Sr., Coastal Carolina; Collin Thacker, Jr., Gardner-Webb; Chris Clare, Jr., High Point; Matt Parrish, Sr., Campbell. **OF**—Connor Owings, Sr., Coastal Carolina; D.J. Artis, Fr., Liberty; Danny Sullivan, Jr., Gardner-Webb. **DH**—G.K. Young, Jr., Coastal Carolina. **UTL**—Andrew Yacyk, Jr., Liberty. **SP**—Andrew Beckwith, Jr., Coastal Carolina; Brad Haymes, Sr., Gardner-Webb; Travis Burnette, Sr., Longwood. **RP**—Mike Morrison, Sr., Coastal Carolina. **Player of the Year:** Connor Owings, Coastal Carolina. **Pitcher of the Year:** Andrew Beckwith, Coastal Carolina. **Freshman of the Year:** D.J. Artis, Liberty. **Coach of the Year:** Gary Gilmore, Coastal Carolina.

INDIVIDUAL BATTING LEADERS
(Minimum 140 At-Bats)

	AVG	OBP	SLG	AB	2B	3B	HR	RBI	SB
Collin Thacker, Gardner-Webb	**.394**	.452	.578	218	**28**	0	4	46	1
Matt Parrish, Campbell	.371	.448	.526	175	14	2	3	41	8
Alex Lewis, Longwood	.369	.409	.528	233	22	0	5	45	5
D.J. Artis, Liberty	.369	**.500**	.464	222	9	3	2	41	23
Tyler Weyenberg, Presbyterian	.358	.407	.466	232	18	2	1	24	16
Connor Owings, Coastal	.352	.458	**.636**	253	20	2	16	57	14
Anthony Paulsen, Winthrop	.352	.415	.441	227	7	2	3	35	11
Danny Sullivan, Gardner-Webb	.348	.393	.548	221	13	2	9	35	4
Chris Clare, High Point	.345	.391	.448	223	15	1	2	27	11
Joe Tietjen, UNC Asheville	.344	.416	.553	215	15	0	10	54	12
Zach Remillard, Coastal	.341	.410	.610	290	17	2	**19**	**72**	15
Weston Jackson, Presbyterian	.341	.419	.613	217	17	1	10	55	9
Roger Gonzalez, Winthrop	.338	.426	.534	204	17	1	7	44	0
G.K. Young, Coastal	.337	.391	.571	**294**	11	2	18	**72**	1
Sly Edwards, Charleston Sou.	.337	.435	.434	196	7	**6**	0	23	7
Connar Bastaich, Longwood	.335	.402	.416	233	10	0	3	34	4
Chris Singleton, Charleston Sou.	.332	.395	.466	193	12	1	4	34	8
Danny Hrbek, Radford	.329	.385	.458	225	11	**6**	2	34	7
Will Shepherd, Liberty	.328	.390	.502	235	17	0	8	46	11
Mark Lowrie, Winthrop	.328	.424	.398	201	8	0	2	38	2
Seth Lancaster, Coastal	.326	.457	.509	175	11	0	7	35	15
Dominic Fazio, High Point	.325	.441	.485	194	16	0	5	42	2
Patrick Graham, Gardner-Webb	.325	.376	.405	200	8	1	2	34	3
Billy Cooke, Coastal	.324	.415	.429	238	16	0	3	36	**27**
Anthony Lopez, Campbell	.319	.368	.515	204	9	5	7	33	7
Tyler Best, Gardner-Webb	.319	.365	.390	182	11	1	0	25	7

INDIVIDUAL PITCHING LEADERS
(Minimum 40 Innings Pitched)

	W	L	ERA	G	SV	IP	H	BB	SO
Mike Morrison, Coastal	8	1	**1.50**	34	11	72	41	27	94
Andrew Beckwith, Coastal	**15**	1	1.85	26	2	117	113	18	75
Erik Dowse, Campbell	2	2	1.93	24	6	47	38	29	59
Brad Haymes, Gardner-Webb	11	3	2.20	15	0	111	87	16	**115**
Travis Burnette, Longwood	8	2	2.35	18	0	100	82	45	85
Grant Yost, Campbell	7	3	2.64	13	0	95	84	15	71
Andrew Gottfried, High Point	6	5	2.65	14	0	71	62	19	48
Tyler Britton, High Point	6	1	2.93	19	4	55	47	10	59
Brian Kehner, Presbyterian	5	7	2.94	15	0	95	80	13	78
Michael Catlin, Longwood	4	1	3.00	25	2	51	50	17	31
Victor Cole, Liberty	3	3	3.12	9	0	52	35	30	56
Michael Horrell, Campbell	5	6	3.18	15	0	74	69	14	43
Austin Kitchen, Coastal	4	1	3.19	21	2	42	**28**	12	36
Evan Raynor, Charleston Sou.	4	6	3.23	13	0	78	66	26	71
Ryan Boelter, Gardner-Webb	4	1	3.25	19	0	64	55	32	67
Wil Sellers, Gardner-Webb	1	3	3.33	25	**12**	51	40	21	52
Zack Ridgely, Radford	4	6	3.34	15	0	97	92	23	69
Shane Quarterley, Liberty	6	4	3.38	29	7	48	55	21	32
Zach Cook, Winthrop	3	3	3.48	30	9	41	40	15	35
Alex Cunningham, Coastal	10	4	3.62	22	1	**119**	116	40	98
Zack Hopeck, Coastal	3	4	3.70	16	1	56	46	14	39
Tyler Poole, Coastal	4	3	3.72	11	0	46	38	26	45
Jeremy Walker, Gardner-Webb	9	5	3.77	15	0	100	102	27	99
Sam Kmiec, Winthrop	6	7	3.82	14	0	97	112	17	72
Evan Mitchell, Liberty	4	2	3.96	15	1	75	73	32	47
Andrew Massey, Gardner-Webb	3	3	5.47	17	1	49	66	**8**	33
Jordan Carr, UNC Ashville	1	**9**	6.01	14	1	70	80	26	35

	AVG	OBP	SLG	AB	2B	3B	HR	RBI	SB
Ronnie Dawson, Ohio State	.331	.419	.611	**257**	25	4	13	51	21
Carmen Benedetti, Michigan	.326	.465	.492	193	19	2	3	33	6
Jake Meyers, Nebraska	.326	.402	.458	227	12	**6**	2	29	10
Scott Schreiber, Nebraska	.325	.391	**.629**	197	10	1	**16**	55	3
Dan Durkin, Michigan State	.324	.402	.454	207	9	0	6	32	5
Tyler Kendall, Penn State	.320	.370	.375	200	9	1	0	33	7
Kyle Johnson, Purdue	.318	.387	.495	214	11	3	7	31	7
Ben Miller, Nebraska	.317	.388	.457	243	16	0	6	46	0
Jim Haley, Penn State	.315	.377	.425	219	12	3	2	27	10
Greg Guers, Penn State	.313	.369	.485	198	12	2	6	38	20
Jason Goldstein, Illinois	.312	.402	.412	170	5	0	4	29	2
Robert Neustrom, Iowa	.307	.389	.405	153	6	3	1	21	4
Nick Riotto, Penn State	.307	.405	.385	179	4	2	2	18	3
Harrison Wenson, Michigan	.289	.345	.491	218	18	1	8	**56**	3
Ryan Boldt, Nebraska	.288	.344	.416	257	14	2	5	30	20
Jawuan Harris, Rutgers	.278	.365	.389	162	5	2	3	22	**37**
Tom Marcinczyk, Rutgers	.270	.384	.446	204	12	**6**	4	47	18

INDIVIDUAL PITCHING LEADERS
(Minimum 40 Innings Pitched)

	W	L	ERA	G	SV	IP	H	BB	SO
Jake Kelzer, Indiana	3	2	**1.32**	22	4	41	**25**	12	48
Jake Meyers, Nebraska	6	1	1.42	9	0	51	37	10	26
Seth Kinker, Ohio State	6	1	1.65	**38**	2	55	50	10	45
Dakota Mekkes, Michigan State	3	2	1.74	28	7	57	26	41	96
Reece Eddins, Nebraska	4	3	1.85	26	1	49	43	21	30
Jack Anderson, Penn State	4	2	2.14	29	**13**	55	50	19	43
Dakota Forsyth, Penn State	2	3	2.28	20	1	43	27	27	28
Cam Vieaux, Michigan State	7	4	2.28	15	0	87	77	19	77
Nick Hedge, Penn State	5	3	2.44	14	1	59	58	12	36
Taylor Bloom, Maryland	6	5	2.46	14	0	102	101	9	60
Thomas Belcher, Indiana	5	3	2.47	28	7	44	36	11	34
Jonathan Stiever, Indiana	1	1	2.48	18	0	40	39	**5**	30
Caleb Baragar, Indiana	4	4	2.49	15	0	87	65	22	74
Cody Sedlock, Illinois	3	3	2.49	14	0	101	80	31	**116**
Keegan Baar, Michigan State	1	3	2.55	19	0	42	31	13	25
Nick Gallagher, Iowa	8	3	2.57	14	0	63	49	22	59
Tanner Tully, Ohio State	8	3	2.59	17	0	**108**	98	23	78
Brian Shaffer, Maryland	8	3	2.60	15	0	104	78	13	75
Ethan Landon, Michigan State	8	3	2.75	15	0	85	77	30	59
Matt Frawley, Purdue	1	5	2.78	14	1	74	65	27	58
Andrew Gonzalez, Mich.State	3	3	2.84	17	0	57	53	19	40
Matt Waldron, Nebraska	7	3	2.87	13	0	75	73	15	56
Derek Burkamper, Nebraska	5	3	3.09	15	0	70	55	34	55
Mike Shawaryn, Maryland	6	4	3.18	15	0	99	69	26	97
Oliver Jaskie, Michigan	7	3	3.19	14	0	79	64	39	69
Kyle Hart, Indiana	**10**	4	3.29	15	0	98	91	15	79
Taylor Lehman, Penn State	2	**9**	4.79	14	0	68	84	31	47

BIG TEN CONFERENCE

	Conference		Overall	
	W	L	W	L
Minnesota	16	7	35	21
Nebraska	16	8	37	22
* **Ohio State**	15	9	44	20
Indiana	15	9	32	24
Michigan	13	10	36	21
Michigan State	13	11	36	20
Maryland	13	11	30	27
Illinois	12	12	28	23
Iowa	12	12	30	26
Penn State	12	12	28	27
Rutgers	9	15	27	28
Northwestern	7	17	15	39
Purdue	2	22	10	44

All-Conference Team: C—Austin Athmann, Jr., Minnesota. **1B**—Schott Schreiber, So., Nebraska. **2B**—Dan Durkin, Jr., Michigan State; Connor Schaefbauer, Sr., Minnesota. **3B**—Nick Sergakis, Sr., Ohio State. **SS**—Nick Roscetti, Sr., Iowa. **OF**—Joel Booker, Sr., Iowa; Cody Bruder, Sr., Michigan; Ronnie Dawson, Jr., Ohio State. **SP**—Cody Sedlock, Jr., Illinois; Kyle Hart, Sr., Indiana; Tanner Tully, Jr., Ohio State. **RP**—Dakota Mekkes, So., Michigan State. **Player of the Year:** Matt Fiedler, Minnesota. **Pitcher of the Year:** Cody Sedlock, Illinois. **Freshman of the Year:** Chad Luensmann, Nebraska. **Coach of the Year:** John Anderson, Minnesota.

INDIVIDUAL BATTING LEADERS
(Minimum 140 At-Bats)

	AVG	OBP	SLG	AB	2B	3B	HR	RBI	SB
R.J. Devish, Rutgers	**.375**	**.524**	.435	168	7	0	1	27	24
Jordan Zimmerman, Mich. State	.374	.461	.594	219	17	2	9	37	10
Matt Fiedler, Minnesota	.372	.417	.534	234	12	1	8	38	14
Cody Bruder, Michigan	.372	.425	.485	231	18	1	2	53	7
Austin Athmann, Minnesota	.370	.440	.615	192	14	0	11	40	0
Joel Booker, Iowa	.370	.421	.532	235	19	2	5	37	23
Jake Bivens, Michigan	.356	.441	.416	233	10	2	0	26	13
Matt Hopfner, Northwestern	.355	.440	.470	200	13	2	2	22	3
Dan Motl, Minnesota	.336	.398	.485	229	19	3	3	31	7
Micah Coffey, Minnesota	.335	.410	.529	206	13	3	7	42	2
Tyler Peyton, Iowa	.335	.412	.507	215	17	4	4	26	8
Nick Sergakis, Ohio State	.332	.451	.542	238	18	1	10	47	15

BIG 12 CONFERENCE

	Conference		Overall	
	W	L	W	L
Texas Tech	19	5	47	20
Oklahoma State	16	8	43	22
* **Texas Christian**	15	9	49	18
West Virginia	12	11	36	22
Oklahoma	11	13	30	27
Baylor	10	14	24	29
Texas	10	14	25	32
Kansas State	8	16	26	31
Kansas	6	17	20	35

All-Conference Team: C—Michael Tinsley, Jr., Kansas. **INF**—Sheldon Neuse, Jr., Oklahoma; J.R. Davis, Jr., Oklahoma State; Donnie Walton, Sr., Oklahoma State; Elliott Barzilli, Jr., Texas Christian; Eric Gutierrez, Jr., Texas Tech. **OF**—Clayton Dalrymple, Sr., Kansas State; Tanner Gardner, So., Texas Tech; Stephen Smith, Jr., Texas Tech. **DH**—Luken Baker, Fr., Texas Christian. **UTL**—Luken Baker, Fr., Texas Christian. **P**—Ben Krauth, Sr., Kansas; Thomas Hatch, So., Oklahoma State; Davis Martin, Fr., Texas Tech; Chad Donato, Jr., West Virginia; Troy Montemayor, So., Baylor; Tyler Buffett, Jr., Oklahoma State. **Player of the Year:** Eric Gutierrez, Texas Tech. **Pitcher of the Year:** Thomas Hatch, Oklahoma State. **Newcomer of the Year:** Jake Scudder, Kansas State. **Freshman**

of the Year: Luken Baker, Texas Christian. **Coach of the Year:** Tim Tadlock, Texas Tech.

INDIVIDUAL BATTING LEADERS
(Minimum 140 At-Bats)

	AVG	OBP	SLG	AB	2B	3B	HR	RBI	SB
Luken Baker, TCU	**.379**	.483	.577	248	16	0	11	**62**	1
Tanner Gardner, Texas Tech	**.379**	.484	.549	235	19	**6**	3	35	6
Michael Tinsley, Kansas	.377	.460	.495	212	15	2	2	42	9
Sheldon Neuse, Oklahoma	.369	.465	**.646**	198	15	5	10	48	12
J.R. Davis, Oklahoma State	.347	.422	.438	219	13	2	1	32	9
Darius Hill, West Virginia	.342	.420	.511	219	20	4	3	40	6
Colby Wright, Kansas	.341	**.466**	.563	176	13	4	6	41	6
Elliott Barzilli, TCU	.339	.418	.518	251	16	4	7	48	14
Donnie Walton, Oklahoma State	.337	.428	.447	246	16	1	4	39	14
Eric Gutierrez, Texas Tech	.333	.465	.581	234	17	1	**13**	60	3
Jake Scudder, Kansas State	.333	.392	.507	219	15	1	7	45	6
Clayton Dalrymple, Kansas State	.325	.414	.421	228	13	3	1	27	16
Cory Raley, Texas Tech	.323	.411	.462	260	14	2	6	53	**21**
Tyler Moore, Kansas State	.321	.390	.444	196	12	0	4	41	2
Dane Steinhagen, TCU	.313	.379	.502	243	20	1	8	51	12
Matt Menard, Baylor	.309	.376	.500	152	11	0	6	25	0
Stephen Smith, Texas Tech	.309	.422	.511	272	19	3	10	42	8
Steven McLean, Baylor	.308	.382	.413	201	9	3	2	24	6
Kameron Esthay, Baylor	.307	.370	.438	192	14	1	3	31	2
Tyler Neslony, Texas Tech	.306	.406	.536	235	**22**	1	10	58	3
Joe Moroney, Kansas	.304	.393	.421	171	11	0	3	18	8
Alex Wise, Oklahoma	.304	.364	.423	227	16	4	1	28	9
Kacy Clemens, Texas	.303	.418	.470	185	14	1	5	31	0
Evan Skoug, TCU	.301	.390	.502	249	21	1	9	51	7
Jake Wodtke, Kansas State	.301	.381	.381	176	5	3	1	29	7
Cam Warner, TCU	.300	.346	.431	**283**	17	1	6	43	10
Jackson Cramer, West Virginia	.300	.416	.535	200	14	3	9	45	7
Travis Jones, Texas	.300	.395	.411	180	7	2	3	22	7
Ryan Merrill, TCU	.298	.353	.410	178	9	4	1	25	11
Justin Arrington, Baylor	.297	.333	.364	165	11	0	0	14	0

INDIVIDUAL PITCHING LEADERS
(Minimum 40 Innings Pitched)

	W	L	ERA	G	SV	IP	H	BB	SO
Thomas Hatch, Oklahoma State	9	3	**2.14**	19	0	**130**	108	33	**112**
Davis Martin, Texas Tech	**10**	1	2.52	19	2	89	75	27	61
Jared Janczak, TCU	7	1	2.60	17	0	83	76	26	80
Tyler Buffett, Oklahoma State	9	3	2.81	**37**	**9**	83	70	32	76
Hayden Howard, Texas Tech	9	3	2.98	35	**9**	85	76	20	54
Trey Cobb, Oklahoma State	4	7	3.09	24	6	82	81	32	100
Steven Gingery, Texas Tech	4	2	3.18	15	0	68	**61**	31	63
Brian Howard, TCU	**10**	2	3.19	17	0	99	80	30	93
Chad Donato, West Virginia	3	4	3.27	15	0	96	86	20	111
Ben Krauth, Kansas	5	6	3.33	15	0	92	86	30	103
Jensen Elliott, Oklahoma State	9	3	3.50	17	0	87	83	35	71
Connor Mayes, Texas	0	4	3.60	21	2	60	**61**	28	53
Kyle Johnston, Texas	3	2	3.72	15	0	68	62	43	64
Ty Culbreth, Texas	8	4	3.74	16	0	87	92	17	78
Morgan Cooper, Texas	3	5	4.03	13	0	67	68	17	70
B.J. Myers, West Virginia	5	3	4.05	17	0	67	55	22	53
Levi MaVorhis, Kansas State	5	6	4.20	14	0	84	89	15	76
Daniel Castano, Baylor	4	5	4.64	14	0	87	93	36	63
Parker Rigler, Kansas State	4	**9**	4.89	16	0	77	78	26	73
Ross Vance, West Virginia	7	2	4.91	14	0	92	89	29	91
Chris Andritsos, Oklahoma	4	6	4.96	15	0	65	62	14	41
Drew Tolson, Baylor	6	4	5.55	14	0	83	102	34	48
Nick Lewis, Baylor	2	5	6.41	18	0	53	70	25	35
Blake Weiman, Kansas	1	7	6.82	17	0	61	85	22	44

BIG WEST CONFERENCE

	Conference		Overall	
	W	L	W	L
* Cal State Fullerton	17	7	36	23
Long Beach State	15	9	38	21
UC Santa Barbara	13	11	43	20
Cal Poly	12	12	32	25
UC Riverside	12	12	26	29

	W	L	W	L
Hawaii	12	12	23	30
Cal State Northridge	11	13	33	22
UC Irvine	11	13	31	25
UC Davis	5	19	17	36

All-Conference Team: C—David Banuelos, So., Long Beach State. **1B**—Tanner Pinkston, Sr., Cal State Fullerton. **2B**—Cole Kreuter, So., UC Irvine. **3B**—Zach Domingues, Sr., Long Beach State. **SS**—Garrett Hampson, Jr., Long Beach State. **OF**—Dalton Blaser, Sr., Cal State Fullerton; Adam Alcantara, Jr., UC Irvine; Vince Fernandez, Jr., UC Riverside. **DH**—Luke Rasmussen, So., Long Beach State. **UTL**—Brett Barbier, Jr., Cal Poly. **SP**—Colton Eastman, Fr., Cal State Fullerton; Darren McCaughan, So., Long Beach State; Shane Bieber, Jr., UC Santa Barbara. **RP**—Austin McGeorge, Jr., Long Beach State; Kyle Nelson, So., UC Santa Barbara. **Player of the Year:** Dalton Blaser, Cal State Fullerton. **Pitcher of the Year:** Darren McCaughan, Long Beach State. **Freshman of the Year:** Nick Meyer, Cal Poly. **Freshman Pitcher of the Year:** Colton Eastman, Cal State Fullerton. **Defensive Player of the Year:** Garrett Hampson, Long Beach State. **Coach of the Year:** Rick Vanderhook, Cal State Fullerton.

INDIVIDUAL BATTING LEADERS
(Minimum 140 At-Bats)

	AVG	OBP	SLG	AB	2B	3B	HR	RBI	SB
Dalton Blaser, CS Fullerton	**.359**	.439	.485	206	14	0	4	38	1
Keston Hiura, UC Irvine	.358	.436	**.539**	204	12	2	7	41	6
Brett Barbier, Cal Poly	.352	**.492**	.482	199	13	2	3	30	8
Vince Fernandez, UC Riverside	.350	.431	.509	220	9	1	8	42	4
Jacob Sheldon-Collins, Hawaii	.349	.407	.405	195	9	1	0	23	6
Adam Alcantara, UC Irvine	.337	.428	.442	172	10	1	2	36	5
Mark Contreras, UC Riverside	.332	.407	.430	193	14	1	1	24	9
Kekai Rios, Hawai'i	.331	.391	.401	157	8	0	1	18	1
Daniel Jackson, Long Beach	.329	.397	.503	155	9	0	6	34	4
Tanner Pinkston, CS Fullerton	.327	.404	.439	214	16	1	2	33	6
Tanner Bily, UC Davis	.318	.403	.373	201	8	1	0	26	17
Fred Smith, CS Northridge	.314	.340	.368	239	10	0	1	19	8
Brock Lundquist, Long Beach	.311	.370	.474	209	**17**	4	3	35	4
Garrett Hampson, Long Beach	.306	.391	.400	**245**	13	2	2	26	**23**
Josh George, Cal Poly	.306	.354	.359	170	7	1	0	16	1
Luke Rasmussen, Long Beach	.301	.376	.440	209	14	0	5	46	3
Nick Meyer, Cal Poly	.301	.374	.370	173	7	1	1	21	2
Mitchell Holland, UC Irvine	.300	.369	.411	207	15	1	2	32	3
Michael Sanderson, Cal Poly	.296	.381	.367	199	12	1	0	33	1
J.J. Muno, UC Santa Barbara	.294	.370	.450	231	15	3	5	31	17
Braden Berry, CS Northridge	.294	.403	.508	197	13	1	9	44	4
Yusuke Akitoshi, CS Northridge	.290	.385	.415	200	11	4	2	22	**23**
John Brontsema, UC Irvine	.289	.364	.389	190	10	3	1	18	7
Zack Domingues, Long Beach	.288	.413	.305	177	1	1	0	15	4
Clay Fisher, UC Santa Barbara	.285	.332	.377	239	15	2	1	24	14
Matt Lococo, Hawaii	.270	.392	.392	204	**9**	5	2	24	5
Josh Vargas, Cal State Fullerton	.268	.354	.399	198	7	**5**	3	25	14
Justin Toerner, CSNorthridge	.266	.402	.399	173	10	**5**	1	24	8
Austin Bush, UC Santa Barbara	.265	.346	.465	230	11	1	**11**	**49**	0
John Schuknecht, Cal Poly	.265	.331	.441	211	15	2	6	**49**	13

INDIVIDUAL PITCHING LEADERS
(Minimum 40 Innings Pitched)

	W	L	ERA	G	SV	IP	H	BB	SO
Austin McGeorge, Long Beach	1	1	**1.02**	**33**	5	53	35	14	76
Scott Serigstad, CS Fullerton	2	1	1.22	27	4	52	**30**	20	55
Darren McCaughan, Long Beach	10	1	2.03	16	0	111	71	16	84
John Gavin, Cal State Fullerton	6	3	2.09	18	1	86	61	31	60
Blake Quinn, Cal State Fullerton	4	3	2.16	17	1	67	40	32	69
Cody Culp, Hawaii		3	2.16	31	5	50	51	**5**	37
Kyle Nelson, UC Santa Barbara	7	2	2.18	33	**10**	74	56	18	87
Colton Eastman, CS Fullerton	8	3	2.24	16	0	101	78	20	100
Alex Fagalde, UC Riverside	3	1	2.47	27	3	44	37	12	51
Connor Seabold, CS Fullerton	7	6	2.48	16	0	83	71	9	96
Austin Sodders, UC Riverside	7	4	2.57	15	0	88	83	37	69
Robert Garcia, UC Davis	3	5	2.73	18	1	86	66	29	78
Shane Bieber, UC Santa Barbara	**12**	4	2.74	18	0	**135**	126	16	109
Jarred Zill, Cal Poly	4	3	2.79	12	0	58	42	16	47
Keaton Leach, UC Riverside	1	1	2.90	18	0	40	38	14	28
Angel Rodriguez, CS Northridge	5	4	3.07	18	0	82	75	18	70
Connor O'Neil, CS Northridge	5	5	3.07	23	**10**	59	45	33	70

	W	L	ERA	G	SV	IP	H	BB	SO
Brendan Hornung, Hawai'i	4	7	3.11	16	0	101	116	22	74
Tanner Brown, Long Beach	8	4	3.16	16	0	91	82	16	60
Andrew Weston, CS Northridge	7	5	3.19	20	0	68	65	19	35
Kenny Rosenberg, CS Northridge	6	1	3.21	15	0	98	70	31	118
Joey Ryan, Cal State Northridge	1	2	3.35	11	0	40	41	11	36
Trevor Bettencourt, UCSB	4	2	3.43	24	4	42	36	21	46
Kyle Von Ruden, Hawaii	7	3	3.44	16	0	107	107	21	50
Chris Mathewson, Long Beach	8	5	3.62	16	0	104	90	43	107
Richard Delgado, UC Riverside	1	8	5.12	16	0	77	81	25	37

COLONIAL ATHLETIC ASSOCIATION

	Conference		Overall	
	W	L	W	L
UNC Wilmington	16	6	41	19
* William & Mary	14	10	31	31
Elon	13	10	25	29
James Madison	13	11	24	31
Northeastern	12	11	31	27
College of Charleston	12	12	31	26
Delaware	10	14	32	22
Towson	10	14	20	35
Hofstra	5	18	15	37

All-Conference Team: C—Nick Feight, So., UNC Wilmington. **1B**—Tyler McVicar, Sr., Elon. **2B**—Brian Mims, So., UNC Wilmington. **3B**—Daniel Stack, Jr., UNC Wilmington. **SS**—Brady Policelli, Jr., Towson. **OF**—Jordan Glover, Jr., Delaware; Steven Linkous, Sr., UNC Wilmington; Ky Parrott, Jr., James Madison. **DH**—C.J. Young, Jr., Elon. **UTL**—Nick Zammarelli, Jr., Elon. **SP**—Aaron Civale, Jr., Northeastern; Ryan Foster, Sr., UNC Wilmington. **RP**—Chris Hall, Jr., Elon. **Player of the Year:** Nick Feight, UNC Wilmington. **Co-Pitchers of the Year:** Aaron Civale, Northeastern; Ryan Foster, UNC Wilmington. **Rookie of the Year:** Richie Palacios, Towson. **Defensive Player of the Year:** Josh Treff, Northeastern. **Coach of the Year:** Mark Scalf, UNC Wilmington.

INDIVIDUAL BATTING LEADERS
(Minimum 140 At-Bats)

	AVG	OBP	SLG	AB	2B	3B	HR	RBI	SB
Brady Policelli, Towson	.375	.502	.620	200	14	4	9	45	22
Steven Linkous, UNCW	.374	.456	.492	254	13	7	1	43	29
Brian Mims, UNCW	.371	.443	.614	259	17	2	14	64	4
Robbie Thorburn, UNCW	.364	.427	.511	225	12	6	3	28	20
Chad Carroll, James Madison	.363	.419	.470	168	9	3	1	24	23
Jordan Glover, Delaware	.360	.443	.555	200	20	2	5	52	22
Nick Feight, UNCW	.349	.412	.726	241	24	2	21	91	1
Gavin Stupienski, UNCW	.347	.444	.590	239	14	1	14	61	3
Kyle Baker, Delaware	.346	.404	.450	191	12	1	2	24	13
Nick Zammarelli, Elon	.342	.425	.590	222	24	2	9	51	12
Nick Tierno, Delaware	.340	.429	.437	206	13	2	1	35	8
Zach Tondi, James Madison	.335	.377	.540	161	12	0	7	36	6
Charley Gould, William & Mary	.329	.431	.483	240	22	0	5	46	1
Richie Palacios, Towson	.329	.415	.480	225	6	5	6	38	32
Brett Johnson, James Madison	.328	.429	.521	192	14	1	7	38	1
Cullen Large, William & Mary	.328	.406	.508	250	20	2	7	46	4
Ky Parrott, James Madison	.318	.496	.495	192	14	4	4	29	15
Cam Walsh, Northeastern	.317	.421	.400	145	3	3	1	17	7
Ryan Hall, William & Mary	.316	.417	.441	247	14	1	5	33	1
Tyler McVicar, Elon	.315	.424	.545	200	15	2	9	46	0
Dupree Hart, Charleston	.314	.443	.414	191	11	1	2	33	10
Ryder Miconi, William & Mary	.314	.425	.425	207	15	1	2	26	1
Casey Golden, UNCW	.311	.400	.554	148	9	0	9	31	2
Zack Canada, UNCW	.308	.376	.447	159	8	1	4	29	2
Kevin Mohollen, Delaware	.300	.395	.456	217	8	7	4	33	21

INDIVIDUAL PITCHING LEADERS
(Minimum 40 Innings Pitched)

	W	L	ERA	G	SV	IP	H	BB	SO
Aaron Civale, Northeastern	9	3	1.73	15	0	114	91	15	121
Ryan Foster, UNCW	13	2	2.46	17	0	117	97	26	69
Austin Magestro, UNCW	5	3	2.59	29	3	49	29	23	66
Michael Evans, James Madison	5	1	2.66	28	4	44	53	14	39
Dustin Hunt, Northeastern	6	3	2.72	14	0	86	68	27	93
Eric Bauer, Charleston	3	2	2.87	19	1	63	67	21	52

	W	L	ERA	G	SV	IP	H	BB	SO
Andrew Misiaszek, Northeastern	5	4	3.29	22	2	52	45	21	53
Bailey Ober, Charleston	7	4	3.53	15	0	97	90	27	96
Brandon Walter, Delaware	7	3	3.63	14	0	89	77	36	85
Austin Easter, UNCW	3	0	3.65	26	0	44	36	20	42
Nathan Helvey, Charleston	4	6	3.77	17	0	91	91	23	62
Kyle Stricker, Towson	6	2	3.86	18	1	42	40	16	27
Matt Golczewski, Towson	3	1	4.08	17	1	57	57	30	32
Nathan Ocker, Charleston	4	1	4.25	20	0	42	45	12	42
Dan Powers, William & Mary	8	6	4.69	17	0	94	120	23	39
Alex Royalty, UNCW	8	2	4.71	15	0	73	74	22	57
David Marriggi, Towson	2	5	4.74	17	2	49	54	18	43
Bodie Sheehan, William & Mary	5	4	4.86	18	0	83	89	34	41
Kevin Milley, Delaware	3	1	4.88	21	1	48	52	23	44
Kevin Ross, Towson	2	7	4.88	14	0	66	87	27	35
Skyler Morris, Towson	2	3	4.89	15	0	53	64	24	28
Ryan Conroy, Elon	4	3	4.93	23	1	49	56	30	34
John Rooney, Hofstra	3	8	5.02	18	0	72	79	32	77
Michael Elefante, Elon	2	2	5.09	15	0	53	46	36	56
Ron Marinaccio, Delaware	7	4	5.18	14	0	82	89	35	73
Bowie Matteson, Hofstra	3	7	5.23	16	0	72	94	14	55
James Mulry, Northeastern	3	7	5.28	14	0	75	75	43	58
Nick Brown, William & Mary	5	7	5.53	16	0	96	99	41	85
Austin Clark, Towson	1	5	6.00	14	0	51	64	11	25

CONFERENCE USA

	Conference		Overall	
	W	L	W	L
Florida Atlantic	21	8	39	19
Marshall	21	9	34	21
* Southern Mississippi	20	10	41	20
Rice	19	10	38	24
Louisiana Tech	19	11	42	20
Old Dominion	15	15	32	24
Florida International	15	15	29	29
Charlotte	12	17	23	32
Alabama-Birmingham	12	18	21	34
Western Kentucky	10	20	24	30
Texas-San Antonio	8	20	17	34
Middle Tennessee State	5	24	20	35

All-Conference Team: C—Chuckie Robinson, Jr., Southern Mississippi. **INF**—C.J. Chatham, Jr., Florida Atlantic; Danny Hudzina, Sr., Western Kentucky; Tommy Lane, Jr., Marshall; Tim Lynch, Sr., Southern Mississippi. **OF**—Dylan Burdeaux, Jr., Southern Mississippi; Jake Sandlin, Sr., Southern Mississippi; D.J. Gee, Sr., Marshall. **DH**—Kaleb Duckworth, So., Western Kentucky. **SP**—Chase Boster, Sr., Marshall; Jon Duplantier, Jr., Rice; Kirk McCarty, Sr., Southern Mississippi; Casey Sutton, Jr., Louisiana Tech. **RP**—Glenn Otto, So., Rice. **Player of the Year:** C.J. Chatham, Florida Atlantic. **Pitcher of the Year:** Jon Duplantier, Rice. **Freshman of the Year:** Ford Proctor, Rice. **Newcomer of the Year:** Tommy Lane, Marshall. **Defensive Player of the Year:** C.J. Chatham, Florida Atlantic. **Coach of the Year:** Jeff Waggoner, Marshall.

INDIVIDUAL BATTING LEADERS
(Minimum 140 At-Bats)

	AVG	OBP	SLG	AB	2B	3B	HR	RBI	SB
Danny Hudzina, Western Ky.	.408	.470	.564	218	18	2	4	32	0
Riley Delgado, Middle Tenn.	.388	.492	.437	206	10	0	0	18	4
Brett Netzer, Charlotte	.384	.461	.555	211	17	2	5	35	6
Tim Lynch, Southern Miss.	.365	.470	.545	233	12	0	10	59	0
T.J. Nichting, Charlotte	.358	.388	.502	229	22	1	3	33	2
C.J. Chatham, Florida Atlantic	.357	.422	.554	249	17	4	8	50	2
Jake Sandlin, Southern Miss.	.353	.436	.540	235	17	3	7	39	2
Charlie Warren, Rice	.341	.408	.379	182	5	1	0	27	6
Raphael Gladu, Louisiana Tech	.339	.429	.466	174	12	2	2	29	5
Ford Proctor, Rice	.336	.428	.471	223	15	3	3	41	6
Logan Sherer, Charlotte	.336	.412	.574	223	15	1	12	52	2
Reece Hampton, Charlotte	.335	.401	.418	239	12	1	2	21	12
Dylan Burdeaux, Southern Miss.	.335	.421	.529	257	13	2	11	41	8
Irving Lopez, Fla. International	.335	.394	.437	197	12	1	2	22	0
Aaron Bossi, Marshall	.333	.380	.484	225	14	1	6	45	8
Kaleb Duckworth, Western Ky.	.329	.421	.473	207	14	2	4	36	3

	AVG	OBP	SLG	AB	2B	3B	HR	RBI	SB
Nick Dawson, Southern Miss.	.328	.432	.473	201	19	2	2	37	6
Tyler Ratliff, Marshall	.327	.368	.579	202	15	0	12	47	2
Bryan Arias, UTSA	.321	.385	.426	190	9	4	1	20	7
Austin Langham, Fla. Atlantic	.320	.421	.392	194	12	1	0	23	1
Steven Kraft, Western Kentucky	.319	.409	.476	210	9	3	6	33	1
Nick Day, Fla. International	.318	.378	.533	195	10	1	10	31	1
Hunter Slater, Southern Miss.	.314	.372	.458	153	10	0	4	26	1
Chase Lunceford, Louisiana Tech	.312	.390	.551	205	10	3	11	51	2
Zach Rutherford, Old Dominion	.311	.372	.409	225	10	3	2	29	12
Corey Bird, Marshall	.300	.375	.335	230	6	1	0	22	34
Tommy Lane, Marshall	.296	.402	.514	216	8	0	13	48	0
Brewer Hicklen, UAB	.289	.413	.408	201	7	4	3	26	22
Dane Myers, Rice	.264	.358	.363	182	4	4	2	21	7

INDIVIDUAL PITCHING LEADERS
(Minimum 40 Innings Pitched)

	W	L	ERA	G	SV	IP	H	BB	SO
Adam Atkins, Louisiana Tech	6	1	1.20	24	9	45	28	12	56
Burris Warner, Marshall	3	1	1.88	26	11	43	37	15	34
Casey Sutton, Louisiana Tech	8	1	1.91	17	0	85	72	24	46
Sean Labsan, Florida Atlantic	5	1	1.96	11	1	46	40	17	39
Glenn Otto, Rice	9	2	2.26	33	8	72	53	30	76
Nick Sandlin, Southern Miss.	3	3	2.38	26	12	42	32	20	44
Blake Fox, Rice	5	7	2.72	17	0	109	92	30	95
Alex Demchak, Fla. International	3	3	2.81	21	3	48	46	20	34
Thomas Lowery, UAB	1	4	2.82	22	8	51	43	21	49
Nate Harris, Louisiana Tech	5	2	2.93	28	5	68	55	21	72
Adam Lamar, UAB	3	4	2.93	22	0	55	42	22	31
Garrett Whitlock, UAB	4	5	3.00	25	0	51	58	21	46
Kirk McCarty, Southern Miss.	8	1	3.15	17	0	89	100	27	89
Garrett Ring, Middle Tenn.	1	4	3.18	16	1	45	49	20	46
Jon Duplantier, Rice	7	7	3.24	17	0	111	77	47	148
Philip Perry, Charlotte	1	1	3.29	25	4	41	36	25	32
Cameron Linck, Louisiana Tech	1	1	3.38	15	0	59	56	21	57
Chase Boster, Marshall	8	3	3.39	16	0	104	91	26	85
Ricardo Salinas, Rice	9	2	3.39	15	0	82	67	33	64
Code Crouse, Fla. International	3	2	3.50	16	1	75	94	24	49
Marc Stewart, Florida Atlantic	6	0	3.58	15	0	78	69	32	45
David McKay, Florida Atlantic	3	6	3.74	14	0	75	62	26	66
Victor Diaz, Old Dominion	6	4	3.78	16	0	69	85	17	33
Holden Capps, Charlotte	5	2	3.79	23	1	62	59	18	43
Sam Sinnen, Old Dominion	6	1	3.81	16	1	78	64	27	59
Sam Higgs, Western Kentucky	3	1	3.83	24	0	40	46	9	29
Cord Cockrell, Southern Miss.	7	2	4.26	15	0	70	77	9	45
Tyler Troutt, Middle Tenn.	1	10	5.74	13	0	63	68	38	33

HORIZON LEAGUE

	Conference		Overall	
	W	L	W	L
* Wright State	23	6	45	16
Wisconsin-Milwaukee	17	11	32	26
Valparaiso	17	12	30	28
Illinois-Chicago	15	12	25	30
Oakland	11	14	23	27
Northern Kentucky	9	21	20	34
Youngstown State	5	21	14	38

All-Conference Team: C—Daulton Varsho, So., Wisconsin-Milwaukee. **1B**—Ricardo, Ramirez, Jr., Illinois-Chicago. **2B**—David Cronin, So., Illinois-Chicago. **3B**—Shea Molitor, Sr., Valparaiso. **SS**—Mike Brosseau, Sr., Oakland. **OF**—Ryan Fucci, Sr., Wright State; Nolan Lodden, Sr., Valparaiso; Luke Meeteer, Sr., Wisconsin-Milwaukee. **DH**—Daniel Delaney, Sr., Valparaiso. **UTL**—Ian Yetsko, Sr., Oakland. **SP**—Brian Keller, Sr., Wisconsin-Milwaukee; Dalton Lundeen, Sr., Valparaiso; Jesse Scholtens, Sr., Wright State. **RP**—Trevor Lane, Sr., Illinois-Chicago. **Player of the Year:** Daulton Varsho, Wisconsin-Milwaukee. **Pitcher of the Year:** Brian Keller, Wisconsin-Milwaukee. **Relief Pitcher of the Year:** Trevor Lane, Illinois-Chicago. **Freshman of the Year:** Caleb Sampen, Wright State. **Coach of the Year:** Greg Lovelady, Wright State.

INDIVIDUAL BATTING LEADERS
(Minimum 140 At-Bats)

	AVG	OBP	SLG	AB	2B	3B	HR	RBI	SB
Daulton Varsho, Milwaukee	.381	.447	.610	231	17	6	8	51	16
Luke Meeteer, Milwaukee	.362	.452	.537	218	16	2	6	44	25
Mike Brosseau, Oakland	.360	.456	.571	186	11	0	10	33	8
David Cronin, Illinois-Chicago	.360	.422	.455	222	12	0	3	28	16
Nolan Lodden, Valparaiso	.356	.451	.472	233	18	3	1	45	16
J.D. Orr, Wright State	.346	.396	.420	205	7	4	0	27	7
Josh Clark, Valparaiso	.338	.399	.464	237	14	2	4	50	12
Mitch Roman, Wright State	.336	.401	.428	250	10	5	1	42	26
Quint Heady, Northern Ky.	.330	.377	.489	182	8	0	7	31	16
Will Haueter, Northern Ky.	.329	.393	.439	164	18	0	0	25	0
Ryan Fucci, Wright State	.326	.412	.525	236	12	1	11	64	26
James Stea, Valparaiso	.322	.398	.412	211	11	3	1	20	18
Logan Spurlin, Northern Ky.	.311	.391	.521	190	10	0	10	40	0
Shea Molitor, Valparaiso	.309	.412	.438	217	17	1	3	53	3
Ben Hart, Oakland	.305	.364	.351	154	4	0	1	29	6
Zach Sterry, Oakland	.303	.365	.466	175	15	1	4	27	5
Alex Dee, Illinois-Chicago	.300	.358	.413	160	9	0	3	31	3
Tyler Pagano, Oakland	.294	.356	.411	187	10	1	3	31	1
Ian Yetsko, Oakland	.294	.354	.466	187	14	2	5	38	3
Conor Philbin, Illinois-Chicago	.293	.416	.431	167	14	0	3	22	8
Peyton Burdick, Wright State	.289	.409	.443	194	14	2	4	31	2
Cody Bohanek, Illinois-Chicago	.286	.367	.397	189	13	1	2	28	15
Trey Ganns, Northern Kentucky	.286	.365	.391	192	17	0	1	21	4
Scott Ota, Illinois-Chicago	.281	.348	.455	167	9	4	4	23	1
John Brodner, Wright State	.280	.376	.415	193	14	3	2	41	3

INDIVIDUAL PITCHING LEADERS
(Minimum 40 Innings Pitched)

	W	L	ERA	G	SV	IP	H	BB	SO
Trevor Lane, Illinois-Chicago	8	5	1.41	26	5	71	41	35	90
Caleb Sampen, Wright State	9	4	2.76	15	0	95	75	23	57
Jesse Scholtens, Wright State	10	1	2.95	16	0	110	89	19	95
Trevor Swaney, Wright State	9	2	3.00	17	0	72	67	9	38
Brian Keller, Milwaukee	10	3	3.10	15	0	107	109	20	103
Robby Sexton, Wright State	7	3	3.15	14	0	74	65	16	58
Jay Peters, Milwaukee	4	5	3.30	17	0	74	73	29	53
Trevor Haas, Valparaiso	5	2	3.38	17	0	93	94	25	43
Connor Ryan, Illinois-Chicago	2	3	3.78	18	0	67	63	25	43
Adam Reuss, Milwaukee	2	4	3.79	14	0	78	70	27	56
Bryce Yoder, Valparaiso	2	3	3.86	32	1	40	46	7	18
Joe Buchalski, Oakland	1	6	3.95	13	0	66	62	35	64
Dalton Lundeen, Valparaiso	7	4	4.13	15	0	98	99	21	70
Tyler Palm, Oakland	4	5	4.43	12	0	63	58	17	37
Logan Blair, Wright State	0	1	4.44	32	4	47	53	18	23
Ian Lewandowski, Ill.-Chicago	4	4	4.52	15	0	94	94	26	67
Mario Losi, Valparaiso	3	6	4.96	12	0	62	74	19	46
Pat Kelley, Northern Kentucky	1	3	4.97	12	0	58	67	23	40
Jeremy Quinlan, Youngstown St.	2	8	5.16	14	0	68	74	36	55
Joe King, Youngstown State	2	7	5.23	14	0	72	83	33	36
Jake Lee, Oakland	5	5	5.31	14	0	59	66	19	37
Jake Dahlberg, Illinois-Chicago	6	8	5.35	14	0	74	63	46	68
Ryan Fritze, Valparaiso	3	5	5.73	25	7	38	56	18	37
Mitchell Schulewitz, Ill.-Chicago	2	5	5.80	19	0	54	57	29	43
Tyler Miller, Northern Kentucky	3	4	5.81	16	0	62	74	26	30

IVY LEAGUE

	Conference		Overall	
Gehrig Division	W	L	W	L
* Princeton	13	7	24	21
Pennsylvania	10	10	19	22
Columbia	10	10	17	24
Cornell	7	13	14	24

	Conference		Overall	
Rolfe Division	W	L	W	L
Dartmouth	11	9	24	21
Yale	11	9	19	22
Harvard	9	11	17	24
Brown	9	11	14	24

All-Conference Team: C—Josh Huntley, Jr., Brown. **1B**—Zak Belski, Jr., Princeton. **2B**—Danny Hoy, Sr., Princeton. **3B**—Bill Arendt, Sr., Princeton. **SS**—Thomas Roulis, Sr., Dartmouth. **OF**—Jesper Horsted, Fr., Princeton; Robb Paller, Sr., Columbia; Gary Tesch, Sr., Pennsylvania. **DH**—Tim Graul, Jr., Pennsylvania. **UT**—Randell Kanemaru, So., Columbia. **SP**—Scott Politz, Fr., Yale; Chad Powers, Jr., Princeton; Duncan Robinson, Sr., Dartmouth. **RP**—Dante Bosnic, So., Brown; Patrick Peterson, So., Dartmouth. **Player of the Year:** Tim Graul, Pennsylvania. **Pitcher of the Year:** Chad Powers, Princeton. **Rookie of the Year:** Matt O'Neill, Pennsylvania. **Coach of the Year:** Scott Bradley, Princeton.

INDIVIDUAL BATTING LEADERS
(Minimum 140 At-Bats)

	AVG	OBP	SLG	AB	2B	3B	HR	RBI	SB
Will Savage, Columbia	**.367**	**.463**	.487	158	11	1	2	15	**20**
Tim Graul, Penn	.364	.443	**.642**	162	21	0	**8**	**35**	2
Ric Slenker, Yale	.342	.443	.513	158	18	0	3	28	7
Gary Tesch, Penn	.335	.399	.445	155	7	2	2	13	12
Danny Hoy, Princeton	.322	.383	.474	171	11	0	5	28	9
Robb Paller, Columbia	.302	.400	.503	149	13	1	5	32	5
Matt Tola, Penn	.301	.340	.371	143	10	0	0	15	1
Dustin Shirley, Dartmouth	.301	.314	.422	166	10	**5**	0	16	8
Harri White, Yale	.293	.369	.479	140	8	3	4	23	4
Nick Hernandez, Princeton	.288	.356	.388	170	6	1	3	33	8
Mitch Klug, Harvard	.286	.396	.421	140	9	2	2	12	4
Bill Arendt, Princeton	.277	.383	.413	155	7	1	4	18	1
Si Whiteman, Yale	.266	.311	.311	**177**	4	2	0	16	17
Rob Henry, Brown	.263	.345	.375	152	3	1	4	18	3
Ryan Mincher, Penn	.257	.366	.450	140	8	2	5	24	2
Michael Ketchmark, Dartmouth	.255	.319	.414	145	8	0	5	28	1
Zack Belski, Princeton	.253	.346	.383	154	11	0	3	28	0
Joseph Flynn, Princeton	.245	.337	.320	147	5	0	2	20	1
Tim DeGraw, Yale	.242	.346	.306	157	4	3	0	23	11
Noah Shulman, Brown	.241	.301	.390	141	10	1	3	17	0

INDIVIDUAL PITCHING LEADERS
(Minimum 40 Innings Pitched)

	W	L	ERA	G	SV	IP	H	BB	SO
Gabe Kleiman, Penn	3	3	**2.24**	9	0	52	43	17	27
Chad Powers, Princeton	**6**	4	2.45	11	0	**77**	61	17	45
Nick Gruener, Harvard	5	4	2.76	9	0	62	59	9	49
Christian Taugner, Brown	5	3	2.79	9	0	58	53	**7**	39
Sean Poppen, Harvard	3	4	3.02	10	0	57	47	21	48
Cole O'Connor, Dartmouth	0	2	3.12	10	0	40	43	8	28
Duncan Robinson, Dartmouth	4	**6**	3.28	11	0	69	71	**7**	**73**
Keelan Smithers, Princeton	4	1	3.46	8	0	42	**39**	17	23
Scott Politz, Yale	**6**	3	3.64	13	0	77	70	14	48
Mike Reitcheck, Penn	2	4	3.96	9	0	52	57	17	27
Adam Bleday, Penn	2	2	3.98	14	0	43	44	17	33
Austin French, Brown	4	4	4.12	9	0	55	50	30	60
Cameron Mingo, Princeton	**6**	4	4.21	11	0	62	62	23	35
Kevin Stone, Harvard	4	2	4.22	8	0	43	40	20	31
Jake Cousins, Penn	4	4	4.23	8	0	45	49	20	45
Luke Strieber, Princeton	2	5	4.67	10	0	54	59	15	31
Chasen Ford, Yale	5	5	5.08	14	1	62	69	21	32
Peter Lannoo, Cornell	3	3	5.15	10	1	44	54	12	25
Billy Lescher, Penn	5	3	5.31	11	1	42	38	16	39
Reid Anderson, Brown	1	5	5.36	9	0	47	62	31	42
Paul Balestrieri, Cornell	2	**6**	5.51	11	0	49	53	22	35
Ma Kukowski, Yale	1	**6**	5.89	**19**	4	44	52	20	27
Adam Cline, Columbia	1	**6**	7.21	9	0	49	62	23	37

METRO ATLANTIC ATHLETIC CONFERENCE

	Conference		Overall	
	W	L	W	L
* **Fairfield**	17	7	32	26
Canisius	16	8	32	27
Monmouth	16	8	30	27
Siena	16	8	25	32
Marist	11	8	22	24
Manhattan	13	11	24	31
Niagara	10	12	15	36

	W	L		W	L
Quinnipiac	10	14		21	31
Rider	9	14		17	33
Iona	5	19		11	39
Saint Peter's	5	19		10	42

All-Conference Team: C—Fabian Pena, Fr., Manhattan. **1B**—Shaine Hughes, So., Monmouth. **2B**—Jordan Bishop, So., Siena. **3B**—Grant Lamberton, Jr., Monmouth. **SS**—Anthony Massicci, Sr., Canisius. **OF**—Jake Salpietro, Sr., Fairfield; Christian Santisteban, Sr., Manhattan; Dan Shea, Sr., Monmouth. **DH**—Frankie Gregoire, Fr., Marist. **UT**—Rob Moore, Sr., Saint Peter's. **P**—Ricky Dennis, Jr., Monmouth; Thomas Jankins, Jr., Quinnipiac; Kyano Cummings, Sr., Siena. **Player of the Year:** Christian Santisteban, Manhattan. **Pitcher of the Year:** Ricky Dennis, Monmouth. **Relief Pitcher of the Year:** Iannick Remillard, Canisius. **Rookie of the Year:** Fabian Pena, Manhattan. **Coach of the Year:** Bill Currier, Fairfield.

INDIVIDUAL BATTING LEADERS
(Minimum 140 At-Bats)

	AVG	OBP	SLG	AB	2B	3B	HR	RBI	SB
Shaine Hughes, Monmouth	**.385**	.457	.522	161	15	2	1	34	1
Christian Santisteban, Manhattan	.367	.453	.570	207	21	0	7	46	1
Michael Fuhrman, Niagara	.360	**.465**	.449	178	13	0	1	24	13
Fabian Pena, Manhattan	.350	.415	.598	214	22	2	9	**54**	3
Jake Salpietro, Fairfield	.344	.432	.571	224	17	2	**10**	42	8
Anthony Massicci, Canisius	.344	.459	.478	209	16	3	2	26	21
Matthew Batten, Quinnipiac	.344	.402	.467	212	10	2	4	25	20
Grant Lamberton, Monmouth	.341	.445	.409	220	8	2	1	22	5
Jake Lumley, Canisius	.339	.437	.431	218	7	2	3	35	12
Michael Conti, Fairfield	.335	.426	.399	158	5	1	1	34	8
Kevin Radziewicz, Fairfield	.330	.401	.399	203	11	0	1	37	4
Rob Moore, Saint Peter's	.327	.423	.484	153	11	2	3	22	8
Tanner Kirwer, Niagara	.319	.407	.458	144	14	0	2	28	18
Jordan Bishop, Siena	.318	.389	.413	223	10	1	3	43	1
Liam Wilson, Canisius	.316	.386	.396	212	14	0	1	34	8
Jose Carrera, Manhattan	.314	.370	.453	**236**	**22**	4	1	26	20
Dan Shea, Monmouth	.312	.429	.490	202	10	1	8	53	8
Dan Swain, Siena	.311	.423	.531	177	13	4	6	33	3
Frank Gregoire, Marist	.309	.374	**.599**	162	15	1	**10**	39	3
Jason Patnick, Manhattan	.307	.355	.440	150	8	3	2	30	5
Greg Cullen, Niagara	.301	.358	.388	206	13	1	1	20	10
Robb Alessandrine, Monmouth	.300	.364	.375	160	10	1	0	22	5
Phil Madonna, Siena	.300	.389	.381	160	11	1	0	19	2
Robert Pescitelli, Quinnipiac	.299	.444	.446	177	7	2	5	26	17
Jason Midkiff, Saint Peter's	.299	.361	.431	144	9	2	2	24	1
Michae Pfenninger, Manhattan	.283	.330	.387	191	10	**5**	0	27	15
Graham McIntire, Marist	.265	.336	.332	211	9	1	1	24	**24**

INDIVIDUAL PITCHING LEADERS
(Minimum 40 Innings Pitched)

	W	L	ERA	G	SV	IP	H	BB	SO
Mike Bonaiuto, Fairfield	4	2	**2.54**	23	5	46	44	**8**	29
Joe DeRosa, Iona	3	3	**2.54**	14	0	60	49	17	26
Shawn Kanwisher, Manhattan	7	3	2.57	22	4	49	39	16	57
Margevicius Nick, Rider	3	6	2.74	13	0	69	78	18	58
John Signore, Fairfield	3	2	2.90	16	0	84	90	**8**	58
Nolan Hunt, Canisius	3	0	2.90	17	0	62	45	23	32
Taylor Luciani, Quinnipiac	4	2	3.13	12	0	69	58	26	42
Aaron Casper, Canisius	7	1	3.19	20	0	54	47	11	48
Thomas Jankins, Quinnipiac	5	6	3.26	14	0	86	82	28	79
Cody Eckerson, Niagara	4	4	3.51	11	0	59	58	14	58
Aaron Howell, Fairfield	6	4	3.68	**26**	5	64	71	24	44
Tom Cosgrove, Manhattan	5	5	3.70	15	0	90	100	31	80
Kyano Cummings, Siena	6	5	3.76	18	5	93	99	48	**91**
Ricky Dennis, Monmouth	**9**	5	3.78	15	0	86	93	22	58
Mike Coss, Marist	1	5	3.86	19	0	47	45	9	43
Joey Rocchietti, Manhattan	4	6	3.90	13	0	83	95	17	48
Charlie Jerla, Marist	6	6	3.96	13	0	73	81	29	53
Tony Romanelli, Marist	2	0	4.04	16	0	42	43	24	35
Kyle Dube, Fairfield	6	4	4.09	15	0	88	94	29	68
Anthon Ciavarella, Monmouth	5	4	4.12	14	0	74	85	21	66
Mike Elwood, Canisius	5	4	4.26	17	0	57	62	17	46
Joe Jacques, Manhattan	5	4	4.30	18	0	75	74	34	63
Sean Keenan, Marist	6	3	4.32	14	0	83	88	26	63
Joe Molettiere, Monmouth	1	2	4.34	18	3	46	52	19	28

	W	L	ERA	G	SV	IP	H	BB	SO
Josh Shepley, Canisius	2	5	4.44	10	0	53	50	21	42
Tyler Smith, Canisius	6	3	4.63	22	1	45	**37**	30	59
Frank Trimarco, Monmouth	7	4	4.72	15	0	**97**	117	26	85

MID-AMERICAN CONFERENCE

	Conference		Overall	
Eastern Division	**W**	**L**	**W**	**L**
Kent State	20	4	43	13
Miami (Ohio)	14	10	27	28
Ohio	8	16	23	29
Buffalo	8	16	21	31
Bowling Green State	7	17	17	37
	Conference		**Overall**	
Western Division	**W**	**L**	**W**	**L**
Ball State	15	9	32	26
Northern Illinois	14	10	24	32
Toledo	13	11	19	37
Central Michigan	12	12	22	36
* Western Michigan	11	13	21	33
Eastern Michigan	10	14	21	35

All-Conference Team: C—Jarett Rindfleisch, Jr., Ball State. **1B**—Caleb Stayton, Jr., Ball State. **2B**—Brad Wood, So., Northern Illinois. **3B**—Mitch McGeein, Sr., Eastern Michigan. **SS**—Deion Tansel, Sr., Toledo. **OF**—Alex Call, Jr., Ball State; Luke Burch, Jr., Kent State; Vinny Mallaro, Jr., Buffalo. **DH**—Zarley Zalewski, Sr., Kent State; Gary Russo, Sr., Miami (Ohio). **SP**—Eric Lauer, Jr., Kent State; Keegan Akin, Jr., Western Michigan; Eli Kraus, So., Kent State; Jake Tuohy, Jr., Buffalo. **RP**—B.J. Butler, Jr., Ball State. **Player of the Year:** Alex Call, Ball State. **Pitcher of the Year:** Eric Lauer, Kent State. **Freshman of the Year:** Connor Smith, Western Michigan. **Freshman Pitcher of the Year:** William Anderson, Northern Illinois. **Defensive Player of the Year:** Deion Tansel, Toledo. **Coach of the Year:** Jeff Duncan, Kent State.

INDIVIDUAL BATTING LEADERS
(Minimum 140 At-Bats)

	AVG	OBP	SLG	AB	2B	3B	HR	RBI	SB
Caleb Stayton, Ball State	**.377**	**.482**	.614	220	17	1	11	**71**	2
Mitch Longo, Ohio	.360	.438	.467	214	14	0	3	22	12
Alex Call, Ball State	.358	.443	**.667**	243	24	**6**	13	44	17
Luke Burch, Kent State	.357	.423	.468	235	12	4	2	37	22
Ross Haffey, Miami (Ohio)	.355	.439	.599	217	20	0	11	48	1
Vinny Mallaro, Buffalo	.351	.438	.649	188	15	1	13	52	0
Zarley Zalewski, Kent State	.349	.449	.507	229	19	1	5	58	5
Connor Smith, Western Mich.	.336	.363	.379	211	6	0	1	24	12
Cody Gaertner, Ohio	.330	.381	.421	221	8	0	4	29	3
Deion Tansel, Toledo	.327	.402	.408	223	12	0	2	29	12
Zach Mckinstry, Central Mich.	.325	.415	.383	**243**	10	2	0	26	12
Bobby Sheppard, Buffalo	.323	.390	.377	220	8	2	0	18	6
Grant Miller, Western Michigan	.321	.410	.386	215	10	2	0	36	4
Rudy Rott, Ohio	.319	.406	.426	204	13	0	3	39	0
Conner Simonetti, Kent State	.311	.373	.599	222	11	1	17	50	1
Brennan Williams, Eastern Mich.	.308	.344	.453	208	11	2	2	25	9
Jaret Rindfleisch, Ball State	.307	.446	.503	179	12	1	7	31	1
Alex Maloney, Ball State	.305	.399	.408	233	14	2	2	32	12
Stephen Letz, Northern Illinois	.304	.376	.486	181	9	0	8	43	4
Mason Mamarella, Kent State	.303	.394	.362	188	11	0	0	13	12
Justin Fletcher, Northern Illinois	.301	.362	.406	229	17	2	1	39	11
Daniel Jipping, Central Mich.	.300	.406	.484	217	16	3	6	42	4
Alex Borglin, Central Michigan	.299	.394	.402	241	12	5	1	27	5
Hunter Prince, Western Mich.	.291	.355	.414	203	17	1	2	32	0
Ryan Heeke, Central Michigan	.291	.361	.371	151	8	2	0	22	7
Gary Russo, Miami (Ohio)	.271	.343	.614	207	8	3	**19**	43	1
Marquise Gill, Eastern Mich.	.250	.310	.301	236	9	0	1	15	**35**

INDIVIDUAL PITCHING LEADERS
(Minimum 40 Innings Pitched)

	W	L	ERA	G	SV	IP	H	BB	SO
Eric Lauer, Kent State	**10**	2	**0.69**	15	0	104	49	28	125
Keegan Akin, Western Mich.	7	4	1.82	17	0	**109**	72	30	**133**
B.J. Butler, Ball State	6	1	1.84	25	9	64	57	14	54
Jake Roehn, Ohio	2	2	2.18	23	7	45	42	**9**	43

	W	L	ERA	G	SV	IP	H	BB	SO
Logan Harasta, Buffalo	1	2	2.33	25	3	46	**31**	23	42
Devin Daugherty, Bowling Grn.	4	2	2.56	30	2	60	55	20	51
Eli Kraus, Kent State	9	1	2.64	14	0	89	78	24	59
Zach Willeman, Kent State	1	3	2.70	23	14	37	33	25	38
Shane Smith, Miami (Ohio)	5	3	2.98	21	1	60	54	15	38
Alec Tuohy, Buffalo	7	4	2.98	14	0	94	83	33	69
C.J. Schildt, Bowling Green	3	6	3.07	11	0	56	53	26	40
Connor Wollersheim, Kent State	3	2	3.10	10	0	41	43	21	25
Ross Achter, Toledo	7	6	3.10	15	0	90	84	35	62
Tyler Butzin, Eastern Michigan	3	5	3.33	15	1	78	73	28	57
Andy Ravel, Kent State	8	4	3.36	15	0	91	96	20	77
Michael Jacob, Toledo	2	5	3.43	25	8	42	42	17	31
Patric Leatherman, Central Mich.	3	4	3.53	15	0	74	73	28	46
Jacob Piechota, Western Mich.	**10**	4	3.75	29	3	60	62	18	37
Cole Gnetz, Miami (Ohio)	4	2	3.75	14	0	70	64	40	67
Jordan Grosjean, Central Mich.	3	4	3.77	26	2	60	55	22	54
Brendan Burns, Ball State	5	4	3.81	14	0	59	61	41	45
Nick Deeg, Central Michigan	4	7	3.95	15	0	98	99	34	86
Matt Haro, Ball State	6	3	4.01	19	0	58	73	22	37
William Anderson, Northern Ill.	5	4	4.08	15	0	86	100	34	49
Tom Colletti, Ohio	3	3	4.11	24	0	50	53	22	39
Kevin Mallwitz, Western Mich.	1	2	5.44	**34**	1	48	62	24	29

MID-EASTERN ATHLETIC CONFERENCE

	Conference		Overall	
Northern Division	**W**	**L**	**W**	**L**
Norfolk State	19	5	29	21
Delaware State	13	10	13	36
Coppin State	8	16	14	38
Maryland-Eastern Shore	7	16	16	32
	Conference		**Overall**	
Southern Division	**W**	**L**	**W**	**L**
Florida A&M	19	5	31	21
* Bethune-Cookman	17	7	29	27
North Carolina Central	11	13	25	30
Savannah State	7	17	12	40
North Carolina A&T.	6	18	13	41

All-Conference Team: C—Clay Middleton, Jr., Bethune-Cookman. **1B**—Brian Davis, So., Florida A&M. **2B**—Alec Wong, Sr., Florida A&M. **3B**—Ben Ellzey, Jr., Florida A&M. **SS**—Milton Rivera, So., North Carolina A&T. **OF**—Nathan Bond, Sr., Bethune-Cookman; Dylan Dillard, Sr., Florida A&M; Carlos Ortiz, Jr., North Carolina Central. **UT**—Michael Cruz, Jr., Bethune-Cookman. **SP**—Matt Outman, Sr., Norfolk State; Jonathan Mauricio, Jr., Norfolk State. **RP**—Andrew Vernon, Sr., North Carolina Central; Alex Mauricio, So., Norfolk State. **Player of the Year:** Dylan Dillard, Florida A&M. **Pitcher of the Year:** Matt Outman, Norfolk State. **Rookie of the Year:** Danny Rodriguez, Bethune-Cookman. **Coach of the Year:** Jamey Shouppe, Florida A&M.

INDIVIDUAL BATTING LEADERS
(Minimum 140 At-Bats)

	AVG	OBP	SLG	AB	2B	3B	HR	RBI	SB
Ben Ellzey, Florida A&M	**.388**	.467	.517	178	11	0	4	42	1
Alec Wong, Florida A&M	.378	**.504**	.528	193	12	1	5	33	5
Brian Davis, Florida A&M	.370	.471	.566	189	14	1	7	44	1
Nathan Bond, Beth.-Cookman	.355	.437	.462	169	7	1	3	30	0
Milton Rivera, N.C. A&T	.349	.405	.553	215	**19**	2	7	26	16
Todd Henry, Delaware State	.336	.420	.388	152	6	1	0	19	6
Dylan Dillard, Florida A&M	.335	.462	.587	179	9	**6**	8	**59**	4
Clay Middleton, Beth.-Cookman	.335	.443	.413	167	4	0	3	31	0
Ellington Hopkins, N.C. Central	.333	.444	.434	198	11	0	3	23	15
Bryant Miranda, Coppin State	.333	.429	.422	192	11	0	2	26	16
Adan Ordonez, N.C. A&T	.332	.420	.449	196	14	0	3	45	1
James Dey, N.C. Central	.329	.407	.459	170	7	0	5	26	1
Jacky Miles Jr., Florida A&M	.328	.420	.477	174	10	2	4	42	0
Michael Cruz, Beth.-Cookman	.325	.461	**.605**	200	6	1	**16**	41	0
Thomas Prospero, N.C. Central	.317	.380	.433	180	8	2	3	29	7
Mike Escanilla, UMES	.316	.396	.435	177	10	4	1	22	18
Roger Hall, Norfolk State	.316	.420	.417	187	17	1	0	31	1
George Dragon, Coppin State	.311	.436	.427	164	8	1	3	36	0
Danny Rodriguez, Beth.-Cookman	.308	.346	.487	**224**	10	0	10	46	0

	AVG	OBP	SLG	AB	2B	3B	HR	RBI	SB
Marlon Gibbs, Florida A&M	.308	.426	.468	201	15	1	5	34	7
Jonathan Moore, Sav. State	.306	.388	.377	183	5	1	2	23	18
Timothy Ravare, N.C. A&T	.306	.374	.372	196	9	2	0	20	0
Carlos Ortiz, N.C. Central	.305	.405	.542	177	9	3	9	42	4
Zachary Marszal, N.C. Central	.301	.385	.409	186	9	1	3	31	9
Trevor Theissen, N.C. Central	.300	.360	.439	180	13	3	2	27	7
Rakeem Quinn, Beth.-Cookman	.298	.401	.319	188	4	0	0	17	**28**

INDIVIDUAL PITCHING LEADERS
(Minimum 40 Innings Pitched)

	W	L	ERA	G	SV	IP	H	BB	SO
Jonathan Mauricio, Norfolk St.	6	2	**2.29**	15	0	59	53	26	59
Ricky Page, Florida A&M	6	3	2.91	14	0	74	71	26	62
Matt Outman, Norfolk State	**7**	4	3.00	14	0	**90**	88	29	71
Ryan McCranie, Savannah State	2	7	3.08	14	1	64	71	**11**	39
Alex Mauricio, Norfolk State	3	1	3.23	16	5	31	22	13	22
Andrew Vernon, N.C. Central	2	3	3.34	19	4	62	54	27	**85**
Devin Hemmerich, Norfolk St.	5	4	3.86	13	0	82	88	19	84
Lane DeLeon, Delaware State	2	5	3.96	14	0	75	83	31	70
Michael Parmentier, Norfolk St.	1	3	4.12	22	4	59	63	24	75
Cooper Jones, Norfolk State	2	4	4.17	18	1	41	**42**	36	51
Tyler Norris, Bethune-Cookman	6	4	4.52	15	0	70	67	22	71
Cameron Scalzo, N.C. Central	5	5	4.66	13	0	75	82	23	47
Alex Dandridge, N.C. Central	4	3	4.73	14	0	67	65	26	58
Alex Seibold, Beth.-Cookman	6	5	4.78	17	0	64	69	21	59
Krystian Negron, Coppin State	5	4	4.81	16	2	77	83	41	62
Chris Melrath, UMES	0	6	5.04	15	0	61	57	34	28
Christian Gonnelli, N.C. Central	3	6	5.15	13	0	58	71	18	54
German Hernandez, B-C	4	5	5.20	15	0	73	93	25	44
Jojo Durden, Florida A&M	2	3	5.25	10	1	48	51	18	43
Chase Jarrell, Florida A&M	6	4	5.45	13	0	66	88	15	39
Trevor McKenna, Sav. State	2	4	5.55	14	0	71	77	38	57
Donte Lindsay, Beth-Cookman	4	3	5.80	16	1	45	56	23	36
Ryan Anderson, Florida A&M	4	1	6.04	13	0	45	66	22	25
Scott Bean, UMES	0	7	6.08	14	0	47	53	31	19
Danny Garrett, N.C. A&T	2	2	8.04	31	0	56	68	34	51
#Kendal Weeks, Florida A&M	1	1	4.38	23	**5**	39	36	14	18

MISSOURI VALLEY CONFERENCE

	Conference		Overall	
	W	L	W	L
*Dallas Baptist	15	5	44	19
Indiana State	13	8	35	21
Bradley	11	9	29	21
Southern Illinois	11	10	31	25
Evansville	9	12	29	27
Wichita State	9	12	21	37
Missouri State	7	13	38	21
Illinois State	7	13	17	37

All-Conference Team: C—Boomer Synek, Sr., Evansville. **1B**—Logan Blackfan, So., Southern Illinois. **2B**—Andy DeJesus, Sr., Indiana State. **3B**—Jake Burger, So., Missouri State. **SS**—Trey Vickers, So., Wichita State. **OF**—Josh Jyawook, Sr., Evansville; David Martinelli, Jr., Dallas Baptist; Hunter Owen, Jr., Indiana State. **DH**—Daniel Sweet, Sr., Dallas Baptist. **UT**—Darick Hall, Jr., Dallas Baptist. **SP**—Michael Baird, So., Southern Illinois; Colin Poche, Jr., Dallas Baptist; Cameron Roegner, Sr., Bradley. **RP**—Seth Elledge, So., Dallas Baptist; Dalton Higgins, So., Dallas Baptist. **Player of the Year:** Darick Hall, Dallas Baptist. **Pitcher of the Year:** Colin Poche, Dallas Baptist. **Co-Freshman of the Year:** Jameson Hannah, Dallas Baptist; Greyson Jenista, Wichita State. **Newcomer of the Year:** Darick Hall, Dallas Baptist. **Defensive Player of the Year:** Jake Burger, Missouri State. **Coach of the Year:** Dan Heefner, Dallas Baptist.

INDIVIDUAL BATTING LEADERS
(Minimum 140 At-Bats)

	AVG	OBP	SLG	AB	2B	3B	HR	RBI	SB
Hunter Owen, Indiana State	**.350**	.430	.527	226	20	1	6	47	5
Jake Burger, Missouri State	.349	.420	.689	235	13	2	21	**72**	3
Boomer Synek, Evansville	.341	.439	.514	214	15	2	6	40	3
Trey Hair, Evansville	.340	.435	.591	215	20	2	10	42	1

	AVG	OBP	SLG	AB	2B	3B	HR	RBI	SB
Spencer Gaa, Bradley	.333	.403	.522	186	14	3	5	31	9
Jameson Hannah, Dal. Baptist	.332	.407	.456	193	8	2	4	37	11
Owen Miller, Illinois State	.328	.368	.498	235	**23**	1	5	44	2
Greyson Jenista, Wichita State	.326	.431	.471	172	8	1	5	32	2
Josh Jyawook, Evansville	.323	.382	.447	226	14	1	4	37	9
Luke Mangieri, Bradley	.322	.424	.423	149	3	3	2	15	3
Matt Duce, Dallas Baptist	.321	.417	.507	134	11	1	4	30	1
Hunter Steinmetz, Mo. State	.317	.419	.443	**246**	14	7	1	27	**14**
Aaron Meyer, Missouri State	.315	.380	.438	203	17	1	2	32	4
Tyler Leffler, Bradley	.313	.402	.474	192	21	2	2	33	1
Kaden Moore, Indiana State	.313	.387	.425	214	15	0	3	50	0
Trooper Reynolds, Dallas Baptist	.312	.380	.418	189	12	1	2	34	0
Greg Lambert, Southern Illinois	.312	.358	.416	231	16	1	2	30	2
Jonathan Ramon, Evansville	.308	.370	.601	143	6	3	10	39	2
Daniel Sweet, Dallas Baptist	.308	**.445**	.410	195	6	4	2	25	11
Trey Vickers, Wichita State	.306	.369	.363	160	6	0	1	19	0
Dayton Dugas, Wichita State	.304	.379	.460	161	11	1	4	24	4
Alec Bohm, Wichita State	.303	.346	.489	178	13	1	6	30	0
Darick Hall, Dallas Baptist	.302	.418	.630	235	17	0	20	**72**	1
David Martinelli, Dallas Baptist	.301	.375	.495	206	14	4	6	37	9
Justin Paulsen, Missouri State	.300	.415	.495	210	16	2	7	48	2
Logan Blackfan, Southern Ill.	.296	.385	.486	216	23	0	6	50	0
Spencer Johnson, Missouri State	.293	.412	**.707**	222	14	3	**24**	70	2
Andy DeJesus, Indiana State	.282	.341	.436	241	15	**8**	2	22	5

INDIVIDUAL PITCHING LEADERS
(Minimum 40 Innings Pitched)

	W	L	ERA	G	SV	IP	H	BB	SO
Michael Baird, Southern Illinois	**9**	4	1.76	15	0	**102**	75	26	58
Ryan Brady, Evansville	2	1	1.99	28	5	41	**27**	12	22
Colin Poche, Dallas Baptist	**9**	1	2.38	16	0	98	75	30	83
Cameron Roegner, Bradley	7	3	2.56	15	0	91	79	12	68
Brent Stong, Bradley	2	2	2.65	13	0	54	51	9	41
Landon Wilson, Dallas Baptist	0	1	2.68	25	3	44	33	26	35
Chad Whitmer, Southern Illinois	7	4	2.77	15	0	94	98	23	66
Sam Perez, Missouri State	8	0	2.86	**36**	1	91	65	35	**112**
Jeremy McKinney, Indiana State	6	4	3.26	25	7	50	45	10	46
Steve Heilenbach, Illinois State	5	4	3.30	15	0	87	82	30	52
Willie Schwanke, Wichita State	5	3	3.40	9	0	53	57	15	35
Ryan Keaffaber, Indiana State	6	4	3.48	15	0	96	98	15	46
Jordan Martinson, Dal. Baptist	3	2	3.68	19	2	71	56	41	59
Darick Hall, Dallas Baptist	**9**	3	3.71	16	0	97	103	21	94
Jake Fromson, Missouri State	6	2	3.71	24	1	70	64	19	74
Joey Marciano, Southern Illinois	4	7	3.78	15	0	83	78	34	59
Dalton Higgins, Dallas Baptist	**9**	4	3.79	27	2	71	77	23	45
Tyler Ward, Indiana State	6	5	3.81	18	1	80	86	13	40
Austin Allinger, Evansville	5	3	3.82	18	0	68	66	25	49
Matt Dennis, Bradley	**9**	3	3.89	15	0	86	78	33	76
Ethan Larrison, Indiana State	2	1	3.97	23	1	45	34	21	29
Weston Rivers, Indiana State	3	1	4.17	13	0	41	39	20	21
Ben Olson, Bradley	1	4	4.20	16	0	41	38	15	45
Patrick Schnieders, Evansville	4	6	4.23	14	0	83	84	37	56
Justin Hill, Indiana State	5	2	4.27	13	0	53	43	38	48
Nathan Stong, Bradley	2	0	5.05	26	2	41	49	**4**	41
Zach Lewis, Wichita State	2	**9**	5.96	23	1	74	76	27	66

MOUNTAIN WEST CONFERENCE

	Conference		Overall	
	W	L	W	L
Fresno State	21	9	36	22
*New Mexico	20	10	39	23
Nevada	20	10	37	24
Nevada-Las Vegas	14	16	24	32
Air Force	12	18	30	26
San Diego State	11	19	21	38
San José State	7	23	17	39

All-Conference Team: Bradley Haslam, Jr., Air Force; Tyler Jones, Jr., Air Force; Aaron Arruda, So., Fresno State; Brody Russell, Sr., Fresno State; T.J. Friedl, So., Nevada; Chris DeVito, Jr., New Mexico; Jared Holley, Sr., New Mexico; Carl Stajduhar, So., New Mexico; Payton Squier, So., Nevada-Las Vegas. **P**—Griffin Jax, Jr., Air Force; Jimmy Lambert, Jr.,

Fresno State; Ricky Tyler Thomas, So., Fresno State; Tyler Stevens, So., New Mexico; D.J. Myers, Jr., Nevada-Las Vegas. **Player of the Year:** Carl Stajduhar, New Mexico. Co-**Pitcher of the Year:** Griffin Jax, Air Force; Jimmy Lambert, Fresno State. **Co-Freshman of the Year:** Nic Ready, Air Force; Kyle Isbel, Nevada-Las Vegas. **Coach of the Year:** Mike Batesole, Fresno State.

INDIVIDUAL BATTING LEADERS
(Minimum 140 At-Bats)

	AVG	OBP	SLG	AB	2B	3B	HR	RBI	SB
Bradley Haslam, Air Force	**.408**	.449	.558	233	22	2	3	57	4
T.J. Friedl, Nevada	.401	**.494**	.563	222	9	**9**	3	35	13
Luis Gonzalez, New Mexico	.381	.470	.575	252	21	5	6	48	18
Adam Groesbeck, Air Force	.378	.453	.583	230	16	8	5	33	**19**
Chris DeVito, New Mexico	.375	.444	.685	232	20	2	16	65	0
Payton Squier, UNLV	.375	.439	.431	216	9	0	1	28	8
Cole Krzmarzick, Nevada	.368	.426	.479	190	16	1	1	37	3
Miles Mastrobuoni, Nevada	.364	.458	.474	228	17	4	0	40	18
Tyler Jones, Air Force	.360	**.438**	**.694**	222	13	2	**19**	64	3
Scott Silva, Fresno State	.357	.400	.521	140	11	0	4	23	1
Justin Bridgman, Nevada	.351	.398	.417	242	14	1	0	37	13
Justin Hazard, Nevada	.339	.378	.476	189	13	2	3	36	2
Jared Holley, New Mexico	.337	.451	.478	184	21	1	1	42	5
Jordan Pearce, Nevada	.332	.391	.522	205	17	5	4	47	1
Carl Stajduhar, New Mexico	.331	.411	.623	**257**	17	2	18	**66**	1
Nic Ready, Air Force	.329	.349	.496	234	17	2	6	53	3
Shane Timmons, San Jose State	.328	.383	.452	186	9	1	4	26	1
Spencer Draws, Air Force	.322	.381	.429	233	16	3	1	32	7
Aaron Arruda, Fresno State	.320	.406	.567	194	15	0	11	44	3
Kyle Isbel, UNLV	.319	.376	.444	232	10	8	1	28	7
Jake Stone, Fresno State	.312	.384	.472	218	18	4	3	35	6
Jack Zoellner, New Mexico	.307	.378	.489	231	16	1	8	46	2
Russell Williams, Air Force	.306	.364	.439	196	9	1	5	31	10
Justin Wylie, San Diego State	.305	.388	.410	239	13	0	4	39	8
Alan Trejo, San Diego State	.305	.357	.360	239	5	1	2	35	7
Tyler Zabojnik, Air Force	.290	.338	.449	214	**24**	2	2	37	1

INDIVIDUAL PITCHING LEADERS
(Minimum 40 Innings Pitched)

	W	L	ERA	G	SV	IP	H	BB	SO
Tim Borst, Fresno State	3	3	**1.72**	**28**	**8**	52	42	26	59
Griffin Jax, Air Force	9	2	2.05	15	0	**105**	94	20	90
Ricky Tyler Thomas, Fresno St.	9	4	2.16	15	0	104	86	16	**108**
Jimmy Lambert, Fresno State	**10**	2	3.13	15	0	98	98	19	78
Dominic Purpura, San Diego St.	4	2	3.25	21	0	69	72	16	27
Dylan Lee, Fresno State	2	2	3.45	27	6	47	41	15	44
Colton Thomson, New Mexico	8	3	3.61	15	0	95	98	27	82
Trevor Charpie, Nevada	5	4	3.74	16	0	75	59	22	52
Edgar Gonzalez, Fresno State	2	3	3.97	16	0	57	62	25	47
Mark Nowaczewski, Nevada	5	1	4.04	22	3	42	**37**	21	24
Tyler Stevens, New Mexico	8	4	4.11	16	0	101	115	42	78
Kenny Oakley, UNLV	4	**9**	4.36	15	0	89	106	35	58
Carson Schneider, New Mexico	4	4	4.68	17	0	100	127	20	44
Matt Hargreaves, Air Force	3	2	4.71	24	2	42	46	14	33
Josh Nashed, San Jose State	0	6	4.79	15	1	88	101	20	45
Brett Seeburger, San Diego St.	1	3	4.81	14	0	67	84	**11**	55
Dean Kremer, UNLV	4	5	4.92	15	0	82	99	21	46
Christian Stolo, Nevada	4	7	5.07	15	0	98	120	23	58
Jacob Devries, Nevada	4	6	5.09	14	0	64	51	52	55
Matt Brown, San Jose State	2	7	5.18	19	2	73	82	36	48
D.J. Myers, UNLV	6	4	5.23	15	0	84	101	29	70
Evan Mcmahan, Nevada	5	2	5.31	25	6	41	50	13	20
Graham Gomez, San Jose State	2	5	5.40	23	2	60	81	16	32
Trenton Brooks, Nevada	6	5	5.56	15	0	78	96	21	55
Hilario Tovar, San Jose State	3	4	5.58	17	0	60	75	16	43

NORTHEAST CONFERENCE

	Conference		Overall	
	W	L	W	L
*Bryant	26	4	47	12
Sacred Heart	18	13	30	28
Fairleigh Dickinson	16	15	28	28
Central Connecticut State	15	17	23	34

	W	L	W	L
Long Island-Brooklyn	13	17	19	35
Wagner	13	19	19	33
Mount St. Mary's	8	24	11	37

All-Conference Team: C—Connor Fitzsimons, Sr., Central Connecticut State. **1B**—Robby Rinn, Sr., Bryant. **2B**—Dean Lockery, So., Central Connecticut State. **3B**—Zach Wood, Sr., Bryant. **SS**—Dan Cellucci, Sr., Bryant. **OF**—Matt Albanese, Jr., Bryant; Ben Ruta, Sr., Wagner; Nick Angelini, Fr., Bryant. **DH**—Brandon Bingel, Jr., Bryant. **SP**—James Karinchak, So., Bryant; Steve Theetge, Fr., Bryant; Andrew Hinckley, Jr., Central Connecticut State. **RP**—Justin Snyder, So., Bryant. **Player of the Year:** Robby Rinn, Bryant. **Pitcher of the Year:** James Karinchak, Bryant. **Rookie of the Year:** Nick Angelini, Bryant. **Coach of the Year:** Steve Owens, Bryant.

INDIVIDUAL BATTING LEADERS
(Minimum 140 At-Bats)

	AVG	OBP	SLG	AB	2B	3B	HR	RBI	SB
Robby Rinn, Bryant	**.378**	.442	.591	**225**	**25**	4	5	**61**	1
Nick Mascelli, Wagner	.374	.414	.472	195	6	2	3	21	2
Matt Albanese, Bryant	.366	**.471**	**.639**	183	13	2	11	52	15
Nick Angelini, Bryant	.356	.467	.494	160	9	2	3	26	9
Trey Nicosia, Wagner	.349	.382	.423	149	11	0	0	18	2
John Giakas, Fairleigh Dickinson	.345	.416	.611	203	15	0	**13**	47	3
Dean Lockery, CCSU	.344	.423	.402	209	10	1	0	21	2
Ben Ruta, Wagner	.343	.406	.439	198	16	0	1	35	9
Ryan Brennan, Fair. Dickinson	.342	.420	.544	158	10	2	6	24	14
Zach Wood, Bryant	.322	.427	.485	171	8	1	6	37	1
Connor Fitzsimons, CCSU	.321	.399	.429	168	10	1	2	29	1
Dan Cellucci, Bryant	.318	.393	.421	195	7	2	3	31	2
Matt McCann, Fairleigh Dickinson	.312	.398	.399	173	13	1	0	14	26
Brian Lamboy, LIU-Brooklyn	.309	.419	.398	181	13	0	1	20	6
Victor Sorrento, Sacred Heart	.307	.354	.484	215	17	**6**	3	44	8
Pat McClure, Fairleigh Dickinson	.307	.391	.393	140	7	1	1	25	0
Bobby Romano, Fair. Dickinson	.303	.384	.465	142	8	3	3	25	11
Jason Fatzinger, Fair. Dickinson	.298	.380	.411	141	5	1	3	27	2
Jayson Sullivan, Sacred Heart	.298	.386	.371	205	10	1	1	27	16
Brandon Bingel, Bryant	.295	.359	.484	190	10	1	8	40	3
Ryan Owens, Mount St. Mary's	.294	.368	.412	170	12	1	2	18	8
Phil Capra, Wagner	.289	.352	.417	180	12	1	3	38	2
Cole Fabio, Bryant	.287	.382	.380	216	8	0	4	38	15
Buck McCarthy, Bryant	.284	.369	.490	204	16	1	8	55	1
Harrison Preschel, LIU-Brooklyn	.282	.383	.366	142	9	0	1	14	6
Tommy Jakubowski, LIU-Brook.	.261	.351	.381	176	8	2	3	29	**28**

INDIVIDUAL PITCHING LEADERS
(Minimum 40 Innings Pitched)

	W	L	ERA	G	SV	IP	H	BB	SO
James Karinchak, Bryant	**12**	3	**2.00**	15	0	95	70	43	**112**
James Taubl, Sacred Heart	5	3	2.16	16	1	67	64	24	27
Justin Snyder, Bryant	2	2	2.18	0	**10**	45	**36**	21	53
Mike Appel, Central Conn. State	2	5	2.44	9	1	59	43	31	23
Steve Theetge, Bryant	9	0	2.84	11	0	70	63	22	43
Baylor LaPointe, LIU-Brooklyn	7	5	3.05	14	0	**89**	78	36	57
Austin Goeke, Wagner	6	4	3.06	13	0	79	60	31	66
Tim Quinn, Fairleigh Dickinson	4	3	3.36	5	1	64	75	16	38
Logan Frati, Fairleigh Dickinson	7	1	3.43	13	0	81	67	38	76
Brandon Bingel, Bryant	9	3	3.52	13	0	69	70	30	60
Chris Kachmar, Fair. Dickinson	6	3	3.57	12	0	68	61	41	63
James Davitt, Bryant	7	2	3.71	13	0	68	66	20	52
Andrew Hinckley, CCSU	8	4	3.73	10	2	80	78	21	58
Corey Zeller, Fairleigh Dickinson	7	3	3.74	11	0	75	69	20	50
Brent Teller, Sacred Heart	4	4	3.91	3	1	46	37	24	29
Casey Brown, Central Conn. St.	4	7	3.98	11	1	86	106	22	56
John Sostarich, Sacred Heart	4	3	3.98	10	0	52	52	34	37
Brett Susi, Central Conn. State	4	6	4.24	12	0	76	80	19	39
Matt Morris, Wagner	4	5	4.60	12	0	59	67	31	35
Michael Kuypers, Mt. St. Mary's	4	2	4.60	1	3	45	45	15	27
Baylor Sundahl, Sacred Heart	3	3	4.81	0	2	43	50	24	30
Brandon Fox, Central Conn. St.	1	5	4.96	8	1	45	57	20	18
Jesus Medina, Sacred Heart	3	4	5.12	9	0	51	61	11	27
James Cooksey, Sacred Heart	5	3	5.27	10	4	70	82	19	27
Mike Adams, Wagner	3	7	5.38	13	0	75	91	37	51
Chad Diehl, Mount St. Mary's	2	**10**	6.92	14	0	66	95	31	49

OHIO VALLEY CONFERENCE

	Conference		Overall	
	W	L	W	L
*Southeast Missouri State	22	8	36	18
Austin Peay State	21	9	34	22
Jacksonville State	20	10	33	22
Morehead State	17	13	32	27
Belmont	17	13	33	27
Tennessee Tech	17	13	31	24
Murray State	15	15	27	29
Eastern Kentucky	13	17	24	31
Tennessee-Martin	9	21	19	35
Eastern Illinois	8	22	15	39
SIU-Edwardsville	6	24	9	40

All-Conference Team: C—Tyler Lawrence, Jr., Murray State. **1B**—Ramsey Scott, Jr., Murray State. **2B**—Clayton Daniel, So., Jacksonville State. **3B**—Mandy Alvarez, Sr., Eastern Kentucky. **SS**—Branden Boggetto, Sr., Southeast Missouri State. **OF**—Kevin Strohschein, Fr., Tennessee Tech; Kyle Nowlin, Sr., Eastern Kentucky; Chris Osborne, Jr., Southeast Missouri State. **DH**—Garrett Gandolfo, Sr., Southeast Missouri State. **UT**—Logan Gray, Jr., Austin Peay State. **SP**—Joey Lucchesi, Southeast Missouri State; Matt Anderson, Morehead State; Robert Beltran, Southeast Missouri State. **RP**—Justin Hoyt, So., Jacksonville State. Co-**Player of the Year:** Mandy Alvarez, Eastern Kentucky; Kevin Strohschein, Tennessee Tech. **Pitcher of the Year:** Joey Lucchesi, Southeast Missouri State. **Rookie of the Year:** Kevin Strohschein, Tennessee Tech. **Coach of the Year:** Steve Bieser, Southeast Missouri State.

INDIVIDUAL BATTING LEADERS
(Minimum 140 At-Bats)

	AVG	OBP	SLG	AB	2B	3B	HR	RBI	SB
Mandy Alvarez, Eastern Ky.	**.409**	.455	.646	237	13	2	13	58	1
Kevin Strohschein, Tenn. Tech	.393	.447	.707	229	21	3	15	**73**	2
Clayton Daniel, Jacksonville St.	.372	.443	.480	**250**	20	2	1	54	7
Chas Hadden, Belmont	.370	**.521**	.495	192	11	2	3	37	8
Chris Osborne, SE Mo. State	.367	.456	**.741**	166	11	3	15	44	2
Keaton Wright, SIU Edwardsville	.362	.420	.530	185	16	0	5	37	0
Logan Gray, Austin Peay State	.356	.454	.687	163	14	2	12	40	7
Garrett Gandolfo, SE Mo. State	.356	.455	.582	239	21	3	9	61	5
Tyler Lawrence, Murray State	.355	.469	.589	214	**22**	2	8	58	1
Zach Lannan, Belmont	.350	.458	.450	20	2	0	0	3	0
Alex Stephens, Morehead State	.349	.385	.519	241	17	3	6	47	12
A.J. Reynolds, Jacksonville State	.347	.362	.542	144	14	4	2	22	3
Reid Leonard, Morehead State	.344	.396	.392	227	11	0	0	32	2
Will Schneider, Morehead State	.343	.402	.559	245	17	3	10	57	4
Adam Bauer, Murray State	.341	.453	.527	220	8	**9**	5	40	8
Patrick Massoni, Austin Peay	.339	.388	.413	189	11	0	1	19	5
Branden Boggetto, SE Mo. State	.339	.435	.508	242	18	4	5	61	9
Taylor Hawthorne, Jacksonville St.	.337	.388	.533	199	14	5	5	52	1
Ramsey Scott, Murray State	.335	.415	.612	206	18	0	13	63	1
Elliot Mccummings, Jville State	.333	.421	.486	210	18	1	4	36	1
Chase Hamilton, Austin Peay	.332	.405	.620	187	14	2	12	47	3
Joseph Duncan, Eastern Illinois	.332	.363	.422	223	16	2	0	22	18
Josh Bobo, Jacksonville State	.330	.352	.586	191	15	2	10	48	2
Chris Brown, Tennessee Tech	.330	.384	.542	212	10	1	11	48	0
Brennan Washington, Belmont	.330	.479	.633	221	14	4	15	52	18
Jake Farr, Tennessee Tech	.330	.420	.463	227	10	1	6	45	1
Gavin Golsan, Jacksonville State	.311	.377	.418	251	14	2	3	36	**27**
Kyle Nowlin, Eastern Kentucky	.300	.435	.657	207	11	0	**21**	61	5

INDIVIDUAL PITCHING LEADERS
(Minimum 40 Innings Pitched)

	W	L	ERA	G	SV	IP	H	BB	SO
Joey Lucchesi, SE Mo. State	**10**	5	**2.19**	17	1	**111**	96	37	**149**
Ethan Roberts, Tennessee Tech	6	1	2.94	17	2	49	44	18	65
Matt Anderson, Morehead State	8	3	2.95	15	0	92	75	42	130
Michael Wood, Tennessee Tech	4	3	3.47	16	1	70	74	14	67
Jared Carkuff, Austin Peay State	6	1	3.57	**32**	6	63	53	23	63
Jake Busiek, SE Mo. State	2	2	3.76	28	1	41	**28**	19	50
Clay Chandler, SE Mo. State	4	5	3.90	16	0	97	92	21	96
Caleb Johnson, Eastern Ky.	3	4	3.93	22	2	55	64	17	44
Caleb Powell, Austin Peay State	7	2	3.96	17	0	75	86	18	50
Tyler Vaughn, Belmont	7	3	4.00	18	1	88	91	25	81

	W	L	ERA	G	SV	IP	H	BB	SO
Nate Sylvester, Jville State	1	2	4.01	23	5	43	49	17	42
Adam Pennington, SE Mo. State	4	1	4.07	19	2	49	53	10	37
Jake Usher, Tennessee Tech	4	0	4.07	14	0	49	36	24	59
Robert Beltran, SE Mo. State	8	1	4.27	17	0	86	91	32	78
Connor Etheridge, Belmont	3	2	4.42	26	0	53	56	21	52
Jacob Lawrence, SE Mo. State	4	1	4.42	14	2	55	57	21	59
Brian Mroz, Eastern Kentucky	0	3	4.43	26	5	41	47	16	36
Aaron Quillen, Belmont	5	5	4.61	15	0	98	97	38	118
Alex Robles, Austin Peay	**10**	6	4.67	16	0	98	103	32	89
Aaron Leasher, Morehead State	5	4	4.69	15	1	81	72	42	107
Patrick Mcguff, Morehead State	5	3	4.73	18	0	59	60	28	63
Curtis Wilson, Morehead State	2	4	4.85	22	0	56	68	**9**	35
Eric Nerl, Eastern Kentucky	6	4	5.14	14	0	77	79	33	46
Ryan Dills, Murray State	5	3	5.20	13	0	62	76	19	76
Hunter Dunn, Eastern Kentucky	3	3	5.36	9	0	42	46	23	29

PACIFIC-12 CONFERENCE

	Conference		Overall	
	W	L	W	L
*Utah	19	11	26	29
Washington	17	13	33	23
Arizona	16	14	49	24
Oregon State	16	14	35	19
Arizona State	16	14	37	23
Stanford	15	15	31	23
Southern California	15	15	28	28
California	14	16	32	21
Oregon	14	16	29	26
UCLA	12	18	25	31
Washington State	11	19	19	35

All-Conference Team: C—Brett Cumberland, So., California; Logan Ice, Jr., Oregon State; Brian Serven, Jr., Arizona State; Jeremy Martinez, Jr., Southern California; Joey Morgan, So., Washington. **1B**—Ryan Aguilar, Sr., Arizona; David Greer, Jr., Arizona State; K.J. Harrison, So., Oregon State. **2B**—Cody Ramer, Sr., Arizona; Nick Madrigal, Fr., Oregon State; Trek Stemp, Jr., Washington State. **3B**—Mitchell Kranson, Sr., California; Dallas Carroll, Jr., Utah; Chris Baker, Jr., Washington. **SS**—Colby Woodmansee, Jr., Arizona State; Tommy Edman, Jr., Stanford; Cody Scaggari, Sr., Utah. **OF**—Zach Gibbons, Jr., Arizona; Christian Donahue, So., Oregon State; Eric Filia, Sr., UCLA; A.J. Ramirez, Sr., Southern California; DaShawn Keirsey, Fr., Utah; Jack Meggs, Jr., Washington. **DH**—David Oppenheim, Sr., Southern California. **SP**—Nathan Bannister, Sr., Arizona; Seth Martinez, Jr., Arizona State; Cole Irvin, Jr., Oregon; Tristan Beck, Fr., Stanford; Jayson Rose, So., Utah. **RP**—Bobby Dalbec, Jr., Arizona; Stephen Nogosek, Jr., Oregon; Troy Rallings, Sr., Washington. **Player of the Year:** Brett Cumberland, California. **Pitcher of the Year:** Troy Rallings, Washington. **Defensive Player of the Year:** Logan Ice, Oregon State. **Freshman of the Year:** Nick Madrigal, Oregon State. **Coach of the Year:** Bill Kinneberg, Utah.

INDIVIDUAL BATTING LEADERS
(Minimum 140 At-Bats)

	AVG	OBP	SLG	AB	2B	3B	HR	RBI	SB
David Oppenheim, USC	**.387**	**.500**	.508	191	9	1	4	25	6
Zach Gibbons, Arizona	.385	.460	.446	278	15	1	0	48	9
Jeremy Martinez, USC	.376	.460	.563	213	18	2	6	42	1
Trek Stemp, Washington State	.355	.393	.388	183	6	0	0	16	12
Cody Ramer, Arizona	.348	.441	.485	**293**	18	**8**	2	40	9
Brett Cumberland, California	.344	.480	**.678**	180	10	1	**16**	51	5
David Greer, Arizona State	.344	.442	.571	224	**23**	2	8	43	4
Christian Donahue, Oregon State	.339	.393	.464	192	11	5	1	29	9
Nick Madrigal, Oregon State	.333	.380	.456	195	11	5	1	29	8
Mitchell Kranson, California	.333	.376	.474	213	15	0	5	36	1
Cody Scaggari, Utah	.330	.380	.502	203	12	4	5	34	6
Frankie Rios, USC	.323	.386	.419	186	6	3	2	20	5
Luke Persico, UCLA	.323	.383	.416	226	10	1	3	30	7
Andrew Shaps, Arizona State	.321	.360	.443	212	12	4	2	27	6
Levi Jordan, Washington	.316	.333	.368	171	6	0	1	26	3
Nick Halamandaris, California	.315	.355	.473	203	15	1	5	43	1
Chris Baker, Washington	.315	.373	.491	216	11	3	7	37	6
Kellen Marruffo, Utah	.314	.392	.432	169	11	0	3	27	0
Logan Ice, Oregon State	.310	.432	.563	174	13	5	7	39	2

	AVG	OBP	SLG	AB	2B	3B	HR	RBI	SB
Ryan Aguilar, Arizona	.310	.384	.495	287	23	3	8	56	12
John Naff, Washington	.301	.423	.466	163	10	1	5	25	1
A.J. Ramirez, USC	.301	.382	.505	196	11	1	9	44	4
Robbie Tenerowicz, California	.299	.353	.485	204	14	3	6	34	3
Sean Bouchard, UCLA	.295	.354	.436	156	8	4	2	36	3
Eric Filia, UCLA	.295	.415	.411	207	11	2	3	32	8
Jared Oliva, Arizona	.240	.293	.378	217	4	7	4	36	13

INDIVIDUAL PITCHING LEADERS
(Minimum 40 Innings Pitched)

	W	L	ERA	G	SV	IP	H	BB	SO
Troy Rallings, Washington	4	1	0.89	28	16	61	32	12	60
Daulton Jefferies, California	7	0	1.08	8	0	50	34	8	53
Stephen Nogosek, Oregon	2	2	1.11	29	16	41	25	14	45
Marc Huberman, USC	2	1	1.94	26	3	42	27	32	45
Colton Hock, Stanford	4	5	2.03	27	6	58	37	24	61
Bryce Fehmel, Oregon State	10	1	2.31	26	2	70	58	23	51
Ryan Walker, Washington State	6	3	2.40	18	5	64	48	25	50
J.C. Cloney, Arizona	8	4	2.45	18	0	110	100	22	61
Tristan Beck, Stanford	6	5	2.48	14	0	83	60	26	76
Joey Matulovich, California	1	1	2.49	21	0	43	32	20	31
Bobby Dalbec, Arizona	11	6	2.50	29	7	101	82	37	96
Nathan Bannister, Arizona	12	2	2.59	22	0	142	104	33	114
Seth Martinez, Arizona State	9	4	2.75	18	1	111	95	35	94
Kevin Ginkel, Arizona	5	1	2.80	25	3	64	53	19	45
Jayson Rose, Utah	8	5	2.89	16	0	109	40	49	106
Andrew Summerville, Stanford	5	2	2.90	16	1	59	49	21	34
Eder Erives, Arizona State	6	2	2.95	23	10	76	50	36	73
Noah Bremer, Washington	4	5	2.98	16	0	103	91	30	66
Cole Irvin, Oregon	6	4	3.17	17	0	105	101	16	93
Ryan Mason, California	8	4	3.21	15	0	87	85	21	65
Kris Bubic, Stanford	0	3	3.26	21	1	47	46	26	38
Travis Eckert, Oregon State	6	4	3.28	14	0	93	82	20	66
Kyle Molnar, UCLA	5	5	3.32	13	0	76	71	20	72
Tanner Dodson, California	4	5	3.36	19	3	62	69	31	29
Tyler Thorne, Stanford	3	2	3.38	29	2	45	40	25	34
Joe Navilhon, USC	5	5	3.38	20	0	83	84	24	71
Cameron Ming, Arizona	3	3	3.59	32	4	80	76	22	59
C.J. Stubbs, USC	2	1	3.86	14	0	42	45	8	27
Ian Hamilton, Washington State	2	10	4.86	15	0	87	96	31	62

PATRIOT LEAGUE

	Conference		Overall	
	W	L	W	L
* Navy	15	5	43	14
Holy Cross	13	7	29	28
Lehigh	9	10	25	29
Bucknell	9	11	19	33
Lafayette	7	13	14	29
Army	6	13	16	32

All-Conference Team: C—Adrian Chinnery, Jr., Navy. **1B**—Anthony Critelli, Jr., Holy Cross. **2B**—Mike Garzillo, Sr., Lehigh. **3B**—Sam Clark, Jr,. Bucknell. **SS**-Kris Lindner, Jr., Army. **OF**—Michael Coniglio, Sr., Lafayette; Robert Currie, Sr., Navy; Connor Deneen, Sr., Navy; Brett Smith, Jr., Bucknell. **DH**—Stephen Born, So., Navy. **SP**—Luke Gillingham, Sr., Navy; Brendan King, Jr., Holy Cross. **RP**—Sam Sorenson, Sr., Navy. **Player of the Year:** Mike Garzillo, Lehigh. **Pitcher of the Year:** Luke Gillingham, Navy. **Rookie of the Year:** Noah Song, Navy. **Coach of the Year:** Paul Kostacopoulos, Navy.

INDIVIDUAL BATTING LEADERS
(Minimum 140 At-Bats)

	AVG	OBP	SLG	AB	2B	3B	HR	RBI	SB
Robert Currie, Navy	.345	.431	.450	220	11	6	0	28	12
Brett Smith, Bucknell	.343	.399	.463	216	6	7	2	16	13
Michael Coniglio, Lafayette	.335	.395	.405	173	8	2	0	20	25
Jacen Nalesnik, Lehigh	.333	.419	.533	210	13	4	7	36	9
Steven Cohen, Lafayette	.327	.421	.453	150	14	1	1	32	9
David Young, Lehigh	.325	.391	.443	194	17	0	2	22	3
Sean Trent, Navy	.319	.357	.475	238	18	5	3	53	2
Kris Lindner, Army	.315	.430	.394	165	8	1	1	16	14
Jon Rosoff, Army	.314	.407	.350	140	3	1	0	16	2

	AVG	OBP	SLG	AB	2B	3B	HR	RBI	SB
Mike Garzillo, Lehigh	.313	.416	.562	201	15	4	9	37	13
Bill Schlich, Holy Cross	.313	.373	.478	182	17	2	3	25	3
James Bleming, Lehigh	.311	.370	.447	190	12	1	4	28	6
Stephen Born, Navy	.310	.390	.433	210	14	3	2	38	7
Logan Knowles, Navy	.307	.426	.361	166	6	0	1	26	9
Spencer Stokes, Bucknell	.305	.343	.442	190	17	3	1	31	5
Adrian Chinnery, Navy	.302	.409	.396	149	6	1	2	22	0
Patrick Donnelly, Lehigh	.299	.329	.430	214	14	1	4	50	1
Connor Deneen, Navy	.296	.389	.432	169	8	6	1	27	5
John McCarthy, Army	.296	.361	.377	162	4	0	3	31	10
Danny Rafferty, Bucknell	.294	.375	.452	197	11	4	4	26	4
Joe Ogren, Bucknell	.293	.402	.479	188	11	6	4	39	8
Bobby Indeglia, Holy Cross	.287	.379	.444	178	13	0	5	23	8
Sam Clark, Bucknell	.282	.344	.411	163	10	1	3	26	2
Cam O'Neill, Holy Cross	.279	.369	.363	201	14	0	1	33	2
Connor Donovan, Lehigh	.272	.357	.435	147	9	0	5	26	0
Anthony Critelli, Holy Cross	.267	.340	.462	225	15	1	9	41	1
Josh Hassell, Holy Cross	.252	.345	.447	206	7	3	9	28	5

INDIVIDUAL PITCHING LEADERS
(Minimum 40 Innings Pitched)

	W	L	ERA	G	SV	IP	H	BB	SO
Sam Sorenson, Navy	5	2	1.72	25	6	47	38	11	44
Mark Washington, Lehigh	6	1	1.80	13	0	45	35	27	24
Luke Gillingham, Navy	8	4	2.35	14	0	92	68	24	93
Noah Song, Navy	9	3	2.75	17	0	75	49	23	57
Brendan King, Holy Cross	7	2	2.84	13	0	82	69	18	74
George Coughlin, Navy	3	4	3.09	16	0	70	67	26	62
George Capen, Holy Cross	3	4	3.15	26	2	54	56	11	38
Daniel Burggraaf, Army	3	2	3.21	11	0	42	39	18	46
Joe Cravero, Holy Cross	6	3	3.24	26	1	50	45	20	48
Andrew Andreychik, Bucknell	5	4	3.58	13	0	75	82	22	57
Kyle Condry, Navy	6	1	3.76	15	0	65	70	19	61
David Bednar, Lafayette	3	5	3.92	10	0	60	54	14	70
Justin Finan, Holy Cross	1	4	4.19	14	0	58	66	20	37
Andrew Bartek, Navy	6	2	4.28	19	1	40	33	18	36
Peter Moore, Lehigh	6	3	4.30	14	0	59	41	29	46
Phil Reese, Holy Cross	4	3	4.59	14	0	69	83	18	41
Dan Keller, Bucknell	3	6	4.74	12	0	63	67	24	38
Jeff Gottesman, Bucknell	2	5	4.80	13	1	45	38	26	34
John Cain, Lafayette	1	5	4.84	10	0	45	52	23	47
Sam Ashey, Lehigh	4	5	4.93	12	0	46	55	17	23
Ethan Friend, Lehigh	2	5	5.13	13	2	40	49	14	22
Jeremy Mortensen, Army	2	4	5.27	11	0	55	68	26	46
Mike Castellani, Bucknell	3	4	5.34	13	0	59	87	19	31
Matt Ball, Army	2	7	5.37	12	0	60	80	20	44
Kevin Long, Lehigh	3	5	5.81	12	0	53	52	29	45

SOUTHEASTERN CONFERENCE

Eastern Division	Conference		Overall	
	W	L	W	L
South Carolina	20	9	46	18
Florida	19	10	52	16
Vanderbilt	18	12	43	19
Kentucky	15	15	32	25
Georgia	11	19	27	30
Missouri	9	21	26	30
Tennessee	9	21	29	28

Western Division	Conference		Overall	
	W	L	W	L
Mississippi State	21	9	44	18
* Texas A&M	20	10	49	16
Louisiana State	19	11	45	21
Mississippi	18	12	43	19
Alabama	15	15	32	26
Auburn	8	22	23	33
Arkansas	7	23	26	29

All-Conference Team: C—Henri Lartigue, Jr., Mississippi. **1B**—Nathaniel Lowe, Jr., Mississippi State. **2B**—Ryne Birk, Jr., Texas A&M. **3B**—Boomer White, Jr., Texas A&M. **SS**—Kramer Robertson, Jr., Louisiana State. **OF**—Jake Mangum, Fr., Mississippi State; J.B.

Woodman, Jr., Mississippi; Gene Cone, Jr., South Carolina. **DH/UT—**Jack Kruger, Jr., Mississippi State; Bryce Jordan, So., Louisiana State. **SP—**Logan Shore, Jr., Florida; Dakota Hudson, Jr., Mississippi State. **RP—**Shaun Anderson, Jr., Florida. **Player of the Year:** Boomer White, Texas A&M. **Pitcher of the Year:** Logan Shore, Florida. **Freshman of the Year:** Jake Mangum, Mississippi State. **Coach of the Year:** John Cohen, Mississippi State.

INDIVIDUAL BATTING LEADERS
(Minimum 140 At-Bats)

	AVG	OBP	SLG	AB	2B	3B	HR	RBI	SB
Jake Mangum, Miss. State	**.408**	.458	.510	206	12	3	1	28	6
Boomer White, Texas A&M	.386	.462	.517	259	19	0	5	46	10
Joshua Palacios, Auburn	.385	.463	.608	143	9	4	5	23	12
Evan White, Kentucky	.376	.419	.535	226	15	3	5	40	10
Peter Alonso, Florida	.374	.469	**.659**	211	18	0	**14**	60	2
Anfernee Grier, Auburn	.366	.457	.576	238	8	3	12	41	19
Gene Cone, South Carolina	.363	**.474**	.498	215	13	2	4	30	7
Austin Homan, Texas A&M	.356	.392	.431	160	7	1	1	26	5
Henri Lartigue, Mississippi	.353	.414	.464	207	11	0	4	31	2
Nick Senzel, Tennessee	.352	.456	.595	210	**25**	1	8	59	25
Nathaniel Lowe, Mississippi	.348	.423	.490	247	20	0	5	49	2
Jack Kruger, Mississippi State	.344	.435	.550	209	19	0	8	40	6
Vincent Jackson, Tennessee	.333	.426	.507	207	10	1	8	57	7
Jeren Kendall, Vanderbilt	.332	.396	.568	250	16	**8**	9	59	**28**
Zach Lavy, Missouri	.332	.403	.214	18	**8**	8	54	4	
Niko Buentello, Auburn	.332	.428	.569	211	15	1	11	55	0
Carson Shaddy, Arkansas	.332	.400	.521	211	12	2	8	35	5
Zach Reks, Kentucky	.331	.425	.500	154	5	0	7	22	3
Bryan Reynolds, Vanderbilt	.330	.461	.603	224	16	3	13	56	8
Cole Freeman, Louisiana State	.329	.427	.403	216	7	3	1	27	26
Derek Lance, Tennessee	.328	.394	.369	198	6	1	0	24	8
Antoine Duplantis, LSU	.327	.404	.419	272	9	5	2	39	13
Jake Fraley, Louisiana State	.326	.408	.464	267	10	6	5	36	**28**
Jordan Ebert, Auburn	.325	.378	.405	237	13	0	2	31	5
Kramer Robertson, LSU	.324	.417	.440	259	20	2	2	39	14
J.B. Woodman, Mississippi	.323	.412	.578	232	15	**1**	**14**	55	12
Dalton Guthrie, Florida	.305	.367	.366	**279**	14	0	1	22	8
Hunter Melton, Texas A&M	.300	.375	.510	253	13	2	12	**67**	2

INDIVIDUAL PITCHING LEADERS
(Minimum 40 Innings Pitched)

	W	L	ERA	G	SV	IP	H	BB	SO
Mark Ecker, Texas A&M	4	2	**0.39**	25	8	47	24	7	56
Shaun Anderson, Florida	3	0	0.97	36	**13**	46	31	7	60
Hunter Martin, Tennessee	3	3	2.03	21	1	40	48	18	20
Josh Reagan, South Carolina	3	2	2.08	29	11	56	34	20	50
Konnor Pilkington, Miss. State	3	1	2.08	14	0	43	38	15	42
Ryan Rigby, Mississippi State	5	1	2.25	20	1	48	37	13	43
Dane Dunning, Florida	6	3	2.29	33	2	79	68	12	88
Nick Eicholtz, Alabama	4	3	2.30	12	0	67	57	22	38
Logan Shore, Florida	12	1	2.31	18	0	105	82	19	96
Andrew Vinson, Texas A&M	4	3	2.32	22	2	50	33	10	57
Matt Ruppenthal, Vanderbilt	5	2	2.33	25	1	46	**24**	27	59
Tyler Johnson, South Carolina	3	2	2.42	29	9	52	34	8	59
Brigham Hill, Texas A&M	9	2	2.51	24	1	97	86	28	99
Turner Larkins, Texas A&M	3	0	2.51	19	1	43	34	16	39
Dakota Hudson, Mississippi St.	9	5	2.55	17	0	**113**	106	35	115
Reed Scott, South Carolina	4	1	2.56	29	2	46	41	15	31
Kyle Simonds, Texas A&M	11	3	2.61	17	0	100	81	26	80
Patrick Raby, Vanderbilt	7	1	2.61	15	2	59	35	19	63
Jake Walters, Alabama	5	4	2.67	15	0	84	79	35	84
Zach Logue, Kentucky	3	2	2.68	17	0	50	48	14	38
David Parkinson, Mississippi	5	3	2.78	22	0	68	74	24	50
Wyatt Short, Mississippi	2	3	2.90	22	11	40	38	10	31
Matt Foster, Alabama	5	3	2.92	25	2	40	33	16	49
Will Stokes, Mississippi	2	1	2.93	30	7	43	37	7	40
Alex Faedo, Florida	**13**	3	3.18	17	0	105	87	21	**133**
Drew Moody, Georgia	2	3	4.47	22	3	44	55	**6**	33
Zack Brown, Kentucky	2	**11**	6.08	14	0	84	106	34	62
#Kirby Snead, Florida	3	1	2.78	**41**	1	36	39	12	33

SOUTHERN CONFERENCE

	Conference		Overall	
	W	L	W	L
Mercer	16	8	38	23
* **Western Carolina**	15	9	31	31
UNC Greensboro	15	9	38	21
Furman	14	10	29	30
East Tennessee State	13	11	27	30
Samford	13	11	35	26
Wofford	12	12	30	28
The Citadel	6	18	17	42
Virginia Military Institute	4	20	5	35

All-Conference Team: C—Hagen Owenby, So., East Tennessee State. **1B—**Matt Smith, Jr., Western Carolina. **2B—**Trey York, Sr., East Tennessee State. **3B—**Collin Woody, Sr., UNC Greensboro. **SS—**Matt Meeder, Jr., Mercer. **OF—**Kyle Lewis, Jr., Mercer; L.J. Kalawaia, Sr., UNC Greensboro; Heath Quinn, Jr., Samford. **DH—**Austin Edens, So., Samford. **SP—**Will Gaddis, So., Furman; Parker Curry, Sr., Samford. **RP—**Andrew Wantz, So., UNC Greensboro. **Player of the Year:** Kyle Lewis, Mercer. **Co-Pitchers of the Year:** Will Gaddis, Furman; Andrew Wantz, UNC Greensboro. **Freshman of the Year:** Jabari Richards, Furman. **Coach of the Year:** Link Jarrett, UNC Greensboro.

INDIVIDUAL BATTING LEADERS
(Minimum 140 At-Bats)

	AVG	OBP	SLG	AB	2B	3B	HR	RBI	SB
Andrew Moritz, UNC Greensboro	**.400**	.454	.570	165	11	**7**	1	33	8
L.J. Kalawaia, UNC Greensboro	.396	.493	.578	225	11	6	6	65	23
Kyle Lewis, Mercer	.395	**.535**	**.731**	223	11	2	20	72	6
Matt Smith, Western Carolina	.388	.495	.582	232	11	2	10	55	6
Ben Spitznagel, UNC Greensboro	.385	.459	.474	247	15	2	1	23	21
Hagen Owenby, East Tenn. State	.374	.426	.660	235	16	0	17	60	1
Derek Hirsch, Wofford	.368	.453	.439	171	4	1	2	27	9
Cesar Trejo, UNC Greensboro	.363	.415	.587	179	7	3	9	30	3
Collin Woody, UNC Greensboro	.349	.418	.571	238	23	0	10	66	3
Trey York, East Tenn. State	.348	.431	.648	233	23	1	15	62	17
Heath Quinn, Samford	.343	.452	.682	242	17	1	**21**	**77**	4
Jabari Richards, Furman	.343	.391	.627	166	11	3	10	25	10
Kramer Ferrell, Western Carolina	.340	.419	.508	238	10	3	8	65	6
Lance Mays, East Tenn. State	.336	.387	.544	143	9	3	4	22	5
Dillon Stewart, UNC Greensboro	.335	.455	.665	209	19	4	14	62	9
Trey Truitt, Mercer	.335	.430	.636	236	16	2	17	54	2
Alex Lee, Samford	.335	.421	.523	239	12	0	11	45	0
Ryne Sigmon, UNC Greensboro	.329	.417	.491	228	12	5	5	56	8
Bryson Bowman, Western Caro.	.326	.442	.661	227	13	3	19	60	10
Matt Pita, VMI	.322	.392	.592	211	16	4	11	40	13
Garrett Brown, Western Caro.	.321	.370	.435	**262**	12	3	4	**34**	**34**
David Geary, VMI	.320	.424	.562	203	21	5	6	45	9
Carter Grote, Furman	.318	.396	.472	195	10	1	6	28	4
Ryan Hagan, Mercer	.316	.419	.488	244	18	0	8	55	10
Aaron Maher, East Tenn. State	.315	.401	.525	219	15	2	9	38	14
Hunter Swilling, Samford	.292	.393	.557	253	**25**	3	12	58	6

INDIVIDUAL PITCHING LEADERS
(Minimum 40 Innings Pitched)

	W	L	ERA	G	SV	IP	H	BB	SO
Chad Sykes, UNC Greensboro	5	2	**2.52**	27	4	50	**31**	40	60
Andrew Wantz, UNC Greensboro	6	1	2.97	34	4	79	55	37	97
Will Gaddis, Furman	**10**	3	3.45	15	0	**102**	95	20	92
Conard Broom, Mercer	4	3	3.57	**41**	4	63	61	25	75
Elliot Lance, Wofford	6	2	3.60	27	0	70	73	17	39
Wyatt Burns, Samford	2	2	3.61	37	8	42	33	15	40
Parker Curry, Samford	7	2	3.69	18	2	78	80	23	60
Ryan Askew, Mercer	6	3	3.90	16	0	**102**	102	18	65
B.J. Nobles, Western Carolina	2	2	4.07	22	5	42	39	14	46
Stephen Jones, Samford	4	2	4.11	17	0	57	57	33	29
Kevin Coulter, Mercer	8	3	4.41	17	0	86	88	23	38
Jack Gomersall, VMI	0	2	4.42	32	1	53	52	22	42
Matthew Milburn, Wofford	6	5	4.47	15	0	99	110	29	**103**
Keaton Haack, UNC Greensboro	4	3	4.60	13	0	45	44	31	31
Josh Rich, Samford	1	3	4.60	26	3	43	47	15	24
Josh Winder, VMI	4	4	4.80	14	0	86	93	16	76
Jared Brasher, Samford	3	4	4.82	19	0	52	37	55	54
Jacob Watcher, Citadel	6	5	4.86	17	0	67	76	23	44

	W	L	ERA	G	SV	IP	H	BB	SO
Matt Frisbee, UNC Greensboro	5	3	4.98	15	0	69	75	31	51
Brendan Nail, Western Carolina	5	6	5.08	18	0	85	85	49	62
Jamin McCann, East Tenn. State	8	4	5.19	26	0	61	56	26	50
Colton Davis, Western Carolina	7	3	5.21	31	2	67	66	40	89
J.P. Sears, Citadel	5	7	5.27	15	0	82	82	36	93
Matthew Quarles, Furman	7	7	5.32	16	0	88	100	42	72
Thomas Byelick, Citadel	1	7	5.32	14	0	71	86	29	51
Matthew Eagle, VMI	5	7	5.74	16	0	64	83	25	51
Taylor Edens, VMI	3	6	5.89	30	6	44	55	11	38
Brandon Barbery, VMI	3	7	6.23	17	0	65	80	25	39
#Will Stillman, Wofford	3	3	3.93	23	9	34	35	19	58

SOUTHLAND CONFERENCE

	Conference		Overall	
	W	L	W	L
* Sam Houston State	24	6	42	22
Southeastern Louisiana	22	8	40	21
Northwestern State	20	10	33	24
Lamar	20	10	34	19
Central Arkansas	16	14	29	27
McNeese State	15	15	31	25
New Orleans	14	16	31	26
Stephen F. Austin	14	16	30	30
Nicholls State	14	16	26	30
Houston Baptist	12	18	24	28
Texas A&M-Corpus Christi	8	20	19	32
Abilene Christian	8	21	16	37
Incarnate Word	5	22	13	38

All-Conference Team: C—Bryndan Arredondo, Jr., Lamar; Kyle Bracey, Sr., New Orleans. **1B**—Jameson Fisher, Jr., Southeastern Louisiana. **2B**—Carson Crites, Jr., Southeastern Louisiana. **3B**—Kyle Thornell, Sr., Stephen F. Austin. **SS**—Stijn van der Meer, Sr., Lamar. **OF**—Reid Russell, Jr., Lamar; Garrett McMullen, Sr., Stephen F. Austin; Conner Fikes, Jr., Stephen F. Austin. **DH**—Hezekiah Randolph, Jr., New Orleans. **P**—Adam Oller, Jr., Northwestern State; Will Hibbs, Sr., Lamar; Mac Sceroler, So., Southeastern Louisiana. **Player of the Year:** Jameson Fisher, Southeastern Louisiana. **Hitter of the Year:** Reid Russell, Lamar. **Pitcher of the Year:** Adam Oller, Northwestern State. **Relief Pitcher of the Year:** Kade Granier, Southeastern Louisiana. **Freshman of the Year:** Brennan Breaud, Southeastern Louisiana. **Newcomer of the Year:** Zac Michener, Stephen F. Austin. **Utility Player of the Year:** Russell Crippen, Abilene Christian. **Coach of the Year:** Matt Deggs, Sam Houston State.

INDIVIDUAL BATTING LEADERS
(Minimum 140 At-Bats)

	AVG	OBP	SLG	AB	2B	3B	HR	RBI	SB
Jameson Fisher, Southeastern La.	.424	.558	.692	198	16	2	11	66	15
Stijn van der Meer, Lamar	.376	.471	.441	213	9	1	1	20	7
Conner Fikes, Stephen F. Austin	.362	.402	.488	213	10	7	1	41	12
Reid Russell, Lamar	.354	.410	.665	209	9	1	18	62	3
Garrett McMullen, S.F. Austin	.353	.425	.555	218	14	3	8	58	15
Lewis Guilbeau, McNeese State	.353	.394	.435	207	12	1	1	31	4
Kyle Knauth, Nicholls State	.347	.395	.486	173	15	0	3	32	0
Bryce Johnson, Sam Houston St.	.345	.401	.418	261	11	1	2	30	20
Kyle Thornell, Stephen F. Austin	.342	.472	.617	196	15	3	11	49	5
Connor Crane, McNeese State	.341	.429	.567	217	18	2	9	45	16
Chris Townsend, Central Arkansas	.340	.414	.375	144	5	0	0	13	10
Tyler Kendrick, Stephen F. Austin	.338	.416	.430	207	16	0	1	21	10
Aaron Palmer, New Orleans	.325	.390	.442	240	12	5	2	37	19
Zach Michener, Stephen F. Austin	.322	.415	.459	205	13	0	5	33	3
Jay Robinson, New Orleans	.322	.392	.404	183	8	2	1	37	9
Casey Thomas, Texas A&M-CC	.322	.368	.394	208	3	6	0	22	5
Dakota Dean, New Orleans	.321	.422	.493	215	10	6	5	45	8
Hezekiah Randolph, New Orleans	.318	.402	.502	223	16	2	7	45	2
Brandon Montalvo, Central Ark.	.315	.417	.450	200	11	2	4	29	7
Bryndan Arredondo, Lamar	.313	.391	.443	194	13	1	3	26	0
Kyle Reese, Nicholls State	.313	.358	.380	150	8	1	0	28	4
Gavin Wehby, Nicholls State	.310	.370	.391	197	7	3	1	27	5
Zacarias Hardy, Texas A&M-CC	.309	.353	.430	207	10	3	3	32	4
Daniel Garner, Northwestern St.	.308	.380	.481	208	21	0	5	38	0

	AVG	OBP	SLG	AB	2B	3B	HR	RBI	SB
Preston Marsh, New Orleans	.308	.370	.403	201	5	1	4	40	2
Zack Gibson, Texas A&M-CC	.279	.390	.480	179	4	7	6	25	7
Andrew Fregia, Sam Houston St.	.274	.328	.516	223	16	7	8	40	9
Nick Heath, Northwestern State	.260	.345	.347	219	11	1	2	27	35

INDIVIDUAL PITCHING LEADERS
(Minimum 40 Innings Pitched)

	W	L	ERA	G	SV	IP	H	BB	SO
Adam Oller, Northwestern State	8	1	1.23	15	0	110	81	32	73
Kaleb Fontenot, McNeese State	6	5	2.02	15	0	107	80	34	108
Domenick Carlini, SE La.	8	2	2.03	16	0	97	71	36	63
Mac Sceroler, Southeastern La.	10	4	2.25	16	0	96	83	33	93
Sam Odom, Sam Houston State	7	0	2.33	12	0	89	67	25	62
Riley Gossett, Sam Houston St.	7	0	2.64	19	1	95	95	24	62
Trent Fontenot, McNeese State	4	2	2.66	30	1	41	32	13	38
Fernando Martinez, Lamar	2	3	2.74	17	3	46	35	13	38
Daniel Martinez, New Orleans	4	4	2.75	32	12	59	54	12	66
Collin Kober, McNeese State	3	4	2.76	23	9	42	33	10	39
Chase Hymel, NW State	5	6	2.84	15	0	79	83	29	53
Chris Falwell, Texas A&M-CC	3	5	2.91	17	0	87	73	29	88
Aaron Mason, Abilene Christian	6	4	2.96	14	0	85	75	13	48
Evan Tidwell, Northwestern St.	5	3	2.97	14	0	76	80	15	25
Greg Belton, Sam Houston State	6	1	3.00	30	13	60	43	18	62
Nathan Jones, Northwestern St.	2	2	3.10	21	5	41	28	12	21
Will Hibbs, Lamar	9	3	3.27	17	0	96	86	29	97
Christian Thames, Hou. Baptist	7	3	3.30	16	0	79	70	23	44
Tyler Gray, Central Arkansas	6	1	3.34	22	1	62	64	22	63
Cody Davenport, Central Ark.	5	2	3.36	13	0	88	101	24	63
Heath Donica, Sam Houston St.	10	4	3.42	18	0	113	99	24	96
Addison Russ, Houston Baptist	8	5	3.44	15	0	99	91	31	66
Jeffrey Stovall, Northwestern St.	4	5	3.48	20	3	62	67	6	31
Cole Stapler, Nicholls State	5	6	3.49	16	0	95	102	18	50
Bryce Kingsley, McNeese State	5	1	3.52	12	0	46	50	16	35
Garrett deMeyere, Ab. Christian	4	9	3.69	15	0	93	92	12	34
Bernie Martinez, Incarnate Word	1	9	7.82	17	0	63	82	27	46

SOUTHWESTERN ATHLETIC CONFERENCE

	Conference		Overall	
Eastern Division	W	L	W	L
* Alabama State	24	0	38	17
Jackson State	14	10	34	26
Alcorn State	10	14	16	36
Alabama A&M	8	16	13	44
Mississippi Valley State	4	20	6	36

	Conference		Overall	
Western Division	W	L	W	L
Arkansas-Pine Bluff	16	5	22	25
Grambling State	15	8	22	27
Texas Southern	13	10	24	26
Southern	6	14	14	32
Prairie View A&M	5	18	10	32

All-Conference Team: C—Hunter Allen, So., Alabama State. **1B**—Chris Biocic, Jr., Alabama State. **2B**—Eriq White, Fr., Alabama State. **3B**—Ray Hernandez, So., Alabama State. **SS**—Cornelius Copeland, Jr., Jackson State. **OF**—Carlos Ocasio, Jr., Alabama State; Yamil Pagan, So., Alabama State; C.J. Newsome, Fr., Jackson State. **DH**—Diandre Amion, Fr., Alabama State. **SP**—Joseph Camacho, Sr., Alabama State; Tyler Howe, Jr., Alabama State. **RP**—Robert Pearson, Jr., Texas Southern; Skyler Henson, Sr., Arkansas-Pine Bluff. **Player of the Year:** Carlos Ocasio, Alabama State. **Pitcher of the Year:** Joseph Camacho, Alabama State. **Newcomer of the Year:** Daniel Barnett, Grambling State. **Freshman of the Year:** Eriq White, Alabama State. **Relief Pitcher of the Year:** Skyler Henson, Arkansas-Pine Bluff. **Coach of the Year:** Mervyl Melendez, Alabama State.

INDIVIDUAL BATTING LEADERS
(Minimum 140 At-Bats)

	AVG	OBP	SLG	AB	2B	3B	HR	RBI	SB
Cornelius Copeland, Jackson St.	.422	.537	.631	187	18	3	5	38	8
Carlos Diaz, Jackson State	.409	.465	.620	171	14	2	6	57	10

	AVG	OBP	SLG	AB	2B	3B	HR	RBI	SB
Daniel Barnett, Grambling St.	.408	.504	**.647**	184	15	1	9	60	0
Bryce Brown, Jackson State	.360	.492	.538	186	10	1	7	43	21
Larry Barraza, Grambling State	.359	.426	.624	181	17	2	9	46	7
Dillon Cooper, Alabama State	.354	.469	.635	192	**22**	1	10	57	6
Aderly Perez, Ark.-Pine Bluff	.353	.402	.497	153	10	0	4	32	4
C.J. Newsome, Jackson State	.351	.417	.469	211	14	4	1	35	20
Jaqueese Moore, Ark.-Pine Bluff	.347	.457	.405	173	7	0	1	33	11
Eriq White, Alabama State	.346	.441	.461	191	13	0	3	41	10
Yamil Pagan, Alabama State	.335	.408	.507	209	11	**5**	5	48	20
Chris Scroggins, Texas Southern	.333	.442	.414	162	7	3	0	32	6
Troy Lewis, Southern	.331	.427	.488	160	11	1	4	26	5
Carlos Ocasio, Alabama State	.330	.418	.593	209	12	2	13	60	19
Diandre Amion, Alabama State	.320	.408	.473	169	5	3	5	40	9
Nolan Ramsey, Alabama A&M	.314	.364	.479	188	16	3	3	26	5
Chris Biocic, Alabama State	.313	.433	.385	182	8	1	1	44	7
Wallace Rios, Alcorn State	.307	.393	.395	205	7	1	3	28	3
Ryan Lazo, Texas Southern	.305	.405	.401	177	8	0	3	27	**40**
Kamren Dukes, Texas Southern	.303	.420	.413	155	5	0	4	22	30
Tony Holton, Jackson State	.302	.368	.431	202	6	4	4	47	9
Arrington Smith, MVSU	.299	.372	.429	147	10	0	3	19	4
Angel Avalos, Prairie View A&M	.297	.369	.459	148	6	0	6	30	0
Patrick McMahon, Alcorn State	.294	.350	.448	143	5	4	3	13	3
Roberto Colon, Ark.-Pine Bluff	.292	.327	.370	154	10	1	0	14	4
Jesus Santana, Jackson State	.278	.410	.594	**212**	16	0	**17**	67	5
Eugene Freeman, Ala. A&M	.219	.302	.331	151	4	**5**	1	12	15
#Anthony Stricklin, Jackson St.	.323	.458	.624	93	6	**5**	4	23	8

INDIVIDUAL PITCHING LEADERS
(Minimum 40 Innings Pitched)

	W	L	ERA	G	SV	IP	H	BB	SO
Tyler Howe, Alabama State	10	3	**1.69**	15	0	80	64	15	82
Joseph Camacho, Ala. State	10	1	2.35	15	1	84	75	23	82
Larry Romero, Texas Southern	9	4	3.15	15	0	**103**	89	38	82
Hunter McIntosh, Ala.State	7	2	3.39	15	0	69	67	28	82
Robert Pearson, Texas Southern	4	4	3.55	18	**5**	51	52	19	44
C.J. Lewington, Ark.-Pine Bluff	2	5	3.73	20	0	60	61	36	32
Brandon Caples, Alabama State	3	1	3.76	12	0	41	**43**	15	31
Jevon Jacobs, Jackson State	6	3	3.98	14	0	72	67	26	52
Anthony Bowmaker, Ark.-PB	6	2	4.10	19	0	59	52	27	59
Daniel Franklin, Southern	4	3	4.19	12	0	69	64	33	49
Jamal Wilson, Jackson State	4	5	4.56	15	0	75	91	33	74
Miguel Yrigoyen, Jackson State	9	3	4.61	16	0	84	79	31	**98**
Issac O'Bear, Grambling State	7	3	4.85	13	0	89	104	21	61
Josh Burchell, Alabama A&M	4	9	5.13	21	1	95	99	48	86
George Helbig, Alcorn State	3	9	5.28	18	0	60	80	20	31
Edgar Sanchez, Prairie View A&M	2	5	5.43	10	0	61	85	19	47
Ryan Rios, Texas Southern	7	2	5.44	17	0	83	104	32	78
Austin Bizzle, Alabama State	2	2	5.53	22	2	42	48	17	46
J'Markus George, Southern	4	6	5.72	12	0	68	77	47	63
Tanner Raiburn, Grambling St.	3	6	5.78	14	0	67	70	30	75
Arrington Smith, Miss. Valley St.	3	11	5.95	16	0	88	111	25	52
Seth Oliver, Texas Southern	2	7	6.03	20	3	63	71	37	55
Tyler Chatman, Alabama A&M	1	4	6.53	16	0	41	51	32	13
Rene Colon, Jackson State	6	5	6.68	17	0	67	87	31	51
Blake Estep, Ark.-Pine Bluff	4	4	6.85	16	0	67	85	28	57
Humberto Medina, Ark.-PB	6	5	6.91	16	1	70	71	41	82
Creighton Hoover, Grambling St.	3	6	7.38	24	2	46	65	**14**	24
Caleb Roberts, Alabama A&M	0	4	9.39	**29**	0	78	123	44	68
#Jesse Anderson, Jackson State	1	3	7.49	20	**5**	34	36	27	34

SUMMIT LEAGUE

	Conference		Overall	
	W	L	W	L
*Oral Roberts	22	8	38	21
Nebraska-Omaha	18	12	28	28
IPFW	14	16	33	26
South Dakota State	13	17	22	35
North Dakota State	12	18	29	25
Western Illinois	11	19	14	36

All-Conference Team: C—Matt Whatley, So., Oral Roberts. 1B—Brent Williams, Jr., Oral Roberts. 2B—Drew Fearing, So., North Dakota State. 3B—Clayton Taylor, Sr., Nebraska-Omaha. SS—Greg Kaiser, Sr., IPFW. OF—Noah Cummings, So., Oral Roberts; Cole Gruber, Sr., Nebraska-Omaha; Brandon Soat, Sr., IPFW, South Dakota State. UT—Ryan Cate, So., Nebraska-Omaha. SP—Tyler Fox, Sr., Nebraska-Omaha; Trevor Storie, Sr., IPFW; Nick Wood, Sr., Oral Roberts. RP—Brady Womacks, Jr., Oral Roberts. **Player of the Year:** Clayton Taylor, Nebraska-Omaha. **Pitcher of the Year:** Tyler Fox, Nebraska-Omaha. **Newcomer of the Year:** Brent Williams, Oral Roberts. **Coach of the Year:** Ryan Folmar, Oral Roberts.

INDIVIDUAL BATTING LEADERS
(Minimum 140 At-Bats)

	AVG	OBP	SLG	AB	2B	3B	HR	RBI	SB
Cole Gruber, Nebraska-Omaha	**.376**	.464	.466	221	13	2	1	30	**43**
Noah Cummings, Oral Roberts	.364	.426	.527	220	18	0	6	44	6
Matt Whatley, Oral Roberts	.363	.469	.562	201	10	3	8	41	5
Luke Ringhofer, S.D. State	.361	**.482**	.465	202	12	0	3	31	2
Roman Visintine, Western Ill.	.345	.391	.421	145	7	2	0	8	8
Drew Fearing, N.D. State	.327	.438	.388	196	10	1	0	26	18
Clayton Taylor, Nebraska-Omaha	.326	.430	.544	215	12	1	11	**66**	10
Brandon Soat, IPFW	.325	.400	.484	246	14	5	5	38	8
Nick Rotola, Oral Roberts	.319	.399	.419	**248**	16	0	3	40	9
Ryan Cate, Nebraska-Omaha	.317	.333	.448	183	7	1	5	31	1
Connor Currier, Western Illinois	.315	.408	.370	162	5	2	0	22	5
Greg Kaiser, IPFW	.313	.372	**.644**	233	20	3	**17**	49	12
Adam Caniglia, Neb.-Omaha	.310	.373	.419	210	10	2	3	24	2
Trevin Sonnier, Oral Roberts	.308	.377	.398	211	13	0	2	22	11
Jesse Munsterman, S.D. State	.308	.372	.430	172	12	0	3	34	2
Rolando Martinez, Oral Roberts	.304	.398	.393	191	9	1	2	24	1
Evan VanSumeren, IPFW	.304	.355	.402	184	12	0	2	24	7
Phil Velez, South Dakota State	.298	.376	.351	188	7	0	1	24	3
Brent Williams, Oral Roberts	.297	.328	.448	232	11	0	8	55	0
Chris Tschida, Western Illinois	.296	.381	.382	199	4	2	3	27	5
Jackson Boyce, IPFW	.294	.356	.401	197	9	3	2	18	15
Cody Sharrow, S.D. State	.293	.350	.425	181	13	1	3	26	4
Taylor Sanders, N.D. State	.290	.354	.345	145	5	0	1	17	0
Michael Hungate, Western Illinois	.285	.331	.437	151	11	0	4	16	8
Mark Garton, Western Illinois	.280	.399	.378	143	8	0	2	17	4
Ben Petersen, N.D. State	.276	.355	.448	192	9	**6**	4	34	15
Chase Stafford, Oral Roberts	.247	.350	.402	194	**21**	0	3	37	4

INDIVIDUAL PITCHING LEADERS
(Minimum 40 Innings Pitched)

	W	L	ERA	G	SV	IP	H	BB	SO
Nick Wood, Oral Roberts	6	3	**2.68**	15	0	77	79	20	60
Tyler Fox, Nebraska-Omaha	**10**	2	3.04	15	0	**101**	108	16	71
Chris Choles, N.D. State	4	0	3.05	21	1	44	44	**8**	27
Jordan Harms, N.D. State	1	3	3.12	14	1	49	**37**	21	48
Brian VanderWoude, N.D. State	8	2	3.18	22	5	51	54	23	61
Jordan Martin, IPFW	3	1	3.30	**29**	2	44	41	19	33
Landon Busch, S.D. State	7	4	3.34	16	1	67	66	30	64
Reed Pfannenstein, N.D. State	2	1	3.56	10	0	43	48	18	27
Cale Tims, Oral Roberts	6	2	3.71	14	0	51	56	21	29
Bryce Howe, Oral Roberts	6	5	3.72	16	0	87	97	40	**84**
Blake Stockert, N.D. State	2	5	3.73	15	1	51	61	16	37
Sam Murphy, Nebraska-Omaha	4	6	3.86	16	1	72	69	23	65
Josh McMinn, Oral Roberts	6	2	4.00	24	0	63	59	17	56
Brandon Pease, IPFW	3	2	4.00	15	0	45	46	17	42
Corey Binger, Nebraska-Omaha	7	3	4.06	15	1	75	79	19	51
Trevor Storie, IPFW	7	5	4.40	16	0	92	84	42	60
Matthew Sturchio, Western Ill.	0	3	4.71	14	0	42	46	17	28
David Flattery, Neb.-Omaha	0	2	4.73	17	2	46	48	24	35
Ian Koch, Western Illinois	3	6	4.73	14	0	67	75	35	34
Kyle Orwig, IPFW	3	2	4.86	13	0	46	52	20	28
Zach Mayo, North Dakota State	2	4	5.51	14	0	47	63	26	57
Will McAffer, S.D. State	2	0	5.75	16	1	41	38	28	30
Andrew Clemen, S.D. State	3	**10**	5.89	15	0	89	105	35	71
Evan Miller, IPFW	4	5	6.35	15	1	72	70	61	71
Mitchell Ley, IPFW	3	2	6.43	16	0	42	57	20	25
#Brady Womacks, Oral Roberts	2	2	1.22	**29**	**14**	37	33	18	29

SUN BELT CONFERENCE

	Conference		Overall	
	W	L	W	L
* Louisiana-Lafayette	21	9	43	21
South Alabama	21	9	42	22
Arkansas-Little Rock	17	13	26	28
Troy	17	13	32	26
Texas State	16	14	31	28
Georgia Southern	16	14	36	24
Texas-Arlington	15	15	30	28
Arkansas State	13	17	28	30
Louisiana-Monroe	10	20	20	35
Georgia State	10	20	24	31
Appalachian State	9	21	18	36

All-Conference Team: C—Brady Cox, Jr., Texas-Arlington. **1B**—Tanner Hill, Sr., Texas State. **2B**—Darien McLemore, Sr., Texas-Arlington. **3B**—Tanner Ring, Sr., Arkansas State. **SS**—Drew LaBounty, So., South Alabama. **OF**—Ryan Scott, Sr., Arkansas-Little Rock; Kyle Clement, Sr., Louisiana-Lafayette; Cole Billingsley, Jr., South Alabama. **DH**—Dalton Thomas, Jr., Arkansas-Little Rock. **UT**—Cory Geisler, Sr., Texas State. **SP**—Gunner Leger, So., Louisiana-Lafayette; Kevin Hill, Sr., South Alabama; Grant Bennett, Sr., Troy. **RP**—Dylan Moore, So., Louisiana-Lafayette. **Player of the Year:** Ryan Scott, Arkansas-Little Rock. **Pitcher of the Year:** Kevin Hill, South Alabama. **Freshman of the Year:** Nick Lee, Louisiana-Lafayette. **Coach of the Year:** Chris Curry, Arkansas-Little Rock.

INDIVIDUAL BATTING LEADERS
(Minimum 140 At-Bats)

	AVG	OBP	SLG	AB	2B	3B	HR	RBI	SB
Ryan Scott, Ark.-Little Rock	**.435**	**.516**	**.713**	216	**20**	2	12	**66**	7
Dalton Thomas, Ark.-Little Rock	.375	.415	.582	232	19	1	9	52	2
Brady Cox, Texas-Arlington	.365	.427	.455	222	12	1	2	41	2
Kyle Clement, La.-Lafayette	.353	.415	.516	184	14	2	4	25	9
Quintin Rohrbaugh, UT-Arlington	.343	.382	.461	230	13	4	2	35	4
Jarrett Hood, Georgia State	.338	.411	.466	204	**20**	0	2	36	0
Hayden Martin, Ark.-Little Rock	.326	.404	.376	181	7	1	0	28	8
Joey Roach, Georgia State	.325	.426	.598	169	13	0	11	45	3
Darien McLemore, UT-Arlington	.324	.402	.468	222	13	1	2	5	44	4
Joey Denison, Troy	.322	.398	.495	214	14	1	7	37	7
Ryan Newman, Texas State	.321	.392	.488	168	3	2	7	24	4
Tanner Hill, Texas State	.321	.369	.583	240	18	0	**15**	42	1
Ty White, Arkansas State	.318	.389	.420	245	7	**6**	2	41	12
Matt Sanders, Troy	.317	.381	.407	167	9	0	2	20	3
Matt Vernon, App. State	.317	.382	.519	189	10	2	8	42	1
Cameron Knight, Ark.-Little Rock	.313	.345	.413	160	10	0	2	28	1
T.J. Binder, Troy	.312	.409	.442	154	9	1	3	22	0
Matt McLean, Texas-Arlington	.307	.411	.407	231	15	4	0	22	7
Tanner Ring, Arkansas State	.304	.333	.496	230	14	2	8	46	8
Logan Baldwin, Ga. Southern	.304	.368	.379	240	12	3	0	32	18
Travis Swaggerty, South Ala.	.303	.431	.422	218	12	1	4	27	20
Jack Thompson, Georgia State	.299	.387	.435	184	7	0	6	35	1
Joe Schrimpf, Arkansas State	.299	.420	.467	214	12	3	6	43	0
Cole Billingsley, South Alabama	.297	.347	.379	**256**	12	3	1	41	**31**
Garrett Rucker, Arkansas State	.295	.375	.420	200	12	2	3	31	10
Nik Gifford, Ark.-Little Rock	.295	.367	.459	220	15	0	7	40	7
Ryan Cleveland, Ga. Southern	.286	.404	.586	227	17	3	**15**	55	12

INDIVIDUAL PITCHING LEADERS
(Minimum 40 Innings Pitched)

	W	L	ERA	G	SV	IP	H	BB	SO
Dylan Moore, La.-Lafayette	6	1	**0.91**	26	**14**	50	**24**	15	59
Anthony Herrera, La.-Monroe	1	4	1.74	22	10	41	27	12	26
Eric Carter, Louisiana-Lafayette	6	2	2.08	26	4	52	37	12	69
Gunner Leger, La.-Lafayette	7	3	2.26	16	0	92	71	24	81
Jacob Moreland, UT-Arlington	6	1	2.27	30	5	71	63	19	40
Grant Bennett, Troy	8	2	2.29	15	0	102	104	19	76
Randy Bell, South Alabama	7	1	2.45	16	0	88	68	20	60
Landon Hughes, Ga. Southern	5	2	2.47	26	4	62	37	14	58
Chase Cohen, Ga. Southern	4	3	2.66	17	0	74	53	27	64
Cory Geisler, Texas State	4	3	2.69	12	0	67	54	21	60
Kevin Hill, South Alabama	8	2	2.86	16	0	**123**	98	31	**126**
Joel Kuhnel, Texas-Arlington	6	4	2.99	12	0	72	76	16	51
Kadon Simmons, UT-Arlington	**9**	4	3.05	16	0	103	95	24	64
Evan Challenger, Ga. Southern	7	5	3.05	16	0	103	81	24	77

(Sun Belt pitching leaders continued, top right)

	W	L	ERA	G	SV	IP	H	BB	SO
Houston Mabray, Troy	5	3	3.05	14	0	59	54	15	28
Lucas Humpal, Texas State	7	5	3.06	15	0	109	94	27	85
Lucas Brown, Troy	8	4	3.10	15	0	102	98	28	71
Corey Childress, Troy	2	4	3.12	26	10	49	45	14	46
Jonathan Hennigan, Texas State	5	2	3.13	13	0	63	52	37	64
Nick Lee, Louisiana-Lafayette	7	1	3.31	16	0	87	69	27	75
Brayden Bouchey, La.-Monroe	5	3	3.73	13	0	70	58	33	72
Brian Eichhorn, Ga. Southern	6	2	3.74	16	0	67	59	19	35
Ryne Long, South Alabama	4	0	3.83	14	1	40	34	**10**	24
Reed Howell, App. State	6	2	3.83	27	0	49	41	20	37
Cory Gill, Troy	3	3	3.88	14	2	46	39	23	45
Coulton Lee, Arkansas State	5	**7**	4.18	26	1	56	62	32	39
Keller Bradford, La.-Monroe	2	3	4.31	**35**	1	48	47	11	35
Wyatt Marks, La.-Lafayette	5	**7**	4.50	15	0	76	75	20	80
Colin Schmid, App. State	2	**7**	5.33	14	0	76	83	31	62
Bobby Hampton, App. State	1	**7**	6.68	14	0	62	75	32	45
Seth Hardin, App. State	1	**7**	8.37	11	0	43	54	33	31

WEST COAST CONFERENCE

	Conference		Overall	
	W	L	W	L
* Saint Mary's	18	9	33	25
Brigham Young	18	9	37	17
Gonzaga	18	9	36	21
Pepperdine	16	11	29	24
San Francisco	14	13	22	34
Loyola Marymount	13	14	26	27
San Diego	13	14	27	29
Pacific	12	15	22	30
Santa Clara	10	17	23	29
Portland	3	24	17	37

All-Conference Team: Jeff Bohling, Jr., Gonzaga; Bryson Brigman, So., San Diego; Gio Brusa, Sr., Pacific; Phil Caufield, Jr., Loyola Marymount; Tyler Frost, So., Gonzaga; Anthony Gonsolin, Sr., Saint Mary's; Zach Kirtley, So., Saint Mary's; Brennon Lund, Jr., Brigham Young; Danny Mayer, Jr., Pacific. **P**—Brandon Bailey, Jr., Gonzaga; Corbin Burnes, Jr., Saint Mary's; Eli Morgan, So., Gonzaga; A.J. Puckett, Jr., Pepperdine; Michael Rucker, Jr., Brigham Young. **Player of the Year:** Jeff Bohling, Gonzaga. **Pitcher of the Year:** A.J. Puckett, Pepperdine. **Freshman of the Year:** Keaton Kringlen, Brigham Young. **Defensive Player of the Year:** Nico Giarratano, San Francisco. **Coach of the Year:** Eric Valenzuela, Saint Mary's.

INDIVIDUAL BATTING LEADERS
(Minimum 140 At-Bats)

	AVG	OBP	SLG	AB	2B	3B	HR	RBI	SB
Brennon Lund, BYU	**.387**	**.454**	.531	243	19	**5**	2	34	15
Bryson Brigman, San Diego	.372	.428	.424	191	8	1	0	22	17
Keaton Kringlen, BYU	.369	.442	.560	141	12	0	5	34	2
Tanner Chauncey, BYU	.348	.373	.427	178	11	0	1	27	3
Gio Brusa, Pacific	.337	.418	**.614**	202	14	0	14	46	1
Colton Shaver, BYU	.335	.452	.582	194	16	1	10	**57**	1
Justin Jacobs, Gonzaga	.333	.442	.392	186	9	1	0	23	3
Taylor Jones, Gonzaga	.332	.399	.509	232	**27**	4	2	36	0
Ross Puskarich, San Francisco	.331	.402	.481	154	8	0	5	29	2
Brennon Anderson, BYU	.329	.418	.510	155	8	1	6	45	4
Riley Adams, San Diego	.327	.443	.512	205	18	1	6	37	4
Cassidy Brown, Loyola Mary.	.325	.394	.502	209	17	1	6	41	4
Zach Kirtley, Saint Mary's	.323	.428	.504	226	20	0	7	43	4
Allen Smoot, San Francisco	.321	.434	.429	156	14	0	1	33	0
Cooper Hummel, Portland	.320	.422	.490	194	14	2	5	29	7
Danny Mayer, Pacific	.314	.346	.590	229	16	1	**15**	40	3
Lucas Halstead, Pacific	.313	.376	.480	179	13	5	1	25	1
Joey Fiske, Saint Mary's	.310	.373	.343	239	6	1	0	25	17
Tyler Frost, Gonzaga	.309	.377	.483	230	15	2	7	49	2
Phil Caufield, Loyola Mary.	.309	.370	.349	149	2	2	0	16	8
Anthony Gonsolin, Saint Mary's	.307	.400	.476	212	9	3	7	26	0
Niko Decolati, Loyola Mary.	.306	.360	.456	147	6	2	4	33	5
Matt Sinatro, San Francisco	.305	.427	.341	167	4	1	0	10	**26**
Eric Urry, BYU	.302	.367	.479	215	12	1	8	53	9
Bronson Larsen, BYU	.301	.405	.514	173	13	0	8	44	0
Jeffrey Bohling, Gonzaga	.298	.360	.522	**245**	23	4	8	50	10

INDIVIDUAL PITCHING LEADERS
(Minimum 40 Innings Pitched)

	W	L	ERA	G	SV	IP	H	BB	SO
Ryan Wilson, Pepperdine	2	0	**0.63**	14	6	43	**18**	14	46
A.J. Puckett, Pepperdine	9	3	1.27	14	0	99	65	26	95
Max Kuhns, Santa Clara	1	4	2.21	28	**14**	41	28	16	37
Brandon Bailey, Gonzaga	10	3	2.42	16	0	100	80	31	**125**
Corbin Burnes, Saint Mary's	9	2	2.48	16	0	102	76	33	120
Michael Rucker, BYU	**11**	1	2.73	16	0	102	80	31	94
Chandle Blanchard, Pepperdine	3	2	3.19	12	1	42	46	**7**	31
Johnny York, Saint Mary's	7	5	3.25	15	0	102	95	21	57
Hayden Rogers, BYU	5	3	3.50	20	0	62	72	18	36
Keaton Cenatiempo, BYU	3	2	3.54	24	3	48	50	16	32
Maverik Buffo, BYU	6	2	3.63	11	0	45	46	17	34
Mitchell White, Santa Clara	3	6	3.72	15	0	92	90	27	118
Eli Morgan, Gonzaga	10	3	3.73	16	0	**111**	109	31	107
Max Gamboa, Pepperdine	2	9	3.74	19	1	53	50	22	52
James Kannenberg, San Fran.	7	5	3.74	16	0	89	77	38	50
Bryce Reichmann, Saint Mary's	0	2	3.77	25	0	45	41	15	34
Jake Jenkins, Pacific	3	4	3.79	16	2	81	92	25	65
Cameron Neff, Saint Mary's	6	3	3.81	18	1	83	75	25	79
Tyler Cohen, Loyola Marymount	3	4	3.84	13	0	61	55	28	42
Anthony Gonsolin, Saint Mary's	3	3	3.86	18	6	42	41	16	39
Steven Wilson, Santa Clara	5	5	3.92	14	0	80	94	28	66
Drew Strotman, Saint Mary's	3	5	3.96	22	2	52	54	31	46
Brenton Arriaga, Loyola Mary.	2	5	4.06	13	1	51	50	9	34
J.D. Busfield, Loyola Marymount	5	4	4.08	13	0	88	102	10	61
Cory Abbott, Loyola Marymount	5	5	4.24	14	0	70	79	22	34
Davis Tominaga, Portland	4	**10**	4.75	14	0	85	93	30	57
#Nick Medeiros, Santa Clara	2	2	3.82	**31**	2	31	23	19	29

INDIVIDUAL BATTING LEADERS
(Minimum 140 At-Bats)

	AVG	OBP	SLG	AB	2B	3B	HR	RBI	SB
Daniel Johnson, N.M. State	**.382**	.434	**.630**	246	11	7	**12**	50	**29**
Dustin Frailey, CS Bakersfield	.376	**.479**	.593	194	12	**9**	4	27	23
Jose Garcia, UTRGV	.369	.447	.477	176	13	3	0	19	16
Paul Panaccione, Grand Canyon	.363	.473	.521	146	9	1	4	26	10
Miles Lewis, North Dakota	.360	.429	.463	175	5	2	3	24	20
Austin Botello, N.M. State	.354	.400	.528	229	10	3	8	50	3
Sheldon Stober, Seattle	.353	.384	.513	238	18	1	6	35	12
Thomas Lerouge, Grand Canyon	.342	.395	.416	231	7	2	2	26	13
Sean Sutton, Seattle	.337	.430	.439	205	13	1	2	32	1
Craig Brinkerhoff, Utah Valley	.330	.408	.561	212	10	3	11	36	1
Mason Fishback, N.M. State	.329	.411	.457	140	6	0	4	28	0
Brock Carpenter, Seattle	.327	.444	.532	205	15	3	7	47	6
Nick Tanner, Northern Colorado	.327	.388	.401	162	7	1	1	15	7
Mark Krueger, Utah Valley	.325	.409	.475	240	11	2	7	45	5
Greg Popylisen, N.M. State	.319	.412	.433	141	7	3	1	15	18
Chris Lewis, Sacramento State	.309	.372	.484	223	16	1	7	42	8
Garrison Schwartz, G. Canyon	.307	.404	.510	202	19	2	6	37	4
Brent Sakurai, N.M. State	.307	.355	.396	192	12	1	1	27	3
Joseph Collazo, UTRGV	.306	.409	.383	183	8	0	2	25	7
David Metzgar, CS Bakersfield	.305	.369	.399	213	12	4	0	47	10
Cole Loncar, UTRGV	.304	.387	.391	161	7	2	1	19	5
Justin Erlandson, Utah Valley	.302	.407	.423	149	8	2	2	23	8
Trevor Howell, Utah Valley	.297	.357	.367	229	13	0	1	28	4
Kody Reynolds, Sac. State	.295	.357	.423	156	11	0	3	14	1
Griffin Andreychuk, Seattle	.293	.397	.386	215	8	3	2	36	11
Greyson Bogden, Utah Valley	.290	.355	.435	**262**	18	1	6	35	11
Trey Stine, New Mexico State	.281	.379	.488	203	**19**	1	7	39	1
Daniel Hetzel, New Mexico State	.278	.348	.424	205	12	0	6	**56**	6

WESTERN ATHLETIC CONFERENCE

	Conference		Overall	
	W	L	W	L
Seattle	21	6	37	21
New Mexico State	20	7	34	23
* Utah Valley	18	9	37	23
Sacramento State	16	11	30	28
Grand Canyon	13	14	25	28
Northern Colorado	11	12	16	34
Cal State Bakersfield	12	14	19	37
Texas-Rio Grande Valley	10	14	21	28
Chicago State	6	21	13	42
North Dakota	4	23	8	37

All-Conference Team: C—Mason Fishback, So., New Mexico State. **1B**—Sean Sutton, So., Seattle. **2B**—Sheldon Stober, Sr. Seattle. **3B**—Brock Carpender, Jr., Seattle. **SS**—Paul Panaccione, Sr., Grand Canyon. **OF**—Daniel Johnson, Jr., New Mexico State; Dustin Frailey, Jr., Cal State Bakersfield; Mark Krueger, Sr., Utah Valley. **At-Large:** Garrison Schwartz, So., Grand Canyon; Greyson Bogden, Sr., Utah Valley; Danny Beddes, Sr., Utah Valley. **SP**—Nick Meservey, So., Seattle; Max Karnos, Jr., Sacramento State. **RP**—Zach Wolf, Fr., Seattle. **Player of the Year:** Daniel Johnson, Nex Mexico State. **Pitcher of the Year:** Nick Meservey, Seattle. **Freshman of the Year:** Miles Lewis, North Dakota. **Coach of the Year:** Donny Harrel, Seattle.

INDIVIDUAL PITCHING LEADERS
(Minimum 40 Innings Pitched)

	W	L	ERA	G	SV	IP	H	BB	SO
Tyler Beardsley, Sac. State	4	2	**1.71**	30	**11**	47	36	16	24
Tarik Skubal, Seattle	6	1	2.11	8	0	43	**32**	17	50
Nick Meservey, Seattle	7	2	2.32	16	1	81	61	43	79
Johnny Gonzalez, UTRGV	5	3	2.83	11	0	64	67	34	67
Connor Moore, Seattle	4	0	2.84	30	4	44	37	13	40
Nick Tanner, Northern Colorado	4	1	2.89	9	0	53	49	13	33
Tyler Erwin, New Mexico State	2	1	3.04	**33**	6	47	47	14	57
Jake Repavich, Grand Canyon	3	3	3.29	17	0	77	89	15	53
Max Karnos, Sacramento State	7	3	3.38	15	0	85	92	28	42
Zach Muckenhirn, North Dakota	3	8	3.59	13	0	93	87	14	99
Andrew Garcia, UTRGV	7	5	3.65	15	0	81	90	29	48
Chad Perry, Sacramento State	2	1	3.74	**33**	0	43	49	15	31
Robert Quinonez, UTRGV	2	1	3.74	11	1	55	47	19	47
Jackson Cofer, Utah Valley	6	5	3.79	14	0	76	86	28	53
Sam Long, Sacramento State	5	8	3.99	16	0	86	81	35	68
Cameron Brendel, Grand Canyon	4	4	4.00	16	0	74	73	14	43
Ted Hammond, Seattle	8	3	4.20	16	0	90	79	26	80
Matthew McHugh, N.M. State	6	3	4.21	17	0	68	75	35	50
Janson Junk, Seattle	6	4	4.21	17	0	68	80	18	59
A.J. Monarrez, CS Bakersfield	4	5	4.23	15	0	79	74	31	64
Jake Mayer, Utah Valley	8	2	4.27	24	1	78	72	25	51
Jake Wong, Grand Canyon	2	3	4.28	18	0	55	52	29	28
Corey Nakakura, Northern Colo.	3	3	4.47	15	0	52	49	18	39
Danny Beddes, Utah Valley	**9**	4	4.56	17	0	**103**	93	55	**99**
Grant Kukuk, Sacramento State	5	4	4.57	16	0	83	89	14	29
Kyle Bradish, New Mexico State	8	3	4.67	17	0	87	84	43	82
Tanner Olson, Sacramento State	3	5	5.22	18	0	50	55	**12**	14
Dillon Engle, Chicago State	2	**11**	5.96	17	0	83	106	38	33

NCAA DIVISION II

BY WILL BRYANT

Nova Southeastern (Fla.) got in its final tune-ups, packed its bags and made its way to North Carolina for the Division II College World Series, just like the other seven teams.

Except, they weren't like the others.

It was their first trip among a sea of experienced teams, but that didn't stop the Sharks from making a splash.

After playing from behind for a majority of its tournament games, Nova Southeastern won the national championship at USA Baseball's National Training Complex, culminated by an 8-6 victory over the Millersville (Pa.) Marauders.

"This team has mentality of being hot, we talked about it being red hot," head coach Greg Brown said. "But they believed in each other."

The Sharks were down to their final out, down by one run against No. 3 seed Franklin Pierce (N.H.), when first baseman Andres Visbal laced a game-tying single up the middle.

A walk-off single in the 12th by leadoff hitter Jancarlos Cintron, the Sharks' second baseman, capped off the comeback for Nova, and the Sharks carried that momentum through the tournament.

Even playing from behind in each of their five games, and facing an assortment of other adversity, the Sharks never dropped their heads. "Our belief was constant," Brown said.

In its next game, Nova erased an early Lander (S.C.) lead with 12 runs across the fourth, fifth and sixth innings but lost starting catcher Michael Hernandez to injury. This left the catching duties in the hands of freshman backstop Jake Anchia.

Anchia did not take long to make his presence felt, delivering a two-run home run in the Sharks' 5-2 win against Cal Poly Pomona to help propel the team into the finals.

While overcoming adversity, Nova Southeastern still had to overcome Millersville, which was 53-5. The Sharks fell behind early in both games of the best-of-three finals, but as they had all season, different guys came through to make the big play for Nova.

In the first game, the Sharks topped Brandon Miller—a top 500 draft prospect—behind a big home run from Brandon Gomez. The next day, a huge game from third baseman Daniel Zardon, and a "Shark tank" (also known as a home run) from Suarez helped erase a 3-0 deficit and beating the previously undefeated Jim McDade.

DIVISION II WORLD SERIES

Site: Cary, N.C.
Participants: Angelo State, Texas (39-20); Cal Poly Pomona (40-17); Central Missouri (42-13); Franklin Pierce, N.H. (48-7); Lander, S.C. (42-14); Millersville, Pa. (50-5); Nova Southeastern, Fla. (39-16); Southern Indiana (37-19).
Champion: Nova Southeastern.
Runner-up: Millersville.
Outstanding player: Devin Raftery, rhp, Nova Southeastern.

FINALS (BEST-OF-THREE)
Nova Southeastern 2, Millersville 1
Nova Southeastern 8, Millersville 6

NATIONAL LEADERS

BATTING AVERAGE (Minimum 100 at-bats)

RK. PLAYER, POS., TEAM	CLASS	AVG	OBP	SLG
1. Patrick O'Donnell, of, Augustana (S.D.)	Jr.	.463	.516	.757
2. Luke Ortel, of, Hillsdale (Mich.)	Sr.	.463	.506	.769
3. Jack Schmidt, of, Northern State (S.D.)	So.	.460	.520	.659
4. Troy Sieber, inf, Saint Leo (Fla.)	Jr.	.457	.553	.873
5. Judd Davis, inf, St. Cloud State (Minn.)	Fr.	.456	.545	.626
6. Jordan Godman, of, Colorado State-Pueblo	Sr.	.454	.495	.691
7. Ryan Snyder, of, Quincy (Ill.)	Sr.	.450	.533	.900
8. Shane Billings, 2b, Wingate (N.C.)	Jr.	.444	.502	.639
9. Nick Vitale, of, Stillman (Ala.)	Sr.	.442	.486	.628
10. Alex Wojciechowski, 1b, Minnesota-Duluth	Sr.	.442	.506	.973

CATEGORY LEADERS: BATTING

DEPT.	PLAYER, POS., TEAM	CLASS	G	TOTAL
OBP *	Troy Sieber, inf, Saint Leo (Fla.)	Jr.	46	.553
SLG *	Alex Wojciechowski, 1b, Minnesota-Duluth	Sr.	55	.973
R	Alex Wojciechowski, 1b, Minnesota-Duluth	Sr.	55	86
H	Luke Ortel, of, Hillsdale (Mich.)	Sr.	56	112
2B	Chance Bowden, 1b, Catawba (N.C.)	So.	55	31
3B	Mike Mastroberti, 2b, Southern N.H.	Sr.	57	13
HR	Alex Wojciechowski, 1b, Minnesota-Duluth	Sr.	55	33
RBI	Alex Wojciechowski, 1b, Minnesota-Duluth	Sr.	55	101
SB	Justin Brock, ss, Franklin Pierce (N.H.)	Sr.	57	47

Minimum 100 at-bats

EARNED RUN AVERAGE (Minimum 40 innings pitched)

RK. PITCHER, TEAM	CLASS	W	L	ERA
1. Placido Torres, Tusculum (Tenn.)	Sr.	11	0	0.70
2. J.R. McDermott, Colorado-Mesa	Fr.	7	0	0.92
3. Brandon Miller, Millersville (Pa.)	Jr.	12	2	1.42
4. Matt Kostalos, St. Thomas Aquinas (N.Y.)	Sr.	8	0	1.46
5. Dylan Stowell, California Baptist	Jr.	9	0	1.52
6. Tanner Bird, Franklin Pierce (N.H.)	Sr.	8	1	1.55
7. Guillaume Blanchette, Lubbock Christian (Texas)	Sr.	12	2	1.73
8. Perry DellaValle, Seton Hill (Pa.)	So.	9	1	1.79
9. Colin McKee, Mercyhurst (Pa.)	Jr.	11	2	1.82
10. Michael Koval, Cal Poly Pomona	Jr.	9	3	1.86

CATEGORY LEADERS: PITCHING

DEPT.	PITCHER, TEAM	CLASS	TOTAL
W	Tre Hobbs, Delta State (Miss.)	Jr.	13
SV	Matt Williams, Grand Valley State (Mich.)	Jr.	20
G	Greg Mason, Washburn (Kan.)	Sr.	38
IP	Placido Torres, Tusculum (Tenn.)	Sr.	116
SO	Placido Torres, Tusculum (Tenn.)	Sr.	162
SO/9 *	Enzo Esposito, Post (Conn.)	So.	15.00
BB/9 *	Connor Hamilton, Cedarville (Ohio)	Sr.	0.53
WHIP *	Brandon Miller, Millersville (Pa.)	Jr.	0.71

Minimum 40 innings pitched

NCAA DIVISION III

Trinity won its first national championship in program history, sweeping through the Division III College World Series in Appleton, Wis.

Making their second straight appearance in the D-III CWS, the Tigers reached the finals first by shutting out Wisconsin-La Crosse, the top hitting team in D-III, and then twice beating SUNY Cortland, the defending national champion. Facing Keystone, which went undefeated in the other bracket, in the best-of-three championship series, the Tigers broke open the first game by scoring in five straight innings from the fourth through the eighth, winning 14-6. Tigers catcher Drew Butler led the offense, going 4-for-6 with six RBIs, and kept it going in Game Two with a 3-for-5 night. Trinity scored three runs in the first inning and never trailed, though Keystone wouldn't go away quietly, closing the gap to one run in the eighth. But Andrew Waters' two-run single in the top of the ninth provided some insurance, and Michael Walker closed out a perfect bottom half to seal the Tigers' title with a 10-7 win.

DIVISION III WORLD SERIES

Site: Appleton, Wis.
Participants: Emory, Ga. (34-10); Keystone, Pa. (37-9); LaRoche, Pa. (41-10); St. John Fisher, N.Y. (38-11); SUNY Cortland (41-6); Trinity, Texas (39-3); Wisconsin-La Crosse (38-8); Wisconsin-Whitewater (35-14).
Champion: Trinity.
Runner-up: Keystone.
Outstanding player: Drew Butler, c, Trinity.

NATIONAL LEADERS

BATTING AVERAGE (Minimum 100 at-bats)

RK. PLAYER, POS., TEAM	CLASS	AVG	OBP	SLG
1. Drake Sykes, of, Knox (Ill.)	Jr.	.487	.583	.846
2. Taylor Kohlwey, of, Wisconsin-La Crosse	Sr.	.485	.549	.823
3. Hayden Tsutsui, c, Carleton (Minn.)	Sr.	.475	.561	.803
4. Kyle Bonicki, inf, Clark (Mass.)	So.	.466	.549	.596
5. Justin Cassinelli, inf, Susquehanna (Pa.)	Sr.	.465	.532	.768

CATEGORY LEADERS: BATTING

DEPT.	PLAYER, POS., TEAM	CLASS	G	TOTAL
OBP *	Drake Sykes, of, Knox (Ill.)	Jr.	33	0.583
SLG *	Justin Taylor, ss, Lancaster Bible (Pa.)	Jr.	36	0.929
HR	Justin Taylor, ss, Lancaster Bible (Pa.)	Jr.	36	17
RBI	Justin Anderson, 1b, Wisconsin-La Crosse	Sr.	49	83
SB	John Rizzi, of, College of New Jersey	Sr.	44	46

Minimum 100 at-bats

EARNED RUN AVERAGE (Minimum 40 innings pitched)

RK. PITCHER, TEAM	CLASS	W	L	ERA
1. Jake Fishman, Union (N.Y.)	Jr.	7	0	0.41
2. T.J. Storer, Ohio Northern	So.	2	0	0.49
3. Seth Lamando, SUNY Cortland	Sr.	10	0	0.72
4. Tom Conclin, Washington & Lee (Va.)	Jr.	8	0	1.03
5. Matt Abrain, Salem State (Mass.)	Sr.	3	3	1.07

CATEGORY LEADERS: PITCHING

DEPT.	PITCHER, TEAM	CLASS	TOTAL
W	Deion Hughes, Westminster (Mo.)	Sr.	12
SV	Eric Dumas, Wheaton (Mass.)	Sr.	13
SO	Felix Baez, Keystone (Pa.)	Sr.	123
SO/9 *	Carson Ferry, Northland (Wis.)	Fr.	13.29
BB/9 *	Coty Franklin, Hope (Mich.)	Sr.	0.43

Minimum 40 innings pitched

NAIA

The NAIA's most successful program returned to the top, as Lewis-Clark State won its national best 18th title and its second straight.

The Warriors did it in dramatic fashion, holding off Faulkner, the tournament's No. 1 seed, in the championship game by a 12-11 score. The final game featured an NAIA World Series record 11 combined home runs, six by Lewis-Clark State. But it ended with a defensive gem, as the Warriors threw out the potential tying run at third base to end the game, the runner trying to advance from first to third on a single.

Lewis-Clark State went 4-1 overall in the Series, led by MVP Jacob Zanon, who hit a three-run homer in the title game and was the outfielder whose throw led to the final out which sealed the title.

Site: Lewiston, Idaho.
Participants: Auburn-Montgomery, Ala. (45-16); Bellevue, Neb. (52-10); Faulkner, Ala. (50-13); Lewis-Clark State, Idaho (49-7); Lindsey Wilson, Ky. (43-23); Point, Ga. (34-30); Science & Arts, Okla. (48-12); Sterling, Kan. (51-14); Tennessee Wesleyan (49-13); The Master's, Calif. (41-18).
Champion: Lewis-Clark State.
Runner-up: Faulkner.
Outstanding player: Jacob Zanon, of, Lewis-Clark State.

NATIONAL LEADERS

BATTING AVERAGE
(Minimum 2.5 PAs per game, 75% of games played)

RK. PLAYER, POS., TEAM	CLASS	AVG	OBP	SLG
1. Javion Randle, of, Jarvis Christian (Texas)	Sr.	.480	.560	.660
2. Gadier Charriez, inf, Bethel (Tenn.)	Sr.	.474	.568	.821
3. Alex Montero, 3b, LSU-Shreveport	Sr.	.459	.546	.890
4. Yariel Gonzalez, inf, Science & Arts (Okla.)	Sr.	.457	.508	.796
5. Ryan Phillips, inf, William Woods (Mo.)	Jr.	.455	.543	.622

EARNED RUN AVERAGE (Minimum 1 IP per team game)

RK. PITCHER, TEAM	CLASS	W	L	ERA
1. Ryan Hartman, Tennessee Wesleyan	Sr.	10	1	0.64
2. Jordan Watson, Science & Arts (Okla.)	Jr.	10	2	1.38
Lucas Daugherty, Mt. Vernon Nazarene (Ohio)	Sr.	8	2	1.38
Alex Webb, British Columbia	Sr.	10	1	1.38
5. Duncan Patterson, Spring Arbor (Mich.)	Fr.	5	3	1.44

NJCAA Division I

Thanks to a 2-run homer by Gavin Johns and a complete game outing by JoJo Romero, Yavapai won the 2016 NJCAA Division I title with a 5-2 win over San Jacinto. The championship is the first for the Roughriders since 1993 and fourth in the program's history.

Romero shone in the tournament, winning three games and striking out 22 batters in 15 innings, including 15 in the championship. Rashaan Kuahaulua was named most outstanding player for the tournament, batting .455 with two home runs and nine runs in the tournament for Yavapai.

The Roughriders finished their first championship season in 23 years with a record of 49-20.

Site: Grand Junction, Colo.
Participants: Chattahoochee Valley, Ala. (49-10); Cisco, Texas (46-14); Cowley County, Kan. (44-16); Darton State, Ga. (43-19); Delgado, La.

(36-14); Harford, Md. (52-9); Iowa Western (50-13); Santa Fe, Fla. (42-8); San Jacinto, Texas (48-10); Yavapai, Ariz. (44-19).
Champion: Yavapai.
Runner-Up: San Jacinto.
Oustanding Player: Rashaan Kuahaulua, ss, Yavapai.

NATIONAL LEADERS

BATTING AVERAGE
(Minimum 2.5 PAs per game, 75% of games played)

RK. PLAYER, TEAM	AVG	OBP	SLG	HR
1. Brylie Ware, Neosho County (Kan.) CC	.560	.660	1.128	29
2. Hosea Nelson, Clarendon (Texas) CC	.531	.606	1.020	20
3. Ryan Toliver, Neosho County (Kan.) CC	.493	.581	.798	13
4. Manuel Mesa, ASA New York CC	.489	.530	.730	4
5. Zachary Rheams, Cisco (Texas) CC	.481	.570	.846	17

EARNED RUN AVERAGE (Minimum 1 IP per team game)

RK. PITCHER, TEAM	W	L	ERA	IP
1. Blair Calvo, Eastern Florida State CC	6	1	0.97	74
2. Hunter Hood, Wallace-Dothan (Ala.) CC	10	2	1.12	81
3. Devin Smeltzer, San Jacinto (Texas) CC	9	3	1.18	92
4. Matthias Dietz, John A. Logan (Ill.) CC	12	1	1.22	103
5. Chase Burks, Chattahoochee Valley (Ala.) CC	14	0	1.34	94

CATEGORY LEADERS: BATTING

DEPT.	PLAYER, TEAM	G	TOTAL
OBP	Brylie Ware, Neosho County (Kan.) CC	62	.660
SLG	Brylie Ware, Neosho County (Kan.) CC	62	1.128
HR	Caden Doga, Hutchinson (Kan.) CC	58	31
RBI	Brylie Ware, Neosho County (Kan.) CC	62	125
SB	David Salgueiro, Kishwaukee (Ill.) CC	54	60

CATEGORY LEADERS: PITCHING

DEPT.	PITCHER, TEAM	G	TOTAL
W	Chase Burks, Chattahoochee Valley (Ala.) CC	15	14
L	Raul Baduel, Frank Phillips (Texas) CC	16	11
SV	Deviner McCray, Gulf Coast State (Fla.) CC	26	16
IP	Jospeh Romero, Yavapai (Ariz.) CC	21	114
SO	Jakob Hernandez, Seward County (Kan.) CC	16	159

NJCAA Division II

Led by five all-tournament freshmen, Jones County won its first-ever national championship with a 7-1 win over GateWay. Tanner Huddleston went 3-for-4 with a home run and Ben Stiglets threw a complete game, striking out eight over 100 pitches.

Tournament MVP Erick Hoard went 3-for-5 in the title game, and finished the tournament 11-for-22 with 11 RBIs. Jones County went 5-1 in the tournament to finish the season 54-9.
Site: Enid, Okla.
Participants: Brunswick, N.C. (40-16); GateWay, Ariz. (40-20); Jones County, Miss. (49-8); McHenry County, Ill. (48-10); Mercer County, N.J. (48-8); Monroe, N.Y. (33-14); North Iowa Area (47-14); Parkland, Co. (45-14); Sinclair, Oh. (49-10); Western Oklahoma State (46-16).
Champion: Jones County.
Runner-Up: GateWay.
Oustanding Player: Erick Hoard, if, Jones County.

NJCAA Division III

Tyler added another chapter to its dominant run, sweeping through the tournament to win its third straight national championship. The Apaches only trailed once in the tournament, coming from behind in the title game to beat Northern Essex 4-3.

Tournament MVP Jonathan Groff won the first game of the tournament with a complete game and ended the last game of the tournament, earning a five-out save by getting five strikeouts.

Tyler outscored its opponents 33-7 in tournament and finished the season with a 42-16 record.
Site: Kinston, N.C.
Participants: Century, Minn. (38-11); Montgomery, Md. (34-15); Niagara County, N.Y. (43-5); Northern Essex, Mass, (22-14); Rowan College, N.J. (39-13); Suffolk County, N.Y. (25-6); Tyler, Texas (38-16); Waubonese, Ill. (37-17).
Champion: Tyler.
Runner-Up: Northern Essex.
Oustanding Player: Jonathan Groff, lhp, Tyler.

California CC Athletic Association

With the championship game tied at 3 in the seventh, Santa Rosa right fielder Zach Hall grounded a single to right to score the go-ahead run, giving the Bear Cubs their third CCCAA championship in school history.

Jake Schneider and Alec Rennard were named co-MVPs for the tournament. Schneider went 10-for-16 in the tournament and drove in five runs. Rennard won Bear Cubs' first game in the tournament and then closed the championship game, picking up his 14th win and first save in doing so.

Santa Rosa previously won the CCCAA title in 1952 and 2005. The Bear Cubs finished the season 38-9.
Site: Fresno, Calif.
Participants: Cypress (30-13), Golden West (29-14), San Joaquin Delta College (31-11), Santa Rosa (35-8).
Champion: Santa Rosa.
Runner-Up: Golden West.
Oustanding Player: Jack Scheiner, ss, Santa Rosa; Alec Rennard, rhp, Santa Rosa.

Northwest Athletic Conference

Yakima Valley (Wash.) JC claimed its NWAC-leading 21st title, but it was the Yaks' first since 1983, ending a three-decade drought. First-year head coach Kyle Krustangel's team went 4-1 in the NWAC tournament, pitching shutouts in each of their first three games and capping it off with a 5-2 win against Everett (Wash.) JC in the finals. Tournament MVP Chris Petrosie threw seven shutout innings in the Yaks' opener, then returned on three days rest to pick up the win in the championship game with six innings of one-run ball.
Site: Longview, Wash.
Participants: Bellevue (35-16); Chemeketa (30-18); Everett (35-11); Lower Columbia (33-12); Mount Hood (26-17); Pierce (31-14); Treasure Valley (33-18); Yakima Valley (33-13).
Champion: Yakima Valley.
Runner-up: Everett.
Outstanding player: Chris Petrosie, rhp, Yakima Valley.

BY TEDDY CAHILL

After the fifth inning of the decisive fifth game between USA Baseball's Collegiate National Team and Cuba, the action paused while the grounds crew raked the infield and the umpires got water. During the brief intermission, manager George Horton gathered his team for a meeting.

Cuba held a 1-0 lead. Team USA was attempting to win its first ever series in Cuba and finish its summer tour on a high note.

"After all the grind we've been through, we've had some challenges," Horton said. "What if I told you we're one run down with four innings to play and the chance to do something that's never been done in USA Baseball history?"

The players agreed they were in a good position. Team USA quickly went to work and tied the game in the sixth when outfielder Jeren Kendall (Vanderbilt) drove in a run on a groundout.

The score was still tied when the eighth inning began. Horton called on Keston Hiura (UC Irvine) to pinch hit to lead off the inning against lefthander Livan Moinelo. Hiura drove a home run over the left field wall to give the CNT the lead in dramatic fashion.

With the lead in hand, lefthander Ricky Tyler Thomas (Fresno State) closed out the victory with two scoreless innings. He earned the win, throwing 5⅓ scoreless innings out of the bullpen. He struck out four batters, walked one and held Cuba to two hits.

For the first time, the CNT won a series in Cuba. The two teams have played an annual series since 2012, alternating home field advantage. In the CNT's first two trips to the island, Cuba won the 2012 series and swept Team USA in 2014. The CNT has won both series played on American soil.

Horton, the 2003 College Coach of the Year, has won two national championships during his coaching career. He said winning the CNT's first series in Cuba felt comparable.

"We didn't dogpile and stuff, but for me, on a personal note, it felt like a national championship to me," Horton said. "I don't think it was on the same level of accomplishment to the players, but they know how good Cuba is and they know what was at stake and they know what they put into it."

Team USA ended the summer 11-7-1, including a 7-7 record in its international tour against Taiwan, Japan and Cuba. The CNT split its series in Taiwan and lost the decisive fifth game of the Japan series in extra innings.

Horton said the tour was taxing, as Team USA travelled from California, where it held its trails in late June, to Taiwan then Japan and then Cuba in the span of four weeks. The travel was exacerbated by some long bus rides in Japan and Cuba because the series moved through multiple locations in the country.

But Horton said the players never complained

COLLEGIATE NATIONAL TEAM STATS

Year indicates 2014-15 class standing

PLAYER, POS.	YEAR	SCHOOL	AVG	OBP	SLG	G	AB	R	H	2B	3B	HR	RBI	BB	SO	SB
Brendan McKay, 1b/lhp	Jr.	Louisville	.326	.434	.372	15	43	8	14	2	0	0	5	6	11	0
Friedl, T.J., of	Jr.	Nevada	.290	.362	.452	18	62	10	18	5	1	1	9	5	2	4
Jeren Kendall, of	Jr.	Vanderbilt	.290	.329	.536	19	69	8	20	5	3	2	14	5	24	5
Keston Hiura, 2b	Jr.	UC Irvine	.289	.356	.553	17	38	7	11	1	0	3	6	5	9	1
Jake Burger, 3b	Jr.	Missouri State	.271	.358	.373	19	59	4	16	4	1	0	3	5	18	2
Evan Skoug, c	Jr.	Texas Christian	.263	.364	.474	15	38	3	10	2	0	2	11	5	8	0
Evan White, 1b/of	Jr.	Kentucky	.250	.298	.288	19	52	8	13	0	1	0	3	3	12	0
Taylor Walls, ss/2b	Jr.	Florida State	.205	.415	.282	19	39	7	8	3	0	0	4	14	12	2
Dalton Guthrie, ss	Jr.	Florida	.191	.240	.213	19	47	8	9	1	0	0	1	2	13	0
Seth Beer, of	So.	Clemson	.178	.315	.267	17	45	3	8	1	0	1	5	7	10	1
K.J. Harrison, 1b/of	Jr.	Oregon State	.103	.188	.103	13	29	1	3	0	0	0	3	2	14	0
Mike Rivera, c	Jr.	Florida	.091	.200	.091	13	22	1	2	0	0	0	1	2	6	1
Devin Hairston, ss	Jr.	Louisville	.000	.130	.00	13	20	2	0	0	0	0	0	3	10	0

PITCHER, POS.	YEAR	SCHOOL	W	L	ERA	G	SV	IP	H	R	ER	BB	SO	AVG
J.B. Bukauskas, rhp	Jr.	North Carolina	1	1	0.00	6	0	22	7	1	0	3	21	.109
Alex Lange, rhp	Jr.	Louisiana State	0	0	0.00	3	0	9	2	0	0	1	7	.074
Alex Faedo, rhp	Jr.	Florida	3	0	0.56	4	0	16	12	1	1	3	21	.214
Ricky Tyler Thomas, lhp	Jr.	Fresno State	1	1	0.95	7	0	19	9	4	2	3	21	.145
Brendan McKay, lhp	Jr.	Louisville	2	1	1.35	4	0	13	6	7	2	7	10	.140
Kyle Wright, rhp	Jr.	Vanderbilt	2	0	2.20	5	1	16	13	4	4	7	16	.228
Tyler Johnson, rhp	Jr.	South Carolina	0	0	2.35	8	3	8	7	2	2	5	7	.280
David Peterson, lhp	Jr.	Oregon	1	1	2.57	6	0	14	10	4	4	7	13	.227
Tanner Houck, rhp	Jr.	Missouri	0	1	2.66	6	0	24	17	7	7	5	8	.205
Zach Warren, lhp	Jr.	Tennessee	0	0	5.40	3	0	7	8	4	4	3	3	.333
Darren McCaughan, rhp	Jr.	Long Beach State	0	1	6.00	4	1	3	6	2	2	0	4	.400
Glenn Otto, rhp	Jr.	Rice	0	1	9.64	6	0	5	7	5	5	5	5	.350

about the grind of the summer.

"I don't know if I've ever been around a group with as tough a mindset and as low maintenance as this group," he said. "They had every right to complain about things that were out of our hands. But not a peep. Not a peep all summer complaining about the food, the bus rides or the challenges of the tour. I tip my cap."

Team USA also had some standout performances on the field. Lefthander/first baseman Brendan McKay (Louisville) led the team in hitting, posting a slash line of .326/.434/.372. Outfielder T.J. Friedl (Nevada) hit .290/.362/.452 and Kendall finished the summer .290/.329/.536.

Pitching was a clear strength of the CNT, as it posted a team ERA of 1.81 and held opponents to a .197 average. Righthander J.B. Bukauskas (North Carolina) held opponents to just one run (unearned) in 21 2/3 innings, striking out 21 batters and walking three. Both righthander Alex Faedo (Florida) and Thomas also struck out 21 batters, and righthander Alex Lange (Louisiana State) didn't allow a run in nine innings all summer.

Y-D Wins Third Straight

Cape Cod was home again to the most talented college summer league in the country, as well as one of college baseball's best dynasties. Yarmouth-Dennis won its third straight Cape Cod League title and sixth in 13 years under manager Scott Pickler. Y-D is the first team to win three straight titles since Cotuit won four straight from 1972-75.

After dropping the first game of the championship series to Falmouth, Y-D rebounded to win the final two games and claim its latest title. Falmouth last won a championship in 1980 and was looking to end the league's longest championship drought but settled for the President's Cup, awarded to the team with the best record in the regular season.

While the Cape's top three prospects a year ago were hitters, this summer the Cape returned to its more typical pitcher-friendly form. After third baseman Nick Senzel, the No. 2 overall pick in June, and outfielder Kyle Lewis, the 2016 College Player of the Year, spent their summer on the Cape last summer, scouts hoping to find more players like them this year were left wanting.

SUMMER LEAGUE ROUNDUP

■ The **Wisconsin Rapids Rafters** captured the first Northwoods League title in team history, sweeping their way through the playoffs with a perfect 4-0 record. The Rafters pulled out a nail-biting 5-4 win against Eau Claire in Game One of the NWL finals, winning it on Rob Calabrese's (Illinois-Chicago) walk-off home run. The second game didn't have quite the same drama, as the Rafters pulled out a big lead by scoring six runs in the top of the sixth and went on to win 11-4. Calabrese had three more hits in the clincher while Joe Wainhouse (Washington) had four RBIs.

■ The **Mat-Su Miners**, the Alaska League's best team in the regular season, finished off a title by sweeping the Peninsula Oilers in two games. Stephen Kolek (Texas A&M), Mick Vorhof (Grand Canyon) and Jordan Floyd (Kansas State) combined to hold the Oilers to just five hits and first baseman Jake Scudder (Kansas State) rapped out three hits and scored twice as the Miners took game one, 3-1. Game two was not as close as designated hitter Jacob Hughey (Long Beach State) and Garrison Schwartz (Grand Canyon) led the way with four hits from the leadoff spot and two RBIs from the three-hole respectively.

■ Once again, the **Santa Barbara Foresters** came out on top in the California Collegiate League. Led by a strong Longhorn core of Texas righthanders Kyle Johnston, Connor Mayes and shortstop Bret Boswell throughout the summer, the Foresters won their 21st California Collegiate League title, defeating the Conejo Oaks, 5-2, in the championship game. However, the Foresters weren't done after the CCL championship. They went on to defeat the Hays Larks—champions of the Jayhawk League—in the National Baseball Congress World Series for their sixth title in 11 years. The sixth championship tied the record for most championships by a single team in the 82-year history of the NBC World Series. It's no coincidence that Santa Barbara and CCL runner-up Conejo players comprise most of this list.

■ In their inaugural season in the Coastal Plain League, the **Savannah Bananas** took home the league crown with a 9-7 victory over the Peninsula Pilots. With the Petit Cup finals tied at one game apiece, the Bananas came out strong in game three as they broke open a five run lead by the third inning. The big blows came on back-to-back home runs in the second from Jameson Hannah (Dallas Baptist)—a three-run blast—and Rylan Bannon (Xavier). The Pilots did not go down quietly though, trading blows with Savannah the rest of the way to keep the game close until Ryan Flores (Richland (Texas) CC) came on to close it out. Savannah was a hit at the box office, averaging 3,630 fans per game.

■ A year after falling in the New England Collegiate League championship to the Vermont Mountaineers, the veteran-heavy **Mystic Schooners** made it all the way back this summer, defeating the Sanford Mainers, 8-2, to win the league crown. The Schooners finished the season with a franchise-best 35-16 record. Lefthander Kevin Magee (St. John's) got the start and victory in the title game, allowing one earned run in five innings.

■ The **Brazos Valley Bombers'** domination of the Texas Collegiate League continued. The Bombers roared to a 48-7 regular-season record and claimed their fourth straight championship with, fittingly, a 4-0 win in the TCL championship game against Acadiana. Tim Lichty (Texas A&M) led the offense in the finale, reaching base in all four of his plate appearances, while five Bomber pitchers combined on a four-hit shutout.

CAPE COD LEAGUE

Eastern Division	W	L	T	PTS
Harwich Mariners	27	15	2	56
Yarmouth-Dennis Red Sox	26	17	1	53
Orleans Firebirds	20	23	1	41
Chatham Anglers	17	26	1	35
Brewster Whitecaps	16	26	2	34

Western Division	W	L	T	PTS
Falmouth Commodores	29	15	0	58
Wareham Gatemen	25	15	4	54
Bourne Braves	21	21	2	44
Hyannis Harbor Hawks	17	27	0	34
Cotuit Kettleers	15	28	1	31

CHAMPIONSHIP: Yarmouth-Dennis defeated Falmouth 2-1 in best-of-three series.

TOP 30 PROSPECTS: 1. Brady Singer, rhp, Falmouth (So., Florida). **2.** Colton Hock, rhp, Cotuit (Jr., Stanford). **3.** Pavin Smith, 1b, Harwich (Jr., Virginia). **4.** Dylan Busby, 3b/1b, Hyannis (Jr., Florida State). **5.** Justin Hooper, lhp, Cotuit (So., UCLA). **6.** Peter Solomon, rhp, Harwich (Jr., Notre Dame). **7.** Brendon Little, lhp, Bourne (So., State JC of Florida). **8.** Joe Dunand, 3b, Harwich (Jr., North Carolina State). **9.** Michael Gigliotti, of, Falmouth (Jr., Lipscomb). **10.** Zach Rutherford, ss/2b, Hyannis (Jr., Old Dominion). **11.** Deon Stafford, c, Yarmouth-Dennis (Jr., St. Joseph's). **12.** Kevin Smith, ss, Yarmouth-Dennis (Jr., Maryland). **13.** Jake Mangum, of, Bourne (So., Mississippi State). **14.** Konnor Pilkington, lhp, Brewster (So., Mississippi State). **15.** Joey Bart, c, Wareham (So., Georgia Tech). **16.** Ford Proctor, ss/2b, Hyannis (So., Rice). **17.** Will Gaddis, rhp, Yarmouth-Dennis (Jr., Furman). **18.** Zac Lowther, lhp, Brewster (Jr., Xavier). **19.** Kade McClure, rhp, Brewster (Jr., Louisville). **20.** Corbin Martin, rhp, Falmouth (Jr., Texas A&M). **21.** J.J. Matijevic, of/1b, Falmouth (Jr., Arizona). **22.** Ernie Clement, 2b/of, Harwich (Jr., Virginia). **23.** Michael Baumann, rhp, Yarmouth-Dennis (Jr., Jacksonville). **24.** Adam Haseley, of, Orleans (Jr., Virginia). **25.** Logan Warmoth, ss/2b, Brewster (Jr., North Carolina). **26.** Hunter Williams, lhp, Harwich (Jr., North Carolina). **27.** Zach Pop, rhp, Wareham (Jr., Kentucky). **28.** Will Toffey, 3b, Yarmouth-Dennis (Jr., Vanderbilt). **29.** Matt Whatley, c, Yarmouth-Dennis (Jr., Oral Roberts). **30.** Garrett Cave, rhp, Hyannis (Jr., Tampa).

INDIVIDUAL BATTING LEADERS

	AVG	AB	R	H	2B	3B	HR	RBI	SB
Cole Freeman, 2b, Wareham	.374	115	23	43	5	0	0	6	13
Ernie Clement, 2b, Harwich	.353	167	25	59	5	1	0	11	19
Brian Miller, of, Orleans	.327	168	25	55	7	0	1	21	15
Quinn Brodey, of, Cotuit	.326	138	22	45	11	1	3	15	3
Joe Dunand, ss, Harwich	.326	135	19	44	8	1	5	24	1
Pavin Smith, 1b, Harwich	.318	151	16	48	7	0	4	18	3
Evan Mendoza, if, Bourne	.315	108	4	34	2	0	2	16	0
Connor Wong, c, Bourne	.313	163	21	51	10	1	3	22	2
Nick Dunn, if, Brewster	.311	164	26	51	8	2	1	25	3
Michael Gigliotti, of, Falmouth	.310	155	31	48	8	2	2	18	11

INDIVIDUAL PITCHING LEADERS

	W	L	ERA	G	SV	IP	H	BB	SO
Jeffrey Passantino, Falmouth	3	0	0.64	7	0	42	20	3	39
Hunter Williams, Harwich	2	2	1.27	8	0	42	23	12	35
Konnor Pilkington, Brewster	2	1	1.37	7	0	39	30	12	33
Brady Puckett, Falmouth	5	1	1.50	8	0	42	26	10	23
Michael Dibrell, Bourne	2	1	1.64	8	0	38	28	18	36
Packy Naughton, Harwich	3	0	1.69	7	0	42	34	6	42
B.J. Myers, Harwich	3	1	1.91	8	0	42	26	7	25
Zac Lowther, Brewster	2	1	2.52	11	1	35	26	4	54
Shane McCarthy, Harwich	1	2	2.75	7	0	39	41	8	25
Jake Bird, Falmouth	3	2	2.78	7	0	35	29	10	29

BOURNE

BATTING	AVG	AB	R	H	2B	3B	HR	RBI	SB
Luis Alvarado, of	.175	40	4	7	0	1	0	3	0
Brennan Breaux, of	.200	55	9	11	0	0	0	0	6
Nate Cardy, c	.000	3	0	0	0	0	0	0	0
Greg Deichmann, if	.182	44	4	8	0	0	0	3	1
Chase DeMars, 2b	.250	8	0	2	0	0	0	0	0

	AVG	AB	R	H	2B	3B	HR	RBI	SB
Jeremy Eierman, ss	.192	104	5	20	5	0	0	8	5
Tyler Friis, ss	.286	14	1	4	0	0	0	1	2
Toby Handley, of	.259	27	3	7	1	0	0	6	1
Robert Henry, of	.222	9	0	2	0	0	0	1	0
Jimmy Herron, of	.222	9	2	2	0	0	0	0	0
John Jones, c	.250	24	3	6	1	0	0	3	0
David MacKinnon, if	.274	146	22	40	6	0	0	20	0
Jake Mangum, of	.300	140	19	42	4	1	0	9	11
Elih Marrero, c	.214	28	1	6	0	0	0	0	1
Connor McVey, 3b	.226	124	11	28	3	0	1	13	3
Evan Mendoza, if	.315	108	4	34	2	0	2	16	0
Kevin Mohollen, of	.100	10	1	1	0	0	0	0	0
Danny Reyes, of	.213	47	4	10	5	0	1	5	0
Will Savage, 2b	.000	0	1	0	0	0	0	0	0
Andrew Shaps, of	.103	29	2	3	1	0	0	3	0
Joey Thomas, c	.300	10	1	3	0	0	0	0	0
Grant Williams, ss	.000	2	0	0	0	0	0	0	0
Garrett Wolforth, c	.107	28	0	3	1	0	0	3	0
Connor Wong, c	.313	163	21	51	10	1	3	22	2
Willy Yahn, 3b	.290	176	29	51	8	2	0	13	3
Justin Yurchak, 3b	.295	146	20	43	3	2	1	17	0

PITCHING	W	L	ERA	G	SV	IP	H	BB	SO
Michael Adams	0	0	0.00	1	0	4	3	2	1
Luis Alvarado	0	0	0.00	1	0	1	2	0	3
Kent Axcell	0	0	0.00	2	0	3	1	0	2
Andrew Cabezas	1	1	6.23	7	0	13	14	8	13
Ty Cohen	0	1	6.23	1	0	4	5	3	1
Zach Cook	1	0	4.50	8	0	10	11	3	10
Michael Dibrell	2	1	1.64	8	0	38	28	18	36
David Drouin	0	0	5.79	2	0	5	6	4	5
Jon Escobar	0	0	1.29	5	2	7	5	1	15
Robert Hitt	0	0	0.00	1	0	1	1	0	2
Christopher Holba	0	0	2.61	7	0	21	23	8	13
Daniel Jagiello	0	0	9.00	2	0	2	2	0	0
Sean Leland	0	0	3.94	7	0	16	15	3	14
Brendon Little	1	0	3.68	12	2	22	18	7	29
Chad Luensmann	4	2	4.87	15	1	20	23	5	23
Brady Miller	0	1	1.48	6	0	24	19	9	25
A.J. Moore	1	6	4.74	8	0	38	41	11	33
Doug Norman	1	1	1.61	8	0	22	12	10	19
Conner Oneil	1	0	1.50	4	1	6	4	2	8
J.T. Perez	0	2	5.88	8	0	34	42	10	28
Patrick Raby	1	2	3.72	4	0	19	19	10	15
Ronnie Rossomando	4	2	2.42	13	0	22	16	9	27
Joshua Shapiro	1	1	3.60	2	0	10	11	3	10
Zach Spangler	2	0	2.40	14	0	15	14	6	11
Dominic Taccolini	0	1	13.50	5	0	7	13	7	7
Andrew Wantz	0	0	2.16	11	4	17	12	3	24
Keith Weisenberg	2	0	3.60	4	0	5	6	5	2
James Ziemba	0	0	3.52	5	0	8	11	4	6

BREWSTER

BATTING	AVG	AB	R	H	2B	3B	HR	RBI	SB
Jared Barnes, c	.149	47	5	7	3	0	0	3	1
Brandon Chapman, c	.333	6	0	2	1	0	0	1	0
Matt Davis, ss	.297	91	20	27	4	2	7	19	4
Nick Dunn, if	.311	164	26	51	8	2	1	25	3
Colby Fitch, c	.214	70	9	15	2	1	1	5	1
Zack Gahagan, 3b	.276	127	21	35	7	0	3	24	3
A.J. Graffanino, ss	.278	72	11	20	5	0	1	10	0
Ryan Gridley, ss	.225	80	11	18	2	1	1	10	1
Julian Infante, 3b	.205	78	9	16	0	0	2	9	0
Kel Johnson, of	.234	77	11	18	2	0	1	11	0
Bryce Jordan, 1b	.330	88	17	29	8	0	0	10	4
Beau Jordane, of	.272	103	14	28	2	0	1	13	1
Brett Langhorne, ss	.250	20	4	5	1	0	0	2	0
Jon Littell, of	.216	37	3	8	1	0	0	4	0
Colby Maiola, of	.263	19	3	5	1	0	0	3	1
Ryan Noda, 1b	.221	131	18	29	5	1	5	17	4
Kekai Rios, c	.295	61	12	18	2	0	1	10	1
Brent Rooker, of	.305	141	17	43	8	0	3	22	4
Logan Warmoth, ss	.270	100	18	27	6	0	4	19	2

PITCHING	W	L	ERA	G	SV	IP	H	BB	SO
Vince Arobio	0	0	12.27	4	0	4	8	3	2
Walter Borkovich	0	2	2.53	8	0	21	30	4	15
Wyatt Burns	0	0	2.46	4	1	4	3	5	2
Hanson Butler	1	2	2.66	13	0	20	20	10	21
Chris Falwell	0	1	12.60	1	0	5	11	0	4
Ryan Feltner	0	3	14.88	5	0	16	30	10	12
Max Herrmann	0	1	3.95	8	1	14	16	3	11
Landon Hughes	1	2	2.20	12	0	16	18	7	17
Bryan Kingr	0	0	2.70	3	0	10	10	5	4
Zacary Lowther	2	1	2.52	11	1	36	26	4	54
Hunter Martin	4	2	2.82	8	0	51	43	17	35
Eric Martinez	0	1	5.01	16	0	23	28	14	17
Kade McClure	0	1	2.84	4	0	19	14	7	22
Joe Mockbee	0	0	3.86	3	0	7	5	3	7
Konnor Pilkington	2	1	1.37	7	0	39	30	12	33
Danny Rafferty	0	0	0.00	2	0	1	3	0	2
Nicholas Rand	0	1	2.25	2	0	4	6	0	3
Aaron Soto	2	1	8.84	4	0	18	31	6	14
Jacob Westphal	1	1	6.75	8	1	8	8	5	7
Jacob Wloczewski	0	5	8.50	12	0	18	23	11	9
Paul Young	0	0	4.50	4	0	4	4	3	9
Tyler Zuber	3	1	5.36	11	0	42	49	17	38

CHATHAM

BATTING	AVG	AB	R	H	2B	3B	HR	RBI	SB
Kyle Adams, c	.207	87	1	18	3	0	0	5	1
John Aiello, ss	.189	106	10	20	0	0	1	6	1
D.J. Artis, of	.271	118	19	32	4	0	1	12	3
Sean Bouchard, ss	.223	112	13	25	6	0	1	8	1
William Boyd, 2b	.000	4	0	0	0	0	0	0	0
Donovan Casey, of	.221	104	7	23	2	0	1	7	2
Matt Cook, of	.000	1	0	0	0	0	0	0	0
Stuart Fairchild, of	.232	112	11	26	6	1	1	11	3
Joseph Freiday, c	.105	19	1	2	1	0	1	3	0
Orlando Garcia, ss	.137	73	4	10	1	0	0	2	1
Tanner Gardner, of	.346	26	2	9	0	0	1	8	0
Cam Hanley, 1b	.231	13	3	3	0	0	0	0	0
Mason Koppens, of	.217	23	5	5	0	0	0	1	0
Hunter Lee, 2b	.189	53	8	10	1	0	0	5	2
Alex LeFevre, c	.091	11	0	1	0	0	0	0	0
Patrick Mathis, of	.217	106	8	23	2	1	4	15	0
Hagen Owenby, c	.241	79	6	19	3	0	1	9	0
Jake Palomaki, if	.215	130	14	28	5	0	1	6	6
Chase Pinder, of	.278	54	7	15	3	1	0	5	1
Jordan Romero, c	.098	51	2	5	2	0	0	2	0
William Shackelford, if	.000	0	0	0	0	0	0	0	0
Joe Tietjen, of	.100	10	1	1	0	0	0	0	0
Gunnar Troutwine, c	.278	79	10	22	2	1	0	11	1
Jeremy Vasquez, 1b	.219	73	8	16	3	0	1	10	0
Matt Vernon, if	.250	20	2	5	1	0	0	0	0

PITCHING	W	L	ERA	G	SV	IP	H	BB	SO
Paul Balestrieria	0	1	2.14	10	0	21	18	7	13
Kale Breaux	0	0	4.82	5	0	9	11	6	9
Jacob Bukauskas	0	1	3.72	2	0	10	10	2	17
Bo Burrup	1	0	3.60	1	0	5	4	3	1
Donovan Casey	0	0	6.00	3	0	3	4	0	6
Moises Ceja	2	2	4.50	14	5	18	16	3	19
Tanner Chock	1	0	1.77	4	0	20	15	8	12
Tom Cosgrove	1	1	8.18	4	0	11	18	4	9
Christopher Farish	0	0	81.00	2	0	1	4	4	1
Michael Fitzgerald	0	1	1.86	15	1	19	17	9	13
Jason Foley	0	0	3.38	4	0	8	10	4	6
Trevor Gay	0	2	6.43	2	0	7	12	2	6
Caleb Gilbert	2	2	7.20	7	0	20	28	8	17
Lincoln Henzman	1	2	5.22	7	0	29	33	8	32
Reed Howell	0	1	3.55	7	0	13	15	5	13
James Karinchak	0	1	9.00	2	0	5	5	3	6
Andrew Karp	1	3	3.99	6	0	29	35	4	22
Austin Magestro	0	0	4.26	6	1	6	5	2	9
Simon Mathews	1	3	4.31	8	0	31	44	6	23
Isaac Mattson	2	1	1.21	13	1	30	27	5	24
Michael McCormick	0	0	9.00	1	0	1	1	2	1
Nick Meservey	1	0	0.00	4	0	11	8	6	13
Connor Moore	1	0	1.47	14	0	18	12	6	19
Alexander Person	0	0	0.00	4	0	5	3	2	4
Matt Pidich	0	1	7.94	5	0	6	6	4	12
Parker Rigler	0	4	4.03	7	0	29	36	10	21
Jacob Stevens	1	1	4.66	2	0	10	7	8	5
Tom Sutera	0	0	8.10	2	0	3	9	1	1
Joe Tietjen	0	0	0.00	1	0	1	1	0	0
Garrett Whitlock	0	0	0.00	4	0	6	2	4	8
Mitchell Zubradt	0	0	2.25	2	0	4	3	1	4

COTUIT

BATTING	AVG	AB	R	H	2B	3B	HR	RBI	SB
A.J. Balta, 2b	.230	100	9	23	7	0	2	14	2
Jake Bivens, ss	.143	7	0	1	0	0	0	0	0
Quinn Brodey, of	.326	138	22	45	11	1	3	15	3
Jason Delay, c	.191	47	7	9	1	0	2	3	0
Patrick Dorrian, ss	.194	93	7	18	4	2	1	12	2
Dayton Dugas, of	.063	16	0	1	0	0	0	0	1
Clay Fisher, ss	.231	52	7	12	3	0	1	5	1
Spencer Gaa, if	.167	12	0	2	0	0	0	1	0
Devon Gradford, of	.100	10	1	1	0	0	0	0	0
Ryan Hagan, 2b	.198	131	7	26	6	0	1	7	5
Marques Inman, 1b	.000	6	0	0	0	0	0	0	0
Greyson Jenista, 1b	.229	140	15	32	6	2	1	8	2
Alonzo Jones Jr., ss	.173	81	8	14	2	2	0	5	2
Jeren Kendall, of	.087	23	0	2	1	0	0	0	0
Jackson Klein, of	.183	120	12	22	3	0	2	8	5
Aaron Maher, of	.000	5	0	0	0	0	0	0	0
Tanner Nishioka, if	.000	3	0	0	0	0	0	0	0
Jordan Pearce, 3b	.193	88	12	17	1	1	2	12	0
Ben Ruta, of	.000	2	0	0	0	0	0	1	0
Josh Shaw, 2b	.194	36	2	7	1	0	0	1	0
Cal Stevenson, of	.254	118	16	30	1	0	0	6	10
Ricky Surum, ss	.400	5	1	2	1	0	0	0	0
Tim Susnara, c	.247	85	7	21	2	0	1	13	1
Cory Voss, c	.151	53	5	8	3	0	2	8	0
T.J. Wardwell, 2b	.000	2	0	0	0	0	0	0	0
Alexander Weiss, c	.192	26	1	5	1	0	1	3	0

PITCHING	W	L	ERA	G	SV	IP	H	BB	SO
Ross Achter	2	1	3.45	9	0	31	32	12	19
Cal Becker	0	1	3.86	7	0	16	13	15	15
Jason Bilous	1	2	5.52	4	0	15	15	14	8
Alec Byrd	0	0	1.62	9	2	17	11	5	23
Jacob Erickson	0	0	2.38	4	2	11	8	1	7
Dave Gerber	0	1	20.25	3	0	4	14	2	4
David Gerics	0	1	6.20	9	0	20	20	12	13
Rio Gomez	1	1	3.98	7	0	20	16	6	24
Colton Hock	1	4	3.44	9	0	37	41	11	31
Justin Hooper	0	2	3.20	8	0	25	21	15	18
Jackson Klein	0	0	6.75	3	0	3	2	0	1
Matt Ladrech	0	1	3.86	2	0	9	12	3	2
Taylor Lehman	3	1	3.19	10	0	31	29	11	17
Aaron Maher	0	0	10.39	2	0	4	5	3	2
Eddie Muhl	3	1	1.84	16	0	29	31	10	21
Jared Padgett	0	0	0.93	5	1	10	8	3	9
Ryan Rigby	1	3	2.16	11	1	17	13	6	12
Josh Roberson	0	1	4.68	13	2	25	27	16	26
Keith Rogalla	0	2	3.94	4	0	16	15	12	14
Matthew Ruppenthal	1	3	3.60	6	0	25	18	13	25
Cameron Sepede	0	0	3.86	3	0	2	1	0	2
Connor Simmons	2	3	5.06	10	0	16	17	13	18
Cal Stevenson	0	0	6.00	3	0	3	3	1	2

FALMOUTH

BATTING	AVG	AB	R	H	2B	3B	HR	RBI	SB
Angel Alicea, p	.000	3	0	0	0	0	0	0	0
Willie Burger, 3b	.227	119	14	27	3	0	4	14	1
Michael Cantu, c	.167	102	8	17	2	0	3	8	0
Ryan Chandler, of	.131	61	9	8	1	0	1	7	5
Zachary Clark, ss	.091	22	2	2	0	0	0	1	1
Matt Duce, c	.236	72	10	17	8	1	1	6	0
Michael Gigliotti, of	.310	155	31	48	8	2	2	18	11
Tristan Gray, ss	.301	103	19	31	8	0	1	13	1

	AVG	AB	R	H	2B	3B	HR	RBI	SB
Cadyn Grenier, ss	.190	116	23	22	4	0	2	14	10
Slade Heggen, c	.000	5	0	0	0	0	0	0	0
Tyler Holton, p	.158	19	1	3	0	0	0	0	0
Bryce Johnson, of	.183	60	7	11	2	0	0	9	3
Trevor Larnach, of	.275	80	13	22	3	0	1	10	1
Tyler Lawrence, c	.312	93	15	29	3	1	7	23	0
Deacon Liput, 2b	.260	73	13	19	2	1	3	15	4
JJ Matijevic, 1b	.376	85	15	32	9	0	2	15	5
Matt McLaughlin, ss	.219	96	16	21	3	0	1	13	5
Kevin Merrell, 2b	.305	59	11	18	1	0	0	2	6
Dylan Morris, of	.133	15	2	2	0	0	0	2	0
Joshua Watson, of	.298	84	10	25	3	2	2	15	4
Ryan Wolfsberg, of	.125	8	0	1	0	0	0	0	0

PITCHING	W	L	ERA	G	SV	IP	H	BB	SO
Keegan Baar	0	0	1.50	4	0	6	8	3	1
Paul Balestrieri	0	1	2.14	10	0	21	18	7	13
Jake Bird	3	2	2.78	7	0	36	29	10	29
George Capen	0	0	0.00	1	0	2	1	1	0
Seth Elledge	0	0	2.63	13	4	14	13	2	19
Brett Gilchrist	2	1	2.74	14	0	23	20	11	22
Jacob Godfrey	1	1	7.88	2	0	8	14	3	2
Tyler Holton	1	1	5.54	6	0	13	19	6	14
Justin Hoyt	1	1	3.21	12	0	14	12	4	16
Tyler Jones	1	1	5.14	6	0	7	8	2	7
Brendan King	4	0	2.92	9	0	37	31	9	44
Turner Larkins	1	0	3.12	6	0	9	7	8	5
Corbin Martin	0	1	1.15	14	6	16	8	3	22
Bryce Montes de Oca	0	0	6.00	7	0	9	13	6	10
Jeffrey Passantino	3	0	0.64	7	0	42	20	3	39
Thomas Ponticelli	3	3	4.77	10	0	28	33	5	16
Brady Puckett	5	1	1.50	8	0	42	26	10	23
Cole Sands	2	0	1.29	6	0	14	7	5	18
Brady Singer	1	0	0.82	5	0	22	16	2	20
John Sparks	0	0	8.10	8	0	10	10	7	5
Stephen Villines	0	1	0.90	20	3	20	16	2	17
Brac Warren	1	1	3.38	6	1	8	3	5	11

HARWICH

BATTING	AVG	AB	R	H	2B	3B	HR	RBI	SB
Johnny Adams, ss	.254	122	12	31	6	1	1	9	0
J.D. Andreessen, c	.000	7	0	0	0	0	0	0	0
Ryan Brown, of	.222	9	1	2	0	0	0	2	0
Max Burt, 2b	.194	93	7	18	3	0	2	9	2
Ernie Clement, 2b	.353	167	25	59	5	1	0	11	19
Anthony Critelli, 1b	.273	99	11	27	11	0	0	6	1
Nicholas Dalesandro, c	.247	89	8	22	5	1	0	6	0
Kyle Davis, of	.175	40	5	7	0	0	2	4	0
Joe Dunand, ss	.326	135	19	44	8	1	5	24	1
Antoine Duplantis, of	.268	112	7	30	3	1	0	7	8
Logan Farrar, of	.286	28	3	8	0	1	0	6	2
Nicholas Feight, c	.270	89	12	24	4	0	3	10	0
Kyle Fiala, if	.000	7	0	0	0	0	0	0	0
Austin Filiere, DH	.248	117	17	29	5	2	7	27	0
Jack Flansburg, 2b	.111	9	0	1	0	0	0	0	0
Steven Foster, of	.128	39	7	5	2	0	0	1	0
Trey Harris, of	.125	32	3	4	1	0	0	4	1
Jonathan India, if	.290	62	11	18	7	0	0	4	5
Tyler Kirkpatrick, of	.350	20	6	7	0	0	0	1	1
Cal Raleigh, c	.204	98	10	20	2	0	1	9	0
Cameron Simmons, of	.000	3	0	0	0	0	0	0	0
Pavin Smith, 1b	.318	151	16	48	7	0	4	18	3
Ryan Tufts, if	.222	9	1	2	0	0	0	0	0

PITCHING	W	L	ERA	G	SV	IP	H	BB	SO
Austin Bain	2	1	2.41	10	0	19	17	8	14
Brad Bass	2	3	1.57	13	0	23	14	4	31
Nick Brown	2	0	0.84	16	2	21	11	6	30
Maddux Conger	0	0	6.14	10	0	15	18	17	14
Tommy DeJuneas	0	1	4.70	12	0	15	14	8	15
Ethan Landon	0	0	0.00	4	0	5	2	2	3
Ryan McAuliffe	3	1	2.76	7	0	29	27	8	20
Shane McCarthy	1	2	2.75	7	0	39	41	8	25
Matthew Minnick	0	0	0.00	2	0	2	0	1	1
B.J. Myers	3	1	1.91	8	0	42	26	7	25

	W	L	ERA	G	SV	IP	H	BB	SO
Packy Naughton	3	0	1.69	7	0	43	34	6	42
Theodore Rodliff	4	1	1.35	15	1	27	20	6	13
Zach Schellenger	1	2	1.33	17	6	20	12	7	32
Peter Solomon	1	0	0.55	10	2	33	9	15	28
Spencer Stockton	0	0	0.00	2	0	3	2	0	3
Speros Varinos	0	0	4.50	2	0	2	3	1	3
Hunter Williams	2	2	1.27	8	0	43	23	12	35
Tyler Wilson	2	1	3.18	4	0	17	20	4	16
John Witkowski	1	0	0.00	1	0	2	1	0	2

HYANNIS

BATTING	AVG	AB	R	H	2B	3B	HR	RBI	SB
Nick Angelini, of	.000	2	0	0	0	0	0	0	0
Joshua Bailey, c	.333	6	0	2	1	0	0	0	0
Dylan Busby, 3b	.322	90	16	29	10	0	4	12	9
Matt Byars, c	.250	4	0	1	0	0	0	0	0
Chris Cullen, c	.333	24	4	8	1	0	0	3	1
Kameron Esthay, LF	.216	88	6	19	3	1	1	7	0
Treg Haberkorn, of	.150	60	6	9	2	1	0	4	1
Cody Henry, 1b	.268	149	17	40	12	3	2	23	2
Christopher Hess, 2b	.000	4	0	0	0	0	0	0	0
Tristan Hildebrandt, ss	.250	8	0	2	1	0	0	0	0
David Hopkins, 2b	.500	4	0	2	0	0	0	1	0
Chris Hudgins, c	.264	91	10	24	5	0	4	15	3
Tanner Kehrer, ss	.500	4	0	2	0	0	0	0	0
Christian Molfetta, c	.167	6	0	1	0	0	0	0	0
Brett Netzer, 2b	.283	99	16	28	4	2	2	13	3
Anthony Pecora, ss	.455	11	1	5	0	0	0	0	0
Ford Proctor, if	.286	140	16	40	6	0	1	5	2
Jordan Rodgers, if	.241	137	21	33	7	2	3	24	3
Nate Rossi, c	.250	8	1	2	0	0	0	0	0
Zachary Rutherford, ss	.278	162	21	45	11	1	4	20	5
Benito Santiago, c	.200	45	4	9	4	0	0	1	1
Richard Smith, c	.000	14	1	0	0	0	0	0	0
Carl Stajduhar, 3b	.149	94	8	14	0	0	2	7	1
Trey Truitt, of	.208	130	11	27	7	0	0	9	10
Drew Wharton, of	.077	13	1	1	0	0	0	0	1
Peter Zyla, if	.250	68	8	17	4	0	0	2	5

PITCHING	W	L	ERA	G	SV	IP	H	BB	SO
Trysten Barlow	1	2	8.22	12	0	15	17	13	7
Charlie Barnes	1	2	4.45	6	0	28	37	9	32
Colie Bowers	0	1	6.52	7	0	10	11	8	9
Garrett Cave	0	2	1.86	20	10	19	10	13	34
Ivan Coutinho	0	0	0.00	1	0	2	1	0	3
Alex Eubanks	2	1	3.21	6	0	34	31	6	22
John Gavin	1	4	6.15	9	0	34	43	13	28
Lucas Gilbreath	0	0	4.59	13	0	18	12	11	19
Andrew Gonzalez	3	2	3.38	9	0	45	42	16	31
James Harrington	2	0	1.86	14	1	19	15	5	19
Alex House	0	3	6.18	9	0	28	34	7	22
Daniel Johnson	0	1	5.68	8	0	13	13	6	15
Thomas Lane	0	0	16.20	1	0	2	4	1	1
Justin Lewis	0	1	4.79	9	0	26	22	13	29
Dominic LoBrutto	0	0	1.93	4	0	5	2	4	3
Matthew Naylor	4	2	2.33	16	0	19	14	6	14
Mark Nowatnick	0	1	7.71	5	1	7	10	2	5
Al Pesto	1	0	3.24	14	0	17	19	9	14
Mac Sceroler	1	3	7.03	6	0	24	36	8	18
Tyler Stevens	1	2	1.96	12	2	18	17	0	21

ORLEANS

BATTING	AVG	AB	R	H	2B	3B	HR	RBI	SB
Riley Adams, c	.333	108	10	36	6	0	1	9	1
Joe Baker, ss	.214	14	2	3	1	0	0	3	1
Garrett Benge, 3b	.321	53	3	17	4	0	0	3	0
Will Golsan, 1b	.235	98	8	23	7	0	1	8	0
Adam Haseley, of	.266	143	19	38	7	1	3	15	6
Scott Hurst, of	.188	96	14	18	2	0	0	3	5
Dane Hutcheon, ss	.333	3	1	1	0	0	0	1	0
Justin Jonesu, ss	.281	96	13	27	2	0	0	6	0
Zach Kirtley, 2b	.217	115	13	25	3	0	3	19	1
Drew Lugbauer, c	.269	78	9	21	3	0	2	10	0
Riley Mahan, ss	.303	165	22	50	7	1	0	17	3

	AVG	AB	R	H	2B	3B	HR	RBI	SB
Keegan McGovern, LF	.156	77	8	12	3	0	3	8	1
Zachary McKinstry, ss	.000	2	0	0	0	0	0	0	0
Brian Miller, of	.327	168	25	55	7	0	1	21	15
Ethan Paul, ss	.252	111	10	28	5	1	3	14	5
Tristan Rojas, of	.000	3	0	0	0	0	0	0	0
Logan Sowers, of	.231	26	0	6	1	0	0	4	0
Payton Squier, of	.277	94	10	26	3	0	0	14	0
Chris Triano, of	.226	53	10	12	6	0	0	3	0

PITCHING	W	L	ERA	G	SV	IP	H	BB	SO
Cory Abbott	0	2	3.38	10	0	32	37	7	24
Connor Alexander	0	0	3.00	1	0	3	4	0	2
Brandon Bielak	2	1	1.54	19	5	23	17	7	29
Chandler Day	0	1	3.91	11	0	23	23	9	21
Sean Guenther	2	3	4.73	9	0	40	41	6	24
Colton Hathcock	0	1	0.00	1	0	4	2	3	4
Calvin LeBrun	0	0	12.27	6	0	7	11	6	8
Zach Logue	1	2	1.98	18	0	27	26	15	26
Kirk McCarty	2	1	1.99	5	0	23	15	6	20
Jason Morgan	3	1	3.68	8	0	37	29	11	24
Eli Morgan	0	2	4.32	8	0	17	15	5	22
John OReilly	1	1	2.84	11	0	25	22	10	11
Logan Roberts	0	0	18.00	1	0	1	2	1	1
Joe Ryan	2	1	2.12	8	0	34	36	13	31
Kit Scheetz	0	2	4.96	14	3	16	13	4	12
Kevin Smith	4	2	2.20	13	0	29	24	6	35
John Sparks	0	0	0.00	1	0	1	1	1	1
Will Stokes	3	1	3.38	15	0	19	14	10	29
Zach Willeman	0	1	4.42	16	0	18	20	9	19
Brooks Wilson	0	1	1.50	2	0	6	6	5	4

WAREHAM

BATTING	AVG	AB	R	H	2B	3B	HR	RBI	SB
Joey Bart, c	.309	97	13	30	2	2	2	21	1
Joey Bartosic, of	.267	176	31	47	2	1	0	12	18
Luke Bonfield, of	.375	8	0	3	1	0	0	1	0
Niko Buentello, 1b	.571	7	1	4	0	0	0	2	0
Colton Burns, 2b	.167	6	1	1	0	0	0	0	0
Alex Destino, of	.250	108	6	27	5	0	1	15	0
Jonathan Engelmann, of	.227	66	6	15	0	0	0	1	3
Trevor Ezell, 2b	.275	40	11	11	2	1	0	4	1
Cole Freeman, 2b	.374	115	23	43	5	0	0	6	13
Nico Giarratano, ss	.204	98	7	20	2	0	1	4	5
Robbie Glendinning, if	.333	3	1	1	1	0	0	0	0
Preston Grand Pre, ss	.178	90	11	16	1	1	0	5	8
Kainoa Harrison, c	.290	31	7	9	2	0	1	6	0
Blake Logan, c	.000	3	0	0	0	0	0	0	0
Robert Metz, 2b	.280	132	17	37	6	0	1	13	13
Dominic Miroglio, c	.103	29	3	3	0	0	0	2	0
Brett Netzer, 2b	.111	18	3	2	1	0	1	3	1
Brian Parreira, 1b	.111	9	0	1	0	0	0	1	0
Jonathan Pryor, of	.167	6	3	1	0	0	0	0	1
Ezequeil Sanchez, LF	.300	10	8	3	1	0	0	1	2
Colton Shaver, 1b	.252	135	16	34	5	0	8	29	0
Gavin Sheets, 1b	.283	152	12	43	4	0	3	25	3
Chase Smartt, c	.000	1	0	0	0	0	0	0	0
Adrian Tovalin, 3b	.217	83	6	18	7	1	3	12	1
Austen Wade, of	.238	21	0	5	1	0	0	1	1
Harrison Wenson, c	.200	40	5	8	3	0	0	1	0

PITCHING	W	L	ERA	G	SV	IP	H	BB	SO
Anthony Alicki	0	0	0.00	1	0	2	1	0	1
Jeff Bain	0	2	5.56	9	0	34	39	7	19
Brett Conine	2	1	3.96	8	0	36	32	11	29
Tom Cosgrove	1	1	8.18	4	0	11	18	4	9
Jake Fishman	1	0	1.80	1	0	5	3	1	3
Robert Garcia	2	1	3.24	8	0	17	16	10	15
Clayton Gelfand	0	1	6.10	4	0	10	9	6	3
Hogan Harris	1	0	4.91	6	0	15	15	7	18
Anthony Herron Jr.	0	0	4.70	2	0	8	10	3	8
Dalton Horton	2	1	2.60	5	0	17	17	5	8
Jackson Lamb	0	0	9.00	1	0	1	3	0	2
Gunner Leger	0	0	0.43	7	0	21	13	1	29
Nick Margevicius	1	0	0.00	1	0	1	0	0	1
Jake Matthys	1	2	3.77	18	7	31	26	6	25

	W	L	ERA	G	SV	IP	H	BB	SO
Casey Mize	1	0	3.00	6	1	12	9	5	11
Zachary Pop	2	3	4.45	9	0	32	31	18	26
Sean Rackoski	0	1	3.00	2	0	6	5	5	4
Phil Reese	0	0	4.50	1	0	4	4	1	0
Joe Romero	0	0	7.71	2	0	2	4	2	0
Jeff Schank	0	0	18.00	1	0	1	3	3	2
Ryan Selmer	2	2	3.18	12	0	23	29	6	12
Cameron Sepede	0	0	0.00	1	0	1	1	0	0
Ethan Small	1	0	1.80	6	1	20	21	8	11
Jake Smith	1	0	0.00	3	0	4	1	2	3
Nick Sprengel	3	0	3.48	9	1	21	21	5	22
Cole Stapler	1	0	3.60	4	0	15	17	2	14
Christian Taugner	2	0	2.70	10	2	17	16	3	10
Jake Walters	1	1	3.54	6	1	20	19	5	16
Ryan Wilson	1	0	0.90	7	2	20	17	4	20
Noah Zavolas	1	0	0.00	2	0	7	3	1	1

YARMOUTH-DENNIS

BATTING	AVG	AB	R	H	2B	3B	HR	RBI	SB
Ashton Bardzell, of	.100	10	0	1	0	0	0	0	0
Korby Batesole, ss	.250	28	6	7	1	0	0	1	2
Nolan Brown, of	.200	85	10	17	4	0	1	6	3
Lukas Burch, of	.000	6	1	0	0	0	0	0	0
Teddy Cillis, of	.000	0	0	0	0	0	0	0	0
Corey Dempster, of	.250	92	12	23	5	1	0	11	5
Brent Diaz, c	.333	24	3	8	2	0	0	4	0
Mikey Diekroeger, 3b	.235	68	4	16	5	0	0	4	0
Tyler Houston, of	.284	102	17	29	6	1	1	17	4
David Leiderman, 3b	.000	1	0	0	0	0	0	0	0
Colin Lyman, of	.227	22	3	5	0	0	0	1	0
Luke Miller, 3b	.000	3	0	0	0	0	0	0	0
Dominic Miroglioo, c	.429	7	1	3	1	0	0	2	0
JJ Muno, if	.304	79	14	24	4	1	0	9	5
Dillon Persinger, 2b	.275	102	13	28	5	0	3	14	4
Dylan Rosa, 3b	.083	12	1	1	0	0	0	1	0
Paul Rufo, ss	.258	31	5	8	0	0	0	1	2
Colby Schultz, ss	.071	14	2	1	0	0	0	1	1
JJ Schwarz, c	.207	29	3	6	0	0	1	5	0
Brendan Skidmore, LF	.253	150	16	38	8	0	3	23	4
Kevin Smith, ss	.301	143	21	43	12	0	2	14	7
Deon Stafford Jr, c	.283	106	18	30	6	0	6	25	5
Joey Thomaso, c	.333	6	0	2	1	0	0	4	0
Will Toffey, 3b	.283	127	31	36	6	0	3	16	9
Connor Wanhanen, of	.143	35	7	5	0	0	0	0	1
Matthew Whatley, c	.198	86	8	17	2	1	1	9	1
Matt Winaker, 1b	.270	115	19	31	5	1	1	17	4
Dylan Woods, 2b	.200	5	0	1	0	0	0	0	1

PITCHING	W	L	ERA	G	SV	IP	H	BB	SO
Sean Barry	0	0	0.00	1	1	2	0	1	3
Michael Baumann	3	3	5.76	8	0	30	35	23	27
Dillon Bray	0	0	3.24	3	0	8	14	4	3
Teddy Cillis	0	0	5.79	4	0	9	5	5	12
Sam Delaplane	0	0	4.29	14	2	21	19	10	23
Michael Fairchild	0	0	0.00	2	0	3	2	0	4
Calvin Faucher	3	1	3.57	16	3	18	8	7	22
Cre Finfrock	0	1	1.98	4	0	14	10	9	11
Will Gaddis	2	1	1.37	4	0	26	17	5	24
Mitchell Hart	2	1	5.57	4	0	21	21	8	20
Jared Janczak	0	1	3.71	5	0	17	15	3	11
Oliver Jaskie	2	0	0.99	6	0	27	17	7	27
Nathan Kuchta	2	1	4.44	14	1	24	25	6	21
William Montgomerie	2	2	1.71	7	0	26	21	10	28
Bryan Pall	1	0	0.69	11	6	13	8	5	15
Bryan Sammons	1	0	1.53	9	0	29	32	8	23
Connor Seabold	1	1	4.50	3	0	10	7	4	5
Sam Sinnen	0	0	11.81	4	0	5	8	4	4
Collin Snider	3	0	6.45	11	0	22	33	14	15
James Taubl	0	0	0.00	1	0	4	0	0	2
Erich Uelmen	2	1	4.88	6	0	24	21	6	24
Pat Vanderslice	2	4	5.34	11	0	30	36	7	25
Nick Vichio	0	0	0.00	3	0	3	2	2	2

ALASKA LEAGUE

	League				Overall			
	W	L	PCT	GB	W	L	PCT	GB
Mat-Su Miners	26	18	.591	—	28	19	.596	—
Peninsula Oilers	24	20	.545	2	30	26	.536	2 ½
Anchorage Glacier Pilots	23	21	.523	3	24	22	.522	3 ½
Anchorage Bucs	20	24	.455	6	22	26	.458	6 ½
Chugiak Chinooks	17	27	.386	9	19	27	.413	8 ½

CHAMPIONSHIP: Mat-Su defeated Peninsula 2-0 in best-of-three series.

TOP 10 PROSPECTS: 1. Stephen Kolek, rhp, Mat-Su (So., Texas A&M). **2.** Cody Deason, rhp, Mat-Su (So., Arizona). **3.** Gage Burland, rhp, Mat-Su (Jr., Gonzaga). **4.** Ryan Lillie, rhp, Peninsula (So., UC Riverside). **5.** Justin Montgomery, rhp, Peninsula (So., California Baptist). **6.** Garrison Schwartz, of, Mat-Su (Jr., Grand Canyon). **7.** Jacob Hughey, lhp/1b, Mat-Su (So., Long Beach State). **8.** Wyatt Mills, rhp, Anchorage Bucs (Sr., Gonzaga). **9.** Kyle Watson, ss, Anchorage Glacier Pilots (Jr., Mississippi). **10.** Jordan Floyd, lhp, Mat-Su (Sr., Kansas State).

INDIVIDUAL BATTING LEADERS

	AVG	AB	R	H	2b	3b	HR	RBI	SB
Jonathan Washam, c, Peninsula	.344	154	17	53	10	0	2	20	4
Michael Donadio, of, Mat-Su	.321	109	23	35	6	3	1	25	2
Levi Jordan, if, Matsu	.316	158	33	50	9	0	0	22	10
Darius Hill, of, Peninsula	.314	191	25	60	5	2	0	17	4
Steven Sensley, of, Bucs	.305	131	23	40	9	1	6	27	7
Hunter Vansau, of, Chugiak	.297	158	17	47	7	3	1	18	4
Brooks Stotler, of, Mat-Su	.284	109	21	31	2	1	1	14	2
Aaron Shackelford, if, Chugiak	.282	142	11	40	6	3	0	7	5
Garrison Schwartz, of, Mat-Su	.277	166	29	46	8	3	2	21	6
Joe Gillette, if, Pilots	.277	137	13	38	9	4	2	22	13

INDIVIDUAL PITCHING LEADERS

	W	L	ERA	G	SV	IP	H	BB	SO
Justin Vernia, Mat-Si	4	3	0.58	8	0	46	29	12	27
Weston Rivers, Pilots	5	1	1.25	8	0	43	33	16	35
Billy Oxford, Peninsula	3	2	1.44	11	0	50	40	20	44
Brody Harris, Chugiak	3	4	1.95	13	0	55	43	24	43
Justin Mulvaney, Bucs	2	5	2.02	10	0	49	43	9	22
Timothy Holdgrafer, Pilots	5	0	2.23	20	4	44	30	3	32
Robert Winslow, Chugiak	1	5	2.34	16	0	50	36	31	43
Connor Lungwitz, Pilots	2	1	2.83	8	0	47	34	5	41
Justin Montgomery, Peninsula	4	2	2.83	12	2	54	24	23	39
Connor Higgins, Mat-Su	4	2	2.95	10	0	42	34	26	28

ATLANTIC COLLEGIATE LEAGUE

	W	L	PCT	GB
Allentown Railers	27	10	.730	—
South Jersey Giants	22	16	.579	5 ½
Staten Island Tide	21	19	.525	7 ½
Quakertown Blazers	21	19	.524	7 ½
North Jersey Eagles	19	19	.500	8 ½
Jersey Pilots	17	22	.438	11
Trenton Generals	15	24	.385	13
Lehigh Valley Catz	11	24	.319	15

CHAMPIONSHIP: Allentown defeated South Jersey 2-1 in best-of-three series.

TOP 10 PROSPECTS: 1. Drew Tumbelty, rhp, South Jersey (Jr., Rider). **2.** Cory Heitler, rhp, North Jersey (So., Wagner). **3.** Joe Zirolli, of/3b, South Jersey (So., Cecil, Md., JC). **4.** Dan Wirchansky, lhp, North Jersey (So., Rockland, N.Y., CC). **5.** Shane Woelfel, of, North Jersey (Jr., Bloomsburg, Pa.). **6.** Anthony Prato, ss, Staten Island (Fr., Connecticut). **7.** Jeff Dixon, rhp, South Jersey (So., Rowan, N.J.). **8.** Karl Blum, rhp, Trenton (Sr., Duke). **9.** Jason McCormick of, Allentown (Sr., Immaculata, Pa.). **10.** Dan Jacobson, rhp, Quakertown (R-So., Delaware).

INDIVIDUAL BATTING LEADERS

	AVG	AB	R	H	2b	3b	HR	RBI	SB
Shane Woelfel, of, North Jersey	.405	131	32	53	7	3	4	20	18
Tom Marcinczyk, of, Jersey	.388	116	23	45	11	0	4	24	12
Bob Barnett, of, Quakertown	.367	120	23	44	4	1	1	14	6

Zach Leone, 1b, Staten Island	.360	139	21	50	18	1	1	30	1
A.J. Wright, if, South Jersey	.351	131	31	46	9	1	5	23	4
Jason McCormick, of, Allentown	.350	117	36	41	12	1	2	13	9
Anthony Gaetaniello, of, LV	.347	124	30	43	4	4	2	13	13
Ivan Rivera, ss, Staten Island	.345	116	16	40	3	0	0	16	7
Austin Pollack, of, Staten Island	.322	121	22	39	3	2	1	19	7
Greg Kocinski, if, Jersey	.317	104	13	33	7	1	3	17	5

INDIVIDUAL PITCHING LEADERS

	W	L	ERA	G	SV	IP	H	BB	SO
Ashton Raines, South Jersey	4	2	1.70	8	0	42	33	11	32
Cory Heitler, North Jersey	5	1	1.78	12	0	50	32	18	60
John Catchmark, Allentown	3	0	2.21	7	0	36	31	8	28
Cole Creighton, Trenton	2	1	2.25	11	1	32	21	6	23
Jerry Dandrea, Staten Island	4	1	2.38	9	1	41	39	14	35
Brett Kosciolek, Allentown	0	1	2.81	7	0	32	42	5	22
Dan Wirchansky, North Jersey	5	1	2.82	9	0	51	37	21	52
Tyler Ksiazek, Quakertown	6	3	2.93	12	0	43	47	16	43
Gabe Mosser, Allentown	5	2	2.93	7	0	43	31	17	52
Michael Hunter, Quakertown	1	2	2.97	20	8	36	32	9	29

CAL RIPKEN COLLEGIATE LEAGUE

Northern Division	W	L	PCT	GB
Baltimore Redbirds	29	11	.725	—
Silver Spring-Takoma T Bolts	20	20	.500	9
Gaithersburg Giants	19	21	.475	10
Rockville Express	17	23	.425	12
Baltimore Dodgers	15	25	.375	14
Southern Division	W	L	PCT	GB
Bethesda Big Train	28	12	.700	—
Alexandria Aces	23	17	.575	5
Herndon Braves	18	22	.450	10
Vienna River Dogs	17	23	.425	11
D.C. Grays	14	26	.350	14

CHAMPIONSHIP: Bethesda defeated Baltimore Redbirds 2-1 in best-of-three series.

TOP 10 PROSPECTS: 1. Mike Rescigno, rhp, Baltimore Redbirds (Sr., Maryland). **2.** Cameron Simmons, of, Baltimore Redbirds (So., Virginia). **3.** Kyle Datres, 3b, Baltimore Redbirds (So., North Carolina). **4.** Logan Gilbert, rhp, Bethesda (So., Stetson). **5.** Marty Costes, of, Baltimore Redbirds (So., Maryland). **6.** Joey Sullivan, rhp, Baltimore Redbirds (Jr., Virginia Tech). **7.** Cole Aker, rhp, Baltimore Redbirds (So., North Carolina). **8.** Hunter Parsons, rhp, Baltimore Redbirds (So., Maryland). **9.** Tyler Blohm, lhp, Baltimore Redbirds (Fr., Maryland). **10.** Nick Cieri, c/1b, Silver Spring-Takoma (Sr., Maryland).

INDIVIDUAL BATTING LEADERS

	AVG	AB	R	H	2b	3b	HR	RBI	SB
Kyle Datres, if, Redbirds	.378	98	25	37	7	1	4	18	22
Evan Alderman, of, Herndon	.371	143	34	53	6	2	0	3	15
Jordan Sergent, of, Vienna	.361	122	25	44	11	1	7	30	4
Tyler Thomas, c, D.C.	.357	98	15	35	6	1	3	13	6
Cameron Simmons, of, Redbirds	.353	116	20	41	5	1	1	17	14
Zachary Racusin, of, SS-T	.352	165	33	58	9	0	0	12	9
Andy Mocahbee, c, Herndon	.351	134	30	47	11	1	7	32	6
Jake Mueller, if, Redbirds	.349	106	18	37	7	0	0	17	14
Clayton Daniel, 2b, Bethesda	.348	158	35	55	5	1	0	22	18
Tyler Galazin, if, Rockville	.345	113	16	39	6	0	1	15	1

INDIVIDUAL PITCHING LEADERS

	W	L	ERA	G	SV	IP	H	BB	SO
Johnny York, Bethesda	4	0	1.36	7	0	33	23	1	29
Hunter Parsons, Redbirds	6	0	1.41	9	0	38	36	7	44
Jacob Erikson, D.C.	4	3	1.66	9	0	48	41	6	24
Matt Chanin, Gaithersburg	6	0	1.76	7	0	46	42	5	30
Sean Barry, Bethesda	4	0	2.17	8	2	37	22	12	42
Mark Curtis, Redbirds	4	1	2.48	11	0	32	32	10	34
Drew Strotman, Bethesda	3	2	2.48	7	0	32	30	8	26
Mason Keen, Vienna	1	2	2.58	7	0	38	40	10	20
Chih-Yuan Lai, SS-T	4	1	2.65	5	0	34	30	3	31
Jonathan Mierzwa, Dodgers	1	3	2.80	6	0	35	36	7	36

COLLEGE

CALIFORNIA COLLEGIATE LEAGUE

Northern Division	W	L	PCT	GB	W	L	PCT
		League				Overall	
Neptune Beach Pearl	17	9	.654	—	24	12	.667
Healdsburg Prune Packers	14	12	.538	3	38	16	.704
Menlo Park Legends	14	12	.538	3	27	17	.614
Walnut Creek Crawdads	4	23	.148	13 ½	6	32	.158

Central Division	W	L	PCT	GB	W	L	PCT
Santa Barbara Foresters	27	12	.692	—	36	14	.716
Conejo Oaks	21	15	.583	4 ½	26	18	.591
San Luis Obispo Blues	16	15	.516	7	24	20	.545
Ventura Halos	12	23	.343	13	20	23	.465

Southern Division	W	L	PCT	GB	W	L	PCT
Academy Barons	24	11	.686	1	29	15	.659
Orange County Riptide	17	19	.472	7 ½	23	24	.490
Southern California Catch	16	20	.444	8 ½	27	22	.551
Long Beach Legends	15	21	.417	9 ½	24	27	.471

CHAMPIONSHIP: Santa Barbara defeated Conejo in championship game.

TOP 10 PROSPECTS: 1. Kyle Johnston, rhp, Santa Barbara (Jr., Texas). 2. Isaiah Campbell, rhp, Conejo (So., Arkansas). 3. Nick Kennedy, lhp, Santa Barbara (So., Texas). 4. Parker Mushinski, lhp, San Luis Obispo (Jr., Texas Tech). 5. Miles Sandum, lhp, Santa Barbara (Fr., San Diego). 6. Bret Boswell, ss/3b, Santa Barbara (R-Jr., Texas). 7. Chad Spanberger, of, Conejo (Jr., Arkansas). 8. Connor Mayes, rhp, Santa Barbara (Jr., Texas). 9. Matt Walker, rhp, San Luis Obispo (R-So., UCLA). 10. Eric Ramirez, 1b, Conejo (Jr., Hawaii).

INDIVIDUAL BATTING LEADERS

	AVG	AB	R	H	2b	3b	HR	RBI	SB
Bret Boswell, if, Santa Barbara	.392	158	41	62	17	2	10	42	4
Ernie De La Trinidad, of, Acad.	.388	147	43	57	8	7	4	27	9
Clayton Andrews, of, Nep. Beach	.376	85	21	32	6	3	0	9	6
Dillon Kelley, c, Orange Cty.	.376	125	37	47	11	0	6	33	2
Lex Kaplan, of, Santa Barbara	.353	139	23	49	11	0	4	23	19
Sean Watkins, of, Menlo Park	.349	109	31	38	15	3	0	25	12
Martin Teague, 1b, Academy	.347	147	25	51	13	0	6	51	3
Eric Ramirez, 1b, Conejo	.347	101	20	35	5	0	2	25	1
Jamey Smart, 1b, Healdsburg	.337	193	40	65	9	5	4	37	1
Andrew Carrillo, if, Orange Cty.	.333	117	24	39	6	2	0	8	18

INDIVIDUAL PITCHING LEADERS

	W	L	ERA	G	SV	IP	H	BB	SO
Kyle Johnston, Santa Barbara	4	1	1.89	9	0	52	34	28	54
Jimmy Gallarda, Southern Calif.	4	2	2.01	9	0	53	39	14	38
Isaiah Campbell, Conejo	5	1	2.11	9	0	47	41	6	45
Connor Mayes, Santa Barbara	4	2	2.17	10	0	49	42	6	49
Alex Trautner, Neptune Beach	4	1	2.18	9	0	41	35	17	31
Addison Pelupessy, Ventura	2	3	2.20	10	0	41	37	10	18
Charlie Brooks, Ventura	1	2	2.25	7	0	40	33	12	17
Kyle Murray, Academy	4	0	2.38	11	0	41	47	12	36
Matt Walker, SLO	3	2	2.46	11	0	55	51	8	48
Noah Gotsis, Neptune Beach	3	1	3.14	8	0	43	37	7	38

COASTAL PLAIN LEAGUE

Eastern Division	W	L	PCT	GB
Peninsula Pilots	38	10	.792	—
Wilmington Sharks	32	22	.593	9
Wilson Tobs	30	24	.556	10
Morehead City Marlins	30	25	.545	10 ½
Edenton Steamers	28	26	.519	13
Holly Springs Salamanders	21	32	.396	19 ½
Fayetteville SwampDogs	18	35	.340	22 ½
Petersburg Generals	16	35	.314	23 ½

Western Division	W	L	PCT	GB
Savannah Bananas	30	20	.600	—
Forest City Owls	32	23	.582	2 ½
High Point-Thomasville HiToms	30	25	.545	2 ½
Asheboro Copperheads	28	26	.519	4
Florence Redwolves	26	29	.473	6 ½

Lexington County Blowfish	26	30	.464	7
Martinsville Mustangs	24	29	.453	7 ½
Gastonia Grizzlies	21	33	.389	11

CHAMPIONSHIP: Savannah defeated Peninsula 2-1 in best-of-three series.

TOP 10 PROSPECTS: 1. Alec Bohm, 3b, Wilmington (So., Wichita State). 2. Jameson Hannah, of, Savannah (So., Dallas Baptist). 3. Barrett Loseke, rhp, Gastonia (So., Arkansas). 4. Will Shepherd, of, Peninsula (Sr., Liberty). 5. Hunter Dolshun, c, Fayetteville (Sr., Maryland-Baltimore County). 6. Ryan Kelly, rhp, Wilmington (Sr., Saint Joseph's). 7. Brady Feigl, rhp, Asheboro (R-So., Mississippi). 8. Luke Watts, rhp, Morehead City (Jr., Appalachian State). 9. Dillon Stewart, of, Holly Springs (Sr., UNC Greensboro). 10. Logan Moody, 1b/of, Savannah (So., Georgia).

INDIVIDUAL BATTING LEADERS

	AVG	AB	R	H	2b	3b	HR	RBI	BB
Will Shepherd, Peninsula	.407	167	39	68	16	1	5	47	23
Jameson Hannah, Savannah	.374	147	35	55	12	1	4	34	24
Clint Hardy, Savannah	.364	176	34	64	12	4	5	36	20
Zachary Files, Florence	.356	104	31	37	14	1	4	23	38
Kyle McPherson, Peninsula	.355	152	34	54	7	4	4	44	16
Rylan Bannon, Savannah	.355	124	33	44	10	0	3	27	34
Mark Donadio, Wilmington	.354	175	32	62	4	0	2	21	31
Hunter Slater, HP-T	.346	133	28	46	4	2	5	21	18
James Latona, Wilson	.342	146	27	50	9	0	4	25	17
Richard Cunningham, Edenton	.341	208	37	71	8	2	6	25	19

INDIVIDUAL PITCHING LEADERS

	W	L	ERA	G	SV	IP	H	BB	SO
Beau Sulser, Savannah	3	1	1.21	12	4	44	27	8	51
Connor Riley, Wilmington	6	3	2.03	12	0	66	40	19	100
Luke Watts, Morehead City	4	1	2.77	10	0	61	51	22	58
John Luke Curtis, Morehead City	5	3	3.02	15	0	47	40	33	72
Nick Yobbi, Fayetteville	3	2	3.07	10	0	44	35	11	35
Ted Christie, Edenton	3	3	3.14	10	0	43	37	13	46
Mike Castellani, Wilmington	6	3	3.16	14	0	68	63	19	51
J.T. Rogoszewski, Holly Springs	6	3	3.29	10	0	54	55	11	42
Nick Spadafino, Petersburg	1	4	3.44	9	0	52	46	20	45
Rodney Hutchison, Holly Springs	1	3	3.44	10	0	49	53	31	26

FLORIDA COLLEGIATE SUMMER LEAGUE

	W	L	PCT	GB
Sanford River Rats	27	16	.628	—
Altamonte Springs Boom	22	19	.537	4
DeLand Suns	20	20	.500	5 ½
Leesburg Lightning	21	23	.477	6 ½
Winter Garden Squeeze	19	23	.452	7 ½
Winter Park Diamond Dawgs	17	25	.405	9 ½

CHAMPIONSHIP: Altamonte Springs defeated Sanford in championship game.

TOP 10 PROSPECTS: 1. Carlos Cortes, 2b/3b, Sanford (Fr., South Carolina). 2. Cody Beckman, lhp, Sanford (R-Jr., North Carolina State). 3. Brant Blaylock, of, Sanford (R-Fr., Mississippi State). 4. Joe Dudek, 1b, DeLand (Signed: Royals). 5. Garrett Wolforth, c, Sanford (So., Dallas Baptist). 6. Jordan Gubelman, rhp, Sanford (So., State JC of Florida). 7. Clay Simmons, ss/3b, Leesburg (R-Jr., Columbia State, Tenn., JC). 8. Reed Hayes, of/rhp, Sanford (R-Jr., Vanderbilt). 9. Codi Heuer, rhp, Altamonte Springs (So., Wichita State). 10. Jacob Billingsley, rhp, Sanford (R-Jr., Mississippi State).

INDIVIDUAL BATTING LEADERS

	AVG	AB	R	H	2b	3b	HR	RBI	SB
Omar Villaman, 2b, Sanford	.430	114	26	49	4	2	1	20	12
Harrison Scanlon, 1b, Leesburg	.381	155	27	59	10	1	6	38	2
Jay Hayes, of, DeLand	.377	130	32	49	10	5	4	32	3
Tyler Halstead, 3b, W. Garden	.372	137	21	51	8	0	4	34	8
Jacob Silverstein, of, W. Park	.358	109	19	39	5	0	1	15	7
Joe Dudek, of, DeLand	.351	114	29	40	11	0	4	22	3
Russell Schwertfeger, of, AS	.349	152	28	53	5	4	0	20	7
Pablo Cabrera, ss, W. Garden	.324	139	24	45	8	0	0	19	11
Kyle Corbin, of, Winter Garden	.322	149	30	48	6	2	1	21	15
Sergio Lopez, of, Sanford	.322	115	30	37	3	0	0	15	20

INDIVIDUAL PITCHING LEADERS

	W	L	ERA	G	SV	IP	H	BB	SO
Brady Mintell, DeLand	2	0	1.40	8	0	38	32	6	21
MacLain Larson, Leesburg	2	0	1.58	19	1	40	38	2	21
Mark Moclair, Alta. Springs	3	0	1.82	7	0	34	24	19	29
Shane Haight, Winter Garden	4	1	1.96	7	0	36	33	18	41
Jarred Neal, Winter Garden	2	2	2.47	13	2	54	47	7	40
Matthew Gulik, DeLand	5	1	2.50	9	0	50	55	4	23
Jordan Gubelman, Sanford	3	0	3.02	10	0	41	30	21	44
Jaylyn Whitehead, Alta. Springs	4	1	3.22	13	0	36	45	3	27
Justin Kortessis, Winter Park	3	1	3.23	8	0	39	37	15	32
Wade McNabb, DeLand	3	5	3.74	13	2	43	47	17	29

FUTURES COLLEGIATE LEAGUE

Eastern Division	W	L	PCT	GB
Seacoast Mavericks	36	18	.667	—
Nashua Silver Knights	34	21	.618	2 ½
North Shore Navigators	29	27	.518	8
Brockton Rox	27	29	.482	10
Marthas Vineyard Sharks	21	35	.375	16

Western Division	W	L	PCT	GB
Worcester Bravehearts	37	18	.673	—
Torrington Titans	24	29	.453	12
Bristol Blues	23	32	.418	14
Pittsfield Suns	22	31	.415	14
Wachusett Dirt Dawgs	21	34	.382	16

CHAMPIONSHIP: Nashua defeated Worcester 2-0 in best-of-three series.

TOP 10 PROSPECTS: 1. Nick Mondak, lhp, Torrington (Fr., St. John's). **2.** Dylan Grove, rhp, Martha's Vineyard (So., Oklahoma). **3.** Ricky Constant, rhp, Nashua (Jr., Massachusetts-Lowell). **4.** Dante Baldelli, of, Nashua (Fr., Boston College). **5.** Jake Nelson, rhp, Nashua (So., Pennsylvania). **6.** Isaiah Musa, rhp, Seacoast (So., Broward, Fla. CC). **7.** Eric Hamilton, 3b/1b, Pittsfield (Sr., Oswego State, N.Y.). **8.** Gavin Hollowell, rhp, Nashua (Fr., St. John's). **9.** Dillon Nelson, of, Martha's Vineyard (So., Indian Hills, Iowa CC). **10.** Mike Hart, of, Seacoast (Sr., Massachusetts).

INDIVIDUAL BATTING LEADERS

	AVG	AB	R	H	2b	3b	HR	RBI	SB
Mickey Gasper, c, Nashua	.421	164	39	69	21	1	9	42	5
Kyle Bonicki, ss, Wachusett	.403	186	37	75	12	0	0	21	17
Michael Hart, of, Seacoast	.364	151	42	55	6	1	10	31	17
Kevin Donati, if, Pittsfield	.344	125	29	43	3	0	1	16	15
Ricky Surum, if, Marthas Vin.	.343	140	22	48	8	2	2	10	15
Austin Chauvin, if, Bristol	.340	147	19	50	5	0	1	22	1
Dillon Nelson, of, Marthas Vin.	.331	163	28	54	11	0	1	25	11
Yanni Thanopoulas, of, Nashua	.328	204	31	67	16	5	6	34	8
Eric Hamilton, if, Pittsfield	.319	207	35	66	18	1	12	63	1
Alex Lewis, if, Marthas Vin.	.319	166	23	53	11	0	5	22	2

INDIVIDUAL PITCHING LEADERS

	W	L	ERA	G	SV	IP	H	BB	SO
Nick Mondak, Torrington	4	1	1.45	9	1	43	32	14	64
Izzy Fuentes, Bristol	6	0	2.20	10	0	57	40	22	70
Clayton Chatham, Seacoast	6	0	2.27	10	0	43	32	14	43
Jake Dexter, North Shore	3	4	2.51	17	2	46	37	13	27
Jeremy Roberts, Nashua	4	2	2.55	9	0	53	48	14	40
Greg Stagani, Worcester	4	3	2.60	8	0	45	45	5	51
Malachi Emond, Torrington	5	1	3.19	15	1	48	35	22	44
Ryan Simpler, Pittsfield	2	1	3.26	10	0	49	47	11	45
Brady Furdon, Worcester	6	2	3.54	9	0	48	48	13	44
Drew Fischer, Nashua	2	3	3.55	9	0	45	33	25	57

GREAT LAKES LEAGUE

Northern Division	W	L	PCT	GB
Lima Locos	28	13	.683	—
Grand Lake Mariners	23	19	.548	5 ½
Irish Hills Leprechauns	22	20	.524	6 ½
Lorain County Ironmen	17	25	.405	11 ½
Lake Erie Monarchs	17	25	.405	11 ½
Galion Graders	12	30	.286	16 ½

Southern Division	W	L	PCT	GB
Xenia Scouts	27	15	.643	—
Hamilton Joes	27	15	.643	—
Licking County Settlers	23	19	.548	4
Cincinnati Steam	23	19	.548	4
Southern Ohio Copperheads	20	22	.476	7
Richmond Jazz	12	29	.293	14 ½

CHAMPIONSHIP: Hamilton defeated Lima 3-2 in best-of-five series.

TOP 10 PROSPECTS: 1. Kevin Woodall, 1b, Lima Locos (Jr., Coastal Carolina). **2.** Ben Spitznagel, 2b/of, Hamilton (Sr., UNC Greensboro). **3.** Dane Tofteland, 3b, Hamilton (R-So., Indiana State). **4.** Cole Murphy, 1b, Cincinnati (So., Cincinnati). **5.** Connor Curlis, lhp, Lima (So., Ohio State). **6.** Kent Axcell, rhp, Galion (R-So., Ohio State). **7.** Jake Richmond, ss, Cincinnati (R-Jr., Northern Kentucky). **8.** Matthew Wade, rhp, Xenia (R-Jr., Southeast Missouri State). **9.** Kyle Moore, of, Hamilton (Sr., Indiana State). **10.** P.J. Piesko, lhp, Licking County (Jr., Oakland).

INDIVIDUAL BATTING LEADERS

	AVG	AB	R	H	2b	3b	HR	RBI	SB
Ben Spitznagel, if, Hamilton	.393	168	52	66	8	3	1	26	20
Dane Tofteland, 3b, Hamilton	.379	140	41	53	11	2	9	38	18
Jeremy Johnson, of, Lima	.368	114	24	42	7	0	0	10	11
Robert Emery, c, Licking Co.	.364	132	29	48	11	0	6	26	3
Ross Haffey, 1b, Lake Erie	.353	136	35	48	12	0	13	40	1
Jackson Boyce, if, Hamilton	.349	146	32	51	5	2	0	30	30
Matthew Malkin, c, Lorain Co.	.345	139	21	48	15	0	5	34	0
Kyle Hubbuch, 1b, Licking Co.	.345	165	27	57	16	0	6	36	2
Connor Callery, if, S. Ohio	.336	149	27	50	9	0	0	17	10
Roger Danison, of, Cincinnati	.333	126	16	42	9	1	2	15	4

INDIVIDUAL PITCHING LEADERS

	W	L	ERA	G	SV	IP	H	BB	SO
Ben Havel, Hamilton	4	0	1.05	7	0	34	26	17	31
Connor Curlis, Lima	6	0	1.06	7	0	42	25	14	39
Jacob Chrysler, Xenia	1	1	1.30	13	1	34	30	9	19
Brandon Phelps, Irish Hills	5	1	1.71	8	0	52	40	15	27
Logan Heffernan, Lorain Co.	3	2	1.76	7	0	41	33	5	25
Cas Silber, Lima	3	2	1.90	6	0	38	24	12	33
Devin Peters, Lake Erie	3	0	2.23	8	0	48	35	23	34
Jorge Lozano, Xenia	5	0	2.27	9	0	51	35	27	36
Bryan Cruse, Licking Co.	5	2	2.48	7	0	40	40	11	40
Adrian Peraza, Xenia	2	1	2.52	10	0	35	34	8	23

HAMPTONS COLLEGIATE LEAGUE

	W	L	T	PCT	GB
Westhampton Aviators	27	14	1	.659	—
North Fork Ospreys	26	16	0	.619	3
Montauk Mustangs	24	18	0	.571	7
Riverhead Tomcats	19	22	1	.463	16
Sag Harbor Whalers	17	24	1	.415	20
Southampton Breakers	17	25	1	.405	21
Shelter Island Bucks	15	26	1	.366	24

CHAMPIONSHIP: Westhampton defeated Montauk 2-1 in best-of-three series.

TOP 10 PROSPECTS: 1. Reiss Knehr, rhp, Westhampton (So., Fordham). **2.** John Rooney, lhp, Southampton (So., Hofstra). **3.** Richie Palacios, ss, North Fork (So., Towson). **4.** Bradley Case, rhp, Montauk (So., Rollins (Fla.). **5.** Josiah Gray, 3b/rhp, Southampton (So., Le Moyne (N.Y.). **6.** Matt Dunlevy, of, Westhampton (Jr., Virginia Military Institute). **7.** Jordan McCrum, if/rhp, Westhampton (So., Monmouth). **8.** Max Smith, of, North Fork (So., Nevada-Las Vegas). **9.** Jamie Galazin, of/rhp, Montauk (Jr., St. John's). **10.** Frank Valentino, rhp, Riverhead (Sr., New York Tech).

INDIVIDUAL BATTING LEADERS

	AVG	AB	R	H	2b	3b	HR	RBI	SB
Matt Dunlevy, of, Westham.	.372	137	34	51	11	0	1	19	12
Daniel Franchi, of, Westham.	.356	104	22	37	3	0	2	23	10
Richard Palacios, if, North Fork.	.347	173	37	60	6	3	8	24	25
Phil Capra, c, Montauk	.342	111	21	38	9	0	5	21	1
Kevin Kolesar, if, Southham.	.339	115	28	39	7	0	1	15	12
Hunter Courson, if, Southham.	.338	160	27	54	9	2	3	26	0
Rob Vani, if, Montauk	.336	131	29	44	9	1	7	30	4

Tim DeGraw, of, Riverhead	.336	110	20	37	7	2	1	11	12
Trey Silvers, if, Westhampton	.336	116	24	39	7	0	7	27	1
Griffin Dey, 1b, Sag Harbor	.336	122	20	41	6	1	5	20	2

INDIVIDUAL PITCHING LEADERS

	W	L	ERA	G	SV	IP	H	BB	SO
Seamus Brazill, Westhampton	4	0	0.73	11	0	37	29	8	38
Reiss Knehr, Westhampton	4	1	1.15	8	0	39	20	16	49
Colman Vila, Sag Harbor	1	3	1.73	12	1	41	39	17	44
Chris Sheehan, Sag Harbor	5	1	1.98	11	2	41	27	24	40
Frank Valentino, Riverhead	5	1	2.63	8	0	41	25	21	48
Joe Molettiere, Montauk	2	3	2.70	6	0	36	33	8	27
Bradley Case, Montauk	5	0	2.87	10	0	37	34	16	51
Tevita Gerber, North Fork	2	3	3.08	8	1	38	35	15	36
Jordan Sheinkop, Sag Harbor	2	4	3.18	8	0	34	34	12	27
Nick Kruel, Sag Harbor	3	0	3.28	12	0	49	47	14	18

JAYHAWK LEAGUE

	W	L	PCT	GB
Hays Larks	33	10	.767	—
El Dorado Broncos	24	16	.600	7 ½
Dodge City A's	26	18	.591	7 ½
Liberal BeeJays	20	21	.488	12
Haysville Aviators	20	22	.476	12 ½
Wellington Heat	17	25	.405	15 ½
Derby Twins	15	27	.357	17 ½
Bethany Bulls	13	29	.310	19 ½

CHAMPIONSHIP: Hays defeated Dodge City 2-0 in best-of-three series.
TOP 10 PROSPECTS: 1. Keegan Curtis, rhp, Hays (Jr., Louisiana-Monroe). **2.** Mike Mioduszewski, of, Hays (R-Sr., Eastern Michigan). **3.** Chase Calabuig, of, Dodge City (Jr., San Diego State). **4.** Tanner Buxton, rhp, Haysville (R-Jr., Texas Tech). **5.** Tony Kjolsing, 3b, El Dorado (Jr., South Dakota State). **6.** J.B. Olson, rhp, Liberal (Sr., Texas-Arlington). **7.** Brady Cox, c, Liberal (Sr., Texas-Arlington). **8.** Austin O'Brien, 1b, Hays (Sr., Oklahoma). **9.** Kyrell Miller, rhp, Haysville (R-Fr., Sam Houston State). **10.** Daniel James, rhp, Hays (Jr., Texas-Arlington).

INDIVIDUAL BATTING LEADERS

	AVG	AB	R	H	2b	3b	HR	RBI	SB
Chase Calabuig, of, Dodge	.421	164	34	69	16	3	4	31	11
Austin O'Brien, if, Hays	.410	166	48	68	17	1	9	48	1
Mike Mioduszewski, of, Hays	.391	156	27	61	8	3	8	43	2
Ian Dawkins, if, Dodge	.367	177	43	65	10	3	2	32	18
Tyler Sutherland, of, El Dorado	.366	142	33	52	9	1	1	23	17
Anthony Gomez, if, Bethany	.355	107	24	38	5	0	0	13	3
Sam Grellner, of, Bethany	.343	105	17	36	7	0	1	18	4
Neil Lambert, if, Haysville	.337	104	21	35	2	0	1	12	15
Mason Pierzchalski, if, Dodge	.336	143	20	48	8	1	4	31	2
Mike Leal, of, El Dorado	.330	103	20	34	4	2	0	15	1

INDIVIDUAL PITCHING LEADERS

	W	L	ERA	G	SV	IP	H	BB	SO
Jake Harrison, Liberal	4	0	2.06	8	0	43	42	17	31
Jake Moore, Haysville	3	0	2.14	14	7	33	17	13	30
Matt Loutzenhister, Dodge	4	0	2.19	6	0	37	30	8	25
Tyson Campbell, El Dorado	2	2	2.40	8	0	41	29	19	42
Nick Burnham, Derby	3	3	2.56	8	0	45	39	17	28
Kevin Torres, Haysville	3	2	2.61	9	1	48	46	15	44
John Pendergast, Dodge	4	0	2.63	10	1	48	41	10	31
Tyler Nelson, Derby	2	3	2.80	9	0	45	42	17	27
Blake Goldsberry, Liberal	3	2	2.91	10	0	43	46	7	22
Blake Haragens, El Dorado	2	1	3.12	11	0	34	28	13	22

MINK LEAGUE

	League				Overall			
Northern Division	W	L	PCT	GB	W	L	PCT	G
Sedalia Bombers	32	14	.696	—	32	14	.696	—
St. Joseph Mustangs	27	16	.628	3 ½	35	17	.673	—
Chillicothe Mudcats	25	16	.610	4 ½	29	17	.630	3
Clarind0a A's	17	25	.405	13	25	26	.490	9 ½
Southern Division	W	L	PCT	GB	W	L	PCT	G
Ozark Generals	25	21	.543	—	27	21	.563	—
Nevada Griffons	22	20	.524	1	24	20	.545	1
Joplin Outlaws	22	21	.512	1 ½	25	21	.543	1
Branson Nationals	2	39	.049	20 ½	2	39	.049	21 ½

CHAMPIONSHIP: Sedalia defeated Ozark 2-1 in best-of-three series.
TOP 10 PROSPECTS: 1. Jacob Ruder, rhp, Branson (So., Cowley County (Kan.) CC). **2.** Jack Burk, rhp, Nevada (So., Louisiana-Lafayette). **3.** Evan McDonald, ss, St. Joseph (Sr., Georgia Southern). **4.** Justin Murphy, rhp, Sedalia (Sr., Southeast Missouri State). **5.** Blake Weiman, lhp, Chillicothe (Jr., Kansas). **6.** Kainalu Pitoy, of, Nevada (Jr., Northwestern Oklahoma State). **7.** Nick Banman, 3b, Chillicothe (Jr., Pittsburgh). **8.** Louis Mele, 3b/1b, St. Joseph (So., NYIT). **9.** Michael Lydon-Lorson, rhp, St. Joseph (Sr., Rockhurst, Mo.). **10.** Justin Holt, of, Sedalia (Sr., Nicholls State).

INDIVIDUAL BATTING LEADERS

	AVG	AB	R	H	2b	3b	HR	RBI	SB
Tyler Pagano, of, Nevada	.343	181	38	62	9	1	6	43	7
Kainalu Pitoy, of, Nevada	.323	158	34	51	10	1	4	18	6
Eric Wagaman, if, Clarinda	.322	199	36	64	14	1	7	46	3
Quade Smith, of, Sedalia	.313	160	40	50	9	2	0	31	11
Cole Johnson, if, Nevada	.307	140	26	43	7	1	0	20	0
Judah Zickafoose, of, Nevada	.291	158	28	46	11	1	3	24	13
Mondesi Gutierrez, if, Clarinda	.278	187	37	52	5	2	0	20	10
Justin Holt, of, Sedalia	.278	151	38	42	2	0	0	23	8
Ethaniel Valdez, if, Nevada	.276	163	32	45	9	0	2	25	20
Nick Gotta, if, Ozark	.270	152	33	41	5	0	1	21	5

INDIVIDUAL PITCHING LEADERS

	W	L	ERA	G	SV	IP	H	BB	SO
John Millan, St. Joseph	5	2	1.51	14	0	41	24	16	30
Justin Murphey, Sedalia	6	1	1.83	8	0	59	26	11	52
Michael Lydon-Lorson, St. Joseph	4	0	2.29	6	0	43	30	7	34
Zach Leban, Chillicothe	2	2	2.34	7	0	42	32	15	46
Doug Molzahn, Nevada	2	2	2.40	9	0	48	35	19	35
Evan Dodd, Sedalia	4	2	2.46	8	0	47	39	25	41
Louis Niemerg, Sedalia	5	2	2.49	10	1	43	40	17	35
Burke Echelmeier, Sedalia	6	0	2.54	7	0	46	37	18	37
J.C. Hatcher, Joplin	2	1	3.00	7	0	42	31	14	42
A.J. Bruner, Ozark	3	3	3.02	10	0	44	42	12	18

NEW ENGLAND COLLEGIATE LEAGUE

Northern Division	W	L	PCT	GB
Sanford Mainers	26	17	.605	—
Valley Blue Sox	24	20	.545	2 ½
North Adams SteepleCats	23	20	.535	3
Upper Valley Nighthawks	21	15	.457	6 ½
Keene Swamp Bats	20	26	.435	7 ½
Vermont Mountaineers	19	26	.422	8
Winnipesaukee Muskrats	19	26	.422	8

Southern Division	W	L	PCT	GB
Mystic Schooners	29	15	.659	—
Newport Gulls	25	19	.568	4
New Bedford Bay Sox	22	23	.489	7 ½
Danbury Westerners	21	23	.477	8
Ocean State Waves	21	24	.467	8 ½
Plymouth Pilgrims	19	25	.432	10

CHAMPIONSHIP: Mystic defeated Sanford 2-0 in best-of-three series.
TOP 10 PROSPECTS: 1. Tommy Doyle, rhp, Keene (Jr., Virginia). **2.** Brandt Stallings, of, Keene (So., Georgia Tech). **3.** Connor Kaiser, ss, Newport (So., Vanderbilt). **4.** Travis Jones, if/of, Valley (Jr., Texas). **5.** Jason Foley, rhp, Mystic (SIGNED: Tigers). **6.** Darrien Ragins, lhp, New Bedford (Jr., Delaware State). **7.** Mark Washington, rhp, Valley (Jr., Lehigh). **8.** Michael Osinski, ss, Vermont (Jr., Longwood). **9.** Troy Dixon, c, Newport (Sr., St. John's). **10.** Stephen Scott, c, Newport (So., Vanderbilt).

INDIVIDUAL BATTING LEADERS

	AVG	AB	R	H	2b	3b	HR	RBI	SB
Troy Dixon, c, Newport	.371	132	25	49	15	0	2	18	1
Nick Mascelli, ss, Mystic	.369	160	43	59	11	1	2	22	13
Joseph Denison, of, Upper Val.	.356	177	29	63	14	2	6	37	4
Michael Osinski, ss, Vermont	.351	148	22	52	5	0	1	11	1
Ryan Wolfsberg, util, N. Bedford	.349	106	22	37	10	1	5	21	3
Richard Slenker, 3b, Mystic	.338	151	24	51	13	2	3	31	7
Daniel Holst, of, Mystic	.336	125	30	42	5	1	2	14	21

COLLEGE

Martin Figueroa, of, Mystic	.336	131	23	44	12	1	8	28	6
Austin Upshaw, 1b, OSW	.327	171	19	56	10	0	1	28	3
Chase Lunceford, 3b, Mystic	.326	135	26	44	10	2	6	28	0

INDIVIDUAL PITCHING LEADERS

	W	L	ERA	G	SV	IP	H	BB	SO
Ryan Testani, Danbury	6	2	1.60	17	0	45	43	7	42
Hunter Schryver, Newport	5	1	1.75	8	0	36	23	13	38
Nicholas Gallagher, Danbury	2	2	1.98	7	0	36.1	26	9	35
George Capen, Ocean State	1	1	2.08	18	0	39	38	4	28
Braxton Wilks, North Adams	7	1	2.13	8	0	42.1	29	20	29
Samuel Nepiarsky, N. Bedford	4	1	2.19	8	0	49.1	36	13	38
Will Jahn, Danbury	5	1	2.25	10	0	48	49	13	36
C.J. Dandeneau, Plymouth	1	3	2.27	13	1	35.2	25	12	39
Doug Domnarski, Mystic	5	1	2.56	10	1	45.2	41	16	42
Nick Margevicius, Plymouth	2	3	2.58	8	0	52.1	43	4	38

NEW YORK COLLEGIATE LEAGUE

Eastern Division	W	L	PCT	GB
Cortland Crush	29	17	.630	—
Syracuse Jr. Chiefs	26	20	.565	3
Syracuse Salt Cats	24	22	.522	5
Sherrill Silversmiths	19	27	.413	10
Rome Generals	18	28	.391	11

Western Division	W	L	PCT	GB
Olean Oilers	39	7	.848	—
Wellsville Nitros	24	22	.522	15
Hornell Dodgers	21	25	.457	18
Genesee Rapids	18	28	.391	21
Rochester Ridgemen	12	34	.261	27

CHAMPIONSHIP: Olean defeated Jr. Chiefs 2-0 in best-of-three series.

INDIVIDUAL BATTING LEADERS

	AVG	AB	R	H	2b	3b	HR	RBI	SB
Aaron Phillips, p, Olean	.395	177	42	70	17	2	5	54	11
Harry Montero Jr., 1b, Wellsville	.388	152	44	59	16	5	10	67	3
Ryan Coulon, 1b, Sherrill	.379	153	26	58	10	1	10	51	3
Ethan Luna, 1b, Rochester	.376	170	31	64	12	6	4	32	1
Anthony Galanoudis, of, S. Cats	.368	117	20	43	6	1	0	12	9
John Ricotta, 1b, Hornell	.361	122	26	44	11	1	2	34	0
Alex Griffith, c, Olean	.361	122	22	44	13	1	4	33	0
Cole Peterson, if, Olean	.356	191	51	68	12	5	0	33	20
David Yanni, if, Olean	.352	142	38	50	9	2	7	35	4
Michael McNicholl, of, Wellsville	.352	125	30	44	7	2	0	22	1

INDIVIDUAL PITCHING LEADERS

	W	L	ERA	G	SV	IP	H	BB	SO
Aaron Phillips, Olean	6	1	1.31	8	0	48	35	17	37
Billy Griffin, Olean	4	1	1.43	8	0	50.1	18	24	45
David Lyskawa, Olean	6	0	1.94	8	0	41.2	33	12	38
Richard Edwards, Rome	4	1	2.01	13	0	49.1	49	5	18
Matthew Sandoval, Chiefs	3	2	2.02	9	0	58	45	26	63
Austin Bizzle, Olean	6	0	2.06	7	0	48	32	7	30
Stephen Witkowski, Cortland	4	0	2.37	8	1	38	32	14	30
Adam Rigney, Olean	4	1	2.39	9	0	49	46	9	28
Carlos Tejeda, Wellsville	5	2	3.09	10	0	46.2	48	15	38
Luke Chevalier, Rochester	1	4	3.38	11	1	50.2	45	20	47

NORTHWOODS LEAGUE

Northern Division	W	L	PCT	GB
St. Cloud Rox	48	23	.676	—
Mankato MoonDogs	46	26	.639	2 ½
Eau Claire Express	45	27	.625	3 ½
Willmar Stingers	41	31	.569	7 ½
La Crosse Loggers	38	33	.535	10
Waterloo Bucks	36	36	.500	12 ½
Duluth Huskies	30	42	.417	18 ½
Thunder Bay Border Cats	21	51	.292	27 ½
Rochester Honkers	20	52	.278	28 ½

Southern Division	W	L	PCT	GB
Wisconsin Rapids Rafters	49	23	.681	—

Madison Mallards	43	29	.597	6
Battle Creek Bombers	39	33	.542	10
Lakeshore Chinooks	35	37	.486	14
Rockford Rivets	33	39	.458	16
Kalamazoo Growlers	33	39	.458	16
Green Bay Bullfrogs	32	40	.444	17
Wisconsin Woodchucks	31	40	.437	17 ½
Kenosha Kingfish	26	46	.361	23

CHAMPIONSHIP: Wisconsin Rapids defeated Eau Claire 2-0 in best-of-three series.

TOP 10 PROSPECTS: 1. Mitchell Kilkenny, rhp, Madison (So., Texas A&M). **2.** T.J. Friedl, of, St. Cloud (SIGNED: Reds). **3.** Daulton Varsho, c, Eau Claire (Jr., Wisconsin-Milwaukee). **4.** Troy Bacon, rhp, Madison (So., Santa Fe JC, Fla.). **5.** Jake Shepski, of, Mankato (Jr., Notre Dame). **6.** Griffin Conine, of, La Crosse (So., Duke). **7.** Luke Shilling, rhp, Madison (So., Illinois). **8.** Drew Ellis, 3b/of, Rochester (R-So., Louisville). **9.** Nick Raquet, lhp, La Crosse (R-So., William & Mary). **10.** Steele Walker, of, Wisconsin (So., Oklahoma).

INDIVIDUAL BATTING LEADERS

	AVG	AB	R	H	2b	3b	HR	RBI	SB
Steele Walker, of, Wisconsin	.406	212	47	86	11	0	7	31	4
Danny Pardo, of, Willmar	.360	264	75	95	13	1	5	42	27
David Metzgar, if, Mankato	.356	225	40	80	10	0	1	38	6
Jake Shepski, of, Mankato	.333	243	52	81	21	2	11	55	8
Anthony Brocato, of, T. Bay	.333	186	27	62	8	1	9	33	2
Greg Lambert, if, Willmar	.330	282	57	93	18	1	9	66	2
Dean Miller, of, Battle Creek	.330	197	37	65	4	1	7	43	22
Justin Toerner, of, Willmar	.330	227	46	75	14	3	5	56	5
Cullen Large, if, La Crosse	.328	204	41	67	20	0	4	38	4
Zach Ashford, of, Eau Claire	.327	208	41	68	6	1	0	26	17

INDIVIDUAL PITCHING LEADERS

	W	L	ERA	G	SV	IP	H	BB	SO
Luke Lind, Green Bay	4	0	1.51	10	0	59	38	19	54
Collin Strall, St. Cloud	3	2	1.53	25	10	58	45	18	46
Marshall Kasowski, Lakeshore	3	1	1.56	12	0	63	41	22	87
Chris Cooper, Wisconsin Rapids	4	2	2.03	10	0	57	47	15	38
Devin Pellien, Kalamazoo	6	1	2.11	13	0	72	58	21	71
Nick Raquet, La Crosse	4	4	2.23	12	0	64	56	30	62
Ricky Digrugilliers, Mankato	6	3	2.31	10	0	62	46	17	38
Caleb Boushley, Eau Claire	8	2	2.95	10	0	61	60	7	47
Scott Sency, Battle Creek	5	3	3.27	12	0	63	73	20	56
Gareth Stroh, Wisconsin Rapids	5	2	3.60	11	0	60	67	13	55

OHIO VALLEY LEAGUE

	W	L	PCT	GB
Hoptown Hoppers	33	9	.786	—
Madisonville Miners	26	14	.650	6
Dubois Co. Bombers	26	15	.634	6 ½
Owensboro Oilers	21	16	.568	9 ½
Fulton Railroaders	16	26	.381	17
Paducah Chiefs	14	26	.350	18
Muhlenberg Co. Stallions	4	34	.105	27

INDIVIDUAL BATTING LEADERS

	AVG	AB	R	H	2b	3b	HR	RBI	SB
Andrew Gross, Hoptown	.442	138	54	61	12	0	22	77	3
Matt Crowder, Hoptown	.390	123	44	48	9	1	5	26	4
Trey Fulton, Dubois Co.	.374	123	21	46	8	0	1	25	4
Nick Lugo, Owensboro	.369	111	34	41	15	0	2	26	19
Seth Woodard, Owensboro	.358	109	32	39	6	3	8	34	10
Genesis Hillard, Madisonville	.352	108	22	38	6	0	3	23	4
Zack Gray, Dubois Co.	.352	128	27	45	11	0	3	35	5
Chase Schmittou, Hoptown	.351	148	41	52	12	0	2	30	2
Grant Robbins, Hoptown	.348	155	27	54	11	2	2	41	5
Andrew Swanson, Fulton	.331	130	24	43	4	0	6	27	7

INDIVIDUAL PITCHING LEADERS

	W	L	ERA	IP	H	R	HR	BB	SO
Casey Queener, Hoptown	4	0	0.29	31	14	7	0	14	37
Renton Poole, Dubois Co.	5	1	0.74	49	24	7	0	23	57
Caleb Wagner, Dubois Co.	3	2	1.09	41	34	11	0	12	30
Seth Oliver, Hoptown	4	0	1.29	35	16	6	2	17	35
Seth Hougsen, Fulton	4	2	1.54	41	31	9	2	16	39

Chase Maddux, Hoptown	6	2	1.84	49	50	16	0	7	27
Austin Morgan, Owensboro	3	2	1.89	38	27	15	1	22	29
Brandon Dusenberry, M'ville.	6	1	2.59	49	39	16	4	8	34
Max Hall, Muhlenberg	0	3	2.64	44	40	22	1	17	35
Austin Schmitt, Owensboro	4	0	2.79	39	30	16	3	19	40

PERFECT GAME LEAGUE

Eastern Division	W	L	PCT	GB
Amsterdam Mohawks	34	15	.694	—
Albany Dutchmen	28	20	.583	5 ½
Mohawk Valley DiamondDawgs	27	20	.574	6
Oneonta Outlaws	24	24	.500	9 ½
Glens Falls Dragons	20	27	.426	13
Saugerties Stallions	14	34	.292	19 ½

Western Division	W	L	PCT	GB
Elmira Pioneers	33	15	.688	—
Utica Blue Sox	31	18	.633	2 ½
Jamestown Jammers	29	20	.592	4 ½
Newark Pilots	29	21	.580	5
Victor RailRiders	23	25	.479	10
Adirondack Trail Blazers	13	35	.271	20
Geneva Red Wings	9	40	.184	24 ½

Championship: Amsterdam defeated Utica 2-0 in best-of-three series.

INDIVIDUAL BATTING LEADERS

	AVG	AB	R	H	2b	3b	HR	RBI	SB
Chris Givin, if, Amsterdam	.383	133	29	51	6	0	2	14	11
Dale Wickham, if, Victor	.376	141	28	53	9	1	2	18	2
Drew Arciuolo, of, Mohawk	.371	140	24	52	3	4	1	23	20
Alex Thrower, of, Saugerties	.354	144	37	51	3	0	0	5	28
J.J. Shimko, of, Albany	.339	168	31	57	11	2	0	16	28
Mac Crispino, of, Mohawk	.336	143	16	48	12	2	0	27	1
Chuck Hooker, of, Adirondack	.329	143	20	47	10	2	1	18	5
Nick Russo, if, Victor	.327	156	26	51	11	1	1	28	5
Tristen Carranza, if, Amsterdam	.325	151	19	49	11	1	5	30	4
Justin Childers, util, Albany	.321	165	24	53	9	0	3	31	14

INDIVIDUAL PITCHING LEADERS

	W	L	ERA	G	SV	IP	H	BB	SO
Cameron Enck, Amsterdam	5	1	0.39	9	0	46	40	9	24
Austin Keen, Amsterdam	4	2	1.01	9	0	44	27	19	39
Brennen Smith, Victor	4	2	1.06	13	0	59	32	39	52
Evan Giles, Albany	3	2	1.50	8	0	42	31	17	37
David Palmer, Mohawk	4	2	1.81	9	0	54	53	10	46
Spencer Kulman, Elmira	3	3	2.03	8	0	40	40	19	27
Jesse Slinger, Adirondack	2	1	2.06	16	3	43	42	13	36
Nate Wrighter, Oneonta	3	3	2.11	11	0	42	38	23	26
Andrew Kneussle, Glens Falls	4	3	2.15	10	0	50	52	8	42
Joe Kelly, Jamestown	3	0	2.17	18	1	45	50	10	20

PROSPECT LEAGUE

Eastern Division	W	L	PCT	GB
West Virginia Miners	34	25	.576	—
Kokomo Jackrabbits	31	29	.517	3 ½
Lafayette Aviators	30	30	.500	4 ½
Butler BlueSox	29	31	.483	5 ½
Champion City Kings	27	33	.450	7 ½
Chillicothe Paints	23	37	.383	11 ½

Western Division	W	L	PCT	GB
Springfield Sliders	39	20	.661	—
DuPage Drones	35	24	.593	4
Terre Haute Rex	35	24	.593	4
Danville Dans	35	25	.583	4 ½
Quincy Gems	27	33	.450	12 ½
Hannibal Cavemen	13	47	.217	26 ½

CHAMPIONSHIP: West Virginia defeated Quincy 2-0 in best-of-three series.

TOP 10 PROSPECTS: 1. T.J. Collett, c, Terre Haute (Fr., Kentucky). **2.** Joey Polak, 3b/1b, Quincy (Fr., South Carolina). **3.** Aaron Meyer, 2b, DuPage (Sr., Missouri State). **4.** Brian Hobbie , rhp, Terra Haute (Jr., Indiana). **5.** Zane Collins, lhp, Champion City (So., Wright State). **6.** Jake Anchia, c, DuPage (So., Nova Southeastern, Fla.). **7.** Connor Coward, rhp, Butler (Jr.,

Virginia Tech). **8.** Tanner Allison, lhp, Chillicothe (Jr., Western Michigan). **9.** Jacob Belinda, rhp, West Virginia (Sr., Lock Haven, Pa.). **10.** Brendan Burns, rhp, Chillicothe (Jr., Ball State).

INDIVIDUAL BATTING LEADERS

	AVG	AB	R	H	2b	3b	HR	RBI	SB
Aaron Meyer, if, DuPage	.423	194	40	82	13	3	5	45	8
Niko Decolati, if, Terre Haute	.374	190	39	71	10	2	5	30	10
Quintin Crandall, if, Springfield	.344	212	45	73	24	2	2	29	17
Dan Ward, if, West Va.	.343	169	27	58	7	2	4	32	12
Will Schneider, of, Butler	.335	212	40	71	14	4	0	27	9
Lee Sponseller, of, Champ. City	.324	148	24	48	9	2	1	16	4
Austin Norman, of, West Va.	.324	219	39	71	19	6	3	45	20
Seth Soto, if, Hannibal	.318	151	17	48	10	0	1	14	3
Joey Fiske, of, Danville	.316	171	30	54	7	1	0	16	21
Griffin Harms, of, Kokomo	.314	207	29	65	5	3	0	18	8

INDIVIDUAL PITCHING LEADERS

	W	L	ERA	G	SV	IP	H	BB	SO
Brian Hobbie, Terre Haute	4	2	0.82	12	1	54	36	11	34
Andy Fisher, Champion City	4	1	1.71	12	0	58	42	16	53
Jacob Belinda, West Va.	5	1	2.06	10	0	52	31	25	69
Connor Coward, Butler	3	1	2.22	9	0	56	40	7	68
Andrew Quinn, Springfield	4	1	2.22	15	2	56	47	18	41
Austin Knight, DuPage	5	2	2.61	9	0	51	35	31	45
Mike Anthony, Kokomo	7	5	2.74	14	0	72	70	11	56
Pavin Parks, Butler	6	2	2.79	10	0	61	59	23	30
Andrew McDonald, Champ. City	2	5	2.80	12	0	70	44	23	68
Jake Haberer, Quincy	4	2	2.86	11	0	56	54	27	54

SUNBELT LEAGUE

Western Division	W	L	PCT	GB
Carrollton	24	9	.727	—
Marietta	16	13	.552	6
Phenix City	14	15	.483	8
Norcross	7	21	.250	14 ½

Eastern Division	W	L	PCT	GB
Atlanta	22	11	.667	—
Gwinnett	18	12	.600	2 ½
Brookhaven	13	16	.448	7
Alpharetta	4	21	.160	14

Prospect Division	W	L	PCT	GB
Titans	12	3	.781	—
Astros	11	5	.688	1 ½
Patriots	6	8	.433	5 ½
Braves	5	8	.385	6
Bucks	1	11	.083	9 ½

CHAMPIONSHIP: Atlanta defeated Carrollton 2-1 in best-of-three series.

INDIVIDUAL BATTING LEADERS

	AVG	AB	R	H	2b	3b	HR	RBI	SB
Nick Piccapietra, of, Astros	.408	49	10	20	6	0	0	11	1
Rodney Tennie, of, Brookhaven	.403	67	24	27	3	0	0	8	19
Austin Jackson, 2b, Braves	.395	38	10	15	2	0	2	4	4
Sylvester Toe Jr., p, Patriots	.385	39	9	15	2	1	1	9	1
Eric Furphy, 2b, Astros	.385	39	14	15	3	0	0	7	2
Jeremy Glore, of, Atlanta	.368	117	29	43	7	0	1	13	10
Jake Franklin, of, Norcross	.367	79	7	29	1	0	0	13	6
Hunter Phillips, of, Titans	.361	36	13	13	3	2	1	16	8
Tony Salvaggio, 3b, Gwinnett	.346	81	19	28	5	0	1	19	6
Jackson Hesterlee, of, Carrollton	.338	80	15	27	4	0	0	17	1

INDIVIDUAL PITCHING LEADERS

	W	L	ERA	G	SV	IP	H	BB	SO
Brooks Buckler, Atlanta	6	1	0.91	9	0	49	32	12	57
Mason LeBlanc, Braves	0	1	1.13	4	0	16	12	3	19
Evan Steele, Marietta	3	1	1.82	6	0	39	25	13	47
Liam Henry, Brookhaven	0	2	1.88	13	0	24	19	10	18
Austin Parrish, Atlanta	3	2	1.91	8	0	37	40	5	27
Zavier Lushington, Braves	1	1	2.08	4	0	21	20	11	17
Kevin Martin, Atlanta	6	2	2.36	9	0	53	47	9	45
Blake Marbut, Atlanta	4	2	2.39	9	0	52	52	5	33
Will Small, Brookhaven	2	2	2.52	8	0	25	20	5	19
Tyler Holcombe, Gwinnett	5	2	2.61	8	0	41	45	6	39

TEXAS COLLEGIATE LEAGUE

	W	L	PCT	GB
Brazos Valley Bombers	48	7	.873	—
Acadiana Cane Cutters	33	24	.579	16
Victoria Generals	28	28	.500	20 ½
Woodlands Strykers	16	40	.286	32 ½
Texas Marshals	15	41	.268	33 ½

CHAMPIONSHIP: Brazos Valley defeated Acadiana in championship game.

TOP 10 PROSPECTS: 1. Nick Anderson, of, Victoria (So., Texas A&M-Corpus Christi). **2.** MacGregor Hines, rhp, Brazos Valley (R-Fr., Florida). **3.** Willy Amador, rhp, Brazos Valley (Jr., Rice). **4.** Cobie Vance, 2b, Acadiana (So., Alabama). **5.** Garrett McCain, of, Brazos Valley (Jr., Oklahoma State). **6.** Mathew Guidry, 1b/3b, Acadiana (R-Fr., Southern Mississippi). **7.** Pedro Barrios, ss, Victoria (Sr., Tennessee Wesleyan). **8.** Zack McGuire, 1b, Brazos Valley (Jr., Michigan State). **9.** Chance Callihan, rhp, Victoria (R-So., Texas). **10.** Anthony Herrera, 2b/rhp, Brazos Valley (Sr., Louisiana-Monroe).

INDIVIDUAL BATTING LEADERS

	AVG	AB	R	H	2b	3b	HR	RBI	SB
Anthony Herrera, 2b, Brazos Val.	.363	171	33	62	20	2	0	30	18
Pedro Barrios, if, Victoria	.340	144	21	49	8	1	0	25	6
Matthew Guidry, if, Acadiana	.331	139	24	46	11	2	0	14	3
Hunter Wilson, ss, Brazos Val.	.324	139	27	45	1	0	0	21	18
Zack McGuire, if, Brazos Val.	.312	157	26	49	12	1	7	37	4
Trey Jimmerson, of, Acadiana	.304	158	23	48	7	0	1	26	7
Cobie Vance, if, Acadiana	.303	145	23	44	6	2	0	22	9
Trenton Buchhorn, if, Acadiana	.292	171	20	50	10	4	0	21	4
Nick Anderson, of, Victoria	.287	157	26	45	6	2	4	24	12
Logan Bottrell, of, Brazos Val.	.285	137	33	39	9	2	0	15	23

INDIVIDUAL PITCHING LEADERS

	W	L	ERA	G	SV	IP	H	BB	SO
Brett Seeburger, Brazos Valley	5	1	1.01	9	0	44	23	11	52
MacGregor Hines, Brazos Valley	5	0	1.16	10	0	46	36	14	43
Chance Callihan, Victoria	7	1	1.80	15	0	60	46	25	60
Hunter Neal, Brazos Valley	5	1	2.05	9	0	48	44	8	39
J.T. Jakubik, Woodlands	4	4	2.10	12	0	68	49	21	54
Wilmer Nunez, Acadiana	3	3	2.50	12	1	54	48	25	34
Michael Brawner, Victoria	6	2	2.67	14	0	54	41	39	48
Danny Garrett, Texas	3	5	2.77	12	0	78	77	24	42
Brian Browning, Acadiana	3	3	3.00	11	0	48	32	29	34
Chase Morris, Texas	2	8	3.57	16	0	75	75	27	26

VALLEY LEAGUE

Northern Division	W	L	PCT	GB
Strasburg Express	30	12	.714	—
Winchester Royals	23	19	.548	7
Front Royal Cardinals	21	21	.500	9
Purcellville Cannons	19	23	.452	11
New Market Rebels	18	24	.429	12
Woodstock River Bandits	11	31	.262	19

Southern Division	W	L	PCT	GB
Waynesboro Generals	30	12	.714	—
Harrisonburg Turks	27	15	.643	3
Covington Lumberjacks	22	20	.524	8
Staunton Braves	15	27	.357	15
Charlottesville TomSox	15	27	.357	15

CHAMPIONSHIP: Strasburg defeated Waynesboro 2-0 in best-of-three series.

TOP 10 PROSPECTS: 1. Corey Childress, rhp, Harrisonburg (Jr., Troy). **2.** Keegan James, rhp, Strasburg (So., Mississippi State). **3.** Brooks Crawford, rhp, Charlottesville (So., Clemson). **4.** Campbell Scholl, rhp, Waynesboro (Sr., Central Florida). **5.** Tanner Poole, of, Waynesboro (R-Jr., Mississippi State). **6.** Tripp Shelton, ss, Harrisonburg (Jr., UNC Greensboro). **7.** Zach Sterry, 1b/3b, Waynesboro (Sr., Oakland). **8.** Adam Sisk, of, Staunton (Jr., James Madison). **9.** Nick Ward, ss/2b, Woodstock (Jr., West Chester, Pa.). **10.** Jonathan Bowlan, rhp, New Market (So., Memphis).

INDIVIDUAL BATTING LEADERS

	AVG	AB	R	H	2b	3b	HR	RBI	SB
Nick Ward, if, Woodstock	.387	150	32	58	13	1	5	24	9
Danton Hyman, of, Woodstock	.360	111	23	40	6	0	0	13	12

Jonathan Pryor, of, Harrisonburg	.358	120	30	43	11	2	1	26	5
Zach Sterry, 1b, Waynesboro	.350	143	33	50	14	1	13	41	4
Carter Pharis, if, Strasburg	.342	155	35	53	13	1	5	30	5
Chase DeMars, 2b, New Market	.336	152	33	51	7	1	5	27	5
Devin Gearhart, 3b, Winchester	.336	149	32	50	8	0	0	25	21
Tanner Poole, of, Waynesboro	.333	156	49	52	7	5	6	27	21
Tripp Shelton, ss, Harrisonburg	.329	146	35	48	10	1	5	24	3
Raul Cabrera, ss, Purcellville	.326	135	18	44	2	1	2	17	2

INDIVIDUAL PITCHING LEADERS

	W	L	ERA	G	SV	IP	H	BB	SO
Campbell Scholl, Waynesboro	2	0	1.04	6	0	34	14	15	13
Erne Valdes, Front Royal	2	1	1.04	6	0	34	16	13	45
Benjamin Dum, Strasburg	4	0	1.42	7	0	38	27	6	32
Terrell McCall, New Market	3	0	1.60	8	0	39	25	13	39
Peyton Plumlee, Strasburg	5	0	2.46	9	0	36	27	17	30
Riley Arnone, Charlottesville	1	1	2.63	7	0	37	43	8	30
Stephen Xirinachs, Front Royal	5	2	2.74	8	0	46	29	19	33
Brandon Caples, Harrisonburg	4	2	2.77	7	0	55	49	9	35
Matthew Sullivan, Charlottesville	3	1	2.84	7	0	38	32	9	41
Corey Childress, Harrisonburg	6	2	2.88	9	1	56	54	10	52

WEST COAST LEAGUE

Northern Division	W	L	PCT	GB
Victoria HarbourCats	40	14	.741	—
Bellingham Bells	32	22	.593	8
Walla Walla Sweets	30	24	.556	10
Kelowna Falcons	25	29	.463	15
Wenatchee AppleSox	19	35	.352	21

Southern Division	W	L	PCT	GB
Corvallis Knights	34	20	.630	—
Yakima Valley Pippins	32	22	.593	2
Gresham GreyWolves	26	28	.481	8
Cowlitz Black Bears	23	31	.427	11
Bend Elks	21	33	.389	13
Kitsap BlueJackets	15	39	.282	19

CHAMPIONSHIP: Corvallis defeated Bellingham 2-1 in best-of-three series.

TOP 10 PROSPECTS: 1. Jared Horn, rhp, Bellingham (Fr., California). **2.** Cameron Bishop, lhp/of, Corvallis (Jr., UC Irvine). **3.** Willie MacIver, c, Walla Walla (So., Washington). **4.** Chris Murphy, lhp, Walla Walla (Fr., San Diego). **5.** Kenyon Yovan, rhp, Cowlitz (Fr., Oregon). **6.** Easton Lucas, lhp, Walla Walla (So., Pepperdine). **7.** Austin Shenton, 3b/of, Bellingham (Fr., Washington). **8.** Ryan Kreidler, ss/3b, Wenatchee (Fr., UCLA). **9.** Michael Toglia, 1b/of, Wenatchee (Fr., UCLA). **10.** Chase Kaplan, lhp, Corvallis (Jr., Kansas).

INDIVIDUAL BATTING LEADERS

	AVG	AB	R	H	2b	3b	HR	RBI	SB
Shane Hanon, of, Bellingham	.331	169	31	56	11	0	2	16	12
Willie MacIver, c, Walla Walla	.327	153	21	50	10	4	4	33	4
Ryan Smith, of, Gresham	.320	175	34	56	11	1	0	23	14
Freddy Smith, if, Yakima Val.	.317	180	28	57	9	1	1	20	16
Jeffrey Mitchell, of, Gresham	.312	141	18	44	7	1	0	11	13
Zak Taylor, c, Corvallis	.309	139	18	43	5	0	1	14	8
Andy Atwood, if, Corvallis	.308	172	26	53	5	0	1	25	19
Billy King, 1b, Bend	.306	147	21	45	5	1	3	22	0
Christian Koss, if, Yakima Val.	.306	180	28	55	9	2	1	22	12
Michael Toglia, util, Wenatchee	.306	170	27	52	10	5	7	40	8

INDIVIDUAL PITCHING LEADERS

	W	L	ERA	G	SV	IP	H	BB	SO
Zach Draper, Yakima Val.	8	0	0.73	12	0	74	57	23	53
Jake Brewer, Kitsap	1	2	1.56	9	0	52	58	9	27
Austin Dondanville, Victoria	6	1	1.72	11	1	52	33	10	43
Ryan Anderson, Walla Walla	3	1	1.84	9	0	44	27	17	30
Josh Mitchell, Victoria	7	0	1.87	13	0	62	51	9	61
Will McAffer, Victoria	6	2	1.99	12	0	54	34	26	58
Aaron Pope, Corvallis	4	2	2.08	10	0	43	29	9	38
Gavin Velasquez, Yakima Val.	7	2	2.12	11	0	76	64	15	38
Bobby Ay, Walla Walla	1	3	2.13	9	0	55	35	15	49
Donavon Ramirez, Gresham	4	3	2.20	11	0	49	37	31	33

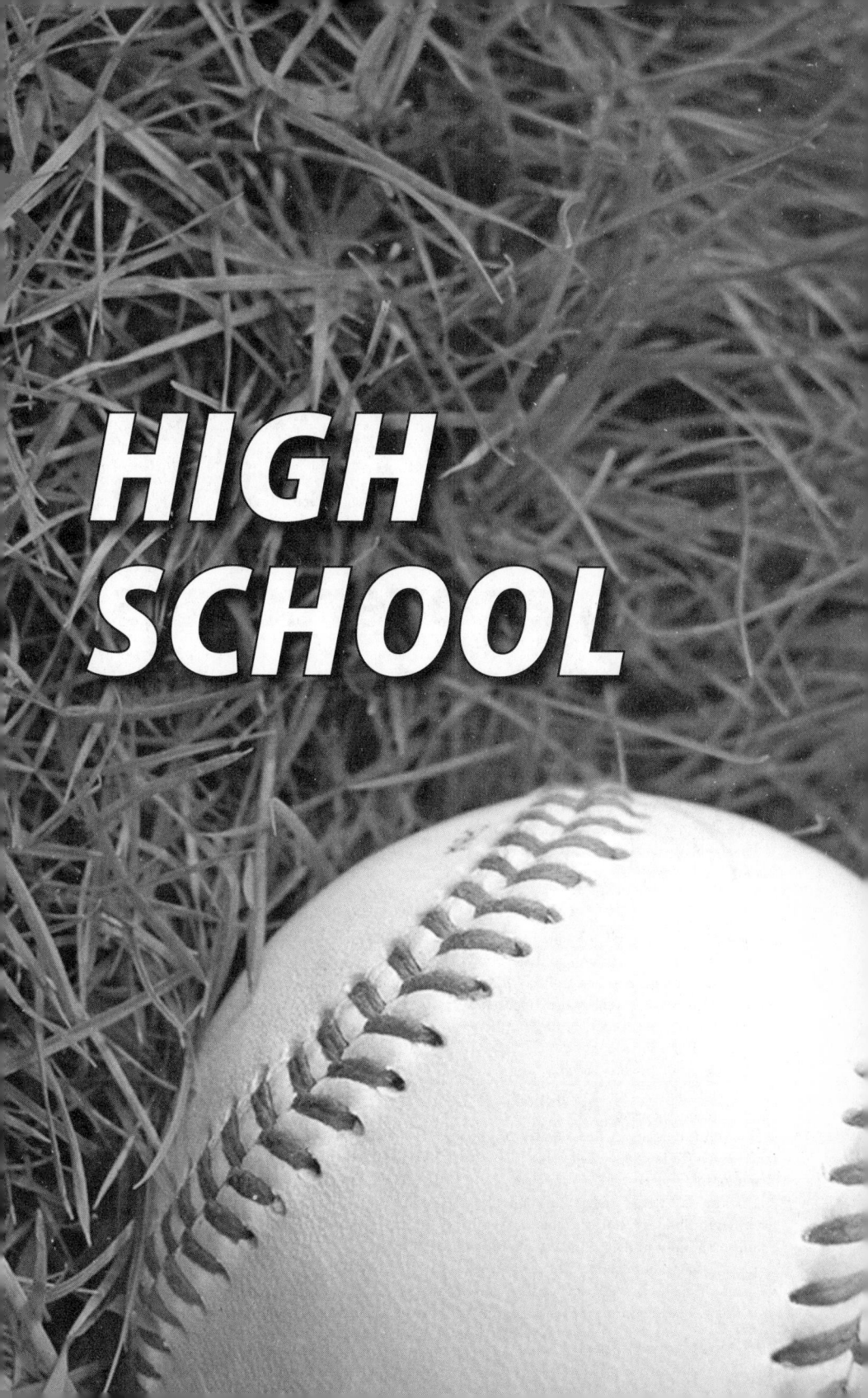

HIGH
SCHOOL

ALYSON V BOYER RODE

Douglas High lost ace Jesus Luzardo early but relied on star third baseman Colton Welker

Douglas overcomes loss to earn top spot

BY WILL BRYANT

A 27-2 record speaks for itself, but that record is more impressive when accomplished without the team's star player.

This is the case for the Baseball America High School Team of the Year, Stoneman Douglas High in Parkland, Fla.

Coming into the season, Stoneman Douglas was poised for a deep playoff run. Led by senior draft prospects Jesus Luzardo, a hard-throwing lefthander, and third baseman Colton Welker, the Eagles were ready. But in his fourth appearance of the season, their ace, Luzardo, injured his throwing arm. His season was done.

This was a tough pill to swallow for the Eagles, but co-captain Luzardo calmed the team's sails with a speech the day after his injury.

"He said, 'I'm gonna be fine—don't worry about me,'" coach Todd Fitz-Gerald said. "'Go win a championship for me and for yourselves.'"

Luzardo was a true leader this season for the Eagles, even without taking the mound. Eventually a third-round pick of the Nationals, Luzardo came to every practice throughout the year and rallied the team through his words and actions. Through his attitude, Luzardo inspired the whole team and gave them an added drive on the field.

"Our guys weren't going to let him go down without a ring," Fitz-Gerald said.

Welker added, "He always told us, 'I wish I could be out there with you,' and 'don't take it for granted.' We listened to him."

The team took these words to heart, becoming a close-knit unit throughout the season.

Coach Fitz-Gerald sees the camaraderie as a key component for the team's development of a winning mentality. From chilling out at home, to hanging together during class change at school, the team stayed close.

"These guys did everything together," Fitz-Gerald said. "They go into battle together, and never once worried or wavered or thought they were going to get beat.

"That is the mentality of a team with great confidence and character."

Still, the coaches and players alike knew the challenges that would come without their ace, but the goal of winning the championship was always there.

"Guys sold out, and bought into what we were doing," Fitz-Gerald said. "I felt like we had all the pieces to the puzzle."

One of the guys who bought in the most was senior utility man Joseph Bullion, whose primary role on the team was serving as a designated pinch-runner.

"He was actually the guy who held our team together," Fitz-Gerald said. "All he cared about was this team."

Bullion, a four-year player for the Eagles, thrived in his pinch-running role. But it was his work on the days without games that made the biggest impact. Fitz-Gerald praised his work ethic and constant effort despite his modest role.

It all paid off for Stoneman Douglas and Bullion—the senior scored the winning run in each of the last seven games for the Eagles. "He's the ultimate team player." Fitz-Gerald said.

Of course, the Eagles had more than just role players like Bullion. They had stars like Welker, a fellow senior.

Following his lead, the Eagles strung together 16 straight wins to end the season on top of the 9A circuit. Welker, a fourth-round pick of the Rockies, led both by example and performance, by hitting a cool .500 to go along with six home runs.

"I just wanted to finish my high school career with a bang and keep the winning tradition going at Douglas," Welker said.

In addition to Welker, the Eagles needed more players to complement Welker and make up for Luzardo's loss if they were going to achieve the championship. One of the more notable among those was Brandon Kaminer.

Kaminer was thrust into the spot of ace this season, a big leap from the being the anchor of the JV staff his sophomore year. The junior flourished in his new role.

"Brandon is competitor, he's fierce. I mean he shows no fear," Welker said. "The work he put in showed this year."

Kaminer went 12-0 this season, including a hard-fought 3-2 win over West Orange in the state semifinals.

"He took the role and ran with it," Fitz-Gerald said.

Behind the spirits of Luzardo, the work ethic of Bullion, and stars such as Kaminer and Welker, Stoneman Douglas rose to the top of Florida high school baseball. Brady Norris was another hero, closing the semifinal win for Kaminer, then tossing a complete-game shutout in the 3-0 state championship game win over Columbus High of Miami.

"It was either destined or meant to be," Welker said. "But we got it done."

The team rose to the top of Baseball America's rankings after not being in the preseason top 50 ranking, thanks in large part to the support and

Rk. School	Record
1. Douglas High, Parkland, Fla.	27-2
2. Buchanan High, Clovis, Calif.	30-1
3. Archbishop McCarthy, Southwest Ranches, Fla.	29-2
4. Walton High, Marietta, Ga.	28-4
5. Basic High, Henderson, Nev.	36-4
6. Bryant (Ark.) High	28-2
7. Canterbury High, Fort Myers, Fla.	31-1
8. Verdigris High, Claremore, Okla.	33-2
9. De La Salle High, Concord, Calif.	25-3
10. Barbe High, Lake Charles, La.	35-6
11. North Davidson High, Lexington, N.C.	28-2
12. Hamilton High, Chandler, Ariz.	27-7
13. Redondo Union High, Redondo Beach, Calif.	31-2
14. Christian Heritage Academy, Del City, Okla.	34-3
15. Houston County High, Warner Robins, Ga.	29-8
16. Steinbrenner High, Lutz, Fla.	27-5
17. Dallas Jesuit Prep	36-8
18. Jefferson High, Shenandoah Junction, W.Va.	33-3
19. Oxford (Miss.) High	28-8
20. Gaither High, Tampa, Fla.	24-6
21. Murrieta (Calif.) Mesa High	27-7
22. McCracken County High, Paducah, Ky.	37-5
23. Teurlings Catholic High, Lafayette, La.	35-4
24. St. Francis High, Mountain View	27-8
25. Cherokee Trail High, Aurora, Colo.	22-5
26. Shawnee Mission East High, Prairie Village, Kan.	21-4
27. Grapevine (Texas) High	35-6
28. Chantilly (Va.) High	27-2
29. Pope High, Marietta, Ga.	28-6
30. El Camino Real High, Woodland Hills, Calif.	28-7
31. Magnolia (Ark.) High	22-6
32. St. Thomas Aquinas High, Overland Park, Kan.	21-4
33. Elk Grove (Calif.) High	26-10
34. Carlsbad (N.M.) High	25-6
35. Shenendehowa High, Clifton Park, N.Y.	21-5
36. Seton Hall Prep, West Orange, N.J.	28-3
37. Locust (Ga.) Grove High	33-5
38. Lady Bird Johnson High, San Antonio	32-6
39. Riverdale Baptist High, Upper Marlboro, Md.	32-3
40. Zionsville (Ind.) High	30-4
41. JSerra High, San Juan Capistrano, Calif.	27-7
42. Madison (Miss.) Central High	27-10
43. St. Mary's Catholic High, Neenah, Wisc.	24-0
44. Creighton Prep, Omaha, Neb.	28-4
45. Calvary Christian High, Fort Lauderdale	21-9
46. Westminster School, Atlanta	30-6
47. Selah (Wash.) High	25-1
48. Mountain Ridge High, Glendale, Ariz.	26-6
49. Defiance (Ohio) High	29-2
50. Buford (Ga.) High	32-5

motivation from coach Fitz-Gerald.

"I pushed this team, cause I really think we're deserving," Fitz-Gerald said.

Fitz-Gerald is no stranger to coaching top-tier teams, having led American Heritage for 10 seasons in a span that included the careers of big leaguers such as Eric Hosmer, Adrian Nieto and Deven Marrero. He found something special in this one, the first state title for the school in baseball.

"I've been doing this a long time man, but this is my most special year," he said.

There has been little down time since the championship, with Luzardo and Welker being drafted

in the third and fourth rounds respectively. But now a few weeks later, Fitz-Gerald can look back.

"I haven't had time to sit back and reflect, and go over whole situation, but I can tell you this," Fitz-Gerald said. "This was probably the best team I've ever had."

He paused for a second, almost replaying the season in his mind.

"Not the most talented—but by far the best team I've ever coached."

Huntington Beach Wins NHSI

When the teams for the 2016 National High School Invitational were unveiled back in January, Huntington Beach (Calif.) High appeared to be the favorite. Huntington had power in the lineup, strong defense up the middle, and a pitching rotation that included three of the nation's most polished high school pitchers.

But one of those pitchers (lefthander Nicholas Pratto) was ineligible for the start of the season, and another (righthander Logan Pouelsen) injured his arm early in the season. After the Oilers lost to strong teams—JSerra Catholic and Orange Lutheran—they slid from No. 1 in the preseason high school rankings, and they were not voted into the Top 25 just before the NHSI started.

It wouldn't have surprised anyone if Huntington Beach struggled at the NHSI, but the team's experience and talent shined, and the Oilers overcame adversity to win the fifth annual NHSI, clinching the trophy with a 7-2 win over Chaminade College Prep (Canoga Park, Calif.). The championship means a lot to the program at Huntington Beach, which has slowly but surely developed into a regional and national force.

"It just keeps getting better and better, and I'm so proud of these guys," coach Benji Medure said. "We worked so hard for it and I think they deserve every bit of it. We beat a really good team; that Chaminade team's a great team."

Many of the Oilers' key contributors are well-known in the high school baseball scene: Hagen Danner's talent has been chronicled for years; Nick Pratto was a rotation stalwart for the 18U National team last summer; Landon Silver has shown excellent power potential for years. But in the NHSI final, a new talent emerged. Sophomore lefthander Nate Madole limited the potent Chaminade offense to two runs over 6.1 innings.

"My whole approach was to pitch to contact, because I knew I wasn't going to be able to blow anyone away," Madole said. "Especially with a great defense behind me like I had, I was really just looking pitch to contact and throw as many strikes as I could."

Madole set the tone for the Oilers, who laid on a steady offensive attack. Huntington Beach had eight hits, all from the first five spots in the lineup. They scored four runs in the bottom of the second, then tacked on one in the third and two more in the sixth.

"This tournament was like the culmination of everything that I've gone through in high school," said senior shortstop Chad Minato, who went 2-for-3 with a pair of runs batted in.

Chaminade made a valiant effort, squaring up Madole a few times, but the Eagles couldn't string hits together. Star outfielder Blake Rutherford went 1-for-3 with a double and a walk in the loss.

"I feel like as a team we were really putting pressure on them today," Minato said. "That's what we've been trying to do this whole year, but I feel like at this tournament we really figured it out, we really came together and started hitting together and putting pressure on the other team."

Use Of Pitch Limits Spreads

In August, the Georgia High School Association adopted new pitch count rules that will take effect for the 2017 season.

It's a decision that high school associations around the country would be making in the coming months after the National High School Federation announced that states must implement pitch count limits for high school pitchers. In the past, most states have relied on innings limits.

The National High School Federation left each individual state organization to create its own pitch limits, but it required all 50 states to create pitch limits of some sort before the 2017 season begins.

Georgia's new rules will limit any varsity pitcher to no more than 110 pitches. Pitchers will be able to finish facing a batter even if that means they go beyond 110 pitches. The new rules for Georgia will also mandate three days of rest after any outing of 86 or more pitches, two days of rest after 61-85 pitches, one day of rest for 35-60 pitches. Pitchers who throw less than 35 pitches can pitch again the next day. According to the Macon (Ga.) Telegraph, pitchers would also be limited to no more than 120 pitches in any postseason tournament unless the series was extended because of poor weather.

The Georgia regulations are less strict than those recommended by USA Baseball's Pitch Smart guidelines that were developed with input from Major League Baseball and doctors. Pitch Smart recommends that no 17-to-18-year-old should throw more than 105 pitches while 15-to-16-year-olds should be limited to 95 or fewer pitches. Pitch Smart's guidelines also recommend four days of rest after any outing where a pitcher throws more

than 76 pitches. GHSA's new rules would allow a pitcher to return after only two days off if they threw 75-80 pitches.

Arkansas also adopted pitch limits. The Arkansas Athletics Activities board's new rules limit pitchers to 110 pitches in any outing. Pitchers throwing more than 86 pitches they are required to have three days of rest before pitching again. Those throwing 61-85 pitches have to have two days of rest, while pitchers need one day of rest after throwing 31-60 pitches.

Some states already adopted pitch count limits before the NHSF's mandate. Alabama went from having very lax innings limits to being ahead of the curve in adopting pitch limits in the fall of 2015. But the majority of states have depended on innings limits. And those limits have often given pitchers and coaches the leeway to throw a heavier workload than any big league pitcher would be allowed to throw today. As Minnesota State High School League associate director Kevin Merkle noted to the Grand Forks (N.D.) Herald, the old rules in Minnesota allowed a high school pitcher to legally throw 35 innings over a seven-day period.

In Kansas, a pitcher threw 157 pitches in a 10-inning outing in the 2015 playoffs. He and his coach were suspended because the 10-inning outing exceeded state rules that at the time limited pitchers to nine innings in any one game. But if he had been pulled after the ninth inning, he would have been within Kansas' current guidelines.

The push for pitch counts to replace innings limits has been going on around amateur baseball for much of the past decade. Little League Baseball replaced innings limits with pitch counts in 2007. In recent years, USA Baseball, Perfect Game, Baseball Factory and multiple summer collegiate leagues have adopted Pitch Smart's guidelines as far as days of rest and pitch limits.

Showcase Season

When Andy Partin arrived in Jupiter, Fla., he believed his team was going to win the World Wood Bat Association Championship. The owner of Dirtbags Baseball and the head coach of the program's top team, Partin knew his roster. He knew they had what it took to win.

Partin had seen his team develop throughout the summer and fall. Some teams might be more talented than his, but Partin believed in the Dirtbags' chemistry and he knew that his players weren't going to go down without a fight. The Dirtbags proved Partin's intuition right, winning the championship with a 4-2 victory over Team Elite Prime.

The WWBA Championship, colloquially known as "Jupiter," is a unique event. Played annually in late October, it's the most heavily scouted tournament in amateur baseball and it's the most prestigious travel baseball event.

There's really no restriction on how teams can be assembled, so many top travel programs will recruit players from around the nation to play for their teams just in Jupiter. There are also scout teams, which are sponsored by major league teams. Scouts build rosters of players who they're interested in seeing, and so they tend to be filled with talent. Teams get to know how players approach game situations and how they handle a competitive environment.

But that's not how the Dirtbags operate. Players primarily from the Carolinas and Tennessee come up through their program for years. Out-of-state players do join the program, but the Dirtbags assemble one team for the summer and fall, and they develop chemistry over the course of months.

"This is our team. This is the team we play with in the summer," Partin said. "It's hard to beat a team like us, because we're a team. We know each other. We know exactly what our guys can do."

This year's Dirtbags brought to Jupiter a unique blend of talent and chemistry. While some of their players lack the prototypical tools or body types to profile as professionals out of high school, the Dirtbags had plenty of players who showed the ability to make a difference in the games.

Davis Schneider (Eastern High, Voorhees, N.J.) proved to be the star of the tournament; following the championship game, he was named the tournament's MVP.

Schneider's dominant week began in the opening game. After doubling in the fifth inning, Schneider reached on a successful bunt to load the bases in the seventh inning. The Dirtbags would score a run and tie that game; without that run, the team's entire week would have been different. Over the course of the week, Schneider went 9-for-22 and swatted two home runs and five doubles.

"Ripping the fastball," Schneider said when asked what was working for him. "I felt like I was seeing the ball really well."

The pitching staff was equally effective, allowing just nine runs in the eight non-exhibition games. The Dirtbags had a talented group, headlined by righthander Mason Hickman, a top prospect who is committed to Vanderbilt. Hickman was named the Co-Most Valuable Pitcher in the tournament, along with Team Elite Prime righthander Ethan Hankins.

■ It's hard to have a better game than Heliot Ramos did at Wrigley Field in the Under Armour All-America Game on July 23. He went 3-for-3 and finished a double short of a cycle to be named

USA BASEBALL

Event	Site	Champion	Runner-up
Tournament of Stars (18 & Under)	Cary, N.C.	Brave	Free
USA Baseball 17U—East	Jupiter, Fla.	Dallas Patriots 17U Stout	ScorpSouth 2018 Prime
USA Baseball 17U—West	Goodyear, Ariz.	CBA Marucci	California Bears
USA Baseball 15U—East	Jupiter, Fla.	US Elite	Elite Squad 15U Prime
USA Baseball 15U—West	Goodyear, Ariz.	Padres Scout Team	Saddleback Cowboys Black
USA Baseball 14U—East	Jupiter, Fla.	Adidas All-American	Florida Legends 14U
USA Baseball 14U—West	Goodyear, Ariz.	Pacific Baseball Academy	First Pitch Gamers

ALL-AMERICAN AMATEUR BASEBALL ASSOCIATION (AAABA)

Event	Site	Champion	Runner-up
World Series (21U)	Johnstown, Pa.	Zanesville Jr. Pioneers	Johnstown-2 Paul Carpenter Capital Advisors

AMATEUR ATHLETIC UNION (AAU)

Event	Site	Champion	Runner-up
9U	Orlando	East Cobb Astros	Tomateros de California
10U	Orlando	PG Select Bluesox	Oakleaf Knights
11U Diamond (70-foot)	Orlando	Florida Pokers	TC Crusaders
11U Gold (70-foot)	Orlando	Georgia Bombers McNellie	West Florida Eagles
12U	Orlando	Bayas Puerto Rico	Panthers OF Kissimmee
13U Diamond (90-foot)	Orlando	Florida Redhawks	CBC Riverhawks Black
13U Gold (90-foot)	Orlando	South Forsyth Giants	Oakleaf Knights
14U	Sarasota, Fla.	API Elite	SBO The Family
15U	Sarasota, Fla.	Cibeco Puerto Rico	Pride Baseball
16/17U	Sarasota, Fla.	Wiregrass Cardinals Red	Boston Blue Jays
18/19U	Sarasota, Fla.	Triton Rays	Georgia Eagles

AMERICAN AMATEUR BASEBALL CONGRESS (AABC)

Event	Site	Champion	Runner-up
Pee Wee Reese (12U)	Toa Baja, P.R.	PL Siege	Indians J.D. Puerto Rico
Sandy Koufax (14U)	Bartlesville, Okla.	Chicago White Sox ACE	Tigres de Puerto Rico
Ken Griffey, Jr. (15U)	Surprise, Ariz.	Colton Nighthawks	Tucson Champs
Mickey Mantle (16U)	Frisco, Texas	Knights Baseball	CT Outlaws
Don Mattingly (17U)	Surprise, Ariz.	D-BAT Robertson	D-BAT Schkade
Connie Mack (18U)	Farmington, N.M.	East Cobb Yankees and Dallas Tigers (Co-Champions)	
Stan Musial (19-and-over)	Waterbury, Conn.	Albany Athletics	Watertown Blaze

AMERICAN LEGION BASEBALL

Event	Site	Champion	Runner-up
World Series (19U)	Shelby, N.C.	Texarkana, Ark., Post 58	Rowan County, N.C., Post 342

BABE RUTH BASEBALL

Event	Site	Champion	Runner-up
Cal Ripken (10U)	Palm Beach Gardens, Fla.	Glen Allen, Va.	Norwalk, Conn.
Cal Ripken 12-year-old (60 feet)	Ocala, Fla.	West Palm Beach, Fla.	Palm Beach Gardens, Fla.
Cal Ripken 13-year-old (70 feet)	Aberdeen, Md.	Japan	Kennewick, Wash.
13-year-old	Ottumwa, Iowa	Mifflin County, Pa.	Pearl City, Hawaii
14-year-old	Westfield, Mass.	Tri-Valley, Calif.	Bismark, N.D.
13-15-year-olds	Williston, N.D.	Torrance, Calif.	Atlantic Shore, N.J.
16-18-year-olds	Ephrata, Wash.	Mobile, Ala.	Columbia Basin, Wash.

CONTINENTAL AMATEUR BASEBALL ASSOCIATION (CABA)

Event	Site	Champion	Runner-up
10U	Mason, Ohio	Chicago W. Englewood	Midland Seminoles
11U	Georgetown, Del.	Mid-Atlantic Shockers	Delaware Blue Hens
12U	Grapevine, Texas	Elite Squad	W. FL Hammerheads
13U (54/80)	Marietta, Ga.	E. Cobb Colt 45	Exposure Baseball
13U (60/90)	Boston	New England Nor'easters	Connecticut Capitals
14U	Boston	New England Ruffnecks	Cross Hit BB
15U (Aluminum)	Jacksonville, Ill.	Michigan Blue Jays	Tennessee Cross Hitters
15U (Wood)	Charleston, S.C.	Midland Tribe	Titans BB

the star of the game. Ramos didn't get a chance to try for a double as rain washed away the final two innings. After two delays, the game was called, giving the National a 5-4 win over the American.

Ramos wasn't the only star of a game that had plenty potential first-round picks in the 2017 draft. Outfielder Royce Lewis evened the game up in the top of the sixth with a home run that almost left the ballpark. But all that did was give Ramos another chance to shine with his home run to take the lead back Righthander Hunter Greene touched 97 mph (98 on the stadium gun) to tie Tyler Kolek's Under Armour game record for velocity in a very quick first inning as the American team starter. Righthander Shane Baz cruised through a scoreless inning of his own while showing very

16U (Aluminum)	Marietta, Ga.	Ontario Blue Jays	Georgia Jackets
16U (Wood)	Marietta, Ga.	East Cobb Astros 15U	East Cobb Athletics
16U (Wood)	Seattle	Enfuego Hawaii	Enfuego Washington
17U (Wood)	Charleston, S.C.	Knoxville Star Blue	Lexington BB
18U (Wood)	Charleston, S.C.	Midwest Prospects	Team Georgia
18U (Wood)	Seattle	Northeast Bandits	Mudville

LITTLE LEAGUE BASEBALL

Event	Site	Champion	Runner-up
Little League (11-12)	Williamsport, Pa.	Maine-Endwell (N.Y.)	South Korea
Junior League (13-14)	Taylor, Mich.	Taiwan	Kawaihau Community (Hawaii)
Senior League (15-16)	Bangor, Maine	Clear Ridge (Ill.)	Australia
Big League (17-18)	Easley, S.C.	Taiwan	Kihei (Hawaii)

NATIONAL AMATEUR BASEBALL FEDERATION (NBAF)

Event	Site	Champion	Runner-up
Rookie (10U)	Tuxedo Park, N.Y.	N.Y. Phenoms	N.Y. Bandits
Freshman (12U)	Hackensack, N.J.	Brooklyn Blue Storm	DB Razorbacks
Sophomore (14U)	Knoxville, Tenn.	Astro Falcons, Ohio	St. Louis Naturals, Mo.
Junior (16U)	Knoxville, Tenn.	Jackson Diamond 96ers, Miss.	Frozen Ropes Outlaws, N.Y.
High School (17U)	Knoxville, Tenn.	HCYP Raiders, Md.	Metro Senators, Va.
Senior (18U)	Struthers, Ohio	Astro Falcons, Ohio	Crab University, Md.

PERFECT GAME/BCS FINALS

Event	Site	Champion	Runner-up
13U	Fort Myers, Fla.	East Cobb Astros	Banditos Black
14U	Fort Myers, Fla.	Florida Stealth 14U Red	Texas Bombers Elite
15U	Fort Myers, Fla.	MVP Banditos	Florida Burn Platinum 2019
16U	Fort Myers, Fla.	Clutch	643 DP Baseball Academy-Mang
17U	Fort Myers, Fla.	Scorpions 2017 Black	Florida Burn Platinum 2017
18U	Fort Myers, Fla.	Team Elite 17's Prime	Florida Stealth 17U Red

PERFECT GAME/WORLD WOOD BAT ASSOCIATION SUMMER CHAMPIONSHIPS

Event	Site	Champion	Runner-up
14U	Emerson, Ga.	Roadrunners Baseball	Banditos Elite
15U	Emerson, Ga.	Banditos Black	EC Sox Prime-Snopek
16U	Emerson, Ga.	Elite Coast Sox Diamond	FTB55 Elite
17U	Emerson, Ga.	FTB Tucci	South Charlotte Panthers 2017
18U	Emerson, Ga.	East Cobb Astros	East Cobb Yankees

PONY BASEBALL

Event	Site	Champion	Runner-up
Mustang 9U	Walnut, Calif.	Emerald, Calif.	Mexico
Mustang 10U	Youngsville, La.	Simi Valley, Calif.	Mexico
Bronco 11U	Chesterfield, Va.	Placentia, Calif.	Richmond, Va.
Bronco 12U	Los Alamitos, Calif.	Taiwan	Puerto Rico
Pony 13U	Whittier, Calif.	El Cajon, Calif.	Panama
Pony 14U	Washington, Pa.	Taiwan	Maui, Hawaii
Colt (15-16)	Lafayette, Ind.	Mexico	Lafayette, Ind.
Palomino (17-18)	Santa Clara, Calif.	Lafayette, L.A.	Santa Clara, Calif.

REVIVING BASEBALL IN INNER CITIES (RBI)

Event	Site	Champion	Runner-up
Junior (13-15)	Cincinnati	Chicago White Sox RBI	Atlanta Metro RBI
Senior (16-18)	Cincinnati	Arizona RBI	Passaic RBI

U.S. SPECIALTY SPORTS ASSOCIATION (USSSA)

Event	Site	Champion	Runner-up
10U/Majors Elite	Orlando	San Diego Show	Wilson MVP
11U/Majors Elite	Orlando	Pico Pride	Cen Cal Prospects
12U/Majors Elite	Orlando	Lamorinda Trojans	Chino Hills Storm 12U
13U/Majors Elite	Orlando	Cali Rays	FCBA Titans Black
14U/Majors Elite	Orlando	SHV Hustle Elite	GBG I.E.

good feel for his 82-84 mph slider.

■ The Yankees' Andrew Papantonis (Delbarton High, Morristown, N.J.) and Rangers lefthander Russell Smith (Midlothian High, Texas) were honored as the outstanding players for the 2016 Area Code Games.

Papantonis finished the Area Codes with four hits and three RBIs, including a home run. But it was his defensive skills at shortstop that set him apart over the five games. According to scouts, Papantonis raised his stock as much as any player over the Area Code Games. Smith struck out eight batters over four innings, while only giving up three hits. The 6-foot-9 lefty was able to translate his physical tools into dominant performances at the ACG.

Moniak's bat does the talking

BY HUDSON BELINSKY

Justin Machado and Matt Moniak go way back. They were high school baseball teammates, and they've remained close. They've even vacationed together. Justin, who is the head coach at La Costa Canyon High in Carlsbad, Calif., remembers fondly one excursion, a surfing trip to Fiji.

The Machado family is really into surfing. Justin's brother Rob is one of the most famous surfers in the world. It would have been easy for Justin to get lost in the waves, but on that particular trip, Justin recalls watching a young Mickey Moniak in his element.

"I actually saw him play Wiffle ball on the beach with a bunch of other kids," Machado said, "and I remember thinking, 'That kid looks pretty damn good.'"

Several years later, Moniak was on his way to being the No. 1 overall pick in the draft, and he was the Baseball America High School Player of the Year for 2016.

In his senior season at La Costa Canyon, Moniak hit .476 (50-for-105), smacking six home runs and barreling a San Diego record 12 triples. In arguably the most competitive high school environment in the country, with hoards of scouts watching every game and every practice, Moniak not only kept his cool, but he elevated his game.

The knock on Moniak entering the spring was that he hadn't hit for much power, but that changed this year. He hit the weight room and packed on additional muscle. "I felt a lot stronger than I have in previous years, and I think that showed a little bit when it came to the power side of things," Moniak said.

Though his six home runs don't necessarily point toward a future of exceptional power, he's able to hit the ball with more authority.

Machado said the dimensions of La Costa Canyon's home field are bigger than many pro parks. "If he played at some other field in our league, he probably would have hit 12-15 (home runs)," Machado said.

With his jolt of power, Moniak became a true five-tool talent. He's a gifted defender in center field. He has speed and he can throw, though some scouts consider his arm fringe-average. His ability to hit is universally lauded, however, and the Phillies chose Moniak with

PLAYER OF THE YEAR

PREVIOUS WINNERS

1992: Preston Wilson, of/rhp, Bamberg-Ehrhardt (S.C.) HS
1993: Trot Nixon, of/lhp, New Hanover HS, Wilmington, N.C.
1994: Doug Million, lhp, Sarasota (Fla.) HS
1995: Ben Davis, c, Malvern (Pa.) Prep
1996: Matt White, rhp, Waynesboro Area (Pa.) HS
1997: Darnell McDonald, of, Cherry Creek HS, Englewood, Colo.
1998: Drew Henson, 3b/rhp, Brighton (Mich.) HS
1999: Josh Hamilton, of/lhp, Athens Drive HS, Raleigh, N.C.
2000: Matt Harrington, rhp, Palmdale (Calif.) HS
2001: Joe Mauer, c, Cretin-Derham Hall HS, St. Paul, Minn.
2002: Scott Kazmir, lhp, Cypress Falls HS, Houston
2003: Jeff Allison, rhp, Veterans Memorial HS, Peabody, Mass.
2004: Homer Bailey, rhp, LaGrange (Texas) HS
2005: Justin Upton, ss, Great Bridge HS, Chesapeake, Va.
2006: Adrian Cardenas, ss/2b, Mons. Pace HS, Opa Locka, Fla.
2007: Mike Moustakas, ss, Chatsworth (Calif.) HS
2008: Ethan Martin, rhp/3b, Stephens County HS, Toccoa, Ga.
2009: Bryce Harper, c, Las Vegas HS
2010: Kaleb Cowart, rhp/3b, Cook HS, Adel, Ga.
2011: Dylan Bundy, rhp, Owasso (Okla.) HS
2012: Byron Buxton, of, Appling County HS, Baxley, Ga.
2013: Clint Frazier, of, Loganville (Ga.) HS
2014: Alex Jackson, of, Rancho Bernardo (Calif.) HS
2015: Kyle Tucker, of, Plant HS, Tampa

the first overall pick of the 2016 draft. He joins three others—Josh Hamilton (1999), Joe Mauer (2001) and Justin Upton (2005)—to win the High School POY award and be selected No. 1 overall in the draft.

Moniak first realized he had potential when he made the varsity squad at La Costa Canyon as a freshman, when he was not in the same place physically as some of his upperclass teammates, either there or with USA Baseball's 15U roster that summer.

Nevertheless, Moniak fit in right away. "He just always let his play do the talking for him, and they respected him right off the bat," Machado said. "He won their respect right off the bat."

No one would blame Moniak lost some humility as a result of his success, but that hasn't happened. In fact, Moniak pointed to maintaining a winning attitude as key to his prep success, which includes gold with USA Baseball's 18U national team in 2015.

"Personally, I'd rather go 0-for-4 and win then go 4-for-4 with four home runs and lose," he said. "I think that whole mindset is what separates the good players from the great players."

ALL-AMERICA TEAM

Thomas Dillard

Taylor Trammell

PHOTOS BY MIKE JANES

FIRST TEAM

Pos.	Name	High School	Yr.	AVG	AB	R	H	2B	3B	HR	RBI	SB	Drafted
C	Payton Henry	Pleasant Grove (Utah) HS	Sr.	.519	52	12	27	6	0	7	30	1	Brewers (6)
1B	Spencer Brickhouse	Bunn (N.C.) HS	Sr.	.516	64	39	33	6	2	13	38	12	Undrafted
MIF	Bo Bichette	Lakewood HS, St. Petersburg, Fla.	Sr.	.576	66	47	38	7	5	13	41	21	Blue Jays (2)
MIF	Gavin Lux	Indian Trail HS, Kenosha, Wis.	Sr.	.524	82	46	43	9	3	6	30	23	Dodgers (1)
3B	Josh Lowe	Pope HS, Marietta, Ga.	Sr.	.383	94	53	36	9	4	11	39	13	Rays (1)
OF	Blake Rutherford	Chaminade College Prep, Canoga Park, Calif.	Sr.	.577	78	34	45	13	1	4	9	17	Yankees (1)
OF	Mickey Moniak	La Costa Canyon HS, Carlsbad, Calif.	Sr.	.476	105	40	50	4	12	7	46	11	Phillies (1)
OF	Taylor Trammell	Mount Paran Christian School, Kennesaw, Ga.	Sr.	.514	72	45	37	7	3	9	26	29	Reds (1s)
UT	Kyle Muller	Dallas Jesuit Prep	Sr.	.390	146	41	57	9	5	15	52	20	Braves (2)

Pos.	Name	High School	Yr.	W	L	ERA	G	SV	IP	H	BB	SO	Drafted
RHP	Gianluca Dalatri	Christian Brothers Academy, Lincroft, N.J.	Sr.	9	0	0.42	10	0	67	27	4	121	Rockies (40)
LHP	Braxton Garrett	Florence (Ala.) HS	Sr.	6	2	0.54	12	0	65	31	15	131	Marlins (1)
RHP	Riley Pint	St. Thomas Aquinas HS, Overland Park, Kan.	Sr.	7	1	0.43	—	0	49	21	25	87	Rockies (1)
RHP	Joey Wentz	Shawnee Mission East HS, Prairie Village, Kan.	Sr.	9	0	0.00	10	0	51	7	12	104	Braves (1s)
RHP	Forrest Whitley	Alamo Heights HS, San Antonio	Sr.	10	1	0.28	12	0	75	23	16	137	Astros (1)
UT	Kyle Muller	Dallas Jesuit Prep	Sr.	9	0	0.25	—	0	83	29	19	142	Braves (2)

SECOND TEAM

Pos.	Name	High School	Yr.	AVG	AB	R	H	2B	3B	HR	RBI	SB	Drafted
C	Thomas Dillard	Oxford (Miss.) HS	Sr.	.438	96	31	42	5	4	16	49	0	Undrafted
1B	Christian Jones	Federal Way (Wash.) HS	Sr.	.431	72	33	31	9	2	6	30	12	Red Sox (31)
MIF	Tyler Fitzgerald	Rochester (Ill.) HS	Sr.	.500	94	54	47	15	2	9	31	41	Red Sox (30)
MIF	Nolan Jones	Holy Ghost Prep, Bensalem, Pa.	Sr.	.630	46	28	29	5	2	6	27	19	Indians (2)
3B	Colton Welker	Douglas HS, Parkland, Fla.	Sr.	.500	86	33	43	11	2	6	24	10	Rockies (4)
OF	Akil Baddoo	Salem HS, Conyers, Ga.	Sr.	.429	77	—	33	5	8	1	—	30	Twins (2s)
OF	Will Benson	The Westminster Schools, Atlanta	Sr.	.454	97	50	44	11	0	8	41	11	Indians (1)
OF	Alex Kirilloff	Plum HS, Pittsburgh	Sr.	.519	79	36	41	15	4	4	28	—	Twins (1)
UT	Grant Gambrell	Buchanan HS, Clovis, Calif.	Sr.	.363	102	21	37	9	0	5	35	0	Undrafted

Pos.	Name	High School	Yr.	W	L	ERA	G	SV	IP	H	BB	SO	Drafted
RHP	Ian Anderson	Shenendehowa HS, Clifton Park, N.Y.	Sr.	4	1	0.60	7	1	35	17	7	47	Braves (1)
RHP	Kevin Gowdy	Santa Barbara (Calif.) HS	Sr.	5	1	1.09	10	0	64	42	6	104	Phillies (2)
LHP	Jason Groome	Barnegat (N.J.) HS	Sr.	2	3	0.77	—	0	40	15	14	90	Red Sox (1)
RHP	Jared Horn	Vintage HS, Napa, Calif.	Sr.	9	2	0.67	13	2	74	34	17	124	Brewers (20)
LHP	Ryan Rolison	University School, Jackson, Tenn.	Sr.	9	0	0.12	9	0	58	10	14	108	Padres (37)
UT	Grant Gambrell	Buchanan HS, Clovis, Calif.	Sr.	12	0	0.69	13	0	71	28	17	72	Undrafted

DRAFT

Phillies nab Moniak with draft's top pick

BY TEDDY CAHILL AND JOHN MANUEL

The Phillies wouldn't confirm it until right up until the eve of the 2016 draft on June 9.

Philadelphia had identified outfielder Mickey Moniak, out of La Costa Canyon High in suburban San Diego, as the potential No. 1 pick for months. And as predicted in Baseball America in the two weeks leading up to the draft, the Phillies executed their plan and selected Moniak first overall, making him the fifth San Diego-area player selected with the top pick since 2000.

"It's indescribable," Moniak said on the draft broadcast on MLB Network. "Kids dream to be drafted by an MLB team, but to be the No. 1 pick, it's insane."

This was the first year the Phillies had the first overall pick since 1998, when they selected Pat Burrell. Moniak is the first high school outfielder to go No. 1 since the Rays made Delmon Young the top overall pick in 2003. In all, eight prep outfielders have been the first overall pick.

Following Moniak off the board was Tennessee third baseman Nick Senzel, who went second overall to the Reds. The top-ranked prospect in the Cape Cod League last summer, Senzel established himself as the best college hitter in the draft.

Even though Senzel heard his name called early in the night, he still found the wait to be interminable,

"I tried to make it as simple as possible and keep myself occupied as much as possible," he

BILL MITCHELL

Picking first for the first time since 2008, the Phillies selected Mickey Moniak

FIRST-ROUND BONUS PROGRESSION

Teams continue to pay a premium for talent at the top of the draft. In 2016, teams paid first rounders an average bonus of $2,897,557, establishing a new record for the second year in a row. That marked an increase of 4.42 percent from last year and the fourth time in five years of this Collective Bargaining Agreement that first-round bonuses have increased.

After the first draft in 1965, first-round bonuses rose by an average of just 0.6 percent annually for the rest of the 1960s and 5.2 percent per year in the 1970s. Bonus inflation picked up in the 1980s, averaging 10.2 percent annually, and soared to 26.9 percent per year in the 1990s.

Below are the annual averages for first-round bonuses since the draft started in 1965. The 1996 total does not include four players who became free agents through a loophole in the draft rules.

YEAR	AVERAGE	CHANGE	YEAR	AVERAGE	CHANGE	YEAR	AVERAGE	CHANGE	YEAR	AVERAGE	CHANGE
1965	$42,516	—	1979	$68,094	0.20%	1993	$613,037	27.20%	2007	$2,098,083	8.50%
1966	$44,430	4.50%	1980	$74,025	8.70%	1994	$790,357	28.90%	2008	$2,458,714	17.20%
1967	$42,898	-3.40%	1981	$78,573	6.10%	1995	$918,019	16.10%	2009	$2,434,800	-1.00%
1968	$43,850	2.20%	1982	$82,615	5.10%	1996*	$944,404	2.90%	2010	$2,220,966	-8.80%
1969	$43,504	-0.80%	1983	$87,236	5.60%	1997	$1,325,536	40.40%	2011	$2,653,375	19.50%
1970	$45,230	3.90%	1984	$105,391	20.80%	1998	$1,637,667	23.10%	2012	$2,475,167	-6.70%
1971	$45,197	-0.10%	1985	$118,115	12.10%	1999	$1,809,767	10.50%	2013	$2,641,538	6.70%
1972	$44,952	-0.50%	1986	$116,300	-1.60%	2000	$1,872,586	3.50%	2014	$2,612,109	-1.10%
1973	$48,832	8.60%	1987	$128,480	10.50%	2001	$2,154,280	15.00%	2015	$2,774,945	6.23%
1974	$53,333	9.20%	1988	$142,540	10.90%	2002	$2,106,793	-2.20%	2016	$2,897,557	4.42%
1975	$49.33	-7.50%	1989	$176,008	23.50%	2003	$1,765,667	-16.20%			
1976	$49,631	0.60%	1990	$252,577	43.50%	2004	$1,958,448	10.90%			
1977	$48,813	-1.60%	1991	$365,396	44.70%	2005	$2,018,000	3.00%			
1978	$67,892	39.10%	1992	$481,893	31.90%	2006	$1,933,333	-4.20%			

DRAFT

said. "Today felt like a long one. It felt like during each pick that four minutes going by felt like the longest four minutes of my entire life. It's been a great week and I'm very, very honored and blessed to be in the position I'm in."

Prep pitchers Ian Anderson and Riley Pint, and Louisville outfielder Corey Ray rounded out the top five.

Moniak joins Adrian Gonzalez (2000), Matt Bush (2004), Stephen Strasburg (2009) and Brady Aiken (2014) as No. 1 overall picks from the San Diego area. He said he patterns his game after another San Diegan, Ted Williams, who coached Moniak's grandfather Bill in a six-year minor league career.

Before the year began, former Phillies general manager and team president Pat Gillick, now a senior advisor to team president Andy MacPhail, had told reporters that the organization's greatest need in the draft was pitching.

"Ultimately it's up to (scouting director) Johnny (Almaraz) and his group," Gillick was quoted as saying, "but if there's someone out there who could advance quickly and be in the big leagues in a short period of time, we should take a look at it."

Gillick was part of the group that worked with Almaraz, a group Moniak swayed to deviate from the pitching plan. Almaraz, in an interview four days after the draft, said the Phillies opened the scouting season with Moniak among a group of 20 players whom he and his staff singled out as potential No. 1 overall picks.

"This was the type of draft with a lot of talent and depth," Almaraz said. "There was good high school and college depth, and also lots of hitters and pitchers. We were looking for that one player to separate himself."

The Phillies eventually winnowed their list to five players who remained contenders. Almaraz later revealed the identity of four of those candidates: Moniak, Florida lefthander A.J. Puk, Mercer outfielder Kyle Lewis—the College Player of the Year—and California prep outfielder Blake Rutherford.

Almaraz, in his second year as Phillies scouting director, was picking No. 1 overall for the first time in his career. The same was true for Pat Gillick, who has been involved in every draft since the first one was held in 1965.

Almaraz's team of top evaluators also included former Phillies manager Charlie Manuel, now a senior advisor to GM Matt Klentak; special assistants to the GM Bart Braun and Charlie Kerfeld, player personnel special assistant Jorge Velandia and Benny Looper, the Phillies' senior advisor for international operations.

BONUS SPENDING BY TEAM

Teams combined to spend $267.4 million on draft bonuses in 2016, eclipsing the mark set last year. Teams' total expenditure on draft bonuses initially fell when a new Collective Bargaining Agreement changed the draft rules when it went into effect in 2012, but bonuses have now exceeded the level they reached under the old system.

The CBA that went into effect in 2012 curtailed spending by instituting harsh penalties for teams that exceed their bonus pools by more than five percent. It also ended the practice of awarding major league contracts to draftees. But as revenues within the game have increased, so too have the bonus pools MLB allocates to teams for the first 10 rounds. As a result, overall spending in the draft has been allowed to increase.

Teams at the top of the draft and those with extra picks get more money in their pools, so it's no surprise the Braves, Phillies and Padres led the industry in spending. The Phillies had the top overall selection, while the Braves picked four times on the first day of the draft and the Padres picked five times. While no team came close to the record for spending under the current CBA, held by the Astros in 2015, the next four highest expenditures all came this year. At the opposite end of the spectrum, none of the four teams that spent the least in this year's draft had a first round selection. The Cubs, Giants, Royals and D-backs all forfeited their top picks due to free agent compensation, shrinking the funds they had available to spend during the draft.

TEAM	2016	2015	2014
Braves	$15,516,300	$12,659,400	$5,069,800
Phillies	$14,990,300	$7,653,200	$7,187,800
Padres	$14,866,045	$4,892,100	$6,637,600
Reds	$14,679,100	$9,018,050	$7,929,900
Rockies	$11,649,200	$14,415,900	$8,853,800
Dodgers	$11,275,800	$7,363,600	$5,901,100
Brewers	$11,136,264	$8,352,600	$8,102,300
Athletics	$11,001,300	$6,381,000	$5,386,000
Cardinals	$10,493,300	$8,247,400	$7,613,800
White Sox	$10,061,500	$5,977,600	$10,460,600
Indians	$8,934,100	$8,461,880	$9,317,800
Nationals	$8,724,000	$4,982,800	$5,188,600
Mets	$8,654,501	$4,268,700	$6,488,800
Twins	$8,532,900	$7,154,400	$8,067,600
Orioles	$8,106,900	$7,031,200	$3,410,600
Red Sox	$7,947,500	$7,589,000	$7,814,800
Blue Jays	$7,871,100	$4,848,800	$9,308,700
Rays	$7,765,700	$7,946,400	$7,141,319
Mariners	$7,574,700	$5,368,600	$8,237,500
Angels	$7,322,600	$5,835,800	$6,387,500
Marlins	$7,219,900	$7,551,400	$13,112,900
Yankees	$7,123,000	$9,442,800	$4,050,200
Astros	$6,910,700	$19,103,000	$6,154,500
Rangers	$6,860,900	$10,728,300	$6,089,200
Tigers	$6,712,300	$7,606,700	$5,405,300
Pirates	$6,472,700	$8,485,000	$8,186,400
D-backs	$6,116,900	$12,270,900	$8,357,900
Royals	$5,047,000	$7,994,300	$9,888,700
Giants	$4,825,200	$8,865,300	$7,275,900
Cubs	$2,959,900	$8,335,700	$9,783,000
Total	**$267,351,610**	**$248,833,845**	**$222,809,919**
Average	**$8,911,720**	**$8,026,898**	**$7,426,997**

Looper was with the Mariners when they picked both Ken Griffey Jr. (1987) and Alex Rodriguez (1993) with the first overall pick, so Almaraz said he leaned on that experience and admitted the final decision wasn't made until hours before the first pick was announced.

"All of these high school hitters, we'd seen previously in the summer at Area Code (Games), and

what have you, and in the fall," Almaraz said.

"(Moniak is) the type of player who from the get-go, his physical maturity, we could see that he had gotten stronger, and he was getting stronger as the year progressed. We felt like he was one of the few middle-of-the-field players in the draft. He can impact the game on both sides because he can play a really good center field.

"We liked him and kept going back. We wanted to make sure we were evaluating efficiently."

Ultimately, Almaraz said, the Phillies took Moniak on talent, not because of financial savings. They bet on Moniak's bat, a hit tool that Almaraz said the Phillies graded as a 70 on the 20-80 scouting scale.

"It definitely started last summer," Moniak said. "I started to get (attention), guys coming to see me. I was going to Tournament of Stars, then I carried it through the fall and into the spring. It's been a fun senior season, and it's come down to this.

"I love to hit. Who doesn't love to hit?"

The other players the Phillies considered at

DANNY PARKER

Nick Senzel was the first college player drafted, going second overall to the Reds

HIGHEST BONUSES EVER

The 2016 draft saw just two players, Nick Senzel and Mickey Moniak, join the list of top bonuses. Three of the top five bonuses in draft history, including the record, came in the 2011 draft. Only seven bonuses from the last four years under the current CBA have made the list that runs 30 players deep.

PLAYER, POS.	TEAM, YEAR (PICK)	BONUS
Gerrit Cole, rhp	Pirates, 2011 (No. 1)	$8,000,000
Stephen Strasburg, rhp	Nationals, 2009 (No. 1)	*$7,500,000
Bubba Starling, of	Royals, 2011 (No. 5)	+$7,500,000
Kris Bryant, 3b	Cubs, 2013 (No. 2)	$6,708,400
Carlos Rodon, lhp	White Sox, 2014 (No. 3)	$6,582,000
Jameson Taillon, rhp	Pirates, 2010 (No. 2)	$6,500,000
Dansby Swanson, ss	D-backs, 2015 (No. 1)	$6,500,000
Danny Hultzen, lhp	Mariners, 2011 (No. 2)	*$6,350,000
Mark Appel, rhp	Astros, 2013 (No. 1	$6,350,000
Donavan Tate, of	Padres, 2009 (No. 3)	+$6,250,000
Bryce Harper, of	Nationals, 2010 (No. 1)	*$6,250,000
Buster Posey, c	Giants, 2008 (No. 5)	$6,200,000
Nick Senzel, 3b	Reds, 2016 (No. 2)	$6,200,000
Tim Beckham, ss	Rays, 2008 (No. 1)	+$6,150,000
Justin Upton, ss	D-backs, 2005 (No. 1)	+$6,100,000
Mickey Moniak, of	Phillies, 2016 (No. 1)	$6,100,000
Matt Wieters, c	Orioles, 2007 (No. 5)	$6,000,000
Pedro Alvarez, 3b	Pirates, 2008 (No. 2)	*$6,000,000
Eric Hosmer, 1b	Royals, 2008 (No. 3)	$6,000,000
Dustin Ackley, of	Mariners, 2009 (No. 2)	*$6,000,000
Anthony Rendon, 3b	Nationals, 2011 (No. 6)	*$6,000,000
Byron Buxton, of	Twins, 2012 (No. 2)	$6,000,000
Tyler Kolek, rhp	Marlins, 2014 (No. 2)	$6,000,000
Alex Bregman, ss	Astros, 2015 (No. 2)	$5,900,000
David Price, lhp	Rays, 2007 (No. 1)	*$5,600,000
Brendan Rodgers, ss	Rockies, 2015 (No. 3)	$5,500,000
Joe Borchard, of	White Sox, 2000 (No. 12)	+$5,300,000
Manny Machado, ss	Orioles, 2010 (No. 3)	$5,250,000
Zach Lee, rhp	Dodgers, 2010 (No. 28)	+$5,250,000
Joe Mauer, c	Twins, 2001 (No. 1)	+$5,150,000

*Part of major league contract.

+Bonus spread over multiple years under MLB provisions for two-sport athletes.

the top of the draft slid after Philadelphia passed. Puk, ranked No. 1 on the Baseball America Top 500 Draft Prospects, wound up falling five spots to the Athletics at No. 6. Lewis went 11th to the Mariners and Rutherford lasted until the Yankees grabbed him at No. 18.

One of the biggest stories on draft day was the slide of New Jersey prep lefthander Jason Groome, who had at one point been considered the top player in the class. He slipped to No. 12, where the Red Sox grabbed the high upside lefty. He said the Red Sox were his favorite team growing up and that "everything happens for a reason."

Puerto Rican shortstop Delvin Perez also fell on draft night after testing positive for a performance enhancing drug in MLB's predraft screening. Ranked No. 8 in the BA 500, Perez lasted until No. 23, where the Cardinals drafted him.

MLB Network analyst Harold Reynolds blasted the selection of Perez for "sending the wrong message" on a night when the sport is supposed to celebrate amateur baseball, but St. Louis, which won

a major league-best 100 games in 2015 and thus had the lowest draft position, saw value in Perez.

The Cardinals, who picked four times on the first night, also grabbed falling college righthanders Dakota Hudson at No. 34 and Connor Jones at No. 70.

The Padres drafted five times on the draft's first night. They started their night by drafting Stanford righthander Cal Quantrill eighth overall. He missed the whole spring as he recovered from Tommy John surgery and was regarded as one of the bigger wild cards in the draft as a result. Later in the night, they added Texas prep shortstop Hudson Sanchez and Kent State lefthander Eric Lauer with the 24th and 25th overall picks.

The first round ended with even splits of 17 high school and 17 college players, as well as 17 pitchers and 17 hitters selected. The most popular demographic wound up being college pitchers, with 10 selected.

Florida led all schools with five players drafted on the first day, which lasted 77 picks. Puk led the Gators, with teammates Dane Dunning (29), Logan Shore (47), Buddy Reed (48) and Peter Alonso (64) following.

Louisville nearly matched Florida, and had a quartet of players drafted on the first day. Ray went fifth overall to the Brewers, followed by Zach Burdi (26), Will Smith (32) and Nick Solak (62). Notably absent was righthander Kyle Funkhouser, who was selected 35th overall last year, but returned to school for his senior year and saw his stock dip. The Tigers drafted him the next day in the fourth round, 115th overall.

Texas A&M led all schools with 13 players drafted total, followed by Southern California's 12. The Aggies' top selection was outfielder Nick Banks, who was drafted in the fourth round by the Nationals. He went just ahead of catcher Jeremy Martinez, who became the Trojans' top pick when the Cardinals drafted him.

Let's Make A Deal

The draft system put into place in 2012 by the Collective Bargaining Agreement has taken much of the suspense out of the mid-July signing deadline, and this year's was the quietest yet. Just three first-round picks came close to the deadline, with only one, Marlins lefthander Braxton Garrett, signing on the July 15 deadline.

Not only did every first-rounder sign, a first since 2007, but the 2016 draft set a record low for unsigned picks in the first 10 rounds. Just two players—No. 41 overall selection Nick Lodolo, picked by the Pirates, and seventh-rounder Tyler Buffet, taken by the Astros—failed to sign.

NO. 1 OVERALL PICKS

YEAR TEAM: PLAYER, POS., SCHOOL	BONUS
1965 Athletics: Rick Monday, of, Arizona State	$100,000
1966 Mets: Steve Chilcott, c, Antelope Valley HS, Lancaster, Calif.	$75,000
1967 Yankees: Ron Blomberg, 1b, Druid Hills HS, Atlanta	$65,000
1968 Mets: Tim Foli, ss, Notre Dame HS, Sherman Oaks, Calif.	$74,000
1969 Senators: Jeff Burroughs, of, Centennial HS, Long Beach	$88,000
1970 Padres: Mike Ivie, c, Walker HS, Atlanta	$75,000
1971 White Sox: Danny Goodwin, c, Peoria (Ill.) HS	Did Not Sign
1972 Padres: Dave Roberts, 3b, Oregon	$70,000
1973 Rangers: David Clyde, lhp, Westchester HS, Texas	*$65,000
1974 Padres: Bill Almon, ss, Brown	*$90,000
1975 Angels: Danny Goodwin, c, Southern	*$125,000
1976 Astros: Floyd Bannister, lhp, Arizona State	$100,000
1977 White Sox: Harold Baines, of, St. Michaels (Md.) HS	$32,000
1978 Braves: Bob Horner, 3b, Arizona State	*$162,000
1979 Mariners: Al Chambers, 1b, Harris HS, Harrisburg, Pa.	$60,000
1980 Mets: Darryl Strawberry, of, Crenshaw HS, Los Angeles	$152,500
1981 Mariners: Mike Moore, rhp, Oral Roberts	$100,000
1982 Cubs: Shawon Dunston, ss, Jefferson HS, New York	$135,000
1983 Twins: Tim Belcher, rhp, Mount Vernon Nazarene (Ohio)	Did Not Sign
1984 Mets: Shawn Abner, of, Mechanicsburg (Pa.) HS	$150,500
1985 Brewers: B.J. Surhoff, c, North Carolina	$150,000
1986 Pirates: Jeff King, 3b, Arkansas	$180,000
1987 Mariners: Ken Griffey Jr., of, Moeller HS, Cincinnati	$160,000
1988 Padres: Andy Benes, rhp, Evansville	$235,000
1989 Orioles: Ben McDonald, rhp, Louisiana State	*$350,000
1990 Braves: Chipper Jones, ss, The Bolles School, Jacksonville	$275,000
1991 Yankees: Brien Taylor, lhp, East Carteret HS, Beaufort, N.C.	$1,550,000
1992 Astros: Phil Nevin, 3b, Cal State Fullerton	$700,000
1993 Mariners: Alex Rodriguez, ss, Westminster Christian HS, Miami	*$1,000,000
1994 Mets: Paul Wilson, rhp, Florida State	$1,550,000
1995 Angels: Darin Erstad, of, Nebraska	$1,575,000
1996 Pirates: Kris Benson, rhp, Clemson	$2,000,000
1997 Tigers: Matt Anderson, rhp, Tigers	$2,505,000
1998 Phillies: Pat Burrell, 3b, Miami	*$3,150,000
1999 Devil Rays: Josh Hamilton, of, Athens Drive HS, Raleigh	$3,960,000
2000 Marlins: Adrian Gonzalez, 1b, Eastlake HS, Chula Vista, Calif.	$3,000,000
2001 Twins: Joe Mauer, c, Cretin-Derham Hall, St. Paul	$5,150,000
2002 Pirates: Bryan Bullington, rhp, Ball State	$4,000,000
2003 Devil Rays: Delmon Young, of, Camarillo (Calif.) HS	*$3,700,000
2004 Padres: Matt Bush, ss, Mission Bay HS, San Diego	$3,150,000
2005 Diamondbacks: Justin Upton, ss, Great Bridge HS, Chesapeake, Va.	$6,100,000
2006 Royals: Luke Hochevar, rhp, Fort Worth (American Association)	*$3,500,000
2007 Devil Rays: David Price, lhp, Vanderbilt	*$5,600,000
2008 Rays: Tim Beckham, ss, Griffin (Ga.) HS	$6,150,000
2009 Nationals: Stephen Strasburg, rhp, San Diego State	*$7,500,000
2010 Nationals: Bryce Harper, of, JC of Southern Nevada	*$6,250,000
2011 Pirates: Gerrit Cole, rhp, UCLA	$8,000,000
2012 Astros: Carlos Correa, ss, Puerto Rico Baseball Academy, Gurabo, P.R.	$4,800,000
2013 Astros: Mark Appel, rhp, Stanford	$6,350,000
2014 Astros: Brady Aiken, lhp, Cathedral Catholic, San Diego	Did Not Sign
2015 Diamondbacks: Dansby Swanson, ss, Vanderbilt	$6,500,000
2016 Phillies: Mickey Moniak, La Costa Canyon HS, Carlsbad, Calif.	$6,100,000

*Part of major league contract.

Lodolo instead will attend Texas Christian, while Buffet will return to Oklahoma State. The Pirates will receive the 42nd overall pick in the 2017 draft as compensation for not signing Lodolo.

The previous record for fewest unsigned picks in the first 10 rounds was six, set last year and in 2014. In contrast, in the last year of the old system in 2011, 28 top-10-rounds picks did not sign, including three first-rounders. The fewest unsigned top-10-round picks before the current CBA was 14 in 2004.

As one scouting director put it: "All the shenanigans and action now take place on draft day."

With bonus pools that totaled more than $234 million, teams spent at least a collective $266,092,996, according to information obtained by Baseball America via industry sources. That includes bonuses in the 11th round and later, where any other signing of $100,000 or less doesn't count against the bonus pools.

The last three first-rounders to sign were all lefthanders, as is Lodolo, the highest unsigned selection. They all had different stories.

Garrett, the No. 7 overall selection, signed with Miami for $4,145,900, nearly $400,000 over the pool allotment for his pick. Signing Garrett and third-rounder Thomas Jones, a prep outfielder from South Carolina for $1 million, meant the Marlins spent their entire pool allotment, the first time they've done that.

Groome, expected by many to be the most contentious draft signing, instead agreed to terms with the Red Sox the night before the deadline for $3.65 million, less than the rumored pre-draft agreement he had with the Padres but well over Boston's allotment for the No. 12 overall pick of $3,192,800.

The only late-signing college first-rounder, Connecticut lefty Anthony Kay, signed for a below-slot deal with the Mets for $1.1 million. The allotment with the No. 31 pick was $1,972,100, but Kay signed the below-slot deal after a medical exam showed a problem with his elbow. He had Tommy John surgery on Oct. 4.

That left Lodolo, out of Damien High in La Verne, Calif., as the highest unsigned player in the draft. He took to Twitter on July 12 to announce, "I'm proud to officially be a Horned Frog!! Let's get back to Omaha."

It's not the first time the Horned Frogs have gotten the highest unsigned pick from the draft class. In 2009, TCU picked up lefthander Matt Purke after he and the Rangers had their deal rejected, and Purke led the Horned Frogs to their first trip to the College World Series the next year. After an injury-plagued career since then, he reached the

THE BONUS RECORD

Rick Monday, the No. 1 overall pick in baseball's first draft in 1965, signed with the Athletics for $100,000—a figure that no draftee bettered for a decade. The record has been broken many times since, with Gerrit Cole setting a new standard in 2011 when he signed for $8 million with the Pirates as the No. 1 overall pick and no draftee under the CBA has eclipsed him in the three years under the new rules. In fact, no signee during that timeframe has topped $7 million.

The list below represents only cash bonuses and doesn't include guaranteed money from major league deals, college scholarship plans or incentives. It also considers only players who signed with the clubs that drafted them and doesn't include draft picks who signed after being granted free agency, such as Bill Bordley ($200,000 from the Giants after the Reds selected him in the January 1979 draft) and Matt White ($10.2 million from the Devil Rays after the Giants chose him in the 1996 draft).

YEAR	PLAYER, POS., CLUB (ROUND)	BONUS
1965	Rick Monday, of, Athletics (1)	$100,000
1975	Danny Goodwin, c, Angels (1)	$125,000
1978	Kirk Gibson, of, Tigers (1)	$150,000
	* Bob Horner, 3b, Braves (1)	$162,000
1979	Todd Demeter, 1b, Yankees (2)	$208,000
1988	Andy Benes, rhp, Padres (1)	$235,000
1989	Tyler Houston, c, Braves (1)	$241,500
	* Ben McDonald, rhp, Orioles (1)	$350,000
	* John Olerud, 1b, Blue Jays (3)	$575,000
1991	Mike Kelly, of, Braves (1)	$575,000
	Brien Taylor, lhp, Yankees (1)	$1,550,000
1994	Paul Wilson, rhp, Mets (1)	$1,550,000
	Josh Booty, 3b, Marlins (1)	$1,600,000
1996	Kris Benson, rhp, Pirates (1)	$2,000,000
1997	Rick Ankiel, lhp, Cardinals (2)	$2,500,000
	Matt Anderson, rhp, Tigers (1)	$2,505,000
1998	* J.D. Drew, of, Cardinals (1)	$3,000,000
	* Pat Burrell, 3b, Phillies (1)	$3,150,000
	Mark Mulder, lhp, Athletics (1)	$3,200,000
	Corey Patterson, of, Cubs (1)	$3,700,000
1999	Josh Hamilton, of, Devil Rays (1)	$3,960,000
2000	Joe Borchard, of, White Sox (1)	$5,300,000
2005	Justin Upton, ss, Diamondbacks (1)	$6,100,000
2008	Tim Beckham, ss, Rays (1)	$6,150,000
	Buster Posey, c, Giants (1)	$6,200,000
2009	Donavan Tate, cf, Padres (1)	$6,250,000
	* Stephen Strasburg, rhp, Nationals (1)	$7,500,000
2011	Gerrit Cole, rhp, Pirates (1)	$8,000,000

*Part of major league contract.

major leagues for the first time in 2016.

Draft Trends And Tidbits

■ Nevada outfielder T.J. Friedl hit .401/.494/.563 this spring as a redshirt sophomore at Nevada, but went undrafted. He was invited to the trials for USA Baseball's Collegiate National Team, where his stellar performance won him a starting job on the team and made him the most coveted undrafted free agent in more than a decade. After he completed Team USA's summer tour through Taiwan, Japan and Cuba, the Reds signed Friedl to a $735,000 bonus, the largest ever for a domestic nondrafted free agent. The bonus is slightly more than the slot value assigned to the 85th overall pick in the draft.

Many of the players in this year's draft had strong family ties to the game, including Moniak and Quantrill. The first round also featured a pair of brother combinations reuniting in professional baseball. The Rays drafted Georgia prep third baseman Josh Lowe 13th overall and later grabbed his older brother, Nathaniel, a first baseman at Mississippi State, in the 13th round. The Nationals drafted Georgia prep shortstop Carter Kieboom, whose older brother, Spencer, made his big league debut for Washington in September. Righthanders Zack Burdi (White Sox first rounder) and Jordan Sheffield (Dodgers supplemental first rounder) also followed their brothers into professional baseball. The Blue Jays drafted in the second round Florida prep infielder Bo Bichette, the son of former all-star Dante Bichette and the younger brother of Dante Bichette Jr. Toronto also drafted Cavan Biggio, the son of Hall of Famer Craig Biggio. The A's selected JaVon Shelby, who follows in his two older brothers' footsteps to the minors and hopes to join his father John Shelby as a big leaguer. Later in the draft, Trey Griffey and Torii Hunter Jr., the football-playing sons of Gold Glove-winning center fielders went in back-to-back rounds. Hunter, who played both baseball and football at Notre Dame, went to the Angels in the 23rd round. The Mariners selected Griffey, who played wide receiver at Arizona, in the 24th round.

A few teams changed scouting directors following the draft. The Angels hired Cardinals crosschecker Matt Swanson to replace Ric Wilson, who was reassigned within the organization. The Blue Jays hired Red Sox assistant scouting director Steve Sanders after firing Brian Parker. The Mariners stayed in house for their replacement for Tom McNamara, who became a special assistant to the GM, promoting international crosschecker Scott Hunter to scouting director. The Brewers reshuffled their scouting department, promoting scouting director Ray Montgomery to vice president of scouting. Assistant scouting director Tod Johnson was promoted to scouting director.

BONUSES VS. PICK VALUES

Signing bonuses and assigned pick values have largely lined up since revamped draft rules were introduced as part of the Collective Bargaining Agreement in 2012. To give the worst teams extra spending power, the values for the selections at the top of the draft have been set higher than the perceived market value. In 2016, Braxton Garrett was the first player selected to receive more than pick value at No. 7. Six of the top 10 picks received less than pick value, and three signed for slot.

Ultimately, the top 50 bonuses added up to $132.3 million, a little more than $4 million more than what MLB assigned to those picks. By comparison, when MLB unilaterally determined slot recommendations in the last year of the previous CBA (2011), the total of the first 50 bonuses ($120.5 million) dwarfed that of the top 50 slots ($70 millon).

PLAYER, POS., TEAM (ROUND/OVERALL PICK)	BONUS	PICK VALUE
1. Nick Senzel, 3b, Reds (1st round/No. 2)	6,200,000	$7,762,900
2. Mickey Moniak, of, Phillies (1st round/No. 1)	6,100,000	$9,015,000
3. Riley Pint, rhp, Rockies (1st round/No. 4)	4,800,000	$5,258,700
4. Braxton Garrett, lhp, Marlins (1st round/No. 7)	4,145,900	$3,756,300
5. Corey Ray, of, Brewers (1st round/No. 5)	4,125,000	$4,382,200
6. A.J. Puk, lhp, Athletics (1st round/No. 6)	4,069,200	$4,069,200
7. Ian Anderson, rhp, Braves (1st round/No. 3)	4,000,000	$6,510,800
8. Cal Quantrill, rhp, Padres (1st round/No. 8)	3,963,045	$3,630,900
9. Jason Groome, lhp, Red Sox (1st round/No. 12)	3,650,000	$3,192,800
10. Matt Manning, rhp, Tigers (1st round/No. 9)	3,505,800	$3,505,800
11. Kevin Gowdy, rhp, Phillies (2nd round/No. 42)	3,500,000	$1,536,200
12. Zack Collins, c, White Sox (1st round/No. 10)	3,380,600	$3,380,600
13. Kyle Lewis, of, Mariners (1st round/No. 11)	3,286,700	$3,286,700
14. Blake Rutherford, of, Yankees (1st round/No. 18)	3,282,000	$2,441,600
15. Taylor Trammell, of, Reds (supp. 1st/No. 35)	3,200,000	$1,837,200
16. Forrest Whitley, rhp, Astros (1st round/No. 17)	3,148,000	$2,504,200
17. Joey Wentz, rhp, Braves (supp. 1st/No. 40)	3,050,000	$1,616,800
18. Alex Kirilloff, of, Twins (1st round/No. 15)	2,817,100	$2,817,100
19. Josh Lowe, 3b, Rays (1st round/No. 13)	2,597,500	$3,098,900
20. Will Benson, of, Indians (1st round/No. 14)	2,500,000	$2,973,700
21. Kyle Muller, rhp, Braves (2nd round/No. 44)	2,500,000	$1,459,700
22. Justin Dunn, rhp, Mets (1st round/No. 19)	2,378,800	$2,378,800
23. Gavin Lux, ss, Dodgers (1st round/No. 20)	2,314,500	$2,316,300
24. Will Craig, 3b, Pirates (1st round/No. 22)	2,253,700	$2,253,700
25. Nolan Jones, ss, Indians (2nd round/No. 55)	2,250,000	$1,159,200
26. Delvin Perez, ss, Cardinals (1st round/No. 23)	2,222,500	$2,222,500
27. T.J. Zeuch, rhp, Blue Jays (1st round/No. 21)	2,175,000	$2,285,100
28. Matt Thaiss, c, Angels (1st round/No. 16)	2,150,000	$2,660,800
29. Zach Burdi, rhp, White Sox (1st round/No. 26)	2,128,500	$2,128,500
30. Cody Sedlock, rhp, Orioles (1st round/No. 27)	2,097,200	$2,097,200
31. Cole Ragans, lhp, Rangers (1st round/No. 30)	2,003,400	$2,003,400
32. Eric Lauer, lhp, Padres (1st round/No. 25)	2,000,000	$2,159,900
33. Carter Kieboom, ss, Nationals (1st round/No. 28)	2,000,000	$2,065,900
34. Dane Dunning, rhp, Nationals (1st round/No. 29)	2,000,000	$2,034,600
35. Dakota Hudson, rhp, Cardinals (1st round/No. 34)	2,000,000	$1,878,000
36. Chris Okey, c, Reds (2nd round/No. 43)	2,000,000	$1,497,500
37. Reggie Lawson, rhp, Padres (supp. 2nd/No. 71)	1,900,000	$905,900
38. Jordan Sheffield, rhp, Dodgers (supp. 1st/No. 36)	1,847,500	$1,791,000
39. Will Smith, c, Dodgers (1st round/No. 32)	1,772,500	$1,940,700
40. Joe Rizzo, 3b, Mariners (2nd round/No. 50)	1,750,000	$1,252,100
41. Mason Thompson, rhp, Padres (3rd round/No. 85)	1,750,000	$730,400
42. Robert Tyler, rhp, Rockies (supp. 1st/No. 38)	1,701,600	$1,701,600
43. Daulton Jefferies, rhp, Athletics (supp. 1st/No. 37)	1,600,000	$1,745,700
44. Ben Bowden, lhp, Rockies (2nd round/No. 45)	1,600,000	$1,422,900
45. Anfernee Grier, of, D-backs (supp. 1st/No. 39)	1,500,000	$1,658,600
46. Logan Shore, rhp, Athletics (2nd round/No. 47)	1,500,000	$1,351,800
47. Brett Cumberland, c, Braves (supp. 2nd/No. 76)	1,500,000	$838,900
48. Jesus Luzardo, lhp, Nationals (3rd round/No. 94)	1,400,000	$635,800
49. Dylan Carlson, of, Cardinals (1st round/No. 33)	1,350,000	$1,909,500
50. Bryan Reynolds, of, Giants (2nd round/No. 59)	1,350,000	$1,090,000
Total	**132,316,045**	**128153600**

TEAM. PLAYER, POS., SCHOOL	BONUS
1. Phillies. Mickey Moniak, of, La Costa Canyon HS, Carlsbad, Calif.	$6,100,000
2. Reds. Nick Senzel, 3b, Tennessee	$6,200,000
3. Braves. Ian Anderson, rhp, Shenendehowa HS, Clifton Park, N.Y.	$4,000,000
4. Rockies. Riley Pint, rhp, St. Thomas Aquinas HS, Overland Park, Kan.	$4,800,000
5. Brewers. Corey Ray, of, Louisville	$4,125,000
6. Athletics. A.J. Puk, lhp, Florida	$4,069,200
7. Marlins. Braxton Garrett, lhp, Florence (Ala.) HS	$4,145,900
8. Padres. Cal Quantrill, rhp, Stanford	$3,963,045
9. Tigers. Matt Manning, rhp, Sheldon HS, Sacramento	$3,505,800
10. White Sox. Zack Collins, c, Miami	$3,380,600
11. Mariners. Kyle Lewis, of, Mercer	$3,286,700
12. Red Sox. Jason Groome, lhp, Barnegat (N.J.) HS	$3,650,000
13. Rays. Josh Lowe, 3b, Pope HS, Marietta, Ga.	$2,597,500
14. Indians. Will Benson, of, The Westminster Schools, Atlanta.	$2,500,000
15. Twins. Alex Kirilloff, of, Plum HS, Pittsburgh	$2,817,100
16. Angels. Matt Thaiss, c, Virginia	$2,150,000
17. Astros. Forrest Whitley, rhp, Alamo Heights HS, San Antonio.	$3,148,000
18. Yankees. Blake Rutherford, of, Chaminade College Prep HS, Canoga Park., Calif.	$3,282,000
19. Mets. Justin Dunn, rhp, Boston College	$2,378,800
20. Dodgers. Gavin Lux, ss, Indian Trail HS, Kenosha, Wis.	$2,314,500
21. Blue Jays. T.J. Zeuch, rhp, Pittsburgh.	$2,175,000
22. Pirates. Will Craig, 3b, Wake Forest	$2,253,700
23. Cardinals. Delvin Perez, ss, International Baseball Academy, Ceiba, P.R.	$2,222,500
24. Padres. Hudson Potts, ss, Carroll HS, Southlake, Texas	$1,000,000
25. Padres. Eric Lauer, lhp, Kent State	$2,000,000
26. White Sox. Zack Burdi, rhp, Louisville	$2,128,500
27. Orioles. Cody Sedlock, rhp, Illinois	$2,097,200
28. Nationals. Carter Kieboom, ss, Walton HS, Marietta, Ga.	$2,000,000
29. Nationals. Dane Dunning, rhp, Florida	$2,000,000
30. Rangers. Cole Ragans, lhp, North Florida Christian HS, Tallahassee, Fla.	$2,003,400
31. Mets. Anthony Kay, lhp, Connecticut	$1,100,000
32. Dodgers. Will Smith, c, Louisville	$1,772,500
33. Cardinals. Dylan Carson, of, Elk Grove (Calif.) HS	$1,350,000
34. Cardinals. Dakota Hudson, rhp, Mississippi State	$2,000,000
35. Reds. Taylor Trammell, of, Mount Paran Christian School, Kennesaw, Ga.	$3,200,000
36. Dodgers. Jordan Sheffield, rhp, Vanderbilt	$1,847,500
37. Athletics. Daulton Jefferies, rhp, California	$1,600,000
38. Rockies. Robert Tyler, rhp, Georgia	$1,701,600
39. D-backs. Anfernee Grier, of, Auburn	$1,500,000
40. Braves. Joey Wentz, lhp, Shawnee Mission East HS, Prairie Village, Kan.	$3,050,000
41. Pirates. Nick Lodolo, lhp, Damien HS, La Verne, Calif.	Did not sign
42. Phillies. Kevin Gowdy, rhp, Santa Barbara (Calif.) HS	$3,500,000
43. Reds. Chris Okey, c, Clemson	$2,000,000
44. Braves. Kyle Muller, lhp, Dallas Jesuit Prep	$2,500,000
45. Rockies. Ben Bowden, lhp, Vanderbilt	$1,600,000
46. Brewers. Lucas Erceg, 3b, Menlo (Calif.)	$1,150,000
47. Athletics. Logan Shore, rhp, Florida	$1,500,000
48. Padres. Buddy Reed, of, Florida.	$1,075,000
49. White Sox. Alec Hansen, rhp, Oklahoma	$1,284,500
50. Mariners. Joe Rizzo, 3b, Oakton HS, Vienna, Va.	$1,750,000
51. Red Sox. C.J. Chatham, ss, Florida Atlantic	$1,100,000
52. D-backs. Andy Yerzy, c, York Mills Collegiate Institute, Toronto	$1,214,100
53. Rays. Ryan Boldt, of, Nebraska.	$997,500
54. Orioles. Keegan Akin, lhp, Western Michigan	$1,177,200
55. Indians. Nolan Jones, ss, Holy Ghost Prep, Bensalem, Pa.	$2,250,000
56. Twins. Ben Rortvedt, c, Verona (Wis.) HS	$900,000
57. Blue Jays. J.B. Woodman, of, Mississippi	$975,000
58. Nationals. Sheldon Neuse, 3b, Oklahoma	$900,000

Kyle Lewis, the College Player of the Year, went 11th overall to the Mariners

TEAM. PLAYER, POS., SCHOOL	BONUS
59. Giants. Bryan Reynolds, of, Vanderbilt	$1,350,000
60. Angels. Brandon Marsh, of, Buford (Ga.) HS	$1,073,300
61. Astros. Ronnie Dawson, of, Ohio State	$1,056,800
62. Yankees. Nick Solak, 2b, Louisville	$950,000
63. Rangers. Alex Speas, rhp, McEachern HS, Powder Springs, Ga.	$1,024,900
64. Mets. Peter Alonso, 1b, Florida	$909,200
65. Dodgers. Mitchell White, rhp, Santa Clara	$588,300
66. Blue Jays. Bo Bichette, ss, Lakewood HS, St. Petersburg, Fla.	$1,100,000
67. Royals. A.J. Puckett, rhp, Pepperdine	$1,200,000
68. Pirates. Travis MacGregor, rhp, East Lake HS, Tarpon Springs, Fla.	$900,000
69. Orioles. Matthias Dietz, rhp, John A. Logan (Ill.) JC	$1,300,000
70. Cardinals. Connor Jones, rhp, Virginia	$1,100,000
71. Padres. Reggie Lawson, rhp, Victor Valley HS, Victorville, Calif.	$1,900,000
72. Indians. Logan Ice, c, Oregon State	$850,000
73. Twins. Jose Miranda, ss, Leadership Christian Academy, Guaynabo, P.R.	$775,000
74. Twins. Akil Baddoo, of, Salem HS, Conyers, Ga.	$750,000
75. Brewers. Mario Feliciano, c, Beltran Baseball Academy, Florida, P.R.	$800,000
76. Braves. Brett Cumberland, c, California	$1,500,000
77. Rays. Jake Fraley, of, Louisiana State	$797,500
78. Phillies. Cole Stobbe, ss, Millard West HS, Omaha	$1,100,000
79. Reds. Nick Hanson, rhp, Prior Lake HS, Savage, Minn.	$925,000
80. Braves. Drew Harrington, lhp, Louisville	$900,000
81. Rockies. Garrett Hampson, ss, Long Beach State	$750,000
82. Brewers. Braden Webb, rhp, South Carolina	$700,000
83. Athletics. Sean Murphy, c, Wright State	$753,100
84. Marlins. Thomas Jones, of, Laurens (S.C.) HS	$1,000,000
85. Padres. Mason Thompson, rhp, Round Rock (Texas) HS	$1,750,000
86. White Sox. Alex Call, of, Ball State	$719,100
87. Mariners. Bryson Brigman, ss, San Diego	$700,000
88. Red Sox. Shaun Anderson, rhp, Florida	$700,000
89. D-backs. Jon Duplantier, rhp, Rice	$686,600
90. Rays. Austin Franklin, rhp, Paxton (Fla.) HS	$597,500
91. Orioles. Austin Hays, of, Jacksonville	$665,800
92. Indians. Aaron Civale, rhp, Northeastern	$625,000
93. Twins. Griffin Jax, rhp, Air Force	$645,600
94. Nationals. Jesus Luzardo, lhp, Douglas HS, Parkland, Fla.	$1,400,000
95. Giants. Heath Quinn, of, Samford	$625,900
96. Royals. Nonnie Williams, ss, Kansas City, Kan. (No school)	$950,000
97. Astros. Jake Rogers, c, Tulane.	$614,000
98. Yankees. Nolan Martinez, rhp, Culver City (Calif.) HS	$1,150,000
99. Rangers. Kole Enright, 3b, West Orange HS, Winter Garden, Fla.	$675,000
100. Mets. Blake Tiberi, 3b, Louisville	$500,000

ORDER OF SELECTION IN PARENTHESES   PLAYERS SIGNED IN BOLD

ARIZONA DIAMONDBACKS (13)

1. (Pick forfeited for signing of free agent Zack Greinke)
1s. **Anfernee Grier, of, Auburn**
2. **Andy Yerzy, c, York Mills Collegiate Institute, Toronto**
3. **Jon Duplantier, rhp, Rice**
4. **Curtis Taylor, rhp, British Columbia**
5. **Joey Rose, 3b, Toms River (N.J.) North HS**
6. **Mack Lemieux, lhp, Palm Beach State (Fla.) JC**
7. **Jordan Watson, lhp, Science and Arts of Oklahoma**
8. **Ryan January, c, San Jacinto (Texas) JC**
9. **Tommy Eveld, rhp, South Florida**
10. **Stephen Smith, of, Texas Tech**
11. **Jake Polancic, rhp, Yale SS, Abbotsford, B.C.**
12. **Gavin Stupienski, c, UNC Wilmington**
13. **Manny Jefferson, 2b, Pepperdine**
14. **Colin Poche, lhp, Dallas Baptist**
15. **Tyler Keele, rhp, Morehead State**
16. **Nick Blackburn, rhp, Illinois**
17. **Jake Winston, rhp, Southern Mississippi**
18. Bowden Francis, rhp, Chipola (Fla.) JC
19. **Mark Karaviotis, ss, Oregon**
20. **Connor Grey, rhp, St. Bonaventure**
21. Cameron Cannon, ss, Mountain Ridge HS, Glendale, Ariz.
22. **Kevin Ginkel, rhp, Arizona**
23. **Luke Van Rycheghem, c, Ursuline College SS, Chatham, Ont.**
24. **Riley Smith, rhp, Louisiana State**
25. **Myles Babitt, of, Cal State East Bay**
26. **Tanner Hill, 1b, Texas State**
27. **Gabe Gonzalez, rhp, JC of Southern Nevada**
28. Edmond Americaan, of, Trinity Christian Academy, Lake Worth, Fla.
29. Hunter Kiel, rhp, Pensacola State (Fla.) JC
30. Brandon Martorano, c, Christian Brothers Academy, Lincroft, N.J.
31. **Williams Durruthy, rhp, Florida International**
32. **Trevor Simms, rhp, Tulane**
33. **Paxton De La Garza, ss, Angelo State (Texas)**
34. **Connor Owings, of, Coastal Carolina**
35. **Billy Endris, of, Florida Atlantic**
36. **Robert Galligan, lhp, Maryland**
37. Welby Malczewski, lhp, Heartland (Ill.) CC
38. Nelson Mompierre, c, Miami-Dade JC
39. Jacob Olson, 2b, West Georgia Tech JC
40. Jordan Wiley, of, Richland HS, North Richland Hills, Texas

ATLANTA BRAVES (3)

1. **Ian Anderson, rhp, Shenendehowa HS, Clifton Park, N.Y.**
1s. **Joey Wentz, lhp, Shawnee Mission East HS, Prairie Village, Kan.** (Competitive balance Round 'A' pick—40th; obtained in trade with Marlins)
2. **Kyle Muller, lhp, Dallas Jesuit Prep**
2s. **Brett Cumberland, c, California** (Competitive balance Round 'B' pick—76th; obtained in trade with Orioles)
3. **Drew Harrington, lhp, Louisville**
4. **Bryse Wilson, rhp, Orange HS, Hillsborough, N.C.**
5. **Jeremy Walker, rhp, Gardner-Webb**
6. **Matt Gonzalez, 2b, Georgia Tech**
7. **J.B. Moss, of, Texas A&M**
8. **Taylor Hyssong, lhp, UNC Wilmington**
9. **Tyler Neslony, of, Texas Tech**
10. **Marcus Mooney, ss, South Carolina**
11. **Matt Rowland, rhp, Pope HS, Marietta, Ga.**
12. **Brandon White, rhp, Lander (S.C.)**
13. **Brandon White, rhp, Davenport (Mich.)**
14. **Ramon Osuna, 1b, Walters State (Tenn.) CC**
15. **Zach Becherer, rhp, Rend Lake (Ill.) JC**
16. Josh Anthony, 3b, Western Oklahoma State JC
17. **Devan Watts, rhp, Tusculum (Tenn.)**
18. **Zach Rice, lhp, North Carolina**
19. **Tucker Davidson, lhp, Midland (Texas) JC**
20. **Gabe Howell, 2b, Trion (Ga.) HS**
21. **Dalton Carroll, rhp, Utah**

22. **Alex Lee, 1b, Samford**
23. **Griffin Benson, 1b, Aledo (Texas) HS**
24. **Matt Hearn, of, Mission (Calif.) JC**
25. **Ryan O'Malley, 3b, Sonoma State (Calif.)**
26. **Alan Crowley, c, Reedley (Calif.) JC**
27. **Corbin Clouse, lhp, Davenport (Mich.)**
28. **Nick Shumpert, 2b, San Jacinto (Texas) JC**
29. **Jackson Pokorney, of, Mater Dei HS, Evansville, Ind.**
30. **Cameron Stanton, rhp, St. Edwards (Texas)**
31. Cameron Jabara, rhp, Newport Harbor HS, Newport Beach, Calif.
32. **Ryan Schlosser, rhp, Century (Minn.) JC**
33. **Handsome Monica, c, Northwest Florida State JC**
34. **Jared James, of, Cal Poly Pomona**
35. Michael Gizzi, rhp, State JC of Florida
36. Andres Perez, c, Pinecrest Academy, Cumming, Ga.
37. Zac Kristofak, rhp, Walton HS, Marietta, Ga.
38. Dayton Tripp, rhp, Rend Lake (Ill.) JC
39. **Parker Danciu, lhp, Marshall**
40. Dylan Beasley, rhp, Rome (Ga.) HS

BALTIMORE ORIOLES (15)

1. (Pick forfeited for signing of free agent Yovani Gallardo)
1. **Cody Sedlock, rhp, Illinois** (Compensation for loss of Wei-Yin Chen as free agent—27th)
2. **Keegan Akin, lhp, Western Michigan**
2. **Matthias Dietz, rhp, John A. Logan (Ill.) JC** (Special compensation for failure to sign 2015 second-round pick Jonathan Hughes—69th)
3. **Austin Hays, of, Jacksonville**
4. **Brenan Hanifee, rhp, Turner Ashby HS, Bridgewater, Va.**
5. **Alexis Torres, ss, Angel David HS, San Juan, P.R.**
6. **Tobias Myers, rhp, Winter Haven (Fla.) HS**
7. **Preston Palmeiro, 1b, North Carolina State**
8. **Ryan Moseley, rhp, Texas Tech**
9. **Lucas Humpal, rhp, Texas State**
10. **Cody Dube, rhp, Keene State (N.H.)**
11. **Zach Muckenhirn, lhp, North Dakota**
12. **Max Knutson, lhp, Nebraska**
13. Brandon Bonilla, lhp, Hawaii Pacific
14. **Ruben Garcia, rhp, Eastern Florida State JC**
15. **Nick Jobst, rhp, South Carolina-Aiken**
16. **Willie Rios, lhp, Florida Southwestern JC**
17. Tyler Blohm, lhp, Archbiship Spalding HS, Severn, Md.
18. **Layne Bruner, lhp, Washington State**
19. **Cole Billingsley, of, South Alabama**
20. **Yelin Rodriguez, lhp, Puerto Rico Baseball Academy, Gurabo, P.R.**
21. **Chris Clare, ss, High Point**
22. **Nick Gruener, rhp, Harvard**
23. **Tyler Erwin, lhp, New Mexico State**
24. **Zach Matson, lhp, Crowder (Mo.) JC**
25. Will Toffey, 3b, Vanderbilt
26. **Jaime Estrada, 1b, Central Arizona JC**
27. Daniel Bakst, 3b, Poly Prep Country Day HS, Brooklyn
28. **Matt De La Rosa, rhp, Lenoir-Rhyne (N.C.)**
29. Wil Dalton, of, Summit HS, Thompson's Station, Tenn.
30. **Garrett Copeland, 2b, Austin Peay State**
31. **Jake Ring, of, Missouri**
32. Ryan Mauch, lhp, South Hills HS, West Covina, Calif.
33. **Markel Jones, of, Brunswick (N.C.) CC**
34. **Lucas Brown, rhp, Troy**
35. **Tanner Kirk, 2b, Wichita State**
36. Ben Brecht, lhp, New Trier HS, Winnetka, Ill.
37. **James Teague, rhp, Arkansas**
38. **Collin Woody, 3b, UNC Greensboro**
39. Seth Shuman, rhp, Valdosta (Ga.) HS
40. **Joe Johnson, rhp, Erskine (S.C.)**

BOSTON RED SOX (12)

1. Jason Groome, lhp, Barnegat (N.J.) HS
2. C.J. Chatham, ss, Florida Atlantic
3. Shaun Anderson, rhp, Florida
4. Bobby Dalbec, 3b, Arizona
5. Mike Shawaryn, rhp, Maryland
6. Steve Nogosek, rhp, Oregon
7. Ryan Scott, of, Arkansas-Little Rock
8. Alan Marrero, c, International Baseball Academy, Ceiba, P.R.
9. Matt McLean, of, Texas-Arlington
10. Santiago Espinal, ss, Miami-Dade JC
11. Nick Quintana, ss, Arbor View HS, Las Vegas
12. Matthew Gorst, rhp, Georgia Tech
13. Brady Bramlett, rhp, Mississippi
14. Robby Sexton, lhp, Wright State
15. Michael Wilson, ss, Colonia (N.J.) HS
16. Alberto Schmidt, c, San Angel David HS, San Juan, P.R.
17. Nick Sciortino, c, Boston College
18. Trevor Stephan, rhp, Hill (Texas) JC
19. Kyle Hart, lhp, Indiana
20. Nick Lovullo, ss, Holy Cross
21. Beau Capanna, ss, Bishop Gorman HS, Las Vegas
22. Granger Studdard, of, Texas State
23. Juan Carlos Abreu, of, Winter Springs (Fla.) HS
24. Hunter Smith, rhp, UNC Greensboro
25. Francisco Soto, rhp, Allen (Kan.) CC
26. Jared Oliver, rhp, Truett-McConnell (Ga.)
27. Vince Arobio, rhp, Pacific
28. Jordan Scheftz, rhp, Saddleback (Calif.) JC
29. Cam Shepherd, ss, Peachtree Ridge HS, Suwanee, Ga.
30. Tyler Fitzgerald, ss, Rochester (Ill.) HS
31. Christian Jones, of, Federal Way (Wash.) HS
32. Jeff Belge, lhp, Henninger HS, Syracuse
33. Chad Hardy, of, Paris (Texas) JC
34. Aaron McGarity, rhp, Virginia Tech
35. John Rave, of, Central Catholic HS, Bloomington, Ill.
36. Jordan Wren, of, Georgia Southern
37. Carter Aldrete, ss, Monterey (Calif.) HS
38. Austin Bergner, rhp, Windermere (Fla.) Prep HS
39. Jake Wilson, of, Nottawasaga Pines SS, Angus, Ont.
40. Carter Henry, rhp, Port Neches-Groves HS, Port Neches, Texas

CHICAGO CUBS (28)

1. (Pick forfeited for signing of free agent John Lackey)
2. (Pick forfeited for signing of free agent Jason Heyward)
3. Thomas Hatch, rhp, Oklahoma State
4. Tyson Miller, rhp, California Baptist
5. Bailey Clark, rhp, Duke
6. Chad Hockin, rhp, Cal State Fullerton
7. Michael Cruz, c, Bethune-Cookman
8. Stephen Ridings, rhp, Haverford (Pa.)
9. Duncan Robinson, rhp, Dartmouth
10. Dakota Mekkes, rhp, Michigan State
11. Michael Rucker, rhp, Brigham Young
12. Trey Cobb, rhp, Oklahoma State
13. Wyatt Short, lhp, Mississippi
14. Parker Dunshee, rhp, Wake Forest
15. Jed Carter, rhp, Auburn-Montgomery (Ala.)
16. Holden Cammack, rhp, Oral Roberts
17. Zack Short, ss, Sacred Heart
18. Marc Huberman, lhp, Southern California
19. Matt Swarmer, rhp, Kutztown (Pa.)
20. Colton Freeman, lhp, Alabama
21. Sam Tidaback, c, North Georgia
22. Dante Biasi, lhp, Hazleton Area HS, Hazle Township, Pa.
23. Delvin Zinn, ss, Itawamba (Miss.) CC
24. Reynaldo Rivera, 1b, Chipola (Fla.) JC
25. Trent Giambrone, 2b, Delta State (Miss.)
26. Austin Jones, rhp, Wisconsin-Whitewater
27. Connor Myers, of, Old Dominion
28. Rian Bassett, rhp, Clark (Wash.) JC
29. Tyler Peyton, rhp, Iowa
30. Montana Parsons, rhp, San Jacinto (Texas) JC
31. Brenden Heiss, rhp, Jacobs HS, Algonquin, Ill.

32. Zach Davis, of, Texas Tech
33. Nathan Sweeney, rhp, Cherry Creek HS, Greenwood Village, Colo.
34. Davis Daniel, rhp, St. James School, Montgomery, Ala.
35. Ryan Kreidler, 3b, Davis (Calif.) HS
36. Jake Slaughter, ss, Ouachita Christian HS, Monroe, La.
37. Davis Moore, rhp, Los Osos HS, Rancho Cucamonga, Calif.
38. Tolly Filotei, of, Faulkner State (Ala.) CC
39. Anthony Block, lhp, Newport HS, Bellevue, Wash.
40. D.J. Roberts, rhp, Atlantic Coast HS, Jacksonville

CHICAGO WHITE SOX (10)

1. Zack Collins, c, Miami
1. Zack Burdi, rhp, Louisville (Compensation for loss of Jeff Samardzija as free agent—26th)
2. Alec Hansen, rhp, Oklahoma
3. Alex Call, of, Ball State
4. Jameson Fisher, of, Southeastern Louisiana
5. Jimmy Lambert, rhp, Fresno State
6. Luis Curbelo, ss, Cocoa (Fla.) HS
7. Bernardo Flores, lhp, Southern California
8. Nate Nolan, c, St. Mary's
9. Max Dutto, ss, Menlo (Calif.)
10. Zach Remillard, 3b, Coastal Carolina
11. Ian Hamilton, rhp, Washington State
12. Mitch Roman, ss, Wright State
13. Michael Hickman, c, Chipola (Fla.) JC
14. Bryan Saucedo, rhp, Davenport (Mich.)
15. Jake Elliott, rhp, Oklahoma
16. Ben Wright, rhp, Nevada-Las Vegas
17. Brad Haymes, rhp, Gardner-Webb
18. Lane Hobbs, rhp, Concordia (Texas)
19. Anthony Villa, 1b, St. Mary's
20. Matt Foster, rhp, Alabama
21. Michael Horejsei, lhp, Ohio State
22. Joel Booker, of, Iowa
23. Sam Dexter, ss, Southern Maine
24. Brady Conlan, 3b, Cal State Dominguez Hills
25. Charlie Madden, c, Mercer
26. Zach Farrar, of, Carroll HS, Southlake, Texas
27. Mike Morrison, rhp, Coastal Carolina
28. Aaron Schnurbusch, of, Pittsburgh
29. Caleb Henderson, 1b, Central Arizona JC
30. Pat Cashman, rhp, Southeastern Louisiana
31. Brandon Bossard, ss, Nazareth Academy, La Grange Park, Ill.
32. Sean Renzi, rhp, Central Michgan
33. Ryan Boelter, lhp, Gardner-Webb
34. Jaxon Shirley, 2b, Lapel (Ind.) HS
35. Garrett Acton, rhp, Lemont (Ill.) HS
36. Reese Cooley, of, Chipola (Fla.) JC
37. Leo Kaplan, of, Harvard-Westlake HS, Los Angeles
38. Tyler Gordon, c, Simeon Career Academy, Chicago
39. Justin Lavey, ss, Tremper HS, Kenosha, Wis.
40. Drew Puglielli, 3b, Gulf Coast HS, Naples, Fla.

CINCINNATI REDS (2)

1. Nick Senzel, 3b, Tennessee
1s. Taylor Trammell, of, Mount Paran Christian School, Kennesaw, Ga. (Competitive balance Round 'A' pick—35th)
2. Chris Okey, c, Clemson
3. Nick Hanson, rhp, Prior Lake HS, Savage, Minn.
4. Scott Moss, lhp, Florida
5. Ryan Hendrix, rhp, Texas A&M
6. Tyler Mondile, rhp, Gloucester Catholic HS, Gloucester City, N.J.
7. Andy Cox, lhp, Tennessee
8. John Sansone, 2b, Florida State
9. Alex Webb, rhp, British Columbia
10. Lucas Benenati, rhp, Kansas State
11. Joel Kuhnel, rhp, Texas-Arlington
12. Cassidy Brown, c, Loyola Marymount
13. Ryan Olson, rhp, Cal Poly Pomona
14. Jesse Adams, lhp, Boston College
15. Jesse Stallings, rhp, Louisiana State

16. **Mauro Conde, of, Cupeyville School, San Juan, P.R.**
17. Mitchell Traver, rhp, Texas Christian
18. J.C. Flowers, of, Trinity Christian Academy, Jacksonville
19. **Matt Blandino, rhp, Felician (N.J.)**
20. Todd Lott, of, Trinity Christian Academy, Jacksonville
21. **Andrew Wright, lhp, Southern California**
22. **Aaron Quillen, rhp, Belmont**
23. **Manny Cruz, ss, Southern New Hampshire**
24. **Bruce Yari, 1b, British Columbia**
25. **Colby Wright, 2b, Kansas**
26. **Patrick Riehl, rhp, Mars Hill (N.C.)**
27. Dion Henderson, lhp, Dearborn, Mich. (no school)
28. Cooper Johnson, c, Carmel HS, Mundelein, Ill.
29. **Daniel Sweet, of, Dallas Baptist**
30. Vincent Byrd, 1b, Long Beach CC
31. Austin Langworthy, of, Williston (Fla.) HS
32. Matt Crohan, lhp, Winthrop
33. Nick Derr, 2b, Sarasota (Fla.) HS
34. Ty Weber, rhp, Menomonie (Wis.) HS
35. Walker Whitworth, 2b, Northern Oklahoma JC
36. **Ty Blankmeyer, 2b, St. John's**
37. Alec Benavides, lhp, Alexander HS, Laredo, Texas
38. John Wilson, lhp, North Hunterdon HS, Annandale, N.J.
39. Otis Statum, of, Bishop O'Dowd HS, Oakland
40. Michael Bienlien, rhp, Great Bridge HS, Chesapeake, Va.

CLEVELAND INDIANS (16)

1. **Will Benson, of, The Westminster Schools, Atlanta**
2. **Nolan Jones, ss, Holy Ghost Prep, Bensalem, Pa.**
2s. **Logan Ice, c, Oregon State** (Competitive balance Round 'B' pick—72nd)
3. **Aaron Civale, rhp, Northeastern**
4. **Shane Bieber, rhp, UC Santa Barbara**
5. **Conner Capel, of, Seven Lakes HS, Katy, Texas**
6. **Ulysses Cantu, 3b, Boswell HS, Fort Worth**
7. **Michael Tinsley, c, Kansas**
8. **Andrew Lantrip, lhp, Houston**
9. **Hosea Nelson, of, Clarendon (Texas) JC**
10. **Samad Taylor, ss, Corona (Calif.) HS**
11. **Andrew Calica, of, UC Santa Barbara**
12. **Zach Plesac, rhp, Ball State**
13. **Gavin Collins, c, Mississippi State**
14. **Mitch Longo, of, Ohio**
15. Zack Smith, c, Eastern Wayne HS, Goldsboro, N.C.
16. **Ben Krauth, lhp, Kansas**
17. **Trenton Brooks, of, Nevada**
18. **Raymond Burgos, lhp, Pedro Falu Orellano HS, Rio Grande, P.R.**
19. **Dakody Clemmer, rhp, Central Arizona JC**
20. Ben Baird, ss, Agoura HS, Agoura Hills, Calif.
21. Wil Crowe, rhp, South Carolina
22. Mason Studstill, rhp, Rockledge (Fla.) HS
23. **Michael Letkewicz, rhp, Augustana (S.D.)**
24. **Skylar Arias, lhp, Tallahassee (Fla.) CC**
25. **Jonathan Laureano, 3b, Connors State (Okla.) JC**
26. **Tanner Tully, lhp, Ohio State**
27. Nelson Alvarez, rhp, Braddock HS, Miami
28. **Jamal Rudledge, ss, Contra Costa (Calif.) JC**
29. Spencer Steer, 3b, Millikan HS, Long Beach
30. **Ryder Ryan, rhp, North Carolina**
31. Chris Farish, rhp, Wake Forest
32. Kramer Robertson, 2b, Louisiana State
33. Blake Sabol, c, Aliso Niguel HS, Aliso Viejo, Calif.
34. Austin Shenton, 3b, Bellingham (Wash.) HS
35. Armani Smith, of, De La Salle HS, Concord, Calif.
36. Andrew Baker, lhp, Ridge Community HS, Davenport, Fla.
37. Mike Amditis, c, Boca Raton (Fla.) HS
38. Jacob DeVries, lhp, Air Force
39. Pedro Alfonseca, of, North Kansas City (Mo.) HS
40. Danny Sinatro, of, Skyline HS, Sammamish, Wash.

COLORADO ROCKIES (4)

1. **Riley Pint, rhp, St. Thomas Aquinas HS, Overland Park, Kan.**
1s. **Robert Tyler, rhp, Georgia** (Competitive balance Round 'A' pick—38th)

2. **Ben Bowden, lhp, Vanderbilt**
3. **Garrett Hampson, ss, Long Beach State**
4. **Colton Welker, 3b, Douglas HS, Parkland, Fla.**
5. **Brian Serven, c, Arizona State**
6. **Willie Abreu, of, Miami**
7. **Reid Humphreys, rhp, Mississippi State**
8. **Ty Culbreth, lhp, Texas**
9. **Justin Calomeni, rhp, Cal Poly**
10. **Vince Fernandez, of, UC Riverside**
11. **Bryan Baker, rhp, North Florida**
12. **Brandon Gold, rhp, Georgia Tech**
13. **Taylor Snyder, ss, Colorado State-Pueblo**
14. **Matt Dennis, rhp, Bradley**
15. **Justin Valdespina, rhp, Southern New Hampshire**
16. **Will Haynie, c, Alabama**
17. **Mike Bunal, rhp, Binghamton**
18. **Hunter Melton, 1b, Texas A&M**
19. **Jacob Bosiokovic, 1b, Ohio State**
20. **Kyle Cedotal, lhp, Southeast Louisiana**
21. **Tyler Bugner, of, Newman (Kan.)**
22. **Steven Linkous, of, UNC Wilmington**
23. **Jared Gesell, rhp, UNC Wilmington**
24. **J.D. Hammer, rhp, Marshall**
25. **Heath Holder, rhp, Georgia**
26. **Austin Moore, rhp, West Texas A&M**
27. **George Thanopoulos, rhp, Columbia**
28. **Ryan Luna, rhp, Sonoma State (Calif.)**
29. **Josh Shelley, rhp, Mobile (Ala.)**
30. **Rico Garcia, rhp, Hawaii Pacific**
31. **Kenny Oakley, rhp, Nevada-Las Vegas**
32. John Hendry, rhp, Notre Dame College Prep, Niles, Ill.
33. **Tyler Orris, ss, Millersville (Pa.)**
34. Wyatt Featherston, of, Green Mountain HS, Lakewood, Colo.
35. Michael Toglia, of, Gig Harbor (Wash.) HS
36. Trevor Edior, of, Carson (Calif.) HS
37. Troy Bacon, rhp, Santa Fe (Fla.) JC
38. Quin Cotton, of, Regis Jesuit HS, Aurora, Colo.
39. Cuba Bess, c, Fruita (Colo.) Monument HS
40. Luca Dalatri, rhp, Christian Brothers Academy, Lincroft, N.J.

DETROIT TIGERS (9)

1. **Matt Manning, rhp, Sheldon HS, Sacramento**
2. (Pick forfeited for signing of free agent Jordan Zimmermann)
3. (Pick forfeited for signing of free agent Justin Upton)
4. **Kyle Funkhouser, rhp, Louisville**
5. **Mark Ecker, rhp, Texas A&M**
6. **Bryan Garcia, rhp, Miami**
7. **Austin Sodders, lhp, UC Riverside**
8. **Jacob Robson, of, Mississippi State**
9. **Daniel Pinero, ss, Virginia**
10. **Sam Machonis, of, Florida Southern**
11. **Zac Houston, rhp, Mississippi State**
12. **Daniel Woodrow, of, Creighton**
13. **Brady Policelli, c, Towson**
14. **Austin Athmann, c, Minnesota**
15. **John Schreiber, rhp, Northwestern Ohio**
16. **Will Savage, 2b, Columbia**
17. **Brandyn Sittinger, rhp, Ashland (Ohio)**
18. **Niko Buentello, 1b, Auburn**
19. **Dustin Frailey, of, Cal State Bakersfield**
20. **Clate Schmidt, rhp, Clemson**
21. **Joe Navilhon, rhp, Southern California**
22. **Burris Warner, rhp, Marshall**
23. **Bryan Torres, c, Beltran Baseball Academy, Florida, P.R.**
24. **Evan Hill, lhp, Michigan**
25. **John Hayes, rhp, Wichita State**
26. **Colyn O'Connell, rhp, Florida Atlantic**
27. **Chad Sedio, ss, Miami (Ohio)**
28. Alex Cunningham, rhp, Coastal Carolina
29. **Hunter Swilling, 3b, Samford**
30. **Dalton Lundeen, lhp, Valparaiso**
31. **Dalton Britt, ss, Liberty**
32. Connor O'Neil, rhp, Cal State Northridge
33. Keegan Thompson, rhp, Auburn
34. Gerardo Gonzalez, ss, Puerto Rico Baseball Academy,

DRAFT

Gurabo, P.R.
35. Jacob White, c, Wakeland HS, Frisco, Texas
36. Drew Mendoza, 3b, Lake Minneola HS, Minneola, Fla.
37. David Fleita, 2b, Maine South HS, Park Ridge, Ill.
38. Josh Smith, ss, Catholic HS, Baton Rouge
39. Garrett Milchin, rhp, The First Academy, Orlando
40. Dalton Feeney, rhp, Century HS, Bismarck, N.D.

HOUSTON ASTROS (21)

1. Forrest Whitley, rhp, Alamo Heights HS, San Antonio
2. Ronnie Dawson, of, Ohio State
3. Jake Rogers, c, Tulane
4. Brett Adcock, lhp, Michigan
5. Abraham Toro, 3b, Seminole State (Okla.) JC
6. Stephen Wrenn, of, Georgia
7. Tyler Buffet, rhp, Oklahoma State
8. Nick Hernandez, rhp, Houston
9. Ryan Hartman, lhp, Tennessee Wesleyan
10. Dustin Hunt, rhp, Northeastern
11. Chad Donato, rhp, West Virginia
12. Carmen Benedetti, lhp, Michigan
13. Ryne Birk, 2b, Texas A&M
14. Carson LaRue, rhp, Cowley County (Kan.) CC
15. Alex DeGoti, ss, Barry (Fla.)
16. Spencer Johnson, of, Missouri State
17. Brian Howard, rhp, Texas Christian
18. Colin McKee, rhp, Mercyhurst (Pa.)
19. Taylor Jones, 1b, Gonzaga
20. L.P. Pelletier, 2b, Seminole State (Okla.) JC
21. Chuckie Robinson, c, Southern Mississippi
22. Ray Henderson, c, Grayson County (Texas) CC
23. Tyler Britton, rhp, High Point
24. Troy Sieber, c, St. Leo (Fla.)
25. Kevin Hill, rhp, South Alabama
26. Avery Tuck, of, Steele Canyon HS, Spring Valley, Calif.
27. Nathan Thompson, lhp, Oklahoma Baptist
28. Johnny Ruiz, 2b, Miami
29. Elliott Barzilli, 3b, Texas Christian
30. Brody Westmoreland, 3b, JC of Southern Nevada
31. Howie Brey, lhp, Rutgers
32. Darius Vines, rhp, St. Bonaventure HS, Ventura, Calif.
33. Toby Handley, of, Stony Brook
34. Stijn Van Der Meer, ss, Lamar
35. Nick Slaughter, c, Klein (Texas) HS
36. Ian Hardman, rhp, Seminole State (Okla.) JC
37. Anthony DeFrancesco, 3b, Red Mountain HS, Mesa, Ariz.
38. Chaz Pal, of, South Carolina-Aiken
39. Tyler Wolfe, 2b, Kansas State
40. Lucas Williams, rhp, Central Missouri

KANSAS CITY ROYALS (27)

1. (Pick forfeited for signing of free agent Ian Kennedy)
2. A.J. Puckett, rhp, Pepperdine
3. Khalil Lee, of, Flint Hill School, Oakton, Va.
4. Jace Vines, rhp, Texas A&M
5. Nicky Lopez, ss, Creighton
6. Cal Jones, of, Dadeville (Ala.) HS
7. Travis Eckert, rhp, Oregon State
8. Chris DeVito, 1b, New Mexico
9. Walker Sheller, rhp, Stetson
10. Richard Lovelady, lhp, Kennesaw State
11. Vance Vizcaino, of, Stetson
12. Jeremy Gwinn, rhp, Colby (Kan.) CC
13. Logan Gray, 2b, Austin Peay State
14. David McKay, rhp, Florida Atlantic
15. Mike Messier, lhp, Bellarmine (Ky.)
16. Nick Heath, of, Northwestern State
17. Dillon Drabble, rhp, Seminole State (Okla.) JC
18. Vance Tatum, lhp, Mississippi State
19. Tyler Fallwell, rhp, Cochise (Ariz.) JC
20. Anthony Bender, rhp, Santa Rosa (Calif.) JC
21. Dalton Griffin, of, South Effingham HS, Guyton, Ga.
22. Cody Nesbit, rhp, San Jacinto (Texas) JC
23. Kort Peterson, of, UCLA

24. Mike McCann, c, Seattle
25. Robby Rinn, 1b, Bryant
26. John Brontsema, 3b, UC Irvine
27. Rex Hill, lhp, Texas Christian
28. Yordany Salva, c, Broward (Fla.) CC
29. Grant Gavin, rhp, Central Missouri
30. Geoffrey Bramblett, rhp, Alabama
31. Malcolm Van Buren, rhp, Hanahan (S.C.) HS
32. Luke Bandy, of, Providence Classical Christian Academy, Rogers, Ark.
33. Kameron Misner, of, Poplar Bluff (Mo.) HS
34. Nathan Webb, rhp, Lee's Summit (Mo.) HS
35. Mark Sanchez, c, California Baptist
36. Alex Massey, rhp, Tulane
37. Justin Camp, rhp, Auburn
38. Joey Fregosi, ss, Murrieta Valley HS, Murrieta, Calif.
39. Chase Livingston, c, Rhode Island
40. Taylor Kaczmarek, rhp, San Diego

LOS ANGELES ANGELS (20)

1. Matt Thaiss, c, Virginia
2. Brandon Marsh, of, Buford (Ga.) HS
3. Nolan Williams, ss, Kansas City, Kan. (no school)
4. Chris Rodriguez, rhp, Pace (Fla.) HS
5. Connor Justus, ss, Georgia Tech
6. Cole Duensing, rhp, Blue Valley NW HS, Overland Park, Kan.
7. Jordan Zimmerman, 2b, Michigan State
8. Troy Montgomery, of, Ohio State
9. Michael Barash, c, Texas A&M
10. Andrew Vinson, rhp, Texas A&M
11. Brennon Lund, of, Brigham Young
12. Bo Tucker, lhp, Georgia
13. Anthony Molina, rhp, West Broward HS, Hollywood, Fla.
14. Francisco Del Valle, of, Puerto Rico Baseball Academy, Gurabo, P.R.
15. Mike Kaelin, rhp, Buffalo
16. Keith Grieshaber, ss, Jefferson (Mo.) JC
17. Zach Gibbons, of, Arizona
18. David Oppenheim, of, Southern California
19. Cody Ramer, ss, Arizona
20. Jack Kruger, c, Mississippi State
21. LJ. Kalawaia, of, UNC Greensboro
22. Troy Rallings, rhp, Washington
23. Torii Hunter Jr., of, Notre Dame
24. Brennan Morgan, c, Kennesaw State
25. Cameron Williams, of, Howard (Texas) JC
26. Derek Jenkins, of, Seton Hall
27. Greg Belton, rhp, Sam Houston State
28. David Hamilton, ss, San Marcos (Texas) HS
29. Blake Smith, rhp, West Virginia
30. Robbie Peto, rhp, Monroe Township (N.J.) HS
31. Johnny Morell, rhp, Basha HS, Chandler, Ariz.
32. Doug Willey, rhp, Arkansas
33. Justin Kelly, lhp, UC Santa Barbara
34. Justin Nielsen, lhp, Illinois
35. Sean Isaac, rhp, Vanguard (Calif.)
36. Jose Rojas, ss, Vanguard (Calif.)
37. John Schuknecht, of, Cal Poly
38. Tyler Bates, of, East Texas Baptist
39. Richard Fecteau, 2b, Salem State (Mass.)
40. Brad Anderson, 1b, Pepperdine

LOS ANGELES DODGERS (25)

1. Gavin Lux, ss, Indian Trail HS, Kenosha, Wis.
1. Will Smith, c, Louisville (Compensation for loss of Zack Greinke as free agent—32nd)
1s. Jordan Sheffield, rhp, Vanderbilt (Special compensation for failure to sign 2015 first-rounder Kyle Funkhouser—36th)
2. Mitchell White, rhp, Santa Clara
3. Dustin May, rhp, Northwest HS, Justin, Texas
4. D.J. Peters, of, Western Nevada CC
5. Devin Smeltzer, lhp, San Jacinto (Texas) JC
6. Errol Robinson, ss, Mississippi
7. Luke Raley, of, Lake Erie (Ohio)
8. Andre Scrubb, rhp, High Point

9. Anthony Gonsolin, rhp, St. Mary's
10. Kevin Lachance, ss, Maryland-Baltimore County
11. A.J. Alexy, rhp, Twin Valley HS, Elverson, Pa.
12. Graham Ashcraft, rhp, Huntsville (Ala.) HS
13. Cody Thomas, of, Oklahoma
14. Dean Kremer, rhp, Nevada-Las Vegas
15. Brayan Morales, of, Hillsborough (Fla.) CC
16. Darien Tubbs, of, Memphis
17. Dillon Persinger, 2b, Golden West (Calif.) JC
18. Cole Freeman, 2b, Louisiana State
19. Chris Mathewson, rhp, Long Beach State
20. Brock Carpenter, 3b, Seattle
21. James Carter, rhp, UC Santa Barbara
22. Jeff Paschke, rhp, Southern California
23. Bailey Ober, rhp, College of Charleston
24. Saige Jenco, of, Virginia Tech
25. Chandler Eden, rhp, Texas Tech
26. Brandon Montgomery, 2b, San Jacinto (Texas) JC
27. Austin French, lhp, Brown
28. Jake Perkins, rhp, Ferrum (Va.)
29. Will Kincanon, rhp, Triton (Ill.) JC
30. Ramon Rodriguez, c, Puerto Rico Baseball Academy, Gurabo, P.R.
31. Stevie Berman, c, Santa Clara
32. Connor Costello, rhp, Oklahoma State
33. Zack McKinstry, ss, Central Michigan
34. Joel Toribio, rhp, Western Oklahoma State JC
35. Nick Yarnall, of, Pittsburgh
36. Cal Stevenson, of, Chabot (Calif.) JC
37. Enrique Zamora, rhp, Calumet College of St. Joseph (Ind.)
38. Kevin Malisheski, rhp, Wauconda (Ill.) HS
39. Ryan Watson, rhp, Auburn (Ala.) HS
40. Zach Taglieri, rhp, Port St. Lucie (Fla.) HS

MIAMI MARLINS (7)

1. Braxton Garrett, lhp, Florence (Ala.) HS
2. (Pick forfeited for signing of free agent Wei-Yin Chen)
3. Thomas Jones, of, Laurens (S.C.) HS
4. Sean Reynolds, of, Redondo Union HS, Redondo Beach, Calif.
5. Sam Perez, rhp, Missouri State
6. Remey Reed, rhp, Oklahoma State
7. Corey Bird, of, Marshall
8. Aaron Knapp, of, California
9. Jarrett Rindfleisch, c, Ball State
10. Dylan Lee, lhp, Fresno State
11. Chad Smith, rhp, Mississippi
12. Mike King, rhp, Boston College
13. Nick Eicholtz, rhp, Alabama
14. Michael Mertz, rhp, Oklahoma State
15. James Nelson, ss, Cisco (Texas) JC
16. Dustin Beggs, rhp, Kentucky
17. Brent Wheatley, rhp, Southern California
18. David Gauntt, c, Washburn (Kan.)
19. Shane Sawczak, lhp, Palm Beach State (Fla.) JC
20. Eric Gutierrez, 1b, Texas Tech
21. Luis Pintor, ss, New Mexico JC
22. Alex Mateo, rhp, Nova Southeastern (Fla.)
23. Hunter Wells, rhp, Gonzaga
24. J.J. Gould, ss, Jacksonville
25. Mike Garzillo, 2b, Lehigh
26. Gunner Pollman, c, Sacramento State
27. Parker Bugg, rhp, Louisiana State
28. Colby Lusignan, 1b, Lander (S.C.)
29. Walker Olis, of, Pacific
30. Garrett Suchey, rhp, Wallace State (Ala.) CC
31. Preston Guillory, rhp, Texas Christian
32. Chevis Hoover, rhp, Tennessee Wesleyan
33. Branden Berry, 1b, Cal State Northridge
34. Trenton Hill, lhp, Lee (Tenn.)
35. Matt Brooks, 2b, Monroe (N.Y.) CC
36. Matt Popowitz, c, Suffern (N.Y.) HS
37. Zach Daly, of, Lander (S.C.)
38. Dustin Demeter, 3b, Dos Pueblos HS, Goleta, Calif.
39. Caleb Scires, of, Fairfield (Texas) HS
40. Evan Douglas, 2b, Spokane Falls (Wash.) CC

MILWAUKEE BREWERS (5)

1. Corey Ray, of, Louisville
2. Lucas Erceg, 3b, Menlo (Calif.)
2s. Mario Feliciano, c, Beltran Baseball Academy, Florida, P.R. (Competitive balance Round 'B' pick—75th)
3. Braden Webb, rhp, South Carolina
4. Corbin Burnes, rhp, St. Mary's
5. Zack Brown, rhp, Kentucky
6. Payton Henry, c, Pleasant Grove (Utah) HS
7. Daniel Brown, lhp, Mississippi State
8. Francisco Thomas, ss, Osceola HS, Kissimmee, Fla.
9. Trey York, 2b, East Tennessee State
10. Blake Fox, lhp, Rice
11. Chad McClanahan, 3b, Brophy Prep, Phoenix
12. Trever Morrison, ss, Oregon State
13. Thomas Jankins, rhp, Quinnipiac
14. Gabriel Garcia, c, Broward (Fla.) CC
15. Scott Serigstad, rhp, Cal State Fullerton
16. Louie Crow, rhp, Buena Park (Calif.) HS
17. Weston Wilson, 3b, Clemson
18. Cooper Hummel, c, Portland
19. Zach Clark, of, Pearl River (Miss.) CC
20. Jared Horn, rhp, Vintage HS, Napa, Calif.
21. Nathan Rodriguez, c, Cypress (Calif.) JC
22. Cam Roegner, lhp, Bradley
23. Ronnie Gideon, 1b, Texas A&M
24. Michael Gonzalez, rhp, Norwalk (Conn.) HS
25. Blake Lillis, lhp, St. Thomas Aquinas HS, Overland Park, Kan.
26. Nick Roscetti, ss, Iowa
27. Nick Cain, of, Faulkner (Ala.)
28. Andrew Vernon, rhp, Noth Carolina Central
29. Brennan Price, rhp, Felician (N.J.)
30. Dalton Brown, rhp, Texas Tech
31. Ryan Aguilar, of, Arizona
32. Wilson Adams, rhp, Alabama-Huntsville
33. Emerson Gibbs, rhp, Tulane
34. Matt Smith, rhp, Georgetown
35. Chase Williams, rhp, Wichita State
36. Parker Bean, rhp, Liberty
37. Jomar Cortes, ss, Beltran Baseball Academy, Florida, P.R.
38. Caleb Whalen, of, Portland
39. Jose Gomez, of, St. Thomas (Fla.)
40. Kyle Serrano, rhp, Tennessee

MINNESOTA TWINS (17)

1. Alex Kirilloff, of, Plum HS, Pittsburgh
2. Ben Rortvedt, c, Verona (Wis.) HS
2s. Jose Miranda, ss, Leadership Christian Academy, Guaynabo, P.R. (Competitive balance Round 'B' pick—73rd)
2s. Akil Baddoo, of, Salem HS, Conyers, Ga. (Special compensation for failure to sign 2015 supplemental second-round pick Kyle Cody—74th)
3. Griffin Jax, rhp, Air Force
4. Tom Hackimer, rhp, St. John's
5. Jordan Balazovic, rhp, St. Martin SS, Mississauga, Ont.
6. Alex Schick, rhp, California
7. Matt Albanese, of, Bryant
8. Shane Carrier, of, Fullerton (Calif.) JC
9. Mitchell Kranson, c, California
10. Brandon Lopez, ss, Miami
11. Tyler Benninghoff, rhp, Rockhurst HS, Kansas City, Mo.
12. Zach Featherstone, of, Tallahassee (Fla.) CC
13. Ryan Mason, rhp, California
14. Andre Jernigan, ss, Xavier
15. Tyler Wells, rhp, Cal State San Bernardino
16. Tyler Beardsley, rhp, Sacramento State
17. Kidany Salva, c, Klein Forest HS, Houston
18. Timmy Richards, ss, Cal State Fullerton
19. Sean Poppen, rhp, Harvard
20. Shamoy Christopher, c, Roane State (Tenn.) CC
21. Domenick Carlini, lhp, Southeast Louisiana
22. Hank Morrison, of, Mercyhurst (Pa.)
23. Caleb Hamilton, ss, Oregon State
24. Matt Byars, c, Michigan State

25. Colton Davis, rhp, Western Carolina
26. Greg Deichmann, 3b, Louisiana State
27. Scott Ogrin, of, Valencia HS, Santa Clarita, Calif.
28. Matt Jones, lhp, Sinclair SS, Whitby, Ont.
29. Dane Hutcheon, ss, Montevallo (Ala.)
30. Quin Grogan, rhp, Lewis-Clark State (Idaho)
31. Juan Gamez, c, North Dakota State
32. Matt Wallner, rhp, Forest Lake (Minn.) HS
33. Clark Beeker, rhp, Davidson
34. Joe Cronin, ss, Boston College
35. Austin Tribby, lhp, Missouri
36. Patrick McGuff, rhp, Morehead State
37. Danny Mayer, of, Pacific
38. Brent Rooker, of, Mississippi State
39. Casey Scoggins, of, Tampa
40. T.J. Collett, c, North Vigo HS, Terre Haute, Ind.

NEW YORK METS (24)

1. Justin Dunn, rhp, Boston College
1. Anthony Kay, lhp, Connecticut (Compensation for loss of Daniel Murphy as free agent—31st)
2. Peter Alonso, 1b, Florida
3. Blake Tiberi, 3b, Louisville
4. Michael Paez, ss, Coastal Carolina
5. Colby Woodmansee, ss, Arizona State
6. Chris Viall, rhp, Stanford
7. Austin McGeorge, rhp, Long Beach State
8. Placido Torres, lhp, Tusculum (Tenn.)
9. Colin Holderman, rhp, Heartland (Ill.) CC
10. Gene Cone, of, South Carolina
11. Cameron Planck, rhp, Rowan County HS, Morehead, Ky.
12. Matt Cleveland, rhp, Windsor (Conn.) HS
13. Dan Rizzie, c, Xavier
14. Christian James, rhp, East Lake HS, Tarpon Springs, Fla.
15. Jacob Zanon, of, Lewis-Clark State (Idaho)
16. Trent Johnson, rhp, Santa Fe (Fla.) CC
17. Jay Jabs, 3b, Franklin Pierce (N.H.)
18. Adam Atkins, rhp, Louisiana Tech
19. Gary Cornish, rhp, San Diego
20. Carlos Cortes, 2b, Lake Howell HS, Winter Park, Fla.
21. Max Kuhns, rhp, Santa Clara
22. Ian Strom, of, Massachusetts-Lowell
23. Nick Sergakis, 2b, Ohio State
24. Dariel Rivera, rhp, Dr. Juan J. Osuna HS, Caguas, P.R.
25. Cody Beckman, lhp, North Carolina State
26. Rylan Thomas, 3b, Windermere (Fla.) Prep HS
27. Joel Urena, lhp, Luperon HS for Math & Science, New York
28. William Sierra, rhp, Edouard Montpetit HS, Montreal
29. Alex Haynes, rhp, Central HS, Knoxville
30. Eric Villanueva, rhp, Josefina Barcelo HS, Guaynabo, P.R.
31. Jeremy Wolf, of, Trinity (Texas)
32. George Kirby, rhp, Rye (N.Y.) HS
33. Duncan Pence, ss, Farragut HS, Knoxville
34. Anthony Herron, rhp, Jefferson (Mo.) JC
35. Andrew Harbin, rhp, Allatoona HS, Acworth, Ga.
36. Garrison Bryant, rhp, Clearwater (Fla.) HS
37. Branden Fryman, ss, Tate HS, Cantonment, Fla.
38. Jaylon McLaughlin, ss, Santa Monica (Calif.) HS
39. Jordan Hand, c, JC of Southern Nevada
40. Michael Chambers, c, John Paul II HS, Plano, Texas

NEW YORK YANKEES (22)

1. Blake Rutherford, of, Chaminade College Prep HS, Canoga Park, Calif.
2. Nick Solak, 2b, Louisville
3. Nolan Martinez, rhp, Culver City (Calif.) HS
4. Nick Nelson, rhp, Gulf Coast State (Fla.) JC
5. Dom Thompson-Williams, of, South Carolina
6. Brooks Kriske, rhp, Southern California
7. Keith Skinner, c, North Florida
8. Dalton Blaser, 1b, Cal State Fullerton
9. Tim Lynch, 1b, Southern Mississippi
10. Trevor Lane, lhp, Illinois-Chicago
11. Connor Jones, lhp, Georgia

12. Taylor Widener, rhp, South Carolina
13. Brian Trieglaff, rhp, Texas Christian
14. Jordan Scott, of, IMG Academy, Bradenton, Fla.
15. Tony Hernandez, lhp, Monroe (N.Y.) JC
16. Zach Linginfelter, rhp, Sevier County HS, Sevierville, Tenn.
17. Mandy Alvarez, 3b, Eastern Kentucky
18. Greg Weissert, rhp, Fordham
19. Evan Alexander, of, Hebron HS, Carrollton, Texas
20. Miles Chambers, rhp, Cal State Fullerton
21. Timmy Robinson, of, Southern California
22. Blair Henley, rhp, Arlington Heights HS, Fort Worth
23. Braden Bristo, rhp, Louisiana Tech
24. Joe Burton, of, Harford (Md.) CC
25. Edel Luaces, of, Hialeah, Fla. (no school)
26. Gage Burland, rhp, Gonzaga
27. Phillip Diehl, lhp, Louisiana Tech
28. Will Jones, rhp, Lander (S.C.)
29. Bo Weiss, rhp, Regis Jesuit HS, Aurora, Colo.
30. Ben Ruta, of, Wagner
31. Miles Sandum, lhp, Granite Hills HS, El Cajon, Calif.
32. Juan Cabrera, rhp, North Canyon HS, Phoenix
33. Bryson Bowman, of, Western Carolina
34. David Clawson, c, Dana Hills HS, Dana Point, Calif.
35. Zack Hess, rhp, Liberty Christian Academy, Lynchburg, Va.
36. Tyler Honahan, lhp, Stony Brook
37. Corey Dempster, of, Southern California
38. Sam Ferri, c, Notre Dame College Prep, Niles, Ill.
39. Brian Keller, rhp, Wisconsin-Milwaukee
40. Nate Brown, rhp, Arrowhead Union HS, Hartland, Wis.

OAKLAND ATHLETICS (6)

1. A.J. Puk, lhp, Florida
1s. Daulton Jefferies, rhp, California (Competitive balance Round 'A' pick—37th)
2. Logan Shore, rhp, Florida
3. Sean Murphy, c, Wright State
4. Skylar Szynski, rhp, Penn HS, Mishawaka, Ind.
5. JaVon Shelby, 3b, Kentucky
6. Brandon Bailey, rhp, Gonzaga
7. Tyler Ramirez, of, North Carolina
8. Will Gilbert, lhp, North Carolina State
9. Dalton Sawyer, lhp, Minnesota
10. Mitchell Jordan, rhp, Stetson
11. Eli White, ss, Clemson
12. Luke Persico, of, UCLA
13. Nate Mondou, 2b, Wake Forest
14. Nolan Blackwood, rhp, Memphis
15. Ty Damron, lhp, Texas Tech
16. Anthony Churlin, of, Island Coast HS, Cape Coral, Fla.
17. Seth Martinez, rhp, Arizona State
18. Skyler Weber, c, Georgia
19. Sam Gilbert, rhp, Kansas
20. Brigham Hill, rhp, Texas A&M
21. Kyle Nowlin, of, Eastern Kentucky
22. Roger Gonzalez, c, Winthrop
23. Christian Young, rhp, Niagara County (N.Y.) CC
24. Robert Bennie, of, East Stroudsburg (Pa.)
25. Jeremiah McCray, of, King HS, Riverside, Calif.
26. Charley Gould, 1b, William & Mary
27. Cole Gruber, of, Nebraska-Omaha
28. Josh Vidales, 2b, Houston
29. Matt Milburn, rhp, Wofford
30. Nick Highberger, rhp, Creighton
31. Sam Sheehan, rhp, Westmont (Calif.)
32. Colin Theroux, c, Oklahoma State
33. Jarrett Costa, c, Westmont (Calif.)
34. Casey Thomas, ss, Texas A&M-Corpus Christi
35. Danny Rafferty, lhp, Bucknell
36. Brady Schanuel, rhp, Parkland (Ill.) JC
37. Michael Farley, of, Chico (Calif.) HS
38. Matthew Fraizer, of, Clovis North HS, Fresno
39. Shane Martinez, ss, North HS, Riverside, Calif.
40. Brett Bittiger, 2b, Pace (N.Y.)

PHILADELPHIA PHILLIES (1)

1. Mickey Moniak, of, La Costa Canyon HS, Carlsbad, Calif.
2. Kevin Gowdy, rhp, Santa Barbara (Calif.) HS
3. Cole Stobbe, ss, Millard West HS, Omaha
4. JoJo Romero, lhp, Yavapai (Ariz.) JC
5. Cole Irvin, lhp, Oregon
6. David Martinelli, of, Dallas Baptist
7. Henri Lartigue, c, Mississippi
8. Grant Dyer, rhp, UCLA
9. Blake Quinn, rhp, Cal State Fullerton
10. Julian Garcia, rhp, Metro State (Colo.)
11. Josh Stephen, of, Mater Dei HS, Santa Ana, Calif.
12. Justin Miller, rhp, Central HS, Fresno
13. Andrew Brown, rhp, Granite Hills HS, El Cajon, Calif.
14. Darick Hall, 1b, Dallas Baptist
15. Alex Wojciechowski, lh, Minnesota-Duluth
16. Brett Barbier, c, Cal Poly
17. Danny Zardon, 3b, Nova Southeastern (Fla.)
18. Jake Kelzer, rhp, Indiana
19. Will Hibbs, rhp, Lamar
20. Caleb Eldridge, 1b, Cowley County (Kan.) CC
21. Jonathan Hennigan, lhp, Texas State
22. Kyle Young, lhp, St. Dominic HS, Oyster Bay, N.Y.
23. Camden Duzenack, ss, Dallas Baptist
24. Tyler Hallead, rhp, JC of Southern Nevada
25. Trevor Bettencourt, rhp, UC Santa Barbara
26. Tyler Kent, of, Otterbein (Ohio)
27. Davis Agle, rhp, Spartanburg Methodist JC (S.C.)
28. Jordan Kurokawa, rhp, Hawaii-Hilo
29. Alexander Kline, lhp, Nova Southeastern (Fla.)
30. Logan Davidson, ss, Providence HS, Charlotte
31. Tyler Frohwirth, rhp, Minnesota State
32. Daniel Garner, c, Northwestern State
33. Jack Klein, rhp, Stanford
34. Luke Maglich, of, South Florida
35. Carter Bins, c, Rodriguez HS, Fairfield, Calif.
36. Mac Sceroler, rhp, Southeastern Louisiana
37. James Ziemba, lhp, Duke
38. Trevor Hillhouse, lhp, Woodstock (Ga.) HS
39. Dante Baldelli, of, Bishop Hendricken HS, Warwick, R.I.
40. Trey Morris, rhp, Taylor HS, Katy, Texas

PITTSBURGH PIRATES (29)

1. Will Craig, 3b, Wake Forest
1s. Nick Lodolo, lhp, Damien HS, La Verne, Calif. (Competitive balance Round 'A' pick—41st)
2. Travis MacGregor, rhp, East Lake HS, Tarpon Springs, Fla.
3. Stephen Alemais, ss, Tulane
4. Braeden Ogle, lhp, Jensen Beach (Fla.) HS
5. Blake Cederlind, rhp, Merced (Calif.) JC
6. Cam Vieaux, lhp, Michigan State
7. Brent Gibbs, c, Central Arizona JC
8. Dylan Prohoroff, rhp, Cal State Fullerton
9. Clark Eagan, of, Arkansas
10. Matt Anderson, rhp, Morehead State
11. Max Kranick, rhp, Valley View HS, Archbald, Pa.
12. Arden Pabst, c, Georgia Tech
13. John Pomeroy, rhp, Oregon State
14. Hagen Owenby, c, East Tennessee State
15. Danny Beddes, rhp, Utah Valley
16. Matt Diorio, of, Central Florida
17. Matt Frawley, rhp, Purdue
18. Kevin Mahala, rhp, George Washington
19. Pearson McMahan, rhp, St. John's River State (Fla.) JC
20. Adam Oller, rhp, Northwestern State
21. Matt Eckelman, rhp, Saint Louis
22. Brandon Bingel, rhp, Bryant
23. Garrett Brown, of, Western Carolina
24. Austin Bodrato, 3b, St. Joseph Regional HS, Montvale, N.J.
25. Hunter Owen, of, Indiana State
26. Robbie Coursel, rhp, Florida Atlantic
27. Tyler Leffler, ss, Bradley
28. Michael Danielak, rhp, Dartmouth
29. Geoff Hartlieb, rhp, Lindenwood (Mo.)

30. Chris Cook, ss, East Tennessee State
31. Jordan Jess, lhp, Minnesota
32. Ben Miller, 1b, Nebraska
33. Austin Shields, rhp, St. Mary Catholic SS, Hamilton, Ont.
34. Craig Dedelow, of, Indiana
35. Pasquale Mazzoccoli, rhp, Texas State
36. Dustin Williams, 1b, Oklahoma State
37. Colin Brockhouse, rhp, Ball State
38. Aaron Maher, of, East Tennessee State
39. Harrison Wenson, c, Michigan
40. Bret Boswell, ss, Texas

ST. LOUIS CARDINALS (30)

1. Delvin Perez, ss, International Baseball Academy, Ceiba, P.R.
1. Dylan Carlson, of, Elk Grove (Calif.) HS (Compensation for loss of John Lackey as free agent—33rd)
1. Dakota Hudson, rhp, Mississippi State (Compensation for loss of Jason Heyward as free agent—34th)
2. Connor Jones, rhp, Virginia
3. Zac Gallen, rhp, North Carolina
4. Jeremy Martinez, c, Southern California
5. Walker Robbins, of, George County HS, Lucedale, Miss.
6. Tommy Edman, ss, Stanford
7. Andrew Knizner, c, North Carolina State
8. Sam Tewes, rhp, Wichita State
9. Matt Fiedler, of, Minnesota
10. Danny Hudzina, 3b, Western Kentucky
11. John Kilichowski, lhp, Vanderbilt
12. Brady Whalen, ss, Union HS, Camas, Wash.
13. Shane Billings, of, Wingate (N.C.)
14. Vincent Jackson, of, Tennessee
15. J.R. Davis, 2b, Oklahoma State
16. Tyler Lancaster, c, Spartanburg Methodist (S.C.) JC
17. Matt Ellis, rhp, UC Riverside
18. Austin Sexton, rhp, Mississippi State
19. Daniel Castano, lhp, Baylor
20. Stefan Trosclair, 1b, Louisiana-Lafayette
21. Cade Cabbiness, of, Bixby (Okla.) HS
22. Mick Fennell, of, California (Pa.)
23. John Crowe, of, Francis Marion (S.C.)
24. Anthony Ciavarella, lhp, Monmouth
25. Spencer Trayner, rhp, North Carolina
26. Eric Carter, rhp, Louisiana-Lafayette
27. Mike O'Reilly, rhp, Flagler (Fla.)
28. Pat Krall, lhp, Clemson
29. Noel Gonzalez, rhp, Lewis-Clark State (Idaho)
30. Josh Burgmann, rhp, Vauxhall (Alberta) Academy of Baseball
31. J.D. Murders, 2b, Bolivar (Mo.) HS
32. Leland Tilley, rhp, Bellevue (Neb.)
33. Caleb Lopes, 2b, West Georgia
34. Jonathan Mulford, rhp, Adelphi (N.Y.)
35. Jackson Lamb, rhp, Michigan
36. Robbie Gordon, rhp, Maryville (Mo.)
37. Andy Young, 3b, Indiana State
38. Robert Calvano, rhp, Nebraska-Omaha
39. Aaron Bond, of, San Jacinto (Texas) JC
40. Jeremy Ydens, of, St. Francis HS, Mountain View, Calif.

SAN DIEGO PADRES (8)

1. Cal Quantrill, rhp, Stanford
1. Hudson Potts, ss, Carroll HS, Southlake, Texas (Compensation for loss of Justin Upton as free agent—24th)
1. Eric Lauer, lhp, Kent State (Compensation for loss of Ian Kennedy as free agent—25th)
2. Buddy Reed, of, Florida
2s. Reggie Lawson, rhp, Victor Valley HS, Victorville, Calif. (Competitive balance Round 'B' pick—71st)
3. Mason Thompson, rhp, Round Rock (Texas) HS
4. Joey Lucchesi, lhp, Southeast Missouri State
5. Lake Bachar, rhp, Wisconsin-Whitewater
6. Will Stillman, rhp, Wofford
7. Dan Dallas, lhp, Canisius HS, Buffalo
8. Ben Sheckler, lhp, Cornerstone (Mich.)
9. Jesse Scholtens, rhp, Wright State

10. Boomer White, 2b, Texas A&M
11. Trevyne Carter, of, Soddy-Daisy (Tenn.) HS
12. Jamie Sara, rhp, West Potomac HS, Alexandria, Va.
13. Joe Galindo, rhp, New Mexico State
14. Jared Poche, lhp, Louisiana State
15. Jack Suwinski, of, Taft HS, Chicago
16. Chris Mattison, c, Southeastern (Fla.)
17. Chris Baker, ss, Washington
18. Jaquez Williams, 1b, East Coweta HS, Sharpsburg, Ga.
19. A.J. Brown, of, Starkville (Miss.) HS
20. Dom DiSabatino, rhp, Harford (Md.) CC
21. Taylor Kohlwey, of, Wisconsin-La Crosse
22. Evan Miller, rhp, Indiana-Purdue Fort Wayne
23. Nate Easley, 2b, Yavapai (Ariz.) JC
24. Hunter Bishop, of, Serra HS, San Mateo, Calif.
25. Luis Anguizola, c, Loyola (Ill.)
26. Grae Kessinger, ss, Oxford (Miss.) HS
27. Chasen Ford, rhp, Yale
28. Ethan Skender, ss, State JC of Florida
29. Collin Sullivan, rhp, Fort Pierce (Fla.) Central HS
30. Dalton Erb, rhp, Chico State (Calif.)
31. G.K. Young, 1b, Coastal Carolina
32. Ariel Burgos Garcia, rhp, Northern Oklahoma JC
33. Mark Zimmerman, rhp, Baldwin-Wallace (Ohio)
34. Denzell Gowdy, 3b, Darton State (Ga.) JC
35. David Bednar, rhp, Lafayette (Pa.)
36. Quinn Hoffman, ss, Cathedral Catholic HS, San Diego
37. Ryan Rolison, lhp, University School, Jackson, Tenn.
38. William Solomon, lhp, Georgia-Gwinnett
39. J.J. Bleday, of, Mosley HS, Lynn Haven, Fla.
40. Chris Burica, lhp, Orange (Calif.) Lutheran HS

SAN FRANCISCO GIANTS (19)

1. (Pick forfeited for signing of free agent Jeff Samardzija)
2. Bryan Reynolds, of, Vanderbilt
3. Heath Quinn, of, Samford
4. Matt Krook, lhp, Oregon
5. Ryan Howard, ss, Missouri
6. Gio Brusa, of, Pacific
7. Garrett Williams, lhp, Oklahoma State
8. Stephen Woods, rhp, Albany
9. Caleb Baragar, lhp, Indiana
10. Alex Bostic, lhp, Clemson
11. Jason Delay, c, Vanderbilt
12. Ryan Kirby, 1b, San Diego
13. Jose Layer, of, Angel David HS, San Juan, P.R.
14. Conner Menez, lhp, The Masters (Calif.)
15. D.J. Myers, rhp, Nevada-Las Vegas
16. Chris Falwell, lhp, Texas A&M-Corpus Christi
17. Reagan Bazar, rhp, Louisiana-Lafayette
18. Jacob Heyward, of, Miami
19. Brandon Van Horn, ss, The Master's (Calif.)
20. Justin Alleman, rhp, Lee (Tenn.)
21. Will Albertson, c, Catawba (N.C.)
22. Malique Ziegler, of, North Iowa Area CC
23. Jacob Greenwalt, rhp, Windsor (Colo.) HS
24. Jeffery Parra, c, Ramapo HS, Wyckoff, N.J.
25. Mike Rescigno, rhp, Maryland
26. Nick Hill, of, Eckerd (Fla.)
27. Pat Ruotolo, rhp, Connecticut
28. Jayden O'Dell, rhp, Angelo State (Texas)
29. Mike Bernal, ss, Arkansas
30. Nick Deeg, lhp, Central Michigan
31. Adam Laskey, lhp, Haddon Heights (N.J.) HS
32. John Timmins, rhp, Bellevue (Neb.)
33. Jarrett Montgomery, rhp, Northwest Florida State JC
34. C.J. Gettman, rhp, Central Washington
35. Sidney Duprey, lhp, Kaskaskia (Ill.) JC
36. Ryan Matranga, c, San Francisco
37. Chris Bono, of, UCLA
38. David Lee, rhp, Santa Fe (Fla.) JC
39. Andrew DiPiazza, rhp, Mercer County (N.J.) CC
40. Nick Bennett, lhp, Moeller HS, Cincinnati

SEATTLE MARINERS (11)

1. Kyle Lewis, of, Mercer
2. Joe Rizzo, 3b, Oakton HS, Vienna, Va.
3. Bryson Brigman, ss, San Diego
4. Thomas Burrows, lhp, Alabama
5. Donnie Walton, ss, Oklahoma State
6. Brandon Miller, rhp, Millersville (Pa.)
7. Matt Festa, rhp, East Stroudsburg (Pa.)
8. Nick Zammarelli, 3b, Elon
9. Jason Goldstein, c, Illinois
10. David Greer, 3b, Arizona State
11. Michael Koval, rhp, Cal Poly Pomona
12. Tim Viehoff, lhp, Southern New Hampshire
13. Reggie McClain, rhp, Missouri
14. Kyle Davis, rhp, Southern California
15. Danny Garcia, lhp, Miami
16. Lyle Lin, c, JSerra HS, San Juan Capistrano, Calif.
17. Dimas Ojeda, of, McLennan (Texas) CC
18. Robert Dugger, rhp, Texas Tech
19. DeAires Moses, of, Volunteer State (Tenn.) CC
20. Eric Filia, of, UCLA
21. Austin Grebeck, of, Oregon
22. Jansiel Rivera, of, Mathuen (Mass.) HS
23. Jack Anderson, rhp, Penn State
24. Trey Griffey, of, Arizona
25. Ryan Fucci, of, Wright State
26. Elliot Surrey, lhp, UC Irvine
27. Paul Covelle, rhp, Franklin Pierce (N.H.)
28. Nathan Bannister, rhp, Arizona
29. Steven Ridings, rhp, Messiah (Pa.)
30. Tyler Duncan, of, Edward Milne SS, Sooke, B.C.
31. Lincoln Henzman, rhp, Louisville
32. Kenyon Yovan, rhp, Westview HS, Portland, Ore.
33. Morgan McCullough, ss, West Seattle HS
34. David Ellingson, rhp, Georgetown
35. Will Ethridge, rhp, Parkview HS, Lilburn, Ga.
36. Joe Venturino, 2b, Ramapo (N.J.)
37. Eli Wilson, c, Garfield HS, Seattle
38. James Reilly, rhp, Magnus HS, Bardonia, N.Y.
39. Camyrn Williams, ss, Gaither HS, Tampa
40. Adley Rutschman, c, Sherwood (Ore.) HS

TAMPA BAY RAYS (14)

1. Josh Lowe, 3b, Pope HS, Marietta, Ga.
2. Ryan Boldt, of, Nebraska
2. Jake Fraley, of, Louisiana State (Competitive balance Round 'B' pick—77th)
3. Austin Franklin, rhp, Paxton (Fla.) HS
4. Easton McGee, rhp, Hopkinsville (Ky.) HS
5. Mikey York, rhp, JC of Southern Nevada
6. Zach Trageton, rhp, Faith Lutheran HS, Las Vegas
7. J.D. Busfield, rhp, Loyola Marymount
8. Kenny Rosenberg, lhp, Cal State Northridge
9. Peter Bayer, rhp, Cal Poly Pomona
10. Spencer Jones, rhp, Washington
11. Zack Thompson, lhp, Wapahani HS, Selma, Ind.
12. Brandon Lawson, rhp, South Florida
13. Nathaniel Lowe, 1b, Mississippi State
14. Miles Mastrobuoni, 2b, Nevada
15. Dalton Moats, lhp, Delta State (Miss.)
16. Dominic Miroglio, c, San Francisco
17. Wyatt Mills, rhp, Gonzaga
18. Sam Long, lhp, Sacramento State
19. Jim Haley, 3b, Penn State
20. Kevin Santiago, ss, Miami-Dade JC
21. John McMillon, 3b, Jasper (Texas) HS
22. Freddy Villarreal, rhp, Veterans Memorial HS, Mission, Texas
23. Isaac Benard, of, Mount Hood (Ore.) CC
24. Joe Serrapica, rhp, Fordham
25. Matt Vogel, rhp, South Carolina
26. Justin Glover, lhp, Buford (Ga.) HS
27. Robbie Tenerowicz, 2b, California
28. Jean Ramirez, c, Illinois State
29. Trek Stemp, 2b, Washington State

30. Kea'von Edwards, ss, Putnam City HS, Oklahoma City
31. Joey Roach, c, Georgia State
32. Deion Tansel, ss, Toledo
33. Hayden Wesneski, rhp, Cy-Fair HS, Cypress, Texas
34. Bobby Melley, 1b, Connecticut
35. Alex Estrella, lhp, New Mexico
36. Anthony Parente, rhp, Fullerton (Calif.) JC
37. Ryan Zeferjahn, rhp, Seaman HS, Topeka, Kan.
38. Brian McAfee, rhp, Duke
39. Joshua Martinez, of, Caguas Military Academy, Gurabo, P.R.
40. Andrew Daschbach, 3b, Sacred Heart Prep, Atherton, Calif.

TEXAS RANGERS (23)

1. Cole Ragans, lhp, North Florida Christian HS, Tallahassee, Fla. (Compensation for loss of Yovani Gallardo as free agent—30th)
2. Alex Speas, rhp, McEachern HS, Powder Springs, Ga.
3. Kole Enright, 3b, West Orange HS, Winter Garden, Fla.
4. Charles LeBlanc, ss, Pittsburgh
5. Kyle Roberts, lhp, Henry Ford (Mich.) JC
6. Kyle Cody, rhp, Kentucky
7. Sam Huff, c, Arcadia HS, Phoenix
8. Tai Tiedemann, rhp, Long Beach CC
9. Hever Bueno, rhp, Arizona State
10. Josh Merrigan, of, Georgia-Gwinnett
11. Joe Barlow, rhp, Salt Lake CC
12. Alex Kowalczyk, c, Pittsburgh
13. Jonah McReynolds, ss, Patrick Henry (Va.) CC
14. Derek Heffel, rhp, Madison (Wis.) JC
15. Kobie Taylor, of, Portsmouth (N.H.) HS
16. Scott Engler, rhp, Cowley County (Kan.) CC
17. Reid Anderson, rhp, Millersville (Pa.)
18. Marcus Mack, of, Bellaire (Texas) HS
19. Alex Daniele, rhp, Oklahoma
20. Stephen Lohr, 3b, California Baptist
21. Kaleb Fontenot, rhp, McNeese State
22. Clayton Middleton, c, Bethune-Cookman
23. Dylan Bice, rhp, Heritage HS, Ringgold, Ga.
24. Kenneth Mendoza, lhp, Clearview Regional HS, Mullica Hill, N.J.
25. Tra'mayne Holmes, 2b, Wallace (Ala.) CC
26. Tyree Thompson, rhp, Karr HS, New Orleans
27. Lucas Jacobsen, lhp, Long Beach State
28. Marc Iseneker, rhp, St. John Fisher (N.Y.)
29. Robert Harris, of, Marietta (Ga.) HS
30. Christian Torres, lhp, Faulkner (Ala.)
31. Blair Calvo, rhp, East Florida State JC
32. Travis Bolin, of, Davenport (Mich.)
33. Mark Vasquez, rhp, Faulkner (Ala.)
34. Preston Scott, of, Fresno Pacific
35. Jean Casanova, rhp, Waukegan (Ill.) HS
36. Herbie Good, rhp, Puyallup, Wash. (no school)
37. Austin O'Banion, of, Fullerton (Calif.) JC
38. Reilly Peltier, rhp, McHenry County (Ill.) JC
39. Tyler Walsh, ss, Belmont
40. Brent Burgess, c, Spartanburg Methodist (S.C.) JC

TORONTO BLUE JAYS (26)

1. T.J. Zeuch, rhp, Pittsburgh
2. J.B. Woodman, of, Mississippi (Special compensation for failure to sign 2015 second-round pick Brady Singer—57th)
2. Bo Bichette, ss, Lakewood HS, St. Petersburg, Fla.
3. Zach Jackson, rhp, Arkansas
4. Josh Palacios, of, Auburn
5. Cavan Biggio, 2b, Notre Dame
6. D.J. Daniels, of, Fike HS, Wilson, N.C.
7. Andy Ravel, rhp, Kent State
8. Kyle Weatherly, rhp, Grayson (Texas) CC
9. Nick Hartman, rhp, Old Dominion
10. Kirby Snead, lhp, Florida
11. Travis Hosterman, lhp, Hagerty HS, Oviedo, Fla.
12. Ridge Smith, c, Austin Peay State
13. Chris Lincoln, rhp, Rancho Verde HS, Moreno Valley, Calif.
14. Chris Hall, rhp, Elon
15. Josh Winckowski, rhp, Estero (Fla.) HS

16. Dominic Taccolini, rhp, Arkansas
17. Clayton Keyes, of, Bishop Carroll HS, Calgary
18. Bradley Jones, 3b, College of Charleston
19. Spencer Van Scoyoc, lhp, Jefferson HS, Cedar Rapids, Iowa
20. Angel Alicea, rhp, Alabama State
21. Mitch McKown, rhp, Seminole State (Fla.) JC
22. Connor Eller, rhp, Ouachita Baptist (Ark.)
23. Dom Abbadessa, of, Huntington Beach (Calif.) HS
24. Mike Ellenbest, rhp, Saginaw Valley State (Mich.)
25. Casey Legumina, rhp, Basha HS, Chandler, Ariz.
26. Ben Anderson, rhp, Shenendehowa HS, Clifton Park, N.Y.
27. Ryan Gold, c, Carolina Forest HS, Myrtle Beach, S.C.
28. Blake Ebo, of, Trenton (N.J.) Catholic Academy
29. Andrew Deramo, rhp, Central Florida
30. Jake Fishman, lhp, Union (N.Y.)
31. Marcus Still, of, Scottsdale (Ariz.) CC
32. David Jacob, 1b, Quincy (Ill.)
33. Brayden Bouchey, rhp, Louisiana-Monroe
34. Shea Langeliers, c, Keller (Texas) HS
35. Jared Carkuff, rhp, Austin Peay State
36. Dustin Skelton, c, Magnolia Heights HS, Senatobia, Miss.
37. Luke Gillingham, lhp, Navy
38. Alex Segal, lhp, Chapparal HS, Scottsdale, Ariz.
39. Chavez Young, of, Faith Baptist Christian Academy, Ludowici, Ga.
40. Carter Loewen, rhp, Yale SS, Abbotsford, B.C.

WASHINGTON NATIONALS (18)

1. (Choice forfeited for signing Daniel Murphy as free agent)
1. Carter Kieboom, ss, Walton HS, Marietta, Ga. (Compensation for loss of Jordan Zimmermann as free agent—28th)
1. Dane Dunning, rhp, Florida (Compensation for loss of Ian Desmond as free agent—29th)
2. Sheldon Neuse, 3b, Oklahoma
3. Jesus Luzardo, lhp, Douglas HS, Parkland, Fla.
4. Nick Banks, of, Texas A&M
5. Daniel Johnson, of, New Mexico State
6. Tres Barrera, c, Texas
7. Jake Noll, 2b, Florida Gulf Coast
8. A.J. Bogucki, rhp, North Carolina
9. Joey Harris, c, Gonzaga
10. Paul Panaccione, ss, Grand Canyon (Ariz.)
11. Armond Upshaw, of, Pensacola State (Fla.) JC
12. Hayden Howard, lhp, Texas Tech
13. Conner Simonetti, 1b, Kent State
14. Kyle Simonds, rhp, Texas A&M
15. Ryan Williamson, lhp, North Carolina State
16. Phil Morse, rhp, Shenandoah (Va.)
17. Tyler Beckwith, ss, Richmond
18. Ben Braymer, lhp, Auburn
19. Jarrett Gonzales, c, Madison HS, Dallas
20. Jake Barnett, lhp, Lewis-Clark State (Idaho)
21. Jacob Howell, rhp, Delta State (Miss.)
22. Sterling Sharpe, rhp, Drury (Mo.)
23. Michael Rishwain, rhp, Westmont (Calif.)
24. Joseph Baltrip, rhp, Wharton County (Texas) JC
25. Branden Boggetto, ss, Southeast Missouri State
26. Jack Sundberg, of, Connecticut
27. Jeremy McDonald, lhp, California Baptist
28. Jonny Reid, lhp, Azusa Pacific (Calif.)
29. Sam Held, rhp, Nevada
30. Tristan Clarke, of, Eastern Oklahoma State JC
31. C.J. Picerni, c, New York
32. Garrett Gonzales, 3b, Madison HS, San Antonio
33. Ryan Wetzel, ss, Heritage Christian Academy, Olathe, Kan.
34. Morgan Cooper, rhp, Texas
35. Tristan Bayless, lhp, Hutto (Texas) HS
36. Jordan McFarland, of, Waterloo (Ill.) HS
37. Cory Voss, c, McLennan (Texas) CC
38. Noah Murdock, rhp, Colonial Heights (Va.) HS
39. Matt Mervis, 1b, Georgetown Prep HS, North Bethesda, Md.
40. Sean Cook, rhp, Whitman HS, Bethesda, Md.

APPENDIX

■ **Gair Allie,** a shortstop who played one season in the big leagues in 1954, died Oct. 4 in San Antonio. He was 84.

■ **Orlando Alvarez,** an outfielder who played in four big league seasons from 1973-76, died March 31 in Canovanas, Puerto Rico. He was 64.

Alvarez got his longest look in the majors following a trade from the Dodgers to the Angels in March 1976. The Angels called him up for parts of May and June of that season, and he played in 15 games and hit .167 (7-for-42).

■ **Steve Arlin,** a righthander who pitched six years in the major leagues from 1969-74, died Aug. 17 in San Diego. He was 70.

Arlin helped Ohio State to two College World Series appearances and the 1966 national championship, the only one in school history. He had a 0.96 ERA in CWS play for his career and won Most Outstanding Player honors at the 1966 CWS. He reached the majors with the expansion Padres in 1969, their first year in the league, and became a full-time member of their rotation in 1971. Although Arlin never won more than 11 games in a season for the fledgling team, he did post a 3.48 ERA in 1971 and a 3.60 in 1972.

■ **Luis Arroyo,** a lefthander who pitched eight years in the majors between 1955 and 1963, died Jan. 13 in Ponce, Puerto Rico. He was 88.

Arroyo pitched five years in the minors before getting the big leagues with the Cardinals in 1955. He bounced from the Cardinals to the Pirates to the Reds over his first four seasons in the majors before settling with the Yankees in 1960. Arroyo's two best seasons came in pinstripes in 1960, when he went 5-1, 2.88 in 41 relief innings, and then in 1961, when he was a vital piece of the Yankees' bullpen on their way to a World Series title. Arroyo led the majors in both saves (29) and appearances (65) in '61 while going 15-5, 2.19 in 119 innings.

■ **Jeff Barton,** a third-generation baseball scout and the Reds' West Coast crosschecker, died Nov. 12, 2015, in Gilbert, Ariz., after a long battle with cancer. He was 50.

■ **Juan Bell,** a second baseman who played seven years from 1989-95, died Aug. 24 in Santo Domingo, Dominican Republic. He was 48.

The younger brother of all-star outfielder George Bell, Juan came up through the Dodgers and Orioles systems as a shortstop. But with Cal Ripken Jr. entrenched at shortstop in Baltimore, Bell shifted to second base upon reaching the majors—he had cups of coffee with Baltimore in 1989 and 1990 and played regularly in 1991. He got back to shortstop after a trade to the Phillies

in August 1992 but had a journeyman's career over the next three seasons, moving from the Phillies to the Brewers, Expos and then Red Sox.

■ **Neil Berry,** a shortstop who played seven years in the big leagues from 1948-54, died Aug. 24 in Kalamazoo, Mich. He was 94.

Berry spent five years in a utility role for the Tigers, playing mostly at shortstop and second base. He hit .242 combined over his five years in Detroit before being traded to the St. Louis Browns after the 1952 season. He split his final two seasons in the majors between the Browns and White Sox, ending in 1954.

■ **Fred Besana,** a lefthander who pitched one season for the Orioles in 1956, died Nov. 7, 2015, in Lincoln, Calif. He was 84.

■ **Alan Brice,** a righthander who pitched briefly in the big leagues in 1961, died July 30 in Bradenton, Fla. He was 78.

Brice played nine years of pro ball, seven of them in the White Sox organization. His lone call-up to the majors came in September 1961, when he made three appearances for Chicago and didn't allow an earned run in three innings of work. He last played professionally in 1964 as part of the Kansas City Athletics organization.

■ **Hal Brown,** a righthander who pitched 14 seasons in the big leagues from 1951-64, died Dec. 17, 2015, in Greensboro, N.C. He was 91.

Brown served in the U.S. Army Air Force during World War II and didn't get to the majors until he was 26 in 1951, when he came up with the White Sox. He worked mainly as a reliever early in his career with the White Sox and Red Sox but came into his own later after moving to a starting role with the Orioles. Brown was a regular in the Orioles' rotation from 1957-61, posting three straight double-digit win seasons form 1959-61. He wound down his career with stints with the Yankees and Astros, ending with an 85-92, 3.81 lifetime record in 358 big league appearances.

■ **Mike Brumley,** a catcher who played three seasons in the major leagues from 1964-66, died Aug. 8 in Grapevine, Texas.

Brumley was the Washington Senators' everyday catcher as a 25-year-old rookie in 1964, batting .244 with two homers in 136 games. However, he moved into a part-time role in 1965 and went back to the minors for most of the 1966 season, appearing in just nine games with Washington. In all, he played in 224 major league games and hit .229 with five homers.

■ **Tom Butters,** a righthander who pitched four seasons in the major leagues from 1962-65, died

March 31 in Durham, N.C. He was 77.

Butters had a couple cups of coffee with Pittsburgh in 1962 and '63 before getting his first extended big league time in '64. He logged 64 innings for the Pirates that summer, going 2-2, 2.38 in 28 appearances, including four starts. However, a car accident ended his playing career in 1965. He went on to serve as Duke's head baseball coach from 1968-70 and, more famously, as the school's athletic director from 1977-1998, during which time he hired Mike Krzyzewski as head basketball coach in 1980.

■ **Carmelo Castillo,** an outfielder who played 10 years in the majors from 1982-91, died Nov. 15, 2015, in Santo Domingo, Dominican Republic. He was 57.

Castillo came up with the Indians in 1982 and maintained a fourth-outfielder's role in Cleveland for the next seven years. He never played 100 games in a big league season but did hit double-digit homers three times. The Indians traded Castillo to the Twins during 1989 spring training and he played parts of three more years in Minnesota. He retired in 1991 as a .252 career hitter in 631 major league games.

■ **Bryan Clutterbuck,** a righthander who pitched in parts of two big league seasons, died Aug. 23 in Milford, Mich. He was 56.

Clutterbuck played nine years in pro ball, with stints in the big leagues in 1986 and 1989, both with the Brewers.

■ **Clarence "Choo-Choo" Coleman,** a catcher who played in four seasons between 1961 and 1966, died Aug. 15 in Orangeburg, S.C. He was 80.

Coleman debuted with the Phillies in 1961, batting .128 in 34 games, then was taken by the Mets in the expansion draft after that season. Coleman played 55 games as a reserve catcher for the inaugural Mets team that lost 120 games, batting .250 in 152 at-bats. He played regularly the following year, appearing in 106 games with a .178 average.

■ **Kevin Collins,** a third baseman who played six years in the majors in the 1960s and '70s, died Feb. 20 in Naples, Fla. He was 69.

Collins was a bonus baby signed by the Mets out of high school in 1964, the last year before the institution of the draft. The bonus baby rules at the time forced New York to bring him up to the majors as a 19-year-old in 1965, and he went 4-for-23 in 11 big league games that September. He got back to New York briefly in 1967 and earned a more regular role in 1968, logging 154 at-bats and hitting .201. Collins played second base, third base and the outfield over the course of

his career, spent mostly with the Mets along with brief stints with the Montreal Expos (1969) and the Tigers (1970-71).

■ **Paul Dade,** an outfielder who played six years in the majors from 1975-80, died Aug. 25 in Seattle. He was 64.

The Angels made Dade the 10th overall pick in the 1970 draft, and he reached the big leagues five years later. He had another brief stint with the Angels in 1976 but was subsequently allowed to leave in free agency, signing with the Indians. Dade hit well in his first season in Cleveland, batting .291 with 45 RBIs and 16 steals, but that would prove to be his best year. He served in a utility role for the remainder of his career.

■ **Jim Davenport,** a third baseman who played 13 years in the majors from 1958-70, died Feb. 18 in Redwood City, Calif. He was 82.

Davenport took over the Giants' everyday third base job as a rookie in 1958, hitting .256 with 12 homers that year, and held the role through 1963. He had his best year in 1962, when he hit .297 with a career-high 14 homers to make his only trip to the All-Star Game. The Giants began using him in more of a utility role in 1964, although he still played in over 100 games in every season through 1969.

Davenport had a long coaching career after his playing days, mostly in the Giants organization at both the major- and minor-league levels. He served as the Giants' big league manager for most of the 1985 season, going 56-88.

■ **Joe DeMaestri,** a shortstop who played 11 years in the big leagues and was an all-star in 1957, died Aug. 26 in San Rafael, Calif. He was 87.

DeMaestri spend the bulk of his career with the Athletics, staying with the franchise following its move to Kansas City in 1954. Although not known for his offense, he twice led AL shortstops in fielding percentage (1957 and '58) and made the AL all-star team in 1957, during a season in which he hit .245 with a career-high nine home runs.

DeMaestri was also part of the trade that sent Roger Maris from the A's to the Yankees after the 1960 season, and he played two seasons in a part-time role for New York.

■ **Bobby Dews,** a minor league shortstop from 1960-70 and a longtime coach with the Braves, died Dec. 26 in Albany, Ga. He was 76.

Dews was a true baseball lifer, working in the game for 53 years, 37 of them for the Braves. Dews played his entire minor league career in the Cardinals system, twice reaching Triple-A. After his playing days, Dews stayed around the sport as a

APPENDIX

Cardinals minor league manager for seven seasons before returning to his native Georgia and joining the Braves in 1974.

Dews worked as a minor league manager for the Braves and had three stints on the major league coaching staff, totaling 14 years. He most recently served as Atlanta's bullpen coach from 1999-2006 and continued to work with the club in an advisory role after his retirement.

■ **Joe Durham,** an outfielder who played in three big league seasons in the 1950s, died April 28 in Randallstown, Md. He was 84.

Durham got his longest run in the majors in 1957, playing in 77 games for the Orioles and hitting .185 with four homers.

■ **Eddie Einhorn,** an executive in the White Sox organization for 35 seasons, died Feb. 24 in Alpine, N.J. He was 80.

Einhorn was prominent in the sports and broadcasting industries for decades. He founded the TVS Television Network in 1965, which proved instrumental in the rise in popularity of college basketball. He was inducted to the National Collegiate Basketball Hall of Fame in Kansas City as a contributor in 2011.

On the baseball side, Einhorn—a longtime friend of White Sox owner Jerry Reinsdorf—served as White Sox team president from 1981-90 and thereafter as the club's vice chairman. During that time, he also helped negotiate some of MLB's national television deals and served on several league committees.

■ **Sammy Ellis,** a righthander who pitched seven years in the majors, died May 13 in Temple Terrace, Fla. He was 75.

Ellis was one of the Reds' best relievers in 1964, going 10-3, 2.57 in 52 appearances. He moved to the rotation the following year and recorded a 20-win season, going 22-10, 3.79 and representing Cincinnati in the All-Star Game. However, arm injuries plagued him thereafter, and he won just 29 games over the next four seasons combined. His playing days ended in 1971, but Ellis went on to a long career as a coach.

■ **Chico Fernandez,** a shortstop who played eight seasons in the majors from 1956-63, died June 11 in Sunrise, Fla. He was 84.

Fernandez, a native of Cuba, came up through the Brooklyn Dodgers system, earning a reputation as a standout defensive prospect. He reached Brooklyn in July 1956 at age 24 but played just 34 games in a Dodgers uniform before being traded to the Phillies. He hit .242 over three seasons as a Phillie from 1957-59 before being dealt to the

Tigers in December 1959. He had a sudden surge in home run power for the Tigers in 1962, mashing 20 homers to go with his .249 average, which accounted for half of the 40 homers he hit in his eight-year career.

■ **Jose Fernandez,** a righthander who was the 2013 Rookie of the Year and a two-time all-star, died Sept. 25 in Miami Beach, Fla., in a boating accident. He was 24.

The 14th overall pick in the 2011 draft by the Marlins, Fernandez was one of the game's best pitchers since he debuted in 2013, when he went 12-6, 2.19 with 187 strikeouts in 172.2 innings. That season, over his final 18 starts from June 1-Sept. 11, Fernandez was the best pitcher in the majors, logging a 1.50 ERA over 120 innings. Tommy John surgery cost Fernandez most of the 2014 and 2015 seasons, but he had returned to form in 2016, going 16-8, 2.86 through 29 starts for Miami, with 253 strikeouts in 182.1 innings.

A night after Fernandez's death, the Marlins resumed play with the first game of a series with the Mets. Every Marlins player wore a jersey bearing both No. 16 and "Fernandez" on the back, and the team announced that they would retire No. 16 effective immediately.

■ **Joe Garagiola,** a longtime big league player and widely renowned broadcaster, died March 23 in Phoenix. He was 90.

Garagiola will be more remembered for his broadcasting career, but he also played nine years in the big leagues as a catcher. He reached the big leagues shortly after getting out of the military in 1946. Garagiola played six seasons for the Cardinals, mostly in a reserve role, before finishing his career with stints with the Pirates (1951-53), Cubs (1953-54) and New York Giants (1954). His best all-around season came in 1952 with Pittsburgh, when he hit .273 with eight homers and a career-high 54 RBIs.

Garagiola began his broadcasting career calling Cardinals games in 1955, and he became widely known for his work with NBC after moving to New York to call Yankees games in 1965. Garagiola called NBC's Game of the Week telecasts for much of the 1970s and '80s. He worked a total of 58 years in broadcasting, doing games for the Diamondbacks in his later years until retiring in 2013. The Hall of Fame honored him with the Buck O'Neil Lifetime Achievement Award in 2014.

■ **George Genovese,** a shortstop who played one year in the big leagues in 1950 and had a lengthy scouting career, died Nov. 15, 2015, in Burbank, Calif. He was 93.

■ **Gus Gil,** a second baseman who played parts of four seasons in the majors between 1967 and 1971, died Dec. 8, 2015, in Phoenix. He was 76.

A native of Venezuela, Gil came up through the Indians and Reds organizations, first reaching the majors with Cleveland in 1967 and appearing in 51 games. He got his most extensive big league time two years later after being sold to the Seattle Pilots, hitting .222 with 17 RBIs in 221 at-bats. He appeared in 78 games over the next two seasons following the Pilots' move to Milwaukee.

■ **Doug Griffin,** a second baseman who played eight years in the major leagues from 1970-77, died July 27 in Clovis, Calif. He was 69.

Griffin came up through the Angels organization, making his debut in September 1970. However, he was part of a six-player trade to the Red Sox after the season, and he spent the rest of his big-league career in Boston. He took over as the Red Sox's everyday second baseman in 1971. Though not an impact offensive player, he did hit over .250 in each of the next three seasons, in addition to winning a Gold Glove award in 1972.

■ **Jim Ray Hart,** a third baseman who played 12 years in the majors from 1963-74, died May 19 in Acampo, Calif. He was 74.

Hart was one of the better home run hitters of the low-offense 1960s, finishing in the top 10 in the National League in homers four times in five years from 1964-68. He burst onto the scene with the Giants in 1964, hitting 31 homers and batting .286 as a 22-year-old rookie. He finished second to Dick Allen in the NL rookie of the year race. He reached the 30-homer mark for a second time in 1966, when he mashed a career-best 33 and made the all-star team for the only time in his career.

■ **Dave Henderson,** an outfielder who played 14 years in the major leagues from 1981-94, died Dec. 27 in Seattle. He was 57.

Henderson had what would've been one of the all-time most memorable postseasons had things ended differently for the Red Sox. Boston was one out from elimination in Game Five of the American League Championship Series when Henderson hit a go-ahead, two-run home run. He then hit .400 (10-for-25) in the World Series against the Mets, and he would have been the hero again after hitting a go-ahead home run in the top of the 10th inning in Game Six that put the Red Sox three outs from the title.

Henderson later became the everyday center fielder for the A's teams that made three straight World Series from 1988-90, winning it all in 1989. Henderson had his best year in 1988 at age

29, hitting .304 with 24 homers and a career-high 94 RBIs, the first of four 20-homer seasons he put up in Oakland. He made his lone All-Star Game appearance in 1991.

■ **Phil Hennigan,** a righthander who pitched five years in the majors from 1969-73, died June 17 in Center, Texas. He was 70.

A fourth-round pick of the Indians in the 1966 January draft, Hennigan reached the majors with Cleveland for the first time in September 1969. He was a regular contributor out of the Indians' bullpen over the next three seasons, his best year coming in 1972 when he went 5-3, 2.67 with six saves in 38 appearances.

■ **Ron Henry,** a catcher who played in parts of two big league seasons for the Twins, died May 14 in Denver. He was 79.

Henry had a 15-year pro career from 1954 to 1968, and he reached the majors for brief stints in Minnesota in 1961 and '64. He appeared in a total of 42 big league games, batting .130 (9-for-69) with two home runs.

■ **Evelio Hernandez,** a righthander who pitched two seasons in the majors from 1956-57, died Dec. 18, 2015, in Miami. He was 83.

Hernandez pitched 11 seasons in pro ball, including a couple brief stints with the Washington Senators. The Cuban native first came up at the tail end of the 1956 season and went 1-1, 4.76 in 23 innings. He got into 14 games the following year, including two starts, and posted a 4.25 ERA in 36 innings without figuring in any decisions.

■ **Jim Hickman,** an outfielder who played 13 years in the big leagues from 1962-74, died June 25 in Jackson, Tenn. He was 79.

Hickman spent five years with the Mets, posting four double-digit home run seasons before a trade sent him to the Dodgers in November 1966. He played only one season in Los Angeles before being dealt again, this time to the Cubs in April 1968. Hickman put up a 21-homer season for the Cubs in 1969—the Cubs team that infamously lost an August nine-game division lead to the Miracle Mets—and had his career year in 1970, when he hit .315 with 32 homers and 115 RBIs to make his first and only All-Star Game appearance. He ended his career with a .252 lifetime average and 159 home runs.

■ **Tim Hill,** longtime head baseball coach at State JC of Florida, died Dec. 25 in Lakeland, Fla. He was 71.

Hill first came to State JC of Florida—known as Manatee CC until 2009—in 1978, serving as an assistant for three seasons before taking over as

head coach. In 31 years running the program, Hill won 1,109 games, making him the winningest coach in Florida junior college baseball history. His teams won 17 conference titles and made five NJCAA World Series appearances.

■ **Hal Hudson,** a lefthander who pitched two years in the big leagues in 1952 and '53, died July 8 in Port St. Lucie, Fla. He was 89.

■ **Monte Irvin,** a Hall of Fame outfielder who played eight years in the majors and was one of the majors' first black players, died Jan. 11 in Houston. He was 96.

In 1949, the New York Giants paid $5,000 for Irvin's contract, making him MLB's fourth black player. He reached the majors that season and was there for good in 1950. In 1951, Irvin finished third in the MVP vote with his best overall season, posting an OPS of .929 and a OPS+ of 147 with a league-leading 121 RBIs as the Giants rallied to overtake the Dodgers in the famous 1951 pennant race which culminated with Bobby Thomson's "Shot Heard 'Round The World." Irvin batted— and popped out—before Thomson's homer off Ralph Branca. He also batted .458 in the World Series against the Yankees, although the Giants lost in six games. Irvin played eight seasons in the majors for the Giants and Cubs and was elected to the Hall of Fame in 1973. Irvin later became a scout for the Mets and then spent 17 years in the commissioner's office. The Giants retired his uniform No. 20 in 2010.

■ **Virgil Jester,** a righthander who pitched two seasons in the majors from 1952-53, died Feb. 15. He was 88.

Jester came up with the Boston Braves in 1952—their final season in Boston—and logged a 3-5, 3.33 mark in 73 innings, including making eight starts among his 19 appearances. He went back to the minors for most of the 1953 season but did make two appearances for the relocated Milwaukee Braves, though arm problems subsequently cut his career short.

■ **Ken Johnson,** a righthander who pitched in the major leagues from 1958-70, died Nov. 21, 2015, in Pineville, La. He was 82.

Johnson had a well-traveled career, pitching for seven different teams over 13 years. He had a couple of quality years as a starter, posting a 2.65 ERA over 224 innings for Houston in 1963 and he went 13-9, 2.74 for the Braves in 1967. Atlanta was where he had his longest stay, pitching there from 1966-69. He finished his career in Montreal in 1970 with a 3.46 lifetime ERA in over 1,700 big league innings.

■ **Tom Knight,** a longtime historian of the Brooklyn Dodgers, died Feb. 17 in Brooklyn. He was 89.

Knight's duties as a historian were largely unofficial, but for three decades he did write a regular baseball history column called "Diamond Reflections," which appeared in The Brooklyn Eagle and other local publications.

■ **Steve Korcheck,** a catcher who played in parts of four seasons between 1954 and 1959, died Aug. 26 in Bradenton, Fla. He was 84.

Korcheck was picked in the third round of the 1954 NFL draft as a center but chose instead to go pro in baseball with the Washington Senators. Korcheck's career was interrupted by two years of military service from 1956-57, although he got back to the majors briefly in 1958. He made a career-high 22 appearances for Washington in his final season in 1959. After his playing career ended, Korcheck coached for five seasons at his alma mater, George Washington, and later in the Royals organization and with Manatee (Fla.) JC.

■ **Bill Law,** a team ambassador for the Durham Bulls and longtime member of the organization, died Aug. 30. He was 88.

Law had been part of the Bulls' organization since the early 1990s, when it still played in the high Class A Carolina League. He served as the team's public address announcer for more than a decade and later as a team representative at various speaking engagements around North Carolina. Law received the Spirit of the International League award in 2013 in recognition for his dedication to the fan experience at league ballparks.

■ **Turk Lown,** a righthander who pitched 11 years in the majors between 1951 and 1962, died July 8 in Pueblo, Colo. He was 92.

Lown spent almost his entire career with the Cubs and White Sox, making more than 500 big league appearances. Lown spent the early portion of his career as a starter but never recorded an ERA better than 4.37 in his three years making starts for the Cubs.

The Cubs dealt him to the Reds in May 1958, but he returned to Chicago a month later when he was claimed on waivers by the White Sox. Pitching on the South Side, he had arguably the best year of his career as a 35-year-old in 1959, going 9-2, 2.89 in 93 innings and with an American League-leading 15 saves. Lown retired with a 4.12 lifetime ERA and 73 saves.

■ **Frank Malzone,** a third baseman who played 12 years in the majors from 1955-66, died Dec. 29, 2015, in Needham, Mass. He was 85.

Malzone took over as the Red Sox's everyday third baseman in 1957 and had a breakout season, hitting .292 with 15 homers and 103 RBIs to earn his first All-Star Game appearance. The '57 season was the first of four straight all-star seasons for Malzone, as he hit a cumulative .282 with 48 home runs over the next three years. He hit a career-high 21 homers in 1962 at age 32, and his .291 average with 15 homers earned him a return to the All-Star Game for a fifth time in 1963. He made a final All-Star Game in 1964 at age 34.

■ **Clyde Mashore,** an outfielder who played five years in the majors from 1969-73, died Jan. 24 in Brentwood, Calif. He was 70.

Mashore stuck in Montreal in a fourth-out-fielder's role, playing all three outfield positions, as well as third base, during his four seasons there. His best year with the bat came in 1972, when he hit .227 with three homers in 176 at-bats. He last played in the majors in 1973, retiring a year later after one more season in Triple-A.

■ **Gordon Massa,** a catcher who played in parts of two seasons in the majors from 1957-58, died July 16 in Cincinnati. He was 80.

■ **Dick McAuliffe,** a second baseman who played 16 years in the majors from 1960-75, died May 13 in Farmington, Conn. He was 76.

A mainstay for the Tigers from the age of 22, McAuliffe set himself apart as a power-hitting middle infielder at a time when such players were rare. He hit 12 home runs as a 22-year-old in 1962, the first of 10 straight years he reached double digits in homers. He broke the 20-homer barrier for the first time in 1964, smacking a career-high 24. In 1965, he began a stretch of three straight all-star seasons, posting his best all-around year when he hit .274 with 23 homers in 1966. The Tigers also used him as their leadoff hitter, and he led the American League in runs scored in 1968 as the Tigers won the World Series. Knee injuries cost McAuliffe much of the 1969 season, and his production tailed off afterward.

■ **Eddie Milner,** an outfielder who played nine years in the majors from 1980-88, died Nov. 2, 2015, in Cincinnati. He was 60.

A 21st-round pick in 1976, Milner came up through the Reds' system, making brief appearances in the majors in 1980 and 1981 before earning a more regular role in 1982. Milner held the Reds' center field role for four years, peaking when he slugged 15 long balls and hit .259 in 1986.

■ **Scott Muckey,** a long-time high school coach at Crespi High in Los Angeles, died March 5 in Westlake Village, Calif. He was 63.

Muckey took over as head coach at Crespi in 1987 and turned it into one of Southern California's most respected programs over a 28-year tenure. He won two Southern Section titles, 11 conference titles, and overall he won 502 games.

■ **Steve Nagy,** a lefthander who pitched two years in the majors in 1947 and 1950, died July 24 in Poulsbo, Wash. He was 97.

■ **Jim O'Toole,** a lefthander who pitched in the major leagues for 10 years from 1958-67, died Dec. 26, 2015, in Cincinnati. He was 78.

O'Toole spent nine years with the Reds, breaking in in 1958 and taking a role in their rotation in 1959. O'Toole won at least 16 games every year from 1961-64, peaking in 1961 when he went 19-9, 3.10 as the Reds won the National League pennant. Two years later, O'Toole started the 1963 All-Star Game for the NL in his lone all-star appearance, in the midst of a season in which he posted a 2.88 ERA in 234 innings. O'Toole was just 26 years old when he made the All-Star Game, but shoulder injuries shortened his career.

■ **Milt Pappas,** a righthander who pitched 17 seasons in the majors and was a two-time all-star, died April 19 in Beecher, Ill. He was 76.

Pappas came up with the Orioles in 1957 and joined their rotation on a regular basis in 1958, going 10-10, 4.06 when he was just 19 years old. He made both of his all-star appearances as an Oriole, in 1962 and 1965, and had the best year of his career in '65, going 13-9, 2.60 in 34 starts. It was that performance that prompted the Reds to trade for him that winter, infamously sending Frank Robinson to Baltimore for Pappas and two other players, a deal regarded as one of the more one-sided in baseball history.

Pappas spent less than three full seasons in Cincinnati, though he did win 16 games for the Reds in 1967. Pappas pitched the last three-plus seasons of his career in Chicago. Pappas won 17 games in back-to-back seasons for the Cubs in 1971 and '72 and finished his career in 1973 with 209 wins. He was the first pitcher to reach the 200-win mark without having a 20-win season.

■ **Harry Perkowski,** a lefthander who pitched eight seasons in the majors between 1947 and 1955, died April 20 in Beckley, W.Va. He was 93.

Perkowski was primarily a reliever in 1950 and '51, but after recording a 2.82 ERA in 102 innings in 1951, the Reds shifted him to the rotation in 1952. Perkowski made 24 starts and 33 appearances overall for Cincinnati that year, going 12-10, 3.80 in 194 innings. That was his best year as a starter, though, and he began transitioning back

into primarily a relief role in 1954. The Reds traded him to the Cubs after the 1954 season, and he went 3-4, 5.29 in 48 innings for Chicago in 1955.

■ **Lee Pfund,** a righthander who pitched for the Dodgers in 1945, died June 2 in Carol Stream, Ill. He was 96.

A knee injury ended his playing career in 1950, but Pfund went on to a long and successful career coaching baseball and basketball at Wheaton (Ill.). He's the winningest coach in school history in both sports, with 249 wins in baseball and 362 in basketball, including the 1957 national championship for the NCAA College Division—the equivalent of Division II today. He retired in 1975.

■ **Tony Phillips,** an outfielder who played 18 years in the majors from 1982-1999, died Feb. 17 in Scottsdale, Ariz. He was 56.

Phillips carved out a lengthy career as a super utility player, best remembered for his time with the "Bash Brothers"-era Athletics from 1982-89. Phillips played six different positions for the 1989 A's team that went on to win the World Series, hitting .262 with four homers and 47 RBIs.

Phillips signed with the Tigers as a free agent after the '89 season and played five years in Detroit, including a year in which he led the majors in walks in 1993. The Tigers traded him to the Angels shortly after the 1994-95 strike ended, and he went on to play for five different teams over his final five seasons before retiring at age 40.

■ **Ruben Quevedo,** a righthander who pitched four years in the majors from 2000-03, died June 7 in Vargas, Venezuela. He was 37.

Pitching in the big leagues as a 21-year-old, Quevedo went 3-10, 7.47 in 88 innings for the Cubs and was dealt to the Brewers in July 2001 while back in the minors. He enjoyed some success in his first stint in Milwaukee, striking out 60 hitters in 57 innings with a 4.61 ERA after the trade, and Quevedo spent most of the 2002 season in the Milwaukee rotation, going 6-11, 5.76. He died of a heart attack in his native Venezuela.

■ **Robert Ramsay,** a lefthander who pitched two seasons in the majors from 1999-2000, died Aug. 4 in Coeur d'Alene, Idaho. He was 42.

Ramsay pitched regularly out of Seattle's bullpen in 2000, going 1-1, 3.40 in 50 innings. Ramsay went back to the minors in 2001, but his career was effectively ended when he was diagnosed with brain cancer later that year. He was able to beat the disease but never pitched in the majors again, though he did make a one-year comeback attempt in 2003. He continued to be plagued by seizures in later years and lost his life to one at age 42.

■ **Vern Rapp,** who managed in the major leagues for parts of three seasons, died Dec. 31, 2015, in Broomfield, Colo. He was 87.

Rapp played 16 years as a catcher in the minor leagues, and the Cardinals hired him as their manager prior to the 1977 season, replacing Red Schoendienst. The Cardinals went 83-79 in what would be Rapp's only full season as a big league manager. He was relieved 17 games into the 1978 season. Rapp worked as a coach with the Expos until getting another chance at managing in the majors, when the Reds hired him in 1984. Cincinnati fired him less than a year later with the club posting a 51-70 record.

■ **Lance Rautzhan,** a lefthander who pitched three years in the major leagues from 1977-79, died Jan. 9 in Myrtle Beach, S.C. He was 63.

Rautzhan reached the majors for the first time in 1977, going 4-1, 4.35 in 21 innings for a Dodger club that went on to win the NL pennant. Rautzhan stayed with the Dodgers, making another trip to the postseason in 1978, until he was sold to the Brewers in May 1979.

■ **H.B. "Spec" Richardson,** a former general manager of the Astros and Giants in the 1960s and '70s, died April 12 in Columbus, Ga. He was 93.

Richardson assumed the reins in Houston in 1967, taking over a fifth-year franchise that had never had a winning season. After winning just 69 games in Richardson's first year in charge, the Astros improved their win totals in each of the next two seasons, finishing at .500 (81-81) in 1969. They had their first-ever winning season in 1972, going 84-69 led by homegrown all-star Cesar Cedeno. The Astros replaced Richardson with Tal Smith in 1975 during a season in which they slipped to a 64-97 record. Richardson landed with the Giants in 1976, beginning a tenure that lasted through midseason 1981.

■ **Jay Ritchie,** a righthander who pitched five years in the big leagues from 1964-68, died Jan. 5 in Salisbury, N.C. He was 79.

Ritchie pitched eight seasons in the minors before getting to make his debut with the Red Sox as a 27-year-old in 1964. He had a solid rookie year, posting a 2.74 ERA in 46 innings, all in relief. The Red Sox traded him to the Braves after the 1965 season, and he pitched two seasons in Atlanta before a trade to the Reds for 1968. He finished his big league career in Cincinnati, going 2-3, 4.61 in 1968. He later spent three years as a Braves area scout in the 1970s before leaving the sport.

■ **Juan C. Rodriguez,** the Marlins beat writer for the Florida Sun Sentinel and Baseball America's